59th Annual Edition

Gun Digest® 2005

Edited by
Ken Ramage

Published by

700 East State Street • Iola, WI 54990-0001
715-445-2214 • 888-457-2873
www.krause.com

Our toll-free number to place an order or obtain a free catalog is 800-258-0929.

Manuscripts, contributions and inquiries, including first class return postage, should be sent to the GUN DIGEST Editorial Offices, Krause Publications, 700 E. State Street, Iola, WI 54990-0001. All materials received will receive reasonable care, but we will not be responsible for their safe return. Material accepted is subject to our requirements for editing and revisions. Author payment covers all rights and title to the accepted material, including photos, drawings and other illustrations. Payment is at our current rates.

CAUTION: Technical data presented here, particularly technical data on the handloading and on firearms adjustment and alteration, inevitably reflects individual experience with particular equipment and components under specific circumstances the reader cannot duplicate exactly. Such data presentations therefore should be used for guidance only and with caution. Krause Publications, Inc., accepts no responsibility for results obtained using this data.

Library of Congress Catalog Number: 0072-9043

ISBN: 0-87349-832-1

Designed by Patsy Howell, Paul Birling and Tom Nelsen
Edited by Ken Ramage

Printed in the United States of America

TWENTY-THIRD ANNUAL

JOHN T. AMBER LITERARY AWARD

John C. Dougan

John C. Dougan in the Ruger Collector's Association display during the 2004 NRA Show in Pittsburgh, Pennsylvania.

John Dougan has won the prestigious John T. Amber Award for his article *"William Batterman Ruger,"* a work meticulously researched and published in the GUN DIGEST 2004, 58TH EDITION.

Born in Amarillo, Texas in 1945, Dougan was fascinated at an early age with guns, gun designs and gun history. Visits to Rock Island Arsenal, Connecticut State Library, Wooloroc, John M. Davis Gun Museum and other renowned firearm collections only served to intensify this interest.

In 1966, he focused on Rugers and, in the following years, assembled a collection of early Ruger guns, artifacts, photographs and research material of national reputation.

He is the President of the Ruger Collectors' Association and long-time Endowment Member of the National Rifle Association. Winner of the 1980 Ross Memorial Literary Award, Dougan has written a continuing series of articles for the *Ruger Collectors' Journal* and has played a key role in Ruger collecting, beginning in the late 1960s.

Mr. Dougan has written for the *American Rifleman*; other writings include several monographs on Ruger firearms and at least four definitive volumes on Ruger single-action revolver history and collecting.

Dougan resides with his wife Nina in El Paso, Texas and is conservator of a comprehensive research library of Ruger material and documents. He has meticulously assembled an advanced collection of Ruger Corp. tools, early autos and single-action revolvers with prototypes and factory-engraved guns dating from 1946 to 1963.

The only juried literary award in the firearms field, the John T. Amber Award replaced the Townsend Whelen Award originated by the late John T. Amber and later re-named in his honor. Now, a $1,000 prize goes to the winner of this annual award.

Nominations for the competition are made by GUN DIGEST Editor Ken Ramage and are judged by a distinguished panel of editors experienced in the firearms field. Entries are evaluated for felicity of expression and illustration, originality and scholarship, and subject importance to the firearms field.

This year's Amber Award nominees, in addition to Dougan, were:

- **Ken Aiken**, *"Bootleg Pistols"*
- **Christopher R. Bartocci**, *"Combat Cartridges of the 20th Century"*
- **Toby Bridges**, *"Evolution of the...High-Performance Muzzleloader"*
- **C. E. "Doc" Ellis**, *"Random Observations...in the Communist Bloc"*
- **Hollis M. Flint**, *"The Winchester Model 12 Heavy Duck Gun"*
- **Jim Foral**, *" The Truth About the 1903 Palma"*
- **Jim Foral**, *"Hudson-Krag Handloads"*
- **M. Kluever/Boots Reynolds**, *"The Lost Sport of Dump Rat Shooting"*
- **George J. Layman**, *"The Maynard Single-Shot Rifle..."*
- **John Sundra/Terry Wieland**, *"Short Magnums: Pro & Con"*

Serving as judges for this year's competition were John D. Acquilino, editor of *Inside Gun News*; Bob Bell, former editor-in-chief of *Pennsylvania Game News*; James W. Bequette, editorial director of Primedia's outdoor group; David Brennan, editor of *Precision Shooting*; Sharon Cunningham, director of Pioneer Press; Pete Dickey, former technical editor of *American Rifleman*; Jack Lewis, former editor and publisher of *Gun World*; Bill Parkerson, former editor of *American Rifleman*, now director of research and information for the National Rifle Association, and Dave Petzal, executive editor of *Field & Stream*.

Introduction

AS THIS EDITION of GUN DIGEST was coming together, I was (again) struck by an appreciation that our shooting sports industry and rather diverse activity is a subtly complex blend of heritage, hardware and circumstance. Each time I come to that realization, there's a moment's recognition, followed by a sense of enrichment. Although I have a reasonably good library of arms and outdoor books *(and have read nearly all of them)*, in no small aspect it is working with the authors who contribute to GUN DIGEST that stimulates new lines of thought for me and, I hope, for you, the reader.

For example, just under a century ago, a debate raged from all points regarding the merits of the lever action vs. the new-fangled bolt action. The debate was waged not only on the pages of the leading national sporting publications, but at shooting ranges across the country as well. Author Jim Foral recognized this fundamental subject, then researched and reported the circumstances of the question, and the national shooting sports personalities that figured prominently in the fulminations. I think you'll enjoy reading his article, "Lever vs. Bolt." Get comfortable, it's a bit lengthy.

In the past year, there has been a certain amount of coverage by the shooting sports press of the tremendous cache of Victorian-era arms just retrieved from Nepal and now being marketed through both International Military Antiques (IMA), and Atlanta Cutlery Corp. The story of these arms is presently being researched and recorded, and a book on the subject should appear later in 2004. The author, familiar to many, is John Walter. Happily, Walter was able to share a portion of his research with us, and you'll find entertaining reading in "The Lost Guns of Nepal."

Once again we have a full color editorial section that, in part, carries the always-excellent photography of some of the finest engraved and custom guns. Rounding out that section this year, we have a well-written and nicely photographed piece by Terry Wieland, entitled " Eibar Revisited." There's just something about a Spanish side-by-side, and Wieland reports on the evolution of modern shotgun manufacturing in Eibar, and the people involved.

This past year has been a good one for new product introductions, and there are some jewels in the bunch. Luckily, our writers were able to borrow samples for a brief workout at the range. You'll find these reports in our "Test Fire" department: "The Pardner Pump," by H. Lea Lawrence (it's a good one). Next, Layne Simpson testfires Remington's new bolt-action rimfire, the Model 504 (another good one). Finally, Larry Sterett wrings out the Ruger No. 1 rifle in the 405 Winchester chambering (yet another good one).

There's more here, of course. More good articles. The GUN DIGEST contributing editors report on the latest products in their respective areas – lots of new products. The "Website Directory" has been updated. So has the catalog of commercial arms and accessories; all the reference section, in fact.

Next year, it's the 60th Anniversary Edition. Mark your calendar: July 2005.

Ken Ramage, Editor

Editorial Comments and Suggestions

We're always looking for feedback on our books. Please let us know what you like about this edition. If you have suggestions for articles you'd like to see in future editions, please contact.

Ken Ramage/Gun Digest
700 East State St.
Iola, WI 54990
email: ramagek@krause.com

About Our Covers...

Two new Ruger pistols appear on the covers of this 59th edition of GUN DIGEST. At first glance, both are familiar, particularly the 22; at second glance, significant differences appear.

Mark III Rimfire Pistol

The company regards the Ruger Standard Pistol, introduced in 1951, as the foundation upon which all else has been built. This year, 2004, Ruger introduces the Mark III generation of the Standard Pistol with significant changes. The first model to be produced is the MKIII512, and this gun appears on our covers.

(Front cover)

While clearly related to the Standard, Mks. I and II, the Mk. III model introduces several welcome and functional refinements.

First, the magazine release has been moved from the base of the pistol butt to the left side of the frame, behind the trigger guard. This refinement puts the release button in a very handy location and will be especially welcome by shooters accustomed to centerfire auto-pistols, the 1911-style family in particular.

Second, along the left side of the receiver lies the innovative loaded chamber indicator, the first to appear on a 22-rimfire pistol. *(Note, this feature, and others, can also be found on the new Mark III models in Ruger's 22/45 rimfire pistol line.)*

Finally, other new features appearing on the Mk III pistols include: recontoured micro-adjustable sights and ejection port, magazine disconnect, and an unobtrusive lock.

Our cover gun is of blued steel, with a 5 1/2-inch bull barrel and checkered synthetic grips. Attached to the top of the frame is the Weaver-style scope base adapter furnished with this model. A nice touch is that the iron sights can be effectively used with the scope base attached. Two 10-round magazines accompany each gun, as well as the usual Ruger inclusions.

P345 Autoloading Pistol

The other gun is one of the new KP345 pistols, a trim and shooter-friendly polymer-frame model chambered for the 45 ACP cartridge. The checkered grip has been slimmed and recontoured to improve handling characteristics, immediately noticeable upon picking up the pistol. The stainless steel slide has also been recontoured to reduce weight.

The P345 pistols include several important features: the loaded-chamber indicator, magazine disconnect, an unobtrusive internal lock, and a new camblock design helps absorb recoil.

The KP345 on the cover is one of two versions to be introduced at this time. The other, designated KP345PR, is similar in all respects to our cover gun–plus it has a molded-in Picatinny-style accessory rail under the front end of the frame to allow mounting popular pistol accessories, such as laser sights and lights.

The P345 on our covers has a black polymer frame mated to a slide and barrel of stainless steel. Sights are of the fixed, white-dot variety and the unloaded weight is reported at just under two pounds. Two 8-round magazines accompany each pistol, plus a gun lock, literature and storage case.

Both the Mk III and the P345 pistols should be available at your gunshop when you read this.

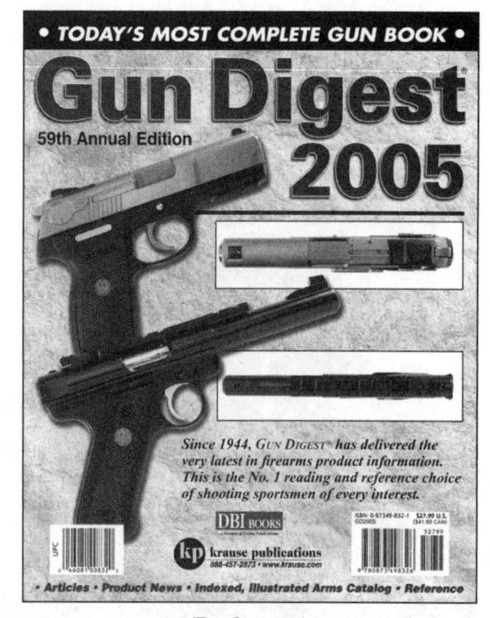

(Back cover)

Gun Digest 2005

The World's Greatest Gun Book

CONTENTS

Page 28

Page 49

REPORTS FROM THE FIELD:

Page 160

Page 206

CATALOG OF ARMS AND ACCESSORIES

Lever vs. Bolt

The debate that bred and nourished one of the most interesting chapters in the history of American arms and ammunition.

by Jim Foral

"It were best that we should not all think alike. It is difference of opinion that makes horse races."

THIS OFT-QUOTED observation of Mark Twain, like most profound quotations, is little more than a gross oversimplification. The opposition of viewpoints is foundational to every conflict in the history of mankind. Difference of opinion is the root source of social and domestic discord and division and its heart-wrenching ripple effect. It remains the core excuse for each religious offshoot ever manufactured and every war ever fought. It is at the cornerstone of politics and law and seems to be the justification for the glut of American lawyers. And difference of opinion is wholly responsible for igniting and fueling a lively exchange in the early years of the sporting press. Let's go back.

From several standpoints, the 1909-1915 era was an interesting stretch. The schuetzen game was still alive. Blackpowder cartridges still had many adherents but were rapidly being phased out. The smokeless powder line was in a perpetual state of expansion and improvement. Independent experimenters had shattered the 3000 fps muzzle velocity barrier with their contrived necked-down cartridges. Older six-gun shooters who had instructed their sons on a cap and ball Colt raised graying eyebrows at the slab-sided Army pistols that loaded themselves. It was an exciting time to be a "crank", the label the gun enthusiast of 90 years ago preferred.

Nestled between the "Moose Hunt in New Brunswick" -type feature articles and the classified advertisements of the outdoor magazines was found the "Arms and Ammunition" column. These columns were editorially intended to be a medium for the exchange and discussion of views, and afforded cranks the opportunity to comment on gun-related matters. The writers and readers contributed articles, letters and other input.

Given the nature and intent of the columns, many interesting opinions concerning all phases of the shooting sports were offered. Naturally, the offering of one man's opinion will automatically invite one of a conflicting nature. The columns, seeking to advance both sides, printed letters and articles from those not in complete agreement.

From time to time, a minor controversy would flare up, occasionally persisting for several issues. In 1912,when the Savage Company introduced the then-new 22 High-Power cartridge in its lever-action Model 1899 rifle, there were followers who viewed it as the shape of things to come—and a sure-fire killer. Others viewed it as a passing fancy and a game-crippler. A well-mannered and disciplined spat ensued—extending the scope of the discussion to include big-bore versus small-bore––but quickly died out. In 1910, the column was host to a mini-feud over the merits of the 12-gauge over 20-gauge as an all-round upland shotgun gauge. While of longer duration, it too was short-lived. A series of articles concerning the "satisfactory game bullet" involved several contributors who seldom shared the same views was printed, but didn't last long.

In 1909, an innocent discussion was beginning to snowball into a full-fledged feud that would occupy space in the columns for the next three years. What began as a friendly exchange quickly evolved into the ugliest row in the history of the sporting press. The multi-faceted, frequently heated discussion—commonly known as the Bolt versus Lever debate.

It began innocently enough. It probably started with a simple statement that the bolt action (or the lever action) was a better sporting rifle than the lever action (or bolt action). As nearly as I've been able to determine, the altercation had its beginnings in late 1908. As often happened in the columns, a statement was made, then objected to, and then defended. By the summer of 1910, a full-scale feud had developed. Letters poured into various magazines, and editors printed what was offered. *Outdoor Life* was the principal magazine used in the discussion, but the editors of *Outers'* permitted the readers to discuss their views on its pages with almost as much freedom. *Arms and The Man*, the forerunner of the *American Rifleman,* allowed a good deal of space and the controversy also spilled over to *Field and Stream* on a very limited basis. By winter of 1910, the Bolt-Lever debate occupied most of the "Arms and Ammunition" column of *Outdoor Life.*

There were four principal combatants. Bolt-action advocate Edward C. Crossman of Los Angeles was a well-rounded crank. Though a champion trap shooter, he was most notably a rifleman. He captured the California State High-Power Rifle Championship in 1907, the same year he started as a magazine columnist. Crossman was a gifted, articulate and prolific writer and reviewer, but a lot of folks took exception to his cross-grained personality. Crossman was deservedly known as "America's Foremost Firearms Authority".

Lt. Townsend Whelen was a pillar in the gunwriting trade. He began his long writing career about 1905, and quickly won both the universal respect of his peers and the profound admiration of his readership. In 1911, Whelen was an Army officer stationed at Fort Jay, New York.

Judging from the abundance of kind–almost reverent–words about him, one can sense a public perception of Whelen as nearly deified; a wingless angel, with a dim halo suspended over his campaign hat. A gentleman who stood mainly above a fray, Lt. Whelen nevertheless supported the bolt action.

Defending the lever action was Ashley A. Haines, a well-liked writer of the day, who lived in the remote British Columbia Rockies, *"miles and miles from the nearest general store."* Haines was a hard and lean logger, farmer, and backwoodsman. More importantly, he was a subsistence hunter, and a user of rifles. He had the practical experience to qualify his opinions, and relied upon his 1886 and 1895 Winchester lever-guns. Haines was a natural-born writer and storyteller.

Captain E. C. Crossman, 1919.

If Haines needed a hand defending the lever action, there was no one more capable than lawyer Chas. Newton of Buffalo, New York. A far-gone rifle crank who shot only targets and woodchucks, Newton lacked the extensive hands-on experience of his associate, but compensated with other significant qualifications. He was a masterful wordsmith and a regular columnist for *Outdoor Life* with a huge following. Newton was rightfully regarded as this country's foremost amateur ballistician.

Ashley Haines observed that bolt-action rifles used as sporting weapons accounted for less than one percent of the total. This is not to suggest that there was not a variety of bolt guns to select from.

Such guns as the Winchester-Lee Straight Pull, the almost unheard-of Remington-Lee, *(which Haines was fond of and Whelen called a "failure in the bolt-action line")*, and the Mannlicher-Schoenauer rifles were available. There was an abundance of Krags and Springfields, which could be purchased through an NRA-affiliated rifle club. The surplus Spanish War Mausers were a flood on the market. Sporterized Springfields by the "name" makers, such as Wundhammer, Adolph, and Pachmayer were just beginning to catch on. Many cranks did their own remodeling of Springfields, Krags, and Mausers, and pictures of the amateur handiwork were published periodically in the columns. Commercial Mauser sporters were gaining in popularity at the time. They were generally accepted as strong, well-built, and superbly finished. They were regarded by many of the affluent sportsmen as hard to beat, and a Mauser sporter was something of a status symbol.

The Canadian Ross, a wonder of the day, enjoyed a good bit of favorable press at the time. It was an expensive rifle, $55 in 1914, and sometimes difficult to obtain. Still, many a lad in knee pants daydreamed of owning one. The dispute began in earnest with a report in the May and June 1909 issues of *Outers Book*. Newton accused Crossman of starting it in an article in *National Sportsman.* Newton and Crossman had been invited by the editor of *Outers* to present both sides of the bolt-lever disagreement, in the hopes of airing it and coming to a swift conclusion. Each writer submitted a carbon copy of his manuscript to the other, so that the opposing view might be printed in the same–or next–issue.

Crossman told his readers that since American people were "creatures of habit," with a "strange dislike to try new things," the bolt-action rifle hadn't caught on, and offered this as the only explanation why people still clung to the "antiquated" lever-gun. Newton, in the July and August issues, pointed out to Crossman and the readers that the bolt action had been around for many years, and that the Franco-German war of 1870 was fought with bolt-action rifles by both sides. The Remington-Lee, the Blake, and the Winchester-Hotchkiss rifles had been available for several years. Newton suggested the reason for their failure to gain acceptance by a rifle-shooting public–despite the efforts of the two greatest rifle factories, Remington and Winchester, to popularize the bolt action–was simply because they were bolt actions. America had used lever actions for too long to try anything new.

Responding to Crossman's accusation that lever actions were constantly prone to jamming problems, Newton stated that he had never had the trouble with a lever action, but had encountered it at times with a Krag, and the Springfield rifle. Newton slyly added that he'd had several misfires in his Krag and Springfield due to not pressing the bolt handle in a fully-closed position, and had *"no such trouble with the lever action."*

Crossman made a point of alleged superiority of the bolt action in its *"simplicity and ease of dismounting."* Newton allowed that if one was talking from the standpoint of taking the rifle entirely apart, the bolt action was clearly superior. However, if we were considering breaking down the rifle for ease of transport, it was hard to beat the lever-action Winchesters in their takedown versions. Newton closed his discussion of this aspect with the words *"Rifles are made to use, not to take apart and put together again."*

Crossman argued sensibly that the bolt action could be cleaned from the breech. Newton countered that the takedown lever action could also be cleaned from the breech, and required a shorter cleaning rod. In summary, Newton pointed out that the selection of action was largely one of personal taste, and freely admitted that each action type has its points of superiority–and drawbacks.

Fairly early in the scrap both factions agreed that their arguments should be confined to the Model 1895 Winchester as the lever action to be compared with any bolt-action rifle. The '95 was chambered for cartridges of high intensity, such as the 30-06, 30-40 Krag, 35 Winchester and 405 Winchester. Performance and pressure of the ammunition compared closely to the chamberings in the then-available bolt-action rifles. Curiously, both Haines and Newton felt the 1886 Winchester was sufficiently strong, and compared favorably to the '95 in terms of strength and reliability. Both conceded, however, that available chamberings for the '86 were not on the same high-pressure level as were the cartridges for the '95, or current bolt actions. The Winchester 1894, as well as its Savage and Marlin counterparts, used cartridges of the 30-30 class, unequal to the 30-06 and the 57mm series of Mauser cartridges. As E.C. Crossman said; *"we find it finally closes into a comparison of the best of the bolt guns and the best of the lever guns which handle cartridges of high concentration as used by the bolt tribe."*

Ashley A. Haines circa 1910, at about 25 to 35 years of age. He was a staunch advocate of the lever-action rifle. ***Stanley Haines photo.***

By the fall of 1909, it was plain the atmosphere in the columns is getting a little warm, and the attacks that heretofore had been confined to the actions, are now taking a different, more personal direction. Critical of Newton's article in the previous month's *Outers*, Crossman states in the October 1909 *Outers* that he *"was unable to find anything that seems to me to accord with the facts."* And here is where Crossman proceeded to confuse the mechanism of the Remington-Lee with the British service rifle, the Lee-Enfield. Newton used the confusion to good advantage: *"Why Mr. Crossman should make the above deliberate misstatement, I am at a loss to understand."*

Crossman further stumbles when he claimed the lever-action rifle had been tested by Ordnance Boards and found to be lacking in strength. Newton asked to be referred to the Ordnance Report "of any nation" who tested the Winchester 1886 model "universally conceded to be the strongest of the lever-action rifles," and accused Crossman of making unqualified "misleading" statements.

The balance of Newton's five-page article was devoted, in the main, to nit-picking Crossman's previously published statements

The 1903 Springfield bolt-action rifle.

that seemed, to him, to be conflicting. Newton found himself defending his own assertions that Crossman advanced and also labeled "misleading." Something that must have really irritated Newton was Crossman's complaint that Newton *"harks continually back to the 1886 Winchester."* Newton pled guilty, for the reason that he considered the '86 to be the *"best of it's type."*

In addition, Crossman said much about the suitability of the British-Lee and the Remington-Lee for military purposes. Newton reaffirmed to Crossman, and whoever might be reading, that the purpose of the series of articles was to discuss the relative merits of the two action types for sporting purposes only. It seems that the viewpoint of the militarist was continually rearing up throughout the entire scrap, always advanced by the bolt-action camp, and the opposing lever-action bunch needed to perpetually remind them of the limited scope of the discussion. As Chas. Newton proclaimed, *"Pick an issue, and stay with it."*

In a closing statement, Newton again offered that the question of bolt action versus lever action resolved itself into a matter of opinion. Also, while he realized that controversies between contributors were wearisome and generally uninteresting, he apologized to the readers for consuming so much space. According Crossman the last word, Newton called the matter closed.

In Crossman's conclusion, he concurred with Mr. Newton on the length of the discussion being dragged out to a "tiresome degree." As to the matter of action choice being one of personal taste, we at last find both writers in agreement.

Crossman also fully expected that any further discussion was unnecessary, and that his last word would be *"the last word"*. But there were others who would also be heard.

In defense of his favorite bolt action, Whelen, in the January 1911 *Outdoor Life,* presented an illustration of the comparative strengths of the bolt- and lever-bolt supporting mechanisms, known and referred to as "Whelen's vise theory". Whelen tells his readers that Figure 1 *"represents a steel bar held in an extremely strong vise". In cut "A," the top of the bar projects about three inches. Consider the vise strong enough to stand any blow. Now take a heavy sledgehammer and strike the bar in cut "A" on its upper end. What happens? The end of the bar may be slightly upset, but otherwise it stands it without injury. Similarly strike the bar in cut "B" and the vise holding fast; if the blow being heavy enough, the three-inch bar of steel will buckle, bend, or split. Now the bar in Cut "A" approximates the way in which the bolt of the Mauser is supported by two heavy locking lugs at its forward end. The bar in Cut "B", on the other hand, represents the method of supporting the breech bolt in lever-action rifles, the locking bolt being from 2 5/8 to 4 1/8 inches from the head of the bolt. It, therefore, is clearly seen that the supporting of the bolt at its head is by far the stronger method. Score one for the bolt action."*

Ashley Haines responded in the same issue that while Whelen was correct in supposing that a bar of steel in a vise would bend, or spring, when struck with a sledge, the bar of steel does not properly represent a bolt- to a lever-action rifle. Moreover, it did not represent what would happen when the rifle was fired.

Reader F. W. Woods wasn't in agreement with the lieutenant's vise theory, and remarked that it was the *"poorest article ever printed from the lieutenant's pen"*. Woods explained that the *"strength of the breech is not found in the strength of the breech bolt, but in the means utilized to lock the bolt in place."* This fact, according to Woods, should be self-evident to *"any man presuming to have anything gray inside his skull."*

Townsend Whelen in his element, at the range during the summer of 1916.

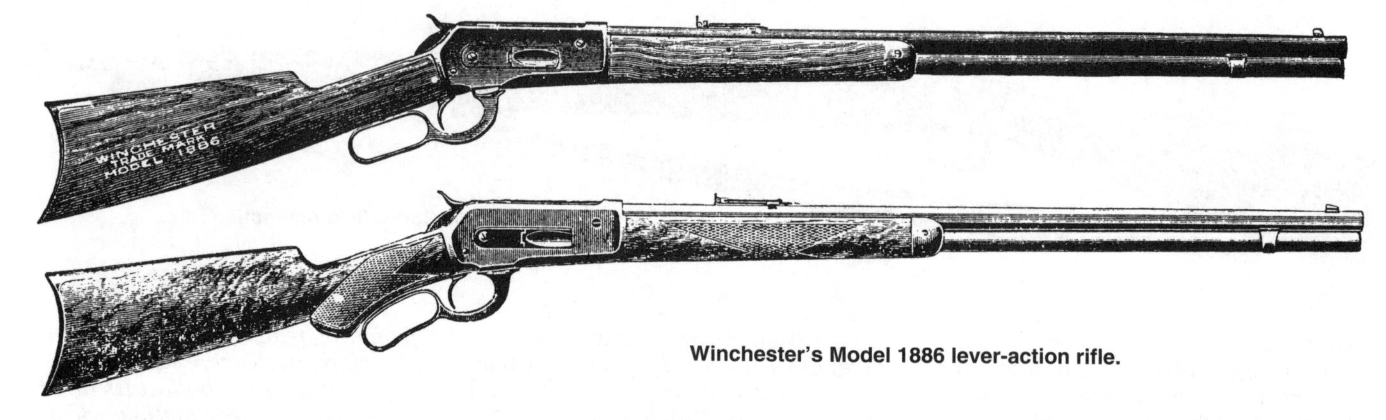

Winchester's Model 1886 lever-action rifle.

An incident occurred at the annual National Matches at Camp Perry in the summer of 1910 that provided the lever-action supporters with some much-needed ammunition. Seven bolts of the service Springfield rifle suffered fractures of the bolt lugs, causing the lugs to break off. An account in the February 1911 issue of *Arms and The Man* of an additional three bolts failing in the same fashion left the bolt-action boys with some explaining to do. An *Arms and The Man* editorial note following the article said: *"Evidently these rifles were of a small lot which were too hard when they were sent out."*

Chas. Newton, in a 1911 article, while allowing that it would be unfair to condemn a design for a lone failure, seven identical failures *"demonstrate clearly that the design of the rifle is weak when it comes to resisting the strain imposed by the explosion of the shell."*

Ashley Haines mentioned the incident in passing, hopeful that Whelen would respond. He did. Whelen, pointing out that no shooters were injured, suggested that if a like number of '95 Winchesters were subjected to the same "strenuous ammunition" *(some of the match loads developed 52,000 psi)*, the rate of failure would be the same or greater. Then he went on to another topic. Crossman, from all indications, sat this one out.

The Ross Model 10 straight-pull rifle, from a 1910 catalog.

Whelen felt that certain guidelines should be drawn as to the essentials of the action of any repeating rifle.

Foremost, he believed, the action should be safe. The bolt action he advocated, the new Springfield and the Mauser, had bolts and receiver vented to allow the escape of gas in the event of a pierced primer or overcharged cartridge. Pointing out the fact that the '95 Winchester was the only lever action similarly vented, Whelen proclaimed *"a standoff"* in this respect. Chas. Newton interpreted Whelen's comments about the '95 Winchester as a recognition of the fact that the '95 was amply safe, and had a sufficient margin for safety, *"which is all we care for in this direction."* Using the Camp Perry incident to good advantage, Newton professed that the "much vaunted" system of locking a rifle at the front end of the bolt was a source of weakness, rather than strength. Newton invited input from a mechanical engineer on the subject, and until such time as he could be proven wrong, Newton insisted that the *"ultimate strength of either the 1886 or 1895 Winchester actions was decidedly superior to that of the Springfield."*

(Ashley Haines took an immediate offense to Whelen's vise theory. He wrote that since the bolts of the levér actions are strongly supported their entire length by the walls of the receiver and can't bend or spring or do *"any of the unreasonable things the bolt-action advocates would have us believe."*)

Secondly, Whelen tells us, it should be sure-fire. Whelen supported the theory that bolt is superior to lever in this regard by the measurement of weight to compress the mainspring of the individual rifles. The Springfield and Mauser require twelve-to-eighteen pounds of pressure to accomplish this compression, while the '95 Winchester required a mere six-to-ten pounds. Reasoning that *"A heavy blow certainly insures a surer ignition of the primer than does a light blow,"* Whelen felt the bolt action should be allowed first place in this essential. Several misfires with lever-actions were pointed out also, due to a piece of twig or other debris caught between the face of the hammer and the rear end of the breech bolt. Whelen maintained that such misfires could only have occurred in a lever action, as there was no such lodging place in a bolt rifle.

Haines, on the other hand, saw the reduced effort required to cock a '95 Winchester as an advantage, noting *"the arm is that much easier to manipulate."* Newton's response was in his typical sarcastic fashion. While he had never seen a rifle fired by compressing the mainsprings, he tells us, he is *"most familiar with those fired by the blow of the firing pin upon the primer, due to the release of the mainspring."* He adds that if the blow isn't powerful enough, simply turn the strain screw under the mainspring a little tighter, *"and all will be well."*

Thirdly, Whelen told his 1911 readers, the arm should positively extract and eject the fired shell. An illustration of the extractive devices of a bolt action and a lever action was included in the text demonstrating that the extractor of the bolt action (Figure A) had nearly four times the surface area of the lever action (Figure B) and using Whelen's reasoning, four times *"as secure a grip on the head of the shell as has the lever action."*

Whelen additionally concedes that sticky, oversized, or reloaded cartridges are much more positively chambered or withdrawn from the chamber of a bolt action than that of a lever action. Extraction in a bolt action is aided by the use of the camming effect of the bolt handle and rotating the bolt. Should a shell stick in a lever-action chamber, Whelen maintains *"the rifle becomes a club incapable of other use."* In his January 1911, rebuttal to Lt. Whelen's criticisms of the lever action, Ashley Haines admits that the extractors of the lever-action rifles could be improved if they were made wider. However, since he uses only factory, and properly handloaded, ammunition in his lever-guns, faulty extraction hadn't been a problem.

Being very brief, Newton falls just short of giving up the positive ejection issue by default, and never addressed the sticky case or faulty handload matter at all. He explained that the '95 Winchester extractor was plenty strong enough, but if it is ever found to be too narrow, it can easily be made wider.

Robert Kane, the "Arms and Ammunition" editor for *Outers Book*, was one of the few Crossman defenders. This photo of Kane fiddling with a Savage Model 1914 22 rimfire appeared in the August, 1914 issue of *Outers*.

Fourth, the rifle should surely load, without undue effort, succeeding cartridges from the magazine into the chamber. The closing movement of the bolt action, forcing the cartridge home in the chamber, is performed by a cam having much more power than the lever action. Whelen told his readers that the cam motion of the bolt is so powerful that it will actually resize the shell, and that the principles involved are similar to those of the Model 1894 Winchester and Ideal reloading tool, which employed the mechanical principles of a cam. Whelen felt that positive, reliable feeding in the lever action was entirely dependent on perfect factory ammunition. The lieutenant proceeded at some length with a description of some tests, using a much-reduced load with Ideal cast bullet #308241 and 11 grains of Marksman powder in a Winchester '95 chambered for the 30-40 Krag cartridge.

Fired shells stuck in the chamber, and the extractor had to cut through, or ride over, the rim of the shells. A cleaning rod and a hammer were needed to withdraw the empty shells. Twenty shots were fired, and *"the action did not extract a single shell."* In Whelen's Krag rifle, the same shells and loads loaded and extracted *"perfectly."* These tests, Whelen concluded, clearly show that the *"bolt action leads,"* at least in this regard.

Newton agreed with Whelen that the cam movement of the Mauser-type of rifle was more positive than the action of the lever rifle, and concluded his brief rebuttal by saying that *" this writer personally prefers a rifle in which speed and ease of operation is not interfered with by an attempt to combine it with a resizing die."*

In dealing with Whelen's experiences with stuck cases in the '95 30-40 rifle, Newton had this to say: *"If that is the kind of shells a sportsman intends using, I should earnestly suggest that he obtain a bolt-action rifle.... or an 1894 loading tool with its resizing capability."*

Intermingled with his responses to Whelen's guidelines, Haines pointed out several quotations

In 1911, lots of guys were getting interested in sporterized Springfields, like S. E. White's Wundhammer sporter shown here in the June, 1911 issue of *Outers*.

Recruited to the lever-action cause by Haines, Ad Topperwein demonstrated the speed of the lever-gun and appeared in the November, 1911 issue of *Outdoor Life*.

from Whelen's previous articles, and compared them to the content of Whelen's January 1911, *Outdoor Life* article. Clearly, Haines was attempting to show that the lieutenant had contradicted himself. Although his remarks were not especially caustic, Haines' obvious frustration and exasperation were very much in evidence. In an altogether uncharacteristic display of anger, Haines lashed out at those–to include Whelen–who would fault the gun for misbehaving, jamming, failing to extract, etc., and not the gun's operator. *"... the gun is at fault, or the factory that made it; the man behind the gun–NEVER! This last man's* (Whelen) *experiences frequently gets in the magazines - but the man who has been around the world and back again and has no trouble from his lever- action—well, you hear very little concerning him, or especially his rifle. There, I'm really ashamed to have written in the above strain, but I have seen firearms abused so much and then so unjustly criticized and by just such men as I had in mind that - well, I couldn't help it. I'll venture to say that Lieut. Whelen has had his blood near the boiling point under similar conditions. If so, he'll forgive me, I'm sure."*

Feeling that he'd been dealt with rather harshly, an obviously hurt Whelen responded in the March number, entitled "A Criticism to a Criticism."

"What a lot of stuff we cranks do write. Mr. Haines and I have been good friends for years. We thought we would enjoy a friendly spat and the editor agreed."

In a refreshingly courteous manner, Whelen adds that he was a *"little disappointed,"* and that Haines had incorrectly estimated the spirit of the article. Turning his attention to the alleged contradictory statements, Whelen said he failed to find any that were *"glaringly contradictory,"* but wisely handled his situation. *"The world moves; we gain more experience as we go on, and it would be strange indeed, if as our experience grows our views did not change to quite a marked extent."*

A conspicuous and openly acknowledged kinship existed among the readers of these "Arms and Ammunition" columns. These were kindred souls, bound by a mutual attraction, who–as often as not–addressed one another as "Brother". There was *camaraderie*. Townsend Whelen noted the mood and referred to our ancestral brethren as *"a rifle fraternity."*

Without question, Crossman and Newton had an intense mutual dislike for one another, and through their writings, came as close to blows as their typewriters and 3000 miles would allow.

Newton wrote endlessly detailing Crossman's contradictions in describing and extolling the Ross rifle, pinpointing inaccuracies in his published

Winchester's Model 1895 lever-action rifle.

statements, and generally downgrading Crossman's experience and authority. In the May, 1912 issue of *Outdoor Life*, Newton wrote that *"... the measure of Mr. Crossman's acquaintance with the twin goddesses of Truth and Veracity is so well known that anyone expecting to find him in their company has but himself to blame for his disappointment."* Elsewhere we find that Newton charged *"... the printed word over the X-Man signature, had failed, most decidedly, to accord with the facts."* The same issue contains an article by Crossman that accuses Newton of *"... deliberately misleading the public."*

Newton used his polished skills as a trial lawyer to undermine Crossman's credibility in a classic courtroom style. Smooth talking to his temporarily captive audience, Newton's shrewd use of the language gave the readers the impression that Crossman was not the infallible expert he appeared to be, and that not every word from the pen of Crossman was some holy nugget. Doubtlessly with good effect, Newton occasionally referred to Crossman as "Eddie", "X-Man" and sarcastically "Bro. Crossman." Moreover, Newton's frequent usage of a scriptural passage, or making a point using a parable-like message, may have left a positive impression

Chauncey Thomas, Editor of *Outdoor Life* magazine.

with the readers, to the detriment and discredit of Crossman.

Robert Kane, editor of *Outers*, was one of the few defenders of Crossman. In one instance, a reader wrote that Crossman's writing was "full of lies," and wondered why a reputable magazine like *Outers* would permit Crossman's contributions. Kane chastised the reader, adding that Crossman was indeed an able and bone-fide–if somewhat controversial–authority and stressed his extensive big-game hunting and rifle match experience.

After the initial confrontation on the pages of *Outers* in 1909, Newton and Crossman went on to establish a highly personal feud that was displayed throughout the columns for the next three years. The Newton-Crossman debate extended past the bolt-lever issue to include an almost endless variety of points. While both parties were generally careful to stop just short of a direct accusation, their writing concerning one another was thick with sarcasm and insinuation, and reeked of innuendo. Newton was certainly not without his critics. Townsend Whelen disagreed violently with Newton on certain areas of interior ballistics. Among the other notables who took Newton to task were Ned Roberts and the Doctors Mann and Hudson.

Advertisements for bolt-action sporters began appearing in U. S. outdoors magazines. This sampling appeared in 1910, 1911 and 1913 issues.

The Remington-Lee bolt-action sporting rifle.

Edward Cathcart Crossman wasn't your chronic people-pleaser. While the charitable wrote *"brother"*, Crossman's pen leaked *"crack-brained," "childish," "Hottentot,"* and *"kindergartner"*. Crossman demonstrated his abrasive demeanor and unhidden maliciousness when he suggested to one critic that he should have some of the *"Maine moss curried off his spine."* Another reader was called a *"cross-eyed caloot."* The collective toes of the schuetzen shooters, which included many of America's most prominent riflemen, were trodden upon when Crossman opined that their style of shooting was *"somewhat effeminate."* Late in 1912, the editor of *Outdoor Life* published two pages of letters headlined "Candid Opinions from Tired Shooters." These letters were bitterly critical of Crossman's impoliteness, and the few printed apparently reflected the views of the mainstream reader.

"Keystone Gun Crank", a Pennsylvanian, wrote: *"E. C. Crossman was born into the gun department of various sporting magazines about 1907. Died at the hand of Chas. Newton in 1912."* He then expressed condolences to the Ross Rifle Co., *"...as it is generally conceded that Mr. X-Man was their best advertising agent and will be difficult to replace."* A Gay's Mill, Wisconsin reader wasted no words sugarcoating his feelings: *"This man Crossman should be barred from your magazine. He is unreliable, and unbelievable and insults every man who does not believe the way he does."* After being publicly chastised by the editor, articles in a less venomous vein by Crossman continued to be published in *Outdoor Life* and *Outers*. There are unconfirmed reports that he was actually barred from the pages of *Arms and The Man* for a time, as Chas. Newton reported *"for reasons of personal dignity."*

Townsend Whelen demonstrated that several well-known hunters of worldwide experience preferred the Mauser system, and left it to the reader to draw their own conclusions. Col. Roosevelt had taken a '95 Winchester in 405-caliber and a remodeled Springfield on an extended African safari and, according to Whelen, is supposed to have preferred the Springfield. Stewart Edward White, on the other hand, said of his '95 405 *"... could not get along without it... it is just the ticket and sure medicine gun for lions,"* but made mention of having killed 78 animals with one shot each with his remodeled Springfield.

Townsend Whelen, a pillar of the gunwriting trade for many years, supported the bolt-action rifle. Here, about 1938, he demonstrates proper positioning of the sling in his book, *The Hunting Rifle.*

By early 1911, Chauncy Thomas of *Outdoor Life* had decided the bolt-lever discussion had been aired to the point of exhaustion, and little could be gained from its continuance. Moreover, other interesting developments had surfaced, and space must be allowed for their discussion. He called for a closing of the feud.

However, members of both camps felt that not all aspects of the controversy had been presented sufficiently. They called for a reopening of the pages of *Outdoor Life* to the consideration of a point both sides felt was too important to ignore; the topic of rapidity of fire of the two actions. Besides, speed trials had already been published in *Arms and The Man,* and elsewhere.

One has to wonder why speed of fire was important enough to warrant re-opening an admittedly boring issue. Presumably the writers involved were unwilling to accept a defeat without a lengthy voicing of their opinions. All of the writers, at one point or another, had expressed the notion that action choice was largely one of personal taste. At this point, the controversy had become basically a standoff. With a victory in the speed trials, one side or the other had an opportunity to appear victorious. Additionally, at the closing of the scrap, no faction had been able to prove that either bolt or lever action was a failure in any major sporting consideration. No side had clearly demonstrated that their favorite action was decidedly superior to the action of the opposition, and saw an opportunity to do so in the speed comparisons.

For the most part in 1911, Americans hadn't warmed up to the auto-loading rifle, then a recent development. Automatics available at the time were underpowered, compared to the lever- and bolt-actions. Thankfully, this factor alone probably kept the autoloader from being involved in another dreaded comparison feud in the columns.

At any rate, the conductor Thomas reluctantly agreed to reopen the discussion for a time to provide an opportunity for both sides to publish results of speed trials.

Townsend Whelen evidently did not put much stock in speed comparisons, and unenthusiastically participated in the writer's trials only through the strong urging of others. In a 1911 article, Whelen admitted that a lever action could be shot faster. He was also quick to point out that there is a *"... great difference between rapidity of fire and rapidity of carefully aimed fire."*

Whelen tells his readers that a 22 lever-action can be fired faster than a 22 bolt-gun, and a 30-30 bolt-gun is a little slower than the 30-30 lever. However, due to the increased *"equilibrium disturbing"* factors caused by more powerful, higher-recoiling cartridges, the bolt action and lever action become equals in this regard at some point. Whelen maintains that both action types can be cycled in the same amount of time while recovering from stiff recoil, and sights can be aligned with equal ease or equal difficulty. The time to recover from the recoil, Whelen computed, was about a half-second. Whelen opined that the lever-action rifle lost its speed advantage at about the 30-40 level of recoil. He offered that he was the owner of three 30-40 rifles: a Krag, a '95 Winchester, and a New Springfield. *(Whelen loaded his Springfield to duplicate the Krag service charge).* Regarding the speed of the three actions, Whelen states: *"In my hands the Krag is the fastest, followed by the Winchester, with the Springfield last."* Whelen submitted his signed and witnessed speed trial report, published in the July 6, 1911, issue of *Arms And The Man*. Firing a meager 20 rounds through his Krag rifle, Whelen offered an apology: *"I am considerably out of practice at this kind of fire."* He further reported that he'd done no rapid-fire practice for the previous two and a half months.

From a standing position, Whelen fired two 5-shot strings in an average of 5-1/4 seconds, all shots hitting a 5-inch bull. The results from the prone position were exactly the same. The distance to the target was 45 feet.

The first of Ashley Haines' extensive spend trials rambled for 15 pages of the September, 1911 *Outdoor Life* magazine. To assist, he had recruited his brother and an assortment of neighbors to shoot a selection of 1886 and 1895 Winchester levers. They proceeded to fire 5-shot strings, under pressure of a stopwatch, at a target 45 feet distant. When all the data was distilled, Haines found that five cartridges could be shot through the lever actions in about 3.4 seconds; each shot hitting a dinner plate-sized mark. Accuracy with times less than three seconds suffered accordingly. Results of further testing was published in the next January and February numbers of *Outdoor Life*. Now practiced at the activity, Haines was able to reduce his time to 2.2 seconds with a 33 WCF '86 rifle.

If there was any question which brand rifle was Crossman's favorite, there was no doubt after the publication of his speed trials. The five rifles Crossman, and his associate, Lt. George Mortimer used were Ross straight-pulls, in their various available chamberings. While apologizing for the large 7-inch group sizes shot with the 35 WCF *(the model 1905 Ross was chambered for this cartridge)*, Crossman explained that the rifle weighed less than

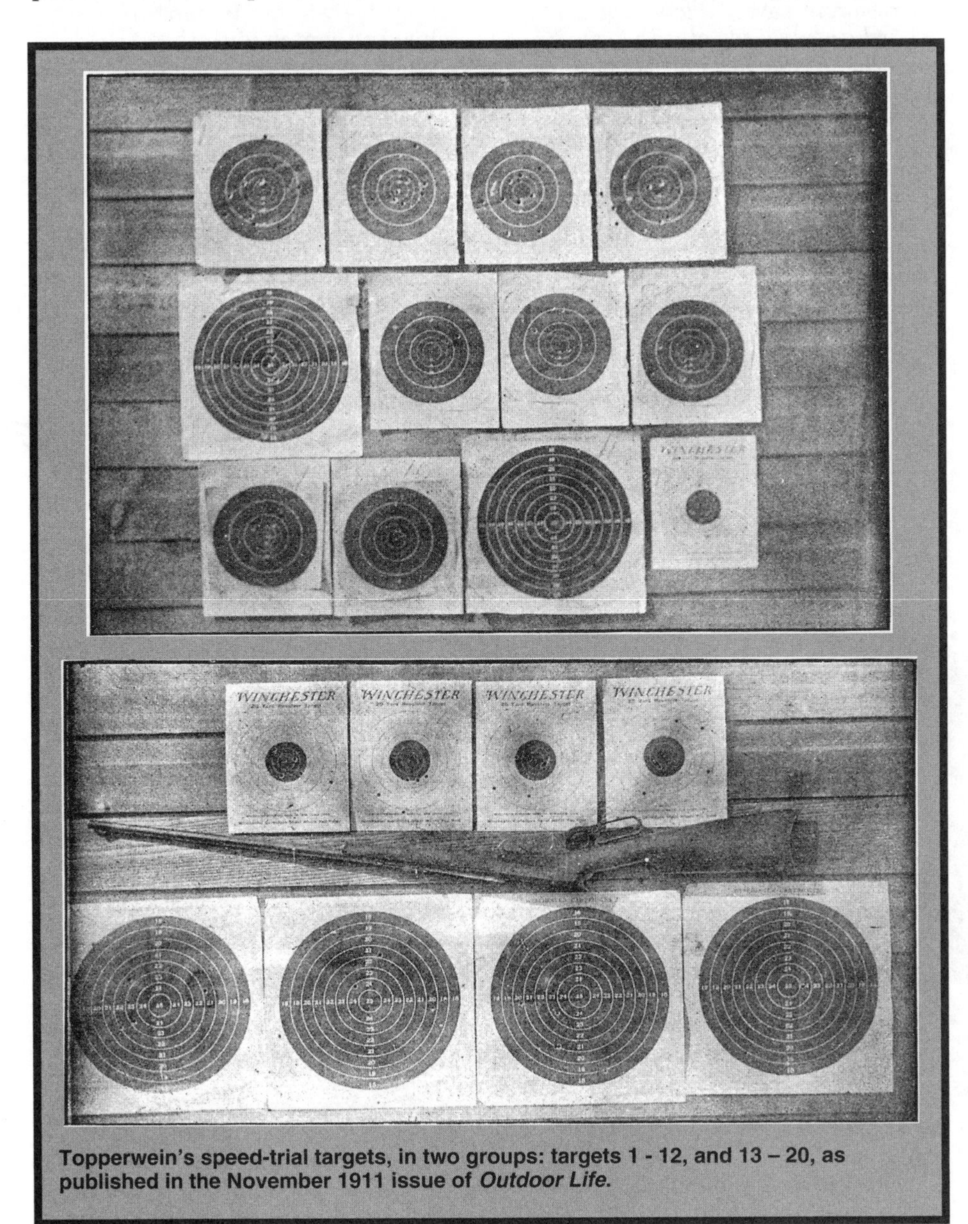

Topperwein's speed-trial targets, in two groups: targets 1 - 12, and 13 – 20, as published in the November 1911 issue of *Outdoor Life*.

Ad Topperwein in 1915.

seven pounds, and that he was *"severely bruised from recoil."* However, he was able to get off five shots in an average of three seconds for four strings. Two rifles were used in 303 British tests; one weighing seven pounds, the other eight and a half. The load, presumably military, burned cordite to launch a 215-grain bullet at 2050 feet-per-second. Several strings were fired in less than 2.5 seconds with an average group size of 7-1/2 inches. Crossman emptied the magazine of his special pet, the 280 Ross, in three seconds.

Lt. Mortimer, evidently familiar with the manipulation of a straight-pull rifle, fired the 280–five shots in 2.4 seconds–and proceeded to fire 10 shots, including reloading, in ten and a half seconds.

Injecting a bit of his typical sarcasm into the issue, Crossman mocked the earlier performance of Ashley Haines' '95 30-40 "Old Calamity", whose record was 3.2 seconds. *"Now, I'm compelled to admit that in print, those five blinding bursts from Old Calamity's red-hot throat, all done in three and a fifth seconds, sounds pretty large. But whenever they get to looming up too large, I squirt two or three strings through my 30-40 Ross, in about two and a half seconds, blinding bursts and all; then all the awe that has crept over me disappear."* Elsewhere in the article Crossman says: *"... whenever my hard lines got too strong for me, I would ramble out and shoot a few reasonably fast strings with the Ross, returning quite cheered up."*

Of the 30 strings fired for speed, only one was fired from the Springfield rifle. Again Crossman apologized for his slowness with the service rifle. He explained that he was so accustomed to the Ross of late, that he had virtually abandoned the Springfield in its favor, and was once again *"unfamiliar with the Springfield."*

Almost as if he expected some criticism, Crossman stated *"any person expressing any sneer as to the authenticity of this performance will be made to apologize."* He further made the offer to furnish the rifle, time, and ammunition to anyone desiring to witness the shooting repeated.

The proceedings were witnessed by seven members of the Los Angeles Rifle and Revolver Club, including its president, C.B. Hubbs. Shortly after the publication of Crossman's article, Ashley Haines referred to the witnesses as *"up the sleeve of the Los Angeles writer."*

Any reader expecting a reply from Newton didn't have long to wait. In an article published in *Outdoor Life*, Newton had this to say of Crossman's speed records: *"The records are not impossible.... By constant practice for a time they might be made honestly."*

In the April 11, 1911 *Arms and The Man* came a challenge to Newton from Crossman. In apparent seriousness, Crossman says: *"This is a challenge to a shooting match, admitted. It is not polite: also admitted."* Crossman urged Newton to take a '95 Winchester, 30-06, and shoot a speed test against Crossman's Springfield. Of course, Crossman added, the results would have to be verified by *"reputable witnesses."* Ordinarily not one to sidestep a challenge, Newton had a brief reply. He wanted no part in a shooting match with the "typewriter of the X-Man."

The speed trials of Chas. Newton were reported in the November 2, 1911 *Arms and The Man.*

Newton commented that there was little excuse for his speed shooting, as the brothers Haines had demonstrated conclusively what the speed possibilities of the lever action were. Newton explained that being a disciplined, deliberate shooter, and accustomed to the *"long, patient hold of the schuetzen rifleman,"* he was inexperienced at any rapid-fire work. In fact, up until September 1911, when he conducted his own speed tests, he'd never attempted to fire a second shot *"rapidly from a repeater."* Borrowing a '95 Winchester 35 WCF, Newton proceeded to the range, box of factory cartridges and stopwatch in hand. Crossman later suggested that Newton had to borrow a '95, *"Presumably because he would not own one."*

At the prescribed distance, Newton fired four strings, the average of which was 4.6 seconds. Group sizes averaged 3-1/2 inches. One string went unrecorded due to

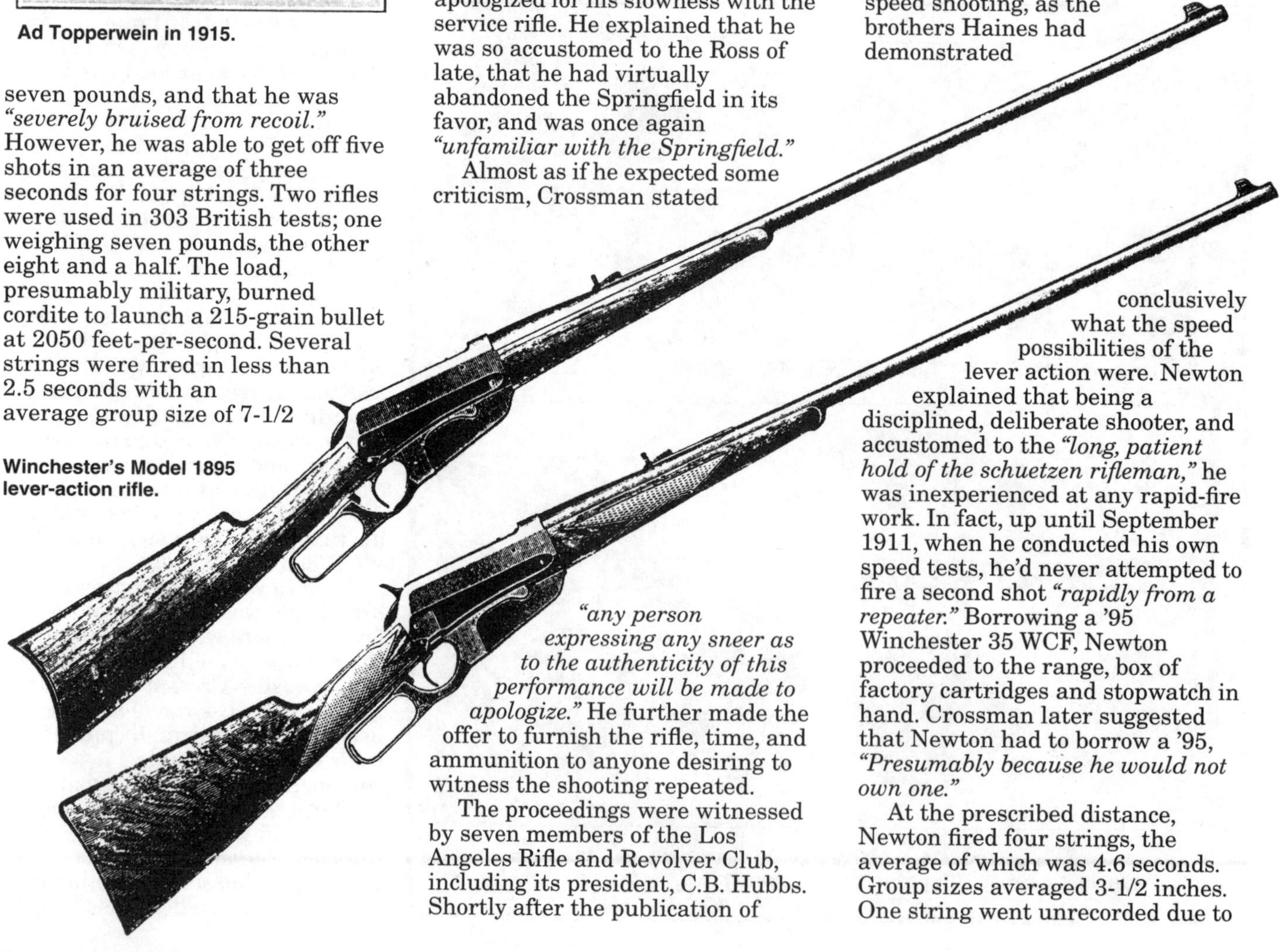

Winchester's Model 1895 lever-action rifle.

a dropped stopwatch. Newton was quick to note that while his shooting was *"no record"* it was significant in that it demonstrated what an ordinary man, totally unfamiliar with rapid-fire work, could do with an unfamiliar rifle having heavy recoil.

Possibly in an effort to emphatically impress the lever action superiority in the speed issue, Ashley Haines recruited the assistance of a "real rifleman." Batting cleanup for the lever-action boys was no less a personality than Winchester's exhibition shooter, Mr. Adolph Topperwein of San Antonio, Texas. One cannot help but wonder if "Topps" participation in the final chapter of the row was with the full endorsement of the Winchester Repeating Arms Co.

Mr. Topperwein would have gladly tested the '95 in the 30-06 chambering, but due to "Mexican troubles" *(an attempt was made to keep rifles and ammunition in a current military caliber out of the thieving hands of Mexican rebels by making them unavailable to anyone in the proximity of the Mexican border)*, he had to obtain a '95 in 30-40 from a local dealer in sporting goods.

Topperwein was comparatively unfamiliar with the 1895 model and stationary targets. The lighter-recoiling 32-20 and 44-40 lever-guns and aerial targets were the tools he preferred. Disregarding the rules, the speed tests were initiated with the 44-40 in the '92 Model, possibly anticipating the shock value of what could be done with a rifle with reduced "equilibrium disturbance."

Six groups were fired with the 44-40. Rather than the customary five shots, ten were fired with this cartridge. The average time was something under five seconds, the best being four seconds. Groups were all in the 8-9 inch range. Next, an 1894 model in 30-30 was dragged out.

Topperwein emptied five shots from this rifle in four seconds or less for the six strings fired. No group exceeded 8 inches.

The trials with the 30-40, which everyone seemed to be the most interested in, were shot at 45 feet, and at fifty yards. Times at the shorter distance were just over four seconds with 4-inch groups. At 50 yards, the stopwatch revealed an average time of just over three and a half seconds, while groups doubled in size from those fired at 45 feet.

In a closing statement, Haines invited the reader to consider Topperwein's work, and compare it to claims repeatedly made by those *"occupying prominent positions"* in the various magazines.

His last remark effectively summarized the tone of the entire bolt-lever scrap:

"Had some of the writers I have in mind devoted as much time to learning the lever gun as they have to the bolt, and been as much interested in dealing in facts – and facts they could have found for the looking – as in making statements which they could not prove, the chances are they would have been spared this report."

Supposedly, the purpose of the debate was to enlighten and educate the readership, but there may have been effects other than this.

Certainly the writers must have been aware that collectively they were influencing potential rifle buyers, especially the impressionable first-time buyer who was not yet bigoted as to action type.

Regarding a well-publicized third-hand account of an 1886 Winchester that had supposedly blown up in an Eskimo's face, Ashley Haines had this to say: *"I will venture the opinion that many inexperienced persons contemplating the purchase of a rifle, their first one, were influenced by the article in which the above statement first appeared to the extent that their money went for some other make of rifle."*

The writers were just as aware that many decisions on which rifle to buy would be based solely on the recommendation of the reader's favorite writer. One reader correctly observed that the "prominence of the author directly increases the confidence of the reader."

The gun factories were keenly aware of what was taking place in the press. Certainly the arms companies, if their lines included only bolt actions or only lever actions, had something to gain from the furthering of the feud. At one point, a disgruntled reader suggested that the arms companies were actually promoting the controversy.

Whether or not a rifle manufacturer ever influenced a writer will never be known. Newton accused Crossman of being a paid publicity agent for the Ross Rifle Co., a statement that Crossman vehemently denied. The Mannlicher and the Mauser rifles that Crossman had formerly so staunchly championed were dropped so suddenly in favor of the Ross, Newton pointed out, that Crossman must surely be on the payroll of the Ross Company.

Probably judging from his mailbag that the bolt-lever discussions end was not yet in sight, and in an apparent effort to bring the feud to a swift conclusion, Chauncy Thomas published a brief notice in the March 1912 issue.

Two examples of the Lee straight-pull rifle: the U.S. Navy model *(above)*, and *(below)* the sporting rifle.

"Strong evidence of smoldering fires in the camps of both the lever- and bolt-action enthusiasts have led us to believe it best to reopen this controversy for the period of a couple months." Contributors were urged to be brief, and Thomas hastened to add that they *"omit all unnecessary sarcasm and personal remarks from their letters"*.

A Texas reader, in an April, 1911 article in *Outdoor Life*, pointed out the popularity aspect of the discussion. While he allowed that the bolt action is universally preferred as a military weapon, *"so immense is the preponderance of lever-action rifles in the hands of hunters that there can be very little doubt that this kind of action is better adapted to the purpose than any other."*

In the May 1912 *Outdoor Life*, Brother Blaize Lorillard Harsell undoubtedly expressed the views of many when he asked: *"Why can't both sides acknowledge the good points of each? What's the use of scrapping?"* Mr. V. G. McMurry made an interesting plug for the lever action when he wrote in 1912: *"I have several times asked British officers, and men in the Army of India why they used American lever-action rifles for sporting purposes to so great an extent, and was always answered,* 'They are more handy and speedy for quick work.' *This from men who daily handled bolt-action rifles in their soldiering work."*

In the minds of many, the bolt/lever dispute was a hair-splitting absurdity. A fair percentage of readers who felt that the Army's adopting of the Colt 45 autoloader marked the beginning of the end of any hand-functioning arm, saw the march of progress headed in a beeline for the self-loading weapon.

Paul Jacklin wrote in April of 1912 that his favorite rifle, the Winchester-Lee Straight Pull, could be fired *"faster than any lever-gun made."*

Two shooters discovered virtues in both actions that were apparently overlooked by the principal writers. Early in 1912, George Brooks, and "Fair Play," a Texan, locked pens in a micro-feud of their own which endured for two issues of *Outdoor Life*.

Brooks contended that the lever-action rifle is difficult to load in the prone position. "Fair Play" responded: *"This has little weight from a sporting viewpoint."*

Brooks particularly stressed the "general beauty" of the Mauser. This beauty evidently was not in

Ashley A. Haines, wearing his 38 Special Colt revolver, with lynx in 1906.

***Outers Book*, February 1914 carried this photo of E. C. Crossman on Catalina Island with slain maverick goat.**

This photo of Crossman at the range, firing the 333 Jeffries Mauser, appeared in *Outers Book*, March 1916.

the eye of the beholder "Fair Play." He says: *"Yet the top of the action is so irregular and cut up, there being four different levels, that when sighting, it's like looking over a relief map of British Columbia."*

Brother Brook was critical of the standard crescent butt of the '95 Winchester, and complained that recoil was especially harsh with this type buttplate. The advice from "Fair Play" was to order the optional shotgun butt that was available "without extra charge."

Sand and dirt will not clog the bolt action to the degree it would bind the lever action, Brooks maintains. "Fair Play" responded that the locking lug recesses of the bolt action receiver is a favorite retreat for dirt and debris, and once there *"as hard to remove as it would be for you to fill your own teeth satisfactorily."*

Brooks said that the '95 Winchester can be loaded but one cartridge at a time, while the Springfield, Mauser, and the Ross could be loaded by means of a clip. He was reminded by "Fair Play" that this was a military and not a sporting consideration.

Evidently, Brooks liked nothing at all about the '95. He even attacked the method of attaching sights on Winchester barrels. *"Notching a barrel makes it whip, and weakens it,"* he claims. Sauer-Mausers and Ross rifles in comparison had their sights attached to the barrels by means of bands or collars.

The long lever and protruding magazine make the '95 unhandy to carry on the shoulder, Brooks maintained. He further stated that when the '95 is carried in the "travel arms" position, the balance is too far to the rear.

The '95 Winchesters are fitted with barrels made of nickel-steel, Brooks pointed out. Since Mausers and Mannlichers had barrels of Krupp steel, the same type used in German heavy ordnance, *"their superiority is manifest."* A broader choice of barrel lengths was available in the bolt-action line as well, Brooks hastens to add. Apparently "Fair Play" failed to note the logic in Brooks' barrel-related allegations, as he failed to respond to them.

The then-current vogue of remodeling Springfield rifles, suggested to Brooks, at least, that the bolt-action lent itself more to refinement than the Model 1895. Another reader saw things exactly oppositely, and preferred the '95 only because its flat-sided receiver had more unbroken area that could be covered with engraving.

One Western reader preferred the '95 from an entirely practical standpoint. He didn't like the way the bolt knob felt under his leg while in a saddle scabbard.

W. Mittendorf, of New Braunfels, Texas, a noted schuetzen riflemen, made a suggestion in the April 1911 *Outdoor Life*, as might be expected from a precision-minded shooter. Mittendorf advanced the notion that a Springfield and a Winchester '95, with duplicated sights and the same 30-1906 ammunition be tested at long range and superiority be judged in this fashion. His suggestion *"applies to the primary essentials of a rifle only, namely accuracy and range."* Evidently no writer or reader saw any merit in Mittendorf's idea, as no further mention was made of it.

Townsend Whelen also felt that there were secondary considerations leading to a choice between the two actions.

Dismounting and cleaning of the Mauser/Springfield actions could be accomplished in *"less than a minute,"* and without tools. The lever action required screwdrivers, and in some cases, drift pins—and much more time to disassemble.

The advocates of the bolt-action maintained that their preferred action offered advantages over the lever action because of its sheer simplicity. According to Crossman, who dissected each action, counted and weighed parts, tells us that the '95 Winchester contained 52 parts, more than twice the number of the Ross, which had 25. The Springfield was comprised of 30 parts, the Mauser, *"fewer than the Springfield."* The '95's parts weighed 65 ounces, compared to 46 ounces for the Springfield. The weight of the parts of the Ross is lighter still, 43 ounces.

And then, in May 1912, with fair warning, it was over. The blackpowder smoke dissipated, the stopwatches were put away and the wiping rods and stronger ammonia were gotten out.

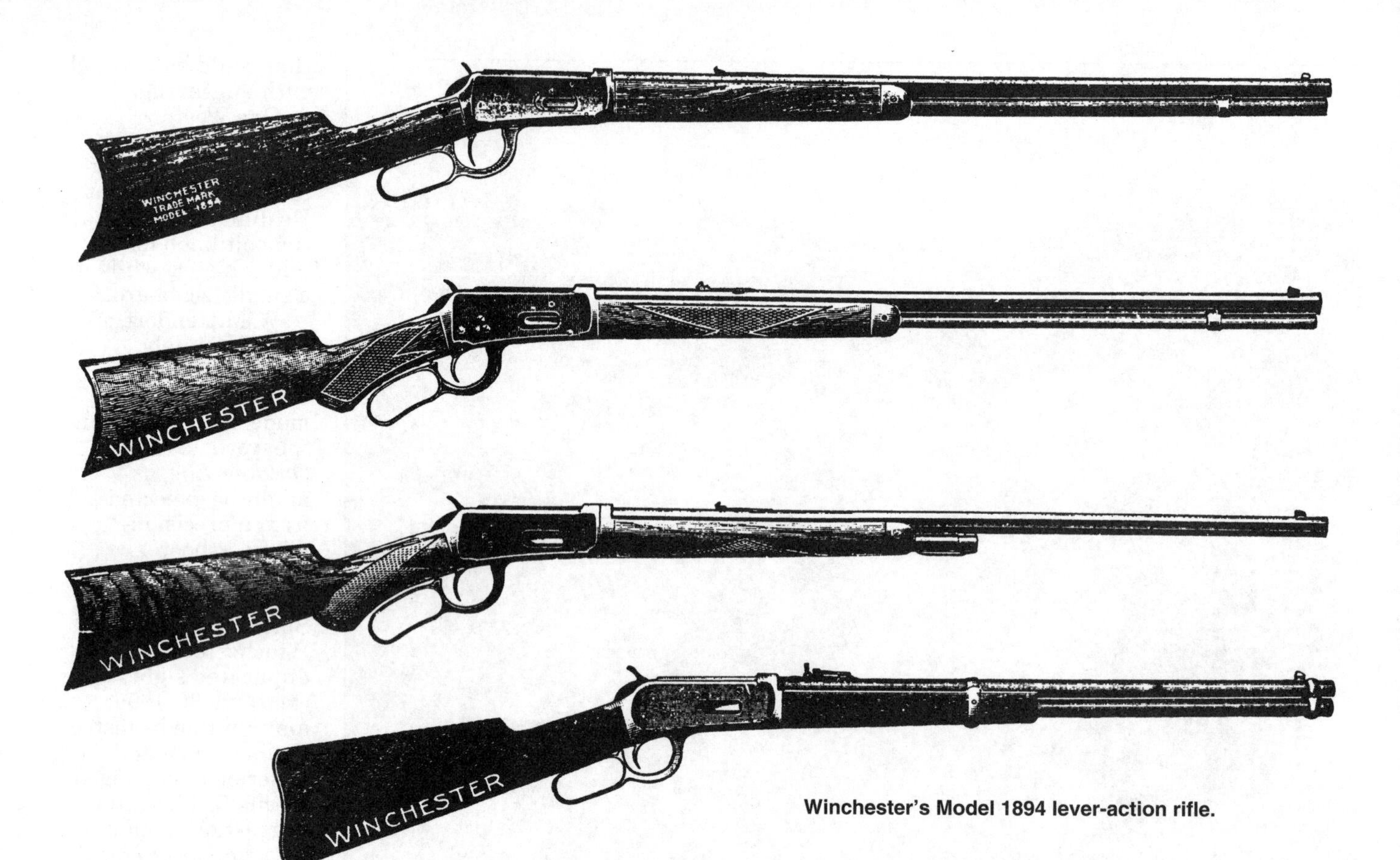

Winchester's Model 1894 lever-action rifle.

In a display of contempt and frustration that reflected the feelings of himself and apparently the bulk of the readership, Chauncy Thomas halted the dispute forever. Thomas printed a woody editorial entitled "The Umpires' Decision," parts of which are well worth quoting here: *"Job remarked some time ago that "All men are liars," so this bolt and lever row must have began early. And it is about time it stopped, for with the holdup in Tripoli, the exchange of flatirons in China and the troubles of Mr. Madero, it won't do to have too much excitement in the world all at one time... It was a jolly row. The bolt men clearly whipped the lever men by hitting them on the end of their right fists with their right eyes, grappling, and going to the floor with them, and holding them there by dexterously getting under them and firmly inserting their noses between their teeth... The lever man failed to prove that a bolt action can trot a mile in 2:16, and displayed their ignorance of firearms by admitting that in July you can fan yourself better with a five-cent palm leaf than with a Winchester. How Teddy kept out of the row I don't see; probably he saw that as all of them were fully qualified for life membership in the Ananias Club there was no need for him to interfere, anyhow."*

"It has done us all good, a great deal of good. We have learned that when you fire a Winchester five thousand times in an afternoon, it causes a great destruction of timber. We have also learned that the bolt action (or is it the lever action) is not as strong as ordinary newspaper, because it (not the newspaper) cannot stand over 75,000 pounds of gas pressure to the square inch. Why! Every writer in the game was working under more pressure than that... well, it is all over but paying the pensions. Some day in the next generation or two, when automatics are all the vogue, and the inky warriors hold an outdoor reunion, we will see their thinning ranks, peg-legged, one-eyed, ragged-eared, come proudly marching down the target range. In the lead will be "Winchester" Haines bearing aloft a bolt of cloth for a banner, and they all will be wearing busted breeches. And right here I want to point out the fact that we six-gun toters don't do such things...we are not bothered by such things as bolts and levers, and some of us even file the front sight. We don't start rows; we end them. There is nothing like having a Peacemaker handy, especially on the present occasion."

There were a few immediate, well-intentioned efforts on the part of some of the readers to revive the discussion, but the general consensus among readers was one of relief.

At any rate, Thomas could not be budged. Readers received an education concerning rifle actions. Editors learned, if nothing else, how damaging permitting a debate of four years could be. Never again would the "Arms and Ammunition" columns be a bulletin board for any mud-slinging writer with an ax to grind. Late in 1912, Bob Kane, editor of *Outers*, printed a notice at the head of each issue's column, restating that the intent of the columns was to be an outlet for the exchange of views pertaining to arms and ammunition. Further he cautioned that opinions should be expressed in a courteous manner and strongly emphasized that *"under no circumstances would personalities be permitted."*

Times were changing. About 1920, the format of the columns was altered in *Outdoor Life* and *Outers*. Rather than a forum for the exchange of ideas they had formerly been, the columns' purpose was redirected. Informative and instructive articles by the recognized experts of the day occupied nearly all the space after the war. Reader input dwindled to non-existence, as did the environment that bred and nourished one of the most interesting chapters in the history of American arms and ammunition. ●

JUST ENOUGH GUN

A Swede in Africa

by Bill Woodward

Zimbabwe, 1999; 4:00 a.m. I lay awake in a thatched hut on the banks of the Nyamishi River. Excited and unable to sleep, I dressed and padded down to the cook tent, settled in a camp chair before a blazing fire and drank a cup of Kenya coffee. A pink sun peeked through the acacia trees as mist rose from the river. Four-pound bream splashed in the pool behind me, and a baboon barked from a distant ridge. I fished in the pocket of my safari jacket and brought out a cartridge. In the half-light the long, round-nose bullet looked outdated and vaguely Victorian. Seventeen days of plains game hunting lay ahead of me. Did I have enough gun? I was about to find out.

I CAME TO this cartridge down a long and dusty road. I had taken more than 50 head of game in America, Africa and Europe with the 243 Winchester, slightly less with everything from the 308 Winchester to the 300 Winchester Magnum. I shot the 243 well, but its performance was uneven on 200-pound game. The 300 Winchester Magnum worked great on large game like elk—but the recoil was no fun.

A lot of reading and the recommendations of friends pointed to one cartridge with gentle recoil and potent killing power—the 6.5x55 Swede.

The Perfect Medium Game Cartridge?

Shooting literature is riddled with praise for specific cartridges. Advocates extol the virtues of the 270 and 30-06, labeling each the "perfect" cartridge for medium game.

Fans of the 375 H & H Magnum quickly point out it's the "only" choice for the one-gun hunter who pursues everything from Cape buffalo to whitetail deer—worldwide. Obviously, there is no "perfect" cartridge. But one cartridge offers surprising performance with gentle recoil—the 6.5x55.

The 6.5x55 is not as flat as the 270, as powerful as the 375 H & H Magnum or as versatile as the 30-06. Yet, this "friendly" cartridge is fully capable of taking everything

Woodward's custom 6.5x55 '98 Mauser and the 160-grain Sierra round nose he used during his 1999 African plains game safari.

from Wyoming elk to African warthog. Fans of the 6.5x55 stress these points:

1. **Moderate Recoil.** Perceived recoil of the 6.5x55 is similar to a 257 Roberts, in rifles of equal weight.
2. **Exceptional Accuracy.** Even in hundred-year-old military rifles, near minute-of-angle groups are common. Accuracy seems to prevail across a wide range of bullet weights.
3. **Sectional Density.** Exceptional bullet length-for-weight is characteristic of the 6.5 bore. The most popular bullet weight—140 grains—has a sectional density of .287, greater than all the 30-calibers in Hornady's line except the lumbering 220-grain round-nose! Sectional density is critical because it is a primary factor in penetration. And penetration is the 6.5's strong suit.
4. **Bullet Selection**. American 6.5 bullets contradict the assumption that the 6.5 is an "odd caliber". Manufacturers (*including premium makers*) offer a dozen weights from 85 to 160 grains.
5. **Flat Trajectory.** A 270 Winchester throws a 140-grain bullet at 2900 fps. Sighted in at 200 yards, the drop is 7.1 inches at 300 yards. In a modern rifle, the 6.5x55 shoots a 140-grain bullet at 2700 fps. With a 200-yard zero, the 6.5x55 drops 8.5 inches at 300 yards—only 1.4 inches more than the 270! (Source: *Hornady Handbook of Cartridge Reloading, Fourth Edition*.)
6. **Killing Power.** Let's compare the same bullets in energy. The 270 retains 1715 foot-pounds at 300 yards; the 6.5x55, 1437 foot-pounds, almost 84 percent of the energy of the 270. What these figures don't reveal is the effectiveness of the 6.5x55. Those who use it will tell you it kills even *better* than its ballistics suggest.

There are several cartridges that will beat the 6.5x55 in any of these six categories—cartridges that are flatter, more powerful, have less recoil. But the 6.5x55 comes *very* close to being the only cartridge that combines *all* these attributes in one package!

6.5s In Africa

The 6.5 caliber is well established in African hunting lore. British firms, including Rigby and Jeffrey, made 6.5x53R sporters based on Dutch Mannlicher rifles. Commercial 6.5x54 Mannlicher-Schoenauer carbines were often the *only* rifle on East African farms and worked on everything from impala to lion. The high sectional density and remarkable penetration of long, 156-grain bullets made the caliber a favorite of famous hunters like Captain Hugh Stigand and "Karamojo" Bell. Bell pushed the envelope by using 6.5 solids on everything—including elephant.

The 6.5x55 was rarely used by early hunters in Africa. Because Norway, Sweden and Denmark had no African colonies, the cartridge's use on the Dark Continent was limited to visiting hunters.

While it has received little press as an African cartridge, the 6.5x55 is fully capable of taking medium-sized plains game, from zebra and kudu on down. Author's custom '98 Mauser is shown with hunting Bowie by Terry Davis of Sumpter, Oregon.

Building a 6.5x55

Intrigued by what I'd read, I decided to make up a rifle using the popular 6.5x55 cartridge on a military '98 Mauser action. Gunsmith Ross Billingsley turned a Douglas premium blank to a slightly heavy sporter barrel 21 inches in length, crowned with a barrel-band front sight. A bolt handle sculpted by knifemaker Terry Davis and a barrel machined to match the contours of a Rigby stalking rifle produced that classic African look. Less-than-classic was a stock salvaged from an old 308 Winchester and reshaped to match the short forearm and slim lines of a plains game rifle. The problem was the pistol grip. When I rasped it back to create that "swept" look, I lost the palm swell. Terry Davis had the answer.

"Fix yourself a drink. Then whip up a batch of epoxy mixed with walnut stain. Sip the drink...for courage. When the epoxy starts to set up, slap a glob on the pistol grip and mold it to fit your hand. It'll look like hell...but it'll work great!"

One of six impala buck taken with Woodward's 6.5x55.

Trackers with decent warthog, taken with Woodward's custom 6.5x55, with the 2350 fps, 160-grain Sierra round nose.

Terry was right. The result was a slim pistol grip with a perfect swell. Fitted with a Pachmayer recoil pad and sling swivels, this stock is the most comfortable I own! The finished rifle, with a 4x Leupold scope, weighs eight pounds, three ounces.

Loading the Swede

As I experimented with handloads I stumbled on what thousands of Americans have discovered. The 6.5x55 Swede is comfortable to shoot and highly accurate! Original Swedish Mausers are the most accurate military rifles ever produced. The right combination of bullet, powder and seating depth usually produces tight groups, even in ancient '94 and '96 Mausers. However, even in modern custom rifles, light bullets may not work—because virtually all commercial 6.5x55 reamers are set up for the long 156- to 160-grain bullets.

Head tracker, with an excellent impala that just makes the book (Rowland Ward's).

A review of four reloading books revealed a consensus: the Swede likes slow-burning powders in the range of IMR 4350 to IMR 7828. Remembering what I'd read about the early Kenya pioneers, I selected a long bullet—the Sierra 160-grain round-nose.

In front of 43 grains of H 4350 the Sierras produced three-shot groups that averaged 1/2-inch on the 75-yard range behind my home. Chronograph readings showed the bullet lumbering along at 2350 fps—right on track with similar loads used by Stigand and Bell in the 6.5x54 Mannlicher-Schoenauer. (*Because this bullet has a longer bearing surface than most 160s [.811- inch], it takes less powder.* ***Do not use powder charges for other 160s as a guide in loading this bullet.***) Unfortunately, I finished the rifle and handloads in January, so I had no chance to test the load on game before my African trip.

As a 6.5x55 reloader I had a lot of company. Charles Benneke (writing in the September 1998 issue of *Rifle* magazine) came up with this fact: the 6.5x55 is the most reloaded cartridge on the planet! When you think about it, Benneke's observation makes sense. Americans load a lot of different cartridges from varmint rounds like the 22 Hornet to brushbusters like the 35 Whelen. In Scandinavia, however, the 6.5x55 dominates the hunting and target shooting scenes. Factories load millions of rounds for rifle clubs, where target shooting is subsidized by the government. (*I've heard that Norma even offers 77-grain bullets specifically for young shooters.*)

A Scandinavian Love Affair

In the late 1960s, as a young Air Force captain, I gained some insight into Scandinavia's love affair with the 6.5x55. I was assigned to *Arctic Express*, a NATO exercise centered in the Arctic city of Bodo, Norway. A Norwegian liaison officer took me to a local rifle club. Shooters waited their turn in a wood plank cabin where an old iron stove fought the subzero Arctic cold. On the walls were photos of Nordic patriarchs with long beards, proudly clutching their 6.5x55 Krag Jørgensens. Outside the clubhouse, the grandsons of these men shot the same rifles at targets set at unknown distances by children on skis. (*Twenty-five years after the war, these targets still bore the likeness of a German paratrooper. The Norwegians have a long memory.*)

Scandinavia is not alone in its love affair with the 6.5x55. Thousands of Swedish '94 and '96 Mausers have been sold in this country (and in Germany) since the late '50s. These rifles made the cartridge so popular that Winchester, Ruger and Remington produced rifles in 6.5x55. Winchester still does! Wayne Wixom of RCBS recently told me that the 6.5x55 is the twentieth most popular caliber in the sale of rifle dies in this country.

At one time the 6.5x55 was the official military cartridge of Norway, Sweden and Denmark. Substantial numbers were used by Finland against the Russians during World War II. Even the tiny state of Luxembourg adopted the 6.5x55 as its military cartridge!

Development of the 6.5x55

Development of the 6.5x55 is often credited to Germany's Mauser factory. However, Mauser scholar Ludwig Olson laid this misconception to rest in a May 1995 article in *Rifle* magazine. Olson's extensive research in Scandinavia established that a joint Norwegian-Swedish committee refined and approved the 6.5x55 cartridge in 1893. On April 21, 1894, Norway adopted the cartridge in the Krag-Jørgensen rifle. (*This same rifle, chambered for the 30-40 Krag cartridge, was once America's primary battle rifle, and was placed in service in 1892.*) Sweden chose the cock-on-closing 1894 Mauser, initially manufactured in Germany. The bulk of Swedish Mausers (Models '94 and '96— and the final version, the Model 38) were manufactured in Sweden at the Carl Gustaf (Royal Armory) and the private firm of Husquavarna. It is these finely-crafted rifles, in a variety of forms (carbines, long rifles and sniper rifles) that were imported into this country. These 6.5x55s earned a unique reputation for exceptional accuracy and potent performance on game.

Swedish Mausers carry an unusual marking device that defines

(*Left to right*): M-38 Swedish Mauser with turned-down bolt for cavalry use, on Ramline synthetic stock; M-38 in original configuration; M-96 Swedish Mauser. Brass disks identify bore diameter and condition. *Courtesy of David Schreiber.*

their accuracy. Circular brass disks on the stocks are armorers' codes that reflect barrel condition. Early "two-screw" disks denote the unit to which the rifle belongs. Later "one-screw" disks tell the actual caliber of the bore; its condition and the aiming point for the "new" pointed M-41 bullet.

Early Scandinavian ball ammo used bullets that were relatively heavy-for-caliber 156-grain roundnoses at a modest velocity of 2296 fps. In 1925 the Norwegians adopted a 139-grain spitzer boattail at 2444 fps. Sweden followed suit in the 1940s with a similar bullet. 6.5mm rifles quickly established a reputation for reliability, accuracy and light recoil. It was this last characteristic—the comfort of the 6.5—that led so many nations to adopt 6.5s. At one time, in addition to the Scandinavian nations, Holland, Greece, Romania, Portugal, Japan and Italy all used 6.5 military cartridges in a variety of cases!

A Wide Range of Bullets

An excellent selection of bullets is available to the American shooter. They range from 85-grain Sierra varmint bullets and 120-grain Speer spire points for deer and antelope, to 160-grain softnoses from Sierra and Hornady. Most versatile are the 140-grain spire points available from Hornady, Speer, Sierra, Nosler and Swift. In between is a cornucopia of options, including the 107-grain Sierra match bullet, the 129-grain Hornady light game bullet and a 125-grain Partition from Nosler.

H 4895 is an excellent choice for the lighter bullets. For heavy bullets, my favorite powder is H 4350. H 4831 seems to offer the *best* combination of accuracy and speed across the wide range of bullets. Special care needs to be taken to gauge loading data to action type. Krag-Jørgensen 6.5s need to be fed loads that do not exceed 43,500 psi. Modern 6.5x55s such as those offered by Winchester and Ruger can withstand the higher pressures of comparable modern cartridges. Owners of Model 1894 and 1896 Mausers will find their ceilings somewhere in-between. I selected a Model 1898 Mauser because it allowed me to use more potent load combinations. ***Always*** check your loading manual with an eye to action type and the bullet manufacturer's recommendations.

Performance on African Plains Game

As I sat on the banks of the Nyamishi River, and contemplated the cartridge in my hand, I wondered if this gentle, civilized cartridge was up to the job at hand. My professional hunter joined me and, over coffee, he explained that the area offered a wide variety of game—from 1500-pound eland down to diminutive 12-pound grysbok.

"What are you shooting?" he asked.

I pulled a cartridge from my pocket and handed it to him.

He held it up against the faint light on the horizon. "Good long bullet. Should work."

He finished his coffee, called for his tracker and picked up his rifle and a box of cartridges. With some chagrin I caught a fleeting glimpse of the cartridge box. It read, *375 Holland and Holland.*

6.5X55
3Shots
75yds
45 grains H4831
129gr Hornady
.315"

The 6.5x55 is an inherently accurate cartridge. Shown here, the author's deer and antelope load: 45 grains of H 4831 behind a 129-grain Hornady spire point.

That first morning we saw lots of game. Big bunches of eland, herds of zebra, two dozen kudu, a mob of wildebeeste, hundreds of impala, a "sounder" of warthog and several giraffe. (*During my two-week stay, I was the only hunter on a block of 30,000 acres. The shooting block was broken hill country crested with mountain acacia and covered with high grass and thick brush.*)

I warmed up on impala, the 120-pound antelope with beautiful lyre-shaped horns. It was on the impala that I first learned my assumptions about the 160-grain round-nose were dead wrong. I was certain that this long bullet at a relatively low speed would hold together and penetrate deeply.

My first impala ram was taken at about 120 yards. I aimed at the point of the shoulder, thinking to upset the long, slow bullet on bone. The ram dropped as if hit by the Hammer of Thor. The bullet had disintegrated, leaving only the jacket and a small amount of lead. Performance on other impala was identical, the bullet producing fierce and violent expansion and dropping them in their tracks the moment it impacted the point of the shoulder.

I took a 35-pound duiker at about 50 yards. Even on this small antelope only part of the jacket exited, the balance of the bullet remained in the animal and weighed 30 grains.

In all, I shot more than nine head of plains game with the 6.5x55, including a kudu and zebra. Zimbabwe has an active market for game meat —so everything shot is used in camp or sold. Non-trophy animals are often available at about a third of the trophy fee of mature males. Non-trophy animals provide an excellent opportunity to test calibers and handloads.

Woodward, tracker and assistant tracker with 53-inch greater kudu taken in Zimbabwe with author's custom 6.5x55.

Recovered 160-grain round noses from (*left to right*) 600-pound kudu, 600-pound zebra and 35-pound duiker.

I found Sierra's 160-grain round-nose an extremely effective bullet on impala, warthog and duiker. While I was surprised at the bullet's ferocious expansion and low retained weight, the litmus test of a bullet's worth is its ability to kill quickly and cleanly. The Sierra did that with great efficiency. On larger game, however, a tough bullet, like a Nosler Partition or Swift might be in order—especially where shoulder shots are required. My kudu expired with one shot; my zebra required a second.

Zimbabwe's high grass and thick brush offered perfect stalking opportunities. We were able to spot herds of impala from a distance, then approach behind a curtain of acacia trees to make the shot. Impala rams stood like tan ghosts in the high golden grass of May. The wind of Africa's autumn carried a hint of winter as the sun fell warm and welcome between our shoulder blades. It was a magic time and it was gratifying to have a rifle that did its job cleanly.

Reflections

The 6.5x55 has received little attention as an African plains game cartridge. That's unfortunate. I think the cartridge is just the ticket for smaller plains game. Light recoil and excellent penetration make for a combination that kills out of all proportion to the cartridge's paper ballistics.

Some African countries require a minimum caliber of 7mm for the larger plains game. But many professional hunters ignore this distinction. After I returned from Africa, I learned that Zimbabwe is one of those countries. Be sure to discuss this issue with your PH—*before* you travel.

As I get older, I tend to gravitate to guns I shoot well. I find the 6.5x55 has a lot in common with the 28-gauge shotgun. The 28 kicks like a .410 and kills like a 20-gauge. The 6.5x55 on the other hand, kills like a 30-06 and kicks like a 243. That's a winning combination for a cartridge that dominates the hunting and shooting scene throughout Northern Europe and is gaining increasing popularity in the U. S. The Swede deserves more attention, here at home—*and* in Africa. ●

Bibliography

CARTRIDGES OF THE WORLD, Revised 4th Edition, Frank C. Barnes (Ed., Ken Warner), DBI Books, Inc., Northfield, IL, 1980.

SIERRA RIFLE RELOADING MANUAL, 4th Edition, Managing Ed., Cliff Callis, Sierra Bullets, L.P., Sedalia, MO, 1995.

HORNADY HANDBOOK OF CARTRIDGE RELOADING, Vol. 1, 4th Edition, Ed., Todd Georgi, Hornady Manufacturing Company, Inc., Grand Island, NE, 1996.

NOSLER RELOADING GUIDE Number Four, Technical Ed., Gail Root, Nosler, Inc., Bend, OR, 1996.

SPEER RELOADING MANUAL: Rifle & Pistol, Number 12, Ed., Allan Jones, Speer, Omark Industries and Blount, Inc., Lewiston, ID, 1995.

AFRICAN RIFLES AND CARTRIDGES, John Taylor, Gun Room Press, Highland Park, NJ, 1977.

"The Ageless 6.5x55", by Ludwig Olson, in *RIFLE* Magazine, Dave Scovill, Editor, Prescott, AZ, May 1995.

"Dear Editor", response to letter by Charles Benneke, in *RIFLE* magazine, Dave Scovill, Editor, Prescott, AZ, September 1998.

Favorite 6.5 x 55 Loads[a,b,c]

Purpose	Bullet	Powder/grs.	Velocity/fps
Varmint, target	100-gr. Sierra HP[d]	IMR 4895/42.0	2800
Antelope, whitetail	129-gr. Hornady Sp[e]	H 4831/45.0	2650
Mule deer, all-around load	140-gr. Hornady Sp[e]	H 4831/44.0	2600
Warthog, impala	160-gr. Sierra round nose[d]	H 4350/43.0	2350

a. CCI 200 large-rifle primers used for all loads.
b. Reduce all loads by 2.0 grains if used in a Krag-Jørgenson.
c. Check these loads against the reloading manuals listed below. **Be alert. Publisher is not responsible for errors in published data.**
d. Source: *Sierra Rifle Reloading Manual, 4th Edition* (50th Anniversary), Sierra Bullets, L.P., 1995
e. Source: *Hornady Handbook of Cartridge Reloading, 4th Edition*, Hornady Manufacturing Company, Inc., 1996.

GUNS OF THE REAL INDIANA JONES

by Roderick S. Carman

THE REAL INDIANA Jones hated adventures. Or so he said. In his book, *On the Trail of Ancient Man,* he writes, "My friend, Stefansson, the Arctic explorer, has a motto, which I am very fond of quoting because it expresses a great deal in a single sentence. He says, 'Adventures are a mark of incompetence.' According to Roy Chapman Andrews, who may have been the real life inspiration for Indiana Jones, the larger-than-life screen hero, adventures can and should be avoided. With careful planning and good equipment one need not suffer undue hardship and peril. As an example of his own success in this regard, he cites the following:

For the last fifteen years I have spent most of the time wandering into the far corners of the world. During the first eight years, I was studying and collecting whales and was at sea a good deal on tiny whaling vessels. Then I gave up that work and began land explorations in Asia. In the fifteen years, I can remember just ten times when I had really narrow escapes from death. Two were from drowning in typhoons, one was when our boat was charged by a wounded whale; once my wife and I were nearly eaten by wild dogs, once we were in great danger from fanatical lama priests; two were close calls when I fell over cliffs, once I was nearly caught by a huge python, and twice I might have been killed by bandits.

One wonders what might have happened with less thorough planning. In fact, it is hard not to suspect that Andrews welcomed a bit of excitement now and then. And, even though he was a serious and dedicated scientist, he loved fast cars, hunting with good guns and the thrill of surviving in the wilderness.

Roy Chapman Andrews in camp, somewhere in southern Mongolia, during the Third Asiatic Expedition (1925). ***J. B. Shackleford photo courtesy the American Museum of Natural History***

Andrews' great expeditions in China and Mongolia in the early 1900s were meant to produce evidence on the origins of humans, and while he failed in this, he did discover spectacular dinosaur fossils, including dinosaur eggs and the first evidence of nesting behavior in these animals. In the process he set new standards for the use of technology, equipment and organization in archeological fieldwork. The first to use motorized transport for scientific expeditions in vast desert regions; he employed "Dodge Brothers'" 28-horsepower automobiles and Fulton trucks. Lightweight motion picture cameras were used for documentation, and short-wave radios for news and navigation.

With meticulous planning and imagination he accomplished what many at the time thought impossible; not only surviving for long periods of time in an extremely hostile environment, but also returning with archeological finds which were stunning at the time and remain impressive today. Joseph Wallace in his book, *Book of Dinosaurs*, says if this explorer extraordinaire wasn't the real-life model for the Spielberg movie character, he should have been.

Roy Chapman Andrews was introduced to firearms and hunting early in life. He states that the greatest event of his early life in Beloit, Wisconsin, occurred when he was given a small single-barrel shotgun for his ninth birthday. Prior to that he had been permitted to shoot his grandfather's muzzleloader, but with its 40-inch barrel it was difficult to manage. After a shaky start on wildfowl (he shot a neighbor's pneumatic decoy), his performance improved, and his father replaced the single barrel with a higher quality double-barrel hammer gun. Andrews says this early introduction to bird hunting led naturally to an interest in taxidermy, and eventually his collection of bird skins found its way to the Department of Ornithology in the American Museum of Natural History in New York.

Later, as the leader of several scientific expeditions in China and Mongolia, Andrews continued to make use of his gun knowledge and skills. Charles Gallenkamp, author of *Dragon Hunter: Roy Chapman Andrews and the Central Asiatic Expeditions,* estimates that there were 10,000 Chinese bandits roaming the Gobi Desert in the 1920s when Andrews was there. These "brigands," to use Andrews' term, were constantly on the lookout for caravans to prey on.

The Savage Model 1920 was designed primarily for the recent 250-3000 Savage cartridge, at the time the only commercial cartridge to exceed 3000 fps. The rifle, Savage's first bolt action, weighed about 6 pounds and continued in production until 1929.

The threat was so great that almost every member of each expedition team had a sidearm, rifle or shotgun nearby at all times. Andrews' constant companion was his 6-inch Colt 38 Army Special that he carried in a Folsom "safety holster." This revolver is still in the possession of a member of the Andrews family, and has three prominent notches on one of its grips. Need we say more?

Firearms were also used on these expeditions to deal with the problem of food supply. It was Andrews' plan to provide high-protein fare for the expedition members by hunting desert antelope. He had with him his favorite Mannlicher-Schoenauer 6.5mm carbine, but also carried one of several new Savage Model 20 bolt actions in the 250-3000 Savage chambering he had obtained especially for these trips. He was very fond of this new high-velocity round, and noted that its flat trajectory and killing power helped ensure success in bagging various gazelles.

Andrews had used a Model 99 Savage 250-3000 on earlier hunting trips in South China with his buddy, the Reverend Harry R. Caldwell, an American missionary, who gained fame with his book, *Blue Tiger*. In this book Caldwell describes the unsuccessful pursuit of a famous man-eater with a distinctive coat of black stripes on a blue-gray ground. The two men once got to within 20 feet of this tiger, but it was frightened off by noise made by nearby woodcutters. Both Andrews and Caldwell were enthusiastic supporters of the new small-bore high-velocity rifles, and Caldwell thought that the Model 99 in 22 Savage Hi-Power was about right for man-eating tigers! He appears in some early Savage ads displaying a large tiger and this cartridge and rifle. Neither he nor Andrews ever got the Blue Tiger and it reportedly killed almost one hundred people over the course of its man-eating career.

There is some indication that Andrews, despite his enthusiasm for the 250, preferred his older Mannlicher for some work. In a letter he wrote in 1934, in response to an inquiry about rifles used on the Asiatic Expeditions he said:

For work in the desert we used 250/3000 Savage Bolt Action rifles. This has a flat trajectory and a long range and was ideal for antelope.

For mountain sheep and ibex, I preferred my 6-1/2mm Mannlicher-Schoenauer. As we were getting no game larger than wild asses, these calibers were quite powerful enough.

The American Museum of Natural History, under whose sponsorship the expeditions were carried out, also required various specimens of wildlife from the region for a display in what was to be called The Great Hall of China. Rifles were used by various members of the group to collect these specimens which were prepared for taxidermy to be done later.

Members of the scientific team were allowed to bring personal firearms with them, but since many came from scientific and academic settings and had little hunting experience, not all could be expected to have appropriate personal armaments. So Andrews, in the course of general fund-raising to support the several expeditions, made a pitch to several gun companies to supply, free of charge, both guns and ammunition.

He first approached the Savage Arms Corporation, and having gotten an agreement from them to supply eight of their Model 20 rifles in 250-3000 Savage, along with eight Model 1907 auto pistols and 6,000 rounds of ammunition, he got the Hunter Arms Company of Fulton, New York, to provide eight field-grade L. C. Smith 12-gauge shotguns. In return, he promised these companies to "give to you advertising which it would be impossible for you to buy." He later provided endorsements for both companies, and was especially enthusiastic about the Savage rifles, notwithstanding the fact that two of them were put out of action in the field with burst barrels. This was apparently due to faulty primers, which failed to completely ignite the powder charge, resulting in bullets lodging in the barrel. According to Andrews, "in the excitement the men did not realize what had happened and fired other shells." Savage quickly shipped two more Model 20s.

In the end, all were pleased with the collaboration and Andrews wrote to the Savage folks in 1926:

Doubtless it would be of interest to you to know of the splendid satisfaction which the Savage 250-3000 rifles have given all of the members of the Third Asiatic Expedition on our recent work in Mongolia. We depend almost entirely on game for our meat while in the field and the long range and flat trajectory of the Savage rifle makes it ideal for our work. Most of our plains shooting is from 300 to 400 yards and we must have a bullet that kills when it hits.

In the last ten years, we have tried the 250-3000 Savage on almost every kind of Asiatic game and I believe it is the finest game cartridge that has ever been invented. I have had many arguments with authorities on ballistics who have said that a little 87-grain bullet could not possibly do certain things. My only reply is that theoretically I know it can't do them, but that actually it does. The rifles have stood up wonderfully under terrible punishment in the desert. As you know, selecting a rifle is very much like picking a wife – everyone has his own individual preferences. It has been interesting to me to see the way in which members of the Expedition who have gone out with other rifles have all given them up in preference for the Savage.

I congratulate you in the splendid weapons you have developed.

At the beginning of the 1922 expedition, Andrews had good reason to be thankful that he was well armed. In his book, *The New Conquest of Central Asia*, he describes what he found in Urga, the capital of Mongolia:

The Minister of War had been executed a few days before we arrived. The former Minister of the Interior, an old friend of mine, was under suspicion. I called upon him one afternoon. The next morning I went again on business and found his house in chaos. That night he had been dragged out and shot. It was not Mongols alone who suffered. Individuals of half a dozen nationalities, including Americans, were in difficulties. Murder and sudden death stalked ahead upon the streets. It was an exceedingly good place to leave.

And things were often not a lot better in the desert. On the 1923 expedition, Andrews, having arrived at a remote location where two Russians had recently been robbed, writes:

As I recognized the spot, I thought to myself, "I wonder if brigands would attempt to hold me up in this same place." Hardly had the thought taken form in my mind when I saw the sun-flash of a gun barrel on the summit of a hill 300 yards away. The head and shoulders of a single mounted horseman were just visible against the sky ... Undoubtedly, the horseman on the hilltop was a sentinel to give warning to others in the valley below. I had no mind to have him in

Chapman's dinosaur finds included this even dozen dinosaur eggs, found in Mongolia during the Third Asiatic Expedition (1925). ***J. B. Shackleford photo courtesy the American Museum of Natural History***

such a position whoever he might be, and drawing my revolver, I fired twice. The bullets must have come too close for comfort, although I did not attempt to hit him, for he instantly disappeared.

Shortly thereafter, Andrews' path was blocked by three more armed horsemen. These he scattered with a full-throttle charge in his Dodge. The horses, if not the horsemen, were unnerved by this tactic and went bucking and leaping into the desert, "while the brigands were endeavoring to unship their rifles which were slung on their backs."

During the 1925 expedition, Andrews reports that "as usual," bandits had been active north of Kalgan, China, his jumping-off point for Mongolia, and that a week before leaving this city, three American cars loaded with sable skins had been robbed. Other automobiles had, according to Andrews, met a similar fate almost every week, and things were so bad that the Foreign Commissioner at Kalgan demanded he sign a statement releasing the Chinese authorities from all responsibility for the safety of the group. Although he thought it a bad precedent, he reluctantly signed the release, commenting that, "I felt quite certain that we were much too strong a party for brigands to attack." On one occasion he describes the vehicles of his group bristling with guns prominently displayed *(and also American flags flying in the best Teddy Roosevelt fashion).*

The Colt Army Special Revolver sprang from an 1884 double-action design adopted by the U. S. Navy in 1889. The Army quickly followed suit and the modifications began in earnest. The predominant chambering for this 38-caliber revolver was the 38 Special cartridge, but some early guns were chambered for the 38 Long Colt.

The American Museum of Natural History "force" might have been too strong for a gang of robbers, but the Chinese Army was something else. In trying to get the 1926 expedition started, Andrews found himself smack in the middle of a Chinese civil war. Attempting to get from Peking, which was under attack by one Army faction, to Tientsin, a city to the south, over roads controlled by the other faction, Andrews and several of his vehicles got caught in the middle. After coming under machinegun and small-arms fire, he did a high speed U-turn and headed back to Peking. He describes what followed:

For three miles we ran the gauntlet of firing from both sides of the road. I would see a soldier standing ready with his rifle at the side waiting until we came opposite. Then 'bang' he would let us have it. Sometimes they fired in squads; sometimes singly. The only reason why we were not riddled with bullets is because the Chinese soldier is the world's worst shot. Most of them aimed directly at the car, when they aimed at all, and the bullets struck just behind us. Every now and then one would zip in close to my head but no one was hit. I really had the best of it because the others could not see what was going on and driving the car kept me busy. I expected every moment that one of the tires would be hit. A blowout at that speed would have turned us over.

At this point, even Roy Chapman Andrews had had enough. After several abortive attempts to get through the fighting to Mongolia, Andrews admitted defeat and called off the 1926 expedition. I suspect this decision was received with almost hysterical relief by most other members of the team. One can only wonder what some of these scientists had come to think of archeological fieldwork in Central Asia with Dr. Roy Chapman Andrews.

It should be noted that not all members of the Central Asiatic expeditions were men. Andrews'

Reverend Harry R. Caldwell with ram taken in October 1919, during the Second Asiatic Expedition in Kivei-hua-cheng, North Shansi Province. ***Yvette B. Andrews photo courtesy the American Museum of Natural History***

The site that yielded the dinosaur eggs was found by an expedition member named Olsen *(left)*. Roy Chapman Andrews *(right)* is later credited with providing the first evidence of nesting behavior among dinosaurs. *J. B. Shackleford photo courtesy the American Museum of Natural History*

first wife, Yvette, was along on some portions of the trips and took many of the wonderful photographs, which are maintained in the American Museum's archival collection. Some of the other wives were also present on some of the treks. While besieged in Peking, the team was joined by a trustee of the museum and his wife, Mr. and Mrs. Douglas Burden of New York, who came over the same road Andrews was turned back on earlier. Andrews advised against the attempt, but they had the good luck to pick up a Chinese air force general on the way, and he was able to get them through. Steady nerves and cool resolve seemed to be the order of the day.

The Savage Model 1907 was the first auto-loading pistol from that arms maker. The 32-caliber pistol held 10 rounds and was a somewhat controversial design.

Incredibly, after all he had been through, the bullet that almost did in Roy Chapman Andrews came from his own Colt. On May 5, 1928, on his next to last expedition to the Gobi, Andrews was headed toward the Shara Murun valley in southern Mongolia, accompanied by J.B. Shackelford, the project's chief photographer, and a navy medical officer, Dr. J.A. Perez. Although Andrews usually carried his 38 on his right side, he occasionally moved it to the left, in cross-draw position. This appears to be the case when, after downing an antelope with one of the Savage 250s, he approached the animal for a finishing shot with the 38. In attempting to release the leather safety catch on this holster, Andrews' finger slipped and a round was fired through the holster and into his left leg. The bullet entered his thigh and exited below the knee, in the process chipping the end of the femur. It was a terrible wound, and according to Andrews, "The heavy bullet struck me such a terrific blow that I went down as though felled by a sledge."

Shackelford ran to fetch Dr. Perez, who was traveling in a companion vehicle. A few hours later Perez performed what was undoubtedly life-saving surgery under the most primitive conditions. Andrews notes that bits of leather from the holster and cloth from his pants were removed from the wound during the procedure. It is a tribute not only to the skills of Dr. Perez, but also to the stamina of Roy Chapman Andrews, that he was not only able to survive the ordeal, but was sitting up within a few days, and in two weeks was making a visit to

Harsh but magnificent vistas were common during the Central Asiatic Expedition in 1928. Here Andrews surveys the badlands at Untyn Obo, Mongolia. ***J. B. Shackleford photo courtesy the American Museum of Natural History***

nearby Baron Sog Lamasery to negotiate with the resident priest for the temporary storage of fossils. He made use of a crutch fabricated from parts of a table taken from Shackelford's portable darkroom. Thus equipped, on May 20th, Andrews resumed his place at the head of the 1928 expedition as it pushed southwestward deeper into the Gobi, with freezing-cold nights, daytime temperatures of 145 degrees Fahrenheit and ferocious sandstorms.

Andrews was to make one more trip to Central Asia in 1930, after which political and military conflicts made further travel and work there impossible. In 1932, Roy Chapman Andrews crated up his belongings in China, his headquarters and jumping off point for all the expeditions, and used them to furnish a luxury apartment just off Central Park West in New York City. He was appointed associate director of the American Museum, and while never truly happy behind a desk, he enjoyed enormous recognition and popularity as a result of his many discoveries and "adventures." He was in constant demand as a lecturer and author, and was a regular participant in a weekly NBC radio program along with Teddy Roosevelt, Lowell Thomas and Admiral Richard Byrd.

Feeling the need for a retreat from his, by now, almost exclusively urban life, in 1937 he and his second wife, Billie, found and purchased a country house in Connecticut, which they named "Pondwood." Eventually finding life as an administrator at the Museum intolerable, Andrews resigned from his position there in 1942, and took up the life of a country squire in the woods of Connecticut. He converted the original living room of the house into a pine-paneled gunroom lined with books, medals and awards. On prominent display was a gun cabinet filled with rifles, shotguns, fishing rods and his favorite 6.5mm Mannlicher. He regularly entertained guests with Skeet shooting, hunting or fishing followed by drinks and gourmet meals. He continued to write, give lectures and do radio programs, and with the onset of WWII he served as a consultant to the military on Asian affairs and advised General George Patton on training troops for desert warfare.

With advancing age and decline in strength, in 1954, at the age of 69, Roy and Billie relocated to the milder climates of Arizona and California. In his 70s, Andrews remained active, doing some writing as well as shooting and conducting field trials for hunting dogs. At age 76, having battled lung cancer and apparently recovered, the old adventurer suffered a massive heart attack and died on March 11, 1960.

With a recent renewal of interest in both his scientific legacy and his intrepid feats of daring and imagination, Roy Chapman Andrews continues to provide us with the thrill of adventure in a time and a world much different from the present. Charles Gallenkamp provides a quote from the book, "*Ever Since Darwin*," by the famous archeologist, Stephen Jay Gould: "The sheer romance (of the Central Asiatic expeditions) fits Hollywood's most heroic mold." And Roy Chapman Andrews seems to fit perfectly the mold of Hollywood's most swashbuckling hero. •

Andrews' Mannlicher-Schoenauer 6.5mm carbine numbers among the most famous rifle models ever built. Introduced in 1903, the lightweight bolt action has an enclosed 5-round rotary magazine similar to that of the Savage Model 1899 lever-action rifle.

Acknowledgement

I would like to thank to thank Matt Pavlick and other staff of the Special Collections Department of the American Museum of Natural History Library for their gracious assistance and support as I worked with the material in the Roy Chapman Andrews Collection.

Bibliography

Andrews, R.C. *On the Trail of Ancient Man: A Narrative of the Field Work of the Central Asiatic Expeditions*. G.P. Putnam's Sons, New York: 1926.

Andrews, R.C. *The New Conquest of Central Asia: A Narrative of the Explorations of the Central Asiatic Expeditions in Mongolia and China, 1921-1930*. The American Museum of Natural History, New York: 1932.

Andrews, R.C. *Under a Lucky Star: A Lifetime of Adventure*. The Viking Press, New York: 1943

Caldwell, H.R. *Blue Tiger*. The Abington Press, New York: 1924.

Gallenkamp, C. *Dragon Hunter: Roy Chapman Andrews and the Central Asiatic Expeditions*. Viking Penguin, New York: 2001.

Wallace, J. *The American Museum of Natural History's Book of Dinosaurs and Other Ancient Creatures*. Simon & Schuster, New York: 1994.

Cast-Bullet Hunting Loads for Deer & Bear

by Harvey T. Pennington

THOSE OF US who use cast-bullet loads for medium-sized big game, are, in a sense, re-discovering at least a part of what hunting was like in the late 1800s and the early 1900s. We select a rifle chambered for a cartridge adequate for the game to be hunted; choose a mould which will cast an appropriate hunting bullet; choose and prepare the bullet alloy; cast the bullets; lubricate the bullets; test the loads; select and assemble the optimum loads; sight in the rifle; and go hunting. Through those extra efforts, we add to the overall enjoyment of the hunt, and—if successful in taking the game we seek—there is a new appreciation of the power those old-style, slow-moving bullets display in the game fields.

One of the most fascinating accounts describing the effectiveness of cast-bullet hunting loads appeared in an article in the December 1906, issue of *Outdoor Life* magazine. [This article was reprinted in *A Treasury of Outdoor Life*, copyright 1975, published by Book Division, Times Mirror Magazines, Inc.] The author was none other than the great writer and outdoorsman, Townsend Whelen, and the title of the article was "Red Letter Days in British Columbia." Whelen and his friend, Bill Andrews, took a six-month hunting trip, on horseback, into an unmapped wilderness area in northern B.C. During that time, they traveled about 1500 miles and lived off the land. In Whelen's words, "*...We took 300 cartridges for*

A 190-grain cast-bullet from author's M71 348 Winchester was used to harvest this 8-point whitetail buck. That bullet, cast from a Lyman mould, was pushed along by a charge of 59 grains of H-4831, and had a muzzle velocity of 2087 fps.

each of our rifles. Bill carried a .38-55 Winchester, model '94, and I had my old .40-72 Winchester, model '95, which had proved too reliable to relinquish for a high-power small bore. Both rifles were equipped with Lyman sights and carefully sighted.... I loaded the ammunition for both rifles myself, with black powder, smokeless priming, and lead bullets. Both rifles proved equal to every emergency...." [Emphasis added.]

Interestingly, Whelen and his friend took bighorn sheep, mountain goats, a mountain lion, coyotes, a wolf, and many deer on that trip. In choosing the 38-55 and 40-72, these two well-informed riflemen—and very experienced hunters—had intentionally bypassed some of the then up-and-coming smokeless high-power cartridges like the 30-30 Winchester and 30-40 Krag, which used jacketed bullets at much higher velocities.

Reading that article by Whelen, along with other such classic accounts, whetted my interest in cast-bullet hunting many years ago. Of course, I have never had the opportunity to take a six-month wilderness hunt, but, on many shorter, annual hunts, I have had the satisfaction of taking medium-sized big game with many different cast-bullet cartridge loads that I assembled.

Three of author's favorite cast-bullet cartridges and bullets. *Left:* 348 WCF and bullet cast from Lyman #350447; that bullet weighs 190 grains when cast of a 1-15 alloy. *Middle:* 38-55 WCF and 276-grain bullet cast from Lyman #375449 mould. *Right:* 405 WCF and 300-grain bullet cast from modified RCBS 40-300-BPS mould.

My own cast-bullet hunting began about 25 years ago. Back in those days, there simply were no other hunters in my home area who used homemade, lead-alloy bullets in their cartridge rifles for deer-sized game,

ith a
aska in

oad
NEI

A nine-point whitetail taken by author during the 2002 Kentucky deer season. Instead of using heavy factory-equivalent, jacketed-bullet loads in his 405 M95 Winchester, author relied on a much milder *(but very effective)* load consisting of a 300-grain cast bullet *(from a modified RCBS mould)* at a muzzle velocity of 1456 fps.

so, at times, it was difficult even to get a good conversation going about the subject.

Things are a little different now. Over the last twenty years or so, there has been a revival in the use of the cast bullet on target ranges all across this country. Certain types of today's popular shooting events *(such as long-range buffalo rifle matches, blackpowder silhouette matches, and the wildly popular "cowboy-action" matches)* require the use of the lead-alloy bullet. Consequently, there seems to be a renewed awareness of the usefulness of cast bullets, and, for an increasing number of shooters, an interest in using cast-bullet cartridge loads for hunting.

One of those who developed a recent interest in cast-bullet hunting is my good friend, Thom Clay. His experience offers a perfect example of how to get started, and it may provide some worthwhile instruction for others who may be inclined to give this type of hunting a try. So, before sharing some of my own experiences, let me quickly review his interesting—and rewarding— introduction to cast-bullet hunting:

Thom *(an old hunting buddy, and a deputy U.S. Marshal)* showed up at my home one day a couple of years ago and asked whether I thought a 38-55, using cast-bullet loads, would be adequate for an Alaskan black bear hunt he had scheduled for the upcoming spring. He had, just recently, purchased a very nice Model 94 Winchester rifle chambered for that old cartridge, and looked upon his planned bear hunt as a good opportunity to put it to use.

Now, Thom already knew the passion I have for hunting deer and other game with cast bullets; he also knew that the 38-55 WCF is one of my favorite cartridges. So, I'm sure it came as no surprise when I offered my opinion that, with a heavyweight cast bullet and a good load, there was no reason the 38-55 couldn't continue doing what it had done for well over 100 years—that is, to cleanly take medium-sized big game.

Thom's old Model '94 was a beauty. The rifle had been manufactured in 1902. It had a 24-inch barrel with a half-magazine; the wood was solid; the metal finish was patinaed, but without pitting; the bore appeared to be in very good condition; it functioned reliably; and it was fitted with a nice (original) Marble's tang sight. My friend had made a wise choice when he bought this rifle.

As yet, Thom didn't have a bullet mould for his rifle, so we took the opportunity to slug the bore of his old Winchester, so we could have an accurate measurement of the bore and groove diameters of the barrel. Since the groove diameter on his rifle was a little on the large side (.381-inch), he decided to order NEI's .379-245-GC (#190) mould. The NEI catalog stated a bullet from this mould would cast .001/.003-inch larger than the listed diameter of .379-inch, so we felt it would fit his needs.

That NEI bullet was designed to be used with a gas-check, and also featured a crimp groove in the proper location so that the overall length of the loaded cartridge would function perfectly through actions

Author's M95 Winchester chambered in 405 WCF. Manufactured in 1915, this rifle is equipped with an original Lyman receiver sight, and a "sourdough" front sight.

One of author's favorite rifles for cast-bullet hunting is this Deluxe M71 348 Winchester. The rear sight is a Williams Foolproof receiver sight; the front sight is the "sourdough"-style *(square-topped post with an angled brass insert on its face).*

Author's 38-55 WCF, which he custom-made using a single-shot Falling Block Works action. This rifle does double-duty as a target rifle, and is pictured with its Parts Unknown long-range tang sight and C. Sharps Arms spirit-level front sight. When used for hunting, this rifle is equipped with an original Lyman 1-A tang sight and a Marble's "ivory bead" front sight.

Author's sporterized 303 British SMLE military rifle; this rifle was extensively customized by the author. It has a five-shot magazine, Williams 5-D receiver sight, Williams ramp with post front sight, a barrel-band front-swivel base, and a custom stock.

having tubular magazines. The broad flat-point (meplat) of the nose of the NEI bullet would permit its use in a rifle having a tubular magazine, and, as a bonus, would add to its effectiveness as a hunting bullet.

When Thom's mould arrived a short time later, he cast some bullets using an alloy of one-part tin to sixteen-parts lead (1:16). The bullets came out of the mould with a diameter of .382-inch —.001-inch larger than the groove diameter of his barrel—which would provide a perfect fit. They weighed 269 grains, complete with gas check and lubricant. Thom pan-lubed the bullets using Tamarack 50/50 (Alox/beeswax) lubricant, and shot them without sizing so as to utilize the full as-cast diameter of the bullets. The gas checks were the Hornady crimp-on style, and were seated on the bullet with the aid of a sizing die. The base of the bullet was inserted into the sizing die just far enough to cause the gas check to be crimped into place, but not deeply enough to reduce the diameter of the driving bands of the bullet.

My friend finally settled on a load of 31 grains of IMR 3031, which gave a velocity of about 1700 fps. One hundred-yard groups were on the order of 2–1/2 inches.

In June of 2001, Thom was off on his Alaskan black bear hunt. Fortunately, on just the second day of that hunt, he got an opportunity for a close shot at a large (6 1/2-foot) black bear. As he intended, his cast bullet from the old 38-5 Winchester struck the bear square in the near (left) shoulder. The bear stumbled, ran about 15 yards, and was dead when Thom and his guide arrived. No recovery of the bullet was possible, since the bullet had penetrated completely, exiting on the opposite side of the chest just behind the bear's right shoulder.

Thom told me that, once the hunt was over, his guide admitted being a little skeptical of the ability of the 38-55 to efficiently take a large black bear, but that his opinion changed after he saw the effect of the shot. When Thom was sharing his account of the hunt with me, it was obvious that the combination of using that old rifle and its cast-bullet load had added immensely to the satisfaction he realized in taking his first black bear—and with good reason.

Of course, the grooved, lead-alloy bullet was not designed for ‘ ultra-high velocities jacketed bullets attain today. The pl cast bullet will ordinaril quite well up to a velocit, 1600 fps; however, when he loads are used to propel the p base cast bullet above that velc level, gas-cutting of the bullet's ba becomes a problem and accuracy disappears. It is at this point that a gas-checked bullet should be chosen. Gas-checked cast bullets will ordinarily retain their accuracy until velocities exceed 1900-2100 fps. So, the cast hunting bullet's useful velocity range is from approximately 1200 fps to about 2000 fps—but, within that range, the properly-alloyed cast bullet *(of adequate caliber, weight and design)* is, without doubt, a supreme hunting bullet for medium-sized big game.

Because of their lower velocities, cast bullet rifles are definitely not flat-shooting rifles. When hunting in densely-wooded areas, where long shots at game would not be expected, I zero my cast-bullet hunting rifles at only 100 yards to prevent overshooting the vital zone of a deer-sized animal when a shot is presented at closer range. So sighted, most of the different cast-bullet loads that I use will strike only 1-1/2 to 3 inches high at 50 yards—not enough to cause a miss on deer-sized game. However, if I will be hunting in open county where I would expect only longer-range shots, and if my loads exceed, say, 1,400 fps, I may opt to sight in for 150 yards. Once the rifle is zeroed, I then spend enough time on the shooting range to become well acquainted with the actual trajectory of my load, at 50-yard intervals, out to 200 yards.

Even with my highest-velocity cast-bullet loads, I refuse to take shots beyond 200 yards. Accurate placement of the shot beyond that distance becomes too difficult because of the high trajectory and the possibility of misjudging the distance over unfamiliar ground. Simply put, it is better not to fire at all than to take a chance on wounding a fine game animal.

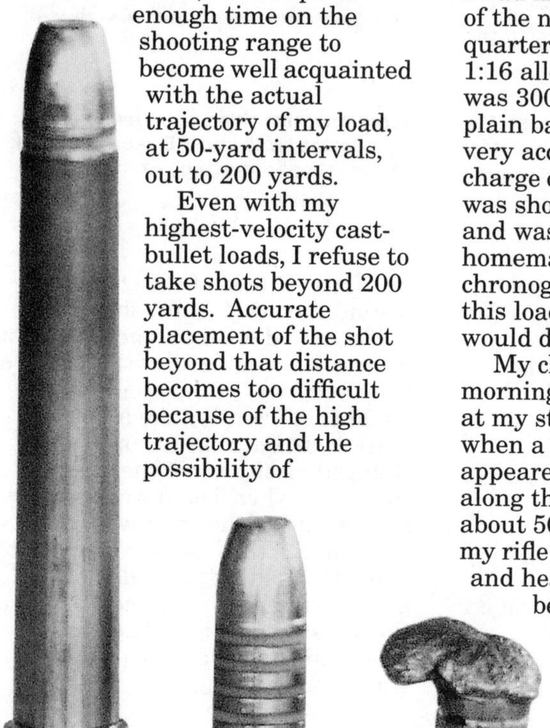

Actually, there are many hunting areas where one does not need to be overly concerned about flat trajectories and long-range shooting, and the cast-bullet hunter is not at all handicapped by his slower-moving bullets. My home area of eastern Kentucky is a good example. We have quite a few whitetail deer—and lots of trees and brush in which the deer spend most of their time. The average distance at which deer are taken in this area would undoubtedly be much less than 100 yards—probably closer to 40 yards—making it practically ideal for the cast-bullet hunter.

For instance, during the 2002 deer season, I was hunting with my Model 95 Winchester, chambered for the 405 W.C.F. But, instead of using the very powerful factory-level 405 load, which fires a jacketed 300-grain bullet at 2200 fps, I was using a cast-bullet load which was much closer, ballistically, to the old 40-72 WCF blackpowder cartridge. My bullet was cast from an RCBS 40-300-CSA mould which I had modified so that the flat point of the nose of the bullet was a full quarter-inch in diameter. Using my 1:16 alloy, the weight of the bullet was 300 grains. The bullet has a plain base *(no gas-check)*, and it is very accurate over my powder charge of 27 grains of XMP-5744. It was shot as-cast *(without sizing)*, and was pan-lubed using a homemade lubricant. The chronographed muzzle velocity of this load was 1456 fps. I figured it would do nicely for deer.

My chance came on the opening morning of the season. I had been at my stand only a couple of hours when a nice 9-point buck quietly appeared, slowly browsing his way along the edge of a hill. He was about 50 yards away. As I brought my rifle up, I could see only his neck and head through the trees between us—and he was looking downhill. Two full steps in that direction would have taken him out of sight, so I decided to fire. At the shot, the buck collapsed from a bullet through the neck. Now, I doubt that buck would ever have regained his feet, but neck shots are notorious for just stunning the deer if the spine is missed. So, upon approaching the downed buck, I fired a finishing shot into the top of his back between his shoulders, on an angle toward the center of his chest.

As expected, my first bullet had passed completely through the buck's heavy neck, and exited. But, upon field-dressing the deer, I found the bullet from my finishing shot just under the hide outside the brisket. Obviously, that second bullet had had a rough journey. It had completely penetrated the heavy bones of the spine, passed through the full depth of the chest, and penetrated the brisket before coming to rest. The recovered bullet had performed superbly, retaining a weight of 220 grains *(of its original 300-grains)*, and expanding to 3/4-inch diameter!

When hunting at close range in wooded areas, I am firmly of the opinion that the cast-bullet hunter has at least a couple of very real advantages over the person hunting with some of the high-velocity loads commonly used by deer hunters these days. The first of these is a virtual guarantee of sufficient depth of penetration to reach the vitals of the animal. It is not uncommon, even on deer-sized game, for the lighter-weight, high-velocity, jacketed bullets to strike a large bone, such as in a shoulder or *(on a quartering-away shot)* a hindquarter, and go to pieces without penetrating into the chest cavity. That is the reason for all of the emphasis these days on "premium-quality" jacketed bullets. But the slow-moving, solid, heavy cast-bullets are already "premium quality" in that respect. I have never had one of them—in solid-point form, with a good tin and lead alloy—give insufficient penetration.

Another obvious advantage of using the slower-moving, flat-point cast bullet is that it possesses great killing power without destroying an excessive amount of meat. Anyone who has examined the amount of wasted meat on a deer shot through the shoulders with one of the high-velocity magnums will know exactly what I mean. On the other hand, with the much milder cast-bullet loads, and the same bullet placement, you can practically "eat right up to the hole", as Elmer Keith was so fond of saying. Meat, after all, is the product of hunting, and there is no need to use loads that are overly destructive in that regard.

Without a doubt, one of my favorite cast-bullet hunting rifles is the lever-action M71, 348 Winchester. I bought it in 1965

Left: **405 WCF cartridge loaded with a bullet cast from a modified RCBS 40-300-BPS mould; the mould, as modified, casts a flat-point on the nose of the bullet that is a full quarter-inch in diameter. *Middle:* unfired RCBS 300-grain cast bullet. *Right:* same type of bullet recovered from a whitetail buck taken by author; the recovered bullet *(cast of a 1:16 alloy)* weighed 220 grains, and had expanded to 3/4-inch diameter!**

when I was in college. Its previous owner simply thought it was more rifle than he needed. For sure, the 348's power was mighty impressive with factory-equivalent, jacketed-bullet handloads *(200-grain bullets at 2500 fps, and 250-grain bullets at 2300 fps)*. But, after having the rifle a few years, I became curious as to how it would perform on game with cast bullets. So, I purchased a Lyman #350447 mould, and cast some bullets using a 1:15 alloy.

These bullets had a flat point and weighed 190 grains, complete with a Lyman gas check. They were sized to .350-inch in my Lyman 450 Lubricator-Sizer, and a 50/50 (Alox/beeswax) lube was used. I proceeded to work up a load using 59 grains of H-4831 powder and a CCI 250 primer. Incredibly, that load had a muzzle velocity of 2087 fps, was decently accurate, and displayed a lot of power. It was almost a ballistic twin to the fine old 33 WCF cartridge.

This 348 rifle and load were used on a deer hunt a few miles from my home, in a thickly wooded area. I was sitting on a stump when an 8-point buck came strolling along. He was only 20 yards away when he paused. I could tell that he was alerted and ready to bolt. From the angle he was facing, my shot had to be directed toward his left shoulder to enter his chest. When I fired, the buck made a quick, 20-foot dash downhill, and fell dead. My bullet had struck him in the left shoulder *(breaking it)*; it then had passed through the chest and exited through the rib cage on his right side.

Indeed, these and other cast-bullet cartridge loads that I have used have proven themselves to be perfect on deer-sized game, at woods-hunting distances. But their use in the western U.S., where shots at game ordinarily take place over longer distances, can be equally effective and satisfying—as long as the hunter maintains the personal discipline to refuse any shot beyond his reasonable ability to ensure adequate bullet placement and a clean kill.

My first western hunt with a cast-bullet cartridge rifle was a mule-deer hunt in 1978. In anticipation of this hunt, I built a 38-55 single-shot rifle, using a Falling Block Works action and a 28-inch Douglas barrel. Using some walnut lumber given to me by a friend, I made the rifle's forend and buttstock. The rear sight that I chose to use was an original Lyman 1-A tang sight; the front sight was a Marble's "ivory bead." When finished, the rifle had the look of an old Winchester High Wall.

For my upcoming mule-deer hunt, I worked up a load for the 38-55 using bullets cast from Lyman's #375449 mould. The alloy used was the approximate hardness of a 1:15 tin-to-lead mixture, and was composed of two parts Lyman's No. 2 alloy and one part lead. Complete with its gas-check and lube, this flat-point bullet weighed 276 grains. In the strong Falling Block Works action of my rifle, I finally settled on a load of 32 grains of IMR 3031, which gave my bullet a muzzle velocity of 1745 fps. This load develops nearly 1900 foot-pounds of muzzle energy (fpe).

Before leaving on the hunt, I did some serious shooting on the range to become familiar with the trajectory of this load and decided on a 150-yard sight setting. With that setting, the bullet would strike about 4-1/2 inches high at 100 yards and about 5-1/2 inches low at 200 yards—my self-imposed maximum shooting distance for hunting purposes.

On the third day of that hunt, from a rock outcropping high in Colorado's Medicine Bow Mountains, I spotted a large buck mule deer. He was grazing in the edge of a small meadow below me and appeared to be less than 150 yards away. *(I later paced the distance to be about 130 yards.)* As calmly as I could, I placed the white bead on the buck as he stood quartering slightly away from me. As the rifle recoiled, the big buck immediately hit the ground—and stayed there! From the buck's reaction to the shot, I thought the bullet from the 38-55 must have struck him in the spine, but I was wrong. After examining him, I saw that the bullet had entered well below the spine and had passed through part of the liver, then forward and through the right lung before exiting.

I was elated with the performance of the 38-55 and its cast bullet. That mulie buck was the largest I have ever taken. He was a 5-by-5, and his antlers had an inside spread of 28 inches. I estimated his live weight at 270 pounds.

My longest shot on a deer, with a cast-bullet load, came during a hunt in southwestern Colorado. I had been working with bullets cast from the Lyman #350482 mould for the 348 WCF. That bullet is a real bruiser—it is a gas-check design that weighs 268 grains when cast of 1:15 alloy. The nose of this bullet has a very blunt, rounded shape *(instead of the flat-point style that I prefer)*, but it was Lyman's heaviest offering for the 348, and I wanted to give it a try. *[Although I don't believe Lyman still offers that mould for this bullet, NEI makes their .348-250-GC (#108) which is a close copy of it.]*

From the very beginning, that bullet showed nice accuracy. Using 31 grains of IMR 4198, at a velocity of 1810 fps, I fired several 100-yard groups of about 2/2-1/2 inches, with one 5-shot group measuring only 1.7 inches. With my iron sights set for 150 yards, that load printed 4 inches high at 100 yards and around 5 inches low at 200 yards. Muzzle energy for this load is 2356 fpe.

Left: **38-40 Win. (38 WCF).** ***Middle:*** **44-40 Win. (44 WCF).** ***Right:*** **45 Colt. These three old *(revolver)* cartridges of the late 1800s, when used in rifles, can be relied on to take deer at close range with well-placed shots. But, beyond 100 yards, their short bullets lose velocity *(and power)* rapidly, and their steep trajectories make precise hits on game animals far too uncertain. The cast-bullet hunter would be much better served with one of the larger rifle cartridges.**

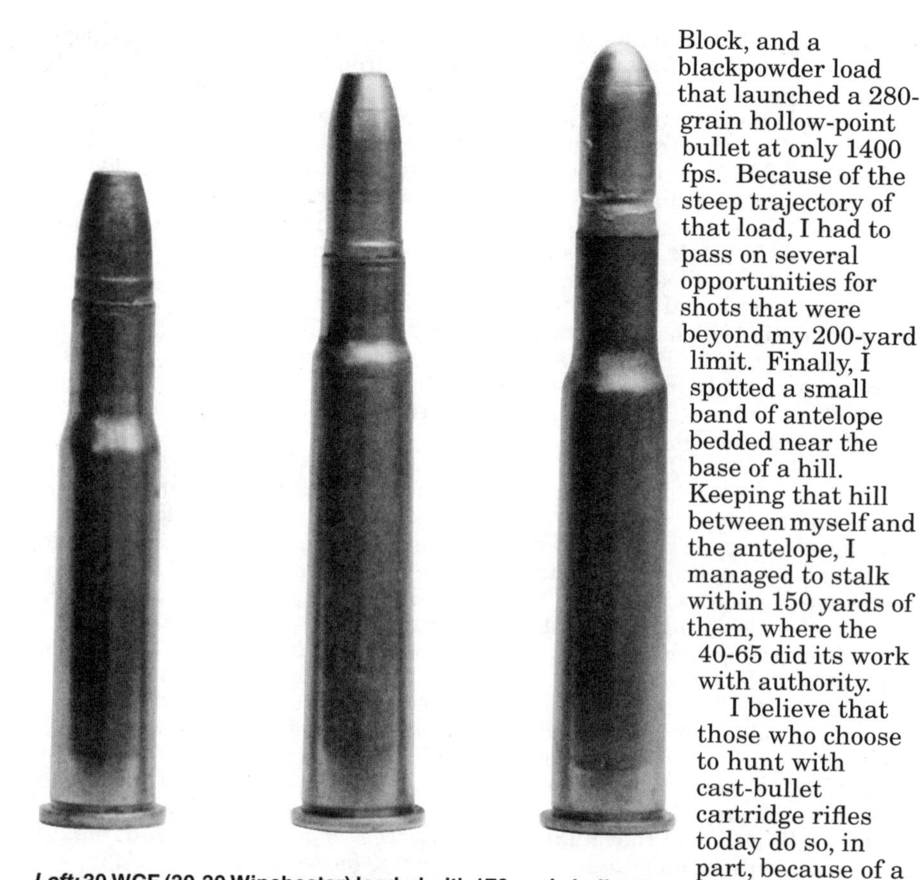

Left: **30 WCF (30-30 Winchester) loaded with 170-grain bullet cast from Lyman #31141 mould.** ***Middle:*** **303 British loaded with 200-grain bullet from modified Lyman #314299 mould.** ***Right:*** **30-40 Krag cartridge with 210-grain bullet cast from Lyman #311284 mould. With good cast-bullet loads, author believes these to be the minimum reliable cartridges for deer-sized game.**

Getting a mule deer proved to be tougher than usual that year, but my chance finally came—at 200 yards—when a young forkhorn buck entered the meadow I was watching. From a solid sitting position, with my back pressed against a large rock, I held the square, gold-faced front sight near the top of the buck's back, and slightly behind his shoulder. Even at that distance, I could plainly see the buck stagger when the bullet struck. He quickly regained his balance, however, and headed into some trees adjacent to the meadow.

My shot had hit the deer high in the lungs and exited. The blood trail was skimpy *(not unusual for high lung shots)*, but sufficient for tracking. He managed to run about 100 yards before dropping.

In all probability, the game animal most commonly associated with long-range shooting in this country is the pronghorn antelope. But even that resident of the open plains is a reasonable target for the cast-bullet hunter who is willing to exercise a little patience. A few years back, I was successful in taking a Montana antelope with my custom 40-65 Remington Rolling Block, and a blackpowder load that launched a 280-grain hollow-point bullet at only 1400 fps. Because of the steep trajectory of that load, I had to pass on several opportunities for shots that were beyond my 200-yard limit. Finally, I spotted a small band of antelope bedded near the base of a hill. Keeping that hill between myself and the antelope, I managed to stalk within 150 yards of them, where the 40-65 did its work with authority.

I believe that those who choose to hunt with cast-bullet cartridge rifles today do so, in part, because of a healthy curiosity to discover—first hand—how those classic old loads perform in the hunting field. Of course, it is also a perfect pursuit for those hunters who like to "sharpen their own tools," or, in this case, cast their own bullets and load their own cartridges.

For the person who might be interested in using a cast-bullet cartridge rifle for medium-sized big game, getting set up can be a lot of fun.

As to the selection of a specific cartridge, perhaps the wisest choice would be one of the old tried-and-true blackpowder rifle cartridges, such as the 38-55, 38-56, 40-65, 40-72, 45-70, 45-110, etc. Those old cartridges have plenty of power for medium-sized game. They can be loaded with blackpowder, Pyrodex *(or other blackpowder substitute)*, or low-level *(blackpowder-equivalent)* smokeless-powder loads. As mentioned earlier, in rifles of adequate strength, the correct smokeless-powder loads in these older cartridges can be used to boost velocities beyond the limits of the original blackpowder loads.

The grand old rifle cartridges of the early smokeless-powder era are also prime candidates for the cast-bullet hunting rifle. In this category, we would find the 30-40 Krag, 303 British, 33 WCF, 35 WCF, and 405 WCF, among others. Of course, these cartridges are right at home when loaded with smokeless powders.

Of the blackpowder-era revolver cartridges that were also chambered in rifles, the ones suitable for deer-sized game—but at short range only—are the 38-40 WCF and 44-40 WCF. *(The 45 Colt cartridge now can be added to that list, since it is presently chambered in rifles currently manufactured by Winchester, Marlin, Uberti and others.)* Anyone who has observed the power of a well-placed shot on a deer, from any of these cartridges, at short range, will be impressed. I have taken two deer with cast bullets from the 44-40 *(one with a rifle and the other with a handgun)*, and one with a 45 Colt handgun; all shots were taken within 30 yards, and none of those deer ran more than 25 yards after being hit. However, beyond 100 yards, the short, flat-pointed bullets of any of these cartridges lose velocity *(and energy)* rapidly, and the trajectory becomes so great that adequate placement of the bullet is far too uncertain for clean kills. In short, although these cartridges perform well within the limits I have described, the beginning cast-bullet hunter would be much better served with one of the larger rifle cartridges.

For those who may be wondering about the minimum reliable cartridge for hunting deer-sized game, the hunting literature of the late 1800s seems to indicate that the 32-40 WCF possessed the minimum ballistics suitable for that task. The standard 32-40 loading used a 165-grain bullet at a velocity of about 1350 fps. Today, those ballistics are easily reached and surpassed by good cast-bullet loads in anything from the 30 WCF (30-30 Winchester) on up. My friend Arville Allen's 30-30 uses a load of 27 grains of IMR 4895, which gives his 170-grain cast bullet a full 1900 fps, and it has performed very satisfactorily. The same can be said for my old 303 British and its 200-grain cast bullets. But, since a line must be drawn somewhere, I believe the 30-caliber cartridges should be considered the absolute minimum for deer-sized game when used with cast bullets.

It must be kept in mind that, with cast-bullet loads, a larger caliber and heavier bullet simply translate into more power. I would much rather see the beginning cast-bullet hunter choose, for instance, a

38-55 WCF over a 30-30 as his first rifle. But, whatever rifle and load is chosen, it is the job of the hunter—first and foremost—to see that his shot is placed accurately, and in a vital spot. Regardless of the cartridge used, nothing can make up for a poorly placed shot.

Once the cartridge and rifle to be used have been chosen, there are several factors to consider when choosing a mould for a proper hunting bullet. Obviously, the first step is to select a mould that will cast a bullet of the proper diameter for the bore of your rifle. For best results, the cast bullet should be .001/.003-inch larger than the groove diameter of your rifle.

If you are unsure about the groove diameter of your rifle, this dimension can be obtained by "slugging" the barrel. This is accomplished by carefully driving a slightly oversized, lightly-lubricated soft lead slug through a clean barrel, and then measuring the slug at its widest point with a micrometer. This measurement will give you the groove diameter of your barrel. *(NOTE: To avoid the possibility of damaging the barrel during this process, I use a leather mallet and a short, wooden dowel rod to start the slug in the muzzle. Once the slug fully enters the bore, I then use the leather mallet—and progressively longer wooden dowel rods—to tap the slug completely through the bore.)*

As to the bullet's style, I strongly recommend that the cast bullet selected for hunting have a broad, solid flat point. Just as handgunners have long recognized that the flat-nosed bullet is much more effective in hunting situations than the round-nosed bullet, the same holds true for the rifle hunter who chooses to use cast bullets. The flat-pointed style has a much greater initial force on impact, cuts a larger entrance wound, and ensures a wider wound-channel than the round-nose style.

The cast bullet selected for use in a rifle having a tubular magazine must have both a flat point, and a properly located crimp groove. Cartridges in a tubular magazine are held "end on end"—that is, the point of the bullet of the cartridge to the rear rests against *(or near)* the primer of the loaded round ahead of it. Thus, when a rifle of sufficient recoil is fired, the primer of the leading cartridge could actually be detonated by being suddenly thrust against a sharply-pointed bullet in the cartridge behind it. Bullets having a wide, flat-nosed design prevent this from happening and are standard for use in tubular magazines. Likewise, the crimp groove on the cast bullet must be properly located so that when the bullet is crimped into place the resulting overall length is standard for the cartridge; this will ensure proper cycling of the cartridge through the magazine and action of the rifle.

The author took this large mule deer with a cast-bullet load from his custom-made 38-55 single-shot rifle at a distance of 130 yards. A single 276-grain bullet, cast from a Lyman #375449 mould was all that was necessary.

For hunting big game, it is best to stay away from the lighter-weight bullets. The heavier bullets, which are standard for the cartridge to be used, should be chosen. *(For example, in a 358 Win., this would be a bullet weighing 200-250 grains; for the 38-55, a bullet weighing 250-280 grains; for the 45-70, bullets from*

350-500 grains.) The hunter needs penetration from his cast bullet, and, all other things being equal, the longer and heavier the bullet, the deeper the penetration.

Because of this need for adequate penetration, I recommend the beginning cast-bullet hunter select a mould that will cast a solid-point *(rather than a hollow-point)* bullet. To be sure, even at the lower blackpowder velocities, a soft, hollow-point cast bullet will provide an amazing amount of expansion, and, on lighter-bodied game such as antelope, will provide dramatically quick kills. But, because of its rapid expansion, the hollow-point cast bullet will have less *(possibly much less)* penetration than the solid-point bullet, and, at times, its penetration may prove inadequate on heavier game. For that reason, the solid, flat-point cast bullet, which has repeatedly proven its reliability and effectiveness, is the choice for nearly all my hunting.

One other decision to be made in selecting the mould is whether to choose a plain-base bullet or one that will permit the use of a gas check. When the shooter will be using only blackpowder loads or low-velocity *(under 1500 fps)* smokeless loads, the plain-base bullet will do just fine. However, as explained earlier, if the shooter plans to boost those velocities much beyond 1500 fps, a gas-check bullet will be required.

Of course, the hardness of the cast bullet is determined by its alloy. Presently, I use only mixtures of pure tin and lead for my bullet alloys. *[I avoid using antimony* (an element present in wheelweights, for instance) *in my bullet alloys because antimony causes the alloy to become brittle and, thus, more likely to shatter when it strikes—a quality that is certainly not appropriate in a hunting bullet.]* For game, I have used bullets cast as soft as 1-part tin to 40-parts lead (1:40), and as hard as 1:15. When the velocity of my loads is on the slow side, say, from 1200-1400 fps, I use the softer alloys (e.g., 1:40 or 1:25) to ensure expansion of the bullet. But, as the velocity of the cast bullet is increased, the alloy should be hardened to maintain accuracy and prevent leading of the barrel. At higher velocities—up to approximately 1700-1900 fps—a gas-check bullet made up of a 1:16 mix usually shoots fine, and will give very satisfactory expansion. As I mentioned earlier, a 1:15 alloy has been used for my highest-velocity hunting loads, and, with certain bullets, those loads have reached 1900 fps, to a little over 2000 fps, with accuracy.

Of course, blackpowder is the traditional propellant for many of the old cartridges, and it does a great job in my 38-55, 40-65, 44-40, and 45-110. Those shooters who are interested in using blackpowder loads—but have never before reloaded blackpowder cartridges—would be wise to invest in one or more of the fine loading manuals available on that subject today. Loading cartridges with blackpowder is actually quite easy, once you understand the basic rules for doing so, but those rules differ in several important respects from those that apply to assembling smokeless- powder loads. The currently available loading manuals written by Mike Venturino, Steve Garbe, Sam Fadala and Paul Matthews, among others, will give the newcomer to blackpowder-cartridge reloading a proper start.

These two 40-caliber bullets illustrate the flat-point and round-nose styles of cast bullets. For hunting, the flat-point style is preferred; it has a greater initial force on impact, cuts a larger entrance wound and wound channel, and promotes greater expansion than the round-nose style.

Should the hunter decide to use smokeless powder for his cast-bullet loads, there are many loading manuals worth having. Two of my favorites have been around for quite a while. The first is the *Lyman Cast Bullet Handbook, 3rd Edition*, copyright 1980, published by Lyman Products Corporation. That volume contains loading information on dozens of current and obsolete rifle cartridges, information on the techniques of casting and the equipment which is used, and has some very helpful tables giving the trajectories of various popular cast bullets. Another great source is *Cartridges of the World*, by Frank C. Barnes. That work has gone through many editions, and still stands as a classic reference work covering handloading data *(as well as technical and historical information)* for almost any cartridge.

Well, I guess it's time to draw the curtain on this little treatise. Certainly, I hope that a strong spark of interest in cast-bullet hunting has fallen on a reader or two. If so, whoever is curious enough to kindle that interest will surely acquire a great respect for the power and effectiveness of a well-designed cast-bullet load—and deservedly greater satisfaction when the next deer is taken and the venison is served. ●

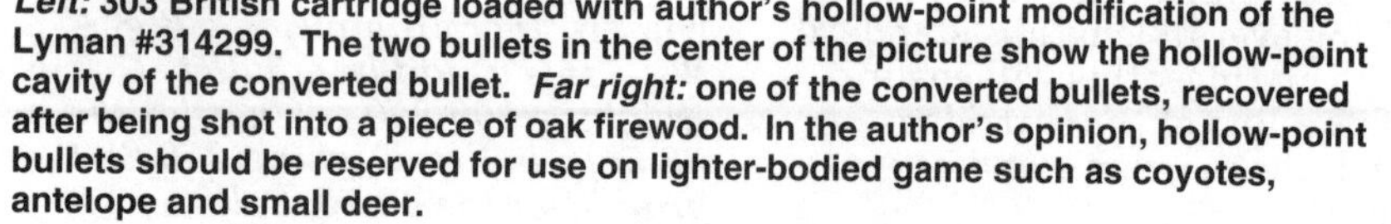

Left: **303 British cartridge loaded with author's hollow-point modification of the Lyman #314299. The two bullets in the center of the picture show the hollow-point cavity of the converted bullet. *Far right:* one of the converted bullets, recovered after being shot into a piece of oak firewood. In the author's opinion, hollow-point bullets should be reserved for use on lighter-bodied game such as coyotes, antelope and small deer.**

THE HANGERS-ON

Handguns and cartridges that refuse to die

Many of these cheaper revolvers are still circulating and okay to shoot if in good condition.

by Ralph Hurne

IN THIS AGE of mega-overkill, so many of the old revolver calibers seem to be on the way out. Why bother with 38 S&W when 38 Special's a bit better, and beyond that the 357 Magnum. As for 38 Long and Short Colt – *finito*. And one hardly dares mention the old European 380 Revolver.

So why lament their demise? Ballistically superceded they may be, but as gun-nuts *(you wouldn't be reading this if you hadn't some of that strange blood in your veins)*, surely it's almost a duty not to let the past slip away.

Revolvers in obsolete and near-obsolete calibers abound, so why relegate them to curio category when most will perform as well as on the day they were made? After all, most of us aren't really likely to be attacked by a 225-pound hulk wielding a machete, or need a handgun for survival. Anyway, should anything nasty happen, there's plenty of modern stuff to choose from even though the old-timers will still do their job.

Not often highlighted is that prolific and widespread group of shooters, the fun brigade. They're not particularly interested in super accuracy or stopping power. With an interest in the Old West they might like reloading precious 41 Long Colt brass for that Colt Bisley. Or the owner might get a box of Fiocchi's 11mm cartridges for his 1873 French Service revolver. Probably too expensive to fire off more than 25 rounds in one session before reloading, so he might use 15 to get an idea where the shots go, then use the remainder to ventilate a few tin cans.

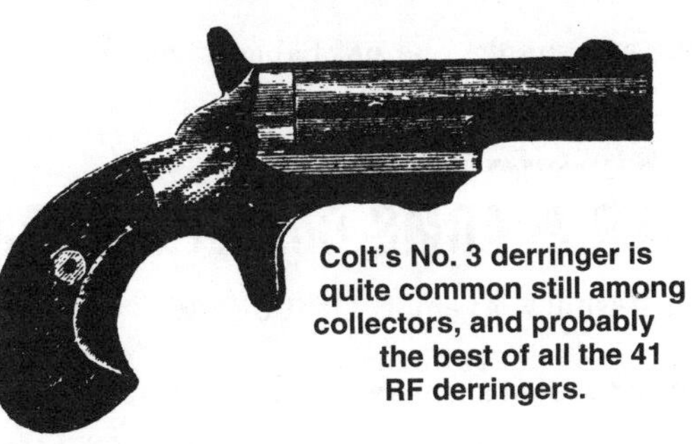

Colt's No. 3 derringer is quite common still among collectors, and probably the best of all the 41 RF derringers.

True, ammo manufacturers are in the business of making money, but the long established concerns must still have what's needed to re-kindle calibers that have passed away. I'm thinking particularly of the rimfire

Typical 19th century European revolver: the tip-up Spirlet (1870), Belgian and of good quality. Often in 450, watch out for those 11mm thick-rim European calibers.

32, 38 and 44. The 41 RF gets catered for very occasionally, but it's hardly a plinking caliber and a few rounds could last a long time. I used to stick a 41 RF Colt No. 3 derringer in my pocket when taking my hound for a woodland walk, and having the odd shot as I went along. This cartridge, and in fact all rimfires, can be made to perform with cases turned from solid brass and a 22 blank (Short) or a 22 cartridge head, seated into a machined primer hole set off-center to coincide with the hammer fall.

The 38 RF revolvers were never as thick on the ground as the 32 RFs, the latter the most prolific. Not long discontinued, the boxes of 32 RF still around are carefully preserved. And 32 RF rifles too – how many Stevens Favorites are still circulating? As expensive as a new short-run production would be to the shooter, would not all those fun shooters stock up while they had the chance? Mainly a rifle cartridge, the 25 Stevens rimfire soon disappeared along with the 32s, ousted by the new 22 Magnum. Yet what a nice accurate cartridge the 25 RF was. I once had a Stevens Lord in this caliber, a dream to shoot.

Many an obsolete revolver is kept going thanks to customer-orientated Fiocchi, even though the old calibers they still manufacture can't be making them a fortune.

Cowboy action shooting has done a lot for some calibers whose futures weren't looking too bright, notably the 32-20 and 38-40. And bringing back the likes of 45 Schofield and 44 Russian was good news indeed. All of which shows that rebirth is possible. Much has been done in recent years to hark back to the past when, to my way of thinking, guns then had more character. One can hope such reborn classics will find a permanent niche.

Almost overlooked now and dating from 1876, the old 38 S&W is such a versatile round. In its standard 145-grain form it's suitable for small revolvers—yet perfectly adequate as a field cartridge. In 1905, and adding a bit of wallop, there appeared a flat-nosed version known as 38 Colt New Police or 38 Colt Police Positive. Many a big revolver has been chambered for it, notably Smith & Wesson's M&P. Once factory-loaded with a 200-grain projectile, it became the Super

THE
WEBLEY-FOSBERY AUTOMATIC REVOLVER

HALF SIZE.

WEBLEY FOSBERY AUTOMATIC
455 CORDITE

Is the only Automatic Pistol or Revolver taking the ·455 Service Cordite Ammunition. None of the Automatic Pistols on the market shoot so large and powerful a cartridge, consequently they all lack the necessary stopping power a Revolver or Pistol should have.

The Mechanism is very strong and simple, and not liable to get out of order.

THE Wholesale at

WEBLEY & SCOTT REVOLVER & ARMS Co., Ltd., BIRMINGHAM

And at 78, Shaftesbury Avenue, LONDON, W.

Webley Fosbery automatic revolver. Interesting and sought after, but hardly a pocket model.

Police, and was adopted by Britain's armed forces before, during, and after WWII. It was still offered as a police caliber up to the 1950s, S&W offering their Regulation Police and Terrier alongside the 38 Specials like the Centennial and Chiefs Special. Yet the M&P continues, listed now as Model 10 M&P HB. Surely the basic heart of S&Ws, the M&P has survived for over a century with relatively few minor changes. Not particularly sought after by collectors/shooters, surely the M&P deserves to be an all-time classic? And the 38 S&W round; a hanger-on if ever there was one!

The long defunct British ammunition makers left revolver owners high and dry with their 320 and 380 Tranters and Webleys. That is, until it was released that the American 32 Short Colt and 38 Short Colt had been originally borrowed from the British 320 and 380. So, luckily, Tranter and Webley owners still have a supply. For a while the British 455 revolver ammo became hard to get until manufacturers finally tumbled that the world was awash with Webleys in this chambering. Today this fine cartridge is not hard to obtain.

None of this is to suggest that a producer brings back, say, 46 RF, 50 Remington, 30 RF, or even 32- and 24-bore shotgun cartridges. But decent runs of 22 Winchester Rim Fire, 22 Automatic, 41 Long Colt and 455 Webley Automatic would not go amiss.

Automatics have fared better than revolvers. Along the way not too many mainstreamers have fallen obsolete. Surprisingly the 8mm Roth-Steyr, 9mm Steyr, 7.65 Luger, 8mm Nambu, 9mm Browning Long are still with us. The main auto scene–prior to the coming of recent varieties–had crystallized into 25, 32 (7.65mm), 380, 38 Colt Automatic, 38 Super Automatic, 9mm Parabellum, 45 ACP. And two original granddaddies are still going strong, sprightly centenarians both predating 1900 – the 7.65 (32 ACP) and the 7.63 Mauser. The latter due to the appeal of the Broomhandle Mauser itself, the former because of its sheer convenience. Disparaged by some as lacking power, the 7.65 blew the lining out of Archduke Ferdinand in 1914, so starting WWI. Puny? It fired the loudest shot in the world! But, optimistically, as long as shooters keep an eye on their heritage, I have faith that not too many fine old-timers will fade away. ●

Webley Pistol Mark I in 455 Webley. Some Colt 1911s were chambered for 455.

A pocket version of the larger 38 ACP Military, an auto that would look right in Humphrey Bogart's hand.

Note the No. 5 Express. This was also a light rifle round, the title meant to imply something more potent. Although most 38 brass will fit, 38 Special brass with flush-seated bullet works well.

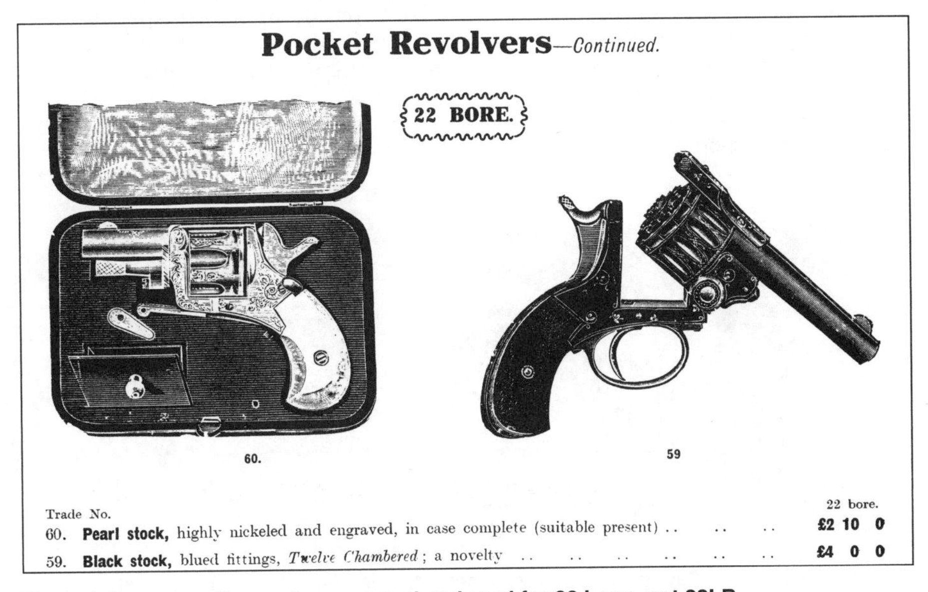

Pocket Revolvers—*Continued.*

22 BORE.

60. 59

Trade No.		22 bore.
60.	**Pearl stock,** highly nickeled and engraved, in case complete (suitable present)	£2 10 0
59.	**Black stock,** blued fittings, *Twelve Chambered*; a novelty	£4 0 0

Most of these novelty revolvers were chambered for 22 Long, not 22LR.

Smokeless Muzzleloader Velocities Without the Smokeless

by Toby Bridges

WHEN THE KNIGHT MK-85 in-line percussion ignition rifle first hit the market back in 1985, the futuristic front-loaded big game rifle was met with immediate opposition from traditionally-minded muzzleloading shooters and hunters. Still, the fast-handling feel, modern lines, sure-fire positive ignition, simplified maintenance, ease of scope installation, and exceptional accuracy with a brand new sabot bullet concept made the Knight rifle–and the many soon-to-follow in-line ignition muzzleloaders–outstanding performers on big game. And it was these benefits that quickly appealed to the modern firearms hunter who had been eyeballing the special muzzleloader seasons as a new hunting opportunity.

Initially, organized efforts by traditional muzzleloading shooters and muzzleloader shooting organizations were successful in getting the modern in-line rifles outlawed in quite a few states. Likewise, the saboted bullets that made the fast rifling twist of these modern muzzleloaders deadly at 150, 175, and even 200 yards were also banned during the special muzzleloader seasons in even more states. Still, the guns and loads continued to appeal to the modern-day hunter wanting all the accuracy and knockdown power a muzzle-loaded hunting rifle could muster. And by the mid-1990s, the majority of these regulations were reversed and the in-line ignition muzzleloaders and equally modern loads became pretty well legalized from coast to coast–because hunters wanted them!

To force these changes, shooters successfully argued that the position of the nipple in the rear center of the breech plug did not make the rifle shoot any faster or any farther than a side-hammer muzzleloader stuffed with a like load. Once game departments permitted in-line muzzleloaders, it was only a matter of time before saboted bullets also became legal in most states.

Things have certainly changed since the early days of the first modern in-line ignition muzzleloading hunting rifles.

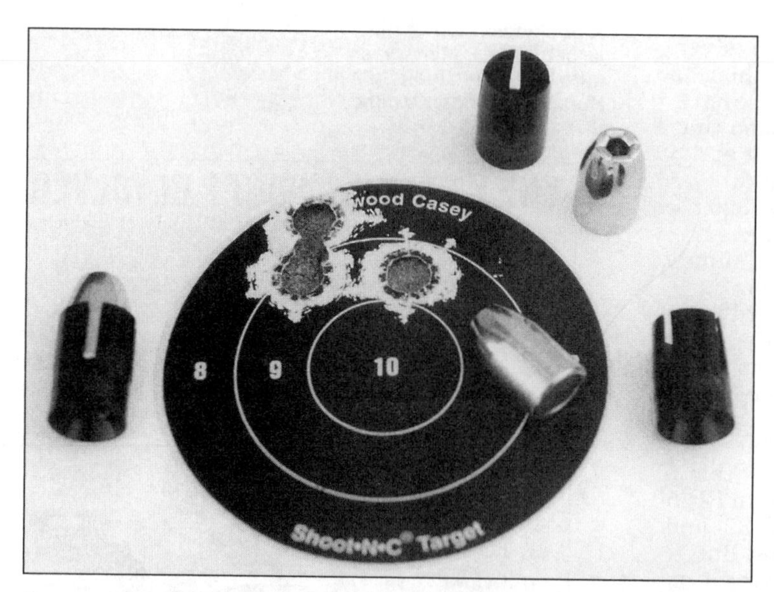

Not only are today's modern in-line ignition rifles capable of exceptional velocities and energy levels, they're also unbelievably accurate with saboted bullets–like the 260-grain Winchester Platinum HP shown here.

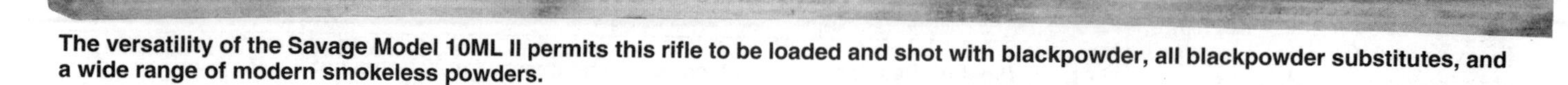
The versatility of the Savage Model 10ML II permits this rifle to be loaded and shot with blackpowder, all blackpowder substitutes, and a wide range of modern smokeless powders.

The light Knight/Barnes all-copper spire-pointed hollow-point "Red Hot" bullets for the 50-caliber bore can be pushed out of the muzzle at speeds well over 2200 fps by hot charges of modern blackpowder substitutes.

Big jacketed hollow-point handgun bullets, like the Hornady 250-grain .452-inch XTP for the 45 Colt, are great for 100- to 150-yard effectiveness on big game. Today's muzzleloading hunter is now demanding a hard-hitting and accurate 200-yard hunting bullet.

The aerodynamic .452-inch Hornady SST (Super Shock Tip) offers the performance-minded muzzleloading hunter a bullet design with a higher ballistic coefficient for improved down-range performance. Bullet shown here with an auxiliary sabot "sub-base" to help contain the pressures of magnum powder charges.

Current models are, without a doubt, the most efficient muzzle-loaded rifles ever manufactured. And thanks to vastly improved ignition systems, better-performing propellants, and newer bullet designs with a high ballistic coefficient, the rifles and loads favored by today's muzzleloading hunter definitely have a true range advantage over any traditionally-styled frontloader and fodder from the past. In fact, the race to have the fastest shooting, hardest hitting and longest-range front-loaded big-game rifle has spurred manufacturers to a new level of muzzleloader performance competition — and boasting.

The 50-caliber Savage Model 10ML II is the rifle that has significantly raised the bar for present muzzleloader velocities and energy levels. Introduced in 2000, this unique muzzleloader holds the distinction of being the first production muzzleloader ever designed and built to be loaded and shot with modern nitrocellulose-based smokeless powders. The company advertises that the Model 10ML II, and loads that can be safely shot out of it, are capable of topping 2300 fps with a saboted 250-grain bullet.

Prior to the Savage muzzleloader, Knight Rifles, of Centerville, Iowa, and Thompson/Center Arms, of Rochester, New Hampshire, were locked in battle to produce the hottest 50-caliber muzzle-loaded rifle on the market.

This 1 1/2-inch 100-yard group was shot with a 150-grain charge of FFFg Triple Seven, a saboted 275-grain Precision Rifle "QT" polymer-tipped lead bullet, and Muzzleload Magnum Products sub-base.

Through the late 1990s, both developed new models that incorporated hot No. 209 shotgun primer ignition for complete burn of the relatively new Pyrodex Pellet charges that were in vogue among muzzleloading hunters. What Knight and T/C also quickly discovered was that the efficiency of the No. 209 primers not only gave better ignition and full consumption of two 50-grain blackpowder-equivalent Pyrodex Pellets, but that the Knight D.I.S.C. Rifle and T/C Encore 209x50 Magnum rifles could effectively burn three of the compressed pellet charges. And that such 150-grain blackpowder-equivalent charges pushed 50-caliber muzzle velocities with a saboted 240- to 250-grain bullet up to around 2000 fps.

These velocities are a good 400 to 500 fps faster than possible with the popular 100-grain Pyrodex "RS/Select" charges widely used ten years prior, in early 50-caliber in-line rifles like the Knight MK-85, T/C Thunderhawk or the CVA Apollo. Modern muzzleloader advocates could no longer claim the in-line ignition rifles were incapable of shooting faster, flatter and farther than traditional muzzleloading rifles and loads. New standards for muzzleloader performance had been established, and in short order just about every in-line percussion rifle manufacturer stepped up to the plate with a model–or several models–capable of producing like velocities with magnum 150-grain charges of Pyrodex Pellets.

With 40- to 45-grain charges of nitrocellulose powders like IMR-4227, Accurate Arms XMP5744 and VihtaVuori N110, the Savage Model 10ML II positively established that a muzzle-loaded 50-caliber rifle could get a saboted 250-grain bullet up over 2300 fps with outstanding accuracy and tremendous knockdown power. However, no matter how much Pyrodex– either super-fine "P" grade or in pellet form–is loaded into a 50-caliber bore, velocities will hardly rise much above 2000 fps. And when they did, accuracy usually suffered. Higher velocities with rifles still requiring blackpowder or Pyrodex meant loading and shooting lighter bullets.

Knight Rifles now offers a line of lightweight all-copper spire-pointed hollow-point saboted projectiles to get more velocity out of their 50-caliber D.I.S.C. Rifle models. Produced by Barnes Bullets, the sleek Knight "Red Hot" bullets are available as 180-, 200- and 220-grain spire-points, plus 250- and

The modern muzzleloading hunter expects more out of the rifle and load used for big game than any muzzleloading hunter in history—today's muzzleloading gun and loading component manufacturers have met that demand.

300-grain bullets with a huge hollow-point nose. With a 150-grain Pyrodex Pellet charge, shooters have discovered they can get the 200-grain saboted .451-inch "Red Hot" bullet out of the muzzle of a primer-ignited 26-inch in-line barrel at just over 2100 fps. And when the still lighter 180-grain spire-point hollow-point bullet is loaded ahead of the same powder charge, velocity rises to around 2175 fps.

A couple of years ago, Thompson/Center Arms introduced their new *"drop action"* Omega with a lengthy 28-inch barrel. In early advertising, the company claimed the added 2 inches of bore *"delivers 250 fps of extra velocity"*. Such claims are nearly impossible to prove, and in a recent catalog, T/C downplayed that boast, instead claiming the slightly longer barrel was capable of *"producing higher velocities over standard length barrels"*. In my testing of the Omega, I found that with three 50-grain Pyrodex Pellets, I could get Knight's 180-grain "Red Hot" bullet out of the muzzle at 2258 fps. Now we're starting to talk real muzzleloader velocities!

Just two years ago (2002), Hodgdon Powder Company introduced a totally new blackpowder substitute known as Triple Seven. Unlike blackpowder or Hodgdon's own Pyrodex powders, the new Triple Seven is formulated without any sulfur whatsoever. The powder burns cleaner than any other traditional muzzleloader propellant to date. While a few shooters have experienced a crusty ring build-up in the bore near the point where the sabot/bullet combination is seated over the powder, for the most part Triple Seven leaves only minor fouling in the bore. And this fouling does not tend to build as badly as blackpowder, or even Pyrodex, having less affect on accuracy.

Another benefit of the new powder is that it is noticeably hotter than Pyrodex, resulting in higher velocities than the earlier blackpowder substitute when loaded in the same volume doses. Hodgdon produces Triple Seven in both pellet and loose grain form. Like the Pyrodex Pellets, each Triple Seven Pellet is supposed to be a 50-grain blackpowder equivalent. However, a Pyrodex Pellet weighs around 42 grains. The new Triple Seven Pellets weigh around 31 grains each. Still, a three-pellet load of each will produce similar velocities with the same weight bullet, with the new compressed Triple Seven pellets producing slightly higher bullet speeds.

During my personal test sessions with Pyrodex Pellet charges, I found that a 150-grain charge (3 pellets) would push a saboted 250-grain

"The Bullet" is a unique saboted muzzle-loaded hunting projectile that features a hole running through the entire length of the bullet. Shown is the 200-grain .451" diameter bullet. The light weight of the design is ideal for obtaining high velocities with heavy charges of Triple Seven.

Hot charges of Triple Seven can get light 150- to 180-grain saboted bullets out of many of today's so-called "Super 45" inline rifles at velocities once reserved for centerfire cartridge rifles. This reading was shot with a 150-grain charge of Pyrodex Pellets and a saboted 155-grain XTP out of a 28-inch barreled 45-caliber Thompson/Center "Omega".

The expanded 250-grain .452-inch Hornady SST here was recovered from a large buck shot at 100 yards with a 48-grain charge of Accurate Arms XMP5744 out of a Savage Model 10ML II. The load clocks 2245 fps at the muzzle, on average just 1 fps faster than with a 150-grain charge of FFFg Triple Seven.

The high ballistic coefficient of modern saboted bullets like the Precision Rifle polymer tipped "QT", coupled with muzzle velocities exceeding 2200 fps ensure high levels of retained energy out to and beyond 200 yards.

Precision Rifle's unique "duplex" sabot (*and .375 BC*) .357-inch 195-grain spire-point bullet can be pushed from the muzzle of the Savage muzzleloader with hot charges of Triple Seven at around 2300 fps. The load retains more than 1500 fpe at 200 yards.

bullet from the muzzle of a No. 209 primer-ignited 24-inch 50-caliber barrel at 1955 fps, for 2125 fpe. The very same rifle loaded with a duplicate sabot and bullet ahead of three Triple Seven Pellets would increase velocity to 2027 fps, for 2275 fpe. On average that is a 72 fps increase with the same 150-grain blackpowder-equivalent powder charge.

A couple of years ago, I learned of a custom in-line riflemaker in Michigan who was building a slick-looking bolt-action rifle on a modern centerfire rifle action. This maker was claiming that due to the design of "his" breech plug, he could get a 300-grain bullet out of the muzzle at well over 2300 fps with four Pyrodex Pellets (a 200-grain charge)...and at 2900 fps with five of the pellets (a 250-grain charge). Fortunately, I had the opportunity to speak with one shooter who had forked out more than $2,500 for one of the rifles, and who could not get velocities anywhere near what the maker was claiming. In fact, this shooter had also bought a Savage Model 10ML II and was getting better velocities (around 2350 fps) with 44 grains of VihtaVuori N110 and the saboted 250-grain Hornady XTP.

Since the Savage was built to contain the higher pressures of smokeless powders, I set out to see just what kind of velocities a shooter could expect with 200- and 250-grain charges of Pyrodex Pellets. As I suspected, the change in velocity was not upward. I first chronographed three pellets behind a saboted 250-grain .452-inch Hornady XTP, and came up with 1955 fps. With four pellets, velocity dropped to 1930 fps, and with five of the 50-grain blackpowder equivalent pellets, I couldn't even break 1900 fps. The only increase was the dramatic jump in recoil!

Once I established that three of the Triple Seven Pellets would produce a muzzle velocity of 2027 fps with the 250-grain .452-inch Hornady XTP and sabot, I loaded the rifle with four of the pellets. Velocity jumped to 2120 fps. The recoil was horrendous, so I didn't attempt loading with five Triple Seven Pellets.

The loading data Hodgdon publishes right on the label of the FFFg Triple Seven canister tells a shooter this powder is significantly hotter than "P"-grade Pyrodex. The powder maker claims that a 100-grain charge of the fine-grain Triple Seven will spit a saboted 250-grain Barnes Expander MZ out of a 50-caliber muzzle at a whopping 1971 fps, faster than possible with a 150-grain three-pellet charge of Pyrodex Pellets. Loose grain "P" is the finest grade of Pyrodex, intended for use in small 20- to 30-grain charges for 36- and 44-caliber percussion revolvers. It took a full 170

Author Toby Bridges took this open country buck at nearly 200 yards with a saboted 180-grain "The Bullet" pushed out of the muzzle of his 50-caliber Savage Model 10ML II at 2347 fps by a hot 150-grain charge of FFFg Triple Seven. The whitetail practically dropped where it stood.

By actual weight, Triple Seven Pellets weigh right at 31 grains each. Still, these three pellets will duplicate the performace of a 150-grain charge of blackpowder. With modern spire-pointeed bullet designs like the saboted Hornady SSt, the new blackpowder sub is capable of outstanding accuracy, and knockdown power.

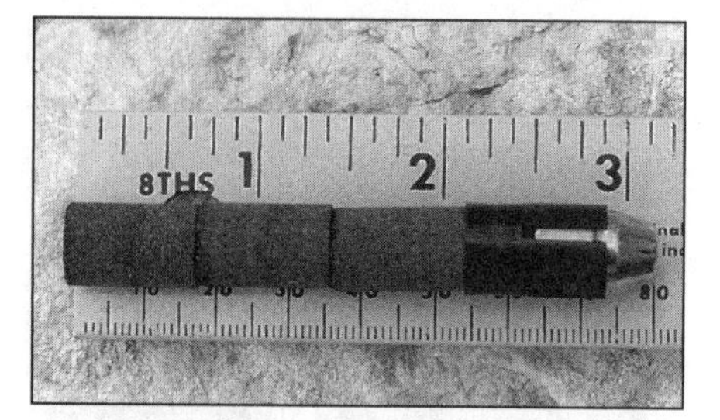

This three Pyrodex Pellet (150-grain) powder charge and saboted 250-grain .452" XTP jacketed hollow-point take up more than 3 inches of a 50-caliber bore.

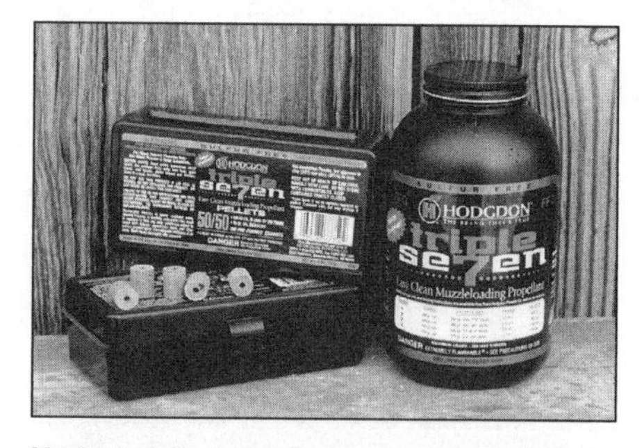

Hodgdon Powder Company's new Triple Seven comes in comressed pellet and loose grain form. Shooters are finding the FFFg grade of Triple Seven hotter than the compressed pellets.

grains of "P"- grade Pyrodex in a 50-caliber Savage Model 10ML II to reach a similar velocity (1973 fps) with a saboted 250-grain bullet.

The quickness of FFFg Triple Seven intrigued me, so I set out to determine just what kind of velocities I could achieve from one of the Model 10ML II rifles with still-heavier loads of the powder. I knew the smokeless powder loads the rifle shoots so well produce far higher pressure levels, so I wasn't concerned about damaging such a well-built muzzleloader. What I did discover was that I could duplicate the smokeless velocities produced by some of the more popular smokeless powder loads commonly shot out of the Savage muzzleloader, but without the smokeless powder.

Right off, I found I could not get the 1971 fps Hodgdon claims with a 100-grain charge behind a saboted 250-grain 45-caliber bullet, but I did get 1948 fps. An additional 10 grains upped velocity to 1992 fps, 120 grains of the FFFg Triple Seven gave me 2085 fps, 130 grains produced 2147 fps and 140 grains brought the velocity of the 250-grain .452-inch Hornady SST up to 2207 fps. When I took the powder charge to a full 150 grains of FFFg Triple Seven, the poly-tipped spire-point bullet was leaving the muzzle at 2244 fps. Interestingly, this hotter load was producing a muzzle velocity just 1 fps slower than my average velocity with the same sabot and bullet pushed from the same rifle by 48 grains of Accurate Arms XMP5744.

At 130 grains, I noticed accuracy was beginning to be affected by the higher pressures created by the hot loads of loose grain Triple Seven, so reverted to loading a simple sub-base between the powder charge and sabot base. This sub-base is nothing more than the gas seal, or obturator cup, cut from the rear of a Winchester 28-gauge "AA" wad. This is loaded atop the powder, cup side-down. Then the sabot and bullet are loaded snugly against the flat-topped surface of the gas seal. This results in added protection of the cupped base of the plastic sabot from the high heat and pressure of magnum charges. Without the sub-base, the Savage would throw the bullets into an 8- to 10-inch "pattern" on 100-yard targets when loaded with 140- to 150-grain charges of FFFg Triple Seven. With the sub-base, a high percentage of the groups shot over the course of several months averaged right at 1-1/2 inches across.

Muzzleload Magnum Products, the company that produces the majority of all sabots packaged by Knight, Thompson/Center, Hornady, Barnes and a few others, picked up on the work I was conducting with a sub-base loaded over the powder charge and began producing one of superior design. The company refers to it as a "ballistic bridge sub-base", and the design they offer features a squat dome on the top side. This fits right into the cupped base of the sabot that's loaded directly over it, providing a very effective double gas seal that will contain some of the hottest muzzleloader pressures. And these pressures are higher than most shooters realize. While conducting some independent testing on a new sabot design for Hornady Manufacturing through the summer and fall of 2003, I learned a 150-grain three-pellet Triple Seven load would produce right at 29,500 psi inside a 50-caliber bore when loaded behind a saboted 250-grain bullet. Pressures with the hotter 150-grain FFFg Triple Seven load would be even higher.

The new MMP sub-base has worked extremely well ahead of hot smokeless charges in the Savage Model 10ML II, and has proven equally beneficial when loading 130 to 150 grains of FFFg Triple Seven. When I initially tested the Savage 10ML II with hot loads of Pyrodex "P" four years ago, I did not attempt loading with a sub-base of any sort. Then, I found that a 100-grain charge of "P" grade would give me 1678 fps with a saboted 250-grain bullet, and even when charges were upped to 150 grains of the very fine Pyrodex powder, velocities only inched up to 1870 fps. So, I went back and retested with the MMP sub-base, and did manage to push velocities with the hottest charge to 1905 fps.

New FFFg Triple Seven shows a definite increase with every additional 10 grains of powder, and

The Traditions Lightning 45 "LD" is just one of a number of hot 45-caliber in-line rifles capable of topping 2500 fps with hot loads of Pyrodex or Triple Seven, and a light saboted bullet.

Many of today's more popular in-line ignition muzzle-loaded rifles rely on hot No. 209 primers for ignition—and better consumption of magnum Pyrodex and Triple Seven charges.

with the sub-base the 140- and 150-grain charges are good for nearly 20 fps more speed than the same charge shot across the chronograph without the sub-base. In other words, with 150 grains of FFFg Triple Seven, the 250-grain SST would speed over the downrange screens of my Shooting Chrony chronograph at 2261 fps. Not bad for a non-smokeless load.

Recoil with the super-hot loads of Triple Seven didn't seem to be any worse than when shooting the three-pellet charges, either Triple Seven or Pyrodex. Even so, felt recoil became noticeably lighter as bullet weight was reduced and, as expected, velocity increased.

With an MMP sub-base over a full 150-grain charge of FFFg Triple Seven, I found I could push a saboted 200-grain Knight "Red Hot" out of the muzzle at 2298 fps, for about 2340 fpe. The lighter 195-grain .357-inch Precision Rifle "Dead Center" bullet, loaded into the 50-caliber using a unique "duplex" sabot arrangement *(sabot-inside-a-sabot)* would leave the muzzle at 2320 fps, with 2330 fpe. And the hefty charge of FFFg Triple Seven would get the novel and light 180-grain "The Bullet" *(the one with the hole running lengthwise through the center)* out of the Savage Model 10ML II at an amazing 2347 fps, for 2200 fpe.

To counter the 2200 to 2300 fps velocities of the 50-caliber Savage Model 10ML II when loaded with smokeless powder loads, Knight, T/C, Traditions, CVA and a few others have brought to market an impressive selection of "Super 45" in-line rifles, designed to be loaded with hot loads of Pyrodex or Triple Seven to get light 150- to 200-grain bullets out of the muzzle at around 2300 to 2500 fps. Some of these rifles, when loaded with bullets having a relatively high ballistic coefficient, are proving to be effective on deer-sized game out to around 200 yards. In fact, the 195-grain .357-inch Precision Rifle bullet is a long cylindrical spire-point with a published BC of .375. Pushed from the muzzle at around 2300 fps/2290 fpe, this extremely aerodynamic poly-tipped bullet would retain more than 1500 foot-pounds of knockdown power slightly past 200 yards.

Many game departments aren't all that comfortable with such muzzleloader performance, claiming that today's guns and loads are just too effective. The smokeless Savage 10ML II is too often singled out in this regard, and attempts to outlaw the rifle are reminiscent of the lobbying efforts we saw back when the in-line rifles first hit the muzzleloader hunting scene. Truth is, with most of the smokeless loads being shot out of this rifle, saboted bullets are being pushed from the muzzle at around 2250 fps. Knight has proudly boasted of 2500+ fps with their 45-caliber DISC Extreme, and T/C brags their Super Encore 209x45 Magnum is capable of producing velocities exceeding 2600 fps. Non-smokeless powders produce these velocities.

Due to the efficiency and long-range capabilities of today's muzzle-loaded big-game rifles, once again we're beginning to hear rumblings that the special muzzleloader seasons are in jeopardy, although they have never been more popular. These seasons exist primarily so game departments can get additional harvest of a still-growing deer herd. And with today's high-performance muzzleloading big-game rifles and loads, more and more deer are being taken out to 200 yards... and farther.

Before attempting to load the hot charges of FFFg Triple Seven discussed here in your muzzleloader, check with the manufacturer to get their written OK. These loads do produce significantly higher pressures. A couple of major manufacturers are already touting the use of 150-grain charges of FFFg Triple Seven in some of their newer models. Check out the latest advertisements for these rifles, or go to the various muzzleloader manufacturers websites to learn more.

(NOTE: Never attempt to load any of the smokeless loads given in this article for the Savage Model 10ML II in any other muzzleloader. While some muzzleloader manufacturers are now recommending the use of heavy loads of Triple Seven, Hodgdon Powder Company does not acknowledge any load heavier than 100 grains.) •

Knight Rifles promotions manager Steve Puppe with a good Montana whitetail, taken with one of the Knight 45-caliber DISC Extreme rifles and 150-grain Pyrodex Pellet charge behind a light 150-grain saboted bullet.

The Engineering of Balance...

Handling Qualities Of Hunting Rifles

by Harold (Hal) Davidson

THE MAY 1991 *American Rifleman* had an article of mine titled "How a Shotgun Handles." A hunting friend offered an opinion that what I wrote about shotgun handling qualities could also apply to rifles, and if so why hadn't the article included any data on rifles? Good question. My answer was that shotgunners seem to be much more interested in the subject than riflemen, so I focused on shotguns. Moreover, there's little reason for competition target shooters to be interested because handling qualities are of no importance in most competitive events. My friend wasn't satisfied.

"What about hunters? If they're not interested, maybe they should be. It could make the difference between getting off a good shot or a poor one; and with dangerous game in heavy cover could make the difference between life and death." He reminded me of Jim Corbett's experience with the Chowgarh man-eating tigress, and some other incidents where a hunter's survival was due to a fast-handling gun. For those who haven't read Corbett's account, he attributed his survival to the handling qualities of the 275 he was carrying instead of his 450/400 double. Based on data for similar rifles, Corbett's 450/400 would have weighed about half again as much as his 275 and its inertia would have been about twice as great.

This is a "re-enactment" of an experience I had while going after a buck. I'd just started to step over one of the numerous windfalls when the buck lurched from his bed.

While the average hunter is unlikely to have a potentially fatal encounter with dangerous game (or, for that matter, to ever have the opportunity of hunting such game), there are occasions when the possibility of making an effective shot on game flushed in heavy cover diminishes with each additional fraction of a second required to get the shot off. That fact is of purely academic interest to those who do all their hunting from stands. However, I've yet to meet anyone who's spent a fair amount of time still-hunting the eastern whitetail without having several experiences of that kind.

They sometimes occur at awkward moments as illustrated in the "re-enactment" photo of an experience I had in going after a buck that my partner and I figured was holed up in an area of blow-downs. I'd just started to step over one of numerous windfalls when the buck lurched from his bed. My right foot came down as the gun was raised from the grip-carry and the left hand came up to complete the mount, even as a finger closed over the trigger.

Timing is critical in such situations, and the key factor (aside from practice) is a gun with the right handling qualities. It should be noted here that handling qualities also have an effect on the condition of a hunter's reflexes at the end of a day's working through rough terrain, heavy cover, or wooded areas with many windfalls.

Handling qualities are directly related to inertia — which is the gun's resistance to movement due to its weight (physicists prefer to speak of "mass") and the way it is distributed relative to the balance point. As a practical matter, differences in balance point location are relatively unimportant, except for situations where it is desirable to have one hand free and still have the gun at ready. This calls for the one-handed grip carry, which is difficult unless the balance point is relatively close to the grip and inertia is on the low side.

My right foot came down as the gun was raised from the grip-carry and the left hand came up to complete the mount, even as a finger closed over the trigger. Timing is critical in such situations, and the key factor *(aside from practice)* is a gun with the right handling qualities.

The influence of weight distribution on handling is easily appreciated by holding a 12-pound bowling ball with the arm straight down and then rotating it with an easy twist of the wrist. Then grasp a 12-pound, heavy-barrel target rifle at the balance point with the arm hanging straight down and swing the muzzle back and forth in an arc. Not only is a greater effort required, but if you attempt to make the back and forth swing with greatest possible speed you'll find that it's impossible to swing the rifle as rapidly as you rotate the ball. The reason is INERTIA.

It is true, of course, that weight is the sole determinant of inertia in any straight-line movement, such as lifting without any turning. However, carrying a rifle in heavy cover or other rough going does involve swinging movements as does the mounting. Thus, handling qualities are directly related to the inertia experienced in these movements, which is designated by the symbol **Icg** (meaning inertial resistance to turning movements about the balance point or center-of-gravity [the technical term is "moment of inertia."])

(It may also be noted that the fast and sustained swings of mounted guns in shotgunning bring the shooter's body inertia into play. My personal experience and opinion is that this complicating factor is not involved in close-range snap-shooting of large game in heavy cover and for that reason is not considered in this article.)

OK, so inertia and not just weight alone makes a difference in handling qualities. How much? Enough to matter? As a preliminary answer to the question: The heaviest of the hunting rifles tested for this article weighed two and a quarter times the lightest, while inertia (Icg*) was <u>four times</u> as great ... enough to matter.

Of course, this knowledge is not of much use to the average hunter unless he has some way of estimating the inertia of the gun he uses, or is considering, and also has some kind of standard or benchmark to compare against. It is the purpose of this article to provide that information.

**As measured by torsion pendulum constructed by author. See illustration and brief description at end of article.*

A big favorite with northwoods hunters from Maine to Minnesota was the Remington Model 141, chambered for the 35 Remington cartridge.

Here's a brush gun for larger game, the Winchester Model 88 chambered for the 358 Winchester.

Let's begin by defining three general categories of hunting rifles and for each category indicating the inertia values, **Icg** (specifically, the moment of inertia about the balance point):

A. Fast-handling brush guns -- **Icg** ideally less than 6500, and not more than 7500 maximum (Note these **Icg** values are comparative figures resulting from calculation with ounce and inch data. If centimeters and grams were used the numbers would be different but the relative differences between the categories would be the same).

B. Easy-handling hunting rifles (most versatile) -- **Icg** in the range of 7500 to 11,000 maximum (including scope).

C. Long-range plains & varmint rifles and large-bore rifles used mainly on African game -- **Icg** ranging from 11,000 to about 25,000 (heavy rifles such as the 460 Weatherby). Guns in this category are chosen by hunters who put handling qualities near the bottom of their "factors to consider" list. Heavy-barrel target rifles also fall in this high inertia category, as do many military rifles (nearly all of WWI & II vintage).

I believe this categorization is realistic for the great majority of hunters. There are exceptions, of course. Almost any gun in the "B" category would be "fast-handling" for an all-pro NFL linebacker. However, as the birthdays accumulate even the super athlete experiences some decline in physical abilities. Senior citizens especially *(at 75 I've been one of them for several years)* should pay attention to handling qualities ... not because we're too feeble to handle the heavier stuff dealers have on their shelves, but because the "fast handling" quality provides some offset to slower reflexes. Hypertension is another reason for favoring rifles with low **Icg**, whatever the hunter's age.

Note, however, that the "fast-handling brush gun" designation has been loosely applied to some arms with handling characteristics much inferior to those of guns shown in the table below. One gun so described in an advertisement is the SKS Simonov 7.62x39mm assault "carbine". As issued it weighs 8.4 pounds with an **Icg** of 10,300 and an overall length of 40.5 inches. Without bayonet the SKS weighs 7.8 pounds, and has an **Icg** of 9300, which is well beyond a reasonable limit for brush guns. Moreover, the 10-shot magazine of the SKS is superfluous - excess baggage - in heavy cover where there is seldom an opportunity for more than one or two shots.

All guns checked to date with **Icg** less than 6500 weighed under 6.75 pounds and were 36 or less inches long overall. Two guns in the 6500 to 7500 range weighed about 6.75 pounds and measured 38 and 39 inches overall. The table following provides data on the four brush

Rifles used in thick cover at close range are often best equipped with an aperture rear sight, leaving the scope sight for rifles used in more open country at longer distances.

The Model 1895 Winchester in 30-40 Krag *(above)* was once favored by some African hunters for lion and other thin-skinned game. The Model 1899 *(below)* in 300 Savage, a lighter gun, matched the ballistic performance of the Model 1895.

guns shown in the accompanying illustrations.

Based on weight, length, and overall configuration Remington's 600 and 660 carbines would fall in the brush gun category, as would most if not all the custom rifles produced by Ultra Light Arms. I have not, however, had the opportunity of making direct measurements on these guns.

The majority of rifles used by North American deer hunters probably fall in the "easy handling" category, of which the nearby table presents a sample. Those marked with asterisk (*) are illustrated in accompanying photos.

The reader may be surprised that a long time favorite of many deer hunters -- the M94 30-30 Winchester carbine — is in this instead of the brush gun category. It's a borderline case. With a half-magazine or shorter barrel the **Icg** would be under 7500. Note that the 358 Mod 88 with 17-inch barrel has a lower **Icg** than the 30-30 Mod 94 although it is heavier by four-tenths of a pound. Also note that while the short-barreled 358 weighs a mere 7% less than the 308 Mod 100 with a 22" barrel, its **Icg** is 28% lower! Short barrels can do wonders for handling qualities. Yes, the muzzle velocity will be lower and the trajectory will be less flat, but not enough to matter if the shooting is at relatively short ranges as in heavy cover. The improvement in handling is well worth the small price.

For other types of hunting where the rifle is often carried on the sling and snap-shooting is not involved -- where speed in mounting the gun is of no advantage -- longer barrels are worth their weight in higher velocity (hence flatter trajectory); and higher inertia is beneficial because it contributes to accuracy. The benefit results from the damping effect of inertia on minor tremors and "shakes", and to a lesser degree from reduced recoil due to additional weight. The benefits are significant in long-range varmint and game shooting; also in some target shooting.

The results on large-bore double rifles may surprise some hunters whose experience with doubles, like mine, is limited to shotguns of 12 and smaller gauge. So, when advocates of the big doubles for dangerous game in heavy cover extol the "quick second shot" and other virtues we tend to assume the handling qualities are much like those of a good Skeet or upland bird gun (**Icg** less than 10,000); which is

BRUSH GUN CHARACTERISTICS

Gun Description	Weight	— Length — Overall	Bbl.	Icg
32-20 Remington M25	4.4 lbs.	34"	16.5"	4400
32 Special Martini	4.5	32"	16.5"	4000
44 Magnum Marlin M1984S	5.8	36"	18.0"	5000
358 Winchester Mod 88 wo/scope	6.7	38"	17.0"	7000

(Note: In many states the 32-20 is no longer legal for deer or other big game. However, my father harvested a good deal of venison still hunting with the 32-20 M25, while an *American Rifleman* article of September 1941 related a chance encounter with a charging leopard that was dispatched with a Winchester M92 in 32-20 caliber that was normally employed in getting camp meat.)

EASY HANDLING

Gun Description	Weight	— Length — Overall	Bbl.	Icg
30-30 Winchester 94 Carbine	6.31bs.	38"	20"	7800
*35 Remington M141	6.7	40"	22"	8000
*22 Hornet Brno Mauser w/scope	6.6	41"	23"	8500
* 8x57 Brno Mauser w/scope	7.3	41"	21"	9100
308 Ruger M77	6.9	42"	22"	9200
358 Winchester M100	7.2	43"	22"	9500
*7mm 08 Custom Sako w/scope	7.7	39"	20"	9600
300 Savage M99 w/scope	7.2	43"	25"	9800
*243 Custom Sako w/scope	7.9	42"	22"	9800
*30-40 Winchester M95	7.9	43"	24"	10,500
458 Winchester M70	8.8	43"	22"	10,800

Three of the author's brush guns. The Marlin 44 Magnum *(top)* has a lightened and shortened barrel and magazine. The Remington Model 25 *(center)* is a 32-20 and the Martini *(below)* was re-chambered for the 32 Winchester Special. Note all three have large-aperture receiver sights.

HIGH INERTIA

Gun		— Length —		
Description	Weight	Overall	Bbl.	Icg
30-06 Browning M78 w/scope	9.21bs.	42"	26"	11,600
7x61 Magnum Custom Enfield w/s	9.7	46"	26"	15,100
220 Swift Win M70 Neidner w/s	10.0	45"	24"	16,300
22rf Winchester M52 Target w/s	9.0	45"	28"	17,300
30-06 1917 Enfield – military as issued	9.7	46"	26"	18,300
375 Weatherby w/4x scope	13.5	47"	26"	21,500
Large Bore Double Rifles	9 to 16	39 to 43	-	14,000 to 28,000

Cast bullets are often useful in both fast-handling and easy-handling rifle classifications. This particular mould, made to the author's design specifications, casts five weights of a plain-base bullet and four weights of a gas-check bullet for the 310 Martini Cadet and the (.318") 8mm Mauser.

to say that not only can you get a quick second shot but you also get on target fast for the first shot ... which could be even more important than a quick second shot. Needless to say, these impressions did not result from any serious study.

Those big doubles with handling characteristics similar to or inferior to those of the issue U.S. 1917 Enfield are not in the same league with upland bird guns when it comes to handling. But, of course, neither are they in the same league when it comes to dishing it out -- on both ends. The inertia data do not deny the virtues of the big doubles in the hands of those who are able to exploit their capabilities. What they do suggest is that hunters who are accustomed to medium-bore rifles in the "easy handling" category might be well advised to select something like the 458 Model 70 if they feel the need for a big bore, rather than one of the big doubles. Alternatively, our editor, who has had some experience with doubles, suggests that medium-bore doubles such as the 9.3x74 and H&H 375—while not exactly light—can be relatively quick depending on how the weight is distributed.

Summing up: the best gun for hunting big game - dangerous or not - in heavy cover is short and light. Such fast-handling guns are available in calibers appropriate to any size of game. They are not, however, the solution to all hunting situations, any more than a sand wedge is the right club for all golfing shots. For some kinds of shooting, high inertia is beneficial.

As seen in the "Easy Handling" chart, the Brno 8x57 Mauser *(top)* with classic European lines and high-mount scope ranks slightly ahead of the custom 7mm-08 Sako.

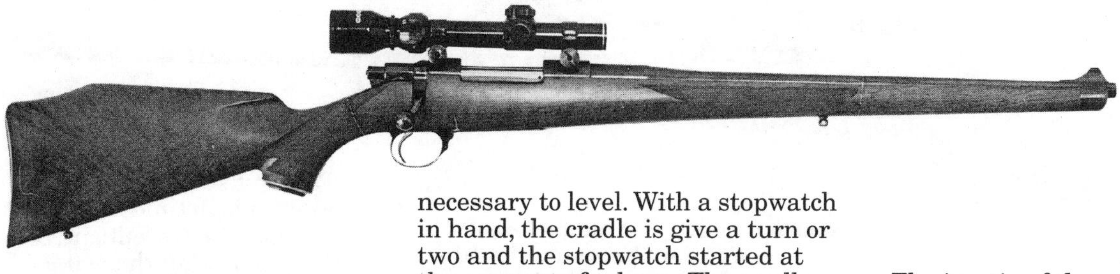

The Torsion Pendulum

The torsion pendulum constructed by the author is a simple cradle to support the gun, with a yoke, which is anchored to the lower end of a five-foot length of 0.03-inch diameter steel spring wire. The upper end of the wire is clamped to a mounting block bolted to an overhead 2x10 floor joist. A bubble level is built into the cradle and is used first to level the cradle with a weighted leveling screw at one end of the cradle. The gun *(see photo)* is then placed in the cradle and shifted as necessary to level. With a stopwatch in hand, the cradle is give a turn or two and the stopwatch started at the moment of release. The cradle will then wind and unwind (i.e. oscillate) back and forth. The time that it takes to return to the approximate beginning position and start another cycle is called the "period" of the pendulum and is determined by the inertia of the cradle plus the gun.

For accuracy, the author times six consecutive cycles and divides by six to get the period (typically 45 to 70 seconds with spring wire of the stated diameter and length).

The inertia of the cradle plus gun is then determined by squaring the period (time for one cycle) and multiplying by a factor 'K' that is found by a simple calibrating procedure that also determines the inertia of the cradle itself (without gun.) Subtracting the cradle inertia from the inertia of cradle plus gun yields **Icg** for the gun.

(Note to shooters with children taking high school physics: ask them if they can explain why the period is always the same whether the cradle is given one, two, three or four turns to start the oscillation.

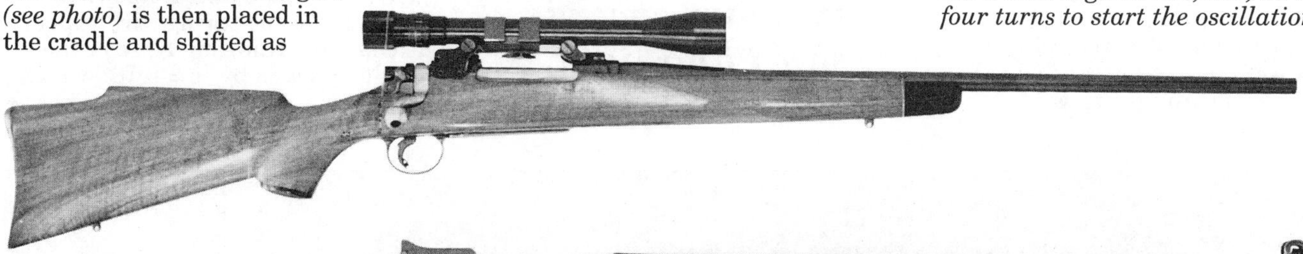

▲Typical of WWI and WWII military bolt actions, the U.S. Model 1917 Enfield in 30-06 ranks in the "High Inertia" class. The long-range 7x61mm Magnum *(top)*, built on an Enfield action with Canjar set-trigger, has the same total weigh (w/scope) and overall length, with 20% lower inertia.

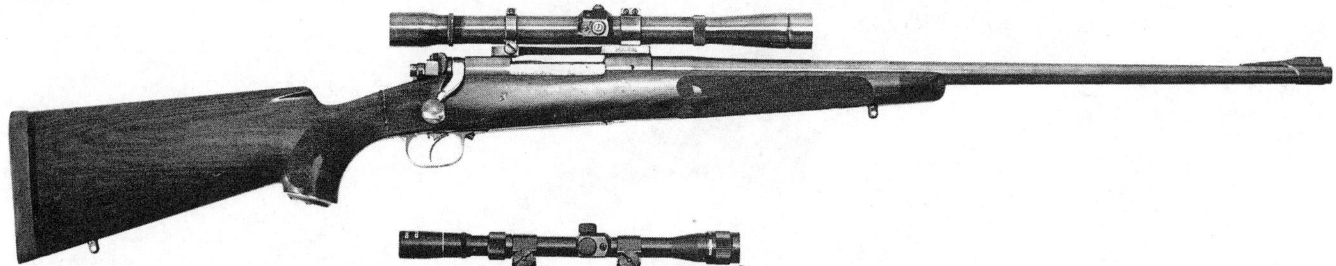

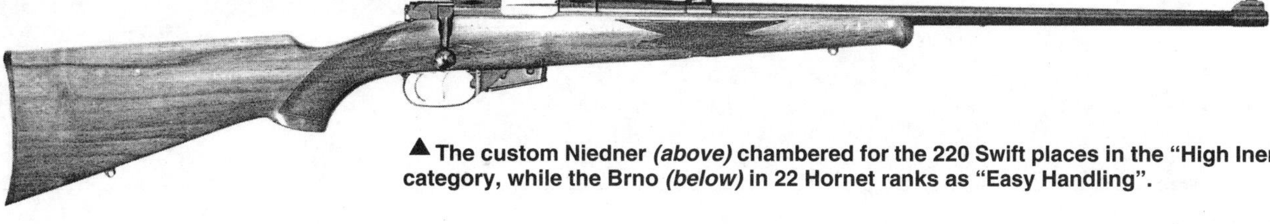

▲The custom Niedner *(above)* chambered for the 220 Swift places in the "High Inertia" category, while the Brno *(below)* in 22 Hornet ranks as "Easy Handling".

The Browning M78 *(above)* in 30-06 inches into the "High Inertia" category because of its heavy 26-inch barrel. On the other hand, the custom Sako in 243 Winchester *(below)* is classified as "Easy Handling".

Can they name a simple, once common device that used this torsion pendulum principle? Answer: an old-fashioned, before-quartz wrist or pocket watch. Another interesting question: would their physics teacher know the answer?)

Construction

Construction is simple and easily accomplished with hand tools. 3/4 x 1/16 aluminum angle was used for the side members (31 inches long), three 4-inch crosspieces, and two vertical members for the yoke. Pop rivets were used for assembly with epoxy at all joining surfaces to insure rigidity. The bubble level is set in epoxy. An aluminum machine screw at the midpoint of the barrel end crosspiece secures leveling weights for the cradle only. Re-leveling with gun in place is accomplished by shifting the gun.

> ***"Summing up: the best gun for hunting big game - dangerous or not - in heavy cover is short and light."***

Calibrating

The first step in calibrating the pendulum is to time its period of oscillation after leveling it, but with nothing in it. Call this value **Tc**. The next step is to place a long object of uniform cross section in the cradle and again time the period of oscillation with cradle leveled. Call this value **Tcc**.

The inertia of the calibrating rod (such as a 6-foot long 1x1 aluminum angle or 1x1 square tube) is given by a standard formula: $I = ml^2/12$ where **m** is the weight in ounces, and **l** is length in inches. We can now compute a calibrating factor **K** for the cradle by the formula $K = I/(Tcc^2 - Tc^2)$. **K** will not change unless length or diameter of the spring wire support is changed. Knowing **K**, **Ic** of the cradle is given by $Ic = KTc^2$, which completes calibration. ●

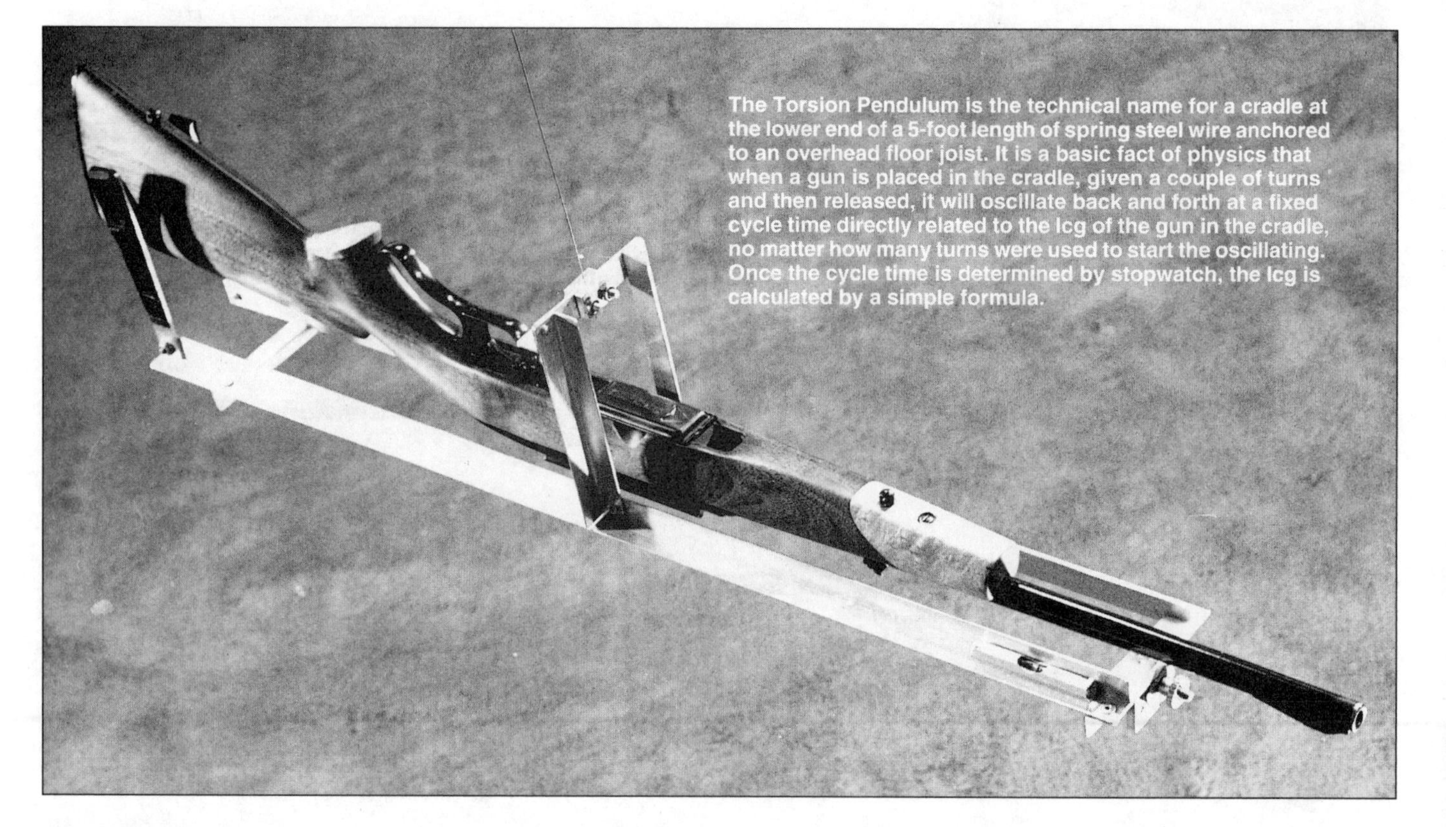

The Torsion Pendulum is the technical name for a cradle at the lower end of a 5-foot length of spring steel wire anchored to an overhead floor joist. It is a basic fact of physics that when a gun is placed in the cradle, given a couple of turns and then released, it will oscillate back and forth at a fixed cycle time directly related to the Icg of the gun in the cradle, no matter how many turns were used to start the oscillating. Once the cycle time is determined by stopwatch, the Icg is calculated by a simple formula.

Why the 17 Hornady Magnum Rimfire?

The Marlin 17 HMR Rifle features a 1:9 twist for the fast-moving 17 and is an accurate shooter.

by C. Rodney James

THE *AMERICAN RIFLEMAN* gave it a cover story and called it: "the little cartridge that could." The initial question that popped into my mind at that point was: could what? This wasn't really explained in the article, and that explanation is the purpose of this article.

In investigating the 17 HMR I availed myself of a Marlin heavy-barrel rifle on the theory it would be a straight-shooter and would draw the most from this cartridge. In that respect I was not disappointed. About everyone I talked with had terrific results in the accuracy department. Additionally, the 17-grain V-max (pointed, boat-tail bullet) ignores wind that drifts 22 rimfires if not quite like thistle seed, enough to be annoying. The 2500 fps-plus velocity yields less than an inch of trajectory at 100 yards. And recoil is zero! I did not fully study the target potential of the HMR, but that might be its strongest suite.

The cartridge box labels the 17 HMR as the "VARMINT EXPRESS" in capital letters yet, indicating it is to be used for varmint shooting. After an impressive sighting-in session with groups well under an inch, I decided to try it on the local varmints, namely woodchucks. A small/medium *(about eight pounds)* chuck made an appearance a few mornings later on a hillside up the road. Conditions were good – good light, very little breeze. The chuck was clearly visible, though down in five-inch grass, and facing me. I took a rest on the window and doorpost of my SUV *(I was off the road)* and centered the crosshairs at the top of the chuck's head. There was a satisfying "plock" when the bullet struck – a good indication of a solid hit. The range was paced at 80 yards. I regularly make one-shot kills at this range with accurate Long Rifle and WMR hollowpoints. This time the chuck went down, but thrashed around in deeper grass, out of clear view. By the time I got to the spot to investigate, the chuck had managed to haul his freight a good five yards to his hole and disappear therein. There was some blood and I have little doubt the chuck subsequently cashed in. This wasn't good news. I had done my part, but as a killer of chucks, the 17 failed miserably. This did not come as a great surprise since the physics of the situation militate against it.

Lethality

In spite of what any number of pundits say about the tremendous "shocking," "stopping," "killing power" of light, small-caliber bullets, it simply isn't so. The requisites for reliable killing include the ability to penetrate deeply enough to reach vital areas and secondarily, to create a large permanent *(not temporary)* wound cavity. The larger and deeper the permanent cavity, the greater the damage to vital organs, arteries and nerves, the higher the level of incapacitation and the quicker the death–assuming a well-placed shot. Lightweight frangible bullets do not penetrate deeply, but fragment very shortly after impact producing a shallow, lacerated, superficial wound.

Many articles include information on bullet penetration in clay or wood. I used to do this until I found, while tests of this sort generate interesting photos, the results are misleading in terms of bullet behavior in tissue. Clay creates expansion where none will occur in tissue. Long Rifle solids will expand in clay.

Results of the water-filled carton test. *L/R:* 17 HMR at 50 and 100 yards. Tiny light fragments have little energy to penetrate. Aguila Super Max LR at 100 yards gives good expansion and penetration. Velocitor and Power Point LRs at 50 yards expand with minimal fragmentation. Semi-hollow-point Winchester failed to expand at 50 yards. TNT 30-grain and Gold Dot 50-grain bullets expanded well. Gold Dot produced more than double the penetration of the TNT at 100 yds.

Wood keeps bullets together that would otherwise fragment. The 17 HMR, for instance, will remain basically intact penetrating 1.92 inches of 1/2-inch pine plywood sheets *(no spaces between)* at 35 yards, expanding to 0.280-inch with a retained weight of 13.4 grains – 78.8 percent. This level of penetration, expansion and retention compares very favorably to high-velocity LRHP rounds in this medium. In tissue and its equivalents, however, the 17 fragments quickly, offering poor penetration and weight retention *(Table 1)*. The standard test for bullet behavior in tissue is penetration in 10 percent ordnance gelatin at 4 C (39.2 F). Gelatin preparation is expensive, tricky and messy. Fellow International Wound Ballistics Association member, Gus Cotey Jr., created an excellent cheap substitute for gelatin blocks by using water-filled, coated-paper 1/2-gallon milk/juice cartons. *Any amateur experimenter with a safe place to shoot can do this. Try asking your local recycling center to save cartons for you.

In the water-carton penetration/expansion tests I ran (Table 1) the 17 HMR, as I had already determined, revealed itself to be a poor performer on woodchuck-size varmints. Penetration is less than the lightest hyper-velocity LR and retained weight is very low – less than 40 percent of the original 17 grains – less than half of a 22 BB cap! While the 17 is moving very fast, its lack of mass deprives it of energy. The best analogy of the action of the ultra-light, high-speed bullet's energy potential is like trying to close the door of a safe by hitting it with a ping-pong ball at 3000 fps. The door will move little if at all with the impact, although the force of one finger giving a gentle push will close that door. The nearest performer to the 17 HMR – Aguila's Super Maximum LR boasts a muzzle velocity of 1700 fps (67 percent of the 17). With nearly double the bullet weight the Max is far more lethal on chucks. It should be added the Max is a poor performer in terms of accuracy, delivering 4-inch groups at 100 yards on a good day through the Winchester 52. The few chucks taken with this round were at ranges less than 50 yards.

The woodchuck is very tough with a high vitality level. The hide is thick and difficult to penetrate as I found in the few attempts I've made to dissect one to study bullet damage. This hide and a layer of fat protect nerves and vital organs. There isn't a lot of blood in them. A Long Rifle hollowpoint is the lightest bullet suitable for taking chucks and shots with the LR must hit the heart *(through the shoulder)*, sever the upper spine or penetrate the brain. The only effective kill possibility with the 17 would be a brain shot. The brain of a woodchuck is about the size of a hickory nut *(without the husk)* or about 3/4-inch in diameter. If someone were skilled enough to make these shots and disciplined enough to pass up all others it could be done, though few chucks will give you the required opportunities.

Just where does the 17 HMR fit in the varmint category? At the bottom end–varmints in the 1 lb. to 3 lb. range. This covers starlings, grackles, crows, gophers, ground squirrels, prairie dogs and rats at the dump. On live targets of this size the explosive effects of the tiny bullet will overcome the stress limits of the varmint, assuring quick kills.

TABLE 1. Comparative Penetration/Expansion Test Results

Cartridge/Rifle			
17 HMR; Marlin 17V; 17-gr. V-MAX BTPP			
Water penetration @ 50 yds. 5.6"	***Exp.*** 0.23"x 0.297"	***Wt.*** 6.4 gr.	***Retained*** 37.64%
Water penetration @ 100 yds. 8.00"	***Exp.*** 0.20"x 0.24"	***Wt.*** 6.5 gr.	***Retained*** 38.24%
22 LR; Winchester 52C			
30-gr. Aguila Super Max HP			
Water penetration @ 100 yds. 11.25"	***Exp.*** .372"	***Wt.*** 30.1 gr.	***Retained*** 100.00%
40-gr. CCI Velocitor 22 LRHP			
Water penetration @ 50 yds. 13.0"	***Exp.*** .340"	***Wt.*** 38.9 gr.	***Retained*** 92.75%
40-gr. Win. Power Pt. 22 LRHP			
Water penetration @ 50 yds. 13.0"	***Exp.*** .275"	***Wt.*** 9.8 gr.	***Retained*** 74.50%
40-gr. Win. Super-X 22 LRSHP			
Water penetration @ 50 yds. 22.5"	***Exp.*** 0.0"	***Wt.*** 40.0 gr.	***Retained*** 100.00%
22 WMR; HK 300			
30-gr. CCI TNT			
Water penetration @ 100 yds. 7.5"	***Exp.*** .325"	***Wt.*** 30.1 gr.	***Retained*** 100.00%
50-gr. CCI Gold Dot			
Water penetration @ 100 yds. 18.75"	***Exp.*** .310"	***Wt***. 50 gr.	***Retained*** 100.00%

Accuracy/Performance

This is where the 17 HMR truly shines! A good rifle will deliver sub-minute of angle groups at 100 yards. Under good conditions, half-minute groups should be possible. Our Marlin rifle was an accurate shooter. The 24-inch barrel features conventional six-groove rifling with a 1:9 twist. The trigger released at a consistent four pounds – about two heavier than I would have liked. Recoil is virtually nothing. The only scope I had available with a tip-on mount was a Burris 4x Mini. This required making the bullseye dimension 1.5 x 2.0 inches in order to see them around the crosshair intersection.

May 27 was the best shooting day so far this year – 70, partly sunny with intermittent breeze 3 to 12 mph. There were no really calm periods throughout the day. Accuracy with our most accurate LR HP (Winchester Power Point) and best WMR HP (Federal Classic 30 gr.) in a bull-barrel Winchester 52 and a Ruger 77VMBZ respectively was below peak performance. These rifles and ammunition have grouped 0.55-inch and 0.50-inch at 100 yards in calm conditions. After sighters and foulers, the 100-yard average for the 52 with Power Point was 1.15 inches, for the Ruger 1.46 inches. Ten groups were tried with this rifle to get better results, and failed. The Marlin 17 averaged 0.73 inch.

17 HMR unfired and as recovered from plywood where it stayed together. Bullet on right passed through a single 1/2-inch plywood slab at 50 yards and was recovered on the ground near the 100-yard target. Wood and clay are unreliable test media.

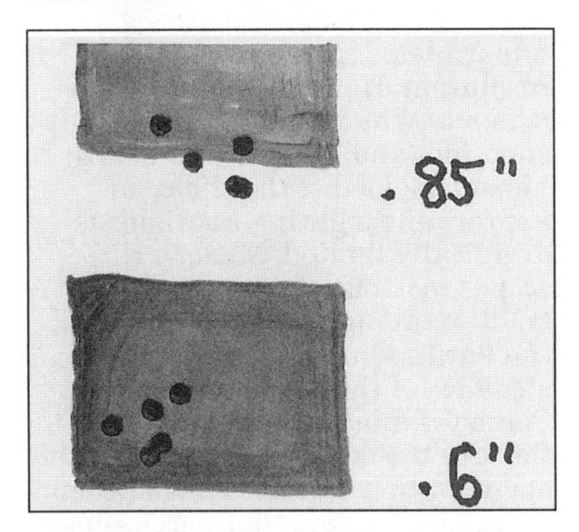

Best and worst 100-yard groups for the 17 HMR–under less than ideal conditions–were well under an inch. Long Rifle and WMR bullets were much more subject to wind drift.

Water-carton testing is cheap and relatively simple. High-powered rifle rounds require more water to stop them and often curve, exiting at the side vs. the back, thus requiring additional rows of cartons.

TABLE 2. Comparative 100yd Accuracy, 5-Shot Groups

	Best	Worst	Avg.
17 HMR Marlin 17V	0.6"	0.85"	0.73"
22 LR Winchester 52C	1.1"	1.2"	1.15"
22 WMR Ruger 77 VMBZ	1.1"	1.8"	1.46"

Temperature 70F. Intermittent crosswind *(r to l)* at 3-12 mph.

TABLE 3. Chronographed Velocities 17 HMR (fps)

Round #	FPS
1.	2601
2.	2604
3.	2548
4.	2554
5.	2562

***MV Highest/Lowest:* 2604; 2548**
***Extreme Spread:* 56 fps.**
***Std. Dev.:* 26 fps.**
***Mean Vel.:* 2573 fps.**

Chronographed velocities for the 5-shot group were taken 12' from muzzle with the Oehler 35P. The 24-inch barrel Marlin exceeded the advertised 2550 fps. Temperature 70F.

Conclusions and the Future of the 17HMR

The light, frangible bullet at high velocity offers the advantage of fewer ricochets in comparison to the LR and WMR cartridges. The tack-driving accuracy and wind-bucking abilities equal–if not surpass–the best 22 LR match rifles and ammunition. The experienced recoil is zero and by comparison the WMR, particularly in my Hk 300 autoloader, produces a real jump. Accuracy is the 17 HMR's strength. Beyond target shooting, though, it isn't really good for much as a varmint round. I rate its effectiveness on a par with the 22 Long. The limitation to varmints well below woodchuck size will restrict varmint shooters to crows, gophers and ground squirrels. This may generate enough interest to keep it alive; along with the fact a number of companies are chambering rifles for it. The reality of the situation is that these pretty little cartridges are priced at $8.75 for 50. With WMRs available at $5.00 to $6.50 and good LR hollowpoints at around $2.50 a box, a lot of shooters will likely stay with the versatility of the wide range of loadings available in the LR and WMR chamberings, as opposed to the 17 HMR's one. I suppose the good news is anyone who buys one of these rifles can easily have the barrel switched for a 22 WMR since the 17 HMR is a bottlenecked WMR, and magazines are identical. The Ruger rifles make this switch especially easy since you can do this at home. If the 17 can qualify for some form of competition status it may find a permanent place on the shooting scene.

* For a full discussion see: "The Limitations of Water-Filled Cardboard Cartons In Predicting Bullet Penetration," *"Wound Ballistics Review"*, Vol. 4 1999 No. 1 pp 30-35. See also Martin L. Fackler MD, "Simplified Bullet Effect Testing", *"Wound Ballistics Review"* Vol. 5 2001 No. 2 pp 21-24 – using a small number of water-filled cartons and a cardboard box filled with polyester fiber (pillow filler) permits capture of the expanded bullet without further damage. •

Unfired 17 HMR and 50- and 100-yard recovered fragments. The bullet on the right is an 18-grain 22 BB cap.

Apertures for Aging Eyes

by Fred Stutzenberger

"The peep or aperture sight is a far more logical and effective type than the open rear sight."
(Jack O'Connor, 1952)

THE HUMAN EYE is a marvel of natural engineering. Its lens focuses images on the concave surface of the retina. This surface is lined with specialized cells (the rods and cones) that transform light energy into nerve impulses that are transmitted to the brain. About three-quarters of our overall perception of the world is transmitted by the eye.

As we get older, the lens of the eye becomes less flexible. Loss of lens flexibility (presbyopia) is relatively unimportant for visualization of distant objects, but our ability to focus on close objects is diminished. Consequently, when shooting a rifle with open sights, the rear sight is blurred *(particularly in dim light)* while the front sight remains well defined. Rifle scores are gradually diminished, while pistol scores may be unimpaired *(at least for some years)* since the pistol is held at arm's length where the sights can still be brought into focus.

For the marksman who uses modern firearms, the loss of visual acuity can be largely compensated by modern rifle scopes that provide magnified sight pictures unparalleled in clarity and resolution. However, for the older rifleman who wants to keep shooting (and shooting well) with his muzzleloader, the choice of appropriate sighting upgrades is drastically limited. Modern rifle scopes look out of place on a traditional muzzleloader and spoil the flowing lines and graceful elegance of the Pennsylvania/Kentucky rifle. Besides the aesthetic objections, the open ignition system of a traditional muzzleloader, whether percussion or flint, will foul and corrode the scope's windage adjustment mechanism–and literally blow the finish off the tube after a few shots.

(Fig. 1) **Strapping metal can be fashioned into an improvised aperture sight that is attached to this flintlock via the tang screw and duct tape.**

Since the modern rifle scope doesn't make a graceful leap back in time, why not consider the advantages of an aperture (peep) sight? The sighting radius *(distance between front and rear sights)* for a tang-mounted aperture sight is much greater than that of the open sight dovetailed way out on the barrel. Secondly, the aging eye does not have to focus on the aperture; rather, it must merely look through it. Also, the aperture provides the advantage of the "pin-hole camera" effect in sharpening definition of viewed objects. One can demonstrate this effect by reading newsprint through a small hole; print that was previously unreadable now becomes sharply defined to the aging presbyope.

(Fig. 4) **This Marble 69W flattop adjustable sight can be folded down out of the line of sight when the aperture is being used.**

There are also disadvantages to the aperture sight.

Competition regulations at muzzleloading rifle events recognize the mechanical advantage of the aperture sight and disqualify it from some matches ("open sights only"). Discrimination against the aperture is not based on authenticity *(some fine old rifles of European origin had aperture sights)*, but on the unfair advantage that it confers. Since the aperture sight is often adjustable, it can also be disqualified on the basis of "fixed sights only". There is also the popular conception that the aperture sight would be useless under low light conditions. However, there are modifications *(described later)* that eliminate, or at least reduce, that problem.

The question for the individual rifleman then becomes: can my shooting be improved, or will I enjoy it more, by using an aperture sight? If you persist in the illusion *"Why, I'm as good as I ever was!"* or think that a peep sight will spoil the lines of your rifle or your macho image with your fellow shooters, then adjust your reading specs and move on to the next article.

For those of you who are still reading, try this simple test, which costs nothing more than a few minutes of your time. Cut an 8-inch piece of black strapping metal *(the kind that lies strewn around a building site after lumber has been unbundled)*. About 1/4-inch from one end, drill a hole with a #60 bit (0.040-inch). About 2 inches from that hole, drill a hole slightly smaller than the head of the tang screw of your muzzleloading rifle. Bend up the end with the small hole to a 90° angle so that you can sight through it down the barrel over your present open sight. Fasten this improvised peep sight to the top of the rifle via the tang screw *(Fig. 1)* and stabilize the forward end with a wrapping of duct tape around the whole rifle. Now sight at some object at least 25 yards away. Don't worry that the circumference of the aperture appears fuzzy—the eye will naturally center the front sight in the center of the sphere of light. If you have a clear sight picture, you are a candidate for an aperture, at least as an alternative to that open sight.

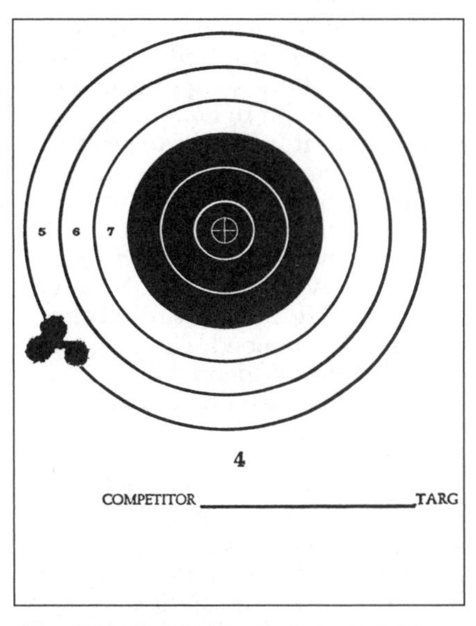

(Fig. 2) **The improvised aperture sight enabled the author to shoot this 3-shot group from the bench at 50 yards.**

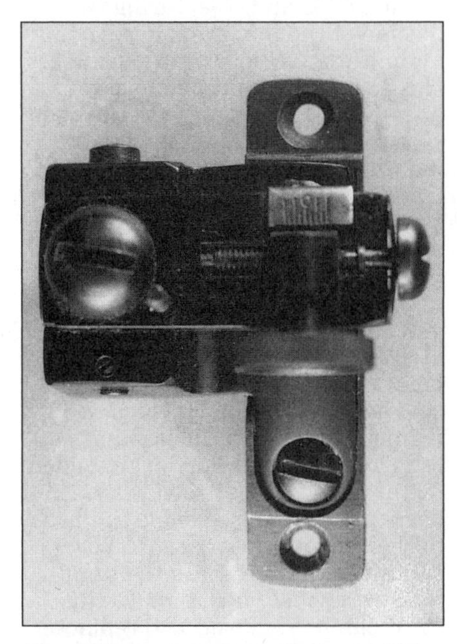

(Fig. 7) **The custom base for the 57 SML sight allows it to be adapted to the screw holes already in the tang.**

If you need further convincing, try out your improvised sight at the rifle range. Black strapping metal is resilient enough to hold quite steady once it is bent into position. If you are careful not to bump it during loading or shooting, it will serve admirably for at least a preliminary test session at the firing line. A 50-yard group, such as the one in *Fig. 2*, might be all the convincing you need. The question now becomes: Which type of aperture sight would be compatible with my style of rifle and its intended use?

For a late-period plains rifle with a long sturdy tang, such as those seen on the late Hawkens, the folding tang sight would be a good bet. These versatile sights, adjustable for elevation *(and some also for windage)*, were standard equipment on the old Sharps and Remington buffalo rifles of the 1860s and '70s during the decline of the muzzleloader. An old mountain man, loathe to give up his Hawken and yet unable to sight accurately any longer with the open sight, just might have resorted to installing a tang sight. Such sights traditionally mount via two 8-32 screws on the wrist of the rifle. The angle of the base is compatible with the long, straight wrists and tangs of the old breechloaders. However, getting the axis of the elevation bar at a 90° angle to the bore may be a bit of a problem on the gently curving wrist of the Hawken or Dimick rifle. The problem was solved on this Hawken by an angled metal sandwich between the sight base and the tang to bring the base to the proper angle *(Fig. 3)*. The sandwich is fastened to the tang *(not merely held between)*, so the sight can be removed and replaced as desired. An open sight that can be folded down out of the way *(Fig. 4)* when the aperture is in use provides the advantages of both systems. Stroebel (1998) has compiled a comprehensive application guide to metallic gunsights, which offers many combinations in this regard.

There is another consideration in the mounting of an adjustable tang-mounted sight. The sight must be mounted so the aperture truly bisects the bore in the vertical plane. Otherwise, during elevation adjustment, a cock-eyed sight will change windage as well. To check vertical alignment, you can set the barrel in a set of V-blocks borrowed from a machinist friend. If you do not have a machinist friend *(or if he is not as good a friend as you thought)*, then sit the barrel on two pieces of square steel stock so as to keep its protruding underlugs off the supporting flat surface beneath. Once the barrel is sitting with top and bottom flats parallel to a supporting flat surface *(such as a clean, straight piece of angle iron)*, a square can be placed aside the barrel and aside the frame of the sight. The frame of the sight must be in alignment with the vertical flats of the barrel. If the alignment is off, shim or grind the base to bring it right. One more consideration: If your Hawken-type rifle has the traditional two-piece hooked breech, the front and rear sights will now be mounted on different pieces of metal. If the standing portion of the hooked breech does not tightly fit the breech hook, shifts in the relationship between the two might prove problematic.

(Fig. 5) **This is a more traditional sight on a Pennsylvania/Kentucky rifle; it consists of a disc atop a threaded post. It should be installed along the curvature of the wrist so that the sight axis closely parallels that of the bore.**

For the Pennsylvania/Kentucky flintlock rifle, the problem is not the possibility of shift between breech and barrel, but rather the aesthetic consideration of detracting from its classic lines. A small, tang-mounted folding aperture, such as that used by Levi Biddle on his Tuscarawas County, Ohio, rifles (Chandler and Whisker, 1993) would not seem terribly obtrusive. A base, mounted on the tang, could be threaded to receive an aperture with a threaded stem. For attachment to a conventional short tang *(which generally is no more than 2-3" long)*, the base would have to mount nearly up to the plane of the top flat of the barrel and aligned so the aperture would be at 90° to the longitudinal axis of the barrel. This alignment could be checked with a small machinist's square set on the top barrel flat *(Fig. 5)*, but if the barrel were tapered or swamped, some shimming of the square might be in order to square the sight with the bore. In any case, the sight can be removed from the permanently mounted base if open sights were required by regulation or circumstance. A convenient feature of some base-mounted sights is that they can be precisely replaced in their same position; this eliminates the need for re-sighting your rifle. If your

(Fig. 3) **This Thompson/Center Vernier tang sight was adapted to a custom Hawken rifle via a machined base, which brought the sighting axis parallel with the bore. A little tension spring *(arrow)* was added to eliminate play in the vertical adjustment.**

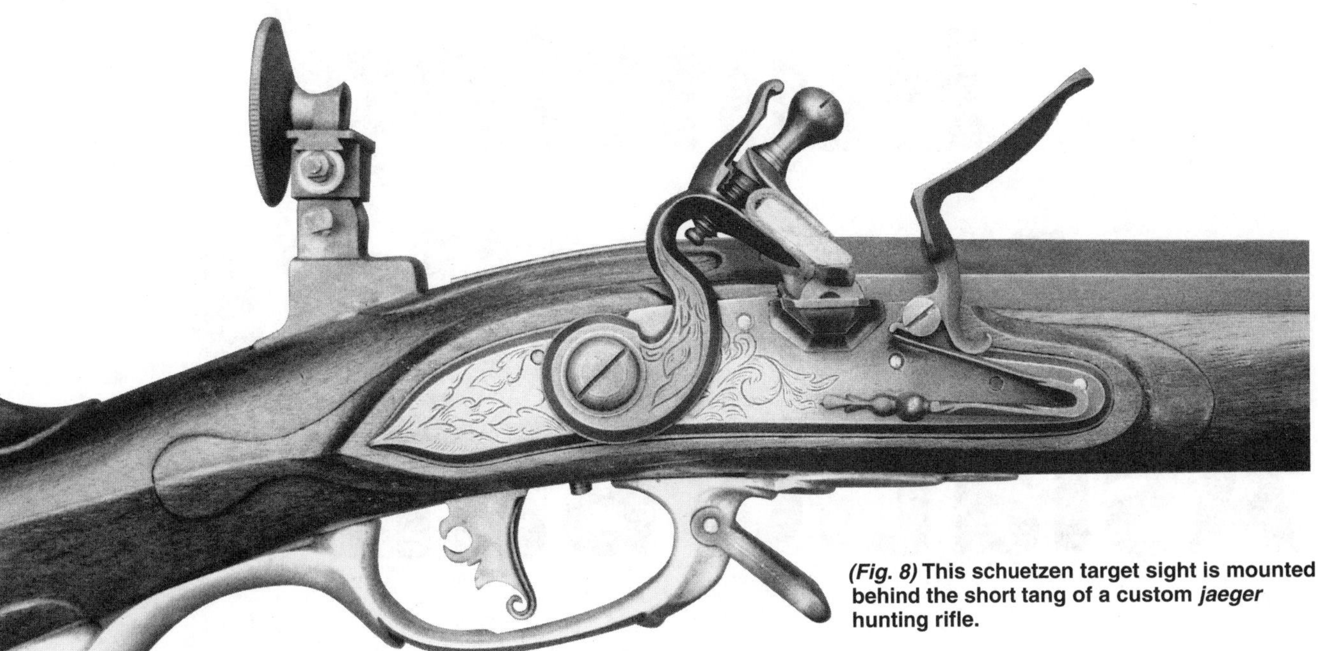

(Fig. 8) **This schuetzen target sight is mounted behind the short tang of a custom *jaeger* hunting rifle.**

muzzleloader is to be confined to the rifle range, you might consider a more contemporary sight such as the Lyman 57 SML. The base of this nifty little sight is machined to hug the rounded wrist of a muzzleloading rifle *(Fig. 6)* and is well adapted for tang installation of muzzleloaders such as the T/C Hawken. Again, if the angle of the wrist does not put the sight axis parallel to that of the bore, a little base *(Fig. 7)* can be machined to bring it into proper alignment.

Fancy aperture sights were a lot more popular in 18th and 19th century Europe than in America, so a schuetzen-type sight with a huge disc *(Fig. 8)* might appropriately show up on a Prussian or Austrian *jaeger* rifle used for target work. While the disc is a full 1-1/2 inches in diameter–ostensibly to block out distractions from the target–the aperture itself is a mere 0.035-inch, which might seem to increase the precision of aiming.

While such a sight might be very effective for target competition, its tiny aperture won't serve you well in a low light hunting situation. No problem. Do what one of my deer hunting associates did—screw out the aperture disc and sight through the threaded hole in the sight housing. He got his deer, using only half a sight, thanks to the tendency of the eye to automatically center the front sight precisely, even in an absurdly large hole. The upper practical limit of effective aperture diameter for hunting under low light conditions has probably never been thoroughly tested. However, when I tested the range of aperture sizes shown in *Fig. 9*, I found that there was negligible difference in group size at 50 yards from the bench. For hunting, a tiny disc *(so as not to obstruct peripheral vision and allow rapid coming to target)* coupled with a large aperture *(to allow maximal definition of a moving target under low light)* would be one way of putting new precision into that old front-stuffer.

Who knows? It might just be a peep show worth watching! •

Acknowledgement

Thanks to John Cummings for assistance in the preparation of this manuscript.

References

Chandler, Roy and James Whisker. *Behold the Longrifle.* Bedford, PA. Old Bedford Village Press. 1993.

O'Conner, Jack. *Sportsman's Arms and Ammunition Manual*. New York, Popular Science Publishing Co. 1952.

Stroebel, N. *Old Gunsights. A Collector's Guide, 1850-1965.* Iola, WI. Krause Publications. 1998.

(Fig. 9) **Custom discs with a variety of aperture sizes can be turned and drilled on a lathe; the author's assortment has apertures ranging from 0.035- to 0.110-inch.**

(Fig. 6) **The Lyman 57 SML adjustable aperture sight makes this little mule-ear caplock rifle a tack-driver at the range.**

Hunting Australia's Asiatic Buffalo

by Layne Simpson

WHEN IN 1770 Captain Cook discovered the great South Seas continent we now know as Australasia, only a small handful of marsupial animals existed there. European colonists changed that during the early 1800s by importing a variety of fauna–such as Asiatic buffalo and banteng–for food along with camels, burros and horses as beasts of burden. Some of those early pioneers eventually abandoned their original settlements in favor of areas having more favorable weather, leaving many of the domesticated livestock to fend for themselves. Those animals rapidly increased in numbers.

Others were introduced to the continent for the sole purpose of sport hunting. Sambar deer, fallow deer and red deer were turned loose in habitat seemingly created just for them. Streams were stocked with trout and salmon. Various game birds, such as Chinese pheasant and Hungarian partridge, were released in the uplands. What was once a vast land inhabited mostly by kangaroos and koala had become a virtual hunter's paradise.

The Asiatic buffalo population increased to the point where, during the 1970s and 1980s, a thriving industry existed among professional market hunters who harvested the animals for foreign commercial markets. Several hundred thousand buffalo hides were salted and shipped to Asian markets each year for the production of leather and gelatin. Portable freezer plants were transported to remote areas where government-employed veterinarians and inspectors made sure the tons of buffalo meat was up to "human consumption" standards. A lot of the meat was exported to the United States, or so Bob Penfold told me.

Penfold, who holds the distinction of being the most famous and most sought-after outfitter in all of Australia, was one of those early buffalo hunters. He began shooting buffalo in 1970 while working for John Barling, a meat contractor operating out of Mudginberry Station in the Northern Territory. He did most of his shooting in a vast wilderness area adjoining the Arnhem Land border. Bob has not told me precisely how many buffaloes he has taken through

This nice bull succumbed to one shot from my 416 Magnum Remington Model 700.

Our camp in the outback had comfortable tents, a hot shower, a flush toilet, a well-equipped kitchen—and crocs in the river just a few steps away.

the years but back in the good old days he averaged over 200 per week and it went on for more than two years. Do the math as I just did and you will come up with about 12,000 tons of steaks, chops and burgers. Needless to say, if anyone knows anything about what rifles and cartridges are best for use on Asiatic buffalo it is Bob Penfold.

Penfold's two favorite rifles are an old BRNO 602 in 375 H&H Magnum and a Remington Model 700 BDL in 308 Winchester. The 375 has long been his No. 1 buffalo gun. As for the 308, he has used it for several years in various government-sponsored culling operations on smaller game. When I asked how many rounds he had fired in those two rifles, he was not sure about the BRNO but figured the Remington had digested right around 300,000 rounds during various culling operations. While Bob has replaced the barrel of the Model 700 several times, not a single part has ever broken. He did replace the extractor, not because it broke but because its claw became worn to the point where it would occasionally slip over the rim of a fired case and leave it in the chamber. As best as he could recall, that happened along about the quarter-million round mark. While the 375 H&H Magnum is Penfold's personal favorite buffalo cartridge, he and most of his guides choose the 458 Winchester Magnum for stopping a buffalo wounded by a client. Several of those rifles, custom-built on 1898 Mauser actions, are used by him and his guides. A couple of the rifles stay in camp as loaners to hunters who had rather not go to the trouble of bringing their own rifles to Australia. Those "community rifles," as I came to call them, have extremely thin 22-inch barrels and wear synthetic stocks. A guide carries his rifle much more than he shoots it so Penfold made his backup rifles extremely light for caliber at about 7-1/2 pounds.

My hunting partner, J.B. Hodgdon, chose to use one of Penfold's loaners. I could see a trace of apprehension in his eyes as he leaned across the hood of the truck, chambered a round, and prepared to squeeze it off as we checked the zeroes of our rifles prior to heading for the hills. The Mag-Na-Port brake at the muzzle surely helped some but 7-1/2 pounds is still a bit on the feathery side when it comes to shoving a 500-grain bullet out the muzzle at over 2000 fps. It is the kind of rifle you'd just as soon see someone else shoot. J.B. Hodgdon is a good hunter and since he is accustomed to shooting hard-kicking rifles, he got along just fine with the lightweight 458.

I asked Penfold and his guides how often their 458 Magnum backup rifles are allowed to join in the fun. Peter Harding said his rifle speaks about once for every 10 buffalo taken by his hunters. Like Penfold, I too am quite fond of the 375 H&H. I took my first African Cape buffalo with it but long ago decided anytime I need to quickly prevent bad things from developing, a bullet of larger caliber is a better choice than staying with the 375 family and selecting a quicker cartridge, such as the 375 Remington Ultra Mag and 378 Weatherby Magnum.

Harding shares my opinion. He went on to say there is a noticeable difference in the effect of cartridges of various calibers on buffalo. In his experience, a buffalo fatally hit by one of the 375s is likely to travel 100 or so yards–and sometimes even farther–before giving up the ghost, whereas the same animal shot with one of the 416s, or the 458, will seldom travel more than 50 yards. He sees no difference in performance between the 416 Remington Magnum and the 458 Winchester Magnum, which rather surprised me. I have used both in Africa while hunting Cape buffalo and it always seems to me that the 458 hammers them a bit harder,

Bob Penfold's favorite meat rifle is the 375 H&H BRNO he is holding here *(at left)* but the '98 Mauser in 458 Winchester Magnum held by J.B. Hodgdon is Penfold's favorite buffalo-stopping rifle.

Hodgdon checks the 458 for zero while his guide anticipates a very loud noise.

especially if the first shot is a bit off its mark.

When hunting Asiatic buffalo with Penfold, I used a Remington Model 700 chambered to 416 Remington Magnum and wearing a Burris 1.75-5X Signature Safari scope. It is one the first pre-production rifles built in that caliber by Remington a few months before the company introduced its new 416 Magnum cartridge. Three other writers and I accompanied several Remington officials on a hunt in Alaska, where we took moose with the new cartridge. Like the other writers, I hung onto my rifle and used it in Africa, before taking it to Australia. The handload I put together for Asiatic buffalo consisted of the Remington case, Remington 9-1/2M primer and the Speer 400-grain African Grand Slam bullet seated atop 77.0 grains of Hodgdon's Varget. Muzzle velocity of that load in the 24-inch barrel of the Model 700 is just over 2425 fps and average group size for three shots from the benchrest at 100 yards usually runs around 1.60 inches.

Unlike most of the professionals I have hunted buffalo with in Africa, Penfold strongly believes in leaving the solids at home and coming to Australia with nothing but premium-grade softnose bullets. Weighing upwards of a ton on the hoof, a buffalo bull is quite large and a bullet has to be capable of penetrating a lot of animal in order to get inside where it lives. Add to this the layer of dried mud likely to be clinging to the animal's hide as a result of its daily wallowing and it is easy to see why only the very best controlled-expansion bullets should be used. The Nosler Partition Gold, Federal Bear Claw, Winchester Fail-Safe, Swift A-Frame and Barnes X in their heaviest weights received the most mentions from Penfold as the ones to use on buffalo. After seeing how well the African Grand Slam I used worked on buffalo, he added it to his list of preferred bullets.

This is one of the smaller termite mounds we saw in Australia.

In the Australian outback, buffalo are found only in the northernmost tips of two regions: the Northern Territory and Western Australia. As for other countries, free-ranging Asian buffalo can be found on Narajo Island at the mouth of the Amazon River in Brazil, and in the Corrientes Province of northern Argentina. Once widespread in Asia where it was first domesticated about 4000 years ago, the wild buffalo has disappeared from most of its original range there. Limited numbers still exist in parts of Nepal and northeastern India, where they are classified as endangered.

The Asiatic buffalo is usually black in color although some of the older bulls can appear gray. Standing as high as six feet at the shoulder, it is an impressive animal to say the least. Mature bulls usually lead a solitary life except during mating season, although a bull will sometimes be seen with a group of juveniles who seem intent on warning him of potential danger. The horns of the buffalo are quite heavy at the base and triangular in cross section, with the wider flat at the top.

Australian buffalo guides divide the giant bulls they hunt into two categories. A "sweeper" has extremely wide horns that curve at their very ends while a "lunar" is not as wide and has more curve over its entire length. A bull is scored for record book purposes by adding the circumferences of both bases of its horns to the overall lengths of both horns. A score of 112 is considered trophy class. The highest-scoring bull ever recorded was taken many years ago by American hunter George Parker, who was a pal of Colonel Charles Askins. A photo of Parker and his great bull appears in Askins' book, *Asian Jungle-African Bush*. With a combined horn length of almost 10 feet, it scored an amazing 162-5/8 inches.

Hodgdon and I were hunting out of a tent camp along the Gan Gan flood plain about 400 miles southwest of Darwin and within half a morning's walk of the Gulf of Carpentaria. Except for our hosts and the inhabitants of an aboriginal village close by, we were the only humans in that particular million-acre hunting concession. I had to keep reminding myself I was in Australia because our camp seemed straight out of Africa. We enjoyed many of life's little pleasures, with a hot shower every night and wonderful meals high up on the list. We even had a flush toilet. Crocodiles had been known to romp and play only a few yards from the tent where I slept each night.

The daily routine was the same as I have experienced in Africa. Breakfast before dawn and the entire day spent bouncing along dusty roads and game trails until something interesting was spotted. Then we made our stalk. One time an old cow became suspicious and

I hold the crosshairs of my 416 on a young bull that approached even closer from upwind after this photo was taken.

the entire herd thundered off into the bush. Another time the wind shifted and spoiled our best-laid plans. Another time, the horns of a bull turned out to be smaller than they had appeared from a distance so we quietly backed away undetected. All were good times.

Then there was the time we got uncomfortably close. It happened the day we made a successful stalk on an old-timer accompanied by three younger bulls. The animals didn't know we were there but one of the juveniles decided to come out of the marsh to investigate the curious bumps out on dry land that had not been there the last time it looked. Sitting there on the ground, I watched the animal in my scope as it slowly walked toward us. Closer and closer the beast came, but it was too small to shoot. At no more than 20 yards, Jones stood up and shouted, *"boo!"* Even then, not a single one of the bulls panicked. They simply began to slowly walk away, with an occasional glance back to make sure we were not following. That's how it sometimes goes in country where hunting pressure ranges from light to nonexistent and the animals seldom see man. Those few moments alone were worth traveling to another continent for.

And by the way, I did not shoot the big bull that was accompanied by the three younger bulls. He was by far the best animal we spotted during the entire hunt but he was also wise enough to stay within a marshy area where the water

Notes on A Guide's Custom Backup Rifle

I have hunted with many guides through the years and most of them were interested in rifles only as tools. Mark Jones, who guided me for buffalo in Australia *(but who lives in New Zealand)*, is an exception. We talked a lot about rifles, cartridges, bullets, scopes and anything else hunters might be interested in and Mark knew as much about the subjects as I. His interest in rifles shows in the one he carries for backup in the outback. It was built around a slicked-up and fine-tuned BRNO 602 action and is chambered for the 416 Rigby cartridge. The barreled action rests in an extremely handsome custom stock, which was carved from a nice piece of New Zealand walnut and then nicely hand-checkered. Extremely durable open sights were also there: a ramped bead of ivory up front and a no-nonsense sight of solid steel at the rear. The wide V of the rear sight was regulated to place the handloaded 400-grain Woodleigh softnose dead on at 100 yards. A very nice rifle, indeed, and one I would love to own.

The screened dining hall also served as an excellent place to relive hunts of the past.

Getting there involves lots of travel, with the last leg by bush plane.

Getting There

Phyllis and I flew from our home in South Carolina to Los Angeles where we hooked up with J.B. and Anne Hodgdon. From there it was about a 12-hour flight to New Zealand where we hunted chamois and Himalayan thar in the Southern Alps *(another story)*. Since Australia is "just down the road" from New Zealand, it takes about the same amount of time to fly from Los Angeles to the Australian cities of Melbourne or Sydney. The gals stayed behind and burned plastic in those two cities while J.B. and I chased buffalo in the Northern Territory. He and I flew from Melbourne and overnighted in Nhulunbuy, then took a bush plane to Penfold's camp near the aboriginal village of Gan Gan.

reached high up on his chest. I had an easy shot from 50 short paces away but turned it down because I would have found it impossible to get decent photos with both the bull and me half-submerged in mud. It was if the old bull knew I would not shoot as long as it stayed belly-deep in water.

Don't think for one minute that any of this implies shooting a wild-ranging Asiatic buffalo is anything less than challenging. It might even be considered a bit risky. Like the Cape buffalo of Africa, the Asiatic buffalo is renowned for its ferocity when wounded, not to mention its ability to hide in sparse cover. I am convinced the reason the Asiatic buffalo of Australia sometimes appear more docile than the African variety is because four-legged predators large enough to do it harm do not exist. On top of that, most of the animals live out their entire lives without ever encountering a white man. The country is dotted with aboriginal villages but since the government welfare recipients who live in them seem to have lost their desire–and perhaps even their ability–to hunt, the buffalo have no reason whatsoever to fear them.

One of Penfold's observations on buffalo behavior through the years has to do with unprovoked charges. Over dinner one night he described the safety zone for a mature bull as 40 to 50 yards. Stay farther away than that and the animal is not likely to charge, so long as it has not been wounded. Step inside 40 or 50 yards and you'd best be prepared to stop a very mad animal before it grinds you into the earth or tosses you into the treetops. He also mentioned that a bull charges with head extended and nose forward, but lowers its nose between its knees with its horns extended forward just before making contact with whatever it has decided to destroy. Penfold is convinced a bull can most definitely count since a too-close encounter by one or two people will almost always result in a charge, while that same bull will seldom charge a party of three or more. Of the many stories he told around the campfire each night, my favorite was the one about the bull charging his Toyota truck—and winning.

I finally took a buffalo during the eleventh hour of my hunt. Time was fast running out when Mark Jones and I turned a corner in the creaky old Toyota and found Lady Luck finally willing to cooperate. We managed to spot the buffalo all alone as it napped in the cool shade of a eucalyptus tree. As I peered intently into my 10x binocular I could see the bull, but a screen of brush just this side of the animal prevented me from getting the look I wanted at its horns. It was not the first buffalo Jones had sized up through the years and he seemed convinced it was the bull I had traveled thousands of miles to collect. "He's a really old bull", he said, "and a few years on the downhill side of his prime, but those horns seem good enough for a closer look." Our stalk would not be an easy one since between the bull and us was about 500 yards of open floodplain covered with short grass. The ground had recently been covered by water from seasonal rains and it made the black earth ankle-deep soft. That, along with the ground being pockmarked by dinner plate-size buffalo tracks, made walking a bit difficult. On the positive side, the wind was right so Jones and I figured we could make it across undetected so long as the great bull did not awaken from its midday snooze.

What to Take

As I mentioned elsewhere in this report, you can choose between bringing your own rifle or using a lightweight 458 furnished by Penfold. I prefer to hunt with my own rifles and actually took two, a lightweight in 243 Winchester *(built by Prairie Gun Works)* for use in New Zealand, and a Remington Model 700 in 416 Magnum for buffalo in Australia. All of my paperwork was in order so I had no problem whatsoever entering and leaving either country with my two rifles. Same goes for ammunition; the 30 rounds of ammo I took for my 416 proved to be far more than I actually needed and I opted to leave what was left in camp rather than haul it back home. Thanks to a rugged case from the Texas firm of Americase, both rifles survived numerous airline flight transfers without suffering a single ding or scratch. The 10x40 Zeiss binocular I used proved ideal, as did the Bushnell Yardage Pro laser rangefinder and the Scopz shooting glasses from Zeiss. To keep weight to a minimum, I chose to not take along a spotting scope but I knew beforehand that my guide would share his with me.

Our buffalo hunt took place in July and the weather could not have been more cooperative. One of the more pleasant things I noticed about northern Australia was the absence of flying insects and no thorns on any of bushes or trees. Green ants love to nest in the foliage of some trees, and while they are not at all bashful about covering anything that brushes against them, I received not a single bite. The staff washes and dries clothing in camp daily so you will not need to take a very large wardrobe. A three-day supply of underwear, along with three shirts and pants will do the trick. A light sweater or jacket will handle the coolest nights and mornings. I could have worn short pants and short-sleeved shirts due to the mild weather but wisely opted for long pants and sleeves for protection against the brush. More specifically, I wore the Serengeti Safari shirt and 7-Pocket cotton pant from Cabela's and liked both so well I will do so again next time. The 10-inch Highlander boots from Irish Setter I left tracks with proved to be just the ticket as well; their light weight made them comfortable to wear on long stalks and their Gore-Tex liner kept my feet dry when walking across muddy ground. I also learned that a wide-brimmed hat or fishing cap with long bill and neck flap is a good thing to have since the sun can become rather intense at times.

We moved along single file and paused every 50 yards or so to take another peek through our binoculars. After what seemed like hours *(but was actually no more than a few minutes)*, we finally made it undetected to the edge of the forest where we did our best to hide behind the trunks of a couple of small trees. From there we would do some serious, up-close glassing. Or so we thought. Only about 50 yards away by now, the buffalo continued to nap, but all was not perfect for the two hunters as a heavy growth of brush and small saplings prevented us from getting a good look at its horns. Then what I had come to Australia for began to happen. Perhaps we made a slight noise or it could have been a whiff of our scent drifting toward the animal. Or maybe something inside the bull's head told it danger had stalked too close for comfort. Suddenly about three-quarters of a ton of hide, bone, muscle and horns was on the alert and staring intently in our direction. But the animal did not flee for its life as it might have done. Rather, the mighty beast lifted its nose into the damp air and began to mosey toward us as if coming to investigate what it was that had disturbed its peace and solitude.

The bull would take a step and then stop to stare in our direction for a minute or so before taking another cautious step and then pausing again for another look. I am sure we stared at each other for a good five minutes. As the bull drew a bit close for comfort I began to wonder why Mark did not tell me to either shoot or back away. I did not realize he was still having trouble sizing up its horns through the extremely thick brush. As the bull stood there–so close in my scope–it looked more than good enough for a last-day buffalo so I had already made up my mind to take a frontal shot into the chest once it came to a rotting tree limb lying on the ground, about 20 yards away. There, clinging to the bottom of the bull's neck, just above its massive chest, was a chunk of dried mud about the size of a silver dollar. That's where I plastered the crosshairs of my scope.

This wild boar was a bonus.

At about 25 yards, caution obviously overcame curiosity and the bull decided the time had come for it to be in another part of the country. Just as the animal turned broadside Jones finally decided the animal had good horns, and whispered *"shoot"*. Shifting the crosshairs to about a third of the way up from bottom and dead center of the shoulder area, I squeezed the trigger and sent 400 grains of death and destruction on its way. As the bull turned away I attempted to hammer more lead home, but even as I pulled the trigger time and again I had my doubts about a single one of the bullets making its way through the wall of saplings. Not a single one of the bullets needed to get through. After taking my first shot low in its shoulder, the bull stumbled along for about 30 yards, then tried to stay on its feet by leaning against a tree. Then it slowly slid to the ground and breathed its last. After making sure the fallen animal was as dead as it appeared to be, Mark and I approached it and then began to retrace the route it took after taking my bullet. We were amazed at the amount of blood the buffalo had lost before dropping. The 416 punches a big hole going in and leaves an even bigger hole going out!

It was estimated that my bull was around 15 years of age, which put it about five years beyond its prime. While its horns would have *"made the book"* when the animal was younger, they had become broomed-off considerably. The fact that the bull scored a bit less than 100 points made it no less magnificent, and the entire affair mattered not to me since I never have had–and never will have–any interest whatsoever in record books. No doubt about it, I will hunt buffalo in Australia again someday for no other reason than I absolutely love hunting buffalo of any kind. Another reason is because Australians love America and Americans, and that makes Australia a safer place for you and me to be than a few other countries I can name. If you have an interest in hunting in Australia, New Zealand or perhaps New Caledonia, Bob Penfold is the man to contact at Hunt Australia Pty. Ltd. His telephone number is 011 61 2 4951 1198 or you can reach him by e-mail at enquiries@huntaust.com.au. He also has a website: www.huntaust.com.au •

Sometimes getting to where the buffalo roamed required travel over water.

The Ballard Single-Shot Rifle...

An Old Favorite of Yesteryear Rides On!

by George J. Layman

Widely advertised, the Ballard No. 8 and No. 9 Union Hill were by far the Marlin company's bestsellers of the entire Ballard line during the mid- to late-1880s. This ad appeared in the July 5th, 1888 issue of *Shooting and Fishing*.

FOR NEARLY 30 years, Charles H. Ballard's design was among the most revered of all single-shot rifles, and today is popular with both collectors and blackpowder shooters.

In the past 15 years, there has been an unprecedented resurgence in the popularity of several different areas of antique gun collecting. It appears this is not restricted to any particular field of antique firearms but, generally speaking, the single-shot metallic cartridge breechloader has reached an all-time high. As far back as the early 1900s, a small but elite group of shooters–including Harry Pope, A.O. Niedner, A.W. Peterson and many others–favored the single-shot rifle for both centerfire and rimfire match shooting. Among their contemporaries, they also maintained the opinion that the graceful mechanics of the butter-smooth Ballard action was a hands-down favorite. In its infancy, however, the Ballard had one of the most convoluted histories of any firearm of its day, but then went on to become one of the most highly regarded single-shot sporting rifles ever conceived.

Patented just as the metallic rimfire cartridge made its debut, its inventor was Charles Henry Ballard of Worcester, Massachusetts. Born in 1822 in Sterling, Massachusetts, Ballard was a professional machinist who began putting his ideas into a single-shot, breechloading rifle design sometime in the late 1850s. During his association with the firm of Ball and Ballard, he had ample time and equipment for such experimentation. Ballard submitted his falling-block action for patent registration and received U.S. Patent # 33,631 on November 5, 1861. His timing could not have been better, as the Civil War had begun a little over six months earlier. Though Ballard was not financially capable of putting his new rifle into full production, he did produce a small number of rifles that were practically handmade. According to his patent drawing, the action had a hammer with a stationary firing pin nose, an internal extractor that functioned on the downward stroke of the lever–and the action was not equipped with a forend.

Ballard had likely envisioned his design would be a worthy contribution to the war effort, and it seemed a pair of New York financial backers thought so as well. Joseph Merwin and Edward P. Bray would soon begin a long affiliation with the Ballard rifle. Entering into a

The first Ballard rifle, serial number one, is chambered for the 32 rimfire and equipped with the early internal extractor per the original patent drawing. The rifle, with its 23 1/4-inch barrel, was also produced sans forend. Interestingly, the rifle was almost entirely handmade.

◀ Markings on the early Ballard rifles as manufactured by Ball and Williams are of two different categories. Those serial-numbered below 9000 *(left)* have the patent, manufacturer, and agent stampings on the octagonal flats just ahead of the rear sight. Those above serial number 9000 *(below)* have the Ball and Williams marking and agent stamping on the left frame, with the Ballard patent on the right side.

contract with Richard Ball and Warren Williams of the Ball and Williams Manufacturing Company of Worcester, Massachusetts ensured production of the Ballard, in both civilian sporting and military variations, would commence almost immediately.

About 50 sporting rifles were initially produced with brass receivers, but the receiver soon changed to iron. When it went into production at the Ball and Williams plant, an unexpected alteration in the design of the Ballard was the elimination of the lever-activated extractor. The design was modified to include a manual extractor, which made it necessary to redesign the forward portion of the frame to allow installation of a forend that housed the spring-operated extractor assembly within. None of these new additions were part of the mechanism indicated on the November 1861 patent drawing.

Prior to the U.S. government order of Ballard carbines, it seems a number of states were eyeing the Ballard for their militias. Among the first purchases of the Ballard for martial usage was the state of Kentucky, whose order of 3000 carbines in 1863 was the first of a long association of the Ballard and the pro-Unionist elements of that state's armed services.

The very first Ballard military carbines were chambered for the 44 rimfire cartridge and were equipped with a 22-inch barrel, sling swivels, and a short carbine-style forend retained by a single barrel band. The April 1863 issue of *Harpers Weekly* advertised that deliveries of various models would be ready in November of that year. The first chamberings of the sporting models were in 32, 38, and 44 rimfire. It was apparent that commercial variations would be available concurrent with military models. With the war escalating, it was hoped the federal government would begin to place orders of an identical frequency and number similar to those of the Spencer or Sharps. The financial backers of the Ballard, Messrs. Merwin and Bray, leaned heavily on the U.S. government to order the rifle. They succeeded in securing a contract for 1500 carbines, but more often than not, it seemed the state of Kentucky would be the most prolific customer for any sizeable military purchases.

In 1863 the Kentucky ordnance department placed an order with Ball and Williams for 3500 rifles, all of which would be chambered for the 56/56 Spencer cartridge, with a 30-inch barrel and short forend. For reasons not clear, the order was changed: they would instead be chambered for the 44 rimfire cartridge. The rifles were received on April 5, 1864 and, not long after, another order of rifles was placed. This time however, it was specified they be chambered for the 46 rimfire cartridge and that the forend of the stock would be a full-length type, secured by three barrel bands. Between July 1864 and March 1865, the Kentuckians received 3500 of these rifles, which in future promotions of the Ballard would become known as the "Kentucky Ballard." It should be mentioned for historical purposes that the 3rd, 6th, 8th, 11th, 12th, and 13th Kentucky cavalry units were issued the Ballard, as was the 45th

Throughout the Civil War, the greatest customer for the Ballard three-band military rifles was the state of Kentucky. So great was their influence that the rifle, when produced by Brown Manufacturing company in 1869, was cataloged as the "Kentucky Model."

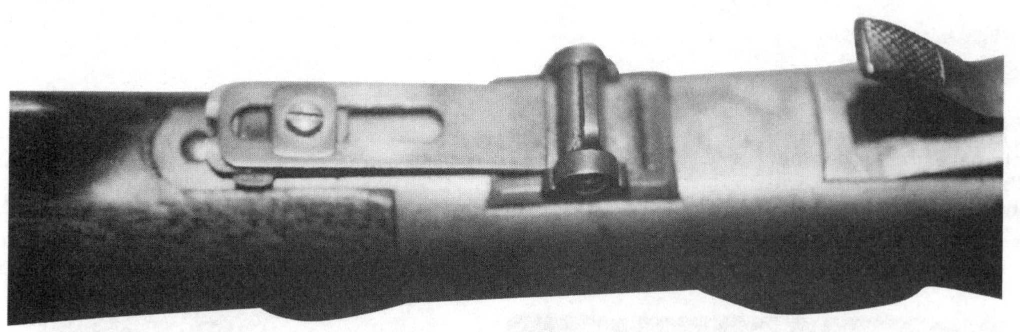

Early Ballard rifles made by Ball and Williams could be ordered with a few special features upon customer request. This early sporting rifle is equipped with a factory-marked tang sight—definitely a rare addition.

Mounted Infantry who, in a number of campaigns, pursued Confederate irregular forces.

By mid-1864, there was little remaining space at the Ball and Williams factory and about this time Merwin and Bray concluded another contract with the federal government for 1000 rifles and 1000 carbines to be chambered in the 56/56 Spencer.

Since the factory in Worcester was working at a prohibitively high capacity, it was decided that the Bridgeport, Connecticut firm of Dwight, Chapin and Company would fulfill this latest order. Not long after, the new contractor ran into all sorts of difficulties and was only able to complete some 115 carbines and a small number of rifles, leaving parts and inventory in all stages of completion. This grave setback occurred during a crucial stage of the war, and upon the speedy completion of all legal proceedings, leftover parts, half-finished rifles, carbines, and machinery were shipped up to the Ball and Williams factory in Massachusetts for finishing, assembly and completion of the contract.

With the government forfeiting the remainder of the order, Kentucky once again bought the leftover carbines, which were finished in the white and had the Dwight, Chapin and Company markings rubbed off the frames.

These Ballard carbines and rifles had a number of unique features compared to the standard Ball and Williams versions: wider dimensions to their breechblocks and frames, with a number of external cosmetic changes such as squarer levers, upswept hammer spurs, and full round barrels *(Ball and Williams carbines had half-round half-octagon barrels)*. The most important deviation was the larger caliber of the 56/56 Spencer. It is estimated that Kentucky bought up 600 of the 835 assembled rifles of the Dwight, Chapin contract.

The two-piece longitudinally divided breechblock was the hallmark of the Ballard throughout its near-30-year production. The breechblock assembly conveniently housed all moving parts within.

Interestingly, 1200 of the 1500 Ballard carbines ordered by the U.S. government were given to the state of Vermont following the daring raid on the St. Albans bank by escaped Confederate prisoners in 1864. Having slipped across the Canadian border, they pulled it off quite successfully, thus the Vermont state militia was given the remaining Ballard carbines as insurance against future incursions.

By 1865 it seems that, outside of a few small orders and the approaching end of the war, production and sales of the Ballard dwindled to a trickle. In July of that same year, Warren Williams decided to retire and left his partner Richard Ball in control of the company. The firm was renamed Richard Ball and Company and continued to manufacture the Ballard rifle.

Built in 1867, this structure located on Merrimack Street in Newburyport, Massachusetts was the site of both the Merrimack Arms Manufacturing Company and, later, the Brown Manufacturing Company. Today the building has been remodeled into condominiums.

This 38-caliber Brown Ballard sporting rifle is an example of the last type of Ballard sporting rifle produced in Massachusetts prior to the foreclosure of the Brown Manufacturing Co. in July of 1873.

Before the Civil War, the Ball and Williams Company was primarily engaged in the production of wood- and metalworking machinery. It seems the Ballard rifle was merely a supplementary operation within the company and the success or failure of the rifle would not have too great an impact on Richard Ball and Company. By 1866, there were only token sales of the Ballard, such as the 100 carbines sold to New York state as well as small, scattered purchases by sporting arms distributors. Both Merwin and Bray were still quite aware that military sales to the U.S. government were impossible since the army was auctioning off surplus guns and equipment at prices that commercial manufacturers could never hope to compete with.

With much of their money still tied up with inventory in Richard Ball's factory, Edward Bray felt that, with continued advertising and a brisk marketing campaign, there was still a market for the Ballard—both commercially and militarily. Thus, in 1866, Bray purchased the entire operation and reorganized it as the Merrimack Arms and Manufacturing Company. The new organization however, was to be relocated in its entirety up north to the seacoast community of Newburyport, Massachusetts, a town at the mouth of the Merrimack River. By the time the Merrimack Arms Co. was created, there were nearly 18,000 Ballards in circulation and Edward Bray made good use of the rifle's established merits with an aggressive sales campaign. Arrival of the new company in Newburyport was greeted with great excitement by the populace, and the *Newburyport Herald* of July 21, 1866 stated about the Merrimack Arms and Manufacturing Company "...they hold the patent of the Ballard rifle, with patents on valuable improvements, also patents on shotguns and pistols, and also a very important wood carving machine ... they have invested in their business $150,000..."

One of those "patents on valuable improvements" was the dual ignition feature that was previously applied on many later Ball and Williams-made Ballard rifles. Patent #41,166 granted to Joseph Merwin and Edward P. Bray on January 5, 1864 was simply a percussion nipple installed on the breechblock just beneath the upper hammer channel. A hollow convex on the center of the hammer's neck met the percussion cap on ignition. The purpose behind this was if the shooter ran out of fixed ammunition, he could literally continue to use the rifle with but a single cartridge case by punching a hole in the base, handloading it with powder and ball, and use a percussion cap for primary ignition. The rifle could even be used as a muzzleloader with this system.

Though considered by many as a regression from a firearms technology standpoint, it was praised by many who often found themselves far away from storekeepers, particularly in the outback of the American West.

Sales of the Ballard were not as lucrative as anticipated, and out of an estimated 2200 pieces made by Merrimack, the majority were sporting rifles; plus about 50 shotguns, slightly less than 200 military carbines, and a very limited number of three-band military rifles. The company had hoped to interest the U.S. government in adopting a special 56/50 Ballard military rifle that housed an external ramrod during the 1868 trials, but the government's "in-house" 2nd Model Allin-Springfield won out over all competition. Probably the only significant "contract" sales by Merrimack was the purchase of 70 carbines by New York state for the prison at Sing-Sing, and the somewhat dubious procurement of some 40 to 60 special 30-inch barreled sporting rifles sold to a Canadian militia group known as the "red sashes" who operated during the Fenian troubles of 1869 and 1870.

Prior to 1881, Marlin-Ballards had the J. M. Marlin address, later changed to Marlin Firearms Co. Also shown is the February 1875 patent date for John M. Marlin's dual firing pin feature. Later production guns dispensed with this marking altogether.

◀ All through the Massachusetts production era, Ballard rifles and carbines utilized the hand-operated manual extractor. After 1864, the dual-ignition feature was added.

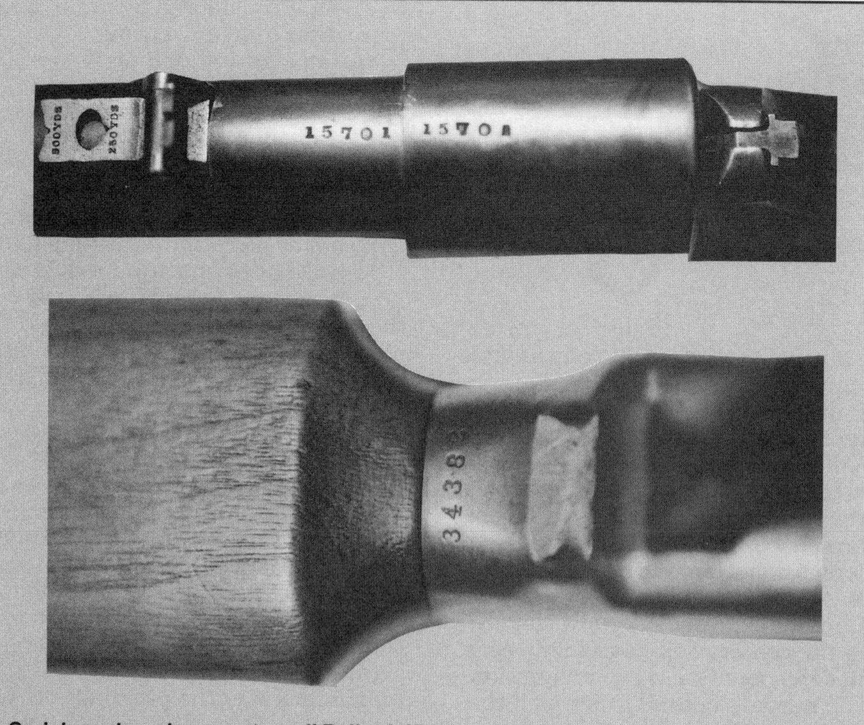

Serial number placement on all Ballard rifles produced in Massachusetts was on the upper frame and barrel *(top)*. All J. M. Marlin and Marlin Firearms Co. Ballards *(bottom)* had their numbers on the lower front of the frame. The only exception was the very first J. M. Marlin, the "Hunter's Model," which had them on the upper frame as in the earlier variants.

It seems the Merrimack company had decided to once again reorganize the firm, and on February 18, 1869, transferred control to Mr. Charles S. Brown of New York City. Thus was created the Brown Manufacturing Company with Mr. Brown as president and Mr. George Merrill as secretary. The Brown Mfg. Co. carried the identical line as Merrimack, but they also produced the Brown bolt-action single-shot rifle, based on James H. Merrill's patent using the 58 Berdan cartridge.

These were apparently made up on surplus Enfield muzzleloading rifles, which were cut at the breech and a new action reinstalled. By 1871, it appeared the company was floundering. It had over-extended its assets, and on May 8th of that year, a mortgage was placed on the company and foreclosure proceedings were drawn up. The company was sold at auction in July 1873.

It is puzzling that between 1869 and 1873, there were a mere 1700 Ballard rifles made up by Brown with about 1,000 of them being three-band military rifles — possibly intended for a failed contract with France during the Franco-Prussian War of 1870. Many of them were sold to the William Read Company of Boston, Massachusetts who cut down the forends on most and converted them to sporting-type rifles. Read advertised them as genuine Ballard "Kentucky" models.

To an observer of the day, the following excerpt from the March 20, 1872, edition of the *Newburyport Daily News* would have convinced one that the Brown Mfg. Co. had a lucrative clientele "...The Brown Manufacturing Company have on hand a contract which they have partially completed in the changing of 2,000 Enfield rifles and making them into the breechloading pattern manufactured by this company... there are now employed 65 hands... there is some of the nicest mechanical work done at Brown Manufacturing Company's works, and their business is continually enlarging ." Such a passage would indicate they were successfully expanding.

A column from the same newspaper on February 13, 1929 paints a different picture, however. An elderly gentleman, Mr. C.W. Adams, presented some interesting facts during an interview; "...When I returned from Boston in early 1870, the firm had changed hands *(author's note: from Merrimack to Brown)* and was then known as the Brown Manufacturing Company, making the 'Southerner' derringer, Ballard rifle, and a military rifle of 50-caliber *(the Brown bolt action)* that was not a success. I secured a job there as one of about 100 men till about January 1872 when this place suddenly closed, and we are still waiting for our last 6 weeks pay..." Quite a contradiction between the two passages. It is obvious that with delinquency in payment to the workforce coupled with the mortgage placed on the property, the Brown Company was in dire financial straits.

Charles Daly, of Schoverling and Daly of New York City, purchased the entire organization and its inventory under foreclosure proceedings and, right then and there, the Ballard took out a new lease on life. Schoverling and Daly's shrewd marketing techniques, coupled with the inventive skills of one John Mahlon Marlin of New Haven, Connecticut, gave the Ballard a whole new identity within the firearms world; it was transformed from just another semi-successful Civil War-era breechloading design to become one of the finest single-shot rifles of all time.

Prior to 1881, Marlin-Ballards had the J. M. Marlin address, later changed to Marlin Firearms Co. Also shown is the February 1875 patent date for John M. Marlin's dual firing pin feature. Later production guns dispensed with this marking altogether.

The Marlin-Ballard No. 4 Perfection was one of the plainer versions that appealed to the outdoorsman of the West due to its availability in larger calibers, such as the 40-65 Everlasting, 44-77, 40-63 Ballard, and the smaller 38-55.

Prior to purchasing any antique firearm, always research and examine the piece, and the Ballard is no exception. This near-excellent No. 6-1/2 Midrange Offhand rifle with light scroll engraving is indeed of interest to the collector. The problem, though, is that the lever is for a pistol-grip Ballard action. Such a mismatch won't terribly affect price, but the buyer should be aware of this–even if the seller is not.

From the very start, gunmaker John Marlin, known for his line of quality pistols and revolvers, made good use of many of the surplus parts and components to produce the Ballard, and in 1875, the very first J.M. Marlin Ballard rifle was ready for the public and was tagged the "Hunters Model." After the first rifle was introduced, one of the first things Marlin made certain of was that an internal extractor would replace its inefficient predecessor, which required two-handed operation. Ironically, this was a return to what Charles Ballard had originally included in his first patent model.

John Marlin was also clever enough to realize that since the rimfire cartridge had a limited efficiency and was basically non-reloadable, it was imperative to begin chambering the new Ballard for centerfire cartridges. Since many early centerfire cartridges had a rimfire counterpart, Marlin patented a useful, dual-purpose, reversible firing pin that could be easily changed depending on what ammunition the shooter had at hand. Patented on February 9, 1875, the pronged firing pin could be changed to either position in a few minutes by removal of a screw on the right upper exposed portion of the breechblock.

The company, until 1881, was the J.M. Marlin Co., which, after reorganization became the Marlin Firearms Company. Between 1875 and the ultimate end of production of the Ballard, over 20 different variations of the rifle were introduced. With each new year, however, the Marlin catalog always seemed to offer something not listed in previous editions. For example, the 1881-1882 Marlin catalog introduced the now super-rare No. 5-1/2 Montana Ballard in a whopping 45-100 chambering, with choice of shotgun buttplate or crescent rifle-type. The 1882 catalog emphasized that the heavy 14-1/2 pound rifle was "well suited to the territory trade," however the rifle proved less popular than anticipated and disappeared from Marlin catalogs by 1883. To include a whole host of rugged, no-nonsense big-bore numbers for the outdoorsman or casual target shooter, Marlin offered a complete series of long-range Creedmoor-style target rifles in 44-100 and 45-100. These were listed as the Numbers 7, 7 A-1 "Long Range", and the 7 A-1 "Extra". As long-range shooting began to wane in popularity by the early 1880s, so did the big-caliber rifles. From 1884 to the demise of the Marlin-Ballard, it seems that both the Ballard Nos. 8 and 9 Union Hill models were destined to become the most well-liked duo ever incorporated into the Marlin-Ballard line. Chambered for the immensely popular 32-40 and 38-55 Ballard cartridges, countless numbers of shooters adored the Union Hill for schuetzen shooting and medium-range target work. This popularity is quite evident today judging by the frequency that both the Number 8 and 9 Ballard are encountered. Though it is estimated there were about 39,000 Ballards manufactured by both J.M. and Marlin Firearms Company, the rifles are not commonly encountered, especially in the higher grades. The Ballard has been so popular with today's shooters that, since 1991, they have been manufactured in reproduction form by Ballard Rifle and Cartridge Company in Cody, Wyoming—a long way from the old Marlin plant in

The upper receiver, on Marlin-Ballards, with a concave configuration is usually indicative of either the 22 rimfire No. 3 Gallery Model or the No. 3F Special Gallery variation. Some larger-caliber No. 2 rifles having this feature have been observed by the author. Shown is a custom-built No. 3F.

The engraving on Marlin-Ballards was often magnificently executed in precise detailing. Ballard rifles with engraved Rigby flats, as shown, with the Ballard logo and arrows that are gold-filled bring a premium on today's market.

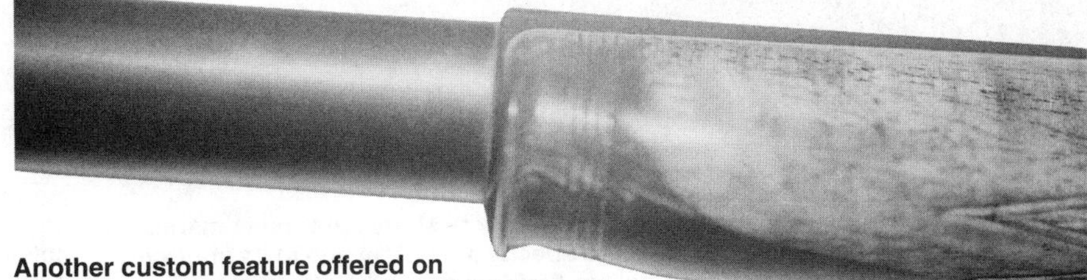

Another custom feature offered on higher grade Marlin-Ballards was a forend tip of horn. Though this material can easily chip or crack, many surviving Ballards show this feature remarkably intact.

The Marlin-Ballard No. 8 Union Hill Model was one of the best-selling variants of the entire line between 1885 and the end of production. Catalogs specified it with a part-round/part-octagonal barrel. The example shown is unusual due to its full-octagonal barrel, indicating it may have been a special-order rifle. ***Robert Gillaspie photo***

New Haven, Connecticut. Though always valued for their glassy-smooth and positive-camming action by shooters, far too many fine Marlin-Ballards have been made into target rifles in more common chamberings; thus numerous complete originals in several of the scarcer models have disappeared altogether.

Specializing in collecting the Ballard can take on many facets: One may specialize solely in the early Massachusetts rimfire variants of either military or sporting models, or focus solely on the J.M. Marlin or Marlin Firearms Company sporting and target models. The areas of Ballard collecting can have a nearly endless theme but with so many of the pristine specimens having been routed out and put into collections, the neophyte will definitely have his work cut out for him. With a near-infinite amount of custom and individual extra features ordered by yesterday's shooters, its no wonder that each Ballard–regardless of having correct *"out of the catalog"* specifications–is often a unique specimen. For those who wish to undertake the Ballard as a collecting theme, the options are practically endless. Having owned dozens of variants over the years, my greatest investigative coup was the discovery of Ballard serial number one in the Worcester Historical Museum in Worcester, Massachusetts. It will probably never be offered for sale to the public, but those who admire the greatest Ballard rifle of them all will always have the satisfaction of knowing exactly where they can visit to admire Charles H. Ballard's inventor's sample when the need arises. ●

References:

Archives, Worcester Historical Museum, Worcester, Massachusetts

Archives, Old Newbury Historical Society, Newburyport, Massachusetts

Flayderman's Guide to Antique American Firearms, 7th Edition, Norm Flayderman, 1998 Krause Publications.

A Guide to the Ballard Breechloader, George J. Layman, Pioneer Press 1997, Union City, TN 38261

The engraving found on Marlin-Ballards is usually executed in the Ulrich style, and variations such as this No. 6-1/2 Rigby Off-Hand rifle are highly sought. This specimen has a deer and bear game scene on both sides of the frame to include heavy scroll engraving.

An example of an unusual Ballard is this No. 3 Gallery Model, profusely marked with British proof marks. The rifle itself is a special order item due to its shotgun buttstock, optional on this model. Also, the 25 Stevens rimfire chambering is most unusual since it was never offered in factory catalogs. The special-order chambering alone puts the rifle in the 1889-1890 period, just prior to Marlin discontinuing the Ballard rifle. ***Frank Kelly collection***

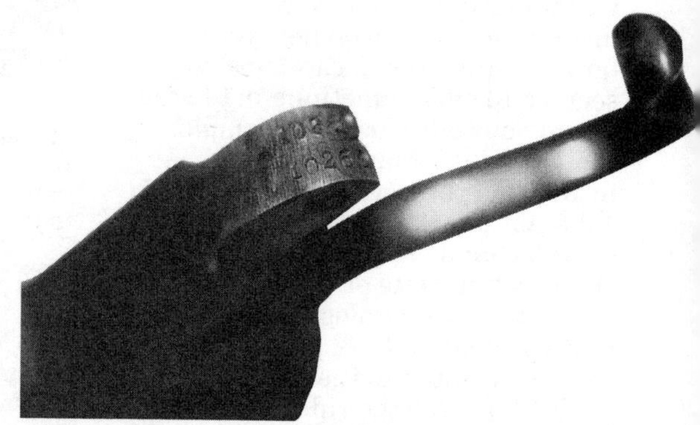

Marlin-Ballards normally have each major component serial-numbered, and serious collectors usually demand all matching numbers. A matching breechblock is especially important and, upon removing the block from the frame, serial numbers are found on both sides of the rear upper shoulder of the block.

Holland & Holland catalog ca 1904

English Black Powder Express Double Rifles

by Thomas D. Schiffer

IN THE LAST half of the nineteenth century and into the twentieth, the British could boast "the sun never sets on the British Empire". In those days, within the geography under their flag, were found some of the most fertile grounds for sport and subsistence hunting known to man. Crown colonies in Africa conjure up thoughts of elephant, rhino, lion, leopard and buffalo—not to mention the plains game—and the control of man-eating lions. India provided leopard and tiger shooting, as well as a plethora of other game. Tigers that developed a taste for human flesh also provided plenty of "sport" for those skillful enough and willing enough to go after them.

A common thread running through much of this landscape was the double rifle from places like London, Birmingham, Dublin and Edinburgh. The names of Rigby, Jeffery, Purdey, Henry, Richards, and Holland–and many others, lesser-known–resonated with numbers like 450/400, 500/450, 577/450, 10-bore and 8-bore. These were the days before the acrid smell of cordite nearly drove blackpowder from the fields. I say nearly, because blackpowder held on for many years, either in its own right, or in nitro-for-black loadings for the older rifles.

A word or two regarding cartridge nomenclature might not be amiss. Just as the 45/70 and 45/2.1-inch are the same thing in America, the 450/400 2 3/8-inch and the 450/400 BPE *(Black Powder Express)* are the same thing in British nomenclature *(but not the same as the 45/70)*. The 450/400 BPE cartridges are 40-caliber cartridges derived from 45-caliber cases. Sometimes the decimal points are used and sometimes not. When the British write a decimal point, it often sits up mid-line. A complete rundown on British cartridges is well beyond the scope of this article. For that, I refer the reader to the current edition of CARTRIDGES OF THE WORLD (Krause Publications) for more information on the topic. As will be seen in one of the cuts, there are sometimes

Matt Middleton shooting "rhino" with a 450 Black Powder Express Alexander Henry. *Al Roberts photo.*

three cartridges that will *fit* in the chamber of blackpowder rifles. I emphasize the word *fit*, because the wrong one could blow up the gun! One is loaded with blackpowder, another with Nitro-for-black *(often marked* LC *for 'light cordite')*. Both of these were designed for use in blackpowder rifles at blackpowder pressures. And then there are Nitro loads, which should *never* be used in a blackpowder rifle because they develop much higher pressures than the other two loads.

Another reference on British cartridges is found in the 16th edition of GUN DIGEST, in an article by that name authored by Ken Waters. Since over 40 years have passed since it was published, the ammunition availability information found in it is seriously outdated. However, the article contains timeless information. Perhaps the most important thing Waters had to say was that anyone thinking about shooting an old British double rifle should take a good look at the proof marks on the barrels. "...[*unless it is*] proved for Nitro powders (either 'NP' or the words 'Nitro" or 'Cordite') do *NOT* use any of the full-charge or magnum cartridges with metal jacketed bullets." Needless to say, *any* such rifle needs to be checked over by a competent person before firing with *any* loads.

Following the U. S. Civil War, the breechloader and metallic cartridges came into full flower. The need to develop rifles that could handle large and dangerous game superceded further development of the as-yet primitive repeating rifles that were, at the time, restricted to pistol-type cartridges. The need was for a rifle that was sufficiently powerful for the largest game, which could provide a quick back-up shot and be extremely reliable. The double rifle filled that need. At the same time, there was a desire to flatten the trajectory curve of blackpowder rifles to extend the effective range. To accomplish this, bullet weight was reduced and powder charges were increased. The increased velocity delivered by this combination extended the effective range to at least 150 yards, in the hands of skilled riflemen.

The theory was that in remote areas, far from civilization and gunsmiths, two rifles joined into one made for good life insurance. Theory further indicated it was not likely that both would go awry at the same time; thus providing a vital second shot in a day when repeating rifles were a novelty and mostly confined to the weaker cartridges. So successful was this format that the double rifle has survived to this day in the face of far cheaper-to-build, more powerful repeating rifles capable of more than one extra shot.

Another development was the Paradox gun. This consisted of a typical side-by-side shotgun having a short section of rifling at the muzzle only *(Fosbery's patent)*. Picture screw-in chokes with rifling in them. However, the rifling in the Paradox was integral with the barrel. Greener reported this allowed the gun to be used with shot and produced better than Cylinder-bore patterns for use in fowling, yet could be used with a cannelured conical bullet against bigger game out to 100 yards. He reported it would produce groups of 4 inches by 3 inches at that distance with blackpowder and that its use against boar or bear was proper. The Paradox gun featured the lightning-fast handling properties of a shotgun that the big-bore double rifle lacked, being perhaps twice the weight of the Paradox gun. Greener didn't think the Paradox was proper for constant use against big game, but would do well in a pinch. Greener had his own version of the Paradox *(Greener's patent)* which differed in detail.

East Enterprise Blackpowder Express Safari

Somewhere west of 85 degrees west longitude and a bit south of 40 degrees north latitude was the

Jack Stoner shooting "elephant" *(in trees)*, with left hand Alexander Henry 450 Black Powder Express. Scorer Linda Drake looks on. "Cobra" is located at end of smoke cloud. *Al Roberts photo.*

Garden (maker) rifle in 500 Black Powder Express.

I. Hollis (maker) rifle in 450 Black Powder Express.

Venables (maker) rifle in 500 Black Powder Express.

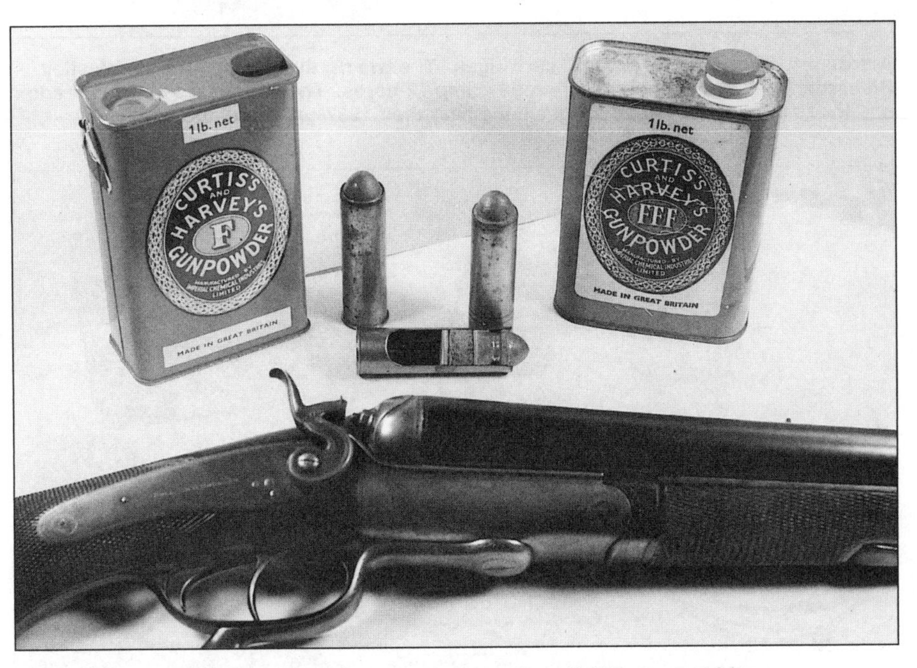

Holland & Holland 10-bore Paradox gun and a sectioned 10-bore cartridge.

scene of a special invitational safari. Targeted at this event were the *Big Five* of African big game: Cape buffalo, rhino, elephant, leopard and lion. This event was held on September 16, 2002. The firearms used– double rifles –were restricted to the blackpowder express loadings from the heyday of African big-game hunting. Names like Holland and Holland, Manton, Purdey, Alexander Henry and Westley Richards were engraved on as fine a collection of double gun hardware to be found afield anywhere in the world on that day.

Among the readers, there will be some that have discerned there is little African big game to be found in the area of 40 degrees north latitude; none at all by the time you arrive at 85 degrees west longitude. These readers will not be surprised to learn that this was a simulated hunt. The guest list was limited to those Midwesterners who had an interest in double rifles. The home states of the participants included Kentucky, Tennessee, Virginia, Ohio, Michigan, Pennsylvania, Alabama and Indiana. A number of those participating had actually been to Africa and taken game there.

Instead of the rolling plains of Africa, we had the rolling hills of southern Indiana. Instead of the tall grasses native to Africa, we had tall fields of corn and millet. Instead of wait-a-bit thorn, we had blackberry and raspberry briers. Instead of the tsetse fly, we had to make do with the mosquito. The targets were silhouettes of the real animals, with a "kill zone" represented by steel swingers fastened where hits could be registered both by sound and by sight. Each silhouette was carefully positioned to give the aspect of a real hunting situation typical of that species. Each species was separated some distance into a separate scenario from the others. None of the animals was hidden completely; they were in high grass or, in the case of the leopard, on a distant tree limb. All were at 100 yards or less.

The "hunters" were to be appropriately attired for an African hunt. They were to be divided into two groups, each lead by a "professional hunter" (PH). Each PH was someone who had actually hunted wild game in Africa. While one hunting party was engaging in somewhat formalized shooting at 50- and 100-yard targets *(no spotting or coaching allowed)*, the other party was out on safari. In mid-afternoon, the parties switched. To stimulate competition, the host announced there was only enough food to feed half of them at dinner, and the winning "team" would eat first! *(As you might guess, there was actually plenty of food for all, even after a hard day in the field.)*

Each hunter on safari was given two minutes to fire four shots at each game scenario. The hunters took turns at this, one at a time. To make things more interesting, the official scorers utilized a computerized random timing sub-event within those two minutes. When the computer said so, the scorer would yell *"COBRA!"* The hunter had to immediately stop shooting at the animal and locate a "cobra"-designated swinger and shoot it, as if a real cobra had threatened his day. Only after shooting–and hitting–the cobra was the hunter allowed to finish his four shots at the game animal. While two minutes is plenty of time to load and fire four aimed shots with

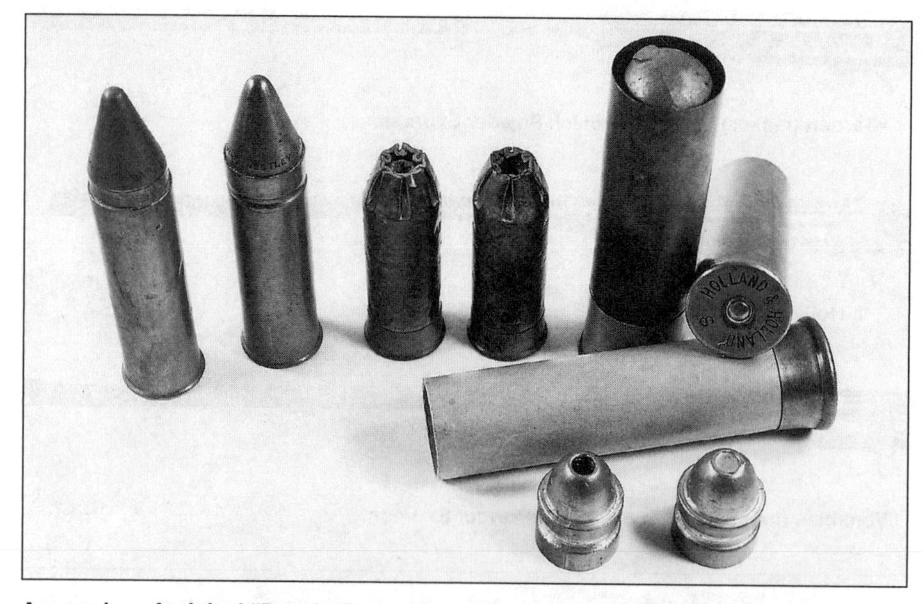

A grouping of original "Paradox" cartridges. The two on the left are 12-bore Westley Richards. The two in the center are rose-crimp 12-bores. The largest is a 4-bore Paradox and those are two 8-bore cartridges lying near their 1257-grain bullets.

These cartridges look the same and measure the same, but they are *NOT* the same. The 500 Nitro Express cartridges from the bottom box would likely wreck a rifle chambered for the 500 Black Powder Express cartridge *(upper right box)*. The Nitro Express cartridge develops 16 tons of pressure per square inch compared to 11 tons for the "Nitro for Black" load *(upper left)* and the Black Powder Express load *(upper right)*.

a double rifle, shooting the cobra consumed valuable time. If the cobra was missed, the hunter had to shoot again until the cobra was dispatched, before returning to the game animal target. Careful thought will reveal that, starting with a loaded rifle, the hunter had to reload once to shoot all four required shots at the game animal. *Any* shot at a cobra put the shooter into a second reloading session; two misses at the cobra put him into a third reloading...not conducive to getting all four shots at the game animal in the two minutes.

There is more than a little pressure for the hunter to perform in an expeditious and precise manner in front of his peers. While nothing of this sort can compete or compare with the heart-pounding experience of a real safari, this experience was unique to say the least. Some real idea of the demands of an actual safari is revealed. The hunter, knowing his performance demanded dexterity, cool deliberation and ability to change priorities quickly, was under some pressure to acquit himself in a creditable manner, with half of his competitors–and the scorers–watching his every move.

While the more formalized shooting at paper targets was not as demanding in terms of decision-making and dexterity as the field shooting, it was demanding in its own way. The shooter knew that each of his ten shots could score points or not, according to the skill with which his cartridges were loaded and the skill with which each was delivered, the chain being no stronger than the weakest link. The 50-yard target was engaged in the offhand position; the 100-yard target from the sitting position.

Double rifle cartridges *must* be a handloading proposition. Factory cartridges from the good old days, with which these rifles were regulated, are now pretty much lost to history. Surviving double rifle cartridges are the stuff of collectors. It needs to be stated again that at this outing and in this article, we deal with the ***blackpowder*** double rifles, not the Nitro loads of later years.

In reloading for these old rifles, five criteria must come together to make a successful double rifle cartridge. The cartridge must be powerful enough to do the job; regulated so that both barrels shoot to nearly the same point of impact; accurate enough to seek out the kill zone on the animal to be hunted; shoot to the point of aim; and last but not least, be a safe load.

None of these rifles can be expected to shoot both barrels to the same point of impact, true to the fixed sights, with light loads designed for target shooting. The rifles were originally regulated to the factory cartridges available at the time the rifles were made—full-power cartridges for game shooting. Double rifles will not tolerate loads that deviate from that criterion. Today, working in the opposite direction, loads must be tailored to the regulation that was built into the rifles when they were created, usually more than a century ago. Keep in mind the sights are fixed and not easily adjusted, and the bulk density of the blackpowder you use must be accommodated in the relatively fixed volume of the cartridge cases available.

Perhaps the biggest anomaly encountered in this "hunt" was that some of the rifles used were designed for taking African plains game, but not the heavier stuff. However, there were some heavy rifles present. While the thin-skinned cats could be laid low with a fair hit with all of the double rifles used, the other game would not be

Army and Navy rifle in 500 Black Powder Express. ***Army and Navy*** **is a term for a class of rifles made by a number of makers and sold for the use of military personnel for personal use.**

Alexander Henry rifle in 450 Black Powder Express.

Garden (maker) rifle in 577 Black Powder Express. This rifle took first place in the shoot.

so easily downed. Karamojo Bell might take exception to this statement. After all, Bell, as an ivory hunter, killed 800 African bull elephants with the little 275 Rigby Mauser. This was about the size of the 7mm Mauser, a cartridge some of today's hunters would consider marginal *(at best)* for elk.

However, if you subscribe to Bell's prescription, you will use a bullet at least four calibers long. A bullet four calibers long, in a .400-inch bore or larger, will fetch you out from under your hat in a hurry. Further, it will have a looping trajectory if propelled by blackpowder. Nevertheless, the double rifles used in this safari preserved the flavor of a real African hunt. And, all of the rifles used in this event were double rifles; one a double-barreled blackpowder muzzleloader. But, even if you concede some of the rifles were a bit on the light side, the Southern Indiana East Enterprise Safari was a resounding success among the participants.

Our host, Bob Woodfill, who has hunted fairly extensively in Africa, had several goals. One was to create a venue for having fun. Another goal was to utilize a specialized tool of the hunter: the double rifle. Yet another goal was to encourage the participants to work up loads that would be effective in these lovely old rifles. Few, if any, of us have the time or inclination to work up loads for all these calibers and rifles. However, pooled information is useful to all.

Getting enough of these rare old double rifles into the hands of the participants was not easy. Some owned their own rifles, but several of us were loaned rifles and it fell upon the host to do a fair amount of the reloading for those loaned rifles. A big job indeed. The writer was one of the beneficiaries of Woodfill's loading and I must give him credit for a fine job on the ammunition for the 450/400 Manton rifle that I used. The fruits of his handloading skill are particularly evident in the scores rung up during the more formal "paper" part of the safari.

Double rifle shooting is not for everybody. There are only a limited number of these fine old rifles out there. New ones being only very rarely produced by custom makers, and none of them likely to fall into the "inexpensive" category. It would take a long purse indeed, not to mention the time involved, to have a new double rifle custom-built in even the plainest configuration. Many of the originals were literal celebrations of the gunmakers' art: Power, weight, balance, and reliability were their long suits. Fine workmanship, fine finish, engraving, and premium wood were considered the norm.

Summary of BPE Loadings used in the EEDRC match. These data are provided for information only. Remember that a competent person must inspect the rifles before firing, and safe loads must be worked up accordingly.

577 BPE: The match winner used a R. S. Garden double rifle with hammers in the 577 x 2 3/4-inch BPE chambering. The load consisted of a 610-grain pure lead bullet twice wrapped with Meade

HOLLAND AND HOLLAND, LIMITED,

8-Bore "Paradox" Elephant Guns.

(Registered)

"Neither of the 4-bores drove as well as the 8-bore 'Paradox,' with steel bullet."—CAPTAIN SWAYNE.
See page 32.

The great success of the 12 and 16-bore "Paradox" Guns has led us to turn our attention to the construction of 8-bores, built on the same principle, and shooting from 8 to 10 drams of powder, and a powerful solid or hollow bullet. They are also regulated for a special steel bullet coated with lead, which gives enormous penetration. Weight of these weapons, 14 to 15 lbs.

8-Bore Bullet. Full Size.

The advantages of the 8-bore "Paradox" over an 8-bore rifle, are:—

I.—The weight is considerably less than that of a rifle.
II.—It is much lighter forward, and handles and comes to the shoulder like an ordinary gun.
III.—Gives a higher velocity and a greater penetration with the same charge of powder.
IV.—Greater accuracy, as is shown in the following notices.
V.—Can be used as a shot gun if desired.

We have supplied a number of these guns to some of our best big game sportsmen, and all the reports we have received speak in the highest terms of the accuracy and penetration of these weapons.

For Cartridges, see page 77. *For Special Requisites for "Paradox" Gun, see page 78.*

Winners of all the "Field" Rifle Trials, London.

30

Holland & Holland catalog ca 1904.

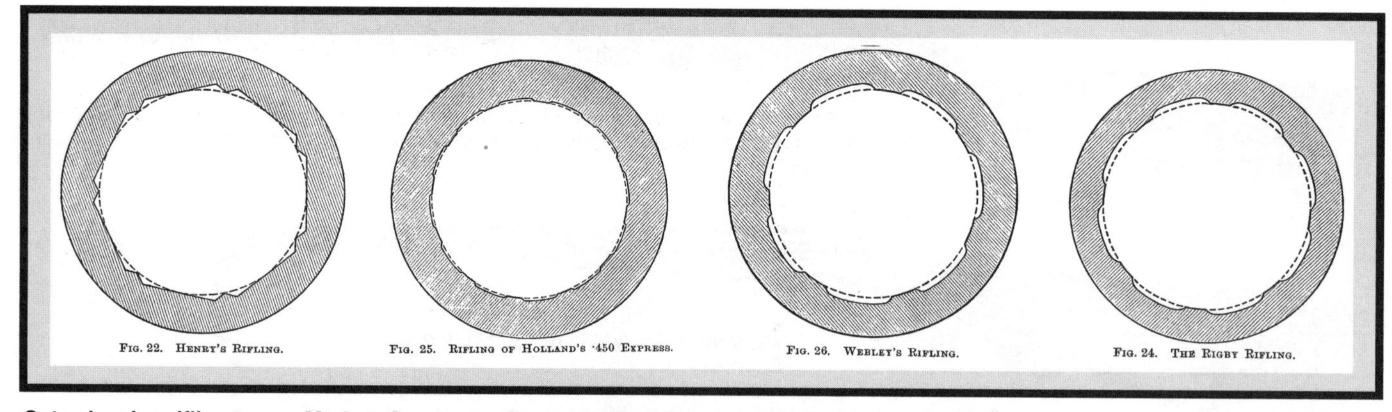

Cuts showing rifling types. *Modern Sportsman Gun and Rifle,* 1882, J. H. Walsh (Stonehenge)

Royal Grade Holland & Holland rifle in 450 Black Powder Express with rare, original, quick-detachable telescope.

Detail of engraving on Royal Grade Holland & Holland rifle in 450 Black Powder Express.

Eraserable Bond paper to a diameter of 0.585-inch, over 140 grains of Elephant 1Fg blackpowder in a Bertram case. A 1/8-inch grease "cookie" of beeswax and Murphy's Oil Soap was loaded between the powder and the 24-gauge Circle Fly Nitro wads under the bullet to keep the blackpowder fouling soft during the match.

500 BPE: Another high-scoring shooter used an Army and Navy double rifle, with hammers, in 500 x 3-inch BPE. His load consisted of a 340-grain, 20:1 *(lead-to-tin ratio)* groove-lubricated bullet, SPG lubricant, over two Walter's vegetable fiber wads and 132 grains of GOEX 3Fg blackpowder in a HDS case.

A Holland & Holland 8-bore Paradox gun produced this grouping at 25 yards, using a 1257-grain bullet like that shown here.

450 BPE: A majority of the shooters including the second and third place winners used 45-caliber BPE double rifles including a mint 500/450 No. 2 Musket Moore and Grey double with hammers, a hammerless 500/450 No. 1 Westley Richards and several 450 x 3 1/4-inch BPE doubles by Braddell, Holland and Holland, Alex Henry, Purdey and Hollis. Most shooters favored 300/330-grain paper-patched bullets, Swiss, GOEX and WANO blackpowders in 2-3Fg granulations and BELL, HDS and Bertram Boxer-primed cases. For authenticity, two shooters used original Kynoch cases, Berdan primers and H&H-type groove-lubricated bullets with success.

400 BPE: Several shooters relied on 40-caliber doubles. Included were a mint Manton hammer double in 450/400 x 2 3/8-inch BPE shooting a 270-grain groove-lubricated bullet, a 400/400 x 3 1/4-inch BPE Kavanagh hammer double with 350-grain groove-lubricated bullets and a 400 (3-inch) Straight Purdey double with 260-grain groove-lubricated bullets. Most cartridge cases were formed from BELL and HDS basic brass using RCBS forming dies. The 400 Purdey cases were made from BELL 405 basic brass. Specialty

Al Roberts with Alexander Henry 450 Black Powder Express. *Al Roberts photo.*

Garden (maker) rifle in 500 Black Powder Express.

Alexander Henry rifle in 450 Black Powder Express. Note this is a left-handed rifle.

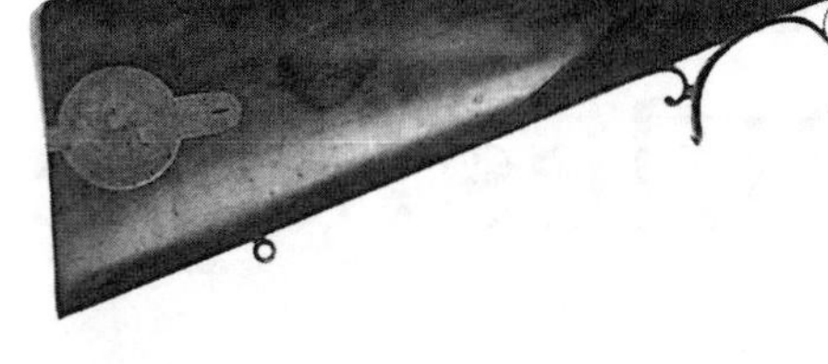

William Moore and Grey rifle in 500/450 No.2 Musket.

brass of almost any kind is also available from Rocky Mountain Cartridge. A chamber cast sent to Rocky Mountain will get you custom-made brass for *your* rifle.

Regulation: Each shooter had developed a full-velocity 1700-1900 fps BPE load consisting of lead bullets and blackpowder *(as required by the rules)* that would duplicate regulation of the rifle barrels to the original express sights. Bullets were restricted to lead and lead alloy, grooved/lubricated or paper-patched. The accuracy of these original BPE double rifles was convincingly demonstrated by the 50- and 100-yard target scores. The best off-hand for 10 shots at 50 yards was 235 out of a possible of 250 points; the best sitting score for 10 shots at 100 yards was 192 out of a possible of 250 points using the standard NMLRA 12-inch bull with a 1 1/2-inch diameter 25-ring. •

References

Baker, Samuel W., 1874, *Ismailia*, London.

Barnes, Frank C., 1989, *Cartridges Of The World,* (Edited by Ken Warner), 6th ed., DBI Books, Inc., Northfield, IL, 448p.

Forsyth, James, 1867, *The Sporting Rifle and its Projectiles*, Smith, Elder, and Co., London, 132p.

Greener, W.W., 1910, *The Gun And Its Development*, 9th Edition, New Orchard Editions, Dorset and London, 804p.

"British Cartridges," by Ken Waters, *Gun Digest, 14th Edition*, Gun Digest Co., 1960.

Hastings, Macdonald, 1969, *English Sporting Guns and Accessories,* Ward Lock & Company Limited, London and Sydney, 96p.

Hoyem, G.A., 1985, *The History and Development of Small Arms Ammunition*, (Vol 3), Armory Publications, Tacoma, 220p.

Sellers, Frank, 1978, *Sharps Firearms,* Beinfeld Publishing, Inc., North Hollywood, CA., 358p.

Roosevelt, Theodore, 1910, *African Game Trails*, Scribners; St. Martins N. Y. reprint 1988, 583p.

Taylor, John, 1948, *African Rifles and Cartridges,* Reprinted edition 1977, The Gun Room Press, Highland Park, NJ, 431p.

Patchbox detail of William Moore and Grey rifle.

Walsh, J.H., 1884, *The Modern Sportsman's Gun And Rifle,* (Vol. II), Horace Cox, London, reprinted 1986, Wolfe Publishing Co., Inc., Prescott, AZ., 582p.

Wright, Graeme, 1999, *Shooting the British Double Rifle,* 2nd Ed., by Graeme Wright, P.O. Box 5085, Kenmore East 4069, Australia, 180p.

Catalogs

Eley Brothers, Limited, 1910-11
Holland & Holland, 1887-90
Kynoch, Ltd., 1902-03
Nobel Industries Limited, 1925

While many contributed by allowing the author to photograph their fine rifles, this article could not have been written without the input of Bob Woodfill. Bob has a vast store of information, backed up by a fine library on the subject. But much of it is from between his ears; he has documented detailed information from many years of shooting, testing and recording, which he is currently expanding and sharing with his peers. My thanks, too, go to Al Roberts for his candid photos of the shoot taken while I was photographing rifles.

These are all original Kynoch cartridges. *(L/R)*: 450/400 Black Powder Express; 500/450 No.1 Black Powder Express; 450 Black Powder Express; 500 Black Powder Express; 577 Black Powder Express LC (light cordite); 577 Black Powder Express.

Ahead of Its Time...

The Cummins "Duplex" Riflescope

by Clarence Anderson

BY THE FINAL decade of the 19th century, the superiority of telescopic sighting for the most demanding requirements of marksmanship in the field—long-range shooting of big game (bison hunting, most notably), precision small game hunting, and military sniping—had been long and conclusively established. To shooters of the preceding generation, those who had fought the Civil War, the new riflescopes advertised in sporting periodicals of this time would have seemed advanced and sophisticated instruments. But broader acceptance was limited by two intractable problems: the high cost of quality optics, and mounting systems deficient in accuracy, convenience, or durability.

Well before the Civil War, the short but optically superior telescopes manufactured for surveying instruments had aroused the interest of many imaginative riflemen, but adapting them to the work of rifle-aiming demanded development of an altogether different mounting arrangement. This was the component of riflescope design that for decades lagged far behind optical improvements, and would in truth continue to do so into the second quarter of the 20th century.

Circa 1890, most American scope manufacturers *(typically, 2- or 3-man shops, not "factories")* mounted their tubes in some variation of the design now commonly labeled "Malcolm-type." Such designs support the rear of the tube in a vertically adjustable clamp (for elevation), which itself pivots on a pin to accommodate the transverse movement of the front mount (for windage); both movements were generally screw-adjustable by 1890, often with micrometer graduations. Some variants of the type located the rear mount (or "hanging," the usual period term) on the side of the receiver, rather than the barrel, but windage and elevation adjustments were similar. *(Credit is indeed due William Malcolm for perfecting this arrangement, but it should be noted that the essential mechanical principals were already in use prior to 1855, when Malcolm began building scopes. Thus, significant as his improvements were, they evidently did not warrant patent protection.)*

This, then, for some 30 years, had been the characteristic American mounting system, but a native son of the Green Mountains, Lawson Cutler Cummins, believed he had a better idea. His scope would be anchored to the barrel in simple ring mounts dovetailed into slots cut for that purpose, because *(according to his first catalog)* "there can be no lost motion where rigidity exists." Instead of moving the tube itself to move the aiming point, Cummins conceived a mechanism for moving the reticle within the tube—"internal adjustment," as it came to be called, although the inventor himself never applied that terminology. The only known precedent for an internally adjustable reticle is a singular Civil War experiment by the great New York rifle maker and telescope pioneer, Morgan James, who built a one-of-a-kind sniper rifle that, because the tube was soldered directly to the barrel, incorporated movable cross-wires. This curiosity *(publicized by Ned Roberts)* is entirely unrelated to Cummins' design, or any subsequent development, and I dredge it up only to be historically punctilious. The daunting complexity of Cummins' design, moreover, is itself a compelling argument for true originality.

For merely to provide the shooter with adjustments for windage and elevation, Cummins was not content: he threw in a separate bore-sighting reticle, and a pendulum, or level, to detect canting! Two patent applications, dated April 30, 1891 and June 24, 1892 attempt to articulate this ambitious agenda. To observe that models of clarity these descriptions are <u>not,</u> is a comic understatement only those who have struggled through their tortured syntax can appreciate.

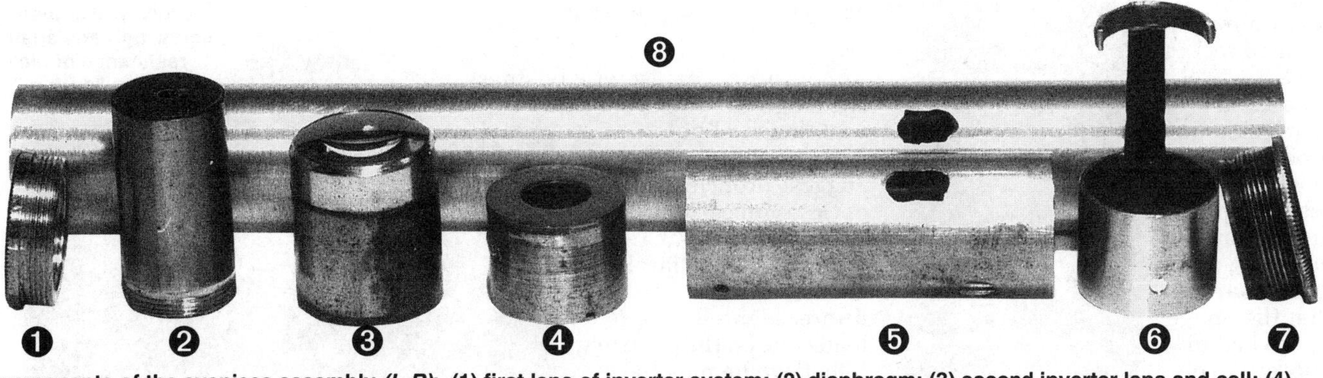

Components of the eyepiece assembly *(L-R)*: (1) first lens of inverter system; (2) diaphragm; (3) second inverter lens and cell; (4) diaphragm supporting fixed vertical wire *(for aligning plumb line)*; (5) crosswire cell with hole for adjusting screw; (6) yoke supporting vertical wire—windage screw bears against flexible arm; (7) ocular lens cell; (8) eyepiece assembly housing. The ocular cell contains both ocular and inverter lenses, along with the horizontal crosswire mechanism.

These documents seem to suggest Cummins viewed the significance of his invention less in terms of replacing external adjustments of the reticle with internal ones, than in providing two independent aiming points: one fixed, one adjustable; hence, a "duplex" sight. The fixed point (a speck of balsam stuck on a single vertical strand of spider silk) was intended to be aligned with the bore when the scope was mounted by shifting the positions of the "hangings" until congruence on the target was achieved—a painstaking procedure, to say the least, but described with care in the Cummins catalog. The tube was next rotated in its mounts until the fixed wire (or silk) was plumb, as determined by a line hung from the target. Finally, "one shot" was fired at a range which allowed the bullet hole to be seen, and the adjustable wires moved to intersect with that hole. "Mathematically perfect range can be secured at one shot," Cummins boasted in his advertising.

In addition to providing elevation adjustment, the horizontal wire, suspended from a "bifurcated pendulum," detected canting by reference to the fixed, plumb, vertical wire: "We have so arranged the parts," Cummins maintained, "that the force of gravitation corrects our errors." Does the sight picture thus described, not to mention the mounting protocol, begin to seem just a touch complex? Patient reader, I must inform you the account I have rendered is in cold truth a simplified and abbreviated one, extracted principally from Cummin's second patent, No. 499160, granted June 6, 1893. The first, No. 476874, awarded June 14, 1892 featured a mechanism of such fragile intricacy that common sense suggests it never entered production. Moreover,

THE DUPLEX TELESCOPE SIGHT.

It is rigidly attached to the rifle barrel with elevation, windage and micrometer level inside. Mathematically perfect range can be secured at one shot, and it will do accurate work with less light than any sight in existence. The lenses are achromatic and power ten to twenty times the human eye. It is manufactured in three grades. Price $12, $15 and $20. Catalogue free.

LAWSON C. CUMMINS,

Montpelier, Vt., U. S. A.

***Shooting & Fishing*, October 6th, 1892.**

Cummin's initial catalog, published Sept. 21, 1892 appears to offer instruments incorporating the "simplifications" of the later patent.

That first catalog *(the only one I've been able to examine, although there are references to others)* presented three models: a 3/4-inch diameter, 12-inch long, 10X "Hunting" model, at $12; a 3/4-inch by 16-inch 20X "Target" model, at $20; and a 1/2-inch by 16-inch 20X "Miniature" model for "pocket rifles," at $15. Each model was "handsomely engraved," and available with tubes of blued steel, or nickeled brass, but only the "Target" model included the "micrometer level." Finally, a 36-inch 60X "Range Telescope" was offered at $12. To place these prices in perspective, Winchester's 1891 catalog listed a standard-grade Model 1873 at $18, or a Model 1886 at $21.

The folly of coupling such high magnifications with such small objective lenses would be patent to any modern scope manufacturer, but up to this time, the "more is better" theory had prevailed among builders and riflemen alike. The majority of scopes used by Civil War snipers, and later by the professional buffalo hunters, were instruments of 10 to 20 power, so Cummins' initial choice of magnifications was not in the least exceptional. However, by the mid to late 1890s, recognition of the practical advantages of lower magnifications seems at long last to have taken root among the rank and file of scope users, and the popularity of the higher magnifications rapidly waned. Suffice it to say that of the half-dozen Cummins scopes I've examined, none were of a power greater than about 8X.

As was true of almost all American builders, Cummins made no pretense of grinding his own lens, noting that "the best quality of achromatic lenses that can be produced are used." This probably meant Bausch & Lomb, principal supplier to the American optics trade. "All [other] parts are made by machinery, the only hand work being in assembling and

Cummins name and patent dates.

inspecting." As Cummins claimed to have consumed a year's time in procuring his machinery, setting up his production facilities, etc., it is apparent that the image he wished to impress upon potential customers was that of a proper, modern, late-Victorian factory, as opposed to an old-fashioned "village gunsmith" sort of operation. Decades would elapse before the Victorian era's fascination with machinery and technology yielded to our modernist reverence for "hand-craftsmanship."

Although Cummins' catalog described in careful detail the complicated mounting and reticle adjusting procedures, it was curiously silent on one critical subject—focusing. Neither did it include any reference to parallax error. As was common with many scopes of the period, the objective lens cell was retained by a large-headed screw passing through a longitudinal slot in the tube, so as to permit focusing by fore and aft adjustment of the cell. In instruments of such high magnification, focusing, and its conjugate, parallax elimination, must be performed with precision. More about this later.

But what about the inventor himself—his educational and professional background, and his previous experience in the optics trade? Such biographical data is often provided in catalogs as a means of establishing the maker's credibility and expertise. Cummins, unfortunately, divulged virtually nothing about himself, or the circumstances that propelled him into such an esoteric business. Although the sheer complexity of his instrument might suggest proficiency in optics science, or engineering, what I suspect to be a "fatal flaw" in his unprecedented design leads me, on the contrary, to believe he may have been mostly, or entirely, self-taught—a circumstance by no means uncommon in the 19th century.

Whatever his academic credentials, Cummins certainly seems to have been a serious shooter, asserting he "had fired more than 7000 shots" *(some of them gross overloads to test for recoil damage)* in developing his "Duplex" system. Even more suggestive of a skilled and thoughtful rifleman is his prescription for achieving 1 MOA groups *(with blackpowder, of course!)*: "That class of targets cannot be bought with rifles [but only with] slate and pencil, bullet mould and sizer, worked under a liberal pressure of perseverance, industry, and good luck." Any blackpowder target shooter competing today will affirm the truth, and wisdom, of that advice!

My *(reluctant)* conclusion that Cummins' design, although truly inspired, was inherently flawed is at present tentative, and further evidence may quite refute it. And I am especially reticent about advancing it in the face of fulsome praise lavished upon these scopes by one of the shooting fraternity's most revered authorities: Ned Roberts, no less. In *The Breech Loading Single Shot Rifle*, surely the best single reference on this "Golden Age" of American riflery, Roberts disclosed that he had owned three of them (6, 8, and 10X), declaring them to be "superior, with more brilliant illumination, to any other scopes we then had, except Sidel." More than any other factor, Robert's enthusiasm precipitated my own interest in acquiring and using a Cummins scope.

Cummins mounts—for security against recoil, Cummins advised drilling holes through tube wall for front mount screws.

Crosswire adjusting screw tightens against resistance of nickel silver "spring."

My first was a 16-inch 6X, bearing the 1893 patent date, and it did indeed exhibit the clarity and brilliance Ned had extolled. Its eye-relief of 2-1/2 inches was quite adequate, and its field of view, 110 inches at 90 yards, was about as wide as lenses of this size will permit. From about 20 feet to infinity, it could be focused very sharply, but, the parallax—it was appalling! Now a bit of parallax error is manageable if the shooter maintains a consistent head position on the stock, but this, this was so extreme as to be quite intolerable. Since some lens systems seem to demand greater precision in focusing than others, I focused over and over again, trying to find some position of the objective that would eliminate the problem; but there was none to be found.

Certain that some former user had meddled with this instrument's "innards," I succeeded in acquiring another specimen, identical except for its power—about 8X, and thus a bit less brilliant. Unbelievably *(and defying coincidence)*, it, too, was possessed by the "parallax demon." Stripping the two, and comparing their internal components side-by-side, revealed identical details of construction and assembly; tampering, therefore, would not appear to be the source of this maddening phenomenon. *(All internal parts, it's worth mentioning, were beautifully machined and finished, with tiny fire-blued screws that still looked sparkling-new.)*

It is at this point germane to introduce a very peculiar anomaly in the Cummins design not heretofore mentioned—the location within the tube of the two adjustable reticle wires. The reticle can be positioned, in theory, at any focal point within the optical system, that of the ocular lens most commonly, but also, as in some European designs, in the focus of the objective. The mechanical novelties of Cummins' design,

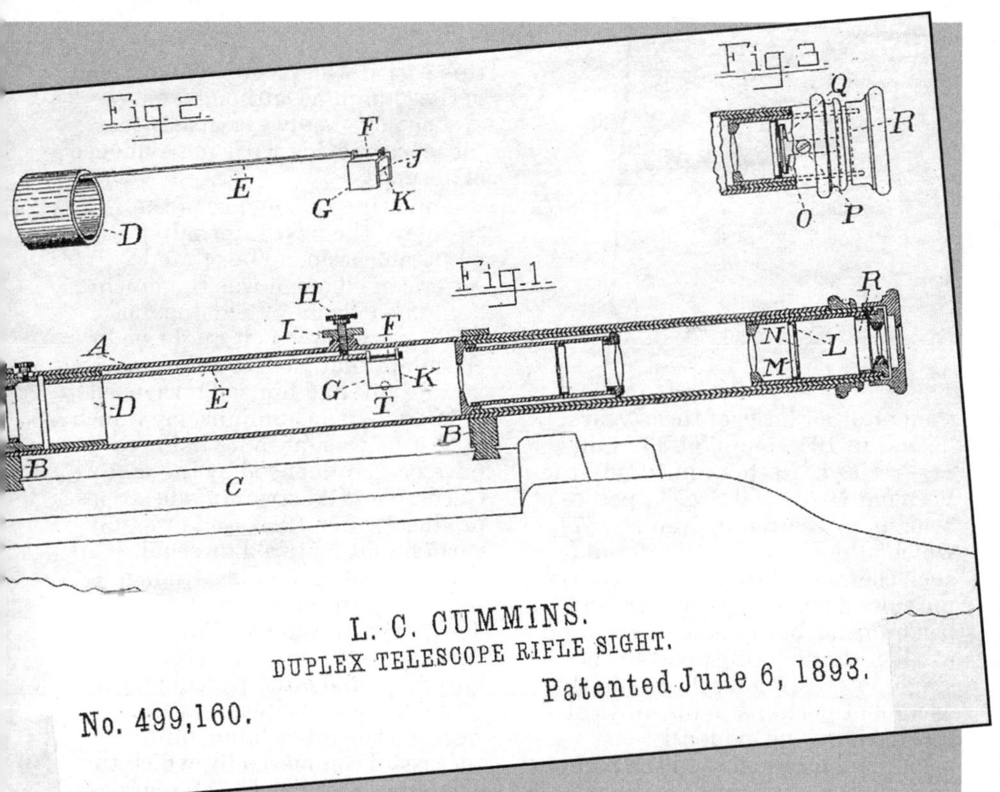

however, obligated him to use both, placing the horizontal wire at the focus of the objective, and the vertical wire at the focus of the ocular, some 8 inches distant. This iconoclastic arrangement I presume to be the consequence of Cummins' infatuation with his "micrometer level," although that complication, thankfully, had been omitted from the two specimens in my possession.

Parallax is eliminated from an optical system by making the target's image and the reticle occupy the same focal plane. This imperative can be achieved in quite different ways, by moving the objective lens (and thus the image it creates) or, as popularized by J. W. Fecker, the inverter lens, or even the reticle itself. What would appear, on the evidence of the testing I conducted, to be optically impossible is parallax elimination when the reticle has been divided so as to occupy two separate focal planes. The failure of an authority as astute as Roberts to make the same observation is as worrisome to me as it is inexplicable, although I deduce that the assessment previously quoted was written by him several decades after his last use of any Cummins scope. *(Moreover, Ned certainly erred in citing 1887 as the first year of Cummins' production—a faux-pas that has been recirculated by commentators using his work as their reference.)*

Seeking opinions contributed by other users of these instruments, I conducted a page-by-page search of *Shooting and Fishing* (predecessor of the *American Rifleman*) from 1892 until the end of publication in 1906. I found but one: an owner of a "Duplex" described as having a remarkable 8-inch eye-relief declared that his Cummins had "withstood many hard hunting trips" which a scope in sliding-type mounts would not, he judged, have survived. Two problems, however, were disclosed: a narrow field *(the obvious optical consequence of such extreme eye-relief)*, and parallax. The latter, as his articulate description makes clear, this shooter well understood, and he claimed to have corrected it, but without, alas, explaining how. If his remedy involved nothing more unusual than a simple focusing adjustment of the objective lens, the matter would not seem worth mentioning, but whether he actually encountered the same difficulty as myself, it is impossible to determine.

Credible evaluations by other users of these instruments, I have not been able to discover, although an incident reported in the Nov. 3, 1892 issue of *Shooting and Fishing* suggests tantalizing possibilities. So confident was Cummins in the performance of his invention, that to the "Camp Perry" of the time–the Walnut Hill Range of the Massachusetts Rifle Ass'n.–he carried several of his scopes, which then "he submitted to the inspection of experts." "These severest of critics examined the glasses with characteristic deliberation, and were loud in their praise of Mr. Cummins' work."

Could such critics have ignored the degree of parallax error I observed? It would not seem likely, but, as sporting periodicals of the time were typically short on "severe criticism," and long on blatant puffery, the reportage is not itself beyond suspicion. *(One of these critics, in all probability, was a director of the Association named Willard, who was at this very time developing the "sliding tube" system of target scope mounting still in use; his honest opinion would indeed be illuminating.)*

The earliest Cummins advertisement I've found appeared in the Oct. 6, 1892 issue of *Shooting and Fishing*—by this time, the pre-eminent medium of communication among American riflemen, and thus the logical venue to promote a new scope. The last ad of which I have certain knowledge appeared in the Dec. 17, 1903 issue of the same.

Production possibly continued after that date, but by the end of 1903, Cummins' innovation had already been caught up in a revolution transforming the American scope market—the introduction of a precedent-setting new line of scopes and mounts by one of the country's largest arms makers, J. Stevens Arms Co. Stevens had announced purchase of the important Cataract Telescope Co. in 1901, and by March of 1902 was producing a limited selection of radically redesigned models under its own name. In 1903, Stevens published a scope catalog which must have dazzled contemporary riflemen; beautifully printed, it offered a stunning selection of models, features, qualities, and prices, including perhaps the earliest variable-power instrument, and the first double-micrometer rear mount. The firm, in addition, was sparing no effort in promoting its new line, not only buying half-page ads in *Shooting and Fishing*, but somehow "persuading" its editor to feature scoped Stevens rifles on many of the magazine's covers.

This advertising blitz did not extinguish such old-line, long respected, makers as Malcolm or Sidel, but it surely fell as a heavy blow on one still struggling to establish a unique identity for itself in the marketplace. Although Stevens offered nothing to compete directly with the "Duplex"—its optics all required external adjustment—scope users of the time did not recognize the modern distinction between the categories "target," and "hunting," except with

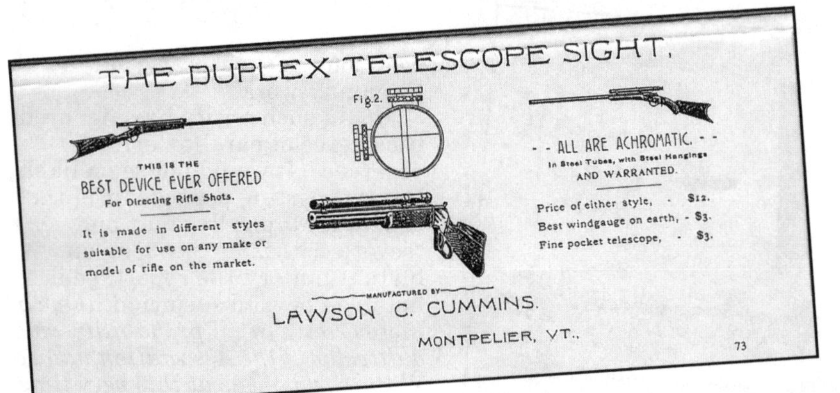

respect to magnification. That distinction Cummins had been striving to define *(hampered by advertising that to me seems unfocused and ineffectual)* when he was overtaken by the Stevens juggernaut. None of the earlier "traditional" scope shops could hope to match the promotional resources of an industry leader like Stevens, in these years at the zenith of its prestige as builder of some of the most highly refined, opulent, target rifles ever produced in this nation. Symbolically, as well as literally, Stevens brought scope manufacturing out of the nineteenth and into the twentieth century.

As to the personal history of my protagonist, embarrassingly meager is the biographical data I can at present provide. His death certificate reveals he was born July 31, 1848 in Montpelier, Vt. and died Aug. 30, 1919 when, according to a funeral notice in the Montpelier *Argus*, "his automobile went over a bank on his way from his farm to the city." His earliest appearance in the Montpelier City Directory was the 1895 edition, where he was listed as "manufacturer rifle telescopes" occupying part of a building at 29 State St. This listing continued unchanged through 1915, then after a hiatus of three years, he was in 1918 found at 33 Main St., "retired." Rather amazingly, the Vermont Historical Society posses a brief diary written by him in 1871, which alludes in no great detail to such common 19th century country pursuits as fishing, trapping, and bee hunting, but makes no mention at all of the shooting sports. The single interesting disclosure in this document pertains to his musical inclinations—he evidently performed frequently on the cornet at local civic and social occasions. As to his livelihood at this time, or any studies, training, etc., in which he might have been engaged, this journal offers not a single clue.

The question thus remains, what inspired a country boy living all his life in one of the most agrarian, least industrialized, sections of the nation to conceive and execute an idea for the most technologically advanced rifle aiming device of the time? Until new evidence emerges, no answer, regrettably, can I suggest.

Although the Cummins "Duplex" must be accorded the distinction of being the world's first internally adjustable scope *(to enter production, at least)*, the often expressed implication that it must therefore be the progenitor of the modern hunting scope lacks entire plausibility, in my opinion. Despite the indelible impression they obviously made upon Ned Roberts, Cummins' scopes were manufactured such a limited time, and in such small numbers, compared to Malcolms, Stevens, and other popular makes of the time, that their influence upon other manufacturers, and the shooting world in general, probably was not great. In truth, I rather suspect it was negligible. Aside from Roberts, I have found no other authority of this period who recorded an opinion of the Cummins, although, as archaeologists always insist, "absence of evidence is not evidence of absence".

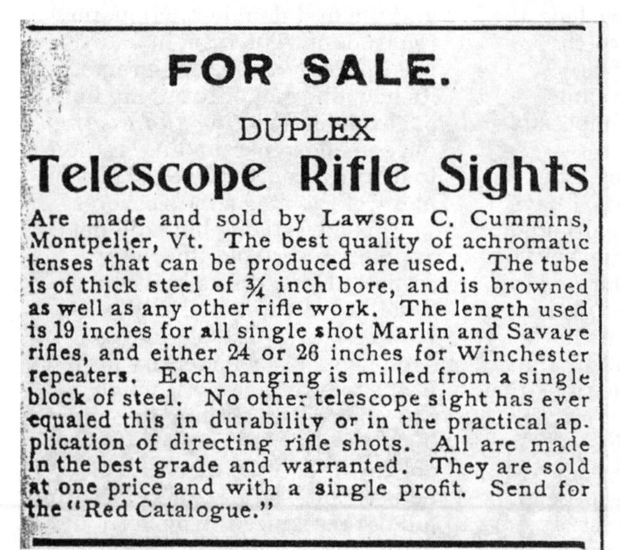

FOR SALE.

DUPLEX

Telescope Rifle Sights

Are made and sold by Lawson C. Cummins, Montpelier, Vt. The best quality of achromatic lenses that can be produced are used. The tube is of thick steel of ¾ inch bore, and is browned as well as any other rifle work. The length used is 19 inches for all single shot Marlin and Savage rifles, and either 24 or 26 inches for Winchester repeaters. Each hanging is milled from a single block of steel. No other telescope sight has ever equaled this in durability or in the practical application of directing rifle shots. All are made in the best grade and warranted. They are sold at one price and with a single profit. Send for the "Red Catalogue."

***Shooting & Fishing*, December 17th, 1903.**

Following the demise of the "Duplex," the next internally adjustable scope to be offered American riflemen was the much-acclaimed Noske "Fieldscope" of 1929. Satisfying as it might be to speculate that Noske, a German immigrant, had himself once used or examined a Cummins, my hunch is that he was far more likely to have been influenced by the many German and Austrian-made scopes produced after 1910, and probably earlier, that featured internal elevation adjustments (windage remaining in their bases). The design shortcomings of all these Teutonic instruments were well known to, and often ridiculed by, American gun writers, but they were, on the other hand, quite successful commercially, which the Cummins, to judge by the scarcity of surviving specimens, was not.

E. C. Crossman, probably the most influential gun writer of the period, discussed the technical problems of internal reticle adjustment in his 1932 masterpiece, *Book of the Springfield*, but did not so much as mention the "Duplex"—dramatic proof of Cummins' precipitous descent into oblivion by that time.

I hope it does not seem too uncharitable to suggest that Cummins became the victim of his own cleverness by miring an advanced idea—move only the reticle, not the entire scope—in complexities that served little or no practical purpose, but added to cost, and subtracted from serviceability. Yet his personal infatuation with gadgetry merely reflected the enthusiasms of his time—an era when, for example, the *Scientific American* was a widely read popular magazine, not an abstruse professional journal. Likewise, his audacity in assuming he could design and manufacture an advanced optical instrument without *(I am persuaded)* appropriate formal training, was certainly no more presumptuous than the conviction of two bicycle mechanics that they could build a "flying machine" when many professional scientists and engineers had already failed dismally. Victorian society was dazzled by the potential of new machines and exciting technologies *(sound familiar?)*, and Cummins seems to have personified the spirit of his age. ●

Dealing with Inaccurate Rifles

by Wilf MacGlais

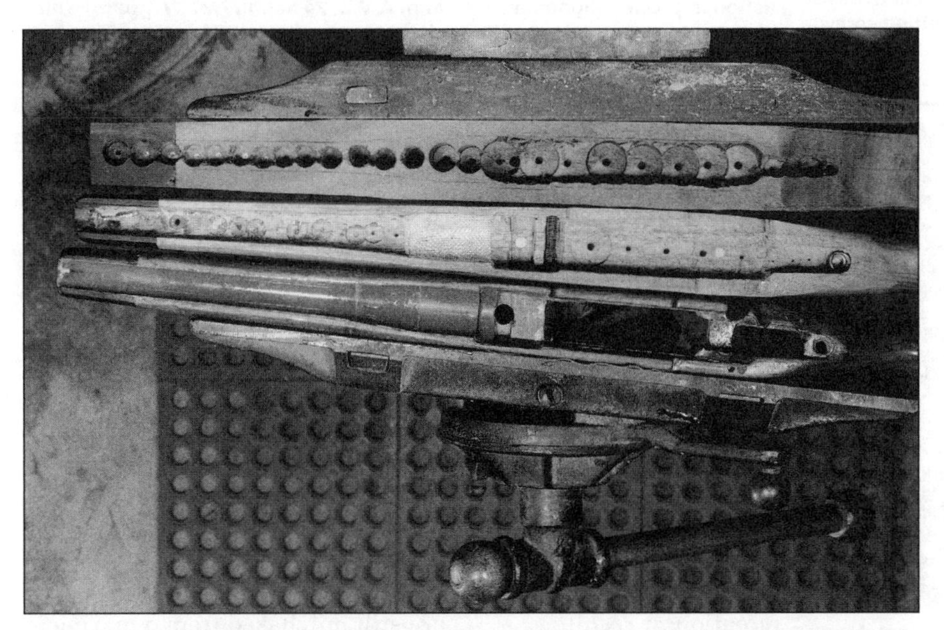

In the author's adjustable patternmaker's vise are *(top)*, the rough-drilled Preslik Claro blank. The project stock *(middle)* being readied for first "pour"–note eye of wrist re-enforcement rod in the tang area. The fiberglass tape in the barrel swell area illustrates how cloth will fit *(full length)* in the undercutting, and *(bottom)* the completed bedding job on the Mark X Mauser stock.

THIRTY-FIVE YEARS after his passing, Colonel Townsend Whelen remains the acknowledged dean (and most quoted) of American gun writers. Though my modest shooting library contains efforts by such notables as Stewart Edward White, Roy Chapman Andrews, Jim Corbett, and John Taylor, an inscribed and autographed copy of the Colonel's 1927 classic *Wilderness Hunting and Wildcraft* is, to me, the library's unchallenged cornerstone.

One of the more frequently seen of the Colonel's opinions advises the aspiring rifleman that he can't go wrong in choosing the 30-06. Another quotation proclaims, "Only accurate rifles are interesting."

With considerable misgiving and apologies to three generations of Whelen fans, I beg to differ with the latter statement. As one who has been the owner of a number of inaccurate rifles, my experience has been that though often time-consuming, and sometimes frustrating, overcoming accuracy problems can be both interesting and rewarding.

Of the 54 centerfire rifles I have owned over the years, only seven have proven beyond redemption. An additional three *(including a Sako Vixen)* have responded to re-barreling.* Of the irredeemable: **I** – A between-the-wars ribbed-barrel 8mm Mauser that produced 10-shot groups averaging over seven minutes of angle; **II** – My late father's Model '95 *(not '99)* Savage with a corrosive primer-ruined barrel–as with the Mauser, we chose not to re-barrel. **III** – Three takedowns, sought after by collectors but notoriously inaccurate. **IV**– An autoloader in 300 Savage: I have long felt the irremediable 6-MOA groups produced by this rifle resulted in large part from the ungodly kick generated by its long-recoil autoloading mechanism. **V** – An expensive Mannlicher-stocked European 22 made up on a "miniature Mauser action" which, in spite of its reputation, ranked second only to the Mauser mentioned.

Some accuracy problems have been rectified by correcting such minor glitches as an overly long *(bottomed out)* front guard screw, loose scope mounts, defective scope, or *(in one instance)* the barrel crowned on the bias. One for the book was my first 25-06 *(of only two)*. Its circa-1970 Zastava-made barrel–later found to be chambered to the pre-standardization dimensions shown in my old Herter's loading manual–produced groups averaging four minutes of angle with handloads made up on the then newly-available factory 25-06 brass.

Said barrel lay idle for several years after being pulled from an F.N. commercial action, but it has recently responded to a pair of remedies. It produces one-minute groups since: *A* – Being paired with a V.Z. 24 action which, thanks in part to a mis-matched bolt, has proven more receptive to the barrel's 25 Niedner chamber. *B* – Being fed handloads built on necked-down *(first in a 270 die)* F.A. 30-06 cases, which are also more compatible with the Niedner chamber.

In the more marginal instances, accuracy has been improved in the finicky eaters *(especially the*

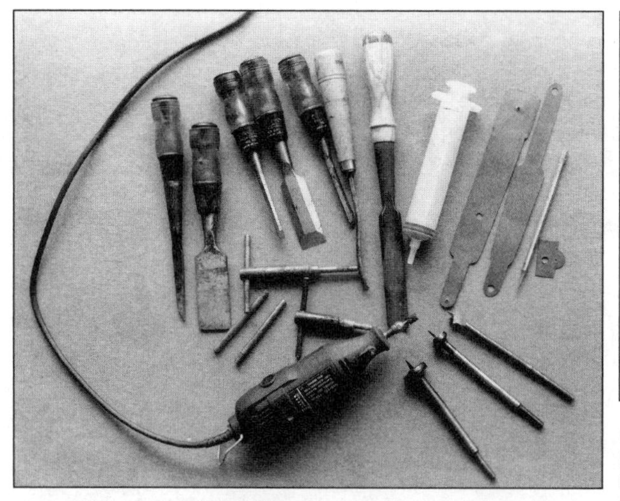

Tools used include: chisels and gouges, glue syringe, patterns and scribe, wormless bits *(last three listed are for blank only)*, Dremel Moto-Tool *(a bonus!)*, inletting screws and stockmaker's hand screws.

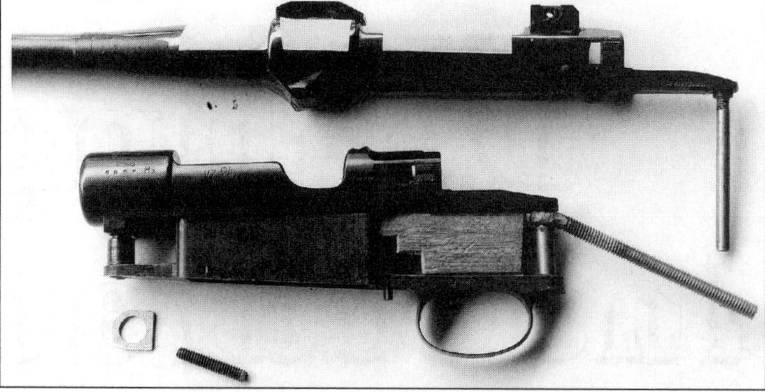

(Top) Mark X barreled action taped up with two layers of P.V.C. tape for first pour. A 1/8-inch gap *(to bare metal)* is left between the P.V.C. tape and our stock line witness mark *(white masking tape)*. On the second pour cellophane tape is used in the free-floated area of the barrel *(forward of the parallel area of the swell)*. The inletting guide screw is a must to hold the action in proper alignment. *(Bottom)* A V.Z. 24 action *(w/F.N. guard)* with wooden trigger mock-up, 5/16-inch threaded wrist re-enforcement rod *(goes in 3/8-inch hole drilled at a 30-degree angle in the stock's wrist)*, threaded blind crossbolt, and dural front tang washer. Not shown are two layers of tape sealing off trigger slot.

Supplies used include 2-inch wide cellophane and P.V.C. tape, fiberglass tape, candle *(drippings are used to seal around receiver plug and fill in areas that might lock in action or guard)*, paste wax *(used as a release agent)*, resin, catalyst, and flock *(shredded fiberglass)*.

smaller bores) by backing off from full loads. Our experience here has been that this is best done *(especially in the smaller bores)* with the use of slower-burning powders.

One of the more commonly encountered and complex accuracy problems results from faulty stock bedding. In my case the complicated part of this equation is, in large part, of my own creation. It results from my having taken the glass bedding process far beyond the simple removal of 1/8-inch of wood at the receiver ring flat, recoil lug abutment, and tang areas, and its replacement with a bit of viscous goop.

Said bedding process has evolved from an early, stumbling, not to say pathetic start–made before bedding kits and their attendant instructions were generally available.

The fact that humidity is likely to cause movement in gun wood has resulted in my glass-bedding any newly acquired rifle prior to range testing. Since relatively large amounts of bedding are used *(as compared to kits)*, materials are still purchased from a marine supply house.

Whether we are inletting and bedding a blank from scratch or re-bedding an existing stock there

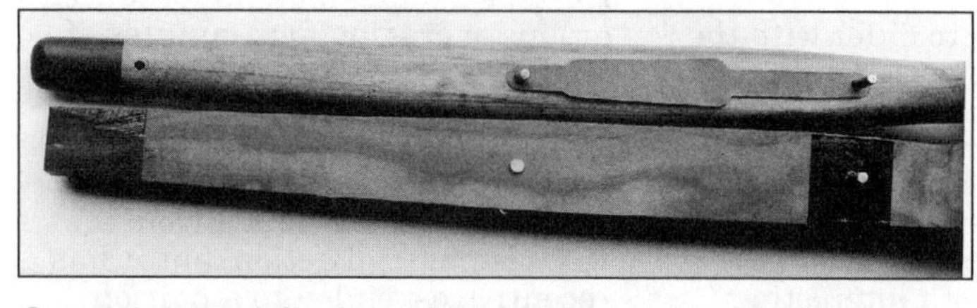

Our project stock (*top)* showing guard template and guide screws in place. Claro blank *(bottom)* shows plugged front guard screw hole and tape *(at rear guide screw)* used to prevent resin drain-off during first pour.

The first pour. The undulations are caused primarily by the P.V.C. tape that moves upon exposure to the resin. During rebedding, the stock's finish and checkering are protected with cellophane tape.

The second pour–note the receiver plug. After alternating between running short *(thus causing voids)* or having a surplus *(massive oozing out)*, it is more practical to make two pours.

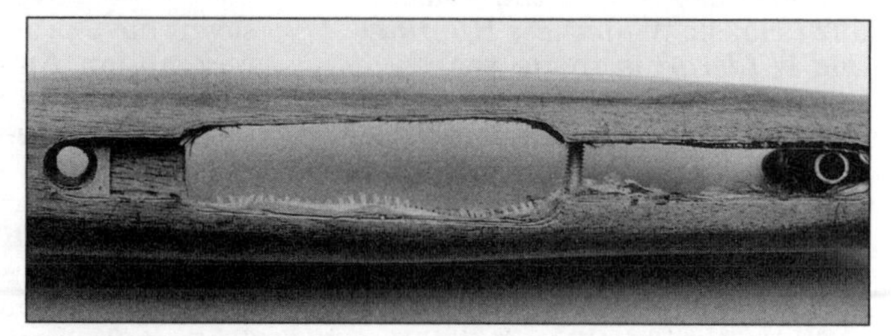

With the glass cloth tacked in place, the undercut guard/trigger area is now ready for the resin/catalyst/flock mixture.

The completed project–a French walnut-stocked 7x57 Mark X Mauser, ready for testing.

is, for the most part, little difference in our approach–and none in the finished product. The bulk of my experience has been with '98 Mausers but I have, with minor changes to suit, successfully used the same technique on a Model 70 Winchester, two Springfields, and three Sakos.

As a result of using a resin with the consistency of 30-weight motor oil–versus that of thick grease as found in the kits–and because that resin is thickened with non-absorbent flock *(fiberglass shreds)*, resin drain-off can be a major problem. In spite of said drawback I continue to use a marine resin because, when used in conjunction with fiberglass cloth and flock and properly applied, it produces a strong and stable stock.

The resin drain-off problem–a product of the combined efforts of Murphy's Law and gravity–is best handled with the judicious use of plugs and tape. This is especially true in re-bedding where the magazine well and trigger areas must be tightly plugged to prevent a major drain-off. In bedding a blank, the wood in these areas is not removed until after the second of our two barreled action pours. In all instances, the slot in the receiver floor must be plugged to prevent formation of voids when resin drains off into the receiver rail area.

To provide room for our bedding materials, the wood in the barreled action, guard/magazine and trigger areas must be undercut. Our undercutting is started from 1/16- to 1/8-inch below the stock's surface and should provide about 3/16-inch clearance *(more in the barrel channel)*.

While *rebedding*, the stock's finish and checkering are protected with cellophane tape. All metal coming in contact with the resin *(including the guide and hand screws)* must be given a *light* coat of paste wax to ensure release. We also wax the bedding of both the action and barrel swell after the second barreled-action pour, to facilitate

Before applying the resin mixture in the trigger/guard area, fit is checked *(as shown)* in the author's versatile patternmaker's vise.

the peeling-off of any stepped-up secondary surface that may result from the guard pour.

Whether bedding a blank or an existing stock, the action is held in alignment with the stockmakers' inletting guide screws. In bedding a blank, a properly padded clamp is used to pull the action down into the bedding material to the "witness mark" *(white tape)* level for both pours.

In bedding the guard, glass cloth is "tacked" in place in the undercut guard/trigger area with a few spots of resin and allowed to set up before generously smearing the entire area with the resin-catalyst-flock mixture. Once the guard is brought up flush, the inletting guide screws are started from below to act as plugs and the bottom of the guard is sealed over with tape. This last is doubly important in stocks suffering from "gaposis."

The wooden trigger mock-up is next dropped into place, and any resin forced up onto the action bedding when the guard was tapped into place is sucked into a glue syringe. Before setting the barreled action in place, the partially full glue syringe is used to replenish those areas around the trigger mock-up and magazine well where the resin level may have subsided.

At this point any traces of resin remaining on the action bedding are thoroughly wiped away with paper towels. The action is then laid in place and the guide screws are screwed into the guard screw holes. When the resin has hardened, a mallet is used to *lightly* tap on the guide screws to free the action.

A hammer and brass punch is used to back the guard out. All that now remains is clean-up and reassembly.

Three things should be noted in conclusion: **I** – Rebedding is not a job that should be undertaken two days before leaving for an out-of-state hunt. **II** – Any attempt to come up with shortcuts or to shirk pre-pour preparation may result in disaster. **III** – No matter how good the bedding job may look, once the rifle is assembled, one's handiwork shows only on the target.

**The Vixen's original barrel was ruined when the previous owner–an ingenious lad–removed a barrel obstruction with acid. It now sports an accurate (1/2-MOA) Flaig-installed Douglas air-gauged barrel.*

***Our project barreled action had previously been glass-bedded in an expensive English walnut blank. Its grouping, which ran about one MOA, has not changed.*

Restoration of a Fraser Side-Lever Express Rifle

by Joel Black

I OWN A large number of English falling block single-shot rifles, many of which are "best quality", but my favorite is a W&C Scott rifle in 500/450 #1 carbine (essentially a 45-75), based on a side-lever Field action. It is relatively plain, but it is in beautiful, totally original condition. Most large-bore British rifles have been restored at least one time. I believe this is because the majority of them were owned by officers stationed in India and Africa. The storage conditions were awful and the British army in general did not stress keeping their arms in a pristine condition. They simply would periodically return them to an arsenal for an "RTF". It should be no surprise that a British officer would use his hunting rifle in deplorable jungle conditions until he could drop it off at Manton's in Calcutta for a restoration. The first four pages of my 1925 Manton's catalog deal specifically with repairs. In 1970, a gentleman at Dickson's in Edinburg told me the restoration of firearms was what was keeping them in business. With this in mind, although I have collected guns for more than 40 years and fully understand the desire for original pieces, I can relate the following story with no sense of guilt.

A few years ago I received a phone call from my good friend, the late Walt Pearson of Rusk Gun Shop in Madison, Wisconsin. An official of the University of Wisconsin Alumni Fund was in the store with two cased British single-shot rifles that had been donated to the fund and they wanted to sell them. I'm sure I broke a few speed laws driving the 25 miles to the store.

When I walked into Walt's office I was disappointed to see two modern cases. The first contained a beautifully engraved model 1897 Westley Richards Farquharson which, sadly, had been made into a 22/250 varmint rifle. Normally I would have passed on it, but this one had been done by Tom Shelhamer and was signed and numbered under the beautifully fitted Niedner buttplate. It has been said that with the exception of Thomas Turner, Shelhamer worked on more Farquharsons than anyone else.

(Fig. 6) **New trigger plate with engraving, in the white.**

The second rifle was an even bigger disappointment. It was a Fraser side-lever in 7x57R, with a second barrel chambered for the 2 1/2-inch 20 gauge. Sadly, a so-called refinisher had butchered both the wood and metal. The Fraser looked as if a coarse wire wheel had been used on it; there wasn't a square edge to be found anywhere on the entire rifle despite the metal still showing obvious pitting *(Figs. 1 & 2)*. Its only redeeming feature was a perfect bore in my favorite caliber, although the take-down barrel was a loose fit. We negotiated a fair price for the rifles based primarily on the value of the Shelhamer.

The Fraser sat ignored in my gunroom until I was fortunate to be introduced to Fred Bowen of Lake Villa, Illinois. He is an amateur gunmaker and engraver who at that time devoted his limited time to making and engraving the most beautiful muzzle-loading firearms I had ever seen. This is not a minor compliment because, back in 1963, I spent an entire afternoon visiting the legendary Cecil Brooks at his Ohio gun shop. It took a while for me to convince Bowen he was the perfect person to attempt resuscitation on the Fraser. There was nothing he could do to make it worse; besides, he worked only with hand tools, just like the great English makers. I know a number of excellent gunsmiths who could easily use a surface grinder to restore the lines of the action, but Bowen would do it with a file, the way it was done originally. I suggested that if the pits were too deep maybe he could incorporate them into an engraving pattern. He gave me a look I'm sure he reserves for lunatics, but was too kind to say anything. He also asked to borrow my collection of Tom Rowe's wonderful books devoted to British single shots and warned me that with the limited time he has after his full-time job as a salesman, it might take him years to complete the project.

(Figs. 1 & 2) **Left & right sides of the Fraser's receiver, stripped of bluing. Pits and wire wheel marks are clearly visible.**

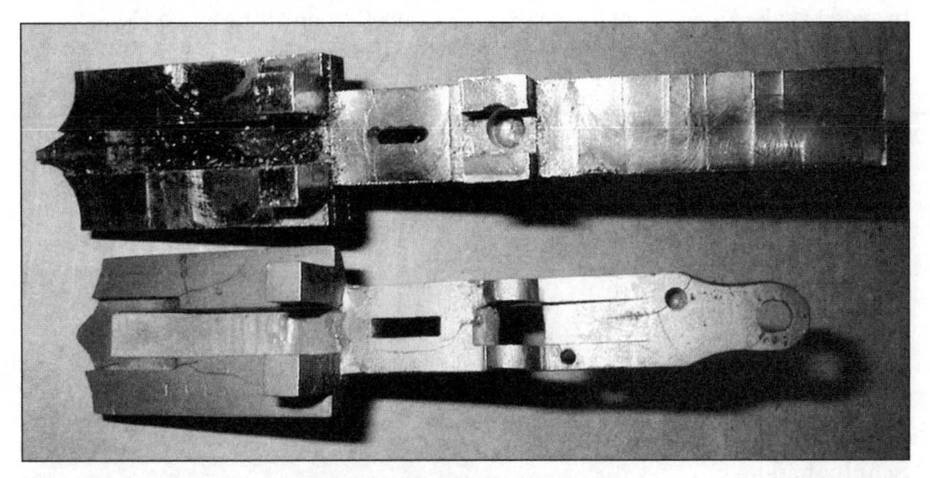

(Fig. 3) **New trigger plate *(above)*, roughed out with blue layout dye on it; *(below)* original trigger plate.**

I explained that it made no difference to me as the rifle was too ugly to sit in my gunroom.

About a month later Fred called to tell me he was ready to start work, but there were some major problems to be dealt with first. Despite the extensive brushing that had ruined the rifle's surface, it still was too hard to be touched by a file. That was easily rectified by having Dave Norin of the Smoking Gun Shop in Waukegan, Illinois anneal it. Norin is a master gunmaker who can do any metal finish, but more about that later. After stripping the

(Fig. 8) **Dave Crowley's Fraser. *(Monty Whitley photo)***

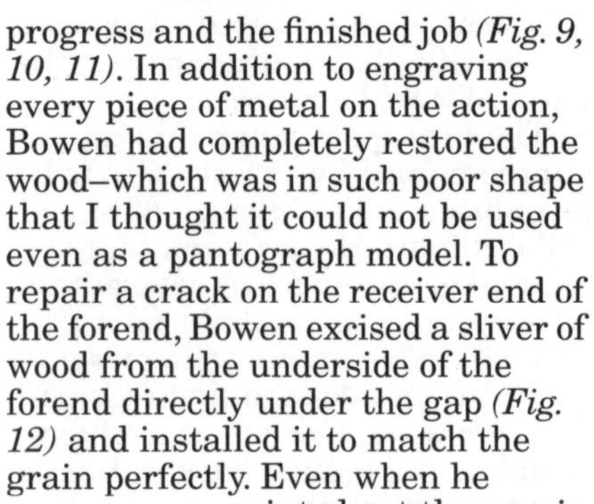

(Figs. 9 & 10) **Left & right side of the receiver, in the white, after Fred Bowen's work.**

trigger plate of its hideous hot blue, he discovered it was an ancient sand casting that Fraser used on their early side levers and it was riddled with flaws and a horribly brazed break *(Fig 3)*. That discovery almost brought the whole endeavor to a screeching halt.

In desperation, I turned to Bill Schultz of Rusk Gun Shop. I've known him for 35 years and knew he had the ability to fabricate anything. The problem was that the shop time required to mill the complicated part from a solid block of steel would have necessitated my mortgaging our farm. As with all the other aspects of the job, I was again very lucky: Schultz had just gotten a new mill at home and decided the trigger plate would be a great project for him to acquaint himself with the nuances of his new toy. While he was working on that phase of the project, Bowen, who had never done any English-style engraving, decided he would practice on blank plates *(Fig. 4 & 5)*. Then, in the middle of that aspect, he bought a GraverMaxt that required months of practice to master–but it really didn't matter since Schultz was still on the early stages of the trigger plate.

I would have completely forgotten about it at this stage if it were not for my wife Merel who likes guns and never forgets anything. About every two months she'd ask "How are Fred and Bill doing with the Fraser?" I was well aware of how much work these jobs entailed and had vowed early on to never ask either of them how they were doing.

Then, about 6 months ago Schultz told me the plate was about done and asked what I wanted to do about the trigger guard *(Fig. 6)*. I explained he needn't concern himself about it because Fraser gave up on the one-piece sand-cast triggerguards and started using shotgun-style guards *(Fig 7)*. I gave him a new one from Galazan's that obviously didn't sit well with him, because he ended up making a separate rifle-style triggerguard.

(Fig. 11) **Detail of Bowen's engraving on the action lever lock.**

I sent Schultz's completed work back to Bowen and tried not to think about it again. However, the following month when I saw Dave Crowley at the CADA show, I knew something was afoot. Crowley told me a guy he had never seen before spent an hour and a half studying his beautiful engraved Fraser *(Fig. 8)* and when asked about it he explained he was working on a similar rifle for a guy named Joel Black! Last week a CD arrived with 30 spectacular photos of the work in progress and the finished job *(Fig. 9, 10, 11)*. In addition to engraving every piece of metal on the action, Bowen had completely restored the wood–which was in such poor shape that I thought it could not be used even as a pantograph model. To repair a crack on the receiver end of the forend, Bowen excised a sliver of wood from the underside of the forend directly under the gap *(Fig. 12)* and installed it to match the grain perfectly. Even when he pointed out the repair to me *(Fig. 13)*, I could not see it.

I could not believe this extraordinary firearm was the same piece of junk I had given him a few years before. He told me he had already turned it over to Dave Norin for metal finishing. Sure enough, that evening I received an e-mail from Norin detailing the finish he proposed for each part and screw. Again I reminded him the barrel threads were loose. Once again he told me not to worry about. When I picked up the completed rifle yesterday the barrel fit as tight as when the rifle was new. With a twinkle in his eye, Norin explained to me that the usual practice of quenching in case hardening is to drop the very hot receiver into the cold bath tang first with spacer blocks in place to keep the tangs from closing. In this case he quenched it receiver front first, which resulted in a slight shrinkage—an elegantly simple solution to what seemed a terrible problem. It is this kind of attention to detail that makes guys like Fred Bowen, Dave Norin and Bill Schultz true craftsmen. ●

ENGRAVED & CUSTOM GUNS

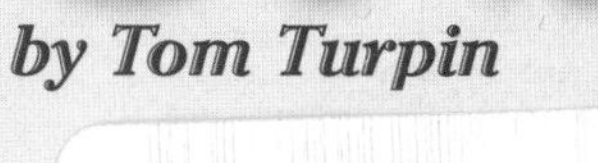

Two views of a beautifully crafted hunting rifle. Starting with a FN commercial Mauser action, all metalwork was executed by the old pro, Tom Burgess. Gary Goudy stocked it in a stick of magnificent seedling English walnut. Goudy also checkered the stock in his well-known fleur-de-lis and ribbon pattern, 24 lines-per-inch. The rifle is chambered for the 280 Remington cartridge.
Photos by Gary Bolster.

▼ Three views of a really wonderful BHE-grade Parker 20-bore. This gun has two sets of barrels and was restocked in the original factory style by Gary Goudy. Goudy also checkered the stock in an original Parker pattern and fitted a skeleton buttplate as was often done on high-grade Parkers. The engraving is original to the gun.
Photos by Gary Bolster.

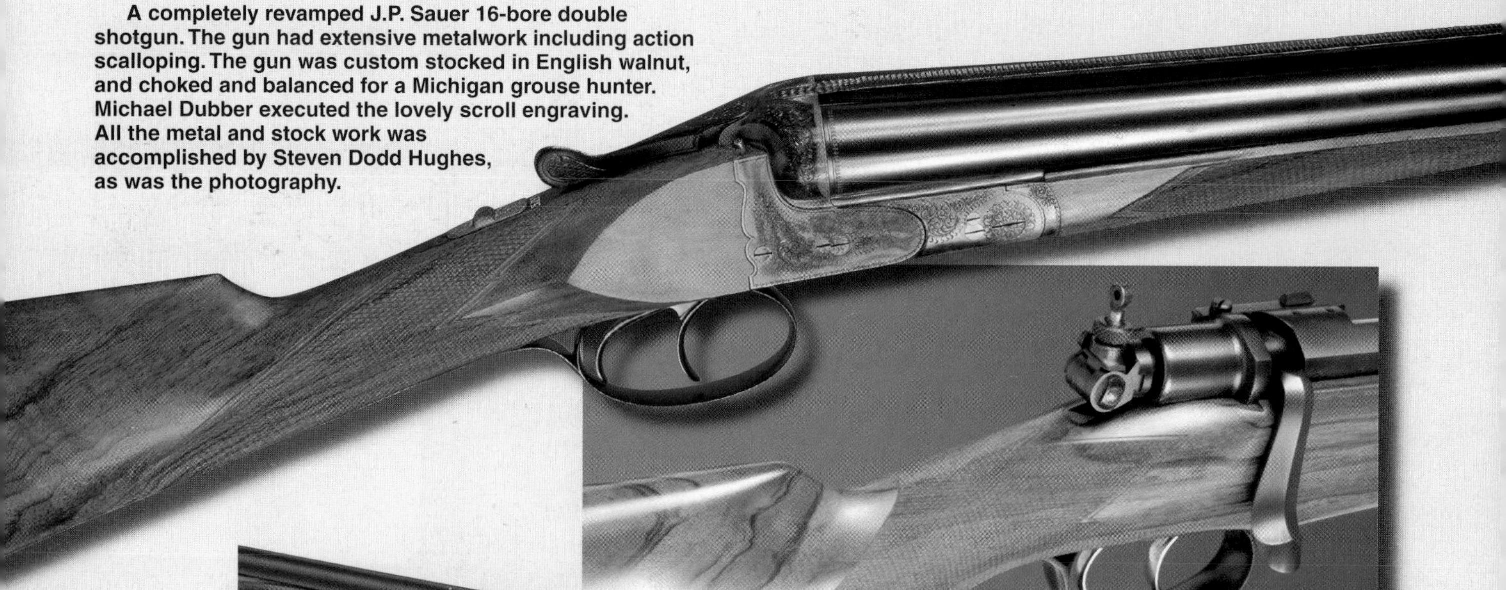

A completely revamped J.P. Sauer 16-bore double shotgun. The gun had extensive metalwork including action scalloping. The gun was custom stocked in English walnut, and choked and balanced for a Michigan grouse hunter. Michael Dubber executed the lovely scroll engraving. All the metal and stock work was accomplished by Steven Dodd Hughes, as was the photography.

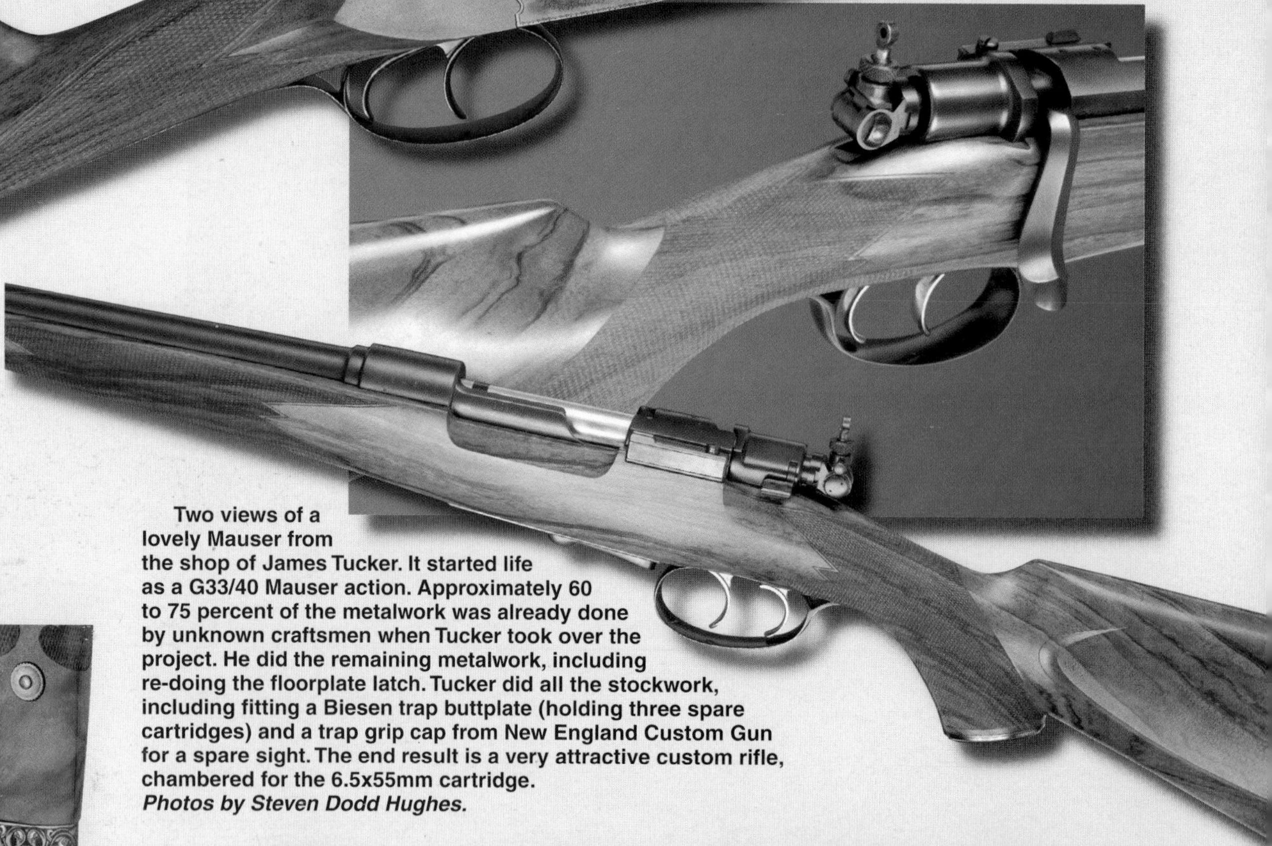

Two views of a lovely Mauser from the shop of James Tucker. It started life as a G33/40 Mauser action. Approximately 60 to 75 percent of the metalwork was already done by unknown craftsmen when Tucker took over the project. He did the remaining metalwork, including re-doing the floorplate latch. Tucker did all the stockwork, including fitting a Biesen trap buttplate (holding three spare cartridges) and a trap grip cap from New England Custom Gun for a spare sight. The end result is a very attractive custom rifle, chambered for the 6.5x55mm cartridge. *Photos by Steven Dodd Hughes.*

Three views of a magnificent Krieghoff O/U competition gun. This engraving is from the Tennessee shop of Kurt Horvath. Kurt was trained in both the Belgian school and the Italian school of engraving. *Photos by Kurt Horvath.*

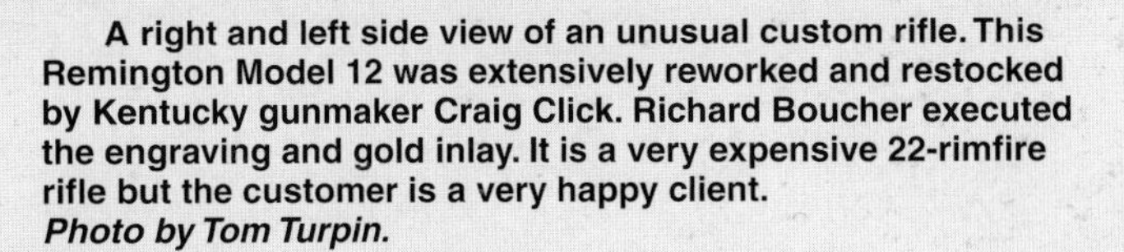

A right and left side view of an unusual custom rifle. This Remington Model 12 was extensively reworked and restocked by Kentucky gunmaker Craig Click. Richard Boucher executed the engraving and gold inlay. It is a very expensive 22-rimfire rifle but the customer is a very happy client. *Photo by Tom Turpin.*

◄ Engraver Roger Sampson executed the excellent engraving work on this Ruger Red Label O/U shotgun. The grouse engraved on the bottom of the gun is done in bulino, with Samson's wonderful fine scrollwork and gold inlay. On one side of the gun is a mallard duck and on the other is a pheasant, also accompanied with scrollwork and gold inlay. The owner of the gun, a very good amateur stockmaker, whittled out the stock and Jim Corpe did the exquisite checkering. *Photo by Tom Alexander.*

► A side and bottom view of an unusual double shotgun. It is marked Central Arms Co., St. Louis although I suspect that Central Arms was a distributor rather than a manufacturer. Starting out, it was typical of the inexpensive doubles marketed during the period of the late nineteenth and early twentieth centuries except for one thing. It is a .410-bore double! Heidi Marsh and her husband Larry completely refurbished the little boxlock double, including a new stock and the engraving and gold inlay work. Heidi did the engraving, inlay and scrimshaw work as well as the stock shaping and bluing of the metalwork. Larry did the stock finish and checkering. A beautiful and unusual double shotgun resulted from all their work. *Photo by Tom Alexander.*

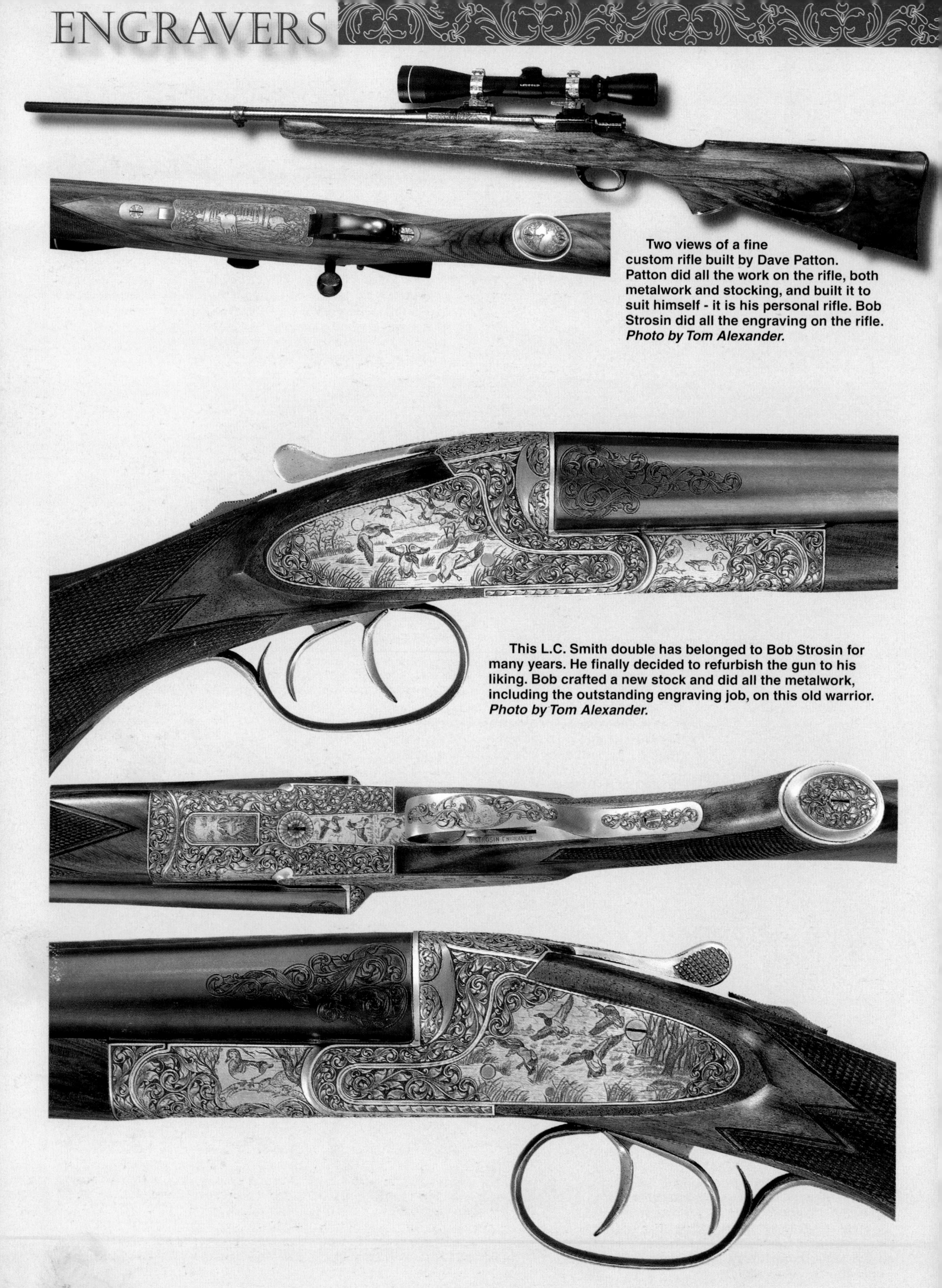

Two views of a fine custom rifle built by Dave Patton. Patton did all the work on the rifle, both metalwork and stocking, and built it to suit himself - it is his personal rifle. Bob Strosin did all the engraving on the rifle. *Photo by Tom Alexander.*

This L.C. Smith double has belonged to Bob Strosin for many years. He finally decided to refurbish the gun to his liking. Bob crafted a new stock and did all the metalwork, including the outstanding engraving job, on this old warrior. *Photo by Tom Alexander.*

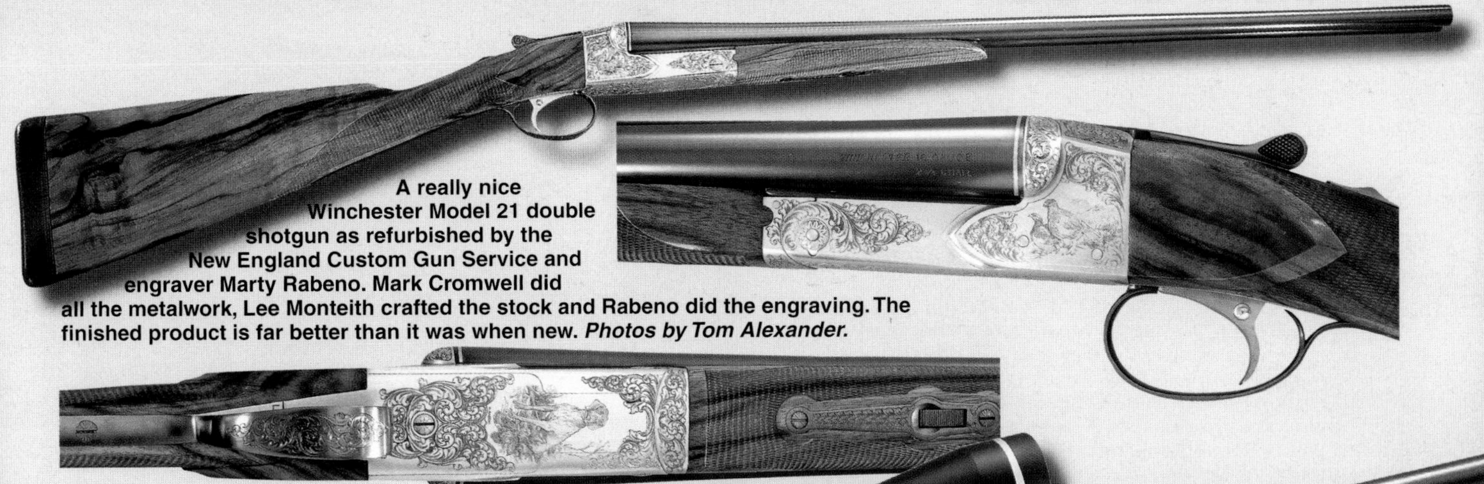

A really nice Winchester Model 21 double shotgun as refurbished by the New England Custom Gun Service and engraver Marty Rabeno. Mark Cromwell did all the metalwork, Lee Monteith crafted the stock and Rabeno did the engraving. The finished product is far better than it was when new. *Photos by Tom Alexander.*

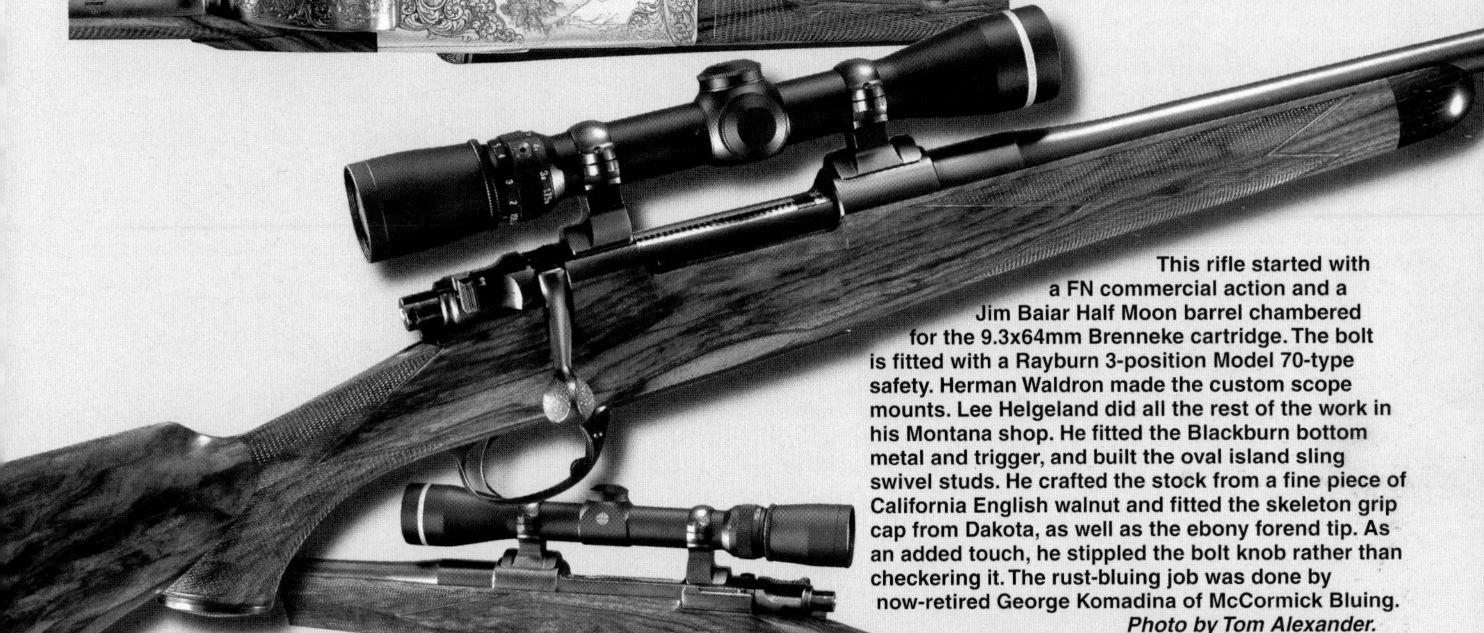

This rifle started with a FN commercial action and a Jim Baiar Half Moon barrel chambered for the 9.3x64mm Brenneke cartridge. The bolt is fitted with a Rayburn 3-position Model 70-type safety. Herman Waldron made the custom scope mounts. Lee Helgeland did all the rest of the work in his Montana shop. He fitted the Blackburn bottom metal and trigger, and built the oval island sling swivel studs. He crafted the stock from a fine piece of California English walnut and fitted the skeleton grip cap from Dakota, as well as the ebony forend tip. As an added touch, he stippled the bolt knob rather than checkering it. The rust-bluing job was done by now-retired George Komadina of McCormick Bluing. *Photo by Tom Alexander.*

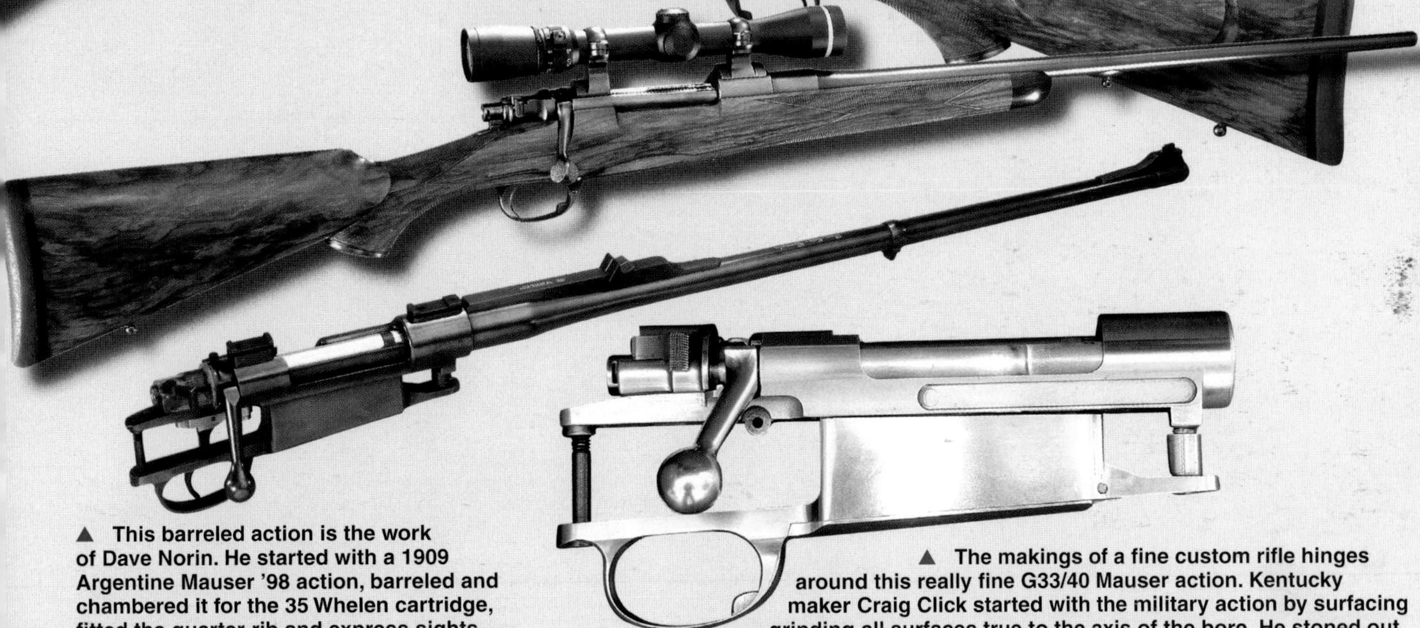

▲ This barreled action is the work of Dave Norin. He started with a 1909 Argentine Mauser '98 action, barreled and chambered it for the 35 Whelen cartridge, fitted the quarter-rib and express sights, fitted the action with a new bolt, installed a Dakota 3-position side-swing safety, reworked the original bottom metal and mounted Talley scope mount bases. Next up is a new stock, also by Norin. *Photo by Tom Alexander.*

▲ The makings of a fine custom rifle hinges around this really fine G33/40 Mauser action. Kentucky maker Craig Click started with the military action by surfacing grinding all surfaces true to the axis of the bore. He stoned out the old tooling marks and welded on a new bolt handle. He installed a Dakota three-position Model 70-type safety and then reworked the bottom metal from a 1909 Argentine Mauser and fitted it to the G33/40. He lapped the locking lugs for full contact, as well as polishing the feed rails and raceway. Next step will involve fitting and chambering a barrel, most likely for the 257 AI Roberts cartridge. *Photo by Tom Turpin.*

The holder of Membership Certificate # 1 in the American Custom Gunmakers Guild is the maker of this fine rifle. John Maxon and Steve Billeb flipped a coin to determine who would get the #1 certificate and who would have to settle for #2—Maxon won the toss. Maxon started with a Remington Model 700 action by completely "blueprinting" it. He then fitted a 2-position Model 70-type safety from New England Custom Gun to the bolt. He installed a Douglas Air Gauge #3 contour chrome-moly 24-inch barrel to the action and chambered it for the 220 Swift cartridge. He then reworked the factory trigger to a crisp 2-1/2 pound break. He crafted the stock from a stick of quarter-sawed Bastogne walnut, fitting a Neidner buttplate and grip cap and checkering the stock 24 lpi with a point pattern and no border. Wearing a Leupold 4.5-14x40 scope, the package weighs 7 lbs., 10 ounces. John built this rifle for himself. *Photo by Tom Alexander.*

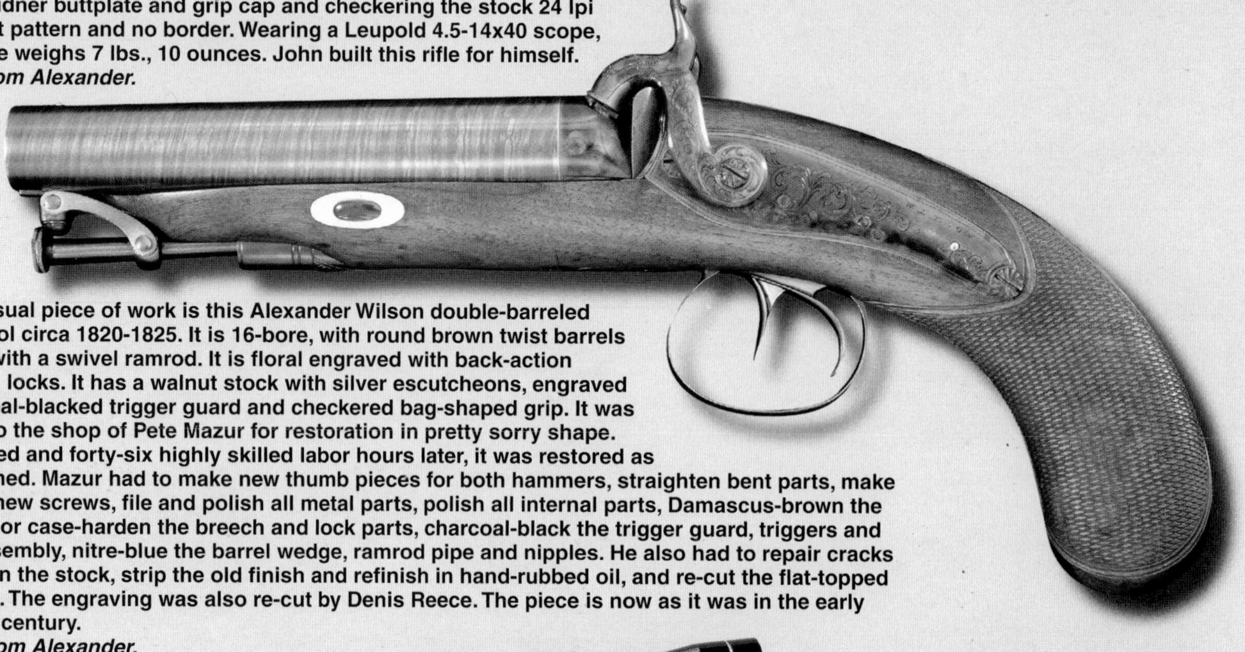

An unusual piece of work is this Alexander Wilson double-barreled Coach pistol circa 1820-1825. It is 16-bore, with round brown twist barrels and fitted with a swivel ramrod. It is floral engraved with back-action percussion locks. It has a walnut stock with silver escutcheons, engraved and charcoal-blacked trigger guard and checkered bag-shaped grip. It was delivered to the shop of Pete Mazur for restoration in pretty sorry shape. One hundred and forty-six highly skilled labor hours later, it was restored as photographed. Mazur had to make new thumb pieces for both hammers, straighten bent parts, make mostly all-new screws, file and polish all metal parts, polish all internal parts, Damascus-brown the barrels, color case-harden the breech and lock parts, charcoal-black the trigger guard, triggers and ramrod assembly, nitre-blue the barrel wedge, ramrod pipe and nipples. He also had to repair cracks and chips in the stock, strip the old finish and refinish in hand-rubbed oil, and re-cut the flat-topped checkering. The engraving was also re-cut by Denis Reece. The piece is now as it was in the early nineteenth century.
Photo by Tom Alexander.

The Mauserlicher - another very unusual piece is this rifle from the shop of Steve Nelson. It started as a 1903 Greek Mannlicher action. Nelson modified it to accept a '98 Mauser bolt, welded the split rear bridge shut, welded on a hanger for a Mauser bolt release and Blackburn trigger. He then installed a Jim Wisner two-position safety. Dough Turnbull did the color case work. It is chambered for the 7x57mm cartridge that required, among other things, modifying the Mannlicher rotary magazine. Steve then stocked his creation in a stick of California English walnut that he acquired from Gilbert "Slim" Swenson many years ago, and then rust-blued it. Ed Peugh did the engraving. No doubt it would have been far easier to have started with a Mauser action in the beginning but, as Steve said, it wouldn't have been as much fun.
Photo by Tom Alexander.

▶ Shown here is an exquisite pair of Holland and Holland shotguns that have been magnificently engraved and embellished by Hoosier engraver Michael Dubber. It just doesn't get a lot better than this work.
Photo by Tom Alexander.

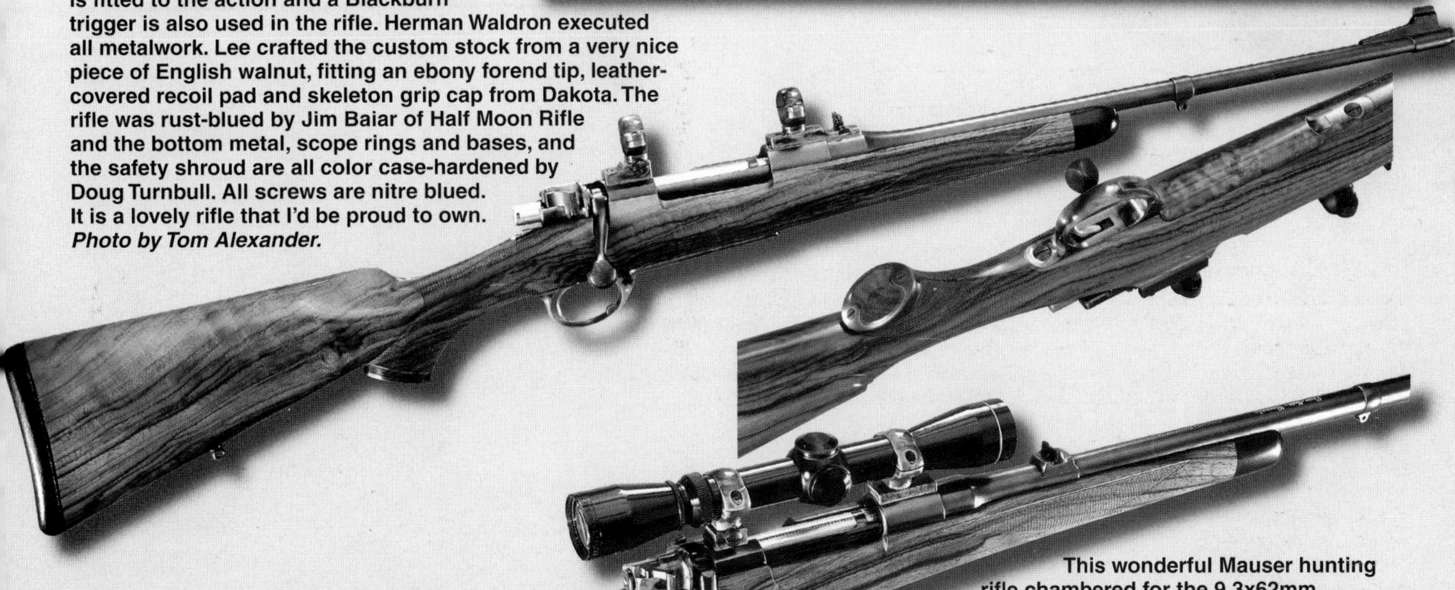

▼ Two views of a superb custom rifle from the Montana shop of Lee Helgeland. A 1909 Argentine Mauser '98 action was used to craft this rifle. It was barreled and chambered for the 7x57mm cartridge and fitted with a two-position side-swing safety. Custom scope bases were machined to fit Leupold rings. Fisher/Blackburn rounded bottom metal is fitted to the action and a Blackburn trigger is also used in the rifle. Herman Waldron executed all metalwork. Lee crafted the custom stock from a very nice piece of English walnut, fitting an ebony forend tip, leather-covered recoil pad and skeleton grip cap from Dakota. The rifle was rust-blued by Jim Baiar of Half Moon Rifle and the bottom metal, scope rings and bases, and the safety shroud are all color case-hardened by Doug Turnbull. All screws are nitre blued. It is a lovely rifle that I'd be proud to own.
Photo by Tom Alexander.

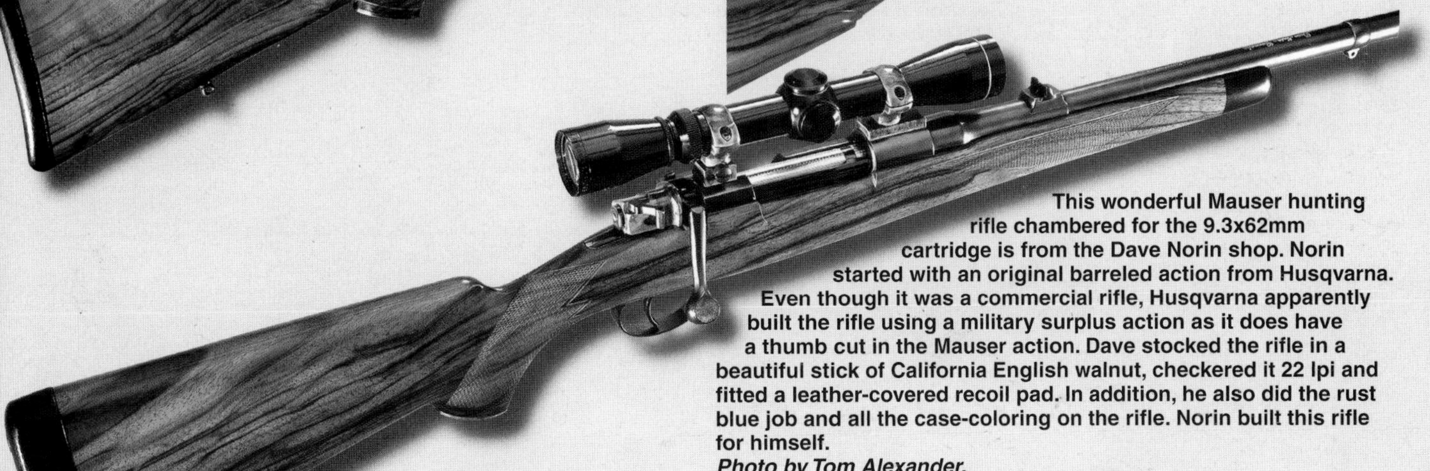

This wonderful Mauser hunting rifle chambered for the 9.3x62mm cartridge is from the Dave Norin shop. Norin started with an original barreled action from Husqvarna. Even though it was a commercial rifle, Husqvarna apparently built the rifle using a military surplus action as it does have a thumb cut in the Mauser action. Dave stocked the rifle in a beautiful stick of California English walnut, checkered it 22 lpi and fitted a leather-covered recoil pad. In addition, he also did the rust blue job and all the case-coloring on the rifle. Norin built this rifle for himself.
Photo by Tom Alexander.

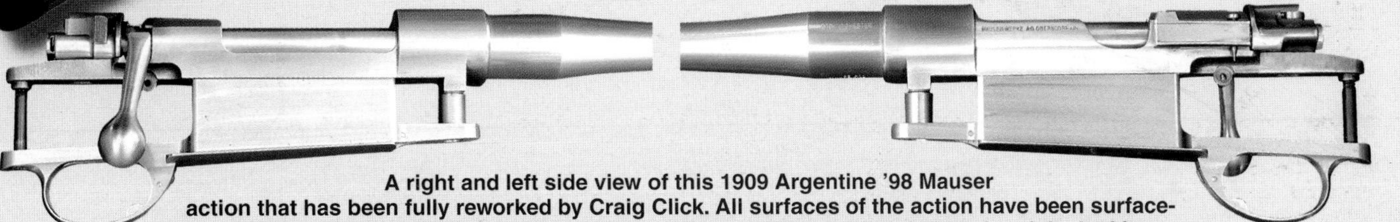

A right and left side view of this 1909 Argentine '98 Mauser action that has been fully reworked by Craig Click. All surfaces of the action have been surface-ground true to the axis of the bore. All surfaces have been polished and stoned and the locking lugs of the bolt have been lapped for full contact. A new bolt knob has been welded onto the military bolt and it has been fitted with a Dakota three-position Model 70-type safety. A new barrel has been installed and chambered for the 338 Winchester Magnum cartridge. Next up will be the crafting of a new stock.
Photo by Tom Turpin.

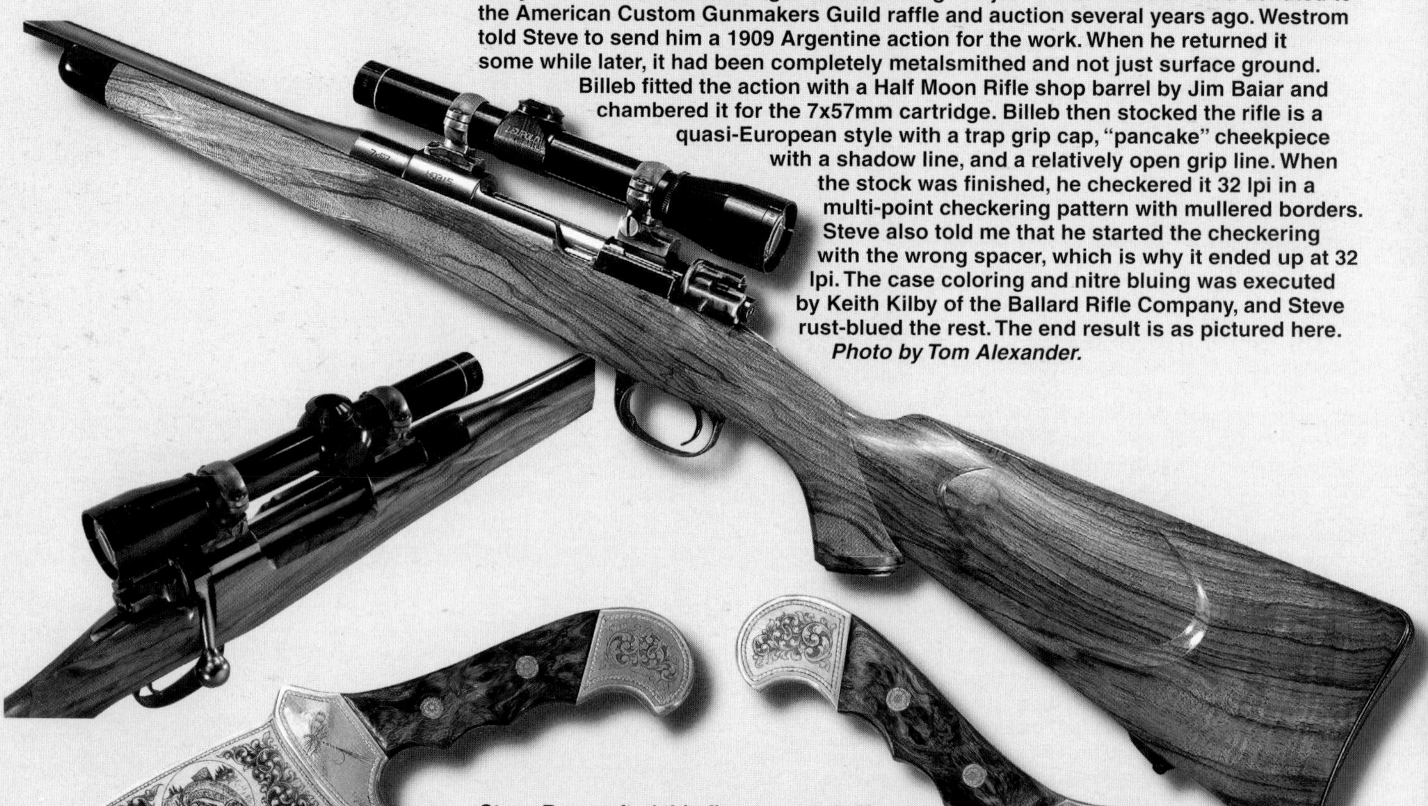

Two views of a fine custom rifle from the shop of Steve Billeb. The '98 Mauser action was completely metalsmithed by the late John Westrom. Billeb told me an interesting story about the metalsmithing. Billeb won a "grind job" which Westrom had donated to the American Custom Gunmakers Guild raffle and auction several years ago. Westrom told Steve to send him a 1909 Argentine action for the work. When he returned it some while later, it had been completely metalsmithed and not just surface ground. Billeb fitted the action with a Half Moon Rifle shop barrel by Jim Baiar and chambered it for the 7x57mm cartridge. Billeb then stocked the rifle is a quasi-European style with a trap grip cap, "pancake" cheekpiece with a shadow line, and a relatively open grip line. When the stock was finished, he checkered it 32 lpi in a multi-point checkering pattern with mullered borders. Steve also told me that he started the checkering with the wrong spacer, which is why it ended up at 32 lpi. The case coloring and nitre bluing was executed by Keith Kilby of the Ballard Rifle Company, and Steve rust-blued the rest. The end result is as pictured here. *Photo by Tom Alexander.*

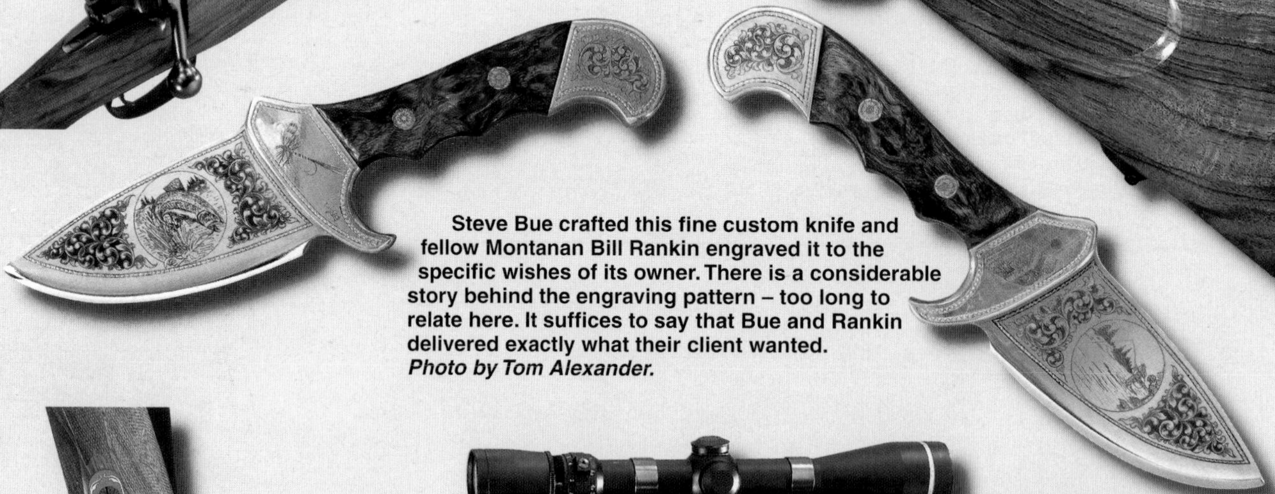

Steve Bue crafted this fine custom knife and fellow Montanan Bill Rankin engraved it to the specific wishes of its owner. There is a considerable story behind the engraving pattern – too long to relate here. It suffices to say that Bue and Rankin delivered exactly what their client wanted. *Photo by Tom Alexander.*

Three views of a wonderful rifle from Keith Heppler. The rifle has a Peruvian Mauser action, and Krieger barrel. It has been fitted with Blackburn bottom metal and a Blackburn trigger. Steve Heilmann did all the metalwork and Pete Mazur did the finishing. Keith crafted the stock from a fine stick of Moroccan walnut to suit himself, as it is his personal rifle. He checkered it 26 lpi in a fleur-de-lis and ribbon pattern. Dennis Reese engraved it. *Photo by Tom Alexander.*

EIBAR REVISITED

by Terry Wieland

In 1968, Jack O'Connor traveled to the Basque gunmaking region of Spain and told of his experiences in the 1969 GUN DIGEST ***("A Visit to Eibar")****. Today, more than 30 years later, Eibar is much the same as it was then. Many of the gunmakers are still in business, and even some of the same craftsmen are at work making fine guns – albeit with greyer hair, and often with their sons and grandsons working at the bench beside them.*

• • •

Jack O'Connor came to Eibar because, bluntly, "there are so many conflicting opinions about shotguns made in Spain…I decided to take a look."

What he found was an industry on the brink. The ancient gunmaking craft of the Basques was facing major changes, although no one knew it at the time. It was a cottage industry of many small companies and shops with one or two workers. Some of the guns they made were excellent quality, selling at bargain prices. Others were no bargain at any price, but sold in great quantities around the world.

Today, that is no longer true. Most of the low-end Spanish gunmakers are gone, swept away by competition from countries with even lower costs – the Philippines, Russia, Brazil.

The major difference, though, is that today more really fine guns are being made in Eibar than ever before. There are more high-quality gunmakers, and their finest models compare well with guns made anywhere. In 1968, the best products from Spain were a secret. Today, they are recognized wherever shotgunning is a religion.

Having said all that, let's return to Jack O'Connor and follow in his footsteps as he wanders the streets of Eibar. What did he see? And what do we see today?

• • •

For his trip, O'Connor rented a car and drove up from Madrid with a mysterious American expatriate by the name of Seymour Siebert. They left the smog-shrouded Spanish capital in the morning and labored north all day through a snowstorm, finally reaching the city of Vitoria that evening. They spent the night there and continued on to Eibar the next day, arriving around noon.

For years, the Garbi Deluxe was the most expensive gun made in Eibar, and is still near the top. It retails in the U.S. for about $25,000. The engraving pattern shown is the original, but now the Deluxe can be had in a range of patterns, from rose and scroll, to deep scroll engraving, to a variety of elaborate patterns and game scenes – anything the client wants, virtually.

These days, you can leave the airport in Madrid, hop onto the N-1 motorway, and be in Eibar in an easy five hours, traversing the plains of Castile at 80 miles per hour in a country where there are no speed limits, and fast driving is a religion. There are comfortable stops along the way, for a frothy espresso and some jamón iberico to fuel your journey.

Even better is a c ommuter flight into Bilbao's shiny new airport, either from Madrid or across the Bay of Biscay from London, then rent a car for a half-hour drive down to Eibar on the A-8.

If you want, you can still see the country as O'Connor did by taking one of the mountain roads. After a couple of hours, however, you will deeply desire to be back on the motorway to make up some time. Twisting through the mountains, doubling back and forth, and crawling along behind a succession of farm wagons, is no more fun now than it was for O'Connor and Siebert.

Seymour Siebert appears in several articles about Eibar, including one written later by John Amber,

This is a rounded-action gun engraved with the pattern of the Arrieta 931, the company's highest-grade gun. It would retail in the U.S. for about $20,000. This particular gun is a 12-gauge, built on a 16-gauge frame, and weighs 6 lbs., 4 oz.

but no one ever explains exactly who he was or how they came to know him. Gregorio Garralda, who worked for AYA in those days, and is now retired after finishing his career with Ignacio Ugartechea, says Siebert was a mystery to the Basques, too.

"He was an American who lived in Madrid – a huge man, with a great girth," Gregorio told me some years ago, during one of our elaborate lunches at Ignacio Ugartechea's club. Gregorio's hands sketched the outline of a large stomach. "And tall, too. At lunch he always ordered a huge pot of alubias (Basque beans). *He ate them in industrial quantities."* Gregorio quickly translated what he had told me, and Ignacio nodded in emphatic agreement. *"Si, si."*

The suspicion was that Siebert worked for the CIA in the days when General Franco was a friend of Washington, opposing the Communists. He died in an equally mysterious accident during a driven-partridge shoot on one of the big estates. Oh, when was it, Ignacio? 1976? 77? *Si, si.* A gun went off. No one knows. He died. Gregorio shrugged. He was a friend of Spain. He was a friend of the gunmakers. More *jamón*? Eat, *eat.*

• • •

Jack O'Connor's first impression of Eibar was a jumble of buildings, tumbled into a narrow mountain valley with steep hills on all sides. The buildings gave the impression they had been there "since Cortez invaded Mexico."

There was an ancient town hall, looking out over a market square; in one direction was the huge sandstone church, so reminiscent of old Mexico in its stark Spanish catholicism. In another direction was the old Eibar proof house, where all the guns were tested, and not far away a tiny bullring. The proof house is gone, replaced by a large parking garage that is a godsend to downtown Eibar, where parking is worse than Manhattan, but the bullring is still there, as is the church. The town hall, a famous building where the Spanish republic was declared in 1931, has been undergoing a major renovation for several years. The market square is still there, though, and people stroll the narrow streets at all hours of day and night.

The first stop for the travelers was the AYA factory, a building huge by Eibar standards, with five floors of machinery and gun parts and gunmakers laboring over their benches. O'Connor met Agustín Aranzabal, son of one of the founders of the company. Aranzabal was one of the great competition shooters of Europe in the 1950s, winning title after title in live-pigeon and trap shooting, going head to head with the scion of the other great gunmaking house, Victor Sarasqueta.

Victor II, grandson of the original Victor, who was himself the godfather of the fine gun trade in Eibar, also won his share of trophies. The two rivals were good friends, but their companies were nothing but rivals. You were a friend of one or the other. Charles Askins, the first American to write about Eibar, was close to AYA, and said little about Sarasqueta. Jack O'Connor was drawn into the same circle, and his article mentions Sarasqueta not at all.

Victor Sarasqueta, the company, was founded in 1881, almost 40 years before AYA was begun by Miguel Aguirre and Nicolas Aranzabal. Although AYA eventually became much larger than Sarasqueta, the older company set the standard for the finest guns, including making guns for the king, Alfonso XIII, who was deposed in 1931. Sarasqueta continued making guns until 1981, when it finally closed its doors, a victim of changing tastes in shotguns, and the ravages of inflation that were tearing the commercial world apart.

Shortly after that shock, the Basque gunmakers tried to bring their cherished industry, which was then almost 500 years old, into the 20th century by amalgamating many small firms into one large one. AYA was the lead company involved, along with the Sarriugarte brothers, makers of over/under competition and game guns. The new company, Diarm, lasted only a year or two before it folded in a cloud of conflict, with half its employees working while the others picketed outside the plant. Organizing the Basque gunmakers is like herding cats.

When Diarm folded, AYA was resurrected as a small custom shop, with a dozen craftsman-owners under Imanol Aranzabal. A few months later, the Sarriugarte brothers resurfaced with a new company of their own, Kemen Armas. Today, both AYA and Kemen are stalwarts of the Basque gun trade, each producing 500 to 1,000 guns a year.

As O'Connor noted, AYA in 1968 made a great variety of guns, and employed several hundred people. They built everything from the most basic single-shot to fine side-by-side and over/under sidelock guns, elaborately engraved and inlaid with gold. Today, AYA limits its production to the finer models from the old days, although they still make both styles of double gun, and in both boxlocks and sidelocks.

O'Connor's particular favorites were the Model 56 and No. 1 sidelock SxS guns. The 56 was *(and is)* a heavy-framed double intended primarily for live-pigeon shooting. It has various refinements to add strength, including sideclips and an extra-wide frame, and normally comes with long barrels, tight chokes, a pistol grip, and single trigger. In 1968, the gun sold for $345 in Eibar; today, ordering one from the U.S., a Model 56 costs about $5000.

The No. 1 was an English-style game gun, discreetly engraved in Purdey-style rose and scroll. AYA developed it for the English market in the 1950s with the help of the King brothers, two Englishmen who established Anglo Spanish Imports. ASI is still AYA's importer in the U.K and their largest export customer. In fact, several other AYA models, including the sidelock No. 2 and the boxlock No. 4, were also made at the behest of the Kings. In the mid-1990s, Edward King persuaded AYA to introduce the No. 1 Deluxe, a spectacular gun in the style of a Holland & Holland, with broad scroll engraving.

The No. 1 Deluxe is AYA's finest side-by-side today, and a delicious gun by any standard.

For many years, AYA also made a specialty of the over/under, especially the Model 37, which was patterned on the famous Merkel with bolsters and a Kersten fastener. Charles Askins called it the finest over/under made in Europe – better, by implication, than the Belgian-made Browning Superposed. While O'Connor did not go that far, he certainly admired the gun.

One other AYA deserves some comment, if only as a eulogy. The Model Senior was a meticulous copy of a Beesley-actioned Purdey, brought to Eibar by the King brothers. It was made for about 20 years but only about 40 were produced altogether. The last Seniors were made in 1987 – a matched set of six guns for a Bilbao banking tycoon. They sold for $15,000 apiece at a time when you could buy an AYA No. 1 for about $2500. The Senior is not made now, and will almost certainly never be made again. Those who own them are not parting with them.

The Model 37 is back in production, though, as is the Model Augusta, a more elaborate version. Very few find their way to the U.S., where the deep-framed, rather archaic-looking Merkel is out of favor in an era of shallow-framed O/U's.

A Pedro Arrizabalaga 12-bore, rounded-action, engraved in the pattern of a Thomas Boss game gun. With a self-opener, it weighs seven pounds. It retails from New England Arms for about $13,500.

O'Connor summed up his impression of AYA with one line: *I have never seen handsomer guns,* he wrote of the No. 1 and the Model 56.

Later, O'Connor owned a matched pair of AYA guns, which are still in his family. He also visited another small gunmaker, Eusebio Arizaga. Arizaga made two guns for him, both side-by-sides – a 20 gauge, and later a 28. Arizaga was one of the companies that merged into Diarm and never came back.

• • •

After Sarasqueta and AYA, the most prominent shotgun maker in Eibar in 1968 was Ignacio Ugartechea, a company founded in 1922

The Model 37 was described by Charles Askins as the best over/under made on the Continent. At one time, it was the most expensive gun made in Eibar. It is modeled on the Merkel, complete with Kersten fastener and three-piece forend. Unlike the Merkel, it is a sidelock, and employs an ingenious AYA exclusive release system on the locks. Traditionally, the locks are gold-plated inside to resist corrosion. The Augusta is the 37 with more expensive engraving. The 16-gauge recently sold, used, in the U.S. for about $10,000.

by the first Ignacio, and carried on by his son, also Ignacio. There is now a third Ignacio in the company, and Ignacio II is in his 70s. He still goes to work every day, to his cluttered office on the fifth floor of his factory on the narrow, twisting Calle Txonta.

Since 1968, Ugartechea has undergone tremendous changes. When O'Connor visited Calle Txonta, the company was the third-largest in Eibar, and made everything from basic boxlocks to fine doubles, including some excellent over/unders. They even made rifles at one time – the last in 1943 for General Franco himself. After a succession of labor problems and the vagaries of international trade and changing tastes, the company now has a work force of little more than a dozen *(compared to a hundred in 1968),* and produces guns strictly to order. Several companies bring Ugartechea boxlocks into the U.S., and there is one, Aspen Outfitting, that imports the high-grade sidelocks. All are side-by-sides.

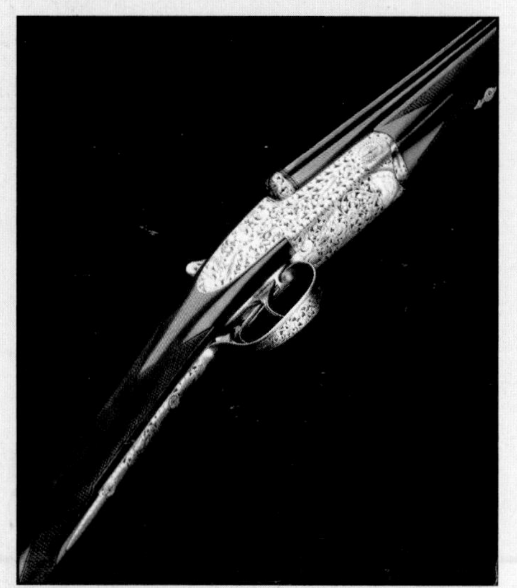

AYA #1 Deluxe, this one is a 16-gauge.

The companies that today produce the majority of the fine Basque guns are the tiny gunmakers who were prospering in the early 1980s, and refused to become part of the Diarm consortium.

The only one mentioned by Jack O'Connor was Armas Garbi, so I will start with them.

Armas Garbi was founded in 1959 by six craftsmen drawn from different larger gunmakers – AYA, Ugartechea, and Luis Arrizabalaga. Together, they began making parts for other companies, handling the overflow, and eventually evolved into a maker of complete guns. After a while, they phased out the cheaper guns and the boxlocks (which have never been regarded in Spain as a true "best" gun) and today they make a half-dozen models of sidelock side-by-sides, as well as a few *(very expensive)* double rifles.

In 1968, according to O'Connor, Garbi would make you a nice gun for $160, and "knock your eye out for $300." They will still knock your eye out with one of their finer models, but it will cost you substantially more than $300. An Armas Garbi Deluxe, today, retails in the United States for about $25,000. William Larkin Moore, who has been their exclusive importer for almost 30 years, says only a handful of these beauties has ever crossed the Atlantic, and few people have even seen one. But they are spectacular guns. Most of the approximately 40 Deluxe models that Garbi makes every year stay in Spain, where they are shot by the nobility and by wealthy friends of King Juan Carlos I, a great Garbi admirer and long-time client.

At the other end of the scale is the Garbi Model 100, a gun that sells for about $3500 here, and is one of the great values to be had in a double shotgun. My personal favorite Garbi is the Model 103A, a Purdey lookalike that begins at about $8,000. If your taste runs to British elegance but your bank account objects to the price, the Garbi 103A may be the answer.

Armas Garbi was not unique, even in 1968. With one exception, all the fine gunmakers of today were in business when O'Connor visited, but he does not mention any of them. Of course, as he points out, at the time there were a hundred or more small companies making guns, many with 20 employees or less, and he could hardly visit them all. It is easier today, when there are only about eight companies in Eibar producing really fine-quality doubles.

In Eibar, you will find AYA, Ugartechea and Armas Garbi, as well as Grulla Armas and Pedro Arrizabalaga. In the adjacent town of Elgoibar is Arrieta, and the new company of the Sarriugarte brothers, Kemen Armas.

In 1968, Grulla was known as Union Armera. It was founded in 1932 by six craftsmen from Victor Sarasqueta who struck out on their own. They followed the usual path, and it is worth taking the time to look at the structure of Basque gunmaking because it applies, more or less, to them all.

The Basque country of Spain is the most industrialized region, being rich in iron ore and hydropower. The Basques were working with iron from the time of the Romans. Gunmaking began almost as soon as gunpowder was introduced, and the small industrial towns that dot the Basque countryside, nestled in the steep mountain valleys, have all had gunmakers of one sort or another. Eibar is the acknowledged center of the trade, and has been for centuries.

Scenes from Eibar as it was in Jack O'Connor's day, and still is. With the exception of the proof house, which has been torn down and replaced by a large parking garage and community recreation area *cum* park in the center of town, overlooking the city hall, everything is as it was in 1968. The new proof house *(above)* is in an industrial park, next to the Greyhound terminal. The church is about 500 years old. Eibar has been incorporated since 1346, and has been the acknowledged center of the Basque gun trade for almost 500 years.

A group of barreled actions in the AYA shop, awaiting the next operation. AYA is one of the few shops in Eibar that is equipped to perform every stage of gunmaking, including making their own lock blanks.

In Britain, firms are founded and carry on under the same name permanently, even if the company changes hands. In Spain, the tradition is that a craftsman will learn the trade at the gunmaker's school, and later during an apprenticeship, then strike out on his own. At first, he will make parts for other companies, and handle their overflow of orders. Eventually, he will make complete guns himself, take in partners and employees, and put his own name on the barrels. And, if the company lasts and his ambition is such, eventually he will make best-quality guns and his name will be murmured by the King of Spain, over a glass of wine during a partridge shoot. Generally, however, when the founder retires or dies, the name dies with him.

With slight variations, that summarizes the history – so far – of Garbi, Grulla, Arrieta, Arrizabalaga, and even Ugartechea and AYA.

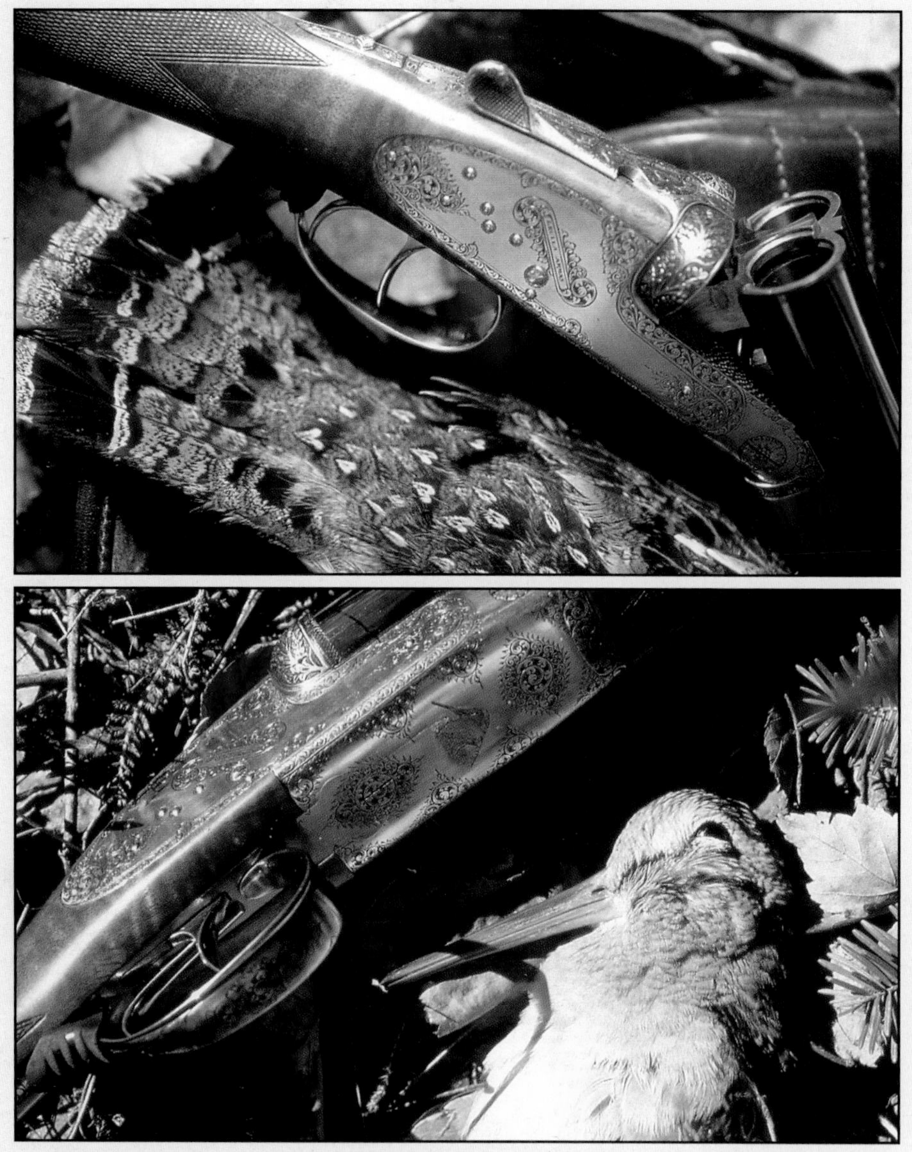

The gun is a Windsor Woodcock, a model created for the author. It is based on the Grulla Windsor, but is a 12-gauge built on a 20-gauge frame. It weighs 6 lbs., 5 oz., with 29-inch chrome-nickel barrels. It is choked Cylinder and Skeet #1, and is intended for grouse and woodcock in thick cover. It works equally well, however, with doves and quail.

Union Armera began by making a range of guns, but none was really best-quality. Gradually, however, they upgraded their line, introducing better models and dropping the cheaper ones. Their trademark was a standing crane – *grulla* – and in 1983 they officially adopted Grulla Armas as their corporate name.

Over the past decade, no company in Eibar has improved as much, or progressed as quickly, as Grulla Armas, and today they make some of the finest guns in Spain. Their highest grade, the Royal, is an exquisite gun, patterned down to the last wrinkle after the very best British shotguns. It is available in any of three standard scroll patterns (H&H, Purdey, or Churchill) at a price of about $12,500, or it can be specially engraved at additional cost. The lower-priced guns in the line, from the Model 215 at about $3000, to the Windsor, at about $8000, reflect the company's determination to be recognized as the best. Anyone contemplating the purchase of a Spanish gun should at least look at the Grullas.

Pedro Arrizabalaga has no such problem, for the simple reason that for many years it has been acclaimed as the finest gunmaker in Spain.

While frame forgings receive their rough shaping on a milling machine, the fine shaping and finishing is done in the traditional way – in a vise, with a file.

The company was founded in 1944 by Pedro Arrizabalaga, an engraver from Ugartechea, and three partners. Today, the company is still small – only four craftsmen and two apprentices. They build no more than 40 guns a year, and only sidelock side-by-sides. But every Pedro Arrizabalaga gun is a "best." Like Purdey, they make only one grade, but they will pattern a gun in just about any way you desire – round action or standard, straight grip or pistol, in any gauge, engraved to your personal tastes. Recently, New England Arms became the exclusive importer of Pedro Arrizabalaga guns, and they retail here for about $12,000 and up.

About three miles down the valley from Eibar lies the town of Elgoibar.

There are two companies there now, producing really fine doubles.

One is Arrieta, probably the best-known name in Spanish guns aside from AYA. Arrieta is family-owned, and run by a third generation. They have about 18 workers and produce perhaps 500 guns a year. They range in price and quality from the Model 557, retailing for around $2500 here, to the Model 931, which would sell for at least $20,000. So few Model 931s have been produced and imported to the U.S. that it is difficult to put an exact price on it, especially since it is not a standard gun in any way except the engraving pattern. The final cost depends on what the buyer wants in terms of engraving, inlay, and walnut.

In between the 557 and the 931 lies the broadest range of quality and style of any Basque gunmaker except AYA. Arrietas are all sidelock side-by-sides. The company stopped making boxlocks about 20 years ago. You can order an Arrieta with standard engraving, or with elaborate scroll and gold inlay done in the traditional Basque *damasquina*.

Arrieta guns are marketed here by some notable companies, including Orvis and Griffin & Howe, and New England Arms is also a longtime importer.

The other Elgoibar gun company is Kemen Armas, founded by the Sarriugarte brothers after the demise of their brainchild, Diarm.

The original company, Francisco Sarriugarte, was founded by their father, a lockmaker who learned the trade at AYA before going out on his own in the 1950s. Eventually, the company came to specialize in over/unders, especially competition guns for trap and live pigeon.

When they started Kemen (Basque for *strength*), the elder brother, Juan Cruz Sarriugarte, designed a gun that incorporated many of the features of the world's foremost competition shotgun, the Perazzi. The basic KM-4 is a boxlock over/under with a detachable trigger group. It is shallow-framed, like the Perazzi, and in appearance the guns are so similar that some have claimed the parts are interchangeable. They are not.

Juan Cruz insists that nothing is interchangeable, and rather coyly adds that nothing was copied, either. Be that as it may, the Kemen guns have many Perazzi-style features. While the Kemen guns are primarily competition pieces, they can be had in a game-gun configuration, even with two triggers, in 12 and 20 gauge. For some years, the great British shooters, George Digweed and Richard Faulds shot Kemen guns, and Digweed used a Kemen when he set a record of shooting almost 700 wood pigeons in a single day.

The Kemen guns obviously shoot well, and they shoot a long time.

Recently, Sarriugarte added a side-by-side to the line, a boxlock with a detachable trigger that retails for around $17,000 – a very high price by Basque standards. Like the company's over/unders, the SxS is a heavy, sturdy gun, designed more for competition than game shooting. All Kemen guns are impressive, and their engraver, Pedro Arreitunandia, is one of the best in the Basque Country.

Kemen guns are all boxlocks, but the over/under can be had in higher grades with sideplates that allow Arreitunandia to really display his skills as an engraver. The most expensive gun, the Suprema AX, has unbelievable Purdey-style rose and scroll, in a severe elegance that screams of money, and retails for upwards of $30,000.

Grulla Armas is one of four (Arrieta, Garbi, and Arrizabalaga being the others) makers now building high-quality double rifles. Grulla has gone further, creating a back-action sidelock (the traditional lock used in large-bore English double rifles) for its E-95 rifle.

• • •

These are the most noteworthy gunmakers working in the Basque country today. Many that O'Connor mentioned in passing, such as the handgun manufacturer Star-Echeverria, have gone out of business. Also gone are historic names such as Llama and Astra, and a host of smaller shotgun makers, like Eusebio Arizaga, that had a brief moment in the sun and then faded.

Ignacio Ugartechea ***(left)*** was in his 40s when Jack O'Connor visited Eibar. Now in his 70s, he goes to work each day, to his office in the factory on Calle Txonta. The firm was founded by his father, also Ignacio, in 1922, and is being carried on by his son, Ignacio the third.

There are fewer makers of low-priced guns in the Basque Country now, because they cannot compete in price with makers in emerging markets like Brazil. Still, there is Lanber, making sound but inexpensive machine-made over/unders, and Laurona, which produces a range of specialty over/unders and even inexpensive double rifles. Armas Ego makes double rifles that are modestly priced, by double-rifle standards – less than $10,000.

The 1030 is the highest-grade traditional action sidelock made by Ignacio Ugartechea today (the slightly more expensive 1042 is a rounded action). The 1030 is the only current Eibar gun with arcaded fences, in the style of a James Woodward. Ugartechea is also the only maker to offer locks with coil springs instead of leaf or V-springs. Ignacio Ugartechea, a noted competition shooter all his life, recommends coil springs because "they don't break."

In the village of Elgueta, about seven miles from Eibar, is Zabala Hermanos, a maker of a range of boxlocks that have been imported to the U.S. by several companies. Zabala is making the new Weatherby side-by-side, which was announced last year. While Zabala guns offer good value for the money, and are strong and dependable, they are not "fine" guns in the traditional sense.

One recent development that deserves mention is the making of true, fine-quality double rifles in the Basque country. Arrieta, Arrizabalaga, Armas Garbi, and Grulla all make rifles in the English style, in calibers up to 500 Nitro Express. Double rifles have been made in the Basque country for many years, but by 1968, only Victor Sarasqueta was still licensed to make them. Now, they are making a comeback, and today's rifles are the finest that have ever come from the region.

In his article, Jack O'Connor dwells at length on the price of guns in Eibar. He quotes an exchange rate of 70 pesetas to the dollar, and says that a Basque craftsman received $5 a day, with a top artisan receiving $8. In that light, a gun that sold for $300 looks quite expensive.

When I first visited Eibar in 1987, the peseta was 110 to the dollar. When the Spanish currency was merged into the Euro in 1999, the exchange rate stood at about 160 to the dollar, so the American currency had more than doubled in relative value since O'Connor's day. So, wages in Spain, while much higher at first glance, are still low compared with other parts of the world.

Today, a top engraver in the Basque country earns about $25,000 a year – vastly less than a comparable artist in London or the United States. Overall, costs in the Basque country are minimal compared to London, and to a great extent this accounts for the difference in price between a London gun and a Basque "best." There are other reasons too, though. One is that a London gun receives about 900 hours of hand labor; an Eibar gun, even a Pedro Arrizabalaga, receives 250 to 300 hours. In Eibar, a considerable amount of the coarse work of gunmaking is done by machine. Forgings are rough-shaped on milling machines, and the barrels come from a specialty barrel-maker who shapes and bores the barrel blanks, and solders the barrels and ribs. Each shop then finishes the barrels to its own standards.

Some makers, such as AYA and Ugartechea, have the capability of carrying out all operations in-house, while others contract out such specialty functions as bore-finishing, bluing, and case hardening. The

The new Kemen side-by-side is expensive, retailing for about $17,000 in the U.S. Again, the sideplates are purely decorative. The gun is a boxlock with detachable trigger group. It is heavy for a SxS, and would make an excellent live-pigeon gun.

Basques are practical people, and see no need to reinvent the wheel. If an operation can be performed more economically by a specialist, they do it -- as long as the quality is up to snuff for a particular gun.

While this is anathema (to hear them tell it) to the British, it is exactly the way gunmaking was carried on for centuries in the second city of English gunmaking, Birmingham. And many excellent guns came out of Birmingham.

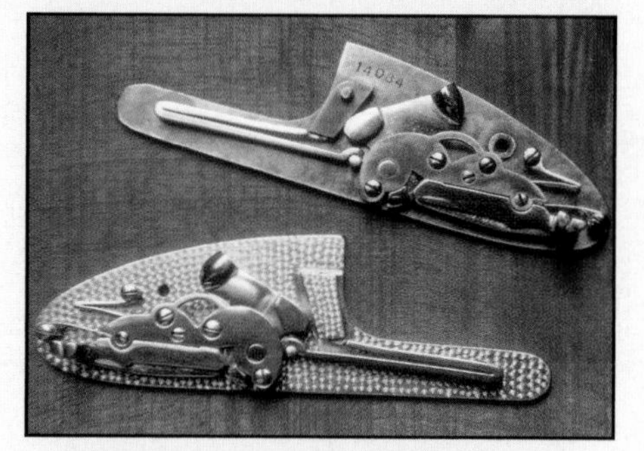

Locks from Pedro Arrizabalaga. The interior of the lock is as much an art form as the exterior. Top is case-hardened and polished, while the bottom lock is jewelled and polished. Locks can also be gold-plated, or with some parts blued. These are questions most American gun buyers have never had to ponder.

• • •

Jack O'Connor acquired several fine guns from the Basque country, including two AYAs and two Arizagas. Although he sold many of his guns and rifles late in his life, he hung onto his Spanish guns until the end, and they are still in his family – a good indication of his high regard for the Basques and their guns.

If O'Connor were to return to Eibar today, he would find a few changes, but only a few. The town is much as he left it, except for the addition of the A-8 motorway that skirts the town and relieves some of the traffic congestion in the narrow streets. The lovely old proof house is gone, relocated to a soul-free industrial park outside of town.

If he walked into Armas Garbi, or Ignacio Ugartechea's office, he would probably notice no difference at all. Many of the same craftsmen would be leaning over the same vise, fashioning guns with the very same tools.

Where O'Connor would see a huge difference is in the United States.

Pedro Arrizabalaga's stockmaker, Pedro Iriondo. His father, Antonio Iriondo, was one of the original partners in the company, and a friend of Charles Askins. The blanks are top-grade English walnut, some from Spain, some from as far away as Turkey.

Today, the Basque country is recognized as one of the great gunmaking centers of the world, and the finest products of Eibar and Elgoibar are displayed here at the best gun shows. There are two-dozen importers, and every year a thousand or more custom-made Spanish guns are delivered to discriminating American shotgunners.

O'Connor had a hand in making that happen, and in preserving the Basque gunmaking tradition. That alone, I suspect, would make him smile.

• • •

Terry Wieland is a regular visitor to Eibar, and author of Spanish Best – The Fine Shotguns of Spain, *recently released in an updated and expanded second edition by Countrysport Press.*

The Lost Guns of Nepal

by John Walter

THE SMALL, LAND-locked kingdom of Nepal, squeezed against the Himalayas by India to the south and China to the north, remains a mysterious place even today. Few Asian states have had such a turbulent past; and not until 1950 was a highway punched through the passes to link Nepal with the modern world.

The area that is now Nepal was once a patchwork of tiny states grouped around settlements in the strategically important Tarai, the fertile central valley. Traditions of enmity ensured that life was often cheap currency. The capture of Kirtipur, in the kingdom of Pathan, was typical of mid-eighteenth century Nepalese life. The inhabitants were promised an amnesty if they surrendered, but the victorious Gorkha king then ordered that the lips and noses of the Pathan men were to be cut off! He even renamed the town *Naskatipur*—'Cut-Nose City'—as a warning to his foes.

The conquest of the Kathmandu valley was successfully completed in 1768. The new King of Nepal, Prithvi Narayan Shah of Gorkha, died in 1775 but expansion careered onward until a reckless invasion of Tibet drew the Chinese into the fray. The Nepalese were forced back in 1792, and, in a remarkable about-turn, requested the help of the British East India Company. However, the conclusion of peace led to the immediate expulsion of the Company's Commissioner from Kathamandu.

In 1799, after King Rana Bahadur Shah had been deposed, a commercial agreement was signed with the East India Company. When the king returned from exile, however, he brought with him a Gorkha noble named Bhimsen Thapa and co-operation with the British once again ceased. Thapa had soon been appointed prime minister, the murder of the king in 1807 allowing him not only to become co-regent but also to expand Nepalese territory into the fertile plains of northern India.

The battle of Gujrat (also 'Gujarat' or 'Goojerat'), fought in February 1849, brought the Second Sikh War to an end. Many guns taken from the Sikh armies seem to have ended their days in Nepal.

The killing in April 1814 of eighteen of its border policemen forced the East India Company to declare war, but the first campaigns simply proved how poorly European-style tactics were adapted to mountain-fighting. The Nepalese beat back three of the four columns sent to face them, inflicting heavy losses in men and materiel, and only General Sir David Ochterlony was able to make progress.

After routing the forces of Amarsing Thapa in the Garwhal valley in 1815, Ochterlony paused. However, when Bhimsen Thapa failed to ratify the peace agreement, the British advanced again and gained important victories around

This flintlock East India Company pistol, dating from 1802, displays the 'bale' mark on the lock plate, the butt and the barrel-top. *Courtesy of auctioneers Weller & Dufty Ltd, Birmingham, England.*

A typical detached lock from Lagan Silekhana. This is one of the 'coat of arms' pattern often mistakenly associated with the Sikhs.

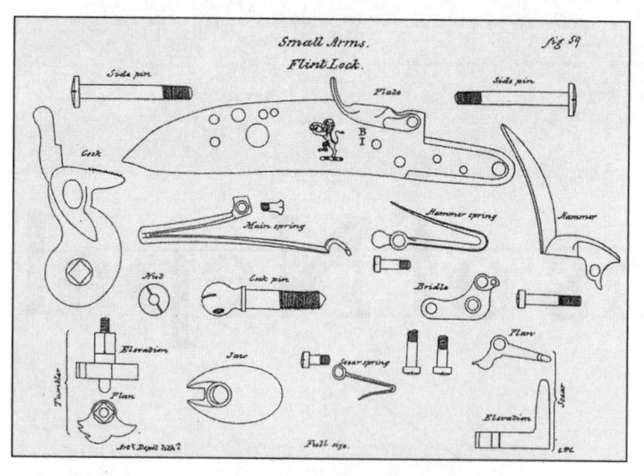

A drawing of a typical East India company flintlock, dismantled into its components. This is a Baker lock, which replaced the Windus pattern after 1818. Note the view mark on the lockplate, which would date this gun to 1838/39.

Makwanpur. Realizing that these successes would soon threaten Kathmandu itself, the Nepalese sued for peace and the Treaty of Sagauli was signed in 1816.

The treaty not only brought an end to the conflict but also allowed the British, greatly impressed by the courage of their opponents, to recruit Nepalese troops of their own—the beginning of a long and honorable tradition of service.[1] The immediate effect on Nepal was catastrophic, with the loss of almost all the fertile Tarai, but much of the sequestered land had been returned within a few years.

By the 1820s, Bhimsen Thapa, realizing that his forces lacked efficient firearms, was determined to modernize the Nepalese arms industry. It is assumed that assistance was provided by the British, probably through the East India Company; guns were undoubtedly provided from Company stores in this period, and an ability to copy them, which has always been a skill in the Indian sub-continent, ensured that surprisingly accurate facsimiles were soon being made.

Bhimsen Thapa's tenure of office lasted until 1837, when he was arraigned on a charge of murdering one of the king's sons. An eight-month trial ended in acquittal, but the appointment of an archenemy to the prime ministership then led to a re-trial. Imprisoned and tortured, Thapa committed suicide in August 1839 when threatened with the public humiliation of his wives and daughters. His senior wife hanged herself from a window in the Thapa palace of Lagan Silekhana, which subsequently became the royal armory.

Nepal's politics reverted to near-anarchy, until the emergence in the 1840s of Jang Bahadur Kunwar, a great-nephew of Bhimsen Thapa. Jang Bahadur visited Britain in 1850-1, strengthening links between the two countries, and was determined to offer his support to British aims—if only to regain land that had been ceded by Nepal in 1816. An offer to supply six regiments to garrison the Punjab in the wake of the First Sikh War was declined, but, when the Indian Mutiny began in 1857, a similar offer was too good to refuse.

The Nepalese contingent was surprisingly large. Several thousand men were employed after the recapture of Delhi, and another large contingent, commanded by Jang Bahadur personally, fought in the vicinity of Gorakhpur and Lucknow before returning home in triumph in March 1858. Most of the Nepalese had been re-armed with East India Company cap-locks. The disbanding of the East India Company armies after the Mutiny may have allowed additional guns to be sent to equip the regiments that had remained in Nepal, the strength of the Nepalese army at this time being reckoned as about 25,000.

The exposure of Nepalese forces to the weapons of a leading European power also encouraged Jang Bahadur to modernize his ordnance department. By this time, the facilities were capable of making surprisingly sophisticated products—including copies of P/53-type 'Enfield' rifle-muskets and, amazingly, Sharps rifles and carbines. Production was undoubtedly substantial, judged by the quantities of guns that have been retrieved from Nepal.

The success of the manufacturing program allowed Snider breech-loaders to be made, and then a large number of dropping-block Gahendra rifles. The Bira Gun, a two-barreled mechanically

The contents of Lagan Silekhana were painstakingly removed, piece by piece. It was reckoned to be dangerous to use the internal stairways, so the guns were passed down from window to window.

1. The Gurkha units of the British Army have had a glorious history, winning 26 Victoria Crosses (the highest British decoration for gallantry, comparable to the U.S. Medal of Honor).

operated machinegun derived from the Gardner Gun, was also made in small numbers in the 1890s.

Recent times

The Nepalese arms-making industry has never been able to supply enough guns to equip the armed forces. There is no doubt that the British Martini-Henry rifle was the most important import statistically, supply amounting to tens of thousands prior to 1914, but later acquisitions included Lee-Enfield rifles; Vickers and British-made Lewis machineguns; Sten and U.S. M3 'Grease Gun' submachine guns; and a broad selection of handguns.

By the late 1990s, left-wing terrorist activity was threatening to become a full-blown civil war and international pressure was applied to modernize the Nepalese army. Acquiring U.S. military equipment, including M16A1 rifles, persuaded the Nepalese government to sell the contents of the principal store-house—the former royal palace of Lagan Silekhana—and it is these that form the basis for the initiative undertaken by Christian Cranmer of International Military Antiques, Inc., and his partner Sudhir Windlass of the Atlanta Cutlery Corporation.

Englishman Cranmer first learned of the antiquated weapons that had accumulated in Lagan Silekhana in 1969, and soon became fascinated by the story. When Interarms announced the purchase of the arsenal in 1973, all seemed lost—until it was realized, some years later, that only a part of the weaponry had been taken. It took time to restore contacts with Nepal, but finally, in the early 1990s, Cranmer and Windlass gained access to Lagan Silekhana to see for themselves what remained in store. Eventually, the offer made by a partnership of International Military Antiques and the Atlanta Cutlery Corporation was accepted; and more than thirty containers were shipped to the U.S.A. and Britain in the summer of 2003.

Much of the material had been undisturbed for more than a hundred years, and there were some exciting surprises. For example, in addition to the firearms and the edged weapons, huge quantities of original British musket flints from the time of the Napoleonic wars were found in a basement…and four tons of original musket balls had been packed in an old latrine!

Recording the colossal amount of information that can be gleaned from such a large number of weapons is a painstaking, time-consuming process that has only just begun. The goal is to produce a detailed study of the subject in the summer of 2004, *The Lost Guns of the Gurkhas*, and also to include some of the information in a new 'overview' book, *British Military Firearms 1776-1945*, which should appear towards the end of the year.

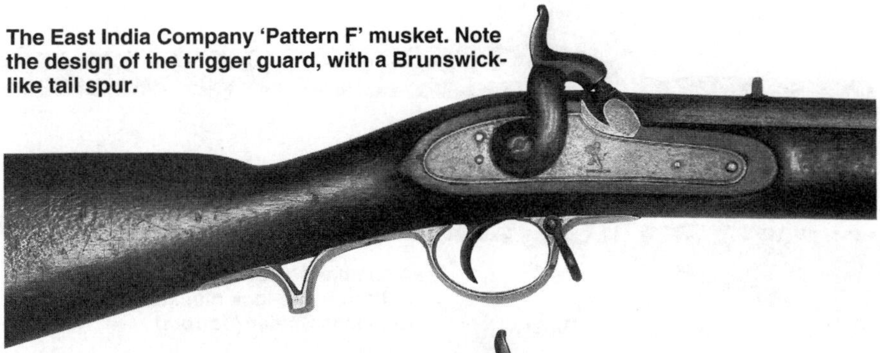

There are far too many questions to be answered in this article, but it is possible—even at this stage—to offer new information about some of the guns, particularly the single-shot designs made prior to 1900.

The East India Company 'Pattern F' musket. Note the design of the trigger guard, with a Brunswick-like tail spur.

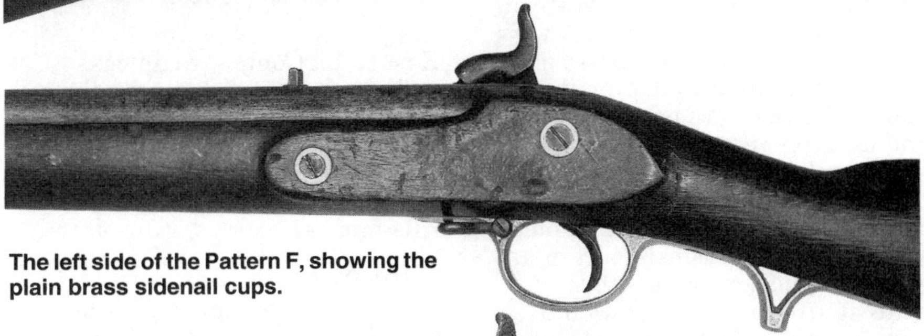

The left side of the Pattern F, showing the plain brass sidenail cups.

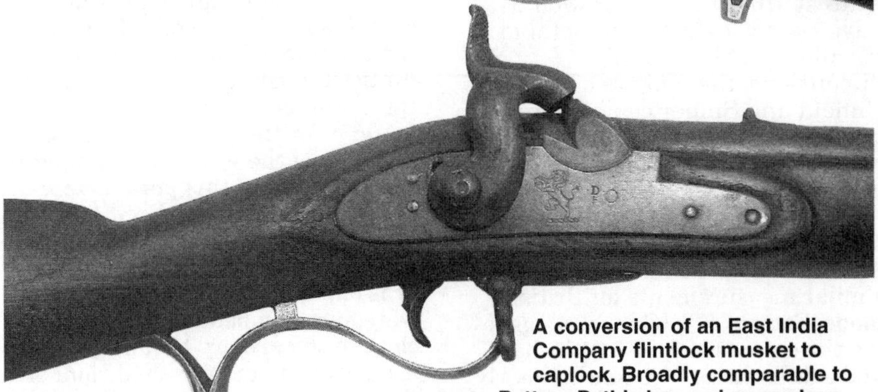

A conversion of an East India Company flintlock musket to caplock. Broadly comparable to Pattern B, this has a view-mark on the lockplate that dates it to 1840/41.

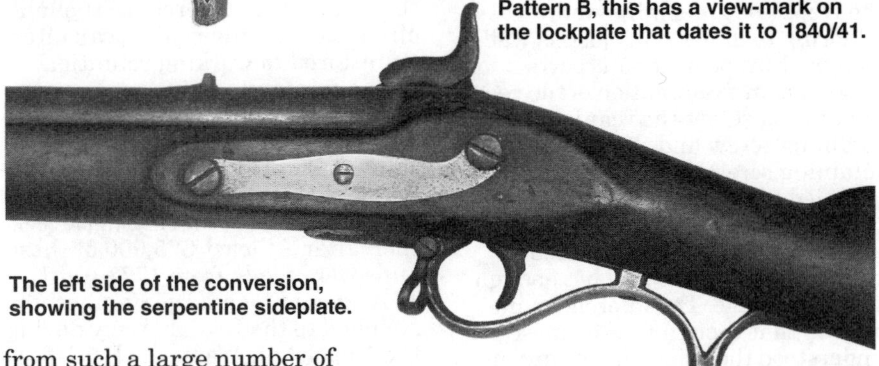

The left side of the conversion, showing the serpentine sideplate.

The guns…

The Indian sub-continent is renowned for its metalwork, and Nepal has been no exception. Edged weapons have been made for centuries, and cannon-founding had been successfully undertaken, but there is as yet no evidence that a large-scale small-arms industry operated prior to the 1820s. It is assumed that the consolidation of the army was initially accomplished with guns that had been purchased in India.

The small-arms made in Nepal are not 'Native Guns', a disparaging term now used to classify 'one-off' products of individual gunsmiths. Of course, few of the guns made in nineteenth-century India offered the consistency of dimensions or repetitive subtleties of design to be expected from service-issue

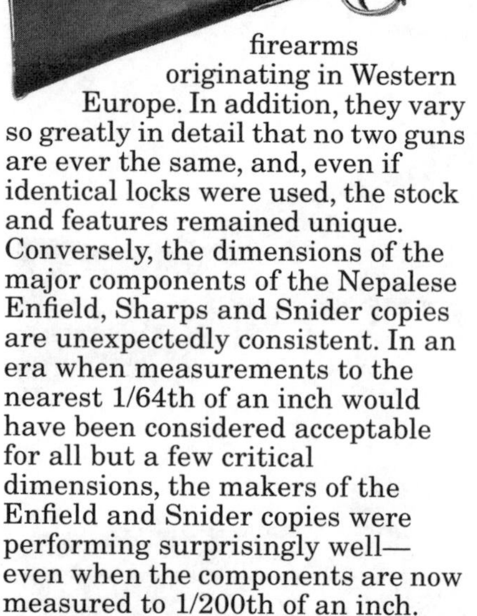

A comparison of the East India Company Pattern F cap-lock musket *(top)* and the Nepalese Snider *(bottom)*.

firearms originating in Western Europe. In addition, they vary so greatly in detail that no two guns are ever the same, and, even if identical locks were used, the stock and features remained unique. Conversely, the dimensions of the major components of the Nepalese Enfield, Sharps and Snider copies are unexpectedly consistent. In an era when measurements to the nearest 1/64th of an inch would have been considered acceptable for all but a few critical dimensions, the makers of the Enfield and Snider copies were performing surprisingly well—even when the components are now measured to 1/200th of an inch.

Measuring the length of five P/53-copy lock plates gave 5.42-5.45 inches, a difference of only 0.03-inch; similar measurements for British-made 'Pattern F' EIC muskets gave measurements of 5.87-5.91 inches and a difference of 0.04-inch. Clearly, the Nepalese gunsmiths were adhering to dimensions just as well as their European counterparts. However, an examination of the rear upper tang screw, the rear lockplate retaining screw and the buttplate retaining screw of a Sharps carbine revealed not only that all three had been hand-forged on an anvil, but also that the slots were pressed-in while the metal was still hot enough to be malleable. The inference can only be that though the Nepalese understood the principles of gauging, and were operating some type of view-system to ensure continuity, their machine tools were limited to pole-lathes and trip hammers.

Another popular misconception that must be corrected concerns the weapons of the East India Company, which are often claimed to have been 'made in India' and condemned as inferior. Company guns were actually assembled in London from parts made largely in Birmingham; were subjected to the rigors of London Gunmakers' Company proof; went through a system of inspection *(called 'View' at the time)* similar to that applied by the British Board of Ordnance; and often incorporated refinements not seen on British regulation firearms of the day. For example, many of the East India Company caplocks embodied a swivel between the mainspring limb and tumbler—a refinement not accepted by the Board of Ordnance until the introduction of the P/1853 Enfield rifle-musket.

Flintlocks

The consignment from Nepal contains a selection of old British Army and East India Company flintlock muskets, captured during the campaigns of 1814-16 or given in aid after the Treaty of Sagauli.

Many of the weapons supplied to the Nepalese in this period were subsequently cannibalized once they had become unserviceable, to retrieve the locks and the valuable brass mounts. Some of these locks were found embedded in the ground close to the armory buildings, and are generally in poor condition; but those from the storerooms, though often superficially rusted, can often be restored to working condition with a minimum of fuss.

Most of the locks prove to be East India Company issue of the so-called 'Windus Pattern', with a rounded lockplate and a swan-neck cock to 1812/13, or a ring-neck cock thereafter. At least 675,000 of these guns were made from 1771 until 1818, including a large number supplied to the British Army during the Napoleonic Wars; the British regulation 'India Pattern', introduced in 1797, was a copy of the Company design.

EIC locks made prior to 1808 were marked with the 'bale', a heart quartered with the letters V E I C beneath the number '4' *(actually the Christian Cross disguised)*. Those made after 1808 displayed a 'rampant guardant' lion holding a globe in its paws—a useful dating aid. British ordnance-pattern locks may be identified by their own special markings, and there are many others displaying nothing but a crude attempt at copying a European coat-of-arms. These marks are said to have been applied to the firearms of the Sikhs during the reign of Ranjit Singh (1801-39); substantial quantities of weapons were then captured by British forces during the Sikh Wars (1845-6; 1848-9), and sent to Nepal. However, they are Nepalese.

1802
4
V
E I
C

A typical pre-1808 mark of the United East India Company: 'V' was an archaism, used as a substitute for 'U', and '4' was actually a cross—camouflaged to avoid overt Christian connotations.

Cap-lock muskets

The P/1842 was the first newly made caplock to be issued throughout the British Army, the preceding P/1839 being a converted flintlock. However, guns with 'India Service' connotations usually prove to have been made for the British East India Company: some were given to the Nepalese units that served the British during the Mutiny of 1857 and others went to Nepal shortly after control of the political and military governance of EIC territories passed to the British Crown. Most of the EIC guns retrieved from Nepal were of 'F' type, interspersed with a small number of 'E' examples—and even an occasional converted flintlock.

The East India Company 'Pattern A' musket of 1840 was a converted flintlock with a nipple lump brazed into the existing barrel, Baker-type brass furniture, and a 'three-motion' or 'Z'-slot bayonet. The 'Pattern B' guns were similar, but the nipple was an integral part of a new plug that replaced the rear of the original barrel.

The conversions are readily recognizable, as they have old flintlock-type lockplates with a squared rise ahead of the nipple. Only about 10,000 of them were made in 1840. 'Pattern C' was the first new gun, but undoubtedly made use of components that were already in existence. Consequently, it amalgamated a plug-type breech with an 'Old Series' side-lock and a two-motion bayonet retained by a spring on the socket body locating against the front-sight block. The furniture duplicated that of the Baker-type light infantry musket. About 43,500 'C'-type caplock muskets were made in 1840-2.

'Pattern D' was similar to the 'C' version, excepting that it usually had a vertically moving 'Hanoverian Spring' bayonet catch beneath the muzzle and a spurred new-type trigger guard. Only about ten thousand guns were made in 1841-2.

'Pattern E' was the first of the entirely new guns, about 61,000 being made in 1842-5 with the 'New Series' side-lock, a hammer-welded nipple lump, and new cast-brass furniture that included a spurred Brunswick-type trigger guard. The tail pipe was replaced by a ramrod-retaining spring let into the forend, and two small brass side-nail cups replaced the serpentine sideplate. The Hanoverian-type bayonet catch protruded from the nose cap beneath the muzzle. About 61,000 guns were made in 1842-5.

The 'Pattern F' musket was the perfected pattern, more than 200,000 being made in 1845-51. It was essentially similar to the 'E'-type, but had a projecting catch beneath the muzzle that passed through a small aperture in the base ring of the bayonet socket. The front sight also took a different form.

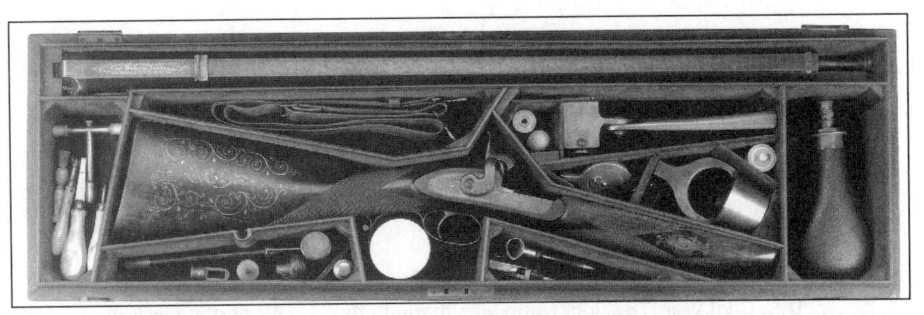

Typical of the sporting guns purchased by individual officers for use in India, this is a 4-bore elephant gun by Charles Osborne of Birmingham.

The EIC bale mark was replaced by a lion-and-globe, pictured here on a typical caplock musket.

Measurements revealed that Pattern F guns average 54.9 inches overall, with 39-inch barrels, and weigh about ten pounds. Bore diameter is difficult to measure accurately, owing to the effects of wear and damage, but an average of five random measurements gave 0.748-inch against a theoretical standard 'musket bore' of 0.753-inch. The standard '14-1/2 to the pound' projectile weighed about 523 grains, and was fired with a 4 1/2-dram (123 grains) charge of blackpowder. No reliable muzzle velocity figures are available for the P/42 or its East India Company equivalents, but were probably about 1500 ft/sec.[2]

The lockplates bear the lion-and-crown crest of the East India Company, adopted in 1808. Close examination reveals the marks to have been stamped, but differences may be seen in the design of each punch owing to the involvement of several 'setters-up' (assemblers).

Nepalese P/53 Enfield copies were found in large numbers.

The guns all display London gunmakers' proof marks—a crown above a 'GP' monogram and a crown above 'V'—in addition to East India Company viewers' marks of the type applied after 1837/8, combining a year-date letter from 'A' to 'Q' (without 'I', 'J' or 'O') with a number denoting an individual inspector. Consequently, two muskets with complete markings can be dated to 1845/6 ('K' above '8') and 1851/2 or later ('Q' above '8'). Without exception, the guns also bear a proliferation of Nagari[3] markings on the buttplates and trigger guards. Often no more than issue numbers, these can sometimes include regimental identifiers.

Caplock rifle-muskets

The layout and individual components of the 577-caliber P/1853 Enfield copies are essentially similar to the guns made for the British Army in the 1850s and 1860s, and also to the many guns supplied by the English gun trade to Federals and Confederates alike during the American Civil War.

Enfield type rifle-muskets fired a 530-grain projectile with a cavity in the base, originally fitted with a boxwood plug to facilitate expansion. The external diameter of the bullet was reduced from 0.568-inch to 0.550-inch for India Service in July 1858, followed by acceptance in the British Army in February 1859. A clay plug—cheaper and easier to make—was substituted for boxwood in December 1863. The standard charge was 2-1/2 drams (68 grains) of RFG powder; no reliable muzzle-velocity figures have been found, but were probably similar to the 58-caliber U.S. M1855 rifle-musket: about 1000 ft/sec.

The barrels are retained by three iron bands held by springs let into the forend. Standard British guns were rifled with three broad grooves, each deepening from 0.05-inch at the muzzle to 0.013-inch at the breech, but the rifling of the Nepalese version is difficult to assess. It appears to share the profile of the original, but the bore *(on some guns at least)* tapers

2. Experiments undertaken in Washington Arsenal in 1843-4, with the standard US Army 69-caliber cap-lock musket (42-inch barrel), gave 1561 ft/sec with British 'Waltham Abbey musket powder'. Trials with U.S.-made Du Pont A4 musket powder gave figures of 1470 and 1499 ft/sec.

3. The Nepali language is written in *Nagari* or 'Nagri' script, derived directly from Devanagari and ultimately from Sanskrit. Consequently, the presence of characters of this type does not necessarily prove direct links with Nepal and supporting evidence must be sought.

Two P/53 Enfield rifle-muskets, of a type that was popular during the U.S. Civil War. The upper gun was made in the U.S.A., and is marked 'WINDSOR' on the lockplate; the lower example is marked 'TOWER'.

sufficiently to make the presence of rifling grooves difficult to detect at the muzzle. This was probably due to difficulties encountered in supporting the barrel during the rifling process.

The furniture is brass, and the side lock is retained by two side nails (screws) set in brass cups. Swivels may be found on the upper band and the front of the trigger guard; a ramrod is carried; there is a tangent-leaf rear sight on the barrel; and a socket bayonet can be locked around the front-sight base. The external barrel diameter was measured as 0.752-inch (average of five measurements).

There is surprisingly delicate two-line engraving around the periphery of the sideplate and on the body of the hammer, and light floral-scroll decoration may be seen on the flat of the cock-head immediately above its junction with the body. Close examination of a gun that had been cleaned revealed no obvious external markings, excepting Nagari characters on the trigger guard, butt, barrel and rear sight. The only marks evident on the 'hidden parts' of the dismantled P/53 were numbers and what could perhaps be the touch-marks of individual inspectors, the most obvious having the appearance of the soles of two feet. These cannot be linked with the British Army issue—no P/1853 Enfields were ever issued to the East India Company—and it is concluded that the rifle-muskets were made in Nepal.

Jang Bahadur Rana is known to have sought 'mainsprings and fore-springs' in Britain in 1860, supposedly to enable the Nepalese to make flintlock muskets, but he also ordered a million percussion caps from London gunmaker James Purdey in the same period. It is probable that P/1853 copies were made instead, circumstantial evidence suggesting that work on the rifle-muskets had already begun by 1862.

Caplock rifles

Distinguished by its barrel, with two deep grooves designed to receive the belt on the ball, the Brunswick Rifle served both the British Army and the forces of the East India Company. Caliber was nominally 0.704, though measurements of a typical example gave a bore diameter of 0.699-inch across the lands and 0.761-inch across grooves that make a turn in the length of the barrel. The perfected bullets, made on a special compressor, weighed '12-1/2 to the pound' (559 grains); the charge was 2-1/2 drams (68 grains) of blackpowder.

The original British guns had back-action locks, designed by George Lovell, that were held by a side nail (bolt) running through the stock from the left and by a small wood screw at the tail of the lockplate. However, the back-action lock proved to be unsatisfactory, weakening the butt-wrist too greatly, and had soon been replaced by a conventional sidelock. Most Brunswick rifles have straight-comb butts with a two-chamber patch box, and a hinged brass lid, let into the right side. The brass trigger guard has a distinctive spur at the tail.

There were four types of East India Company Brunswick. The earliest of these 'Two-Grooved Percussion Rifles', dating from 1840-2, had a back-action lock, a twist-steel barrel, and a bar at the muzzle for a Baker-type sword bayonet with a blade of about 22-3/4in. The guns were about 46in long, with thirty-inch barrels, and weighed 9lb 6oz. Production is estimated to have totaled about 3800 guns.

The second-type EIC gun, the most common of the sub-varieties with a total output of about 8500 (1843-6), had a swivel-type sidelock. A large disc-headed rammer replaced the original reversible cup-head design at this time. The third version—exceptionally rare—had the bayonet bar set back from the muzzle, receiving a Brunswick-type sword bayonet with a waisted blade; and the fourth type, otherwise identical with its immediate predecessor, had a barrel of plain iron instead of twist-steel. Little more than a hundred third-type guns were made in 1846, followed by two thousand of the fourth type in 1848-9.

Meager production, owing to the specialized nature of the issue of Brunswick Rifles, restricted the distribution of guns in Nepal. There were undoubtedly some full-length rifles, but also a handful of carbine conversions with their barrels cut to 21-11/16 inches, giving an overall length of 37-11/16 inches and a weight of 7lbs 12oz. The front sights have been re-attached to the muzzle, but the original bayonet bars have been discarded.

A smoothbore version of the Brunswick was developed in Britain in 1841, possibly developed for serjeants of infantry regiments, to complement the P/39 and P/42 muskets. Guns of this type were similar to the standard rifled pattern externally, accepting a large brass-hilted sword bayonet with a knuckle bow, but had plain trigger guards and simple standing-block rear sights. No details have yet been found in Board of Ordnance

The lock and rear sight of a Nepalese P/53 copy, difficult to distinguish at a glance from the British guns.

The left side of the Nepalese P/53, showing the lugged sidenail cups.

This smoothbore version of the Brunswick rifle was only made in small numbers, allegedly for trials as a serjeants' fusil. However, substantial quantities of essentially similar guns have been found in Nepal.

records, but the retrieval of two hundred ex-Nepalese guns fitting this general description may indicate that enough were made to allow large-scale field trials.

Caplock carbines

The consignment purchased in Nepal contained a variety of guns that lie outside regulation British and East India Company patterns. Some of these were undoubtedly acquired by individuals—usually officers—but others were made in quantity for irregular units, often financed privately by their colonels.

The carbines are all short-barreled, with conventional sidelocks and full-length stocks retained by keys. The position and design of the sling swivels vary, there is some variety in the sights, and the sling bars *(where present)* take differing forms.

There are at least ten recognizably different patterns among the ex-Nepalese guns, and, presumably more to find once the inventory has been completed. They include standard East India Company Victoria (cavalry) carbines, about 5820 being made from 1842/3 to 1846/7. The gun examined in detail is 37-7/16 inches long, with a 21 5/8-inch smooth-bored iron barrel, and weighs 7lbs., 3oz. The barrel is held in the stock by a plug-type breech and two keys entering laterally from the left side. The bore measures 0.743-inch.

A fixed standing-block rear sight is brazed to the barrel and the sidelock is a typical East India Company pattern with a swivel between the tumbler and the mainspring. The gun has a spurred trigger guard; a flanged nose cap; a swivel rammer; sling swivels through the butt, trigger-guard bow and forend; and a wrought-iron sling bar on the left side of the breech.

The lion-and-globe mark is pressed into the lockplate ahead of the cock, and repeated, rather crudely, on the right side of the butt; there are London proof marks on the barrel; and a view mark reading 'F' above '13' shows that the gun was set-up in the 1842/3 financial year.

The breech of the carbine supplied by William Garden of London to the Bengal XIII Irregular Cavalry, probably about 1850. Note the leather sweatband around the butt-wrist and the lugged cup for the sling-bar retaining screw.

The left side of the Bengal cavalry carbine, showing the sling bar.

Typical of the non-regulation patterns is a carbine supplied by William Garden[4] of London to the 13th Bengal Irregular Cavalry, which gained this particular designation in September 1847. A lightweight version of the regulation EIC cavalry carbine, this elegant little gun is stocked to the muzzle and has a 21 1/32-inch Damascus-twist smooth-bored barrel with a caliber of 0.735-inch. It is about 37 inches long and weighs only 5lb 7oz. The rear sight, a standing block at the junction of the breech-plug tang and the barrel, is used in conjunction with a small front sight made as part of a saddle that has been brazed to the muzzle.

The sidelock displays the double-line and floral-scroll decoration that

Some of the Sharps rifles retrieved from Lagan Silekhana.

4. William Garden was a 'furnisher', more of an entrepreneur than a gunsmith, and it is assumed that the carbine was made elsewhere in London. His marks have also been found on a variety of caplocks supplied to the Scinde Irregular Horse in the East India Company's Bombay Presidency—including single-barrelled carbines, and single- and double-barrelled pistols.

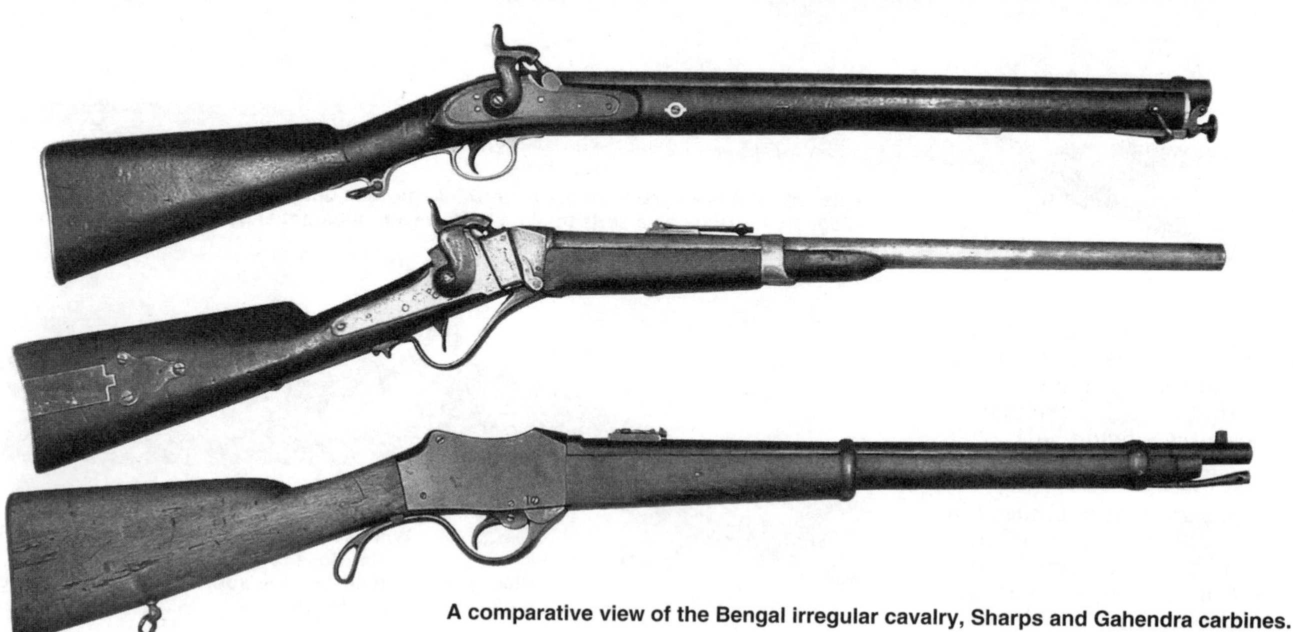

A comparative view of the Bengal irregular cavalry, Sharps and Gahendra carbines.

typified British military firearms of this period, and the trigger lever is attractively blued. A wrought-iron sling bar, complete with two iron split-rings, lies on the left side of the breech.

The walnut stock has a leather sweatband around the wrist, and good-quality 'white brass' mounts. The round-ended trigger guard has a tail spur, and, interestingly, the flared front rammer-pipe is formed integrally with the nose cap. The rammer is a swivel pattern.

The barrel has London proof marks, and the mark of the supplier, *GARDEN. 200. PICCADILLY. LONDON*, running from the breech to the muzzle. The lockplate is clearly marked IRREGULAR above XIII and CAVALRY, the large roman numerals being much the same width as the other two lines. No Nagari marks are to be seen.

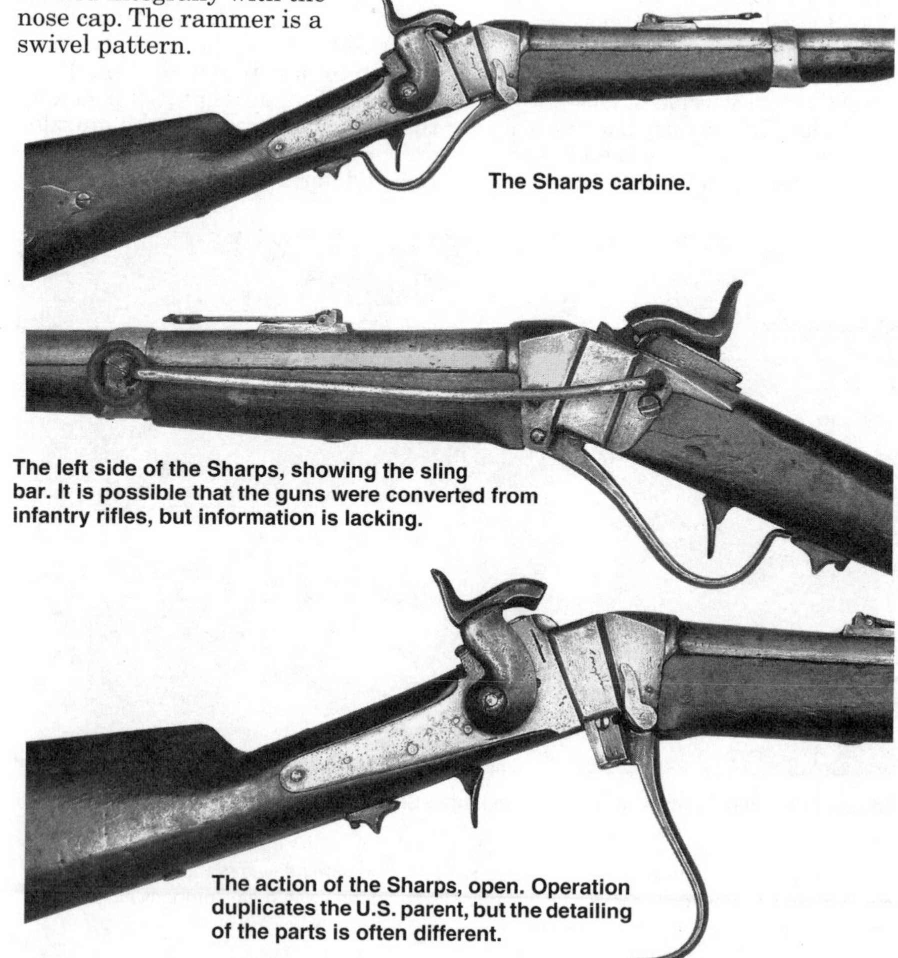

The Sharps carbine.

The left side of the Sharps, showing the sling bar. It is possible that the guns were converted from infantry rifles, but information is lacking.

The action of the Sharps, open. Operation duplicates the U.S. parent, but the detailing of the parts is often different.

Sharps breech-loaders

These fascinating guns were found in Nepal in two types, a full-length infantry rifle and a short-barreled carbine. With one or two insignificant exceptions, the features are common to both types.

Patented in the U.S.A. in 1848 by Christian Sharps, production of these guns began on a small scale in the late 1840s, and, by 1851, most of the development problems had been overcome. Large-scale series production began in 1852, and a succession of improved patterns followed until the 'New Model' appeared in 1859. Most of the early guns were made by Robbins & Lawrence under contract to Sharps, but the partnership failed in 1856.

At much the same time, Christian Sharps lost patience with Richard Lawrence, who was also acting as the superintendent of the Hartford, Connecticut, manufactory, and moved on to other things; most of the improvements made in the Sharps rifle from the mid-1850s onwards, therefore, were due to Lawrence—including a perfected gas-seal, an automatic priming-pellet feeder system, and the change from a slanting breech to a vertical design.

The Nepalese rifle is essentially the 1853-type Sharps, but its history is obscure. Breech-loading cavalry carbines (*Panchadi bata bhamya risala banduk*) were being made in 1863 for a 'new cavalry unit', but this does not explain the chronology and issue of the rifles. However, the men of the special "prime minister's bodyguard", the *Bijuli garad*, may have been the intended recipients. During his visit to Britain in 1850-1, Jang Bahadur is known to have purchased sufficient firearms from the gunmakers Purdey and

Lancaster to equip a corps of 150-200 men,[5] and the Sharps, then 'cutting-edge' technology, may have been replacements for these particular muzzleloaders in the 1860s.

Inspiration probably came from the issues of Sharps carbines to five British Army cavalry regiments in India, part of an order for 6000 that had been placed in the U.S.A. in January, 1856 and fulfilled by March, 1858. However, U.S. participation in the manufacturing process cannot be entirely ruled out.

The overall design of the Nepalese Sharps approximates closely to the original U.S.-made guns, with a breechblock (or 'slide') that runs diagonally down and forward in the iron receiver as the action opens. A back-action lock is set in the right side of the stock immediately behind the receiver.

The similarities extend to fitting a pellet-feed system and duplicating the distinctive flat-comb butt, but the breechblock or 'slide' housing (rectangular on U.S.-made guns) has a distinctly wedge-shape appearance. U.S.-made Sharps rifles and carbines also had an elegant extension to the operating-lever pivot pin to prevent the pin being detached accidentally, yet allow it to be removed readily when required. This feature is absent from the Nepalese Sharps rifles, which have an operating-lever pin doubling as the rear sling-swivel retainer. The carbines do have an extension to the operating-lever pivot pin, but the design and construction, and the position of the 'retaining stud', suggests that the manufacturer of the carbines did not understand the purpose of the original components.

'A Gurkha picket in Afghanistan, 1878', an engraving published in the *Illustrated London News* after an illustration by the renowned British military artist Richard Caton Woodville. The gun appears to be a P/53 Enfield, though some 'artistic license' has been taken by the engraver!

The Nepalese guns have surprisingly heavy barrels, with far thicker walls than, for example, the P/1853-type copies or the Sniders. A typical rifle is 56.9 inches long, with a 40.4-inch barrel; a typical carbine measures 37.7 inches overall and has a 21.7-inch barrel. Bore diameter was measured as 0.520-inch for a typical rifle and 0.527-inch for a representative carbine, with three grooves turning to the right. The diameter of the carbine muzzle is greater than the rifle, suggesting that a full-length barrel may have been cut-down to carbine length either during the manufacturing process or at a later date. The comparative crudity of the barrel band may support the idea of conversion, but scientific comparison of the wood of the butt and forend has yet to be completed.

Detaching the lock plate from the carbine revealed a standard 1853-pattern Sharps mechanism, with a separate sear spring. The tumbler and the sear are supported by a bridle, and the trigger is pivoted on the plate let into the underside of the butt. The main spring, which presses upward on the heel of the hammer, is still in working order.

The brass shoulder plate is retained by two screws, and the forend is held by a combination of three iron bands, secured by springs, and a bolt that runs up into the underside of the barrel. It is assumed that a socket bayonet could be locked around the front sight. The rifles also have a rear sight consisting of a standing block, with a shallow 'V', and an exceptionally long *(and very flimsy)* leaf that pivots backwards to lie on the barrel surface. The carbine sight is similar, but the leaf is shorter and pivots forward.

The half-stocked carbine is similar mechanically to the rifle, but a patch-box, let into the right side of the butt, has a brass lid that pivots outward to reveal a small chamber. A sling bar on the left side of the breech screws directly into the frame at the rear and is held at the front by a screw in a brass cup.

Snider breech-loaders

François Eugène Schneider of Paris and Jacob Snider, Jr, 'of the United States of America' jointly received British Patent 1828 in June 1862 for their breech-loading system, and the British government ultimately decided that it was the best method of converting cap-locks to fire self-contained cartridges. The U.S. Army tested two carbine-like Snider short rifles in 1865-6, as 'Guns No. 62' and 'Gun No. 63', but preferred the Allin conversion of the Springfield rifle musket.[6]

Officially accepted in September 1866, after substantial quantities had been issued for field trials, the British rifles first saw large-scale service in the Abyssinian campaign of 1868. They proved to be sturdy and serviceable, until the spring-loaded detent in the standing breech wore far enough to allow the breechblock to spring open as the gun fired. Though this was not especially dangerous, it was too unnerving to be permissible; a search for a satisfactory breech-lock was resolved when Edward Bond, Managing Director of the London Small Arms Company, submitted a suitable design. This was adopted for the Mark III or 'Bolted Action' rifle in January 1869.

The ammunition was less successful. The trials guns had chambered cartridges with bodies of papier-mâché, but these were soon replaced by metal-case rounds with Pottet-style bases. These also failed to impress the authorities, until Colonel Edward Boxer of the Royal Laboratory perfected a case of rolled brass sheet with a strengthened base. By the introduction of the Mark IX ball round in 1871, most of the early problems had been overcome.

The short straight-case cartridge was about 2.45 inches long, containing 70 grains of RFG powder and a 0.573-inch diameter 480-grain lead bullet lubricated with beeswax. The bullet had a hollow cavity in the nose, hidden by a covering of spun lead, and a clay plug in the base to assist expansion. According to the 1888 edition of the

---

5. One Purdey-made caplock pistol has been found, with an octagonal Damascus-type barrel of 'swamped' form (increasing in width towards the muzzle) and refinements such as a platinum plug in the nipple bolster. Caliber is probably 0.442 (54 Bore). Nagari marks on the butt, once their significance is properly understood, may show if it is one of the guns purchased in 1850/1.
6. The only U.S. Patent, 69941, was granted to Snider's widow Angeline in October 1867 to protect the perfected British-type design.

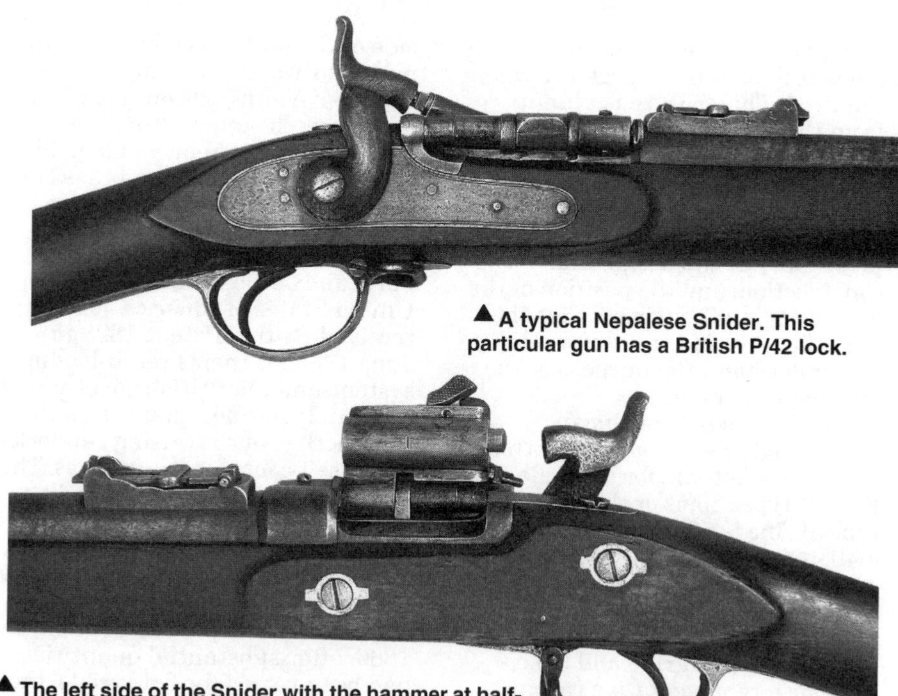

▲ A typical Nepalese Snider. This particular gun has a British P/42 lock.

▲ The left side of the Snider with the hammer at half-cock and the breech open, showing the locking catch and the lugged sidenail cups.

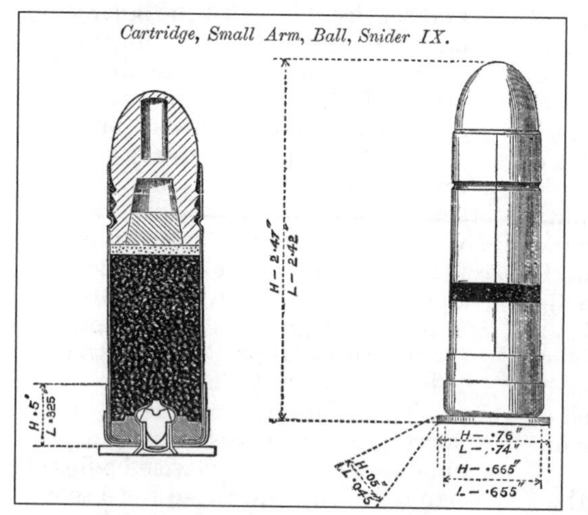

The British 0.577 Mark IX ball round.

Treatise on Military Small Arms and Ammunition, the British Army's textbook, a velocity of 1240 ft/sec at the muzzle had dropped to only 458 ft/sec at 1000 yards; the time of flight and the maximum height of the trajectory at this range were 4.33 seconds and 76 feet, respectively.

Sniders were made in huge quantities, the earliest being converted from rifle muskets, short rifles, serjeants' rifles and carbines. By March 31 1871, according to a memorandum written by Colonel William Dixon, Superintendent of the Royal Small Arms Factory, 458,000 conversions and 192,000 new guns had been made by the Enfield small-arms factory,[7] the Birmingham Small Arms Co. Ltd ('BSA') and the London Small Arms Co. Ltd ('LSA'). Snider-type rifles were supplied in quantity to India, and used in Denmark, France, Portugal and Spain. Some Turkish 1855-type Springfield rifle-muskets were also converted to accept the Snider breech.

The British Snider was little more than a P/1853 Enfield rifle-musket with the barrel cut away at the breech to receive a wrought-iron receiver or 'box' containing a breech-block or 'shoe' that could be lifted up and to the right around a longitudinal pivot on the right side of the feed way, then pulled backwards to extract the spent case. The nose of the hammer was twisted inward to strike a spring-loaded firing pin running through the breechblock.

The Nepalese Snider breech mechanism duplicates the 'Bolted Action' introduced with the British Pattern No. 3, which shows that the copies date no earlier than 1870. Dimensions include an overall length of 55.3 inches, with a 36.6-inch barrel rifled with three broad grooves turning to the right. A typical bore diameter measures 0.578-inch.

Stripping one lock of encrusted grease revealed that it had come from an old British P/1842 musket. In addition to the customary two-line engraving around the edge of the lockplate and on the body of the cock, with scroll engraving on the side of the cock-head and checkering on the cock-spur, V.R. above TOWER are struck faintly into the lock plate immediately ahead of the cock, with 'crown/12' and '7' inside the plate. The plate also bears a mark that, though tiny and exceptionally difficult to read, appears to be R. & W. A.—the lock maker, R. & W. Aston of Birmingham—and the absence of a date suggests origins prior to 1844. Examination of another gun revealed that its lock, externally difficult to distinguish from the P/42, had been made in Nepal. The finish is not as good as the British-made version, and the shape of the sear spring is recognizably different.

In common with the P/1853 copies, markings on these Sniders are few and far between. There is nothing but an alignment mark on

▲ A top view of the Snider breech.

▲ The Snider trigger guard, a brass casting. Note the Nagari characters.

7. The few thousand P/1855 Engineers Carbines, with Lancaster oval-bore rifling, were converted in the short-lived factory in Pimlico, London, instead of Enfield.

the junction of the breech-plug and the new receiver; and signs of Nepalese issue can be restricted to Nagari numerals on the back sight. However, one of the sample guns is numbered on the buttplate, on the nocksform *(the 'shoulder' on the barrel in front of the receiver, named after gunmaker Henry Nock)* behind the retaining screw, and on the nose band. Nagari characters on the rear tang of the trigger guard, combinations of letters and numerals, can also often reveal the identity of a specific unit.

▲ The 'Trials Martini' rifle found in the consignment. This is a most unusual gun, as only little over 200 were made in 1869.

▲ A standard Martini-Henry Mark II rifle.

▲ The left side of the action body of the Martini rifle, showing the marks of Alex Henry. Note the length of the action compared to the standard Martini-Henry infantry rifle, and the exceptionally short operating lever.

Martini-Henry Mark II rifles

This was the principal service rifle of the British Army from June 1871 until the advent of the magazine rifle in 1888, though teething troubles delayed the first large-scale issues until 1874. The most unexpected find among the guns from Lagan Silekhana was a survivor of the 'long-action' trials pattern of 1869, bearing the marks of Alexander Henry, most of the guns proving to be Mark II or Mark IV rifles (though there are also a few hundred carbines).

The Martini-Henry breechblock pivots downward within a sturdy open-box receiver ('action body' or 'shoe' in official British terminology) around a transverse axis at the upper rear. This was originally a threaded pin, retained by a small keeper screw on the left side of the breech, but was soon replaced by a self-retaining split pin.

The Mark I rifle had undergone several major changes before the advent of the Mark II, including the removal of the safety catch and the replacement of the original checkered shoulder plate with a plain version. The Mark II also lacked the 'tumbler rest' *(effectively a sear)*, and the trigger was shrouded to prevent accumulated debris allowing the striker to fall as the breechblock closed.

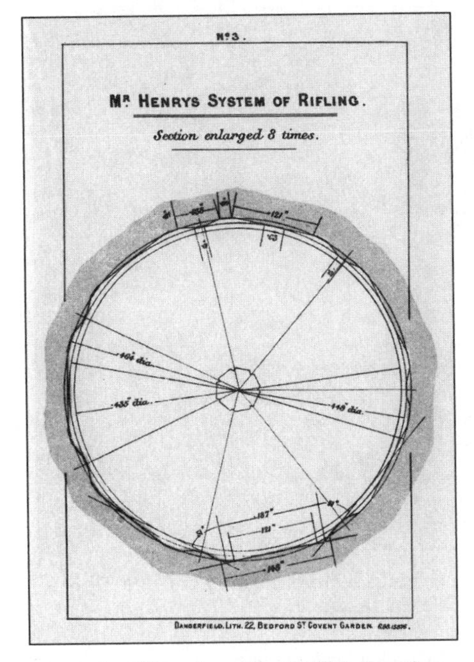

Henry's rifling, from the *British Treatise on Small Arms and Ammunition*, 1888.

However, virtually all Mark I rifles were rebuilt to Mark II standards simply by replacing the entire trigger sub-group—one of the advantages of the Martini-Henry breech. These guns, altered to be identical mechanically with the purpose-built Mark II, can usually be distinguished only by their markings.

The Mark II rifle is 4ft 1-1/2 inches overall (with the long butt) and weighs 8lb 12oz with the bayonet in place. A 1450-yard rear sight is used in conjunction with a small open 'barleycorn' (inverted-'V') at the muzzle. The barrel is 33 – 3/16 inches long, rifled with seven grooves making a turn in 22 inches. Each groove was 0.009-inch deep at the breech, reducing to a constant 0.007-inch at a distance of eleven inches from the breech. The bore was slightly enlarged for the first eight inches, accepting a 0.451-inch plug, and the chamber was tapered by 0.018-inch to facilitate extraction. Henry rifling was a curious hybrid, derived from the Whitworth and other polygonal designs of the 1850s, but was notoriously difficult to make.

The guns have straight-wrist butts and separate forends of Italian walnut. The tip of the butt is squared to enter a socket in the rear of the body, where it is held by a massive stock-screw running up through the wrist. This gives great strength; though the Martini-Henry butt can work loose, it rarely breaks away entirely.

The forend of the Mark II is held by a shallow tenon that enters the hollow face of the action body, by a cross pin through the barrel lug, and by two wrought-iron bands. The front band, which lies behind the small iron nose cap, carries a lug for a sword bayonet. However, only some of the Martini-Henry rifles were issued with sword bayonets, as the rank-and-file infantrymen carried adapted P/1853 or new P/1876 socket bayonets that locked around the squared base of the front sight. The blade lengths were 17 inches and 22-1/8 inches respectively. About 225,000 socket and 104,000 saber bayonets were bushed for the Martini-Henry in the 1870s and 1880s. The external muzzle diameter of the rifles was about 0.700-inch, compared with 0.760-inch for the P/53 Enfield and the Snider.

Swivels were usually attached to the front of the trigger guard and

A sectional drawing of the breech of the Mark III Martini action, which was substantially the same as the Mark II except for an alteration to the extractor.

The breech of the Martini-Henry in its open position. Note how the cocking indicator *(above the rear of the trigger guard)* has been rocked backward.

the front band, though an additional swivel was fitted under the butt prior to 1875. This fitting was subsequently abandoned, excepting on guns issued to the Rifle Brigade and the 60th Rifles, and the butts of guns made prior to this date will now often be found with a hardwood plug where the swivel had been.

The earliest Martini-Henry trials rifles chambered an elongated cartridge with a straight, slightly tapering case; predictably shown to be flimsy, this was replaced by a necked design credited to William Eley of the renowned ammunition-making business. The earliest rolled-case cartridges were also too flimsy, but the Mark III of 1873 was efficient enough to remain in service for many years. Made of 0.004-inch sheet brass with a strengthening strip and a built-up base, the 'Rolled Mark III' round was about 3.15 inches long. The crimped-neck case was 2.32 inches long, with a rim diameter of 0.75-inch and contained 85 grains of RFG[2] powder; the 480-grain bullet was 1.04 inches long and had a shallow, hollowed base.[8] Velocity at the muzzle, according to the *Treatise on Military Small Arms and Ammunition* (1888), was 1315 ft/sec, reducing to 664 ft/sec at 1000 yards. At this distance, the time of flight was about 3.5 seconds and the bullet was nearly 48ft above the line of sight at the peak of its trajectory.

Though the Martini-Henry worked satisfactorily under most service conditions, problems arose when rapid fire was required in excessively hot and dusty conditions. The extractor then often simply tore the case-head away to leave the remainder of the case jammed in the chamber. Disastrous experience in the Sudan in the mid-1880s led to the introduction of a solid drawn-case cartridge and an improved Mark III extractor, which was fitted retrospectively to many surviving guns—beginning with those serving with the units engaged in Egypt and the Sudan. Guns of this type display 'S-X' or 'S.X.' (strengthened extractor) above the chamber.

Large numbers of Martini-Henry rifles and carbines were converted to 303-caliber in the 1890s, the design of the rifling determining whether they were classified as 'Martini-Metford' (seven grooves) or 'Martini-Enfield' (five grooves). Very few guns of this type were sent to India and, to date, only a couple of sporting-rifle conversions have been retrieved from Nepal.

The date and origin of a Martini-Henry rifle can usually be determined from the marks on the right side of the action body. These consist of a crown over 'V.R.' (for *Victoria Regina*), above the place of manufacture, the date, an inverted Broad Arrow beneath a small crown, and the 'Mark of Arm'. This will read 'II' or 'IV' on the guns retrieved from Nepal, but the Mark II guns often prove to be Mark I rebuilt to Mark II standards, and the 'II' mark will be seen to consist of 'I.' added to the original 'I'. A 'Class of Arm' designator will usually be found beneath the Mark, 'I' or '1' signifying First-Class (issued to regular units) and 'II' or '2' showing a Second-Class gun destined for Militia, Volunteers or Yeomanry.[9]

A roundel containing a Broad Arrow and the factory name, and sometimes also the date, will lie on the right side of the butt. There are British military proof marks on the barrel and the receiver, and separate viewers' marks appear on many of the parts. The view marks

Photographed in 1896, this British cavalry trooper holds a Martini-Henry carbine. Only a few guns of this type were found in the Lagan Silekhana cache.

8. Carbine loads contained only 70 grains of propellant, and had 410-grain bullets to reduce recoil in the lightweight guns.
9. Mark and Class designators may also be found on the right side of the butt below the roundel.

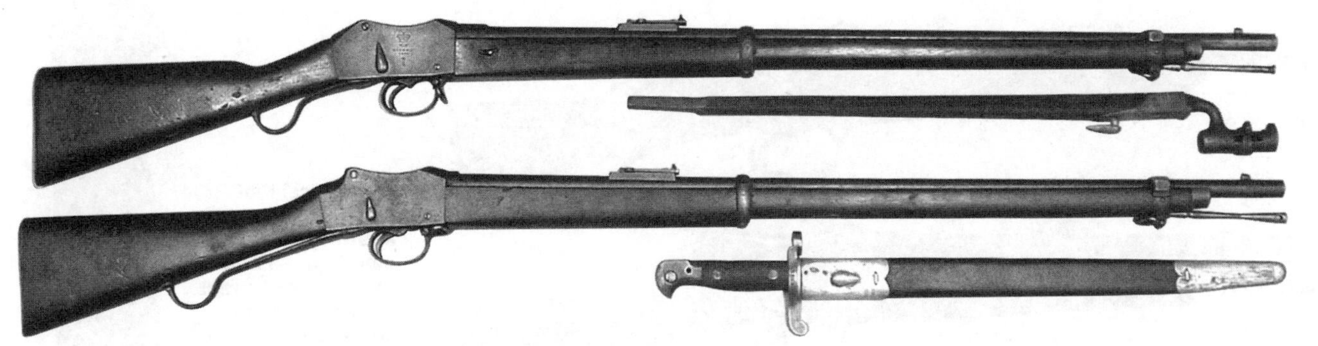

A comparison of the principal Nepalese Martini-Henry rifles, Mark II *(top)* and Mark IV *(bottom)*, with their bayonets.

can be used to identify the source of the guns—assumed to have been entirely rebuilt—that have had the marks on the action-body wholly or partially erased. The code is 'E' for Enfield, 'B' for Birmingham (BSA&M Co. Ltd, Small Heath), 'BR' for 'Birmingham Repair' (Royal Small Arms Repair Factory, Bagot Street, prior to 1894) and 'X' for London (LSA Co. Ltd, Bow).

Most of the Mark II rifles retrieved from Nepal have additional Nagari characters on the butt and beneath the trigger guard, which usually prove to be combinations of unit identifiers and rack numbers. None has yet been found with India Service re-issue or refurbishment marks dated later than 1894, and it is suggested, therefore, that they were sent to Nepal *c.* 1895-1900. The left side of the barrels usually displays 'N ! S' and 'N E P' beneath the rear-sight base.

Martini-Henry Mark IV rifles

The long-lever 450 'Mark IV' gun was adopted in September 1887 to succeed the abortive 402-calibre Enfield-Martini, but the advent of the magazine rifle ensured that even the perfected Martini-Henry had a short front-line life. Most of the guns, therefore, ended their days in India and the other British colonies.

The Mark IV Martini-Henry had an elongated operating lever, changes to the rear of the action body, and a combless butt.

The left side of the Mark IV Martini-Henry.

Distinguished by the shape of the action body, with the rear upper surface cut away to provide a more comfortable grip, the Mark IV 'Pattern A' was a conversion of the original 0.402 Enfield Martini—though only a few of the original parts were used. It has an ultra-short nocksform and a filled hole on the under-edge of the butt where the seat for the original short operating lever was once placed.

The 'Pattern B' and 'Pattern C' Mark IV rifles had new butts, long levers, and ramped front sights instead of the original squared block. Barrels were either taken from old guns ('B') or newly drawn from store ('C'). As the old barrels had to be slightly shortened from the breech, the Pattern B nocksform is only 1-7/64 inches long compared with 1-15/64 inches for Pattern C; this makes the 'C' barrel 33-3/16 inches long instead of 33-1/8 inches for the 'B' type.

Only 21,755 Pattern A conversions were made in Enfield in 1888-9, making them the rarest of the Mark IV variants. Production of Patterns B and C amounted to 42,902 and 35,344 respectively. They were all issued with the Pattern 1887 sword bayonet, with an 18 3/8-inch straight-edged straight blade.

Adopted in May 1887, the P/87 Mark I had a leaf spring for the locking catch and four grip rivets; the Mark II of July 1888 had a coil spring in the pommel and two rivets through the grips; the Mark III (June 1888) had a plain blade without fullers; and the Mark IV, accepted in June 1891, was a conversion of earlier sabre bayonets. The muzzle ring of the Mk IV is measurably nearer the tang of the grip than the others, the blade has a slight-but-perceptible curve, and the markings will include 'C/' followed by a two-digit date.

The Mk II is the rarest of these bayonets, as only a little over 2000 were made, compared with about 24,000 Mk IV, 50,000 Mk 3 and 52,000 Mk I. Bayonets sent to Nepal usually have 'N E P' and a number on the pommel.

The Mark IV Martini-Henry rifles are marked similarly to their predecessors, excepting that the

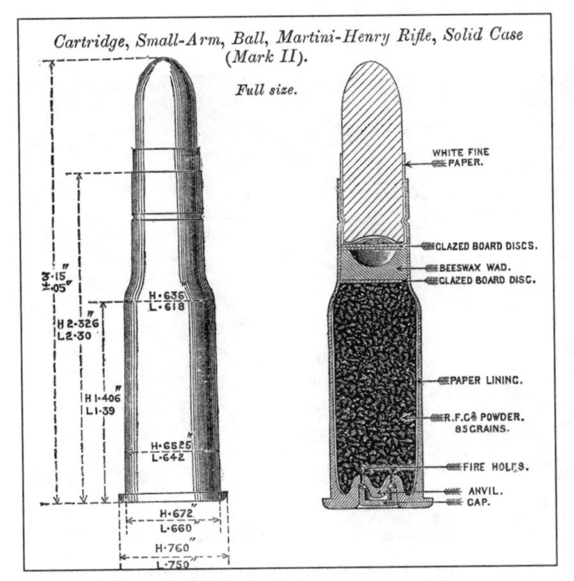

The solid, or rolled-case Martini-Henry rifle cartridge.

Taken from the catalogue published by the gun-dealer A.L. Frank ('Alfa') of Hamburg in 1911, these Martini-Henry rifles have been altered to sporting guise. Guns of this type have been brought back from Nepal, including one with markings in Arabic.

►A typical P/87 sword bayonet, showing Nagari markings—a unit identifier and a rack number—on the crossguard.

'Mark of Arm' reads IV instead of II. The guns retrieved from Nepal usually show signs of India Service, in the form of stock roundels reading FORT WILLIAM or ALLAHABAD, and inspection dates that read typically '11 08' (November 1908). Consequently, it is assumed that they were sent to Nepal in *c.* 1910-14. Nagari characters, which may include regimental identifiers, are usually struck into the underside of the trigger guard.

Gahendra breechloaders

These interesting rifles have been identified as 'Nepalese Martini' or even 'Peabody-Wessely' designs, but were the work of General Gahendra Shamsher Jang Bahadur Rana (1871-1905), an adoptive grandson of Jang Bahadur Rana. A member of the aristocratic ruling family, Gahendra was renowned as a scientist and engineer. He was also responsible for the Bira Gun, and for improvements in artillery.

A typical Gahendra Rifle is 49.7 inches long, with a 33 1/4-inch barrel held in the stock by two bands and a pinned nose cap; caliber is 0.450-inch, and the barrel is rifled with three broad grooves turning to the right. The guns weigh about 9lb 5oz. A copy of the British P/76 socket bayonet locked around the front-sight base, though the external diameter of the muzzle is larger than the Mark II Martini-Henry. Consequently, the British bayonets will not fit over the Nepalese rifle muzzle; and the Gahendra bayonets are much too loose for the Martini-Henry. Measurement suggests that the external diameter of the Gahendra muzzle can vary greatly (0.728/0.767-inch on the samples), and that the internal dimensions of the bayonet sockets, which seem much more consistent, would often have resulted in a 'rattle fit'. The Nepalese-made scabbards—which bear a fascinating amount of markings—will undoubtedly be the key to the eventual transcription of unit designators.

The Gahendra rifle resembles the Martini-Henry externally, the butt plate, the forend and the rear sight being virtually identical. The front swivel lies on the nose band; the rear swivel not only runs through the trigger plate, but has also been greatly enlarged to allow the lever to be opened without fouling the loop.

The carbine is similar to the rifle, but considerably shorter (37.9 inches overall, with a 21.4-inch barrel), weighs 7lb 10oz, and does not accept a bayonet. The rear sight is graduated only to 1000 yards; the front sight, on a post, is a barleycorn flanked by two low protective wings. The forend has two iron bands and a separate nose cap, and the iron barrel, with a nocksform merely 0.41-inch long, is additionally held by a large pin through the barrel lug. The rear swivel lies under the butt, and the contours of the upper body immediately behind the breech are noticeably refined.

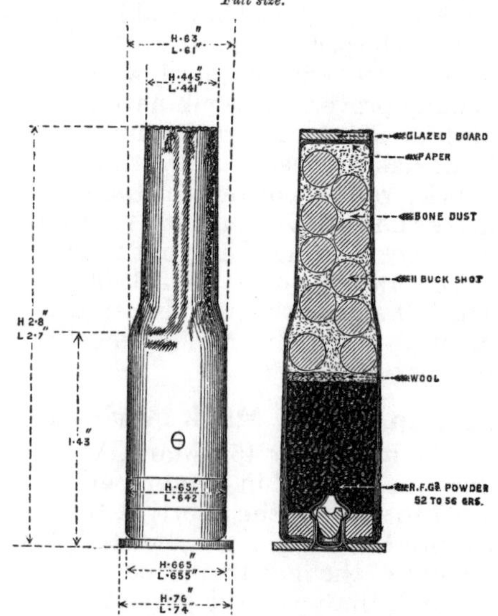

British buckshot-loaded ammunition for the Martini-Henry.

A line of Mark II Martini-Henry rifles, showing Nagari unit markings and numbers on their trigger guards.

The resemblance to the Martini-Henry is less obvious when attention is paid to detail. The Gahendra operating lever has a distinctive down-curving loop, and runs up into the action ahead of the trigger instead of behind it. Two arms of a single piece of spring steel anchored to the trigger plate, bent into an inverted 'U', are used to hold the lever closed. In addition, the butt is held by one large bolt running down through the tang and a large screw running up through the trigger plate—not nearly as desirable as the Martini system, as it needs careful inletting and is comparatively weak.

Internally, the Gahendra shows quite clearly that its parentage is different from any Martini. Though it retains a pivoting-block action, the block is supported at the front instead of towards the rear; and the striker of the British rifle has been replaced by a hammer. There are only two springs in the Nepalese gun—a large hammer spring, hooked to engage with a link pivoted in the back of the hammer body, and a small plain leaf spring that presses down on the tail of the trigger. Both are mounted on the elongated trigger plate.

Gahendra clearly drew his inspiration from Westley Richards patent of 1869, just as his Bira Gun was derived from the Gardner. The Richards rifle had been entered in the British trials, but was withdrawn when the inventor realized that it was likely to be placed third behind the Martini and the Henry. Richards thereafter became a vocal critic of the Martini-Henry rifle, and, though the claim that he was directly involved with the production of the Gahendra rifle in Nepal lacks credence, the retrieval of a least one Richards dropping-block rifle from Lagan Silekhana may show that the source of inspiration was the collection of sporting guns amassed by Jang Bahadur Rana.

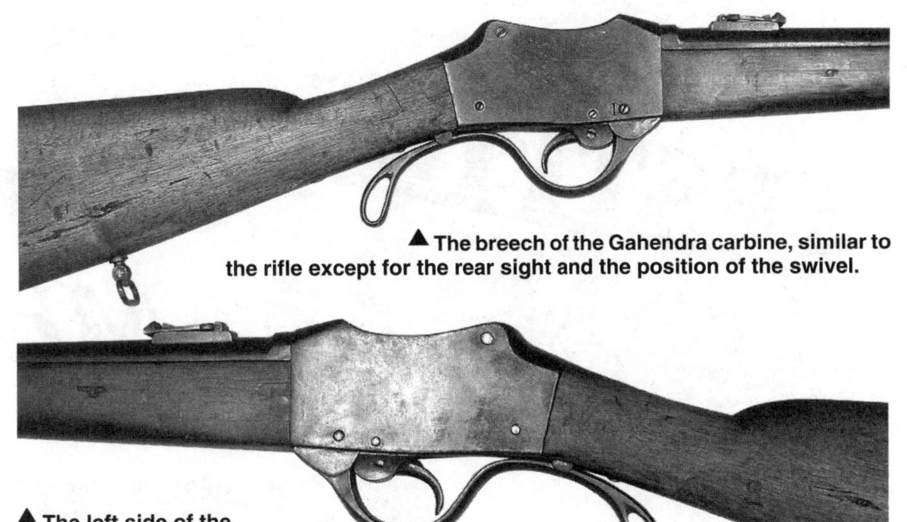
▲ The breech of the Gahendra carbine, similar to the rifle except for the rear sight and the position of the swivel.

▲ The left side of the Gahendra carbine.

The most important mark is a string of Nagari characters that runs at an angle across the rear top left side of the body, which contains Gahendra's full name preceded by the honorific *tin sri* ('3 sri'). The characters on the underside of the lever read '3-sri Ga[hendra] rifle', and a serial number, sometimes accompanied by a unit identifier, lies on the lower back of the body.

Production was substantial, but this was camouflaged by a system of serial-number suffixes similar to that commonly encountered on German weapons such as Mauser rifles and Luger pistols. Each block contained 999 guns, but the sequence of suffixes is still unknown. A survey of seven rifles revealed four different Nagari characters—*ga*, *ja*, *na* and *ra*. These are far enough apart in the syllabary to suggest that they had been chosen at random.

A two-barreled Bira Gun, a mechanical machinegun derived from the Gardner, stands framed in a gateway in Lagan Silekhana. This particular example dates from 1897.

Dating the Gahendra rifle is also difficult; however, the Bira Guns are dated 1896-7, and it is likely that the rifles originated in the same era. The marks on the receiver of the carbine differ from those on the rifle, and their significance is still being investigated. But it seems that only a few of these short-barreled guns were made, perhaps in a single experimental batch: those that have been retrieved from Nepal are numbered between '1' and '15'. ●

Epilogue

The thousands of guns found in Nepal not only give a fascinating glimpse into the colorful history of the military firearms of the Gurkhas, but also facilitate the recovery of details that could otherwise have been lost. In addition, the ability of the Nepalese to copy up-to-the-minute designs such as the P/1853 rifle-musket and the Sharps breechloaders, before proceeding to the Snider copy and then the Gahendra, force us rewrite the ordnance history of the period. It also allows the authentication of a whole new range of collectable guns!

Many people have provided me with information, but I would particularly like to thank David Harding of London, author of the standard history of the firearms of the East India Company; Chris Fox and Guy Marner of Fire Power International, the UK offshoot of International Military Antiques; David Penn, Keeper of Exhibits, Imperial War Museum, London; Peter Smithurst of the Royal Armouries, Leeds, England; Phillip McGrath, Curator of Fort Nelson, Portsmouth, England; the Gurkha Museum, Winchester, England; Dr. Jonathan Minns, Director, and Peter Fagg, Chief Engineer, of the British Engineerium, Hove, England; the Patent Offices in Britain and the U.S.A.; and, above all, Christian Cranmer of IMA for underwriting the research into the origins of the Nepalese guns…

The guns imported from Nepal are historically significant and are sold only as collectables. They have been stored for many years and, in the absence of re-proof facilities in the U.S.A., no warranty is expressed or implied that they are fit to shoot. Additional information may be obtained from the websites of the promoters, International Military Antiques, Inc., PO Box 256, Millington, New Jersey 07946 (http://www.ima-usa.com), and the Atlanta Cutlery Corporation, 2143 Gees Mill Road, Conyers, Georgia 30208 (http://www.atlantacutlery.com).

by Layne Simpson

TESTFIRE
TESTFIRE
TESTFIRE

Remington Model 504

I WON'T BEAT around the bush; the new Model 504 is the finest standard-production 22 rimfire ever created by Remington. Built at Remington's Mayfield, Kentucky factory, it will surely go on to rank right up there with other Remington classics such as the Model 700 centerfire rifle, the Model 870 pump gun and the Model 1100 autoloader. For now the Model 504 is available only in 22 Long Rifle, but the 22 WMR and 17 HMR are bound to follow in 2005. They say the 22 Hornet is also a possibility but it is probably a long way off, if indeed it ever does happen.

The nickel-plated bolt of the Model 504 has a 90-degree lift, travels 1-1/4 inches during its cycle and locks up at two points. When the bolt is rotated to its locked position, the root of its handle and a smaller lug on the opposite side of the bolt body engage their respective slots in the receiver. The bolt is equipped with dual extractors, and out back it wears a Mark V Weatherby-style bolt shroud. The tail of the firing pin serves as a cocking indicator by protruding through the rear surface of the bolt shroud just enough to be seen by the eye or felt by a finger. The bolt handle is nicely shaped and attached to a metal sleeve, which is held in place on the bolt body by the bolt shroud. I found cocking the firing pin during bolt lift to be smooth and effortless due to well-designed cam surface angles. The bolt is easily disassembled by hand with no tools required.

The Model 504 receiver is machined from a bar of carbon steel. Cylindrical in shape, it reminds me of the Model 700 receiver although, at 1.20 inches, it is a bit smaller than the 1.35-inch receiver ring diameter of the Model 700. The bolt is just over 0.600-inch in diameter so the walls of the receiver are extremely thick for strength and rigidity, and yet at only six pounds the rifle is plenty light for carrying over hill and dale all day long.

Regardless of whether you use a 22 rimfire for small-game hunting or plinking, the Model 504 is an excellent choice.

The receiver is just over seven inches long, or about three-quarters of an inch shorter than the receiver of the short action Model 700. The spring-loaded bolt release located on the left-hand side of the receiver is unobtrusive and works flawlessly. The magazine housing *(which also contains the magazine release and spent case ejector)* is bolted to the bottom of the receiver, as are the fire-control assembly and a cylindrical recoil lug, the latter drilled and threaded for acceptance of one of two bolts that hold barreled action and stock together. The third bolt serves only to hold the rear of the trigger guard against the stock. Removing the trigger assembly from the receiver for cleaning is easily accomplished by turning out two hex-headed retention bolts. A receiver drilled and tapped for easy scope attachment comes as no surprise on a rifle designed during an era when just about all hunters and shooters use telescopic sights, a receiver drilled and tapped for easy scope attachment. My rifle wore a Warne mount.

Capacity of the staggered-column detachable magazine is six rounds.

My trusty RCBS trigger-pull scale indicated weights ranging from three pounds, nine ounces to an even four pounds for a maximum variation of seven ounces for 10 pulls. That's good enough for a hunting rifle. Trigger pull was quite smooth and, while my finger detected a slight amount of creep, there was no overtravel. The trigger is fully adjustable for overtravel, pull weight and sear engagement. Minimum weight adjustment is around two pounds and the design prevents sear engagement from being reduced below a safe level. Keep in mind that trigger adjustments are to be made only by a Remington authorized repair center and the one nearest you can be found by visiting the Remington website at www.remington.com or by e-mailing your request for information to info@remington.com.

A two-position safety lever is located at the right-hand side of the receiver tang. When in its extreme rearward position, the trigger fingerpiece is blocked from travel. The bolt can be rotated with the safety engaged, allowing removal of a cartridge from the chamber while the rifle is in its *"safe"* mode.

The 20-inch barrel measures one inch in diameter at the receiver and tapers to 0.600-inch at the muzzle. It has a recessed crown and Remington's famous 5-R rifling, which is the same type of rifling used in barrels made in the custom shop for the 40X rifle. Rifling twist rate is 1:14-1/2 inches. The chamber is reamed to semi-match dimensions, making it tighter than the chambers of some economy-grade rifles but generous enough to accept any 22 Long Rifle cartridge. Only those who have lived in caves for the past few years do not know that a popular thing to do is to replace the factory barrels of certain 22 rimfire rifles with aftermarket barrels. Ruger started it all with the 10/22, and Remington engineers kept the switch-barrel concept rolling when designing the Model 597 autoloader. They did likewise when creating the Model 504, although it differs from the rest.

The barrel is attached to the receiver by a clamping system which consists of a crossbolt that, when tightened, squeezes the split bottomside of the receiver tightly around the barrel shank. In addition, a setscrew running through the wall of the receiver ring and against the barrel increases tensile strength to the point where barrel and receiver are all but impossible to separate unless screw

Capacity of the staggered-column detachable magazine is six rounds.

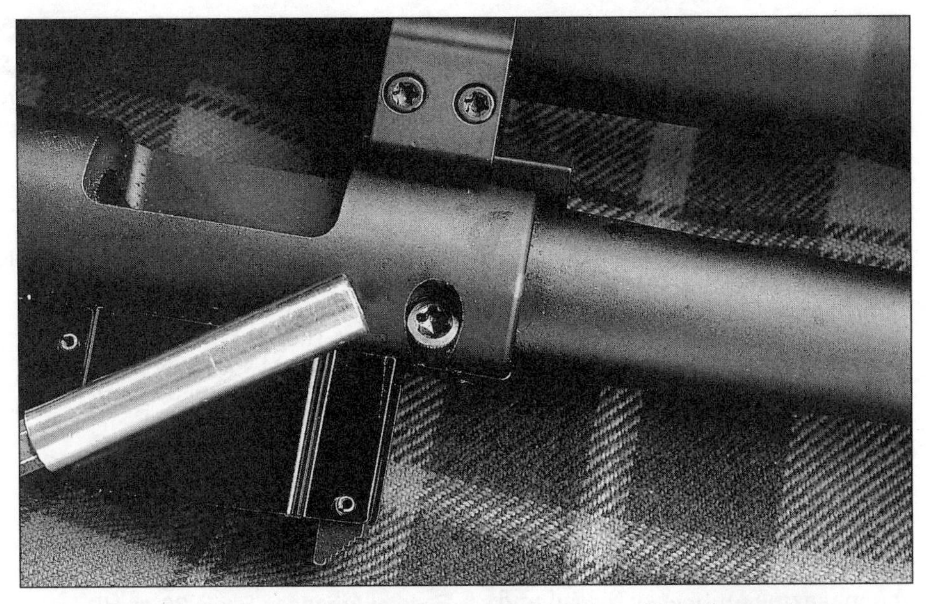

Split receiver is clamped tightly around the shank of the barrel by this crossbolt.

Bolt release is located on left-hand side of receiver.

Laser-cut checkering was very nicely executed.

and crossbolt are loosened. This arrangement allows the barrel to be easily replaced by a gunsmith who has a tool especially designed to loosen and retighten the crossbolt. It also simplifies headspace adjustment at the factory and that results in a slight reduction in production cost. If you believe threading and then screwing a 22 rimfire barrel into the receiver is in some way superior to clamping it into place, I will remind you that the barrels of Anschutz rifles are press-fitted and cross-pinned into their receivers—and we all know how accurate they are.

The detachable magazine of the Model 504 holds six rounds in a staggered fashion and fits flush with the bottom of the stock. It is easily disassembled for cleaning. I found the magazine quite easy to load and it fed cartridges smoothly during my testing. Pressing a lever located at the front of the magazine allows it to drop into the hand. The release lever is convenient to reach and yet its flush fit with the magazine housing prevents it from being bumped against something in the field.

The classical-style stock was carved from a rather plain block of American walnut. It has 17-line laser-cut checkering, a 1/2-inch rubber buttpad, quick-detach sling swivel posts and a steel grip cap attached with two screws and adorned with the "Golden R" logo. Except for a small area at the right-hand side of the barrel channel, wood-to-metal fit is quite good. Same goes for the application of the satin finish. Stock dimensions worked great for me. I tried the Model 504 with medium-height Warne Maxima rings and two scopes, a Bushnell 6-24X 4200 Elite and the new 2-7x rimfire scope from Kahles, and found the amount of drop in the stock to be just right. The 14-1/4 inch length of pull represents a workable compromise for seasonal changes in hunting clothing ranging from light to everything you own. The stock just plain feels good in my hands.

During my accuracy tests I pitted the new Model 504 against my old 40X-BR and the results proved most enlightening. The ammunition consisted of a mixture of low-velocity match loads and high-velocity hunting loads, and the two rifles were equipped with scopes of the same magnification: a 6-24X Bushnell Elite 4200 on the Model 504, a Weaver T24 on the 40X-BR. I fired five, 5-shot groups with each of 25 different loads at 50 yards during near-perfect range conditions. After firing a 25-shot string with one of the rifles I would allow its barrel to cool while firing the same number of groups with the other rifle. As you can see in my accuracy results, the Model 504 proved to be accurate enough for head shots on cottontail rabbits out to 50 yards and it equaled the accuracy of the 40X-BR rifle with several loads.

The folks at Remington are convinced that everyone who owns or will own a Model 700 will want to also own a Remington Model 504 since it is the perfect small-game companion to that big-game rifle. I believe they have something there. ●

ACCURACY TEST RESULTS

Remington Model 504 versus Remington 40X-BR

Five, 5-shot groups fired at 50 yards from a benchrest with each load.
Range conditions: ideal, with no wind.

Load		—Accuracy (Inches)—	
	Velocity (fps)	40X-BR	Model 504
Remington/Eley Match Xtra Plus 40-gr. SN	1074	0.55	0.58
Remington/Eley Club Xtra 40-gr. SN	1058	0.47	1.02
Remington/Eley Target Rifle 40-gr. SN	1066	0.51	1.24
Remington Thunderbolt 40-gr. SN	1232	1.10	1.35
Remington Target 40-gr. SN	1143	0.74	0.87
Remington Yellow Jacket 33-gr. HP	1404	0.79	0.88
Remington Cyclone 36-gr. HP	1251	1.22	1.14
Remington Subsonic 38-gr. HP	1018	0.57	0.62
Remington High Velocity 40-gr. SN	1160	1.14	1.42
Remington High Velocity 36-gr. HP	1210	0.84	1.12
Eley Tenex 40-gr. SN	1082	0.58	0.59
Federal Gold Medal Match 40-gr. SN	1130	0.45	0.74
Federal Classic Hyper 31-gr. HP	1462	0.70	0.76
Federal American Eagle 36-gr. HP	1302	0.65	1.04
Federal Classic High Velocity 40-gr. SN	1251	0.78	1.02
CCI Green Tag 40-gr. SN	1085	0.53	0.85
CCI Mini-Group 40-gr. SN	1130	0.78	1.43
CCI MinMag 36-gr. HP	1314	0.63	1.08
CCI Mini-Mag +V 32-gr. HP	1432	1.18	1.23
CCI Mini-Mag 40-gr. SN	1262	0.62	0.88
CCI SGB 40-gr. SN	1241	0.55	0.90
CCI Sub-Sonic 40-gr. SN	1026	0.68	0.84
CCI Stinger 32-gr. HP	1607	0.78	1.00
Winchester Power Point 40-gr. HP	1222	0.65	0.74
Winchester Super-X 40-gr. SN	1224	0.66	1.07
OVERALL AVERAGE		0.72	0.97

Receiver is drilled and tapped for scope mounting.

Cocking indicator protruding through rear of bolt shroud is easily seen by the eye and felt with a finger.

TESTFIRE TESTFIRE TESTFIRE

Ruger's No. 1 in 405 Winchester

by Larry Sterett

THE RIMMED 405 Winchester cartridge was introduced in 1895, and when former President Theodore Roosevelt took it and a lever-action Winchester M1895 rifle so chambered to Africa in 1909 on his year-long safari, he called it his *big medicine* gun. Both the cartridge and the rifle eventually went into decline among hunters and Winchester discontinued rifle production around 1936, although stocks were available on dealer's shelves for some years afterwards.

The 405 Winchester cartridges and the M1895 Winchester rifles became more or less collectors' items, although ammunition was available for another couple of decades after rifle production was discontinued. Later, diehard fans handloaded their fired 405 cases for hunting purposes. *(Barnes Bullets and a few custom bullet manufacturers produced bullets for loading the 405 cases, and toward the end of the twentieth century new cases were available through RCBS and Huntington Supplies as produced by Bertram Bullet Co. Ltd. of Victoria, Australia, and Bell Brass in the U.S. Loading dies for the 405 Winchester were not a problem. C-H had them. So did RCBS. Today, Hornady, RCBS, and probably other firms have dies for the 405 cartridge.)*

Then, four years ago Browning Arms reintroduced the M1895 in this chambering, even though Winchester did not reintroduce loaded 405 ammunition. In 2002 Hornady Manufacturing in Grand Island, Nebraska, introduced new loaded 405 Winchester ammunition under their own label. *(For several years prior to Hornady's announcement this shooter had considered having a Ruger No.1 rifle rebarreled for the 405 Winchester cartridge, and handloading ammunition for it using Bertram and Bell brass and Barnes bullets. The problem was solved in 2002 when Sturm, Ruger & Co. announced the firm would be chambering the No. 1 for the 405.)*

The Hornady 405 ammunition is loaded with 300-grain jacketed softpoint round-nose bullets. It is packaged 20 rounds per box, the flaps and one side of which are perforated, permitting separation into two 10-round packs. Each 10-round pack is complete with plastic inserts retaining the cartridges; the fit in a jacket pocket is handier than the usual 20-round box.

Current ballistics show the 300-grain softpoint exiting the muzzle at 2200 feet-per-second (fps) or the same as 170-grain flat point jacketed bullet from the 30-30 Winchester, or 100 fps faster than the jacketed 350-grain flat-point bullet from the 450 Marlin Magnum. *(In 1953 Winchester listed the 300-grain softpoint as having a muzzle velocity of 2260 fps.)* However, at 100 yards the 405 bullet has 2282 foot-pounds of retained energy (fpe), while the bullet of the 30-30 has only 1355 fpe, and the 450 Marlin bullet at 2286 has only four fpe more than the 405. At 100 yards the Hornady 405 bullet strikes the target with only 14 fpe less energy than does the 150-grain jacketed softpoint from a 30-06 with a muzzle velocity of 2910 fps. Not bad for a cartridge nearly 110 years old.

Although announced in 2002, the Ruger No 1 in 405 Winchester did not actually become available until mid-2003. The wait was warranted. Tipping the scales at 8 pounds 3 ounces, empty, the 405 No. 1 features a 24-inch barrel and an overall length of 40-3/8 inches. It has all the features of the regular No. 1-H, with the band on the barrel forward of the

The slim 405 Winchester round slides into the chamber of the Ruger No. 1 as though the rifle was designed with this cartridge in mind. Ejection of fired casings is excellent.

forearm for attaching a sling swivel, quarter-rib on the barrel with open rear sight and provisions for mounting a scope, if desired. The front sight consisted of a 0.065-inch brass bead front on a barrel band ramp, with a Lyman-type folding rear sight on the quarter-rib. *(The rear sight leaf featured a 0.070-inch wide U-shape notch and can be removed and inverted to provide a 0.090-inch wide shallow square notch.)* The face of the leaf featured a white diamond in line with the sight notch, and the right side of the sight was indexed. It is adjustable for elevation by loosening two small screws and moving the leaf up or down. *(A three-leaf English-style shallow V-notch sight with white or gold-colored vertical line in the center would be ideal as an option on the rib.)* Sight radius measured 17-1/2 inches on the test gun.

Trigger let-off on the test gun measured a crisp four pounds. The trigger is well shaped, adjustable using a hex wrench, and the face is ridged to reduce finger slippage.

There's no Monte Carlo on the straight comb pistol-grip stock, and the forearm is the Henry style, which helps in giving the rifle a 'British Empire' appearance. The forearm and pistol grip feature borderless cut checkering, and the pistol grip base is graced with a metal cap having in the center a small gold-colored medallion bearing the Ruger logo.

Length of pull measured 13-13/16 inches on the test gun, including the 1/2-inch thick solid rubber buttpad. The face of the pad features a leather-grained surface with the Ruger logo in the center. *(Any shooter wanting to have a bit more cushion than the buttpad offers might consider a slip-on recoil pad such as those by Uncle Mike. Just remember it will increase the length of pull by 1/2-inch or more.)*

The small of the stock in the pistol grip area is slightly oval in cross-section and a comfortable 4-7/8 inches in circumference at its smallest. Coupled with the rounded comb nose, fluted slightly on each side, the No. 1 stock is well suited for either right- or left-hand shooters.

Left to right: **Unfired 300-grain Hornady jacketed flat nose softpoint bullet, similar bullet recovered from 13 inches of saturated *Wall Street Journal* wet pack, 300-grain Barnes "XFB" bullet recovered from 14 inches of saturated *Wall Street Journal* wet pack, and unfired 300-grain Barnes "XFB" bullet. Both bullets exhibit near-perfect expansion.**

The slide safety on the upper tang is non-automatic as it should be. When the rifle is cocked, the safety can be moved to the rear, exposing the word *SAFE* at the forward edge. The raised center portion of the safety slide is ridged to reduce thumb slippage, and moving the slide forward to 'off' or rearward to *SAFE* is quick and easy.

After examination, the No. 1 was taken to the range to determine how it would perform with the Hornady ammunition. Since T.R. would have been using open sights in Africa back in 1909 it was decided to stick with the open sights on the Ruger and limit shots to 75 yards. *(Since the No. 1 has provisions for mounting a scope, it will probably be mounted with a 1-4X variable when this shooter takes it afield.)* Three-shot groups were fired for accuracy from the bench with the hand grasping the forearm resting on a sandbag.

The 405 Winchester is not considered a target round, but it is accurate, or at least the Hornady loading did well. The smallest three-shot group measured 0.594-inch, center-to-center, in a nice cloverleaf, in the three o'clock position on the target. All of the groups measured less than 2-1/2 inches center-to-center, more than adequate accuracy for most North American big game, as long as the range is reasonable. *(Shortly after the testing was finished, Hornady announced another 405 Winchester load, with a pointed bullet especially intended for use with the No. 1. Unfortunately, no cartridges were available in time to include.)*

No problems were encountered other than the test rifle tended to group slightly to the right of the point-of-aim. The first group was low and off the target, but still on the backing sheet with the rear sight as it came set from the factory. Loosening the two screws on the leaf and raising it to its highest location moved the groups up to the bull, but still left them in the three o'clock position. Later the leaf was inverted to permit use of the square notch.

The 405 Winchester cartridge can handle any game available on this side of the big pond and most, if not all, of the game in Africa. *(Kermit Roosevelt killed at least two elephant with the 405, and may have judiciously used it on the Cape buffalo. His father preferred the 577 on buffalo.)* Hornady has two loads currently available, the Old Western Scrounger has at least one, and A-Square and Buffalo Arms did have loads. Loading data can be found in *Cartridges of the World* (Krause), *The Handloader's Manual of Cartridge Conversions* (Stoeger), Volume I of the *Hornady Handbook of Cartridge Reloading*, and a couple of others to mention a few, plus many of the older Lyman manuals. Thus, a great old (109 years) cartridge has a new lease on life. It and the Ruger No. 1 make a great combination. ●

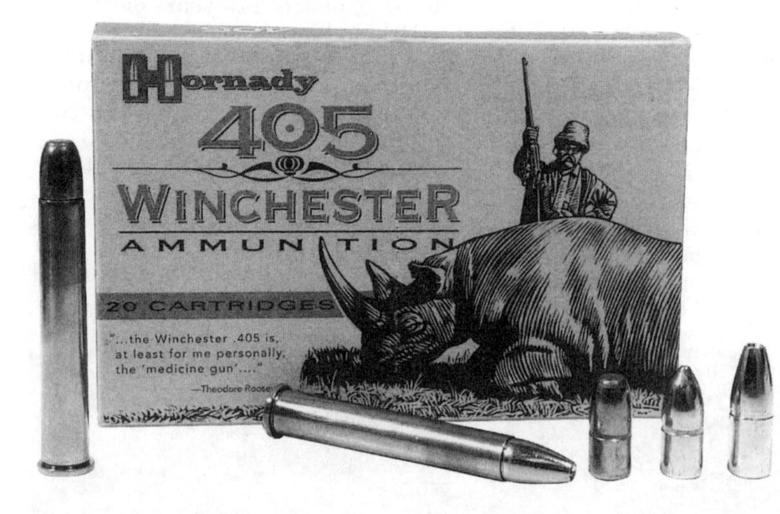

Hornady packaging of the 405 Winchester load features T.R. with his M1895 in 405 and the rhino he bagged with it. *Left to right:* Hornady 405 Winchester with 300-grain flat-nose bullet, 405 Winchester loaded with Barnes "XFB" bullet, and Hornady flat-nose softpoint, pointed softpoint, and Barnes "XFB" hollow-point bullet, respectively, all 300-grain weights.

The Pardner Pump

by H. Lea Lawrence & photos by Aubrey Watson

ONE OF THE most interesting shotguns to appear on the market in recent years is the 12-gauge Pardner Pump, built in China and distributed through New England Firearms. I was made aware of it long before it was officially announced, and I must admit that in not knowing what to expect, I was somewhat apprehensive. When the real thing was delivered, it didn't take long to dispel that feeling.

Had someone handed me the shotgun without identifying it, my initial impression would have been that I was looking at a Remington Model 870, because the shotgun's outline is the same, and as I discovered as I examined it further, many of its features are identical. I remember thinking that the Chinese technicians couldn't have picked a better shotgun design to emulate. It also quickly became apparent that quality had been foremost in their minds.

At present, the Pardner Pump is available in 12-gauge only, with the possibility of a 20-gauge model sometime in the future.

All features of the shotgun assure safe and smooth operation. The take-down mechanism is identical to that of the Model 870, and features double action bars. The magazine cap is removed and the forearm brought all the way down to detach the barrel. As with the Model 870, the breech bolt locks itself into the top of the barrel extension, and because it locks directly behind the casing, the possibility of headspace problems developing is minimal.

Function of the action with two rounds in the magazine and one in the chamber is flawless. The cross-bolt safety is to the rear of the trigger guard, and the slide release is forward of the trigger guard and to the left just behind the loading port.

Weight of the Pardner Pump is 7-1/2 pounds, and the length is 48-1/2 inches. Length of pull is 14-1/2 inches. Drop at the comb is 1-1/2 inches, and drop at the heel is 2-1/2 inches.

The 28-inch barrel is chambered for up to 3-inch shells, and appears to be well bored and polished, with a

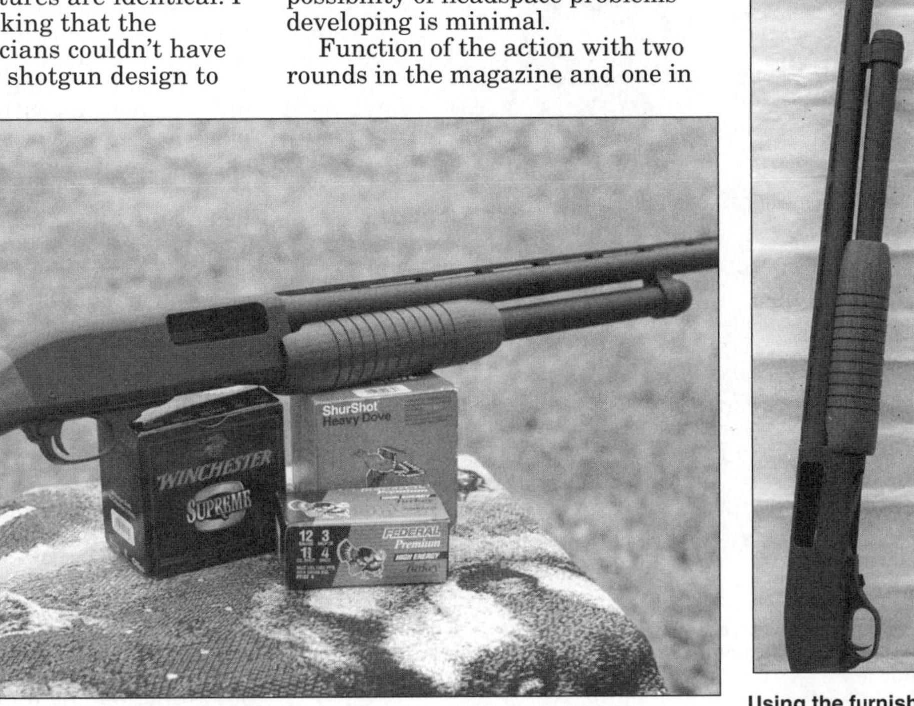

The Pardner Pump bears a close resemblance to the Remington 870, and the workmanship and function is equal to that of shotguns of a far higher price range.

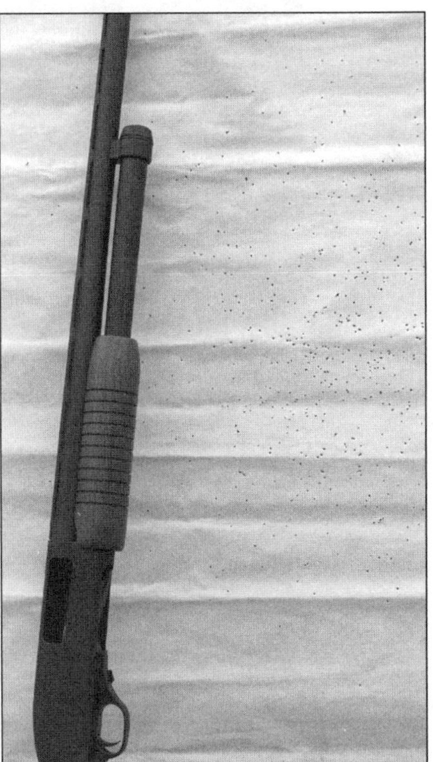

Using the furnished Modified choke tube, the gun placed 50 percent of the pattern above the bead.

Two of the finest pumps ever built are the Model 12 Winchester *(left)*, and the Remington 870 *(center)*. The Pardner Pump can easily compete with either of its predecessors in all respects.

1/4-inch wide ventilated rib and brass bead. The Modified choke tube is smoothly threaded and fitted, and with the minimal amount of shooting I did, the choke tube hits where it is looking. Only one choke comes with the gun, but they are of the Winchester/Mossberg design, and are readily available at sporting goods stores.

The tubular magazine has a capacity of 5 shells, and the cap on the magazine spring is orange, making it easy to tell when it is empty. A 2-shot plug is included with the gun.

The forearm grip is just under 7-1/2 inches. It is well shaped and grooved in a manner typical on many pump guns in the early days. This adds a nice aesthetic touch, as well as a dependable grip.

The stock is very attractive, made of American black walnut with a medium brown finish, and it is well finished and fitted to the receiver. This is much better than we encounter in a gun of this price range, and as good as that found in guns of a considerably higher price. I would rate the wood and the way it is finished as very good to excellent. Actually the overall fitting of wood to metal, and metal to wood is also very good. The finish on the metal parts is a subdued black.

One slight drawback lies in the positioning of the forearm, since a shooter with short arms is unable to fully grip it. Either lengthening it, or moving it farther back on the magazine tube will eliminate this problem.

While extensive pattern testing was not done, enough was conducted to make it clear that the gun shoots where it looks. Using Remington low brass dove loads with No. 8 shot, it placed about 50 percent of the pellets above the bead at a distance of 30 yards.

The Modified choke was very suitable for skeet, but for trap, the stock configuration made it necessary to hold the bead on the bird instead of under it. In both cases, different chokes would have been preferable for testing purposes.

While the suggested retail price of the Pardner Pump is $223.00, buyers can depend on purchasing it for well under $200.00.

Equipped with a selection of choke tubes ranging from Improved Cylinder to Extra Full, this can be a very good choice for an all-around shotgun, one that compares favorably with almost any standard-grade pump gun on the market in both function and appearance. ●

OLD NEVER-MISS

by Eric L. Matherne

IT STARTED A long time ago. Reading Jack O'Connor's columns planted the seed and the desire to own something different made it grow. I knew that one day I had to have a 257 Roberts, come hell or high water. The final push was N. E. Nelson, Jr.'s article in the 1965 GUN DIGEST, titled simply, "The 257 Roberts."

This fine piece of writing put it all together for me and forever removed any doubts I may have entertained.

Chance, and a hardware store, would provide the essential item to start the fulfillment of my wish.

As I walked into the local Western Auto one day, I glanced at their used gun rack, which was located near the front door. There stood a disreputable-looking piece of wood *(painted red)* and metal *(not too rusty)* that turned out to be a '98 Mauser. On closer examination, it was all-milled and coded byf42. The bore of the military barrel resembled, in the words of Bill Brinkley, "a hand-dug well," but it was going to be pulled, so that didn't matter. Putting on my best gun-dealing face, I asked the store manager how much he would take for that worthless piece of junk.

"Got to get fifty dollars for it," came his reply.

This was in the mid-60s when a factory-built rifle was $100 or less, depending on make and model. I assumed my "you must be nuts" stance and left the store.

Over the next several months, I had many occasions to visit the store and on every visit the dialogue was the same:

"How much?"

"Fifty bucks."

"Too much."

One day, things changed:

"How much?"

"Nothin', take the blankety-blank thing and don't ever mention it again. You hear?"

"Yes sir; thank you sir!"

Let this be a lesson to all on the power of persistence or applied aggravation. A free '98 action was a great start on my new rifle.

Being financially one notch above a church mouse, it took a while to scratch up the money to build the rifle. The first order of the day was a Douglas barrel, 24 inches, medium-heavy, which I decided to buy from Flaig's and have them install. They installed it, headspaced and test-fired it, and returned the rifle with a fired Norma case still in the

Years later, the rifle now wears an MPI stock and Leupold 2-7x variable as it rests on author's backyard shooting bench.

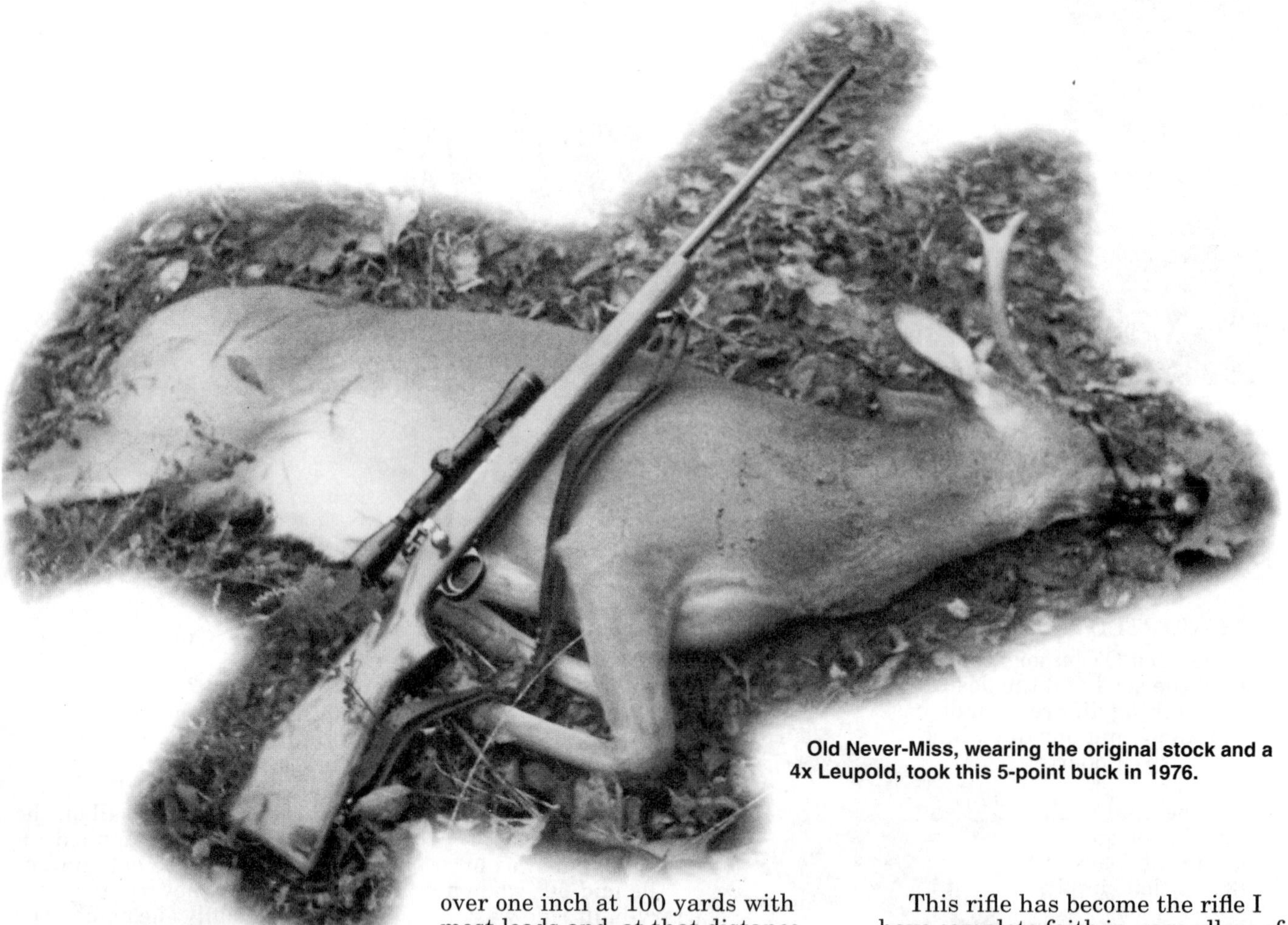

Old Never-Miss, wearing the original stock and a 4x Leupold, took this 5-point buck in 1976.

chamber. The total cost was the grand sum of $41 *(don't forget, its 1968)*. The issue trigger was replaced with a Sako #2 adjustable trigger from Herter's - cost: $12. I had a rough-turned, semi-inletted '98 stock, also from Herter's, and that was inletted and shaped. I had the action drilled and tapped, the bolt altered, and mounted a Leupold M8-4x in Leupold Detacho mounts before I finished shaping the comb and the length of the stock. This made the scope line up with my eye and the target as soon as the butt touched my shoulder.

As the project moved along, I picked up 25-caliber bullets whenever I ran across them. Cases were as scarce as hen's teeth and I had to buy a couple of boxes of factory loads to get started. A friend loaned me a set of C-H dies, and I was in business. I don't have any idea how many times I loaded and fired those first 40 cases before hunting season rolled around.

The rifle was a joy to shoot, compared to my DCM '03-A3, and was accurate to boot. It averaged just over one inch at 100 yards with most loads and, at that distance, would put five different bullet weights into a 1 1/2-inch group.

Over the next couple of seasons, I killed a few deer with it, but I didn't like the fact that the 100-grain bullets I used wouldn't always come out the other side. I decided to get the chamber throated for a three-inch overall length cartridge so I could load heavier bullets without encroaching on the powder space. This task was accomplished by a gunsmith named Lucius Lazurus and let me make the switch to 117-grain bullets seated to the base of the case neck. Instant success: bullet in/bullet out. The load that worked the best was a hefty charge of H4831 and a Sierra 117-grain spitzer, either flat-base or boattail. It gives an honest 2752 fps through the Chrony and kills deer with authority.

My son-in-law, Craig Cifreo, hung the name "Old Never Miss" on the Roberts after we hunted together in the Atchafalaya Basin, and reaffirmed it when we made a mule deer hunt in Colorado. The name is correct in that it never missed any deer that offered a decent shot, but I did lose the first deer I shot with it. Found the next day, it was spoiled.

This rifle has become the rifle I have complete faith in, regardless of the hunting situation. It has become an extension of me and even after 35 years, a few thousand rounds in load-testing and practice, and hunting in all kinds of weather, it will still shoot 1 1/2- to 1 3/4-inch 5-shot groups from the bench. We have combined for 34 deer at distances from 25 yards to just over 300 yards. My load notes show four swamp rabbits that ended up in the gumbo pot and I remember a cottonmouth moccasin, a yellow coyote, a black coyote and a big raccoon that I grazed on the skull. Dennis found out he wasn't quite gone when he tried to pick him up. Didn't take long to let him go.

Over the years, we've both changed, but the rifle still looks good. The scope mounts are now Weaver bases and Burris Zee rings. The scope is a Leupold Vari-X II 2-7 and the stock is an MPI fiberglass, painted in a camouflage pattern.

I have owned several deer rifles over the years, some of them real gems. They have all been sold or traded for other gems, which in turn, have been sold or traded, but "Old Never-Miss" will always be my pet. My one good gun. ●

by JOHN MALLOY

HANDGUNS TODAY:

AUTOLOADERS

IT IS SOMETIMES difficult to understand some of the factors that influence the world of autoloading handguns.

Certainly, the purchase of sidearms by various governmental bodies is a factor. Companies who make service-type pistols would naturally like to get a contract for a large number of guns of the same type. A number of companies have supplied semiautomatic pistols to various police and military organizations, and then make similar models for commercial sale.

Sometimes, things are not so straightforward. In November 2002, President George Bush approved arming of the pilots of commercial passenger aircraft. The Transportation Security Administration (TSA) apparently opposed the program and set up requirements that tended to discourage participation. A year later, in November 2003, only some 200 pilots had reportedly been armed. Yet, in July 2003, the TSA contracted for up to 9600 40-caliber pistols to arm pilots who completed the program.

The economy appears to be improving, and according to one report, handgun sales are up, and about three-quarters of all new handguns sold now are semiautomatics. Most autoloading handguns can be used for personal protection, and many–perhaps most–are bought with this factor in mind. Personal protection is a valid reason for handgun use, and most states now recognize this fact.

"License to carry" or "carry of concealed weapons" (CCW) legislation continues to grow across the country. Forty-seven states are reported to allow some sort of concealed carry. Only Vermont and Alaska have true "right-to-carry" provisions, under which citizens do not need the government's permission to be armed. (New Hampshire, at the time of this writing, is considering a similar program). In the other states, those with "shall issue," license provisions avoid the bias and favoritism that characterizes states with "may issue" provisions.

How many "shall issue" states are there? Probably about 37 at the time of this writing. Hard to tell at any given moment, though, as anti-gun forces are constantly trying to undermine such laws, and things keep changing.

In Missouri, the legislature passed a CCW law, then the Governor vetoed it, then the legislature overrode the veto, then a judge struck down the law, then the Missouri Supreme Court upheld the law...except in four counties! In addition, the court decided the law imposed an unfounded mandate, and at the time of this writing, no permits have been issued.

In Wisconsin, the legislature passed a CCW law, then the Governor vetoed it, then the state Senate overrode the veto, but then one of the Representatives who had originally cosponsored the legislation changed his mind and the state House failed to override the veto by one vote.

In Ohio, after ten years of effort, a "shall issue" law was passed by the legislature and signed by the Governor, but it contained some ludicrous provisions. Motorists who carry must wear the handgun visible to law enforcement (and everyone else) while in a vehicle, then must immediately put on a concealing outer garment when exiting the vehicle.

Texas has had a "shall issue" law for some time, but anti-gun municipal leaders, with disregard for the law, have held that any public property—including municipal transit and parking areas—is off-limits for concealed carry. Such municipalities have had to be taken to court, one by one, and forced to obey the law. In Houston, the mayor conceded that licensed people could carry concealed on city property, but required that armed citizens wear a special red identification badge.

Georgia also has had CCW for some years, the Metropolitan Atlanta Rapid Transit Authority (MARTA) has required that legally-carried handguns must be separate from their ammunition (illegally-carried handguns are apparently not restricted). I guess, in a way, such a ridiculous provision actually favors autoloading handguns for honest people. In an emergency, it is generally easier to charge a semiauto with a loaded magazine than to draw, open and load a revolver.

In spite of these occasional setbacks and absurdities, we should take heart. Public acceptance of individual carry is growing, as people realize that Wild West shootouts do not occur, and that crime rates go down.

Autoloading handguns are used for many purposes other than for military and police use, or for personal protection. Competitive target shooting of many kinds, small game and/or big game hunting, informal target shooting and plinking, collecting, or just for pride of ownership—all these are reasons for semiautomatic pistols. At times, decorated pistols have been used as a way of raising money for worthy causes.

So, what are the trends in autoloading handguns today?

The Colt/Browning 1911 design seems to be going stronger than ever. Most new pistols introduced are variations on the 1911 theme. However, long-time manufacturers of other types of autoloading pistols now also offer their own 1911 models.

The 22 Long Rifle cartridge remains immensely popular, and new 22 pistols—and conversion kits for centerfire pistols—continue to be introduced.

In a sense, cartridge choices remain the same. The 45 Automatic Colt Pistol (45 ACP) cartridge celebrates its 100th birthday in 2005, and still seems to be king of the hill. 9mm and 40 S&W are very popular. Pocket pistols are still mostly 32 and 380.

In another sense, however, cartridge innovation has seldom offered a wider range of calibers than this year's new offerings. New cartridges ranging from 17- to 50-caliber were introduced, with new 25-, 32- and 45-caliber options in between.

The stainless-steel Accu-Tek AT380 pistol has a new longer grip frame and a magazine that provides an additional round.

The 38 Super cartridge, never a first choice for military or police use, has maintained a certain popularity since its introduction in 1929. It seems to be undergoing a small rejuvenation now, as several companies are bringing out new 38 Super pistols.

The resurrection of good things from the past continues to the guns themselves. Two names too long absent from the pistol scene are now back. Look for them in the report below.

Collectable and commemorative pistols seem to find a following, and a number have appeared this year. An interesting new twist consists of pistols with grips made of the wood of historic trees. Some special pistols offer a way of contributing to worthy causes.

Pistol-carbines are popular. Lacking a better definition, let's include pistols that can be made into carbines, and carbines based on pistols. Not really the proper subjects for this report, perhaps, but related and certainly interesting.

Much is going on. Let's take a look at what the companies are doing:

ADCO is importing the TT 45, a new 45 ACP polymer-frame pistol made in the Czech Republic. This is a peek at one of the first to be displayed.

The new nickel-plated Beretta Cheetah has wood grips and comes in 380 ACP.

ADCO

ADCO, a Massachusetts firm, is now offering a 45-caliber pistol. The new TT 45 is being imported from the Czech Republic. The original CZ firearms factory, established in 1919, began making firearms again after the end of the Soviet Union. That Czech company is now producing the TT 45, and ADCO describes the new pistols as "original CZ."

The mechanism is basically that of the CZ-75, in a polymer-frame package. The design allows carrying the pistol hammer down *(for a double-action first shot)* or cocked-and-locked with the frame-mounted thumb safety. The pistol has a 3.77-inch barrel and measures 7.6 x 5.9 inches. Unloaded weight is about 26 ounces.

The new 45 will probably be followed by other variants in other calibers, and various accessories are available.

Advantage Arms

Advantage Arms has offered, for several years, 22 Long Rifle (22 LR) conversion kits for most models of Glock pistols. Now, the company has introduced a new 22 LR conversion kit for 1911-type pistols. The conversion features Millett adjustable Sights, and has last-round hold-open. Availability was scheduled for summer 2004.

Beretta

Beretta has introduced a number of new models, primarily modifications of the company's basic pistol line.

The Model 92/96 STEEL 1 is designed for the competitive shooter. It has a heavier steel frame, vertex grip, a heavier "Brigadier" slide, and a nickel-alloy finish. With a frame-mounted safety, the STEEL 1 can be carried cocked-and-locked. Recall that Model 92 pistols are 9mm, and Model 96 pistols are 40 Smith & Wesson (40 S&W).

The Model 92 / 96 FS Olive Drab pistols are similar to the United States' M9 military pistol, with an OD finish.

The 92 INOX Lasergrips model is a 9mm in stainless-steel finish with a laser-aiming device contained in the grip panels.

New Cougar INOX pistols are stainless steel with checkered wood grips, a nice-looking combination. The new pistols feature the Cougar's rotating-barrel locking system and are available in 9mm and 40 S&W.

The 84 / 85 FS Cheetah Nickel variant has wood grips and comes in 380 ACP. The Model 84 has a 10-shot magazine. The lighter Model 85 has an 8-shot magazine.

The U22 NEOS carbine kit is now available to convert the NEOS 22-caliber pistol into a light semiautomatic carbine for plinking or small-game hunting. Simply removing the pistol's grip frame and barrel allows installation of the carbine stock and barrel.

A kit is now available to convert the Beretta NEOS 22 pistol into a light carbine. A carbine barrel and grip/buttstock component are furnished, and extra stock combs and extensions are available.

Bernardelli

The Bernardelli polymer-frame pistol, based on the CZ-75 mechanism, is now in full production, and a new variant has been introduced. Resurrecting the company's former "Baby" terminology, the new compact version is called the Bernardelli 2000 Baby.

Bersa

New versions of the Thunder 45 and Thunder 9 Ultra Compact pistols are now available with stainless-steel

Ever wonder if Ken Ramage, the editor of this publication, can shoot a handgun well? He proves that he can at a windswept range in Nevada. The pistol is Beretta's new stainless-steel Cougar in 40 S&W.

Bersa has brought out a version of its Thunder 45 polymer-frame pistol with a stainless-steel slide. A similar 9mm is also available.

The Browning Hi-Power pistol, gone for a while, is back in the lineup, in 9mm and 40 calibers.

▲The smallest of Charles Daly's 1911 pistols, the Ultra X, hopes to join the line soon, as modifications to permit its importation are planned.

slides. The new Bersa pistols have alloy frames with polymer grips, and are of the tilting-barrel locking system. Barrel length is 3.6 inches, and the pistols measure 4.9 x 6.7 inches. Weight is about 27 ounces. Bersa pistols are made in Argentina and are imported by Eagle Imports.

Browning

The standby Browning Hi-Power pistol was absent for a while, but is now back in the Browning lineup. It is available in 9mm and 40 S&W, in several options.

The PRO-9 and PRO-40 double-action-only (DAO) polymer-frame pistols were introduced last year. The 9mm version, the PRO-9, is now in production. The 40-caliber variant may arrive soon.

At the 2004 SHOT Show, Browning also displayed a "Liberty Tree" Hi-Power pistol. The grips of the pistol are made from the wood of the last surviving Liberty Tree. The Liberty Tree story is an interesting part of American history. In the 1770s, Great Britain sought to prevent rebellion by forbidding private meetings in the colonies. Each colony selected a tree, a "Liberty Tree," as a meeting place, in order to get around the British order. The last tree, a tulip poplar in Maryland, came down during a hurricane in 1999. The wood was harvested and preserved by the American Forests organization, and the wood has been used for the grips. For each of the 228 pistols sold (numbered 1776 to 2004) trees will be planted in environmental restoration projects.

Bushmaster

Late in 2003, Bushmaster Firearms, Inc. acquired the Professional Ordnance firm. Professional Ordnance's 223-caliber Carbon 15 pistols (and rifles) now are part of Bushmaster's product line. The former Professional Ordnance facility in Arizona has become Bushmaster's western division. The Carbon 15 arms are made on the AR-15 pattern, but are built from a carbon composition material instead of aluminum. The weight reduction allows pistols that weigh about 46 ounces.

The new Bushmaster Carbon 15 pistols are designated Type 97 (fluted barrel) or Type 21 (unfluted barrel). Two variants of the Type 21, mechanically the same, are offered. The commercial version has a bright stainless-steel barrel and comes with a 10-round magazine. The law-enforcement pistol has a black-coated stainless-steel barrel, and can be had with a 30-round magazine.

Century

New additions to Century's line of Philippine-made 45-caliber 1911-type pistols are twofold. The first type has most of the features modern shooters seem to like—beavertail grip safety, low profile rear sight and round spur hammer. Another variant has these features, but in addition, the top of the slide is flat and the front of the frame is squared. This treatment adds weight, mostly forward, to help control recoil and muzzle rise. The new 45s were scheduled for mid-2004 availability.

Century is importing the Korean Daewoo pistols, which have been absent for a while. Recall that these pistols use the "tri-fire" system that allows the pistol to be carried hammer-down for a double-action (DA) first shot, or cocked-and-locked for a single-

The new polymer-frame Browning PRO 9 pistol, announced last year, is in full production.

◀The Korean Daewoo pistol, absent for some time, is now being imported by Century International Arms. This is the compact DP51C in 9mm. Full-size variants in 9mm and 40 S&W are also available.

Daewoo "tri-fire" pistols can be carried hammer-down for double-action use or cocked-and-locked. For a third option, a cocked hammer can also simply be pushed forward for safe carry and instant readiness.

▲A highly-polished stainless version of the new Colt 38 Super has early-style parts and resembles the bright nickel pistols of the past.

▲Colt has brought back the 38 Super, and a blued version with enhancements is standard.

▲A brand-new Colt Model 1911, in the pattern of the WWI pistols, is now a catalog item.

action (SA) first shot. In addition, a third method may be used. A cocked hammer can simply be pushed forward for safe carry, after which a light pull on the trigger will cock the hammer again.

Century also offers newly-manufactured Egyptian 9mm Helwan pistols, and also Arcus 9mm pistols in several variations.

Charles Daly

Brand new in the Charles Daly lineup is the ZDA pistol, which bears something of a resemblance to the SIG P 226, both in looks and function. The new ZDA has a 4-inch barrel and will be available in 9mm and 40 S&W.

A new variant added to the HP (Hi-Power) line has a chrome finish and express sights. This pistol will probably be cataloged as an Empire Grade entry.

The M-5 line of 1911-type polymer-frame pistols has a new addition. A 5-inch bull-barrel version is now available, made on the 10-round high-capacity frame. The Ultra X version of the Daly M-5, the little 3-inch barrel variant, was announced last year but will probably not make an appearance until late in 2004. It ran afoul of the BATF's absurd point system and could not be imported. The company hopes that by adding features such as a loaded-chamber indicator, the Ultra X will gain approval.

Colt

The 38 Super is back in the Colt lineup! Introduced in 1929, Colt's 38 Super pistol for a time held the position of being the most powerful handgun made, in terms of energy and penetration. The pistol and cartridge developed a following among lawmen and outdoorsmen. More recently, the 38 Super has become a favorite for action- and practical-style shooting competition.

Colt offers the 38 Super in three different models, all full-size with 5-inch barrels. The blued version has a Commander hammer, aluminum trigger and rubber composite grips. The stainless variant has these same features in a stainless-steel pistol. The top of the line Super is made of stainless steel, polished bright to resemble the early nickel finishes. It features a traditional spur hammer and checkered "big diamond" wood grips.

The World War I-style 1911 pistol, displayed in prototype last year at the 2003 SHOT Show, is now a standard catalog item. A WWI-type screwdriver and copy of an original manual are included with each pistol.

CZ USA

The new CZ Model 2075 "RAMI" is a compact little pistol based on the CZ 75 mechanism. This version is the smallest yet made, with a 3-inch barrel and weight of less than 25 ounces. At

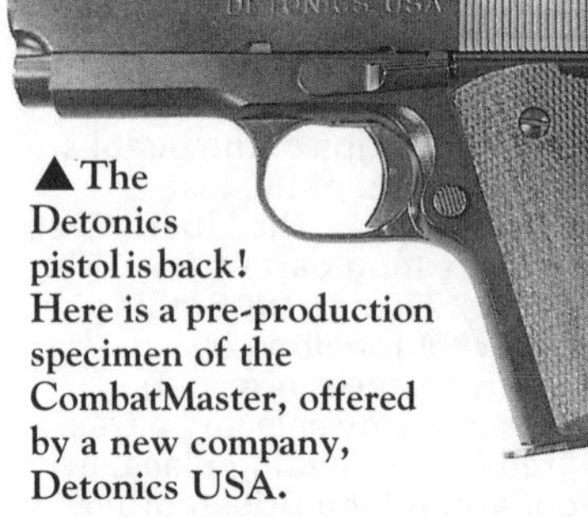

▲The Detonics pistol is back! Here is a pre-production specimen of the CombatMaster, offered by a new company, Detonics USA.

Principals of the original Detonics company are involved with Detonics USA. Sid Woodcock *(left)* the original designer, and Peter Dunn, gunsmith, hold variants that will be offered by the new company.

▲The new CZ 2075 "Rami" pistol is the most compact version of the CZ 75 mechanism offered.

▲Ed Brown's Executive Carry pistol is a "commander-size" 1911-type 45 with the "bobtail" grip treatment.

New offerings by Excel Arms: Richard Gilliam holds the 17 HRM carbine, Kathy Gilliam shows the Accu-Tek AT 380 II pistol, and Excel President Larry Gilliam displays the 17 HRM pistol.

4.7 x 6.5 inches, it falls just between our arbitrary categories of compact (5 x 7) and subcompact (4 x 6). The pistol is offered in 9mm and 40 S&W. The staggered-column magazine gives 10+1 capacity in 9mm and 8+1 in 40.

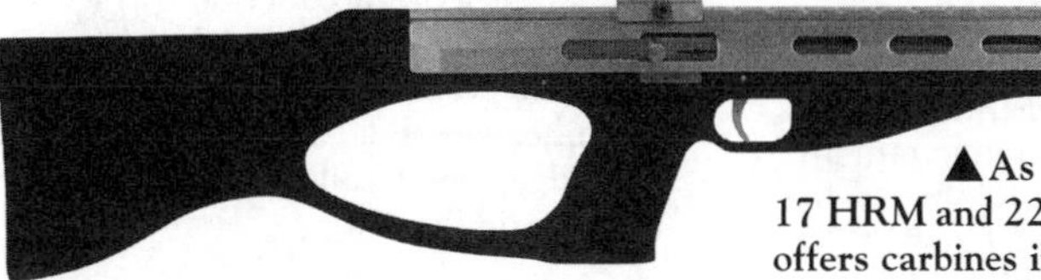

▲As companions to their new 17 HRM and 22 WMR pistols, Excel Arms offers carbines in the same calibers.

Detonics

Detonics is back! The original Detonics company was formed in Washington state about 1976 and stayed in business until 1988. It was sold to another group in Phoenix, AZ who did business as New Detonics Manufacturing Co. Within a few years, however, at least by 1992, that company had ceased to do business.

Now a new company, Detonics USA, has been formed in Atlanta, GA by some of the principals of the original firm. Designer Sid Woodcock and gunsmith Peter Dunn are back making Detonics pistols. Author Jerry Ahern, an early proponent of the Detonics design, is also involved with the company.

Woodcock, with his background in explosives, named the first pistol "Detonics," a word related to the science of explosives. That early pistol, the first compact 45-caliber pistol, introduced a number of concepts that are widely used today. The cone-shaped bushingless barrel, captive counter-wound recoil spring and enlarged ejection port were all introduced with the early Detonics pistols. The company was also one of the early users of stainless steel as a suitable material for autoloading pistols.

Detonics USA will offer the small version—the 3 1/2-inch barrel CombatMaster—as its first product, because "that is the Detonics that people remember." The mid-size ServiceMaster and full-size ScoreMaster—also produced by the original company—will be offered later. Initial production was scheduled for October 2004.

EAA

European American Armory (EAA) has added a few new variants to its popular Witness line of Tanfoglio-made pistols.

A Witness P variant with a polymer frame and stainless-steel slide is now available in 10mm chambering with the short 3.6-inch barrel. A Witness PS can be had in 9mm with an accessory rail on the forward part of the frame.

The Witness Limited target pistol, a big single-action pistol in chrome finish and with adjustable Sights, is now available in 38 Super chambering.

Ed Brown

Ed Brown Products of Perry, MO, offers the Executive Elite (5-inch barrel) and Executive Carry (4 1/4-inch barrel) lines. These 1911-type pistols are offered in three finishes—blue, stainless steel, and blue slide on a stainless-steel frame. Front straps and mainspring housings are checkered at 25 lines per inch (lpi), and grips are checkered Cocobolo wood.

The larger Elite pistols have straight mainspring housings. The smaller Carry guns feature the Ed Brown "Bobtail" treatment, in which the end of the mainspring housing and grip frame angles forward. The Bobtail shape makes concealment easier, and many like the feel of the modified grip.

Excel

Excel Industries makes the Accu-Tek AT-380 pistol, and for 2004, the Accu-Tek was designed with a slightly longer grip and a magazine holding an extra round. Measuring just over 4 x 6 inches, the little stainless-steel 380 is still in the subcompact class, and has 6+1 capacity. Each new AT-380 pistol comes with two 6-round magazines, a hard case and a lock.

A totally new pistol, the Accelerator, is now offered, chambered for either the 17 Hornady Magnum Rimfire (17 HMR) or 22 Winchester Magnum Rimfire (22 WMR). Model numbers are MP-17 and MP-22, respectively. Either pistol has an 8 1/2-inch barrel and

▲A new full-size 1911-type offering from Ed Brown is the Executive Elite 45.

▶The Excel Arms MP 17 is a new semiauto pistol for the 17 HRM cartridge. A similar pistol is also made for the 22WMR.

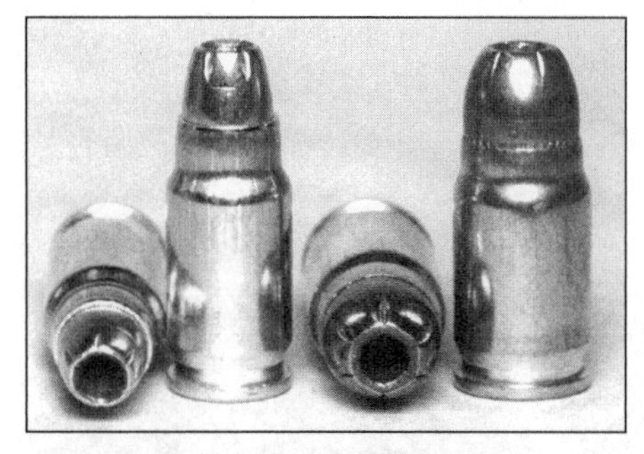

After several years of development, the hot new 25 NAA version of North American Arms' Guardian series has been introduced.

▲Glock or 1911 pistols can be converted into carbines with Mech-Tech's Carbine Conversion Unit. This is a Glock conversion.

▲Here is a pre-production version of the Glock Model 37. The production model has a heavier slide, and the cartridge is now called the 45 GAP (45 Glock Automatic Pistol).

weight of about 54 ounces. The big pistols are constructed from stainless steel, with a polymer grip. An aluminum top rib contains fully adjustable sights and allows mounting of optical or other types of Sighting devices. The Excel Accelerator is the second semiautomatic pistol to be offered for the 17 HMR cartridge.

A carbine with a related mechanism is also offered in the same calibers. This will not convert to a pistol, or vice versa, but it uses the same ammunition and same 9-shot magazine, and would make a neat companion piece with the pistol.

Excel also makes a conversion kit that will adapt a 1911 pistol to use either the 17 HMR or the 22 WMR cartridges, in 8-round magazines. This is a serious conversion, with an 8 1/2-inch barrel and fully adjustable Sights.

FNH

FNH USA is the American arm of FN Herstal, offering some firearms similar to those sold under the Browning name.

The 9mm FNP-9 was introduced last year, and it has now been joined by the FNP-40, in 40 S&W caliber. The pistol is a conventional double action with a high-capacity polymer frame and an ambidextrous decocker. With a 4-inch barrel, the FNP-40 is only 7 inches long, and weighs about 25 ounces.

Glock

The Glock Model 37—chambered for the new 45 Glock Automatic Pistol (45 GAP) cartridge—was introduced last year and is now in production. The 45 GAP uses a shorter case (about 0.750") and shorter overall length (about 1.10") than the standard 45 Automatic Colt Pistol (45 ACP) cartridge. Some changes have been made since the introduction of the Model 37, noticeably the use of a heavier slide—a modified Model 21 slide. However, the Model 37 is still about the same general size as the original Model 17 9mm pistol. The shorter 45 GAP cartridge allows the use of a smaller frame, but limits the loadings to the shorter-length 45-caliber bullets. Chamber pressure of the 45 GAP is somewhat higher than that of the 45 ACP, but several companies have begun to produce it, and at least one other manufacturer plans to offer a 45 GAP chambering in its pistol line.

Olive-drab (OD) frames are now available on some Glock pistols. Available only through Acusport, Models 17, 19, 21, 22, 23 and 27 can be had in OD after June 2004.

Guncrafter Industries

Displayed for the first time at the February 2004 SHOT Show, the GI Model No. 1 from Guncrafter Industries attracted considerable attention. At first glance, the new pistol appears to be another modernized full-size 1911 of normal size and weight. Until one notices the size of the bore. It is a 50-caliber!

The new GI pistol is chambered for the new 50 GI cartridge. The cartridge is a new one, with a case slightly shorter in length than a 45 ACP, and with a rebated rim the same diameter as the 45 ACP. The loaded 50-caliber round is about the same overall length as the 45 ACP. Ammunition, brass, bullets and reloading dies *(dies made by Hornady and Lee Precision)* are available from the company. The 50 GI ammunition, as loaded, features a light

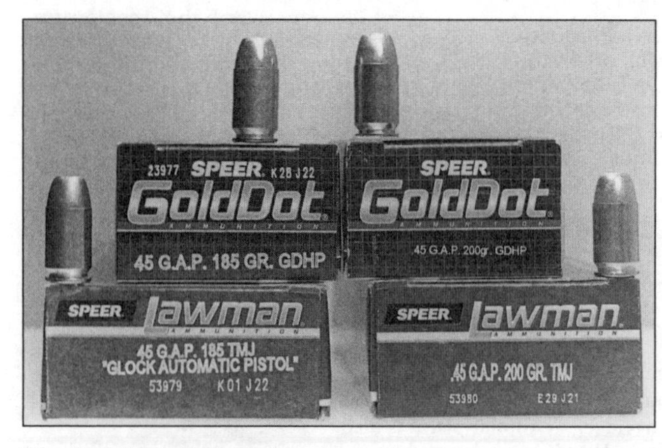

The 45 GAP (45 Glock Automatic Pistol) cartridge, introduced last year, already has a number of different loads offered for it.

▲It looks like an enhanced 45-caliber 1911, but it is a 50-caliber! Guncrafter Industries GI Model No. 1 is chambered for the powerful new 50 GI cartridge.

Three different loadings of 50 GI cartridges are offered. The rebated rims are the same diameter as that of the 45 ACP, and the overall length is about the same. A 45 ACP is on the right for comparison.

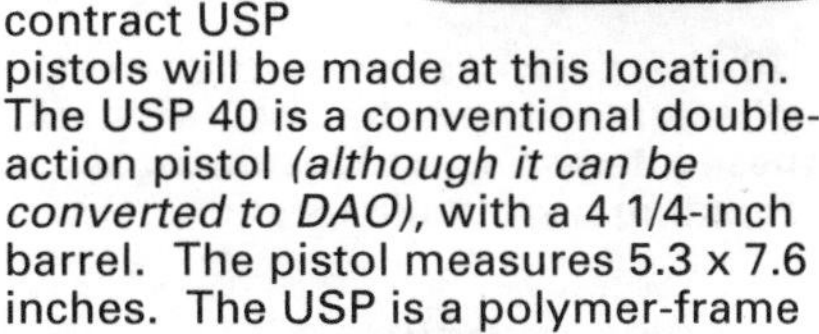

The new Hi-Point polymer-frame 40 and 45-caliber pistols have undergone some refinements and are now in full production. Adjustable Sights and accessory rails are standard.

load (300-grain bullet at 725 fps) and a heavier load (300-grain bullet at 900 fps). At the introduction, three bullet types—jacketed flat point, soft point and hollow point—were displayed.

Although the pistol is externally the same as a 45-caliber 1911, there are internal dimensional differences. The pistol uses a cone barrel that is fitted directly into the front of the slide. The magazine well in the frame is machined larger to accept the fatter 50-caliber magazine. These changes preclude using those standard 1911 parts, but GI offers a conversion kit of their special parts to convert their Model No. 1 to 45 ACP.

Heckler & Koch

In July 2003, the Transportation Security Administration (TSA) made plans to acquire up to 9600 40-caliber pistols. The pistols were to be used to arm U. S. commercial airline pilots who passed the Federal Flight Deck Officer (FFDO) program administered by the TSA. The contract was awarded to Heckler & Koch (HK) for their USP 40 pistol. In August 2003, HK announced its first U. S. factory, which would be at a site at Columbus, GA. The official groundbreaking for the plant was on October 14, 2003. Reportedly, the contract USP pistols will be made at this location. The USP 40 is a conventional double-action pistol *(although it can be converted to DAO)*, with a 4 1/4-inch barrel. The pistol measures 5.3 x 7.6 inches. The USP is a polymer-frame pistol with a blued slide.

Newly introduced at the February 2004 SHOT Show were two variants of the P 2000 K subcompact pistol, in 9mm and 40 S&W. Smaller and lighter than the USP series, the P 2000 series pistols have different trigger mechanisms. With 3.6-inch barrels, the pistols measure 5 x 7 inches.

High Standard

High Standard and Aguila worked together, and last year introduced the 17 Hi-Standard cartridge, basically a 22 Long Rifle case necked down to 17-caliber, and loaded with a 20-grain bullet. The new round worked perfectly in rebarreled Hi-Standard semiautomatic pistols. However, High Standard has held off marketing the 17-caliber pistols.

In February 2004, a new 17-caliber cartridge based on the 22 LR case was announced. Hornady and CCI worked together to develop a similar—but not quite the same—short 17 round, the 17 Mach 2, with a 17-grain bullet. Eley also plans to make the ammunition. There seems to be a substantial amount of interest in a Long Rifle-length 17, and it will be interesting to see how this situation plays out.

High Standard continues its line of 22 LR target pistols, 45-caliber 1911-type pistols and conversion kits to adapt the 1911 to 22 LR.

Among the new items is the Shea Custom 10X pistol, a 22 target pistol to be hand-built in small quantities by High Standard gunsmith Bob Shea. Shea worked for High Standard from 1943 to 1984, then as an independent gunsmith specializing in Hi-Standard pistols after that. He apparently knows what he is doing.

Another new item is the Marine Corps Trial Pistol, a 45-caliber 1911-type pistol that has the features of the pistol that High Standard submitted for the United States Marine Corps (USMC) sidearm trials.

Hi-Point

Last year, Hi-Point introduced new polymer-frame 40- and 45-caliber pistols. Some minor refinements have been made, and the pistols are now in full production. These are the least expensive new handguns made in these calibers, but seem to work fine and shoot well. Recall that these are blowback pistols, yet are rated for +P ammunition, and have a lifetime warranty.

The 17-caliber rimfire scene has seen a surprising amount of activity. From left, a 17 Hi-Standard, made by Aguila; a 17 Mach 2, made by CCI and the 17 Mach 2 as made by Eley. The earlier 17 Hornady Magnum Rimfire is at the right for comparison.

The 40 and 45-caliber polymer-frame Hi-Point pistols are in full production. Here, Malloy shoots the new 45.

Best-known for replicas of 1800s firearms, IAR also offers a small number of 45 ACP Chinese copies of the Mauser "broomhandle" pistol. IAR president Will Hanson holds a specimen.

The 7-ounce Kel-Tec 380-caliber pistol, the Model P3AT, is now in full production.

New for 2004 is the Hi-Point carbine in 40 S&W. The carbine, of course, belongs in another report, but is mentioned here because the 10-shot magazine is identical to, and interchangeable with, that of the new 40-caliber pistol. In the Old West, it was an advantage to have a carbine and a handgun that used the same ammunition. Hi-Point offers that advantage with the added factor that extra magazines will work in either carbine or pistol.

IAR

One thinks of the IAR (International Antique Reproductions) firm as a source of shooting replicas of 19th century historical firearms. However, they have a small quantity of the original big 45 ACP Chinese "broomhandle Mauser" copies made in the 20th century. It may be of interest to collectors to know that a small stock of these interesting and historical autoloading pistols still exists.

Kahr

Kahr has introduced a number of new models, all variations of the company's patented DAO mechanism. As the number of models has grown, so have the designations for these models. Here is a breakdown that may help in understanding the Kahr offerings: "K" alone before a number indicates the original stainless-steel Kahr offering, a mid-size pistol with a 3.5-inch barrel. The numbers 9 or 40 following always indicate the caliber. A "P" prefix indicates a polymer-frame pistol. "M" indicates a Micro Compact, with a 3-inch barrel. "T" represents target or tactical pistols, which have 4-inch barrels.

With this in mind, the new PM 40 pistol is a small 40-caliber, polymer-frame pistol with a 3-inch barrel. The slide is matte stainless steel, and the pistol comes with two magazines—one flush, one elongated for extended grip and an extra round.

The TP 9 is a new 4-inch barrel, polymer-frame 9mm pistol. The polymer frame is black and the slide is matte stainless steel. Either 3-dot sights or tritium night sights are available. Delivery was scheduled for mid-2004.

Impress your friends by being able to tell the difference between the P3AT *(left)* and the earlier P-32. The P-32 *(right)* has narrower grasping grooves and a lightening cut at the front of the slide.

The T 40 is a 29-ounce 40-caliber stainless-steel frame pistol with a 4-inch barrel. Checkered wood Hogue grips offset the matte-finish stainless steel, and make a sharp-looking pistol. This variant began shipping in February 2004.

Recall that Kahr also offers the Auto-Ordnance line of Thompson 45-caliber pistols. The Custom 1911 pistol, announced last year, is now a catalog item. It is all stainless steel, a full-size pistol with a 5-inch barrel. It features a beavertail grip safety, lightened hammer, adjustable trigger and other niceties. Grips are laminate with big-diamond checkering and have the Thompson bullet logo inlaid.

Kel-Tec

Kel-Tec's little 380 pistol, the P-3AT, which was introduced last year, is now in full production. Like its predecessor, the P-32, it uses a tilting-barrel locked-breech system.

The 380 is very slightly longer than the 32, and weight has gone up a bit over 1/2-ounce to 7.3 ounces. Visually, about all that distinguishes the new 380 are the wider spacing of the grasping grooves and the absence of some lightening cuts on the slide.

Mechanically, the P-3AT does not have the internal slide lock of the P-32. This apparently was omitted to make space for the larger-diameter 380 cartridge and still keep the width to 3/4-inch. The greater diameter of the cartridge also decreases the magazine to six rounds (6+1 total) capacity. However, a magazine extension is available as an accessory to increase the capacity by an extra round.

Other accessories avail for the P-3AT are a belt clip *(very useful in some carry situations)* and a lanyard kit. The lanyard kit includes an attachment unit for the rear of the pistol, and an elastic lanyard with a latching hook. Handgun guru Jeff Cooper pointed out the benefits of using a lanyard over 40 years ago, and it is interesting that Kel-Tec is offering the option.

Kimber

In 2004, Kimber celebrated its 25th anniversary. To commemorate this special event, the company decided that a number of special 1911 pistols would be made. A total of 1,911 *(a logical number)* 25th Anniversary "Custom" pistols would be made. In addition, 500 25th Anniversary "Gold Match" pistols would be produced. 250 pairs of one each of the Custom and Gold Match pistols, with matching serial numbers, would also be put up in wood presentation cases.

In their regular line, the company offers the Stainless TLE II pistol, a 45 ACP version of the Kimber selected for duty carry by the LAPD's SWAT team. The gun is a full-size 1911-type pistol with a 5-inch barrel. It has tritium night sights.

From the Kimber Custom Shop, the 22 LR pistol introduced last year now is available in a "Rimfire Super" version, with two-tone finish, adjustable Sights, ambidextrous thumb safety, big diamond wood grips and other niceties. Performance has not taken a back seat to looks, though—the 22 pistol has turned in 1 1/2-inch groups at 25 yards.

As of February 2004, Kimber had donated $200,000 to the USA Shooting team. Kimber is thus the largest firearms corporate donor in USA Shooting Team history. The money comes from the sales of special guns, and goes straight to benefit the team. Way to go, Kimber!

Korth

Willi Korth began business by making blank revolvers in 1954, so 2004 became the 50th anniversary of the German Korth company. The firm now has a reputation for making very fine *(and very expensive)* handguns. To commemorate this 50-year milestone, a few specially–embellished Korth pistols and revolvers were scheduled. Five semiautomatic pistols, in 9mm, and five 357 Magnum revolvers will be available, Korth USA reports.

Ammunition for the potent 32NAA is in production. Cor-Bon now produces two loads—a zippy 60-grain jacketed hollow-point, and a 71-grain full-metal-jacket "target load."

Les Baer

New from Les Baer Custom are two 1911-type 45-caliber pistols in the Thunder Ranch series, which was introduced last year. The Commanche is a serious self-defense pistol with a 4 1/4-inch barrel. It is chrome-plated.

The Home Defense pistol is designed for use in dark environments. It has an M3 tactical illuminator mounted to the front of the "Monolith" frame. The light can be selected to be on for constant or momentary time periods. Night Sights are also provided.

Lone Star

In February 2003, Lone Star Armament introduced a new series of 1911-type pistols. In November 2003, it was announced that Lone Star had been acquired by STI. ***(see STI)***

Mech-Tech

Mech-Tech offers a Carbine Conversion Unit (CCU) that uses the frame of a 1911 or Glock pistol to form a pistol-caliber carbine. Pistol-carbines seem to be of interest now, and this is an interesting device.

Mitchell

The new 1911-type pistols shown in prototype last year are now in production. The first display of production models was at the February 2004 SHOT Show in Las Vegas, NV. The guns are called "Mitchell Gold Series" 1911s, and combine the original 1911 mechanism with 21st century enhancements.

Chamberings have been expanded from the original 45 ACP to also include 40 S&W, 9mm and 38 Super. Standard features include beavertail grip safety, lowered ejection port, skeletonized hammer and trigger, extended thumb safety, walnut big-diamond grips and other niceties.

North American

North American Arms (NAA) has introduced a new pistol in its Guardian series, chambered for the new 25 NAA cartridge. The pistol is the same size as their 13-ounce 32 ACP Guardian, and has been in development for several years. The first concept was to neck down the semi-rimmed 32 ACP to 25-caliber. That approach was tried, but did not give the 100-percent reliability desired. Working with Cor-Bon, NAA developed a new rimless case with a longer body, and the body diameter of the 32 Harrington & Richardson Magnum (32 H&R Magnum). Although this newer case is longer than that of the 32 ACP, the overall length of the loaded cartridge is about the same.

The performance of the 25 NAA is of some interest. A 35-grain Hornady XTP bullet screams out of its 2.2-inch barrel at about 1200 feet per second (fps). Considering that the case is about three-quarters of an inch long, the bullet only has about 1-1/2 inches to get up to speed. Pretty impressive.

The 25 NAA cartridge was developed for a small 32-size pistol. From left, a 32 ACP; an experimental 25 formed by necking down the 32 ACP; and the final 25 NAA with a longer rimless case, but of about the same overall length as the 32.

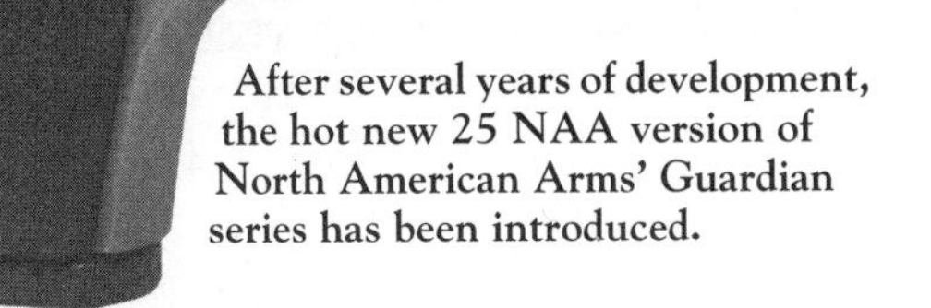

After several years of development, the hot new 25 NAA version of North American Arms' Guardian series has been introduced.

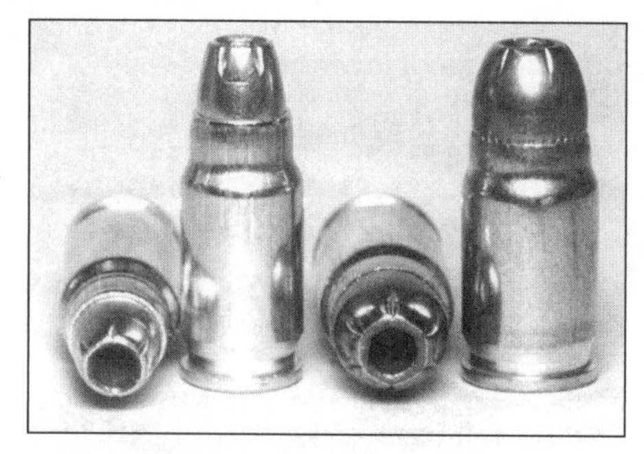

North American Arms has provided two new cartridges for pocket pistols. The 32NAA has been joined this year by the new 25NAA round.

North American has also introduced an optional 10-shot extended magazine adapter for its 32 ACP and 380 ACP Guardians. Made by Hogue, the adaptor uses the original magazine and floorplate. It increases capacity, while providing additional grip surface.

Olympic Arms

The Whitney is back! At the February 2004 SHOT Show, Olympic Arms announced the return of the Whitney Wolverine. As many old-timers may remember, the original Whitney pistol appeared about 1955 or 1956. Its streamlined, futuristic styling and light aluminum-alloy frame made it stand out from other postwar pistols. The company, however, ran into financial problems, and production stopped after fewer than 14,000 pistols had been produced.

Olympic Arms has improved the Whitney design, and displayed a pre-production specimen at the show. Handguns with aluminum-alloy frames were a novel idea in the 1950s. Now, half a century later, polymer plastics have gained acceptance, and Olympic has updated the Whitney with a new polymer frame. Other additions will be a ventilated rib, a dovetailed rear Sight, and better distinction of the manual safety positions.

The Whitney name was on the pre-production specimen, and is planned to appear on the final production model.

The new Para "Power Extractor" was introduced in the new PXT 1911 full-size pistol.

The original designer, Bob Hillberg, reportedly requested that the name be retained. Production was scheduled to begin in mid-2004.

Many older shooters liked the original Whitney pistol and hoped for its return to production. Olympic's new version should please them, and introduce younger generations to the Whitney.

Pacific Armament

Pacific Armament has introduced a line of Argentine-made FM Hi-Power 9mm pistols. These have the original-style round hammer spurs of the early Belgian-made Hi-Powers, and come with 10-round magazines. The standard "Military" model has a 4.65-inch barrel. A more compact version, the "Detective" model, has a 3.65-inch barrel. Kits to convert existing pistols to Detective configuration are offered. Also, a conversion kit to adapt the Hi-Power pistols to 22 LR is available.

The company also imports a line of Philippine-made 45-caliber 1911-style pistols in full-size (5-inch barrel), mid-size (4-inch barrel) and compact (3 1/2-inch barrel) variants. These pistols are offered in the United States under the Rock Island Armory name.

Para-Ordnance

Para-Ordnance's big news is the introduction of its new "Power Extractor." In the past several years, many makers of 1911-type pistols have begun using coil-spring-loaded external extractors instead of the tempered-steel internal extractor of the original 1911 design.

Para's answer was a new internal extractor, spring-loaded, that reportedly maintains constant pressure against the rim of the cartridge case and has twice the surface area of the original 1911 design. The rear of the Power Extractor is the same size as that of the original, and thus maintains the classic 1911 appearance.

The first two Para pistols with the new extractor are the 5-inch barrel PXT 1911, and the 4 1/4-inch barrel PXT LTC. The Power Extractor will soon become standard on all Para models. Both new PXT pistols also have ramped barrels and supported chambers, features that have been made standard on all Para pistols. As with all Para-Ordnance pistols, they are shipped with two magazines.

The company has a number of new introductions. Of interest to those who favor small, big-bore pistols with as many shots as possible is the new Warthog. It is a 3-inch barrel 10-shot 45 that weighs only 24 ounces. Para is coming up with so many new

Olympic Arms is planning to reintroduce the futuristic Whitney pistol of the 1950s. Here is a peek at a pre-production specimen.

▲This cutaway slide shows the enlarged gripping surfaces of the new Para Power Extractor.

Para-Ordnance's CCW pistol introduced "Griptor" grooves on the frame front strap and sides of the slide.

options that the company plans to publish two catalogs a year to keep shooters current on their offerings.

Para-Ordnance is proud that the Para CCW pistol was chosen as the winner of the *Guns & Ammo* "Gun of the Year" award for 2003. This makes the fourth time one of the company's products has won the award. The Para CCW introduced "Griptor" grasping grooves on the frame front strap and sides of the slide.

World Champion shooter Todd Jarrett has used different Para pistols to win all four United States Practical Shooting Association (USPSA) national championships—Open, Limited, Limited 10 and Production. This seems to speak well for Para's accuracy and functioning.

Phoenix

Phoenix Arms, maker of affordable 22- and 25-caliber pistols for personal protection and informal target shooting, is working on a larger-caliber 380 pistol. No prototype was available for observation at the February 2004 SHOT Show. However, a representative said the pistol would probably be similar in design to the present pistols in the Phoenix line. The new 380 was expected to be announced during Summer 2004.

Professional Ordnance

Late in 2003, Professional Ordnance was acquired by Bushmaster Firearms, Inc. Professional Ordnance's Carbon 15 pistols (and rifles) will be manufactured under the Bushmaster name. ***(see Bushmaster)***

Rock River Arms

Rock River has added a new "basic carry" pistol to its offerings of 1911-type pistols. This is a lower-priced model in Parkerized finish, but still includes a beavertail grip safety, and ventilated trigger and hammer.

A 9mm long-slide version with a 6-inch barrel is also new. This configuration is aimed toward PPC shooters, and has a supported chamber.

For those who want to build their own pistols, a frame and slide kit is available. Most of the fitting is done, and a shooter can build a 1911 to his own specifications.

Rohrbaugh

The little DAO Rohrbaugh R9 pistol, introduced as a prototype two years ago, and as a pre-production specimen one year ago, is now in production. Several hundred guns had been made by early 2004.

Recall that the pistol uses standard 9mm ammunition, and has a tilting-barrel locked breech action. It is all metal, with 7075 aluminum frame and 17-4 stainless-steel slide and barrel. With a 2.9-inch barrel, the pistol measures only 3.7 x 5.2 inches, putting it in the smallest part of the subcompact class. Weight is 12.8 ounces, and capacity is 6 +1. The R9 is available with or without Sights.

Ruger

All Ruger adjustable-sight 22-caliber pistols will now be drilled and tapped for a Weaver-type base, and the base itself will be included with each drilled pistol. The base fits in front of the rear sight, and does not interfere with the pistol's metallic sights, but allows easy mounting of optical or electronic sights.

The Ruger NRA pistol has special markings and simulated ivory grips. For each pistol sold, a donation is made to NRA's training programs.

Two special model 22 pistols were scheduled for production during 2004. The first, the William B. Ruger Endowment Special NRA Edition pistol, is a blued Mark II with simulated ivory grips, with red eagle Ruger grip medallions. William B. Ruger's signature is rollmarked on the top of the receiver, along with the Ruger and NRA crests. For every pistol sold, a donation is made to the National Rifle Association's basic marksmanship training program.

The U. S. A. Shooting commemorative is a Mark II with gold plating on the bolt, and black laminate grip panels. For every pistol sold, a donation is made to the United States Shooting Team, which is preparing for the Olympic contests in Athens, Greece. As of February 2004, Ruger had contributed $30,000 to the U. S. A. Shooting Team. Bravo!

A "commander-size" Para pistol, the PXT LTC, comes with the new Power Extractor.

SIGARMS

Will the popularity of the 1911 design ever level out? Last year, Smith & Wesson added a 1911 to that company's offerings. In February 2004, SIGARMS unveiled their own 1911.

SIGARMS realized that American practical shooting is dominated by the 1911, and in order to be competitive, the company needed to add a 1911 to their line. The result was the GSR pistol. "GSR" stands for "Granite Series Rail," and denotes the accessory rail on the front portion of the slide. The rail is one thing that makes the SIG 1911 GSR visually distinctive from some other 1911s. Another factor is the shape of the slide's top and side cuts, which make the GSR look a little bit more "SIGgy." The GSR is a high-end pistol, and has an external extractor and many of the enhancements that are now in favor. It comes as a stainless-steel, or a blued stainless-steel finish.

Other SIGARMS models now have variants that incorporate an accessory rail. Among them are the P 220, P 226 and P 229. The single-action P 210 is now available with a U. S.-style magazine release on the left side of the frame.

An interesting new development is the "K trigger" option for some of the company's pistols. The K trigger is a new DAO with a pull similar to the best double-action revolver triggers. The frame of the pistol has to be changed to accommodate the new trigger mechanism, which involves new parts, spring rates and cam angles.

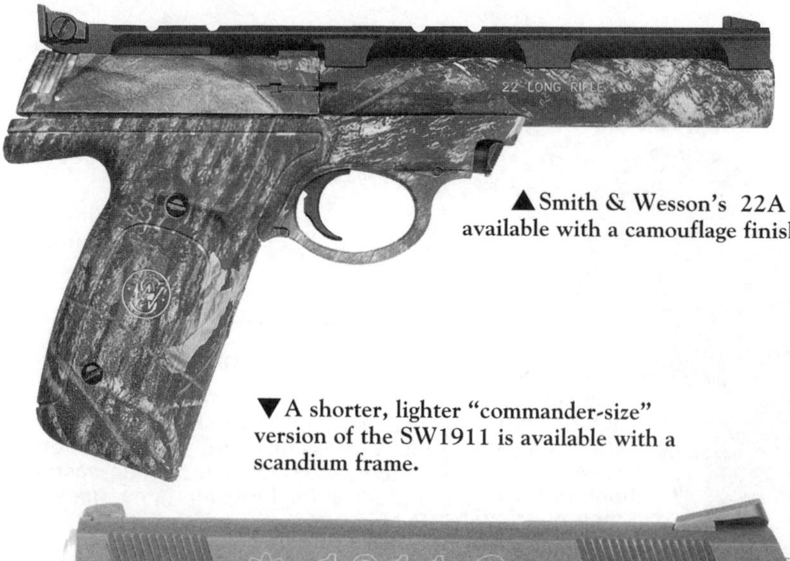

▲Smith & Wesson's 22A pistol is now available with a camouflage finish.

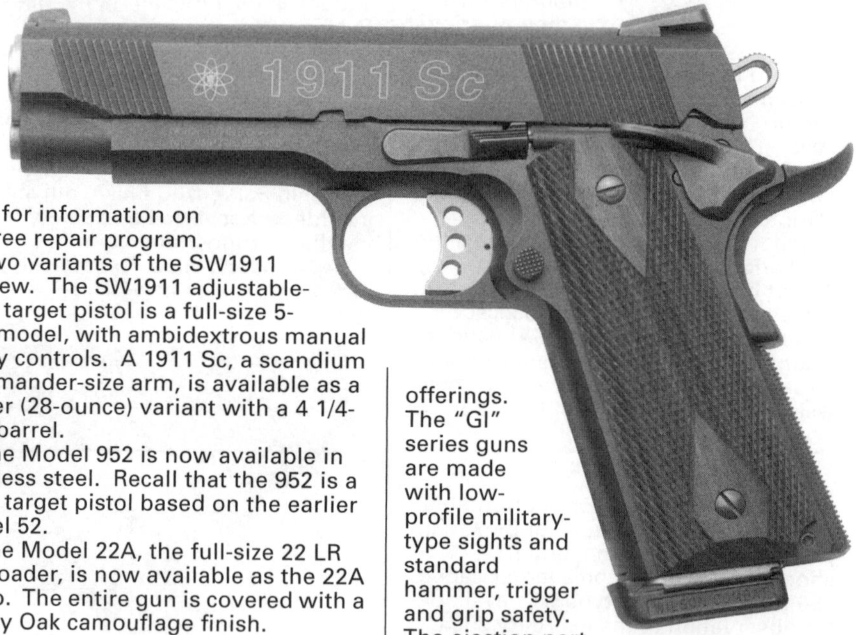

▼A shorter, lighter "commander-size" version of the SW1911 is available with a scandium frame.

Smith & Wesson

The SW1911, introduced last year, has been out long enough to warrant a minor recall. Some specimens might need to have the firing pin safety plunger repaired. If you have an SW1911 between the numbers JRD 0000 and JRD 4750, call 1-800-331-0852 for information on the free repair program.

Two variants of the SW1911 are new. The SW1911 adjustable-sight target pistol is a full-size 5-inch model, with ambidextrous manual safety controls. A 1911 Sc, a scandium Commander-size arm, is available as a lighter (28-ounce) variant with a 4 1/4-inch barrel.

The Model 952 is now available in stainless steel. Recall that the 952 is a 9mm target pistol based on the earlier Model 52.

The Model 22A, the full-size 22 LR autoloader, is now available as the 22A Camo. The entire gun is covered with a Mossy Oak camouflage finish.

Springfield

It is back to basics for part of Springfield Armory's new 1911A1 offerings. The "GI" series guns are made with low-profile military-type sights and standard hammer, trigger and grip safety. The ejection port is standard, not lowered, and a lanyard loop again appears at the rear of the butt. Slide serrations are the older narrow vertical type. Some concessions have been made to the modern era, as the barrels have ramped barrels with fully supported chambers. Except for the big-diamond walnut grips, the 5-inch Parkerized version is a dead ringer for the World War II 1911A1 configuration. There are also other versions in the GI line—a 5-inch OD green Armory Kote, a 5-inch stainless steel variant, and 3-inch and 4-inch Parkerized variants. It is good to have these basic models available again, so that new shooters do not think that every 1911 has to look like a racegun.

In the XD line of polymer-frame pistols, some variants now will be available in the 45 Glock Auto Pistol (45 GAP) chambering from Springfield's Custom Shop.

A special edition "Sergeant York" 1911 has been prepared by Springfield in connection with Investment Arms.

▲A stainless-steel version of the S&W Model 952 9mm target pistol is now available.

▶A target version of the SW1911 pistol is now offered, with adjustable sights.

▲A 4-inch barrel Parkerized version of Springfield's new "GI" series is available.

▼Springfield's new "GI" series includes a stainless-steel version.

These special pistols honor Sgt. Alvin C. York, an excellent marksman with both rifle and pistol, who almost single-handedly captured 132 German prisoners during World War I. His actions stopped a German counterattack in France's Argonne Forest. York was awarded the Medal of Honor and the French Croix de Guerre, and became the most decorated soldier of that war. The commemorative pistols are special because the grips are made from the wood of trees that actually grew on York's land. A nonprofit conservation organization, American Forests, kept track of the trees on the York farm and harvested the wood when the trees died. For every pistol sold, new trees will be planted in special Liberty Forests.

▲A full-size Parkerized 45 with a 5-inch barrel, Springfield's new "GI" pistol resembles previous military pistols.

▲Springfield has introduced "GI" series pistols. This is a Parkerized version with a 3-inch barrel.

▲Springfield's two special Sgt. York commemorative pistols, the Peerless Grade and the Issue Grade, rest on a piece of cherry wood from the York farm, from which the grips of the Peerless pistols are made.

132 Peerless Grade pistols, plated and engraved, and with grips made of cherry wood from York's farm will be made. 5000 additional Issue Grade pistols, with grips made from the black walnut tree that actually shaded the cabin in which York was born, will also be made.

STI

STI, of Georgetown, TX, in November 2003 acquired Lone Star Armament of Stephenville, TX. The acquisition essentially doubled STI's capacity for producing 1911-type pistols and parts. Beside the increase in pistol production, STI planned to begin providing a full line of parts to other manufacturers.

◀ The Taurus 24/7 service pistol, introduced last year in 9mm and 40, is now offered in 45 ACP.

▼ A Taurus pistol in 38 Super, the Model PT38S, is now available.

The Lone Star name has been phased out. Recall, however, that Lone Star offered two basic single-column 1911 pistols—the 5-inch Lawman and the 4-inch Ranger. The Ranger has been dropped, but the full-size pistol continues on as the STI Lawman. The Lawman is suitable for IDPA competition as well as IPSC and USPSA.

Taurus

In mid-2003, Taurus announced its new polymer-frame DAO service pistol, the 24/7. It was introduced in 9mm and 40 S&W, and those options are now available. In the meantime, Taurus developed a larger-bore version, and the 24/7 in 45 ACP was introduced at the February 2004 SHOT Show. The new 45 has a bushingless flared barrel and a captive flat-coil recoil spring. An accessory rail is present at the front of the frame. The 45-caliber was scheduled for production in late 2004.

The nice PT 922 22-caliber pistol has undergone some revisions in the past two years, and is now in final form. It has a 6-inch barrel, 10+1 capacity and weighs 29 ounces. The polymer frame has a slanty "Woodsman" look and feel, and the pistol has an adjustable rear sight and fiber-optic front sight.

The 38 Super cartridge came on the scene in 1929, and although it has never been a standard military or police service round, it has remained popular. Taurus has introduced its first 38 Super pistol, the PT 38S. The pistol is conventional double-action, and comes in either blue or stainless steel finishes. With a 4 1/4-inch barrel, it weighs 30 ounces. Availability was scheduled for late 2004.

Uselton

A new line of 1911-style pistols was presented for the first time at the February 2004 SHOT Show, under the name Uselton Arms. Made on Caspian steel frames, the pistols have Uselton stainless-steel slides, barrels and triggers. The Uselton trigger is very distinctive, and has a flat vertical front surface. Other features now in vogue, such as beavertail grip safeties and extended manual safety levers, are also present.

Variants with 5-inch, 4 1/4-inch, 3 1/2-inch and 3-inch barrels are offered. Special features such as titanium frames and Damascus slides are also offered on select models. Calibers are 45 ACP, 40 S&W and 357 SIG. In some versions, interchangeable barrels are provided to make the pistol both a 40 S&W and a 357 SIG, at the choice of the shooter.

Uselton considers their pistols "totally customized" out of the box.

Volquartsen

Known for their Ruger-style 22-caliber pistols, Volquartsen plans to introduce a new lightweight version. The pistol will have a steel receiver and a barrel of 12mm diameter sleeved in titanium. They will offer it in 22 LR, and tentatively plan to offer the 17 Aguila (17 Hi-Standard) when the ammunition becomes available.

Walther

Walther didn't really offer anything new in the autoloading pistol line this year. However, they introduced a 22 LR carbine. It is not really a pistol-carbine, but it is related, so let's give it a quick look. The new G22 carbine is of the bullpup design, so the action is under the stock's cheekpiece. With a 20-inch barrel, the overall length is only 28 inches. The grip of the polymer stock is similar to that of Walther's P22 rimfire pistol, and the carbine can use the same magazines.

After several years of development, the 22-caliber Taurus PT922 is now in final form.

Uselton Arms president Rick Uselton holds one of his company's 1911 variants, built with a titanium frame and a Damascus slide.

▲The Walther 22-caliber G22 carbine has a grip similar to that of the P22 pistol and uses the same magazines.

▶Optical sights can be added to the Walther G22 carbine.

Wilson

Wilson Combat has added the Professional Model to its line of 1911-based pistols. It has a full-size frame with a compact slide and matching 4.1-inch barrel. Features such as beavertail grip safety, lightened hammer and extended thumb safety are standard. It is available in all-black, gray-and-black, and green-and-black. Available in 45 ACP, it weighs 35 ounces. The match barrel is hand-fitted, and the accuracy guarantee is an impressive one inch at 25 yards.

Wildey

Wildey is working with the government of Jordan on the Jordanian Armament Weapons Systems (JAWS) pistol project, and the new pistol, introduced last year, is well into development. Recall that the pistol is service-type, with a conventional double-action trigger system. One of its distinctive features is the ability to convert from 9mm to 40 S&W to 45 ACP with the change of a few parts. The replaceable bolt face can be changed by removing the extractor. The rotating barrel and the magazine can both be readily replaced when the pistol is stripped for cleaning. Internal parts can be reached by removing a frame sideplate, which is retained by the slide.

The pistol has a name now. It will be called the JAWS "Viper." A standard model will have a stainless-steel frame, either natural or blackened, and a lightweight version will have an aluminum-alloy frame and shorter barrel. The design has a true ambidextrous magazine catch, which can be pressed from either side.

POSTSCRIPT

As this is written in 2004, a number of things lie ahead in the remainder of this year and into 2005 that hold great importance for the industry and for the shooters involved with autoloading handguns. Things unknown to me now—such as the fate of the 1994 "Assault Weapon" and magazine ban (due to sunset in September 2004), and the results of the November 2004 elections—may be history when you read this. Regardless of the outcomes, we know we will face continuing battles over license-to-carry legislation and reciprocity, and the enemies of freedom continue to call for greater restrictions on firearms. Please resolve to know where your legislators stand, and to let your legislators know where you stand. ●

The pistol developed by Wildey and the country of Jordan has been given a name, and will appear as the Jaws Viper.

▲The Wilson Combat Professional Model has a full-size frame with a 4.1-inch barrel and shorter slide.

by JOHN TAFFIN

HANDGUNS TODAY:

SIXGUNS & OTHERS

IT WAS 50 years ago, in 1955, when Smith & Wesson produced the first 44 Magnum. Everyone knew we had reached the top; there was simply no way six-guns could ever be made more powerful. Then, in 1983 Freedom Arms produced their first 454 Casull. John Linebaugh arrived on the scene giving us the 475 and 500 Linebaughs and then stretching both to approximately 1.60 inches for "Maximum" versions of the same two cartridges. Custom revolver-builders offered heavy-duty, five-shot 45 Colt six-guns to allow heavy loading of this grand old cartridge, and Hornady and Ruger collaborated on the 480. Had we reached the end of powerful six-gun cartridge development?

Not quite. The big news last year was the 500 S&W Magnum cartridge and the new Smith & Wesson X-frame revolver. We have now had a year to test this largest of all double-action six-guns, as well as the 500 cartridge. Other manufacturers have joined with Smith & Wesson in supplying 500-chambered revolvers–with Magnum Research offering a single action BFR revolver while Taurus has countered with their Raging Bull version in 500 S&W Magnum. Two custom makers, Gary Reeder Custom Guns and SSK Industries, have offered their 500 Magnums in revolver and single-shot form, respectively. It has been my good (?) fortune to have test-fired the 500 Magnum extensively over the past year, chambered in the original 8 3/8-inch Smith & Wesson Model 500, a 10 1/2-inch BFR, an SSK Custom Encore, and a Gary Reeder single action. The cartridge has proven to be extremely accurate, as well as speaking with authority and finality when used on game.

One might think this would be the end of cartridge development; however, I have been shown three new cartridges that will be arriving on the scene this year. As this is written they must remain as "mystery cartridges", however I can share the fact that two of them will be standard length 50-caliber cartridges for use in single-action revolvers, while the other will be a "Maximum"-length 45-caliber cartridge. We are still looking and hoping for a five-shot Ruger single action in 480 Ruger or 50-caliber, however none of these will be in handguns marked with the Ruger label. Once again it is time for our annual alphabetical trip down the path labeled "Six-guns, Single Shots, and Others."

American Western Arms: AWA has been offering both the Longhorn and Peacekeeper traditionally-styled SAAs for several years. Available in most of the standard frontier calibers, these six-guns were offered in the blue and case-colored finish, as well as in hard chrome. Normally, I would say chrome belongs on the bumpers of a '49 Ford Club Coupe. However, I must admit AWA's hard chrome is very attractive, much like brushed stainless steel. The combination of hard chrome and 45 Colt make an excellent outdoorsman's revolver.

Last year AWA made a major change in their Peacekeeper and Longhorn revolvers. As one takes a close look at the back to the hammer, one notices something quite strange for a traditionally-styled single action. The area of the hammer between the two ears of the back strap is slotted to accept a strut. AWA began fitting their revolvers–on special order–with a coil mainspring system, as well as offering a kit consisting of a new hammer with an attached strut, a coil spring, and a shelf that attaches to the back strap to accept the strut. Changing from a flat mainspring to a coil spring is not quite a drop-in, as the inside of the back of the front strap must be milled out to accept the coil spring. With a coil spring-operated hand and hammer mated up with a Wolff trigger and bolt spring, the action of a single action comes very close to being indestructible. Now AWA has made another significant change. The Longhorn and Peacekeeper have been dropped and replaced by The Ultimate featuring the new coil mainspring system. These revolvers are made by Matiba and can be specially ordered with one-piece *faux* ivory grips by Tru-Art. Those six-guns I have seen have been very well finished and timed.

The Ultimate by AWA features a coil mainspring.

Beretta's Stampede is now offered with a Lightning-style grip frame.

The Stampede by Beretta carries a transfer bar safety and is a very attractive single-action revolver, whether finished in blue/case coloring or nickel-plated as shown.

Beretta: This is not only the oldest firearms manufacturer in existence, it is the oldest company of any kind–dating back nearly 500 years. In the early 1990s it was my pleasure to be escorted through the Beretta factory, which included a personally conducted tour of their private museum housing several centuries of firearms development. We've all known Beretta as a manufacturer of high quality semi-automatic pistols and shotguns. Then the unexpected happened. Beretta, of semi-automatic fame, purchased Uberti, known for producing replicas of 19th-century firearms. Suddenly, Beretta was in the business of producing single-action six-guns.

In addition to now owning Uberti, Beretta is also offering a revolver under the Beretta name. That single-action six-gun is known as the Stampede. Although traditionally sized and styled, it contains a transfer bar safety, making it safe to carry with six rounds. Available in both the standard grip frame style as well as the Lightning grip frame, the well-built and smoothly operating Stampede has been warmly accepted by single-action shooters. Currently it is available in both 45 Colt and 357 Magnum, in either the standard blue and case-coloring, or nickel finishes.

Bond Arms: Most of us six-gunners will probably admit a fascination with derringers. When I was the kid growing up, one could still find original Remington 41RF derringers at very reasonable prices. They were, of course, chambered for hard-to-get rimfire ammunition. Then Great Western came along and, in addition to bringing out the first true replica single action army, also duplicated the Remington double-barreled derringer in 38 Special. Great Western Arms is long gone now and in the intervening years several companies have offered derringers that run the gamut from excellent quality all the way down to extremely poor. Unfortunately the latter is what too many folks have purchased to use for self-defense.

Bond Arms offers extremely high quality double-barreled derringers in both the spur trigger and trigger guard style. All Bond Arms derringers are made of stainless steel with a spring-loaded extractor, rebounding firing pin, cross-bolt safety, and a nearly endless list of available chamberings. Barrels are interchangeable, allowing the use of 26 different cartridges—all the way from 22 Long Rifle up to the 45 Colt—as well as a special rendition that not only accepts the 45 Colt but .410 shotshells as well. The standard offering, looking much like the traditional Remington Derringer, is known as the Cowboy Defender. Add a trigger guard and it becomes the Texas Defender. For those desirous of the ultimate in snake protection, there is the Century 2000, which handles 3-inch .410 shells. I have been in some places, while hunting, where I would have felt a lot more comfortable packing a Century 2000.

Cimarron Firearms (CFA): Cimarron recently celebrated its 20th year as a leader in supplying authentic replica revolvers, leverguns, and single-shot rifles to cowboy action shooters and those who appreciate the firearms of the Old West. Cimarron's Model P, a traditionally styled SAA, is now offered in stainless steel as well as blue/case-coloring and nickel. Barrel lengths are 4 3/4- and 5 1/2- with 7 1/2-inch versions now arriving. Thus far, chamberings offered are 45 Colt and 357 Magnum.

For those desiring a specially tuned and smoothed single action for cowboy action shooting, Cimarron offers the Evil Roy Model P. Evil Roy is one of the top shooters in CAS and has incorporated his ideas of the perfect single action in this latest Model P including easy-to-see square-shaped sights. All of the special guns feature Evil Roy's signature on the barrel. Cimarron says of this revolver: "Featuring internal parts produced exclusively for Cimarron, and springs from U.S. manufacturers. The rear sight notch is large and square while the front sight is wide–with no taper–giving the shooter the finest sight picture.... Grips are hand-checkered or smooth walnut; very slim and trim for fast and safe handling. The actions are set up in the U.S.A. to function safely with lighter hammer action, no creep, and safe but

The Bond Arms Cowboy Defender is offered in 26 chamberings, including the easy-handling 32 H&R Magnum.

This Texas rattler met up with a .410-chambered Bond Arms Cowboy Defender.

Cimarron's Model P Jr. is an easy-to-handle, lightweight single action chambered in 38 Special/38LC and 32-20.

crisp trigger pull. Each revolver is regulated to shoot dead-center left and right windage." Shooters have a choice of the standard finish or a special U.S.A. premium finish with case-coloring by Doug Turnbull.

Normally I am known for shooting the biggest six-guns available; however, I have a kinder, gentler side that has been indulged by shooting Cimarron's Model P Jr. These little six-guns have the standard single-action grip frame of the Model P with a smaller frame and cylinder. Chambered in 38 Special/38 Long Colt, or 32-20, they are not only fun guns for experienced six-gunners, they are also just the ticket for younger shooters—or anyone who cannot handle the recoil of larger six-guns.

There are several classes of shooters under the banner of cowboy action shooting. One group looks to authenticity in their costumes and firearms, especially their six-guns. For these folks, Cimarron offers their Model P with what they call an Original Finish, which is actually no finish at all, or perhaps we should say a specially-induced finish to make a six-gun look like it has been in use since the 1870s—although literally brand-new and in perfect mechanical shape. Original Finish six-guns may be used with either smokeless or blackpowder loads; however, they are an excellent choice for those who shoot blackpowder as they not only sound like the Old West, they also look like a six-gun with a definite story to tell.

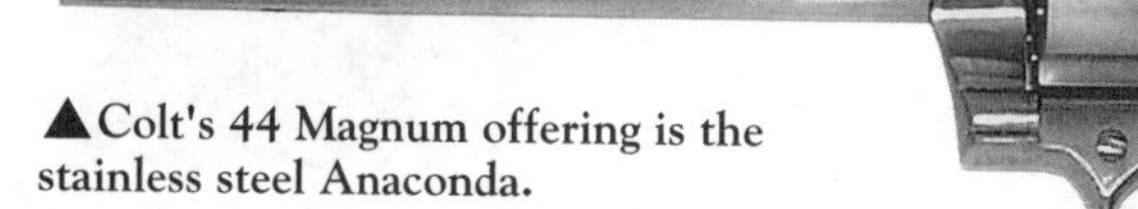

▲Colt's 44 Magnum offering is the stainless steel Anaconda.

▲The Colt Single Action Army is once again offered with a 7 1/2-inch barrel in 45 Colt, 44-40, 38-40, 38 Special, 357 Magnum, and 32-20.

Colt: Colt has made a lot of drastic, and very welcome, changes over the past few years. Three years ago Colt Single Actions were offered only in 45 Colt and 44-40, only in barrel lengths of 4-3/4 and 5-1/2 inches, and with a price tag coming very close to $2000! The last two years the price was reduced to make it more competitive with replica single actions, while still remaining a genuine Colt Single Action. Now, for this year, the Single Action part of the catalog has been greatly expanded as to calibers offered and barrel lengths. Shooters now have a choice of the three standard barrel lengths of 4-3/4, 5-1/2, and 7-1/2 inches, in either the traditional blue/case-colored finish or full nickel finish; chambered for the 45 Colt, 44-40, 38-40, 38 Special, 357 Magnum, and—for the first time in nearly three-quarters of a century—32-20. Just to prove shooters can never be satisfied, I have to ask, "Where is the 44 Special?"

Every day, in nearly every way and every location, single-action shooters argue the merits of replica single actions and the original Colt Single Action Army. When all the arguing and debating is through—there is only one genuine Single Action Army that says COLT on the barrel. No replica, no matter how well it is finished and tuned, can make that statement. While

The top and middle 44-40s are original Colt Single Actions; the bottom six-gun is Cimarron's Model P with the antique-looking Original Finish.

Colt's Python celebrates its 50th anniversary this year as the Python Elite.

▲ ▶ EMF offers the Great Western II in both blue/case-coloring and nickel-plated finishes.

the Colt Single Action Army remains in 36 different versions when one considers calibers, barrel lengths, and finish, the Colt Cowboy is no more.

At one time Colt had a whole stable full of snakes. The Viper, Cobra, King Cobra, and Diamondback are all gone; however, the Anaconda and the Python remain. Although originally offered in both 45 Colt and 44 Magnum, currently the Anaconda is offered only in a stainless steel 44 Magnum with barrel lengths of 4, 6, and 8 inches, complete with fully adjustable sights and finger-groove rubber grips. It has proven to be a sturdy, reliable, accurate hunting handgun. Many shooters would argue that the Python is the finest double-action revolver ever offered at any time. I don't argue; I just enjoy shooting the Python. It continues in the Colt lineup as the Python Elite, in either blue or stainless with a 4- or 6-inch barrel.

Early And Modern Firearms (EMF): Last year EMF introduced the Great Western II. The Great Western originally appeared in 1954 as a totally American-made replica of the Colt Single Action Army. EMF was one of the early distributors of the Great Western, which disappeared in the early 1960s. The Great Western II line has been greatly expanded this year. The Custom Great Western is offered in nickel, satin nickel, blue/case colored, and all-blue finish, in the three standard barrel lengths of 4-3/4, 5-1/2, and 7-1/2 inches; in 45 Colt, 44-40, and 357 Magnum with other calibers–as well as engraving–available on special order. All Custom Series Great Westerns are fitted with one-piece ivory-style grips.

In addition to the Great Western, which is made by Pietta, EMF also offers the Hartford Premiere in the three standard barrel lengths and chambered in 45 Colt, 44-40, 44 Special, 38-40, and 32-20. Special versions offered include the Bisley Model in all three barrel lengths, a 3-inch ejectorless Sheriff's Model, the round-butted 4-inch Pinkerton Model, and the 3 1/2-inch Deputy Model—all chambered in 45 Colt. Both the 1875 and 1890 Remingtons are offered and the Remington and the SAA models are also offered with the Antique Finish, making them appear to have experienced more than a century of service. Finally, EMF also offers a Buntline Special version of their 1873 six-guns.

Freedom Arms: Last year Freedom Arms introduced their Model 97 five-shot 44 Special, which I have now had a pleasurable year shooting. In addition, two more six-shot Model 97s have arrived on the scene. One is a 32 Magnum *(with an extra 32-20 cylinder available)*, while the other is chambered in the hot new 17 HMR. Since its inception in 1907, the 44 Special has been chambered in some of the finest revolvers ever produced. From Smith & Wesson we have the Triple-Lock, the Model 1926, the 1950 Target and, in more recent times, the Model 24 and Model 624—as well as a five-shot 296 and 696. Colt waited a while to chamber the 44 Special; however, when they finally moved in that direction they gave us the New Service, the Single Action Army, and the New Frontier. All great six-guns; however, the 44 Special Triple-Lock is most often considered the finest 44 Special—if not the finest revolver-period—ever manufactured. It now has a rival. The 44 Special Model 97 from Freedom Arms is surely the finest single-action 44 Special ever

50 years separates these two Great Westerns. The top six-gun is an original Great Western, while the bottom revolver is EMF's Pietta-manufactured Great Western II.

The two greatest 44 Specials of all times? The S&W 1907 Triple-Lock and the Freedom Arms Model 97.

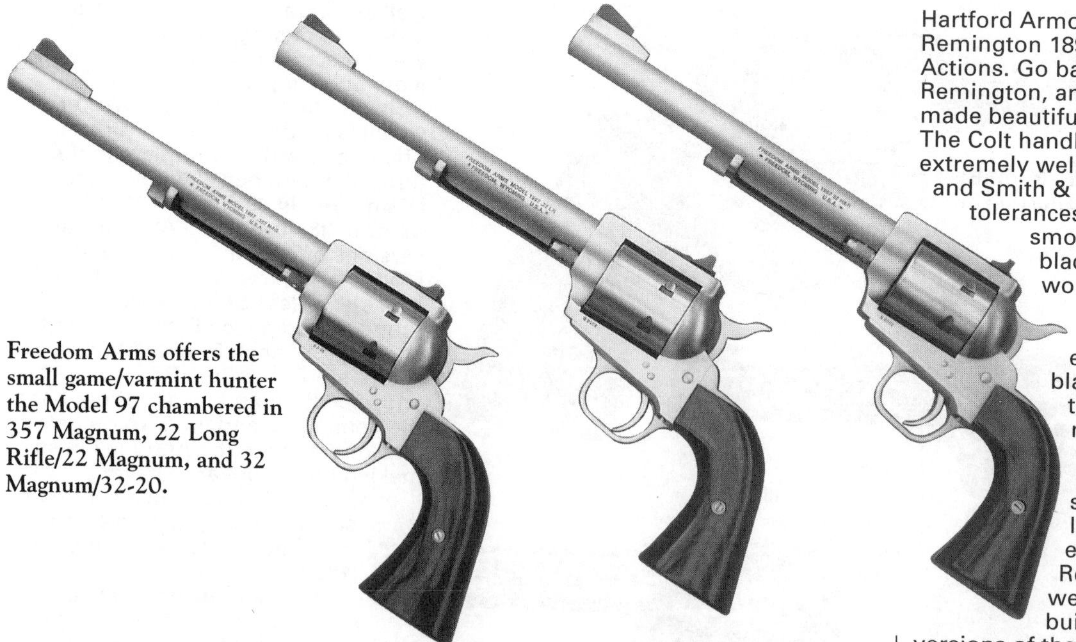

Freedom Arms offers the small game/varmint hunter the Model 97 chambered in 357 Magnum, 22 Long Rifle/22 Magnum, and 32 Magnum/32-20.

offered, and may just be every bit as good as that first Special 44.

Freedom Arms spent a long time studying barrel twists and different loads in both the 32 Magnum and the 32-20 before deciding to offer this combination in their Model 97. I personally supplied some loads for testing, and spent time with Bob Baker of Freedom Arms shooting the prototype model–both on paper for accuracy and over Oehler's Model 35P chronograph for muzzle velocity. Shooting 32s is always educational and this was no exception as some loads that were expected to do well performed poorly, while others gave surprisingly better results than expected.

The Freedom Arms Model 97 32 is superbly accurate. All testing was done with a 2x Leupold in place to remove as much human sighting error as possible. Five-shot groups, with either the 32 Magnum or 32-20 cylinder in place, were exceptionally small with groups of well under one inch at 25 yards being commonplace. When it comes to varmints and small game one can cover all the bases with three 7 1/2-inch Model 97s chambered in 357 Magnum, 32 Magnum/32-20, and 22 Long Rifle/22 Magnum. While excellent ammunition abounds in both the 357 Magnum and both 22s, the 32 Magnum and 32-20 require handloading for the best results. The most accurate load in 32 Magnum has proven to be Sierra's 90-grain JHC over 10 grains of H110 for five shots in 1/2-inch and a muzzle velocity of 1260 fps, while the 32-20 shoots best *(thus far)* with Speer's 100-grain JHP over 10.0 grains of #2400 for slightly under 1200 fps and five shots in 5/8-inch. This year the Model 97 chambered in 17 HMR has joined the three small game/varmint-gathering Model 97 six-guns.

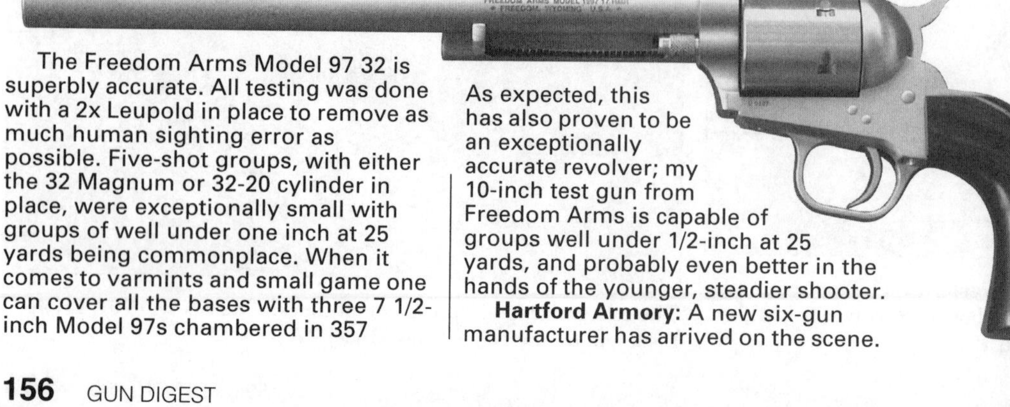

As expected, this has also proven to be an exceptionally accurate revolver; my 10-inch test gun from Freedom Arms is capable of groups well under 1/2-inch at 25 yards, and probably even better in the hands of the younger, steadier shooter.

Hartford Armory: A new six-gun manufacturer has arrived on the scene.

Hartford Armory is now offering the Remington 1890 and 1875 Single Actions. Go back 125 years. Colt, Remington, and Smith & Wesson all made beautiful single-action revolvers. The Colt handled blackpowder extremely well, while the Remington and Smith & Wesson had such tight tolerances they were actually smokeless-powder guns in a blackpowder age. In other words, they were so tightly fitted and closely machined they fouled easily when used with blackpowder. Fast-forward to today and we have the return of the Remington at a time when most shooters use them with smokeless powder. At last we will find out what excellent six-guns the Remingtons actually were. Hartford Armory is building truly authentic versions of the originals that have, at least in my hand, a different feel from the Italian replicas. Both the 1875 and 1890 will be offered in a full blue finish, classified as Hartford Armory Dark Blue, or with a Turnbull case-colored frame; and also in stainless steel. Stocks are two-piece walnut.

Now comes the real surprise: this new version of the old Remington Single Action is chambered in 45 Colt and rated for +P loads; and is also offered in 44 Magnum. Other calibers will be 357 Magnum and 44-40. Although sights are the traditionally fixed single-action style; the front sight, which screws into the barrel, will be offered in different heights for sighting-in heavy-duty hunting loads.

I am definitely looking forward to fully testing of this new/old revolver.

▲Magnum Research's BFR is now chambered in 500 S&W Magnum.

▼The newest offering from Freedom Arms is the Model 97 chambered in 17 HMR.

The BFR from Magnum Research has proven to be an exceptionally accurate revolver.

Magnum Research: Magnum Research offers the all-stainless steel BFR *(Biggest Finest Revolver)*. The BFR looks much like a Ruger Super Blackhawk; the grip frames will accept the same grips—however, unlike Ruger six-guns, the BFR has a freewheeling cylinder that rotates either clockwise or counter-clockwise when the loading gate is opened. It is offered in two versions: the Short Cylinder chambered in 454 Casull and 480 Ruger/475 Linebaugh, and 22 Hornet; the Long Cylinder is offered in 444 Marlin, 450 Marlin, 45-70, a special 45 Colt that also accepts 3-inch .410 shotgun shells, and–new for this year–500 S&W Magnum.

All BFR revolvers are American-made with cut-rifled, hand-lapped, recessed-muzzle-crowned barrels; tight tolerances; soft brushed stainless steel finish; and are normally equipped with an adjustable rear sight mated with a front sight with interchangeable blades of differing heights. They can be ordered from the factory set up with a scope and an SSK base. The SSK mounting system is the strongest available anywhere for scoping hard-kicking handguns. For the past year I have been extensively testing two BFR six-guns in 480/475 Linebaugh and 500 S&W Magnum. They have proven to be exceptionally accurate and have performed flawlessly.

Navy Arms: When it comes to replica firearms, Val Forgett of Navy Arms started it all. With the passing of Val Forgett this past year, Navy Arms is now headed up by his son, Val Forgett III. The leadership may have changed, but Navy Arms continues to offer some of the finest replicas available. These include The Gunfighter, a specially-tuned single-action army offered in the three standard barrel lengths, chambered in 357 Magnum, 44-40, and 45 Colt. Finish is blue with a case-colored frame and the German silver-plated back strap and trigger guard. Springs are all U.S.-made Wolff springs, and the standard grips are black-checkered gunfighter style.

Navy Arms has also added the stainless steel Gunfighter with the same barrel lengths and chamberings. Stainless steel may not be authentic Old West, however it sure makes a lot of sense for shooting blackpowder loads. Navy Arms also continues to offer the standard 1873 Cavalry six-gun, the 1895 Artillery Model, the Bisley Model, and the two great Smith

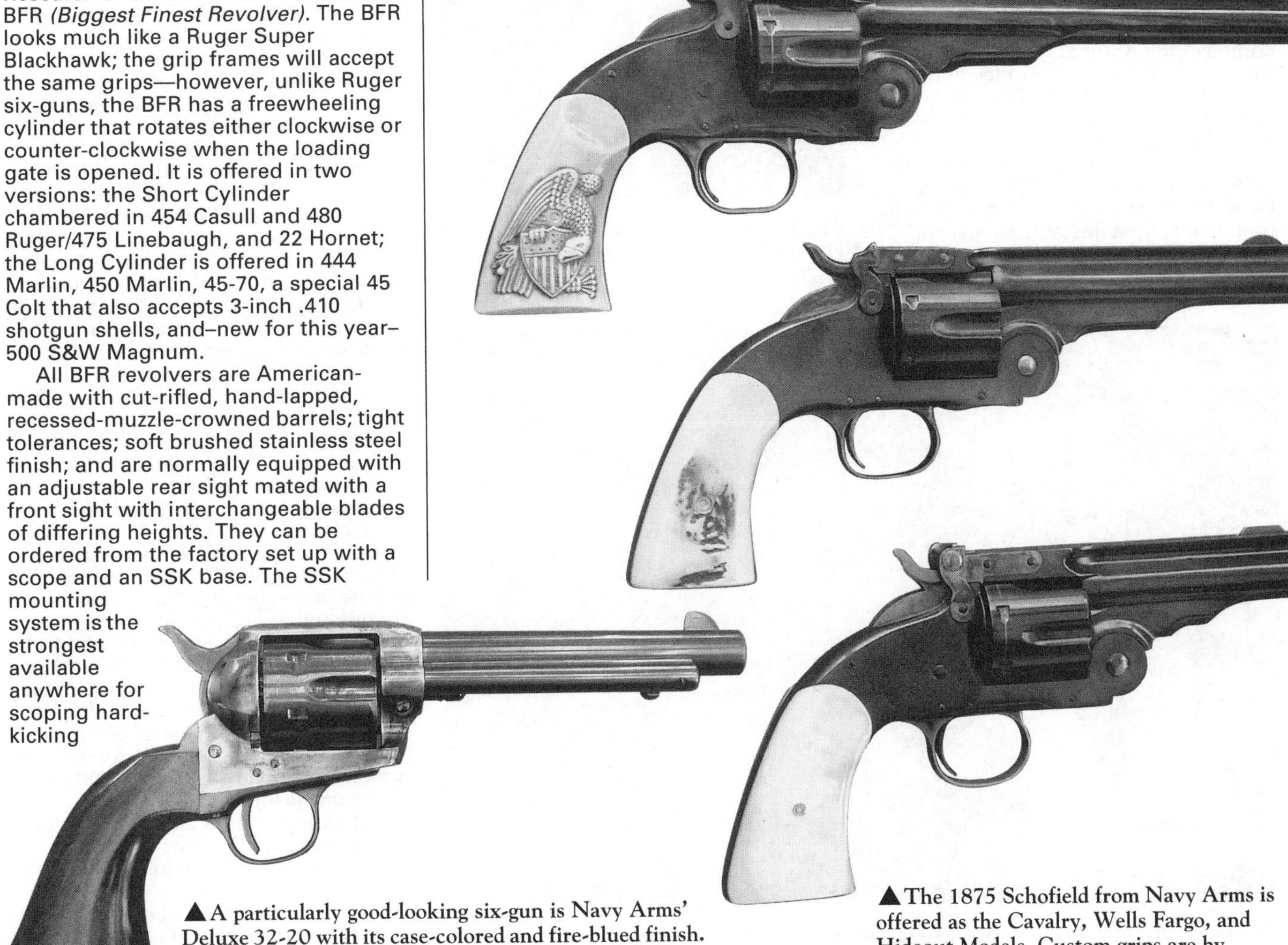

▲A particularly good-looking six-gun is Navy Arms' Deluxe 32-20 with its case-colored and fire-blued finish. It also shoots great.

▲The 1875 Schofield from Navy Arms is offered as the Cavalry, Wells Fargo, and Hideout Models. Custom grips are by Buffalo Brothers and Eagle Grips.

◀ ▼ Navy Arms Gunfighter features a specially-tuned action, gunfighter grips, blue/case colored finish, and a German silver-plated backstrap and trigger guard.

◀ Ruger's Single-Six chambered in 17 HMR has proven to be an accurate varmint pistol.

& Wesson single actions: the 1875 Schofield and the New Model Russian. The latter is offered only in 44 Russian with a 6 1/2-inch barrel, while the Schofield comes in the original 7-inch version, the 5-inch Wells Fargo Model, and a 3 1/2-inch Hideout Model. Navy Arm's Schofields are available in both 45 Colt and 38 Special.

Ruger: In 1953 Ruger resurrected the SAA six-gun with their 22 Single-Six. Over the years it has been offered with both fixed and adjustable sights, and barrel lengths of 4-5/8, 5-1/2, 6-1/2, and 9-1/2 inches. For whatever reason, my preferred barrel length for a hunting handgun — 7-1/2 inches — has never been offered during the first 50 years of the 22 Single-Six. However, Ruger starts off their second half-century with the most popular 22 single-action revolver ever offered by correcting this mistake.

Ruger's Ken Jorgensen with the new Ruger Hunter Model 22 Long Rifle/22 Magnum version.

Ruger single actions have always been favorites of handgun hunters—especially their Hunter Models which continue to be offered in both the Super Blackhawk and Bisley models, in stainless steel, chambered in 44 Magnum, and wearing 7 1/2-inch heavy-ribbed barrels set up to accept Ruger scope rings. These are exceptionally popular hunting handguns and it is proper and fitting that they are now joining by a 22 RF model. The newest Hunter Model is a 7 1/2-inch 22 Long Rifle/22 Magnum version with a heavy-ribbed barrel set up to accept Ruger scope rings.

For those of us who have been shooting the original 22 Single-Six since the 1950s, a longer-barrel scope-sighted version has arrived none too soon. I don't know what goes on in the gun safe but something causes those sights to become a little fuzzier every year. The scope-sighted 22 Hunter Model can take care of this problem. This new Hunter Model is also being offered in 17 HMR. There is still no word from Ruger on a five-shot, large-bore single-action six-gun. *Maybe next year....*

Ruger continues to offer their excellent lineup of six-guns: the Blackhawk, the Bisley Model, the Vaquero, the Bisley Vaquero, the Redhawk, the Super Redhawk, the GP-100, and the Single-Six. This year marks the Golden Anniversary of the immensely popular Ruger 357 Blackhawk. Also new this year from Ruger is the Ruger Studio Of Art and Decoration for providing engraved versions of Ruger firearms. There will be no set patterns; rather, each firearm will be individually embellished to fit the desires of the owner. The work will be performed only on new Ruger firearms. In the past this service has only been available for special presentations or occasions, and for Bill Ruger's personal collection.

Savage: Savage continues to offer their excellent Striker series of bolt-action pistols. The Sport Striker, designed for small game and varmints is chambered in 17 HMR, 22 LR, and 22 Magnum. The stainless steel Striker comes with a black synthetic stock, muzzle brake, left-hand bolt, and chambered in 223 Remington, 270 WSM, 7-08 Remington, 7mm WSM, 308 Winchester, and 300 WSM

Smith & Wesson: Thousands of the Model 500 X-Frame 500 S&W Magnum were sold in its first year of production and now a new, easier-packing version is offered. The newest Model 500 has a 4-inch barrel–actually 3 inches of barrel, plus a compensator. This could be just the ticket for those who regularly travel areas where four-legged beasts can be mean and nasty. This new version also wears the finger-grooved rubber grips of the original 8 3/8-inch Model 500. As far as grips

Two of the greatest bargains offered to handgun hunters are Ruger's Hunter Model 44 Magnum in the Bisley and Super Blackhawk versions.

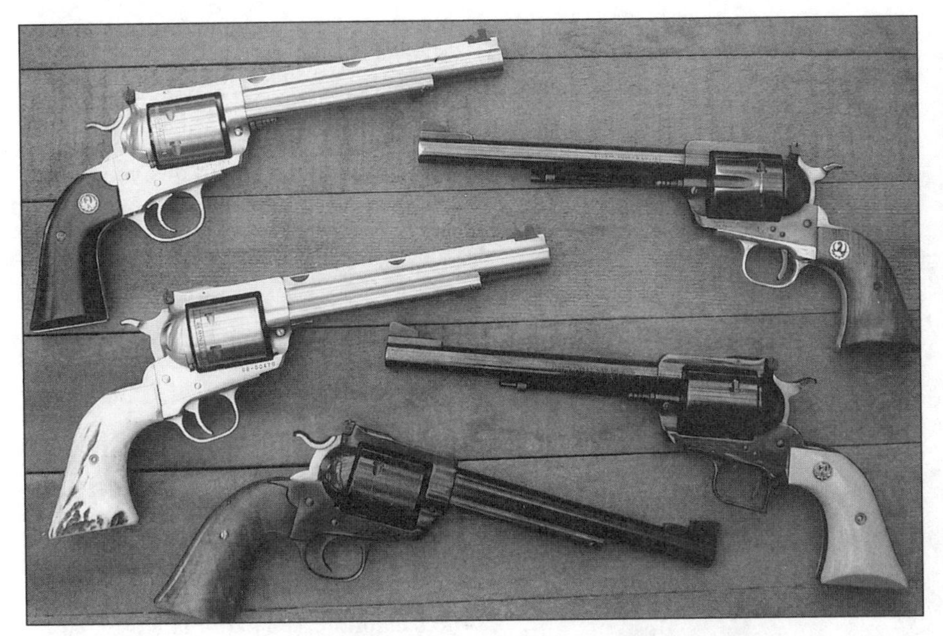

A half-century of Ruger 44 Magnums. *From top right*: original Flattop, Super Blackhawk, Bisley Model, Super Blackhawk Hunter, and the Bisley Hunter.

Herrett's Jordan stocks improve the handling of Smith & Wesson's Model 500.

▶ The Savage Striker is a stainless steel, synthetic-stocked, bolt-action pistol chambered for such cartridges as the 7-08 Remington and 308 Winchester.

◀ Senior citizens rejoice! At last we have a J-framed Smith & Wesson chambered in 22 Magnum.

go, I have found a better way—I should say the better way has been shown to me by Rod Herrett of Herrett's Stocks.

Some shooters experience a phenomenon when shooting the 500 Magnum in that the cylinder unlocks and rotates backwards. One of the reasons for this–and it does not happen with every shooter–is the rubber grips cause the Model 500 to bounce off the web of the hand, resulting in the trigger hitting the trigger finger–which naturally causes the trigger to start backwards and the cylinder to unlock. The solution from Rod Herrett was a pair of smooth-finished walnut Jordan stocks. These grips fill in the backstrap and do not bounce off the hand, as the rubber grips have a tendency to do with some shooters.

Other new offerings from Smith & Wesson this year include the Model 325PD, a lightweight, 21 1/2-ounce scandium and titanium 45 ACP revolver with a 2 1/2-inch barrel and Hi-Viz front sight. Used with full-moon clips, this lightweight but powerful revolver should become very popular for those with concealed weapons permits. When it comes to concealed firearms, one of the most neglected groups has been senior citizens. The AARP, which should be doing everything they can to protect their vulnerable members, instead is rabidly anti-gun. Quite often, senior citizens have a hard time finding a firearm they can easily handle. Smith & Wesson has greatly solved this problem by offering their Air-Lite PD in a seven-shot 22 Magnum version. Bill Jordan often asked for a J-Frame 22 Magnum, and it is now reality.

Smith & Wesson also offers two other special CCW packages with the

Smith & Wesson now offers an Airweight 38 Special, paired with a Kydex holster.

Recoil is heavy with Cor-Bon's 440-grain 500 Magnum load; however accuracy is excellent.

J-Frame Model 642 hammerless 38 Special equipped with Crimson Trace Laser Grips and the Model 637 Airweight 38 Special matched up with a Kydex holster. The Smith & Wesson Performance Center offers several versions every year and this year is no exception. The extremely popular Mountain Gun with its tapered 4-inch barrel is back, this time as a 45 Colt with the Model 25; the Model 686 is offered as a seven-shot 357 Magnum with a 5-inch standard barrel *sans* the heavy underlug; the Model 327 is offered as an eight-shot 357 Magnum with a 2-inch barrel. Hopefully, these special 25 and 686 Models will start a trend back to standard barrels.

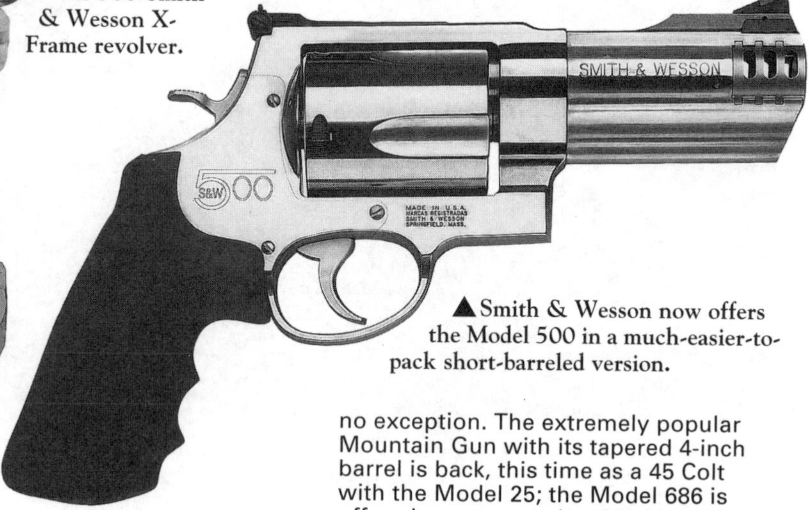

◀ Taffin shooting the 500 Smith & Wesson X-Frame revolver.

▲ Smith & Wesson now offers the Model 500 in a much-easier-to-pack short-barreled version.

▲ Eight shots and a 2-inch barrel––Smith & Wesson's latest 357 Magnum.

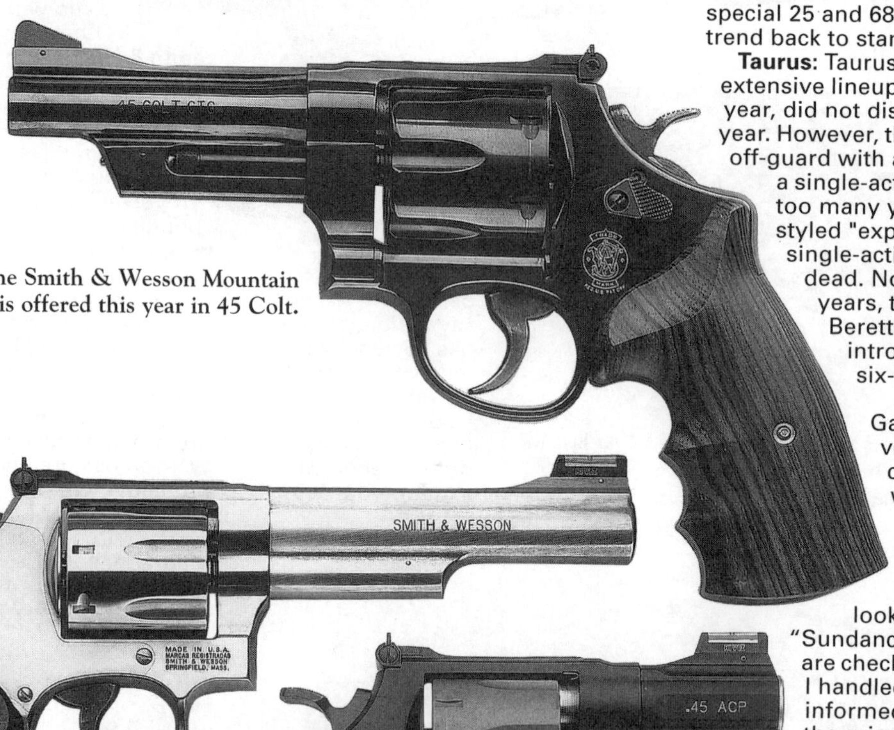

▶ The Smith & Wesson Mountain Gun is offered this year in 45 Colt.

▲ One of the special offerings this year from Smith & Wesson is a 5-inch Model 686 357 Magnum with a standard profile barrel. Great lookin' six-gun!

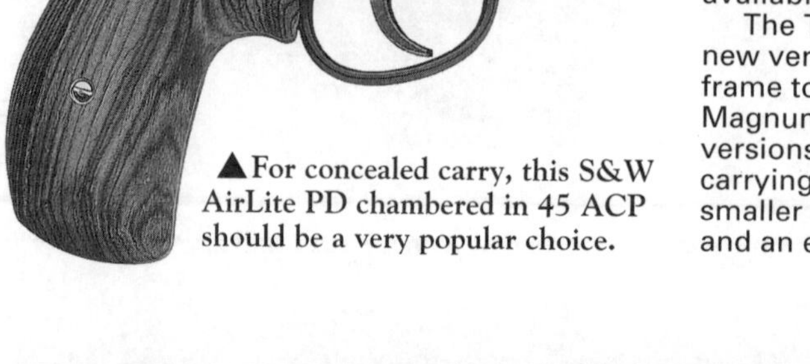

▲ For concealed carry, this S&W AirLite PD chambered in 45 ACP should be a very popular choice.

Taurus: Taurus, which always has an extensive lineup of new firearms each year, did not disappoint shooters this year. However, they caught everybody off-guard with a totally new offering, a single-action revolver. It wasn't too many years ago that self-styled "experts" told us the single-action revolver was dead. Now in two successive years, two major companies, Beretta and Taurus, have introduced single-action six-guns.

Taurus' version is the Gaucho. Original versions are chambered in 45 Colt with 5-1/2-inch barrels and four finish choices: blue, blue/case color, stainless, and nickel-looking polished "Sundance" stainless. Grips are checkered wood and when I handled the Gaucho I informed the folks at Taurus the grips were 'way too thick. They responded that this problem has already been taken care of. Although the Gaucho has a transfer bar safety it also has a traditional half-cock notch and trigger. The Gaucho is scheduled to be available about the time you read this.

The Taurus Raging Bull arrives in a new version with a longer cylinder and frame to accommodate the 500 S&W Magnum, and a couple of lightweight versions are now offered for easy carrying, with the Instant Backup smaller Model 85 in a five-shot 9mm and an eight-shot 17 HMR—viable options for senior citizens' defensive use. At the other end of the power spectrum, Taurus offers the Hip Carry, a 28-ounce, 4-inch barreled Raging Bull chambered in 44 Magnum. Grips are the recoil-reducing cushioned insert grips found on the standard Raging Bull.

Taylor's & Co.: Last year we mentioned that Taylor's & Co. was offering R&D Conversion Cylinders for both the Remington 1858 and the Ruger Old Army. I have now had plenty of time to use these conversion cylinders in a pair of Ruger Old Armies. My particular 5 1/2-inch Rugers shoot right to point of aim with the conversion cylinders and 255-grain 45 Colt bullets. Not only do they shoot to the right spot, they also do it with excellent accuracy.

This year Taylor's has expanded their line of conversion cylinders with the 32 S&W Short for the 1849 Wells Fargo, 45 Colt cylinders for the Colt Dragoon and 1860 Army, 38 Long Colt cylinders for the 1851 and 1861 Navy, and 38 Special cylinders for the 36-caliber 1858 Remington. The cylinders, of course, are for cowboy action shooting-level loads only.

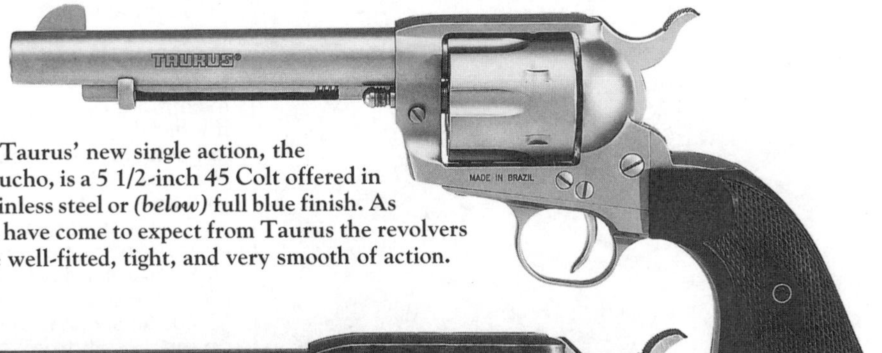

▲Taurus' new single action, the Gaucho, is a 5 1/2-inch 45 Colt offered in stainless steel or *(below)* full blue finish. As we have come to expect from Taurus the revolvers are well-fitted, tight, and very smooth of action.

▼The 500 S&W Magnum has now found a home in the stainless-steel Raging Bull from Taurus.

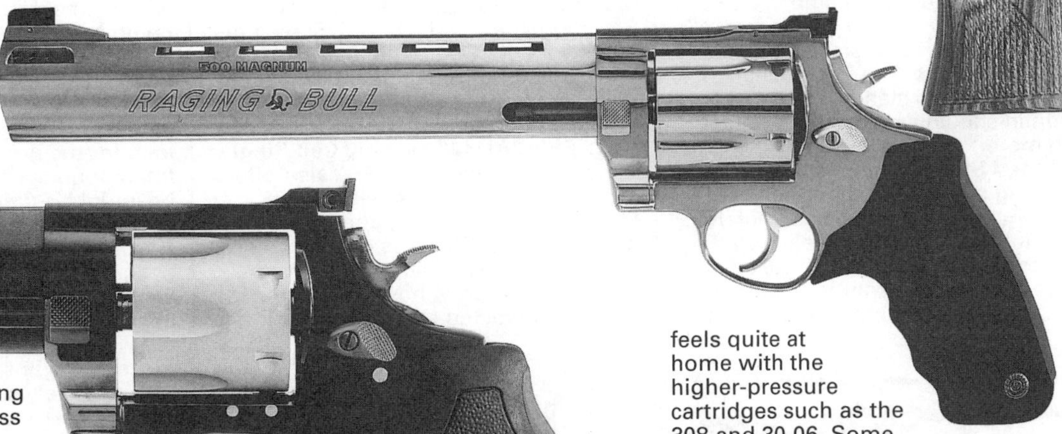

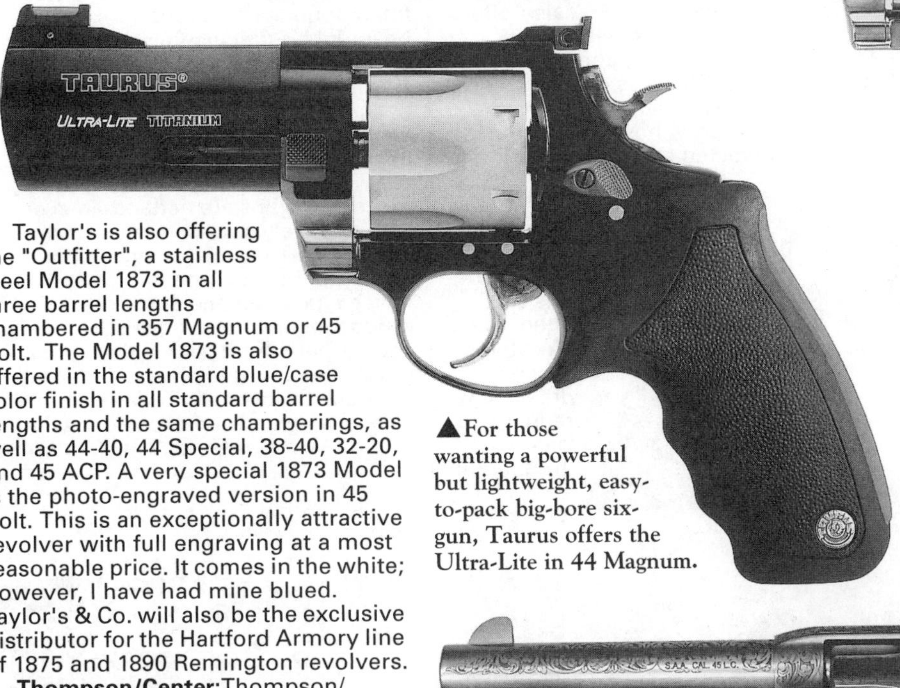

Taylor's is also offering the "Outfitter", a stainless steel Model 1873 in all three barrel lengths chambered in 357 Magnum or 45 Colt. The Model 1873 is also offered in the standard blue/case color finish in all standard barrel lengths and the same chamberings, as well as 44-40, 44 Special, 38-40, 32-20, and 45 ACP. A very special 1873 Model is the photo-engraved version in 45 Colt. This is an exceptionally attractive revolver with full engraving at a most reasonable price. It comes in the white; however, I have had mine blued. Taylor's & Co. will also be the exclusive distributor for the Hartford Armory line of 1875 and 1890 Remington revolvers.

Thompson/Center:Thompson/ Center single-shot pistols have long been favorites both at long-range silhouette matches and in the hunting field. They have been chambered for dozens of factory and wildcat cartridges for those looking for long-range accuracy and adequate power for either target shooting or taking big game. T/C offers two versions of their break-open, single-shot pistols: the standard Contender now in its second phase with the easier-opening G2, and the Encore. The G2 will handle cartridges in the 30-30 and 44 Magnum range, while the larger, heavier Encore feels quite at home with the higher-pressure cartridges such as the 308 and 30-06. Some cartridges, such as the 45-70, are offered in both versions.

▲For those wanting a powerful but lightweight, easy-to-pack big-bore six-gun, Taurus offers the Ultra-Lite in 44 Magnum.

Two new cartridges have been added this year, both chambered in the Contender and the Encore. The first cartridge is the new 20-caliber varmint cartridge, the 204 Ruger; while the second is capable of taking any big-game animal found anywhere in the world. The latter cartridge is the 375 JDJ, designed by J.D. Jones of SSK Industries. J.D. is a longtime friend and the absolute authority when it comes to many things concerned with firearms, especially with single-shot pistol cartridges.

The 375 JDJ is to single-shot pistols what the 375 H&H is

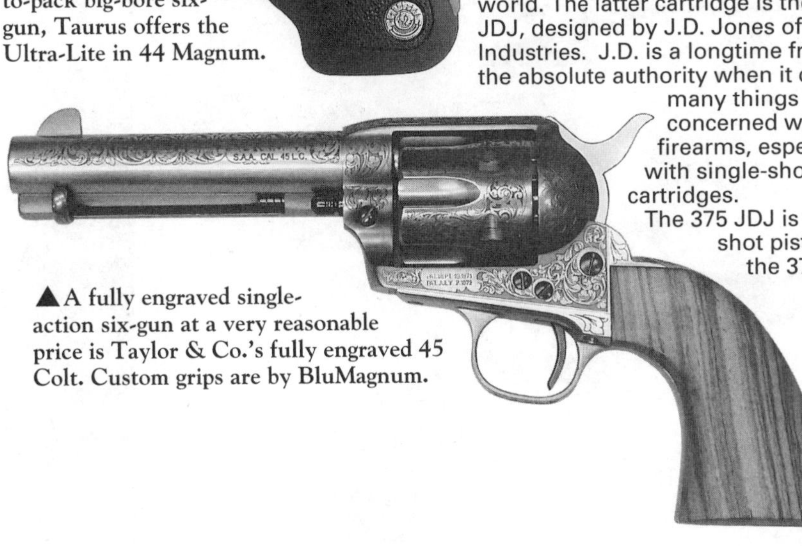

▲A fully engraved single-action six-gun at a very reasonable price is Taylor & Co.'s fully engraved 45 Colt. Custom grips are by BluMagnum.

Thompson/Center's Encore is now offered in 375 JDJ.

These three "Mystery Cartridges" should be revealed by the time you read this. The first two are 50-caliber for standard-sized single actions, while the Maximum length 45 is for use in stretch-framed, long-cylindered revolvers.

to bolt-action rifles. It may be larger than necessary for some critters and a little light for others, but in capable hands it will always do the job with authority. If I could have only one–and wouldn't that be terrible–single-shot pistol for hunting big game, it would be chambered in 375 JDJ. I have been using my custom SSK 375 JDJ with great satisfaction for nearly two decades now. The introduction of this cartridge in a standard factory handgun should increase its popularity even more.

United States Firearms (USFA): The first thing most notice about the USFA Single Action Army is the absolutely beautiful finish with the main frame and the hammer beautifully case-colored by Doug Turnbull. Standard grips, of checkered hard rubber with a "US" molded into the top part of the grip, are perfectly fitted to the frame and feel exceptionally good to my hand. Custom grips are available in smooth or checkered walnut, as well as ivory and pearl.

For the past year I have been shooting two USFA SAAs, a 4 3/4-inch 45 Colt and a 7 1/2-inch 38-40. All six chambers on the 45 Colt from USFA measure a uniform and perfect 0.452-inch, and the 38-40 is also uniform and correct at 0.400-inch. Trigger pulls on both six-guns are set at three pounds. Cylinders lock up tight when the hammer is down on an empty chamber, as well as when the hammer is in the cocked position.

All USFA six-guns are available with a V- or square-notch rear sight and a choice of a cross pin or screw-in blackpowder-style cylinder pin latch. Standard chamberings for USFA single actions are 45 Colt as well as 32-20, 41 Long Colt, 38 Special, 38-40, 44-40, 45 ACP, and 44 Special/44 Russian. The latter can be marked "RUSSIAN AND S&W SPECIAL 44" as early Colt Single Actions were marked. USFA also offers the Rodeo in 45 Colt, 44-40, and 38 Special in 4 3/4-, 5 1/2-, and 7 1/2-inch barrel lengths. This less expensive six-gun is the same basic revolver as the single action army; however, it comes with bead-blasted satin blue finish instead of the beautiful finish of the standard revolver.

Last year, as the switch to all American-made parts was completed, the USFA catalog line was drastically reduced to only traditional single action army six-guns with the three standard barrel lengths. However, this year the Bisley, the Flat-Top Target, and the Omnipotent have all returned with all the parts, finishing, and fitting being totally American.

It has been another most interesting handgun year with many new models and cartridges being offered. It is easy, at least at my age, to wax nostalgic and long for the good old days with hand-fitted double-action revolvers with beautiful bright blue finishes. *(Remember S&W Bright Blue and Colt Royal Blue?)* I still look for such guns at gun shows–especially if offered at bargain prices. We will never see guns like this again. The upside is that with today's machinery and manufacturing processes, guns are better than ever and, relatively speaking, much less expensive. They are stronger, built to tighter tolerances, and in every case in which I have run one of the new production revolvers against one of its counterparts from back in the "good old days", the new gun always wins in the accuracy department. Today's shooters have a wide and varied choice of the best guns ever offered. Yep, it looks like another great six-gunnin' year! ●

▲USFA offers their SAA in the three traditional barrel lengths, with case-colored frames by Doug Turnbull.

Gary Germaine of United States Firearms with a pair of USFA's SAAs.

by LAYNE SIMPSON

RIFLE REVIEW

Anschutz

LIKE A NUMBER of other companies who build 22 rimfire rifles, Anschutz is, as I write this, feverishly working toward the day when it will begin the delivery of rifles in 17 Mach 2, a co-development of CCI and Hornady. Announced in February of 2004, it is basically the CCI 22 Long Rifle Stinger case necked down. Rated at a muzzle velocity of 2100 fps with a 17-grain bullet, the 17 Mach 2 is said to shoot three inches flatter and deliver 50 percent more energy at 100 yards than the standard-velocity loading of the 22 Long Rifle. How it will fare in the field when pitted against hyper-velocity loadings of the 22 Long Rifle *(such as the CCI Stinger)* remains to be seen. Can the 17 Mach 1 on the 22 Short case or perhaps even the 17 Mach 1/2 on the 22 CB case be far behind?

New sporters from Anschutz for 2004 are the Model 1717DKL with Model 54 action and 23-inch, standard-weight barrel and Model 1517D with a left-hand Model 64 action and heavy 23-inch barrel, both in 17 HMR. Their triggers are set at the factory to pull 34 ounces. The Model 1712 Silhouette Sporter wears no sights, weighs 7.3 pounds and has a relatively light barrel in 22 Long Rifle only.

Armalite

The new AR-10T Ultra Mag from Armalite is chambered for Remington's 300 Short Action Ultra Mag cartridge. It is available as a complete rifle or as a top assembly designed to convert the AR-10 you already own to that powerful cartridge.

Benelli

Last year, the sleek R1 autoloading rifle from Benelli was available in 30-06 and 300 Winchester Magnum. This year, the 308 Winchester chambering has been added to the list but, unfortunately, the 7mm-08 Remington has not.

Ed Brown

I recently examined the new lightweight Damara from Ed Brown and found it to be a very nice rifle. Built on Brown's short action, it has a McMillan fiberglass stock and 22-inch barrel and it weighs just over six pounds. Available chamberings include about anything you can squeeze into a short-action rifle, from the 243 Winchester to the short magnums from Remington and Winchester. You can buy this one with a right- or left-hand action.

Browning

With their racy European styling, the new ShortTrac and LongTrac versions of the BAR autoloader were obviously spooked from the bushes by last year's introduction of the R1 rifle by Benelli. As you might have guessed, one is chambered for short cartridges such as the 243 Winchester, 308 Winchester and the three WSM cartridges in 270, 7mm and 300 calibers while the other is offered in 270 Winchester, 30-06, 7mm Remington Magnum and 300 Winchester Magnum. Both variations have lightweight aluminum receivers and their trigger guards and floorplates are synthetic. Depending on caliber and barrel length, nominal weights range from 6-3/4 to 7-1/2 pounds. Weights for the standard BAR run from 7-1/4 to 8-1/2 pounds.

With its titanium receiver, lightweight 23-inch stainless steel barrel and synthetic stock, the new Mountain Ti version of the A-Bolt rifle is rated at only 5-1/2 pounds. Add a sensible-size scope, a magazine full of

A titanium receiver keeps the weight of the new A-Bolt Mountain Ti at only 5-1 /2 pounds.

ShortTrac *(top)* and LongTrac *(bottom)* versions of the Browning BAR have European styling and weigh less than eight pounds.

cartridges and a lightweight nylon carrying sling and the one you decide to carry up the tallest sheep mount should not weigh much over 7-1/4 pounds. For now, it is available in the three WSM chamberings of 270, 7mm and 300. As other Browning A-Bolts go, the 223 Remington, 223 WSSM and the 25 WSSM are now available in the Hunter, the Varmint Stalker, the Composite Stalker and the Medallion. Why Browning chose to chamber the new 25 WSSM in 22-inch barrels rather than something longer is a question to which I do not have the answer.

Browning's lever-action 22, the BL-22 is now available with a nitride finish on its engraved receiver and octagon barrel. Called the Classic Series, Grade II Octagon, its tubular magazine holds 15 Long Rifles, 17 Longs or 22 Shorts. Its receiver is grooved for scope mounting.

Chipmunk vs. Crickett

A big question on the minds of world-traveled hunters and shooters these past few years has been which is the cutest 22 rimfire rifle—the Chipmunk from Rogue Rifles or the Crickett from Keystone Arms. The Crickett began to pull away in the race when none other than Davey Crickett became its official spokesbug *(quite devastating since this happened not long after Chipmunk spokesrodent, Chipper Chipmunk, hung up his guns and retired)*. Then came a candy-pink laminate stock built especially for girl kids and the Chipmunk started eating even more dust kicked up by the four *(or is it six?)* heels of Davey Crickett. While the spunky Chipmunk may be down, it most certainly is not out of the race and the new .410 shotgun is sure to get plenty of attention from toddling bunny hunters. On top of that, the Chipmunk is also available in 17 HMR and 22 WMR while the Crickett is not. As you may have guessed by now, both of those tiny little rifles are made for tiny little people who consider a length of pull of 11-1/2 inches plenty long. Single-shots both, they weigh 2-1/2 pounds. Barrel length is just over 16 inches and they measure around 30 inches overall. Regardless of what we grownups have to say, only kids and their tremendous buying power will determine in the end which is cutest, the Chipmunk or Crickett.

CZ-USA

New chamberings you will soon see added to the CZ rifle lineup are 17 Remington, 221 Remington Fire Ball, 458 Lott and three WSMs in 270, 7mm and 300 calibers. I particularly like the idea of the 17 Remington in the 527 Varmint with its heavy, 24-inch barrel and Turkish walnut stock. And if that's not enough, "American-pattern" wood stocks are now available on sporter- and varmint-weight rifles in both centerfire and rimfire persuasions. Same goes for the 550 Safari Magnum in two grades of American walnut as well as a tri-color laminate. Another rifle I saw had a Winchester Model 70-style bolt action *(complete with three-position safety)* and from five yards away it even looked a lot like a Winchester Model 70–but it was not a Winchester Model 70. They say it was designed specifically for the families of short magnums introduced during the past few years by Remington and Winchester.

Daisy

Like many who grew up during the very best of times in America, my first rifle was a Daisy, the Red Ryder version to be exact. The Red Ryder offered by Daisy today differs a bit from the one I once used to terrorize the sparrows in our neighborhood but it is close enough to make me yearn for those innocent days of yesteryear. The one I recently shot weighs 2.2 pounds, measures 29 inches overall, holds 650 BBs, has a maximum range of 195 yards *(honest)* and is fully capable of minute-of-tomato soup-can accuracy if you can hold that close. The genuine wood stock of the Model 1938 has Red Ryder galloping across the prairie; put there, no doubt, by a red-hot branding iron. Just like on my old Daisy, the ever-familiar saddle ring with leather thong makes this one easy to tie onto the saddle of your favorite broomstick steed. The Model 1938 has something my old Red Ryder did not have—a crossbolt safety. It also comes in an attractive cardboard box decorated with Old West scenes that would make Red Ryder and his sidekick, Little Beaver, feel right at home on the range. The same rifle is also available in a bubble-pack kit replete with carrying case, shooting glasses, ShatterBlast reactive targets, a supply of PrecisionMax BBs for shooting and a smaller quantity in a tin for collecting. Add one youngster to those ingredients, stir gently, and you will become an instant hero. There was a time when every kid in America wanted a Red Ryder. I'm betting a lot still do. After all—It's a Daisy.

Harrington & Richardson/NEF

The break-action H&R single-shot Handi-Rifle is now available in a varmint version chambered in 22-250. Equally new are both adult and youth rifles in 7mm-08 and stainless steel rifles in 30-06 and 270 Winchester. Then we have the Huntsman Combos. The Pardner and Handi-Rifle sets come with interchangeable shotgun and muzzleloader barrels in 12-gauge and 50-caliber, while the Handi-Rifle set has barrels in 243 Winchester and 50-caliber. Regardless of which you choose, all represent excellent buys and are surprisingly accurate considering their cost. In my report on new rifles from Marlin I tell about taking a nice caribou bull in the Northwest Territories of Canada with a Model 1895 lever action in the 444 chambering. My license allowed me to take two bulls on that hunt so I decided to go after the second one with an H&R Ultra Rifle in 308 Winchester. Like the Marlin lever action, it wore a Burris 3-9x Fullfield II scope. One shot at just under 200 yards was all it took.

Henry Repeating Arms

A knockabout lever-action rifle in 22 rimfire, the Henry is now available with an oversized finger lever, similar to those worn by Winchester rifles used in the past by John Wayne and Chuck Connors to settle the accounts of untold numbers of bad guys. The Model H001L has an 18 1/4-inch barrel, holds 15 Long Rifle cartridges and weighs 5-1/4 pounds. Same goes for the Golden Boy with its "Brasslite" receiver. Other chamberings include 17 HMR and 22 WMR. Henry also offers an economy-grade slide-action 22 with an 18 1/4-inch barrel; it weighs 5-1/2 pounds.

H-S Precision

Long known for its super-accurate *(but relatively heavy)* big-game rifles, H-S Precision now brings us one that no sheep hunter would mind toting up the steepest mountain. Called the ProHunter Lightweight, it weighs 5–1/2 pounds and comes with a right- or left-hand action. Barrel lengths are 20 or 22 inches, depending on caliber and that includes the entire family of Remington and Winchester short magnums. All metal is Teflon-coated for rust resistance.

Kimber

New from Kimber for 2004 is the Pro Varmint on the Kimber 22 action in 22 Long Rifle and on the Model 84M action in 22-250. Both have stainless steel barrels and laminated wood stocks. The rimfire version has a 20-inch barrel and weighs 6-3/4 pounds while its centerfire mate has a 24-inch barrel and weighs 7-1/4 pounds. The new Rimfire Super from the custom shop comes with a test-target proving it is capable of shooting a 0.400-inch group at 50 yards on an indoor range. Commemorating Kimber's 25th anniversary is the Custom Match Limited Edition in 22 rimfire with 22-inch barrel and a weight of 6-1/2 pounds. Among other very nice things, it has a stock of triple-A grade French walnut, 24-line cut checkering and ebony forend tip.

The 6-1/2 pound Howa Model 1500 Mountain Rifle has a 20-inch barrel in 243 Winchester, 7mm-08 Remington or 308 Winchester.

Legacy Sports International

The 6-1/2 pound Howa Model 1500 Mountain Rifle is available with a 20-inch barrel in 243 Winchester, 7mm-08 Remington and 308 Winchester. The action has a hollowed bolt handle knob

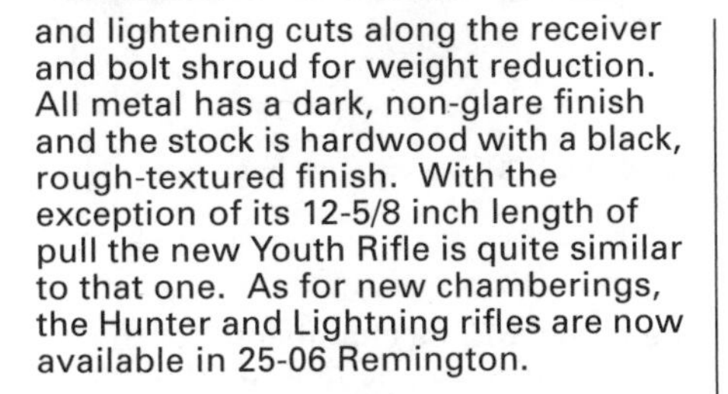

Marlin Model 60DL

and lightening cuts along the receiver and bolt shroud for weight reduction. All metal has a dark, non-glare finish and the stock is hardwood with a black, rough-textured finish. With the exception of its 12-5/8 inch length of pull the new Youth Rifle is quite similar to that one. As for new chamberings, the Hunter and Lightning rifles are now available in 25-06 Remington.

Marlin

The New Model Marlin 1895 is now available in five chamberings. Joining the 444 Marlin, 45-70 Government and 450 Marlin are the 480 Ruger and 475 Linebaugh. Called the Model 1895RL, it has an 18 1/2-inch barrel with six-groove rifling with a 1:20 twist and its magazine holds six 480s or five 475s. Nominal weight is seven pounds, same as for rifles in the other three calibers.

The new T-900 fire control system, now on all 900-series Marlin bolt-action single-shots and repeaters in 22 Long Rifle, 22 WMR and 17 HMR, features a wide fingerpiece with serrated surface and a two-position safety lever with positive stops in its *"Safe"* and *"Fire"* positions. The trigger is noticeably smoother than the old design. A red dot at the top of the bolt shroud is exposed when the striker is cocked. Beginning in 2004, the receivers of all Marlin bolt guns will be drilled and tapped for scope mounting. Bases that take Weaver-style rings are available from Marlin, as well as Burris and Warne.

I hunted barren ground caribou in the Northwest Territories of Canada in September of 2003 and, since I was allowed to take two bulls, I decided to double my fun by using a different rifle when hunting each of them. I took the first bull with a Marlin Model 444 and a handload that pushed the 280-grain Swift A-Frame along at 2200 fps. Realizing I might have no choice but to shoot at relatively long range, I equipped the rifle with a Burris 3-9X Signature scope with the Ballistic Plex reticle. And since my handload averaged around five inches at 300 yards, I decided to chart the trajectory of the Swift bullet in 50-yard increments out to that range. With the rifle zeroed to place its bullets three inches above the intersection of the crosshairs at 100 yards it was only slightly low at 200. Then by using the first and second tick marks of the special reticle, I could hold dead on at 250 and 300 yards. Knowing the range precisely was important so I took along a Bushnell Yardage Pro Scout laser rangefinder. As it turned out, all that range time prior to the hunt was time well spent. When the Bushnell rangefinder read 248 yards I was as close as I could possibly get–but it was close enough, and I got my bull.

Remington

Biggest news from Remington for 2004 is the introduction of a new bolt-action 22-rimfire sporter called the Model 504. It gets its name from the old 500 series of Remington rifles, along with the year of its introduction. Since I have filed a "Testfire" report elsewhere I will say no more on the 504 here and now.

For several years now I have urged Remington decision-makers to offer the 8x57mm Mauser chambering in the limited edition Model 700 Classic. After all, what could be more classic than an old cartridge that continues to be more popular among American hunters than a whole slew of American-designed cartridges. I finally get my wish in 2004. Number 24 in a series that started back in 1981 with the 7x57mm Mauser, the Model 700 Classic in 8x57mm has a 24-inch barrel and weighs just over seven pounds.

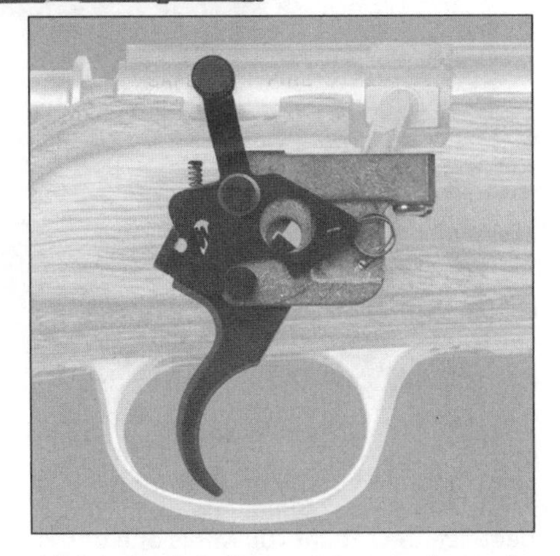

All Marlin bolt-action 22s now have the new T-900 fire control system.

Remington describes the new short-action Model 700 LVSF (Light Varmint, Stainless-Fluted) as the ideal walking varmint rifle. With a weight of less than seven pounds, along with 17 Remington, 221 FireBall, 223 Remington and 22–250 chambering options, few would argue. The 22-inch medium-heavy stainless steel barrel measures a nominal 0.657-inch at the muzzle and has six lightening flutes for weight reduction. Other features include a stainless-steel action with blind magazine, pillar-bedded receiver, semi-beavertail forearm and R3 recoil pad.

They call it the Model 700 CDL (Classic Deluxe) but to me it looks like a

The New Model 1895 from Marlin is now available in 480 Ruger and 475 Linebaugh.

Not many people hunt caribou with lever-action rifles these days but the Marlin 1895 in 444 did a great job on this Northwest Territories bull.

Biggest news from Remington is the new Model 502 in 22 rimfire.

From Remington's custom shop comes this Model 700C, a rifle we have not seen for many years.

reintroduction of the original Model 700 Mountain Rifle. Which is okay by me because the Model 700 MR is one of the best-looking, best-handling and best-feeling big-game rifles I have ever carried in the field. The new version does have a longer barrel: 24 inches in 243 Winchester, 7mm-08, 270 Winchester and 30-06, and 26 inches in 7mm Remington Magnum, 7mm Remington Ultra Mag, 300 Winchester Magnum and 300 Remington Ultra Mag. Weights run around 7-1/2 pounds in standard chamberings and 7-3/4 pounds for the magnums. All metal has a satin blued finish and the classically styled stock has cut checkering, black forearm tip and gripcap and Remington's own R3 recoil pad.

The Model 700 Titanium, which is America's first affordable rifle with a titanium receiver, is now available in a short-action magnum version with 24-inch barrel in 7mm and 300 Remington Short Action Ultra Mag. Nominal weight is 6-3/8 pounds which means that its field-ready weight with scope, lightweight carrying sling and loaded magazine should not greatly exceed eight pounds. That's darned light for a rifle capable of squeezing maximum performance from Remington's two ultra-short magnum cartridges.

For the fourth consecutive year, a portion of the proceeds from the sale of a special edition of the Model 700 rifle will go to the Rocky Mountain Elk Foundation. Called the Model 700 BDL/SS Camo, it is offered only with a 26-inch barrel in 300 Winchester Magnum. The barreled action is stainless steel while the synthetic stock wears the Hardwoods Gray HD camo pattern from Realtree. Other features include a laser engraving on the hinged floorplate, and the highly efficient R3 recoil pad. Nominal weight is 7-1/2 pounds.

The original Model 600 Magnum was available in 350 and 6.5 Remington Magnum so it stands to reason that the latest version of that old classic called the Model 673 be chambered for the same cartridges. Remington did the 350 last year and this year the 6.5 Magnum has been added, along with a resurrection of the old factory load with a 120-grain bullet at 3200 fps. I once owned a Model 660 in 6.5 Magnum and believe me when I say when it comes to hunting game the size of deer and pronghorn antelope, the 6.5 will do anything the 270 Winchester can do–and it will do it from a short-action rifle. And just as I predicted last year, you can now buy a Model 673 in 308 Winchester as well. Who knows, we may eventually see the 7mm-08 added to its list of options.

Considered by many who own it to offer the most performance for the least amount of money, the Model 710 is now available in a magnum version with a 24-inch barrel in 7mm Remington Magnum or 300 Winchester Magnum. Its detachable magazine holds three rounds and the rifle comes with a Bushnell 3-9X Sharpshooter scope riding up top. Nominal weight is 7-1/4 pounds.

As its name implies, the Model Seven YS (Youth Synthetic) has a synthetic stock and a 12 3/8-inch length of pull for short arms. Surface texturing on the grip and forearm are just the thing for slippery hands and the R3 recoil pads tames what little recoil is generated by the 223 Remington, 243 Winchester, and 7mm-08 cartridges. The satin-blued barrel is 20 inches long and nominal weight is 6-1/4 pounds. A long-action version with a 22-inch barrel in 270 Winchester and 30-06 might represent the best of all deals. The young hunter can start out with Remington's new Managed Recoil loadings of those two cartridges and then after a few deer seasons have come and gone he or she can graduate to standard-power loadings.

I enjoy hunting with vintage firearms so you can bet the smile on my face reached from ear to ear when I was recently invited on a mule deer hunt in Colorado and told I could use any Remington firearm so long as I teamed it up with Remington ammo loaded with the relatively new Core-Lokt Ultra bullet. So I opted for a Model 700 BDL I bought in 1963, about a year after the Model 700 was introduced. It is chambered for the 7mm Remington Magnum *(which was*

A super-light rifle like the Remington Model 700 Titanium in 243 Winchester is just the thing to have when hunting chamois at 10,000 feet in the Southern Alps of New Zealand.

Bolt-action *(top)* and single-shot *(bottom)* rifles from Ruger are now chambered for a new cartridge called 204 Ruger.

also introduced in 1962) and if I told you about all the times, good and bad, that old rifle and I have shared in the field, there would be room left for nothing else in this issue of GUN DIGEST. My old Model 700 averaged close to an inch for three-shot groups at 100 yards with the 140-grain CLU load, not too shabby for a 40-year-old rifle with hundreds of rounds of wear on its barrel. It still works nicely on mule deer too, or I should say it does when it is fed ammo with the Core-Lokt Ultra bullet. One shot at about 150 yards did it. I still like that rifle a lot and I am beginning to like the new Remington bullet equally well.

Another old Model 700 I hunted with during 2003 was one of the first built by Remington in 416 Magnum several months before that cartridge was officially introduced. Remington took us and our new 416 Magnum rifles to Alaska where we each shot a gigantic moose. All were one-shot kills. Sixteen years later, in 2003, I took that same rifle to Australia where it accounted for one very large Asiatic buffalo, again with a single shot. One of the things I like about a rifle in 416 Remington Magnum is that it does not use up a lot of ammo.

Rifles, Incorporated

Among my proudest possessions is a trio of Lightweight Strata rifles built by Lex Webernick on Remington Model 700 actions in 257 STW, 6.5 STW and 7mm STW. Those rifles weigh around five pounds each. Even lighter at 4-1/2 pounds is the Titanium Strata built on the Model 700 titanium action in most chamberings up to and including the 300 Weatherby Magnum. One of those rifles on the short action in 243 Winchester, 6mm Remington or 257 Roberts would be especially nice for rough-country deer hunting and, in 7mm-08 Remington, would tough to beat for sheep hunting. Moving on up in weight to 5-3/4 pounds we have the Lightweight 70 on the Winchester Model 70 action. You can order this one in most any commercial chambering up to 375 H&H Magnum. With its slightly heavier barrel and synthetic stock, the Classic weighs 6-1/2 pounds and is available in the same calibers. When I start planning my next trip to Africa my plans might just include the Safari on the Model 70 action in 416 Remington Magnum. It weighs 8-1/2 pounds, has express-style open sights and is also available in 375 H&H Magnum, 458 Winchester Magnum and 458 Lott. Last but not least is the Master Series in most calibers up to the 300 Remington Ultra Mag. This rifle weighs 7-3/4 pounds and is guaranteed to shoot half-minute-of-angle with loads developed for it by Webernick.

Rossi

Last year, Rossi introduced its "Matched Pairs" combo set version of its single-shot gun with both centerfire rifle and shotgun barrels. This year, you can buy a three-barrel set with those–plus a muzzleloader barrel. One combination is made up of barrels in 17 HMR, 270 Winchester and 50-caliber. In case you are not familiar with the Rossi, it is an economy-grade, break-action, knockabout gun with exposed hammer *(replete with hammer-block safety)*. To break down its barrel for loading and unloading you simply press down on a lever located at the side of its receiver.

Ruger

Biggest news from Ruger is the 204 Ruger chambering. Developed by–and presently loaded only by–Hornady, the 204 Ruger pretty much duplicates the performance of the 223 Remington when that cartridge is loaded with a 40-grain bullet. The new chambering is slated for availability in three Model 77 Mark II variations and two versions of the No. 1 single-shot. Also new from Ruger is a 40th Anniversary edition of the 10/22 carbine and a "rifle" version of the 10/22 carbine. The former will be manufactured only during 2004 and comes with a special transparent rotary magazine replete with red rotor. The latter has a 20-inch barrel and is available in 22 Long Rifle and 17 HMR.

Sako

New Model 75 variants from Sako for 2004 include the Hunter and Stainless Synthetic in 270 WSM and 300 WSM. Three additional chambering options for the Model 75 Deluxe are 416 Remington Magnum and the two just-mentioned Winchester shorty magnums. Also new is the Custom Single-Shot in 308 Winchester with heavy, fluted, stainless-steel barrel, laminated wood stock replete with beavertail forearm. Why it is not also available in 22-250 and 243 Winchester is a question Sako and Beretta officials do not–at the moment–have an answer for. What is the most handsome of all Sako rifles is a question I have the answer for. It is the Anniversary Limited Edition in 375 H&H Magnum. But then, at a price of $16,500 it cannot be anything but handsome.

Savage

The Model 40 and Model 340 rifles once offered by Savage were economy-grade rifles, a description that fits the new Model 40 Varmint

The new Model 40 Varmint Hunter in 22 Hornet and 223 from Savage brings back old memories of the Model 40 and Model 340 of yesteryear.

The new Savage Model 12 Varminter Low Profile in 223 and 22-250 has the AccuTrigger.

Hunter equally well. It has a tubular receiver and is available in 223 and 22 Hornet. The 24-inch, heavy barrel is button-rifled and it free-floats in a laminated wood stock replete with Monte Carlo at the rear and beavertail forearm up front. A third sling swivel stud on the forearm is correctly positioned for use with a Harris folding bipod. The fact that this rifle does not wear Savage's relatively new AccuTrigger is to be expected, considering its low price.

I am no great fan of muzzle brakes but if ever I become one the adjustable brake from Savage is the one my rifles will wear. Twist the brake one way to open its gas ports and your rifle is ready for a shooting session at the benchrest or practice range. Twist it in the opposite direction and you are ready to head for the field. The AMB is presently available on the Model 116SAK and the Safari Express. The relatively new AccuTrigger is something Savage bolt guns have needed for a very long time and I am glad to see it standard issue on practically every model variation, including the in-line muzzleloader. Weight of pull on most rifles is owner-adjustable from 2-1/2 to 6 pounds, although the triggers on the varmint and law enforcement series can be adjusted down to 24 ounces. Latest rifle to wear the new trigger is the Model 12 Varminter Low Profile with its 26-inch heavy fluted stainless-steel barrel, in 223 and 22-250.

A 26-inch barrel in 6mm-06 for my Encore rifle from the T/C custom shop and the new 90-grain Scirocco from Swift Bullets were the perfect combination for this New Mexico pronghorn.

Schuerman Arms, Ltd.

For the second year in a row, the Model SA40 from Schuerman Arms has received my vote as the bolt-action rifle with the smoothest action. Somewhat like the Colt Sauer rifle of yesteryear, it has three pivoting locking lugs–but in this case they are located quite close to the front of the bolt. The bolt glides to and fro in the receiver like hot grease on glass. It is available in about any chambering you can think of, from 22-250 to 416 Remington Magnum.

Taurus

The new pump-action Thunderbolt from Taurus is a Brazilian-made knockoff of the old Colt Lightning in 45 Colt only. It is available in two styles: Model C45BR in blued steel and Model C45SSR in polished stainless. Both have 26-inch barrels, 14-round magazines, adjustable open sights and hardwood stocks with curved steel buttplates. Weight is just over eight pounds.

SIGARMS

Several custom options are now available on Blaser rifles. The R93 Lexus Plus, as an example, comes with a black receiver and a choice of sideplate finishes, including color casehardening by Doug Turnbull. The R93 Synthetic wears a Mossy Oak camo finish and the R93/SRHS (Steel Receiver Heavy Safari) has an "American-style" stock and heavy barrel in 375 H&H and 416 Remington Magnum.

Springfield, Inc.

The SOCOM 16 is the latest version of Springfield's M1A rifle, with a 16-inch barrel in 308 Winchester. Other features include a muzzle brake, hooded front sight, synthetic stock and forward-positioned scope mount.

Thompson/Center

The Classic in 22 Long Rifle from T/C has quickly earned a reputation for excellent accuracy. As autoloaders go, the one I have been shooting for about a year is second in accuracy only to custom 10/22s built by Volquartsen, Clark, Briley and a few others. On top of that, with its blued steel and real walnut, it looks the way many of us like to see a rifle look. Those who march to a different drummer will like the looks of a new variation called the Silver Lynx. Even I will have to admit its stainless steel barreled action and synthetic stock make a lot of sense for rough-weather hunting. The 17 Hornady Mach 2 is a new chambering for this rifle.

The G2 Contender rifle will be offered in 375 JDJ and 204 Ruger and the Encore rifle is now available in 280 Remington, 375 JDJ, and 405 Winchester. Also available from Thompson/Center is 375 JDJ ammo loaded with a 220-grain flatnose bullet at about 2200 fps in Encore and Contender pistols, and 2300 to 2400 fps in rifle versions of those guns. The new carbine variation of the Encore 209x50 muzzleloader has a 20-inch barrel.

I had never hunted with the Encore in anything except its handgun form until the performance I was getting out of a 26-inch custom shop barrel in 6mm-06 and the new 90-grain Swift Scirocco bullet indicated it was time I did. My handload consisted of cases formed by simply necking down Remington 25-06 brass, the Remington 9-1/2M primer and 58.0 grains of H4831SC for a velocity of 3450 fps. So I took the rig antelope hunting. I had been chasing that particular New Mexico pronghorn on foot all morning long of the last day and

Thompson/Center's new Silver Lynx version of its Classic 22 autoloader is now available in 17 Hornady Mach 2.

The Winchester Model 70 Ultimate Shadow comes in three variations: blued *(top)*, stainless *(middle)*, and camouflage *(bottom)*.

when it suddenly paused momentarily from chasing a doe, I dropped to the prone position and rested the rifle atop my daypack. I was zeroed three inches high at 100 yards and when the trusty Bushnell laser rangefinder indicated 365 yards away, I held about four inches high and about as much into the light breeze I felt against the side of my face and squeezed the trigger. The bullet struck caught the buck in the shoulder, dropping it where it stood. After seeing how much damage that tiny 90-grain bullet did to all that shoulder bone I decided then and there that I would be using Scirocco bullets on more hunts in the future. I later used that same Encore receiver and stock along with a 205x50 muzzleloader barrel to take a 140s-class whitetail while hunting with Judd Cooney in Iowa.

Tikka

The T3 Lite Stainless is my favorite Tikka big-game rifle. It has a stainless-steel barreled action, a black synthetic stock and weighs a mere 6-1/4 pounds in standard chamberings, and 6-1/2 pounds in the magnums. Barrel lengths are 22-1/2 and 24-1/2 inches. Chambering options range from the 223 Remington to the 338 Winchester Magnum. My pick for this rifle is the 7mm-08 Remington. Latest in the lineup is the T3 Laminated Stainless with those same barrel lengths and calibers. Just as new is the T3 Varmint with synthetic stock and heavy 23-1/2 inch blued or stainless steel barrel in 223 Remington, 22-250 and 308. The shape of the stock on this one makes it just about ideal for shooting over sandbags. According to the catalog, no T3 rifle is allowed to depart Finland and head our way until it has fired a one-inch, 3-shot group at 100 yards.

U.S. Firearms

One of the more interesting firearms I have seen lately is the slide-action Lightning Rifle in 45 Colt, 44-40 Winchester and 38-40 Winchester from United States Firearms. Similar in appearance to the Colt Lightning of yesteryear, it is available with a 20- or 26-inch barrel and wears a walnut stock with curved steel buttplate. The 15-round magazine of the rifle will surely make this one a winner among cowboy action shooters. A fancy-grade version with half-octagon barrel, figured wood and pistol grip-style stock is also available. If what they say about it being made in America is true, every would-be cowpoke in America owes it to himself to sell his foreign-made replica to some unsuspecting greenhorn and buy one of these.

USRAC

U.S. Repeating Arms has announced the availability of Winchester's new 25 WSSM cartridge in three Model 70 Ultimate Shadow variations, blued, stainless and camo. Oddly enough, all have 22-inch barrels. The new chambering is also available in the Classic Featherweight and it too has a too-short barrel. In case you are not familiar with the 25 WSSM, it is a super-short magnum capable of duplicating the 25-06 Remington in a short-action rifle. Like the old 25-06, the new 25 WSSM will be seen at its best when used in barrels no shorter than 24 inches.

Those who shoot from the left shoulder will surely be pleased to learn that the Featherweight and Sporter versions of the Model 70 now come with the bolt handle over on their side. The left-hand Featherweight is available in three WSM chamberings: 270, 7mm and 300, while Sporter options include those three, plus 270 Winchester, 30-06, 7mm Remington Magnum and 300 Winchester Magnum. Believe it or not, USRAC now offers seven variations of the Model 9410 with the Semi-Fancy Traditional being the latest. It gets its name from–you guessed it–its stock of semi-fancy walnut. The latest version of the Model 94 lever action is called the Timber *(who comes up with these names?)*. It has an 18-inch ported barrel in 450 Marlin and, even more interesting, it comes from the factory wearing an aperture sight.

Winchester Model 94 Timber.

Winchester Model 9410 Semi-Fancy Traditional.

Tom Volquartsen's new super-accurate centerfire autoloader is initially chambered to 204 Ruger and 223 Remington.

Volquartsen Custom

I have shot Tom Volquartsen's rifles enough to become thoroughly convinced that they have no peer when it comes to squeezing maximum accuracy from autoloaders. The one in 22 Long Rifle I own shoots five-shot groups at 50 yards averaging just over 1/4-inch with Remington/Eley ammunition. The other rifle in 22 WMR will consistently shoot five bullets inside 3/4-inch at 100 yards with Federal ammo loaded with the Speer 30-grain TNT. I have not tried Tom's new switch-barrel gun in 17 HMR and 22 WMR but I plan to this summer and expect it to be superbly accurate. Its two barrels are quickly switched in mere seconds by loosening a collar just in front of the receiver. Volquartsen will be chambering his rifles for the new 17 Mach 2 and will also offer a switch-barrel rifle with one barrel in that caliber and the other barrel in 22 Long Rifle. He has also moved into the centerfire field with a new super-accurate, semiautomatic rifle chambered for the 223 Remington and 204 Ruger.

Weatherby

Who'd ever have thought we'd see a Weatherby big-game rifle with a fully adjustable trigger priced at $476? That's retail for the Vanguard Synthetic and I've seen them go for a bit less. The one in 22-250 I took on a deer hunt in Texas proved to be better than accurate enough with Federal Premium ammo loaded with the 55-grain Bear Claw bullet. The latest Vanguard synthetic stock is the Monte Carlo style and it is injection-molded of lightweight composite materials for maximum durability and stability. Also new for 2004 is the Vanguard Sporter with walnut stock replete with rosewood forend tip, 18 lines-per-inch cut checkering and a nice rubber recoil pad. It has a 24-inch barrel and is chambered for a variety of cartridges. Both new variations have Monte Carlo-style stocks simply because a Weatherby doesn't look or feel like a Weatherby unless it has a Monte Carlo stock. Others have attempted to copy the design but nobody has managed to capture the true essence of the Monte Carlo stock like Weatherby.

Up until now the Vanguard has been available in 223 Remington, 22-250, 243 Winchester, 270 Winchester, 308 Winchester, 30-06, 7mm Remington Magnum, 300 Winchester Magnum, 300 Winchester Short Magnum, 300 Weatherby Magnum and 338 Winchester Magnum. A new chambering this year is the 257 Magnum–which just happens to be one of the most popular Weatherby cartridges. Loaded to respective velocities of 3825, 3600 and 3400 fps with 87-, 100- and 117-grain bullets, it also just happens to be the fastest 25-caliber factory cartridge available. I simply cannot imagine a better long-range antelope/deer/caribou/sheep/goat rifle for the money than the Weatherby Vanguard in 257 Weatherby Magnum.

For those who simply cannot be satisfied by an off-the-shelf rifle, the Weatherby custom shop offers a number of modifications to the Vanguard. They include hand-bedded synthetic stocks in various camo patterns, replete with pillar bedding. Special metal finishes such as black Teflon and titanium nitride are also available.

One of my very best hunts ever took place in August of 2003 when I hunted Dall sheep in the Wrangell mountain range of Alaska with outfitter Terry Overly of Pioneer Outfitters *(907-734-0007)*. I took a very nice ram on the seventh day with a Weatherby Super Big GameMaster in 280 Remington. Wearing a Zeiss 3-9X scope, a lightweight Weatherby nylon sling and a magazine full of cartridges, the entire outfit weighed just 7-1/2 pounds. It was a tough hunt but I loved every minute of it and I would go back tomorrow if given the opportunity. I especially appreciated the lightweight of the Weatherby rifle on that hunt. It proved to be tough as nails, too. Mine lost a lot of its finish on rocks during many steep climbs but it and its scope managed to hold zero perfectly. My hunting partner also took his ram with a Super Big GameMaster, but in 240 Weatherby Magnum. When his horse fell and rolled over the rifle three times we both thought it was a goner, but it held its zero perfectly. That's the kind of rifle you most definitely want to be carrying in country where the nearest gunsmith is hundreds of miles away.

Before leaving the subject of things Weatherby I must mention that I survived another cold winter hunting season in large part due to the warmth of excellent wool clothing sold by this company. Its most severe test of 2003

The Weatherby Vanguard wears a new Monte Carlo style stock and is now available in 257 Weatherby Magnum.

This Vanguard, with it pillar-bedded Outfitter stock, is available from Weatherby's custom shop.

came during a muzzleloader hunt for deer in Iowa. Sitting on a deer stand all day long in temperatures that drop below zero is not very high up on my list of fun things to do and had I not been wearing extremely warm wool clothing I could not have done it. I managed to survive by wearing the Double Yoke Shirt, the Heavyweight Parka and the Late Season Cargo Pant over several layers of long underwear. Anytime it snowed or the wind blew I wore a Browning rain jacket and pant on the outside. I also wore the Weatherby Heavyweight Gloves with chemical warmers placed inside. Like Ralphie's little brother in "The Christmas Story", I had on so much clothing I could hardly lower my arms but I stayed warm and just as important, I got my buck. ●

NOTE: Autographed copies of Layne's full-color, hardback books, "Shotguns and Shotgunning" and "Rifles and Cartridges For Large Game", are available for $39.95 plus $6 for shipping and handling each from High Country Press, 306 Holly Park Lane, Dept. GD, Simpsonville, SC 29681. Also available is a softcover edition of his "The Custom 1911 Pistol" for $30.95 plus $4 s&h.

I took this Dall sheep with a Weatherby Super Big GameMaster in 280 Remington while hunting in the Wrangell mountain range of Alaska with outfitter Terry Overly.

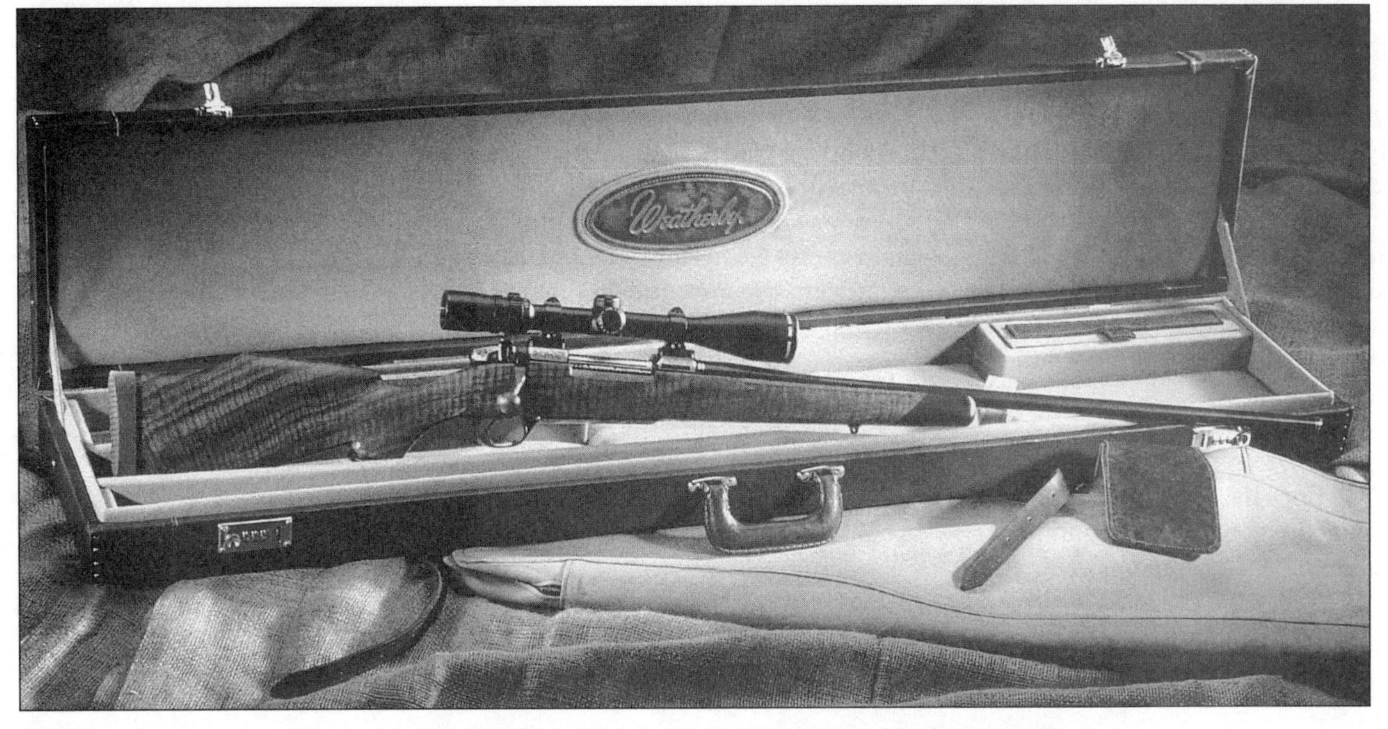

This rifle, along with another just like it, raised $40,000 for the National High School Rodeo Association.

THE 2005 GUN DIGEST WEB DIRECTORY

by Holt Bodinson

How old is the World Wide Web that is the basis of so much firearms e-commerce? Hard as it might be to believe, the World Wide Web did not debut until 1991—a mere 14 years ago.

This past year was significant because the person who created the World Wide Web, who never claimed a penny or royalty for his creation, was knighted. Tim Berners-Lee, a 25-year-old graduate of Oxford at the time, had a vision. "Suppose," he wrote, "all the information stored on computers everywhere was linked. Suppose I could program my computer to create a space in which every computer...on the planet would be available to me and to anyone else."

Sir Berners-Lee went on to do it, giving us the coding system HTML (HyperTextMarkup Language), the Web page address system or URL (Univeral Resource Locator), a set of rules or HTTP (HyperText Transfer Protocol) to link documents across the Internet, and the first rudimentary Web browser, permitting users to view other users' files.

And look where we are 14 years later!

The firearms industry has done a remarkably good job of adapting to e-commerce. More and more firearm related businesses are striking out and creating their own discrete web pages, and it's never been easier with the inexpensive software programs now available.

Firearm auction sites like Auction Arms or Gun Broker have brought together collectors from around the world. But beware! If you are buying a firearm over the Internet, insist on a 3-day inspection privilege. Speaking from personal experience, "a bright and shiny bore" often arrives as a "bright, shiny, and pitted bore!"

The GUN DIGEST Web Directory is in its sixth year of publication. The Internet is proving to be a dynamic environment and since our last edition, there have been numerous changes. Companies have consolidated and adopted a new owner's web site address. New companies have appeared and old companies have disappeared. Search engines are now more powerful than ever and seem to root out even the most obscure reference to a product name or manufacturer.

The following index of current web addresses is offered to our readers as a convenient jumping-off point. Half the fun is just exploring what's out there. Considering that most of the web pages have hot links to other firearm-related web pages, the Internet trail just goes on-and-on once you've taken the initial step to go online.

Here are a few pointers:

If the web site you desire is not listed, try using the full name of the company or product, typed without spaces, between www.-and-.com, for example, www.krause.com. Probably 95 percent of current Web sites are based on this simple, self-explanatory format.

Try a variety of search engines like Microsoft Internet Explorer, Metacrawler, GoTo.com, Yahoo, HotBot, AltaVista, Lycos, Excite, InfoSeek, Looksmart, Google, and WebCrawler while using key words such as gun, firearm, rifle, pistol, blackpowder, shooting, hunting–frankly, any word that relates to the sport. Each search engine seems to comb through the World Wide Web in a different fashion and produces different results. We find Google to be among the best. Accessing the various search engines is simple. Just type www.google.com for example, and you're on your way.

Welcome to the digital world of firearms. Enjoy our Directory!

WEB DIRECTORY

Ammunition and Components

3-D Ammunition www.3dammo.com
Accurate Arms Co. Inc www.accuratepowder.com
ADCO/Nobel Sport Powder www.adcosales.com
Aguila Ammunition www.aguilaammo.com
Alliant Powder www.alliantpowder.com
American Ammunition www.a-merc.com
Ammo Depot www.ammodepot.com
Arizona Ammunition, Inc. www.arizonaammunition.com
A-Zoom Ammo www.a-zoom.com
Ballistic Products, Inc. www.ballisticproducts.com
Barnes Bullets www.barnesbullets.com
Baschieri & Pellagri www.baschieri-pellagri.com
Beartooth Bullets www.beartoothbullets.com
Bell Brass www.bellbrass.com
Berger Bullets, Ltd. www.bergerbullets.com
Berry's Mfg., Inc. www.berrysmfg.com
Big Bore Bullets of Alaska www.awloo.com/bbb/index.htm
Big Bore Express www.bigbore.com
Bismuth Cartridge Co. www.bismuth-notox.com
Black Dawge Cartridge www.blackdawgecartridge.com
Black Hills Ammunition, Inc. www.black-hills.com
Brenneke of America Ltd. www.brennekeusa.com
Buffalo Arms www.buffaloarms.com
Calhoon, James, Bullets www.jamescalhoon.com
Cartuchos Saga www.saga.es
Cast Performance Bullet www.castperformance.com
CCI www.cci-ammunition.com
Century Arms www.centuryarms.com
Cheaper Than Dirt www.cheaperthandirt.com
Cheddite France www.cheddite.com
Claybuster Wads www.claybusterwads.com
Clean Shot Powder www.cleanshot.com
Cole Distributing www.cole-distributing.com
Combined Tactical Systems www.less-lethal.com
Cor-Bon/Glaser www.cor-bon.com
Cowboy Bullets www.cowboybullets.com
Denver Bullet Co. denbullets@aol.com
Dillon Precision www.dillonprecision.com
DKT, Inc. www.dktinc.com
Dynamit Nobel RWS Inc. www.dnrws.com
Elephant/Swiss Black Powder www.elephantblackpowder.com
Eley Ammunition www.remington.com
Eley Hawk Ltd. www.eleyhawk.com
Eley Limited www.eley.co.uk
Estate Cartridge www.estatecartridge.com
Extreme Shock Munitions www.extremeshockusa.com
Federal Cartridge Co. www.federalpremium.com
Fiocchi of America www.fiocchiusa.com
Fowler Bullets www.benchrest.com/fowler
Garrett Cartridges www.garrettcartridges.com
Gentner Bullets www.benchrest.com/gentner/
Glaser Safety Slug, Inc. www.corbon.com
GOEX Inc. www.goexpowder.com
Graf & Sons www.grafs.com
Hawk Bullets www.hawkbullets.com
Hevi.Shot www.hevishot.com
Hi-Tech Ammunition www.iidbs.com/hitech
Hodgdon Powder www.hodgdon.com
Hornady www.hornady.com
Hull Cartridge www.hullcartridge.com
Huntington Reloading Products www.huntingtons.com
Impact Bullets www.impactbullets.com
IMR Smokeless Powders www.imrpowder.com
International Cartridge Corp www.internationalcartridgecorp.com
Israel Military Industries www.imisammo.co.il
ITD Enterprise www.itdenterpriseinc.com
Jada Enterprise www.jadaenterprise.com
Kent Cartridge America www.kentgamebore.com
Knight Bullets www.benchrest.com/knight/
Kynoch Ammunition www.kynochammunition.com
Lapua www.lapua.com
Lawrence Brand Shot www.metalico.com
Lazzeroni Arms Co. www.lazzeroni.com
Leadheads Bullets www.proshootpro.com
Liberty Shooting Supplies www.libertyshootingsupplies.com
Lightfield Ammunition Corp www.lightfield-ammo.com
Lomont Precision Bullets www.klomont.com/kent
Lost River Ballistic Technologies,Inc. www.lostriverballistic.com
Lyman www.lymanproducts.com
Magnus Bullets www.magnusbullets.com
MagSafe Ammunition www.realpages.com/magsafeammo
Magtech www.magtechammunition.com
Mast Technology www.bellammo.com
Masterclass Bullet Co. www.mastercast.com
Meister Bullets www.meisterbullets.com
Midway USA www.midwayusa.com
Miltex,Inc. www.miltexusa.com
Mitchell Mfg. Co. www.mitchellsales.com
MK Ballistic Systems www.mkballistics.com
Mullins Ammunition www.mullinsammunition.com
National Bullet Co. www.nationalbullet.com
Nobel Sport www.adcosales.com
Nobel Sport www.snpe.com
Norma www.norma.cc
North Fork Technologies www.northforkbullets.com
Nosler Bullets Inc www.nosler.com
Old Western Scrounger www.ows-ammunition.com
Oregon Trail/Trueshot Bullets www.trueshotbullets.com
Pattern Control www.patterncontrol.com
PMC-Eldorado Cartridge www.pmcammo.com
Polywad www.polywad.com
PowerBelt Bullets www.powerbeltbullets.com
Precision Ammunition www.precisionammo.com
Precision Reloading www.precisionreloading.com
Pro Load Ammunition www.proload.com
Rainier Ballistics www.rainierballistics.com
Ram Shot Powder www.ramshot.com
Reloading Specialties Inc. www.reloadingspecialties.com
Remington www.remington.com
Roc Imports (GPA bullets) www.roc-import.com
Sellier & Bellot USA inc. www.sb-usa.com
Shilen www.shilen.com
Sierra www.sierrabullets.com
Speer Bullets www.speer-bullets.com
Sporting Supplies Int'l Inc. www.ssiintl.com
Starline www.starlinebrass.com
Triton Cartridge www.tritonammo.com
Trueshot Bullets www.trueshotbullets.com
Tru-Tracer www.trutracer.com
Vihtavuori Lapua www.lapua.com
West Coast Bullets www.westcoastbullet.com
Western Powders Inc. www.westernpowders.com
Widener's Reloading & Shooters Supply www.wideners.com
Winchester Ammunition www.winchester.com
Wolf Ammunition www.wolfammo.com
Woodleigh Bullets www.woodleighbullets.com.au
Zanders Sporting Goods www.gzanders.com

Cases, Safes, Gun Locks, and Cabinets

Ace Case Co. www.acecase.com
AG English Sales Co. www.agenglish.com
All Americas' Outdoors www.innernet.net/gunsafe
Alpine Cases www.alpinecases.com
Aluma Sport by Dee Zee www.deezee.com
American Security Products www.amsecusa.com
Americase www.americase.com
Avery Outdoors, Inc. www.averyoutdoors.com
Bear Track Cases www.beartrackcases.com
Boyt Harness Co. www.boytharness.com
Bulldog Gun Safe Co. www.gardall.com
Cannon Safe Co. www.cannonsafe.com

WEB DIRECTORY

CCL Security Products www.cclsecurity.com
Concept Development Corp. www.saf-t-blok.com
Doskocil Mfg. Co. www.doskocilmfg.com
Fort Knox Safes www.ftknox.com
Franzen Security Products www.securecase.com
Frontier Safe Co. www.frontiersafe.com
Granite Security Products www.granitesafe.com
Gunlocker Phoenix USA Inc. www.gunlocker.com
GunVault www.gunvault.com
Hakuba USA Inc. www.hakubausa.com
Heritage Safe Co. www.heritagesafecompany.com
Hide-A-Gun www.hide-a-gun.com
Homak Safes www.homak.com
Hunter Company www.huntercompany.com
Kalispel Case Line www.kalispelcaseline.com
Knouff & Knouff, Inc. www.kkair.com
Knoxx Industries www.knoxx,com
Kolpin Mfg. Co. www.kolpin.com
Liberty Safe & Security www.libertysafe.com
New Innovative Products www.starlightcases
Noble Security Systems Inc. www.noble.co.ll
Phoenix USA Inc. www.gunlocker.com
Plano Molding Co. www.planomolding.com
Rhino Gun Cases www.rhinoguns.com
Safe Tech, Inc. www.safrgun.com
Saf-T-Hammer www.saf-t-hammer.com
Saf-T-Lok Corp. www.saf-t-lok.com
San Angelo All-Aluminum Products Inc. sasptuld@x.netcom.com
Securecase www.securecase.com
Shot Lock Corp. www.shotlock.com
Smart Lock Technology Inc. www.smartlock.com
Sportsmans Steel Safe Co. www.sportsmansteelsafes.com
Stack-On Products Co. www.stack-on.com
Sun Welding www.sunwelding.com
T.Z. Case Int'l www.tz-case.com
Versatile Rack Co. www.versatilegunrack.com
V-Line Industries www.vlineind.com
Winchester Safes www.fireking.com
Ziegel Engineering www.ziegeleng.com
Zonetti Armor www.zonettiarmor.com

Choke Devices, Recoil Reducers, and Accuracy Devices

100 Straight Products www.100straight.com
Answer Products Co. www.answerrifles.com
Briley Mfg www.briley.com
Carlson's www.carlsonschokes.com
Colonial Arms www.colonialarms.com
Comp-N-Choke www.comp-n-choke.com
Hastings www.hastingsbarrels.com
Kick's Industries www.kicks-ind.com
Mag-Na-Port Int'l Inc. www.magnaport.com
Sims Vibration Laboratory www.limbsaver.com
Truglo www.truglo.com

Chronographs and Ballistic Software

Barnes Ballistic Program www.barnesbullets.com
Ballisticard Systems www.ballisticards.com
Competitive Edge Dynamics www.cedhk.com
Hodgdon Shotshell Program www.hodgdon.com
Lee Shooter Program www.leeprecision.com
Load From A Disk www.loadammo.com
Oehler Research Inc. www.oehler-research.com
PACT www.pact.com
ProChrony www.competitionelectronics.com
Quickload www.neconos.com
RCBS Load www.rcbs.com
Shooting Chrony Inc www.chrony.com
Sierra Infinity Ballistics Program www.sierrabullets.com

Cleaning Products

Accupro www.accupro.com
Ballistol USA www.ballistol.com
Birchwood Casey www.birchwoodcasey.com
Bore Tech www.boretech.com
Break-Free, Inc. www.break-free.com
Bruno Shooters Supply www.brunoshooters.com
Butch's Bore Shine www.lymanproducts.com
C.J. Weapons Accessories www.cjweapons,com
Clenzoil www.clenzoil.com
Corrosion Technologies www.corrosionx.com
Dewey Mfg. www.deweyrods.com
Eezox Inc. www.xmission.com
G 96 www.g96.com
Hollands Shooters Supply www.hollandgun.com
Hoppes www.hoppes.com
Hydrosorbent Products www.dehumidify.com
Inhibitor VCI Products www.inhibitor.com
Iosso Products www.iosso.com
KG Industries www.kgcoatings.com
Kleen-Bore Inc. www.kleen-bore.com
L&R Mfg. www.lrultrasonics.com
Militec-1 www.militec-1.com
Mpro7 Gun Care www.mp7.com
Otis Technology, Inc. www.otisgun.com
Outers www.outers-guncare.com
Ox-Yoke Originals Inc. www.oxyoke.com
Parker-Hale Ltd. www.parker-hale.com
Prolix Lubricant www.prolixlubricant.com
ProShot Products www.proshotproducts.com
ProTec Lubricants www.proteclubricants.com
Rusteprufe Labs www.rusteprufe.com
Sagebrush Products www.sagebrushproducts.com
Sentry Solutions Ltd. www.sentrysolutions.com
Shooters Choice Gun Care www.shooters-choice.com
Silencio www.silencio.com
Slip 2000 www.slip2000.com
Stony Point Products www.stoneypoint.com
Tetra Gun www.tetraproducts.com
World's Fastest Gun Bore Cleaner www.michaels-oregon.com

Firearm Manufacturers and Importers

AAR, Inc. www.iar-arms.com
Accuracy Int'l North America www.accuracyinternational.org
Accuracy Rifle Systems www.mini-14.net
Ace Custom 45's www.acecustom45.com
Advanced Weapons Technology www.AWT-Zastava.com
AIM www.aimsurplus.com
AirForce Airguns www.airforceairguns.com
Airguns of Arizona www.airgunsofarizona.com
Airgun Express www.airgunexpress.com
Alchemy Arms www.alchemyltd.com
Alexander Arms www.alexanderarms.com
American Derringer Corp. www.amderringer.com
American Spirit Arms Corp. www.gunkits.com
American Western Arms www.awaguns.com
Anics Corp. www.anics.com
Answer Products Co. www.answerrifles.com
AR-7 Industries, LLC www.ar-7.com
Armalite www.armalite.com
Armsco www.armsco.net
Armscorp USA Inc. www.armscorpusa.com
Arnold Arms www.arnoldarms.com
Arsenal USA www.arsenalusa.com
Arthur Brown Co. www.eabco.com
Austin & Halleck www.austinhalleck.com
Autauga Arms, Inc. www.autaugaarms.com
Auto-Ordnance Corp. www.tommygun.com
AWA Int'l www.awaguns.com
Axtell Rifle Co. www.riflesmith.com
AyA www.aya-fineguns.com

WEB DIRECTORY

Baikal www.baikalinc.ru/eng/
Ballard Rifle & Cartridge LLC www.ballardrifles.com
Barrett Firearms Mfg. www.barrettrifles.com
Beeman Precision Airguns www.beeman.com
Benelli USA Corp. www.benelliusa.com
Benjamin Sheridan www.crosman.com
Beretta U.S.A. Corp. www.berettausa.com
Bernardelli www.bernardelli.com
Bill Hanus Birdguns www.billhanusbirdguns.com
Bleiker www.bleiker.ch
Bond Arms www.bondarms.com
Borden's Rifles, Inc. www.bordensrifles.com
Boss & Co. www.bossguns.co.uk
Bowen Classic Arms www.bowenclassicarms.com
Briley Mfg. www.briley.com
BRNO Arms www.zbrojovka.com
Brown, David McKay www.mckaybrown.com
Brown, Ed Products www.brownprecision.com
Browning www.browning.com
BSA Guns www.bsaguns.com
BUL Ltd. www.bultransmark.com
Bushmaster Firearms/Quality Parts www.bushmaster.com
BWE Firearms www.bwefirearms.com
Cape Outfitters www.doublegun.com
Carbon 15 www.professional-ordnance.com
Caspian Arms, Ltd. www.caspianarmsltd.8m.com
Casull Arms Corp. www.casullarms.com
CDNN Investments, Inc. www.cdnninvestments.com
Century Arms www.centuryarms.com
Chadick's Ltd. www.chadicks-ltd.com
Champlin Firearms www.champlinarms.com
Chapuis Arms www.doubleguns.com/chapuis.htm
Charles Daly www.charlesdaly.com
Charter 2000, Inc. www.charterfirearms.com
Christensen Arms www.christensenarms.com
Cimarron Firearms Co. www.cimarron-firearms.com
Clark Custom Guns www.clarkcustomguns.com
Cobra Enterprises www.cobrapistols.com
Cogswell & Harrison www.cogswell.co.uk/home.htm
Colt Mfg Co. www.colt.com
Compasseco, Inc. www.compasseco.com
Connecticut Valley Arms www.cva.com
Cooper Firearms www.cooperfirearms.com
Crosman www.crosman.com
Crossfire, L.L.C. www.crossfirelle.com
C. Sharp Arms Co. www.csharparms.com
CZ USA www.cz-usa.com
Daisy Mfg Co. www.daisy.com
Dakota Arms Inc. www.dakotaarms.com
Dan Wesson Firearms www.danwessonfirearms.com
Davis Industries www.davisindguns.com
Dixie Gun Works www.dixiegun.com
Dlask Arms Corp. www.dlask.com
D.S. Arms, Inc. www.dsarms.com
Dumoulin www.dumoulin-herstal.com
Dynamit Noble www.dnrws.com
Eagle Imports, Inc. www.bersa-llama.com
EDM Arms www.edmarms.com
E.M.F. Co. www.emf-company.com
Enterprise Arms www.enterprise.com
European American Armory Corp. www.eaacorp.com
Evans, William www.williamevans.com
Fabarm www.fabarm.com
FAC-Guns-N-Stuff www.gunsnstuff.com
Falcon Pneumatic Systems www.falcon-airguns.com
Fausti Stefano www.faustistefanoarms.com
Firestorm www.firestorm-sgs.com
Flodman Guns www.flodman.com
FN Herstal www.fnherstal.com
FNH USA www.fnhusa.com
Franchi www.franchiusa.com
Freedom Arms www.freedomarms.com
Gambo Renato www.renatogamba.it
Gamo www.gamo.com
Gary Reeder Custom Guns www.reeder-customguns.com
Gazelle Arms www.gazellearms.com
Gibbs Rifle Company www.gibbsrifle.com
Glock www.glock.com
Griffin & Howe www.griffinhowe.com
Grizzly Big Boar Rifle www.largrizzly.com
GSI Inc. www.gsifirearms.com
Hammerli www.hammerli.com
Hatsan Arms Co. www.hatsan.com.tr
Heckler and Koch www.hecklerkoch-usa.com
Henry Repeating Arms Co. www.henryrepeating.com
Heritage Mfg. www.heritagemfg.com
Heym www.heym-waffenfabrik.de
High Standard Mfg. www.highstandard.com
Hi-Point Firearms www.hi-pointfirearms.com
Holland & Holland www.hollandandholland.com
H&R Firearms www.marlinfirearms.com
H-S Precision www.hsprecision.com
Hunters Lodge Corp. www.hunterslodge.com
IAR Inc. www.iar-arms.com
Imperial Miniature Armory www.1800miniature.com
Interarms www.interarms.com
International Military Antiques, Inc. www.ima-usa.com
Inter Ordnance www.interordnance.com
Intrac Arms International LLC www.hsarms.com
Israel Arms www.israelarms.com
Ithaca Gun Co. www.ithacagun.com
Izhevsky Mekhanichesky Zavod www.baikalinc.ru
Jarrett Rifles, Inc. www.jarrettrifles.com
J&G Sales, Ltd. www.jgsales.com
Johannsen Express Rifle www.johannsen-jagd.de
JP Enterprises, Inc. www.jpar15.com
Kahr Arms/Auto-Ordnance www.kahr.com
K.B.I. www.kbi-inc.com
Kel-Tec CNC Ind., Inc. www.kel-tec.com
Kifaru www.kifaru.net
Kimber www.kimberamerica.com
Knight's Armament Co. www.knightsarmament.com
Knight Rifles www.knightrifles.com
Korth www.korthwaffen.de
Krieghoff GmbH www.krieghoff.de
KY Imports, Inc. www.kyimports.com
Krieghoff Int'l www.krieghoff.com
L.A.R Mfg www.largrizzly.com
Lazzeroni Arms Co. www.lazzeroni.com
Legacy Sports International www.legacysports.com
Les Baer Custom, Inc. www.lesbaer.com
Linebaugh Custom Sixguns www.sixgunner.com/linebaugh
Ljutic www.ljuticgun.com
Lone Star Rifle Co. www.lonestarrifle.com
Magnum Research www.magnumresearch.com
Markesbery Muzzleloaders www.markesbery.com
Marksman Products www.marksman.com
Marlin www.marlinfirearms.com
Mauser www.mauserwaffen.de
McMillan Bros Rifle Co. www.mcfamily.com
Meacham Rifles www.meachamrifles.com
Merkel www.gsifirearms.com
Miltech www.miltecharms.com
Miltex, Inc. www.miltexusa.com
Mitchell's Mausers www.mitchellsales.com
MK Ballistic Systems www.mkballistics.com
M-Mag www.mmag.com
Montana Rifle Co. www.montanarifleman.com
Navy Arms www.navyarms.com
Nesika Actions www.nesika.com
New England Arms Corp. www.newenglandarms.com
New England Custom Gun Svc, Ltd. www.newenglandcustomgun.com
New England Firearms www.hr1871.com
New Ultra Light Arms www.newultralight.com

WEB DIRECTORY

North American Arms www.naaminis.com
Nowlin Mfg. Inc. www.nowlinguns.com
O.F. Mossberg & Sons www.mossberg.com
Ohio Ordnance Works www.ohioordnanceworks.com
Olympic Arms www.olyarms.com
Panther Arms www.dpmsinc.com
Para-Ordnance www.paraord.com
Pedersoli Davide & Co. www.davide-pedersoli.com
Perazzi www.perazzi.com
Power Custom www.powercustom.com
Purdey & Sons www.purdey.com
Remington www.remington.com
Republic Arms Inc. www.republicarmsinc.com
Rigby www.johnrigbyandco.com
Rizzini Di Rizzini www.rizzini.it
Robar Companies, Inc. www.robarguns.com
Robinson Armament Co. www.robarm.com
Rock River Arms, Inc. www.rockriverarms.com
Rogue Rifle Co. Inc. www.chipmunkrifle.com
Rohrbaugh Firearms www.rohrbaughfirearms.com
Rossi Arms www.rossiusa.com
RPM www.rpmxlpistols.com
RWS www.dnrws.com
Sabatti SPA www.sabatti.com
Saco Defense www.sacoinc.com
Safari Arms www.olyarms.com
Sako www.berettausa.com
Samco Global Arms Inc. www.samcoglobal.com
Sarco Inc. www.sarcoinc.com
Savage Arms Inc. www.savagearms.com
Scattergun Technologies Inc. www.wilsoncombat.com
Searcy Enterprises www.searcyent.com
Shiloh Sharps www.shilohrifle.com
SIG Arms, Inc. www.sigarms.com
Simpson Ltd. www.simpsonltd.com
SKB Shotguns www.skbshotguns.com
Smith & Wesson www.smith-wesson.com
SOG International, Inc. soginc@go-concepts.com
Sphinx System www.sphinxarms.com
Springfield Armory www.springfield-armory.com
SSK Industries www.sskindustries.com
Steyr Mannlicher www.gsifirearms.com
Strayer-Voigt Inc. www.sviguns.com
Sturm, Ruger & Company www.ruger-firearms.com
Tar-Hunt Slug Guns, Inc. www.tar-hunt.com
Taser Int'l www.taser.com
Taurus www.taurususa.com
Tennessee Guns www.tennesseeguns.com
The 1877 Sharps Co. www.1877sharps.com
Thompson Center Arms www.tcarms.com
Tikka www.berettausa.com
TNW, Inc. tncorp@aol.com
Traditions www.traditionsfirearms.com
Uberti www.stoegerindustries.com
U.S. Firearms Mfg. Co. www.usfirearms.com
U.S. Repeating Arms Co. www.winchester-guns.com
Valkyrie Arms www.valkyriearms.com
Vektor Arms www.vektorarms.com
Volquartsen Custom Ltd. www.volquartsen.com
Walther USA www.waltheramerica.com
Weatherby www.weatherby.com
Webley and Scott Ltd. www.webley.co.uk
Westley Richards www.westleyrichards.com
Wildey www.wildeyguns.com
Wild West Guns www.wildwestguns.com
William Larkin Moore & Co. www.doublegun.com
Wilson's Gun Shop Inc. www.wilsoncombat.com
Winchester Firearms www.winchester-guns.com

Gun Parts, Barrels, After-Market Accessories

300 Below www.300below.com
Accuracy International of North America www.accuracyinternational.org
Accuracy Speaks, Inc. www.accuracyspeaks.com
Advanced Barrel Systems www.carbonbarrels.com
AK-USA www.ak-103.com
American Spirit Arms Corp. www.gunkits.com
AMT Gun Parts www.amt-gunparts.com
Badger Barrels, Inc. www.badgerbarrels.com
Bar-Sto Precision Machine www.barsto.com
Battenfeld Technologies www.battenfeldtechnologies.com
Belt Mountain Enterprises www.beltmountain.com
Brownells www.brownells.com
Buffer Technologies www.buffertech.com
Bullberry Barrel Works www.bullberry.com
Bushmaster Firearms/Quality Parts www.bushmaster.com
Butler Creek Corp www.butler-creek.com
Cape Outfitters Inc. www.capeoutfitters.com
Caspian Arms Ltd. www.caspianarmsltd.8m.com
Cheaper Than Dirt www.cheaperthandirt.com
Chesnut Ridge www.chestnutridge.com/
Chip McCormick Corp www.chipmccormickcorp.com
Choate Machine & Tool Co. www.riflestock.com
Colonial Arms www.colonialarms.com
Comp-N-Choke www.comp-n-choke.com
Cylinder & Slide Shop www.cylinder-slide.com
Digi-Twist www.fmtcorp.com
Dixie Gun Works www.dixiegun.com
Douglas Barrels www.benchrest.com/douglas/
DPMS www.dpmsinc.com
D.S. Arms, Inc. www.dsarms.com
Ed Brown Products www.edbrown.com
EFK Marketing/Fire Dragon Pistol Accessories www.flmfire.com
Federal Arms www.fedarms.com
Forrest Inc. www.gunmags.com
Fulton Armory www.fulton-armory.com
Galazan www.connecticutshotgun.com
Gemtech www.gem-tech.com
Gentry, David www.gentrycustom.com
GG&G www.gggaz.com
Green Mountain Rifle Barrels www.gmriflebarrel.com
Gun Parts Corp. www.e-gunparts.com
Harris Barrels wwharris@msn.com
Hart Rifle Barrels www.hartbarrels.com
Hastings Barrels www.hastingsbarrels.com
Heinie Specialty Products www.heinie.com
Holland Shooters Supply www.hollandgun.com
100 Straight Products www.100straight.com
I.M.A. www.ima-usa.com
Jarvis, Inc. www.jarvis-custom.com
J&T Distributing www.jtdistributing.com
Jonathan Arthur Ciener, Inc. www.22lrconversions.com
JP Enterprises www.jpar15.com
King's Gunworks www.kingsgunworks.com
Knoxx Industries www.knoxx.com
Krieger Barrels www.kriegerbarrels.com
Les Baer Custom, Inc. www.lesbaer.com
Lilja Barrels www.riflebarrels.com
Lone Star Rifle Co. www.lonestarrifles.com
Lone Wolf Dist. www.lonewolfdist.com
Lothar Walther Precision Tools Inc. www.lothar-walther.de
M&A Parts, Inc. www.m-aparts.com
MAB Barrels www.mab.com.au
Marvel Products, Inc. www.marvelprod.com
MEC-GAR SrL www.mec-gar.com
Michaels of Oregon Co. www.michaels-oregon.com
North Mfg. Co. www.rifle-barrels.com
Numrich Gun Parts Corp. www.e-gunparts.com
Pachmayr www.pachmayr.com
Pac-Nor Barrels www.pac-nor.com
Para Ordinance Pro Shop www.ltms.com

WEB DIRECTORY

Point Tech Inc. pointec@ibm.net
Promag Industries www.promagindustries.com
Power Custom, Inc. www.powercustom.com
Red Star Arms www.redstararms.com
Rocky Mountain Arms www.rockymountainarms.com
Royal Arms Int'l www.royalarms.com
R.W. Hart www.rwhart.com
Sarco Inc. www.sarcoinc.com
Scattergun Technologies Inc. www.wilsoncombat.com
Schuemann Barrels www.schuemann.com
Seminole Gunworks Chamber Mates www.chambermates.com
Shilen www.shilen.com
Sims Vibration Laboratory www.limbsaver.com
Smith & Alexander Inc. www.smithandalexander.com
Speed Shooters Int'l www.shooternet.com/ssi
Sprinco USA Inc. sprinco@primenet.com
S&S Firearms www.ssfirearms.com
SSK Industries www.sskindustries.com
Sunny Hill Enterprises www.sunny-hill.com
Tapco www.tapco.com
Trapdoors Galore www.trapdoors.com
Triple K Manufacturing Co. Inc. www.triplek.com
U.S.A. Magazines Inc. www.usa-magazines.com
Verney-Carron SA www.verney-carron.com
Volquartsen Custom Ltd. www.volquartsen.com
W.C. Wolff Co. www.gunsprings.com
Waller & Son www.wallerandson.com
Weigand Combat Handguns www.weigandcombat.com
Western Gun Parts www.westerngunparts.com
Wilson Arms www.wilsonarms.com
Wilson Combat www.wilsoncombat.com
Wisner's Inc. www.gunpartsspecialist.com
Z-M Weapons www.zmweapons.com/home.htm

Gunsmithing Supplies and Instruction

American Gunsmithing Institute www.americangunsmith.com
Battenfeld Technologies www.battenfeldtechnologies.com
Brownells, Inc. www.brownells.com
B-Square Co. www.b-square.com
Clymer Mfg. Co. www.clymertool.com
Craftguard Metal Finishing crftgrd@aol.com
Dem-Bart www.dembartco.com
Doug Turnbull Restoration www.turnbullrestoration,com
Du-Lite Corp. www.dulite.com
Dvorak Instruments www.dvorakinstruments.com
Gradient Lens Corp. www.gradientlens.com
Gunline Tools www.gunline.com
JGS Precision Tool Mfg. LLC www.jgstools.com
Mag-Na-Port International www.magnaport.com
Manson Precision Reamers www.mansonreamers.com
Midway www.midwayusa.com
Olympus America Inc. www.olympus.com
Trinidad State Junior College www.trinidadstate.edu

Handgun Grips

Ajax Custom Grips, Inc. www.ajaxgrips.com
Altamont Co. www.altamontco.com
Badger Grips www.pistolgrips.com
Barami Corp. www.hipgrip.com
Blu Magnum Grips www.blumagnum.com
Buffalo Brothers www.buffalobrothers.com
Crimson Trace Corp. www.crimsontrace.com
Eagle Grips www.eaglegrips.com
Falcon Industries www.ergogrips.net
Hogue Grips www.getgrip.com
Kirk Ratajesak www.kgratajesak.com
Lett Custom Grips www.lettgrips.com
N.C. Ordnance www.gungrip.com
Nill-Grips USA www.nill-grips.com
Pachmayr www.pachmayr.com
Pearce Grips www.pearcegrip.com
Trausch Grips Int.Co. www.trausch.com
Uncle Mike's: www.uncle-mikes.com

Holsters and Leather Products

Akah www.akah.de
Aker Leather Products www.akerleather.com
Alessi Distributor R&F Inc. www.alessiholsters.com
Alfonso's of Hollywood www.alfonsogunleather.com
Armor Holdings www.holsters.com
Bagmaster www.bagmaster.com
Bianchi International www.bianchi-int.com
Blackhills Leather www.blackhillsleather.com
BodyHugger Holsters www.nikolais.com
Boyt Harness Co. www.boytharness.com
Brigade Gun Leather www.brigadegunleather.com
Chimere www.chimere.com
Classic Old West Styles www.cows.com
Conceal It www.conceal-it.com
Concealment Shop Inc. www.theconcealmentshop.com
Coronado Leather Co. www.coronadoleather.com
Creedmoor Sports, Inc. www.creedmoorsports.com
Custom Leather Wear www.customleatherwear.com
Defense Security Products www.thunderwear.com
Dennis Yoder www.yodercustomleather.com
DeSantis Holster www.desantisholster.com
Dillon Precision www.dillonprecision.com
Don Hume Leathergoods, Inc. www.donhume.com
Ernie Hill International www.erniehill.com
Fist www.fist-inc.com
Fobus USA www.fobusholster.com
Front Line Ltd. frontlin@internet-zahav.net
Galco www.usgalco.com
Gilmore's Sports Concepts www.gilmoresports.com
Gould & Goodrich www.goulduse.com
Gunmate Products www.gun-mate.com
Hellweg Ltd. www.hellwegltd.com
Hide-A-Gun www.hide-a-gun.com
Holsters.Com www.holsters.com
Horseshoe Leather Products www.horseshoe.co.uk
Hunter Co. www.huntercompany.com
Kirkpatrick Leather Company www.kirkpatrickleather.com
KNJ www.knjmfg.com
Kramer Leather www.kramerleather.com
Law Concealment Systems www.handgunconcealment.com
Levy's Leathers Ltd. www.levysleathers.com
Michaels of Oregon Co. www.michaels-oregon.com
Milt Sparks Leather www.miltsparks.com
Mitch Rosen Extraordinary Gunleather www.mitchrosen.com
Old World Leather www.gun-mate.com
Pacific Canvas & Leather Co. paccanadleather@directway.com
Pager Pal www.pagerpal.com
Phalanx Corp. www.phalanxarms.com
PWL www.pwlusa.com
Rumanya Inc. www.rumanya.com
S.A. Gunleather www.elpasoleather.com
Safariland Ltd. Inc. www.safariland.com
Shooting Systems Group Inc. www.shootingsystems.com
Strictly Anything Inc. www.strictlyanything.com
Strong Holster Co. www.strong-holster.com
The Belt Co. www.conceal-it.com
The Leather Factory Inc. lflandry@flash.net
The Outdoor Connection www.outdoorconnection.com
Top-Line USA inc. www.toplineusa.com
Triple K Manufacturing Co. www.triplek.com
Wilson Combat www.wilsoncombat.com

Miscellaneous Shooting Products

10X Products Group www.10Xwear.com
Aero Peltor www.aearo.com
Beartooth www.beartoothproducts.com
Dalloz Safety www.cdalloz.com

WEB DIRECTORY

Deben Group Industries Inc. www.deben.com
Decot Hy-Wyd Sport Glasses www.sportyglasses.com
E.A.R., Inc. www.earinc.com
First Choice Armor www.firstchoicearmor.com
Gunstands www.gunstands.com
Howard Leight Hearing Protectors www.howardleight.com
Hunters Specialties www.hunterspec.com
Johnny Stewart Wildlife Calls www.hunterspec.com
North Safety Products www.northsafety-brea.com
Pro-Ears www.pro-ears.com
Second Chance Body Armor Inc. www.secondchance.com
Silencio www.silencio.com
Smart Lock Technologies www.smartlock.com
Surefire www.surefire.com
Walker's Game Ear Inc. www.walkersgameear.com

Muzzleloading Firearms and Products

American Pioneer Powder www.americanpioneerpowder.com
Austin & Halleck, Inc. www.austinhalleck.com
CVA www.cva.com
Davis, Vernon C. & Co. www.mygunroom/vcdavis&co/
Dixie Gun Works, Inc. www.dixiegun.com
Elephant/Swiss Black Powder www.elephantblackpowder.com
Goex Black Powder www.goexpowder.com
Jedediah Starr Trading Co. www.jedediah-starr.com
Jim Chambers Flintlocks www.flintlocks.com
Kahnke Gunworks www.powderandbow.com/kahnke/
Knight Rifles www.knightrifles.com
Log Cabin Shop www.logcabinshop.com
Lyman www.lymanproducts.com
Millennium Designed Muzzleloaders www.mdm-muzzleloaders.com
Mountain State Muzzleloading www.mtnstatemuzzleloading.com
MSM, Inc. www.msmfg.com
Muzzleload Magnum Products www.mmpsabots.com
Muzzleloading Technologies, Inc. www.mtimuzzleloading.com
Navy Arms www.navyarms.com
October Country Muzzleloading www.oct-country.com
Ox-Yoke Originals Inc. www.oxyoke.com
Palmetto Arms www.palmetto.it
Rightnour Mfg. Co. Inc. www.rmcsports.com
The Rifle Shop trshoppe@aol.com
Thompson Center Arms www.tcarms.com
Traditions Performance Muzzleloading www.traditionsfirearms.com

Publications, Videos, and CDs

A&J Arms Booksellers www.ajarmsbooksellers.com
Airgun Letter www.airgunletter.com
American Firearms Industry www.amfire.com
American Handgunner www.americanhandgunner.com
American Hunter www.nrapublications.org
American Rifleman www.nrapublications.org
American Shooting Magazine www.americanshooting.com
Blacksmith sales@blacksmithcorp.com
Blackpowder Hunting www.blackpowderhunting.org
Black Powder Cartridge News www.blackpowderspg.com
Black Powder Journal www.blackpowderjournal.com
Blue Book Publications www.bluebookinc.com
Combat Handguns www.combathandguns.com
Countrywide Press www.countrysport.com
DBI Books/Krause Publications www.krause.com
Delta Force www.infogo.com/delta
Gun List www.gunlist.com
Gun Video www.gunvideo.com
GUNS Magazine www.gunsmagazine.com
Guns & Ammo www.gunsandammomag.com
Gunweb Magazine WWW Links www.imags.com
Gun Week www.gunweek.com
Gun World www.gunworld.com
Harris Publications www.harrispublications.com
Heritage Gun Books www.gunbooks.com
Krause Publications www.krause.com
Moose Lake Publishing MooselakeP@aol.com
Munden Enterprises Inc. www.bob-munden.com
Outdoor Videos www.outdoorvideos.com
Precision Shooting www.precisionshooting.com
Ray Riling Arms Books www.rayrilingarmsbooks.com
Rifle and Handloader Magazines www.riflemagazine.com
Safari Press Inc. www.safaripress.com
Shoot! Magazine www.shootmagazine.com
Shooters News www.shootersnews.com
Shooting Illustrated www.nrapublications.org
Shooting Industry www.shootingindustry.com
Shooting Sports Retailer ssretailer@ad.com
Shooting Sports USA www.nrapublications.org
Shotgun News www.shotgunnews.com
Shotgun Report www.shotgunreport.com
Shotgun Sports Magazine www.shotgun-sports.com
Small Arms Review www.smallarmsreview.com
Sporting Clays Web Edition www.sportingclays.com
Sports Afield www.sportsafield.comm
Sports Trend www.sportstrend.com
Sportsmen on Film www.sportsmenonfilm.com
The Gun Journal www.shooters.com
The Shootin Iron www.off-road.com/4x4web/si/si.html
The Single Shot Exchange Magazine singleshot@earthlink.net
The Sixgunner www.sskindustries.com
Voyageur Press www.voyageurpress.com
VSP Publications www.gunbooks.com
Vulcan Outdoors Inc. www.vulcanpub.com

Reloading Tools and Supplies

Ballisti-Cast Mfg. www.ballisti-cast.com
Bruno Shooters Supply www.brunoshooters.com
CH Tool & Die www.cdhd.com
Colorado Shooters Supply www.hochmoulds.com
Corbin Mfg & Supply Co. www.corbins.com
Dillon Precision www.dillonprecision.com
Forster Precision Products www.forsterproducts.com
Hanned Line www.hanned.com
Harrell's Precision www.harrellsprec.com
Holland's Shooting Supplies www.hollandgun.com
Hornady www.hornady.com
Huntington Reloading Products www.huntingtons.com
J & J Products Co. www.jandjproducts.com
Lead Bullet Technology LBTisaccuracy@Imbris.net
Lee Precision, Inc. www.leeprecision.com
Littleton Shotmaker www.leadshotmaker.com
Load Data www.loaddata.com
Lyman www.lymanproducts.com
Magma Engineering www.magmaengr.com
Mayville Engineering Co. (MEC) www.mecreloaders.com
Midway www.midwayusa.com
Moly-Bore www.molybore.com
MTM Case-Guard www.mtmcase-guard.com
NECO www.neconos.com
NEI www.neihandtools.com
Neil Jones Custom Products www.neiljones.com
Ponsness/Warren www.reloaders.com
Ranger Products www.pages.prodigy.com/rangerproducts.home.htm
Rapine Bullet Mold Mfg Co. www.customloads.com/rapine.html
RCBS www.rcbs.com
Redding Reloading Equipment www.redding-reloading.com
Russ Haydon's Shooting Supplies www.shooters-supply.com
Sinclair Int'l Inc. www.sinclairintl.com
Stoney Point Products Inc www.stoneypoint.com
Thompson Bullet Lube Co. www.thompsonbulletlube.com
Vickerman Seating Die www.castingstuff.com
Wilson (L.E. Wilson) www.lewilson.com

Rests–Bench, Portable, Attachable

Bench Master www.bench-master.com
B-Square www.b-square.com

WEB DIRECTORY

Bullshooter www.bullshooterssightingin.com
Desert Mountain Mfg. www.bench-master.com
Harris Engineering Inc. www.cyberteklabs.com/harris/main/htm
Kramer Designs www.snipepod.com
L Thomas Rifle Support www.ltsupport.com
Level-Lok www.levellok.com
Midway www.midwayusa.com
Ransom International www.ransom-intl.com
R.W. Hart www.rwhart.com
Sinclair Intl, Inc. www.sinclairintl.com
Stoney Point Products www.stoneypoint.com
Target Shooting www.targetshooting.com
Varmint Masters www.varmintmasters.com
Versa-Pod www.versa-pod.com

Scopes, Sights, Mounts and Accessories

Accusight www.accusight.com
ADCO www.shooters.com/adco/index/htm
Adirondack Optics www.adkoptics.com
Aimpoint www.aimpoint.com
Aim Shot, Inc. www.miniosprey.com
Aimtech Mount Systems www.aimtech-mounts.com
Alpec Team, Inc. www.alpec.com
Alpen Outdoor Corp. www.alpenoutdoor.com
American Technologies Network, Corp. www.atncorp.com
AmeriGlo, LLC www.ameriglo.net
AO Sight Systems Inc. www.aosights.com
Ashley Outdoors, Inc. www.ashleyoutdoors.com
ATN www.atncorp.com
BSA Optics www.bsaoptics.com
B-Square Company, Inc. www.b-square.com
Burris www.burrisoptics.com
Bushnell Performance Optics www.bushnell.com
Carl Zeiss Optical Inc. www.zeiss.com
Carson Optical www.carson-optical.com
C-More Systems www.cmore.com
Conetrol Scope Mounts www.conetrol.com
Crimson Trace Corp. www.crimsontrace.com
Crossfire L.L.C. www.amfire.com/hesco/html
DCG Supply Inc. www.dcgsupply.com
D&L Sports www.dlsports.com
EasyHit, Inc. www.easyhit.com
EAW www.eaw.de
Electro-Optics Technologies www.eotechmdc.com/holosight
Europtik Ltd. www.europtik.com
Fujinon, Inc. www.fujinon.com
Gilmore Sports www.gilmoresports.com
Hakko Co. Ltd. www.hakko-japan.co.jp
Hesco www.hescosights.com
Hitek Industries www.nightsight.com
HIVIZ www.hivizsights.com
Horus Vision www.horusvision.com
Hunter Co. www.huntercompany.com
Innovative Weaponry,Inc. www.ptnightsights.com
Ironsighter Co. www.ironsighter.com
ITT Night Vision www.ittnightvision.com
Kahles www.kahlesoptik.com
Kowa Optimed Inc. www.kowascope.com
Laser Bore Sight www.laserboresight.com
Laser Devices Inc. www.laserdevices.com
Lasergrips www.crimsontrace.com
LaserLyte www.laserlyte.com
LaserMax Inc. www.lasermax-inc.com
Laser Products www.surefire.com
Leapers, Inc. www.leapers.com
Leatherwood www.leatherwoodoptics.com
Leica Camera Inc. www.leica-camera.com/usa
Leupold www.leupold.com
LightForce/NightForce USA www.nightforcescopes.com
Lyman www.lymanproducts.com
Lynx www.b-square.com
Marble's Outdoors www.marbleoutdoors.com
MDS, Inc. www.mdsincorporated.com
Meprolight www.kimberamerica.com
Micro Sight Co. www.microsight.com
Millett www.millettsights.com
Miniature Machine Corp. www.mmcsight.com
Montana Vintage Arms www.montanavintagearms.com
Mounting Solutions Plus www.mountsplus.com
NAIT www.nait.com
Newcon International Ltd. newconsales@newcon-optik.com
Night Owl Optics www.nightowloptics.com
Nikon Inc. www.nikonusa.com
North American Integrated Technologies www.nait.com
O.K. Weber, Inc. www.okweber.com
Pentax Corp. www.pentaxlightseeker.com
Premier Reticle www.premierreticles.com
Redfield www.redfieldoptics.com
R&R Int'l Trade www.nightoptic.com
Schmidt & Bender www.schmidt-bender.com
Scopecoat www.scopecoat.com
Scopelevel www.scopelevel.com
Segway Industries www.segway-industries.com
Shepherd Scope Ltd. www.shepherdscopes.com
Sightron www.sightron.com
Simmons www.simmonsoptics.com
S&K www.scopemounts.com
Springfield Armory www.springfield-armory.com
Sure-Fire www.surefire.com
Swarovski/Kahles www.swarovskioptik.com
Swift Instruments Inc. www.swift-optics.com
Talley Mfg. Co. www.talleyrings.com
Tasco www.tascosales.com
Trijicon Inc. www.trijicon-inc.com
Truglo Inc. www.truglo.com
US Night Vision www.usnightvision.com
U.S. Optics Technologies Inc. www.usoptics.com
Valdada-IOR Optics www.valdada.com
Warne www.warnescopemounts.com
Weaver Scopes www.weaveroptics.com
Wilcox Industries Corp www.wilcoxind.com
Williams Gun Sight Co. www.williamsgunsight.com
Zeiss www.zeiss.com

Shooting Organizations, Schools and Ranges

Amateur Trapshooting Assoc. www.shootata.com
American Custom Gunmakers Guild www.acgg.org
American Gunsmithing Institute www.americangunsmith.com
American Pistolsmiths Guild www.americanpistol.com
American Shooting Sports Council www.assc.com
Assoc. of Firearm & Tool Mark Examiners www.afte.org
BATF www.atf.ustreas.gov
Blackwater Lodge and Training Center www.blackwaterlodge.com
Boone and Crockett Club www.boone-crockett.org
Buckmasters, Ltd. www.buckmasters.com
Citizens Committee for the Right to Keep & Bear Arms www.ccrkba.org
Civilian Marksmanship Program www.odcmp.com
Colorado School of Trades www.gunsmith-school.com
Ducks Unlimited www.ducks.org
Fifty Caliber Shooters Assoc. www.fcsa.org
Firearms Coalition www.nealknox.com
Front Sight Firearms Training Institute www.frontsight.com
German Gun Collectors Assoc. www.germanguns.com
Gun Clubs www.associatedgunclubs.org
Gun Owners' Action League www.goal.org
Gun Owners of America www.gunowners.org
Gun Trade Assoc. Ltd. www.brucepub.com/gta
Gunsite Training Center, Inc. www.gunsite.com
Handgun Hunters International www.sskindustries.com
Hunting and Shooting Sports Heritage Fund www.hsshf.org
International Defense Pistol Assoc. www.idpa.com
International Handgun Metallic Silhouette Assoc. www.ihmsa.org

WEB DIRECTORY

International Hunter Education Assoc. www.ihea.com
Jews for the Preservation of Firearms Ownership www.jpfo.org
Murray State College(gunsmithing)darnold@msc.cc.ok.us
National 4-H Shooting Sports www.4-hshootingsports.org
National Benchrest Shooters Assoc. www.benchrest.com
National Muzzle Loading Rifle Assoc. www.nmlra.org
National Reloading Manufacturers Assoc www.reload-nrma.com
National Rifle Assoc. www.nra.org
National Rifle Assoc. ILA www.nraila.org
National Shooting Sports Foundation www.nssf.org
National Skeet Shooters Association www.nssa-nsca.com
National Sporting Clays Assoc. www.nssa-nsca.com
National Wild Turkey Federation www.nwtf.com
North American Hunting Club www.huntingclub.com
Pennsylvania Gunsmith School www.pagunsmith.com
Quail Unlimited www.qu.org
Right To Keep and Bear Arms www.rkba.org
Rocky Mountain Elk Foundation www.rmef.org
SAAMI www.saami.org
Second Amendment Foundation www.saf.org
Second Amendment Sisters www.2asisters.org
Shooting Ranges Int'l www.shootingranges.com
Single Action Shooting Society www.sassnet.com
S&W Academy and Nat'l Firearms Trng. Center www.sw-academy.com
Tactical Defense Institute www.tdiohio.com
Ted Nugent United Sportsmen of America www.tnugent.com
Thunder Ranch www.thunderranchinc.com
Trapshooters Homepage www.trapshooters.com
Trinidad State Junior College www.trinidadstate.edu
U.S. Int'l Clay Target Assoc. www.usicta.com
United States Fish and Wildlife Service www.fws.gov
U.S. Practical Shooting Assoc. www.uspsa.org
USA Shooting www.usashooting.com
Varmint Hunters Assoc. www.varminthunter.org
U.S. Sportsmen's Alliance www.ussportsmen.org
Women Hunters www.womanhunters.com
Women's Shooting Sports Foundation www.wssf.org

Stocks

Advanced Technology www.atigunstocks.com
Bell & Carlson, Inc. www.bellandcarlson.com
Boyd's Gunstock Industries, Inc. www.boydboys.com
Butler Creek Corp www.butler-creek.com
Calico Hardwoods, Inc. www.calicohardwoods.com
Choate Machine www.riflestock.com
Elk Ridge Stocks www.reamerrentals.com/elk_ridge.htm
Fajen www.battenfeldtechnologies.com
Great American Gunstocks www.gunstocks.com
Herrett's Stocks www.herrettstocks.com
High Tech Specialties www.bansnersrifle.com/hightech
Holland's Shooting Supplies www.hollandgun.com
Lone Wolf www.lonewolfriflestocks.com
McMillan Fiberglass Stocks www.mcmfamily.com
MPI Stocks www.mpistocks.com
Precision Gun Works www.precisiongunstocks.com
Ram-Line www.outers-guncare.com
Rimrock Rifle Stock www.rimrockstocks.com
Royal Arms Gunstocks www.imt.net/~royalarms
Speedfeed, Inc. www.speedfeedinc.com
Tiger-Hunt Curly Maple Gunstocks www.gunstockwood.com
Wenig Custom Gunstocks Inc. www.wenig.com

Targets and Range Equipment

Action Target Co. www.actiontarget.com
Advanced Interactive Systems www.ais-sim.com
Birchwood Casey www.birchwoodcasey.com
Caswell Detroit Armor Companies www.caswellintl.com
Laser Shot www.lasershot.com
MTM Products www.mtmcase-gard.com
National Target Co. www.nationaltarget.com
Newbold Target Systems www.newboldtargets.com
Porta Target, Inc. www.portatarget.com
Range Management Services Inc. www.casewellintl.com
Range Systems www.shootingrangeproducts.com
Reactive Target Systems Inc. chrts@primenet.com
ShatterBlast Targets www.daisy.com
Super Trap Bullet Containment Systems www.supertrap.com
Thompson Target Technology www.thompsontarget.com
Visible Impact Targets www.crosman.com
White Flyer www.whiteflyer.com

Trap and Skeet Shooting Equipment, and Accessories

Auto-Sporter Industries www.auto-sporter.com
10X Products Group www.10Xwear.com
Claymaster Traps www.claymaster.com
Do-All Traps, Inc. www.do-alltraps.com
Laporte USA www.laporte-shooting.com
Outers www.blount.com
Trius Products Inc. www.triustraps.com
White Flyer www.whiteflyer.com

Triggers

Brownells www.brownells.com
Shilen www.shilen.com
Timney Triggers www.timneytrigger.com

Major Shooting Web Sites and Links

24 Hour Campfire www.24hourcampfire.com
Alphabetic Index of Links www.gunsgunsguns.com
Auction Arms www.auctionarms.com
Benchrest Central www.benchrest.com
Bullseye Pistol www.bullseyepistol.com
Dave Kopel Articles www.davekoppel.org/DavePage.htm
Firearms History www.researchpress.co.uk/firearms
Firearm News www.firearmnews.com
For The Hunt www.forthehunt.com
Gun Broker Auctions www.gunbroker.com
Gun Index www.gunindex.com
Gun Industry www.gunindustry.com
Gun Blast www.gunblast.com
Gun Boards www.gunboards.com
Gun Law www.gunlaw.com
GunLinks www.gunlinks.com
Gun Manuals www.gunmanuals.ch/manuals.htm
Gun Nuts www.gunuts.com
Guns For Sale www.gunsamerica.com
Gun Show Auction www.gunshowauction.com
GunXchange www.gunxchange.com
Hunting Digest www.huntingdigest.com
Hunting Information (NSSF) www.huntinfo.org
Hunting Net www.hunting.net
Hunting Network www.huntingnetwork.com
John Lott Articles www.tsra.com/LottPage.htm
Keep and Bear Arms www.keepandbeararms.com
Leverguns www.leverguns.com
Outdoor Yellow Pages www.outdoorsyp.com
Real Guns www.realguns.com/links/glinks.htm
Rec.Guns www.recguns.com
Shooters' Gun Calendar www.guncalendar.com/index.cfm
Shooter's Online Services www.shooters.com
Shooters Search www.shooterssearch.com
Shotgun Sports Resource Guide www.shotgunsports.com
Sixgunner www.sixgunner.com
Sportsman's Web www.sportsmansweb.com
Surplus Rifles www.surplusrifle.com
Surplus Pistols www.surpluspistol.com
Where To Shoot www.wheretoshoot.com

by JOHN HAVILAND

SHOTGUN REVIEW

IN 2004 SHOTGUN companies have added refinements and camouflage patterns to their existing lines of guns, with Browning leading the way with its new Cynergy over/under that incorporates a new locking and trigger system—all wrapped up in futuristic styling. Meanwhile, the 16-gauge is continuing its comeback with four new guns this year.

Beretta

The Silver Pigeon III has more extensive floral and scroll decorations and hunting scenes on its frame than the Silver Pigeon S and II. The Pigeon III features ducks and pheasants in flight on the 12-gauge and quail and woodcock on the 20- and 28-gauge guns. A TRUGLO fiber-optic front sight is standard. For about $800 more, the Silver Pigeon V showcases the embellishments of a color case-hardened frame and gold inlays of ducks in flight and flushing pheasants on the 12-gauge gun, or quail and grouse on the 20 and 28. High-grade wood finishes the guns.

The AL391 Urika and A391 Xtrema 3.5 go discrete with MAX-4 HD camo on their synthetic stocks. The A391 Xtrema 3.5 autoloader Turkey Package comes in several camo patterns, with a Weaver base for optical sights, TRUGLO fiber-optic sights, sling and a ported extended turkey choke tube.

DT10 Trident line has added the L Sporting 12-gauge. The gun features floral engraving and fancy walnut. Like all Trident guns, it can be ordered with a palm swell on the left side of the grip for left-hand shooters.

The White Onyx Sporting 12-gauge joins the 686 line of sporting over/unders, distinguishing itself with a nickel-alloy finish on the receiver with a jeweled surface. An oiled finish and schnabel forearm finish the gun.

Benelli

The light weight and recoil-operating system of Benelli's Super Black Eagle and M1 shotguns have always kicked more than gas-operated guns. Benelli has addressed that concern with its new ComforTech system that it claims reduces recoil by 30 percent. The ComforTech system reduces recoil three ways: with a gel recoil butt pad, gel pad on the comb and 11 gel inserts placed diagonally in the buttstock that absorb recoil and also allow the buttstock to flex.

Shooting the Benelli M2 12-gauge in the Arkansas swamps.

▲The new Benelli M4 shotgun is available with MAX4 camouflage covering the entire gun.

The new Benelli Super Black Eagle II features the ComforTech recoil reduction system; the synthetic stock comes plain or covered in HD Timber camouflage.

The ComforTech system is available on the new Benelli M4 Field with synthetic stock. Other features include a wide loop trigger guard, dimpled surface on the grip; a set of shims between the receiver and buttstock adjusts comb height.

The new Benelli M2 shotgun is available with Timber camouflage covering the entire gun.

Benelli M2 took these Arkansas mallards.

To determine how well the ComfoTech system worked, I first shot the old M1 and then the new M2 with the ComforTech system at clay targets with Federal's Gold Medal Target shells firing 1-1/8 ounces of shot. The M1's recoil built to a sharp snap against my cheek and shoulder, then trailed off. The ComforTech system incorporated in the M2 removed that jolt, and recoil was more of a long push. Switching my concentration to the clay targets, I noticed the M2's muzzle jump was also somewhat less than that of the old M1.

The ComforTech system is available on the Benelli new Super Black Eagle II, M2 and the SuperSport. These three new guns have additional features:

* A wider loop trigger guard allows easier access for a gloved finger.
* AirTouch is a dimpled surface molded on the grip that provides a sure hold even in the wettest day in the duck marsh.
* A set of shims between the receiver and buttstock adjusts comb height. Adjusting the steel recoil rod in the buttstock tailors buttstock cast.
* A new design adds more flats and flowing lines to the receiver. The new forearm has a pear-shape to its belly to fill the palm of your hand and a full-length scallop along the top for fingers to grip, allowing a sure grip anywhere along the forend.
* A stainless steel recoil tube in the buttstock is corrosion-resistant and is easily removed for cleaning by detaching the gel recoil pad and removing the lock nut.

Bill Hanus Birdguns

Hanus is selling a limited run of Browning Citori Lightning Feather over/unders in 16-gauge. The gun features a round knob, half-pistol grip and aluminum receiver with a steel breech face. The guns weigh about six pounds. Barrels are 26 or 28 inches, and back-bored with chromed chambers. Browning furnishes Improved Cylinder, Modified and Full screw-in choke tubes. Hanus adds two Skeet chokes and a bottle of Colonial Arms Choke Tube Lube.

The 28-gauge Bill Hanus Birdgun model over/under is built on B. Rizzini's new small frame and weighs only five pounds, 12 ounces. It's stocked in two configurations: 28-inch barrels choked Skeet 1/Skeet 2, or with 26-inch barrels and screw-in chokes. Cylinder, Skeet, Improved Cylinder, Modified and Full choke tubes are included. A custom .410 is also available. These guns feature a schnabel forend and a half- or semi-pistol grip, with an initial plate in the butt stock. All the guns come with snap caps, a bottle of Clenzoil and cloth protective sheaths in a lockable case.

Boss & Company

Boss & Company's roots in shotgun-making date back to 1773 when William Boss began his gun-making apprenticeship in Birmingham, England. In 1891 John Robertson took over the business and added to the reputation of Boss by inventing the famous Boss single trigger in 1894, the Boss ejector in 1898 and an over-and-under gun in 1909. Boss still makes guns today and one of their side-by-sides will set you back at least $55,000 and an over/under $75,000.

Gary Clark manned the Boss booth at the 2004 SHOT Show in Las Vegas to show a few of Boss's best guns. But mainly, Clark was there to determine what features Americans want and like in a shotgun in hopes of entering the American market. "We have started

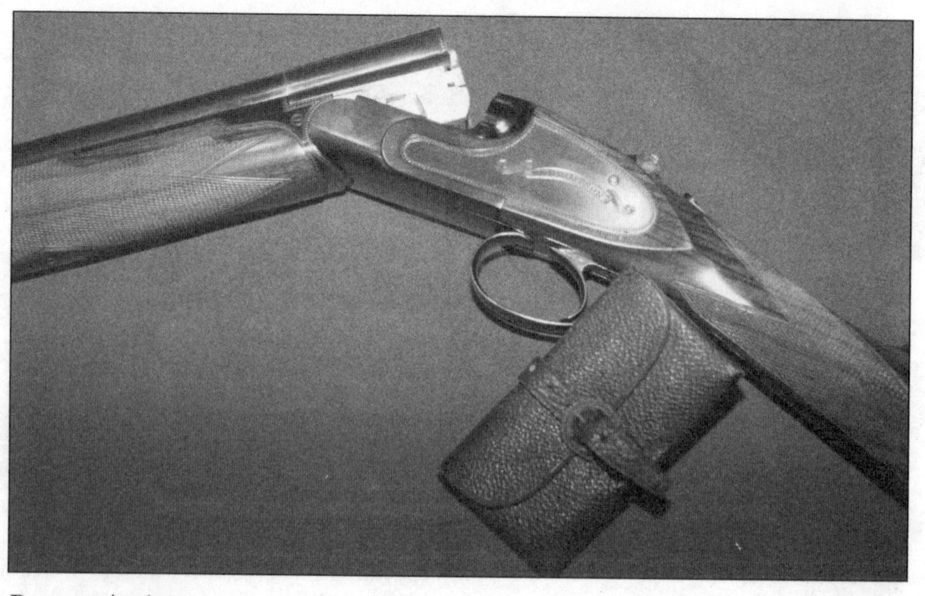

Boss over/under.

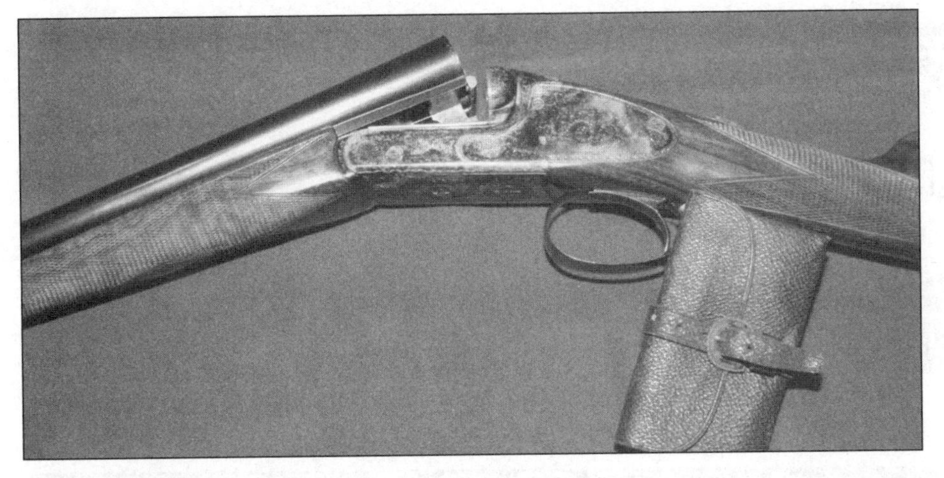

Boss side-by-side.

Browning over/under Cynergy.

making designs of these guns so they can be produced on CNC machines and that has enabled us to reduce the price to around $10,000," Clark said.

Send Clark your ideas of what Americans want in a shotgun to: mail@Bossguns.com.

Browning

I knew Browning's Cynergy shotgun was something special when the Perazzi people showed up to study the shotgun at the Browning booth during the SHOT Show last February. Browning states the Cynergy has the lowest profile of any over/under shotgun. That was partially accomplished by a trigger system similar to a rifle. The firing pin springs lay forward of the trigger and a "Reverse Striker," as Browning calls it, reverses the springs' energy to power the firing pins. Doing away with hammers to hit the firing pins meant the Cynergy's profile could be lowered. The gun's MonoLock Hinge also makes the receiver more compact. The Cynergy's barrels pivot on a pair of C-shaped humps in the receiver that lock into matching cuts in the monoblock. "The MonoLock Hinge pivots on significantly more surface area... resulting in less wear over time," according to Browning.

The Cynergy's butt pad is odd-looking, to say the least. But the Inflex Recoil Pad soaks up recoil like a shock absorber. Browning states the pad and the ported barrels reduce felt recoil by 25 percent. Three pad lengths are available in 1/2-inch increments to adjust length of pull. A 1/4-inch spacer further regulates length of pull.

The Cynergy's styling is based on straight lines. The front of the trigger guard, back and front of the forearm, receiver outline, checkering pattern and lines cut here and there in the stocks are all straight lines. Its appearance grows on you, after awhile.

The Cynergy is available with wood or synthetic stock, in Field and Sporting models. The synthetic stock also has an adjustable comb.

The Cynergy will not replace Browning's Citori. The Citori Lightning, White Lightning and Gran Lightning have new engraving patterns on their receivers. The Citori XS Special target gun features a light contour and ported barrels with ventilated side rib. An adjustable comb and Triple Trigger System, which slightly adjusts length of pull, fits the gun to you.

The BT-99 Micro joins the two other BT-99 single-barrel target guns. The Micro has a 13 3/4-inch length of pull and six ounces shaved off the weight of the regular BT-99 to better fit smaller shooters. Barrels are 30 or 32 inches.

The Gold Evolve autoloader differs from the standard Gold with a slightly altered receiver, magazine cap and full checkering pattern and sculpting to the forearm that provide a sure grip. The Evolve also has a HiViz TriComp sight mounted on a 26-, 28- or 30-inch barrel.

Franchi

The new Model 712 (12-gauge) and 720 (20-gauge) autoloaders have a more rounded receiver top than the established 612 and 620s. The 712 and 720 wood stock models also wear the Franchi WeatherCoat, which provides a water-resistant finish with matching blued metal. A synthetic stock in black or several camo patterns is also available with a matte metal finish. The 712 has a 24-, 26- or 28-inch barrel and three screw-in choke tubes. The 712 weighs a light seven pounds. The 720 has all the same features as the

The Escort Turkey pump gun wears a 24-inch barrel with FH TriViz sights and a polymer stock covered with Mossy Oak Break-up camo.

The Escort pump Hunter wears a 28-inch barrel threaded for choke tubes, and a black polymer stock.

The Escort pump Camo comes with a 28-inch barrel threaded for choke tubes and wears a metal and polymer stock covered with Mossy Oak camo.

The Aimguard pump is designed for personal defense, and is fitted with a 20-inch Cylinder-bore barrel, 5-shot magazine, and a dovetail rib on the receiver for mounting accessory sights.

The 12-gauge Field Hunter weighs seven pounds, and is fitted with a 28-inch barrel threaded for choke tubes, and a synthetic stock.

712, but weighs six pounds. The 720 Short Stock has length of pull shortened 1-1/2 inches.

The Alcione over/under Field Classic has a blued receiver. The SX Classic has a blued frame with gold inlays of pheasants and quail.

Legacy Sports

The Escort line of Field Hunter pump and semi-auto guns will be covered in Mossy Oak Shadow Grass and Obsession camo. In a few months, all models in the Escort line will add a lightweight 20-gauge. The Escort semi-auto AimGuard 12 gauge has a 20-inch Cylinder-bore barrel with a five-shot magazine and studs for a sling. A dovetail milled in the top of the receiver accepts various sights.

Ithaca

Ithaca is celebrating its 125th anniversary with a 125-gun edition of the Model 37 pump shotgun. The guns feature a walnut stock and forearm with 22 lines per inch checkering, engraving on the blued receiver that depicts Ithaca's history and products and a 26-inch ventilated rib barrel with a set of interchangeable choke tubes. To further customize the gun, length of pull can be chosen, a medallion inlaid in the stock and your name or initials engraved upon the receiver.

For slug shooters, Ithaca has a rifled 24-inch barrel with a 1:34 twist that fits Remington, Browning and Benelli shotguns. The barrels have either a steel cantilever scope mount or TRUGLO fiber-optic sights. Ithaca states two-inch groups at 100 yards should not be uncommon.

Last year's introduction of the Storm series of 12-gauge guns was so well received that a 20-gauge "lite" version is now available. The Deerslayer has a 24-inch rifled barrel with open sights. All metal parts have a Parkerized finish to go along with a black synthetic stock and forearm. A Sims Limb Saver recoil pad takes the sting out of recoil. The Turkeyslayer wears a 24-inch ported barrel with TRUGLO fiber-optic sights and a screw-in Full choke tube designed for Remington's Hevi-Shot loads. The camo pattern is HD Hardwoods Green. The Upland wears a 26-inch ventilated rib barrel with a Raybar front sight. The Parkerized metal and synthetic stock and forearm will withstand any foul weather. The gun can also be cloaked in Realtree Advantage MAX-4 HD camo.

Mossberg

The 935 Magnum is Mossberg's new gas-operated autoloader, which handles the 12-gauge 3 1/2-inch shell. The 935's synthetic stocks come in basic black or dressed in various camo patterns. The gun includes a ventilated rib on a 22-, 24-, 26-, or 28-inch barrel with three screw-in Accu-Mag choke tubes. Nice touches include stock spacers, a button to quickly empty the magazine and a fiber-optic front bead.

The Grand Slam series includes the 935 and the 835 Ultra-Mag and 500 pumps. The 935 Grand Slam has a 22-inch barrel; 20-inch barrels are on the 835s and 500s. All the guns are covered in a variety of camouflage patterns and come with a camo-colored sling. Adjustable fiber-optic sights are standard, along with an Extra Full extended choke tube for turkey hunting.

The 835 pump 12-gauge comes in several additional models. The Field wears hardwood stocks and a 26-inch ventilated rib barrel. The Synthetic is the same gun with a matte metal finish and synthetic stocks. The Turkey/Waterfowl Combo is dressed in camo with 24- and 28-inch barrels. Adjustable fiber-optic sights are attached to the shorter barrel. The longer barrel wears a fiber-optic front bead. The Turkey/Deer Combo comes with a 24-inch barrel with an Ulti-Full choke tube screwed in. The deer barrel is 24 inches long, rifled for slugs and has a cantilever scope ring base.

The 500 pump Waterfowl wears Mossy Oak Obsession camo with a 20-gauge 28-inch barrel and Advantage Max 4 camo with the 12-gauge's 28-inch barrel. The Bantam Slug 20-gauge has a rifled barrel 24 inches long. The stock has a 13-inch length of pull, grip closer to the trigger and forearm set closer to the receiver. The Bantam Field/Slug Combo has a 20-gauge 22-inch barrel for birds, and a 24-inch rifled slug barrel. The regular size Field/Slug Combo 12-gauge has a 24-inch rifled barrel with adjustable sights and a 28-inch smoothbore barrel that accepts choke tubes. The Muzzleloader/Slug Combo has a 50-caliber muzzleloader barrel and a 24-inch rifled slug barrel.

New England Arms Corporation

F.A.I.R.- I. Rizzini guns are imported by New England. The Model 400 and 400 Gold over/unders are new and include a boxlock action, chrome-lined bores with a ventilated top rib and screw in choke tubes. The 12-, 16-, 20- and 28-gauge guns are fit to proportionally sized frames. The .410 shares the 28's frame. Stocks of Turkish walnut are finished with a wood buttplate, straight or curved grip and a schnabel forend. The Gold model features gold inlays of pheasants and quail. Meltas Marangos, of New England, said the 16 is by far the most popular gauge–across the board–in New England's shotguns.

New England Firearms

A pump-action shotgun is always the right choice. NEF thinks so and has introduced the 12-gauge Pardner Pump. The Pardner includes an American walnut forearm and stock with a cushioned recoil pad. The steel receiver has a matte finish, double action bars and a cross-bolt safety at the rear of the trigger guard. The

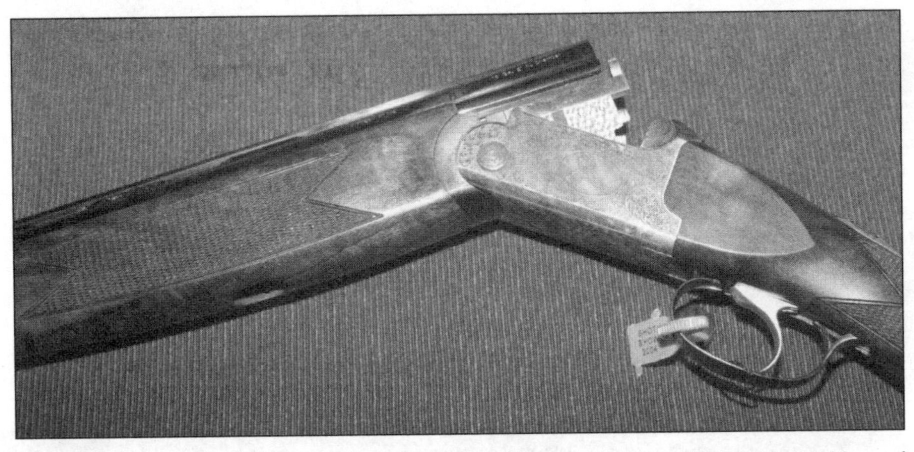

F.A.I.R.- I. Rizzini guns are imported by New England Arms. The Model 400 Gold over/under features a boxlock action, chromed bores, plus a ventilated top rib and screw-in choke tubes. The 12-, 16-, 20- and 28-gauge guns are built on proportionally sized frames.

28-inch ventilated rib barrel slips out of the receiver by removing the magazine cap for easy takedown. The barrel muzzle is threaded for choke tubes and comes with a Modified tube.

Remington

The Model 332 over/under, introduced last year, is now offered in an enhanced version with a high-gloss American walnut stock.

The 20-gauge has been added to the Model 1100 Classic Field, which features white-line spacers on the grip cap and butt plate, and the Model 1100 Tournament Skeet with a 26-inch barrel and twin sight beads. The 28-gauge and .410 bore have also been added to the Model 1100 Sporting with a 27-inch barrel.

The 20-gauge is also the choice for the Dale Earnhardt Limited Edition 11-87 Premier autoloader for 2004. This is the second gun in a four-year series. The gun wears a 28-inch light contoured barrel, blued receiver engraved with Earnhardt's likeness and signature and "Seven Time Winston Cup Champion" in 24-karat gold.

A Model 11-87 decked out in Mossy Oak Shadow Grass camo is called the Waterfowl Camo. The gun comes with a fiber optic front sight with interchangeable light pipes. The loading carrier has also been lengthened to speed loading.

The Model 870 pump has been around in one version or another since ducks were invented. This year an 870 Special Purpose Shotgun in 20-gauge has a fully rifled 18 1/2-inch barrel, black synthetic stocks, R3 recoil pad and a cantilever scope base that is attached to the barrel and reaches back over the receiver to allow using a scope, or other optic sight with normal eye relief.

Rizzini USA

The Aurum Classic over/under is now chambered in 16-gauge. Jack Dudley, the national sales manager for Rizzini USA, said the gun's frame is scaled to fit the 16-gauge. The gun has a single trigger, walnut wood and 28-inch barrels with fixed chokes. Rizzini now offers five models in 16-gauge.

The Aurum Small Action is available in 28-gauge or .410. It weighs about half a pound less than other steel-frame Rizzini over/unders.

Rossi

Rossi has added a fully rifled 12-gauge barrel to its hinge action. To take the sting out of shooting slugs, the barrel is ported back of the front sight. Adjustable rear and front dot TRUGLO fiber-optic sights are standard, as is a scope ring base.

Stoeger

The three models of Coach Gun Supreme double barrels will help you guard the strongbox in the stagecoach coming from the gold mine during cowboy action shoots. The Coach Gun offers the choice of blued barrels and receiver, blued barrels and stainless receiver or nickel-plated barrels and receiver. The Coach Gun is chambered in 12, 20 or .410, with 20- or 24-inch barrels. The .410 has fixed Improved Cylinder and Modified chokes. The 12 and 20 have screw-in chokes and come with Improved Cylinder and Modified choke tubes. The Supreme name comes from the nice American walnut stock and soft rubber recoil pad.

The Combo joins the Condor over/under line. It has a 12-gauge 28-inch barrel set and a 26-inch 20-gauge barrel set to fit one forearm and receiver. Both sets have a bead sight and screw-in Improved Cylinder and Modified chokes.

The Special joins the Single Barrel line with a matte stainless steel receiver.

Traditions

Traditions imports over/under shotguns made by Fausti Stefano in Brescia, Italy. The rising popularity of the 16-gauge has prompted Traditions to introduce the Real 16 and Real 16 Gold over/unders. These guns are built on a receiver proportioned to the 16-gauge shells and weigh 6 3/4-pounds; the same weight as the Fausti 20-gauge Field guns. The 16-gauge guns have chrome-lined bores, ventilated ribs and three screw-in choke tubes. The barrels lock with a cross bolt. Refinements include a barrel selector inside the trigger guard, engraved game scenes on the receiver flats and point pattern checkering on the grip and forearm. The Gold comes in a hard case.

Like its name implies, the Field II 20/.410 Combo is a two-barrel set with 20-gauge and .410 barrels. Weight is six pounds with 26-inch barrels.

Tristar

Tristar imports a variety of shotguns from Europe as follows:

Breda Shotguns from Italy include the Grizzly Mag inertia-operated autoloading shotguns chambered for the 3 1/2-inch 12-gauge. The Grizzly has a synthetic stock and forend, either in black or covered with Advantage Timber HD camo. The gun wears a 28-inch barrel and comes in a hard case.

The Pegaso Sporting over/under has 30-inch barrels chambered in 3-inch 12-gauge and ventilated top and side ribs. The trigger is adjustable and the whole trigger assembly is easily removed. The blued receiver sports the Breda logo inlaid in gold to match the walnut

The Winchester Select Field over/under features oval checkering panels, an engraved receiver, and 26- or 28-inch barrels.

For the rough world of waterfowling, the Super X2 3-1/2 inch gun wears Mossy Oak's Shadow Grass camo from butt to muzzle.

The Select Traditional Elegance has engraved bird scenes on its receiver and trigger guard, and panels of traditional point-pattern checkering on the grip and forearm.

The Extreme Elegance is similar to the Traditional, but has the oval checkering panels.

The Winchester Energy Trap has a comb that adjusts for height and cast, and a fiber-optic front sight.

stocks. The Pegaso Hunter is similar, except it has a silver receiver and is also chambered in 20-gauge.

The HP and HP Marine join the TR-Diana line of semi-autos. Both models have synthetic black handles and a 19-inch barrel with three extended 12-gauge choke tubes. An adjustable rear sight and front blade are for shooting slugs and buckshot. Metal of the standard HP model is finished in black chrome. The Marine is finished in white chrome.

The four models of the TR-Diana pumps are all new. The Synthetic is chambered in 12-gauge three-inch and the Synthetic Mag in 3 1/2-inch 12-gauge. Both guns have a 20-inch barrel with a fixed Cylinder choke, and barrel and receiver finished in black chrome. The Synthetic VR and Mag VR are similar to the standard Synthetic and Mag, except have a 28-inch barrel with a ventilated top rib and a front bead. The barrel is threaded for choke tubes and comes with a Modified tube. The Field is similar to the VR, but with a walnut stock and forearm handle. A 20-gauge has a scaled-down stock for smaller shooters. The Camo Mag is masked in Mossy Oak Breakup camo and its 24-inch barrel is chambered in 3 1/2-inch 12-gauge. Sights include an adjustable rear and front blade. A Full choke tube is supplied.

The Silver II series of over/unders has added a youth/ladies model in 20-gauge, at six pounds, ten ounces. The gun's grip is one inch closer to the trigger and its stock has slightly more drop on the comb and a 7/8-inch shorter length of pull.

Winchester

The Winchester Model 9410 is too much fun. It's a grouse and rabbit-potting machine. The Packer Compact lets the kids in on the fun with its shorter 12 1/2-inch length of pull and 20-inch barrel. At six pounds, the Compact weighs 3/4-pound less than the regular 9410. A semi-fancy Traditional model sports a figured walnut stock.

The Select over/unders are a big makeover of Winchester's previous Supreme Select guns. The Select Energy models all have ported barrels, vented top- and side- ribs and adjustable trigger shoes. The Energy Trap's comb adjusts for height and cast and also has a fiber-optic front sight. The Energy Sporting comes with a regular buttstock, or one with an adjustable comb. Barrel lengths are 28, 30 or 32 inches. The checkering is a pattern of small ovals. The Monte Carlo comb on the Energy Trap keeps your head up.

The Select Field features the same checkering ovals and an engraved receiver. The 26- or 28-inch barrels are not ported. The Select Traditional Elegance has engraved bird scenes on the receiver and trigger guard. More traditional panels of point pattern checkering adorn the grip and forearm. The Extreme Elegance is similar to the Traditional, but has the oval checkering.

For the rough world of waterfowl, the Super X2 wears Mossy Oak's Shadow Grass camo from butt to muzzle. So does the Model 1300 pump. For those who like to look at their gun, not look for it, the 1300 Walnut Field has a gloss-finished walnut stock. The 1300 Upland Special Field wears the same stock finish, but with a straight grip and 24-inch barrel, in 12- or 20-gauge, and weighs 1/2-pound less than the standard 1300. Just right to carry after mountain grouse. ●

The Winchester 1300 Upland Special Field wears a gloss-finish, straight-grip walnut stock, has a 24-inch barrel in either 12- or 20-gauge, and weighs a half-pound less than the standard 1300—just right to carry after mountain grouse.

The Winchester Model 9410 Semi-Fancy Traditional sports a figured walnut stock and is a grouse- and rabbit-potting machine. The related Packer Compact lets the kids in on the fun with it's shorter 12-1/2 inch length of pull and 20-inch barrel. At six pounds, the Compact weighs 3/4-pound less than the full-size 9410.

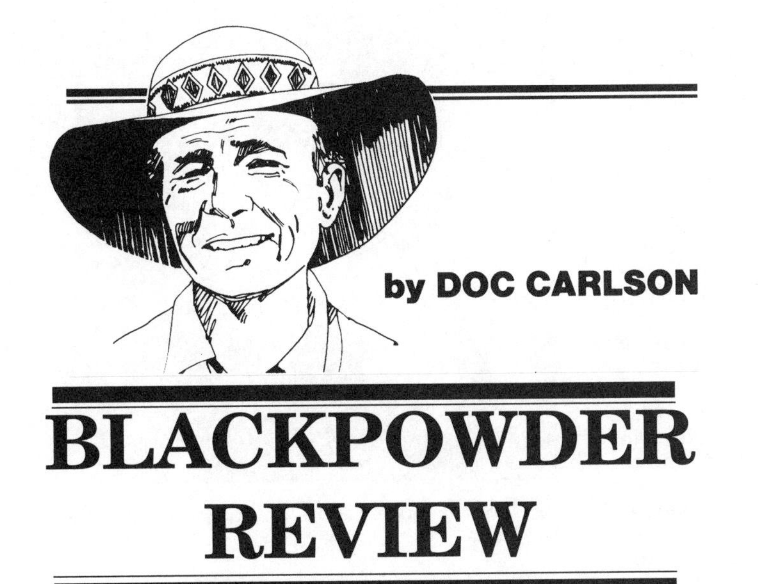

by DOC CARLSON

BLACKPOWDER REVIEW

A COUPLE OF hundred years ago, a couple of captains headed up the Missouri River to its source, hoping to find the Northwest Passage to the Pacific Ocean. The captains were, of course, Lewis and Clark. The bicentennial of the expedition has fostered a renewed interest in the history of the era, and the guns involved. After several years of the blackpowder market being driven primarily by the requirements of hunters, it appears traditional guns are making a comeback. The same phenomenon occurred back in the 1960s when the centennial of the Civil War was celebrated. There was a great deal of interest in Civil War guns which, in turn, sparked interest in other firearms of the era—and muzzleloaders in general. I'm sure we'll see the same pattern over the next few years.

Interest in the guns of the Lewis and Clark Expedition is hampered, to some extent, by a lack of information as to exactly what the guns were. There is very sketchy information contained in the Lewis and Clark journals, but details of the firearms are lacking. We know that Lewis took delivery of 15 rifles from the Harpers Ferry Armory, along with powder horns, knives, tomahawks and other accoutrements. He also had shooting bags made for the expedition. Exactly what they all looked like remains elusive. Unfortunately all the equipment belonging to the government that remained when the expedition returned to St. Louis, was sold at auction and the money returned to the U.S. Treasury—so there are no known Lewis and Clark guns in existence.

However, a great deal of research has been done on the guns of the Corps of Discovery and some pretty solid conclusions can be drawn. The 1803 Harpers Ferry rifle has often been promoted as the rifle carried by the Corps. Unfortunately for the promoters of the 1803, the design for the rifle was not finalized until May of 1803, after Lewis had received his rifles. The likely rifle carried by the expedition was probably made up from 1792-1794 Contract Rifles that were in storage at Harpers Ferry at the time. These were full-stocked rifles of 49-caliber that had been made up to government specifications by private gunsmiths in the late 1700s. Lewis had the rifles fitted with new Harpers Ferry locks and sling swivels for carrying straps, a very practical addition for the trip. The locks were of a common pattern, and interchangeable. Also furnished were replacement locks and parts. The lock was probably the same as was used on the Harpers Ferry 1803 Rifle.

Village Restorations & Consulting, Inc., of Claysburg, PA is reproducing a rifle that is likely correct for the rifle that the expedition carried. The full-stocked rifle is 49-caliber, with a typical 1803-type Harpers Ferry flintlock. The brass patchbox is what is found on the 1803 also; the few surviving 1792-94 contract rifles have this type of

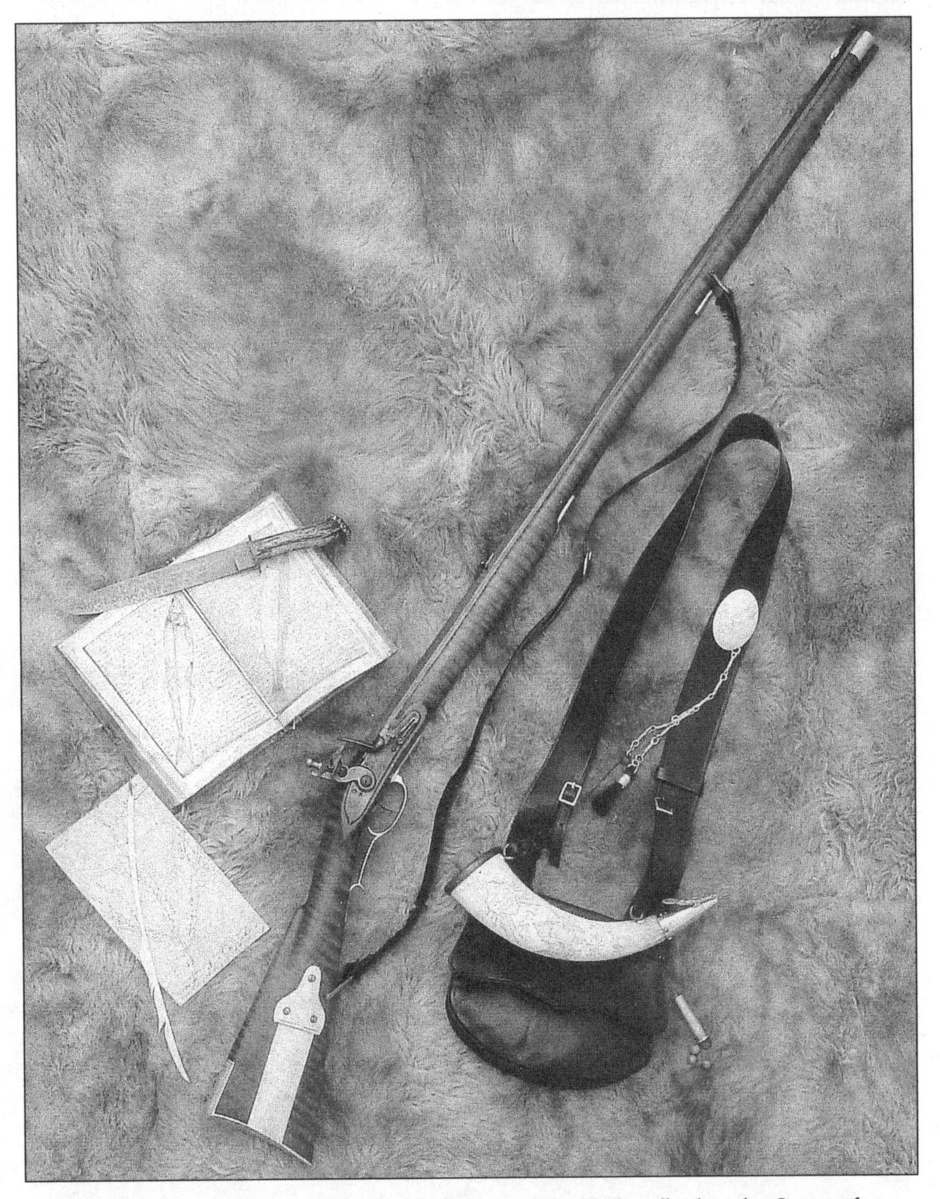

Village Restorations & Consulting reproduction of the likely rifle that the Corps of Discovery requisitioned from the Harpers Ferry Arsenal for the trip up the Missouri.

patchbox. The patchbox release button is in the top of the typical Harpers Ferry brass buttplate and the brass trigger guard is reminiscent of the 1803, again typical of the 1792-94 series of rifle. The ramrod pipes are brass with the entry pipe having a rounded tail, typical of the 1803 but unusual on full-stock Kentucky-type rifles. The ramrod is wood, whereas the 1803 utilized a steel ramrod. The stock is of seasoned maple. These guns are hand-built from standardized parts by some of the more notable contemporary custom gunsmiths in the United States. The rifles are supplied with a hand-made horn with a spring-loaded brass cutoff. The horn is copied from an infantry horn, which appears in a painting of Lewis done shortly after the expedition returned home. The horn holds 1/2-pound of powder and is made by well-known contemporary horn makers. Also supplied with the rifle is a reproduction shot pouch, patterned after a military rifleman's pouch of the correct period in the Smithsonian collection. The shot pouch is also handmade by custom leather workers. All in all, this is probably as close to duplicating the guns and accoutrements Lewis acquired for the trip as is possible, without original artifacts to examine.

The rifles are offered in two grades: The Presentation Grade features a highly-figured curly maple stock; the powder horn having a federal eagle, panoply of arms, and personalized cartouche engraved. The shot pouch has a silver cross belt-plate, with federal eagle, fitted to it. The Standard Issue has a plain maple stock, non-engraved horn, and shot pouch with a brass plate installed. The Standard Issue rifle would be pretty much what the Corps carried up the Missouri. For the Lewis and Clark *aficionado* or re-enactor, these rifles would be the ultimate.

Another gun of interest to the Lewis and Clark re-enactor is a reproduction of the 1795 U.S. Musket. This firearm would have undoubtedly made up the rest of the guns the expedition carried. The 1795 was the first standardized "official" military musket the new nation produced. Various contractors made parts and the guns were assembled at the Springfield Armory, the first military arms to be made there. They were, basically, an updated copy of the French Charleville musket that was issued in quantity during the Revolutionary War. France supplied a large quantity of these muskets to the colonies, and it was logical that the first U.S. musket would follow the lines of this gun.

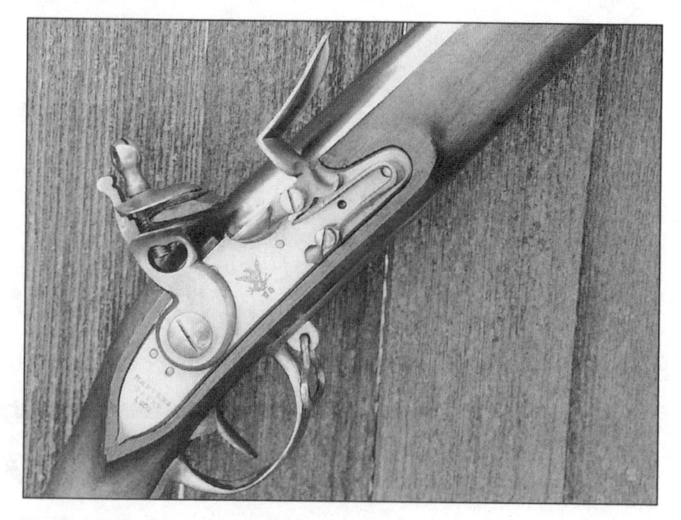

Lock of the Dixie 1795 U.S. Musket reproduction; a very well done copy.

A few details were changed to reflect American thinking. The major change was to give the buttstock more drop so the gun could be properly aimed. The Charleville stock was very straight; it was difficult to get one's head down on the comb enough to sight along the barrel. The Charleville was intended for heads-up volley fire, not aimed shots. *As an aside, the 1795 musket used metric screws, as did the Charleville, setting a trend for military arms that continued through most of the 19th century—through the 1873 trapdoor. The French gun utilized both a gooseneck and a double-throated hammer. The Americans went with the double-throated hammer for its greater strength.* The basic design and shape of this musket remained little changed through U.S. military musket models for the next 50 years.

Dixie Gun Works is importing the 1795 repro, made in Italy by Pedersoli. The gun is a faithful copy and shows good quality. The tapered barrel is 69-caliber, smoothbore, and 44-3/4 inches long, finished "bright" (polished, with no blue or browned finish). The steel buttplate, trigger guard, sideplate and barrel bands are also finished "bright". The walnut oil-finished stock is 60 inches overall. There is a bayonet stud on top of the muzzle, and a front sight is incorporated into the front barrel band. The ramrod is steel. The "bright"-finished lock features a thinner pan than the Charleville and is marked with the federal eagle, and "US" is script in front of the hammer, with "Springfield" and a date on the tail of the lock. There is no rear sight, in keeping with the thinking of the time. A number of these muskets, along with spare parts, would have undoubtedly been a major part of the expedition's armament. The Corps went through drills and marching to impress the various Indian tribes along the way, and this military musket would have played a part in those demonstrations, I'm sure. Lewis and Clark *aficionados* would do well to give this well-made musket a look.

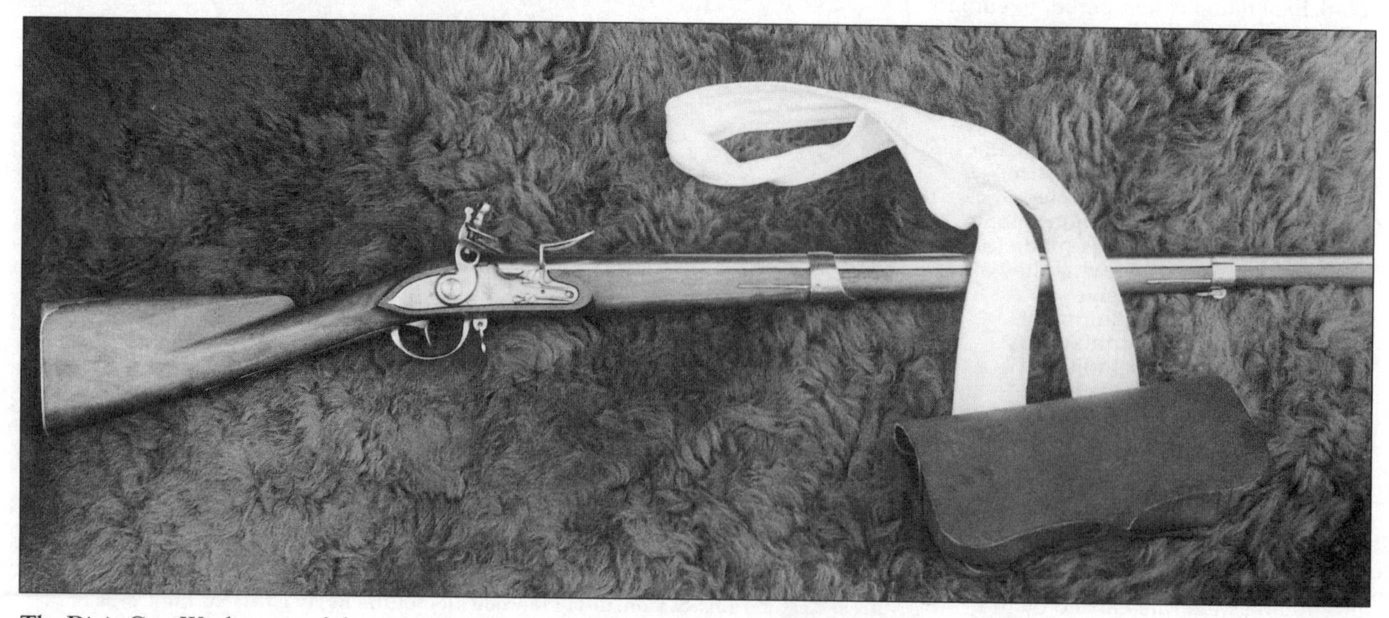

The Dixie Gun Works copy of the 1795 U.S. Musket produced at the Springfield Armory.

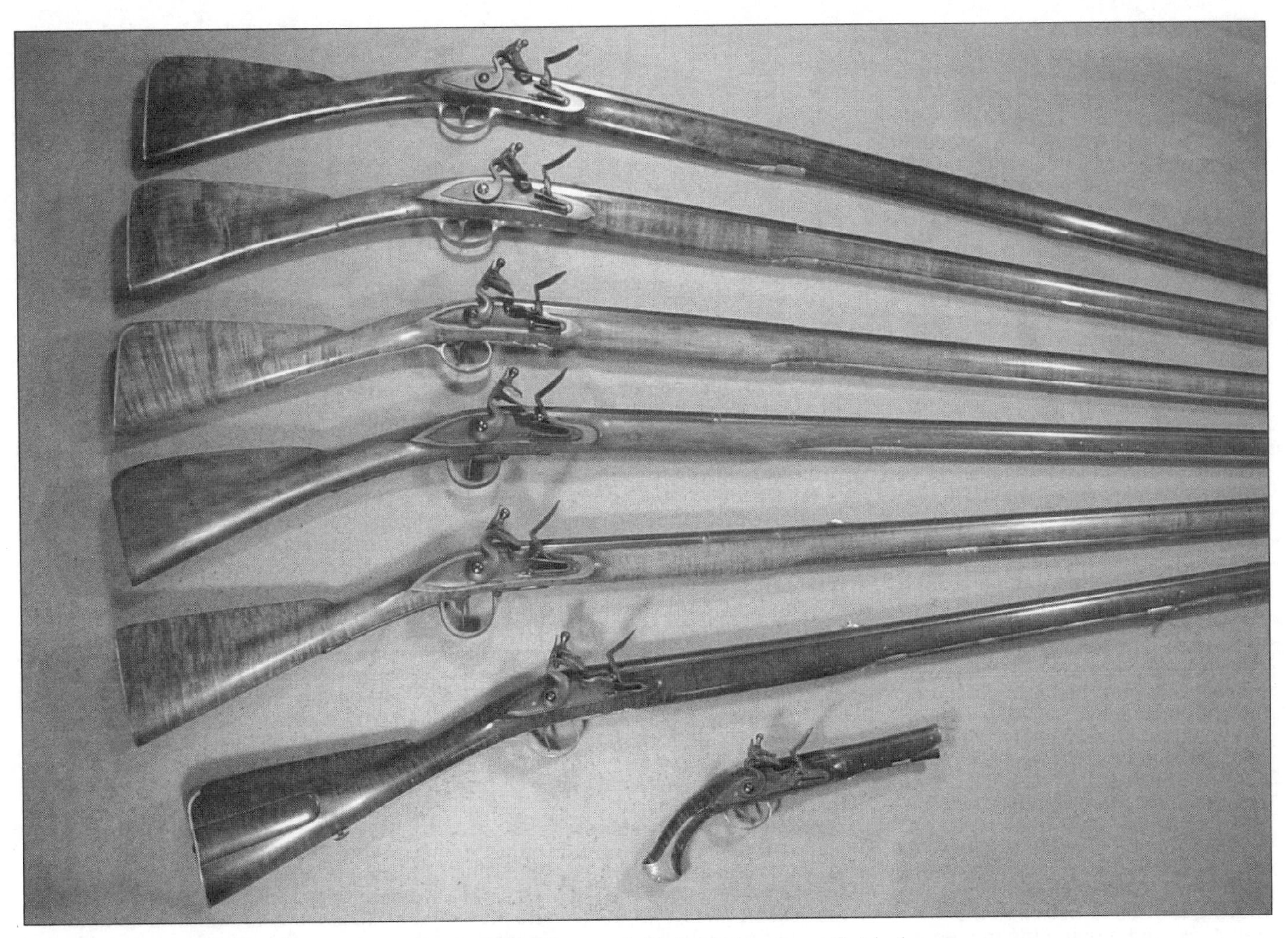

Caywood Gunmakers line of semi-custom flintlock fusils are available in kit form or as finished guns.

There is a relatively new company making some very nice semi-custom traditional guns. **Caywood Gunmakers** is offering a line of fusils that include a Wilson chiefs-grade trade gun, a typical English Northwest trade gun, two French-type trade guns (types C and D), an English sporting fowler and a French-type pistol. The guns are available with 20-gauge (62-cal), 24-gauge (58-cal) and 28-gauge (55-cal.) smoothbore, and 50-, 54- and 58-caliber rifled barrels. All the guns are available with interchangeable barrels, so a great variety of calibers–in both smoothbore and rifled–can be installed on the same gun for versatility. The furniture on the fusils: buttplates, trigger guards etc. carry tasteful engraving patterns correct for the particular gun and its time period.

The flintlocks used on the guns are of very high quality, a fundamental requirement for a flintlock firearm. The lock is the heart of the firing system and a good lock is necessary for fast, sure ignition. All the internal parts of the locks are made of low carbon steel that is case-hardened. This gives a relatively soft, tough interior and a wear-resistant hard skin, ideal for protecting critical parts from wear and breakage. The frizzens of the locks are made of a high-carbon steel hardened all the way through, so they will never wear out and quit throwing good, hot sparks–essential for reliable ignition. The locks feature a single-position sear bar, meaning the sear bar is in the same place whether the lock is in full cock, half cock or fired position. This allows a trigger position that never changes, and never has excessive slack and "rattle".

One can order these traditional firearms as kits, which include all parts and an inletted stock, with whatever amount of work remaining the craftsman feels comfortable doing. Parts must be fitted to the wood, although the inlets require very little work. Some shaping of the stock, such as lock panels etc. remains to be done. The next step up is the semi-finished kit that has the stock smoothed more, and lock and tang panels shaped. Also available is the assembled-in-the-white kit, which consists of a basically completed rifle left unfinished. Or the guns can be ordered completed and finished with a full warranty. Prices are very reasonable, considering quality. These fusils, both as kits and completed guns, are done on a semi-custom basis. Machine-inlet stocks, etc. are used but there is much hand-fitting involved, depending upon the percent of finish done on the kit. For this reason, there is a waiting period of two to four months after ordering.

Want something different? Caywood Gunmakers is doing a run of David Crockett rifles. This run of rifles, limited to 100 units, is a reproduction of Davy Crockett's first rifle. This is a high-dollar gun with a beautiful curly maple stock featuring extensive relief carving. It has all brass furniture and an engraved four-piece patchbox. Each rifle is personalized with a sterling silver plate inside the patchbox engraved "David Crockett-Freedom Fighter" and the number of the gun out of the 100. An additional sterling patchbox plate is engraved with the customer's name, and a framed signed & numbered certificate of authenticity is included with each firearm.

These are top-drawer custom rifles. Each gun comes with a hard case, fire-

The Prairie River Arms "Bull Pup" inline; note the nipple access door in the buttstock.

blued bag-type mould, screwdriver, David Crockett's autobiography, Crockett and Boone videos by Native Sun Productions and a document of ownership history. The 49-caliber guns weigh in at 9 lbs. and have an overall length of 62-1/2 inches. This is a rifle that can be shot, hunted with and handed down as a family heirloom.

For those more interested in the modern-type muzzleloader, there are several new guns coming into the market that will be well-received, I believe. The greatly increasing deer herds in many states have resulted in expanded hunting opportunities, many of which are available to the muzzleloading hunter. The ranks of hunters using muzzle-loading guns is increasing and, while many of these hunters are using traditional arms, the majority seem to be interested in the high-performance, non-traditional guns.

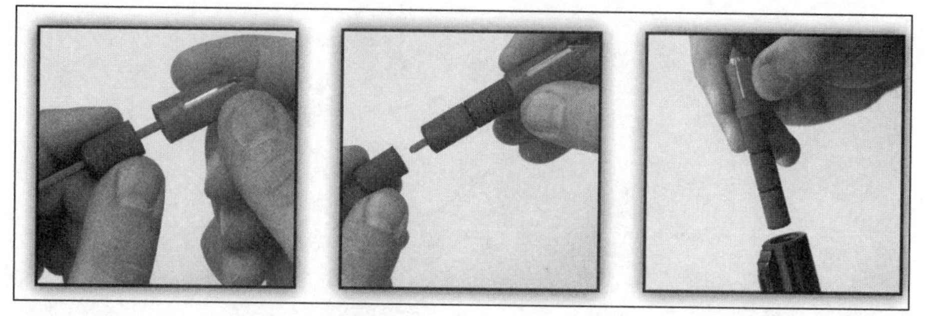

Hornady's new Lock and Load Speed Sabot.

Prairie River Arms is marketing a modern-type muzzleloader that is about as far from the traditional long rifle as one can get. They have incorporated the inline principal into a bullpup design that is truly innovative. The bullpup design, where the action is moved back into the buttstock under the shooter's cheek, surfaced in the mid-1900s in custom centerfire varmint rifles. It is most recently seen in the current British military assault rifle. The advantage is a standard length barrel in a very short rifle.

The Prairie River rifle features a 28-inch barrel, and an overall length of 31-1/2 inches. This is accomplished by moving the action back into the buttstock, and moving the trigger forward. The stock design is a thumbhole type: very straight, putting the shoulder directly in line with the barrel. This makes recoil very manageable with little or no muzzle raise on firing. Balance is very good, putting the weight of the gun between the hands. The short length makes it a very handy gun in brush or tree stands. The rifle is available with a hardwood stock in either a natural or an "all weather" black epoxy finish. It can be had in either 50- or 54-caliber. The 1:28 rifling twist is correct for conical bullets or sabotted projectiles.

The rifle uses standard #11 caps. The nipple is reached by pushing up a door in the offside of the buttstock. After capping, this door is pushed back down, effectively sealing the ignition system from moisture, dirt, etc.— as well as containing any cap fragmentation or blowback. The nipple sets in a drum that protrudes from the bottom of the barrel, which assures the drum will fill with powder via gravity when the gun is loaded. The cocking handle is just to the rear of the trigger and has two safety positions. There is an additional safety inside the trigger guard that blocks trigger movement. An anodized hard aluminum ramrod fits into the stock under the barrel. The mechanism is very simple, just two moving parts, and takedown is by the removal of one screw.

The guns are available with Williams Guide-type sights, front and rear, or an optional M-16-type carrying handle that contains a M-16 national match sight, matched with a Williams front. The carrying handle will also accept standard M-16/AR-15 scope mounts, if you are so inclined. With the carrying handle installed and the tall front sight–*ala* assault rifles–this one is certainly not your grandfather's muzzleloader!

Knight Rifles has a couple of things for the in-line shooter also. First, they have added something to their Disc Extreme rifles. The new offering is a 52-caliber with a totally redesigned breech plug called the Power Stem. The breech plug is made with a thin, hollow extension on the front that channels the fire from the 209 primer to the front of the powder charge. By igniting the front of the powder charge first, the bullet gains more uniform acceleration, yielding higher velocities, increased energy and less punishing recoil, according to Knight. To further add to shooter comfort, the gun comes with an Xcoil recoil pad by HiViz shooting systems. This pad is said to dampen felt recoil by 33 percent more than conventional recoil pads. The recommended charge of 150 grains of FFg loose blackpowder, or its equivalent, gives velocities approaching 2000 fps with a 375-grain bullet. Pellets or charges less than 90 grains are not recommended. The 52-caliber outperforms the 54-caliber due to the bullet/sabot fit. The thinner petals on the 52-cal. sabot allow it to release from the bullet quicker, enhancing accuracy. The rifle uses the Full Plastic Jacket ignition system, with 209 primers, found on the other Disc Supreme rifles.

The other new offering from Knight is a revolutionary in-line that looks, at first glance, like a Winchester High Wall without a hammer. This rotating-block action is activated by pulling the trigger guard down and forward to expose the breech plug. A full plastic jacket is inserted into the breechblock and raising the trigger guard closes the action. The gun, assuming a loaded barrel, is ready to fire. The hammer is enclosed in the swinging-action block.

For cleaning, the trigger guard is rotated forward and the entire action block — trigger, hammer, springs, etc.––can be removed from the rifle without tools. Called the Knight Revolution, the new rifle features a 27-inch barrel in either blued or stainless finish, a two-piece synthetic stock and fully adjustable metallic fiber optic sights. Caliber is .50. The trigger is fully adjustable for both creep and pull weight. With an overall length of 43-1/2 inches and a weight of just under 8 lbs., this is a handy rifle that will find favor with hunters everywhere, I predict.

Hornady Manufacturing Co., a Nebraska-based outfit that has been one of the leaders in developing projectiles for the muzzle-loading hunter, is out

The Knight Disc Extreme in 52-caliber gives superior ballistics at ranges of 200 yards.

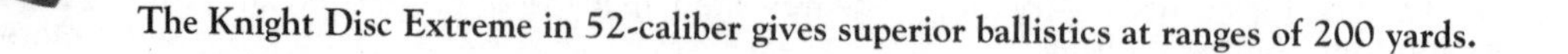

The Knight Disc Extreme in 52-caliber gives superior ballistics at ranges of 200 yards.

Hornady packages their Speed Sabot in handy 5-shot packages.

with a new sabot that should simplify things in the hunting field. Called the Lock and Load Speed Sabot, this is a typical plastic sabot–but with a "tail." A plastic stem, cast in the center of the bottom of the sabot, is designed to fit into the hole in the center of the Pyrodex or new Triple 7 pellets from Hodgdon. The stem will hold three of the 50-grain pellets or it can be cut off if two pellets are required for the favorite load. This is the closest anyone has come to bringing the convenience of cartridge loading to muzzleloading since the days of combustible paper cartridges. The sabots are combined with Hornady's SST-ML bullet. This bullet, developed specifically for muzzleloading, features a polymer tip that increases ballistic efficiency and initiates expansion of the jacketed bullet to twice its diameter upon impact. Hornady claims true 200-yard performance from this bullet, properly loaded. The Lock and Load Speed Sabot is available in 50-caliber with two 45-caliber bullet weights, 250- and 300-grain. It is packaged in 5-load pocket field packs that will hold the sabots, with pellets attached; keeping them clean and moisture-free until needed. A real handy system for the hunter.

Every year at the Shooting, Hunting and Outdoor Trade Show, I always look forward to stopping by the **Taylor's & Company** display. Over the years they have imported reproductions of many muzzleloading and cartridge guns of a bygone era. The quality and authenticity of their entire line is top-drawer, and they usually have something new and interesting to see. This year was no exception. They had a few things that will be of interest to cowboy action shooters—or anyone interested in replica or antique firearms.

While several companies are importing very nice copies of the venerable Winchester '92, Taylor's is doing a takedown version. Something over a million '92s were produced by Winchester but the takedown version was somewhat rare.

The Taylor's reproduction of this classic firearm is of top quality, as are all their offerings. It is available with an octagon barrel in either 20- or 24-inch length. To take the gun down, a folding handle is lifted at the muzzle end of the magazine tube, the tube is screwed out of the receiver and the barrel, magazine and forearm unit is turned out of the receiver unit, exactly as with the original Winchester. This allows the gun to be packed into either a 20- or 24-inch space, depending upon barrel length. The little rifle is offered in 32/20, 32 H&R Magnum, 357 Magnum, 38 Special, 38/40, 44/40, 44 S&W and 45 Colt chamberings, which pretty well covers things. This one should be popular with the cowboy action shooters, as well as anyone who likes a light, handy rifle that can be packed into a small space while traveling.

Another new "must have" from Taylor's is a Uberti-made, steel frame copy of the 31-caliber Colt Pocket Model 1849 cap-and-ball revolver, with an interchangeable cylinder to allow it to fire 32 S&W Short. The conversion cylinder is available separately, if you already have the gun. This conversion cylinder joins the others offered in 45 Colt for Remington and Ruger 44/45 revolvers, in 38 Special for the Remington 36 Navy, and 38 LC for the 1851/1861 Navies. Other than Ruger, the cylinders are sold to convert either Uberti or Pietta steel-frame revolvers only. They also offer conversion cylinders for Rogers & Spencer revolvers by the same makers in various calibers.

Something else new this year that will delight both cowboy action shooters and blackpowder cartridge silhouette shooters who are interested in the new scope class, is a scope and mounts of correct timeframe for Sharps and other single-shot blackpowder cartridge rifles. The 6X scope will be made with either a brass or steel tube and is 32-1/2 inches long. There will also be a shorter version in 4X, 26 inches long for shorter barreled guns. Both scopes should meet NRA Silhouette rules and can be used in BRCS competition.

Taylor's can supply arms for anyone interested in reenacting from the 1700s period through the Civil War era to the cowboy action shooters. Their fine line of guns and equipment is worth a serious look.

A remake of a famous old rifle that should "trip the trigger" of cowboy action shooters is the reproduction Colt Lightning pump rifle from **American Western Arms.** This faithful copy of the centerfire Lightning is nicely reproduced with round or octagon barrel in 32/20, 38 Special, 38/40, 44/40 and 45 Colt. Both rifle and carbine versions are available, with 24- and 20-inch barrels, respectively. Stocks are American walnut, as were the originals. Sights are a standard blade front, paired with an elevation-adjustable semi-buckhorn rear. A firing pin block safety has been added as a concession to modern life. The guns all sport the engraved logo of American Western Arms, so there is little chance of these guns being passed off as originals. As Colt brought out these guns in the early 1880s, they will fit the time period covered by the cowboy action game.

One can't help but be amazed by the wide selection of both traditional and modern-type blackpowder guns being made. It seems that every year we see major improvements in the modern hunting muzzleloading firearms and the ammunition available for them. Manufacturers and suppliers are continually improving and upgrading. We have taken the muzzleloading firearm to levels never dreamed of by our forefathers. The muzzleloading hunter has a vast selection of guns and supplies to choose from – a larger selection than at any time in our history, including the era when the muzzleloader reigned supreme. Traditional firearm reproductions also cover darn near everything that was made during the heyday of this type firearm. Quality and authenticity of these reproductions is very good. If you are a muzzleloading hunter, re-enactor, or lover of these old guns, it's a great time to be alive. Life is good. •

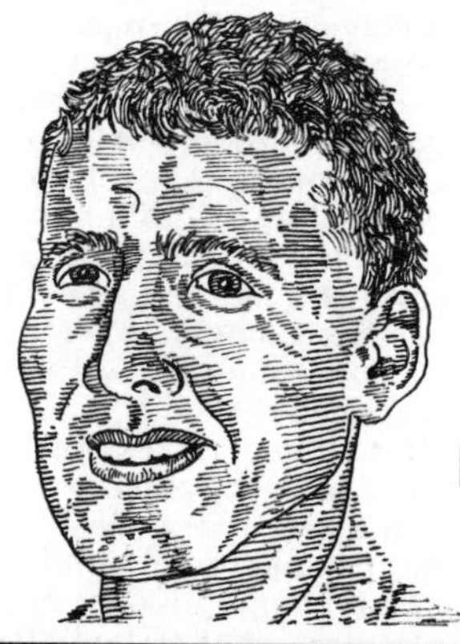

by **WAYNE VAN ZWOLL**

SCOPES AND MOUNTS

EACH YEAR, A flood of new riflescopes, binoculars and spotting scopes washes into catalogs and display cases. Sportsmen must sift old from new, then decide if the new is really better. Here I've distilled news from most of the major optics firms. Regrettably, not all specifications, prices and photos for 2004's optics crop were available at this writing. And space compelled me to be selective. Some products that were new last year didn't survive the cut, though have yet to get much field time. The fine 8x32 Swarvoski EL binocular comes to mind. So do Predator binoculars from Steiner, which have phase-corrected optics treated to enhance brown and red, so these colors are easier to pick out in foliage. A dearth of new optics can make a company vulnerable to editors. The new Vartac scope, a 4-16x50 from Western Powders, for instance, has a lot to interest varminters, with 66 percent of the elevation adjustment range on the top-side so you can zero long, and 1/8-minute clicks for precise shooting. But Western Powders (Ramshot) doesn't market an extensive line of optics. Minox now catalogs a 10x32 roof-prism binocular with aspheric lenses, and is using argon instead of nitrogen to prevent fogging. Worthy news. But other than a mini-night vision device, it is the only news from Minox. Thompson/Center imports scopes to brand for its Contender and Encore firearms; Remington optics are likewise contracted by a brand licensee. Both lines include useful glass. Leatherwood's "Tactikal" scope is patterned on Leatherwood's ART range-compensating sight that earned plaudits from Vietnam snipers. Leatherwood also imports a full line of conventional scopes....

Well, you see where I'm going. There's really no end to the news. But our space is limited.

Aimpoint

Some firms are busy designing new models before current products see the shelf. An unspoken mandate to push new items in front of consumers annually brings us innovative thinking on deadline. But it also saddles the market with products that aren't needed. Some aren't even new. When existing optics appear in a different camo finish with *NEW* emblazoned on the page, my heart goes out to that R&D team.

Some companies, however, trundle along with a different focus: providing top-quality items while working constantly to improve them. When improvements can be implemented, a new model appears. But not until then. Kenneth Mardklint, a Swedish engineer, remembers the first Aimpoint sights. He helped design them 30 years ago, and he's still with the firm.

"Gunnar Sandberg came up with what he called the single-point sight. You couldn't look through it at all; you saw the dot with one eye, the target with the other." The Aimpoint Electronic that followed sat high on Weaver-style bases, windage and elevation dials underneath. In 1978 a second generation of sights appeared, with a detachable 3x or 1-4x lens. These were the first Aimpoints sold in the U.S. Six years later a Mark III came along, with internal adjustments and a dot that automatically dimmed for dark conditions.

Aimpoint 7000SC.

In 1985 the Aimpoint 2000 featured a tube that could be mounted in standard rings. The Model 1000 appeared in 1987. It offered nine click-stop light settings and an integral base. Two years later came the more compact Aimpoint 3000, with 2x magnification and 1-inch tube. The 3000 was replaced in 1991 by the 5000, with a 30mm tube. In 1998 Aimpoint announced its XD (extreme duty) diode with three times the brightness of the old diode. Battery life soared from 100 to 500 hours! Aimpoint's current Model 7000 offers up to 20,000 hours at low setting – all from a single 3-volt lithium cell.

Aimpoint uses an expensive doublet instead of a single lens up front, so even if your eye is not in line with the sight's axis, you'll hit where the dot appears. No parallax problems. Excepting models with magnification, Aimpoint sights offer almost unlimited eye relief. Your eye can be 3 inches back, or 8. You can shoot as you might with a shotgun bead, both eyes wide open. The Comp 7000 has double the range of windage and elevation adjustment of earlier sights: more than 140 inches at 100 yards!

Military sales now account for 75 percent of Aimpoint's total revenues, but the firm's American representative Mike Kingston points out that one of every 10 Swedish hunters using optical sights carries an Aimpoint, and the company exports them to 40 countries. New Aimpoints are always on the drawing board, but don't expect one every year.

Alpen Outdoor Corporation

Established in 1977, Alpen is a relative newcomer to the field of sporting optics. But the company has busily built its binocular line and continues adding to a core of popularly priced spotting scopes. This year, Alpen Optics has

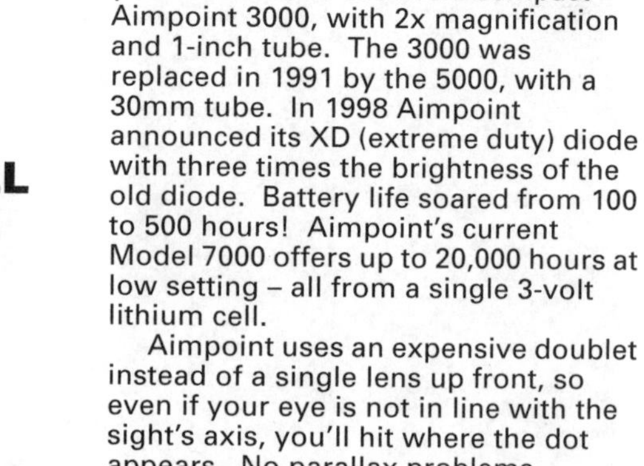

Red dot sights, like the Redfield on this Remington, afford fast aim with a single bright aiming point.

Kodiak 3-9x44mm riflescope.

also introduced its first riflescopes, comprising 11 models in two series. Three top-end Apex variables feature fully multi-coated lens systems, plus re-settable finger-adjustable windage and elevation adjustments with 1/4-minute clicks. Choose a 3-9x42, 3.5-10x50 or 6-24x50. All have fast-focus eyepieces and the Alpen AccuPlex reticle, plus a lifetime warranty. Prices start at just $300. The second-tier Alpen line is Kodiak. These scopes are also fully waterproof, fog-proof and warranted, but only some of the lenses are multi-coated. The eight models include only one fixed-power, retail for as little as $75.

Alpen's Apex roof-prism binocular clan has two new members for 2004: an 8x32 and 8.5x50. Like the 8x42 and 10x42 *(both now in Mossy Oak as well as standard colors)*, these center-focus models feature fully multi-coated optics and BaK4 prisms. They're color phase-corrected and waterproof as well. Twist-up eyepieces lock in position. At 20 ounces, the 8x32 is a top pick for long hikes. Prices start at just $395. But outdoorsmen on tighter budgets should consider the new Alpen Shasta Ridge binoculars. There are only two: an 8x42 and a 10x42. Four ounces heavier than Apex counterparts, they have very nearly the same specs but list for about $100 less.

Three new spotting scopes joined the Alpen stable this year: a 20-60x80 and rubber-armored 15-30x50 and 18-36x60 models. The high-powered model comes with 45-degree eyepiece, while the 15-30 and 18-36x60 have straight eyepieces. All are waterproof and feature fully multi-coated lenses. Carrying cases included. Prices start at just under $100.

Browning

One of the most widely known manufacturers and importers in the hunting and shooting industry, Browning has until now stayed out of the optics market. That changed this year, when Bushnell agreed to bring the Browning brand onto riflescopes, spotting scopes and binoculars. The riflescope series includes predictable models: 2-7x32, 3-9x40, 3-9x50 and 5-15x40. Distinctive in appearance, they wear Browning's buck logo. People at Browning claim 94 percent light transmission *(that's very high)* and point out the fast-focus eyepiece, finger-friendly click adjustments and a one-piece tube. Waterproof and fully multi-coated, the new Browning scopes list from $336 to $490. Rounding out this optics line are three binoculars and a spotting scope.

The roof-prism 8x32, 8x42 and 10x42 binoculars feature BaK4 prisms and phase-corrected optics with a locking diopter. They focus as close as 6 feet (the 8x32 to 5 feet). At 29 ounces, the 42mm glasses are still light enough to use without harness. The 8x32 weighs just 24 ounces. Browning's spotting scope is a 15-45x65 with ED (extra-low dispersion) glass. Like the binoculars, it boasts fully multi-coated optics. A shooters' tripod, soft case and hard case are included.

Burris

Short years ago, Burris announced its Black Diamond 30mm scopes. Optically good, they were bulky and heavy. They've since been refined, and the latest version with side-mounted parallax correction is quite handsome. Choose a 4-16x, 6-24x or 8-32x, all with 50mm objectives. The 3-12x alone wears a traditional parallax ring. This spring, a new 30mm series joined the Black Diamond at Burris. The Euro Diamond 1.5-6x40, 3-10x40, 2.5-10x44 and 3-12x50 riflescopes come in matte black finish, with fully multi-coated lenses and 1/4-minute clicks on resettable dials. Eye relief is a generous 3-1/2 to 4 inches. The eyepiece and power ring are integrated, for quick and easy power change. A helical rear ocular ring focuses the reticle with a turn of your wrist. The German 3P#4 reticle is standard, but on the three most powerful scopes you can specify a Ballistic Plex. An illuminated reticle is available on all but the 2.5-10x. Made in the U.S., the Burris Euro Diamond scopes list for $728 to $1254.

Burris EuroDiamond 1.5-6x riflescope.

The Colorado-based optics company is also upgrading its flagship Signature scope series, with seven new Signature Selects, from 1.75-5x32 to 8-32x44. They feature center-located turrets for more convenient ring spacing, deep-grooved power and parallax rings and integrated eyepieces. Ballistic Plex, Ballistic Mil Dot and a new Taper Plex reticle are available on various models. MSRP: $601-$965.

Burris also has a laser range-finding binocular, a 7x40 powered by a 9-volt battery and capable of reading reflective targets to 1500 yards. Hence the moniker: B-1500. Figure a reach of 600 yards to deer and other targets with low reflectivity. The new device has automatic rain and scan modes, a target quality indicator and an accuracy indicator. Also, for the forgetful, a 10-second automatic shut-off. It weighs little more than an ordinary 7x42 binocular – about 34

▲Burris Laser Rangefinder.

Too much binocular power won't let you glass offhand. Heavy binocs keep you out of places like this.

Long-range target scopes appeal to varmint hunters, even on AR-15s. New models are proliferating.

Tactical-style adjustments with resettable zeros help with distant targets, when you have time to dial.

ounces – and lists for $1017. In the same weight and price range you can also get a Burris 12x32 image-stabilizing binocular. Gyro-driven, with multi-coated optics, this waterproof, center-focus glass has a stabilizer button. Press it, and high-frequency vibration goes out of the picture. There's also a 16x32 model for about $100 more. In traditional offerings, Burris has a new Landmark II binocular, 8x42 or 10x42, with BaK4 prisms, fully multi-coated lenses and twist-up eyecups. Waterproof and lighter in weight than its predecessor, the Landmark II retails for $226 and $243.

Following the recent introduction of an ultra-lightweight fixed-power scope, the Burris company now has a 12-24x50 variable. It scales less than a pound and focuses down to 40 feet but boasts a 145-foot field of view at 12x and a 100-foot field at 24x (1000 yards). MSRP is just $210.

Bushnell Performance Optics

Few optics firms can match Bushnell for covering the needs of hunters and shooters. Very few even approach Bushnell's volume of sales. New products appear every year at this Kansas City firm. For 2004 a 2-7x32 scope will be added to the mid-priced Legend line, and the Firefly reticle installed on more Elite models. *(The Firefly operates on the principle of a luminous watch dial, "storing" illumination so you get an illuminated reticle without a battery. Shine a flashlight beam briefly into the ocular lens of the scope just before dusk, and as the surrounding light fades, the reticle will begin to glow, helping you aim clearly at dark targets.)* A red-dot sight at Bushnell comes under the Tasco label that the company acquired last year. ProPoint features a red or green 5-minute dot – you choose the color that suits conditions. There's also a new Tasco target/varmint scope, an 8-32x44 with 1/4-minute dot. And a 4-16x40. Three Golden Antler scopes include a 2.5x32 for crossbows. Bushnell's own Elite 3200 line is bigger, with a 2-6x32 pistol (LER) scope. A 3-9x40 Banner will give shotgunners 6 inches of eye relief, for forward mounting on a cantilever bar. The 6-24x40 Banner qualifies as a bona fide varmint scope but costs much less than most.

For up-close shooting, nothing beats the Bushnell HOLOsight. Rather than showing a dot inside the unit, it projects the reticle in front of the sight – at least, that's where it appears to be. The workings of holography were hard to explain long before Bushnell used them in HOLOsights, which are now available with AA power. This new version weighs 9 ounces; the original with smaller batteries scales 6.5. Either is ideal for shotguns and handguns, as well as for rifles in thick cover. For shotgunning, you must raise your cheek off the comb, which is akin to deliberately running a red light. But looking through the HOLOsight, you can break targets from your weak-side

▲New Black Diamond scopes have sleek profiles. Euro Diamonds were announced this year.

Your aim is only as good as your sight. New models offer brighter images, more sophistication.

shoulder that you'd miss shooting with your eye on the rib.

Bushnell's Elite spotting scopes now come with Rainguard lens coatings to prevent sheeting when you're out in the wet. There's a 20-60x80 with either straight or angled eyepiece, and a 20-60x70 and 15-45x60 with straight tubes. Weights: 53, 40 and 27 ounces. The 80mm scopes feature ED glass and can be fitted with optional 20x and 30x long-eye-relief eyepieces. All Elite models are waterproof.

While the Bushnell binocular line is already the most extensive in the industry, three new models have appeared for 2004. The NatureView 8x42 and 10x42 glasses are of roof-prism, center-focus design, with BaK4 prisms and twist-up eyecups. They focus down to 15 feet. One level up is the new Legacy series, comprising six porro-prism models and two roof-prism compacts. The 24-ounce 8x40 will be of most interest to hunters. Most unusual is the 8-24x50 variable, scaling just 31 ounces. All have fully multi-coated optics. In compact binoculars, Bushnell is also offering a new 7x26 Custom that's pocket-ready at 12 ounces – high-quality glass in a small package. Tradition gets left behind in the Image View group, with three new 8x30s and a tiny 7x18 to complement the 10x25. All incorporate a camera, so you can take digital photos of what you're viewing. More sophisticated is the 8x32 Instant Replay binocular, with video capabilities. It will record a 30-second loop or snap digital photos. You can store up to 30 video segments and edit them to make room for more, then download clips to a computer. Bushnell's Laura Olinger cites a QVC television ad that brought 7000 orders for Image View binoculars in an hour.

Bushnell's Yardage Pro Quest, an 8x36 binocular with integral rangefinder, has sold well since its introduction last year. Bushnell now owns about 90 percent of the market in laser rangefinders because, says Olinger, "Since our first in 1995 we've kept improving them without jacking prices beyond reach. The Trophy is the latest model.

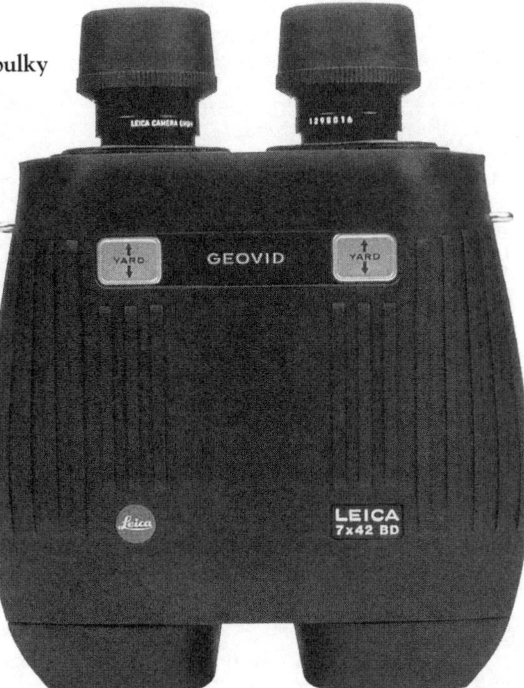

This original Leica Geovid was optically excellent, but heavy, bulky and very expensive.

It sells for as little as $200 but can range reflective objects to 800 yards. To cut costs, we eliminated the zip mode, but we kept the scan." (You can't shoot through brush to a distant target across a field; but you *can* range a *moving* target.) The 6x Yardage Pro Trophy weighs 9 ounces. It's one of half a dozen laser rangefinders in the Bushnell line.

Kahles North America

There's no visible battery housing with a new Helia CSX daylight illuminated reticle for 1.1-4x24 and 1.5-6x42 scopes in the Kahles 30mm line. A knob on the turret contains the light unit and brightness control. Choose the intensity that fits the situation. A red bulb indicates when the illumination is activated, and a safety switch prevents accidental operation. Two reticle styles are available: an illuminated circle dot and an illuminated dot on top of a post. Fully multi-coated optics are standard on all Kahles scopes. These high-quality variables weigh 14.6 and 16.4 ounces and retail at $1443 and $1666, respectively.

Leica

A decade ago the venerable German optics firm Leica introduced the Geovid, a 7x42 binocular with a laser rangefinder built in. Optically excellent, the standard model weighed a hefty 47 ounces, the version with integral compass 52. They retailed for almost as much as a compact car, a reflection of that great Leica glass and sophisticated circuitry. Sales were predictably modest.

The new Geovid BRF announced this year comes as an 8x42 or a 10x42, with a rangefinder that reaches reflective objects at 1300 yards with .05 percent accuracy. "You'll come within 2 yards of actual distance out to nearly 800 yards," adds Terry Moore, long-time Leica representative in the U.S. "A high-visibility LED display automatically adjusts for light conditions, so it's always easy to read. There's just one button to press. Hit it once to activate, and a second time to get a read. Eyecups adjust for glasses." The new Geovid has an aluminum housing, with a soft rubber jacket. It's waterproof to 16 feet and weighs just 32 ounces – a third less than its forebear. List price is about half: $1800 for the 8x, $1850 for the 10x.

Leica's LRF 900 and 1200 are considered among the best laser rangefinders available.

Companies with a reputation for top-end optics often lag in bringing to market the latest electronic products. "Customers expect the very best, and we must deliver," observes Terry. "A firm with products at lower price points can afford to offer new technology before all the bugs are worked out, because the consumers are buying the technology, not primarily optics. Any company with a reputation for excellence will protect that reputation by making sure a new item passes muster." He told me that Leica considered developing an image-stabilizing binocular but backed out because it could not hew to its own high optical standards, ensure ruggedness and price it to compete with stabilized binoculars from Canon, Nikon and kin. Leica *has*, however, succeeded in the rangefinder field. The LRF Rangemaster 800, launched in 2000, has been upgraded. Current LRF 900 and 1200 models reach farther; their lightweight composite bodies measure just 4 inches square and weigh only 11 ounces with battery. Both come with scan modes.

Leupold & Stevens, Inc.

The Vari-X III line that defined Leupold for thousands of hunters who cherished these scopes, is no more. The company has replaced it with the VX-III. The designation is a follow-up to the VX-II and VX-I scopes that emerged a couple of years ago when the firm shelved the old Vari-X II series. The new VX-III scopes look like the Vari-X IIIs at a glance, but new lens coatings make them better, say the folks from the Beaverton, Oregon plant. An improvement even over the Multicoat 4 that distinguished Vari-X IIIs from lesser scopes? Yep. The new coatings are called, collectively, an Index Matched Lens System. In simple terms the IMLS matches coatings to the different types of glass used in a scope's lens system. Rather than use a single recipe that might permit higher reflectivity *(and light loss)* from one lens than from another, engineers specified coatings for individual lenses. The result: up to 98 percent light transmission to your eye. Other refinements in the VX-III include a fast-focus, lockable eyepiece that combines the best attributes of conventional and European ocular housings, and a 30mm tube for scopes with side-mounted focus (parallax correction) dials – to deliver more windage and elevation latitude. The finger-adjustable dials have re-settable pointers to indicate zero. Thirteen models of VX-III scopes are available, from a 1.5-5x20 to a 8.5-25x50. Three offer illuminated reticles. Standard reticles include a "Varmint Hunter's" and a "Boone and Crockett" for long shots. List prices for VX-IIIs range from $500 to $1115.

The VX-II has been improved this year, with the Multicoat 4 lens coatings that such a short time ago came only on Vari-X III and LPS scopes. The power ring on the new VX-II has bump you can feel, and a lockable, fast-focus eyepiece like that of the VX-III. You'll still find 1/4-minute click adjustments – no soft dials at this level since the demise of the Vari-X II. Priced from $325 to 615, six VX-IIs appear in Leupold's current catalog. Magnification ranges: 1-4x to 6-18x. Even the VX-I has undergone surgery for 2004. The 2-7x33, 3-9x40 and 4-12x40, now all come in matte black finish. At $250, $275 and $340, they cost $25 to $30 more than their glossy counterparts. Another change is the Micro-friction windage and elevation dials. You can get new VX-Is with a Wide Duplex reticle that has a more open center (between posts). And finally, a clarification: While the Rifleman scope that popped up in the wake of the VX-I appears to be the same scope, it isn't. Magnification choices and housings are identical, but the Rifleman has no gloss-finish option; matte black is your only choice. The friction dials differ from the VX-1's too; and lenses aren't all multi-coated. The Rifleman costs the same as the glossy VX-1s: $225, $250 and $310. So what inside a scope has the same value as a dull finish?

Leupold's Wind River binocular family has a new member. The Katmai replaces the Denali. Its compact profile and quick-twist eyecups should endear it to hunters. Featuring "L-coated" prisms and fully multi-coated lenses, the Katmai comes in three magnifications: 6x, 8x and 10x. All have 32mm objectives.

Forward mounting puts this Leupold IER scope out of reach of your brow. Expect a smaller field.

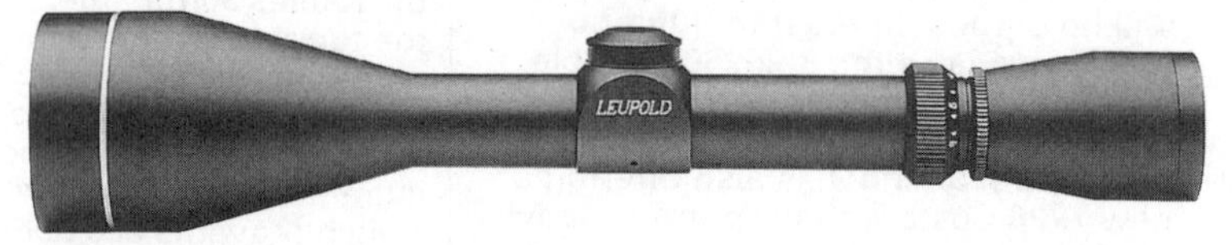

Leupold's VX-II series, new last year, is improved for 2004, with Multicoat 4 lens treatment.

The 6x might remind old-timers of B&L's 6x30 porro prism glasses of long ago. The new glass will be a lot brighter, and you'll still get 5mm of exit pupil. An excellent glass for hunting in mixed cover. Also in Leupold's new line-up: an 8x32 range-finding binocular. The RB800 can range reflective objects out to 900 yards, deer to 550. The RB800C includes a digital compass. Both are waterproof and feature scan modes.

Strong market response to the Leupold Golden Ring Compact 10-20x40, announced last year, prompted the company to offer a 15-30x50 Compact for 2004. At 11 inches and 22 ounces, it's a natural for backpack hunters. The power range is as useful as you'll find; more magnification is hardly ever needed afield.

Nickel

Nickel, a German name in optics that dates back decades, has new life in a scope line that includes illuminated reticles. A standard three-bar black reticle brings your eye to center, where an arrow-shaped dot can be illuminated by turning a left-side dial on the turret. But this ordinary-looking dial is not: Pull

▲Leupold's new VX-III scope line replaces the old Vari-X line, well known to American hunters. The new line appears similar to its predecessors, but has a superior lens coating system.

Wayne likes this Burris 6x; only Leupold and Weaver among other firms offer series of fixed-power sights.

The adjustable objective on this scope enables a rimfire shooter to correct for parallax up close.

it out, and the reticle goes black. So if you're hunting in dim light but don't want to maintain battery contact, dial up the degree of illumination you want, then pull the dial a fraction of an inch to a stop. When you're ready to shoot, you need only hit the dial with your forward thumb as you raise the rifle, instead of having to look at the dial and turn it. Fast. Simple. Good idea. I viewed the Nickel sights at the 2004 IWA Show (the European equivalent of SHOT) in Frankfurt, where I was also impressed by a very slender Nickel 1.5-6x scope delivering 5 full inches of eye relief. Some of the scope tubes were 30mm in diameter, but others had 26mm pipes – just over an inch. This size was once popular not only on the Continent but with makers in the States. The Lyman Challenger, as I recall, had a 26mm tube.

▼The 6-18x40AO joins Nikon's Buckmasters riflescope series; a 4-12x50AO is also new this year.

Nikon, Inc.

New to the Nikon riflescope line is a 6-8x40AO in the Buckmaster series. Its fully multi-coated optics deliver up to 92 percent light transmission. Tall target stems with caps offer 1/8-minute adjustments. Parallax correction is via a ring on the objective bell. Also new to the Buckmasters category is a 4-12x50, again with a front-mounted parallax ring. These two scopes each list for $330. They join five other sights in the Buckmaster stable: 1x20 Black Powder, 4x40, 3-9x40, 3-9x50 and 4.5-14x40. Nikon's economy-class Pro Staff line remains unchanged this year. So too the top-end Monarch UCC family, which includes some of the brightest scopes available. Nikon Monarch Gold 30mm scopes (1.5-6x42, 2.5-10x50 and 2.5-10x56) incorporate turret-mounted parallax dials. The 30mm tactical series offers mil-dot reticles, turret parallax knobs and exceptionally wide adjustment ranges. The 2.5-10x44 is available with illuminated reticle. Tactical models range in price from $900 to $1050.

Nikon binoculars come in several price ranges. The mid-level ATB series has six new Action EX models this year, all of center-focus Porro-prism design. The 7x35 and 8x40 are most portable and feature 490-foot fields of view at 1000 yards. For low-light glassing, pick the 7x50. Long-distance viewing calls for the 10x, 12x or 16x, all with 50mm objectives. These are all waterproof. Corresponding binoculars in the less expensive Action series (also new), plus 7-15x35 and 10-22x50 Action Zooms, feature aspherical ocular lenses. Nikon is also introducing a new waterproof spotting scope, a modestly priced 16-48x60 in both black and Realtree camo finishes. It features phase-corrected prism coatings and fully multi-coated lenses, plus a sliding sunshade and quick-sight notch.

Pentax USA, Inc.

The Pentax line of riflescopes has a new moniker. The XL suffix hints of changes not all clearly described in the catalog. One that's obvious: centered turrets for additional ring space. "PentaBright" technology, plus internal lenses "up to

Minox offers big binoculars like this 8.5x52, and this year a compact new aspheric 10x32.

▲Nikon has several new models in the mid-priced Action EX and economy Action binocular lines.

Nikon's 15-45x60 Spotter has a useful power range, an objective the right size for all-around hunting.

Springfield Armory specializes in military guns. Its powerful scopes have "tactical" features.

▼Camouflage finishes, as on this Nikon TurkeyPro 1.5-4x20, are popular on sights for deer, gobblers.

40% larger than the competition" are harder to confirm. But Pentax scopes do deliver extraordinarily bright images. The new Lightseeker-XL 2.5-10x50, 3-9x43, 3-9x50 and 4-16x44 are priced from $495 to $682. The Lightseeker 30s, from 3-10x40 *(new for 2004)* to 8.5-32x50, list from $599 to $865. Economical Whitetails Unlimited variables continue to offer value. There's a new 4.5-14x42, at $497. Others, from 3-9x40 to 6.5-20x50, retail from $348 to $698.

Pentax binoculars now include a pair of new hunting glasses: DCF XP 8x33 and 10x33. They're roof-prism models, phase-corrected with center focus, click-stop diopter ring and twist-up eyecups. Fully multi-coated and waterproof, they complement new UCF-X and UCF-WP compact Porro-prism binoculars, both available in 8x25 and 10x25 versions. Suggested list for the DCF XPs is $558. The compacts range in price from $127 to $182.

Schmidt & Bender, Inc.

Among riflescopes for big game hunting, none is more versatile than a 1.5-6x42. At Germany's prestigious firm of Schmidt & Bender, that scope has been fitted with a Flash Dot, S&B's luminous reticle. Battery powered, the Flash Dot is controlled by a knob on the left side of the turret. Turn the knob from stops 1 through 6, and you get an increasingly bright dot to use against a dark target or when light levels are low. A neutral click between stop 6 and 7 alerts you to a change in dot intensity. From stops 7 through 11, the dot is noticeably brighter, for use on well-illuminated targets. You can turn the dot off and use the standard black cross-wire by itself. Like other Zenith scopes, the 1.5-6x has Posicon adjustment dials. Each shows where the reticle is in relation to the tube, so you're aware of erector tube position before movement of the vertical dial restricts movement of the horizontal dial and vice versa. Each can be calibrated and set to zero.

The 30mm tube gives you a wide adjustment range. The 7mm exit pupil at 6x is as big as you can use in the poorest light, while the company's multi-coat lens treatments deliver bright, sharp images under all conditions. A replacement battery for the Flash Dot is cleverly hidden under the lateral adjustment cap. At 21 ounces, the S&B 1.5-6x Zenith FD is not lightweight. And the $1699 list price will challenge some budgets. But this is a superlative sight for all-around big game hunting.

▲Pentax Lightseeker-LX 2.5-10x50mm riflescope.

▼Pentax Lightseeker-30: 3-10x40mm riflescope.

Sightron, Inc.

Sightron's latest SII scopes are of sensible dimensions and useful magnification. The 3-9x36AO model also features a parallax ring up front. Its compact profile and close-up focus distance of 30 feet make this 3-9 an ideal mate for a 22 rimfire rifle or an air gun. The scope retails for $356. Also new: an SII 3-9x32RF, specifically designed for rimfire shooting with zero parallax at 50 yards. Lighter and even trimmer than its AO companion, it's a natural for slim, lightweight rifles. Price: $156. Another Sightron introduction: SI 3-9x40GL in high gloss finish at $205. The Sightron catalog features many other scopes, plus red dot sights, binoculars and spotting scopes.

Springfield Armory

Significant design changes mark the 2004 riflescopes listed by Springfield Armory. But a tactical heritage is still obvious. From the 6x40 to the 6-20x50, they feature range-finding reticles, ballistic drop compensators, illuminated cross-wires, mil dots. Only the 3-9x42 and the 3.5-10x50 look like the hunting sights you might get from manufacturers focused on the domestic market. That isn't to say Springfield's sophisticated scopes can't be used on hunting rifles. Their multi-coated optics and click adjustments, fast-focus eyepieces and patented gear zoom systems benefit sportsmen, too. Four of the 15 scopes in this line have 1-inch tubes; the others are all 30mm. A clever device found in each is an internal bubble level at the bottom of the scope field to tell you if you're canting. Target knobs are standard on 4-16x50 models, BDC knobs on 6-20x50 scopes. Prices for this new generation of Springfield optics range from $419 to $899. The Geneseo, Illinois firm is perhaps best known for its series of M1A rifles and autoloading pistols. But the optics offer value – and features you'll find in few other sights.

Swarovski Optik N.A.

Americans used to clamping scopes in rings might take a tip from Europeans, who've been putting rails on scopes for a long time. The mount grips the rail, so the scope isn't pressured or damaged. Squeezing a tube by tightening rings can impair the mountings of internal lenses and actually change inter-lens distances, affecting focus. Alas, mounts for rails are costly and hard to find in the U.S. But Swarovski is betting that some shooters will buy into its new SR scope line. The integral toothed rail on PH 1.25x24, PH 1-6x42 and PH 3-12x50 scopes actually makes the tube stronger. With these scopes (all retailing for over $1000), you'll have no ring scars, and the scope won't slip, no matter how stiff the recoil.

Swarovski has also engineered a clever and lightweight bracket for its STS spotting scopes. The new device allows you to mount a camera on the scope and photograph what you see through the lens. A full range of adjustments permits exact positioning. The mount also allows you to swing the camera away, then return it to its preset place.

Another long-awaited development from the Austrian firm is its 8x30 laser rangefinder. Called the Laser Guide, it lists for $888 and will instantly show distances to targets as far as any hunter has any business shooting – and beyond. A quick-draw hip pouch is available. It holds the unit securely, even when you run, but gives immediate and easy access when you need it. The Laser Guide has a scan mode but no extra buttons. "We kept it simple," says Jim Morey, president of Swarovski of North America. "Like all Swarovski products, quality was a priority. The optics in this rangefinder are peerless. It's the kind of instrument a serious hunter will want."

Swift Instruments, Inc.

The Swift line of riflescopes includes both variable and fixed-power models in magnifications of 1.5x-4x5x to 8-32x. New on the charts are variables with mil-dot reticles: a 4.5-14x and a 6-18x, both with 44mm objectives. Also for 2004, you'll find a 3-9x40 airgun scope, and a 6.5-20x44. They have target turrets, adjustable objectives and sunshades. Handgunners should like the 2-6x32 LER scope. As with the Swift 4x32 and 2x20 pistol sights, it's zeroed for parallax at 50 yards. Swift scopes are priced from $50 to $290. Illuminated reticles, available on two riflescopes, are extra.

Weaver Optics

You'll recall that Weaver, an all-American name for decades, became like many small companies a subsidiary of larger firms. It last sold to Meade Optical, which at the same time got the Simmons and Redfield brands. Weaver's scope selection hasn't changed much in the ensuing year, which is a good thing if you like these sights. Most shooters see them as excellent values. Weaver scopes have the blessing of history, and the fixed-power "K" sight has survived (hallelujah!) a number of corporate restructurings.

Among new releases, there's a T-10 target model (no AO) with quarter-minute click adjustments and a 1/8-minute dot reticle. It weighs just one pound, has a 40mm objective lens and comes in black satin finish. The other notable offering is a T-24, also with a 40mm front end. The parallax (AO) adjustment is via a traditional forward ring. At 17 ounces, the T-24 is very lightweight for its magnification. Choose a 1/8-minute dot or a 1/2-minute dot. The new T-10 retails for $420, the T-24 for $450.

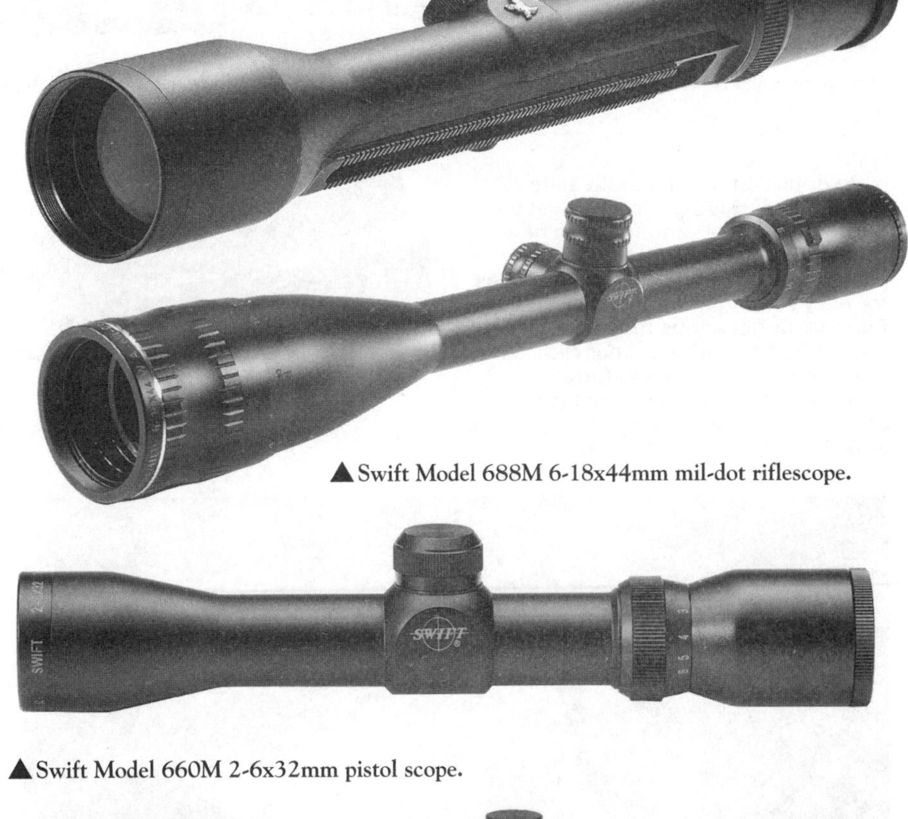

Swarovski's new rail mount scope tube promotes a rigid, no-slip connection to the rifle.

▲ Swift Model 688M 6-18x44mm mil-dot riflescope.

▲ Swift Model 660M 2-6x32mm pistol scope.

▲ Swift Model 687M 4.5-14x44mm mil-dot riflescope.

Zeiss

Four years ago, Zeiss brought a new line of scopes to market. The Conquests offered high optical quality at a relatively modest price. They've been followed now by three new Conquests, all with 50mm objectives for enhanced light transmission at dawn and dusk. The 3-9x50, 3.5-10x50 and 4.5-14x50 have 1-inch alloy tubes and reticles in the second focal plane *(where it stays the same apparent size through the power range)*. All Conquest scopes have Zeiss MC multicoating on every air-to-glass surface, to minimize light loss inside the tube. Available in black matte and stainless finishes, they're waterproof, fog-proof, and come with a plex reticle. The new 3-9x, 3.5-10x and 4.5-14x Conquests weigh 17, 18 and 20 ounces and list for $550, $700 and $800. In addition, Zeiss is listing a high-powered variable under the Conquest label. The 3-12x56 comes in response to continued demand for sights that match the reach of magnum rifles. With 3.2 inches of eye relief, this Zeiss is shooter-friendly, but unlike its stablemates, the 3-12x56 features a 30mm alloy tube. That big pipe helps deliver more than 30 inches of windage and elevation adjustment. Field of view is 9.9 to 27.6 feet at 100 yards. The scope weighs 25.8 ounces and retails for $1050. Add $20 for a brushed-stainless finish.

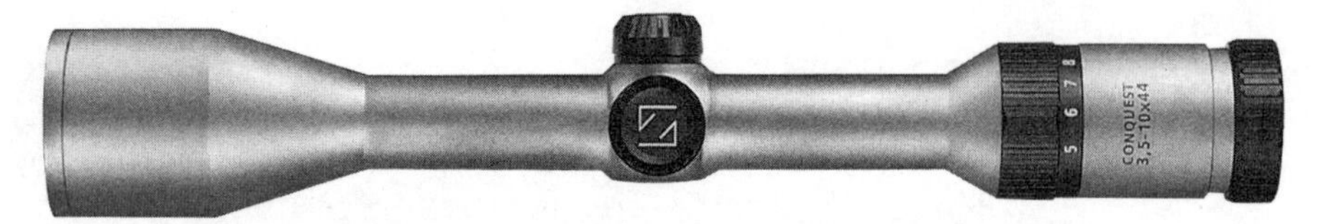

The popular Zeiss Conquest riflescope line is now expanded to include models with 50mm objectives.

In optics, prices generally reflect quality; and truly few scopes rival the Zeiss VM/V. This year, there's a new model. The 6-24x56 has the largest elevation range in its class: 57.6 inches for easy zeroing at long distance. External target knobs move point of impact half a centimeter per click. A quick-focus eyepiece and turret-mounted parallax adjustment (55 yards to infinity) deliver a perfect sight picture almost instantly. To trim weight without compromising optical quality, Zeiss equipped this scope with "Advanced Optical System" lenses – thin, lead- and arsenic-free glass. Zeiss T* coatings ensure top light transmission, especially in the blue wavelengths incident at dawn and dusk. Eye relief is 3.1 inches. With a 5.2-foot field at 24x and an 18.6-foot field at 6x, the VM/V 6-24x56 is available in black and stainless finishes for $1500 ($1900 with an illuminated reticle).

At the other end of the magnification range is the Zeiss Z-Point, a red-dot sight announced last year but not available until recently. Just 1.7 inches high, 1.4 inches wide and 2.5 inches long, it weighs only 3.5 ounces and is designed to mount on a 1913 Picatinny rail. A side-mounted button gives you a choice of three brightness ranges. After you select one, the diode automatically adjusts to light conditions. The dot operates on a 3-volt lithium battery but also has a solar cell to provide extended illumination. At home on slug-shooting shotguns and rifles built for fast game up close, the Z-Point lists for $450.

The Zeiss VM/V shown here is a predecessor to the new 6-24x56.

Zeiss is keen to compete in the mid-priced binocular arena and has this year fielded a companion line to its Conquest riflescopes. Conquest binoculars include 8x30, 10x30, 12x45 and 15x45 models, all with Pechan prisms and phase-correction coatings. The company's proprietary T* lens coatings maximize light transmission. Pull-out eyecups can be locked in position. All models feature center focusing, with a close-focus range of 10 feet for the 8x and 10x, 16 feet for the others. Prices: $550, $600, $700 and $750.

Also at Zeiss this year; the QCA or Quick Camera Adaptor. It's a mechanical device that fits on your Zeiss Diascope FL65 or FL85 spotting scope, allowing you to photograph through the lens. It offers a full range of adjustments so you can position almost any popular camera in just the right spot. A stop knob allows you to preset lens-to-lens distance so you can reposition a camera in seconds. Want to use camera and scope alternately? The QCA's swinging arm gets the camera out of the way when you don't need it. A tilt feature allows use of this adapter on both angled and straight eyepieces. Listing for $350, the QCA is a lot less expensive than a camera lens to match the power and clarity of a Diascope! ●

Thompson/Center made this G2 Contender rifle in 375 JDJ, but the scope was imported for T/C.

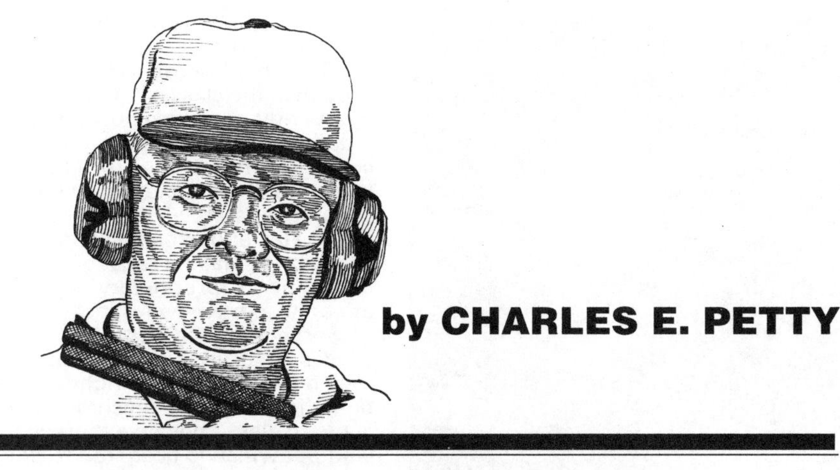

by CHARLES E. PETTY

HANDLOADING UPDATE

TO BE BLUNT there haven't been too many things in handloading over the last few years that have made a lasting impression on my loading habits. New cartridges come along and I almost always work with them for a while, but the guns normally end up in the back corner of the safe or, more commonly, being returned to the manufacturer. Somehow I always end up with time-tested guns and cartridges.

One area where new products have truly, permanently, changed the way I do things is in the powders I use all the time. When I learned how to reload there weren't very many choices. Handguns were loaded with Bullseye, Unique and 2400 and shotguns used Red Dot. Rifles were a bit more complex but whenever possible I used surplus Hodgdon 4831 or IMR 4895.

Today I rarely use any of those. Hodgdon Varget is very similar to 4895 and is useful in a wide range of cartridges. It's not the only rifle powder I use but is often the starting point when I work up loads for moderate-size cases.

Almost every handgun cartridge that I shoot regularly with cast bullets is loaded with Hodgdon Titegroup. Those cartridges include: 32 S&W Long, 32-20, 38-40, 44-40, 44 Special and 45 Colt. Jacketed bullets in either 45 ACP or 9mm Luger get Alliant Power Pistol. I got to this point over a long period of time based upon two basic criteria: accuracy and consistent velocity. Some folks think those two are closely related. I don't, for I have seen superb accuracy with loads that had velocity spreads of 100 fps or more. It is obviously desirable to have things as consistent as possible, but that alone does not guarantee accuracy.

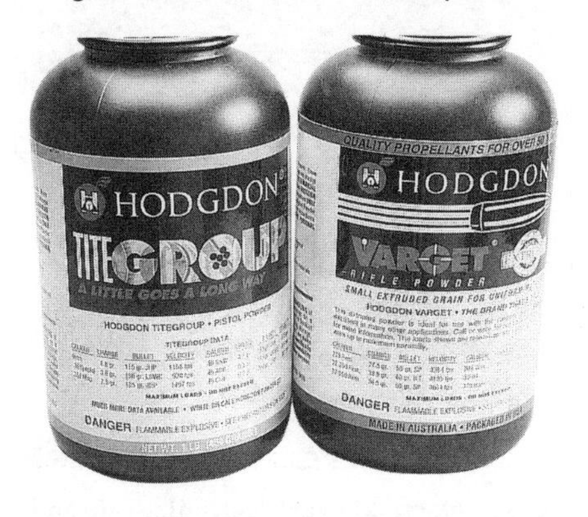

Hodgdon Titegroup and Varget.

Titegroup and Power Pistol are different as night and day. Titegroup is a fast-burning powder that is a bit slower than Bullseye in burning rate although it is, by Hodgdon's nomenclature, a "Spherical" powder it looks suspiciously like powders sold by Winchester. It should. It is made in the same place. Olin Corporation sold their St. Marks, Florida plant and it is now known as St. Marks Powder Co. and the identifier begins with, "SMP" followed by some numbers. They make many commercial powders used throughout the industry in addition to the canister powders sold by Winchester and Hodgdon.

Alliant Power Pistol is an extruded, small-grain powder that is a little slower than Unique. It began life as a commercial powder called Bullseye 84. Commercial powders are sold within the industry and are a bit different from the canister powders you and I can buy. The ammo factories routinely do pressure and velocity testing during the day and, when they open a new can of powder, test and make adjustments–if they need to. If there is a little variation from one batch to the next it's no big deal for them, but we don't have that facility so the stuff we buy needs to be very consistent so we can use standard loading data.

One event of last year could either pass unnoticed or produce sweeping change in the way we think of powders. "IMR" stands for improved military rifle and for generations if you said "IMR"

Tom Shepherd of Hodgdon introduces IMR powder.

everyone knew you were getting a powder made by the legendary DuPont family of companies that, of course, also included Remington Arms. It was completely logical for DuPont to make powder since it was a core business dating back to 1802 and a little powder mill on Brandywine Creek near Wilmington, Delaware. In the shadow of the Great Depression, Remington was purchased and operated until 1993. DuPont had begun, in what some called a move toward political correctness, to distance themselves from things that went *bang* or *boom*. Most folks didn't know that the manufacture of IMR powder had moved to Canada, at least partly because of an explosion at the U.S. plant. IMR Powder Co. was formed but manufacturing was done by Expro-Tec in Valley Field Canada, a suburb of Montreal. It has been that way for a long time and consumers who weren't paying attention might have missed it because all the packaging was exactly the same—except for the company name, and that was in small print.

In late 2003 Hodgdon purchased the IMR Powder Company. This is one of those deals that hadn't generated any rumors until one day a press release came out announcing the purchase. Hodgdon has purchased the IMR trademark, powder formulas and intellectual property—and has exclusive marketing rights for the states. All packaging has moved to Kansas. Hodgdon did not buy as much as a brick, and manufacturing will continue in Canada. Hodgdon will be able to tweak powder specifications, and there are hints that we'll see some new powders in the future.

According to Hodgdon president Tom Shepherd the only change the consumer will notice will be a shift from the metal cans we're so used to, to the plastic containers Hodgdon is already

Allan Jones of Speer shows the new 38 Special bullet to John Taffin.

using. The labeling will be the same and the color scheme will be preserved. One of the best things about DuPont and IMR powders was that each had a distinctive color all its own. I always liked that because one quickly learned the color of the powders used most often and I could grab them off the shelf without having to sort through a bunch of similar-looking cans.

There are a few new powders intended for some specialized niches within the broad spectrum of canister powders. **Alliant** has two shotgun powders that will almost surely find a place in handgun loads as well. First is "410" designed specifically for the .410-bore shotgun. If this works as well in small cases like the 221 Fireball, as does Hodgdon's competing "Lil'Gun," it is going to be lots of fun. The other has a name that will need explanation. It is called "e3" and is a faster-burning propellant intended for 12-gauge target loads. The name is derived from characteristics of "energy, efficiency and excellence". Alliant reports it should do very well in target-level handgun loads, too.

Western Powder is introducing Ramshot Hunter, an imported ball-type powder. It is geared toward the assorted short, and super short, magnum cartridges and should also do nicely in medium-size cases, up to and including 280 Remington and 30-06 Springfield.

Bullet Stuff

Everyone who sells component bullets always has "new" offerings-usually just a different weight of the same bullet types-but there are some innovations to report.

One of the real gaps in the bullet market is for a 38 Special bullet that will perform well from the 2-inch barrels that almost everyone uses for small carry guns. The "good ole boys" at **Speer** have three of their Gold Dot bullets crafted especially for the snubguns. There are 110-, 135- and 147-grain offerings, but Speer seems to be most proud of the 135. Samples loaded to +P levels fired from a 2-inch barrel are reported to penetrate the magic 12" and expand to over 50-caliber.

The Gold Dot is one of the best of the premium hollowpoints and takes advantage of Speer's ability to plate lots of copper onto a swaged lead core. This is exactly the same process they use to make their TMJ *(totally metal jacketed)* bullets—but then they poke a hole in the nose to create a hollowpoint. The Gold Dot is actually the remnant of the plating that is driven to the bottom of the hollowpoint.

The other hot topic in bullets is the growth in the class of "bonded" bullets. Everybody has some now and there is a definite appeal to this type of construction. The idea is to bond the lead core to the bullet jacket so the two will not separate as the bullet penetrates and expands in game. The process for making most of them is described as "proprietary" but there are only so many ways it can be done.

Some might call Speer's Hot-Cor process a form of bonding because they pour molten lead right into the bullet jacket on the machine. Actually, it's very clever because there is a lead pot which is triggered to pour a fixed amount every time a jacket comes by. Technically speaking, it is not bonding but the procedure does reduce what is called "slippage" between core and jacket.

Another variation is in the manufacture of **"Trophy Bonded Bear Claw"** bullets. In this one a bit of flux and a lead core are inserted in jackets arranged in a plate with lots of holes. Then the entire unit goes into a furnace and is heated almost red-hot. This "solders" the lead to the jacket and makes a strong physical bond. The bullet then goes through traditional forming operations. The appeal of bonded bullets is that they lose very little weight as they expand and penetrate.

The **Barnes X-bullet** has always been a great game bullet, but sometimes was a challenge because of the large bearing surface. Barnes has now introduced the "Triple-shock X-bullet" that has three grooves in the shank of the solid copper bullet. This doesn't seem to change the way the bullet expands but has significantly reduced the bearing surface to allow for higher velocities at standard pressures. The grooves also appear to be beneficial in the accuracy department for some limited shooting I've done found them to be very accurate.

The Year of the Scale

Digital electronic scales are one of the best things to happen to reloaders

Speer Gold Dot 38 Special bullets in 110-, 135- and 147-grain weights. The expanded bullet is the new 135-grain Gold Dot fired from a 2-inch barrel.

RCBS Charge Master electronic scale and powder dispenser.

Lyman's array of scales with the Powder Pal combination weighing pan/powder funnel.

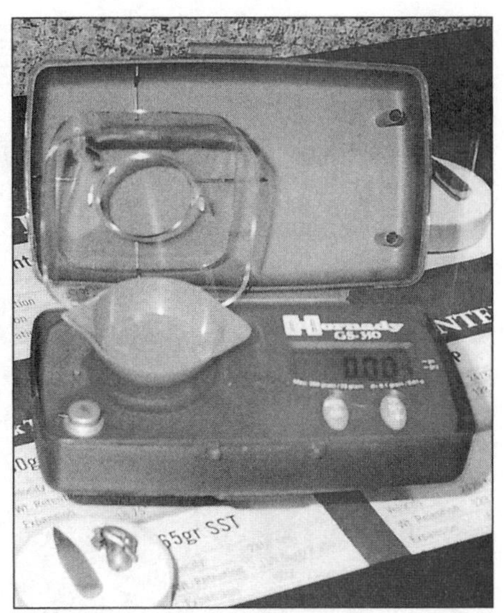

Hornady's new scale.

in a long time. At first they were terribly expensive, but as it is with all electronic gadgets the price has been cut in half–and then half again–to the point where some cost very little more than a good-quality beam balance.

This year Lyman, Hornady and RCBS all have at least one addition, and Lyman has two. Most of these are relatively small units that have the advantage of portability. The idea of being able to take one to the range with you is surely appealing but requires considerable care to have everything come out right. First of all is the great sensitivity of the electronic scales that makes them subject to wild swings with just a little breeze. It is surely possible to shield them from wind, but that's a bit troublesome. Another issue is that electronic scales can be caused to drift by changes in temperature. This doesn't mean that you can't use them outdoors, for you surely can, but it does mean it is a very good idea to check the calibration frequently.

Last year we saw Lyman enter the digital powder dispenser market with their 1200 Digital Powder System to compete with units sold by RCBS and PACT. The only difference between them was the color of the box—both were made by PACT. Now RCBS is showing a unit of their own, called the Charge Master, which is being made offshore. The only criticism I ever had with the original was that it seemed to be pretty slow. PACT has gone through a complete re-design to produce a unit that is twice as fast. It's in the same box as the original but all the innards are new. I'm not sure that we really need to weigh each and every powder charge, but the improved speed makes it much more convenient to do so if you wish.

New Cartridges and Dies

We've got at least three new cartridges that were shown at the SHOT Show in February. Hornady is making the 204 Ruger and Winchester has the latest addition to the WSSM family, a 25-caliber that looks just like the others. And then there is the 50GI, a proprietary 50-caliber cartridge designed to work in a Government Model-size pistols, that looks exactly like the old 45 we know and love. Guncrafter Industries is offering the gun, ammo, brass and loading dies. There are two factory loads at this writing, both using Speer's 300-grain TMJ bullet. One is loaded to around 700 fps, with recoil comparable to 45 ACP ball ammo; another at around 900 fps. that feels a lot like the early 10mm Auto ammo. Neither is as severe in recoil as the bigger 50s. It is an interesting concept, but very early in the process right now.

Of course, the 500 S&W is still getting lots of interest. The latest wrinkle is the availability of carbide sizing dies from RCBS. I'm sure the carbide is going to be an improvement, but the case is so big and has so much area to size that RCBS recommends lubricant still be applied to the case, anyhow. They also offer carbide sizing dies for the 480 Ruger and 475 Linebaugh cartridges. Redding has added steel dies, as has Lyman.

RCBS Charge Master on left; Baby Grand shotshell press on right.

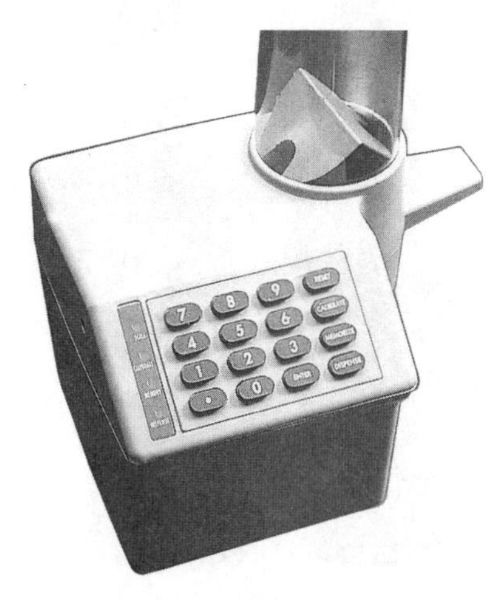

PACT digital powder dispenser.

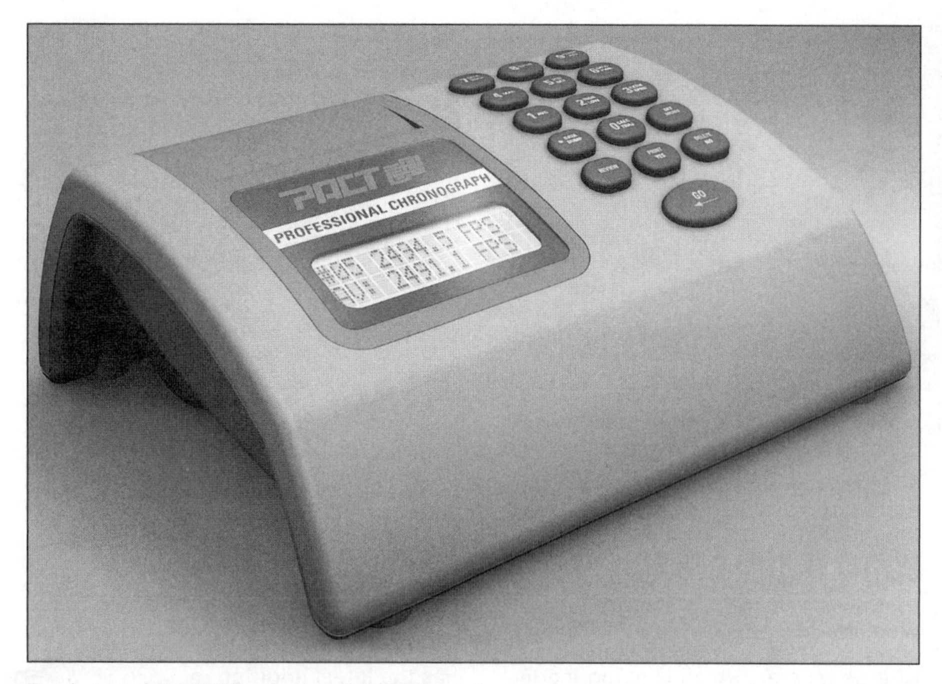

Re-designed PACT Professional Chronograph.

Redding's Imperial Sizing Die Wax.

We've got new .500" jacketed bullets from Hornady (350-grain XTP) and Sierra (400-grain JSP and 350-grain JHP), and Barnes has added to their solid copper offerings with 325- and 385-grain spitzer styles. The big .50 also lends itself very well to big, fat lead bullets and **Cast Performance Bullet Company,** the original supplier for factory ammo, has 370-, 400- and 440-grain in the LBT style with gas checks. **Liberty Shooting Supplies** also offers a 430-grain flatnose with a plain base. These things really don't need to be driven flat-out to be effective hunting loads for most anything in North America, and I found the 400-grain offering to be super-accurate and easy to shoot at around 1100 fps.

Everyone seems to have dies for the WSSM family of cartridges and Hornady showed the new 204 Ruger. It's funny how things catch your eye sometimes and that's what happened at the **Forster** booth. They've always had super dies and now they've really improved the box they come in.

This isn't really new, and in fact is so old odds are good that the current generation of reloaders have never heard of it. The product is Imperial Sizing Die Wax and it is now being manufactured and sold by **Redding Reloading Equipment.** We've got umpteen various case-sizing lubricants—and for general purpose use most work just fine, but if you're going to do any aggressive case-forming or have something that, for some reason, is hard to size, this is the stuff to use. It comes in a small tin that is probably a lifetime supply for most users and the only thing different is that it is green now. *(I'm sure you've noticed that manufacturers of reloading stuff are incredibly color conscious)* The best way to use it is to just smear a little on your fingers and then rub the case. It doesn't take much and it's pretty hard to over-lube with it, although I'm sure you can. With liquid lubricants it is easy to leave too much on the case and end up with a dimple at the bottleneck. I found that a rag dampened with rubbing alcohol easily takes off the lube.

Another gadget that isn't new but is so handy that it deserves more mention is **Lyman's "Powder Pal"** scale pan and powder funnel. This is only for digital scales. One side has a funnel that seems to fit just about everything *(I've used it for 45-70)* and all you do is dispense the charge into the pan and then go straight to the case. It's one of those inexpensive little things that helps a bunch and makes you wonder why nobody thought of it before.

It seems as if this is a year with something for everyone. We've got a couple of new cartridges from Winchester and Hornady that will keep folks like me off the streets but probably the most important news is that we've got lots of stuff to make the job of loading a little easier. I really do like electronic scales and powder dispensers. Only a prototype of RCBS's new Charge Master was available at the SHOT Show but I've been using the improved PACT model for awhile and find it to be much improved.

Rest Well, Old Friend

Any of you who called the RCBS customer service line over the last 20-30 years probably spoke to Jay Postman. He was the voice of RCBS to generations of reloaders... myself included... and the guy with the Santa Claus beard that was in RCBS print ads for years. Never have I known anyone with such an encyclopedic memory. Even after I became reasonably proficient at this stuff, tough questions were often most easily answered by getting Jay on the phone. He delighted in telling me where to find answers in GUN DIGEST or *The American Rifleman* ––right down to the issue and even page number. Never once was he wrong. Jay died unexpectedly not long ago and there's a little empty space in the world now that will never be filled. ●

25 WSSM

Robert Ruch of Forster, with their new die box.

Reference

Guncrafter Industries
171 Madison 1510
Huntsville, AR 72740
(479)-665-2466
www.guncrafterindustries.com

by RAYMOND CARANTA

THE GUNS OF EUROPE

SIG SAUER

A European Technological Venture

SIG-SAUER IS a partnership between two European companies: SIG (Schweizerische Industrie Gesellschaft) in Switzerland, and Germany's J.P. SAUER & SOHN for the design, development and production of an original line of automatic pistols and rifles. This partnership developed as a result of international events beyond the control of the two managements.

For SIG, it was a Swiss political decision prohibiting the export of war materiel from the Helvetic Confederation territory where they were developing a new sophisticated pistol, the P220. For Sauer & Sohn, it was the German collapse of 1945—and the subsequent Soviet occupation—that led to the company's relocation, in 1951, to Eckernförde, in western Germany, a Baltic Sea island located 20 miles north of Kiel. There, the renovated company, employing 500 people in 1953, focused on the manufacture of deluxe sporting rifles and shotguns. However, management was reminiscing about the time they made some of the best pistols of the period... Obviously, it was time for a meeting!

SIG, the Schweizerische Industrie Gesellschaft

It was founded in 1853 as the "Swiss Railway Truck Company" near "Schaffhausen", for building cars and trucks. Then, the workforce consisted of 150 people (1). Seven years later, it included a gunmaking department responsible for the manufacture(under license) and maintenance of the Belgian Prelaz-Burnand percussion rifle Model 1842/59, adopted by the Swiss army.

Subsequently, the company took its current name of SIG in 1863. Later, in 1866, the gunmaking department became a 'division' when its second manager, Frederic Vetterli, invented a successful military bolt-action repeating rimfire rifle, the "Vetterli"—featuring a Winchester-style 12-shot tubular magazine. The following year, this gun became the Swiss service model until 1889, when it was superseded by the Schmidt-Rubin that fired smokeless powder cartridges.

Subsequently, SIG and others participated in the development and production of all Swiss military rifles in connection with the Bern Waffenfabrik, up to 1955.

Among the gun design achievements for which SIG is responsible, let us mention the development of the Mexican Mondragon semi-automatic rifles—1893 to 1911; several advanced families of submachine guns over 40 years—1920 to 1960; plus the design and production of the delayed-blowback Stgw 57 (Swiss service model from 1957 to 1982), and the SG 510 assault rifles.

More recently, in the '60s, SIG shifted to gas operation for their 5.56 mm assault rifles of the SG 530, SG 540 and SG 550 lines; the latter currently in production as the SG 552 "Commando." However, the most famous SIG gun is an automatic pistol, the 30-caliber and 9mm Luger P210, adopted by the Danish and

▶ The Sauer & Sohn model 1913 was a very compact and accurate blowback 32 ACP pistol (*oal = 5.63"*) featuring a fixed barrel. It was used by the German military during World War I and became a favorite police model thereafter.

The Sauer & Sohn 32 ACP model 38 (H) featured both a selective double-action lock and a convenient drop-hammer lever located behind the trigger guard opening.

Swiss armies in 1949. The accuracy and workmanship of this exceptional pistol are such that it is still in such demand by gun enthusiasts that new sporting versions have been developed and introduced in 2001 and 2003. Introduced in 1956 on the American market at $98.50, a basic P210-1 in excellent condition now brings over $2250, second-hand!

▶ The famous SIG P210 9mm Luger eight-shot single-action Swiss and Danish service pistol was designed for 50-meter offhand shooting.

▶ An engraved and gold inlaid SIG P210 pistol.

▶ The current Swiss army 9mm Luger 9 + 1 shot SIG Sauer P220 selective double-action pistol. Note the skeleton magazine catch under the grip.

J.P. Sauer & Sohn

This famous German company, a family affair, was founded in Suhl, Thuringia, in 1751 (2). It was already singled out by the fact that J.P. Sauer & Sohn was a genuine gun manufactory rather than a custom gunmaking business, as it was then often the case with most German gunsmithing centers.

While specialized for quite a long time in the manufacture of wheel-lock, flint-lock, and—later—percussion rifles and shotguns, the J.P. Sauer & Sohn/ Gewehrfabrik received its first published mention in 1880, for their double shotguns.

Their introduction to the modern handgun world was as a subcontractor in the production of the German military Reichsrevolver Model 1879, in 1883. Sauer & Sohn then introduced a tiny "Bär" repeating pistol, chambered for a special 7mm round, that was manufactured from 1899 to 1911—and perhaps a bit longer.

The company entered the modern autoloading pistol age in 1904, with a sophisticated long recoil-operated Roth-Sauer model chambered for another special cartridge, this time in 32-caliber (71-grain jacketed bullet @ 1070 fps). This expensive gun (58 gold Marks in 1911, or $14.40 ex works), patented in 1905 by Mr. Georg Roth, was a refinement of an 1895 Karel Krnka design.

It was followed, in 1913, by an original Sauer-patented blowback seven-shot pistol chambered for the popular 32 ACP (71-grain jacketed bullet @ 900/950 fps). Used by the German military during World War I, and by many police organizations thereafter, this compact Sauer model 1913 was perfected in 1930, and culminated in a Behorden modell featuring a trigger automatic safety. During that same period, J.P. Sauer & Sohn also made three variations of small 25 ACP automatic pistols: the two WTM, and the Model 33. Their total production exceeded 200,000 guns at the eve of World War II.

However, during the 1930s, J.P. Sauer & Sohn, like their other German competitors, was severely affected by the blazing success of the Walther PP and PPK selective double-action pistols. Therefore, the company started in 1932 the development of what was to become the famous Sauer 38 (H) model of 1938.

This Sauer 38 (H) was a hammerless blowback selective double-action pistol chambered in 32 ACP, with an 8-shot magazine capacity. However, its leading feature was a drop-hammer safety, still one of the most advanced yet designed.

This model was released too late — just before the war— to realize the large commercial distribution it deserved, but approximately 140,000 of these Sauer 38 (H) pistols were produced before the 1945 Armistice.

This clever drop-hammer device was operated by a side lever, conveniently located on the receiver behind the trigger guard opening, thus avoiding the sophisticated firing pin of the Walther slide safety design. Of course, it was to be used again for the SIG Sauer P220 pistol family.

A 9mm Luger German police P6 SIG Sauer compact pistol.

The SIG Sauer P220 pistol requirements

By the end of the '60s, the Swiss services were fully equipped with P210 pistols, while new selective double-action designs were under study in several engineering departments of the United States, Germany, Italy, Austria and Czechoslovakia.

Moreover, directly related to the continuous Swiss currency appreciation, cost of the precision-machined SIG pistol was becoming prohibitive for the export market *($220 for the basic P210-1 on the American market in 1970, against $125 for a Colt "Government" or "Commander", and $110 for a Smith & Wesson Model 39!).*

For SIG to remain competitive, the Swiss designers had to dramatically reduce product costs, while providing customers with a simple, light, and compact multi-caliber pistol design meeting the stringent 50-meter (55 yards) accuracy and 10,000 rounds endurance requirements of their national services, and featuring a drop-hammer safety device potentially better than the P-38 type, then considered as the best for the last 30 years!

The SIG Sauer P220 Pistol Design

In short, the SIG Sauer designers were able to reduce costs by using a light alloy receiver, a stamped sheet-metal slide with an inside-pinned breechblock, and by simplifying the former P210 Browning/Colt-style expensive tilting barrel design, which featured a dual ramp at the breech end. By remaining faithful to a tilting barrel design, they still had a reliable and basically economical construction but by shifting to a square breech —self-centering in a matching square slide recess — they were able to satisfactorily increase the accuracy level up to the 50-meter requirement. Moreover, thanks to the new barrel design—featuring a single ramp and a single upper shoulder—cost was reduced further.

Concerning the 10,000-round service life with a light alloy receiver design, they protected the barrel ramp recess by fitting a sturdy hollow steel block in it, against which the recoil spring guide bottomed. Also, the slide grooves of the receiver were duly enlarged so as to increase the bearing surface.

As previously mentioned, the excellent Sauer 38 (H) drop-hammer lever was adapted to the SIG Sauer P220 rebounding outside-hammer design, providing it with one of the most advanced safety devices to date!

The P220—released in 1973—featured a single-stack magazine with the release located under the grip, as dictated by the European World War II experience. Being 7.8 inches long x 5.63 inches high x 1.34 inches wide, it weighed 29.6 oz. empty and could be chambered in 22 Long Rifle (10 + 1 rounds), 30 Luger, 9mm Luger, 38 Super Auto (9 + 1 rounds), and 45 ACP (7 + 1 rounds).

The dual-mode trigger let-off was also lighter than that of typical P-38s at 3.75-lb. SA and 10-lb. DA for the basic version. Now, 30 years later, the magazine catch has been relocated on the left side of the receiver, behind the trigger guard opening, in the American way. Solid stainless steel receivers and slides are optional and only the 9mm Luger and 45 ACP (8 + 1 rounds) chamberings are available.

Meanwhile, 160,000 units of the basic 9mm Luger design have been made for the Swiss services and the P220 model has been exported the world over, with more than 100,000 units sold in the United States alone, mostly in 45 ACP.

A heavy IPSC 45 ACP version with 5.47-inch barrel, counter-weight and micrometer rear sight, featuring 3.5lb (SA) and 9.5lb (DA) trigger pulls, called "P220 Sport SL" in the United States and "P220 X-Zone" in Europe, is now available for Practical shooting.

The SIG Suer P226 large-capacity 9mm Luger pistol, a British service model since December 1990.

The SIG Sauer P225 (German Police P6)

Designed in response to a German police requirement of 1974, a compact version of the SIG Sauer P220 *(7.08" long x 5.15" high x 1.34" wide, weighing 29 oz. empty)* was selected in 1980 as the P6 9mm Luger service model, with an 8-shot magazine capacity.

The magazine catch was now located on the side of the frame, and dual concentric recoil springs were fitted to this model, which is highly accurate and the most widely used among German police departments.

The SIG Sauer P226 High-Capacity Family

The 15-shot basic 9mm SIG Sauer P226, released in 1983 (7.7" long x 5.63" high x 1.37" wide, 31-oz empty) was the company's submission to the American "XM9" specification of that same year. It was rejected on cost criteria, which however did not prevent its selection by the British services in December 1990 and by many military and police organizations the world over, including the American DEA in 1999, and other U.S. services.

This year, seven versions of the P226 are listed in the factory catalog.

In my opinion, this gun is one of the most accurate in its class today!

The SIG Sauer P228, P229, P230, P232, P239 and P245 Compact

The SIG Sauer P228 is a compact 13-shot 9mm Luger version of the large-capacity P226 released in 1989 and adopted by the British army and police in 1990—which also became the U.S. M-11 in 1992.

The P228 is 7.08 inches long, 5.35 inches high and 1.22 inches thick; it weighs 29.46 oz., empty. During the U.S. Army selection tests, three specimens, firing a total of 15,000 rounds, had only a single malfunction attributable to the gun (out of 17 allowed)!

The P229 is a similar pistol featuring a solid stainless steel slide, introduced in 1991 following introduction of the 40 SW chambering in 1990. This model is available in 9mm Luger, 357 SIG and 40 SW. The P229 X-Range, known as the P229-Sport in the United States, is a heavy IPSC version of this pistol marketed in 1996 with a 5.15" barrel, in the same chamberings.

The P230 was an elegant blowback double-action pistol principally chambered in 32 ACP and 380 ACP, made from 1973 to 1997. It was superseded in 1997 by the P232, with either a light alloy, or stainless steel receiver, in the two same calibers (6.6" long x 4.68" high x 1.22" thick. 18 or 22.7 oz empty).

The P239 is a smaller and lighter successor to the P225 (6.6" long x 5.12" high x 1.26" wide; 27.5 oz., empty), featuring the solid stainless steel slide design of the P229 and chambered for the same cartridges (8 + 1 shots for 9mm Luger; 7 + 1 shots for 357 SIG and 40 S&W). It was introduced in 1995.

The P245 Compact, introduced in 1999, is a similar version of the 45-caliber P220-1 (6 + 1 shots. 7.28" long x 5.31" high x 1.38" wide. 29 oz., empty).

A compact SIG Sauer P228 9mm Luger 13-shot pistol (U.S. M-11 service model) with the original two-piece slide unit.

The SIG PRO SP 2009, SPC 2009, SP 2022 and SP 2340

All are chambered in 9mm Luger, with the exception of the SP 2340, which is available in 357 SIG and 40 SW. These pistols, mostly intended for police duty, feature polymer receivers, interchangeable lockplates and wrap-around grips of three different sizes, combined with a new slide mounting. They are more economical than the remainder of the SIG Sauer line *(in 2003, $596 in the U.S. vs. $830 for the basic P226).*

The SP 2009, SP 2022 and SP 2340 have the large capacity of the P226 service model *(15 + 1 shots in 9mm Luger and 12 + 1 shots in 40 SW),* but are both smaller *(7.36" long x 5.67" high x 1.38" wide)* and 3.93 oz. lighter, empty.

The SPC 2009, only available in 9mm Luger with a 15 + 1 capacity, is approximately the size of the P228 and P229 models but carries two additional rounds and weighs, respectively, 4 and 5.4 oz. less, empty.

The SP 2022, with the same 9mm magazine capacity, was designed in 2003 to meet specifications of the French police, customs and Gendarmerie. These services have ordered 201,000 units of this model as their unique standard (99,000 for police, 95,000 for Gendarmerie and 7,000 for customs). The SP 2022 differs principally from the basic SP 2009 by its square trigger-guard, a lanyard ring under the grip, a loaded chamber indicator above the ejection port, a transponder registering the handgun service life and a Picatinny rail in front of the trigger guard.

The P229 is a similar pistol, but fitted with an American-made solid stainless steel slide that handles the high-pressure 357 SIG and 40 S&W ammunition.

SIG Sauer Today

As of the first of December 2000, SIG Sauer became a German company, following the sale of the Swiss SIG Arms assets to two Endsdetten investors, Messrs. Michael Lüke and Thomas Ortmeier. The corporate headquarters of the concern is now located at the J.P.

Sauer & Sohn factory of Eckernförde (Schleswig Holstein).

Further to this reorganization, SIG Sauer consists of J.P. Sauer & Sohn in Eckernförde; SIGARMS Inc. (Exeter, New Hampshire U.S.A.); Blaser Jagdwaffen GmbH at Isny Im Allgau, Germany; Hämmerli (Lenzburg, Switzerland) and SAN Swiss Arms AG at Neuhausen-am-Rheinfall, in Switzerland. Overall, 779 people are employed, generating yearly revenue of 139,700,000 Euro.

The current line of SIG Sauer firearms is listed, with specifications and prices, in the catalog section of the GUN DIGEST. Readers having a good command of the French language and wishing to learn more details about this company may find some interest in consulting reference (1) of the bibliography. Reference (2) recalls, in English, the J.P. Sauer & Sohn story in Suhl, up to 1945. •

The SIG Sauer P245 is a compact version of the P220-1 model chambered in 45 ACP, with a 6-round magazine capacity.

Field-stripping a SIG PRO pistol shows the removable lock mechanism.

Bibliography:

SIG SAUER, une épopée technologique européene by Raymond Caranta (in French). Crépin-Leblond Editeur, 52902 CHAUMONT CEDEX 9, France. 2003.

J.P. Sauer & Sohn Suhl (Waffenstadt), by Jim Cate and Martin Krause (in English). Volume II. Walsworth Publishing Co. Marceline, Missouri 64658 U.S.A. 2000.

JP SAUER & SOHN GMBH
Sauerstrasse 2-6
D-24340 - ECKERNFÖRDE
GERMANY

by HOLT BODINSON

AMMUNITION, BALLISTICS & COMPONENTS

HODGDON BUYS THE IMR Powder Company. Imagine what Bruce Hodgdon would have thought. Here was an entrepreneur at the end of WWII, shoveling surplus 4831 out of a boxcar and selling it in paper bags, whose company has gone on to acquire one of Dupont's former crown jewels, IMR. It's a great American business story.

The varmint cartridge rage just keeps raging with the announcement of yet another 17-caliber rimfire, the wee Hornady 17 Mach2, plus the legitimization of the 20-caliber in the form of the 204 Ruger, said to be the fastest commercial cartridge ever offered.

Winchester surprised us once again with the roll out of their 25 WSSM (Winchester Super Short Magnum), following so closely on the heels of the 223 WSSM and the 243 WSSM. Making another rather dramatic, surprise appearance was the short 45 Glock Automatic Pistol (G.A.P.) cartridge that permits Glock to pack the punch of the 45 ACP into a smaller framed pistol.

"Low-recoil," " Managed- recoil," whatever the name, Remington and Federal are actively promoting reduced-power centerfire rifle loads that are aimed at those under 18, over 50, and the female sector of the shooting and hunting public.

In the "Why didn't I think of it" category is Hodgdon's "Xperimental Pack." The same innovative marketing and packaging concept is apparent in Ballistic Products' "Hull Integrated Technology System" packs. There may be a trend developing here—small samples of various reloading components that allow handloaders to develop the best load at the least cost for each firearm.

The commercial bullet makers are doing well as more and more Barnes, Hornady, Nosler, Sierra, Swift and Woodleigh bullets are integrated into the major ammunition lines.

Did you know that Norma–along with RWS, Geco, SM and Hirtenberg–is owned by RUAG of Thun, Switzerland? It's a fascinating story covered in Norma's first real reloading manual released this year.

It's been a busy year in ammunition, ballistics and components.

Aguila

The race is on at Aguila to get their little 17-caliber rimfire, the 17 Aguila, into production and into the marketplace after the surprise introduction by Hornady of its 17-caliber Mach 2 cartridge that is also based on the 22 Long Rifle case.
www.aguilaammo.com

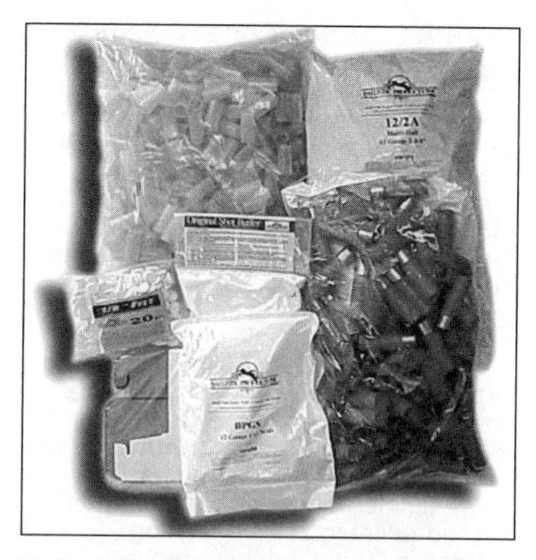

Ballistic Products Prepackaged: Just add powder and shot to Ballistic Products' prepackaged components and you'll produce a true Master load.

Alliant

No new formulations this year in a line that now includes ten shotgun powders, three pistol powders and six rifle powders; however, there is a new, free reloading manual this year chock-full of recipes for the E3 shotgun powder, as well as international shotgun, cowboy action and silhouette competition loadings.
www.alliantpowder.com

American Pioneer Powder

Offering a sulfurless, volume-for-volume, replacement for blackpowder that cleans up with water, American Pioneer is supplying its FFG and FFFG formulas as granular powder, as 100- and 150-grain pre-measured loads, and as 45- and 50-caliber compressed stick charges. Ballistics and accuracy data

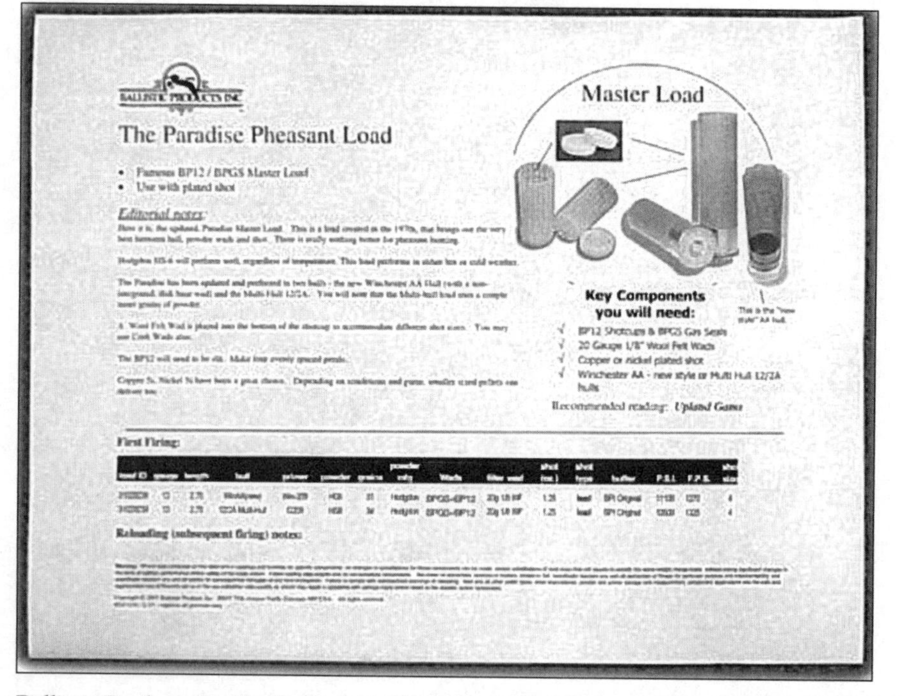

The Paradise Pheasant Load
- Famous BP12 / BPGS Master Load
- Use with plated shot

Editorial notes:

Master Load

Key Components you will need:
- BP12 Shotcups & BPGS Gas Seals
- 20 Gauge 1/8" Wool Felt Wads
- Copper or nickel plated shot
- Winchester AA - new style or Multi Hull 12/2A hulls

Recommended reading: Upland Game

First Firing:

Reloading (subsequent firing) notes:

Ballistic Products Guide: Ballistic Products is now issuing a simple to follow recipe guide for assembling Master loads.

Ocalcombo: Barnes streamlined 50-caliber spitzer boattail is the latest addition to its successful Expander line of muzzleloading bullets.

for muzzle-stuffers and cowboy action cartridges look very good. www.americanpioneerpowder.com

Ballistic Products

Here is the most specialized shotshell component headquarters in the field. If Ballistic Products doesn't stock it or hasn't invented it, it probably doesn't exist. Having access to their own in-house ballistics laboratory, the company has issued a series of "Master Load" recommendations over the years. These loads were the best that could be assembled for a specific purpose such as sporting clays or pheasant hunting, but, of course, you had to have exactly the right components on hand to duplicate them. Well, why not box up the specific components and market them as a package? They've done it. Called HITS—Hull Integrated Technology System—you can now buy the pre-packaged components with instructions for assembling "Master" steel duck/goose, pheasant, sporting clays, and 20-gauge field loads. All you need to add is the shot and powder. If you reload shotshells, don't miss their fascinating catalog. www.ballisticproducts.com

In their premium Gold line, Black Hills is introducing a 60-grain Nosler Partition in the 22-250 Rem. for those who wish to use this high performance 224-caliber for light big game.

Barnes

Building on the phenomenal success they have had with the performance, accuracy and shooter acceptance of the "Triple-Shock" X-bullet, Barnes is adding six new bullets to the line: a 53-grain 224; 85-grain 6mm; 130-grain 6.5mm; 200-grain 308; and a 185- and 225-grain 338. *(Note: Lazzeroni is also offering a proprietary plated version of the Triple-Shock bullet under the trade name, "LazerHead.")* Imagine a 50-caliber spitzer boattail projectile for muzzleloaders. Barnes just made it. Called the Spit-Fire MZ and offered in both 245- and 285-grain weights with matching sabots, these streamlined bullets are part of the successful Expander MZ line that features solid copper HP projectiles, delivering 100 percent weight retention. If you do try the Expander line, be sure to buy Barnes "Aligner" jags that conform to the ogive of the bullets and insure concentric seating. Speaking of spitzers, over in their XPB pistol bullet line, which is also based on a solid copper, HP, design, there are two new 500 S&W spitzers in 325- and 375-grain weights. In their more conventional XPB pistol designs, new offerings include a 115-grain 9mm; 155-grain 40 S&W; 185-grain 45 ACP; and 275-grain 500 S&W. Finally, for the big, booming 577 Nitro Express, there is a 750-grain XLC coated X-Bullet. *Kudos* has to go to Barnes this year for their imaginative advertising campaign based on the gasoline pump grades: "Leaded," "Unleaded," and "Premium." Refreshing! www.barnesbullets.com

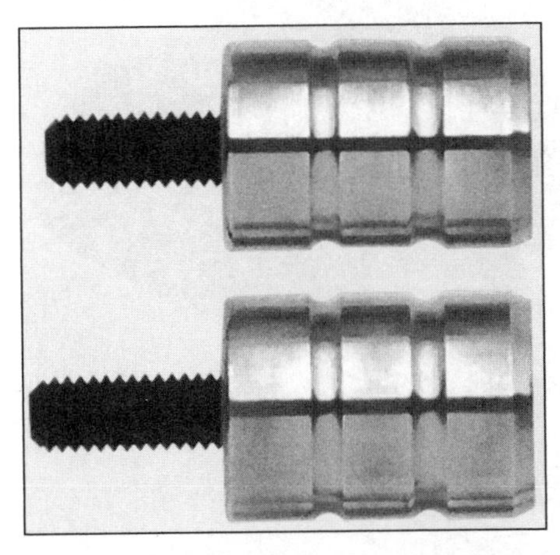

If you shoot Barnes sabot muzzleloading bullets, you'll want to add their Aligner tip to your ramrod.

Berger Bullets

Focused on filling all the niches in the 17- and 20-caliber classes, Berger now offers seven 17-caliber bullets in weights ranging from 15 to 30 grains and five 20-caliber pills weighing from 30 to 50 grains. And that pretty well covers the waterfront. www.bergerbullets.com

Berry's Manufacturing

This is the home of the copper plated, swaged lead core bullet readily available in all popular handgun and rifle calibers. They're inexpensive, too. New in the line this year is a 350-grain 500 S&W bullet and a 150-grain 30-30 Win. bullet. The latter is sized after

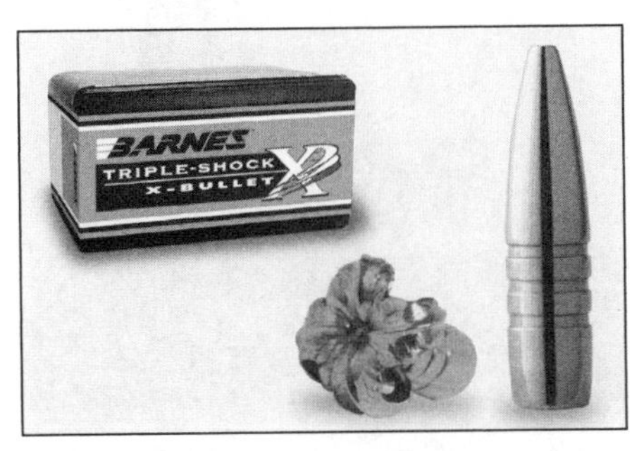

TripleShockSlide: Barnes accurate and deadly "Triple Shock" X bullet line is being expanded this year with new 224, 6mm, 6.5mm, 308, and 338-caliber offerings.

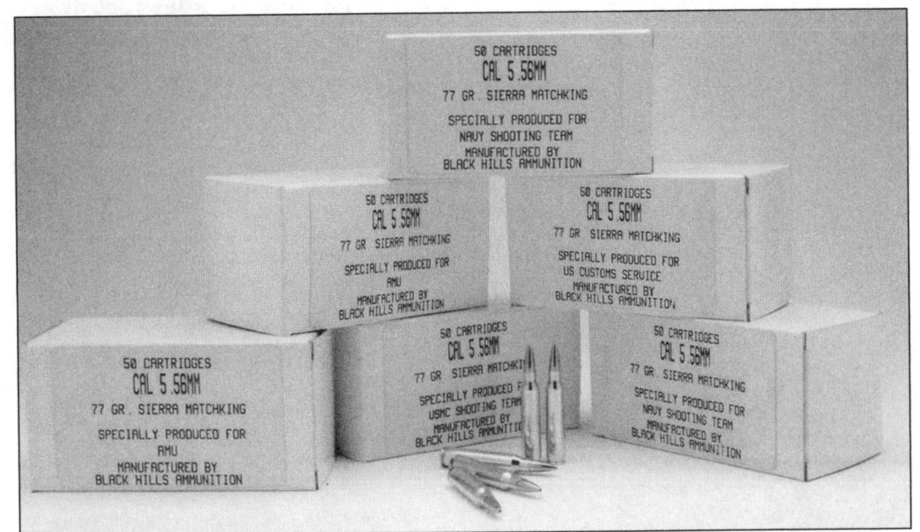

The highly accurate and effective 77-grain bullet loaded in the 223 Rem/5.56mm by Black Hills has proven to be their most popular match, varmint and military loading.

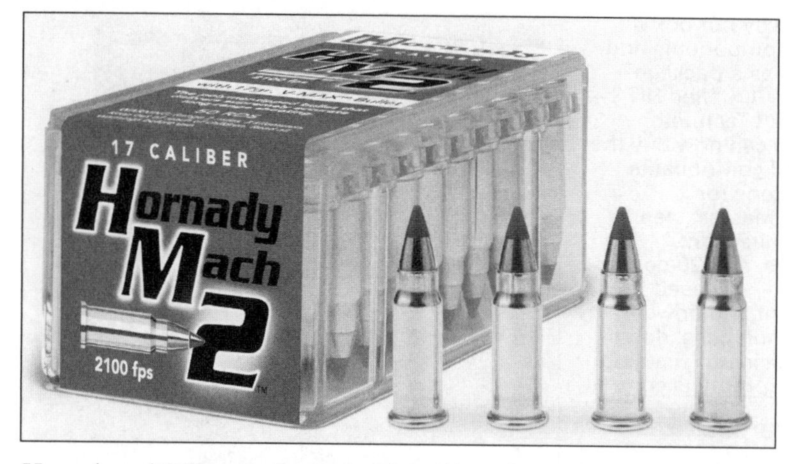

Hornady and CCI teamed up to build the Hornady Mach2—an exciting 17-caliber rimfire based on a necked-down 22 LR case.

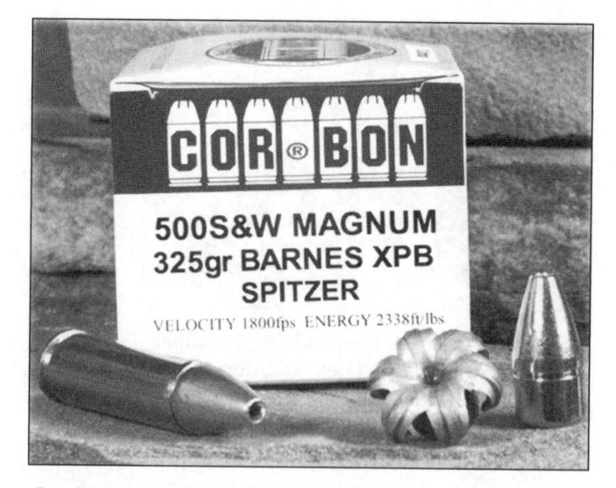

Cor-Bon now offers the 325-grain Barnes XPB spitzer in their extensive 500 S&W ammunition line.

plating to insure absolute concentricity. www.berrysmfg.com

Black Hills Ammunition

Can the 22-250 be an effective deer and antelope cartridge? With care, yes it can, with Black Hills newest 60-grain Nosler Partition loading. The 77-grain Sierra MatchKing has proved to be the most accurate and effective bullet that can be loaded in the 223 Rem./5.56mm. Black Hills currently provides all the 5.56mm match ammunition for the military branches, and you can buy it, too. The Black Hills are famous for gold, and the Black Hills Gold line is famous for being one of the greatest premium hunting ammunition lines ever assembled. It's the product of a careful selection of bullets and methodical loading practices. See it at www.black-hills.com

Buffalo Arms Co.

Some great new bullets for the blackpowder silhouette competitor. From a 20:1 alloy, Buffalo Arms is swaging a variety of grease-groove bullets in .410" and .459" diameter.

The grease grooves are actually machined into the bearing surface of the swaged slug, and the bullets are being held to a tolerance of plus-or-minus 2-1/2 tenths of a grain. In 40-caliber, there are 400- and 427-grain Creedmoor designs. In 45-caliber, there are 510-, 545- and 575-grain Creedmoor designs and a 545-grain Postell. Nice company to do business with as well. www.buffaloarms.com

Calhoon

Prolific varmint bullet maker, James Calhoon, is entering the 20-caliber race with two new .204" bullets featuring his proprietary double hollowpoint and electro-chemically applied "Slick Silver" plating. Look for 33- and 39-grain pills this year in his famous 250-count boxes. www.jamescalhoon.com

CCI

Combine CCI's mastery in the rimfire world with a Hornady 17-caliber V-Max bullet and what do you get? The Hornady 17 Mach2, that's what. Based on a CCI 22 LR case, this new little varmint cartridge pushes a 17-grain V-Max along at 2100 fps. Accuracy is reported to be exceptional, and the target price for the ammo affordable. Gun makers are lining up to chamber this little mosquito. What happened to last year's 17 HMR? Well, CCI just made it more lethal with the addition of a 17-grain TNT hollowpoint. Look for reloadable brass cases in CCI's

Built on the 32 ACP case by Cor-Bon, the 25 NAA propels a 35-grain JHP at 1200 fps from NAA's little Guardian automatic.

Cor-Bon has developed an entirely new Deep Penetrating X line of bullets for its high-velocity handgun cartridge line.

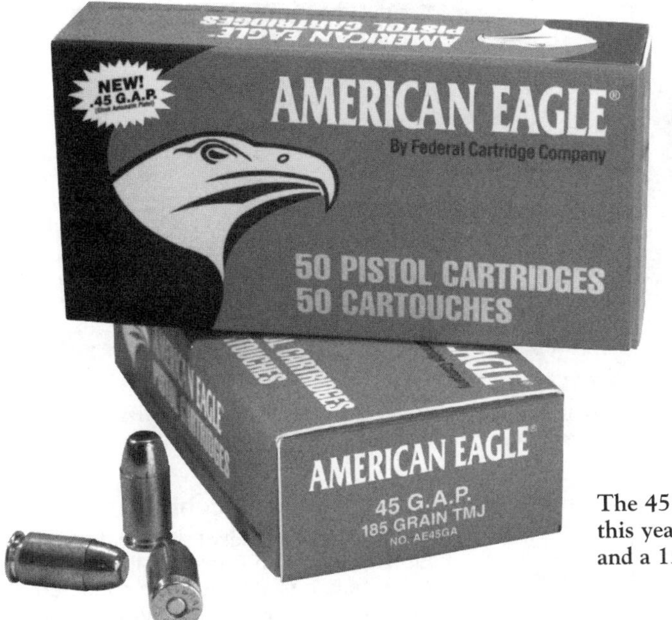

The 45 G.A.P. cartridge in the Federal line this year gets a 150-grain Hydra-Shok JHP and a 150-grain FMG at 1090 fps.

inexpensive Blazer line. The throwaway aluminum cases will still be with us while the reloadable brass cases will prove a boon to reloaders. www.cci-ammunition.com

Cor-Bon

When Smith & Wesson went looking for a new magnum handgun cartridge, Cor-Bon designed the 500 S&W Magnum cartridge. This year Cor-Bon has focused on hunting loads for the big fifty that include a 325-grain Barnes XPB spitzer at 1800 fps; a 350-grain JHP at 1600 fps; and a heavy bonded-core 385-grain spitzer at 1725 fps, just right for those African safaris. For those of us who like to carry *(and shoot!)* the new titanium lightweights, Cor-Bon has added three new loadings based on their light-kicking 100-grain "Pow'Rball" bullet--a 38 Special+P at 1400 fps; a 9x23 at 1600 fps; and a 357 Mag. at 1600 fps. Teaming up with Barnes, Cor-Bon has created an entirely new DPX (Deep Penetrating X) line. The DPX bullets are a proprietary design and are currently available as a 115-grain 9mm+P at 1275 fps, a 140-grain 40 S&W at 1300 fps and a 185-grain 45ACP+P at 1075 fps. It really has happened. Cor-Bon, in concert with North American Arms, has released the 25NAA—a 25-caliber cartridge based on the 32 ACP case and chambered in NAA's little Guardian automatic. Ballistics of the wee round are pretty hot—a 35-grain JHP at 1200 fps. Cor-Bon also loads rifle cartridges–lots of them. Two new loadings this year are long range tactical loads for the 223 Rem. featuring a 69-grain BTHP match bullet at 3000 fps and for the 308 Win, a 175-grain BTHP match bullet at 2600 fps. In the pipeline are a variety of new Cor-Bon recipes for the 45 G.A.P. www.corbon.com

Federal

Federal's rifle ammunition lines have expanded exponentially with the addition of numerous new loadings using Nosler's Partition, Solid Base, Accubond and Ballistic Tip bullets. Just as an example, in their Premium Vital-Shok line, Federal has introduced the following loadings for the 270 Win. Short Magnum: 130-grain Nosler Solid Base; 130-grain Nosler Ballistic Tip; 140-grain Nosler Accubond; and 150-grain Nosler Partition. Plus, the company is filling in other niches with the Barnes Triple-Shock X bullet and Federal's own Trophy Bonded Bear Claw. At last count, there were 80 new rifle loads this year, so be sure to send for the latest catalog. While everything seems to be getting faster in the cartridge field, Federal decided to slow things down with the introduction of a "Low Recoil"

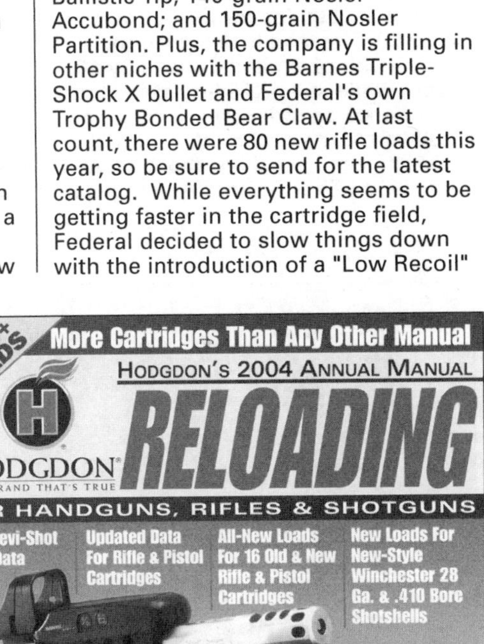

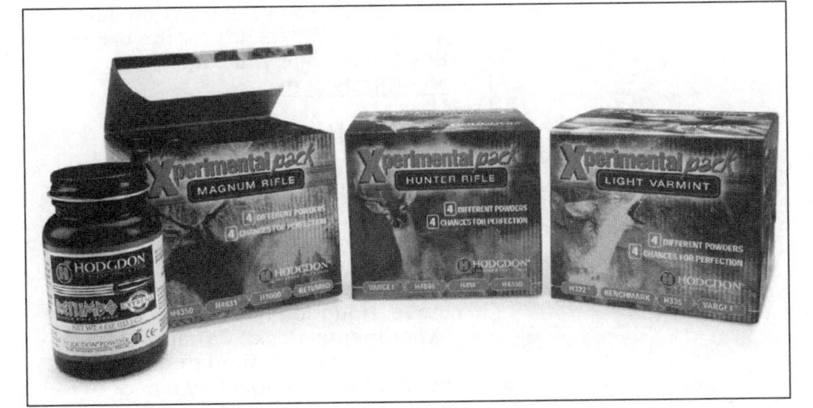

Designed to lower the cost of load development, Hodgdon's Xperimental Pack of four quarter-pound samples of powder is sure to prove popular with reloaders.

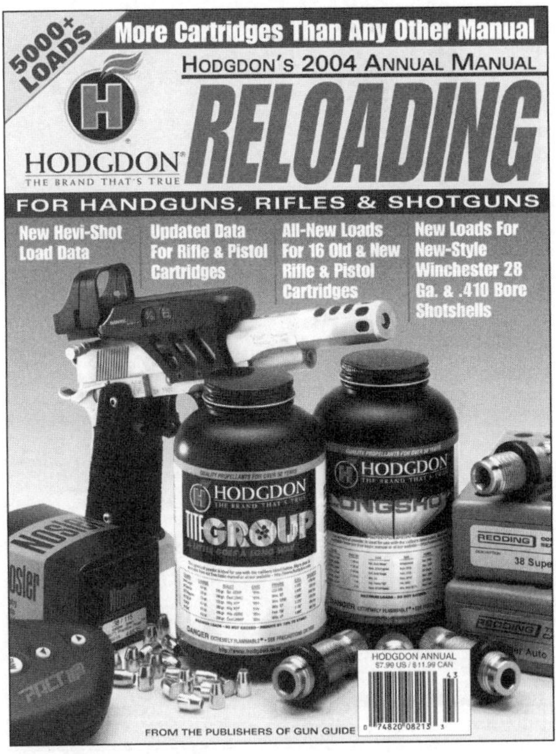

Hodgdon's latest and best "Handloading Annual" is packed with 5000+ loads for even the most recent factory cartridges.

Hodgdon's popular Triple Seven powder is now available in easy loading pellet form for muzzleloaders and metallic cartridges.

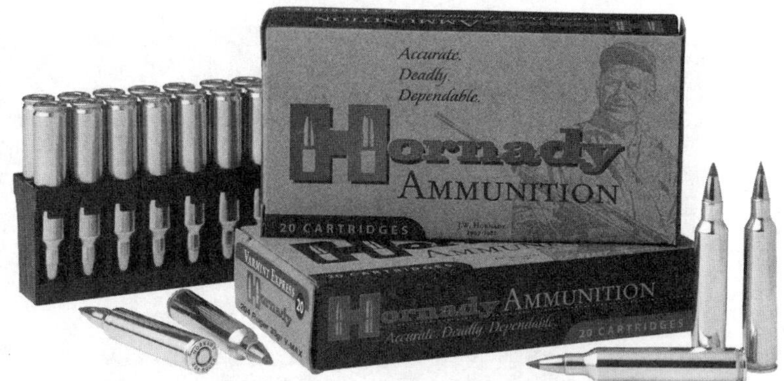

The Ruger 204 loaded by Hornady delivers 4225 fps from a 32-grain V-Max bullet and is the fastest factory cartridge currently offered.

deer load featuring a 170-grain softpoint at 2000 fps for the 308 Win. and 30-06. The load is designed to reduce recoil of a standard load by 50 percent while still providing excellent performance on medium-size game out to 200 yards. It's a great idea for new shooters, recoil-sensitive shooters, and youngsters. The 45 Glock Automatic Pistol (G.A.P.) cartridge is a hot new item this year, and Federal is fielding a 150-grain Hydra-Shok JHP and 150-grain FMJ at 1090 fps. In the Premium line, there are two V-Shok loadings for the 17 HMR–a 17-grain Speer TNT and a 17-grain Hornady V-Max bullet. Velocity of both loads is a sizzling 2550 fps. And who would have thought the 20-gauge slug gun would have come back in vogue? It has, and Federal has brought out a 5/8-oz. Barnes Sabot round at 1900 fps. It appears that the marriage between Federal and ATK is working very well! www.federalcartridge.com

Fiocchi

Loaded with nickel-plated shot, Fiocchi's Golden Pheasant line of shotshells has always been considered premium upland game ammunition. It just got better with a new 12-gauge load consisting of 1-3/8 oz. of #'s 4, 5, or 6 at 1485 fps! Fiocchi has also added a 28-gauge loading to the Golden Pheasant line consisting of 7/8-oz. of #'s 6, 7-1/2 or 8 at 1300 fps. Pheasants beware. There's a new 20-gauge steel, low-recoil load of 7/8-oz. of #7s at 1225. Finally, there's an interesting 9mm Luger leadless loading featuring a 100-grain, truncated cone, encapsulated base bullet at 1400 fps. Delivering less recoil, the new cartridge is also said to be more accurate than standard 9mm ammunition. www.fiocchiusa.com

Graf & Sons

For everyone who enjoys shooting the military warhorses, Graf has done an outstanding job of supplying obsolete cases and bullets being produced under contract by Hornady. You can now buy loaded ammunition or components for the 6.5x52 Carcano, 7.5x55 Swiss and 7.65x53 Argentine. Brass only is available for the 7.5x54 MAS, 455 Webley and 9mm Steyr. Awaiting production are the 6.5x50 Jap, 7.7x58 Jap, and 8x56R Mannlicher. Available component bullets include a unique 123-grain V-Max bullet for the 7.62x39, a 160-grain round nose (.268") bullet for the 6.5 Carcano, a 123-grain SP (.300") for the 7.35mm Carcano, and a 205-grain SP (.330") for the 8x56R. Buy them while you can. www.grafs.com

Hodgdon Powder

The BIG news this year is Hodgdon's acquisition of the IMR Powder Company. It's too soon to know what the future holds, but it's certainly an exciting development for both companies. In a brilliant marketing move, Hodgdon has developed the "Xperimental Pack." For approximately the price of one pound of powder, the handloader can now buy a pack of four 4-oz. canisters of Hodgdon powders organized by burning rate. For example, the Magnum Rifle pack contains H4350, H4831, H1000 and

Lightfield is entering the less lethal shotgun ammunition market with rubber buckshot, rubber slugs, and their unique, rubber spider-looking projectiles called Tri-Star and Super Star.

Retumbo. The Light Varmint pack--H322, Benchmark, H335, and Varget. The Xperimental Packs enable the handloader to test a variety of powders without having to buy, and possibly never use again, full pounds of powder. Building on the success of their Triple Seven blackpowder substitute, there are two new Triple Seven pellet loads this year–a 45-caliber 50-grain and a 50-caliber 30-grain. Hodgdon's latest and best *Handloading Annual* is packed with 5000+ loads for even the most recent factory cartridges and contains some great, old stories by Elmer Keith and Bill Jordan. www.hodgdon.com

Hornady

The creative cartridge designers at Hornady seem to generate a new cartridge each year. This year there are two surprises. The 20-caliber, 204 Ruger varmint cartridge has emerged as the fastest factory cartridge currently loaded with a 32-grain V-Max bullet at 4225 fps and a 40-grain V-Max at 3900 fps. Then there's the 17 Hornady Mach2 rimfire that is a petite bottleneck cartridge based on the 22 Long Rifle case. The Mach2 was developed cooperatively with CCI. It zips a 17-grain V-Max bullet down range at 2100 fps and tests indicate that its accuracy exceeds that of its 22 LR parent. Wheel out your Model 1895 Winchesters in 405 Win. Hornady now offers a factory load with a 300-grain SP at 2200 fps. And while we're discussing big bores, Hornady has introduced a new loading for the 500 S&W--a 350-grain XTP Mag. bullet at 1900 fps. And for the muzzle-stuffers, Hornady has come up with a neat idea–the Lock-N-Load Speed Sabot. Take the SST-ML bullet, place it in a sabot that has a soda straw-looking projecting tail, and slide three Pyrodex or Triple Seven pellets onto that tail. It's a complete round–bullet, sabot, and attached powder charge. Look for it initially in 50-caliber with a choice of either 250- or 300-grain SST-ML's. www.hornady.com

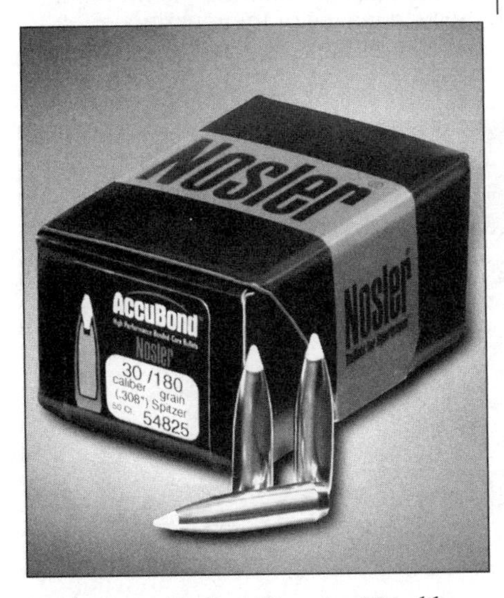

Nosler has added a 180-grain, 30-caliber bonded core bullet to its successful AccuBond line.

Huntington

If you need brass, bullets, or RCBS products, Huntington is the first stop. They are particularly strong in the rare and obsolete caliber department. For example, this year they're adding brass for the 6.5x68mm, 8x68mm, 6.5 Rem SPC, 7.62 Nagant Revolver, 7.92x33 Kurtz, 8x50R Lebel, 50 Alaskan and 50-110 Win. New custom jacketed bullets include 200-grain SP's for the 9x57mm (.352" and .356"), and a 200-grain SP for the 9.3x72R (.364"). Huntington has them plus they offer a unique service for cartridge collectors and handloaders. They will sell you a single case in every conceivable caliber for a very reasonable price. See their extensive catalog at www.huntington.com

Igman

Just beginning to appear on dealers' shelves are sporting rifle and pistol cartridges produced by Igman, a Bosnian company. Igman International USA is the importer. Phone number (203) 375-8544.

International Cartridge Corp.

International is a 100-percent "green" cartridge maker using copper/tin composites and sintered, powder metal technology to create bullets, slugs and shot. They offer a full range of tactical, duty, and special application handgun, rifle and shotgun ammunition for the law enforcement community. www.internationalcartridge.com

Jada Enterprise

Here's an interesting development. Daun Suarez of Jada Enterprise is marketing a homogeneous bullet with a hole through it. He claims it delivers superior velocity, accuracy and penetration from muzzleloading or cartridge rifles. Available in .429", .452", .454", and .458" diameters, the bullet with a hole in it is loaded in a ML with a sabot or seated in a cartridge case with a lexan insert under the base. www.jadaenterprise.com

Lightfield

Well known for their shotgun slugs, Lightfield is making a major push into the non-lethal shotgun ammunition market with the introduction of rubber buckshot, rubber slugs and some unique, rubber spider looking projectiles called the Tri-Star and Super Star. The primary applications for their new ammunition lines are law enforcement and wildlife control. www.lightfieldslugs.com

First Defense Box: "First Defense" is Magtech's latest line of 100-percent copper hollowpoint ammunition in 9mm, 40 S&W, and 45 ACP.

Magtech

"First Defense" is the label for Magtech's latest line of 100% copper hollowpoint ammunition for law enforcement and personal defense. It's available in 9mm, 40 S&W and 45 ACP. There's a new 400-grain semi-jacketed

Oregon Trail has expanded its silver alloy True Shot cast bullet line to include new gas check designs in 308-, 41-, 44-, 45-, 480-, and 500-caliber.

softpoint loading for the 500 S&W, a selection of solid brass shotshells for the cowboy action crowd, and a completely new line of rimfire ammunition.
www.magtechammunition.com

Meister Bullets

This well-known brand of hard cast bullets is expanding this year to include 167-grain 30-30 Win.; 170-grain 32-40 Win.; and 330-grain 500 S&W bullets. www.meisterbullets.com

Natec

It's an idea whose time has come again—polymer cased rifle ammunition. Combining a solid brass head and a special, engineered polymer from Dupont, Natec is currently producing 223 and 308 ammunition. The claimed benefits for the polymer-cased ammo are reduced weight and, because of its insulating qualities, improved propellant combustion and reduced heat transference to the firearm.
www.natec-us.com

Norma

Finally, Norma has produced a complete and thoroughly fascinating reloading manual. The history of the Norma Company and the technical manufacturing and ballistics data contained in the first 150 pages are worth the price of the book alone.

Excellent text and illustrations, and very clearly written. The loading data is right up-to-date to include the Winchester short magnums as well as less covered cartridges like the 9.3x74mm, 404 Jeffery and 505 Gibbs. Of course, the powders are all Norma, but the bullets span the spectrum of makers including Hornady, Nosler, Sierra, Swift and Woodleigh. There's a new Norma component bullet this year,

Sierra has designed a true light big game bullet for the high velocity 22 centerfires--a 65-grain SBT GameKing.

a 7mm 175-grain Oryx, featuring a bonded core and long bearing surface to promote improved alignment and stability. Don't miss this new manual.
www.norma.cc

Nosler

Building on the success and industry acceptance of their Accubond bullets, Nosler has added two new bonded-core bullets to the line—a 7mm 140-grain and a 30-caliber 180-grain.
www.nosler.com

Oregon Trail Bullet Co.

Home of those beautiful, accurate "True Shot" silver alloy bullets, Oregon Trail has developed eight new gas-checked designs: 30-caliber 170-grain RNFP and 200-grain RN; 41-caliber 265-grain WNFP; 44-caliber 310-grain WNFP; 45 Colt (.452) 360-grain WNFP; 45-70 (.459) 430-grain FP; 480-caliber 355-grain WNFP; and a 500 S&W 370-grain WNFP. Top quality. Great folks.
www.trueshotbullets.com

Powerbelt

This popular copper-clad muzzleloading bullet line that features an attached plastic gas seal has expanded to include a 45-caliber 175-grain and a 50-caliber 223-grain. Both bullets feature a poly tip named the "Aerotip."
www.powerbeltbullets.com

Precision Reloading, Inc.

Here's a great source for a variety of common and hard-to-find reloading components. The company has just released their first shotshell reloading manual, entitled "Blanks to Supersonics." There are articles and loading data on environmentally friendly loads; sub-sonic loads; international target loads; as well as 42 tables covering every subject from Ed Lowry's shotshell ballistics charts to Italian proof marks.
www.precisionreloading.com

Precision Reloading's first shotshell manual covers environmentally friendly loads, subsonic loads, international target loads as well as 42 invaluable reference tables.

Remington

"Managed recoil" has become an industry trend, and Remington has it covered. There are three new reduced centerfire loads designed to be lethal on big game out to 200 yards, as well as reduced-recoil 12-ga. slug and buckshot loads. The rifle loads consist of a 115-grain bullet at 2710 fps in the 270 Win; a 125-grain bullet at 2660 fps in the 30-06; and a 140-grain bullet at 2710 fps in the 7mm Rem. Mag. Over in the shotshell area, the managed recoil loadings in the 2-3/4"/ 12-gauge case are a 1-oz. slug and 9 pellets of OO buck at 1200 fps. At the beefier end of the new shotshell lineup are a 1-3/8 oz. "BuckHammer" slug at 1500 fps from the 3-inch 12-gauge case and a 1-oz. 20-gauge slug at 1550 fps in the 2-3/4" hull. Tactical has become practical overnight with the public release of Remington's special operational cartridge, the 6.8mm Rem. SPC (Special Purpose Cartridge). This is a 270-caliber cartridge based on the old 30 Remington case. It fits a M-15/16 magazine box and modified bolt face and was designed to provide increased incapacitation at ranges out to 500 meters. The BTHP or FMJ 115-grain bullets have a muzzle velocity of 2800 fps. Old Remington cases? Here's another one. The 6.5 Rem. Mag. cartridge has been revived. It's good and hot featuring a 120-grain Core-Lokt bullet at 3210 fps. Remington's highly successful bonded bullet, the Core-Lokt Ultra, and the varmint weight AccuTip bullet are being loaded in a number of new cartridges this year. The Premier Match ammunition line is being expanded to include Sierra MatchKings in the 6.8 Rem. SPC, 300 Win. Mag. and 300 Rem. SA Ultra Mag. There's even a new shotgun wad design this year in which the petals of the Fig8 and TGT12 wads are connected by a thin tab of plastic at the mouth of the wad. The "stitching" prevents wads from sticking together in bags and eliminates folded petals during the loading process. The stitched petals separate the moment the wad leaves of the muzzle.
www.remington.com

Winchester selected the classic 230-grain bullet for their line of 45 G.A.P. cartridges that includes four commercial and two law enforcement loads.

After introducing the 223 and 243 WSSMs last year, Winchester surprised everyone with their new 25 WSSM designed for varmints and medium size game.

Designed to appeal to the high-volume, cost conscious shooter, Winchester's new Super Target loads in 12- and 20-gauge are available in competitively priced case lots.

Sellier & Bellot

S&B is loading Barnes XLC bullets across most of its big game centerfire line this year. There's a hot, new 30-30 loading consisting of a 140-grain SP bullet at 2388 fps.

The 32 S&W Long loaded with a 100-grain bullet at 886 fps has been added to the pistol line, and a 22 WMR with a 45-grain bullet at 1562 fps to the rimfire offerings. www.sb-usa.com

Sierra Bullets

There has always been a market for a stout deer bullet for the 22 centerfires. For years, Sierra's 63-grain semi-pointed Varminter bullet served that purpose well. Sierra has taken the challenge one step further with the release of a true GameKing spitzer BT bullet weighing 65 grains. It will take a 1:10" or faster twist to stabilize the new bullet, but for game up to the size of deer, it should be a dilly. www.sierrabullets.com

Speer

Finally, a carefully crafted cartridge is available for 38-caliber snubbies. Speer is offering a 38 Special +P loading featuring a 135-grain Gold Dot HP bullet at 975 fps. The load is designed to provide optimal ballistics from a 2" barrel. New to the Gold Dot Hunting ammunition line is the 41 Mag. loaded with a 210-grain Gold Dot HP at 1280 fps. The 45 Glock Automatic Pistol round gets four new loadings—a 185-grain Gold Dot HP at 1050 fps, a 200-grain GDHP at 950 fps and two similar weight FMJ loadings for training purposes. New component bullets this year in the Gold Dot HP handgun line include 110-, 135- and 145-grain bullets for the 38 Spl.; the 210-grain 41 Mag.; and in the Trophy Bonded Bear Claw rifle line, a 250-grain 375-caliber; and a 500-grain 470 NE (.474") bullet. www.speer-bullets.com

Winchester is adding bonded core Accubond CT bullets to its popular Supreme rifle line in 270 Win., 270 WSM, 7mm WSM, 30-06 Spfld, 300 WSM, 300 Win. Mag, and 338 Win. Mag.

Starline

At the request of S&W and Cor-Bon, Starline has re-designed the 500 S&W case to accept a large magnum rifle primer to eliminate pierced primer problems that have occurred with the big boomer. The new cases are clearly marked with an "R" after the word "MAG" on the head stamp, so be forewarned. www.starlinebrass.com

Swift

Swift has announced that they intend on adding 224-, 257- and 6.5mm caliber bullets to their Scirocco line. Stay tuned. www.swiftbullets.com

Vihtavuori and Lapua

Vihtavuori and Lapua have created a new website this year. See their products at www.vihtavuori-lapua.com.

Winchester Ammunition

Winchester did it again. They caught all of us by surprise when they announced the creation of the 25 WSSM

Loaded with five OOO buckshot, Winchester's new .410 round is designed for hunting and home defense.

Own a classic English double with 2 1/2-inch chambers? Zanders carries a complete line of 2 1/2-inch shotshell loads.

(Winchester Super Short Magnum). Designed for varmints and medium-size game, the 25 WSSM will be loaded with an 85-grain Ballistic Silvertip at 3470 fps; a 115-grain Ballistic Silvertip at 3060 fps; and a 120-grain Positive Expanding Point at 2990 fps. Teamed together with super short action Winchester Model 70s and Browning A Bolts, the 25 WSSM is sure to generate a lot of excitement in the hunting field. Should be an ideal combination for women and beginning shooters. Nosler's successful bonded core, AccuBond bullet has been given a Lubalox coating by Winchester and will be loaded in eight Supreme rifle calibers: 270 Win., 270 WSM, 7mm WSM, 7mm Rem. Mag., 30-06, 300 WSM, 300 Win. Mag. and the 338 Win. Mag. The 45 G.A.P. is getting quite a play this year. In their economically priced "USA" line, Winchester is fielding a 230-grain FMJ round at 850 fps and a 230 JHP loading at an impressive 880 fps. For target ranges, there is a lead-free Winclean loading featuring a 230-grain FMJ at 875 fps. Then for personal protection purposes, there is a hot 185-grain Silvertip HP loading at 1000 fps on your dealer's shelf. For the high volume, cost-conscious target shooter who doesn't reload, Winchester is introducing a new "Super-Target line of 12- and 20-gauge loads with a suggested retail price of $57 a case. The 12-gauge line includes both 2-3/4 and 3-dram level loadings plus a 1-1/8 oz. #7 steel shot load retailing for $84 a case. The smaller bores, and particularly the 28-gauge, are growing in popularity for target shooting and upland game. To maximize the effectiveness of the 28-gauge on larger species of upland game, Winchester is adding a 1-oz. loading of hard #5s to its Super-X High Brass Game line. There is a new 3-inch .410 load carrying five OOO buck pellets at a velocity of 1135 fps. The HS hull based AA Super Sport line is being expanded with a 12-gauge, 1-1/8 oz. load of #9s at 1300 fps and a .410-bore 2-1/2" load carrying 1/2-oz. of #8s at 1300 fps. There are several new screaming 1550 fps steel shot shells for the 3-1/2", 3", and 2-3/4" 12-gauge in #'s BB, 2, 3, 4 appearing in time for the next waterfowling season in the affordable Xpert line. And finally, for those tough, old, fall roosters, Winchester is introducing two Super-X Super Pheasant loadings—a 2-3/4" 12-gauge load consisting of 1-3/8 oz. of copper-plated hard lead shot in #s 4, 5, 6 at 1300 fps and a 20-gauge 2-3/4" load of 1 oz of #s 5, 6 at the same, sizzling 1300 fps. The folks at Winchester Ammunition have been very busy this year! www.winchester.com

Woodleigh Bullets

Long respected for their bonded core, big caliber, big game bullets, Woodleigh is applying its experience and technology to a number of new smaller caliber bullets including a 140-grain 6.5mm; a 250-grain 8mm (.323"); a 200-grain 8x57 (.318"); 286- and 320-grain 9.3mm; as well as some heavies, a 400-grain 416-caliber; 500-grain 458-caliber; 600-grain 505 Gibbs; 600-grain 500 Jeffery; and 650-grain 577 Nitro. See them at www.woodleighbullets.com.

Wolf Ammunition

Expect to see FMJ loads for the 308 Win., 30-06, and 30 Carbine added to this popular and inexpensive line sometime during the year. www.wolfammo.com

Zanders Sporting Goods

Zanders is importing a new line of 2-1/2" English Classic 12-gauge shells with 1-1/16 or 1 oz. of #s 6, 7-1/2 and 8 manufactured by Nobel Sport Martignoni. Zanders is also stocking a new line of Eley Tenex and Eley Match 22 LR loads engineered specifically for semi-auto pistols and rifles. The new Eley ammunition features a special round nose bullet profile and lubricant that facilitate feeding while reducing fouling build-up. www.gzanders.com ●

Zanders is importing Eley's new semi-auto 22 LR cartridges featuring a special round-nose bullet and lubricant to facilitate feeding and reduce fouling in semi-auto 22s.

With the increasing popularly of the 28-gauge for upland game, Winchester has added #5 shot to its 28-gauge Super-X line.

Average Centerfire Rifle Cartridge Ballistics and Prices

Many manufacturers do not supply suggested retail prices. Others did not get their pricing to us before press time. All pricing can vary dependent on the exact brand and style of ammo selected and/or the retail outlet from which you make your purchase. Pricing has been rounded to the nearest dollar and represents our best estimate of average pricing. An * after the cartridge means these loads are available with Nosler Partition or Swift A-Frame bullets. Listed pricing may or may not reflect this bullet type. ** = these are packed 50 to box, all others are 20 to box. Wea. Mag.= Weatherby Magnum. Spfd. = Springfield. A-A-Sq. = A-Square. N.E.=Nitro Express.

Cartridge	Bullet Weight Grains	VELOCITY (fps)					ENERGY (ft. lbs.)					TRAJ. (in.)				Est. Price/ box
		Muzzle	100 yds.	200 yds.	300 yds.	400 yds.	Muzzle	100 yds.	200 yds.	300 yds.	400 yds.	100 yds.	200 yds.	300 yds.	400 yds.	
17 Remington	25	4040	3284	2644	2086	1606	906	599	388	242	143	+2.0	+1.7	-4.0	-17.0	$17
204 Ruger	32	4225	3632	3114	2652	2234	1268	937	689	500	355	.6	0.0	-4.2	-13.4	NA
204 Ruger	40	3900	3451	3046	2677	2336	1351	1058	824	636	485	.7	0.0	-4.5	-13.9	NA
221 Fireball	50	2800	2137	1580	1180	988	870	507	277	155	109	+0.0	-7.0	-28.0	0.0	$14
22 Hornet	34	3050	2132	1415	1017	852	700	343	151	78	55	+0.0	-6.6	-15.5	-29.9	NA
22 Hornet	35	3100	2278	1601	1135	929	747	403	199	100	67	+2.75	0.0	-16.9	-60.4	NA
22 Hornet	45	2690	2042	1502	1128	948	723	417	225	127	90	+0.0	-7.7	-31.0	0.0	$27**
218 Bee	46	2760	2102	1550	1155	961	788	451	245	136	94	+0.0	-7.2	-29.0	0.0	$46**
222 Remington	40	3600	3117	2673	2269	1911	1151	863	634	457	324	+1.07	0.0	-6.13	-18.9	NA
222 Remington	50	3140	2602	2123	1700	1350	1094	752	500	321	202	+2.0	-0.4	-11.0	-33.0	$11
222 Remington	55	3020	2562	2147	1773	1451	1114	801	563	384	257	+2.0	-0.4	-11.0	-33.0	$12
22 PPC	52	3400	2930	2510	2130	NA	1335	990	730	525	NA	+2.0	1.4	-5.0	0.0	NA
223 Remington	40	3650	3010	2450	1950	1530	1185	805	535	340	265	+2.0	+1.0	-6.0	-22.0	$14
223 Remington	40	3800	3305	2845	2424	2044	1282	970	719	522	371	0.84	0.0	-5.34	-16.6	NA
223 Remington	50	3300	2874	2484	2130	1809	1209	917	685	504	363	1.37	0.0	-7.05	-21.8	NA
223 Remington	52/53	3330	2882	2477	2106	1770	1305	978	722	522	369	+2.0	+0.6	-6.5	-21.5	$14
223 Remington	55	3240	2748	2305	1906	1556	1282	922	649	444	296	+2.0	-0.2	-9.0	-27.0	$12
223 Remington	60	3100	2712	2355	2026	1726	1280	979	739	547	397	+2.0	+0.2	-8.0	-24.7	$16
223 Remington	64	3020	2621	2256	1920	1619	1296	977	723	524	373	+2.0	-0.2	-9.3	-23.0	$14
223 Remington	69	3000	2720	2460	2210	1980	1380	1135	925	750	600	+2.0	+0.8	-5.8	-17.5	$15
223 Remington	75	2790	2554	2330	2119	1926	1296	1086	904	747	617	2.37	0.0	-8.75	-25.1	NA
223 Remington	77	2750	2584	2354	2169	1992	1293	1110	948	804	679	1.93	0.0	-8.2	-23.8	NA
223 WSSM	55	3850	3438	3064	2721	2402	1810	1444	1147	904	704	0.7	0.0	-4.4	-13.6	NA
223 WSSM	64	3600	3144	2732	2356	2011	1841	1404	1061	789	574	1.0	0.0	-5.7	-17.7	NA
222 Rem. Mag.	55	3240	2748	2305	1906	1556	1282	922	649	444	296	+2.0	-0.2	-9.0	-27.0	$14
225 Winchester	55	3570	3066	2616	2208	1838	1556	1148	836	595	412	+2.0	+1.0	-5.0	-20.0	$19
224 Wea. Mag.	55	3650	3192	2780	2403	2057	1627	1244	943	705	516	+2.0	+1.2	-4.0	-17.0	$32
22-250 Rem.	40	4000	3320	2720	2200	1740	1420	980	660	430	265	+2.0	+1.8	-3.0	-16.0	$14
22-250 Rem.	50	3725	3264	2641	2455	2103	1540	1183	896	669	491	0.89	0.0	-5.23	-16.3	NA
22-250 Rem.	52/55	3680	3137	2656	2222	1832	1654	1201	861	603	410	+2.0	+1.3	-4.0	-17.0	$13
22-250 Rem.	60	3600	3195	2826	2485	2169	1727	1360	1064	823	627	+2.0	+2.0	-2.4	-12.3	$19
220 Swift	40	4200	3678	3190	2739	2329	1566	1201	904	666	482	+0.51	0.0	-4.0	-12.9	NA
220 Swift	50	3780	3158	2617	2135	1710	1586	1107	760	506	325	+2.0	+1.4	-4.4	-17.9	$20
220 Swift	50	3850	3396	2970	2576	2215	1645	1280	979	736	545	0.74	0.0	-4.84	-15.1	NA
220 Swift	55	3800	3370	2990	2630	2310	1765	1390	1090	850	650	0.8	0.0	-4.7	-14.4	NA
220 Swift	55	3650	3194	2772	2384	2035	1627	1246	939	694	506	+2.0	+2.0	-2.6	-13.4	$19
220 Swift	60	3600	3199	2824	2475	2156	1727	1364	1063	816	619	+2.0	+1.6	-4.1	-13.1	$19
22 Savage H.P.	71	2790	2340	1930	1570	1280	1225	860	585	390	190	+2.0	-1.0	-10.4	-35.7	NA
6mm BR Rem.	100	2550	2310	2083	1870	1671	1444	1185	963	776	620	+2.5	-0.6	-11.8	0.0	$22
6mm Norma BR	107	2822	2667	2517	2372	2229	1893	1690	1506	1337	1181	+1.73	0.0	-7.24	-20.6	NA
6mm PPC	70	3140	2750	2400	2070	NA	1535	1175	895	665	NA	+2.0	+1.4	-5.0	0.0	NA
243 Winchester	55	4025	3597	3209	2853	2525	1978	1579	1257	994	779	+0.6	0.0	-4.0	-12.2	NA
243 Winchester	60	3600	3110	2660	2260	1890	1725	1285	945	680	475	+2.0	+1.8	-3.3	-15.5	$17
243 Winchester	70	3400	3040	2700	2390	2100	1795	1435	1135	890	685	1.1	0.0	-5.9	-18.0	NA
243 Winchester	75/80	3350	2955	2593	2259	1951	1993	1551	1194	906	676	+2.0	+0.9	-5.0	-19.0	$16
243 Winchester	85	3320	3070	2830	2600	2380	2080	1770	1510	1280	1070	+2.0	+1.2	-4.0	-14.0	$18
243 Winchester	90	3120	2871	2635	2411	2199	1946	1647	1388	1162	966	1.4	0.0	-6.4	-18.8	NA
243 Winchester*	100	2960	2697	2449	2215	1993	1945	1615	1332	1089	882	+2.5	+1.2	-6.0	-20.0	$16
243 Winchester	105	2920	2689	2470	2261	2062	1988	1686	1422	1192	992	+2.5	+1.6	-5.0	-18.4	$21
243 Light Mag.	100	3100	2839	2592	2358	2138	2133	1790	1491	1235	1014	+1.5	0.0	-6.8	-19.8	NA
243 WSSM	55	4060	3628	3237	2880	2550	2013	1607	1280	1013	794	0.6	0.0	-3.9	-12.0	NA
243 WSSM	95	3250	3000	2763	2538	2325	2258	1898	1610	1359	1140	1.2	0.0	-5.7	-16.9	NA
243 WSSM	100	3110	2838	2583	2341	2112	2147	1789	1481	1217	991	1.4	0.0	-6.6	-19.7	NA
6mm Remington	80	3470	3064	2694	2352	2036	2139	1667	1289	982	736	+2.0	+1.1	-5.0	-17.0	$16
6mm Remington	100	3100	2829	2573	2332	2104	2133	1777	1470	1207	983	+2.5	+1.6	-5.0	-17.0	$16
6mm Remington	105	3060	2822	2596	2381	2177	2105	1788	1512	1270	1059	+2.5	+1.1	-3.3	-15.0	$21
6mm Rem. Light Mag.	100	3250	2997	2756	2528	2311	2345	1995	1687	1418	1186	1.59	0.0	-6.33	-18.3	NA
6.17(.243) Spitfire	100	3350	3122	2905	2698	2501	2493	2164	1874	1617	1389	2.4	3.20	0.0	-8.0	NA
240 Wea. Mag.	87	3500	3202	2924	2663	2416	2366	1980	1651	1370	1127	+2.0	+2.0	-2.0	-12.0	$32
240 Wea. Mag.	100	3395	3106	2835	2581	2339	2559	2142	1785	1478	1215	+2.5	+2.8	-2.0	-11.0	$43

AVERAGE CENTERFIRE RIFLE CARTRIDGE BALLISTICS & PRICES, *continued*

Cartridge	Bullet Weight Grains	VELOCITY (fps)					ENERGY (ft. lbs.)					TRAJ. (in.)				Est. Price/box
		Muzzle	100 yds.	200 yds.	300 yds.	400 yds.	Muzzle	100 yds.	200 yds.	300 yds.	400 yds.	100 yds.	200 yds.	300 yds.	400 yds.	
25-20 Win.	86	1460	1194	1030	931	858	407	272	203	165	141	0.0	-23.5	0.0	0.0	$32**
25-35 Win.	117	2230	1866	1545	1282	1097	1292	904	620	427	313	+2.5	-4.2	-26.0	0.0	$24
250 Savage	100	2820	2504	2210	1936	1684	1765	1392	1084	832	630	+2.5	+0.4	-9.0	-28.0	$17
257 Roberts	100	2980	2661	2363	2085	1827	1972	1572	1240	965	741	+2.5	-0.8	-5.2	-21.6	$20
257 Roberts+P	117	2780	2411	2071	1761	1488	2009	1511	1115	806	576	+2.5	-0.2	-10.2	-32.6	$18
257 Roberts+P	120	2780	2560	2360	2160	1970	2060	1750	1480	1240	1030	+2.5	+1.2	-6.4	-23.6	$22
257 Roberts	122	2600	2331	2078	1842	1625	1831	1472	1169	919	715	+2.5	0.0	-10.6	-31.4	$21
257 Light Mag.	117	2940	2694	2460	2240	2031	2245	1885	1572	1303	1071	+1.7	0.0	-7.6	-21.8	NA
25-06 Rem.	87	3440	2995	2591	2222	1884	2286	1733	1297	954	686	+2.0	+1.1	-2.5	-14.4	$17
25-06 Rem.	90	3440	3043	2680	2344	2034	2364	1850	1435	1098	827	+2.0	+1.8	-3.3	-15.6	$17
25-06 Rem.	100	3230	2893	2580	2287	2014	2316	1858	1478	1161	901	+2.0	+0.8	-5.7	-18.9	$17
25-06 Rem.	117	2990	2770	2570	2370	2190	2320	2000	1715	1465	1246	+2.5	+1.0	-7.9	-26.6	$19
25-06 Rem.*	120	2990	2730	2484	2252	2032	2382	1985	1644	1351	1100	+2.5	+1.2	-5.3	-19.6	$17
25-06 Rem.	122	2930	2706	2492	2289	2095	2325	1983	1683	1419	1189	+2.5	+1.8	-4.5	-17.5	$23
25 WSSM	85	3470	3156	2863	2589	2331	2273	1880	1548	1266	1026	1.0	0.0	-5.2	-15.7	NA
25 WSSM	115	3060	284	2639	2442	2254	2392	2066	1778	1523	1398	1.4	0.0	-6.4	-18.6	NA
25 WSSM	120	2990	2717	2459	2216	1987	2383	1967	1612	1309	1053	1.6	0.0	-7.4	-21.8	NA
257 Wea. Mag.	87	3825	3456	3118	2805	2513	2826	2308	1870	1520	1220	+2.0	+2.7	-0.3	-7.6	$32
257 Wea. Mag.	100	3555	3237	2941	2665	2404	2806	2326	1920	1576	1283	+2.5	+3.2	0.0	-8.0	$32
257 Scramjet	100	3745	3450	3173	2912	2666	3114	2643	2235	1883	1578	+2.1	+2.77	0.0	-6.93	NA
6.5x50mm Jap.	139	2360	2160	1970	1790	1620	1720	1440	1195	985	810	+2.5	-1.0	-13.5	0.0	NA
6.5x50mm Jap.	156	2070	1830	1610	1430	1260	1475	1155	900	695	550	+2.5	-4.0	-23.8	0.0	NA
6.5x52mm Car.	139	2580	2360	2160	1970	1790	2045	1725	1440	1195	985	+2.5	0.0	-9.9	-29.0	NA
6.5x52mm Car.	156	2430	2170	1930	1700	1500	2045	1630	1285	1005	780	+2.5	-1.0	-13.9	0.0	NA
6.5x55mm Light Mag.	129	2750	2549	2355	2171	1994	2166	1860	1589	1350	1139	+2.0	0.0	-8.2	-23.9	NA
6.5x55mm Swe.	140	2550	NA	NA	NA	NA	2020	NA	NA	NA	NA	0.0	0.0	0.0	0.0	$18
6.5x55mm Swe.*	139/140	2850	2640	2440	2250	2070	2525	2170	1855	1575	1330	+2.5	+1.6	-5.4	-18.9	$18
6.5x55mm Swe.	156	2650	2370	2110	1870	1650	2425	1950	1550	1215	945	+2.5	0.0	-10.3	-30.6	NA
260 Remington	125	2875	2669	2473	2285	2105	2294	1977	1697	1449	1230	1.71	0.0	-7.4	-21.4	NA
260 Remington	140	2750	2544	2347	2158	1979	2351	2011	1712	1448	1217	+2.2	0.0	-8.6	-24.6	NA
6.5-284 Norma	142	3025	2890	2758	2631	2507	2886	2634	2400	2183	1982	1.13	0.0	-5.7	-16.4	NA
6.71 (264) Phantom	120	3150	2929	2718	2517	2325	2645	2286	1969	1698	1440	+1.3	0.0	-6.0	-17.5	NA
6.5 Rem. Mag.	120	3210	2905	2621	2353	2102	2745	2248	1830	1475	1177	+2.5	+1.7	-4.1	-16.3	Disc.
264 Win. Mag.	140	3030	2782	2548	2326	2114	2854	2406	2018	1682	1389	+2.5	+1.4	-5.1	-18.0	$24
6.71 (264) Blackbird	140	3480	3261	3053	2855	2665	3766	3307	2899	2534	2208	+2.4	+3.1	0.0	-7.4	NA
6.8mm Rem.	115	2800	2535	2285	2049	1828	2002	1641	1333	1072	853	.8	-2.3	-12.1	-30.2	NA
270 Winchester	100	3430	3021	2649	2305	1988	2612	2027	1557	1179	877	+2.0	+1.0	-4.9	-17.5	$17
270 Win. (Rem.)	115	2710	2482	2265	2059	NA	1875	1485	1161	896	NA	0.0	4.8	-17.3	0.0	NA
270 Winchester	130	3060	2776	2510	2259	2022	2702	2225	1818	1472	1180	+2.5	+1.4	-5.3	-18.2	$17
270 Win. Supreme	130	3150	2881	2628	2388	2161	2865	2396	1993	1646	1348	1.3	0.0	-6.4	-18.9	NA
270 Winchester	135	3000	2780	2570	2369	2178	2697	2315	1979	1682	1421	+2.5	+1.4	-6.0	-17.6	$23
270 Winchester*	140	2940	2700	2480	2260	2060	2685	2270	1905	1590	1315	+2.5	+1.8	-4.6	-17.9	$20
270 Win. Light Magnum	130	3215	2998	2790	2590	2400	2983	2594	2246	1936	1662	1.21	0.0	-5.83	-17.0	NA
270 Winchester*	150	2850	2585	2336	2100	1879	2705	2226	1817	1468	1175	+2.5	+1.2	-6.5	-22.0	$17
270 Win. Supreme	150	2930	2693	2468	2254	2051	2860	2416	2030	1693	1402	1.7	0.0	-7.4	-21.6	NA
270 WSM	130	3275	3041	2820	2609	2408	3096	2669	2295	1564	1673	1.1	0.0	-5.5	-16.1	NA
270 WSM	140	3125	2865	2619	2386	2165	3035	2559	2132	1769	1457	1.4	0.0	-6.5	-19.0	NA
270 WSM	150	3120	2923	2734	2554	2380	3242	2845	2490	2172	1886	1.3	0.0	-5.9	-17.2	NA
270 Wea. Mag.	100	3760	3380	3033	2712	2412	3139	2537	2042	1633	1292	+2.0	+2.4	-1.2	-10.1	$32
270 Wea. Mag.	130	3375	3119	2878	2649	2432	3287	2808	2390	2026	1707	+2.5	-2.9	-0.9	-9.9	$32
270 Wea. Mag.*	150	3245	3036	2837	2647	2465	3507	3070	2681	2334	2023	+2.5	+2.6	-1.8	-11.4	$47
7mm BR	140	2216	2012	1821	1643	1481	1525	1259	1031	839	681	+2.0	-3.7	-20.0	0.0	$23
7mm Mauser*	139/140	2660	2435	2221	2018	1827	2199	1843	1533	1266	1037	+2.5	0.0	-9.6	-27.7	$17
7mm Mauser	145	2690	2442	2206	1985	1777	2334	1920	1568	1268	1017	+2.5	+0.1	-9.6	-28.3	$18
7mm Mauser	154	2690	2490	2300	2120	1940	2475	2120	1810	1530	1285	+2.5	+0.8	-7.5	-23.5	$17
7mm Mauser	175	2440	2137	1857	1603	1382	2313	1774	1340	998	742	+2.5	-1.7	-16.1	0.0	$17
7x57 Light Mag.	139	2970	2730	2503	2287	2082	2722	2301	1933	1614	1337	+1.6	0.0	-7.2	-21.0	NA
7x30 Waters	120	2700	2300	1930	1600	1330	1940	1405	990	685	470	+2.5	-0.2	-12.3	0.0	$18
7mm-08 Rem.	120	3000	2725	2467	2223	1992	2398	1979	1621	1316	1058	+2.0	0.0	-7.6	-22.3	$18
7mm-08 Rem.*	140	2860	2625	2402	2189	1988	2542	2142	1793	1490	1228	+2.5	+0.8	-6.9	-21.9	$18
7mm-08 Rem.	154	2715	2510	2315	2128	1950	2520	2155	1832	1548	1300	+2.5	+1.0	-7.0	-22.7	$23
7mm-08 Light Mag.	139	3000	2790	2590	2399	2216	2777	2403	2071	1776	1515	+1.5	0.0	-6.7	-19.4	NA
7x64mm Bren.	140	Not Yet Announced														$17
7x64mm Bren.	154	2820	2610	2420	2230	2050	2720	2335	1995	1695	1430	+2.5	+1.4	-5.7	-19.9	NA
7x64mm Bren.*	160	2850	2669	2495	2327	2166	2885	2530	2211	1924	1667	+2.5	+1.6	-4.8	-17.8	$24

Cartridge	Bullet Weight Grains	VELOCITY (fps)					ENERGY (ft. lbs.)					TRAJ. (in.)				Est. Price/ box
		Muzzle	100 yds.	200 yds.	300 yds.	400 yds.	Muzzle	100 yds.	200 yds.	300 yds.	400 yds.	100 yds.	200 yds.	300 yds.	400 yds.	
7x64mm Bren.	175	Not Yet Announced														$17
284 Winchester	150	2860	2595	2344	2108	1886	2724	2243	1830	1480	1185	+2.5	+0.8	-7.3	-23.2	$24
280 Remington	120	3150	2866	2599	2348	2110	2643	2188	1800	1468	1186	+2.0	+0.6	-6.0	-17.9	$17
280 Remington	140	3000	2758	2528	2309	2102	2797	2363	1986	1657	1373	+2.5	+1.4	-5.2	-18.3	$17
280 Remington*	150	2890	2624	2373	2135	1912	2781	2293	1875	1518	1217	+2.5	+0.8	-7.1	-22.6	$17
280 Remington	160	2840	2637	2442	2556	2078	2866	2471	2120	1809	1535	+2.5	+0.8	-6.7	-21.0	$20
280 Remington	165	2820	2510	2220	1950	1701	2913	2308	1805	1393	1060	+2.5	+0.4	-8.8	-26.5	$17
7x61mm S&H Sup.	154	3060	2720	2400	2100	1820	3200	2520	1965	1505	1135	+2.5	+1.8	-5.0	-19.8	NA
7mm Dakota	160	3200	3001	2811	2630	2455	3637	3200	2808	2456	2140	+2.1	+1.9	-2.8	-12.5	NA
7mm Rem. Mag. (Rem.)	140	2710	2482	2265	2059	NA	2283	1915	1595	1318	NA	0.0	-4.5	-1.57	0.0	NA
7mm Rem. Mag.*	139/140	3150	2930	2710	2510	2320	3085	2660	2290	1960	1670	+2.5	+2.4	-2.4	-12.7	$21
7mm Rem. Hvy Mag	139	3250	3044	2847	2657	2475	3259	2860	2501	2178	1890	1.1	0.0	-5.5	-16.2	NA
7mm Rem. Mag.	150/154	3110	2830	2568	2320	2085	3221	2667	2196	1792	1448	+2.5	+1.6	-4.6	-16.5	$21
7mm Rem. Mag.*	160/162	2950	2730	2520	2320	2120	3090	2650	2250	1910	1600	+2.5	+1.8	-4.4	-17.8	$34
7mm Rem. Mag.	165	2900	2699	2507	2324	2147	3081	2669	2303	1978	1689	+2.5	+1.2	-5.9	-19.0	$28
7mm Rem Mag.	175	2860	2645	2440	2244	2057	3178	2718	2313	1956	1644	+2.5	+1.0	-6.5	-20.7	$21
7mm Rem. SA ULTRA MAG	140	3175	2934	2707	2490	2283	3033	2676	2277	1927	1620	1.3	0.0	-6	-17.7	NA
7mm Rem. SA ULTRA MAG	150	3110	2828	2563	2313	2077	3221	2663	2188	1782	1437	2.5	2.1	-3.6	-15.8	NA
7mm Rem. SA ULTRA MAG	160	2960	2762	2572	2390	2215	3112	2709	2350	2029	1743	2.6	2.2	-3.6	-15.4	NA
7mm Rem. WSM	140	3225	3008	2801	2603	2414	3233	2812	2438	2106	1812	1.2	0.0	-5.6	-16.4	NA
7mm Rem. WSM	160	2990	2744	2512	2081	1883	3176	2675	2241	1864	1538	1.6	0.0	-7.1	-20.8	NA
7mm Wea. Mag.	140	3225	2970	2729	2501	2283	3233	2741	2315	1943	1621	+2.5	+2.0	-3.2	-14.0	$35
7mm Wea. Mag.	154	3260	3023	2799	2586	2382	3539	3044	2609	2227	1890	+2.5	+2.8	-1.5	-10.8	$32
7mm Wea. Mag.*	160	3200	3004	2816	2637	2464	3637	3205	2817	2469	2156	+2.5	+2.7	-1.5	-10.6	$47
7mm Wea. Mag.	165	2950	2747	2553	2367	2189	3188	2765	2388	2053	1756	+2.5	+1.8	-4.2	-16.4	$43
7mm Wea. Mag.	175	2910	2693	2486	2288	2098	3293	2818	2401	2033	1711	+2.5	+1.2	-5.9	-19.4	$35
7.21(.284) Tomahawk	140	3300	3118	2943	2774	2612	3386	3022	2693	2393	2122	2.3	3.20	0.0	-7.7	NA
7mm STW	140	3325	3064	2818	2585	2364	3436	2918	2468	2077	1737	+2.3	+1.8	-3.0	-13.1	NA
7mm STW Supreme	160	3150	2894	2652	2422	2204	3526	2976	2499	2085	1727	1.3	0.0	-6.3	-18.5	NA
7mm Rem. Ultra Mag.	140	3425	3184	2956	2740	2534	3646	3151	2715	2333	1995	1.7	1.60	-2.6	-11.4	NA
7mm Firehawk	140	3625	3373	3135	2909	2695	4084	3536	3054	2631	2258	+2.2	+2.9	0.0	-7.03	NA
7.21 (.284) Firebird	140	3750	3522	3306	3101	2905	4372	3857	3399	2990	2625	1.6	2.4	0.0	-6.0	NA
30 Carbine	110	1990	1567	1236	1035	923	977	600	373	262	208	0.0	-13.5	0.0	0.0	$28**
303 Savage	190	1890	1612	1327	1183	1055	1507	1096	794	591	469	+2.5	-7.6	0.0	0.0	$24
30 Remington	170	2120	1822	1555	1328	1153	1696	1253	913	666	502	+2.5	-4.7	-26.3	0.0	$20
7.62x39mm Rus.	123/125	2300	2030	1780	1550	1350	1445	1125	860	655	500	+2.5	-2.0	-17.5	0.0	$13
30-30 Win.	55	3400	2693	2085	1570	1187	1412	886	521	301	172	+2.0	0.0	-10.2	-35.0	$18
30-30 Win.	125	2570	2090	1660	1320	1080	1830	1210	770	480	320	-2.0	-2.6	-19.9	0.0	$13
30-30 Win.	150	2390	1973	1605	1303	1095	1902	1296	858	565	399	+2.5	-3.2	-22.5	0.0	$13
30-30 Win. Supreme	150	2480	2095	1747	1446	1209	2049	1462	1017	697	487	0.0	-6.5	-24.5	0.0	NA
30-30 Win.	160	2300	1997	1719	1473	1268	1879	1416	1050	771	571	+2.5	-2.9	-20.2	0.0	$18
30-30 PMC Cowboy	170	1300	1198	1121			638	474				0.0	-27.0	0.0	0.0	NA
30-30 Win.*	170	2200	1895	1619	1381	1191	1827	1355	989	720	535	+2.5	-5.8	-23.6	0.0	$13
300 Savage	150	2630	2354	2094	1853	1631	2303	1845	1462	1143	886	+2.5	-0.4	-10.1	-30.7	$17
300 Savage	180	2350	2137	1935	1754	1570	2207	1825	1496	1217	985	+2.5	-1.6	-15.2	0.0	$17
30-40 Krag	180	2430	2213	2007	1813	1632	2360	1957	1610	1314	1064	+2.5	-1.4	-13.8	0.0	$18
7.65x53mm Arg.	180	2590	2390	2200	2010	1830	2685	2280	1925	1615	1345	+2.5	0.0	-27.6	0.0	NA
307 Winchester	150	2760	2321	1924	1575	1289	2530	1795	1233	826	554	+2.5	-1.5	-13.6	0.0	Disc.
307 Winchester	180	2510	2179	1874	1599	1362	2519	1898	1404	1022	742	+2.5	-1.6	-15.6	0.0	$20
7.5x55 Swiss	180	2650	2450	2250	2060	1880	2805	2390	2020	1700	1415	+2.5	+0.6	-8.1	-24.9	NA
308 Winchester	55	3770	3215	2726	2286	1888	1735	1262	907	638	435	-2.0	+1.4	-3.8	-15.8	$22
308 Winchester	150	2820	2533	2263	2009	1774	2648	2137	1705	1344	1048	+2.5	+0.4	-8.5	-26.1	$17
308 Winchester	165	2700	2440	2194	1963	1748	2670	2180	1763	1411	1199	+2.5	0.0	-9.7	-28.5	$20
308 Winchester	168	2680	2493	2314	2143	1979	2678	2318	1998	1713	1460	+2.5	0.0	-8.9	-25.3	$18
308 Win. (Fed.)	170	2000	1740	1510	NA	NA	1510	1145	860	NA	NA	0.00	0.0	0.0	0.0	NA
308 Winchester	178	2620	2415	2220	2034	1857	2713	2306	1948	1635	1363	+2.5	0.0	-9.6	-27.6	$23
308 Winchester*	180	2620	2393	2178	1974	1782	2743	2288	1896	1557	1269	+2.5	-0.2	-10.2	-28.5	$17
308 Light Mag.*	150	2980	2703	2442	2195	1964	2959	2433	1986	1606	1285	+1.6	0.0	-7.5	-22.2	NA
308 Light Mag.	165	2870	2658	2456	2263	2078	3019	2589	2211	1877	1583	+1.7	0.0	-7.5	-21.8	NA
308 High Energy	165	2870	2600	2350	2120	1890	3020	2485	2030	1640	1310	+1.8	0.0	-8.2	-24.0	NA
308 Light Mag.	168	2870	2658	2456	2263	2078	3019	2589	2211	1877	1583	+1.7	0.0	-7.5	-21.8	NA
308 High Energy	180	2740	2550	2370	2200	2030	3000	2600	2245	1925	1645	+1.9	0.0	-8.2	-23.5	NA
30-06 Spfd.	55	4080	3485	2965	2502	2083	2033	1483	1074	764	530	+2.0	+1.9	-2.1	-11.7	$22

AVERAGE CENTERFIRE RIFLE CARTRIDGE BALLISTICS & PRICES, *continued*

Cartridge	Bullet Weight Grains	VELOCITY (fps)					ENERGY (ft. lbs.)					TRAJ. (in.)				Est. Price/ box
		Muzzle	100 yds.	200 yds.	300 yds.	400 yds.	Muzzle	100 yds.	200 yds.	300 yds.	400 yds.	100 yds.	200 yds.	300 yds.	400 yds.	
30-06 Spfd. (Rem.)	125	2660	2335	2034	1757	NA	1964	1513	1148	856	NA	0.0	-5.2	-18.9	0.0	NA
30-06 Spfd.	125	3140	2780	2447	2138	1853	2736	2145	1662	1279	953	+2.0	+1.0	-6.2	-21.0	$17
30-06 Spfd.	150	2910	2617	2342	2083	1853	2820	2281	1827	1445	1135	+2.5	+0.8	-7.2	-23.4	$17
30-06 Spfd.	152	2910	2654	2413	2184	1968	2858	2378	1965	1610	1307	+2.5	+1.0	-6.6	-21.3	$23
30-06 Spfd.*	165	2800	2534	2283	2047	1825	2872	2352	1909	1534	1220	+2.5	+0.4	-8.4	-25.5	$17
30-06 Spfd.	168	2710	2522	2346	2169	2003	2739	2372	2045	1754	1497	+2.5	+0.4	-8.0	-23.5	$18
30-06 Spfd. (Fed.)	170	2000	1740	1510	NA	NA	1510	1145	860	NA	NA	0.0	0.0	0.0	0.0	NA
30-06 Spfd.	178	2720	2511	2311	2121	1939	2924	2491	2111	1777	1486	+2.5	+0.4	-8.2	-24.6	$23
30-06 Spfd.*	180	2700	2469	2250	2042	1846	2913	2436	2023	1666	1362	-2.5	0.0	-9.3	-27.0	$17
30-06 Spfd.	220	2410	2130	1870	1632	1422	2837	2216	1708	1301	988	+2.5	-1.7	-18.0	0.0	$17
30-06 Light Mag.	150	3100	2815	2548	2295	2058	3200	2639	2161	1755	1410	+1.4	0.0	-6.8	-20.3	NA
30-06 Light Mag.	180	2880	2676	2480	2293	2114	3316	2862	2459	2102	1786	+1.7	0.0	-7.3	-21.3	NA
30-06 High Energy	180	2880	2690	2500	2320	2150	3315	2880	2495	2150	1845	+1.7	0.0	-7.2	-21.0	NA
300 REM SA ULTRA MAG	150	3200	2901	2622	2359	2112	3410	2803	2290	1854	1485	1.3	0.0	-6.4	-19.1	NA
300 REM SA ULTRA MAG	165	3075	2792	2527	2276	2040	3464	2856	2339	1898	1525	1.5	0.0	-7	-20.7	NA
300 REM SA ULTRA MAG	180	2960	2761	2571	2389	2214	3501	3047	2642	2280	1959	2.6	2.2	-3.6	-15.4	NA
7.82 (308) Patriot	150	3250	2999	2762	2537	2323	3519	2997	2542	2145	1798	+1.2	0.0	-5.8	-16.9	NA
300 WSM	150	3300	3061	2834	2619	2414	3628	3121	2676	2285	1941	1.1	0.0	-5.4	-15.9	NA
300 WSM	180	2970	2741	2524	2317	2120	3526	3005	2547	2147	1797	1.6	0.0	-7.0	-20.5	NA
300 WSM	180	3010	2923	2734	2554	2380	3242	2845	2490	2172	1886	1.3	0	-5.9	-17.2	NA
308 Norma Mag.	180	3020	2820	2630	2440	2270	3645	3175	2755	2385	2050	+2.5	+2.0	-3.5	-14.8	NA
300 Dakota	200	3000	2824	2656	2493	2336	3996	3542	3131	2760	2423	+2.2	+1.5	-4.0	-15.2	NA
300 H&H Magnum*	180	2880	2640	2412	2196	1990	3315	2785	2325	1927	1583	+2.5	+0.8	-6.8	-21.7	$24
300 H&H Magnum	220	2550	2267	2002	1757	NA	3167	2510	1958	1508	NA	-2.5	-0.4	-12.0	0.0	NA
300 Peterson	180	3500	3319	3145	2978	2817	4896	4401	3953	3544	3172	+2.3	+2.9	0.0	-6.8	NA
300 Win. Mag.	150	3290	2951	2636	2342	2068	3605	2900	2314	1827	1424	+2.5	+1.9	-3.8	-15.8	$22
300 Win. Mag.	165	3100	2877	2665	2462	2269	3522	3033	2603	2221	1897	+2.5	+2.4	-3.0	-16.9	$24
300 Win. Mag.	178	2900	2760	2568	2375	2191	3509	3030	2606	2230	1897	+2.5	+1.4	-5.0	-17.6	$29
300 Win. Mag.*	180	2960	2745	2540	2344	2157	3501	3011	2578	2196	1859	+2.5	+1.2	-5.5	-18.5	$22
300 W.M. High Energy	180	3100	2830	2580	2340	2110	3840	3205	2660	2190	1790	+1.4	0.0	-6.6	-19.7	NA
300 W.M. Light Mag.	180	3100	2879	2668	2467	2275	3840	3313	2845	2431	2068	+1.39	0.0	-6.45	-18.7	NA
300 Win. Mag.	190	2885	1691	2506	2327	2156	3511	3055	2648	2285	1961	+2.5	+1.2	-5.7	-19.0	$26
300 W.M. High Energy	200	2930	2740	2550	2370	2200	3810	3325	2885	2495	2145	+1.6	0.0	-6.9	-20.1	NA
300 Win. Mag.*	200	2825	2595	2376	2167	1970	3545	2991	2508	2086	1742	-2.5	+1.6	-4.7	-17.2	$36
300 Win. Mag.	220	2680	2448	2228	2020	1823	3508	2927	2424	1993	1623	+2.5	0.0	-9.5	-27.5	$23
300 Rem. Ultra Mag.	150	3450	3208	2980	2762	2556	3964	3427	2956	2541	2175	1.7	1.5	-2.6	-11.2	NA
300 Rem. Ultra Mag.	180	3250	3037	2834	2640	2454	4221	3686	3201	2786	2407	2.4	0.0	-3.0	-12.7	NA
300 Wea. Mag.	100	3900	3441	3038	2652	2305	3714	2891	2239	1717	1297	+2.0	+2.6	-0.6	-8.7	$32
300 Wea. Mag.	150	3600	3307	3033	2776	2533	4316	3642	3064	2566	2137	+2.5	+3.2	0.0	-8.1	$32
300 Wea. Mag.	165	3450	3210	3000	2792	2593	4360	3796	3297	2855	2464	+2.5	+3.2	0.0	-7.8	NA
300 Wea. Mag.	178	3120	2902	2695	2497	2308	3847	3329	2870	2464	2104	+2.5	-1.7	-3.6	-14.7	$43
300 Wea. Mag.	180	3330	3110	2910	2710	2520	4430	3875	3375	2935	2540	+1.0	0.0	-5.2	-15.1	NA
300 Wea. Mag.	190	3030	2830	2638	2455	2279	3873	3378	2936	2542	2190	+2.5	+1.6	-4.3	-16.0	$38
300 Wea. Mag.	220	2850	2541	2283	1964	1736	3967	3155	2480	1922	1471	+2.5	+0.4	-8.5	-26.4	$35
300 Warbird	180	3400	3180	2971	2772	2582	4620	4042	3528	3071	2664	+2.59	+3.25	0.0	-7.95	NA
300 Pegasus	180	3500	3319	3145	2978	2817	4896	4401	3953	3544	3172	+2.28	+2.89	0.0	-6.79	NA
32-20 Win.	100	1210	1021	913	834	769	325	231	185	154	131	0.0	-32.3	0.0	0.0	$23**
303 British	150	2685	2441	2210	1992	1787	2401	1984	1627	1321	1064	+2.5	+0.6	-8.4	-26.2	$18
303 British	180	2460	2124	1817	1542	1311	2418	1803	1319	950	687	+2.5	-1.8	-16.8	0.0	$18
303 Light Mag.	150	2830	2570	2325	2094	1884	2667	2199	1800	1461	1185	+2.0	0.0	-8.4	-24.6	NA
7.62x54mm Rus.	146	2950	2730	2520	2320	NA	2820	2415	2055	1740	NA	+2.5	+2.0	-4.4	-17.7	NA
7.62x54mm Rus.	180	2580	2370	2180	2000	1820	2650	2250	1900	1590	1100	+2.5	0.0	-9.8	-28.5	NA
7.7x58mm Jap.	180	2500	2300	2100	1920	1750	2490	2105	1770	1475	1225	+2.5	0.0	-10.4	-30.2	NA
8x57mm JS Mau.	165	2850	2520	2210	1930	1670	2965	2330	1795	1360	1015	+2.5	+1.0	-7.7	0.0	NA
32 Win. Special	170	2250	1921	1626	1372	1175	1911	1393	998	710	521	+2.5	-3.5	-22.9	0.0	$14
8mm Mauser	170	2360	1969	1622	1333	1123	2102	1464	993	671	476	+2.5	-3.1	-22.2	0.0	$18
8mm Rem. Mag.	185	3080	2761	2464	2186	1927	3896	3131	2494	1963	1525	+2.5	+1.4	-5.5	-19.7	$30
8mm Rem. Mag.	220	2830	2581	2346	2123	1913	3912	3254	2688	2201	1787	+2.5	+0.6	-7.6	-23.5	Disc.
338-06	200	2750	2553	2364	2184	2011	3358	2894	2482	2118	1796	+1.9	0.0	-8.22	-23.6	NA
330 Dakota	250	2900	2719	2545	2378	2217	4668	4103	3595	3138	2727	+2.3	+1.3	-5.0	-17.5	NA
338 Lapua	250	2963	2795	2640	2493	NA	4842	4341	3881	3458	NA	+1.9	0.0	-7.9	0.0	NA
338 Win. Mag.	200	2960	2658	2375	2110	1862	3890	3137	2505	1977	1539	+2.5	+1.0	-6.7	-22.3	$27
338 Win. Mag.*	210	2830	2590	2370	2150	1940	3735	3130	2610	2155	1760	+2.5	+1.4	-6.0	-20.9	$33
338 Win. Mag.*	225	2785	2517	2266	2029	1808	3871	3165	2565	2057	1633	+2.5	+0.4	-8.5	-25.9	$27
338 W.M. Heavy Mag.	225	2920	2678	2449	2232	2027	4259	3583	2996	2489	2053	+1.75	0.0	-7.65	-22.0	NA

Cartridge	Bullet Weight Grains	VELOCITY (fps)					ENERGY (ft. lbs.)					TRAJ. (in.)				Est. Price/ box
		Muzzle	100 yds.	200 yds.	300 yds.	400 yds.	Muzzle	100 yds.	200 yds.	300 yds.	400 yds.	100 yds.	200 yds.	300 yds.	400 yds.	
338 W.M. High Energy	225	2940	2690	2450	2230	2010	4320	3610	3000	2475	2025	+1.7	0.0	-7.5	-22.0	NA
338 Win. Mag.	230	2780	2573	2375	2186	2005	3948	3382	2881	2441	2054	+2.5	+1.2	-6.3	-21.0	$40
338 Win. Mag.*	250	2660	2456	2261	2075	1898	3927	3348	2837	2389	1999	+2.5	+0.2	-9.0	-26.2	$27
338 W.M. High Energy	250	2800	2610	2420	2250	2080	4350	3775	3260	2805	2395	+1.8	0.0	-7.8	-22.5	NA
338 Ultra Mag.	250	2860	2645	2440	2244	2057	4540	3882	3303	2794	2347	1.7	0.0	-7.6	-22.1	NA
8.59(.338) Galaxy	200	3100	2899	2707	2524	2347	4269	3734	3256	2829	2446	3	3.80	0.0	-9.3	NA
340 Wea. Mag.*	210	3250	2991	2746	2515	2295	4924	4170	3516	2948	2455	+2.5	+1.9	-1.8	-11.8	$56
340 Wea. Mag.*	250	3000	2806	2621	2443	2272	4995	4371	3812	3311	2864	+2.5	+2.0	-3.5	-14.8	$56
338 A-Square	250	3120	2799	2500	2220	1958	5403	4348	3469	2736	2128	+2.5	+2.7	-1.5	-10.5	NA
338-378 Wea. Mag.	225	3180	2974	2778	2591	2410	5052	4420	3856	3353	2902	3.1	3.80	0.0	-8.9	NA
338 Titan	225	3230	3010	2800	2600	2409	5211	4524	3916	3377	2898	+3.07	+3.80	0.0	-8.95	NA
338 Excalibur	200	3600	3361	3134	2920	2715	5755	5015	4363	3785	3274	+2.23	+2.87	0.0	-6.99	NA
338 Excalibur	250	3250	2922	2618	2333	2066	5863	4740	3804	3021	2370	+1.3	0.0	-6.35	-19.2	NA
348 Winchester	200	2520	2215	1931	1672	1443	2820	2178	1656	1241	925	+2.5	-1.4	-14.7	0.0	$42
357 Magnum	158	1830	1427	1138	980	883	1175	715	454	337	274	0.0	-16.2	-33.1	0.0	$25**
35 Remington	150	2300	1874	1506	1218	1039	1762	1169	755	494	359	+2.5	-4.1	-26.3	0.0	$16
35 Remington	200	2080	1698	1376	1140	1001	1921	1280	841	577	445	+2.5	-6.3	-17.1	-33.6	$16
356 Winchester	200	2460	2114	1797	1517	1284	2688	1985	1434	1022	732	+2.5	-1.8	-15.1	0.0	$31
356 Winchester	250	2160	1911	1682	1476	1299	2591	2028	1571	1210	937	+2.5	-3.7	-22.2	0.0	$31
358 Winchester	200	2490	2171	1876	1619	1379	2753	2093	1563	1151	844	+2.5	-1.6	-15.6	0.0	$31
358 STA	275	2850	2562	2292	2039	NA	4958	4009	3208	2539	NA	+1.9	0.0	-8.6	0.0	NA
350 Rem. Mag.	200	2710	2410	2130	1870	1631	3261	2579	2014	1553	1181	+2.5	-0.2	-10.0	-30.1	$33
35 Whelen	200	2675	2378	2100	1842	1606	3177	2510	1958	1506	1145	+2.5	-0.2	-10.3	-31.1	$20
35 Whelen	225	2500	2300	2110	1930	1770	3120	2650	2235	1870	1560	+2.6	0.0	-10.2	-29.9	NA
35 Whelen	250	2400	2197	2005	1823	1652	3197	2680	2230	1844	1515	+2.5	-1.2	-13.7	0.0	$20
358 Norma Mag.	250	2800	2510	2230	1970	1730	4350	3480	2750	2145	1655	+2.5	+1.0	-7.6	-25.2	NA
358 STA	275	2850	2562	229*2	2039	1764	4959	4009	3208	2539	1899	+1.9	0.0	-8.58	-26.1	NA
9.3x57mm Mau.	286	2070	1810	1590	1390	1110	2710	2090	1600	1220	955	+2.5	-2.6	-22.5	0.0	NA
9.3x62mm Mau.	286	2360	2089	1844	1623	NA	3538	2771	2157	1670	1260	+2.5	-1.6	-21.0	0.0	NA
9.3x64mm	286	2700	2505	2318	2139	1968	4629	3984	3411	2906	2460	+2.5	+2.7	-4.5	-19.2	NA
9.3x74Rmm	286	2360	2089	1844	1623	NA	3538	2771	2157	1670	NA	+2.5	-2.0	-11.0	0.0	NA
38-55 Win.	255	1320	1190	1091	1018	963	987	802	674	587	525	0.0	-23.4	0.0	0.0	$25
375 Winchester	200	2200	1841	1526	1268	1089	2150	1506	1034	714	527	+2.5	-4.0	-26.2	0.0	$27
375 Winchester	250	1900	1647	1424	1239	1103	2005	1506	1126	852	676	+2.5	-6.9	-33.3	0.0	$27
376 Steyr	225	2600	2331	2078	1842	1625	3377	2714	2157	1694	1319	2.5	0.0	-10.6	-31.4	NA
376 Steyr	270	2600	2372	2156	1951	1759	4052	3373	2787	2283	1855	2.3	0.0	-9.9	-28.9	NA
375 Dakota	300	2600	2316	2051	1804	1579	4502	3573	2800	2167	1661	+2.4	0.0	-11.0	-32.7	NA
375 N.E. 2-1/2"	270	2000	1740	1507	1310	NA	2398	1815	1362	1026	NA	+2.5	-6.0	-30.0	0.0	NA
375 Flanged	300	2450	2150	1886	1640	NA	3998	3102	2369	1790	NA	+2.5	-2.4	-17.0	0.0	NA
375 H&H Magnum	250	2670	2450	2240	2040	1850	3955	3335	2790	2315	1905	+2.5	-0.4	-10.2	-28.4	NA
375 H&H Magnum	270	2690	2420	2166	1928	1707	4337	3510	2812	2228	1747	+2.5	0.0	-10.0	-29.4	$28
375 H&H Magnum*	300	2530	2245	1979	1733	1512	4263	3357	2608	2001	1523	+2.5	-1.0	-10.5	-33.6	$28
375 H&H Hvy. Mag.	270	2870	2628	2399	2182	1976	4937	4141	3451	2150	1845	+1.7	0.0	-7.2	-21.0	NA
375 H&H Hvy. Mag.	300	2705	2386	2090	1816	1568	4873	3793	2908	2195	1637	+2.3	0.0	-10.4	-31.4	NA
375 Rem. Ultra Mag.	270	2900	2558	2241	1947	1678	5041	3922	3010	2272	1689	1.9	2.7	-8.9	-27	NA
375 Rem. Ultra Mag.	300	2760	2505	2263	2035	1822	5073	4178	3412	2759	2210	2.0	0.0	-8.8	-26.1	NA
375 Wea. Mag.	300	2700	2420	2157	1911	1685	4856	3901	3100	2432	1891	+2.5	-.04	-10.7	0.0	NA
378 Wea. Mag.	270	3180	2976	2781	2594	2415	6062	5308	4635	4034	3495	+2.5	+2.6	-1.8	-11.3	$71
378 Wea. Mag.	300	2929	2576	2252	1952	1680	5698	4419	3379	2538	1881	+2.5	+1.2	-7.0	-24.5	$77
375 A-Square	300	2920	2626	2351	2093	1850	5679	4594	3681	2917	2281	+2.5	+1.4	-6.0	-21.0	NA
38-40 Win.	180	1160	999	901	827	764	538	399	324	273	233	0.0	-33.9	0.0	0.0	$42**
405 WIN	300	2200	1851	1545	1296		3224	2282	1589	1119		4.6	0.0	-19.5	0.0	NA
450/400-3"	400	2150	1932	1730	1545	1379	4105	3316	2659	2119	1689	+2.5	-4.0	-9.5	-30.0	NA
416 Dakota	400	2450	2294	2143	1998	1859	5330	4671	4077	3544	3068	+2.5	-0.2	-10.5	-29.4	NA
416 Taylor	400	2350	2117	1896	1693	NA	4905	3980	3194	2547	NA	+2.5	-1.2	15.0	0.0	NA
416 Hoffman	400	2380	2145	1923	1718	1529	5031	4087	3285	2620	2077	+2.5	-1.0	-14.1	0.0	NA
416 Rigby	350	2600	2449	2303	2162	2026	5253	4661	4122	3632	3189	+2.5	-1.8	-10.2	-26.0	NA
416 Rigby	400	2370	2210	2050	1900	NA	4990	4315	3720	3185	NA	+2.5	-0.7	-12.1	0.0	NA
416 Rigby	410	2370	2110	1870	1640	NA	5115	4050	3165	2455	NA	+2.5	-2.4	-17.3	0.0	$110
416 Rem. Mag.*	350	2520	2270	2034	1814	1611	4935	4004	3216	2557	2017	+2.5	-0.8	-12.6	-35.0	$82
416 Rem. Mag.*	400	2400	2175	1962	1763	1579	5115	4201	3419	2760	2214	+2.5	-1.5	-14.6	0.0	$80
416 Wea. Mag.*	400	2700	2397	2115	1852	1613	6474	5104	3971	3047	2310	+2.5	0.0	-10.1	-30.4	$96
10.57 (416) Meteor	400	2730	2532	2342	2161	1987	6621	5695	4874	4147	3508	+1.9	0.0	-8.3	-24.0	NA
404 Jeffrey	400	2150	1924	1716	1525	NA	4105	3289	2614	2064	NA	+2.5	-4.0	-22.1	0.0	NA
425 Express	400	2400	2160	1934	1725	NA	5115	4145	3322	2641	NA	+2.5	-1.0	-14.0	0.0	NA
44-40 Win.	200	1190	1006	900	822	756	629	449	360	300	254	0.0	-33.3	0.0	0.0	$36**
44 Rem. Mag.	210	1920	1477	1155	982	880	1719	1017	622	450	361	0.0	-17.6	0.0	0.0	$14

Cartridge	Bullet Weight Grains	VELOCITY (fps)					ENERGY (ft. lbs.)					TRAJ. (in.)				Est. Price/ box
		Muzzle	100 yds.	200 yds.	300 yds.	400 yds.	Muzzle	100 yds.	200 yds.	300 yds.	400 yds.	100 yds.	200 yds.	300 yds.	400 yds.	
44 Rem. Mag.	240	1760	1380	1114	970	878	1650	1015	661	501	411	0.0	-17.6	0.0	0.0	$13
444 Marlin	240	2350	1815	1377	1087	941	2942	1753	1001	630	472	+2.5	-15.1	-31.0	0.0	$22
444 Marlin	265	2120	1733	1405	1160	1012	2644	1768	1162	791	603	+2.5	-6.0	-32.2	0.0	Disc.
444 Marlin Light Mag	265	2335	1913	1551	1266		3208	2153	1415	943		2.0	-4.90	-26.5	0.0	NA
45-70 Govt.	300	1810	1497	1244	1073	969	2182	1492	1031	767	625	0.0	-14.8	0.0	0.0	$21
45-70 Govt. Supreme	300	1880	1558	1292	1103	988	2355	1616	1112	811	651	0.0	-12.9	-46.0	-105.0	NA
45-70 Govt. CorBon	350	1800	1526	1296			2519	1810	1307			0.0	-14.6	0.0	0.0	NA
45-70 Govt.	405	1330	1168	1055	977	918	1590	1227	1001	858	758	0.0	-24.6	0.0	0.0	$21
45-70 Govt. PMC Cowboy	405	1550	1193				1639	1280				0.0	-23.9	0.0	0.0	NA
45-70 Govt. Garrett	415	1850					3150					3.0	-7.0	0.0	0.0	NA
45-70 Govt. Garrett	530	1550	1343	1178	1062	982	2828	2123	1633	1327	1135	0.0	-17.8	0.0	0.0	NA
450 Marlin	350	2100	1774	1488	1254	1089	3427	2446	1720	1222	922	0.0	-9.7	-35.2	0.0	NA
458 Win. Magnum	350	2470	1990	1570	1250	1060	4740	3065	1915	1205	870	+2.5	-2.5	-21.6	0.0	$43
458 Win. Magnum	400	2380	2170	1960	1770	NA	5030	4165	3415	2785	NA	+2.5	-0.4	-13.4	0.0	$73
458 Win. Magnum	465	2220	1999	1791	1601	NA	5088	4127	3312	2646	NA	+2.5	-2.0	-17.7	0.0	NA
458 Win. Magnum	500	2040	1823	1623	1442	1237	4620	3689	2924	2308	1839	+2.5	-3.5	-22.0	0.0	$61
458 Win. Magnum	510	2040	1770	1527	1319	1157	4712	3547	2640	1970	1516	+2.5	-4.1	-25.0	0.0	$41
450 Dakota	500	2450	2235	2030	1838	1658	6663	5544	4576	3748	3051	+2.5	-0.6	-12.0	-33.8	NA
450 N.E. 3-1/4"	465	2190	1970	1765	1577	NA	4952	4009	3216	2567	NA	+2.5	-3.0	-20.0	0.0	NA
450 N.E. 3-1/4"	500	2150	1920	1708	1514	NA	5132	4093	3238	2544	NA	+2.5	-4.0	-22.9	0.0	NA
450 No. 2	465	2190	1970	1765	1577	NA	4952	4009	3216	2567	NA	+2.5	-3.0	-20.0	0.0	NA
450 No. 2	500	2150	1920	1708	1514	NA	5132	4093	3238	2544	NA	+2.5	-4.0	-22.9	0.0	NA
458 Lott	465	2380	2150	1932	1730	NA	5848	4773	3855	3091	NA	+2.5	-1.0	-14.0	0.0	NA
458 Lott	500	2300	2062	1838	1633	NA	5873	4719	3748	2960	NA	+2.5	-1.6	-16.4	0.0	NA
450 Ackley Mag.	465	2400	2169	1950	1747	NA	5947	4857	3927	3150	NA	+2.5	-1.0	-13.7	0.0	NA
450 Ackley Mag.	500	2320	2081	1855	1649	NA	5975	4085	3820	3018	NA	+2.5	-1.2	-15.0	0.0	NA
460 Short A-Sq.	500	2420	2175	1943	1729	NA	6501	5250	4193	3319	NA	+2.5	-0.8	-12.8	0.0	NA
460 Wea. Mag.	500	2700	2404	2128	1869	1635	8092	6416	5026	3878	2969	+2.5	+0.6	-8.9	-28.0	$72
500/465 N.E.	480	2150	1917	1703	1507	NA	4926	3917	3089	2419	NA	+2.5	-4.0	-22.2	0.0	NA
470 Rigby	500	2150	1940	1740	1560	NA	5130	4170	3360	2695	NA	+2.5	-2.8	-19.4	0.0	NA
470 Nitro Ex.	480	2190	1954	1735	1536	NA	5111	4070	3210	2515	NA	+2.5	-3.5	-20.8	0.0	NA
470 Nitro Ex.	500	2150	1890	1650	1440	1270	5130	3965	3040	2310	1790	+2.5	-4.3	-24.0	0.0	$177
475 No. 2	500	2200	1955	1728	1522	NA	5375	4243	3316	2573	NA	+2.5	-3.2	-20.9	0.0	NA
505 Gibbs	525	2300	2063	1840	1637	NA	6166	4922	3948	3122	NA	+2.5	-3.0	-18.0	0.0	NA
500 N.E.-3"	570	2150	1928	1722	1533	NA	5850	4703	3752	2975	NA	+2.5	-3.7	-22.0	0.0	NA
500 N.E.-3"	600	2150	1927	1721	1531	NA	6158	4947	3944	3124	NA	+2.5	-4.0	-22.0	0.0	NA
495 A-Square	570	2350	2117	1896	1693	NA	5850	4703	3752	2975	NA	+2.5	-1.0	-14.5	0.0	NA
495 A-Square	600	2280	2050	1833	1635	NA	6925	5598	4478	3562	NA	+2.5	-2.0	-17.0	0.0	NA
500 A-Square	600	2380	2144	1922	1766	NA	7546	6126	4920	3922	NA	+2.5	-3.0	-17.0	0.0	NA
500 A-Square	707	2250	2040	1841	1567	NA	7947	6530	5318	4311	NA	+2.5	-2.0	-17.0	0.0	NA
500 BMG PMC	660	3080	2854	2639	2444	2248	13688	500 yd. zero				+3.1	+3.9	+4.7	+2.8	NA
577 Nitro Ex.	750	2050	1793	1562	1360	NA	6990	5356	4065	3079	NA	+2.5	-5.0	-26.0	0.0	NA
577 Tyrannosaur	750	2400	2141	1898	1675	NA	9591	7633	5996	4671	NA	+3.0	0.0	-12.9	0.0	NA
600 N.E.	900	1950	1680	1452	NA	NA	7596	5634	4212	NA	NA	+5.6	0.0	0.0	0.0	NA
700 N.E.	1200	1900	1676	1472	NA	NA	9618	7480	5774	NA	NA	+5.7	0.0	0.0	0.0	NA

Centerfire Handgun Cartridges — Ballistics & Prices

Notes: Blanks are available in 32 S&W, 38 S&W and 38 Special. "V" after barrel length indicates test barrel was vented to produce ballistics similar to a revolver with a normal barrel-to-cylinder gap. Ammo prices are per 50 rounds except when marked with an ** which signifies a 20 round box; *** signifies a 25-round box. Not all loads are available from all ammo manufacturers. Listed loads are those made by Remington, Winchester, Federal, and others. DISC. is a discontinued load. Prices are rounded to nearest whole dollar and will vary with brand and retail outlet. † = new bullet weight this year; "c" indicates a change in data.

Cartridge	Bullet Wgt. Grs.	VELOCITY (fps)			ENERGY (ft. lbs.)			Mid-Range Traj. (in.)		Bbl. Lgth. (in).	Est. Price/ box
		Muzzle	50 yds.	100 yds.	Muzzle	50 yds.	100 yds.	50 yds.	100 yds.		
221 Rem. Fireball	50	2650	2380	2130	780	630	505	0.2	0.8	10.5"	$15
25 Automatic	35	900	813	742	63	51	43	NA	NA	2"	$18
25 Automatic	45	815	730	655	65	55	40	1.8	7.7	2"	$21
25 Automatic	50	760	705	660	65	55	50	2.0	8.7	2"	$17
7.5mm Swiss	107	1010	NA	NA	240	NA	NA	NA	NA	NA	NEW
7.62mmTokarev	87	1390	NA	NA	365	NA	NA	0.6	NA	4.5"	NA
7.62 Nagant	97	790	NA	NA	134	NA	NA	NA	NA	NA	NEW
7.63 Mauser	88	1440	NA	NA	405	NA	NA	NA	NA	NA	NEW
30 Luger	93†	1220	1110	1040	305	255	225	0.9	3.5	4.5"	$34
30 Carbine	110	1790	1600	1430	785	625	500	0.4	1.7	10"	$28
30-357 AeT	123	1992	NA	NA	1084	NA	NA	NA	NA	10"	NA
32 S&W	88	680	645	610	90	80	75	2.5	10.5	3"	$17
32 S&W Long	98	705	670	635	115	100	90	2.3	10.5	4"	$17
32 Short Colt	80	745	665	590	100	80	60	2.2	9.9	4"	$19
32 H&R Magnum	85	1100	1020	930	230	195	165	1.0	4.3	4.5"	$21
32 H&R Magnum	95	1030	940	900	225	190	170	1.1	4.7	4.5"	$19
32 Automatic	60	970	895	835	125	105	95	1.3	5.4	4"	$22
32 Automatic	60	1000	917	849	133	112	96			4"	NA
32 Automatic	65	950	890	830	130	115	100	1.3	5.6	NA	NA
32 Automatic	71	905	855	810	130	115	95	1.4	5.8	4"	$19
8mm Lebel Pistol	111	850	NA	NA	180	NA	NA	NA	NA	NA	NEW
8mm Steyr	112	1080	NA	NA	290	NA	NA	NA	NA	NA	NEW
8mm Gasser	126	850	NA	NA	200	NA	NA	NA	NA	NA	NEW
380 Automatic	60	1130	960	NA	170	120	NA	1.0	NA	NA	NA
380 Automatic	85/88	990	920	870	190	165	145	1.2	5.1	4"	$20
380 Automatic	90	1000	890	800	200	160	130	1.2	5.5	3.75"	$10
380 Automatic	95/100	955	865	785	190	160	130	1.4	5.9	4"	$20
38 Super Auto +P	115	1300	1145	1040	430	335	275	0.7	3.3	5"	$26
38 Super Auto +P	125/130	1215	1100	1015	425	350	300	0.8	3.6	5"	$26
38 Super Auto +P	147	1100	1050	1000	395	355	325	0.9	4.0	5"	NA
9x18mm Makarov	95	1000	NA	NA	NA	NA	NA	NA	NA	NA	NEW
9x18mm Ultra	100	1050	NA	NA	240	NA	NA	NA	NA	NA	NEW
9x23mm Largo	124	1190	1055	966	390	306	257	0.7	3.7	4"	NA
9x23mm Win.	125	1450	1249	1103	583	433	338	0.6	2.8	NA	NA
9mm Steyr	115	1180	NA	NA	350	NA	NA	NA	NA	NA	NEW
9mm Luger	88	1500	1190	1010	440	275	200	0.6	3.1	4"	$24
9mm Luger	90	1360	1112	978	370	247	191	NA	NA	4"	$26
9mm Luger	95	1300	1140	1010	350	275	215	0.8	3.4	4"	NA
9mm Luger	100	1180	1080	NA	305	255	NA	0.9	NA	4"	NA
9mm Luger	115	1155	1045	970	340	280	240	0.9	3.9	4"	$21
9mm Luger	123/125	1110	1030	970	340	290	260	1.0	4.0	4"	$23
9mm Luger	140	935	890	850	270	245	225	1.3	5.5	4"	$23
9mm Luger	147	990	940	900	320	290	265	1.1	4.9	4"	$26
9mm Luger +P	90	1475	NA	NA	437	NA	NA	NA	NA	NA	NA
9mm Luger +P	115	1250	1113	1019	399	316	265	0.8	3.5	4"	$27
9mm Federal	115	1280	1130	1040	420	330	280	0.7	3.3	4"V	$24
9mm Luger Vector	115	1155	1047	971	341	280	241	NA	NA	4"	NA
9mm Luger +P	124	1180	1089	1021	384	327	287	0.8	3.8	4"	NA
38 S&W	146	685	650	620	150	135	125	2.4	10.0	4"	$19
38 Short Colt	125	730	685	645	150	130	115	2.2	9.4	6"	$19
39 Special	100	950	900	NA	200	180	NA	1.3	NA	4"V	NA
38 Special	110	945	895	850	220	195	175	1.3	5.4	4"V	$23
38 Special	110	945	895	850	220	195	175	1.3	5.4	4"V	$23
38 Special	130	775	745	710	175	160	120	1.9	7.9	4"V	$22

Centerfire Handgun Cartridges — Ballistics & Prices, *continued*

Notes: Blanks are available in 32 S&W, 38 S&W and 38 Special. "V" after barrel length indicates test barrel was vented to produce ballistics similar to a revolver with a normal barrel-to-cylinder gap. Ammo prices are per 50 rounds except when marked with an ** which signifies a 20 round box; *** signifies a 25-round box. Not all loads are available from all ammo manufacturers. Listed loads are those made by Remington, Winchester, Federal, and others. DISC. is a discontinued load. Prices are rounded to nearest whole dollar and will vary with brand and retail outlet. † = new bullet weight this year; "c" indicates a change in data.

Cartridge	Bullet Wgt. Grs.	VELOCITY (fps)			ENERGY (ft. lbs.)			Mid-Range Traj. (in.)		Bbl. Lgth. (in).	Est. Price/ box
		Muzzle	50 yds.	100 yds.	Muzzle	50 yds.	100 yds.	50 yds.	100 yds.		
38 Special Cowboy	140	800	767	735	199	183	168			7.5" V	NA
38 (Multi-Ball)	140	830	730	505	215	130	80	2.0	10.6	4"V	$10**
38 Special	148	710	635	565	165	130	105	2.4	10.6	4"V	$17
38 Special	158	755	725	690	200	185	170	2.0	8.3	4"V	$18
38 Special +P	95	1175	1045	960	290	230	195	0.9	3.9	4"V	$23
38 Special +P	110	995	925	870	240	210	185	1.2	5.1	4"V	$23
38 Special +P	125	975	929	885	264	238	218	1	5.2	4"	NA
38 Special +P	125	945	900	860	250	225	205	1.3	5.4	4"V	#23
38 Special +P	129	945	910	870	255	235	215	1.3	5.3	4"V	$11
38 Special +P	130	925	887	852	247	227	210	1.3	5.50	4"V	NA
38 Special +P	147/150(c)	884	NA	NA	264	NA	NA	NA	NA	4"V	$27
38 Special +P	158	890	855	825	280	255	240	1.4	6.0	4"V	$20
357 SIG	115	1520	NA	NA	593	NA	NA	NA	NA	NA	NA
357 SIG	124	1450	NA	NA	578	NA	NA	NA	NA	NA	NA
357 SIG	125	1350	1190	1080	510	395	325	0.7	3.1	4"	NA
357 SIG	150	1130	1030	970	420	355	310	0.9	4.0	NA	NA
356 TSW	115	1520	NA	NA	593	NA	NA	NA	NA	NA	NA
356 TSW	124	1450	NA	NA	578	NA	NA	NA	NA	NA	NA
356 TSW	135	1280	1120	1010	490	375	310	0.8	3.50	NA	NA
356 TSW	147	1220	1120	1040	485	410	355	0.8	3.5	5"	NA
357 Mag., Super Clean	105	1650									NA
357 Magnum	110	1295	1095	975	410	290	230	0.8	3.5	4"V	$25
357 (Med.Vel.)	125	1220	1075	985	415	315	270	0.8	3.7	4"V	$25
357 Magnum	125	1450	1240	1090	585	425	330	0.6	2.8	4"V	$25
357 (Multi-Ball)	140	1155	830	665	420	215	135	1.2	6.4	4"V	$11**
357 Magnum	140	1360	1195	1075	575	445	360	0.7	3.0	4"V	$25
357 Magnum	145	1290	1155	1060	535	430	360	0.8	3.5	4"V	$26
357 Magnum	150/158	1235	1105	1015	535	430	360	0.8	3.5	4"V	$25
357 Mag. Cowboy	158	800	761	725	225	203	185				NA
357 Magnum	165	1290	1189	1108	610	518	450	0.7	3.1	8-3/8"	NA
357 Magnum	180	1145	1055	985	525	445	390	0.9	3.9	4"V	$25
357 Magnum	180	1180	1088	1020	557	473	416	0.8	3.6	8"V	NA
357 Mag. CorBon F.A.	180	1650	1512	1386	1088	913	767	1.66	0.0		NA
357 Mag. CorBon	200	1200	1123	1061	640	560	500	3.19	0.0		NA
357 Rem. Maximum	158	1825	1590	1380	1170	885	670	0.4	1.7	10.5"	$14**
40 S&W	135	1140	1070	NA	390	345	NA	0.9	NA	4"	NA
40 S&W	155	1140	1026	958	447	362	309	0.9	4.1	4"	$14***
40 S&W	165	1150	NA	NA	485	NA	NA	NA	NA	4"	$18***
40 S&W	180	985	936	893	388	350	319	1.4	5.0	4"	$14***
40 S&W	180	1015	960	914	412	368	334	1.3	4.5	4"	NA
400 Cor-Bon	135	1450	NA	NA	630	NA	NA	NA	NA	5"	NA
10mm Automatic	155	1125	1046	986	436	377	335	0.9	3.9	5"	$26
10mm Automatic	170	1340	1165	1145	680	510	415	0.7	3.2	5"	$31
10mm Automatic	175	1290	1140	1035	650	505	420	0.7	3.3	5.5"	$11**
10mm Auto. (FBI)	180	950	905	865	361	327	299	1.5	5.4	4"	$16**
10mm Automatic	180	1030	970	920	425	375	340	1.1	4.7	5"	$16**
10mm Auto H.V.	180†	1240	1124	1037	618	504	430	0.8	3.4	5"	$27
10mm Automatic	200	1160	1070	1010	495	510	430	0.9	3.8	5"	$14**
10.4mm Italian	177	950	NA	NA	360	NA	NA	NA	NA	NA	NEW
41 Action Exp.	180	1000	947	903	400	359	326	0.5	4.2	5"	$13**
41 Rem. Magnum	170	1420	1165	1015	760	515	390	0.7	3.2	4"V	$33
41 Rem. Magnum	175	1250	1120	1030	605	490	410	0.8	3.4	4"V	$14**

Notes: Blanks are available in 32 S&W, 38 S&W and 38 Special. "V" after barrel length indicates test barrel was vented to produce ballistics similar to a revolver with a normal barrel-to-cylinder gap. Ammo prices are per 50 rounds except when marked with an ** which signifies a 20 round box; *** signifies a 25-round box. Not all loads are available from all ammo manufacturers. Listed loads are those made by Remington, Winchester, Federal, and others. DISC. is a discontinued load. Prices are rounded to nearest whole dollar and will vary with brand and retail outlet. † = new bullet weight this year; "c" indicates a change in data.

Cartridge	Bullet Wgt. Grs.	VELOCITY (fps)			ENERGY (ft. lbs.)			Mid-Range Traj. (in.)		Bbl. Lgth. (in).	Est. Price/ box
		Muzzle	50 yds.	100 yds.	Muzzle	50 yds.	100 yds.	50 yds.	100 yds.		
41 (Med. Vel.)	210	965	900	840	435	375	330	1.3	5.4	4"V	$30
41 Rem. Magnum	210	1300	1160	1060	790	630	535	0.7	3.2	4"V	$33
41 Rem. Magnum	240	1250	1151	1075	833	706	616	0.8	3.3	6.5V	NA
44 S&W Russian	247	780	NA	NA	335	NA	NA	NA	NA	NA	NA
44 S&W Special	180	980	NA	NA	383	NA	NA	NA	NA	6.5"	NA
44 S&W Special	180	1000	935	882	400	350	311	NA	NA	7.5"V	NA
44 S&W Special	200†	875	825	780	340	302	270	1.2	6.0	6"	$13**
44 S&W Special	200	1035	940	865	475	390	335	1.1	4.9	6.5"	$13**
44 S&W Special	240/246	755	725	695	310	285	265	2.0	8.3	6.5"	$26
44-40 Win. Cowboy	225	750	723	695	281	261	242				NA
44 Rem. Magnum	180	1610	1365	1175	1035	745	550	0.5	2.3	4"V	$18**
44 Rem. Magnum	200	1400	1192	1053	870	630	492	0.6	NA	6.5"	$20
44 Rem. Magnum	210	1495	1310	1165	1040	805	635	0.6	2.5	6.5"	$18**
44 (Med. Vel.)	240	1000	945	900	535	475	435	1.1	4.8	6.5"	$17
44 R.M. (Jacketed)	240	1180	1080	1010	740	625	545	0.9	3.7	4"V	$18**
44 R.M. (Lead)	240	1350	1185	1070	970	750	610	0.7	3.1	4"V	$29
44 Rem. Magnum	250	1180	1100	1040	775	670	600	0.8	3.6	6.5"V	$21
44 Rem. Magnum	250	1250	1148	1070	867	732	635	0.8	3.3	6.5"V	NA
44 Rem. Magnum	275	1235	1142	1070	931	797	699	0.8	3.3	6.5"	NA
44 Rem. Magnum	300	1200	1100	1026	959	806	702	NA	NA	7.5"	$17
44 Rem. Magnum	330	1385	1297	1220	1406	1234	1090	1.83	0.00	NA	NA
440 CorBon	260	1700	1544	1403	1669	1377	1136	1.58	NA	10"	NA
450 Short Colt/450 Revolver	226	830	NA	NA	350	NA	NA	NA	NA	NA	NEW
45 S&W Schofield	180	730	NA	NA	213	NA	NA	NA	NA	NA	NA
45 S&W Schofield	230	730	NA	NA	272	NA	NA	NA	NA	NA	NA
45 G.A.P.	185	1090	970	890	490	385	320	1	4.7	5	NA
45 G.A.P.	230	880	842	NA	396	363	NA	NA	NA	NA	NA
45 Automatic	165	1030	930	NA	385	315	NA	1.2	NA	5"	NA
45 Automatic	185	1000	940	890	410	360	325	1.1	4.9	5"	$28
45 Auto. (Match)	185	770	705	650	245	204	175	2.0	8.7	5"	$28
45 Auto. (Match)	200	940	890	840	392	352	312	2.0	8.6	5"	$20
45 Automatic	200	975	917	860	421	372	328	1.4	5.0	5"	$18
45 Automatic	230	830	800	675	355	325	300	1.6	6.8	5"	$27
45 Automatic	230	880	846	816	396	366	340	1.5	6.1	5"	NA
45 Automatic +P	165	1250	NA	NA	573	NA	NA	NA	NA	NA	NA
45 Automatic +P	185	1140	1040	970	535	445	385	0.9	4.0	5"	$31
45 Automatic +P	200	1055	982	925	494	428	380	NA	NA	5"	NA
45 Super	185	1300	1190	1108	694	582	504	NA	NA	5"	NA
45 Win. Magnum	230	1400	1230	1105	1000	775	635	0.6	2.8	5"	$14**
45 Win. Magnum	260	1250	1137	1053	902	746	640	0.8	3.3	5"	$16**
45 Win. Mag. CorBon	320	1150	1080	1025	940	830	747	3.47			NA
455 Webley MKII	262	850	NA	NA	420	NA	NA	NA	NA	NA	NA
45 Colt	200	1000	938	889	444	391	351	1.3	4.8	5.5"	$21
45 Colt	225	960	890	830	460	395	345	1.3	5.5	5.5"	$22
45 Colt + P CorBon	265	1350	1225	1126	1073	884	746	2.65	0.0		NA
45 Colt + P CorBon	300	1300	1197	1114	1126	956	827	2.78	0.0		NA
45 Colt	250/255	860	820	780	410	375	340	1.6	6.6	5.5"	$27
454 Casull	250	1300	1151	1047	938	735	608	0.7	3.2	7.5"V	NA
454 Casull	260	1800	1577	1381	1871	1436	1101	0.4	1.8	7.5"V	NA
454 Casull	300	1625	1451	1308	1759	1413	1141	0.5	2.0	7.5"V	NA
454 Casull CorBon	360	1500	1387	1286	1800	1640	1323	2.01	0.0		NA
475 Linebaugh	400	1350	1217	1119	1618	1315	1112	NA	NA	NA	NA
480 Ruger	325	1350	1191	1076	1315	1023	835	2.6	0.0	7.5"	NA
50 Action Exp.	325	1400	1209	1075	1414	1055	835	0.2	2.3	6"	$24**
500 S&W	275	1665	1392	1183	1693	1184	854	1.5	NA	8.375	NA
500 S&W	400	1675	1472	1299	2493	1926	1499	1.3	NA	8.375	NA
500 S&W	440	1625	1367	1169	2581	1825	1337	1.6	NA	8.375	NA

RIMFIRE AMMUNITION — BALLISTICS & PRICES

Note: The actual ballistics obtained with your firearm can vary considerably from the advertised ballistics. Also, ballistics can vary from lot to lot with the same brand and type load.

Cartridge	Bullet Wt. Grs.	Velocity (fps) 22-1/2" Bbl.		Energy (ft. lbs.) 22-1/2" Bbl.		Mid-Range Traj. (in.)	Muzzle Velocity
		Muzzle	100 yds.	Muzzle	100 yds.	100 yds.	6" Bbl.
17 Aguila	20	1850	1267	NA	NA	NA	NA
17 Hornady Mach 2	17	2100	1530	166	88	0.7	NA
17 Aguila	20	1850	NA	NA	NA	NA	NA
17 HMR	17	2550	1902	245	136	NA	NA
22 Short Blank	—	—	—	—	—	—	—
22 Short CB	29	727	610	33	24	NA	706
22 Short Target	29	830	695	44	31	6.8	786
22 Short HP	27	1164	920	81	50	4.3	1077
22 Colibri	20	375	183	6	1	NA	NA
22 Super Colibri	20	500	441	11	9	NA	NA
22 Long CB	29	727	610	33	24	NA	706
22 Long HV	29	1180	946	90	57	4.1	1031
22 LR Ballistician	25	1100	760	65	30	NA	NA
22 LR Pistol Match	40	1070	890	100	70	4.6	940
22 LR Sub Sonic HP	38	1050	901	93	69	4.7	NA
22 LR Standard Velocity	40	1070	890	100	70	4.6	940
22 LR HV	40	1255	1016	140	92	3.6	1060
22 LR Silhoutte	42	1220	1003	139	94	3.6	1025
22 SSS	60	950	802	120	86	NA	NA
22 LR HV HP	40	1280	1001	146	89	3.5	1085
22 Velocitor GDHP	40	1435	0	0	0	NA	NA
22 LR Hyper HP	32/33/34	1500	1075	165	85	2.8	NA
22 LR Stinger HP	32	1640	1132	191	91	2.6	1395
22 LR Hyper Vel	30	1750	1191	204	93	NA	NA
22 LR Shot #12	31	950	NA	NA	NA	NA	NA
22 WRF LFN	45	1300	1015	169	103	3	NA
22 Win. Mag.	30	2200	1373	322	127	1.4	1610
22 Win. Mag. V-Max BT	33	2000	1495	293	164	0.60	NA
22 Win. Mag. JHP	34	2120	1435	338	155	1.4	NA
22 Win. Mag. JHP	40	1910	1326	324	156	1.7	1480
22 Win. Mag. FMJ	40	1910	1326	324	156	1.7	1480
22 Win. Mag. Dyna Point	45	1550	1147	240	131	2.60	NA
22 Win. Mag. JHP	50	1650	1280	300	180	1.3	NA
22 Win. Mag. Shot #11	52	1000	—	NA	—	—	NA

SHOTSHELL LOADS & PRICES

NOTES: * = 10 rounds per box. ** = 5 rounds per box. Pricing variations and number of rounds per box can occur with type and brand of ammunition. Listed pricing is the average nominal cost for load style and box quantity shown. Not every brand is available in all shot size variations. Some manufacturers do not provide suggested list prices. All prices rounded to nearest whole dollar. The price you pay will vary dependent upon outlet of purchase. # = new load spec this year; "C" indicates a change in data.

10 Gauge 3-1/2" Magnum

Dram Equiv.	Shot Ozs.	Load Style	Shot Sizes	Brands	Avg. Price/box	Velocity (fps)
4-1/2	2-1/4	premium	BB, 2, 4, 5, 6	Win., Fed., Rem.	$33	1205
Max	2	premium	4, 5, 6	Fed., Win.	NA	1300
4-1/4	2	high velocity	BB, 2, 4	Rem.	$22	1210
Max	18 pellets	premium	00 buck	Fed., Win.	$7**	1100
Max	1-7/8	hevi. shot	4, 5, 6	Rem.	NA	1225
Max	1-7/8	Bismuth	BB, 2, 4	Bis.	NA	1225
Max	1-3/4	hevi. shot	2, 4	Rem.	NA	1300
4-1/4	1-3/4	steel	TT, T, BBB, BB, 1, 2, 3	Win., Rem.	$27	1260
Mag	1-5/8	steel	T, BBB	Win.	$27	1285
Max	1-5/8	Tungsten - Iron	BBB, BB, 2, 4	Fed.		1300
Max	1-5/8	Bismuth	BB, 2, 4	Bismuth	NA	1375
Max	1-1/2	steel	T, BBB, BB, 1, 2, 3	Fed.	NA	1450
Max	1-3/8	steel	T, BBB, BB, 1, 2, 3	Fed.	NA	1500
Max	1-3/8	steel	T, BBB, BB, 2	Fed., Win.	NA	1450
Max	1-3/8	Tungsten - Iron	BBB, BB, 2, 4	Fed.		1450
Max	1-3/4	slug, rifled	slug	Fed.	NA	1280
Max	24 pellets	Buckshot	1 Buck	Fed.	NA	1100
Max	54 pellets	Super-X	4 Buck	Win.	NA	1150

12 Gauge 3-1/2" Magnum

Dram Equiv.	Shot Ozs.	Load Style	Shot Sizes	Brands	Avg. Price/box	Velocity (fps)
Max	2-1/4	premium	4, 5, 6	Fed., Rem., Win.	$13*	1150
Max	2	Lead	4, 5, 6	Fed.	NA	1275
Max	2	Copper plated turkey	4, 5	Rem.	NA	1300
Max	18 pellets	premium	00 buck	Fed., Win., Rem.	$7**	1100
Max	1-7/8	hevi. shot	4, 5, 6	Rem.	NA	1225
Max	1-3/4	hevi. shot	4, 5, 6	Rem.	NA	1300
Max	1-7/8	Bismuth	BB, 2, 4	Bis.	NA	1225
Max	1-3/8	steel	T, BBB, BB, 2, 4	Fed., Win., Rem.	NA	1450
Max	1-3/8	Tungsten - Iron	BBB, BB, 2, 4	Fed.	NA	1450
Max	24 pellets	Premium	1 Buck	Fed.	NA	1100
Max	54 pellets	Super-X	4 Buck	Win.	NA	1050

12 Gauge 3" Magnum

Dram Equiv.	Shot Ozs.	Load Style	Shot Sizes	Brands	Avg. Price/box	Velocity (fps)
4	2	premium	BB, 2, 4, 5, 6	Win., Fed., Rem.	$9*	1175
4	1-7/8	premium	BB, 2, 4, 6	Win., Fed., Rem.	$19	1210
4	1-7/8	duplex	4x6	Rem.	$9*	1210
Max	1-3/4	turkey	4, 5, 6	Fed., Fio., Win., Rem.	NA	1300
Max	1-5/8	hevi. shot	4, 5, 6	Rem.	NA	1225
4	1-5/8	premium	2, 4, 5, 6	Win., Fed., Rem.	$18	1290
Max	1-1/2	hevi. shot	4, 5, 6	Rem.	NA	1300
Max	1-5/8	Bismuth	BB, 2, 4, 5, 6	Bis.	NA	1250
4	24 pellets	buffered	1 buck	Win., Fed., Rem.	$5**	1040
4	15 pellets	buffered	00 buck	Win., Fed., Rem.	$6**	1210
4	10 pellets	buffered	000 buck	Win., Fed., Rem.	$6**	1225
4	41 pellets	buffered	4 buck	Win., Fed., Rem.	$6**	1210
Max	1-3/8	Tungsten-Iron	4	Fed.	NA	1300
Max	1-3/8	slug	slug	Bren.	NA	1476
Max	1-1/4	slug, rifled	slug	Fed.	NA	1600
Max	1-3/16	saboted slug	copper slug	Rem.	NA	1500
Max	7/8	slug, rifled	slug	Rem.	NA	1875
Max	1-1/8	Tungsten - Iron	BBB, BB, 2, 4	Fed.	NA	1400

12 Gauge 3" Magnum (cont.)

Dram Equiv.	Shot Ozs.	Load Style	Shot Sizes	Brands	Avg. Price/box	Velocity (fps)
Max	1-1/8	steel	BB, 2, 3, 4	Fed., Win.	NA	1550
Max	1	steel	4, 6	Fed.	NA	1330
Max	1-3/8	buckhammer	slug	Rem.	NA	1500
Max	1	slug, rifled	slug, magnum	Win., Rem.	$5**	1760
Max	1	saboted slug	slug	Rem., Win., Fed.	$10**	1550
Max	385 grs.	partition gold	slug	Win.	NA	2000
3-5/8	1-3/8	steel	BBB, BB, 1, 2, 3, 4	Win., Fed., Rem.	$19	1275
Max	1-1/8	steel	BB, 2, 4	Rem.	NA	1500
Max	1-1/8	steel	T, BBB, BB, 2, 4, 5, 6	Fed., Win.	NA	1450
Max	1-1/8	steel	BB, 2	Fed.	NA	1400
4	1-1/4	steel	T, BBB, BB, 1, 2, 3, 4, 6	Win., Fed., Rem.	$18	1400

12 Gauge 2-3/4"

Dram Equiv.	Shot Ozs.	Load Style	Shot Sizes	Brands	Avg. Price/box	Velocity (fps)
Max	1-5/8	magnum	4, 5, 6	Win., Fed.	$8*	1250
Max	1-3/8	lead	4, 5, 6	Fiocchi	NA	1485
Max	1-3/8	turkey	4, 5, 6	Fio.	NA	1250
Max	1-3/8	steel	4, 5, 6	Fed.	NA	1400
Max	1-3/8	Bismuth	BB, 2, 4, 5, 6	Bis.	NA	1300
Max	1-3/8	hevi. shot	4, 5, 6	Rem.	NA	1250
3-3/4	1-1/2	magnum	BB, 2, 4, 5, 6	Win., Fed., Rem.	$16	1260
Max	1-1/4	Supreme H-V	4, 5, 6, 7-1/2	Win. Rem.	NA	1400
3-3/4	1-1/4	high velocity	BB, 2, 4, 5, 6, 7-1/2, 8, 9	Win., Fed., Rem., Fio.	$13	1330
Max	1-1/4	hevi. shot	4, 6, 7-1/2	Rem.	NA	1325
3-1/2	1-1/4	mid-velocity	7, 8, 9	Win.	Disc.	1275
3-1/4	1-1/4	standard velocity	6, 7-1/2, 8, 9	Win., Fed., Rem., Fio.	$11	1220
3-1/4	1-1/8	standard velocity	4, 6, 7-1/2, 8, 9	Win., Fed., Rem., Fio.	$9	1255
Max	1-1/8	steel	2, 4	Rem.	NA	1390
Max	1	steel	BB, 2	Fed.	NA	1450
Max	1	Tungsten - Iron	BB, 2, 4	Fed.	NA	1450
3-1/4	1	standard velocity	6, 7-1/2, 8	Rem., Fed., Fio., Win.	$6	1290
3-1/4	1-1/4	target	7-1/2, 8, 9	Win., Fed., Rem.	$10	1220
3	1-1/8	spreader	7-1/2, 8, 8-1/2, 9	Fio.	NA	1200
3	1-1/8	target	7-1/2, 8, 9, 7-1/2x8	Win., Fed., Rem., Fio.	$7	1200
2-3/4	1-1/8	target	7-1/2, 8, 8-1/2, 9, 7-1/2x8	Win., Fed., Rem., Fio.	$7	1145
2-3/4	1-1/8	low recoil	7-1/2, 8	Rem.	NA	1145
2-1/2	26 grams	low recoil	8	Win.	NA	980
2-1/4	1-1/8	target	7-1/2, 8, 8-1/2, 9	Rem., Fed.	$7	1080
Max	1	spreader	7-1/2, 8, 8-1/2, 9	Fio.	NA	1300
3-1/4	28 grams (1 oz)	target	7-1/2, 8, 9	Win., Fed., Rem., Fio.	$8	1290
3	1	target	7-1/2, 8, 8-1/2, 9	Win., Fio.	NA	1235
2-3/4	1	target	7-1/2, 8, 8-1/2, 9	Fed., Rem., Fio.	NA	1180
3-1/4	24 grams	target	7-1/2, 8, 9	Fed., Win., Fio.	NA	1325
3	7/8	light	8	Fio.	NA	1200
3-3/4	8 pellets	buffered	000 buck	Win., Fed., Rem.	$4**	1325
4	12 pellets	premium	00 buck	Win., Fed., Rem.	$5**	1290
3-3/4	9 pellets	buffered	00 buck	Win., Fed., Rem., Fio.	$19	1325
Max	9 pellets	hevi. shot	00 buck	Rem.	NA	1325
3-3/4	12 pellets	buffered	0 buck	Win., Fed., Rem.	$4**	1275

SHOTSHELL LOADS & PRICES, *continued*

12 Gauge 2-3/4" (cont.)

Dram Equiv.	Shot Ozs.	Load Style	Shot Sizes	Brands	Avg. Price/box	Velocity (fps)
4	20 pellets	buffered	1 buck	Win., Fed., Rem.	$4**	1075
3-3/4	16 pellets	buffered	1 buck	Win., Fed., Rem.	$4**	1250
4	34 pellets	premium	4 buck	Fed., Rem.	$5**	1250
3-3/4	27 pellets	buffered	4 buck	Win., Fed., Rem., Fio.	$4**	1325
Max	1	saboted slug	slug	Win., Fed., Rem.	$10**	1450
Max	1-1/4	slug, rifled	slug	Fed.	NA	1520
Max	1-1/4	slug	slug	Lightfield		1440
Max	1-1/4	saboted slug	attached sabot	Rem.	NA	1550
Max	1	slug, rifled	slug, magnum	Rem., Fio.	$5**	1680
Max	1	slug, rifled	slug	Win., Fed., Rem.	$4**	1610
Max	1	sabot slug	slug	Sauvestre		1640
Max	7/8	slug, rifled	slug	Rem.	NA	1800
Max	400	plat. tip	sabot slug	Win.	NA	1700
Max	385 grains	Partition Gold Slug	slug	Win.	NA	1900
Max	385 grains	Core-Lokt bonded	sabot slug	Rem.	NA	1900
Max	325 grains	Barnes Sabot	slug	Fed.	NA	1900
3	1-1/8	steel target	6-1/2, 7	Rem.	NA	1200
2-3/4	1-1/8	steel target	7	Rem.	NA	1145
3	1#	steel	7	Win.	$11	1235
3-1/2	1-1/4	steel	T, BBB, BB, 1, 2, 3, 4, 5, 6	Win., Fed., Rem.	$18	1275
3-3/4	1-1/8	steel	BB, 1, 2, 3, 4, 5, 6	Win., Fed., Rem., Fio.	$16	1365
3-3/4	1	steel	2, 3, 4, 5, 6, 7	Win., Fed., Rem., Fio.	$13	1390
Max	7/8	steel	7	Fio.	NA	1440

16 Gauge 2-3/4"

Dram Equiv.	Shot Ozs.	Load Style	Shot Sizes	Brands	Avg. Price/box	Velocity (fps)
3-1/4	1-1/4	magnum	2, 4, 6	Fed., Rem.	$16	1260
3-1/4	1-1/8	high velocity	4, 6, 7-1/2	Win., Fed., Rem., Fio.	$12	1295
Max	1-1/8	Bismuth	4, 5	Bis.	NA	1200
2-3/4	1-1/8	standard velocity	6, 7-1/2, 8	Fed., Rem., Fio.	$9	1185
2-1/2	1	dove	6, 7-1/2, 8, 9	Fio., Win.	NA	1165
2-3/4	1		6, 7-1/2, 8	Fio.	NA	1200
Max	15/16	steel	2, 4	Fed., Rem.	NA	1300
Max	7/8	steel	2, 4	Win.	$16	1300
3	12 pellets	buffered	1 buck	Win., Fed., Rem.	$4**	1225
Max	4/5	slug, rifled	slug	Win., Fed., Rem.	$4**	1570
Max	.92	sabot slug	slug	Sauvestre	NA	1560

20 Gauge 3" Magnum

Dram Equiv.	Shot Ozs.	Load Style	Shot Sizes	Brands	Avg. Price/box	Velocity (fps)
3	1-1/4	premium	2, 4, 5, 6, 7-1/2	Win., Fed., Rem.	$15	1185
3	1-1/4	turkey	4, 6	Fio.	NA	1200
Max	1-1/4	hevi. shot	4, 5, 6	Rem.	NA	1175
Max	1-1/8	hevi. shot	4, 6, 7-1/2	Rem.	NA	1300
Max	18 pellets	buck shot	2 buck	Fed.	NA	1200
Max	24 pellets	buffered	3 buck	Win.	$5**	1150
2-3/4	20 pellets	buck	3 buck	Rem.	$4**	1200
3-1/4	1	steel	1, 2, 3, 4, 5, 6	Win., Fed., Rem.	$15	1330
Max	7/8	steel	2, 4	Win.	MA	1300
Max	1-1/16	Bismuth	2, 4, 5, 6	Bismuth	NA	1250
Max	7/8	Tungsten - Iron	2, 4	Fed.	NA	1375
Mag	5/8	saboted slug	275 gr.	Fed.	NA	1900

20 Gauge 2-3/4"

Dram Equiv.	Shot Ozs.	Load Style	Shot Sizes	Brands	Avg. Price/box	Velocity (fps)
2-3/4	1-1/8	magnum	4, 6, 7-1/2	Win., Fed., Rem.	$14	1175
2-3/4	1	high velocity	4, 5, 6, 7-1/2, 8, 9	Win., Fed., Rem., Fio.	$12	1220
Max	1	Bismuth	4, 6	Bis.	NA	1200
Max	1	hevi-shot	4, 6, 7-1/2	Rem.	NA	1275
Max	1	Supreme H-V	4, 6, 7-1/2	Win. Rem.	NA	1300
Max	7/8	Steel	2, 3, 4	Fio.	NA	1500
2-1/2	1	standard velocity	6, 7-1/2, 8	Win., Rem., Fed., Fio.	$6	1165
2-1/2	7/8	clays	8	Rem.	NA	1200
2-1/2	7/8	promotional	6, 7-1/2, 8	Win., Rem., Fio.	$6	1210
2-1/2	1	target	8, 9	Win., Rem.	$8	1165
Max	7/8	clays	7-1/2, 8	Win.	NA	1275
2-1/2	7/8	target	8, 9	Win., Fed., Rem.	$8	1200
Max	3/4	steel	2, 4	Rem.	NA	1425
2-1/2	7/8	steel - target	7	Rem.	NA	1200
Max	1	buckhammer	slug	Rem.	NA	1500
Max	5/8	Saboted Slug	Copper Slug	Rem.	NA	1500
Max	20 pellets	buffered	3 buck	Win., Fed.	$4	1200
Max	5/8	slug, saboted	slug	Win.,	$9**	1400
2-3/4	5/8	slug, rifled	slug	Rem.	$4**	1580
Max	3/4	saboted slug	copper slug	Fed., Rem.	NA	1450
Max	3/4	slug, rifled	slug	Win., Fed., Rem., Fio.	$4**	1570
Max	.9	sabot slug	slug	Sauvestre		1480
Max	260 grains	Partition Gold Slug	slug	Win.	NA	1900
Max	260 grains	Core-Lokt Ultra	slug	Rem.	NA	1900
Max	260 grains	saboted slug	platinum tip	Win.	NA	1700
Max	3/4	steel	2, 3, 4, 6	Win., Fed., Rem.	$14	1425
Max	1/2	rifled, slug	slug	Rem.	NA	1800

28 Gauge 2-3/4"

Dram Equiv.	Shot Ozs.	Load Style	Shot Sizes	Brands	Avg. Price/box	Velocity (fps)
2	1	high velocity	6, 7-1/2, 8	Win.	$12	1125
2-1/4	3/4	high velocity	6, 7-1/2, 8, 9	Win., Fed., Rem., Fio.	$11	1295
2	3/4	target	8, 9	Win., Fed., Rem.	$9	1200
Max	3/4	sporting clays	7-1/2, 8-1/2	Win.	NA	1300
Max	5/8	Bismuth	4, 6	Bis.	NA	1250

410 Bore 3"

Dram Equiv.	Shot Ozs.	Load Style	Shot Sizes	Brands	Avg. Price/box	Velocity (fps)
Max	11/16	high velocity	4, 5, 6, 7-1/2, 8, 9	Win., Fed., Rem., Fio.	$10	1135
Max	9/16	Bismuth	4	Bis.	NA	1175

410 Bore 2-1/2"

Dram Equiv.	Shot Ozs.	Load Style	Shot Sizes	Brands	Avg. Price/box	Velocity (fps)
Max	1/2	high velocity	4, 6, 7-1/2	Win., Fed., Rem.	$9	1245
Max	1/5	slug, rifled	slug	Win., Fed., Rem.	$4**	1815
1-1/2	1/2	target	8, 8-1/2, 9	Win., Fed., Rem., Fio.	$8	1200
Max	1/2	sporting clays	8-1/2	Win.	NA	1300
Max		Buckshot	5-000 Buck	Win.		1135

SHOOTER'S MARKETPLACE

INTERESTING PRODUCT NEWS FOR THE ACTIVE SHOOTING SPORTSMAN

The companies represented on the following pages will be happy to provide additional information – feel free to contact them.

HIGH QUALITY OPTICS

One of the best indicators of quality is a scope's resolution number. The smaller the number, the better. Our scope has a resolution number of 2.8 seconds of angle. This number is about 20% smaller (better) than other well-known scopes costing much more. It means that two .22 caliber bullets can be a hair's breadth apart and edges of each still be clearly seen. With a Shepherd at 800 yards, you will be able to tell a four inch antler from a four inch ear and a burrowing owl from a prairie dog. Bird watchers will be able to distinguish a Tufted Titmouse from a Ticked-Off Field Mouse. Send for free catalog.

SHEPHERD ENTERPRISES, INC.

Box 189, Waterloo, NE 68069

Phone: 402-779-2424 • Fax: 402-779-4010

E-mail: shepherd@shepherdscopes.com • Web: www.shepherdscopes.com

BEAR TRACK CASES

Designed by an Alaskan bush pilot! Polyurethane coated, zinc plated corners and feet, zinc plated—spring loaded steel handles, stainless steel hinges, high density urethane foam inside with a neoprene seal. Aluminum walls are standard at .070 with riveted ends. Committed to quality that will protect your valuables regardless of the transportation method you use. Exterior coating also protects other items from acquiring "aluminum black."

Many styles, colors and sizes available. Wheels come on large cases and special orders can be accommodated. Call for a brochure or visit online.

Bear Track Cases when top quality protection is a must.

BEAR TRACK CASES

314 Highway 239, Freedom, WY 83120

Phone: 307-883-2468 • Fax: 307-883-2005

Web: www.beartrackcases.com

SHOOTER'S MARKETPLACE

ULTIMATE 500

Gary Reeder Custom Guns, builder of full custom guns for over 25 years, and with over 50 different series of custom hunting handguns, cowboy guns, custom Encores and large caliber hunting rifles, has a free brochure for you. Or visit their website. One of the most popular is their Ultimate 500, chambered in the 500 S&W Magnum. This beefy 5-shot revolver is for the serious handgun hunter and is one of several series of large caliber handguns, such as 475 Linebaugh and 475 Maximum, 500 Linebaugh and 500 Maximum. For more information, contact:

GARY REEDER CUSTOM GUNS

2601 E. 7th Avenue, Flagstaff, AZ 86004
Phone: 928-527-4100 or 928-526-3313
Website: www.reedercustomguns.com

NYLON COATED GUN CLEANING RODS

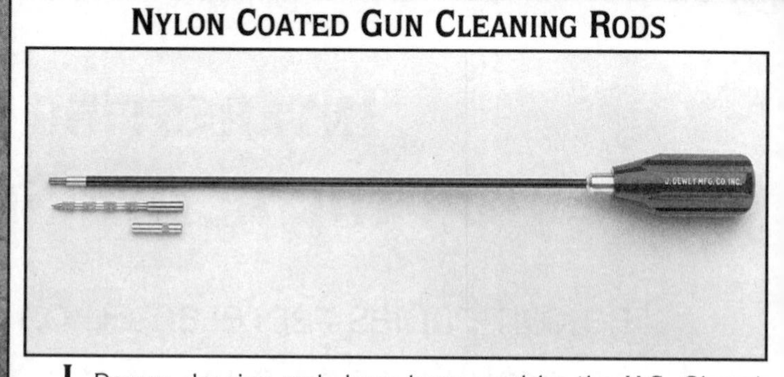

J. Dewey cleaning rods have been used by the U.S. Olympic shooting team and the benchrest community for over 20 years. These one-piece, spring-tempered, steel-base rods will not gall delicate rifling or damage the muzzle area of front-cleaned firearms. The nylon coating elmininates the problem of abrasives adhering to the rod during the cleaning operation. Each rod comes with a hard non-breakable plastic handle supported by ball-bearings, top and bottom, for ease of cleaning.

The brass cleaning jags are designed to pierce the center of the cleaning patch or wrap around the knurled end to keep the patch centered in the bore.

Coated rods are available from 17-caliber to shotgun bore size in several lengths to meet the needs of any shooter. Write for more information.

J. DEWEY MFG. CO., INC.

P.O. Box 2014, Southbury, CT 06488
Phone: 203-264-3064 • Fax: 203-262-6907
Web: www.deweyrods.com

FINE GUN STOCKS

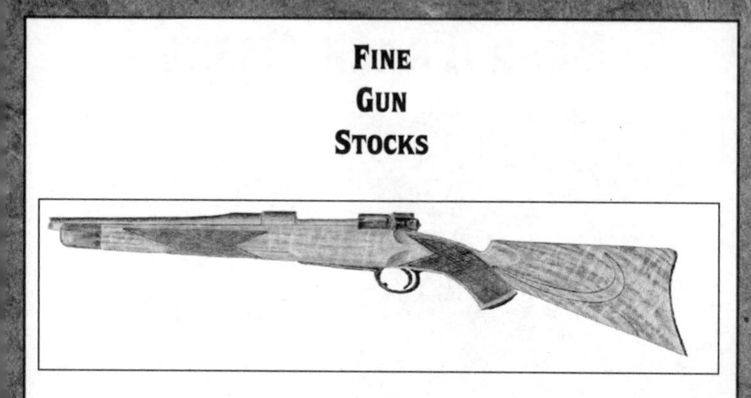

Manufacturing custom and production gunstocks for hundreds of models of rifles and shotguns—made from the finest stock woods and available in all stages of completion.

Visit www.gunstocks.com to view their bargain list of fine custom gunstocks. Each displayed in full color.

GREAT AMERICAN GUNSTOCK COMPANY

3420 Industrial Drive
Yuba City, CA 95993
Phone: 530-671-4570
Fax: 530-671-3906
Gunstock Hotline: 800-784-GUNS (4867)
Web: www.gunstocks.com
E-mail: gunstox@syix.com

COMBINATION RIFLE AND OPTICS REST

The Magna-Pod weighs less than two pounds, yet firmly supports more than most expensive tripods. It will hold 50 pounds at its low 9-inch height and over 10 pounds extended to 17 inches. It sets up in seconds where there is neither time nor space for a tripod and keeps your expensive equipment safe from knock-overs by kids, pets, pedestrians, or even high winds. It makes a great mono-pod for cam-corders, etc., and its carrying box is less than 13" x 13" x 3 1/4" high for easy storage and access.

Attached to its triangle base it becomes an extremely stable table pod or rifle bench rest. The rifle yoke pictured in photo is included.

It's 5 pods in 1: Magna-Pod, Mono-Pod, Table-Pod, Shoulder-Pod and Rifle Rest. Send for free catalog.

SHEPHERD ENTERPRISES, INC.

Box 189, Waterloo, NE 68069
Phone: 402-779-2424 • Fax: 402-779-4010
E-mail: shepherd@shepherdscopes.com • Web: www.shepherdscopes.com

Gary Levine Fine Knives
A Dealer of Handmade Knives

Gary's goal is to offer the collector the best custom knives available, in stock and ready for delivery. He has the best makers as well as the rising stars at fair prices. Gary enjoys working with collectors who want to enhance their collections, as well as someone who just wants a great knife to carry. Gary is also always on the lookout for collections, as well as single custom knives to purchase. Please stop by his website.

GARY LEVINE FINE KNIVES

P.O. Box 382, Chappaqua, NY 10514
Phone: 914-238-5748 • Fax: 914-238-6524
Web: http://www.levineknives.com
Email: gary@levineknives.com

Border Classic

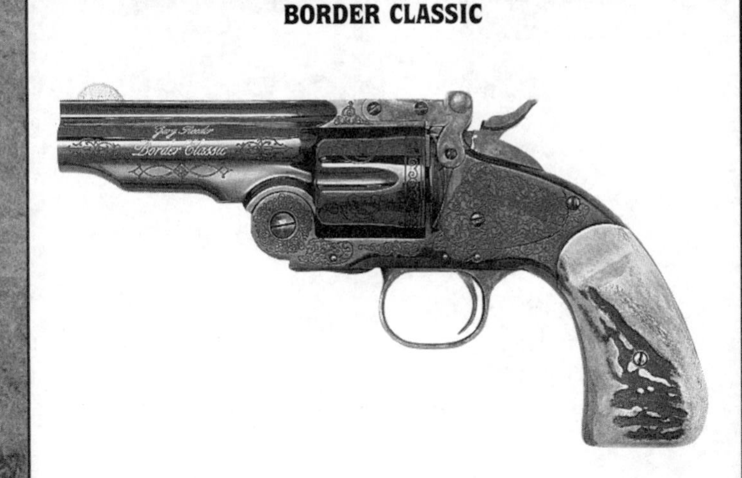

Gary Reeder Custom Guns, builder of full custom guns including hunting handguns, custom Encores, large caliber hunting rifles and over 20 different series of cowboy guns, including our Border Classic, shown. This beauty is the first ever snubbie Schofield, and can be built on any current Schofield. Fully engraved, round butted, with their Black Chromex finish and a solid silver Mexican coin for the front sight, this one is truly a masterpiece. See them all at their website, or call for a brochure.

GARY REEDER CUSTOM GUNS

2601 E. 7th Avenue, Flagstaff, AZ 86004
Phone: 928-527-4100 or 928-526-3313
Website: www.reedercustomguns.com

Quality Gunstock Blanks

Cali'co Hardwoods has been cutting superior-quality shotgun and rifle blanks for more than 31 years. Cali'co supplies blanks to many of the major manufacturers—Browning, Weatherby, Ruger, Holland & Holland, to name a few—as well as custom gunsmiths the world over.

Profiled rifle blanks are available, ready for inletting and sanding. Cali'co sells superior California hardwoods in Claro walnut, French walnut, Bastogne, maple and myrtle.

Cali'co offers good, serviceable blanks and some of the finest exhibition blanks available. Satisfaction guaranteed.

Color catalog, retail and dealer price list (FFL required) free upon request.

CALI'CO HARDWOODS, INC.

3580 Westwind Blvd., Santa Rosa, CA 95403
Phone: 707-546-4045 • Fax: 707-546-4027

Black Hills Gold Ammunition

Black Hills Ammunition has introduced a new line of premium performance rifle ammunition. Calibers available in the Black Hills Gold Line are .243, .270, .308, .30-06, and .300 Win Mag. This line is designed for top performance in a wide range of hunting situations. Bullets used in this ammunition are the Barnes X-Bullet with XLC coating and the highly accurate Nosler Ballistic-Tip™.

Black Hills Ammunition is sold dealer direct. The Gold line is packaged in 20 rounds per box, 10 boxes per case. Black Hills pays all freight to dealers in the continental United States. Minimum dealer order is only one case.

BLACK HILLS AMMUNITION

P.O. Box 3090, Rapid City, SD 57709
Phone: 1-605-348-5150 • Fax: 1-605-348-9827
Web: www.black-hills.com

SHOOTER'S MARKETPLACE

FOLDING BIPODS

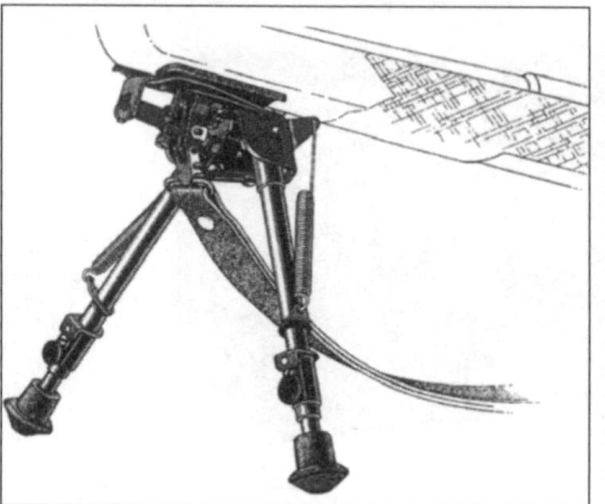

Harris Bipods clamp securely to most stud-equipped bolt-action rifles and are quick-detachable. With adapters, they will fit some other guns. On all models except the Model LM, folding legs have completely adjustable spring-return extensions. The sling swivel attaches to the clamp. This time-proven design is manufactured with heat-treated steel and hard alloys and has a black anodized finish.

Series S Bipods rotate 35° for instant leveling on uneven ground. Hinged base has tension adjustment and buffer springs to eliminate tremor or looseness in crotch area of bipod. They are otherwise similar to non-rotating Series 1A2.

Thirteen models are available from Harris Engineering; literature is free.

HARRIS ENGINEERING INC.

Dept: GD54, Barlow, KY 42024
Phone: 270-334-3633 • Fax: 270-334-3000

GATCO 5-STONE SHARPENING SYSTEM

The GATCO 5-Stone Sharpening System is the only fixed-angle sharpening kit needed to restore a factory perfect edge on even the most well-used knives.

Instructions are permanently mounted inside the storage case to make the job easy.

Just secure the blade in the polymer vise, select the proper angle guide, insert one of the five hone-stone angle guide bars into the guide slot, then put a few drops of mineral oil on the stone and start sharpening.

The GATCO 5-Stone Sharpening System includes extra coarse, coarse, medium and fine honing stones that are made from high-density aluminum oxide for long wear. The fifth, triangular-shaped hone is used for serrated blades.

All stones are mounted in color-coded grips.

To locate a GATCO dealer, call 1-800-LIV-SHARP.

GATCO SHARPENERS

P.O. Box 600, Getzville, NY 14068-0600
Phone: 716-877-2200 • Fax: 716-877-2591
E-mail: gatco@buffnet.net • www.gatcosharpeners.com

RUGER 10-22® COMPETITION MATCHED HAMMER AND SEAR KIT

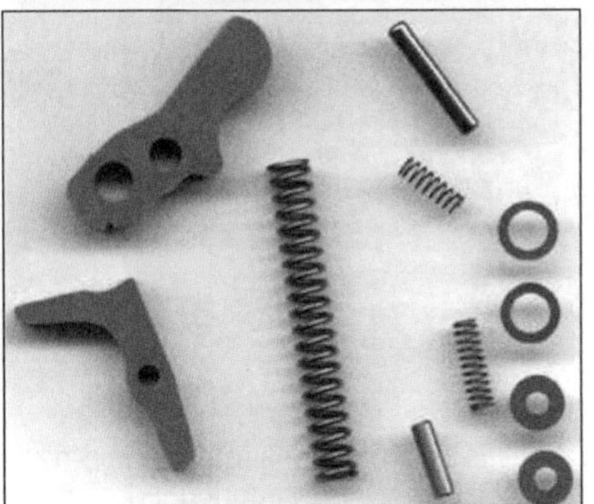

Precision EDM/CNC machined custom hammer and sear for your Ruger 10-22®. Both parts are machined from a solid billet of steel. Case hardened to RC-58-60. These are the highest quality drop in parts available on the market. They will produce a crisp 2-1/2 lbs. trigger pull. They are precision ground with Vapor hand honed engagement surfaces. Includes an Extra Power hammer spring, Extra Power disconnector spring, replacement trigger return spring, 2 hammer shims, and 2 trigger shims.

Price $55.95 plus $3.85 Priority Mail

POWER CUSTOM, INC.

29739 Hwy. J, Dept. KP, Gravois Mills, MO 65037
Phone: 1-573-372-5684 • Fax: 1-573-372-5799
Web: www.powercustom.com • E-mail: rwpowers@laurie.net

PRECISION RIFLE REST

Bald Eagle Precision Machine Co. offers a rifle rest perfect for the serious benchrester or dedicated varminter.

"The Slingshot" or Next Generation has 60° front legs. The rest is constructed of aircraft-quality aluminum or fine grain cast iron and weighs 12 to 20 lbs. The finish is 3 coats of Imron clear. Primary height adjustments are made with a rack and pinion gear. Secondary adjustment uses a mariner wheel with thrust bearings for smooth operation. A hidden fourth leg allows for lateral movement on the bench.

Bald Eagle offers approximately 150 rest combinations to choose from, including windage adjustable, right or left hand, cast aluminum or cast iron.

Prices: $175.00 to $345.00

BALD EAGLE PRECISION MACHINE CO.

101-K Allison Street, Lock Haven, PA 17745
Phone: 570-748-6772 — Fax: 570-748-4443
Web: www.baldeaglemachine.com

SHOOTER'S MARKETPLACE

10-22® Hammer and Sear Pac

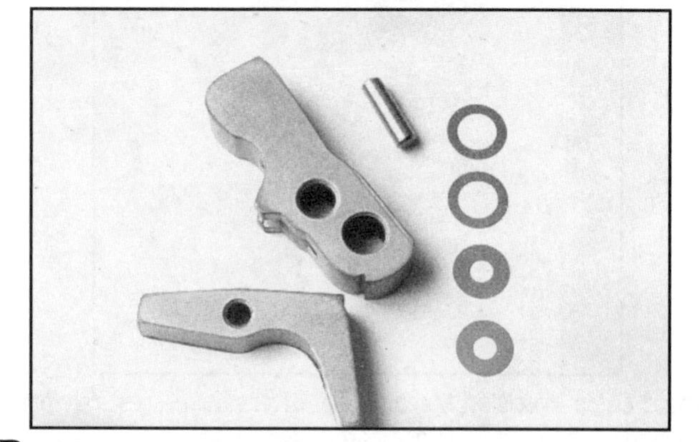

Power Custom introduces a new Ruger 10-22® Matched Hammer & Sear to reduce the triggevr pull weight for your 10-22® & 10-22 Magnum. This allows for a 2 1/2lb. trigger pull. Manufactured by the E.D.M. process out of carbon steel and heat treated to a 56-58 Rc and precision ground with honed engagement surfaces. Kit includes extra power hammer & sear disconnector spring, 2 precision trigger shims, 2 precision hammer shims, and a replacement trigger return spring. Price $55.95.

10-22® is a registered trademark of Sturm, Ruger & Co. Inc.

POWER CUSTOM, INC.
29739 Hwy J, Dept GD,
Gravois Mills, MO 65037
Phone: 573-372-5684 • Fax: 573-372-5799
Website: www.powercustom.com

For the Serious Reloader...

Rooster Labs' line of professional-quality high-performance lubricants and polishes for the shooting industry now includes:

- **ZAMBINI** 220° Pistol Bullet Lubricant (1x4 & 2x6)
- **HVR** 220° High Velocity Rifle Bullet Lube (1x4)
- **ROOSTER JACKET** Waterproof Liquid Bullet Film Lube
- **BP-7 BLACK POWDER** Bullet Lube 210° melt (1x4)
- **PL-16 BLACK POWDER** Patch Lube 265° melt (2 oz tin)
- **ROOSTER BRIGHT** Brass Case Polish Media Additive!
- **CFL-56** Radical Case Forming Lube...for the Wildcatter
- **PDQ-21** Spray Case Sizing Lube...quick, no contamination
- **DF-7303 DEEP DRAWING FLUID** (commercial concentrate)

Rooster LABORATORIES®
P.O. Box 414605, Kansas City, MO 64141
Phone: 816-474-1622 • Fax: 816-474-7622
E-mail: roosterlabs@aol.com
Web: www.roosterlabs.com

The oldest mail order knife company, celebrating over 40 years in the knife industry, has a tradition of offering the finest quality knives and accessories worldwide. Lines include Randall, Dozier, William Henry, Leatherman, Case, Gerber, SOG, Ka-Bar, Kershaw, CRKT, Al Mar, Klotzli, Boker, Marbles, Schatt & Morgan, A. G. Russell and more. Call for a free catalog or shop online to see the entire inventory.

A. G. RUSSELL KNIVES
1920 North 26th Street, Dept. KA04, Lowell, AR 72745-8489
Phone: 479-571-6161 • Fax: 479-631-8493
E-mail: ag@agrussell.com • Web: www.agrussell.com

New Catalog!

Catalog #26 is Numrich's latest edition! This 1,216 page catalog features more than 500 schematics for use in identifying obsolete and current commercial, military, antique and foreign guns. Edition #26 contains 180,000 items from their inventory of over 550 million parts and accessories and is a necessity for any true gunsmith or hobbyist. It has been the industry's leading reference book for firearm parts and identification for over 50 years!

Order Item #YP-26 $12.95
U.S. Orders: Bulk mail, shipping charges included.
Foreign Orders: Air mail, 30-day delivery; or surface 90-day delivery. Shipping charges additional.

NUMRICH GUN PARTS CORPORATION
226 Williams Lane, P.O. Box 299, West Hurley, NY 12491
Orders Toll-Free: 866-NUMRICH (866-686-7424)
Customer Service: (845) 679-4867
Toll-Free Fax: (877) GUNPART
Web: e-GunParts.com • E-mail: info@gunpartscorp.com

2005 GUN DIGEST Complete Compact CATALOG

A

GUNDEX

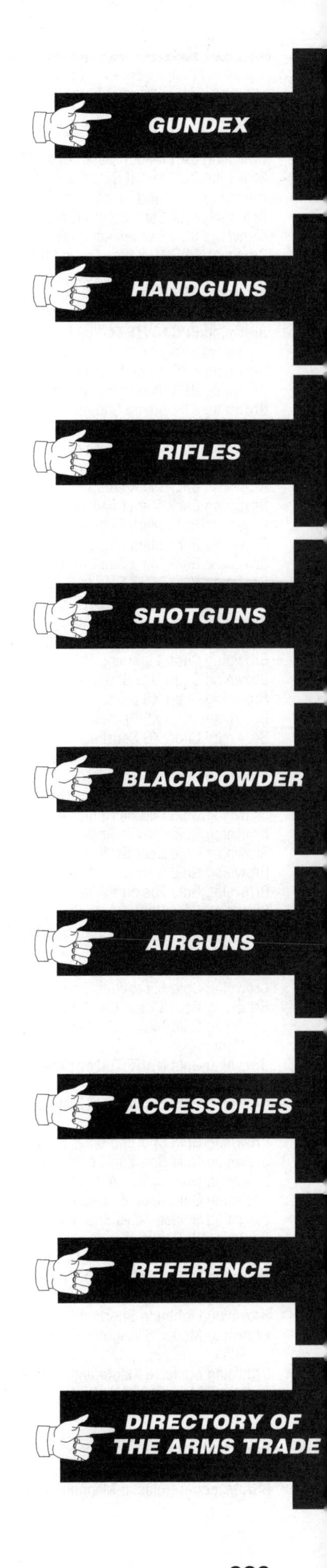

GUNDEX
HANDGUNS
RIFLES
SHOTGUNS
BLACKPOWDER
AIRGUNS
ACCESSORIES
REFERENCE
DIRECTORY OF THE ARMS TRADE

GUNDEX

C

GUNDEX

GUNDEX

F

G

H

I

J

K

GUNDEX

L

M

N

GUNDEX

GUNDEX

S

GUNDEX

T

GUNDEX

U

V

W

Z

NUMBERS

HANDGUNS — AUTOLOADERS, SERVICE & SPORT

Includes models suitable for several forms of competition and other sporting purposes.

Accu-Tek HC-380

Accu-Tek XL-9

Auto-Ordnance 1911A1 Standard

Baer Custom Carry

Auto-Ordnance Deluxe

Baer Premium II

ACCU-TEK MODEL HC-380 AUTO PISTOL

Caliber: 380 ACP, 10-shot magazine. **Barrel:** 2.75". **Weight:** 26 oz. **Length:** 6" overall. **Grips:** Checkered black composition. **Sights:** Blade front, rear adjustable for windage. **Features:** External hammer; manual thumb safety with firing pin and trigger disconnect; bottom magazine release. Stainless steel construction. Introduced 1993. Price includes cleaning kit and gun lock. Made in U.S.A. by Accu-Tek.

Price: Satin stainless **$249.00**

ACCU-TEK XL-9 AUTO PISTOL

Caliber: 9mm Para., 5-shot magazine. **Barrel:** 3". **Weight:** 24 oz. **Length:** 5.6" overall. **Grips:** Black pebble composition. **Sights:** Three-dot system; rear adjustable for windage. **Features:** Stainless steel construction; double-action-only mechanism. Introduced 1999. Price includes cleaning kit and gun lock, two magazines. Made in U.S.A. by Accu-Tek.

Price: **$267.00**

AMERICAN DERRINGER LM-5 AUTOMATIC PISTOL

Caliber: 25 ACP, 5-shot magazine. **Barrel:** 2-1/4". **Weight:** 15 oz. **Length:** NA. **Grips:** Wood. **Sights:** Fixed. **Features:** Compact, stainless, semi-auto, single-action hammerless design. Hand assembled and fitted.

Price: **$425.00**

AUTO-ORDNANCE 1911A1 AUTOMATIC PISTOL

Caliber: 45 ACP, 7-shot magazine. **Barrel:** 5". **Weight:** 39 oz. **Length:** 8-1/2" overall. **Grips:** Checkered plastic with medallion. **Sights:** Blade front, rear adjustable for windage. **Features:** Same specs as 1911A1 military guns-parts interchangeable. Frame and slide blued; each radius has non-glare finish. Made in U.S.A. by Auto-Ordnance Corp.

Price: 45 ACP, blue **$511.00**

Price: 45 ACP, Parkerized **$515.00**

Price: 45 ACP Deluxe (three-dot sights, textured rubber wraparound grips) **$525.00**

AUTAUGA 32 AUTO PISTOL

Caliber: 32 ACP, 6-shot magazine. **Barrel:** 2". **Weight:** 11.3 oz. **Length:** 4.3" overall. **Grips:** Black polymer. **Sights:** Fixed. **Features:** Double-action-only mechanism. Stainless steel construction. Uses Winchester Silver Tip ammunition.

Price: . . . . **NA**

BAER 1911 CUSTOM CARRY AUTO PISTOL

Caliber: 45 ACP, 7- or 10-shot magazine. **Barrel:** 5". **Weight:** 37 oz. **Length:** 8.5" overall. **Grips:** Checkered walnut. **Sights:** Baer improved ramp-style dovetailed front, Novak low-mount rear. **Features:** Baer forged NM frame, slide and barrel with stainless bushing; fitted slide to frame; double serrated slide (full-size only); Baer speed trigger with 4-lb. pull; Baer deluxe hammer and sear, tactical-style extended ambidextrous safety, beveled magazine well; polished feed ramp and throated barrel; tuned extractor; Baer extended ejector, checkered slide stop; lowered and flared ejection port, full-length recoil guide rod; recoil buff. Partial listing shown. Made in U.S.A. by Les Baer Custom, Inc.

Price: Standard size, blued **$1,640.00**

Price: Standard size, stainless **$1,690.00**

Price: Comanche size, blued **$1,640.00**

Price: Comanche size, stainless **$1,690.00**

Price: Comanche size, aluminum frame, blued slide **$1,923.00**

Price: Comanche size, aluminum frame, stainless slide **$1,995.00**

BAER 1911 PREMIER II AUTO PISTOL

Caliber: 9x23, 38 Super, 400 Cor-Bon, 45 ACP, 7- or 10-shot magazine. **Barrel:** 5". **Weight:** 37 oz. **Length:** 8.5" overall. **Grips:** Checkered rosewood, double diamond pattern. **Sights:** Baer dovetailed front, low-mount Bo-Mar rear with hidden leaf. **Features:** Baer NM forged steel frame and barrel with stainless bushing; slide fitted to frame; double serrated slide; lowered, flared ejection port; tuned, polished extractor; Baer extended ejector, checkered slide stop, aluminum speed trigger with 4-lb. pull, deluxe Commander hammer and sear, beavertail grip safety with pad, beveled magazine well, extended ambidextrous safety; flat mainspring housing; polished feed ramp and throated barrel; 30 lpi checkered front strap. Made in U.S.A. by Les Baer Custom, Inc.

Price: Blued **$1,428.00**

Price: Stainless **$1,558.00**

Price: 6" model, blued, from **$1,595.00**

BAER 1911 S.R.P. PISTOL

Caliber: 45 ACP. **Barrel:** 5". **Weight:** 37 oz. **Length:** 8.5" overall. **Grips:** Checkered walnut. **Sights:** Trijicon night sights. **Features:** Similar to the F.B.I. contract gun except uses Baer forged steel frame. Has Baer match barrel with supported chamber, Wolff springs, complete tactical action job. All parts Mag-na-fluxed; deburred for tactical carry. Has Baer Ultra Coat finish. Tuned for reliability. Contact Baer for complete details. Introduced 1996. Made in U.S.A. by Les Baer Custom, Inc.

Price: Government or Comanche length **$2,240.00**

Beretta M8000/8040 Cougar

Beretta 96

Beretta U22 Neos

Bersa Thunder 380

BERETTA MODEL 92FS PISTOL

Caliber: 9mm Para., 10-shot magazine. **Barrel:** 4.9". **Weight:** 34 oz. **Length:** 8.5" overall. **Grips:** Checkered black plastic. **Sights:** Blade front, rear adjustable for windage. Tritium night sights available. **Features:** Double action. Extractor acts as chamber loaded indicator, squared trigger guard, grooved front and backstraps, inertia firing pin. Matte or blued finish. Introduced 1977. Made in U.S.A. and imported from Italy by Beretta U.S.A.

Price: With plastic grips **$712.00**
Price: Vertec with access rail **$751.00**
Price: Vertec Inox **$801.00**

Beretta Model 92FS/96 Brigadier Pistols

Similar to the Model 92FS/96 except with a heavier slide to reduce felt recoil and allow mounting removable front sight. Wrap-around rubber grips. Three-dot sights dovetailed to the slide, adjustable for windage. Weighs 35.3 oz. Introduced 1999.

Price: 9mm or 40 S&W, 10-shot **$772.00**
Price: Inox models (stainless steel) **$822.00**

Beretta Model 96 Pistol

Same as the Model 92FS except chambered for 40 S&W. Ambidextrous safety mechanism with passive firing pin catch, slide safety/decocking lever, trigger bar disconnect. Has 10-shot magazine. Available with three-dot sights. Introduced 1992.

Price: Model 96, plastic grips **$712.00**
Price: Stainless, rubber grips **$772.00**
Price: Vertec with access rail **$751.00**
Price: Vertec Inox **$801.00**

BERETTA MODEL 80 CHEETAH SERIES DA PISTOLS

Caliber: 380 ACP, 10-shot magazine (M84); 8-shot (M85); 22 LR, 7-shot (M87). **Barrel:** 3.82". **Weight:** About 23 oz. (M84/85); 20.8 oz. (M87). **Length:** 6.8" overall. **Grips:** Glossy black plastic (wood optional at extra cost). **Sights:** Fixed front, drift-adjustable rear. **Features:** Double action, quick takedown, convenient magazine release. Introduced 1977. Imported from Italy by Beretta U.S.A.

Price: Model 84 Cheetah, plastic grips **$615.00**
Price: Model 85 Cheetah, plastic grips, 8-shot **$579.00**
Price: Model 87 Cheetah, wood, 22 LR, 7-shot **$615.00**
Price: Model 87 Target, plastic grips **$708.00**

Beretta Model 86 Cheetah

Similar to the 380-caliber Model 85 except has tip-up barrel for first-round loading. Barrel length is 4.4", overall length of 7.33". Has 8-shot magazine, walnut grips. Introduced 1989.

Price: **$615.00**

Beretta Model 21 Bobcat Pistol

Similar to the Model 950 BS. Chambered for 22 LR or 25 ACP. Both double action. Has 2.4" barrel, 4.9" overall length; 7-round magazine on 22 cal.; 8 rounds in 25 ACP, 9.9 oz., available in nickel, matte, engraved or blue finish. Plastic grips. Introduced in 1985.

Price: Bobcat, 22 or 25, blue **$300.00**
Price: Bobcat, 22, stainless **$329.00**
Price: Bobcat, 22 or 25, matte **$265.00**

BERETTA MODEL 3032 TOMCAT PISTOL

Caliber: 32 ACP, 7-shot magazine. **Barrel:** 2.45". **Weight:** 14.5 oz. **Length:** 5" overall. **Grips:** Checkered black plastic. **Sights:** Blade front, drift-adjustable rear. **Features:** Double action with exposed hammer; tip-up barrel for direct loading/unloading; thumb safety; polished or matte blue finish. Imported from Italy by Beretta U.S.A. Introduced 1996.

Price: Blue **$393.00**
Price: Matte **$358.00**
Price: Stainless **$443.00**
Price: With Tritium sights **$436.00**

BERETTA MODEL 8000/8040/8045 COUGAR PISTOL

Caliber: 9mm Para., 10-shot, 40 S&W, 10-shot magazine; 45 ACP, 8-shot. **Barrel:** 3.6". **Weight:** 33.5 oz. **Length:** 7" overall. **Grips:** Checkered plastic. **Sights:** Blade front, rear drift adjustable for windage. **Features:** Slide-mounted safety; rotating barrel; exposed hammer. Matte black Bruniton finish. Announced 1994. Imported from Italy by Beretta U.S.A.

Price: 8000 and 8000L **$729.00**
Price: D model, 9mm, 40 S&W **$729.00**
Price: D model, 45 ACP **$779.00**
Price: Inox **$794.00**

BERETTA MODEL 9000S COMPACT PISTOL

Caliber: 9mm Para., 40 S&W; 10-shot magazine. **Barrel:** 3.4". **Weight:** 26.8 oz. **Length:** 6.6". **Grips:** Soft polymer. **Sights:** Windage-adjustable white-dot rear, white-dot blade front. **Features:** Glass-reinforced polymer frame; patented tilt-barrel, open-slide locking system; chrome-lined barrel; external serrated hammer; automatic firing pin and manual safeties. Introduced 2000. Imported from Italy by Beretta USA.

Price: 9000S Type F (single and double action, external hammer) **$472.00**

BERETTA MODEL U22 NEOS

Caliber: 22 LR, 10-shot magazine. **Barrel:** 4.2"; 6". **Weight:** 32 oz.; 36 oz. **Length:** 8.8"; 10.3". **Sights:** Target. **Features:** Integral rail for standard scope mounts, light, perfectly weighted, 100% American made by Beretta.

Price: **$265.00**
Price: Inox **$315.00**
Price: DLX **$336.00**
Price: Inox **$386.00**

BERSA THUNDER LITE 380 AUTO PISTOLS

Caliber: 380 ACP, 7-shot (Thunder 380 Lite), 9-shot magazine (Thunder 380 DLX). **Barrel:** 3.5". **Weight:** 23 oz. **Length:** 6.6" overall. **Grips:** Black polymer. **Sights:** Blade front, notch rear adjustable for windage; three-dot system. **Features:** Double action; firing pin and magazine safeties. Available in blue, nickel, or duo tone. Introduced 1995. Distributed by Eagle Imports, Inc.

Price: Thunder 380, 7-shot, deep blue finish **$266.95**
Price: Thunder 380 Deluxe, 9-shot, satin nickel **$299.95**
Price: Thunder 380 Gold, 7-shot **$299.95**

Browning Buck Mark Standard

Browning Buck Mark Challenge

Bersa Thunder 45 Ultra Compact Pistol

Similar to the Bersa Thunder 380 except in 45 ACP. Available in three finishes. Introduced 2003. Imported from Argentina by Eagle Imports, Inc.

Price: Thunder 45, matte blue ... **$400.95**
Price: Thunder 45, Duotone ... **$424.95**
Price: Thunder 45, Satin nickel ... **$441.95**

BLUE THUNDER/COMMODORE 1911-STYLE AUTO PISTOLS

Caliber: 45 ACP, 7-shot magazine. **Barrel:** 4-1/4", 5". **Weight:** NA. **Length:** NA. **Grips:** Checkered hardwood. **Sights:** Blade front, drift-adjustable rear. **Features:** Extended slide release and safety, spring guide rod, skeletonized hammer and trigger, magazine bumper, beavertail grip safety. Imported from the Philippines by Century International Arms Inc.

Price: ... **$464.80 to $484.80**

AUTOBOND 450

Caliber: 450 Autobond (also 45 ACP). Model 1911-style. **Barrel:** 5 inches.

Price: ... **$1150.00**

BROWNING HI-POWER 9mm AUTOMATIC PISTOL

Caliber: 9mm Para.,10-shot magazine. **Barrel:** 4-21/32". **Weight:** 32 oz. **Length:** 7-3/4" overall. **Grips:** Walnut, hand checkered, or black Polyamide. **Sights:** 1/8" blade front; rear screw-adjustable for windage and elevation. Also available with fixed rear (drift-adjustable for windage). **Features:** External hammer with half-cock and thumb safeties. A blow on the hammer cannot discharge a cartridge; cannot be fired with magazine removed. Fixed rear sight model available. Includes gun lock. Imported from Belgium by Browning.

Price: Fixed sight model, walnut grips ... **$680.00**
Price: Fully adjustable rear sight, walnut grips ... **$730.00**
Price: Mark III, standard matte black finish, fixed sight, moulded grips, ambidextrous safety ... **$662.00**

Browning Hi-Power Practical Pistol

Similar to the standard Hi-Power except has silver-chromed frame with blued slide, wrap-around Pachmayr rubber grips, round-style serrated hammer and removable front sight, fixed rear (drift-adjustable for windage). Available in 9mm Para. Includes gun lock. Introduced 1991.

Price: ... **$717.00**

BROWNING BUCK MARK STANDARD 22 PISTOL

Caliber: 22 LR, 10-shot magazine. **Barrel:** 5-1/2". **Weight:** 32 oz. **Length:** 9-1/2" overall. **Grips:** Black moulded composite with checkering. **Sights:** Ramp front, Browning Pro Target rear adjustable for windage and elevation. **Features:** All steel, matte blue finish or nickel, gold-colored trigger. Buck Mark Plus has laminated wood grips. Includes gun lock. Made in U.S.A. Introduced 1985. From Browning.

Price: Buck Mark Standard, blue ... **$310.00**
Price: Buck Mark Nickel, nickel finish with contoured rubber grips **$366.00**
Price: Buck Mark Plus, matte blue with laminated wood grips ... **$379.00**
Price: Buck Mark Plus Nickel, nickel finish, laminated wood grips **$415.00**

Browning Buck Mark Camper

Similar to the Buck Mark except 5-1/2" bull barrel. Weight is 34 oz. Matte blue finish, molded composite grips. Introduced 1999. From Browning.

Price: ... **$279.00**
Price: Camper Nickel, nickel finish, molded composite grips ... **$311.00**

Browning Buck Mark Challenge

Similar to the Buck Mark except has a lightweight barrel and smaller grip diameter. Barrel length is 5-1/2", weight is 25 oz. Introduced 1999. From Browning.

Price: ... **$346.00**

Browning Buck Mark Micro

Same as the Buck Mark Standard and Buck Mark Plus except has 4" barrel. Available in blue or nickel. Has 16-click Pro Target rear sight. Introduced 1992.

Price: Micro Standard, matte blue finish ... **$310.00**
Price: Micro Nickel, nickel finish ... **$366.00**
Price: Buck Mark Micro Plus Nickel ... **$415.00**

Browning Buck Mark Bullseye

Same as the Buck Mark Standard except has 7-1/4" fluted barrel, matte blue finish. Weighs 36 oz.

Price: Bullseye Standard, molded composite grips ... **$420.00**
Price: Bullseye Target, contoured rosewood grips ... **$541.00**

Browning Buck Mark 5.5

Same as the Buck Mark Standard except has a 5-1/2" bull barrel with integral scope mount, matte blue finish.

Price: 5.5 Field, Pro-Target adj. rear sight, contoured walnut grips ... **$459.00**
Price: 5.5 Target, hooded adj. target sights, contoured walnut grips ... **$459.00**

BROWNING PRO-9

Caliber: 9mm Luger, 10-round magazine. **Barrel:** 4". **Weight:** 30 oz. **Overall length:** 7 1/4". **Features:** Double-action, ambidextrous decocker and safety. Fixed, three-dot-style sights, 6" sight radius. Molded composite grips with interchangeable backstrap inserts.

Price: ... **$628.00**

BROWNING HI-POWER

Caliber: 9mm, 40 S&W. **Barrel:** 4 3/4". **Weight:** 32 to 35 oz. **Overall length:** 7 3/4". **Features:** Blued, matte, polymer or silver-chromed frame; molded, wraparound Pachmayr or walnut grips; Commander-style or spur-type hammer.

Price: Practical model, fixed sights ... **$791.00**
Price: Mark II model, epoxy finish ... **$730.00**
Price: HP Standard, blued, fixed sights, walnut grips ... **$751.00**
Price: HP Standard, blued, adj. sights ... **$805.00**

CHARLES DALY M-1911-A1P AUTOLOADING PISTOL

Caliber: 45 ACP, 7- or 10-shot magazine. **Barrel:** 5". **Weight:** 38 oz. **Length:** 8-3/4" overall. **Grips:** Checkered. **Sights:** Blade front, rear drift adjustable for windage; three-dot system. **Features:** Skeletonized combat hammer and trigger; beavertail grip safety; extended slide release; oversize thumb safety; Parkerized finish. Introduced 1996. Imported from the Philippines by K.B.I., Inc.

Price: ... **$469.95**

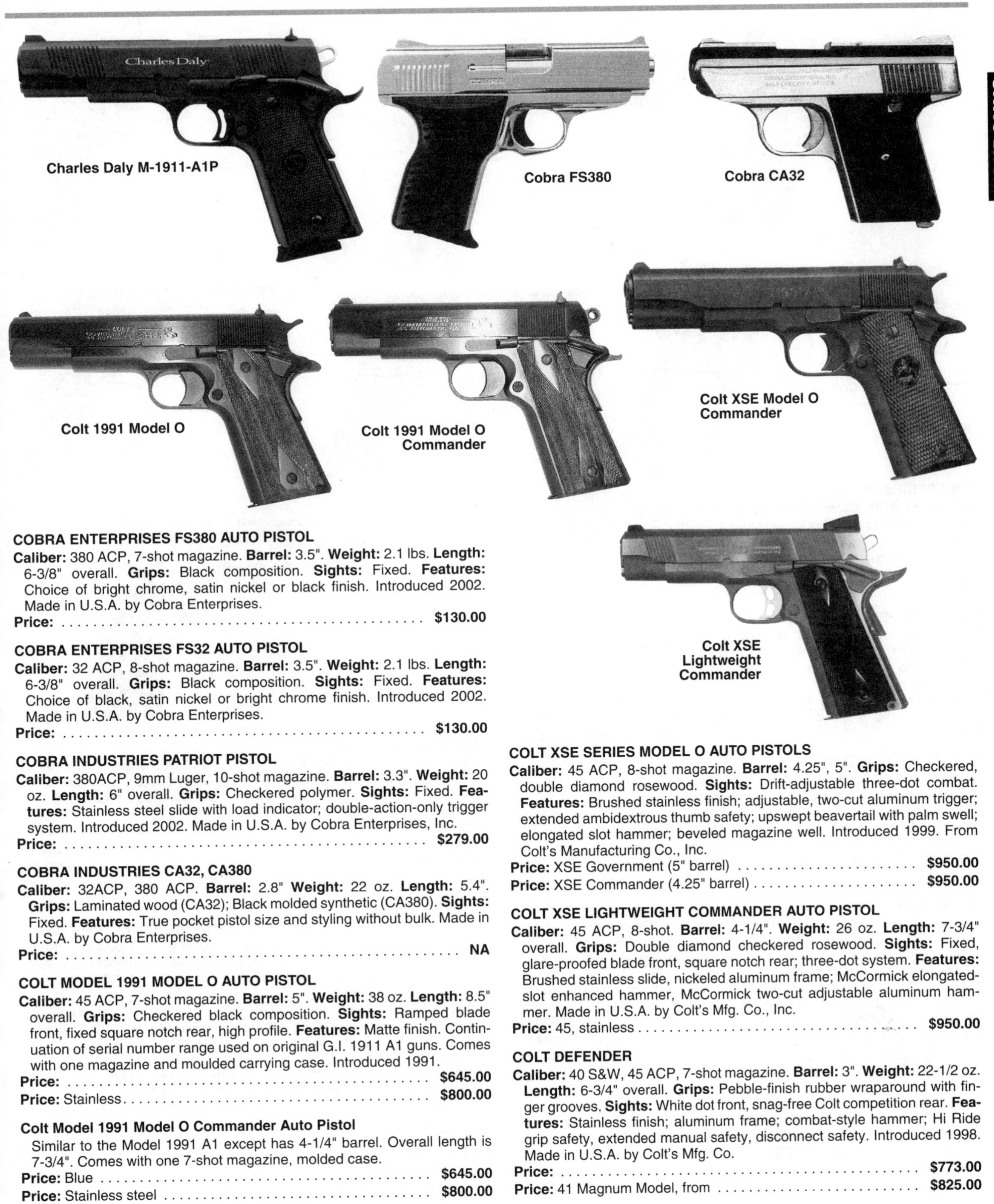

Charles Daly M-1911-A1P

Cobra FS380

Cobra CA32

Colt 1991 Model O

Colt 1991 Model O Commander

Colt XSE Model O Commander

Colt XSE Lightweight Commander

COBRA ENTERPRISES FS380 AUTO PISTOL

Caliber: 380 ACP, 7-shot magazine. **Barrel:** 3.5". **Weight:** 2.1 lbs. **Length:** 6-3/8" overall. **Grips:** Black composition. **Sights:** Fixed. **Features:** Choice of bright chrome, satin nickel or black finish. Introduced 2002. Made in U.S.A. by Cobra Enterprises.

Price: **$130.00**

COBRA ENTERPRISES FS32 AUTO PISTOL

Caliber: 32 ACP, 8-shot magazine. **Barrel:** 3.5". **Weight:** 2.1 lbs. **Length:** 6-3/8" overall. **Grips:** Black composition. **Sights:** Fixed. **Features:** Choice of black, satin nickel or bright chrome finish. Introduced 2002. Made in U.S.A. by Cobra Enterprises.

Price: **$130.00**

COBRA INDUSTRIES PATRIOT PISTOL

Caliber: 380ACP, 9mm Luger, 10-shot magazine. **Barrel:** 3.3". **Weight:** 20 oz. **Length:** 6" overall. **Grips:** Checkered polymer. **Sights:** Fixed. **Features:** Stainless steel slide with load indicator; double-action-only trigger system. Introduced 2002. Made in U.S.A. by Cobra Enterprises, Inc.

Price: **$279.00**

COBRA INDUSTRIES CA32, CA380

Caliber: 32ACP, 380 ACP. **Barrel:** 2.8" **Weight:** 22 oz. **Length:** 5.4". **Grips:** Laminated wood (CA32); Black molded synthetic (CA380). **Sights:** Fixed. **Features:** True pocket pistol size and styling without bulk. Made in U.S.A. by Cobra Enterprises.

Price: . . . . **NA**

COLT MODEL 1991 MODEL O AUTO PISTOL

Caliber: 45 ACP, 7-shot magazine. **Barrel:** 5". **Weight:** 38 oz. **Length:** 8.5" overall. **Grips:** Checkered black composition. **Sights:** Ramped blade front, fixed square notch rear, high profile. **Features:** Matte finish. Continuation of serial number range used on original G.I. 1911 A1 guns. Comes with one magazine and moulded carrying case. Introduced 1991.

Price: **$645.00**

Price: Stainless **$800.00**

Colt Model 1991 Model O Commander Auto Pistol

Similar to the Model 1991 A1 except has 4-1/4" barrel. Overall length is 7-3/4". Comes with one 7-shot magazine, molded case.

Price: Blue **$645.00**

Price: Stainless steel **$800.00**

COLT XSE SERIES MODEL O AUTO PISTOLS

Caliber: 45 ACP, 8-shot magazine. **Barrel:** 4.25", 5". **Grips:** Checkered, double diamond rosewood. **Sights:** Drift-adjustable three-dot combat. **Features:** Brushed stainless finish; adjustable, two-cut aluminum trigger; extended ambidextrous thumb safety; upswept beavertail with palm swell; elongated slot hammer; beveled magazine well. Introduced 1999. From Colt's Manufacturing Co., Inc.

Price: XSE Government (5" barrel) **$950.00**

Price: XSE Commander (4.25" barrel) **$950.00**

COLT XSE LIGHTWEIGHT COMMANDER AUTO PISTOL

Caliber: 45 ACP, 8-shot. **Barrel:** 4-1/4". **Weight:** 26 oz. **Length:** 7-3/4" overall. **Grips:** Double diamond checkered rosewood. **Sights:** Fixed, glare-proofed blade front, square notch rear; three-dot system. **Features:** Brushed stainless slide, nickeled aluminum frame; McCormick elongated-slot enhanced hammer, McCormick two-cut adjustable aluminum hammer. Made in U.S.A. by Colt's Mfg. Co., Inc.

Price: 45, stainless **$950.00**

COLT DEFENDER

Caliber: 40 S&W, 45 ACP, 7-shot magazine. **Barrel:** 3". **Weight:** 22-1/2 oz. **Length:** 6-3/4" overall. **Grips:** Pebble-finish rubber wraparound with finger grooves. **Sights:** White dot front, snag-free Colt competition rear. **Features:** Stainless finish; aluminum frame; combat-style hammer; Hi Ride grip safety, extended manual safety, disconnect safety. Introduced 1998. Made in U.S.A. by Colt's Mfg. Co.

Price: **$773.00**

Price: 41 Magnum Model, from **$825.00**

Colt Defender

Colt Series 70

Colt 38 Super

Colt Gunsite

CZ 75B 9mm

CZ 75B Decocker

CZ 85

COLT SERIES 70

Caliber: 45 ACP. **Barrel:** 5". **Weight:** NA **Length:** NA **Grips:** Rosewood with double diamond checkering pattern. **Sights:** Fixed. **Features:** A custom replica of the Original Series 70 pistol with a Series 70 firing system, original rollmarks. Introduced 2002. Made in U.S.A. by Colt's Manufacturing.

Price: . . . . **NA**

COLT 38 SUPER

Caliber: 38 Super **Barrel:** 5" **Weight:** NA. **Length:** 8-1/2" **Grips:** Checkered rubber (Stainless and blue models); Wood with double diamond checkering pattern (Bright stainless model). **Sights:** 3-dot. **Features:** Beveled magazine well, standard thumb safety and service-style grip safety. Introduced 2003. Made in U.S.A. by Colt's Mfg. Co.

Price: . . . . (Blue) **$864.00** (Stainless steel) **$943.00**

Price: . . . . (Bright stainless steel) **$1,152.00**

COLT GUNSITE PISTOL

Caliber: 45 ACP **Barrel:** 5". **Weight:** NA. **Length:** NA. **Grips:** Rosewood. **Sights**: Heinie, front; Novak, rear. **Features:** Contains most all of the Gunsite school recommended features such as Series 70 firing system, Smith & Alexander metal grip safety w/palm swell, serrated flat mainspring housing, dehorned all around. Available in blue or stainless steel. Introduced 2003. Made in U.S.A. by Colt's Mfg. Co.

Price: . . . . **NA**

CZ 75B AUTO PISTOL

Caliber: 9mm Para., 40 S&W, 10-shot magazine. **Barrel:** 4.7". **Weight:** 34.3 oz. **Length:** 8.1" overall. **Grips:** High impact checkered plastic. **Sights:** Square post front, rear adjustable for windage; three-dot system. **Features:** Single action/double action design; firing pin block safety; choice of black polymer, matte or high-polish blue finishes. All-steel frame. Imported from the Czech Republic by CZ-USA.

Price: Black polymer. **$529.00**

Price: Glossy blue. **$559.00**

Price: Dual tone or satin nickel **$559.00**

Price: 22 LR conversion unit. **$399.00**

CZ 75B Decocker

Similar to the CZ 75B except has a decocking lever in place of the safety lever. All other specifications are the same. Introduced 1999. Imported from the Czech Republic by CZ-USA.

Price: 9mm, black polymer **$559.00**

Price: 40 S&W **$569.00**

CZ 75B Compact Auto Pistol

Similar to the CZ 75 except has 10-shot magazine, 3.9" barrel and weighs 32 oz. Has removable front sight, non-glare ribbed slide top. Trigger guard is squared and serrated; combat hammer. Introduced 1993. Im-ported from the Czech Republic by CZ-USA.

Price: 9mm, black polymer **$559.00**

Price: Dual tone or satin nickel **$569.00**

Price: D Compact, black polymer **$569.00**

Price: CZ2075 Sub-compact RAMI **$559.00**

CZ 75M IPSC Auto Pistol

Similar to the CZ 75B except has a longer frame and slide, slightly larger grip to accommodate new heavy-duty magazine. Ambidextrous thumb safety, safety notch on hammer; two-port in-frame compensator; slide racker; frame-mounted Firepoint red dot sight. Introduced 2001. Imported from the Czech Republic by CZ USA.

Price: 40 S&W, 10-shot mag. **$1,551.00**

Price: CZ 75 Standard IPSC (40 S&W, adj. sights) **$1,038.00**

CZ 85B Auto Pistol

Same gun as the CZ 75 except has ambidextrous slide release and safety-levers; non-glare, ribbed slide top; squared, serrated trigger guard; trigger stop to prevent overtravel. Introduced 1986. Imported from the Czech Republic by CZ-USA.

Price: Black polymer. **$483.00**

Price: Combat, black polymer. **$540.00**

Price: Combat, dual tone **$487.00**

Price: Combat, glossy blue. **$499.00**

CZ 97B

CZ 75/85 Kadet

CZ 100

Dan Wesson Firearms Pointman Major

Dan Wesson Firearms Major Aussie

CZ 85 Combat

Similar to the CZ 85B (9mm only) except has an adjustable rear sight, adjustable trigger for overtravel, free-fall magazine, extended magazine catch. Does not have the firing pin block safety. Introduced 1999. Imported from the Czech Republic by CZ-USA.

Price: 9mm, black polymer **$540.00**
Price: 9mm, glossy blue **$566.00**
Price: 9mm, dual tone or satin nickel **$586.00**

CZ 83B DOUBLE-ACTION PISTOL

Caliber: 9mm Makarov, 32 ACP, 380 ACP, 10-shot magazine. **Barrel:** 3.8". **Weight:** 26.2 oz. **Length:** 6.8" overall. **Grips:** High impact checkered plastic. **Sights:** Removable square post front, rear adjustable for windage; three-dot system. **Features:** Single action/double action; ambidextrous magazine release and safety. Blue finish; non-glare ribbed slide top. Imported from the Czech Republic by CZ-USA.

Price: Blue **$378.00**
Price: Nickel **$397.00**

CZ 97B AUTO PISTOL

Caliber: 45 ACP, 10-shot magazine. **Barrel:** 4.85". **Weight:** 40 oz. **Length:** 8.34" overall. **Grips:** Checkered walnut. **Sights:** Fixed. **Features:** Single action/double action; full-length slide rails; screw-in barrel bushing; linkless barrel; all-steel construction; chamber loaded indicator; dual transfer bars. Introduced 1999. Imported from the Czech Republic by CZ-USA.

Price: Black polymer. **$625.00**
Price: Glossy blue. **$641.00**

CZ 75/85 KADET AUTO PISTOL

Caliber: 22 LR, 10-shot magazine. **Barrel:** 4.88". **Weight:** 36 oz. **Grips:** High impact checkered plastic. **Sights:** Blade front, fully adjustable rear. **Features:** Single action/double action mechanism; all-steel construction. Duplicates weight, balance and function of the CZ 75 pistol. Introduced 1999. Imported from the Czech Republic by CZ-USA.

Price: Black polymer. **$486.00**

CZ 100 AUTO PISTOL

Caliber: 9mm Para., 40 S&W, 10-shot magazine. **Barrel:** 3.7". **Weight:** 24 oz. **Length:** 6.9" overall. **Grips:** Grooved polymer. **Sights:** Blade front with dot, white outline rear drift adjustable for windage. **Features:** Double action only with firing pin block; polymer frame, steel slide; has laser sight mount. Introduced 1996. Imported from the Czech Republic by CZ-USA.

Price: 9mm Para. **$405.00**
Price: 40 S&W **$424.00**

DAN WESSON FIREARMS POINTMAN MAJOR AUTO PISTOL

Caliber: 45 ACP. **Barrel:** 5". **Grips:** Rosewood checkered. **Features:** Blued or stainless steel frame and serrated slide; Chip McCormick match-grade trigger group, sear and disconnect; match-grade barrel; high-ride beavertail safety; checkered slide release; **Sights:** High rib; interchangeable sight system; laser engraved. Introduced 2000. Made in U.S.A. by Dan Wesson Firearms.

Price: Model PM1-B (blued) **$799.00**
Price: Model PM1-S (stainless) **$699.00**

Dan Wesson Firearms Pointman Seven Auto Pistols

Similar to Pointman Major, dovetail adjustable target rear sight and dovetail target front sight. Available in blued or stainless finish. Introduced 2000. Made in U.S.A. by Dan Wesson Firearms.

Price: PM7 (blued frame and slide) **$999.00**
Price: PM7S (stainless finish). **$799.00**

Dan Wesson Firearms Pointman Guardian Auto Pistols

Similar to Pointman Major, more compact frame with 4.25" barrel. Avaiable in blued or stainless finish with fixed or adjustable sights. Introduced 2000. Made in U.S.A. by Dan Wesson Firearms.

Price: PMG-FS, all new frame (fixed sights). **$769.00**
Price: PMG-AS (blued frame and slide, adjustable sights). **$799.00**
Price: PMGD-FS Guardian Duce, all new frame (stainless frame and blued slide, fixed sights) **$829.00**
Price: PMGD-AS Guardian Duce (stainless frame and blued slide, adj. sights). **$799.00**

Dan Wesson Firearms Major Tri-Ops Packs

Similar to Pointman Major. Complete frame assembly fitted to 3 match grade complete slide assemblied (9mm, 10mm, 40 S&W). Includes recoil springs and magazines that come in hard cases fashioned after high-grade European rifle case. Constructed of navy blue cordura stretched over hardwood with black leather trim and comfortable black leather wrapped handle. Brass corner protectors, dual combination locks, engraved presentation plate on the lid. Inside, the Tri-Ops Pack components are nested in precision die-cut closed cell foam and held sercurely in place by convoluted foam in the inside of the lid. Introduced 2002. Made in U.S.A. by Dan Wesson Firearms.

Price: TOP1B (blued), TOP1-S (stainless) **$2,459.00**

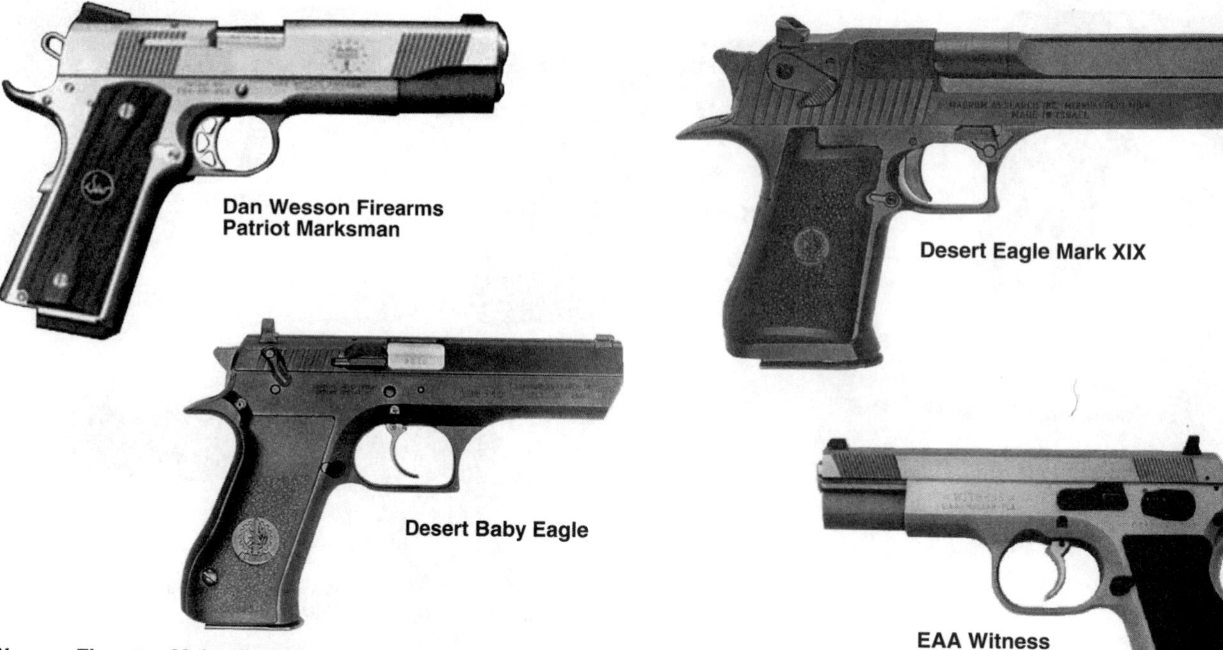

Dan Wesson Firearms Patriot Marksman

Desert Eagle Mark XIX

Desert Baby Eagle

EAA Witness

Dan Wesson Firearms Major Aussie

Similar to Pointman Major. Available in 45 ACP. Features Bomar-style adjustable rear target sight, unique slide top configuration exclusive to this model (features radius from the flat side surfaces of the slide to a narrow flat on top and then a small redius and reveal ending in a flat, low (1/16" high) sight rib 3/8" wide with lengthwise serrations). Clearly identified by the Southern Cross flag emblem laser engraved on the sides of the slide (available in 45 ACP only). Introduced 2002. Made in U.S.A. by Dan Wesson Firearms.

Price: PMA-B (blued) **$799.00**
Price: PMA-S (stainless). **$799.00**

Dan Wesson Firearms Pointman Minor Auto Pistol

Similar to Pointman Major. Full size (5") entry level IDPA or action pistol model with blued carbon alloy frame and round top slide, bead blast matte finish on frame and slide top and radius, satin-brushed polished finish on sides of slide, chromed barrel, dovetail mount fixed rear target sight and tactical/target ramp front sight, match trigger, skeletonized target hammer, high ride beavertail, fitted extractor, serrations on thumb safety, slide release and mag release, lowered and relieved ejection port, beveled mag well, exotic hardwood grips, serrated mainspring housing, laser engraved. Introduced 2000. Made in U.S.A. by Dan Wesson Firearms.

Price: Model PM2-P **$599.00**

Dan Wesson Firearms Pointman Hi-Cap Auto Pistol

Similar to Pointman Minor, full-size high-capacity (10-shot) magazine with 5" chromed barrel, blued finish and dovetail fixed rear sight. Match adjustable trigger, ambidextrous extended thumb safety, beavertail safety. Introduced 2001. From Dan Wesson Firearms.

Price: PMHC (Pointman High-Cap) **$689.00**

Dan Wesson Firearms Pointman Dave Pruitt Signature Series

Similar to other full-sized Pointman models, customized by Master Pistolsmith and IDPA Grand Master Dave Pruitt. Alloy carbon-steel with black oxide bluing and bead-blast matte finish. Front and rear chevron cocking serrations, dovetail mount fixed rear target sight and tactical/target ramp front sight, ramped match barrel with fitted match bushing and link, Chip McCormick (or equivalent) match grade trigger group, serrated ambidextrous tactical/carry thumb safety, high ride beavertail, serrated slide release and checkered mag release, match grade sear and hammer, fitted extractor, lowered and relieved ejection port, beveled mag well, full length 2-piece recoil spring guide rod, cocobolo double diamond checkered grips, serrated steel mainspring housing, special laser engraving. Introduced 2001. From Dan Wesson Firearms.

Price: PMDP (Pointman Dave Pruitt) **$899.00**

DAN WESSON FIREARMS PATRIOT 1911 PISTOL

Caliber: 45 ACP. **Grips:** Exotic exhibition grade cocobolo, double diamond hand cut checkering. **Sights:** New innovative combat/carry rear sight that completely encloses the dovetail. **Features:** The new Patriot Expert and Patriot Marksman are full size match grade series 70 1911s machined from steel forgings. Available in blued chome moly steel or stainless steel. Beveled mag well, lowered and flared ejection port, high sweep beavertail safety. Introduced June 2002.

Price: Model PTM-B (blued) **$797.00**
Price: Model PTM-S (stainless) **$898.00**
Price: Model PTE-B (blued) **$864.00**
Price: Model PTE-S (stainless). **$971.00**

DESERT EAGLE MARK XIX PISTOL

Caliber: 357 Mag., 9-shot; 44 Mag., 8-shot; 50 AE, 7-shot. **Barrel:** 6", 10", interchangeable. **Weight:** 357 Mag.-62 oz.; 44 Mag.-69 oz.; 50 AE - 72 oz. **Length:** 10-1/4" overall (6" bbl.). **Grips:** Polymer; rubber available. **Sights:** Blade on ramp front, combat-style rear. Adjustable available. **Features:** Interchangeable barrels; rotating three-lug bolt; am-bidextrous safety; adjustable trigger. Military epoxy finish. Satin, bright nickel, chrome, brushed, matte or black finishes available. 10" barrel extra. Imported from Israel by Magnum Research, Inc.

Price: 357, 6" bbl., standard pistol **$1,249.00**
Price: 44 Mag., 6", standard pistol **$1,249.00**
Price: 50 Magnum, 6" bbl., standard pistol. **$1,249.00**

DESERT BABY EAGLE PISTOLS

Caliber: 9mm Para., 40 S&W, 45 ACP, 10-round magazine. **Barrel:** 3.5", 3.7", 4.72". **Weight:** 26.8 - 39.8 oz. **Length:** 7.25" to 8.25" overall. **Grips:** Polymer. **Sights:** Drift-adjustable rear, blade front. **Features:** Steel frame and slide; polygonal rifling to reduce barrel wear; slide safety; decocker. Reintroduced in 1999. Imported from Israel by Magnum Research Inc.

Price: Standard (9mm or 40 cal.; 4.72" barrel, 8.25" overall) **$499.00**
Price: Semi-Compact (9mm, 40 or 45 cal.; 3.7" barrel, 7.75" overall) **$499.00**
Price: Compact (9mm or 40 cal.; 3.5" barrel, 7.25" overall) **$499.00**
Price: Polymer (9mm or 40 cal; polymer frame; 3.25" barrel, 7.25" overall) **$499.00**

Ed Brown Commander Bobtail

Ed Brown Kobra Carry

Entréprise Elite P500

EAA WITNESS DA AUTO PISTOL

Caliber: 9mm Para., 10-shot magazine; 38 Super, 40 S&W, 10-shot magazine; 45 ACP, 10-shot magazine. **Barrel:** 4.50". **Weight:** 35.33 oz. **Length:** 8.10" overall. **Grips:** Checkered rubber. **Sights:** Undercut blade front, open rear adjustable for windage. **Features:** Double-action trigger system; round trigger guard; frame-mounted safety. Introduced 1991. Imported from Italy by European American Armory.

Price: 9mm, blue **$449.00**
Price: 9mm, Wonder finish **$459.00**
Price: 9mm Compact, blue, 10-shot **$449.00**
Price: As above, Wonder finish **$459.00**
Price: 38 Super, blue **$449.00**
Price: 38 Super, Wonder finish **$459.00**
Price: 40 S&W, blue **$449.00**
Price: As above, Wonder finish **$459.00**
Price: 40 S&W Compact, 9-shot, blue **$449.00**
Price: As above, Wonder finish **$459.00**
Price: 45 ACP, blue **$449.00**
Price: As above, Wonder finish **$459.00**
Price: 45 ACP Compact, 8-shot, blue **$449.00**
Price: As above, Wonder finish **$459.00**

ED BROWN CLASSIC CUSTOM

Caliber: 45 ACP, 7 shots. **Barrel:** 5 inches. **Weight:** 39 oz. **Stocks:** Cocobolo wood. **Sights:** Bo-Mar adjustable rear, dovetail front. **Features:** Single-action, M1911 style, custom made to order, stainless frame and slide available.

Price: **$2,895.00**

ED BROWN COMMANDER BOBTAIL

Caliber: 45 ACP, 400 Cor-Bon, 40 S&W, 357 SIG, 38 Super, 9mm Luger, 7-shot magazine. **Barrel:** 4.25". **Weight:** 34 oz. **Grips:** Hogue exotic wood. **Sights:** Customer preference front; fixed Novak low-mount, rear. Optional night inserts available. **Features:** Checkered forestrap and bobtailed mainspring housing. Other options available.

Price: Executive Carry **$2,295.00**
Price: Executive Elite **$2,195.00**

ED BROWN KOBRA

Caliber: 45 ACP, 7-shot magazine. **Barrel:** 5" (Kobra); 4.25" (Kobra Carry). **Weight:** 39 oz. (Kobra); 34 oz. (Kobra Carry). **Grips:** Hogue exotic wood. **Sights:** Ramp, front; fixed Novak low-mount night sights, rear. **Features:** Has snakeskin pattern serrations on forestrap and mainspring housing, denorned edges, beavertail grip safety.

Price: Kobra **$1,895.00**
Price: Kobra Carry **$1,995.00**

ENTRÉPRISE ELITE P500 AUTO PISTOL

Caliber: 45 ACP, 10-shot magazine. **Barrel:** 5". **Weight:** 40 oz. **Length:** 8.5" overall. **Grips:** Black ultra-slim, double diamond, checkered synthetic. **Sights:** Dovetailed blade front, rear adjustable for windage; three-dot system. **Features:** Reinforced dust cover; lowered and flared ejection port; squared trigger guard; adjustable match trigger; bolstered front strap; high grip cut; high ride beavertail grip safety; steel flat mainspring housing; extended thumb lock; skeletonized hammer, match grade sear, disconnector; Wolff springs. Introduced 1998. Made in U.S.A. by Entréprise Arms.

Price: **$739.90**

Entréprise Boxer P500

Entréprise Tactical 500

Entréprise Boxer P500 Auto Pistol

Similar to the Medalist model except has adjustable Competizione "melded" rear sight with dovetailed Patridge front; high mass chiseled slide with sweep cut; machined slide parallel rails; polished breech face and barrel channel. Introduced 1998. Made in U.S.A. by Entréprise Arms.

Price: **$1,399.00**

Entréprise Medalist P500 Auto Pistol

Similar to the Elite model except has adjustable Competizione "melded" rear sight with dovetailed Patridge front; machined slide parallel rails with polished breech face and barrel channel; front and rear slide serrations; lowered and flared ejection port; full-length one-piece guide rod with plug; National Match barrel and bushing; stainless firing pin; tuned match extractor; oversize firing pin stop; throated barrel and polished ramp; slide lapped to frame. Introduced 1998. Made in U.S.A. by Entréprise Arms.

Price: 45 ACP **$979.00**
Price: 40 S&W **$1,099.00**

Entréprise Tactical P500 Auto Pistol

Similar to the Elite model except has Tactical2 Ghost Ring sight or Novak lo-mount sight; ambidextrous thumb safety; front and rear slide serrations; full-length guide rod; throated barrel, polished ramp; tuned match extractor; fitted barrel and bushing; stainless firing pin; slide lapped to frame; dehorned. Introduced 1998. Made in U.S.A. by Entréprise Arms.

Price: **$979.90**
Price: Tactical Plus (full-size frame, Officer's slide). **$1,049.00**

ERMA KGP68 AUTO PISTOL

Caliber: 32 ACP, 6-shot, 380 ACP, 5-shot. **Barrel:** 4". **Weight:** 22-1/2 oz. **Length:** 7-3/8" overall. **Grips:** Checkered plastic. **Sights:** Fixed. **Features:** Toggle action similar to original "Luger" pistol. Action stays open after last shot. Has magazine and sear disconnect safety systems.

Price: **$499.95**

FEG PJK-9HP
Felk MTF 450
Firestorm Mini
Firestorm 45 Gov't
Glock 17C
Glock 22

FEG PJK-9HP AUTO PISTOL

Caliber: 9mm Para., 10-shot magazine. **Barrel:** 4.75". **Weight:** 32 oz. **Length:** 8" overall. **Grips:** Hand-checkered walnut. **Sights:** Blade front, rear adjustable for windage; three dot system. **Features:** Single action; polished blue or hard chrome finish; rounded combat-style serrated hammer. Comes with two magazines and cleaning rod. Imported from Hungary by K.B.I., Inc.

Price: Blue **$259.95**
Price: Hard chrome. **$259.95**

FEG SMC-380 AUTO PISTOL

Caliber: 380 ACP, 6-shot magazine. **Barrel:** 3.5". **Weight:** 18.5 oz. **Length:** 6.1" overall. **Grips:** Checkered composition with thumbrest. **Sights:** Blade front, rear adjustable for windage. **Features:** Patterned after the PPK pistol. Alloy frame, steel slide; double action. Blue finish. Comes with two magazines, cleaning rod. Imported from Hungary by K.B.I., Inc.

Price: **$224.95**

FELK MTF 450 AUTO PISTOL

Caliber: 9mm Para. (10-shot); 40 S&W (8-shot); . 357 Mag, 45 ACP (9-shot magazine). **Barrel:** 3.5". **Weight:** 19.9 oz. **Length:** 6.4" overall. **Grips:** Checkered. **Sights:** Blade front; adjustable rear. **Features:** Double-action only trigger, striker fired; polymer frame; trigger safety, firing pin safety, trigger bar safety; adjustable trigger weight; fully interchangeable slide/barrel to change calibers. Introduced 1998. Imported by Felk Inc.

Price: **$395.00**
Price: 45 ACP pistol with 9mm and 40 S&W slide/barrel assemblies **$999.00**

FIRESTORM AUTO PISTOL

Features: 7 or 10 rd. double action pistols with matte, duotone or nickel finish. Distributed by SGS Importers International.

Price: 22 LR 10 rd, 380 7 rd. matte. **$264.95**
Price: Duotone **$274.95**
Price: Mini 9mm, 40 S&W, 10 rd. matte **$383.95**
Price: Duotone **$391.95**
Price: Nickel **$408.95**
Price: Mini 45, 7 rd. matte. **$383.95**
Price: Duotone 45. . . . . **$399.95**
Price: Nickel 45. . . . . **$416.95**
Price: 45 Government, Compact, 7 rd. matte **$324.95**
Price: Duotone **$333.95**
Price: Extra magazines. **$29.95-49.95**

GLOCK 17 AUTO PISTOL

Caliber: 9mm Para., 10-shot magazine. **Barrel:** 4.49". **Weight:** 22.04 oz. (without magazine). **Length:** 7.32" overall. **Grips:** Black polymer. **Sights:** Dot on front blade, white outline rear adjustable for windage. **Features:** Polymer frame, steel slide; double-action trigger with "Safe Action" system; mechanical firing pin safety, drop safety; simple takedown without tools; locked breech, recoil operated action. Adopted by Austrian armed forces 1983. NATO approved 1984. Imported from Austria by Glock, Inc.

Price: Fixed sight, extra magazine, magazine loader, cleaning kit. . **$641.00**
Price: Adjustable sight **$671.00**
Price: Model 17L (6" barrel) **$800.00**
Price: Model 17C, ported barrel (compensated) **$646.00**

Glock 19 Auto Pistol

Similar to the Glock 17 except has a 4" barrel, giving an overall length of 6.85" and weight of 20.99 oz. Magazine capacity is 10 rounds. Fixed or adjustable rear sight. Introduced 1988.

Price: Fixed sight **$641.00**
Price: Adjustable sight **$671.00**
Price: Model 19C, ported barrel **$646.00**

Glock 20 10mm Auto Pistol

Similar to the Glock Model 17 except chambered for 10mm Automatic cartridge. Barrel length is 4.60", overall length is 7.59", and weight is 26.3 oz. (without magazine). Magazine capacity is 10 rounds. Fixed or adjust-able rear sight. Comes with an extra magazine, magazine loader, clean-ing rod and brush. Introduced 1990. Imported from Austria by Glock, Inc.

Price: Fixed sight **$700.00**
Price: Adjustable sight **$730.00**

Glock 21 Auto Pistol

Similar to the Glock 17 except chambered for 45 ACP, 10-shot magazine. Overall length is 7.59", weight is 25.2 oz. (without magazine). Fixed or adjustable rear sight. Introduced 1991.

Price: Fixed sight **$700.00**
Price: Adjustable sight **$730.00**

Glock 22 Auto Pistol

Similar to the Glock 17 except chambered for 40 S&W, 10-shot magazine. Overall length is 7.28", weight is 22.3 oz. (without magazine). Fixed or adjustable rear sight. Introduced 1990.

Price: Fixed sight **$641.00**
Price: Adjustable sight **$671.00**
Price: Model 22C, ported barrel **$646.00**

Glock 23 Auto Pistol

Similar to the Glock 19 except chambered for 40 S&W, 10-shot magazine. Overall length is 6.85", weight is 20.6 oz. (without magazine). Fixed or adjustable rear sight. Introduced 1990.

Price: Fixed sight **$641.00**
Price: Model 23C, ported barrel **$646.00**
Price: Adjustable sight **$671.00**

GLOCK 26, 27 AUTO PISTOLS

Caliber: 9mm Para. (M26), 10-shot magazine; 40 S&W (M27), 9-shot magazine. **Barrel:** 3.46". **Weight:** 21.75 oz. **Length:** 6.29" overall. **Grips:** Integral. Stippled polymer. **Sights:** Dot on front blade, fixed or fully adjustable white outline rear. **Features:** Subcompact size. Polymer frame, steel slide; double-action trigger with "Safe Action" system, three safeties. Matte black Tenifer finish. Hammer-forged barrel. Imported from Austria by Glock, Inc. Introduced 1996.

Price: Fixed sight **$641.00**
Price: Adjustable sight **$671.00**

GLOCK 29, 30 AUTO PISTOLS

Caliber: 10mm (M29), 45 ACP (M30), 10-shot magazine. **Barrel:** 3.78". **Weight:** 24 oz. **Length:** 6.7" overall. **Grips:** Integral. Stippled polymer. **Sights:** Dot on front, fixed or fully adjustable white outline rear. **Features:** Compact size. Polymer frame steel slide; double-recoil spring reduces recoil; Safe Action system with three safeties; Tenifer finish. Two magazines supplied. Introduced 1997. Imported from Austria by Glock, Inc.

Price: Fixed sight **$700.00**
Price: Adjustable sight **$730.00**

Glock 31/31C Auto Pistols

Similar to the Glock 17 except chambered for 357 Auto cartridge; 10-shot magazine. Overall length is 7.32", weight is 23.28 oz. (without magazine). Fixed or adjustable sight. Imported from Austria by Glock, Inc.

Price: Fixed sight **$641.00**
Price: Adjustable sight **$671.00**
Price: Model 31C, ported barrel **$646.00**

Glock 32/32C Auto Pistols

Similar to the Glock 19 except chambered for the 357 Auto cartridge; 10-shot magazine. Overall length is 6.85", weight is 21.52 oz. (without magazine). Fixed or adjustable sight. Imported from Austria by Glock, Inc.

Price: Fixed sight **$616.00**
Price: Adjustable sight **$644.00**
Price: Model 32C, ported barrel **$646.00**

Glock 33 Auto Pistol

Similar to the Glock 26 except chambered for the 357 Auto cartridge; 9-shot magazine. Overall length is 6.29", weight is 19.75 oz. (without magazine). Fixed or adjustable sight. Imported from Austria by Glock, Inc.

Price: Fixed sight **$641.00**
Price: Adjustable sight **$671.00**

GLOCK 34, 35 AUTO PISTOLS

Caliber: 9mm Para. (M34), 40 S&W (M35), 10-shot magazine. **Barrel:** 5.32". **Weight:** 22.9 oz. **Length:** 8.15" overall. **Grips:** Integral. Stippled polymer. **Sights:** Dot on front, fully adjustable white outline rear. **Features:** Polymer frame, steel slide; double-action trigger with "Safe Action" system; three safeties; Tenifer finish. Imported from Austria by Glock, Inc.

Price: Model 34, 9mm. **$770.00**
Price: Model 35, 40 S&W **$770.00**

GLOCK 36 AUTO PISTOL

Caliber: 45 ACP, 6-shot magazine. **Barrel:** 3.78". **Weight:** 20.11 oz. **Length:** 6.77" overall. **Grips:** Integral. Stippled polymer. **Sights:** Dot on front, fully adjustable white outline rear. **Features:** Polymer frame, steel slide; double-action trigger with "Safe Action" system; three safeties; Tenifer finish. Imported from Austria by Glock, Inc.

Price: Fixed sight **$700.00**
Price: Adj. sight **$730.00**

HAMMERLI "TRAILSIDE" TARGET PISTOL

Caliber: 22 LR. **Barrel:** 4.5", 6". **Weight:** 28 oz. **Grips:** Synthetic. **Sights:** Fixed. **Features:** 10-shot magazine. Imported from Switzerland by Sigarms. Distributed by Hammerli U.S.A.

Price: **$579.00**

HECKLER & KOCH USP AUTO PISTOL

Caliber: 9mm Para., 10-shot magazine, 40 S&W, 10-shot magazine, 357 Mag. **Barrel:** 4.25". **Weight:** 28 oz. (USP40). **Length:** 6.9" overall. **Grips:** Non-slip stippled black polymer. **Sights:** Blade front, rear adjustable for windage. **Features:** New HK design with polymer frame, modified Browning action with recoil reduction system, single control lever. Special "hostile environ-ment" finish on all metal parts. Available in SA/DA, DAO, left- and right- hand versions. Introduced 1993. Imported from Germany by Heckler & Koch, Inc.

Price: Right-hand **$769.00**
Price: Left-hand **$794.00**

Heckler & Koch USP Compact Auto Pistol

Similar to the USP except has 3.58" barrel, measures 6.81" overall, and weighs 1.60 lbs. (9mm). Available in 9mm Para. 357 SIG or 40 S&W with 10-shot magazine. Introduced 1996. Imported from Germany by Heckler & Koch, Inc.

Price: Blue **$799.00**
Price: Blue with control lever on right **$824.00**
Price: Same as USP Compact DAO, enhanced trigger performance **$799.00**

Heckler & Koch USP Compact

Heckler & Koch USP45

Heckler & Koch USP45 Compact

Heckler & Koch USP45 Tactical

Heckler & Koch Elite

Heckler & Koch Mark 23 Special Operations

Heckler & Koch P7M8

Heckler & Koch USP45 Auto Pistol

Similar to the 9mm and 40 S&W USP except chambered for 45 ACP, 10-shot magazine. Has 4.13" barrel, overall length of 7.87" and weighs 30.4 oz. Has adjustable three-dot sight system. Available in SA/DA, DAO, left- and right-hand versions. Introduced 1995. Imported from Germany by Heckler & Koch, Inc.

Price: Right-hand **$839.00**
Price: Left-hand **$864.00**

Heckler & Koch USP45 Compact

Similar to the USP45 except has stainless slide; 8-shot magazine; modified and contoured slide and frame; extended slide release; 3.80" barrel, 7.09" overall length, weighs 1.75 lbs.; adjustable three-dot sights. Introduced 1998. Imported from Germany by Heckler & Koch, Inc.

Price: With control lever on left, stainless **$909.00**
Price: As above, blue **$857.00**
Price: With control lever on right, stainless. **$944.00**
Price: As above, blue **$892.00**

HECKLER & KOCH USP45 TACTICAL PISTOL

Caliber: 45 ACP, 10-shot magazine. **Barrel:** 4.92". **Weight:** 2.24 lbs. **Length:** 8.64" overall. **Grips:** Non-slip stippled polymer. **Sights:** Blade front, fully adjustable target rear. **Features:** Has extended threaded barrel with rubber O-ring; adjustable trigger; extended magazine floorplate; adjustable trigger stop; polymer frame. Introduced 1998. Imported from Germany by Heckler & Koch, Inc.

Price: **$1,115.00**

HECKLER & KOCH MARK 23 SPECIAL OPERATIONS PISTOL

Caliber: 45 ACP, 10-shot magazine. **Barrel:** 5.87". **Weight:** 43 oz. **Length:** 9.65" overall. **Grips:** Integral with frame; black polymer. **Sights:** Blade front, rear drift adjustable for windage; three-dot. **Features:** Polymer frame; double action; exposed hammer; short recoil, modified Browning action. Civilian version of the SOCOM pistol. Introduced 1996. Imported from Germany by Heckler & Koch, Inc.

Price: **$2,112.00**

Heckler & Koch USP Expert Pistol

Combines features of the USP Tactical and HK Mark 23 pistols with a new slide design. Chambered for 45 ACP, .40 S&W & 9mm; 10-shot magazine. Has adjustable target sights, 5.20" barrel, 8.74" overall length, weighs 1.87 lbs. Match-grade single- and double-action trigger pull with adjustable stop; ambidextrous control levers; elongated target slide; barrel O-ring that seals and centers barrel. Suited to IPSC competition. Introduced 1999. Imported from Germany by Heckler & Koch, Inc.

Price: **$1,869.00**

Heckler & Koch Elite

A long slide version of the USP combining features found on standard-sized and specialized models of the USP. Most noteworthy is the 6.2-inch-barrel, making it the most accurate of the USP series. In 9mm and .45 ACP. Imported from Germany by Heckler & Koch, Inc. Introduced 2003.

Price: **$1,569.00**

HECKLER & KOCH P7M8 AUTO PISTOL

Caliber: 9mm Para., 8-shot magazine. **Barrel:** 4.13". **Weight:** 29 oz. **Length:** 6.73" overall. **Grips:** Stippled black plastic. **Sights:** Blade front, adjustable rear; three dot system. **Features:** Unique "squeeze cocker" in frontstrap cocks the action. Gas-retarded action. Squared combat-type trigger guard. Blue finish. Compact size. Imported from Germany by Heckler & Koch, Inc.

Price: P7M8, blued **$1,515.00**

HECKLER & KOCH P2000 GPM PISTOL

Caliber: 9mmx19; 10-shot magazine. 13- or 16-round law enforcment/military magazines. **Barrel:** 3.62". **Weight:** 21.87 ozs. **Length:** 7". **Grips:** Interchangeable panels. **Sights:** Fixed partridge style, drift adjustable for windage, standard 3-dot. **Features:** German Pistol Model incorporating features of the HK USP Compact such as the pre-cocked hammer system which combines the advantages of a cocked striker with the double action hammer system. Introduced 2003. Imported from Germany by Heckler & Koch, Inc.

Price: **$887.00**

HECKLER & KOCK P2000SK SUBCOMPACT

Caliber: 9mm and 40 S&W. **Barrel:** 2.48". **Weight:** 1.49 lbs. (9mm) or 1.61 lbs. (40 S&W). **Sights:** Fixed partridge style, drift adjustable. **Features:** Standard accessory rails, ambidextrous slide release, polymer frame, polygonal bore profile.

Price: **$887.00**

Hi-Point 9MM Comp

Kahr K9

Kahr MK40

Kel-Tec P-11

HI-POINT FIREARMS 9MM COMP PISTOL

Caliber: 9mm, Para., 10-shot magazine. **Barrel:** 4". **Weight:** 39 oz. **Length:** 7.72" overall. **Grips:** Textured acetal plastic. **Sights:** Adjustable; low pro-file. **Features:** Single-action design. Scratch-resistant, non-glare blue fin-ish, alloy frame. Muzzle brake/compensator. Compensator is slotted for laser or flashlight mounting. Introduced 1998. From MKS Supply, Inc.

Price: Matte black **$159.00**

HI-POINT FIREARMS MODEL 9MM COMPACT PISTOL

Caliber: 9mm Para., 8-shot magazine. **Barrel:** 3.5". **Weight:** 29 oz. **Length:** 6.7" overall. **Grips:** Textured acetal plastic. **Sights:** Combat-style adjust-able three-dot system; low profile. **Features:** Single-action design; frame- mounted magazine release; polymer or alloy frame. Scratch-resistant matte finish. Introduced 1993. Made in U.S.A. by MKS Supply, Inc.

Price: Black, alloy frame **$149.00**

Price: With polymer frame (29 oz.), non-slip grips **$149.00**

Price: Aluminum with polymer frame **$149.00**

Hi-Point Firearms Model 380 Polymer Pistol

Similar to the 9mm Compact model except chambered for 380 ACP, 8-shot magazine, adjustable three-dot sights. Weighs 29 oz. Polymer frame. Introduced 1998. Made in U.S.A. by MKS Supply.

Price: **$114.00**

Hi-Point Firearms 380 Comp Pistol

Similar to the 380 Polymer Pistol except has a 4" barrel with muzzle compensator; action locks open after last shot. Includes a 10-shot and an 8-shot magazine; trigger lock. Introduced 2001. Made in U.S.A. by MKS Supply Inc.

Price: **$135.00**

Price: With laser sight **$229.00**

HI-POINT FIREARMS 45 POLYMER FRAME

Caliber: 45 ACP, 9-shot, 40 S&W . **Barrel:** 4.5". **Weight:** 35 oz. **Sights:** Adjustable 3-dot. **Features:** Last round lock-open, grip mounted magazine release, magazine disconnect safety, integrated accessory rail. Introduced 2002. Made in U.S.A. by MKS Supply Inc.

Price: **$179.00**

IAI M-2000 PISTOL

Caliber: 45 ACP, 8-shot. **Barrel:** 5", (Compact 4.25"). **Weight:** 36 oz. **Length:** 8.5", (6" Compact). **Grips:** Plastic or wood. **Sights:** Fixed. **Features:** 1911 Government U.S. Army-style. Steel frame and slide parkerized. GI grip safety. Beveled feed ramp barrel. By IAI, Inc.

Price: **$465.00**

KAHR K9, K40 DA AUTO PISTOLS

Caliber: 9mm Para., 7-shot, 40 S&W, 6-shot magazine. **Barrel:** 3.5". **Weight:** 25 oz. **Length:** 6" overall. **Grips:** Wrap-around textured soft polymer. **Sights:** Blade front, rear drift adjustable for windage; bar-dot combat style. **Features:** Trigger-cocking double-action mechanism with passive firing pin block. Made of 4140 ordnance steel with matte black finish. Contact maker for complete price list. Introduced 1994. Made in U.S.A. by Kahr Arms.

Price: E9, black matte finish **$425.00**

Price: Matte black, night sights 9mm **$668.00**

Price: Matte stainless steel, 9mm. . . **$638.00**

Price: 40 S&W, matte black **$580.00**

Price: 40 S&W, matte black, night sights **$668.00**

Price: 40 S&W, matte stainless **$638.00**

Price: K9 Elite 98 (high-polish stainless slide flats, Kahr combat trigger), from **$694.00**

Price: As above, MK9 Elite 98, from **$694.00**

Price: As above, K40 Elite 98, from **$694.00**

Price: Covert, black, stainless slide, short grip **$599.00**

Price: Covert, black, tritium nite sights **$689.00**

Kahr K9 9mm Compact Polymer Pistol

Similar to K9 steel frame pistol except has polymer frame, matte stainless steel slide. Barrel length 3.5"; overall length 6"; weighs 17.9 oz. Includes two 7-shot magazines, hard polymer case, trigger lock. Introduced 2000. Made in U.S.A. by Kahr Arms.

Price: **$599.00**

Kahr MK9/MK40 Micro Pistol

Similar to the K9/K40 except is 5.5" overall, 4" high, has a 3" barrel. Weighs 22 oz. Has snag-free bar-dot sights, polished feed ramp, dual recoil spring system, DA-only trigger. Comes with 6- and 7-shot magazines. Introduced 1998. Made in U.S.A. by Kahr Arms.

Price: Matte stainless **$638.00**

Price: Elite 98, polished stainless, tritium night sights **$791.00**

KAHR PM9 PISTOL

Caliber: 9x19. **Barrel:** 3", 1:10 twist. **Weight:** 15.9 oz. **Length:** 5.3" overall. **Features:** Lightweight black polymer frame, polygonal rifling, stainless steel slide, DAO with passive striker block, trigger lock, hard case, 6 and 7 rd. mags.

Price: Matte stainless slide **$622.00**

Price: Tritium night sights **$719.00**

KEL-TEC P-11 AUTO PISTOL

Caliber: 9mm Para., 10-shot magazine. **Barrel:** 3.1". **Weight:** 14 oz. **Length:** 5.6" overall. **Grips:** Checkered black polymer. **Sights:** Blade front, rear adjustable for windage. **Features:** Ordnance steel slide, aluminum frame. Double-action-only trigger mechanism. Introduced 1995. Made in U.S.A. by Kel-Tec CNC Industries, Inc.

Price: Blue **$314.00**

Price: Hard chrome. **$368.00**

Price: Parkerized **$355.00**

KEL-TEC P-32 AUTO PISTOL

Caliber: 32 ACP, 7-shot magazine. **Barrel:** 2.68". **Weight:** 6.6 oz. **Length:** 5.07" overall. **Grips:** Checkered composite. **Sights:** Fixed. **Features:** Double-action-only mechanism with 6-lb. pull; internal slide stop. Textured composite grip/frame. Now available in 380 ACP. Made in U.S.A. by Kel-Tec CNC Industries, Inc.

Price: Blue **$300.00**

Price: Hard chrome. **$340.00**

Price: Parkerized **$355.00**

Kel-Tec P-32

Kimber Custom II

Kimber Pro Carry II

Kimber Ultra Carry II

Kimber Ten II High Capacity Polymer

Kimber Gold Match II

KIMBER CUSTOM II AUTO PISTOL

Caliber: 45 ACP, 40 S&W, .38 Super, 9 mm. **Barrel:** 5", match grade; 9 mm, .40 S&W, .38 Super barrels ramped. **Weight:** 38 oz. **Length:** 8.7" overall. **Grips:** Checkered black rubber, walnut, rosewood. **Sights:** Dovetail front and rear, Kimber low profile adj. or fixed three dot (green) Meprolight night sights. **Features:** Slide, frame and barrel machined from steel or stainless steel. Match grade barrel, chamber and trigger group. Extended thumb safety, beveled magazine well, beveled front and rear slide serrations, high ride beavertail grip safety, checkered flat mainspring housing, kidney cut under trigger guard, high cut grip, match grade stainless steel barrel bushing, polished breech face, Commander-style hammer, lowered and flared ejection port, Wolff springs, bead blasted black oxide finish. Intro-duced in 1996. Made in U.S.A. by Kimber Mfg., Inc.

Price: Custom **$745.00**
Price: Custom Walnut (double-diamond walnut grips) **$767.00**
Price: Custom Stainless **$848.00**
Price: Custom Stainless 40 S&W **$799.00**
Price: Custom Stainless Target 45 ACP (stainless, adj. sight) . . . **$989.00**
Price: Custom Stainless Target 38 Super **$994.00**

Kimber Stainless II Auto Pistol

Similar to Custom II except has stainless steel frame, 4-inch bbl., grip is .400" shorter than standard, no front ser-rations. Weighs 34 oz. 45 ACP only. Introduced in 1998. Made in U.S.A. by Kimber Mfg., Inc.

Price: **$964.00**

Kimber Pro Carry II Auto Pistol

Similar to Custom II, has aluminum frame, 4" bull barrel fitted directly to the slide without bushing. HD with stainless steel frame. Introduced 1998. Made in U.S.A. by Kimber Mfg., Inc.

Price: Pro Carry **$789.00**
Price: Pro Carry w/night sights **$893.00**
Price: Pro Carry Stainless w/night sights **$862.00**
Price: Pro Carry HD II 38 Super **$936.00**

Kimber Ultra Carry II Auto Pistol

Similar to Compact Stainless II, lightweight aluminum frame, 3" match grade bull barrel fitted to slide without bushing. Grips .400" shorter. Special slide stop. Low effort recoil. Weighs 25 oz. Introduced in 1999. Made in U.S.A. by Kimber Mfg., Inc.

Price: **$783.00**
Price: Stainless **$858.00**
Price: Stainless 40 S&W **$903.00**

Kimber Ten II High Capacity Polymer Pistol

Similar to Custom II, Pro Carry II and Ultra Carry II depending on barrel length. Ten-round magazine capacity (double stack and flush fitting). Polymer grip frame molded over stainless steel or aluminum (BP Ten pistols only) frame insert. Checkered front strap and belly of trigger guard. All models have fixed sights except Gold Match Ten II, which has adjustable sight. Frame grip dimensions approximate that of the standard 1911 for natural aiming and better recoil control. **Weight:** 24 to 34 oz. Improved version of the Kimber Polymer series. Made in U.S.A. by Kimber Mfg., Inc.

Price: Pro Carry Ten II **$828.00**
Price: Stainless Ten II **$812.00**

Kimber Gold Match II Auto Pistol

Similar to Custom II models. Includes stainless steel barrel with match grade chamber and barrel bushing, ambidextrous thumb safety, adjustable sight, premium aluminum trigger, hand-checkered double diamond rosewood grips. Barrel hand-fitted to bushing and slide for target accuracy. Made in U.S.A. by Kimber Mfg., Inc.

Price: Gold Match II **$1,192.00**
Price: Gold Match Stainless II 45 ACP **$1,342.00**
Price: Gold Match Stainless II 40 S&W **$1,373.00**

Kimber Gold Match Ten II Polymer Auto Pistol

Similar to Stainless Gold Match II. High capacity polymer frame with ten-round magazine. No ambi thumb safety. Polished flats add elegant look. Introduced 1999. Made in U.S.A. by Kimber Mfg., Inc.

Price: **$1,373.00**

Kimber Gold Combat II Auto Pistol

Similar to Gold Match II except designed for concealed carry. Extended and beveled magazine well, Meprolight tritium night sights; premium aluminum trigger; 30 lpi front strap checkering; special Custom Shop markings; KimPro premium finish. Introduced 1999. Made in U.S.A. by Kimber Mfg., Inc.

Price: 45 ACP **$1,716.00**
Price: Stainless (stainless frame and slide, special markings) . . **$1,657.00**

Kimber Gold Combat II

Kimber CDP II

Kimber Eclipse II

Kimber Eclipse Pro II

Kimber LTP II

Llama Micromax 380

Kimber CDP II Series Auto Pistol

Similar to Custom II, but designed for concealed carry. Aluminum frame. Standard features include stainless steel slide, Meprolight tritium three dot (green) dovetail-mounted night sights, match grade barrel and cham-ber, 30 LPI front strap checkering, two tone finish, ambidextrous thumb safety, hand-checkered double diamond rosewood grips. Introduced in 2000. Made in U.S.A. by Kimber Mfg., Inc.

Price: Ultra CDP II 40 S&W **$1,165.00**
Price: Ultra CDP II (3' barrel, short grip) **$1,165.00**
Price: Compact CDP II (4' barrel, short grip) **$1,165.00**
Price: Pro CDP II (4' barrel, full length grip) **$1,165.00**
Price: Custom CDP II (5' barrel, full length grip) **$1,203.00**

Kimber Eclipse II Series Auto Pistol

Similar to Custom II and other stainless Kimber pistol.s Stainless slide and frame, black anodized, two tone finish. Gray/black laminated grips. 30 LPI front strap checkering. All have night sights, with Target versions having Meprolight adjustable Bar/Dot version. Made in U.S.A. by Kimber Mfg., Inc.

Price: Eclipse Ultra II (3' barrel, short grip) **$1,074.00**
Price: Eclipse Pro II (4' barrel, full length grip) **$1,074.00**
Price: Eclipse Pro Target II (4' barrel, full length grip, adjustable sight) **$1,177.00**
Price: Eclipse Custom II (5' barrel, full length grip) **$1,077.00**
Price: Eclipse Target II (5' barrel, full length grip, adjustable sight) **$1,177.00**

Kimber LTP II Auto Pistol

Similar to Gold Match II. Built for Limited Ten competition. First Kimber pistol with new, innovative Kimber external extractor. KimPro premium finish. Stainless steel match grade barrel. Extended and beveled magazine well. Checkered front strap and trigger guard belly. Tungsten full length guide rod. Premium aluminum trigger. Ten-round single stack magazine. Wide ambidextrous thumb safety. Made in U.S.A. by Kimber Mfg., Inc.

Price: **$2,078.00**

Kimber Super Match II Auto Pistol

Similar to Gold Match II. Built for target and action shotting competition. Tested for accuracy. Target included. Stainless steel barrel and chamber. KimPro finish on stainless steel slide. Stainless steel frame. 30 LPI checkered front strap, premium aluminum trigger, Kimber adjustable sight. Introduced in 1999.

Price: **$1,966.00**

KORTH PISTOL

Llama Minimax

Caliber: .40 S&W, .357 SIG (9-shot); 9mm Para, 9x21 (10-shot). **Barrel:** 4" (standard), 5" (optional). Trigger **Weight:** 3.3 lbs. (single Action), 11 lbs. (double action). **Sights:** Fully adjustable. **Features:** All parts of surface-hardened steel; recoil-operated action, mechanically-locked via large pivoting bolt block maintaining parallel positioning of barrel during the complete cycle. Accessories include sound suppressor for qualified buyers. A masterpiece of German precision. Imported by Korth USA.

Price: **$5,602.00**

LLAMA MICROMAX 380 AUTO PISTOL

Caliber: 32 ACP, 8-shot, 380 ACP, 7-shot magazine. **Barrel:** 3-11/16". **Weight:** 23 oz. **Length:** 6-1/2" overall. **Grips:** Checkered high impact polymer. **Sights:** 3-dot combat. **Features:** Single-action design. Mini custom extended slide release; mini custom extended beavertail grip safety; combat-style hammer. Introduced 1997. Distributed by Import Sports, Inc.

Price: Matte blue. **$291.95**
Price: Satin chrome (380 only) **$308.95**

LLAMA MINIMAX SERIES

Caliber: 40 S&W, 7-shot; 45 ACP, 6-shot magazine. **Barrel:** 3-1/2". **Weight:** 35 oz. **Length:** 7-1/3" overall. **Grips:** Checkered rubber. **Sights:** Three-dot combat. **Features:** Single action, skeletonized combat-style hammer, extended slide release, cone-style barrel, flared ejection port. Introduced 1996. Distributed by Import Sports, Inc.

Price: Blue **$341.95**
Price: Duo-Tone finish (45 only) **$349.95**
Price: Satin chrome **$358.95**

Llama Minimax Sub-Compact Auto Pistol

Similar to the Minimax except has 3.14" barrel, weighs 31 oz.; 6.8" overall length; has 10-shot magazine with finger extension; beavertail grip safety. Introduced 1999. Distributed by Import Sports, Inc.

Price: 45 ACP, matte blue. **$358.95**
Price: As above, satin chrome **$374.95**
Price: Duo-Tone finish (45 only) **$366.95**

HANDGUNS — AUTOLOADERS, SERVICE & SPORT

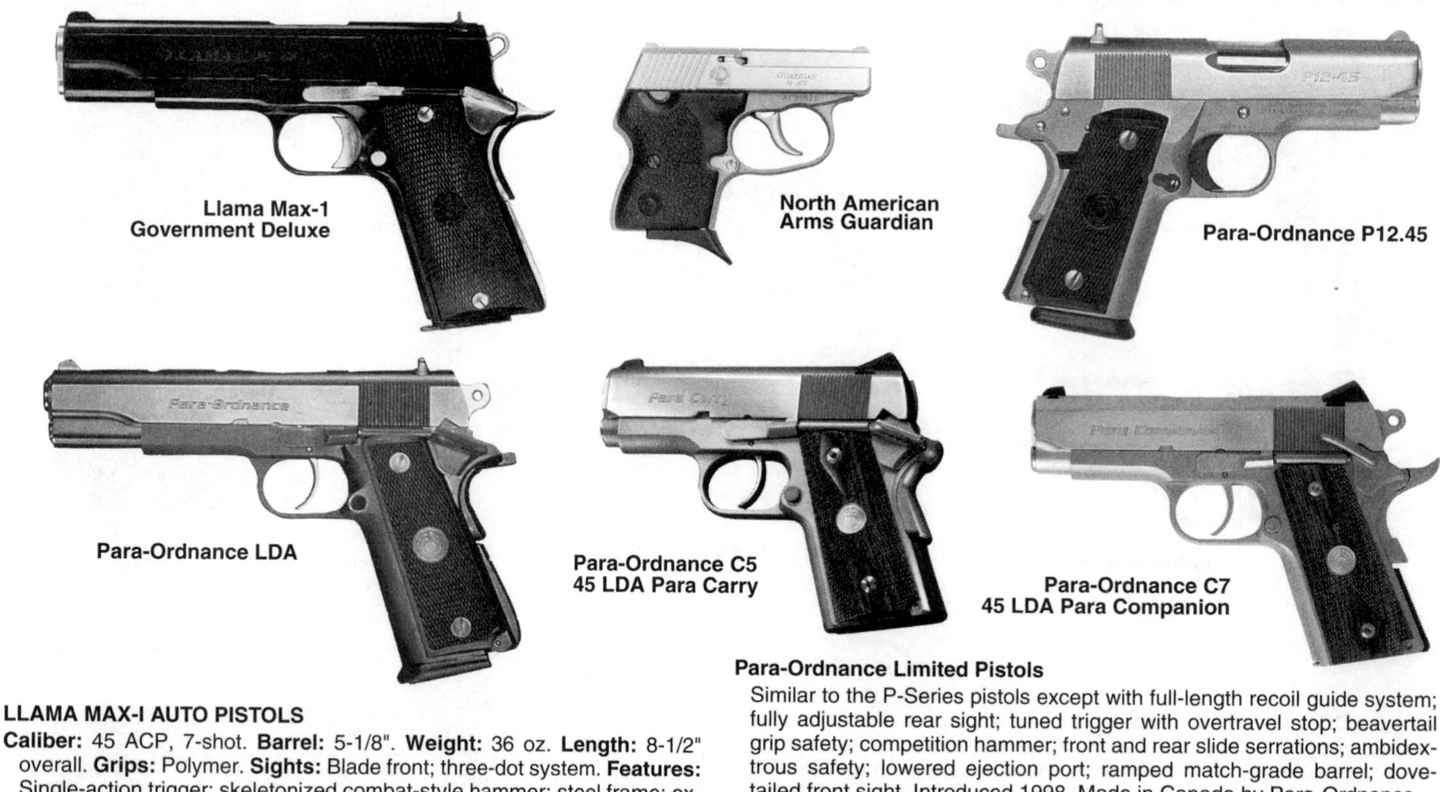

Llama Max-1 Government Deluxe

North American Arms Guardian

Para-Ordnance P12.45

Para-Ordnance LDA

Para-Ordnance C5 45 LDA Para Carry

Para-Ordnance C7 45 LDA Para Companion

LLAMA MAX-I AUTO PISTOLS

Caliber: 45 ACP, 7-shot. **Barrel:** 5-1/8". **Weight:** 36 oz. **Length:** 8-1/2" overall. **Grips:** Polymer. **Sights:** Blade front; three-dot system. **Features:** Single-action trigger; skeletonized combat-style hammer; steel frame; extended manual and grip safeties, matte finish. Introduced 1995. Distributed by Import Sports, Inc.

Price: 45 ACP, 7-shot, Government model **$358.95**

NORTH AMERICAN ARMS GUARDIAN PISTOL

Caliber: 32 ACP, 380 ACP, 32NAA, 6-shot magazine. **Barrel:** 2.1". **Weight:** 13.5 oz. **Length:** 4.36" overall. **Grips:** Black polymer. **Sights:** Fixed. **Features:** Double-action-only mechanism. All stainless steel construction; snag-free. Introduced 1998. Made in U.S.A. by North American Arms.

Price: . . . . **$402.00 to $479.00**

OLYMPIC ARMS OA-96 AR PISTOL

Caliber: 223. **Barrel:** 6", 8", 4140 chrome-moly steel. **Weight:** 5 lbs. **Length:** 15-3/4" overall. **Grips:** A2 stowaway pistol grip; no buttstock or receiver tube. **Sights:** Flat-top upper receiver, cut-down front sight base. **Features:** AR-15-type receivers with special bolt carrier; short aluminum hand guard; Vortex flash hider. Introduced 1996. Made in U.S.A. by Olympic Arms, Inc.

Price: **$858.00**

Olympic Arms OA-98 AR Pistol

Similar to the OA-93 except has removable 7-shot magazine, weighs 3 lbs. Introduced 1999. Made in U.S.A. by Olympic Arms, Inc.

Price: **$990.00**

PARA-ORDNANCE P-SERIES AUTO PISTOLS

Caliber: 9mm Para., 40 S&W, 45 ACP, 10-shot magazine. **Barrel:** 3", 3-1/2", 4-1/4", 5". **Weight:** From 24 oz. (alloy frame). **Length:** 8.5" overall. **Grips:** Textured composition. **Sights:** Blade front, rear adjustable for windage. High visibility three-dot system. **Features:** Available with alloy, steel or stainless steel frame with black finish (silver or stainless gun). Steel and stainless steel frame guns weigh 40 oz. (P14.45), 36 oz. (P13.45), 34 oz. (P12.45). Grooved match trigger, rounded combat-style hammer. Beveled magazine well. Manual thumb, grip and firing pin lock safeties. Solid barrel bushing. Contact maker for full details. Introduced 1990. Made in Canada by Para-Ordnance.

Price: Steel frame **$795.00**

Price: Alloy frame **$765.00**

Price: Stainless steel **$865.00**

Para-Ordnance Limited Pistols

Similar to the P-Series pistols except with full-length recoil guide system; fully adjustable rear sight; tuned trigger with overtravel stop; beavertail grip safety; competition hammer; front and rear slide serrations; ambidextrous safety; lowered ejection port; ramped match-grade barrel; dovetailed front sight. Introduced 1998. Made in Canada by Para-Ordnance.

Price: 9mm, 40 S&W, 45 ACP . . . . **$945.00 to $999.00**

Para-Ordnance LDA Auto Pistols

Similar to P-series except has double-action trigger mechanism. Steel frame with matte black finish, checkered composition grips. Available in 9mm Para., 40 S&W, 45 ACP. Introduced 1999. Made in Canada by Para-Ordnance.

Price: **$775.00**

Para-Ordnance LDA Limited Pistols

Similar to LDA, has ambidextrous safety, adjustable rear sight, front slide serrations and full-length recoil guide system. Made in Canada by Para-Ordnance.

Price: Black finish **$975.00**

Price: Stainless. **$1,049.00**

PARA-ORDNANCE C5 45 LDA PARA CARRY

Caliber: 45 ACP. **Barrel:** 3", 6+1 shot. **Weight:** 30 oz. **Length:** 6.5". **Grips:** Double diamond checkered Cocobolo. **Features:** Stainless finish and receiver, "world's smallest DAO 45 auto." Para LDA trigger system and safeties.

Price: **$899.00**

PARA-ORDNANCE C7 45 LDA PARA COMPANION

Caliber: 45 ACP. **Barrel:** 3.5", 7+1 shot. **Weight:** 32 oz. **Length:** 7". **Grips:** Double diamond checkered Cocobolo. **Features:** Para LDA trigger system with Para LDA 3 safeties (slide lock, firing pin block and grip safety). Lightning speed, full size capacity.

Price: **$899.00**

PETERS STAHL AUTOLOADING PISTOLS

Caliber: 9mm Para., 45 ACP. **Barrel:** 5" or 6". **Grips:** Walnut or walnut with rubber wrap. **Sights:** Fully adjustable rear, blade front. **Features:** Stainless steel extended slide stop, safety and extended magazine release button; speed trigger with stop and approx. 3-lb. pull; polished ramp. Introduced 2000. Imported from Germany by Phillips & Rogers.

Price: High Capacity (accepts 15-shot magazines in 45 cal.; includes 10-shot magazine) **$1,695.00**

Price: Trophy Master (blued or stainless, 7-shot in 45, 8-shot in 9mm) **$1,995.00**

Price: Millennium Model (titanium coating on receiver and slide) **$2,195.00**

HANDGUNS — AUTOLOADERS, SERVICE & SPORT

Peters Stahl High Capacity

Peters Stahl Trophy Master

Peters Stahl Millennium

Phoenix Arms HP22

Ruger P89

Ruger P90

Rock River Standard Match

PHOENIX ARMS HP22, HP25 AUTO PISTOLS

Caliber: 22 LR, 10-shot (HP22), 25 ACP, 10-shot (HP25). **Barrel:** 3". **Weight:** 20 oz. **Length:** 5-1/2" overall. **Grips:** Checkered composition. **Sights:** Blade front, adjustable rear. **Features:** Single action, exposed hammer; manual hold-open; button magazine release. Available in satin nickel, polished blue finish. Introduced 1993. Made in U.S.A. by Phoenix Arms.

Price: With gun lock and cable lanyard. **$130.00**

Price: HP Rangemaster kit with 5" bbl., locking case and assessories **$171.00**

Price: HP Deluxe Rangemaster kit with 3" and 5" bbls., 2 mags., case **$210.00**

ROCK RIVER ARMS STANDARD MATCH AUTO PISTOL

Caliber: 45 ACP. **Barrel:** NA. **Weight:** NA. **Length:** NA. **Grips:** Cocobolo, checkered. **Sights:** Heine fixed rear, blade front. **Features:** Chrome-moly steel frame and slide; beavertail grip safety with raised pad; checkered slide stop; ambidextrous safety; polished feed ramp and extractor; aluminum speed trigger with 3.5 lb. pull. Made in U.S.A. From Rock River Arms.

Price: **$1,025.00**

ROCKY MOUNTAIN ARMS PATRIOT PISTOL

Caliber: 223, 10-shot magazine. **Barrel:** 7", with muzzle brake. **Weight:** 5 lbs. **Length:** 20.5" overall. **Grips:** Black composition. **Sights:** None furnished. **Features:** Milled upper receiver with enhanced Weaver base; milled lower receiver from billet plate; machined aluminum National Match handguard. Finished in DuPont Teflon-S matte black or NATO green. Comes with black nylon case, one magazine. Introduced 1993. From Rocky Mountain Arms, Inc.

Price: With A-2 handle top . . . . **$2,500.00 to $2,800.00**

Price: Flat top model. . . . . **$3,000.00 to $3,500.00**

RUGER P89 AUTOLOADING PISTOL

Caliber: 9mm Para., 10-shot magazine. **Barrel:** 4.50". **Weight:** 32 oz. **Length:** 7.84" overall. **Grips:** Grooved black synthetic composition. **Sights:** Square post front, square notch rear adjustable for windage, both with white dot inserts. **Features:** Double action, ambidextrous slide-mounted safety-levers. Slide 4140 chrome-moly steel or 400-series stainless steel, frame lightweight aluminum alloy. Ambidextrous magazine release. Blue, stainless steel. Introduced 1986; stainless 1990.

Price: P89, blue, extra mag and mag loader, plastic case locks . **$475.00**

Price: KP89, stainless, extra mag and mag loader, plastic case locks **$525.00**

Ruger P89D Decocker Autoloading Pistol

Similar to standard P89 except has ambidextrous decocking levers in place of regular slide-mounted safety. Decocking levers move firing pin inside slide where hammer can not reach, while simultaneously blocking firing pin from forward movement-allows shooter to decock cocked pis-tol without manipulating trigger. Conventional thumb decocking proce-dures are therefore unnecessary. Blue, stainless steel. Introduced 1990.

Price: P89D, blue, extra mag and mag loader, plastic case locks **$475.00**

Price: KP89D, stainless, extra mag and mag loader, plastic case locks **$525.00**

Ruger P89 Double-Action-Only Autoloading Pistol

Same as KP89 except operates only in double-action mode. Has spurless hammer, gripping grooves on each side of rear slide; no external safety or decocking lever. Internal safety prevents forward movement of firing pin unless trigger is pulled. Available 9mm Para., stainless steel only. In-tro-duced 1991.

Price: Lockable case, extra mag and mag loader. **$525.00**

RUGER P90 MANUAL SAFETY MODEL AUTOLOADING PISTOL

Caliber: 45 ACP, 8-shot magazine. **Barrel:** 4.50". **Weight:** 33.5 oz. **Length:** 7.75" overall. **Grips:** Grooved black synthetic composition. **Sights:** Square post front, square notch rear adjustable for windage, both with white dot. **Features:** Double action ambidextrous slide-mounted safety-levers move firing pin inside slide where hammer can not reach, simultaneously blocking firing pin from forward movement. Stainless steel only. Introduced 1991.

Price: KP90 with extra mag, loader, case and gunlock. **$565.00**

Price: P90 (blue). **$525.00**

Ruger P93D

Ruger KP94D

Ruger KP95DAO

Ruger KP90 Decocker Autoloading Pistol

Similar to the P90 except has a manual decocking system. The ambidextrous decocking levers move the firing pin inside the slide where the hammer can not reach it, while simultaneously blocking the firing pin from forward movement-allows shooter to decock a cocked pistol without manipulating the trigger. Available only in stainless steel. Overall length 7.75", weighs 33.5 oz. Introduced 1991.

Price: KP90D with case, extra mag and mag loading tool **$565.00**

RUGER P93 COMPACT AUTOLOADING PISTOL

Caliber: 9mm Para., 10-shot magazine. **Barrel:** 3.9". **Weight:** 31 oz. **Length:** 7.25" overall. **Grips:** Grooved black synthetic composition. **Sights:** Square post front, square notch rear adjustable for windage. **Features:** Front of slide crowned with convex curve; slide has seven finger grooves; trigger guard bow higher for better grip; 400-series stainless slide, lightweight alloy frame; also blue. Decocker-only or DAO-only. Includes hard case and lock. Introduced 1993. Made in U.S.A. by Sturm, Ruger & Co.

Price: KP93DAO, double-action-only **$575.00**
Price: KP93D ambidextrous decocker, stainless **$575.00**
Price: P93D, ambidextrous decocker, blue **$495.00**

Ruger KP94 Autoloading Pistol

Sized midway between full-size P-Series and compact P93. 4.25" barrel, 7.5" overall length, weighs about 33 oz. KP94 manual safety model; KP94DAO double-action-only (both 9mm Para., 10-shot magazine); KP94D is decocker-only in 40-caliber with 10-shot magazine. Slide gripping grooves roll over top of slide. KP94 has ambidextrous safety-levers; KP94DAO has no external safety, full-cock hammer position or decocking lever; KP94D has ambidextrous decocking levers. Matte finish stainless slide, barrel, alloy frame. Also blue. Includes hard case and lock. Introduced 1994. Made in U.S.A. by Sturm, Ruger & Co.

Price: P94, P944, blue (manual safety) **$495.00**
Price: KP94 (9mm), KP944 (40-caliber) (manual safety-stainless) **$575.00**
Price: KP94DAO (9mm), KP944DAO (40-caliber) **$575.00**
Price: KP94D (9mm), KP944D (40-caliber)-decock only **$575.00**

RUGER P95 AUTOLOADING PISTOL

Caliber: 9mm Para., 10-shot magazine. **Barrel:** 3.9". **Weight:** 27 oz. **Length:** 7.25" overall. **Grips:** Grooved; integral with frame. **Sights:** Blade front, rear drift adjustable for windage; three-dot system. **Features:** Moulded polymer grip frame, stainless steel or chrome-moly slide. Suitable for +P+ ammunition. Safety model, decocker or DAO. Introduced 1996. Made in U.S.A. by Sturm, Ruger & Co. Comes with lockable plastic case, spare magazine, loader and lock.

Price: P95 DAO double-action-only **$425.00**
Price: P95D decocker only **$425.00**
Price: KP95D stainless steel decocker only **$475.00**
Price: KP95DAO double-action only, stainless steel. **$475.00**
Price: KP95 safety model, stainless steel. **$475.00**
Price: P95 safety model, blued finish **$425.00**

RUGER P97 AUTOLOADING PISTOL

Caliber: 45 ACP 8-shot magazine. **Barrel:** 4-1/8". **Weight:** 30-1/2 oz. **Length:** 7-1/4" overall. Grooved: Integral with frame. **Sights:** Blade front, rear drift adjustable for windage; three dot system. **Features:** Moulded polymer grip frame, stainless steel slide. Decocker or DAO. Introduced 1997. Made in U.S.A. by Sturm, Ruger & Co. Comes with lockable plastic case, spare magazine, loading tool.

Ruger KMK 4

Ruger 22/45-P4

Price: KP97D decocker only. **$495.00**
Price: KP97DAO double-action only **$495.00**
Price: P97D decocker only, blued **$460.00**

RUGER MARK II STANDARD AUTOLOADING PISTOL

Caliber: 22 LR, 10-shot magazine. **Barrel:** 4-3/4" or 6". **Weight:** 35 oz. (4-3/4" bbl.). **Length:** 8-5/16" (4-3/4" bbl.). **Grips:** Checkered composition grip panels. **Sights:** Fixed, wide blade front, fixed rear. **Features:** Updated design of original Standard Auto. New bolt hold-open latch. 10-shot magazine, magazine catch, safety, trigger and new receiver contours. Introduced 1982.

Price: Blued (MK 4, MK 6) **$289.00**
Price: In stainless steel (KMK 4, KMK 6) **$379.00**

Ruger 22/45 Mark II Pistol

Similar to other 22 Mark II autos except has grip frame of Zytel that matches angle and magazine latch of Model 1911 45 ACP pistol. Available in 4" bull, 4-3/4" standard and 5-1/2" bull barrels. Comes with extra magazine, plastic case, lock. Introduced 1992.

Price: P4, 4" bull barrel, adjustable sights **$290.00**
Price: KP 4 (4-3/4" barrel), stainless steel, fixed sights **$315.00**
Price: KP512 (5-1/2" bull barrel), stainless steel, adj. sights **$380.00**
Price: P512 (5-1/2" bull barrel, all blue), adj. sights **$290.00**

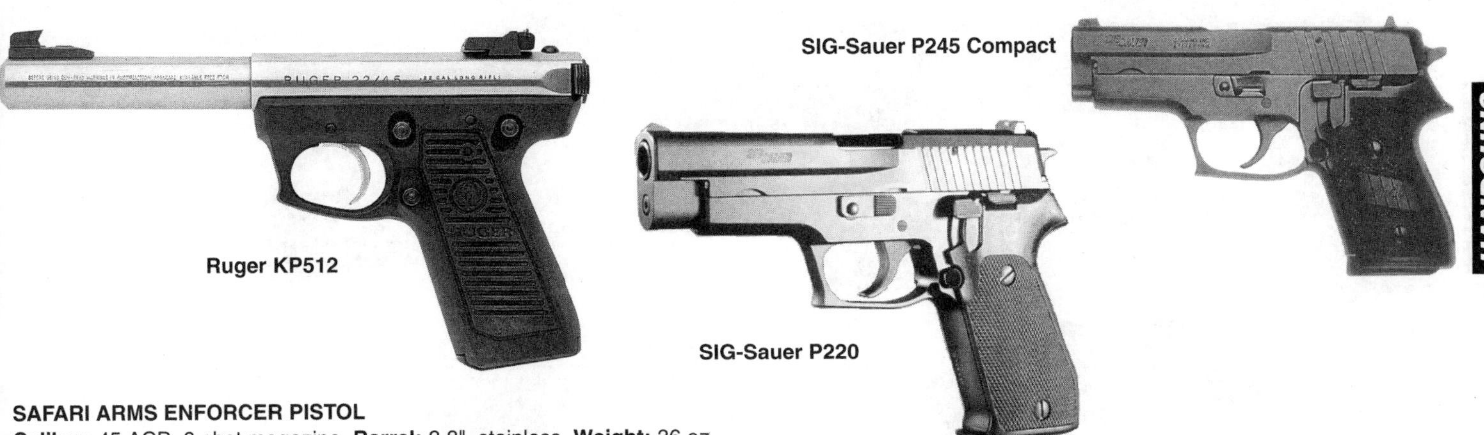
Ruger KP512

SIG-Sauer P220

SIG-Sauer P245 Compact

SAFARI ARMS ENFORCER PISTOL

Caliber: 45 ACP, 6-shot magazine. **Barrel:** 3.8", stainless. **Weight:** 36 oz. **Length:** 7.3" overall. **Grips:** Smooth walnut with etched black widow spider logo. **Sights:** Ramped blade front, LPA adjustable rear. **Features:** Extended safety, extended slide release; Commander-style hammer; beavertail grip safety; throated, polished, tuned. Parkerized matte black or satin stainless steel finishes. Made in U.S.A. by Safari Arms.

Price: **$630.00**

SAFARI ARMS GI SAFARI PISTOL

Caliber: 45 ACP, 7-shot magazine. **Barrel:** 5", 416 stainless. **Weight:** 39.9 oz. **Length:** 8.5" overall. **Grips:** Checkered walnut. **Sights:** G.I.-style blade front, drift-adjustable rear. **Features:** Beavertail grip safety; extended thumb safety and slide release; Commander-style hammer. Parkerized finish. Reintroduced 1996.

Price: **$439.00**

SAFARI ARMS CARRIER PISTOL

Caliber: 45 ACP, 7-shot magazine. **Barrel:** 6", 416 stainless steel. **Weight:** 30 oz. **Length:** 9.5" overall. **Grips:** Wood. **Sights:** Ramped blade front, LPA adjustable rear. **Features:** Beavertail grip safety; extended controls; full-length recoil spring guide; Commander-style hammer. Throated, polished and tuned. Satin stainless steel finish. Introduced 1999. Made in U.S.A. by Safari Arms, Inc.

Price: **$714.00**

SAFARI ARMS COHORT PISTOL

Caliber: 45 ACP, 7-shot magazine. **Barrel:** 3.8", 416 stainless. **Weight:** 37 oz. **Length:** 8.5" overall. **Grips:** Smooth walnut with laser-etched black widow logo. **Sights:** Ramped blade front, LPA adjustable rear. **Features:** Combines the Enforcer model, slide and MatchMaster frame. Beavertail grip safety; extended thumb safety and slide release; Commander-style hammer. Throated, polished and tuned. Satin stainless finish. Introduced 1996. Made in U.S.A. by Safari Arms, Inc.

Price: **$654.00**

SAFARI ARMS MATCHMASTER PISTOL

Caliber: 45 ACP, 7-shot. **Barrel:** 5" or 6", 416 stainless steel. **Weight:** 38 oz. (5" barrel). **Length:** 8.5" overall. **Grips:** Smooth walnut. **Sights:** Ramped blade, LPA adjustable rear. **Features:** Beavertail grip safety; extended controls; Commander-style hammer; throated, polished, tuned. Parkerized matte-black or satin stainless steel. Made in U.S.A. by Olympic Arms, Inc.

Price: 5" barrel **$594.00**

Price: 6" barrel **$654.00**

Safari Arms Carry Comp Pistol

Similar to the Matchmaster except has Wil Schueman-designed hybrid compensator system. Made in U.S.A. by Olympic Arms, Inc.

Price: **$1,067.00**

SEECAMP LWS 32 STAINLESS DA AUTO

Caliber: 32 ACP Win. Silvertip, 6-shot magazine. **Barrel:** 2", integral with frame. **Weight:** 10.5 oz. **Length:** 4-1/8" overall. **Grips:** Glass-filled nylon. **Sights:** Smooth, no-snag, contoured slide and barrel top. **Features:** Aircraft quality 17-4 PH stainless steel. Inertia-operated firing pin. Hammer fired double-action-only. Hammer automatically follows slide down to safety rest position after each shot-no manual safety needed. Magazine safety disconnector. Polished stainless. Introduced 1985. From L.W. Seecamp.

Price: **$425.00**

SEMMERLING LM-4 SLIDE-ACTION PISTOL

Caliber: 45 ACP, 4-shot magazine. **Barrel:** 2". **Weight:** 24 oz. **Length:** NA. **Grips:** NA. **Sights:** NA. **Features:** While outwardly appearing to be a semi-automatic, the Semmerling LM-4 is a unique and super compact pistol employing a thumb activated slide mechanism (the slide is manually retracted between shots). Hand-built and super reliable, it is intended for professionals in law enforcement and for concealed carry by licensed and firearms knowledgeable private citizens. From American Derringer Corp.

Price: **$2,635.00**

SIG-SAUER P220 SERVICE AUTO PISTOL

Caliber: 45 ACP, (7- or 8-shot magazine). **Barrel:** 4-3/8". **Weight:** 27.8 oz. **Length:** 7.8" overall. **Grips:** Checkered black plastic. **Sights:** Blade front, drift adjustable rear for windage. Optional Siglite nightsights. **Features:** Double action. Decocking lever permits lowering hammer onto locked firing pin. Squared combat-type trigger guard. Slide stays open after last shot. Imported from Germany by SIGARMS, Inc.

Price: Blue SA/DA or DAO **$790.00**

Price: Blue, Siglite night sights **$880.00**

Price: K-Kote or nickel slide **$830.00**

Price: K-Kote or nickel slide with Siglite night sights. **$930.00**

SIG-Sauer P220 Sport Auto Pistol

Similar to the P220 except has 4.9" barrel, ported compensator, all-stainless steel frame and slide, factory-tuned trigger, adjustable sights, extended competition controls. Overall length is 9.9", weighs 43.5 oz. Introduced 1999. From SIGARMS, Inc.

Price: **$1,320.00**

SIG-Sauer P245 Compact Auto Pistol

Similar to the P220 except has 3.9" barrel, shorter grip, 6-shot magazine, 7.28" overall length, and weighs 27.5 oz. Introduced 1999. From SIGARMS, Inc.

Price: Blue **$780.00**

Price: Blue, with Siglite sights. **$850.00**

Price: Two-tone. **$830.00**

Price: Two-tone with Siglite sights **$930.00**

Price: With K-Kote finish. **$830.00**

Price: K-Kote with Siglite sights **$930.00**

SIG-Sauer P229 DA Auto Pistol

Similar to the P228 except chambered for 9mm Para., 40 S&W, 357 SIG. Has 3.86" barrel, 7.08" overall length and 3.35" height. Weight is 30.5 oz. Introduced 1991. Frame made in Germany, stainless steel slide assembly made in U.S.; pistol assembled in U.S. From SIGARMS, Inc.

Price: **$795.00**

Price: With nickel slide **$890.00**

Price: Nickel slide Siglite night sights **$935.00**

SIG-Sauer Pro 2009

SIG-Sauer P229 Sport

SIG-Sauer P232

Smith & Wesson 457 TDA

Smith & Wesson 908

Smith & Wesson 4013 TSW

SIG PRO AUTO PISTOL

Caliber: 9mm Para., 40 S&W, 10-shot magazine. **Barrel:** 3.86". **Weight:** 27.2 oz. **Length:** 7.36" overall. **Grips:** Composite and rubberized one-piece. **Sights:** Blade front, rear adjustable for windage. Optional Siglite night sights. **Features:** Polymer frame, stainless steel slide; integral frame accessory rail; replaceable steel frame rails; left- or right-handed magazine release. Introduced 1999. From SIGARMS, Inc.

Price: SP2340 (40 S&W) **$596.00**
Price: SP2009 (9mm Para.) **$596.00**
Price: As above with Siglite night sights **$655.00**

SIG-Sauer P226 Service Pistol

Similar to the P220 pistol except has 4.4" barrel, and weighs 28.3 oz. 357 SIG or 40 S&W. Imported from Germany by SIGARMS, Inc.

Price: Blue SA/DA or DAO **$830.00**
Price: With Siglite night sights **$930.00**
Price: Blue, SA/DA or DAO 357 SIG....................... **$830.00**
Price: With Siglite night sights **$930.00**
Price: K-Kote finish, 40 S&W only or nickel slide **$830.00**
Price: K-Kote or nickel slide Siglite night sights **$930.00**
Price: Nickel slide 357 SIG.............................. **$875.00**
Price: Nickel slide, Siglite night sights **$930.00**

SIG-Sauer P229 Sport Auto Pistol

Similar to the P229 except available in 357 SIG only; 4.8" heavy barrel; 8.6" overall length; weighs 40.6 oz.; vented compensator; adjustable target sights; rubber grips; extended slide latch and magazine release. Made of stainless steel. Introduced 1998. From SIGARMS, Inc.

Price: **$1,320.00**

SIG-SAUER P232 PERSONAL SIZE PISTOL

Caliber: 380 ACP, 7-shot. **Barrel:** 3-3/4". **Weight:** 16 oz. **Length:** 6-1/2" overall. **Grips:** Checkered black composite. **Sights:** Blade front, rear adjustable for windage. **Features:** Double action/single action or DAO. Blowback operation, stationary barrel. Introduced 1997. Imported from Germany by SIGARMS, Inc.

Price: Blue SA/DA or DAO **$505.00**
Price: In stainless steel................................ **$545.00**
Price: With stainless steel slide, blue frame **$525.00**
Price: Stainless steel, Siglite night sights, Hogue grips **$585.00**

SIG-SAUER P239 PISTOL

Caliber: 9mm Para., 8-shot, 357 SIG 40 S&W, 7-shot magazine. **Barrel:** 3.6". **Weight:** 25.2 oz. **Length:** 6.6" overall. **Grips:** Checkered black composite. **Sights:** Blade front, rear adjustable for windage. Optional Siglite night sights. **Features:** SA/DA or DAO; blackened stainless steel slide, aluminum alloy frame. Introduced 1996. Made in U.S.A. by SIGARMS, Inc.

Price: SA/DA or DAO **$620.00**
Price: SA/DA or DAO with Siglite night sights................ **$720.00**
Price: Two-tone finish **$665.00**
Price: Two-tone finish, Siglite sights **$765.00**

SMITH & WESSON MODEL 22A SPORT PISTOL

Caliber: 22 LR, 10-shot magazine. **Barrel:** 4", 5-1/2", 7". **Weight:** 29 oz. **Length:** 8" overall. **Grips:** Two-piece polymer. **Sights:** Patridge front, fully adjustable rear. **Features:** Comes with a sight bridge with Weaver-style integral optics mount; alloy frame; .312" serrated trigger; stainless steel slide and barrel with matte blue finish. Introduced 1997. Made in U.S.A. by Smith & Wesson.

Price: 4" **$264.00**
Price: 5-1/2" **$292.00**
Price: 7" **$331.00**

SMITH & WESSON MODEL 457 TDA AUTO PISTOL

Caliber: 45 ACP, 7-shot magazine. **Barrel:** 3-3/4". **Weight:** 29 oz. **Length:** 7-1/4" overall. **Grips:** One-piece Xenoy, wrap-around with straight backstrap. **Sights:** Post front, fixed rear, three-dot system. **Features:** Aluminum alloy frame, matte blue carbon steel slide; bobbed hammer; smooth trigger. Introduced 1996. Made in U.S.A. by Smith & Wesson.

Price: **$591.00**

SMITH & WESSON MODEL 908 AUTO PISTOL

Caliber: 9mm Para., 8-shot magazine. **Barrel:** 3-1/2". **Weight:** 26 oz. **Length:** 6-13/16". **Grips:** One-piece Xenoy, wrap-around with straight backstrap. **Sights:** Post front, fixed rear, three-dot system. **Features:** Aluminum alloy frame, matte blue carbon steel slide; bobbed hammer; smooth trigger. Introduced 1996. Made in U.S.A. by Smith & Wesson.

Price: **$535.00**

SMITH & WESSON MODEL 4013, 4053 TSW AUTOS

Caliber: 40 S&W, 9-shot magazine. **Barrel:** 3-1/2". **Weight:** 26.4 oz. **Length:** 6-7/8" overall. **Grips:** Xenoy one-piece wrap-around. **Sights:** Novak three-dot system. **Features:** Traditional double-action system; stainless slide, alloy frame; fixed barrel bushing; ambidextrous decocker; reversible magazine catch, equipment rail. Introduced 1997. Made in U.S.A. by Smith & Wesson.

Price: Model 4013 TSW **$886.00**
Price: Model 4053 TSW, double-action-only................. **$886.00**

Smith & Wesson 410 DA

Smith & Wesson 910 DA

Smith & Wesson 3913 LadySmith

Smith & Wesson 4006

Smith & Wesson 4566 TSW

SMITH & WESSON MODEL 22S SPORT PISTOLS

Similar to the Model 22A Sport except with stainless steel frame. Available only with 5-1/2" or 7" barrel. Introduced 1997. Made in U.S.A. by Smith & Wesson.

Price: 5-1/2" standard barrel **$358.00**
Price: 5-1/2" bull barrel, wood target stocks with thumbrest **$434.00**
Price: 7" standard barrel **$395.00**
Price: 5-1/2" bull barrel, two-piece target stocks with thumbrest . **$353.00**

SMITH & WESSON MODEL 410 DA AUTO PISTOL

Caliber: 40 S&W, 10-shot magazine. **Barrel:** 4". **Weight:** 28.5 oz. **Length:** 7.5 oz. **Grips:** One-piece Xenoy, wrap-around with straight backstrap. **Sights:** Post front, fixed rear; three-dot system. **Features:** Aluminum alloy frame; blued carbon steel slide; traditional double action with left-side slide-mounted decocking lever. Introduced 1996. Made in U.S.A. by Smith & Wesson.

Price: Model 410 . . . . **$591.00**
Price: Model 410, HiViz front sight **$612.00**

SMITH & WESSON MODEL 910 DA AUTO PISTOL

Caliber: 9mm Para., 10-shot magazine. **Barrel:** 4". **Weight:** 28 oz. **Length:** 7-3/8" overall. **Grips:** One-piece Xenoy, wrap-around with straight backstrap. **Sights:** Post front with white dot, fixed two-dot rear. **Features:** Alloy frame, blue carbon steel slide. Slide-mounted decocking lever. Introduced 1995.

Price: Model 910 . . . . **$535.00**
Price: Model 410, HiViz front sight **$535.00**

SMITH & WESSON MODEL 3913 TRADITIONAL DOUBLE ACTION

Caliber: 9mm Para., 8-shot magazine. **Barrel:** 3-1/2". **Weight:** 26 oz. **Length:** 6-13/16" overall. **Grips:** One-piece Delrin wrap-around, textured surface. **Sights:** Post front with white dot, Novak LoMount Carry with two dots. **Features:** Aluminum alloy frame, stainless slide (M3913) or blue steel slide (M3914). Bobbed hammer with no half-cock notch; smooth .304" trigger with rounded edges. Straight backstrap. Equipment rail. Extra magazine included. Introduced 1989.

Price: **$760.00**

Smith & Wesson Model 3913-LS Ladysmith Auto

Similar to the standard Model 3913 except has frame that is upswept at the front, rounded trigger guard. Comes in frosted stainless steel with matching gray grips. Grips are ergonomically correct for a woman's hand. Novak LoMount Carry rear sight adjustable for windage, smooth edges for snag resistance. Extra magazine included. Introduced 1990.

Price: **$782.00**

Smith & Wesson Model 3953 DAO Pistol

Same as the Model 3913 except double-action-only. Model 3953 has stainless slide with alloy frame. Overall length 7"; weighs 25.5 oz. Extra magazine included. Equipment rail. Introduced 1990.

Price: **$760.00**

Smith & Wesson Model 3913TSW/3953TSW Auto Pistols

Similar to the Model 3913 and 3953 except TSW guns have tighter tolerances, ambidextrous manual safety/decocking lever, flush-fit magazine, delayed-unlock firing system; magazine disconnector. Compact alloy frame, stainless steel slide. Straight backstrap. Introduced 1998. Made in U.S.A. by Smith & Wesson.

Price: Single action/double action **$760.00**
Price: Double action only **$760.00**

SMITH & WESSON MODEL 4006 TDA AUTO

Caliber: 40 S&W, 10-shot magazine. **Barrel:** 4". **Weight:** 38.5 oz. **Length:** 7-7/8" overall. **Grips:** Xenoy wrap-around with checkered panels. **Sights:** Replaceable post front with white dot, Novak LoMount Carry fixed rear with two white dots, or micro. click adjustable rear with two white dots. **Features:** Stainless steel construction with non-reflective finish. Straight backstrap, quipment rail. Extra magazine included. Introduced 1990.

Price: With adjustable sights **$944.00**
Price: With fixed sight **$907.00**
Price: With fixed night sights **$1,040.00**
Price: With Saf-T-Trigger, fixed sights **$927.00**

SMITH & WESSON MODEL 4006 TSW

Caliber: 40, 10-shot. **Barrel:** 4". **Grips:** Straight back strap grip. **Sights:** Fixed Novak LoMount Carry. **Features:** Traditional double action, ambidextrous safety, Saf-T-Trigger, equipment rail, satin stainless.

Price: **$927.00**

Smith & Wesson Model 4043, 4046 DA Pistols

Similar to the Model 4006 except is double-action-only. Has a semi-bobbed hammer, smooth trigger, 4" barrel; Novak LoMount Carry rear sight, post front with white dot. Overall length is 7-1/2", weighs 28 oz. Model 4043 has alloy frame, equipment rail. Extra magazine included. Introduced 1991.

Price: Model 4043 (alloy frame) **$886.00**
Price: Model 4046 (stainless frame) **$907.00**
Price: Model 4046 with fixed night sights **$1,040.00**

Smith & Wesson Sigma SW40V

Smith & Wesson 99

SMITH & WESSON MODEL 4500 SERIES AUTOS

Caliber: 45 ACP, 8-shot magazine. **Barrel:** 5" (M4506). **Weight:** 41 oz. (4506). **Length:** 8-1/2" overall. **Grips:** Xenoy one-piece wrap-around, arched or straight backstrap. **Sights:** Post front with white dot, adjustable or fixed Novak LoMount Carry on M4506. **Features:** M4506 has serrated hammer spur, equipment rail. All have two magazines. Contact Smith & Wesson for complete data. Introduced 1989.

Price: Model 4566 (stainless, 4-1/4", traditional DA, ambidextrous safety, fixed sight) **$942.00**
Price: Model 4586 (stainless, 4-1/4", DA only) **$942.00**
Price: Model 4566 (stainless, 4-1/4" with Saf-T-Trigger, fixed sight) **$961.00**

SMITH & WESSON MODEL 4513TSW/4553TSW PISTOLS

Caliber: 45 ACP, 7-shot magazine. **Barrel:** 3-3/4". **Weight:** 28 oz. (M4513TSW). **Length:** 6-7/8 overall. **Grips:** Checkered Xenoy; straight backstrap. **Sights:** White dot front, Novak LoMount Carry 2-Dot rear. **Features:** Model 4513TSW is traditional double action, Model 4553TSW is double action only. TSW series has tighter tolerances, ambidextrous manual safety/decocking lever, flush-fit magazine, delayed-unlock firing system; magazine disconnector. Compact alloy frame, stainless steel slide, equipment rail. Introduced 1998. Made in U.S.A. by Smith & Wesson.

Price: Model 4513TSW. **$924.00**
Price: Model 4553TSW. **$924.00**

SMITH & WESSON MODEL 4566 TSW

Caliber: 45 ACP. **Barrel:** 4-1/4", 8-shot . **Grips:** Straight back strap grip. **Sights:** Fixed Novak LoMount Carry. **Features:** Ambidextrous safety, equipment rail, Saf-T-Trigger, satin stainless finish. Traditional double action.

Price: **$961.00**

SMITH & WESSON MODEL 5900 SERIES AUTO PISTOLS

Caliber: 9mm Para., 10-shot magazine. **Barrel:** 4". **Weight:** 28-1/2 to 37-1/2 oz. (fixed sight); 38 oz. (adjustable sight). **Length:** 7-1/2" overall. **Grips:** Xenoy wrap-around with curved backstrap. **Sights:** Post front with white dot, fixed or fully adjustable with two white dots. **Features:** All stainless, stainless and alloy or carbon steel and alloy construction. Smooth .304" trigger, .260" serrated hammer. Equipment rail. Introduced 1989.

Price: Model 5906 (stainless, traditional DA, adjustable sight, ambidextrous safety) **$904.00**
Price: As above, fixed sight. **$841.00**
Price: With fixed night sights. **$995.00**
Price: With Saf-T-Trigger. **$882.00**
Price: Model 5946 DAO (as above, stainless frame and slide). . . **$863.00**

SMITH & WESSON ENHANCED SIGMA SERIES DAO PISTOLS

Caliber: 9mm Para., 40 S&W, 10-shot magazine. **Barrel:** 4". **Weight:** 26 oz. **Length:** 7.4" overall. **Grips:** Integral. **Sights:** White dot front, fixed rear; three-dot system. Tritium night sights available. **Features:** Ergonomic polymer frame; low barrel centerline; internal striker firing system; corrosion-resistant slide; Teflon-filled, electroless-nickel coated magazine, equipment rail. Introduced 1994. Made in U.S.A. by Smith & Wesson.

Price: SW9E, 9mm, 4" barrel, black finish, fixed sights **$447.00**
Price: SW9V, 9mm, 4" barrel, satin stainless, fixed night sights . . **$447.00**
Price: SW9VE, 4" barrel, satin stainless, Saf-T-Trigger, fixed sights **$466.00**
Price: SW40E, 40 S&W, 4" barrel, black finish, fixed sights **$657.00**
Price: SW40V, 40 S&W, 4" barrel, black polymer, fixed sights . . . **$447.00**
Price: SW40VE, 4" barrel, satin stainless, Saf-T-Trigger, fixed sights **$466.00**

SMITH & WESSON MODEL CS9 CHIEF'S SPECIAL AUTO

Caliber: 9mm Para., 7-shot magazine. **Barrel:** 3". **Weight:** 20.8 oz. **Length:** 6-1/4" overall. **Grips:** Hogue wrap-around rubber. **Sights:** White dot front, fixed two-dot rear. **Features:** Traditional double-action trigger mechanism. Alloy frame, stainless or blued slide. Ambidextrous safety. Introduced 1999. Made in U.S.A. by Smith & Wesson.

Price: Blue or stainless. **$680.00**

Smith & Wesson Model CS40 Chief's Special Auto

Similar to CS9, chambered for 40 S&W (7-shot magazine), 3-1/4" barrel, weighs 24.2 oz., measures 6-1/2" overall. Introduced 1999. Made in U.S.A. by Smith & Wesson.

Price: Blue or stainless. **$717.00**

Smith & Wesson Model CS45 Chief's Special Auto

Similar to CS40, chambered for 45 ACP, 6-shot magazine, weighs 23.9 oz. Introduced 1999. Made in U.S.A. by Smith & Wesson.

Price: Blue or stainless. **$717.00**

SMITH & WESSON MODEL 99

Caliber: 9mm Para. 4" barrel; 40 S&W 4-1/8" barrel; 10-shot, adj. sights. **Features:** Traditional double action satin stainless, black polymer frame, equipment rail, Saf-T-Trigger.

Price: 4" barrel **$648.00**
Price: 4-1/8" barrel **$648.00**

SPRINGFIELD, INC. FULL-SIZE 1911A1 AUTO PISTOL

Caliber: 9mm Para., 9-shot; 38 Super, 9-shot; 40 S&W, 9-shot; 45 ACP, 7-shot. **Barrel:** 5". **Weight:** 35.6 oz. **Length:** 8-5/8" overall. **Grips:** Cocobolo. **Sights:** Fixed three-dot system. **Features:** Beveled magazine well; lowered and flared ejection port. All forged parts, including frame, barrel, slide. All new production. Introduced 1990. From Springfield, Inc.

Price: Mil-Spec 45 ACP, Parkerized **$559.00**
Price: Standard, 45 ACP, blued, Novak sights **$824.00**
Price: Standard, 45 ACP, stainless, Novak sights. **$828.00**
Price: Lightweight 45 ACP (28.6 oz., matte finish, night sights) . . **$877.00**
Price: 40 S&W, stainless **$860.00**
Price: 9mm, stainless **$837.00**

Springfield, Inc. TRP Pistols

Similar to 1911A1 except 45 ACP only, checkered front strap and mainspring housing, Novak Night Sight combat rear sight and matching dovetailed front sight, tuned, polished extractor, oversize barrel link; lightweight speed trigger and combat action job, match barrel and bush-ing, extended ambidextrous thumb safety and fitted beavertail grip safety. Carry bevel on entire pistol; checkered cocobolo wood grips, comes with two Wilson 7-shot magazines. Frame is engraved "Tactical," both sides of frame with "TRP." Introduced 1998. From Springfield, Inc.

Price: Standard with Armory Kote finish. **$1,395.00**
Price: Standard, stainless steel **$1,370.00**
Price: Standard with Operator Light Rail Armory Kote **$1,473.00**

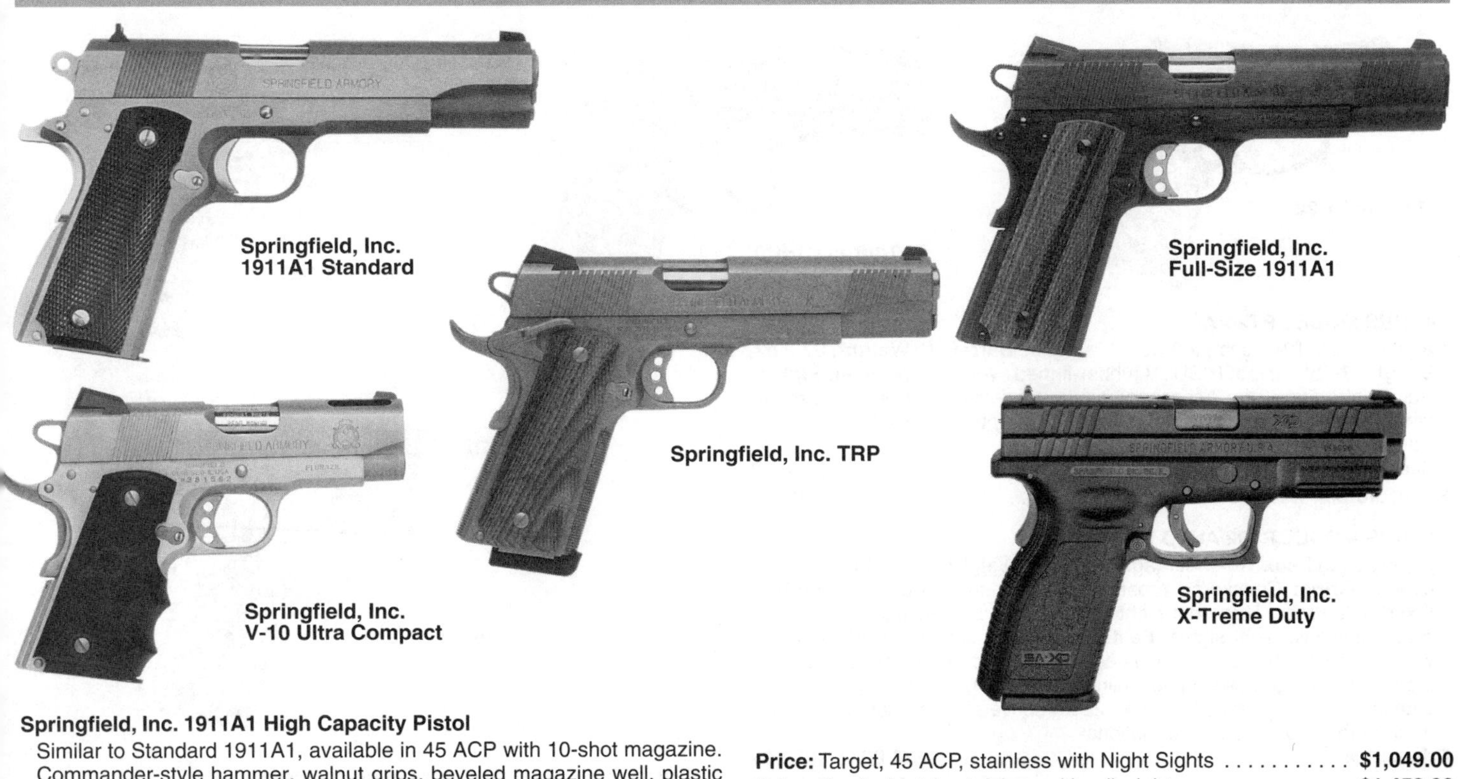

Springfield, Inc. 1911A1 Standard

Springfield, Inc. TRP

Springfield, Inc. Full-Size 1911A1

Springfield, Inc. V-10 Ultra Compact

Springfield, Inc. X-Treme Duty

Springfield, Inc. 1911A1 High Capacity Pistol

Similar to Standard 1911A1, available in 45 ACP with 10-shot magazine. Commander-style hammer, walnut grips, beveled magazine well, plastic carrying case. Can accept higher-capacity Para-Ordnance magazines. Introduced 1993. From Springfield, Inc.

Price: Mil-Spec 45 ACP **$756.00**
Price: 45 ACP Ultra Compact (3-1/2" bbl.) **$909.00**

Springfield, Inc. 1911A1 V-Series Ported Pistols

Similar to standard 1911A1, scalloped slides with 10, 12 or 16 matching barrel ports to redirect powder gasses and reduce recoil and muzzle flip. Adjustable rear sight, ambi thumb safety, Videki speed trigger, and beveled magazine well. Checkered walnut grips standard. Available in 45 ACP, stainless or bi-tone. Introduced 1992.

Price: V-16 Long Slide, stainless **$1,121.00**
Price: Target V-12, stainless **$878.00**
Price: V-10 (Ultra-Compact, bi-tone). **$853.00**
Price: V-10 stainless **$863.00**

Springfield, Inc. 1911A1 Champion Pistol

Similar to standard 1911A1, slide is 4". Novak Night Sights. Delta hammer and cocobolo grips. Available in 45 ACP only; Parkerized or stainless. Introduced 1989.

Price: Stainless. **$849.00**

Springfield, Inc. Ultra Compact Pistol

Similar to 1911A1 Compact, shorter slide, 3.5" barrel, beavertail grip safety, beveled magazine well, Novak Low Mount or Novak Night Sights, Videki speed trigger, flared ejection port, stainless steel frame, blued slide, match grade barrel, rubber grips. Introduced 1996. From Springfield, Inc.

Price: Parkerized 45 ACP, Night Sights **$589.00**
Price: Stainless 45 ACP, Night Sights. **$849.00**
Price: Lightweight, 9mm, stainless **$837.00**

Springfield, Inc. Compact Lightweight

Mates a Springfield Inc. Champion length slide with the shorter Ultra-Compact forged alloy frame for concealability. In 45 ACP.

Price: **$733.00**

Springfield, Inc. Long Slide 1911 A1 Pistol

Similar to Full Size model, 6" barrel and slide for increased sight radius and higher velocity, fully adjustable sights, muzzle-forward weight distribution for reduced recoil and quicker shot-to-shot recovery. From Springfield Inc.

Price: Target, 45 ACP, stainless with Night Sights **$1,049.00**
Price: Trophy Match, stainless with adj. sights **$1,452.00**
Price: V-16 stainless steel **$1,121.00**

SPRINGFIELD, INC. MICRO-COMPACT 1911A1 PISTOL

Caliber: 45 ACP, 40 S&W 6+1 capacity. **Barrel:** 3" 1:16 LH. **Weight:** 24 oz. **Length:** 5.7". **Sights:** Novak LoMount tritium. Dovetail front. **Features:** Forged frame and slide, ambi thumb safety, extreme carry bevel treatment, lockable plastic case, 2 magazines.

Price: . . . . **$993.00 to $1,021.00**

SPRINGFIELD, INC. X-TREME DUTY

Caliber: 9mm, 40 S&W, 357 Sig. **Barrel:** 4.08". **Weight:** 22.88 oz. **Length:** 7.2". **Sights:** Dovetail front and rear. **Features:** Lightweight, ultra high-impact polymer frame. Trigger, firing pin and grip safety. Two 10-rod steel easy glide magazines. Imported from Croatia.

Price: . . . . **$489.00 to $1,099.00**

STEYR M & S SERIES AUTO PISTOLS

Caliber: 9mm Para., 40 S&W, 357 SIG; 10-shot magazine. **Barrel:** 4" (3.58" for Model S). **Weight:** 28 oz. (22.5 oz. for Model S). **Length:** 7.05" overall (6.53" for Model S). **Grips:** Ultra-rigid polymer. **Sights:** Drift-adjustable, white-outline rear; white-triangle blade front. **Features:** Polymer frame; trigger-drop firing pin, manual and key-lock safeties; loaded chamber indicator; 5.5-lb. trigger pull; 111-degree grip angle enhances natural pointing. Introduced 2000. Imported from Austria by GSI Inc.

Price: Model M (full-sized frame with 4" barrel) **$609.95**
Price: Model S (compact frame with 3.58" barrel) **$609.95**
Price: Extra 10-shot magazines (Model M or S) **$39.00**

TAURUS MODEL PT 22/PT 25 AUTO PISTOLS

Caliber: 22 LR, 8-shot (PT 22); 25 ACP, 9-shot (PT 25). **Barrel:** 2.75". **Weight:** 12.3 oz. **Length:** 5.25" overall. **Grips:** Smooth rosewood or mother-of-pearl. **Sights:** Fixed. **Features:** Double action. Tip-up barrel for loading, cleaning. Blue, nickel, duotone or blue with gold accents. Introduced 1992. Made in U.S.A. by Taurus International.

Price: 22 LR, 25 ACP, blue, nickel or with duo-tone finish with rosewood grips **$219.00**
Price: 22 LR, 25 ACP, blue with gold trim, rosewood grips. **$234.00**
Price: 22 LR, 25 ACP, blue, nickel or duotone finish with checkered wood grips. **$219.00**
Price: 22 LR, 25 ACP, blue with gold trim, mother of pearl grips . **$250.00**

Taurus PT 22

Taurus PT-911

Taurus PT-938

Taurus PT-940

TAURUS MODEL PT24/7

Caliber: 9mm, 10+1 shot; .40 Cal., 10+1 shot. **Barrel:** 4". **Weight:** 27.2 oz. **Length**: 7-18". **Grips:** RIBBER rubber-finned overlay on polymer. **Sights:** Adjustable. **Features:** Accessory rail, four safeties, blue or stainless finish, consistent trigger pull weight and travel. Introduced 2003. Imported from Brazil by Taurus International.

Price: 9mm **$578.00**
Price: .40 Cal. **$594.00**

TAURUS MODEL PT92 AUTO PISTOL

Caliber: 9mm Para., 10-shot mag. **Barrel:** 5". **Weight:** 34 oz. **Length:** 8.5" overall. **Grips:** Checkered rubber, rosewood, mother-of-pearl. **Sights:** Fixed notch rear. Three-dot sight system. Also offered with micrometer-click adjustable night sights. **Features:** Double action, ambidextrous 3-way hammer drop safety, allows cocked & locked carry. Blue, stainless steel, blue with gold highlights, stainless steel with gold highlights, forged aluminum frame, integral key-lock. .22 LR conversion kit available. Imported from Brazil by Taurus International.

Price: Blue . . . . **$578.00 to $672.00**

Taurus Model PT99 Auto Pistol

Similar to PT92, fully adjustable rear sight.

Price: Blue . . . . **$575.00 to $670.00**
Price: 22 Conversion kit for PT 92 and PT99 (includes barrel and slide) **$266.00**

TAURUS MODEL PT-100/101 AUTO PISTOL

Caliber: 40 S&W, 10-shot mag. **Barrel:** 5". **Weight:** 34 oz. **Length:** 8-1/2". **Grips:** Checkered rubber, rosewood, mother-of-pearl. **Sights:** 3-dot fixed or adjustable; night sights available. **Features:** Single/double action with three-position safety/decocker. Re-introduced in 2001. Imported by Taurus International.

Price: PT100. . . . . **$578.00 to $672.00**
Price: PT101. . . . . **$594.00 to $617.00**

TAURUS MODEL PT-111 MILLENNIUM PRO AUTO PISTOL

Caliber: 9mm Para., 10-shot mag. **Barrel:** 3.25". **Weight:** 18.7 oz. **Length:** 6-1/8" overall. **Grips:** Polymer. **Sights:** 3-dot fixed; night sights available. Low profile, three-dot combat. **Features:** Double action only, polymer frame, matte stainless or blue steel slide, manual safety, integral key-lock. Deluxe models with wood grip inserts. Now issued in a third generation series with many cosmetic and internal improvements.

Price: . . . . **$445.00 to $539.00**

Taurus Model PT-111 Millennium Titanium Pistol

Similar to PT-111, titanium slide, night sights.

Price: **$586.00**

TAURUS PT-132 MILLENIUM PRO AUTO PISTOL

Caliber: 32 ACP, 10-shot mag. **Barrel:** 3.25". **Weight:** 18.7 oz. **Grips:** Polymer. **Sights:** 3-dot fixed; night sights available. **Features:** Double action only, polymer frame, matte stainless or blue steel slide, manual safety, integral key-lock action. Introduced 2001.

Price: . . . . **$445.00 to $461.00**

TAURUS PT-138 MILLENIUM PRO SERIES

Caliber: 380 ACP, 10-shot mag. **Barrel:** 3.25". **Weight:** 18.7 oz. **Grips:** Polymer. **Sights:** Fixed 3-dot fixed. **Features:** Double action only, polymer frame, matte stainless or blue steel slide, manual safety, integral key-lock.

Price: . . . . **$445.00 to $461.00**

TAURUS PT-140 MILLENIUM PRO AUTO PISTOL

Caliber: 40 S&W, 10-shot mag. **Barrel:** 3.25". **Weight:** 18.7 oz. **Grips:** Checkered polymer. **Sights:** 3-dot fixed; night sights available. **Features:** Double-action only; matte stainless or blue steel slide, black polymer frame, manual safety, integral key-lock action. From Taurus International.

Price: . . . . **$484.00 to $578.00**

TAURUS PT-145 MILLENIUM AUTO PISTOL

Caliber: 45 ACP, 10-shot mag. **Barrel:** 3.27". **Weight:** 23 oz. **Stock:** Checkered polymer. **Sights:** 3-dot fixed; night sights available. **Features:** Double-action only, matte stainless or blue steel slide, black polymer frame, manual safety, integral key-lock. From Taurus International.

Price: . . . . **$484.00 to $578.00**

TAURUS MODEL PT-911 AUTO PISTOL

Caliber: 9mm Para., 10-shot mag. **Barrel:** 4". **Weight:** 28.2 oz. **Length:** 7" overall. **Grips:** Checkered rubber, rosewood, mother-of-pearl. **Sights:** Fixed, three-dot blue or stainless; night sights optional. **Features:** Double action, semi-auto ambidextrous 3-way hammer drop safety, allows cocked and locked carry. Blue, stainless steel, blue with gold highlights, or stainless steel with gold highlights, forged aluminum frame, integral key-lock.

Price: . . . . **$523.00 to $617.00**

TAURUS MODEL PT-938 AUTO PISTOL

Caliber: 380 ACP, 10-shot mag. **Barrel:** 3.72". **Weight:** 27 oz. **Length:** 6.5" overall. **Grips:** Checkered rubber. **Sights:** Fixed, three-dot. **Features:** Double action, ambidextrous 3-way hammer drop allows cocked & locked carry. Forged aluminum frame. Integral key-lock. Imported by Taurus International.

Price: Blue **$516.00**
Price: Stainless. **$531.00**

TAURUS MODEL PT-940 AUTO PISTOL

Caliber: 40 S&W, 10-shot mag. **Barrel:** 3-5/8". **Weight:** 28.2 oz. **Length:** 7" overall. **Grips:** Checkered rubber, rosewood or mother-of-pearl. **Sights:** Fixed, three-dot blue or stainless; night sights optional. **Features:** Double action, semi-auto ambidextrous 3-way hammer drop safety, allows cocked & locked carry. Blue, stainless steel, blue with gold highlights, or stainless steel with gold hightlights, forged aluminum frame, integral key-lock.

Price: . . . . **$523.00 to $617.00**

Taurus PT-945

Taurus PT-957

Walther PPK/S

Walther P22

Walther P99

Walther PPK

Wilkinson Sherry

TAURUS MODEL PT-945 SERIES

Caliber: 45 ACP, 8-shot mag. **Barrel:** 4.25". **Weight:** 28.2/29.5 oz. **Length:** 7.48" overall. **Grips:** Checkered rubber, rosewood or mother-of-pearl. **Sights:** Fixed, three-dot; night sights optional. **Features:** Double-action with ambidextrous 3-way hammer drop safety allows cocked & locked carry. Forged aluminum frame, PT-945C has poarted barrel/slide. Blue, stainless, blue with gold highlights, stainless with gold highlights, integral key-lock. Introduced 1995. Imported by Taurus International.

Price: .... **$563.00 to $641.00**

TAURUS MODEL PT-957 AUTO PISTOL

Caliber: 357 SIG, 10-shot mag. **Barrel:** 4". **Weight:** 28 oz. **Length:** 7" overall. **Grips:** Checkered rubber, rosewood or mother-of-pearl. **Sights:** Fixed, three-dot blue or stainless; night sights optional. **Features:** Double-action, blue, stainless steel, blue with gold accents or stainless with gold accents, ported barrel/slide, three-position safety with decocking lever and ambidextrous safety. Forged aluminum frame, integral key-lock. Introduced 1999. Imported by Taurus International.

Price: .... **$525.00 to $620.00**

Price: Non-ported .... **$525.00 to $535.00**

TAURUS MODEL 922 SPORT PISTOL

Caliber: .22 LR, 10-shot magazine. **Barrel:** 6". **Weight:** 24.8 oz. **Length:** 9-1/8". **Grips:** Polymer. **Sights:** Adjustable. **Features:** Matte blue steel finish, machined target crown, polymer frame, single and double action, easy disassembly for cleaning.

Price: .... (blue) **$310.00**

Price: .... (stainless) **$328.00**

WALTHER PPK/S AMERICAN AUTO PISTOL

Caliber: 380 ACP, 7-shot magazine. **Barrel:** 3.27". **Weight:** 23-1/2 oz. **Length:** 6.1" overall. **Stocks:** Checkered plastic. **Sights:** Fixed, white markings. **Features:** Double action; manual safety blocks firing pin and drops hammer; chamber loaded indicator on 32 and 380; extra finger rest magazine provided. Made entirely in the United States. Introduced 1980.

Price: 380 ACP only, blue **$540.00**

Price: As above, 32 ACP or 380 ACP, stainless **$540.00**

Walther PPK American Auto Pistol

Similar to Walther PPK/S except weighs 21 oz., has 6-shot capacity. Made in the U.S. Introduced 1986.

Price: Stainless, 32 ACP or 380 ACP **$540.00**

Price: Blue, 380 ACP only **$540.00**

WALTHER P99 AUTO PISTOL

Caliber: 9mm Para., 9x21, 40 S&W,10-shot magazine. **Barrel:** 4". **Weight:** 25 oz. **Length:** 7" overall. **Grips:** Textured polymer. **Sights:** Blade front (comes with three interchangeable blades for elevation adjustment), micrometer rear adjustable for windage. **Features:** Double-action mechanism with trigger safety, decock safety, internal striker safety; chamber loaded indicator; ambidextrous magazine release levers; polymer frame with interchangeable backstrap inserts. Comes with two magazines. Introduced 1997. Imported from Germany by Carl Walther USA.

Price: **$799.00**

Walther P990 Auto Pistol

Similar to the P99 except is double action only. Available in blue or silver tenifer finish. Introduced 1999. Imported from Germany by Carl Walther USA.

Price: **$749.00**

WALTHER P22 PISTOL

Caliber: 22 LR. **Barrel:** 3.4", 5". **Weight:** 19.6 oz. (3.4"), 20.3 oz. (5"). **Length:** 6.26", 7.83". **Grips:** NA. **Sights:** Interchangeable white dot, front, 2-dot adjustable, rear. **Features:** A rimfire version of the Walther P99 pistol, available in nickel slide with black frame, or green frame with black slide versions. Made in Germany and distributed in the U.S. by Smith & Wesson.

Price: .... **NA**

WILKINSON SHERRY AUTO PISTOL

Caliber: 22 LR, 8-shot magazine. **Barrel:** 2-1/8". **Weight:** 9-1/4 oz. **Length:** 4-3/8" overall. **Grips:** Checkered black plastic. **Sights:** Fixed, groove. **Features:** Cross-bolt safety locks the sear into the hammer. Available in all blue finish or blue slide and trigger with gold frame. Introduced 1985.

Price: **$280.00**

WILKINSON LINDA AUTO PISTOL

Caliber: 9mm Para. **Barrel:** 8-5/16". **Weight:** 4 lbs., 13 oz. **Length:** 12-1/4" overall. **Grips:** Checkered black plastic pistol grip, walnut forend. **Sights:** Protected blade front, aperture rear. **Features:** Fires from closed bolt. Semi-auto only. Straight blowback action. Cross-bolt safety. Removable barrel. From Wilkinson Arms.

Price: **$675.00**

Includes models suitable for several forms of competition and other sporting purposes.

Baer 1911 Ultimate Master

Baer 1911 Bullseye Wadcutter

BF Ultimate

Browning Buck Mark Target 5.5

BAER 1911 ULTIMATE MASTER COMBAT PISTOL

Caliber: 9x23, 38 Super, 400 Cor-Bon 45 ACP (others available), 10-shot magazine. **Barrel:** 5", 6"; Baer NM. **Weight:** 37 oz. **Length:** 8.5" overall. **Grips:** Checkered rosewood. **Sights:** Baer dovetail front, low-mount Bo-Mar rear with hidden leaf. **Features:** Full-house competition gun. Baer forged NM blued steel frame and double serrated slide; Baer triple port, tapered cone compensator; fitted slide to frame; lowered, flared ejection port; Baer reverse recoil plug; full-length guide rod; recoil buff; beveled magazine well; Baer Commander hammer, sear; Baer extended ambidextrous safety, extended ejector, checkered slide stop, beavertail grip safety with pad, extended magazine release button; Baer speed trigger. Made in U.S.A. by Les Baer Custom, Inc.

Price: Compensated, open sights. **$2,476.00**
Price: 6" Model 400 Cor-Bon **$2,541.00**

BAER 1911 NATIONAL MATCH HARDBALL PISTOL

Caliber: 45 ACP, 7-shot magazine. **Barrel:** 5". **Weight:** 37 oz. **Length:** 8.5" overall. **Grips:** Checkered walnut. **Sights:** Baer dovetail front with undercut post, low-mount Bo-Mar rear with hidden leaf. **Features:** Baer NM forged steel frame, double serrated slide and barrel with stainless bushing; slide fitted to frame; Baer match trigger with 4-lb. pull; polished feed ramp, throated barrel; checkered front strap, arched mainspring housing; Baer beveled magazine well; lowered, flared ejection port; tuned extractor; Baer extended ejector, checkered slide stop; recoil buff. Made in U.S.A. by Les Baer Custom, Inc.

Price: **$1,335.00**

Baer 1911 Bullseye Wadcutter Pistol

Similar to National Match Hardball except designed for wadcutter loads only. Polished feed ramp and barrel throat; Bo-Mar rib on slide; full-length recoil rod; Baer speed trigger with 3-1/2-lb. pull; Baer deluxe hammer and sear; Baer beavertail grip safety with pad; flat mainspring housing checkered 20 lpi. Blue finish; checkered walnut grips. Made in U.S.A. by Les Baer Custom, Inc.

Price: From **$1,495.00**
Price: With 6" barrel, from. **$1,690.00**

BF ULTIMATE SILHOUETTE HB SINGLE SHOT PISTOL

Caliber: 7mm U.S., 22 LR Match and 100 other chamberings. **Barrel:** 10.75" Heavy Match Grade with 11-degree target crown. **Weight:** 3 lbs., 15 oz. **Length:** 16" overall. **Grips:** Thumbrest target style. **Sights:** Bo-Mar/Bond ScopeRib I Combo with hooded post front adjustable for height and width, rear notch available in .032", .062", .080" and .100" widths; 1/2-MOA clicks. **Features:** Designed to meet maximum rules for IHMSA Production Gun. Falling block action gives rigid barrel-receiver mating. Hand fitted and headspaced. Etched receiver; gold-colored trigger. Introduced 1988. Made in U.S.A. by E. Arthur Brown Co. Inc.

Price: **$669.00**

BF Classic Hunting Pistol

Similar to BF Ultimate Silhouette HB Single Shot Pistol, except no sights; drilled and tapped for scope mount. Barrels from 8" to 15". Variety of options offered. Made in U.S.A. by E. Arthur Brown Co. Inc.

Price: **$599.00**

BROWNING BUCK MARK TARGET 5.5

Caliber: 22 LR, 10-shot magazine. **Barrel:** 5-1/2" barrel with .900" diameter. **Weight:** 35-1/2 oz. **Length:** 9-5/8" overall. **Grips:** Contoured walnut grips with thumbrest, or finger-groove walnut. **Sights:** Hooded sights mounted on scope base that accepts optical or reflex sight. Rear sight is Browning fully adjustable Pro Target, front sight is adjustable post that customizes to different widths, can be adjusted for height. **Features:** Matte blue finish. Introduced 1990. From Browning.

Price: **$496.00**

BROWNING BUCK MARK FIELD 5.5

Same as Target 5.5, hoodless ramp-style front sight and low profile rear sight. Matte blue finish, contoured or finger-groove walnut stocks. Introduced 1991.

Price: **$496.00**

BROWNING BUCK MARK BULLSEYE

Similar to Buck Mark Silhouette, 7-1/4" heavy barrel with three flutes per side; trigger adjusts from 2-1/2 to 5 lbs.; specially designed rosewood target or three-finger-groove stocks with competition-style heel rest, or with contoured rubber grip. Overall length 11-5/16", weighs 36 oz. Introduced 1996. Made in U.S.A. From Browning.

Price: With ambidextrous moulded composite stocks. **$454.00**
Price: With rosewood stocks, or wrap-around finger groove. **$586.00**

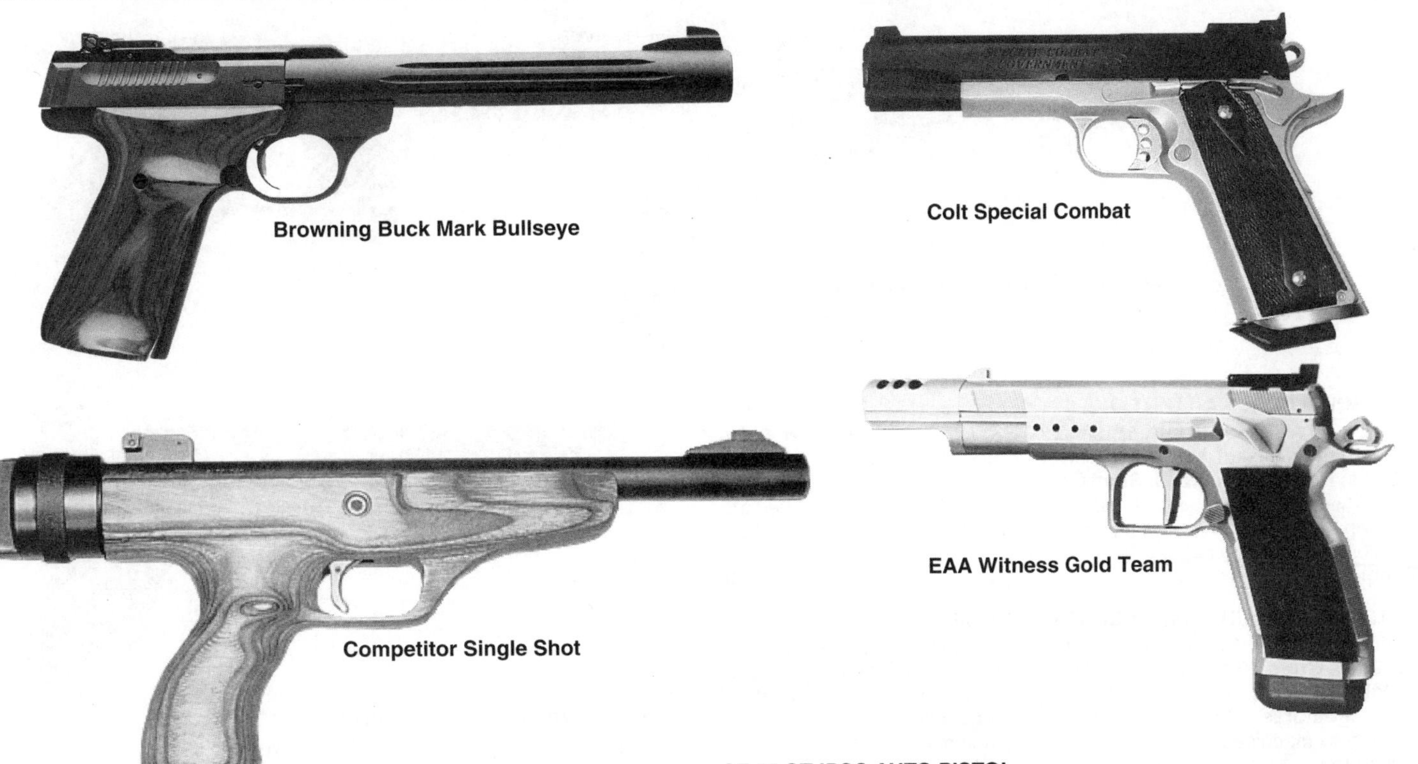

Browning Buck Mark Bullseye

Colt Special Combat

EAA Witness Gold Team

Competitor Single Shot

COLT GOLD CUP MODEL O PISTOL

Caliber: 45 ACP, 8-shot magazine. **Barrel:** 5", with new design bushing. **Weight:** 39 oz. **Length:** 8-1/2". **Grips:** Checkered rubber composite with silver-plated medallion. **Sights:** Patridge-style front, Bomar-style rear adjustable for windage and elevation, sight radius 6-3/4". **Features:** Arched or flat housing; wide, grooved trigger with adjustable stop; ribbed-top slide, hand fitted, with improved ejection port.

Price: Blue **$1,050.00**

Price: Stainless. **$1,116.00**

COLT SPECIAL COMBAT GOVERNMENT

Caliber: 45 ACP. **Barrel:** 5" **Weight:** NA. **Length:** 8-1/2" **Grips:** Rosewood w/double diamond checkering pattern. **Sights:** Clark dovetail, front; Bomar adjustable, rear. **Features:** A competition ready pistol with enhancements such as skeletonized trigger, upswept grip safety, custom tuned action, polished feed ramp. Blue or satin nickel finish. Introduced 2003. Made in U.S.A. by Colt's Mfg. Co.

Price: **$1,640.00**

COMPETITOR SINGLE SHOT PISTOL

Caliber: 22 LR through 50 Action Express, including belted magnums. **Barrel:** 14" standard; 10.5" silhouette; 16" optional. **Weight:** About 59 oz. (14" bbl.). **Length:** 15.12" overall. **Grips:** Ambidextrous; synthetic (standard) or laminated or natural wood. **Sights:** Ramp front, adjustable rear. **Features:** Rotary canon-type action cocks on opening; cammed ejector; interchangeable barrels, ejectors. Adjustable single stage trigger, sliding thumb safety and trigger safety. Matte blue finish. Introduced 1988. From Competitor Corp., Inc.

Price: 14", standard calibers, synthetic grip **$414.95**

Price: Extra barrels, from **$159.95**

CZ 75 CHAMPION COMPETITION PISTOL

Caliber: 9mm Para., 9x21, 40 S&W, 10-shot mag. **Barrel:** 4.49". **Weight:** 35 oz. **Length:** 9.44" overall. **Grips:** Black rubber. **Sights:** Blade front, fully adjustable rear. **Features:** Single-action trigger mechanism; three-port compensator (40 S&W, 9mm have two port) full-length guide rod; extended magazine release; ambidextrous safety; flared magazine well; fully adjustable match trigger. Introduced 1999. Imported from the Czech Republic by CZ USA.

Price: 9mm Para., 9x21, 40 S&W, dual-tone finish. **$1,551.00**

CZ 75 ST IPSC AUTO PISTOL

Caliber: 40 S&W, 10-shot magazine. **Barrel:** 5.12". **Weight:** 2.9 lbs. **Length:** 8.86" overall. **Grips:** Checkered walnut. **Sights:** Fully adjustable rear. **Features:** Single-action mechanism; extended slide release and ambidextrous safety; full-length slide rail; double slide serrations. Introduced 1999. Imported from the Czech Republic by CZ-USA.

Price: Dual-tone finish **$1,038.00**

EAA/BAIKAL IZH35 AUTO PISTOL

Caliber: 22 LR, 5-shot mag. **Barrel:** 6". **Grips:** Walnut; fully adjustable right-hand target-style. **Sights:** Fully adjustable rear, blade front; detachable scope mount. **Features:** Hammer-forged target barrel; machined steel receiver; adjustable trigger; manual slide hold back, grip and manual trigger-bar disconnect safeties; cocking indicator. Introduced 2000. Imported from Russia by European American Armory.

Price: Blued finish. **$489.00**

EAA WITNESS GOLD TEAM AUTO

Caliber: 9mm Para., 9x21, 38 Super, 40 S&W, 45 ACP. **Barrel:** 5.1". **Weight:** 44 oz. **Length:** 10.5" overall. **Grips:** Checkered walnut, competition style. **Sights:** Square post front, fully adjustable rear. **Features:** Triple-chamber cone compensator; competition SA trigger; extended safety and magazine release; competition hammer; beveled magazine well; beavertail grip. Hand-fitted major components. Hard chrome finish. Match-grade barrel. From E.A.A. Custom Shop. Introduced 1992. From European American Armory.

Price: **$1,699.00**

EAA Witness Silver Team Auto

Similar to Witness Gold Team, double-chamber compensator, oval magazine release, black rubber grips, double-dip blue finish. Super Sight and drilled and tapped for scope mount. Built for the intermediate competition shooter. Introduced 1992. From European American Armory Custom Shop.

Price: 9mm Para., 9x21, 38 Super, 40 S&W, 45 ACP. **$968.00**

ED BROWN CLASSIC CUSTOM PISTOL

Caliber: 45 ACP. **Barrel:** 5". **Weight:** 39 oz. **Grips:** Hogue exotic wood. **Sights:** Modified ramp or post, front; fully-adjustable Bo-Mar, rear. **Features:** Highly-polished slide, two-piece guide rod, oversize mag release, ambidextrous safety.

Price: **$2,895.00**

Freedom Arms 83 22 Silhouette Class

Hammerli SP 20

High Standard Trophy

ED BROWN CLASS A LIMITED

Caliber: 45 ACP, 400 Cor-Bon, 10mm, 40 S&W, 357 SIG, 38 Super, 9x23, 9mm Luger, 7-shot magazine. **Barrel:** 4.25", 5". **Weight:** 34 to 39 oz. **Grips:** Hogue exotic wood. **Sights:** Customer preference, front; fixed Novak low-mount or fully-adjustable Bo-Mar, rear. **Features:** Checkered forestrap and mainspring housing, matte finished top sighting surface. Many options available.

Price: **$2,250.00**

ENTRÉPRISE TOURNAMENT SHOOTER MODEL I

Caliber: 45 ACP, 10-shot mag. **Barrel:** 6". **Weight:** 40 oz. **Length:** 8.5" overall. **Grips:** Black ultra-slim double diamond checkered synthetic. **Sights:** Dovetailed Patridge front, adjustable Competizione "melded" rear. **Features:** Oversized magazine release button; flared magazine well; fully machined parallel slide rails; front and rear slide serrations; serrated top of slide; stainless ramped bull barrel with fully supported chamber; full-length guide rod with plug; stainless firing pin; match extractor; polished ramp; tuned match extractor; black oxide. Introduced 1998. Made in U.S.A. by Entréprise Arms.

Price: **$2,300.00**

Price: TSMIII (Satin chrome finish, two-piece guide rod) **$2,700.00**

EXCEL INDUSTRIES CP-45, XP-45 AUTO PISTOL

Caliber: 45 ACP, 6-shot & 10-shot mags. **Barrel:** 3-1/4". **Weight:** 31 oz. & 25 oz. **Length:** 6-3/8" overall. **Grips:** Checkered black nylon. **Sights:** Fully adjustable rear. **Features:** Stainless steel frame and slide; single action with external hammer and firing pin block, manual thumb safety; last-shot hold open. Includes gun lock and cleaning kit. Introduced 2001. Made in U.S.A. by Excel Industries Inc.

Price: CP-45 .... **$425.00**

Price: XP-45 .... **$465.00**

FEINWERKEBAU AW93 TARGET PISTOL

Caliber: 22. **Barrel:** 6". **Grips:** Fully adjustable orthopaedic. **Sights:** Fully adjustable micrometer. **Features:** Advanced Russian design with German craftmanship. Imported from Germany by Nygord Precision Products.

Price: **$1,495.00**

FREEDOM ARMS MODEL 83 22 FIELD GRADE SILHOUETTE CLASS

Caliber: 22 LR, 5-shot cylinder. **Barrel:** 10". **Weight:** 63 oz. **Length:** 15.5" overall. **Grips:** Black Micarta. **Sights:** Removable patridge front blade; Iron Sight Gun Works silhouette rear, click adjustable for windage and elevation (optional adj. front sight and hood). **Features:** Stainless steel, matte finish, manual sliding-bar safety system; dual firing pins, lightened hammer for fast lock time, pre-set trigger stop. Introduced 1991. Made in U.S.A. by Freedom Arms.

Price: Silhouette Class **$1,901.75**

Price: Extra fitted 22 WMR cylinder **$264.00**

FREEDOM ARMS MODEL 83 CENTERFIRE SILHOUETTE MODELS

Caliber: 357 Mag., 41 Mag., 44 Mag.; 5-shot cylinder. **Barrel:** 10", 9" (357 Mag. only). **Weight:** 63 oz. (41 Mag.). **Length:** 15.5", 14-1/2" (357 only). **Grips:** Pachmayr Presentation. **Sights:** Iron Sight Gun Works silhouette rear sight, replaceable adjustable front sight blade with hood. **Features:** Stainless steel, matte finish, manual sliding-bar safety system. Made in U.S.A. by Freedom Arms.

Price: Silhouette Models **$1,634.85**

GAUCHER GP SILHOUETTE PISTOL

Caliber: 22 LR, single shot. **Barrel:** 10". **Weight:** 42.3 oz. **Length:** 15.5" overall. **Grips:** Stained hardwood. **Sights:** Hooded post on ramp front, open rear adjustable for windage and elevation. **Features:** Matte chrome barrel, blued bolt and sights. Other barrel lengths available on special order. Introduced 1991. Imported by Mandall Shooting Supplies.

Price: **$425.00**

HAMMERLI SP 20 TARGET PISTOL

Caliber: 22 LR, 32 S&W. **Barrel:** 4.6". **Weight:** 34.6-41.8 oz. **Length:** 11.8" overall. **Grips:** Anatomically shaped synthetic Hi-Grip available in five sizes. **Sights:** Integral front in three widths, adjustable rear with changeable notch widths. **Features:** Extremely low-level sight line; anatomically shaped trigger; adjustable JPS buffer system for different recoil characteristics. Receiver available in red, blue, gold, violet or black. Introduced 1998. Imported from Switzerland by SIGARMS, Inc and Hammerli Pistols USA.

Price: Hammerli 22 LR **$1,668.00**

Price: Hammerli 32 S&W **$1,743.00**

HAMMERLI X-ESSE SPORT PISTOL

An all-steel .22 LR target pistol with a Hi-Grip in a new anatomical shape and an adjustable hand rest. Made in Switzerland. Introduced 2003.

Price: **$710.00**

HARRIS GUNWORKS SIGNATURE JR. LONG RANGE PISTOL

Caliber: Any suitable caliber. **Barrel:** To customer specs. **Weight:** 5 lbs. **Stock:** Gunworks fiberglass. **Sights:** None furnished; comes with scope rings. **Features:** Right- or left-hand benchrest action of titanium or stainless steel; single shot or repeater. Comes with bipod. Introduced 1992. Made in U.S.A. by Harris Gunworks, Inc.

Price: **$2,700.00**

HIGH STANDARD TROPHY TARGET PISTOL

Caliber: 22 LR, 10-shot mag. **Barrel:** 5-1/2" bull or 7-1/4" fluted. **Weight:** 44 oz. **Length:** 9.5" overall. **Stock:** Checkered hardwood with thumbrest. **Sights:** Undercut ramp front, frame-mounted micro-click rear adjustable for windage and elevation; drilled and tapped for scope mounting. **Features:** Gold-plated trigger, slide lock, safety-lever and magazine release; stippled front grip and backstrap; adjustable trigger and sear. Barrel weights optional. From High Standard Manufacturing Co., Inc.

Price: 5-1/2", scope base **$540.00**

Price: 7.25" **$689.00**

Price: 7.25", scope base **$625.00**

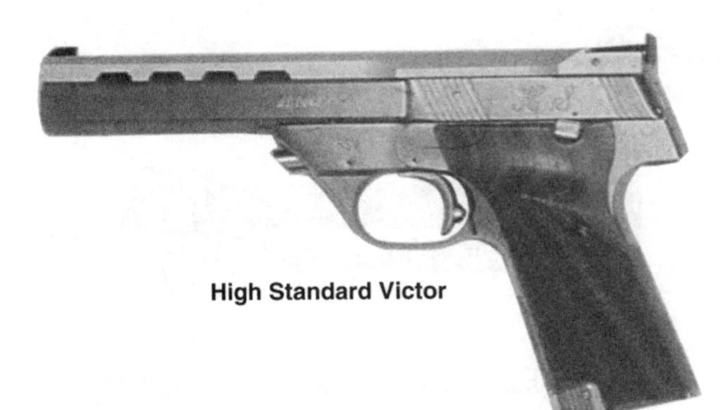
High Standard Victor

Ruger Mark II Target

Ruger Mark II Government Target

HIGH STANDARD VICTOR TARGET PISTOL

Caliber: 22 LR, 10-shot magazine. **Barrel:** 4-1/2" or 5-1/2"; push-button takedown. **Weight:** 46 oz. **Length:** 9.5" overall. **Stock:** Checkered hardwood with thumbrest. **Sights:** Undercut ramp front, micro-click rear adjustable for windage and elevation. Also available with scope mount, rings, no sights. **Features:** Stainless steel construction. Full-length vent rib. Gold-plated trigger, slide lock, safety-lever and magazine release; stippled front grip and backstrap; polished slide; adjustable trigger and sear. Comes with barrel weight. From High Standard Manufacturing Co., Inc.

Price: 4-1/2" scope base **$564.00**
Price: 5-1/2", sights **$625.00**
Price: 5-1/2" scope base **$564.00**

KIMBER SUPER MATCH II

Caliber: 45 ACP, 7-shot magazine. **Barrel:** 5". **Weight:** 38 oz. **Length:** 18.7" overall. **Sights:** Blade front, Kimber fully adjustable rear. **Features:** Guaranteed to have shot 3" group at 50 yards. Stainless steel frame, black KimPro slide; two-piece magazine well; premium aluminum match-grade trigger; 30 lpi front strap checkering; stainless match-grade barrel; ambidextrous safety; special Custom Shop markings. Introduced 1999. Made in U.S.A. by Kimber Mfg., Inc.

Price: **$1,927.00**

KORTH MATCH REVOLVER

Caliber: 357 Mag., 38 Special, 32 S&W Long, 9mm Para., 22 WMR, 22 LR. **Barrel:** 5-1/4", 6". **Grips:** Adjustable match of oiled walnut with matte finish. **Sights:** Fully adjustable with rear sight leaves (wide th of sight notch: 3.4 mm, 3.5 mm, 3.6 mm), rear; undercut partridge, front. Trigger: Equipped with completely machined trigger shoe. Interchangeable caliber cylinders available as well as a variety of finishes. Made in Germany.

Price: .... From **$5,632.00**

MORINI MODEL 84E FREE PISTOL

Caliber: 22 LR, single shot. **Barrel:** 11.4". **Weight:** 43.7 oz. **Length:** 19.4" overall. **Grips:** Adjustable match type with stippled surfaces. **Sights:** Interchangeable blade front, match-type fully adjustable rear. **Features:** Fully adjustable electronic trigger. Introduced 1995. Imported from Switzerland by Nygord Precision Products.

Price: **$1,450.00**

PARDINI MODEL SP, HP TARGET PISTOLS

Caliber: 22 LR, 32 S&W, 5-shot magazine. **Barrel:** 4.7". **Weight:** 38.9 oz. **Length:** 11.6" overall. **Grips:** Adjustable; stippled walnut; match type. **Sights:** Interchangeable blade front, interchangeable, fully adjustable rear. **Features:** Fully adjustable match trigger. Introduced 1995. Imported from Italy by Nygord Precision Products.

Price: Model SP (22 LR) **$995.00**
Price: Model HP (32 S&W) **$1,095.00**

PARDINI GP RAPID FIRE MATCH PISTOL

Caliber: 22 Short, 5-shot magazine. **Barrel:** 4.6". **Weight:** 43.3 oz. **Length:** 11.6" overall. **Grips:** Wrap-around stippled walnut. **Sights:** Interchangeable post front, fully adjustable match rear. Introduced 1995. Imported from Italy by Nygord Precision Products.

Price: Model GP **$1,095.00**
Price: Model GP-E Electronic, has special parts **$1,595.00**

PARDINI K22 FREE PISTOL

Caliber: 22 LR, single shot. **Barrel:** 9.8". **Weight:** 34.6 oz. **Length:** 18.7" overall. **Grips:** Wrap-around walnut; adjustable match type. **Sights:** Interchangeable post front, fully adjustable match open rear. **Features:** Removable, adjustable match trigger. Toggle bolt pushes cartridge into chamber. Barrel weights mount above the barrel. New upgraded model introduced in 2002. Imported from Italy by Nygord Precision Products.

Price: **$1,295.00**

PARDINI GT45 TARGET PISTOL

Caliber: 45, 9mm, 40 S&W. **Barrel:** 5", 6". **Grips:** Checkered fore strap. **Sights:** Interchangeable post front, fully adjustable match open rear. **Features:** Ambi-safeties, trigger pull adjustable. Fits Helweg Glock holsters for defense shooters. Imported from Italy by Nygord Precision Products.

Price: 5" **$1,050.00**
Price: 6" **$1,125.00**
Price: Frame mount available .... **$75.00 extra**
Price: Slide mount available .... **$35.00 extra**

PARDINI/NYGORD "MASTER" TARGET PISTOL

Caliber: 22 cal. **Barrel:** 5-1/2". **Grips:** Semi-wrap-around. **Sights:** Micrometer rear and red dot. **Features:** Elegant NRA "Bullseye" pistol. Superior balance of Pardini pistols. Revolutionary recirpcating internal weight barrel shroud. Imported from Italy by Nygord Precision Products.

Price: **$1,145.00**

RUGER MARK II TARGET MODEL AUTOLOADING PISTOL

Caliber: 22 LR, 10-shot magazine. **Barrel:** 6-7/8". **Weight:** 42 oz. **Length:** 11-1/8" overall. **Grips:** Checkered composition grip panels. **Sights:** .125" blade front, micro-click rear, adjustable for windage and elevation. Sight radius 9-3/8". Plastic case with lock included.

Features: Introduced 1982.

Price: Blued (MK-678) **$349.00**
Price: Stainless (KMK-678) **$439.00**

Ruger Mark II Government Target Model

Same gun as Mark II Target Model except has 6-7/8" barrel, higher sights and is roll marked "Government Target Model" on right side of receiver below rear sight. Identical in all aspects to military model used for training U.S. Armed Forces except for markings. Comes with factory test target, also lockable plastic case. Introduced 1987.

Price: Blued (MK-678G) **$425.00**
Price: Stainless (KMK-678G) **$509.00**

Ruger Mark II Bull Barrel - MK10

Safari Arms Big Deuce

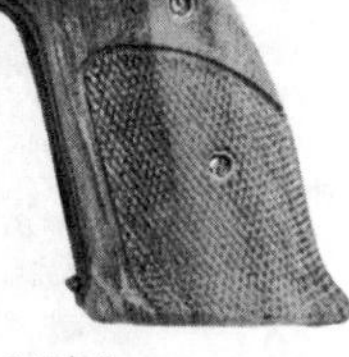

Smith & Wesson Model 41

Springfield, Inc. 1911A1 Bullseye Wadcutter

Ruger Stainless Competition Model Pistol

Similar to Mark II Government Target Model stainless pistol, 6-7/8" slab- sided barrel; receiver top is fitted with Ruger scope base of blued, chrome moly steel; has Ruger 1" stainless scope rings for mounting variety of op-tical sights; checkered laminated grip panels with right-hand thumbrest. Blued open sights with 9-1/4" radius. Overall length 11-1/8", weight 45 oz. Case and lock included. Introduced 1991.

Price: KMK-678GC **$529.00**

Ruger Mark II Bull Barrel

Same gun as Target Model except has 5-1/2" or 10" heavy barrel (10" meets all IHMSA regulations). Weight with 5-1/2" barrel is 42 oz., with 10" barrel, 51 oz. Case with lock included.

Price: Blued (MK-512) **$349.00**
Price: Blued (MK-10) **$357.00**
Price: Stainless (KMK-10) **$445.00**
Price: Stainless (KMK-512) **$439.00**

SAFARI ARMS BIG DEUCE PISTOL

Caliber: 45 ACP, 7-shot magazine. **Barrel:** 6", 416 stainless steel. **Weight:** 40.3 oz. **Length:** 9.5" overall. **Grips:** Smooth walnut. **Sights:** Ramped blade front, LPA adjustable rear. **Features:** Beavertail grip safety; extended thumb safety and slide release; Commander-style hammer. Throated, polished and tuned. Parkerized matte black slide with satin stainless steel frame. Introduced 1995. Made in U.S.A. by Safari Arms, Inc.

Price: **$714.00**

SMITH & WESSON MODEL 41 TARGET

Caliber: 22 LR, 10-shot clip. **Barrel:** 5-1/2", 7". **Weight:** 44 oz. (5-1/2" barrel). **Length:** 9" overall (5-1/2" barrel). **Grips:** Checkered walnut with modified thumbrest, usable with either hand. **Sights:** 1/8" Patridge on ramp base; micro-click rear adjustable for windage and elevation. **Features:** 3/8" wide, grooved trigger; adjustable trigger stop drilled and tapped.

Price: S&W Bright Blue, either barrel **$958.00**

SMITH & WESSON MODEL 22A TARGET PISTOL

Caliber: 22 LR, 10-shot magazine. **Barrel:** 5-1/2" bull. **Weight:** 38.5 oz. **Length:** 9-1/2" overall. **Grips:** Dymondwood with ambidextrous thumbrests and flared bottom or rubber soft touch with thumbrest. **Sights:** Patridge front, fully adjustable rear. **Features:** Sight bridge with Weaver-style integral optics mount; alloy frame, stainless barrel and slide; blue finish. Introduced 1997. Made in U.S.A. by Smith & Wesson.

Price: **$367.00**
Price: HiViz front sight **$387.00**
Price: Camo model **$355.00**

Smith & Wesson Model 22S Target Pistol

Similar to the Model 22A except has stainless steel frame. Introduced 1997. Made in U.S.A. by Smith & Wesson.

Price: **$434.00**
Price: HiViz front sight **$453.00**

SPRINGFIELD, INC. 1911A1 BULLSEYE WADCUTTER PISTOL

Caliber: 38 Super, 45 ACP. **Barrel:** 5". **Weight:** 45 oz. **Length:** 8.59" overall (5" barrel). **Grips:** Checkered walnut. **Sights:** Bo-Mar rib with undercut blade front, fully adjustable rear. **Features:** Built for wadcutter loads only. Has full-length recoil spring guide rod, fitted Videki speed trigger with 3.5-lb. pull; match Commander hammer and sear; beavertail grip safety; lowered and flared ejection port; tuned extractor; fitted slide to frame; recoil buffer system; beveled and polished magazine well; checkered front strap and steel mainspring housing (flat housing standard); polished and throated National Match barrel and bushing. Comes with two magazines with slam pads, plastic carrying case, test target. Introduced 1992. From Springfield, Inc.

Price: **$1,499.00**
Price: Adj. Target **$1,049.00**
Price: M1911SC, Commander style **$1,029.00**

Springfield, Inc. Basic Competition Pistol

Has low-mounted Bo-Mar adjustable rear sight, undercut blade front; match throated barrel and bushing; polished feed ramp; lowered and flared ejection port; fitted Videki speed trigger with tuned 3.5-lb. pull; fitted slide to frame; recoil buffer system; checkered walnut grips; serrated, arched mainspring housing. Comes with two magazines with slam pads, plastic carrying case. Introduced 1992. From Springfield, Inc.

Price: 45 ACP, blue, 5" only **$1,295.00**

Springfield, Inc. Expert

Springfield, Inc. Distinguished

Springfield, Inc. N.M. Hardball

Springfield, Inc. 1911A1 Trophy Match

Springfield, Inc. Expert Pistol

Similar to the Competition Pistol except has triple-chamber tapered cone compensator on match barrel with dovetailed front sight; lowered and flared ejection port; fully tuned for reliability; fitted slide to frame; extended ambidextrous thumb safety, extended magazine release button; beavertail grip safety; Pachmayr wrap-around grips. Comes with two magazines, plastic carrying case. Introduced 1992. From Springfield, Inc.

Price: 45 ACP, Duotone finish **$1,724.00**
Price: Expert Ltd. (non-compensated) **$1,624.00**

Springfield, Inc. Distinguished Pistol

Has all the features of the 1911A1 Expert except is full-house pistol with deluxe Bo-Mar low-mounted adjustable rear sight; full-length recoil spring guide rod and recoil spring retainer; checkered frontstrap; S&A magazine well; walnut grips. Hard chrome finish. Comes with two magazines with slam pads, plastic carrying case. From Springfield, Inc.

Price: 45 ACP **$2,445.00**
Price: Distinguished Limited (non-compensated) **$2,345.00**

Springfield, Inc. 1911A1 N.M. Hardball Pistol

Has Bo-Mar adjustable rear sight with undercut front blade; fitted match Videki trigger with 4-lb. pull; fitted slide to frame; throated National Match barrel and bushing, polished feed ramp; recoil buffer system; tuned extractor; Herrett walnut grips. Comes with two magazines, plastic carrying case, test target. Introduced 1992. From Springfield, Inc.

Price: 45 ACP, blue **$1,336.00**

Springfield, Inc. Leatham Legend TGO Series Pistols

Three models of 5" barrel, .45 ACP 1911 pistols built for serious competition. TGO 1 has deluxe low mount BoMar rear sight, Dawson fiber optics front sight, 3.5 lb. trigger pull. TGO 2 has BoMar low mount adjustable rear sight, Dawson fiber optic front sight, 4.5 to 5 lb. trigger pull. TGO 3 has Springfield Armory fully adjustable rear sight with low mount BoMar cut Dawson fiber optic front sight, 4.5 to 5 lb. trigger.

Price: TGO 1 .... **$2,999.00**
Price: TGO 2 .... **$1,899.00**
Price: TGO 3 .... **$1,295.00**

Springfield, Inc. Trophy Match Pistol

Similar to Springfield, Inc.'s Full Size model, but designed for bullseye and action shooting competition. Available with a Service Model 5" frame with matching slide and barrel in 5" and 6" lengths. Fully adjustable sights, checkered frame front strap, match barrel and bushing. In 45 ACP only. From Springfield Inc.

Price: **$1,248.00**

STI EAGLE 5.0, 6.0 PISTOL

Caliber: 9mm, 9x21, 38 & 40 Super, 40 S&W, 10mm, 45 ACP, 10-shot magazine. **Barrel:** 5", 6" bull. **Weight:** 34.5 oz. **Length:** 8.62" overall. **Grips:** Checkered polymer. **Sights:** STI front, Novak or Heine rear. **Features:** Standard frames plus 7 others; adjustable match trigger; skeletonized hammer; extended grip safety with locator pad; match-grade fit of all parts. Many options available. Introduced 1994. Made in U.S.A. by STI International.

Price: .... (5.0 Eagle) **$1,794.00**, (6.0 Eagle) **$1,894.00**

STI EXECUTIVE PISTOL

Caliber: 40 S&W. **Barrel:** 5" bull. **Weight:** 39 oz. **Length:** 8-5/8". **Grips:** Gray polymer. **Sights:** Dawson fiber optic, front; STI adjustable rear. **Features:** Stainless mag. well, front and rear serrations on slide. Made in U.S.A. by STI.

Price: **$2,389.00**

STI TROJAN

Caliber: 9mm, 38 Super, 40S&W, 45 ACP. **Barrel:** 5", 6". **Weight:** 36 oz. **Length:** 8.5". **Grips:** Rosewood. **Sights:** STI front with STI adjustable rear. **Features:** Stippled front strap, flat top slide, one-piece steel guide rod.

Price: (Trojan 5") **$1,024.00**
Price: (Trojan 6", not available in 38 Super) **$1,232.50**

WALTHER GSP MATCH PISTOL

Caliber: 22 LR, 32 S&W Long (GSP-C), 5-shot magazine. **Barrel:** 4.22". **Weight:** 44.8 oz. (22 LR), 49.4 oz. (32). **Length:** 11.8" overall. **Grips:** Walnut. **Sights:** Post front, match rear adjustable for windage and elevation. **Features:** Available with either 2.2-lb. (1000 gm) or 3-lb. (1360 gm) trigger. Spare magazine, barrel weight, tools supplied. Imported from Germany by Nygord Precision Products.

Price: GSP, with case **$1,495.00**
Price: GSP-C, with case **$1,595.00**

Includes models suitable for hunting and competitive courses of fire, both police and international.

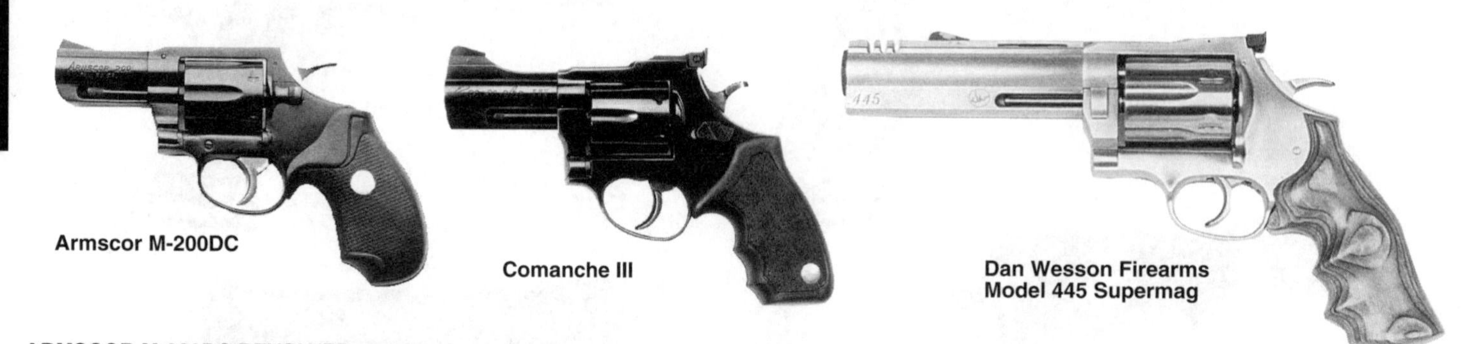
Armscor M-200DC

Comanche III

Dan Wesson Firearms Model 445 Supermag

ARMSCOR M-200DC REVOLVER

Caliber: 38 Spec., 6-shot cylinder. **Barrel:** 2-1/2", 4". **Weight:** 22 oz. (2-1/2" barrel). **Length:** 7-3/8" overall (2-1/2" barrel). **Grips:** Checkered rubber. **Sights:** Blade front, fixed notch rear. **Features:** All-steel construction; floating firing pin, transfer bar ignition; shrouded ejector rod; blue finish. Reintroduced 1996. Imported from the Philippines by K.B.I., Inc.

Price: 2-1/2" **$199.99**
Price: 4" **$205.00**

ARMSPORT MODEL 4540 REVOLVER

Caliber: 38 Special. **Barrel:** 4". **Weight:** 32 oz **Length:** 9" overall. **Sights:** Fixed rear, blade front. **Features:** Ventilated rib; blued finish. Imported from Argentina by Armsport Inc.

Price: **$140.00**

COMANCHE I, II, III DA REVOLVERS

Features: Adjustable sights. Blue or stainless finish. Distributed by SGS Importers.

Price: I 22 LR, 6" bbl, 9-shot, blue **$236.95**
Price: I 22LR, 6" bbl, 9-shot, stainless **$258.95**
Price: II 38 Special, 3", 4" bbl, 6-shot, blue. **$219.95**
Price: II 38 Special, 4" bbl, 6-shot, stainless. **$236.95**
Price: III 357 Mag, 3", 4", 6" bbl, 6-shot, blue **$253.95**
Price: III 357 Mag, 3", 4", 6" bbl, 6-shot, stainless **$274.95**
Price: II 38 Special, 3" bbl, 6-shot, stainless steel **$236.95**

DAN WESSON FIREARMS MODEL 722 SILHOUETTE REVOLVER

Caliber: 22 LR, 6-shot. **Barrel:** 10", vent heavy. **Weight:** 53 oz. **Grips:** Combat style. **Sights:** Patridge-style front, .080" narrow notch rear. **Features:** Single action only. Satin brushed stainless finish. Reintroduced 1997. Made in U.S.A. by Dan Wesson Firearms.

Price: 722 VH10 (vent heavy 10" bbl.) **$888.00**
Price: 722 VH10 SRS1 (Super Ram Silhouette, Bo-Mar sights, front hood, trigger job). **$1,164.00**

DAN WESSON FIREARMS MODEL 3220/73220 TARGET REVOLVER

Caliber: 32-20, 6-shot. **Barrel:** 2.5", 4", 6", 8", 10" standard vent, vent heavy. **Weight:** 47 oz. (6" VH). **Length:** 11.25" overall. **Grips:** Hogue Gripper rubber (walnut, exotic hardwoods optional). **Sights:** Red ramp interchangeable front, fully adjustable rear. **Features:** Bright blue (3220) or stainless (73220). Reintroduced 1997. Made in U.S.A. by Dan Wesson Firearms.

Price: 3220 VH2.5 (blued, 2.5" vent heavy bbl.) **$643.00**
Price: 73220 VH10 (stainless 10" vent heavy bbl.) **$873.00**

DAN WESSON FIREARMS MODEL 40/740 REVOLVERS

Caliber: 357 Maximum, 6-shot. **Barrel:** 4", 6", 8", 10". **Weight:** 72 oz. (8" bbl.). **Length:** 14.3" overall (8" bbl.). **Grips:** Hogue Gripper rubber (walnut or exotic hardwood optional). **Sights:** 1/8" serrated front, fully adjustable rear. **Features:** Blue or stainless steel. Made in U.S.A. by Dan Wesson Firearms.

Price: Blue, 4". **$702.00**
Price: Blue, 6". **$749.00**
Price: Blue, 8". **$795.00**
Price: Blue, 10". **$858.00**
Price: Stainless, 4" **$834.00**
Price: Stainless, 6" **$892.00**
Price: Stainless, 8" slotted **$1,024.00**
Price: Stainless, 10" **$998.00**
Price: 4", 6", 8" Compensated, blue . . . . **$749.00 to $885.00**
Price: As above, stainless. . . . . **$893.00 to $1,061.00**

Dan Wesson Firearms Model 414/7414 and 445/7445 SuperMag Revolvers

Similar size and weight as Model 40 revolvers. Chambered for 414 SuperMag or 445 SuperMag cartridge. Barrel lengths of 4", 6", 8", 10". Contact maker for complete price list. Reintroduced 1997. Made in the U.S. by Dan Wesson Firearms.

Price: 4", vent heavy, blue or stainless **$904.00**
Price: 8", vent heavy, blue or stainless **$1,026.00**
Price: 10", vent heavy, blue or stainless **$1,103.00**
Price: Compensated models . . . . **$965.00 to $1,149.00**

DAN WESSON FIREARMS MODEL 22/722 REVOLVERS

Caliber: 22 LR, 22 WMR, 6-shot. **Barrel:** 2-1/2", 4", 6", 8" or 10"; interchangeable. **Weight:** 36 oz. (2-1/2"), 44 oz. (6"). **Length:** 9-1/4" overall (4" barrel). **Grips:** Hogue Gripper rubber (walnut, exotic woods optional). **Sights:** 1/8" serrated, interchangeable front, white outline rear adjustable for windage and elevation. **Features:** Built on the same frame as the Wesson 357; smooth, wide trigger with over-travel adjustment, wide spur hammer, with short double-action travel. Available in blue or stainless steel. Reintroduced 1997. Contact Dan Wesson Firearms for complete price list.

Price: 22 VH2.5/722 VH2.5 (blued or stainless 2-1/2" bbl.) **$551.00**
Price: 22VH10/722 VH10 (blued or stainless 10" bbl.) **$750.00**

Dan Wesson 722M Small Frame Revolver

Similar to Model 22/722 except chambered for 22 WMR. Blued or stainless finish, 2-1/2", 4", 6", 8" or 10" barrels.

Price: Blued or stainless finish . . . . **$643.00 to $873.00**

DAN WESSON FIREARMS MODEL 15/715 and 32/732 REVOLVERS

Caliber: 32-20, 32 H&R Mag. (Model 32), 357 Mag. (Model 15). **Barrel:** 2-1/2", 4", 6", 8" (M32), 2-1/2", 4", 6", 8", 10" (M15); vent heavy. **Weight:** 36 oz. (2-1/2" barrel). **Length:** 9-1/4" overall (4" barrel). **Grips:** Checkered, interchangeable. **Sights:** 1/8" serrated front, fully adjustable rear. **Features:** New Generation Series. Interchangeable barrels; wide, smooth trigger, wide hammer spur; short double-action travel. Available in blue or stainless. Reintroduced 1997. Made in U.S.A. by Dan Wesson Firearms. Contact maker for full list of models.

Price: Model 15/715, 2-1/2" (blue or stainless). **$551.00**
Price: Model 15/715, 8" (blue or stainless). **$612.00**
Price: Model 15/715, compensated . . . . **$704.00 to $827.00**
Price: Model 32/732, 4" (blue or stainless). **$674.00**
Price: Model 32/732, 8" (blue or stainless). **$766.00**

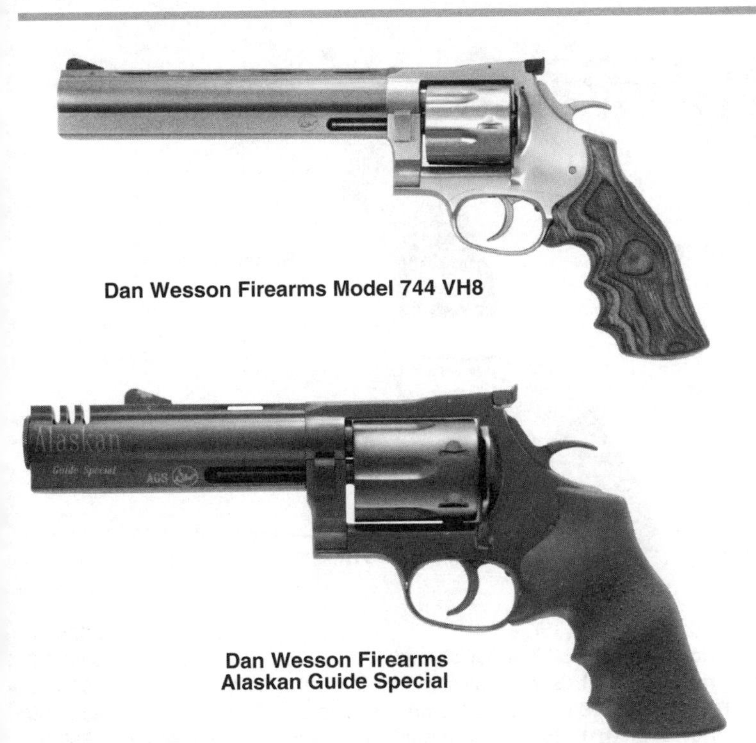

Dan Wesson Firearms Model 744 VH8

Dan Wesson Firearms
Alaskan Guide Special

Dan Wesson Firearms
Super Ram Silhouette

DAN WESSON FIREARMS MODEL 41/741, 44/744 and 45/745 REVOLVERS

Caliber: 41 Mag., 44 Mag., 45 Colt, 6-shot. **Barrel:** 4", 6", 8", 10"; interchangeable; 4", 6", 8" Compensated. **Weight:** 48 oz. (4"). **Length:** 12" overall (6" bbl.) **Grips:** Smooth. **Sights:** 1/8" serrated front, white outline rear adjustable for windage and elevation. **Features:** Available in blue or stainless steel. Smooth, wide trigger with adjustable over-travel, wide hammer spur. Available in Pistol Pac set also. Reintroduced 1997. Contact Dan Wesson Firearms for complete price list.

Price: 41 Mag., 4", vent heavy (blue or stainless). **$643.00**
Price: 44 Mag., 6", vent heavy (blue or stainless). **$689.00**
Price: 45 Colt, 8", vent heavy (blue or stainless) **$766.00**
Price: Compensated models (all calibers) . . . . **$812.00 to $934.00**

DAN WESSON FIREARMS LARGE FRAME SERIES REVOLVERS

Caliber: 41, 741/41 Magnum; 44, 744/44 Magnum; 45, 745/45 Long Colt; 360, 7360/357; 460, 7460/45. **Barrel:** 2"-10". **Weight:** 49 oz.-69 oz. **Grips:** Standard, Hogue rubber Gripper Grips. **Sights:** Standard front, serrated ramp with color insert. Standard rear, adustable wide notch. Other sight options available. **Features:** Available in blue or stainless steel. Smooth, wide trigger with overtravel, wide hammer spur. Double and single action.

Price: . . . . **$769.00 to $889.00**

DAN WESSON FIREARMS MODEL 360/7360 REVOLVERS

Caliber: 357 Mag. **Barrel:** 4", 6", 8", 10"; vent heavy. **Weight:** 64 oz. (8" barrel). **Grips:** Hogue rubber finger groove. **Sights:** Interchangeable ramp or Patridge front, fully adjustable rear. **Features:** New Generation Large Frame Series. Interchangeable barrels and grips; smooth trigger, wide hammer spur. Blue (360) or stainless (7360). Introduced 1999. Made in U.S.A. by Dan Wesson Firearms.

Price: 4" bbl., blue or stainless **$735.00**
Price: 10" bbl., blue or stainless **$873.00**
Price: Compensated models . . . . **$858.00 to $980.00**

DAN WESSON FIREARMS MODEL 460/7460 REVOLVERS

Caliber: 45 ACP, 45 Auto Rim, 45 Super, 45 Winchester Magnum and 460 Rowland. **Barrel:** 4", 6", 8", 10"; vent heavy. **Weight:** 49 oz. (4" barrel). **Grips:** Hogue rubber finger groove; interchangeable. **Sights:** Interchangeable ramp or Patridge front, fully adjustable rear. **Features:** New Generation Large Frame Series. Shoots five cartridges (45 ACP, 45 Auto Rim, 45 Super, 45 Winchester Magnum and 460 Rowland; six half-moon clips for auto cartridges included). Interchangeable barrels and grips. Available with non-fluted cylinder and Slotted Lightweight barrel shroud. Introduced 1999. Made in U.S.A. by Dan Wesson Firearms.

Price: 4" bbl., blue or stainless **$735.00**
Price: 10" bbl., blue or stainless **$888.00**
Price: Compensated models . . . . **$919.00 to $1,042.00**

DAN WESSON FIREARMS STANDARD SILHOUETTE REVOLVERS

Caliber: 357 SuperMag/Maxi, 41 Mag., 414 SuperMag, 445 SuperMag. **Barrel:** 8", 10". **Weight:** 64 oz. (8" barrel). **Length:** 14.3" overall (8" barrel). **Grips:** Hogue rubber finger groove; interchangeable. **Sights:** Patridge front, fully adjustable rear. **Features:** Interchangeable barrels and grips, fluted or non-fluted cylinder, satin brushed stainless finish. Introduced 1999. Made in U.S.A. by Dan Wesson Firearms.

Price: 357 SuperMag/Maxi, 8" **$1,057.00**
Price: 41 Mag., 10" **$888.00**
Price: 414 SuperMag., 8" **$1,057.00**
Price: 445 SuperMag., 8" **$1,057.00**

Dan Wesson Firearms Super Ram Silhouette Revolver

Similar to Standard Silhouette except has 10 land and groove Laser Coat barrel, Bo-Mar target sights with hooded front, special laser engraving. Fluted or non-fluted cylinder. Introduced 1999. Made in U.S.A. by Dan Wesson Firearms.

Price: 357 SuperMag/Maxi, 414 SuperMag., 445 SuperMag., 8", blue or stainless **$1,364.00**
Price: 41 Magnum, 44 Magnum, 8", blue or stainless **$1,241.00**
Price: 41 Magnum, 44 Magnum, 10", blue or stainless **$1,333.00**

DAN WESSON FIREARMS ALASKAN GUIDE SPECIAL

Caliber: 445 SuperMag, 44 Magnum. **Barrel:** Compensated 4" vent heavy barrel assembly. **Features:** Stainless steel with baked on, non-glare, matte black coating, special laser engraving.

Price: Model 7445 VH4C AGS **$995.00**
Price: Model 744 VH4C AGS **$855.00**

EAA WINDICATOR REVOLVERS

Caliber: 38 Spec., 6-shot; 357 magnum, 6-shot. **Barrel:** 2", 4". **Weight:** 38 oz. (22 rimfire, 4"). **Length:** 8.5" overall (4" bbl.). **Grips:** Rubber with finger grooves. **Sights:** Blade front, fixed or adjustable on rimfires; fixed only on 32, 38. **Features:** Swing-out cylinder; hammer block safety; blue finish. Introduced 1991. Imported from Germany by European American Armory.

Price: 38 Special 2" **$249.00**
Price: 38 Special, 4" **$259.00**
Price: 357 Magnum, 2" **$259.00**
Price: 357 Magnum, 4" **$279.00**

KORTH COMBAT REVOLVER

Caliber: .357 Mag., .32 S&W Long, 9mm Para., .22 WMR, .22 LR. **Barrel:** 3", 4", 5-1/4", 6"; 8". **Sights:** Fully-adjustable, rear; Baughman ramp, front. **Grips:** Walnut (checkered or smooth). Also available as a Target model in .22 LR, .38 Spl., .32 S&W Long, .357 Mag. with undercut partridge front sight; fully-adjustable rear. Made in Germany. Imported by Korth USA.

Price: . . . . From **$5,442.00**

Medusa Model 47

Ruger GP-161

Ruger KGP-141

KORTH TROJA REVOLVER

Caliber: .357 Mag. **Barrel:** 6". **Finish:** Matte blue. **Grips:** Smooth, oversized finger contoured walnut. **Features:** Maintaining all of the precision German craftsmanship that has made this line famous, the final surface finish is not as finely polished as the firm's other products - thus the lower price. Introduced 2003. Imported from Germany by Korth USA.

Price: . . . . From **$3,995.00**

MEDUSA MODEL 47 REVOLVER

Caliber: Most 9mm, 38 and 357 caliber cartridges; 6-shot cylinder. **Barrel:** 2-1/2", 3", 4", 5", 6"; fluted. **Weight:** 39 oz. **Length:** 10" overall (4" barrel). **Grips:** Gripper-style rubber. **Sights:** Changeable front blades, fully adjustable rear. **Features:** Patented extractor allows gun to chamber, fire and extract over 25 different cartridges in the .355 to .357 range, without half-moon clips. Steel frame and cylinder; match quality barrel. Matte blue finish. Introduced 1996. Made in U.S.A. by Phillips & Rogers, Inc.

Price: **$899.00**

ROSSI MODEL 351/352 REVOLVERS

Caliber: 38 Special +P, 5-shot. **Barrel:** 2". **Weight:** 24 oz. **Length:** 6-1/2" overall. **Grips:** Rubber. **Sights:** Blade front, fixed rear. **Features:** Patented key-lock Taurus Security System; forged steel frame handles +P ammunition. Introduced 2001. Imported by BrazTech/Taurus.

Price: Model 351 (blued finish) **$298.00**
Price: Model 352 (stainless finish) **$345.00**

ROSSI MODEL 461/462 REVOLVERS

Caliber: 357 Magnum +P, 6-shot. **Barrel:** 2". **Weight:** 26 oz. **Length:** 6-1/2" overall. **Grips:** Rubber. **Sights:** Fixed. **Features:** Single/double action. Patented key-lock Taurus Security System; forged steel frame handles +P ammunition. Introduced 2001. Imported by BrazTech/Taurus.

Price: Model 461 (blued finish) **$298.00**
Price: Model 462 (stainless finish) **$345.00**

ROSSI MODEL 971/972 REVOLVERS

Caliber: 357 Magnum +P, 6-shot. **Barrel:** 4", 6". **Weight:** 40-44 oz. **Length:** 8-1/2" or 10-1/2" overall. **Grips:** Rubber. **Sights:** Fully adjustable. **Features:** Single/double action. Patented key-lock Taurus Security System; forged steel frame handles +P ammunition. Introduced 2001. Imported by BrazTech/Taurus.

Price: Model 971 (blued finish, 4" barrel) **$345.00**
Price: Model 972 (stainless steel finish, 6" barrel) **$391.00**

Rossi Model 851

Similar to Model 971/972, chambered for 38 Special +P. Blued finish, 4" barrel. Introduced 2001. From BrazTech/Taurus.

Price: **$298.00**

RUGER GP-100 REVOLVERS

Caliber: 38 Spec., 357 Mag., 6-shot. **Barrel:** 3", 3" full shroud, 4", 4" full shroud, 6", 6" full shroud. **Weight:** 3" barrel-35 oz., 3" full shroud-36 oz., 4" barrel-37 oz., 4" full shroud-38 oz. **Sights:** Fixed; adjustable on 4" full shroud, all 6" barrels. **Grips:** Ruger Santoprene Cushioned Grip with Goncalo Alves inserts. **Features:** Uses action, frame incorporating improvements and features of both the Security-Six and Redhawk revolvers. Full length, short ejector shroud. Satin blue and stainless steel.

Price: GP-141 (357, 4" full shroud, adj. sights, blue) **$499.00**
Price: GP-160 (357, 6", adj. sights, blue) **$499.00**
Price: GP-161 (357, 6" full shroud, adj. sights, blue), 46 oz. **$499.00**
Price: GPF-331 (357, 3" full shroud) **$495.00**

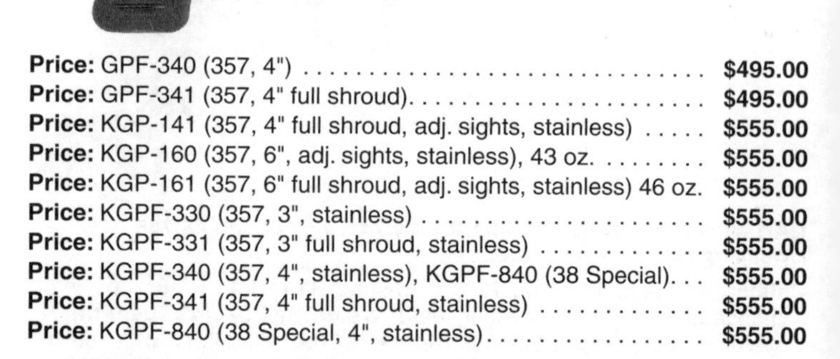

Ruger KSP-331X

Price: GPF-340 (357, 4") **$495.00**
Price: GPF-341 (357, 4" full shroud) **$495.00**
Price: KGP-141 (357, 4" full shroud, adj. sights, stainless) **$555.00**
Price: KGP-160 (357, 6", adj. sights, stainless), 43 oz. **$555.00**
Price: KGP-161 (357, 6" full shroud, adj. sights, stainless) 46 oz. **$555.00**
Price: KGPF-330 (357, 3", stainless) **$555.00**
Price: KGPF-331 (357, 3" full shroud, stainless) **$555.00**
Price: KGPF-340 (357, 4", stainless), KGPF-840 (38 Special). . . **$555.00**
Price: KGPF-341 (357, 4" full shroud, stainless) **$555.00**
Price: KGPF-840 (38 Special, 4", stainless) **$555.00**

Ruger SP101 Double-Action-Only Revolver

Similar to standard SP101 except double-action-only with no single-action sear notch. Spurless hammer for snag-free handling, floating firing pin and Ruger's patented transfer bar safety system. Available with 2-1/4" barrel in 357 Magnum. Weighs 25 oz., overall length 7.06". Natural brushed satin, high-polish stainless steel. Introduced 1993.

Price: KSP321XL (357 Mag.) **$495.00**

RUGER SP101 REVOLVERS

Caliber: 22 LR, 32 H&R Mag., 6-shot; 38 Spec. +P, 357 Mag., 5-shot. **Barrel:** 2-1/4", 3-1/16", 4". **Weight:** (38 & 357 mag models) 2-1/4"-25 oz.; 3-1/16"-27 oz. **Sights:** Adjustable on 22, 32, fixed on others. **Grips:** Ruger Cushioned Grip with inserts. **Features:** Incorporates improvements and features found in the GP-100 revolvers into a compact, small frame, double-action revolver. Full-length ejector shroud. Stainless steel only. Introduced 1988.

Price: KSP-821X (2-1/4", 38 Spec.) **$495.00**
Price: KSP-831X (3-1/16", 38 Spec.) **$495.00**
Price: KSP-241X (4" heavy bbl., 22 LR), 34 oz. **$495.00**
Price: KSP-3231X (3-1/16", 32 H&R), 30 oz. **$495.00**
Price: KSP-321X (2-1/4", 357 Mag.). **$495.00**
Price: KSP-331X (3-1/16", 357 Mag.). **$495.00**
Price: KSP-3241X (32 Mag., 4" bbl) **$495.00**

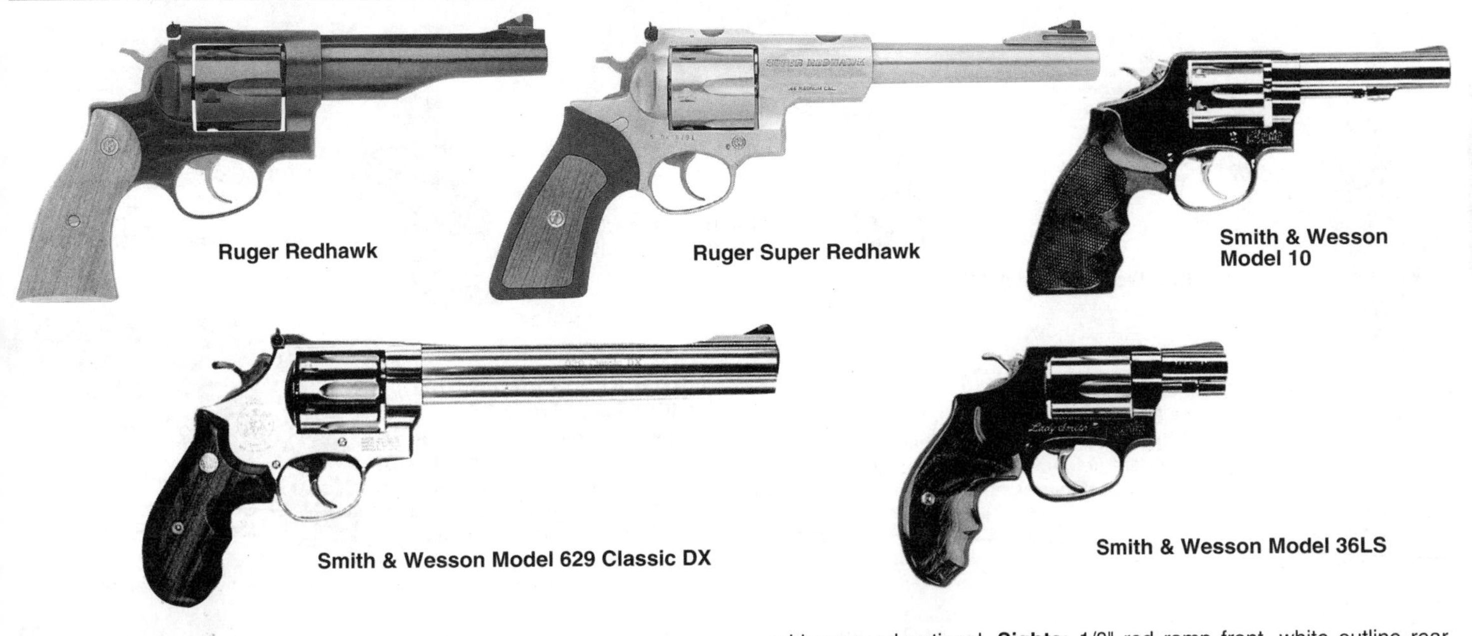

Ruger Redhawk

Ruger Super Redhawk

Smith & Wesson Model 10

Smith & Wesson Model 629 Classic DX

Smith & Wesson Model 36LS

RUGER REDHAWK

Caliber: 44 Rem. Mag., 45 Colt, 6-shot. **Barrel:** 5-1/2", 7-1/2". **Weight:** About 54 oz. (7-1/2" bbl.). **Length:** 13" overall (7-1/2" barrel). **Grips:** Square butt cushioned grip panels. **Sights:** Interchangeable Patridge-type front, rear adjustable for windage and elevation. **Features:** Stainless steel, brushed satin finish, blued ordnance steel. 9-1/2" sight radius. Introduced 1979.

Price: Blued, 44 Mag., 5-1/2" RH-445, 7-1/2" RH-44 .... **$585.00**
Price: Blued, 44 Mag., 7-1/2" RH44R, with scope mount, rings .. **$625.00**
Price: Stainless, 44 Mag., KRH445, 5-1/2", 7-1/2" KRH-44 ..... **$645.00**
Price: Stainless, 44 Mag., 7-1/2", with scope mount, rings KRH-44R **$685.00**
Price: Stainless, 45 Colt, KRH455, 5-1/2", 7-1/2" KRH-45 ...... **$645.00**
Price: Stainless, 45 Colt, 7-1/2", with scope mount and rings KRH-45R **$685.00**

Ruger Super Redhawk Revolver

Similar to standard Redhawk except has heavy extended frame with Ruger Integral Scope Mounting System on wide topstrap. Also available 454 Casull and 480 Ruger. Wide hammer spur lowered for better scope clearance. Incorporates mechanical design features and improvements of GP-100. Choice of 7-1/2" or 9-1/2" barrel, both ramp front sight base with Redhawk-style Interchangeable Insert sight blades, adjustable rear sight. Comes with Ruger "Cushioned Grip" panels with wood panels. Target gray stainless steel. Introduced 1987.

Price: KSRH-7 (7-1/2"), KSRH-9 (9-1/2"), 44 Mag **$685.00**
Price: KSRH-7454 (7-1/2") 454 Casull, 9-1/2 KSRH-9454 ...... **$775.00**
Price: KSRH-7480 (7-1/2") 480 Ruger **$775.00**
Price: KSRH-9480 (9-1/2") 480 Ruger **$775.00**

SMITH & WESSON MODEL 10 M&P HB REVOLVER

Caliber: 38 Spec., 6-shot. **Barrel:** 4". **Weight:** 33.5 oz. **Length:** 9-5/16" overall. **Grips:** Uncle Mike's Combat soft rubber; square butt. **Sights:** Fixed; ramp front, square notch rear.

Price: Blue **$496.00**

SMITH & WESSON COMMEMORATIVE MODEL 29

Features: Reflects original Model 29: 6-1/2" barrel, four-screw side plate, over-sized target grips, red vamp front and black blade rear sights, 150th Anniversary logo, engraved, gold-plated, blue, in wood presentation case. Limited.

Price: .... **NA**

SMITH & WESSON MODEL 629 REVOLVERS

Caliber: 44 Magnum, 44 S&W Special, 6-shot. **Barrel:** 5", 6", 8-3/8". **Weight:** 47 oz. (6" bbl.). **Length:** 11-3/8" overall (6" bbl.). **Grips:** Soft rubber; wood optional. **Sights:** 1/8" red ramp front, white outline rear, internal lock, adjustable for windage and elevation.

Price: Model 629, 4" **$717.00**
Price: Model 629, 6" **$739.00**
Price: Model 629, 8-3/8" barrel **$756.00**

Smith & Wesson Model 629 Classic Revolver

Similar to standard Model 629, full-lug 5", 6-1/2" or 8-3/8" barrel, chamfered front of cylinder, interchangeable red ramp front sight with adjustable white outline rear, Hogue grips with S&W monogram, frame is drilled and tapped for scope mounting. Factory accurizing and endurance packages. Overall length with 5" barrel is 10-1/2"; weighs 51 oz. Introduced 1990.

Price: Model 629 Classic (stainless), 5", 6-1/2" **$768.00**
Price: As above, 8-3/8" **$793.00**
Price: Model 629 with HiViz front sight **$814.00**

Smith & Wesson Model 629 Classic DX Revolver

Similar to Model 629 Classic, offered only with 6-1/2" or 8-3/8" full-lug barrel, five front sights: red ramp, black Patridge, black Patridge with gold bead, black ramp, black Patridge with white dot, white outline rear sight, adjustable sight, internal lock. Hogue combat-style and wood round butt grip. Introduced 1991.

Price: Model 629 Classic DX, 6-1/2" **$986.00**
Price: As above, 8-3/8" **$1,018.00**

SMITH & WESSON MODEL 37 CHIEF'S SPECIAL & AIRWEIGHT

Caliber: 38 Spec. +P, 5-shot. **Barrel:** 1-7/8". **Weight:** 19-1/2 oz. (2" bbl.); 13-1/2 oz. (Airweight). **Length:** 6-1/2" (round butt). **Grips:** Round butt soft rubber. **Sights:** Fixed, serrated ramp front, square notch rear. Glass beaded finish.

Price: Model 37 .... **$523.00**

Smith & Wesson Model 637 Airweight Revolver

Similar to the Model 37 Airweight except has alloy frame, stainless steel barrel, cylinder and yoke; rated for 38 Spec. +P; Uncle Mike's Boot Grip. Weighs 15 oz. Introduced 1996. Made in U.S.A. by Smith & Wesson.

Price: **$548.00**

SMITH & WESSON MODEL 36LS, 60LS LADYSMITH

Caliber: .38 S&W Special +P, 5-shot. **Barrel:** 1-7/8". **Weight:** 20 oz. **Length:** 6-5/16 overall (1-7/8" barrel). **Grips:** Combat Dymondwood® grips with S&W monogram. **Sights:** Serrated ramp front, fixed notch rear. **Features:** Speedloader cutout. Comes in a fitted carry/storage case. Introduced 1989.

Price: Model 36LS **$518.00**
Price: Model 60LS, 2-1/8" barrel stainless, 357 Magnum **$566.00**

Smith & Wesson Model 65LS

Smith & Wesson Model 317 AirLite

Smith & Wesson Model 625

Smith & Wesson Model 340 PD Airlite Sc

SMITH & WESSON MODEL 60 CHIEF'S SPECIAL

Caliber: 357 Magnum, 5-shot. **Barrel:** 2-1/8" or 3". **Weight:** 24 oz. **Length:** 7-1/2 overall (3" barrel). **Grips:** Rounded butt synthetic grips. **Sights:** Fixed, serrated ramp front, square notch rear. **Features:** Stainless steel construction. 3" full lug barrel, adjustable sights, internal lock. Made in U.S.A. by Smith & Wesson.

Price: 2-1/8" barrel **$541.00**
Price: 3" barrel **$574.00**

SMITH & WESSON MODEL 65

Caliber: 357 Mag. and 38 Spec., 6-shot. **Barrel:** 4". **Weight:** 34 oz. **Length:** 9-5/16" overall (4" bbl.). **Grips:** Uncle Mike's Combat. **Sights:** 1/8" serrated ramp front, fixed square notch rear. **Features:** Heavy barrel. Stainless steel construction. Internal lock.

Price: **$531.00**

SMITH & WESSON MODEL 317 AIRLITE, 317 LADYSMITH REVOLVERS

Caliber: 22 LR, 8-shot. **Barrel:** 1-7/8" 3". **Weight:** 9.9 oz. **Length:** 6-3/16" overall. **Grips:** Dymondwood Boot or Uncle Mike's Boot. **Sights:** Serrated ramp front, fixed notch rear. **Features:** Aluminum alloy, carbon and stainless steels, and titanium construction. Short spur hammer, smooth combat trigger. Clear Cote finish. Introduced 1997. Made in U.S.A. by Smith & Wesson.

Price: With Uncle Mike's Boot grip **$550.00**
Price: With DymondWood Boot grip, 3" barrel, HiViz front sight, internal lock **$600.00**
Price: Model 317 LadySmith (DymondWood only, comes with display case) **$596.00**

SMITH & WESSON MODEL 351PD

Caliber: 22 Mag. **Barrel:** 2". **Features:** Seven-shot, Scandium alloy.

Price: **$625.00**

SMITH & WESSON MODEL 64 STAINLESS M&P

Caliber: 38 Spec. +P, 6-shot. **Barrel:** 2", 3", 4". **Weight:** 34 oz. **Length:** 9-5/16" overall. **Grips:** Soft rubber. **Sights:** Fixed, 1/8" serrated ramp front, square notch rear. **Features:** Satin finished stainless steel, square butt.

Price: 2" **$522.00**
Price: 3", 4" **$532.00**

SMITH & WESSON MODEL 65LS LADYSMITH

Caliber: 357 Magnum, 38 Spec. +P, 6-shot. **Barrel:** 3". **Weight:** 31 oz. **Length:** 7.94" overall. **Grips:** Rosewood, round butt. **Sights:** Serrated ramp front, fixed notch rear. **Features:** Stainless steel with frosted finish. Smooth combat trigger, service hammer, shrouded ejector rod. Comes with case. Introduced 1992.

Price: **$584.00**

SMITH & WESSON MODEL 66 STAINLESS COMBAT MAGNUM

Caliber: 357 Mag. and 38 Spec. +P, 6-shot. **Barrel:** 2-1/2", 4", 6". **Weight:** 36 oz. (4" barrel). **Length:** 9-9/16" overall. **Grips:** Soft rubber. **Sights:** Red ramp front, micro-click rear adjustable for windage and elevation. **Features:** Satin finish stainless steel. Internal lock.

Price: 2-1/2" **$590.00**
Price: 4" **$579.00**
Price: 6" **$608.00**

SMITH & WESSON MODEL 67 COMBAT MASTERPIECE

Caliber: 38 Special, 6-shot. **Barrel:** 4". **Weight:** 32 oz. **Length:** 9-5/16" overall. **Grips:** Soft rubber. **Sights:** Red ramp front, micro-click rear ad-justable for windage and elevation. **Features:** Stainless steel with satin finish. Smooth combat trigger, semi-target hammer. Introduced 1994.

Price: **$585.00**

Smith & Wesson Model 686 Magnum PLUS Revolver

Similar to the Model 686 except has 7-shot cylinder, 2-1/2", 4" or 6" barrel. Weighs 34-1/2 oz., overall length 7-1/2" (2-1/2" barrel). Hogue rubber grips. Internal lock. Introduced 1996. Made in U.S.A. by Smith & Wesson.

Price: 2-1/2" barrel **$631.00**
Price: 4" barrel **$653.00**
Price: 6" barrel **$663.00**

SMITH & WESSON MODEL 625 REVOLVER

Caliber: 45 ACP, 6-shot. **Barrel:** 5". **Weight:** 46 oz. **Length:** 11.375" overall. **Grips:** Soft rubber; wood optional. **Sights:** Patridge front on ramp, S&W micrometer click rear adjustable for windage and elevation. **Features:** Stainless steel construction with .400" semi-target hammer, .312" smooth combat trigger; full lug barrel. Glass beaded finish. Introduced 1989.

Price: 5" **$745.00**
Price: 4" with internal lock **$745.00**

SMITH & WESSON MODEL 640 CENTENNIAL DA ONLY

Caliber: 357 Mag., 38 Spec. +P, 5-shot. **Barrel:** 2-1/8". **Weight:** 25 oz. **Length:** 6-3/4" overall. **Grips:** Uncle Mike's Boot Grip. **Sights:** Serrated ramp front, fixed notch rear. **Features:** Stainless steel. Fully concealed hammer, snag-proof smooth edges. Internal lock. Introduced 1995 in 357 Magnum.

Price: **$599.00**

SMITH & WESSON MODEL 617 K-22 MASTERPIECE

Caliber: 22 LR, 6- or 10-shot. **Barrel:** 4", 6", 8-3/8". **Weight:** 42 oz. (4" barrel). **Length:** NA. **Grips:** Soft rubber. **Sights:** Patridge front, adjustable rear. Drilled and tapped for scope mount. **Features:** Stainless steel with satin finish; 4" has .312" smooth trigger, .375" semi-target hammer; 6" has either .312" combat or .400" serrated trigger, .375" semi-target or .500" target hammer; 8-3/8" with .400" serrated trigger, .500" target hammer. Introduced 1990.

Price: 4" **$644.00**
Price: 6", target hammer, target trigger **$625.00**
Price: 6", 10-shot **$669.00**
Price: 8-3/8", 10 shot **$679.00**

SMITH & WESSON MODEL 610 CLASSIC HUNTER REVOLVER

Caliber: 10mm, 40 S&W, 6-shot cylinder. **Barrel:** 6-1/2" full lug. **Weight:** 52 oz. **Length:** 12" overall. **Grips:** Hogue rubber combat. **Sights:** Interchangeable blade front, micro-click rear adjustable for windage and elevation. **Features:** Stainless steel construction; target hammer, target trigger; unfluted cylinder; drilled and tapped for scope mounting. Introduced 1998.

Price: **$785.00**

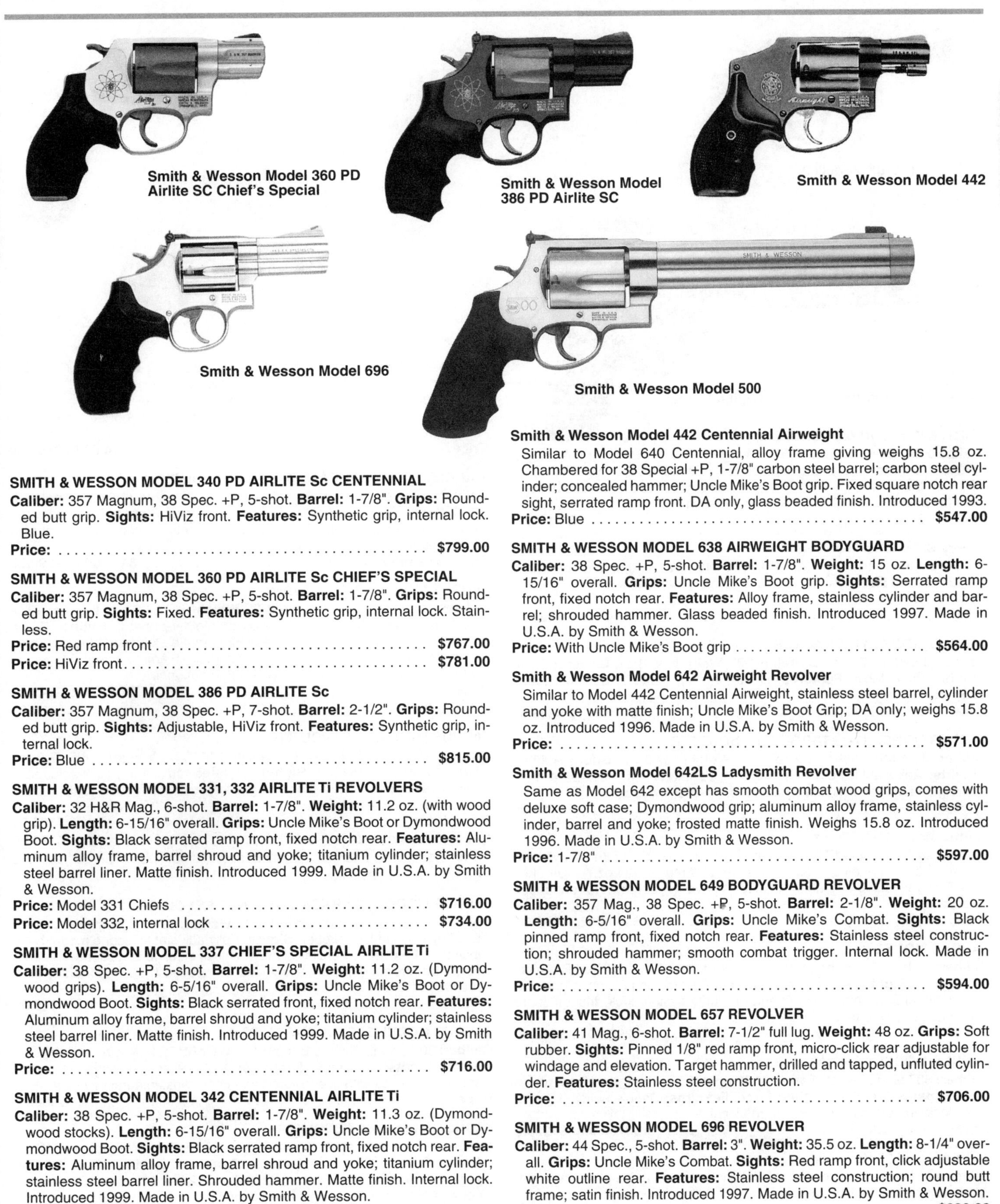

Smith & Wesson Model 360 PD Airlite SC Chief's Special

Smith & Wesson Model 386 PD Airlite SC

Smith & Wesson Model 442

Smith & Wesson Model 696

Smith & Wesson Model 500

SMITH & WESSON MODEL 340 PD AIRLITE Sc CENTENNIAL

Caliber: 357 Magnum, 38 Spec. +P, 5-shot. **Barrel:** 1-7/8". **Grips:** Rounded butt grip. **Sights:** HiViz front. **Features:** Synthetic grip, internal lock. Blue.

Price: **$799.00**

SMITH & WESSON MODEL 360 PD AIRLITE Sc CHIEF'S SPECIAL

Caliber: 357 Magnum, 38 Spec. +P, 5-shot. **Barrel:** 1-7/8". **Grips:** Rounded butt grip. **Sights:** Fixed. **Features:** Synthetic grip, internal lock. Stainless.

Price: Red ramp front **$767.00**
Price: HiViz front **$781.00**

SMITH & WESSON MODEL 386 PD AIRLITE Sc

Caliber: 357 Magnum, 38 Spec. +P, 7-shot. **Barrel:** 2-1/2". **Grips:** Rounded butt grip. **Sights:** Adjustable, HiViz front. **Features:** Synthetic grip, internal lock.

Price: Blue **$815.00**

SMITH & WESSON MODEL 331, 332 AIRLITE Ti REVOLVERS

Caliber: 32 H&R Mag., 6-shot. **Barrel:** 1-7/8". **Weight:** 11.2 oz. (with wood grip). **Length:** 6-15/16" overall. **Grips:** Uncle Mike's Boot or Dymondwood Boot. **Sights:** Black serrated ramp front, fixed notch rear. **Features:** Aluminum alloy frame, barrel shroud and yoke; titanium cylinder; stainless steel barrel liner. Matte finish. Introduced 1999. Made in U.S.A. by Smith & Wesson.

Price: Model 331 Chiefs **$716.00**
Price: Model 332, internal lock **$734.00**

SMITH & WESSON MODEL 337 CHIEF'S SPECIAL AIRLITE Ti

Caliber: 38 Spec. +P, 5-shot. **Barrel:** 1-7/8". **Weight:** 11.2 oz. (Dymondwood grips). **Length:** 6-5/16" overall. **Grips:** Uncle Mike's Boot or Dymondwood Boot. **Sights:** Black serrated front, fixed notch rear. **Features:** Aluminum alloy frame, barrel shroud and yoke; titanium cylinder; stainless steel barrel liner. Matte finish. Introduced 1999. Made in U.S.A. by Smith & Wesson.

Price: **$716.00**

SMITH & WESSON MODEL 342 CENTENNIAL AIRLITE Ti

Caliber: 38 Spec. +P, 5-shot. **Barrel:** 1-7/8". **Weight:** 11.3 oz. (Dymondwood stocks). **Length:** 6-15/16" overall. **Grips:** Uncle Mike's Boot or Dymondwood Boot. **Sights:** Black serrated ramp front, fixed notch rear. **Features:** Aluminum alloy frame, barrel shroud and yoke; titanium cylinder; stainless steel barrel liner. Shrouded hammer. Matte finish. Internal lock. Introduced 1999. Made in U.S.A. by Smith & Wesson.

Price: **$734.00**

Smith & Wesson Model 442 Centennial Airweight

Similar to Model 640 Centennial, alloy frame giving weighs 15.8 oz. Chambered for 38 Special +P, 1-7/8" carbon steel barrel; carbon steel cylinder; concealed hammer; Uncle Mike's Boot grip. Fixed square notch rear sight, serrated ramp front. DA only, glass beaded finish. Introduced 1993.

Price: Blue **$547.00**

SMITH & WESSON MODEL 638 AIRWEIGHT BODYGUARD

Caliber: 38 Spec. +P, 5-shot. **Barrel:** 1-7/8". **Weight:** 15 oz. **Length:** 6-15/16" overall. **Grips:** Uncle Mike's Boot grip. **Sights:** Serrated ramp front, fixed notch rear. **Features:** Alloy frame, stainless cylinder and barrel; shrouded hammer. Glass beaded finish. Introduced 1997. Made in U.S.A. by Smith & Wesson.

Price: With Uncle Mike's Boot grip **$564.00**

Smith & Wesson Model 642 Airweight Revolver

Similar to Model 442 Centennial Airweight, stainless steel barrel, cylinder and yoke with matte finish; Uncle Mike's Boot Grip; DA only; weighs 15.8 oz. Introduced 1996. Made in U.S.A. by Smith & Wesson.

Price: **$571.00**

Smith & Wesson Model 642LS Ladysmith Revolver

Same as Model 642 except has smooth combat wood grips, comes with deluxe soft case; Dymondwood grip; aluminum alloy frame, stainless cylinder, barrel and yoke; frosted matte finish. Weighs 15.8 oz. Introduced 1996. Made in U.S.A. by Smith & Wesson.

Price: 1-7/8" **$597.00**

SMITH & WESSON MODEL 649 BODYGUARD REVOLVER

Caliber: 357 Mag., 38 Spec. +P, 5-shot. **Barrel:** 2-1/8". **Weight:** 20 oz. **Length:** 6-5/16" overall. **Grips:** Uncle Mike's Combat. **Sights:** Black pinned ramp front, fixed notch rear. **Features:** Stainless steel construction; shrouded hammer; smooth combat trigger. Internal lock. Made in U.S.A. by Smith & Wesson.

Price: **$594.00**

SMITH & WESSON MODEL 657 REVOLVER

Caliber: 41 Mag., 6-shot. **Barrel:** 7-1/2" full lug. **Weight:** 48 oz. **Grips:** Soft rubber. **Sights:** Pinned 1/8" red ramp front, micro-click rear adjustable for windage and elevation. Target hammer, drilled and tapped, unfluted cylinder. **Features:** Stainless steel construction.

Price: **$706.00**

SMITH & WESSON MODEL 696 REVOLVER

Caliber: 44 Spec., 5-shot. **Barrel:** 3". **Weight:** 35.5 oz. **Length:** 8-1/4" overall. **Grips:** Uncle Mike's Combat. **Sights:** Red ramp front, click adjustable white outline rear. **Features:** Stainless steel construction; round butt frame; satin finish. Introduced 1997. Made in U.S.A. by Smith & Wesson.

Price: **$620.00**

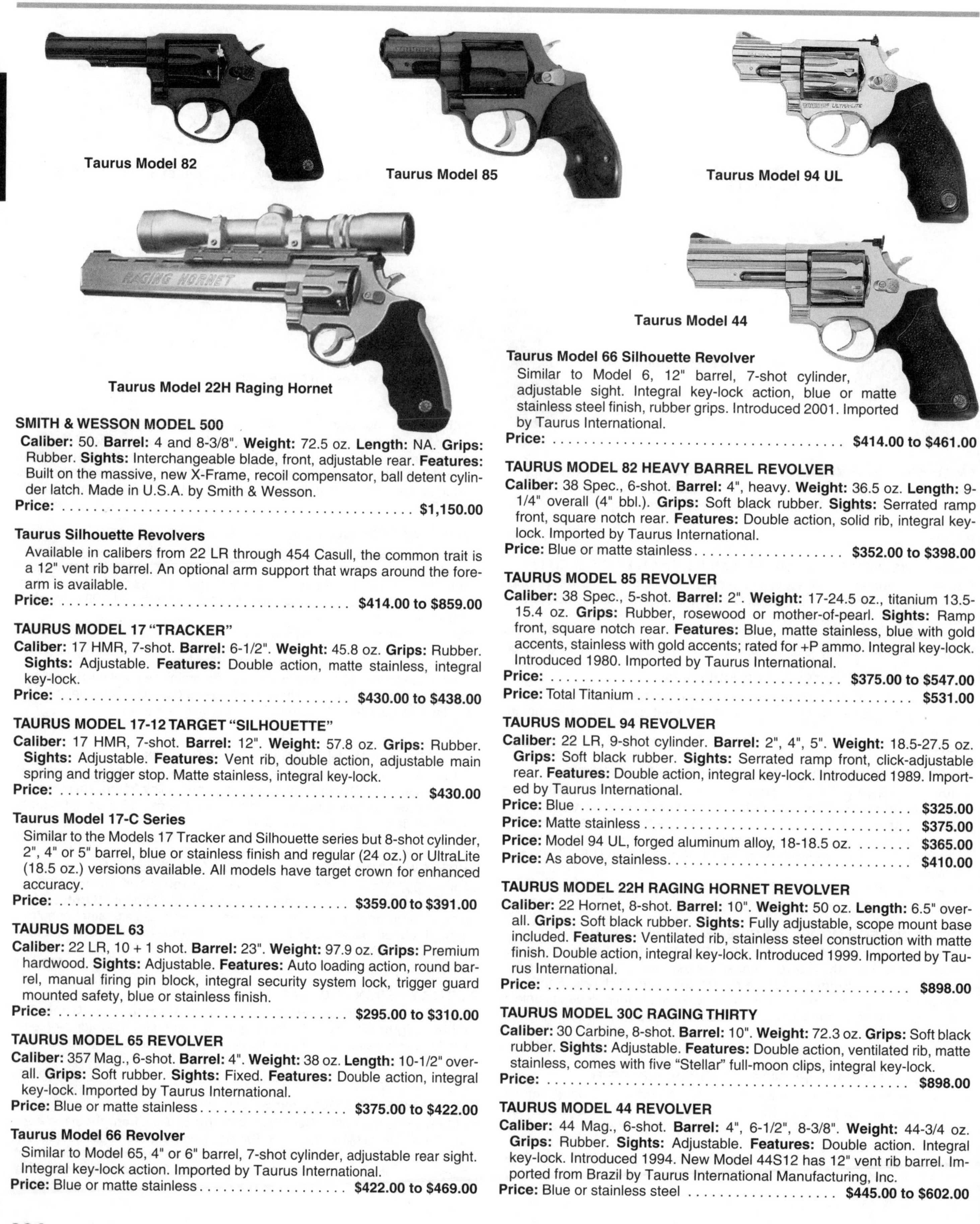

Taurus Model 82

Taurus Model 85

Taurus Model 94 UL

Taurus Model 44

Taurus Model 22H Raging Hornet

SMITH & WESSON MODEL 500

Caliber: 50. **Barrel:** 4 and 8-3/8". **Weight:** 72.5 oz. **Length:** NA. **Grips:** Rubber. **Sights:** Interchangeable blade, front, adjustable rear. **Features:** Built on the massive, new X-Frame, recoil compensator, ball detent cylinder latch. Made in U.S.A. by Smith & Wesson.

Price: **$1,150.00**

Taurus Silhouette Revolvers

Available in calibers from 22 LR through 454 Casull, the common trait is a 12" vent rib barrel. An optional arm support that wraps around the forearm is available.

Price: .... **$414.00 to $859.00**

TAURUS MODEL 17 "TRACKER"

Caliber: 17 HMR, 7-shot. **Barrel:** 6-1/2". **Weight:** 45.8 oz. **Grips:** Rubber. **Sights:** Adjustable. **Features:** Double action, matte stainless, integral key-lock.

Price: .... **$430.00 to $438.00**

TAURUS MODEL 17-12 TARGET "SILHOUETTE"

Caliber: 17 HMR, 7-shot. **Barrel:** 12". **Weight:** 57.8 oz. **Grips:** Rubber. **Sights:** Adjustable. **Features:** Vent rib, double action, adjustable main spring and trigger stop. Matte stainless, integral key-lock.

Price: **$430.00**

Taurus Model 17-C Series

Similar to the Models 17 Tracker and Silhouette series but 8-shot cylinder, 2", 4" or 5" barrel, blue or stainless finish and regular (24 oz.) or UltraLite (18.5 oz.) versions available. All models have target crown for enhanced accuracy.

Price: .... **$359.00 to $391.00**

TAURUS MODEL 63

Caliber: 22 LR, 10 + 1 shot. **Barrel:** 23". **Weight:** 97.9 oz. **Grips:** Premium hardwood. **Sights:** Adjustable. **Features:** Auto loading action, round barrel, manual firing pin block, integral security system lock, trigger guard mounted safety, blue or stainless finish.

Price: .... **$295.00 to $310.00**

TAURUS MODEL 65 REVOLVER

Caliber: 357 Mag., 6-shot. **Barrel:** 4". **Weight:** 38 oz. **Length:** 10-1/2" overall. **Grips:** Soft rubber. **Sights:** Fixed. **Features:** Double action, integral key-lock. Imported by Taurus International.

Price: Blue or matte stainless .... **$375.00 to $422.00**

Taurus Model 66 Revolver

Similar to Model 65, 4" or 6" barrel, 7-shot cylinder, adjustable rear sight. Integral key-lock action. Imported by Taurus International.

Price: Blue or matte stainless .... **$422.00 to $469.00**

Taurus Model 66 Silhouette Revolver

Similar to Model 6, 12" barrel, 7-shot cylinder, adjustable sight. Integral key-lock action, blue or matte stainless steel finish, rubber grips. Introduced 2001. Imported by Taurus International.

Price: .... **$414.00 to $461.00**

TAURUS MODEL 82 HEAVY BARREL REVOLVER

Caliber: 38 Spec., 6-shot. **Barrel:** 4", heavy. **Weight:** 36.5 oz. **Length:** 9-1/4" overall (4" bbl.). **Grips:** Soft black rubber. **Sights:** Serrated ramp front, square notch rear. **Features:** Double action, solid rib, integral key-lock. Imported by Taurus International.

Price: Blue or matte stainless .... **$352.00 to $398.00**

TAURUS MODEL 85 REVOLVER

Caliber: 38 Spec., 5-shot. **Barrel:** 2". **Weight:** 17-24.5 oz., titanium 13.5-15.4 oz. **Grips:** Rubber, rosewood or mother-of-pearl. **Sights:** Ramp front, square notch rear. **Features:** Blue, matte stainless, blue with gold accents, stainless with gold accents; rated for +P ammo. Integral key-lock. Introduced 1980. Imported by Taurus International.

Price: .... **$375.00 to $547.00**

Price: Total Titanium **$531.00**

TAURUS MODEL 94 REVOLVER

Caliber: 22 LR, 9-shot cylinder. **Barrel:** 2", 4", 5". **Weight:** 18.5-27.5 oz. **Grips:** Soft black rubber. **Sights:** Serrated ramp front, click-adjustable rear. **Features:** Double action, integral key-lock. Introduced 1989. Imported by Taurus International.

Price: Blue **$325.00**

Price: Matte stainless **$375.00**

Price: Model 94 UL, forged aluminum alloy, 18-18.5 oz. **$365.00**

Price: As above, stainless **$410.00**

TAURUS MODEL 22H RAGING HORNET REVOLVER

Caliber: 22 Hornet, 8-shot. **Barrel:** 10". **Weight:** 50 oz. **Length:** 6.5" overall. **Grips:** Soft black rubber. **Sights:** Fully adjustable, scope mount base included. **Features:** Ventilated rib, stainless steel construction with matte finish. Double action, integral key-lock. Introduced 1999. Imported by Taurus International.

Price: **$898.00**

TAURUS MODEL 30C RAGING THIRTY

Caliber: 30 Carbine, 8-shot. **Barrel:** 10". **Weight:** 72.3 oz. **Grips:** Soft black rubber. **Sights:** Adjustable. **Features:** Double action, ventilated rib, matte stainless, comes with five "Stellar" full-moon clips, integral key-lock.

Price: **$898.00**

TAURUS MODEL 44 REVOLVER

Caliber: 44 Mag., 6-shot. **Barrel:** 4", 6-1/2", 8-3/8". **Weight:** 44-3/4 oz. **Grips:** Rubber. **Sights:** Adjustable. **Features:** Double action. Integral key-lock. Introduced 1994. New Model 44S12 has 12" vent rib barrel. Imported from Brazil by Taurus International Manufacturing, Inc.

Price: Blue or stainless steel .... **$445.00 to $602.00**

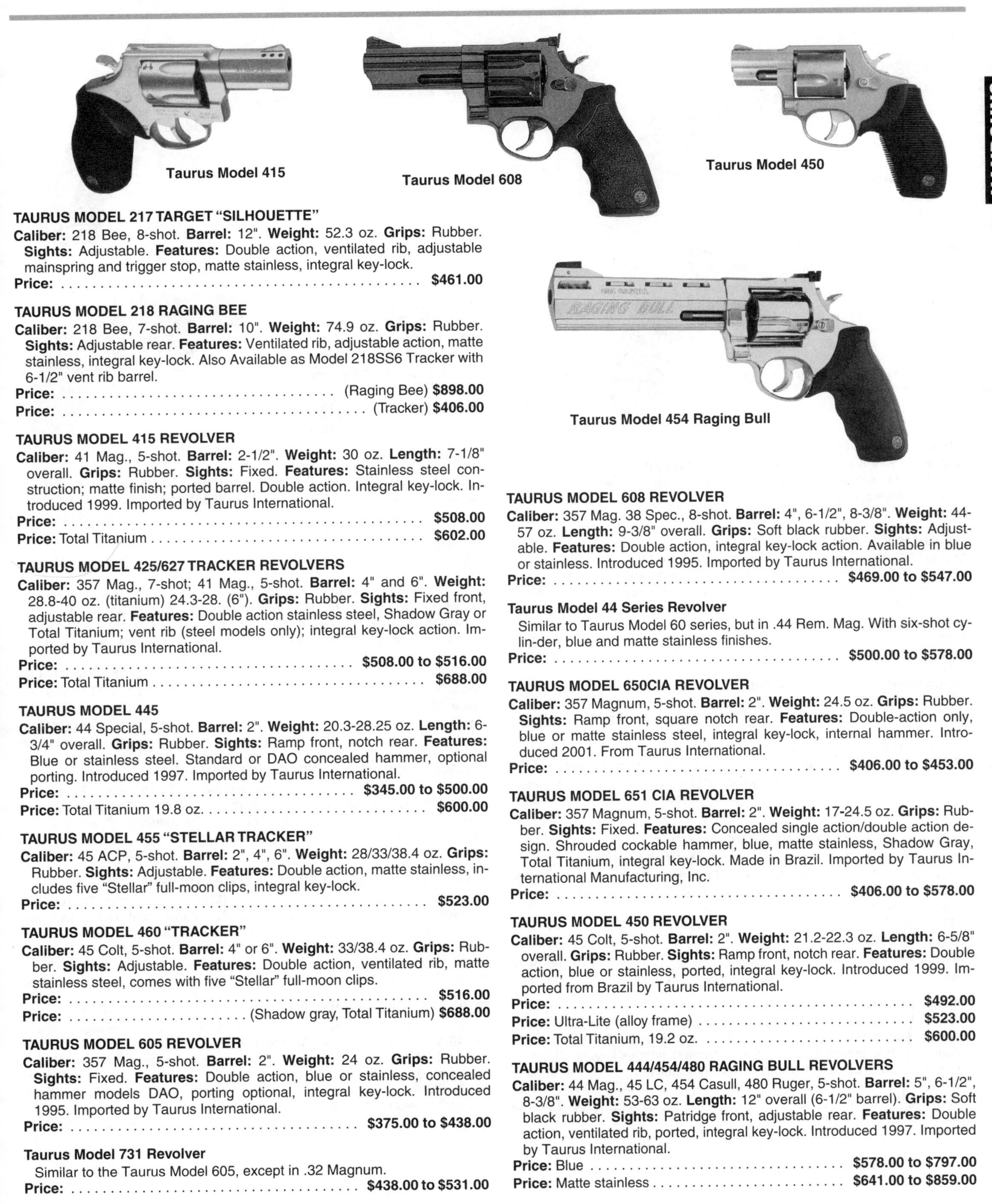

Taurus Model 415

Taurus Model 608

Taurus Model 450

Taurus Model 454 Raging Bull

TAURUS MODEL 217 TARGET "SILHOUETTE"

Caliber: 218 Bee, 8-shot. **Barrel:** 12". **Weight:** 52.3 oz. **Grips:** Rubber. **Sights:** Adjustable. **Features:** Double action, ventilated rib, adjustable mainspring and trigger stop, matte stainless, integral key-lock.

Price: **$461.00**

TAURUS MODEL 218 RAGING BEE

Caliber: 218 Bee, 7-shot. **Barrel:** 10". **Weight:** 74.9 oz. **Grips:** Rubber. **Sights:** Adjustable rear. **Features:** Ventilated rib, adjustable action, matte stainless, integral key-lock. Also Available as Model 218SS6 Tracker with 6-1/2" vent rib barrel.

Price: . . . . (Raging Bee) **$898.00**

Price: . . . . (Tracker) **$406.00**

TAURUS MODEL 415 REVOLVER

Caliber: 41 Mag., 5-shot. **Barrel:** 2-1/2". **Weight:** 30 oz. **Length:** 7-1/8" overall. **Grips:** Rubber. **Sights:** Fixed. **Features:** Stainless steel construction; matte finish; ported barrel. Double action. Integral key-lock. Introduced 1999. Imported by Taurus International.

Price: **$508.00**

Price: Total Titanium **$602.00**

TAURUS MODEL 425/627 TRACKER REVOLVERS

Caliber: 357 Mag., 7-shot; 41 Mag., 5-shot. **Barrel:** 4" and 6". **Weight:** 28.8-40 oz. (titanium) 24.3-28. (6"). **Grips:** Rubber. **Sights:** Fixed front, adjustable rear. **Features:** Double action stainless steel, Shadow Gray or Total Titanium; vent rib (steel models only); integral key-lock action. Imported by Taurus International.

Price: . . . . **$508.00 to $516.00**

Price: Total Titanium **$688.00**

TAURUS MODEL 445

Caliber: 44 Special, 5-shot. **Barrel:** 2". **Weight:** 20.3-28.25 oz. **Length:** 6-3/4" overall. **Grips:** Rubber. **Sights:** Ramp front, notch rear. **Features:** Blue or stainless steel. Standard or DAO concealed hammer, optional porting. Introduced 1997. Imported by Taurus International.

Price: . . . . **$345.00 to $500.00**

Price: Total Titanium 19.8 oz. **$600.00**

TAURUS MODEL 455 "STELLAR TRACKER"

Caliber: 45 ACP, 5-shot. **Barrel:** 2", 4", 6". **Weight:** 28/33/38.4 oz. **Grips:** Rubber. **Sights:** Adjustable. **Features:** Double action, matte stainless, includes five "Stellar" full-moon clips, integral key-lock.

Price: **$523.00**

TAURUS MODEL 460 "TRACKER"

Caliber: 45 Colt, 5-shot. **Barrel:** 4" or 6". **Weight:** 33/38.4 oz. **Grips:** Rubber. **Sights:** Adjustable. **Features:** Double action, ventilated rib, matte stainless steel, comes with five "Stellar" full-moon clips.

Price: **$516.00**

Price: . . . . (Shadow gray, Total Titanium) **$688.00**

TAURUS MODEL 605 REVOLVER

Caliber: 357 Mag., 5-shot. **Barrel:** 2". **Weight:** 24 oz. **Grips:** Rubber. **Sights:** Fixed. **Features:** Double action, blue or stainless, concealed hammer models DAO, porting optional, integral key-lock. Introduced 1995. Imported by Taurus International.

Price: . . . . **$375.00 to $438.00**

Taurus Model 731 Revolver

Similar to the Taurus Model 605, except in .32 Magnum.

Price: . . . . **$438.00 to $531.00**

TAURUS MODEL 608 REVOLVER

Caliber: 357 Mag. 38 Spec., 8-shot. **Barrel:** 4", 6-1/2", 8-3/8". **Weight:** 44-57 oz. **Length:** 9-3/8" overall. **Grips:** Soft black rubber. **Sights:** Adjustable. **Features:** Double action, integral key-lock action. Available in blue or stainless. Introduced 1995. Imported by Taurus International.

Price: . . . . **$469.00 to $547.00**

Taurus Model 44 Series Revolver

Similar to Taurus Model 60 series, but in .44 Rem. Mag. With six-shot cylin-der, blue and matte stainless finishes.

Price: . . . . **$500.00 to $578.00**

TAURUS MODEL 650CIA REVOLVER

Caliber: 357 Magnum, 5-shot. **Barrel:** 2". **Weight:** 24.5 oz. **Grips:** Rubber. **Sights:** Ramp front, square notch rear. **Features:** Double-action only, blue or matte stainless steel, integral key-lock, internal hammer. Introduced 2001. From Taurus International.

Price: . . . . **$406.00 to $453.00**

TAURUS MODEL 651 CIA REVOLVER

Caliber: 357 Magnum, 5-shot. **Barrel:** 2". **Weight:** 17-24.5 oz. **Grips:** Rubber. **Sights:** Fixed. **Features:** Concealed single action/double action design. Shrouded cockable hammer, blue, matte stainless, Shadow Gray, Total Titanium, integral key-lock. Made in Brazil. Imported by Taurus International Manufacturing, Inc.

Price: . . . . **$406.00 to $578.00**

TAURUS MODEL 450 REVOLVER

Caliber: 45 Colt, 5-shot. **Barrel:** 2". **Weight:** 21.2-22.3 oz. **Length:** 6-5/8" overall. **Grips:** Rubber. **Sights:** Ramp front, notch rear. **Features:** Double action, blue or stainless, ported, integral key-lock. Introduced 1999. Imported from Brazil by Taurus International.

Price: **$492.00**

Price: Ultra-Lite (alloy frame) **$523.00**

Price: Total Titanium, 19.2 oz. **$600.00**

TAURUS MODEL 444/454/480 RAGING BULL REVOLVERS

Caliber: 44 Mag., 45 LC, 454 Casull, 480 Ruger, 5-shot. **Barrel:** 5", 6-1/2", 8-3/8". **Weight:** 53-63 oz. **Length:** 12" overall (6-1/2" barrel). **Grips:** Soft black rubber. **Sights:** Patridge front, adjustable rear. **Features:** Double action, ventilated rib, ported, integral key-lock. Introduced 1997. Imported by Taurus International.

Price: Blue . . . . **$578.00 to $797.00**

Price: Matte stainless . . . . **$641.00 to $859.00**

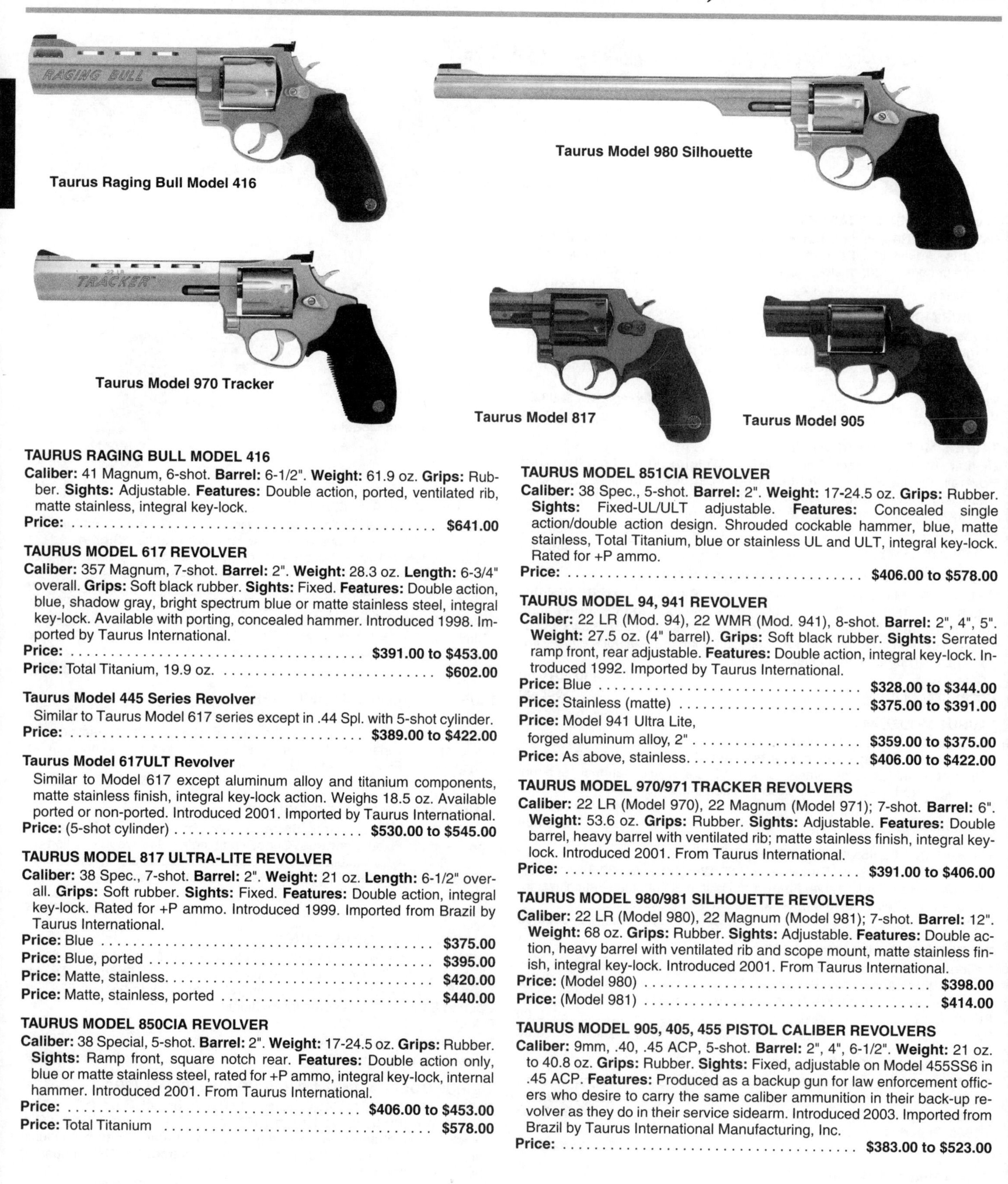

Taurus Raging Bull Model 416

Taurus Model 980 Silhouette

Taurus Model 970 Tracker

Taurus Model 817

Taurus Model 905

TAURUS RAGING BULL MODEL 416

Caliber: 41 Magnum, 6-shot. **Barrel:** 6-1/2". **Weight:** 61.9 oz. **Grips:** Rubber. **Sights:** Adjustable. **Features:** Double action, ported, ventilated rib, matte stainless, integral key-lock.

Price: **$641.00**

TAURUS MODEL 617 REVOLVER

Caliber: 357 Magnum, 7-shot. **Barrel:** 2". **Weight:** 28.3 oz. **Length:** 6-3/4" overall. **Grips:** Soft black rubber. **Sights:** Fixed. **Features:** Double action, blue, shadow gray, bright spectrum blue or matte stainless steel, integral key-lock. Available with porting, concealed hammer. Introduced 1998. Imported by Taurus International.

Price: .... **$391.00 to $453.00**

Price: Total Titanium, 19.9 oz. **$602.00**

Taurus Model 445 Series Revolver

Similar to Taurus Model 617 series except in .44 Spl. with 5-shot cylinder.

Price: .... **$389.00 to $422.00**

Taurus Model 617ULT Revolver

Similar to Model 617 except aluminum alloy and titanium components, matte stainless finish, integral key-lock action. Weighs 18.5 oz. Available ported or non-ported. Introduced 2001. Imported by Taurus International.

Price: (5-shot cylinder) .... **$530.00 to $545.00**

TAURUS MODEL 817 ULTRA-LITE REVOLVER

Caliber: 38 Spec., 7-shot. **Barrel:** 2". **Weight:** 21 oz. **Length:** 6-1/2" overall. **Grips:** Soft rubber. **Sights:** Fixed. **Features:** Double action, integral key-lock. Rated for +P ammo. Introduced 1999. Imported from Brazil by Taurus International.

Price: Blue **$375.00**

Price: Blue, ported **$395.00**

Price: Matte, stainless. **$420.00**

Price: Matte, stainless, ported **$440.00**

TAURUS MODEL 850CIA REVOLVER

Caliber: 38 Special, 5-shot. **Barrel:** 2". **Weight:** 17-24.5 oz. **Grips:** Rubber. **Sights:** Ramp front, square notch rear. **Features:** Double action only, blue or matte stainless steel, rated for +P ammo, integral key-lock, internal hammer. Introduced 2001. From Taurus International.

Price: .... **$406.00 to $453.00**

Price: Total Titanium **$578.00**

TAURUS MODEL 851CIA REVOLVER

Caliber: 38 Spec., 5-shot. **Barrel:** 2". **Weight:** 17-24.5 oz. **Grips:** Rubber. **Sights:** Fixed-UL/ULT adjustable. **Features:** Concealed single action/double action design. Shrouded cockable hammer, blue, matte stainless, Total Titanium, blue or stainless UL and ULT, integral key-lock. Rated for +P ammo.

Price: .... **$406.00 to $578.00**

TAURUS MODEL 94, 941 REVOLVER

Caliber: 22 LR (Mod. 94), 22 WMR (Mod. 941), 8-shot. **Barrel:** 2", 4", 5". **Weight:** 27.5 oz. (4" barrel). **Grips:** Soft black rubber. **Sights:** Serrated ramp front, rear adjustable. **Features:** Double action, integral key-lock. Introduced 1992. Imported by Taurus International.

Price: Blue .... **$328.00 to $344.00**

Price: Stainless (matte) .... **$375.00 to $391.00**

Price: Model 941 Ultra Lite, forged aluminum alloy, 2" .... **$359.00 to $375.00**

Price: As above, stainless. .... **$406.00 to $422.00**

TAURUS MODEL 970/971 TRACKER REVOLVERS

Caliber: 22 LR (Model 970), 22 Magnum (Model 971); 7-shot. **Barrel:** 6". **Weight:** 53.6 oz. **Grips:** Rubber. **Sights:** Adjustable. **Features:** Double barrel, heavy barrel with ventilated rib; matte stainless finish, integral key-lock. Introduced 2001. From Taurus International.

Price: .... **$391.00 to $406.00**

TAURUS MODEL 980/981 SILHOUETTE REVOLVERS

Caliber: 22 LR (Model 980), 22 Magnum (Model 981); 7-shot. **Barrel:** 12". **Weight:** 68 oz. **Grips:** Rubber. **Sights:** Adjustable. **Features:** Double action, heavy barrel with ventilated rib and scope mount, matte stainless finish, integral key-lock. Introduced 2001. From Taurus International.

Price: (Model 980) **$398.00**

Price: (Model 981) **$414.00**

TAURUS MODEL 905, 405, 455 PISTOL CALIBER REVOLVERS

Caliber: 9mm, .40, .45 ACP, 5-shot. **Barrel:** 2", 4", 6-1/2". **Weight:** 21 oz. to 40.8 oz. **Grips:** Rubber. **Sights:** Fixed, adjustable on Model 455SS6 in .45 ACP. **Features:** Produced as a backup gun for law enforcement officers who desire to carry the same caliber ammunition in their back-up revolver as they do in their service sidearm. Introduced 2003. Imported from Brazil by Taurus International Manufacturing, Inc.

Price: .... **$383.00 to $523.00**

HANDGUNS — SINGLE ACTION REVOLVERS

Both classic six-shooters and modern adaptations for hunting and sport.

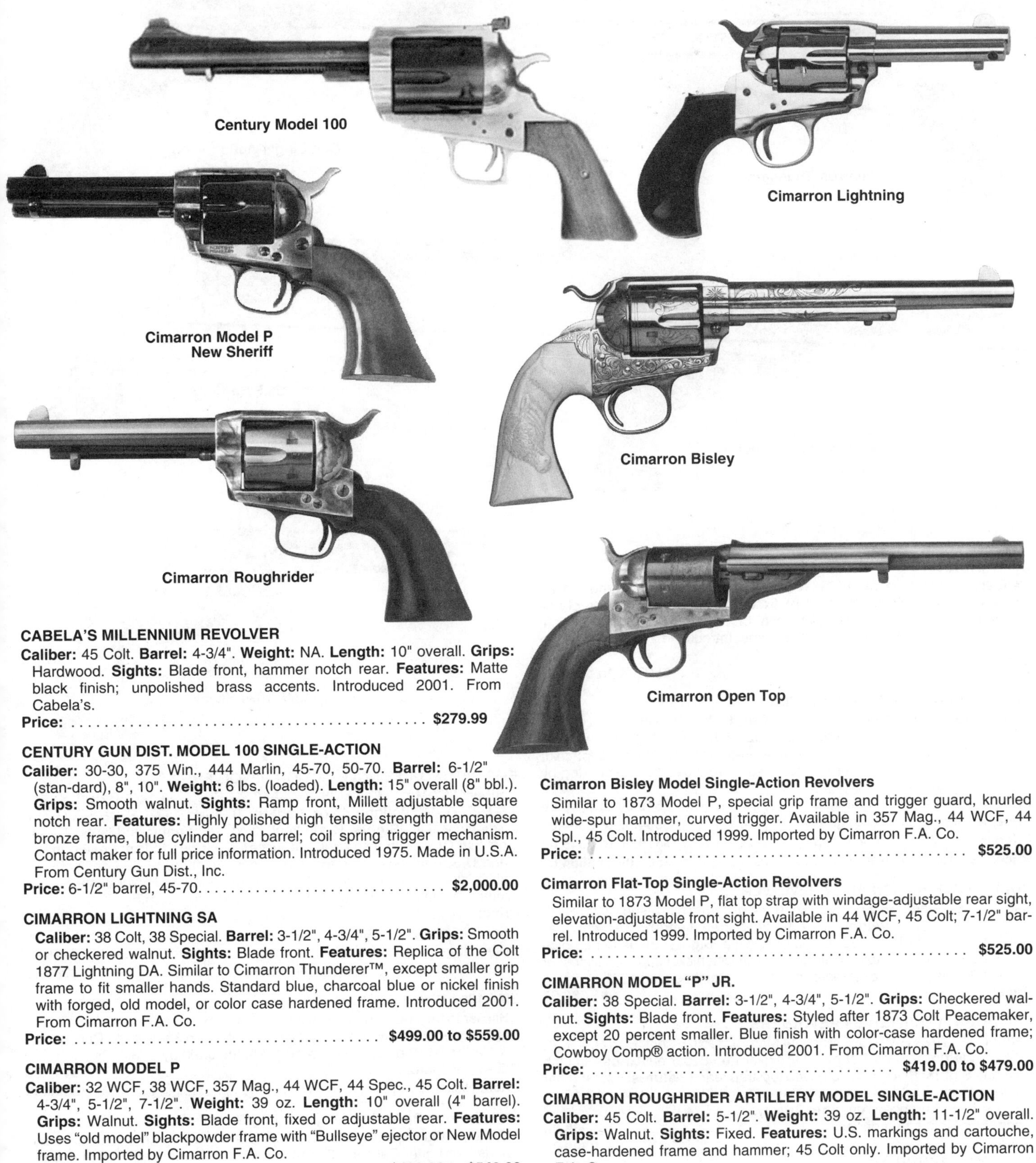

Century Model 100

Cimarron Lightning

Cimarron Model P New Sheriff

Cimarron Bisley

Cimarron Roughrider

Cimarron Open Top

CABELA'S MILLENNIUM REVOLVER

Caliber: 45 Colt. **Barrel:** 4-3/4". **Weight:** NA. **Length:** 10" overall. **Grips:** Hardwood. **Sights:** Blade front, hammer notch rear. **Features:** Matte black finish; unpolished brass accents. Introduced 2001. From Cabela's.

Price: **$279.99**

CENTURY GUN DIST. MODEL 100 SINGLE-ACTION

Caliber: 30-30, 375 Win., 444 Marlin, 45-70, 50-70. **Barrel:** 6-1/2" (stan-dard), 8", 10". **Weight:** 6 lbs. (loaded). **Length:** 15" overall (8" bbl.). **Grips:** Smooth walnut. **Sights:** Ramp front, Millett adjustable square notch rear. **Features:** Highly polished high tensile strength manganese bronze frame, blue cylinder and barrel; coil spring trigger mechanism. Contact maker for full price information. Introduced 1975. Made in U.S.A. From Century Gun Dist., Inc.

Price: 6-1/2" barrel, 45-70. . . . . **$2,000.00**

CIMARRON LIGHTNING SA

Caliber: 38 Colt, 38 Special. **Barrel:** 3-1/2", 4-3/4", 5-1/2". **Grips:** Smooth or checkered walnut. **Sights:** Blade front. **Features:** Replica of the Colt 1877 Lightning DA. Similar to Cimarron Thunderer™, except smaller grip frame to fit smaller hands. Standard blue, charcoal blue or nickel finish with forged, old model, or color case hardened frame. Introduced 2001. From Cimarron F.A. Co.

Price: . . . . **$499.00 to $559.00**

CIMARRON MODEL P

Caliber: 32 WCF, 38 WCF, 357 Mag., 44 WCF, 44 Spec., 45 Colt. **Barrel:** 4-3/4", 5-1/2", 7-1/2". **Weight:** 39 oz. **Length:** 10" overall (4" barrel). **Grips:** Walnut. **Sights:** Blade front, fixed or adjustable rear. **Features:** Uses "old model" blackpowder frame with "Bullseye" ejector or New Model frame. Imported by Cimarron F.A. Co.

Price: . . . . **$489.00 to $549.00**

Price: New Sheriff . . . . **$489.00 to $564.00**

Cimarron Bisley Model Single-Action Revolvers

Similar to 1873 Model P, special grip frame and trigger guard, knurled wide-spur hammer, curved trigger. Available in 357 Mag., 44 WCF, 44 Spl., 45 Colt. Introduced 1999. Imported by Cimarron F.A. Co.

Price: **$525.00**

Cimarron Flat-Top Single-Action Revolvers

Similar to 1873 Model P, flat top strap with windage-adjustable rear sight, elevation-adjustable front sight. Available in 44 WCF, 45 Colt; 7-1/2" barrel. Introduced 1999. Imported by Cimarron F.A. Co.

Price: **$525.00**

CIMARRON MODEL "P" JR.

Caliber: 38 Special. **Barrel:** 3-1/2", 4-3/4", 5-1/2". **Grips:** Checkered walnut. **Sights:** Blade front. **Features:** Styled after 1873 Colt Peacemaker, except 20 percent smaller. Blue finish with color-case hardened frame; Cowboy Comp® action. Introduced 2001. From Cimarron F.A. Co.

Price: . . . . **$419.00 to $479.00**

CIMARRON ROUGHRIDER ARTILLERY MODEL SINGLE-ACTION

Caliber: 45 Colt. **Barrel:** 5-1/2". **Weight:** 39 oz. **Length:** 11-1/2" overall. **Grips:** Walnut. **Sights:** Fixed. **Features:** U.S. markings and cartouche, case-hardened frame and hammer; 45 Colt only. Imported by Cimarron F.A. Co.

Price: . . . . **$549.00 to $599.00**

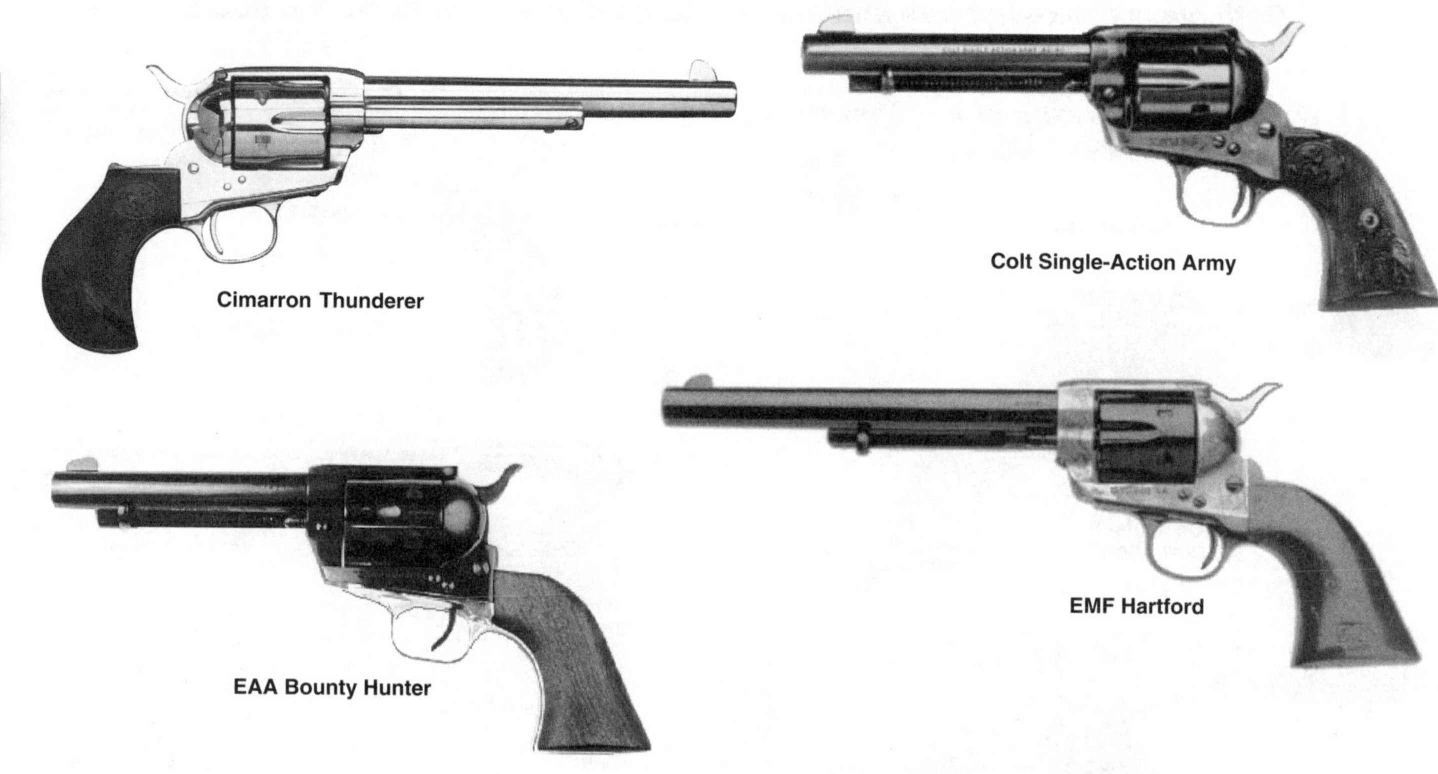
Cimarron Thunderer

Colt Single-Action Army

EMF Hartford

EAA Bounty Hunter

CIMARRON 1872 OPEN TOP REVOLVER

Caliber: 38, 44 Special, 45 S&W Schofield. **Barrel:** 5-1/2" and 7-1/2". **Grips:** Walnut. **Sights:** Blade front, fixed rear. **Features:** Replica of first cartridge-firing revolver. Blue, charcoal blue, nickel or Original® finish; Navy-style brass or steel Army-style frame. Introduced 2001 by Cimarron F.A. Co.

Price: .... **$529.00 to $599.00**

CIMARRON THUNDERER REVOLVER

Caliber: 357 Mag., 44 WCF, 44 Spl, 45 Colt, 6-shot. **Barrel:** 3-1/2", 4-3/4", 5-1/2", 7-1/2", with ejector. **Weight:** 38 oz. (3-1/2" barrel). **Grips:** Smooth walnut. **Sights:** Blade front, notch rear. **Features:** Thunderer grip; color case-hardened frame with balance blued. Introduced 1993. Imported by Cimarron F.A. Co.

Price: 3-1/2", 4-3/4", smooth grips .... **$519.00 to $549.00**
Price: As above, checkered grips .... **$564.00 to $584.00**
Price: 5-1/2", 7-1/2", smooth grips .... **$519.00 to $549.00**
Price: As above, checkered grips .... **$564.00 to $584.00**

COLT SINGLE-ACTION ARMY REVOLVER

Caliber: 357 Mag., 38 Special, .32/20, 44-40, 45 Colt, 6-shot. **Barrel:** 4-3/4", 5-1/2", 7-1/2". **Weight:** 40 oz. (4-3/4" barrel). **Length:** 10-1/4" overall (4-3/4" barrel). **Grips:** Black Eagle composite. **Sights:** Blade front, notch rear. **Features:** Available in full nickel finish with nickel grip medallions, or Royal Blue with color case-hardened frame. Reintroduced 1992.

Price: **$1,380.00**

EAA BOUNTY HUNTER SA REVOLVERS

Caliber: 22 LR/22 WMR, 357 Mag., 44 Mag., 45 Colt, 6-shot. **Barrel:** 4-1/2", 7-1/2". **Weight:** 2.5 lbs. **Length:** 11" overall (4-5/8" barrel). **Grips:** Smooth walnut. **Sights:** Blade front, grooved topstrap rear. **Features:** Transfer bar safety; three position hammer; hammer forged barrel. Introduced 1992. Imported by European American Armory.

Price: Blue or case-hardened........................... **$369.00**
Price: Nickel **$399.00**
Price: 22LR/22WMR, blue **$269.00**
Price: As above, nickel **$299.00**

EMF 1894 Bisley

EMF HARTFORD SINGLE-ACTION REVOLVERS

Caliber: 357 Mag., 32-20, 38-40, 44-40, 44 Spec., 45 Colt. **Barrel:** 4-3/4", 5-1/2", 7-1/2". **Weight:** 45 oz. **Length:** 13" overall (7-1/2" barrel). **Grips:** Smooth walnut. **Sights:** Blade front, fixed rear. **Features:** Identical to the original Colts with inspector cartouche on left grip, original patent dates and U.S. markings. All major parts serial numbered using original Colt-style lettering, numbering. Bullseye ejector head and color case-hardening on frame and hammer. Introduced 1990. From E.M.F.

Price: **$500.00**
Price: Cavalry or Artillery **$390.00**
Price: Nickel plated, add.............................. **$125.00**
Price: Casehardened New Model frame.................... **$365.00**

EMF 1894 Bisley Revolver

Similar to the Hartford single-action revolver except has special grip frame and trigger guard, wide spur hammer; available in 38-40 or 45 Colt, 4-3/4", 5-1/2" or 7-1/2" barrel. Introduced 1995. Imported by E.M.F.

Price: Casehardened/blue **$400.00**
Price: Nickel **$525.00**

EMF Hartford Pinkerton Single-Action Revolver

Same as the regular Hartford except has 4" barrel with ejector tube and birds head grip. Calibers: 357 Mag., 45 Colt. Introduced 1997. Imported by E.M.F.

Price: **$375.00**

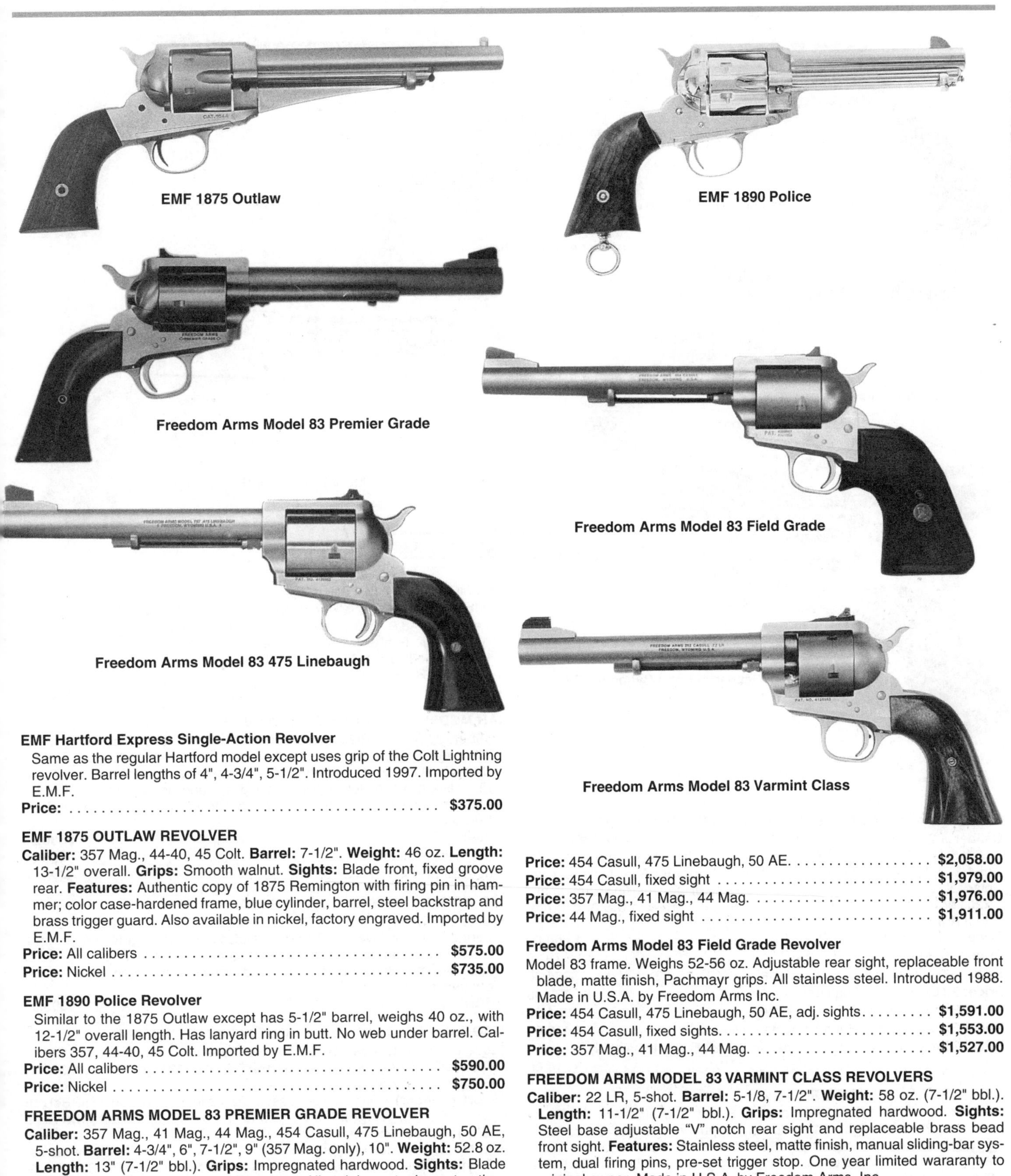

EMF 1875 Outlaw

EMF 1890 Police

Freedom Arms Model 83 Premier Grade

Freedom Arms Model 83 Field Grade

Freedom Arms Model 83 475 Linebaugh

Freedom Arms Model 83 Varmint Class

EMF Hartford Express Single-Action Revolver

Same as the regular Hartford model except uses grip of the Colt Lightning revolver. Barrel lengths of 4", 4-3/4", 5-1/2". Introduced 1997. Imported by E.M.F.

Price: **$375.00**

EMF 1875 OUTLAW REVOLVER

Caliber: 357 Mag., 44-40, 45 Colt. **Barrel:** 7-1/2". **Weight:** 46 oz. **Length:** 13-1/2" overall. **Grips:** Smooth walnut. **Sights:** Blade front, fixed groove rear. **Features:** Authentic copy of 1875 Remington with firing pin in hammer; color case-hardened frame, blue cylinder, barrel, steel backstrap and brass trigger guard. Also available in nickel, factory engraved. Imported by E.M.F.

Price: All calibers **$575.00**

Price: Nickel **$735.00**

EMF 1890 Police Revolver

Similar to the 1875 Outlaw except has 5-1/2" barrel, weighs 40 oz., with 12-1/2" overall length. Has lanyard ring in butt. No web under barrel. Calibers 357, 44-40, 45 Colt. Imported by E.M.F.

Price: All calibers **$590.00**

Price: Nickel **$750.00**

FREEDOM ARMS MODEL 83 PREMIER GRADE REVOLVER

Caliber: 357 Mag., 41 Mag., 44 Mag., 454 Casull, 475 Linebaugh, 50 AE, 5-shot. **Barrel:** 4-3/4", 6", 7-1/2", 9" (357 Mag. only), 10". **Weight:** 52.8 oz. **Length:** 13" (7-1/2" bbl.). **Grips:** Impregnated hardwood. **Sights:** Blade front, notch or adjustable rear. **Features:** All stainless steel construction; sliding bar safety system. Lifetime warranty. Made in U.S.A. by Freedom Arms, Inc.

Price: 454 Casull, 475 Linebaugh, 50 AE. **$2,058.00**

Price: 454 Casull, fixed sight **$1,979.00**

Price: 357 Mag., 41 Mag., 44 Mag. **$1,976.00**

Price: 44 Mag., fixed sight **$1,911.00**

Freedom Arms Model 83 Field Grade Revolver

Model 83 frame. Weighs 52-56 oz. Adjustable rear sight, replaceable front blade, matte finish, Pachmayr grips. All stainless steel. Introduced 1988. Made in U.S.A. by Freedom Arms Inc.

Price: 454 Casull, 475 Linebaugh, 50 AE, adj. sights. **$1,591.00**

Price: 454 Casull, fixed sights. **$1,553.00**

Price: 357 Mag., 41 Mag., 44 Mag. **$1,527.00**

FREEDOM ARMS MODEL 83 VARMINT CLASS REVOLVERS

Caliber: 22 LR, 5-shot. **Barrel:** 5-1/8, 7-1/2". **Weight:** 58 oz. (7-1/2" bbl.). **Length:** 11-1/2" (7-1/2" bbl.). **Grips:** Impregnated hardwood. **Sights:** Steel base adjustable "V" notch rear sight and replaceable brass bead front sight. **Features:** Stainless steel, matte finish, manual sliding-bar system, dual firing pins, pre-set trigger stop. One year limited wararanty to original owner. Made in U.S.A. by Freedom Arms, Inc.

Price: Varmint Class **$1,828.00**

Price: Extra fitted 22 WMR cylinder **$264.00**

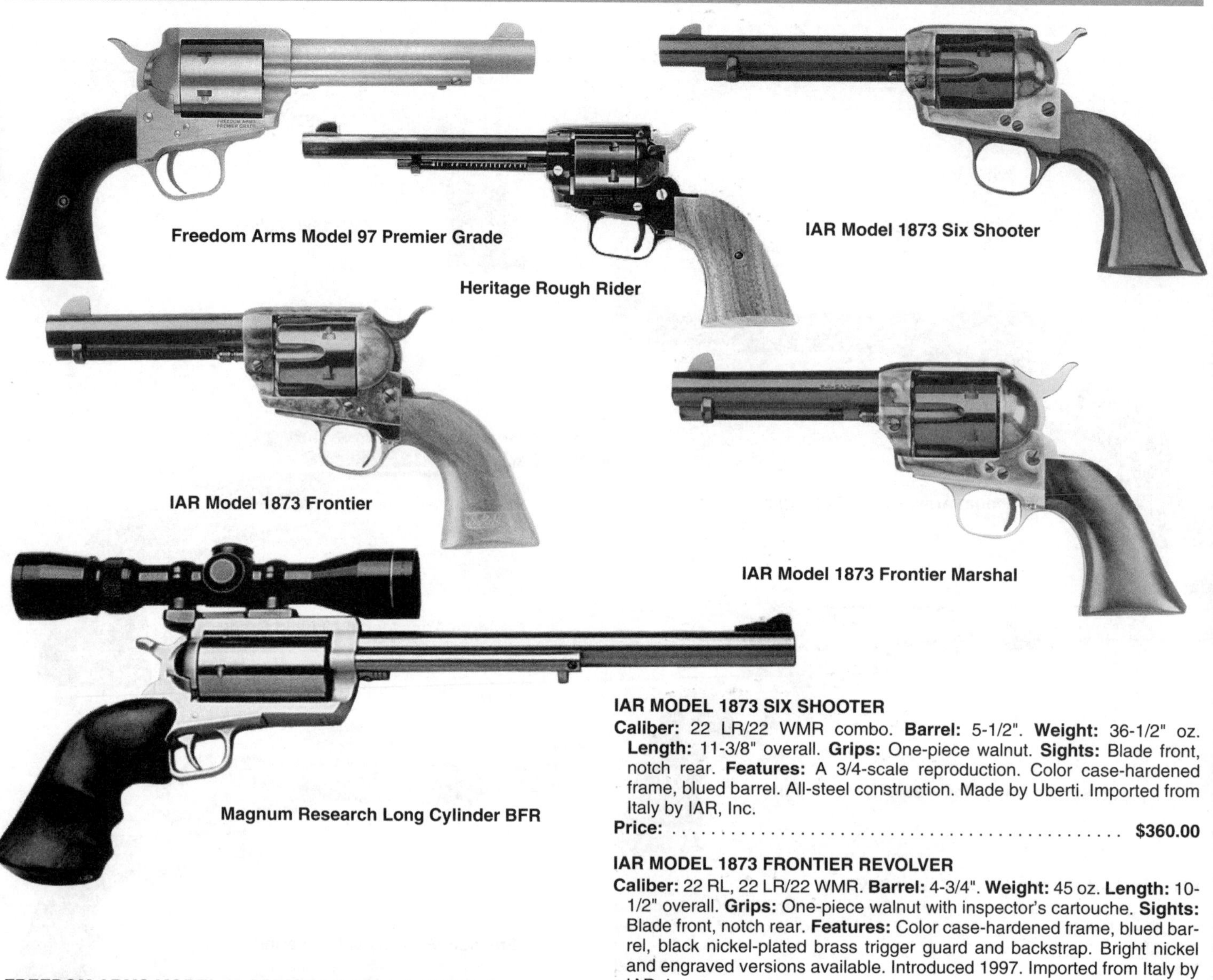

Freedom Arms Model 97 Premier Grade

Heritage Rough Rider

IAR Model 1873 Six Shooter

IAR Model 1873 Frontier

IAR Model 1873 Frontier Marshal

Magnum Research Long Cylinder BFR

FREEDOM ARMS MODEL 97 PREMIER GRADE REVOLVER

Caliber: 22 LR, 357 Mag., 41 Mag., 44 Special, 45 Colt, 5-shot. **Barrel:** 4-1/2", 5-1/2", 7-1/2", 10". **Weight:** 37 oz. (45 Colt 5-1/2"). **Length:** 10-3/4" (5-1/2" bbl.). **Grips:** Impregnated hardwood. **Sights:** Adjustable rear, replaceable blade front. **Features:** Stainless steel, brushed finish, automatic transfer bar safety system. Introduced in 1997. Made in U.S.A. by Freedom Arms.

Price: 357 Mag., 41 Mag., 45 Colt **$1,668.00**
Price: 357 Mag., 45 Colt, fixed sight **$1,576.00**
Price: Extra fitted cylinders 38 Special, 45 ACP **$264.00**
Price: 22 LR with sporting chambers **$1,732.00**
Price: Extra fitted 22 WMR cylinder **$264.00**
Price: Extra fitted 22 LR match grade cylinder **$476.00**
Price: 22 match grade chamber instead of 22 LR sport chamber **$214.00**

HERITAGE ROUGH RIDER REVOLVER

Caliber: 22 LR, 22 LR/22 WMR combo, 6-shot. **Barrel:** 2-3/4", 3-1/2", 4-3/4", 6-1/2", 9". **Weight:** 31 to 38 oz. **Length:** NA. **Grips:** Exotic hardwood, laminated wood or mother of pearl; bird's head models offered. **Sights:** Blade front, fixed rear. Adjustable sight on 6-1/2" only. **Features:** Hammer block safety. High polish blue or nickel finish. Introduced 1993. Made in U.S.A. by Heritage Mfg., Inc.

Price: . . . . **$184.95 to $239.95**

IAR MODEL 1873 SIX SHOOTER

Caliber: 22 LR/22 WMR combo. **Barrel:** 5-1/2". **Weight:** 36-1/2" oz. **Length:** 11-3/8" overall. **Grips:** One-piece walnut. **Sights:** Blade front, notch rear. **Features:** A 3/4-scale reproduction. Color case-hardened frame, blued barrel. All-steel construction. Made by Uberti. Imported from Italy by IAR, Inc.

Price: **$360.00**

IAR MODEL 1873 FRONTIER REVOLVER

Caliber: 22 RL, 22 LR/22 WMR. **Barrel:** 4-3/4". **Weight:** 45 oz. **Length:** 10-1/2" overall. **Grips:** One-piece walnut with inspector's cartouche. **Sights:** Blade front, notch rear. **Features:** Color case-hardened frame, blued barrel, black nickel-plated brass trigger guard and backstrap. Bright nickel and engraved versions available. Introduced 1997. Imported from Italy by IAR, Inc.

Price: **$380.00**
Price: Nickel-plated. **$425.00**
Price: 22 LR/22WMR combo **$420.00**

IAR MODEL 1873 FRONTIER MARSHAL

Caliber: 357 Mag., 45 Colt. **Barrel:** 4-3/4", 5-1/2, 7-1/2". **Weight:** 39 oz. **Length:** 10-1/2" overall. **Grips:** One-piece walnut. **Sights:** Blade front, notch rear. **Features:** Bright brass trigger guard and backstrap, color case-hardened frame, blued barrel and cylinder. Introduced 1998. Imported from Italy by IAR, Inc.

Price: **$395.00**

MAGNUM RESEARCH BFR SINGLE-ACTION REVOLVER

(Long cylinder) Caliber: 30/30, 45/70 Government, 444 Marlin, 45 LC/410, 450 Marlin, 50 AE, .500 S&W. **Barrel:** 7.5", 10". **Weight:** 4 lbs., 4.36 lbs. **Length:** 15", 17.5".

(Short cylinder) Caliber: 454 Casull, 22 Hornet, BFR 480/475. **Barrel:** 6.5", 7.5", 10". **Weight:** 3.2 lbs, 3.5 lbs., 4.36 lbs. (10"). **Length:** 12.75 (6"), 13.75", 16.25"

Sights: All have fully adjustable rear, black blade ramp front. **Features:** Stainless steel construction, rubber grips, all 5-shot capacity. Barrels are stress-relieved and cut rifled. Made in U.S.A. From Magnum Research, Inc.

Price: **$999.00**

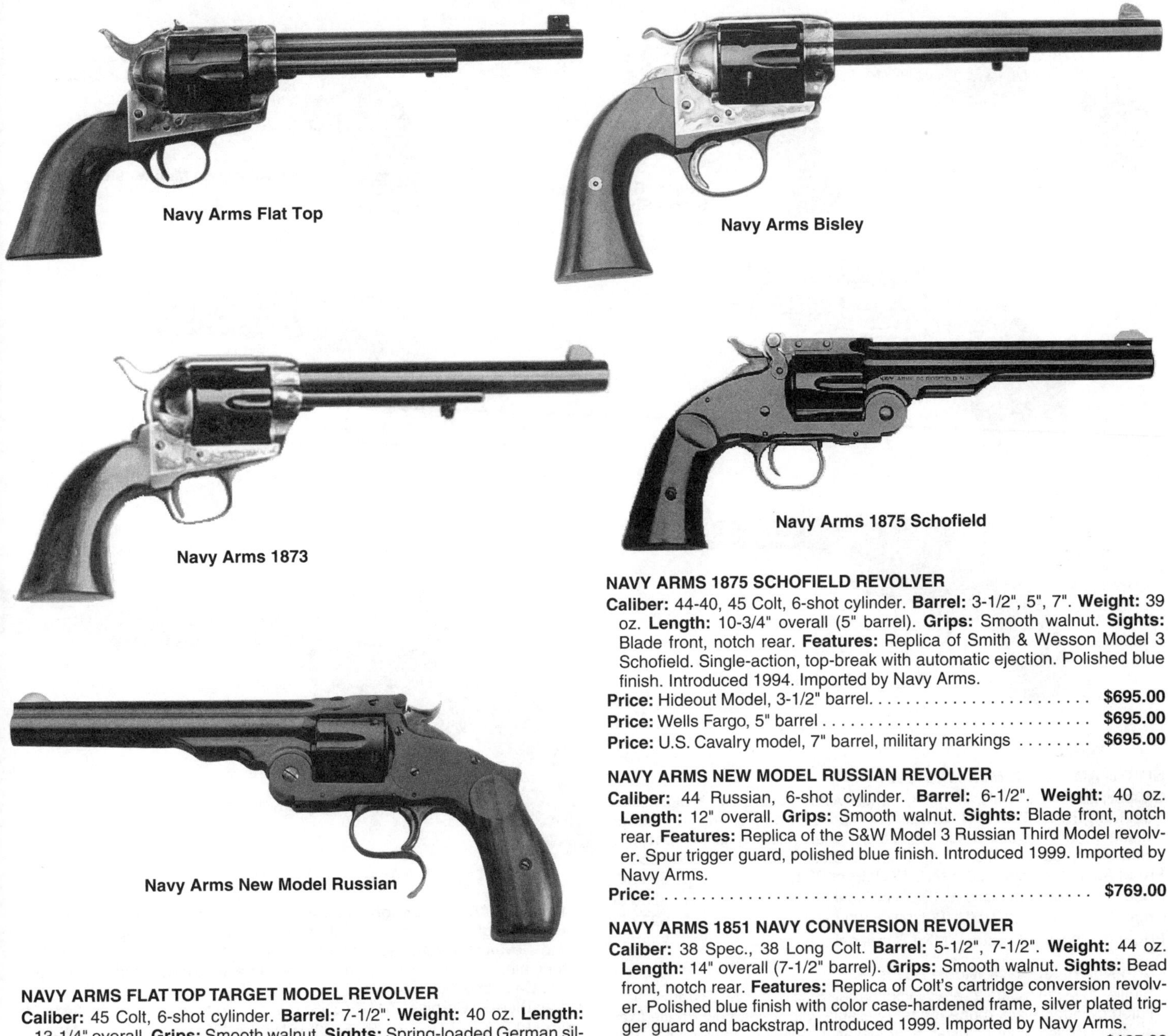

Navy Arms Flat Top

Navy Arms Bisley

Navy Arms 1873

Navy Arms 1875 Schofield

Navy Arms New Model Russian

NAVY ARMS FLAT TOP TARGET MODEL REVOLVER

Caliber: 45 Colt, 6-shot cylinder. **Barrel:** 7-1/2". **Weight:** 40 oz. **Length:** 13-1/4" overall. **Grips:** Smooth walnut. **Sights:** Spring-loaded German silver front, rear adjustable for windage. **Features:** Replica of Colt's Flat Top Frontier target revolver made from 1888 to 1896. Blue with color case-hardened frame. Introduced 1997. Imported by Navy Arms.

Price: **$450.00**

NAVY ARMS BISLEY MODEL SINGLE-ACTION REVOLVER

Caliber: 44-40 or 45 Colt, 6-shot cylinder. **Barrel:** 4-3/4", 5-1/2", 7-1/2". **Weight:** 40 oz. **Length:** 12-1/2" overall (7-1/2" barrel). **Grips:** Smooth walnut. **Sights:** Blade front, notch rear. **Features:** Replica of Colt's Bisley Model. Polished blue finish, color case-hardened frame. Introduced 1997. Imported by Navy Arms.

Price: .... **$425.00 to $460.00**

NAVY ARMS 1873 SINGLE-ACTION REVOLVER

Caliber: 357 Mag., 44-40, 45 Colt, 6-shot cylinder. **Barrel:** 4-3/4", 5-1/2", 7-1/2". **Weight:** 36 oz. **Length:** 10-3/4" overall (5-1/2" barrel). **Grips:** Smooth walnut. **Sights:** Blade front, notch rear. **Features:** Blue with color case-hardened frame. Introduced 1991. Imported by Navy Arms.

Price: **$405.00**

NAVY ARMS 1875 SCHOFIELD REVOLVER

Caliber: 44-40, 45 Colt, 6-shot cylinder. **Barrel:** 3-1/2", 5", 7". **Weight:** 39 oz. **Length:** 10-3/4" overall (5" barrel). **Grips:** Smooth walnut. **Sights:** Blade front, notch rear. **Features:** Replica of Smith & Wesson Model 3 Schofield. Single-action, top-break with automatic ejection. Polished blue finish. Introduced 1994. Imported by Navy Arms.

Price: Hideout Model, 3-1/2" barrel....................... **$695.00**

Price: Wells Fargo, 5" barrel........................... **$695.00**

Price: U.S. Cavalry model, 7" barrel, military markings **$695.00**

NAVY ARMS NEW MODEL RUSSIAN REVOLVER

Caliber: 44 Russian, 6-shot cylinder. **Barrel:** 6-1/2". **Weight:** 40 oz. **Length:** 12" overall. **Grips:** Smooth walnut. **Sights:** Blade front, notch rear. **Features:** Replica of the S&W Model 3 Russian Third Model revolver. Spur trigger guard, polished blue finish. Introduced 1999. Imported by Navy Arms.

Price: **$769.00**

NAVY ARMS 1851 NAVY CONVERSION REVOLVER

Caliber: 38 Spec., 38 Long Colt. **Barrel:** 5-1/2", 7-1/2". **Weight:** 44 oz. **Length:** 14" overall (7-1/2" barrel). **Grips:** Smooth walnut. **Sights:** Bead front, notch rear. **Features:** Replica of Colt's cartridge conversion revolver. Polished blue finish with color case-hardened frame, silver plated trigger guard and backstrap. Introduced 1999. Imported by Navy Arms.

Price: **$165.00**

NAVY ARMS 1860 ARMY CONVERSION REVOLVER

Caliber: 38 Spec., 38 Long Colt. **Barrel:** 5-1/2", 7-1/2". **Weight:** 44 oz. **Length:** 13-1/2" overall (7-1/2" barrel). **Grips:** Smooth walnut. **Sights:** Blade front, notch rear. **Features:** Replica of Colt's conversion revolver. Polished blue finish with color case-hardened frame, full-size 1860 Army grip with blued steel backstrap. Introduced 1999. Imported by Navy Arms.

Price: **$190.00**

NORTH AMERICAN MINI REVOLVERS

Caliber: 22 Short, 22 LR, 22 WMR, 5-shot. **Barrel:** 1-1/8", 1-5/8". **Weight:** 4 to 6.6 oz. **Length:** 3-5/8" to 6-1/8" overall. **Grips:** Laminated wood. **Sights:** Blade front, notch fixed rear. **Features:** All stainless steel construction. Polished satin and matte finish. Engraved models available. From North American Arms.

Price: 22 Short, 22 LR **$193.00**

Price: 22 WMR, 1-1/8" or 1-5/8" bbl. **$193.00**

Price: 22 WMR, 1-1/8" or 1-5/8" bbl. with extra 22 LR cylinder... **$193.00**

North American Mini

Ruger "Bird's Head" Single Six

North American Mini-Master

North American Black Widow

Ruger Blackhawk

Ruger SSMBH-4F

Ruger Bisley Single-Action

NORTH AMERICAN MINI-MASTER

Caliber: 22 LR, 22 WMR, 17 HMR, 5-shot cylinder. **Barrel:** 4". **Weight:** 10.7 oz. **Length:** 7.75" overall. **Grips:** Checkered hard black rubber. **Sights:** Blade front, white outline rear adjustable for elevation, or fixed. **Features:** Heavy vent barrel; full-size grips. Non-fluted cylinder. Introduced 1989.

Price: Adjustable sight, 22 WMR, 17 HMR or 22 LR **$301.00**
Price: As above with extra WMR/LR cylinder **$330.00**
Price: Fixed sight, 22 WMR, 17 HMR or 22 LR $272.00
Price: As above with extra WMR/LR cylinder **$330.00**

North American Black Widow Revolver

Similar to Mini-Master, 2" heavy vent barrel. Built on 22 WMR frame. Non-fluted cylinder, black rubber grips. Available with Millett Low Profile fixed sights or Millett sight adjustable for elevation only. Overall length 5-7/8", weighs 8.8 oz. From North American Arms.

Price: Adjustable sight, 22 LR, 17 HMR or 22 WMR **$287.00**
Price: As above with extra WMR/LR cylinder **$316.00**
Price: Fixed sight, 22 LR, 17 HMR or 22 WMR **$287.00**
Price: As above with extra WMR/LR cylinder **$287.00**

RUGER NEW MODEL SINGLE SIX REVOLVER

Caliber: 32 H&R. **Barrel:** 4-5/8", 6-shot. **Grips:** Black Micarta "birds head", rosewood with color case. **Sights:** Fixed. **Features:** Instruction manual, high impact case, gun lock standard.

Price: Stainless, KSSMBH-4F, birds head **$576.00**
Price: Color case, SSMBH-4F, birds head **$576.00**
Price: Color case, SSM-4F-S, rosewood **$576.00**

RUGER NEW MODEL BLACKHAWK AND BLACKHAWK CONVERTIBLE

Caliber: 30 Carbine, 357 Mag./38 Spec., 41 Mag., 45 Colt, 6-shot. **Barrel:** 4-5/8" or 5-1/2", either caliber; 7-1/2" (30 Carbine and 45 Colt). **Weight:** 42 oz. (6-1/2" bbl.). **Length:** 12-1/4" overall (5-1/2" bbl.). **Grips:** American walnut. **Sights:** 1/8" ramp front, micro-click rear adjustable for windage and elevation. **Features:** Ruger transfer bar safety system, independent firing pin, hardened chrome-moly steel frame, music wire springs throughout. Case and lock included.

Price: Blue 30 Carbine, 7-1/2" (BN31) **$435.00**
Price: Blue, 357 Mag., 4-5/8", 6-1/2" (BN34, BN36) **$435.00**
Price: As above, stainless (KBN34, KBN36) **$530.00**
Price: Blue, 357 Mag./9mm Convertible, 4-5/8", 6-1/2" (BN34X, BN36X) includes extra cylinder **$489.00**
Price: Blue, 41 Mag., 4-5/8", 6-1/2" (BN41, BN42)............ **$435.00**
Price: Blue, 45 Colt, 4-5/8", 5-1/2", 7-1/2" (BN44, BN455, BN45) **$435.00**
Price: Stainless, 45 Colt, 4-5/8", 7-1/2" (KBN44, KBN45) **$530.00**
Price: Blue, 45 Colt/45 ACP Convertible, 4-5/8", 5-1/2" (BN44X, BN455X) includes extra cylinder **$489.00**

Ruger Bisley Single-Action Revolver

Similar to standard Blackhawk, hammer is lower with smoothly curved, deeply checkered wide spur. The trigger is strongly curved with wide smooth surface. Longer grip frame has hand-filling shape. Adjustable rear sight, ramp-style front. Unfluted cylinder and roll engraving, adjustable sights. Chambered for 357, 44 Mags. and 45 Colt; 7-1/2" barrel; overall length of 13"; weighs 48 oz. Plastic lockable case. Introduced 1985.

Price: RB-35W, 357Mag, RBD-44W, 44Mag, RB-45W, 45 Colt . . **$535.00**

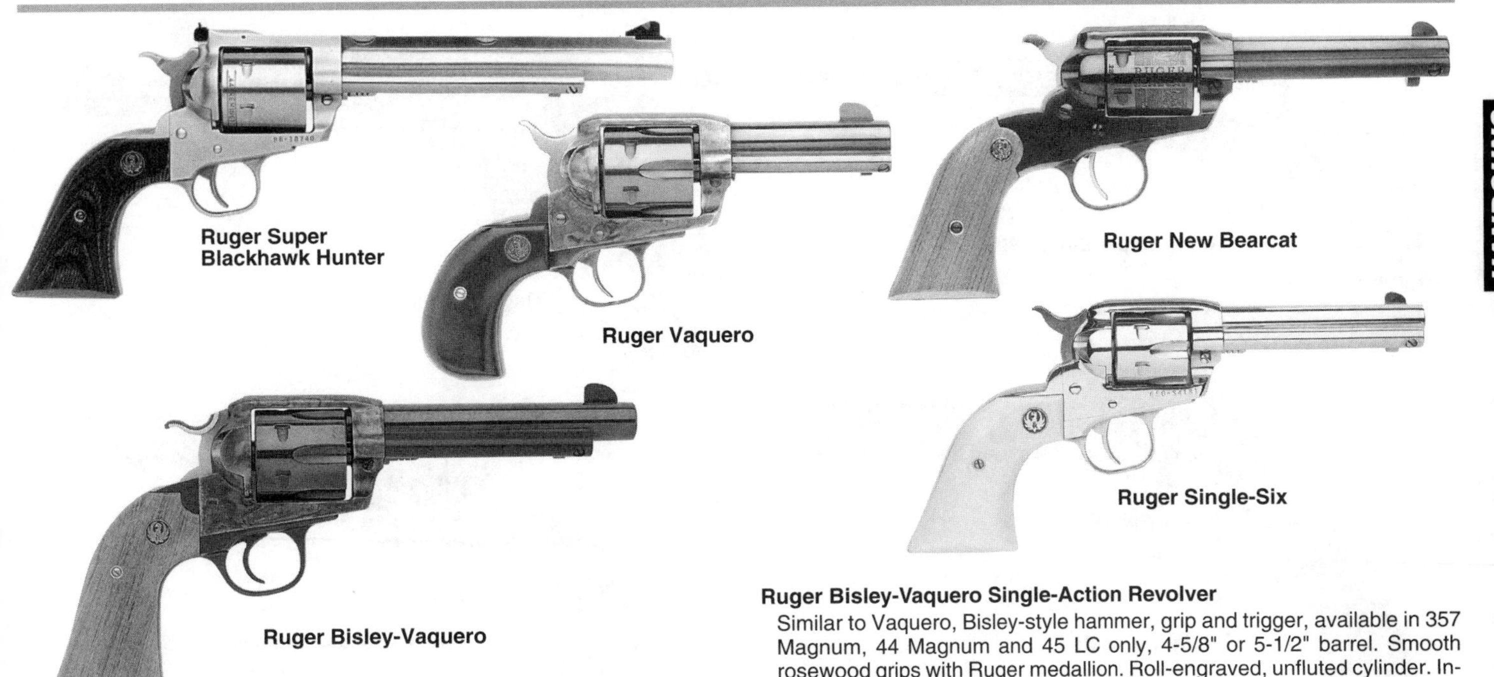
Ruger Super Blackhawk Hunter
Ruger Vaquero
Ruger New Bearcat
Ruger Single-Six
Ruger Bisley-Vaquero

RUGER NEW MODEL SUPER BLACKHAWK

Caliber: 44 Mag., 6-shot. Also fires 44 Spec. **Barrel:** 4-5/8", 5-1/2", 7-1/2", 10-1/2" bull. **Weight:** 48 oz. (7-1/2" bbl.), 51 oz. (10-1/2" bbl.). **Length:** 13-3/8" overall (7-1/2" bbl.). **Grips:** American walnut. **Sights:** 1/8" ramp front, micro-click rear adjustable for windage and elevation. **Features:** Ruger transfer bar safety system, fluted or un-fluted cylinder, steel grip and cylinder frame, round or square back trigger guard, wide serrated trigger, wide spur hammer. With case and lock.

Price: Blue, 4-5/8", 5-1/2", 7-1/2" (S458N, S45N, S47N) **$519.00**
Price: Blue, 10-1/2" bull barrel (S411N) **$529.00**
Price: Stainless, 4-5/8", 5-1/2", 7-1/2" (KS458N, KS45N, KS47N) **$535.00**
Price: Stainless, 10-1/2" bull barrel (KS411N) **$545.00**

RUGER NEW MODEL SUPER BLACKHAWK HUNTER

Caliber: 44 Mag., 6-shot. **Barrel:** 7-1/2", full-length solid rib, unfluted cylinder. **Weight:** 52 oz. **Length:** 13-5/8". **Grips:** Black laminated wood. **Sights:** Adjustable rear, replaceable front blade. **Features:** Reintroduced Ultimate SA revolver. Includes instruction manual, high-impact case, set 1" medium scope rings, gun lock, ejector rod as standard.

Price: **$639.00**

RUGER VAQUERO SINGLE-ACTION REVOLVER

Caliber: 357 Mag., 44-40, 44 Mag., 45 LC, 6-shot. **Barrel:** 4-5/8", 5-1/2", 7-1/2". **Weight:** 38-41 oz. **Length:** 13-1/8" overall (7-1/2" barrel). **Grips:** Smooth rosewood with Ruger medallion. **Sights:** Blade front, fixed notch rear. **Features:** Uses Ruger's patented transfer bar safety system and loading gate interlock with classic styling. Blued model color case-hardened finish on frame, rest polished and blued. Stainless has high-gloss. Introduced 1993. From Sturm, Ruger & Co.

Price: 357 Mag. BNV34, KBNV34 (4-5/8"), BNV35, KBNV35 (5-1/2") **$535.00**
Price: 44-40 BNV40, KBNV40 (4-5/8"). BNV405, KBNV405 (5-1/2"). BNV407, KBNV407 (7-1/2") **$535.00**
Price: 44 Mag., BNV474, KBNV474 (4-5/8"). BNV475, KBNV475 (5-1/2"). BNV477, KBNV477 (7-1/2") **$535.00**
Price: 45 LC, BN444, KBNV44 (4-5/8"). BNV455, KBNV455 (5-1/2"). BNV45, KBNV45 (7-1/2") **$535.00**
Price: 45 LC, BNVBH453, KBNVBH453 3-3/4" with "birds head" grip **$576.00**
Price: 357 Mag., RBNV35 (5-1/2") **$535.00**; KRBNV35 (5-1/2") . **$555.00**
Price: 45 LC, RBNV44 (4-5/8"), RBNV455 (5-1/2") **$535.00**
Price: 45 LC, KRBNV44 (4-5/8"), KRBNV455 (5-1/2") **$555.00**

Ruger Bisley-Vaquero Single-Action Revolver

Similar to Vaquero, Bisley-style hammer, grip and trigger, available in 357 Magnum, 44 Magnum and 45 LC only, 4-5/8" or 5-1/2" barrel. Smooth rosewood grips with Ruger medallion. Roll-engraved, unfluted cylinder. Introduced 1997. From Sturm, Ruger & Co.

Price: Color case-hardened frame, blue grip frame, barrel and cylinder, RBNV-475, RBNV-474, 44 Mag. **$535.00**
Price: High-gloss stainless steel, KRBNV-475, KRBNV-474 . . . . **$555.00**
Price: For simulated ivory grips add . . . . **$41.00 to $44.00**

RUGER NEW BEARCAT SINGLE-ACTION

Caliber: 22 LR, 6-shot. **Barrel:** 4". **Weight:** 24 oz. **Length:** 8-7/8" overall. **Grips:** Smooth rosewood with Ruger medallion. **Sights:** Blade front, fixed notch rear. **Features:** Reintroduction of the Ruger Bearcat with slightly lengthened frame, Ruger patented transfer bar safety system. Available in blue only. Introduced 1993. With case and lock. From Sturm, Ruger & Co.

Price: SBC4, blue **$379.00**
Price: KSBC-4, ss **$429.00**

RUGER MODEL SINGLE-SIX REVOLVER

Caliber: 32 H&R Magnum. **Barrel:** 4-5/8", 6-shot. **Weight:** 33 oz. **Length:** 10-1/8". **Grips:** Blue, rosewood, stainless, simulated ivory. **Sights:** Blade front, notch rear fixed. **Features:** Transfer bar and loading gate interlock safety, instruction manual, high impact case and gun lock.

Price: **$576.00**
Price: Blue, SSM4FS **$576.00**
Price: SS, KSSM4FSI **$576.00**

RUGER SINGLE-SIX AND SUPER SINGLE-SIX CONVERTIBLE

Caliber: 22 LR, 6-shot; 22 WMR in extra cylinder; 17 HMR. **Barrel:** 4-5/8", 5-1/2", 6-1/2", 9-1/2" (6-groove). **Weight:** 35 oz. (6-1/2" bbl.). **Length:** 11-13/16" overall (6-1/2" bbl.). **Grips:** Smooth American walnut. **Sights:** Improved Patridge front on ramp, fully adjustable rear protected by integral frame ribs (super single-six); or fixed sight (single six). **Features:** Ruger transfer bar safety system, loading gate interlock, hardened chrome-moly steel frame, wide trigger, music wire springs throughout, independent firing pin.

Price: 4-5/8", 5-1/2", 6-1/2", 9-1/2" barrel, blue, adjustable sight NR4, NR5, NR6, NR9 . . . . **$399.00**
Price: 5-1/2", 6-1/2" bbl. only, stainless steel, adjustable sight KNR5, KNR6 . . . . **$485.00**
Price: 5-1/2", 6-1/2" barrel, blue fixed sights **$399.00**
Price: 6-1/2" barrel, NR 617, 17 HMR **$399.00**
Price: Ruger 50th Anniversary Single Six with 4-5/8" barrel and a gold-colored rollmark "50 years of Single Six 1953 to 2003," blued steel finish, Cocobolo wood grips with red Ruger medallions and both .22 LR and .22 WMR cylinders **$599.00**
Price: Stainless Hunter **$650.00**

Ruger Super Single-Six

Ruger Bisley

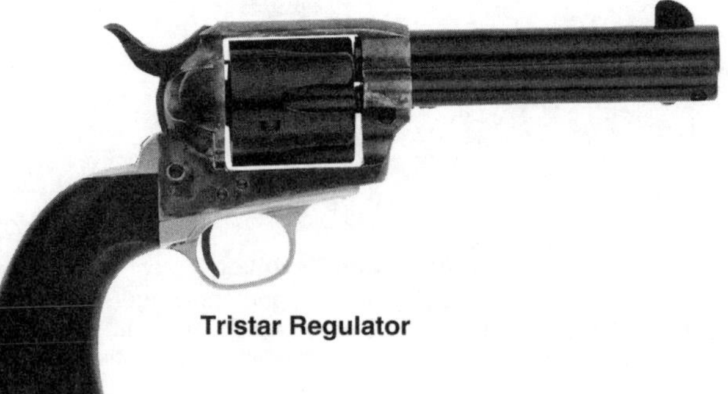

Tristar Regulator

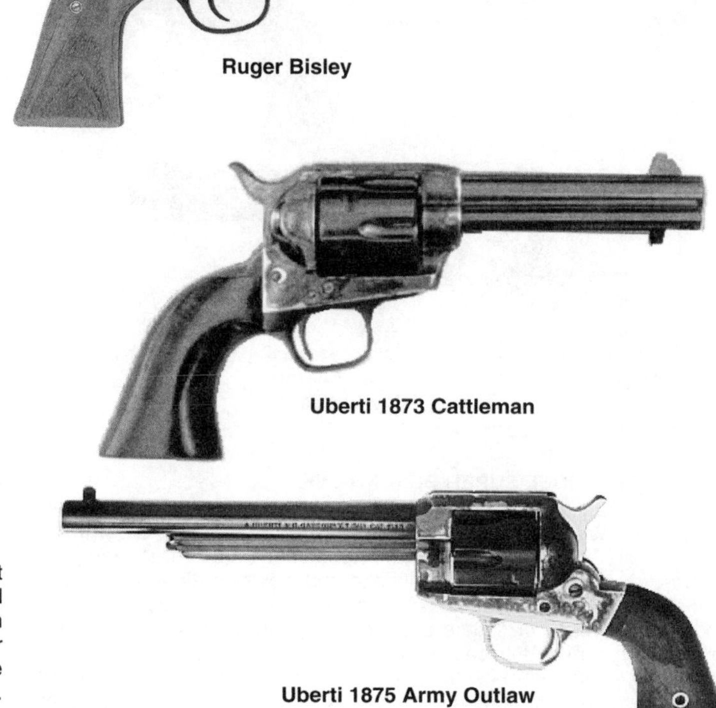

Uberti 1873 Cattleman

Uberti 1875 Army Outlaw

Ruger Bisley Small Frame Revolver

Similar to Single-Six, frame is styled after classic Bisley "flat-top." Most mechanical parts are unchanged. Hammer is lower and smoothly curved with deeply checkered spur. Trigger is strongly curved with wide smooth surface. Longer grip frame designed with hand-filling shape, and trigger guard is a large oval. Adjustable dovetail rear sight; front sight base accepts interchangeable square blades of various heights and styles. Unfluted cylinder and roll engraving. Weighs 41 oz. Chambered for 22 LR, 6-1/2" barrel only. Plastic lockable case. Introduced 1985.

Price: RB-22AW **$422.00**

SMITH & WESSON COMMEMORATIVE MODEL 2000

Caliber: 45 S&W Schofield. **Barrel:** 7". **Features:** 150th Anniversary logo, engraved, gold-plated, walnut grips, blue, original style hammer, trigger, and barrel latch. Wood presentation case. Limited.

Price: . . . . **NA**

TRISTAR/UBERTI REGULATOR REVOLVER

Caliber: 45 Colt. **Barrel:** 4-3/4", 5-1/2". **Weight:** 32-38 oz. **Length:** 8-1/4" overall (4-3/4" bbl.) **Grips:** One-piece walnut. **Sights:** Blade front, notch rear. **Features:** Uberti replica of 1873 Colt Model "P" revolver. Color-case hardened steel frame, brass backstrap and trigger guard, hammer-block safety. Imported from Italy by Tristar Sporting Arms.

Price: Regulator **$335.00**

Price: Regulator Deluxe (blued backstrap, trigger guard). **$367.00**

UBERTI 1873 CATTLEMAN SINGLE-ACTION

Caliber: 22 LR/22 WMR, 38 Spec., 357 Mag., 44 Spec., 44-40, 45 Colt/45 ACP, 6-shot. **Barrel:** 4-3/4", 5-1/2", 7-1/2"; 44-40, 45 Colt also with 3", 3-1/2", 4". **Weight:** 38 oz. (5-1/2" bbl.). **Length:** 10-3/4" overall (5-1/2" bbl.). **Grips:** One-piece smooth walnut. **Sights:** Blade front, groove rear; fully adjustable rear available. **Features:** Steel or brass backstrap, trigger guard; color case-hardened frame, blued barrel, cylinder. Imported from Italy by Uberti U.S.A.

Price: Steel backstrap, trigger guard, fixed sights. **$410.00**

Price: Brass backstrap, trigger guard, fixed sights **$359.00**

Price: Bisley model. **$435.00**

Uberti 1873 Buckhorn Single-Action

A slightly larger version of the Cattleman revolver. Available in 44 Magnum or 44 Magnum/44-40 convertible, otherwise has same specs.

Price: Steel backstrap, trigger guard, fixed sights. **$410.00**

UBERTI 1875 SA ARMY OUTLAW REVOLVER

Caliber: 357 Mag., 44-40, 45 Colt, 45 Colt/45 ACP convertible, 6-shot. **Barrel:** 5-1/2", 7-1/2". **Weight:** 44 oz. **Length:** 13-3/4" overall. **Grips:** Smooth walnut. **Sights:** Blade front, notch rear. **Features:** Replica of the 1875 Remington S.A. Army revolver. Brass trigger guard, color case-hardened frame, rest blued. Imported by Uberti U.S.A.

Price: **$483.00**

Price: 45 Colt/45 ACP convertible **$525.00**

UBERTI 1890 ARMY OUTLAW REVOLVER

Caliber: 357 Mag., 44-40, 45 Colt, 45 Colt/45 ACP convertible, 6-shot. **Barrel:** 5-1/2", 7-1/2". **Weight:** 37 oz. **Length:** 12-1/2" overall. **Grips:** American walnut. **Sights:** Blade front, groove rear. **Features:** Replica of the 1890 Remington single-action. Brass trigger guard, rest is blued. Imported by Uberti U.S.A.

Price: **$483.00**

UBERTI NEW MODEL RUSSIAN REVOLVER

Caliber: 44 Russian, 6-shot cylinder. **Barrel:** 6-1/2". **Weight:** 40 oz. **Length:** 12" overall. **Grips:** Smooth walnut. **Sights:** Blade front, notch rear. **Features:** Repica of the S&W Model 3 Russian Third Model revolver. Spur trigger guard, polished blue finish. Introduced 1999. Imported by Uberti USA.

Price: **$800.00**

UBERTI 1875 SCHOFIELD-STYLE BREAK-TOP REVOLVER

Caliber: 44-40, 45 Colt, 6-shot cylinder. **Barrel:** 5", 7". **Weight:** 39 oz. **Length:** 10-3/4" overall (5" barrel). **Grips:** Smooth walnut. **Sights:** Blade front, notch rear. **Features:** Replica of Smith & Wesson Model 3 Schofield. Single-action, top-break with automatic ejection. Polished blue finish. Introduced 1994. Imported by Uberti USA.

Price: **$750.00**

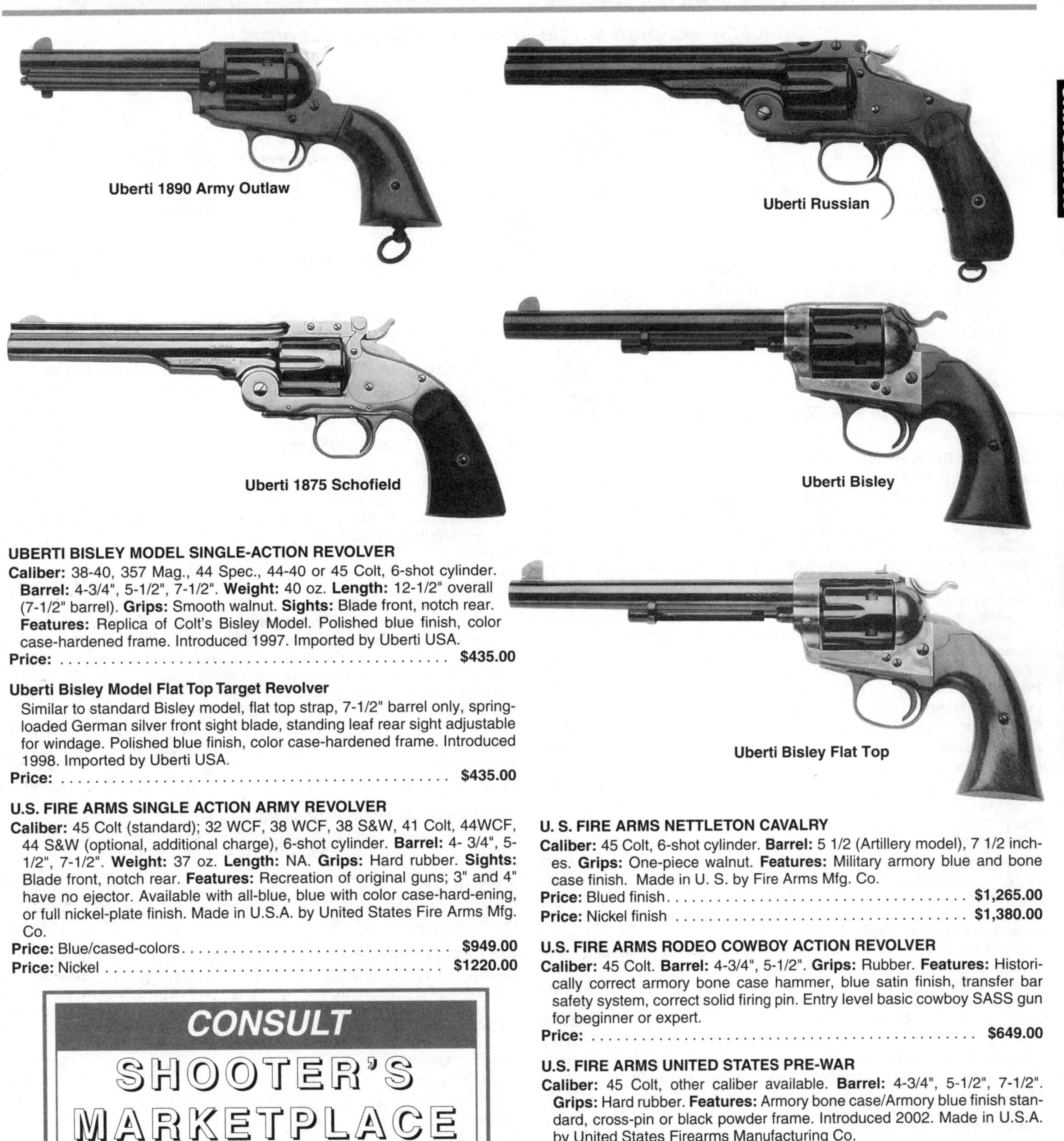

Uberti 1890 Army Outlaw

Uberti Russian

Uberti 1875 Schofield

Uberti Bisley

Uberti Bisley Flat Top

UBERTI BISLEY MODEL SINGLE-ACTION REVOLVER

Caliber: 38-40, 357 Mag., 44 Spec., 44-40 or 45 Colt, 6-shot cylinder. **Barrel:** 4-3/4", 5-1/2", 7-1/2". **Weight:** 40 oz. **Length:** 12-1/2" overall (7-1/2" barrel). **Grips:** Smooth walnut. **Sights:** Blade front, notch rear. **Features:** Replica of Colt's Bisley Model. Polished blue finish, color case-hardened frame. Introduced 1997. Imported by Uberti USA.

Price: **$435.00**

Uberti Bisley Model Flat Top Target Revolver

Similar to standard Bisley model, flat top strap, 7-1/2" barrel only, spring-loaded German silver front sight blade, standing leaf rear sight adjustable for windage. Polished blue finish, color case-hardened frame. Introduced 1998. Imported by Uberti USA.

Price: **$435.00**

U.S. FIRE ARMS SINGLE ACTION ARMY REVOLVER

Caliber: 45 Colt (standard); 32 WCF, 38 WCF, 38 S&W, 41 Colt, 44WCF, 44 S&W (optional, additional charge), 6-shot cylinder. **Barrel:** 4- 3/4", 5-1/2", 7-1/2". **Weight:** 37 oz. **Length:** NA. **Grips:** Hard rubber. **Sights:** Blade front, notch rear. **Features:** Recreation of original guns; 3" and 4" have no ejector. Available with all-blue, blue with color case-hard-ening, or full nickel-plate finish. Made in U.S.A. by United States Fire Arms Mfg. Co.

Price: Blue/cased-colors **$949.00**

Price: Nickel **$1220.00**

U. S. FIRE ARMS NETTLETON CAVALRY

Caliber: 45 Colt, 6-shot cylinder. **Barrel:** 5 1/2 (Artillery model), 7 1/2 inches. **Grips:** One-piece walnut. **Features:** Military armory blue and bone case finish. Made in U. S. by Fire Arms Mfg. Co.

Price: Blued finish **$1,265.00**

Price: Nickel finish **$1,380.00**

U.S. FIRE ARMS RODEO COWBOY ACTION REVOLVER

Caliber: 45 Colt. **Barrel:** 4-3/4", 5-1/2". **Grips:** Rubber. **Features:** Historically correct armory bone case hammer, blue satin finish, transfer bar safety system, correct solid firing pin. Entry level basic cowboy SASS gun for beginner or expert.

Price: **$649.00**

U.S. FIRE ARMS UNITED STATES PRE-WAR

Caliber: 45 Colt, other caliber available. **Barrel:** 4-3/4", 5-1/2", 7-1/2". **Grips:** Hard rubber. **Features:** Armory bone case/Armory blue finish standard, cross-pin or black powder frame. Introduced 2002. Made in U.S.A. by United States Firearms Manufacturing Co.

Price: **$1,195.00**

HANDGUNS — MISCELLANEOUS

Specially adapted single-shot and multi-barrel arms.

American Derringer Model 1

American Derringer Model 4

American Derringer Model 6

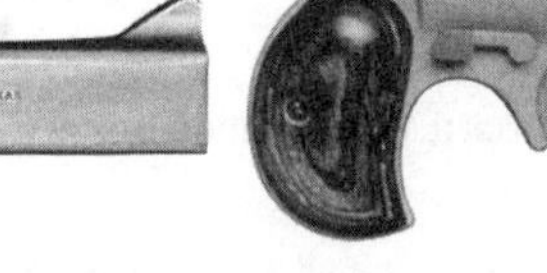

American Derringer Model 7

American Derringer Lady Derringer

American Derringer DA 38

AMERICAN DERRINGER MODEL 1

Caliber: 22 LR, 22 WMR, 30 Carbine, 30 Luger, 30-30 Win., 32 H&R Mag., 32-20, 380 ACP, 38 Super, 38 Spec., 38 Spec. shotshell, 38 Spec. +P, 9mm Para., 357 Mag., 357 Mag./45/410, 357 Maximum, 10mm, 40 S&W, 41 Mag., 38-40, 44-40 Win., 44 Spec., 44 Mag., 45 Colt, 45 Win. Mag., 45 ACP, 45 Colt/410, 45-70 single shot. **Barrel:** 3". **Weight:** 15-1/2 oz. (38 Spec.). **Length:** 4.82" overall. **Grips:** Rosewood, Zebra wood. **Sights:** Blade front. **Features:** Made of stainless steel with high-polish or satin finish. Two-shot capacity. Manual hammer block safety. Introduced 1980. Available in almost any pistol caliber. Contact the factory for complete list of available calibers and prices. From American Derringer Corp.

Price: 22 LR . . . . POR
Price: 38 Spec. . . . . POR
Price: 357 Maximum . . . . POR
Price: 357 Mag. . . . . POR
Price: 9mm, 380 . . . . POR
Price: 40 S&W . . . . POR
Price: 44 Spec. . . . . POR
Price: 44-40 Win. . . . . POR
Price: 45 Colt . . . . POR
Price: 30-30, 45 Win. Mag. . . . . POR
Price: 41, 44 Mags. . . . . POR
Price: 45-70, single shot . . . . POR
Price: 45 Colt, 410, 2-1/2" . . . . POR
Price: 45 ACP, 10mm Auto . . . . POR

American Derringer Model 4

Similar to the Model 1 except has 4.1" barrel, overall length of 6", and weighs 16-1/2 oz.; chambered for 357 Mag., 357 Maximum, 45-70, 3" 410-bore shotshells or 45 Colt or 44 Mag. Made of stainless steel. Manual hammer block safety. Introduced 1980.

Price: 3" 410/45 Colt **$425.00**
Price: 45-70 . . . . **$560.00**
Price: 44 Mag. with oversize grips **$515.00**
Price: Alaskan Survival model (45-70 upper barrel, 410 or 45 Colt lower) **$475.00**

American Derringer Model 6

Similar to the Model 1 except has 6" barrel chambered for 3" 410 shotshells or 22 WMR, 357 Mag., 45 ACP, 45 Colt; rosewood stocks; 8.2" o.a.l. and weighs 21 oz. Shoots either round for each barrel. Manual ham-mer block safety. Introduced 1980.

Price: 22 WMR **$440.00**
Price: 357 Mag. **$440.00**
Price: 45 Colt/410 . . . . **$450.00**
Price: 45 ACP **$440.00**

American Derringer Model 7 Ultra Lightweight

Similar to Model 1 except made of high strength aircraft aluminum. Weighs 7-1/2 oz., 4.82" o.a.l., rosewood stocks. Available in 22 LR, 22 WMR, 32 H&R Mag., 380 ACP, 38 Spec., 44 Spec. Introduced 1980.

Price: 22 LR, WMR **$325.00**
Price: 38 Spec. **$325.00**
Price: 380 ACP **$325.00**
Price: 32 H&R Mag/32 S&W Long **$325.00**
Price: 44 Spec. **$565.00**

American Derringer Model 10 Ultra Lightweight

Similar to the Model 1 except frame is of aluminum, giving weight of 10 oz. Stainless barrels. Available in 38 Spec., 45 Colt or 45 ACP only. Matte gray finish. Introduced 1980.

Price: 45 Colt **$385.00**
Price: 45 ACP **$330.00**
Price: 38 Spec. **$305.00**

American Derringer Lady Derringer

Same as the Model 1 except has tuned action, is fitted with scrimshawed synthetic ivory grips; chambered for 32 H&R Mag. and 38 Spec.; 357 Mag., 45 Colt, 45/410. Deluxe Grade is highly polished; Deluxe Engraved is engraved in a pattern similar to that used on 1880s derringers. All come in a French fitted jewelry box. Introduced 1989.

Price: 32 H&R Mag. **$375.00**
Price: 357 Mag. **$405.00**
Price: 38 Spec. **$360.00**
Price: 45 Colt, 45/410 . . . . **$435.00**

American Derringer Texas Commemorative

A Model 1 Derringer with solid brass frame, stainless steel barrel and rosewood grips. Available in 38 Spec., 44-40 Win., or 45 Colt. Introduced 1980.

Price: 38 Spec. **$365.00**
Price: 44-40 . . . . **$420.00**
Price: Brass frame, 45 Colt **$450.00**

AMERICAN DERRINGER DA 38 MODEL

Caliber: 22 LR, 9mm Para., 38 Spec., 357 Mag., 40 S&W. **Barrel:** 3". **Weight:** 14.5 oz. **Length:** 4.8" overall. **Grips:** Rosewood, walnut or other hardwoods. **Sights:** Fixed. **Features:** Double-action only; two-shots. Manual safety. Made of satin-finished stainless steel and aluminum. Introduced 1989. From American Derringer Corp.

Price: 22 LR **$435.00**
Price: 38 Spec. **$460.00**
Price: 9mm Para. **$445.00**
Price: 357 Mag. **$450.00**
Price: 40 S&W **$475.00**

ANSCHUTZ MODEL 64P SPORT/TARGET PISTOL

Caliber: 22 LR, 22 WMR, 5-shot magazine. **Barrel:** 10". **Weight:** 3 lbs., 8 oz. **Length:** 18-1/2" overall. **Stock:** Choate Rynite. **Sights:** None furnished; grooved for scope mounting. **Features:** Right-hand bolt; polished blue finish. Introduced 1998. Imported from Germany by AcuSport.

Price: 22 LR **$455.95**
Price: 22 WMR **$479.95**

HANDGUNS — MISCELLANEOUS

Bond Arms Texas Defender

Bond Arms Century 2000 Defender

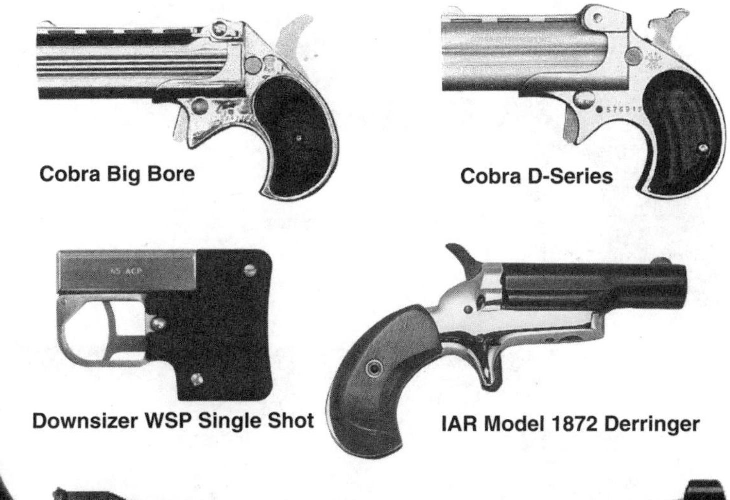

Cobra Big Bore

Cobra D-Series

Downsizer WSP Single Shot

IAR Model 1872 Derringer

Comanche Super Single Shot

Gaucher GN1 Silhouette

BOND ARMS DEFENDER DERRINGER

Caliber: 410 Buckshot or slug, 45 Colt/45 Schofield (2.5" chamber), 45 Colt (only), 450 Bond Super/45 ACP/45 Super, 44 Mag./44 Special/44 Russian, 10mm, 40 S&W, 357 SIG, 357 Maxi-mum/357 Mag./38 Special, 357 Mag/38 Special & 38 Long Colt, 38 Short Colt, 9mm Luger (9x19), 32 H&R Mag./38 S&W Long/32 Colt New Police, 22 Mag., 22 LR., 38-40, 44-40. **Barrel:** 3", 3-1/2". **Weight:** 20-21 oz. **Length:** 5"-5-1/2". **Grips:** Exotic woods or animal horn. **Sights:** Blade front, fixed rear. **Features:** Interchangeable barrels, retractingand rebounding firing pins, cross-bolt safety, automatic extractor for rimmed calibers. Stainless steel construction. Right or left hand.

Price: Texas (with TG) 3" bbl. **$379.00**

Price: Super (with TG) 3" bbl., 450 Bond Super and 45 ACP . . . **$379.00**

Price: Cowboy (no TG) **$379.00**

Price: Century 2000 (with TG), Cowboy Century 2000 (no TG), 3-1/2" bbls., 410/45 Colt **$394.00**

Price: Additional calibers - available separately

BROWN CLASSIC SINGLE SHOT PISTOL

Caliber: 17 Ackley Hornet through 375x444. **Barrel:** 15" airgauged match grade. **Weight:** About 3 lbs., 7 oz. **Grips:** Walnut; thumbrest target style. **Sights:** None furnished; drilled and tapped for scope mounting. **Features:** Falling block action gives rigid barrel-receiver mating; hand-fit-ted and headspaced. Introduced 1998. Made in U.S.A. by E.A. Brown Mfg.

Price: **$589.00**

COBRA BIG BORE DERRINGERS

Caliber: 22 WMR, 32 H&R Mag, 38 Spec., 9mm Para. **Barrel:** 2.75". **Weight:** 11.5 oz. **Length:** 4.65" overall. **Grips:** Textured black synthetic. **Sights:** Blade front, fixed notch rear. **Features:** Alloy frame, steel-lined barrels, steel breech block. Plunger-type safety with integral hammer block. Chrome or black Teflon finish. Introduced 2002. Made in U.S.A. by Cobra Enterprises.

Price: **$98.00**

Price: 9mm Para **$136.00**

COBRA LONG-BORE DERRINGERS

Caliber: 22 WMR, 38 Spec., 9mm Para. **Barrel:** 3.5". **Weight:** 13 oz. **Length**: 5.65" overall. **Grips:** Textured black synthetic. **Sights:** Fixed. **Features:** Chrome or black Teflon finish. Larger than Davis D-Series models. Introduced 2002. Made in U.S.A. by Cobra Enterprises.

Price: **$136.00**

Price: 9mm Para. **$136.00**

Price: Big-Bore models (same calibers, 3/4" shorter barrels). . . . **$136.00**

COBRA STARBIRD-SERIES DERRINGERS

Caliber: 22 LR, 22 WMR, 25 ACP, 32 ACP. **Barrel:** 2.4". **Weight:** 9.5 oz. **Length**: 4" overall. **Grips:** Laminated wood or pearl. **Sights:** Blade front, fixed notch rear. **Features:** Choice of black powder coat, satin nickel or chrome finish; spur trigger. Introduced 2002. Made in U.S.A. by Cobra Enterprises.

Price: **$112.00**

COMANCHE SUPER SINGLE SHOT PISTOL

Caliber: 45 LC, 410 ga. **Barrel:** 10." **Sights:** Adjustable. **Features:** Blue finish, not available for sale in CA, MA. Distributed by SGS Importers International, Inc.

Price: **$174.95**

Price: Satin nickel **$191.95**

Price: Duo tone **$185.95**

DOWNSIZER WSP SINGLE SHOT PISTOL

Caliber: 357 Magnum, 45 ACP, 38 Special. **Barrel:** 2.10." **Weight:** 11 oz. **Length:** 3.25" overall. **Grips:** Black polymer. **Sights:** None. **Features:** Single shot, tip-up barrel. Double action only. Stainless steel construction. Measures .900" thick. Introduced 1997. From Downsizer Corp.

Price: **$499.00**

GAUCHER GN1 SILHOUETTE PISTOL

Caliber: 22 LR, single shot. **Barrel:** 10". **Weight:** 2.4 lbs. **Length:** 15.5" overall. **Grips:** European hardwood. **Sights:** Blade front, open adjustable rear. **Features:** Bolt action, adjustable trigger. Introduced 1990. Imported from France by Mandall Shooting Supplies.

Price: About **$525.00**

Price: Model GP Silhouette **$425.00**

IAR MODEL 1872 DERRINGER

Caliber: 22 Short. **Barrel:** 2-3/8". **Weight:** 7 oz. **Length:** 5-1/8" overall. **Grips:** Smooth walnut. **Sights:** Blade front, notch rear. **Features:** Gold or nickel frame with blue barrel. Reintroduced 1996 using original Colt designs and tooling for the Colt Model 4 Derringer. Made in U.S.A. by IAR, Inc.

Price: **$109.00**

Price: Single cased gun **$125.00**

Price: Double cased set **$215.00**

IAR MODEL 1866 DOUBLE DERRINGER

Caliber: 38 Special. **Barrel:** 2-3/4". **Weight:** 16 oz. **Grips:** Smooth walnut. **Sights:** Blade front, notch rear. **Features:** All steel construction. Blue barrel, color case-hardened frame. Uses original designs and tooling for the Uberti New Maverick Derringer. Introduced 1999. Made in U.S.A. by IAR, Inc.

Price: **$395.00**

Maximum Single Shot

RPM XL Pistol

Thompson/Center C2 Contender

MAXIMUM SINGLE SHOT PISTOL

Caliber: 22 LR, 22 Hornet, 22 BR, 22 PPC, 223 Rem., 22-250, 6mm BR, 6mm PPC, 243, 250 Savage, 6.5mm-35M, 270 MAX, 270 Win., 7mm TCU, 7mm BR, 7mm-35, 7mm INT-R, 7mm-08, 7mm Rocket, 7mm Super-Mag., 30 Herrett, 30 Carbine, 30-30, 308 Win., 30x39, 32-20, 350 Rem. Mag., 357 Mag., 357 Maximum, 358 Win., 375 H&H, 44 Mag., 454 Casull. **Barrel:** 8-3/4", 10-1/2", 14". **Weight:** 61 oz. (10-1/2" bbl.); 78 oz. (14" bbl.). **Length:** 15", 18-1/2" overall (with 10-1/2" and 14" bbl., respectively). **Grips:** Smooth walnut stocks and forend. Also available with 17" finger groove grip. **Sights:** Ramp front, fully adjustable open rear. **Features:** Falling block action; drilled and tapped for M.O.A. scope mounts; integral grip frame/receiver; adjustable trigger; Douglas barrel (interchangeable). Introduced 1983. Made in U.S.A. by M.O.A. Corp.

Price: Stainless receiver, blue barrel **$799.00**
Price: Stainless receiver, stainless barrel **$883.00**
Price: Extra blued barrel **$254.00**
Price: Extra stainless barrel **$317.00**
Price: Scope mount **$60.00**

RPM XL SINGLE SHOT PISTOL

Caliber: 22 LR through 45-70. **Barrel:** 8", 10-3/4", 12", 14". **Weight:** About 60 oz. **Grips:** Smooth Goncalo Alves with thumb and heel rests. **Sights:** Hooded front with interchangeable post, or Patridge; ISGW rear adjustable for windage and elevation. **Features:** Barrel drilled and tapped for scope mount. Visible cocking indicator. Spring-loaded barrel lock, positive hammer-block safety. Trigger adjustable for weight of pull and over-travel. Contact maker for complete price list. Made in U.S.A. by RPM.

Price: XL Hunter model (action only) **$1,045.00**
Price: Extra barrel, 8" through 10-3/4" **$407.50**
Price: Extra barrel, 12" through 14" **$547.50**
Price: Muzzle brake **$160.00**
Price: Left hand action, add **$50.00**

SAVAGE STRIKER BOLT-ACTION HUNTING HANDGUN

Caliber: 223, 243, 7mm-08, 308, 300 WSM 2-shot mag. **Barrel:** 14". **Weight:** About 5 lbs. **Length:** 22-1/2" overall. **Stock:** Black composite ambidextrous mid-grip; grooved forend; "Dual Pillar" bedding. **Sights:** None furnished; drilled and tapped for scope mounting. **Features:** Short left-hand bolt with right-hand ejection; free-floated barrel; uses Savage Model 110 rifle scope rings/bases. Introduced 1998. Made in U.S.A. by Savage Arms, Inc.

Price: Model 503 (blued barrel and action) **$285.00**
Price: Model 503 R17FSS (stainless barrel and action) **$281.00**
Price: Model 516FSAK black stock (ss, aMB, 300WSM) **$260.00**

SAVAGE SPORT STRIKER BOLT-ACTION HUNTING HANDGUN

Similar to Striker, but chambered in 22 LR and 22 WMR. Detachable, 10-shot magazine (5-shot magazine for 22 WMR). Overall length 19", weighs 4 lbs. Ambidextrous fiberglass/graphite composite rear grip. Drilled and tapped, scope mount installed. Introduced 2000. Made in U.S.A. by Savage Arms Inc.

Price: Model 501F (blue finish, 22LR) **$236.00**
Price: Model 501FXP with soft case, 1.25-4x28 scope **$258.00**
Price: Model 502F (blue finish, 22 WMR) **$238.00**

SPRINGFIELD M6 SCOUT PISTOL

Caliber: 22 LR/45 LC/.410, 22 Hornet, 45 LC/.410. **Barrel:** 10". **Weight:** NA. **Length:** NA. **Grips:** NA. **Sights:** NA. **Features:** Adapted from the U.S. Air Force M6 Survival Rifle, it is also available as a carbine with 16" barrel.

Price: .... **$169.00 to $197.00**
Price: Pistol/Carbine .... **$183.00 to $209.00**

THOMPSON/CENTER ENCORE PISTOL

Caliber: 22-250, 223, 260 Rem., 7mm-08, 243, 308, 270, 30-06, 375 JDJ, 204 Ruger, 44 Mag., 454 Casull, 480 Ruger, 444 Marlin single shot, 450 Marlin with muzzle tamer, no sights. **Barrel:** 12", 15", tapered round. **Weight:** NA. **Length:** 21" overall with 12" barrel. **Grips:** American walnut with finger grooves, walnut forend. **Sights:** Blade on ramp front, adjustable rear, or none. **Features:** Interchangeable barrels; action opens by squeezing the trigger guard; drilled and tapped for scope mounting; blue finish. Announced 1996. Made in U.S.A. by Thompson/Center Arms.

Price: .... **$578.00 to $641.00**
Price: Extra 12" barrels **$260.00**
Price: Extra 15" barrels **$267.00**
Price: 45 Colt/410 barrel, 12" **$289.00**
Price: 45 Colt/410 barrel, 15" **$297.00**

Thompson/Center Stainless Encore Pistol

Similar to blued Encore, made of stainless steel, available with 15" barrel in 223, 22-250, 243 Win., 7mm-08, 308, 30/06 Sprgfld., 45/70 Gov't., 45/410 VR. With black rubber grip and forend. Made in U.S.A. by Thompson/Center Arms.

Price: .... **$633.00 to $670.00**

Thompson/Center G2 Contender Pistol

A second generation Contender pistol maintaining the same barrel interchangeability with older Contender barrels and their corresponding forends (except Herrett forend). The G2 frame will not accept old-style grips due to the change in grip angle. Incorporates an automatic hammer block safety with built-in interlock. Features include trigger adjustable for overtravel, adjustable rear sight; ramp front sight blade, blued steel finish.

Price: **$566.75**

UBERTI ROLLING BLOCK TARGET PISTOL

Caliber: 22 LR, 22 WMR, 22 Hornet, 357 Mag., 45 Colt, single shot. **Barrel:** 9-7/8", half-round, half-octagon. **Weight:** 44 oz. **Length:** 14" overall. **Stock:** Walnut grip and forend. **Sights:** Blade front, fully adjustable rear. **Features:** Replica of the 1871 rolling block target pistol. Brass trigger guard, color case-hardened frame, blue barrel. Imported by Uberti U.S.A.

Price: **$410.00**

CENTERFIRE RIFLES — AUTOLOADERS

Both classic arms and recent designs in American-style repeaters for sport and field shooting.

Armalite M15A2

Armalite AR-10A4

Armalite AR-180B

Auto-Ordnance 1927 A-1 Thompson

ARMALITE M15A2 CARBINE

Caliber: 223, 7-shot magazine. **Barrel:** 16" heavy chrome lined; 1:9" twist. **Weight:** 7 lbs. **Length:** 35-11/16" overall. **Stock:** Green or black composition. **Sights:** Standard A2. **Features:** Upper and lower receivers have push-type pivot pin; hard coat anodized; A2-style forward assist; M16A2-type raised fence around magazine release button. Made in U.S.A. by ArmaLite, Inc.

Price: Green **$930.00**

Price: Black **$945.00**

ARMALITE AR-10A4 SPECIAL PURPOSE RIFLE

Caliber: 308 Win., 10-shot magazine. **Barrel:** 20" chrome-lined, 1:12" twist. **Weight:** 9.6 lbs. **Length:** 41" overall **Stock:** Green or black composition. **Sights:** Detachable handle, front sight, or scope mount available; comes with international style flattop receiver with Picatinny rail. **Features:** Proprietary recoil check. Forged upper receiver with case deflector. Receivers are hard-coat anodized. Introduced 1995. Made in U.S.A. by ArmaLite, Inc.

Price: Green **$1,383.00**

Price: Black **$1,383.00**

Price: Green or black with match trigger **$1,483.00**

Price: Green or Black with match trigger and stainless barrel . . **$1,583.00**

Armalite AR-10(T)

Similar to the Armalite AR-10A4 but with stainless steel, barrel, machined tool steel, two-stage National Match trigger group and other features.

Price: AR-10(T) Rifle **$2,080.00**

Price: AR-10(T) Carbine **$2,080.00**

Armalite AR-10A2

Utilizing the same 20" double-lapped, heavy barrel as the Armalite AR-10A4 Special Purpose Rifle, the AR-10A2 has a clamping front sight base allowing the removeable front sight to be rotated to zero the front sight. This assures the rear sight is centered and full left and right windage movement is available when shooting in strong winds. Offered in 308 caliber only. Made in U.S.A. by Armalite, Inc.

Price: AR-10A2 Rifle or Carbine. **$1,435.00**

Price: AR-10A2 Rifle or Carbine with match trigger **$1,535.00**

Price: AR-10A2 Rifle with stainless steel barrel **$1,535.00**

ARMALITE AR-180B RIFLE

Caliber: 223, 10-shot magazine. **Barrel:** 19.8" **Weight:** 6 lbs. **Length:** 38". **Stock:** Synthetic. **Sights:** Rear sight adjustable for windage, small and large apertures. **Features:** Lower receiver made of polymer, upper formed of sheet metal. Uses standard AR-15 magazines. Made in U.S.A. by Armalite. **Price: $650.00**

Price: With match trigger **$750.00**

ARSENAL USA SSR-56

Caliber: 7.62x39mm **Barrel:** 16.25" **Weight:** 7.4 lbs. **Length:** 35.5" **Stock:** Black polymer. **Sights:** Adjustable rear. **Features:** An AK-47 style rifle built on a hardened Hungarian FEG receiver with the required six U.S. made parts to make it legal for use with all extra-capacity magazines. From Arsenal I, LLC.

Price: **$565.00**

Barrett Model 82A-1

Browning Mark II Safari

ARSENAL USA SSR-74-2

Caliber: 5.45x39mm **Barrel:** 16.25" **Weight:** 7 lbs. **Length:** 36.75" **Stock:** Polymer or wood. **Sights:** Adjustable. **Features:** Built with parts from an unissued Bulgarian AK-74 rifle, it has a Buffer Technologies recoil buffer, and enough U.S.-made parts to allow pistol grip stock, and use with all extra-capacity magazines. Assembled in U.S.A. From Arsenal I, LLC.

Price: **$499.00**

ARSENAL USA SSR-85C-2

Caliber: 7.62x39mm **Barrel:** 16.25" **Weight:** 7.1 lbs. **Length:** 35.5" **Stock:** Polymer or wood. **Sights:** Adjustable rear calibrated to 800 meters. **Features:** Built from parts obtained from unissued Polish AK-47 rifles, the gas tube is vented and the receiver cover is plain. Rifle contains enough U.S.-sourced parts to allow pistol grip stock and use with all extra-capacity magazines. Assembled in U.S.A. by Arsenal USA I, LLC.

Price: **$499.00**

AUTO-ORDNANCE 1927 A-1 THOMPSON

Caliber: 45 ACP. **Barrel:** 16-1/2". **Weight:** 13 lbs. **Length:** About 41" overall (Deluxe). **Stock:** Walnut stock and vertical forend. **Sights:** Blade front, open rear adjustable for windage. **Features:** Recreation of Thompson Model 1927. Semi-auto only. Deluxe model has finned barrel, adjustable rear sight and compensator; Standard model has plain barrel and military sight. From Auto-Ordnance Corp.

Price: Deluxe **$950.00**

Price: 1927A1C Lightweight model (9-1/2 lbs.) **$950.00**

Auto-Ordnance Thompson M1/M1-C

Similar to the 1927 A-1 except is in the M-1 configuration with side cocking knob, horizontal forend, smooth unfinned barrel, sling swivels on butt and forend. Matte black finish. Introduced 1985.

Price: M1 semi-auto carbine. **$950.00**

Price: M1-C lightweight semi-auto **$925.00**

Auto-Ordnance 1927A1 Commando

Similar to the 1927A1 except has Parkerized finish, black-finish wood butt, pistol grip, horizontal forend. Comes with black nylon sling. Introduced 1998. Made in U.S.A. by Auto-Ordnance Corp.

Price: **$950.00**

BARRETT MODEL 82A-1 SEMI-AUTOMATIC RIFLE

Caliber: 50 BMG, 10-shot detachable box magazine. **Barrel:** 29". **Weight:** 28.5 lbs. **Length:** 57" overall. **Stock:** Composition with energy-absorbing recoil pad. **Sights:** Scope optional. **Features:** Semi-automatic, recoil operated with recoiling barrel. Three-lug locking bolt; muzzle brake. Adjustable bipod. Introduced 1985. Made in U.S.A. by Barrett Firearms.

Price: From **$7,200.00**

BENELLI RI RIFLE

Caliber: 300 Win. Mag., 30-06 Springfield. **Barrel:** 20", 22", 24". **Weight:** 7.1 lbs. **Length:** 43.75" **Stock:** Select satin walnut. **Sights:** None. **Features:** Auto-regulating gas-operated system, three-lugged rotary bolt, interchangeable barrels. Introduced 2003. Imported from Italy by Benelli USA.

Price: . . . . **$1065.00 to $1,080.00**

BROWNING BAR MARK II SAFARI SEMI-AUTO RIFLE

Caliber: 243, 25-06, 270, 30-06, 308, 270 WSM, 7mm WSM. **Barrel:** 22" round tapered. **Weight:** 7-3/8 lbs. **Length:** 43" overall. **Stock:** French walnut pistol grip stock and forend, hand checkered. **Sights:** Gold bead on hooded ramp front, click adjustable rear, or no sights. **Features:** Has new bolt release lever; removable trigger assembly with larger trigger guard; redesigned gas and buffer systems. Detachable 4-round box magazine. Scroll-engraved receiver is tapped for scope mounting. BOSS barrel vibration modulator and muzzle brake system available only on models without sights. Mark II Safari introduced 1993. Imported from Belgium by Browning.

Price: Safari, with sights **$833.00**

Price: Safari, no sights **$815.00**

Price: Safari, 270 and 30-06, no sights, BOSS. **$891.00**

Browning BAR Mark II Safari Rifle (Magnum)

Same as the standard caliber model, except weighs 8-3/8 lbs., 45" overall, 24" bbl., 3-round mag. Cals. 7mm Mag., 300 Win. Mag., 338 Win. Mag. BOSS barrel vibration modulator and muzzle brake system available only on models without sights. Introduced 1993.

Price: Safari, no sights **$908.00**

Price: Safari, no sights, BOSS **$1,007.00**

BROWNING BAR SHORT TRAC/LONG TRAC AUTO RIFLES

Caliber: (Short Trac models): 270 WSM, 7mm WSM, 300 WSM, 243 Win., 308 WIn.; (Long Trac models)270 Win., 30-06 Sprfld., 7mm Rem. Mag., 300 Win. Mag. **Barrel:** 23". **Weight:** 6 lbs., 10 oz. to 7 lbs., 4 oz. **Length:** 41 1/2" to 44". **Stock:** Satif-finish walnut, pistol-grip, fluted forend. **Sights:** Adj. rear, bead front standard, no sights on BOSS models (optional). **Features:** Designed to handle new WSM chamberings. Gas-operated, blued finish, rotary bolt design (Long Trac models)

Price: Short Trac, WSM calibers **$902.00**

Price: Short Trac, 243, 308. . . . . **$827.00**

Price: Long Trac calibers . . . . **$827.00 to 902.00**

Bushmaster M17S Bullpup

Bushmaster XM15 E2S Carbine

Bushmaster Varminter

Colt Match Target Lightweight

BROWNING BAR STALKER AUTO RIFLES

Caliber: 243, 308, 270, 30-06, 7mm Rem. Mag., 300 Win. Mag., 338 Win. Mag., 270 WSM< 7mm WSM. **Barrel:** 20", 22" and 24". **Weight:** 6 lbs., 12 oz. (243) to 8 lbs., 2 oz. (magnum cals.) **Length:** 41" to 45" overall. **Stock:** Black composite stock and forearm. **Sights:** Hooded front and adjustable rear or none. **Features:** Optional BOSS (no sights); gas-operated action with seven-lug rotary bolt; dual action bars; 3- or 4-shot magazine (depending on caliber). Introduced 2001. Imported by Browning.

Price: BAR Stalker, open sights (243, 308, 270, 30-06) **$825.00**

Price: BAR Stalker, open sights (7mm, 300 Win. Mag., 338 Win. Mag.) **$901.00**

BUSHMASTER M17S BULLPUP RIFLE

Caliber: 223, 10-shot magazine. **Barrel:** 21.5", chrome lined;1:9" twist. **Weight:** 8.2 lbs. **Length:** 30" overall. **Stock:** Fiberglass-filled nylon. **Sights:** Designed for optics-carrying handle incorporates scope mount rail for Weaver-type rings; also includes 25-meter open iron sights. **Features:** Gas-operated, short-stroke piston system; ambidextrous magazine release. Introduced 1993. Made in U.S.A. by Bushmaster Firearms, Inc./Quality Parts Co.

Price: **$765.00**

BUSHMASTER SHORTY XM15 E2S CARBINE

Caliber: 223,10-shot magazine. **Barrel:** 16", heavy; 1:9" twist. **Weight:** 7.2 lbs. **Length:** 34.75" overall. **Stock:** A2 type; fixed black composition. **Sights:** Fully adjustable M16A2 sight system. **Features:** Patterned after Colt M-16A2. Chrome-lined barrel with manganese phosphate finish. "Shorty" handguards. Has forged aluminum receivers with push-pin. Made in U.S.A. by Bushmaster Firearms Inc.

Price: (A2) **$985.00**

Price: (A3) **$1,085.00**

Bushmaster XM15 E2S Dissipator Carbine

Similar to the XM15 E2S Shorty carbine except has full-length "Dissipator" handguards. Weighs 7.6 lbs.; 34.75" overall; forged aluminum receivers with push-pin style takedown. Made in U.S.A. by Bushmaster Firearms, Inc.

Price: (A2 type) **$995.00**

Price: (A3 type) **$1,095.00**

Bushmaster XM15 E25 AK Shorty Carbine

Similar to the XM15 E2S Shorty except has 14.5" barrel with an AK muzzle brake permanently attached giving 16" barrel length. Weighs 7.3 lbs. Introduced 1999. Made in U.S.A. by Bushmaster Firearms, Inc.

Price: (A2 type) **$1,005.00**

Price: (A3 type) **$1,105.00**

Bushmaster M4/M4A3 Post-Ban Carbine

Similar to the XM15 E2S except has 14.5" barrel with Mini Y compensator, and fixed tele-stock. MR configuration has fixed carry handle; M4A3 has removeable carry handle.

Price: (M4) **$1,065.00**

Price: (M4A3) **$1,165.00**

BUSHMASTER VARMINTER RIFLE

Caliber: 223 Rem., 5-shot. **Barrel:** 24", 1:9" twist, fluted, heavy, stainless. **Weight:** 8/3/4 lbs. **Length:** 42-1/4". **Stock:** Rubberized pistol grip. **Sights:** 1/2" scope risers. **Features:** Gas-operated, semi-auto, 2 stage trigger, slotted free floater forend, lockable hard case.

Price: **$1,245.00**

COLT MATCH TARGET RIFLE

Caliber: 223 Rem., 5-shot magazine. **Barrel:** 16.1" or 20". **Weight:** 7.1 to 8-1/2 lbs. **Length:** 34-1/2" to 39" overall. **Stock:** Composition stock, grip, forend. **Sights:** Post front, rear adjustable for windage and elevation. **Features:** 5-round detachable box magazine, flash suppressor, sling swivels. Forward bolt assist included. Introduced 1991. Made in U.S.A. by Colt's Manufacturing Co. Inc.

Price: Colt Light Rifle **$779.00**

Price: Match Target HBAR, from **$1,194.00**

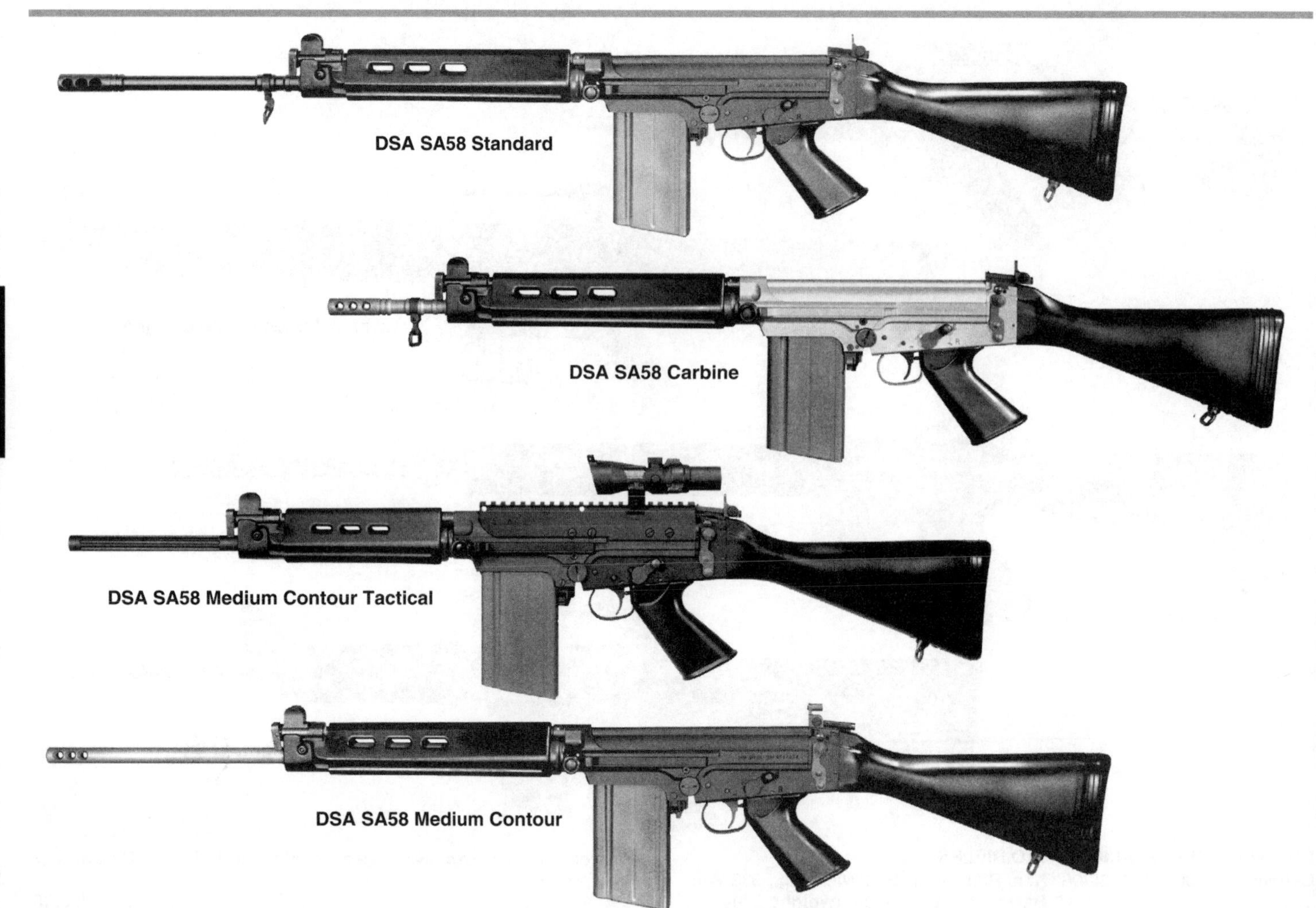

DSA SA58 Standard

DSA SA58 Carbine

DSA SA58 Medium Contour Tactical

DSA SA58 Medium Contour

DPMS PANTHER ARMS A-15 RIFLES

Caliber: 223 Rem., 7.62x39. **Barrel:** 16" to 24". **Weight:** 7-3/4 to 11-3/4 lbs. **Length:** 34-1/2 to 42-1/4" overall. **Stock:** Black Zytel® composite. **Sights:** Square front post, adjustable A2 rear. **Features:** Steel or stainless steel heavy or bull barrel; hard-coat anodized receiver; aluminum free-float tube handguard; many options. From DPMS Panther Arms.

Price: Panther Bull A-15 (20" stainless bull barrel) **$915.00**
Price: Panther Bull Twenty-Four (24" stainless bull barrel) **$945.00**
Price: Bulldog (20" stainless fluted barrel, flat top receiver) **$1,219.00**
Price: Panther Bull Sweet Sixteen (16" stainless bull barrel) **$885.00**
Price: DCM Panther (20" stainless heavy bbl., n.m. sights) **$1,099.00**
Price: Panther 7.62x39 (20" steel heavy barrel) **$849.00**

DSA SA58 CONGO, PARA CONGO

Caliber: 308 Win. **Barrel:** 18" w/short muzzle brake. **Weight:** 8.6 lbs. (Congo); 9.85 lbs. (Para Congo). **Length:** 39.75" **Stock:** Synthetic w/military grade furniture (Congo); Synthetic with non-folding steel para stock (Para Congo). **Sights:** Post, front, windage adjustable peep, rear (Congo); Belgian style para flip peep, rear (Para Congo). **Features:** Fully-adjustable gas system, high-grade steel upper receiver with carry handle. Made in U.S.A. by DSA, Inc.

Price: . . . . **$1,695.00** (Congo); **$1,995.00** (Para Congo)

DSA SA58 GRAY WOLF

Caliber: 308 Win., 300 WSM. **Barrel:** 21" match-grade bull w/target crown. **Weight:** 13 lbs. **Length:** 41.75" **Stock:** Synthetic. **Sights:** Elevation adjustable post, front; windage adjustable match peep, rear. **Features:** Fully-adjustable gas system, high-grade steel upper receiver, Picatinny scope mount, DuraCoat finish. Made in U.S.A. by DSA, Inc.

Price: **$2,120.00**

DSA SA58 PREDATOR

Caliber: 260 Rem., 243 Win., 308 Win. **Barrel:** 16" and 19" w/target crown. **Weight:** 9 to 9.3 lbs. **Length:** 36.25" to 39.25". **Stock:** Synthetic. **Sights:** Elevation adjustable post, front; windage adjustable match peep, rear. **Features:** Fully-adjustable gas system, high-grade steel upper receiver, Picatinny scope mount, DuraCoat solid and camo finishes.

Price: . . . . **$1,595.00** (308 win.); **$1,695.00** (243 Win., 260 Rem.)

DSA SA58 T48

Caliber: 308 Win. **Barrel:** 16.25" with Browning replica flash hider. **Weight:** 9.3 lbs. **Length:** 44.5". **Stock:** European walnut. **Sights:** Adjustable post front, adjustable rear peep. **Features:** Gas-operated semi-auto with fully adjustable gas system, high grade steel upper receiver. DuraCoat finishes. Made in U.S.A. by DSA, Inc.

Price: **$1,795.00**

DSA SA58 GI

Similar to the SA58 T48, except has steel bipod cut handguard with hardwood stock and synthetic pistol grip, original GI steel lower receiver with GI bipod. Made in U.S.A. by DSA, Inc.

Price: **$1,695.00**

DSA SA58 TACTICAL CARBINE, CARBINE

Caliber: 308 Win., limited 243 and 260. **Barrel:** 16.25" with integrally machined muzzle brake. **Weight:** 8.75 lbs. **Length:** 38.25". **Stock:** Fiberglass reinforced synthetic handguard. **Sights:** Adjustable post front, adjustable rear peep. **Features:** Gas-operated semi-auto with fully adjustable gas system, high grade steel or 416 stainless upper receiver. In variety of camo finishes. Made in U.S.A. by DSA, Inc.

Price: Tactical Fluted bbl. **$1,475.00**
Price: Carbine stainless steel bbl. **$1,645.00**
Price: Carbine high-grade steel bbl. **$1,395.00**

DSA SA58 Bull

DSA SA58 T48

DSA SA58 OSW

Heckler & Koch USC

DSA SA58 MEDIUM CONTOUR

Caliber: 308 Win., limited 243 and 260. **Barrel:** 21" with integrally machined muzzle brake. **Weight:** 9.75 lbs. **Length:** 43". **Stock:** Fiberglass reinforced synthetic handguard. **Sights:** Adjustable post front with match rear peep. **Features:** Gas-operated semi-auto with fully adjustable gas system, high grade steel or 416 stainless upper receiver. In variety of camo finishes. Made in U.S.A. by DSA, Inc.

Price: chrome moly **$1,475.00**
Price: stainless steel **$1,725.00**

DSA SA58 21" OR 24" BULL BARREL RIFLE

Caliber: 308 Win., 300 WSM. **Barrel:** 21" or 24". **Weight:** 11.1 and 11.5 lbs. **Length:** 41.5" and 44.5". **Stock:** Synthetic, free floating handguard. **Sights:** Elevation adjustable protected post front, match rear peep. **Features:** Gas-operated semi-auto with fully adjustable gas system, high grade steel or stainless upper receiver. Made in U.S.A. by DSA, Inc.

Price: 21", 24" **$1,745.00**
Price: 24" fluted bbl. **$1,795.00**

DSA SA58 MINI OSW

Caliber: 7.62 NATO. **Barrel:** 11" or 13" with muzzle brake. **Weight:** 9 to 9.35 lbs. **Length:** 33". **Stock:** Synthetic. **Features:** Gas-operated semi-auto or select fire with fully adjustable short gas system, optional FAL Rail Interface Handguard, SureFire Vertical Foregrip System, EOTech HOLOgraphic Sight and ITC Cheekrest. Made in U.S.A. by DSA, Inc.

Price: **$1,525.00**

EAA/SAIGA SEMI-AUTO RIFLE

Caliber: 7.62x39, 308, 223. **Barrel:** 20.5", 22", 16.3". **Weight:** 7 to 8-1/2 lbs. **Length:** 43". **Stock:** Synthetic or wood. **Sights:** Adjustable, sight base. **Features:** Based on AK Combat rifle by Kalashnikov. Imported from Russia by EAA Corp.

Price: 7.62x39 (syn.) **$239.00**
Price: 308 (syn. or wood) **$429.00**
Price: 223 (syn.) **$389.00**

EAGLE ARMS AR-10 RIFLE

Caliber: 308. **Barrel:** 20", 24". **Weight:** NA **Length:** NA **Stock:** Synthetic. **Sights:** Adjustable A2, front, Std. A2, rear; Flat top and Match Rifle have no sights but adjustable Picatinny rail furnished. **Features:** A product of the latest in manufacturing technology to provide a quality rifle at a reasonable price. Introduced 2003. Made in U.S.A. by Eagle Arms.

Price: AR-10 Service Rifle **$1,055.00**
Price: AR-10 Flat Top Rifle **$999.95**
Price: AR-10 Match Rifle **$1,480.00**

EAGLE ARMS M15 RIFLE

Caliber: 223. **Barrel:** 16", 20". **Weight:** NA **Length:** NA **Stock:** Synthetic. **Sights:** Adjustable A2, front; Std. A2, rear; Flat Top Rifle & Carbine versions, no sights furnished. **Features:** Available in 4 different configurations, the latest manufacturing technology has been employed to keep the price reasonable. Introduced 2003. Made in U.S.A. by Eagle Arms.

Price: A2 Rifle **$795.00**
Price: A2 Carbine **$795.00**
Price: Flat Top Rifle **$835.00**
Price: Flat Top Carbine **$835.00**

HECKLER & KOCH USC CARBINE

Caliber: 45 ACP, 10-shot magazine. **Barrel:** 16". **Weight:** 8.6 lb. **Length:** 35.4" overall. **Stock:** Skeletonized polymer thumbhole. **Sights:** Blade front with integral hood, fully adjustable diopter. **Features:** Based on German UMP submachine gun. Blowback operation; almost entirely constructed of carbon fiber-reinforced polymer. Free-floating heavy target barrel. Introduced 2000. From H&K.

Price: **$1,249.00**

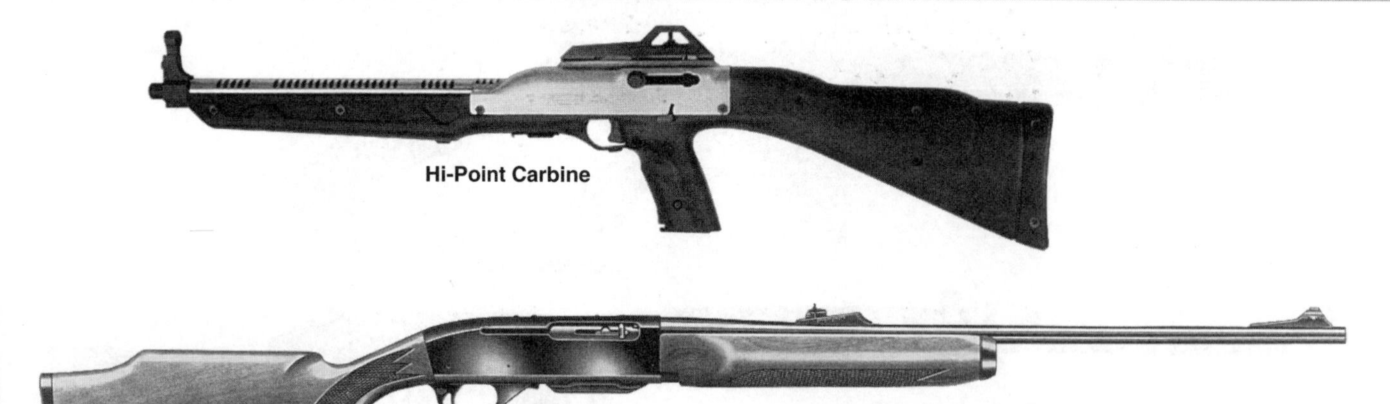

Hi-Point Carbine

Remington Model 7400

HI-POINT 9MM CARBINE

Caliber: 9mm Para., 40 S&W, 10-shot magazine. **Barrel:** 16-1/2" (17-1/2" for 40 S&W). **Weight:** 4-1/2 lbs. **Length:** 31-1/2" overall. **Stock:** Black polymer, camouflage. **Sights:** Protected post front, aperture rear. Integral scope mount. **Features:** Grip-mounted magazine release. Black or chrome finish. Sling swivels. Available with laser or red dot sights. Introduced 1996. Made in U.S.A. by MKS Supply, Inc.

Price: Black or chrome, 9mm **$199.00**
Price: 40 S&W **$225.00**
Price: Camo stock. **$210.00**

IAI M-333 M1 GARAND

Caliber: 30-06, 8-shot clip. **Barrel:** 24". **Weight:** 9-1/2 lbs. **Length:** 43.6" overall. **Stock:** Hardwood. **Sights:** Blade front, aperture adjustable rear. **Features:** Parkerized finish; gas-operated semi-automatic; remanufactured to military specifications. From IAI.

Price: **$971.75**

IAI M-888 M1 CARBINE SEMI-AUTOMATIC RIFLE

Caliber: 22, 30 Carbine. **Barrel:** 18"-20". **Weight:** 5-1/2 lbs. **Length:** 35"-37" overall. **Stock:** Laminate, walnut or birch. **Sights:** Blade front, adjustable rear. **Features:** Gas-operated, air cooled, manufactured to military specifications. 10/15/30 rnd. mag. scope available. From IAI.

Price: 30 cal. . . . . **$556.00 to $604.00**
Price: 22 cal. . . . . **$567.00 to $654.00**

Intrac Arms IAI-65 Rifle

A civilian-legal version of the original HKM rifle manufactured in Hungary. Manufactured by Gordon Technologies using an original AMD-65 matching parts kit built on an AKM receiver. The original wire stock is present, but it is welded in the open position as per BATF regulations. Furnished with a 12.6" barrel with large weld-in-place muzzle brake to bring its length over the 16" federal minimum. This rifle accepts all 7.62x39mm magazines and drums. Introduced 2002. From Intrac Arms International, Inc.

Price: **$799.00**

LES BAER CUSTOM ULTIMATE AR 223 RIFLES

Caliber: 223. **Barrel:** 18", 20", 22", 24". **Weight:** 7-3/4 to 9-3/4 lb. **Length:** NA. **Stock:** Black synthetic. **Sights:** None furnished; Picatinny-style flat top rail for scope mounting. **Features:** Forged receiver; Ultra single-stage trigger (Jewell two-stage trigger optional); titanium firing pin; Versa-Pod bipod; chromed National Match carrier; stainless steel, hand-lapped and cryo-treated barrel; guaranteed to shoot 1/2 or 3/4 MOA, depending on model. Made in U.S.A. by Les Baer Custom Inc.

Price: Super Varmint Model **$1,989.00**
Price: M4 Flattop Model **$2,195.00**
Price: IPSC Action Model **$2,195.00**

LR 300 SR LIGHT SPORT RIFLE

Caliber: 223. **Barrel:** 16-1/4"; 1:9" twist. **Weight:** 7.2 lbs. **Length:** 36" overall (extended stock), 26-1/4" (stock folded). **Stock:** Folding, tubular steel, with thumbhold-type grip. **Sights:** Trijicon post front, Trijicon rear. **Features:** Uses AR-15 type upper and lower receivers; flattop receiver with weaver base. Accepts all AR-15/M-16 magazines. Introduced 1996. Made in U.S.A. from Z-M Weapons.

Price: **$2,550.00**

OLYMPIC ARMS CAR-97 RIFLES

Caliber: 223, 7-shot; 9mm Para., 45 ACP, 40 S&W, 10mm, 10-shot. **Barrel:** 16". **Weight:** 7 lbs. **Length:** 34.75" overall. **Stock:** A2 stowaway grip, telescoping-look butt. **Sights:** Post front, fully adjustable aperature rear. **Features:** Based on AR-15 rifle. Post-ban version of the CAR-15. Made in U.S.A. by Olympic Arms, Inc.

Price: 223 . . . . **$780.00**
Price: 9mm Para., 45 ACP, 40 S&W, 10mm **$840.00**
Price: PCR Eliminator (223, full-length handguards) **$803.00**

OLYMPIC ARMS PCR-4 RIFLE

Caliber: 223, 10-shot magazine. **Barrel:** 20". **Weight:** 8 lbs., 5 oz. **Length:** 38.25" overall. **Stock:** A2 stowaway grip, trapdoor buttstock. **Sights:** Post front, A1 rear adjustable for windage. **Features:** Based on the AR-15 rifle. Barrel is button rifled with 1:9" twist. No bayonet lug. Introduced 1994. Made in U.S.A. by Olympic Arms, Inc.

Price: **$792.00**

OLYMPIC ARMS PCR-6 RIFLE

Caliber: 7.62x39mm (PCR-6), 10-shot magazine. **Barrel:** 16". **Weight:** 7 lbs. **Length:** 34" overall. **Stock:** A2 stowaway grip, trapdoor buttstock. **Sights:** Post front, A1 rear adjustable for windage. **Features:** Based on the CAR-15. No bayonet lug. Button-cut rifling. Introduced 1994. Made in U.S.A. by Olympic Arms, Inc.

Price: **$845.00**

REMINGTON MODEL 7400 AUTO RIFLE

Caliber: 243 Win., 270 Win., 308 Win., 30-06, 4-shot magazine. **Barrel:** 22" round tapered. **Weight:** 7-1/2 lbs. **Length:** 42-5/8" overall. **Stock:** Walnut, deluxe cut checkered pistol grip and forend. Satin or high-gloss finish. **Sights:** Gold bead front sight on ramp; step rear sight with windage adjustable. **Features:** Redesigned and improved version of the Model 742. Positive cross-bolt safety. Receiver tapped for scope mount. Introduced 1981.

Price: **$624.00**
Price: Carbine (18-1/2" bbl., 30-06 only) **$624.00**
Price: With black synthetic stock, matte black metal, rifle or carbine **$520.00**
Price: Weathermaster, nickel-plated w/synthetic stock and forend, 270, 30-06. . . . . **$624.00**

ROCK RIVER ARMS STANDARD A2 RIFLE

Caliber: 45 ACP. **Barrel:** NA. **Weight:** 8.2 lbs. **Length:** NA. **Stock:** Thermoplastic. **Sights:** Standard AR-15 style sights. **Features:** Two-stage, national match trigger; optional muzzle brake. Made in U.S.A. From River Rock Arms.

Price: **$925.00**

Ruger Deerfield 99/44 Carbine

Ruger PC4 Carbine

Ruger Ranch Mini 14/5R

Springfield M1A

RUGER DEERFIELD 99/44 CARBINE

Caliber: 44 Mag., 4-shot rotary magazine. **Barrel:** 18-1/2". **Weight:** 6-1/4 lbs. **Length:** 36-7/8" overall. **Stock:** Hardwood. **Sights:** Gold bead front, folding adjustable aperture rear. **Features:** Semi-automatic action; dual front-locking lugs lock directly into receiver; integral scope mount; push-button safety; includes 1" rings and gun lock. Introduced 2000. Made in U.S.A. by Sturm, Ruger & Co.

Price: $675.00

RUGER PC4, PC9 CARBINES

Caliber: 9mm Para., 40 cal., 10-shot magazine. **Barrel:** 16.25". **Weight:** 6 lbs., 4 oz. **Length:** 34.75" overall. **Stock:** Black high impact synthetic checkered grip and forend. **Sights:** Blade front, open adjustable rear; integral Ruger scope mounts. **Features:** Delayed blowback action; manual push-button cross bolt safety and internal firing pin block safety automatic slide lock. Introduced 1997. Made in U.S.A. by Sturm, Ruger & Co.

Price: PC9, PC4, (9mm, 40 cal.) $605.00
Price: PC4GR, PC9GR, (40 auto, 9mm, post sights, ghost ring) $628.00

RUGER MINI-14/5 AUTOLOADING RIFLE

Caliber: 223 Rem., 5-shot detachable box magazine. **Barrel:** 18-1/2". Rifling twist 1:9". **Weight:** 6.4 lbs. **Length:** 37-1/4" overall. **Stock:** American hardwood, steel reinforced. **Sights:** Ramp front, fully adjustable rear. **Features:** Fixed piston gas-operated, positive primary extraction. New buffer system, redesigned ejector system. Ruger S100RM scope rings included on Ranch Rifle.

Price: Mini-14/5R, Ranch Rifle, blued, scope rings. $695.00
Price: K-Mini-14/5R, Ranch Rifle, stainless, scope rings. $770.00
Price: Mini-14/5, blued. $655.00
Price: K-Mini-14/5, stainless. $715.00
Price: K-Mini-14/5P, stainless, synthetic stock. $715.00
Price: K-Mini-14/5RP, Ranch Rifle, stainless, synthetic stock. . . . $770.00

Ruger Mini Thirty Rifle

Similar to the Mini-14 Ranch Rifle except modified to chamber the 7.62x39 Russian service round. Weight is about 6-7/8 lbs. Has 6-groove barrel with 1:10" twist, Ruger Integral Scope Mount bases and folding peep rear sight. Detachable 5-shot staggered box magazine. Blued finish. Introduced 1987.

Price: Blue, scope rings $695.00
Price: Stainless, scope rings $770.00

SPRINGFIELD, INC. M1A RIFLE

Caliber: 7.62mm NATO (308), 5- or 10-shot box magazine. **Barrel:** 25-1/16" with flash suppressor, 22" without suppressor. **Weight:** 9-3/4 lbs. **Length:** 44-1/4" overall. **Stock:** American walnut with walnut-colored heat-resistant fiberglass handguard. Matching walnut handguard available. Also available with fiberglass stock. **Sights:** Military, square blade front, full click-adjustable aperture rear. **Features:** Commercial equivalent of the U.S. M-14 service rifle with no provision for automatic firing. From Springfield, Inc.

Price: Standard M1A, black fiberglass stock $1,319.00
Price: Standard M1A, black fiberglass stock, stainless $1,629.00
Price: Standard M1A, black stock, carbon barrel $1,379.00
Price: Standard M1A, Mossy Oak stock, carbon barrel $1,443.00
Price: Scout Squad M1A . . . . $1,529 to $1,639.00
Price: National Match . . . . $1,995.00 to $2,040.00
Price: Super Match (heavy premium barrel), about $2,449.00
Price: M21 Tactical Rifle (adj. cheekpiece), about $2,975.00
Price: M25 White Feather Tactical Rifle $4,195.00

SPRINGFIELD M1 GARAND RIFLE

Caliber: 308, 30-06. **Barrel:** 24". **Weight:** 9.5 lbs. **Length:** 43-3/5". **Stock:** Walnut. **Sights:** Military aperture with MOA adjustments for both windage and elevation, rear; military square post, front. **Features:** Original U.S. government-issue parts on a new walnut stock.

Price: . . . . $1,099 to $1,129.00

Springfield National Match M1A

Springfield Super Match with Camo M1A

STONER SR-15 M-5 RIFLE

Caliber: 223. **Barrel:** 20". **Weight:** 7.6 lbs. **Length:** 38" overall. **Stock:** Black synthetic. **Sights:** Post front, fully adjustable rear (300-meter sight). **Features:** Modular weapon system; two-stage trigger. Black finish. Introduced 1998. Made in U.S.A. by Knight's Mfg.

Price: **$1,650.00**

Price: M-4 Carbine (16" barrel, 6.8 lbs) **$1,555.00**

STONER SR-25 CARBINE

Caliber: 7.62 NATO, 10-shot steel magazine. **Barrel:** 16" free-floating **Weight:** 7-3/4 lbs. **Length:** 35.75" overall. **Stock:** Black synthetic. **Sights:** Integral Weaver-style rail. Scope rings, iron sights optional. **Features:** Shortened, non-slip handguard; removable carrying handle. Matte black finish. Introduced 1995. Made in U.S.A. by Knight's Mfg. Co.

Price: **$3,345.00**

WILKINSON LINDA CARBINE

Caliber: 9mm Para. **Barrel:** 16-3/16". **Weight:** 7 lbs. Stocks: Fixed tubular with wood pad. **Sights:** Aperture rear sight. **Features:** Aluminum receiver, pre-ban configuration (limited supplies), vent. barrel shroud, small wooden forearm, 18 or 31 shot mag. Many accessories.

Price: **$1,800.00**

Wilkinson Linda L2 Limited Edition

Manufactured from the last 600 of the original 2,200 pre-ban Linda Carbines, includes many upgrades and accessories. New 2002.

Price: **$4,800.00**

WILKINSON TERRY CARBINE

Caliber: 9mm Para. **Barrel:** 16-3/16". **Weight:** 7 lbs. Stocks: Black or maple. **Sights:** Adjustable. **Features:** Blowback semi-auto action, 31 shot mag., closed breech.

Price: . . . . **NA**

Centerfire Rifles — Lever and Slide

Both classic arms and recent designs in American-style repeaters for sport and field shooting.

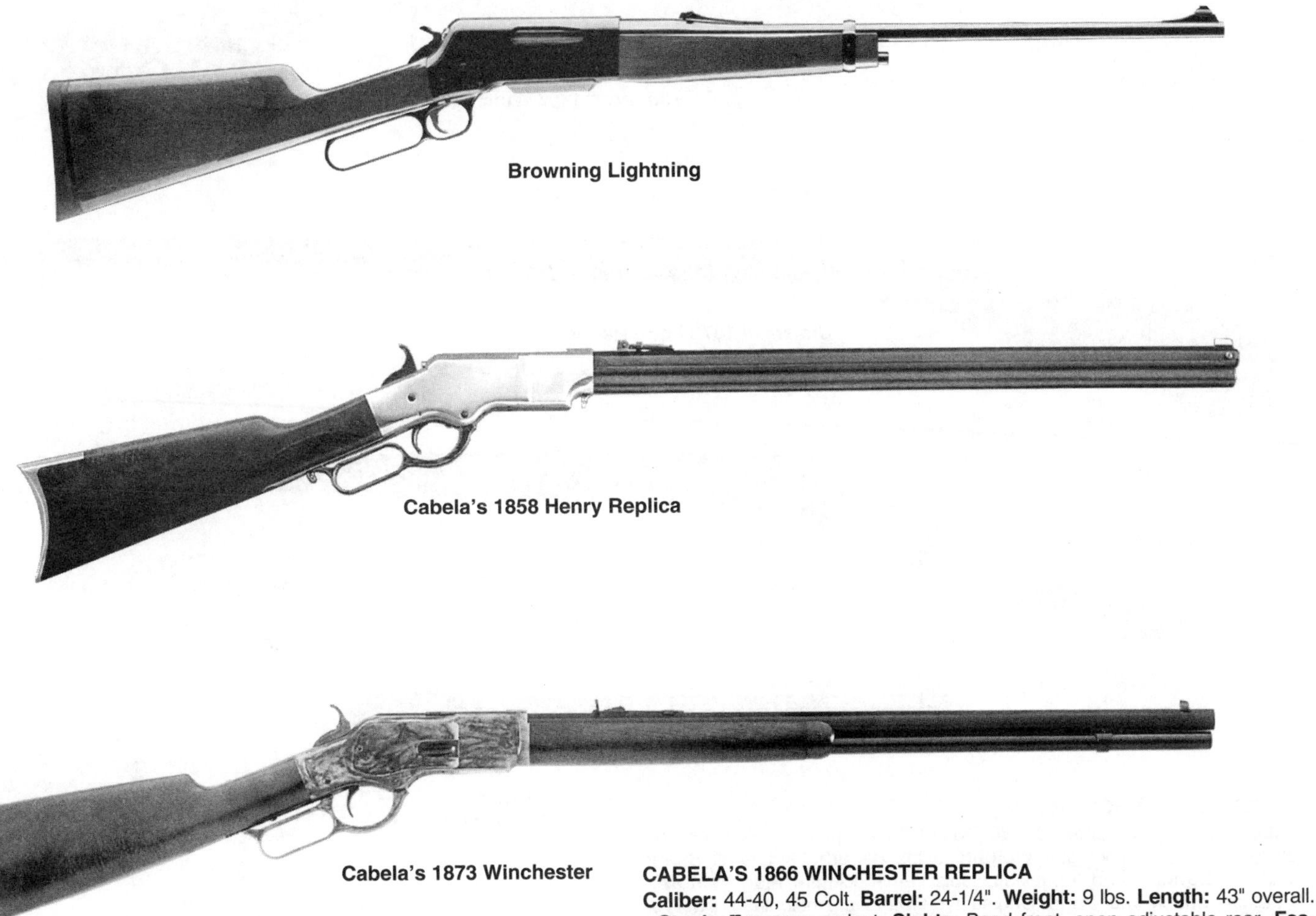

Browning Lightning

Cabela's 1858 Henry Replica

Cabela's 1873 Winchester

BROWNING MODEL '81 LIGHTNING LEVER-ACTION RIFLE

Caliber: 22-250, 243, 7mm-08, 308 Win., 270 WSM, 7mm WSM, 300 WSM, 358 Win., 450 Marlin, 270 Win., 30-06 Sprg., 7mm Rem. Mag., 300 Win. Mag. 4-shot detachable magazine. **Barrel:** 20" round tapered. **Weight:** 6 lbs., 8 oz. **Length:** 39-1/2" overall. **Stock:** Walnut. Checkered grip and forend, high-gloss finish. **Sights:** Gold bead on ramp front; low profile square notch adjustable rear. **Features:** Wide, grooved trigger; half-cock hammer safety; fold-down hammer. Receiver tapped for scope mount. Recoil pad installed. Introduced 1996. Imported from Japan by Browning.

Price: **$710.00**

BROWNING MODEL '81 LIGHTNING LONG ACTION

Similar to the standard Lightning BLR except has long action to accept 30-06, 270, 7mm Rem. Mag. and 300 Win. Mag. Barrel lengths are 22" for 30-06 and 270, 24" for 7mm Rem. Mag. and 300 Win. Mag. Has six-lug rotary bolt; bolt and receiver are full-length fluted. Fold-down hammer at half-cock. Weighs about 7 lbs., overall length 42-7/8" (22" barrel). Introduced 1996.

Price: **$686.00**

CABELA'S 1858 HENRY REPLICA

Caliber: 44-40, 45 Colt. **Barrel:** 24-1/4". **Weight:** 9.3 lbs. **Length:** 43.75" overall. **Stock:** American walnut. **Sights:** Bead front, open adjustable rear. **Features:** Brass receiver and buttplate. Uses original Henry loading system. Faithful to the original rifle. Introduced 1994. Imported by Cabela's.

Price: **$999.99**

CABELA'S 1866 WINCHESTER REPLICA

Caliber: 44-40, 45 Colt. **Barrel:** 24-1/4". **Weight:** 9 lbs. **Length:** 43" overall. **Stock:** European walnut. **Sights:** Bead front, open adjustable rear. **Features:** Solid brass receiver, buttplate, forend cap. Octagonal barrel. Faithful to the original Winchester '66 rifle. Introduced 1994. Imported by Cabela's.

Price: **$799.99**

CABELA'S 1873 WINCHESTER REPLICA

Caliber: 44-40, 45 Colt. **Barrel:** 24-1/4", 30". **Weight:** 8.5 lbs. **Length:** 43-1/4", 50" overall. **Stock:** European walnut. **Sights:** Bead front, open adjustable rear; globe front, tang rear. **Features:** Color case-hardened steel receiver. Faithful to the original Model 1873 rifle. Introduced 1994. Imported by Cabela's.

Price: Sporting model, 30" barrel, 44-40, 45 Colt. **$999.99**

Price: Sporting model, 24" or 25" barrel **$899.99**

CIMARRON 1860 HENRY REPLICA

Caliber: 44 WCF, 13-shot magazine. **Barrel:** 24-1/4" (rifle), 22" (carbine). **Weight:** 9-1/2 lbs. **Length:** 43" overall (rifle). **Stock:** European walnut. **Sights:** Bead front, open adjustable rear. **Features:** Brass receiver and buttplate. Uses original Henry loading system. Faithful to the original rifle. Introduced 1991. Imported by Cimarron F.A. Co.

Price: **$1,029.00**

CIMARRON 1866 WINCHESTER REPLICAS

Caliber: 22 LR, 22 WMR, 38 Spec., 44 WCF. **Barrel:** 24-1/4" (rifle), 19" (carbine). **Weight:** 9 lbs. **Length:** 43" overall (rifle). **Stock:** European walnut. **Sights:** Bead front, open adjustable rear. **Features:** Solid brass receiver, buttplate, forend cap. Octagonal barrel. Faithful to the original Winchester '66 rifle. Introduced 1991. Imported by Cimarron F.A. Co.

Price: Rifle **$839.00**

Price: Carbine. **$829.00**

Cimarron 1866 Winchester Replica

Cimarron 1873 Long Range

Dixie 1873

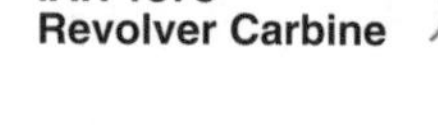
IAR 1873 Revolver Carbine

CIMARRON 1873 SHORT RIFLE

Caliber: 357 Mag., 38 Spec., 32 WCF, 38 WCF, 44 Spec., 44 WCF, 45 Colt. **Barrel:** 20" tapered octagon. **Weight:** 7.5 lbs. **Length:** 39" overall. **Stock:** Walnut. **Sights:** Bead front, adjustable semi-buckhorn rear. **Features:** Has half "button" magazine. Original-type markings, including caliber, on barrel and elevator and "Kings" patent. From Cimarron F.A. Co.

Price: . . . . **$949.00 to $999.00**

CIMARRON 1873 LONG RANGE RIFLE

Caliber: 44 WCF, 45 Colt. **Barrel:** 30", octagonal. **Weight:** 8-1/2 lbs. **Length:** 48" overall. **Stock:** Walnut. **Sights:** Blade front, semi-buckhorn ramp rear. Tang sight optional. **Features:** Color case-hardened frame; choice of modern blue-black or charcoal blue for other parts. Barrel marked "Kings Improvement." From Cimarron F.A. Co.

Price: . . . . **$999.00 to $1,199.00**

Cimarron 1873 Sporting Rifle

Similar to the 1873 Short Rifle except has 24" barrel with half-magazine.

Price: . . . . **$949.00 to $999.00**

DIXIE ENGRAVED 1873 RIFLE

Caliber: 44-40, 11-shot magazine. **Barrel:** 20", round. **Weight:** 7-3/4 lbs. **Length:** 39" overall. **Stock:** Walnut. **Sights:** Blade front, adjustable rear. **Features:** Engraved and case-hardened frame. Duplicate of Winchester 1873. Made in Italy. From 21 Gun Works.

Price: **$1,350.00**

Price: Plain, blued carbine **$850.00**

E.M.F. 1860 HENRY RIFLE

Caliber: 44-40 or 45 Colt. **Barrel:** 24.25". **Weight:** About 9 lbs. **Length:** About 43.75" overall. **Stock:** Oil-stained American walnut. **Sights:** Blade front, rear adjustable for elevation. **Features:** Reproduction of the original Henry rifle with brass frame and buttplate, rest blued. From E.M.F.

Price: Brass frame **$850.00**

Price: Steel frame **$950.00**

E.M.F. 1866 YELLOWBOY LEVER ACTIONS

Caliber: 38 Spec., 44-40. **Barrel:** 19" (carbine), 24" (rifle). **Weight:** 9 lbs. **Length:** 43" overall (rifle). **Stock:** European walnut. **Sights:** Bead front, open adjustable rear. **Features:** Solid brass frame, blued barrel, lever, hammer, buttplate. Imported from Italy by E.M.F.

Price: Rifle **$690.00**

Price: Carbine **$675.00**

E.M.F. HARTFORD MODEL 1892 LEVER-ACTION RIFLE

Caliber: 45 Colt. **Barrel:** 24", octagonal. **Weight:** 7-1/2 lbs. **Length:** 43" overall. **Stock:** European walnut. **Sights:** Blade front, open adjustable rear. **Features:** Color case-hardened frame, lever, trigger and hammer with blued barrel, or overall blue finish. Introduced 1998. Imported by E.M.F.

Price: Standard **$590.00**

E.M.F. MODEL 1873 LEVER-ACTION RIFLE

Caliber: 32/20, 357 Mag., 38/40, 44-40, 44 Spec., 45 Colt. **Barrel:** 24". **Weight:** 8 lbs. **Length:** 43-1/4" overall. **Stock:** European walnut. **Sights:** Bead front, rear adjustable for windage and elevation. **Features:** Color case-hardened frame (blue on carbine). Imported by E.M.F.

Price: Rifle **$865.00**

Price: Carbine, 19" barrel **$865.00**

IAR MODEL 1873 REVOLVER CARBINE

Caliber: 357 Mag., 45 Colt. **Barrel:** 18". **Weight:** 4 lbs., 8 oz. **Length:** 34" overall. **Stock:** One-piece walnut. **Sights:** Blade front, notch rear. **Features:** Color case-hardened frame, blue barrel, backstrap and trigger-guard. Introduced 1998. Imported from Italy by IAR, Inc.

Price: Standard **$490.00**

Marlin 336C

Marlin 336 Cowboy

Marlin 336Y Spikehorn

Marlin 444P Outfitter

MARLIN MODEL 336C LEVER-ACTION CARBINE

Caliber: 30-30 or 35 Rem., 6-shot tubular magazine. **Barrel:** 20" Micro-Groove®. **Weight:** 7 lbs. **Length:** 38-1/2" overall. **Stock:** Checkered American black walnut, capped pistol grip. Mar-Shield® finish; rubber butt pad; swivel studs. **Sights:** Ramp front with Wide-Scan hood, semi-buckhorn folding rear adjustable for windage and elevation. **Features:** Hammer-block safety. Receiver tapped for scope mount, offset hammer spur; top of receiver sandblasted to prevent glare. Includes safety lock.

Price: **$529.00**

Marlin Model 336 Cowboy

Similar to the Model 336C except chambered for 38-55 Win., 24" tapered octagon barrel with deep-cut Ballard-type rifling; straight-grip walnut stock with hard rubber buttplate; blued steel forend cap; weighs 7-1/2 lbs.; 42-1/2" overall. Introduced 1999. Includes safety lock. Made in U.S.A. by Marlin.

Price: **$735.00**

Marlin Model 336A Lever-Action Carbine

Same as the Marlin 336C except has cut-checkered, walnut-finished hardwood pistol grip stock with swivel studs, 30-30 only, 6-shot. Hammer-block safety. Adjustable rear sight, brass bead front. Includes safety lock.

Price: **$451.00**

Price: With 4x scope and mount **$501.00**

Marlin Model 336CC Lever-Action Carbine

Same as the Marlin 336A except has Mossy Oak® Break-Up camouflage stock and forearm. 30-30 only, 6-shot; receiver tapped for scope mount or receiver sight. Introduced 2001. Includes safety lock. Made in U.S.A. by Marlin.

Price: **$503.00**

Marlin Model 336SS Lever-Action Carbine

Same as the 336C except receiver, barrel and other major parts are machined from stainless steel. 30-30 only, 6-shot; receiver tapped for scope. Includes safety lock.

Price: **$640.00**

Marlin Model 336W Lever-Action Rifle

Similar to the Model 336CS except has walnut-finished, cut-checkered Maine birch stock; blued steel barrel band has integral sling swivel; no front sight hood; comes with padded nylon sling; hard rubber butt plate. Introduced 1998. Includes safety lock. Made in U.S.A. by Marlin.

Price: **$457.00**

Price: With 4x scope and mount **$506.00**

Marlin Model 336 Y "Spikehorn"

Similar to the Models in the 336 series except in a compact format with 16-1/2" barrel measuring only 34" in overall length. Weight is 6-1/2 lbs., length of pull 12-1/2". Blued steel barrel and receiver. Chambered for 30/30 cartridge. Introduced 2003.

Price: **$536.00**

MARLIN MODEL 444 LEVER-ACTION SPORTER

Caliber: 444 Marlin, 5-shot tubular magazine. **Barrel:** 22" deep cut Ballard rifling. **Weight:** 7-1/2 lbs. **Length:** 40-1/2" overall. **Stock:** Checkered American black walnut, capped pistol grip, rubber rifle butt pad. Mar-Shield® finish; swivel studs. **Sights:** Hooded ramp front, folding semi-buckhorn rear adjustable for windage and elevation. **Features:** Hammer-block safety. Receiver tapped for scope mount; offset hammer spur. Includes safety lock.

Price: **$618.00**

Marlin Model 444P Outfitter Lever-Action

Similar to the 444SS with deep-cut Ballard-type rifling; weighs 6-3/4 lbs.; overall length 37". Available only in 444 Marlin. Introduced 1999. Includes safety lock. Made in U.S.A. by Marlin.

Price: **$631.00**

MARLIN MODEL 1894 LEVER-ACTION CARBINE

Caliber: 44 Spec./44 Mag., 10-shot tubular magazine. **Barrel:** 20" Ballard-type rifling. **Weight:** 6 lbs. **Length:** 37-1/2" overall. **Stock:** Checkered American black walnut, straight grip and forend. Mar-Shield® finish. Rubber rifle butt pad; swivel studs. **Sights:** Wide-Scan hooded ramp front, semi-buckhorn folding rear adjustable for windage and elevation. **Features:** Hammer-block safety. Receiver tapped for scope mount, offset hammer spur, solid top receiver sand blasted to prevent glare. Includes safety lock.

Price: **$544.00**

CENTERFIRE RIFLES — LEVER AND SLIDE

Marlin Model 1894PG/1894FG

Pistol-gripped versions of the Model 1894. Model 1894PG is chambered for .44 Magnum; Model 1894FG is chambered for .41 Magnum.

Price: (Model 1894PG) **$610.00**
Price: (Model 1894FG) **$610.00**

Marlin Model 1894C Carbine

Similar to the standard Model 1894S except chambered for 38 Spec./357 Mag. with full-length 9-shot magazine, 18-1/2" barrel, hammer-block safety, hooded front sight. Introduced 1983. Includes safety lock.

Price: **$556.00**

MARLIN MODEL 1894 COWBOY

Caliber: 357 Mag., 44 Mag., 45 Colt, 10-shot magazine. **Barrel:** 20" except .45 Colt which has a 24" tapered octagon, deep cut rifling. **Weight:** 7-1/2 lbs. **Length:** 41-1/2" overall. **Stock:** Straight grip American black walnut, hard rubber buttplate, Mar-Shield® finish. **Sights:** Marble carbine front, adjustable Marble semi-buckhorn rear. **Features:** Squared finger lever; straight grip stock; blued steel forend tip. Designed for Cowboy Shooting events. Introduced 1996. Includes safety lock. Made in U.S.A. by Marlin.

Price: **$820.00**

Marlin Model 1894 Cowboy Competition Rifle

Similar to Model 1894 except 20" barrel, 37-1/2" long, weighs only 6 lbs., antique finish on receiver, lever and bolt. Factory-tuned for competitive cowboy action shooting.Available in .38 Spl. And .45 Colt.

Price: **$986.00**

Marlin Model 1894SS

Similar to Model 1894 except has stainless steel barrel, receiver, lever, guard plate, magazine tube and loading plate. Nickel-plated swivel studs.

Price: **$680.00**

MARLIN MODEL 1895 LEVER-ACTION RIFLE

Caliber: 45-70, 4-shot tubular magazine. **Barrel:** 22" round. **Weight:** 7-1/2 lbs. **Length:** 40-1/2" overall. **Stock:** Checkered American black walnut, full pistol grip. Mar-Shield® finish; rubber butt pad; quick detachable swivel studs. **Sights:** Bead front with Wide-Scan hood, semi-buckhorn folding rear adjustable for windage and elevation. **Features:** Hammer- block safety. Solid receiver tapped for scope mounts or receiver sights; offset hammer spur. Includes safety lock.

Price: **$631.00**

Marlin Model 1895G Guide Gun Lever-Action Rifle

Similar to Model 1895 with deep-cut Ballard-type rifling; straight-grip walnut stock. Overall length is 37", weighs 7 lbs. Introduced 1998. Includes safety lock. Made in U.S.A. by Marlin.

Price: **$646.00**

Marlin Model 1895GS Guide Gun

Similar to Model 1895G except receiver, barrel and most metal parts are machined from stainless steel. Chambered for 45-70, 4-shot, 18-1/2" barrel. Overall length is 37", weighs 7 lbs. Introduced 2001. Includes safety lock. Made in U.S.A. by Marlin.

Price: **$760.00**

Marlin Model 1895 Cowboy Lever-Action Rifle

Similar to Model 1895 except has 26" tapered octagon barrel with Ballard-type rifling, Marble carbine front sight and Marble adjustable semi-buckhorn rear sight. Receiver tapped for scope or receiver sight. Overall length is 44-1/2", weighs about 8 lbs. Introduced 2001. Includes safety lock. Made in U.S.A. by Marlin.

Price: **$802.00**

Marlin Model 1895M Lever-Action Rifle

Similar to Model 1895 except has an 18-1/2" barrel with Ballard-type cut rifling. New Model 1895MR variant has 22" barrel, pistol grip. Chambered for 450 Marlin. Includes safety lock.

Price: (Model 1895M) **$695.00**
Price: (Model 1895MR) **$761.00**

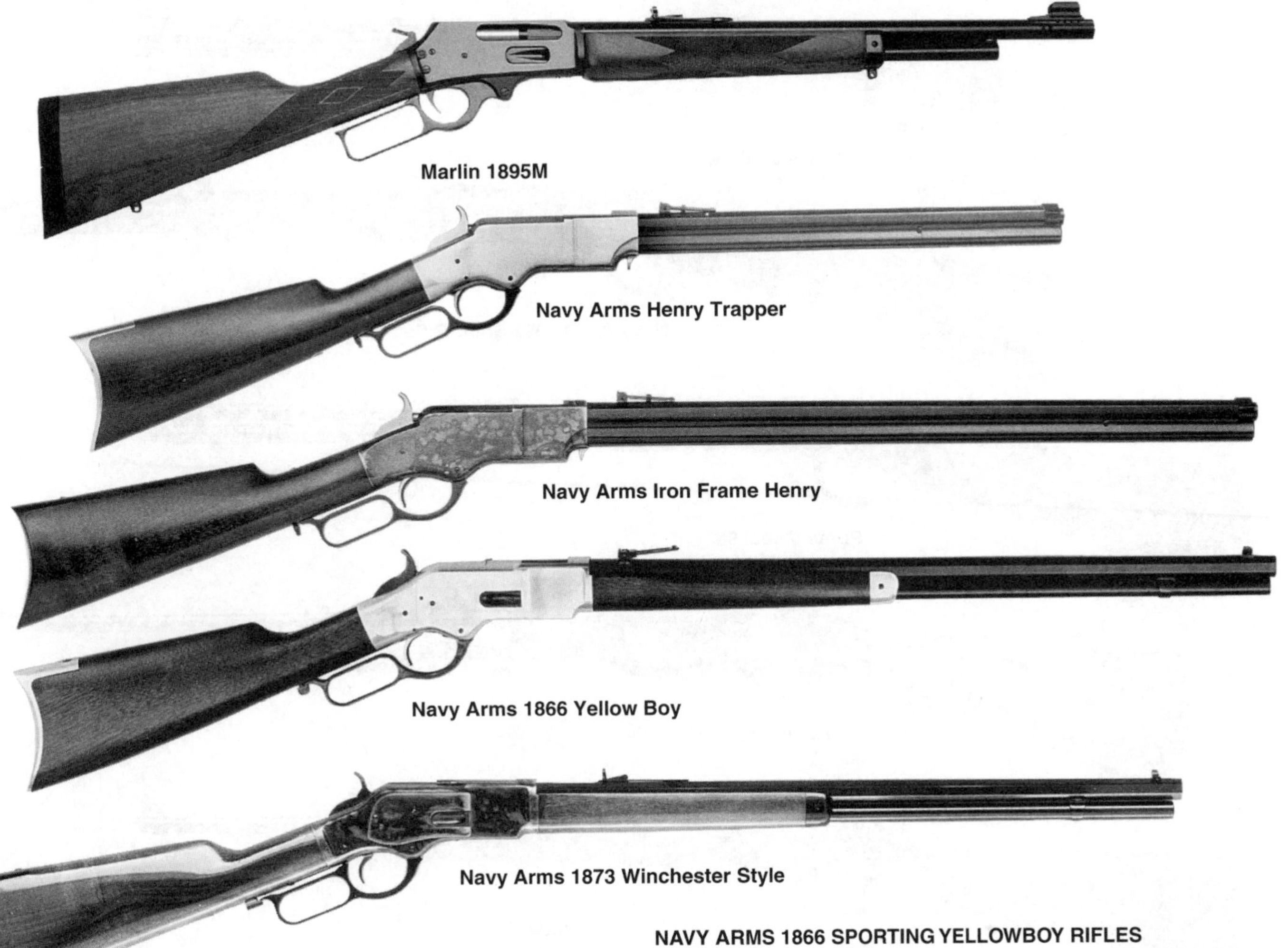

Marlin 1895M

Navy Arms Henry Trapper

Navy Arms Iron Frame Henry

Navy Arms 1866 Yellow Boy

Navy Arms 1873 Winchester Style

NAVY ARMS MILITARY HENRY RIFLE

Caliber: 44-40 or 45 Colt, 12-shot magazine. **Barrel:** 24-1/4". **Weight:** 9 lbs., 4 oz. **Stock:** European walnut. **Sights:** Blade front, adjustable ladder-type rear. **Features:** Brass frame, buttplate, rest blued. Recreation of the model used by cavalry units in the Civil War. Has full-length magazine tube, sling swivels; no forend. Imported from Italy by Navy Arms.

Price: **$989.00**

Navy Arms Iron Frame Henry

Similar to the Military Henry Rifle except receiver is blued or color case-hardened steel. Imported by Navy Arms.

Price: **$1,035.00**

NAVY ARMS 1860 HENRY RIFLES

Caliber: 45 Colt. **Barrel:** 24-1/4" octagonal; 1:16" twist. **Weight:** 9.26 lbs. **Length:** 43-3/4" overall. **Stock:** Walnut. **Sights:** Blade front, adjustable folding rear. **Features:** Steel color-case hardened or brass receiver; 13-shot magazine. Introduced 2001. Imported from Uberti by Navy Arms.

Price: (steel color-case hardened receiver) **$984.00**

Price: (brass receiver). **$1,035.00**

NAVY ARMS 1866 YELLOW BOY RIFLE

Caliber: 38 Spec., 44-40, 45 Colt, 12-shot magazine. **Barrel:** 20" or 24", full octagon. **Weight:** 8-1/2 lbs. **Length:** 42-1/2" overall. **Stock:** Walnut. **Sights:** Blade front, adjustable ladder-type rear. **Features:** Brass frame, forend tip, buttplate, blued barrel, lever, hammer. Introduced 1991. Imported from Italy by Navy Arms.

Price: **$761.00**

Price: Carbine, 19" barrel **$746.00**

NAVY ARMS 1866 SPORTING YELLOWBOY RIFLES

Caliber: 45 Colt. **Barrel:** 24-1/4" octagonal; 1:16" twist. **Weight:** 8.16 lbs. **Length:** 43-3/4"overall. **Stock:** Walnut. **Sights:** Blade front, adjustable folding rear. **Features:** Brass receiver; blued or white barrel; 13-shot magazine. Introduced 2001. Imported from Uberti by Navy Arms.

Price: (blued barrel) **$761.00**

NAVY ARMS 1873 WINCHESTER-STYLE RIFLE

Caliber: 357 Mag., 44-40, 45 Colt, 12-shot magazine. **Barrel:** 24-1/4". **Weight:** 8-1/4 lbs. **Length:** 43" overall. **Stock:** European walnut. **Sights:** Blade front, buckhorn rear. **Features:** Color case-hardened frame, rest blued. Full-octagon barrel. Imported by Navy Arms.

Price: **$890.00**

Price: 1873 Carbine, 19" barrel **$869.00**

Price: 1873 Sporting Rifle (full oct. bbl., checkered walnut stock and forend) **$1,005.00**

Price: 1873 Border Model, 20" octagon barrel **$890.00**

Price: 1873 Deluxe Border Model. **$1,005.00**

NAVY ARMS 1892 RIFLE

Caliber: 357 Mag., 44-40, 45 Colt. **Barrel:** 24-1/4" octagonal. **Weight:** 7 lbs. **Length:** 42" overall. **Stock:** American walnut. **Sights:** Blade front, semi- buckhorn rear. **Features:** Replica of Winchester's early Model 1892 with octagonal barrel, forend cap and crescent buttplate. Blued or color case-hardened receiver. Introduced 1998. Imported by Navy Arms.

Price: **$545.00**

Navy Arms 1892 Stainless Carbine

Similar to the 1892 Rifle except stainless steel, has 20" round barrel, weighs 5-3/4 lbs., and is 37-1/2" overall. Introduced 1998. Imported by Navy Arms.

Price: **$585.00**

Navy Arms 1892 Rifle
Navy Arms 1892 Short Rifle
Puma Model 92
Remington 7600 Rifle
Ruger Model 96/44

Navy Arms 1892 Short Rifle

Similar to the 1892 Rifle except has 20" octagonal barrel, weighs 6-1/4 lbs., and is 37-3/4" overall. Replica of the rare, special order 1892 Winchester nicknamed the "Texas Special." Blued or color case-hardened receiver and furniture. Introduced 1998. Imported by Navy Arms.

Price: **$545.00**
Price: (stainless steel, 20" octagon barrel) **$585.00**

NAVY ARMS 1892 STAINLESS RIFLE

Caliber: 357 Mag., 44-40, 45 Colt. **Barrel:** 24-1/4" octagonal. **Weight:** 7 lbs. **Length:** 42". **Stock:** American walnut. **Sights:** Brass bead front, semi- buckhorn rear. **Features:** Designed for the Cowboy Action Shooter. Stain-less steel barrel, receiver and furniture. Introduced 2000. Imported by Navy Arms.

Price: **$585.00**

PUMA MODEL 92 RIFLES & CARBINES

Caliber: 38 Spec./357 Mag., 44 Mag., 45 Colt, 454 Casull (20" carbine only), 480 Ruger. **Barrel:** 20" round, 24"octagonal. **Weight:** 6.1-7.7 lbs. **Stock:** Walnut-stained hardwood. **Sights:** Open, buckhorn front & rear available. **Features:** Blue, case-hardened, stainless steel and brass receivers, matching buttplates. Blued, stainless steel barrels, full-length magazines. Thumb safety on top of both. 454 Casull carbine loads through magazine tube, has rubber recoil pad. 45 Colt brass-framed, saddle-ring rifle and 454 Casull carbine introduced 2002. The 480 Ruger version was introduced in 2003. Imported from Brazil by Legacy Sports International.

Price: Octagonal barrel.... **$500.00 to $561.00**
Price: Round barrel.... **$407.00 to $549.00**

REMINGTON MODEL 7600 PUMP ACTION

Caliber: 243, 270, 30-06, 308. **Barrel:** 22" round tapered. **Weight:** 7--1/2 lbs. **Length:** 42-5/8" overall. **Stock:** Cut-checkered walnut pistol grip and forend, Monte Carlo with full cheekpiece. Satin or high-gloss finish. **Sights:** Gold bead front sight on matted ramp, open step adjustable sporting rear. **Features:** Redesigned and improved version of the Model 760. Detachable 4-shot clip. Cross-bolt safety. Receiver tapped for scope mount. Introduced 1981.

Price: **$588.00**
Price: Carbine (18-1/2" bbl., 30-06 only) **$588.00**
Price: With black synthetic stock, matte black metal, rifle or carbine **$484.00**

RUGER MODEL 96/44 LEVER-ACTION RIFLE

Caliber: 44 Mag., 4-shot rotary magazine. **Barrel:** 18-1/2". **Weight:** 5-7/8 lbs. **Length:** 37-5/16" overall. **Stock:** American hardwood. **Sights:** Gold bead front, folding leaf rear. **Features:** Solid chrome-moly steel receiver. Manual cross-bolt safety, visible cocking indicator; short-throw lever action; integral scope mount; blued finish; color case-hardened lever. Introduced 1996. Made In U.S. by Sturm, Ruger & Co.

Price: 96/44M, 44 Mag **$525.00**

TRISTAR/UBERTI 1873 SPORTING RIFLE

Caliber: 44-40, 45 Colt. **Barrel:** 24-1/4", 30", octagonal. **Weight:** 8.1 lbs. **Length:** 43-1/4" overall. **Stock:** Walnut. **Sights:** Blade front adjustable for windage, open rear adjustable for elevation. **Features:** Color case-hardened frame, blued barrel, hammer, lever, buttplate, brass elevator. Imported from Italy by Tristar Sporting Arms Ltd.

Price: 24-1/4" barrel **$925.00**
Price: 30" barrel **$969.00**

Tristar 1873 Sporting Rifle

Tristar 1866 Yellowboy Carbine

Tristar 1860 Henry

Winchester 94 Traditional

TRISTAR/UBERTI 1866 SPORTING RIFLE, CARBINE

Caliber: 22 LR, 22 WMR, 38 Spec., 44-40, 45 Colt. **Barrel:** 24-1/4", octagonal. **Weight:** 8.1 lbs. **Length:** 43-1/4" overall. **Stock:** Walnut. **Sights:** Blade front adjustable for windage, rear adjustable for elevation. **Features:** Frame, buttplate, forend cap of polished brass, balance charcoal blued. Imported by Tristar Sporting Arms Ltd.

Price: **$779.00**

Price: Yellowboy Carbine (19" round bbl.) **$739.00**

TRISTAR/UBERTI 1860 HENRY RIFLE

Caliber: 44-40, 45 Colt. **Barrel:** 24-1/4", half-octagon. **Weight:** 9.2 lbs. **Length:** 43-3/4" overall. **Stock:** American walnut. **Sights:** Blade front, rear adjustable for elevation. **Features:** Frame, elevator, magazine follower, buttplate are brass, balance blue. Imported by Tristar Sporting Arms Ltd. Arms, Inc.

Price: **$989.00**

Tristar/Uberti 1860 Henry Trapper Carbine

Similar to the 1860 Henry Rifle except has 18-1/2" barrel, measures 37-3/4" overall, and weighs 8 lbs. Introduced 1999. Imported from Italy by Tristar Sporting Arms Ltd.

Price: Brass frame, blued barrel **$989.00**

U.S. FIRE-ARMS LIGHTNING MAGAZINE RIFLE

Caliber: 45 Colt, 44 WCF, 44 Spl., 38 WCF, 32 WCF, 15-shot. **Barrel:** 26" (rifle); 20" carbine, round or octagonal. **Stock:** Oiled walnut. Finish: Dome blue. Introduced 2002. Made in U.S.A. by United States Fire Arms Manufacturing Co.

Price: **$995.00**

VEKTOR H5 SLIDE-ACTION RIFLE

Caliber: 223 Rem., 5-shot magazine. **Barrel:** 18", 22". **Weight:** 9 lbs., 15 oz. **Length:** 42-1/2" overall (22" barrel). **Stock:** Walnut thumbhole. **Sights:** Comes with 1" 4x32 scope with low-light reticle. **Features:** Rotating bolt mechanism. Matte black finish. Introduced 1999. Imported from South Africa by Vektor USA.

Price: **$849.95**

WINCHESTER TIMBER CARBINE

Caliber: Chambered for 450 Marlin. **Barrel:** 18" barrel, ported. **Weight:** 6 lbs. **Length:** 36-1/4" overall. **Stock:** Half-pistol grip stock with butt pad; checkered grip and forend. **Sights:** XS ghost-ring sight. **Features:** Introduced 1999. Made in U.S.A. by U.S. Repeating Arms Co., Inc.

Price: **$610.00**

WINCHESTER MODEL 94 TRADITIONAL-CW

Caliber: 30-30 Win., 6-shot; 44 Mag., 11-shot tubular magazine. **Barrel:** 20". **Weight:** 6-1/2 lbs. **Length:** 37-3/4" overall. **Stock:** Straight grip checkered walnut stock and forend. **Sights:** Hooded blade front, semi-buckhorn rear. Drilled and tapped for scope mount. Post front sight on Trapper model. **Features:** Solid frame, forged steel receiver; side ejection, exposed rebounding hammer with automatic trigger-activated transfer bar. Introduced 1984.

Price: 30-30 .... **$469.00**

Price: 44 Mag. **$492.00**

Price: Traditional (no checkering, 30-30 only) **$435.00**

Winchester Model 94 Trapper

Similar to Model 94 Traditional except has 16" barrel, 5-shot magazine in 30-30, 9-shot in 357 Mag., 44 Magnum/44 Special, 45 Colt. Has stainless steel claw extractor, saddle ring, hammer spur extension, smooth walnut wood.

Price: 30-30 .... **$459.00**

Price: 44 Mag., 357 Mag., 45 Colt **$459.00**

Winchester Model 94 Trapper

Winchester Model 94 Trails End

Winchester Model 94 Legacy

Winchester Model 94 Ranger

Winchester Model 94 Ranger Compact

Winchester Model 94 Trails End

Similar to the Model 94 Walnut except octagon-barrel version available, chambered only for 357 Mag., 44-40, 44 Mag., 45 Colt; 11-shot magazine. Available with standard lever loop. Introduced 1997. From U.S. Repeating Arms Co., Inc.

Price: With standard lever loop **$474.00**

Winchester Model 94 Legacy

Similar to the Model 94 Traditional-CW except has half-pistol grip walnut stock, checkered grip and forend. Chambered for 30-30, 357 Mag., 44 Mag., 45 Colt; 24" barrel. Introduced 1995. Made in U.S.A. by U.S. Repeating Arms Co., Inc.

Price: With 24" barrel **$487.00**

Winchester Model 94 Ranger

Similar to the Model 94 Traditional except has a hardwood stock, post-style front sight and hammer-spur extension.

Price: (20" barrel) **$379.00**

Price: Trail's End octagon **$757.00**

Price: Trail's End octagon, case color **$815.00**

Winchester Model 94 Ranger Compact

Similar to the Model 94 Ranger except 357, 30-30 calibers, has 16" barrel and 12-1/2" length of pull, rubber recoil pad, post front sight. Introduced 1998. Made in U.S.A. by U.S. Repeating Arms Co., Inc.

Price: **$402.00**

WINCHESTER MODEL 1895 LEVER-ACTION RIFLE

Caliber: 405 Win, 4-shot magazine. **Barrel:** 24", round. **Weight:** 8 lbs. **Length:** 42" overall. **Stock:** American walnut. **Sights:** Gold bead front, buckhorn rear adjustable for elevation. **Features:** Recreation of the original Model 1895. Polished blue finish. Two-piece cocking lever, schnabel forend, straight-grip stock. Introduced 1995. From U.S. Repeating Arms Co., Inc.

Price: Grade I **$1,116.00**

CENTERFIRE RIFLES — BOLT ACTION

Includes models for a wide variety of sporting and competitive purposes and uses.

Anschutz 1733D

Barrett Model 95

Blaser R93 Classic

ANSCHUTZ 1743D BOLT-ACTION RIFLE

Caliber: 222 Rem., 3-shot magazine. **Barrel:** 19.7". **Weight:** 6.4 lbs. **Length:** 39" overall. **Stock:** European walnut. **Sights:** Hooded blade front, folding leaf rear. **Features:** Receiver grooved for scope mounting; single stage trigger; claw extractor; sling safety; sling swivels. Imported from Germany by AcuSport Corp.

Price: **$1,588.95**

ANSCHUTZ 1740 MONTE CARLO RIFLE

Caliber: 22 Hornet, 5-shot clip; 222 Rem., 3-shot clip. **Barrel:** 24". **Weight:** 6-1/2 lbs. **Length:** 43.25" overall. **Stock:** Select European walnut. **Sights:** Hooded ramp front, folding leaf rear; drilled and tapped for scope mounting. **Features:** Uses match 54 action. Adjustable single stage trigger. Stock has roll-over Monte Carlo cheekpiece, slim forend with Schnabel tip, Wundhammer palm swell on grip, rosewood gripcap with white diamond insert. Skip-line checkering on grip and forend. Introduced 1997. Imported from Germany by AcuSport Corp.

Price: From **$1,439.00**

Price: Model 1730 Monte Carlo, as above except in 22 Hornet **$1,439.00**

Anschutz 1733D Rifle

Similar to the 1740 Monte Carlo except has full-length, walnut, Mannlicher-style stock with skip-line checkering, rosewood Schnabel tip, and is chambered for 22 Hornet. Weighs 6.4 lbs., overall length 39", barrel length 19.7". Imported from Germany by AcuSport Corp.

Price: **$1,588.95**

BARRETT MODEL 95 BOLT-ACTION RIFLE

Caliber: 50 BMG, 5-shot magazine. **Barrel:** 29". **Weight:** 22 lbs. **Length:** 45" overall. **Stock:** Energy-absorbing recoil pad. **Sights:** Scope optional. **Features:** Bolt-action, bullpup design. Disassembles without tools; extendable bipod legs; match-grade barrel; high efficiency muzzle brake. Introduced 1995. Made in U.S.A. by Barrett Firearms Mfg., Inc.

Price: From **$4,950.00**

BLASER R93 BOLT-ACTION RIFLE

Caliber: 22-250, 243, 6.5x55, 270, 7x57, 7mm-08, 308, 30-06, 257 Wea. Mag., 7mm Rem. Mag., 300 Win. Mag., 300 Wea. Mag., 338 Win Mag., 375 H&H, 416 Rem. Mag. **Barrel:** 22" (standard calibers), 26" (magnum). **Weight:** 7 lbs. **Length:** 40" overall (22" barrel). **Stock:** Two-piece European walnut. **Sights:** None furnished; drilled and tapped for scope mounting. **Features:** Straight pull-back bolt action with thumb-activated safety slide/cocking mechanism; interchangeable barrels and bolt heads. Introduced 1994. Imported from Germany by SIGARMS.

Price: R93 Classic **$3,680.00**

Price: R93 LX **$1,895.00**

Price: R93 Synthetic (black synthetic stock) **$1,595.00**

Price: R93 Safari Synthetic (416 Rem. Mag. only) **$1,855.00**

Price: R93 Grand Lux **$4,915.00**

Price: R93 Attaché **$5,390.00**

BRNO 98 BOLT-ACTION RIFLE

Caliber: 7x64, 243, 270, 308, 30-06, 300 Win. Mag., 9.3x62. Barrrel: 23.6". **Weight:** 7.2 lbs. **Length:** 40.9" overall. **Stock:** European walnut. **Sights:** Blade on ramp front, open adjustable rear. **Features:** Uses Mauser 98-type action; polished blue. Announced 1998. Imported from the Czech Republic by Euro-Imports.

Price: Standard calibers **$507.00**

Price: Magnum calibers **$547.00**

Price: With set trigger, standard calibers **$615.00**

Price: As above, magnum calibers **$655.00**

Price: With full stock, set trigger, standard calibers **$703.00**

Price: As above, magnum calibers **$743.00**

Price: 300 Win. Mag., with BOSS **$933.00**

BROWNING A-BOLT RIFLES

Caliber: 223, 22-250, 243, 7mm-08, 308, 25-06, 260, 270, 30-06, 260 Rem., 7mm Rem. Mag., 300 Win. Short Mag., 300 Win. Mag., 338 Win. Mag., 375 H&H Mag, 223 WSSM, 243 WSSM, 270 WSM, 7mm WSM, 300 WSM. **Barrel:** 22" medium sporter weight with recessed muzzle; 26" on mag. cals. **Weight:** 6-1/2 to 7-1/2 lbs. **Length:** 44-3/4" overall (magnum and standard); 41-3/4" (short action). **Stock:** Classic style American walnut; recoil pad standard on magnum calibers. **Features:** Short-throw (60") fluted bolt, three locking lugs, plunger-type ejector; adjustable trigger is grooved and gold-plated. Hinged floorplate, detachable box magazine (4 rounds std. cals., 3 for magnums). Slide tang safety. BOSS barrel vibration modulator and muzzle brake system not available in 375 H&H. Introduced 1985. Imported from Japan by Browning.

Price: Hunter, no sights **$672.00**

Price: Hunter, no sights, magnum calibers **$698.00**

Price: For BOSS add **$80.00**

Browning A-Bolt Hunter

Browning A-Bolt Medallion

Browning A-Bolt White Gold Medallion

Browning A-Bolt Eclipse M-1000

BROWNING A-BOLT MEDALLION

Similar to standard A-Bolt except has glossy stock finish, rosewood grip and forend caps, engraved receiver, high-polish blue, no sights. New calibers include 223 WSSM, 243 WSSM< 270 WSM, 7mm WSM.

Price: Short-action calibers. **$782.00**
Price: Long-action calibers **$782.00**
Price: Medallion, 375 H&H Mag., open sights **$811.00**
Price: 300 Win. Short Magnum. **$811.00**
Price: For BOSS, add **$80.00**

BROWNING A-BOLT MEDALLION Left-Hand

Same as the Medallion model A-Bolt except has left-hand action and is available in 270, 30-06, 7mm Rem. Mag., 300 Win. Mag. Introduced 1987.

Price: 270, 30-06 (no sights) **$813.00**
Price: 7mm Mag., 300 Win. Mag. (no sights) **$840.00**
Price: For BOSS, add **$80.00**

BROWNING A-BOLT WHITE GOLD MEDALLION

Similar to the standard A-Bolt except has select walnut stock with brass spacers between rubber recoil pad and between the rosewood gripcap and forend tip; gold-filled barrel inscription; palm-swell pistol grip, Monte Carlo comb, 22 lpi checkering with double borders; engraved receiver flats. In 270, 30-06, 7mm Rem. Mag. and 300 Win. Mag. Introduced 1988.

Price: 270, 30-06 . . . . **$1,121.00**
Price: 7mm Rem. Mag, 300 Win. Mag. **$1,149.00**
Price: For BOSS, add **$80.00**

BROWNING A-BOLT WHITE GOLD RMEF

Caliber: 7mm Rem. Mag. Similar to the A-Bolt Medallion except has select walnut stock with rosewood forend cap, RMEF-engraved grip cap: continental cheekpiece; gold engraved, stainless receiver and bbl. Introduced 2004. Imported from Japan by Browning.

Price: **$1,224.00**

BROWNING A-BOLT ECLIPSE HUNTER

Similar to the A-Bolt II except has gray/black laminated, thumbhole stock, BOSS barrel vibration modulator and muzzle brake. Available in long and short action with heavy barrel. In 270 Win., 30-06, 7mm Rem. Mag. Introduced 1996. Imported from Japan by Browning.

Price: 270, 30-06, with BOSS. **$1,101.00**
Price: 7mm Rem. Mag, with BOSS. **$1,128.00**

BROWNING A-BOLT ECLIPSE M-1000

Similar to the A-Bolt II Eclipse except has long action and heavy target barrel. Chambered only for 300 Win. Mag. Adjustable trigger, bench-style forend, 3-shot magazine; laminated thumbhold stock; BOSS system standard. Introduced 1997. Imported for Japan by Browning.

Price: **$1,134.00**

BROWNING A-BOLT MICRO HUNTER

Similar to the A-Bolt II Hunter except has 13-5/16" length of pull, 20" barrel, and comes in 260 Rem., 243, 308, 7mm-08, 223, 22-250, 22 Hornet, 270 WSM, 7mm WSM, 300 WSM. Weighs 6 lbs., 1 oz. Introduced 1999. Imported by Browning. Also available in left-hand version.

Price: (no sights). **$664.00**

BROWNING A-BOLT CLASSIC HUNTER

Similar to the A-Bolt unter except has low-luster bluing and walnut stock with Monte Carlo comb, pistol grip palm swell, double-border checkering. Available in 223 WSSM, 243 WSSM. Introduced 1999. Imported by Browning.

Price: WSM. **$784.00**
Price: WSSM **$805.00**

CENTERFIRE RIFLES — BOLT ACTION

Browning A-Bolt Stalker

Charles Daly Superior

CZ 527 Lux

CZ 550 Lux

BROWNING A-BOLT STAINLESS STALKER

Similar to the Hunter model A-Bolt except receiver and barrel are made of stainless steel; the rest of the exposed metal surfaces are finished with a durable matte silver-gray. Graphite-fiberglass composite textured stock. No sights are furnished. Available in 260, 243, 308, 7mm-08, 270, 280,30-06, 7mm Rem. Mag., 300 WSM, 300 Rem. Ultra Mag., 338 Win. Mag., 338 Rem. Ultra Mag., 375 H&H, 223 WSSM, 243 WSSM, 270 WSM, 7mm WSM. Introduced 1987.

Price: Short-action calibers. **$871.00**
Price: Magnum calibers **$899.00**
Price: 300 Win. Short Magnum. **$899.00**
Price: For BOSS, add **$80.00**
Price: Left-hand, 270, 30-06. . . . . **$898.00**
Price: Left-hand, 7mm, 300 Win. Mag., 338 Win. Mag.. . . . . **$926.00**
Price: Left-hand, 375 H&H, with sights. **$926.00**
Price: Left-hand, for BOSS, add **$80.00**

BROWNING A-BOLT COMPOSITE STALKER

Similar to the A-Bolt Hunter except has black graphite-fiberglass stock with textured finish. Matte blue finish on all exposed metal surfaces. Available in 223, 22-250, 243, 7mm-08, 308, 30-06, 270, 280, 25-06, 7mm Rem. Mag., 300 WSM, 300 Win. Mag., 338 Win. Mag, 223 WSSM, 243 WSSM, 270 WSM, 7mm WSM. BOSS barrel vibration modulator and muzzle brake system offered in all calibers. Introduced 1994.

Price: Standard calibers, no sights **$684.00**
Price: Magnum calibers, no sights **$713.00**
Price: For BOSS, add **$80.00**

CARBON ONE BOLT-ACTION RIFLE

Caliber: 22-250 to 375 H&H. **Barrel:** Up to 28". **Weight:** 5-1/2 to 7-1/4 lbs. **Length:** Varies. **Stock:** Synthetic or wood. **Sights:** None furnished. **Features:** Choice of Remington, Browning or Winchester action with free-floated Christensen graphite/epoxy/steel barrel, trigger pull tuned to 3 to 3-1/2 lbs. Made in U.S.A. by Christensen Arms.

Price: Carbon One Hunter Rifle, 6-1/2 to 7 lbs. **$1,499.00**
Price: Carbon One Custom, 5-1/2 to 6-1/2 lbs., Shilen trigger . . **$2,750.00**
Price: Carbon Ranger, 50 BMG, 5-shot repeater **$4,750.00**
Price: Carbon Ranger, 50 BMG, single shot. **$3,950.00**

CHARLES DALY SUPERIOR BOLT-ACTION RIFLE

Caliber: 22 Hornet, 5-shot magazine. **Barrel:** 22.6". **Weight:** 6.6 lbs. **Length:** 41.25" overall. **Stock:** Walnut-finished hardwood with Monte Carlo comb and cheekpiece. **Sights:** Ramped blade front, fully adjustable open rear. **Features:** Receiver dovetailed for tip-off scope mount. Introduced 1996. Imported by K.B.I., Inc.

Price: **$364.95**

Charles Daly Empire Grade Rifle

Similar to the Superior except has oil-finished American walnut stock with 18 lpi hand checkering; black hardwood gripcap and forend tip; highly polished barreled action; jewelled bolt; recoil pad; swivel studs. Imported by K.B.I., Inc.

Price: **$469.95**

CZ 527 LUX BOLT-ACTION RIFLE

Caliber: 22 Hornet, 222 Rem., 223 Rem., detachable 5-shot magazine. **Barrel:** 23-1/2"; standard or heavy barrel. **Weight:** 6 lbs., 1 oz. **Length:** 42-1/2" overall. **Stock:** European walnut with Monte Carlo. **Sights:** Hooded front, open adjustable rear. **Features:** Improved mini-Mauser action with non-rotating claw extractor; single set trigger; grooved receiver. Imported from the Czech Republic by CZ-USA.

Price: **$566.00**
Price: Model FS, full-length stock, cheekpiece **$658.00**

CZ 527 American Classic Bolt-Action Rifle

Similar to the CZ 527 Lux except has classic-style stock with 18 l.p.i. checkering; free-floating barrel; recessed target crown on barrel. No sights furnished. Introduced 1999. Imported from the Czech Republic by CZ-USA.

Price: 22 Hornet, 222 Rem., 223 Rem. . . . . **$586.00 to $609.00**

CZ 550 LUX BOLT-ACTION RIFLE

Caliber: 22-250, 243, 6.5x55, 7x57, 7x64, 308 Win., 9.3x62, 270 Win., 30-06. **Barrel:** 20.47". **Weight:** 7.5 lbs. **Length:** 44.68" overall. **Stock:** Turkish walnut in Bavarian style or FS (Mannlicher). **Sights:** Hooded front, adjustable rear. **Features:** Improved Mauser-style action with claw extractor, fixed ejector, square bridge dovetailed receiver; single set trigger. Imported from the Czech Republic by CZ-USA.

Price: Lux . . . . **$566.00 to $609.00**
Price: FS (full stock) **$706.00**

CZ 550 American Classic

CZ 550 Magnum

Dakota 76 Classic

Dakota 76 Safari

CZ 550 American Classic Bolt-Action Rifle

Similar to CZ 550 Lux except has American classic-style stock with 18 l.p.i. checkering; free-floating barrel; recessed target crown. Has 25.6" barrel; weighs 7.48 lbs. No sights furnished. Introduced 1999. Imported from the Czech Republic by CZ-USA.

Price: .... **$586.00 to $609.00**

CZ 550 Medium Magnum Bolt-Action Rifle

Similar to the CZ 550 Lux except chambered for the 300 Win. Mag. and 7mm Rem. Mag.; 5-shot magazine. Adjustable iron sights, hammer-forged barrel, single-set trigger, Turkish walnut stock. Weighs 7.5 lbs. Introduced 2001. Imported from the Czech Republic by CZ USA.

Price: **$621.00**

CZ 550 Magnum Bolt-Action Rifle

Similar to CZ 550 Lux except has long action for 300 Win. Mag., 375 H&H, 416 Rigby, 458 Win. Mag. Overall length is 46.45"; barrel length 25"; weighs 9.24 lbs. Hooded front sight, express rear with one standing, two folding leaves. Imported from the Czech Republic by CZ-USA.

Price: 300 Win. Mag. **$717.00**

Price: 375 H&H..................................... **$756.00**

Price: 416 Rigby **$809.00**

Price: 458 Win. Mag..................................... **$744.00**

CZ 700 M1 SNIPER RIFLE

Caliber: 308 Winchester, 10-shot magazine. **Barrel:** 25.6". **Weight:** 11.9 lbs. **Length:** 45" overall. **Stock:** Laminated wood thumbhole with adjustable buttplate and cheekpiece. **Sights:** None furnished; permanently attached Weaver rail for scope mounting. **Features:** 60-degree bolt throw; oversized trigger guard and bolt handle for use with gloves; full-length equipment rail on forend; fully adjustable trigger. Introduced 2001. Imported from the Czech Republic by CZ USA.

Price: **$2,097.00**

DAKOTA 76 TRAVELER TAKEDOWN RIFLE

Caliber: 257 Roberts, 25-06, 7x57, 270, 280, 30-06, 338-06, 35 Whelen (standard length); 7mm Rem. Mag., 300 Win. Mag., 338 Win. Mag., 416 Taylor, 458 Win. Mag. (short magnums); 7mm, 300, 330, 375 Dakota Magnums. **Barrel:** 23". **Weight:** 7-1/2 lbs. **Length:** 43-1/2" overall. **Stock:** Medium fancy-grade walnut in classic style. Checkered grip and forend; solid butt pad. **Sights:** None furnished; drilled and tapped for scope mounts. **Features:** Threadless disassembly-no threads to wear or stretch, no interrupted cuts, and headspace remains constant. Uses mod-ified Model 76 design with many features of the Model 70 Winchester. Left-hand model also available. Introduced 1989. Made in U.S.A. by Dakota Arms, Inc.

Price: Classic **$4,495.00**

Price: Safari **$5,495.00**

Price: Extra barrels..................................... **$1,650.00 to $1,950.00**

DAKOTA 76 CLASSIC BOLT-ACTION RIFLE

Caliber: 257 Roberts, 270, 280, 30-06, 7mm Rem. Mag., 338 Win. Mag., 300 Win. Mag., 375 H&H, 458 Win. Mag. **Barrel:** 23". **Weight:** 7-1/2 lbs. **Length:** 43-1/2" overall. **Stock:** Medium fancy grade walnut in classic style. Checkered pistol grip and forend; solid butt pad. **Sights:** None furnished; drilled and tapped for scope mounts. **Features:** Has many features of the original Model 70 Winchester. One-piece rail trigger guard assembly; steel gripcap. Model 70-style trigger. Many options available. Left-hand rifle available at same price. Introduced 1988. From Dakota Arms, Inc.

Price: **$3,595.00**

DAKOTA 76 SAFARI BOLT-ACTION RIFLE

Caliber: 270 Win., 7x57, 280, 30-06, 7mm Dakota, 7mm Rem. Mag., 300 Dakota, 300 Win. Mag., 330 Dakota, 338 Win. Mag., 375 Dakota, 458 Win. Mag., 300 H&H, 375 H&H, 416 Rem. **Barrel:** 23". **Weight:** 8-1/2 lbs. **Length:** 43-1/2" overall. **Stock:** XXX fancy walnut with ebony forend tip; point-pattern with wrap-around forend checkering. **Sights:** Ramp front, standing leaf rear. **Features:** Has many features of the original Model 70 Winchester. Barrel band front swivel, inletted rear. Cheekpiece with shadow line. Steel gripcap. Introduced 1988. From Dakota Arms, Inc.

Price: Wood stock..................................... **$4,595.00**

Dakota Longbow

Dakota 97 Lightweight Hunter

Dakota Hunter

Ed Brown 702 Savanna

Dakota African Grade

Similar to 76 Safari except chambered for 338 Lapua Mag., 404 Jeffery, 416 Rigby, 416 Dakota, 450 Dakota, 4-round magazine, select wood, two stock cross-bolts. 24" barrel, weighs 9-10 lbs. Ramp front sight, standing leaf rear. Introduced 1989.

Price: **$4,995.00**

DAKOTA LONGBOW TACTICAL E.R. RIFLE

Caliber: 300 Dakota Magnum, 330 Dakota Magnum, 338 Lapua Magnum. **Barrel:** 28", .950" at muzzle **Weight:** 13.7 lbs. **Length:** 50" to 52" overall. **Stock:** Ambidextrous McMillan A-2 fiberglass, black or olive green color; adjustable cheekpiece and buttplate. **Sights:** None furnished. Comes with Picatinny one-piece optical rail. **Features:** Uses the Dakota 76 action with controlled-round feed; three-position firing pin block safety, claw extractor; Model 70-style trigger. Comes with bipod, case tool kit. Introduced 1997. Made in U.S.A. by Dakota Arms, Inc.

Price: **$4,250.00**

DAKOTA 97 LIGHTWEIGHT HUNTER

Caliber: 22-250 to 330. **Barrel:** 22"-24". **Weight:** 6.1-6.5 lbs. **Length:** 43" overall. **Stock:** Fiberglass. **Sights:** Optional. **Features:** Matte blue finish, black stock. Right-hand action only. Introduced 1998. Made in U.S.A. by Dakota Arms, Inc.

Price: **$1,995.00**

DAKOTA LONG RANGE HUNTER RIFLE

Caliber: 25-06, 257 Roberts, 270 Win., 280 Rem., 7mm Rem. Mag., 7mm Dakota Mag., 30-06, 300 Win. Mag., 300 Dakota Mag., 338 Win. Mag., 330 Dakota Mag., 375 H&H Mag., 375 Dakota Mag. **Barrel:** 24", 26", match-quality; free-floating. **Weight:** 7.7 lbs. **Length:** 45" to 47" overall. **Stock:** H-S Precision black synthetic, with one-piece bedding block system. **Sights:** None furnished. Drilled and tapped for scope mounting. **Features:** Cylindrical machined receiver controlled round feed; Mauser-style extractor; three-position striker blocking safety; fully adjustable match trigger. Right-hand action only. Introduced 1997. Made in U.S.A. by Dakota Arms, Inc.

Price: **$1,995.00**

ED BROWN MODEL 702, SAVANNA

Caliber: (long action) 25-06, 270 Win., 280 Rem., 7mm Rem. Mag., 7STW, 30-06, 300 Win. Mag., 300 Weatherby, 338 Win. Mag. (Short action) 223, 22-250, 243, 6mm, 260 Rem. 7mm-08, 308, 300 WSM, 270 WSM, 7mm WSM. **Barrel:** 23" (standard calibers) light weight #3 contour; medium weight 24", 26" with #4 contour on medium calibers. **Weight:** 8 to 8.5-lbs. **Stock:** Fully glass-bedded McMillan fiberglass sporter. **Sights:** None furnished. Talley scope mounts utilzing heavy duty 8-40 screws. **Features:** Custom action with machined steel trigger guard and hinged floor plate. Available in left-hand version.

Price: From **$2,800.00**

Ed Brown 702 Ozark

Ed Brown 702 Bushveld

Ed Brown 702 Varmint

Harris Gunworks Alaskan

Ed Brown Model 702 Denali, Ozark

Similar to the Ed Brown Model 702 Savanna but the Denali is a lighter weight rifle designed specifically for mountain hunting, especially suited to the 270 and 280 calibers. Right hand only. Weighs about 7.75 lbs. The Model 702 Ozark is another lighter weight rifle made on a short action with a very light weight stock. Ozark calibers are 223, 243, 6mm, 260 Rem., 7mm-08, 308. Weight 6.5 lbs.

Price: From (either model) **$2,800.00**

ED BROWN MODEL 702 BUSHVELD

Caliber: 338 Win. Mag., 375 H&H, 416 Rem. Mag., 458 Win. Mag. And all Ed Brown Savanna long action calibers. **Barrel:** 24" medium or heavy weight. **Weight:** 8.25 lbs. **Stock:** Fully bedded McMillan fiberglass with Monte Carlo style cheekpiece, Pachmayr Decelerator recoil pad. **Sights:** None furnish. Talley scope mounts utilizing heavy duty 8-40 screws. **Features:** A dangerous game rifle with options including left-hand action, stainless steel barrel, additional calibers, iron sights.

Price: From **$2,900.00**

ED BROWN MODEL 702 VARMINT

Caliber: 223, 22-250, 220 Swift, 243, 6mm, 308. **Barrel:** Medium weight #5 contour 24"; heavy weight #17 contour 24"; 26" optional. **Weight:** 9 lbs. **Stock:** Fully glass-bedded McMillan fiberglass with recoil pad. **Sights:** None furnished. Talley scope mounts with heavy duty 8-40 screws. **Features:** Fully-adjustable trigger, steel trigger guard and floor plate, many options available.

Price: From **$2,500.00**

HARRIS GUNWORKS SIGNATURE CLASSIC SPORTER

Caliber: 22-250, 243, 6mm Rem., 7mm-08, 284, 308 (short action); 25-06, 270, 280 Rem., 30-06, 7mm Rem. Mag., 300 Win. Mag., 300 Wea. (long action); 338 Win. Mag., 340 Wea., 375 H&H (magnum action). **Barrel:** 22", 24", 26". **Weight:** 7 lbs. (short action). **Stock:** Fiberglass in green, beige, brown or black. Recoil pad and 1" swivels installed. Length of pull up to 14-1/4". **Sights:** None furnished. Comes with 1" rings and bases. **Features:** Uses right- or left-hand action with matte black finish. Trigger pull set at 3 lbs. Four-round magazine for standard calibers; three for magnums. Aluminum floorplate. Wood stock optional. Introduced 1987. From Harris Gunworks, Inc.

Price: **$2,700.00**

Harris Gunworks Signature Classic Stainless Sporter

Similar to Signature Classic Sporter except action is made of stainless steel. Same calibers, in addition to 416 Rem. Mag. Fiberglass stock, right- or left-hand action in natural stainless, glass bead or black chrome sulfide finishes. Introduced 1990. From Harris Gunworks, Inc.

Price: **$2,900.00**

Harris Gunworks Signature Alaskan

Similar to Classic Sporter except match-grade barrel with single leaf rear sight, barrel band front, 1" detachable rings and mounts, steel floorplate, electroless nickel finish. Wood Monte Carlo stock with cheekpiece, palm-swell grip, solid butt pad. Chambered for 270, 280 Rem., 30-06, 7mm Rem. Mag., 300 Win. Mag., 300 Wea., 358 Win., 340 Wea., 375 H&H. Introduced 1989.

Price: **$3,800.00**

Harris Gunworks Signature Titanium Mountain

Harris Gunworks Signature Super Varminter

Harris Gunworks Talon Safari

Howa Lightning

Harris Gunworks Signature Titanium Mountain Rifle

Similar to Classic Sporter except action made of titanium alloy, barrel of chrome-moly steel. Stock is graphite reinforced fiberglass. Weight is 5-1/2 lbs. Chambered for 270, 280 Rem., 30-06, 7mm Rem. Mag., 300 Win. Mag. Fiberglass stock optional. Introduced 1989.

Price: **$3,300.00**
Price: With graphite-steel composite light weight barrel **$3,700.00**

Harris Gunworks Signature Varminter

Similar to Signature Classic Sporter except has heavy contoured barrel, adjustable trigger, field bipod and special hand-bedded fiberglass stock. Chambered for 223, 22-250, 220 Swift, 243, 6mm Rem., 25-06, 7mm-08, 7mm BR, 308, 350 Rem. Mag. Comes with 1" rings and bases. Introduced 1989.

Price: **$2,700.00**

HARRIS GUNWORKS TALON SAFARI RIFLE

Caliber: 300 Win. Mag., 300 Wea. Mag., 300 Phoenix, 338 Win. Mag., 30/378, 338 Lapua, 300 H&H, 340 Wea. Mag., 375 H&H, 404 Jeffery, 416 Rem. Mag., 458 Win. Mag. (Safari Magnum); 378 Wea. Mag., 416 Rigby, 416 Wea. Mag., 460 Wea. Mag. (Safari Super Magnum). **Barrel:** 24". **Weight:** About 9-10 lbs. **Length:** 43" overall. **Stock:** Gunworks fiberglass Safari. **Sights:** Barrel band front ramp, multi-leaf express rear. **Features:** Uses Harris Gunworks Safari action. Has quick detachable 1" scope mounts, positive locking steel floorplate, barrel band sling swivel. Match-grade barrel. Matte black finish standard. Introduced 1989. From Harris Gunworks, Inc.

Price: Talon Safari Magnum **$3,900.00**
Price: Talon Safari Super Magnum **$4,200.00**

HARRIS GUNWORKS TALON SPORTER RIFLE

Caliber: 22-250, 243, 6mm Rem., 6mm BR, 7mm BR, 7mm-08, 25-06, 270, 280 Rem., 284, 308, 30-06, 350 Rem. Mag. (long action); 7mm Rem. Mag., 7mm STW, 300 Win. Mag., 300 Wea. Mag., 300 H&H, 338 Win. Mag., 340 Wea. Mag., 375 H&H, 416 Rem. Mag. **Barrel:** 24" (standard). **Weight:** About 7-1/2 lbs. **Length:** NA. **Stock:** Choice of walnut or fiberglass. **Sights:** None furnished; comes with rings and bases. Open sights optional. **Features:** Uses pre-'64 Model 70-type action with cone breech, controlled feed, claw extractor and three-position safety. Barrel and action are of stainless steel; chrome-moly optional. Introduced 1991. From Harris Gunworks, Inc.

Price: **$2,900.00**

HOWA LIGHTNING BOLT-ACTION RIFLE

Caliber: 223, 22-250, 243, 6.5x55, 270, 308, 30-06, 7mm Rem. Mag., 300 Win. Mag., 338 Win. Mag, 300 WSM, 7mm WSM, 270 WSM. **Barrel:** 22", 24" magnum calibers. **Weight:** 7-1/2 lbs. **Length:** 42" overall (22" barrel). **Stock:** Black Bell & Carlson Carbelite composite with Monte Carlo comb; checkered grip and forend. **Sights:** None furnished. Drilled and tapped for scope mounting. **Features:** Sliding thumb safety; hinged floorplate; polished blue/black finish. Introduced 1993. From Legacy Sports International.

Price: Blue, standard calibers **$479.00**
Price: Blue, magnum calibers **$502.00**
Price: Stainless, standard calibers **$585.00**
Price: Stainless, magnum calibers **$612.00**

Howa M-1500 Hunter Bolt-Action Rifle

Similar to Lightning Model except has walnut-finished hardwood stock. Polished blue finish or stainless steel. Introduced 1999. From Legacy Sports International.

Price: Blue, standard calibers **$539.00**
Price: Stainless, standard calibers **$638.00**
Price: Blue, magnum calibers **$560.00**
Price: Stainless, magnum calibers **$662.00**

Howa M-1500 Hunter

Howa M-1500 Ultralight

Howa M-1500 Varmint Supreme

Kimber 84M Classic

Kimber 84M Varmint

Howa M-1500 Supreme Rifles

Similar to Howa M-1500 Lightning except stocked with JRS Classic or Thumbhole Sporter laminated wood stocks in Nutmeg (brown/black) or Pepper (gray/black) colors. Barrel 22"; 24" magnum calibers. Weights are JRS stock 8 lbs., THS stock 8.3 lbs. Introduced 2001. Imported from Japan by Legacy Sports International.

Price: Blue, standard calibers, JRS stock **$616.00**
Price: Blue, standard calibers, THS stock **$668.00**
Price: Blue, magnum calibers, JRS stock **$638.00**
Price: Blue, magnum calibers, THS stock **$638.00**
Price: Stainless, standard calibers, JRS stock **$720.00**
Price: Stainless, standard calibers, THS stock **$771.00**
Price: Stainless, magnum calibers, JRS stock **$720.00**
Price: Stainless, magnum calibers, THS stock **$742.00**

Howa M-1500 Ultralight

Similar to Howa M-1500 Lightning except receiver milled to reduce weight, tapered 22" barrel; 1-10" twist. Chambered for 243 Win. Stocks are black texture-finished hardwood. Weighs 6.4 lbs. Length 40"overall.

Price: Blued **$511.00**

Howa M-1500 Varmint and Varmint Supreme Rifles

Similar to M-1500 Lightning except has heavy 24" hammer-forged barrel. Chambered for 223, 22-250, 308. Weighs 9.3 lbs.; overall length 44.5". Introduced 1999. Imported from Japan by Interarms/Howa. Varminter Supreme has heavy barrel, target crown muzzle. Heavy 24" barrel, laminated wood with raised comb stocks, rollover cheekpiece, vented beavertail forearm; available in 223 Rem., 22-250 Rem., 308 Win. Weighs 9.9 lbs. Introduced 2001. Imported from Japan by Legacy Sports International.

Price: Varminter, blue, polymer stock **$517.00**
Price: Varminter, stainless, polymer stock **$626.00**
Price: Varminter, blue, wood stock **$575.00**
Price: Varminter, stainless, wood stock. **$677.00**
Price: Varminter Supreme, blued . . . . **$612.00 to $641.00**
Price: Varminter Supreme, stainless. . . . . **$714.00 to $743.00**

KIMBER MODEL 84M BOLT-ACTION RIFLE

Caliber: 22-250, 243, 260 Rem., 7mm-08, 308, 5-shot. **Barrel:** 22", 24", 26". **Weight:** 5 lbs., 10 oz. to 10 lbs. **Length:** 41"-45". **Stock:** Claro walnut, checkered with steel grip cap or gray laminate. **Sights:** None; drilled and tapped for bases. **Features:** Mauser claw extractor, two-position wing safety, action bedded on aluminum pillars, free-floated barrel, match-grade trigger set at 4 lbs., matte blue finish. Includes cable lock. Introduced 2001. Made in U.S.A. by Kimber Mfg. Inc.

Price: Classic (243, 260, 7mm-08, 308) **$917.00**
Price: Varmint (22-250). **$1,001.00**

L.A.R. Grizzly

Magnum Research Tactical

Raptor Bolt-Action

Remington 673 Guide

L.A.R. GRIZZLY 50 BIG BOAR RIFLE

Caliber: 50 BMG, single shot. **Barrel:** 36". **Weight:** 30.4 lbs. **Length:** 45.5" overall. **Stock:** Integral. Ventilated rubber recoil pad. **Sights:** None furnished; scope mount. **Features:** Bolt-action bullpup design, thumb and bolt stop safety. All-steel construction. Unsurpassed accuracy and impact. Introduced 1994. Made in U.S.A. by L.A.R. Mfg., Inc.

Price: **$2,195.00**

MAGNUM RESEARCH MAGNUM LITE TACTICAL RIFLE

Caliber: 223 Rem., 22-250, 308 Win., 300 Win. Mag., 300 WSM. **Barrel:** 26" Magnum Lite™ graphite. **Weight:** 8.3 lbs. **Length:** NA. **Stock:** H-S Precision™ tactical black synthetic. **Sights:** None furnished; drilled and tapped for scope mount. **Features:** Accurized Remington 700 action; adjustable trigger; adjustable comb height. Tuned to shoot 1/2" MOA or better. Introduced 2001. From Magnum Research Inc.

Price: **$2,400.00**

MOUNTAIN EAGLE MAGNUM LITE RIFLE

Caliber: 22-250, 223 Rem. (Varmint); 280, 30-06 (long action); 7mm Rem. Mag., 300 Win. Mag., (magnum action). **Barrel:** 24", 26", free floating. **Weight:** 7 lbs., 13 oz. **Length:** 44" overall (24" barrel). **Stock:** Kevlar-graphite with aluminum bedding block, high comb, recoil pad, swivel studs; made by H-S Precision. **Sights:** None furnished; accepts any Remington 700-type base. **Features:** Special Sako action with one-piece forged bolt, hinged steel floorplate, lengthened receiver ring; adjustable trigger. Krieger cut-rifled benchrest barrel. Introduced 1996. From Magnum Research, Inc.

Price: Magnum Lite (graphite barrel) **$2,295.00**

NEW ULTRA LIGHT ARMS BOLT-ACTION RIFLES

Caliber: 17 Rem. to 416 Rigby (numerous calibers available). **Barrel:** Douglas, length to order. **Weight:** 4-3/4 to 7-1/2 lbs. **Length:** Varies. **Stock:** Kevlar®/ graphite composite, variety of finishes. **Sights:** None furnished; drilled and tapped for scope mount. **Features:** Timney trigger, hand-lapped action, button-rifled barrel, hand-bedded action, recoil pad, sling-swivel studs, optional Jewell Trigger. Made in U.S.A. by New Ultra Light Arms.

Price: Model 20 (short action). **$2,500.00**
Price: Model 24 (long action) **$2,600.00**
Price: Model 28 (magnum action). **$2,900.00**
Price: Model 40 (300 Wea. Mag., 416 Rigby) **$2,900.00**
Price: Left-hand models, add **$100.00**

RAPTOR BOLT-ACTION RIFLE

Caliber: 270, 30-06, 243, 25-06, 308; 4-shot magazine. **Barrel:** 22". **Weight:** 7 lbs., 6 oz. **Length:** 42.5" overall. **Stock:** Black synthetic, fiberglass reinforced; checkered grip and forend; vented recoil pad; Monte Carlo cheekpiece. **Sights:** None furnished; drilled and tapped for scope mounts. **Features:** Rust-resistant "Taloncote" treated barreled action; pillar bedded; stainless bolt with three locking lugs; adjustable trigger. Announced 1997. Made in U.S.A. by Raptor Arms Co., Inc.

Price: **$249.00**

Remington Model 673 Guide Rifle

Available in 350 Rem. Mag., 300 Rem. SAUM with 22" magnum contour barrel with machined steel ventilated rib, iron sights, wide laminate stock.

Price: **$825.00**

Remington 700 Classic

Remington 700 ADL Synthetic

Remington 700 BDL

Remington 700 BDL Left Hand

REMINGTON MODEL 700 CLASSIC RIFLE

Caliber: 300 Savage. **Barrel:** 24". **Weight:** About 7-1/4 lbs. **Length:** 44-1/2" overall. **Stock:** American walnut, 20 lpi checkering on pistol grip and forend. Classic styling. Satin finish. **Sights:** None furnished. Receiver drilled and tapped for scope mounting. **Features:** A "classic" version of the BDL with straight comb stock. Fitted with rubber recoil pad. Sling swivel studs installed. Hinged floorplate. Limited production in 2003 only.

Price: **$683.00**

REMINGTON MODEL 700 ADL DELUXE RIFLE

Caliber: 270, 30-06. **Barrel:** 22" round tapered. **Weight:** 7-1/4 lbs. **Length:** 41-5/8" overall. **Stock:** Walnut. Satin-finished pistol grip stock with fine-line cut checkering, Monte Carlo. **Sights:** Gold bead ramp front; removable, step-adjustable rear with windage screw. **Features:** Side safety, receiver tapped for scope mounts.

Price: **$580.00**

Remington Model 700 ADL Synthetic

Similar to the 700 ADL except has a fiberglass-reinforced synthetic stock with straight comb, raised cheekpiece, positive checkering, and black rubber butt pad. Metal has matte finish. Available in 22-250, 223, 243, 270, 308, 30-06 with 22" barrel, 300 Win. Mag., 7mm Rem. Mag. with 24" barrel. Introduced 1996.

Price: From .... **$500.00 to $527.00**

Remington Model 700 ADL Synthetic Youth

Similar to the Model 700 ADL Synthetic except has 1" shorter stock, 20" barrel. Chambered for 243, 308. Introduced 1998.

Price: **$500.00**

Remington Model 700 BDL Custom Deluxe Rifle

Same as 700 ADL except chambered for 222, 223 (short action, 24" barrel), 7mm-08, 280, 22-250, 25-06. (short action, 22" barrel), 243, 270, 30-06, skip-line checkering, black forend tip and gripcap with white line spacers. Matted receiver top, quick-release floorplate. Hooded ramp front sight, quick detachable swivels.

Price: **$683.00**

Also available in 17 Rem., 7mm Rem. Mag., 7mm Rem. Ultra Mag., 300 Win. Mag. (long action, 24" barrel); 300 Rem. Ultra Mag. (26" barrel). Overall length 44-1/2", weight about 7-1/2 lbs.

Price: .... **$709.00 to $723.00**

Remington Model 700 BDL Left Hand Custom Deluxe

Same as 700 BDL except mirror-image left-hand action, stock. Available in 270, 30-06, 7mm Rem. Mag., 300 Rem. Ultra Mag, 338 Rem. Ultra Mag., 7mm Rem. Ultra Mag.

Price: .... **$709.00 to $749.00**

Remington Model 700 BDL DM Rifle

Same as 700 BDL except detachable box magazine (4-shot, standard calibers, 3-shot for magnums). Glossy stock finish, open sights, recoil pad, sling swivels. Available in 270, 30-06, 7mm Rem. Mag., 300 Win. Mag. Introduced 1995.

Price: From .... **$749.00 to $776.00**

Remington Model 700 BDL SS Rifle

Similar to 700 BDL rifle except hinged floorplate, 24" standard weight barrel in all calibers; magnum calibers have magnum-contour barrel. No sights supplied, but comes drilled and tapped. Corrosion-resistant follower and fire control, stainless BDL-style barreled action with fine matte finish. Synthetic stock has straight comb and cheekpiece, textured finish, positive checkering, plated swivel studs. Calibers-270, 30-06; mag-nums-7mm Rem. Mag., 7mm Rem. UltraMag., 300 Rem. Ultra Mag. (26" barrel) 300 Win. Mag., 338 Rem. Ultra Mag., 7mm Rem. SAUM, 300 Rem. SAUM. Weighs 7-3/8 to 7-1/2 lbs. Introduced 1993.

Price: From .... **$735.00 to $775.00**

Remington 700 BDL SS

Remington 700 BDL SS DM

Remington 700 LSS Mountain

Remington 700 Safari KS

Remington Model 700 BDL SS DM Rifle

Same as 700 BDL SS except detachable box magazine. Barrel, receiver and bolt made of #416 stainless steel; black synthetic stock, fine-line engraving. Available in 270, 30-06, 7mm Rem. Mag., 300 Win. Mag. Introduced 1995.

Price: From .... **$801.00 to $828.00**

Remington Model 700 Custom KS Mountain Rifle

Similar to 700 BDL except custom finished with aramid fiber reinforced resin synthetic stock. Available in left- and right-hand versions. Chambered 270 Win., 280 Rem., 30-06, 7mm Rem. Mag., 7mm STW, 300 Rem. Ultra Mag., 338 Rem. Ultra Mag., 300 Win. Mag., 300 Wea. Mag., 35 Whelen, 338 Win. Mag., 8mm Rem. Mag., 375 H&H, with 24" barrel (except 300 Rem. Ultra Mag., 26"), 7mm RUM, 375 RUM. Weighs 6 lbs., 6 oz. Introduced 1986.

Price: Right-hand **$1,314.00**
Price: Left-hand **$1,393.00**
Price: Stainless............................ **$1,500 to $1,580.00**

Remington Model 700 LSS Mountain Rifle

Similar to Model 700 Custom KS Mountain Rifle except stainless steel 22" barrel and two-tone laminated stock. Chambered in 260 Rem., 7mm-08, 270 Winchester and 30-06. Overall length 42-1/2", weighs 6-5/8 oz. Introduced 1999.

Price: **$800.00**

Remington Model 700 Safari Grade

Similar to 700 BDL aramid fiber reinforced fiberglass stock, blued carbon steel bbl. and action, or stainless, w/cheekpiece, custom finished and tuned. In 8mm Rem. Mag., 375 H&H, 416 Rem. Mag. or 458 Win. Mag. calibers only with heavy barrel. Right- and left-hand versions.

Price: Safari KS .... **$1,520.00 to $1,601.00**
Price: Safari KS (stainless right-hand only) **$1,697.00**

Remington Model 700 AWR Alaskan Wilderness Rifle

Similar to the 700 BDL except has stainless barreled action finishBlack Teflon 24" bbl. 26" Ultra Mag raised cheekpiece, magnum-grade black rubber recoil pad. Chambered for 7mm RUM., 375 RUM, 7mm STW, 300 Rem. Ultra Mag., 300 Win. Mag., 300 Wea. Mag., 338 Rem. Ultra Mag., 338 Win. Mag., 375 H&H. Aramid fiber reinforced fiberglass stock. Introduced 1994.

Price: .... **$1,593.00** (right-hand); **$1,673.00** (left-hand)

Remington Model 700 APR African Plains Rifle

Similar to Model 700 BDL except magnum receiver and specially contoured 26" Custom Shop barrel with satin blued finish, laminated wood stock with raised cheekpiece, satin finish, black butt pad, 20 lpi cut checkering. Chambered for 7mm Rem. Mag., 7mm RUM, 375 RUM, 300 Rem. Ultra Mag., 300 Win. Mag., 300 Wea. Mag., 338 Win. Mag., 338 Rem. Ultra Mag., 375 H&H. Introduced 1994.

Price: **$1,716.00**

Remington Model 700 LSS Rifle

Similar to 700 BDL except stainless steel barreled action, gray laminated wood stock with Monte Carlo comb and cheekpiece. No sights furnished. Available in (RH) 7mm Rem. Mag., 300 Win. Mag., 300 RUM, 338 RUM, 7mm Rem. Ultra Mag., 375 Rem. Ultra Mag., (LH) 7mm Rem. Ultra Mag., 300 Rem. Ultra Mag., and 338 Rem. RUM. Introduced 1996.

Price: From .... (Right-hand) **$820.00 to $840.00**; (LH) **$867.00**

Remington Model 700 MTN DM Rifle

Similar to 700 BDL except weighs 6-1/2 to 6-5/8 lbs., 22" tapered barrel. Redesigned pistol grip, straight comb, contoured cheekpiece, hand-rubbed oil stock finish, deep cut checkering, hinged floorplate and magazine follower, two-position thumb safety. Chambered for 260 Rem., 270 Win., 7mm-08, 25-06, 280 Rem., 30-06, 4-shot detachable box magazine. Overall length is 41-5/8"-42-1/2". Introduced 1995.

Price: **$728.00**

Remington 700 APR African Plains

Remington 700 Titanium

Remington 700 VLS

Remington 700 VS

Remington 700 VS SF

Remington 700 Sendero SF

Remington Model 700 Titanium

Similar to 700 BDL except has titanium receiver, spiral-cut fluted bolt, skeletonized bolt handle and carbon-fiber and aramid fiber reinforced stock with sling swivel studs. Barrel 22"; weighs 5-1/4 lbs. (short action) or 5-1/2 lbs. (long action). Satin stainless finish. 260 Rem., 270 Win., 7mm-08, 30-06, 308 Win. Introduced 2001.

Price: **$1,239.00**

Remington Model 700 VLS Varmint Laminated Stock

Similar to 700 BDL except 26" heavy barrel without sights, brown laminated stock with beavertail forend, gripcap, rubber butt pad. Available in 223 Rem., 22-250, 6mm, 243, 308. Polished blue finish. Introduced 1995.

Price: From **$705.00**

Remington Model 700 VS SF Rifle

Similar to Model 700 Varmint Synthetic except satin-finish stainless barreled action with 26" fluted barrel, spherical concave muzzle crown. Chambered for 223, 220 Swift, 22-250. Introduced 1994.

Price: **$976.00**

Remington Model 700 VS Varmint Synthetic Rifles

Similar to 700 BDL Varmint Laminated except composite stock reinforced with aramid fiber reinforced, fiberglass and graphite. Aluminum bedding block that runs full length of receiver. Free-floating 26" barrel. Metal has black matte finish; stock has textured black and gray finish and swivel studs. Available in 223, 22-250, 308. Right- and left-hand. Introduced 1992.

Price: . . . . **$811.00 to $837.00**

Remington Model 700 EtronX VSSF Rifle

Similar to Model 700 VS SF except features battery-powered ignition system for near-zero lock time and electronic trigger mechanism. Requires ammunition with EtronX electrically fired primers. Aluminum-bedded 26" heavy, stainless steel, fluted barrel; overall length 45-7/8"; weight 8 lbs., 14 oz. Black, Kevlar-reinforced composite stock. Light-emitting diode display on grip top indicates fire or safe mode, loaded or unloaded chamber, battery condition. Introduced 2000.

Price: 220 Swift, 22-250 or 243 Win. **$1,332.00**

Remington Model 700 Sendero SF Rifle

Similar to 700 Sendero except stainless steel action and 26" fluted stainless barrel. Weighs 8-1/2 lbs. Chambered for 7mm Rem. SAUM, 300 Rem. SAUM, 7mm Rem. Mag., 7mm STW, 300 Rem. Ultra Mag., 338 Rem. Ultra Mag., 300 Win. Mag., 7mm Rem. Ultra Mag. Introduced 1996.

Price: . . . . **$1,003.00 to $1,016.00**

REMINGTON MODEL 700 RMEF

Caliber: 300 Rem. SAUM. **Barrel:** 26". **Weight:** 7-5/8 lbs. **Length:** 46.5". **Stock:** Synthetic, Realtree Hardwoods HD finish. **Sights:** None; drilled and tapped. **Features:** Special Edition (sold one year only), Rocky Mountain Elk Foundation rifle, 416 stainless bolt, varrel, receiver. Portion of proceeds to RMEF.

Price: **$835.00**

Remington Seven LS

Remington Model Seven LS Mag

Remington Model Seven SS Mag

Remington Model Seven Custom MS

Remington Seven Custom KS

REMINGTON MODEL 710 BOLT-ACTION RIFLE

Caliber: 270 Win., 30-06. **Barrel:** 22". **Weight:** 7-1/8 lbs. **Length:** 42-1/2" overall. **Stock:** Gray synthetic. **Sights:** Bushnell Sharpshooter 3-9x scope mounted and bore-sighted. **Features:** Unique action locks bolt directly into barrel; 60-degree bolt throw; 4-shot dual-stack magazine; key-operated Integrated Security System locks bolt open. Introduced 2001. Made in U.S.A. by Remington Arms Co.

Price: **$425.00**

REMINGTON MODEL SEVEN LS

Caliber: 223 Rem., 243 Win., 7mm-08 Rem., 308 Win. **Barrel:** 20". **Weight:** 6-1/2 lbs. **Length:** 39-1/4" overall. **Stock:** Brown laminated, satin finished. **Features:** Satin finished carbone steel barrel and action, 4-round magazine, hinged magazine floorplate. Furnished with iron sights and sling swivel studs, drilled and tapped for scope mounts.

Price: **$701.00**

Price: 7mmRSAUM, 300RSAUM, LS Magnum, 22" bbl. **$741.00**

Remington Model Seven SS

Similar to Model Seven LS except stainless steel barreled action and black synthetic stock, 20" barrel. Chambered for 243, 260 Rem., 7mm-08, 308. Introduced 1994.

Price: **$729.00**

Price: 7mmRSAUM, 300RSAUM, Model Seven SS Magnum, 22" bbl. **$769.00**

Remington Model Seven Custom MS Rifle

Similar to Model Seven LS except full-length Mannlicher-style stock of laminated wood with straight comb, solid black recoil pad, black steel forend tip, cut checkering, gloss finish. Barrel length 20", weighs 6-3/4 lbs. Available in 222 Rem., 223, 22-250, 243, 6mm Rem., 260 Rem., 7mm-08 Rem., 308, 350 Rem. Mag. Calibers 250 Savage, 257 Roberts, 35 Rem. Polished blue finish. Introduced 1993. From Remington Custom Shop.

Price: From **$1,332.00**

Remington Model Seven Youth Rifle

Similar to Model Seven LS except hardwood stock, 1" shorter length of pull, chambered for 223, 243, 260 Rem., 7mm-08. Introduced 1993.

Price: **$547.00**

Remington Model Seven Custom KS

Similar to Model Seven LS except gray aramid fiber reinforced stock with 1" black rubber recoil pad and swivel studs. Blued satin carbon steel barreled action. No sights on 223, 260 Rem., 7mm-08, 308; 35 Rem. and 350 Rem. have iron sights.

Price: **$1,314.00**

RUGER MAGNUM RIFLE

Caliber: 375 H&H, 416 Rigby, 458 Lott. **Barrel:** 23". **Weight:** 9-1/2 to 10-1/4 lbs. **Length:** 44". **Stock:** AAA Premium Grade Circassian walnut with live-rubber recoil pad, metal grip cap, and studs for mounting sling swivels. **Sights:** Blade, front; V-notch rear express sights (one stationary, two folding) drift-adjustable for windage. **Features:** Patented floorplate latch secures the hinged floorplate against accidental dumping of cartridges; one-piece bolt has a non-rotating Mauser-type controlled-feed extractor; fixed-blade ejector.

Price: M77RSMMKII **$1,695.00**

Ruger Magnum

Ruger 77/22 Hornet Varmint

Ruger M77 Mark II

Ruger KM77RLFP MKII

Ruger KM77RSFP MKII

RUGER 77/22 HORNET BOLT-ACTION RIFLE

Caliber: 22 Hornet, 6-shot rotary magazine. **Barrel:** 20". **Weight:** About 6 lbs. **Length:** 39-3/4" overall. **Stock:** Checkered American walnut, black rubber butt pad. **Sights:** Brass bead front, open adjustable rear; also available without sights. **Features:** Same basic features as rimfire model except slightly lengthened receiver. Uses Ruger rotary magazine. Three-position safety. Comes with 1" Ruger scope rings. Introduced 1994.

Price: 77/22RH (rings only) **$589.00**

Price: 77/22RSH (with sights).......... **$609.00**

Price: K77/22VHZ Varmint, laminated stock, no sights.......... **$625.00**

RUGER M77 MARK II RIFLE

Caliber: 223, 220 Swift, 22-250, 243, 6mm Rem., 257 Roberts, 25-06, 6.5x55 Swedish, 270, 7x57mm, 260 Rem., 280 Rem., 308, 30-06, 7mm Rem. Mag., 7mm Rem. Short Ultra Mag., 300 Rem. Short Ultra Mag., 300 WSM, 300 Win. Mag., 338 Win. Mag., 4-shot magazine. **Barrel:** 20", 22"; 24" (magnums). **Weight:** About 7 lbs. **Length:** 39-3/4" overall. **Stock:** Synthetic American walnut; swivel studs, rubber butt pad. **Sights:** None furnished. Receiver has Ruger integral scope mount base, Ruger 1" rings. Some with iron sights. **Features:** Short action with new trigger, 3-position safety. Steel trigger guard. Left-hand available. Introduced 1989.

Price: M77RMKII (no sights).......... **$675.00**

Price: M77RSMKII (open sights) **$759.00**

Price: M77LRMKII (left-hand, 270, 30-06, 7mm Rem. Mag.,300 Win. Mag.) **$675.00**

Price: KM77REPMKII (Shorts) **$675.00**

Ruger M77RSI International Carbine

Same as standard Model 77 except 18" barrel, full-length International-style stock, steel forend cap, loop-type steel sling swivels. Integral-base receiver, open sights, Ruger 1" steel rings. Improved front sight. Available in 243, 270, 308, 30-06. Weighs 7 lbs. Length overall is 38-3/8".

Price: M77RSIMKII.......... **$769.00**

Ruger M77 Mark II All-Weather and Sporter Model Stainless Rifle

Similar to wood-stock M77 Mark II except all metal parts are stainless steel, has an injection-moulded, glass-fiber-reinforced polymer stock. Laminated wood stock. Chambered for 223, 243, 270, 308, 30-06, 7mm Rem. Mag., 300 Win. Mag., 338 Win. Mag. Fixed-blade-type ejector, 3-position safety, new trigger guard with patented floorplate latch. Integral Scope Base Receiver, 1" Ruger scope rings, built-in sling swivel loops. Introduced 1990.

Price: K77RFPMKII **$675.00**

Price: K77RLFPMKII Ultra-Light, synthetic stock, rings, no sights **$675.00**

Price: K77LRBBZMKII, left-hand bolt, rings, no sights, laminated stock **$729.00**

Price: K77RSFPMKII, synthetic stock, open sights **$759.00**

Price: K77RBZMKII, no sights, laminated wood stock, 223, 22/250, 243, 270, 280 Rem., 7mm Rem. Mag., 30-06, 308, 300 Win. Mag., 338 Win. Mag. **$729.00**

Price: K77RSBZMKII, open sights, laminated wood stock, 243, 270, 7mm Rem. Mag., 30-06, 300 Win. Mag., 338 Win. Mag.... **$799.00**

Price: KM77RFPMKII (Shorts), M77RMKII.......... **$675.00**

Ruger M77RL Ultra Light

Similar to standard M77 except weighs 6 lbs., chambered for 223, 243, 308, 270, 30-06, 257 Roberts, barrel tapped for target scope blocks, 20" Ultra Light barrel. Overall length 40". Ruger's steel 1" scope rings supplied. Introduced 1983.

Price: M77RLMKII **$729.00**

Ruger M77 Mark II Compact Rifles

Similar to standard M77 except reduced 16-1/2" barrel, weighs 5-3/4 lbs. Chambered for 223, 243, 260 Rem., 308, and 7mm-08.

Price: M77CR MKII (blued finish, walnut stock) **$675.00**

Price: KM77CRBBZ MkII (stainless finish, black laminated stock) **$729.00**

Ruger KM77RFP MKII

Ruger 77/44

Ruger M77VT Target

Sako TRG-S

Sako 75 Hunter

RUGER 77/44 BOLT-ACTION RIFLE

Caliber: 44 Magnum, 4-shot magazine. **Barrel:** 18-1/2". **Weight:** 6 lbs. **Length:** 38-1/4" overall. **Stock:** American walnut with rubber butt pad and swivel studs or black polymer (stainless only). **Sights:** Gold bead front, folding leaf rear. Comes with Ruger 1" scope rings. **Features:** Uses same action as the Ruger 77/22. Short bolt stroke; rotary magazine; three-position safety. Introduced 1997. Made in U.S.A. by Sturm, Ruger & Co.

Price: Blue, walnut, 77/44RS **$605.00**

Price: Stainless, polymer, stock, K77/44RS **$605.00**

RUGER M77VT TARGET RIFLE

Caliber: 22-250, 220 Swift, 223, 243, 25-06, 308. **Barrel:** 26" heavy stainless steel with target gray finish. **Weight:** 9-3/4 lbs. **Length:** Approx. 44" overall. **Stock:** Laminated American hardwood with beavertail forend, steel swivel studs; no checkering or gripcap. **Sights:** Integral scope mount bases in receiver. **Features:** Ruger diagonal bedding system. Ruger steel 1" scope rings supplied. Fully adjustable trigger. Steel floorplate and trigger guard. New version introduced 1992.

Price: K77VTMKII **$819.00**

SAKO TRG-S BOLT-ACTION RIFLE

Caliber: 338 Lapua Mag., 30-378 Weatherby, 3-shot magazine. **Barrel:** 26". **Weight:** 7.75 lbs. **Length:** 45.5" overall. **Stock:** Reinforced polyurethane with Monte Carlo comb. **Sights:** None furnished. **Features:** Resistance-free bolt with 60-degree lift. Recoil pad adjustable for length. Free-floating barrel, detachable magazine, fully adjustable trigger. Matte blue metal. Introduced 1993. Imported from Finland by Beretta USA.

Price: **$896.00**

Sako TRG-42 Bolt-Action Rifle

Similar to TRG-S except 5-shot magazine, fully adjustable stock and competition trigger. Offered in 338 Lapua Mag. and 300 Win. Mag. Im-ported from Finland by Beretta USA.

Price: **$2,829.00**

SAKO 75 HUNTER BOLT-ACTION RIFLE

Caliber: 17 Rem., 222, 223, 22-250, 243, 7mm-08, 308 Win., 25-06, 270, 280, 30-06; 270 Wea. Mag., 7mm Rem. Mag., 7mm STW, 7mm Wea. Mag., 300 Win. Mag., 300 Wea. Mag., 338 Win. Mag., 340 Wea. Mag., 375 H&H, 416 Rem. Mag. **Barrel:** 22", standard calibers; 24", 26" magnum calibers. **Weight:** About 6 lbs. **Length:** NA. **Stock:** European walnut with matte lacquer finish. **Sights:** None furnished; dovetail scope mount rails. **Features:** New design with three locking lugs and a mechanical ejector, key locks firing pin and bolt, cold hammer-forged barrel is free-floating, 2-position safety, hinged floorplate or detachable magazine that can be loaded from the top, short 70 degree bolt lift. Five action lengths. Introduced 1997. Imported from Finland by Beretta USA.

Price: Standard calibers **$1,129.00**

Price: Magnum Calibers **$1,163.00**

Sako 75 Stainless Synthetic Rifle

Similar to 75 Hunter except all metal is stainless steel, synthetic stock has soft composite panels moulded into forend and pistol grip. Available in 22-250, 243, 308 Win., 25-06, 270, 30-06 with 22" barrel, 7mm Rem. Mag., 7mm STW, 300 Win. Mag., 338 Win. Mag. and 375 H&H Mag. with 24" barrel and 300 Wea. Mag., 300 Rem.Ultra Mag. with 26" barrel. Introduced 1997. Imported from Finland by Beretta USA.

Price: Standard calibers **$1,212.00**

Price: Magnum calibers **$1,246.00**

CENTERFIRE RIFLES — BOLT ACTION

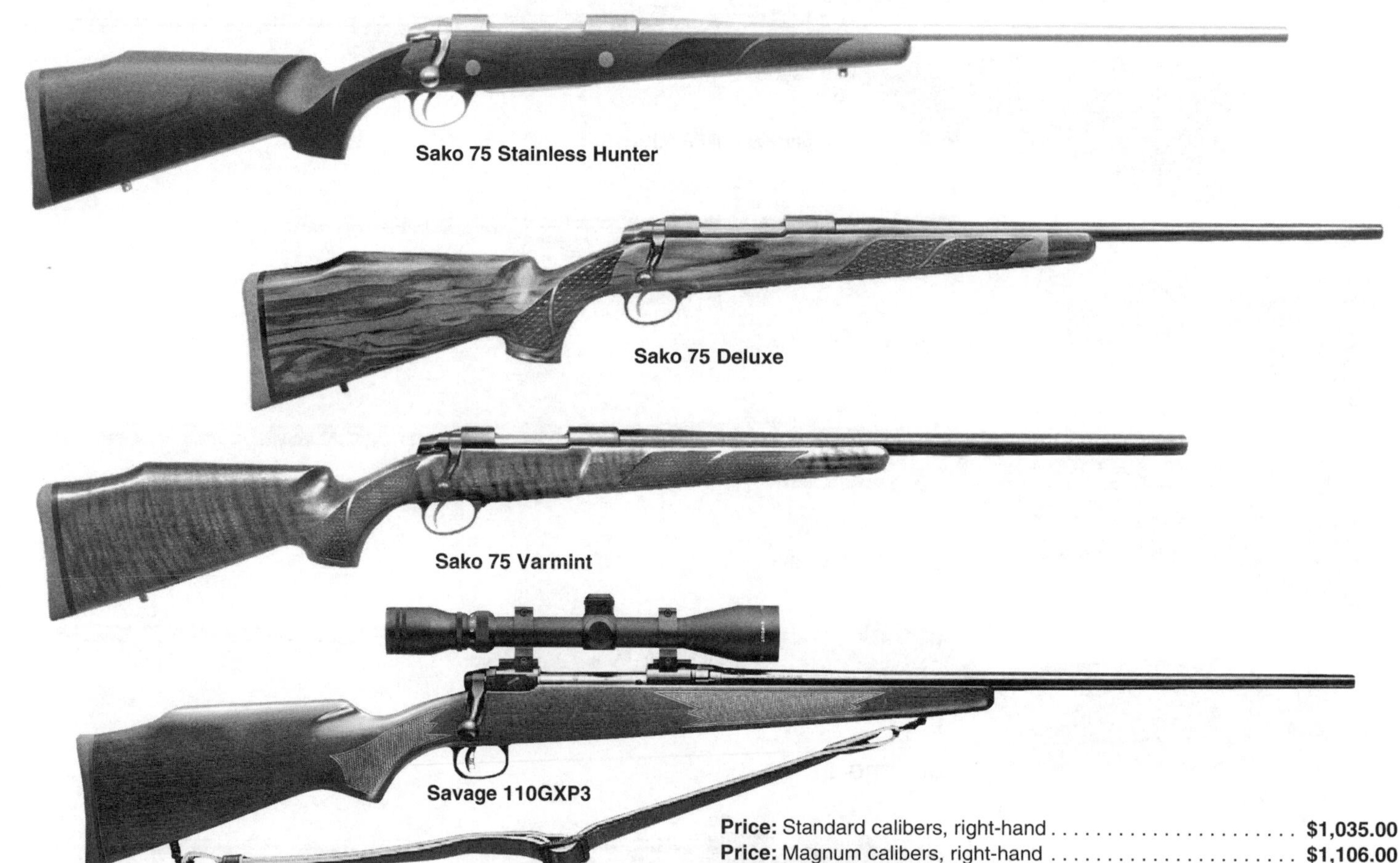

Sako 75 Stainless Hunter

Sako 75 Deluxe

Sako 75 Varmint

Savage 110GXP3

Sako 75 Deluxe Rifle

Similar to 75 Hunter except select wood rosewood gripcap and forend tip. Available in 17 Rem., 222, 223, 25-06, 243, 7mm-08, 308, 25-06, 270, 280, 30-06; 270 Wea. Mag., 7mm Rem. Mag., 7mm STW, 7mm Wea. Mag., 300 Win. Mag., 300 Wea. Mag., 338 Win. Mag., 340 Wea. Mag., 375 H&H, 416 Rem. Mag. Introduced 1997. Imported from Finland by Beretta USA.

Price: Standard calibers **$1,653.00**
Price: Magnum calibers **$1,688.00**

Sako 75 Varmint Stainless Laminated Rifle

Similar to Sako 75 Hunter except chambered only for 222, 223, 22-250, 22 PPC USA, 6mm PPC, heavy 24" barrel with recessed crown, all metal is stainless steel, laminated wood stock with beavertail forend. Introduced 1999. Imported from Finland by Beretta USA.

Price: **$1,448.00**

Sako 75 Varmint Rifle

Similar to Model 75 Hunter except chambered only for 17 Rem., 222 Rem., 223 Rem., 22-250 Rem., 22 PPC and 6mm PPC, 24" heavy barrel with recessed crown, beavertail forend. Introduced 1998. Imported from Finland by Beretta USA.

Price: **$1,337.00**

SAUER 202 BOLT-ACTION RIFLE

Caliber: Standard-243, 6.5x55, 270 Win., 308 Win., 30-06; magnum-7mm Rem. Mag., 300 Win. Mag., 300 Wea. Mag., 375 H&H. **Barrel:** 23.6" (standard), 26" (magnum). **Weight:** 7.7 lbs. (standard). **Length:** 44.3" overall (23.6" barrel). **Stock:** Select American Claro walnut with high-gloss epoxy finish, rosewood grip and forend caps; 22 lpi checkering. Synthetic also available. **Sights:** None furnished; drilled and tapped for scope mounting. **Features:** Short 60" bolt throw; detachable box magazine; six-lug bolt; quick-change barrel; tapered bore; adjustable two-stage trigger; firing pin cocking indicator. Introduced 1994. Imported from Germany by SIGARMS, Inc.

Price: Standard calibers, right-hand **$1,035.00**
Price: Magnum calibers, right-hand **$1,106.00**
Price: Standard calibers, synthetic stock **$985.00**
Price: Magnum calibers, synthetic stock. **$1,056.00**

SAVAGE MODEL 10GXP3, 110GXP3 PACKAGE GUNS

Caliber: 223 Rem., 22-250 Rem., 243 Win., 7mm-08 Rem., 308 Win., 300 WSM (10GXP3). 25-06 Rem., 270 Win., 30-06 Spfld., 7mm Rem. Mag., 300 Win. Mag., 300 Rem. Ultra Mag. (110GXP3). **Barrel:** 22" 24", 26". **Weight:** 7.5 lbs. average. **Length:** 43"-47". **Stock:** Walnut Monte Carlo with checkering. **Sights:** 3-9X40mm scope, mounted & bore sighted. **Features:** Blued, free floating and button rifled, internal box magazines, swivel studs, leather sling. Left-hand available.

Price: **$495.00**

SAVAGE MODEL 11FXP3, 111FXP3, 111FCXP3, 11FYXP3 (Youth) PACKAGE GUNS

Caliber: 223 Rem., 22-250 Rem., 243 Win., 308 Win., 300 WSM (11FXP3). 270 Win., 30-06 Spfld., 25-06 Rem., 7mm Rem. Mag., 300 Win. Mag., 338 Win. Mag., 300 Rem. Ultra Mag. (11FCXPE & 111FXP3). **Barrel:** 22"-26". **Weight:** 6.5 lbs. **Length:** 41"-47". **Stock:** Synthetic checkering, dual pillar bed. **Sights:** 3-9X40mm scope, mounted & bore sighted. **Features:** Blued, free floating and button rifled, Top loading internal box mag (except 111FXCP3 has detachable box mag.). Nylon sling and swivel studs. Some left-hand available.

Price: Model 11FXP3 . . . . **$505.00**
Price: Model 111FCXP3 . . . . **$425.00**
Price: Model 11FYXP3, 243 Win., 12.5" pull (youth) **$471.00**

SAVAGE MODEL 16FXP3, 116FXP3 SS ACTION PACKAGE GUNS

Caliber: 223 Rem., 243 Win., 308 Win., 300 WSM, 270 Win., 30-06 Spfld., 7mm Rem. Mag., 300 Win. Mag., 338 Win. Mag., 375 H&H, 7mm S&W, 7mm Rem. Ultra Mag., 300 Rem. Ultra Mag. **Barrel:** 22", 24", 26". **Weight:** 6.75 lbs. average. **Length:** 41"-46". **Stock:** Synthetic checkering, dual pillar bed. **Sights:** 3-9X40mm scope, mounted & bore sighted. **Features:** Free floating and button rifled. Internal box mag., nylon sling and swivel studs.

Price: **$556.00**

SAVAGE MODEL 10FM SIERRA ULTRA LIGHT RIFLE

Caliber: 223, 243, 308. **Barrel:** 20". **Weight:** 6 lbs. **Length:** 41-1/2". **Stock:** "Dual Pillar" bedding in black synthetic stock with silver medallion in grip-cap. **Sights:** None furnished; drilled and tapped for scope mounting. **Features:** True short action. Comes with sling and quick-detachable swivels. Introduced 1998. Made in U.S.A. by Savage Arms, Inc.

Price: **$495.00**

SAVAGE MODEL 10FCM SCOUT ULTRA LIGHT RIFLE

Caliber: 7mm-08 Rem., 308 Win. **Barrel:** 20", 4-shot. **Weight:** 6.25 lbs. **Length:** 39.75" overall. **Stock:** Synthetic checkering, dual pillar bed. **Sights:** Ghost ring rear, gold bead front. **Features:** Blued, detachable box magazine, Savage shooting sling/carry strap. Quick detach swivels.

Price: **$581.00**

SAVAGE MODEL 10/110FP LONG RANGE RIFLE

Caliber: 223, 25-06, 308, 30-06, 300 Win. Mag., 7mm Rem. Mag., 4-shot magazine. **Barrel:** 24", heavy; recessed target muzzle. **Weight:** 8-1/2 lbs. **Length:** 45.5" overall. **Stock:** Black graphite/fiberglass composition; positive checkering. **Sights:** None furnished. Receiver drilled and tapped for scope mounting. **Features:** Pillar-bedded stock. Black matte finish on all metal parts. Double swivel studs on the forend for sling and/or bipod mount. Right or left-hand. Introduced 1990. From Savage Arms, Inc.

Price: Right- or left-hand. **$558.00**

Savage Model 10FP Tactical Rifle

Similar to the Model 110FP except has true short action, chambered for 223, 308; black synthetic stock with "Dual Pillar" bedding. Introduced 1998. Made in U.S.A. by Savage Arms, Inc.

Price: **$558.00**
Price: Model 10FLP (left-hand). **$558.00**
Price: Model 10FP-LE1 (20"), 10FPLE2 (26") **$566.00**
Price: Model 10FPXP-LE w/Burris 3.5-10X50 scope, Harris bipod package **$1,632.00**

Savage Model 10FP-LE1A Tactical Rifle

Similar to the Model 110FP except weighs 10.75 lbs. and has overall length of 39.75". Chambered for 223 Rem., 308 Win. Black synthetic Choate™ adjustable stock with accessory rail and swivel studs.

Price: **$684.00**

Savage Model 10FPXP-LE

Savage Model 111F

Savage Model 11FNS

Savage Model 11G

Savage Model 10GY

SAVAGE MODEL 111 CLASSIC HUNTER RIFLES

Caliber: 25-06 Rem., 270 Win., 30-06 Spfld., 7mm Rem. Mag, 300 Win. Mag., 7mm RUM, 300 RUM. **Barrel:** 22", 24", 26" (magnum calibers). **Weight:** 6.5 to 7.5 lbs. **Length:** 42.75" to 47.25". **Stock:** Walnut-finished hardwood (M111G, GC); graphite/fiberglass filled composite. **Sights:** Ramp front, open fully adjustable rear; drilled and tapped for scope mounting. **Features:** Three-position top tang safety, double front locking lugs, free-floated button-rifled barrel. Comes with trigger lock, target, ear puffs. Introduced 1994. Made in U.S.A. by Savage Arms, Inc.

Price: Model 111F (270 Win., 30-06 Spfld., 7mm Rem. Mag., 300 win. Mag.) **$411.00**

Price: Model 111F (25-06 Rem., 338 Win. Mag., 7mm Rem. Ultra Mag, 300 Rem. Ultra Mag.) **$461.00**

Price: Model 111G (wood stock, top-loading magazine, right- or left-hand) **$436.00**

Price: Model 111GNS (wood stock, top-loading magazine, no sights, right-hand only) **$428.00**

Savage Model 11 Classic Hunter Rifles, Short Action

Similar to the Model 111F except has true short action, chambered for 22-250, Rem., 243 Win., 7mm-08 Rem., 308 Win.; black synthetic stock with "Dual Pillar" bedding, positive checkering. Introduced 1998. Made in U.S.A. by Savage Arms, Inc.

Price: Model 11F **$461.00**

Price: Model 11FL (left-hand) **$461.00**

Price: Model 11FNS (right-hand, no sights) **$453.00**

Price: Model 11G (wood stock) **$436.00**

Price: Model 11GL (as above, left-hand) **$436.00**

Price: Model 11FC (right hand, open sights) **$487.00**

Savage Model 10GY

Similar to the Model 111G except weighs 6.3 lbs., is 42-1/2" overall, and the stock is scaled for ladies, small-framed adults and youths. Chambered for 223, 243, 308. Ramp front sight, open adjustable rear; drilled and tapped for scope mounts. Made in U.S.A. by Savage Arms, Inc.

Price: Model 10GY (short action, calibers 223, 243, 308) **$436.00**

Savage Model 114U

Savage Model 12FV

Savage Model 12VSS

Savage Model 116SE Safari Express

SAVAGE MODEL 114U ULTRA RIFLE

Caliber: 270 Win., 30-06 Spfld., 7mm Rem. Mag., 7mm STW, 300 Win. Mag. **Barrel:** 22"-24". **Weight:** 7-7.5 lbs. **Length:** 43.25"-45.25" overall. **Stock:** Ultra high gloss American walnut with black tip and custom cut checkering. **Sights:** None furnished; drilled and tapped for scope mounting. **Features:** High-luster blued barrel action, internal box magazine.

Price: **$552.00**

SAVAGE MODEL 112 LONG RANGE RIFLES

Caliber: 22-250, 223, 5-shot magazine. **Barrel:** 26" heavy. **Weight:** 8.8 lbs. **Length:** 47.5" overall. **Stock:** Black graphite/fiberglass filled composite with positive checkering. **Sights:** None furnished; drilled and tapped for scope mounting. **Features:** Pillar-bedded stock. Blued barrel with recessed target-style muzzle. Double front swivel studs for attaching bipod. Introduced 1991. Made in U.S.A. by Savage Arms, Inc.

Price: Model 112FVSS (cals. 223, 22-250, 25-06, 7mm Rem. Mag., 300 Win. Mag., stainless barrel, bolt handle, trigger guard), right- or left-hand. **$626.00**

Price: Model 112FVSS-S (as above, single shot). **$675.00**

Price: Model 112BVSS (heavy-prone laminated stock with high comb, Wundhammer swell, fluted stainless barrel, bolt handle, trigger guard) **$675.00**

Price: Model 112BVSS-S (as above, single shot) **$675.00**

Savage Model 12 Long Range Rifles

Similar to the Model 112 Long Range except with true short action, chambered for 223, 22-250, 308. Models 12FV, 12FVSS have black synthetic stocks with "Dual Pillar" bedding, positive checkering, swivel studs; model 12BVSS has brown laminated stock with beavertail forend, fluted stainless barrel. Introduced 1998. Made in U.S.A. by Savage Arms, Inc.

Price: Model 12FV (223, 22-250, 243 Win., 308 Win., blue). **$515.00**

Price: Model 12FVSS (blue action, fluted stainless barrel). **$626.00**

Price: Model 12FLVSS (as above, left-hand) **$626.00**

Price: Model 12FVSS-S (blue action, fluted stainless barrel, single shot). **$934.00**

Price: Model 12BVSS (laminated stock). **$675.00**

Price: Model 12BVSS-S (as above, single shot) **$675.00**

Price: Model 12BVSS-XP (hard case, Burris 6-18X37) **$1,100.00**

Savage Model 12VSS Varminter Rifle

Similar to other Model 12s except blue/stainless steel action, fluted stainless barrel, Choate full pistol-grip, adjustable synthetic stock, Sharp Shooter trigger. Overall length 47-1/2 inches, weighs appx. 15 lbs. No sights; drilled and tapped for scope mounts. Chambered in 223, 22-250, 308 Win. Made in U.S.A. by Savage Arms Inc.

Price: **$934.00**

SAVAGE MODEL 116SE SAFARI EXPRESS RIFLE

Caliber: 458 Win. Mag. **Barrel:** 24". **Weight:** 8.5 lbs. **Length:** 45.5" overall. **Stock:** Classic-style select walnut with ebony forend tip, deluxe cut checkering. Two cross bolts; internally vented recoil pad. **Sights:** Bead on ramp front, three-leaf express rear. **Features:** Controlled-round feed design; adjustable muzzle brake; one-piece barrel band stud. Satin-finished stainless steel barreled action. Introduced 1994. Made in U.S.A. by Savage Arms, Inc.

Price: **$1,013.00**

SAVAGE MODEL 116 WEATHER WARRIORS

Caliber: 375 H&H, 300 Rem. Ultra Mag., 308 Win., 300 Rem. Ultra Mag., 300 WSM, 7mm Rem. Ultra Mag., 7mm Rem. Short Ultra Mag., 7mm S&W, 7mm-08 Rem. **Barrel:** 22", 24" for 7mm Rem. Mag., 300 Win. Mag., 338 Win. Mag. (M116FSS only). **Weight:** 6.25 to 6.5 lbs. **Length:** 41"-47". **Stock:** Graphite/fiberglass filled composite. **Sights:** None furnished; drilled and tapped for scope mounting. **Features:** Stainless steel with matte finish; free-floated barrel; quick-detachable swivel studs; laser-etched bolt; scope bases and rings. Left-hand models available in all models, calibers at same price. Model 116FSS introduced 1991; 116FSAK introduced 1994. Made in U.S.A. by Savage Arms, Inc.

Price: Model 116FSS (top-loading magazine) **$520.00**

Price: Model 116FSAK (top-loading magazine, Savage Adjustable Muzzle Brake system) **$601.00**

Price: Model 16BSS (brown laminate, 24") **$668.00**

Price: Model 116BSS (brown laminate, 26") **$668.00**

Savage Model 16FSS

Savage Model 116FSAK

Sigarms SHR 970

Steyr Mannlicher SBS

Steyr SBS Forester

Steyr SBS Prohunter

Savage Model 16FSS Rifle

Similar to Model 116FSS except true short action, chambered for 223, 243, 22" free-floated barrel; black graphite/fiberglass stock with "Dual Pillar" bedding. Also left-hand. Introduced 1998. Made in U.S.A. by Savage Arms, Inc.

Price: **$520.00**

SIGARMS SHR 970 SYNTHETIC RIFLE

Caliber: 270, 30-06. **Barrel:** 22". **Weight:** 7.2 lbs. **Length:** 41.9" overall. **Stock:** Textured black fiberglass or walnut. **Sights:** None furnished; drilled and tapped for scope mounting. **Features:** Quick takedown; interchangeable barrels; removable box magazine; cocking indicator; three-position safety. Introduced 1998. Imported by Sigarms, Inc.

Price: Synthetic stock **$499.00**

Price: Walnut stock **$550.00**

STEYR CLASSIC MANNLICHER SBS RIFLE

Caliber: 243, 25-06, 308, 6.5x55, 6.5x57, 270, 7x64 Brenneke, 7mm-08, 7.5x55, 30-06, 9.3x62, 6.5x68, 7mm Rem. Mag., 300 Win. Mag., 8x685, 4-shot magazine. **Barrel:** 23.6" standard; 26" magnum; 20" full stock standard calibers. **Weight:** 7 lbs. **Length:** 40.1" overall. **Stock:** Hand-checkered fancy European oiled walnut with standard forend. **Sights:** Ramp front adjustable for elevation, V-notch rear adjustable for windage. **Features:** Single adjustable trigger; 3-position roller safety with "safe-bolt" setting; drilled and tapped for Steyr factory scope mounts. Introduced 1997. Imported from Austria by GSI, Inc.

Price: Full-stock, standard calibers....................... **$1,749.00**

STEYR SBS FORESTER RIFLE

Caliber: 243, 25-06, 270, 7mm-08, 308 Win., 30-06, 7mm Rem. Mag., 300 Win. Mag. Detachable 4-shot magazine. **Barrel:** 23.6", standard calibers; 25.6", magnum calibers. **Weight:** 7.5 lbs. **Length:** 44.5" overall (23.6" barrel). **Stock:** Oil-finished American walnut with Monte Carlo cheekpiece. Pachmayr 1" swivels. **Sights:** None furnished. Drilled and tapped for Browning A-Bolt mounts. **Features:** Steyr Safe Bolt systems, three-position ambidextrous roller tang safety, for Safe, Loading Fire. Matte finish on barrel and receiver; adjustable trigger. Rotary cold-hammer forged barrel. Introduced 1997. Imported by GSI, Inc.

Price: Standard calibers **$799.00**

Price: Magnum calibers **$829.00**

STEYR SBS PROHUNTER RIFLE

Similar to the SBS Forester except has ABS synthetic stock with adjustable butt spacers, straight comb without cheekpiece, palm swell, Pachmayr 1" swivels. Special 10-round magazine conversion kit available. Introduced 1997. Imported by GSI.

Price: Standard calibers **$769.00**

Price: Magnum calibers **$799.00**

Steyr Scout Rifle

Tikka T-3 Hunter

STEYR SCOUT BOLT-ACTION RIFLE

Caliber: 308 Win., 5-shot magazine. **Barrel:** 19", fluted. **Weight:** NA. **Length:** NA. **Stock:** Gray Zytel. **Sights:** Pop-up front & rear, Leupold M8 2.5x28 IER scope on Picatinny optic rail with Steyr mounts. **Features:** luggage case, scout sling, two stock spacers, two magazines. Introduced 1998. From GSI.

Price: From **$1,969.00**

STEYR SSG BOLT-ACTION RIFLE

Caliber: 308 Win., detachable 5-shot rotary magazine. **Barrel:** 26" **Weight:** 8.5 lbs. **Length:** 44.5" overall. **Stock:** Black ABS Cycolac with spacers for length of pull adjustment. **Sights:** Hooded ramp front adjustable for elevation, V-notch rear adjustable for windage. **Features:** Sliding safety; NATO rail for bipod; 1" swivels; Parkerized finish; single or double-set triggers. Imported from Austria by GSI, Inc.

Price: SSG-PI, iron sights. **$1,699.00**

Price: SSG-PII, heavy barrel, no sights **$1,699.00**

Price: SSG-PIIK, 20" heavy barrel, no sights **$1,699.00**

Price: SSG-PIV, 16.75" threaded heavy barrel with flash hider . **$2,659.00**

TIKKA WHITETAIL HUNTER LEFT-HAND BOLT-ACTION RIFLE

Caliber: 22-250, 223, 243, 7mm-08, 25-06, 270, 308, 30-06, 7mm Rem. Mag., 300 Win. Mag., 338 Win. Mag. **Barrel:** 22-1/2" (std. cals.), 24-1/2" (magnum cals.). **Weight:** 7-1/8 lbs. **Length:** 43" overall (std. cals.). **Stock:** European walnut with Monte Carlo comb, rubber butt pad, checkered grip and forend. **Sights:** None furnished. **Features:** Detachable four-shot magazine (standard calibers), three-shot in magnums. Receiver dovetailed for scope mounting. Reintroduced 1996. Imported from Finland by Beretta USA.

Price: Left-hand **$710.00**

Tikka Continental Varmint Rifle

Similar to the standard Tikka rifle except has 26" heavy barrel, extra-wide forend. Chambered for 17 Rem., 22-250, 223, 308. Reintroduced 1996. Made in Finland by Sako. Imported by Beretta USA.

Price: **$720.00**

Tikka Continental Long Range Hunting Rifle

Similar to the Whitetail Hunter except has 26" heavy barrel. Available in 25-06, 270 Win., 7mm Rem. Mag., 300 Win. Mag. Introduced 1996. Imported from Finland by Beretta USA.

Price: 25-06, 270 Win. **$720.00**

Price: 7mm Rem. Mag., 300 Win. Mag. **$750.00**

Tikka Whitetail Hunter Stainless Synthetic

Similar to the Whitetail Hunter except all metal is of stainless steel, and it has a black synthetic stock. Available in 22-250, 223, 243, 7mm-08, 25-06, 270, 308, 30-06, 7mm Rem. Mag., 300 Win. Mag., 338 Win. Mag. Introduced 1997. Imported from Finland by Beretta USA.

Price: Standard calibers **$775.00**

Price: Magnum calibers **$745.00**

VEKTOR BUSHVELD BOLT-ACTION RIFLE

Caliber: 243, 308, 7x57, 7x64 Brenneke, 270 Win., 30-06, 300 Win. Mag., 300 H&H, 9.3x62. **Barrel:** 22"-26". **Weight:** NA. **Length:** NA. **Stock:** Turkish walnut with wrap-around hand checkering. **Sights:** Blade on ramp front, fixed standing leaf rear. **Features:** Combines the best features of the Mauser 98 and Winchester 70 actions. Controlled-round feed; Mauser-type extractor; no cut-away through the bolt locking lug; M70-type three-position safety; Timney-type adjustable trigger. Introduced 1999. Imported from South Africa by Vektor USA.

Price: . . . . **$1,595.00 to $1,695.00**

VEKTOR MODEL 98 BOLT-ACTION RIFLE

Caliber: 243, 308, 7x57, 7x64 Brenneke, 270 Win., 30-06, 300 Win. Mag., 300 H&H, 375 H&H, 9.3x62. **Barrel:** 22"-26". **Weight:** NA. **Length:** NA. **Stock:** Turkish walnut with hand-checkered grip and forend. **Sights:** None furnished; drilled and tapped for scope mounting. **Features:** Bolt has guide rib; non-rotating, long extractor enhances positive feeding; polished blue finish. Updated Mauser 98 action. Introduced 1999. Imported from South Africa by Vektor USA.

Price: . . . . **$1,149.00 to $1,249.00**

WEATHERBY MARK V DELUXE BOLT-ACTION RIFLE

Caliber: All Weatherby calibers plus 22-250, 243, 25-06, 270 Win., 280 Rem., 7mm-08, 30-06, 308 Win. **Barrel:** 24" barrel on standard calibers. **Weight:** 8-1/2 to 10-1/2 lbs. **Length:** 46-5/8" to 46-3/4" overall. **Stock:** Walnut, Monte Carlo with cheekpiece; high luster finish; checkered pistol grip and forend; recoil pad. **Sights:** None furnished. **Features:** Cocking indicator; adjustable trigger; hinged floorplate, thumb safety; quick detachable sling swivels. Made in U.S.A. From Weatherby.

Price: 257, 270, 7mm. 300, 340 Wea. Mags., 26" barrel. **$1,767.00**

Price: 416 Wea. Mag. with Accubrake, 28" barrel. **$2,079.00**

Price: 460 Wea. Mag. with Accubrake, 28" barrel. **$2,443.00**

Price: 24" barrel **$1,715.00**

Weatherby Mark V Lazermark Rifle

Same as Mark V Deluxe except stock has extensive oak leaf pattern laser carving on pistol grip and forend. Introduced 1981.

Price: 257, 270, 7mm Wea. Mag., 300, 340, 26" **$1,923.00**

Price: 378 Wea. Mag., 28" **$2,266.00**

Price: 416 Wea. Mag., 28", Accubrake **$2,266.00**

Price: 460 Wea. Mag., 28", Accubrake **$2,661.00**

CENTERFIRE RIFLES — BOLT ACTION

Weatherby Mark V Lazermark

Weatherby Mark V Sporter

Weatherby Mark V Stainless

Weatherby Mark V Synthetic

Weatherby Mark V Accumark

Weatherby Mark V Sporter Rifle

Same as the Mark V Deluxe without the embellishments. Metal has low-luster blue, stock is Claro walnut with matte finish, Monte Carlo comb, recoil pad. Introduced 1993. From Weatherby.

Price: 22-250, 243, 240 Wea. Mag., 25-06, 7mm-08, 270 WCF, 280, 30-06, 308; 24" **$1,091.00**

Price: 257 Wea., 270, 7 mm Wea., 7mm Rem., 300 Wea., 300 Win., 340 Wea., 338 Win. Mag., 26" barrel for Wea. Calibers; 24" for non-Wea. Calibers. **$1,143.00**

Weatherby Mark V Stainless Rifle

Similar to the Mark V Deluxe except made of 410-series stainless steel. Also available in 30-378 Wea. Mag. Has lightweight injection-moulded synthetic stock with raised Monte Carlo comb, checkered grip and forend, custom floorplate release. Right-hand only. Introduced 1995. Made in U.S.A. From Weatherby.

Price: 22-250 Rem., 243 Win., 240 Wby. Mag., 25-06 Rem., 270 Win., 280 Rem., 7mm-08 Rem., 30-06 Spfld., 308 Win., 24" barrel. . **$1,018.00**

Price: 257, 270, 7mm, 300, 340 Wby. Mag., 26" barrel. **$1,070.00**

Price: 7mm Rem. Mag., 300 Win. Mag., 338 Win. Mag., 375 H&H Mag., 24" barrel. **$1,070.00**

Weatherby Mark V Synthetic

Similar to the Mark V Stainless except made of matte finished blued steel. Injection moulded synthetic stock. Weighs 6-1/2 lbs., 24" barrel. Available in 22-250, 240 Wea. Mag., 243, 25-06, 270, 7mm-08, 280, 30-06, 308. Introduced 1997. Made in U.S.A. From Weatherby.

Price: **$923.00**

Price: 257, 270, 7mm, 300, 340 Wea. Mags., 26" barrel **$975.00**

Price: 7mm STW, 7mm Rem. Mag., 300, 338 Win. Mags. **$975.00**

Price: 375 H&H, 24" barrel **$975.00**

Price: 30-378 Wea. Mag., 338-378 Wea 28" barrel. **$1,151.00**

WEATHERBY MARK V ACCUMARK RIFLE

Caliber: 257, 270, 7mm, 300, 340 Wea. Mags., 338-378 Wea. Mag., 30-378 Wea. Mag., 7mm STW, 7mm Rem. Mag., 300 Win. Mag. **Barrel:** 26", 28". **Weight:** 8-1/2 lbs. **Length:** 46-5/8" overall. **Stock:** Bell & Carlson with full length aluminum bedding block. **Sights:** None furnished. Drilled and tapped for scope mounting. **Features:** Uses Mark V action with heavy-contour stainless barrel with black oxidized flutes, muzzle diameter of .705". Introduced 1996. Made in U.S.A. From Weatherby.

Price: 26" **$1,507.00**

Price: 30-378 Wea. Mag., 338-378 Wea. Mag., 28", Accubrake **$1,724.00**

Price: 223, 22-250, 243, 240 Wea. Mag., 25-06, 270, 280 Rem., 7mm-08, 30-06, 308; 24". **$1,455.00**

Price: Accumark Left-Hand 257, 270, 7mm, 300, 340 Wea. Mag., 7mm Rem. Mag., 7mm STW, 300 Win. Mag. **$1,559.00**

Price: Accumark Left-Hand 30-378, 333-378 Wea. Mags. **$1,788.00**

Weatherby Mark V SVR

Weatherby Mark V Fibermark

Weatherby Mark V Dangerous Game Rifle

Weatherby Mark V Accumark Ultra Lightweight Rifles

Similar to the Mark V Accumark except weighs 5-3/4 lbs, 6-3/4 lbs. in Mag. calibers.; 24", 26" fluted barrel with recessed target crown; hand- laminated stock with CNC-machined aluminum bedding plate and faint gray "spider web" finish. Available in 257, 270, 7mm, 300 Wea. Mags., (26"); 243, 240 Wea. Mag., 25-06, 270 Win., 280 Rem., 7mm-08, 7mm Rem. Mag., 30-06, 338-06 A-Square, 308, 300 Win. Mag. (24"). Intro-duced 1998. Made in U.S.A. by Weatherby.

Price: . . . . **$1,459.00 to $1,517.00**

Price: Left-hand models **$1,559.00**

Weatherby Mark V Special Varmint Rifle (SVR)

A new entrant in the Mark V series similar to the Super VarmintMaster and Accumark with 22", #3 contour chrome moly 4140 steel Krieger Cri-terion botton-rifled barrel with 1-degree target crown and hand-laminated composite stock. Available in .223 Rem. (5+1 magazine capacity) and .22-250 Rem. (4+1 magazine capacity) in right-hand models only.

Price: **$999.00**

Weatherby Mark V SVM/SPM Rifles

Similar to the Mark V Accumark except has 26" fluted (SVM) or 24" fluted Krieger barrel, spiderweb-pattern tan laminated synthetic stock. SVM has a fully adjustable trigger. Chambered for 223, 22-250, 220 Swift (SVM only), 243, 7mm-08 and 308. Made in U.S.A. by Weatherby.

Price: SVM (Super VarmintMaster), repeater or single-shot. . . . **$1,517.00**

New! **Price:** SPM (Super PredatorMaster) **$1,459.00**

Weatherby Mark V Fibermark Rifles

Similar to other Mark V models except has black Kevlar® and fiberglass composite stock and bead-blast blue or stainless finish. Chambered for 19 standard and magnum calibers. Introduced 1983; reintroduced 2001. Made in U.S.A. by Weatherby.

Price: Fibermark. . . . . **$1,070.00 to $1,347.00**

Price: Fibermark Stainless . . . . **$1,165.00 to $1,390.00**

WEATHERBY MARK V DANGEROUS GAME RIFLE

Caliber: 375 H&H, 375 Wea. Mag., 378 Wea. Mag., 416 Rem. Mag., 416 Wea. Mag., 458 Win. Mag., .458 Lott, 460 Wea. Mag. 300 Win. Mag., 300 Wby., Mag., 338 Win. Mag., 340 Wby. Mag., 24" only **Barrel:** 24" or 26". **Weight:** 8-3/4 to 9-1/2 lbs. **Length:** 44-5/8" to 46-5/8" overall. **Stock:** Kevlar® and fiberglass composite. **Sights:** Barrel-band hooded front with large gold bead, adjustable ramp/shallow "V" rear. **Features:** Designed for dangerous-game hunting. Black oxide matte finish on all metalwork; Pachmayr Decelerator™ recoil pad, short-throw Mark V action. Introduced 2001. Made in U.S.A. by Weatherby.

Price: . . . . **$2,703.00 to $2,935.00**

WEATHERBY MARK V SUPER BIG GAMEMASTER DEER RIFLE

Caliber: 240 Wby. Mag., 25-06 Rem., 270 Win., 280 Rem., 30-06 Spfld., 257 Wby. Mag., 270 Wby. Mag., 7mm Rem., Mag., 7mm Wby. Mag., 338-06 A-Square, 300 Win. Mag., 300 Wby. Mag. **Barrel:** 26", target crown. **Weight:** 5-3/4 lbs., (6-3/4 lbs. Magnum). **Stock:** Raised comb Monte Carlo composite. **Features:** Fluted barrel, aluminum bedding block, Pachmayr decelerator, 54-degree bolt lift, adj. trigger.

Price: **$1,459.00**

Price: Magnum **$1,517.00**

WEATHERBY MARK V ROYAL CUSTOM RIFLE

Caliber: 257, 270, 7mm, 300, 340 all Wby. Mags. Other calibers available upon request. **Barrel:** 26". **Stock:** Monte Carlo hand-checkered claro walnut with high gloss finish. **Features:** Bolt and follower are damascened with checkered knob. Engraved receiver, bolt sleeve and floorplate sport scroll pattern. Animal images on floorplate optional. High gloss blue, 24-karat gold and nickel-plating. Made in U.S.A. From Weatherby.

Price: **$5,831.00**

WEATHERBY THREAT RESPONSE RIFLES (TRR) SERIES

Caliber: TRR 223 Rem., 300 Win. TRR Magnum and Magnum Custom 300 Win. Mag., 300 Wby. Mag., 30-378 Wby. Mag., 328-378 Wby. Mag. **Barrel:** 22", 26", target crown. **Stock:** Hand-laminated composite. TTR & TRR Magnum have raised comb Monte Carlo style. TRR Magnum Custom adjustable ergonomic stock. **Features:** Adjustable trigger, aluminum bedding block, beavertail forearms dual tapered, flat-bottomed. "Rocker Arm" lockdown scope mounting. 54 degree bolt. Pachmayr decelerator pad. Made in U.S.A.

Price: TRR Magnum Custom 300 . . . . **$2,699.00**

Price: 30-378, 338-378 with accubrake **$2,861.00**

WILDERNESS EXPLORER MULTI-CALIBER CARBINE

Caliber: 22 Hornet, 218 Bee, 44 Magnum, 50 A.E. (interchangeable). **Barrel:** 18", match grade. **Weight:** 5.5 lbs **Length:** 38-1/2" overall. **Stock:** Synthetic or wood. **Sights:** None furnished; comes with Weaver-style mount on barrel. **Features:** Quick-change barrel and bolt face for caliber switch. Removable box magazine; adjustable trigger with side safety; detachable swivel studs. Introduced 1997. Made in U.S.A. by Phillips & Rogers, Inc.

Price: **$995.00**

Wilderness Explorer

Winchester Model 70 Classic

Winchester Model 70 Classic Stainless

Winchester Model 70 Classic Featherweight

Winchester Model 70 Classic Compact

WINCHESTER MODEL 70 CLASSIC SPORTER LT

Caliber: 25-06, 270 Win., 30-06, 7mm STW, 7mm Rem. Mag., 300 Win. Mag., 338 Win. Mag., 3-shot magazine; 5-shot for 25-06, 270 Win., 30-06. **Barrel:** 24", 26" for magnums. **Weight:** 7-3/4 to 8 lbs. **Length:** 46-3/4" overall (26" bbl.). **Stock:** American walnut with cut checkering and satin finish. Classic style with straight comb. **Sights:** None furnished. Drilled and tapped for scope mounting. **Features:** Uses pre-64-type action with controlled round feeding. Three-position safety, stainless steel magazine follower; rubber butt pad; epoxy bedded receiver recoil lug. From U.S. Repeating Arms Co.

Price: 25-06, 270, 30-06 .... **$727.00**
Price: Other calibers **$756.00**
Price: Left-hand, 270 or 30-06 .... **$762.00**
Price: Left-hand, 7mm Rem. Mag or 300 Win. Mag. **$793.00**

Winchester Model 70 Classic Stainless Rifle

Same as Model 70 Classic Sporter except stainless steel barrel and pre-64-style action with controlled round feeding and matte gray finish, black composite stock impregnated with fiberglass and graphite, contoured rubber recoil pad. No sights (except 375 H&H). Available in 270 Win., 30-06, 7mm STW, 7mm Rem. Mag., 300 Win. Mag., 300 Ultra Mag., 338 Win. Mag., 375 H&H Mag. (24" barrel), 3- or 5-shot magazine. Weighs 7-1/2 lbs. Introduced 1994.

Price: 270, 30-06 .... **$800.00**
Price: 375 H&H Mag., with sights **$924.00**
Price: Other calibers **$829.00**

Winchester Model 70 Classic Featherweight

Same as Model 70 Classic except action bedded in standard-grade walnut stock. Available in 22-250, 243, 6.5x55, 308, 7mm-08, 270 Win., 30-06. Drilled and tapped for scope mounts. Weighs 7 lbs. Introduced 1992.

Price: **$726.00**

Winchester Model 70 Classic Compact

Similar to Classic Featherweight except scaled down for smaller shooters. 20" barrel, 12-1/2" length of pull. Pre-'64-type action. Available in 243, 308 or 7mm-08. Introduced 1998. Made in U.S.A. by U. S. Repeating Arms Co.

Price: **$740.00**

Winchester Model 70 Coyote

Winchester Model 70 Stealth

Winchester Model 70 Classic Super Grade

Winchester Model 70 Safari Express

Winchester Model 70 WSM

Winchester Model 70 Coyote

Similar to Model 4 Ranger except laminated wood stock, 24" me-dium-heavy stainless steel barrel Available in223 Rem., 22-250 Rem., 243 Win., or 308 Win.

Price: **$705.00**

WINCHESTER MODEL 70 STEALTH RIFLE

Caliber: 223, 22-250, 308 Win. **Barrel:** 26". **Weight:** 10-3/4 lbs. **Length:** 46" overall. **Stock:** Kevlar/fiberglass/graphite Pillar Plus Accu-Block with full-length aluminum bedding block. **Sights:** None furnished. **Features:** Push-feed bolt design; matte finish. Introduced 1999. Made in U.S.A. by U.S. Repeating Arms Co.

Price: **$785.00**

WINCHESTER MODEL 70 CLASSIC SUPER GRADE

Caliber: 25-06, 270, 30-06, 5-shot magazine; 7mm Rem. Mag., 300 Win. Mag., 338 Win. Mag., 3-shot magazine. **Barrel:** 24", 26" for magnums. **Weight:** 7-3/4 lbs. to 8 lbs. **Length:** 44-1/2" overall (24" bbl.) **Stock:** Walnut with straight comb, sculptured cheekpiece, wrap-around cut checkering, tapered forend, solid rubber butt pad. **Sights:** None furnished; comes with scope bases and rings. **Features:** Controlled round feeding with stainless steel claw extractor, bolt guide rail, three-position safety; all steel bottom metal, hinged floorplate, stainless magazine follower. Introduced 1994. From U.S. Repeating Arms Co.

Price: 25-06, 270, 30-06 . . . . **$995.00**

Price: Other calibers **$1,024.00**

WINCHESTER MODEL 70 CLASSIC SAFARI EXPRESS

Caliber: 375 H&H Mag., 416 Rem. Mag., 458 Win. Mag., 3-shot magazine. **Barrel:** 24". **Weight:** 8-1/4 to 8-1/2 lbs. **Stock:** American walnut with Monte Carlo cheekpiece. Wrap-around checkering and finish. **Sights:** Hooded ramp front, open rear. **Features:** Controlled round feeding. Two steel cross bolts in stock for added strength. Front sling swivel stud mounted on barrel. Contoured rubber butt pad. From U.S. Repeating Arms Co.

Price: **$1,124.00**

Price: Left-hand, 375 H&H only **$1,163.00**

WINCHESTER MODEL 70 WSM RIFLES

Caliber: 300 WSM, 3-shot magazine. **Barrel:** 24". **Weight:** 7-1/4 to 7-3/4 lbs. **Length:** 44" overall. **Stock:** Checkered walnut, black synthetic or laminated wood. **Sights:** None. **Features:** Model 70 designed for the new 300 Winchester Short Magnum cartridge. Short-action receiver, three-position safety, knurled bolt handle. Introduced 2001. From U.S. Repeating Arms Co.

Price: Classic Featherweight WSM (checkered walnut stock and forearm) **$769.00**

Price: Classic Stainless WSM (black syn. stock, stainless steel bbl.) **$829.00**

Price: Classic Laminated WSM (laminated wood stock). **$793.00**

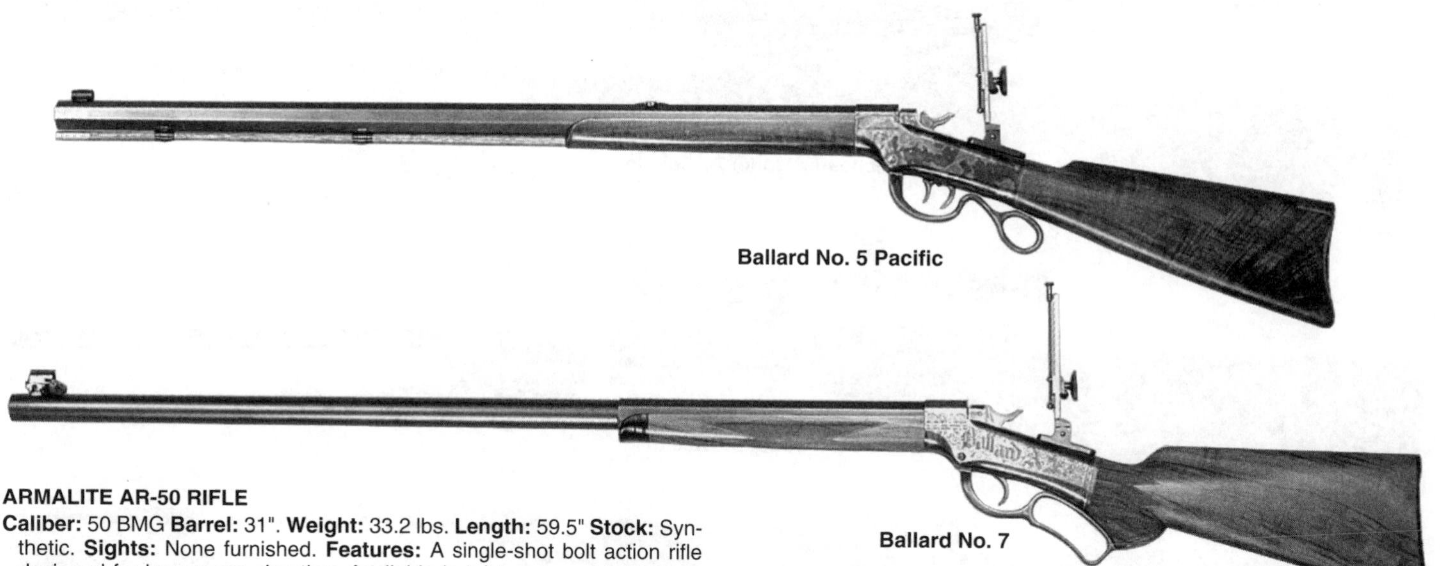

Ballard No. 5 Pacific

Ballard No. 7

ARMALITE AR-50 RIFLE

Caliber: 50 BMG **Barrel:** 31". **Weight:** 33.2 lbs. **Length:** 59.5" **Stock:** Synthetic. **Sights:** None furnished. **Features:** A single-shot bolt action rifle designed for long range shooting. Available in left-hand model. Made in U.S.A. by Armalite.

Price: $2,745.00

ARMSPORT 1866 SHARPS RIFLE, CARBINE

Caliber: 45-70. **Barrel:** 28", round or octagonal. **Weight:** 8.10 lbs. **Length:** 46" overall. **Stock:** Walnut. **Sights:** Blade front, folding adjustable rear. Tang sight set optionally available. **Features:** Replica of the 1866 Sharps. Color case-hardened frame, rest blued. Imported by Armsport.

Price: $865.00

Price: With octagonal barrel $900.00

Price: Carbine, 22" round barrel $850.00

BALLARD NO. 1 3/4 FAR WEST RIFLE

Caliber: 22 LR, 32-40, 38-55, 40-65, 40-70, 45-70, 45-110, 50-70, 50-90. **Barrel:** 30" std. or heavyweight. **Weight:** 10-1/2 lbs. (std.) or 11-3/4 lbs. (heavyweight bbl.) **Length:** NA. **Stock:** Walnut. **Sights:** Blade front, Rocky Mountain rear. **Features:** Single or double-set triggers, S-lever or ring-style lever; color case-hardened finish; hand polished and lapped Badger barrel. Made in U.S.A. by Ballard Rifle & Cartridge Co.

Price: $2,250.00

BALLARD NO. 4 PERFECTION RIFLE

Caliber: 22 LR, 32-40, 38-55, 40-65, 40-70, 45-70, 45-90, 45-110, 50-70, 50-90. **Barrel:** 30" or 32" octagon, standard or heavyweight. **Weight:** 10-1/2 lbs. (standard) or 11-3/4 lbs. (heavyweight bbl.). **Length:** NA. **Stock:** Smooth walnut. **Sights:** Blade front, Rocky Mountain rear. **Features:** Rifle or shotgun-style buttstock, straight grip action, single or double-set trigger, "S" or right lever, hand polished and lapped Badger barrel. Made in U.S.A. by Ballard Rifle & Cartridge Co.

Price: $2,250.00

BALLARD NO. 5 PACIFIC SINGLE-SHOT RIFLE

Caliber: 32-40, 38-55, 40-65, 40-90, 40-70 SS, 45-70 Govt., 45-110 SS, 50-70 Govt., 50-90 SS. **Barrel:** 30", or 32" octagonal. **Weight:** 10-1/2 lbs. **Length:** NA. **Stock:** High-grade walnut; rifle or shotgun style. **Sights:** Blade front, Rocky Mountain rear. **Features:** Standard or heavy barrel; double-set triggers; under-barrel wiping rod; ring lever. Introduced 1999. Made in U.S.A. by Ballard Rifle & Cartridge Co.

Price: $2,575.00

BALLARD NO. 7 LONG RANGE RIFLE

Caliber: 32-40, 38-55, 40-65, 40-70 SS, 45-70 Govt., 45-90, 45-110. **Barrel:** 32", 34" half-octagon. **Weight:** 11-3/4 lbs. **Length:** NA. **Stock:** Walnut; checkered pistol grip shotgun butt, ebony forend cap. **Sights:** Globe front. **Features:** Designed for shooting up to 1000 yards. Standard or heavy barrel; single or double-set trigger; hard rubber or steel buttplate. Introduced 1999. Made in U.S.A. by Ballard Rifle & Cartridge Co.

Price: From $2,475.00

BALLARD NO. 8 UNION HILL RIFLE

Caliber: 22 LR, 32-40, 38-55, 40-65 Win., 40-70 SS. **Barrel:** 30" half-octagon. **Weight:** About 10-1/2 lbs. **Length:** NA. **Stock:** Walnut; pistol grip butt with cheekpiece. **Sights:** Globe front. **Features:** Designed for 200-yard offhand shooting. Standard or heavy barrel; double-set triggers; full loop lever; hook Schuetzen buttplate. Introduced 1999. Made in U.S.A. by Bal-lard Rifle & Cartridge Co.

Price: From $2,500.00

BALLARD MODEL 1885 HIGH WALL SINGLE SHOT RIFLE

Caliber: 17 Bee, 22 Hornet, 218 Bee, 219 Don Wasp, 219 Zipper, 22 Hi-Power, 225 Win., 25-20 WCF, 25-35 WCF, 25 Krag, 7mmx57R, 30-30, 30-40 Krag, 303 British, 33 WCF, 348 WCF, 35 WCF, 35-30/30, 9.3x74R, 405 WCF, 50-110 WCF, 500 Express, 577 Express. **Barrel:** Lengths to 34". **Weight:** NA. **Length:** NA. **Stock:** Straight-grain American walnut. **Sights:** buckhorn or flat top rear, blade front. **Features:** Faithful copy of original Model 1885 High Wall; parts interchange with original rifles; variety of options available. Introduced 2000. Made in U.S.A. by Ballard Rifle & Cartridge LLC.

Price: From $2,255.00

Price: With single set trigger from $2,355.00

BARRETT MODEL 99 SINGLE SHOT RIFLE

Caliber: 50 BMG. **Barrel:** 33". **Weight:** 25 lbs. **Length:** 50.4" overall. **Stock:** Anodized aluminum with energy-absorbing recoil pad. **Sights:** None furnished; integral M1913 scope rail. **Features:** Bolt action; detachable bipod; match-grade barrel with high-efficiency muzzle brake. Introduced 1999. Made in U.S.A. by Barrett Firearms.

Price: From $3,000.00

BROWN MODEL 97D SINGLE SHOT RIFLE

Caliber: 17 Ackley Hornet through 45-70 Govt. **Barrel:** Up to 26", air gauged match grade. **Weight:** About 5 lbs., 11 oz. **Stock:** Sporter style with pistol grip, cheekpiece and Schnabel forend. **Sights:** None furnished; drilled and tapped for scope mounting. **Features:** Falling block action gives rigid barrel-receiver matting; polished blue/black finish. Hand-fitted action. Many options. Made in U.S.A. by E. Arthur Brown Co. Inc.

Price: From $699.00

BROWNING MODEL 1885 HIGH WALL SINGLE SHOT RIFLE

Caliber: 22-250, 30-06, 270, 7mm Rem. Mag., 454 Casull, 45-70. **Barrel:** 28". **Weight:** 8 lbs., 12 oz. **Length:** 43-1/2" overall. **Stock:** Walnut with straight grip, Schnabel forend. **Sights:** None furnished; drilled and tapped for scope mounting. **Features:** Replica of J.M. Browning's high-wall falling block rifle. Octagon barrel with recessed muzzle. Imported from Japan by Browning. Introduced 1985.

Price: $1,027.00

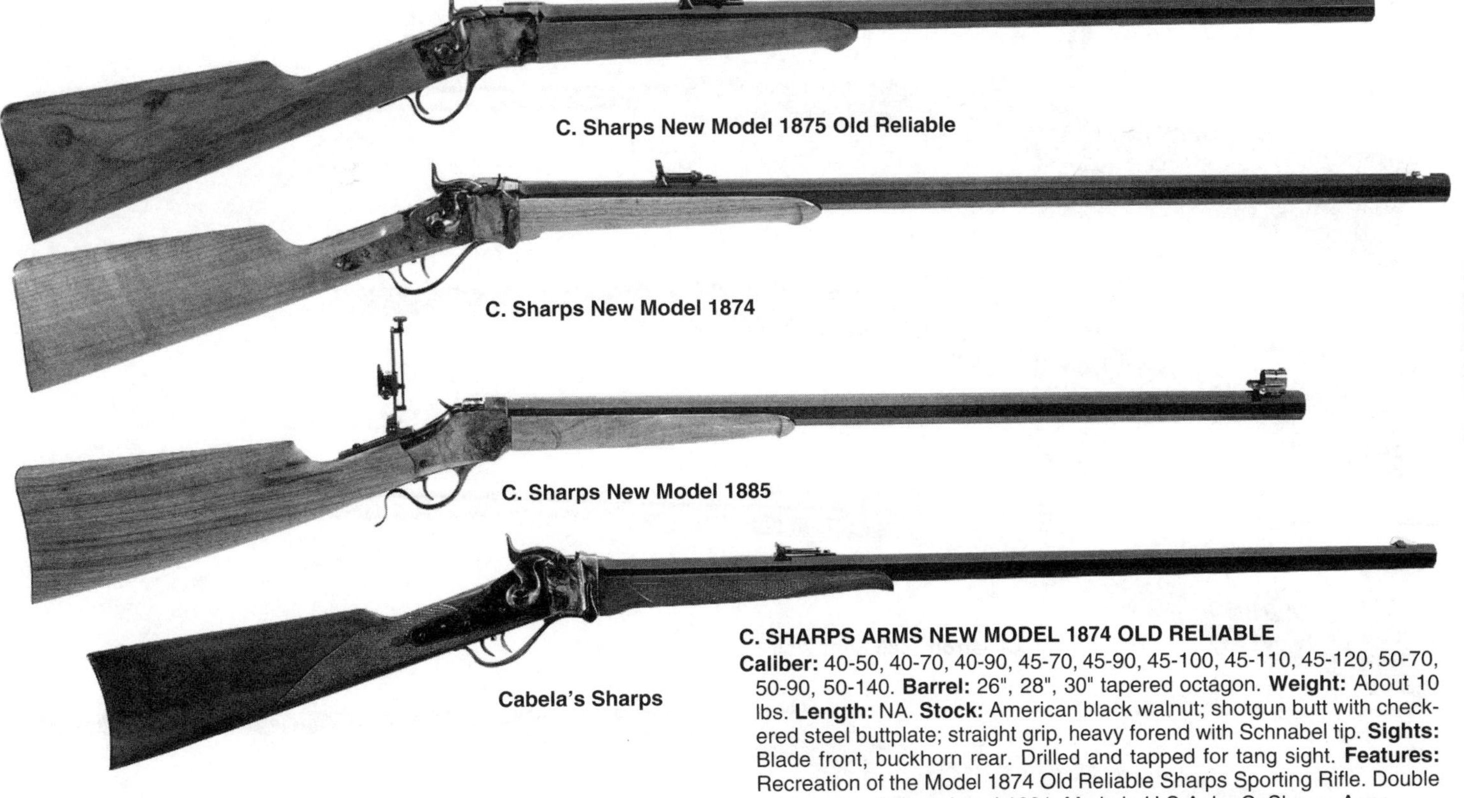

C. Sharps New Model 1875 Old Reliable

C. Sharps New Model 1874

C. Sharps New Model 1885

Cabela's Sharps

BRNO ZBK 110 SINGLE SHOT RIFLE

Caliber: 222 Rem., 5.6x52R, 22 Hornet, 5.6x50 Mag., 6.5x57R, 7x57R, 8x57JRS. **Barrel:** 23.6". **Weight:** 5.9 lbs. **Length:** 40.1" overall. **Stock:** European walnut. **Sights:** None furnished; drilled and tapped for scope mounting. **Features:** Top tang opening lever; cross-bolt safety; polished blue finish. Announced 1998. Imported from The Czech Republic by Euro-Imports.

Price: Standard calibers **$223.00**
Price: 7x57R, 8x57JRS **$245.00**
Price: Lux model, standard calibers **$311.00**
Price: Lux model, 7x57R, 8x57JRS **$333.00**

C. SHARPS ARMS NEW MODEL 1875 OLD RELIABLE RIFLE

Caliber: 22LR, 32-40 & 38-55 Ballard, 38-56 WCF, 40-65 WCF, 40-90 3-1/4", 40-90 2-5/8", 40-70 2-1/10", 40-70 2-1/4", 40-70 2-1/2", 40-50 1-11/16", 40- 50 1-7/8", 45-90, 45-70, 45-100, 45-110, 45-120. Also available on special order only in 50-70, 50-90, 50-140. **Barrel:** 24", 26", 30" (standard), 32", 34" optional. **Weight:** 8-12 lbs. **Stock:** Walnut, straight grip, shotgun butt with checkered steel buttplate. **Sights:** Silver blade front, Rocky Mountain buck-horn rear. **Features:** Recreation of the 1875 Sharps rifle. Production guns will have case colored receiver. Available in Custom Sporting and Target versions upon request. Announced 1986. From C. Sharps Arms Co.

Price: 1875 Sporting Rifle (30" tapered oct. bbl.) **$1,185.00**

C. Sharps Arms 1875 Classic Sharps

Similar to New Model 1875 Sporting Rifle except 26", 28" or 30" full octagon barrel, crescent buttplate with toe plate, Hartford-style forend with cast German silver nose cap. Blade front sight, Rocky Mountain buckhorn rear. Weighs 10 lbs. Introduced 1987. From C. Sharps Arms Co.

Price: **$1,470.00**

C. Sharps Arms New Model 1875 Target & Long Range

Similar to New Model 1875 in all listed calibers except 22 LR; 34" tapered octagon barrel; globe with post front sight, Long Range Vernier tang sight with windage adjustments. Pistol grip stock with cheek rest; checkered steel buttplate. Introduced 1991. From C. Sharps Arms Co.

Price: **$1,549.50**

C. SHARPS ARMS NEW MODEL 1874 OLD RELIABLE

Caliber: 40-50, 40-70, 40-90, 45-70, 45-90, 45-100, 45-110, 45-120, 50-70, 50-90, 50-140. **Barrel:** 26", 28", 30" tapered octagon. **Weight:** About 10 lbs. **Length:** NA. **Stock:** American black walnut; shotgun butt with checkered steel buttplate; straight grip, heavy forend with Schnabel tip. **Sights:** Blade front, buckhorn rear. Drilled and tapped for tang sight. **Features:** Recreation of the Model 1874 Old Reliable Sharps Sporting Rifle. Double set triggers. Reintroduced 1991. Made in U.S.A. by C. Sharps Arms.

Price: **$1,584.00**

C. SHARPS ARMS NEW MODEL 1885 HIGHWALL RIFLE

Caliber: 22 LR, 22 Hornet, 219 Zipper, 25-35 WCF, 32-40 WCF, 38-55 WCF, 40-65, 30-40-Krag, 40-50 ST or BN, 40-70 ST or BN, 40-90 ST or BN, 45-70 2-1/10" ST, 45-90 2-4/10" ST, 45-100 2-6/10" ST, 45-110 2-7/8" ST, 45-120 3-1/4" ST. **Barrel:** 26", 28", 30", tapered full octagon. **Weight:** About 9 lbs., 4 oz. **Length:** 47" overall. **Stock:** Oil-finished American walnut; Schnabel-style forend. **Sights:** Blade front, buckhorn rear. Drilled and tapped for optional tang sight. **Features:** Single trigger; octagonal receiver top; checkered steel buttplate; color case-hardened receiver and buttplate, blued barrel. Many options available. Made in U.S.A. by C. Sharps Arms Co

Price: From **$1,439.00**

C. SHARPS ARMS CUSTOM NEW MODEL 1877 LONG RANGE TARGET RIFLE

Caliber: 44-90 Sharps/Rem., 45-70, 45-90, 45-100 Sharps. **Barrel:** 32", 34" tapered round with Rigby flat. **Weight:** Appx. 10 lbs. **Stock:** Walnut checkered. Pistol grip/forend. **Sights:** Classic long range with windage. **Features:** Elegant single shot, limited to custom production only.

Price: . . . . **$5,550.00 and up**

CABELA'S SHARPS BASIC RIFLE

Caliber: .45-70. **Barrel:** 28" tapered round. **Weight:** 8.7 lbs. **Length:** 44" overall. **Stock:** European walnut. **Sights:** Buckhorn rear, blade front. **Features:** Utilitarian look of the original with single trigger and 1-in-18 twist rate. Imported by Cabela's.

Price: **$799.99**

CABELA'S SHARPS SPORTING RIFLE

Caliber: 45-70, 45-120, .45-110, .50-70. **Barrel:** 32", tapered octagon. **Weight:** 9 lbs. **Length:** 47-1/4" overall. **Stock:** Checkered walnut. **Sights:** Blade front, open adjustable rear. **Features:** Color case-hardened receiver and hammer, rest blued. Introduced 1995. Imported by Cabela's.

Price: **$949.99**
Price: (Deluxe engraved Sharps, .45-70) **$1,599.99**
Price: (Heavy target Sharps, 45-70, 45-120, .50-70) **$1,099.99**
Price: (Quigley Sharps, 45-70, 45-120, 45-110). **$1,399.99**

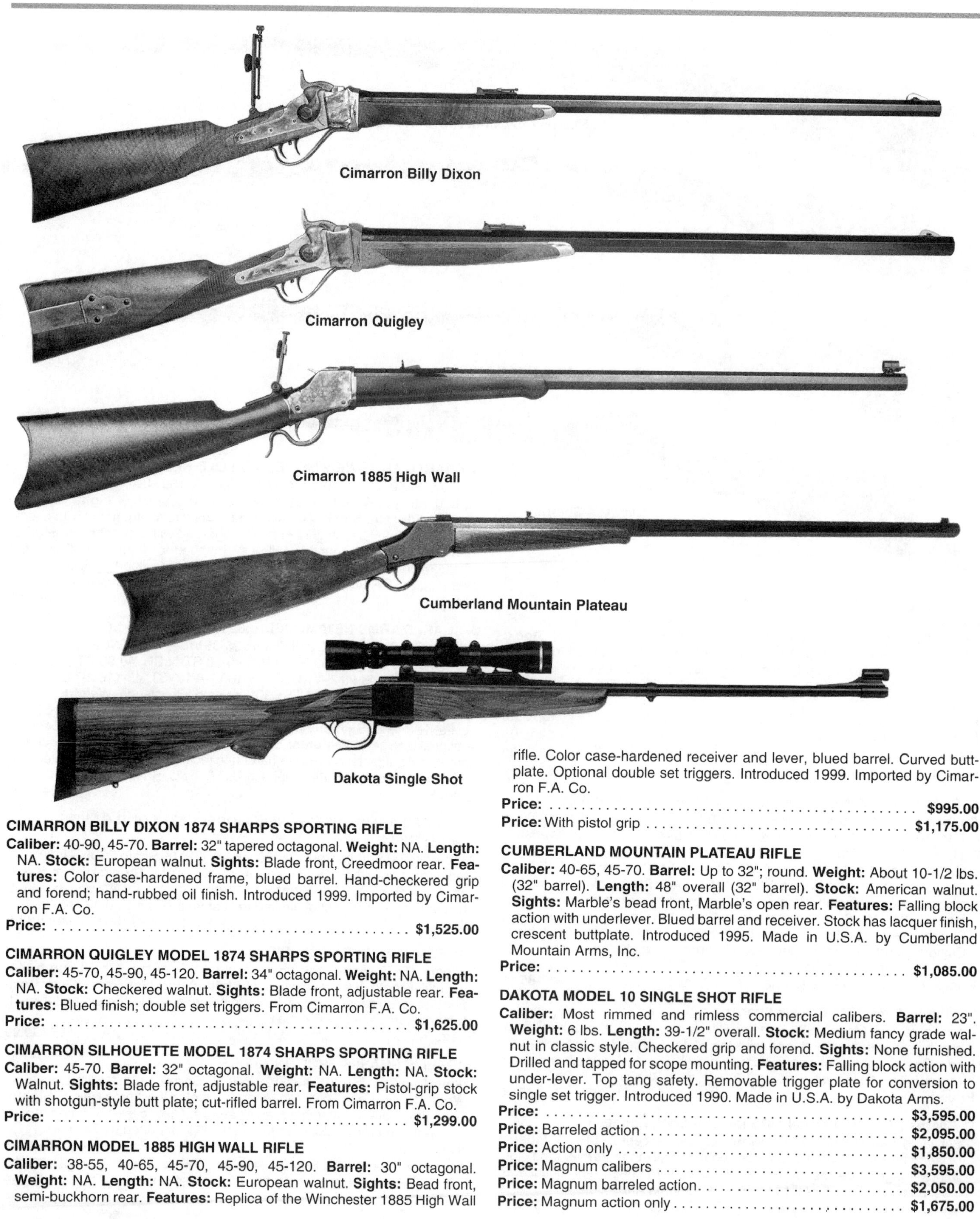

Cimarron Billy Dixon

Cimarron Quigley

Cimarron 1885 High Wall

Cumberland Mountain Plateau

Dakota Single Shot

CIMARRON BILLY DIXON 1874 SHARPS SPORTING RIFLE

Caliber: 40-90, 45-70. **Barrel:** 32" tapered octagonal. **Weight:** NA. **Length:** NA. **Stock:** European walnut. **Sights:** Blade front, Creedmoor rear. **Features:** Color case-hardened frame, blued barrel. Hand-checkered grip and forend; hand-rubbed oil finish. Introduced 1999. Imported by Cimarron F.A. Co.

Price: **$1,525.00**

CIMARRON QUIGLEY MODEL 1874 SHARPS SPORTING RIFLE

Caliber: 45-70, 45-90, 45-120. **Barrel:** 34" octagonal. **Weight:** NA. **Length:** NA. **Stock:** Checkered walnut. **Sights:** Blade front, adjustable rear. **Features:** Blued finish; double set triggers. From Cimarron F.A. Co.

Price: **$1,625.00**

CIMARRON SILHOUETTE MODEL 1874 SHARPS SPORTING RIFLE

Caliber: 45-70. **Barrel:** 32" octagonal. **Weight:** NA. **Length:** NA. **Stock:** Walnut. **Sights:** Blade front, adjustable rear. **Features:** Pistol-grip stock with shotgun-style butt plate; cut-rifled barrel. From Cimarron F.A. Co.

Price: **$1,299.00**

CIMARRON MODEL 1885 HIGH WALL RIFLE

Caliber: 38-55, 40-65, 45-70, 45-90, 45-120. **Barrel:** 30" octagonal. **Weight:** NA. **Length:** NA. **Stock:** European walnut. **Sights:** Bead front, semi-buckhorn rear. **Features:** Replica of the Winchester 1885 High Wall rifle. Color case-hardened receiver and lever, blued barrel. Curved buttplate. Optional double set triggers. Introduced 1999. Imported by Cimarron F.A. Co.

Price: **$995.00**

Price: With pistol grip **$1,175.00**

CUMBERLAND MOUNTAIN PLATEAU RIFLE

Caliber: 40-65, 45-70. **Barrel:** Up to 32"; round. **Weight:** About 10-1/2 lbs. (32" barrel). **Length:** 48" overall (32" barrel). **Stock:** American walnut. **Sights:** Marble's bead front, Marble's open rear. **Features:** Falling block action with underlever. Blued barrel and receiver. Stock has lacquer finish, crescent buttplate. Introduced 1995. Made in U.S.A. by Cumberland Mountain Arms, Inc.

Price: **$1,085.00**

DAKOTA MODEL 10 SINGLE SHOT RIFLE

Caliber: Most rimmed and rimless commercial calibers. **Barrel:** 23". **Weight:** 6 lbs. **Length:** 39-1/2" overall. **Stock:** Medium fancy grade walnut in classic style. Checkered grip and forend. **Sights:** None furnished. Drilled and tapped for scope mounting. **Features:** Falling block action with under-lever. Top tang safety. Removable trigger plate for conversion to single set trigger. Introduced 1990. Made in U.S.A. by Dakota Arms.

Price: **$3,595.00**

Price: Barreled action **$2,095.00**

Price: Action only **$1,850.00**

Price: Magnum calibers **$3,595.00**

Price: Magnum barreled action **$2,050.00**

Price: Magnum action only **$1,675.00**

Dixie 1874 Sharps Silhouette

H&R Ultra Hunter

H&R Buffalo

DIXIE 1874 SHARPS BLACKPOWDER SILHOUETTE RIFLE

Caliber: 45-70. **Barrel:** 30"; tapered octagon; blued; 1:18" twist. **Weight:** 10 lbs., 3 oz. **Length:** 47-1/2" overall. **Stock:** Oiled walnut. **Sights:** Blade front, ladder-type hunting rear. **Features:** Replica of the Sharps #1 Sporter. Shotgun-style butt with checkered metal buttplate; color case-hardened receiver, hammer, lever and buttplate. Tang is drilled and tapped for tang sight. Double-set triggers. Meets standards for NRA blackpowder cartridge matches. Introduced 1995. Imported from Italy by Dixie Gun Works.

Price: $1,025.00

Dixie 1874 Sharps Lightweight Hunter/Target Rifle

Same as the Dixie 1874 Sharps Blackpowder Silhouette model except has a straight-grip buttstock with military-style buttplate. Based on the 1874 military model. Introduced 1995. Imported from Italy by Dixie Gun Works.

Price: $995.00

E.M.F. 1874 METALLIC CARTRIDGE SHARPS RIFLE

Caliber: 45-70, 45/120. **Barrel:** 28", octagon. **Weight:** 10-3/4 lbs. **Length:** NA. **Stock:** Oiled walnut. **Sights:** Blade front, flip-up open rear. **Features:** Replica of the 1874 Sharps Sporting rifle. Color case-hardened lock; double-set trigger; blue finish. Imported by E.M.F.

Price: From $700.00

Price: With browned finish $1,000.00

Price: Military Carbine $650.00

HARRINGTON & RICHARDSON ULTRA VARMINT RIFLE

Caliber: 223, 243. **Barrel:** 24", heavy. **Weight:** About 7.5 lbs. **Stock:** Hand-checkered laminated birch with Monte Carlo comb. **Sights:** None furnished. Drilled and tapped for scope mounting. **Features:** Break-open action with side-lever release, positive ejection. Scope mount. Blued receiver and barrel. Swivel studs. Introduced 1993. From H&R 1871, Inc.

Price: $332.00

Harrington & Richardson Ultra Hunter Rifle

Similar to Ultra Varmint rifle except chambered for 25-06 with 26" barrel, or 308 Win., 450 Marlin with 22" barrel. Stock and forend are of cinnamon-colored laminate; hand-checkered grip and forend. Introduced 1995. Made in U.S.A. by H&R 1871, LLC.

Price: $332.00

HARRINGTON & RICHARDSON BUFFALO CLASSIC RIFLE

Caliber: 45-70. **Barrel:** 32" heavy. **Weight:** 8 lbs. **Length:** 52" overall. **Stock:** American black walnut. **Sights:** Williams receiver sight; Lyman target front sight with 8 aperture inserts. **Features:** Color case-hardened Handi-Rifle action with exposed hammer; color case-hardened crescent buttplate; 19th century checkering pattern. Introduced 1995. Made in U.S.A. by H&R 1871, LLC.

Price: About $418.00

Harrington & Richardson 38-55 Target Rifle

Similar to the Buffalo Classic rifle except chambered for 38-55 Win., has 28" barrel. The barrel, steel trigger guard and forend spacer, are highly polished and blued. Color case-hardened receiver and buttplate. Williams receiver sight; Lyman target front sight with 8 aperture inserts. Introduced 1998. Made in U.S.A. by H&R 1871, LLC.

Price: $418.00

HARRIS GUNWORKS ANTIETAM SHARPS RIFLE

Caliber: 40-65, 45-75. **Barrel:** 30", 32", octagon or round, hand-lapped stainless or chrome-moly. **Weight:** 11.25 lbs. **Length:** 47" overall. **Stock:** Choice of straight grip, pistol grip or Creedmoor with Schnabel forend; pewter tip optional. Standard wood is A Fancy; higher grades available. **Sights:** Montana Vintage Arms #111 Low Profile Spirit Level front, #108 mid-range tang rear with windage adjustments. **Features:** Recreation of the 1874 Sharps sidehammer. Action is color case-hardened, barrel satin black. Chrome-moly barrel optionally blued. Optional sights include #112 Spirit Level Globe front with windage, #107 Long Range rear with windage. Introduced 1994. Made in U.S.A. by Harris Gunworks.

Price: $2,400.00

KRIEGHOFF HUBERTUS SINGLE-SHOT RIFLE

Caliber: 222, 243, 270, 308, 30-06, 5.6x50R Mag., 5.6x52R, 6x62R Freres, 6.5x57R, 6.5x65R, 7x57R, 7x65R, 8x57JRS, 8x75RS, 7mm Rem. Mag., 300 Win. Mag. **Barrel:** 23-1/2". **Weight:** 6-1/2 lbs. **Length:** NA. **Stock:** High-grade walnut. **Sights:** Blade front, open rear. **Features:** Break-loading with manual cocking lever on top tang; take-down; extractor; schnabel forearm; many options. Imported from Germany by Krieghoff International Inc.

Price: Hubertus single shot, from $5,850.00

Price: Hubertus, magnum calibers $6,850.00

LONE STAR NO. 5 REMINGTON PATTERN ROLLING BLOCK RIFLE

Caliber: 25-35, 30-30, 30-40 Krag. **Barrel:** 26" to 34". **Weight:** NA. **Length:** NA **Stock:** American walnut. **Sights:** Beech style, Marble bead, Rocky Mountain-style, front; Buckhorn, early or late combination, rear. **Features:** Round, tapered round, octagon, tapered octagon, half octagon-half round barrels; bone-pack color case-hardened actions; single, single set, or double set triggers. Made in U.S.A. by Lone Star Rifle Co., Inc.

Price: $1,595.00

Lonestar Silhouette

Model 1885 High Wall

Mossberg SSi-One Sporter

Mossberg SSi-One Varminter

Lone Star Cowboy Action Rifle

Similar to the Lone Star No. 5 rifle, but designed for Cowboy Action Shooting with 28-33" barrel, buckhorn rear sight.

Price: $1,595.00

Lone Star Standard Silhouette Rifle

Similar to the Lone Star No. 5 rifle but designed for silhouette shooting with 30-34" barrel.

Price: $1,595.00

MEACHAM HIGHWALL SILHOUETTE RIFLE

Caliber: 40-65 Match, 45-70 Match. **Barrel:** 30", 34" octagon. **Stock:** Black walnut with cheekpiece. **Weight:** 11.5 to 11.9 lbs. **Sights:** None. Tang drilled for Win. base, 3/8" dovetail notch, front. Length of pull: 13-5/8". **Features:** Parts interchangeable copy of '85 Winchester. Available with single trigger, single set trigger, or Schuetzen-style double set triggers. Color case-hardened action. Introduced 2002. From Meacham T&H, Inc.

Price: $2,999.00

MERKEL K-1 MODEL LIGHTWEIGHT STALKING RIFLE

Caliber: 243 Win., 270 Win., 7x57R, 308 Win., 30-06, 7mm Rem. Mag., 300 Win. Mag., 9.3x74R. **Barrel:** 23.6". **Weight:** 5.6 lbs. unscoped. **Stock:** Satin-finished walnut, fluted and checkered; sling-swivel studs. **Sights:** None (scope base furnished). **Features:** Franz Jager single-shot break-open action, cocking/uncocking slide-type safety, matte silver receiver, selectable trigger pull weights, integrated, quick detach 1" or 30mm optic mounts (optic not included). Imported from Germany by GSI.

Price: Standard, simple border engraving $3,795.00

Price: Premium, light arabesque scroll $3,795.00

Price: Jagd, fine engraved hunting scenes $4,395.00

MODEL 1885 HIGH WALL RIFLE

Caliber: 30-40 Krag, 32-40, 38-55, 40-65 WCF, 45-70. **Barrel:** 26" (30-40), 28"-30" all others. Douglas Premium #3 tapered octagon. **Weight:** 9 lbs, 4 oz. **Length:** 47" overall. **Stock:** Premium American black walnut. **Sights:** Marble's standard ivory bead front, #66 long blade top rear with reversible notch and elevator. **Features:** Receiver with octagon top, thick-wall High Wall with coil spring action. Tang drilled, tapped for High Wall tang sight. Receiver, lever, hammer and breechblock color case-hardened. Available from Montana Armory, Inc.

Price: $1,350.00

MOSSBERG SSi-ONE SINGLE SHOT RIFLE

Caliber: 223 Rem., 22-250 Rem., 243 Win., 270 Win., 308 Rem., 30-06. **Barrel:** 24". **Weight:** 8 lbs. **Length:** 40". **Stock:** Satin-finished walnut, fluted and checkered; sling-swivel studs. **Sights:** None (scope base furnished). **Features:** Frame accepts interchangeable barrels, including 12-gauge, fully rifled slug barrel and 12 ga., 3-1/2" chambered barrel with Ulti-Full Turkey choke tube. Lever-opening, break-action design; single-stage trigger; ambidextrous, top-tang safety; internal eject/extract selector. Introduced 2000. From Mossberg.

Price: SSi-One Sporter (standard barrel) or 12 ga., 3-1/2" chamber $459.00

Price: SSi-One Varmint (bull barrel, 22-250 Rem. only; weighs 10 lbs.) $480.00

Price: SSi-One 12-gauge Slug (fully rifled barrel, no sights, scope base) $480.00

NAVY ARMS 1873 SHARPS "QUIGLEY"

Caliber: 45/70. Barrel: 34" heavy octagonal. Stock: Walnut. Features: Case-hardened receiver and military patchbox. Exact reproduction from "Quigley Down Under."

Price: $1,390.00

NAVY ARMS 1873 SHARPS NO. 2 CREEDMOOR RIFLE

Caliber: 45/70. **Barrel:** 30" tapered round. **Stock:** Walnut. **Sights:** Front globe, "soule" tang rear. **Features:** NIckel receiver and action. Lightweight sporting rifle.

Price: $1,300.00

NAVY ARMS 1874 SHARPS CAVALRY CARBINE

Caliber: 45-70. **Barrel:** 22". **Weight:** 7 lbs., 12 oz. **Length:** 39" overall. **Stock:** Walnut. **Sights:** Blade front, military ladder-type rear. **Features:** Replica of the 1874 Sharps miltary carbine. Color case-hardened receiver and furniture. Imported by Navy Arms.

Price: **$1,000.00**

NAVY ARMS 1874 SHARPS BUFFALO RIFLE

Caliber: 45-70, 45-90. **Barrel:** 28" heavy octagon. **Weight:** 10 lbs., 10 oz. **Length:** 46" overall. **Stock:** Walnut; checkered grip and forend. **Sights:** Blade front, ladder rear; tang sight optional. **Features:** Color case-hardened receiver, blued barrel; double-set triggers. Imported by Navy Arms.

Price: **$1,160.00**

Navy Arms Sharps Plains Rifle

Similar to Sharps Buffalo rifle except 45-70 only, 32" medium-weight barrel, weighs 9 lbs., 8 oz., and is 49" overall. Imported by Navy Arms.

Price: $1,125.00

Navy Arms Sharps Sporting Rifle

Same as the Navy Arms Sharps Plains Rifle except has pistol grip stock. Introduced 1997. Imported by Navy Arms.

Price: 45-70 only.................................. **$1,160.00**

NAVY ARMS 1885 HIGH WALL RIFLE

Caliber: 45-70; others available on special order. **Barrel:** 28" round, 30" octagonal. **Weight:** 9.5 lbs. **Length:** 45-1/2" overall (30" barrel). **Stock:** Walnut. **Sights:** Blade front, vernier tang-mounted peep rear. **Features:** Replica of Winchester's High Wall designed by Browning. Color case-hardened receiver, blued barrel. Introduced 1998. Imported by Navy Arms.

Price: 28", round barrel, target sights..................... **$920.00**

Price: 30" octagonal barrel, target sights **$995.00**

NAVY ARMS 1873 SPRINGFIELD CAVALRY CARBINE

Caliber: 45-70. **Barrel:** 22". **Weight:** 7 lbs. **Length:** 40-1/2" overall. **Stock:** Walnut. **Sights:** Blade front, military ladder rear. **Features:** Blued lockplate and barrel; color case-hardened breechblock; saddle ring with bar. Replica of 7th Cavalry gun. Imported by Navy Arms.

Price: **$930.00**

NAVY ARMS ROLLING BLOCK RIFLE

Caliber: 45-70. **Barrel:** 26", 30". **Stock:** Walnut. **Sights:** Blade front, adjustable rear. **Features:** Reproduction of classic rolling block action. Available with full-octagon or half-octagon-half-round barrel. Color case- hardened action, steel fittings. From Navy Arms.

Price: Buffalo **$825.00**

Price: Special Sporting, 26" half round bbl. **$730.00**

NAVY ARMS "JOHN BODINE" ROLLING BLOCK RIFLE

Caliber: 45-70. **Barrel:** 30" heavy octagonal. **Stock:** Walnut. **Sights:** Globe front, "soule" tang rear. **Features:** Double set triggers.

Price: **$1,385.00**

CENTERFIRE RIFLES — SINGLE SHOT

New England Firearms Handi-Rifle

New England Firearms Super Light

New England Firearms Survivor

Remington No. 1 Mid-Range

NAVY ARMS SHARPS NO. 3 LONG RANGE RIFLE

Caliber: 45-70, 45-90. **Barrel:** 34" octagon. **Weight:** 10 lbs., 12 oz. **Length:** 51-1/2". **Stock:** Deluxe walnut. **Sights:** Globe target front and match grade rear tang. **Features:** Shotgun buttplate, German silver forend cap, color case hardenend receiver. Imported by Navy Arms.

Price: **$1,885.00**

NEW ENGLAND FIREARMS HANDI-RIFLE

Caliber: 22 Hornet, 223, 243, 30-30, 270, 280 Rem., 308, 30-06, 357 Mag., 44 Mag., 45-70. **Barrel:** 22", 24"; 26" for 280 Rem. **Weight:** 7 lbs. **Stock:** Walnut-finished hardwood; black rubber recoil pad. **Sights:** Ramp front, folding rear (22 Hornet, 30-30, 45-70). Drilled and tapped for scope mount; 223, 243, 270, 280, 30-06 have no open sights, come with scope mounts. **Features:** Break-open action with side-lever release. The 223, 243, 270 and 30-06 have recoil pad and Monte Carlo stock for shooting with scope. Swivel studs on all models. Blue finish. Introduced 1989. From New England Firearms.

Price: **$270.00**

Price: 280 Rem., 26" barrel **$270.00**

Price: Synthetic Handi-Rifle (black polymer stock and forend, swivels, recoil pad) **$281.00**

Price: Handi-Rifle Youth (223, 243)...................... **$270.00**

Price: Stainless Handi-Rifle (223 Rem., 243 Rem.) **$337.00**

New England Firearms Super Light Rifle

Similar to Handi-Rifle except new barrel taper, shorter 20" barrel with recessed muzzle, special lightweight synthetic stock and forend. No sights furnished on 223 and 243 versions, but have factory-mounted scope base and offset hammer spur; Monte Carlo stock; 22 Hornet has ramp front, fully adjustable open rear. Overall length 36", weight is 5.5 lbs. Introduced 1997. Made in U.S.A. by New England Firearms.

Price: 22 Hornet, 223 Rem. or 243 Win.................... **$281.00**

NEW ENGLAND FIREARMS SURVIVOR RIFLE

Caliber: 223, 308 Win., single shot. **Barrel:** 22". **Weight:** 6 lbs. **Length:** 36" overall. **Stock:** Black polymer, thumbhole design. **Sights:** None furnished; scope mount provided. **Features:** Receiver drilled and tapped for scope mounting. Stock and forend have storage compartments for ammo, etc.; comes with integral swivels and black nylon sling. Introduced 1996. Made in U.S.A. by New England Firearms.

Price: Blue finish.................................... **$284.00**

REMINGTON NO. 1 ROLLING BLOCK MID-RANGE SPORTER

Caliber: 45-70. **Barrel:** 30" round. **Weight:** 8-3/4 lbs. **Length:** 46-1/2" overall. **Stock:** American walnut with checkered pistol grip and forend. **Sights:** Beaded blade front, adjustable center-notch buckhorn rear. **Features:** Recreation of the original. Polished blue metal finish. Many options available. Introduced 1998. Made in U.S.A. by Remington.

Price: **$1,450.00**

Price: Silhouette model with single-set trigger, heavy barrel ... **$1,560.00**

ROSSI SINGLE SHOT CENTERFIRE RIFLE

Caliber: 308 Win., 270 Win., 30-06 Spfld., 223 Rem., 243 Win. **Barrel:** 23". **Weight:** 6-6.5 lbs. **Stock:** Monte carlo, exotic woods, walnut finish & swivels with white line space and recoil pad. **Sights:** None, scope rails and hammer extension included. **Features:** Break Open, positive ejection, internal transfer bar mechanism and manual external safety. Trigger block system included.

Price: **$179.95**

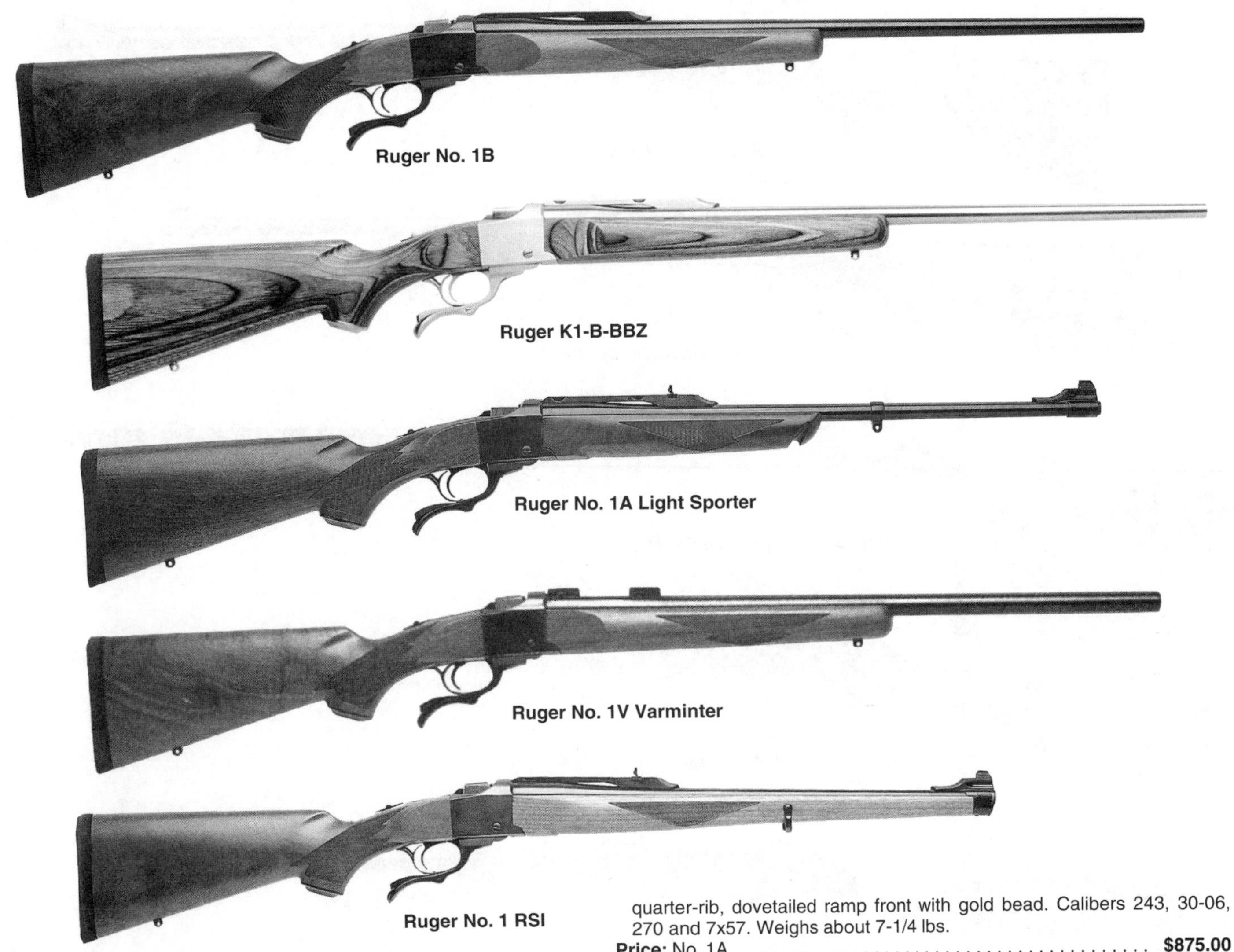
Ruger No. 1B

Ruger K1-B-BBZ

Ruger No. 1A Light Sporter

Ruger No. 1V Varminter

Ruger No. 1 RSI

ROSSI CENTERFIRE/SHOTGUN "MATCHED PAIRS"

Caliber: 12 ga./223 Rem., full size, 20 ga./223 Rem. full & youth, 12 ga./342 Win. full, 20 ga./243 Win., full & youth, 12 ga./308 Win. full, 20 ga./308 Win. full & youth, 12 ga./30-06 Spfld. full, 20 ga./30-06 Spfld. full, 12 ga./270 Win. full, 20 ga./270 Win. full. **Barrel:** 28"/23" full, 22"/22" youth. **Weight:** 5-7 lbs. **Stock:** Straight, exotic woods, walnut finish and swivels wtih white line space and recoil pad. **Sights:** Bead front shotgun, fully adjustable rifle, drilled and tapped. **Features:** Break Open, positive ejection, internal transfer bar mechanism and manual external safety. Trigger block system included.

Price: 350.00

RUGER NO. 1B SINGLE SHOT

Caliber: 218 Bee, 22 Hornet, 220 Swift, 22-250, 223, 243, 6mm Rem., 25-06, 257 Roberts, 270, 280, 30-06, 7mm Rem. Mag., 300 Win. Mag., 308 Win., 338 Win. Mag., 270 Wea., 300 Wea. **Barrel:** 26" round tapered with quarter-rib; with Ruger 1" rings. **Weight:** 8 lbs. **Length:** 42-1/4" overall. **Stock:** Walnut, two-piece, checkered pistol grip and semi-beavertail forend. **Sights:** None, 1" scope rings supplied for integral mounts. **Features:** Under-lever, hammerless falling block design has auto ejector, top tang safety.

Price: 1B **$875.00**

Price: Barreled action **$600.00**

Price: K1-B-BBZ Stainless steel, laminated stock 25-06, 7MM mag, 7MM STW, 300 Win Mag., 243 Win., 30-06, 308 Win. **$910.00**

Ruger No. 1A Light Sporter

Similar to the No. 1B Standard Rifle except has lightweight 22" barrel, Alexander Henry-style forend, adjustable folding leaf rear sight on quarter-rib, dovetailed ramp front with gold bead. Calibers 243, 30-06, 270 and 7x57. Weighs about 7-1/4 lbs.

Price: No. 1A **$875.00**

Price: Barreled action **$600.00**

Ruger No. 1V Varminter

Similar to the No. 1B Standard Rifle except has 24" heavy barrel. Semi-beavertail forend, barrel ribbed for target scope block, with 1" Ruger scope rings. Calibers 22-250, 220 Swift, 223, 25-06, 6mm Rem. Weight about 9 lbs.

Price: No. 1V **$875.00**

Price: Barreled action **$600.00**

Price: K1-V-BBZ stainless steel, laminated stock 22-250 . . . . **$910.00**

Ruger No. 1 RSI International

Similar to the No. 1B Standard Rifle except has lightweight 20" barrel, full-length International-style forend with loop sling swivel, adjustable folding leaf rear sight on quarter-rib, ramp front with gold bead. Calibers 243, 30-06, 270 and 7x57. Weight is about 7-1/4 lbs.

Price: No. 1 RSI **$890.00**

Price: Barreled action **$600.00**

Ruger No. 1H Tropical Rifle

Similar to the No. 1B Standard Rifle except has Alexander Henry forend, adjustable folding leaf rear sight on quarter-rib, ramp front with dovetail gold bead, 24" heavy barrel. Calibers 375 H&H, 416 Rem. Mag., 416 Rigby, and 458 Win. Mag. (weighs about 9 lbs.).

Price: No. 1H **$875.00**

Price: Barreled action **$600.00**

Price: K1-H-BBZ, S/S, 375 H&H, 416 Rigby **$910.00**

Ruger No. 1H Tropical

Ruger No. 1S Medium Sporter

Shiloh 1874 Long Range Express

Shiloh 1874 Quigley

Shiloh 1874 Saddle

Ruger No. 1S Medium Sporter

Similar to the No. 1B Standard Rifle except has Alexander Henry-style forend, adjustable folding leaf rear sight on quarter-rib, ramp front sight base and dovetail-type gold bead front sight. Calibers 218 Bee, 7mm Rem. Mag., 338 Win. Mag., 300 Win. Mag. with 26" barrel, 45-70 with 22" barrel. Weighs about 7-1/2 lbs. In 45-70.

Price: No. 1S **$875.00**
Price: Barreled action **$600.00**
Price: K1-S-BBZ, S/S, 45-70 .... **$910.00**

SHILOH RIFLE CO. SHARPS 1874 LONG RANGE EXPRESS

Caliber: 40-50 BN, 40-70 BN, 40-90 BN, 45-70 ST, 45-90 ST, 45-110 ST, 50-70 ST, 50-90 ST, 38-55, 40-70 ST, 40-90 ST. **Barrel:** 34" tapered octagon. **Weight:** 10-1/2 lbs. **Length:** 51" overall. **Stock:** Oil-finished semi-fancy walnut with pistol grip, shotgun-style butt, traditional cheek rest, Schnabel forend. **Sights:** Globe front, sporting tang rear. **Features:** Recreation of the Model 1874 Sharps rifle. Double set triggers. Made in U.S.A. by Shiloh Rifle Mfg. Co.

Price: **$1,796.00**
Price: Sporting Rifle No. 1 (similar to above except with 30" bbl., blade front, buckhorn rear sight) **$1,706.00**
Price: Sporting Rifle No. 3 (similar to No. 1 except straight-grip stock, standard wood) **$1,504.00**
Price: 1874 Hartford (Hartford collar, pewter tip) **$1,702.00**
Price: 1874 Sporter #1 (30" bbl, blade, buckhorn sights) **$1,706.00**
Price: 1874 Sporter #3 (walnut, shotgun or military stock) **$1,504.00**

SHILOH RIFLE CO. SHARPS 1874 QUIGLEY

Caliber: 45-70, 45-110. **Barrel:** 34" heavy octagon. **Stock:** Military-style with patch box, standard grade American walnut. **Sights:** Semi buckhorn, interchangeable front and midrange vernier tang wight with windage. **Features:** Gold inlay initials, pewter tip, hartford collar, case color or antique finish. Double set triggers.

Price: **$2,860.00**

SHILOH RIFLE CO. SHARPS 1874 SADDLE RIFLE

Caliber: 38-55, 40-50 BN, 40-65 Win., 40-70 BN, 40-70 ST, 40-90 BN, 40-90 ST, 44-77 BN, 44-90 BN, 45-70 ST, 45-90 ST, 45-100 ST, 45-110 ST, 45-120 ST, 50-70 ST, 50-90 ST. **Barrel:** 26" full or half octagon. **Stock:** Semi fancy American walnut. Shotgun style with cheekrest. **Sights:** Buckhorn and blade. **Features:** Double set trigger, numerous custom features can be added.

Price: **$1,504.00**

SHILOH RIFLE CO. SHARPS 1874 MONTANA ROUGHRIDER

Caliber: 38-55, 40-50 BN, 40-65 Win., 40-70 BN, 40-70 ST, 40-90 BN, 40-90 ST, 44-77 BN, 44-90 BN, 45-70 ST, 45-90 ST, 45-100 ST, 45-110 ST, 45-120 ST, 50-70 ST, 50-90 ST. **Barrel:** 30" full or half octagon. **Stock:** American walnut in shotgun or military style. **Sights:** Buckhorn and blade. **Features:** Double set triggers, numerous custom features can be added.

Price: **$1,504.00**

Shiloh 1874 Montana Roughrider

Shiloh 1874 Creedmoor

Thompson/Center Encore

Thompson/Center Encore "Katahdin"

Thompson/Center Encore

SHILOH RIFLE CO. SHARPS CREEDMOOR TARGET

Caliber: 38-55, 40-50 BN, 40-65 Win., 40-70 BN, 40-70 ST, 40-90 BN, 40-90 ST, 44-77 BN, 44-90 BN, 45-70 ST, 45-90 ST, 45-100 ST, 45-110 ST, 45-120 ST, 50-70 ST, 50-90 ST. **Barrel:** 32", half round-half octagon. **Stock:** Extra fancy American walnut. Shotgun style with pistol grip. **Sights:** Customer's choice. **Features:** Single trigger, AA finish on stock, polished barrel and screws, pewter tip.

Price: **$2,442.00**

THOMPSON/CENTER ENCORE RIFLE

Caliber: 22-250, 223, 243, 25-06, 270, 7mm-08, 308, 30-06, 7mm Rem. Mag., 300 Win. Mag. **Barrel:** 24", 26". **Weight:** 6 lbs., 12 oz. (24" barrel). **Length:** 38-1/2" (24" barrel). **Stock:** American walnut. Monte Carlo style; Schnabel forend or black composite. **Sights:** Ramp-style white bead front, fully adjustable leaf-type rear. **Features:** Interchangeable barrels; action opens by squeezing trigger guard; drilled and tapped for T/C scope mounts; polished blue finish. Introduced 1996. Made in U.S.A. by Thompson/Center Arms.

Price: .... **$599 to $632.00**

Price: Extra barrels **$270.00**

Thompson/Center Stainless Encore Rifle

Similar to blued Encore except stainless steel with blued sights, black composite stock and forend. Available in 22-250, 223, 7mm-08, 30-06, 308. Introduced 1999. Made in U.S.A. by Thompson/Center Arms.

Price: .... **$670.00 to $676.00**

THOMPSON/CENTER ENCORE "KATAHDIN" CARBINE

Caliber: 45-70 Gov't., 444 Marlin, 450 Marlin. **Barrel:** 18" with muzzle tamer. **Stock:** Composite.

Price: **$619.00**

Thompson/Center G2 Contender Rifle

Similar to the G2 Contender pistol, but in a compact rifle format. **Features:** interchangeable 23" barrels, chambered for 17 HMR, 22LR, 223 Rem., 30/30 Win. and 45/70 Gov't; plus a 45 Cal. Muzzleloading barrel. All of the 16-1/4" and 21" barrels made for the old style Contender will fit. **Weight:** 5-1/2 lbs. Introduced 2003. Made in U.S.A. by Thompson/Center Arms.

Price: .... **$592.40 to $607.00**

Traditions 1874 Sharps Deluxe

Traditions 1874 Sharps Sporting Deluxe

Tristar/Uberti 1885 Single Shot

TRADITIONS 1874 SHARPS DELUXE RIFLE

Caliber: 45-70. **Barrel:** 32" octagonal; 1:18" twist. **Weight:** 11.67 lbs. **Length:** 48.8" overall. **Stock:** Checkered walnut with German silver nose cap and steel butt plate. **Sights:** Globe front, adjustable creedmore rear with 12 inserts. **Features:** Color-case hardened receiver; double-set triggers. Introduced 2001. Imported from Pedersoli by Traditions.

Price: **$999.00**

Traditions 1874 Sharps Sporting Deluxe Rifle

Similar to Sharps Deluxe but custom silver engraved receiver, European walnut stock and forend, satin finish, set trigger, fully adjustable.

Price: **$1,999.00**

Traditions 1874 Sharps Standard Rifle

Similar to 1874 Sharps Deluxe Rifle, except has blade front and adjustable buckhorn-style rear sight. Weighs 10.67 pounds. Introduced 2001. Imported from Pedersoli by Traditions.

Price: **$769.00**

TRADITIONS ROLLING BLOCK SPORTING RIFLE

Caliber: 45-70. **Barrel:** 30" octagonal; 1:18" twist. **Weight:** 11.67 lbs. **Length:** 46.7" overall. **Stock:** Walnut. **Sights:** Blade front, adjustable rear. **Features:** Antique silver, color-case hardened receiver, drilled and tapped for tang/globe sights; brass butt plate and trigger guard. Introduced 2001. Imported from Pedersoli by Traditions.

Price: **$769.00**

TRADITIONS
ROLLING BLOCK SPORTING RIFLE IN 30-30 WINCHESTER

Caliber: 30-30. **Barrel:** 28" round, blued. **Weight:** 8.25 lbs. **Stock:** Walnut. **Sights:** Fixed front, adjustable rear. **Features:** Steel butt plate, trigger guard, barrel band.

Price: **$769.00**

TRISTAR/SHARPS 1874 SPORTING RIFLE

Caliber: 45-70. **Barrel:** 28", 32", 34" octagonal. **Weight:** 9.75 lbs. **Length:** 44.5" overall. **Stock:** Walnut. **Sights:** Dovetail front, adjustable rear. **Features:** Cut checkering, case colored frame finish.

Price: **$795.00**

TRISTAR/UBERTI 1885 SINGLE SHOT

Caliber: 45-70. **Barrel:** 28". **Weight:** 8.75 lbs. **Length:** 44.5" overall. **Stock:** European walnut. **Sights:** Bead on blade front, open step-adjustable rear. **Features:** Recreation of the 1885 Winchester. Color case-hardened receiver and lever, blued barrel. Introduced 1998. Imported from Italy by Tristar Sporting Arms Ltd.

Price: **$765.00**

UBERTI BABY ROLLING BLOCK CARBINE

Caliber: 22 LR, 22 WMR, 22 Hornet, 357 Mag., single shot. **Barrel:** 22". **Weight:** 4.8 lbs. **Length:** 35-1/2" overall. **Stock:** Walnut stock and forend. **Sights:** Blade front, fully adjustable open rear. **Features:** Resembles Remington New Model No. 4 carbine. Brass trigger guard and buttplate; color case-hardened frame, blued barrel. Imported by Uberti USA Inc.

Price: **$490.00**

Price: Baby Rolling Block Rifle, 26" bbl. **$590.00**

DRILLINGS, COMBINATION GUNS, DOUBLE GUNS

Designs for sporting and utility purposes worldwide.

Beretta Express SSO

Beretta Model 455 SxS

Charles Daly Superior

Charles Daly Empire Combo

BERETTA EXPRESS SSO O/U DOUBLE RIFLES

Caliber: 375 H&H, 458 Win. Mag., 9.3x74R. **Barrel:** 25.5". **Weight:** 11 lbs. **Stock:** European walnut with hand-checkered grip and forend. **Sights:** Blade front on ramp, open V-notch rear. **Features:** Sidelock action with color case-hardened receiver (gold inlays on SSO6 Gold). Ejectors, double triggers, recoil pad. Introduced 1990. Imported from Italy by Beretta U.S.A.

Price: SSO6 . . . . **$21,000.00**
Price: SSO6 Gold **$23,500.00**

BERETTA MODEL 455 SxS EXPRESS RIFLE

Caliber: 375 H&H, 458 Win. Mag., 470 NE, 500 NE 3", 416 Rigby. **Barrel:** 23-1/2" or 25-1/2". **Weight:** 11 lbs. **Stock:** European walnut with hand-checkered grip and forend. **Sights:** Blade front, folding leaf V-notch rear. **Features:** Sidelock action with easily removable sideplates; color case-hardened finish (455), custom big game or floral motif engraving (455EELL). Double triggers, recoil pad. Introduced 1990. Imported from Italy by Beretta U.S.A.

Price: Model 455. . . . . **$36,000.00**
Price: Model 455EELL **$47,000.00**

BRNO 500 COMBINATION GUNS

Caliber/Gauge: 12 (2-3/4" chamber) over 5.6x52R, 5.6x50R, 222 Rem., 243, 6.x55, 308, 7x57R, 7x65R, 30-06. **Barrel:** 23.6". **Weight:** 7.6 lbs. **Length:** 40.5" overall. **Stock:** European walnut. **Sights:** Bead front, V-notch rear; grooved for scope mounting. **Features:** Boxlock action; double set trigger; blue finish with etched engraving. Announced 1998. Imported from The Czech Republic by Euro-Imports.

Price: **$1,023.00**
Price: O/U double rifle, 7x57R, 7x65R, 8x57JRS **$1,125.00**

BRNO ZH 300 COMBINATION GUN

Caliber/Gauge: 22 Hornet, 5.6x50R Mag., 5.6x52R, 7x57R, 7x65R, 8x57JRS over 12, 16 (2-3/4" chamber). **Barrel:** 23.6". **Weight:** 7.9 lbs. **Length:** 40.5" overall. **Stock:** European walnut. **Sights:** Blade front, open adjustable rear. **Features:** Boxlock action; double triggers; automatic safety. Announced 1998. Imported from The Czech Republic by Euro-Imports.

Price: **$724.00**

BRNO ZH Double Rifles

Similar to ZH 300 combination guns except double rifle barrels. Available in 7x65R, 7x57R and 8x57JRS. Announced 1998. Imported from The Czech Republic by Euro-Imports.

Price: **$1,125.00**

CHARLES DALY SUPERIOR COMBINATION GUN

Caliber/Gauge: 12 ga. over 22 Hornet, 223 Rem., 22-250, 243 Win., 270 Win., 308 Win., 30-06. **Barrel:** 23.5", shotgun choked Imp. Cyl. **Weight:** About 7.5 lbs. **Stock:** Checkered walnut pistol grip buttstock and semi-beavertail forend. **Features:** Silvered, engraved receiver; chrome-moly steel barrels; double triggers; extractors; sling swivels; gold bead front sight. Introduced 1997. Imported from Italy by K.B.I. Inc.

Price: **$1,249.95**

Charles Daly Empire Combination Gun

Same as the Superior grade except has deluxe wood with European-style comb and cheekpiece; slim forend. Introduced 1997. Imported from Italy by K.B.I., Inc.

Price: **$1,789.95**

CZ 584 SOLO COMBINATION GUN

Caliber/Gauge: 7x57R; 12, 2-3/4" chamber. **Barrel:** 24.4". **Weight:** 7.37 lbs. **Length:** 45.25" overall. **Stock:** Circassian walnut. **Sights:** Blade front, open rear adjustable for windage. **Features:** Kersten-style double lump locking system; double-trigger Blitz-type mechanism with drop safety and adjustable set trigger for the rifle barrel; auto safety, dual extractors; receiver dovetailed for scope mounting. Imported from the Czech Republic by CZ-USA.

Price: **$851.00**

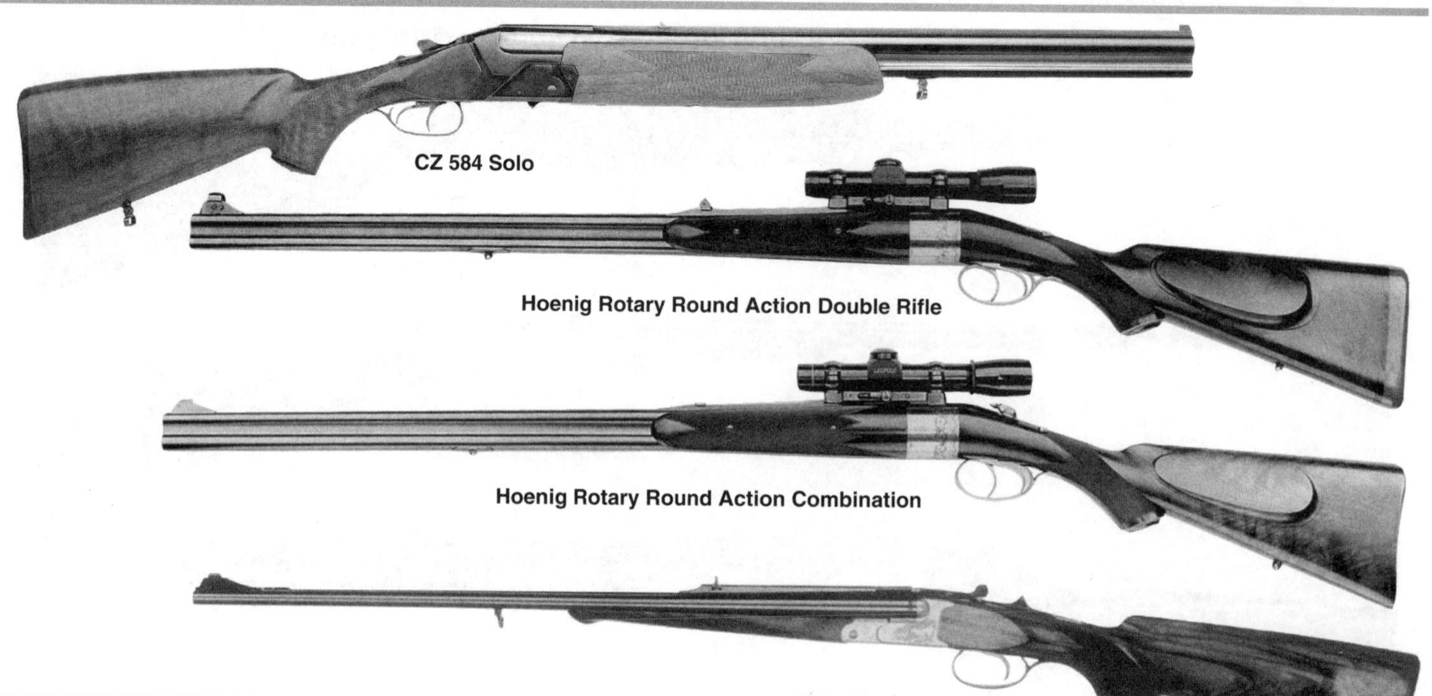

CZ 584 Solo

Hoenig Rotary Round Action Double Rifle

Hoenig Rotary Round Action Combination

Krieghoff Classic Double Rifle

CZ 589 STOPPER OVER/UNDER GUN

Caliber: 458 Win. Magnum. Barrels: 21.7". **Weight:** 9.3 lbs. **Length:** 37.7" overall. **Stock:** Turkish walnut with sling swivels. **Sights:** Blade front, fixed rear. **Features:** Kersten-style action; Blitz-type double trigger; hammer-forged, blued barrels; satin-nickel, engraved receiver. Introduced 2001. Imported from the Czech Republic by CZ USA.

Price: **$2,999.00**

Price: Fully engraved model **$3,999.00**

DAKOTA DOUBLE RIFLE

Caliber: 470 Nitro Express, 500 Nitro Express. **Barrel:** 25". **Stock:** Exhibition-grade walnut. **Sights:** Express. **Features:** Round action; selective ejectors; recoil pad; Americase. From Dakota Arms Inc.

Price: **$25,000.00**

EAA/BAIKAL IZH-94 COMBINATION GUN

Caliber/Gauge: 12, 3" chamber; 222 Rem., 223, 5.6x50R, 5.6x55E, 7x57R, 7x65R, 7.62x39, 7.62x51, 308, 7.62x53R, 7.62x54R, 30-06. **Barrel:** 24", 26"; imp., mod. and full choke tubes. **Weight:** 7.28 lbs. **Stock:** Walnut; rubber butt pad. **Sights:** Express style. **Features:** Hammer-forged barrels with chrome-lined bores; machined receiver; single-selective or double triggers. Imported by European American Armory.

Price: Blued finish **$549.00**

Price: 20 ga./22 LR, 20/22 Mag, 3" **$629.00**

GARBI EXPRESS DOUBLE RIFLE

Caliber: 7x65R, 9.3x74R, 375 H&H. **Barrel:** 24-3/4". **Weight:** 7-3/4 to 8-1/2 lbs. **Length:** 41-1/2" overall. **Stock:** Turkish walnut. **Sights:** Quarter-rib with express sight. **Features:** Side-by-side double; H&H-pattern sidelock ejector with reinforced action, chopper lump barrels of Boehler steel; double triggers; fine scroll and rosette engraving, or full coverage ornamental; coin-finished action. Introduced 1997. Imported from Spain by Wm. Larkin Moore.

Price: **$19,900.00**

HOENIG ROTARY ROUND ACTION DOUBLE RIFLE

Caliber: Most popular calibers from 225 Win. to 9.3x74R. **Barrel:** 22"-26". **Stock:** English Walnut; to customer specs. **Sights:** Swivel hood front with button release (extra bead stored in trap door gripcap), express-style rear on quarter-rib adjustable for windage and elevation; scope mount. **Features:** Round action opens by rotating barrels, pulling forward. Inertia extractor system, rotary safety blocks strikers. single lever quick-detachable scope mount. Simple takedown without removing forend. Introduced 1997. Made in U.S.A. by George Hoenig.

Price: **$24,975.00**

HOENIG ROTARY ROUND ACTION COMBINATION

Caliber: 28 ga. **Barrel:** 26". **Weight:** 7 lbs. **Stock:** English Walnut to customer specs. **Sights:** Front ramp with button release blades. Foldable aperture tang sight windage and elevation adjustable. Quarter rib with scope mount. **Features:** Round action opens by rotating barrels, pulling forward. Inertia extractor; rotary safety blocks strikers. Simple takedown without removing forend. Made in U.S.A. by George Hoenig.

Price: **$24,975.00**

KRIEGHOFF CLASSIC DOUBLE RIFLE

Caliber: 7x65R, 308 Win., 30-06, 8x57 JRS, 8x75RS, 9.3x74R. **Barrel:** 23.5". **Weight:** 7.3 to 8 lbs. **Stock:** High grade European walnut. Standard has conventional rounded cheekpiece, Bavaria has Bavarian-style cheekpiece. **Sights:** Bead front with removable, adjustable wedge (375 H&H and below), standing leaf rear on quarter-rib. **Features:** Boxlock action; double triggers; short opening angle for fast loading; quiet extractors; sliding, self-adjusting wedge for secure bolting; Purdey-style barrel extension; horizontal firing pin placement. Many options available. Introduced 1997. Imported from Germany by Krieghoff International.

Price: With small Arabesque engraving **$7,850.00**

Price: With engraved sideplates **$9,800.00**

Price: For extra barrels **$4,500.00**

Price: Extra 20-ga., 28" shotshell barrels **$3,200.00**

Krieghoff Classic Big Five Double Rifle

Similar to the standard Classic excpet available in 375 Flanged Mag. N.E., 500/416 N.E., 470 N.E., 500 N.E. 3". Has hinged front trigger, non-removable muzzle wedge (larger than 375-caliber), Universal Trigger System, Combi Cocking Device, steel trigger guard, specially weighted stock bolt for weight and balance. Many options available. Introduced 1997. Imported from Germany by Krieghoff International.

Price: **$9,450.00**

Price: With engraved sideplates **$11,400.00**

LEBEAU - COURALLY EXPRESS RIFLE SxS

Caliber: 7x65R, 8x57JRS, 9.3x74R, 375 H&H, 470 N.E. **Barrel:** 24" to 26". **Weight:** 7-3/4 to 10-1/2 lbs. **Stock:** Fancy French walnut with cheekpiece. **Sights:** Bead on ramp front, standing left express rear on quarter-rib. **Features:** Holland & Holland-type sidelock with automatic ejectors; double triggers. Built to order only. Imported from Belgium by Wm. Larkin Moore.

Price: **$41,000.00**

Merkel 96K Engraved

Merkel 140-1

Rizzini Express

Savage 24F Combination

Springfield M6 Scout

MERKEL DRILLINGS

Caliber/Gauge: 12, 20, 3" chambers, 16, 2-3/4" chambers; 22 Hornet, 5.6x50R Mag., 5.6x52R, 222 Rem., 243 Win., 6.5x55, 6.5x57R, 7x57R, 7x65R, 308, 30-06, 8x57JRS, 9.3x74R, 375 H&H. **Barrel:** 25.6". **Weight:** 7.9 to 8.4 lbs. depending upon caliber. **Stock:** Oil-finished walnut with pistol grip; cheekpiece on 12-, 16-gauge. **Sights:** Blade front, fixed rear. **Features:** Double barrel locking lug with Greener cross-bolt; scroll-engraved, case-hardened receiver; automatic trigger safety; Blitz action; double triggers. Imported from Germany by GSI.

Price: Model 96K (manually cocked rifle system), from **$7,495.00**

Price: Model 96K Engraved (hunting series on receiver) **$8,595.00**

Merkel Boxlock Double Rifles

Similar to the Model 160 double rifle except with Anson & Deely boxlock action with cocking indicators, double triggers, engraved color case-hardened receiver. Introduced 1995. Imported from Germany by GSI.

Price: Model 140-1, from **$6,695.00**

Price: Model 140-1.1 (engraved silver-gray receiver), from **$7,795.00**

RIZZINI EXPRESS 90L DOUBLE RIFLE

Caliber: 30-06, 7x65R, 9.3x74R. **Barrel:** 24". **Weight:** 7-1/2 lbs. **Length:** 40" overall. **Stock:** Select European walnut with satin oil finish; English-style cheekpiece. **Sights:** Ramp front, quarter-rib with express sight. **Features:** Color case-hardened boxlock action; automatic ejectors; single selective trigger; polished blue barrels. Extra 20-gauge shotshell barrels available. Imported for Italy by Wm. Larkin Moore.

Price: With case **$3,850.00**

SAVAGE 24F PREDATOR O/U COMBINATION GUN

Caliber/Gauge: 22 Hornet, 223, 30-30 over 12 (24F-12) or 22 LR, 22 Hornet, 223, 30-30 over 20-ga. (24F-20); 3" chambers. **Action:** Takedown, low re-bounding visible hammer. Single trigger, barrel selector spur on hammer. **Barrel:** 24" separated barrels; 12-ga. has mod. choke tubes, 20-ga. has fixed Mod. choke. **Weight:** 8 lbs. **Length:** 40-1/2" overall. **Stock:** Black Rynite composition. **Sights:** Blade front, rear open adjustable for eleva-tion. **Features:** Introduced 1989.

Price: 24F-12 .... **$586.00**

Price: 24F-20 .... **$556.00**

SPRINGFIELD, INC. M6 SCOUT RIFLE/SHOTGUN

Caliber/Gauge: 22 LR or 22 Hornet over 410-bore. **Barrel:** 18.25". **Weight:** 4 lbs. **Length:** 32" overall. **Stock:** Folding detachable with storage for 15 22 LR, four 410 shells. **Sights:** Blade front, military aperture for 22; V-notch for 410. **Features:** All-metal construction. Designed for quick disas-sembly and minimum maintenance. Folds for compact storage. Intro-duced 1982; reintroduced 1996. Imported from the Czech Republic by Springfield, Inc.

Price: Parkerized **$185.00**

Price: Stainless steel **$219.00**

RIMFIRE RIFLES — AUTOLOADERS

Designs for hunting, utility and sporting purposes, including training for competition

Armscor M-20C Carbine

Browning Buck Mark Target

Browning Semi-Auto 22

CZ 511 Auto

AR-7 EXPLORER CARBINE

Caliber: 22 LR, 8-shot magazine. **Barrel:** 16". **Weight:** 2-1/2 lbs. **Length:** 34-1/2" / 16-1/2" stowed. **Stock:** Moulded Cycolac; snap-on rubber butt pad. **Sights:** Square blade front, aperture rear. **Features:** Takedown design stores barrel and action in hollow stock. Light enough to float. Reintroduced 1999. From AR-7 Industries, LLC.

Price: Black matte finish **$150.00**
Price: AR-20 Sporter (tubular stock, barrel shroud) **$200.00**
New! **Price:** AR-7 camo- or walnut-finish stock. **$164.95**

ARMSCOR MODEL AK22 AUTO RIFLE

Caliber: 22 LR, 10-shot magazine. **Barrel:** 18.5". **Weight:** 7.5 lbs. **Length:** 38" overall. **Stock:** Plain mahogany. **Sights:** Adjustable post front, leaf rear adjustable for elevation. **Features:** Resembles the AK-47. Matte black finish. Introduced 1987. Imported from the Philippines by K.B.I., Inc.

Price: About **$219.95**

ARMSCOR M-1600 AUTO RIFLE

Caliber: 22 LR, 10-shot magazine. **Barrel:** 18.25". **Weight:** 6.2 lbs. **Length:** 38.5" overall. **Stock:** Black finished mahogany. **Sights:** Post front, aper-ture rear. **Features:** Resembles Colt AR-15. Matte black finish. Introduced 1987. Imported from the Philippines by K.B.I., Inc.

Price: About **$199.95**

ARMSCOR M-20C AUTO CARBINE

Caliber: 22 LR, 10-shot magazine. **Barrel:** 18.25". **Weight:** 6.5 lbs. **Length:** 38" overall. **Stock:** Walnut-finished mahogany. **Sights:** Hooded front, rear adjustable for elevation. **Features:** Receiver grooved for scope mounting. Blued finish. Introduced 1990. Imported from the Philippines by K.B.I., Inc.

Price: **$154.95**

BROWNING BUCK MARK SEMI-AUTO RIFLES

Caliber: 22 LR, 10-shot magazine. **Barrel:** 18" tapered (Sporter), heavy bull (Target), or carbon composite barrel (Classic Carbon). **Weight:** 4 lbs., 2 oz. (Sporter) or 5 lbs., 4 oz. (Target). **Length:** 34" overall. **Stock:** Walnut stock and forearm with full pistol grip. **Sights:** Hi-Viz adjustable (Sporter). **Features:** A rifle version of the Buck Mark Pistol; straight blowback action; machined aluminum receiver with integral rail scope mount; recessed muzzle crown; manual thumb safety. Introduced 2001. From Browning.

Price: Sporter (adj. sights) **$518.00**
Price: Target (heavy bbl., no sights) **$518.00**

BROWNING SEMI-AUTO 22 RIFLE

Caliber: 22 LR, 11-shot. **Barrel:** 19-1/4". **Weight:** 5 lbs., 3 oz. **Length:** 37" overall. **Stock:** Checkered select walnut with pistol grip and semi-beavertail forend. **Sights:** Gold bead front, folding leaf rear. **Features:** Engraved receiver with polished blue finish; cross-bolt safety; tubular magazine in buttstock; easy takedown for carrying or storage. Imported from Japan by Browning.

Price: Grade I **$479.00**

Browning Semi-Auto 22, Grade VI

Same as the Grade I Auto-22 except available with either grayed or blued receiver with extensive engraving with gold-plated animals: right side pictures a fox and squirrel in a woodland scene; left side shows a beagle chasing a rabbit. On top is a portrait of the beagle. Stock and forend are of high-grade walnut with a double-bordered cut checkering design. Introduced 1987.

Price: Grade VI, blue or gray receiver. **$1,028.00**

BRNO ZKM 611 AUTO RIFLE

Caliber: 22 WMR, 6- or 10-shot magazine. **Barrel:** 20.4". **Weight:** 5.9 lbs. **Length:** 38.9" overall. **Stock:** European walnut. **Sights:** Hooded blade front, open adjustable rear. **Features:** Removable box magazine; polished blue finish; cross-bolt safety; grooved receiver for scope mounting; easy takedown for storage. Imported from The Czech Republic by Euro-Imports.

Price: **$475.00**

CZ 511 AUTO RIFLE

Caliber: 22 LR, 8-shot magazine. **Barrel:** 22.2". **Weight:** 5.39 lbs. **Length:** 38.6" overall. **Stock:** Walnut with checkered pistol grip. **Sights:** Hooded front, adjustable rear. **Features:** Polished blue finish; detachable magazine; sling swivel studs. Imported from the Czech Republic by CZ-USA.

Price: **$351.00**

Rimfire Rifles — Autoloaders

CZ 511 Auto

Henry U.S. Survival

Marlin Model 60

Marlin Model 60SSK

Marlin Model 70PSS

Marlin 7000

HENRY U.S. SURVIVAL RIFLE .22

Caliber: 22 LR, 8-shot magazine. **Barrel:** 16" steel lined. **Weight:** 2.5 lbs. **Stock:** ABS plastic. **Sights:** Blade front on ramp, aperture rear. **Features:** Takedown design stores barrel and action in hollow stock. Light enough to float. Silver, black or camo finish. Comes with two magazines. Introduced 1998. From Henry Repeating Arms Co.

Price: **$165.00**

MARLIN MODEL 60 AUTO RIFLE

Caliber: 22 LR, 14-shot tubular magazine. **Barrel:** 19" round tapered. **Weight:** About 5-1/2 lbs. **Length:** 37-1/2" overall. **Stock:** Press-checkered, walnut-finished Maine birch with Monte Carlo, full pistol grip; Mar-Shield® finish. **Sights:** Ramp front, open adjustable rear. **Features:** Matted receiver is grooved for scope mount. Manual bolt hold-open; automatic last-shot bolt hold-open. Model 60C is similar except has hardwood Monte Carlo stock with Mossy Oak Break-Up camouflage pattern. From Marlin.

Price: **$185.00**

Price: With 4x scope **$193.00**

Price: (Model 60C) $220.00

Marlin Model 60SS Self-Loading Rifle

Same as the Model 60 except breech bolt, barrel and outer magazine tube are made of stainless steel; most other parts are either nickel-plated or coated to match the stainless finish. Monte Carlo stock is of black/gray Maine birch laminate, and has nickel-plated swivel studs, rubber butt pad. Introduced 1993. From Marlin.

Price: **$297.00**

Price: Model 60SSK (black fiberglass-filled stock) **$257.00**

Price: Model 60SB (walnut-finished birch stock) **$235.00**

Price: Model 60SB with 4x scope **$251.00**

MARLIN 70PSS PAPOOSE STAINLESS RIFLE

Caliber: 22 LR, 7-shot magazine. **Barrel:** 16-1/4" stainless steel, Micro-Groove® rifling. **Weight:** 3-1/4 lbs. **Length:** 35-1/4" overall. **Stock:** Black fiberglass-filled synthetic with abbreviated forend, nickel-plated swivel studs, moulded-in checkering. **Sights:** Ramp front with orange post, cutaway Wide Scan® hood; adjustable open rear. Receiver grooved for scope mounting. **Features:** Takedown barrel; cross-bolt safety; manual bolt hold-open; last shot bolt hold-open; comes with padded carrying case. Introduced 1986. Made in U.S.A. by Marlin.

Price: **$304.00**

MARLIN MODEL 7000 AUTO RIFLE

Caliber: 22 LR, 10-shot magazine **Barrel:** 18" heavy target with 12-groove Micro-Groove® rifling, recessed muzzle. **Weight:** 5-1/2 lbs. **Length:** 37" overall. **Stock:** Black fiberglass-filled synthetic with Monte Carlo combo, swivel studs, moulded-in checkering. **Sights:** None furnished; comes with ring mounts. **Features:** Automatic last-shot bolt hold-open, manual bolt hold-open; cross-bolt safety; steel charging handle; blue finish, nickel-plated magazine. Introduced 1997. Made in U.S.A. by Marlin Firearms Co.

Price: **$249.00**

Marlin Model 795 Auto Rifle

Similar to Model 7000 except standard-weight 18" barrel with 16-groove Micro-Groove rifling. Ramp front sight with brass bead, screw adjustable open rear. Receiver grooved for scope mount. Introduced 1997. Made in U.S.A. by Marlin Firearms Co.

Price: **$176.00**

RIMFIRE RIFLES — AUTOLOADERS

Marlin 795

Marlin 552 BDL Speedmaster

Remington 597

Ruger 10/22 International

Ruger 10/22 Deluxe Sporter

Marlin Model 795SS Auto Rifle

Similar to Model 795 excapt stainless steel barrel. Most other parts nickel-plated. Adjustable folding semi-buckhorn rear sights, ramp front high-visibility post and removeable cutaway wide scan hood.

Price: **$235.00**

REMINGTON MODEL 552 BDL DELUXE SPEEDMASTER RIFLE

Caliber: 22 S (20), L (17) or LR (15) tubular mag. **Barrel:** 21" round tapered. **Weight:** 5-3/4 lbs. **Length:** 40" overall. **Stock:** Walnut. Checkered grip and forend. **Sights:** Big game. **Features:** Positive cross-bolt safety, receiver grooved for tip-off mount.

Price: **$393.00**

REMINGTON 597 AUTO RIFLE

Caliber: 22 LR, 10-shot clip. **Barrel:** 20". **Weight:** 5-1/2 lbs. **Length:** 40" overall. **Stock:** Black synthetic. **Sights:** Big game. **Features:** Matte black finish, nickel-plated bolt. Receiver is grooved and drilled and tapped for scope mounts. Introduced 1997. Made in U.S.A. by Remington.

Price: **$169.00**
Price: Model 597 Magnum, 22 WMR, 8-shot clip **$335.00**
Price: Model 597 LSS (laminated stock, stainless). **$279.00**
Price: Model 597 SS
(22 LR, stainless steel, black synthetic stock). **$224.00**
Price: Model 597 LS Heavy Barrel (22 LR, laminated stock) **$265.00**
Price: Model 597 Magnum LS Heavy Barrel
(22 WMR, lam. stock) **$399.00**
Price: Model 597 Magnum 17 HMR, 8-shot clip **$361.00**

RUGER 10/22 AUTOLOADING CARBINE

Caliber: 22 LR, 10-shot rotary magazine. **Barrel:** 18-1/2" round tapered. **Weight:** 5 lbs. **Length:** 37-1/4" overall. **Stock:** American hardwood with pistol grip and barrel band or synthetic. **Sights:** Brass bead front, folding leaf rear adjustable for elevation. **Features:** Detachable rotary magazine fits flush into stock, cross-bolt safety, receiver tapped and grooved for scope blocks or tip-off mount. Scope base adaptor furnished with each rifle.

Price: Model 10/22 RB (blue) **$239.00**
Price: Model K10/22RB (bright finish stainless barrel) **$279.00**
Price: Model 10/22RPF (blue, synthetic stock). **$239.00**

Ruger 10/22 International Carbine

Similar to the Ruger 10/22 Carbine except has full-length International stock of American hardwood, checkered grip and forend; comes with rubber butt pad, sling swivels. Reintroduced 1994.

Price: Blue (10/22RBI) **$279.00**
Price: Stainless (K10/22RBI) **$299.00**

Ruger 10/22 Deluxe Sporter

Same as 10/22 Carbine except walnut stock with hand checkered pistol grip and forend; straight buttplate, no barrel band, has sling swivels.

Price: Model 10/22 DSP **$299.00**

Ruger 10/22T Target Rifle

Similar to the 10/22 except has 20" heavy, hammer-forged barrel with tight chamber dimensions, improved trigger pull, laminated hardwood stock dimensioned for optical sights. No iron sights supplied. Introduced 1996. Made in U.S.A. by Sturm, Ruger & Co.

Price: 10/22T **$425.00**
Price: K10/22T, stainless steel **$485.00**

Ruger 10/22 Target

Ruger 10/22 International

Savage Model 64FV

Ruger K10/22RPF All-Weather Rifle

Similar to the stainless K10/22/RB except has black composite stock of thermoplastic polyester resin reinforced with fiberglass; checkered grip and forend. Brushed satin, natural metal finish with clear hardcoat finish. Weighs 5 lbs., measures 36-3/4" overall. Introduced 1997. From Sturm, Ruger & Co.

Price: $279.00

RUGER 10/22 MAGNUM AUTOLOADING CARBINE

Caliber: 22 WMR, 9-shot rotary magazine. **Barrel:** 18-1/2". **Weight:** 6 lbs. **Length:** 37-1/4" overall. **Stock:** Birch. **Sights:** Gold bead front, folding rear. **Features:** All-steel receiver has integral Ruger scope bases for the included 1" rings. Introduced 1999. Made in U.S.A. by Sturm, Ruger & Co.

Price: 10/22RBM $499.00

SAVAGE MODEL 64G AUTO RIFLE

Caliber: 22 LR, 10-shot magazine. **Barrel:** 20", 21". **Weight:** 5-1/2 lbs. **Length:** 40", 41". **Stock:** Walnut-finished hardwood with Monte Carlo-type comb, checkered grip and forend. **Sights:** Bead front, open adjustable rear. Receiver grooved for scope mounting. **Features:** Thumb-operated rotating safety. Blue finish. Side ejection, bolt hold-open device. Introduced 1990. Made in Canada, from Savage Arms.

Price: $151.00
Price: Model 64FSS, stainless $196.00
Price: Model 64F, black synthetic stock $135.00
Price: Model 64GXP Package Gun includes 4x15 scope and mounts $156.00
Price: Model 64FXP (black stock, 4x15 scope) $144.00
Price: Model 64F Camo $166.00

Savage Model 64FV Auto Rifle

Similar to the Model 64F except has heavy 21" barrel with recessed crown; no sights provided-comes with Weaver-style bases. Introduced 1998. Imported from Canada by Savage Arms, Inc.

Price: $182.00
Price: Model 64FVSS, stainless $235.00

THOMPSON/CENTER 22 LR CLASSIC RIFLE

Caliber: 22 LR, 8-shot magazine. **Barrel:** 22" match-grade. **Weight:** 5-1/2 pounds. **Length:** 39-1/2" overall. **Stock:** Satin-finished American walnut with Monte Carlo-type comb and pistol grip cap, swivel studs. **Sights:** Ramp-style front and fully adjustable rear, both with fiber optics. **Features:** All-steel receiver drilled and tapped for scope mounting; barrel threaded to receiver; thumb-operated safety; trigger guard safety lock included. New .22 Classic Benchmark TGT target rifle variant has 18" heavy barrel, brown laminated target stock, blued with matte finish, 10-shot magazine and no sights; drilled and tapped.

Price: T/C 22 LR Classic (blue) $370.00
Price: T/C 22 LR Classic Benchmark $472.00

TAURUS MODEL 63 RIFLE

Caliber: 22 LR, 10-shot tube-fed magazine. **Barrel:** 23". **Weight:** 72 oz. **Length:** 32-1/2". **Stock:** Hand-fitted walnut-finished hardwood. **Sights:** Adjustable rear, fixed front. **Features:** Manual safety, metal buttplate, can accept Taurus tang sight. Charged and cocked with operating plunger at front of forend. Available in blue or polished stainless steel.

Price: 63 .... $295.00
Price: 63SS $311.00

RIMFIRE RIFLES — LEVER & SLIDE ACTION

Classic and modern models for sport and utility, including training.

Browning BL-22

Henry Lever-Action 22

Henry Golden Boy 22

Henry Pump-Action 22

Marlin Model 39AS

BROWNING BL-22 LEVER-ACTION RIFLE

Caliber: 22 S (22), L (17) or LR (15), tubular magazine. **Barrel:** 20" round tapered. **Weight:** 5 lbs. **Length:** 36-3/4" overall. **Stock:** Walnut, two-piece straight grip Western style. **Sights:** Bead post front, folding-leaf rear. **Features:** Short throw lever, half-cock safety, receiver grooved for tip-off scope mounts, gold-colored trigger. Imported from Japan by Browning.

Price: Grade I **$415.00**
Price: Grade II (engraved receiver, checkered grip and forend) . . **$471.00**
Price: Classic, Grade I (blued trigger, no checkering) **$415.00**
Price: Classic, Grade II (cut checkering, satin wood finish, polished blueing) **$471.00**

HENRY LEVER-ACTION 22

Caliber: 22 Long Rifle (15-shot). **Barrel:** 18-1/4" round. **Weight:** 5-1/2 lbs. **Length:** 34" overall. **Stock:** Walnut. **Sights:** Hooded blade front, open adjustable rear. **Features:** Polished blue finish; full-length tubular magazine; side ejection; receiver grooved for scope mounting. Introduced 1997. Made in U.S.A. by Henry Repeating Arms Co.

Price: **$239.95**
Price: Youth model (33" overall, 11-rounds 22 LR) **$229.95**

HENRY GOLDEN BOY 22 LEVER-ACTION RIFLE

Caliber: 22 LR, 22 Magnum, 16-shot. **Barrel:** 20" octagonal. **Weight:** 6.25 lbs. **Length:** 38" overall. **Stock:** American walnut. **Sights:** Blade front, open rear. **Features:** Brasslite receiver, brass buttplate, blued barrel and lever. Introduced 1998. Made in U.S.A. from Henry Repeating Arms Co.

Price: **$379.95**
Price: Magnum **$449.95**

HENRY PUMP-ACTION 22 PUMP RIFLE

Caliber: 22 LR, 15-shot. **Barrel:** 18.25". **Weight:** 5.5 lbs. **Length:** NA. **Stock:** American walnut. **Sights:** Bead on ramp front, open adjustable rear. **Features:** Polished blue finish; receiver groved for scope mount; grooved slide handle; two barrel bands. Introduced 1998. Made in U.S.A. from Henry Repeating Arms Co.

Price: **$249.95**

MARLIN MODEL 39A GOLDEN LEVER-ACTION RIFLE

Caliber: 22, S (26), L (21), LR (19), tubular mag. **Barrel:** 24" Micro-Groove®. **Weight:** 6-1/2 lbs. **Length:** 40" overall. **Stock:** Checkered American black walnut; Mar-Shield® finish. Swivel studs; rubber butt pad. **Sights:** Bead ramp front with detachable Wide-Scan™ hood, folding rear semi-buckhorn adjustable for windage and elevation. **Features:** Hammer block safety; rebounding hammer. Takedown action, receiver tapped for scope mount (supplied), offset hammer spur, gold-plated steel trigger. From Marlin Firearms.

Price: **$552.00**

Remington Model 572 BDL Deluxe Fieldmaster

Ruger Model 96/22

Taurus 62R

Taurus 72C-SS

Winchester 9422 Legacy

REMINGTON 572 BDL DELUXE FIELDMASTER PUMP RIFLE

Caliber: 22 S (20), L (17) or LR (15), tubular mag. **Barrel:** 21" round tapered. **Weight:** 5-1/2 lbs. **Length:** 40" overall. **Stock:** Walnut with checkered pistol grip and slide handle. **Sights:** Big game. **Features:** Cross-bolt safety; removing inner magazine tube converts rifle to single shot; receiver grooved for tip-off scope mount.

Price: **$407.00**

RUGER MODEL 96 LEVER-ACTION RIFLE

Caliber: 22 LR, 10 rounds; 22 WMR, 9 rounds; 44 Magnum, 4 rounds; 17 HMR 9 rounds. **Barrel:** 18-1/2". **Weight:** 5-1/4 lbs**. Length:** 37-1/4" overall. **Stock:** Hardwood. **Sights:** Gold bead front, folding leaf rear. **Features:** Sliding cross button safety, visible cocking indicator; short-throw lever action. Introduced 1996. Made in U.S.A. by Sturm, Ruger & Co.

Price: 96/22 (22 LR) **$349.00**
Price: 96/22M (22 WMR) **$375.00**
Price: 96/22M (44 Mag.) **$525.00**
***New!* Price:** 96/17M (17 HMR) **$375.00**

TAURUS MODEL 62 PUMP RIFLE

Caliber: 22 LR, 12- or 13-shot. **Barrel:** 16-1/2" or 23" round. **Weight:** 72 oz-80 oz. **Length:** 39" overall. **Stock:** Premium hardwood. **Sights:** Adjustable rear, bead blade front, optional tang. **Features:** Blue, case hardened or stainless, bolt-mounted safety, pump action, manual firing pin block, integral security lock system. Imported from Brazil by Taurus International.

Price: M62C (blue) **$280.00**
Price: M62C-CH (case hardened-blue) **$280.00**
Price: M62CCH-T (case hardened-blue) **$358.00**
Price: M62C-SS (stainless steel) **$295.00**
Price: M62CSS-T (stainless steel) **$373.00**
Price: M62C-SS-Y (stainless steel) **$327.00**
Price: M62C-T (blue) **$358.00**
Price: M62C-Y (blue) **$311.00**
Price: M62R (blue) **$280.00**
Price: M62R-CH (case hardened-blue) **$280.00**
Price: M62RCH-T (case hardened-blue) **$358.00**
Price: M62R-SS (stainless steel) **$295.00**
Price: M62RSS-T (stainless steel) **$373.00**
Price: M62R-T (blue) **$358.00**

Taurus Model 72 Pump Rifle

Same as Model 62 except chambered in 22 Magnum or .17 HMR; 16-1/2" bbl. holds 10-12 shots, 23" bbl. holds 11-13 shots. Weighs 72 oz.-80 oz. Introduced 2001. Imported from Brazil by Taurus International.

Price: M72C (blue) **$295.00**
Price: M72C-CH (case hardened-blue) **$295.00**
Price: M72CCH-T (case hardened-blue) **$373.00**
Price: M72C-SS (stainless steel) **$311.00**
Price: M72CSS-T (stainless steel) **$389.00**
Price: M72C-T (blue) **$373.00**
Price: M72R (blue) **$295.00**
Price: M72R-CH (case hardened-blue) **$295.00**
Price: M72RCH-T (case hardened-blue) **$373.00**
Price: M72R-SS (stainless steel) **$311.00**
Price: M72RSS-T (stainless steel) **$389.00**
Price: M72R-T (blue) **$373.00**

WINCHESTER MODEL 9422 LEVER-ACTION RIFLES

Caliber: 22 LR, 22 WMR, tubular magazine. **Barrel:** 20-1/2". **Weight:** 6-1/4 lbs. **Length:** 37-1/8" overall. **Stock:** American walnut, two-piece, straight grip (Traditional) or semi-pistol grip (Legacy). **Sights:** Hooded ramp front, adjustable semi-buckhorn rear. **Features:** Side ejection, receiver grooved for scope mounting, takedown action. From U.S. Repeating Arms Co.

Price: Traditional, 22 LR 15-shot **$465.00**
Price: Traditional, 22WMR, 11-shot **$487.00**
Price: Legacy, 22 LR 15-shot **$498.00**
Price: Legacy 22 WMR, 11-shot **$521.00**

RIMFIRE RIFLES — BOLT ACTIONS & SINGLE SHOTS

Includes models for a variety of sports, utility and competitive shooting.

Anschutz 1518D Luxus

Anschutz 1710D

Chipmunk Deluxe

CZ 452 Lux

ANSCHUTZ 1416D/1516D CLASSIC RIFLES

Caliber: 22 LR (1416D), 5-shot clip; 22 WMR (1516D), 4-shot clip. **Barrel:** 22-1/2". **Weight:** 6 lbs. **Length:** 41" overall. **Stock:** European hardwood with walnut finish; classic style with straight comb, checkered pistol grip and forend. **Sights:** Hooded ramp front, folding leaf rear. **Features:** Uses Match 64 action. Adjustable single stage trigger. Receiver grooved for scope mounting. Imported from Germany by AcuSport Corp.

Price: 1416D, 22 LR **$755.95**
Price: 1516D, 22 WMR **$779.95**
Price: 1416D Classic left-hand **$679.95**

Anschutz 1416D/1516D Walnut Luxus Rifles

Similar to the Classic models except have European walnut stocks with Monte Carlo cheekpiece, slim forend with Schnabel tip, cut checkering on grip and forend. Introduced 1997. Imported from Germany by AcuSport Corp.

Price: 1416D (22 LR) **$755.95**
Price: 1516D (22 WMR) **$779.95**

ANSCHUTZ 1518D LUXUS BOLT-ACTION RIFLE

Caliber: 22 WMR, 4-shot magazine. **Barrel:** 19-3/4". **Weight:** 5-1/2 lbs. **Length:** 37-1/2" overall. **Stock:** European walnut. **Sights:** Blade on ramp front, folding leaf rear. **Features:** Receiver grooved for scope mounting; single stage trigger; skip-line checkering; rosewood forend tip; sling swivels. Imported from Germany by AcuSport Corp.

Price: **$1,186.95**

ANSCHUTZ 1710D CUSTOM RIFLE

Caliber: 22 LR, 5-shot clip. **Barrel:** 24-1/4". **Weight:** 7-3/8 lbs. **Length:** 42-1/2" overall. **Stock:** Select European walnut. **Sights:** Hooded ramp front, folding leaf rear; drilled and tapped for scope mounting. **Features:** Match 54 action with adjustable single-stage trigger; roll-over Monte Carlo cheekpiece, slim forend with Schnabel tip, Wundhammer palm swell on pistol grip, rosewood gripcap with white diamond insert; skip-line checker-ing on grip and forend. Introduced 1988. Imported from Germany by AcuSport Corp.

Price: **$1,289.95**

CHIPMUNK SINGLE SHOT RIFLE

Caliber: 22 LR, 22 WMR, single shot. **Barrel:** 16-1/8". **Weight:** About 2-1/2 lbs. **Length:** 30" overall. Stocks: American walnut. **Sights:** Post on ramp front, peep rear adjustable for windage and elevation. **Features:** Drilled and tapped for scope mounting using special Chipmunk base ($13.95). Engraved model also available. Made in U.S.A. Introduced 1982. From Rogue Rifle Co., Inc.

Price: Standard. **$194.25**
Price: Standard 22 WMR **$209.95**
Price: Deluxe (better wood, checkering). **$246.95**
Price: Deluxe 22 WMR **$262.95**
Price: Laminated stock **$209.95**
Price: Laminated stock, 22 WMR **$225.95**
Price: Bull barrel models of above, add **$16.00**

CHIPMUNK TM (TARGET MODEL)

Caliber: 22 S, L, or LR. **Barrel:** 18" blue. **Weight:** 5 lbs. **Length:** 33". Stocks: Walnut with accessory rail. **Sights:** 1/4 minute micrometer adjustable. **Features:** Manually cocking single shot bolt action, blue receiver, adjustable butt plate and butt pad.

Price: **$329.95**

COOPER MODEL 57-M BOLT-ACTION RIFLE

Caliber: 22 LR, 22 WMR, 17 HMR. **Barrel:** 23-3/4" stainless steel or 41-40 match grade. **Weight:** 6.6 lbs. **Stock:** Claro walnut, 22 lpi hand checkering. **Sights:** None furnished. **Features:** Three rear locking lug, repeating bolt-action with 5-shot mag. Fully adjustable trigger. Many options. Made 100% in the U.S.A. by Cooper Firearms of Montana, Inc.

Price: Classic **$1,100.00**
Price: LVT **$1,295.00**
Price: Custom Classic **$1,895.00**
Price: Western Classic **$2,495.00**

CZ 452 LUX BOLT-ACTION RIFLE

Caliber: 22 LR, 22 WMR, 5-shot detachable magazine. **Barrel:** 24.8". **Weight:** 6.6 lbs. **Length:** 42.63" overall. **Stock:** Walnut with checkered pistol grip. **Sights:** Hooded front, fully adjustable tangent rear. **Features:** All-steel construction, adjustable trigger, polished blue finish. Imported from the Czech Republic by CZ-USA.

Price: 22 LR, 22 WMR **$378.00**

CZ 452 Varmint

CZ 452 American Classic

Henry "Mini" Bolt 22

Kimber 22 Classic

Kimber 22 SuperAmerica

CZ 452 Varmint Rifle

Similar to the Lux model except has heavy 20.8" barrel; stock has beavertail forend; weighs 7 lbs.; no sights furnished. Available only in 22 LR. Imported from the Czech Republic by CZ-USA.

Price: **$407.00**

CZ 452 American Classic Bolt-Action Rifle

Similar to the CZ 452 M 2E Lux except has classic-style stock of Circassian walnut; 22.5" free-floating barrel with recessed target crown; receiver dovetail for scope mounting. No open sights furnished. Introduced 1999. Imported from the Czech Republic by CZ-USA.

Price: 22 LR, 22 WMR **$420.00**

HARRINGTON & RICHARDSON ULTRA HEAVY BARREL 22 MAG RIFLE

Caliber: 22 WMR, single shot. **Barrel:** 22" bull. **Stock:** Cinnamon laminated wood with Monte Carlo cheekpiece. **Sights:** None furnished; scope mount rail included. **Features:** Hand-checkered stock and forend; deep-crown rifling; tuned trigger; trigger locking system; hammer extension. Introduced 2001. From H&R 1871 LLC.

Price: **$193.00**

HENRY "MINI" BOLT 22 RIFLE

Caliber: 22 LR, single shot. **Barrel:** 16" stainless, 8-groove rifling. **Weight:** 3.25 lbs. **Length:** 30", LOP 11-1/2". **Stock:** Synthetic, pistol grip, wraparound checkering and beavertail forearm. **Sights:** William Fire sights. **Features:** One piece bolt configuration manually operated safety. Ideal for beginners or ladies.

Price: **$169.95**

KIMBER 22 CLASSIC BOLT-ACTION RIFLE

Caliber: 22 LR, 5-shot magazine. **Barrel:** 18", 22", 24" match grade; 11-degree target crown. **Weight:** 5-8 lbs. **Length:** 35"-43". **Stock:** Classic Claro walnut, hand-cut checkering, steel gripcap, swivel studs. **Sights:** None, drilled and tapped. **Features:** All-new action with Mauser-style full-length claw extractor, two-position wing safety, match trigger, pillar-bedded action with recoil lug. Introduced 1999. Made in U.S.A. by Kimber Mfg., Inc.

Price: New Classic **$1,085.00**
Price: Classic **$949.00**
Price: Hunter **$678.00**
Price: Youth **$746.00**

Kimber 22 SuperAmerica Bolt-Action Rifle

Similar to 22 Classic except has AAA Claro walnut stock with wraparound 22 l.p.i. hand-cut checkering, ebony forened tip, beaded cheekpiece. Introduced 1999. Made in U.S.A. by Kimber Mfg., Inc.

Price: **$1,764.00**

Kimber 22 SVT Bolt-Action Rilfe

Similar to 22 Classic except has 18" stainless steel, fluted bull barrel, gray laminated, high-comb target-style stock with deep pistol grip, high comb, beavertail forend with bipod stud. Weighs 7.5 lbs., overall length 36.5". Matte finish on action. Introduced 1999. Made in U.S.A. by Kimber Mfg., Inc.

Price: **$949.00**

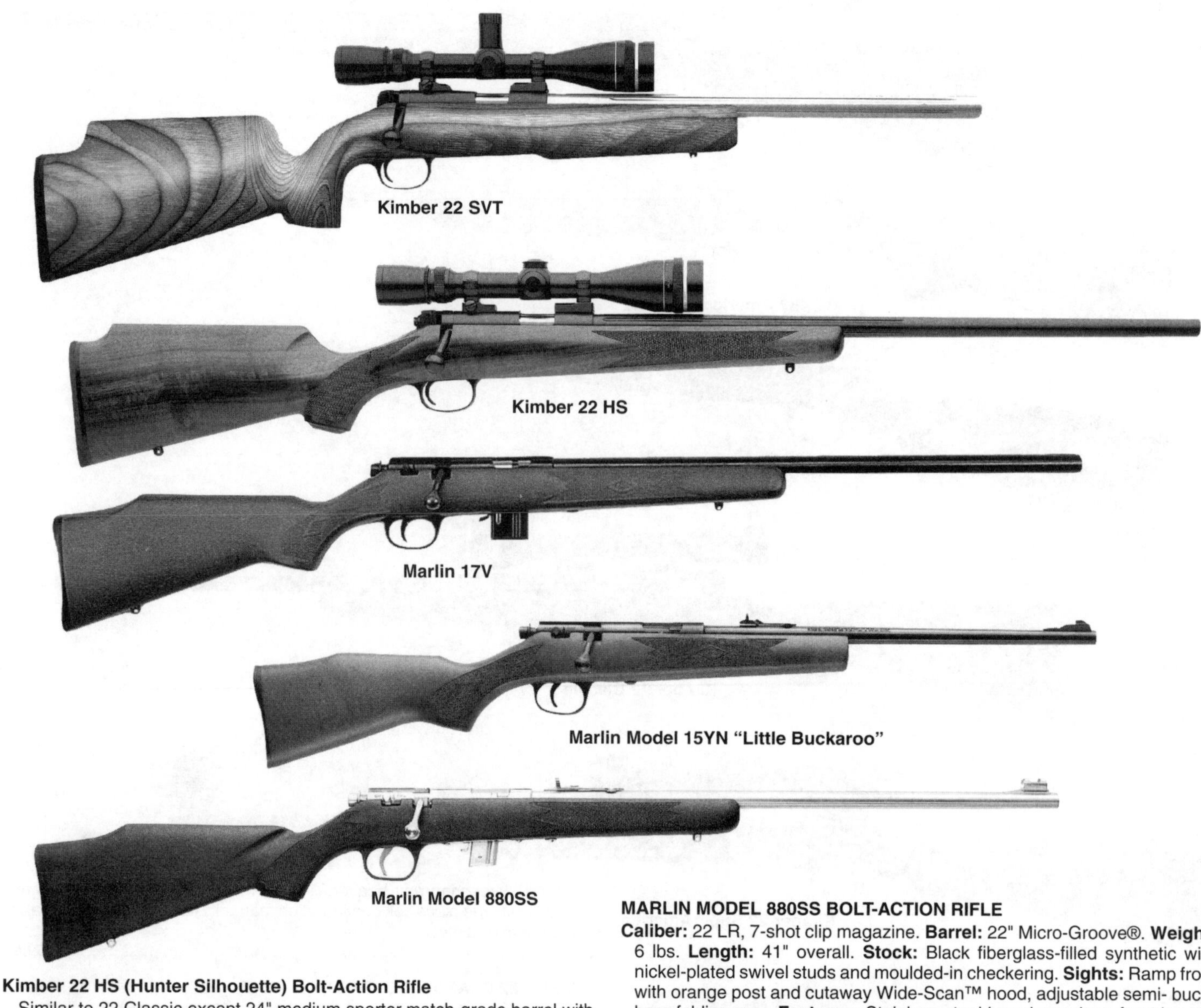

Kimber 22 SVT

Kimber 22 HS

Marlin 17V

Marlin Model 15YN "Little Buckaroo"

Marlin Model 880SS

Kimber 22 HS (Hunter Silhouette) Bolt-Action Rifle

Similar to 22 Classic except 24" medium sporter match-grade barrel with half-fluting; high comb, walnut, Monte Carlo target stock with 18 l.p.i. checkering; matte blue metal finish. Introduced 1999. Made in U.S.A. by Kimber Mfg., Inc.

Price: **$814.00**

MARLIN MODEL 17V HORNADY MAGNUM

Caliber: 17 Magnum, 7-shot. **Barrel:** 22. **Weight:** 6 lbs., stainless 7 lbs. **Length:** 41". **Stock:** Checkered walnut Monte Carlo SS, laminated black/grey. **Sights:** No sights but receiver grooved. **Features:** Swivel studs, positive thumb safety, red cocking indicator, safety lock, SS 1" brushed aluminum scope rings.

Price: **$269.00**

Price: Bead blasted SS barrel & receiver **$402.00**

MARLIN MODEL 15YN "LITTLE BUCKAROO"

Caliber: 22 S, L, LR, single shot. **Barrel:** 16-1/4" Micro-Groove®. **Weight:** 4-1/4 lbs. **Length:** 33-1/4" overall. **Stock:** One-piece walnut-finished, press-checkered Maine birch with Monte Carlo; Mar-Shield® finish. **Sights:** Ramp front, adjustable open rear. **Features:** Beginner's rifle with thumb safety, easy-load feed throat, red cocking indicator. Receiver grooved for scope mounting. Introduced 1989.

Price: **$209.00**

Price: Stainless steel with fire sights...................... **$233.00**

MARLIN MODEL 880SS BOLT-ACTION RIFLE

Caliber: 22 LR, 7-shot clip magazine. **Barrel:** 22" Micro-Groove®. **Weight:** 6 lbs. **Length:** 41" overall. **Stock:** Black fiberglass-filled synthetic with nickel-plated swivel studs and moulded-in checkering. **Sights:** Ramp front with orange post and cutaway Wide-Scan™ hood, adjustable semi- buckhorn folding rear. **Features:** Stainless steel barrel, receiver, front breech bolt and striker; receiver grooved for scope mounting. Introduced 1994. Model 880SQ (Squirrel Rifle) is similar but has heavy 22" barrel. Made in U.S.A. by Marlin.

Price: (Model 880SS) **$316.00**

Price: (Model 880SQ) **$330.00**

Marlin Model 81TS Bolt-Action Rifle

Same as Marlin 880SS except blued steel, tubular magazine, holds 17 Long Rifle cartridges. Weighs 6 lbs.

Price: **$213.00**

Marlin Model 880SQ Squirrel Rifle

Similar to Model 880SS except uses heavy target barrel. Black synthetic stock with moulded-in checkering, double bedding screws, matte blue finish. Without sights, no dovetail or filler screws; receiver grooved for scope mount. Weighs 7 lbs. Introduced 1996. Made in U.S.A. by Marlin.

Price: **$322.00**

Marlin Model 25N Bolt-Action Repeater

Similar to Marlin 880, except walnut-finished hardwood stock, adjustable open rear sight, ramp front.

Price: **$212.00**

Price: With 4x scope and mount.............................. **$220.00**

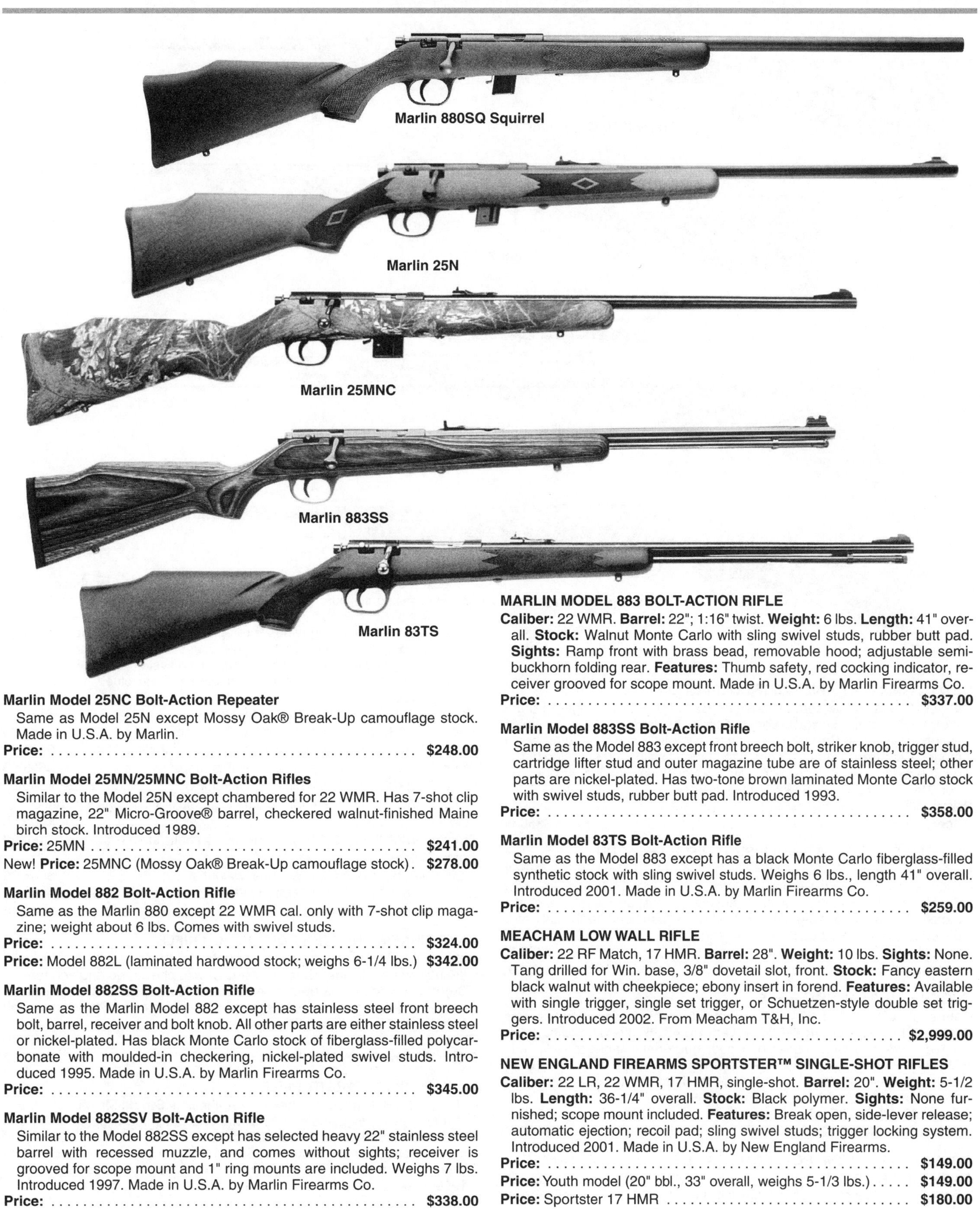

Marlin 880SQ Squirrel

Marlin 25N

Marlin 25MNC

Marlin 883SS

Marlin 83TS

Marlin Model 25NC Bolt-Action Repeater

Same as Model 25N except Mossy Oak® Break-Up camouflage stock. Made in U.S.A. by Marlin.

Price: **$248.00**

Marlin Model 25MN/25MNC Bolt-Action Rifles

Similar to the Model 25N except chambered for 22 WMR. Has 7-shot clip magazine, 22" Micro-Groove® barrel, checkered walnut-finished Maine birch stock. Introduced 1989.

Price: 25MN **$241.00**

New! **Price:** 25MNC (Mossy Oak® Break-Up camouflage stock) . **$278.00**

Marlin Model 882 Bolt-Action Rifle

Same as the Marlin 880 except 22 WMR cal. only with 7-shot clip magazine; weight about 6 lbs. Comes with swivel studs.

Price: **$324.00**

Price: Model 882L (laminated hardwood stock; weighs 6-1/4 lbs.) **$342.00**

Marlin Model 882SS Bolt-Action Rifle

Same as the Marlin Model 882 except has stainless steel front breech bolt, barrel, receiver and bolt knob. All other parts are either stainless steel or nickel-plated. Has black Monte Carlo stock of fiberglass-filled polycarbonate with moulded-in checkering, nickel-plated swivel studs. Introduced 1995. Made in U.S.A. by Marlin Firearms Co.

Price: **$345.00**

Marlin Model 882SSV Bolt-Action Rifle

Similar to the Model 882SS except has selected heavy 22" stainless steel barrel with recessed muzzle, and comes without sights; receiver is grooved for scope mount and 1" ring mounts are included. Weighs 7 lbs. Introduced 1997. Made in U.S.A. by Marlin Firearms Co.

Price: **$338.00**

MARLIN MODEL 883 BOLT-ACTION RIFLE

Caliber: 22 WMR. **Barrel:** 22"; 1:16" twist. **Weight:** 6 lbs. **Length:** 41" overall. **Stock:** Walnut Monte Carlo with sling swivel studs, rubber butt pad. **Sights:** Ramp front with brass bead, removable hood; adjustable semi-buckhorn folding rear. **Features:** Thumb safety, red cocking indicator, receiver grooved for scope mount. Made in U.S.A. by Marlin Firearms Co.

Price: **$337.00**

Marlin Model 883SS Bolt-Action Rifle

Same as the Model 883 except front breech bolt, striker knob, trigger stud, cartridge lifter stud and outer magazine tube are of stainless steel; other parts are nickel-plated. Has two-tone brown laminated Monte Carlo stock with swivel studs, rubber butt pad. Introduced 1993.

Price: **$358.00**

Marlin Model 83TS Bolt-Action Rifle

Same as the Model 883 except has a black Monte Carlo fiberglass-filled synthetic stock with sling swivel studs. Weighs 6 lbs., length 41" overall. Introduced 2001. Made in U.S.A. by Marlin Firearms Co.

Price: **$259.00**

MEACHAM LOW WALL RIFLE

Caliber: 22 RF Match, 17 HMR. **Barrel:** 28". **Weight:** 10 lbs. **Sights:** None. Tang drilled for Win. base, 3/8" dovetail slot, front. **Stock:** Fancy eastern black walnut with cheekpiece; ebony insert in forend. **Features:** Available with single trigger, single set trigger, or Schuetzen-style double set triggers. Introduced 2002. From Meacham T&H, Inc.

Price: **$2,999.00**

NEW ENGLAND FIREARMS SPORTSTER™ SINGLE-SHOT RIFLES

Caliber: 22 LR, 22 WMR, 17 HMR, single-shot. **Barrel:** 20". **Weight:** 5-1/2 lbs. **Length:** 36-1/4" overall. **Stock:** Black polymer. **Sights:** None furnished; scope mount included. **Features:** Break open, side-lever release; automatic ejection; recoil pad; sling swivel studs; trigger locking system. Introduced 2001. Made in U.S.A. by New England Firearms.

Price: **$149.00**

Price: Youth model (20" bbl., 33" overall, weighs 5-1/3 lbs.) **$149.00**

Price: Sportster 17 HMR **$180.00**

Ruger K77/22 Varmint

Ruger 77/22R

Sako Finnfire

Savage Mark I-G

NEW ULTRA LIGHT ARMS 20RF BOLT-ACTION RIFLE

Caliber: 22 LR, single shot or repeater. **Barrel:** Douglas, length to order. **Weight:** 5-1/4 lbs. **Length:** Varies. **Stock:** Kevlar®/graphite composite, variety of finishes. **Sights:** None furnished; drilled and tapped for scope mount. **Features:** Timney trigger, hand-lapped action, button-rifled barrel, hand-bedded action, recoil pad, sling-swivel studs, optional Jewell Trigger. Made in U.S.A. by New Ultra Light Arms.

Price: 20 RF single shot **$800.00**
Price: 20 RF repeater **$850.00**

ROSSI MATCHED PAIR SINGLE-SHOT RIFLE/SHOTGUN

Caliber: 22 LR or 22 Mag. **Barrel:** 18-1/2" or 23". **Weight:** 6 lbs. **Stock:** Hardwood (brown or black finish). **Sights:** Fully adjustable front and rear. **Features:** Break-open breech, transfer-bar manual safety, includes matched 410-, 20- or 12-gauge shotgun barrel with bead front sight. Introduced 2001. Imported by BrazTech/Taurus.

Price: blue **$139.95**
Price: stainless steel **$169.95**

RUGER K77/22 VARMINT RIFLE

Caliber: 22 LR, 10-shot, 22 WMR, 9-shot detachable rotary magazine. **Barrel:** 24", heavy. **Weight:** 6-7/8 lbs. **Length:** 43.25" overall. **Stock:** Laminated hardwood with rubber butt pad, quick-detachable swivel studs. **Sights:** None furnished. Comes with Ruger 1" scope rings. **Features:** Stainless steel or blued finish. Three-position safety, dual extractors. Stock has wide, flat forend. Introduced 1993.

Price: K77/22VBZ, 22 LR **$645.00**
Price: K77/22VMBZ, 22 WMR **$645.00**

RUGER 77/22 RIMFIRE BOLT-ACTION RIFLE

Caliber: 22 LR, 10-shot rotary magazine; 22 WMR, 9-shot rotary magazine. **Barrel:** 20". **Weight:** About 5-3/4 lbs. **Length:** 39-3/4" overall. **Stock:** Checkered American walnut, laminated hardwood, or synthetic stocks, stainless sling swivels. **Sights:** Brass bead front, adjustable folding leaf rear or plain barrel with 1" Ruger rings. **Features:** Mauser-type action uses Ruger's rotary magazine. Three-position safety, simplified bolt stop, patented bolt locking system. Uses the dual-screw barrel attachment system of the 10/22 rifle. Integral scope mounting system with 1" Ruger rings. Blued model introduced 1983. Stainless steel and blued with synthetic stock introduced 1989.

Price: 77/22R (no sights, rings, walnut stock). **$580.00**
Price: 77/22RS (open sights, rings, walnut stock) **$605.00**
Price: K77/22RP (stainless, no sights, rings, synthetic stock) . . . **$580.00**
Price: K77/22RSP (stainless, open sights, rings, synthetic stock) **$605.00**
Price: 77/22RM (22 WMR, blue, walnut stock) **$580.00**
Price: K77/22RSMP (22 WMR, stainless, open sights, rings, synthetic stock) **$605.00**
Price: K77/22RMP (22 WMR, stainless, synthetic stock) **$580.00**
Price: 77/22RSM (22 WMR, blue, open sights, rings, walnut stock) **$585.00**
New!! **Price:** K77/17RM, 17RMP, 17VMBBZ (17 HMR, walnut, synthetic or laminate stocks, no sights, rings, blued or stainless) **$580.00 to $645.00**

SAKO FINNFIRE HUNTER BOLT-ACTION RIFLE

Caliber: 22 LR, 5-shot magazine. **Barrel:** 22". **Weight:** 5.75 lbs. **Length:** 39-1/2" overall. **Stock:** European walnut with checkered grip and forend. **Sights:** Hooded blade front, open adjustable rear. **Features:** Adjustable single-stage trigger; has 50-degree bolt lift. Introduced 1994. Imported from Finland by Beretta USA.

Price: **$854.00**
Price: Varmint (heavy barrel) **$896.00**

SAKO FINNFIRE TARGET RIFLE

Caliber: 22 LR. **Barrel:** 22"; heavy, free-floating. **Stock:** Match style of European walnut; adjustable cheekpiece and buttplate; stippled pistol grip and forend. **Sights:** None furnished; has 11mm integral dovetail scope mount. **Features:** Based on the Sako P94S action with two bolt locking lugs, 50-degree bolt lift and 30mm throw; adjustable trigger. Introduced 1999. Imported from Finland by Beretta USA.

Price: **$951.00**

Savage Mark I-Y

Savage Mark II-BV

Savage Mark II-FXP

Savage Mark II-FSS

Savage Model 93G

SAVAGE MARK I-G BOLT-ACTION RIFLE

Caliber: 22 LR, single shot. **Barrel:** 20-3/4". **Weight:** 5-1/2 lbs. **Length:** 39-1/2" overall. **Stock:** Walnut-finished hardwood with Monte Carlo-type comb, checkered grip and forend. **Sights:** Bead front, open adjustable rear. Receiver grooved for scope mounting. **Features:** Thumb-operated rotating safety. Blue finish. Rifled or smooth bore. Introduced 1990. Made in Canada, from Savage Arms Inc.

Price: Mark IG, rifled or smooth bore, right- or left-handed **$144.00**
Price: Mark I-GY (Youth), 19" bbl., 37" overall, 5 lbs. **$144.00**
Price: Mark I-LY (Youth), 19" bbl., color laminate **$175.00**
Price: Mark I-Y (Youth), 19" bbl., camo **$174.00**
Price: Mark I-GYXP (Youth), with scope **$162.00**
Price: Mark I-GSB (22 LR shot cartridge) **$144.00**

SAVAGE MARK II BOLT-ACTION RIFLE

Caliber: 22 LR, 10-shot magazine. **Barrel:** 20-1/2". **Weight:** 5-1/2 lbs. **Length:** 39-1/2" overall. **Stock:** Walnut-finished hardwood with Monte Carlo-type comb, checkered grip and forend. **Sights:** Bead front, open adjustable rear. Receiver grooved for scope mounting. **Features:** Thumb-operated rotating safety. Blue finish. Introduced 1990. Made in Canada, from Savage Arms, Inc.

Price: Mark II-BV **$248.00**
Price: Mark II Camo **$174.00**
Price: Mark II-GY (youth), 19" barrel, 37" overall, 5 lbs. **$156.00**
Price: Mark II-GL, left-hand **$156.00**
Price: Mark II-GLY (youth) left-hand $156.00
Price: Mark II-GXP Package Gun (comes with 4x15 scope), right- or left-handed **$164.00**
Price: Mark II-FXP (as above with black synthetic stock) **$151.00**
Price: Mark II-F (as above, no scope) **$144.00**
Price: Mark II-FVXP (as above, with scope and rings) **$252.00**

Savage Mark II-FSS Stainless Rifle

Similar to the Mark II-G except has stainless steel barreled action and graphite/polymer filled stock; free-floated barrel. Weighs 5 lbs. Introduced 1997. Imported from Canada by Savage Arms, Inc.

Price: **$205.00**

SAVAGE MODEL 93G MAGNUM BOLT-ACTION RIFLE

Caliber: 22 WMR, 5-shot magazine. **Barrel:** 20-3/4". **Weight:** 5-3/4 lbs. **Length:** 39-1/2" overall. **Stock:** Walnut-finished hardwood with Monte Carlo-type comb, checkered grip and forend. **Sights:** Bead front, adjustable open rear. Receiver grooved for scope mount. **Features:** Thumb-operated rotary safety. Blue finish. Introduced 1994. Made in Canada, from Savage Arms.

Price: **$182.00**
Price: Model 93F (as above with black graphite/fiberglass stock) **$175.00**

Savage Model 93FSS Magnum Rifle

Similar to Model 93G except stainless steel barreled action and black synthetic stock with positive checkering. Weighs 5-1/2 lbs. Introduced 1997. Imported from Canada by Savage Arms, Inc.

Price: **$236.00**

Savage Model 93FVSS Magnum Rifle

Similar to Model 93FSS Magnum except 21" heavy barrel with recessed target-style crown, satin-finished stainless barreled action, black graphite/fiberglass stock. Drilled and tapped for scope mounting; comes with Weaver-style bases. Introduced 1998. Imported from Canada by Savage Arms, Inc.

Price: .... **$252.00**, With scope **$287.00**

Savage Model 93FSS

Savage Model 93FVSS

Savage Model 30G Stevens "Favorite"

Savage Cub G Youth

Winchester Model 52B

Winchester Model 1885 Low Wall

SAVAGE MARK 30G STEVENS "FAVORITE"

Caliber: 22 LR, 22WMR - Model 30GM, 17 HMR - Model 30R17. **Barrel:** 21". **Weight:** 4.25 lbs. **Length:** 36.75". **Stock:** Walnut, straight grip, Schnabel forend. **Sights:** Adjustable rear, bead post front. **Features:** Lever action falling block, inertia firing pin system, Model 30G half octagonal bbl. Model 30GM full octagonal bbl.

Price: Model 30G **$221.00**

Price: Model 30GM **$258.00**

Price: Model 30R17 . . . . **$284.00**

SAVAGE CUB G YOUTH

Caliber: 22 S, L, LR. **Barrel:** 16.125" **Weight:** 3.3 lbs. **Length:** 33" **Stock:** Walnut finished hardwood. **Sights:** Bead post, front; peep, rear. **Features:** Mini single shot bolt action, free-floating button-rifled barrel, blued finish. From Savage Arms.

Price: **$149.00**

WINCHESTER MODEL 52B BOLT-ACTION RIFLE

Caliber: 22 Long Rifle, 5-shot magazine. **Barrel:** 24". **Weight:** 7 lbs. **Length:** 41-3/4" overall. **Stock:** Walnut with checkered grip and forend. **Sights:** None furnished; grooved receiver and drilled and tapped for scope mounting. **Features:** Has Micro Motion trigger adjustable for pull and over-travel; match chamber; detachable magazine. Reintroduced 1997. From U.S. Repeating Arms Co.

Price: **$662.00**

WINCHESTER MODEL 1885 LOW WALL RIMFIRE

Caliber: 17 HMR, single-shot. **Barrel:** 24-1/2"; half-octagon. **Weight:** 8 lbs. **Length:** 41" overall. **Stock:** Walnut. **Sights:** Blade front, semi-buckhorn rear. **Features:** Drilled and tapped for scope mount or tang sight; target chamber. From U.S. Repeating Arms Co.

Price: Grade I **$965.00**

COMPETITION RIFLES — CENTERFIRE & RIMFIRE

Includes models for classic American and ISU target competition and other sporting and competitive shooting.

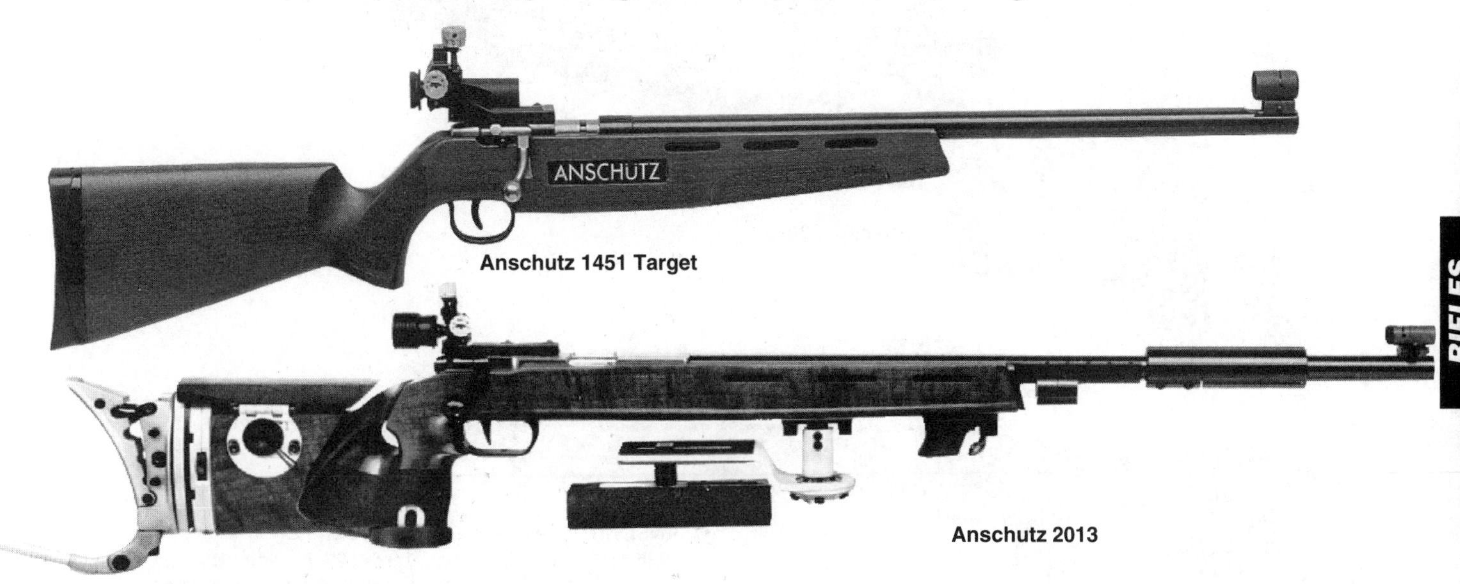

Anschutz 1451 Target

Anschutz 2013

RIFLES

ANSCHUTZ 1451R SPORTER TARGET RIFLE

Caliber: 22 LR, 5-shot magazine. **Barrel:** 22" heavy match. **Weight:** 6.4 lbs. **Length:** 39.75" overall. **Stock:** European hardwood with walnut finish. **Sights:** None furnished. Grooved receiver for scope mounting or Anschutz micrometer rear sight. **Features:** Sliding safety, two-stage trigger. Adjustable buttplate; forend slide rail to accept Anschutz accessories. Imported from Germany by AcuSport Corp.

Price: **$549.00**

ANSCHUTZ 1451 TARGET RIFLE

Caliber: 22 LR. **Barrel:** 22". **Weight:** About 6.5 lbs. **Length:** 40". **Sights:** Optional. Receiver grooved for scope mounting. **Features:** Designed for the beginning junior shooter with adjustable length of pull from 13.25" to 14.25" via removable butt spacers. Two-stage trigger factory set at 2.6 lbs. Introduced 1999. Imported from Germany by Gunsmithing, Inc.

Price: **$347.00**

Price: #6834 Match Sight Set **$227.10**

ANSCHUTZ 1808D-RT SUPER RUNNING TARGET RIFLE

Caliber: 22 LR, single shot. **Barrel:** 32-1/2". **Weight:** 9 lbs. **Length:** 50" overall. **Stock:** European walnut. Heavy beavertail forend; adjustable cheekpiece and buttplate. Stippled grip and forend. **Sights:** None furnished. Grooved for scope mounting. **Features:** Designed for Running Target competition. Nine-way adjustable single-stage trigger, slide safety. Introduced 1991. Imported from Germany by Accuracy International, Gunsmithing, Inc.

Price: Right-hand **$1,364.10**

ANSCHUTZ 1903 MATCH RIFLE

Caliber: 22 LR, single shot. **Barrel:** 25.5", .75" diameter. **Weight:** 10.1 lbs. **Length:** 43.75" overall. **Stock:** Walnut-finished hardwood with adjustable cheekpiece; stippled grip and forend. **Sights:** None furnished. **Features:** Uses Anschutz Match 64 action and #5098 two-stage trigger. A medium weight rifle for intermediate and advanced Junior Match competition. Introduced 1987. Imported from Germany by Accuracy International, Gunsmithing, Inc.

Price: Right-hand **$720.40**

Price: Left-hand **$757.90**

ANSCHUTZ 64-MS R SILHOUETTE RIFLE

Caliber: 22 LR, 5-shot magazine. **Barrel:** 21-1/2", medium heavy; 7/8" diameter. **Weight:** 8 lbs. **Length:** 39.5" overall. **Stock:** Walnut-finished hardwood, silhouette-type. **Sights:** None furnished. **Features:** Uses Match 64 action. Designed for metallic silhouette competition. Stock has stippled checkering, contoured thumb groove with Wundhammer swell. Two-stage #5098 trigger. Slide safety locks sear and bolt. Introduced 1980. Imported from Germany by AcuSport Corp., Accuracy International, Gunsmithing, Inc.

Price: 64-MS R **$704.30**

ANSCHUTZ 2013 BENCHREST RIFLE

Caliber: 22 LR, single shot. **Barrel:** 19.6". **Weight:** About 10.3 lbs. **Length:** 37.75" to 42.5" overall. **Stock:** Benchrest style of European hardwood. Stock length adjustable via spacers and buttplate. **Sights:** None furnished. Receiver grooved for mounts. **Features:** Uses the Anschutz 2013 target action, #5018 two-stage adjustable target trigger factory set at 3.9 oz. Introduced 1994. Imported from Germany by Accuracy International, Gunsmithing, Inc.

Price: **$1,757.20**

Anschutz 2007 Match Rifle

Uses same action as the Model 2013, but has a lighter barrel. European walnut stock in right-hand, true left-hand or extra-short models. Sights optional. Available with 19.6" barrel with extension tube, or 26", both in stainless or blue. Introduced 1998. Imported from Germany by Gunsmithing, Inc., Accuracy International.

Price: Right-hand, blue, no sights **$1,766.60**

Price: Right-hand, blue, no sights, extra-short stock **$1,756.60**

Price: Left-hand, blue, no sights **$1,856.80**

ANSCHUTZ 1827 BIATHLON RIFLE

Caliber: 22 LR, 5-shot magazine. **Barrel:** 21-1/2". **Weight:** 8-1/2 lbs. with sights. **Length:** 42-1/2" overall. **Stock:** European walnut with cheekpiece, stippled pistol grip and forend. **Sights:** Optional globe front specially designed for Biathlon shooting, micrometer rear with hinged snow cap. **Features:** Uses Super Match 54 action and nine-way adjustable trigger; adjustable wooden buttplate, Biathlon butthook, adjustable hand-stop rail. Introduced 1982. Imported from Germany by Accuracy International, Gunsmithing, Inc.

Price: Right-hand, with sights, about . . . . **$1,500.50 to $1,555.00**

Anschutz 1827BT Fortner Biathlon Rifle

Similar to the Anschutz 1827 Biathlon rifle except uses Anschutz/Fortner system straight-pull bolt action, blued or stainless steel barrel. Introduced 1982. Imported from Germany by Accuracy International, Gunsmithing, Inc.

Price: Right-hand, with sights . . . . **$1,908.00 to $2,210.00**

Price: Left-hand, with sights . . . . **$2,099.20 to $2,395.00**

Price: Right-hand, sights, stainless barrel (Gunsmithing, Inc.) . . **$2,045.20**

Anschutz 2012

Anschutz 54.18MS REP

ANSCHUTZ SUPER MATCH SPECIAL MODEL 2013 RIFLE

Caliber: 22 LR, single shot. **Barrel:** 25.9". **Weight:** 13 lbs. **Length:** 41.7-42.9". **Stock:** A thumbhole version made of European walnut, both the cheekpiece and buttplate are highly adjustable. **Sights:** None furnished. **Features:** Developed by Anschütz for women to shoot in the sport rifle category. Stainless or blue. This top of the line rifle was introduced in 1997.

Price: Right-hand, blue, no sights, walnut **$2,219.30**
Price: Right-hand, stainless, no sights, walnut **$2,345.30**
Price: Left-hand, blue, no sights, walnut **$2,319.50**

ANSCHUTZ 2012 SPORT RIFLE

Caliber: 22 LR, 5-shot magazine. **Barrel:** 22.4" match; detachable muzzle tube. **Weight:** 7.9 lbs. **Length:** 40.9" overall. **Stock:** European walnut, thumbhole design. **Sights:** None furnished. **Features:** Uses Anschutz 54.18 barreled action with two-stage match trigger. Introduced 1997. Imported from Germany by Accuracy International, AcuSport Corp.

Price: . . . . **$1,425.00 to $2,219.95**

ANSCHUTZ 1911 PRONE MATCH RIFLE

Caliber: 22 LR, single shot. **Barrel:** 27-1/4". **Weight:** 11 lbs. **Length:** 46" overall. **Stock:** Walnut-finished European hardwood; American prone-style with adjustable cheekpiece, textured pistol grip, forend with swivel rail and adjustable rubber buttplate. **Sights:** None furnished. Receiver grooved for Anschutz sights (extra). **Features:** Two-stage #5018 trigger adjustable from 2.1 to 8.6 oz. Extremely fast lock time. Stainless or blue barrel. Imported from Germany by Accuracy International, Gunsmithing, Inc.

Price: Right-hand, no sights **$1,714.20**

ANSCHUTZ 1912 SPORT RIFLE

Caliber: 22 LR, single shot. **Barrel:** 25.9". **Weight:** About 11.4 lbs. **Length:** 41.7-42.9". **Stock:** European walnut or aluminum. **Sights:** None furnished. **Features:** Light weight sport rifle version. Still uses the 54 match action like the 1913 but weighs 1.5 pounds less. Stainless or blue barrel. Introduced 1997.

Price: Right-hand, blue, no sights, walnut **$1,789.50**
Price: Right-hand, blue, no sights, aluminum **$2,129.80**
Price: Right-hand, stainless, no sights, walnut **$1,910.30**
Price: Left-hand, blue, no sights, walnut **$1,879.00**

ANSCHUTZ 1913 SUPER MATCH RIFLE

Caliber: 22 LR, single shot. **Barrel:** 27.1". **Weight:** About 14.3 lbs. **Length:** 44.8-46". **Stock:** European walnut, color laminate, or aluminum. **Sights:** None furnished. **Features:** Two-stage #5018 trigger. Extremely fast lock time. Stainless or blue barrel.

Price: Right-hand, blue, no sights, walnut stock **$2,262.90**
Price: Right-hand, blue, no sights, color laminate stock **$2,275.10**
Price: Right-hand, blue, no sights, aluminum stock **$2,262.90**
Price: Left-hand, blue, no sights, walnut stock **$2,382.20**

Anschutz 1913 Super Match Rifle

Same as the Model 1911 except European walnut International-type stock with adjustable cheekpiece, or color laminate, both available with straight or lowered forend, adjustable aluminum hook buttplate, adjustable hand stop, weighs 15.5 lbs., 46" overall. Stainless or blue barrel. Imported from Germany by Accuracy International, Gunsmithing, Inc.

Price: Right-hand, blue, no sights, walnut stock . . **$2,139.00 to $2,175.00**
Price: Right-hand, blue, no sights, color laminate stock **$2,199.40**
Price: Right-hand, blue, no sights, walnut, lowered forend **$2,181.80**
Price: Right-hand, blue, no sights, color laminate, lowered forend **$2,242.20**
Price: Left-hand, blue, no sights, walnut stock . . . **$2,233.10 to $2,275.00**

Anschutz 54.18MS REP Deluxe Silhouette Rifle

Same basic action and trigger specifications as the Anschutz 1913 Super Match but with removable 5-shot clip magazine, 22.4" barrel extendable to 30" using optional extension and weight set. Weight is 8.1 lbs. Receiver drilled and tapped for scope mounting. Stock is thumbhole silhouette version or standard silhouette version, both are European walnut. Introduced 1990. Imported from Germany by Accuracy International, Gunsmithing, Inc.

Price: Thumbhole stock **$1,461.40**
Price: Standard stock **$1,212.10**

Anschutz 1907 Standard Match Rifle

Same action as Model 1913 but with 7/8" diameter 26" barrel (stainless or blue). Length is 44.5" overall, weighs 10.5 lbs. Choice of stock configurations. Vented forend. Designed for prone and position shooting ISU requirements; suitable for NRA matches. Also available with walnut flat-forend stock for benchrest shooting. Imported from Germany by Accuracy International, Gunsmithing, Inc.

Price: Right-hand, blue, no sights, hardwood stock . . . . **$1,253.40 to $1,299.00**
Price: Right-hand, blue, no sights, colored laminated stock . . . . **$1,316.10 to $1,375.00**
Price: Right-hand, blue, no sights, walnut stock **$1,521.10**
Price: Left-hand, blue barrel, no sights, walnut stock **$1,584.60**

Anschutz 1907

Armalite AR-10 (T)

Bushmaster XM15

ARMALITE AR-10 (T) RIFLE

Caliber: 308, 10-shot magazine. **Barrel:** 24" target-weight Rock 5R custom. **Weight:** 10.4 lbs. **Length:** 43.5" overall. **Stock:** Green or black compostion; N.M. fiberglass handguard tube. **Sights:** Detachable handle, front sight, or scope mount available. Comes with international-style flattop receiver with Picatinny rail. **Features:** National Match two-stage trigger. Forged upper receiver. Receivers hard-coat anodized. Introduced 1995. Made in U.S.A. by ArmaLite, Inc.

Price: Green **$2,075.00**
Price: Black **$2,090.00**
Price: AR-10 (T) Carbine, lighter 16" barrel, single stage trigger, weighs 8.8 lbs. Green **$1,970.00**
Price: Black **$1,985.00**

ARMALITE M15A4 (T) EAGLE EYE RIFLE

Caliber: 223, 7-shot magazine. **Barrel:** 24" heavy stainless; 1:8" twist. **Weight:** 9.2 lbs. **Length:** 42-3/8" overall. **Stock:** Green or black butt, N.M. fiberglass handguard tube. **Sights:** One-piece international-style flattop receiver with Weaver-type rail, including case deflector. **Features:** Detachable carry handle, front sight and scope mount (30mm or 1") avail-able. Upper and lower receivers have push-type pivot pin, hard coat anodized. Made in U.S.A. by ArmaLite, Inc.

Price: Green **$1,378.00**
Price: Black **$1,393.00**

ARMALITE M15A4 ACTION MASTER RIFLE

Caliber: 223, 7-shot magazine. **Barrel:** 20" heavy stainless; 1:9" twist. **Weight:** 9 lbs. **Length:** 40-1/2" overall. **Stock:** Green or black plastic; N.M. fiberglass handguard tube. **Sights:** One-piece international-style flattop receiver with Weaver-type rail. **Features:** Detachable carry handle, front sight and scope mount available. National Match two-stage trigger group; Picatinny rail; upper and lower receivers have push-type pivot pin; hard coat anodized finish. Made in U.S.A. by ArmaLite, Inc.

Price: **$1,175.00**

BLASER R93 LONG RANGE RIFLE

Caliber: 308 Win., 10-shot detachable box magazine. **Barrel:** 24". **Weight:** 10.4 lbs. **Length:** 44" overall. **Stock:** Aluminum with synthetic lining. **Sights:** None furnished; accepts detachable scope mount.**Features:** Straight-pull bolt action with adjustable trigger; fully adjustable stock; quick takedown; corrosion resistant finish. Introduced 1998. Imported from Germany by Sigarms.

Price: **$2,360.00**

BUSHMASTER XM15 E2S TARGET MODEL RIFLE

Caliber: 223. **Barrel:** 20", 24"; 1:9" twist; heavy. **Weight:** 8.3 lbs. **Length:** 38.25" overall (20" barrel). **Stock:** Black composition; A2 type. **Sights:** Adjustable post front, adjustable aperture rear. **Features:** Patterned after Colt M-16A2. Chrome-lined barrel with manganese phosphate exterior. Forged aluminum receivers with push-pin takedown. Available in stainless barrel and camo stock versions. Made in U.S.A. by Bushmaster Firearms Co.

Price: 20" match heavy barrel (A2 type) **$965.00**
Price: (A3 type) **$1,095.00**

BUSHMASTER DCM COMPETITION RIFLE

Similar to the XM15 E2S Target Model except has 20" extra-heavy (1" diameter) barrel with 1.8" twist for heavier competition bullets. Weighs about 12 lbs. with balance weights. Has special competition rear sight with interchangeable apertures, extra-fine 1/2- or 1/4-MOA windage and elevation adjustments; specially ground front sight post in choice of three widths. Full-length handguards over free-floater barrel tube. Introduced 1998. Made in U.S.A. by Bushmaster Firearms, Inc.

Price: **$1,495.00**

Bushmaster DCM

Bushmaster XM15 E2S V-Match Carbine

Colt Accurized

Colt Match Target HBAR

Colt Match Target HBAR II

BUSHMASTER XM15 E2S V-MATCH RIFLE

Caliber: 223. **Barrel:** 20", 24""; 1:9" twist; heavy. **Weight:** 8.1 lbs. **Length:** 38.25" overall (20" barrel). **Stock:** Black composition. A2 type. **Sights:** None furnished; upper receiver has integral scope mount base. **Features:** Chrome-lined .950" heavy barrel with counter-bored crown, manganese phosphate finish, free-floating aluminum handguard, forged aluminum receivers with push-pin takedown, hard anodized mil-spec finish. Competition trigger optional. Made in U.S.A. by Bushmaster Firearms, Inc.

Price: 20" Match heavy barrel.......................... **$1,055.00**
Price: 24" Match heavy barrel.......................... **$1,065.00**
Price: V-Match Carbine (16" barrel) **$1,045.00**

COLT MATCH TARGET MODEL RIFLE

Caliber: 223 Rem., 8-shot magazine. **Barrel:** 20". **Weight:** 7.5 lbs. **Length:** 39" overall. **Stock:** Composition stock, grip, forend. **Sights:** Post front, aperture rear adjustable for windage and elevation. **Features:** Five-round detachable box magazine, standard-weight barrel, sling swivels. Has forward bolt assist. Military matte black finish. Model introduced 1991.

Price: **$1,144.00**
Price: With compensator............................. **$1,150.00**

Colt Accurized Rifle

Similar to the Colt Match Target Model except has 24" stainless steel heavy barrel with 1.9" rifling, flattop receiver with scope mount and 1" rings, weighs 9.25 lbs. Introduced 1998. Made in U.S.A. by Colt's Mfg. Co., Inc.

Price: **$1,424.00**

Colt Match Target HBAR Rifle

Similar to the Target Model except has heavy barrel, 800-meter rear sight adjustable for windage and elevation. Introduced 1991.

Price: **$1,194.00**

Colt Match Target Competition HBAR Rifle

Similar to the Sporter Target except has flat-top receiver with integral Weaver-type base for scope mounting. Counter-bored muzzle, 1:9" rifling twist. Introduced 1991.

Price: Model R6700 .... **$1,199.00**

Colt Match Target Competition HBAR II Rifle

Similar to the Match Target Competition HBAR except has 16:1" barrel, weighs 7.1 lbs., overall length 34.5"; 1:9" twist barrel. Introduced 1995.

Price: **$1,172.00**

EAA/IZHMASH URAL 5.1

EAA/IZHMASH Biathlon

EAA/IZHMASH Biathlon Target

Ed Brown Model 702 Light Tactical

Ed Brown Model 702 Tactical

EAA/HW 660 MATCH RIFLE

Caliber: 22 LR. **Barrel:** 26". **Weight:** 10.7 lbs. **Length:** 45.3" overall. **Stock:** Match-type walnut with adjustable cheekpiece and buttplate. **Sights:** Globe front, match aperture rear. **Features:** Adjustable match trigger; stip-pled pistol grip and forend; forend accessory rail. Introduced 1991. Import-ed from Germany by European American Armory.

Price: About **$999.00**
Price: With laminate stock. **$1,159.00**

EAA/IZHMASH URAL 5.1 TARGET RIFLE

Caliber: 22 LR. **Barrel:** 26.5". **Weight:** 11.3 lbs. **Length:** 44.5". **Stock:** Wood, international style. **Sights:** Adjustable click rear, hooded front with inserts. **Features:** Forged barrel with rifling, adjustable trigger, aluminum rail for accessories, hooked adjustable butt plate. Adjustable comb, adjustable large palm rest. Hand stippling on grip area.

Price: . . . . **NA**

EAA/Izhmash Biathlon Target Rifle

Similar to URAL with addition of snow covers for barrel and sights, stock holding extra mags, round trigger block. Unique bolt utilizes toggle action. Designed to compete in 40 meter biathlon event. 22 LR, 19.5" bbl.

Price: **$979.00**

EAA/Izhmash Biathalon Basic Target Rifle

Same action as Biathlon but designed for plinking or fun. Beech stock, heavy barrel with Weaver rail for scope mount. 22 LR, 19.5" bbl.

Price: **$339.00**

ED BROWN MODEL 702 LIGHT TACTICAL

Caliber: 223, 308. **Barrel:** 21". **Weight:** 8.75 lbs. **Stock:** Fully glass-bedded fiberglass with recoil pad. Wide varmint-style forend. **Sights:** None furnished. Talley scope mounts utilizing heavy duty 8-40 screws. **Features:** Compact and super accurate, it is ideal for police, military and varmint hunters.

Price: From **$2,800.00**

ED BROWN MODEL 702 TACTICAL

Caliber: 308, 300 Win. Mag. **Barrel:** 26". **Weight:** 11.25 lbs. **Stock:** Hand bedded McMillan A-3 fiberglass tactical stock with recoil pad. **Sights:** None furnished. Leupold Mark 4 30mm scope mounts utilizing heavy-duty 8-40 screws. **Features:** Custom short or long action, steel trigger guard, hinged floor plate, additional caliber available.

Price: From **$2,900.00**

Ed Brown 702

Harris Gunworks Long Range

Harris Gunworks M-86

ED BROWN MODEL 702, M40A2 MARINE SNIPER

Caliber: 308 Win., 30-06 Springfield. **Barrel:** Match-grade 24". **Weight:** 9.25 lbs. **Stock:** Hand bedded McMillan GP fiberglass tactical stock with recoil pad in special Woodland Camo molded-in colors. **Sights:** None furnished. Leupold Mark 4 30mm scope mounts with heavy-duty 8-40 screws. **Features:** Steel trigger guard, hinged floor plate, three position safety. Left-hand model available.

Price: From **$2,900.00**

HARRIS GUNWORKS NATIONAL MATCH RIFLE

Caliber: 7mm-08, 308, 5-shot magazine. **Barrel:** 24", stainless steel. **Weight:** About 11 lbs. (std. bbl.). **Length:** 43" overall. **Stock:** Fiberglass with adjustable buttplate. **Sights:** Barrel band and Tompkins front; no rear sight furnished. **Features:** Gunworks repeating action with clip slot, Canjar trigger. Match-grade barrel. Available in right-hand only. Fiberglass stock, sight installation, special machining and triggers optional. Introduced 1989. From Harris Gunworks, Inc.

Price: **$3,500.00**

HARRIS GUNWORKS LONG RANGE RIFLE

Caliber: 300 Win. Mag., 7mm Rem. Mag., 300 Phoenix, 338 Lapua, single shot. **Barrel:** 26", stainless steel, match-grade. **Weight:** 14 lbs. **Length:** 46-1/2" overall. **Stock:** Fiberglass with adjustable buttplate and cheekpiece. Adjustable for length of pull, drop, cant and cast-off. **Sights:** Barrel band and Tompkins front; no rear sight furnished. **Features:** Uses Gunworks solid bottom single shot action and Canjar trigger. Barrel twist 1:12". Introduced 1989. From Harris Gunworks, Inc.

Price: **$3,620.00**

HARRIS GUNWORKS M-86 SNIPER RIFLE

Caliber: 308, 30-06, 4-shot magazine; 300 Win. Mag., 3-shot magazine. **Barrel:** 24", Gunworks match-grade in heavy contour. **Weight:** 11-1/4 lbs. (308), 11-1/2 lbs. (30-06, 300). **Length:** 43-1/2" overall. **Stock:** Specially designed McHale fiberglass stock with textured grip and forend, recoil pad. **Sights:** None furnished. **Features:** Uses Gunworks repeating action. Comes with bipod. Matte black finish. Sling swivels. Introduced 1989. From Harris Gunworks, Inc.

Price: **$2,700.00**

HARRIS GUNWORKS M-89 SNIPER RIFLE

Caliber: 308 Win., 5-shot magazine. **Barrel:** 28" (with suppressor). **Weight:** 15 lbs., 4 oz. **Stock:** Fiberglass; adjustable for length; recoil pad. **Sights:** None furnished. Drilled and tapped for scope mounting. **Features:** Uses Gunworks repeating action. Comes with bipod. Introduced 1990. From Harris Gunworks, Inc.

Price: Standard (non-suppressed) **$3,200.00**

HARRIS GUNWORKS COMBO M-87 SERIES 50-CALIBER RIFLES

Caliber: 50 BMG, single shot. **Barrel:** 29, with muzzle brake. **Weight:** About 21-1/2 lbs. **Length:** 53" overall. **Stock:** Gunworks fiberglass. **Sights:** None furnished. **Features:** Right-handed Gunworks stainless steel receiver, chrome-moly barrel with 1:15" twist. Introduced 1987. From Harris Gunworks, Inc.

Price: **$3,885.00**

Price: M87R 5-shot repeater **$4,000.00**

Price: M-87 (5-shot repeater) "Combo" **$4,300.00**

Price: M-92 Bullpup (shortened M-87 single shot with bullpup stock) **$4,770.00**

Price: M-93 (10-shot repeater with folding stock, detachable magazine) **$4,150.00**

OLYMPIC ARMS PCR-SERVICEMATCH RIFLE

Caliber: 223, 10-shot magazine. **Barrel:** 20", broach-cut 416 stainless steel. **Weight:** About 10 lbs. **Length:** 39.5" overall. **Stock:** A2 stowaway grip and trapdoor buttstock. **Sights:** Post front, E2-NM fully adjustable aperture rear. **Features:** Based on the AR-15. Conforms to all DCM standards. Free-floating 1:8.5" or 1:10" barrel; crowned barrel; no bayonet lug. Introduced 1996. Made in U.S.A. by Olympic Arms, Inc.

Price: **$1,062.00**

OLYMPIC ARMS PCR-1 RIFLE

Caliber: 223, 10-shot magazine. **Barrel:** 20", 24"; 416 stainless steel. **Weight:** 10 lbs., 3 oz. **Length:** 38.25" overall with 20" barrel. **Stock:** A2 stowaway grip and trapdoor butt. **Sights:** None supplied; flattop upper receiver, cut-down front sight base. **Features:** Based on the AR-15 rifle. Broach-cut, free-floating barrel with 1:8.5" or 1:10" twist. No bayonet lug. Crowned barrel; fluting available. Introduced 1994. Made in U.S.A. by Olympic Arms, Inc.

Price: **$1,038.00**

Remington 40-XB Rangemaster

Remington 40-XC KS

Springfield, Inc. M1A Super Match

Springfield, Inc.
M1A/M-21

Olympic Arms PCR-2, PCR-3 Rifles

Similar to the PCR-1 except has 16" barrel, weighs 8 lbs., 2 oz.; has post front sight, fully adjustable aperture rear. Model PCR-3 has flattop upper receiver, cut-down front sight base. Introduced 1994. Made in U.S.A. by Olympic Arms, Inc.

Price: **$958.00**

REMINGTON 40-XB RANGEMASTER TARGET CENTERFIRE

Caliber: 15 calibers from 220 Swift to 300 Win. Mag. **Barrel:** 27-1/4". **Weight:** 11-1/4 lbs. **Length:** 47" overall. **Stock:** American walnut, laminated thumbhole or Kevlar with high comb and beavertail forend stop. Rubber non-slip buttplate. **Sights:** None. Scope blocks installed. **Features:** Adjustable trigger. Stainless barrel and action. Receiver drilled and tapped for sights.

Price: Standard single shot. . . . . **$1,636.00** (right-hand)
. . . . **$1,761.00** (left-hand)

Price: Repeater. **$1,734.00**

REMINGTON 40-XBBR KS

Caliber: Five calibers from 22 BR to 308 Win. **Barrel:** 20" (light varmint class), 24" (heavy varmint class). **Weight:** 7-1/4 lbs. (light varmint class); 12 lbs. (heavy varmint class). **Length:** 38" (20" bbl.), 42" (24" bbl.). **Stock:** Aramid fiber. **Sights:** None. Supplied with scope blocks. **Features:** Unblued benchrest with stainless steel barrel, trigger adjustable from 1-1/2 lbs. to 3-1/2 lbs. Special 2-oz. trigger extra cost. Scope and mounts extra.

Price: Single shot **$1,876.00**

REMINGTON 40-XC KS TARGET RIFLE

Caliber: 7.62 NATO, 5-shot. **Barrel:** 24", stainless steel. **Weight:** 11 lbs. without sights. **Length:** 43-1/2" overall. **Stock:** Aramid fiber. **Sights:** None furnished. **Features:** Designed to meet the needs of competitive shooters. Stainless steel barrel and action.

Price: **$1,821.00**

REMINGTON 40-XR CUSTOM SPORTER

Caliber: 22 LR, 22 WM. **Features:** Model XR-40 Target rifle action with craftsmanship of Model 700 Custom. Many options available.

Price: Single shot **$3,383.00**

SAKO TRG-22 BOLT-ACTION RIFLE

Caliber: 308 Win., 10-shot magazine. **Barrel:** 26". **Weight:** 10-1/4 lbs. **Length:** 45-1/4" overall. **Stock:** Reinforced polyurethane with fully adjustable cheekpiece and buttplate. **Sights:** None furnished. Optional quick-detachable, one-piece scope mount base, 1" or 30mm rings. **Features:** Resistance-free bolt, free-floating heavy stainless barrel, 60-degree bolt lift. Two-stage trigger is adjustable for length, pull, horizontal or vertical pitch. Introduced 2000. Imported from Finland by Beretta USA.

Price: Green **$2,898.00**

Price: Model TRG-42, as above except in 338 Lapua Mag or 300 Win. Mag. **$2,829.00**

Price: Green (new) **$3,243.00**

SPRINGFIELD, INC. M1A SUPER MATCH

Caliber: 308 Win. **Barrel:** 22", heavy Douglas Premium. **Weight:** About 11 lbs. **Length:** 44.31" overall. **Stock:** Heavy walnut competition stock with longer pistol grip, contoured area behind the rear sight, thicker butt and forend, glass bedded. **Sights:** National Match front and rear. **Features:** Has figure-eight-style operating rod guide. Introduced 1987. From Springfield, Inc.

Price: About **$2,479.00**

Springfield, Inc. M1A/M-21 Tactical Model Rifle

Similar to M1A Super Match except special sniper stock with adjustable cheekpiece and rubber recoil pad. Weighs 11.6 lbs. From Springfield, Inc.

Price: **$2,975.00**

SPRINGFIELD, INC. M-1 GARAND AMERICAN COMBAT RIFLES

Caliber: 30-06, 308 Win., 8-shot. **Barrel:** 24". **Weight:** 9.5 lbs. **Length:** 43.6". **Stock:** American walnut. **Sights:** Military square post front, military aperture, MOA adjustable rear. **Features:** Limited production, certificate of authenticity, all new receiver, barrel and stock with remaining parts USGI mil-spec. 2-stage military trigger.

Price: About **$2,479.00**

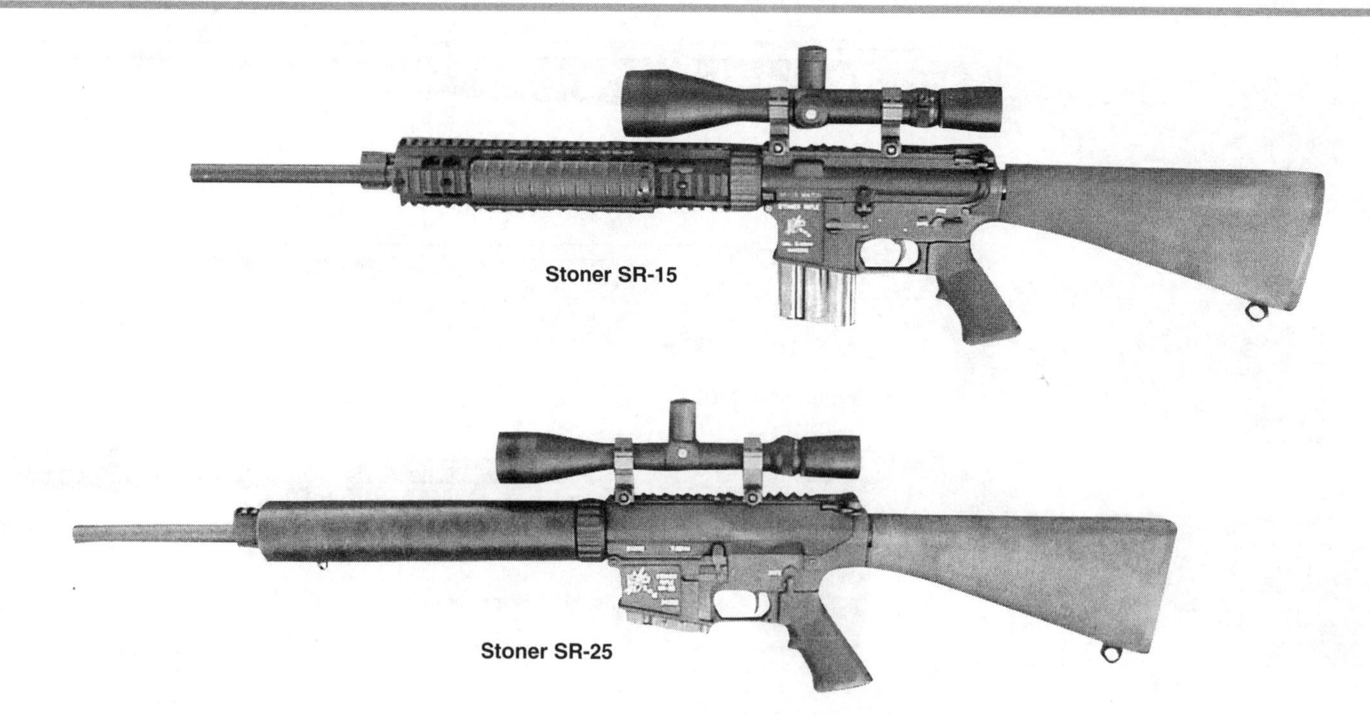

Stoner SR-15

Stoner SR-25

STONER SR-15 MATCH RIFLE

Caliber: 223. **Barrel:** 20". **Weight:** 7.9 lbs. **Length:** 38" overall. **Stock:** Black synthetic. **Sights:** None furnished; flat-top upper receiver for scope mounting. **Features:** Short Picatinny rail, two-stage match trigger. Introduced 1998. Made in U.S.A. by Knight's Mfg.Co.

Price: **$1,650.00**

STONER SR-25 MATCH RIFLE

Caliber: 7.62 NATO, 10-shot steel magazine, 5-shot optional. **Barrel:** 24" heavy match; 1:11.25" twist. **Weight:** 10.75 lbs. **Length:** 44" overall. **Stock:** Black synthetic AR-15A2 design. Full floating forend of Mil-spec synthetic attaches to upper receiver at a single point. **Sights:** None furnished. Has integral Weaver-style rail. Rings and iron sights optional. **Features:** Improved AR-15 trigger, AR-15-style seven-lug rotating bolt. Gas block rail mounts detachable front sight. Introduced 1993. Made in U.S.A. by Knight's Mfg. Co.

Price: **$3,345.00**

Price: SR-25 Lightweight Match (20" medium match target contour barrel, 9.5 lbs., 40" overall) **$3,345.00**

TIKKA TARGET RIFLE

Caliber: 223, 22-250, 308, detachable 5-shot magazine. **Barrel:** 23-1/2" heavy. **Weight:** 9 lbs. **Length:** 43-5/8" overall. **Stock:** European walnut with adjustable comb, adjustable buttplate; stippled grip and forend. **Sights:** None furnished; drilled and tapped for scope mounting. **Features:** Buttplate adjustable for distance, angle, height and pitch, adjustable trigger, free-floating barrel. Introduced 1998. Imported from Finland by Beretta USA.

Price: **$950.00**

SHOTGUNS — AUTOLOADERS

Includes a wide variety of sporting guns and guns suitable for various competitions.

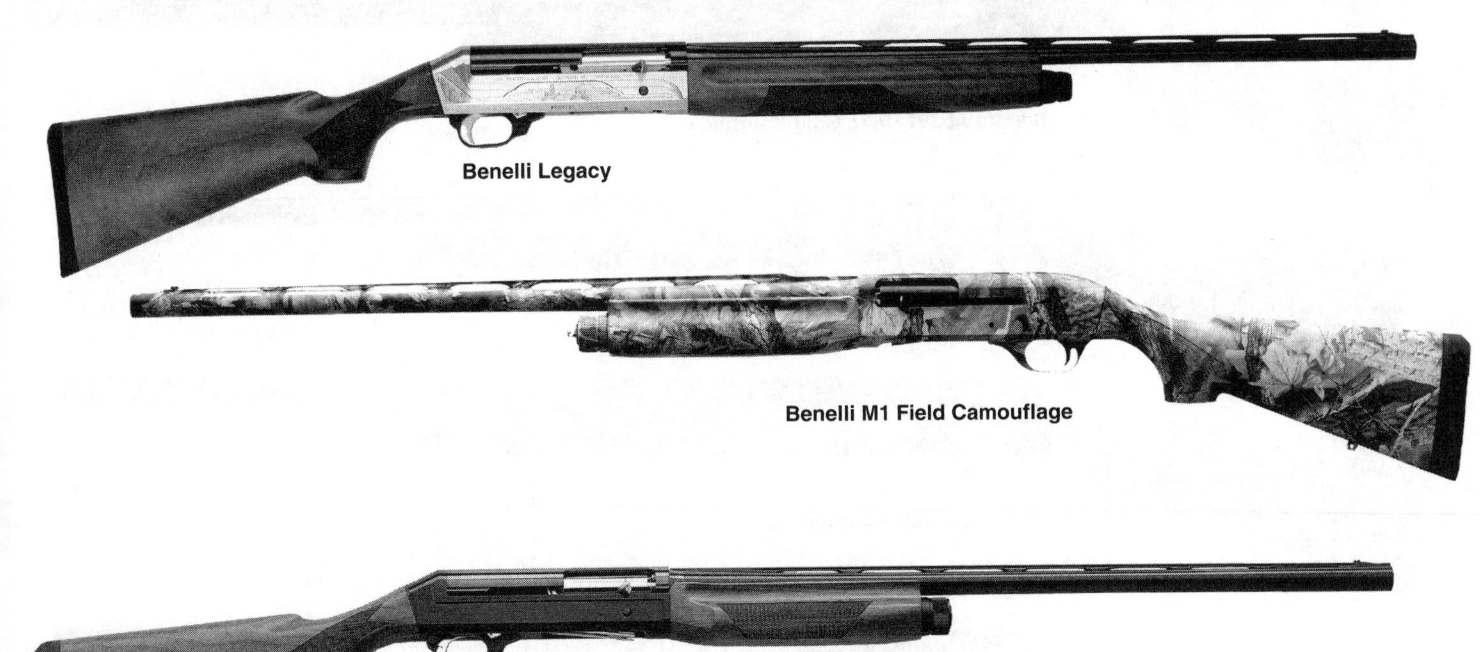

Benelli Legacy

Benelli M1 Field Camouflage

Benelli Super Black Eagle

BENELLI LEGACY SHOTGUN

Gauge: 12, 20, 2-3/4" and 3" chamber. **Barrel:** 24", 26", 28" (Full, Mod., Imp. Cyl., Imp. Mod., cylinder choke tubes). Mid-bead sight. **Weight:** 5.8 to 7.6 lbs. **Length:** 49-5/8" overall (28" barrel). **Stock:** Select European walnut with satin finish. **Features:** Uses the rotating bolt inertia recoil operating system with a two-piece steel/aluminum etched receiver (bright on lower, blue upper). Drop adjustment kit allows the stock to be custom fitted without modifying the stock. Introduced 1998. Imported from Italy by Benelli USA, Corp.

Price: **$1,400.00**

Benelli Sport II Shotgun

Similar to the Legacy model except has dual tone blue/silver receiver, two carbon fiber interchangeable ventilated ribs, adjustable butt pad, adjustable buttstock, and functions with ultra-light target loads. Walnut stock with satin finish. Introduced 1997. Imported from Italy by Benelli U.S.A.

Price: **$1,400.00**

BENELLI M1 FIELD SHOTGUN

Gauge: 12, 20 ga. **Barrel:** 21", 24", 26", 28". **Weight:** 7 lbs., 4 oz. **Stock:** High impact polymer; wood on 26", 28". **Sights:** Red bar. **Features:** Sporting version of the military & police gun. Uses the rotating Montefeltro bolt system. Ventilated rib; blue finish. Comes with set of five choke tubes. Imported from Italy by Benelli U.S.A.

Price: ... (Synthetic) **$985.00**; (Wood) **$1,000.00**; (Timber HD) **$1,085.00**

Price: 24" rifled barrel ..... (Synthetic) **$1,060.00**; Timber HD **$1,165.00**

Price: Synthetic stock, left-hand version (24", 26", 28" brls.) ... **$1,005.00**

Price: Timber HD camo left-hand, 21", 24" barrel............ **$1,105.00**

Price: MI Field Steadygrip **$1,175.00**

Benelli Montefeltro Shotgun

Similar to the M1 Super except has checkered walnut stock with satin finish. Uses the Montefeltro rotating bolt system with a simple inertia recoil design. Full, Imp. Mod, Mod., Imp. Cyl. choke tubes, 12 and 20 ga. Weighs 6.8-7.1 lbs. Finish is blue. Introduced 1987.

Price: 24", 26", 28" **$1,005.00**

Price: Left-hand, 26", 28" **$1,020.00**

BENELLI SUPER BLACK EAGLE SHOTGUN

Gauge: 12, 3-1/2" chamber. **Barrel:** 24", 26", 28" (Cyl. Imp. Cyl., Mod., Imp. Mod., Full choke tubes). **Weight:** 7 lbs., 5 oz. **Length:** 49-5/8" overall (28" barrel). **Stock:** European walnut with satin finish, or polymer. Adjustable for drop. **Sights:** Red bar front. **Features:** Uses Montefeltro inertia recoil bolt system. Fires all 12 gauge shells from 2-3/4" to 3-1/2" magnums, vent rib. Introduced 1991. Imported from Italy by Benelli U.S.A.

Price: With 26" and 28" barrel, wood stock................ **$1,300.00**

Price: Timber HD Camo 24", 26", 28" barrel............... **$1,385.00**

Price: With 24", 26" and 28" barrel, polymer stock........... **$1,290.00**

Price: Left-hand, 24", 26", 28", polymer stock **$1,345.00**

Price: Left-hand, 24", 26", 28", camo stock **$1,435.00**

Price: Steadygrip Turkey Gun.......................... **$1,465.00**

Benelli Super Black Eagle Slug Gun

Similar to the Benelli Super Black Eagle except has 24" rifled barrel with 2-3/4" and 3" chamber, drilled and tapped for scope. Uses the inertia recoil bolt system. Matte-finish receiver. Weight is 7.5 lbs., overall length 45.5". Wood or polymer stocks available. Introduced 1992. Imported from Italy by Benelli U.S.A.

Price: With wood stock **$1,345.00**

Price: With polymer stock............................. **$1,335.00**

Price: 24" barrel, Timber HD Camo **$1,460.00**

Benelli Executive Series Shotgun

Similar to the Legacy except has grayed steel lower receiver, hand-engraved and gold inlaid (Grade III), and has highest grade of walnut stock with drop adjustment kit. Barrel lengths 26" or 28"; 2-3/4" and 3" chamber. Special order only. Introduced 1995. Imported from Italy by Benelli U.S.A.

Price: Grade I (engraved game scenes).................. **$5,465.00**

Price: Grade II (game scenes with scroll engraving) **$6,135.00**

Price: Grade III (full coverage, gold inlays)................. **$7,065.00**

BERETTA AL391 TEKNYS

Gauge: 12, 20 gauge; 3" chamber, semi-auto. **Barrel:** 26", 28". **Weight:** 5.9 lbs. (20 ga.), 7.3 lbs. (12 ga.). **Length:** N/A. **Stock:** X-tra wood (special process wood enhancement). **Features:** Flat 1/4 rib, TruGlo Tru-Bead sight, recoil reducer, stock spacers, overbored bbls., flush choke tubes. Comes with fitted, lined case.

Price: **$1,194.00**

Price: Teknys Gold (green enamel inlays, oil-finished walnut... **$1,515.00**

Price: Teknys Gold Sporting (blue inlays, select walnut) **$1,653.00**

Beretta AL391 Urika Gold Sporting

Beretta AL391 Urika Sporting

Beretta A391 Xtrema 3.5

Browning Gold Deer Hunter

BERETTA AL391 URIKA AUTO SHOTGUNS

Gauge: 12, 20 gauge; 3" chamber. **Barrel:** 22", 24", 26", 28", 30"; five Mobilchoke choke tubes. **Weight:** 5.95 to 7.28 lbs. **Length:** Varies by model. **Stock:** Walnut, black or camo synthetic; shims, spacers and interchangeable recoil pads allow custom fit. **Features:** Self-compensating gas operation handles full range of loads; recoil reducer in receiver; enlarged trigger guard; reduced-weight receiver, barrel and forend; hard-chromed bore. Introduced 2000. Imported from Italy by Beretta USA.

Price: AL391 Urika (12 ga., 26", 28", 30" barrels) **$1,035.00**
Price: AL391 Urika (20 ga., 24", 26", 28" barrels) **$1,035.00**
Price: AL391 Urika Synthetic (12 ga., 24", 26", 28", 30" barrels) **$1,035.00**
Price: AL391 Urika Camo. (12 ga., Realtree Hardwoods or Max 4-HD) **$1,139.00**

Beretta AL391 Urika Gold and Gold Sporting Auto Shotguns

Similar to AL391 Urika except features deluxe wood, jeweled bolt and carrier, gold-inlaid receiver with black or silver finish. Introduced 2000. Imported from Italy by Beretta USA.

Price: AL391 Urika Gold Sporting (12 or 20, black receiver, engraving) **$1,377.00**
Price: AL391 Urika Gold Sporting (12 ga., silver receiver, engraving) **$1,377.00**

Beretta AL391 Urika Sporting Auto Shotguns

Similar to AL391 Urika except has competition sporting stock with rounded rubber recoil pad, wide ventilated rib with white front and mid-rib beads, satin-black receiver with silver markings. Available in 12 and 20 gauge. Introduced 2000. Imported from Italy by Beretta USA.

Price: AL391 Urika Sporting. **$1,101.00**

Beretta AL391 Urika Trap Auto Shotguns

Similar to AL391 Urika except in 12 ga. only, has wide ventilated rib with white front and mid-rib beads, Monte Carlo stock and special trap recoil pad. Gold Trap features highly figured walnut stock and forend, gold-filled Beretta logo and signature on receiver. Optima bore and Optima choke tubes. Introduced 2000. Imported from Italy by Beretta USA.

Price: AL391 Urika Trap **$1,101.00**

Beretta AL391 Urika Parallel Target RL and SL Auto Shotguns

Similar to AL391 Urika except has parallel-comb, Monte Carlo stock with tighter grip radius to reduce trigger reach and stepped ventilated rib. SL model has same features but with 13.5" length of pull stock. Introduced 2000. Imported from Italy by Beretta USA.

Price: AL391 Urika Parallel Target RL **$1,101.00**
Price: AL391 Urika Parallel Target SL **$1,101.00**

Beretta AL391 Urika Youth Shotgun

Similar to AL391 except has a 24" or 26" barrel with 13.5" stock for youth and smaller shooters. Introduced 2000. From Beretta USA.

Price: **$1,035.00**

BERETTA A391 XTREMA 3.5 AUTO SHOTGUNS

Gauge: 12 ga. 3-1/2" chamber. **Barrel:** 24", 26", 28". **Weight:** 7.8 lbs. **Stock:** Synthetic. **Features:** Semi-auto goes with two-lug rotating bolt and self-compensating gas valve, extended tang, cross bolt safety, self-cleaning, with case.

Price: Synthetic **$1,035.00**
Price: Realtree Hardwood HD Camo and Max 4-HD **$1,139.00**

BROWNING GOLD HUNTER AUTO SHOTGUN

Gauge: 12, 3" or 3-1/2" chamber; 20, 3" chamber. **Barrel:** 12 ga.-26", 28", 30", Invector Plus choke tubes; 20 ga.-26", 30", Invector choke tubes. **Weight:** 7 lbs., 9 oz. (12 ga.), 6 lbs., 12 oz. (20 ga.). **Length:** 46-1/4" overall (20 ga., 26" barrel). **Stock:** 14"x1-1/2"x2-1/3"; select walnut with gloss finish; palm swell grip. **Features:** Self-regulating, self-cleaning gas system shoots all loads; lightweight receiver with special non-glare deep black finish; large reversible safety button; large rounded trigger guard, gold trigger. The 20 gauge has slightly smaller dimensions; 12 gauge have back-bored barrels, Invector Plus tube system. Introduced 1994. Imported by Browning.

Price: 12 or 20 gauge, 3" chamber **$894.00**
Price: 12 ga., 3-1/2" chamber **$1,038.00**
Price: Extra barrels .... **$336.00 to $415.00**

Browning Gold Sporting Golden Clays

Browning NWTF Mossy Oak Break-Up

Browning Gold Classic Stalker

Browning Gold Fusion

Browning Gold Rifled Deer Hunter Auto Shotgun

Similar to the Gold Hunter except 12 or 20 gauge, 22" rifled barrel with cantilever scope mount, walnut stock with extra-thick recoil pad. Weighs 7 lbs., 12 oz., overall length 42-1/2". Sling swivel studs fitted on the magazine cap and butt. Introduced 1997. Imported by Browning.

Price: 12 gauge $887.00
Price: With Mossy Oak Break-up camouflage $1,046.00
Price: 20 ga. (satin-finish walnut stock, 3" chamber) $987.00

Browning Gold Deer Stalker

Similar to the Gold Deer Hunter except has black composite stock and forend, fully rifled barrel, cantilever scope mount. Introduced 1999. Imported by Browning.

Price: 12 gauge $967.00

Browning Gold Sporting Clays Auto Shotgun

Similar to the Gold Hunter except 12 gauge only with 28" or 30" barrel; front Hi-Viz Pro-Comp and center bead on tapered ventilated rib; ported and back-bored Invector Plus barrel; 2-3/4" chamber; satin-finished stock with solid, radiused recoil pad with hard heel insert; non-glare black alloy receiver has "Sporting Clays" inscribed in gold. Introduced 1996. Imported from Japan by Browning.

Price: $984.00

Browning Gold Sporting Golden Clays

Similar to the Sporting Clays except has silvered receiver with gold engraving, high grade wood. Introduced 1999. Imported by Browning.

Price: $1,457.00

Browning Gold Ladies'/Youth Sporting Clays Auto

Similar to the Gold Sporting Clays except has stock dimensions of 14-1/4"x1-3/4"x2" for women and younger shooters. Introduced 1999. Imported by Browning.

Price: $920.00

Browning Gold Micro Auto Shotgun

Similar to the Gold Hunter except has a 26" barrel, 13-7/8" pull length and smaller pistol grip for youths and other small shooters. Weighs 6 lbs., 10 oz. Introduced 2001. From Browning.

Price: $894.00

Browning Gold Stalker Auto Shotgun

Similar to the Gold Hunter except has black composite stock and forend. Choice of 3" or 3-1/2" chamber.

Price: 12 ga. with 3" chamber............................ $856.00
Price: With 3-1/2" chamber............................ $1,002.00

Browning Gold Mossy Oak® Shadow Grass Shotgun

Similar to the Gold Hunter except 12 gauge only, completely covered with Mossy Oak® Shadow Grass camouflage. Choice of 3" or 3-1/2" chamber and 26" or 28" barrel. Introduced 1999. Imported by Browning.

Price: 12 ga. 3" chamber $967.00
Price: 12 ga., 3-1/2" chamber.......................... $1,146.00

Browning Gold Mossy Oak® Break-up Shotgun

Similar to the Gold Hunter except 12 gauge only, completely covered with Mossy Oak® Break-Up camouflage. Imported by Browning.

Price: 3" chamber.................................. $1,069.00
Price: 3-1/2" chamber............................... $1,282.00
Price: NWTF model, 3" chamber, 24" bbl. with Hi-Viz sight $998.00
Price: NWTF model, 3-1/2" chamber, 24" bbl. with Hi-Viz sight . $1,177.00
Price: Gold Rifled Deer (22" rifled bbl., Cantilever scope mount) $1,046.00

Browning Gold Classic Hunter Auto Shotgun

Similar to the Gold Hunter 3" except has semi-hump back receiver, magazine cut-off, adjustable comb, and satin-finish wood. Introduced 1999. Imported by Browning.

Price: 12 or 20 gauge $912.00
Price: Classic High Grade (silvered, gold engraved receiver, high-grade wood) $1,750.00

Browning Gold Waterfowl

Browning Gold Light 10 Gauge

EAA/Baikal MP-153

Escort Model AS

Browning Gold Classic Stalker

Similar to the Gold Classic Hunter except has adjustable composite stock and forend. Introduced 1999. Imported by Browning.

Price: **$856.00**

Browning Gold Fusion™ Auto Shotgun

Similar to the Gold Hunter except is 1/2 lb. lighter, has a new-style vent rib, adjustable comb system, Hi-Viz Pro-Comp front sight and five choke tubes. Offered with 26", 28" or 30" barrel, 12 gauge, 3" chamber only. Includes hard case. Introduced 2001. Imported by Browning.

Price: **$1,055.00**

Browning Gold NWTF Turkey Series Camo Shotgun

Similar to the Gold Hunter except 10- or 12-gauge (3" or 3-1/2" chamber), 24" barrel with extra-full choke tube, Hi-Viz fiber-optic sights and complete gun coverage in Mossy Oak Break-Up camouflage with National Wild Turkey Federation logo on stock. Introduced 2001. From Browning.

Price: 10 gauge **$1,378.00**

Price: 12 gauge, 3-1/2" chamber Ultimate **$1,330.00**

Price: 12 gauge, 3" chamber **$1,101.00**

Browning Gold Upland Special Auto Shotgun

Similar to the Gold Classic Hunter except has straight-grip walnut stock, 12 or 20 gauge, 3" chamber. Introduced 2001. From Browning

Price: 12-gauge model (24" bbl., weighs 7 lbs.) **$958.00**

Price: 20-gauge model (26" bbl., weighs 6 lbs., 12 oz.) **$958.00**

Browning Gold Light 10 Gauge Auto Shotgun

Similar to the Browning Gold 10, except has an alloy receiver that is 1 lb. lighter than standard model. Offered in 26" or 28" bbls. With Mossy Oak Break-Up or Shadow Grass coverage; 5-shot magazine. Weighs 9 lbs., 10 oz. (28" bbl.). Introduced 2001. Imported by Browning.

Price: Camo model only **$1,297.00**

Browning Gold Evolve Shotgun

Similar to Browning Gold auto shotguns with new rib design, HiViz sights, three bbl. lengths (12 ga. only, 26", 28" or 30").

Price: **$1,118.00**

DIAMOND SEMI-AUTO SHOTGUNS

Gauge: 12 ga., 2-3/4" and 3" chambers. **Barrel:** 20"-30". **Stock:** Walnut, synthetic. **Features:** One-piece receiver, rotary butt, gas ejection, high strength steel. Gold, Silver Marine, Elite and Panther series with vented barrels and all but Silver have 3 chokes. Slug guns available, all but Panther with sights. Imported from Istanbul by Adco Sales, Inc.

Price: Gold, 28", walnut **$549.00**

Price: Gold, 28", synthetic **$499.00**

Price: Gold Slug, 24", w/sights, walnut **$549.00**

Price: Gold Slug, 24", w/sights, synthetic **$499.00**

Price: Silver Mariner, 22", synthetic **$499.00**

Price: Silver Mariner, 20" slug w/sights, synthetic **$479.00**

Price: Elite, 22" Slug, 24"-28", walnut . . . . **$429.00 to $449.00**

Price: Panther, 22" slug; 26", 28", vent rin w/3 chokes, synthetic . . . . **$379.00 to $399.00**

Price: Imperial 12, 20 ga., 24" slug w/sights, 26", 28" vent rib w/3 chokes, walnut . . . . **$479.00 to $499.00**

Price: Imperial, 12 ga., 28" vent rib w/3 chokes, 3.5" chamber, walnut **$499.00**

EAA/BAIKAL MP-153 AUTO SHOTGUN

Gauge: 12, 3-1/2" chamber. **Barrel:** 24", 26", 28"; imp., mod. and full choke tubes. **Weight:** 7.8 lbs. **Stock:** Walnut. **Features:** Gas-operated action with automatic gas-adjustment valve allows use of light and heavy loads interchangeably; 4-round magazine; rubber recoil pad. Introduced 2000. Imported by European American Armory.

Price: MP-153 (blued finish, walnut stock and forend) **$459.00**

Price: MP-153 (field grade, synthetic stock) **$349.00**

EAA/SAIGA AUTO SHOTGUN

Gauge: 12, 20, .410, 3" chamber. **Barrel:** 19", 21", 24". **Weight:** 6.6-7.6 lbs. **Length:** 40"-45". **Stock:** Synthetic. **Features:** Retains best features of the AK Rifle by Kalashnikov as the semi-auto shotgun. Magazine fed. Imported from Russia by EAA Corp.

Price: .410 ga. **$299.00**

Price: 20 ga. **$389.00**

Price: 12 ga. . . . . **$409.00 to $439.00**

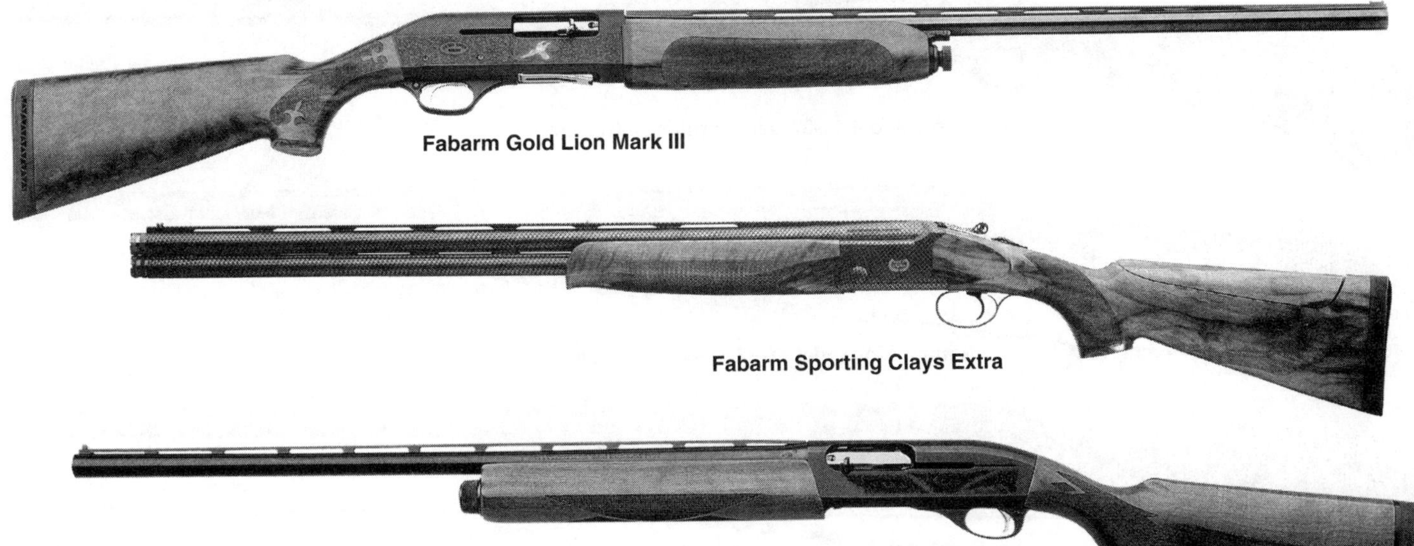

Fabarm Gold Lion Mark III

Fabarm Sporting Clays Extra

Remington Model 11-87 Premier

ESCORT SEMI-AUTO SHOTGUN

Gauge: 12. **Barrel:** 28", 24", 20" (AimGuard model); 3" chambers. **Weight:** 7 lbs. **Stock:** Polymer, black, or camo finish; also Turkish walnut. **Features:** Black chrome finish; top of receiverdovetailed for sight mounting. Gold-plated trigger, trigger-guard safety, magazine cut-off. Three choke tubes (IC, M, F - except AimGuard); 24" bbl. model comes with turkey choke tube. **Sights:** Optional HiVIz Spark and TriViz fiber optic sights. Introduced 2002. Camo model introduced 2003. Imported from Turkey by Legacy Sports Interna-tional.

Price: Walnut stock **$386.00**
Price: Model PS, black polymer stock. **$363.00**
Price: Camo polymer stock, Spark sight. **$407.00**
Price: Camo, 24" bbl, TriViz sight, turkey choke **$444.00**
Price: AimGuard, 20" bbl., black stock, cyl bore **$363.00**
Price: Waterfowl/turkey combo, camo, 2 bbls **$519.00**

FABARM GOLD LION MARK III AUTO SHOTGUN

Gauge: 12, 3" chamber. **Barrel:** 24", 26", 28", choke tubes. **Weight:** 7 lbs. **Length:** 45.5" overall. **Stock:** European walnut with gloss finish; olive wood grip cap. **Features:** TriBore barrel, reversible safety; gold-plated trigger and carrier release button; leather-covered rubber recoil pad. Introduced 1998. Imported from Italy by Heckler & Koch, Inc.

Price: **$939.00**

Fabarm Sporting Clays Extra Auto Shotgun

Similar to Gold Lion except 28" TriBore ported barrel with interchangeable colored front-sight beads, mid-rib bead, 10mm channeled vent rib, carbon-fiber finish, oil-finished walnut stock and forend with olive wood grip-cap. Stock dimensions are 14.58"x1.58"x2.44". Distinctive gold-colored receiver logo. Available in 12 gauge only, 3" chamber. Introduced 1999. Imported from Italy by Heckler & Koch, Inc.

Price: **$1,249.00**

FRANCHI 48AL SHOTGUN

Gauge: 20 or 28, 2-3/4" chamber. **Barrel:** 24", 26", 28" (Full, cyl., mod., choke tubes). **Weight:** 5.5 lbs. (20 gauge). **Length:** 44"-48.". **Stock:** 14-1/4"x1-5/ 8"x2-1/2". Walnut with checkered grip and forend. **Features:** Long recoil-operated action. Chrome-lined bore; cross-bolt safety. Imported from Italy by Benelli U.S.A.

Price: 20 ga. **$715.00**
Price: 28 ga. **$825.00**

Franchi 48AL Deluxe Shotgun

Similar to 48AL but with select walnut stock and forend and high-polish blue finish with gold trigger. Introduced 2000.

Price: (20 gauge, 26" barrel). **$940.00**
Price: (28 gauge, 26" barrel). **$990.00**

Franchi 48AL English

Similar to 48AL Deluxe but with straight grip "English style" stock. 20 ga., 28 ga., 26" bbl, ICMF tubes.

Price: 20 gauge **$940.00**
Price: 28 gauge **$990.00**

Franchi 48AL Short Stock Shotgun

Similar to 48AL but with stock shortened to 12-1/2" length of pull.

Price: (20 gauge, 26" barrel) **$715.00**

FRANCHI 612 AND 620 SHOTGUNS

Gauge: 12, 20, 3" chamber. **Barrel:** 24", 26", 28", IC, MF tubes. **Weight:** 7 lbs. **Stock:** European walnut, synthetic and Timber HD. **Features:** Alloy frame with matte black finish; gas-operated with Vario System, four-lug rotating bolt. Introduced 1996. Imported from Italy by Benelli U.S.A.

Price: Walnut wood **$750.00**
Price: Camo, Timber HD **$875.00**
Price: Synthetic (black synthetic stock, forend) **$710.00**
Price: 20 ga., 24", 26", 28", walnut. **$750.00**
Price: Variopress 620 (Timber HD Camo) **$875.00**

Franchi 612 Defense Shotgun

Similar to 612 except has 18-1/2", cylinder-bore barrel with black, synthetic stock. Available in 12 gauge, 3" chamber only. Weighs 6-1/2 lbs. 2-shot magazine extension available. Introduced 2000.

Price: **$635.00**

Franchi 612 Sporting Shotgun

Similar to 612 except has 30" ported barrel to reduce muzzle jump. Available in 12 gauge, 3" chamber only. Introduced 2000.

Price: **$1,275.00**

Franchi 620 Short Stock Shotgun

Similar to 620 but with stock shortened to 12-1/2" length of pull for smaller shooters. Introduced 2000.

Price: (20 gauge, 26" barrel). **$730.00**

FRANCHI MODEL 912

Gauge: 12. **Barrel:** 24", 26", 28", 30". **Weight:** 7.5 to 7.8lbs. **Length:** 46" to 52". **Stock:** Satin walnut; synthetic. **Sights:** White bead, front. **Features:** Chambered for 3-1/2" magnum shells with Dual-Recoil-Reduction-System, multi-lugged rotary bolt. Made in Italy and imported by Benelli USA.

Price: (Walnut) . . . . **$1,000.00**; (Synthetic) **$940.00**
Price: Timber HD Camo **$1,050.00**

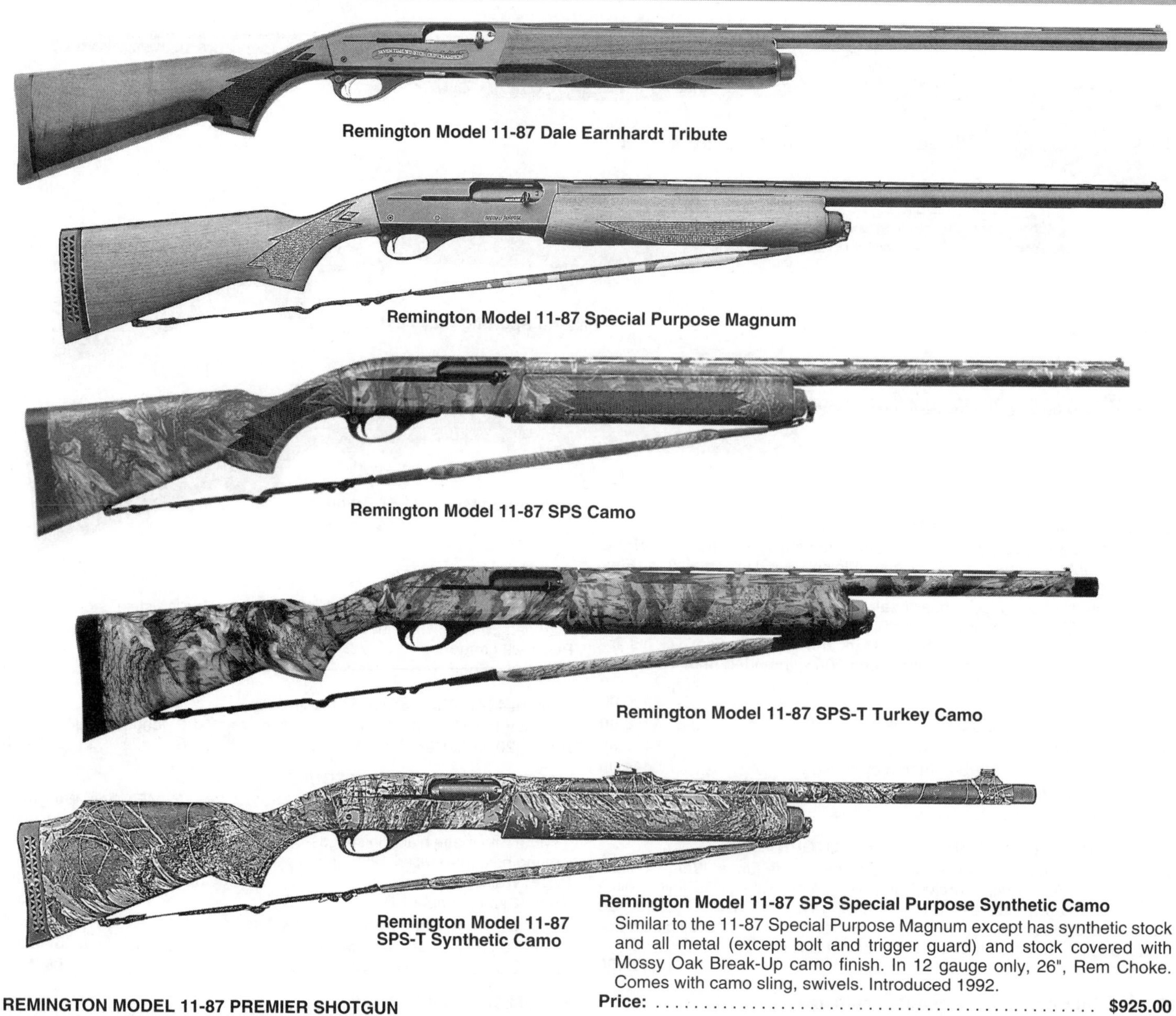

Remington Model 11-87 Dale Earnhardt Tribute

Remington Model 11-87 Special Purpose Magnum

Remington Model 11-87 SPS Camo

Remington Model 11-87 SPS-T Turkey Camo

Remington Model 11-87 SPS-T Synthetic Camo

REMINGTON MODEL 11-87 PREMIER SHOTGUN

Gauge: 12, 20, 3" chamber. **Barrel:** 26", 28", 30" Rem Choke tubes. Light Contour barrel. **Weight:** About 7-3/4 lbs. **Length:** 46" overall (26" bbl.). **Stock:** Walnut with satin or high-gloss finish; cut checkering; solid brown buttpad; no white spacers. **Sights:** Bradley-type white-faced front, metal bead middle. **Features:** Pressure compensating gas system allows shooting 2-3/4" or 3" loads interchangeably with no adjustments. Stainless magazine tube; redesigned feed latch, barrel support ring on operating bars; pinned forend. Introduced 1987.

Price: Light contour barrel **$777.00**
Price: Left-hand, 28" barrel.......... **$831.00**
Price: Premier cantilever deer barrel, fully-rifled, 21" sling, swivels, Monte Carlo stock.......... **$859.00**
Price: 3-1/2" Super Magnum, 28" barrel **$865.00**
Price: Dale Earnhardt Tribute, 12 ga., 28" barrel **$972.00**

Remington Model 11-87 Special Purpose Magnum

Similar to the 11-87 Premier except has dull stock finish, Parkerized exposed metal surfaces. Bolt and carrier have dull blackened coloring. Comes with 26" or 28" barrel with Rem Chokes, padded Cordura nylon sling and quick detachable swivels. Introduced 1987.

Price: With synthetic stock and forend (SPS) **$791.00**

Remington Model 11-87 SPS Special Purpose Synthetic Camo

Similar to the 11-87 Special Purpose Magnum except has synthetic stock and all metal (except bolt and trigger guard) and stock covered with Mossy Oak Break-Up camo finish. In 12 gauge only, 26", Rem Choke. Comes with camo sling, swivels. Introduced 1992.

Price: **$925.00**

Remington Model 11-87 SPS-T Turkey Camo

Similar to the 11-87 Special Purpose Magnum except with synthetic stock, 21" vent. rib barrel with Rem Choke tube. Completely covered with Mossy Oak Break-Up Brown camouflage. Bolt body, trigger guard and recoil pad are non-reflective black.

Price: **$905.00**
Price: Model 11-87 SPS-T Camo CL cantilever **$907.00**

Remington Model 11-87 SPS-T Super Magnum Synthetic Camo

Similar to the 11-87 SPS-T Turkey Camo except has 23" vent rib barrel with Turkey Super full choke tube, chambered for 12 ga., 3-1/2", TruGlo rifle sights. Version available without TruGlo sights. Introduced 2001.

Price: **$963.00**

Remington Model 11-87 SPS-Deer Shotgun

Similar to the 11-87 Special Purpose Camo except has fully-rifled 21" barrel with rifle sights, black non-reflective, synthetic stock and forend, black carrying sling. Introduced 1993.

Price: **$824.00**
Price: With wood stock (Model 11-87 SP Deer Gun) Rem choke, 21" barrel w/rifle sights **$756.00**

Remington Model 11-87 SPS-Deer

Remington Model 11-87 SPS Cantilever

Remington Model 11-87 SP

Remington Model 1100 Youth Turkey Camo

Remington 1100 LT-20 Deer

Remington Model 11-87 SPS Cantilever Shotgun

Similar to the 11-87 SPS except has fully rifled barrel; synthetic stock with Monte Carlo comb; cantilever scope mount deer barrel. Comes with sling and swivels. Introduced 1994.

Price: **$872.00**

Remington Model 11-87 SP and SPS Super Magnum Shotguns

Similar to Model 11-87 Special Purpose Magnum except has 3-1/2" chamber. Available in flat-finish American walnut or black synthetic stock, 26" or 28" black-matte finished barrel and receiver; imp. cyl., modified and full Rem Choke tubes. Overall length 45-3/4", weighs 8 lbs., 2 oz. Introduced 2000. From Remington Arms Co.

Price: 11-87 SP Super Magnum (walnut stock) **$865.00**

Price: 11-87 SPS Super Magnum (synthetic stock) **$879.00**

Price: 11-87 SPS Super Magnum, 28" (camo) **$963.00**

Remington Model 11-87 Upland Special Shotgun

Similar to 11-87 Premier except has 23" ventilated rib barrel with straight-grip, English-style walnut stock. Available in 12 or 20 gauge. Overall length 43-1/2", weighs 7-1/4 lbs. (6-1/2 lbs. in 20 ga.). Comes with imp. cyl., modified and full choke tubes. Introduced 2000.

Price: 12 or 20 gauge **$777.00**

REMINGTON MODEL 1100 SYNTHETIC LT-20 SHOTGUN

Gauge: 20. **Barrel:** 26" Rem Chokes. **Weight:** 6-3/4 lbs. **Stock:** 14"x1-1/2"x2-1/2". Black synthetic, checkered pistol grip and forend. **Fea-tures:** Matted receiver top with scroll work on both sides of receiver.

Price: **$549.00**

Price: Youth Gun LT-20 (21" Rem Choke).................. **$549.00**

Price: Remington Model 1100 Synthetic, 12 gauge, black synthetic stock; vent. rib 28" barrel, Mod. Rem Choke tube. Weighs about 7-1/2 lbs. Introduced 1996............................. **$549.00**

Remington Model 1100 Youth Synthetic Turkey Camo

Similar to the Model 1100 LT-20 except has 1" shorter stock, 21" vent rib barrel with Full Rem Choke tube; 3" chamber; synthetic stock and forend are covered with Skyline Excel camo, and barrel and receiver have non-reflective, black matte finish. Introduced 2003.

Price: **$612.00**

Remington Model 1100 LT-20 Synthetic Deer Shotgun

Similar to the Model 1100 LT-20 except has 21" fully rifled barrel with rifle sights, 2-3/4" chamber, and fiberglass-reinforced synthetic stock. Introduced 1997. Made in U.S. by Remington.

Price: **$583.00**

Remington Model 1100 Sporting 28

Remington Model 1100 Classic Trap

Remington Model 1100 Sporting 12

Remington Model SP-10

Remington Model SP-10 Camo

Remington Model 1100 Sporting 28

Similar to the 1100 LT-20 except in 28 gauge with 25" barrel; comes with Skeet, Imp. Cyl., Light Mod., Mod. Rem Choke tube. Semi-Fancy walnut with gloss finish, Sporting rubber butt pad. Made in U.S. by Remington. Introduced 1996.

Price: **$901.00**

Remington Model 1100 Sporting 20 Shotgun

Similar to Model 1100 LT-20 except tournament-grade American walnut stock with gloss finish and sporting-style recoil pad, 28" Rem choke barrel for Skeet, Imp. Cyl., Light Modified and Modified. Introduced 1998.

Price: **$868.00**

Remington Model 1100 Classic Trap Shotgun

Similar to Standard Model 1100 except 12 gauge with 30", low-profile barrel, semi-fancy American walnut stock, high-polish blued receiver with engraving and gold eagle inlay. Singles, mid handicap and long handicap choke tubes. Overall length 50-1/2", weighs 8 lbs., 4 oz. Introduced 2000. From Remington Arms Co.

Price: **$895.00**

Remington Model 1100 Sporting 12 Shotgun

Similar to Model 1100 Sporting 20 Shotgun except in 12 gauge, 28" ventilated barrel with semi-fancy American walnut stock, gold-plated trigger. Overall length 49", weighs 8 lbs. Introduced 2000. From Remington Arms Co.

Price: **$901.00**

Remington Model 1100 Synthetic Deer Shotgun

Similar to Model 1100 LT-20 except 12 gauge, 21" fully rifled barrel with cantilever scope mount and fiberglass-reinforced synthetic stock with Monte Carlo comb. Introduced 1997. Made in U.S. by Remington.

Price: **$629.00**

REMINGTON MODEL SP-10 MAGNUM SHOTGUN

Gauge: 10, 3-1/2" chamber, 2-shot magazine. **Barrel:** 26", 30" (full and mod. Rem chokes). **Weight:** 10-3/4 to 11 lbs. **Length:** 47-1/2" overall (26" barrel). **Stock:** Walnut with satin finish or black synthetic with 26" barrel. Checkered grip and forend. **Sights:** Twin bead. **Features:** Stainless steel gas system with moving cylinder; 3/8" ventilated rib. Receiver and barrel have matte finish. Brown recoil pad. Comes with padded Cordura nylon sling. Introduced 1989.

Price: **$1,317.00**

Remington Model SP-10 Magnum Camo Shotgun

Similar to SP-10 Magnum except buttstock, forend, receiver, barrel and magazine cap are covered with Mossy Oak Break-Up camo finish; bolt body and trigger guard have matte black finish. Rem choke tube, 26" vent. rib barrel with mid-rib bead and Bradley-style front sight, swivel studs and quick-detachable swivels, non-slip Cordura carrying sling in same camo pattern. Introduced 1993.

Price: **$1,453.00**

Stoeger Model 2000

Tristar CD Diana

Traditions ALS 2100

SARSILMAZ SEMI-AUTOMATIC SHOTGUN

Gauge: 12, 3" chamber. **Barrel:** 26" or 28"; fixed chokes. **Stock:** Walnut or synthetic. **Features:** Handles 2-3/4" or 3" magnum loads. Introduced 2000. Imported from Turkey by Armsport Inc.

Price: With walnut stock **$969.95**
Price: With synthetic stock **$919.95**

STOEGER MODEL 2000

Gauge: 12, 3" chamber, set of 5 choke tubes. **Barrel:** 24", 26", 28", 30". **Stock:** Walnut, deluxe, synthetic, and Timber HD. **Sights:** White bar. **Features:** Inertia-recoil for light target to turkey leads. Single trigger combo 26"/24" pack with optional 24" slug barrel.

Price: Walnut, 26", 28", 30" bbl. **$499.00**
Price: Synthetic, 24", 26", 28" bbl. **$480.00**
Price: Synthetic combo, 26"/24" bbl. **$560.00**
Price: Optional slug bbl., 26" **$105.00**
Price: Timber HD, 24", 26", 28" bbl. **$550.00**

TRADITIONS ALS 2100 SERIES SEMI-AUTOMATIC SHOTGUNS

Gauge: 12, 3" chamber; 20, 3" chamber. **Barrel:** 24", 26", 28" (imp. cyl., mod. and full choke tubes). **Weight:** 5 lbs., 10 oz. to 6 lbs., 5 oz. **Length:** 44" to 48" overall. **Stock:** Walnut or black composite. **Features:** Gas-operated; vent-rib barrel with Beretta-style threaded muzzle. Introduced 2001 by Traditions.

Price: (12 or 20 ga., 26" or 28" barrel, walnut stock) **$479.00**
Price: (12 or 20 ga., 24" barrel Youth Model, walnut stock) **$479.00**
Price: (12 or 20 ga., 26" or 28" barrel, composite stock) **$459.00**

Traditions ALS 2100 Turkey Semi-Automatic Shotgun

Similar to ALS 2100 Field Model except chambered in 12 gauge, 3" only with 26" barrel and Mossy Oak® Break Up™ camo finish. Weighs 6 lbs., 46" overall.

Price: **$519.00**

Traditions ALS 2100 Waterfowl Semi-Automatic Shotgun

Similar to ALS 2100 Field Model except chambered in 12 gauge, 3" only with 28" barrel and Advantage® Wetlands™ camo finish. Weighs 6.25 lbs.; 48" overall. Multi chokes.

Price: **$529.00**

Traditions ALS 2100 Hunter Combo

Similar to ALS 2100 Field Model except 2 barrels, 28" vent rib and 24" fully rifled deer. Weighs 6-6.5 lbs.; 48" overall. Choice TruGlo adj. sights or fixed cantilever mount on rifled barrel. Multi chokes.

Price: Walnut, rifle barrel **$609.00**
Price: Walnut, cantilever **$629.00**
Price: Synthetic **$579.00**

Traditions ALS 2100 Slug Hunter

Similar to ALS 2100 Field Model, 12 ga., 24" barrel, overall length 44", weighs 6.25 lbs. Designed specificaly for the deer hunter. Rifled barrel has 1 in 36" twist. Fully adjustable sights are fiber optic.

Price: Walnut, rifle barrel. **$529.00**
Price: Synthetic, rifle barrel. **$499.00**
Price: Walnut, cantilever **$549.00**
Price: Synthetic, cantilever **$529.00**

Traditions ALS 2100 Home Security

Similar to ALS 2100 Field Model, 12 ga., 20" barrel, overall length 40", weighs 6 lbs. Can be reloaded with one hand while shouldered and on-target. Swivel studs installed in stock.

Price: **$399.00**

TRISTAR CD DIANA AUTO SHOTGUNS

Gauge: 12, shoots 2-3/4" or 3" interchangeably. **Barrel:** 24", 26", 28" (Imp. Cyl., Mod., Full choke tubes). **Stock:** European walnut or black synthetic. **Features:** Gas-operated action; blued barrel; checkered pistol grip and forend; vent rib barrel. Available with synthetic and camo stock and in slug model. First introduced 1999 under the name "Tristar Phantom." Imported by Tristar Sporting Arms Ltd.

Price: . . . . **$399.00 to $576.00**

VERONA MODEL SX400 SEMI AUTO SHOTGUN

Gauge: 12. **Barrel:** 26", 30". **Weight:** 6-1/2 lbs. **Stock:** Walnut, black composite. **Sights:** Red dot. **Features:** Aluminum receivers, gas-operated, 2-3/4" or 3" Magnum shells without adj. or mod., 4 screw-in chokes and wrench included. Sling swivels, gold trigger. Blued barrel. Imported from Italy by B.C. Outdoors.

Price: 401S, 12 ga. **$398.40**
Price: 405SDS, 12 ga. **$610.00**
Price: 405L, 12 ga. **$331.20**

WEATHERBY SAS (SEMI-AUTOMATIC SHOTGUNS)

6 Models: SAS Field, SAS Sporting Clays, SAS Shadow Grass, SAS Break-Up, SAS Synthetic and a Slug Gun.

Gauge: 12 ga. **Barrel:** Vent ribbed, 24"-30". **Stock:** SAS Field and Sporting Clays, walnut. SAS Shadow Grass, Break-Up, Synthetic, composite. **Sights:** SAS Sporting Clays, frass front and mid-point back. SAS Shadow Grass and Break-Up, HiViz front and brass mid. Synthetic has brass front. **Features:** Easy to shoot, load, clean, lightweight, lessened recoil, IMC system includes 3 chrome moly screw-in choke tubes. Slug gun has 22" rifled barrel with matte blue finish and cantilever base for scope mounting.

Price: . . . . **$699.00 to 849.00**

SHOTGUNS — AUTOLOADERS

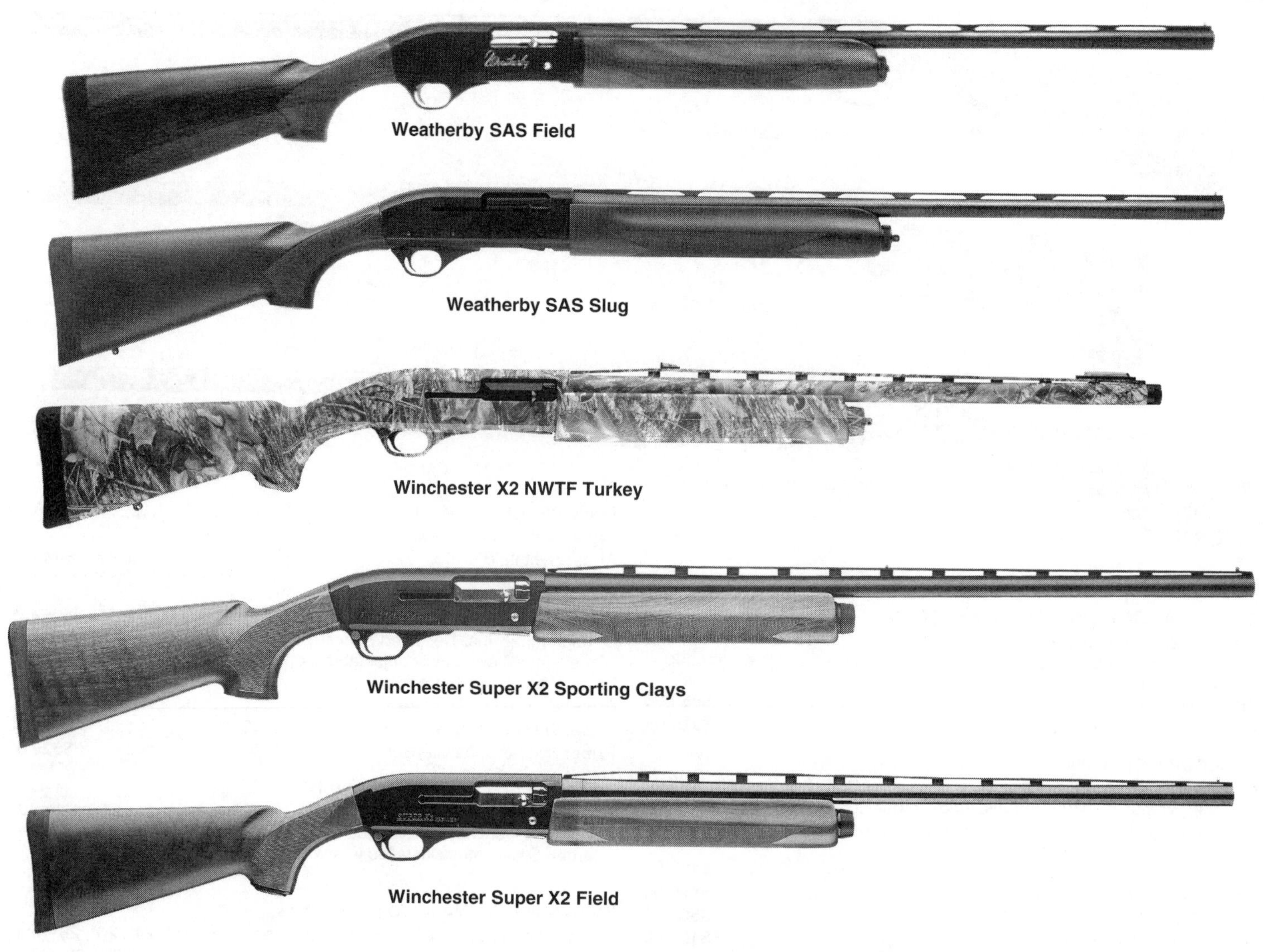
Weatherby SAS Field

Weatherby SAS Slug

Winchester X2 NWTF Turkey

Winchester Super X2 Sporting Clays

Winchester Super X2 Field

WINCHESTER SUPER X2 AUTO SHOTGUN

Gauge: 12, 3", 3-1/2" chamber. **Barrel:** Belgian, 24", 26", 28"; Invector Plus choke tubes. **Weight:** 7-1/4 to 7-1/2 lbs. **Stock:** 14-1/4"x1-3/4"x2". Walnut or black synthetic. **Features:** Gas-operated action shoots all loads without adjustment; vent. rib barrels; 4-shot magazine. Introduced 1999. Assembled in Portugal by U.S. Repeating Arms Co.

Price: Field, walnut or synthetic stock, 3" **$874.00**
Price: Magnum, 3-1/2", synthetic stock, 26" or 28" bbl. **$988.00**
Price: Camo Waterfowl, 3-1/2", Mossy Oak Shadow Grass **$1,139.00**
Price: NWTF Turkey, 3-1/2", Mossy Oak Break-Up camo. **$1,165.00**
Price: Universal Hunter Model **$1,139.00**

WINCHESTER SUPER X2 SPORTING CLAYS AUTO SHOTGUN

Similar to the Super X2 except has two gas pistons (one for target loads, one for heavy 3" loads), adjustable comb system and high-post rib. Back-bored barrel with Invector Plus choke tubes. Offered in 28" and 30" barrels. Introduced 2001. From U.S. Repeating Arms Co.

Price: Super X2 Sporting Clays **$959.00**
Price: Signature red stock **$976.00**

Winchester Super X2 Field 3" Auto Shotgun

Similar to the Super X2 except has a 3" chamber, walnut stock and forearm and high-profile rib. Back-bored barrel and Invector Plus choke tubes. Introduced 2001. From U.S. Repeating Arms Co.

Price: Super X2 Field 3", 26" or 28" bbl. **$874.00**

SHOTGUNS — SLIDE & LEVER ACTIONS

Includes a wide variety of sporting guns and guns suitable for competitive shooting.

Armscor M-30F Field

Benelli Nova Pump

Benelli Nova Pump Slug

Browning BPS 10 gauge

Browning BPS 10 gauge Mossy Oak® Shadow Grass

ARMSCOR M-30F FIELD PUMP SHOTGUN

Gauge: 12, 3" chamber. **Barrel:** 28" fixed Mod., or with Mod. and Full choke tubes. **Weight:** 7.6 lbs. **Stock:** Walnut-finished hardwood. **Features:** Dou-ble action slide bars; blued steel receiver; damascened bolt. Introduced 1996. Imported from the Philippines by K.B.I., Inc.

Price: With fixed choke **$239.00**
Price: With choke tubes **$269.00**

BENELLI NOVA PUMP SHOTGUN

Gauge: 12, 20. **Barrel:** 24", 26", 28". **Stock:** Synthetic, X-tra Brown 12 ga., Timber HD 20 ga. **Sights:** Red bar. **Features:** 2-3/4", 3" chamber (3-2/1" 12 ga. only). Montefeltro rotating bolt design with dual action bars, magazine cut-off, synthetic trigger assembly, 4-shot magazine. Introduced 1999. Imported from Italy by Benelli USA.

Price: Synthetic **$335.00**
Price: Timber HD **$400.00**
Price: Youth model **$415.00**

Benelli Nova Pump Slug Gun

Similar to the Nova except has 18.5" barrel with adjustable rifle-type or ghost ring sights; weighs 7.2 lbs.; black synthetic stock. Introduced 1999. Imported from Italy by Benelli USA.

Price: With rifle sights **$355.00**
Price: With ghost-ring sights **$395.00**

Benelli Nova Pump Rifled Slug Gun

Similar to Nova Pump Slug Gun except has 24" barrel and rifled bore; open rifle sights; synthetic stock; weighs 8.1 pounds.

Price: . . . . (Synthetic) **$500.00**; Timber HD **$575.00**

BROWNING BPS PUMP SHOTGUN

Gauge: 10, 12, 3-1/2" chamber; 12 or 20, 3" chamber (2-3/4" in target guns), 28, 2-3/4" chamber, 5-shot magazine, .410, 3" chamber. **Barrel:** 10 ga.- 24" Buck Special, 28", 30", 32" Invector; 12, 20 ga.-22", 24", 26", 28", 30", 32" (Imp. Cyl., mod. or full). .410-26" barrel. (Imp. Cyl., mod. and full choke tubes.) Also available with Invector choke tubes, 12 or 20 ga.; Upland Special has 22" barrel with Invector tubes. BPS 3" and 3-1/2" have back-bored barrel. **Weight:** 7 lbs., 8 oz. (28" barrel). **Length:** 48-3/4" overall (28" barrel). **Stock:** 14-1/4"x1-1/2"x2-1/2". Select walnut, semi-beavertail forend, full pistol grip stock. **Features:** All 12 gauge 3" guns except Buck Special and game guns have back-bored barrels with Invector Plus choke tubes. Bottom feeding and ejection, receiver top safety, high post vent. rib. Double action bars eliminate binding. Vent. rib barrels only. All 12 and 20 gauge guns with 3" chamber available with fully engraved receiver flats at no extra cost. Each gauge has its own unique game scene. Introduced 1977. Imported from Japan by Browning.

Price: 12 ga., 3-1/2" Magnum Stalker (black syn. stock). **$562.00**
Price: 12, 20 ga., Hunter, Invector Plus **$494.00**
Price: 12 ga. Deer Hunter (22" rifled bbl., cantilever mount). **$606.00**
Price: 28 ga., Hunter, Invector **$528.00**
Price: .410, Hunter, Invector **$528.00**

Browning BPS 10 Gauge Shotguns

Chambered for the 10 gauge, 3-1/2" load. Offered in 24", 26" and 28" barrels. Offered with walnut, black composite (Stalker models) or camouflage stock and forend. Introduced 1999. Imported by Browning.

Price: Stalker (composite). **$562.00**
Price: Mossy Oak® Shadow Grass or Break-Up Camo **$668.00**

Browning BPS 10 Gauge Camo Pump Shotgun

Similar to the BPS 10 gauge Hunter except completely covered with Mossy Oak Shadow Grass camouflage. Available with 24", 26", 28" barrel. Introduced 1999. Imported by Browning.

Price: **$668.00**

EAA/Baikal MP-133

Escort AimGuard

Escort FieldHunter

Fabarm Field Pump

Browning BPS Waterfowl Camo Pump Shotgun

Similar to the BPS Hunter except completely covered with Mossy Oak Shadow Grass camouflage. Available in 12 gauge, with 24", 26" or 28" barrel, 3" chamber. Introduced 1999. Imported by Browning.

Price: **$652.00**

Browning BPS Game Gun Deer Hunter

Similar to the standard BPS except has newly designed receiver/magazine tube/barrel mounting system to eliminate play, heavy 20.5" barrel with rifle-type sights with adjustable rear, solid receiver scope mount, "rifle" stock dimensions for scope or open sights, sling swivel studs. Gloss or matte finished wood with checkering, polished blue metal. Introduced 1992.

Price: **$568.00**

Browning BPS Game Gun Turkey Special

Similar to the standard BPS except has satin-finished walnut stock and dull-finished barrel and receiver. Receiver is drilled and tapped for scope mounting. Rifle-style stock dimensions and swivel studs. Has Extra-Full Turkey choke tube. Introduced 1992.

Price: **$500.00**

Browning BPS Stalker Pump Shotgun

Same gun as the standard BPS except all exposed metal parts have a matte blued finish and the stock has a durable black finish with a black recoil pad. Available in 10 ga. (3-1/2") and 12 ga. with 3" or 3-1/2" chamber, 22", 28", 30" barrel with Invector choke system. Introduced 1987.

Price: 12 ga., 3" chamber, Invector Plus. **$448.00**

Price: 10, 12 ga., 3-1/2" chamber. **$537.00**

Browning BPS NWTF Turkey Series Pump Shotgun

Similar to the BPS Stalker except has full coverage Mossy Oak® Break-Up camo finish on synthetic stock, forearm and exposed metal parts. Offered in 10 and 12 gauge, 3" or 3-1/2" chamber; 24" bbl. has extra-full choke tube and Hi-Viz fiber optic sights. Introduced 2001. From Browning.

Price: 10 ga., 3-1/2" chamber. **$637.00**

Price: 12 ga., 3-1/2" chamber. **$637.00**

Price: 12 ga., 3" chamber. **$549.00**

Browning BPS Micro Pump Shotgun

Same as BPS Upland Special except 20 ga. only, 22" Invector barrel, stock has pistol grip with recoil pad. Length of pull is 13-1/4"; weighs 6 lbs., 12 oz. Introduced 1986.

Price: **$482.00**

DIAMOND 12 GA. PUMP SHOTGUN

Gauge: 12, 2-3/4" and 3" chambers. **Barrel:** 18"-30". **Weight:** 7 lbs. **Stock:** Walnut, synthetic. **Features:** Aluminum one-piece receiver sculpted for lighter weight. Double locking on fixed bolt. Gold, Elite and Panther series with vented barrels and 3 chokes. All series slug guns available (Gold and Elite with sights). Imported from Istanbul by ADCO Sales.

Price: Gold, 28" vent rib w/3 chokes, walnut **$359.00**

Price: Gold, 28", synthetic **$329.00**

Price: Gold Slug, 24" w/sights, walnut or synthetic . . **$329.00 to $359.00**

Price: Silver Mariner 18.5" Slug, synthetic **$399.00**

Price: Silver Mariner 22" vent rib w/3 chokes **$419.00**

Price: Elite, 22" slug w/sights; 24", 28" ventib w/3 chokes, walnut . . . . **$329.00 to $349.00**

Price: Panther, 28", 30" vent rib w/3 chokes, synthetic. **$279.00**

Price: Panther,18.5", 22" Slug, synthetic . . . . **$209.00 to $265.00**

Price: Imperial 12 ga., 28" vent rib w/3 chokes, 3.5" chamber, walnut **$399.00**

EAA/BAIKAL MP-133 PUMP SHOTGUN

Gauge: 12, 3-1/2" chamber. **Barrel:** 18-1/2", 20", 24", 26", 28"; imp., mod. and full choke tubes. **Weight:** NA. **Stock:** Walnut; checkered grip and grooved forearm. **Features:** Hammer-forged, chrome-lined barrel with ventilated rib; machined steel parts; dual action bars; trigger-block safety; 4-shot magazine tube; handles 2-3/4" through 3-1/2" shells. Introduced 2000. Imported by European American Armory.

Price: MP-133 (blued finish, walnut stock and forend) **$359.00**

ESCORT PUMP SHOTGUN

Gauge: 12, 3" chamber. **Barrel:** 20", fixed (AimGuard model); 24" and 28" (Field Hunter models), choke tubes (M, IC, F); turkey choke w/ 24" bbl. **Weight:** 6.4 to 7 lbs. **Stock:** Polymer, black chrome or camo finish. **Features:** Alloy receiver w/ dovetail for sight mounting. Two stock adjusting spacers included. Introduced 2003. From Legacy Sports International.

Price: Field Hunter, black stock **$224.00**

Price: Field Hunter, camo stock **$271.00**

Price: Camo, 24" bbl. **$444.00**

Price: AimGuard, 20" bbl., black stock **$199.00**

Ithaca Model 37 Waterfowl

Ithaca Model 37 Deerslayer II

Mossberg Model 835
Mossy Oak Camo

FABARM FIELD PUMP SHOTGUN

Gauge: 12, 3" chamber. **Barrel:** 28" (24" rifled slug barrel available). **Weight:** 76.6 lbs. **Length:** 48.25" overall. **Stock:** Polymer. **Features:** Similar to Fabarm FP6 Pump Shotgun. Alloy receiver; twin action bars; available in black or Mossy Oak Break-Up™ camo finish. Includes cyl., mod. and full choke tubes. Introduced 2001. Imported from Italy by Heckler & Koch Inc.

Price: Matte black finish **$399.00**
Price: Mossy Oak Break-Up™ finish **$469.00**

ITHACA MODEL 37 DELUXE PUMP SHOTGUN

Gauge: 12, 16, 20, 3" chamber. **Barrel:** 26", 28", 30" (12 gauge), 26", 28" (16 and 20 gauge), choke tubes. **Weight:** 7 lbs. **Stock:** Walnut with cut-checkered grip and forend. **Features:** Steel receiver; bottom ejection; brushed blue finish, vent rib barrels. Reintroduced 1996. Made in U.S. by Ithaca Gun Co.

Price: **$633.00**
Price: With straight English-style stock **$803.00**
Price: Model 37 New Classic (ringtail forend, sunburst recoil pad, hand-finished walnut stock, 26" or 28" barrel) **$803.00**

ITHACA MODEL 37 WATERFOWL

Similar to Model 37 Deluxe except in 12 gauge only with 24", 26", or 30" barrel, special extended steel shot choke tube system. Complete coverage of Advantage Wetlands or Hardwoods camouflage. Introduced 1999. Made in U.S. by Ithaca Gun Co. Storm models have synthetic stock.

Price: . . . . **$499.00 to $549.00**

ITHACA MODEL 37 DEERSLAYER II PUMP SHOTGUN

Gauge: 12, 16, 20; 3" chamber. **Barrel:** 24", 26", fully rifled. **Weight:** 11 lbs. **Stock:** Cut-checkered American walnut with Monte Carlo comb. **Sights:** Rifle-type. **Features:** Integral barrel and receiver. Bottom ejection. Brushed blue finish. Reintroduced 1997. Made in U.S. by Ithaca Gun Co. Storm models have synthetic stock.

Price: **$633.00**
Price: Smooth Bore Deluxe **$582.00**
Price: Rifled Deluxe **$582.00**
Price: Storm **$399.00**

ITHACA MODEL 37 DEERSLAYER III PUMP SHOTGUN

Gauge: 12, 20, 2-3/4" and 3" chambers. **Barrel:** 26" free floated. **Weight:** 9 lbs. **Stock:** Monte Carlo laminate. **Sights:** Rifled. **Features:** Barrel length gives increased velocity. Trigger and sear set hand filed and stoned for creep free operation. Weaver-style scope base. Swivel studs. Matte blue.

Price: . . . . **Custom order only**

ITHACA MODEL 37 RUFFED GROUSE SPECIAL EDITION

Gauge: 20 ga. **Barrel:** 22", 24", interchangeable choke tubes. **Weight:** 5.25 lbs. **Stock:** American black walnut. **Features:** Laser engraved stock with line art drawing. Bottom eject. Vent rib and English style. Right- or left-hand thru simple safety change. Aluminum receiver. Made in U.S.A. by Ithaca Gun Co.

Price: **$840.00**

ITHACA TURKEYSLAYER STORM

Gauge: 12 or 20 ga., 3" chamber. **Barrel:** 24" ported. **Stock:** Composite. **Sights:** TruGlo front and rear. **Features:** Itha-Choke full turkey choke tube. Matte metal, Realtree Hardwoods pattern, swivel studs.

Price: Storm **$459.00**

ITHACA MODEL 37 ULTRALIGHT DELUXE

Gauge: 16 ga. 2-3/4" chamber. **Barrel:** 24", 26", 28". **Weight:** 5.25 lbs. **Stock:** Standard deluxe. **Sights:** Raybar. **Features:** Vent rib, drilled and tapped, interchangeable barrel. F, M, IC choke tubes.

Price: Deluxe **$649.00**
Price: Classic/English **$824.00**
Price: Classic/Pistol **$824.00**

MARLIN PARDNER PUMP

Gauge: 12 ga., 3". **Barrel:** 28" vent rib, screw-in modified choke tube. **Weight:** 7 1/2 pounds. **Length:** 48 1/2". **Stock:** American walnut, grooved forend, ventilated recoil pad. **Sights:** Bead front. **Features:** Machined steel receiver, double action bars, five-shot magazine.

Price: **$200.00**

MOSSBERG MODEL 835 ULTI-MAG PUMP

Gauge: 12, 3-1/2" chamber. **Barrel:** Ported 24" rifled bore, 24", 28", Accu-Mag choke tubes for steel or lead shot. **Weight:** 7-3/4 lbs. **Length:** 48-1/2" overall. **Stock:** 14"x1-1/2"x2-1/2". Dual Comb. Cut-checkered hardwood or camo synthetic; both have recoil pad. **Sights:** White bead front, brass mid-bead; Fiber Optic. **Features:** Shoots 2-3/4", 3" or 3-1/2" shells. Back-bored and ported barrel to reduce recoil, improve patterns. Ambidextrous thumb safety, twin extractors, dual slide bars. Mossberg Cablelock included. Introduced 1988.

Price: 28" vent. rib, hardwood stock **$394.00**
Price: Combos, 24" rifled or smooth bore, rifle sights, 24" vent. rib Accu-Mag Ulti-Full choke tube, Mossy Oak camo finish **$556.00**
Price: RealTree Camo Turkey, 24" vent. rib, Accu-Mag Extra-Full tube, synthetic stock **$460.00**
Price: Mossy Oak Camo, 28" vent. rib, Accu-Mag tubes, synthetic stock **$460.00**
Price: OFM Camo, 28" vent. rib, Accu-Mag Mod. tube, synthetic stock **$438.00**

SHOTGUNS — SLIDE & LEVER ACTIONS

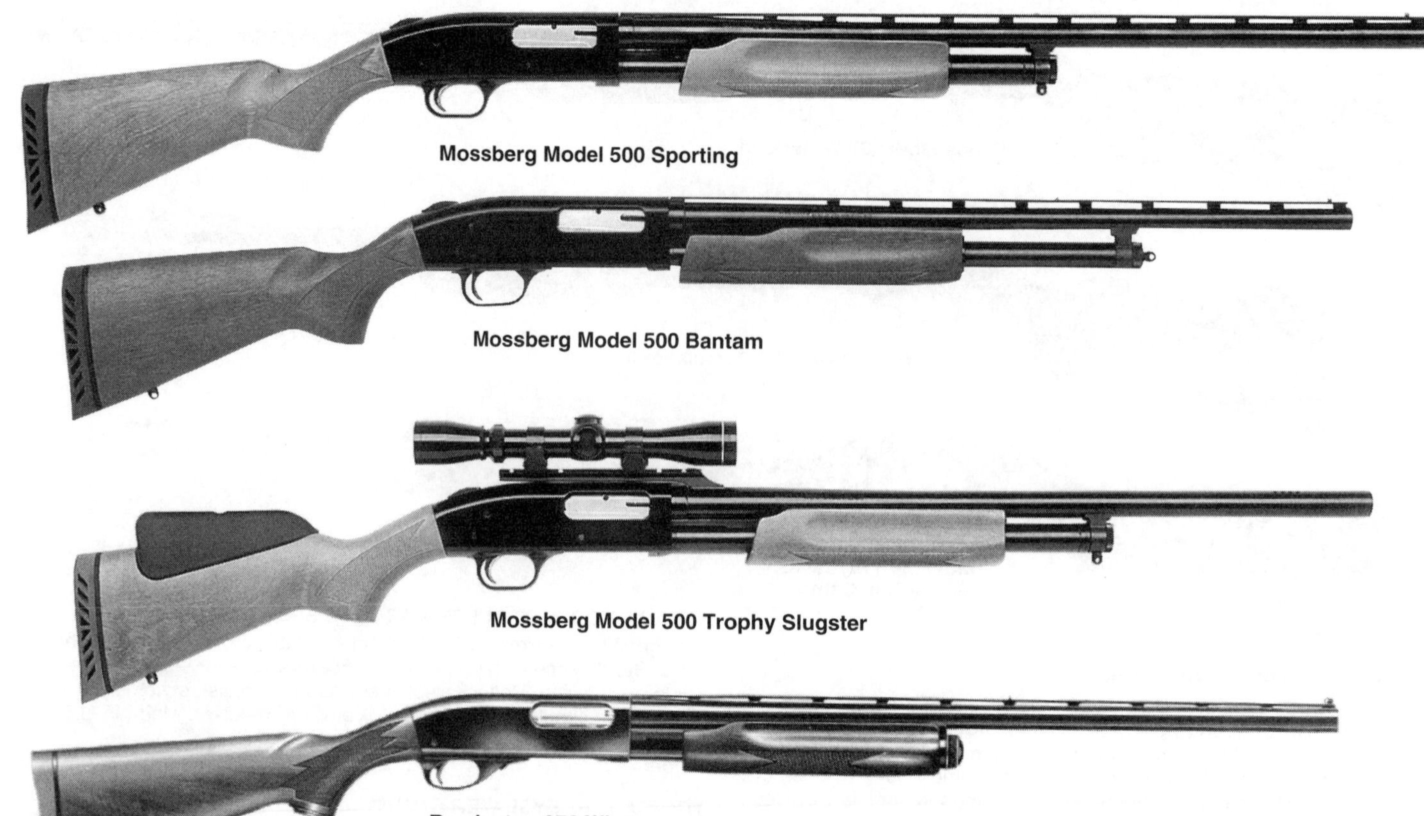

Mossberg Model 500 Sporting

Mossberg Model 500 Bantam

Mossberg Model 500 Trophy Slugster

Remington 870 Wingmaster

Mossberg Model 835 Synthetic Stock

Similar to the Model 835, except with 28" ported barrel with Accu-Mag Mod. choke tube, Parkerized finish, black synthetic stock and forend. Introduced 1998. Made in U.S. by Mossberg.

Price: **$394.00**

MOSSBERG MODEL 500 SPORTING PUMP

Gauge: 12, 20, .410, 3" chamber. **Barrel:** 18-1/2" to 28" with fixed or Accu-Choke, plain or vent. rib. **Weight:** 6-1/4 lbs. (.410), 7-1/4 lbs. (12). **Length:** 48" overall (28" barrel). **Stock:** 14"x1-1/2"x2-1/2". Walnut-stained hardwood. Cut-checkered grip and forend. **Sights:** White bead front, brass mid-bead; Fiber Optic. **Features:** Ambidextrous thumb safety, twin extractors, disconnecting safety, dual action bars. Quiet Carry forend. Many barrels are ported. Mossberg Cablelock included. From Mossberg.

Price: From about **$316.00**

Price: Sporting Combos (field barrel and Slugster barrel), from . . **$381.00**

Mossberg Model 500 Bantam Pump

Same as the Model 500 Sporting Pump except 12 (new for 2001) or 20 gauge, 22" vent. rib Accu-Choke barrel with choke tube set; has 1" shorter stock, reduced length from pistol grip to trigger, reduced forend reach. Introduced 1992.

Price: **$316.00**

Price: With Realtree Hardwoods camouflage finish (20 ga. only) . **$364.00**

Mossberg Model 500 Camo Pump

Same as the Model 500 Sporting Pump except 12 gauge only and entire gun is covered with Mossy Oak Advantage camouflage finish. Receiver drilled and tapped for scope mounting. Comes with quick detachable swivel studs, swivels, camouflage sling, Mossberg Cablelock.

Price: From about **$364.00**

MOSSBERG MODEL 500 PERSUADER/CRUISER SHOTGUN

Similar to Mossberg Model 500 except has 18-1/2" or 20" barrel with cylinder bore choke, synthetic stock and blue or Parkerized finish. Available in 12, 20 and .410 with bead or ghost ring sights, 6- or 8-shot mag-azines. From Mossberg.

Price: 12 gauge, 20" barrel, 8-shot, bead sight. **$391.00**

Price: 20 gauge or .410, 18-1/2" barrel, 6-shot, bead sight **$353.00**

Price: 12 gauge, parkerized finish, 6-shot, 18-1/2" barrel, ghost ring sights **$468.00**

Price: Home Security 410 (.410, 18-1/2" barrel with spreader choke) **$335.00**

Mossberg Model 590 Special Purpose Shotgun

Similar to Model 500 except has parkerized or Marinecote finish, 9-shot magazine and black synthetic stock (some models feature Speed Feed. Available in 12 gauge only with 20", cylinder bore barrel. Weighs 7-1/4 lbs. From Mossberg.

Price: Bead sight, heat shield over barrel **$417.00**

Price: Ghost ring sight, Speed Feed stock. **$586.00**

MOSSBERG MODEL 500 SLUGSTER

Gauge: 12, 20, 3" chamber. **Barrel:** 24", ported rifled bore. Integral scope mount. **Weight:** 7-1/4 lbs. **Length:** 44" overall. **Stock:** 14" pull, 1-3/8" drop at heel. Walnut; Dual Comb design for proper eye positioning with or without scoped barrels. Recoil pad and swivel studs. **Features:** Ambidextrous thumb safety, twin extractors, dual slide bars. Comes with scope mount. Mossberg Cablelock included. Introduced 1988.

Price: Rifled bore, integral scope mount, 12 or 20 ga. **$361.00**

Price: Fiber Optic, rifle sights **$361.00**

Price: Rifled bore, rifle sights **$338.00**

Price: 20 ga., Standard or Bantam, from **$338.00**

REMINGTON MODEL 870 WINGMASTER

Gauge: 12ga., 16 ga., 3" chamber. **Barrel:** 26", 28", 30" (Rem chokes). **Weight:** 7-1/4 lbs.. **Length:** 46", 48". **Stock:** Walnut, hardwood, synthetic. **Sights:** Single bead (Twin bead Wingmaster). **Features:** Balistically balanced performance, milder recoil. Light contour barrel. Double action bars, cross-bolt safety, blue finish.

Price: Wingmaster, walnut, blued, 26", 28", 30" **$584.00**

Price: 870 Wingmaster Super Magnum, 3-1/2" chamber, 28" . . . **$665.00**

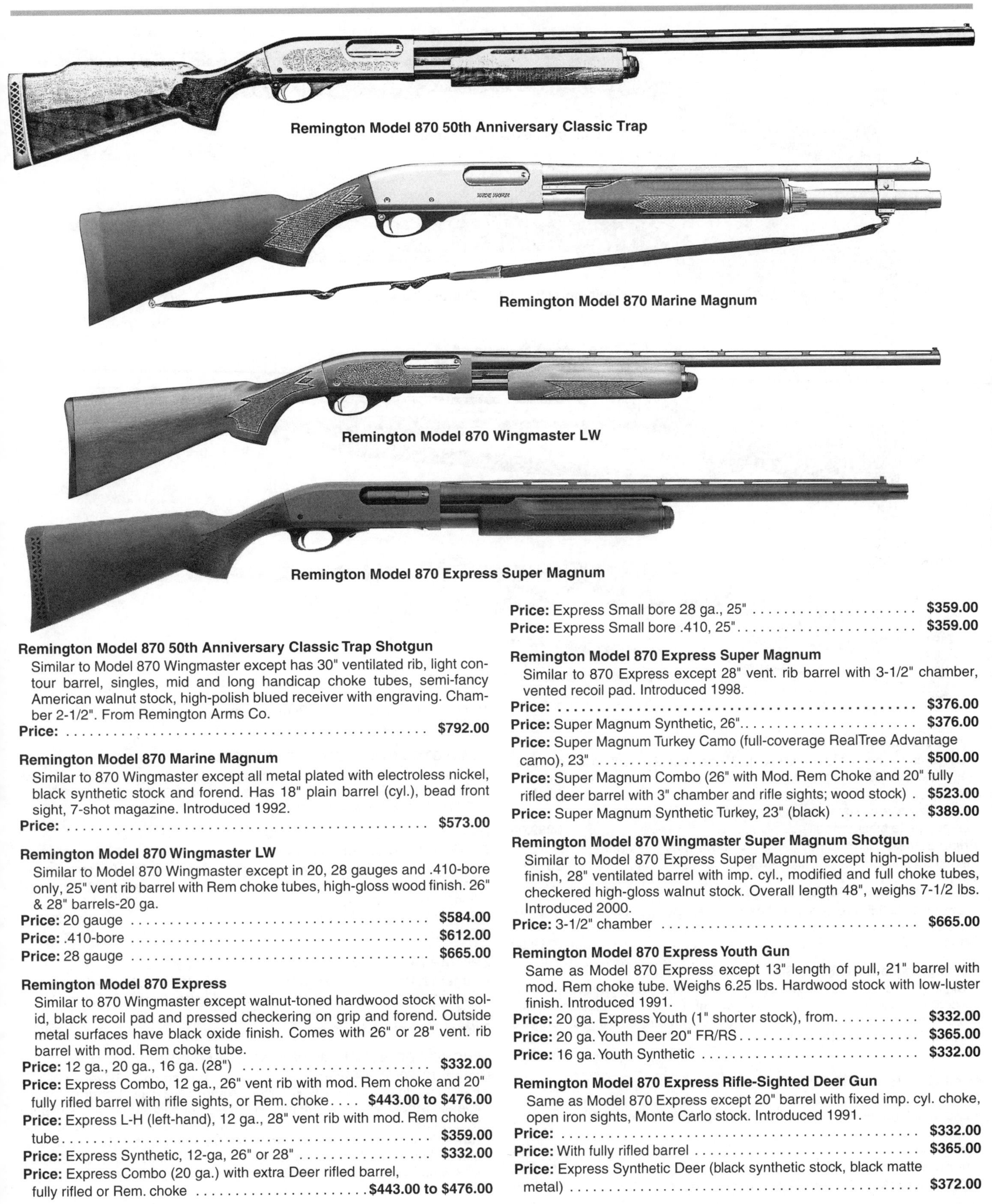

Remington Model 870 50th Anniversary Classic Trap

Remington Model 870 Marine Magnum

Remington Model 870 Wingmaster LW

Remington Model 870 Express Super Magnum

Remington Model 870 50th Anniversary Classic Trap Shotgun

Similar to Model 870 Wingmaster except has 30" ventilated rib, light contour barrel, singles, mid and long handicap choke tubes, semi-fancy American walnut stock, high-polish blued receiver with engraving. Chamber 2-1/2". From Remington Arms Co.

Price: **$792.00**

Remington Model 870 Marine Magnum

Similar to 870 Wingmaster except all metal plated with electroless nickel, black synthetic stock and forend. Has 18" plain barrel (cyl.), bead front sight, 7-shot magazine. Introduced 1992.

Price: **$573.00**

Remington Model 870 Wingmaster LW

Similar to Model 870 Wingmaster except in 20, 28 gauges and .410-bore only, 25" vent rib barrel with Rem choke tubes, high-gloss wood finish. 26" & 28" barrels-20 ga.

Price: 20 gauge **$584.00**
Price: .410-bore **$612.00**
Price: 28 gauge **$665.00**

Remington Model 870 Express

Similar to 870 Wingmaster except walnut-toned hardwood stock with solid, black recoil pad and pressed checkering on grip and forend. Outside metal surfaces have black oxide finish. Comes with 26" or 28" vent. rib barrel with mod. Rem choke tube.

Price: 12 ga., 20 ga., 16 ga. (28") **$332.00**
Price: Express Combo, 12 ga., 26" vent rib with mod. Rem choke and 20" fully rifled barrel with rifle sights, or Rem. choke . . . . **$443.00 to $476.00**
Price: Express L-H (left-hand), 12 ga., 28" vent rib with mod. Rem choke tube **$359.00**
Price: Express Synthetic, 12-ga, 26" or 28" **$332.00**
Price: Express Combo (20 ga.) with extra Deer rifled barrel, fully rifled or Rem. choke . . . . **$443.00 to $476.00**
Price: Express Small bore 28 ga., 25" **$359.00**
Price: Express Small bore .410, 25" **$359.00**

Remington Model 870 Express Super Magnum

Similar to 870 Express except 28" vent. rib barrel with 3-1/2" chamber, vented recoil pad. Introduced 1998.

Price: **$376.00**
Price: Super Magnum Synthetic, 26" **$376.00**
Price: Super Magnum Turkey Camo (full-coverage RealTree Advantage camo), 23" **$500.00**
Price: Super Magnum Combo (26" with Mod. Rem Choke and 20" fully rifled deer barrel with 3" chamber and rifle sights; wood stock) . **$523.00**
Price: Super Magnum Synthetic Turkey, 23" (black) **$389.00**

Remington Model 870 Wingmaster Super Magnum Shotgun

Similar to Model 870 Express Super Magnum except high-polish blued finish, 28" ventilated barrel with imp. cyl., modified and full choke tubes, checkered high-gloss walnut stock. Overall length 48", weighs 7-1/2 lbs. Introduced 2000.

Price: 3-1/2" chamber **$665.00**

Remington Model 870 Express Youth Gun

Same as Model 870 Express except 13" length of pull, 21" barrel with mod. Rem choke tube. Weighs 6.25 lbs. Hardwood stock with low-luster finish. Introduced 1991.

Price: 20 ga. Express Youth (1" shorter stock), from. **$332.00**
Price: 20 ga. Youth Deer 20" FR/RS **$365.00**
Price: 16 ga. Youth Synthetic **$332.00**

Remington Model 870 Express Rifle-Sighted Deer Gun

Same as Model 870 Express except 20" barrel with fixed imp. cyl. choke, open iron sights, Monte Carlo stock. Introduced 1991.

Price: **$332.00**
Price: With fully rifled barrel **$365.00**
Price: Express Synthetic Deer (black synthetic stock, black matte metal) **$372.00**

Remington Model 870 Express Deer Gun

Remington Model 870 Express Turkey

Remington Model 870 SPS Super Slug Deer Gun

Remington Model 870 SPS-T Camo

Remington Model 870 Express Turkey

Same as Model 870 Express except 3" chamber, 21" vent rib turkey barrel and extra-full Rem. choke turkey tube; 12 ga. only. Introduced 1991.

Price: $345.00

Price: Express Turkey Camo stock has Skyline Excel camo, matte black metal $399.00

Price: Express Youth Turkey camo (as above with 1" shorter length of pull), 20 ga., Skyline Excel camo $399.00

Remington Model 870 Express Synthetic 18"

Similar to 870 Express with 18" barrel except synthetic stock and forend; 7-shot. Introduced 1994.

Price: $319.00

Remington Model 870 SPS Super Slug Deer Gun

Similar to the Model 870 Express Synthetic except has 23" rifled, modified contour barrel with cantilever scope mount. Comes with black synthetic stock and forend with swivel studs, black Cordura nylon sling. Introduced 1999. Fully rifled centilever barrel.

Price: $580.00

Remington Model 870 SPS-T Synthetic Camo Shotgun

Chambered for 12 ga., 3" shells, has Mossy Oak Break-Up® synthetic stock and metal treatment, TruGlo fiber optic sights. Introduced 2001.

Price: 20" RS, Rem. choke $595.00

Price: Youth version $595.00

Price: Super Magnum Camo, 23", CL Rem. Choke $609.00

Price: Super Magnum Camo 23", VT Rem. Choke $591.00

Price: 20 ga., Truglo sights, Rem. Choke, Mossy Oak Break-Up Camo $595.00

REMINGTON MODEL 870 SPS SUPER MAGNUM CAMO

Has synthetic stock and all metal (except bolt and trigger guard) and stock covered with Mossy Oak Break-Up camo finish. In 12 gauge 3-1/2", 26", 28" vent rib, Rem choke. Comes with camo sling, swivels.

Price: $591.00

SARSILMAZ PUMP SHOTGUN

Gauge: 12, 3" chamber. **Barrel:** 26" or 28". Stocks: Oil-finished hardwood. **Features:** Includes extra pistol-grip stock. Introduced 2000. Imported from Turkey by Armsport Inc.

Price: With pistol-grip stock $299.95

Price: With metal stock $349.95

TRISTAR MODEL 1887

Gauge: 12. **Barrel:** 22". **Weight:** 8.75 lbs. **Length:** 40-1/2". Stocks: Walnut. **Features:** Imp. cylinder choke, 5 shell, oil finish. Introduced 2002. Made in Australia. Available through AcuSport Corp.

Price: With pistol-grip stock $299.95

WINCHESTER MODEL 1300 WALNUT FIELD PUMP

Gauge: 12, 20, 3" chamber, 5-shot capacity. **Barrel:** 26", 28", vent. rib, with Full, Mod., Imp. Cyl. Winchoke tubes. **Weight:** 6-3/8 lbs. **Length:** 42-5/8" overall. **Stock:** American walnut, with deep cut checkering on pistol grip, traditional ribbed forend; high luster finish. **Sights:** Metal bead front. **Features:** Twin action slide bars; front-locking rotary bolt; roll-engraved receiver; blued, highly polished metal; cross-bolt safety with red indicator. Introduced 1984. From U.S. Repeating Arms Co., Inc.

Price: $439.00

Winchester 1300 Walnut Field Pump

Winchester 1300 Black Shadow Field Gun

Winchester 1300 Deer Black Shadow Gun

Winchester 1300 Ranger Compact

Winchester 9410

Winchester Model 1300 Upland Pump Shotgun

Similar to Model 1300 Walnut except straight-grip stock, 24" barrel. Introduced 1999. Made in U.S. by U.S. Repeating Arms Co.

Price: **$439.00**

Winchester Model 1300 Black Shadow Field Shotgun

Similar to Model 1300 Walnut except black composite stock and forend, matte black finish. Has vent rib 26" or 28" barrel, 3" chamber, mod. Win-Choke tube. Introduced 1995. From U.S. Repeating Arms Co., Inc.

Price: 12 or 20 gauge **$353.00**

Winchester Model 1300 Deer Black Shadow Shotgun

Similar to Model 1300 Black Shadow Turkey Gun except ramp-type front sight, fully adjustable rear, drilled and tapped for scope mounting. Black composite stock and forend, matte black metal. Smoothbore 22" barrel with one imp. cyl. WinChoke tube; 12 gauge only, 3" chamber. Weighs 6-3/4 lbs. Introduced 1994. From U.S. Repeating Arms Co., Inc.

Price: With rifled barrel **$377.00**
Price: With cantilever scope mount. **$422.00**
Price: Combo (22" rifled and 28" smoothbore bbls.). **$455.00**
Price: Wood stock (20 ga., 22" rifled barrel) **$377.00**

WINCHESTER MODEL 1300 RANGER PUMP SHOTGUN

Gauge: 12, 20, 3" chamber, 5-shot magazine. **Barrel:** 28" vent. rib with Full, Mod., Imp. Cyl. Winchoke tubes. **Weight:** 7 to 7-1/4 lbs. **Length:** 48-5/8" to 50-5/8" overall. **Stock:** Walnut-finished hardwood with ribbed forend. **Sights:** Metal bead front. **Features:** Cross-bolt safety, black rubber recoil pad, twin action slide bars, front-locking rotating bolt. From U.S. Repeating Arms Co., Inc.

Price: Vent. rib barrel, Winchoke. **$367.00**
Price: Model 1300 Compact, 24" vent. rib **$367.00**
Price: Compact wood model, 20 ga. **$392.00**

Winchester Model 1300 Turkey, Universal Hunter Shotgun

Rotary bolt action. Durable Mossy oak break-up finish on 26" VR barrel extra full turkey improved cylinder, modified and full WinChoke tubes included. 3", 12 gauge chamber.

Price: Universal Hunter **$515.00**
Price: Buck and Tom **$554.00**
Price: Short Turkey **512.00**

WINCHESTER MODEL 9410 LEVER-ACTION SHOTGUN

Gauge: .410, 2-1/2" chamber. **Barrel:** 24" cyl. bore, also Invector choke system. **Weight:** 6-3/4 lbs. **Length:** 42-1/8" overall. **Stock:** Checkered walnut straight-grip; checkered walnut forearm. **Sights:** Adjustable "V" rear, TruGlo® front. **Features:** Model 94 rifle action (smoothbore) chambered for .410 shotgun. Angle Controlled Eject extractor/ejector; choke tubes; 9-shot tubular magazine; 13-1/2" length of pull. Introduced 2001. From U.S. Repeating Arms Co.

Price: 9410 fixed choke **$579.00**
Price: 9410 Packer w/chokes **$600.00**
Price: 9410 w/Invector, traditional model **$645.00**
Price: 9410 w/Invector, Packer model. **$667.00**
Price: 9410 w/Invector, semi-fancy traditional **$789.00**

SHOTGUNS — OVER/UNDERS

Includes a variety of game guns and guns for competitive shooting.

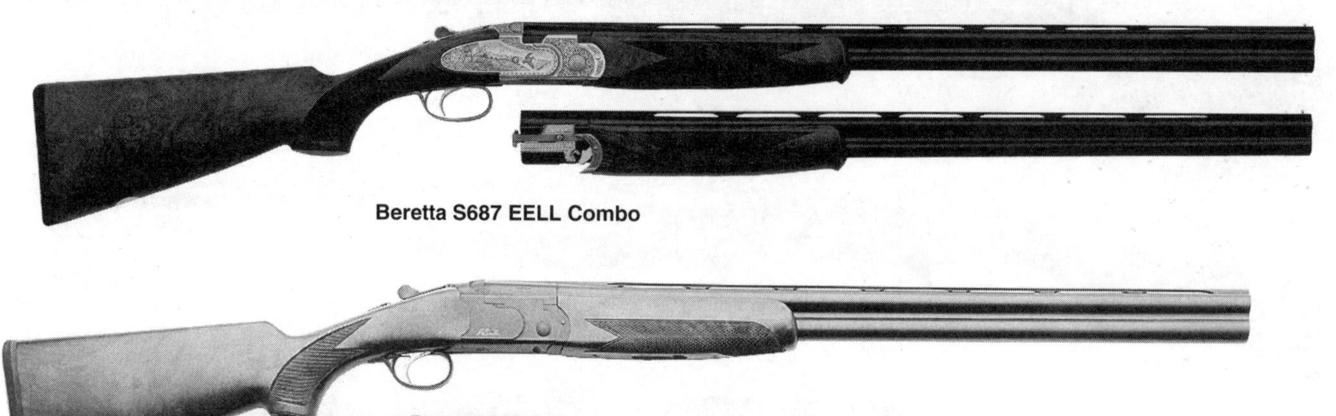

Beretta S687 EELL Combo

Beretta 686 Onyx

Beretta S686 Silver Pigeon

BERETTA DT10 TRIDENT SHOTGUNS

Gauge: 12, 2-3/4", 3" chambers. **Barrel:** 28", 30", 32", 34"; competition-style vent rib; fixed or Optima Choke tubes. **Weight:** 7.9 to 9 lbs. **Stock:** High-grade walnut stock with oil finish; hand-checkered grip and forend, adjustable stocks available. **Features:** Detachable, adjustable trigger group, raised and thickened receiver, forend iron has replaceable nut to guarantee wood-to-metal fit, Optima Bore to improve shot pattern and reduce felt recoil. Introduced 2000. Imported from Italy by Beretta USA.

Price: DT10 Trident Trap (selective, lockable single trigger, adjustable stock) **$6,686.00**
Price: DT10 Trident Top Single **$6,686.00**
Price: DT10 Trident X Trap Combo (single and o/u barrels) . . . . **$9,005.00-$9,557.00**
Price: DT10 Trident Skeet (skeet stock with rounded recoil pad, tapered rib) **$6,866.00**
Price: DT10 Trident Sporting (sporting clays stock with rounded recoil pad) **$6,383.00**
Price: DT10L Sporting **$7,797.00**

BERETTA SERIES 682 GOLD E SKEET, TRAP, SPORTING OVER/UNDERS

Gauge: 12, 2-3/4" chambers. **Barrel:** Skeet-28"; trap-30" and 32", imp. mod. & full and Mobilchoke; trap mono shotguns-32" and 34" Mobilchoke; trap top single guns-32" and 34" full and Mobilchoke; trap combo sets-from 30" O/U, to 32" O/U, 34" top single. **Stock:** Close-grained walnut, hand checkered. **Sights:** White Bradley bead front sight and center bead. **Features:** Receiver has Greystone gunmetal gray finish with gold accents. Trap Monte Carlo stock has deluxe trap recoil pad. Various grades available; contact Beretta USA for details. Imported from Italy by Beretta USA.

Price: 682 Gold E Trap with adjustable stock **$3,933.00**
Price: 682 Gold E Trap Top Combo . . . . **$3,485..00**
Price: 682 Gold E Sporting **$3,937.00**
Price: 682 Gold E Skeet, adjustable stock **$3,905.00**
Price: 682 Gold E Double Trap . . . . **NA**
Price: 687 EELL Diamond Pigeon Sporting **$6,207.00**

BERETTA 686 ONYX O/U SHOTGUN

Gauge: 12, 3" chambers. **Barrel:** 28", 30" (Mobilchoke tubes). **Weight:** 7.7 lbs. **Stock:** Checkered American walnut. **Features:** Intended for the beginning Sporting Clays shooter. Has wide, vented 12.5mm target rib, radiused recoil pad. Polished black finish on receiver and barrels. Introduced 1993. Imported from Italy by Beretta U.S.A.

Price: White Onyx **$1,718.00**
Price: Onyx Pro **$1,856.00**
Price: Onyx Pro 3.5 . . . . **$1,929.00**

BERETTA 686 SILVER PIGEON O/U SHOTGUN

Gauge: 12, 20, 28, 3" chambers (2-3/4" 28 ga.). **Barrel:** 26", 28". **Weight:** 6.8 lbs. **Stock:** Checkered walnut. **Features:** Interchangeable barrels (20 and 28 ga.), single selective gold-plated trigger, boxlock action, auto safety, schnabel forend.

Price: Silver Pigeon S **$1,994.00**
Price: Silver Pigeon S Combo **$2,757.00**

BERETTA ULTRALIGHT OVER/UNDER

Gauge: 12, 2-3/4" chambers. **Barrel:** 26", 28", Mobilchoke choke tubes. **Weight:** About 5 lbs., 13 oz. **Stock:** Select American walnut with checkered grip and forend. **Features:** Low-profile aluminum alloy receiver with titanium breech face insert. Electroless nickel receiver with game scene engraving. Single selective trigger; automatic safety. Introduced 1992. Imported from Italy by Beretta U.S.A.

Price: **$1,931.00**
Price: Silver Pigeon II **$2,270.00**
Price: Silver Pigeon II Combo **$3.098.00**
Price: Silver Pigeon III **$2,408.00**
Price: Silver Pigeon IV **$2,684.00**
Price: Silver Pigeon V **$3,171.00**

Beretta Over/Under Field Shotgun

Beretta SO9

Browning Citori White Lightning

Beretta Ultralight Deluxe Over/Under Shotgun

Similar to the Ultralight except has matte electroless nickel finish receiver with gold game scene engraving; matte oil-finished, select walnut stock and forend. Imported from Italy by Beretta U.S.A.

Price: $2,323.00

BERETTA OVER/UNDER FIELD SHOTGUNS

Gauge: 12, 20, 28, and .410 bore, 2-3/4", 3" and 3-1/2" chambers. **Barrel:** 26" and 28" (Mobilchoke tubes). **Stock:** Close-grained walnut. **Features:** Highly-figured, American walnut stocks and forends, and a unique, weather-resistant finish on barrels. Silver designates standard 686, 687 models with silver receivers; 686 Silver Pigeon has enhanced engraving pattern, schnabel forend; 686 Silver Essential has matte chrome finish; Gold indicates higher grade 686EL, 687EL models with full sideplates; Diamond is for 687EELL models with highest grade wood, engraving. Case provided with Gold and Diamond grades. Imported from Italy by Beretta U.S.A.

Price: S686 Silver Pigeon two-bbl. set $2,587.00
Price: S686 Silver Pigeon $1,817.00
Price: S687 Silver Pigeon II Sporting $2,196.00
Price: Combo 29" and 30" $3,151.00
Price: S687EL Gold Pigeon (gold inlays, sideplates) $4,099.00
Price: S687EL Gold Pigeon, .410, 26"; 28 ga., 28". $4,273.00
Price: S687 EL Gold Pigeon II (deep relief engraving) $4,513.00
Price: S687 EL Gold Pigeon II Sporting (D.R. engraving). $4,554.00

BERETTA MODEL SO5, SO6, SO9 SHOTGUNS

Gauge: 12, 2-3/4" chambers. **Barrel:** To customer specs. **Stock:** To customer specs. **Features:** SO5-Trap, Skeet and Sporting Clays models SO5; SO6- SO6 and SO6 EELL are field models. SO6 has a case-hardened or silver receiver with contour hand engraving. SO6 EELL has hand-engraved receiver in a fine floral or "fine English" pattern or game scene, with bas-relief chisel work and gold inlays. SO6 and SO6 EELL are available with sidelocks removable by hand. Imported from Italy by Beretta U.S.A.

Price: SO5 Trap, Skeet, Sporting $13,000.00
Price: SO6 Trap, Skeet, Sporting $17,500.00
Price: SO6 EELL Field, custom specs $28,000.00
Price: SO9 (12, 20, 28, .410, 26", 28", 30", any choke) $31,000.00

Beretta S687EL Gold Pigeon Sporting O/U

Similar to S687 Silver Pigeon Sporting except sideplates with gold inlay game scene, vent side and top ribs, bright orange front sight. Stock and forend are high grade walnut with fine-line checkering. Available in 12 gauge only with 28" or 30" barrels and Mobilchoke tubes. Weighs 6 lbs., 13 oz. Imported from Italy by Beretta USA.

Price: $4,971.00
Price: Combo (28 and .410) $5,520.00

BRNO ZH 300 OVER/UNDER SHOTGUN

Gauge: 12, 2-3/4" chambers. **Barrel:** 26", 27-1/2", 29" (Skeet, Imp. Cyl., Mod., Full). **Weight:** 7 lbs. **Length:** 44.4" overall. **Stock:** European walnut. **Features:** Double triggers; automatic safety; polished blue finish engraved receiver. Announced 1998. Imported from the Czech Republic by Euro-Imports.

Price: ZH 301, field $594.00
Price: ZH 302, skeet $608.00
Price: ZH 303, 12 ga. trap $608.00
Price: ZH 321, 16 ga. $595.00

BRNO 501.2 OVER/UNDER SHOTGUN

Gauge: 12, 2-3/4" chambers. **Barrel:** 27.5" (Full & Mod.). **Weight:** 7 lbs. **Length:** 44" overall. **Stock:** European walnut. **Features:** Boxlock action with double triggers, ejectors; automatic safety; hand-cut checkering. Announced 1998. Imported from The Czech Republic by Euro-Imports.

Price: $850.00

BROWNING CITORI O/U SHOTGUNS

Gauge: 12, 20, 28 and .410. **Barrel:** 26", 28" in 28 and .410. Offered with In-vector choke tubes. All 12 and 20 gauge models have back-bored barrels and Invector Plus choke system. **Weight:** 6 lbs., 8 oz. (26" .410) to 7 lbs., 13 oz. (30" 12 ga.). **Length:** 43" overall (26" bbl.). **Stock:** Dense walnut, hand checkered, full pistol grip, beavertail forend. Field-type recoil pad on 12 ga. field guns and trap and Skeet models. **Sights:** Medium raised beads, German nickel silver. **Features:** Barrel selector integral with safe-ty, automatic ejectors, three-piece takedown. Imported from Japan by Browning. Contact Browning for complete list of models and prices.

Price: Grade I, Hunter, Invector, 12 and 20 . . . . $1,486.00
Price: Grade I, Lightning, 28 and .410, Invector $1,594.00
Price: Grade III, Lightning, 28 and .410, Invector $2,570.00
Price: Grade VI, 28 and .410 Lightning, Invector $3,780.00
Price: Grade I, Lightning, Invector Plus, 12, 20 . . . . $1,534.00
Price: Grade I, Hunting, 28", 30" only, 3-1/2", Invector Plus $1,489.00
Price: Grade III, Lightning, Invector, 12, 20 . . . . $2,300.00
Price: Grade VI, Lightning, Invector, 12, 20 . . . . $3,510.00
Price: Gran Lightning, 26", 28", Invector, 12, 20. . . . . $2,184.00
Price: Gran Lightning, 28, .410. . . . . $2,302.00
Price: Micro Lightning, 20 ga., 24" bbl., 6 lbs., 4 oz.. . . . . $1,591.00
Price: White Lightning (silver nitride receiver w/engraving, 12 or 20 ga., 26", 28") $1,583.00
Price: White Lightning, 28 or .410 gauge $1,654.00
Price: Citori Satin Hunter (12 ga., satin-finished wood, matte-finished barrels and receiver) 3-1/2" chambers. $1,535.00

SHOTGUNS

Browning Lightning Feather

Browning Citori XT Trap

Browning Citori XS Special

BROWNING LIGHTNING FEATHER CITORI OVER/UNDER

Similar to the standard Citori except available in 12, 20, 28 or .410 with, 26" or 28" barrels choked Imp. Cyl., Mod. and Full. Has pistol grip stock, rounded forend. Lightning Feather 12 weighs 7 lbs., 15 oz. (26" barrels); Lightning Feather 20 weighs 6 lbs., 10 oz. (26" barrels). Introduced 2004.

Price: Lightning, 28 or .410. . . . . **$1,659.00**
Price: Lightning 12 or 20. . . . . **$1,597.00**
Price: White Lightning, 28 or .410. . . . . **$1,738.00**
Price: White Lightning, 12 or 20 . . . . **$1,664.00**
Price: Citori 525 Field, 28 or .410. . . . . **$1,914.00**
Price: Citori 525 Field, 12 or 20 . . . . **$1,885.00**
Price: Citori Superlight Feather, 12 or 20 . . . . **$1,882.00**
Price: Citori Lightning Feather, 12 or 20. . . . . **$1,815.00**
Price: Citori Lightning Feather Combo (20 & 28) **$2,949.00**

Browning Citori XT Trap Over/Under

Similar to the Citori Special Trap except has engraved silver nitride receiver with gold highlights, vented side barrel rib. Available In 12 gauge with 30" or 32" barrels, Invector-Plus choke tubes. Introduced 1999. Imported by Browning.

Price: **$1,834.00**
Price: With adjustable-comb stock **$2,054.00**

Browning Citori Lightning Feather O/U

Similar to the 12 gauge Citori Grade I except has 2-3/4" chambers, rounded pistol grip, lightning-style forend, and lightweight alloy receiver. Weighs 6 lbs. 15 oz. with 26" barrels (12 ga.); 6 lbs., 2 oz. (20 ga., 26" bbl.), sil-vered, engraved receiver. Introduced 1999. Imported by Browning.

Price: 12 or 20 ga., 26" or 28" barrels **$1,693.00**
Price: Lightning Feather Combo
(20 and 28 ga. bbls., 27" each) **$2,751.00**

Browning Citori XS Skeet

Similar to other Citori Ultra models except features a semi-beavertail forearm with deep finger grooves, ported barrels and triple system. Adjustable comb is optional. Introduced 2000.

Price: 12 ga., 28" or 30" barrel **$2,363.00**
Price: 20 ga., 28" or 30" barrel **$2,363.00**

Browning Citori XS Trap

Similar to other Citori Ultra models except offered in 12 ga. only with 30" or 32" ported barrel, high-post rib, ventilated side ribs, triple trigger system™ and silver nitride receiver. Includes full, modified and imp. cyl. choke tubes. From Browning.

Price: 30" or 32" barrel **$2,209.00**
Price: Adjustable-comb Model **$2,475.00**

Browning Citori XS Special

Similar to other Citori XS models except offered in 12 gauge ony, silver nitride receiver with new Special engraving, adjustable comb, low profile rib, right-hand palm swell, Triple Trigger™ system, HiViz® Pro-Comb sight with mid bead, Invector-Plus™ choke system with five Midas chokes. From Browning.

Price: **$2,727.00**

Browning Citori XS Sporting

Similar to other Citori XS models except offered in 12 and 20 gauge. silver nitride receiver, schnabel forearm, ventilated side rib. Imported by Browning.

Price: 12 or 20 ga. **$2,400.00**

Browning Citori Feather Shotgun

Similar to the standard Citori. Available in Lightning and Superlight models only. Introduced 2000.

Price: 28" or 30" barrel . . . . **$2,266.00 To $2,338.00**

Browning Citori High Grade Shotguns

Similar to standard Citori except has engraved hunting scenes and gold inlays, High-grade, Hand-oiled walnut stock and forearm. Introduced 2000. From Browning.

Price: Citori VI Lightning blue or gray (gold inlays of ducks and pheasants) From **$3,797.00**
Price: Citori Grade III Superlight (bird scene engraving on grayed receiver, gold inlays) **$2,464.00**
Price: Citori 525 Golden Clays (engraving of game bird-clay bird transition, gold accents), 12 or 20 ga. **$4,236.00**

Browning Citori XS Sporting Clays

Similar to the Citori Grade I except has silver nitride receiver with gold accents, stock dimensions of 14-3/4"x1-1/2"x2-1/4" with satin finish, right-hand palm swell, schnabel forend. Comes with modified, imp. cyl. and skeet invector-plus choke tubes. Back-bored barrels; vented side ribs. Introduced 1999. Imported by Browning.

Price: 12, 20 ga. **$2,400.00**

Browning 525 Sporting Clays

Charles Daly Superior Trap

Charles Daly Field Hunter

Browning Lightning Sporting Clays

Similar to the Citori Lightning with rounded pistol grip and classic forend. Has high post tapered rib or lower hunting-style rib with 30" back-bored Invector Plus barrels, ported or non-ported, 3" chambers. Gloss stock finish, radiused recoil pad. Has "Lightning Sporting Clays Edition" engraved and gold filled on receiver. Introduced 1989.

Price: Low-rib, ported **$1,691.00**
Price: High-rib, ported. **$1,770.00**

BROWNING 525 SPORTING CLAYS

Gauge: 12, 20, 2-3/4" chambers. **Barrel:** 12 ga.-28", 30", 32" (Invector Plus tubes), back-bored; 20 ga.-28", 30" (Invector Plus tubes). **Weight:** 7 lbs., 13 oz. (12 ga., 28"). **Stock:** 14-13/16" (1/8")x1-7/16"x2-3/16" (12 ga.). Select walnut with gloss finish, cut checkering, schnabel forend. **Features:** Grayed receiver with engraving, blued barrels. Barrels are ported on 12 gauge guns. Has low 10mm wide vent rib. Comes with three interchangeable trigger shoes to adjust length of pull. Introduced in U.S. 1993. Imported by Browning.

Price: Grade I, 12, 20 ga., Invector Plus. **$2,645.00**
Price: Golden Clays, 12, 20 ga., Invector Plus **$4,236.00**

CHARLES DALY SUPERIOR TRAP AE MC

Gauge: 12, 2-3/4" chambers. **Barrel:** 30" choke tubes. **Weight:** About 7 lbs. **Stock:** Checkered walnut; pistol grip, semi-beavertail forend. **Features:** Silver engraved receiver, chrome moly steel barrels; gold single selective trigger; automatic safety, automatic ejectors; red bead front sight, metal bead center; recoil pad. Introduced 1997. Imported from Italy by K.B.I., Inc.

Price: **$1,339.00**

CHARLES DALY FIELD HUNTER OVER/UNDER SHOTGUN

Gauge: 12, 20, 28 and .410 bore (3" chambers, 28 ga. has 2-3/4"). **Barrel:** 28" Mod & Full, 26" Imp. Cyl. & Mod (.410 is Full & Full). **Weight:** About 7 lbs. **Length:** NA. **Stock:** Checkered walnut pistol grip and forend. **Features:** Blued engraved receiver, chrome moly steel barrels; gold single selective trigger; automatic safety; extractors; gold bead front sight. Introduced 1997. Imported from Italy by K.B.I., Inc.

Price: 12 or 20 ga. **$799.00**
Price: 28 ga. **$879.00**
Price: .410 bore **$919.00**

Charles Daly Field Hunter AE Shotgun

Similar to the Field Hunter except 28 gauge only; 26" (Imp. Cyl. & Mod., 28 gauge), 26" (Full & Full, .410); automatic; ejectors. Introduced 1997. Imported from Italy by K.B.I., Inc.

Price: 28 . . . . **$999.00**

Charles Daly Superior Hunter AE Shotgun

Similar to the Field Hunter AE except has silvered, engraved receiver. Introduced 1997. Imported from Italy by F.B.I., Inc.

Price: 28 ga. **$1,129.00**
Price: .410 bore **$1,129.00**

Charles Daly Field Hunter AE-MC

Similar to the Field Hunter except in 12 or 20 only, 26" or 28" barrels with five multichoke tubes; automatic ejectors. Introduced 1997. Imported from Italy by K.B.I., Inc.

Price: 12 or 20 . . . . **$979.95**

Charles Daly Superior Sporting O/U

Similar to the Field Hunter AE-MC except 28" or 30" barrels; silvered, engraved receiver; five choke tubes; ported barrels; red bead front sight. Introduced 1997. Imported from Italy by K.B.I., Inc.

Price: **$1,259.95**

CHARLES DALY DIAMOND REGENT GTX DL HUNTER O/U

Gauge: 12, 20, .410, 3" chambers, 28, 2-3/4" chambers. **Barrel:** 26", 28", 30" (choke tubes), 26" (Imp. Cyl. & Mod. in 28, 26" (Full & Full) in .410. **Weight:** About 7 lbs. **Stock:** Extra select fancy European walnut with 24" hand checkering, hand rubbed oil finish. **Features:** Boss-type action with internal side lumps. Deep cut hand-engraved scrollwork and game scene set in full sideplates. GTX detachable single selective trigger system with coil springs; chrome moly steel barrels; automatic safety; automatic ejectors, white bead front sight, metal bead center sight. Introduced 1997. Imported from Italy by K.B.I., Inc.

Price: 12 or 20 . . . . **Special order only**
Price: 28 . . . . **Special order only**
Price: .410 . . . . **Special order only**
Price: Diamond Regent GTX EDL Hunter (as above with engraved scroll and birds, 10 gold inlays), 12 or 20. . . . . **Special order only**
Price: As above, 28. . . . . **Special order only**
Price: As above, .410 . . . . **Special order only**

CHARLES DALY EMPIRE EDL HUNTER O/U

Gauge: 12, 20, .410, 3" chambers, 28 ga., 2-3/4". **Barrel:** 26", 28" (12, 20, choke tubes), 26" (Imp. Cyl. & Mod., 28 ga.), 26" (Full & Full, .410). **Weight:** About 7 lbs. Stocks: Checkered walnut pistol grip buttstock, semi-beaver-tail forend; recoil pad. **Features:** Silvered, engraved receiver; chrome moly barrels; gold single selective trigger; automatic safety; automatic ejectors; red bead front sight, metal bead middle sight. Introduced 1997. Imported from Italy by K.B.I., Inc.

Price: Empire EDL (dummy sideplates) 12 or 20 . . . . **$1,559.95**
Price: Empire EDL, 28 . . . . **$1,559.95**
Price: Empire EDL, .410. . . . . **$1,599.95**

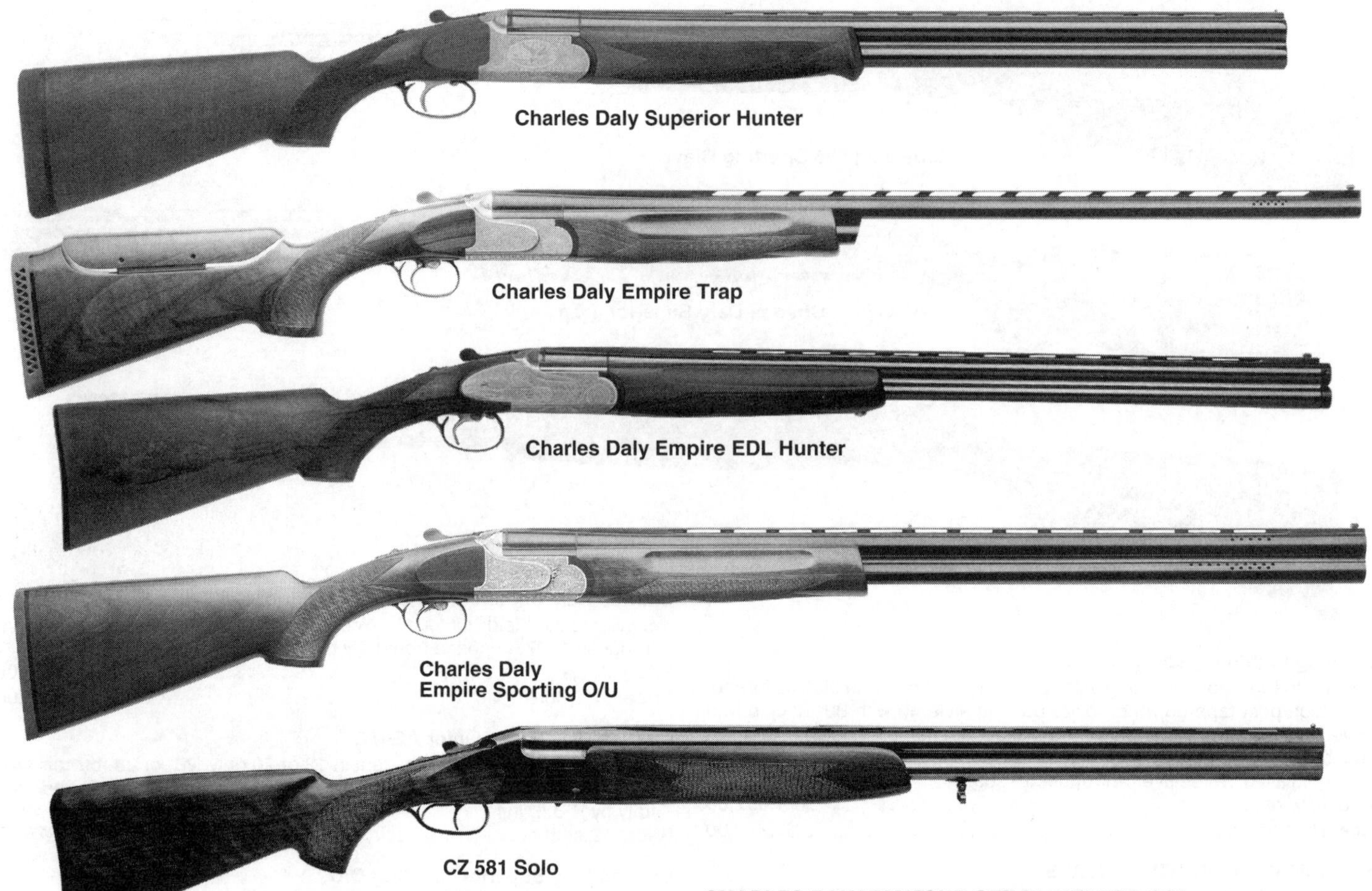

Charles Daly Superior Hunter

Charles Daly Empire Trap

Charles Daly Empire EDL Hunter

Charles Daly Empire Sporting O/U

CZ 581 Solo

Charles Daly Empire Sporting O/U

Similar to the Empire EDL Hunter except 12 or 20 gauge only, 28", 30" barrels with choke tubes; ported barrels; special stock dimensions. Introduced 1997. Imported from Italy by K.B.I., Inc.

Price: **$1,499.95**

CHARLES DALY EMPIRE TRAP AE MC

Gauge: 12, 2-3/4" chambers. **Barrel:** 30" choke tubes. **Weight:** About 7 lbs. **Stock:** Checkered walnut; pistol grip, semi-beavertail forend. **Features:** Silvered, engraved, reinforced receiver; chrome moly steel barrels; gold single selective trigger; automatic safety, automatic ejector; red bead front sight, metal bead center; recoil pad. Imported from Italy by K.B.I., Inc.

Price: **$1,539.95**

CHARLES DALY DIAMOND GTX SPORTING O/U SHOTGUN

Gauge: 12, 20, 3" chambers. **Barrel:** 28", 30" with choke tubes. **Weight:** About 8.5 lbs. **Stock:** Checkered deluxe walnut; Sporting clays dimensions. Pistol grip; semi-beavertail forend; hand rubbed oil finish. **Features:** Chromed, hand-engraved receiver; chrome moly steel barrels; GTX detachable single selective trigger system with coil springs, automatic safety; automatic ejectors; red bead front sight; ported barrels. Introduced 1997. Imported from Italy by K.B.I., Inc.

Price: . . . . **Price on request**

CHARLES DALY DIAMOND GTX TRAP AE-MC O/U SHOTGUN

Gauge: 12, 2-3/4" chambers. **Barrel:** 30" (Full & Full). **Weight:** About 8.5 lbs. **Stock:** Checkered deluxe walnut; pistol grip; trap dimensions; semi-beaver-tail forend; hand-rubbed oil finish. **Features:** Silvered, hand-engraved receiver; chrome moly steel barrels; GTX detachable single selective trigger system with coil springs, automatic safety, automatic-ejectors, red bead front sight, metal bead middle; recoil pad. Imported from Italy by K.B.I., Inc.

Price: . . . . **Price on request**

CHARLES DALY DIAMOND GTX DL HUNTER O/U

Gauge: 12, 20, .410, 3" chambers, 28, 2-3/4" chambers. **Barrel:** 26, 28", choke tubes in 12 and 20 ga., 26" (Imp. Cyl. & Mod.), 26" (Full & Full) in .410-bore. **Weight:** About 8.5 lbs. **Stock:** Select fancy European walnut stock, with 24 lpi hand checkering; hand-rubbed oil finish. **Features:** Boss-type action with internal side lugs, hand-engraved scrollwork and game scene. GTX detachable single selective trigger system with coil springs; chrome moly steel barrels, automatic safety, automatic ejectors, red bead front sight, recoil pad. Introduced 1997. Imported from Italy by K.B.I., Inc.

Price: . . . . **Special order only**

CZ 581 SOLO OVER/UNDER SHOTGUN

Gauge: 12, 2-3/4" chambers. **Barrel:** 27.6" (Mod. & Full). **Weight:** 7.37 lbs. **Length:** 44.5" overall. **Stock:** Circassian walnut. **Features:** Automatic ejectors; double triggers; Kersten-style double lump locking system. Imported from the Czech Republic by CZ-USA.

Price: **$799.00**

EAA BAIKAL IZH27 OVER/UNDER SHOTGUN

Gauge: 12 (3" chambers), 16 (2-3/4" chambers), 20 (3" chambers), 28 (2-3/4" chambers), .410 (3"). **Barrel:** 26-1/2", 28-1/2" (imp., mod. and full choke tubes for 12 and 20 gauges; improved cylinder and modified for 16 and 28 gauges; improved modified and full for .410; 16 also offered in mod. and full). **Weight:** NA. **Stock:** Walnut, checkered forearm and grip. Imported by European American Armory.

Price: IZH-27 (12, 16 and 20 gauge) **$509.00**

Price: IZH-27 (28 gauge and .410) **$569.00**

EAA Baikal IZH27 Sporting O/U

Basic IZH-27 with barrel porting, wide vent rib with double sight beads, engraved nickel receiver, checkered walnut stock and forend with palm swell and semi beavertail, 3 screw chokes, SS trigger, selectable ejectors, auto tang safety

Price: 12 ga., 29" bbl. **$589.00**

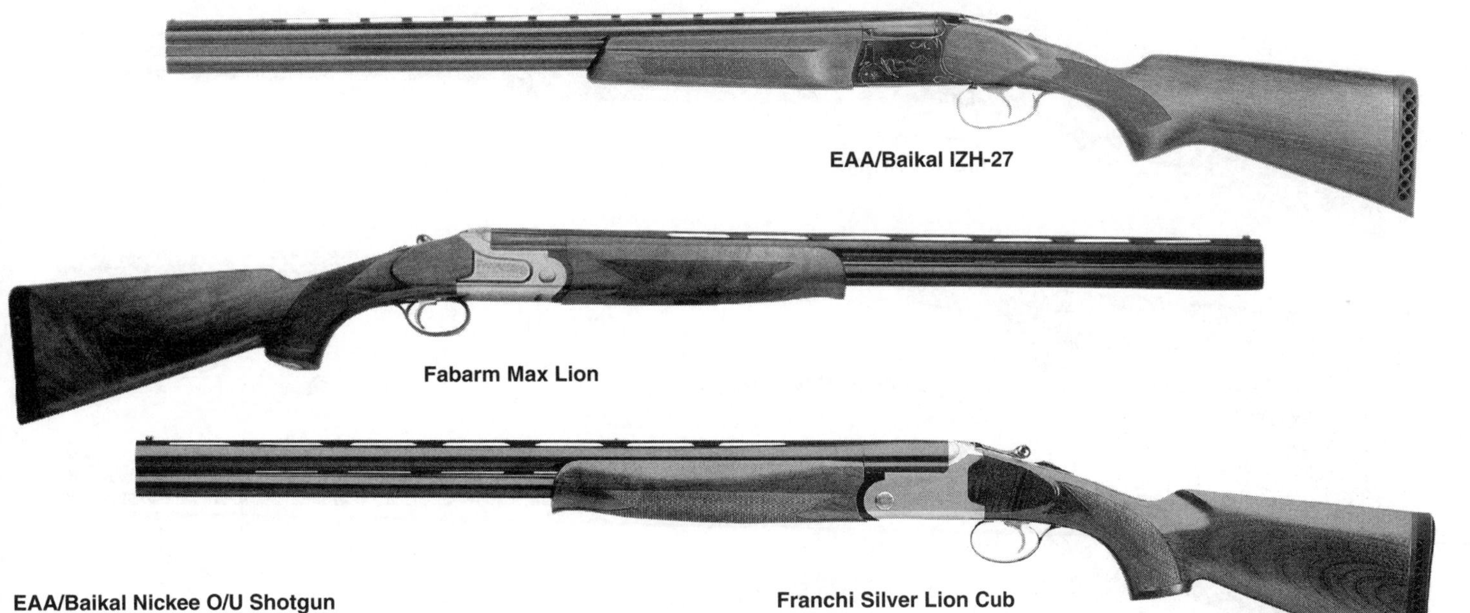
EAA/Baikal IZH-27

Fabarm Max Lion

Franchi Silver Lion Cub

EAA/Baikal Nickee O/U Shotgun

Same as IZH27 but with polished nickel receiver.

Price: $529.00

FABARM MAX LION OVER/UNDER SHOTGUNS

Gauge: 12, 3" chambers, 20, 3" chambers. **Barrel:** 26", 28", 30" (12 ga.); 26", 28" (20 ga.), choke tubes. **Weight:** 7.4 lbs. **Length:** 47.5" overall (26" barrel). **Stock:** European walnut; leather-covered recoil pad. **Features:** TriBore barrel, boxlock action with single selective trigger, manual safety, automatic ejectors; chrome-lined barrels; adjustable trigger. Silvered, engraved receiver. Comes with locking, fitted luggage case. Introduced 1998. Imported from Italy by Heckler & Koch, Inc.

Price: 12 or 20 . . . . $1,799.00

FABARM ULTRA CAMO MAG LION O/U SHOTGUN

Gauge: 12, 3-1/2" chambers. **Barrel:** 28" (cyl., imp. cyl., mod., imp. mod., full, SS-mod., SS-full choke tubes). **Weight:** 7.9 lbs. **Length:** 50" overall. **Stock:** Camo-colored walnut. **Features:** TriBore barrel, Wetlands Camo finished metal surfaces, single selective trigger, non-auto ejectors, leather-covered recoil pad. Locking hard plastic case. Introduced 1998. Imported from Italy by Heckler & Koch, Inc.

Price: $1,229.00

FABARM MAX LION PARADOX

Gauge: 12, 20, 3" chambers. **Barrel:** 24". **Weight:** 7.6 lbs. **Length:** 44.5" overall. **Stock:** Walnut with special enhancing finish. **Features:** TriBore upper barrel, both wood and receiver are enhanced with special finishes, color-case hardened type finish.

Price: 12 or 20 . . . . $1,129.00

FABARM SILVER LION OVER/UNDER SHOTGUNS

Gauge: 12, 3" chambers, 20, 3" chambers. **Barrel:** 26", 28", 30" (12 ga.); 26", 28" (20 ga.), choke tubes. **Weight:** 7.2 lbs. **Length:** 47.5" overall (26" barrels). **Stock:** Walnut; leather-covered recoil pad. **Features:** TriBore barrel, boxlock action with single selective trigger; silvered receiver with engraving; automatic ejectors. Comes with locking hard plastic case. Introduced 1998. Imported from Italy by Heckler & Koch, Inc.

Price: 12 or 20 . . . . $1,229.00

Fabarm Silver Lion Cub Model O/U

Similar to the Silver Lion except has 12.5" length of pull, is in 20 gauge only (3-1/2" chambers), and comes with 24" TriBore barrel system. Weight is 6 lbs. Introduced 1999. Imported from Italy by Heckler & Koch, Inc.

Price: $1,229.00

FABARM CAMO TURKEY MAG O/U SHOTGUN

Gauge: 12, 3-1/2" chambers. **Barrel:** 20" TriBore (Ultra-Full ported tubes). **Weight:** 7.5 lbs. **Length:** 46" overall. **Stock:** 14.5"x1.5"x2.29". Walnut. **Sights:** Front bar, Picatinny rail scope base. **Features:** Completely covered with Xtra Brown camouflage finish. Unported barrels. Introduced 1999. Imported from Italy by Heckler & Koch, Inc.

Price: $1,199.00

FABARM SPORTING CLAYS COMPETITION EXTRA O/U

Gauge: 12, 20, 3" chambers. **Barrel:** 12 ga. has 30", 20 ga. has 28"; ported TriBore barrel system with five tubes. **Weight:** 7 to 7.8 lbs. **Length:** 49.6" overall (20 ga.). **Stock:** 14.50"x1.38"x2.17" (20 ga.); deluxe walnut; leather-covered recoil pad. **Features:** Single selective trigger, auto ejectors; 10mm channeled rib; carbon fiber finish. Introduced 1999. Imported from Italy by Heckler & Koch, Inc.

Price: $1,749.00

FRANCHI ALCIONE FIELD OVER/UNDER SHOTGUN

Gauge: 12, 20, 3" chambers. **Barrel:** 26", 28"; IC, M, F tubes. **Weight:** 7.5 lbs. **Length:** 43" overall with 26" barrels. **Stock:** European walnut. **Features:** Boxlock action with ejectors, barrel selector mounted on trigger; silvered, engraved receiver, vent center rib, automatic safety, interchangeable 20 ga. bbls., left-hand available. Imported from Italy by Benelli USA. Hard case included.

Price: $1,275.00

Price: (20 gauge barrel set) $460.00

Franchi Alcione SX O/U Shotgun

Similar to Alcione Field model with high grade walnut stock and forend. Gold engraved removeable sideplates, interchangeable barrels.

Price: $1,800.00

Price: (12 gauge barrel set) . . . . $450.00 to $500.00

Price: (20 gauge barrel set) $450.00

Franchi Alcione Sport SL O/U Shotgun

Similar to Alcione except 2-3/4" chambers, elongated forcing cones and porting for Sporting Clays shooting. 10mm vent rib, tightly curved pistol grip, manual safety, removeable sideplates. Imported from Italy by Benelli USA.

Price: $1,650.00

FRANCHI ALCIONE TITANIUM OVER/UNDER SHOTGUN

Gauge: 12, 20, 3" chambers. **Barrel:** 26", 28"; IC, M, F tubes. **Weight:** 6.8 lbs. **Length:** 43", 45". **Stock:** Select walnut. **Sights:** Front/mid. **Features:** Receiver (titanium inserts) made of aluminum alloy. 7mm vent rib. Fast locking triggers. Left-hand available.

Price: $1,425.00

SHOTGUNS — OVER/UNDERS

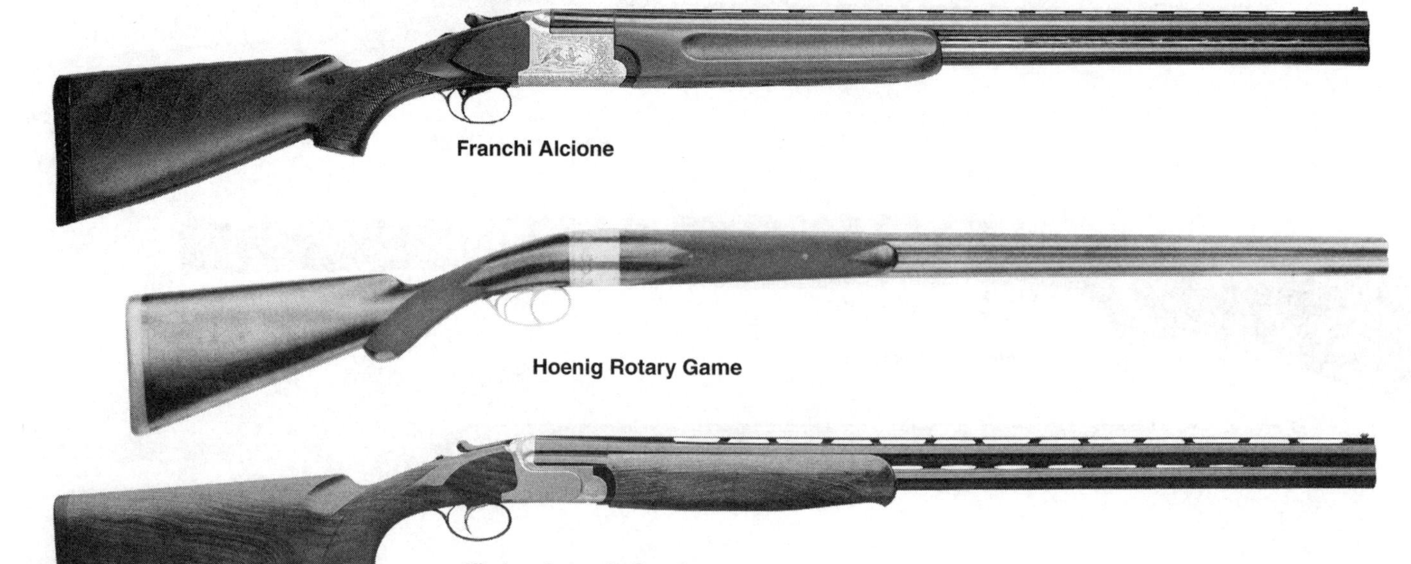

Franchi Alcione

Hoenig Rotary Game

Kimber Augusta Sport

FRANCHI 912 SHOTGUN

Gauge: 12 ga., 2-3/4", 3", 3-1/2"" chambers. **Barrel:** 24"-30". **Weight:** Appx. 7.6 lbs. **Length:** 46"-52". **Stock:** Walnut, synthetic, Timber HD. **Sights:** White bead front. **Features:** Based on 612 design, magazine cut-off, stepped vent rib, dual-recoil-reduction system.

Price: Satin walnut $1,000.00
Price: Synthetic $940.00
Price: Timber HD Camo $1,050.00

FRANCHI VELOCE OVER/UNDER SHOTGUN

Gauge: 20, 28. **Barrel:** 26", 28"; IC, M, F tubes. **Weight:** 5.5-5.8 lbs. **Length:** 43"-45". **Stock:** High grade walnut. **Features:** Aluminum receiver with steel reinforcement scaled to 20 gauge for light weight. Pistol grip stock with slip recoil pad. Imported by Benelli USA. Hard case included.

Price: $1,425.00
Price: 28 ga. $1,500.00

FRANCHI VELOCE ENGLISH OVER/UNDER SHOTGUN

Similar to Veloce standard model with straight grip English-style stock. Available with 26" barrels in 20 and 28 gauge. Hard case included.

Price: $1,425.00
Price: 28 ga. $1,500.00

HOENIG ROTARY ROUND ACTION GAME GUN

Gauge: 20, 28. **Barrel:** 26", 28", solid tapered rib. **Weight:** 6 lbs. and 6 1/4 lbs.**Stock:** English walnut to customer specifications. **Features:** Round action opens by rotating barrels, pulling forward. Inertia extraction system, rotary wing safety blocks strikers. Simple takedown without removing forend. Introduced 1997. Made in U.S.A. by George Hoenig.

Price: $19,980.00

Kimber Augusta Shotgun

Premium over/under, Boss type action. 12 ga. only. Tri-alloy barrel with choke tubes. Backbored 736. Long forcing cones. HiViz sight with center bead on vent ribl. Available with many features. Custom dimensions available. Imported from Italy by Kimber Mfg., Inc.

Price: $6,000.00

KOLAR SPORTING CLAYS O/U SHOTGUN

Gauge: 12, 2-3/4" chambers. **Barrel:** 30", 32", 34"; extended choke tubes. **Stock:** 14-5/8"x2-1/2"x1-7/8"x1-3/8". French walnut. Four stock versions available. **Features:** Single selective trigger, detachable, adjustable for length; overbored barrels with long forcing cones; flat tramline rib; matte blue finish. Made in U.S. by Kolar.

Price: Standard. $7,995.00
Price: Elite $10,990.00
Price: Elite Gold $12,990.00
Price: Legend $13,990.00
Price: Select $15,990.00
Price: Custom. . . . . Price on request

Kolar AAA Competition TRAP O/U Shotgun

Similar to the Sporting Clays gun except has 32" O/U /34" Unsingle or 30" O/U /34" Unsingle barrels as an over/under, unsingle, or combination set. Stock dimensions are 14-1/2"x2-1/2"x1-1/2"; American or French walnut; step parallel rib standard. Contact maker for full listings. Made in U.S. by Kolar.

Price: Over/under, choke tubes, Standard $8,220.00
Price: Unsingle, choke tubes, Standard $8.600.00
Price: Combo (30"/34", 32"/34"), Standard. $10,995.00

Kolar AAA Competition SKEET O/U Shotgun

Similar to the Sporting Clays gun except has 28" or 30" barrels with Kolarite AAA sub gauge tubes; stock of American or French walnut with matte finish; flat tramline rib; under barrel adjustable for point of impact. Many options available. Contact maker for complete listing. Made in U.S. by Kolar.

Price: Standard, choke tubes $8,645.00
Price: Standard, choke tubes, two-barrel set $10,995.00

KRIEGHOFF K-80 SPORTING CLAYS O/U

Gauge: 12. **Barrel:** 28", 30" or 32" with choke tubes. **Weight:** About 8 lbs. **Stock:** #3 Sporting stock designed for gun-down shooting. **Features:** Standard receiver with satin nickel finish and classic scroll engraving. Selective mechanical trigger adjustable for position. Choice of tapered flat or 8mm parallel flat barrel rib. Free-floating barrels. Aluminum case. Imported from Germany by Krieghoff International, Inc.

Price: Standard grade with five choke tubes, from $8,150.00

KRIEGHOFF K-80 SKEET SHOTGUN

Gauge: 12, 2-3/4" chambers. **Barrel:** 28", 30", (Skeet & Skeet), optional choke tubes). **Weight:** About 7-3/4 lbs. **Stock:** American Skeet or straight Skeet stocks, with palm-swell grips. Walnut. **Features:** Satin gray receiver finish. Selective mechanical trigger adjustable for position. Choice of ventilated 8mm parallel flat rib or ventilated 8-12mm tapered flat rib. Introduced 1980. Imported from Germany by Krieghoff International, Inc.

Price: Standard, Skeet chokes $6,900.00
Price: Skeet Special (28" or 30", tapered flat rib, Skeet & Skeet choke tubes) $7,575.00

SHOTGUNS — OVER/UNDERS

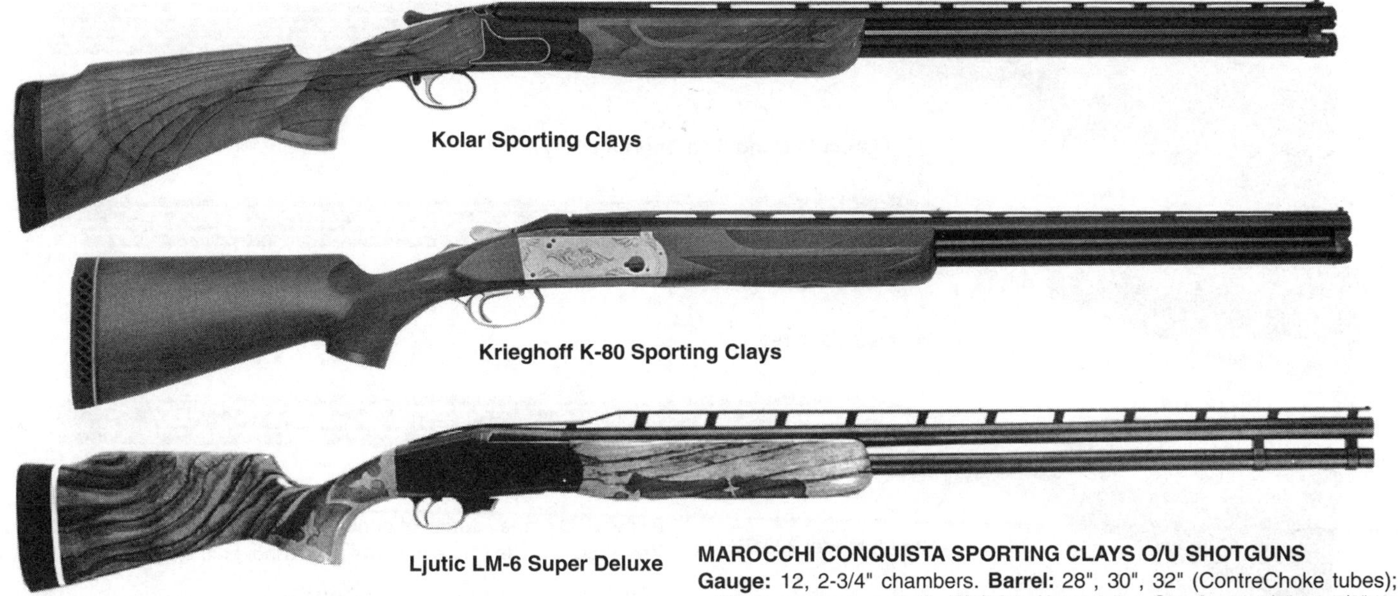

Kolar Sporting Clays

Krieghoff K-80 Sporting Clays

Ljutic LM-6 Super Deluxe

KRIEGHOFF K-80 O/U TRAP SHOTGUN

Gauge: 12, 2-3/4" chambers. **Barrel:** 30", 32" (Imp. Mod. & Full or choke tubes). **Weight:** About 8-1/2 lbs. **Stock:** Four stock dimensions or adjustable stock available; all have palm swell grips. Checkered European walnut. **Features:** Satin nickel receiver. Selective mechanical trigger, adjustable for position. Ventilated step rib. Introduced 1980. Imported from Germany by Krieghoff International, Inc.

Price: K-80 O/U (30", 32", Imp. Mod. & Full), from **$7,375.00**
Price: K-80 Unsingle (32", 34", Full), Standard, from **$7,950.00**
Price: K-80 Combo (two-barrel set), Standard, from **$10,475.00**

Krieghoff K-20 O/U Shotgun

Similar to the K-80 except built on a 20-gauge frame. Designed for skeet, sporting clays and field use. Offered in 20, 28 and .410, 28" and 30" barrels. Imported from Germany by Krieghoff International Inc.

Price: K-20, 20 gauge, from **$8,150.00**
Price: K-20, 28 gauge, from **$8,425.00**
Price: K-20, .410, from **$8,425.00**

LEBEAU - COURALLY BOSS-VEREES O/U

Gauge: 12, 20, 2-3/4" chambers. **Barrel:** 25" to 32". **Weight:** To customer specifications. **Stock:** Exhibition-quality French walnut. **Features:** Boss-type sidelock with automatic ejectors; single or double triggers; chopper lump barrels. A custom gun built to customer specifications. Imported from Belgium by Wm. Larkin Moore.

Price: From **$96,000.00**

LJUTIC LM-6 SUPER DELUXE O/U SHOTGUN

Gauge: 12. **Barrel:** 28" to 34", choked to customer specs for live birds, trap, International Trap. **Weight:** To customer specs. **Stock:** To customer specs. Oil finish, hand checkered. **Features:** Custom-made gun. Hollow-milled rib, pull or release trigger, pushbutton opener in front of trigger guard. From Ljutic Industries.

Price: Super Deluxe LM-6 O/U **$17,995.00**
Price: Over/Under Combo (interchangeable single barrel, two trigger guards, one for single trigger, one for doubles). **$24,995.00**
Price: Extra over/under barrel sets, 29"-32" **$5,995.00**

LUGER CLASSIC O/U SHOTGUNS

Gauge: 12, 3" and 3-1/2" chambers. **Barrel:** 26", 28", 30"; imp. cyl. mod. and full choke tubes. **Weight:** 7-1/2 lbs. **Length:** 45" overall (28" barrel) **Stock:** Select-grade European walnut, hand-checkered grip and forend. **Features:** Gold, single selective trigger; automatic ejectors. Introduced 2000.

Price: Classic (26", 28" or 30" barrel; 3-1/2" chambers) **$919.00**
Price: Classic Sporting (30" barrel; 3" chambers). **$964.00**

MAROCCHI CONQUISTA SPORTING CLAYS O/U SHOTGUNS

Gauge: 12, 2-3/4" chambers. **Barrel:** 28", 30", 32" (ContreChoke tubes); 10mm concave vent rib. **Weight:** About 8 lbs. **Stock:** 14-1/2"-14-7/8"x2-3/16"x1-7/16"; American walnut with checkered grip and forend; Sporting Clays butt pad. **Sights:** 16mm luminescent front. **Features:** Lower monoblock and frame profile. Fast lock time. Ergonomically-shaped trigger adjustable for pull length. Automatic selective ejectors. Coin-finished receiver, blued barrels. Five choke tubes, hard case. Available as true left-hand model-opening lever operates from left to right; stock has left-hand cast. Introduced 1994. Imported from Italy by Precision Sales International.

Price: Grade I, right-hand **$1,490.00**
Price: Grade I, left-hand **$1,615.00**
Price: Grade II, right-hand **$1,828.00**
Price: Grade II, left-hand **$2,180.00**
Price: Grade III, right-hand, from **$3,093.00**
Price: Grade III, left-hand, from **$3,093.00**

Marocchi Conquista TRAP O/U Shotgun

Similar to Conquista Sporting Clays model except 30" or 32" barrels choked Full & Full, stock dimensions of 14-1/2"-14-7/8"x1-11/16"x1-9/32"; weighs about 8-1/4 lbs. Introduced 1994. Imported from Italy by Precision Sales International.

Price: Grade I, right-hand **$1,490.00**
Price: Grade II, right-hand **$1,828.00**
Price: Grade III, right-hand, from **$3,093.00**

Marocchi Conquista Skeet O/U Shotgun

Similar to Conquista Sporting Clays except 28" (Skeet & Skeet) barrels, stock dimensions of 14-3/8"-14-3/4"x2-3/16"x1-1/2". Weighs about 7-3/4 lbs. Introduced 1994. Imported from Italy by Precision Sales International.

Price: Grade I, right-hand **$1,490.00**
Price: Grade II, right-hand **$1,828.00**
Price: Grade III, right-hand, from **$3,093.00**

MAROCCHI MODEL 99 SPORTING TRAP AND SKEET

Gauge: 12, 2-3/4", 3" chambers. **Barrel:** 28", 30", 32". **Stock:** French walnut. **Features:** Boss Locking system, screw-in chokes, low recoil, lightweight monoblock barrels and ribs. Imported from Italy by Precision Sales International.

Price: Grade I **$2,350.00**
Price: Grade II **$2,870.00**
Price: Grade II Gold **$3,025.00**
Price: Grade III **$3,275.00**
Price: Grade III Gold. **$3,450.00**
Price: Blackgold **$4,150.00**
Price: Lodestar **$5,125.00**
Price: Brittania **$5,125.00**
Price: Diana **$6,350.00**

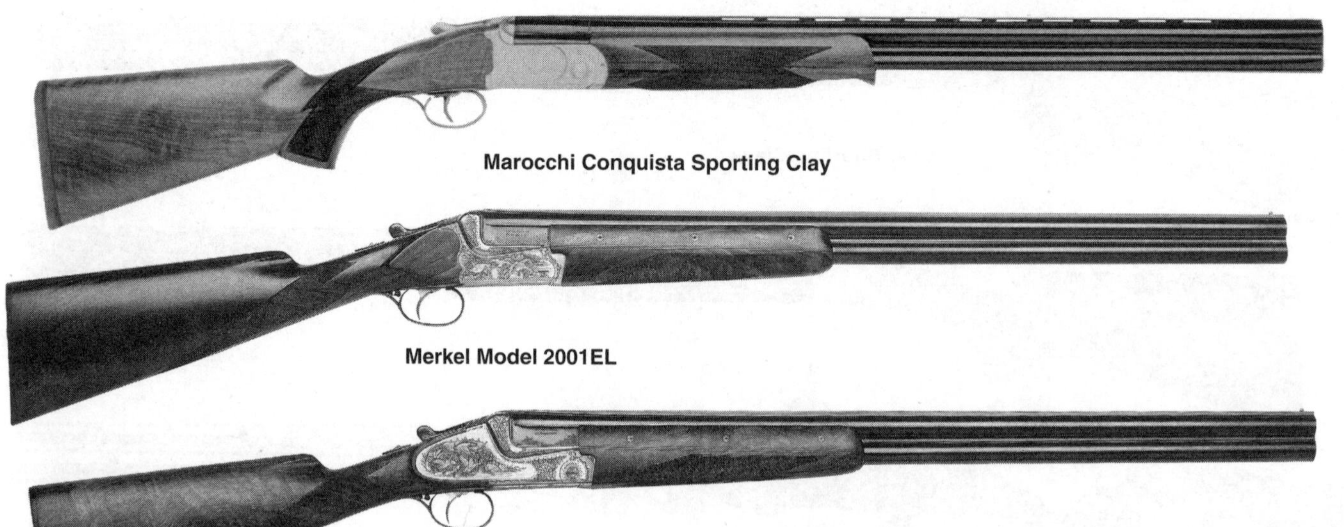

Marocchi Conquista Sporting Clay

Merkel Model 2001EL

Merkel Model 2001EL

MAROCCHI CONQUISTA USA MODEL 92 SPORTING CLAYS O/U SHOTGUN

Gauge: 12, 3" chambers. **Barrel:** 30"; back-bored, ported (ContreChoke Plus tubes); 10 mm concave ventilated top rib, ventilated middle rib. **Weight:** 8 lbs. 2 oz. **Stock:** 14-1/4"-14-5/8"x 2-1/8"x1-3/8"; American walnut with checkered grip and forend; Sporting Clays butt pad. **Features:** Low profile frame; fast lock time; automatic selective ejectors; blued receiver and barrels. Comes with three choke tubes. Ergonomically shaped trigger adjustable for pull length without tools. Barrels are back-bored and ported. Introduced 1996. Imported from Italy by Precision Sales International.

Price: **$1,490.00**

MERKEL MODEL 2001EL O/U SHOTGUN

Gauge: 12, 20, 3" chambers, 28, 2-3/4" chambers. **Barrel:** 12-28"; 20, 28 ga.-26-3/4". **Weight:** About 7 lbs. (12 ga.). **Stock:** Oil-finished walnut; English or pistol grip. **Features:** Self-cocking Blitz boxlock action with cocking indicators; Kersten double cross-bolt lock; silver-grayed receiver with engraved hunting scenes; coil spring ejectors; single selective or double triggers. Imported from Germany by GSI, Inc.

Price: 12, 20 . . . . **$7,295.00**

Price: 28 ga. **$7,295.00**

Price: Model 2000EL (scroll engraving, 12, 20 or 28). **$5,795.00**

MERKEL MODEL 303EL O/U SHOTGUN

Similar to Model 2001 EL except Holland & Holland-style sidelock action with cocking indicators; English-style Arabesque engraving. Available in 12, 20, 28 gauge. Imported from Germany by GSI, Inc.

Price: **$19,995.00**

Merkel Model 2002 EL O/U Shotgun

Similar to Model 2001 EL except dummy sideplates, Arabesque engraving with hunting scenes; 12, 20, 28 gauge. Imported from Germany by GSI, Inc.

Price: **$10,995.00**

PERAZZI MX8 OVER/UNDER SHOTGUNS

Gauge: 12, 2-3/4" chambers. **Barrel:** 28-3/8" (Imp. Mod. & Extra Full), 29-1/2" (choke tubes). **Weight:** 7 lbs., 12 oz. **Stock:** Special specifications. **Features:** Has single selective trigger; flat 7/16"x5/16" vent. rib. Many options available. Imported from Italy by Perazzi U.S.A., Inc.

Price: Sporting **$10,800.00**

Price: Trap Double Trap (removable trigger group) **$9,560.00**

Price: Skeet **$9,560.00**

Price: SC3 grade (variety of engraving patterns) . . . . **$16,200+**

Price: SCO grade (more intricate engraving, gold inlays). . . . . . **$26,000+**

PERAZZI MX12 HUNTING OVER/UNDER

Gauge: 12, 2-3/4" chambers. **Barrel:** 26-3/4", 27-1/2", 28-3/8", 29-1/2" (Mod. & Full); choke tubes available in 27-5/8", 29-1/2" only (MX12C). **Weight:** 7 lbs., 4 oz. **Stock:** To customer specs; Interchangeable. **Features:** Single selective trigger; coil springs used in action; schnabel forend tip. Imported from Italy by Perazzi U.S.A., Inc.

Price: From **$10,841.00**

Price: MX12C (with choke tubes), from **$11,612.00**

Perazzi MX20 Hunting Over/Under

Similar to the MX12 except 20 ga. frame size. Non-removable trigger group. Available in 20, 28, .410 with 2-3/4" or 3" chambers. 26" standard, and choked Mod. & Full. Weight is 6 lbs., 6 oz. Imported from Italy by Perazzi U.S.A., Inc.

Price: From **$10,841.00**

Price: MX20C (as above, 20 ga. only, choke tubes), from **$11,612.00**

PERAZZI MX8/MX8 SPECIAL TRAP, SKEET

Gauge: 12, 2-3/4" chambers. **Barrel:** Trap-29-1/2" (Imp. Mod. & Extra Full), 31-1/2" (Full & Extra Full). Choke tubes optional. Skeet-27-5/8" (Skeet & Skeet). **Weight:** About 8-1/2 lbs. (Trap); 7 lbs., 15 oz. (Skeet). **Stock:** Interchangeable and custom made to customer specs. **Features:** Has detachable and interchangeable trigger group with flat V springs. Flat 7/16" ventilated rib. Many options available. Imported from Italy by Perazzi U.S.A., Inc.

Price: From **$10,841.00**

Price: MX8 Special (adj. four-position trigger), from **$11,476.00**

Price: MX8 Special Combo (o/u and single barrel sets), from . **$15,127.00**

Perazzi MX8 Special Skeet O/U Shotgun

Similar to the MX8 Skeet except has adjustable four-position trigger, Skeet stock dimensions. Imported from Italy by Perazzi U.S.A., Inc.

Price: From **$10,841.00**

Perazzi MX8/20 Over/Under Shotgun

Similar to the MX8 except has smaller frame and has a removable trigger mechanism. Available in trap, Skeet, sporting or game models with fixed chokes or choke tubes. Stock is made to customer specifications. Introduced 1993. Imported from Italy by Perazzi U.S.A., Inc.

Price: From **$10,841.00**

PERAZZI MX10 OVER/UNDER SHOTGUN

Gauge: 12, 2-3/4" chambers. **Barrel:** 29.5", 31.5" (fixed chokes). **Weight:** NA. **Stock:** Walnut; cheekpiece adjustable for elevation and cast. **Features:** Adjustable rib; vent. side rib. Externally selective trigger. Available in single barrel, combo, over/under trap, Skeet, pigeon and sporting models. Introduced 1993. Imported from Italy by Perazzi U.S.A., Inc.

Price: MX200410 . . . . **$13,608.00**

Perazzi MX8

Perazzi MX28

Piotti Boss

Rizzini S790 Emel

PERAZZI MX28, MX410 GAME O/U SHOTGUNS

Gauge: 28, 2-3/4" chambers, .410, 3" chambers. **Barrel:** 26" (Imp. Cyl. & Full). **Weight:** NA. **Stock:** To customer specifications. **Features:** Made on scaled-down frames proportioned to the gauge. Introduced 1993. Imported from Italy by Perazzi U.S.A., Inc.

Price: From **$19,120.00**

PIOTTI BOSS OVER/UNDER SHOTGUN

Gauge: 12, 20. **Barrel:** 26" to 32", chokes as specified. **Weight:** 6.5 to 8 lbs. **Stock:** Dimensions to customer specs. Best quality figured walnut. **Features:** Essentially a custom-made gun with many options. Introduced 1993. Imported from Italy by Wm. Larkin Moore.

Price: From **$48,000.00**

REMINGTON MODEL 332 O/U SHOTGUN

Gauge: 12, 3" chambers. **Barrel:** 26", 28", 30". **Weight:** 7.75 lbs. **Length:** 42"-47" **Stock:** Satin-finished American walnut. **Sights:** Twin bead. **Features:** Light-contour, vent rib, Rem chock barrel, blued, traditional M-32 experience with M-300 Ideal performance, standard auto ejectors, set trigger. Proven boxlock action.

Price: **$1,624.00**

RIZZINI S790 EMEL OVER/UNDER SHOTGUN

Gauge: 20, 28, .410. **Barrel:** 26", 27.5" (Imp. Cyl. & Imp. Mod.). **Weight:** About 6 lbs. **Stock:** 14"x1-1/2"x2-1/8". Extra-fancy select walnut. **Features:** Boxlock action with profuse engraving; automatic ejectors; single selective trigger; silvered receiver. Comes with Nizzoli leather case. Introduced 1996. Imported from Italy by Wm. Larkin Moore & Co.

Price: From **$9,725.00**

RIZZINI S792 EMEL OVER/UNDER SHOTGUN

Similar to S790 EMEL except dummy sideplates with extensive engraving coverage. Nizzoli leather case. Introduced 1996. Imported from Italy by Wm. Larkin Moore & Co.

Price: From **$9,075.00**

RIZZINI UPLAND EL OVER/UNDER SHOTGUN

Gauge: 12, 16, 20, 28, .410. **Barrel:** 26", 27-1/2", Mod. & Full, Imp. Cyl. & Imp. Mod. choke tubes. **Weight:** About 6.6 lbs. **Stock:** 14-1/2"x1-1/2"x2-1/4". **Features:** Boxlock action; single selective trigger; ejectors; profuse engraving on silvered receiver. Comes with fitted case. Introduced 1996. Imported from Italy by Wm. Larkin Moore & Co.

Price: From **$3,350.00**

Rizzini Artemis Over/Under Shotgun

Same as Upland EL model except dummy sideplates with extensive game scene engraving. Fancy European walnut stock. Fitted case. Introduced 1996. Imported from Italy by Wm. Larkin Moore & Co.

Price: From **$2,100.00**

RIZZINI S782 EMEL OVER/UNDER SHOTGUN

Gauge: 12, 2-3/4" chambers. **Barrel:** 26", 27.5" (Imp. Cyl. & Imp. Mod.). **Weight:** About 6.75 lbs. **Stock:** 14-1/2"x1-1/2"x2-1/4". Extra fancy select walnut. **Features:** Boxlock action with dummy sideplates, extensive engraving with gold inlaid game birds, silvered receiver, automatic ejectors, single selective trigger. Nizzoli leather case. Introduced 1996. Imported from Italy by Wm. Larkin Moore & Co.

Price: From **$11,450.00**

SHOTGUNS — OVER/UNDERS

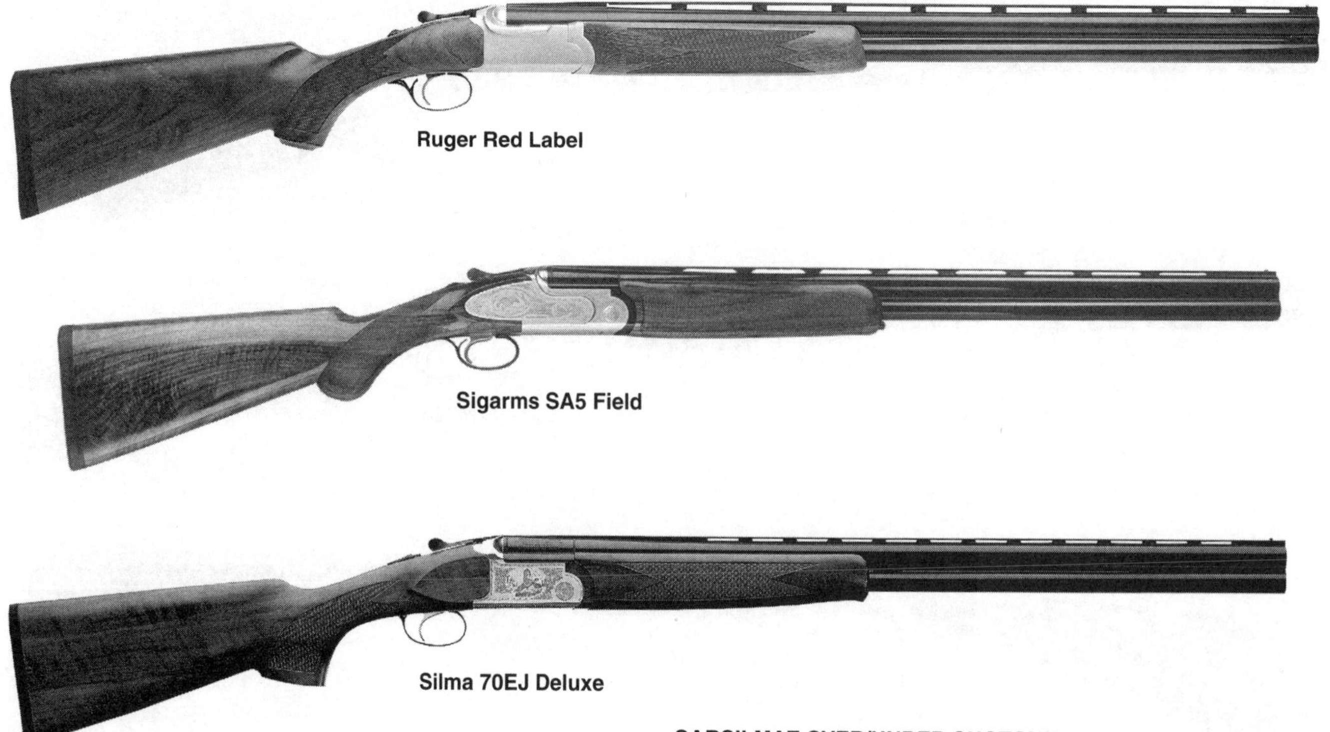

Ruger Red Label

Sigarms SA5 Field

Silma 70EJ Deluxe

RUGER RED LABEL O/U SHOTGUN

Gauge: 12, 20, 3" chambers; 28 2-3/4" chambers. **Barrel:** 26", 28" (Skeet [two], Imp. Cyl., Full, Mod. screw-in choke tubes). Proved for steel shot. **Weight:** About 7 lbs. (20 ga.); 7-1/2 lbs. (12 ga.). **Length:** 43" overall (26" barrels). **Stock:** 14"x1-1/2"x2-1/2". Straight grain American walnut or black synthetic. Checkered pistol grip and forend, rubber butt pad. **Features:** Stainless steel receiver. Single selective mechanical trigger, selective automatic ejectors; serrated free-floating vent. rib. Comes with two Skeet, one Imp. Cyl., one Mod., one Full choke tube and wrench. Made in U.S. by Sturm, Ruger & Co.

Price: Red Label with pistol grip stock **$1,489.00**
Price: English Field with straight-grip stock **$1,489.00**
Price: All-Weather Red Label with black synthetic stock. . . . . **$1,489.00 to $1,545.00**
Price: Factory engraved All-Weather models . . . . **$1,650.00 to $1,725.00**

Ruger Engraved Red Label O/U Shotgun

Similar to Red Label except scroll engraved receiver with 24-carat gold game bird (pheasant in 12 gauge, grouse in 20 gauge, woodcock in 28 gauge, duck on All-Weather 12 gauge). Introduced 2000.

Price: Engraved Red Label (12 gauge, 30" barrel). **$1,725.00**
Price: Engraved Red Label (12, 20 and 28 gauge in 26" and 28" barrels). **$1,650.00**
Price: Engraved Red Label, All-Weather (synthetic stock, 12 gauge only; 26" and 28" brls.) **$1,650.00**
Price: Engraved Red Label, All-Weather (synthetic stock, 12 gauge only, 30" barrel) **$1,650.00**

Ruger Sporting Clays O/U Shotgun

Similar to Red Label except 30" back-bored barrels, stainless steel choke tubes. Weighs 7.75 lbs., overall length 47". Stock dimensions of 14-1/8"x1-1/ 2"x2-1/2". Free-floating serrated vent rib with brass front and mid-rib beads. No barrel side spacers. Comes with two Skeet, one imp. cyl., one mod. + full choke tubes. 12 ga. introduced 1992, 20 ga. introduced 1994.

Price: 12 or 20 . . . . **$1,545.00**
Price: All-Weather with black synthetic stock **$1,545.00**

SARSILMAZ OVER/UNDER SHOTGUN

Gauge: 12, 3" chambers. **Barrel:** 26", 28"; fixed chokes or choke tubes. **Weight:** NA. **Length:** NA. **Stock:** Oil-finished hardwood. **Features:** Double or single selective trigger, wide ventilated rib, chrome-plated parts, blued finish. Introduced 2000. Imported from Turkey by Armsport Inc.

Price: Double triggers; mod. and full or imp. cyl. and mod. fixed chokes. **$499.95**
Price: Single selective trigger; imp. cyl. and mod. or mod. and full fixed chokes **$575.00**
Price: Single selective trigger; five choke tubes and wrench **$695.00**

SIGARMS SA5 OVER/UNDER SHOTGUN

Gauge: 12, 20, 3" chamber. **Barrel:** 26-1/2", 27" (Full, Imp. Mod., Mod., Imp. Cyl., Cyl. choke tubes). **Weight:** 6.9 lbs. (12 gauge), 5.9 lbs. (20 gauge). **Stock:** 14-1/2" x 1-1/2" x 2-1/2". Select grade walnut; checkered 20 l.p.i. at grip and forend. **Features:** Single selective trigger, automatic ejectors; hand-engraved detachable sideplated; matte nickel receiver, rest blued; ta-pered bolt lock-up. Introduced 1997. Imported by Sigarms, Inc.

Price: Field, 12 gauge. **$2,670.00**
Price: Sporting Clays **$2,800.00**
Price: Field 20 gauge **$2,670.00**

SILMA MODEL 70EJ DELUXE

Gauge: 12 (3-1/2" chambers), 20, .410 (3" chambers), 28 (2-3/4" chambers). **Barrel:** 28" (12 and 20 gauge, fixed and tubed, 28 and .410 fixed), 26" (12 and 20 fixed). **Weight:** 7.6 lbs 12 gauge, 6.9 lbs, 20, 28 and .410. **Stock:** Checkered select European walnut, pistol grip, solid rubber recoil pad. **Features:** Monobloc construction, chrome-moly blued steel barrels, raised vent rib, automatic safety and ejectors, single selective trigger, gold plated, bead front sight. Brushed, engraved receiver. Introduced 2002. Clays models introduced 2003. Imported from Italy by Legacy Sports International.

Price: 12 gauge **$1,020.00**
Price: 20 gauge **$945.00**
Price: 28, .410 . . . . **$1,060.00**

Silma Model 70 EJ Superlight

Similar to Silma 70EJ Deluxe except 12 gauge, 3" chambers, alloy receiver, weighs 5.6 lbs.

Price: 12, 20 multichokes (IC, M, F) **$1,105.00**

Stoeger Condor

Tristar Silver Sporting O/U

Silma Model 70 EJ Standard

Similar to Silma 70EJ Deluxe except 12 and 20 gauge only, standard walnut stock, light engraving, silver-plated trigger.

Price: 12 gauge **$940.00**
Price: 20 gauge **$865.00**
Price: Sporting Clays model **$1,305.00**

SKB MODEL 85TSS OVER/UNDER SHOTGUN

Gauge: 12, 20, .410 - 3"; 28, 2-3/4".**Barrel:** Chrome lined 26", 28", 30", 32" (w/choke tubes). **Weight:** 7 lbs., 7 oz. to 8 lbs, 14 oz. **Stock:** Hand-checkered American walnut with matte finish, schnabel or grooved forend. Target stocks available in various styles. **Sights:** Metal bead front or HiViz competition sights. **Features:** Low profile boxlock action with Greener-style cross bolt; single selective trigger; manual safety. Back-bored barrels with lengthened forcing cones. Introduced 2004. Imported from Japan by G.U. Inc.

Price: Sporting Clays, 12 or 20. . . . . **$1,949.00**
Price: Sporting Clays, 28 . . . . **$1,949.00**
Price: Sporting Clays set, 12 and 20 . . . . **$3,149.00**
Price: Skeet, 12 or 20. . . . . **$1,949.00**
Price: Skeet, 28 or .410 . . . . **$2,129.00 to $2,179.00**
Price: Skeet, three-barrel set, 20, 28, .410. . . . . **$4,679.00**
Price: Trap, standard or Monte Carlo **$1,499.00**
Price: Trap adjustable comb **$2,129.00**

SKB MODEL 585 OVER/UNDER SHOTGUN

Gauge: 12 or 20, 3"; 28, 2-3/4"; .410, 3". **Barrel:** 12 ga.-26", 28", 30", 32", 34" (Inter-Choke tubes); 20 ga.-26", 28" (Inter-Choke tube); 28-26", 28" (Inter-Choke tubes); .410-26", 28" (Inter-Choke tubes). Ventilated side ribs. **Weight:** 6.6 to 8.5 lbs. **Length:** 43" to 51-3/8" overall. **Stock:** 14- 1/8"x1-1/ 2"x2-3/16". Hand checkered walnut with high-gloss finish. Tar-get stocks available in standard and Monte Carlo. **Sights:** Metal bead front (field), target style on Skeet, trap, Sporting Clays. **Features:** Boxlock action; silver nitride finish with Field or Target pattern engraving; manual safety, automatic ejectors, single selective trigger. All 12 gauge barrels are back-bored, have lengthened forcing cones and longer choke tube system. Sporting Clays models in 12 gauge with 28" or 30" barrels avail-able with optional 3/8" step-up target-style rib, matte finish, nickel center bead, white front bead. Introduced 1992. Imported from Japan by G.U., Inc.

Price: Field **$1,499.00**
Price: Two-barrel Field Set, 12 & 20 . . . . **$2,399.00**
Price: Two-barrel Field Set, 20 & 28 or 28 & .410. . . . . **$2,469.00**

SKB Model 585 Gold Package

Similar to Model 585 Field except gold-plated trigger, two gold-plated game inlays, schnabel forend. Silver or blue receiver. Introduced 1998. Imported from Japan by G.U. Inc.

Price: 12, 20 ga. **$1,689.00**
Price: 28, .410 . . . . **$1,749.00**

SKB Model 505 Shotguns

Similar to Model 585 except blued receiver, standard bore diameter, standard Inter-Choke system on 12, 20, 28, different receiver engraving. Imported from Japan by G.U. Inc.

Price: Field, 12 (26", 28"), 20 (26", 28") **$1,229.00**

STOEGER CONDOR SPECIAL

Gauge: 12, 20, 2-3/4" 3" chambers. **Barrel:** 26", 28". **Weight:** 7.7 lbs. **Sights:** Brass bead. **Features:** IC and M screw-in choke trubes with each gun. Oil finished hardwood with pistol grip and forend. Auto safety, single trigger, automatic extractors.

Price: **$390.00**
Price: Condor Special **$440.00**
Price: Supreme Deluxe w/SS and red bar sights **$500.00**

TRADITIONS CLASSIC SERIES O/U SHOTGUNS

Gauge: 12, 3"; 20, 3"; 16, 2-3/4"; 28, 2-3/4"; .410, 3". **Barrel:** 26" and 28". **Weight:** 6 lbs., 5 oz. to 7 lbs., 6 oz. **Length:** 43" to 45" overall. **Stock:** Walnut. **Features:** Single-selective trigger; chrome-lined barrels with screw-in choke tubes; extractors (Field Hunter and Field I models) or automatic ejectors (Field II and Field III models); rubber butt pad; top tang safety. Imported from Fausti of Italy by Traditions.

Price: (Field Hunter - blued receiver; 12 or 20 ga.; 26" bbl. has I.C. and mod. tubes, 28" has mod. and full tubes) **$669.00**
Price: (Field I - blued receiver; 12, 20, 28 ga. or .410; fixed chokes [26" has I.C. and mod., 28" has mod. and full]) **$619.00**
Price: (Field II - coin-finish receiver; 12, 16, 20, 28 ga. or .410; gold trigger; choke tubes) **$789.00**
Price: (Field III - coin-finish receiver; gold engraving and trigger; 12 ga.; 26" or 28" bbl.; choke tubes) **$999.00**
Price: (Upland II - blued receiver; 12 or 20 ga.; English-style straight walnut stock; choke tubes) **$839.00**
Price: (Upland III - blued receiver, gold engraving; 20 ga.; high-grade pistol grip walnut stock; choke tubes) **$1,059.00**
Price: (Upland III - blued, gold engraved receiver, 12 ga. Round pistol grip stock, choke tubes) **$1,059.00**
Price: (Sporting Clay II - silver receiver; 12 ga.; ported barrels with skeet, i.c., mod. and full extended tubes) **$959.00**
Price: (Sporting Clay III - engraved receivers, 12 and 20 ga., walnut stock, vent rib, extended choke tubes) **$1,189.00**

TRADITIONS MAG 350 SERIES O/U SHOTGUNS

Gauge: 12, 3-1/2". Barrels: 24", 26" and 28". **Weight:** 7 lbs. to 7 lbs., 4 oz. **Length:** 41" to 45" overall. **Stock:** Walnut or composite with Mossy Oak® Break-Up™ or Advantage® Wetlands ™ camouflage. **Features:** Black matte, engraved receiver; vent rib; automatic ejectors; single-selective trigger; three screw-in choke tubes; rubber recoil pad; top tang safety. Imported from Fausti of Italy by Traditions.

Price: (Mag Hunter II - 28" black matte barrels, walnut stock, includes I.C., Mod. and Full tubes) **$799.00**
Price: (Turkey II - 24" or 26" camo barrels, Break-Up camo stock, includes Mod., Full and X-Full tubes) **$889.00**
Price: (Waterfowl II - 28" camo barrels, Advantage Wetlands camo stock, includes I.C., Mod. and Full tubes) **$899.00**

TRISTAR SILVER SPORTING O/U

Gauge: 12, 2-3/4" chambers, 20 3" chambers. **Barrel:** 28", 30" (Skeet, Imp. Cyl., Mod., Full choke tubes). **Weight:** 7-3/8 lbs. **Length:** 45-1/2" overall. **Stock:** 14-3/8"x1-1/2"x2-3/8". Figured walnut, cut checkering; Sporting Clays quick-mount buttpad. **Sights:** Target bead front. **Features:** Boxlock action with single selective trigger, automatic selective ejectors; special broadway channeled rib; vented barrel rib; chrome bores. Chrome-nickel finish on frame, with engraving. Introduced 1990. Imported from Italy by Tristar Sporting Arms Ltd.

Price: **$799.00**

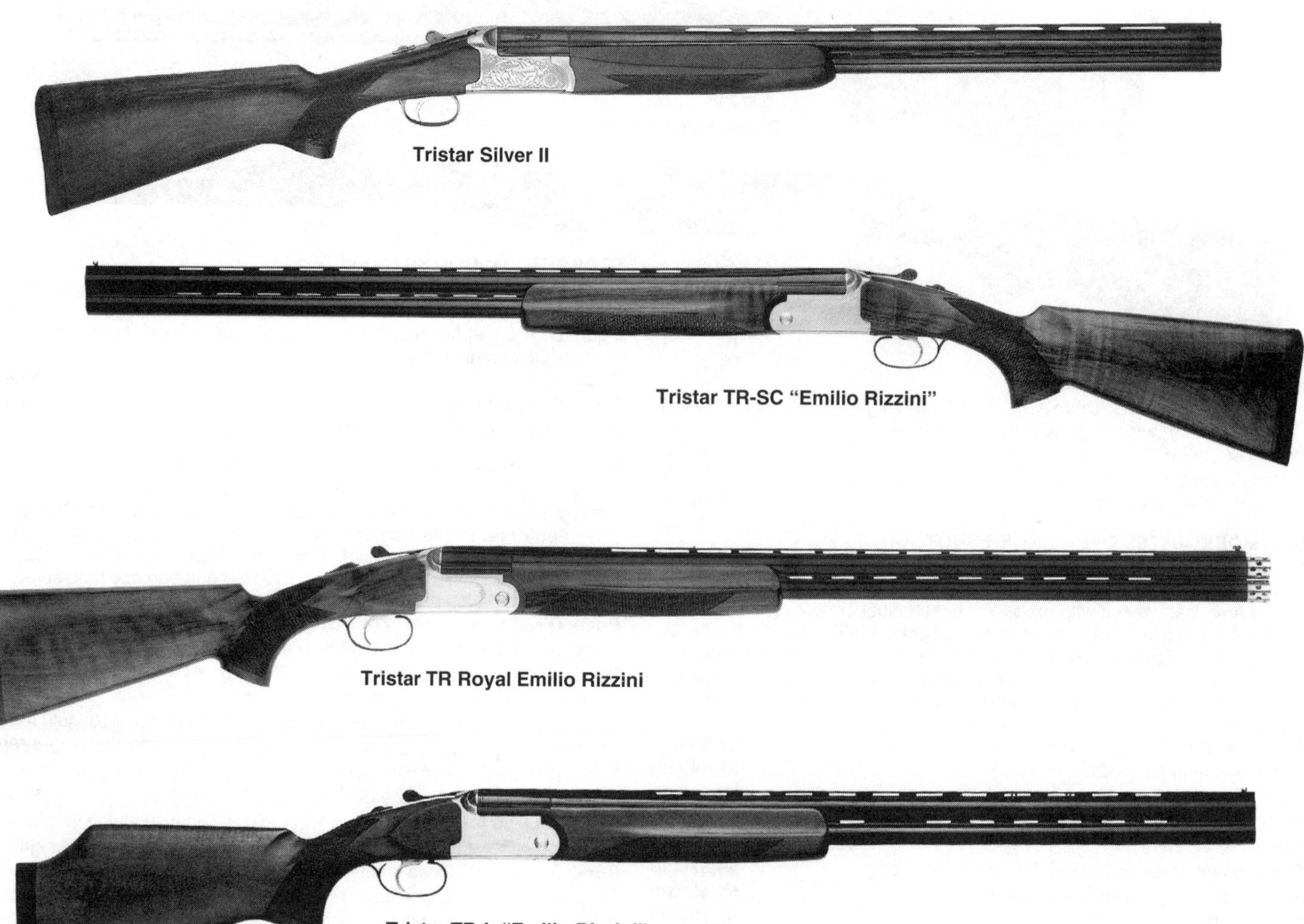

Tristar Silver II

Tristar TR-SC "Emilio Rizzini"

Tristar TR Royal Emilio Rizzini

Tristar TR-L "Emilio Rizzini"

Tristar Silver II Shotgun

Similar to the Silver I except 26" barrel (Imp. Cyl., Mod., Full choke tubes, 12 and 20 ga.), 28" (Imp. Cyl., Mod., Full choke tubes, 12 ga. only), 26" (Imp. Cyl. & Mod. fixed chokes, 28 and .410), automatic selective ejectors. Weight is about 6 lbs., 15 oz. (12 ga., 26").

Price: **$669.00**

TRISTAR TR-SC "EMILIO RIZZINI" OVER/UNDER

Gauge: 12, 20, 3" chambers. **Barrel:** 28", 30" (Imp. Cyl., Mod., Full choke tubes). **Weight:** 7-1/2 lbs. **Length:** 46" overall (28" barrel). **Stock:** 1-1/2"x2-3/ 8"x14-3/8". Semi-fancy walnut; pistol grip with palm swell; semi- beavertail forend; black Sporting Clays recoil pad. **Features:** Silvered boxlock action with Four Locks locking system, auto ejectors, single selec-tive (inertia) trigger, auto safety. Hard chrome bores. Vent. 10mm rib with target-style front and mid-rib beads. Introduced 1998. Imported from Italy by Tristar Sporting Arms, Ltd.

Price: Sporting Clay model **$1,047.00**
Price: 20 ga. **$1,127.00**

Tristar TR-Royal "Emilio Rizzini" O/U Shotgun

Similar to the TR-SC except has special parallel stock dimensions (1-1/2"x1-5/8"x14-3/8") to give low felt recoil; Rhino ported, extended choke tubes; solid barrel spacer; has "TR-Royal" gold engraved on the silvered receiver. Available in 12 gauge (28", 30") 20 and 28 gauge (28" only). Introduced 1999. Imported from Italy by Tristar Sporting Arms, Ltd.

Price:12, 20, 28 ga. **$1,319.00**

Tristar TR-L "Emilio Rizzini" O/U Shotgun

Similar to the TR-SC except has stock dimensions designed for female shooters (1-1/2" x 3" x 13-1/2"). Standard grade walnut. Introduced 1998. Imported from Italy by Tristar Sporting Arms, Ltd.

Price: **$1,063.00**

TRISTAR TR-I, II "EMILIO RIZZINI" O/U SHOTGUN

Gauge: 12, 20, 3" chambers (TR-I); 12, 16, 20, 28, .410 3" chambers. **Barrel:** 12 ga., 26" (Imp. Cyl. & Mod.), 28" (Mod. & Full); 20 ga., 26" (Imp. Cyl. & Mod.), fixed chokes. **Weight:** 7-1/2 lbs. **Stock:** 1-1/2"x2-3/8"x14-3/8". Walnut with palm swell pistol grip, hand checkering, semi-beavertail forend, black recoil pad. **Features:** Boxlock action with blued finish, Four Locks locking system, gold single selective (inertia) trigger system, automatic safety, extractors. Introduced 1998. Imported from Italy by Tristar Sporting Arms, Ltd.

Price: TR-I. **$779.00**
Price: TR-II (automatic ejectors, choke tubes) 12, 16 ga. **$919.00**
Price: 20, 28 ga., .410 . . . . **$969.00**

Tristar TR-Mag "Emilio Rizzini" O/U Shotgun

Similar to TR-I, 3-1/2" chambers; choke tubes; 24" or 28" barrels with three choke tubes; extractors; auto safety. Matte blue finish on all metal, non-reflective wood finish. Introduced 1998. Imported from Italy by Tristar Sporting Arms, Ltd.

Price: **$799.00**
Price: Mossy Oak® Break-Up camo. **$969.00**
Price: Mossy Oak® Shadow Grass camo **$969.00**
Price: 10 ga., Mossy Oak® camo patterns. **$1,132.10**

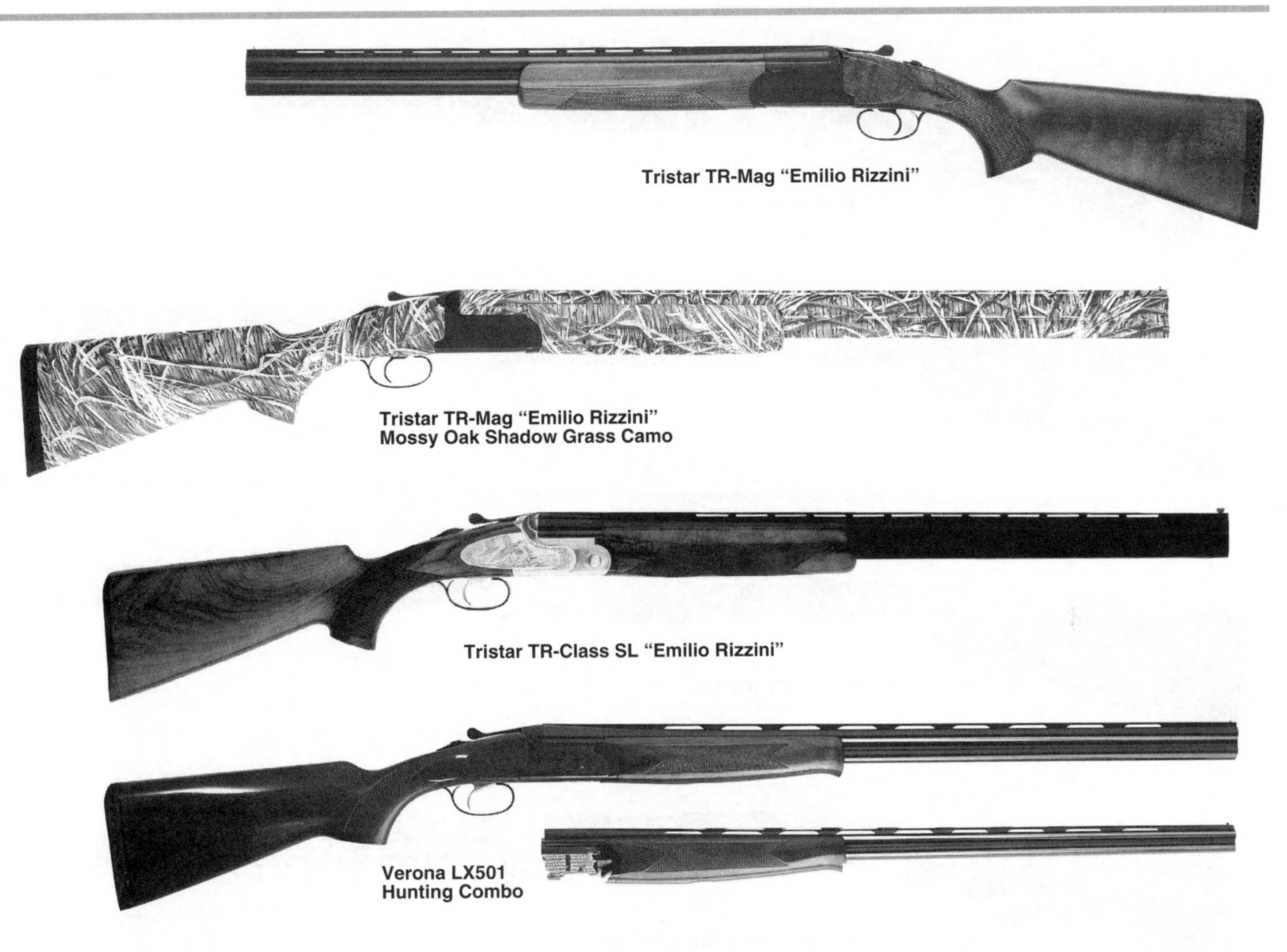

Tristar TR-Mag "Emilio Rizzini"

Tristar TR-Mag "Emilio Rizzini" Mossy Oak Shadow Grass Camo

Tristar TR-Class SL "Emilio Rizzini"

Verona LX501 Hunting Combo

TRISTAR TR-CLASS SL EMILIO RIZZINI O/U

Gauge: 12, 2-3/4" chambers. **Barrel:** 28", 30". **Weight:** 7-3/4 lbs. **Stock:** Fancy walnut, hand checkering, semi-beavertail forend, black recoil pad, gloss finish. **Features:** Boxlock action with silvered, engraved sideplates; Four Lock locking system; automatic ejectors; hard chrome bores; vent tapered 7mm rib with target-style front bead. hand-fitted gun. Introduced 1999. Imported from Italy by Tristar Sporting Arms, Ltd.

Price: **$1,775.00**

TRISTAR WS/OU 12 SHOTGUN

Gauge: 12, 3-1/2" chambers. **Barrel:** 28" or 30" (imp. cyl., mod., full choke tubes). **Weight:** 6 lbs., 15 oz. **Length:** 46" overall. **Stock:** 14-1/8"x1-1/8"x2-3/8". European walnut with cut checkering, black vented recoil pad, matte finish. **Features:** Boxlock action with single selective trigger, automatic selective ejectors; chrome bores. Matte metal finish. Imported by Tristar Sporting Arms Ltd.

Price: **$645.00**

VERONA LX501 HUNTING O/U SHOTGUNS

Gauge: 12, 20, 28, .410 (2-3/4", 3" chambers). **Barrel:** 28"; 12, 20 ga. have Interchoke tubes, 28 ga. and .410 have fixed Full & Mod. **Weight:** 6-7 lbs. **Stock:** Matte-finished walnut with machine-cut checkering. **Features:** Gold-plated single-selective trigger; ejectors; engraved, blued receiver, non-automatic safety; coil spring-operated firing pins. Introduced 1999. Imported from Italy by B.C. Outdoors.

Price: 12 and 20 ga. **$878.08**
Price: 28 ga. and .410. .... **$926.72**
Price: .410 .... **$907.01**
Price: Combos 20/28, 28/.410 .... **$1,459.20**

Verona LX692 Gold Hunting O/U Shotgun

Similar to Verona LX501 except engraved, silvered receiver with false sideplates showing gold-inlaid bird hunting scenes on three sides; Schnabel forend tip; hand-cut checkering; black rubber butt pad. Available in 12 and 20 gauge only, five InterChoke tubes. Introduced 1999. Imported from Italy by B.C. Outdoors.

Price: **$1,295.00**
Price: LX692G Combo 28/.410. .... **$2,192.40**

Verona LX680 Sporting O/U Shotgun

Similar to Verona LX501 except engraved, silvered receiver; ventilated middle rib; beavertail forend; hand-cut checkering; available in 12 or 20 gauge only with 2-3/4" chambers. Introduced 1999. Imported from Italy by B.C. Outdoors.

Price: **$1,159.68**

Verona LX680 Skeet/Sporting/Trap O/U Shotgun

Similar to Verona LX501 except skeet or trap stock dimensions; beavertail forend, palm swell on pistol grip; ventilated center barrel rib. Introduced 1999. Imported from Italy by B.C. Outdoors.

Price: **$1,736.96**

Verona LX692 Gold Sporting O/U Shotgun

Similar to Verona LX680 except false sideplates have gold-inlaid bird hunting scenes on three sides; red high-visibility front sight. Introduced 1999. Imported from Italy by B.C. Outdoors.

Price: Skeet/Sporting **$1,765.12**
Price: Trap (32" barrel, 7-7/8 lbs.). **$1,594.80**

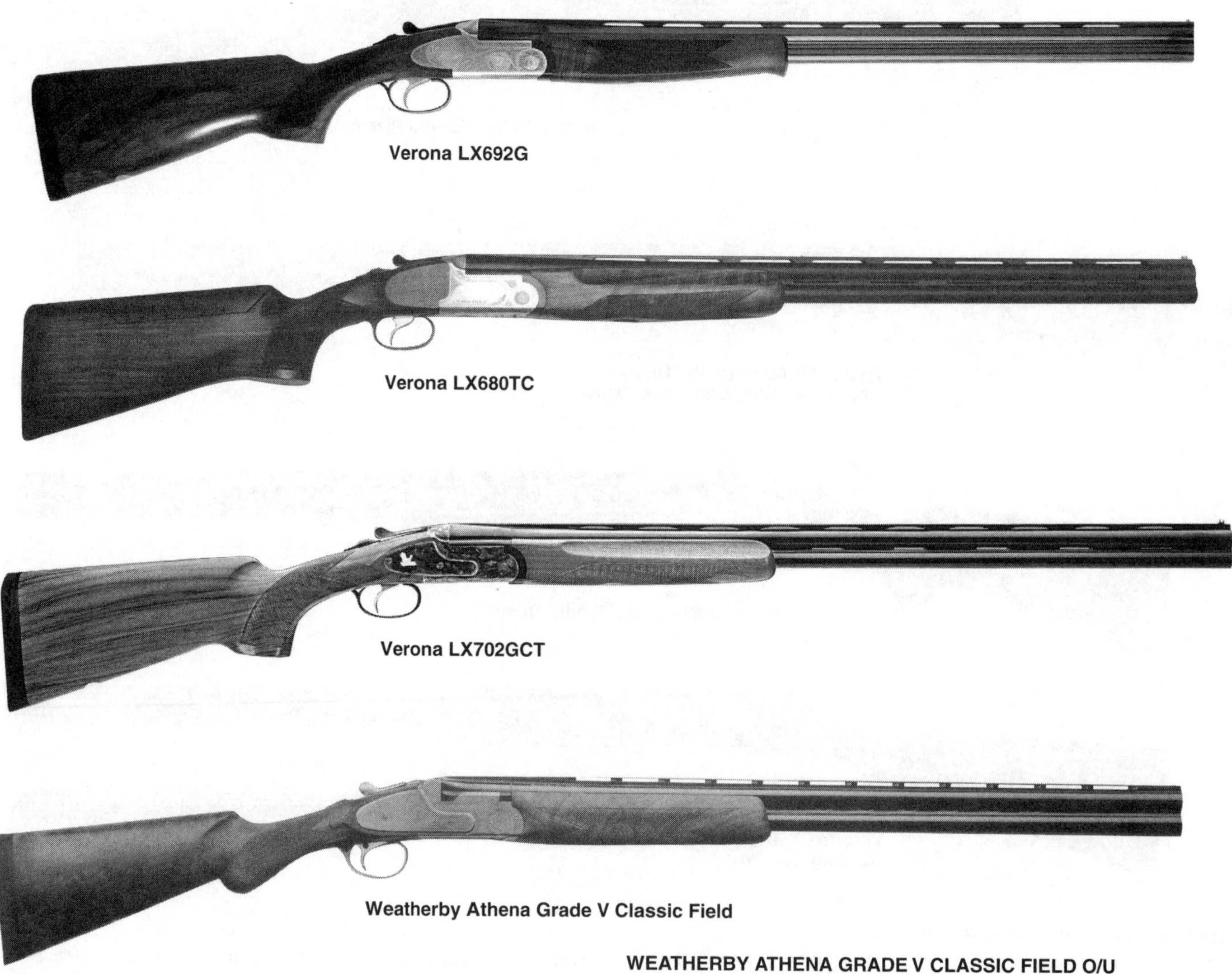

Verona LX692G

Verona LX680TC

Verona LX702GCT

Weatherby Athena Grade V Classic Field

VERONA LX680 COMPETITION TRAP

Gauge: 12. **Barrel:** 30" O/U, 32" single bbl. **Weight:** 8-3/8 lbs. combo, 7 lbs. single. **Stock:** Walnut. **Sights:** White front, mid-rib bead. **Features:** Interchangeable barrels switch from O/U to single configurations. 5 Briley chokes in combo, 4 in single bbl. extended forcing cones, parted barrels 32" with raised rib. By B.C. Outdoors.

Price: Trap Single (LX680TGTSB) **$1,736.96**

Price: Trap Combo (LX680TC) **$2,553.60**

VERONA LX702 GOLD TRAP COMBO

Gauge: 20/28, 2-3/4"chamber. **Barrel:** 30". **Weight:** 7 lbs. **Stock:** Turkish walnut with beavertail forearm. **Sights:** White front bead. **Features:** 2-barrel competition gun. Color case-hardened side plates and receiver with gold inlaid pheasant. Ventilated rib between barrels. 5 interchokes. Imported from Italy by B.C. Outdoors.

Price: Combo **$2,467.84**

Price: 20 ga. **$1,829.12**

Verona LX702 Skeet/Trap O/U Shotgun

Similar to Verona LX702. Both are 12 gauge and 2-3/4" chamber. Skeet has 28" barrel and weighs 7-3/4 lbs. Trap has 32" barrel and weighs 7-7/8 lbs. By B.C. Outdoors.

Price: Skeet **$1,829.12**

Price: Trap. **$1,829.12**

WEATHERBY ATHENA GRADE V CLASSIC FIELD O/U

Gauge: 12, 20, 3" chambers. **Barrel:** 26", 28", IMC Multi-Choke tubes. **Weight:** 12 ga., 7-1/4-8 lbs.; 20 ga. 6-1/2-7-1/4 lbs. **Stock:** Oil-finished American Claro walnut with fine-line checkering, rounded pistol grip and slender forend. **Features:** Old English recoil pad. Sideplate receiver has rose and scroll engraving.

Price: **$3,037.00**

Weatherby Athena Grade III Classic Field O/U

Similar to Athena Grade V, has Grade III Claro walnut with oil finish, rounded pistol grip, slender forend; silver nitride/gray receiver has rose and scroll engraving with gold-overlay upland game scenes. Introduced 1999. Imported from Japan by Weatherby.

Price: 12, 20, 28 ga. **$2,173.00**

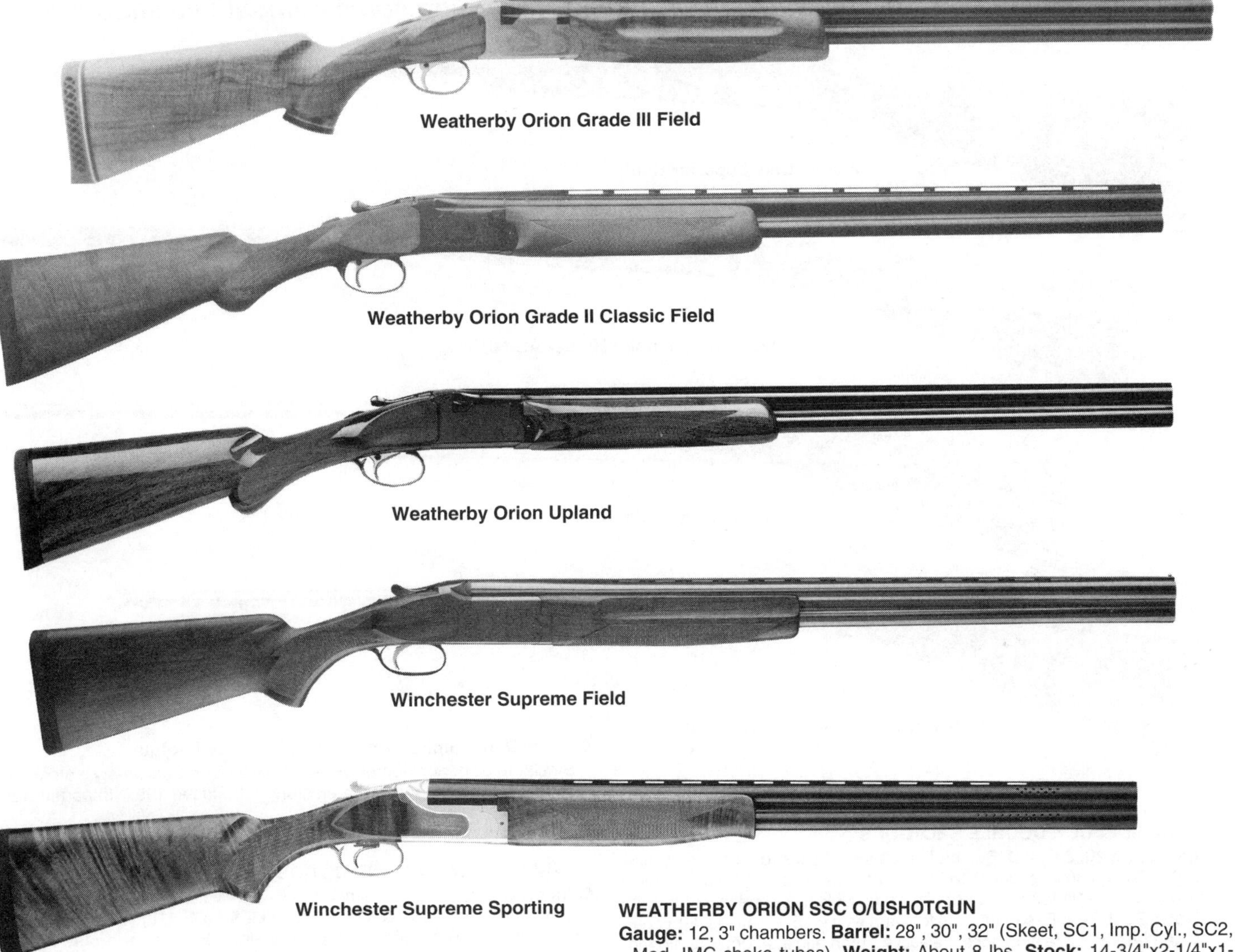

Weatherby Orion Grade III Field

Weatherby Orion Grade II Classic Field

Weatherby Orion Upland

Winchester Supreme Field

Winchester Supreme Sporting

WEATHERBY ORION GRADE III FIELD O/U SHOTGUNS

Gauge: 12, 20, 3" chambers. **Barrel:** 26", 28", IMC Multi-Choke tubes. **Weight:** 6-1/2 to 8 lbs. **Stock:** 14-1/4"x1-1/2"x2-1/2". American walnut, checkered grip and forend. Rubber recoil pad. **Features:** Selective automatic ejectors, single selective inertia trigger. Top tang safety, Greener cross bolt. Has silver-gray receiver with engraving and gold duck/pheasant. Imported from Japan by Weatherby.

Price: Orion III, Field, 12, IMC, 26", 28" **$1,955.00**

Price: Orion III, Field, 20, IMC, 26", 28" **$1,955.00**

Weatherby Orion Grade II Classic Field O/U

Similar to Orion III Classic Field except stock has high-gloss finish, and bird on receiver is not gold. Available in 12 gauge, 26", 28", 30" barrels, 20 gauge, 26" 28", both with 3" chambers, 28 gauge, 26", 2-3/4" chambers. All have IMC choke tubes. Imported from Japan by Weatherby.

Price: **$1,622.00**

Weatherby Orion Upland O/U

Similar to Orion Grade I. Plain blued receiver, gold W on trigger guard; rounded pistol grip, slender forend of Claro walnut with high-gloss finish; black butt pad. Available in 12 and 20 gauge with 26" and 28" barrels. Introduced 1999. Imported from Japan by Weatherby.

Price: **$1,299.00**

WEATHERBY ORION SSC O/USHOTGUN

Gauge: 12, 3" chambers. **Barrel:** 28", 30", 32" (Skeet, SC1, Imp. Cyl., SC2, Mod. IMC choke tubes). **Weight:** About 8 lbs. **Stock:** 14-3/4"x2-1/4"x1-1/2". Claro walnut with satin oil finish; schnabel forend tip; Sporter-style pistol grip; Pachmayr Decelerator recoil pad. **Features:** Designed for Sporting Clays competition. Has lengthened forcing cones and back-boring; ported barrels with 12mm grooved rib with mid-bead sight; mechanical trigger is adjustable for length of pull. Introduced 1998. Imported from Japan by Weatherby.

Price: SSC (Super Sporting Clays). **$2,059.00**

WINCHESTER SELECT O/U SHOTGUNS

Gauge: 12, 2-3/4", 3" chambers. **Barrel:** 28", 30", Invector Plus choke tubes. **Weight:** 7 lbs. 6 oz. to 7 lbs. 12. oz. **Length:** 45" overall (28" barrel). **Stock:** Checkered walnut stock. **Features:** Chrome-plated chambers; back-bored barrels; tang barrel selector/safety; deep-blued finish. Introduced 2000. From U.S. Repeating Arms. Co.

Price: Select Field (26" or 28" barrel, 6mm ventilated rib) **$1,438.00**

Price: Select Energy. **$1,871.00**

Price: Select Eleganza **$2,227.00**

Price: Select Energy Trap **$1,871.00**

Price: Select Energy Trap adjustable **$2,030.00**

Price: Select Energy Sporting adjustable. **$2,030.00**

SHOTGUNS — SIDE-BY-SIDES

Variety of models for utility and sporting use, including some competitive shooting.

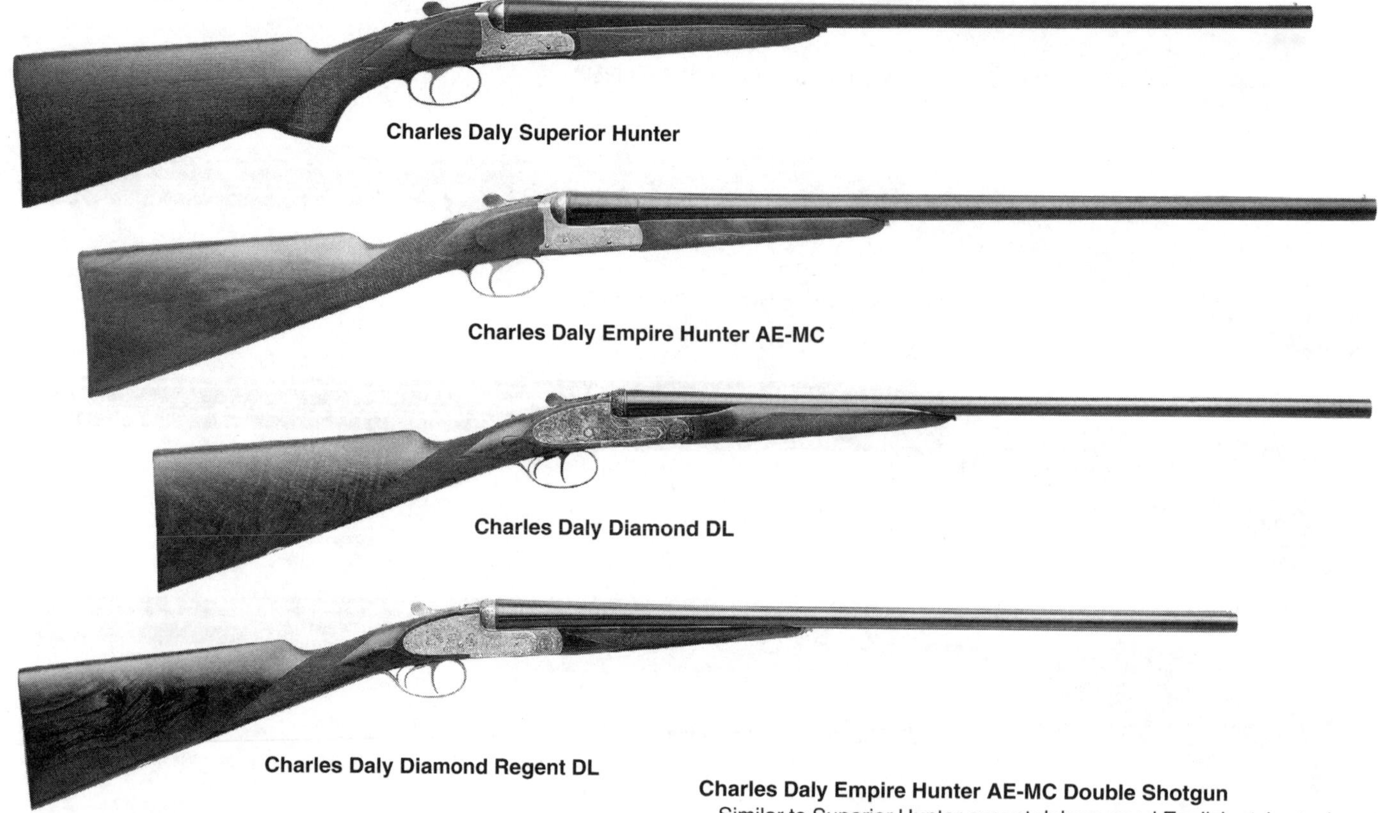
Charles Daly Superior Hunter

Charles Daly Empire Hunter AE-MC

Charles Daly Diamond DL

Charles Daly Diamond Regent DL

ARRIETA SIDELOCK DOUBLE SHOTGUNS

Gauge: 12, 16, 20, 28, .410. **Barrel:** Length and chokes to customer specs. **Weight:** To customer specs. **Stock:** To customer specs. Straight English with checkered butt (standard), or pistol grip. Select European walnut with oil finish. **Features:** Essentially custom gun with myriad options. H&H pattern hand-detachable sidelocks, selective automatic ejectors, double triggers (hinged front) standard. Some have self-opening action. Finish and engraving to customer specs. Imported from Spain by Wingshooting Adventures.

Price: Model 557, auto ejectors, from **$3,250.00**
Price: Model 570, auto ejectors, from **$3,950.00**
Price: Model 578, auto ejectors, from **$4,350.00**
Price: Model 600 Imperial, self-opening, from **$6,050.00**
Price: Model 601 Imperial Tiro, self-opening, from **$6,950.00**
Price: Model 801, from **$9,135.00**
Price: Model 802, from **$9,135.00**
Price: Model 803, from **$6,930.00**
Price: Model 871, auto ejectors, from **$5,060.00**
Price: Model 872, self-opening, from **$12,375.00**
Price: Model 873, self-opening, from **$8,200.00**
Price: Model 874, self-opening, from **$9,250.00**
Price: Model 875, self-opening, from **$14,900.00**

CHARLES DALY SUPERIOR HUNTER AND SUPERIOR MC DOUBLE SHOTGUN

Gauge: 12, 20, 3" chambers, 28, 2-3/4" chambers. **Barrel:** 28" (Mod. & Full) 26" (Imp. Cyl. & Mod.). **Weight:** About 7 lbs. **Stock:** Checkered walnut pis-tol grip buttstock, splinter forend. **Features:** Silvered, engraved receiver; chrome-lined barrels; gold single trigger; automatic safety; extractors; gold bead front sight. Introduced 1997. Imported from Italy by K.B.I., Inc.

Price: Superior Hunter, 28 gauge and .410 .... **$1,029.00**
Price: Superior Hunter MC 26"-28" **$1,059.00**

Charles Daly Empire Hunter AE-MC Double Shotgun

Similar to Superior Hunter except deluxe wood English-style stock, game scene engraving, automatic ejectors. Introduced 1997. Imported from Italy by K.B.I., Inc.

Price: 12 or 20 .... **$1,349.00**

CHARLES DALY DIAMOND DL DOUBLE SHOTGUN

Gauge: 12, 20, .410, 3" chambers, 28, 2-3/4" chambers. **Barrel:** 28" (Mod. & Full), 26" (Imp. Cyl. & Mod.), 26" (Full & Full, .410). **Weight:** About 5-7 lbs. **Stock:** Select fancy European walnut, English-style butt, beavertail forend; hand-checkered, hand-rubbed oil finish. **Features:** Drop-forged action with gas escape valves; demiblock barrels with concave rib; selective automatic ejectors; hand-detachable double safety sidelocks with hand-engraved rose and scrollwork. Hinged front trigger. Color case-hardened receiver. Introduced 1997. Imported from Spain by K.B.I., Inc.

Price: .... **Special order only**

CHARLES DALY DIAMOND REGENT DL DOUBLE SHOTGUN

Gauge: 12, 20, .410, 3" chambers, 28, 2-3/4" chambers. **Barrel:** 28" (Mod. & Full), 26" (Imp. Cyl. & Mod.), 26" (Full & Full, .410). **Weight:** About 5-7 lbs. **Stock:** Special select fancy European walnut, English-style butt, splinter forend; hand-checkered; hand-rubbed oil finish. **Features:** Drop-forged action with gas escape valves; demiblock barrels of chrome-nickel steel with concave rib; selective automatic-ejectors; hand-detachable, double-safety H&H sidelocks with demi-relief hand engraving; H&H pattern easy-opening feature; hinged trigger; coin finished action. Introduced 1997. Imported from Spain by K.B.I., Inc.

Price: Special Custom Order .... **NA**

CHARLES DALY FIELD II, AE-MC HUNTER DOUBLE SHOTGUN

Gauge: 12, 20, 28, .410 (3" chambers; 28 has 2-3/4"). **Barrel:** 32" (Mod. & Mod.), 28, 30" (Mod. & Full), 26" (Imp. Cyl. & Mod.) .410 (Full & Full). **Weight:** 6 lbs. to 11.4 lbs. **Stock:** Checkered walnut pistol grip and forend. **Features:** Silvered, engraved receiver; gold single selective trigger in 10-, 12, and 20 ga.; double triggers in 28 and .410; automatic safety; extractors; gold bead front sight. Introduced 1997. Imported from Spain by K.B.I., Inc.

Price: 28 ga., .410-bore **$729.00**
Price: 12 or 20 AE-MC **$799.00**

SHOTGUNS — SIDE-BY-SIDES

Charles Daly Field Hunter

EAA/Baikal IZH-43 Bounty Hunter

EAA/Baikal MP-213

Fabarm Classic Lion

Fabarm Classic Lion Elite

DAKOTA PREMIER GRADE SHOTGUNS

Gauge: 12, 16, 20, 28, .410. **Barrel:** 27". **Weight:** NA. **Length:** NA. **Stock:** Exhibition-grade English walnut, hand-rubbed oil finish with straight grip and splinter forend. **Features:** French grey finish; 50 percent coverage engraving; double triggers; selective ejectors. Finished to customer specifications. Made in U.S. by Dakota Arms.

Price: 12, 16, 20 gauge **$13,950.00**

Price: 28 gauge and .410 . . . . **$15,345.00**

Dakota Legend Shotgun

Similar to Premier Grade except has special selection English walnut, full-coverage scroll engraving, oak and leather case. Made in U.S. by Dakota Arms.

Price: 12, 16, 20 gauge **$18,000.00**

Price: 28 gauge and .410 . . . . **$19,800.00**

EAA BAIKAL BOUNTY HUNTER IZH43K SHOTGUN

Gauge: 12, 3-inch chambers. **Barrel:** 18-1/2", 20", 24", 26", 28", three choke tubes. **Weight:** 7.28 lbs. Overall length: NA. **Stock:** Walnut, checkered forearm and grip. **Features:** Machined receiver; hammer-forged barrels with chrome-line bores; external hammers; double triggers (single, selective trigger available); rifle barrel inserts optional. Imported by European American Armory.

Price: . . . . **$379.00 to 399.00**

EAA BAIKAL IZH43 BOUNTY HUNTER SHOTGUN

Gauge: 12, 3-inch chambers.**Barrel:** 20", 24", 26", 28"; imp., mod. and full choke tubes. **Stock:** Hardwood or walnut; checkered forend and grip. **Features:** Hammer forged barrel; internal hammers; extractors; engraved receiver; automatic tang safety; non-glare rib. Imported by European American Armory.

Price: IZH-43 Bounty Hunter (12 gauge, 2-3/4" chambers, 20" brl., dbl. triggers, hardwood stock) **$329.00**

Price: IZH-43 Bounty Hunter (20 gauge, 3" chambers, 20" bbl., dbl. triggers, walnut stock). **$359.00**

E.M.F. HARTFORD MODEL COWBOY SHOTGUN

Gauge: 12. **Barrel:** 20". **Weight:** NA. **Length:** NA. **Stock:** Checkered walnut. **Sights:** Center bead. **Features:** Exposed hammers; color-case hardened receiver; blued barrel. Introduced 2001. Imported from Spain by E.M.F. Co. Inc.

Price: **$625.00**

FABARM CLASSIC LION DOUBLE SHOTGUN

Gauge: 12, 3" chambers. **Barrel:** 26", 28", 30" (Cyl., Imp. Cyl., Mod., Imp. Mod., Full choke tubes). **Weight:** 7.2 lbs. **Length:** 44.5"-48.5. **Stock:** English-style or pistol grip oil-finished European walnut. **Features:** Boxlock action with double triggers, automatic ejectors, automatic safety. Introduced 1998. Imported from Italy by Heckler & Koch, Inc.

Price: Grade I **$1,499.00**

Price: Grade II **$2,099.00**

Price: Elite (color-case hardened type finish, 44.5"). **$1,689.00**

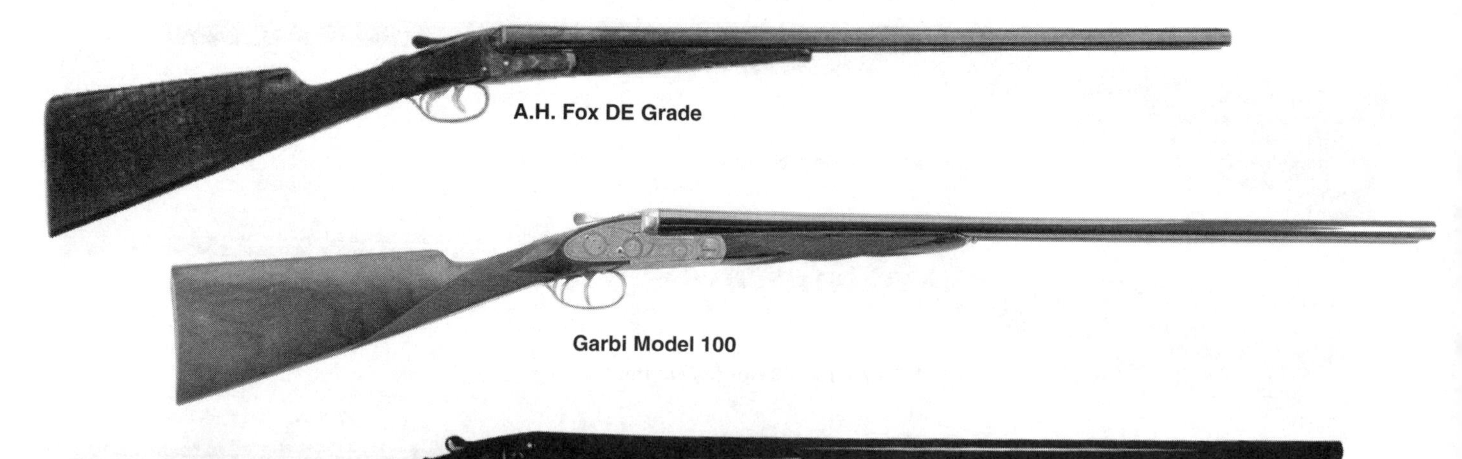

A.H. Fox DE Grade

Garbi Model 100

Bill Hanus Birdgun

FOX, A.H., SIDE-BY-SIDE SHOTGUNS

Gauge: 16, 20, 28, .410. **Barrel:** Length and chokes to customer specifications. Rust-blued Chromox or Krupp steel. **Weight:** 5-1/2 to 6-3/4 lbs. **Stock:** Dimensions to customer specifications. Hand-checkered Turkish Circassian walnut with hand-rubbed oil finish. Straight, semi or full pistol grip; splinter, schnabel or beavertail forend; traditional pad, hard rubber buttplate or skeleton butt. **Features:** Boxlock action with automatic ejectors; double or Fox single selective trigger. Scalloped, rebated and color case-hardened receiver; hand finished and hand-engraved. Grades differ in engraving, inlays, grade of wood, amount of hand finishing. Add $1,500 for 28 or .410-bore. Introduced 1993. Made in U.S. by Connecticut Shotgun Mfg.

Price: CE Grade **$11,000.00**
Price: XE Grade **$12,500.00**
Price: DE Grade **$15,000.00**
Price: FE Grade **$20,000.00**
Price: Exhibition Grade **$30,000.00**
Price: 28/.410 CE Grade. **$12,500.00**
Price: 28/.410 XE Grade. **$14,000.00**
Price: 28/.410 DE Grade. **$16,500.00**
Price: 28/.410 FE Grade. **$21,500.00**
Price: 28/.410 Exhibition Grade **$30,000.00**

GARBI MODEL 100 DOUBLE

Gauge: 12, 16, 20, 28. **Barrel:** 26", 28", choked to customer specs. **Weight:** 5-1/2 to 7-1/2 lbs. **Stock:** 14-1/2"x2-1/4"x1-1/2". European walnut. Straight grip, checkered butt, classic forend. **Features:** Sidelock action, automatic ejectors, double triggers standard. Color case-hardened action, coin finish optional. Single trigger; beavertail forend, etc. optional. Five other models are available. Imported from Spain by Wm. Larkin Moore.

Price: From **$4,850.00**

Garbi Model 200 Side-by-Side

Similar to the Garbi Model 100 except has heavy-duty locks, magnum proofed. Very fine Continental-style floral and scroll engraving, well figured walnut stock. Other mechanical features remain the same. Imported from Spain by Wm. Larkin Moore.

Price: **$11,200.00**

Garbi Model 101 Side-by-Side

Similar to the Garbi Model 100 except is hand engraved with scroll engraving, select walnut stock. Better overall quality than the Model 100. Imported from Spain by Wm. Larkin Moore.

Price: From **$6,250.00**

Garbi Model 103 A & B Side-by-Side

Similar to the Garbi Model 100 except has Purdey-type fine scroll and rosette engraving. Better overall quality than the Model 101. Model 103B has nickel-chrome steel barrels, H&H-type easy opening mechanism; other mechanical details remain the same. Imported from Spain by Wm. Larkin Moore.

Price: Model 103A, from **$8,000.00**
Price: Model 103B, from **11,800.00**

HANUS BIRDGUN

Gauge: 16, 20, 28. **Barrel:** 27", 20 and 28 ga.; 28", 16 ga. (Skeet 1 & Skeet 2). **Weight:** 5 lbs., 4 oz. to 6 lbs., 4 oz. **Stock:** 14-3/8"x1-1/2"x2-3/8", with 1/4" cast-off. Select walnut. **Features:** Boxlock action with ejectors; splinter forend, straight English grip; checkered butt; English leather-covered handguard and AyA snap caps included. Made by AyA. Introduced 1998. Imported from Spain by Bill Hanus Birdguns.

Price: **$2,495.00**

ITHACA CLASSIC DOUBLES SKEET GRADE SxS

Gauge: 20, 28, 2-3/4" chambers, .410, 3". **Barrel:** 26", 28", 30", fixed chokes. **Weight:** 5 lbs., 14 oz. (20 gauge). **Stock:** 14-1/2"x2-1/4"x1-3/8". High-grade American black walnut, hand-rubbed oil finish; splinter or beavertail forend, straight or pistol grip. **Features:** Double triggers, ejectors; color case-hardened, engraved action body with matted top surfaces. Introduced 1999. Made in U.S. by Ithaca Classic Doubles.

Price: From **$5,999.00**

Ithaca Classic Doubles Grade 4E Classic SxS Shotgun

Gold-plated triggers, jeweled barrel flats and hand-turned locks. Feather crotch and flame-grained black walnut hand-checkered 28 lpi with fleur de lis pattern. Action body engraved with three game scenes and bank note scroll, color case-hardened. Introduced 1999. Made in U.S. by Ithaca Classic Doubles.

Price: From **$7,500.00**

Ithaca Classic Doubles Grade 7E Classic SxS Shotgun

Engraved with bank note scroll and flat 24k gold game scenes: gold setter and gold pointer on opposite action sides, American bald eagle inlaid on bottom plate. Hand-timed, polished, jeweled ejectors and locks. Exhibition grade American black walnut stock and forend with eight-panel fleur de lis borders. Introduced 1999. Made in U.S. by Ithaca Classic Doubles.

Price: From **$11,000.00**

Ithaca Classic Doubles Grade 5E SxS Shotgun

Completely hand-made, it is based on the early Ithaca engraving patterns of master engraver William McGraw. The hand engraving is at 90% coverage in deep chiseled floral scroll with game scenes in 24kt gold inlays. Stocks are of high-grade Turkish and American walnut and are hand-checkered. Available in 12, 16, 20, 28 gauges and .410 bore including two barrel combination sets in 16/20 ga. and 28/.410 bore. Introduced 2003. Made in U.S.A. by Ithaca Classic Doubles.

Price: From **$8,500.00**

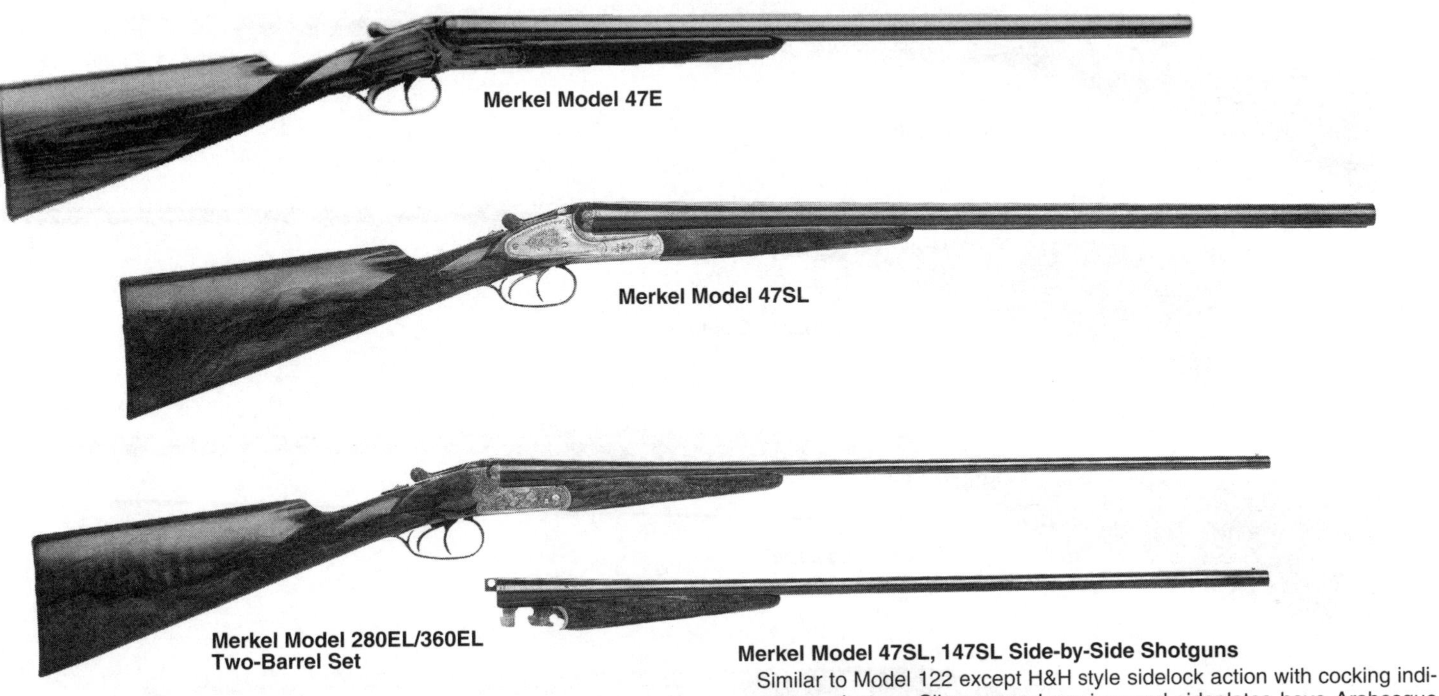

Merkel Model 47E

Merkel Model 47SL

Merkel Model 280EL/360EL Two-Barrel Set

Ithaca Classic Doubles Grade 6e Side-by-Side Shotgun

Features hand engraving of fine English scroll coupled with game scenes and 24kt gold inlays. Stockare hand-made of best quality American, Turkish or English walnut with hand checkering. All metal work is finished in traditional bone and charcoal color case hardening and deep rust blue. Available in 12, 16, 20, 28 gauges and .410 bore. Introduced 2003. Made in U.S.A. by Ithaca Classic Doubles.

Price: From **$9,999.00**

Ithaca Classic Doubles Sousa Grade Side-by-Side Shotgun

Presentation grade American black walnut, hand-carved and checkered; hand-engraving with 24-karat gold inlays; tuned action and hand-applied finishes. Made in U.S. by Ithaca Classic Doubles.

Price: From **$18,000.00**

LEBEAU - COURALLY BOXLOCK SIDE-BY-SIDE SHOTGUN

Gauge: 12, 16, 20, 28, .410-bore. **Barrel:** 25" to 32". **Weight:** To customer specifications. **Stock:** French walnut. **Features:** Anson & Deely-type action with automatic ejectors; single or double triggers. Essentially a custom gun built to customer specifications. Imported from Belgium by Wm. Larkin Moore.

Price: From **$25,500.00**

LEBEAU - COURALLY SIDELOCK SIDE-BY-SIDE SHOTGUN

Gauge: 12, 16, 20, 28, .410-bore. **Barrel:** 25" to 32". **Weight:** To customer specifications. **Stock:** Fancy French walnut. **Features:** Holland & Holland-type action with automatic ejectors; single or double triggers. Essentially a custom gun built to customer specifications. Imported from Belgium by Wm. Larkin Moore.

Price: From **$56,000.00**

MERKEL MODEL 47E, 147E SIDE-BY-SIDE SHOTGUNS

Gauge: 12, 3" chambers, 16, 2-3/4" chambers, 20, 3" chambers. **Barrel:** 12, 16 ga.-28"; 20 ga.-26-3/4" (Imp. Cyl. & Mod., Mod. & Full). **Weight:** About 6-3/4 lbs. (12 ga.). **Stock:** Oil-finished walnut; straight English or pistol grip. **Features:** Anson & Deeley-type boxlock action with single selective or double triggers, automatic safety, cocking indicators. Color case-hardened receiver with standard Arabesque engraving. Imported from Germany by GSI.

Price: Model 47E (H&H ejectors) **$3,295.00**

Price: Model 147E (as above with ejectors) **$3,995.00**

Merkel Model 47SL, 147SL Side-by-Side Shotguns

Similar to Model 122 except H&H style sidelock action with cocking indicators, ejectors. Silver-grayed receiver and sideplates have Arabesque engraving, engraved border and screws (Model 47S), or fine hunting scene engraving (Model 147S). Imported from Germany by GSI.

Price: Model 47SL **$5,995.00**

Price: Model 147SL **$7,995.00**

Price: Model 247SL (English-style engraving, large scrolls). . . . **$7,995.00**

Price: Model 447SL (English-style engraving, small scrolls) . . . **$9,995.00**

Merkel Model 280EL, 360EL Shotguns

Similar to Model 47E except smaller frame. Greener cross bolt with double under-barrel locking lugs, fine engraved hunting scenes on silver-grayed receiver, luxury-grade wood, Anson and Deely box-lock action. H&H ejectors, single-selective or double triggers. Introduced 2000. From Merkel.

Price: Model 280EL (28 gauge, 28" barrel, imp. cyl. and mod. chokes) 4 mod. chokes) **$5,795.00**

Price: Model 360EL (.410, 28" barrel, mod. and full chokes). **$5,795.00**

Price: Model 280/360EL two-barrel set (28 and .410 gauge as above) **$8,295.00**

Merkel Model 280SL and 360SL Shotguns

Similar to Model 280EL and 360EL except has sidelock action, double triggers, English-style Arabesque engraving. Introduced 2000. From Merkel.

Price: Model 280SL (28 gauge, 28" barrel, imp. cyl. and mod. chokes) **$8,495.00**

Price: Model 360SL (.410, 28" barrel, mod. and full chokes) **$8,495.00**

Price: Model 280/360SL two-barrel set **$11,995.00**

PIOTTI KING NO. 1 SIDE-BY-SIDE

Gauge: 12, 16, 20, 28, .410. **Barrel:** 25" to 30" (12 ga.), 25" to 28" (16, 20, 28, .410). To customer specs. Chokes as specified. **Weight:** 6-1/2 lbs. to 8 lbs. (12 ga. to customer specs.). **Stock:** Dimensions to customer specs. Finely figured walnut; straight grip with checkered butt with classic splinter forend and hand-rubbed oil finish standard. Pistol grip, beavertail forend. **Features:** Holland & Holland pattern sidelock action, automatic ejectors. Double trigger; non-selective single trigger optional. Coin finish standard; color case-hardened optional. Top rib; level, file-cut; concave, ventilated optional. Very fine, full coverage scroll engraving with small floral bouquets. Imported from Italy by Wm. Larkin Moore.

Price: From **$29,600.00**

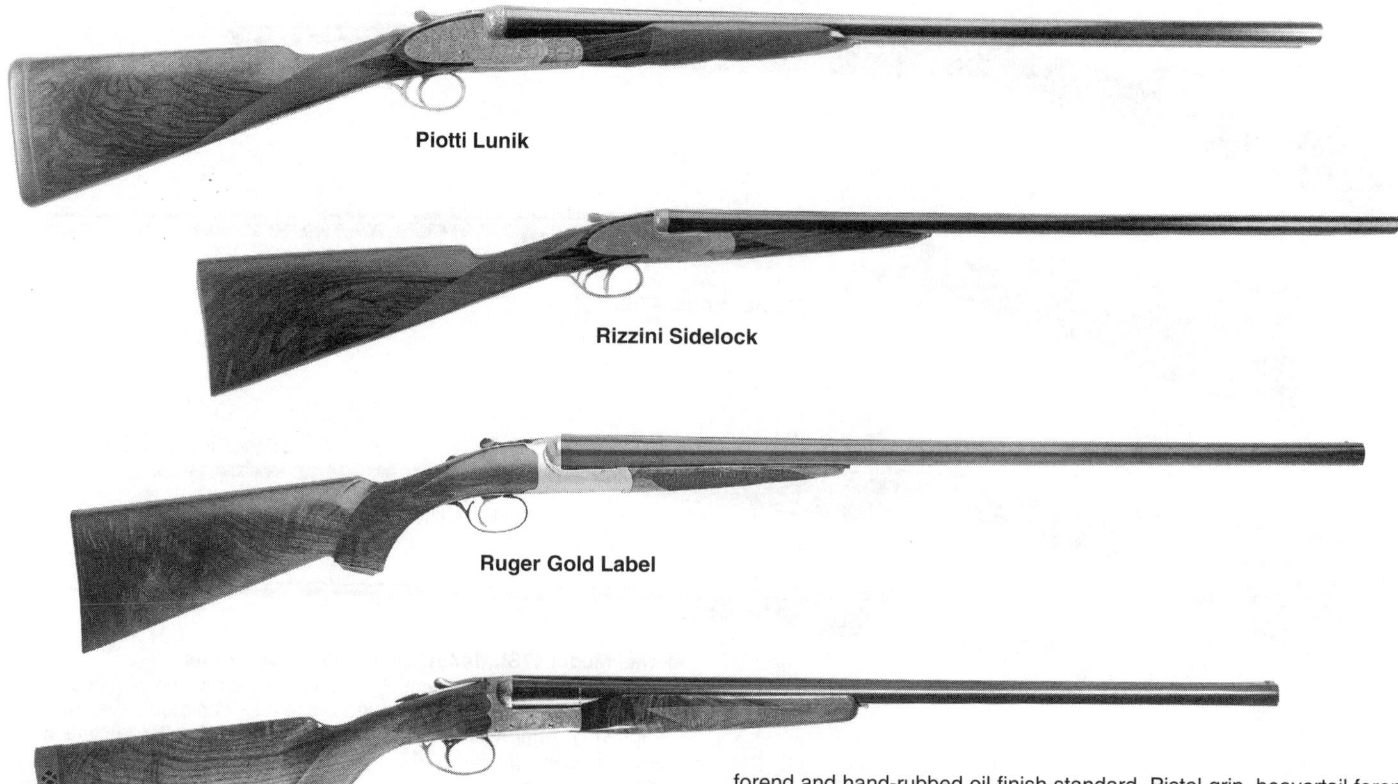

Piotti Lunik

Rizzini Sidelock

Ruger Gold Label

SKB Model 385

Piotti King Extra Side-by-Side

Similar to the Piotti King No. 1 except with upgraded engraving. Choice of any type of engraving, including bulino game scene engraving and game scene engraving with gold inlays. Engraved and signed by a master engraver. Other mechanical specifications remain the same. Imported from Italy by Wm. Larkin Moore.

Price: From **$35,000.00**

Piotti Lunik Side-by-Side

Similar to the Piotti King No. 1 in overall quality. Has Renaissance-style large scroll engraving in relief. Best quality Holland & Holland-pattern sidelock ejector double with chopper lump (demi-bloc) barrels. Other mechanical specifications remain the same. Imported from Italy by Wm. Larkin Moore.

Price: From **$30,900.00**

PIOTTI PIUMA SIDE-BY-SIDE

Gauge: 12, 16, 20, 28, .410. **Barrel:** 25" to 30" (12 ga.), 25" to 28" (16, 20, 28, .410). **Weight:** 5-1/2 to 6-1/4 lbs. (20 ga.). **Stock:** Dimensions to customer specs. Straight grip stock with walnut checkered butt, classic splinter forend, hand-rubbed oil finish are standard; pistol grip, beavertail forend, satin luster finish optional. **Features:** Anson & Deeley boxlock ejector double with chopper lump barrels. Level, file-cut rib, light scroll and rosette engraving, scalloped frame. Double triggers; single non-selective optional. Coin finish standard, color case-hardened optional. Imported from Italy by Wm. Larkin Moore.

Price: From **$14,800.00**

RIZZINI SIDELOCK SIDE-BY-SIDE

Gauge: 12, 16, 20, 28, .410. **Barrel:** 25" to 30" (12, 16, 20 ga.), 25" to 28" (28, .410). To customer specs. Chokes as specified. **Weight:** 6-1/2 lbs. to 8 lbs. (12 ga. to customer specs). **Stock:** Dimensions to customer specs. Finely figured walnut; straight grip with checkered butt with classic splinter forend and hand-rubbed oil finish standard. Pistol grip, beavertail forend. **Features:** Sidelock action, auto ejectors. Double triggers or non-selective single trigger standard. Coin finish standard. Imported from Italy by Wm. Larkin Moore.

Price: 12, 20 ga., from **$66,900.00**

Price: 28, .410 bore, from **$75,500.00**

RUGER GOLD LABEL SIDE-BY-SIDE SHOTGUN

Gauge: 12, 3" chambers. **Barrel:** 28" with skeet tubes. **Weight:** 6-1/2 lbs. **Length:** 45". **Stock:** American walnut straight or pistol grip. **Sights:** Gold bead front, full length rib, serrated top. **Features:** Spring-assisted break-open, SS trigger, auto eject. 5 interchangeable screw-in choke tubes, combination safety/barrel selector with auto safety reset.

Price: **$1,950.00**

SKB MODEL 385 SIDE-BY-SIDE

Gauge: 12, 20, 3" chambers; 28, 2-3/4" chambers. **Barrel:** 26" (Imp. Cyl., Mod., Skeet choke tubes). **Weight:** 6-3/4 lbs. **Length:** 42-1/2" overall. **Stock:** 14-1/8"x1-1/2"x2-1/2" American walnut with straight or pistol grip stock, semi-beavertail forend. **Features:** Boxlock action. Silver nitrided receiver with engraving; solid barrel rib; single selective trigger, selective automatic ejectors, automatic safety. Introduced 1996. Imported from Japan by G.U. Inc.

Price: **$2,159.00**

Price: Field Set, 20, 28 ga., 26" or 28", English or pistol grip . . . **$3,059.00**

SKB Model 385 Sporting Clays

Similar to the Field Model 385 except 12 gauge only; 28" barrel with choke tubes; raised ventilated rib with metal middle bead and white front. Stock dimensions 14-1/4"x1-7/16"x1-7/8". Introduced 1998. Imported from Japan by G.U. Inc.

Price: **$2,159.00**

Price: Sporting Clays set, 20, 28 ga. **$3,059.00**

SKB Model 485 Side-by-Side

Similar to the Model 385 except has dummy sideplates, raised ventilated rib with metal middle bead and white front, extensive upland game scene engraving, semi-fancy American walnut English or pistol grip stock. Imported from Japan by G.U. Inc.

Price: **$2,769.00**

Price: Field set, 20, 28 ga., 26" **$2,769.00**

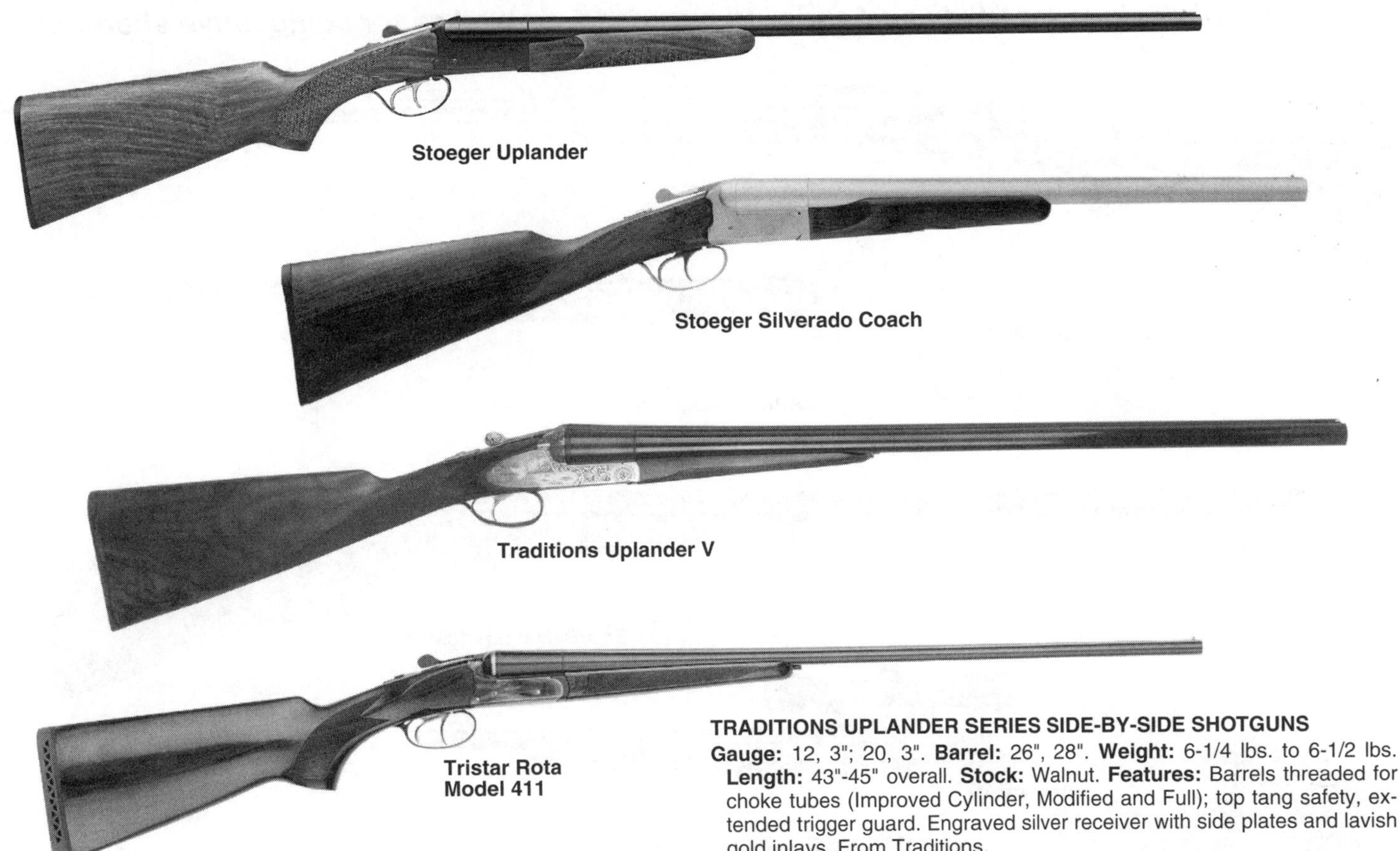

Stoeger Uplander

Stoeger Silverado Coach

Traditions Uplander V

Tristar Rota Model 411

STOEGER UPLANDER SIDE-BY-SIDE SHOTGUN

Gauge: 16, 28, 2-3/4 chambers. 12, 20, .410, 3" chambers. **Barrel:** 26", 28". **Weight:** 7.3 lbs. **Sights:** Brass bead. **Features:** Double trigger, IC, M fixed choke tubes with gun.

Price: ..... (With fixed chokes) **$335.00**; (With screw-in chokes) **$350.00**
Price: With English stock .... **$335.00 to $350.00**
Price: Upland Special **$375.00**
Price: Upland Supreme with SST, red bar sights **$445.00**
Price: Upland Short Stock (Youth) **$335.00**

STOEGER COACH GUN SIDE-BY-SIDE SHOTGUN

Gauge: 12, 20, .410, 2-3/4", 3" chambers. **Barrel:** 20". **Weight:** 6-1/2 lbs. **Stock:** Brown hardwood, classic beavertail forend. **Sights:** Brass bead. **Features:** IC & M fixed chokes, tang auto safety, auto extractors, black plastic butt plate. 12 ga. and 20 ga. also with English style stock.

Price: .... **$320.00**; (Nickel) **$375.00**
Price: Silverado .... **$375.00**; (With English stock) **$375.00**

TRADITIONS ELITE SERIES SIDE-BY-SIDE SHOTGUNS

Gauge: 12, 3"; 20, 3"; 28, 2-3/4"; .410, 3". **Barrel:** 26". **Weight:** 5 lbs., 12 oz. to 6-1/2 lbs. **Length:** 43" overall. **Stock:** Walnut. **Features:** Chrome-lined barrels; fixed chokes (Elite Field III ST, Field I DT and Field I ST) or choke tubes (Elite Hunter ST); extractors (Hunter ST and Field I models) or au-tomatic ejectors (Field III ST); top tang safety. Imported from Fausti of Italy by Traditions.

Price: (Elite Field I DT - 12, 20, 28 ga. or .410; I.C. and Mod. fixed chokes [F and F on .410]; double triggers) .... **$789.00 to $969.00**
Price: (Elite Field I ST - 12, 20, 28 ga. or .410; same as DT but with single trigger)................................. **$969.00 to $1,169.00**
Price: (Elite Field III ST - 28 ga. or .410; gold-engraved receiver; high-grade walnut stock)................................ **$2,099.00**
Price: (Elite Hunter ST - 12 or 20 ga.; blued receiver; I.C. and Mod. choke tubes) **$999.00**

TRADITIONS UPLANDER SERIES SIDE-BY-SIDE SHOTGUNS

Gauge: 12, 3"; 20, 3". **Barrel:** 26", 28". **Weight:** 6-1/4 lbs. to 6-1/2 lbs. **Length:** 43"-45" overall. **Stock:** Walnut. **Features:** Barrels threaded for choke tubes (Improved Cylinder, Modified and Full); top tang safety, extended trigger guard. Engraved silver receiver with side plates and lavish gold inlays. From Traditions.

Price: Uplander III Silver 12, 20 ga. **$2,699.00**
Price: Uplander V Silver 12, 20 ga. **$3,199.00**

TRISTAR ROTA MODEL 411 SIDE-BY-SIDE

Gauge: 12, 16, 20, .410, 3" chambers; 28, 2-3/4". **Barrel:** 12 ga., 26", 28"; 16, 20, 28 ga., .410-bore, 26"; 12 and 20 ga. have three choke tubes, 16, 28 (Imp. Cyl. & Mod.), .410 (Mod. & Full) fixed chokes. **Weight:** 6-1/2 to 7- 1/4 lbs. **Stock:** 14-3/8" l.o.p. Standard walnut with pistol grip, splinter-style forend; hand checkered. **Features:** Engraved, color case-hardened box-lock action; double triggers, extractors; solid barrel rib. Introduced 1998. Imported from Italy by Tristar Sporting Arms, Ltd.

Price: **$849.00**

Tristar Rota Model 411D Side-by-Side

Similar to Model 411 except automatic ejectors, straight English-style stock, single trigger. Solid barrel rib with matted surface; chrome bores; color case-hardened frame; splinter forend. Introduced 1999. Imported from Italy by Tristar Sporting Arms, Ltd.

Price: **$1,110.00**

Tristar Rota Model 411R Coach Gun Side-by-Side

Similar to Model 411 except in 12 or 20 gauge only with 20" barrels and fixed chokes (Cyl. & Cyl.). Double triggers, extractors, choke tubes. Introduced 1999. Imported from Italy by Tristar Sporting Arms, Ltd.

Price: **$745.00**

Tristar Rota Model 411F Side-by-Side

Similar to Model 411 except silver, engraved receiver, ejectors, IC, M and F choke tubes, English-style stock, single gold trigger, cut checkering. Imported from Italy by Tristar Sporting Arms Ltd.

Price: **$1,608.00**

TRISTAR DERBY CLASSIC SIDE-BY-SIDE

Gauge: 12. **Barrel:** 28" Mod. & Full fixed chokes. **Features:** Sidelock action, engraved, double trigger, auto ejectors, English straight stock. Made in Europe for Tristar Sporting Arms Ltd.

Price: **$1,059.00**

Shotguns — Bolt Actions & Single Shots

Variety of designs for utility and sporting purposes, as well as for competitive shooting.

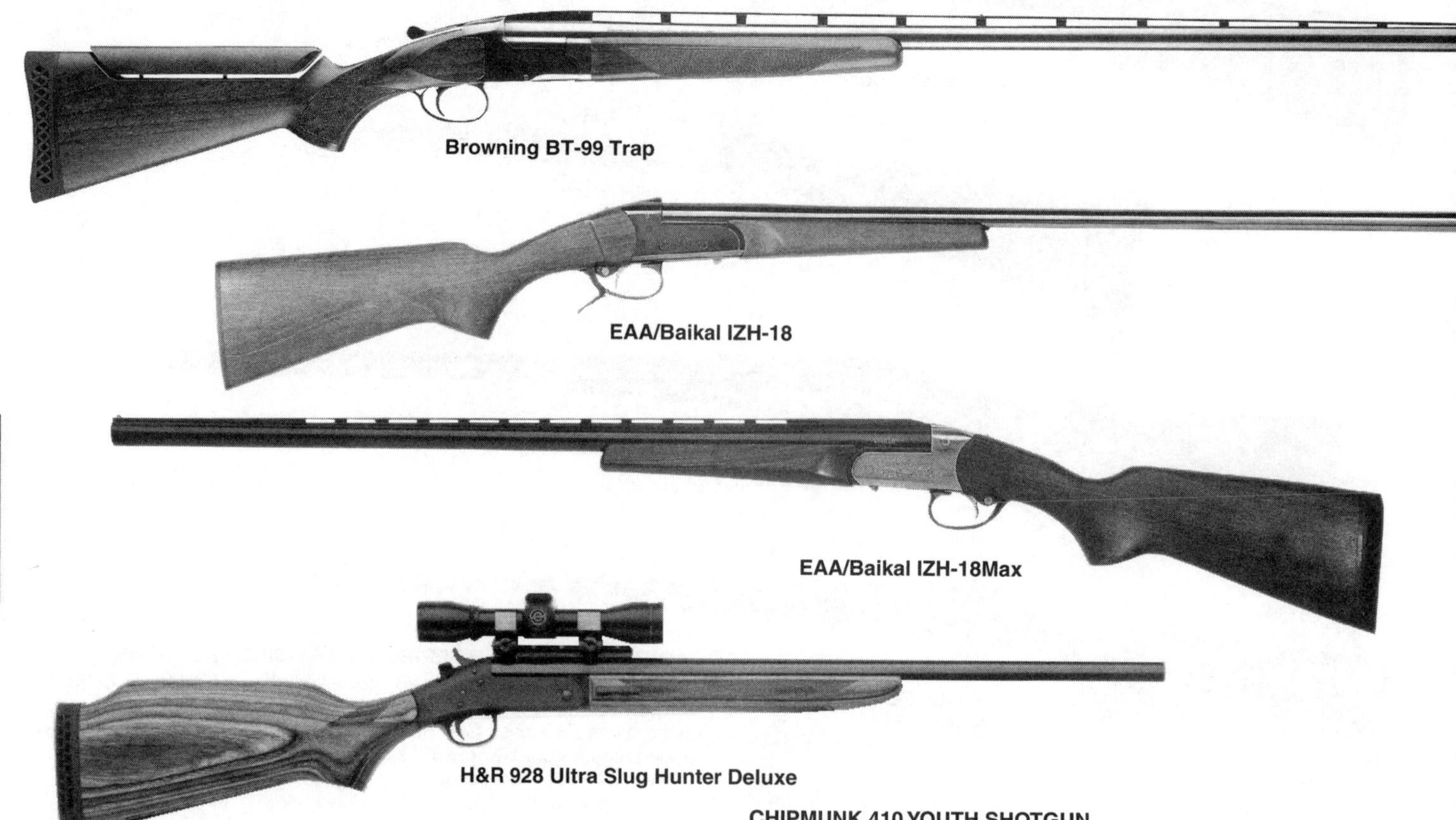

Browning BT-99 Trap

EAA/Baikal IZH-18

EAA/Baikal IZH-18Max

H&R 928 Ultra Slug Hunter Deluxe

BERETTA DT10 TRIDENT TRAP TOP SINGLE SHOTGUN

Gauge: 12, 3" chamber. **Barrel:** 34"; five Optima Choke tubes (full, full, imp. modified, mod. and imp. cyl.). **Weight:** 8.8 lbs. **Stock:** High-grade walnut; adjustable. **Features:** Detachable, adjustable trigger group; Optima Bore for improved shot pattern and reduced recoil; slim Optima Choke tubes; raised and thickened receiver for long life. Introduced 2000. Imported from Italy by Beretta USA.

Price: **$8,500.00**

BRNO ZBK 100 SINGLE BARREL SHOTGUN

Gauge: 12 or 20. **Barrel:** 27.5". **Weight:** 5.5 lbs. **Length:** 44" overall. **Stock:** Beech. **Features:** Polished blue finish; sling swivels. Announced 1998. Imported from The Czech Republic by Euro-Imports.

Price: **$185.00**

BROWNING BT-99 TRAP SHOTGUN

Gauge: 12, 2-3/4" chamber. **Barrel:** 32" or 34"; Invector choke system (full choke tube only included); High Post Rib; back-bored. **Weight:** 8 lbs., 10 oz. (34" bbl.). **Length:** 50-1/2" overall (34" bbl.). **Stock:** Conventional or adjustable-comb. **Features:** Re-introduction of the BT-99 Trap Shotgun. Full beavertail forearm; checkered walnut stock; ejector; rubber butt pad. Re-introduced 2001. Imported by Browning.

Price: Conventional stock, 32" or 34" barrel **$1,290.00**

Price: Adj.-comb stock, 32" or 34" barrel **$1,558.00**

Price: Micro (for small-framed shooters) **$1,290.00**

BROWNING GOLDEN CLAYS SHOTGUN

Gauge: 12, 3" chamber. **Barrel:** 32", 34" with Full, Improved Modified, Modified tubes. **Weight:** 8 lbs. 14 oz. to 9 lbs. **Length:** 49" to 51" overall. **Stock:** Adjustable comb; Walnut with high gloss finish; cut checkering. GraCoil recoil reduction system. Imported from Japan by Browning.

Price: 34" bbl. **$3,407.00**

Price: 32" bbl. **$3,407.00**

CHIPMUNK 410 YOUTH SHOTGUN

Gauge: .410. **Barrel:** 18-1/4" tapered, blue. **Weight:** 3.25 lbs. **Length:** 33". **Stock:** Walnut. **Features:** Manually cocking single shot bolt, blued receiver.

Price: **$225.95**

EAA BAIKAL IZH-18 SINGLE BARREL SHOTGUN

Gauge: 12 (2-3/4" and 3" chambers), 20 (2-3/4" and 3"), 16 (2-3/4"), .410 (3"). **Barrel:** 26-1/2", 28-1/2"; modified or full choke (12 and 20 gauge); full only (16 gauge), improved cylinder (20 gauge) and full or improved modified (.410). **Stock:** Walnut-stained hardwood; rubber recoil pad. **Features:** Hammer-forged steel barrel; machined receiver; cross-block safety; cocking lever with external cocking indicator; optional automatic ejector, screw- in chokes and rifle barrel. Imported by European American Armory.

Price: IZH-18 (12, 16, 20 or .410). **$109.00**

Price: IZH-18 (20 gauge w/imp. cyl. or .410 w/imp. mod.). **$109.00**

EAA BAIKAL IZH-18MAX SINGLE BARREL SHOTGUN

Gauge: 12, 3"; 20, 3"; 410, 3". **Barrel:** 24" (.410), 26" (.410 or 20 ga.) or 28" (12 ga.). **Weight:** 6.4 to 6.6 lbs. **Stock:** Walnut. **Features:** Polished nickel receiver; ventilated rib; I.C., Mod. and Full choke tubes; titanium-coated trigger; internal hammer; selectable ejector/extractor; rubber butt pad; decocking system. Imported by European American Armory.

Price: (12 or 20 ga., choke tubes). **$229.00**

Price: (.410, full choke only) **$239.00**

Price: Sporting, 12 ga., ported, Monte Carlo stock **$219.00**

HARRINGTON & RICHARDSON SB2-980 ULTRA SLUG

Gauge: 12, 20, 3" chamber. **Barrel:** 22" (20 ga. Youth) 24", fully rifled. **Weight:** 9 lbs. **Length:** NA. **Stock:** Walnut-stained hardwood. **Sights:** None furnished; comes with scope mount. **Features:** Uses the H&R 10 gauge action with heavy-wall barrel. Monte Carlo stock has sling swivels; comes with black nylon sling. Introduced 1995. Made in U.S. by H&R 1871, LLC.

Price: **$259.00**

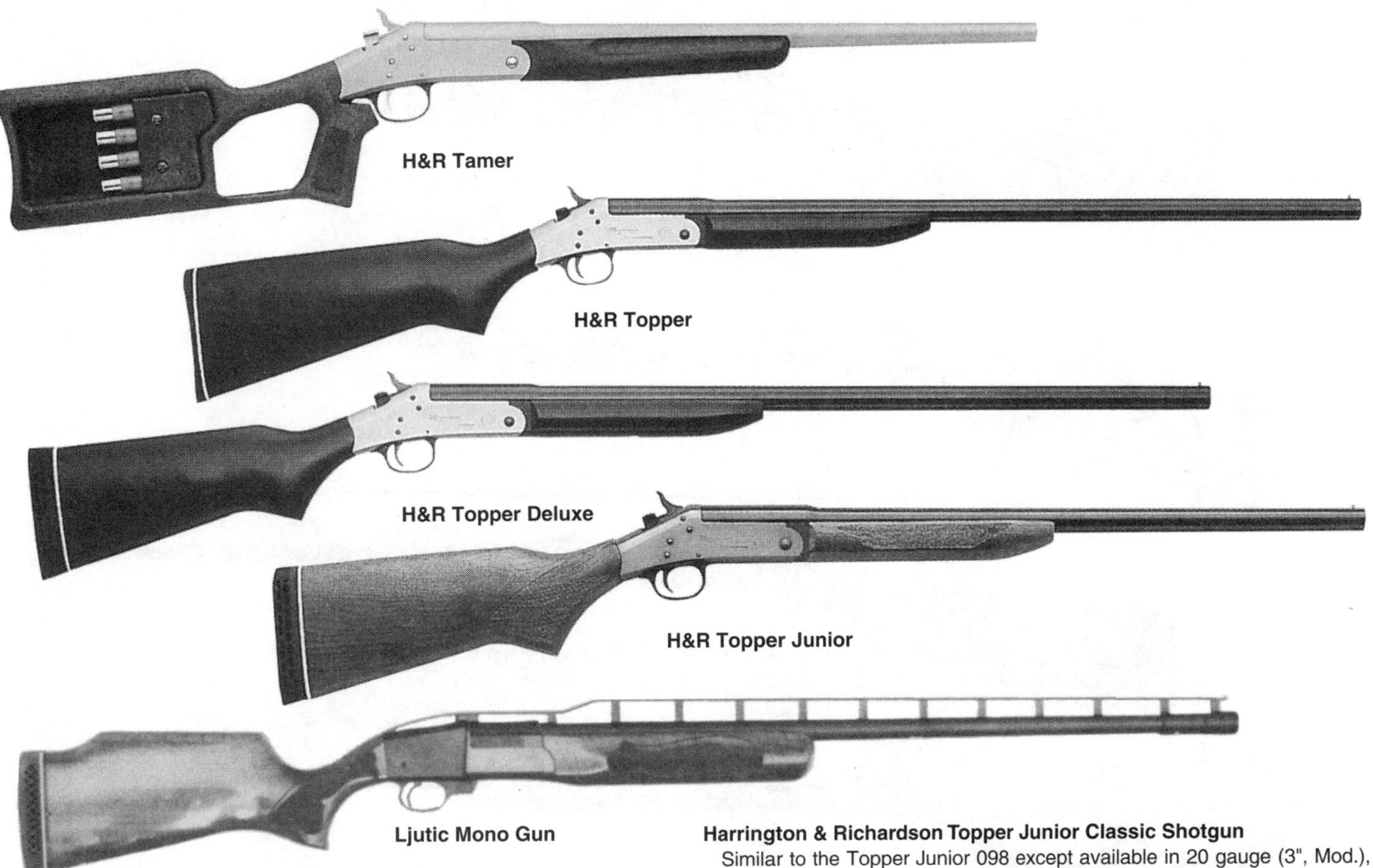

H&R Tamer

H&R Topper

H&R Topper Deluxe

H&R Topper Junior

Ljutic Mono Gun

Harrington & Richardson Model 928 Ultra Slug Hunter Deluxe

Similar to the SB2-980 Ultra Slug except uses 12 gauge action and 12 gauge barrel blank bored to 20 gauge, then fully rifled with 1:28" twist. Has hand-checkered camo laminate Monte Carlo stock and forend. Comes with Weaver-style scope base, offset hammer extension, ventilat-ed recoil pad, sling swivels and nylon sling. Introduced 1997. Made in U.S. by H&R 1871 LLC.

Price: **$315.00**

HARRINGTON & RICHARDSON TAMER SHOTGUN

Gauge: .410, 3" chamber. **Barrel:** 20" (Full). **Weight:** 5-6 lbs. **Length:** 33" overall. **Stock:** Thumbhole grip of high density black polymer. **Features:** Uses H&R Topper action with matte electroless nickel finish. Stock holds four spare shotshells. Introduced 1994. From H&R 1871, LLC.

Price: **$164.00**

HARRINGTON & RICHARDSON TOPPER MODEL 098

Gauge: 12, 16, 20, 28 (2-3/4"), .410, 3" chamber. **Barrel:** 12 ga.-28" (Mod.); 16 ga.- 28" (Full.); 20 ga.-26" (Mod.); 28 ga.-26" (Mod.); .410 bore- 26" (Full). **Weight:** 5-6 lbs. **Stock:** Black-finish hardwood with full pistol grip; semi-beavertail forend. **Sights:** Gold bead front. **Features:** Break-open action with side-lever release, automatic ejector. Satin nickel frame, blued barrel. Reintroduced 1992. From H&R 1871, LLC.

Price: **$145.00**

Price: Topper Junior 098 (as above except 22" barrel, 20 ga. (Mod.), .410-bore (Full), 12-1/2" length of pull) **$152.00**

Harrington & Richardson Topper Deluxe Model 098

Similar to the standard Topper 098 except 12 gauge only with 3-1/2" chamber, 28" barrel with choke tube (comes with Mod. tube, others optional). Satin nickel frame, blued barrel, black-finished wood. Introduced 1992. From H&R 1871, LLC.

Price: **$169.00**

Harrington & Richardson Topper Junior Classic Shotgun

Similar to the Topper Junior 098 except available in 20 gauge (3", Mod.), .410-bore (Full) with 3" chamber; all have 22" barrel. Stock is American black walnut with cut-checkered pistol grip and forend. Ventilated rubber recoil pad. Blued barrel, blued frame. Introduced 1992. From H&R 1871, LLC.

Price: **$184.00**

Ithaca Classic Doubles Knickerbocker Trap Gun

A reissue of the famous Ithaca Knickerbocker Trap Gun. Built on a custom basis only. Introduced 2003. Made in U.S.A. by Ithaca Classic Doubles.

Price: From **$9,000.00**

KRIEGHOFF K-80 SINGLE BARREL TRAP GUN

Gauge: 12, 2-3/4" chamber. **Barrel:** 32" or 34" Unsingle. Fixed Full or choke tubes. **Weight:** About 8-3/4 lbs. **Stock:** Four stock dimensions or adjustable stock available. All hand-checkered European walnut. **Features:** Satin nickel finish. Selective mechanical trigger adjustable for finger position. Tapered step vent. rib. Adjustable point of impact.

Price: Standard grade full Unsingle, from **$7,950.00**

KRIEGHOFF KX-5 TRAP GUN

Gauge: 12, 2-3/4" chamber. **Barrel:** 34"; choke tubes. **Weight:** About 8-1/2 lbs. **Stock:** Factory adjustable stock. European walnut. **Features:** Ventilated tapered step rib. Adjustable position trigger, optional release trigger. Fully adjustable rib. Satin gray electroless nickel receiver. Fitted aluminum case. Imported from Germany by Krieghoff International, Inc.

Price: **$4,200.00**

LJUTIC MONO GUN SINGLE BARREL

Gauge: 12 only. **Barrel:** 34", choked to customer specs; hollow-milled rib, 35-1/2" sight plane. **Weight:** Approx. 9 lbs. **Stock:** To customer specs. Oil finish, hand checkered. **Features:** Totally custom made. Pull or release trigger; removable trigger guard contains trigger and hammer mechanism; Ljutic pushbutton opener on front of trigger guard. From Ljutic Industries.

Price: Std., med. or Olympic rib, custom bbls., fixed choke. **$5,795.00**

Price: As above with screw-in choke barrel **$6,095.00**

Price: Stainless steel mono gun **$6,795.00**

Mossberg SSi One

New England Firearms Camo Turkey

New England Firearms Tracker II

New England Firearms Special Purpose

Ljutic LTX Pro 3 Deluxe Mono Gun

Deluxe, lightweight version of the Mono Gun with high quality wood, upgrade checkering, special rib height, screw-in chokes, ported and cased.

Price: $8,995.00

Price: Stainless steel model **$9,995.00**

MOSSBERG SSi-ONE 12 GAUGE SLUG SHOTGUN

Gauge: 12, 3" chamber. **Barrel:** 24", fully rifled. **Weight:** 8 pounds. **Length:** 40" overall. **Stock:** Walnut, fluted and cut checkered; sling-swivel studs; drilled and tapped for scope base. **Sights:** None (scope base supplied). **Features:** Frame accepts interchangeable rifle barrels (see Mossberg SSi-One rifle listing); lever-opening, break-action design; ambidextrous, top-tang safety; internal eject/extract selector. Introduced 2000. From Mossberg.

Price: **$480.00**

Mossberg SSi-One Turkey Shotgun

Similar to SSi-One 12 gauge Slug Shotgun, but chambered for 12 ga., 3-1/2" loads. Includes Accu-Mag Turkey Tube. Introduced 2001. From Mossberg.

Price: **$459.00**

NEW ENGLAND FIREARMS CAMO TURKEY SHOTGUNS

Gauge: 10, 3-1/2"; 12, 20, 3" chamber. **Barrel:** 24"; extra-full, screw-in choke tube (10 ga.); fixed full choke (12, 20). **Weight:** NA. **Stock:** American hardwood, green and black camouflage finish with sling swivels and ventilated recoil pad. **Sights:** Bead front. **Features:** Matte metal finish; stock counterweight to reduce recoil; patented transfer bar system for hammer-down safety; includes camo sling and trigger lock. Accepts other factory-fitted barrels. Introduced 2000. From New England Firearms.

Price: . . . . 10 ga. **$278.00**; 12 ga., **$189.00**

Price: 20 ga. youth model (22" bbl.) **$189.00**

NEW ENGLAND FIREARMS TRACKER II SLUG GUN

Gauge: 12, 20, 3" chamber. **Barrel:** 24" (Cyl.), rifle bore. **Weight:** 5-1/4 lbs. **Length:** 40" overall. **Stock:** Walnut-finished hardwood with full pistol grip, recoil pad. **Sights:** Blade front, fully adjustable rifle-type rear. **Features:** Break-open action with side-lever release; blued barrel, color case-hardened frame. Introduced 1992. From New England Firearms.

Price: Tracker II **$187.00**

NEW ENGLAND FIREARMS SPECIAL PURPOSE SHOTGUNS

Gauge: 10, 3-1/2" chamber. **Barrel:** 28" (Full), 32" (Mod.). **Weight:** 9.5 lbs. **Length:** 44" overall (28" barrel). **Stock:** American hardwood with walnut or matte camo finish; ventilated rubber recoil pad. **Sights:** Bead front. **Features:** Break-open action with side-lever release; ejector. Matte finish on metal. Introduced 1992. From New England Firearms.

Price: Walnut-finish wood sling and swivels **$215.00**

Price: Camo finish, sling and swivels **$278.00**

Price: Camo finish, 32", sling and swivels **$272.00**

Price: Black matte finish, 24", Turkey Full choke tube, sling and swivels **$251.00**

NEW ENGLAND FIREARMS SURVIVOR

Gauge: .410/45 Colt, 3" chamber. **Barrel:** 22" (Mod.); 20" (.410/45 Colt, rifled barrel, choke tube). **Weight:** 6 lbs. **Length:** 36 overall. **Stock:** Black polymer with thumbhole/pistol grip, sling swivels; beavertail forend. **Sights:** Bead front. **Features:** Buttplate removes to expose storage for extra ammunition; forend also holds extra ammunition. Black or nickel finish. Introduced 1993. From New England Firearms.

Price: .410/45 Colt, black **$203.00**

Price: .410/45 Colt, nickel **$221.00**

New England Firearms Survivor

New England Firearms Standard Pardner

Rossi Single-Shot

Rossi Matched Pair

Ruger KTS-1234-BRE

NEW ENGLAND FIREARMS STANDARD PARDNER

Gauge: 12, 20, .410, 3" chamber; 16, 28, 2-3/4" chamber. **Barrel:** 12 ga.-28" (Full, Mod.), 32" (Full); 16 ga.-28" (Full), 32" (Full); 20 ga.-26" (Full, Mod.); 28 ga.-26" (Mod.); .410-bore-26" (Full). **Weight:** 5-6 lbs. **Length:** 43" overall (28" barrel). **Stock:** Walnut-finished hardwood with full pistol grip. **Sights:** Bead front. **Features:** Transfer bar ignition; break-open action with side-lever release. Introduced 1987. From New England Firearms.

Price: **$132.00**
Price: Youth model (12, 20, 28 ga., .410, 22" barrel, recoil pad). . **$141.00**

ROSSI SINGLE-SHOT SHOTGUN

Gauge: 12, 20, 2-3/4" chamber; .410, 3" chamber. **Barrel:** 28" full, 22" Youth. **Weight:** 5 lbs. **Stock:** Stained hardwood. **Sights:** Bead. **Features:** Break-open, positive ejection, internal transfer bar, trigger block.

Price: **$101.00**

ROSSI MATCHED PAIR SINGLE-SHOT SHOTGUN/RIFLE

Gauge: .410, 20 or 12. **Barrel:** 22" (18.5" Youth), 28" (23"full). **Weight:** 4-6 lbs **Stock:** Hardwood (brown or black finish). **Sights:** Bead front. **Features:** Break-open internal transfer bar manual external safety; blued or stainless steel finish; sling-swivel studs; includes matched 22 LR or 22 Mag. barrel with fully adjustable front and rear sight. Trigger block system. Introduced 2001. Imported by BrazTech/Taurus.

Price: Blue **$139.95**
Price: Stainless steel **$169.95**

RUGER KTS-1234-BRE TRAP MODEL SINGLE-BARREL SHOTGUN

Gauge: 12, 2-3/4" chamber. **Barrel:** 34". **Weight:** 9 lbs. **Length:** 50-1/2" overall. **Stock:** Select walnut checkered; adjustable pull length 13"-15". **Features:** Fully adjustable rib for pattern position; adjustable stock comb cast for right- or left-handed shooters; straight grooves the length of barrel to keep wad from rotating for pattern improvement. Full and modified choke tubes supplied. Gold inlaid eagle and Ruger name on receiver. Introduced 2000. From Sturm Ruger & Co.

Price: **$2,850.00**

Shotguns — Bolt Actions & Single Shots

Savage 210F Master Shot Slug Warrior

Stoeger Single-Shot

Tar-Hunt RSG-20 Mountaineer

Thompson/Center Encore Rifled Slug

Thompson/Center Encore Turkey

SAVAGE MODEL 210F SLUG WARRIOR

Gauge: 12, 3" chamber; 2-shot magazine. **Barrel:** 24" 1:35" rifling twist. **Weight:** 7-1/2 lbs. **Length:** 43.5" overall. **Stock:** Glass-filled polymer with positive checkering. **Features:** Based on the Savage Model 110 action; 60 bolt lift; controlled round feed; comes with scope mount. Introduced 1996. Made in U.S. by Savage Arms.

Price: **$458.00**

Price: (Camo) **$495.00**

STOEGER SINGLE-SHOT SHOTGUN

Gauge: 12, 20, .410, 2-3/4", 3" chambers. **Barrel:** 26", 28". **Weight:** 5.4 lbs. **gth:** 40-1/2" to 42-1/2" overall. **Sights:** Brass bead. **Features:** .410, full fixed choke tubes, rest M, screw-in. .410 12 ga. hardwood pistol-grip stock and forend. 20 ga. 26" bbl., hardwood forend.

Price: Blue; Youth **$109.00**

Price: Youth with English stock **$119.00**

TAR-HUNT RSG-12 PROFESSIONAL RIFLED SLUG GUN

Gauge: 12, 16 & 20, 2-3/4" or 3" chamber, 1-shot magazine. **Barrel:** 23", fully rifled with muzzle brake. **Weight:** 7-3/4 lbs. **Length:** 41-1/2" overall. **Stock:** Matte black McMillan fiberglass with Pachmayr Decelera-tor pad. **Sights:** None furnished; comes with Leupold windage or Weaver bases. **Features:** Uses rifle-style action with two locking lugs; two-position safety; Shaw barrel; single-stage, trigger; muzzle brake. Many options available. Right- and left-hand models at same prices. Introduced 1991. Made in U.S. by Tar-Hunt Custom Rifles, Inc.

Price: 12 ga. Professional model, right- or left-hand; Elite 16 ga. **$2,395.00**

Price: Millennium/10th Anniversary models (limited to 25 guns): NP-3 nickel/Teflon metal finish, black McMillan Fibergrain stock, Jewell adj. trigger. **$2,300.00**

Tar-Hunt RSG-20 Mountaineer Slug Gun

Similar to the RSG-12 Professional except chambered for 20 gauge (3" shells); 23" Shaw rifled barrel, with muzzle brake; two-lug bolt; one- shot blind magazine; matte black finish; McMillan fiberglass stock with Pach-mayr Decelerator pad; receiver drilled and tapped for Rem. 700 bases. Weighs 6-1/2 lbs. Introduced 1997. Made in U.S. by Tar-Hunt Cus-tom Ri-fles, Inc.

Price: **$2,395.00**

THOMPSON/CENTER ENCORE RIFLED SLUG GUN

Gauge: 20, 3" chamber. **Barrel:** 26", fully rifled. **Weight:** About 7 pounds. **Length:** 40-1/2" overall. **Stock:** Walnut with walnut forearm. **Sights:** Steel, click-adjustable rear and ramp-style front, both with fiber optics. **Features:** Encore system features a variety of rifle, shotgun and muzzle-loading rifle barrels interchangeable with the same frame. Break-open de-sign operates by pulling up and back on trigger guard spur. Composite stock and forearm available. Introduced 2000.

Price: **$665.00**

THOMPSON/CENTER ENCORE TURKEY GUN

Gauge: 12 ga. **Barrel:** 24". **Features:** All-camo finish, high definition Real-tree Hardwoods HD camo.

Price: **$740.00**

SHOTGUNS — MILITARY & POLICE

Designs for utility, suitable for and adaptable to competitions and other sporting purposes.

Benelli M3 Convertible

Benelli M1 Tactical

Benelli M1 Practical

Fabarm Tactical

BENELLI M3 CONVERTIBLE SHOTGUN

Gauge: 12, 2-3/4", 3" chambers, 5-shot magazine. **Barrel:** 19-3/4" (Cyl.). **Weight:** 7 lbs., 4oz. **Length:** 41" overall. **Stock:** High-impact polymer with sling loop in side of butt; rubberized pistol grip on stock. **Sights:** Open rifle, fully adjustable. Ghost ring and rifle type. **Features:** Combination pump/auto action. Alloy receiver with inertia recoil rotating locking lug bolt; matte finish; automatic shell release lever. Introduced 1989. Imported by Benelli USA. Price with pistol grip, open rifle sights.

Price: With standard stock, open rifle sights **$1,135.00**
Price: With ghost ring sight system, standard stock **$1,185.00**
Price: With ghost ring sights, pistol grip stock. **$1,200.00**

BENELLI M1 TACTICAL SHOTGUN

Gauge: 12, 2-3/4", 3" chambers, 5-shot magazine. **Barrel:** 18.5" IC, M, F choke tubes. **Weight:** 6.7 lbs. **Length:** 39.75" overall. **Stock:** Black polymer. **Sights:** Rifle type with ghost ring system, tritium night sights optional. **Features:** Semi-auto intertia recoil action. Cross-bolt safety; bolt release button; matte-finish metal. Introduced 1993. Imported from Italy by Benelli USA.

Price: With rifle sights, standard stock **$945.00**
Price: With ghost ring rifle sights, standard stock **$1,015.00**
Price: With ghost ring sights, pistol grip stock. **$1,030.00**
Price: With rifle sights, pistol grip stock. **$960.00**
Price: MI Entry, 14" barrel (law enforcement only) . . **$980.00 to $1,060.00**

Benelli M1 Practical

Similar to M1 Field Shotgun, Picatinny receiver rail for scope mounting, nine-round magazine, 26" compensated barrel and ghost ring sights. Designed for IPSC competition.

Price: **$1,265.00**

CROSSFIRE SHOTGUN/RIFLE

Gauge/Caliber: 12, 2-3/4" Chamber: 4-shot/223 Rem. (5-shot). **Barrel:** 20" (shotgun), 18" (rifle). **Weight:** About 8.6 lbs. **Length:** 40" overall. **Stock:** Composite. **Sights:** Meprolight night sights. Integral Weaver-style scope rail. **Features:** Combination pump-action shotgun, rifle; single selector, single trigger; dual action bars for both upper and lower actions; ambidextrous selector and safety. Introduced 1997. Made in U.S. From Hesco.

Price: About **$1,895.00**
Price: With camo finish **$1,995.00**

FABARM TACTICAL SEMI-AUTOMATIC SHOTGUN

Gauge: 12, 3" chamber. **Barrel:** 20". **Weight:** 6.6 lbs. **Length:** 41.2" overall. **Stock:** Polymer or folding. **Sights:** Ghost ring (tritium night sights optional). **Features:** Gas operated; matte receiver; twin forged action bars; over-sized bolt handle and safety button; Picatinny rail; includes cylinder bore choke tube. New features include polymer pistol grip stock. Introduced 2001. Imported from Italy by Heckler & Koch Inc.

Price: **$999.00**

Fabarm FP6

Mossberg Model 500 Persuader

Mossberg Model 500 Persuader

Mossberg Ghost Ring

Mossberg Model HS410

FABARM FP6 PUMP SHOTGUN

Gauge: 12, 3" chamber. **Barrel:** 20" (Cyl.); accepts choke tubes. **Weight:** 6.6 lbs. **Length:** 41.25" overall. **Stock:** Black polymer with textured grip, grooved slide handle. **Sights:** Blade front. **Features:** Twin action bars; anodized finish; free carrier for smooth reloading. Introduced 1998. New features include ghost-ring sighting system, low profile Picatinny rail, and pistol grip stock. Imported from Italy by Heckler & Koch, Inc.

Price: (Carbon fiber finish) **$499.00**

Price: With flip-up front sight, Picatinny rail with rear sight, oversize safety button **$499.00**

MOSSBERG MODEL 500 PERSUADER SECURITY SHOTGUNS

Gauge: 12, 20, .410, 3" chamber. **Barrel:** 18-1/2", 20" (Cyl.). **Weight:** 7 lbs. **Stock:** Walnut-finished hardwood or black synthetic. **Sights:** Metal bead front. **Features:** Available in 6- or 8-shot models. Top-mounted safety, double action slide bars, swivel studs, rubber recoil pad. Blue, Parkerized, Marinecote finishes. Mossberg Cablelock included. From Mossberg.

Price: 12 ga., 18-1/2", blue, wood or synthetic stock, 6-shot **$353.00**

Price: Cruiser, 12 ga., 18-1/2", blue, pistol grip, heat shield. **$357.00**

Price: As above, 20 ga. or .410 bore. **$345.00**

Mossberg Model 500, 590 Mariner Pump

Similar to the Model 500 or 590 Security except all metal parts finished with Marinecote metal finish to resist rust and corrosion. Synthetic field stock; pistol grip kit included. Mossberg Cablelock included.

Price: 6-shot, 18-1/2" barrel **$497.00**

Price: 9-shot, 20" barrel **$513.00**

Mossberg Model 500, 590 Ghost-Ring Shotguns

Similar to the Model 500 Security except has adjustable blade front, adjustable Ghost-Ring rear sight with protective "ears." Model 500 has 18.5" (Cyl.) barrel, 6-shot capacity; Model 590 has 20" (Cyl.) barrel, 9-shot capacity. Both have synthetic field stock. Mossberg Cablelock included. Introduced 1990. From Mossberg.

Price: 500 parkerized **$468.00**

Price: 590 parkerized **$543.00**

Price: 590 parkerized Speedfeed stock. **$586.00**

Mossberg Model HS410 Shotgun

Similar to the Model 500 Security pump except chambered for 20 gauge or .410 with 3" chamber; has pistol grip forend, thick recoil pad, muzzle brake and has special spreader choke on the 18.5" barrel. Overall length is 37.5", weight is 6.25 lbs. Blue finish; synthetic field stock. Mossberg Cablelock and video included. Introduced 1990.

Price: HS 410 . . . . **$355.00**

Tactical Response TR-870

Winchester Model 1300 Defender

Winchester Model 1300 Marine

Winchester Model 1300 Camp Defender®

MOSSBERG MODEL 590 SHOTGUN

Gauge: 12, 3" chamber. **Barrel:** 20" (Cyl.). **Weight:** 7-1/4 lbs. **Stock:** Synthetic field or Speedfeed. **Sights:** Metal bead front. **Features:** Top-mounted safety, double slide action bars. Comes with heat shield, bayonet lug, swivel studs, rubber recoil pad. Blue, Parkerized or Marinecote finish. Mossberg Cablelock included. From Mossberg.

Price: Blue, synthetic stock **$417.00**
Price: Parkerized, synthetic stock **$476.00**
Price: Parkerized, Speedfeed stock **$519.00**

TACTICAL RESPONSE TR-870 STANDARD MODEL SHOTGUN

Gauge: 12, 3" chamber, 7-shot magazine. **Barrel:** 18" (Cyl.). **Weight:** 9 lbs. **Length:** 38" overall. **Stock:** Fiberglass-filled polypropolene with non-snag recoil absorbing butt pad. Nylon tactical forend houses flashlight. **Sights:** Trak-Lock ghost ring sight system. Front sight has tritium insert. **Features:** Highly modified Remington 870P with Parkerized finish. Comes with nylon three-way adjustable sling, high visibility non-binding follower, high performance magazine spring, Jumbo Head safety, and Side Saddle extended 6-shot shell carrier on left side of receiver. Introduced 1991. From Scattergun Technologies, Inc.

Price: Standard model **$815.00**
Price: FBI model **$770.00**
Price: Patrol model **$595.00**
Price: Border Patrol model **$605.00**
Price: K-9 model (Rem. 11-87 action) **$995.00**
Price: Urban Sniper, Rem. 11-87 action **$1,290.00**
Price: Louis Awerbuck model **$705.00**
Price: Practical Turkey model **$725.00**
Price: Expert model **$1,350.00**
Price: Professional model **$815.00**
Price: Entry model **$840.00**
Price: Compact model **$635.00**
Price: SWAT model **$1,195.00**

WINCHESTER MODEL 1300 DEFENDER PUMP GUN

Gauge: 12, 20, 3" chamber, 5- or 8-shot capacity. **Barrel:** 18" (Cyl.). **Weight:** 6-3/4 lbs. **Length:** 38-5/8" overall. **Stock:** Walnut-finished hardwood stock and ribbed forend, synthetic or pistol grip. **Sights:** Metal bead front or TRUGLO® fiber-optic. **Features:** Cross-bolt safety, front-locking rotary bolt, twin action slide bars. Black rubber butt pad. From U.S. Repeating Arms Co.

Price: 8-Shot (black synthetic stock, TRUGLO® sight) **$343.00**
Price: 8-Shot Pistol Grip (pistol grip synthetic stock) **$343.00**

Winchester Model 1300 Coastal Pump Gun

Same as the Defender 8-Shot except has bright chrome finish, nickel-plated barrel, bead front sight. Phosphate coated receiver for corrosion resistance.

Price: **$576.00**

Winchester Model 1300 Camp Defender®

Same as the Defender 8-Shot except has hardwood stock and forearm, fully adjustable open sights and 22" barrel with WinChoke® choke tube system (cylinder choke tube included). Weighs 6-7/8 lbs. Introduced 2001. From U.S. Repeating Arms Co.

Price: Camp Defender® **$392.00**

BLACKPOWDER SINGLE SHOT PISTOLS — FLINT & PERCUSSION

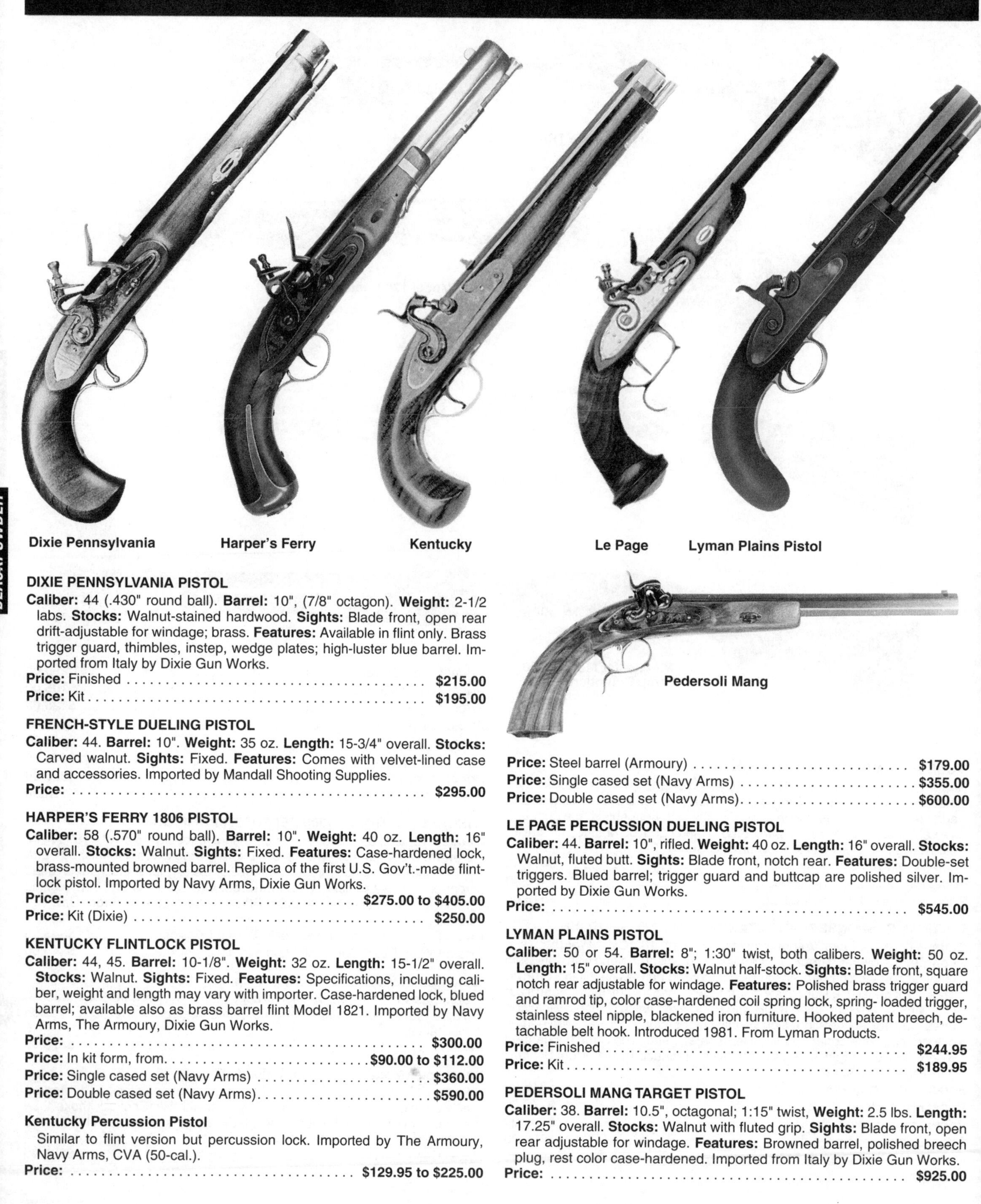

Dixie Pennsylvania Harper's Ferry Kentucky Le Page Lyman Plains Pistol

Pedersoli Mang

DIXIE PENNSYLVANIA PISTOL

Caliber: 44 (.430" round ball). **Barrel:** 10", (7/8" octagon). **Weight:** 2-1/2 labs. **Stocks:** Walnut-stained hardwood. **Sights:** Blade front, open rear drift-adjustable for windage; brass. **Features:** Available in flint only. Brass trigger guard, thimbles, instep, wedge plates; high-luster blue barrel. Imported from Italy by Dixie Gun Works.

Price: Finished **$215.00**

Price: Kit **$195.00**

FRENCH-STYLE DUELING PISTOL

Caliber: 44. **Barrel:** 10". **Weight:** 35 oz. **Length:** 15-3/4" overall. **Stocks:** Carved walnut. **Sights:** Fixed. **Features:** Comes with velvet-lined case and accessories. Imported by Mandall Shooting Supplies.

Price: **$295.00**

HARPER'S FERRY 1806 PISTOL

Caliber: 58 (.570" round ball). **Barrel:** 10". **Weight:** 40 oz. **Length:** 16" overall. **Stocks:** Walnut. **Sights:** Fixed. **Features:** Case-hardened lock, brass-mounted browned barrel. Replica of the first U.S. Gov't.-made flintlock pistol. Imported by Navy Arms, Dixie Gun Works.

Price: . . . . **$275.00 to $405.00**

Price: Kit (Dixie) **$250.00**

KENTUCKY FLINTLOCK PISTOL

Caliber: 44, 45. **Barrel:** 10-1/8". **Weight:** 32 oz. **Length:** 15-1/2" overall. **Stocks:** Walnut. **Sights:** Fixed. **Features:** Specifications, including caliber, weight and length may vary with importer. Case-hardened lock, blued barrel; available also as brass barrel flint Model 1821. Imported by Navy Arms, The Armoury, Dixie Gun Works.

Price: **$300.00**

Price: In kit form, from. . . . . **$90.00 to $112.00**

Price: Single cased set (Navy Arms) **$360.00**

Price: Double cased set (Navy Arms). **$590.00**

Kentucky Percussion Pistol

Similar to flint version but percussion lock. Imported by The Armoury, Navy Arms, CVA (50-cal.).

Price: . . . . **$129.95 to $225.00**

Price: Steel barrel (Armoury) **$179.00**

Price: Single cased set (Navy Arms) **$355.00**

Price: Double cased set (Navy Arms). **$600.00**

LE PAGE PERCUSSION DUELING PISTOL

Caliber: 44. **Barrel:** 10", rifled. **Weight:** 40 oz. **Length:** 16" overall. **Stocks:** Walnut, fluted butt. **Sights:** Blade front, notch rear. **Features:** Double-set triggers. Blued barrel; trigger guard and buttcap are polished silver. Imported by Dixie Gun Works.

Price: **$545.00**

LYMAN PLAINS PISTOL

Caliber: 50 or 54. **Barrel:** 8"; 1:30" twist, both calibers. **Weight:** 50 oz. **Length:** 15" overall. **Stocks:** Walnut half-stock. **Sights:** Blade front, square notch rear adjustable for windage. **Features:** Polished brass trigger guard and ramrod tip, color case-hardened coil spring lock, spring- loaded trigger, stainless steel nipple, blackened iron furniture. Hooked patent breech, detachable belt hook. Introduced 1981. From Lyman Products.

Price: Finished **$244.95**

Price: Kit **$189.95**

PEDERSOLI MANG TARGET PISTOL

Caliber: 38. **Barrel:** 10.5", octagonal; 1:15" twist, **Weight:** 2.5 lbs. **Length:** 17.25" overall. **Stocks:** Walnut with fluted grip. **Sights:** Blade front, open rear adjustable for windage. **Features:** Browned barrel, polished breech plug, rest color case-hardened. Imported from Italy by Dixie Gun Works.

Price: **$925.00**

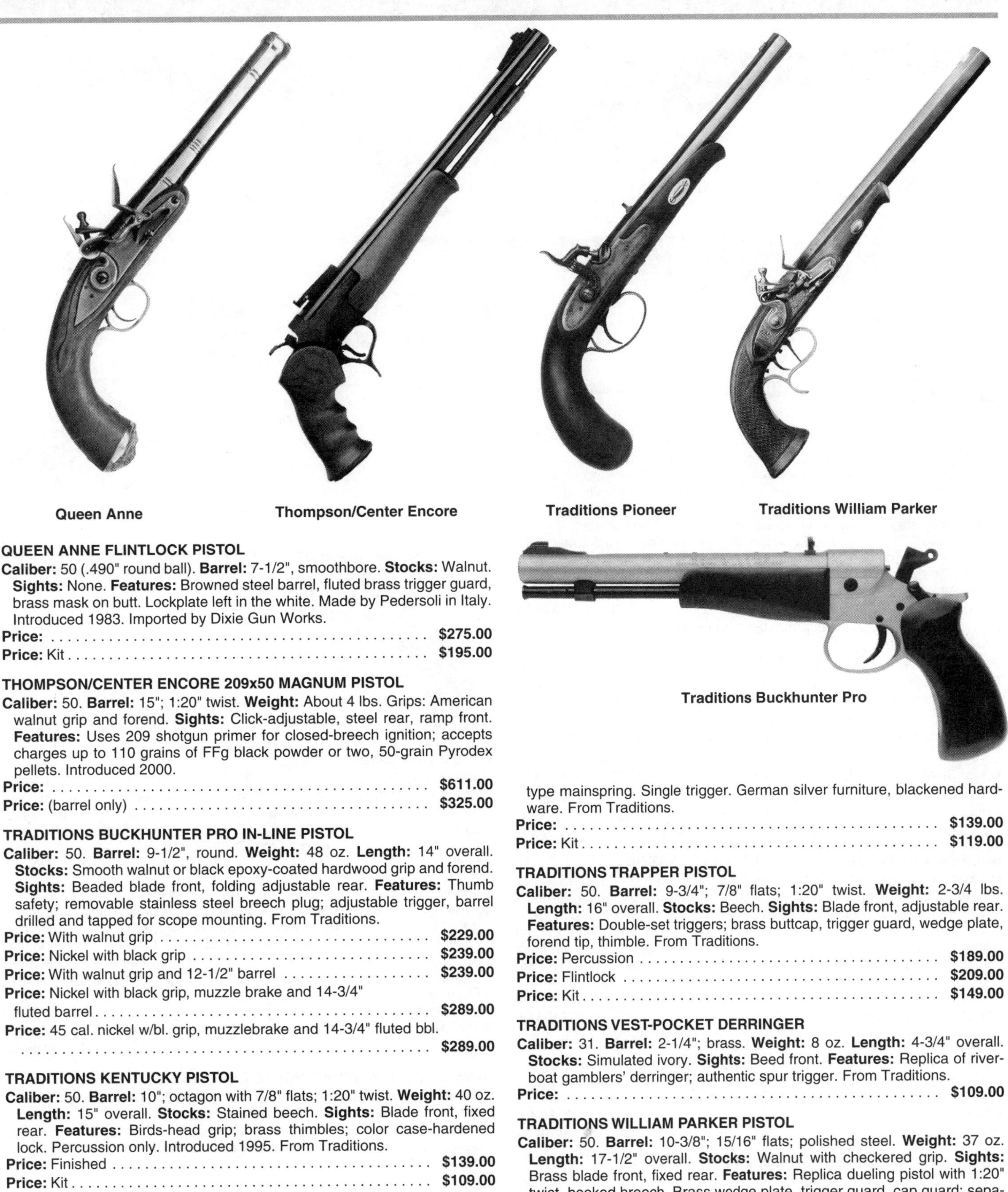

Queen Anne

Thompson/Center Encore

Traditions Pioneer

Traditions William Parker

Traditions Buckhunter Pro

QUEEN ANNE FLINTLOCK PISTOL

Caliber: 50 (.490" round ball). **Barrel:** 7-1/2", smoothbore. **Stocks:** Walnut. **Sights:** None. **Features:** Browned steel barrel, fluted brass trigger guard, brass mask on butt. Lockplate left in the white. Made by Pedersoli in Italy. Introduced 1983. Imported by Dixie Gun Works.

Price: **$275.00**
Price: Kit **$195.00**

THOMPSON/CENTER ENCORE 209x50 MAGNUM PISTOL

Caliber: 50. **Barrel:** 15"; 1:20" twist. **Weight:** About 4 lbs. Grips: American walnut grip and forend. **Sights:** Click-adjustable, steel rear, ramp front. **Features:** Uses 209 shotgun primer for closed-breech ignition; accepts charges up to 110 grains of FFg black powder or two, 50-grain Pyrodex pellets. Introduced 2000.

Price: **$611.00**
Price: (barrel only) **$325.00**

TRADITIONS BUCKHUNTER PRO IN-LINE PISTOL

Caliber: 50. **Barrel:** 9-1/2", round. **Weight:** 48 oz. **Length:** 14" overall. **Stocks:** Smooth walnut or black epoxy-coated hardwood grip and forend. **Sights:** Beaded blade front, folding adjustable rear. **Features:** Thumb safety; removable stainless steel breech plug; adjustable trigger, barrel drilled and tapped for scope mounting. From Traditions.

Price: With walnut grip **$229.00**
Price: Nickel with black grip **$239.00**
Price: With walnut grip and 12-1/2" barrel **$239.00**
Price: Nickel with black grip, muzzle brake and 14-3/4" fluted barrel **$289.00**
Price: 45 cal. nickel w/bl. grip, muzzlebrake and 14-3/4" fluted bbl. **$289.00**

TRADITIONS KENTUCKY PISTOL

Caliber: 50. **Barrel:** 10"; octagon with 7/8" flats; 1:20" twist. **Weight:** 40 oz. **Length:** 15" overall. **Stocks:** Stained beech. **Sights:** Blade front, fixed rear. **Features:** Birds-head grip; brass thimbles; color case-hardened lock. Percussion only. Introduced 1995. From Traditions.

Price: Finished **$139.00**
Price: Kit **$109.00**

TRADITIONS PIONEER PISTOL

Caliber: 45. **Barrel:** 9-5/8"; 13/16" flats, 1:16" twist. **Weight:** 31 oz. **Length:** 15" overall. **Stocks:** Beech. **Sights:** Blade front, fixed rear. **Features:** V-type mainspring. Single trigger. German silver furniture, blackened hardware. From Traditions.

Price: **$139.00**
Price: Kit **$119.00**

TRADITIONS TRAPPER PISTOL

Caliber: 50. **Barrel:** 9-3/4"; 7/8" flats; 1:20" twist. **Weight:** 2-3/4 lbs. **Length:** 16" overall. **Stocks:** Beech. **Sights:** Blade front, adjustable rear. **Features:** Double-set triggers; brass buttcap, trigger guard, wedge plate, forend tip, thimble. From Traditions.

Price: Percussion **$189.00**
Price: Flintlock **$209.00**
Price: Kit **$149.00**

TRADITIONS VEST-POCKET DERRINGER

Caliber: 31. **Barrel:** 2-1/4"; brass. **Weight:** 8 oz. **Length:** 4-3/4" overall. **Stocks:** Simulated ivory. **Sights:** Beed front. **Features:** Replica of riverboat gamblers' derringer; authentic spur trigger. From Traditions.

Price: **$109.00**

TRADITIONS WILLIAM PARKER PISTOL

Caliber: 50. **Barrel:** 10-3/8"; 15/16" flats; polished steel. **Weight:** 37 oz. **Length:** 17-1/2" overall. **Stocks:** Walnut with checkered grip. **Sights:** Brass blade front, fixed rear. **Features:** Replica dueling pistol with 1:20" twist, hooked breech. Brass wedge plate, trigger guard, cap guard; separate ramrod. Double-set triggers. Polished steel barrel, lock. Imported by Traditions.

Price: **$269.00**

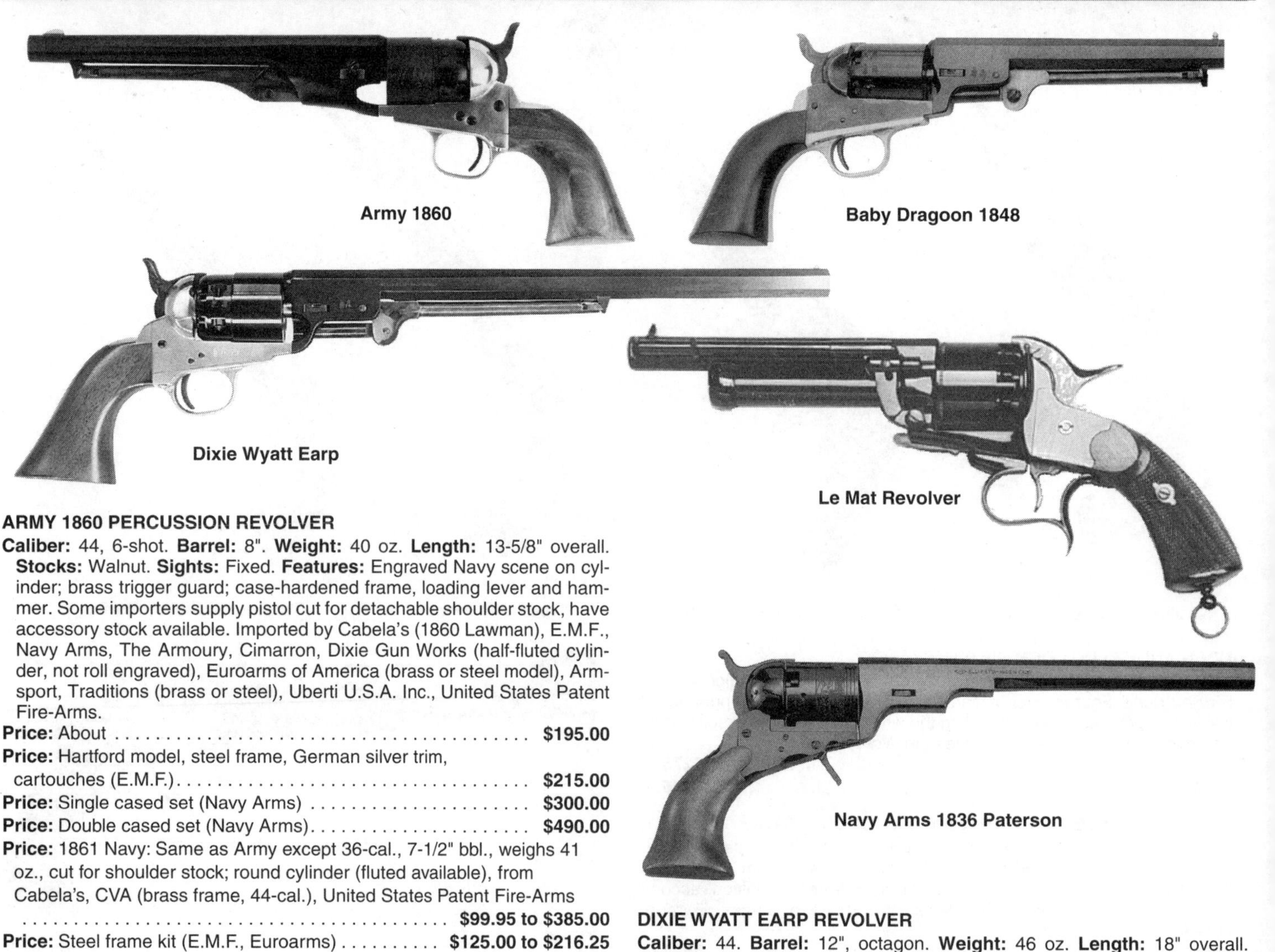

Army 1860

Baby Dragoon 1848

Dixie Wyatt Earp

Le Mat Revolver

Navy Arms 1836 Paterson

ARMY 1860 PERCUSSION REVOLVER

Caliber: 44, 6-shot. **Barrel:** 8". **Weight:** 40 oz. **Length:** 13-5/8" overall. **Stocks:** Walnut. **Sights:** Fixed. **Features:** Engraved Navy scene on cylinder; brass trigger guard; case-hardened frame, loading lever and hammer. Some importers supply pistol cut for detachable shoulder stock, have accessory stock available. Imported by Cabela's (1860 Lawman), E.M.F., Navy Arms, The Armoury, Cimarron, Dixie Gun Works (half-fluted cylinder, not roll engraved), Euroarms of America (brass or steel model), Armsport, Traditions (brass or steel), Uberti U.S.A. Inc., United States Patent Fire-Arms.

Price: About **$195.00**

Price: Hartford model, steel frame, German silver trim, cartouches (E.M.F.) **$215.00**

Price: Single cased set (Navy Arms) **$300.00**

Price: Double cased set (Navy Arms)..................... **$490.00**

Price: 1861 Navy: Same as Army except 36-cal., 7-1/2" bbl., weighs 41 oz., cut for shoulder stock; round cylinder (fluted available), from Cabela's, CVA (brass frame, 44-cal.), United States Patent Fire-Arms .... **$99.95 to $385.00**

Price: Steel frame kit (E.M.F., Euroarms) .... **$125.00 to $216.25**

Price: Colt Army Police, fluted cyl., 5-1/2", 36-cal. (Cabela's).... **$124.95**

Price: With nickeled frame, barrel and backstrap, gold-tone fluted cylinder, trigger and hammer, simulated ivory grips (Traditions) **$199.00**

BABY DRAGOON 1848, 1849 POCKET, WELLS FARGO

Caliber: 31. **Barrel:** 3", 4", 5", 6"; seven-groove; RH twist. **Weight:** About 21 oz. **Stocks:** Varnished walnut. **Sights:** Brass pin front, hammer notch rear. **Features:** No loading lever on Baby Dragoon or Wells Fargo models. Unfluted cylinder with stagecoach holdup scene; cupped cylinder pin; no grease grooves; one safety pin on cylinder and slot in hammer face; straight (flat) mainspring. From Armsport, Cimarron F.A. Co., Dixie Gun Works, Uberti U.S.A. Inc.

Price: 6" barrel, with loading lever (Dixie Gun Works) **$275.00**

Price: 4" (Uberti USA Inc.) **$335.00**

CABELA'S 1860 ARMY SNUBNOSE REVOLVER

Caliber: .44. **Barrel:** 3". **Weight:** 2 lbs., 3 oz. **Length:** 9" overall. **Grips:** Hardwood. **Sights:** Blade front, hammer notch near. **Features:** Shortened barrels w/o loading lever. Separate brass loading tool included.

Price: Revolver only **$189.99**

Price: W/starter kit **$289.99**

CABELA'S 1862 POLICE SNUBNOSE REVOLVER

Caliber: .36. **Barrel:** 3". **Weight:** 2 lbs., 3 oz. **Length:** 8.5" overall. **Grips:** Hardwood. **Sights:** Blade front, hammer notch rear. **Features:** Shortened barrel, removed loading lever. Separate brass loading tool included.

Price: .... **$169.99** (revolver only); **$209.99** (with starter kit).

DIXIE WYATT EARP REVOLVER

Caliber: 44. **Barrel:** 12", octagon. **Weight:** 46 oz. **Length:** 18" overall. **Stocks:** Two-piece walnut. **Sights:** Fixed. **Features:** Highly polished brass frame, backstrap and trigger guard; blued barrel and cylinder; case-hardened hammer, trigger and loading lever. Navy-size shoulder stock ($45) will fit with minor fitting. From Dixie Gun Works.

Price: **$160.00**

LE MAT REVOLVER

Caliber: 44/65. **Barrel:** 6-3/4" (revolver); 4-7/8" (single shot). **Weight:** 3 lbs., 7 oz. **Stocks:** Hand-checkered walnut. **Sights:** Post front, hammer notch rear. **Features:** Exact reproduction with all-steel construction; 44-cal. 9-shot cylinder, 65-cal. single barrel; color case-hardened hammer with selector; spur trigger guard; ring at butt; lever-type barrel release. From Navy Arms.

Price: Cavalry model (lanyard ring, spur trigger guard) **$595.00**

Price: Army model (round trigger guard, pin-type barrel release) **$595.00**

Price: Naval-style (thumb selector on hammer) **$595.00**

NAVY ARMS NEW MODEL POCKET REVOLVER

Caliber: 31, 5-shot. **Barrel:** 3-1/2", octagon. **Weight:** 15 oz. **Length:** 7-3/4". **Stocks:** Two-piece walnut. **Sights:** Fixed. **Features:** Replica of the Remington New Model Pocket. Available with polisehd brass frame or nickel plated finish. Introduced 2000. Imported by Navy Arms.

Price: **$300.00**

NAVY ARMS 1836 PATERSON REVOLVER

Features: Hidden trigger, 36 cal., blued barrel, replica of 5-shooter, roll-engraved with stagecoach hold-up.

Price: .... **$340.00 to $499.00**

Blackpowder Revolvers

North American Companion

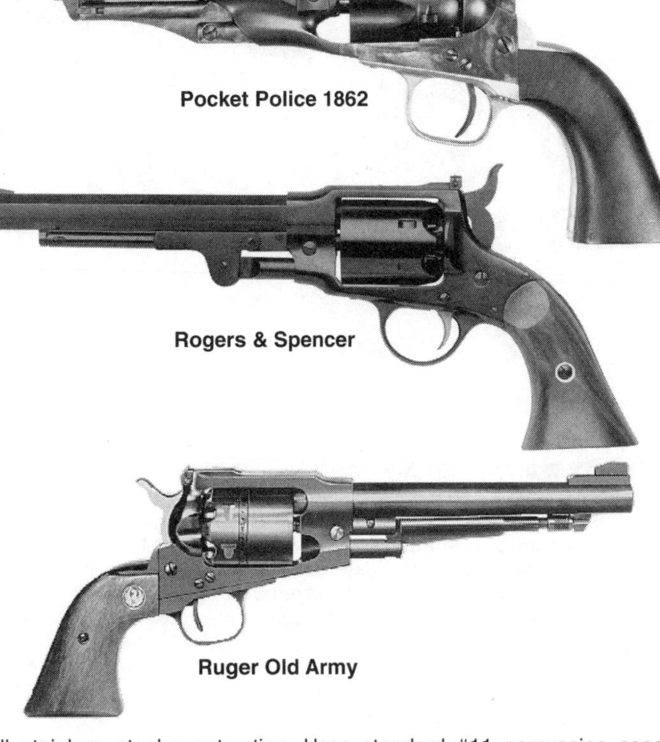

Pocket Police 1862

Rogers & Spencer

Ruger Old Army

Navy Arms
1858 Army Percussion

NAVY MODEL 1851 PERCUSSION REVOLVER

Caliber: 36, 44, 6-shot. **Barrel:** 7-1/2". **Weight:** 44 oz. **Length:** 13" overall. **Stocks:** Walnut finish. **Sights:** Post front, hammer notch rear. **Features:** Brass backstrap and trigger guard; some have 1st Model squareback trigger guard, engraved cylinder with navy battle scene; case-hardened frame, hammer, loading lever. Imported by The Armoury, Cabela's, Cimarron F.A. Co., Navy Arms, E.M.F., Dixie Gun Works, Euroarms of America, Armsport, CVA (44-cal. only), Traditions (44 only), Uberti U.S.A. Inc., United States Patent Fire-Arms.

Price: Brass frame . . . . **$99.95 to $385.00**
Price: Steel frame . . . . **$130.00 to $285.00**
Price: Kit form . . . . **$110.00 to $123.95**
Price: Engraved model (Dixie Gun Works) **$182.50**
Price: Single cased set, steel frame (Navy Arms) **$280.00**
Price: Double cased set, steel frame (Navy Arms) **$455.00**
Price: Confederate Navy (Cabela's) **$89.99**
Price: Hartford model, steel frame, German silver trim, cartouche (E.M.F.) **$190.00**

NEW MODEL 1858 ARMY PERCUSSION REVOLVER

Caliber: 36 or 44, 6-shot. **Barrel:** 6-1/2" or 8". **Weight:** 38 oz. **Length:** 13-1/2" overall. **Stocks:** Walnut. **Sights:** Blade front, groove-in-frame rear. **Features:** Replica of Remington Model 1858. Also available from some importers as Army Model Belt Revolver in 36-cal., a shortened and light-ened version of the 44. Target Model (Uberti U.S.A. Inc., Navy Arms) has fully adjustable target rear sight, target front, 36 or 44. Imported by Cabe-la's, Cimarron F.A. Co., CVA (as 1858 Army, brass frame, 44 only), Dixie Gun Works, Navy Arms, The Armoury, E.M.F., Euroarms of America (engraved, stainless and plain), Armsport, Traditions (44 only), Uberti U.S.A. Inc.

Price: Steel frame, about . . . . **$99.95 to $280.00**
Price: Steel frame kit (Euroarms, Navy Arms) . . . . . . **$115.95 to $150.00**
Price: Single cased set (Navy Arms) **$290.00**
Price: Double cased set (Navy Arms) **$480.00**
Price: Stainless steel Model 1858 (Euroarms, Uberti U.S.A. Inc., Cabela's, Navy Arms, Armsport, Traditions) . . . . **$169.95 to $380.00**
Price: Target Model, adjustable rear sight (Cabela's, Euroarms, Uberti U.S.A. Inc., Stone Mountain Arms) . . . . **$95.95 to $399.00**
Price: Brass frame (CVA, Cabela's, Traditions, Navy Arms) . . . . **$79.95 to $159.95**
Price: As above, kit (Dixie Gun Works, Navy Arms) . . **$145.00 to $188.95**
Price: Buffalo model, 44-cal. (Cabela's) **$119.99**
Price: Hartford model, steel frame, German silver trim, cartouche (E.M.F.) **$215.00**

NORTH AMERICAN COMPANION PERCUSSION REVOLVER

Caliber: 22. **Barrel:** 1-1/8". **Weight:** 5.1 oz. **Length:** 4-5/10" overall. **Stocks:** Laminated wood. **Sights:** Blade front, notch fixed rear. **Features:** All stainless steel construction. Uses standard #11 percussion caps. Comes with bullets, powder measure, bullet seater, leather clip holster, gun rug. Long Rifle or Magnum frame size. Introduced 1996. Made in U.S. by North American Arms.

Price: Long Rifle frame **$156.00**

North American Magnum Companion Percussion Revolver

Similar to the Companion except has larger frame. Weighs 7.2 oz., has 1-5/8" barrel, measures 5-7/16" overall. Comes with bullets, powder measure, bullet seater, leather clip holster, gun rag. Introduced 1996. Made in U.S. by North American Arms.

Price: **$215.00**

POCKET POLICE 1862 PERCUSSION REVOLVER

Caliber: 36, 5-shot. **Barrel:** 4-1/2", 5-1/2", 6-1/2", 7-1/2". **Weight:** 26 oz. **Length:** 12" overall (6-1/2" bbl.). **Stocks:** Walnut. **Sights:** Fixed. **Features:** Round tapered barrel; half-fluted and rebated cylinder; case-hardened frame, loading lever and hammer; silver or brass trigger guard and backstrap. Imported by Dixie Gun Works, Navy Arms (5-1/2" only), Uberti U.S.A. Inc. (5-1/2", 6-1/2" only), United States Patent Fire-Arms and Cimarron F.A. Co.

Price: About . . . . **$139.95 to $335.00**
Price: Single cased set with accessories (Navy Arms) **$365.00**
Price: Hartford model, steel frame, German silver trim, cartouche (E.M.F.) **$215.00**

ROGERS & SPENCER PERCUSSION REVOLVER

Caliber: 44. **Barrel:** 7-1/2". **Weight:** 47 oz. **Length:** 13-3/4" overall. **Stocks:** Walnut. **Sights:** Cone front, integral groove in frame for rear. **Features:** Accurate reproduction of a Civil War design. Solid frame; extra large nipple cut-out on rear of cylinder; loading lever and cylinder easily removed for cleaning. From Dixie Gun Works, Euroarms of America (standard blue, engraved, burnished, target models), Navy Arms.

Price: . . . . **$160.00 to $299.95**
Price: Nickel-plated **$215.00**
Price: Engraved (Euroarms) **$287.00**
Price: Kit version . . . . **$245.00 to $252.00**
Price: Target version (Euroarms) . . . . **$239.00 to $270.00**
Price: Burnished London Gray (Euroarms) . . . . **$245.00 to $270.00**

BLACKPOWDER REVOLVERS

Spiller & Burr

3rd U.S. Model Dragoon

Texas Paterson

Walker

RUGER OLD ARMY PERCUSSION REVOLVER

Caliber: 45, 6-shot. Uses .457" dia. lead bullets or 454 conical. **Barrel:** 7-1/2" (6-groove; 1:16" twist). **Weight:** 2-7/8 lbs. **Length:** 13-1/2" overall. **Stocks:** Rosewood. **Sights:** Ramp front, rear adjustable for windage and elevation; or fixed (groove). **Features:** Stainless steel; standard size nipples, chrome-moly steel cylinder and frame, same lockwork as original Super Blackhawk. Also stainless steel. Includes hard case and lock. Made in USA. From Sturm, Ruger & Co.

Price: Blued steel, fixed sight (Model BP-5F) **$499.00**
Price: Stainless steel, fixed sight (Model KBP-5F-I) **$576.00**
Price: Stainless steel (Model KBP-7) **$535.00**
Price: Blued steel (Model BP-7) **$499.00**
Price: Blued steel, fixed sight (BP-7F) **$499.00**
Price: Stainless steel, fixed sight (KBP-7F) **$535.00**

SHERIFF MODEL 1851 PERCUSSION REVOLVER

Caliber: 36, 44, 6-shot. **Barrel:** 5". **Weight:** 40 oz. **Length:** 10-1/2" overall. **Stocks:** Walnut. **Sights:** Fixed. **Features:** Brass backstrap and trigger guard; engraved navy scene; case-hardened frame, hammer, loading lever. Imported by E.M.F.

Price: Steel frame **$169.95**
Price: Brass frame **$140.00**

SPILLER & BURR REVOLVER

Caliber: 36 (.375" round ball). **Barrel:** 7", octagon. **Weight:** 2-1/2 lbs. **Length:** 12-1/2" overall. **Stocks:** Two-piece walnut. **Sights:** Fixed. **Features:** Reproduction of the C.S.A. revolver. Brass frame and trigger guard. Also available as a kit. From Dixie Gun Works, Navy Arms.

Price: **$150.00**
Price: Kit form (Dixie) **$125.00**
Price: Single cased set (Navy Arms) **$270.00**
Price: Double cased set (Navy Arms) **$430.00**

TEXAS PATERSON 1836 REVOLVER

Caliber: 36 (.375" round ball). **Barrel:** 7-1/2". **Weight:** 42 oz. **Stocks:** One-piece walnut. **Sights:** Fixed. **Features:** Copy of Sam Colt's first commercially-made revolving pistol. Has no loading lever but comes with loading tool. From Cimarron F.A. Co., Dixie Gun Works, Navy Arms, Uber-ti U.S.A. Inc.

Price: About **$495.00**
Price: With loading lever (Uberti U.S.A. Inc.) **$450.00**
Price: Engraved (Navy Arms) **$485.00**

UBERTI 1861 NAVY PERCUSSION REVOLVER

Caliber: 36. **Barrel:** 7-1/2", round. **Weight:** 40-1/2 oz. **Stocks:** One-piece oiled American walnut. **Sights:** Brass pin front, hammer notch rear. **Features:** Rounded trigger guard, German silver blade front sight, "creeping" loading lever. Available with fluted or round cylinder. Imported by Uberti U.S.A. Inc.

Price: Steel backstrap, trigger guard, cut for stock **$265.00**

1ST U.S. MODEL DRAGOON

Caliber: 44. **Barrel:** 7-1/2", part round, part octagon. **Weight:** 64 oz. **Stocks:** One-piece walnut. **Sights:** German silver blade front, hammer notch rear. **Features:** First model has oval bolt cuts in cylinder, square- back flared trigger guard, V-type mainspring, short trigger. Ranger and Indian scene roll-engraved on cylinder. Color case-hardened frame, loading lever, plunger and hammer; blue barrel, cylinder, trigger and wedge. Available with old-time charcoal blue or standard blue-black finish. Polished brass backstrap and trigger guard. From Cimarron F.A. Co., Dixie Gun Works, Uberti U.S.A. Inc., Navy Arms.

Price: . . . . **$295.00 to $435.00**

2nd U.S. Model Dragoon Revolver

Similar to the 1st Model except distinguished by rectangular bolt cuts in the cylinder. From Cimarron F.A. Co., Uberti U.S.A. Inc., United States Patent Fire-Arms, Navy Arms, Dixie Gunworks.

Price: . . . . **$295.00 to $435.00**

3rd U.S. Model Dragoon Revolver

Similar to the 2nd Model except for oval trigger guard, long trigger, modifications to the loading lever and latch. Imported by Cimarron F.A. Co., Uberti U.S.A. Inc., United States Patent Fire-Arms, Dixie Gunworks.

Price: Military model (frame cut for shoulder stock, steel backstrap) . . . . **$295.00 to $435.00**
Price: Civilian (brass backstrap, trigger guard) . . . . . . **$295.00 to $325.00**

1862 POCKET NAVY PERCUSSION REVOLVER

Caliber: 36, 5-shot. **Barrel:** 5-1/2", 6-1/2", octagonal, 7-groove, LH twist. **Weight:** 27 oz. (5-1/2" barrel). **Length:** 10-1/2" overall (5-1/2" bbl.). **Stocks:** One-piece varnished walnut. **Sights:** Brass pin front, hammer notch rear. **Features:** Rebated cylinder, hinged loading lever, brass or silver-plated backstrap and trigger guard, color-cased frame, hammer, loading lever, plunger and latch, rest blued. Has original-type markings. From Cimarron F.A. Co., Uberti U.S.A. Inc., Dixie Gunworks.

Price: With brass backstrap, trigger guard . . . . **$260.00 to $310.00**

1861 Navy Percussion Revolver

Similar to Colt 1851 Navy except has round 7-1/2" barrel, rounded trigger guard, German silver blade front sight, "creeping" loading lever. Fluted or round cylinder. Imported by Cimarron F.A. Co., Uberti U.S.A. Inc., Dixie Gunworks.

Price: Steel backstrap, trigger guard, cut for stock . . . **$255.00 to $300.00**

WALKER 1847 PERCUSSION REVOLVER

Caliber: 44, 6-shot. **Barrel:** 9". **Weight:** 84 oz. **Length:** 15-1/2" overall. **Stocks:** Walnut. **Sights:** Fixed. **Features:** Case-hardened frame, loading lever and hammer; iron backstrap; brass trigger guard; engraved cylinder. Imported by Cabela's, Cimarron F.A. Co., Navy Arms, Dixie Gun Works, Uberti U.S.A. Inc., E.M.F., Cimarron, Traditions, United States Patent Fire-Arms.

Price: About . . . . **$225.00 to $445.00**
Price: Single cased set (Navy Arms) **$405.00**
Price: Deluxe Walker with French fitted case (Navy Arms) **$540.00**
Price: Hartford model, steel frame, German silver trim, cartouche (E.M.F.) **$295.00**

Austin & Halleck 420 LR In-Line

Austin & Halleck 320 LR In-Line

Austin & Halleck Mountain

Cabela's Blue Ridge

Cabela's Traditional Hawken

ARMOURY R140 HAWKEN RIFLE

Caliber: 45, 50 or 54.**Barrel:** 29". **Weight:** 8-3/4 to 9 lbs. **Length:** 45-3/4" overall. **Stock:** Walnut, with cheekpiece. **Sights:** Dovetail front, fully adjustable rear. **Features:** Octagon barrel, removable breech plug; double set triggers; blued barrel, brass stock fittings, color case-hardened percussion lock. From Armsport, The Armoury.

Price: . . . . $225.00 to $245.00

AUSTIN & HALLECK MODEL 420 LR IN-LINE RIFLE

Caliber: 50. **Barrel:** 26", 1" octagon to 3/4" round; 1:28" twist. **Weight:** 7-7/8 lbs. **Length:** 47-1/2" overall. **Stock:** Lightly figured maple in Classic or Monte Carlo style. **Sights:** Ramp front, fully adjustable rear. **Features:** Blue or electroless nickel finish; in-line percussion action with removable weather shroud; Timney adjustable target trigger with sear block safety. Introduced 1998. Made in U.S. by Austin & Halleck.

Price: Blue $549.00
Price: Stainless steel $549.00
Price: Blue, hand-select highly figured stock $709.00
Price: Stainless steel, select stock $739.00

Austin & Halleck Model 320 LR In-Line Rifle

Similar to the Model 420 LR except has black resin synthetic stock with checkered grip and forend. Introduced 1998. Made in U.S. by Austin & Halleck.

Price: Blue $419.00
Price: Stainless steel $449.00

AUSTIN & HALLECK MOUNTAIN RIFLE

Caliber: 50. **Barrel:** 32"; 1:28" or 1:66" twist; 1" flats. **Weight:** 7-1/2 lbs. **Length:** 49" overall. **Stock:** Curly maple. **Sights:** Silver blade front, buckhorn rear. **Features:** Available in percussion or flintlock; double throw adjustable set triggers; rust brown finish. Made in U.S. by Austin & Halleck.

Price: Flintlock, fancy wood $589.00
Price: Flintlock, select wood $769.00
Price: Percussion, fancy wood $539.00
Price: Percussion, select wood $719.00

BOSTONIAN PERCUSSION RIFLE

Caliber: 45. **Barrel:** 30", octagonal. **Weight:** 7-1/4 lbs. **Length:** 46" overall. **Stock:** Walnut. **Sights:** Blade front, fixed notch rear. **Features:** Color case-hardened lock, brass trigger guard, buttplate, patchbox. Imported from Italy by E.M.F.

Price: $285.00

CABELA'S BLUE RIDGE RIFLE

Caliber: 32, 36, 45, 50, .54. **Barrel:** 39", octagonal. **Weight:** About 7-3/4 lbs. **Length:** 55" overall. **Stock:** American black walnut. **Sights:** Blade front, rear drift adjustable for windage. **Features:** Color case-hardened lockplate and cock/hammer, brass trigger guard and buttplate, double set, double-phased triggers. From Cabela's.

Price: Percussion $409.99
Price: Flintlock $519.99

CABELA'S TRADITIONAL HAWKEN

Caliber: 50, 54. **Barrel:** 29". **Weight:** About 9 lbs. **Stock:** Walnut. **Sights:** Blade front, open adjustable rear. **Features:** Flintlock or percussion. Adjustable double-set triggers. Polished brass furniture, color case-hardened lock. Imported by Cabela's.

Price: Percussion, right-hand $269.99
Price: Percussion, left-hand $269.99
Price: Flintlock, right-hand $299.99

Cook & Brother

Cabela's Sporterized Hawken Hunter Rifle

Similar to the Traditional Hawken except has more modern stock style with rubber recoil pad, blued furniture, sling swivels. Percussion only, in 50- or 54-caliber.

Price: Carbine or rifle, right-hand **$329.99**

CABELA'S KODIAK EXPRESS DOUBLE RIFLE

Caliber: 50, 54, 58, 72. **Barrel:** Length n/a; 1:48" twist. **Weight:** 9.3 lbs. **Length:** 45-1/4" overall. **Stock:** European walnut, oil finish. **Sights:** Fully adjustable double folding-leaf rear, ramp front. **Features:** Percussion. Barrels regulated to point of aim at 75 yards; polished and engraved lock, top tang and trigger guard. From Cabela's.

Price: 50, 54, 58 calibers **$899.99**

Price: 72 caliber **$929.99**

COOK & BROTHER CONFEDERATE CARBINE

Caliber: 58. **Barrel:** 24". **Weight:** 7-1/2 lbs. **Length:** 40-1/2" overall. **Stock:** Select walnut. **Features:** Recreation of the 1861 New Orleans-made artillery carbine. Color case-hardened lock, browned barrel. Buttplate, trigger guard, barrel bands, sling swivels and nosecap of polished brass. From Euroarms of America.

Price: **$513.00**

Price: Cook & Brother rifle (33" barrel) **$552.00**

KODIAK MAGNUM RIFLE

NEW!

Caliber: 45, 50. No. 209 primer ignition. **Barrel:** 28"; 1:28" twist. **Stock:** Ambidextrous black or Mossy Oak camo. **Sights:** Fiber optic. **Features:** Blue or nickel finish, recoil pa, lifetime warranty. From CVA.

Price: Mossy Oak camo; nickel barrel **$329.95**

Price: Mossy Oak camo; blued barrel **$309.95**

Price: Black stock; nickel barrel **$289.95**

Price: Black stock; blued barrel **$259.95**

CVA BOBCAT RIFLE

Caliber: 50 percussion. **Barrel:** 26"; 1:48" twist, octagonal. **Weight:** 6 lbs. **Length:** 42" overall. **Stock:** Dura-Grip synthetic or wood. **Sights:** Blade front, open rear. **Features:** Oversize trigger guard; wood ramrod; matte black finish. From CVA.

Price: (Wood stock) **$99.95**

Price: (Black synthetic stock) **$69.95**

CVA MOUNTAIN RIFLE

Caliber: 50. **Barrel:** 32"; 1:48" rifling. **Weight:** 8-1/2 lbs. **Length:** NA. **Sights:** Blade front, buckhorn rear. **Features:** Browned steel furniture, patchbox. Made in U.S. From CVA.

Price: **$259.95**

CVA ST. LOUIS HAWKEN RIFLE

Caliber: 50, 54. **Barrel:** 28", octagon; 15/16" across flats; 1:48" twist. **Weight:** 8 lbs. **Length:** 44" overall. **Stock:** Select hardwood. **Sights:** Beaded blade front, fully adjustable open rear. **Features:** Fully adjustable double-set triggers; synthetic ramrod (kits have wood); brass patchbox, wedge plates, nosecap, thimbles, trigger guard and buttplate; blued barrel; color case-hardened, engraved lockplate. V-type mainspring. Button breech. Introduced 1981. From CVA.

Price: St. Louis Hawken, finished (50- , 54-cal.) **$229.95**

CVA FIREBOLT MUSKETMAG BOLT-ACTION IN-LINE RIFLES

Caliber: 45 or 50. **Barrel:** 26". **Weight:** 7 lbs. **Length:** 44". **Stock:** Rubber-coated black or Mossy Oak® Break-Up™ camo synthetic. **Sights:** CVA Illuminator Fiber Optic Sight System. **Features:** Bolt-action, inline ignition system handles up to 150 grains blackpowder or Pyrodex; Nickel or matte blue barrel; removable breech plug; trigger-block safety. Three-way ignition system. From CVA.

Price: FiberGrip/nickel, 50 cal. **$294.95**

Price: Breakup/nickel, 50 cal. **$259.95**

Price: FiberGrip/nickel, 45 cal. **$294.95**

Price: Breakup/nickel, 45 cal. **$259.95**

Price: FiberGrip/blue, 50 cal. **$199.95**

Price: Breakup/blue, 50 cal. **$239.95**

Price: FiberGrip/blue, 45 cal. **$199.95**

Price: Breakup/blue, 45 cal. **$239.95**

CVA Hunterbolt209 Magnum Rifle

Similar to the Firebolt except has 26" barrel and black or Mossy Oak® Break-Up™ synthetic stock. Three-way ignition system. Weighs 6 lbs. From CVA.

Price: 45 or 50 cal. .... **$179.95 to $234.95**

CVA OPTIMA PRO BREAK-ACTION RIFLE

Caliber: 45, 50. **Barrel:** 29" fluted, blue or nickel. **Weight:** 8.8 lbs. **Stock:** Ambidextrous Mossy Oak camo or black Fiber-Grip. **Sights:** Adj. Fiber Optic. **Features:** Break-action, stainless No. 209 breech plug, aluminum loading rod, cocking spur, lifetime warranty.

Price: Mossy Oak Camo/nickel **$364.95**

Price: Mossy Oak Camo/blued **$329.95**

Price: Black/nickel **$309.95**

Price: Black/blued **$279.95**

Price: Blued fluted bbl. **$94.95**

Price: Nickel fluted bbl. **$109.95**

CVA Optima Magnum Break-Action Rifle

Similar to Optima Pro but with 26" bbl., nickel or blue finish

Price: Mossy Oak Camo/nickel **$299.95**

Price: Mossy Oak Camo/blue **$279.95**

Price: Black/nickel **$254.95**

Price: Black/blued **$224.95**

DIXIE EARLY AMERICAN JAEGER RIFLE

Caliber: 54. **Barrel:** 27-1/2" octagonal; 1:24" twist. **Weight:** 8-1/4 lbs. **Length:** 43-1/2" overall. **Stock:** American walnut; sliding wooden patchbox on on butt. **Sights:** Notch rear, blade front. **Features:** Flintlock or percussion. Browned steel furniture. Imported from Italy by Dixie Gun Works.

Price: Flintlock or percussion **$795.00**

DIXIE DELUXE CUB RIFLE

Caliber: 40. **Barrel:** 28". **Weight:** 6-1/2 lbs. **Stock:** Walnut. **Sights:** Fixed. **Features:** Short rifle for small game and beginning shooters. Brass patchbox and furniture. Flint or percussion. From Dixie Gun Works.

Price: Finished **$450.00**

Price: Kit **$390.00**

Price: Super Cub (50-caliber) **$485.00**

DIXIE 1863 SPRINGFIELD MUSKET

Caliber: 58 (.570" patched ball or .575" Minie). **Barrel:** 50", rifled. **Stock:** Walnut stained. **Sights:** Blade front, adjustable ladder-type rear. **Features:** Bright-finish lock, barrel, furniture. Reproduction of the last of the regulation muzzleloaders. Imported from Japan by Dixie Gun Works.

Price: Finished **$625.00**

Price: Kit **$550.00**

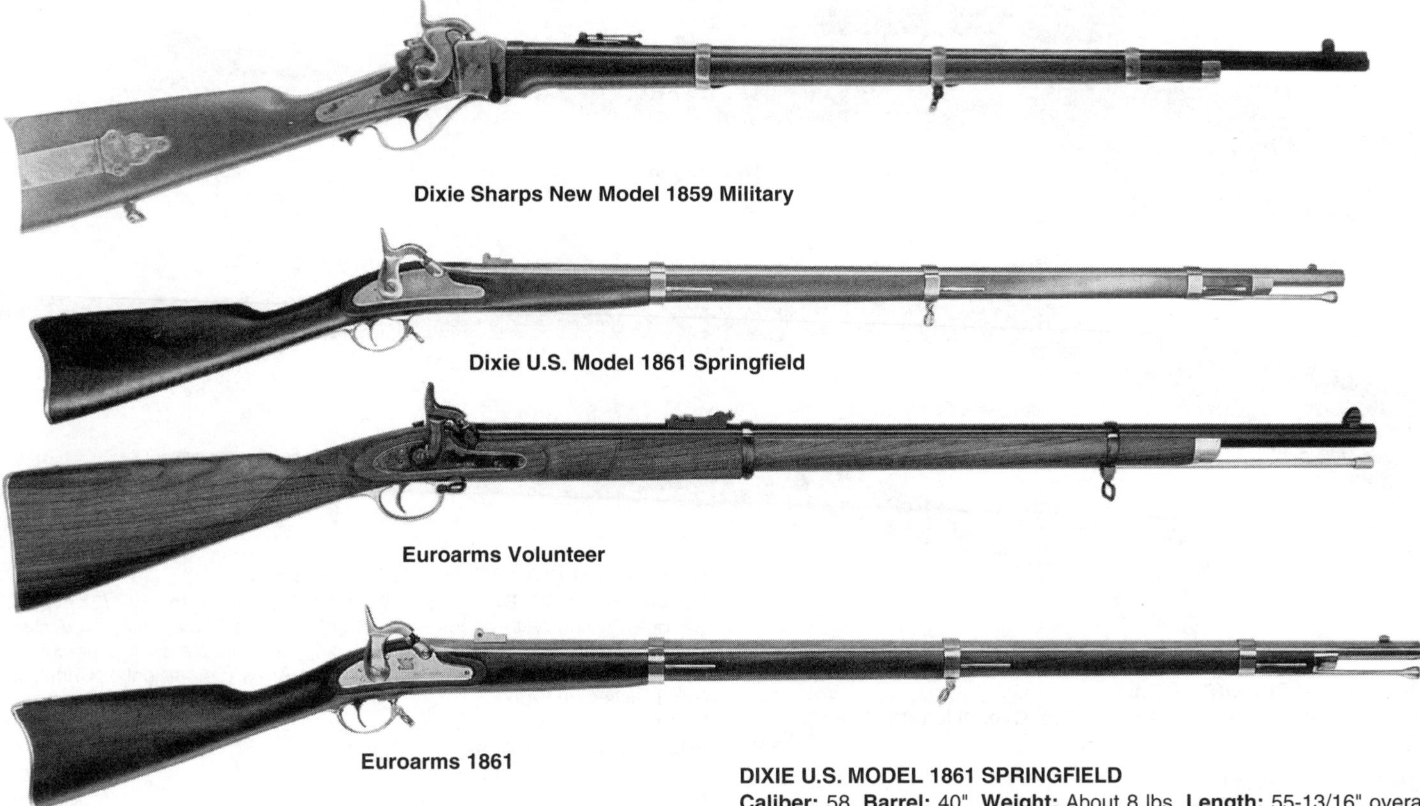

Dixie Sharps New Model 1859 Military

Dixie U.S. Model 1861 Springfield

Euroarms Volunteer

Euroarms 1861

DIXIE INLINE CARBINE

Caliber: 50, 54. **Barrel:** 24"; 1:32" twist. **Weight:** 6.5 lbs. **Length:** 41" overall. **Stock:** Walnut-finished hardwood with Monte Carlo comb. **Sights:** Ramp front with red insert, open fully adjustable rear. **Features:** Sliding "bolt" fully encloses cap and nipple. Fully adjustable trigger, automatic safety. Aluminum ramrod. Imported from Italy by Dixie Gun Works.

Price: **$375.00**

DIXIE PEDERSOLI 1857 MAUSER RIFLE

Caliber: 54. **Barrel:** 39-3/8". **Weight:** N/A. **Length:** 52" overall. **Stock:** European walnut with oil finish, sling swivels. **Sights:** Fully adjustable rear, lug front. **Features:** Percussion (musket caps). Armory bright finish with color case-hardened lock and barrel tang, engraved lockplate, steel ramrod. Introduced 2000. Imported from Italy by Dixie Gun Works.

Price: **$950.00**

DIXIE PEDERSOLI 1766 CHARLEVILLE MUSKET

Caliber: 69. **Barrel:** 44-3/4". **Weight:** 10-1/2 lbs. **Length:** 57-1/2" overall. **Stock:** European walnut with oil finish. **Sights:** Fixed rear, lug front. **Features:** Smoothbore flintlock. Armory bright finish with steel furniture and ramrod. Introduced 2000. Imported from Italy by Dixie Gun Works.

Price: **$895.00**

DIXIE SHARPS NEW MODEL 1859 MILITARY RIFLE

Caliber: 54. **Barrel:** 30", 6-groove; 1:48" twist. **Weight:** 9 lbs. **Length:** 45-1/2" overall. **Stock:** Oiled walnut. **Sights:** Blade front, ladder-style rear. **Features:** Blued barrel, color case-hardened barrel bands, receiver, hammer, nosecap, lever, patchbox cover and buttplate. Introduced 1995. Imported from Italy by Dixie Gun Works.

Price: **$995.00**

DIXIE U.S. MODEL 1816 FLINTLOCK MUSKET

Caliber: 69. **Barrel:** 42", smoothbore. **Weight:** 9.75 lbs. **Length:** 56.5" overall. **Stock:** Walnut with oil finish. **Sights:** Blade front. **Features:** All metal finished "National Armory Bright"; three barrel bands with springs; steel ramrod with button-shaped head. Imported by Dixie Gun Works.

Price: **$875.00**

DIXIE U.S. MODEL 1861 SPRINGFIELD

Caliber: 58. **Barrel:** 40". **Weight:** About 8 lbs. **Length:** 55-13/16" overall. **Stock:** Oil-finished walnut. **Sights:** Blade front, step adjustable rear. **Features:** Exact recreation of original rifle. Sling swivels attached to trigger guard bow and middle barrel band. Lockplate marked "1861" with eagle motif and "U.S. Springfield" in front of hammer; "U.S." stamped on top of buttplate. From Dixie Gun Works.

Price: Kit **$550.00**

E.M.F. 1863 SHARPS MILITARY CARBINE

Caliber: 54. **Barrel:** 22", round. **Weight:** 8 lbs. **Length:** 39" overall. **Stock:** Oiled walnut. **Sights:** Blade front, military ladder-type rear. **Features:** Color case-hardened lock, rest blued. Imported by E.M.F.

Price: **$600.00**

EUROARMS VOLUNTEER TARGET RIFLE

Caliber: .451. **Barrel:** 33" (two-band), 36" (three-band). **Weight:** 11 lbs. (two-band). **Length:** 48.75" overall (two-band). **Stock:** European walnut with checkered wrist and forend. **Sights:** Hooded bead front, adjustable rear with interchangeable leaves. **Features:** Alexander Henry-type rifling with 1:20" twist. Color case-hardened hammer and lockplate, brass trigger guard and nosecap, rest blued. Imported by Euroarms of America, Dixie Gun Works.

Price: Two-band **$795.00**

Price: (Three-band) **$845.00**

EUROARMS 1861 SPRINGFIELD RIFLE

Caliber: 58. **Barrel:** 40". **Weight:** About 10 lbs. **Length:** 55.5" overall. **Stock:** European walnut. **Sights:** Blade front, three-leaf military rear. **Features:** Reproduction of the original three-band rifle. Lockplate marked "1861" with eagle and "U.S. Springfield." Metal left in the white. Imported by Euroarms of America.

Price: **$530.00**

EUROARMS ZOUAVE RIFLE

Caliber: 58 percussion. **Barrel:** 33 inches. **Overall length:** 49 inches.

Price: **$469.00**

EUROARMS HARPERS FERRY RIFLE

Caliber: 54 flintlock. **Barrel:** 35 inches. **Overall length:** 50 1/2 inches.

Price: **$735.00**

Gonic Model 93 Thumbhole

Harper's Ferry 1803

J.P. Murray

EUROARMS RICHMOND RIFLE

Caliber: 58 percussion. **Barrel:** 40 inches. **Overall length:** 49 inches.
Price: **$579.00**

GONIC MODEL 93 M/L RIFLE

Caliber: 45, 50. **Barrel:** 26"; 1:24" twist. **Weight:** 6-1/2 to 7 lbs. **Length:** 43" overall. **Stock:** American hardwood with black finish. **Sights:** Adjustable or aperture rear, hooded post front. **Features:** Adjustable trigger with side safety; unbreakable ram rod; comes with A. Z. scope bases installed. Introduced 1993. Made in U.S. by Gonic Arms, Inc.
Price: Model 93 Standard (blued barrel). **$720.00**
Price: Model 93 Standard (stainless brl., 50 cal. only) **$782.00**

Gonic Model 93 Deluxe M/L Rifle

Similar to the Model 93 except has classic-style walnut or gray laminated wood stock. Introduced 1998. Made in U.S. by Gonic Arms, Inc.
Price: Blue barrel, sights, scope base, choice of stock. **$902.00**
Price: Stainless barrel, sights, scope base, choice of stock (50 cal. only) **$964.00**

Gonic Model 93 Mountain Thumbhole M/L Rifles

Similar to the Model 93 except has high-grade walnut or gray laminate stock with extensive hand-checkered panels, Monte Carlo cheekpiece and beavertail forend; integral muzzle brake. Introduced 1998. Made in U.S. by Gonic Arms, Inc.
Price: Blued or stainless. **$2,700.00**

H&R SIDEKICK

Caliber: 50, 209 primer ignition. **Barrel:** 24 or 26 (magnum). **Weight:** 6 1/2 lbs. **Length:** 39-1/4 to 41-1/4. **Stock:** Black matte polymer or hardwood. **Sights:** Adjustable fiber optic open, tapped for scope mounts. **Features:** Break-action single-shot. Uses No. 209 shotgun primer held in place by special primer carrier. Telescoping brass ramrod. Introduced 2004.
Price: (Wood stock, blued finish, case-hardened frame) . . . . **N/A**
Price: (Stainless, polymer stock) . . . . **N/A**

H&R HUNTSMAN

Caliber: 50, 209 primer ignition. **Barrel:** 24". **Weight:** 6 1/2 lbs. **Length:** 40". **Stock:** Black matte polymer or hardwood. **Sights:** Fiber optic open sights, tapped for scope mounts. **Features:** Break-open action, transfer-bar safety system, breech plug removable for cleaning. Introduced 2004.
Price: Stainless model . . . . **N/A**
Price: Blued finish. . . . . **N/A**
Price: Combo model (12 ga., . 50 cal. muzzleloader, .243 Win). . . . . . **N/A**

HARPER'S FERRY 1803 FLINTLOCK RIFLE

Caliber: 54 or 58. **Barrel:** 35". **Weight:** 9 lbs. **Length:** 59-1/2" overall. **Stock:** Walnut with cheekpiece. **Sights:** Brass blade front, fixed steel rear. **Features:** Brass trigger guard, sideplate, buttplate; steel patchbox. Imported by Euroarms of America, Navy Arms (54-cal. only), Cabela's, and Dixie Gun Works.
Price: . . . . **$495.95 to $729.00**
Price: 54-cal. (Navy Arms) **$625.00**
Price: 54-caliber (Cabela's) **$599.99**
Price: 54-caliber (Dixie Gun Works) **$795.00**
Price: 54 and 58 caliber (Euroarms). **$575.00**

HAWKEN RIFLE

Caliber: 45, 50, 54 or 58. **Barrel:** 28", blued, 6-groove rifling. **Weight:** 8-3/4 lbs. **Length:** 44" overall. **Stock:** Walnut with cheekpiece. **Sights:** Blade front, fully adjustable rear. **Features:** Coil mainspring, double-set triggers, polished brass furniture. From Armsport and E.M.F.
Price: . . . . **$220.00 to $345.00**

J.P. MURRAY 1862-1864 CAVALRY CARBINE

Caliber: 58 (.577" Minie). **Barrel:** 23". **Weight:** 7 lbs., 9 oz. **Length:** 39" overall. **Stock:** Walnut. **Sights:** Blade front, rear drift adjustable for windage. **Features:** Browned barrel, color case-hardened lock, blued swivel and band springs, polished brass buttplate, trigger guard, barrel bands. From Euroarms of America.
Price: . . . . **$405.00 to $453.00**

J.P. HENRY TRADE RIFLE

Caliber: 54. **Barrel:** 34"; 1" flats. **Weight:** 8-1/2 lbs. **Length:** 45" overall. **Stock:** Premium curly maple. **Sights:** Silver blade front, fixed buckhorn rear. **Features:** Brass buttplate, side plate, trigger guard and nosecap; browned barrel and lock; L&R Large English percussion lock; single trigger. Made in U.S. by J.P. Gunstocks, Inc.
Price: **$965.50**

KENTUCKIAN RIFLE

Caliber: 44. **Barrel:** 35". **Weight:** 7 lbs. (Rifle), 5-1/2 lbs. (Carbine). **Length:** 51" overall (Rifle), 43" (Carbine). **Stock:** Walnut stain. **Sights:** Brass blade front, steel V-ramp rear. **Features:** Octagon barrel, case-hardened and engraved lockplates. Brass furniture. Imported by Dixie Gun Works.
Price: Flintlock or Percussion **$395.00**

KENTUCKY FLINTLOCK RIFLE

Caliber: 44, 45, or 50. **Barrel:** 35". **Weight:** 7 lbs. **Length:** 50" overall. **Stock:** Walnut stained, brass fittings. **Sights:** Fixed. **Features:** Available in carbine model also, 28" bbl. Some variations in detail, finish. Kits also available from some importers. Imported by The Armoury.
Price: About . . . . **$217.95 to $345.00**

Kentucky Flintlock

Knight 50 Caliber Disc In-Line

Knight Master Hunter Disc Extreme

London Armory 1861

Kentucky Percussion Rifle

Similar to flintlock except percussion lock. Finish and features vary with importer. Imported by The Armoury and CVA.

Price: About $259.95
Price: 45 or 50 cal. (Navy Arms)........................ $425.00
Price: Kit, 50 cal. (CVA) $189.95

KNIGHT 50 CALIBER DISC IN-LINE RIFLE

Caliber: 50. **Barrel:** 24", 26". **Weight:** 7 lbs., 14 oz. **Length:** 43" overall (24" barrel). **Stock:** Checkered synthetic with palm swell grip, rubber recoil pad, swivel studs; black, Advantage or Mossy Oak Break-Up camouflage. **Sights:** Bead on ramp front, fully adjustable open rear. **Features:** Bolt-action in-line system uses #209 shotshell primer for ignition; primer is held in plastic drop-in Primer Disc. Available in blued or stainless steel. Made in U.S. by Knight Rifles (Modern Muzzleloading).

Price: .... $439.95 to $632.45

Knight Master Hunter II DISC In-Line Rifle

Similar to Knight 50 caliber DISC rifle except features premier, wood laminated two-tone stock, gold-plated trigger and engraved trigger guard, jeweled bolt and fluted, air-gauged Green Mountain 26" barrel. Length 45" overall, weighs 7 lbs., 7 oz. Includes black composite thumbhole stock. Introduced 2000. Made in U.S. by Knight Rifles (Modern Muzzleloading).

Price: $1,099.95

KNIGHT MUZZLELOADER DISC EXTREME

Caliber: 45 fluted, 50. **Barrel:** 26". **Stock:** Stainless steel laminate, blued walnut, black composite thumbhole with blued or SS. **Sights:** Fully adjustable metallic. **Features:** New full plastic jacket ignition system.

Price: 50 SS laminate................................ $703.95
Price: 45 SS laminate................................ $769.95
Price: 50 blue walnut $626.95
Price: 45 blue walnut $703.95
Price: 50 blue composite $549.95
Price: 45 blue composite $632.45
Price: 50 SS composite $632.45
Price: 45 SS composite $703.95

Knight Master Hunter DISC Extreme

Similar to DISC Extreme except fluted barrel, two-tone laminated thumbhole Monte Carlo-style stock, black composite thumbhole field stock included. Jeweled bolt, adjustable premium trigger.

Price: 50 .... $1,044.95

KNIGHT AMERICAN KNIGHT M/L RIFLE

Caliber: 50. **Barrel:** 22"; 1:28" twist. **Weight:** 6 lbs. **Length:** 41" overall. **Stock:** Black composite. **Sights:** Bead on ramp front, open fully adjustable rear. **Features:** Double safety system; one-piece removable hammer assembly; drilled and tapped for scope mounting. Introduced 1998. Made in U.S. by Knight Rifles.

Price: blued, black comp.................................. $197.95
Price: blued, black comp VP $225.45

KNIGHT WOLVERINE 209

Caliber: 50. **Barrel:** 22". **Stock:** HD stock with SS barrel, break-up stock blued, black composite thumbhole with stainless steel, standard black composite with blued or SS. **Sights:** Metallic with fiber optic. **Features:** Double safety system, adjustable match grade trigger, left-hand model available. Full plastic jacket ignition system.

Price: Starting at $302.45

KNIGHT REVOLUTION

NEW

Caliber: 50, 209 primer ignition. **Barrel:** Stainless, 27". **Weight:** 7 lbs., 14 oz. **Stock:** Walnut, laminated, black composite, Mossy Oak Breakup or Hardwoods Green finish. **Features:** Blued or stainless finish, adjustable trigger and sights.

Price: .... N/A

Lyman Trade

Lyman Deerstalker

Lyman Great Plains

Markesbery KM Colorado

LONDON ARMORY 2-BAND 1858 ENFIELD

Caliber: .577" Minie, .575" round ball. **Barrel:** 33". **Weight:** 10 lbs. **Length:** 49" overall. **Stock:** Walnut. **Sights:** Folding leaf rear adjustable for elevation. **Features:** Blued barrel, color case-hardened lock and hammer, polished brass buttplate, trigger guard, nosecap. From Navy Arms, Euroarms of America, Dixie Gun Works.

Price: .... **$385.00 to $600.00**

LONDON ARMORY 1861 ENFIELD MUSKETOON

Caliber: 58, Minie ball. **Barrel:** 24", round. **Weight:** 7 - 7-1/2 lbs. **Length:** 40-1/2" overall. **Stock:** Walnut, with sling swivels. **Sights:** Blade front, graduated military-leaf rear. **Features:** Brass trigger guard, nosecap, buttplate; blued barrel, bands, lockplate, swivels. Imported by Euroarms of America, Navy Arms.

Price: .... **$300.00 to $515.00**

Price: Kit .... **$365.00 to $373.00**

LONDON ARMORY 3-BAND 1853 ENFIELD

Caliber: 58 (.577" Minie, .575" round ball, .580" maxi ball). **Barrel:** 39". **Weight:** 9-1/2 lbs. **Length:** 54" overall. **Stock:** European walnut. **Sights:** Inverted "V" front, traditional Enfield folding ladder rear. **Features:** Recreation of the famed London Armory Company Pattern 1853 Enfield Musket. One- piece walnut stock, brass buttplate, trigger guard and nosecap. Lock-plate marked "London Armoury Co." and with a British crown. Blued Badde-ley barrel bands. From Dixie Gun Works, Euroarms of America, Navy Arms.

Price: About .... **$350.00 to $645.00**

Price: Assembled kit (Dixie, Euroarms of America) **$495.00**

LYMAN TRADE RIFLE

Caliber: 50, 54. **Barrel:** 28" octagon;1:48" twist. **Weight:** 8-3/4 lbs. **Length:** 45" overall. **Stock:** European walnut. **Sights:** Blade front, open rear adjustable for windage or optional fixed sights. **Features:** Fast twist rifling for conical bullets. Polished brass furniture with blue steel parts, stainless steel nipple. Hook breech, single trigger, coil spring percussion lock. Steel barrel rib and ramrod ferrules. Introduced 1980. From Lyman.

Price: 50 cal. Percussion **$581.80**

Price: 50 cal. Flintlock **$652.80**

Price: 54 cal. Percussion **$581.80**

Price: 54 cal. Flintlock **$652.80**

LYMAN DEERSTALKER RIFLE

Caliber: 50, 54. **Barrel:** 24", octagonal; 1:48" rifling. **Weight:** 7-1/2 lbs. **Stock:** Walnut with black rubber buttpad. **Sights:** Lyman #37MA beaded front, fully adjustable fold-down Lyman #16A rear. **Features:** Stock has less drop for quick sighting. All metal parts are blackened, with color case-hardened lock; single trigger. Comes with sling and swivels. Available in flint or percussion. Introduced 1990. From Lyman.

Price: 50 cal. flintlock **$652.80**

Price: 50- or 54-cal., percussion, left-hand, carbine **$695.40**

Price: 50- or 54-cal., flintlock, left-hand **$645.00**

Price: 54 cal. flintlock **$780.50**

Price: 54 cal. percussion **$821.80**

Price: Stainless steel **$959.80**

LYMAN GREAT PLAINS RIFLE

Caliber: 50- or 54-cal. **Barrel:** 32"; 1:60" twist. **Weight:** 9 lbs. **Stock:** Walnut. **Sights:** Steel blade front, buckhorn rear adjustable for windage and elevation and fixed notch primitive sight included. **Features:** Blued steel furniture. Stainless steel nipple. Coil spring lock, Hawken-style trigger guard and double-set triggers. Round thimbles recessed and sweated into rib. Steel wedge plates and toe plate. Introduced 1979. From Lyman.

Price: Percussion **$469.95**

Price: Flintlock **$494.95**

Price: Percussion kit **$359.95**

Price: Flintlock kit **$384.95**

Price: Left-hand percussion **$474.95**

Price: Left-hand flintlock **$499.95**

Lyman Great Plains Hunter Model

Similar to Great Plains model except 1:32" twist shallow-groove barrel and comes drilled and tapped for Lyman 57GPR peep sight.

Price: **$959.80**

Mississippi 1841

Navy Arms Charleville

Navy Arms 1859 Sharps

MARKESBERY KM BLACK BEAR M/L RIFLE

Caliber: 36, 45, 50, 54. **Barrel:** 24"; 1:26" twist. **Weight:** 6-1/2 lbs. **Length:** 38-1/2" overall. **Stock:** Two-piece American hardwood, walnut, black laminate, green laminate, black composition, X-Tra or Mossy Oak Break-Up camouflage. **Sights:** Bead front, open fully adjustable rear. **Features:** Interchangeable barrels; exposed hammer; Outer-Line Magnum ignition system uses small rifle primer or standard No. 11 cap and nipple. Blue, black matte, or stainless. Made in U.S. by Markesbery Muzzle Loaders.

Price: American hardwood walnut, blue finish **$536.63**
Price: American hardwood walnut, stainless **$553.09**
Price: Black laminate, blue finish **$539.67**
Price: Black laminate, stainless **$556.27**
Price: Camouflage stock, blue finish. **$556.46**
Price: Camouflage stock, stainless. **$573.73**
Price: Black composite, blue finish **$532.65**
Price: Black composite, stainless **$549.93**
Price: Green laminate, blue finish. **$539.00**
Price: Green laminate, stainless **$556.27**

MARKESBERY KM COLORADO ROCKY MOUNTAIN RIFLE

Caliber: 36, 45, 50, 54. **Barrel:** 24"; 1:26" twist. **Weight:** 6-1/2 lbs. **Length:** 38-1/2" overall. **Stock:** American hardwood walnut, green or black laminate. **Sights:** Firesight bead on ramp front, fully adjustable open rear. **Features:** Replicates Reed/Watson rifle of 1851. Straight grip stock with or without two barrel bands, rubber recoil pad, large-spur hammer. Made in U.S. by Markesbery Muzzle Loaders, Inc.

Price: American hardwood walnut, blue finish **$545.92**
Price: Black or green laminate, blue finish **$548.30**
Price: American hardwood walnut, stainless **$563.17**
Price: Black or green laminate, stainless **$566.34**

Markesberry KM Brown Bear Rifle

Similar to KM Black Bear except one-piece thumbhole stock with Monte Carlo comb. Stock in Crotch Walnut composite, green or black laminate, black composite or X-Tra or Mossy Oak Break-Up camouflage. Contact maker for complete price listing. Made in U.S. by Markesberry Muzzle Loaders, Inc.

Price: Black composite, blue finish **$658.83**
Price: Crotch Walnut, blue finish. **$658.83**
Price: Camo composite, blue finish **$682.64**
Price: Walnut wood **$662.81**
Price: Black wood **$662.81**
Price: Black laminated wood. **$662.81**
Price: Green laminated wood **$662.81**
Price: Camo wood **$684.69**
Price: Black composite, stainless **$676.11**
Price: Crotch Walnut composite, stainless **$676.11**
Price: Camo composite, stainless. **$697.69**
Price: Walnut wood, stainless **$680.07**
Price: Black wood, stainless **$680.07**
Price: Black laminated wood, stainless. **$680.07**
Price: Green laminate, stainless **$680.07**
Price: Camo wood, stainless **$702.76**

Markesberry KM Grizzly Bear Rifle

Similar to KM Black Bear except thumbhole buttstock with Monte Carlo comb. Stock in Crotch Walnut composite, green or black laminate, black composite or X-Tra or Mossy Oak Break-Up camouflage. Contact maker for complete price listing. Made in U.S. by Markesbury Muzzle Loaders, Inc.

Price: Black composite, blue finish **$642.96**
Price: Crotch Walnut, blue finish. **$642.96**
Price: Camo composite, blue finish **$666.67**
Price: Walnut wood **$646.93**
Price: Black wood **$646.93**
Price: Black laminate wood. **$646.93**
Price: Green laminate wood **$646.93**
Price: Camo wood **$670.74**
Price: Black composite, stainless **$660.98**
Price: Crotch Walnut composite, stainless **$660.98**
Price: Black laminate wood, stainless. **$664.20**
Price: Green laminate, stainless **$664.20**
Price: Camo wood, stainless **$685.74**
Price: Camo composite, stainless. **$684.04**
Price: Walnut wood, stainless **$664.20**
Price: Black wood, stainless **$664.20**

Markesberry KM Polar Bear Rifle

Similar to KM Black Bear except one-piece stock with Monte Carlo comb. Stock in American Hardwood walnut, green or black laminate, black composite, or X-Tra or Mossy Oak Break-Up camouflage. Interchangeable barrel system, Outer-Line ignition system, cross-bolt double safety. Available in 36, 45, 50, 54 caliber. Contact maker for full price listing. Made in U.S. by Markesbery Muzzle Loaders, Inc.

Price: American Hardwood walnut , blue finish **$539.01**
Price: Black composite, blue finish **$536.63**
Price: Black laminate, blue finish **$541.17**
Price: Green laminate, blue finish. **$541.17**
Price: Camo, blue finish **$560.43**
Price: American Hardwood walnut, stainless **$556.27**
Price: Black composite, stainless **$556.04**
Price: Black laminate, stainless **$570.56**
Price: Green laminate, stainless. **$570.56**
Price: Camo, stainless **$573.94**

Navy Arms Berdan

Navy Arms Whitworth

Navy Arms Smith Carbine

Navy Arms 1863 C.S. Richmond

MDM BUCKWACKA IN-LINE RIFLES

Caliber: 45, 50. **Barrel:** 23", 25". **Weight:** 7 to 7-3/4 lbs. **Stock:** Black, walnut, laminated and camouflage finishes. **Sights:** Williams Fire Sight blade front, Williams fully adjustable rear with ghost-ring peep aperture. **Features:** Break-open action; Incinerating Ignition System incorporates 209 shotshell primer directly into breech plug; 50-caliber models handle up to 150 grains of Pyrodex; synthetic ramrod; transfer bar safety; stainless or blued finish. Made in U.S. by Millennium Designed Muzzleloaders Ltd.

Price: 50 cal., blued finish **$309.95**

Price: 50 cal., stainless **$339.95**

Price: Camouflage stock . . . . **$359.95 to $389.95**

MDM M2K In-Line Rifle

Similar to Buckwacka except adjustable trigger and double-safety mechanism designed to prevent misfires. Made in U.S. by Millennium Designed Muzzleloaders Ltd.

Price: . . . . **$529.00 to $549.00**

Mississippi 1841 Percussion Rifle

Similar to Zouave rifle but patterned after U.S. Model 1841. Caliber: 54, 58. Imported by Dixie Gun Works, Euroarms of America, Navy Arms.

Price: About **$595.00**

NAVY ARMS 1763 CHARLEVILLE

Caliber: 69. **Barrel:** 44-5/8". **Weight:** 8 lbs., 12 oz. **Length:** 59-3/8" overall. **Stock:** Walnut. **Sights:** Brass blade front. **Features:** Replica of French musket used by American troops during the Revolution. Imported by Navy Arms.

Price: **$1,020.00**

NAVY ARMS PARKER-HALE VOLUNTEER RIFLE

Caliber: .451. **Barrel:** 32". **Weight:** 9-1/2 lbs. **Length:** 49" overall. **Stock:** Walnut, checkered wrist and forend. **Sights:** Globe front, adjustable ladder-type rear. **Features:** Recreation of the type of gun issued to volunteer regiments during the 1860s. Rigby-pattern rifling, patent breech, detented lock. Stock is glass bedded for accuracy. Imported by Navy Arms.

Price: **$905.00**

NAVY ARMS 1859 SHARPS CAVALRY CARBINE

Caliber: 54. **Barrel:** 22". **Weight:** 7-3/4 lbs. **Length:** 39" overall. **Stock:** Walnut. **Sights:** Blade front, military ladder-type rear. **Features:** Color case-hardened action, blued barrel. Has saddle ring. Introduced 1991. Imported from Navy Arms.

Price: **$1,000.00**

NAVY ARMS BERDAN 1859 SHARPS RIFLE

Caliber: 54. **Barrel:** 30". **Weight:** 8 lbs., 8 oz. **Length:** 46-3/4" overall. **Stock:** Walnut. **Sights:** Blade front, folding military ladder-type rear. **Features:** Replica of the Union sniper rifle used by Berdan's 1st and 2nd Sharpshooter regiments. Color case-hardened receiver, patchbox, furniture. Double-set triggers. Imported by Navy Arms.

Price: **$1,165.00**

Price: 1859 Sharps Infantry Rifle (three-band) **$1,100.00**

NAVY ARMS PARKER-HALE WHITWORTH MILITARY TARGET RIFLE

Caliber: 45. **Barrel:** 36". **Weight:** 9-1/4 lbs. **Length:** 52-1/2" overall. **Stock:** Walnut. Checkered at wrist and forend. **Sights:** Hooded post front, open step-adjustable rear. **Features:** Faithful reproduction of Whitworth rifle, only bored for 45-cal. Trigger has detented lock, capable of being adjusted very finely without risk of the sear nose catching on the half-cock bent and damaging both parts. Introduced 1978. Imported by Navy Arms.

Price: **$930.00**

NAVY ARMS SMITH CARBINE

Caliber: 50. **Barrel:** 21-1/2". **Weight:** 7-3/4 lbs. **Length:** 39" overall. **Stock:** American walnut. **Sights:** Brass blade front, folding ladder-type rear. **Features:** Replica of breech-loading Civil War carbine. Color case-hardened receiver, rest blued. Cavalry model has saddle ring and bar, Artillery model has sling swivels. Imported by Navy Arms.

Price: Cavalry model **$645.00**

Price: Artillery model **$645.00**

NAVY ARMS 1863 C.S. RICHMOND RIFLE

Caliber: 58. **Barrel:** 40". **Weight:** 10 lbs. **Length:** NA. **Stocks:** Walnut. **Sights:** Blade front, adjustable rear. **Features:** Copy of three-band rifle musket made at Richmond Armory for the Confederacy. All steel polished bright. Imported by Navy Arms.

Price: **$590.00**

NAVY ARMS 1861 SPRINGFIELD RIFLE

Caliber: 58. **Barrel:** 40" **Weight:** 10 lbs., 4 oz. **Length:** 56" overall. **Stock:** Walnut. **Sights:** Blade front, military leaf rear. **Features:** Steel barrel, lock and all furniture have polished bright finish. Has 1855-style hammer. Imported by Navy Arms.

Price: **$590.00**

BLACKPOWDER MUSKETS & RIFLES

New England Firearms Huntsman

Peifer TS-93

Remington Model 700 ML

NAVY ARMS 1863 SPRINGFIELD

Caliber: 58, uses .575 Minie. **Barrel:** 40", rifled. **Weight:** 9-1/2 lbs. **Length:** 56" overall. **Stock:** Walnut. **Sights:** Open rear adjustable for elevation. **Features:** Full-size, three-band musket. Polished bright metal, including lock. From Navy Arms.

Price: Finished rifle **$590.00**

NEW ENGLAND FIREARMS HUNTSMAN

Caliber: 50. **Barrel:** 24". **Weight:** 6-1/2 lbs. **Length:** 40". **Stock:** Walnut-finished American hardwood with pistol grip. **Sights:** Adjustable fiber optics open sights, tapped for scope base. **Features:** Break-open action, color case-hardened frame, black oxide barrel. Made in U.S.A. by New England Firearms.

Price: **$188.00**

New England Firearms Stainless Huntsman

Similar to Huntsman, but with matte nickel finish receiver and stainless bbl. Introduced 2003. From New England Firearms.

Price: **81.00**

PACIFIC RIFLE MODEL 1837 ZEPHYR

Caliber: 62. **Barrel:** 30", tapered octagon. **Weight:** 7-3/4 lbs. **Length:** NA. **Stock:** Oil-finished fancy walnut. **Sights:** German silver blade front, semi-buckhorn rear. Options available. **Features:** Improved underhammer action. First production rifle to offer Forsyth rifle, with narrow lands and shallow rifling with 1:144" pitch for high-velocity round balls. Metal finish is slow rust brown with nitre blue accents. Optional sights, finishes and integral muzzle brake available. Introduced 1995. Made in U.S. by Pacific Rifle Co.

Price: From **$995.00**

Pacific Rifle Big Bore African Rifles

Similar to the 1837 Zephyr except in 72-caliber and 8-bore. The 72-caliber is available in standard form with 28" barrel, or as the African with flat buttplate, checkered upgraded wood; weight is 9 lbs. The 8-bore African has dual-cap ignition, 24" barrel, weighs 12 lbs., checkered English walnut, engraving, gold inlays. Introduced 1998. Made in U.S. by Pacific Rifle Co.

Price: 72-caliber, from. **$1,150.00**

Price: 8-bore from. **$2,500.00**

PEIFER MODEL TS-93 RIFLE

Caliber: 45, 50. **Barrel:** 24" Douglas premium; 1:20" twist in 45; 1:28" in 50. **Weight:** 7 lbs. **Length:** 43-1/4" overall. **Stock:** Bell & Carlson solid composite, with recoil pad, swivel studs. **Sights:** Williams bead front on ramp, fully adjustable open rear. Drilled and tapped for Weaver scope mounts with dovetail for rear peep. **Features:** In-line ignition uses #209 shotshell primer; extremely fast lock time; fully enclosed breech; adjustable trigger; automatic safety; removable primer holder. Blue or stainless. Made in U.S. by Peifer Rifle Co. Introduced 1996.

Price: Blue, black stock. **$730.00**

Price: Blue, wood or camouflage composite stock, or stainless with black composite stock **$803.00**

Price: Stainless, wood or camouflage composite stock **$876.00**

PRAIRIE RIVER ARMS PRA BULLPUP RIFLE

Caliber: 50. **Barrel:** 28"; 1:28" twist. **Weight:** 7-1/2 lbs. **Length:** 31-1/2" overall. **Stock:** Hardwood or black all-weather. **Sights:** Blade front, open adjustable rear. **Features:** Bullpup design thumbhole stock. Patented internal percussion ignition system. Left-hand model available. Dovetailed for scope mount. Introduced 1995. Made in U.S. by Prairie River Arms, Ltd.

Price: 4140 alloy barrel, hardwood stock **$199.00**

Price: All Weather stock, alloy barrel **$205.00**

REMINGTON MODEL 700 ML, MLS RIFLES

Caliber: 50, new 45 (MLS Magnum).**Barrel:** 24"; 1:28" twist, 26" (Magnum). **Weight:** 7-3/4 lbs. **Length:** 42"-44-1/2" overall. **Stock:** Black fiberglass-reinforced synthetic with checkered grip and forend; magnum-style buttpad. **Sights:** Ramped bead front, open fully adjustable rear. Drilled and tapped for scope mounts. **Features:** Uses the Remington 700 bolt action, stock design, safety and trigger mechanisms; removable stainelss steel breech plug, No. 11 nipple; solid aluminum ramrod. Comes with cleaning tools and accessories; 3-way ignition.

Price: ML, blued, 50-caliber only **$415.00**

Price: MLS, stainless, 45 Magnum, 50-caliber **$533.00**

Price: MLS, stainless, Mossy Oak Break-Up camo stock. **$569.00**

RICHMOND, C.S., 1863 MUSKET

Caliber: 58. **Barrel:** 40". **Weight:** 11 lbs. **Length:** 56-1/4" overall. **Stock:** European walnut with oil finish. **Sights:** Blade front, adjustable folding leaf rear. **Features:** Reproduction of the three-band Civil War musket. Sling swivels attached to trigger guard and middle barrel band. Lockplate marked "1863" and "C.S. Richmond." All metal left in white. Brass buttplate and forend cap. Imported by Euroarms of America, Navy Arms, and Dixie Gun Works.

Price: Euroarms **$530.00**

Price: Dixie Gun Works **$675.00**

RUGER 77/50 IN-LINE PERCUSSION RIFLE

Caliber: 50. **Barrel:** 22"; 1:28" twist. **Weight:** 6-1/2 lbs. **Length:** 41-1/2" overall. **Stock:** Birch with rubber buttpad and swivel studs. **Sights:** Gold bead front, folding leaf rear. Comes with Ruger scope mounts. **Features:** Shares design features with Ruger 77/22 rifle. Stainless steel bolt and nipple/breech plug; uses #11 caps, three-position safety, blued steel ramrod. Introduced 1997. Made in U.S. by Sturm, Ruger & Co.

Price: 77/50RS **$434.00**

Price: 77/50RSO Officer's (straight-grip checkered walnut stock, blued) **$555.00**

Price: K77/50RSBBZ (stainless steel, black laminated stock) . . . **$601.00**

Price: K77/50RSP All-Weather (stainless steel, synthetic stock) . **$580.00**

Price: 77/50 RSP (blued, synthetic stock) **$434.00**

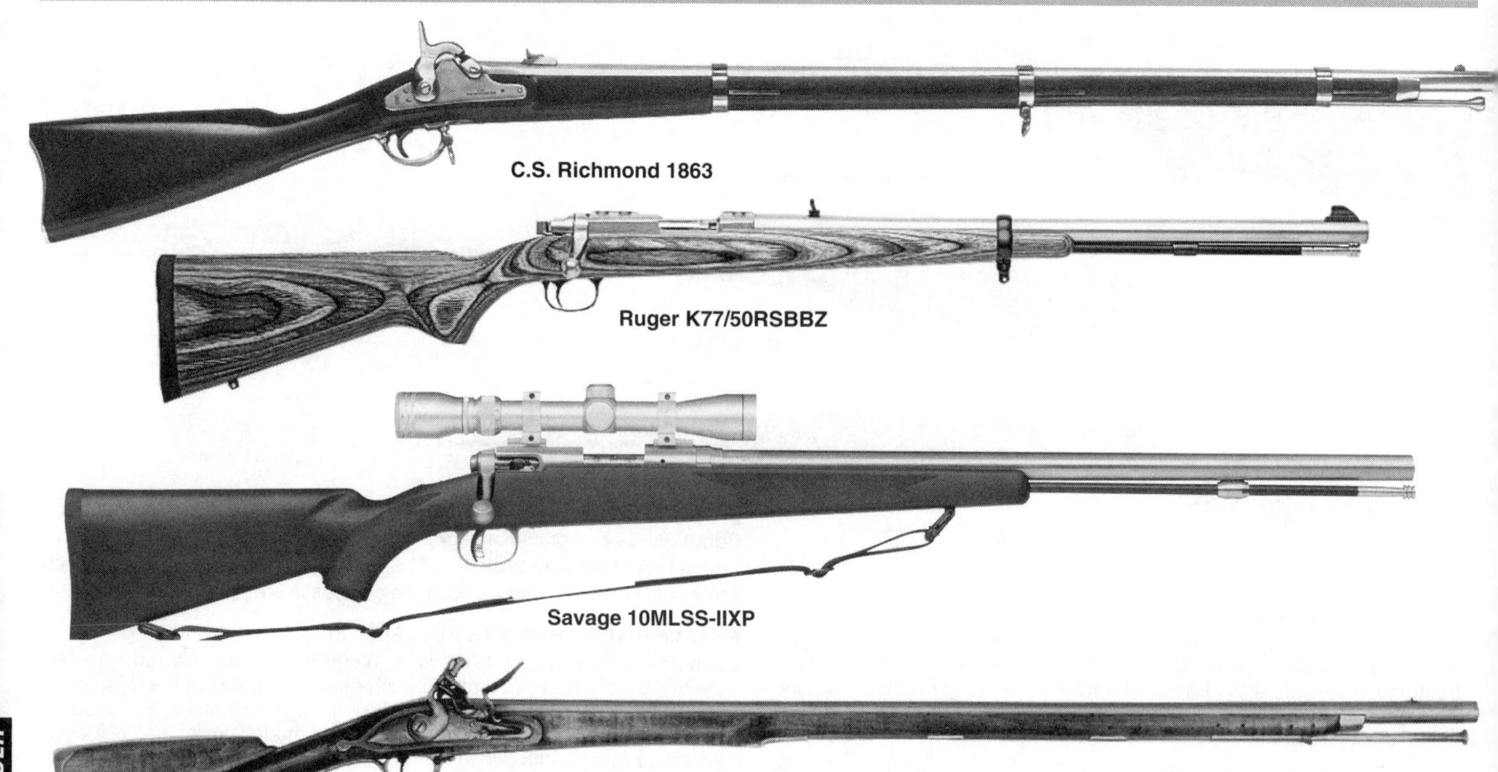

C.S. Richmond 1863

Ruger K77/50RSBBZ

Savage 10MLSS-IIXP

Second Model Brown Bess

SAVAGE MODEL 10ML MUZZLELOADER RIFLE SERIES

Caliber: 50. **Barrel:** 24", 1:24 twist, blue or stainless. **Weight:** 7.75 lbs. **Stock:** Black synthetic, Realtree Hardwood JD Camo, brown laminate. **Sights:** Green adjustable rear, Red FiberOptic front. **Features:** XP Models scoped, no sights, smokeless powder, "easy to prime", #209 primer ignition. Removeable breech plut and vent liner.

Price: Model 10ML-II **$512.00**
Price: Model 10ML-II Camo **$549.00**
Price: Model 10MLSS-II Camo **$607.00**
Price: Model 10MLBSS-II **$645.00**
Price: Model 10ML-IIXP **$549.00**
Price: Model 10MLSS-IIXP **$607.00**

SECOND MODEL BROWN BESS MUSKET

Caliber: 75, uses .735" round ball. **Barrel:** 42", smoothbore. **Weight:** 9-1/2 lbs. **Length:** 59" overall. **Stock:** Walnut (Navy); walnut-stained hardwood (Dixie). **Sights:** Fixed. **Features:** Polished barrel and lock with brass trigger guard and buttplate. Bayonet and scabbard available. From Navy Arms, Dixie Gun Works, Cabela's.

Price: Finished .... **$475.00 to $850.00**
Price: Kit (Dixie Gun Works, Navy Arms) .... **$575.00 to $625.00**
Price: Carbine (Navy Arms) **$835.00**
Price: Dixie Gun Works **$765.00**

THOMPSON/CENTER FIRE STORM RIFLE

Caliber: 50. **Barrel:** 26"; 1:28" twist. **Weight:** 7 lbs. **Length:** 41-3/4" overall. **Stock:** Black synthetic with rubber recoil pad, swivel studs. **Sights:** Click-adjustable steel rear and ramp-style front, both with fiber optic inserts. **Features:** Side hammer lock is the first designed for up to three 50-grain Pyrodex pellets; patented Pyrodex Pyramid breech directs ignition fire 360 degrees around base of pellet. Quick Load Accurizor Muzzle System; aluminum ramrod. Flintlock only. Introduced 2000. Made in U.S. by Thomson/Center Arms.

Price: Blue finish, flintlock model with 1:48" twist for round balls, conicals **$423.00**
Price: SST, flintlock **$473.00**

THOMPSON/CENTER ENCORE 209x50 MAGNUM

Caliber: 50. **Barrel:** 26"; interchangeable with centerfire calibers. **Weight:** 7 lbs. **Length:** 40-1/2" overall. **Stock:** American walnut butt and forend, or black composite. **Sights:** Tru-Glo Fiber Optic front, Tru-Glo Fiber Optic rear. **Features:** Blue or stainless steel. Uses the stock, frame and forend of the Encore centerfire pistol; break-open design using trigger guard spur; stainless steel universal breech plug; uses #209 shotshell primers. Introduced 1998. Made in U.S. by Thompson/Center Arms.

Price: Stainless wtih camo stock **$765.00**
Price: Blue, walnut stock and forend **$665.00**
Price: Blue, composite stock and forend **634.00**
Price: Stainless, composite stock and forend **$706.00**
Price: All camo Realtree Hardwoods **$723.00**

THOMPSON/CENTER BLACK DIAMOND RIFLE XR

Caliber: 50. **Barrel:** 26" with QLA; 1:28" twist. **Weight:** 6 lbs., 9 oz. **Length:** 41-1/2" overall. **Stock:** Black Rynite with moulded-in checkering and grip cap, or walnut. **Sights:** Tru-Glo Fiber Optic ramp-style front, Tru-Glo Fiber Optic open rear. **Features:** In-line ignition system for musket cap, No. 11 cap, or 209 shotshell primer; removable universal breech plug; stain-less steel construction. Selected models available in .45 cal. Made in U.S. by Thompson/Center Arms.

Price: With composite stock, blued **$337.00**
Price: With walnut stock **$412.00**

THOMPSON/CENTER HAWKEN RIFLE

Caliber: 50. **Barrel:** 28" octagon, hooked breech. **Stock:** Ameri-can walnut. **Sights:** Blade front, rear adjustable for windage and elevation. **Features:** Solid brass furniture, double-set triggers, button rifled barrel, coil-type mainspring. From Thompson/Center Arms.

Price: Percussion model **$545.00**
Price: Flintlock model **$570.00**

TRADITIONS BUCKSKINNER CARBINE

Caliber: 50. **Barrel:** 21"; 15/16" flats, half octagon, half round; 1:20" or 1:66" twist. **Weight:** 6 lbs. **Length:** 37" overall. **Stock:** Beech or black laminated. **Sights:** Beaded blade front, fiber optic open rear click adjustable for windage and elevation or fiber optics. **Features:** Uses V-type mainspring, single trigger. Non-glare hardware; sling swivels. From Traditions.

Price: Flintlock **$249.00**
Price: Flintlock, laminated stock **$303.00**

T/C Hawken

Traditions Deerhunter

Traditions Pursuit

TRADITIONS DEERHUNTER RIFLE SERIES

Caliber: 32, 50 or 54. **Barrel:** 24", octagonal; 15/16" flats; 1:48" or 1:66" twist. **Weight:** 6 lbs. **Length:** 40" overall. **Stock:** Stained hardwood or All-Weather composite with rubber buttpad, sling swivels. **Sights:** Lite Optic blade front, adjustable rear fiber optics. **Features:** Flint or percussion with color case-hardened lock. Hooked breech, oversized trigger guard, blackened furniture, PVC ramrod. All-Weather has composite stock and C-Nickel barrel. Drilled and tapped for scope mounting. Imported by Traditions, Inc.

Price: Percussion, 50; blued barrel; 1:48" twist. **$189.00**
Price: Percussion, 54 . . . . **$169.00**
Price: Flintlock, 50 caliber only; 1:48" twist. **$179.00**
Price: Flintlock, All-Weather, 50-cal. **$239.00**
Price: Redi-Pak, 50 cal. flintlock **$219.00**
Price: Flintlock, left-handed hardwood, 50 cal. **$209.00**
Price: Percussion, All-Weather, 50 or 54 cal. **$179.00**
Price: Percussion, 32 cal. **$199.00**

Traditions Panther Sidelock Rifle

Similar to Deerhunter rifle, but has blade front and windage-adjustable-only rear sight, black composite stock.

Price: **$129.00**

TRADITIONS PURSUIT BREAK-OPEN MUZZLELOADER

Caliber: 45, 54 and 12 gauge. **Barrel:** 28", tapered, fluted; blued, stainless or Hardwoods Green camo. **Stock:** Synthetic black or Hardwoods Green. **Sights:** Steel fiber optic rear, bead front. **Weight:** 8 1/4 lbs. **Overall length:** 44". Introduced 2004 by Traditions, Inc.

Price: Steel, blued, 45 or 50 cal., synthetic stock **$279.00**
Price: Steel, nickel, 45 or 50 cal., synthetic stock. **$309.00**
Price: Steel, nickel w/Hardwoods Green stock **$359.00**
Price: Matte blued; 12 ga., synthetic stock **$369.00**
Price: Matte blued; 12 ga. w/Hardwoods Green stock **$439.00**
Price: Lightweight model, blued, synthetic stock **$199.00**
Price: Lightweight model, blued, Mossy Oak Breakup Camo stock. **$239.00**
Price: Lightweight model, nickel, Mossy Oak Breakup Camo stock. **$279.00**

TRADITIONS EVOLUTION BOLT-ACTION BLACKPOWDER RIFLE

Caliber: 50 percussion. **Barrel:** 26", fluted with porting. **Sights:** Steel fiber optic. **Weight:** 7 lbs. to 7 1/4 lbs. **Overall length:** 45". **Features:** Bolt-action, cocking indicator, thumb safety, aluminum ramrod, sling studs. Wide variety of stocks and metal finishes. Introduced 2004 by Traditions, Inc.

Price: Synthetic stock **$279.00**
Price: Walnut X-wood **$349.00**
Price: Brown laminated. **$469.00**
Price: Advantage Timber **$369.00**
Price: Synthetic, Tru-Glo sights. **$249.00**
Price: Mossy Oak Breakup. **$279.00**
Price: Nickel finish **$309.00**
Price: Beech/nickel, Advantage/nickel, Advantage 54 cal. **$289.00**

TRADITIONS PA PELLET FLINTLOCK

Caliber: 50. **Barrel:** 26", blued, nickel. **Weight:** 7 lbs. **Stock:** Hardwood, synthetic and synthetic break-up. **Sights:** FO. **Features:** Removeable breech plug, left-hand model with hardwood stock. 1:48" twist.

Price: Hardwood, blued **$259.00**
Price: Hardwood left, blued. **$269.00**

TRADITIONS HAWKEN WOODSMAN RIFLE

Caliber: 50 and 54. **Barrel:** 28"; 15/16" flats. **Weight:** 7 lbs., 11 oz. **Length:** 44-1/2" overall. **Stock:** Walnut-stained hardwood. **Sights:** Beaded blade front, hunting-style open rear adjustable for windage and elevation. **Features:** Percussion only. Brass patchbox and furniture. Double triggers. From Traditions.

Price: 50 or 54 . . . . **$299.00**
Price: 50-cal., left-hand. **$279.00**
Price: 50-caliber, flintlock **$299.00**

TRADITIONS KENTUCKY RIFLE

Caliber: 50. **Barrel:** 33-1/2"; 7/8" flats; 1:66" twist. **Weight:** 7 lbs. **Length:** 49" overall. **Stock:** Beech; inletted toe plate. **Sights:** Blade front, fixed rear. **Features:** Full-length, two-piece stock; brass furniture; color case-hardened lock. From Traditions.

Price: **$279.00**

TRADITIONS PENNSYLVANIA RIFLE

Caliber: 50. **Barrel:** 40-1/4"; 7/8" flats; 1:66" twist, octagon. **Weight:** 9 lbs. **Length:** 57-1/2" overall. **Stock:** Walnut. **Sights:** Blade front, adjustable rear. **Features:** Brass patchbox and ornamentation. Double-set triggers. From Traditions.

Price: Flintlock **$529.00**
Price: Percussion **$519.00**

TRADITIONS SHENANDOAH RIFLE

Caliber: 36, 50. **Barrel:** 33-1/2" octagon; 1:66" twist. **Weight:** 7 lbs., 3 oz. **Length:** 49-1/2" overall. **Stock:** Walnut. **Sights:** Blade front, buckhorn rear. **Features:** V-type mainspring; double-set trigger; solid brass buttplate, patchbox, nosecap, thimbles, trigger guard. Introduced 1996. From Traditions.

Price: Flintlock **$419.00**
Price: Percussion **$399.00**
Price: 36 cal. Flintlock, 1:48"twist **$419.00**
Price: 36 cal. Percussion, 1:48"twist **$449.00**

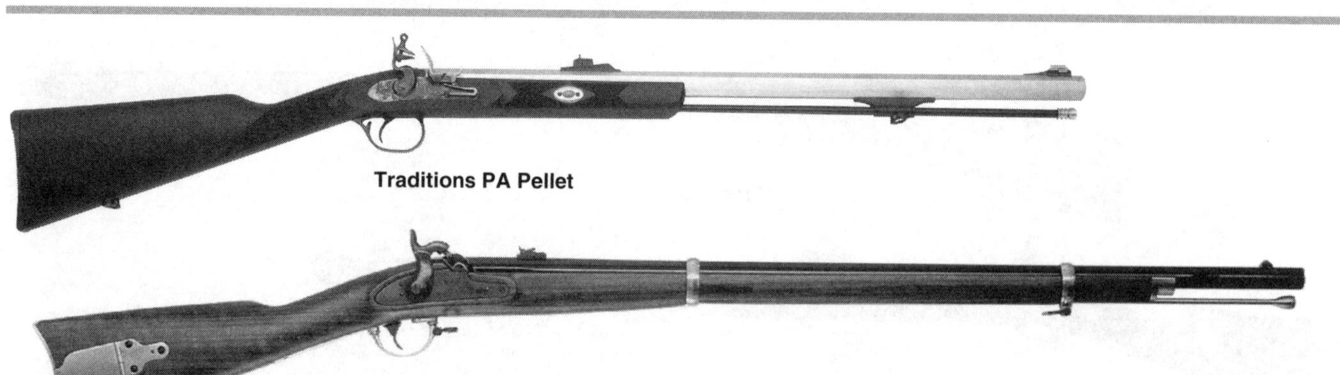

Traditions PA Pellet

Zouave Percussion

TRADITIONS TENNESSEE RIFLE

Caliber: 50. **Barrel:** 24", octagon; 15/16" flats; 1:66" twist. **Weight:** 6 lbs. **Length:** 40-1/2" overall. **Stock:** Stained beech. **Sights:** Blade front, fixed rear. **Features:** One-piece stock has inletted brass furniture, cheekpiece; double-set trigger; V-type mainspring. Flint or percussion. From Traditions.

Price: Flintlock **$339.00**

Price: Percussion **$329.00**

TRADITIONS TRACKER 209 IN-LINE RIFLES

Caliber: 45, 50. **Barrel:** 22" blued or C-Nickel finish; 1:28" twist, 50 cal. 1:20" 45 cal. **Weight:** 6 lbs., 4 oz. **Length:** 41" overall. **Stock:** Black, Advantage Timber® composite, synthetic. **Sights:** Lite Optic blade front, adjustable rear. **Features:** Thumb safety; adjustable trigger; rubber butt pad and sling swivel studs; takes 150 grains of Pyrodex pellets; one-piece breech system takes 209 shotshell primers. Drilled and tapped for scope. From Traditions.

Price: (Black composite or synthetic stock, 22" blued barrel) **$129.00**

Price: (Black composite or synthetic stock, 22" C-Nickel barrel) . **$139.00**

Price: (Advantage Timber® stock, 22" C-Nickel barrel) **$189.00**

Price: (Redi-Pak, black stock and blued barrel, powder flask, capper, ball starter, other accessories) **$179.00**

Price: (Redi-Pak, synthetic stock and blued barrel, with scope) . . **$229.00**

WHITE MODEL 97 WHITETAIL HUNTER RIFLE

Caliber: 45, 50. **Barrel:** 22", 1:20 twist (45 cal.); 1:24 twist (50 cal.). **Weight:** 7.7 lbs. **Length:** 40" overall. **Stock:** Black laminated or black composite. **Sights:** Marble TruGlo fully adjustable, steel rear with white diamond, red bead front with high-visibility inserts. **Features:** In-line ignition with FlashFire one-piece nipple and breech plug that uses standard or magnum No. 11 caps, fully adjustable trigger, double safety system, aluminum ramrod; drilled and tapped for scope. Hard gun case. Made in U.S.A. by Split Fire Sporting Goods.

Price: Whitetail w/laminated or composite stock. **$499.95**

Price: Adventurer w/26" stainless barrel & thumbhole stock) . . . **$699.95**

Price: Odyssey w/24" carbon fiber wrapped barrel & thumbhole stock **$1,299.95**

WHITE MODEL 98 ELITE HUNTER RIFLE

Caliber: 45, 50. **Barrel:** 24", 1:24" twist (50 cal). **Weight:** 8.6 lbs. **Length:** 43-1/2" overall. **Stock:** Black laminate wtih swivel studs. **Sights:** TruGlo fully adjustable, steel rear with white diamond, red bead front with high-visibility inserts. **Features:** In-line ignition with FlashFire one-piece nipple and breech plug that uses standard or magnum No. 11 caps, fully adjustable trigger, double safety system, aluminum ramrod, drilled and taped for scope, hard gun case. Made in U.S.A. by Split Fire Sporting Goods.

Price: Composite or laminate wood stock. **$499.95**

White Thunderbolt Rifle

Similar to the Elite Hunter but is designed to handle 209 shotgun primers only. Has 26" stainless steel barrel, weighs 9.3 lbs. and is 45-1/2" long. Composite or laminate stock.

Price: **$599.95**

WHITE MODEL 2000 BLACKTAIL HUNTER RIFLE

Caliber: 50. **Barrel:** 22", 1:24" twist (50 cal.). **Weight:** 7.6 lbs. **Length:** 39-7/8" overall. **Stock:** Black laminated with swivel studs with laser engraved deer or elk scene. **Sights:** TruGlo fully adjustable, steel rear with white diamond, red bead front with high-visibility inserts. **Features:** Teflon finished barrel, in-line ignition with FlashFire one-piece nipple and breech plug that uses standard or magnum No. 11 caps, fully adjustable trigger, double safety system, aluminum ramrod, drilled and tapped for scope. Hard gun case. Made in U.S.A. by Split Fire Sporting Goods.

Price: Laminate wood stock, w/laser engraved game scene **$599.95**

WHITE LIGHTNING II RIFLE

Caliber: 45 and 50 percussion. **Barrel:** 24", 1:32 twist. **Sights:** Adj. rear. **Stock:** Black polymer. **Weight:** 6 lbs. **Features:** In-line, 209 primer ignition system, blued or nickel-plated bbl., adj. trigger, Delrin ramrod, sling studs, recoil pad.

Price: **$299.95**

WHITE ALPHA RIFLE

Caliber: 45, 50 percussion. **Barrel:** 27" tapered, stainless. **Sights:** Marble TruGlo rear, fiber optic front. **Stock:** Laminated. **Features:** Lever action rotating block, hammerless; adj. trigger, positive safety. All stainless metal, including trigger.

Price: **$449.95**

WINCHESTER APEX SWING-ACTION MAGNUM RIFLE

Caliber: 45, 50. **Barrel:** 28". **Stock:** Mossy Oak Camo, Black Fleck. **Sights:** Adj. Fiber Optic. **Weight:** 7 lbs., 12 oz. **Overall length:** 42". **Features:** Monte Carlo cheekpiece, swing-action design, external hammer.

Price: Mossy Oak/stainless **$489.95**

Price: Black Fleck/stainless **$449.95**

Price: Full Mossy Oak. **$469.95**

Price: Black Fleck/blued **$364.95**

WINCHESTER X-150 BOLT-ACTION MAGNUM RIFLE

Caliber: 45, 50. **Barrel:** 26". **Stock:** Hardwoods or Timber HD, Black Fleck, Breakup. **Weight:** 8 lbs., 3 oz. **Sights:** Ajd. Fiber Optic. **Features:** No. 209 shotgun primer ignition, stainless steel bolt, stainless fluted bbl.

Price: Mossy Oak, Timber, Hardwoods/stainless **$349.95**

Price: Black Fleck/stainless **$299.95**

Price: Mossy Oak, Timber, Hardwoods/blued. **$279.95**

Price: Black Fleck/blued **$229.95**

ZOUAVE PERCUSSION RIFLE

Caliber: 58, 59. **Barrel:** 32-1/2". **Weight:** 9-1/2 lbs. **Length:** 48-1/2" overall. **Stock:** Walnut finish, brass patchbox and buttplate. **Sights:** Fixed front, rear adjustable for elevation. **Features:** Color case-hardened lockplate, blued barrel. From Navy Arms, Dixie Gun Works, E.M.F., Cabela's, Euroarms of America.

Price: . . . . **$415.00 to $515.00**

BLACKPOWDER SHOTGUNS

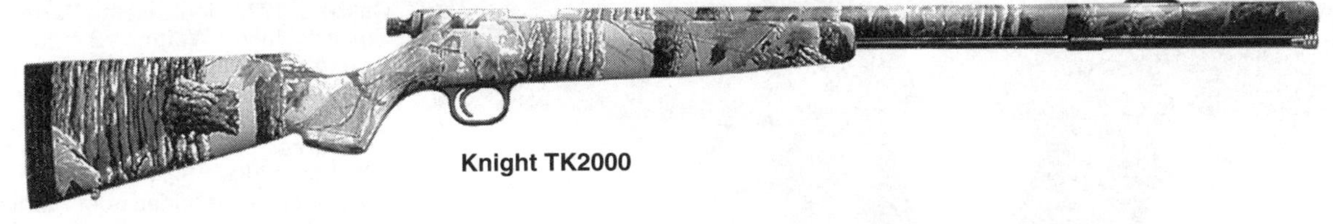

Knight TK2000

CABELA'S BLACKPOWDER SHOTGUNS

Gauge: 10, 12, 20. **Barrel:** 10-ga., 30"; 12-ga., 28-1/2" (Extra-Full, Mod., Imp. Cyl. choke tubes); 20-ga., 27-1/2" (Imp. Cyl. & Mod. fixed chokes). **Weight:** 6-1/2 to 7 lbs. **Length:** 45" overall (28-1/2" barrel). **Stock:** American walnut with checkered grip; 12- and 20-gauge have straight stock, 10-gauge has pistol grip. **Features:** Blued barrels, engraved, color case-hardened locks and hammers, brass ramrod tip. From Cabela's.

Price: 10-gauge **$799.99**
Price: 12-gauge **$649.99**
Price: 20-gauge **$659.99**

DIXIE MAGNUM PERCUSSION SHOTGUN

Gauge: 10, 12, 20. **Barrel:** 30" (Imp. Cyl. & Mod.) in 10-gauge; 28" in 12-gauge. **Weight:** 6-1/4 lbs. **Length:** 45" overall. **Stock:** Hand-checkered walnut, 14" pull. **Features:** Double triggers; light hand engraving; case-hardened locks in 12-gauge, polished steel in 10-gauge; sling swivels. From Dixie Gun Works.

Price: Upland **$650.00**
Price: 12-ga. kit. **$445.00**
Price: 20-ga. **$525.00**
Price: 10-ga. **$575.00**
Price: 10-ga. kit. **$445.00**

KNIGHT TK2000 MUZZLELOADING SHOTGUN (209)

Gauge: 12. **Barrel:** 26", extra-full choke tube. **Weight:** 7 lbs., 9 oz. **Length:** 45" overall. **Stock:** Synthetic black or Advantage Timber HD; recoil pad; swivel studs. **Sights:** Fully adjustable rear, blade front with fiber optics. **Features:** Receiver drilled and tapped for scope mount; in-line ignition; adjustable trigger; removable breech plug; double safety system; imp. cyl. choke tube available. Made in U.S. by Knight Rifles.

Price: . . . . **$349.95 to $399.95**

KNIGHT VERSATILE TK2002

Gauge: 12. **Stock:** Black composite, blued, Advantage Timber HD finish. Both with sling swivel studs installed. **Sights:** Adjustable metallic TruGol fiber optic. **Features:** Full plastic jacket ignition system, screw-on choke tubes, load without removing choke tubes, incredible shot density with jug-chocked barrel design. Improved cylinder and modified choke tubes available.

Price: . . . . **$349.95 to $399.95**

NAVY ARMS STEEL SHOT MAGNUM SHOTGUN

Gauge: 10. **Barrel:** 28" (Cyl. & Cyl.). **Weight:** 7 lbs., 9 oz. **Length:** 45-1/2" overall. **Stock:** Walnut, with cheekpiece. **Features:** Designed specifically for steel shot. Engraved, polished locks; sling swivels; blued barrels. Imported by Navy Arms.

Price: **$605.00**

NAVY ARMS T&T SHOTGUN

Gauge: 12. **Barrel:** 28" (Full & Full). **Weight:** 7-1/2 lbs. **Stock:** Walnut. **Sights:** Bead front. **Features:** Color case-hardened locks, double triggers, blued steel furniture. From Navy Arms.

Price: **$580.00**

WHITE TOMINATOR SHOTGUN

Caliber: 12. **Barrel:** 25" blue, straight, tapered stainless steel. **Weight:** NA. **Length:** NA. **Stock:** Black laminated or black wood. **Sights:** Drilled and tapped for easy scope mounting. **Features:** Internchangeable choke tubes. Custom vent-rib with high visibility front bead. Double safeties. Fully adjustable custom trigger. Recoil pad and sling swivel studs.

Price: **$349.95**

AIRGUNS — HANDGUNS

Gamo PT-80

Daisy 662X

AIR FORCE CONDOR

Caliber: 177, 22. **Barrel:** 24" rifled. **Weight:** 6.5 lbs. **Overall length:** 38.75". **Sights:** None, integral mount supplied. **Features:** 600-1,300 fps. 3,000 psi fill pressure. Automatic safety. Air tank volume: 490cc.

Price: 22 w/refill clamp and open sights **$649.95**
Price: 177 w/refill clamp and open sights **$599.95**
Price: Gun only (22 or 177) **$549.95**

AIR FORCE TALON SS

Caliber: 177, 22. **Barrel:** 12". **Weight:** 5.25 lbs. **Overall length:** 32.75". **Sights:** None, integral mount supplied. **Features:** 400-1000 fps. Fill pressure: 3000 psi. Air tank volume: 490cc.

Price: 22 w/refill clamp, open sights **$559.95**
Price: 177 w/refill clamp, open sights **$559.95**
Price: Gun only (22 or 177) **$459.95**

AIR FORCE TALON

Same as Talon SS but 32.6" long, weight: 5.5 lbs.

Price: 22 w/refill clamp, open sights **$539.95**
Price: 177 w/refill clamp, open sights **$539.95**
Price: Gun only **$439.95**

ARS HUNTING MASTER AR6 PISTOL

Caliber: 22 (177 +20 special order). **Barrel:** 12" rifled. **Weight:** 3 lbs. **Length:** 18.25 overall. **Stock:** Indonesian walnut with checkered grip. **Sights:** Adjustable rear, blade front. **Features:** 6 shot repeater with rotary magazine, single or double action, receiver grooved for scope, hammer block and trigger block safeties.

Price: .... **NA**

BEEMAN P1 MAGNUM AIR PISTOL

Caliber: 177, 5mm, single shot. **Barrel:** 8.4". **Weight:** 2.5 lbs. **Length:** 11" overall. **Power:** Top lever cocking; spring-piston. **Stocks:** Checkered walnut. **Sights:** Blade front, square notch rear with click micrometer adjustments for windage and elevation. Grooved for scope mounting. **Features:** Dual power for 177 and 20-cal.: low setting gives 350-400 fps; high setting 500-600 fps. Rearward expanding mainspring simulates firearm recoil. All Colt 45 auto grips fit gun. Dry-firing feature for practice. Optional wooden shoulder stock. Imported by Beeman.

Price: 177, 5mm **$440.00**

BEEMAN P3 AIR PISTOL

Caliber: 177 pellet, single shot. **Barrel:** N/A. **Weight:** 1.7 lbs. **Length:** 9.6" overall. **Power:** Single-stroke pneumatic; overlever barrel cocking. **Grips:** Reinforced polymer. **Sights:** Adjustable rear, blade front. **Features:** Velocity 410 fps. Polymer frame; automatic safety; two-stage trigger; built-in muzzle brake.

Price: **$180.00**
Price: Combo **$285.00**

BEEMAN/FEINWERKBAU 103 PISTOL

Caliber: 177, single shot. **Barrel:** 10.1", 12-groove rifling. **Weight:** 2.5 lbs. **Length:** 16.5" overall. **Power:** Single-stroke pneumatic, underlever cocking. **Stocks:** Stippled walnut with adjustable palm shelf. **Sights:** Blade front, open rear adjustable for windage and elevation. Notch size adjustable for width. Interchangeable front blades. **Features:** Velocity 510 fps. Fully adjustable trigger. Cocking effort of 2 lbs. Imported by Beeman.

Price: Right-hand **$1,236.00**
Price: Left-hand **$1,275.00**

BEEMAN/FWB P34 MATCH AIR PISTOL

Caliber: 177, single shot. **Barrel:** 10-5/16", with muzzlebrake. **Weight:** 2.4 lbs. **Length:** 16.5" overall. **Power:** Pre-charged pneumatic. **Stocks:** Stippled walnut; adjustable match type. **Sights:** Undercut blade front, fully adjustable match rear. **Features:** Velocity to 525 fps; up to 200 shots per CO2 cartridge. Fully adjustable trigger; built-in muzzlebrake. Imported from Germany by Beeman.

Price: Right-hand **$1,395.00**
Price: Left-hand **$1,440.00**

BEEMAN HW70A AIR PISTOL

Caliber: 177, single shot. **Barrel:** 6-1/4", rifled. **Weight:** 38 oz. **Length:** 12-3/4" overall. **Power:** Spring, barrel cocking. **Stocks:** Plastic, with thumbrest. **Sights:** Hooded post front, square notch rear adjustable for windage and elevation. Comes with scope base. **Features:** Adjustable trigger, 31-lb. cocking effort, 440 fps MV; automatic barrel safety. Imported by Beeman.

Price: **$190.00**

BEEMAN/WEBLEY TEMPEST AIR PISTOL

Caliber: 177, 22, single shot. **Barrel:** 6-7/8". **Weight:** 32 oz. **Length:** 8.9" overall. **Power:** Spring-piston, break barrel. **Stocks:** Checkered black plastic with thumbrest. **Sights:** Blade front, adjustable rear. **Features:** Velocity to 500 fps (177), 400 fps (22). Aluminum frame; black epoxy finish; manual safety. Imported from England by Beeman.

Price: **$205.00**

Beeman/Webley Hurricane Air Pistol

Similar to the Tempest except has extended frame in the rear for a click-adjustable rear sight; hooded front sight; comes with scope mount. Imported from England by Beeman.

Price: **$255.00**

BENJAMIN SHERIDAN CO2 PELLET PISTOLS

Caliber: 177, 20, 22, single shot. **Barrel:** 6-3/8", rifled brass. **Weight:** 29 oz. **Length:** 9.8" overall. **Power:** 12-gram CO2 cylinder. **Stocks:** Walnut. **Sights:** High ramp front, fully adjustable notch rear. **Features:** Velocity to 500 fps. Turnbolt action with cross-bolt safety. Gives about 40 shots per CO2 cylinder. Black or nickel finish. Made in U.S. by Benjamin Sheridan Co.

Price: Black finish, EB17 (177), EB20 (20), ... **$190.00**

BENJAMIN SHERIDAN PNEUMATIC PELLET PISTOLS

Caliber: 177, 20, 22, single shot. **Barrel:** 9-3/8", rifled brass. **Weight:** 38 oz. **Length:**13-1/8" overall. **Power:** Underlever pnuematic, hand pumped. **Stocks:** Walnut stocks and pump handle. **Sights:** High ramp front, fully adjustable notch rear. **Features:** Velocity to 525 fps (variable). Bolt action with cross-bolt safety. Choice of black or nickel finish. Made in U.S. by Benjamin Sheridan Co.

Price: Black finish, HB17 (177), HB20 (20) **$190.00**
Price: HB22 (22) **$199.00**

BRNO TAU-7 CO2 MATCH PISTOL

Caliber: 177. **Barrel:** 10.24". **Weight:** 37 oz. **Length:** 15.75" overall. **Power:** 12.5-gram CO2 cartridge. **Stocks:** Stippled hardwood with adjustable palm rest. **Sights:** Blade front, open fully adjustable rear. **Features:** Comes with extra seals and counterweight. Blue finish. Imported by Great Lakes Airguns.

Price: **$299.50**

CROSMAN BLACK VENOM PISTOL

Caliber: 177 pellets, BB, 17-shot magazine; darts, single shot. **Barrel:** 4.75" smooth-bore. **Weight:** 16 oz. **Length:** 10.8" overall. **Power:** Spring. **Sights:** Blade front, adjustable rear. **Features:** Velocity to 270 fps (BBs), 250 fps (pellets). Spring-fed magazine; cross-bolt safety. Made in U.S.A. by Crosman Corp.

Price: **$60.00**

CROSMAN MODEL 1377 AIR PISTOLS

Caliber: 177, single shot. **Barrel:** 8", rifled steel. **Weight:** 39 oz. **Length:** 13-5/8". **Power:** Hand pumped. **Sights:** Blade front, rear adjustable for windage and elevation. **Features:** Bolt action moulded plastic grip, hand size pump forearm. Cross-bolt safety. From Crosman.

Price: **$60.00**

CROSMAN AUTO AIR II PISTOL

Caliber: BB, 17-shot magazine, 177 pellet, single shot. **Barrel:** 8-5/8" steel, smooth-bore. **Weight:** 13 oz. **Length:** 10-3/4" overall. **Power:** CO2 Powerlet. **Sights:** Blade front, adjustable rear; highlighted system. **Features:** Velocity to 480 fps (BBs), 430 fps (pellets). Semi-automatic action with BBs, single shot with pellets. Black. From Crosman.

Price: AAIIB **$38.00**
Price: AAIIBRD . . . . . . **NA**

CROSMAN MODEL 1008 REPEAT AIR

Caliber: 177, 8-shot pellet clip. **Barrel:** 4.25", rifled steel. **Weight:** 17 oz. **Length:** 8.625" overall. **Power:** CO2 Powerlet. **Stocks:** Checkered black plastic. **Sights:** Post front, adjustable rear. **Features:** Velocity about 430 fps. Break-open barrel for easy loading; single or double semi-automatic action; two 8-shot clips included. Optional carrying case available. From Crosman.

Price: **$60.00**
Price: Model 1008SB (silver and black finish), about **$60.00**

CROSMAN SEMI AUTO AIR PISTOL

Caliber: 177, pellets. **Barrel:** Rifled steel. **Weight:** 40 oz. **Length:** 8.63". **Power:** CO2. **Sights:** Blade front, rear adjustable. **Features:** Velocity up to 430 fps. Synthetic grips, zinc alloy frame. From Crosman.

Price: C40. . . . . . **NA**

CROSMAN MAGNUM AIR PISTOLS

Caliber: 177, pellets. **Barrel:** Rifled steel. **Weight:** 27 oz. **Length:** 9.38". **Power:** CO2. **Sights:** Blade front, rear adjustable. **Features:** Single/double action accepts sights and scopes with standard 3/8" dovetail mount. Model 3576W features 6" barrel for increased accuracy. From Crosman.

Price: 3574W . . . . . . **NA**
Price: 3576W . . . . . . **NA**

DAISY/POWERLINE MODEL 15XT AIR PISTOL

Caliber: 177 BB, 15-shot built-in magazine. **Barrel:** NA. **Weight:** NA. **Length:** 7.21". **Power:** CO2. **Stocks:** NA. **Sights:** NA. **Features:** Velocity 425 fps. Made in the U.S.A. by Daisy Mfg. Co.

Price: **$36.95**
New! Price: 15XK Shooting Kit **$59.95**

DAISY/POWERLINE 717 PELLET PISTOL

Caliber: 177, single shot. **Barrel:** 9.61". **Weight:** 2.25 lbs. **Length:** 13-1/2" overall. **Stocks:** Moulded wood-grain plastic, with thumbrest. **Sights:** Blade and ramp front, micro-adjustable notch rear. **Features:** Single pump pneumatic pistol. Rifled steel barrel. Cross-bolt trigger block. Muzzle velocity 385 fps. From Daisy Mfg. Co.

Price: **$71.95**

DAISY/POWERLINE 1270 CO2 AIR PISTOL

Caliber: BB, 60-shot magazine. **Barrel:** Smoothbore steel. **Weight:** 17 oz. **Length:** 11.1" overall. **Power:** CO2 pump action. **Stocks:** Moulded black polymer. **Sights:** Blade on ramp front, adjustable rear. **Features:** Velocity to 420 fps. Crossbolt trigger block safety; plated finish. Made in U.S. by Daisy Mfg. Co.

Price: **$39.95**

DAISY/POWERLINE 93 AIR PISTOL

Caliber: BB, 15-shot magazine. **Barrel:** Smoothbore steel. **Weight:** 1.1 lbs. **Length:** 7.9" overall. **Power:** CO2 powered semi-auto. **Stocks:** Moulded brown checkered. **Sights:** Blade on ramp front, fixed open rear. **Features:** Velocity to 400 fps. Manual trigger block. Made in U.S.A. by Daisy Mfg. Co.

Price: **$48.95**

Daisy/Powerline 693 Air Pistol

Similar to Model 93 except has velocity to 235 fps.

Price: **$52.95**

DAISY/POWERLINE 622X PELLET PISTOL

Caliber: 22 (5.5mm), 6-shot. **Barrel:** Rifled steel. **Weight:** 1.3 lbs. **Length:** 8.5". **Power:** CO2. **Grips:** Molded black checkered. **Sights:** Fiber optic front, fixed open rear. **Features:** Velocity 225 fps. Rotary hammer block. Made by Daisy Mfg. Co.

Price: **$69.95**

DAISY/POWERLINE 45 AIR PISTOL

Caliber: BB, 13-shot magazine. **Barrel:** Rifled steel. **Weight:** 1.25 lbs. **Length:** 8.5" overall. **Power:** CO2 powered semi-auto. **Stocks:** Moulded black checkered. **Sights:** TRUGLO® fiber optic front, fixed open rear. **Features:** Velocity to 224 fps. Manual trigger block. Made in U.S.A. by Daisy Mfg. Co.

Price: **$54.95**

EAA MP651K

Daisy/Powerline 645 Air Pistol

Similar to Model 93 except has distinctive black and nickel-finish.

Price: **$59.95**

EAA/BAIKAL IZH-M46 TARGET AIR PISTOL

Caliber: 177, single shot. **Barrel:** 10". **Weight:** 2.4 lbs. **Length:** 16.8" overall. **Power:** Underlever single-stroke pneumatic. **Grips:** Adjustable wooden target. **Sights:** Micrometer fully adjustable rear, blade front. **Features:** Velocity about 420 fps. Hammer-forged, rifled barrel. Imported from Russia by European American Armory.

Price: **$349.00**

GAMO AUTO 45

Caliber: .177 (12-shot). **Barrel:** 4.25". **Weight:** 1.10 lbs. **Length:** 7.50". **Power:** CO2 cartridge, semi-automatic, 410 fps. **Stock:** Plastic. **Sights:** Rear sights adjusts for windage. **Features:** Looking very much like a Glock cartridge pistol, it fires in the double-action model and has a manual safety. Imported from Spain by Gamo.

Price: **$99.95**

GAMO COMPACT TARGET PISTOL

Caliber: .177, single shot. **Barrel:** 8.26". **Weight:** 1.95 lbs. **Length:** 12.60. **Power:** Spring-piston, 400 fps. **Stock:** Walnut. **Sights:** Micro-adjustable. **Features:** Rifle steel barrel, adjustable match trigger, recoil and vibration-free. Imported from Spain by Gamo.

Price: **$229.95**

GAMO P-23, P-23 LASER PISTOL

Caliber: .177 (12-shot). **Barrel:** 4.25". **Weight:** 1 lb. **Length:** 7.5". **Power:** CO2 cartridge, semi-automatic, 410 fps. **Stock:** Plastic. **Sights:** NA. **Features:** Style somewhat like a Walther PPK cartridge pistol, an optional laser allows fast sight acquisition. Imported from Spain by Gamo.

Price: . . . . . . **$89.95**, (with laser) **$129.95**

GAMO PT-80, PT-80 LASER PISTOL

Caliber: .177 (8-shot). **Barrel:** 4.25". **Weight:** 1.2 lbs. **Length:** 7.2". **Power:** CO2 cartridge, semi-automatic, 410 fps. **Stock:** Plastic. **Sights:** 3-dot. **Features:** Available with optional laser sight and with optional walnut grips. Imported from Spain by Gamo.

Price: . . . . . . **$108.95,** (with laser) **$129.95**, (with walnut grip) **$119.95**

"GAT" AIR PISTOL

Caliber: 177, single shot. **Barrel:** 7-1/2" cocked, 9-1/2" extended. **Weight:** 22 oz. **Power:** Spring-piston. **Stocks:** Cast checkered metal. **Sights:** Fixed. **Features:** Shoots pellets, corks or darts. Matte black finish. Imported from England by Stone Enterprises, Inc.

Price: **$24.95**

HAMMERLI AP40 AIR PISTOL

Caliber: 177. **Barrel:** 10". **Stocks:** Adjustable orthopaedic. **Sights:** Fully adjustable micrometer. **Features:** Sleek, light, well balanced and accurate. Imported from Switzerland by Nygord Precision Products.

Price: **$1,195.00**

MARKSMAN 2000 REPEATER PISTOL

Caliber: 177, 18-shot BB repeater. **Barrel:** 2-1/2", smoothbore. **Weight:** 24 oz. **Length:** 8-1/4" overall. **Power:** Spring. **Features:** Velocity to 200 fps. Thumb safety. Uses BBs, darts, bolts or pellets. Repeats with BBs only. From Marksman Products.

Price: **$27.00**

MARKSMAN 2005 LASERHAWK SPECIAL EDITION AIR PISTOL

Caliber: 177, 24-shot magazine. **Barrel:** 3.8", smoothbore. **Weight:** 22 oz. **Length:** 10.3" overall. **Power:** Spring-air. **Stocks:** Checkered. **Sights:** Fixed fiber optic front sight. **Features:** Velocity to 300 fps with Hyper-Velocity pellets. Square trigger guard with skeletonized trigger; extended barrel for greater velocity and accuracy. Shoots BBs, pellets, darts or bolts. Made in the U.S. From Marksman Products.

Price: **$32.00**

MORINI 162E MATCH AIR PISTOL

Caliber: 177, single shot. **Barrel:** 9.4". **Weight:** 32 oz. **Length:** 16.1" overall. **Power:** Scuba air. **Stocks:** Adjustable match type. **Sights:** Interchangeable blade front, fully adjustable match-type rear. **Features:** Power mechanism shuts down when pressure drops to a preset level. Adjustable electronic trigger. Imported from Switzerland by Nygord Precision Products.

Price: **$825.00**
Price: 162 EI **$1,075.00**

MORINI SAM K-11 AIR PISTOL

Caliber: 177. **Barrel:** 10". **Weight:** 38 oz. **Stocks:** Fully adjustable. **Sights:** Fully adjustable. **Features:** Improved trigger, more angle adjustment on grip. Sophisticated counter balance system. Deluxe aluminum case, two cylinders and manometer. Imported from Switzerland by Nygord Precision Products.

Price: **$975.00**

PARDINI K58 MATCH AIR PISTOL

Caliber: 177, single shot. **Barrel:** 9". **Weight:** 37.7 oz. **Length:** 15.5" overall. **Power:** Precharged compressed air; single-stroke cocking. **Stocks:** Adjustable match type; stippled walnut. **Sights:** Interchangeable post front, fully adjustable match rear. **Features:** Fully adjustable trigger. Short version K-2 available. Imported from Italy by Nygord Precision Products.

Price: **$795.00**
Price: K2S model, precharged air pistol, introduced in 1998 . . . . **$945.00**

RWS 9B/9N AIR PISTOLS

Caliber: 177, single shot. **Grips:** Plastic with thumbrest. **Sights:** Adjustable. **Features:** Spring-piston powered; 550 fps. Black or nickel finish. Imported from Spain by Dynamit Nobel-RWS.

Price: 9B **$169.00**
Price: 9N **$185.00**

STEYR LP 5CP MATCH AIR PISTOL

Caliber: 177, 5-shot magazine. **Weight:** 40.7 oz. **Length:** 15.2" overall. **Power:** Precharged air cylinder. **Stocks:** Adjustable match type. **Sights:** Interchangeable blade front, fully adjustable match rear. **Features:** Adjustable sight radius; fully adjustable trigger. Barrel compensator. One-shot magazine available. Imported from Austria by Nygord Precision Products.

Price: **$1,100.00**

STEYR LP10P MATCH PISTOL

Caliber: 177, single shot. **Barrel:** 9". **Weight:** 38.7 oz. **Length:** 15.3" overall. **Power:** Scuba air. **Stocks:** Fully adjustable Morini match, palm shelf, stippled walnut. **Sights:** Interchangeable blade in 4mm, 4.5mm or 5mm widths, fully adjustable open rear, interchangeable 3.5mm or 4mm leaves. **Features:** Velocity about 500 fps. Adjustable trigger, adjustable sight radius from 12.4" to 13.2". With compensator. New "absorber" eliminates recoil. Imported from Austria by Nygord Precision Products.

Price: **$1,175.00**

TECH FORCE SS2 OLYMPIC COMPETITION AIR PISTOL

Caliber: 177 pellet, single shot. **Barrel:** 7.4". **Weight:** 2.8 lbs. **Length:** 16.5" overall. **Power:** Spring piston, sidelever. **Grips:** Hardwood. **Sights:** Extended adjustable rear, blade front accepts inserts. **Features:** Velocity 520 fps. Recoilless design; adjustments allow duplication of a firearm's feel. Match-grade, adjustable trigger; includes carrying case. Imported from China by Compasseco Inc.

Price: **$295.00**

TECH FORCE 35 AIR PISTOL

Caliber: 177 pellet, single shot. **Weight:** 2.86 lbs. **Length:** 14.9" overall. **Power:** Spring piston, underlever. **Grips:** Hardwood. **Sights:** Micrometer adjustable rear, blade front. **Features:** Velocity 400 fps. Grooved for scope mount; trigger safety. Imported from China by Compasseco Inc.

Price: **$39.95**

Tech Force 8 Air Pistol

Similar to Tech Force 35, but with break-barrel action, ambidextrous polymer grips.

Price: **$59.95**

Tech Force S2-1 Air Pistol

Similar to Tech Force 8, more basic grips and sights for plinking.

Price: **$29.95**

WALTHER LP300 MATCH PISTOL

Caliber: 177. **Barrel:** 236mm. **Weight:** 1.018g. **Length:** NA. **Power:** NA. **Stocks:** NA. **Sights:** Integrated front with three different widths, adjustable rear. **Features:** Adjustable grip and trigger. Imported from Germany by Nygord Precision Products.

Price: **$1,095.00**

Crosman 2289G

Daisy 7840 Buckmaster

AIR FORCE TALON AIR RIFLE

Caliber: .177, .22, single-shot. **Barrel:** 18". **Weight:** 5.5 lbs. **Length:** 32.6". **Power:** Precharged pneumatic. **Sights:** Intended for scope use, fiber optic open sights optional. **Features:** Lothar Walther match barrel, adjustable power levels from 400-1000 FPS, operates on high pressure air from scuba tank or hand pump. Wide variety of accessories easily attach to multiple dovetail mounting rails. Manufactured in the U.S.A. by AirForce Airguns.

Price: **$439.95**

AIR FORCE TALON SS AIR RIFLE

Caliber: 177, 22, single-shot. **Barrel:** 12". **Weight:** 5.25 lbs. **Length:** 32.75". **Power:** Precharged pneumatic. **Sights:** Intended for scope use, fiber optic open sights optional. **Features:** Lothar Walther match barrel, adjustable power levels from 400-1000 FPS. Chamber in front of barrel strips away air turbulence, protects muzzle and reduces firing report. Operates on high pressure air from scuba tank or hand pump. Wide variety of accessories easily attach to multiple dovetail mounting rails. Manufactured in the U.S.A. by AirForce Airguns.

Price: **$439.95**

AIRROW MODEL A-8SRB STEALTH AIR GUN

Caliber: 177, 22, 25, 9-shot. **Barrel:** 20"; rifled. **Weight:** 6 lbs. **Length:** 34" overall. **Power:** CO2 or compressed air; variable power. **Stock:** Telescoping CAR-15-type. **Sights:** Variable 3.5-10x scope. **Features:** Velocity 1100 fps in all calibers. Pneumatic air trigger. All aircraft aluminum and stainless steel construction. Mil-spec materials and finishes. From Swivel Machine Works, Inc.

Price: About **$2,299.00**

AIRROW MODEL A-8S1P STEALTH AIR GUN

Caliber: #2512 16" arrow. **Barrel:** 16". **Weight:** 4.4 lbs. **Length:** 30.1" overall. **Power:** CO2 or compressed air; variable power. **Stock:** Telescoping CAR-15-type. **Sights:** Scope rings only. 7 oz. rechargeable cylinder and valve. **Features:** Velocity to 650 fps with 260-grain arrow. Pneumatic air trigger. Broadhead guard. All aircraft aluminum and stainless steel construction. Mil-spec materials and finishes. A-8S Models perform to 2,000 PSIG above or below water levels. Waterproof case. From Swivel Machine Works, Inc.

Price: **$1,699.00**

ARS HUNTING MASTER AR6 AIR RIFLE

Caliber: 22, 6-shot repeater. **Barrel:** 25-1/2". **Weight:** 7 lbs. **Length:** 41-1/4" overall. **Power:** Pre-compressed air from 3000 psi diving tank. **Stock:** Indonesian walnut with checkered grip; rubber buttpad. **Sights:** Blade front, adjustable peep rear. **Features:** Velocity over 1000 fps with 32-grain pellet. Receiver grooved for scope mounting. Has 6-shot rotary magazine. Imported by Air Rifle Specialists.

Price: **$580.00**

ARS/CAREER 707 AIR RIFLE

Caliber: 22, 6-shot repeater. **Barrel:** 23". **Weight:** 7.75 lbs. **Length:** 40.5" overall. **Power:** Pre-compressed air; variable power. **Stock:** Indonesian walnut with checkered grip, gloss finish. **Sights:** Hooded post front with interchangeable inserts, fully adjustable diopter rear. **Features:** Velocity to 1000 fps. Lever-action with straight feed magazine; pressure gauge in lower front air reservoir; scope mounting rail included. Imported from the Philippines by Air Rifle Specialists.

Price: **$580.00**

ANSCHUTZ 2002 MATCH AIR RIFLE

Caliber: 177, single shot. **Barrel:** 25.2". **Weight:** 10.4 lbs. **Length:** 44.5" overall. **Stock:** European walnut, blonde hardwood or colored laminated hardwood; stippled grip and forend. Also available with flat-forend walnut stock for benchrest shooting and aluminum. **Sights:** Optional sight set #6834. **Features:** Muzzle velocity 575 fps. Balance, weight match the 1907 ISU smallbore rifle. Uses #5021 match trigger. Recoil and vibration free. Fully adjustable cheekpiece and buttplate; accessory rail under forend. Available in Pneumatic and Compressed Air versions. Imported from Germany by Gunsmithing, Inc., Accuracy International, Champion's Choice.

Price: Right-hand, blonde hardwood stock, with sights **$1,275.00**
Price: Right-hand, walnut stock **$1,275.00**
Price: Right-hand, color laminate stock **$1,300.00**
Price: Right-hand, aluminum stock, butt plate **$1,495.00**
Price: Left-hand, color laminate stock **$1,595.00**
Price: Model 2002D-RT Running Target, right-hand, no sights . **$1,248.90**
Price: #6834 Sight Set **$227.10**

BEEMAN CROW MAGNUM AIR RIFLE

Caliber: 20, 22, 25, single shot. **Barrel:** 16"; 10-groove rifling. **Weight:** 8.5 lbs. **Length:** 46" overall. **Power:** Gas-spring; adjustable power to 32 foot pounds muzzle energy. Barrel-cocking. **Stock:** Classic-style hardwood; hand checkered. **Sights:** For scope use only; built-in base and 1" rings included. **Features:** Adjustable two-stage trigger. Automatic safety. Available in 22-caliber on special order. Imported by Beeman.

Price: **$1,290.00**

BEEMAN KODIAK AIR RIFLE

Caliber: 25, single shot. **Barrel:** 17.6". **Weight:** 9 lbs. **Length:** 45.6" overall. **Power:** Spring-piston, barrel cocking. **Stock:** Stained hardwood. **Sights:** Blade front, open fully adjustable rear. **Features:** Velocity to 820 fps. Up to 30 foot pounds muzzle energy. Imported by Beeman.

Price: **$670.00**

BEEMAN MAKO MKII AIR RIFLE

Caliber: 177, 22 single shot. **Barrel:** 20", with compensator. **Weight:** 5.5 to 7.8 lbs. **Length:** 39" overall. **Power:** Pre-charged pneumatic. **Stock:** Stained beech; Monte Carlo cheekpiece; checkered grip. **Sights:** None furnished. **Features:** Velocity to 930 fps. Gives over 50 shots per charge. Manual safety; brass trigger blade; vented rubber butt pad. Requires scuba tank for air. Imported from England by Beeman.

Price: **$999.00**

BEEMAN R1 AIR RIFLE

Caliber: 177, 20 or 22, single shot. **Barrel:** 19.6", 12-groove rifling. **Weight:** 8.5 lbs. **Length:** 45.2" overall. **Power:** Spring-piston, barrel cocking. **Stock:** Walnut-stained beech; cut-checkered pistol grip; Monte Carlo comb and cheekpiece; rubber buttpad. **Sights:** Tunnel front with interchangeable inserts, open rear click-adjustable for windage and elevation. Grooved for scope mounting. **Features:** Velocity of 940-1000 fps (177), 860 fps (20), 800 fps (22). Non-drying nylon piston and breech seals. Adjustable metal trigger. Milled steel safety. Right- or left-hand stock. Adjustable cheekpiece and buttplate at extra cost. Custom and Super Laser versions available. Imported by Beeman.

Price: Right-hand, 177, 20, 22 . . . . **$605.00**
Price: Left-hand, 177, 20, 22 . . . . **$680.00**

BEEMAN R7 AIR RIFLE

Caliber: 177, 20, single shot. **Barrel:** 17". **Weight:** 6.1 lbs. **Length:** 40.2" overall. **Power:** Spring piston. **Stock:** Stained beech. **Sights:** Hooded front, fully adjustable micrometer click open rear. **Features:** Velocity to 700 fps (177), 620 fps (20). Receiver grooved for scope mounting; double-jointed cocking lever; fully adjustable trigger; checkered grip. Imported by Beeman.

Price: **$330.00**

AIRGUNS—LONG GUNS

BEEMAN R9 AIR RIFLE

Caliber: 177, 20, single shot. **Barrel:** NA. **Weight:** 7.3 lbs. **Length:** 43" overall. **Power:** Spring-piston, barrel cocking. **Stock:** Stained hardwood. **Sights:** Tunnel post front, fully adjustable open rear. **Features:** Velocity to 1000 fps (177), 800 fps (20). Adjustable Rekord trigger; automatic safety; receiver dovetailed for scope mounting. Imported from Germany by Beeman Precision Airguns.

Price: **$360.00**

Beeman R9 Deluxe Air Rifle

Same as R9 except has extended forend stock, checkered pistol grip, grip cap, carved Monte Carlo cheekpiece. Globe front sight with inserts. Imported by Beeman.

Price: **$440.00**

BEEMAN R11 MKII AIR RIFLE

Caliber: 177, single shot. **Barrel:** 19.6". **Weight:** 8.6 lbs. **Length:** 43.5" overall. **Power:** Spring-piston, barrel cocking. **Stock:** Walnut-stained beech; adjustable buttplate and cheekpiece. **Sights:** None furnished. Has dovetail for scope mounting. **Features:** Velocity 910-940 fps. All-steel barrel sleeve. Imported by Beeman.

Price: **$620.00**

BEEMAN SUPER 12 AIR RIFLE

Caliber: 22, 25, 12-shot magazine. **Barrel:** 19", 12-groove rifling. **Weight:** 7.8 lbs. **Length:** 41.7" overall. **Power:** Pre-charged pneumatic; external air reservoir. **Stock:** European walnut. **Sights:** None furnished; drilled and tapped for scope mounting; scope mount included. **Features:** Velocity to 850 fps (25-caliber). Adjustable power setting gives 30-70 shots per 400 cc air bottle. Requires scuba tank for air. Imported by Beeman.

Price: **$1,940.00**

BEEMAN RX-2 GAS-SPRING MAGNUM AIR RIFLE

Caliber: 177, 20, 22, 25, single shot. **Barrel:** 19.6", 12-groove rifling. **Weight:** 8.8 lbs. **Power:** Gas-spring piston air; single stroke barrel cocking. **Stock:** Walnut-finished hardwood, hand checkered, with cheekpiece. Adjustable cheekpiece and buttplate. **Sights:** Tunnel front, click-adjustable rear. **Features:** Velocity adjustable to about 1200 fps. Uses special sealed chamber of air as a mainspring. Gas-spring cannot take a set. Imported by Beeman.

Price: 177, 20, 22 or 25 regular, right-hand **$670.00**

Price: 177, 20, 22, 25, left-hand **$670.00**

BEEMAN R1 CARBINE

Caliber: 177, 20, 22, 25, single shot. **Barrel:** 16.1". **Weight:** 8.6 lbs. **Length:** 41.7" overall. **Power:** Spring-piston, barrel cocking. **Stock:** Stained beech; Monte Carlo comb and checkpiece; cut checkered pistol grip; rubber buttpad. **Sights:** Tunnel front with interchangeable inserts, open adjustable rear; receiver grooved for scope mounting. **Features:** Velocity up to 1000 fps (177). Non-drying nylon piston and breech seals. Adjustable metal trigger. Machined steel receiver end cap and safety. Right- or left-hand stock. Imported by Beeman.

Price: 177, 20, 22, 25, right-hand **$605.00**

Price: As above, left-hand............................. **$680.00**

BEEMAN/FEINWERKBAU 603 AIR RIFLE

Caliber: 177, single shot. **Barrel:** 16.6". **Weight:** 10.8 lbs. **Length:** 43" overall. **Power:** Single stroke pneumatic. **Stock:** Special laminated hardwoods and hard rubber for stability. Multi-colored stock also available. **Sights:** Tunnel front with interchangeable inserts, click micrometer match aperture rear. **Features:** Velocity to 570 fps. Recoilless action; double supported barrel; special, short rifled area frees pellet form barrel faster so shooter's motion has minimum effect on accuracy. Fully adjustable match trigger with separately adjustable trigger and trigger slack weight. Trigger and sights blocked when loading latch is open. Imported by Beeman.

Price: Right-hand **$1,625.00**

Price: Left-hand **$1,775.00**

Price: Junior **$1,500.00**

BEEMAN/FEINWERKBAU 300-S AND 300 JUNIOR MINI-MATCH

Caliber: 177, single shot. **Barrel:** 17-1/8". **Weight:** 8.8 lbs. **Length:** 40" overall. **Power:** Spring-piston, single stroke sidelever cocking. **Stock:** Walnut. Stippled grip, adjustable buttplate. Scaled-down for youthful or slightly built shooters. **Sights:** Globe front with interchangeable inserts, micro. adjustable rear. Front and rear sights move as a single unit. **Features:** Recoilless, vibration free. Grooved for scope mounts. Steel piston ring. Cocking effort about 9-1/2 lbs. Barrel sleeve optional. Left-hand model available. Imported by Beeman.

Price: Right-hand **$1,680.00**

Price: Left-hand **$1,825.00**

BEEMAN/FEINWERKBAU P70 AND P70 JUNIOR AIR RIFLE

Caliber: 177, single shot. **Barrel:** 16.6". **Weight:** 10.6 lbs. **Length:** 42.6" overall. **Power:** Precharged pneumatic. **Stock:** Laminated hardwoods and hard rubber for stability. Multi-colored stock also available. **Sights:** Tunnel front with interchangeable inserts, click micormeter match aperture rear. **Features:** Velocity to 570 fps. Recoilless action; double supported barrel; special short rifled area frees pellet from barrel faster so shooter's motion has minimum effect on accuracy. Fully adjustable match trigger with separately adjustable trigger and trigger slack weight. Trigger and sights blocked when loading latch is open. Imported by Beeman.

Price: P70, pre-charged, right-hand **$1,600.00**

Price: P70, pre-charged, left-hand **$1,690.00**

Price: P70, pre-charged, Junior **$1,600.00**

Price: P70, pre-charged, right-hand, multi **$1,465.00**

BEEMAN/HW 97 AIR RIFLE

Caliber: 177, 20, single shot. **Barrel:** 17.75". **Weight:** 9.2 lbs. **Length:** 44.1" overall. **Power:** Spring-piston, underlever cocking. **Stock:** Walnut-stained beech; rubber buttpad. **Sights:** None. Receiver grooved for scope mounting. **Features:** Velocity 830 fps (177). Fixed barrel with fully opening, direct loading breech. Adjustable trigger. Imported by Beeman Precision Airguns.

Price: Right-hand only **$605.00**

BENJAMIN SHERIDAN PNEUMATIC (PUMP-UP) AIR RIFLES

Caliber: 177 or 22, single shot. **Barrel:** 19-3/8", rifled brass. **Weight:** 5-1/2 lbs. **Length:** 36-1/4" overall. **Power:** Underlever pneumatic, hand pumped. **Stock:** American walnut stock and forend. **Sights:** High ramp front, fully adjustable notch rear. **Features:** Variable velocity to 800 fps. Bolt action with ambidextrous push-pull safety. Black or nickel finish. Made in the U.S. by Benjamin Sheridan Co.

Price: Black finish, Model 397 (177), Model 392 (22) **$224.00**

Price: Nickel finish, Model S397 (177), Model S392 (22) **$245.00**

BRNO TAU-200 AIR RIFLE

Caliber: 177, single shot. **Barrel:** 19", rifled. **Weight:** 7-1/2 lbs. **Length:** 42" overall. **Power:** 6-oz. CO2 cartridge. **Stock:** Wood match style with adjustable comb and buttplate. **Sights:** Globe front with interchangeable inserts, fully adjustable open rear. **Features:** Adjustable trigger. Comes with extra seals, large CO2 bottle, counterweight. Imported by Great Lakes Airguns. Available in Standard Universal, Deluxe Universal, International and Target Sporter versions.

Price: Standard Universal (ambidex. stock with buttstock extender, adj. cheekpiece).. .... **$349.50**

Price: Deluxe Universal (as above but with micro-adj. aperture sight) **$449.50**

Price: International (like Deluxe Universal but with right- or left-hand stock) **$454.50**

Price: Target Sporter (like Std. Universal but with 4X scope, no sights) **$412.50**

BSA MAGNUM SUPERSTAR™ MK2 MAGNUM AIR RIFLE, CARBINE

Caliber: 177, 22, 25, single shot. **Barrel:** 18-1/2". **Weight:** 8 lbs., 8 oz. **Length:** 43" overall. **Power:** Spring-air, underlever cocking. **Stock:** Oil-finished hardwood; Monte Carlo with cheekpiece, checkered at grip; recoil pad. **Sights:** Ramp front, micrometer adjustable rear. Maxi-Grip scope rail. **Features:** Velocity 950 fps (177), 750 fps (22), 600 fps (25). Patented rotating breech design. Maxi-Grip scope rail protects optics from recoil; automatic anti-beartrap plus manual safety. Imported from U.K. by Precision Sales International, Inc.

Price: **$349.95**

Price: MKII Carbine (14" barrel, 39-1/2" overall).............. **$349.95**

AIRGUNS—LONG GUNS

BSA MAGNUM SUPERSPORT™ AIR RIFLE

Caliber: 177, 22, 25, single shot. **Barrel:** 18-1/2". **Weight:** 6 lbs., 8 oz. **Length:** 41" overall. **Power:** Spring-air, barrel cocking. **Stock:** Oil-finished hardwood; Monte Carlo with cheekpiece, recoil pad. **Sights:** Ramp front, micrometer adjustable rear. Maxi-Grip scope rail. **Features:** Velocity 950 fps (177), 750 fps (22), 600 fps (25). Patented Maxi-Grip scope rail protects optics from recoil; automatic anti-beartrap plus manual tang safety. Muzzle brake standard. Imported for U.K. by Precision Sales International, Inc.

Price: **$194.95**
Price: Carbine, 14" barrel, muzzle brake **$214.95**

BSA MAGNUM GOLDSTAR MAGNUM AIR RIFLE

Caliber: 177, 22, 10-shot repeater. **Barrel:** 17-1/2". **Weight:** 8 lbs., 8 oz. **Length:** 42.5" overall. **Power:** Spring-air, underlever cocking. **Stock:** Oil-finished hardwood; Monte Carlo with cheekpiece, checkered at grip; recoil pad. **Sights:** Ramp front, micrometer adjustable rear; comes with Maxi-Grip scope rail. **Features:** Velocity 950 fps (177), 750 fps (22). Patented 10-shot indexing magazine; Maxi-Grip scope rail protects optics from recoil; automatic anti-beartrap plus manual safety; muzzlebrake standard. Imported from U.K. by Precision Sales International, Inc.

Price: **$499.95**

BSA MAGNUM SUPERTEN AIR RIFLE

Caliber: 177, 22 10-shot repeater. **Barrel:** 17-1/2". **Weight:** 7 lbs., 8 oz. **Length:** 37" overall. **Power:** Precharged pneumatic via buddy bottle. **Stock:** Oil-finished hardwood; Monte Carlo with cheekpiece, cut checkering at grip; adjustable recoil pad. **Sights:** No sights; intended for scope use. **Features:** Velocity 1000+ fps (177), 1000+ fps (22). Patented 10-shot indexing magazine, bolt-action loading. Left-hand version also available. Imported from U.K. by Precision Sales International, Inc.

Price: **$599.95**

BSA METEOR MK6 AIR RIFLE

Caliber: 177, 22, single shot. **Barrel:** 18-1/2". **Weight:** 6 lbs. **Length:** 41" overall. **Power:** Spring-air, barrel cocking. **Stock:** Oil-finished hardwood. **Sights:** Ramp front, micrometer adjustable rear. **Features:** Velocity 650 fps (177), 500 fps (22). Automatic anti-beartrap; manual tang safety. Receiver grooved for scope mounting. Imported from U.K. by Precision Sales International, Inc.

Price: Rifle **$144.95**
Price: Carbine **$164.95**

CROSMAN MODEL 66 POWERMASTER

Caliber: 177 (single shot pellet) or BB, 200-shot reservoir. **Barrel:** 20", rifled steel. **Weight:** 3 lbs. **Length:** 38-1/2" overall. **Power:** Pneumatic; hand pumped. **Stock:** Wood-grained ABS plastic; checkered pistol grip and forend. **Sights:** Fiber optic front, fully adjustable open rear. **Features:** Velocity about 645 fps. Bolt action, cross-bolt safety. From Crosman.

Price: Model 66BX **$60.00**
Price: Model 664X (as above, with 4x scope). **$70.00**
Price: Model 664SB (as above with silver and black finish), about. **$75.00**

CROSMAN REMINGTON GENESIS AIR RIFLE

Caliber: 177 **Barrel:** Break-action. **Sights:** Fiber optic front, adj. rear. Dovetailed for scope. **Stock:** Synthetic, thumbhole pistol grip. **Weight:** 6.5 lbs. **Overall length:** 43".

Price: **$249.99**
Price: W 3-9x40 scope **$279.99**

CROSMAN MODEL 760 PUMPMASTER

Caliber: 177 pellets (single shot) or BB (200-shot reservoir). **Barrel:** 19-1/2", rifled steel. **Weight:** 2 lbs., 12 oz. **Length:** 33.5" overall. **Power:** Pneumatic, hand pumped. **Stock:** Walnut-finished ABS plastic stock and forend. **Features:** Velocity to 590 fps (BBs, 10 pumps). Short stroke, power determined by number of strokes. Fiber optic front sight and adjustable rear sight. Cross-bolt safety. From Crosman.

Price: Model 760B **$40.00**
Price: Model 764SB (silver and black finish), about **$55.00**
Price: Model 760SK . . . . **NA**
Price: Model 760BRO . . . . **NA**

CROSMAN MODEL 1077 REPEAT AIR RIFLE

Caliber: 177 pellets, 12-shot clip. **Barrel:** 20.3", rifled steel. **Weight:** 3 lbs., 11 oz. **Length:** 38.8" overall. **Power:** CO2 Powerlet. **Stock:** Textured synthetic or hardwood. **Sights:** Blade front, fully adjustable rear. **Features:** Velocity 590 fps. Removable 12-shot clip. True semi-automatic action. From Crosman.

Price: **$75.00**
Price: 1077W (walnut stock) **$110.00**

CROSMAN 2260 AIR RIFLE

Caliber: 22, single shot. **Barrel:** 24". **Weight:** 4 lbs., 12 oz. **Length:** 39.75" overall. **Power:** CO2 Powerlet. **Stock:** Hardwood. **Sights:** Blade front, adjustable rear open or peep. **Features:** About 600 fps. Made in U.S. by Crosman Corp.

Price: . . . . **NA**

CROSMAN MODEL 2100 CLASSIC AIR RIFLE

Caliber: 177 pellets (single shot), or BB (200-shot BB reservoir). **Barrel:** 21", rifled. **Weight:** 4 lbs., 13 oz. **Length:** 39-3/4" overall. **Power:** Pump-up, pneumatic. **Stock:** Wood-grained checkered ABS plastic. **Features:** Three pumps give about 450 fps, 10 pumps about 755 fps (BBs). Cross-bolt safety; concealed reservoir holds over 200 BBs. From Crosman.

Price: Model 2100B **$75.00**

CROSMAN MODEL 2200 MAGNUM AIR RIFLE

Caliber: 22, single shot. **Barrel:** 19", rifled steel. **Weight:** 4 lbs., 12 oz. **Length:** 39" overall. **Stock:** Full-size, wood-grained ABS plastic with checkered grip and forend or American walnut. **Sights:** Ramp front, open step-adjustable rear. **Features:** Variable pump power; three pumps give 395 fps, six pumps 530 fps, 10 pumps 595 fps (average). Full-size adult air rifle. Has white line spacers at pistol grip and buttplate. From Crosman.

Price: **$75.00**

DAISY 1938 RED RYDER 60th ANNIVERSARY CLASSIC

Caliber: BB, 650-shot repeating action. **Barrel:** Smoothbore steel with shroud. **Weight:** 2.2 lbs. **Length:** 35.4" overall. **Stock:** Walnut stock burned with Red Ryder lariat signature. **Sights:** Post front, adjustable V-slot rear. **Features:** Walnut forend. Saddle ring with leather thong. Lever cocking. Gravity feed. Controlled velocity. One of Daisy's most popular guns. From Daisy Mfg. Co.

Price: **$39.95**

DAISY MODEL 840 GRIZZLY

Caliber: 177 pellet single shot; or BB 350-shot. **Barrel:** 19", smoothbore, steel. **Weight:** 2.25 lbs. **Length:** 36.8" overall. **Power:** Pneumatic, single pump. **Stock:** Moulded wood-grain stock and forend. **Sights:** Ramp front, open, adjustable rear. **Features:** Muzzle velocity 320 fps (BB), 300 fps (pellet). Steel buttplate; straight pull bolt action; cross-bolt safety. Forend forms pump lever. From Daisy Mfg. Co.

Price: **$32.95**
Price: 840C Mossy Oak® Break Up™ camo **$49.95**

DAISY MODEL 7840 BUCKMASTER

Caliber: 177 pellets, or BB. **Barrel:** Smoothbore steel. **Weight:** 2.25 lbs. **Length:** 36.8" overall. **Power:** Single-pump pneumatic. **Stock:** Moulded with checkering and woodgrain. **Sights:** Ramp and blade front, adjustable open rear plus Electronic Point Sight. **Features:** Velocity to 320 fps (BB), 300fps (pellet). Cross-bolt trigger block safety. From Daisy Mfg. Co.

Price: **$54.95**

DAISY MODEL 105 BUCK

Caliber: 177 or BB. **Barrel:** Smoothbore steel. **Weight:** 1.6 lbs. **Length:** 29.8" overall. **Power:** Lever cocking, spring air. **Stock:** Stained solid wood. **Sights:** TRUGLO® Fiber Optic, open fixed rear. **Features:** Velocity to 275. Cross-bolt trigger block safety. From Daisy Mfg. Co.

Price: . . . . **NA**

Daisy Model 95 Timberwolf

Similar to the 105 Buck except velocity to 325 fps. Weighs 2.4 lbs, overall length 35.2".

Price: **$38.95**

DAISY/POWERLINE 853

Caliber: 177 pellets, single shot. **Barrel:** 20.9"; 12-groove rifling, high-grade solid steel by Lothar Waltherô, precision crowned; bore size for precision match pellets. **Weight:** 5.08 lbs. **Length:** 38.9" overall. **Power:** Single-pump pneumatic. **Stock:** Full-length select American hardwood, stained and finished; black buttplate with white spacers. **Sights:** Globe front with four aperture inserts; precision micrometer adjustable rear peep sight mounted on a standard 3/8" dovetail receiver mount.

Price: **$225.00**

AIRGUNS—LONG GUNS

DAISY/POWERLINE 856 PUMP-UP AIRGUN

Caliber: 177 pellets (single shot) or BB (100-shot reservoir). **Barrel:** Rifled steel with shroud. **Weight:** 2.7 lbs. **Length:** 37.4" overall. **Power:** Pneumatic pump-up. **Stock:** Moulded wood-grain with Monte Carlo cheekpiece. **Sights:** Ramp and blade front, open rear adjustable for elevation. **Features:** Velocity from 315 fps (two pumps) to 650 fps (10 pumps). Shoots BBs or pellets. Heavy die-cast metal receiver. Cross-bolt trigger-block safety. From Daisy Mfg. Co.

Price: **$39.95**
Price: 856C. **$59.95**

DAISY/POWERLINE 1170 PELLET RIFLE

Caliber: 177, single shot. **Barrel:** Rifled steel. **Weight:** 5.5 lbs. **Length:** 42.5" overall. **Power:** Spring-air, barrel cocking. **Stock:** Hardwood. **Sights:** Hooded post front, micrometer adjustable open rear. **Features:** Velocity to 800 fps. Monte Carlo comb. From Daisy Mfg. Co.

Price: **$129.95**
Price: Model 131 (velocity to 600 fps). **$117.95**
Price: Model 1150 (black copolymer stock, velocity to 600 fps) . . . **$77.95**

DAISY/POWERLINE EAGLE 7856 PUMP-UP AIRGUN

Caliber: 177 (pellets), BB, 100-shot BB magazine. **Barrel:** Rifled steel with shroud. **Weight:** 3.3 lbs. **Length:** 37.4" overall. **Power:** Pneumatic pump-up. **Stock:** Moulded wood-grain plastic. **Sights:** Ramp and blade front, open rear adjustable for elevation. **Features:** Velocity from 315 fps (two pumps) to 650 fps (10 pumps). Finger grooved forend. Cross-bolt trigger-block safety. From Daisy Mfg. Co.

Price: With 4x scope, about **$49.95**

DAISY/POWERLINE 880

Caliber: 177 pellet or BB, 50-shot BB magazine, single shot for pellets. **Barrel:** Rifled steel. **Weight:** 3.7 lbs. **Length:** 37.6" overall. **Power:** Multi-pump pneumatic. **Stock:** Moulded wood grain; Monte Carlo comb. **Sights:** Hooded front, adjustable rear. **Features:** Velocity to 685 fps. (BB). Variable power (velocity, range) increase with pump strokes; resin receiver with dovetail scope mount. Made in U.S.A. by Daisy Mfg. Co.

Price: **$50.95**

DAISY/POWERLINE 1000 AIR RIFLE

Caliber: 177, single shot. **Barrel:** NA. **Weight:** 6.15 lbs. **Length:** 43" overall. **Power:** Spring-air, barrel cocking. **Stock:** Stained hardwood. **Sights:** Hooded blade front on ramp, fully adjustable micrometer rear. **Features:** Velocity to 1000 fps. Blued finish; trigger block safety. From Daisy Mfg. Co.

Price: **$208.95**

DAISY/YOUTHLINE MODEL 105 AIR RIFLE

Caliber: BB, 400-shot magazine. **Barrel:** 13-1/2". **Weight:** 1.6 lbs. **Length:** 29.8" overall. **Power:** Spring. **Stock:** Moulded woodgrain. **Sights:** Blade on ramp front, fixed rear. **Features:** Velocity to 275 fps. Blue finish. Cross-bolt trigger block safety. Made in U.S. by Daisy Mfg. Co.

Price: **$28.95**

DAISY/YOUTHLINE MODEL 95 AIR RIFLE

Caliber: BB, 700-shot magazine. **Barrel:** 18". **Weight:** 2.4 lbs. **Length:** 35.2" overall. **Power:** Spring. **Stock:** Stained hardwood. **Sights:** Blade on ramp front, open adjustable rear. **Features:** Velocity to 325 fps. Cross-bolt trigger block safety. Made in U.S. by Daisy Mfg. Co.

Price: **$38.95**

EAA/BAIKAL MP-512 AIR RIFLE

Caliber: 177, single shot. **Barrel:** 17.7". **Weight:** 6.2 lbs. **Length:** 41.3" overall. **Power:** Spring-piston, single stroke. **Stock:** Black synthetic. **Sights:** Adjustable rear, hooded front. **Features:** Velocity 490 fps. Hammer-forged, rifled barrel; automatic safety; scope mount rail. Imported from Russia by European American Armory.

Price: 177 caliber **$49.00**
Price: 512M (590 fps) **$65.00**

EAA/BAIKAL IZH-61 AIR RIFLE

Caliber: 177 pellet, 5-shot magazine. **Barrel:** 17.8". **Weight:** 6.4 lbs. **Length:** 31" overall. **Power:** Spring piston, side-cocking lever. **Stock:** Black plastic. **Sights:** Adjustable rear, fully hooded front. **Features:** Velocity 490 fps. Futuristic design with adjustable stock. Imported from Russia by European American Armory.

Price: **$99.00**

EAA/BAIKAL IZHMP-532 AIR RIFLE

Caliber: 177 pellet, single shot. **Barrel:** 15.8". **Weight:** 9.3 lbs. **Length:** 46.1" overall. **Power:** Single-stroke pneumatic. **Stock:** One- or two-piece competition-style stock with adjustable butt pad, pistol grip. **Sights:** Fully adjustable rear, hooded front. **Features:** Velocity 460 fps. Five-way adjustable trigger. Imported from Russia by European American Armory.

Price: **$599.00**

GAMO DELTA AIR RIFLE

Caliber: 177. **Barrel:** 15.7". **Weight:** 4.2 lbs. **Length:** 37.8". **Power:** Single-stroke pneumatic, 525 fps. **Stock:** Synthetic. **Sights:** Truglo fiber optic.

Price: **$89.95**

GAMO YOUNG HUNTER AIR RIFLE

Caliber: 177. **Barrel:** 17.7". **Weight:** 5.5 lbs. **Length:** 41". **Power:** Single-stroke pneumatic, 640 fps. **Stock:** Wood. **Sights:** Truglo fiber optic adjustable. **Features:** Excellent for young adults, it has a rifled steel barrel, hooded front sight, grooved receiver for scope. Imported from Spain by Gamo.

Price: **$129.95**
Price: Combo packed with BSA 4x32 scope and rings **$169.95**

GAMO SPORTER AIR RIFLE

Caliber: 177. **Barrel:** NA **Weight:** 5.5 lbs. **Length:** 42.5". **Power:** Single-stroke pneumatic, 760 fps. **Stock:** Wood. **Sights:** Adjustable Truglo fiber optic. **Features:** Intended to bridge the gap between Gamo's Young Hunter model and the adult-sized Hunter 440. Imported from Spain by Gamo.

Price: **$159.95**

GAMO HUNTER 440 AIR RIFLE

Caliber: 177, 22. **Barrel:** NA. **Weight:** 6.6 lbs. **Length:** 43.3". **Power:** Single-stroke pneumatifc, 1,000 fps (177), 750 fps (22). **Stock:** Wood. **Sights:** Adjustable Truglo fiber optic. **Features:** Adjustable two-stage trigger, rifled barrel, raised scope ramp on receiver. Realtree camo model available.

Price: **$229.95**
Price: Hunter 440 Combo with BSA 4x32mm scope **$259.95**

HAMMERLI AR 50 AIR RIFLE

Caliber: 177. **Barrel:** 19.8". **Weight:** 10 lbs. **Length:** 43.2" overall. **Power:** Compressed air. **Stock:** Anatomically-shaped universal and right-hand; match style; multi-colored laminated wood. **Sights:** Interchangeable element tunnel front, fully adjustable Hammerli peep rear. **Features:** Vibration-free firing release; fully adjustable match trigger and trigger stop; stainless air tank, built-in pressure gauge. Gives 270 shots per filling. Imported from Switzerland by Sigarms, Inc.

Price: **$1,653.00**

HAMMERLI MODEL 450 MATCH AIR RIFLE

Caliber: 177, single shot. **Barrel:** 19.5". **Weight:** 9.8 lbs. **Length:** 43.3" overall. **Power:** Pneumatic. **Stock:** Match style with stippled grip, rubber buttpad. Beach or walnut. **Sights:** Match tunnel front, Hammerli diopter rear. **Features:** Velocity about 560 fps. Removable sights; forend sling rail; adjustable trigger; adjustable comb. Imported from Switzerland by Sigarms, Inc.

Price: Beech stock **$1,355.00**
Price: Walnut stock **$1,395.00**

MARKSMAN BB BUDDY AIR RIFLE

Caliber: 177, 20-shot magazine. **Barrel:** 10.5" smoothbore. **Weight:** 1.6 lbs. **Length:** 33" overall. **Power:** Spring-air. **Stock:** Moulded composition. **Sights:** Blade on ramp front, adjustable V-slot rear. **Features:** Velocity 275 fps. Positive feed; automatic safety. Youth-sized lightweight design. Made in U.S. From Marksman Products.

Price: **$27.95**

MARKSMAN 2015 LASERHAWK™ BB REPEATER AIR RIFLE

Caliber: 177 BB, 20-shot magazine. **Barrel:** 10.5" smoothbore. **Weight:** 1.6 lbs. **Length:** Adjustable to 33", 34" or 35" overall. **Power:** Spring-air. **Stock:** Moulded composition. **Sights:** Fixed fiber optic front sight, adjustable elevation V-slot rear. **Features:** Velocity about 275 fps. Positive feed; automatic safety. Adjustable stock. Made in the U.S. From Marksman Products.

Price: **$33.00**

RWS/DIANA MODEL 24 AIR RIFLE

Caliber: 177, 22, single shot. **Barrel:** 17", rifled. **Weight:** 6 lbs. **Length:** 42" overall. **Power:** Spring-air, barrel cocking. **Stock:** Beech. **Sights:** Hooded front, adjustable rear. **Features:** Velocity of 700 fps (177). Easy cocking effort; blue finish. Imported from Germany by Dynamit Nobel-RWS, Inc.

Price: 24, 24C **$215.00**

RWS/Diana Model 34 Air Rifle

Similar to the Model 24 except has 19" barrel, weighs 7.5 lbs. Gives velocity of 1000 fps (177), 800 fps (22). Adjustable trigger, synthetic seals. Comes with scope rail.

Price: 177 or 22 . . . . **$290.00**

Price: Model 34N (nickel-plated metal, black epoxy-coated wood stock) **$350.00**

Price: Model 34BC (matte black metal, black stock, 4x32 scope, mounts) **$510.00**

RWS/DIANA MODEL 36 AIR RIFLE

Caliber: 177, 22, single shot. **Barrel:** 19", rifled. **Weight:** 8 lbs. **Length:** 45" overall. **Power:** Spring-air, barrel cocking. **Stock:** Beech. **Sights:** Hooded front (interchangeable inserts available), adjustable rear. **Features:** Velocity of 1000 fps (177-cal.). Comes with scope mount; two-stage adjustable trigger. Imported from Germany by Dynamit Nobel-RWS, Inc.

Price: 36, 36C **$435.00**

RWS/DIANA MODEL 52 AIR RIFLE

Caliber: 177, 22, 25, single shot. **Barrel:** 17", rifled. **Weight:** 8-1/2 lbs. **Length:** 43" overall. **Power:** Spring-air, sidelever cocking. **Stock:** Beech, with Monte Carlo, cheekpiece, checkered grip and forend. **Sights:** Ramp front, adjustable rear. **Features:** Velocity of 1100 fps (177). Blue finish. Solid rubber buttpad. Imported from Germany by Dynamit Nobel-RWS, Inc.

Price: 177, 22 . . . . **$565.00**

Price: 25 . . . . **$605.00**

Price: Model 52 Deluxe (177) **$810.00**

Price: Model 48B (as above except matte black metal, black stock) **$535.00**

Price: Model 48 (same as Model 52 except no Monte Carlo, cheekpiece or checkering) **$520.00**

RWS/DIANA MODEL 45 AIR RIFLE

Caliber: 177, single shot. **Weight:** 8 lbs. **Length:** 45" overall. **Power:** Spring-air, barrel cocking. **Stock:** Walnut-finished hardwood with rubber recoil pad. **Sights:** Globe front with interchangeable inserts, micro. click open rear with four-way blade. **Features:** Velocity of 820 fps. Dovetail base for either micrometer peep sight or scope mounting. Automatic safety. Imported from Germany by Dynamit Nobel-RWS, Inc.

Price: **$350.00**

RWS/DIANA MODEL 46 AIR RIFLE

Caliber: 177, 22, single shot. **Barrel:** 18". **Weight:** 8.2 lbs. **Length:** 45" overall. **Stock:** Hardwood Monte Carlo. **Sights:** Blade front, adjustable rear. **Features:** Underlever cocking spring-air (950 fps in 177, 780 fps in 22); extended scope rail, automatic safety, rubber buttpad, adjustable trigger. Imported from Germany by Dynamit Nobel-RWS Inc.

Price: **$470.00**

Price: Model 46E (as above except matte black metal, black stock) **$430.00**

RWS/DIANA MODEL 54 AIR RIFLE

Caliber: 177, 22, single shot. **Barrel:** 17". **Weight:** 9 lbs. **Length:** 43" overall. **Power:** Spring-air, sidelever cocking. **Stock:** Walnut with Monte Carlo cheekpiece, checkered grip and forend. **Sights:** Ramp front, fully adjustable rear. **Features:** Velocity to 1000 fps (177), 900 fps (22). Totally recoilless system; floating action absorbs recoil. Imported from Germany by Dynamit Nobel-RWS, Inc.

Price: **$785.00**

RWS/DIANA MODEL 92/93/94 AIR RIFLES

Caliber: 177, 22, single shot. **Barrel:** N/A. **Weight:** N/A. **Length:** N/A. **Stock:** Beechwood; Monte Carlo. **Sights:** Hooded front, fully adjustable rear. **Features:** Break-barrel, spring-air; receiver grooved for scope; adjustable trigger; lifetime warranty. Imported from Spain by Dynamit Nobel-RWS Inc.

Price: Model 92 (auto safety, 700 fps in 177) . . . . **NA**

Price: Model 93 (manual safety, 850 fps in 177) . . . . **NA**

Price: Model 94 (auto safety, 1,000 fps in 177) . . . . **NA**

RWS/DIANA MODEL 350 MAGNUM AIR RIFLE

Caliber: 177, 22, single shot. **Barrel:** 19-1/2". **Weight:** 8 lbs. **Length:** 48". **Stock:** Beechwood; Monte Carlo. **Sights:** Hooded front, fully adjustable rear. **Features:** Break-barrel, spring-air; 1,250 fps. Imported from Germany by Dynamit Nobel-RWS Inc.

Price: Model 350 . . . . **NA**

TECH FORCE BS4 OLYMPIC COMPETITION AIR RIFLE

Caliber: 177 pellet, single shot. **Barrel:** N/A. **Weight:** 10.8 lbs. **Length:** 43.3" overall. **Power:** Spring piston, sidelever action. **Stock:** Wood with semi-pistol grip, adjustable butt plate. **Sights:** Micro-adjustable competition rear, hooded front. **Features:** Velocity 640 fps. Recoilless action; adjustable trigger. Includes carrying case. Imported from China by Compasseco Inc.

Price: **$595.00**

Price: Optional diopter rear sight **$79.95**

TECH FORCE 6 AIR RIFLE

Caliber: 177 pellet, single shot. **Barrel:** 14". **Weight:** 6 lbs. **Length:** 35.5" overall. **Power:** Spring piston, sidelever action. **Stock:** Paratrooper-style folding, full pistol grip. **Sights:** Adjustable rear, hooded front. **Features:** Velocity 800 fps. All-metal construction; grooved for scope mounting. Imported from China by Compasseco Inc.

Price: **$69.95**

Tech Force 51 Air Rifle

Similar to Tech Force 6, but with break-barrel cocking mechanism and folding stock fitted with recoil pad. Overall length, 36". Weighs 6 lbs. From Compasseco Inc.

Price: **$69.95**

TECH FORCE 25 AIR RIFLE

Caliber: 177, 22 pellet; single shot. **Barrel:** N/A. **Weight:** 7.5 lbs. **Length:** 46.2" overall. **Power:** Spring piston, break-action barrel. **Stock:** Oil-finished wood; Monte Carlo stock with recoil pad. **Sights:** Adjustable rear, hooded front with insert. **Features:** Velocity 1,000 fps (177); grooved receiver and scope stop for scope mounting; adjustable trigger; trigger safety. Imported from China by Compasseco Inc.

Price:177 or 22 caliber **$125.00**

Price: Includes rifle and Tech Force 96 red dot point sight **$164.95**

TECH FORCE 36 AIR RIFLE

Caliber: 177 pellet, single shot. **Barrel:** N/A. **Weight:** 7.4 lbs. **Length:** 43" overall. **Power:** Spring piston, underlever cocking. **Stock:** Monte Carlo hardwood stock; recoil pad. **Sights:** Adjustable rear, hooded front. **Features:** Velocity 900 fps; grooved receiver and scope stop for scope mounting; auto-reset safety. Imported from China by Compasseco Inc.

Price: **$89.95**

WHISCOMBE JW SERIES AIR RIFLES

Caliber: 177, 20, 22, 25, single shot. **Barrel:** 15", Lothar Walther. Polygonal rifling. **Weight:** 9 lbs., 8 oz. **Length:** 39" overall. **Power:** Dual spring-piston, multi-stroke; underlever cocking. **Stock:** Walnut with adjustable buttplate and cheekpiece. **Sights:** None furnished; grooved scope rail. **Features:** Velocity 660-1000 (JW80) fps (22-caliber, fixed barrel) depending upon model. Interchangeable barrels; automatic safety; muzzle weight; semi-floating action; twin opposed pistons with counter-wound springs; adjustable trigger. All models include H.O.T. System (Harmonic Optimization Tunable System). Imported from England by Pelaire Products.

Price: JW50, MKII fixed barrel only **$2,085.00**

Price: JW65, MKII **$2,085.00**

Price: JW80, MKII **$2,195.00**

METALLIC CARTRIDGE PRESSES

CH4D Heavyduty Champion

Frame: Cast iron
Frame Type: O-frame
Die Thread: 7/8-14 or 1-14
Avg. Rounds Per Hour: NA
Ram Stroke: 3-1/4"
Weight: 26 lbs.
Features: 1.185" diameter ram with 16 square inches of bearing surface; ram drilled to allow passage of spent primers; solid steel handle; toggle that slightly breaks over the top dead center. Includes universal primer arm with large and small punches. From CH Tool & Die/4D Custom Die.
Price: **$220.00**

CH4D No. 444 4-Station "H" Press

Frame: Aluminum alloy
Frame Type: H-frame
Die Thread: 7/8-14
Avg. Rounds Per Hour: 200
Ram Stroke: 3-3/4"
Weight: 12 lbs.
Features: Two 7/8" solid steel shaft "H" supports; platen rides on permanently lubed bronze bushings; loads smallest pistol to largest magnum rifle cases and has strength to full-length resize. Includes four rams, large and small primer arm and primer catcher. From CH Tool & Die/4D Custom Die, Co.
Price: **$195.00**

CH4D No. 444

CH4D No. 444-X Pistol Champ

Frame: Aluminum alloy
Frame Type: H-frame
Die Thread: 7/8-14
Avg. Rounds Per Hour: 200
Ram Stroke: 3-3/4"
Weight: 12 lbs.
Features: Tungsten carbide sizing die; Speed Seater seating die with tapered entrance to automatically align bullet on case mouth; automatic primer feed for large or small primers; push-button powder measure with easily changed bushings for 215 powder/load combinations; taper crimp die. Conversion kit for caliber changeover available. From CH Tool & Die/4D Custom Die, Co.
Price: . . . . **$292.00-$316.50**

CH4D 444-X Pistol Champ

CORBIN CSP-2 MEGA MITE

Frame: N/A
Frame Type: N/A
Die Thread: 1-1/2 x 12
Avg. Rounds Per Hour: N/A
Ram Stroke: 6"
Weight: 70 lbs.
Features: Roller bearing linkage, hardened tool steel pivots, precision bush bushings glide on polished steel guide rods. Made for use with -H type (hydraulic) swage dies, it is capable of swaging rifle calibers up to .600 Nitro, lead shotgun slugs up to 12 gauge and the reloading of .50 BMG ammo. From Corbin Manufacturing.
Price: **$750.00**

FORSTER Co-Ax Press B-2

Frame: Cast iron
Frame Type: Modified O-frame
Die Thread: 7/8-14
Avg. Rounds Per Hour: 120
Ram Stroke: 4"
Weight: 18 lbs.
Features: Snap in/snap out die change; spent primer catcher with drop tube threaded into carrier below shellholder; automatic, handle-activated, cammed shellholder with opposing spring-loaded jaws to contact extractor groove; floating guide rods for alignment and reduced friction; no torque on the head due to design of linkage and pivots; shellholder jaws that float with die permitting case to center in the die; right- or left-hand operation; priming device for seating to factory specifications. "S" shellholder jaws included. From Forster Products.
Price: **$318.30**
Price: Extra LS shellholder jaws **$27.80**

Forster Co-Ax

HOLLYWOOD Senior Press

Frame: Ductile iron
Frame Type: O-frame
Die Thread: 7/8-14
Avg. Rounds Per Hour: 50-100
Ram Stroke: 6-1/2"
Weight: 50 lbs.
Features: Leverage and bearing surfaces ample for reloading cartridges or swaging bullets. Precision ground one-piece 2-1/2" pillar with base; operating handle of 3/4" steel and 15" long; 5/8" steel tie-down rod fro added strength when swaging; heavy steel toggle and camming arms held by 1/2" steel pins in reamed holes. The 1-1/2" steel die bushing takes standard threaded dies; removed, it allows use of Hollywood shotshell dies. From Hollywood Engineering.
Price: **$600.00**

Hollywood Senior

HOLLYWOOD Senior Turret Press

Frame: Ductile iron
Frame Type: H-frame
Die Thread: 7/8-14
Avg. Rounds Per Hour: 50-100
Ram Stroke: 6-1/2"
Weight: 50 lbs.
Features: Same features as Senior press except has three-position turret head; holes in turret may be tapped 1-1/2" or 7/8" or four of each. Height, 15". Comes complete with one turret indexing handle; one operating handle and three turret indexing handles; one 5/8" tie down bar for swaging. From Hollywood Engineering.
Price: **$700.00**

Hollywood Senior Turret

METALLIC CARTRIDGE PRESSES

Hornady Lock-N-Load Classic

Lee Hand Press

Lee Reloader

Lee Challenger

Lee Turret

Lyman 310

HORNADY Lock-N-Load Classic

Frame: Die cast heat-treated aluminum alloy
Frame Type: O-frame
Die Thread: 7/8-14
Avg. Rounds Per Hour: NA
Ram Stroke: 3-5/8"
Weight: 14 lbs.
Features: Features Lock-N-Load bushing system that allows instant die changeovers. Solid steel linkage arms that rotate on steel pins; 30° angled frame design for improved visibility and accessibility; primer arm automatically moves in and out of ram for primer pickup and solid seating; two primer arms for large and small primers; long offset handle for increased leverage and unobstructed reloading; lifetime warranty. Comes as a package with primer catcher, PPS automatic primer feed and three Lock-N-Load die bushings. Dies and shellholder available separately or as a kit with primer catcher, positive priming system, automatic primer feed, three die bushings and reloading accessories. From Hornady Mfg. Co.
Price: Press and Three Die Bushings **$99.95**
Price: Classic Reloading Kit **$259.95**

LEE Hand Press

Frame: ASTM 380 aluminum
Frame Type: NA
Die Thread: 7/8-14
Avg. Rounds Per Hour: 100
Ram Stroke: 3-1/4"
Weight: 1 lb., 8 oz.
Features: Small and lightweight for portability; compound linkage for handling up to 375 H&H and case forming. Dies and shellholder not included. From Lee Precision, Inc.
Price: **$26.98**

LEE Challenger Press

Frame: ASTM 380 aluminum
Frame Type: O-frame
Die Thread: 7/8-14
Avg. Rounds Per Hour: 100
Ram Stroke: 3-1/2"
Weight: 4 lbs., 1 oz.
Features: Larger than average opening with 30° offset for maximum hand clearance; steel connecting pins; spent primer catcher; handle adjustable for start and stop positions; handle repositions for left- or right-hand use; shortened handle travel to prevent springing the frame from alignment. Dies and shellholders not included. From Lee Precision, Inc.
Price: **$45.00**

LEE Classic Cast

Features: Cast iron, O-type. Adjustable handle moves from right to left, start and stop position is adjustable. Large 1 1/8" diameter hollow ram catches primers for disposal. Automatic primer arm with bottom of stroke priming. Two assembled primer arms included. From Lee Precision, Inc.
Price: **$90.00**

LEE Reloader Press

Frame: ASTM 380 aluminum
Frame Type: C-frame
Die Thread: 7/8-14
Avg. Rounds Per Hour: 100
Ram Stroke: 3"
Weight: 1 lb., 12 oz.
Features: Balanced lever to prevent pinching fingers; unlimited hand clearance; left- or right-hand use. Dies and shellholders not included. From Lee Precision, Inc.
Price: **$26.98**

LEE Turret Press

Frame: ASTM 380 aluminum
Frame Type: O-frame
Die Thread: 7/8-14
Avg. Rounds Per Hour: 300
Ram Stroke: 3"
Weight: 7 lbs., 2 oz.
Features: Replaceable turret lifts out by rotating 30°; T-primer arm reverses for large or small primers; built-in primer catcher; adjustable handle for right- or left-hand use or changing angle of down stroke; accessory mounting hole for Lee Auto-Disk powder measure. Optional Auto-Index rotates die turret to next station for semi-progressive use. Safety override prevents overstressing should turret not turn. From Lee Precision, Inc.
Price: **$69.98**
Price: With Auto-Index **$83.98**
Price: Four-Hole Turret with Auto-Index **$85.98**

LYMAN 310 Tool

Frame: Stainless steel
Frame Type: NA
Die Thread: 7/8-14
Avg. Rounds Per Hour: NA
Ram Stroke: NA
Weight: 10 oz.
Features: Compact, portable reloading tool for pistol or rifle cartridges. Adapter allows loading rimmed or rimless cases. Die set includes neck resizing/decapping die, primer seating chamber; neck expanding die; bullet seating die; and case head adapter. From Lyman Products Corp.
Price: Dies **$45.00**
Price: Handles **$47.50**
Price: Carrying pouch **$9.95**

METALLIC CARTRIDGE PRESSES

LYMAN AccuPress

Frame: Die cast
Frame Type: C-frame
Die Thread: 7/8-14
Avg. Rounds Per Hour: 75
Ram Stroke: 3.4"
Weight: 4 lbs.
Features: Reversible, contoured handle for bench mount or hand-held use; for rifle or pistol; compound leverage; Delta frame design. Accepts all standard powder measures. From Lyman Products Corp.
Price: $34.95

LYMAN Crusher II

Frame: Cast iron
Frame Type: O-frame
Die Thread: 7/8-14
Avg. Rounds Per Hour: 75
Ram Stroke: 3-7/8"
Weight: 19 lbs.
Features: Reloads both pistol and rifle cartridges; 1" diameter ram; 4-1/2" press opening for loading magnum cartridges; direct torque design; right- or left-hand use. New base design with 14 square inches of flat mounting surface with three bolt holes. Comes with priming arm and primer catcher. Dies and shellholders not included. From Lyman Products Corp.
Price: $116.50

LYMAN T-Mag II

Frame: Cast iron with silver metalflake powder finish
Frame Type: Turret
Die Thread: 7/8-14
Avg. Rounds Per Hour: 125
Ram Stroke: 3-13/16"
Weight: 18 lbs.
Features: Reengineered and upgraded with new turret system for ease of indexing and tool-free turret removal for caliber changeover; new flat machined base for bench mounting; new nickel-plated non-rust handle and links; and new silver hammertone powder coat finish for durability. Right- or left-hand operation; handles all rifle or pistol dies. Comes with priming arm and primer catcher. Dies and shellholders not included. From Lyman Products Corp.
Price: $164.95
Price: Extra turret $37.50

MEACHAM ANYWHERE PORTABLE RELOADING PRESS

Frame: Anodized 6061 T6 aircraft aluminum
Frame Type: Cylindrical
Die Thread: 7/8-14
Avg. Rounds Per Hour: N/A
Ram Stroke: 2.7"
Weight: 2 lbs. (hand held); 5 lbs. (with docking kit)
Features: A light weight, portable press that can be used hand-held (or with a docking kit) can be clamped to a table top up to 9.75" thick. Docking kit includes a threaded powder measure mount and holder for the other die. Designed for neck sizing abd bullet seating of short action cartridges, it can be used for long action cartridges with the addition of an Easy Seater straight line seating die. Dies not included.
Price: $99.95
Price: (with docking kit) $144.95
Price: Easy Seater $114.95
Price: Re-De-Capper .... N/A

PONSNESS/WARREN Metal-Matic P-200

Frame: Die cast aluminum
Frame Type: Unconventional
Die Thread: 7/8-14
Avg. Rounds Per Hour: 200+
Weight: 18 lbs.
Features: Designed for straight-wall cartridges; die head with 10 tapped holes for holding dies and accessories for two calibers at one time; removable spent primer box; pivoting arm moves case from station to station. Comes with large and small primer tool. Optional accessories include primer feed, extra die head, primer speed feeder, powder measure extension and dust cover. Dies, powder measure and shellholder not included. From Ponsness/Warren.
Price: $215.00
Price: Extra die head $44.95
Price: Powder measure extension $29.95
Price: Primer feed $44.95
Price: Primer speed feed $14.50
Price: Dust cover $21.95

RCBS Partner

Frame: Aluminum
Frame Type: O-frame
Die Thread: 7/8-14
Avg. Rounds Per Hour: 50-60
Ram Stroke: 3-5/8"
Weight: 5 lbs.
Features: Designed for the beginning reloader. Comes with primer arm equipped with interchangeable primer plugs and sleeves for seating large and small primers. Shellholder and dies not included. Available in kit form (see Metallic Presses-Accessories). From RCBS.
Price: $69.95

Turret handle disconnector

Lyman T-Mag II

Lyman Crusher II

Meacham Re-De-Capper

Ponsness/Warren Metal-Matic P-200

RCBS AmmoMaster Single

METALLIC CARTRIDGE PRESSES

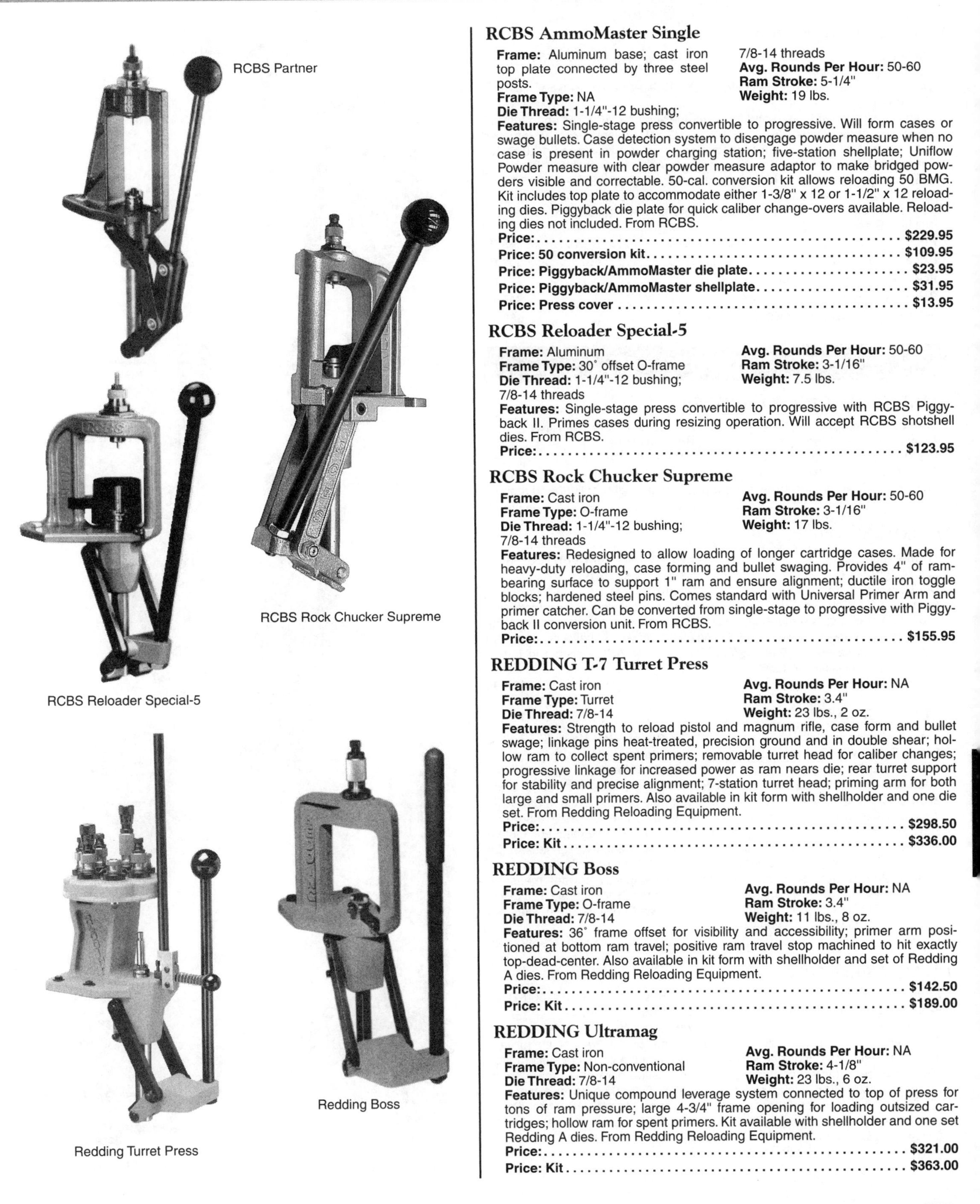

RCBS Partner

RCBS Rock Chucker Supreme

RCBS Reloader Special-5

Redding Boss

Redding Turret Press

RCBS AmmoMaster Single

Frame: Aluminum base; cast iron top plate connected by three steel posts.
Frame Type: NA
Die Thread: 1-1/4"-12 bushing; 7/8-14 threads
Avg. Rounds Per Hour: 50-60
Ram Stroke: 5-1/4"
Weight: 19 lbs.
Features: Single-stage press convertible to progressive. Will form cases or swage bullets. Case detection system to disengage powder measure when no case is present in powder charging station; five-station shellplate; Uniflow Powder measure with clear powder measure adaptor to make bridged powders visible and correctable. 50-cal. conversion kit allows reloading 50 BMG. Kit includes top plate to accommodate either 1-3/8" x 12 or 1-1/2" x 12 reloading dies. Piggyback die plate for quick caliber change-overs available. Reloading dies not included. From RCBS.
Price: **$229.95**
Price: 50 conversion kit **$109.95**
Price: Piggyback/AmmoMaster die plate **$23.95**
Price: Piggyback/AmmoMaster shellplate **$31.95**
Price: Press cover **$13.95**

RCBS Reloader Special-5

Frame: Aluminum
Frame Type: 30˚ offset O-frame
Die Thread: 1-1/4"-12 bushing; 7/8-14 threads
Avg. Rounds Per Hour: 50-60
Ram Stroke: 3-1/16"
Weight: 7.5 lbs.
Features: Single-stage press convertible to progressive with RCBS Piggyback II. Primes cases during resizing operation. Will accept RCBS shotshell dies. From RCBS.
Price: **$123.95**

RCBS Rock Chucker Supreme

Frame: Cast iron
Frame Type: O-frame
Die Thread: 1-1/4"-12 bushing; 7/8-14 threads
Avg. Rounds Per Hour: 50-60
Ram Stroke: 3-1/16"
Weight: 17 lbs.
Features: Redesigned to allow loading of longer cartridge cases. Made for heavy-duty reloading, case forming and bullet swaging. Provides 4" of ram-bearing surface to support 1" ram and ensure alignment; ductile iron toggle blocks; hardened steel pins. Comes standard with Universal Primer Arm and primer catcher. Can be converted from single-stage to progressive with Piggyback II conversion unit. From RCBS.
Price: **$155.95**

REDDING T-7 Turret Press

Frame: Cast iron
Frame Type: Turret
Die Thread: 7/8-14
Avg. Rounds Per Hour: NA
Ram Stroke: 3.4"
Weight: 23 lbs., 2 oz.
Features: Strength to reload pistol and magnum rifle, case form and bullet swage; linkage pins heat-treated, precision ground and in double shear; hollow ram to collect spent primers; removable turret head for caliber changes; progressive linkage for increased power as ram nears die; rear turret support for stability and precise alignment; 7-station turret head; priming arm for both large and small primers. Also available in kit form with shellholder and one die set. From Redding Reloading Equipment.
Price: **$298.50**
Price: Kit **$336.00**

REDDING Boss

Frame: Cast iron
Frame Type: O-frame
Die Thread: 7/8-14
Avg. Rounds Per Hour: NA
Ram Stroke: 3.4"
Weight: 11 lbs., 8 oz.
Features: 36˚ frame offset for visibility and accessibility; primer arm positioned at bottom ram travel; positive ram travel stop machined to hit exactly top-dead-center. Also available in kit form with shellholder and set of Redding A dies. From Redding Reloading Equipment.
Price: **$142.50**
Price: Kit **$189.00**

REDDING Ultramag

Frame: Cast iron
Frame Type: Non-conventional
Die Thread: 7/8-14
Avg. Rounds Per Hour: NA
Ram Stroke: 4-1/8"
Weight: 23 lbs., 6 oz.
Features: Unique compound leverage system connected to top of press for tons of ram pressure; large 4-3/4" frame opening for loading outsized cartridges; hollow ram for spent primers. Kit available with shellholder and one set Redding A dies. From Redding Reloading Equipment.
Price: **$321.00**
Price: Kit **$363.00**

METALLIC CARTRIDGE PRESSES

ROCK CRUSHER Press

Frame: Cast iron
Frame Type: O-frame
Die Thread: 2-3/4"-12 with bushing reduced to 1-1/2"-12
Avg. Rounds Per Hour: 50
Ram Stroke: 6"
Weight: 67 lbs.
Features: Designed to load and form ammunition from 50 BMG up to 23x115 Soviet. Frame opening of 8-1/2"x3-1/2"; 1-1/2"x12"; bushing can be removed and bushings of any size substituted; ram pressure can exceed 10,000 lbs. with normal body weight; 40mm diameter ram. Angle block for bench mounting and reduction bushing for RCBS dies available. Accessories for Rock Crusher include powder measure, dies, shellholder, bullet puller, priming tool, case gauge and other accessories found elsewhere in this catalog. From The Old Western Scrounger.
Price: **$795.00**
Price: Angle block **$57.95**
Price: Reduction bushing **$21.00**
Price: Shellholder **$47.25**
Price: Priming tool, 50 BMG, 20 Lahti **$65.10**

PROGRESSIVE PRESSES

CORBIN BENCHREST S-PRESS

Frame: All steel
Frame Type: O-Frame
Die Thread: 7/8-14 and T-slot adapter
Avg. Rounds Per Hour: NA
Ram Stroke: 4"
Weight: 22 lbs.
Features: Roller bearing linkage, removeable head, right- or left-hand mount.
Price: **$298.00**

DILLON AT 500

Frame: Aluminum alloy
Frame Type: NA
Die Thread: 7/8-14
Avg. Rounds Per Hour: 200-300
Ram Stroke: 3-7/8"
Weight: NA
Features: Four stations; removable tool head to hold dies in alignment and allow caliber changes without die adjustment; manual indexing; capacity to be upgraded to progressive RL 550B. Comes with universal shellplate to accept 223, 22-250, 243, 30-06, 9mm, 38/357, 40 S&W, 45 ACP. Dies not included. From Dillon Precision Products.
Price: **$193.95**

DILLON RL 550B

Frame: Aluminum alloy
Frame Type: NA
Die Thread: 7/8-14
Avg. Rounds Per Hour: 500-600
Ram Stroke: 3-7/8"
Weight: 25 lbs.
Features: Four stations; removable tool head to hold dies in alignment and allow caliber changes without die adjustment; auto priming system that emits audible warning when primer tube is low; a 100-primer capacity magazine contained in DOM steel tube for protection; new auto powder measure system with simple mechanical connection between measure and loading platform for positive powder bar return; a separate station for crimping with star-indexing system; 220 ejected-round capacity bin; 3/4-lb. capacity powder measure. Height above bench, 35"; requires 3/4" bench overhang. Will reload 120 different rifle and pistol calibers. Comes with one caliber conversion kit. Dies not included. From Dillon Precision Products, Inc.
Price: **$329.95**

DILLON Super 1050

Frame: Ductile iron
Frame Type: Platform type
Die Thread: 7/8-14
Avg. Rounds Per Hour: 1000-1200
Ram Stroke: 2-5/16"
Weight: 62 lbs.
Features: Eight stations; auto case feed; primer pocket swager for military cartridge cases; auto indexing; removable tool head; auto prime system with 100-primer capacity; low primer supply alarm; positive powder bar return; auto powder measure; 515 ejected round bin capacity; 500-600 case feed capacity; 3/4-lb. capacity powder measure. Has lengthened frame and short-stroke crank to accommodate long calibers. Loads all pistol rounds as well as 30 M1 Carbine, 223, and 7.62x39 rifle rounds. Height above the bench, 43". Dies not included. From Dillon Precision Products, Inc.
Price: **$1,399.95**

Redding Ultramag

Rock Crusher

Dillon RL 550B

Dillon Square Deal B

Dillon RL 1050

METALLIC CARTRIDGE PRESSES

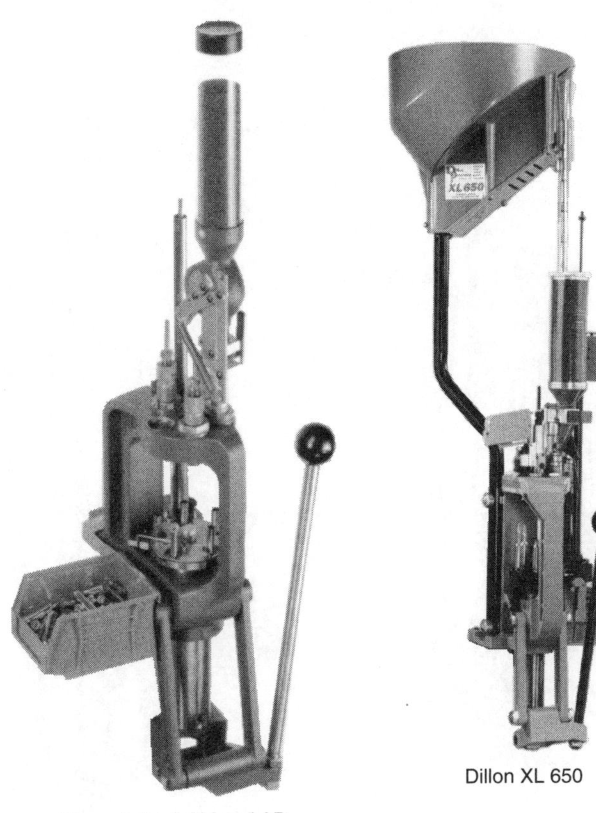

Hornady Lock-N-Load AP

Dillon XL 650

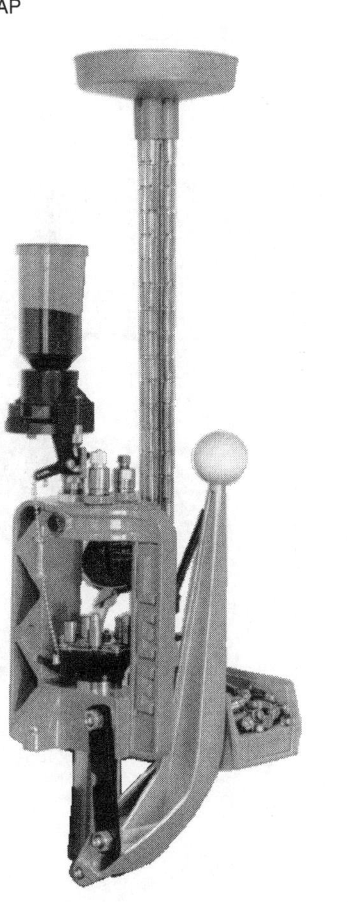

Lee Load-Master

DILLON Square Deal B

Frame: Zinc alloy
Frame Type: NA
Die Thread: None (unique Dillon design)
Avg. Rounds Per Hour: 400-500
Ram Stroke: 2-5/16"
Weight: 17 lbs.
Features: Four stations; auto indexing; removable tool head; auto prime system with 100-primer capacity; low primer supply alarm; auto powder measure; positive powder bar return; 170 ejected round capacity bin; 3/4-lb. capacity powder measure. Height above the bench, 34". Comes complete with factory adjusted carbide die set. From Dillon Precision Products, Inc.
Price: **$252.95**

DILLON XL 650

Frame: Aluminum alloy
Frame Type: NA
Die Thread: 7/8-14
Avg. Rounds Per Hour: 800-1000
Ram Stroke: 4-9/16"
Weight: 46 lbs.
Features: Five stations; auto indexing; auto case feed; removable tool head; auto prime system with 100-primer capacity; low primer supply alarm; auto powder measure; positive powder bar return; 220 ejected round capacity bin; 3/4-lb. capacity powder measure. 500-600 case feed capacity with optional auto case feed. Loads all pistol/rifle calibers less than 3-1/2" in length. Height above the bench, 44"; 3/4" bench overhang required. From Dillon Precision Products, Inc.
Price: Less dies **$443.95**

HORNADY Lock-N-Load AP

Frame: Die cast heat-treated aluminum alloy
Frame Type: O-frame
Die Thread: 7/8-14
Avg. Rounds Per Hour: NA
Ram Stroke: 3-3/4"
Weight: 26 lbs.
Features: Features Lock-N-Load bushing system that allows instant die changeovers; five-station die platform with option of seating and crimping separately or adding taper-crimp die; auto prime with large and small primer tubes with 100-primer capacity and protective housing; brass kicker to eject loaded rounds into 80-round capacity cartridge catcher; offset operating handle for leverage and unobstructed operation; 2" diameter ram driven by heavy-duty cast linkage arms rotating on steel pins. Comes with five Lock-N-Load die bushings, shellplate, deluxe powder measure, auto powder drop, and auto primer feed and shut-off, brass kicker and primer catcher. Lifetime warranty. From Hornady Mfg. Co.
Price: **$367.65**

LEE Load-Master

Frame: ASTM 380 aluminum
Frame Type: O-frame
Die Thread: 7/8-14
Avg. Rounds Per Hour: 600
Ram Stroke: 3-1/4"
Weight: 8 lbs., 4 oz.
Features: Available in kit form only. A 1-3/4" diameter hard chrome ram for han-dling largest magnum cases; loads rifle or pistol rounds; five station press to fac-tory crimp and post size; auto indexing with wedge lock mechanism to hold one ton; auto priming; removable turrets; four- tube case feeder with optional case collator and bullet feeder (late 1995); loaded round ejector with chute to optional loaded round catcher; quick change shellplate; primer catcher. Dies and shell-holder for one caliber included. From Lee Precision, Inc.
Price: Rifle **$320.00**
Price: Pistol **$330.00**
Price: Extra turret **$14.98**
Price: Adjustable charge bar **$9.98**

LEE Pro 1000

Frame: ASTM 380 aluminum and steel
Frame Type: O-frame
Die Thread: 7/8-14
Avg. Rounds Per Hour: 600
Ram Stroke: 3-1/4"
Weight: 8 lbs., 7 oz.
Features: Optional transparent large/small or rifle case feeder; deluxe auto-disk case-activated powder measure; case sensor for primer feed. Comes complete with carbide die set (steel dies for rifle) for one caliber. Optional accessories include: case feeder for large/small pistol cases or rifle cases; shell plate carrier with auto prime, case ejector, auto-index and spare parts; case collator for case feeder. From Lee Precision, Inc.
Price: **$199.98**

METALLIC CARTRIDGE PRESSES

PONSNESS/WARREN Metallic II

Frame: Die cast aluminum
Frame Type: H-frame
Die Thread: 7/8-14
Avg. Rounds Per Hour: 150+
Ram Stroke: NA
Weight: 32 lbs.
Features: Die head with five tapped 7/8-14 holes for dies, powder measure or other accessories; pivoting die arm moves case from station to station; depriming tube for removal of spent primers; auto primer feed; interchangeable die head. Optional accessories include additional die heads, powder measure extension tube to accommodate any standard powder measure, primer speed feeder to feed press primer tube without disassembly. Comes with small and large primer seating tools. Dies, powder measure and shellholder not included. From Ponsness/ Warren.
Price: **$375.00**
Price: Extra die head **$56.95**
Price: Primer speed feeder **$14.50**
Price: Powder measure extension **$29.95**
Price: Dust cover **$27.95**

RCBS Pro 2000™

Frame: Cast iron
Frame Type: H-Frame
Die Thread: 7/8 x 14
Avg. Rounds Per Hour: 500-600
Ram Stroke: NA
Weight: NA
Features: Five-station manual indexing; full-length sizing; removable die plate; fast caliber conversion. Uses APS Priming System. From RCBS.
Price: **$42.95**

RCBS Turret Press

Frame: Cast iron
Frame Type: NA
Die Thread: 7/8x14
Avg. Rounds Per Hour: 50 to 200
Ram Stroke: NA
Weight: NA
Features: Six-station turret head; positive alignment; on-press priming.
Price: **$214.95**

STAR Universal Pistol Press

Frame: Cast iron with aluminum base
Frame Type: Unconventional
Die Thread: 11/16-24 or 7/8-14
Avg. Rounds Per Hour: 300
Ram Stroke: NA
Weight: 27 lbs.
Features: Four or five-station press depending on need to taper crimp; handles all popular handgun calibers from 32 Long to 45 Colt. Comes completely assembled and adjusted with carbide dies (except 30 Carbine) and shellholder to load one caliber. Prices slightly higher for 9mm and 30 Carbine. From Star Machine Works.
Price: With taper crimp **$1,055.00**
Price: Without taper crimp **$1,025.00**
Price: Extra tool head, taper crimp **$425.00**
Price: Extra tool head, w/o taper crimp **$395.00**

RCBS AmmoMaster

Lee Pro 1000

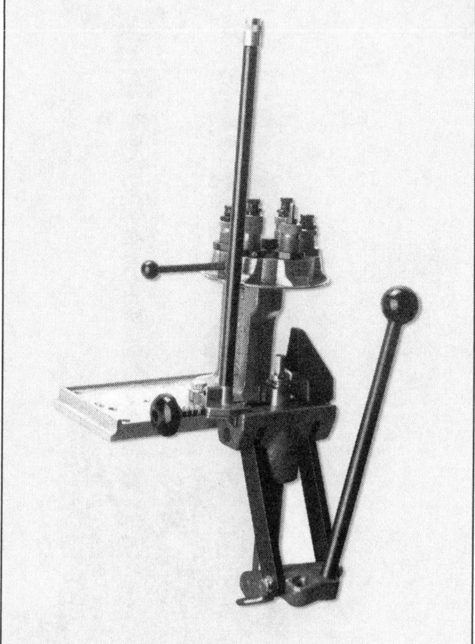

RCBS Turret

Fully-automated Star Universal

Dillon SL 900

Hollywood Automatic

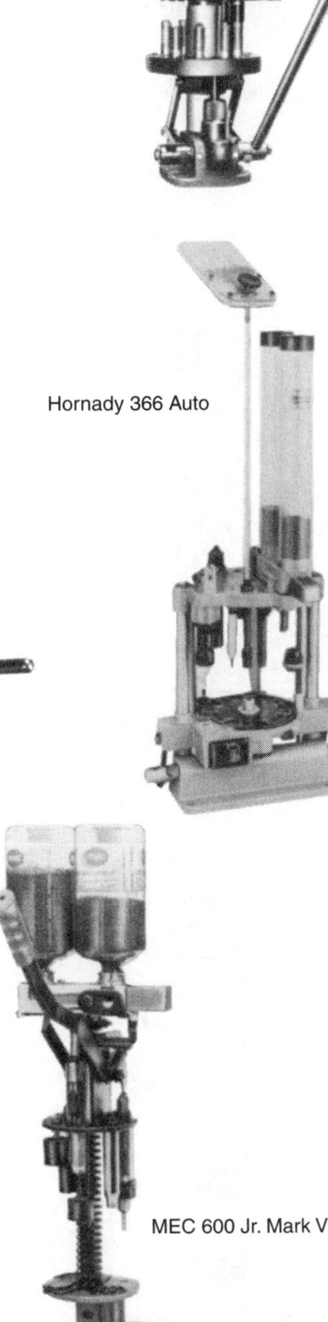

Hollywood Senior Turret Press

Hornady 366 Auto

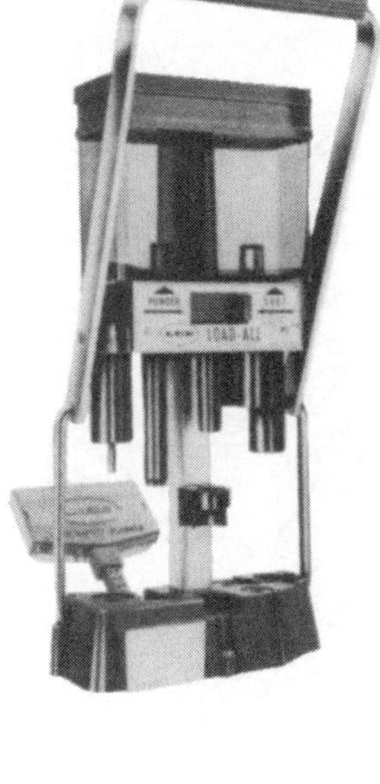

MEC 600 Jr. Mark V

DILLON SL 900

Press Type: Progressive
Avg. Rounds Per Hour: 700-900
Weight: 51 lbs.
Features: 12-ga. only; factory adjusted to load AA hulls; extra large 25-pound capacity shot hopper; fully-adjustable case-activated shot system; hardened steel starter crimp die; dual-action final crimp and taper die; tilt-out wad guide; auto prime; auto index; strong mount machine stand. From Dillon Precision Products.
Price: $819.95

HOLLYWOOD Automatic Shotshell Press

Press Type: Progressive
Avg. Rounds Per Hour: 1,800
Weight: 100 lbs.
Features: Ductile iron frame; fully automated press with shell pickup and ejector; comes completely set up for one gauge; one starter crimp; one finish crimp; wad guide for plastic wads; decap and powder dispenser unit; one wrench for inside die lock screw; one medium and one large spanner wrench for spanner nuts; one shellholder; powder and shot measures. Available for 10, 12, 20, 28 or 410. From Hollywood Engineering.
Price: $3,600.00

HOLLYWOOD Senior Turret Press

Press Type: Turret
Avg. Rounds Per Hour: 200
Weight: 50 lbs.
Features: Multi-stage press constructed of ductile iron comes completely equipped to reload one gauge; one starter crimp; one finish crimp; wad guide for plastic wads; decap and powder dispenser unit; one wrench for inside die lock screw; one medium and one large spanner wrench for spanner nuts; one shellholder; powder and shot measures. Available for 10, 12, 16, 20, 28 or 410. From Hollywood Engineering.
Price: Press only $700.00
Price: Dies $195.00

HORNADY 366 Auto

Press Type: Progressive
Avg. Rounds Per Hour: NA
Weight: 25 lbs.
Features: Heavy-duty die cast and machined steel body and components; auto primer feed system; large capacity shot and powder tubes; adjustable for right- or left-hand use; automatic charge bar with shutoff; swing-out wad guide; primer catcher at base of press; interchangeable shot and powder bushings; life-time warranty. Available for 12, 20, 28 2-3/4" and 410 2-1/2. From Hornady Mfg. Co.
Price: $434.95
Price: Die set, 12, 20, 28 .... $196.86
Price: Magnum conversion dies, 12, 20 .... $43.25

LEE Load-All II

Press Type: Single stage
Avg. Rounds Per Hour: 100
Weight: 3 lbs., 3 oz.
Features: Loads steel or lead shot; built-in primer catcher at base with door in front for emptying; recesses at each station for shell positioning; optional primer feed. Comes with safety charge bar with 24 shot and powder bushings. Available for 12-, 16- or 20-gauge. From Lee Precision, Inc.
Price: $49.98

MEC 600 Jr. Mark V

Press Type: Single stage
Avg. Rounds Per Hour: 200
Weight: 10 lbs.
Features: Spindex crimp starter for shell alignment during crimping; a cam-action crimp die; Pro-Check to keep charge bar properly positioned; adjustable for three shells. Available in 10, 12, 16, 20, 28 gauges and 410 bore. Die set not included. From Mayville Engineering Company, Inc.
Price: $112.35
Price: Die set $59.97

Shotshell Reloading Presses

MEC 650

Press Type: Progressive
Avg. Rounds Per Hour: 400
Weight: 19 lbs.
Features: Six-station press; does not resize except as separate operation; auto primer feed standard; three crimping stations for starting, closing and tapering crimp. Die sets not available. Available in 12, 16, 20, 28 and 410. From Mayville Engineering Company, Inc.
Price: $213.10

MEC 8567 Grabber

Press Type: Progressive
Avg. Rounds Per Hour: 400
Weight: 22 lbs.
Features: Six-station press; auto primer feed; auto-cycle charging; three-stage crimp; power ring resizer returns base to factory specs; resizes high and low base shells; optional kits to reload three shells and steel shot. Available in 12, 16, 20, 28 gauge and 410 bore. From Mayville Engineering Company, Inc.
Price: $306.05
Price: 3" kit, 12-ga. $70.70
Price: 3" kit, 20-ga. $40.40
Price: Steel shot kit $35.35

MEC 9000 Grabber

Press Type: Progressive
Avg. Rounds Per Hour: 400
Weight: 26 lbs.
Features: All same features as the MEC Grabber, but with auto-indexing and auto-eject. Finished shells automatically ejected from shell carrier to drop chute for boxing. Available in 12, 16, 20, 28 and 410. From Mayville Engineering Company, Inc.
Price: $371.70
Price: 3" kit, 12-ga. $70.70
Price: 3" kit, 20-ga. $40.40
Price: Steel shot kit $35.35

MEC 9000 Hustler

Press Type: Progressive
Avg. Rounds Per Hour: 400
Weight: 30 lbs.
Features: Same features as 9000G with addition of foot pedal-operated hydraulic system for complete automation. Operates on standard 110V household current. Comes with bushing-type charge bar and three bushings. Available in 12, 16, 20, 28 gauge and 410 bore. From Mayville Engineering Company, Inc.
Price: $896.90
Price: Steel shot kit $35.35

MEC Sizemaster

Press Type: Single stage
Avg. Rounds Per Hour: 150
Weight: 20 lbs.
Features: Power ring eight-fingered collet resizer returns base to factory specs; handles brass or steel, high or low base heads; auto primer feed; adjustable for three shells. Available in 10, 12, 16, 20, 28 gauges and 410 bore. From Mayville Engineering Company, Inc.
Price: $170.10
Price: Die set, 12, 16, 20, 28, 410 .... $89.56
Price: Die set, 10-ga. $105.10
Price: Steel shot kit $20.20
Price: Steel shot kit, 12-ga. 3-1/2" $70.97

MEC Steelmaster

Press Type: Single stage
Avg. Rounds Per Hour: 150
Weight: 20 lbs.
Features: Same features as Sizemaster except can load steel shot. Press is available for 3-1/2" 10-ga. and 12-ga. 2-3/4", 3" or 3-1/2". For loading lead shot, die sets available in 10, 12, 16, 20, 28 and 410. From Mayville Engineering Company, Inc.
Price: $183.75
Price: 12 ga. 3-1/2" $205.80

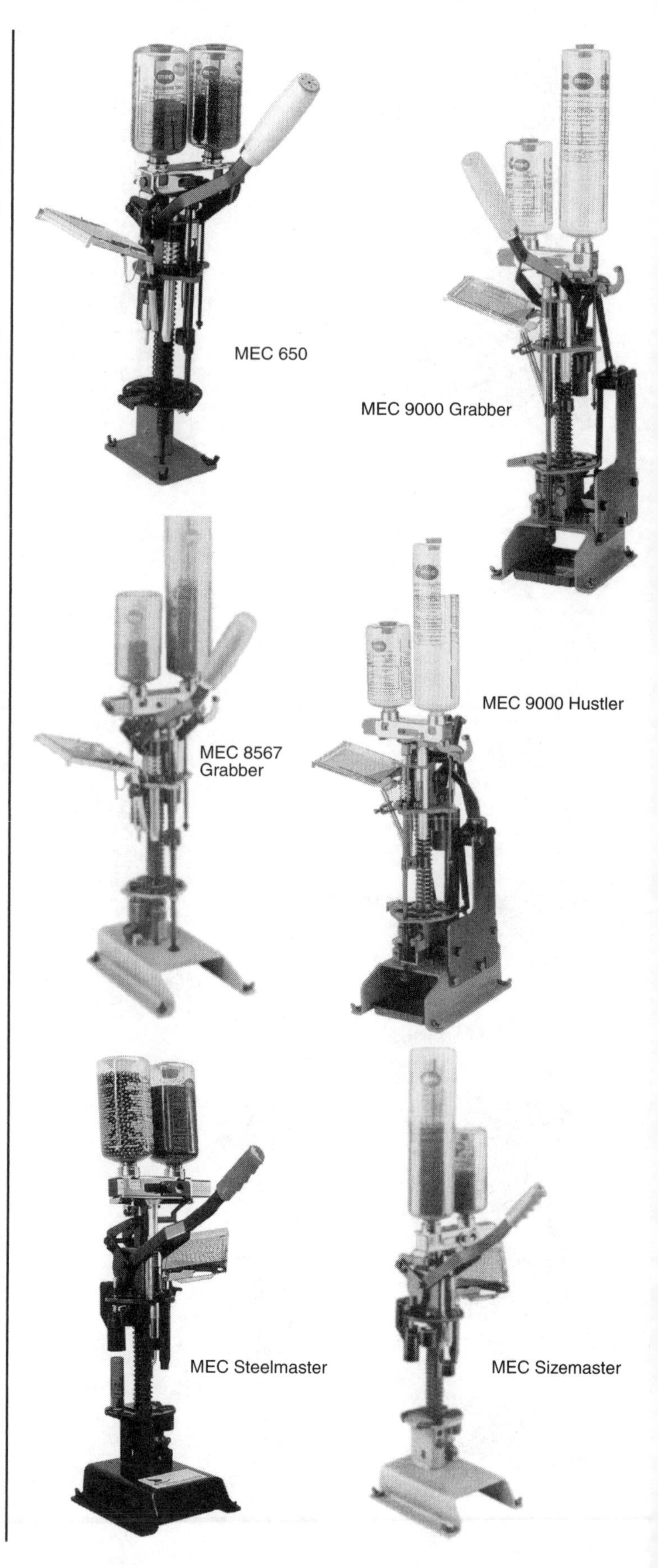
MEC 650
MEC 9000 Grabber
MEC 8567 Grabber
MEC 9000 Hustler
MEC Steelmaster
MEC Sizemaster

Shotshell Reloading Presses

Ponsness/Warren
Du-O-Matic 375C

Ponsness/Warren
Hydro-Multispeed

Ponsness/Warren
Size-O-Matic
900 Elite

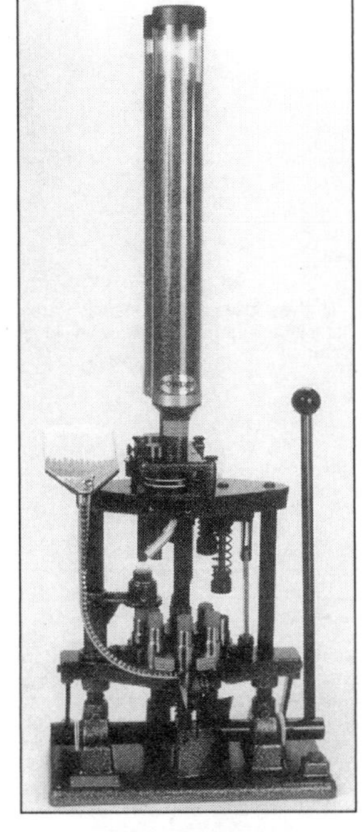

Ponsness/Warren
Platinum 2000

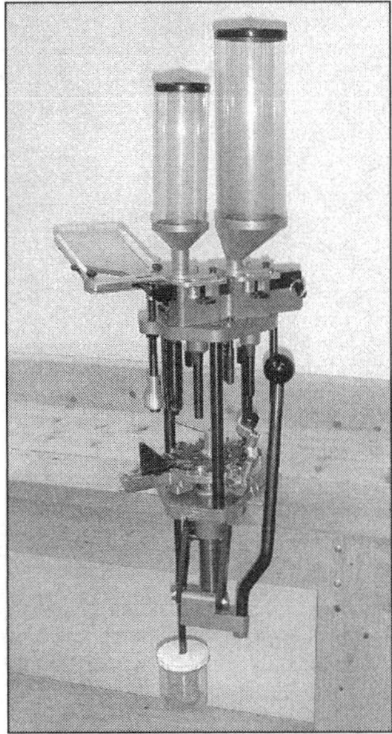

RCBS The Grand

PONSNESS/WARREN Du-O-Matic 375C

Press Type: Progressive
Avg. Rounds Per Hour: NA
Weight: 31 lbs.
Features: Steel or lead shot reloader; large shot and powder reservoirs; bushing access plug for dropping in shot buffer or buckshot; positive lock charging ring to prevent accidental flow of powder; double-post construction for greater leverage; removable spent primer box; spring-loaded ball check for centering size die at each station; tip-out wad guide; two-gauge capacity tool head. Available in 10 (extra charge), 12, 16, 20, 28 and 410 with case lengths of 2-1/2, 2-3/4, 3 and 3-1/2 inches. From Ponsness/ Warren.
Price: 12-, 20-, and 28-ga., 2-3/4" and 410, 2-1/2" **$289.00**
Price: 12-ga. 3-1/2"; 3" 12, 20, 410 . . . . **$305.00**
Price: 12, 20 2-3/4" **$383.95**
Price: 10-ga. press **$315.00**

PONSNESS/WARREN Hydro-Multispeed

Hydraulic system developed for Ponsness/Warren L/S-1000. Usable for the 950, 900 and 800 series presses. Three reloading speed settings operated with variable foot pedal control. Features stop/reverse at any station; automatic shutdown with pedal control release; fully adjustable hydraulic cylinder rod to prevent racking or bending of machine; quick disconnect hoses for ease of installation. Preassembled with step-by-step instructions. From Ponsness/Warren.
Price: **$879.00**
Price: Cylinder kit **$399.95**

PONSNESS/WARREN L/S-1000

Frame: Die cast aluminum
Avg. Rounds Per Hour: NA
Weight: 55 lbs.
Features: Fully progressive press to reload steel, bismuth or lead shot. Equipped with new Uni-Drop shot measuring and dispensing system which allows the use of all makes of shot in any size. Shells automatically resized and deprimed with new Auto-Size and De-Primer system. Loaded rounds drop out of shellholders when completed. Each shell pre-crimped and final crimped with Tru-Crimp system. Available in 10-gauge 3-1/2" or 12-gauge 2-3/4" and 3". 12-gauge 3-1/2" conversion kit also available. 20-gauge 2-3/4" and 3" special order only. From Ponsness/Warren.
Price: 12 ga. **$849.00**
Price: 10 ga. **$895.00**
Price: Conversion kit **$199.00**

PONSNESS/WARREN Size-O-Matic 900 Elite

Press Type: Progressive
Avg. Rounds Per Hour: 500-800
Weight: 49 lbs.
Features: Progressive eight-station press; frame of die cast aluminum; center post design index system ensures positive indexing; timing factory set, drilled and pinned. Automatic features include index, deprime, reprime, powder and shot drop, crimp start, tapered final crimp, finished shell ejection. Available in 12, 20, 28 and 410. 16-ga. special order. Kit includes new shellholders, seating port, resize/primer knockout assembly, new crimp assembly. From Ponsness/Warren.
Price: **$749.00**
Price: Conversion tooling, 12, 20, 28, 410 . . . . **$189.00**

PONSNESS/WARREN Platinum 2000

Press Type: Progressive
Avg. Rounds Per Hour: 500-800
Weight: 52 lbs.
Features: Progressive eight-station press, similar to 900 and 950 except has die removal system that allows removal of any die component during reloading cycle. Comes standard with 25-lb. shot tube, 19" powder tube, brass adjustable priming feed allows adjustment of primer seating depth. From Ponsness/Warren.
Price: **$889.00**

RCBS The Grand

Press Type: Progressive
Avg. Rounds Per Hour: NA
Weight: NA
Features: Constructed from a high-grade aluminum casting, allows complete resizing of high and low base hulls. Available for 12 and 20 gauge.
Price: **$688.95**

SCOPES / HUNTING, TARGET & VARMINT

ADCO

Maker and Model	Magn.	Field at 100 Yds. (feet)	Eye Relief (in.)	Length (in.)	Tube Dia. (in.)	W & E Adjustments	Weight (ozs.)	Price
Magnum 50 mm[5]	0			4.1	45 mm	Int.	6.8	**$269.00**
MIRAGE Ranger 1"	0			5.2	1	Int.	3.9	**159.00**
MIRAGE Ranger 30mm	0			5.5	30mm	Int.	5	**159.00**
MIRAGE Competitor	0			5.5	30mm	Int.	5.5	**229.00**
IMP Sight[2]	0			4.5		Int.	1.3	**17.95**
Square Shooter 2[3]	0			5		Int.	5	**99.00**
MIRAGE Eclipse[1]	0			5.5	30mm	Int.	5.5	**229.00**
Champ Red Dot	0			4.5		Int.	2	**33.95**
Vantage 1"	0			3.9	1	Int.	3.9	**129.00**
Vantage 30mm	0			4.2	30mm	Int.	4.9	**159.00**
Vision 2000[6]	0	60		4.7		Int.	6.2	**79.00**
e-dot ESB[1]	0			4.12	1	Int.	3.7	**139.00**
e-dot E1B	0			4.12	1	Int.	3.7	**99.00**
e-dot ECB	0			3.8	30mm	Int.	6.4	**99.00**
e-dot E30B	0			4.3	30mm	Int.	4.6	**99.00**

Other Data: [1]Multi-Color Dot system changes from red to green. [2]For airguns, paint ball, rimfires. Uses common lithium water battery. [3]Comes with standard dovetail mount. [4].75" dovetail mount; poly body; adj. intensity diode. [5]10 MOA dot; black or nickel. [6]Square format; with mount battery. From ADCO Sales.

AIMPOINT

Maker and Model	Magn.	Field at 100 Yds. (feet)	Eye Relief (in.)	Length (in.)	Tube Dia. (in.)	W & E Adjustments	Weight (ozs.)	Price
Comp	0			4.6	30mm	Int.	4.3	**331.00**
Comp M[4]	0			5	30mm	Int.	6.1	**409.00**
Series 5000[3]	0			6	30mm	Int.	6	**297.00**
Series 3000 Universal[2]	0			6.25	1	Int.	6	**232.00**
Series 5000/2x[1]	2			7	30mm	Int.	9	**388.00**

Other Data: Illuminates red dot in field of view. Noparallax (dot does not need to be centered). Unlimited field of view and eye relief. On/off, adj. intensity. Dot covers 3" @100 yds. [1]Comes with 30mm rings, battery, lense cloth. [2]Requires 1" rings. Black finish. AP Comp avail. in black, blue, SS, camo. [3]Black finish (AP 5000-B) ; avail. with regular 3-min. or 10-min. Mag Dot as B2 or S2. [4]Band pass reflection coating for compatibility with night vision equipment; U.S. Army contract model; with anti-reflex coated lenses (Comp ML), **$359.00**. From Aimpoint U.S.A.

ARMSON O.E.G.

Maker and Model	Magn.	Field at 100 Yds. (feet)	Eye Relief (in.)	Length (in.)	Tube Dia. (in.)	W & E Adjustments	Weight (ozs.)	Price
Standard	0			5.125	1	Int.	4.3	**202.00**
22 DOS[1]	0			3.75		Int.	3	**127.00**
22 Day/Night	0			3.75		Int.	3	**169.00**
M16/AR-15	0			5.125		Int.	5.5	**226.00**

Other Data: Shown red dot aiming point. No batteries needed. Standard model fits 1" ring mounts (not incl.). Other O.E.G. models for shotguns and rifles can be special ordered. [1]Daylight Only Sight with .375" dovetail mount for 22s. Does not contain tritium. From Trijicon, Inc.

ARTEMIS 2000

Maker and Model	Magn.	Field at 100 Yds. (feet)	Eye Relief (in.)	Length (in.)	Tube Dia. (in.)	W & E Adjustments	Weight (ozs.)	Price
4x32	4	34.4	3.15	10.7	1	Int.	17.5	**215.00**
6x42	6	23	3.15	13.7	1	Int.	17.5	**317.00**
7x50	7	18.7	3.15	13.9	1	Int.	17.5	**329.00**
1.5-6x42	1.5-6	40-12.8	2.95	12.4	30mm	Int.	19.4	**522.00**
2-8x42	2-8	31-9.5	2.95	13.1	30mm	Int.	21.1	**525.00**
3-9x42	3-9	24.6-8.5	2.95	12.4	30mm	Int.	19.4	**466.00**
3-12x50	3-12	20.6-6.2	2.95	14	30mm	Int.	22.9	**574.00**

Other Data: Click-stop windage and elevation adjustments; constantly centered reticle; rubber eyepiece ring; nitrogen filled. Imported from the Czech Republic by CZ-USA.

BEC

Maker and Model	Magn.	Field at 100 Yds. (feet)	Eye Relief (in.)	Length (in.)	Tube Dia. (in.)	W & E Adjustments	Weight (ozs.)	Price
EuroLux								
EL2510x56	2.5-10	39.4-11.5	3.25-2	15.1	30mm	Int.	25.4	**249.90**
EL39x42	3-9	34.1-13.2	3.5-3	12.3	30mm	Int.	17.7	**99.80**
EL28x36	2-8	44.9-11.5	3.8-3	12.2	30mm	Int.	15.9	**149.50**
ELA39x40RB[2]	3-9	39-13	3	12.7	30mm	Int.	14.3	**95.95**
EL6x42	6	21	3	12.6	30mm	Int.	14.8	**69.00**
EL4x42	4	29	3	12.6	30mm	Int.	14.8	**59.60**
EL4x36	4	29	3	12	30mm	Int.	14	**49.90**
EL4x25	4	26	3	7	30mm	Int.	7.6	**37.00**
AR4x22WA[1]	4	24	3	7	34mm	Int.	13.6	**109.97**
Goldlabel[3]								
GLI 624x50	6-24	16-4	3.5-3	15.3	1	Int.	22.5	**139.00**
GLI 416x50	4-16	25-6	3.5-3	13.5	1	Int.	21.8	**135.00**
GLI 39x40R[2]	3-9	39-13	3.5-3	12.7	28mm	Int.	18.5	**99.00**
GLC 5x42BD[4]	5	24	3.5	8.7	1	Int.	16.5	**79.00**

Other Data: Black matte finish. Multi-coated lenses; 1/4-MOA click adjustments (1/2-MOA on EL4x25, AR4x22WA); fog and water-proof. [1]For AR-15; bullet drop compensator; q.d. mount. [2]Rubber armored. Imported by BEC Inc. Partial listing shown. Contact BEC for complete details. [3]All Goldlabel scopes feature lighted reticles and finger-adjustable windage and elevation adjustments. [4]Bullet-drop compensator system for Mini-14 and AR-15 rifles.

BEEMAN

Maker and Model	Magn.	Field at 100 Yds. (feet)	Eye Relief (in.)	Length (in.)	Tube Dia. (in.)	W & E Adjustments	Weight (ozs.)	Price
Rifle Scopes								
5045[1]	4-12	26.9-9	3	13.2	1	Int.	15	**275.00**
5046[1]	6-24	18-4.5	3	16.9	1	Int.	20.2	**395.00**
5050[1]	4	26	3.5	11.7	1	Int.	11	**80.00**
5055[1]	3-9	38-13	3.5	10.75	1	Int.	11.2	**90.00**
5060[1]	4-12	30-10	3	12.5	1	Int.	16.2	**210.00**
5065[1]	6-18	17-6	3	14.7	1	Int.	17.3	**265.00**
5066RL[2]	2-7	58-15	3	11.4	1	Int.	17	**380.00**
5047L[2]	4	25	3.5	7	1	Int.	13.7	**NA**
Pistol Scopes								
5021	2	19	10-24	9.1	1	Int.	7.4	**85.50**
5020	1.5	14	11-16	8.3	.75	Int.	3.6	**NA**

Other Data: All scopes have 5 point reticle, all glass fully coated lenses. [1]Parallel adjustable. [2]Reticle lighted by ambient light. [3]Available with lighted Electro-Dot reticle. Imported by Beeman.

BSA

Maker and Model	Magn.	Field at 100 Yds. (feet)	Eye Relief (in.)	Length (in.)	Tube Dia. (in.)	W & E Adjustments	Weight (ozs.)	Price
Catseye[1]								
CE1545x32	1.5-4.5	78-23	4	11.25	1	Int.	12	**91.95**
CE310x44	3-10	39-12	3.25	12.75	1	Int.	16	**151.95**
CE3510x50	3.5-10	30-10.5	3.25	13.25	1	Int.	17.25	**171.95**
CE416x50	4-16	25-6	3	15.25	1	Int.	22	**191.95**
CE624x50	6-24	16-3	3	16	1	Int.	23	**222.95**
CE1545x32IR	1.5-4.5	78-23	5	11.25	1	Int.	12	**121.95**
Deer Hunter[2]								
DH25x20	2.5	72	6	7.5	1	Int.	7.5	**59.95**
DH4x32	4	32	3	12	1	Int.	12.5	**49.95**
DH39x32	3-9	39-13	3	12	1	Int.	11	**69.95**

Other Data: [1]Waterproof, fogproof; multi-coated lenses; finger-adjustable knobs. [2]Waterproof, fogproof; matte black finish. [3]With 4" sunshade; target knobs; 1/8-MOA click adjustments. [4]Adjustable for parallax; with sun shades; target knobs, 1/8-MOA adjustments. Imported by BSA. [5]Illuminated reticle model; also available in 3-10x, 3.5-10x, and 3-9x. [6]Red dot sights also available in 42mm and 50mm versions. [7]Includes Universal Bow Mount. [8]Five other models offered. From BSA.

Maker and Model	Magn.	Field at 100 Yds. (feet)	Eye Relief (in.)	Length (in.)	Tube Dia. (in.)	W & E Adjustments	Weight (ozs.)	Price	Other Data
DH39x40	3-9	39-13	3	13	1	Int.	12.1	**89.95**	
DH39x50	3-9	41-15	3	12.75	1	Int.	13	**109.95**	
DH2510x44	2.5-10	42-12	3	13	1	Int.	12.5	**99.95**	
DH1545x32	1.5-4.5	78-23	5	11.25	1	Int.	12	**79.95**	
Contender[3]									
CT24x40TS	24	6	3	15	1	Int.	18	**129.95**	
CT36x40TS	36	3	3	15.25	1	Int.	19	**139.95**	
CT312x40TS	3-12	28-7	3	13	1	Int.	17.5	**129.95**	
CT416x40TS	4-16	21-5	3	13.5	1	Int.	18	**131.95**	
CT624x40TS	6-24	16-4	3	15.5	1	Int.	20	**149.95**	
CT832x40TS	8-32	11-3	3	15.5	1	Int.	20	**171.95**	
CT312x50TS	3-12	28-7	3	13.75	1	Int.	21	**131.95**	
CT416x50TS	4-16	21-5	3	15.25	1	Int.	22	**151.95**	
CT624x50TS	6-24	16-4	3	16	1	Int.	23	**171.95**	
CT832x50TS	8-32	11-3	3	16.5	1	Int.	24	**191.95**	
Pistol									
P52x20	2	N/A	N/A	N/A	N/A	Int.	N/A	**89.95**	
Platinum[4]									
PT24x44TS	24	4.5	3	16.25	1	Int.	17.9	**189.55**	
PT36x44TS	36	3	3	14.9	1	Int.	17.9	**199.95**	
PT624x44TS	6-24	15-4.5	3	15.25	1	Int.	18.5	**221.95**	
PT832x44TS	8-32	11-3.5	3	17.25	1	Int.	19.5	**229.95**	
.22 Special									
S39x32WR	3-9	37.7-14.1	3	12	1	Int.	12.3	**89.95**	
S4x32WR	4	26	3	10.75	1	Int.	9	**39.95-44.95**	
Air Rifle									
AR4x32	4	33	3	13	1	Int.	14	**69.95**	
AR27x32	2-7	48	3	12.25	1	Int.	14	**79.95**	
AR312x44	3-12	36	3	12.25	1	Int.	15	**109.95**	
Red Dot									
RD30[6]	0			3.8	30mm	Int.	5	**59.95**	
PB30[6]	0			3.8	30mm	Int.	4.5	**79.95**	
Bow30[7]	0			N/A	30mm	Int.	5	**89.95**	
Big Cat									
BIgCat[8]	3.5-10	30-11	5	9.7	1	Int.	16.8	**219.95**	

BURRIS

Maker and Model	Magn.	Field at 100 Yds. (feet)	Eye Relief (in.)	Length (in.)	Tube Dia. (in.)	W & E Adjustments	Weight (ozs.)	Price
Mr. T Black Diamond Titanium								
2.5-10x50A	2.5-10	4.25-4.75		13.6			29	**1,518.00**
4-16x50	4-16	27-7.5	3.3-3.8	13.6	30mm	Int.	27	**1,594.00**
Black Diamond								
3-12x50[3,4,6]	3.2-11.9	34-12	3.5-4	13.8	30mm	Int.	25	**974.00**
6-24x50	6-24	18-6	3.5-4	16.2	30mm	Int.	25	**1,046.00**
Fullfield II								
2.5x9	2.5	55	3.5-3.75	10.25	1	Int.	9	**307.00**
1.75-5x[1,2,9,10]	1.7-4.6	66-25	3.5-3.75	10.875	1	Int.	13	**400.00**
3-9x40[1,2,3,10]	3.3-8.7	38-15	3.5-3.75	12.625	1	Int.	15	**336.00**
3-9x50	3-9	35-15	3.5-3.75	13	1	Int.	18	**481.00**
3.5-10x50mm[3,5,10]	3.7-9.7	29.5-11	3.5-3.75	14	1	Int.	19	**542.00**
4.5-14x[1,4,8,11]	4.4-11.8	27-10	3.5-3.75	15	1	Int.	18	**585.00**
6.5-20x[1,3,4,6,7,8]	6.5-17.6	16.7	3.5-3.75	15.8	1	Int.	18.5	**656.00**
Compact Scopes								
1x XER[3]	1	51	4.5-20	8.8	1	Int.	7.9	**320.00**
4x[4,5]	3.6	24	3.75-5	8.25	1	Int.	7.8	**397.00**
6x[1,4]	5.5	17	3.75-5	9	1	Int.	8.2	**397.00**
6x HBR[1,5,8]	6	13	4.5	11.25	1	Int.	13	**415.00**
1-4x XER[3]	1-3.8	53-15	4.25-30	8.8	1	Int.	10.3	**467.00**
3-9x[4,5]	3.6-8.8	25-11	3.75-5	12.625	1	Int.	11.5	**442.00**
4-12x[1,4,6]	4.5-11.6	19-8	3.75-4	15	1	Int.	15	**534.00**
Signature Series								
1.5-6x[2,3,5,9,10]	1.7-5.8	70-20	3.5-4	10.8	1	Int.	13	**601.00**
8x3[2,5,11]	2.1-7.7	53-17	3.5-4	11.75	1	Int.	14	**840.00**
3-10x[3,5,10,13]	3.3-8.8	36-14	3.5-4	12.875	1	Int.	15.5	**665.00**
3-12x[3,10]	3.3-11.7	34-9	3.5-4	14.25	1	Int.	21	**701.00**
4-16x[1,3,5,6,8,10]	4.3-15.7	33-9	3.5-4	15.4	1	Int.	23.7	**760.00**
6-24x[1,3,5,6,8,10,13]	6.6-23.8	17-6	3.5-4	16	1	Int.	22.7	**787.00**
8-32x[8,10,12]	8.6-31.4	13-3.8	3.5-4	17	1	Int.	24	**840.00**
Speeddot 135[14]								
Red Dot	1			4.85	35mm	Int.	5	**291.00**
Handgun								
1.50-4x LER[1,5,10]	1.6-3	16-11	11-25	10.25	1	Int.	11	**411.00**
2-7x LER[3,4,5,10]	2-6.5	21-7	7-27	9.5	1	Int.	12.6	**458.00**
2x LER[4,5,6]	1.7	21	10-24	8.75	1	Int.	6.8	**286.00**
4x LER[1,4,5,6,10]	3.7	11	10-22	9.625	1	Int.	9	**338.00**
3x12x LER[1,4,6]	9.5	4	8-12	13.5	1	Int.	14	**558.00**
Scout Scope								
1xXER[3,9]	1.5	32	4-24	9	1	Int.	7.0	**320.00**
2.75x[3,9]	2.7	15	7-14	9.375	1	Int.	7.0	**356.00**

Available in Carbon Black, Titanium Gray and Autumn Gold finishes. **Black Diamond & Fullfield:** All scopes avail. with Plex reticle. Steel-on-steel click adjustments. [1]Dot reticle on some models. [2]Post crosshair reticle extra. [3]Matte satin finish. [4]Available with parallax adjustment (standard on 10x, 12x, 4-12x, 6-12x, 6-18x, 6x HBR and 3-12x Signature). [5]Silver matte finish extra. [6]Target knobs extra, standard on silhouette models. LER and XER with P.A., 6x HBR. [7]Sunshade avail. [8]Avail. with Fine Plex reticle. [9]Available with Heavy Plex reticle. [10]Available with Posi-Lock. [11]Available with Peep Plex reticle. [12]Also avail. for rimfires, airguns. [13]Selected models available with camo finish.
Signature Series: LER=Long Eye Relief; IER=Intermediate Eye Relief; XER=Extra Eye Relief.
Speeddot 135: [14]Waterproof, fogproof, coated lenses, 11 bright ness settings; 3-MOA or 11-MOA dot size; includes Weaver-style rings and battery.
Partial listing shown. Contact Burris for complete details.

Plex

Fine Plex

Heavy Plex & Electro-Dot Plex

Peep Plex

Ballistic Mil-Dot

Target Dot

Mil-Dot

BUSHNELL (Bausch & Lomb Elite rifle scopes now sold under Bushnell brand)

Maker and Model	Magn.	Field at 100 Yds. (feet)	Eye Relief (in.)	Length (in.)	Tube Dia. (in.)	W & E Adjustments	Weight (ozs.)	Price	Other Data
Elite 4200 RainGuard									
42-6244M[1]	6-24	18-6	3	16.9	1	Int.	20.2	**639.95**	
42-2104G[2]	2.5-10	41.5-10.8	3	13.5	1	Int.	16	**563.95**	
42-2151M[6, 9]	2.5-10	40.3-10.8	3.3	14.3	1	Int.	18	**699.95**	
42-1636M[3]	1.5-6	61.8-16.1	3	12.8	1	Int.	15.4	**533.95**	
42-4164M[5, 6]	4-16	26-7	3.5	18.6	1	Int.	18.6	**565.95**	

SCOPES / HUNTING, TARGET & VARMINT

Maker and Model	Magn.	Field at 100 Yds. (feet)	Eye Relief (in.)	Length (in.)	Tube Dia. (in.)	W & E Adjustments	Weight (ozs.)	Price	Other Data
42-4165M[5]	4-16	26-7	3	15.6	1	Int.	22	**731.95**	(Bushnell Elite) [1]Adj. objective, sunshade; with 1/4-MOA dot or Mil Dot reticle. [2]Also in matte and silver finish. [3]Only in matte finish. [4]Also in matte and silver finish. [5]Adjustable objective. [6]50mm objective; also in matte finish. [7]Also in silver finish. [8]40mm. [9]Ill. dot reticle. **Partial listings shown. Contact Bushnell Performance Optics for details.** (Bushnell) [1]Wide Angle. [2]Also silver finish. [3]Also silver finish. [4]Matte finish. [5]Also silver finish. [7]Adj. obj. [8]Variable intensity; fits Weaver-style base. [9]Blackpowder scope; extended eye relief, Circle-X reticle. [10]50mm objective. [11]With Circle-X reticle, matte finish. [12]Matte finish, adjustable objective.
42-8324M	8-32	14-3.75	3.3	18	1	Int.	22	**703.95**	
Elite 3200 RainGuard									
32-5155M	5-15	21-7	3	15.9	1	Int.	19	**463.95**	
32-4124A[1]	4-12	26.9-9	3	13.2	1	Int.	15	**411.95**	
32-1040M	10	11	3.5	11.7	1	Int.	15.5	**279.95**	
32-3940G[4]	3-9	33.8-11.5	3	12.6	1	Int.	13	**279.95**	
32-2732M	2-7	44.6-12.7	3	11.6	1	Int.	12	**265.95**	
32-39544G[6]	3-9	31.5-10.5	3	15.7	1	Int.	19	**335.95**	
32-3955E	3-9	31.5-10.5	3	15.6	30mm	Int.	22	**561.95**	
Elite 3200 Handgun RainGuard									
32-2632M[7]	2-6	10-4	20	9	1	Int.	10	**389.95**	
32-2636[10]	2-6	10-4	20	9	1	Int.	10	**431.95**	
Trophy									
73-0134	1	68	Unlimited	5.5	1	Int.	6	**119.95**	
73-1500[1]	1.75-5	68-23	3.5	10.8	1	Int.	12.3	**155.95**	
73-4124[1]	4-12	32-11	3	12.5	1	Int.	16.1	**263.95**	
73-3940[2]	3-9	42-14	3	11.7	1	Int.	13.2	**139.95**	
73-6184[7]	6-18	17.3-6	3	14.8	1	Int.	17.9	**331.95**	
Turkey & Brush									
73-1421[11]	1.75-4	73-30	3.5	10.8	32mm	Int.	10.9	**149.95**	
HOLOsight Model[8]	1			6		Int.	8.7	**389.95**	
Trophy Handgun									
73-2632[3]	2-6	21-7	9-26	9.1	1	Int.	10.9	**251.95**	
Banner									
71-1545	1.5-4.5	67-23	3.5	10.5	1	Int.	10.5	**101.95**	
71-3944[9]	3-9	36-13	4	11.5	1	Int.	12.5	**109.95**	
71-3950[10]	3-9	26-10	3	16	1	Int.	19	**163.95**	
71-4124[7]	4-12	29-11	3	12	1	Int.	15	**138.95**	
71-6185[10]	6-18	17-6	3	16	1	Int.	18	**209.95**	
Sportsman									
72-0038	3-9	37-14	3.5	12	1	Int.	6	**69.95**	
72-0039	3-9	38-13	3.5	10.75	1	Int.	11.2	**101.95**	
72-0412[7]	4-12	27-9	3.2	13.1	1	Int.	14.6	**123.95**	
72-1393[6]	3-9	35-12	3.5	11.75	1	Int.	10	**59.95**	
72-1545	1.5-4.5	69-24	3	10.7	1	Int.	8.6	**75.95**	
72-1548[11]	1.5-4.5	71-25	3.5	10.4	1	Int.	11.8	**95.95**	
72-1403	4	29	4	11.75	1	Int.	9.2	**49.95**	
72-3940M	3-9	42-14	3	12.7	1	Int.	12.5	**83.95**	
22 Rimfire									
76-2239	3-9	40-13	3	11.75	1	Int.	11.2	**53.95**	
76-2243	4	30	3	11.5	1	Int.	10	**45.95**	

A RETICLE IS THE CROSSHAIR OR PATTERN PLACED IN THE EYEPIECE OF THE SCOPE WHICH ESTABLISHES THE GUN'S POSITION ON THE TARGET.

MULTI-X

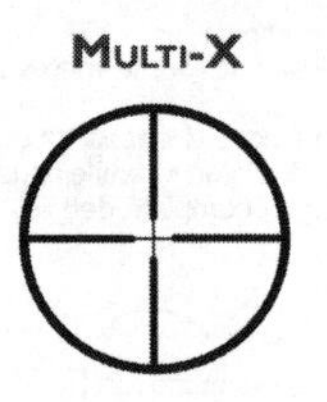

CIRCLE-X

MIL DOT

3-2-1 LOW-LIGHT

¼ M.O.A.

EUROPEAN

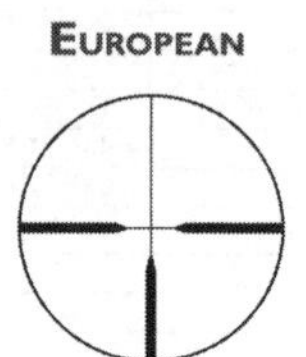

EUROPTIK SUPREME

Maker and Model	Magn.	Field at 100 Yds. (feet)	Eye Relief (in.)	Length (in.)	Tube Dia. (in.)	W & E Adjustments	Weight (ozs.)	Price	Other Data
4x36K	4	39	3.5	11.6	26mm	Int.	14	**795.00**	[1]Military scope with adjustable parallax. Fixed powers have 26mm tubes, variables have 30mm tubes. Some models avail. with steel tubes. All lenses multi-coated. Dust and water tight. From Europtik.
6x42K	6	21	3.5	13	26mm	Int.	15	**875.00**	
8x56K	8	18	3.5	14.4	26mm	Int.	20	**925.00**	
1.5-6x42K	1.5-6	61.7-23	3.5	12.6	30mm	Int.	17	**1,095.00**	
2-8x42K	2-8	52-17	3.5	13.3	30mm	Int.	17	**1,150.00**	
2.5-10x56K	2.5-10	40-13.6	3.5	15	30mm	Int.	21	**1,295.00**	
3-12x56 Super	3-12	10.8-34.7	3.5-2.5	15.2	30mm	Int.	24	**1,495.00**	
4-16x56 Super	4-16	9.8-3.9	3.1	18	30mm	Int.	26	**1,575.00**	
3-9x40 Micro	3-9	3.2-12.1	2.7	13	1	Int.	14	**1,450.00**	
2.5-10x46 Micro	2.5-10	13.7-33.4	2.7	14	30mm	Int.	20	**1,395.00**	
4-16x56 EDP[1]	4-16	22.3-7.5	3.1	18	30mm	Int.	29	**1,995.00**	
7-12x50 Target	7-12	8.8-5.5	3.5	15	30mm	Int.	21	**1,495.00**	

JAEGER

Maker and Model	Magn.	Field at 100 Yds. (feet)	Eye Relief (in.)	Length (in.)	Tube Dia. (in.)	W & E Adjustments	Weight (ozs.)	Price	Other Data
ST-10		10, 17	Varies	13	30mm, 35mm		34	**895.00**	All scopes available w/standard and extra-long eye relief eyepiece. Variable power military and police tactical scope systems are also available. Offers scope rings and bases. By U.S.O. Jaeger.
SN-1 Long Range		17, 22, 42	12.35 (10x)	Varies	30mm, 35mm, 40mm		36	**2,395.00**	
SN6 2d Perimeter		10, 17, 22	12.35 (10x)	Varies	30mm, 35mm, 40mm		34	**1,295.00**	
SN-9 Extreme Range		22, 42	6.2 (22x)	Varies			62.4	**2,600.00**	
SN-12 CQB		3, 4	38 (3x)	7.5	1		34	**865.00**	
USMC 10x Sniper		10	10.36	12.5	1		34	**2,500.00**	
USMC M40A3		10	10.36	12.5	1		34	**NA**	
JH-4 Safari		1-4	119-34	9.25	30mm		31	**1,195.00**	
JH-3 Denali		1.8-10x	48.7-12.35	13	30mm		32	**1,695.00**	
JH-3 Serengeti		3.2-17x		14.5	30mm		33	**1,895.00**	
JH-T-PAL Chucker		3.8-22x	30-6.2	17.5	30mm		34	**1,995.00**	

SCOPES / HUNTING, TARGET & VARMINT

KAHLES

Maker and Model	Magn.	Field at 100 Yds. (feet)	Eye Relief (in.)	Length (in.)	Tube Dia. (in.)	W & E Adjustments	Weight (ozs.)	Price
4x36	4	34.5	3.15	11.2	1	Int.	12.7	**555.00**
6x42	6	23	3.15	12.4	1	Int.	14.4	**694.00**
8x50[1]	8	17.3	3.15	13	1	Int.	16.5	**749.00**
1.1-4x24	1.1-4	108-31.8	3.5	10.8	30mm	Int.	12.7	**722.00**
1.5-6x42[1]	1.5-6	72-21.3	3.5	12.0	30mm	Int.	15.8	**832.00**
2.5-10x50[1]	2.5-10	43.5-12.9	3.5	12.8	30mm	Int.	15.8	**1,353.00**
3-9x42	3-9	43-16	3.5	12	1	Int.	13	**621.06**
3-9x42AH	3-9	43-15	3.5	12.36	1	Int.	12.7	**665.00**
3-12x56[1]	3-12	30-11	3.5	15.4	30mm	Int.	18	**1,377.72**

Other Data: Aluminum tube. Multi-coated, waterproof. [1]Also available with illuminated reticle. Imported from Austria by Swarovski Optik.

No. 4A **No. 7A** **Plex** **Illuminated No. 4N** **Illuminated Plex N** **TD Smith**

LEATHERWOOD

Maker and Model	Magn.	Field at 100 Yds. (feet)	Eye Relief (in.)	Length (in.)	Tube Dia. (in.)	W & E Adjustments	Weight (ozs.)	Price
Uni-Dial*								
U3510x50 3.5-10	50	36.7-12.8	3.25	13.11			18.7	**299.00**
U412-50 4-12	50	30.6-10.2	3.25	14.53			22.1	**339.00**
U618-50 6-18	50	20.4-7.5	3.25	15.35			22	**367.50**
U6520x50 6.5-20	50	18.8-6.3	3.25	15.43			23.5	**375.00**
U3501x50MD 3.5-10	50	36.7-12.8	3.25	13.11			18.7	**437.50**
Distinguished								
D3510x50 3.5-10	50	36.7-12.8	3.25	13.11			17.2	**199.00**
D412x50 4-12	50	30.6-10.2	3.25	14.53			20.6	**239.00**
D618x5- 6-18	50	20.4-7.5	3.25	15.35			21.5	**267.00**
D6520x50 6.5-20	50	18.8-6.3	3.35	15.43			22	**275.00**
D3510x50MD 3.5-10	50	36.7-12.8	3.25	13.11			17.2	**337.00**
Expert								
E412x44 4-12	44	30.6-10.7	3.25	14.53			19.7	**149.00**
E618x44 6-18	44	20.4-6.8	3.25	15.35			20.2	**159.00**
E6520x44 6.5-20	44	18.8-6.28	3.25	15.43			21.2	**169.00**
E6520x44MD 4-12	44	30.6-10.7	3.25	14.53			19.7	**223.50**
Sharpshooter								
S39x40 3-9	40	41-15	3.25	13			13.5	**95.00**
S39x40IR 3-9	40	39-13	3.25	12.75			14	**105.00**
S39x50 3-9	50	41-13	3.25	12.75			14.5	**112.00**
S3510x50 3.5-10	50	36.7-12.8	3.25	13.11			16.2	**119.00**
S310x44 3-10	44	40.8-12.8	3.25	13.11			15.2	**107.00**
S55-16x44 5.5-16	44	21.9-7.5	3.25	14.41			19.9	**149.00**
S6520x44 6.5-20	44	18.8-6.28	3.25	15.43			21.7	**145.00**
Long Eye Relief								
LER2732 2-7	32	18.88-6.28	11.2-8.7	11.08			11.57	**185.00**
Double Duce Rimfire								
RF4x32 4	32	26	3	12			11	**49.50**
RF39x32 3-9	32	38.5-13	3	12.5			12	**69.50**

Other Data: *Elevation adjustment is 1/8" and windage adjustment is 1/4". All air-glass surfaces are fully multi-coated to maximize light transmission.

LEICA

Maker and Model	Magn.	Field at 100 Yds. (feet)	Eye Relief (in.)	Length (in.)	Tube Dia. (in.)	W & E Adjustments	Weight (ozs.)	Price
Ultravid 1.75-6x32	1.75-6	47-18	4.8-3.7	11.25	30mm	Int.	14	**749.00**
Ultravid 3.5-10x42	3.5-10	29.5-10.7	4.6-3.6	12.62	30mm	Int.	16	**849.00**
Ultravid 4.5-14x42	4.5-14	20.5-7.4	5-3.7	12.28	30mm	Int.	18	**949.00**

Other Data: Aluminum tube with hard anodized matte black finish with titanium accents; finger-adjustable windage and elevation with 1/4-MOA clicks. Made in U.S. From Leica.

Leicaplex Standard **Leica Dot** **Standard Dot** **Crosshair** **Euro** **Post & Plex**

LEUPOLD

Maker and Model	Magn.	Field at 100 Yds. (feet)	Eye Relief (in.)	Length (in.)	Tube Dia. (in.)	W & E Adjustments	Weight (ozs.)	Price
M8-3.5x10	3.2-9.5	29.9	4.7	13.5	30mm	Int.	19.5	**1,124.99**
M8-2.7-28	2.66	41	3.8	9.9	1	Int.	8.2	**299.99**
M8-4X Compact RF	3.6	25.5	4.5	9.2	1	Int.	7.5	**289.99**
Vari-X 2-7x	2.5-6.5	41.7-17.3	4.2	10.8	1	Int.	10	**299.99**
Vari-X 3-9x	3.3-8.5	32-13.1	4.2	12.2	1	Int.	12	**314.99**
M8-4X	4	24	4	10.5	1	Int.	9.3	**249.99**
M8-6x36mm	5.9	17.7	4.3	11.3	1	Int.	10	**469.99**
M8-6x42mm	6	17	4.5	11.9	1	Int.	11.3	**424.99**
M8-12x40	11.6	9.1	4.2	13	1	Int.	13.5	**474.99**
Vari-X 3-9x	3.5-8.6	32.9-13.1	4-2	12.2	1	Int.	12	**454.99**
Vari-X-III 1.5-5x20	1.5-4.5	65-17	4.4-3.6	9.4	1	Int.	9.7	**499.99**
Vari-X-III 1.75-6x32	1.9-5.6	51	4.4-3.2	11.4	1	Int.	11.6	**499.99**
Vari-X-III 2.5x8	2.6-7.8	37-13.5	4.4-3.5	11.4	1	Int.	11.6	**499.99**
Vari-X-III 3.5-10x40	3.9-9.6	29.7-11	4.4-3.5	12.6	1	Int.	13	**549.99**
Vari-X-III 3.5-10x50	3.3-9.5	29.8-11	4.4-3.5	12.2	1	Int.	15.1	**624.99**
Vari-X-III 4.5-14x40	4.8-14.2	19.9	4.4-3.6	12.6	1	Int.	13.2	**699.99**
*Vari-X-III 4.5-14x50	4.9-14.4	19.1	4.4-3.6	12.6	1	Int.	16	**789.99**
Vari-X III 4.5-14x50 LRT[4]	4.9-14.3	19-6	5-3.7	12.1	30mm	Int.	17.5	**999.00**
Vari-X-III 6.5-20 A.O.	6.5-19.2	14.3-5.6	5-3.6	14.3	1	Int.	16	**749.99**
Vari-X III 6.5-20xLRT	6.5-19.2	14.3-5.5	4.4	14.2	1	Int.	21	**974.99**

Other Data: Constantly centered reticles, choice of Duplex, tapered CPC, Leupold Dot, Crosshair and Dot. CPC and Dot reticles extra. [1]2x and 4x scopes have from 12"-24" of eye relief and are suitable for handguns, top ejection arms and muzzleloaders. [2]3x9 Compact, 6x Compact, 12x, 3x9, and 6.5x20 come with adjustable objective. Sunshade available for all adjustable objective scopes, **$23.20-$41.10**. [3]Long Range scopes have side focus parallax adjustment, additional windage and elevation travel. Partial listing shown. **Contact Leupold for complete details.**

Duplex **CPC** **Post & Duplex** **Leupold Dot** **Dot**

SCOPES / HUNTING, TARGET & VARMINT

Maker and Model	Magn.	Field at 100 Yds. (feet)	Eye Relief (in.)	Length (in.)	Tube Dia. (in.)	W & E Adjustments	Weight (ozs.)	Price	Other Data
Vari-X III 8.5-25x40 LRT	8.3-24.3	11.3-4.3	5.2	14.3	1	Int.	21	**1,039.99**	
Vari-X III 8.5-25x 50 LRT[4]	8.3-24.3	11.3-4.3	5.2-7	14.4	30mm	Int.	21	**1,149.99**	
Mark 4 M1-10x40	10	11.1	3.6	13.125	30mm	Int.	21	**1,124.99**	
Mark 4 M1-16x40	16	6.6	4.1	12.875	30mm	Int.	22	**1,509.99**	
Mark 4 M3-10x40LRT	10	13.1	3.4	13.125	30mm	Int.	21	**939.99**	
Mark 4 6.5x20[2]	6.5-19.5	14.3-5.5	5.5-3.8	11.2	30mm	Int.	16	**1,198.99**	
LPS 1.5-6x42	1.5-6	58.7-15.7	4	11.2	30mm	Int.	16	**1,198.99**	
LPS 2.5-10x45	2.6-9.8	37.2	4.5-3.8		1	Int.	17.2	**1,119.99**	
LPS 3.5-14x52	3.5-14	28-7.2	4	13.1	30mm	Int.	22	**1,249.99**	
Rimfire									
Vari-X 2-7x RF Special	3.6	25.5	4.5	9.2	1	Int.	7.5	**299.99**	
Shotgun									
M8 2.5x20	2.3	39.5	4.9	8.4	1	Int.	6	**249.99**	
LYMAN									
Super TargetSpot[1]	10, 12, 15, 20, 25, 30	5.5	2	24.3	.75	Int.	27.5	**685.00**	Made under license from Lyman to Lyman's orig. specs. Blue steel. Three-point suspension rear mount with .25-min. click adj. Data listed for 20x model. [1]Price appx. Made in U.S. by Parsons Optical Mfg. Co.
McMILLAN									
Vision Master 2.5-10x	2.5-10	14.2-4.4	4.3-3.3	13.3	30mm	Int.	17	**1,250.00**	42mm obj. lens; .25-MOA clicks; nitrogen filled, fogproof, waterproof; etched duplex-type reticle. [1]Tactical Scope with external adj. knobs, military reticle; 60+ min. adj.
Vision Master Model 1[1]	2.5-10	14.2-4.4	4.3-3.3	13.3	30mm	Int.	17	**1,250.00**	
MEOPTA									
Artemis									
4x32A[1]	4	34	3.15	11	1	Int.	14.7	**194.00**	Steel tubes are waterproof, dustproof, and shockproof; nitrogen filled. Anti-reflective coatings, protective rubber eye piece, clear caps. Made in Czech Replublic by Meopta. [1]Range finder reticles available. Partial listing shown.
6x42A[1]	6	23	3.15	13.6	1	Int.	18.2	**267.00**	
7x50A[1]	7	18	3.15	14.1	1	Int.	19	**278.00**	
MEPROLIGHT									
Meprolight Reflex Sights 14-21 5.5 MOA 1x30[1]	1			4.4	30mm	Int.	5.2	**335.00**	[1]Also available with 4.2 MOA dot. Uses tritium and fiber optics-no batteries required. From Hesco, Inc.
MILLETT									
Buck 3-9x44	3-9	38-14	3.25-4	13	1	Int.	16.2	**238.00**	[1]3-MOA dot. 25-MOA dot. 33- , 5- , 8- , 10-MOA dots. 410-MOA dot. All have click adjustments; waterproof, shockproof; 11 dot intensity settings. All avail. in matte/black or silver finish. From Millett Sights.
Buck 3.5-10x50	3.5-10	NA	NA	NA	1	NA	NA	**258.00**	
Buck 3-12x44 A/O	3-12	NA	NA	NA	1	NA	NA	**258.00**	
Buck 4-16x44 A/O	4-16	NA	NA	NA	1	NA	NA	**270.00**	
Buck Varmint 4-16x56	4-16	NA	NA	NA	30mm	NA	NA	**318.00**	
Buck Varmint 6-25x56	6-25	NA	NA	NA	30mm	NA	NA	**338.00**	
Buck Varmint 6-25x56	6-25	NA	NA	NA	30mm	NA	NA	**370.00**	
Buck Lightning 1.5-6x44	1.5-6	NA	NA	NA	1	NA	NA	**270.00**	
Buck Lightning 3-9x44	3-9	NA	NA	NA	1	NA	NA	**270.00**	
Buck Silver 3-9x40	3-9	NA	NA	NA	1	NA	NA	**129.95**	
Buck Silver 4-12x40 A/O	4-12	NA	NA	NA	1	NA	NA	**172.00**	
Buck Silver 6-18x40 A/O	6-18	NA	NA	NA	1	NA	NA	**172.00**	
Buck Silver Compact 2x20	2	NA	NA	NA	1	NA	NA	**99.50**	
Buck Silver Compact 4x32	4	NA	NA	NA	1	NA	NA	**105.00**	
Buck Silver Compact 1.5-4x32	1.5-4	NA	NA	NA	1	NA	NA	**136.00**	
SP-1 Compact[1] Red Dot	1	36.65		4.1	1	Int.	3.2	**147.45**	
SP-2 Compact[2] Red Dot	1	58		4.5	30mm	Int.	4.3	**147.45**	
MultiDot SP[3]	1	50		4.8	30mm	Int.	5.3	**179.45**	
30mm Wide View[4]	1	60		5.5	30mm	Int.	5	**179.45**	
MIRADOR									
RXW 4x40[1]	4	37	3.8	12.4	1	Int.	12	**179.95**	[1]Wide angle scope. Multi-coated objective lens. Nitrogen filled; waterproof; shockproof. From Mirador Optical Corp.
RXW 1.5-5x20[1]	1.5-5	46-17.4	4.3	11.1	1	Int.	10	**188.95**	
RXW 3-9x40	3-9	43-14.5	3.1	12.9	1	Int.	13.4	**251.95**	
NIGHTFORCE									
3.5-15x50	3.5-15	27.6-9.7.3		14.7	30mm		30	**1,278.90**	Lighted reticles with eleven intensity levels. Most scopes have choice of reticles. From Lightforce U.S.A.
3.5-15x56	3.5-15	27.6-7	3	14.8	30mm	Int.	31	**1,309.77**	
5.5-22x56	5.5-22	17.5-4.47		15	30mm	Int.	31	**1,385.90**	
5.5-22x56	5.5-22	17.5-4.7		15.2	30mm	Int.	32	**1,300.18**	
8-32x56	8-32	12.1-3.1		15.9	30mm	Int.	34	**1,519.25**	
12-42x56	12-42	8.2-2.4		16.1	30mm	Int.	34	**1,648.24**	
3.5-15x36	3.5-15	24.5-6.9		15.8	30mm	Int.	32	**1,000.83**	
8-32x56	8-32	9.4-3.1	3	16.6	30mm	Int.	36	**997.90**	
12-42x56	12-42	6.7-2.3	3	17	30mm	Int.	36	**1,053.64**	
NIKON									
Monarch UCC									
4x40[2]	4	26.7	3.5	11.7	1	Int.	11.7	**229.99**	
1.5-4.5x20[3]	1.5-4.5	67.8-22.5	3.7-3.2	10.1	1	Int.	9.5	**239.99**	
2-7x32	2-7	46.7-13.7	3.9-3.3	11.3	1	Int.	11.3	**259.99**	
3-9x40[1]	3-9	33.8-11.3	3.6-3.2	12.5	1	Int.	12.5	**299.99**	

SCOPES / HUNTING, TARGET & VARMINT

Maker and Model	Magn.	Field at 100 Yds. (feet)	Eye Relief (in.)	Length (in.)	Tube Dia. (in.)	W & E Adjustments	Weight (ozs.)	Price
3.5-10x50	3.5-10	25.5-8.9	3.9-3.8	13.7	1	Int.	15.5	**429.99**
4-12x40 A.O.	4-12	25.7-8.6	3.6-3.2	14	1	Int.	16.6	**369.99**
6.5-20x44	6.5-19.4	16.2-5.4	3.5-3.1	14.8	1	Int.	19.6	**459.99**
2x20 EER	2	22	26.4	8.1	1	Int.	6.3	**169.99**
Buckmasters								
4x40	4	30.4	3.3	12.7	1	Int.	11.8	**159.99**
3-9x40[4]	3.3-8.6	33.8-11.3	3.5-3.4	12.7	1	Int.	13.4	**209.99**
3-9x50	3.3-8.6	33.8-11.3	3.5-3.4	12.9	1	Int.	18.2	**299.99**

Super multi-coated lenses and blackening of all internal metal parts for maximum light gathering capability; positive .25-MOA; fogproof; waterproof; shockproof; luster and matte finish. [1]Also available in matte silver finish. [2]Available in silver matte finish. [3]Available with TurkeyPro or Nikoplex reticle. [4]Silver Shadow finish; black matte **$296.95**. Partial listing shown. From Nikon, Inc.

NORINCO

Maker and Model	Magn.	Field at 100 Yds. (feet)	Eye Relief (in.)	Length (in.)	Tube Dia. (in.)	W & E Adjustments	Weight (ozs.)	Price
N2520	2.5	44.1	4		1	Int.		**52.28**
N420	4	29.3	3.7		1	Int.		**52.70**
N640	6	20	3.1		1	Int.		**67.88**
N154520	1.5-4.5	63.9-23.6	4.1-3.2			Int.		**80.14**
N251042	2.5-10	27-11	3.5-2.8		1	Int.		**206.60**
N3956	3-9	35.1-6.3	3.7-2.6		1	Int.		**231.88**
N31256	3-12	26-10	3.5-2.8		1	Int.		**290.92**
NC2836M	2-8	50.8-14.8	3.6-2.7		1	Int.		**255.60**

Partial listing shown. Some with Ruby Lens coating, blue/black and matte finish. Imported by Nic Max, Inc.

PARSONS

Maker and Model	Magn.	Field at 100 Yds. (feet)	Eye Relief (in.)	Length (in.)	Tube Dia. (in.)	W & E Adjustments	Weight (ozs.)	Price
Parsons Long Scope	6	10	2	28-34+	.75	Ext.	13	**475.00-525.00**

Adj. for parallax, focus. Micrometer rear mount with .25-min. click adjust ments. Price is approximate. Made in U.S. by Parsons Optical Mfg. Co.

PENTAX

Maker and Model	Magn.	Field at 100 Yds. (feet)	Eye Relief (in.)	Length (in.)	Tube Dia. (in.)	W & E Adjustments	Weight (ozs.)	Price
Lightseeker 1.75-6x[1]	1.75-6	71-20	3.5-4	10.8	1	Int.	13	**546.00**
Lightseeker 2-8x[2]	2-8	53-17	3.5-4	11.7	1	Int.	14	**594.00**
Lightseeker 3-9x[3,4,10,11]	3-9	36-14	3.5-4	12.7	1	Int.	15	**594.00**
Lightseeker 3.5-10x[5]	3.5-10	29.5-11	3.5-4	14	1	Int.	19.5	**630.00**
Lightseeker 4-16x[6,9]	4-16	33-9	3.5-4	15.4	1	Int.	22.7	**888.00**
Lightseeker 6-24x[7,12]	6-24	18-5.5	3.5-4	16	1	Int.	23.7	**1,028.00**
Lightseeker 8.5-32x[8]	8.5-32	13-3.8	3.5-4	17.2	1	Int.	24	**968.00**
Shotgun								
Lightseeker 2.5x1[3]	2.5	55	3.5-4	10	1	Int.	9	**398.00**
Lightseeker Zero-X SG Plus	0	51	4.5-15	8.9	1	Int.	7.9	**372.00**
Lightseeker Zero-X/ V Still-Target	0-4	53.8-15	3.5-7	8.9	1	Int.	10.3	**476.00**
Lightseeker Zero X/ V	0-4	53.8-15	3.5-7	8.9	1	Int.	10.3	**454.00**

[1]Glossy finish; Matte finish, Heavy Plex or Penta-Plex, **$546.00**. [2]Glossy finish; Matte finish, **$594.00**. [3]Glossy finish; Matte finish, **$628.00**; Heavy Plex, add **$20.00**. [4]Matte finish; Mil-Dot, **$798.00**. [5]Glossy finish; Matte finish, **$652.00**; Heavy Plex, add **$10.00**. [6]Glossy finish; Matte finish, **$816.00**; with Heavy Plex, **$830.00**; with Mil-Dot, **$978.00**. [7]Matte finish; with Mil-Dot, **$1,018.00**. [8]Matte finish, with Mil-Dot, **$1098.00**. [9]Lightseeker II, Matte finish, **$844.00**. [10]Lightseeker II, Glossy finish, **$636.00**. [11]Lightseeker II, Matte finish, **$660.00**. [12]Lightseeker II, Matte finish, **$878.00**. [13]Matte finish; Advantage finish, Break-up Mossy Oak finish, Treestand Mossy Oak finish, **$364.00**. From Pentax Corp.

Pentax Reticles

Heavy Plex | Fine Plex | Penta-Plex | Deepwoods Plex | Comp-Plex | Mil-dot

RWS

Maker and Model	Magn.	Field at 100 Yds. (feet)	Eye Relief (in.)	Length (in.)	Tube Dia. (in.)	W & E Adjustments	Weight (ozs.)	Price
300	4	36	3.5	11.75	1	Int.	13.2	**170.00**
450	3-9	43-14	3.5	12	1	Int.	14.3	**215.00**

SCHMIDT & BENDER

Maker and Model	Magn.	Field at 100 Yds. (feet)	Eye Relief (in.)	Length (in.)	Tube Dia. (in.)	W & E Adjustments	Weight (ozs.)	Price
Fixed								
4x36	4	30	3.25	11	1	Int.	14	**859.00**
6x42	6	21	3.25	13	1	Int.	17	**999.00**
8x56	8	16.5	3.25	14	1	Int.	22	**1,099.00**
10x42	10	10.5	3.25	13	1	Int.	18	**999.00**
Variables								
1.25-4x20[5]	1.25-4	96-16	3.75	10	30mm	Int.	15.5	**1,199.00**
1.5-6x42[1,5]	1.5-6	60-19.5	3.70	12	30mm	Int.	19.7	**1,299.00**
2.5-10x56[1,5]	2.5-10	37.5-12	3.90	14	30mm	Int.	24.6	**1,479.00**
3-12x42[2]	3-12	34.5-11.5	3.90	13.5	30mm	Int.	19	**1,479.00**
3-12x50[1,5]	3-12	33.3-12.6	3.90	13.5	30mm	Int.	22.9	**1,499.00**
4-16x50 Varmint[4,6]	4-16	22.5-7.5	3.90	14	30mm	Int.	26	**1,799.00**
Police/Marksman II								
3-12x507	3-12	33.3-12.6	3.74	13.9	34mm	Int.	18.5	**2,799.00**

All scopes have 30-yr. warranty, click adjustments, centered reticles, rotation indicators. [1]Glass reticle; aluminum. Available in aluminum with mounting rail. [2]Aluminum only. [3]Aluminum tube. Choice of two bullet drop compensators, choice of two sunshades, two range find ing reticles. From Schmidt & Bender, Inc. [4]Parallax adjustment in third turret; extremely fine crosshairs. [5]Available with illuminated ret icle that glows red; third turret houses on/off switch, dimmer and bat tery. [6]4-16x50/Long Range. [7]Also with Long Eye Relief. From Schmidt & Bender, Inc. Available with illuminated crosshairs and parallax adjustment.

SCHMIDT & BENDER ZENITH SERIES

Maker and Model	Magn.	Field at 100 Yds. (feet)	Eye Relief (in.)	Length (in.)	Tube Dia. (in.)	W & E Adjustments	Weight (ozs.)	Price
3-12x50	3-12	33.3-11.4	3.70	13.71	NA	NA	23.4	**1,599.00-1,795.00**
2.5-10x56	2.5-10	39.6-12	3.70	14.81	NA	NA	24	**1,490.00-1,795.00**

No 1 (fixed) | No. 1 variable | No. 2 | No. 3 | No. 4 | No. 6 | No. 7 | No. 8 | No. 8 Dot | No. 9

ACCESSORIES

SCOPES / HUNTING, TARGET & VARMINT

SIGHTRON

Maker and Model	Magn.	Field at 100 Yds. (feet)	Eye Relief (in.)	Length (in.)	Tube Dia. (in.)	W & E Adjustments	Weight (ozs.)	Price
Variables								
SII 1.56x42	1.5-6	50-15	3.8-4	11.69	1	Int.	15.35	**287.95**
SII 2.58x42	2.5-8	36-12	3.6-4.2	11.89	1	Int.	12.82	**261.95**
SII 39x42[4, 6, 7]	3-9	34-12	3.6-4.2	12.00	1	Int.	13.22	**274.95**
SII 312x42[6]	3-12	32-9	3.6-4.2	11.89	1	Int.	12.99	**311.95**
SII 3.510x42	3.5-10	32-11	3.6	11.89	1	Int.	13.16	**324.95**
SII 4.514x42[1]	4.5-14	22-7.9	3.6	13.88	1	Int.	16.07	**371.95**
Target								
SII 24x44	24	4.1	4.33	13.30	1	Int.	15.87	**341.95**
SII 416x42[1, 4, 5,6, 7]	4-16	26-7	3.6	13.62	1	Int.	16	**371.95**
SII 624-42[1, 4, 5, 7]	6-24	16-5	3.6	14.6	1	Int.	18.7	**393.95**
SII1040x42	10-40	8.9-4	3.6	16.1	1	Int.	19	**563.95**
Compact								
SII 4x32	4	25	4.5	9.69	1	Int.	9.34	**205.95**
SII2.5-10x32	2.5-10	41-10.5	3.75-3.5	10.9	1	Int.	10.39	**260.95**
Shotgun								
SII 2.5x20SG	2.5	41	4.3	10.28	1	Int.	8.46	**194.95**
Pistol								
SII 1x28P[4]	1	30	9-24	9.49	1	Int.	8.46	**212.95**
SII 2x28P[4]	2	16-10	9-24	9.49	1	Int.	8.28	**212.95**

Other Data: [1]Adjustable objective. [2]3MOA dot; also with 5 or 10 MOA dot. [3]Variable 3, 5, 10 MOA dot; black finish; also stainless. [4]Satin black; also stainless. Electronic Red Dot scopes come with ring mount, front and rear extension tubes, polarizing filter, battery, haze filter caps, wrench. Rifle, pistol, shotgun scopes have aluminum tubes, Exac Trak adjustments. Lifetime warranty. From Sightron, Inc. 53" sun shade. [6]Mil Dot or Plex reticle. [7]Dot or Plex reticle. [8]Double Diamond reticle.

SIMMONS

Maker and Model	Magn.	Field at 100 Yds. (feet)	Eye Relief (in.)	Length (in.)	Tube Dia. (in.)	W & E Adjustments	Weight (ozs.)	Price
22 Mag.								
80102[2]	4	29.5	3	11.75			11	**49.99**
80103[1]	4	23.5	3	7.25			8.25	**49.99**
80103[7]	3-9	29.5	3.3	11.5			10	**59.99**
AETEC								
2100[8]	2.8-10	44-14	5	11.9	1	Int.	15.5	**189.99**
210416[6]	3.8-12	33-11	4	13.5	1	Int.	20	**199.99**
44Mag								
M-1044[3]	3-10	34-10.5	3	12.75	1	Int.	15.5	**149.99**
M-1045[3]	4-12	29.5-9.5	3	13.2	1	Int.	18.25	**169.99**
M-1047[3]	6.5-20	14-.5	2.6-3.4	12.8	1	Int.	19.5	**199.99**
1048[3,20] (3)	6.5-20	16-5.5	2.6-3.4	14.5	1	Int.	20	**219.99**
M-1050DM[3,19]	3.8-12	26-9	3	13.08	1	Int.	16.75	**189.99**
8-Point								
4-12x40mmAO[3]	4-12	29-10	3-2 7/8	13.5	1	Int.	15.75	**99.99**
4x32mm[3]	4	28.75	3	11.625	1	Int.	14.25	**34.99**
3-9x32mm[3]	3-9	37.5-13	3-2 7/8	11.875	1	Int.	11.5	**39.99**
3-9x40mm[18]	3-9	37-13	3-2 7/8	12.25	1	Int.	12.25	**49.99-79.99**
3-9x50mm[3]	3-9	32-11.75	3-2 7/8	13	1	Int.	15.25	**79.99**
Prohunter								
7700	2-7	53-16.25	3	11.5	1	Int.	12.5	**79.99**
7710[2]	3-9	36-13	3	12.6	1	Int.	13.5	**89.99**
7716	4-12	26-9	3	12.6	1	Int.	16.75	**129.99**
7721	6-18	18.5-6	3	13.75	1	Int.	16	**144.99**
7740[3]	6	21.75	3	12.5	1	Int.	12	**99.99**
Prohunter Handgun								
7732[18]	2	22	9-17	8.75	1	Int.	7	**109.99**
7738[18]	4	15	11.8- 17.6	8.5	1	Int.	8	**129.99**
82200[9]	2-6							**159.99**
Whitetail Classic								
WTC 11[4]	1.5-5	75-23	3.4-3.2	9.3	1	Int.	9.7	**184.99**
WTC 12[4]	2.5-8	45-14	3.2-3	11.3	1	Int.	13	**199.99**
WTC 13[4]	3.5-10	30-10.5	3.2-3	12.4	1	Int.	13.5	**209.99**
WTC 15[4]	3.5-10	29.5-11.5	3.2	12.75	1	Int.	13.5	**289.99**
WTC 45[4]	4.5-14	22.5-8.6	3.2	13.2	1	Int.	14	**265.99**
Whitetail Expedition								
1.5-6x32mm[3]	1.5-6	72-19	3	11.16	1	Int.	15	**259.99**
3-9x42mm[3]	3-9	40-13.5	3	13.2	1	Int.	17.5	**269.99**
4-12x42mm[3]	4-12	29-9.6	3	13.46	1	Int.	21.25	**299.99**
6-18x42mm[3]	6-18	18.3-6.5	3	15.35	1	Int.	22.5	**319.99**
Pro50								
8800[10]	4-12	27-9	3.5	13.2	1	Int.	18.25	**179.99**
8810[10]	6-18	17-5.8	3.6	13.2	1	Int.	18.25	**174.99**
808825	3.5-10	32-8.75	3.5	3.25			14.5	**179.99**
808830	2.5-10	39-12.2	2.75	12.75			15.9	**179.99**
Shotgun								
2100[4]	4	16	5.5	8.8	1	Int.	9.1	**84.99**
2100[5]	2.5	24	6	7.4	1	Int.	7	**59.99**
7789D	2	31	5.5	8.8	1	Int.	8.75	**99.99**
7790D	4	17	5.5	8.5	1	Int.	8.75	**114.99**
7791D	1.5-5	76-23.5	3.4	9.5	1	Int.	10.75	**138.99**
Blackpowder								
BP0420M17	4	19.5	4	7.5	1	Int.	8.3	**59.99**
BP2732M12	2-7	57.7-16.6	3	11.6	1	Int.	12.4	**129.99**
Red Dot								
5100421	1			4.8	30mm	Int.	4.7	**44.99**
5111222	1			5.25	42mm	Int.	6	**49.99**
Pro Air Gun								
21608 A.O.	4	25	3.5	12	1	Int.	11.3	**99.99**
21613 A.O.	4-12	25-9	3.1-2.9	13.1	1	Int.	15.8	**179.99**
21619 A.O.	6-18	18-7	2.9-2.7	13.8	1	Int.	18.2	**189.99**

Other Data: [1]Matte; also polished finish. [2]Silver; also black matte or polished. [3]Black matte finish. [4]Granite finish. [5]Camouflage. [6]Black polish. [7]With ring mounts. [8]Silver; black polish avail. [10]50mm obj.; black matte. [11]Black or silver matte. [12]75-yd. par allax; black or silver matte. [13]TV view. [14]Adj. obj. [15]Silver matte. [16]Adj. objective; 4" sunshade; black matte. [17]Octagon body; rings included; black matte or silver finish. [18]Black matte finish; also available in silver. [19]Smart reticle. [20]Target turrets. [21]With dovetail rings. [23]With 3V lithium battery, extension tube, polarizing filter, Weaver rings. **Only selected models shown.** Contact Simmons Outdoor Corp. for complete details.

Truplex™ **Smart** **ProDiamond®** **Crossbow**

Maker and Model	Magn.	Field at 100 Yds. (feet)	Eye Relief (in.)	Length (in.)	Tube Dia. (in.)	W & E Adjustments	Weight (ozs.)	Price	Other Data
SPRINGFIELD ARMORY									
	6		3.5	13	1	Int.	14.7	**379.00**	[1]Range finding reticle with automatic bullet drop compensator for 308 match ammo to 700 yds. [2]Range finding reticle with automatic bullet drop compensator for 223 match ammo to 700 yds. [3]Also avail. as 2nd Gen. with target knobs and adj. obj., **$549.00**; as 3rd Gen. with illuminated reticle, **$749.00**; as Mil Dot model with illuminated Target Tracking reticle, target knobs, adj. obj., **$698.00**. [4]Unlimited range finding, target knobs, adj. obj., illuminated Target Tracking green reticle. All scopes have matte black finish, internal bubble level, 1/4-MOA clicks. From Springfield, Inc.
4-14x70 Tactical Government Model[2]	4-14		3.5	14.25	1	Int.	15.8	**395.00**	
4-14x56 1st Gen. Government Model[3]	4-14		3.5	14.75	30mm	Int.	23	**480.00**	
10x56 Mil Dot Government Model[4]	10		3.5	14.75	30mm	Int.	28	**672.00**	
6-20x56 Mil Dot Government Model	6-20		3.5	18.25	30mm	Int.	33	**899.00**	
SWAROVSKI OPTIK									
PF Series									
8x50[1,3]	8	17	3.15	13.9	30mm	Int.	21.5	**987.78**	
8x56[1,3]	8	17	3.15	14.29	30mm	Int.	24	**1,054.44**	
PH Series									
1.25-4x24[1]	1.25-4	98.4-31.2	3.15	10.63	30mm	Int.	16.2	**1,198.89**	
1.5-6x42[1]	1.5-6	65.4-21	3.15	12.99	30mm	Int.	20.8	**1,332.22**	
2.5-10x42[1,2]	2.5-10	39.6-12.6	3.15	13.23	30mm	Int.	19.8	**1,487.78**	
3-12x50[1]	3-12	33-10.5	3.15	14.33	30mm	Int.	22.4	**1,576.67**	
4-16x50	4-16	30-8.5	3.15	14.22	30mm	Int.	22.3	**1,643.33**	
6-24x50	6-24	18.6-5.4	3.15	15.4	30mm	Int.	23.6	**1,854.33**	
A-Line Series									
3-9x36AV[4]	3-9	39-13.5	3.35	11.8	1	Int.	11.7	**798.89**	
3-10x42AV[4]	3-10	33-11.7	3.35	12.44	1	Int.	12.7	**876.67**	
4-12x50AV[4]	4-12	29.1-9.9	3.35	13.5	1	Int.	13.9	**921.11**	
6-18x50	6-18	17.4-6.6	3.5	14.84	1	Int.	20.3	**976.67**	

TDS **No. 4** **No. 4A** **No. 7A** **Plex** **No. 24**

Maker and Model	Magn.	Field at 100 Yds. (feet)	Eye Relief (in.)	Length (in.)	Tube Dia. (in.)	W & E Adjustments	Weight (ozs.)	Price	Other Data
SWIFT									
600 4x15	4	17	2.8	10.6	.75	Int.	3.5	**15.00**	All Swift scopes, with the exception of the 4x15, have Quadraplex reticles and are fogproof and waterproof. The 4x15 has crosshair reticle and is non-waterproof. [1]Available in regular matte black or silver finish. [2]Comes with ring mounts, wrench, lens caps, extension tubes, filter, battery. [3]Regular and matte black finish. [4]Speed Focus scopes. Partial listing shown. From Swift Instruments.
601 3-7x20	3-7	25-12	3-2.9	11	.75	Int.	5.6	**35.00**	
650 4x32	4	26	4	12	1	Int.	9.1	**75.00**	
653 4x40WA[1]	4	35	4	12.2	1	Int.	12.6	**125.00**	
654 3-9x32	3-9	35-12	3.4-2.9	12	1	Int.	9.8	**125.00**	
656 3-9x40WA[1]	3-9	40-14	3.4-2.8	12.6	1	Int.	12.3	**140.00**	
657 6x40	6	28	4	12.6	1	Int.	10.4	**125.00**	
658 2-7x40WA[3]	2-7	55-18	3.3-3	11.6	1	Int.	12.5	**160.00**	
659 3.5-10x44WA	3.5-10	34-12	3-2.8	12.8	1	Int.	13.5	**230.00**	
665 1.5-4.5x21	1.5-4.5	69-24.5	3.5-3	10.9	1	Int.	9.6	**125.00**	
665M 1.5-4.5x21	1.5-4.5	69-24.5	3.5-3	10.9	1	Int.	9.6	**125.00**	
666M Shotgun 1x20	1	113	3.2	7.5	1	Int.	9.6	**130.00**	
667 Fire-Fly[2]	1	40		5.4	30mm	Int.	5	**220.00**	
668M 4x32	4	25	4	10	1	Int.	8.9	**120.00**	
669M 6-18x44	6-18	18-6.5	2.8	14.5	1	Int.	17.6	**220.00**	
680M	3.9	43-14	4	18	40mm	Int.	17.5	**399.95**	
681M	1.5-6	56-13	4	11.8	40mm	Int.	17.5	**399.95**	
682M	4-12	33-11	4	15.4	50mm	Int.	21.7	**499.95**	
683M	2-7	55-17	3.3	11.6	32mm	Int.	10.6	**499.95**	
Premier Rifle Scopes									
648M[1] 1.5-4.5	32	71-25	3.05-3.27	10.41	1	Int.	12.7	**179.95**	
649R 4-12	50	29.5-9.5	3.3-3	13.8	1	Int.	15.8	**245.00**	
658M 2-7	40	55-18	3.3-3	11.6	1	Int.	12.5	**175.00**	
659S 3.5-10	44	34-12	3-2.8	12.8	1	Int.	13.5	**215.00**	
669M 6-18	44	18-6.5	2.8	14.5	1	Int.	17.6	**230.00**	
671M 3-9	50	35-25	3.24- 3.12	15.5	1	Int.	18.2	**250.00**	
672M 6-18	50	19-6.7	3.25-3	15.8	1	Int.	20.9	**260.00**	
674M 3-9	40	40-14.2	3.6-2.9	12	1	Int.	13.1	**170.00**	
676S 4-12	40	29.3-10.5	3.15-2.9	12.4	1	Int.	15.4	**180.00**	
677M 6-24	50	18-5	3.1-3.2	15.9	1	Int.	20.8	**280.00**	
678M 8-32	50	13-3.5	3.13-2.94	16.9	1	Int.	21.5	**290.00**	
685M[3] 3-9	40	39-13.5	3.7-2.8	12.4	1	Int.	20.5	**189.95**	
686M[3] 6.5-20	44	19-6.5	2.7	15.6	1	Int.	23.6	**249.95**	
687M[2] 4.5-14	44	25.5-8.5	3.2	14.1	1	Int.	21.5	**220.00**	
688M[2] 6-18	44	19.597	2.8	15.4	1	Int.	22.6	**240.00**	
Standard Rifle Scopes									
5875[5] 4	32	25	3.1	11.7	1	Int.	13	**50.00**	
653M 4	40	35	4	12.2	1	Int.	12.6	**128.00**	
654M 3-9	32	35-12	3.4-2.9	12	1	Int.	9.8	**125.00**	
656 3-9	40	40-14	3.4-2.8	12.6	1	Int.	12.3	**140.00**	
657M 6	40	28	4	12.6	1	Int.	10.4	**125.00**	
660M[4] 2-6	32	14-4.5	20-12.6	5.5	1	Int.	10.6	**241.80**	
661M[4] 4	32	6.6	13.8	9.4	1	Int.	9.9	**130.00**	
663S[4] 4	32	9.8	7.3	7.2	1	Int.	8.5	**130.00**	
665M 1.5-4.5	21	69-24.5	3.5-3	10.8	1	Int.	9.6	**125.00**	
668M 4	32	25	4	10	1	Int.	8.9	**120.00**	

TASCO

*for .22 rimfire

Maker and Model	Magn.	Field at 100 Yds. (feet)	Eye Relief (in.)	Length (in.)	Tube Dia. (in.)	W & E Adjustments	Weight (ozs.)	Price	Other Data
Titan									
DWCP3510	50	30-10.5	3.75	13	1	Int.	17.1	191.95	
DWCP39X	44	39-14	305	12.75	1	Int.	16.5	173.95	
T156X	42N	59-20	3.5	12	1	Int.	16.4	293.95	
T14526N4A	1.25-4.5	59.20	3.5	12	1	Int.	16.4	293.95	
T14526N4A	1.25-4.5	77.5-22	3.25	10.5	1	Int.	15.2	335.95	
T312X52N	3-12	27-10	4.5	14	1	Int.	20.7	335.95	
T312X52N4A	3-12	27-10	4.5	14	1	Int.	20.7	335.95	
T39X42N	3-9	37-13	3.5	12.5	1	Int.	16	281.95	
T39X42N4A	3-9	37-13	3.5	12.5	1	Int.	16	281.95	
Target & Varmint									
VAR211042M	1.5-10	35.9	3	14	1	Int.	19.1	89.95	
MAG624X40	6-24	17-4	3	16	1	Int.	19.1	113.95	
VAR624X42M	6-24	13-3.7	7	16	1	Int.	19.6	113.95	
TG624X44DS	15-4.5	15-4.5	3	16.5	1	Int.	19.6	199.95	
TG104040DS	10-40	11-2.5	3.25	15.5	1	Int.	25.5	211.95	
TG832X44DS	8-32	11-3.5	3.25	17	1	Int.	20	219.95	
World Class									
BA1545X32	1.5-4.5	77-23	4	11.25	1	Int.	12	59.95	
DWC28x32	2-8	50-17	4	10.5	1	Int.	12.5	69.96	
DWC39X40N	3-9	41-15	3.5	12.75	1	Int.	13	73.95	
WA39X40N	3-9	41-15	3.5	12.75	1	Int.	13	73.95	
WA39X40STN	3-9	41-15	3.5	12.75	1	Int.	13	73.95	
DWC39X50N	3-9	41-13	3	12.5	1	Int.	15.8	87.95	
DWC39X40M	3-9	41-15	3.5	12.75	1	Int.	13	73.95	
MAG321X40	3-12	26.5-7.3	3	14	1	Int.	18	95.95	
DWC416X40	4-16	22.5-5-9	3.7	14	1	Int.	16	103.95	
DWC416X50	4-16	28-7	3	16	1	Int.	20.5	123.95	
ProPoint									
PDP2	1	40	Un.	5	1	Int.	5.5	117.95	
PDP3CMP	1	68	Un.	4.75	1	Int.	5.4	157.95	
PDP3	1	52	Un.	5	1	Int.	5.5	137.95	
PD3ST1	1	52	Un.	5	1	Int.	5.5	143.95	
PDPRGD	1	60	Un.	5.4	1	Int.	5.7	91.95	
Golden Antler									
DMGA39X32T	3-9	39-13	3	13.5	1	Int.	12.2	49.95	
DMGA4X32T	4	32	3	13.25	1	Int.	11	37.95	
GA3940	3-9	41-15	3	12.75	1	Int.	13	57.95	
GA2532CB	2.5	43	3.2	11.4	1	Int.	10.1	43.95	
GA3932AGD	3-9	39	3	13.25	1	Int.	12	43.95	
Pronghhorn									
PH39X40D	3-9	39-13	3	13	1	Int.	12.1	47.95	
PH39X32S	3-9	39-13	3	12	1	Int.	11	41.95	
PH4X32D	4	32	3	12	1	Int.	11	32.95	
PH2533	2.5	43	3.2	11.4	1	Int.	10.1	31.95	
PH3950D	3-9	33	3.3	13	1	Int.	14.8	57.95	
.22 Riflescopes									
MAG39X32D	3-9	17.75-6	3	12.75	1	Int.	11.3	55.95	
MAG38X32SD	3-9	17.75-6	3	12.75	1	Int.	11.3	55.95	
MAG4X32SD	4	13.5	3	12.75	1	Int.	12.1	43.95	
MAG4X32STD	4	13.5	3	12.75	1	Int.	21.1	43.95	
Rimfire									
EZ01D	1	35	Un.	4.75	1	Int.	2.5	17.95	
RF37X20D	3-7	24	2.5	11.5	1	Int.	5.7	23.95	
RF4X15D	4	20.5	2.5	11	1	Int.	3.8	7.95	
RF4X20WAD	4	23	2.5	10.5	1	Int.	3.8	9.95	
Red Dot									
BKR30	1	57	Un.	3.75	1	Int.	6	45.95	
BKR3022*	1	57	Un.	3.75	1	Int.	6	45.95	
BKR42	1	62	Un.	3.75	1	Int.	6.7	57.95	

THOMPSON/CENTER RECOIL PROOF SERIES

Maker and Model	Magn.	Field at 100 Yds. (feet)	Eye Relief (in.)	Length (in.)	Tube Dia. (in.)	W & E Adjustments	Weight (ozs.)	Price	Other Data
Pistol Scopes									
8315[2]	2.5-7	15-5	8-21, 8-11	9.25	1	Int.	9.2	349.00	[1]Black finish; silver optional. [2]Black; lighted reticle. From Thompson/Center Arms.
8326[4]	2.5-7	15-5	8-21, 8-11	9.25	1	Int.	10.5	416.00	
Muzzleloader Scopes									
8658	1	60	3.8	9.125	1	Int.	10.2	149.00	
8662	4	16	3	8.8	1	Int.	9.1	141.00	

TRIJICON

Maker and Model	Magn.	Field at 100 Yds. (feet)	Eye Relief (in.)	Length (in.)	Tube Dia. (in.)	W & E Adjustments	Weight (ozs.)	Price	Other Data
ReflexII 1x24	1			4.25		Int.	4.2	425.00	[1]Advanced Combat Optical Gunsight for AR-15, M16, with integral mount. Other mounts available. All models feature tritium and fiber optics duallighting system that requires no batteries. From Trijicon, Inc.
TA44 1.5x16[1]	1.5	39	2.4	5.34		Int.	5.31	895.00	
TA45 1.5x24[1]	1.5	25.6	3.6	5.76		Int.	5.92	950.00	
TA47 2x20[1]	2	33.1	2.1	5.3		Int.	5.82	950.00	
TA50 3x24[1]	3	29.5	1.4	5		Int.	5.89	950.00	
TA11 3.5x35[1]	3.5	25.6	2.4	8		Int.	14	1,295.00	
TA01 4x32[1]	4	36.8	1.5	5.8		Int.	9.9	950.00	
Variable AccuPoint									
3-9x40	3-9	33.8-11.3	3.6-3.2	12.2	1	Int.	12.8	720.00	
1.25-4x24	1.25-4	61.6-20.5	4.8-3.4	10.2	1	Int.	11.4	700.00	

Maker and Model	Magn.	Field at 100 Yds. (feet)	Eye Relief (in.)	Length (in.)	Tube Dia. (in.)	W & E Adjustments	Weight (ozs.)	Price	Other Data
ULTRA DOT									
Micro-Dot Scopes[1]									
1.5-4.5x20 Rifle	1.5-4.5	80-26	3	9.8	1	Int.	10.5	**297.00**	[1]Brightness-adjustable fiber optic red dot reticle. Waterproof, nitrogen-filled one-piece tube. Tinted see-through lens covers and battery included. [2]Parallax adjustable. [3]Ultra Dot sights include rings, battery, polarized filter, and 5-year warranty. All models available in black or satin finish. [4]Illuminated red dot has eleven brightness settings. Shock-proof aluminum tube. From Ultra Dot Distribution.
2-7x32	2-7	54-18	3	11	1	Int.	12.1	**308.00**	
3-9x40	3-9	40-14	3	12.2	1	Int.	13.3	**327.00**	
4x-12x56[2]	4-12	30-10	3	14.3	1	Int.	18.3	**417.00**	
Ultra-Dot Sights[3]									
Ultra-Dot 25[4]	1			5.1	1	Int.	3.9	**159.00**	
Ultra-Dot 30[4]	1			5.1	30mm	Int.	4	**179.00**	
UNERTL									
1" Target	6, 8, 10	16-10	2	21.5	.75	Ext.	21	**675.00**	[1]Dural .25-MOA click mounts. Hard coated lenses. Non-rotating objective lens focusing. [2].25-MOA click mounts. [3]With target mounts. [4]With calibrated head. [5]Same as 1" Target but without objective lens focusing. [6]With new Posa mounts. [7]Range focus unit near rear of tube. Price is with Posa or standard mounts. Magnum clamp. From Unertl.
10X	10	10.3	3	12.5	1	Ext.	35	**2,500.00**	
1.25" Target[1]	8, 10, 12, 14	12-16	2	25	.75	Ext.	21	**715.00**	
1.5" Target	10, 12, 14, 16, 18, 20	11.5-3.2	2.25	25.5	.75	Ext.	31	**753.50**	
2" Target[2]	10, 12, 14, 16, 18, 24, 30, 32, 36,	8	2.25	26.25	1	Ext.	44	**918.50**	
Varmint, 1.25"[3] 3" Ultra Varmint, 2"[4]	15	12.6-7	2.25	24	1	Ext.	34	**918.50**	
Small Game[5]	3, 4, 6	25-17	2.25	18	.75	Ext.	16	**550.00**	
Programmer 200[7]	10, 12, 14, 16, 18, 20, 24, 30, 36	11.3-4		26.5	1	Ext.	45	**1,290.00**	
B8									
Tube Sight				17		Ext.		**420.00**	
U.S. OPTICS									
SN-1/TAR Fixed Power System									
16.2x	15	8.6	4.3	16.5	30mm	Int.	27	**1,700.00**	Prices shown are estimates; scopes built to order; choice of reticles; choice of front or rear focal plane; extra-heavy MIL-SPEC construction; extra-long turrets; individual w&e rebound springs; up to 100mm dia. objectives; up to 50mm tubes; all lenses multi-coated. Other magnifications available. [1]Modular components allow a variety of fixed or variable magnifications, night vision, etc. Made in U.S. by U.S. Optics.
22.4x	20	5.8	3.8	18	30mm	Int.	29	**1,800.00**	
26x	24	5	3.4	18	30mm	Int.	31	**1,900.00**	
31x	30	4.6	3.5	18	30mm	Int.	32	**2,100.00**	
37x	36	4	3.6	18	30mm	Int.	32	**2,300.00**	
48x	50	3	3.8	18	30mm	Int.	32	**2,500.00**	
Variables									
SN-2	4-22	26.8-5.8	5.4-3.8	18	30mm	Int.	24	**1,762.00**	
SN-3	1.6-8		4.4-4.8	18.4	30mm	Int.	36	**1,435.00**	
SN-4	1-4	116-31.2	4.6-4.9	18	30mm	Int.	35	**1,065.00**	
Fixed Power									
SN-6	8, 10, 17, 22	14-8.5	3.8-4.8	9.2	30mm	Int.	18	**1,195.00**	
SN-8 Modular[1]	4, 10, 20, 40	32	3.3	7.5	30mm	Int.	11.1	**890.00-4,000.00**	
WEAVER									
Riflescopes									
K2.5[1]	2.5	35	3.7	9.5	1	Int.	7.3	**132.86**	[1]Gloss black. [2]Matte black. [3]Silver. [4]Satin. [5]Silver and black (slightly higher in price). [6]Field of view measured at 18" eye relief. .25 MOA click adjustments, except T-Series which vary from .125 to .25 clicks. One-piece tubes with multi-coated lenses. All scopes are shock-proof, waterproof, and fogproof. Dual-X reticle available in all except V24 which has a fine X-hair and ot; T-Series in which certain models are available in fine X-hair and dots; Qwik-Point red dot scopes which are available in fixed 4 or 12 MOA, or variable 4-8-12 MOA. V16 also avail able with fine X-hair, dot or Dual-X reticle. T-Series scopes have Micro-Trac® adjustments. From Weaver Products.
K4[1,2]	3.7	26.5	3.3	11.3	1	Int.	10	**149.99**	
K6[1]	5.7	18.5	3.3	11.4	1	Int.	10	**154.99**	
KT15[1]	14.6	7.5	3.2	12.9	1	Int.	14.7	**281.43**	
V3[1,2]	1.1-2.8	88-32	3.9-3.7	9.2	1	Int.	8.5	**189.99**	
V9[1,2]	2.8-8.7	33-11	3.5-3.4	12.1	1	Int.	11.1	**249.99-299.99**	
V9x50[1,2]	3-9	29.4-9.9	3.6-3	13.1	1	Int.	14.5	**239.99**	
V10[1-3]	2.2-9.6	38.5-9.5	3.4-3.3	12.2	1	Int.	11.2	**259.99-269.99**	
V10-50[1-3]	2.3-9.7	40.2-9.2	2.9-2.8	13.75	1	Int.	15.2	**279.99**	
V16 MDX[2,3]	3.8-15.5	26.8-6.8	3.1	13.9	1	Int.	16.5	**329.99**	
V16 MFC[2,3]	3.8-15.5	26.8-6.8	3.1	13.9	1	Int.	16.5	**329.99**	
V16 MDT[2,3]	3.8-15.5	26.8-6.8	3.1	13.9	1	Int.	16.5	**329.99**	
V24 Varmint[2]	6-24	15.3-4	3.15	14.3	1	Int.	17.5	**379.99-399.99**	
Handgun									
H2[1-3]	2	21	4-29	8.5	1	Int.	6.7	**161.43**	
H4[1-3]	4	18	11.5-18	8.5	1	Int.	6.7	**175.00**	
VH4[1-3]	1.5-4	13.6-5.8	11-17	8.6	1	Int.	8.1	**215.71**	
VH8[1-3]	2.5-8	8.5-3.7	12.16	9.3	1	Int.	8.3	**228.57**	
Rimfire									
RV7[2]	2.5-7	37-13	3.7-3.3	10.75	1	Int.	10.7	**148.57**	
Grand Slam									
6-20x40mm Varminter Reticle[2]	6-20X	16.5-5.25	2.75-3	14.48	1	Int.	17.75	**419.99**	
6-20x40mm Fine Crosshairs w/Dot[2]	6-20X	16.5-5.25	2.75-3	14.48	1	Int.	17.75	**419.99**	
1.5-5x32mm[2]	1.5-5X	71-21	3.25	10.5	1	Int.	10.5	**349.99**	
4.75x40mm[2]	4.75X	14.75	3.25	11	1	Int.	10.75	**299.99**	
3-10x40mm[2]	3-10X	35-11.33	3.5-3	12.08	1	Int.	12.08	**329.99**	
3.5-10x50mm[2]	3.5-10X	30.5-10.8	3.5-3	12.96	1	Int.	16.25	**389.99**	
4.5-14x40mm	4.5-14X	22.5-10.5	3.5-3	14.48	1	Int.	17.5	**399.99**	
T-Series									
T-64	614	14	3.58	12.75	1	Int.	14.9	**424.95**	
T-36[3-4]	36	3	3	15.1	1	Int.	16.7	**489.99**	

SCOPES / HUNTING, TARGET & VARMINT

Maker and Model	Magn.	Field at 100 Yds. (feet)	Eye Relief (in.)	Length (in.)	Tube Dia. (in.)	W & E Adjustments	Weight (ozs.)	Price	Other Data
ZEISS									
ZM/Z									
6x42MC	6	22.9	3.2	12.7	1	Int.	13.4	**749.00**	[1]Also avail. with illuminated reticle. [2]Illuminated Vari-point reticle. Black matte finish. All scopes have .25-min. click-stop adjustments. Choice of Z-Plex or fine crosshair reticles. Rubber armored objective bell, rubber eyepiece ring. Lenses have T-Star coating for highest light transmission. VM/V scopes avail. with rail mount. Partial listing shown. From Carl Zeiss Optical, Inc.
8x56MC	8	18	3.2	13.8	1	Int.	17.6	**829.00**	
1.25-4x24MC	1.25-4	105-33	3.2	11.46	30mm	Int.	17.3	**779.00**	
1.5-6x42MC	1.5-6	65.5-22.9	3.2	12.4	30mm	Int.	18.5	**899.00**	
2.5-10x48MC[1]	2.5-10	33-11.7	3.2	14.5	30mm	Int.	24	**1,029.00**	
3-12x56MC[1]	3-12	27.6-9.9	3.2	15.3	30mm	Int.	25.8	**1,099.00**	
Conquest									[1]Stainless. [2]Turkey reticle. [3]Black matte finish. All scopes have .25-min. click-stop adjustments. Choice of Z-Plex, Turkey or fine crosshair reticles. Coated lenses for highest light transmisison. Partial listing shown. From Carl Zeiss Optical, Inc.
3-9x40MC[3]	3-9	37.5	3.34	12.36	1	Int.	17.28	**499.99**	
3-9x40MC[1]	3-9	37.5	3.34	12.36	1	Int.	17.28	**529.99**	
3-9x40S[3]	3-9	37.5	3.34	12.36	1	Int.	17.28	**499.99**	
3-9x40S[2,3]	3-9	37.5	3.34	12.36	1	Int.	17.28	**529.99**	
3-12x56MC[3]	2.5-10	27.6	3.2	15.3	30mm	Int.	25.8	**1,049.00**	
3-12x56MC[1]	3-12	27.6	3.2	15.3	30mm	Int.	25.8	**1,079.00**	
VM/V									
1.1-4x24 VariPoint T[2]	1.1-4	120-34	3.5	11.8	30mm	Int.	15.8	**1,699.00**	
1.5-6x42T*	1.5-6	65.5-22.9	3.2	12.4	30mm	Int.	18.5	**1,299.00**	
2.5-10x50T*[1]	2.5-10	47.1-13	3.5	12.5	30mm	Int.	16.25	**1,499.00**	
3-12x56T*	3-12	37.5-10.5	3.5	13.5	30mm	Int.	19.5	**1,499.00**	
3-9x42T*	3-9	42-15	3.74	13.3	1	Int.	15.3	**1,999.00**	
5-15x42T*	5-15	25.7-8.5	3.74	13.3	1	Int.	15.4	**1,399.00**	

Hunting scopes in general are furnished with a choice of reticlecrosshairs, post with crosshairs, tapered or blunt post, or dot crosshairs, etc. The great majority of target and varmint scopes have medium or fine crosshairs but post or dot reticles may be ordered. Wwindage EElevation MOAMinute of Angle or 1" (approx.) at 100 yards.

LASER SIGHTS

Lasergrips LG-206

Alpec Mini Shot

Laser Devices ULS 2001 with TLS 8R light

Maker and Model	Wave length (nm)	Beam Color	Lens	Operating Temp. (degrees F.)	Weight (ozs.)	Price	Other Data
ALPEC							[1]Range 1000 yards. [2]Range 300 yards. Mini Shot II range 500 yards, output 650mm, **$129.95**. [3]Range 300 yards; Laser Shot II 500 yards; Super Laser Shot 1000 yards. Black or stainless finish aluminum; removable pressure or push-button switch. Mounts for most handguns, many rifles and shotguns. From Alpec Team, Inc.
Power Shot[1]	635	Red	Glass	NA	2.5	**$199.95**	
Mini Shot[2]	670	Red	Glass	NA	2.5	**99.95**	
Laser Shot[3]	670	Red	Glass	NA	3.0	**99.95**	
BEAMSHOT							[1]Black or silver finish; adj. for windage and elevation; 300-yd. range; also M1000/S (500-yd. range), M1000/u (800-yd.). [2]Black finish; 300-, 500-, 800-yd. models. All come with removable touch pad switch, 5" cable. Mounts to fit virtually any firearm. From Quarton USA Co.
1000[1]	670	Red	Glass		3.8	**NA**	
3000[2]	635/670	Red	Glass		2	**NA**	
1001/u	635	Red	Glass		3.8	**NA**	
780	780	Red	Glass		3.8	**NA**	
BSA							[1]Comes with mounts for 22/air rifle and Weaver-style bases.
LS650[1]	N/A	Red	NA	NA	NA	**49.95**	
LASERAIM							[1]Red dot/laser combo; 300-yd. range: LA3xHD Hotdot has 500-yd. range **$249.00**; [4] MOA dot size, laser gives 2" dot size at 100 yds. 230mm obj. lens: [4]MOA dot at 100 yds: fits Weaver base. 3300-yd range; 2" dot at 100 yds.; rechargeable Nicad battery 41.5-mile range; 1" dot at 100 yds.; 20+ hrs. batt. life. [5]1.5-mile range; 1" dot at 100 yds; rechargeable Nicad battery (comes with in-field charger); [6]Black or satin finish. With mount, **$169.00.** [7]Laser projects 2" dot at 100 yds.: with rotary switch; with Hotdot **$237.00**; with Hotdot touch switch **$357.00.** [8]For Glock 17-27; G1 Hotdot **$299.00**; price installed. 10Fits std. Weaver base, no rings required; 6-MOA dot; seven brightness settings. All have w&e adj.; black or satin silver finish. From Laser aim Technologies, Inc.
LA10 Hotdot[4]					NA	**199.00**	
Lasers							
MA-35RB Mini Aimer[7]					1.0	**129.00**	
G1 Laser[8]					2.0	**229.00**	
LASER DEVICES							[1]For S&W P99 semi-auto pistols; also BA-2, 5 oz., **$339.00**. [2]For revolvers. [3]For HK, Walther P99. [4]For semi-autos. [5]For rifles; also FA-4/ULS, 2.5 oz., **$325.00**. [6]For HK sub guns. [7]For military rifles. [8]For shotguns. [9]For SIG-Pro pistol. [10]Universal, semi-autos. [11]For AR-15 variants. All avail. with Magnum Power Point (650nM) or daytime-visible Super Power Point (632nM) diode. Infrared diodes avail. for law enforcement. From Laser Devices, Inc.
BA-1[1]	632	Red	Glass		2.4	**372.00**	
BA-3[2]	632	Red	Glass		3.3	**332.50**	
BA-5[3]	632	Red	Glass		3.2	**372.00**	
Duty-Grade[4]	632	Red	Glass		3.5	**372.00**	
FA-4[5]	632	Red	Glass		2.6	**358.00**	
LasTac[1]	632	Red	Glass		5.5	**298.00 to 477.00**	
MP-5[6]	632	Red	Glass		2.2	**495.00**	
MR-2[7]	632	Red	Glass		6.3	**485.00**	
SA-2[8]	632	Red	Glass		3.0	**360.00**	
SIG-Pro[9]	632	Red	Glass		2.6	**372.00**	
ULS-2001[10]	632	Red	Glass		4.5	**210.95**	
Universal AR-2A	632	Red	Glass		4.5	**445.00**	
LASERGRIPS							Replaces existing grips with built-in laser high in the right grip panel. Integrated pressure sensi tive pad in grip activates the laser. Also has master on/off switch. [1]For Colt 1911/Commander. [2]For all Glock models. Option on/off switch. Requires factory installation. [3]For S&W K, L, N frames, round or square butt (LG-207); [4]For Taurus small-frame revolvers. [5]For Ruger SP-101. [6]For SIG Sauer P226. From Crimson Trace Corp. [7]For Beretta 92/96. [8]For Ruger MK II. [9]For S&W J-frame. [10]For Sig Sauer P228/229. [11]For Colt 1911 full size, wraparound. [12]For Beretta 92/96, wraparound. [13]For Colt 1911 compact, wraparound. [14]For S&W J-frame, rubber.
LG-201[1]	633	Red- Orange	Glass	NA		**299.00**	
LG-206[3]	633	Red- Orange	Glass	NA		**229.00**	
LG-085[4]	633	Red- Orange	Glass	NA		**229.00**	
LG-101[5]	633	Red- Orange	Glass	NA		**229.00**	
LG-226[6]	633	Red- Orange	Glass	NA		**229.00**	
GLS-630[2]	633	Red- Orange	Glass	NA		**595.00**	
LG202[7]	633	Red- Orange	Glass	NA		**299.00**	
LG203[8]	633	Red- Orange	Glass	NA		**299.00**	
LG205[9]	633	Red- Orange	Glass	NA		**299.00**	
LG229[10]	633	Red- Orange	Glass	NA		**299.00**	
LG301[11]	633	Red- Orange	Glass	NA		**329.00**	
LG302[12]	633	Red- Orange	Glass	NA		**329.00**	
LG304[13]	633	Red- Orange	Glass	NA		**329.00**	
LG305[14]	633	Red- Orange	Glass	NA		**299.00**	
LASERLYTE							[1]Dot/circle or dot/crosshair projection; black or stainless. [2]Also 635/645mm model. From Tac Star Laserlyte. in grip activates the laser. Also has master on/off switch.
LLX-0006-140/090[1]	635/645	Red			1.4	**159.95**	
WPL-0004-140/090[2]	670	Red			1.2	**109.95**	
TPL-0004-140/090[2]	670	Red			1.2	**109.95**	
T7S-0004-140[2]	670	Red			0.8	**109.95**	
LASERMAX							Replaces the recoil spring guide rod; includes a customized takedown lever that serves as the laser's insta in grip activates the laser. Also has master on/off switch. [1]For Colt 1911/Commant on/off switch. For Glock, Smith & Wesson, Sigarms, Beretta, Colt, Kimber, Springfield Gov't. Model 1911, Heckler & Koch and select Taurus models. Installs in most pistols without gunsmithing. Battery life 1/2 hour to 2 hours in continuous use. From Laser Max.
LMS-1000 Internal Guide Rod	635	Red- Orange	Glass	40-120	.25	**389.00**	
NIGHT STALKER							Waterproof; LCD panel displays power remaining; programmable blink rate; con stant or memory on. From Wilcox Industri in grip activates the laser. Also has master on/off switch. [1]For Colt 1911/Commaes Corp.
S0 Smart	635	Red	NA	NA	2.46	**515.00**	

SCOPE RINGS & BASES

Maker, Model, Type	Adjust.	Scopes	Price
ADCO			
Std. Black or nickel		1"	$13.95
Std. Black or nickel		30mm	13.95
Rings Black or nickel		30mm w/ 3/8" grv.	13.95
Rings Black or nickel		1" raised 3/8" grv.	13.95
AIMTECH			
AMT Auto Mag II .22 Mag.	No	Weaver rail	$56.99
Astra .44 Mag Revolver	No	Weaver rail	63.25
Beretta/Taurus 92/99	No	Weaver rail	63.25
Browning Buckmark/Challenger II	No	Weaver rail	56.99
Browning Hi-Power	No	Weaver rail	63.25
Glock 17, 17L, 19, 23, 24 etc. no rail	No	Weaver rail	63.25
Glock 20, 21 no rail	No	Weaver rail	63.25
Glock 9mm and .40 with access. rail	No	Weaver rail	74.95
Govt. 45 Auto/.38 Super	No	Weaver rail	63.25
Hi-Standard (Mitchell version) 107	No	Weaver rail	63.25
H&K USP 9mm/40 rail mount	No	Weaver rail	74.95
Rossi 85/851/951 Revolvers	No	Weaver rail	63.25
Ruger Mk I, Mk II	No	Weaver rail	49.95
Ruger P85/P89	No	Weaver rail	63.25
S&W K, L, N frames	No	Weaver rail	63.25
S&W K. L, N with tapped top strap*	No	Weaver rail	69.95
S&W Model 41 Target 22	No	Weaver rail	63.25
S&W Model 52 Target 38	No	Weaver rail	63.25
S&W Model 99 Walther frame rail mount	No	Weaver rail	74.95
S&W 2nd Gen. 59/459/659 etc.	No	Weaver rail	56.99
S&W 3rd Gen. full size 5906 etc.	No	Weaver rail	69.95
S&W 422, 622, 2206	No	Weaver rail	56.99
S&W 645/745	No	Weaver rail	56.99
S&W Sigma	No	Weaver rail	64.95
Taurus PT908	No	Weaver rail	63.25
Taurus 44 6.5" bbl.	No	Weaver rail	69.95
Walther 99	No	Weaver rail	74.95
Shotguns			
Benelli M-1 Super 90	No	Weaver rail	44.95
Benelli Montefeltro	No	Weaver rail	44.95
Benelli Nova	No	Weaver rail	69.95
Benelli Super Black Eagle	No	Weaver rail	49.95
Browning A-5 12-ga.	No	Weaver rail	40.95
Browning BPS 12-ga.	No	Weaver rail	40.95
Browning Gold Hunter 12-ga.	No	Weaver rail	44.95
Browning Gold Hunter 20-ga.	No	Weaver rail	49.95
Browning Gold Hunter 10-ga.	No	Weaver rail	49.95
Beretta 303 12-ga.	No	Weaver rail	44.95
Beretta 390 12-ga.	No	Weaver rail	44.95
Beretta Pintail	No	Weaver rail	44.95
H&K Fabarms Gold/SilverLion	No	Weaver rail	49.95
Ithaca 37/87 12-ga.	No	Weaver rail	40.95
Ithaca 37/87 20-ga.	No	Weaver rail	40.95
Mossberg 500/Maverick 12-ga.	No	Weaver rail	40.95
Mossberg 500/Maverick 20-ga.	No	Weaver rail	40.95
Mossberg 835 3.5" Ulti-Mag	No	Weaver rail	40.95
Mossberg 5500/9200	No	Weaver rail	40.95
Remington 1100/1187 12-ga.	No	Weaver rail	42.80
Remington 1100/1187 12-ga. LH	No	Weaver rail	42.80
Remington 1100/1187 20-ga.	No	Weaver rail	40.95
Remington 1100/1187 20-ga. LH	No	Weaver rail	40.95
Remington 870 12-ga.	No	Weaver rail	40.95
Remington 870 12-ga. LH	No	Weaver rail	40.95
Remington 870 20-ga.	No	Weaver rail	42.80
Remington 870 20-ga. LH	No	Weaver rail	42.80
Remington 870 Express Magnum	No	Weaver rail	40.95
Remington SP-10 10-ga.	No	Weaver rail	49.95
Winchester 1300 12-ga.	No	Weaver rail	40.95
Winchester 1400 12-ga.	No	Weaver rail	40.95
Winchester Super X2	No	Weaver rail	44.95
"Rib Rider" Ultra Low Profile Mounts Non See Through 2-piece rib attached			
Mossberg 500/835/9200	No	Weaver rail	29.95
Remington 1100/1187/870	No	Weaver rail	29.95
Winchester 1300	No	Weaver rail	29.95
1-Piece Rib Rider Low Rider Mounts			
Mossberg 500/835/9200	No	Weaver rail	29.95
Remington 1100/1187/870	No	Weaver rail	29.95
Winchester 1300	No	Weaver rail	29.95
2-Piece Rib Rider See-Through			
Mossberg 500/835/9200	No	Weaver rail	29.95
Remington 1100/1187/87	No	Weaver rail	29.95
Winchester 1300	No	Weaver rail	29.95
1-Piece Rib Rider See-Through			
Mossberg 500/835/9200	No	Weaver rail	29.95
Remington 1100/1187/870	No	Weaver rail	29.95
Winchester 1300	No	Weaver rail	29.95

Maker, Model, Type	Adjust.	Scopes	Price
AIMTECH (cont.)			
Rifles			
AR-15/M16	No	Weaver rail	21.95
Browning A-Bolt	No	Weaver rail	21.95
Browning BAR	No	Weaver rail	21.95
Browning BLR	No	Weaver rail	21.95
CVA Apollo	No	Weaver rail	21.95
Marlin 336	No	Weaver rail	21.95
Mauser Mark X	No	Weaver rail	21.95
Modern Muzzleloading	No	Weaver rail	21.95
Remington 700 Short Action	No	Weaver rail	21.95
Remington 700 Long Action	No	Weaver rail	21.95
Remington 7400/7600	No	Weaver rail	21.95
Ruger 10/22	No	Weaver rail	21.95
Ruger Mini 14 Scout Rail**	No	Weaver rail	89.50
Savage 110, 111, 113, 114, 115, 116	No	Weaver rail	21.95
Thompson Center Thunderhawk	No	Weaver rail	21.95
Traditions Buckhunter	No	Weaver rail	21.95
White W Series	No	Weaver rail	21.95
White G Series	No	Weaver rail	21.95
White WG Series	No	Weaver rail	21.95
Winchester Model 70	No	Weaver rail	21.95
Winchester 94 AE	No	Weaver rail	21.95

All mounts no-gunsmithing, iron sight usable. Rifle mounts are solid see-through bases. All mounts accommodate standard Weaver-style rings of all makers. From Aimtech division, L&S Technologies, Inc. *3-blade sight mount combination. **Replacement handguard and mounting rail.

Maker, Model, Type	Adjust.	Scopes	Price
A.R.M.S.			
M16A1,A2,AR-15	No	Weaver rail	$59.95
Multibase	No	Weaver rail	59.95
#19 ACOG Throw Lever Mt.	No	Weaver rail	150.00
#19 Weaver/STANAG Throw Lever Rail	No	Weaver rail	140.00
STANAG Rings	No	30mm	75.00
Throw Lever Rings	No	Weaver rail	99.00
Ring Inserts	No	1", 30mm	29.00
#22M68 Aimpoint Comp Ring Throw Lever	No	Weaver rail	99.00
#38 Std. Swan Sleeve[1]	No		180.00
#39 A2 Plus Mod. Mt.	No	#39T rail	125.00

[1]Avail. in three lengths. From A.R.M.S., Inc.

Maker, Model, Type	Adjust.	Scopes	Price
ARMSON			
AR-15[1]	No	1"	45.00
Mini-14[2]	No	1"	66.00
H&K[3]	No	1"	82.00

[1]Fastens with one nut. [2]Models 181, 182, 183, 184, etc. [3]Claw mount. From Trijicon, Inc.

Maker, Model, Type	Adjust.	Scopes	Price
ARMSPORT			
100 Series [1]	No	1" rings, Low, med., high	10.75
104 22-cal.	No	1"	10.75
201 See-Thru	No	1"	13.00
1-Piece Base[2]	No		5.50
2-Piece Base[2]	No		2.75

[1]Weaver-type ring. [2]Weaver-type base; most popular rifles. Made in U.S. From Arm Sport.

Maker, Model, Type	Adjust.	Scopes	Price
AO			
AO/Lever Scout Scope	No	Weaver rail	50.00

No gunsmithing required for lever-action rifles with 8" Weaver-style rails; surrounds barrel shank; 6" long; low profile. AO Sight Systems Inc.

Maker, Model, Type	Adjust.	Scopes	Price
B-SQUARE			
Pistols (centerfire)			
Beretta 92, 96/Taurus 99	No	Weaver rail	69.95
Colt M1911	E only	Weaver rail	69.95
Desert Eagle	No	Weaver rail	69.95
Glock	No	Weaver rail	69.95
H&K USP, 9mm and 40 S&W	No	Weaver rail	69.95
Ruger P85/89	E only	Weaver rail	69.95
SIG Sauer P226	E only	Weaver rail	69.95
Pistols (rimfire)			
Browning Buck Mark	No	Weaver rail	32.95
Colt 22	No	Weaver rail	49.95
Ruger Mk I/II, bull or taper	No	Weaver rail	32.95-49.95
Smith & Wesson 41, 2206	No	Weaver rail	36.95-49.95
Revolvers			
Colt Anaconda/Python	No	Weaver rail	35.95-74.95
Ruger Single-Six	No	Weaver rail	64.95
Ruger GP-100	No	Weaver rail	64.95

SCOPE RINGS & BASES

Maker, Model, Type	Adjust.	Scopes	Price
B-SQUARE (cont.)			
Ruger Blackhawk, Super	No	Weaver rail	**64.95**
Ruger Redhawk, Super	No	Weaver rail	**64.95**
Smith & Wesson K, L, N	No	Weaver rail	**36.95-74.95**
Taurus 66, 669, 607, 608	No	Weaver rail	**64.95**
Rifles (sporting)			
Browning BAR, A-Bolt	No	Weaver rail	**45.90**
Marlin MR7	No	Weaver rail	**45.90**
Mauser 98 Large Ring	No	Weaver rail	**45.90**
Mauser 91/93/95/96 Small Ring	No	Weaver rail	**45.90**
Remington 700, 740, 742, 760	No	Weaver rail	**45.90**
Remington 7400, 7600	No	Weaver rail	**45.90**
Remington Seven	No	Weaver rail	**45.90**
Rossi 62, 59 and 92	No	Weaver rail	**44.95**
Ruger Mini-14	W&E	Weaver rail	**66.95**
Ruger 96/22	No	Weaver rail	**45.90**
Ruger M77 (short and long)	No	Weaver rail	**62.95**
Ruger 10/22 (reg. and See-Thru)	No	Weaver rail	**45.90**
Savage 110-116, 10-16	No	Weaver rail	**45.90**
Modern Military (rings incl.)			
AK-47/MAC 90	No	Weaver rail	**49.95**
Colt AR-15	No	Weaver rail	**66.95-81.95**
FN/FAL/LAR (See-Thru rings)	No	Weaver rail	**81.95**
Classic Military (rings incl.)			
FN 49	No	Weaver rail	**72.95**
Hakim	No	Weaver rail	**72.95**
Mauser 38, 94, 96, 98	E only	Weaver rail	**72.95**
Mosin-Nagant (all)	E only	Weaver rail	**72.95**
Air Rifles			
RWS, Diana, BSA, Gamo	W&E	11mm rail	**49.95-59.95**
Weihrauch, Anschutz, Beeman, Webley	W&E	11mm rail	**59.95-69.95**
Shotguns/Slug Guns			
Benelli Super 90 (See-Thru)	No	Weaver rail	**53.95**
Browning BPS, A-5 9 (See-Thru)	No	Weaver rail	**53.95**
Browning Gold 10/12/20-ga. (See- Thru)	No	Weaver rail	**53.95**
Ithaca 37, 87	No	Weaver rail	**53.95**
Mossberg 500/Mav. 88	No	Weaver rail	**53.95**
Mossberg 835/Mav. 91	No	Weaver rail	**53.95**
Remington 870/1100/11-87	No	Weaver rail	**53.95**
Remington SP10	No	Weaver rail	**53.95**
Winchester 1200-1500	No	Weaver rail	**53.95**

Prices shown for anodized black finish; add $10 for stainless finish. Partial listing of mounts shown here. Contact B-Square for complete listing and details.

Maker, Model, Type	Adjust.	Scopes	Price
BEEMAN			
Two-Piece, Med.	No	1"	**31.50**
Deluxe Two-Piece, High	No	1"	**33.00**
Deluxe Two-Piece	No	30mm	**41.00**
Deluxe One-Piece	No	1"	**50.00**
Dampa Mount	No	1"	**120.00**

All grooved receivers and scope bases on all known air rifles and 22-cal. rimfire rifles (1/2" to 5/8" 6mm to 15mm).

Maker, Model, Type	Adjust.	Scopes	Price
BOCK			
Swing ALK[1]	W&E	1", 26mm, 30mm	**349.00**
Safari KEMEL[2]	W&E	1", 26mm, 30mm	**149.00**
Claw KEMKA[3]	W&E	1", 26mm, 30mm	**224.00**
ProHunter Fixed[4]	No	1", 26mm, 30mm	**95.00**

[1]Q.D.: pivots right for removal. For Steyr-Mannlicher, Win. 70, Rem. 700, Mauser 98, Dakota, Sako, Sauer 80, 90. Magnum has extra-wide rings, same price. [2]Heavy-duty claw-type reversible for front or rear removal. For Steyr-Mannlicher rifles. [3]True claw mount for bolt-action rifles. Also in extended model. For Steyr-Mannlicher, Win. 70, Rem. 700. Also avail. as Gunsmith Bases, not drilled or contoured same price. [4]Extra-wide rings. Imported from Germany by GSI, Inc.

Maker, Model, Type	Adjust.	Scopes	Price
BSA			
AA Airguns	Yes	Super Ten, 240 Magnum, Maxi gripped scope rail equipped air rifles	**59.99 (adj). 29.99 (fixed)**
BURRIS			
Supreme (SU) One-Piece (T)[1]	W only	1" split rings, 3 heights	**1-piece base - 23.00-27.00**
Trumount (TU) Two-Piece (T)	W only	1" split rings, 3 heights	**2-piece base - 21.00-30.00**
Trumount (TU) Two-Piece Ext.	W only	1" split rings	**26.00**
Browning 22-cal. Auto Mount[2]	No	1" split rings	**20.00**
1" 22-cal. Ring Mounts[3]	No	1" split rings	**1"rings - 24.00-41.00**
L.E.R. (LU) Mount Bases[4]	W only	1" split rings	**24.00-52.00**
BURRIS (cont.)			
L.E.R. No Drill-No Tap Bases[4,7,8]	W only	1" split rings	**48.00-52.00**
Extension Rings[5]	No	1" scopes	**28.00-46.00**
Ruger Ring Mount[6,9]	W only	1" split rings	**50.00-68.00**
Std. 1" Rings[9]		Low, medium, high heights	**29.00-43.00**
Zee Rings[9]		Fit Weaver bases; medium and high heights	**29.00-44.00**
Signature Rings	No	30mm split rings	**68.00**
Rimfire/Airgun Rings	W only	1" split rings, med. & high	**24.00-41.00**
Double Dovetail (DD) Bases	No	30mm Signature	**23.00-26.00**

[1]Most popular rifles. Universal rings, mounts fit Burris, Universal, Redfield, Leupold and Browning bases. Comparable prices. [2]Browning Standard 22 Auto rifle. [3]Grooved receivers. [4]Universal dovetail; accepts Burris, Universal, Redfield, Leupold rings. For Dan Wesson, S&W, Virginian, Ruger Blackhawk, Win. 94. [5]Medium standard front, extension rear, per pair. Low standard front, extension rear per pair. [6]Compact scopes, scopes with 2" bell for M77R. [7]Selected rings and bases available with matte Safari or silver finish. [8]For S&W K, L, N frames, Colt Python, Dan Wesson with 6" or longer barrels. [9]Also in 30mm.

Maker, Model, Type	Adjust.	Scopes	Price
CATCO			
Enfield Drop-In	No	1"	**39.95**

Uses Weaver-style rings (not incl.). No gunsmithing required. See-Thru design. From CATCO.

Maker, Model, Type	Adjust.	Scopes	Price
CLEAR VIEW			
Universal Rings, Mod. 101[1]	No	1" split rings	**21.95**
Standard Model[2]	No	1" split rings	**21.95**
Broad View[3]	No	1"	**21.95**
22 Model[4]	No	3/4", 7/8", 1"	**13.95**
SM-94 Winchester[5]	No	1" spllit rings	**23.95**
94 EJ[6]	No	1" split rings	**21.95**

[1]Most rifles by using Weaver-type base; allows use of iron sights. [2]Most popular rifles; allows use of iron sights. [3]Most popular rifles; low profile, wide field of view. [4]22 rifles with grooved receiver. [5]Side mount. [6]For Win. A.E. From Clear View Mfg.

Maker, Model, Type	Adjust.	Scopes	Price
CONETROL			
Huntur[1] (base & rings)	W only	1", split rings, 3 heights	**99.96**
Gunnur[2] (base & rings)	W only	1", split rings, 3 heights	**119.88**
Custum[3] (base & rings)	W only	1", split rings, 3 heights	**149.88**
One-Piece Side Mount Base[4]	W only		
DapTar Bases[5]	W only		
Pistol Bases, 2-or 3-ring[6]	W only		
Fluted Bases[7]	W only		**149.88**
Metric Rings[8]	W only	26mm, 26.5mm, 30mm	**99.96-149.88**

[1]All popular rifles, including metric-drilled foreign guns. Price shown for base, two rings. Matte finish. [2]Gunnur grade has mirror-finished rings to match scopes. Satin-finish base to match guns. Price shown for base, two rings. [3]Custom grade has mirror-finished rings and mirror-finished, streamlined base. Price shown for base, two rings. [4]Win. 94, Krag, older split-bridge Mannlicher-Schoenauer, Mini-14, etc. Prices same as above. [5]For all popular guns with integral mounting provision, including Sako, BSA Ithacagun, Ruger, Tikka, H&K, BRNO and many others. Also for grooved-receiver rimfires and air rifles. Prices same as above. [6]For XP-100, T/C Contender, Colt SAA, Ruger Blackhawk, S&W and others. [7]Sculptured two-piece bases as found on fine custom rifles. Price shown is for base alone. Also available unfinished **$99.96**, or finished but unblued **$119.88.** [8]26mm, 26.5mm, and 30mm rings made in projectionless style, in three heights. Three-ring mount for T/C Contender and other pistols in Conetrol's three grades. Any Conetrol mount available in stainless steel add 50 percent. Adjust-Quik-Detach (AQD) mounting is now available from Conetrol. Jam screws return the horizontal-split rings to zero. Adjustable for windage. AQD bases: **$89.94.** AQD rings: **$99.96.** (Total cost of complete setup, rings and 2-piece base, is **$179.88**).

Maker, Model, Type	Adjust.	Scopes	Price
CUSTOM QUALITY			
Custom See-Thru	No	Up to 44mm	**29.95**
Dovetail 101-1 See-Thru	No	1"	**29.95**
Removable Rings	No	1"	**29.95**
Solid Dovetail	No	1", 30mm vertically split	**29.95**
Dovetail 22 See-Thru	No	1"	**29.95**

Mounts for many popular rifles. From Custom Quality Products, Inc.

Maker, Model, Type	Adjust.	Scopes	Price
EAW			
Quick-Loc Mount	W&E	1", 26mm	**315.00**
	W&E	30mm	**325.00**
Magnum Fixed Mount	W&E	1", 26mm	**270.00**
	W&E	30mm	**285.00**

Fit most popular rifles. Avail. in 4 heights, 4 extensions. Reliable return to zero. Stress-free mounting. Imported by New England Custom Gun Svc.

Maker, Model, Type	Adjust.	Scopes	Price
EXCEL INDUSTRIES, INC.			
Titanium Weaver-Style Rings	No	1" and 30mm, low and high	**179.00**
Steel Weaver-Style Rings	No	1" and 30mm, low and high	**149.00**
Flashlight Mounts - Titanium and Steel	No	1" and 30mm, low and high	**89.50/75.00**

Scope Rings & Bases

Maker, Model, Type	Adjust.	Scopes	Price
GENTRY			
Feather-Light Rings and Bases	No	1", 30mm	90.00-125.00

Bases for Rem. Seven, 700, Mauser 98, Browning A-Bolt, Weatherby Mk. V, Win. 70, HVA, Dakota. Two-piece base for Rem. Seven, chrome moly or stainless. Rings in matte or regular blue, or stainless gray; four heights. From David Gentry.

Maker, Model, Type	Adjust.	Scopes	Price
GRIFFIN & HOWE			
Topmount[1]	No	1", 30mm	625.00
Sidemount[2]	No	1", 30mm	255.00
Garand Mount[3]	No	1"	255.00

[1]Quick-detachable, double-lever mount with 1" rings, installed; with 30mm rings **$875.00**. [2]Quick-detachable, double-lever mount with 1" rings; with 30mm rings **$375.00**; installed, 1" rings. **$405.00**; installed, 30mm rings **$525.00**. [3]Price installed, with 1" rings **$405.00**. From Griffin & Howe.

Maker, Model, Type	Adjust.	Scopes	Price
G. G. & G.			
Remington 700 Rail	No	Weaver base	135.00
Sniper Grade Rings	No	30mm	159.95
M16/AR15 F.I.R.E. Std.[1]	No	Weaver rail	75.00
M16/AR15 F.I.R.E. Scout	No	Weaver rail	82.95
Aimpoint Standard Ring	No		164.95
Aimpoint Cantilever Ring	No	Weaver rail	212.00

1For M16/A3, AR15 flat top receivers; also in extended length. [2]For Aimpoint 5000 and Comp; quick detachable; spare battery compartment. [3]Low profile; quick release. From G. G. & G.

Maker, Model, Type	Adjust.	Scopes	Price
IRONSIGHTER			
Ironsighter See-Through Mounts[1]	No	1" split rings	29.40-64.20
Ironsighter S-9[4]	No	1" split rings	45.28
Ironsighter AR-15/M-16[8]	No	1", 30mm	70.10
Ironsighter 22-Cal.Rimfire[2]	No	1"	18.45
Model #570[9]	No	1" split rings	29.40
Model #573[9]	No	30mm split rings	45.28
Model #727[3]	No	.875" split rings	18.45
Blackpowder Mount[7]	No	1"	34.20-78.25

[1]Most popular rifles. Rings have oval holes to permit use of iron sights. [2]For 1" dia. scopes. [3]For .875 dia. scopes. [4]For 1" dia. extended eye relief scopes. [7]Fits most popular blackpowder rifles; two-piece (CVA, Knight, Marlin and Austin & Halleck) and one-piece integral (T/C). [8]Model 716 with 1" #540 rings; Fits Weaver-style bases. Some models in stainless finish. [9]New detachable Weaver style rings fit all Weaver style bases. **Price: $26.95.** From Ironsighter Co.

Maker, Model, Type	Adjust.	Scopes	Price
K MOUNT By KENPATABLE			
Shotgun Mount	No	1", laser or red dot device	49.95
SKS1	No	1"	39.95

Wrap-around design; no gunsmithing required. Models for Browning BPS, A-5 12-ga., Sweet 16, 20, Rem. 870/1100 (LTW, and L.H.), S&W 916, Mossberg 500, Ithaca 37 & 51 12- ga., S&W 1000/3000, Win. 1400. 1Requires simple modification to gun. From KenPatable Ent.

Maker, Model, Type	Adjust.	Scopes	Price
KRIS MOUNTS			
Side-Saddle[1]	No	1",26mm split rings	12.98
Two-Piece (T)[2]	No	1", 26mm split rings	8.98
One Piece (T)[3]	No	1", 26mm split rings	12.98

[1]One-piece mount for Win. 94. [2]Most popular rifles and Ruger. [3]Blackhawk revolver. Mounts have oval hole to permit use of iron sights.

Maker, Model, Type	Adjust.	Scopes	Price
KWIK-SITE			
Adapter	No	1"	27.95-57.95
KS-W2[2]	No	1"	21.95
KS-W94[3]	No	1"	42.95
KS-WEV (Weaver-style rings)	No	1"	19.95
KS-WEV-HIGH	No	1"	19.95
KS-T22 1"[4]	No	1"	17.95
KS-FL Flashlite[5]	No	Mini or C cell flash light	37.95
KS-T88[6]	No	1"	21.95
KS-T89	No	30mm	21.95
KSN 22 See-Thru	No	1", 7/8"	17.95
KSN-T22	No	1", 7/8"	17.95
KSN-M-16 See-Thru (for M16 + AR- 15)	No	1"	49.95
KS-202[1]	No	1"	27.97
KS-203	No	30mm	42.95
KSBP[7]	No	Integral	76.95
KSB Base Set			5.95
Combo Bases & Rings	No	1"	21.95

Bases interchangeable with Weaver bases. [1]Most rifles. Allows use of iron sights. [2]22-cal. rifles with grooved receivers. Allows use of iron sights. [3]Model 94, 94 Big Bore. No drilling or tapping. Also in adjustable model **$57.95**. [4]Non-See-Thru model for grooved receivers. [5]Allows C-cell or, Mini Mag Lites to be mounted atop See-Thru mounts. [6]Fits any Redfield, Tasco, Weaver or Universal-style Kwik-Site dovetail base. [7]Blackpowder mount with integral rings and sights. [8]Shotgun side mount. Bright blue, black matte or satin finish. Standard, high heights.

Maker, Model, Type	Adjust.	Scopes	Price
LASER AIM	No	Laser Aim	19.99-69.00

Mounts Laser Aim above or below barrel. Avail. for most popular hand guns, rifles, shotguns, including militaries. From Laser Aim Technologies, Inc.

Maker, Model, Type	Adjust.	Scopes	Price
LEUPOLD			
STD Bases[1]	W only	One- or two-piece bases	25.40
STD Rings[2]		1" super low, low, medium, high	33.60
DD RBH Handgun Mounts[2]	No		34.00
Dual Dovetail Bases[3]	No		25.40
Dual Dovetail Rings[8]		1", low, med, high	33.60
Ring Mounts[4,5,6]	No	7/8", 1"	102.80
22 Rimfire[8]	No	7/8", 1"	73.60
Gunmaker Base[7]	W only	1"	73.60
Quick Release Rings		1", low, med., high	43.00-81.00
Quick Release Bases[9]	No	1", one- or two- piece	73.60

[1]Base and two rings; Casull, Ruger, S&W, T/C; add $5.00 for silver finish. [2]Rem. 700, Win. 70-type actions. For Ruger No. 1, 77, 77/22; interchangeable with Ruger units. For dovetailed rimfire rifles. Sako; high, medium, low. [7]Must be drilled, tapped for each action. [8]13mm dovetail receiver. [9]BSA Monarch, Rem. 40x, 700, 721, 725, Ruger M77, S&W 1500, Weatherby Mark V, Vanguard, Win. M70.

Maker, Model, Type	Adjust.	Scopes	Price
MARLIN			
One-Piece QD (T)	No	1" split rings	10.10

Most Marlin lever actions.

Maker, Model, Type	Adjust.	Scopes	Price
MILLETT			
Black Onyx Smooth		1", low, medium, high	32.71
Chaparral Engraved		engraved	50.87
One-Piece Bases[6]	Yes	1"	26.41
Universal Two-Piece Bases			
700 Series	W only	Two-piece bases	26.41
FN Series	W only	Two-piece bases	26.41
70 Series[1]	W only	1", two-piece bases	26.41
Angle-Loc Rings[2]	W only	1", low, medium, high	35.49
Ruger 77 Rings[3]		1"	38.14
Shotgun Rings[4]		1"	32.55
Handgun Bases, Rings[5]		1"	36.07-80.38
30mm Rings[7]		30mm	20.95-41.63
Extension Rings[8]		1"	40.43-56.44
See-Thru Mounts[9]	No	1"	29.35-31.45
Shotgun Mounts[10]	No	1"	52.45
Timber Mount	No	1"	81.90

BRNO, Rem. 40x, 700, 722, 725, 7400 Ruger 77 (round top), Marlin, Weatherby, FN Mauser, FN Brownings, Colt 57, Interarms Mark X, Parker-Hale, Savage 110, Sako (round receiver), many others. [1]Fits Win. M70 70XTR, 670, Browning BBR, BAR, BLR, A-Bolt, Rem. 7400/7600, Four, Six, Marlin 336, Win. 94 A. E., Sav. 110. [2]To fit Weaver-type bases. [3]Engraved. Smooth **$34.60**. [4]For Rem. 870, 1100; smooth. [5]Two- and three-ring sets for Colt Python, Trooper, Diamondback, Peacekeeper, Dan Wesson, Ruger Redhawk, Super Redhawk. [6]Turn-in bases and Weaver-style for most popular rifles and T/C Contender, XP-100 pistols. [7]Both Weaver and turn-in styles; three heights. [8]Med. or high; ext. front std. rear, ext. rear std. front, ext. front ext. rear; **$40.90** for double extension. [9]Many popular rifles, Knight MK-85, T/C Hawken, Renegade, Mossberg 500 Slugster, 835 slug. [10]For Rem. 879/1100, Win. 1200, 1300/1400, 1500, Mossberg 500. Some models available in nickel at extra cost. New Angle-Loc two-piece bases fit all Weaver-style rings. In smooth, matte and nickel finishes, they are available for: Browning A-Bolt, Browning BAR/BLR, Interarms MK X, FN, Mauser 98, CVA rifles with octagon barrels, CVA rifles with round receiver, Knight MK-85, Knight Wolverine, Remington 700, Sauer SHR 970, Savage 110, Winchester 70. **$24.95 to $28.95.** From Millett Sights.

Maker, Model, Type	Adjust.	Scopes	Price
MMC			
AK[1]	No		39.95
FN FAL/LAR[2]	No		59.95

[1]Fits all AK derivative receivers; Weaver-style base; low-profile scope position. [2]Fits all FAL versions; Weaver-style base. From MMC.

Maker, Model, Type	Adjust.	Scopes	Price
REDFIELD			
JR-SR (T)1. One/two-piece bases.	W only	3/4", 1", 26mm, 30mm	JR-15.99-46.99 SR-15.99-33.49
Ring (T)[2]	No	3/4" and 1"	27.95-29.95
Widefield See-Thru Mounts	No	1"	15.95
Ruger Rings[4]	No	1", med., high	30.49-36.49
Ruger 30mm[5]	No	1"	37.99-40.99

[1]Low, med. & high, split rings. Reversible extension front rings for 1". 2-piece bases for Sako. Colt Sauer bases **$39.95**. Med. Top Access JR rings nickel-plated, **$28.95**. SR two-piece ABN mount nickel-plated **$22.95**. [2]Split rings for grooved 22s; 30mm, black matte **$42.95**. [3]Used with MP scopes for; S&W K, L or N frame, XP-100, T/C Contender, Ruger receivers. [4]For Ruger Model 77 rifles, medium and high; medium only for M77/22. [5]For Model 77. Also in matte finish **$45.95**. [6]Aluminun 22 groove mount **$14.95**; base and medium rings **$18.95**. Scout mounts available for Mosin Nagant, Schmidt Rubin K-31, 98K Mauser, Husqvarna Mauser, Persian Mauser, Turkish Mauser.

Scope Rings & Bases

Maker, Model, Type	Adjust.	Scopes	Price
S&K			
Insta-Mount (T) Bases and Rings[1]	W only	Uses S&K rings only	**47.00-117.00**
Conventional Rings and Bases[2]	W only	1" split rings	**From 65.00**
Sculptured Bases, Rings[2]	W only	1", 26mm, 30mm	**From 65.00**
Smooth Contoured Rings[3]	Yes	1", 26mm, 30mm	**90.00-120.00**

[1]1903, A3, M1 Carbine, Lee Enfield #1. Mk.III, #4, #5, M1917, M98 Mauser, AR-15, AR-180, M-14, M-1, Ger. K-43, Mini-14, M1-A, Krag, AKM, Win. 94, SKS Type 56, Daewoo, H&K. [2]Most popular rifles already drilled and tapped and Sako, Tikka dovetails. [3]No projections; weigh 1/2-oz. each; matte or gloss finish. Horizontally and vertically split rings, matte or high gloss.

Maker, Model, Type	Adjust.	Scopes	Price
SAKO			
QD Dovetail	W only	1"	**70.00-155.00**

Sako, or any rifle using Sako action, 3 heights available. Stoeger, importer.

Maker, Model, Type	Adjust.	Scopes	Price
SPRINGFIELD, INC.			
M1A Third Generation	No	1" or 30mm	**123.00**
M1A Standard	N0	1" or 30mm	**77.00**
M6 Scout Mount	No		**29.00**

Weaver-style bases. From Springfield, Inc.

Maker, Model, Type	Adjust.	Scopes	Price
TALBOT			
QD Bases	No		**180.00-190.00**
Rings	No	1", 30mm	**50.00-70.00**

Blue or stainless steel; standard or extended bases; rings in three heights. For most popular rifles. From Talbot QD Mounts.

Maker, Model, Type	Adjust.	Scopes	Price
TASCO			
Centerfire rings	Integral	1", 30mm, matte black	**5.95**
High centerfire rings	Special high	1", matte black aluminum	**5.95**
.22/airgun rings	Yes	1", matte black aluminum	**5.95**
.22/airgun "Quick Peep" rings	Yes	1", matte black aluminum	**5.95**

Maker, Model, Type	Adjust.	Scopes	Price
THOMPSON/CENTER			
Duo-Ring Mount[1]	No	1"	**73.80**
Weaver-Style Bases	No		**13.00–42.50**
Weaver-Style Rings[2]	No	1"	**36.00**
Weaver-Style See-Thru Rings[3]	No	1"	**36.00**

[1]Attaches directly to T/C Contender bbl., no drilling/tapping; also for T/C M/L rifles, needs base adapter; blue or stainless. [2]Medium and high; blue or silver finish. [3]For T.C FireHawk, ThunderHawk; blue; silver **$29.80**. From Thompson/Center.

Maker, Model, Type	Adjust.	Scopes	Price
UNERTL			
1/4 Click[1]	Yes	3/4", 1" target scopes	**Per set 285.00**

[1]Unertl target or varmint scopes. Posa or standard mounts, less bases. From Unertl.

Maker, Model, Type	Adjust.	Scopes	Price
WARNE			
Premier Series (all steel)			
T.P.A. (Permanently Attached)	No	1", 4 heights 30mm, 2 heights	**87.75-98.55**
Premier Series Rings fit Premier Series Bases			
Premier Series (all-steel Q.D. rings)			
Premier Series (all steel) Quick detachable lever	No	1", 4 heights 26mm, 2 heights 30mm, 3 heights	**131.25-129.95** **142.00**
BRNO 19mm	No	1", 3 heights 30mm, 2 heights	**125.00-136.70**
BRNO 16mm		1", 2 heights	**125.00**
Ruger	No	1", 4 heights 30mm, 3 heights	**125.00-136.70**
Ruger M77	No	1", 3 heights 30mm, 2 heights	**125.00-136.70**
Sako Medium & Long Action	No	1", 4 heights 30mm, 3 heights	**125.00-136.70**
Sako Short Action	No	1", 3 heights	**125.00**
All-Steel One-Piece Base, ea.			**38.50**
All-Steel Two-Piece Base, ea.			**14.00**
Maxima Series (fits all Weaver-style bases)			
Permanently Attached[1]	No	1", 3 heights 30mm, 3 heights	**25.50** **36.00**
Adjustable Double Lever[2]	No	1", 3 heights 30mm, 3 heights	**72.60** **80.75**
Thumb Knob	No	1", 3 heights 30mm, 3 heights	**59.95** **68.25**
Stainless-Steel Two-Piece Base, ea.			**15.25**

Vertically split rings with dovetail clamp, precise return to zero. Fit most popular rifles, handguns. Regular blue, matte blue, silver finish. [1]All-Steel, non-Q.D. rings. [2]All-steel, Q.D. rings. From Warne Mfg. Co.

Maker, Model, Type	Adjust.	Scopes	Price
WEAVER			
Top Mount	No	7/8", 1", 30mm, 33mm	**24.95-38.95**
Side Mount	No	1", 1" long	**14.95-34.95**
Tip-Off Rings	No	7/8", 1"	**24.95-32.95**
Pivot Mounts	No	1"	**38.95**
Complete Mount Systems			
Pistol	No	1"	**75.00-105.00**
Rifle	No	1"	**32.95**
SKS Mount System	No	1"	**49.95**
Pro-View (no base required)	No	1"	**13.95-15.95**
Converta-Mount, 12-ga. (Rem. 870, Moss. 500)	No	1", 30mm	**74.95**
See-Thru Mounts			
Detachable	No	1"	**27.00-32.00**
System (no base required)	No	1"	**15.00-35.00**
Tip-Off	No	1"	**15.00**

Nearly all modern rifles, pistols, and shotguns. Detachable rings in standard, See-Thru, and extension styles, in Low, Medium, High or X- High heights; gloss (blued), silver and matte finishes to match scopes. Extension rings are only available in 1" High style and See- Thru X-tensions only in gloss finish. Tip-Off rings only for 3/8" grooved receivers or 3/8"grooved adaptor bases; no base required. See-Thru & Pro-View mounts for most modern big bore rifles, some in silver. No Drill & Tap Pistol systems in gloss or silver for: Colt Python, Trooper, 357, Officer's Model; Ruger Single-Six, Security- Six (gloss finish only), Blackhawk, Super Blackhawk, Blackhawk SRM 357, Redhawk, Mini-14 Series (not Ranch), Ruger 22 Auto Pistols, Mark II; Smith & Wesson I- and current K-frames with adj. rear sights. Converta-Mount Systems in Standard and See-Under for: Mossberg 500 (12- and 20-ga.); Remington 870, 11-87 (12- and 20- ga. lightweight); Winchester 1200, 1300, 1400, 1500. Converta Brackets, Bases, Rings also avail. for Beretta A303 and A390; Browning A-5, BPS Pump; Ithaca 37, 87. From Weaver.

Maker, Model, Type	Adjust.	Scopes	Price
WEIGAND			
Browning Buck Mark[1]	No		**29.95**
Integra Mounts[2]	No		**39.95-69.00**
S&W Revolver[3]	No		**29.95**
Ruger 10/22[4]	No		**14.95-39.95**
Ruger Revolver[5]	No		**29.95**
Taurus Revolver[4]	No		**29.95-65.00**
Lightweight Rings	No	1", 30mm	**29.95-39.95**
1911			
SM36	No	Weaver rail	**99.95**
APCMNT[7]	No		**69.95**

[1]No gunsmithing. [2]S&W K, L, N frames; Taurus vent rib models; Colt Anaconda/ Python; Ruger Redhawk; Ruger 10/22. [3]K, L, N frames. [4]Three models. [5]Redhawk, Blackhawk, GP-100. [6]3rd Gen.; drill and tap; without slots **$59.95**. [7]For Aimpoint Comp. Red Dot scope, silver only. From Weigand Combat Handguns, Inc.

Maker, Model, Type	Adjust.	Scopes	Price
WIDEVIEW			
Premium 94 Angle Eject and side mount	No	1"	**18.70**
Premium See-Thru	No	1"	**18.70**
22 Premium See-Thru	No	3/4", 1"	**13.60**
Universal Ring Angle Cut	No	1"	**18.70**
Universal Ring Straight Cut	No	1"	**18.70**
Solid Mounts			
Lo Ring Solid[1]	No	1"	**13.60**
Hi Ring Solid[1]	No	1"	**13.60**
SR Rings		1", 30mm	**13.60**
22 Grooved Receiver	No	1"	**13.60**
Blackpowder Mounts[2]	No	1"	**18.70-37.40**
High, extra-high ring mounts with base	No	up to 60mm	**18.70**
Desert Eagle Pistol Mount	No	1", 30mm	**34.95-44.95**

[1]For Weaver-type base. Models for many popular rifles. Low ring, high ring and grooved receiver types. [2]No drilling, tapping, for T/C Renegade, Hawken, CVA, Knight Traditions guns. From Wideview Scope Mount Corp.

Maker, Model, Type	Adjust.	Scopes	Price
WILLIAMS			
Side Mount with HCO Rings[1]	No	1", split or exten sion rings	**74.35**
Side Mount, Offset Rings[2]	No	Same	**61.45**
Sight-Thru Mounts[3]	No	1", 7/8" sleeves	**19.50**
Streamline Mounts	No	1" (bases form rings)	**26.50**

[1]Most rifles, Br. S.M.L.E. (round rec.) **$14.41** extra. [2]Most rifles including Win. 94 Big Bore. [3]Many modern rifles, including CVA Apollo, others with 1" octagon barrels.

Maker, Model, Type	Adjust.	Scopes	Price
YORK			
M-1 Garand	Yes	1"	**39.95**

Centers scope over the action. No drilling, tapping or gunsmithing. Uses standard dovetail rings. From York M-1 Conversions.

NOTES

(S)Side Mount; (T)Top Mount; 22mm=.866"; 25.4mm=1.024"; 26.5mm=1.045"; 30mm=1.81".

METALLIC SIGHTS

Sporting Leaf and Open Sights

AUTOMATIC DRILLING REAR SIGHT Most German and Austrian drillings have this kind of rear sight. When rifle barrel is selected, the rear sight automatically comes to the upright position. Base length 2.165", width .472", folding leaf height .315". From New England Custom Gun Service.
Price: **$48.50**

CLASSIC MARBLE/WILLIAMS STYLE FULLY ADJUSTABLE REAR SPORTING SIGHTS Screw-on attachment. Dovetailed graduated windage and elevation adjustment. Elevation and windage lock with set screws. Available in steel or lightweight alloy construction. From Sarco, Inc.
Price: **$13.50**

ERA MASTERPIECE ADJUSTABLE REAR SIGHTS Precision-machined, all-steel, polished and blued. Attaches with 8-36 socket head screw. Use small screwdriver to adjust windage and elevation. Available for various barrel widths. From New England Custom Gun Service.
Price: **$82.00**

ERA CLASSIC ADJUSTABLE REAR SIGHT Similar to the Masterpiece unit except windage is adjusted by pushing sight sideways, then locking it with a reliable clamp. Precision machined all steel construction, polished, with 6-48 fastening screw and Allen wrench. Shallow "V" and "U" notch. Length 2.170", width .550". From New England Custom Gun Service.
Price: **$55.00**

ERA EXPRESS SIGHTS A wide variety of open sights and bases for custom installation. Partial listing shown. From New England Custom Gun Service.
Price: One-leaf express. **$66.00**
Price: Two-leaf express. **$71.50**
Price: Three-leaf express. **$77.00**
Price: Bases for above **$27.50**
Price: Standing rear sight, straight. **$13.25**
Price: Base for above. **$16.50**

ERA CLASSIC EXPRESS SIGHTS Standing or folding leaf sights are securely locked to the base with the ERA Magnum Clamp, but can be loosened for sighting in. Base can be attached with two socket-head cap screws or soldered. Finished and blued. Barrel diameters from .600" to .930". From New England Custom Gun Service.
Price: Standing leaf. **$54.00**
Price: One-leaf express. **$96.00**
Price: Two-leaf express. **$101.00**
Price: Three-leaf express. **$120.00**

ERA MASTERPIECE REAR SIGHT Adjustable for windage and elevation, and adjusted and locked with a small screwdriver. Comes with 8-36 socket-head cap screw and wrench. Barrel diameters from .600" to .930".
Price: **$75.00**

G.G. & G. SAME PLANE APERTURE M-16/AR-15 A2-style dual aperture rear sight with both large and small apertures centered on the same plane.
Price: **$45.00**

LYMAN No.16 Middle sight for barrel dovetail slot mounting. Folds flat when scope or peep sight is used. Sight notch plate adjustable for elevation. White triangle for quick aiming. Designed to fit 3/8" dovetail slots. Three heights: A-.400" to.500", B-.345" to .445", C-.500" to .600". A slot blank designed to fill dovetail notch when sight is removed is available
Price: **$5.00**
Price: **$13.25**

MARBLE FALSE BASE #76, #77, #78 New screw-on base for most rifles replaces factory base. 3/8" dovetail slot permits installation of any folding rear sight. Can be had in sweat-on models also.
Price: **$8.00**

MARBLE FOLDING LEAF Flattop or semi-buckhorn style. Folds down when scope or peep sights are used. Reversible plate gives choice of "U" or "V" notch. Adjustable for elevation.
Price: **$16.00**
Price: Also available with both windage and elevation adjustment. **$18.00**

MARBLE SPORTING REAR With white enamel diamond, gives choice of two "U" and two "V" notches or different sizes. Adjustment in height by means of double step elevator and sliding notch piece. For all rifles; screw or dovetail installation.
Price: . . . . **$16.00 to $17.00**

MARBLE #20 UNIVERSAL New screw or sweat-on base. Both have .100" elevation adjustment. In five base sizes. Three styles of U-notch, square notch, peep. Adjustable for windage and elevation.
Price: Screw-on. **$23.00**
Price: Sweat-on. **$21.00**

MILLETT SPORTING & BLACKPOWDER RIFLE Open click adjustable rear fits 3/8" dovetail cut in barrel. Choice of white outline, target black or open express V rear blades. Also available is a replacement screw-on sight with express V, .562" hole centers. Dovetail fronts in white or blaze orange in seven heights (.157"-.540").
Price: Dovetail or screw-on rear. **$58.38**
Price: Front sight. **$12.96**

MILLETT SCOPE-SITE Open, adjustable or fixed rear sights dovetail into a base integral with the top scope-mounting ring. Blaze orange front ramp sight is integral with the front ring half. Rear sights have white outline aperture. Provides fast, short-radius, Patridge-type open sights on the top of the scope. Can be used with all Millett rings, Weaver-style bases, Ruger 77 (also fits Redhawk), Ruger Ranch Rifle, No. 1, No. 3, Rem. 870, 1100; Burris, Leupold and Redfield bases.
Price: Scope-Site top only, windage only. **$31.15**
Price: As above, fully adjustable. **$66.10**
Price: Scope-Site Hi-Turret, fully adjustable, low, medium, high. **$66.10**

RUGER WINDAGE ADJUSTABLE FOLDING REAR SIGHT Fits all Ruger rifles produced with standard folding rear sights. Available in low (.480"), medium (.503") and high (.638") heights. From Sturm, Ruger & Co., Inc.
Price: **$19.80**

TRIJICON 3-DOT NIGHT SIGHTS Self-luminous and machined from steel. Available for the M16/AR-15, H&K rifles. Front and rear sets and front only.
Price: . . . . **$50.00 to $84.00**

WHITWORTH STYLE ENGLISH 3 LEAF EXPRESS SIGHTS Folding leafs marked in 100, 200 and 300 yard increments. Slide assembly is dovetailed in base. Available in four different styles: 3 folding leaves, flat bottom; 1 fixed, 2 folding leaves, flat bottom; 3 folding leaves, round bottom; 1 fixed, 2 folding leaves, round bottom. Available from Sarco, Inc.
Price: **$49.95**

WICHITA MULTI RANGE SIGHT SYSTEM Designed for silhouette shooting. System allows you to adjust the rear sight to four repeatable range settings, once it is pre-set. Sight clicks to any of the settings by turning a serrated wheel. Front sight is adjustable for weather and light conditions with one adjustment. Specify gun when ordering.
Price: Rear sight. **$125.00**
Price: Front sight. **$95.00**

WILLIAMS DOVETAIL OPEN SIGHT (WDOS) Open rear sight with windage and elevation adjustment. Furnished "U" notch or choice of blades. Slips into dovetail and locks with gib lock. Heights from .281" to .531".
Price:With blade. **$19.50**
Price:Less blade. **$12.45**
Price:Rear sight blades, each. **$7.05**

WILLIAMS GUIDE OPEN SIGHT (WGOS) Open rear sight with windage and elevation adjustment. Bases to fit most military and commercial barrels. Choice of square "U" or "V" notch blade, 3/16", 1/4", 5/16", or 3/8" high.
Price: Less blade. **$19.50**
Price: Extra blades, each. **$7.05**

WILLIAMS WGOS OCTAGON Open rear sight for 1" octagonal barrels. Installs with two 6-48 screws and uses same hole spacing as most T/C muzzleloading rifles. Four heights, choice of square, U, V, or B blade.
Price: **$26.55**

WILLIAMS WSKS, WAK47 Replaces original military-type rear sight. Adjustable for windage and elevation. No drilling or tapping. Peep aperture or open. For SKS carbines, AK-47-style rifles.
Price: Aperture. **$25.95**
Price: Open. **$24.95**

WILLIAMS WM-96 Fits Mauser 96-type military rifles. Replaces original rear sight with open blade or aperture. Fully adjustable for windage and elevation. No drilling or tapping.
Price: Aperture. **$25.95**
Price: Open. **$24.95**

WILLIAMS FIRE RIFLE SETS Replacement front and rear fiber optic sights. Red bead front, two green elements in the fully-adjustable rear. Made of CNC-machined metal.
Price: For Ruger 10/22. . . . . **$24.95**
Price: For most Marlin and Win. (3/8" dovetail). **$34.95**
Price: For Remington (newer style sight base). **$28.95**

Aperture and Micrometer Receiver Sights

A2 REAR SIGHT KIT Featuring an exclusive numbered windage knob. For .223 AR-style rifles. From ArmaLite, Inc.
Price: **$55.00**

AO GHOST RING HUNTING SIGHT Fully adjustable for windage and elevation. Available for most rifles, including blackpowder guns. Minimum gunsmithing required for most installations; matches most mounting holes. From AO Sight Systems, Inc.
Price: **$90.00**

AO AR-15/M-16 APERTURE Drop-in replacement of factory sights. Both apertures are on the same plane. Large ghost ring has .230" inside diameter; small ghost ring has .100" inside diameter. From AO Sight Systems, Inc.
Price: **$30.00**

AO BACKUP GHOST RING SIGHTS Mounts to scope base and retains zero when reinstalled in the field. Affords same elevation/windage adjustability as AO Hunting Ghost Rings. Included are both .191" and .230" apertures and test posts. Available for Ruger, Sako, Remington 700 and other rifles. From AO Sight Systems, Inc.
Price: **$65.00**

AO Ghost Ring

AO TACTICAL SIGHTS For HK UMP/USC/G36/SL8/MP5. The Big Dot Tritium or standard dot tritium is mated with a large .300" diameter rear ghost ring. The "same plane" rear aperture flips from the .300" to a .230" diameter ghost ring. From AO Sight Systems, Inc.
Price: . . . . **$90.00 to $120.00**

BEEMAN/FEINWERKBAU 5454 MATCH APERTURE SIGHT Small size, new-design sight uses constant-pressure flat springs to eliminate point of impact shifts.
Price: **$350.00**

BEEMAN SPORT APERTURE SIGHT Positive click micrometer adjustments. Standard units with flush surface screwdriver adjustments. Deluxe version has target knobs. For air rifles with grooved receivers.
Price: Standard. **$40.00**
Price: Deluxe. **$50.00**

METALLIC SIGHTS

BUSHMASTER COMPETITION A2 REAR SIGHT ASSEMBLY Elevation and windage mechanism feature either 1/2 or 1/4 minute of adjustment. Long distance aperture allows screw-in installation of any of four interchangeable micro-apertures.
Price: 1/2 M.O.A.. . . . . **$109.95**
Price: 1/4 M.O.A.. . . . . **$114.95**

DPMS NATIONAL MATCH Replaces the standard A2 rear sight on M16/AR-15 rifles. Has 1/4-minute windage and 1/2-minute elevation adjustments. Includes both a .052" and .200" diameter aperture.
Price: **$92.99**

ENFIELD No. 4 TARGET/MATCH SIGHT Originally manufactured by Parker-Hale, has adjustments up to 1,300 meters. Micrometer click adjustments for windage. Adjustable aperture disc has six different openings from .030" to .053". From Sarco, Inc.
Price: **$49.95**

EAW RECEIVER SIGHT A fully adjustable aperture sight that locks securely into the EAW quick-detachable scope mount rear base. Made by New England Custom Gun Service.
Price:. **$80.00**

ERA SEE-THRU Contains fiber optic center dot. Fits standard 3/8" American dovetails. Locks in place with set screw. Ideal for use on moving targets. Width 19.5mm. Available in low (.346", medium .425" and high **.504**" models. From New England Custom Gun Service.
Price:. **$27.50**

G. G.& G. MAD IRIS Multiple Aperture Device is a four sight, rotating aperture disk with small and large apertures on the same plane. Mounts on M-16/AR-15 flattop receiver. Fully adjustable.
Price:. **$141.95**
Price: A2 IRIS, two apertures, full windage adjustments. **$124.95**

KNIGHT'S ARMAMENT 600 METER FOLDING REAR SIGHT Click adjustable from 200 to 600 meters with clearly visible range markings. Intermediate clicks allows for precise zero at known ranges. Allows use of optical scopes by folding don. Mounts on rear of upper receiver rail on SR-25 and similar rifles. From Knight's Armament Co.
Price:. **$181.00**

KNIGHT'S ARMAMENT FOLDING 300M SIGHT Mounts on flat-top upper receivers on SR-25 and similar rifles. May be used as a back-up iron sight for a scoped rifle/carbine or a primary sight. Peep insert may be removed to expose the 5mm diameter ghost ring aperture. From Knight's Armament Co.
Price:. **$144.00**

LYMAN NO. 2 TANG SIGHT Designed for the Winchester Model 94. Has high index marks on aperture post; comes with both .093" quick sighting aperture, .040" large disk aperture, and replacement mounting screws.
Price:. **$76.00**
Price: For Marlin lever actions. **$76.00**

LYMAN No. 57 1/4-minute clicks. Stayset knobs. Quick-release slide, adjustable zero scales. Made for almost all modern rifles.
Price:. **$67.50**
Price: No. 57SME, 57SMET (for White Systems Model 91 and Whitetail rifles). **$62.50**

LYMAN 57GPR Designed especially for the Lyman Great Plains Rifle. Mounts directly onto the tang of the rifle and has 1/4-minute micrometer click adjustments.
Price: **$62.50**

Lyman No. 57

LYMAN No. 66 Fits close to the rear of flat-sided receivers, furnished with Stayset knobs. Quick-release slide, 1/4-min. adjustments. For most lever or slide action or flat-sided automatic rifles.
Price:. **$67.50**
Price: No. 66MK (for all current versions of the Knight MK-85 in-line rifle with flat-sided receiver). **$67.50**
Price: No. 66 SKS fits Russian and Chinese SKS rifles; large and small apertures. **$67.50**
Price: No. 66 WB for Model 1886 Winchester lever actions. **$67.50**

LYMAN No. 66U Light weight, designed for most modern shotguns with a flat-sided, round-top receiver. 1/4-minute clicks. Requires drilling, tapping. Not for Browning A-5, Rem. M11.
Price: **$71.50**

LYMAN 90MJT RECEIVER SIGHT Mounts on standard Lyman and Williams FP bases. Has 1/4-minute audible micrometer click adjustments, target knobs with direction indicators. Adjustable zero scales, quick-release slide. Large 7/8" diameter aperture disk.
Price: Right- or left-hand. **$74.95**

LYMAN RECEIVER SIGHT Audible-click adjustments for windage and elevation, coin-slotted "stayset" knobs and two interchangeable apertures. For Mauser, Springfield, Sako, T/C Hawken, Rem. 700, Win. 70, Savage 110, SKS, Win. 94, Marlin 336 and 1894.
Price:. **$53.99**

LYMAN 1886 #2 TANG SIGHT Fits the Winchester 1886 lever action rifle and replicas thereof not containing a tang safety. Has height index marks on the aperture post and an .800" maximum elevation adjustment. Included is a .093" x 1/2" quick-sighting aperture and .040 x 5/8" target disk.
Price:. **$76.00**

MARBLE PEEP TANG SIGHT All-steel construction. Micrometer-like click adjustments for windage and elevation. For most popular old and new lever-action rifles.
Price:. **$125.00**

MILLETT PEEP RIFLE SIGHTS Fully adjustable, heat-treated nickel steel peep aperture receiver sight for the Mini-14. Has fine windage and elevation adjustments; replaces original.
Price: Rear sight, Mini-14. . . . . **$51.45**
Price: Front sight, Mini-14. . . . . **$19.69**
Price: Front and rear combo with hood. **$67.20**

NATIONAL MATCH REAR SIGHT KIT For AR-15 style rifles. From Armalite, Inc.
Price: 1/2 W, 1/2E. **$80.00**
Price: 1/4 W, 1/2 E **$80.00**

NECG PEEP SIGHT FOR WEAVER SCOPE MOUNT BASES Attaches to Weaver scope mount base. Windage adjusts with included Allen wrenches, elevation with a small screwdriver. Furnished with two apertures (.093" and .125" diameter hole) and two interchangeable elevation slides for high or low sight line. From New England Custom Gun Service.
Price:. **$85.00**

NECG RUGER PEEP SIGHT Made for Ruger M-77 and No. 1 rifles, it is furnished with .093" and .125" opening apertures. Can be installed on a standard Ruger rear mount base or quarter rib. Tightening the aperture disk will lock the elevation setting in place. From New England Custom Gun Service.
Price:. **$85.00**

T/C HUNTING STYLE TANG PEEP SIGHT Compact, all steel construction, with locking windage and elevation adjustments. For use with "bead style" and fiber optic front sights. Models available to fit all traditional T/C muzzleloading rifles. From Thompson/Center Arms.
Price:. **$58.00**

T/C CONTENDER CARBINE PEEP SIGHT All-steel, low profile, click-adjustable unit mounting on the pre-drilled tapped scope mount holes on the T/C Contender Carbine. From Thompson/Center Arms.
Price:. **$56.00**

WILLIAMS APERTURE SIGHT Made to fit SKS rifles.
Price:. **$23.49**

WILLIAMS FIRE SIGHT PEEP SETS Combines the Fire Sight front bead with Williams fully adjustable metallic peep rear.
Price: For SKS. **$39.95**
Price: For Ruger 10/22. . . . . **$39.95**
Price: For Marlin or Winchester lever actions. **$73.95**

WILLIAMS FP Internal click adjustments. Positive locks. For virtually all rifles, T/C Contender, Heckler & Koch HK-91, Ruger Mini-14, plus Win., Rem., and Ithaca shotguns.
Price: From. **$69.95**
Price: With Target Knobs. **$71.20**
Price: FP-GR (for dovetail-grooved receivers, .22s and air guns). **$59.95**
Price: FP-94BBSE (for Win. 94 Big Bore A.E.; uses top rear scope mount holes). **$59.95**

WILLIAMS TARGET FP Similar to the FP series but developed for most bolt-action rimfire rifles. Target FP High adjustable from 1.250" to 1.750" above centerline of bore; Target FP Low adjustable from .750" to 1.250". Attaching bases for Rem. 540X, 541-S, 580, 581, 582 (#540); Rem. 510, 511, 512, 513-T, 521-T (#510); Win. 75 (#75); Savage/ Anschutz 64 and Mark 12 (#64). Some rifles require drilling, tapping.
Price: High or Low. **$79.95**
Price: Base only. **$13.75**
mount holes). $59.**95**

WILLIAMS 5-D SIGHT Low cost sight for shotguns, 22s and the more popular big game rifles. Adjustment for windage and elevation. Fits most guns without drilling and tapping. Also for British SMLE, Winchester M94 Side Eject.
Price: From. **$36.95**
Price: With Shotgun Aperture **$36.95**

WILLIAMS 5D RECEIVER SIGHT Alloy construction and similar design to the FP model except designed to fit Win. 94, Marlin 336, Marlin 1895, Mauser 98.
Price: **$34.50**

WILLIAMS GUIDE (WGRS) Receiver sight for 30 M1 Carbine, M1903A3 Springfield, Savage 24s, Savage-Anschutz and Weatherby XXII. Utilizes military dovetail; no drilling. Double-dovetail windage adjustment, sliding dovetail adjustment for elevation.
Price:. . . . . **$34.95 to $47.95**

Vernier Tang Sights

BALLARD TANG SIGHTS Available in variety of models including short & long staff hunter, Pacific & Montana, custom units allowing windage & elevation adjustments. Uses 8x40 base screws with screw spacing of 1.120". From Axtell Rifle Co.
Price:. . . . . **$175.00 to $325.00**

LYMAN TANG SIGHT Made for Win. 94, 1886, Marlin 30, 336 and 1895.
Price:. . . . . **$59.99 to $64.99**

MARLIN TANG SIGHTS Available in short and long staff hunter models using 8x40 base screws and screw spacing of 1.120". From Axtell Rifle Co.
Price:. . . . . **$170.00 to $180.00**

PEDERSOLI CREEDMORE Adjustable for windage and elevation, fits Traditions by Pedersoli rifles and other brands. From Dixie Gun Works.
Price:. **$110.00**

REMINGTON TANG SIGHTS Available in short-range hunter and vernier, mid- and long-range vernier and custom models with windage and elevation adjustments. Uses 10x28 base screws, with screw spacing of 1.940". Eye disk has .052" hole with 10x40 thread. From Axtell Rifle Co.
Price:. . . . . **$175.00 to $325.00**

METALLIC SIGHTS

SHARPS TANG SIGHTS Reproduction tang sights as manufactured for various Sharps rifles through the years 1859 -1878. Wide variety of models available including Standard Issue Sporting Peep, Hartford Transition Mid and Long Range, and Custom Express Sights. From Axtell Rifle Co.
Price:. . . . . **$150.00 to $340.00**
STEVENS CUSTOM Available in thin base short and long staff hunter, mid and long range sporting vernier, custom mid and long range (custom models allow windage and elevation adjustments) models. Uses 5x40 base screws with screw spacing of 1.485". From Axtell Rifle Co.
Price:. . . . . **$170.00 to $325.00**
TAURUS TANG SIGHT Made of blue steel, available for Taurus Models 62, 72, 172, 63, 73 and 173. Folds down, aperture disk sight, height index marks on aperture post.
Price:. **$77.00**
WINCHESTER & BROWNING TANG SIGHTS Available in variety of models, including thin & thick base short & long staff hunter, mid & long range sporting vernier and custom units. Screw spacing of 2.180" on all models. From Axtell Rifle Co.
Price:. . . . . **$170.00 to $325.00**

Globe Target Front Sights

AXTELL CUSTOM GLOBE Designed similar to the original Winchester #35 sight, it contains five inserts. Also available with spirit level. From Axtell Rifle Co.
Price: . . . . **$125.00 to $175.00**
BALLARD FRONT SIGHTS Available in windgauge with spirit level, globe with clip, and globe with spirit level (all with five inserts) and beach combination with gold plated rocker models. Dovetail of .375" for all. From Axtell Rifle Co.
Price:. . . . . **$125.00 to $240.00**
LYMAN 20 MJT TARGET FRONT Has 7/8" diameter, one-piece steel globe with 3/8" dovetail base. Height is .700" from bottom of dovetail to center of aperture; height on 20 LJT is .750". Comes with seven Anschutz-size steel inserts-two posts and five apertures .126" through .177".
Price: 20 MJT or 20 LJT. **$33.75**

Lyman No. 17A Target

LYMAN No. 17A TARGET Includes seven interchangeable inserts: four apertures, one transparent amber and two posts .50" and .100" in width.
Price: **$28.25**
Price: Insert set. **$13.25**
LYMAN 17AEU Similar to the Lyman 17A except has a special dovetail design to mount easily onto European muzzleloaders such as CVA, Traditions and Investarm. All steel, comes with eight inserts.
Price: **$26.00**
LYMAN No. 93 MATCH Has 7/8" diameter, fits any rifle with a standard dovetail mounting block. Comes with seven target inserts and accepts most Anschutz accessories. Hooked locking bolt and nut allows quick removal, installation. Base available in .860" (European) and .562" (American) hole spacing.
Price: **$45.00**
MAYNARD FRONT SIGHTS Custom globe with five inserts and clip. Also available with spirit level bracket and windgauge styles. From Axtell Rifle Co.
Price: **$125.00 to $240.00**
PEDERSOLI GLOBE A tunnel front sight with 12 interchangeable inserts for high precision target shooting. Fits Traditions by Pedersoli and other rifles.
Price: **$69.95**
REMINGTON FRONT SIGHTS Available in windgauge with spirit level, custom globe with clip and custom globe with spirit level (all with five inserts) and beach combination with gold plated rocker models. Dovetail .460". From Axtell Rifle Co.
Price: **$125.00 to $250.00**
SHARPS FRONT SIGHTS Original-style globe with non-moveable post and pinhead. Also available with windgauge and spirit level. From Axtell Rifle Co.
Price:. . . . . **$100.00 to $265.00**
WILLIAMS TARGET GLOBE FRONT Adapts to many rifles. Mounts to the base with a knurled locking screw. Height is .545" from center, not including base. Comes with inserts.
Price:. **$47.95**
Price: Dovetail base (low) .220". **$18.95**
Price: Dovetail base (high) .465". **$18.95**
Price: Screw-on base, .300" height, .300" radius. **$16.95**
Price: Screw-on base, .450" height, .350" radius. **$16.95**
Price: Screw-on base, .215" height, .400" radius. **$16.95**
WINCHESTER & BROWNING FRONT SIGHTS Available in windgauge with spirit level, globe with clip, globe with spirit level (all with five inserts) and beach combination with gold plated rocker models. From Axtell Rifle Co.
Price:. . . . . **$125.00 to $240.00**

Front Sights

AO TACTICAL SIGHTS Three types of drop-in replacement front posts - round top or square top night sight posts in standard and Big Dot sizes, or white stripe posts in .080 and .100 widths. For AR15 and M16 rifles. From AO Sight Systems, Inc.
Price: . . . . **$30.00 to $90.00**
AO RIFLE TEST POSTS Allows easy establishment of correct front post height. Provides dovetail post with .050" segments to allow shooter to "shoot-n-snip", watching point- of-impact walk into point of aim. Available for 3/8" standard dovetail, Ruger-style or Mauser. From AO Sight Systems, Inc.
Price:. **$5.00**
AR-10 DETACHABLE FRONT SIGHT Allows use of the iron rear sight, but are removable for use of telescopic sights with no obstruction to the sight line, For AR-style rifles. From ArmaLite, Inc.
Price: . . . . **$50.00 to $70.00**
ASHLEY AR-15/M-16 FRONT SIGHTS Drop-in replacement sight post. Double faced so it can be rotated 180 degrees for 2.5 MOA elevation adjustment. Available in .080" width with .030" white stripe, or .100" with .040" stripe. From Ashley Outdoors, Inc.
Price:. **$30.00**
Price: Tritium Dot Express. **$60.00**
LYMAN AR-15 FIRE SIGHTS Front metallic sight, fully adjustable for elevation, no gunsmithing required.
Price: **$41.95**
BUSHMASTER FLIP-UP FRONT SIGHT Made for V Match AR-style rifles, this sight unit slips over milled front sight bases and clamps around barrel. Locks with the push of a button. For use with flip-up style rear sights or the A3 removable carry handle. From Bushmaster Firearms.
Price: **$99.95**
BUSHMASTER A2 COMPETITION FRONT SIGHT POST Surface ground on three sides for optimum visual clarity. Available in two widths: .052"; and .062". From Bushmaster Firearms.
Price: **$12.95**
CLASSIC STREAMLINED FRONT SPORTER RAMP SIGHT Comes with blade and sight cover. Serrated and contoured ramp. Screw-on attachment. Slide-on sight cover is easily detachable. Gold bead. From Sarco, inc.
Price:. **$13.50**
ERA BEADS FOR RUGER RIFLES White bead and fiber optic front sights that replace the standard sights on M-77 and No. 1 Ruger rifles. Using 3/32" beads, they are available in heights of .330", .350", .375", .415" and .435". From New England Custom Gun Service.
Price:. . . . . **$16.00 to $24.00**
ERA FRONT SIGHTS European-type front sights inserted from the front. Various heights available. From New England Custom Gun Service.
Price: 1/16" silver bead. **$11.50**
Price: 3/32" silver bead. **$16.00**
Price: Sourdough bead. **$14.50**
Price: Fiber optic. **$24.00**
Price: Folding night sight with ivory bead. **$39.50**

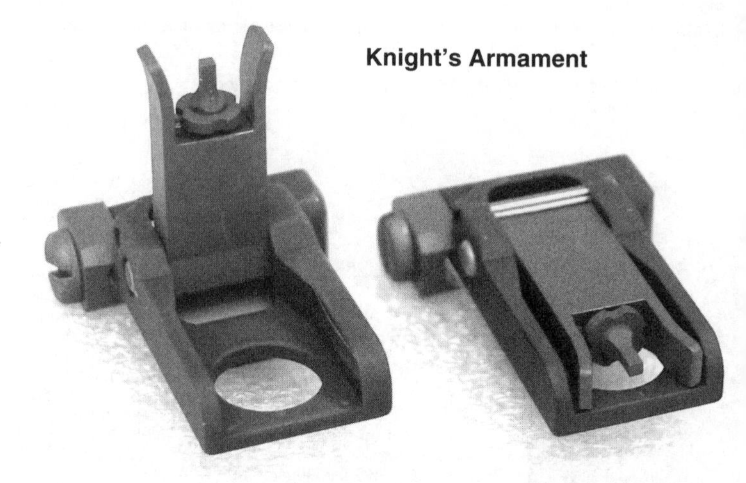
Knight's Armament

KNIGHT'S ARMAMENT FRONT STANDING/FOLDING SIGHT Mounts to the SR-25 rifle barrel gas block's MilStd top rail. Available in folding sight model. From Knight's Armament Co.
Price:. . . . . **$145.00 to $175.00**
KNIGHT'S ARMAMENT CARRYING HANDLE SIGHT Rear sight and carry handle for the SR-25 rifle. Has fixed range and adjustable windage. From Knight's Armament Co.
Price: **$181.15**
KNIGHT'S ARMAMENT MK II FOLDING FRONT SIGHT For the SR-25 rifle. Requires modified handguard. From Knight's Armament Co.
Price: **$175.00**
KNIGHT'S ARMAMENT FOR FREE-FLOATING RAS Mounts to free-floating SR-25 and SR-15 RAS (rail adapter system) rifle forends. Adjustable for elevation. Made of aluminum. From Knight's Armament Co.
Price:. **$155.25**
KNS PRECISION SYSTEMS SIGHT Screws into front base. Hooded for light consistency; precision machined with fine wire crosshairs measuring .010-inches thick. Aperture measures .240-inches diameter. Standard and duplex reticles. Available for AK-47, MAK-90, AR-15, M16, FN-FAL, H&K 91, 93, 94, MP5, SP89, L1A1, M1 Garand.
Price:. **$25.99**

METALLIC SIGHTS

LYMAN HUNTING SIGHTS Made with gold or white beads 1/16" to 3/32" wide and in varying heights for most military and commercial rifles. Dovetail bases.
Price: **$8.95**

MARBLE STANDARD Ivory, red, or gold bead. For all American-made rifles, 1/16" wide bead with semi-flat face that does not reflect light. Specify type of rifle when ordering.
Price: **$10.00**

MARBLE CONTOURED Has 3/8" dovetail base, .090" deep, is 5/8" long. Uses standard 1/16" or 3/32" bead, ivory, red, or gold. Specify rifle type.
Price: **$11.50**

NATIONAL MATCH FRONT SIGHT POST Has .050" blade. For AR-style rifle. From ArmaLite, Inc.
Price: **$12.00**

T/C FIBER OPTIC FRONT MUZZLELOADER SIGHT Ramp-style steel with fiber optic bead for all tradition cap locks, both octagonal and round barrels with dovetail, and most T/C rifles. From Thompson/Center Arms.
Price: . . . . **$16.95 to $36.00**

TRIJICON NIGHT SIGHT Self-luminous tritium gas-filled front sight for the M16/AR-15 series.
Price: **$60.00**

WILLIAMS STREAMLINED HOODLESS RAMP Available in 3/16", 5/16", 3/8", and 7/16" models.
Price: Less blade. **$15.49**

WILLAMS SHORTY RAMPS Available in 1/8", 3/16", 9/32" and 3/8" models.
Price: Less blade. **$15.49**

WILLIAMS GOLD BEAD Available in .312", .343", and .406" high models all with 3/32" bead.
Price: **$8.49**

WILLIAMS RISER BLOCKS For adding .250" height to front sights when using a receiver sight. Two widths available: .250" for Williams Streamlined Ramp or .340" on all standard ramps having this base width. Uses standard 3/8" dovetail.
Price: **$5.46**

WILLIAMS AR-15 FIRESIGHT Fiber optic unit attaches to any standard AR-15-style front sight assembly. Machined from aircraft-strength aluminum. Adjustable for elevation. Green-colored light-gathering fiber optics. From Williams Gun Sight Co.
Price: . . . . **NA**

Ramp Sights

ERA MASTERPIECE Banded ramps; 21 sizes; hand-detachable beads and hood; beads inserted from the front. Various heights available. From New England Custom Gun Service.
Price: Banded ramp. **$54.00**
Price: Hood. **$10.50**
Price: 1/16" silver bead. **$11.50**
Price: 3/32" silver bead. **$16.00**
Price: Sourdough bead. **$14.50**
Price: Fiber optic. **$22.00**
Price: Folding night sight with ivory bead. **$39.50**

HOLLAND & HOLLAND STYLE FRONT SIGHT RAMPS Banded and screw-on models in the Holland & Holland-style night sight. Flips forward to expose a .0781" silver bead. Flip back for use of the .150" diameter ivory bead for poor light or close-up hunting. Band thickness .040", overall length 3.350", band length 1.180". From New England Custom Gun Service.
Price: . . . . **$90.00 to $115.00**

LYMAN NO. 18 SCREW-ON RAMP Used with 8-40 screws but may also be brazed on. Heights from .10" to .350". Ramp without sight.
Price: **$13.75**

MARBLE FRONT RAMPS Available in polished or dull matte finish or serrated style. Standard 3/8x.090" dovetail slot. Made for MR-width (.340") front sights. Can be used as screw-on or sweat-on. Heights: .100", .150", .300".
Price: Polished or matte. **$14.00**
Price: Serrated **$10.00**

NECG UNIVERSAL FRONT SIGHTS Available in five ramp heights and three front sight heights. Sights can be adjusted up or down .030" with an Allen wrench. Slips into place and then locks into position with a set screw. Six different front sight shapes are offered, including extra large and fiber optic. All hoods except the extra low ramp slide on from the rear and click in place. Extra low ramp has spring-loaded balls to lock hood. Choose from three hood sizes. From New England Custom Gun Service.
Price: **$25.50**

T/C TARGET SIGHT FOR OCTAGON BARREL MUZZLELOADERS A precision rear sight with click adjustments (via knurled knobs) for windage and elevation. Available for 15/16-inch and 1-inch octagon barrels with a screw hole spacing of .836-inch between centers. From Thompson/Center Arms.
Price: **$56.00**

T/C FIBER OPTIC MUZZLELOADER SIGHT Click adjustable for windage and elevation. Steel construction fitted with Tru-Glo™ fiber optics. Models available for most T/C muzzleloading rifles. Fits others with 1-inch and 15/16-inch octagon barrels with a hole spacing of .836-inch between screws. From Thompson/Center Arms.
Price: **$36.00**

WILLIAMS SHORTY RAMP Companion to "Streamlined" ramp, about 1/2" shorter. Screw-on or sweat-on. It is furnished in 1/8", 3/16", 9/32", and 3/8" heights without hood only. Also for shotguns.
Price: **$18.25**
Price: With dovetail lock. **$20.35**

WILLIAMS STREAMLINED RAMP Available in screw-on or sweat-on models. Furnished in 9/16", 7/16", 3/8", 5/16", 3/16" heights.
Price: **$21.95**
Price: Sight hood. **$4.95**

WILLIAMS STREAMLINED FRONT SIGHTS Narrow (.250" width) for Williams Streamlined ramps and others with 1/4" top width; medium (.340" width) for all standard factory ramps. Available with white, gold or fluorescent beads, 1/16" or 3/32".
Price: . . . . **$10.50 to $10.95**

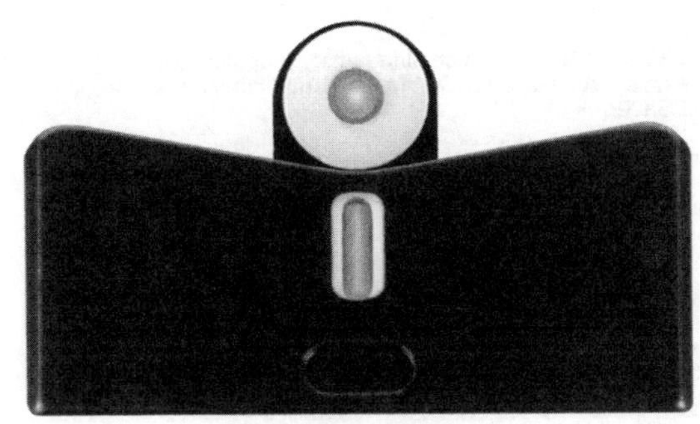

AO Express

Handgun Sights

AO EXPRESS SIGHTS Low-profile, snag-free express-type sights. Shallow V rear with white vertical line, white dot front. All-steel, matte black finish. Rear is available in different heights. Made for most pistols, many with double set-screws. From AO Sight Systems, Inc.
Price: Standard Set, front and rear. **$60.00**
Price: Big Dot Set, front and rear. **$60.00**
Price: Tritium Set, Standard or Big Dot. **$90.00**
Price: 24/7 Pro Express, Std. or Big Dot Tritium **$120.00**

BO-MAR DELUXE BMCS Gives 3/8" windage and elevation adjustment at 50 yards on Colt Gov't 45; sight radius under 7". For GM and Commander models only. Uses existing dovetail slot. Has shield-type rear blade.
Price: **$65.95**
Price: BMCS-2 (for GM and 9mm). **$68.95**
Price: Flat bottom. **$65.95**
Price: BMGC (for Colt Gold Cup), angled serrated blade, rear. **$68.95**
Price: BMGC front sight. **$12.95**
Price: BMCZ-75 (for CZ-75,TZ-75, P-9 and most clones). Works with factory front. **$68.95**

BO-MAR FRONT SIGHTS Dovetail style for S&W 4506, 4516, 1076; undercut style (.250", .280", 5/16" high); Fast Draw style (.210", .250", .230" high).
Price: **$12.95**

BO-MAR BMU XP-100/T/C CONTENDER No gunsmithing required; has .080" notch.
Price: **$77.00**

BO-MAR BMML For muzzleloaders; has .062" notch, flat bottom.
Price: **$65.95**
Price: With 3/8" dovetail. **$65.95**

BO-MAR RUGER "P" ADJUSTABLE SIGHT Replaces factory front and rear sights.
Price: Rear sight. **$65.95**
Price: Front sight. **$12.00**

BO-MAR BMR Fully adjustable rear sight for Ruger MKI, MKII Bull barrel autos.
Price: Rear. **$65.95**
Price: Undercut front sight. **$12.00**

BO-MAR GLOCK Fully adjustable, all-steel replacement sights. Sight fits factory dovetail. Longer sight radius. Uses Novak Glock .275" high, .135" wide front, or similar.
Price: Rear sight. **$68.95**
Price: Front sight. **$20.95**

BO-MAR LOW PROFILE RIB & ACCURACY TUNER Streamlined rib with front and rear sights; 7 1/8" sight radius. Brings sight line closer to the bore than standard or extended sight and ramp. Weight 5 oz. Made for Colt Gov't 45, Super 38, and Gold Cup 45 and 38.
Price: **$140.00**

BO-MAR COMBAT RIB For S&W Model 19 revolver with 4" barrel. Sight radius 5 3/4", weight 5 1/2 oz.
Price: **$127.00**

BO-MAR WINGED RIB For S&W 4" and 6" length barrels-K-38, M10, HB 14 and 19. Weight for the 6" model is about 7 1/4 oz.
Price: **$140.00**

BO-MAR COVER-UP RIB Adjustable rear sight, winged front guards. Fits right over revolver's original front sight. For S&W 4" M-10HB, M-13, M-58, M-64 & 65, Ruger 4" models SDA-34, SDA-84, SS-34, SS-84, GF-34, GF-84.
Price: **$130.00**

CHIP MCCORMICK "DROP-IN" A low mount sight that fits any 1911-style slide with a standard military-type dovetail sight cut (60x.290"). Dovetail front sights also available. From Chip McCormick Corp.
Price: **$47.95**

CHIP MCCORMICK FIXED SIGHTS Same sight picture (.110" rear - .110" front) that's become the standard for pro combat shooters. Low mount design with rounded edges. For 1911-style pistols. May require slide machining for installation. From Chip McCormick Corp.
Price: **$24.95**

METALLIC SIGHTS

C-MORE SIGHTS Replacement front sight blades offered in two types and five styles. Made of Du Pont Acetal, they come in a set of five high-contrast colors: blue, green, pink, red and yellow. Easy to install. Patridge style for Colt Python (all barrels), Ruger Super Blackhawk (7 1/2"), Ruger Blackhawk (4 5/8"); ramp style for Python (all barrels), Blackhawk (4 5/8"), Super Blackhawk (7 1/2" and 10 1/2"). From C-More Systems.
Price: Per set. **$19.95**
G.G. & G. GHOST RINGS Replaces the factory rear sight without gunsmithing. Black phosphate finish. Available for Colt M1911 and Commander, Beretta M92F, Glock, S&W, SIG Sauer.
Price:. **$65.00**

Heinie Slant Pro

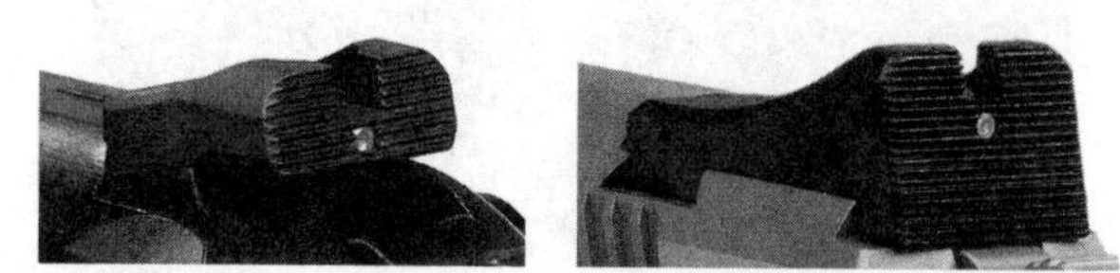

HEINIE SLANT PRO Made with a slight forward slant, the unique design of these rear sights is snag free for unimpeded draw from concealment. The combination of the slant and the rear serrations virtually eliminates glare. Made for most popular handguns. From Heinie Specialty Products.
Price: . . . . **$50.35 to $122.80**
HEINIE STRAIGHT EIGHT SIGHTS Consists of one tritium dot in the front sight and a slightly smaller Tritium dot in the rear sight. When aligned correctly, an elongated 'eight' is created. The Tritium dots are green in color. Designed with the belief that the human eye can correct vertical alignment faster than horizontal. Available for most popular handguns. From Heinie Specialty Products.
Price: . . . . **$104.95 to $122.80**
HEINIE CROSS DOVETAIL FRONT SIGHTS Made in a variety of heights, the standard dovetail is 60 degrees x .305" x .062" with a .002 taper. From Heinie Specialty Products.
Price:. . . . . **$20.95 to $47.20**
JP GHOST RING Replacement bead front, ghost ring rear for Glock and M1911 pistols. From JP Enterprises.
Price:. **$79.95**
Price: Bo-Mar replacement leaf with JP dovetail front bead. **$99.95**
LES BAER CUSTOM ADJUSTABLE LOW MOUNT REAR SIGHT Considered one of the top adjustable sights in the world for target shooting with 1911-style pistols. Available with Tritium inserts. From Les Baer Custom.
Price:. . . . . **$49.00** (standard); **$99.00** (tritium)
LES BAER DELUXE FIXED COMBAT SIGHT A tactical-style sight with a very low profile. Incorporates a no-snag design and has serrations on sides. For 1911-style pistols. Available with Tritium inserts for night shooting. From Les Baer Custom.
Price:. . . . . **$26.00** (standard); **$67.00** (with Tritium)
LES BAER DOVETAIL FRONT SIGHT Blank dovetail sight machined from bar stock. Can be contoured to many different configurations to meet user's needs. Available with Tritium insert. From Les Baer Custom.
Price:. . . . . **$17.00** (standard); **$47.00** (with Tritium insert)
LES BAER FIBER OPTIC FRONT SIGHT Dovetail .330x65 degrees, .125" wide post, .185" high, .060" diameter. Red and green fiber optic. From Les Baer Custom.
Price: **$24.00**
LES BAER PPC-STYLE ADJUSTABLE REAR SIGHT Made for use with custom built 1911-style pistols, allows the user to preset three elevation adjustments for PPC-style shooting. Milling required for installation. Made from 4140 steel. From Les Baer Custom.
Price:. **$120.00**
LES BAER DOVETAIL FRONT SIGHT WITH TRITIUM INSERT This fully contoured and finished front sight comes ready for gunsmith installation. From Les Baer Custom.
Price: **$47.00**
MMC TACTICAL ADJUSTABLE SIGHTS Low-profile, snag free design. Twenty-two click positions for elevation, drift adjustable for windage. Machined from 4140 steel and heat treated to 40 RC. Tritium and non-tritium. Ten different configurations and colors. Three different finishes. For 1911s, all Glock, HK USP, S&W, Browning Hi-Power.
Price: Sight set, tritium. **$144.92**
Price: Sight set, white outline or white dot. **$99.90**
Price: Sight set, black. **$93.90**
MEPROLIGHT TRITIUM NIGHT SIGHTS Replacement sight assemblies for low-light conditions. Available for pistols (fixed and adj.),rifles, shotguns. 12-year warranty for useable illumination, while non-TRU-DOT have a 5-year warranty. Distributed in American by Kimber.
Price: Kahr K9, K40, fixed, TRU-DOT. **$100.00**
Price: Ruger P85, P89, P94, adjustable, TRU-DOT. **$156.00**
Price: Ruger Mini-14R sights. **$140.00**
Price: SIG Sauer P220, P225, P226, P228, adjustable, TRU-DOT. **$156.00**
Price: Smith&Wesson autos, fixed or adjustable, TRU-DOT. **$100.00**
Price: Taurus PT92, PT100, adjustable, TRU-DOT. **$156.00**
Price: Walther P-99, fixed, TRU-DOT. **$100.00**
Price: Shotgun bead. **$32.00**
Price: Beretta M92, Cougar, Brigadier, fixed, TRU-DOT. **$100.00**
Price: Browning Hi-Power, adjustable, TRU-DOT. **$156.00**
Price: Colt M1911 Govt., adjustable, TRU-DOT. **$156.00**

MILLETT SERIES 100 REAR SIGHTS All-steel highly visible, click adjustable. Blades in white outline, target black, silhouette, 3-dot. Fit most popular revolvers and autos.
Price:. . . . . **$51.77 to $84.00**
MILLETT BAR-DOT-BAR TRITIUM NIGHT SIGHTS Replacement front and rear combos fit most automatics. Horizontal tritium bars on rear, dot front sight.
Price:. **$152.25**
MILLETT BAR/DOT Made with orange or white bar or dot for increased visibility. Available for Beretta 84, 85, 92S, 92SB, Browning, Colt Python & Trooper, Ruger GP 100, P85, Redhawk, Security Six.
Price:. . . . . **$14.99 to $24.99**
MILLETT 3-DOT SYSTEM SIGHTS The 3-Dot System sights use a single white dot on the front blade and two dots flanking the rear notch. Fronts available in Dual-Crimp and Wide Stake-On styles, as well as special applications. Adjustable rear sight available for most popular auto pistols and revolvers including Browning Hi-Power, Colt 1911 Government and Ruger P85.
Price: Front, from. **$16.80**
Price: Adjustable rear. **$55.60**
MILLETT REVOLVER FRONT SIGHTS All-steel replacement front sights with either white or orange bar. Easy to install. For Ruger GP-100, Redhawk, Security-Six, Police- Six, Speed-Six, Colt Trooper, Diamondback, King Cobra, Peacemaker, Python, Dan Wesson 22 and 15-2.
Price:. . . . . **$13.60 to $16.00**
MILLETT DUAL-CRIMP FRONT SIGHT Replacement front sight for automatic pistols. Dual-Crimp uses an all-steel two-point hollow rivet system. Available in eight heights and four styles. Has a skirted base that covers the front sight pad. Easily installed with the Millett Installation Tool Set. Available in Blaze Orange Bar, White Bar, Serrated Ramp, Plain Post. Available in heights of .185", .200", .225", .275", .312", .340" and .410".
Price:. **$16.80**
MILLETT STAKE-ON FRONT SIGHT Replacement front sight for automatic pistols. Stake-On sights have skirted base that covers the front sight pad. Easily installed with the Millet Installation Tool Set. Available in seven heights and four styles-Blaze Orange Bar, White Bar, Serrated Ramp, Plain Post. Available for Glock 17L and 24, others.
Price:. **$16.80**
MILLETT ADJUSTABLE TARGET Positive light-deflection serration and slant to eliminate glare and sharp edge sight notch. Audible "click" adjustments. For AMT Hardballer, Beretta 84, 85, 92S, 92SB, Browning Hi-Power, Colt 1911 Government and Gold Cup, Colt revolvers, Dan Wesson 15, 41, 44, Ruger revolvers, Glock 17, 17L, 19, 20, 21, 22, 23.
Price:. **$44.99**
MILLETT ADJUSTABLE WHITE OUTLINE Similar to the Target sight, except has a white outline on the blade to increase visibility. Available for the same handguns as the Target model, plus BRNO CZ-75/TZ-75/TA-90 without pin on front sight, and Ruger P85.
Price:. . . . . **$44.99 to $49.99**
OMEGA OUTLINE SIGHT BLADES Replacement rear sight blades for Colt and Ruger single action guns and the Interarms Virginian Dragoon. Standard Outline available in gold or white notch outline on blue metal. From Omega Sales, Inc.
Price:. **$10.00**
OMEGA MAVERICK SIGHT BLADES Replacement "peep-sight" blades for Colt, Ruger SAs, Virginian Dragoon. Three models available-No. 1, Plain; No. 2, Single Bar; No. 3, Double Bar Rangefinder. From Omega Sales, Inc.
Price: Each. **$10.00**
ONE RAGGED HOLE Replacement rear sight ghost ring sight for Ruger handguns. Fits Blackhawks, Redhawks, Super Blackhawks, GP series and Mk. II target pistols with adjustable sights. From One Ragged Hole, Tallahassee, Florida.
Price:. . . . . **NA**
PACHMAYR ACCU-SET Low-profile, fully adjustable rear sight to be used with existing front sight. Available with target, white outline or 3-dot blade. Blue finish. Uses factory dovetail and locking screw. For Browning, Colt, Glock, SIG Sauer, S&W and Ruger autos. From Pachmayr.
Price:. **$59.98**
P-T TRITIUM NIGHT SIGHTS Self-luminous tritium sights for most popular handguns, Colt AR-15, H&K rifles and shotguns. Replacement handgun sight sets available in 3- Dot style (green/green, green/yellow, green/orange) with bold outlines around inserts; Bar-Dot available in green/green with or without white outline rear sight. Functional life exceeds 15 years. From Innovative Weaponry, Inc.
Price: Handgun sight sets. **$99.95**
Price: Rifle sight sets. **$99.95**
Price: Rifle, front only. **$49.95**
Price: Shotgun, front only. **$49.95**
T/C ENCORE FIBER OPTIC SIGHT SETS Click adjustable, steel rear sight and ramp-style front sight, both fitted with Tru-GloTM fiber optics. Specifically-designed for the T/C Encore pistol series. From Thompson/Center Arms.
Price:. **$49.35**
T/C ENCORE TARGET REAR SIGHT Precision, steel construction with click adjustments (via knurled knobs) for windage and elevation. Models available with low, medium and high blades. From Thompson/Center Arms.
Price:' **$54.00**
TRIJICON NIGHT SIGHTS Three-dot night sight system uses tritium lamps in the front and rear sights. Tritium "lamps" are mounted in silicone rubber inside a metal cylinder. A polished crystal

Trijicon BE-03

sapphire provides protection and clarity. Inlaid white outlines provide 3-dot aiming in daylight also. Available for most popular handguns including Glock 17, 19, 20, 21, 23, 24, 25, 26, 29, 30, H&K USP, Ruger P94, SIG P220, P225, 226, Colt 1911. Front and rear sets available. From Trijicon, Inc.
Price: . . . . **$80.00 to $299.00**

TRIJICON 3-DOT Self-luminous front iron night sight for the Ruger SP101.
Price: **$50.00**

WICHITA SERIES 70/80 SIGHT Provides click windage and elevation adjustments with precise repeatability of settings. Sight blade is grooved and angled back at the top to reduce glare. Available in Low Mount Combat or Low Mount Target styles for Colt 45s and their copies, S&W 645, Hi-Power, CZ 75 and others.
Price: Rear sight, target or combat. **$75.00**
Price: Front sight, Patridge or ramp. **$18.00**

WICHITA GRAND MASTER DELUXE RIBS Ventilated rib has wings machined into it for better sight acquisition and is relieved for Mag-Na-Porting. Milled to accept Weaver see-thru-style rings. Made of stainless; front and rear sights blued. Has Wichita Multi-Range rear sight system, adjustable front sight. Made for revolvers with 6" barrel.
Price: Model 301S, 301B (adj. sight K frames with custom bbl. of 1" to 1.032" dia. L and N frame with 1.062" to 1.100" dia. bbl.). **$225.00**
Price: Model 303S, 303B (adj. sight K, L, N frames with factory barrel) **$225.00**

WICHITA MULTI-RANGE QUICK CHANGE SIGHTING SYSTEM Multi-range rear sight can be pre-set to four positive repeatable range settings. Adjustable front sight allows compensation for changing lighting and weather conditions with just one front sight adjustment. Front sight comes with Lyman 17A Globe and set of apertures.
Price: Rear sight **$125.00**
Price: Front, sight **$95.00**

WILLIAMS FIRE SIGHT SETS Red fiber optic metallic sight replaces the original. Rear sight has two green fiber optic elements. Made of CNC-machined aluminum. Fits all Glocks, Ruger P-Series (except P-85), S&W 910, Colt Gov't. Model Series 80, Ruger GP 100 and Redhawk, and SIG Sauer (front only).
Price: Front and rear set **$39.95**
Price: SIG Sauer front. **$22.95**
Price: Browning BuckMark sight set **$44.95**
Price: Taurus PT111,PT140, PT145, PT1232, PT138 . . . . **$44.95**
Price: Ruger P Series, Glock, S&W 910, Colt Gov't. Series 80, Springfield XD . **$44.95**

WILSON ADJUSTABLE REAR SIGHTS Machined from steel, the click adjustment design requires simple cuts and no dovetails for installation. Available in several configurations: matte black standard blade with .128" notch; with .110" notch; with Tritium dots and .128" square or "U" shaped notch; and Combat Pyramid. From Wilson Combat.
Price: . . . . **$24.95 to $69.95**

WILSON NITE-EYES SIGHTS Low-profile, snag free design with green and yellow Tritium inserts. For 1911-style pistols. From Wilson Combat.
Price: **$119.95**

WILSON TACTICAL COMBAT SIGHTS Low-profile and snag-free in design, the sight employs the Combat Pyramid shape. For many 1911-style pistols and some Glock models. From Wilson Combat.
Price: **$139.95**

Shotgun Sights

AO SHOTGUN SIGHTS 24/7 Pro Express sights fit Remington rifle sighted barrels. Front sight divetails into existing ramp, rear installs on Remington rear ramp. Available in Big Dot Tritium or Standard Dot Tritium. Three other styles (for pedestal base, beaded, and ribbed barrels) provide a Big Dot Tritium front that epoxies over the existing bead front sight. From AO Sight Systems, Inc.
Price: 24/7 Tritium Sets. . . . . **$90.00 to $120.00**
Price: Big Dot Tritium (front only). **$60.00**

ACCURA-SITE For shooting shotgun slugs. Three models to fit most shotguns-"A" for vent. rib barrels, "B" for solid ribs, "C" for plain barrels. Rear sight has windage and elevation provisions. Easily removed and replaced. Includes front and rear sights. From All's, The Jim Tembeils Co.
Price: . . . . **$27.95 to $34.95**

BRADLEY SHOTGUN SIGHTS Front beads available in sizes of 1/8" and 5/32" in thread sizes of #3-56, #6-48, and #8-40. From 100 Straight Products.
Price: **$5.00**

BRADLEY CENTER SIGHTS Available in 1/16" bead size and #3-56 thread or taper. Plain brass, bright silver and white finishes. From 100 Straight Products.
Price: . . . . **$2.50 to $6.00 each**

BRADLEY SHOTGUN SIGHT ASSORTMENT An assortment of the most frequently used sights including six each of 18-3, 18-6,532-3, 532-7, 532-9, MB-01 and MB-11. From 100 Straight Products.
Price: **$119.95**

CARLSON SHOTGUN SIGHT A brilliant orange bead securely held by two bands. Used for low light conditions. Bead size .150", thread size 6-48. From Carlson's and 100 Straight Products.
Price: **$7.50**

FIRE FLY EM-109 SL SHOTGUN SIGHT Made of aircraft-grade aluminum, this 1/4-oz. "channel" sight has a thick, sturdy hollowed post between the side rails to give a Patridge sight picture. All shooting is done with both eyes open, allowing the shooter to concentrate on the target, not the sights. The hole in the sight post gives reduced-light shooting capability and allows for fast, precise aiming. For sport or combat shooting. Model EM-109 fits all vent. rib and double barrel shotguns and muzzleloaders with octagon barrel. Model MOC-110 fits all plain barrel shotguns without screw-in chokes. From JAS, Inc.
Price: **$35.00**

LYMAN Three sights of over-sized ivory beads. No. 10 Front (press fit) for double barrel or ribbed single barrel guns **$4.50**; No. 10D Front (screw fit) for non-ribbed single barrel guns (comes with wrench) **$5.50**; No. 11 Middle (press fit) for double and ribbed single barrel guns
Price: **$4.75**

MMC M&P COMBAT SHOTGUN SIGHT SET A durable, protected ghost ring aperture, combat sight made of steel. Fully adjustable for windage and elevation.
Price: M&P Sight Set (front and rear). **$73.45**
Price: As above, installed. **$83.95**

MMC TACTICAL GHOST RING SIGHT Click adjustable for elevation with 30 MOA total adjustment in 3 MOA increments. Click windage adjustment. Machined from 4140 steel, heat-treated to 40 RC. Front sight available in banded tactical or serrated ramp. Front and rear sights available with or without tritium. Available in three different finishes.
Price: Rear Ghost Ring with tritium. **$119.95**
Price: Rear Ghost Ring without tritium. **$99.95**
Price: Front Banded Tactical with tritium. **$59.95**
Price: Front Banded Tactical without tritium. **$39.95**
Price: Front serrated ramp. **$24.95**

MARBLE SHOTGUN BEAD SIGHTS No. 214-Ivory front bead, 11/64", tapered shank **$4.40**; No. 223-Ivory rear bead, .080", tapered shank **$4.40**; No. 217- Ivory front bead, 11/64", threaded shank **$4.75**; No. 223-T-Ivory rear bead, .080, threaded shank **$5.95.** Reamers, taps and wrenches available from Marble Arms.

MEPROLIGHT Ghost ring sight set for Benelli tactical shotguns. From Meprolight, Inc.
Price: **$100.00**

MILLETT SHURSHOT SHOTGUN SIGHT A sight system for shotguns with ventilated rib. Rear sight attaches to the rib, front sight replaces the front bead. Front has an orange face, rear has two orange bars. For 870, 1100 or other models.
Price: Rear, fixed. **$13.81**
Price: Adjustable front and rear set. **$32.55**
Price: Front. **$13.60**

NECG IVORY SHOTGUN BEAD Genuine ivory shotgun beads with 6-48 thread. Available in heights of .157" and .197". From New England Custom Gun Service.
Price: **$9.00**

POLY-CHOKE Replacement front shotgun sights in four styles-Xpert, Poly Bead, Xpert Mid Rib sights, and Bev-L-Block. Xpert Front available in 3x56, 6x48 thread, 3/32" or 5/32" shank length, gold, ivory **$4.70**; or Sun Spot orange bead **$5.95**; Poly Bead is standard replacement 1/8" bead, 6x48 **$2.95**; Xpert Mid Rib in tapered carrier (ivory only) **$5.95**, or 3x56 threaded shank (gold only) **$2.95**; Hi and Lo Blok sights with 6x48 thread, gold or ivory **$5.25**. From Marble Arms.

SLUG SIGHTS Made of non-marring black nylon, front and rear sights stretch over and lock onto barrel. Sights are low profile with blaze orange front blade. Adjustable for windage and elevation. For plain-barrel (non-ribbed) guns in 12-, 16- and 20-gauge, and for shotguns with 5/16" and 3/8" ventilated ribs. From Innovision Ent.
Price: **$11.95**

TRIJICON 3-DOT NIGHT SIGHTS Self-luminous and machined from steel. Available for Remington 870, 1100, 1187.
Price: . . . . **$75.00 to $175.00**

WILLIAMS GUIDE BEAD SIGHT Fits all shotguns, 1/8" ivory, red or gold bead. Screws into existing sight hole. Various thread sizes and shank lengths.
Price: **$4.77**

WILLIAMS SLUGGER SIGHTS Removable aluminum sights attach to the shotgun rib. High profile front, fully adjustable rear. Fits 1/4", 5/16" or 3/8" (special) ribs.
Price: **$34.95**

WILLIAMS UNIVERSAL SLUGGER shotgun fire sight set. Fiber optic, front and rear metallic sights attach to most vent ribs. Adjustable for windage and elevation. No gunsmithing required.
Price: **$39.95**

WILLIAMS FIRE SIGHTS Fiber optic light gathering front sights in red or yellow, glow with natural light. Fit 1/4", 5/16" or 3/8" vent. ribs, most popular shotguns.
Price: **$13.95**

WILLIAMS SIGHT KITS Contains over 36 beads to fit any shotgun (with drills and taps).
Price: **$102.99**

Sight Attachments

MERIT ADJUSTABLE APERTURES Eleven clicks give 12 different apertures. No. 3 Disc and Master, primarily target types, 0.22" to .125"; No. 4, 1/2" dia. hunting type, .025" to .155". Available for all popular sights. The Master, with flexible rubber light shield, is particularly adapted to extension, scope height, and tang sights. All models have internal click springs; are hand fitted to minimum tolerance.
Price: No. 3 Master Disk. **$66.00**
Price: No. 3 Target Disc (Plain Face). **$56.00**
Price: No. 4 Hunting Disc. **$48.00**

MERIT LENS DISC Similar to Merit Iris Shutter (Model 3 or Master) but incorporates provision for mounting prescription lens integrally. Lens may be obtained locally from your optician. Sight disc is 7/16" wide (Model 3), or 3/4" wide (Master).
Price: No. 3 Target Lens Disk. **$68.00**
Price: No. 3 Master Lens Disk. **$78.00**

MERIT OPTICAL ATTACHMENT For iron sight shooting with handgun or rifle. Instantly attached by rubber suction cup to prescription or shooting glasses. Swings aside. Aperture adjustable from .020" to .156".
Price: **$65.00**

WILLIAMS APERTURES Standard thread, fits most sights. Regular series 3/8" to 1/2" O.D., .050" to .125" hole. "Twilight" series has white reflector ring.
Price: Regular series. **$4.97**
Price: Twilight series. **$6.79**
Price: Wide open 5/16" aperture for shotguns fits 5-D or Foolproof sights (specify model). **$8.77**

SPOTTING SCOPES

Bushnell Collapsible Spotting Scope

BROWNING 15-45x zoom, 65mm objective lens. Weight: 48 oz. Waterproof, fogproof. Tripod, soft and hard cases included.
Price:. $559.95

BUSHNELL DISCOVERER 15x to 60x zoom, 60mm objective. Constant focus throughout range. Field at 1000 yds. 38 ft (60x), 150 ft. (15x). Comes with lens caps. Length 17 1/2"; weight 48.5 oz.
Price:. $342.95

BUSHNELL ELITE 15x to 45x zoom, 60mm objective. Field at 1000 yds., 125-65 ft. Length is 12.2"; weight, 26.5 oz. Waterproof, armored. Tripod mount. Comes with black case.
Price:. $559.95

BUSHNELL ELITE ZOOM 20x-60x, 70mm objective. Roof prism. Field at 1000 yds. 90-50 ft. Length is 16"; weight 40 oz. Waterproof, armored. Tripod mount. Comes with black case.
Price: $769.95

BUSHNELL 80MM ELITE 20x-60x zoom, 80mm objective. Field of view at 1000 yds. 98-50 ft. (zoom). Weight 51 oz. (20x, 30x), 54 oz. (zoom); length 17". Interchangeable bayonet-style eyepieces. Built-in peep sight.
Price: With EDPrime Glass $1,119.95

BUSHNELL TROPHY 65mm objective, 20x-60x zoom. Field at 1000 yds. 90ft. (20x), 45 ft. (60x). Length 12.7"; weight 20 oz. Black rubber armored, waterproof. Case included.
Price: $297.95

BUSHNELL COMPACT TROPHY 50mm objective, 20x-50x zoom. Field at 1000 yds. 92 ft. (20x), 52 ft. (50x). Length 12.2"; weight 17 oz. Black rubber armored, waterproof. Case included.
Price:. $257.95

BUSHNELL SENTRY 16-32 zoom, 50mm objective. Field at 1000 yds. 140-65 ft. Length 8.7", weight 21.5 oz. Black rubber armored. Built-in peep sight. Comes with tripod and hardcase.
Price:. $199.95

BUSHNELL SPACEMASTER 20x-45x zoom. Long eye relief. Rubber armored, prismatic. 60mm objective. Field at 1000 yds. 90-58 ft. Minimum focus 20 ft. Length 12.7"; weight 43 oz.
Price: With tripod, carrying case and 20x-45x LER eyepiece. $491.95

BUSHNELL SPACEMASTER COLLAPSIBLE 15-45x zoom, 50mm objective lens. Field of view at 1000 yds., 113 ft. (15x) 52 ft. (45x). Length: 8". Weight: 22.8 oz. Comes with tripod, window mount and case.
Price:. $209.95

BUSHNELL SPORTVIEW 15x-45x zoom, 50mm objective. Field at 100 yds. 103 ft. (15x), 35 ft. (45x). Length 17.4"; weight 34.4 oz.
Price: With tripod and carrying case $91.95

HERMES 1 70mm objective, 16x, 25x, 40x. Field at 1000 meters 160 ft. (16x), 75ft. (40x). Length 12.2"; weight 33 oz. From CZ-USA.
Price: Body. $359.00
Price: 25x eyepiece $86.00
Price: 40x eyepiece $128.00

KOWA TS-500 SERIES Offset 45° or straight body. Comes with 20-40x zoom eyepiece or 20x fixed eyepiece. 50mm obj. Field of view at 1000 yds.: 171 ft. (20x fixed), 132-74 ft. (20-40x zoom). Length 8.9-10.4", weight 13.4-14.8 oz.
Price: TS-501 (offset 45° body w/20x fixed eyepiece) $258.00
Price: TS-502 (straight body w/20x fixed eyepiece) $231.00
Price: TS-501Z (offset 45° body w/20-40x zoom eyepiece). $321.00
Price: TS-502Z (straight body w/20-40x zoom eyepiece). $290.00

KOWA TS-660 SERIES Offset 45° or straight body. Fully waterproof. Available with ED lens.Sunshade and rotating tripod mount. 66mm obj. Field of view at 1000 yds.: 177 ft. (20xW), 154 ft. (27xW), 131 ft. (30xW), 102 ft. (25x), 92 ft. (25xLER), 108-79 ft. (20-40x multi-coated zoom), 98-62 ft. (20-60x high grade zoom). Length 12.3"; weight 34.9-36.7 oz. Note: Eyepieces for TSN 77mm series, TSN-660 series, 661 body (45° offset) **$660.00**
Price: TSN-662 body (straight). $610.00
Price: TSN-663 body (45 offset, ED lens) $1,070.00
Price: TSN-664 body (straight, ED lens) $1,010.00
Price: TSE-Z6 (20-40x multi-coatedzoom eyepiece). $378.00
Price: TSE-17HB (25x long eye relief eyepiece) $240.00
Price: TSE-14W (30x wide angle high-grade eyepiece) $288.00
Price: TSE-21WB (20x wide-angle eyepiece) $230.00
Price: TSE-15 WM (27x wide-angle eyepiece) $182.00
Price: TSE-16 PM (25x eyepiece). $108.00
Price: TSN-DA1 digital photo adapter $105.00
Price: DA1 adapter rings. $43.00
Price: TSN-PA2 (800mm photo adapter). $269.00
Price: TSN-PA4 (1200mm photo adapter). $330,00
Price: Camera mounts (for use with photo adapter) $30.00

KOWA TSN-660 SERIES Offset 45° or straight body. Fully waterproof. Available with fluorite lens. Sunshade and rotating tripod mount. 66mm obj., field of view at 1000 yds: 177 ft. (20x@), 154 ft. (27xW), 131 ft. (30xW), 102 ft. (25x), 92 ft. (25xLER), 62 ft. (40x), 108-79 ft. (20-40x Multi-Coated Zoom), 102-56 ft. (20-60x Zoom), 98-62 ft. (20-60x High Grade Zoom). Length 12.3"; weight 34.9-36.7 oz. Note: Eyepieces for TSN 77mm Series, TSN-660 Series, and TSN610 Series are interchangeable.
Price: TSN-661 body (45° offset) $660.00
Price: TSN-662 body (straight). $610.00
Price: TSN-663 body (45° offset, fluorite lens). $1,070.00
Price: TSN-664 body (straight, fluorite lens) $1,010.00
Price: TSE-Z4 (20-60x high-grade zoom eyepiece) $378.00
Price: TSE-Z6 (20-40x multi-coated zoom eyepiece) $250.00
Price: TSE-17HB (25x long eye relief eyepiece) $240.00
Price: TSE-14W (30x wide angle eyepiece) $288.00
Price: TSE-21WB (20x wide angle eyepiece) $230.00
Price: TSE-15PM (27x wide angle eyepiece) $182.00
Price: TSE-10PM (40x eyepiece). $108.00
Price: TSE-16PM (25x eyepiece) $105.00
Price: TSN-DA1 (digital photo adapter) $105.00
Price: Adapter rings for DA1. . . . . $43.00
Price: TSN-PA2 (800mm photo adapter). $269.00
Price: TSN-PA4 (1200mm photo adapter). $330.00
Price: Camera mounts (for use with photo adapter) $30.00

KOWA TSN-820M SERIES Offset 45° or straight body. Fully waterproof. Available with fluorite lens. Sunshade and rotating tripod mount. 82mm obj., field of view at 1000 yds: 75 ft (27xLER, 50xW), 126 ft. (32xW), 115-58 ft. (20-60xZoom). Length 15"; weight 49.4-52.2 oz.
Price: TSN-821M body (45° offset) $850.00
Price: TSN-822M body (straight) $770.00
Price: TSN-823M body (45° offset, fluorite lens) $1,850.00
Price: TSN-824M body (straight, fluorite lens). $1,730.00
Price: TSE-Z7 (20-60x zoom eyepiece). $433.00
Price: TSE-9W (50x wide angle eyepiece) $345.00
Price: TSE-14WB (32x wide angle eyepiece) $366.00
Price: TSE-17HC (27x long eye relief eyepiece) $248.00
Price: TSN-DA1 (digital photo adapter) $105.00
Price: Adapter rings for DA1. . . . . $43.00
Price: TSN-PA2C (850mm photo adapter) $300.00
Price: Camera mounts (for use with photo adapter) $30.00

LEUPOLD 10-20x40mm COMPACT 40mm objective, 10-20x. Field at 100 yds. 19.9-13.6ft.; eye relief 18.5mm (10x). Overall length 7.5", weight 15.8 oz. Rubber armored.
Price:. $439.95

LEUPOLD 55-30x50 COMPACT 50mm objective, 15-30x. Field at 100 yds. 13.6ft.; eye relief 17.5mm; length overall 11"; weight 1.5 oz.
Price: $564.99

LEUPOLD Wind River Sequoia 15-30x60mm, 60mm objective, 15-30x. Field at 100 yards: 13.1 ft.; eye relief: 16.5mm. Overall length: 13 inches. Weight: 35.1 oz.
Price: $294.99

LEUPOLD Wind River Sequoia 15-45x60mm Angled. Armored, 15-45x. Field at 100 yards: 13.1-6.3 ft.; eye relief: 16.5-13.0. Overall length: 12.5". Weight: 35.1 oz.
Price: $309.99

LEUPOLD Golden Ring 12-40x60mm; 12.7x38.1x. Field at 100 yards: 16.8-5.2 ft.; eye relief: 30.0; Overall length: 12.4". Weight: 37.0 oz.
Price: $1,124.99

LEUPOLD Golden Ring15-30x50mm Compact Armored; 15.2-30.4x; field at 100 yards: 13.6-8.9; eye relief: 17.5-17.1; overall length: 11.0". Weight: 21.5 oz.
Price:. $564.99

MIRADOR TTB SERIES Draw tube armored spotting scopes. Available with 75mm or 80mm objective. Zoom model (28x-62x, 80mm) is 11 7/8" (closed), weighs 50 oz. Field at 1000 yds. 70-42 ft. Comes with lens covers.
Price: 28-62x80mm. $1,133.95
Price: 32x80mm $971.95
Price: 26-58x75mm. $989.95
Price: 30x75mm $827.95

SPOTTING SCOPES

MIRADOR SSD SPOTTING SCOPES 60mm objective, 15x, 20x, 22x, 25x, 40x, 60x, 20-60x; field at 1000 yds. 37 ft.; length 10 1/4"; weight 33 oz.
Price: 25x **$575.95**
Price: 22x Wide Angle **$593.95**
Price: 20-60x Zoom **$746.95**
Price: As above, with tripod, case **$944.95**

MIRADOR SIA SPOTTING SCOPES Similar to the SSD scopes except with 45° eyepiece. Length 12 1/4"; weight 39 oz.
Price: 25x **$809.95**
Price: 22x Wide Angle **$827.95**
Price: 20-60x Zoom **$980.95**

MIRADOR SSR SPOTTING SCOPES 50mm or 60mm objective. Similar to SSD except rubber armored in black or camouflage. Length 11 1/8"; weight 31 oz.
Price: Black, 20x. **$521.95**
Price: Black, 18x Wide Angle. **$539.95**
Price: Black, 16-48x Zoom. **$692.95**
Price: Black, 20x, 60mm, EER **$692.95**
Price: Black, 22x Wide Angle, 60mm **$701.95**
Price: Black, 20-60x Zoom. **$854.95**

MIRADOR SSF FIELD SCOPES Fixed or variable power, choice of 50mm, 60mm, 75mm objective lens. Length 9 3/4"; weight 20 oz. (15-32x50).
Price: 20x50mm. **$359.95**
Price: 25x60mm. **$440.95**
Price: 30x75mm. **$584.95**
Price: 15-32x50mm Zoom **$548.95**
Price: 18-40x60mm Zoom **$629.95**
Price: 22-47x75mm Zoom **$773.95**

MIRADOR SRA MULTI ANGLE SCOPES Similar to SSF Series except eyepiece head rotates for viewing from any angle.
Price: 20x50mm. **$503.95**
Price: 25x60mm. **$647.95**
Price: 30x75mm. **$764.95**
Price: 15-32x50mm Zoom **$692.95**
Price: 18-40x60mm Zoom **$836.95**
Price: 22-47x75mm Zoom **$953.95**

MIRADOR SIB FIELD SCOPES Short-tube, 45° scopes with porro prism design. 50mm and 60mm objective. Length 10 1/4"; weight 18.5 oz. (15-32x50mm); field at 1000 yds. 129-81 ft.
Price: 20x50mm. **$386.95**
Price: 25x60mm. **$449.95**
Price: 15-32x50mm Zoom **$575.95**
Price: 18-40x60mm Zoom **$638.95**

NIKON FIELDSCOPES 60mm and 78mm lens. Field at 1000 yds. 105 ft. (60mm, 20x), 126 ft. (78mm, 25x). Length 12.8" (straight 60mm), 12.6" (straight 78mm); weight 34.5- 47.5 oz. Eyepieces available separately.
Price: 60mm straight body. **$499.99**
Price: 60mm angled body **$519.99**
Price: 60mm straight ED body. **$779.99**
Price: 60mm angled ED body **$849.99**
Price: 78mm straight ED body. **$899.99**
Price: 78mm angled ED body **$999.99**
Price: Eyepieces (15x to 60x) . . . . . . **$146.95 to $324.95**
Price: 20-45x eyepiece (25-56x for 78mm). **$320.55**

NIKON SPOTTING SCOPE 60mm objective, 20x fixed power or 15-45x zoom. Field at 1000 yds. 145 ft. (20x). Gray rubber armored. Straight or angled eyepiece. Weighs 44.2 oz., length 12.1" (20x).
Price: 20x60 fixed (with eyepiece). **$290.95**
Price: 15-45x zoom (with case, tripod, eyepiece) **$578.95**

PENTAX PF-80ED spotting scope 80mm objective lens available in 18x, 24x, 36x, 48x, 72x and 20-60x. Length 15.6", weight 11.9 to 19.2 oz.
Price: **$1,320.00**

SIGHTRON SII 2050X63 63mm objective lens, 20x-50x zoom. Field at 1000 yds 91.9 ft. (20x), 52.5 ft. (50x). Length 14"; weight 30.8 oz. Black rubber finish. Also available with 80mm objective lens.
Price: 63mm or 80mm **$339.95**

SIMMONS 1280 50mm objective, 15-45x zoom. Black matte finish. Ocular focus. Peep finder sight. Waterproof. FOV 95-51 ft. @ 1000 yards. Wgt. 33.5 oz., length 12".
Price: With tripod **$189.99**

SIMMONS 1281 60mm objective, 20-60x zoom. Black matte finish. Ocular focus. Peep finder sight. Waterproof. FOV 78-43 ft. @ 1000 yards. Wgt. 34.5 oz. Length 12".
Price: With tripod **$209.99**

SIMMONS 77206 PROHUNTER 50mm objectives, 25x fixed power. Field at 1000 yds. 113 ft.; length 10.25"; weighs 33.25 oz. Black rubber armored.
Price: With tripod case. **$160.60**

SIMMONS 41200 REDLINE 50mm objective, 15x-45x zoom. Field at 1000 yds. 104-41 ft.; length 16.75"; weighs 32.75 oz.
Price: With hard case and tripod **$74.99**
Price: 20-60x, 60mm objective **$99.99**

SWAROVSKI CTC and **CTS EXTENDIBLE SCOPES**. 30x75 mm or 85mm objective, 20-60x zoom or fixed 20x, 30x or 45x eyepieces. Field at 1000 yards: 180 ft. (20xSW), 126 ft. (30xSW), 84 ft. (45xSW), 108-60 ft. (20-60xS) for zoom. Length 12.2" (closed), 19.3" (open) for the CTC; 9.7"/17.2" for theCTS. Weight 42.3 oz. (CTC), 49.4 oz. (CTS). Green rubber armored.
Price: CTC 30x75 body. **$1,032.22**
Price: CTS-85 body. **$1,298.89**

SWAROVSKI ATS-65 SCOPES. 65mm or 80mm objective, 20-60x zoom, or fixed 20x, 30x 45x eyepieces. Field at 1000 yds. 180 ft.(20xSW). 126 ft. (30xSW), 84 ft. (45xSW), 108-60 ft. (20-60xS) for zoom. Length: 13.98" (ATS/STS 80), 12.8" (ATS/STS 65); weight: 45.93 oz. (ATS 80), 47.70 oz. (ATS 80HD), 45.23 oz., (STS 80), 46.9 oz. (STS 80 HD), 38.3 oz. (ATS 65), 39.9 oz. (ATS 65HD) 38.1 oz. (STS 65), 39.2 oz. (STS 65 HD). Available with HD (high density) glass add approximately **$450**.
Price: ATS65 (angled eyepiece) **$1,087.78**
Price: STS 65 (straight eyepiece). **$1,087.78**
Price: ATS-80 (angled eyepiece) **$1,321.11**
Price: ATS-80 (straight eyepiece) **$1,321.11**
Price: 20xSW **$310.00**
Price: 30xSW **$310.00**
Price: 45xSW **$376.67**

SWIFT LYNX M836 15x-45x zoom, 60mm objective. Weight 7 lbs., length 14". Has 45° eyepiece, sunshade.
Price: **$315.00**

SWIFT NIGHTHAWK M849U 80mm objective, 20x-60x zoom, or fixed 19, 25x, 31x, 50x, 75x eyepieces. Has rubber armored body, 1.8x optical finder, retractable lens hood, 45° eyepiece. Field at 1000 yds. 60 ft. (28x), 41 ft. (75x). Length 13.4 oz.; weight 39 oz.
Price: Body only **$870.00**
Price: 20-68x eyepiece **$370.00**
Price: Fixed eyepieces . . . . . . **$130.00 to $240.00**
Price: Model 849 (straight) body. **$795.00**

SWIFT LYNX 60mm objective, 15-45X zoom, 45-degree inclined roof prism, magenta coated on all air-to-glass surfaces, rubber armored body, length 14 inches, weighs 30 ounces. Equipped with sun shade, threaded dust covers and low level tripod.
Price: complete **$330.00**

SWIFT TELEMASTER M841 60mm objective. 15x to 60x variable power. Field at 1000 yds. 160 feet (15x) to 40 feet (60x). Weight 3.25 lbs.; length 18" overall.
Price: **$399.50**

SWIFT PANTHER M844 15x-45x zoom or 22x WA, 15x, 20x, 40x. 60mm objective. Field at 1000 yds. 141 ft. (15x), 68 ft. (40x), 95-58 ft. (20x-45x).
Price: Body only **$380.00**
Price: 15x-45x zoom eyepiece **$120.00**
Price: 20x-45x zoom (long eye relief) eyepiece. **$140.00**
Price: 15x, 40x eyepiece. **$65.00**
Price: 22x WA eyepiece **$80.00**

SWIFT M700T 12x-36x, 50mm objective. Field of view at 100 yds. 16 ft. (12x), 9 ft. (36x). Length 14"; weight with tripod 3.22 lbs.
Price: **$30.00**

TASCO 15-45x Zoom, 50mm objective lens, 20x-60x zoom. Field of view at 100 yds. 19 ft (15x) Length: 16". Weight: 19 oz. Matte black finish.
Price: **$67.95**

TASCO 20-60x zoom, 60mm objective, 12-36x zoom. Field of view at 100 yds. 12 ft. (20x). Length: 20". Weight: 50 oz. Black finish.
Price: **$95.95**

TASCO 18-36x zoom 50mm objective. Field of view at 100 yds. 12 ft. (18x). Length: 14.5". Weight: 31 oz. Camo or black rubber armor. Includes carrying case.
Price: **$131.95**

UNERTL "FORTY-FIVE" 54mm objective. 20x (single fixed power). Field at 100 yds. 10',10"; eye relief 1"; focusing range infinity to 33 ft. Weight about 32 oz.; overall length 15 3/4". With lens covers.
Price: With mono-layer magnesium coating **$810.00**

UNERTL STRAIGHT PRISMATIC 24x63. 63.5mm objective, 24x. Field at 100 yds., 7 ft. Relative brightness, 6.96. Eye relief 1/2". Weight 40 oz.; length closed 19". Push-pull and screw-focus eyepiece. 16x and 32x eyepieces **$125.00 each.**
Price: **$786.00**

UNERTL 20x STRAIGHT PRISMATIC 54mm objective, 20x. Field at 100 yds. 8.5 ft. Relative brightness 6.1. Eye relief 1/2". Weight 36 oz.; length closed 13 1/2". Complete with lens covers.
Price: **$695.00**

UNERTL TEAM SCOPE 100mm objective. 15x, 24x, 32x eyepieces. Field at 100 yds. 13 to 7.5 ft. Relative brightness, 39.06 to 9.79. Eye relief 2" to 1 1/2". Weight 13 lbs.; length 29 7/8" overall. Metal tripod, yoke and wood carrying case furnished (total weight 80 lbs.).
Price: **$3,624.50**

WEAVER 20x50 50mm objective. Field of view 124 ft. at 100 yds. Eye relief .85"; weighs 21 oz.; overall length 10". Waterproof, armored.
Price: **$249.99**

WEAVER 15-40x60 ZOOM 60mm objective. 15x-40x zoom. Field at 100 yds. 119 ft. (15x), 66 ft. (60x). Overall length 12.5", weighs 26 oz. Waterproof, armored.
Price: **$399.99**

CHOKES & BRAKES

Briley Screw-In Chokes

Installation of these choke tubes requires that all traces of the original choking be removed, the barrel threaded internally with square threads and then the tubes are custom fitted to the specific barrel diameter. The tubes are thin and, therefore, made of stainless steel. Cost of installation for single-barrel guns (pumps, autos), lead shot, 12-gauge, **$149.00**, 20-gauge **$159.00**; steel shot **$179.00** and **$189.00**, all with three chokes; un-single target guns run **$219.00**; over/unders and side-by-sides, lead shot, 12-gauge, **$369.00**, 20-gauge **$389.00**; steel shot **$469.00** and **$489.00**, all with five chokes. For 10-gauge auto or pump with two steel shot chokes, **$189.00**; over/unders, side-by-sides with three steel shot chokes, **$349.00**. For 16-gauge auto or pump, three lead shot chokes, **$179.00**; over/unders, side-by-sides with five lead shot chokes, **$449.00**. The 28 and 410-bore run **$179.00** for autos and pumps with three lead shot chokes, **$449.00** for over/unders and side-by-sides with five lead shot chokes.

Carlson's Choke Tubes

Manufactures choke tubes for Beretta, Benelli, Remington, Winchester, Browning Invector and Invector Plus, TruChokes, FranChokes, American Arms, Ruger and more. All choke tubes are manufactured from corrosion resistant stainless steel. Most tubes are compatible with lead, steel, Hevi-shot, etc. Available in flush mount, extended sporting clay and extended turkey designs, ported and non-ported. Also offers sights, rifled choke tubes and other accessories for most shotgun models. Prices range from **$18.95** to **$36.95**.

Cutts Compensator

The Cutts Compensator is one of the oldest variable choke devices available. Manufactured by Lyman Gunsight Corporation, it is available with a steel body. A series of vents allows gas to escape upward and downward. For the 12-ga. Comp body, six fixed-choke tubes are available: the Spreader-popular with Skeet shooters; Improved Cylinder; Modified; Full; Superfull, and Magnum Full. Full, Modified and Spreader tubes are available for 12 or 20. Cutts Compensator, complete with wrench, adaptor and any single tube **$87.50**. All single choke tubes **$26.00** each. No factory installation available.

Dayson Automatic Brake System

This system fits most single barrel shotguns threaded for choke tubes, and cuts away 30 grooves on the exterior of a standard one-piece wad as it exits the muzzle. This slows the wad, allowing shot and wad to separate faster, reducing shot distortion and tightening patterns. The A.B.S. Choke Tube is claimed to reduce recoil by about 25 percent, and with the Muzzle Brake up to 60 percent. Ventilated Choke Tubes available from .685" to .725", in .005" increments. Model I Ventilated Choke Tube for use with A.B.S. Muzzle Brake, **$49.95**; for use without Muzzle Brake, **$52.95**; A.B.S. Muzzle Brake, from **$69.95**. Contact Dayson Arms for more data.

Gentry Quiet Muzzle Brake

Developed by gunmaker David Gentry, the "Quiet Muzzle Brake" is said to reduce recoil by up to 85 percent with no loss of accuracy or velocity. There is no increase in noise level because the noise and gases are directed away from the shooter. The barrel is threaded for installation and the unit is blued to match the barrel finish. Price, installed, is **$150.00**. Add **$15.00** for stainless steel, **$45.00** for knurled cap to protect threads. Shipping extra.

JP Muzzle Brake

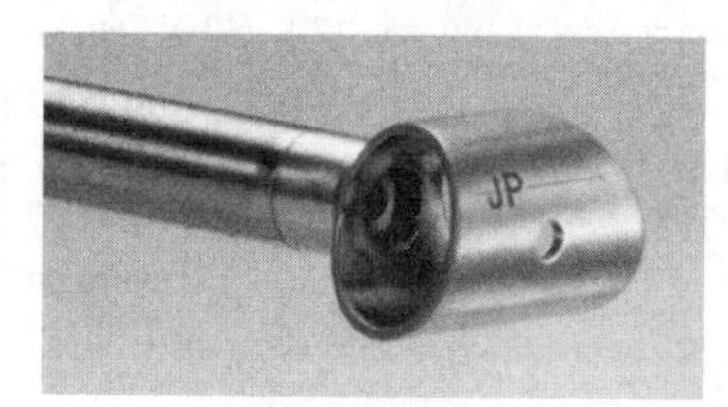

JP Muzzle Brake

Designed for single shot handguns, AR-15, Ruger Mini-14, Ruger Mini Thirty and other sporting rifles, the JP Muzzle Brake redirects high pressure gases against a large frontal surface which applies forward thrust to the gun. All gases are directed up, rearward and to the sides. Priced at **$79.95** (AR-15 or sporting rifles), **$89.95** (bull barrel and SKS, AK models), **$89.95** (Ruger Minis), Dual Chamber model **$79.95**. From JP Enterprises, Inc.

KDF Slim Line Muzzle Brake

This threaded muzzle brake has 30 pressure ports that direct combustion gases in all directions to reduce felt recoil up to a claimed 80 percent without affecting accuracy or ballistics. It is said to reduce felt recoil of a 30-06 to that of a 243. Price, installed, is **$179.00**. From KDF, Inc.

Laseraim

Simple, no-gunsmithing compensator reduces felt recoil and muzzle flip by up to 30 percent. Machined from single piece of Stainless Steel (Beretta/Taurus model made of aircraft aluminum). In black and polished finish. For Colt Government/Commander and Beretta/Taurus full-size pistols. Weighs 1 ounce. **$49.00**. From Laseraim Arms Inc.

Mag-Na-Port

Electrical Discharge Machining works on any firearm except those having non-conductive shrouded barrels. EDM is a metal erosion technique using carbon electrodes that control the area to be processed. The Mag-Na-Port venting process utilizes small trapezoidal openings to direct powder gases upward and outward to reduce recoil. No effect is had on bluing or nickeling outside the Mag-Na-Port area so no refinishing is needed. Rifle-style porting on single shot or large caliber handguns with barrels 7 1/2" or longer is **$115.00**; Dual Trapezoidal porting on most handguns with minimum barrel length of 3", **$115.00**; standard revolver porting, **$88.50**; porting through the slide and barrel for semi-autos, **$129.50**; traditional rifle porting, **$135.00**. Prices do not include shipping, handling and insurance. From Mag-Na-Port International.

Mag-Na-Brake

A screw-on brake under 2" long with progressive integrated exhaust chambers to neutralize expanding gases. Gases dissipate with an opposite twist to prevent the brake from unscrewing, and with a 5-degree forward angle to minimize sound pressure level. Available in blue, satin blue, bright or satin stainless. Standard and Light Contour installation cost **$195.00** for bolt-action rifles, many single action and single shot handguns. A knurled thread protector supplied at extra cost. Also available in Varmint style with exhaust chambers covering 220 degrees for prone-position shooters. From Mag-Na-Port International.

Poly-Choke

Marble Arms Corp., manufacturer of the Poly-Choke adjustable shotgun choke, now offers two models in 12-, 16-, 20-, and 28-gauge-the Ventilated and Standard style chokes. Each provides nine choke settings including Xtra-Full and Slug. The Ventilated model reduces 20 percent of a shotgun's recoil, the company claims, and is priced at **$135.00**. The Standard Model is **$125.00**. Postage not included. Contact Marble Arms for more data.

Pro-port

A compound ellipsoid muzzle venting process similar to Mag-Na-Porting, only exclusively applied to shotguns. Like Mag-Na-Porting, this system reduces felt recoil, muzzle jump, and shooter fatigue. Very helpful for trap doubles shooters. Pro-Port is a patented process and installation is available in both the U.S. and Canada. Cost for the Pro-Port process is **$139.00** for over/unders (both barrels); **$110.00** for only the top or bottom barrel; and **$88.50** for single-barrel shotguns. Optional pigeon porting costs **$25.00** extra per barrel. Prices do not include shipping and handling. From Pro-port Ltd.

Que Industries Adjustable Muzzle Brake

The Que Brake allows for fine-tuning of a rifle's accuracy by rotating the brake to one of 100 indexed stops. Mounts in minutes without barrel modification with heat-activated tensioning ring. The slotted exhaust ports reduce recoil by venting gases sideways, away from rifle. **$189.50**. From Que Industries.

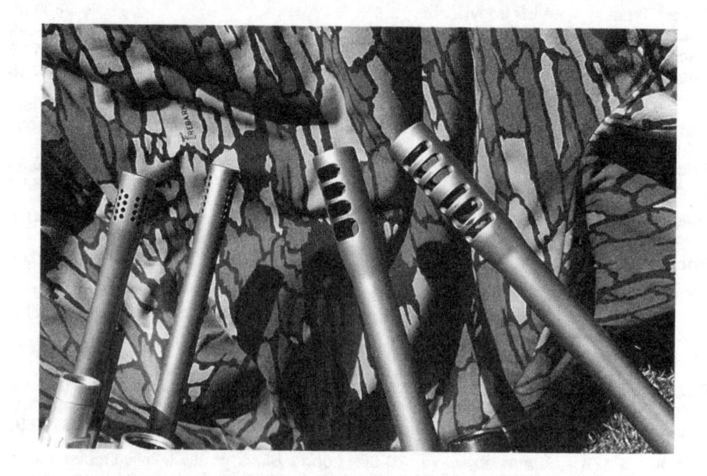
SSK Arrestor muzzle brakes

SSK Arrestor Brake

This is a true muzzle brake with an expansion chamber. It takes up about 1" of barrel and reduces velocity accordingly. Some Arrestors are added to a barrel, increasing its length. Said to reduce the felt recoil of a 458 to that approaching a 30-06. Can be set up to give zero muzzle rise in any caliber, and can be added to most guns. For handgun or rifle. Prices start at **$95.00**. Contact SSK Industries for full data.

PERIODICAL PUBLICATIONS

AAFTA News (M)
5911 Cherokee Ave., Tampa, FL 33604. Official newsletter of the American Airgun Field Target Assn.

The Accurate Rifle
Precisions Shooting, Inc., 222 Mckee Street, Manchester CT 06040. $37 yr. Dedicated to the rifle accuracy enthusiast.

Action Pursuit Games Magazine (M)
CFW Enterprises, Inc., 4201 W. Vanowen Pl., Burbank, CA 91505 818-845-2656. $4.99 single copy U.S., $5.50 Canada. Editor: Dan Reeves. World's leading magazine of paintball sports.

Air Gunner Magazine
4 The Courtyard, Denmark St., Wokingham, Berkshire RG11 2AZ, England/011-44-734-771677. $U.S. $44 for 1 yr. Leading monthly airgun magazine in U.K.

Airgun Ads
Box 33, Hamilton, MT 59840/406-363-3805; Fax: 406-363-4117. $35 1 yr. (for first mailing; $20 for second mailing; $35 for Canada and foreign orders.) Monthly tabloid with extensive For Sale and Wanted airgun listings.

The Airgun Letter
Gapp, Inc., 4614 Woodland Rd., Ellicott City, MD 21042-6329/410-730-5496; Fax: 410-730-9544; e-mail: staff@airgnltr.net; http://www.airgunletter.com. $21 U.S., $24 Canada, $27 Mexico and $33 other foreign orders, 1 yr. Monthly newsletter for airgun users and collectors.

Airgun World
4 The Courtyard, Denmark St., Wokingham, Berkshire RG40 2AZ, England/011-44-734-771677. Call for subscription rates. Oldest monthly airgun magazine in the U.K., now a sister publication to *Air Gunner.*

Alaska Magazine
Morris Communications, 735 Broad Street, Augusta, GA 30901/706-722-6060. Hunting, Fishing and Life on the Last Frontier articles of Alaska and western Canada.

American Firearms Industry
Nat'l. Assn. of Federally Licensed Firearms Dealers, 2455 E. Sunrise Blvd., Suite 916, Ft. Lauderdale, FL 33304. $35.00 yr. For firearms retailers, distributors and manufacturers.

American Guardian
NRA, 11250 Waples Mill Rd., Fairfax, VA 22030. Publications division. $15.00 1 yr. Magazine features personal protection; home-self-defense; family recreation shooting; women's issues; etc.

American Gunsmith
Belvoir Publications, Inc., 75 Holly Hill Lane, Greenwich, CT 06836-2626/203-661-6111. $49.00 (12 issues). Technical journal of firearms repair and maintenance.

American Handgunner*
Publisher's Development Corp., 591 Camino de la Reina, Suite 200, San Diego, CA 92108/800-537-3006 $16.95 yr. Articles for handgun enthusiasts, competitors, police and hunters.

American Hunter (M)
National Rifle Assn., 11250 Waples Mill Rd., Fairfax, VA 22030 (Same address for both.) Publications Div. $35.00 yr. Wide scope of hunting articles.

American Rifleman (M)
National Rifle Assn., 11250 Waples Mill Rd., Fairfax, VA 22030 (Same address for both). Publications Div. $35.00 yr. Firearms articles of all kinds.

American Survival Guide
McMullen Angus Publishing, Inc., 774 S. Placentia Ave., Placentia, CA 92670-6846. 12 issues $19.95/714-572-2255; FAX: 714-572-1864.

Armes & Tir*
c/o FABECO, 38, rue de Trévise 75009 Paris, France. Articles for hunters, collectors, and shooters. French text.

Arms Collecting (Q)
Museum Restoration Service, P.O. Box 70, Alexandria Bay, NY 13607-0070. $22.00 yr.; $62.00 3 yrs.; $112.00 5 yrs.
Australian Shooter *(formerly Australian Shooters Journal)*
Sporting Shooters' Assn. of Australia, Inc., P.O. Box 2066, Kent Town SA 5071, Australia. $60.00 yr. locally; $65.00 yr. overseas surface mail. Hunting and shooting articles.

The Backwoodsman Magazine
P.O. Box 627, Westcliffe, CO 81252. $16.00 for 6 issues per yr.; $30.00 for 2 yrs.; sample copy $2.75. Subjects include muzzle-loading, woodslore, primitive survival, trapping, homesteading, blackpowder cartridge guns, 19th century how-to.

Black Powder Cartridge News (Q)
SPG, Inc., P.O. Box 761, Livingston, MT 59047/Phone/Fax: 406-222-8416. $17 yr. (4 issues) ($6 extra 1st class mailing). For the blackpowder cartridge enthusiast.

Blackpowder Hunting (M)
Intl. Blackpowder Hunting Assn., P.O. Box 1180Z, Glenrock, WY 82637/307-436-9817. $20.00 1 yr., $36.00 2 yrs. How-to and where-to features by experts on hunting; shooting; ballistics; traditional and modern blackpowder rifles, shotguns, pistols and cartridges.

Black Powder Times
P.O. Box 234, Lake Stevens, WA 98258. $20.00 yr.; add $5 per year for Canada, $10 per year other foreign. Tabloid newspaper for blackpowder activities; test reports.

Blade Magazine
Krause Publications, 700 East State St., Iola, WI 54990-0001. $25.98 for 12 issues. Foreign price (including Canada-Mexico) $50.00. A magazine for all enthusiasts of handmade, factory and antique knives.

Caliber
GFI-Verlag, Theodor-Heuss Ring 62, 50668 Koln, Germany. For hunters, target shooters and reloaders.

The Caller (Q) (M)
National Wild Turkey Federation, P.O. Box 530, Edgefield, SC 29824. Tabloid newspaper for members; 4 issues per yr. (membership fee $25.00)

Cartridge Journal (M)
Robert Mellichamp, 907 Shirkmere, Houston, TX 77008/713-869-0558. Dues $12 for U.S. and Canadian members (includes the newsletter); 6 issues.

The Cast Bullet*(M)
Official journal of The Cast Bullet Assn. Director of Membership, 203 E. 2nd St., Muscatine, IA 52761. Annual membership dues $14, includes 6 issues.

Cibles
14, rue du Patronage-Laique, BP 2057, 52902 Chaumont, cedex 9, France. French-language arms magazine also carries a small amount of arms-related and historical content. 12 issues per year. Tel/03-25-03-87-47/Email cibeles@graphycom.com; Website: www.graphycom.com

COLTELLI, che Passione (Q)
Casella postale N.519, 20101 Milano, Italy/Fax:02-48402857. $15 1 yr., $27 2 yrs. Covers all types of knives—collecting, combat, historical. Italian text.

Combat Handguns*
Harris Publications, Inc., 1115 Broadway, New York, NY 10010.

Deer & Deer Hunting Magazine
Krause Publications, 700 E. State St., Iola, WI 54990-0001. $19.95 yr. (9 issues). For the serious deer hunter. Website: www.krause.com

The Derringer Peanut (M)
The National Association of Derringer Collectors, P.O. Box 20572, San Jose, CA 95160. A newsletter dedicated to developing the best derringer information. Write for details.

Deutsches Waffen Journal
Journal-Verlag Schwend GmbH, Postfach 100340, D-74503 Schwäbisch Hall, Germany/0791-404-500; FAX:0791-404-505 and 404-424. DM102 p. yr. (interior); DM125.30 (abroad), postage included. Antique and modern arms and equipment. German text.

Double Gun Journal
P.O. Box 550, East Jordan, MI 49727/800-447-1658. $35 for 4 issues.

Ducks Unlimited, Inc. (M)
1 Waterfowl Way, Memphis, TN 38120

The Engraver (M) (Q)
P.O. Box 4365, Estes Park, CO 80517/970-586-2388; Fax: 970-586-0394. Mike Dubber, editor. The journal of firearms engraving.

The Field
King's Reach Tower, Stamford St., London SE1 9LS England. £36.40 U.K. 1 yr.; 49.90 (overseas, surface mail) yr.; £82.00 (overseas, air mail) yr. Hunting and shooting articles, and all country sports.

Field & Stream
Time4 Media, Two Park Ave., New York, NY 10016/212-779-5000. 12 issues/$19.97. Monthly shooting column. Articles on hunting and fishing.

Field Tests
Belvoir Publications, Inc., 75 Holly Hill Lane; P.O. Box 2626, Greenwich, CT 06836-2626/203-661-6111; 800-829-3361 (subscription line). U.S. & Canada $29 1 yr., $58 2 yrs.; all other countries $45 1 yr., $90 2 yrs. (air).

Fur-Fish-Game
A.R. Harding Pub. Co., 2878 E. Main St., Columbus, OH 43209. $15.95 yr. Practical guidance regarding trapping, fishing and hunting.

The Gottlieb-Tartaro Report
Second Amendment Foundation, James Madison Bldg., 12500 NE 10th Pl., Bellevue, WA 98005/206-454-7012;Fax:206-451-3959. $30 for 12 issues. An insiders guide for gun owners.

Gray's Sporting Journal
Gray's Sporting Journal, P.O. Box 1207, Augusta, GA 30903. $36.95 per yr. for 6 issues. Hunting and fishing journals. Expeditions and Guides Book (Annual Travel Guide).

Gun List†
700 E. State St., Iola, WI 54990. $37.98 yr. (26 issues); $66.98 2 yrs. (52 issues). Indexed market publication for firearms collectors and active shooters; guns, supplies and services. Website: www.krause.com

Gun News Digest (Q)
Second Amendment Fdn., P.O. Box 488, Station C, Buffalo, NY 14209/716-885-6408; Fax:716-884-4471. $10 U.S.; $20 foreign.

The Gun Report
World Wide Gun Report, Inc., Box 38, Aledo, IL 61231-0038. $33.00 yr. For the antique and collectable gun dealer and collector.

Gunmaker (M) (Q)
ACGG, P.O. Box 812, Burlington, IA 52601-0812. The journal of custom gunmaking.

The Gunrunner
Div. of Kexco Publ. Co. Ltd., Box 565G, Lethbridge, Alb., Canada T1J 3Z4. $23.00 yr., sample $2.00. Monthly newspaper, listing everything from antiques to artillery.

Gun Show Calendar (Q)
700 E. State St., Iola, WI 54990. $14.95 yr. (4 issues). Gun shows listed; chronologically and by state. Website: www.krause.com

Gun Tests
11 Commerce Blvd., Palm Coast, FL 32142. The consumer resource for the serious shooter. Write for information.

Gun Trade News
Bruce Publishing Ltd., P.O. Box 82, Wantage, Ozon OX12 7A8, England/44-1-235-771770; Fax: 44-1-235-771848. Britain's only "trade only" magazine exclusive to the gun trade.

Gun Week†
Second Amendment Foundation, P.O. Box 488, Station C, Buffalo, NY 14209. $35.00 yr. U.S. and possessions; $45.00 yr. other countries. Tabloid paper on guns, hunting, shooting and collecting (36 issues).

Gun World
Y-Visionary Publishing, LP 265 South Anita Drive, Ste. 120, Orange, CA 92868. $21.97 yr.; $34.97 2 yrs. For the hunting, reloading and shooting enthusiast.

Guns & Ammo
Primedia, 6420 Wilshire Blvd., Los Angeles, CA 90048/213-782-2780. $23.94 yr. Guns, shooting, and technical articles.

Guns
Publishers Development Corporation, P.O. Box 85201, San Diego, CA 92138/800-537-3006. $19.95 yr. In-depth articles on a wide range of guns, shooting equipment and related accessories for gun collectors, hunters and shooters.

Guns Review
Ravenhill Publishing Co. Ltd., Box 35, Standard House, Bonhill St., London EC 2A 4DA, England. £20.00 sterling (approx. U.S. $38 USA & Canada) yr. For collectors and shooters.

H.A.C.S. Newsletter (M)
Harry Moon, Pres., P.O. Box 50117, South Slope RPO, Burnaby BC, V5J 5G3, Canada/604-438-0950; Fax:604-277-3646. $25 p. yr. U.S. and Canada. Official newsletter of The Historical Arms Collectors of B.C. (Canada).

Handgunner*
Richard A.J. Munday, Seychelles house, Brightlingsen, Essex CO7 ONN, England/012063-305201. £18.00 (sterling).

Handguns*
Primedia, 6420 Wilshire Blvd., Los Angeles, CA 90048/323-782-2868. For the handgunning and shooting enthusiast.

Handloader*
Wolfe Publishing Co., 2626 Stearman Road, Ste. A, Prescott, AZ 86301/520-445-7810;Fax:520-778-5124. $22.00 yr. The journal of ammunition reloading.

INSIGHTS*
NRA, 11250 Waples Mill Rd., Fairfax, VA 22030. Editor, John E. Robbins. $15.00 yr., which includes NRA junior membership; $10.00 for adult subscriptions (12 issues). Plenty of details for the young hunter and target shooter; emphasizes gun safety, marksmanship training, hunting skills.

International Arms & Militaria Collector (Q)
Arms & Militaria Press, P.O. Box 80, Labrador, Qld. 4215, Australia. A$39.50 yr. (U.S. & Canada), 2 yrs. A$77.50; A$37.50 (others), 1 yr., 2 yrs. $73.50 all air express mail; surface mail is less. Editor: Ian D. Skennerton.

International Shooting Sport*/UIT Journal
International Shooting Union (UIT), Bavariaring 21, D-80336 Munich, Germany. Europe: (Deutsche Mark) DM44.00 yr., 2 yrs. DM83.00; outside Europe: DM50.00 yr., 2 yrs. DM95.00 (air mail postage included.) For international sport shooting.

Internationales Waffen-Magazin
Habegger-Verlag Zürich, Postfach 9230, CH-8036 Zürich, Switzerland. SF 105.00 (approx. U.S. $73.00) surface mail for 10 issues. Modern and antique arms, self-defense. German text; English summary of contents.

The Journal of the Arms & Armour Society (M)
A. Dove, P.O. Box 10232, London, SW19 2ZD England. £15.00 surface mail; £20.00 airmail sterling only yr. Articles for the historian and collector.

Journal of the Historical Breechloading Smallarms Assn.
Published annually. P.O. Box 12778, London, SE1 6XB, England. $21.00 yr. Articles for the collector plus mailings of short articles on specific arms, reprints, newsletters, etc.

Knife World
Knife World Publications, P.O. Box 3395, Knoxville, TN 37927. $15.00 yr.; $25.00 2 yrs. Published monthly for knife enthusiasts and collectors. Articles on custom and factory knives; other knife-related interests, monthly column on knife identification, military knives.

Man At Arms*
P.O. Box 460, Lincoln, RI 02865. $27.00 yr., $52.00 2 yrs. plus $8.00 for foreign subscribers. The N.R.A. magazine of arms collecting-investing, with excellent articles for the collector of antique arms and militaria.

The Mannlicher Collector (Q)(M)
Mannlicher Collectors Assn., Inc., P.O. Box 7144, Salem Oregon 97303. $20/ yr. subscription included in membership.

MAGNUM
Rua Madre Rita Amada de Jesus, 182 , Granja Julieta, Sao Paulo – SP – 04721-050 Brazil. No details.

---

*Published bi-monthly
† Published weekly
‡Published three times per month. All others are published monthly.

M=Membership requirements; write for details.
Q=Published Quarterly.

PERIODICAL PUBLICATIONS

MAN/MAGNUM
S.A. Man (Pty) Ltd., P.O. Box 35204, Northway, Durban 4065, Republic of South Africa. SA Rand 200.00 for 12 issues. Africa's only publication on hunting, shooting, firearms, bushcraft, knives, etc.

The Marlin Collector (M)
R.W. Paterson, 407 Lincoln Bldg., 44 Main St., Champaign, IL 61820.

Muzzle Blasts (M)
National Muzzle Loading Rifle Assn., P.O. Box 67, Friendship, IN 47021/812-667-5131. $35.00 yr. annual membership. For the blackpowder shooter.

Muzzleloader Magazine*
Scurlock Publishing Co., Inc., Dept. Gun, Route 5, Box 347-M, Texarkana, TX 75501. $18.00 U.S.; $22.50 U.S./yr. for foreign subscribers. The publication for blackpowder shooters.

National Defense (M)*
American Defense Preparedness Assn., Two Colonial Place, Suite 400, 2101 Wilson Blvd., Arlington, VA 22201-3061/703-522-1820; FAX: 703-522-1885. $35.00 yr. Articles on both military and civil defense field, including weapons, materials technology, management.

National Knife Magazine (M)
Natl. Knife Coll. Assn., 7201 Shallowford Rd., P.O. Box 21070, Chattanooga, TN 37424-0070. Membership $35 yr.; $65.00 International yr.

National Rifle Assn. Journal (British) (Q)
Natl. Rifle Assn. (BR.), Bisley Camp, Brookwood, Woking, Surrey, England. GU24, OPB. £24.00 Sterling including postage.

National Wildlife*
Natl. Wildlife Fed., 1400 16th St. NW, Washington, DC 20036, $16.00 yr. (6 issues); *International Wildlife*, 6 issues, $16.00 yr. Both, $22.00 yr., includes all membership benefits. Write attn.: Membership Services Dept., for more information.

New Zealand GUNS*
Waitekauri Publishing, P.O. 45, Waikino 3060, New Zealand. $NZ90.00 (6 issues) yr. Covers the hunting and firearms scene in New Zealand.

New Zealand Wildlife (Q)
New Zealand Deerstalkers Assoc., Inc., P.O. Box 6514, Wellington, N.Z. $30.00 (N.Z.). Hunting, shooting and firearms/game research articles.

North American Hunter* (M)
P.O. Box 3401, Minnetonka, MN 55343/612-936-9333; e-mail: huntingclub@pclink.com. $18.00 yr. (7 issues). Articles on all types of North American hunting.

Outdoor Life
Time4 Media, Two Park Ave., New York, NY 10016. $14.97/10 issues. Extensive coverage of hunting and shooting. Shooting column by Jim Carmichel.

La Passion des Courteaux (Q)
Phenix Editions, 25 rue Mademoiselle, 75015 Paris, France. French text.

Paintball Games International Magazine
Aceville Publications, Castle House, 97 High St., Colchester, Essex, England CO1 1TH/011-44-206-564840. Write for subscription rates. Leading magazine in the U.K. covering competitive paintball activities.

Paintball News
PBN Publishing, P.O. Box 1608, 24 Henniker St., Hillsboro, NH 03244/603-464-6080. $35 U.S. 1 yr. Bi-weekly. Newspaper covering the sport of paintball, new product reviews and industry features.

Paintball Sports (Q)
Paintball Publications, Inc., 540 Main St., Mount Kisco, NY 10549/941-241-7400. $24.75 U.S. 1 yr., $32.75 foreign. Covering the competitive paintball scene.

Performance Shooter
Belvoir Publications, Inc., 75 Holly Hill Lane, Greenwich, CT 06836-2626/203-661-6111. $45.00 yr. (12 issues). Techniques and technology for improved rifle and pistol accuracy.

Petersen's HUNTING Magazine
Primedia, 6420 Wilshire Blvd., Los Angeles, CA 90048. $19.94 yr.; Canada $29.34 yr.; foreign countries $29.94 yr. Hunting articles for all game; test reports.

P.I. Magazine
America's Private Investigation Journal, 755 Bronx Dr., Toledo, OH 43609. Chuck Klein, firearms editor with column about handguns.

Pirsch
BLV Verlagsgesellschaft GmbH, Postfach 400320, 80703 Munich, Germany/089-12704-0;Fax:089-12705-354. German text.

Point Blank
Citizens Committee for the Right to Keep and Bear Arms (sent to contributors), Liberty Park, 12500 NE 10th Pl., Bellevue, WA 98005

POINTBLANK (M)
Natl. Firearms Assn., Box 4384 Stn. C, Calgary, AB T2T 5N2, Canada. Official publication of the NFA.

The Police Marksman*
6000 E. Shirley Lane, Montgomery, AL 36117. $17.95 yr. For law enforcement personnel.

Police Times (M)
3801 Biscayne Blvd., Miami, FL 33137/305-573-0070.

Popular Mechanics
Hearst Corp., 224 W. 57th St., New York, NY 10019. Firearms, camping, outdoor oriented articles.

Precision Shooting
Precision Shooting, Inc., 222 McKee St., Manchester, CT 06040. $37.00 yr. U.S. Journal of the International Benchrest Shooters, and target shooting in general. Also considerable coverage of varmint shooting, as well as big bore, small bore, schuetzen, lead bullet, wildcats and precision reloading.

Rifle*
Wolfe Publishing Co., 2626 Stearman Road, Ste. A, Prescott, AZ 86301/520-445-7810; Fax: 520-778-5124. $19.00 yr. The sporting firearms journal.

Rifle's Hunting Annual
Wolfe Publishing Co., 2626 Stearman Road, Ste. A, Prescott, AZ 86301/520-445-7810; Fax: 520-778-5124. $4.99 Annual. Dedicated to the finest pursuit of the hunt.

Rod & Rifle Magazine
Lithographic Serv. Ltd., P.O. Box 38-138, Wellington, New Zealand. $50.00 yr. (6 issues). Hunting, shooting and fishing articles.

Safari* (M)
Safari Magazine, 4800 W. Gates Pass Rd., Tucson, AZ 85745/602-620-1220. $55.00 (6 times). The journal of big game hunting, published by Safari Club International. Also publish *Safari Times*, a monthly newspaper, included in price of $55.00 national membership.

Second Amendment Reporter
Second Amendment Foundation, James Madison Bldg., 12500 NE 10th Pl., Bellevue, WA 98005. $15.00 yr. (non-contributors).

Shoot! Magazine*
Shoot! Magazine Corp., 1770 West State Stret PMB 340, Boise ID 83702/208-368-9920; Fax: 208-338-8428. Website: www.shootmagazine.com; $32.95 (6 times/yr.). Articles of interest to the cowboy action shooter, or others interested the Western-era firearms and ammunition.

Shooter's News
23146 Lorain Rd., Box 349, North Olmsted, OH 44070/216-979-5258;Fax:216-979-5259. $29 U.S. 1 yr., $54 2 yrs.; $52 foreign surface. A journal dedicated to precision riflery.

Shooting Industry
Publisher's Dev. Corp., 591 Camino de la Reina, Suite 200, San Diego, CA 92108. $50.00 yr. To the trade. $25.00.

Shooting Sports USA
National Rifle Assn. of America, 11250 Waples Mill Road, Fairfax, VA 22030. Annual subscriptions for NRA members are $5 for classified shooters and $10 for non-classified shooters. Non-NRA member subscriptions are $15. Covering events, techniques and personalities in competitive shooting.

Shooting Sportsman*
P.O. Box 11282, Des Moines, IA 50340/800-666-4955 (for subscriptions). Editorial: P.O. Box 1357, Camden, ME 04843. $19.95 for six issues. The magazine of wingshooting and fine guns.

The Shooting Times & Country Magazine (England)†
IPC Magazines Ltd., King's Reach Tower, Stamford St, 1 London SE1 9LS, England/0171-261-6180;Fax:0171-261-7179. £65 (approx. $98.00) yr.; £79 yr. overseas (52 issues). Game shooting, wild fowling, hunting, game fishing and firearms articles. Britain's best selling field sports magazine.

Shooting Times
Primedia, 2 News Plaza, P.O. Box 1790, Peoria, IL 61656/309-682-6626. $16.97 yr. Guns, shooting, reloading; articles on every gun activity.

The Shotgun News‡
Primedia, 2 News Plaza, P.O. Box 1790, Peoria, IL 61656/800-495-8362. 36 issues/ yr. @ $28.95; 12 issues/yr. @ $19.95. foreign subscription call for rates. Sample copy $4.00. Gun ads of all kinds.

SHOT Business
National Shooting Sports Foundation, Flintlock Ridge Office Center, 11 Mile Hill Rd., Newtown, CT 06470-2359/203-426-1320; FAX: 203-426-1087. For the shooting, hunting and outdoor trade retailer.

Shotgun Sports
P.O. Box 6810, Auburn, CA 95604/916-889-2220; FAX:916-889-9106. $31.00 yr. Trapshooting how-to's, shotshell reloading, shotgun patterning, shotgun tests and evaluations, Sporting Clays action, waterfowl/upland hunting. Call 1-800-676-8920 for a free sample copy.

The Single Shot Exhange Magazine
PO box 1055, York SC 29745/803-628-5326 phone/fax. $31.50/yr., monthly. Articles of interest to the blackpowder cartridge shooter and antique arms collector.

Single Shot Rifle Journal* (M)
Editor John Campbell, PO Box 595, Bloomfield Hills, MI 48303/248-458-8415. Email: jcampbel@dmbb.com Annual dues $35 for 6 issues. Journal of the American Single Shot Rifle Assn.

The Sixgunner (M)
Handgun Hunters International, P.O. Box 357, MAG, Bloomingdale, OH 43910

The Skeet Shooting Review
National Skeet Shooting Assn., 5931 Roft Rd., San Antonio, TX 78253. $20.00 yr. (Assn. membership includes mag.) Competition results, personality profiles of top Skeet shooters, how-to articles, technical, reloading information.

Soldier of Fortune
Subscription Dept., P.O. Box 348, Mt. Morris, IL 61054. $29.95 yr.; $39.95 Canada; $50.95 foreign.
Sporting Classics

Sporting Classics, Inc.
PO Box 23707, Columbia, SC 29223/1-800-849-1004. 1 yr./6 issues/$23.95; 2 yrs./12 issues/$38.95; 3 yrs./18 issues/$47.95. Firearms & outdoor articles and columns.

Sporting Clays Magazine
Patch Communications, 5211 South Washington Ave., Titusville, FL 32780/407-268-5010; FAX: 407-267-7216. $29.95 yr. (12 issues). Official publication of the National Sporting Clays Association.

Sporting Goods Business
Miller Freeman, Inc., One Penn Plaza, 10th Fl., New York, NY 10119-0004. Trade journal.

Sporting Goods Dealer
Two Park Ave., New York, NY 10016. $100.00 yr. Sporting goods trade journal.

Sporting Gun
Bretton Court, Bretton, Peterborough PE3 8DZ, England. £27.00 (approx. U.S. $36.00), airmail £35.50 yr. For the game and clay enthusiasts.

Sports Afield
15621 Chemical Lane, Huntington Beach CA 92648. U.S./800-234-3537. International/714-894-9080. Nine issues for $29.97. Website: www.sportsafield.com. America's oldest outdoor publication is now devoted to high-end sporting pursuits, especially in North America and Africa.

The Squirrel Hunter
P.O. Box 368, Chireno, TX 75937. $14.00 yr. Articles about squirrel hunting.

Stott's Creek Calendar
Stott's Creek Printers, 2526 S 475 W, Morgantown, IN 46160/317-878-5489. 1 yr (3 issues) $11.50; 2 yrs. (6 issues) $20.00. Lists all gun shows everywhere in convenient calendar form; call for information.

Super Outdoors
2695 Aiken Road, Shelbyville, KY 40065/502-722-9463; 800-404-6064; Fax: 502-722-8093. Mark Edwards, publisher. Contact for details.

TACARMI
Via E. De Amicis, 25; 20123 Milano, Italy. $100.00 yr. approx. Antique and modern guns. (Italian text.)

Territorial Dispatch—1800s Historical Publication (M)
National Assn. of Buckskinners, 4701 Marion St., Suite 324, Livestock Exchange Bldg., Denver, CO 80216. Michael A. Nester & Barbara Wyckoff, editors. 303-297-9671.

Trap & Field
1000 Waterway Blvd., Indianapolis, IN 46202. $25.00 yr. Official publ. Amateur Trapshooting Assn. Scores, averages, trapshooting articles.

Turkey Call* (M)
Natl. Wild Turkey Federation, Inc., P.O. Box 530, Edgefield, SC 29824. $25.00 with membership (6 issues per yr.)

Turkey & Turkey Hunting*
Krause Publications, 700 E. State St., Iola, WI 54990-0001. $13.95 (6 issue p. yr.). Magazine with leading-edge articles on all aspects of wild turkey behavior, biology and the successful ways to hunt better with that info. Learn the proper techniques to calling, the right equipment, and more.

The U.S. Handgunner* (M)
U.S. Revolver Assn., 40 Larchmont Ave., Taunton, MA 02780. $10.00 yr. General handgun and competition articles. Bi-monthly sent to members.

U.S. Airgun Magazine
P.O. Box 2021, Benton, AR 72018/800-247-4867; Fax: 501-316-8549. 10 issues a yr. Cover the sport from hunting, 10-meter, field target and collecting. Write for details.

The Varmint Hunter Magazine (Q)
The Varmint Hunters Assn., Box 759, Pierre, SD 57501/800-528-4868. $24.00 yr.

Waffenmarkt-Intern
GFI-Verlag, Theodor-Heuss Ring 62, 50668 K"ln, Germany. Only for gunsmiths, licensed firearms dealers and their suppliers in Germany, Austria and Switzerland.

Wild Sheep (M) (Q)
Foundation for North American Wild Sheep, 720 Allen Ave., Cody, WY 82414. Website: http://iigi.com/os/non/fnaws/fnaws.htm; e-mail: fnaws@wyoming.com. Official journal of the foundation.

Wisconsin Outdoor Journal
Krause Publications, 700 E. State St., Iola, WI 54990-0001. $17.97 yr. (8 issues). For Wisconsin's avid hunters and fishermen, with features from all over that state with regional reports, legislative updates, etc. Website: www.krause.com

Women & Guns
P.O. Box 488, Sta. C, Buffalo, NY 14209. $24.00 yr. U.S.; $72.00 foreign (12 issues). Only magazine edited by and for women gun owners.

World War II*
Cowles History Group, 741 Miller Dr. SE, Suite D-2, Leesburg, VA 20175-8920. Annual subscriptions $19.95 U.S.; $25.95 Canada; 43.95 foreign. The title says it—WWII; good articles, ads, etc.

---

*Published bi-monthly
† Published weekly
‡Published three times per month. All others are published monthly.

M=Membership requirements; write for details.
Q=Published Quarterly.

THE ARMS LIBRARY

FOR COLLECTOR ◆ HUNTER ◆ SHOOTER ◆ OUTDOORSMAN

IMPORTANT NOTICE TO BOOK BUYERS

Books listed here may be bought from Ray Riling Arms Books Co., 6844 Gorsten St., Philadelphia, PA 19119, Phone 215-438-2456; FAX: 215-438-5395. E-Mail: sales@rayrilingarmsbooks.com. Larry Riling is the researcher and compiler of "The Arms Library" and a seller of gun books for over 32 years. The Riling stock includes books classic and modern, many hard-to-find items, and many not obtainable elsewhere. These pages list a portion of the current stock. They offer prompt, complete service, with delayed shipments occurring only on out-of-print or out-of-stock books.

Visit our web site at **www.rayrilingarmsbooks.com** and order all of your favorite titles on line from our secure site.

NOTICE FOR ALL CUSTOMERS: Remittance in U.S. funds must accompany all orders. For your convenience we accept VISA, MasterCard, Discover Card & American Express. For shipments in the U.S. add $7.00 for the 1st book and $2.00 for each additional book for postage and insurance. Minimum order $10.00. International Orders add $13.00 for the 1st book and $5.00 for each additional book. All International orders are shipped at the buyer's risk unless an additional $5 for insurance is included. USPS does not offer insurance to all countries unless shipped Air-Mail please e-mail or call for pricing.

Payments in excess of order or for "Backorders" are credited or fully refunded at request. Books "As-Ordered" are not returnable except by permission and a handling charge on these of 10% or $2.00 per book which ever is greater is deducted from refund or credit. Only Pennsylvania customers must include current sales tax.

A full variety of arms books also available from Rutgers Book Center, 127 Raritan Ave., Highland Park, NJ 08904/908-545-4344; FAX: 908-545-6686 or I.D.S.A. Books, 1324 Stratford Drive, Piqua, OH 45356/937-773-4203; FAX: 937-778-1922.

BALLISTICS AND HANDLOADING

ABC's of Reloading, 6th Edition, by C. Rodney James and the editors of Handloader's Digest, DBI Books, a division of Krause Publications, Iola, WI, 1997. 288 pp., illus. Paper covers. $21.95

The definitive guide to every facet of cartridge and shotshell reloading.

Accurate Arms Loading Guide Number 2, by Accurate Arms. McEwen, TN: Accurate Arms Company, Inc., 2000. Paper Covers. $22.95

Includes new data on smokeless powders XMR4064 and XMP5744 as well as a special section on Cowboy Action Shooting. The new manual includes 50 new pages of data. An appendix includes nominal rotor charge weights, bullet diameters.

The American Cartridge, by Charles Suydam, Borden Publishing Co. Alhambra, CA, 1986. 184 pp., illus. Softcover $24.95

An illustrated study of the rimfire cartridge in the United States.

Ammo and Ballistics II, by Robert W. Forker, Safari Press, Inc., Huntington Beach, CA., 2002. 298 pp., illustrated. Paper covers. $19.95

Ballistic data on 125 calibers and 1,400 loads out to 500 yards.

Ammunition: Grenades and Projectile Munitions, by Ian V. Hogg, Stackpole Books, Mechanicsburg, PA, 1998. 144 pp., illus. $24.00

Concise guide to modern ammunition. International coverage with detailed specifications and illustrations.

Barnes Reloading Manual #3, Barnes Bullets, American Fork, UT, 2003. 668 pp., illus. $29.95

Features data and trajectories on the new weight X, XBT and Solids in calibers from .22 to .50 BMG.

Blackpowder Loading Manual, 3rd Edition, by Sam Fadala, DBI Books, a division of Krause Publications, Iola, WI, 1995. 368 pp., illus. Paper covers. $20.95

Revised and expanded edition of this landmark blackpowder loading book. Covers hundreds of loads for most of the popular blackpowder rifles, handguns and shotguns.

Cartridges of the World, 10th Edition, by Frank Barnes, Krause Publications, Iola, WI, 2003. 512 pp., illus. Paper covers. $27.99

Completely revised edition of the general purpose reference work for which collectors, police, scientists and laymen reach first for answers to cartridge identification questions.

Cartridge Reloading Tools of the Past, by R.H. Chamberlain and Tom Quigley, Tom Quigley, Castle Rock, WA, 1998. 167 pp., illustrated. Paper covers. $25.00

A detailed treatment of the extensive Winchester and Ideal line of handloading tools and bullet molds, plus Remington, Marlin, Ballard, Browning, Maynard, and many others.

Cast Bullets for the Black Powder Rifle, by Paul A. Matthews, Wolfe Publishing Co., Prescott, AZ, 1996. 133 pp., illus. Paper covers. $22.50

The tools and techniques used to make your cast bullet shooting a success.

Complete Blackpowder Handbook, 4th Edition, by Sam Fadala, DBI Books, a division of Krause Publications, Iola, WI, 2001. 400 pp., illus. Paper covers. $22.95

Expanded and completely rewritten edition of the definitive book on the subject of blackpowder.

Complete Reloading Guide, by Robert & John Traister, Stoeger Publishing Co., Wayne, NJ, 1997. 608 pp., illus. Paper covers. $34.95

Perhaps the finest, most comprehensive work ever published on the subject of reloading.

Complete Reloading Manual, One Book / One Caliber. California: Load Books USA, 2000. $7.95 each

Containing unabridged information from U. S. Bullet and Powder Makers. With thousands of proven and tested loads, plus dozens of various bullet designs and different powders. Spiral bound. Available in all Calibers.

Designing and Forming Custom Cartridges for Rifles and Handguns, by Ken Howell. Precision Shooting, Manchester, CT. 2002. 600 pages, illus. $59.95

The classic work in its field, out of print for the last few years, and virtually unobtainable on the used book market, now returns in an exact reprint of the original. Some 600 pages, full size (8 1/2" x 11"), hard covers. Dozens of cartridge drawings never published anywhere before-dozens you've never heard of (guaranteed!). Precisely drawn to the dimensions specified by men who designed them, the factories that made them, and the authorities that set the standards. All drawn to the same format and scale (1.5x)-for most, how to form them from brass. Some 450 pages of them, two to a page. Plus other practical information.

Early Loading Tools & Bullet Molds, Pioneer Press, 1988. 88 pages, illustrated. Softcover. $7.50

German 7.9MM Military Ammunition 1888-1945, by Daniel Kent, Ann Arbor, MI: Kent, 1990. 153 pp., plus appendix. illus., b&w photos. $35.00

Handbook for Shooters and Reloaders, by P.O. Ackley, Salt Lake City, UT, 1998, (Vol. I), 567 pp., illus. Includes a separate exterior ballistics chart. $21.95; (Vol. II), a new printing with specific new material. 495 pp., illus. $20.95

Handgun Stopping Power; The Definitive Study, by Marshall & Sandow. Boulder, CO: Paladin Press, 1992. 240 pages. $45.00

Offers accurate predictions of the stopping power of specific loads in calibers from .380 Auto to .45 ACP, as well as such specialty rounds as the Glaser Safety Slug, Federal Hydra-Shok, MagSafe, etc. This is the definitive methodology for predicting the stopping power of handgun loads, the first to take into account what really happens when a bullet meets a man.

Handloader's Digest, 18th Edition, edited by Ken Ramage. Krause Publications, Iola, WI, 2003. 256 pp., illustrated. Paper covers. $22.95

Top writers in the field contribute helpful information on techniques and components. Greatly expanded and fully indexed catalog of all currently available tools, accessories and components for metallic, blackpowder cartridge, shotgun reloading and swaging.

Handloader's Manual of Cartridge Conversions, 2nd Revised Edition by John J. Donnelly, Stoeger Publishing Co., So. Hackensack, NJ, 2002. Unpaginated. $39.95

From 14 Jones to 70-150 Winchester in English and American cartridges, and from 4.85 U.K. to 15.2x28R Gevelot in metric cartridges. Over 900 cartridges described in detail.

Hatcher's Notebook, by S. Julian Hatcher, Stackpole Books, Harrisburg, PA, 1992. 488 pp., illus. $39.95

A reference work for shooters, gunsmiths, ballisticians, historians, hunters and collectors.

History and Development of Small Arms Ammunition; Volume 2 Centerfire: Primitive, and Martial Long Arms. by George A. Hoyem. Oceanside, CA: Armory Publications, 1991. 303 pages, illustrated. $60.00

Covers the blackpowder military centerfire rifle, carbine, machine gun and volley gun ammunition used in 28 nations and dominions, together with the firearms that chambered them.

History and Development of Small Arms Ammunition; Volume 4, American Military Rifle Cartridges. Oceanside, CA: Armory Publications, 1998. 244pp., illus. $60.00

Carries on what Vol. 2 began with American military rifle cartridges. Now the sporting rifle cartridges are at last organized by their originators-235 individual case types designed by eight makers of single shot rifles and four of magazine rifles from .50-140 Winchester Express to .22-15-60 Stevens. plus experimentals from .70-150 to .32-80. American Civil War enthusiasts and European collectors will find over 150 primitives in Appendix A to add to those in Volumes One and Two. There are 16 pages in full color of 54 box labels for Sharps, Remington and Ballard cartridges. There are large photographs with descriptions of 15 Maynard, Sharps, Winchester, Browning, Freund, Remington-Hepburn, Farrow and other single shot rifles, some of them rare one of a kind specimens.

Hornady Handbook of Cartridge Reloading, 6th Edition, Vol. I and II, Edited by Larry Steadman, Hornady Mfg. Co., Grand Island, NE, 2003., illus. $49.95

2 Volumes; Volume 1, 773 pp.; Volume 2, 717 pp. New edition of this famous reloading handbook covers rifle and handgun reloading data and ballistic tables.

Latest loads, ballistic information, etc.

How-To's for the Black Powder Cartridge Rifle Shooter, by Paul A. Matthews, Wolfe Publishing Co., Prescott, AZ, 1995. 45 pp. Paper covers. $22.50

Covers lube recipes, good bore cleaners and over-powder wads. Tips include compressing powder charges, combating wind resistance, improving ignition and much more.

The Illustrated Reference of Cartridge Dimensions, edited by Dave Scovill, Wolfe Publishing Co., Prescott, AZ, 1994. 343 pp., illus. Paper covers. $19.00

A comprehensive volume with over 300 cartridges. Standard and metric dimensions have been taken from SAAMI drawings and/or fired cartridges.

Loading the Black Powder Rifle Cartridge, by Paul A Matthews, Wolfe Publishing Co., Prescott, AZ, 1993. 121 pp., illus. Paper covers. $22.50

Author Matthews brings the blackpowder cartridge shooter valuable information on the basics, including cartridge care, lubes and moulds, powder charges and developing and testing loads in his usual authoritative style.

THE ARMS LIBRARY

Lyman Cast Bullet Handbook, 3rd Edition, edited by C. Kenneth Ramage, Lyman Publications, Middlefield, CT, 1980. 416 pp., illus. Paper covers. $19.95

Information on more than 5000 tested cast bullet loads and 19 pages of trajectory and wind drift tables for cast bullets.

Lyman Black Powder Handbook, 2nd Edition, edited by Sam Fadala, Lyman Products for Shooters, Middlefield, CT, 2000. 239 pp., illus. Paper covers. $19.95

Comprehensive load information for the modern blackpowder shooter.

Lyman Pistol & Revolver Handbook, 2nd Edition, edited by Thomas J. Griffin, Lyman Products Co., Middlefield, CT, 1996. 287 pp., illus. Paper covers. $18.95

The most up-to-date loading data available including the hottest new calibers, like 40 S&W, 9x21, 9mm Makarov, 9x25 Dillon and 454 Casull.

Lyman Reloading Handbook No. 48, edited by Thomas J. Griffin, Lyman Publications, Middlefield, CT, 2003. 480 pp., illus. Paper covers. $26.95

A comprehensive reloading manual complete with "How to Reload" information. Expanded data section with all the newest rifle and pistol calibers.

Lyman Shotshell Handbook, 4th Edition, edited by Edward A. Matunas, Lyman Products Co., Middlefield, CT, 1996. 330 pp., illus. Paper covers. $24.95

Has 9000 loads, including slugs and buckshot, plus feature articles and a full color I.D. section.Superb reference text.

Modern Combat Ammunition, by Duncan Long, Paladin Press, Boulder, CO, 1997, soft cover, photos, illus., 216 pp. $34.00

Now, Paladin's leading weapons author presents his exhaustive evaluation of the stopping power of modern rifle, pistol, shotgun and machine gun rounds based on actual case studies of shooting incidents. He looks at the hot new cartridges that promise to dominate well into the next century .40 S&W, 10mm auto, sub-sonic 9mm's - as well as the trusted standbys. Find out how to make your own exotic tracers, fléchette and sabot rounds, caseless ammo and fragmenting bullets.

Modern Exterior Ballistics, by Robert L. McCoy, Schiffer Publishing Co., Atglen, PA, 1999. 128 pp. $95.00

Advanced students of exterior ballistics and flight dynamics will find this comprehensive textbook on the subject a useful addition to their libraries.

Modern Reloading 2nd Edition, by Richard Lee, Inland Press, 2003. 623 pp., illus. $29.95

The how-to's of rifle, pistol and shotgun reloading plus load data for rifle and pistol calibers.

Modern Sporting Rifle Cartridges, by Wayne van Zwoll, Stoeger Publishing Co., Wayne, NJ, 1998. 310 pp., illustrated. Paper covers. $21.95

Illustrated with hundreds of photos and backed up by dozens of tables and schematic drawings, this four-part book tells the story of how rifle bullets and cartridges were developed and, in some cases, discarded.

Mr. Single Shot's Cartridge Handbook, by Frank de Haas, Mark de Haas, Orange City, IA, 1996. 116 pp., illus. Paper covers. $21.50

This book covers most of the cartridges, both commercial and wildcat, that the author has known and used.

Nosler Reloading Manual #5, edited by Gail Root, Nosler Bullets, Inc., Bend, OR, 2002. 516 pp., illus. $29.99

Combines information on their Ballistic Tip, Partition and Handgun bullets with traditional powders and new powders never before used, plus trajectory information from 100 to 500 yards.

The Paper Jacket, by Paul Matthews, Wolfe Publishing Co., Prescott, AZ, 1991. Paper covers. $14.50

Up-to-date and accurate information about paper-patched bullets.

Reloading Tools, Sights and Telescopes for S/S Rifles, by Gerald O. Kelver, Brighton, CO, 1982. 163 pp., illus. Softcover. $15.00

A listing of most of the famous makers of reloading tools, sights and telescopes with a brief description of the products they manufactured.

Reloading for Shotgunners, 4th Edition, by Kurt D. Fackler and M.L. McPherson, DBI Books, a division of Krause Publications, Iola, WI, 1997. 320 pp., illus. Paper covers. $19.95

Expanded reloading tables with over 11,000 loads. Bushing charts for every major press and component maker. All new presentation on all aspects of shotshell reloading by two of the top experts in the field.

The Rimfire Cartridge in the United States and Canada, Illustrated history of rimfire cartridges, manufacturers, and the products made from 1857-1984, by John L. Barber, Thomas Publications, Gettysburg, PA 2000. 1st edition. Profusely illustrated. 221 pages. $50.00

The author has written an encyclopedia of rimfire cartridges from the .22 to the massive 1.00 in. Gatling. Fourteen chapters, six appendices and an excellent bibliography make up a reference volume that all cartridge collectors should aquire.

Shotshells & Ballistics, Safari Press, 2002. 275pp, photos. Softcover, $19.95

There is a bewildering array of commercially loaded shotgun shells for sale, from the .410 to the 10-gauge. In fact, there are more types of shells and shot sizes on the market now than ever before. With this overwhelming selection of shells available, here, finally, is a practical, reasonably priced book that makes sense of it all. It lists commercially available shotshell loads from the .410-bore to the 10-gauge, in all shot sizes available, different shot types (lead, steel, bismuth, tungsten, and others) so that the shooter or hunter can quickly find what will be best for the gun he has and the game or targets he wants to shoot. Each shotgun shell with each loading has its own table--over 1,600 tables!!--showing shot size; weight of shot; recoil; average number of pellets in the shell; manufacturer's order number; shell length and type of hull; type of wad; and whether the shot is buffered or not. In addition, each table contains data that details velocity (in 10-yard intervals from 0 to 70 yards); average pellet energy; and time of flight in seconds. This book includes complete listings and tables of every load made from the following manufacturers: Aguilla, Armscorp, ARMUSA, Baschieri & Pellagri, Bismuth Cartridge Company, Clever, Dionisi, Dynamit Nobel, Eley Hawk, Federal, Fiocchi, Hevi-Shot (now loaded exclusively by Remington), Kent, Lightfield, Nobel Sport, PMC, RIO, Remington, Rotweil, Sellier & Bellot, RST, RWS, and Winchester. In addition, this informative reference contains authoritative articles on the history and development of shotshells, the components and technical data that govern production of shotshells, what load and shot size to use for what type of game or target, and much more. Never before has so much information on shotshells and ballistics been placed in a single book. Accentuated with photos from the field and the range, this is a reference book unlike any other.

Sierra Reloading Manual, 5th Edition: Rifle and Handgun Manual of Reloading Data. Sedalia, MO: Sierra Bullets, 2003. 5th edition. Hardcover. $39.95

This 1152 page manual retains the popular three-ring binder format and has been modernized with new cartridge information, histories and reloading recommendations. New bullets, new cartridges and new powders make this manual a necessity in every reloader's library.

Sixgun Cartridges and Loads, by Elmer Keith, The Gun Room Press, Highland Park, NJ, 1986. 151 pp., illus. $24.95

A manual covering the selection, uses and loading of the most suitable and popular revolver cartridges. Originally published in 1936. Reprint.

Speer Reloading Manual No. 13, edited by members of the Speer research staff, Omark Industries, Lewiston, ID, 1999. 621 pp., illustrated. $24.95

With thirteen new sections containing the latest technical information and reloading trends for both novice and expert in this latest edition. More than 9,300 loads are listed, including new propellant powders from Accurate Arms, Alliant, Hodgdon and Vihtavuori.

Stopping Power: A Practical Analysis of the Latest Handgun Ammunition, by Marshall & Sanow. Boulder, CO: Paladin Press, 2002. 1st edition. 600+ photos, 360 pp. Softcover. $49.95

If you want to know how handgun ammunition will work against human targets in the future, you must look at how similar ammo has worked against human targets in the past. Stopping Power bases its conclusions on real-world facts from real-world gunfights. It provides the latest street results of actual police and civilian shootings in all of the major handgun calibers, from .22 LR to .45 ACP, plus more than 30 chapters of vital interest to all gun owners. The only thing worse than being involved in a gunfight is losing one. The info. in this book will help you choose the right bullets for your gun so you don't lose.

Street Stoppers, The Latest Handgun Stopping Power Street Results, by Marshall & Lanow. Boulder, CO, Paladin Press, 1996. 374 pages, illus. Softcover. $42.95

Street Stoppers is the long-awaited sequel to Handgun Stopping Power. It provides the latest results of real-life shootings in all of the major handgun calibers, plus more than 25 thought-provoking chapters that are vital to anyone interested in firearms, would ballistics, and combat shooting. This book also covers the street results of the hottest new caliber to hit the shooting world in years, the .40 Smith & Wesson. Updated street results of the latest exotic ammunition including Remington Golden Saber and CCI-Speer Gold Dot, plus the venerable offerings from MagSafe, Glaser, Cor-Bon and others. A fascinating look at the development of Hydra-Shok ammunition is included.

Understanding Ballistics, Revised 2nd Edition by Robert A. Rinker, Mulberry House Publishing Co., Corydon, IN, 2000. 430 pp., illus Paper covers. New, Revised and Expanded. 2nd Edition. $24.95

Explains basic to advanced firearm ballistics in understandable terms.

Why Not Load Your Own?, by Col. T. Whelen, Gun Room Press, Highland Park, NJ 1996, 4th ed., rev. 237 pp., illus. $20.00

A basic reference on handloading, describing each step, materials and equipment. Includes loads for popular cartridges.

Wildcat Cartridges Volumes 1 & 2 Combination, by the editors of Handloaders magazine, Wolfe Publishing Co., Prescott, AZ, 1997. 350 pp., illus. Paper covers. $39.95

A profile of the most popular information on wildcat cartridges that appeared in the Handloader magazine.

COLLECTORS

18th Century Weapons of the Royal Welsh Fuziliers from Flixton Hall, by Goldstein, Erik. Thomas Publications, Gettysburg, PA: 2002. 1st edition. 126 pages, illustrated with b&w photos. Softcover. $19.95

A Glossary of the Construction, Decoration and Use of Arms and Armor in All Countries and in All Times, by George Cameron Stone., Dover Publishing, New York 1999. Softcover. $39.95

An exhaustive study of arms and armor in all countries through recorded history - from the stone age up to the second world war. With over 4500 b&w illustrations. This Dover edition is an unabridged republication of the work originally published in 1934 by the Southworth Press, Portland MA. A new Introduction has been specially prepared for this edition.

Ackermann Military Prints: Uniforms of the British and Indian Armies 1840-1855, by Carman, William Y. with Robert W. Kenny Jr. Schiffer Publications, Atglen, PA: 2002. 1st edition. 176 pages, with over 160 color images. $69.95

Accoutrements of the United States Infantry, Riflemen, and Dragoons 1834-1839, by R.T. Huntington, Historical Arms Series No. 20. Canada: Museum Restoration. 58 pp. illus. Softcover. $8.95

Although the 1841 edition of the U.S. Ordnance Manual provides ample information on the equipment that was in use during the 1840s, it is evident that the patterns of equipment that it describes were not introduced until 1838 or 1839. This guide is intended to fill this gap in our knowledge by providing an overview of what we now know about the accoutrements that were issued to the regular infantryman, rifleman, and dragoon, in the 1830's with excursions into earlier and later years.

Age of the Gunfighter; Men and Weapons on the Frontier 1840-1900, by Joseph G. Rosa, University of Oklahoma Press, Norman, OK, 1999. 192 pp., illustrated. Paper covers. $21.95

Stories of gunfighters and their encounters and detailed descriptions of virtually every firearm used in the old West.

Air Guns, by Eldon G. Wolff, Duckett's Publishing Co., Tempe, AZ, 1997. 204 pp., illus Paper covers. $35.00

Historical reference covering many makers, European and American guns, canes and more.

All About Southerners, by Lionel J. Bogut; including a detailed look at the characteristics & design of the "Best Little Pistol in the World," Sun City, CA: White Star, Inc., 2002. A limited edition of 1,000 copies. Signed and Numbered. 114 pages, including bibliography, and plenty of b&w photographs and detailed drawings. Hardcover. $29.95

Allied and Enemy Aircraft: May 1918; Not to be Taken from the Front Lines, Historical Arms Series No. 27. Canada: Museum Restoration. Softcover. $8.95

The basis for this title is a very rare identification manual published by the French government in 1918 that illustrated 60 aircraft with three or more views: French, English American, German, Italian, and Belgian, which might have been seen over the trenches ofFrance. Each is describe in a text translated from the original French. This is probably the most complete collection of illustrations of WW1 aircraft which has survived.

THE ARMS LIBRARY

American Beauty; The Prewar Colt National Match Government Model Pistol, by Timothy J. Mullin, Collector Grade Publications, Cobourg, Ontario, Canada. 72 pp., illustrated. $34.95
Includes over 150 serial numbers, and 20 spectacular color photos of factory engraved guns and other authenticated upgrades, including rare "double-carved" ivory grips.

American Civil War Artillery 1861-65: Field Artillery, by Katcher, Philip Oxford, United Kingdom: Osprey Publishing, 2001. 1st edition. 48 pages. Softcover. $14.95
Perhaps the most influential arm of either army in the prosecution of the American Civil War, the artillery of both sides grew to be highly professional organisations. This book covers all the major artillery pieces employed, including the Napoleon, Parrott Rifle and Mountain Howitzer.

American Military And Naval Belts, 1812-1902, by Dorsey, R. Stephen. Eugene, OR: Collectors Library, 2002. 1st edition. Hardcover. $80.00
With introduction by Norm Flayderman, this massive work is the NEW key reference on Sword Belts, Waist Belts, Sabre Belts, Shoulder Belts and Cartridge Belts (looped and non-looped). At over 460 pages, this 8.5x 11 inch book offers over 840 photos (primarily in color) and original period drawings. In addition, this work offers the first, comprehensive research on the Anson Mills Woven Cartridge Belts: the man, the company and its personalities, the belt-related patents and the government contracts from 1880 through 1902. This book is a "must" for all accoutrements collectors, military historians and museums

American Military Belt Plates, by O'Donnell, Michael J. and J. Duncan Campbell. Alexandria, VA: O'Donnell Publishing, 2000. 2nd edition. 614 pages, illus. Hardcover $49.00
At last available and well worth the wait! This massive study encompasses all the known plates from the Revolutionary War through the Spanish-American conflict. A sweeping, handsomely presented study that covers 1776 through 1910. Over 1,025 specimens are illustrated front and back along with many images of soldiers wearing various plates.

The American Military Saddle, 1776-1945, by R. Stephen Dorsey & Kenneth L. McPheeters, Collector's Library, Eugene, OR, 1999. 400 pp., illustrated. $67.00
The most complete coverage of the subject ever writeen on the American Military Saddle. Nearly 1000 actual photos and official drawings, from the major public and private collections in the U.S. and Great Britain.

American Police Collectibles; Dark Lanterns and Other Curious Devices, by Matthew G. Forte, Turn of the Century Publishers, Upper Montclair, NJ, 1999. 248 pp., illustrated. $24.95
For collectors of police memorabilia (handcuffs, police dark lanterns, mechanical and chain nippers, rattles, billy clubs and nightsticks) and police historians.

Ammunition; Small Arms, Grenades, and Projected Munitions, by Greenhill Publishing. 144 pp., Illustrated. 144 pp. As new – Hardcover.$22.95
The best concise guide to modern ammunition available today. Covers ammo for small arms, grenades, and projected munitions.

Antique Guns, the Collector's Guide, 2nd Edition, edited by John Traister, Stoeger Publishing Co., So. Hackensack, NJ, 1994. 320 pp., illus. Paper covers. $19.95
Covers a vast spectrum of pre-1900 firearms: those manufactured by U.S. gunmakers as well as Canadian, French, German, Belgian, Spanish and other foreign firms.

Arming the Glorious Cause; Weapons of the Second War for Independence, by James B. Whisker, Daniel D. Hartzler and Larry W. Tantz, Old Bedford Village Press, Bedford, PA., 1998. 175 pp., illustrated. $45.00
A photographic study of Confederate weapons.

Arms & Accoutrements of the Mounted Police 1873-1973, by Roger F. Phillips and Donald J. Klancher, Museum Restoration Service, Ont., Canada, 1982. 224 pp., illus. $49.95
A definitive history of the revolvers, rifles, machine guns, cannons, ammunition, swords, etc. used by the NWMP, the RNWMP and the RCMP during the first 100 years of the Force.

Arms and Armor in the Art Institute of Chicago, by Waltler J. Karcheski, Bulfinch, New York 1999. 128 pp., 103 color photos, 12 black & white illustrations. $50.00
The George F. Harding Collection of arms and armor is the most visited installation at the Art Institute of Chicago - a testament to the enduring appeal of swords, muskets and the other paraphernalia of medieval and early modern war. Organized both chronologically and by type of weapon, this book captures the best of this astonishing collection in 115 striking photographs - most in color - accompanied by illuminating text. Here are intricately filigreed breastplates and ivory-handled crossbows, samurai katana and Toledo-steel scimitars, elaborately decorated maces and beautifully carved flintlocks - a treat for anyone who has ever been beguiled by arms, armor and the age of chivalry.

Arms and Armor in Colonial America 1526-1783, by Harold Peterson, Dover Publishing, New York, 2000. 350 pages with over 300 illustrations, index, bibliography & appendix. Softcover. $34.95
Over 200 years of firearms, ammunition, equipment & edged weapons.

Arms and Armor: The Cleveland Museum of Art, by Stephen N. Fliegel, Abrams, New York, 1998. 172 color photos, 17 halftones. 181 pages. $49.50
Intense look at the culture of the warrior and hunter, with an intriguing discussion of the decorative arts found on weapons and armor, set against the background of political and social history. Also provides information on the evolution of armor, together with manufacture and decoration, and weapons as technology and art.

Arms Makers of Maryland, by Daniel D. Hartzler, George Shumway, York, PA, 1975. 200 pp., illus. $50.00
A thorough study of the gunsmiths of Maryland who worked during the late 18th and early 19th centuries.

Arms Makers of Western Pennsylvania, by James B. Whisker, Old Bedford Village Press. 1st edition. This deluxe hard bound edition has 176 pages, $50.00
Printed on fine coated paper, with many large photographs, and detailed text describing the period, lives, tools, and artistry of the Arms Makers of Western Pennsylvania.

Arsenal Of Freedom: The Springfield Armory 1890-1948, by Lt. Col. William Brophy, Andrew Mowbray, Inc., Lincoln, RI,1997. 20 pgs. of photos. 400 pages. As new - Softcover. $29.95
A year by year account drawn from offical records. Packed with reports, charts, tables, line drawings, and 20 page photo section.

Artistic Ingredients of the Longrifle, by George Shumway Publisher, 1989 102 pp., with 94 illus. $20.00
After a brief review of Pennsylvania-German folk art and architecture, to establish the artistic enviroment in which the longrifle was made, the author demonstrates that the sophisticated rococo decoration on the many of the finer longrifles is comparable to the best rococo work of Philadelphia cabinet makers and silversmiths.

Art of Miniature Firearms: Centuries of Craftsmanship, by Miniature Arms Society. Plainfield, IL: MAS Publications, 1999. Hardcover. $100.00
This volume of miniature arms includes some of the finest collector's items in existence, from antique replicas to contemporary pieces made by premium craftsmen working today, many of whom are members of the Miniature Arms Society. Beautiful color photographs highlight details of miniature firearms, including handguns, shoulder guns, and machine guns; cannon weaponry; weapons systems such as suits of armor, crossbows, and Gatling guns; and hand weapons, which include bows and arrows, daggers, knives, swords, maces, and spears. Also featured are exquisite replicas of accessories, from gun cases to cavalry saddles. 335 pages, full color photos.

The Art of Gun Engraving, by Claude Gaier and Pietro Sabatti, Knickerbocker Press, N.Y., 1999. 160 pp., illustrated. $34.95
The richness and detail lavished on early firearms represents a craftmanship nearly vanished. Beginning with crossbows in the 100's, hunting scenes, portraits, or mythological themes are intricately depicted within a few square inches of etched metal. The full-color photos contained herein recaptures this lost art with exquisite detail.

Artillery Fuses of the Civil War, by Charles H. Jones, O'Donnell Publishing, Alexandria, VA: 2001. Hardcover. $34.00
Chuck Jones has been recognized as the leading authority on Civil War fuses for decades. Over the course of "Artillery Fuses" 167 pages Mr. Jones imparts the reader with the culmination of his life-long study of the subject with well-researched text and hundreds of photographs of every type of Civil War fuse known. The book is hardbound, color cover format, printed on lustrous glossy paper. A valuable reference for every serious Civil War collector.

Astra Automatic Pistols, by Leonardo M. Antaris, FIRAC Publishing Co., Sterling, CO, 1989. 248 pp., illus. $55.00
Charts, tables, serial ranges, etc. The definitive work on Astra pistols.

Austrian & German Guns And Rifles (Fucili Da Caccia Austriaci E Tedeschi), by Marco E. Nobili, Italy: Il Volo Srl, 2000. 1st printing. 304 pages, illustrated with b&w photographs, plus 16 full color plates. Text in Italian and English. Hardcover. New in very good dust jacket. $189.95

Ballard: The Great American Single Shot Rifle, by John T. Dutcher. Denver, CO: Privately printed, 2002. 1st edition. 380 pages, illustrated with black & white photos, with 8-page color insert. Hardcover. New in new dust jacket. $79.95

Basic Documents on U.S. Martial Arms, commentary by Col. B. R. Lewis, reissue by Ray Riling, Phila., PA, 1956 and 1960. Rifle Musket Model 1855. Each $10.00
The first issue rifle of musket caliber, a muzzle loader equipped with the Maynard Primer, 32 pp. Rifle Musket Model 1863. The typical Union muzzle-loader of the Civil War, 26 pp. Breech-Loading Rifle Musket Model 1866. The first of our 50-caliber breechloading rifles, 12 pp. Remington Navy Rifle Model 1870. A commercial type breech-loader made at Springfield, 16 pp. Lee Straight Pull Navy Rifle Model 1895. A magazine cartridge arm of 6mm caliber. 23 pp. Breech-Loading Arms (five models) 27 pp. Ward-Burton Rifle Musket 1871-16 pp.

Battle Weapons of the American Revolution, by George C. Neuman, Scurlock Publishing Co., Texarkana, TX, 2001. 400 pp. Illus. Softcovers. $34.95
The most extensive photographic collection of Revolutionary War weapons ever in one volume. More than 1,600 photos of over 500 muskets, rifles, swords, bayonets, knives and other arms used by both sides in America's War for Independence.

The Bedford County Rifle and Its Makers, by George Shumway. 40pp. illustrated, Softcover. $10.00
The authors study of the graceful and distinctive muzzle-loading rifles made in Bedford County, Pennsylvania. Stands as a milestone on the long path to the understanding of America's longrifles.

The Belgian Rattlesnake; The Lewis Automatic Machine Gun, by William M. Easterly, Collector Grade Publications, Cobourg, Ontario, Canada, 1998. 584 pp., illustrated. $79.95
The most complete account ever published on the life and times of Colonel Isaac Newton Lewis and his crowning invention, the Lewis Automatic machine gun.

Beretta Automatic Pistols, by J.B. Wood, Stackpole Books, Harrisburg, PA, 1985. 192 pp., illus. $24.95
Only English-language book devoted to the Beretta line. Includes all important models.

Best Of Holland & Holland, England's Premier Gunmaker, by Michael McIntosh & Jan G. Roosenburg. Safari Press, Inc., Long Beach, CA: 2002. 1st edition. 298 pages. Profuse color illustrations. $69.95
Holland & Holland has had a long history of not only building London's "best" guns but also providing superior guns--the ultimate gun in finish, engraving, and embellishment. From the days of old in which a maharaja would order 100 fancifully engraved H&H shotguns for his guests to use at his duck shoot to the recent elaborately decorated sets depicting the Apollo 11 moon landing or the history of the British Empire, all of these guns represent the zenith in the art and craft of gunmaking and engraving. These and other H&H guns in the series named "Products of Excellence" are a cut above the ordinary H&H gun and hark back to a time when the British Empire ruled over one-third of the globe--a time when rulers, royalty, and the rich worldwide came to H&H for a gun that would elevate them above the crowd. In this book master gunwriter and acknowledged English gun expert Michael McIntosh and former H&H director Jan Roosenburg show us in words and pictures the finest products ever produced by H&H and, many would argue, by any gun company on earth. From a dainty and elegant .410 shotgun with gold relief engraving of scenes from Greek and Roman antiquity to the massive .700 Nitro Express double rifle, some of the most expensive and opulent guns ever produced on earth parade through these pages. An overview of the Products of Excellence series is given as well as a description and history of these special H&H guns. Never before have so many superlative guns from H&H--or any other maker for that manner--been displayed in one book. Many photos shown are firearms from private collections, which cannot be seen publicly anywhere except in this book. In addition, many interesting details and a general history of H&H are provided.

The Big Guns, Civil War Siege, Seacoast, and Naval Cannon, by Edwin Olmstead, Wayne E. Stark, and Spencer C. Tucker, Museum Restoration Service, Bloomfield, Ontario, Canada, 1997. 360 pp., illustrated. $80.00
This book is designed to identify and record the heavy guns available to both sides by the end of the Civil War.

Blue Book of Air Guns, 3rd Edition, edited by S.P. Fjestad, Blue Book Publications, Inc. Minneapolis, MN 2003. $24.95
This new 3rd Edition simply contains more airgun values and information than any other single publication.

THE ARMS LIBRARY

Blue Book of Gun Values, 25th Edition, edited by S.P. Fjestad, Blue Book Publications, Inc. Minneapolis, MN 2004. $39.95

This new 25th Edition simply contains more firearms values and information than any other single publication. Expanded to over 1,600 pages featuring over 100,000 firearms prices, the new Blue Book of Gun Values also contains over Ω million words of text – no other book is even close! Most of the information contained in this publication is simply not available anywhere else, for any price!

Blue Book of Modern Black Powder Values, 3rd Edtion by Dennis Adler, Blue Book Publications, Inc. Minneapolis, MN 2003. 271 pp., illustrated. 41 color photos. Softcover. $24.95

This new title contains more up-to-date black powder values and related information than any other single publication. This new book will keep you up to date on modern black powder models and prices, including most makes & models introduced this year!

The Blunderbuss 1500-1900, by James D. Forman, Historical Arms Series No. 32. Canada: Museum Restoration, 1994.

An excellent and authoritative booklet giving tons of information on the Blunderbuss, a very neglected subject. 40 pages, illustrated. Softcover. $8.95

Boarders Away I: With Steel-Edged Weapons & Polearms, by William Gilkerson, Andrew Mowbray, Inc. Publishers, Lincoln, RI, 1993. 331 pages. $48.00

Contains the essential 24 page chapter 'War at Sea' which sets the historical and practical context for the arms discussed. Includeds chapters on, Early Naval Weapons, Boarding Axes, Cutlasses, Officers Fighting Swords and Dirks, and weapons at hand of Random Mayhem.

Boarders Away, Volume II: Firearms of the Age of Fighting Sail, by William Gilkerson, Andrew Mowbray, Inc. Publishers, Lincoln, RI, 1993. 331 pp., illus. $65.00

Covers the pistols, muskets, combustibles and small cannon used aboard American and European fighting ships, 1626-1826.

Boston's Gun Bible, by Boston T. Party, Ignacio, CO: Javelin Press, August 2000. Expanded Edition. Softcover. $28.00

This mammoth guide for gun owners everywhere is a completely updated and expanded edition (more than 500 new pages!) of Boston T. Party's classic Boston on Guns and Courage. Pulling no punches, Boston gives new advice on which shoulder weapons and handguns to buy and why before exploring such topics as why you should consider not getting a concealed carry permit, what guns and gear will likely be outlawed next, how to spend within your budget, why you should go to a quality defensive shooting academy now, which guns and gadgets are inferior and why, how to stay off illegal government gun registration lists, how to spot an undercover agent trying to entrap law-abiding gun owners and much more.

The Bren Gun Saga, by Thomas B. Dugelby, Collector Grade Publications, Cobourg, Ontario, Canada, 1999, revised and expanded edition. 406 pp., illustrated. $65.95

A modern, definitive book on the Bren in this revised expanded edition, which in terms of numbers of pages and illustrations is nearly twice the size of the original.

British Board of Ordnance Small Arms Contractors 1689-1840, by De Witt Bailey, Rhyl, England: W. S. Curtis, 2000. 150 pp. $18.00

Thirty years of research in the Archives of the Ordnance Board in London has identified more than 600 of these suppliers. The names of many can be found marking the regulation firearms of the period. In the study, the contractors are identified both alphabetically and under a combination of their date period together with their specialist trade.

The British Enfield Rifles, Volume 1, The SMLE Mk I and Mk III Rifles, by Charles R. Stratton, North Cape Pub. Tustin, CA, 1997. 150 pp., illus. Paper covers. $16.95

A systematic and thorough examination on a part-by-part basis of the famous British battle rifle that endured for nearly 70 years as the British Army's number one battle rifle.

British Enfield Rifles, Volume 2, No.4 and No.5 Rifles, by Charles R. Stratton, North Cape Publications, Tustin, CA, 1999. 150 pp., illustrated. Paper covers. $16.95

The historical background for the development of both rifles describing each variation and an explanation of all the "marks", "numbers" and codes found on most parts.

British Enfield Rifles, Volume 4, The Pattern 1914 and U. S. Model 1917 Rifles, by Charles R. Stratton, North Cape Publications, Tustin, CA, 2000. Paper covers. $16.95

One of the lease know American and British collectible military rifles is analyzed on a part by part basis. All markings and codes, refurbishment procedures and WW 2 upgrade are included as are the various sniper rifle versions.

The British Falling Block Breechloading Rifle from 1865, by Jonathan Kirton, Tom Rowe Books, Maynardsville, TN, 2nd edition, 1997. 380 pp., illus. $70.00

Expanded 2nd edition of a comprehensive work on the British falling block rifle.

British Gun Engraving, by Douglas Tate, Safari Press, Inc., Huntington Beach, CA, 1999. 240 pp., illustrated. Limited, signed and numbered edition, in a slipcase. $80.00

A historic and photographic record of the last two centuries.

British Military Flintlock Rifles 1740-1840, with a remarkable weath of data about the Rifleman and Regiments that carried these weapons, by Bailey, De Witt. Andrew Mowbray, Inc. Lincoln, RI:, 2002. 1st edition. 264 pages with over 320 photographs. Hardcover. $47.95

Pattern 1776 Rifles, The Ferguson Breechloader, The famous Baker Rifle, rifles of the Hessians and other German Mercenaries, American Loylist Rifles, rifles given to Indians, Cavalry Rifles and rifled carbines, bayonets, accoutrements, ammunition and more.

British Service Rifles and Carbines 1888-1900, by Alan M. Petrillo, Excaliber Publications, Latham, NY, 1994. 72 pp., illus, Paper covers. $11.95

A complete review of the Lee-Metford and Lee-Enfield rifles and carbines.

British Single Shot Rifles, Volume 1, Alexander Henry, by Wal Winfer, Tom Rowe, Maynardsville, TN, 1998, 200 pp., illus. $50.00

Detailed Study of the single shot rifles made by Henry. Illustrated with hundreds of photographs and drawings.

British Single Shot Rifles Volume 2, George Gibbs, by Wal Winfer, Tom Rowe, Maynardsville, TN, 1998. 177 pp., illus. $50.00

Detailed study of the Farquharson as made by Gibbs. Hundreds of photos.

British Single Shot Rifles, Volume 3, Jeffery, by Wal Winfer, Rowe Publications, Rochester, N.Y., 1999. 260 pp., illustrated. $60.00

The Farquharsen as made by Jeffery and his competitors, Holland & Holland, Bland, Westley, Manton. Large section on the development of nitro cartridges including the .600.

British Single Shot Rifles, Vol. 4; Westley Richards, by Wal Winfer, Rowe Publications, Rochester, N.Y., 2000. 265 pages, illustrated, photos. $60.00

In his 4th volume Winfer covers a detailed study of the Westley Richards single shot rifles, including Monkey Tails, Improved Martini, 1872,1873, 1878,1881, 1897 Falling Blocks. He also covers Westley Richards Cartridges, History and Reloading information.

The British Soldier's Firearms from Smoothbore to Rifled Arms, 1850-1864, by Dr. C.H. Roads, R&R Books, Livonia, NY, 1994. 332 pp., illus. $49.00

A reprint of the classic text covering the development of British military hand and shoulder firearms in the crucial years between 1850 and 1864.

British Sporting Guns & Rifles, compiled by George Hoyem, Armory Publications, Coeur d'Alene, ID, 1997. 1024 pp., illus. In two volumes. $250.00

Eighteen old sporting firearms trade catalogs and a rare book reproduced with their color covers in a limited, signed and numbered edition.

Broad Arrow: British & Empire Factory Production, Proof, Inspection, Armourers, Unit & Issue Markings, by Ian Skennerton. Australia: Arms & Militaria Press, 2001. 140 pp, circa 80 illus. Stiff paper covers. $29.95

Thousands of service markings are illustrated and their applications described. Invaluable reference on units, also ideal for medal collectors.

Browning Dates of Manufacture, compiled by George Madis, Art and Reference House, Brownsboro, TX, 1989. 48 pp. $10.00

Gives the date codes and product codes for all models from 1824 to the present.

Browning Sporting Firearms: Dates Of Manufacture, by D. R. Morse. Phoenix, AZ: Firing Pin Enterprizes, 2003. 37 pages. Softcover. New. $6.95

Covers their pistols, revolvers, rifles, shotguns and commemoratives. Plus, Models & Serial Numbers.

Bullard Firearms, by G. Scott Jamieson, Schiffer Publications, Atglen, PA 2002. 1st edition. 400 pages, with over 1100 color and b&w photographs, charts, diagrams. Hardcover. $100.00

Bullard Firearms is the story of a mechanical genius whose rifles and cartridges were the equal of any made in America in the 1880s, yet little of substance had been written about James H. Bullard or his arms prior to 1988 when the first edition called Bullard Arms was published. This greatly expanded volume with over 1,000 b&w and 150 color plates, most not previously published answers many of the questions posed in the first edition. The book is divided into eleven chapters each covering a different aspect of the Bullard story. Each model is covered in depth with many detailed photographs of the interior parts and workings of the repeaters. Chapter nine covers the fascinating and equally unknown world of Bullard cartridges and reloading tools. The final chapter outlines in chart form almost 500 Bullard rifles by serial number, caliber and type. Quick and easy to use, this book is a real benefit for collectors and dealers alike.

Burning Powder, compiled by Major D.B. Wesson, Wolfe Publishing Company, Prescott, AZ, 1992. 110 pp. Soft cover. $10.95

A rare booklet from 1932 for Smith & Wesson collectors.

The Burnside Breech Loading Carbines, by Edward A. Hull, Andrew Mowbray, Inc., Lincoln, RI, 1986. 95 pp., illus. $16.00

No. 1 in the "Man at Arms Monograph Series." A model-by-model historical/technical examination of one of the most widely used cavalry weapons of the American Civil War based upon important and previously unpublished research.

Cacciare A Palla: Uso E Tecnologia Dell'arma Rigata, by Marco E. Nobili. Italy: Il Volo Srl, 1994. 4th Edition - 1st printing. 397 pages, illustrated with b&w photographs. Hardcover. New in new dust jacket. $75.00

Camouflage Uniforms of European and NATO Armies; 1945 to the Present, by J. F. Borsarello, Atglen, PA: Schiffer Publications. Over 290 color and b&w photographs, 120 pages. Softcover. $29.95

This full-color book covers nearly all of the NATO, and other European armies' camouflaged uniforms, and not only shows and explains the many patterns, but also their efficacy of design. Described and illustrated are the variety of materials tested in over forty different armies, and includes the history of obsolete trial tests from 1945 to the present time. More than two hundred patterns have been manufactured since World War II using various landscapes and seasonal colors for their look. The Vietnam and Gulf Wars, African or South American events, as well as recent Yugoslavian independence wars have been used as experimental terrains to test a variety of patterns. This book provides a superb reference for the historian, reenactor, designer, and modeler.

Camouflage Uniforms of the Waffen-SS A Photographic Reference, by Michael Beaver, Schiffer Publishing, Atglen, PA. Over 1,000 color and b&w photographs and illustrations, 296 pages. $69.95

Finally a book that unveils the shroud of mystery surrounding Waffen-SS camouflage clothing. Illustrated here, both in full color and in contemporary b&w photographs, this unparalleled look at Waffen-SS combat troops and their camouflage clothing will benefit both the historian and collector.

Canadian Colts for the Boer War, by Col. Robert D. Whittington III. Hooks, TX: Brownlee Books, 2003. A limited edition of 1,000 copies. Numbered. 5 pages. Paper Covers. New. $15.00

A study of Colt Revolvers issued to the First and Second Canadian Contingents Special Service Force.

Canadian Gunsmiths from 1608: A Checklist of Tradesmen, by John Belton, Historical Arms Series No. 29. Canada: Museum Restoration, 1992. 40 pp., 17 illustrations. Softcover. $8.95

This Checklist is a greatly expanded version of HAS No. 14, listing the names, occupation, location, and dates of more than 1,500 men and women who worked as gunmakers, gunsmiths, armorers, gun merchants, gun patent holders, and a few other gun related trades. A collection of contemporary gunsmiths' letterhead have been provided to add color and depth to the study.

Cap Guns, by James Dundas, Schiffer Publishing, Atglen, PA, 1996. 160 pp., illus. Paper covers. $29.95

Over 600 full-color photos of cap guns and gun accessories with a current value guide.

Carbines of the Civil War, by John D. McAulay, Pioneer Press, Union City, TN, 1981. 123 pp., illus. Paper covers. $12.95

A guide for the student and collector of the colorful arms used by the Federal cavalry.

Carbines of the U.S. Cavalry 1861-1905, by John D. McAulay, Andrew Mowbray Publishers, Lincoln, RI, 1996. $35.00

Covers the crucial use of carbines from the beginning of the Civil War to the end of the cavalry carbine era in 1905.

Cartridge Carbines of the British Army, by Alan M. Petrillo, Excalibur Publications, Latham, NY, 1998. 72 pp., illustrated. Paper covers. $11.95

Begins with the Snider-Enfield which was the first regulation cartridge carbine introduced in 1866 and ends with the .303 caliber No.5, Mark 1 Enfield.

THE ARMS LIBRARY

Cartridge Reloading Tools of the Past, by R.H. Chamberlain and Tom Quigley, Tom Quigley, Castle Rock, WA, 1998. 167 pp., illustrated. Paper covers. $25.00

A detailed treatment of the extensive Winchester and Ideal lines of handloading tools and bulletmolds plus Remington, Marlin, Ballard, Browning and many others.

Cartridges for Collectors, by Fred Datig, Pioneer Press, Union City, TN, 1999. In three volumes of 176 pp. each. Vol.1 (Centerfire); Vol.2 (Rimfire and Misc.) types. Volume 1, softcover only, $19.95. Volumes 2 & 3, Hardcover. $19.95

Vol.3 (Additional Rimfire, Centerfire, and Plastic.). All illustrations are shown in full-scale drawings.

Civil War Arms Makers and Their Contracts, edited by Stuart C. Mowbray and Jennifer Heroux, Andrew Mowbray Publishing, Lincoln, RI, 1998. 595 pp. $39.50

A facsimile reprint of the Report by the Commissioner of Ordnance and Ordnance Stores, 1862.

Civil War Arms Purchases and Deliveries, edited by Stuart C. Mowbray, Andrew Mowbray Publishing, Lincoln, RI, 1998. 300pp., illus. $39.50

A facsimile reprint of the master list of Civil War weapons purchases and deliveries including Small Arms, Cannon, Ordnance and Projectiles.

Civil War Breech Loading Rifles, by John D. McAulay, Andrew Mowbray, Inc., Lincoln, RI, 1991. 144 pp., illus. Paper covers. $15.00

All the major breech-loading rifles of the Civil War and most, if not all, of the obscure types are detailed, illustrated and set in their historical context.

Civil War Cartridge Boxes of the Union Infantryman, by Paul Johnson, Andrew Mowbray, Inc., Lincoln, RI, 1998. 352 pp., illustrated. $45.00

There were four patterns of infantry cartridge boxes used by Union forces during the Civil War. The author describes the development and subsequent pattern changes to these cartridge boxes.

Civil War Collector's Price Guide; Expanded Millennium Edition, by North South Trader. Orange, VA: Publisher's Press, 2000. 9th edition. 260 pps., illus. Softcover. $29.95

All updated prices, scores of new listings, and hundreds of new pictures! It's the one reference work no collector should be without. An absolute must.

Civil War Commanders, by Dean Thomas, Thomas Publications, Gettysburg, PA. 1998. 72 pages, illustrated, photos. Paper Covers. $9.95

138 photographs and capsule biographies of Union and Confederate officers. A convenient personalities reference guide.

Civil War Guns, by William B. Edwards, Thomas Publications, Gettysburg, PA, 1997. 444 pp., illus. $40.00

The complete story of Federal and Confederate small arms; design, manufacture, identifications, procurement issue, employment, effectiveness, and postwar disposal by the recognized expert.

Civil War Infantryman: In Camp, On the March, and in Battle, by Dean Thomas, Thomas Publications, Gettysburg, PA. 1998. 72 pages, illustrated, Softcovers. $12.95

Uses first-hand accounts to shed some light on the "common soldier" of the Civil War from enlistment to muster-out, including camp, marching, rations, equipment, fighting, and more.

Civil War Pistols, by John D. McAulay, Andrew Mowbray Inc., Lincoln, RI, 1992. 166 pp., illus. $38.50

A survey of the handguns used during the American Civil War.

Civil War Projectiles II; Small Arms & Field Artillery, with Supplement, by McKee, W. Reid, and M. E. Mason, Jr. Orange, VA: Publisher's Press, 2001. The standard reference work is now available. 202 pages, illus. Hardcover. $40.00

Essential for every Civil War bullet collector.

Civil War Sharps Carbines and Rifles, by Earl J. Coates and John D. McAulay, Thomas Publications, Gettysburg, PA, 1996. 108 pp., illus. Paper covers. $12.95

Traces the history and development of the firearms including short histories of specific serial numbers and the soldiers who received them.

Civil War Small Arms of the U.S. Navy and Marine Corps, by John D. McAulay, Mowbray Publishing, Lincoln, RI, 1999. 186 pp., illustrated. $39.00

The first reliable and comprehensive guide to the firearms and edged weapons of the Civil War Navy and Marine Corps.

The W.F. Cody Buffalo Bill Collector's Guide with Values, by James W. Wojtowicz, Collector Books, Paducah, KY, 1998. 271 pp., illustrated. $24.95

A profusion of colorful collectibles including lithographs, programs, photographs, books, medals, sheet music, guns, etc. and today's values.

Col. Burton's Spiller & Burr Revolver, by Matthew W. Norman, Mercer University Press, Macon, GA, 1997. 152 pp., illus. $22.95

A remarkable archival research project on the arm together with a comprehensive story of the establishment and running of the factory.

Collector's Guide to Colt .45 Service Pistols Models of 1911 and 1911A1, Enlarged and revised 3rd edition. Clawson Publications, Fort Wayne, IN, 2004. 146 pp., illustrated. $39.95

From 1911 to the end of production in 1945 with complete military identification including all contractors.

A Collector's Guide to United States Combat Shotguns, by Bruce N. Canfield, Andrew Mowbray Inc., Lincoln, RI, 1992. 184 pp., illus. Paper covers. $24.00

This book provides full coverage of combat shotguns, from the earliest examples right up to the Gulf War and beyond.

A Collector's Guide to Winchester in the Service, by Bruce N. Canfield, Andrew Mowbray, Inc., Lincoln, RI, 1991. 192 pp., illus. Paper covers. $24.00

The firearms produced by Winchester for the national defense. From Hotchkiss to the M14, each firearm is examined and illustrated.

A Collector's Guide to the '03 Springfield, by Bruce N. Canfield, Andrew Mowbray Inc., Lincoln, RI, 1989. 160 pp., illus. Paper covers. $24.00

A comprehensive guide follows the '03 through its unparalleled tenure of service. Covers all of the interesting variations, modifications and accessories of this highly collectible military rifle.

Collector's Illustrated Encyclopedia of the American Revolution, by George C. Neumann and Frank J. Kravic, Rebel Publishing Co., Inc., Texarkana, TX, 1989. 286 pp., illus. $36.95

A showcase of more than 2,300 artifacts made, worn, and used by those who fought in the War for Independence.

Colonial Frontier Guns, by T.M. Hamilton, Pioneer Press, Union City, TN, 1988. 176 pp., illus. Paper covers. $17.50

A complete study of early flint muskets of this country.

Colt and its Collectors Exhibition Catalog for Colt: The Legacy of a Legend, Buffalo Bill Historical Center, Cody, Wyoming, by Paul Goodwin and the Colt Collectors Association (Andrus, Fees, Fjestad, Houze, Newman, Roes, and Winchester) Colt Collectors Association, 2003. 1st edition. More than 400 color pages and a comprehensive index. Hardcover. New in new dust jacket. $125.00

Colt and Its Collectors accompanies the upcoming special exhibition, Colt: The Legacy of a Legend, opening at the Buffalo Bill Historical Center in May 2003. Numerous essays, over 750 color photographs by Paul Goodwin.

The Colt Engraving Book, Volumes I & II, by R. L. Wilson. Privately Printed, 2001. Each volume is appx. 500 pages, with 650 illustrations, most in color. $390.00

This third edition from the original texts of 1974 and 1982 has been fine-tuned and dramatically expanded, and is by far the most illuminating and complete. With over 1,200 illustrations, more than 2/3 of which are in color, this book joins the author's The Book of Colt Firearms, and Fine Colts as companion volumes. Approximately 1,000 pages in two volumes, each signed by the author, serial numbered, and strictly limited to 3000 copies. Volume I covers from the Paterson and pre-Paterson period through c.1921 (end of the Helfricht period). Volume II commences with Kornbrath, and Glahn, and covers Colt embellished arms from c.1919 through 2000.

The Colt Armory, by Ellsworth Grant, Man-at-Arms Bookshelf, Lincoln, RI, 1996. 232 pp., illus. $35.00

A history of Colt's Manufacturing Company.

The Colt Model 1905 Automatic Pistol, by John Potocki, Andrew Mowbray Publishing, Lincoln, RI, 1998. 191 pp., illus. $28.00

Covers all aspects of the Colt Model 1905 Automatic Pistol, from its invention by the legendary John Browning to its numerous production variations.

Colt Peacemaker British Model, by Keith Cochran, Cochran Publishing Co., Rapid City, SD, 1989. 160 pp., illus. $35.00

Covers those revolvers Colt squeezed in while completing a large order of revolvers for the U.S. Cavalry in early 1874, to those magnificent cased target revolvers used in the pistol competitions at Bisley Commons in the 1890s.

Colt Peacemaker Encyclopedia, by Keith Cochran, Keith Cochran, Rapid City, SD, 1986. 434 pp., illus. $60.00

A must book for the Peacemaker collector.

Colt Peacemaker Encyclopedia, Volume 2, by Keith Cochran, Cochran Publishing Co., SD, 1992. 416 pp., illus. $60.00

Included in this volume are extensive notes on engraved, inscribed, historical and noted revolvers, as well as those revolvers used by outlaws, lawmen, movie and television stars.

Colt Presentations: From The Factory Ledgers 1856-1869, by Herbert G. Houze. Lincoln, RI: Andrew Mowbray, Inc., 2003. 112 pages, 45 b&w photos. Softcover. $21.95

Samuel Colt was a generous man. He also used gifts to influence government decision makers. But after Congress investigated him in 1854, Colt needed to hide the gifts from prying eyes, which makes it very difficult for today's collectors to document the many revolvers presented by Colt and the factory. Using the original account journals of the Colt's Patent Fire Arms Manufacturing Co., renowned arms authority Herbert G. Houze finally gives us the full details behind hundreds of the most exciting Colts ever made.

Colt Revolvers and the Tower of London, by Joseph G. Rosa, Royal Armouries of the Tower of London, London, England, 1988. 72 pp., illus. Soft covers. $15.00

Details the story of Colt in London through the early cartridge period.

Colt's SAA Post War Models, by George Garton, The Gun Room Press, Highland Park, NJ, 1995. 166 pp., illus. $39.95

Complete facts on the post-war Single Action Army revolvers. Information on calibers, production numbers and variations taken from factory records.

Colt Single Action Army Revolvers: The Legend, the Romance and the Rivals, by "Doc" O'Meara, Krause Publications, Iola, WI, 2000. 160 pp., illustrated with 250 photos in b&w and a 16 page color section. $34.95

Production figures, serial numbers by year, and rarities.

Colt Single Action Army Revolver Study: New Discoveries, by Kenneth Moore, Lincoln, RI: Andrew Mowbray, Inc., 2003. 1st edition. 200 pages, with 77 photos and illustrations. Hardcover. New. $49.95

25 years after co-authoring the classic Study of the Colt Single Action Army Revolver, Ken fills in the gaps and sets the record straight. Decades in the making, this impressive new study brings us entirely up to date, including all the new research that the author has painstakingly gathered over the years. The serial number data alone will astound you. Includes, ejector models, special section on low serial numbers, U.S. Army testing data, new details about militia S.A.A.'s plus a true wealth of cartridge info.

Colt Single Action Army Revolvers and Alterations, by C. Kenneth Moore, Mowbray Publishers, Lincoln, RI, 1999. 112 pp., illustrated. $35.00

A comprehensive history of the revolvers that collectors call "Artillery Models." These are the most historical of all S.A.A. Colts, and this new book covers all the details.

Colt Single Action Army Revolvers and the London Agency, by C. Kenneth Moore, Andrew Mowbray Publishers, Lincoln, RI, 1990. 144 pp., illus. $35.00

Drawing on vast documentary sources, this work chronicles the relationship between the London Agency and the Hartford home office.

The Colt U.S. General Officers' Pistols, by Horace Greeley IV, Andrew Mowbray Inc., Lincoln, RI, 1990. 199 pp., illus. $38.00

These unique weapons, issued as a badge of rank to General Officers in the U.S. Army from WWII onward, remain highly personal artifacts of the military leaders who carried them. Includes serial numbers and dates of issue.

Colts from the William M. Locke Collection, by Frank Sellers, Andrew Mowbray Publishers, Lincoln, RI, 1996. 192 pp., illus. $55.00

This important book illustrates all of the famous Locke Colts, with captions by arms authority Frank Sellers.

Colt's Dates of Manufacture 1837-1978, by R.L. Wilson, published by Maurie Albert, Coburg, Australia; N.A. distributor Madis Books, TX, 1997. 61 pp. $7.50

An invaluable pocket guide to the dates of manufacture of Colt firearms up to 1978.

Colt's Pocket '49: Its Evolution Including the Baby Dragoon and Wells Fargo, by Robert Jordan and Darrow Watt, privately printed, Loma Mar, CA 2000. 304 pages, with 984 color photos, illus. Beautifully bound in a deep blue leather like case. $125.00

Detailed information on all models and covers engaving, cases, accoutrements, holsters, fakes, and much more. Included is a summary booklet containing information such as serial numbers, production ranges & identifing photos. This book is a masterpiece on its subject.

Colt Sporting Firearms: Dates Of Manufacture, by Morse, D. R. Phoenix, AZ: Firing Pin Enterprizes, 2003. 82 pages. Softcover. New. $6.95

Covers their pistols, revolvers, rifles, shotguns and commemoratives. Plus models & serial numbers.

THE ARMS LIBRARY

Combat Helmets Of The Third Reich: A Study In Photographs, by Kibler, Thomas Pottsboro, TX: Reddick Enterprises, 2003. 1st edition. 96 pages, illustrated in full color. Pictorial softcover. New. $19.95

Complete Guide to all United States Military Medals 1939 to Present, by Colonel Frank C. Foster, Medals of America Press, Fountain Inn, SC, 2000. 121 pp,.illustrated, photos. $29.95

Complete criteria for every Army, Navy, Marines, Air Force, Coast Guard, and Merchant Marine awards since 1939. All decorations, service medals, and ribbons shown in full-color and accompanied by dates and campaigns as well as detailed descriptions on proper wear and display.

Complete Guide to the M1 Garand and the M1 Carbine, by Bruce N. Canfield, 2nd printing, Andrew Mowbray Inc., Lincoln, RI, 1999. 296 pp., illus. $39.50

Expanded and updated coverage of both the M1 Garand and the M1 Carbine, with more than twice as much information as the author's previous book on this topic.

The Complete Guide to U.S. Infantry Weapons of the First War, by Bruce Canfield, Andrew Mowbray, Publisher, Lincoln, RI, 2000. 304 pp., illus. $39.95

The definitive study of the U.S. Infantry weapons used in WW1.

The Complete Guide to U.S. Infantry Weapons of World War Two, by Bruce Canfield, Andrew Mowbray, Publisher, Lincoln, RI, 1995. 303 pp., illus. $39.95

A definitive work on the weapons used by the United States Armed Forces in WWII.

Confederate Belt Buckles & Plates by Mullinax, Steve E. O'Donnell Publishing, Alexandria, VA: 1999. Expanded edition. Hardbound, 247 pages, illus. Hardcover. $34.00

Hundreds of crisp photographs augment this classic study of Confederate accoutrement plates.

Confederate Carbines & Musketoons: Cavalry Small Arms manufactured in and for the Southern Confederacy 1861-1865, by Murphy, John M. Santa Ana, CA: Privately printed, 2002. Reprint. 320 pages, illustrated with b&w drawings and photos. Color front is by Don Troiani. Hardcover. $79.95

This is Dr. Murphy's first work on Confederate arms. See also "Confederate Rifles & Muskets". Exceptional photography compliments the text. John Murphy has one of the finest collections of Confederate arms known.

Confederate Rifles & Muskets: Infantry Small Arms Manufactured in the Southern Confederacy 1861-1865, by John M. Murphy. Santa Ana, CA: Privately printed, 1996. Reprint. 768pp, 8pp color plates, profusely illustrated. Hardcover. $119.95

The first in-depth and academic analysis and discussion of the "long" longarms produced in the South by and for the Confederacy during the American Civil War. The collection of Dr. Murphy is doubtless the largest and finest grouping of Confederate longarms in private hands today.

Confederate Saddles & Horse Equipment, by Knopp, Ken R. Orange, VA: Publisher's Press, 2002. 194 pps., illus. Hardcover. $39.95

Confederate Saddles & Horse Equipment is a pioneer work on the subject. After ten years of research Ken Knopp has compiled a thorough and fascinating study of the little-known field of Confederate saddlery and equipment. His analysis of ordnance operations coupled with his visual presentation of surviving examples offers an indispensable source for collectors and historians.

A Concise Guide to the Artillery at Gettysburg, by Gregory Coco, Thomas Publications, Gettysburg, PA, 1998. 96 pp., illus. Paper Covers. $10.00

Coco's tenth book on Gettysburg is a beginner's guide to artillery and its use at the battle. It covers the artillery batteries describing the types of cannons, shells, fuses, etc.using interesting narrative and human interest stories.

Cooey Firearms, Made in Canada 1919-1979, by John A. Belton, Museum Restoration, Canada, 1998. 36pp., with 46 illus. Paper Covers. $8.95

More than 6 million rifles and at least 67 models, were made by this small Canadian riflemaker. They have been identified from the first 'Cooey Canuck' through the last variations made by the 'Winchester-Cooey'. Each is descibed and most are illustrated in this first book on The Cooey.

Cowboy Collectibles and Western Memorabilia, by Bob Bell and Edward Vebell, Schiffer Publishing, Atglen, PA, 1992. 160 pp., illus. Paper covers. $29.95

The exciting era of the cowboy and the wild west collectibles including rifles, pistols, gun rigs, etc.

Cowboy Culture: The Last Frontier of American Antiques, by Michael Friedman, Schiffer Publishing, Ltd., West Chester, PA, 2002. 300 pp., illustrated. $89.95

Covers the artful aspects of the old west, the antiques and collectibles. Illustrated with clear color plates of over 1,000 items such as spurs, boots, guns, saddles etc.

Cowboy and Gunfighter Collectible, by Bill Mackin, Mountain Press Publishing Co., Missoula, MT, 1995. 178 pp., illus. Paper covers. $25.00

A photographic encyclopedia with price guide and makers' index.

Cowboys and the Trappings of the Old West, by William Manns and Elizabeth Clair Flood, Zon International Publishing Co., Santa Fe, NM, 1997, 1st edition. 224 pp., illustrated. $45.00

A pictorial celebration of the cowboys dress and trappings.

C. S. Armory Richmond: History of the Confederate States Armory, Richmond, VA and the Stock Shop at the C.S. Armory, Macon, GA., by Paul Davies. Privately printed, 2000. 368 pages, illustrated with black & white photos. Hardcover. $89.95

The American Society of Arms Collectors is pleased to recommend C.S. Armory Richmond as a useful and valuable reference for collectors and scholars in the field of antique firearms. Gives fantastic explanations of machinery, stocks, barrels, and every facet of the production process during the timeframe covered in this book. He taught us that the SA cartouche on some long arms does not stand for Springfield Armory. Instead, it stands for Sam Adams. We also know about high-hump locks and low-hump locks. In his research for his book, which represents a true labor of love, he found one-half of the original payrolls from the Richmond Armory and the last official letter sent from the Armory in February 1865.

Custom Firearms Engraving, by Tom Turpin, Krause Publications, Iola, WI, 1999. 208 pp., illustrated. $49.95

Over 200 four-color photos with more than 75 master engravers profiled. Engravers Directory with addresses in the U.S. and abroad.

Daisy Air Rifles & BB Guns: The First 100 Years, by Neal Punchard. St. Paul, MN: Motorbooks, 2002. 1st edition. Hardcover, 10 x 10, 156 pp, 300 color. Hardcover. $29.95

Flash back to the days of your youth and recall fond memories of your Daisy. Daisy Air Rifles and BB Guns looks back fondly on the first 100 years of Daisy BB rifles and pistols, toy and cork guns, accessories, packaging, period advertising and literature. Wacky ads and catalogs conjure grins of pure nostalgia as chapters reveal how Daisy used a combination of savvy business sense and quality products to dominate the market.

The Decorations, Medals, Ribbons, Badges and Insignia of the United States Army; World War 2 to Present, by Col. Frank C. Foster, Medals of America Press, Fountain Inn, SC. 2001. 145 pages, illustrated. $29.95

The most complete guide to United States Army medals, ribbons, rank, insignia nad patches from WWII to the present day. Each medal and insignia shown in full color. Includes listing of respective criteria and campaigns.

The Decorations, Medals, Ribbons, Badges and Insignia of the United States Navy; World War 2 to Present, by James G. Thompson, Medals of America Press, Fountain Inn, SC. 2000. 123 pages, illustrated. $29.95

The most complete guide to United States Army medals, ribbons, rank, insignia nad patches from WWII to the present day. Each medal and insignia shown in full color. Includes listing of respective criteria and campaigns.

Defending The Dominion, Canadian Military Rifles, 1855-1955, by David Edgecombe. Service Publications, Ont. Canada, 2003. 168 pages, with 60+ illustrations. Hardcover. $39.95

This book contains much new information on the Canadian acquisition, use and disposal of military rifles during the most significant century in the development of small arms. In addition to the venerable Martini-Henry, there are chapters on the Winchester, Snider, Starr, Spencer, Peabody, Enfield rifles and others.

The Derringer in America, Volume 1, The Percussion Period, by R.L. Wilson and L.D. Eberhart, Andrew Mowbray Inc., Lincoln, RI, 1985. 271 pp., illus. $48.00

A long awaited book on the American percussion deringer.

The Derringer in America, Volume 2, The Cartridge Period, by L.D. Eberhart and R.L. Wilson, Andrew Mowbray Inc., Publishers, Lincoln, RI, 1993. 284 pp., illus. $65.00

Comprehensive coverage of cartridge deringers organized alphabetically by maker. Includes all types of deringers known by the authors to have been offered to the American market.

The Devil's Paintbrush: Sir Hiram Maxim's Gun, by Dolf Goldsmith, 3rd Edition, expanded and revised, Collector Grade Publications, Toronto, Canada, 2002. 384 pp., illus. $79.95

The classic work on the world's first true automatic machine gun.

Die Wehrmacht, Volume One, by Uwe Feist, Ryton Publications, Bellingham, WA, 2000. Large format (8-3/4" x 11-1/2") hardbound book with over 250 b&w photos and 240 color prints, all on high quality coated paper. Hardcover. $65.00

This is a great reference book, the first in a new series dedicated to the weapons, uniforms and equipment of the German Wehrmacht in World War II. This first volume deals exclusively with over three dozen infantry assult weapons including the Mk b-42, P-38, P.P.K., MG-42, MP-28/11, and many, many more. Beautifully illustrated with hundreds of color and b&w photos of the various weapons, ammunition, and accessories. Includes color photos of each weapon, plus hundreds of wartime photos.

Dr. Josephus Requa Civil War Dentist and the Billinghurst-Requa Volley Gun, by John M. Hyson, Jr., & Margaret Requa DeFrancisco, Museum Restoration Service, Bloomfield, Ont., Canada, 1999. 36 pp., illus. Paper covers. $8.95

The story of the inventor of the first practical rapid-fire gun to be used during the American Civil War.

The Dutch Luger (Parabellum) A Complete History, by Bas J. Martens and Guus de Vries, Ironside International Publishers, Inc., Alexandria, VA, 1995. 268 pp., illus. $49.95

The history of the Luger in the Netherlands. An extensive description of the Dutch pistol and trials and the different models of the Luger in the Dutch service.

The Eagle on U.S. Firearms, by John W. Jordan, Pioneer Press, Union City, TN, 1992. 140 pp., illus. Paper covers. $17.50

Stylized eagles have been stamped on government owned or manufactured firearms in the U.S. since the beginning of our country. This book lists and illustrates these various eagles in an informative and refreshing manner.

Early Gunpowder Artillery 1300-1600, by Norris, John. London: The Crowood Press, 2003. 1st edition. 141 pages, with 160 b&w photos. Hardcover. $34.95

In the 300-year time span covered by this book, gunpowder artillery was developed from a novelty to a serious weapon of war. By 1600 the cannon was to be found in large numbers on the battlefield, on board ship and on defensive positions on buildings and city walls. Illustrated with contemporary and modern photographs of surviving and recreated weapons, Early Gunpowder Artillery 1300-1600 sheds light on these earliest ancestors of the modern cannon and field gun. Looking not only at the weapons themselves, but also at the men who made and used them, and the tactics with which they were deployed, this is the ideal introduction for anyone interested in medieval warfare.

E. F.Lli Piotti Italian Fine Gun Maker, by Nobili, Marco Italy: Il Volo Srl, 2000. 1st Printing. 221 pages, illustrated with b&w photographs, plus 22 full color plates. Text in Italian and English. Hardcover. New in new dust jacket. $189.95

Encyclopedia of Rifles & Handguns; A Comprehensive Guide to Firearms, edited by Sean Connolly, Chartwell Books, Inc., Edison, NJ., 1996. 160 pp., illustrated. $26.00

A lavishly illustrated book providing a comprehensive history of military and civilian personal firepower.

Eprouvettes: A Comprehensive Study of Early Devices for the Testing of Gunpowder, by R.T.W. Kempers, Royal Armouries Museum, Leeds, England, 1999. 352 pp., illustrated with 240 black & white and 28 color plates. $125.00

The first comprehensive study of eprouvettes ever attempted in a single volume.

Fifteen Years in the Hawken Lode, by John D. Baird, The Gun Room Press, Highland Park, NJ, 1976. 120 pp., illus. $24.95

A collection of thoughts and observations gained from many years of intensive study of the guns from the shop of the Hawken brothers.

'51 Colt Navies, by Nathan L. Swayze, The Gun Room Press, Highland Park, NJ, 1993. 243 pp., illus. $59.95

The Model 1851 Colt Navy, its variations and markings.

Fighting Iron, by Art Gogan, Andrew Mowbray, Inc., Lincoln, R.I., 2002. 176 pp., illustrated. $28.00

It doesn't matter whether you collect guns, swords, bayonets or accountrement— sooner or later you realize that it all comes down to the metal. If you don't understand the metal you don't understand your collection.

THE ARMS LIBRARY

Fine Colts, The Dr. Joseph A. Murphy Collection, by R.L. Wilson, Sheffield Marketing Associates, Inc., Doylestown, PA, 1999. 258 pp., illustrated. Limited edition signed and numbered. $99.00
This lavish new work covers exquisite, deluxe and rare Colt arms from Paterson and other percussion revolvers to the cartridge period and up through modern times.

Firearms, by Derek Avery, Desert Publications, El Dorado, AR, 1999. 95 pp., illustrated. $9.95
The firearms included in this book are by necessity only a selection, but nevertheless one that represents the best and most famous weapons seen since the Second World War.

Firearms and Tackle Memorabilia, by John Delph, Schiffer Publishing, Ltd., West Chester, PA, 1991. 124 pp., illus. $39.95
A collector's guide to signs and posters, calendars, trade cards, boxes, envelopes, and other highly sought after memorabilia. With a value guide.

Firearms of the American West 1803-1865, Volume 1, by Louis A. Garavaglia and Charles Worman, University of Colorado Press, Niwot, CO, 1998. 402 pp., illustrated. $79.95
Traces the development and uses of firearms on the frontier during this period.

Firearms of the American West 1866-1894, Volume 2, by Louis A. Garavaglia and Charles G. Worman, University of Colorado Press, Niwot, CO, 1998. 416 pp., illus. $79.95
A monumental work that offers both technical information on all of the important firearms used in the West during this period and a highly entertaining history of how they were used, who used them, and why.

Firearms from Europe, 2nd Edition, by David Noe, Larry W. Yantz, Dr. James B. Whisker, Rowe Publications, Rochester, N.Y., 2002. 192 pp., illustrated. $45.00
A history and description of firearms imported during the American Civil War by the United States of America and the Confederate States of America.

Firepower from Abroad, by Wiley Sword, Andrew Mowbray Publishing, Lincoln, R.I., 2000. 120 pp., illustrated. $23.00
The Confederate Enfield and the LeMat revolver and how they reached the Confederate market.

Flayderman's Guide to Antique American Firearms and Their Values, 8th Edition, edited by Norm Flayderman, Krause Publications, Iola, WI, 2001. 692 pp., illus. Paper covers. $34.95
A completely updated and new edition with more than 3,600 models and variants extensively described with all marks and specifications necessary for quick identification.

The FN-FAL Rifle, et al, by Duncan Long, Paladin Press, Boulder, CO, 1999. 144 pp., illustrated. Paper covers. $18.95
Detailed descriptions of the basic models produced by Fabrique Nationale and the myriad variants that evolved as a result of the firearms universal acceptance.

The .45-70 Springfield; Book 1, by Frasca, Albert and Robert Hill. Frasca, Albert and Robert Hill . Frasca Publishing, 2000. Memorial Edition. Hardback with gold embossed cover and spine. $95.00
The Memorial Edition reprint of The .45-70 SPRINGFIELD was done to honor Robert H. Hill who was an outstanding Springfield collector, historian, researcher, and gunsmith. Only 1000 of these highly regarded books were printed using the same binding and cover material as the original 1980 edition. The book is considered The Bible for .45-70 Springfield Trapdoor collectors.

The .45-70 Springfield Book II 1865-1893, by Frasca, Albert. Frasca Publishing, Springfield, Ohio 1997 Hardback with gold embossed cover and spine. The book has 400+ pages and 400+ photographs which cover ALL the trapdoor Springfield models. Hardback with gold embossed cover and spine. $85.00
A MUST for the trapdoor collector!

The .45-70 Springfield, by Joe Poyer and Craig Riesch, North Cape Publications, Tustin, CA, 1996. 150 pp., illus. Paper covers. $16.95
A revised and expanded second edition of a best-selling reference work organized by serial number and date of production to aid the collector in identifying popular "Trapdoor" rifles and carbines.

Freund & Bro. Pioneer Gunmakers to the West, by F.J. Pablo Balentine, Graphic Publishers, Newport Beach, CA, 1997. 380 pp., illustrated $69.95
The story of Frank W. and George Freund, skilled German gunsmiths who plied their trade on the Western American frontier during the final three decades of the nineteenth century.

The Fusil de Tulole in New France, 1691-1741, by Russel Bouchard, Museum Restorations Service, Bloomfield, Ontario, Canada, 1997. 36 pp., illus. Paper covers. $8.95
The development of the company and the identification of their arms.

The Gas Trap Garand, by Billy Pyle, Collector Grade Publications, Cobourg, Ontario, Canada, 1999 316 pp., illustrated. $59.95
The in-depth story of the rarest Garands of them all, the initial 80 Model Shop rifles made under the personal supervision of John Garand himself in 1934 and 1935, and the first 50,000 plus production "gas trap" M1's manufactured at Springfield Armory between August, 1937 and August, 1940.

George Schreyer, Sr. and Jr., Gunmakers of Hanover, Pennsylvania, by George Shumway, George Shumway Publishers, York, PA, 1990. 160pp., illus. $50.00
This monograph is a detailed photographic study of almost all known surviving long rifles and smoothbore guns made by highly regarded gunsmiths George Schreyer, Sr.

The German Assault Rifle 1935-1945, by Peter R. Senich, Paladin Press, Boulder, CO, 1987. 328 pp., illus. $60.00
A complete review of machine carbines, machine pistols and assault rifles employed by Hitler's Wehrmacht during WWII.

German Cross in Gold - Holders of the SS and Police, by Mark Yerger. San Jose, CA: Bender Publishing, 2004. 1st edition. 432 pages - 295 photos / illustrations - deluxe binding. Hardcover. New. $44.95
Commencing an unprecedented study detailing all SS and Police holders of the German Cross in Gold by unit, the first of two volumes of this new series examines the holders of the 2.SS-Panzer-Division "Das Reich." More than twenty years of research provide comprehensive information for the holders of this prestigious decoration to include the combat narrative that actually resulted in the award. Also included are all other awards, promotions, and known service history. Aside from full information on each individual, detailed data is provided for the various elements they were assigned to within the Division and other postings held in the course of their often diverse careers. Heavily illustrated with rare photos and documents, many were provided by the recipients themselves who fully supported the research. The actual award recommendation documents are seen and the approval process fully examined, adding tho an invaluable study for the historian. The illustrations also provide a wealth of information for collectors of uniforms, insignia, medals, documents, and autographs. An appendix includes the most detailed Order of Battle listing of commands compiled to date, as well as new data on the Division's Roll of Honor Clasp and Close Combat Clasp in Gold holders. Foreward by "Das Reich" Knight's Cross and German Cross in Gold winner Siegfried Brosow.

The German K98k Rifle, 1934-1945: The Backbone of the Wehrmacht, by Richard D. Law, Collector Grade Publications, Toronto, Canada, 1993. 336 pp., illus. $69.95
The most comprehensive study ever published on the 14,000,000 bolt-action K98k rifles produced in Germany between 1934 and 1945.

German Machine Guns, by Daniel D. Musgrave, revised edition, Ironside International Publishers, Inc. Alexandria, VA, 1992. 586 pp., 650 illus. $49.95
The most definitive book ever written on German machineguns. Covers the introduction and development of machineguns in Germany from 1899 to the rearmament period after WWII.

German Military Rifles and Machine Pistols, 1871-1945, by Hans Dieter Gotz, Schiffer Publishing Co., West Chester, PA, 1990. 245 pp., illus. $35.00
This book portrays in words and pictures the development of the modern German weapons and their ammunition including the scarcely known experimental types.

The Government Models, by William H.D. Goddard, Andrew Mowbray Publishing, Lincoln, RI, 1998. 296 pp., illustrated. $58.50
The most authoritative source on the development of the Colt model of 1911.

Grasshoppers and Butterflies, by Adrian B. Caruana, Museum Restoration Service, Alexandria, Bay, N.Y., 1999. 32 pp., illustrated. Paper covers. $8.95
No.39 in the Historical Arms Series. The light 3 pounders of Pattison and Townsend.

The Greener Story, by Graham Greener, Quiller Press, London, England, 2000. 256 pp., illustrated with 32 pages of color photos. $69.95
W.W. Greener, his family history, inventions, guns, patents, and more.

The Greenhill Dictionary of Guns and Gunmakers: From Colt's First Patent to the Present Day, 1836-2001, by John Walter, Greenhill Publishing, 2001, 1st edition, 576 pages, illustrated with 200 photos, 190 trademarks and 40 line drawings, Hardcover: $59.95
Covers military small arms, sporting guns and rifles, air and gas guns, designers, inventors, patentees, trademarks, brand names and monograms.

Grenade - British and Commonwealth Hand and Rifle Grenades, by Rick Landers, Norman Bonney & Gary Oakley. Australia: Privately Printed, 2001. 1st edition. 294 pages, illustrated with b&w photos drawings. Hardcover. New in New Dust Jacket. $69.95
Covers from type no.1 to no. 95 includes dischargers, fuzes, markings, equipment.

A Guide to American Trade Catalogs 1744-1900, by Lawrence B. Romaine, Dover Publications, New York, NY. 422 pp., illus. Paper covers. $12.95

A Guide to Ballard Breechloaders, by George J. Layman, Pioneer Press, Union City, TN, 1997. 261 pp., illus. Paper covers. $19.95
Documents the saga of this fine rifle from the first models made by Ball & Williams of Worchester, to its production by the Marlin Firearms Co, to the cessation of 19th century manufacture in 1891, and finally to the modern reproductions made in the 1990's.

A Guide To Civil War Artillery Projectiles, by Jack W. Melton, and Lawrence E. Pawl. Kennesaw, GA: Kennesaw Mounton Press, 1996. 96 pps., illus. Softcover. $9.95
The concise pictorial study belongs on the shelf of every enthusiast. Hundreds of crisp photographs and a wealth of rich, well-researched information.

A Guide to the Maynard Breechloader, by George J. Layman, George J. Layman, Ayer, MA, 1993. 125 pp., illus. Paper covers. $11.95
The first book dedicated entirely to the Maynard family of breech-loading firearms. Coverage of the arms is given from the 1850s through the 1880s.

A Guide to U. S. Army Dress Helmets 1872-1904, by Kasal and Moore, North Cape Publications, 2000. 88 pp., illus. Paper covers. $15.95
This thorough study provides a complete description of the Model 1872 & 1881 dress helmets worn by the U.S. Army. Including all componets from bodies to plates to plumes & shoulder cords and tells how to differentiate the originals from reproductions. Extensively illustrated with photographs, '8 pages in full color' of complete helmets and their components.

The Gun And Its Development, by W.W. Greener, New York: Lyons Press, 2002. 9th Edition. Rewritten, and with many Additional Illustrations. 804 pages plus advertising section. Contains over 700 illustrations plus many tables. Softcover. $19.95
A famed book of great value, truly encyclopedic in scope and sought after by firearms collectors.

Gun Collecting, by Geoffrey Boothroyd, Sportsman's Press, London, 1989. 208 pp., illus. $29.95
The most comprehensive list of 19th century British gunmakers and gunsmiths ever published.

Gunmakers of London 1350-1850 with Supplement, by Howard L. Blackmore, Museum Restoration Service, Alexandria Bay, NY, 1999. 222 pp., illus. 2 volumes. Slipcased. $135.00
A listing of all the known workmen of gun making in the first 500 years, plus a history of the guilds, cutlers, armourers, founders, blacksmiths, etc. 260 gunmarks are illustrated. Supplement is 156 pages, and Begins with an introductory chapter on "foreighn" gunmakers followed by records of all the new information found about previously unidentified armourers, gunmakers and gunsmiths.

The Guns that Won the West: Firearms of the American Frontier, 1865-1898, by John Walter, Stackpole Books, Inc., Mechanicsburg, PA.,1999. 256 pp., illustrated. $34.95
Here is the story of the wide range of firearms from pistols to rifles used by plainsmen and settlers, gamblers, native Americans and the U.S. Army.

Gunsmiths of Illinois, by Curtis L. Johnson, George Shumway Publishers, York, PA, 1995. 160 pp., illus. $50.00
Genealogical information is provided for nearly one thousand gunsmiths. Contains hundreds of illustrations of rifles and other guns, of handmade origin, from Illinois.

The Gunsmiths of Manhattan, 1625-1900: A Checklist of Tradesmen, by Michael H. Lewis, Museum Restoration Service, Bloomfield, Ont., Canada, 1991. 40 pp., illus. Paper covers. $8.95
This listing of more than 700 men in the arms trade in New York City prior to about the end of the 19th century will provide a guide for identification and further research.

The Guns of Dagenham: Lanchester, Patchett, Sterling, by Peter Laidler and David Howroyd, Collector Grade Publications, Inc., Cobourg, Ont., Canada, 1995. 310 pp., illus. $39.95
An in-depth history of the small arms made by the Sterling Company of Dagenham, Essex, England, from 1940 until Sterling was purchased by British Aerospace in 1989 and closed.

THE ARMS LIBRARY

Guns of the Western Indian War, by R. Stephen Dorsey, Collector's Library, Eugene, OR, 1997. 220 pp., illus. Paper covers. $30.00

The full story of the guns and ammunition that made western history in the turbulent period of 1865-1890.

Gun Powder Cans & Kegs, by Ted & David Bacyk and Tom Rowe, Rowe Publications, Rochester, NY, 1999. 150 pp., illus. $65.00

The first book devoted to powder tins and kegs. All cans and kegs in full color. With a price guide and rarity scale.

The Guns of Remington: Historic Firearms Spanning Two Centuries, compiled by Howard M. Madaus, Biplane Productions, Publisher, in cooperation with Buffalo Bill Historical Center, Cody, WY, 1998. 352 pp., illustrated with over 800 color photos. $79.95

A complete catalog of the firearms in the exhibition, "It Never Failed Me: The Arms & Art of Remington Arms Company" at the Buffalo Bill Historical Center, Cody, Wyoming.

Gun Tools, Their History and Identification by James B. Shaffer, Lee A. Rutledge and R. Stephen Dorsey, Collector's Library, Eugene, OR, 1992. 375 pp., illus. $30.00

Written history of foreign and domestic gun tools from the flintlock period to WWII.

Gun Tools, Their History and Identifications, Volume 2, by Stephen Dorsey and James B. Shaffer, Collectors' Library, Eugene, OR, 1997. 396 pp., illus. Paper covers. $30.00

Gun tools from the Royal Armouries Museum in England, Pattern Room, Royal Ordnance Reference Collection in Nottingham and from major private collections.

Gunsmiths of the Carolinas 1660-1870, by Daniel D. Hartzler and James B. Whisker, Old Bedford Village Press, Bedford, PA, 1998. 176 pp., illustrated. $40.00

This deluxe hard bound edition of 176 pages is printed on fine coated paper, with about 90 pages of large photographs of fine longrifles from the Carolinas, and about 90 pages of detailed research on the gunsmiths who created the highly prized and highly collectable longrifles. Dedicated to serious students of original Kentucky rifles, who may seldom encounter fine longrifles from the Carolinas.

Gunsmiths of Maryland, by Daniel D. Hartzler and James B. Whisker, Old Bedford Village Press, Bedford, PA, 1998. 208 pp., illustrated. $45.00

Covers firelock Colonial period through the breech-loading patent models. Featuring longrifles.

Gunsmiths of Virginia, by Daniel D. Hartzler and James B. Whisker, Old Bedford Village Press, Bedford, PA, 1992. 206 pp., illustrated. $40.00

A photographic study of American longrifles.

Gunsmiths of West Virginia, by Daniel D. Hartzler and James B. Whisker, Old Bedford Village Press, Bedford, PA, 1998. 176 pp., illustrated. $40.00

A photographic study of American longrifles.

Gunsmiths of York County, Pennsylvania, by Daniel D. Hartzler and James B. Whisker, Old Bedford Village Press, Bedford, PA, 1998. 160 pp., illus. $40.00

160 pages of photographs and research notes on the longrifles and gunsmiths of York County, Pennsylvania. Many longrifle collectors and gun builders have noticed that York County style rifles tend to be more formal in artistic decoration than some other schools of style. Patriotic themes, and folk art were popular design elements.

Hall's Military Breechloaders, by Peter A. Schmidt, Andrew Mowbray Publishers, Lincoln, RI, 1996. 232 pp., illus. $55.00

The whole story behind these bold and innovative firearms.

Harrington & Richardson Sporting Firearms: Dates of Manufacture 1871-1991, by D. R. Morse. Phoenix, AZ: Firing Pin Enterprizes, 2003. 14 pages. Softcover. NEW. $6.95

Covers their pistols, revolvers, rifles, shotguns and commemoratives. Plus models.

The Hawken Rifle: Its Place in History, by Charles E. Hanson, Jr., The Fur Press, Chadron, NE, 1979. 104 pp., illus. Paper covers. $15.00

A definitive work on this famous rifle.

Hi-Standard Sporting Firearms: Dates of Manufacture, by D. R. Morse. 1926-1992. Phoenix, AZ: Firing Pin Enterprizes, 2003. Plus models & serial numbers. 22 pages. Softcover. New. $6.95

Covers their pistols, revolvers, rifles, shotguns and commemoratives.

High Standard: A Collector's Guide to the Hamden & Hartford Target Pistols, by Tom Dance, Andrew Mowbray, Inc., Lincoln, RI, 1991. 192 pp., illus. Paper covers. $24.00

From Citation to Supermatic, all of the production models and specials made from 1951 to 1984 are covered according to model number or series.

Historical Hartford Hardware, by William W. Dalrymple, Colt Collector Press, Rapid City, SD, 1976. 42 pp., illus. Paper covers. $10.00

Historically associated Colt revolvers.

The History and Development of Small Arms Ammunition, Volume 2, by George A. Hoyem, Armory Publications, Oceanside, CA, 1991. 303 pp., illus. $65.00

Covers the blackpowder military centerfire rifle, carbine, machine gun and volley gun ammunition used in 28 nations and dominions, together with the firearms that chambered them.

The History and Development of Small Arms Ammunition, Volume 4, by George A. Hoyem, Armory Publications, Seattle, WA, 1998. 200 pp., illustrated $65.00

A comprehensive book on American black powder and early smokeless rifle cartridges.

The History of Colt Firearms, by Dean Boorman, Lyons Press, New York, NY, 2001. 144 pp., illus. $29.95

Discover the fascinating story of the world's most famous revolver, complete with more than 150 stunning full-color photographs.

History of the German Steel Helmet: 1916-1945, by Ludwig Baer. Bender Publishing, San Jose, CA, 2001. 448 pages, nearly 1,000 photos & illustrations. $54.95

This publication is the most complete and detailed German steel helmet book ever produced, with in-depth documentated text and nearly 1,000 photographs and illustrations encompassing all German steel helmets from 1916 through 1945. The regulations, modifications and use of camouflage are carefully clarified for the Imperial Army, Reichswehr and the numerous 3rd Reich organizations.

History of Modern U.S. Military Small Arms Ammunition. Volume 1, 1880-1939, revised by F.W. Hackley, W.H. Woodin and E.L. Scranton, Thomas Publications, Gettysburg, PA, 1998. 328 pp., illus. $49.95

This revised edition incorporates all publicly available information concerning military small arms ammunition for the period 1880 through 1939 in a single volume.

Based on decades of original research conducted at the National Archives, numerous military, public and private museums and libraries, as well as individual collections, this edition incorporates all publicly available information concerning military small arms ammunition for the period 1940 through 1945.

The History Of Smith & Wesson Firearms, by Dean Boorman, Lyons Press, New York, NY, 2002. 44 pages, illustrated in full color. Hardcover. New in new dust jacket. $29.95

The definitive guide to one of the world's best-known firearms makers. Takes the story through the years of the Military & Police .38 & of the Magnum cartridge, to today's wide range of products for law-enforcement customers.

The History of Winchester Rifles, by Dean Boorman, Lyons Press, New York, NY, 2001. 144 pp., illus. 150 full-color photos. $29.95

A captivating and wonderfully photographed history of one of the most legendary names in gun lore.

HK Heckler & Koch, by Manfred Kersten and Walter Schmid. The official history of the Oberndorf company of Heckler & Koch. Sterling, VA: Privately Printed, 2001. 1st edition. 383pp, profuse color photos, charts, large format. Hardcover. New in new dust jacket. $150.00

No other German gunmaker has the admiration and repect that the Heckler & Koch firearms company has. Covers, historical insights, descriptions of weapons and technology.

Honour Bound: The Chauchat Machine Rifle, by Gerard Demaison and Yves Buffetaut, Collector Grade Publications, Inc., Cobourg, Ont., Canada, 1995. $39.95

The story of the CSRG (Chauchat) machine rifle, the most manufactured automatic weapon of World War One.

Hunting Weapons From the Middle Ages to the Twentieth Century, by Howard L. Blackmore, Dover Publications, Meneola, NY, 2000. 480 pp., illustrated. Paper covers. $16.95

Dealing mainly with the different classes of weapons used in sport—swords, spears, crossbows, guns, and rifles—from the Middle Ages until the present day.

Identification Handbook of British Grenades 1900-1960 (Numerical Series). Australia: by Landers, Rick & Bonney, Norman & Oakley, Gary Privately Printed, 2001. 1st edition. 48 pages, illustrated with b&w photos drawings. Softcover. New. $10.95

Description, illustration and identification details of all British grenades in the numerical series.

Illustrations of United States Military Arms 1776-1903 and Their Inspector's Marks, compiled by Turner Kirkland, Pioneer Press, Union City, TN, 1988. 37 pp., illus. Paper covers. $7.00

Reprinted from the 1949 Bannerman catalog. Valuable information for both the advanced and beginning collector.

Indian War Cartridge Pouches, Boxes and Carbine Boots, by R. Stephen Dorsey, Collector's Library, Eugene, OR, 1993. 156 pp., illus. Paper Covers. $20.00

The key reference work to the cartridge pouches, boxes, carbine sockets and boots of the Indian War period 1865-1890.

International Armament: With History, Data, Technical Information And Photographs Of Over 800 Weapons, by George Johnson. Alexandria, VA: Ironside International, 2002. Over 947 pages, illustrated with over 800 photos. 2nd edition, new printing. Hardcover. $59.95

The development and progression of modern military small arms. All significant weapons have been included and examined in depth. Over 800 photographs and illustrations with both historical and technical data. Two volumes are now bound in to 1 book.

An Introduction to the Civil War Small Arms, by Earl J. Coates and Dean S. Thomas, Thomas Publishing Co., Gettysburg, PA, 1990. 96 pp., illus. Paper covers. $10.00

The small arms carried by the individual soldier during the Civil War.

Islamic Weapons Maghrib To Mohul, by Tirri, Anthony C. Canada: John Denner, 2003. 1st edition. 483 pages. Hardcover. New in new dust jacket. $149.95

This book is the most important work on the Islamic and Eastern arms ever written on the subject. It almost makes redundant "Stone's Glossary", "Elgood's- Firearms of the Islamic World", and "Egreton's books on Eastern Weapons". This book is a capsulated geography and history of the entire Islamic world. The 800 plus color photos are exceptional. There are over 1350 weapons and accessories, all are accurately described and photographed. I can not recommend this book highly enough to both the serious collector of Islamic arms or to anyone with a passing interest. This is an absolute must in the library of every dealer. This book will be the benchmark for all those who follow.

Jaeger Rifles, Shumway, George. Collected Articles Published in Muzzle Blasts. York, PA: George Shumway, 2003. Reprint. 108 pages, illustrated. Stiff paper covers. New. $30.00

Thirty-six articles previously published in Muzzle Blast are reproduced here.

Japanese Rifles of World War Two, by Duncan O. McCollum, Excalibur Publications, Latham, NY, 1996. 64 pp., illus. Paper covers. $18.95

A sweeping view of the rifles and carbines that made up Japan's arsenal during the conflict.

Kalashnikov "Machine Pistols, Assault Rifles, and Machine Guns, 1945 to the Present", by John Walter, Stackpole Books, Mechanicsburg, PA 1999, hardcover, photos, illus., 146 pp. $22.95

This exhaustive work published by Greenhill Military Manuals features a gun-by-gun directory of Kalashnikov variants. Technical specifications and illustrations are provided throughout, along with details of sights, bayonets, markings and ammunition. A must for the serious collector and historian.

The Kentucky Pistol, by Roy Chandler and James Whisker, Old Bedford Village Press, Bedford, PA, 1997. 225 pp., illus. $60.00

A photographic study of Kentucky pistols from famous collections.

The Kentucky Rifle, by Captain John G.W. Dillin, George Shumway Publisher, York, PA, 1993. 221 pp., illus. $50.00

This well-known book was the first attempt to tell the story of the American longrifle. This edition retains the original text and illustrations with supplemental footnotes provided by Dr. George Shumway.

Know Your Broomhandle Mausers, by R.J. Berger, Blacksmith Corp., Southport, CT, 1996. 96 pp., illus. Paper covers. $14.95

An interesting story on the big Mauser pistol and its variations.

Law Enforcement Memorabilia Price and Identification Guide, by Monty McCord, DBI Books a division of Krause Publications, Inc. Iola, WI, 1999. 208 pp., illustrated. Paper covers. $19.95

Lebeau And Courally Guns & Rifles Maker Since 1865, by Nobili, Marco E. Italy: Il Volo Srl, 1997. 1st Printing. 176 pages, illustrated with b&w photographs, plus 16 full color plates. Text in Italian and English. Hardcover. New in New Dust Jacket. $189.95

THE ARMS LIBRARY

Legendary Sporting Guns, by Eric Joly, Abbeville Press, New York, N.Y., 1999. 228 pp., illustrated. $65.00

A survey of hunting through the ages and relates how many different types of firearms were created and refined for use afield.

Legends and Reality of the AK, by Val Shilin and Charlie Cutshaw, Paladen Press, Boulder, CO, 2000. 192 pp., illustrated. Paper covers. $35.00

A behind-the-scenes look at history, design and impact of the Kalashnikov family of weapons.

The Light 6-Pounder Battalion Gun of 1776, by Adrian Caruana, Museum Restoration Service, Bloomfield, Ontario, Canada, 2001. 76 pp., illus. Paper covers. $8.95

The London Gun Trade, 1850-1920, by Joyce E. Gooding, Museum Restoration Service, Bloomfield, Ontario, Canada, 2001. 48 pp., illus. Paper covers. $8.95

Names, dates and locations of London gunmakers working between 1850 and 1920 are listed. Compiled from the original Kelly's Post Office Directories of the City of London.

The London Gunmakers and the English Duelling Pistol, 1770-1830, by Keith R. Dill, Museum Restoration Service, Bloomfield, Ontario, Canada, 1997. 36 pp., illus. Paper covers. $8.95

Ten gunmakers made London one of the major gunmaking centers of the world. This book examines how the design and construction of their pistols contributed to that reputation and how these characteristics may be used to date flintlock arms.

Longrifles of Pennsylvania, Volume 1, Jefferson, Clarion & Elk Counties, by Russel H. Harringer, George Shumway Publisher, York, PA, 1984. 200 pp., illus. $50.00

First in series that will treat in great detail the longrifles and gunsmiths of Pennsylvania.

The Luger Handbook, by Aarron Davis, Krause Publications, Iola, WI, 1997. 112 pp., illus. Paper covers. $9.95

Quick reference to classify Luger models and variations with complete details including proofmarks.

Lugers at Random, by Charles Kenyon, Jr., Handgun Press, Glenview, IL, 1990. 420 pp., illus. $59.95

A new printing of this classic, comprehensive reference for all Luger collectors.

The Luger Story, by John Walter, Stackpole Books, Mechanicsburg, PA, 2001. 256 pp., illus. Paper Covers $19.95

The standard history of the world's most famous handgun.

M1 Carbine, by Larry Ruth, Gun room Press, Highland Park, NJ, 1987. 291 pp., illus. Paper $19.95

The origin, development, manufacture and use of this famous carbine of World War II.

The M-1 Carbine - A Revolution in Gun-Stocking, by Grafton H. Cook II and Barbara W. Cook. Lincoln, RI: Andrew Mowbray, Inc., 2002. 1st edition. 208 pages, heavily illustrated with 157 rare photographs of the guns and the men and women who made them. Softcover. $29.95

Shows you, step by step, how M1 Carbine stocks were made, right through to assembly with the hardware. Learn about M1 Carbine development, and how the contracting and production process actually worked. Also contains lots of detailed information about other military weapons, like the M1A1, the M1 Garand, the M14 and much, much more. Includes more than 200 short biographies of the people who made M1 Carbines. The depth of this information will amaze you. Shows and explains the machinery used to make military rifle stocks during World War II, with photos of these remarkable machines and data about when they were invented and shipped. Explains why walnut gunstocks are so very difficult to make, and why even large gun manufacturers are usually unable to do this specialized work.

The M1 Carbine: Owner's Guide, by Scott A. Duff, Scott A. Duff, Export, PA, 1997. 126 pp., illus. Paper covers. $21.95

This book answers the questions M1 owners most often ask concerning maintenance activities not encounted by military users.

The M1 Garand: Owner's Guide, by Scott A. Duff, Scott A. Duff, Export, PA, 1998. 132 pp., illus. Paper covers. $21.95

This book answers the questions M1 owners most often ask concerning maintenance activities not encounted by military users.

The M1 Garand Serial Numbers and Data Sheets, by Scott A. Duff, Export, PA, 1995. 101 pp., illus. Paper covers. $11.95

Provides the reader with serial numbers related to dates of manufacture and a large sampling of data sheets to aid in identification or restoration.

The M1 Garand 1936 to 1957, by Joe Poyer and Craig Riesch, North Cape Publications, Tustin, CA, 1996. 216 pp., illus. Paper covers. $19.95

Describes the entire range of M1 Garand production in text and quick-scan charts.

The M1 Garand: Post World War, by Scott A. Duff, Scott A. Duff, Export, PA, 1990. 139 pp., illus. Soft covers. $21.95

A detailed account of the activities at Springfield Armory through this period. International Harvester, H&R, Korean War production and quantities delivered. Serial numbers.

The M1 Garand: World War 2, by Scott A. Duff, Scott A. Duff, Export, PA, 2001. 210 pp., illus. Paper covers. $34.95

The most comprehensive study available to the collector and historian on the M1 Garand of World War II.

Machine Guns, by Ian V. Hogg. Iola, WI: Krause Publications, 2002. 1st edition. A detailed history of the rapid-fire gun, 14th century to present. 336 pages, illustrated with b&w photos with a 16 page color section. Softcover. $29.95

Covers the development, history and specifications.

Maine Made Guns and Their Makers, by Dwight B. Demeritt Jr., Maine State Museum, Augusta, ME, 1998. 209 pp., illustrated. $55.00

An authoritative, biographical study of Maine gunsmiths.

Marlin Firearms: A History of the Guns and the Company That Made Them, by Lt. Col. William S. Brophy, USAR, Ret., Stackpole Books, Harrisburg, PA, 1989. 672 pp., illus. $80.00

The definitive book on the Marlin Firearms Co. and their products.

Martini-Henry .450 Rifles & Carbines, by Dennis Lewis, Excalibur Publications, Latham, NY, 1996. 72 pp., illus. Paper covers. $11.95

The stories of the rifles and carbines that were the mainstay of the British soldier through the Victorian wars.

Mauser Bolt Rifles, by Ludwig Olson, F. Brownell & Son, Inc., Montezuma, IA, 1999. 364 pp., illus. $64.95

The most complete, detailed, authoritative and comprehensive work ever done on Mauser bolt rifles. Completely revised deluxe 3rd edition.

Mauser Military Rifles of the World, 3rd Edition, by Robert Ball, Krause Publications, Iola, WI, 2003. 304 pp., illustrated with 1,000 b&w photos and a 48 page color section. $44.95

This 3rd edition brings more than 100 new photos of these historic rifles and the wars in which they were carried.

Mauser Military Rifle Markings, by Terence W. Lapin, Arlington, VA: Hyrax Publishers, LLC, 2001. 167 pages, illustrated. 2nd edition. revised and expanded. Softcover. $22.95

A general guide to reading and understanding the often mystifying markings found on military Mauser Rifles. Includes German Regimental markings as well as German police markings and W.W. 2 German Mauser subcontractor codes. A handy reference to take to gun shows.

Mauser Smallbores Sporting, Target and Training Rifles, by Jon Speed, Collector Grade Publications, Cobourg, Ontario, Canada 1998. 349 pp., illustrated. $67.50

A history of all the smallbore sporting, target and training rifles produced by the legendary Mauser-Werke of Obendorf Am Neckar.

Metallic Cartridge Conversions: The History Of The Guns And Modern Reproductions, by Dennis Adler, Foreword by R. L. Wilson. Krause Publications, 2003. 208 pages, 250 color photos. Hardcover. $39.95

Collectors and enthusiasts will track the history of the original conversions of the 1800s through historic text and both new and archival photographs. All current modern reproductions are represented with photos, technical details, and performance test results. In-depth coverage of the original revolvers includes models from Colt, Remington, Smith & Wesson, Rollin White, Richards, and Richards-Mason. Modern guns from American Western Arms, Navy Arms, and Cimarron F.A. Co. are highlighted. Color section highlights engraved and presentation models.

Military Holsters of World War 2, by Eugene J. Bender, Rowe Publications, Rochester, NY, 1998. 200 pp., illustrated. $45.00

A revised edition with a new price guide of the most definitive book on this subject.

Military Pistols of Japan, by Fred L. Honeycutt, Jr., Julin Books, Palm Beach Gardens, FL, 1997. 168 pp., illus. $42.00

Covers every aspect of military pistol production in Japan through WWII.

The Military Remington Rolling Block Rifle, by George Layman, Pioneer Press, TN, 1998. 146 pp., illus. Paper covers. $24.95

A standard reference for those with an interest in the Remington rolling block family of firearms.

Military Rifles of Japan, 5th Edition, by F.L. Honeycutt, Julin Books, Lake Park, FL, 1999. 208 pp., illus. $42.00

A new revised and updated edition. Includes the early Murata-period markings, etc.

Military Small Arms Data Book, by Ian V. Hogg, Stackpole Books, Mechanicsburg, PA, 1999. 336 pp., illustrated. $44.95

Data on more than 1,500 weapons. Covers a vast range of weapons from pistols to anti-tank rifles. Essential data, 1870-2000, in one volume.

The MP38, 40, 40/1 & 41 Submachine Gun, by de Vries & Martens. Propaganda Photo Series, Volume II. Alexandria, VA: Ironside International, 2001. 1st edition. 150 pages, illustrated with 200 high quality b&w photos. Hardcover. $34.95

Covers all essential information on history and development, ammunition and accessories, codes and markings, and contains photos of nearly every model and accessory. Includes a unique selection of original German WWII propoganda photos, most never published before.

Modern Beretta Firearms, by Gene Gangarosa, Jr., Stoeger Publishing Co., So. Hackensack, NJ, 1994. 288 pp., illus. Paper covers. $16.95

Traces all models of modern Beretta pistols, rifles, machine guns and combat shotguns.

Greatly updated and expanded edition describing and valuing over 7,000 firearms manufactured from 1900 to 1996. The standard for valuing modern firearms.

Modern Gun Identification & Value Guide, 13th Edition, by Russell and Steve Quertermous, Collector Books, Paducah, KY, 1998. 504 pp., illus. Paper covers. $14.95

Features current values for over 2,500 models of rifles, shotguns and handguns, with over 1,800 illustrations.

More Single Shot Rifles, by James C. Grant, The Gun Room Press, Highland Park, NJ, 1976. 324 pp., illus. $35.00

Details the guns made by Frank Wesson, Milt Farrow, Holden, Borchardt, Stevens, Remington, Winchester, Ballard and Peabody-Martini.

Mortimer, the Gunmakers, 1753-1923, by H. Lee Munson, Andrew Mowbray Inc., Lincoln, RI, 1992. 320 pp., illus. $65.00

Seen through a single, dominant, English gunmaking dynasty this fascinating study provides a window into the classical era of firearms artistry.

The Mosin-Nagant Rifle, by Terence W. Lapin, North Cape Publications, Tustin, CA, 1998. 30 pp., illustrated. Paper covers. $19.95

The first ever complete book on the Mosin-Nagant rifle written in English. Covers every variation.

The Navy Luger, by Joachim Gortz and John Walter, Handgun Press, Glenview, IL, 1988. 128 pp., illus. $24.95

The 9mm Pistole 1904 and the Imperial German Navy. A concise illustrated history.

The New World of Russian Small Arms and Ammunition, by Charlie Cutshaw, Paladin Press, Boulder, CO, 1998. 160 pp., illustrated. $42.95

Detailed descriptions, specifications and first-class illustrations of the AN-94, PSS silent pistol, Bizon SMG, Saifa-12 tactical shotgun, the GP-25 grenade launcher and more cutting edge Russian weapons.

The Number 5 Jungle Carbine, by Alan M. Petrillo, Excalibur Publications, Latham, NY, 1994. 32 pp., illus. Paper covers. $7.95

A comprehensive treatment of the rifle that collectors have come to call the "Jungle Carbine"—the Lee-Enfield Number 5, Mark 1.

Observations on Colt's Second Contract, November 2, 1847, by G. Maxwell Longfield and David T. Basnett, Museum Restoration Service, Bloomfield, Ontario, Canada, 1997. 36 pp., illus. Paper covers. $6.95

This study traces the history and the construction of the Second Model Colt Dragoon supplied in 1848 to the U.S. Cavalry.

The Official Soviet SVD Manual, by Major James F. Gebhardt (Ret.) Paladin Press, Boulder, CO, 1999. 112 pp., illustrated. Paper covers. $22.00

Operating instructions for the 7.62mm Dragunov, the first Russian rifle developed from scratch specifically for sniping.

Old Gunsights: A Collector's Guide, 1850 to 2000, by Nicholas Stroebel, Krause Publications, Iola, WI, 1998. 320 pp., illus. Paper covers. $29.95

An in-depth and comprehensive examination of old gunsights and the rifles on which they were used to get accurate feel for prices in this expanding market.

THE ARMS LIBRARY

Ordnance Tools, Accessories & Appendages of the M1 Rifle, by Billy Pyle. Houston, TX: Privately Printed, 2002. 2nd edition. 206 pages, illustrated with b&w photos. Softcover $40.00

This is the new updated second edition with over 350 pictures and drawings - 30 of which are new. Part I contains accessories, appendages, and equipment including such items as bayonets, blank firing attachments, cheek pads, cleaning equipment, clips, flash hiders, grenade launchers, scabbards, slings, telescopes and mounts, winter triggers, and much more. Part II covers ammunition, grenades, and pyrotechnics. Part III shows the inspection gages. Part IV presents the ordnance tools, fixtures, and assemblies. Part V contains miscellaneous items related to the M1 Rifle such as arms racks, rifle racks, clip loading machine, and other devices.

Orders, Decorations and Badges of the Socialist Republic of Vietnam and the National Front for the Liberation of South Vietnam, by Edward J. Emering. Schiffer Publications, Atglen, PA. 2000. 96 pages, 190 color and b&w photographs, line drawings. $24.95

The Orders and Decorations of the "enemy" during the Vietnam War have remained shrouded in mystery for many years. References to them are scarce and interrogations of captives during the war often led to the proliferation of misinformation concerning them. Includes value guide.

Packing Iron, by Richard C. Rattenbury, Zon International Publishing, Millwood, NY, 1993. 216 pp., illus. $45.00

The best book yet produced on pistol holsters and rifle scabbards. Over 300 variations of holster and scabbards are illustrated in large, clear plates.

Painted Steel, Steel Pots Volume 2, by Chris Armold. Bender Publishing, San Jose, CA, 2001. 384 pages - 1,053 photos (hundreds in color) $57.95

From the author of "Steel Pots: The History of America's Steel Combat Helmets" comes "Painted Steel: Steel Pots, Vol. II." This companion volume features detailed chapters on painted and unit marked helments of WWI and WWII, plus a variety of divisional, regimental and subordinate markings. Special full-color plates detail subordinate unit markings such as the tactical markings used by the U.S. 2nd Division in WWI. In addition, insignia and specialty markings such as USN beach battalion, Army engineers, medics, MP and airborne division tactical markings are examined. For those interested in American armored forces, a complete chapter is devoted to the history of the U.S. tank and combat vehicle crewman's helmet from WWI to present. Other chapters provide tips on reproductions and fake representations of U.S. helmets and accessories. With over 1,000 photos and images (many in color), "Painted Steel" will be a prized addition to any collector's reference bookshelf.

The P-08 Parabellum Luger Automatic Pistol, edited by J. David McFarland, Desert Publications, Cornville, AZ, 1982. 20 pp., illus. Paper covers. $11.95

Covers every facet of the Luger, plus a listing of all known Luger models.

Pattern Dates for British Ordnance Small Arms, 1718-1783, by DeWitt Bailey, Thomas Publications, Gettysburg, PA, 1997. 116 pp., illus. Paper covers. $20.00

The weapons discussed in this work are those carried by troops sent to North America between 1737 and 1783, or shipped to them as replacement arms while in America.

Percussion Ammunition Packets 1845-1888 Union, Confederate & European, by John J. Malloy, Dean S. Thomas & Terry A. White with Foreward by Norm Flayderman. Gettysburg, PA: Thomas Publications, 2003. 1st edition. 134 pages, illustrated with color photos. Hardcover. New. $75.00

Finally a means to recognize the untold variety of labeled types of ammunition box labels.

Peters & King, by Thomas D. Schiffer. Krause Publications, Iola, WI 2002. 1st edition. 256 pages, 200+ b&w photos with a 32 page color section. Hardcover. $44.95

Discover the history behind Peters Cartridge and King Powder and see how they shaped the arms industry into what it is today and why their products fetch hundreds and even thousands of dollars at auctions. Current values are provided for their highly collectible product packaging and promotional advertising premiums such as powder kegs, tins, cartridge boxes, and calendars.

The Pitman Notes on U.S. Martial Small Arms and Ammunition, 1776-1933, Volume 2, Revolvers and Automatic Pistols, by Brig. Gen. John Pitman, Thomas Publications, Gettysburg, PA, 1990. 192 pp., illus. $29.95

A most important primary source of information on United States military small arms and ammunition.

Plates and Buckles of the American Military 1795-1874, by Sydney C. Kerksis, Orange, VA: Publisher's Press, 1998. 5th edition. 568 pages, illustrated with 100's of b&w photos. Hardcover. $39.00

The single most comprehensive reference for U.S. and Confederate plates.

The Plains Rifle, by Charles Hanson, Gun Room Press, Highland Park, NJ, 1989. 169 pp., illus. $35.00

All rifles that were made with the plainsman in mind, including pistols.

The Presentation And Commercial Colt Walker Pistols, by Col. Robert D. Whittington III, Hooks, TX: Brownlee Books, 2003. A limited edition of 1,000 copies. Numbered. 21 pages. Paper covers. New. (9997) $15.00

A study of events at the Whitneyville Armoury and Samuel Colt's Hartford Factory from 1 June 1847 to 29 November 1848.

Proud Promise: French Autoloading Rifles, 1898-1979, by Jean Huon, Collector Grade Publications, Inc., Cobourg, Ont., Canada, 1995. 216 pp., illus. $39.95

The author has finally set the record straight about the importance of French contributions to modern arms design.

E. C. Prudhomme's Gun Engraving Review, by E. C. Prudhomme, R&R Books, Livonia, NY, 1994. 164 pp., illus. $60.00

As a source for engravers and collectors, this book is an indispensable guide to styles and techniques of the world's foremost engravers.

Purdey Gun and Rifle Makers: The Definitive History, by Donald Dallas, Quiller Press, London, 2000. 245 pp., illus. Color throughout. $99.95

A limited edition of 3,000 copies. Signed and Numbered. With a PURDEY book plate.

The Queen Anne Pistol, 1660-1780: A History of the Turn-Off Pistol, by John W. Burgoyne, Bloomfield, Ont. CANADA: Museum Restoration Service, 2002. 1st edition - Historical Arms New Series No. 1. 120 pages, a detailed, fast moving, thoroughly researched text and almost 200 cross-referenced illustrations. Pictorial hardcover. $35.00

This distinctive breech-loading arm was developed in the middle years of the 17th century but found popularity during the reign of the monarch (1702-1714), by whose name it is known.

Red Shines The Sun: A Pictorial History of the Fallschirm-Infantrie, by Eric Queen. San Jose, CA: R. James Bender Publishing, 2003. 1st edition. Hardcover. $69.95

A culmination of 12 years of research, this reference work traces the history of the Army paratroopers of the Fallschirm-Infanterie from their origins in 1937, to the expansion to battalion strength in 1938, then on through operations at Wola Gulowska (Poland), and Moerdijk (Holland). This 240 page comprehensive look at their history is supported by 600 images, many of which are in full color, and nearly 90% are previously unpublished. This work also features original examples of nearly all documents awarded to the Army paratroopers, as well as the most comprehensive study to date of the Army paratrooper badge or Fallschirmschützenabzeichen (Heer). Original examples of all known variations (silver, aluminum, cloth, feinzink) are pictured in full color. If you are interested in owning one of these badges, this book can literally save you from making a $2,000.00 mistake.

Reloading Tools, Sights and Telescopes for Single Shot Rifles, by Gerald O. Kelver, Brighton, CO, 1982. 163 pp., illus. Paper covers. $13.95

A listing of most of the famous makers of reloading tools, sights and telescopes with a brief description of the products they manufactured.

The Remington-Lee Rifle, by Eugene F. Myszkowski, Excalibur Publications, Latham, NY, 1995. 100 pp., illus. Paper covers. $22.50

Features detailed descriptions, including serial number ranges, of each model from the first Lee Magazine Rifle produced for the U.S. Navy to the last Remington-Lee Small Bores shipped to the Cuban Rural Guard.

Remington 'America's Oldest Gunmaker', The Official Authorized History Of The Remington Arms Company, by Roy Marcot. Madison, NC: Remington Arms Company, 1999. 1st edition. 312 pages, with 167 b&w illustrations, plus 291 color plates. $79.95

This is without a doubt the finest history of that firm ever to have been compiled. Based on firsthand research in the Remington companies archives, it is extremely well written.

Remington Sporting Firearms: Dates of Manufacture, by Morse, D. R. Phoenix, AZ: Firing Pin Enterprizes, 2003. 43 pages. Softcover. New. $6.95

Covers their pistols, revolvers, rifles, shotguns and commemoratives. Plus models & serial numbers.

Remington's Vest Pocket Pistols, by Hatfield, Robert E. Lincoln, RI: Andrew Mowbray, Inc., 2002. 117 pages. Hardcover. $29.95

While Remington Vest Pocket Pistols have always been popular with collectors, very little solid information has been available about them. Such simple questions such as "When were they made?"..."How many were produced?"...and "What calibers were they available in?" have all remained unanswered. This new book, based upon years of study and a major survey of surviving examples, attempts to answer these critical questions. Specifications, markings, mechanical design and patents are also presented here. Inside you will find 100+ photographs, serial number data, exploded views of all four Remington Vest Pocket Pistol sizes, component parts lists and a guide to disassembly and reassembly. Also includes a discussion of Vest Pocket Wire-Stocked Buggy/Bicycle rifles. plus the documented serial number story.

Revolvers of the British Services 1854-1954, by W.H.J. Chamberlain and A.W.F. Taylerson, Museum Restoration Service, Ottawa, Canada, 1989. 80 pp., illus. $27.50

Covers the types issued among many of the United Kingdom's naval, land or air services.

Rifles Of The U. S. Army 1861-1906, by McAulay, John D Lincoln, RI: Andrew Mowbray, Inc., 2003. 1st edition. Over 40 rifles covered, 278 pages, illustrated. Hardcover. New. $47.95

There have been several excellent books written about the manufacture of rifles for the U.S. Army from the time of the Civil War to the early 20th century. However, few of these books have focused upon what happened to these rifles after they were issued. This exciting new book by renowned authority John McAulay fills this gap. It gives the reader detailed coverage of the issue and actual field service of American's fighting rifles, both in peacetime and in war, including their military service with the infantry, artillery, cavalry and engineers. Calling upon his thousands of hours of research in the National Archives and elsewhere, the author will show you how these rifles fared in field tests, what their strengths and failings were, which units carried them and how they performed in battle. When possible, actual serial numbers and other exciting details have been included, which are sure to thrill collectors and historians. One feature that all readers will value is the impressive number of historian photos, taken during the Civil War, the Mexican War, the Indian Wars, the Spanish-American War, the Philippine Insurrection and more, showing these rifles in the hands of them men who fought with them. Procurement information, issue details and historical background.

Rifles of the World, by Oliver Achard, Chartwell Books, Inc., Edison, NJ, 141 pp., illus. $24.95

A unique insight into the world of long guns, not just rifles, but also shotguns, carbines and all the usual multi-barreled guns that once were so popular with European hunters, especially in Germany and Austria.

Round Ball to Rimfire, Vol. 1, by Dean Thomas, Thomas Publications, Gettysburg, PA, 1997. 144 pp., illus. $40.00

The first of a two-volume set of the most complete history and guide for all small arms ammunition used in the Civil War. The information includes data from research and development to the arsenals that created it.

Round Ball to Rimfire: A History of Civil War Small Arms Ammunition, Vol. 2. by Dean Thomas, Thomas Publications, Gettysburg, PA 2002. 528 pages. Hardcover. $49.95

Completely discusses the ammunition for Federal Breechloading Carbines and Rifles. The seven chapters with eighteen appendices detailing the story of the twenty-seven or so different kinds of breechloaders actually purchased or ordered by the Ordnance Department during the Civil War. The book is conveniently divided by the type of priming — external or internal — and then alphabetically by maker or supplier. A wealth of new information and research has proven that these weapons either functioned properly or were inadequate relative to the design and ingenuity of the proprietary cartridges.

Round Ball to Rimfire, Vol. 3, by Dean Thomas, Thomas Publications, Gettysburg, PA, 2003. 488 pages, illus. $49.95

Completely discusses the ammunition for Federal Pistols and Revolvers. The seven chapters with eighteen appendices detailing the story of the twenty-seven or so different kinds of breechloaders actually purchased or ordered by the Ordnance Department during the Civil War. The book is conveniently divided by the type of priming — external or internal — and then alphabetically by maker or supplier. A wealth of new information and research has proven that these weapons either functioned properly or were inadequate relative to the design and ingenuity of the proprietary cartridges.

Ruger and his Guns, by R.L. Wilson, Simon & Schuster, New York, NY, 1996. 358 pp., illus. $65.00

A history of the man, the company and their firearms.

Russell M. Catron and His Pistols, by Warren H. Buxton, Ucross Books, Los Alamos, NM, 1998. 224 pp., illustrated. Paper covers. $49.50

An unknown American firearms inventor and manufacturer of the mid twentieth century. Military, commerical, ammunition.

The SAFN-49 and The FAL, by Joe Poyer and Dr. Richard Feirman, North Cape Publications, Tustin, CA, 1998. 160 pp., illus. Paper covers. $14.95

The first complete overview of the SAFN-49 battle rifle, from its pre-World War 2 beginnings to its military service in countries as diverse as the Belgian Congo and Argentina. The FAL was "light" version of the SAFN-49 and it became the Free World's most adopted battle rifle.

Savage Sporting Firearms: Dates of Manufacture 1907-1997, by D. R. Morse. Phoenix, AZ: Firing Pin Enterprizes, 2003. 22 pages. Softcover. New. $6.95

Covers their pistols, revolvers, rifles, shotguns and commemoratives. Plus models & serial numbers.

J. P. Sauer & Sohn, Sauer "Dein Waffenkamerad" Volume 2, by Cate & Krause, Walsworth Publishing, Chattanooga, TN, 2000. 440 pp., illus. $69.95

A historical study of Sauer automatic pistols. This new volume includes a great deal of new knowledge that has surfaced about the firm J.P. Sauer. You will find new photos, documentation, serial number ranges and historial facts which will expand the knowledge and interest in the oldest and best of the German firearms companies.

Scale Model Firearms, by Joseph D. Kramer. Pittsburgh, PA: Privately Printed, 1999. 1st edition. 136 pages, oversize, photos, many color, index. Softcover. New. $35.00

Each of the models, which are nearly all in one-half scale require a year or more to complete, and in most cases only one example was made. Mr. R. E. Hutchens uncompromising devotion to the producing of these models, is a tribute to a man who is known internationally, to be the finest maker of model firearms in the world.

Scottish Firearms, by Claude Blair and Robert Woosnam-Savage, Museum Restoration Service, Bloomfield, Ont., Canada, 1995. 52 pp., illus. Paper covers. $8.95

This revision of the first book devoted entirely to Scottish firearms is supplemented by a register of surviving Scottish long guns.

Sharps Firearms, by Frank Seller, Frank M. Seller, Denver, CO, 1998. 358 pp., illus. $59.95

Traces the development of Sharps firearms with full range of guns made including all martial variations.

Silk And Steel: Women at Arms, by R. L. Wilson. New York: Random House, 2003. 1st edition. 300+ Striking four-color images; 11x8.5 inches, 320 pgs. Hardcover. New in New Dust Jacket. (9775). $65.00

Beginning with Artemis & Diana, goddesses of hunting, evolving through modern times, here is the first comprehensive presentation on the subject of women & firearms. No object has had a greater impact on world history over the past 650 years than the firearm, & a surprising number of women have been keen on the subject: as shooters, hunters, collectors, engravers, & even gunmakers.

The SKS Carbine, by Steve Kehaya and Joe Poyer, North Cape Publications, Tustin, CA, 1997. 150 pp., illus. Paper covers. $16.95

The first comprehensive examination of a major historical firearm used through the Vietnam conflict to the diamond fields of Angola.

The SKS Type 45 Carbines, by Duncan Long, Desert Publications, El Dorado, AZ, 1992. 110 pp., illus. Paper covers. $19.95

Covers the history and practical aspects of operating, maintaining and modifying this abundantly available rifle.

Smith & Wesson 1857-1945, by Robert J. Neal and Roy G. Jinks, R&R Books, Livonia, NY, 1996. 434 pp., illus. $50.00

The bible for all existing and aspiring Smith & Wesson collectors.

Smith & Wesson Sporting Firearms: Dates Of Manufacture, by D. R. Morse. Phoenix, AZ: Firing Pin Enterprizes, 2003. 76 pages. Softcover. New. $6.95

Covers their pistols, revolvers, rifles, shotguns and commemoratives. Plus models & serial numbers.

Sniper Variations of the German K98k Rifle, by Richard D. Law, Collector Grade Publications, Ontario, Canada, 1997. 240 pp., illus. $47.50

Volume 2 of "Backbone of the Wehrmacht" the author's in-depth study of the German K98k rifle. This volume concentrates on the telescopic-sighted rifle of choice for most German snipers during World War 2.

Southern Derringers of the Mississippi Valley, by Turner Kirkland, Pioneer Press, Tenn., 1971. 80 pp., illus., paper covers. $4.00

A guide for the collector, and a much-needed study.

Soviet Russian Postwar Military Pistols and Cartridges, by Fred A. Datig, Handgun Press, Glenview, IL, 1988. 152 pp., illus. $29.95

Thoroughly researched, this definitive sourcebook covers the development and adoption of the Makarov, Stechkin and the new PSM pistols. Also included in this source book is coverage on Russian clandestine weapons and pistol cartridges.

Soviet Russian Tokarev "TT" Pistols and Cartridges 1929-1953, by Fred Datig, Graphic Publishers, Santa Ana, CA, 1993. 168 pp., illus. $39.95

Details of rare arms and their accessories are shown in hundreds of photos. It also contains a complete bibliography and index.

Spencer Repeating Firearms, by Roy M. Marcot. New York: Rowe Publications, 2002. 316 pages; numerous B&W photos & illustrations. Hardcover. $65.00

Sporting Collectibles, by Jim and Vivian Karsnitz, Schiffer Publishing Ltd., West Chester, PA, 1992. 160 pp., illus. Paper covers. $29.95

The fascinating world of hunting related collectibles presented in an informative text.

The Springfield 1903 Rifles, by Lt. Col. William S. Brophy, USAR, Ret., Stackpole Books Inc., Harrisburg, PA, 1985. 608 pp., illus. $75.00

The illustrated, documented story of the design, development, and production of all the models, appendages, and accessories.

Springfield Model 1903 Service Rifle Production and Alteration, 1905-1910, by C.S. Ferris and John Beard, Arvada, CO, 1995. 66 pp., illus. Paper covers. $12.50

A highly recommended work for any serious student of the Springfield Model 1903 rifle.

Springfield Shoulder Arms 1795-1865, by Claud E. Fuller, S. & S. Firearms, Glendale, NY, 1996. 76 pp., illus. Paper covers. $14.95

Exact reprint of the scarce 1930 edition of one of the most definitive works on Springfield flintlock and percussion muskets ever published.

SS Headgear, by Kit Wilson. Johnson Reference Books, Fredericksburg, VA. 72 pages, 15 full-color plates and over 70 b&w photos. $16.50

An excellent source of information concerning all types of SS headgear, to include Allgemeine-SS, Waffen-SS, visor caps, helmets, overseas caps, M-43's and miscellaneous headgear. Also included is a guide on the availability and current values of SS headgear. This guide was compiled from auction catalogs, dealer price lists, and input from advanced collectors in the field.

SS Helmets: A Collector's Guide, Vol 1, by Kelly Hicks. Johnson Reference Books, Fredericksburg, VA. 96 pages, illustrated. $17.50

Deals only with SS helmets and features some very nice color close-up shots of the different SS decals used. Also, has some nice color shots of entire helmets. Over 85 photographs, 27 in color. The author has documented most of the known types of SS helmets, and describes in detail all of the vital things to look for in determining the originality, style type, and finish. Complete descriptions of each helmet are provided along with detailed close-ups of interior and exterior views of the markings and insignia. Also featured are several period photos of helmets in wear.

SS Helmets: A Collector's Guide, Vol 2, by Kelly Hicks. Johnson Reference Books, Fredericksburg, VA. 2000. 128 pages. 107 full-color photos, 14 period photos. $25.00

Volume II contains dozen of highly detailed, full-color photos of rare and original SS and Field Police helmets, featuring both sides as well as interior view. The very best graphics techniques ensure that these helmets are presented in such a way that the reader can 'almost feel' the different paint textures of the camo and factory finishes. The outstanding decal section offers detailed close-ups of original SS and Police decals, and in conjunction with Volume I, completes the documentation of virtually all types of original decal variations used between 1934 and 1945.

SS Uniforms, Insignia and Accoutrements, by A. Hayes. Schiffer Publications, Atglen, PA. 1996. 248 pages, with over 800 color and b&w photographs. $69.95

This new work explores in detailed color the complex subject of Allgemeine and Waffen-SS uniforms, insignia, and accoutrements. Hundreds of authentic items are extensively photographed in close-up to enable the reader to examine and study.

Steel Pots: The History of America's Steel Combat Helmets, by Chris Armold. Bender Publishing, San Jose, CA, 2000. $47.95

Packed with hundreds of color photographs, detailed specification diagrams and supported with meticulously researched data, this book takes the reader on a fascinating visual journey covering 80 years of American helmet design and development. From the classic Model 1917 "Doughboy" helmet to the distinctive ballistic "Kelvar" helmet, Steel Pots will introduce you to over 50 American helmet variations. Also, rare WWI experimental helmets to specialized WWII aircrew anti-flak helmets, plus liners, suspensions, chinstraps, camouflage covers, nets and even helmet radios!

Standard Catalog of Firearms, 14th Edition, by Ned Schwing, Krause Publications, Iola, WI, 2004.1422 Pages, illustrated. 6,000+ b&w photos plus a 16-page color section. Paper covers. $34.95

This is the largest, most comprehensive and best-selling firearm book of all time! And this year's edition is a blockbuster for both shooters and firearm collectors. More than 14,000 firearms are listed and priced in up to six grades of condition. That's almost 100,000 prices! Gun enthusiasts will love the new full-color section of photos highlighting the finest firearms sold at auction this past year.

Steel Canvas: The Art of American Arms, by R.L. Wilson, Random House, NY, 1995, 384 pp., illus. $65.00

Presented here for the first time is the breathtaking panorama of America's extraordinary engravers and embellishers of arms, from the 1700s to modern times.

A Study of Remington's Smoot Patent and Number Four Revolvers, by Parker Harry, Parker Ora Lee, and Reisch, Joan. (Foreword by Roy M. Marcot) Santa Ana, CA: Armslore Press - Graphic Publishers, 2003. 1st edition. 120 pages, profusely illustrated, plus an 8-page color section. Softcover. $17.95

A detailed, pictorial essay on Remington's early metallic cartridge-era pocket revolvers: their design, development, patents, models, identification and variations. Includes the biography of arms inventor Wm. S. Smoot--for the first time ever!--as well as a mini-history of the Remington Arms Company.

The Sumptuous Flaske, by Herbert G. Houze, Andrew Mowbray, Inc., Lincoln, RI, 1989. 158 pp., illus. Soft covers. $35.00

Catalog of a recent show at the Buffalo Bill Historical Center bringing together some of the finest European and American powder flasks of the 16th to 19th centuries.

The Swedish Mauser Rifles, by Steve Kehaya and Joe Poyer, North Cape Publications, Tustin, CA, 1999. 267 pp., illustrated. Paper covers. $19.95

Every known variation of the Swedish Mauser carbine and rifle is described, all match and target rifles and all sniper fersions. Includes serial number and production data.

System Lefaucheaux, by Chris C. Curtis, with a Foreword by Norm Flayderman. Armslore Press, 2002. 312 pages, heavily illustrated with b&w photos. Hardcover. $44.95

The study of pinfire cartridge arms including their role in the American Civil War.

Thompson: The American Legend, by Tracie L. Hill, Collector Grade Publications, Ontario, Canada, 1996. 584 pp., illus. $85.00

The story of the first American submachine gun. All models are featured and discussed.

Thoughts on the Kentucky Rifle in its Golden Age, by Joe K. Kindig, III. York, PA: George Shumway Publisher, 2002. Annotated second edition. 561pp; Illustrated. This scarce title, long out of print, is once again available. Hardcover. $85.00

The definitive book on the Kentucky Rifle, illustrating 266 of these guns in 856 detailed photographs.

Toys That Shoot and Other Neat Stuff, by James Dundas, Schiffer Books, Atglen, PA, 1999. 112 pp., illustrated. Paper covers. $24.95

Shooting toys from the twentieth century, especially 1920's to 1960's, in over 420 color photographs of BB guns, cap shooters, marble shooters, squirt guns and more. Complete with a price guide.

Trade Guns of the Hudson's Bay Company 1670-1970, Historical Arms New Series No. 2. by Gooding, S. James Bloomfield, Ont. CANADA: Museum Restoration Service, 2003. 1st edition. 158 pages, thoroughly researched text. Includes bibliographical references. Pictorial Hardcover. NEW. (9312) $35.00

The Trapdoor Springfield, by M.D. Waite and B.D. Ernst, The Gun Room Press, Highland Park, NJ, 1983. 250 pp., illus. $39.95

The first comprehensive book on the famous standard military rifle of the 1873-92 period.

Treasures of the Moscow Kremlin: Arsenal of the Russian Tsars, A Royal Armories and the Moscow Kremlin exhibition. HM Tower of London 13, June 1998 to 11 September, 1998. BAS Printers, Over Wallop, Hampshire, England. xxii plus 192 pp. over 180 color illustrations. Text in English and Russian. $65.00

For this exhibition catalog each of the 94 objects on display are photographed and described in detail to provide a most informative record of this important exhibition.

U. S. Army Headgear 1812-1872, by Langellier, John P. and C. Paul Loane. Atglen, PA: Schiffer Publications, 2002. 167 pages, with over 350 color and b&w photos. Hardcover. $69.95

This profusely illustrated volume represents more than three decades of research in public and private collections by military historian John P. Langellier and Civil War authority C. Paul Loane.

THE ARMS LIBRARY

U.S. Army Rangers & Special Forces Of World War 2 Their War In Photographs, by Robert Todd Ross. Atglen, PA: Schiffer Publications, 2002. 216 pages, over 250 b&w & color photographs. Hardcover. $59.95

Never before has such an expansive view of World War II elite forces been offered in one volume. An extensive search of public and private archives unearthed an astonishing number of rare and never before seen images, including color. Most notable are the nearly twenty exemplary photographs of Lieutenant Colonel William O. Darby's Ranger Force in Italy, taken by Robert Capa, considered by many to be the greatest combat photographer of all time. Complementing the period photographs are numerous color plates detailing the rare and often unique items of insignia, weapons, and equipment that marked the soldiers whose heavy task it was to Lead the Way. Includes rare, previously unpublished photographs by legendary combat photographer Robert Capa.

U.S. Breech-Loading Rifles and Carbines, Cal. 45, by Gen. John Pitman, Thomas Publications, Gettysburg, PA, 1992. 192 pp., illus. $29.95

The third volume in the Pitman Notes on U.S. Martial Small Arms and Ammunition, 1776-1933. This book centers on the "Trapdoor Springfield" models.

U.S. Handguns of World War 2: The Secondary Pistols and Revolvers, by Charles W. Pate, Andrew Mowbray, Inc., Lincoln, RI, 1998. 515 pp., illus. $39.00

This indispensable new book covers all of the American military handguns of World War 2 except for the M1911A1 Colt automatic.

United States Martial Flintlocks, by Robert M. Reilly, Mowbray Publishing Co., Lincoln, RI, 1997. 264 pp., illus. $40.00

A comprehensive history of American flintlock longarms and handguns (mostly military) c. 1775 to c. 1840.

U.S. Martial Single Shot Pistols, by Daniel D. Hartzler and James B. Whisker, Old Bedford Village Pess, Bedford, PA, 1998. 128 pp., illus. $45.00

A photographic chronicle of military and semi-martial pistols supplied to the U.S. Government and the several States.

U.S. Military Arms Dates of Manufacture from 1795, by George Madis, David Madis, Dallas, TX, 1995. 64 pp. Soft covers. $9.95

Lists all U.S. military arms of collector interest alphabetically, covering about 250 models.

U.S. Military Small Arms 1816-1865, by Robert M. Reilly, The Gun Room Press, Highland Park, NJ, 1983. 270 pp., illus. $39.95

Covers every known type of primary and secondary martial firearms used by Federal forces.

U.S. M1 Carbines: Wartime Production, by Craig Riesch, North Cape Publications, Tustin, CA, 1994. 72 pp., illus. Paper covers. $16.95

Presents only verifiable and accurate information. Each part of the M1 Carbine is discussed fully in its own section; including markings and finishes.

U.S. Naval Handguns, 1808-1911, by Fredrick R. Winter, Andrew Mowbray Publishers, Lincoln, RI, 1990. 128 pp., illus. $26.00

The story of U.S. Naval Handguns spans an entire century—included are sections on each of the important naval handguns within the period.

Uniform and Dress Army and Navy of the Confederate States of America. (Official Regulations), by Confederate States of America. Ray Riling Arms Books, Philadelphia, PA. 1960. $20.00

A portfolio containing a complete set of nine color plates expecially prepared for framing Reproduced in exactly 200 sets from the very rare Richmond, VA., 1861 regulations.

Uniform Buttons of the United States 1776-1865, by Warren K. Tice. Thomas Publications, Gettysburg, PA. 1997. 520 pages over 3000 illustrations. $60.00

A timely work on US uniform buttons for a growing area of collecting. This work interrelates diverse topics such as manufacturing proceses, history of manufacturing companies, known & recently discovered button patterns and the unist that wore them.

Uniforms & Equipment of the Imperial German Army 1900-1918: A Study in Period Photographs, by Charles Woolley. Schiffer Publications, Atglen, PA. 2000. 375 pages, over 500 b&w photographs and 50 color drawings. $69.95

Features formal studio portraits of pre-war dress and wartime uniforms of all arms. Also contains photo postal cards taken in the field of Infantry, Pionier, Telegraph-Signal, Landsturm, and Mountain Troops, vehicles, artillery, musicians, the Bavarian Leib Regiment, specialized uniforms and insignia, small arms close-ups, unmotorized transport, group shots and Balloon troops and includes a 60 page full-color uniform section reproduced from rare 1914 plates. Fully illustrated.

Uniforms & Equipment of the Imperial German Army 1900-1918: A Study in Period Photographs, Volume 2, by Charles Woolley. Schiffer Publications, Atglen, PA. 2000. 320 pages, over 500 b&w photographs and 50 color drawings. $69.95

Contains over 500 never before published photographic images of Imperial German military subjects. This initial volume, of a continuing study, features formal studio portraits of pre-war dress and wartime uniforms of all arms. It also contains photo postal cards taken in the field of Infantry, Pionier, Telegraph-Signal, Landsturm and Mountain Troops, Vehicles, Artillery, Musicians, the Bavarian Leib Regiment, specialized uniforms and insignia, small arms close-ups, unmotorized transport, group shots and Balloon troops.

Uniforms of the Third Reich: A Study in Photographs, by Maguire Hayes. Schiffer Publications, Atglen, PA. 1997. 200 pages, with over 400 color photographs. $69.95

This new book takes a close look at a variety of authentic World War II era German uniforms including examples from the Army, Luftwaffe, Kriegsmarine, Waffen-SS, Allgemeine-SS, Hitler Youth and Political Leaders. The pieces are shown in large full frame front and rear shots, and in painstaking detail to show tailors tags, buttons, insignia detail etc. and allow the reader to see what the genuine article looks like. Various accoutrements worn with the uniforms are also included to aid the collector.

Uniforms Of The United States Army, 1774-1889, by Henry Alexander Ogden. Dover Publishing, Mineola, NY. 1998. 48 pages of text plus 44 color plates. Softcover. $9.95

A republication of the work published by the quarter-master general, United States army in 1890. A striking collection of lithographs and a marvelous archive of military, social, and costume history portraying the gamut of U.S. Army uniforms from fatigues to full dress, between 1774 and 1889.

Uniforms, Organization, and History of the NSKK/NSFK, by John R. Angolia & David Littlejohn. Bender Publishing, San Jose, CA, 2000. $44.95

This work is part of the on-going study of political organizations that formed the structure of the Hitler hierarchy, and is authored by two of the most prominent authorities on the subject of uniforms and insignia of the Third Reich. This comprehensive book covers details on the NSKK and NSFK such as history, organization, uniforms, insignia, special insignia, flags and standards, gorgets, daggers, awards, "day badges," and much more!

Uniforms of the Waffen-SS; Black Service Uniform - LAH Guard Uniform - SS Earth-Grey Service Uniform - Model 1936 Field Service Uniform - 1939-1940 - 1941 Volume 1, by Michael D. Beaver. Schiffer Publications, Atglen, PA. 2002. 272 pages, with 500 color, and b&w photos. $79.95

This spectacular work is a heavily documented record of all major clothing articles of the Waffen-SS. Hundreds of unpublished photographs were used in production. Original and extremely rare SS uniforms of various types are carefully photographed and presented here. Among the subjects covered in this multi volume series are field-service uniforms, sports, drill, dress, armored personnel, tropical, and much more. A large updated chapter on SS camouflage clothing is also provided. Special chapters on the SD and concentration camp personnel assist the reader in differentiating these elements from combat units of the Waffen-SS. Difficult areas such as mountain and ski troops, plus ultra-rare pre-war uniforms are covered. Included are many striking and exquisite uniforms worn by such men as Himmler, Dietrich, Ribbentrop (father and son), Wolff, Demelhuber, and many others. From the enlisted man to the top of the SS empire, this book covers it all. This book is indispensable and an absolute must-have for any serious historian of World War II German uniforms.

Uniforms of the Waffen-SS; 1942- 1943 - 1944-1945 - Ski Uniforms - Overcoats - White Service Uniforms -Tropical Clothing, Volume 2, by Michael D. Beaver. Schiffer Publications, Atglen, PA. 2002. 272 pages, with 500 color, and b&w photos. $79.95

Uniforms of the Waffen-SS; Sports and Drill Uniforms - Black Panzer Uniform - Camouflage - Concentration Camp Personnel-SD-SS Female Auxiliaries, Volume 3, by Michael D. Beaver. Schiffer Publications, Atglen, PA. 2002. 272 pages, with 500 color, and b&w photos. $79.95

U.S. Silent Service - Dolphins & Combat Insignia 1924-1945, by David Jones. Bender Publishing, San Jose, CA, 2001. 224 pages, 532 photos. (most in full color) $39.95

After eight years of extensive research, the publication of this book is a submarine buff and collectorᴤs dream come true. This beautiful full-color book chronicles, with period letters and sketches, the developmental history of US submarine insignia prior to 1945. It also contains many rare and never before published photographs, plus interviews with WWII submarine veterans, from enlisted men to famous skippers. Each insignia is photographed (obverse and reverse) and magnified in color. All known contractors are covered plus embroidered versions, mess dress variations, the Roll of Honor, submarine combat insignia, battleflags, launch memorabilia and related submarine collectibles (postal covers, match book covers, jewelry, posters, advertising art, postcards, etc.)

Variations Of Colt's New Model Police And Pocket Breech Loading Pistols, by Breslin, John D., Pirie, William Q., & Price, David E.: Lincoln, RI: Andrew Mowbray Publishers, 2002. 1st edition. 158 pages, heavily illustrated with over 160 photographs and superb technical detailed drawings and diagrams. Pictorial hardcover. $37.95

A type-by-type guide to what collectors call small frame conversions.

The Walker's Walkers Controversy is Solved, by Whittington III, Col. Robert D. Hooks, TX: Brownlee Books, 2003. A limited edition of 1,000 copies. Numbered. 17 pages. Paper covers. New. $15.00

The truth about serial numbers on the Colt Whitneyville-Walker Pistols presented to Captain Samuel Hamilton Walker by Sam Colt and J. B. Colt on July 28th, 1847.

Walther: A German Legend, by Manfred Kersten, Safari Press, Inc., Huntington Beach, CA, 2000. 400 pp., illustrated. $85.00

This comprehensive book covers, in rich detail, all aspects of the company and its guns, including an illustrious and rich history, the WW2 years, all the pistols (models 1 through 9), the P-38, P-88, the long guns, .22 rifles, centerfires, Wehrmacht guns, and even a gun that could shoot around a corner.

Walther Pistols: Models 1 Through P99, Factory Variations and Copies, by Dieter H. Marschall, Ucross Books, Los Alamos, NM. 2000. 140 pages, with 140 b&w illustrations, index. Paper Covers. $19.95

This is the English translation, revised and updated, of the highly successful and widely acclaimed German language edition. This book provides the collector with a reference guide and overview of the entire line of the Walther military, police, and self-defense pistols from the very first to the very latest. Models 1-9, PP, PPK, MP, AP, HP, P.38, P1, P4, P38K, P5, P88, P99 and the Manurhin models. Variations, where issued, serial ranges, calibers, marks, proofs, logos, and design aspects in an astonishing quantity and variety are crammed into this very well researched and highly regarded work.

The Walther Handgun Story: A Collector's and Shooter's Guide, by Gene Gangarosa, Steiger Publications, 1999. 300., illustrated. Paper covers. $21.95

Covers the entire history of the Walther empire. Illustrated with over 250 photos.

Walther P-38 Pistol, by Maj. George Nonte, Desert Publications, Cornville, AZ, 1982. 100 pp., illus. Paper covers. $12.95

Complete volume on one of the most famous handguns to come out of WWII. All models covered.

Walther Models PP & PPK, 1929-1945 – Volume 1, by James L. Rankin, Coral Gables, FL, 1974. 142 pp., illus. $40.00

Complete coverage on the subject as to finish, proofmarks and Nazi Party inscriptions.

Walther Volume II, Engraved, Presentation and Standard Models, by James L. Rankin, J.L. Rankin, Coral Gables, FL, 1977. 112 pp., illus. $40.00

The new Walther book on embellished versions and standard models. Has 88 photographs, including many color plates.

Walther, Volume III, 1908-1980, by James L. Rankin, Coral Gables, FL, 1981. 226 pp., illus. $40.00

Covers all models of Walther handguns from 1908 to date, includes holsters, grips and magazines.

Warman's Civil War Collectibles (Encyclopedia Of Antiques And Collectibles), by John F. Graf, Iola, WI: Krause Publications, 2003. 1st edition. This new volume is a huge 518 pages, full of the information on the Civil War memorabilia that you'll thrill to as there are more than 1,000 images plus over 3,000 price listings! Softcover. $24.95

18 of the most popular collectibles areas are covered, and collecting tips will help the reader to add to their collection! Here are just a few of the MANY items you will find in this book, along with their prices on the collectibles market of today: Carbines Ephemera Flags & Musical Equipment Insignia, badges, buttons Firearms, Muskets, Revolvers Swords Uniforms Artillery, Bayonets, Accoutrements, and more! Photographs in black & white are found throughout the book; the actual items are shown. This is a really comprehensive book that collectors of Civil War Memorabilia will absolutely be thrilled with!

THE ARMS LIBRARY

Winchester Bolt Action Military & Sporting Rifles 1877 to 1937, by Herbert G. Houze, Andrew Mowbray Publishing, Lincoln, RI, 1998. 295 pp., illus. $45.00
Winchester was the first American arms maker to commercially manufacture a bolt action repeating rifle, and this book tells the exciting story of these Winchester bolt actions.

The Winchester Book, by George Madis, David Madis Gun Book Distributor, Dallas, TX, 2000. 650 pp., illus. $54.50
A new, revised 25th anniversary edition of this classic book on Winchester firearms. Complete serial ranges have been added.

Winchester Commemoratives, by Tom Troland. Coos Bay, OR: Commemorative Investments Press Library, 2003. 2nd printing - Limited to 1500 copies. Signed by the Author. Brown leatherette binding, decorative pictorial cover; illustrated in full color. Oblong, 8 3/4" x 11", 183 pages. Hardcover. New in new dust jacket. $109.95
Includes index to the rifles, with production figures & original prices.

Winchester Dates of Manufacture 1849-1984, by George Madis, Art & Reference House, Brownsboro, TX, 1984. 59 pp. $9.50
A most useful work, compiled from records of the Winchester factory.

The Winchester Model 1876 "Centennial" Rifle, by Herbert G. Houze. Lincoln, RI: Andrew Mowbray, Inc., 2001. Illustrated with over 180 b&w photographs. 192 Pages. Hardcover. $45.00
The first authoritative study of the Winchester Model 1876 written using the company's own records. This book dispels the myth that the Model 1876 was merely a larger version of the Winchester company's famous Model 1873 and instead traces its true origins to designs developed immediately after the American Civil War. The specifics of the model-such as the numbers made in its standard calibers, barrel lengths, finishes and special order features-are fully listed here for the first time. In addition, the actual processes and production costs involved in its manufacture are also completely documented. For Winchester collectors, and those interested in the mechanics of the 19th-century arms industry, this book provides a wealth of previously unpublished information.

Winchester Engraving, by R.L. Wilson, Beinfeld Books, Springs, CA, 1989. 500 pp., illus. $135.00
A classic reference work of value to all arms collectors.

The Winchester Handbook, by George Madis, Art & Reference House, Lancaster, TX, 1982. 287 pp., illus. $26.95
The complete line of Winchester guns, with dates of manufacture, serial numbers, etc.

The Winchester-Lee Rifle, by Eugene Myszkowski, Excalibur Publications, Tucson, AZ 2000. 96 pp., illustrated. Paper Covers. $22.95
The development of the Lee Straight Pull, the cartridge and the approval for military use. Covers details of the inventor and memorabilia of Winchester-Lee related material.

Winchester Lever Action Repeating Firearms, Vol. 1, The Models of 1866, 1873 and 1876, by Arthur Pirkle, North Cape Publications, Tustin, CA, 1995. 112 pp., illus. Paper covers. $19.95
Complete, part-by-part description, including dimensions, finishes, markings and variations throughout the production run of these fine, collectible guns.

Winchester Lever Action Repeating Rifles, Vol. 2, The Models of 1886 and 1892, by Arthur Pirkle, North Cape Publications, Tustin, CA, 1996. 150 pp., illus. Paper covers. $19.95
Describes each model on a part-by-part basis by serial number range complete with finishes, markings and changes.

Winchester Lever Action Repeating Rifles, Volume 3, The Model of 1894, by Arthur Pirkle, North Cape Publications, Tustin, CA, 1998. 150 pp., illus. Paper covers. $19.95
The first book ever to provide a detailed description of the Model 1894 rifle and carbine.

The Winchester Lever Legacy, by Clyde "Snooky" Williamson, Buffalo Press, Zachary, LA, 1988. 664 pp., illustrated. $75.00
A book on reloading for the different calibers of the Winchester lever action rifle.

The Winchester Single-Shot- Volume 1; A History and Analysis, by John Campbell, Andrew Mowbray, Inc., Lincoln RI, 1995. 272 pp., illus. $55.00
Covers every important aspect of this highly-collectible firearm.

The Winchester Single-Shot-Volume 2; Old Secrets and New Discoveries, by John Campbell, Andrew Mowbray, Inc., Lincoln RI, 2000. 280 pp., illus. $55.00
An exciting follow-up to the classic first volume.

Winchester Sporting Firearms: Dates Of Manufacture, by Morse, D. R. Phoenix, AZ: Firing Pin Enterprizes, 2003. Covers their pistols, revolvers, rifles, shotguns and commemoratives. Plus models & serial numbers. 45 pages. Softcover. NEW. $6.95

World War One Collectors Handbook Volumes 1 and 2 Schulz, Paul and Otoupalik, Hayes and Gordon, Dennis Uniforms, Insignia, Equipment, Weapons, Souvenirs and Miscellaneous. Missoula, MT: Privately Printed, 2002. Two volumes in one edition. 110 pages, loaded with b&w photos. Includes price guide. Softcover. New. $21.95
Covers, uniforms, insignia, equipment, weapons, souvenirs and miscellaneous. For all of you Doughboy collectors, this is a must.

Worldwide Webley and the Harrington and Richardson Connection, by Stephen Cuthbertson, Ballista Publishing and Distributing Ltd., Gabriola Island, Canada, 1999. 259 pp., illus. $50.00
A masterpiece of scholarship. Over 350 photographs plus 75 original documents, patent drawings, and advertisements accompany the text.

EDGED WEAPONS

A Photographic Supplement of Confederate Swords, with addendum, by William A. Albaugh III. Broadfoot Publishing, Wilmington, NC. 1999. $45.00. 205 plus 54 pages of the addendum, illustrated with b&w photos.

Advertising Cutlery; With Values, by Richard White, Schiffer Publishing, Ltd., Atglen, PA. 176 pages, with over 400 color photos. Softcover. $29.95
Advertising Cutlery is the first-ever publication to deal exclusively with the subject of promotional knives. Containing over 400 detailed color photographs, this book explores over one hundred years of advertisements stamped into the sides of knives. In addition to the book's elegant photographic presentation, extensive captions and text give the reader the background information necessary for evaluating collectible advertising knives. Significant examples of advertising specimens are described in detailed stories. Evaluative schemes are included, and all captions contain accurate pricing information. Future trends are also discussed.

Allied Military Fighting Knives; And The Men Who Made Them Famous, by Robert A. Buerlein, Paladin Press, Boulder, CO: 2001. 185 pages, illustrated with b&w photos. Softcover. $35.00

The American Eagle Pommel Sword: The Early Years 1794-1830, by Andrew Mowbray, Manrat Arms Publications, Lincoln, RI, 1997. 244 pp., illus. $65.00
The standard guide to the most popular style of American sword.

American Knives; The First History and Collector's Guide, by Harold L. Peterson, The Gun Room Press, Highland Park, NJ, 1980. 178 pp., illus. $24.95
A reprint of this 1958 classic. Covers all types of American knives.

American Military Bayonets of the 20th Century, by Gary M. Cunningham, Scott A. Duff Publications, Export, PA, 1997. 116 pp., illus. Paper covers. $21.95
A guide for collectors, including notes on makers, markings, finishes, variations, scabbards, and production data.

American Primitive Knives 1770-1870, by G.B. Minnes, Museum Restoration Service, Ottawa, Canada, 1983. 112 pp., illus. $24.95
Origins of the knives, outstanding specimens, structural details, etc.

American Socket Bayonets and Scabbards, by Robert M. Reilly, 2nd printing, Andrew Mowbray, Inc., Lincoln, RI, 1998. 208 pp., illustrated. $45.00
Full coverage of the socket bayonet in America, from Colonial times through the post-Civil War.

The American Sword, 1775-1945, by Harold L. Peterson, Ray Riling Arms Books, Co., Phila., PA, 2001. 286 pp. plus 60 pp. of illus. $49.95
1977 reprint of a survey of swords worn by U.S. uniformed forces, plus the rare "American Silver Mounted Swords, (1700-1815)."

American Swords and Sword Makers, by Richard H. Bezdek, Paladin Press, Boulder, CO, 1994. 648 pp., illus. $79.95
The long-awaited definitive reference volume to American swords, sword makers and sword dealers from Colonial times to the present.

American Swords & Sword Makers Volume 2, by Richard H. Bezdek, Paladin Press, Boulder, CO, 1999. 376 pp., illus. $69.95
More than 400 stunning photographs of rare, unusual and one-of-a-kind swords from the top collections in the country

American Swords from the Philip Medicus Collection, edited by Stuart C. Mowbray, with photographs and an introduction by Norm Flayderman, Andrew Mowbray Publishers, Lincoln, RI, 1998. 272 pp., with 604 swords illustrated. $55.00
Covers all areas of American sword collecting.

The Ames Sword Company Catalog: An Exact Reprint of the Original 19th Century Military and Fraternal Sword Catalog, by Mowbray, Stuart C. (Intro. by). Lincoln, RI: Andrew Mowbray, Inc., 2003. 1st edition. 200 pp, 541 swords illustrated with original prices and descriptions. Pictorial Hardcover. $37.50
The level of detail in these original catalog images will surprise you. Dealers who sold Ames swords used this catalog in their stores, and every feature is clearly shown. Reproduced directly from the incredibly rare originals, Military, Fraternal and more! The key to identifying hundreds of Ames Swords! Shows the whole Ames line, including swords from the Civil War and even earlier. Lots of related military items like belts, bayonets, etc.

The Ames Sword Company, 1829-1935, by John D. Hamilton, Andrew Mowbray Publisher, Lincoln, RI, 1995. 255 pp., illus. $45.00.
An exhaustively researched and comprehensive history of America's foremost sword manufacturer and arms supplier during the Civil War.

Antlers & Iron II, by Krause Publications, Iola, WI, 1999. 40 Pages, illustrated with 100 photos. Paper covers. $12.00
Lays out actual plans so you can build your mountain man folding knife using ordinary hand tools. Step-by-step instructions, with photos, design, antler slotting and springs.

The Art of Throwing Weapons, by James W. Madden, Paladin Press, Boulder, CO, 1993. 102 pp., illus. $14.00
This comprehensive manual covers everything from the history and development of the five most common throwing weapons--spears, knives, tomahawks, shurikens and boomerangs--to their selection or manufacture, grip, distances, throwing motions and advanced combat methods.

Arte Of Defence An Introduction To The Use Of The Rapier, by Wilson, William E. Union City, CA: Chivalry Bookshelf, 2002. 1st edition. 167 pages, illustrated with over 300 photographs. Softcover $24.95

Battle Blades: A Professional's Guide to Combat Fighting Knives, by Greg Walker; Foreword by Al Mar, Paladin Press, Boulder, CO, 1993. 168 pp., illus. $40.95
The author evaluates daggers, Bowies, switchblades and utility blades according to their design, performance, reliability and cost.

The Bayonet in New France, 1665-1760, by Erik Goldstein, Museum Restoration Service, Bloomfield, Ontario, Canada, 1997. 36 pp., illus. Paper covers. $8.95
Traces bayonets from the recently developed plug bayonet, through the regulation socket bayonets which saw service in North America.

Bayonets From Janzen's Notebook, by Jerry Jansen. Cedar Ridge Publications, Tulsa, Ok 2000. 6th printing. 258 pages, illus. Hardcover. $45.00
This collection of over 1000 pieces is one of the largest in the U.S.

Bayonets, Knives & Scabbards; United States Army Weapons Report 1917 Thru 1945, edited by Frank Trzaska, Knife Books, Deptford, NJ, 1999. 80 pp., illustrated. Paper covers. $15.95
Follows the United States edged weapons from the close of World War 1 through the end of World War 2. Manufacturers involved, dates, numbers produced, problems encountered, and production data.

The Best of U.S. Military Knives, Bayonets & Machetes, by M. H. Cole, (edited by) Michael W. Silvey. IDSA Books, 2002. 335 pages, illustrated. $59.95
This book consolidates Cole's four books into one usable text that includes drawings and information about all the significant U.S. issue and private purchase knives, bayonets, and machetes.

The Book of the Sword, by Richard F. Burton, Dover Publications, New York, NY, 1987. 199 pp., illus. Paper covers. $12.95
Traces the swords origin from its birth as a charged and sharpened stick through diverse stages of development.

Borders Away, Volume 1: With Steel, by William Gilkerson, Andrew Mowbray, Inc., Lincoln, RI, 1991. 184 pp., illus. $48.00
A comprehensive study of naval armament under fighting sail. This first voume covers axes, pikes and fighting blades in use between 1626-1826.

Borders Away, Volume 2: Firearms of the Age of Fighting Sail, by William Gilkerson, Andrew Mowbray, Inc., Lincoln, RI, 1999. 331 pp., illus. $65.00
Completing a two volume set, this impressive work covers the pistols, muskets, combustibles, and small cannon once employed aboard American and European fightng ships. 200 photos, 16 color plates.

THE ARMS LIBRARY

Bowie And Big-Knife Fighting System, by Dwight C. McLemore. Bouder, CO: Paladin Press, 2003. 200+ pen-and-ink drawings are so skillfully executed that they vividly convey the movement of the training sequences. 240 pages, illustrated. Softcover. $35.00

Bowie Knives and Bayonets of the Ben Palmer Collection, 2nd Edition, by Ben Palmer, Bill Moran and Jim Phillips. Williamstown, NJ: Phillips Publications, 2002. Hardcover. $49.95

Vastly expanded with more than 300 makers, distributors & dealers added to the makers list; chapter on Bowie knife photograph with 50 image photo gallery of knife holders from the Mexican War, Civil War, & the West; contains a chapter on Bowie Law; includes several unpublished Bowie documents, including the first account of the Alamo. 224 pages, illustrated with photos. As things stand, it is a 'must' read for collectors, particularly if you're looking for photos of some knives not often seen, or curious about what Bill Moran might have to say about some of the old bowie designs.

Bowies, Big Knives, and the Best of Battle Blades, by Bill Bagwell, Paladin Press, Boulder, CO. 2001. 184 pp., illus. Paper covers. $30.00

This book binds the timeless observations and invaluable advice of master bladesmith and blade combat expert Bill Bagwell under one cover for the first time. As the outspoken author of Soldier of Fortune's "Battle Blades" column from 1984 to 1988, Bagwell was considered both outrageous and revolutionary in his advocacy of carrying fighting knives as long as 10 inches and his firm belief that the Bowie was the most effective and efficient fighting knife ever developed. Here, you'llfind all of Bagwell's classic SOF columns, plus all-new material linking his early insights with his latest conclusions. Must reading for serious knife fans.

British & Commonwealth Bayonets, by Ian D. Skennerton and Robert Richardson, I.D.S.A. Books, Piqua, OH, 1986. 404 pp., 1300 illus. $40.00

Civil War Cavalry & Artillery Sabers, 1833-1865, by Thillmann, John H., Andrew Mowbray, Inc. Lincoln, RI: 2002. 1st edition. 500+ pages, over 50 color photographs, 1,373 B&W illustrations, coated paper, dust jacket, premium hardcover binding. Hardcover $79.95

Collecting the Edged Weapons of Imperial Germany, by Johnson & Wittmann, Johnson Reference Books, Fredericksburg, VA, 1989. 363 pp., illus. $39.50

An in-depth study of the many ornate military, civilian, and government daggers and swords of the Imperial era.

Clandestine Edged Weapons, by Windrum, William. Phillips Publications, Williamstown, NJ 2001. 74 pages, illustrated with b&w photographs. Pictorial Softcover $9.95

Collecting Indian Knives, 2nd Edition, by Lar Hothem, Krause Publications, Iola, WI, 2000. 176 pp., illustrated. Paper covers. $19.95

Expanded and updated with new photos and information, this 2nd edition will be a must have for anyone who collects or wants to learn about chipped Indian artifacts in the knife family. With an emphasis on prehistoric times, the book is loaded with photos, values and identification guidelines to help identify blades as to general time-period and, in many cases, help date sites where such artifacts are found. Includes information about different regional materials and basic styles, how knives were made and for what they were probably used.

Collector's Guide to Ames U.S. Contract Military Edged Weapons: 1832-1906, by Ron G. Hickox, Pioneer Press, Union City, IN, 1993. 70 pp., illus. Paper covers. $17.50

While this book deals primarily with edged weapons made by the Ames Manufacturing Company, this guide refers to other manufactureres of United States swords.

Collectors Guide To Switchblade Knives, An Illustrated Historical and Price Reference, by Richard V. Langston. Paladin Press, Boulder, CO. 2001. 224 pp., illus. $49.95

It has been more than 20 years since a major work on switchblades has been published, and never has one showcased as many different types as Rich Langston's welcome new book. The Collector's Guide to Switchblade Knives contains a history of the early cutlery industry in America; a detailed examination of the evolution of switchblades; and a user-friendly, up-to-the-minute, illustrated reference section that helps collectors and novices alike identify all kinds of knives, from museum-quality antiques to Granddad's old folder that's been hidden in the attic for decades. Langston, a life-long knife lover and collector, provides an honest appraisal of more than 160 autos based on maker, condition, markings, materials, functioning and availability.

Collector's Handbook of World War 2 German Daggers, by LtC. Thomas M. Johnson, Johnson Reference Books, Fredericksburg, VA, 2nd edition, 1991. 252 pp., illus. Paper covers. $25.00

Concise pocket reference guide to Third Reich daggers and accoutrements in a convenient format. With value guide.

Collins Machetes and Bowies 1845-1965, by Daniel E. Henry, Krause Publications, Iola, WI, 1996. 232 pp., illus. Paper covers. $19.95

A comprehensive history of Collins machetes and bowies including more than 1200 blade instruments and accessories.

The Complete Bladesmith: Forging Your Way to Perfection, by Jim Hrisoulas, Paladin Press, Boulder, CO, 1987. 192 pp., illus. $42.95

Novice as well as experienced bladesmith will benefit from this definitive guide to smithing world-class blades.

The Complete Book of Pocketknife Repair, by Ben Kelly, Jr., Krause Publications, Iola, WI, 1995. 130 pp., illus. Paper covers. $10.95

Everything you need to know about repairing knives can be found in this step-by-step guide to knife repair.

Confederate Edged Weapons, by W.A. Albaugh, R&R Books, Lavonia, NY, 1994. 198 pp., illus. $40.00

The master reference to edged weapons of the Confederate forces. Features precise line drawings and an extensive text.

The Connoisseur's Book of Japanese Swords, by Nagayama, Kodauska International, Tokyo, Japan, 1997. 348pp., illustrated. $75.00

Translated by Kenji Mishina. A comprehensive guide to the appreciation and appraisal of the blades of Japanese swords. The most informative guide to the blades of Japanese swords ever to appear in English.

Counterfeiting Antique Cutlery, by Gerald Witcher. National Brokerage And Sales, Inc., Brentwood, TN. 1997. 512 pages, illustrated with 1500-2000 b&w photographs. $24.95

Daggers and Bayonets a History, by Logan Thompson, Paladin Press, Boulder, CO, 1999. 128 pp., illustrated. $40.00

This authoritative history of military daggers and bayonets examines all patterns of daggers in detail, from the utilitarian Saxon scamasax used at Hastings to lavishly decorated Cinquedas, Landsknecht and Holbein daggers of the late high Renaissance.

Daggers and Fighting Knives of the Western World: From the Stone Age til 1900, by Harold Peterson, Dover Publishing, Mineola, NY, 2001. 96 pages, plus 32 pages of matte stock. Over 100 illustrations. Softcover. $9.95

The only full-scale reference book devoted entirely to the subject of fighting knives: flint knives, daggers of all sorts, scramasaxes, hauswehren, dirks and more. 108 plates, bibliography and Index.

The Earliest Commando Knives, by William Windrum. Phillips Publications, Williamstown, NJ. 2001. 74 pages, illustrated. Softcover. $9.95

Edged Weapon Accouterments Of Germany 1800-1945, by Kreutz, Hofmann, Johnson, Reddick. Pottsboro, TX: Reddick Enterprises, 2002. 1st edition. Profusely illustrated, with 160 pages. 54 full color plates of illustrations, 26 pages of full color photos and over 125 b&w photos, including over 90 period in wear photos. Hardcover. $49.90

Eickhorn Edged Weapons Exports, Vol. 1: Latin America, by A.M. de Quesada, Jr & Ron G. Hicock, Pioneer Press, Union City, TN, 1996. 120 pp., illus. Softcovers. $15.00

This research studies the various Eickhorn edged weapons and accessories manufactured for various countries outside of Germany.

Exploring the Dress Daggers of the German Army, by Thomas T. Wittmann, Johnson Reference Books, Fredericksburg, VA, 1995. 350 pp., illus. $69.95

The first in-depth analysis of the dress daggers worn by the German Army.

Exploring the Dress Daggers of the German Luftwaffe, by Thomas T. Wittmann, Johnson Reference Books, Fredericksburg, VA, 1998. 350 pp., illus. $79.95

Examines the dress daggers and swords of the German Luftwaffe. The designs covered include the long DLV patterns, the Glider Pilot designs of the NSFK and DLV, 1st and 2nd model Luftwaffe patterns, the Luftwaffe sword and the General OFficer Dengen. Many are pictured for the first time in color.

Exploring The Dress Daggers Of The German Navy, by Thomas T. Wittmann, Johnson Reference Books, Fredericksburg, VA, 2000. 560 pp., illus. $89.95

Explores the dress daggers and swords of the Imperial, Weimar, and Third Reich eras, from 1844-1945. Provides detailed information, as well as many superb b&w and color photographs of individual edged weapons. Many are pictured for the first time in full color.

Exploring the Dress Daggers and Swords of the SS, by Thomas T. Wittmann, Johnson Reference Books, Fredericksburg, VA, 2003. 1st edition. 750 pages, illustrated with nearly 1000 photographs, many in color. $150.00

Covers all model SS Service Daggers, Chained SS Officer Daggers, Himmler & Rohm Inscriptions, Damascus presentations, SS Officer Degen, Himmler Birthday Degen, Silver Lionhead Swords, Blade etch study & much more. Profusely illustrated with historically important period in-wear photographs. Most artifacts appearing for the first time in reference.

The First Commando Knives, by Prof. Kelly Yeaton and Col. Rex Applegate, Phillips Publications, Williamstown, NJ, 1996. 115 pp., illus. Paper covers. $12.95

Here is the full story of the Shanghai origins of the world's best known dagger.

German Clamshells and Other Bayonets, by G. Walker and R.J. Weinard, Johnson Reference Books, Fredericksburg, VA, 1994. 157 pp., illus. $22.95

Includes unusual bayonets, many of which are shown for the first time. Current market values are listed.

German Etched Dress Bayonets (Extra-Seitengewehr) 1933-1945, by Wayne H. Techet. Printed by the Author, Las Vegas, NV. 2002. $55.00

Photographs of over 200 Obverse and Reverse motifs. Rare SS and Panzer patterns pictured for the first time, with an extensive chapter on Reproductions and Red Flags. Close-up photography revealing design details within patterns, plus many more details, insights, and observations relating to collecting the etched dress bayonets of the Third Reich. Color section, and value guide. 262 pages. A limited edition of 1,300 copies. Signed and Numbered.

German Swords and Sword Makers: Edged Weapons Makers from the 14th to the 20th Centuries, by Richard H. Bezdek, Paladin Press, Boulder, CO, 2000. 248 pp., illustrated. $59.95

This book contains the most informations ever published on German swords and edged weapons makers from the Middle Ages to the present.

A Guide to Military Dress Daggers, Volume 1, by Kurt Glemser, Johnson Reference Books, Fredericksburg, VA, 1991. 160 pp., illus. Softcover. $26.50

Very informative guide to dress daggers of foreign countries, to include an excellent chapter on DDR daggers. There is also a section on reproduction Third Reich period daggers. Provides, for the first time, identification of many of the war-time foreign dress daggers. There is also a section on Damascus blades. Good photographic work. Mr. Glemser is certainly to be congratulated on this book on such a neglected area of militaria.

A Guide to Military Dress Daggers, Volume 2, by Kurt Glemser, Johnson Reference Books, Fredericksburg, VA, 1993. 160 pp., illus. $32.50

As in the first volume, reproduction daggers are covered in depth (Third Reich, East German, Italian, Polish and Hungarian). American Navy dirks are featured for the first time. Bulgarian Youth daggers, Croatioan daggers and Imperial German Navy dagger scabbards all have chapters devoted to them. Continues research initiated in Volume I on such subjects as dress daggers, Solingen export daggers, East German daggers and Damascus Smith Max Dinger.

A Guide to Military Dress Daggers, Volume 3, by Kurt Glemser, Johnson Reference Books, Fredericksburg, VA, 1996. 260 pp., illus. $39.50

Includes studies of Swedish daggers, Italian Cadet daggers, Rumanian daggers, Austrian daggers, Dress daggers of the Kingdom of Yugoslavia, Czechoslovakian daggers, Paul Dinger Damastschmied, Swiss Army daggers, Polish daggers (1952-1994), and Hungarian Presentation daggers.

A Guide to Military Dress Daggers, Volume 4, by Kurt Glemser, Johnson Reference Books, Fredericksburg, VA, 2001. 252 pp., illus. $49.50

Several chapters dealing with presentation daggers to include a previously unknown series of East German daggers. Other chapters cover: Daggers in wear; Czech & Slovak daggers; Turkish daggers; swiss Army daggers; Solingen Export daggers; Miniature daggers, Youth knives.

The Halberd and other European Polearms 1300-1650, by George Snook, Museum Restoration Service, Bloomfield, Ontario, Canada, 1998.

A comprehensive introduction to the history, use, and identification of the staff weapons of Europe. 40 pp., illus. Paper covers. $8.95

THE ARMS LIBRARY

Highland Swordsmanship: Techniques of the Scottish Swordmasters, edited by Mark Rector. Chivalry Bookshelf, Union City, CA 2001. 208 pages, Includes more than 100 illustrative photographs. Softcover $29.95

Rector has done a superb job at bringing together two influential yet completely different 18th century fencing manuals from Scotland. Adding new interpretative plates, Mark offers new insights and clear presentations of many useful techniques. With contributions by Paul MacDonald and Paul Wagner, this book promises to be a treat for students of historical fencing, Scottish history and reenactors.

How to Make Folding Knives, by Ron Lake, Frank Centofante and Wayne Clay, Krause Publications, Iola, WI, 1995. 193 pp., illus. Paper covers. $13.95

With step-by-step instructions, learn how to make your own folding knife from three top custom makers.

How to Make Knives, by Richard W. Barney and Robert W. Loveless, Krause Publications, Iola, WI, 1995. 182 pp., illus. Paper covers. $13.95

Complete instructions from two premier knife makers on making high-quality, handmade knives.

How to Make Multi-Blade Folding Knives, by Eugene Shadley & Terry Davis, Krause Publications, Iola, WI, 1997. 192 pp., illus. Paper covers. $19.95

This step-by-step instructional guide teaches knifemakers how to craft these complex folding knives.

How to Make a Tactical Folder, by Bob Tetzuola, Krause Publications, Iola, WI, 2000. 160 pp., illustrated. Paper covers. $16.95

Step-by-step instructions and outstanding photography guide the knifemaker from start to finish.

The Modern Swordsman, by Fred Hutchinson, Paladin Press, Boulder, CO, 1999. 80 pp., illustrated. Paper covers. $22.00

Realistic training for serious self-defense.

The Wonder of Knifemaking, by Wayne Goddard, Krause Publications, Iola, WI, 2000. 160 pp., illustrated with 150 b&w photos and a 16 page color section. $19.95

Tips for Knifemakers of all skill levels. Heat treating and steel selection.

KA-BAR: The Next Generation of the Ultimate Fighting Knife, by Greg Walker, Paladin Press, Boulder, CO, 2001. 88 pp., illus. Soft covers. $16.00

The KA-BAR Fighting/Utility Knife is the most widely recognized and popular combat knife ever to be produced in the United States. Since its introduction on 23 November 1942, the KA-BAR has performed brilliantly on the battlefields of Europe, the South Pacific, Korea, Southeast Asia, Central America and the Middle East, earning its moniker as the "ultimate fighting knife." In this book, Greg Walker gives readers an inside view of the exacting design criteria, cutting-edge materials, extensivefactory tests and exhaustive real-life field tests that went into the historic redesign of the blade, handguard, handle, pommel, and sheath of the ultimate fighting knife of the future. The new knife excelled at these rigorous tests, earning the right tobe called a KA-BAR.

Kalashnikov Bayonets: The Collector's Guide to Bayonets for the AK and its Variations, by Martin D. Ivie, Texas: Diamond Eye Publications, 2002. 1st edition. 220 pages, with over 250 color photos and illustrations. Hardcover. $59.95

Knife and Tomahawk Throwing: The Art of the Experts, by Harry K. McEvoy, Charles E. Tuttle, Rutland, VT, 1989. 150 pp., illus. Soft covers. $8.95

The first book to employ side-by-side the fascinating art and science of knives and tomahawks.

The Knife in Homespun America and Related Items: Its Construction And Material, As Used by Woodsmen, Farmers, Soldiers, Indians And General Population, by Madison Grant,. York, PA: Privately Printed, 1984. 1st edition. 187 pages, profusely illustrated. $45.00

Shows over 300 examples of knives and related items made and used by woodsman, farmers, soldiers, indians and the general frontier population.

Knife Talk, The Art and Science of Knifemaking, by Ed. Fowler, Krause Publications, Iola, WI, 1998. 158 pp., illus. Paper covers. $14.95

Valuable how-to advice on knife design and construction plus 20 years of memorable articles from the pages of "Blade" Magazine.

Knifemakers of Old San Francisco, by Bernard Levine, 2nd edition, Paladin Press, Boulder, CO, 1998. 150 pp., illus. $39.95

The definitive history of the knives and knife-makers of 19th century San Francisco.

Knives Of The United States Military - World War II, by Michael W. Silvey. Privately Printed, Sacramento, CA 1999. 250 pages, illustrated with full color photos. $60.00

240 full page color plates depicting the knives of World War II displayed against a background of wartime accoutrements and memorabilia. The book focuses on knives and their background.

Knives Of The United States Military In Vietnam: 1961-1975, by Michael W. Silvey. Privately Printed, Sacramento, CA., 139 pp. Hardcover. $45.00

A beautiful color celebration of the most interesting and rarest knives of the Vietnam War, emphasizing SOG knives, Randalls, Gerbers, Eks, and other knives of this era. Shown with these knives are the patches and berets of the elite units who used them.

Knives 2004, 24th Annual Edition, edited by Joe Kertzman, Krause Publications, Iola, WI, 2003. 320 pp., illustrated. Paper covers. $22.95

More than 1,200 photos and listings of new knives plus articles from top writers in the field.

Les Baionnettes Reglementaires Francises de 1840 a 1918 'The Bayonets; Military Issue 1840-1918, by French Assoc.of Bayonet Collectors, 2000. 77 pp. illus. $24.95

Profusely illustrated. By far the most comprehenive guide to French military bayonets done for this period. Includes hundreds of illustrations. 77 large 8 1/4 x ll 1/2 inch pages. French Text. Color photos are magnificant!

The Master Bladesmith: Advanced Studies in Steel, by Jim Hrisoulas, Paladin Press, Boulder, CO, 1990. 296 pp., illus. $49.95

The author reveals the forging secrets that for centuries have been protected by guilds.

Medieval Swordsmanship, Illustrated Methods and Techniques, by John Clements, Paladin Press, Boulder, CO, 1998. 344 pp., illustrated. $40.00

The most comprehensive and historically accurate view ever written of the lost fighting arts of Medieval knights.

The Military Knife & Bayonet Book, by Homer Brett. World Photo Press, Japan. 2001. 392 pages, illus. $69.95

Professional studio color photographs, with more than 1,000 military knives and knife-bayonets illustrated. Both the U.S. and foreign sections are extensive, and includes standard models, prototypes and experimental models. Many of the knives and bayonets photographed have never been previously illustrated in any other book. The U.S. section also includes the latest developments in military Special Operations designs. Written in Japanese and English. This book is a must for any collector.

Military Knives: A Reference Book, by Frank Trzaska (editor), Knife Books, Deptford, NJ, 2001. 255 pp., illustrated. Softcover. $17.95

A collection of your favorite Military Knive articles fron the pages of Knife World Magazine. 67 articles ranging from the Indian Wars to the present day modern military knives.

Modern Combat Blades, by Duncan Long, Paladin Press, Boulder, CO, 1993. 128 pp., illus. $30.00

Long discusses the pros and cons of bowies, bayonets, commando daggers, kukris, switchblades, butterfly knives, belt-buckle blades and many more.

Officer Swords of the German Navy 1806-1945, Claus P. Stefanski & Dirk. Schiffer Publications, Atglen, PA, 2002. 1st edition. 176 pages, with over 250 b&w and color photos. Hardcover. $59.95

On Damascus Steel, by Dr. Leo S. Figiel, Atlantis Arts Press, Atlantis, FL, 1991. 145 pp., illus. $65.00

The historic, technical and artistic aspects of Oriental and mechanical Damascus. Persian and Indian sword blades, from 1600-1800, which have never been published, are illustrated.

The Pattern-Welded Blade: Artistry in Iron, by Jim Hrisoulas, Paladin Press, Boulder, CO, 1994. 120 pp., illus. $44.95

Reveals the secrets of this craft—from the welding of the starting billet to the final assembly of the complete blade.

The Plug Bayonet: An Identification Guide For Collectors, by R.D.C. Evans. West Yorkshire, UK: Privately Printed, 2002. 1st edition. 263 pages, illustrated. 507 Plug Bayonets are covered. Hardcover. $67.95

This volume is intended to allow the collector to place a particular plug bayonet in its correct time period & country of origin. Separate countries covered British Isles, France, Germanic countries, Italian states, Low countries, Russia, E. Europe, America, India, Spain & Portugal. Cutler's marks found on bayonets are covered in detail.

Pocket Knives Of The United States Military, by Michael W. Silvey. Sacramento, CA: Privately printed, 2002. 135 pages. Hardcover. $34.95

This beautiful new full color book is the definitive reference on U.S. Military folders. Pocket Knives of the United States Military is organized into the following sections: Introduction, The First Folders, World War I, World War II, and Postwar (which covers knives up through the late 1980s). Coverage ranges from the expected pages of TL-29s and 4-blade utility knives to rare switchblades, demolition knives, OSS and CIA folders, and far, far more U.S. Navy rope knives than I ever knew existed. The photos are as beautiful as expected, and the knives pictured the finest that could be procured. A bibliography is included as an added bonus. Essential reading for pocketknife and military knife collectors alike!

The Randall Chronicles, by Hamilton, Pete. Privately printed, 2002. 160 pages, profusely illustrated in color. Hardcover in Dust Jacket. $79.95

Randall Fighting Knives In Wartime: WWII, Korea, and Vietnam, by Robert E. Hunt. Sacramento, CA: Privately Printed, 2002. 1st edition. 192 pages. Hardcover. $44.95

While other books on Randall knives have been published, this new title is the first to focus specifically on Randalls with military ties. There are three main sections, containing more than 80 knives from the WWII, Korea, and Vietnam War periods. Each knife is featured in a high quality, full page, full color photograph, with the opposing page carrying a detailed description of the knife and its history or other related information. Some interesting military accessories can be found in the photos as well. One of the most useful parts of the book is the section in the back devoted to explaining such complexities as wrist thong attachments for model #1 and #2 knives, sheath snaps, Springfield fighters, small stamps, Johnson split-back sheaths with small rivets, and "fighter sets." All of this is important information for the Randall devotee. A price guide is also included, which I thought a nice touch. My complaints about the book are minor: the abbreviations used should have been better explained, and some additional photos would have been very useful in helping the reader understand the plethora of variations described in the text. Page after page of classic Randall fighting knives from WWII, Korea, and Vietnam, all in beautiful full color.

Randall Made Knives, by Robert L. Gaddis, Paladin Press, Boulder, CO, 2000. 292 pp., illus. $59.95

Plots the designs of all 24 of Randall's unique knives. This step-by-step book, seven years in the making, is worth every penny and moment of your time.

The Razor Anthology, by Krause Publications, Iola, WI. 1998. 246 pp., illustrated. Paper covers. $14.95

Razor Anthology is a cut above the rest. Razor aficionados will find this collection of articles about razors both informative and interesting.

Razor Edge, by John Juranitch, Krause Publications, Iola, WI. 1998. 132 pp., illustrated. Paper covers. $15.00

Reveals step-by-step instructions for sharpening everything from arrowheads, to blades, to fish hooks.

Renaissance Swordsmanship, by John Clements, Paladin Press, Boulder, CO, 1997. 152 pp., illus. Paper covers. $25.00

The illustrated use of rapiers and cut-and-thrust swords.

Rice's Trowel Bayonet, reprinted by Ray Riling Arms Books, Co., Phila., PA, 1968. 8 pp., illus. Paper covers. $3.00

A facsimile reprint of a rare circular originally published by the U.S. government in 1875 for the information of U.S. troops.

The Scottish Dirk, by James D. Forman, Museum Restoration Service, Bloomfield, Ont., Canada, 1991. 60 pp., illus. Paper covers. $8.95

More than 100 dirks are illustrated with a text that sets the dirk and Sgian Dubh in their socio-historic content following design changes through more than 300 years of evolution.

Seitengewehr: History of the German Bayonet, 1919-1945, by George T. Wheeler, Johnson Reference Books, Fredericksburg, VA, 2000. 320 pp., illus. $44.95

Provides complete information on Weimar and Third Reich bayonets, as well astheir accompanying knots and frogs. Illustrates re-issued German and foreign bayonets utilized by both the Reichswehr and the Wehrmacht, and details the progression ofnewly manufactured bayonets produced after Hitler's rise to power. Photos illustrate rarely seen bayonets worn by the Polizei, Reichsbahn, Postschutz, Hitler Jugend, and other civil and political organiztions. German modified bayonets from other countries are pictured and described. Book contains an up-to-date price guide including current valuations of various Imperial, Weimar, and Third Reich bayonets.

Silver Mounted Swords: The Lattimer Family Collection; Featuring Silver Hilts Through the Golden Age, by Daniel Hartzler, Rowe Publications, New York, 2000. 300 pages, with over 1000 illustrations and 1350 photo's. Oversize 9x12. $75.00

The world's largest Silver Hilt collection.

Small Arms Identification Series, No. 6-British Service Sword & Lance Patterns, by Ian Skennerton, I.D.S.A. Books, Piqua, OH, 1994. 48 pp. $12.50

Small Arms Series, No. 2. The British Spike Bayonet, by Ian Skennerton, I.D.S.A. Books, Piqua, OH, 1982. 32 pp., 30 illus. $9.00

THE ARMS LIBRARY

The Socket in the British Army 1667-1783, by Erik Goldstein, Andrew Mowbray, Inc., Lincoln, RI, 2001. 136 pp., illus. $23.00
The spectacle of English "redcoats" on the attack, relentlessly descending upon enemy lines with fixed bayonets, is one of the most chilling images from European history and the American Revolution. The bayonets covered in this book stood side by side with the famous "Brown Bess" as symbols of English military power throughout the world. Drawing upon new information from archaeological digs and archival records, the author explains how to identify each type of bayonet and shows which bayonets were used where and with which guns. No student of military history or weapons development can afford to do without this useful new book.

Socket Bayonets of the Great Powers, by Robert W. Shuey, Excalibur Publications, Tucson, AZ, 2000 96 pp., illus. Paper covers $22.95
With 175 illustrations the author brings together in one place, many of the standard socket arrnagements used by some of the " Great Powers". With an illustrated glossary of blade shape and socket design.

Spyderco Story: The New Shape of Sharp, by Kenneth T. Delavigne, Paladin Press, Boulder, CO, 1998. 312 pp., illus. $69.95
Discover the history and inner workings of the company whose design innovations have redefined the shape of the modern folding knife and taken high-performance cutting to a new level.

Swords and Sword Makers of the War of 1812, by Richard Bezdek, Paladin Press, Boulder, CO, 1997. 104 pp., illus. $49.95
The complete history of the men and companies that made swords during and before the war. Includes examples of cavalry and artillery sabers.

Swords And Sabers of the Armory at Springfield, by Burton A. Kellerstedt, Burton A. Kellerstedt, New Britain, CT, 1998. 121 pp, illus. Softcover. $29.95
The basic and most important reference for it's subject, and one that is unlikely to be surpassed for comprehensiveness and accuracy.

Swords and Blades of the American Revolution, by George C. Neumann, Rebel Publishing Co., Inc., Texarkana, TX, 1991. 288 pp., illus. $36.95
The encyclopedia of bladed weapons—swords, bayonets, spontoons, halberds, pikes, knives, daggers, axes—used by both sides, on land and sea, in America's struggle for independence.

Swords and Sword Makers of England and Scotland, by Richard H. Bezdek, Boulder, CO: Paladin Press, 2003. 1st edition. 424 pages, illustrated. Hardcover. $69.95
Covers English sword makers from the 14th century and Scottish makers from the 16th century all the way through the renowned Wilkinson Sword Company and other major sword manufacturers of today. The important early English sword- and blade-making communities of Hounslow Heath and Shotley Bridge, and the influential Cutlers Company of London. The many types of craftsmen associated with sword production, including hilt, blade and scabbard makers and decorators; and goldsmiths and silversmiths who decorated, mounted, assembled and sold swords. Cutlers, merchants, outfitters and exporters who sold swords, including those who exported swords to the United States. The book concludes with dozens of beautiful illustrations of hilt designs taken directly from famed sword hilt maker Matthew Boulton's 18th-century pattern book and more than 450 spectacular photographs of English and Scottish swords of every type and era from some of the world's major collections.

Swords of Imperial Japan, 1868-1945, by Jim Dawson, Published by the Author. 160 Pages, illustrated with 263 b&w photos. Paper covers. $29.95
Details the military, civilian, diplomatic and civil, police and colonial swords and the post-Samurai era as well as the swords of Manchukuo, the Japanese independent territory.

Tactical Knives, by Dietmar Pohl, Iola, WI: Krause Publications, 2003. 1st edition. 191 Pages, illustrated with 170 color photos. Softcover. $24.95
The 1980s gave birth to combat knives, a type of knife developed specifically for police and military Special Forces. This comprehensive reference is the first to illustrate the development, varieties, and applications of this advanced type of knife from its origins through today. Dozens of knife styles are identified and showcased, including survival knives, multi-tool, tantos, Bowie, machetes, and other trench, commando, boot, and neck knives. Special attention is given to knives that served troops in WWII and Vietnam, as well as those carried by today's Special Forces.

Tactical Folding Knife; A Study of the Anatomy and Construction of the Liner-Locked Folder, by Terzuola, Krause Publications, Iola, WI. 2000. 160 Pages, 200 b&w photos, illustrated. Paper covers. $16.00
Step-by-step instructions and outstanding photography guide the knifemaker from start to finish. This book details everything from the basic definition of a tactical folder to the final polishing as the knife is finished.

The U.S. M3 Trench Knife of World War II, by Coniglio and Laden. Privately Printed, 2003. Reprint. 41 pages, illustrated. Softcover. $18.00
A superb reference book on that hot WWII collectable.

U.S. Military Knives, Bayonets and Machetes Price Guide, 4th ed. by Frank Trzaska (editor), Knife Books, Deptford, NJ, 2001. 80 pp., illustrated. Softcover. $7.95
This volume follows in the tradition of the previous three versions of using major works on the subject as a reference to keep the price low to you.

Wayne Goddard's $50 Knife Shop, by Wayne Goddard, Krause Publications, Iola, WI. 2000. 160 Pages, illus. Soft covers. $19.95
This new book expands on information from Goddard's popular column in Blade magazine to show knifemakers of all skill levels how to create helpful gadgets and supply their shop on a shoestring.

Wonder of Knifemaking, by Wayne Goddard, Krause Publications, Iola, WI. 2000. 160 Pages, illus. Soft covers. $19.95
Master bladesmith Wayne Goddard draws on his decades of experience to answer questions of knifemakers at all levels. As a columnist for Blade magazine, Goddard has been answering real questions from real knifemakers for the past eight years. Now, all the details are compiled in one place as a handy reference for every knifemaker, amateur or professional.

The Working Folding Knife, by Steven Dick, Stoeger Publishing Co., Wayne, NJ, 1998. 280 pp., illus. Paper covers. $21.95
From the classic American Barlow to exotic folders like the spanish Navaja this book has it all.

GENERAL

2004 Standard Catalog of Firearms, 14th Edition, The Collector's Price & Reference Guide, by Ned Schwing, Iola, WI: Krause Publishing, 2003. 14th edition. 1,384 Pages, illustrated. 6,000+ b&w photos plus a 16-page color section. Softcover. $34.95
This is the largest, most comprehensive and best-selling firearm book of all time! And this year's edition is a blockbuster for both shooters and firearm collectors. More than 25,000 firearms are listed and priced in up to six grades of condition. That's almost 110,000 prices! Gun enthusiasts will love the new full-color section of photos highlighting the finest firearms sold at auction this past year.

Action Shooting: Cowboy Style, by John Taffin, Krause Publications, Iola, WI, 1999. 320 pp., illustrated. $39.95
Details on the guns and ammunition. Explanations of the rules used for many events. The essential cowboy wardrobe.

Advanced Muzzleloader's Guide, by Toby Bridges, Stoeger Publishing Co., So. Hackensack, NJ, 1985. 256 pp., illus. Paper covers. $14.95
The complete guide to muzzle-loading rifles, pistols and shotguns—flintlock and percussion.

Aids to Musketry for Officers & NCOs, by Capt. B.J. Friend, Excalibur Publications, Latham, NY, 1996. 40 pp., illus. Paper covers. $7.95
A facsimile edition of a pre-WWI British manual filled with useful information for training the common soldier.

Airgun Odyssey, by Steve Hanson. Manchester, CT: Precision Shooting, Inc., 2004. 1st edition. 175 pages. Pictorial softcover. $28.95
The evolution of today's precision air rifle is traced from the early (and recent) lever action B-B guns to the cost-in-four-figures target and hunting guns now available. The pros and cons of the airgun calibers are discussed in depth for both hunting and target applications. Airguns from foreign manufacturers are given in-depth review as are the popular airgun-specializing gunsmiths operating today. The book's chapter titles give a capsule of the book's contents: Airgun Evolution & Trends... Airgun Propulsion Systems... Airgun Varmint Hunting & Pest Control... American Field Target... Introduction to BR 4000 ... Airgun Tests/Current Production Guns... Airgun Tests/Classic & Discontinued Guns ... Spring-Piston Airgun Tuning... Building A New PCP Airgun for the Sport of American Field Target... Supplier's Index (Airgun Periodicals, Suppliers, Services, Parts & Accessories.

American Air Rifles, by James E. House. Krause Publications, Iola, WI. 2002. 1st edition. 208 pages, with 198 b&w photos. Softcover. $22.95
Air rifle ballistics, sights, pellets, games, and hunting caliber recommendations are thoroughly explained to help shooters get the most out of their American air rifles. Evaluation of more than a dozen American-made and American-imported air rifle models.

The American B.B. Gun: A Collector's Guide, by Arni T. Dunathan. A.S. Barnes and Co., Inc., South Brunswick. 2001. 154 pages, illustrated with nearly 200 photographs, drawings and detailed diagrams. Hardcove. $35.00

American and Imported Arms, Ammunition and Shooting Accessories, Catalog No. 18 of the Shooter's Bible, Stoeger, Inc., reprinted by Fayette Arsenal, Fayetteville, NC, 1988. 142 pp., illus. Paper covers. $10.95
A facsimile reprint of the 1932 Stoeger's Shooter's Bible.

America's Great Gunmakers, by Wayne van Zwoll, Stoeger Publishing Co., So. Hackensack, NJ, 1992. 288 pp., illus. Paper covers. $16.95
This book traces in great detail the evolution of guns and ammunition in America and the men who formed the companies that produced them.

Annie Oakley of the Wild West, by Walter Havighurst. New York: Castle Books, 2000. 246 pages. Hardcover. $10.00
This book brings to life the complete story of "Little Sureshot"—not only her phenomenal sharp-shooting techniques and career in the Wild West Show, but also her fifty-year marriage to Frank Butler, himself a professional marksman.

Armed and Female, by Paxton Quigley, E.P. Dutton, New York, NY, 2001. 237 pp., illus. Softcover $9.95
The first complete book on one of the hottest subjects in the media today, the arming of the American woman.

Arming the Glorious Cause: Weapons of the Second War for Independence, by James B. Whisker, Daniel D. Hartzler and Larry W. Yantz, R & R Books, Livonia, NY, 1998. 175 pp., illustrated. $45.00
A photographic study of Confederate weapons.

Arms & Armor in the Art Institute of Chicago, by Walter J. Karcheski, Jr., Bulfinch Press, Boston, MA, 1995. 128 pp., illus. $35.00
Now, for the first time, the Art Institute of Chicago's arms and armor collection is presented in the visual delight of 103 color illustrations.

Arms for the Nation: Springfield Longarms, edited by David C. Clark, Scott A. Duff, Export, PA, 1994. 73 pp., illus. Paper covers. $9.95
A brief history of the Springfield Armory and the arms made there.

Arsenal of Freedom, The Springfield Armory, 1890-1948: A Year-by-Year Account Drawn from Official Records, compiled and edited by Lt. Col. William S. Brophy, USAR Ret., Andrew Mowbray, Inc., Lincoln, RI, 1991. 400 pp., illus. Soft covers. $29.95
A "must buy" for all students of American military weapons, equipment and accoutrements.

Arrowmaker Frontier Series Volume 1, by Roy Chandler. Jacksonville, NC: Iron Brigade Armory, 2000. 390 pages. Hardcover. $38.95
Those who have read or reviewed Arrowmaker claim the story is better than even the frontier classics "Drums Along the Mohawk" and. "The Last of the Mohicans." We, the publishers agree. There has never been such a fulfilling tale of the colonial frontier. Arrowmaker leaves a reader satisfied. Things come out the way they should, and in these days of confused and irresolute writing that alone is gratifying. Arrowmaker is filled with exploring, building and fighting. The story is based on facts including actual incidents that occurred in the areas depicted. If a reader chose, he could go to the land described and walk the ground while recognizing the physical features written about. Arrowmaker is replete with the danger and violence of the times, but the warring is believable and much of it really happened. Readers develop a unique empathy with the frontiersman, Rob Shatto, and when finished each reader will have gained a new friend that he will cherish as if Rob's great wilderness home had been just down the road. In this volume you will meet frontiersmen and Indians who reappear in succeeding books of this frontier series, but you must read Arrowmaker first. It is the soul-the heart-of all that comes after, and believe us, you will wait with impatience the coming of the next book and each thereafter. We know it is so because we (including the author) have experienced it.

Assault Pistols, Rifles and Submachine Guns, by Duncan Long, Paladin Press, Boulder, CO, 1997, 8 1/2 x 11, soft cover, photos, illus. 152 pp. $21.95
This book offers up-to-date, practical information on how to operate and field-strip modern military, police and civilian combat weapons. Covers new developments and trends such as the use of fiber optics, liquid-recoil systems and lessening of barrel length are covered. Troubleshooting procedures, ballistic tables and a list of manufacturers and distributors are also included.

THE ARMS LIBRARY

Assault Weapons, 5th Edition, The Gun Digest Book of, edited by Jack Lewis and David E. Steele, DBI Books, a division of Krause Publications, Iola, WI, 2000. 256 pp., illustrated. Paper covers. $21.95

This is the latest word on true assault weaponry in use today by international military and law enforcement organizations.

The Belgian Rattlesnake: The Lewis Automatic Machine Gun, by William M. Easterly, Collector Grade Publications, Inc., Cobourg, Ont. Canada, 1998. 542 pp., illus. $79.95

A social and technical biography of the Lewis automatic machine gun and its inventors.

The Benchrest Shooting Primer, by Brennan, Dave (Editor). Precision Shooting, Inc., Manchester, CT 2000. 2nd edition. 420 pages, illustrated with b&w photographs, drawings and detailed diagrams. Pictorial softcover. $24.95

The very best articles on shooting and reloading for the most challenging of all the rifle accuracy disciplines...benchrest shooting.

The Big Guns: Civil War Siege, Seacoast, and Naval Cannon, by Edwin Olmstead, Wayne E. Stark and Spencer C. Tucker, Museum Restoration Service, Bloomfield, Ontario, Canada, 1997. 360 pp., illus. $80.00

This book is designed to identify and record the heavy guns available to both sides during the Civil War.

Blackpowder Loading Manual, 3rd Edition, by Sam Fadala, DBI Books, a division of Krause Publications, Iola, WI, 1995. 368 pp., illus. Paper covers. $20.95

Revised and expanded edition of this landmark blackpowder loading book. Covers hundreds of loads for most of the popular blackpowder rifles, handguns and shotguns.

Black Powder, Pig Lead And Steel Silhouettes, by Paul A. Matthews. Wolfe Publishing, Prescott, AZ, 2002. 132 pages, illustrated with b&w photographs and detailed drawings and diagrams. Softcover. $16.95

The Black Rifle Frontier Series Volume 2, by Roy Chandler. Jacksonville, NC: Iron Brigade Armory, 2002. 226 pages. Hardcover. New in new dust jacket. $42.95

In 1760, inexperienced Jack Elan settles in Sherman's Valley, suffers tragedy, is captured by hostiles, escapes, and fights on. This is the "2nd" book in the Frontier Series.

Bolt Action Rifles, 4th Edition, by Frank de Haas, DBI Books, a division of Krause Publications, Iola, WI, 2004. 628 pp., illus. Paper covers. $27.95

A revised edition of the most definitive work on all major bolt-action rifle designs.

British Small Arms of World War 2, by Ian D. Skennerton, Arms & Militaria Press, Australia 1988. 110 pp., 37 illus. $25.00.

Carbine And Shotgun Speed Shooting: How To Hit Hard And Fast In Combat, by Steve Moses. Paladin Press, Boulder, CO. 2002. 96 pages, illus. Softcover $18.00

In this groundbreaking book, he breaks down the mechanics of speed shooting these weapons, from stance and grip to sighting, trigger control and more, presenting them in a concise and easily understood manner. Whether you wish to further your defensive, competitive or recreational shooting skills, you will find this book a welcome resource for learning to shoot carbines and shotguns with the speed and accuracy that are so critical at short distances.

Co2 Pistols and Rifles, by James E. House. Iola, WI: Krause Publications, 2004. 1st edition. 240 pages, with 198 b&w photos. Softcover. $24.95

In this new guide to CO2-powered pistols and rifles, James E. House offers a comprehensive history of CO2 guns, dating back to the 1930s, and a discussion of propulsion, pellets, and sights. Beginning shooters are introduced to the market with a complete analysis on performance and accuracy of currently available products. Airgun enthusiasts are reunited with CO2 classics no longer being manufactured. This book also offers additional sections on target shooting, games, and varmints. Offers a comprehensive history of CO2 pistols and rifles dating back to the 1930s. Includes a categorical review of BB pistols, .177 caliber pistols, .20 and .22 caliber pistols, and rifles. Discover products currently available only on the secondary market.

Combat Handgunnery, 5th Edition, The Gun Digest Book of, by Chuck Taylor, DBI Books, a division of Krause Publications, Iola, WI, 2002. 256 pp., illus. Paper covers. $21.95

This edition looks at real world combat handgunnery from three different perspectives—military, police and civilian.

The Complete Blackpowder Handbook, 4th Edition, by Sam Fadala, DBI Books, a division of Krause Publications, Iola, WI, 2002. 400 pp., illus. Paper covers. $21.95.

Expanded and completely rewritten edition of the definitive book on the subject of blackpowder.

The Complete Guide to Game Care and Cookery, 4th Edition, by Sam Fadala, Krause Publications, Iola, WI, 2003. 320 pp., illus. Paper covers. $21.95

Over 500 photos illustrating the care of wild game in the field and at home with a separate recipe section providing over 400 tested recipes.

The Complete .50-caliber Sniper Course, by Dean Michaelis, Paladin Press, Boulder, CO, 2000. 576 pp, illustrated, $60.00

The history from German Mauser T-Gewehr of World War 1 to the Soviet PTRD and beyond. Includes the author's Program of Instruction for Special Operations Hard-Target Interdiction Course.

Cowgirls: Women of the Wild West, by Elizabeth Clair Flood, Manns, William, Sage, Helene (edited by). Santa Fe, NM: ZON International Publishing Company, 2000. 1st edition. 224 pages. Foreword by Dale Evans. Hardcover. $45.00

Pays tribute to the women of the frontier. With over 450 color photos and historic images, the spirit, lore and relics of these colorful cowgirls are gloriously depicted. Fashion, ranch life, Hollywood cowgirls, rodeo stars, dude ranches, women of the Wild West Shows, gear, Girls of the Golden West, Western romance and much more.

Cowboys & the Trappings of the Old West, by William Manns & Elizabeth Clair Flood. Santa Fe, NM: ZON International Publishing Company, 1997. 224 pages, 550 colorful photos. With a forewordby Roy Rogers. Hardcover. $45.00

Big & beautiful book covering: Hats, boots, spurs, chaps, guns, holsters, saddles and more. It's really a pictorial cele bration of the old time buckaroo. This exceptional book presents all the accoutrements of the cowboy life in a comprehensive tribute to the makers. The history of the craftsmen and the evolution of the gear are lavishly illustrated.

Custom Firearms Engraving, by Tom Turpin, Krause Publications, Iola, WI, 1999. 208 pp., illustrated. $49.95

Provides a broad and comprehensive look at the world of firearms engraving. The exquisite styles of more than 75 master engravers are shown on beautiful examples of handguns, rifles, shotguns, and other firearms, as well as knives.

Dark Horse Six: A Memoir of the Korean War 1950-1951, Williamstown, NJ: Phillips Publications, 2003. 1st edition. 286 pages, illustrated with photos. Hardcover. $29.95

Dark Horse Six, is the combat memoir of Colonel Robert D. Taplett. He was the commander of one of the USMC's most famed battalions, the 3rd Battalion of the 5th Marine Regiment, during the first year of fighting in Korea. His battalion's radio call sign during the bitter fighting against the Chinese was Dark Horse. After 50 years he has decided to tell his story. He wants the deeds of his Marine's put into the record. The mistakes of combat, planning and egos are here as well. His experience was on the front lines, not theorizing behind some desk. This is a warrior's story!

Dead On, by Tony Noblitt and Warren Gabrilska, Paladin Press, Boulder, CO, 1998. 176 pp., illustrated. Paper covers. $22.00

The long-range marksman's guide to extreme accuracy.

Early American Flintlocks, by Daniel D. Hartzler and James B. Whisker, Bedford Valley Press, Bedford, PA 2000. 192 pp., Illustrated. $45.00

Covers early Colonial Guns, New England Guns, Pennsylvania Guns and Souther Guns.

Elmer Keith: The Other Side Of A Western Legend, by Gene Brown., Precision Shooting, Inc., Manchester, CT 2002. 1st edition. 168 pages, illustrated with b&w photographs. Softcover. $19.95

An updated and expanded edition of his original work, incorporating new tales and information that has come to light in the past six years. Additional photos have been added, and the expanded work has been professionally edited and formatted. Gene Brown was a long time friend of Keith, and today is unquestionably the leading authority on Keith's books. The chapter on the topic is worth the price of admission by itself.

Encyclopedia of Native American Bows, Arrows and Quivers, by Steve Allely and Jim Hamm, The Lyons Press, N.Y., 1999. 160 pp., illustrated. $29.95

A landmark book for anyone interested in archery history, or Native Americans.

Fort Robinson, by Roy Chandler. Frontier Series Volume 4. Jacksonville, NC: Iron Brigade Armory, 2003. 1st edition. 560 pages. Hardcover. $39.95

The Exercise of Armes, by Jacob de Gheyn, Dover Publications, Inc., Mineola, NY, 1999. 144 pp., illustrated. Paper covers. $14.95

Republications of all 117 engravings from the 1607 classic military manual. A meticulously accurate portrait of uniforms and weapons of the 17th century Netherlands.

The Federal Civil War Shelter Tent, by Frederick C. Gaede, Alexandria, VA: O'Donnell Publishing, 2001. 1st edition. This is a great monograph for all Civil War collectors. 134 pages, and illustrated. Softcover $20.00

The text covers everything from government patents, records, and contract data to colorful soldier's descriptions. In addition, it is extensively illustrated with drawings and photos of over 30 known examples with close-ups of stitching, fastening buttons, and some that were decorated with soldier's art. This book is a well-presented study by a leading researcher, collector, and historian.

Fighting Iron; A Metals Handbook for Arms Collectors, by Art Gogan, Mowbray Publishers, Inc., Lincoln, RI, 2002. 176 pp., illustrated. $28.00

A guide that is easy to use, explains things in simple English and covers all of the different historical periods that we are interested in.

The Fighting Submachine Gun, Machine Pistol, and Shotgun, by Timothy J. Mullin, Paladin Press, Boulder, CO, 1999. 224 pp., illustrated. Paper covers. $35.00

An invaluable reference for military, police and civilian shooters who may someday need to know how a specific weapon actually performs when the targets are shooting back and the margin of errors is measured in lives lost.

Firearms Assembly Disassembly; Part 4 : Centerfire Rifles (2nd Edition), by J. B. Wood, Iola, WI: Krause Publications, 2004. 2nd edition. 576 pages, 1,750 b&w photos. Softcover. $24.95

The increasing cost of gunsmithing services has caused enthusiasts to perform minor repairs, refinishing, and deep cleaning on their own firearms. This updated edition shows how to easily disassemble and reassemble centerfire rifles and the correct tools needed. Sixty-six popular guns are taken apart and individually photographed. The cross-reference index identifies more than 400 similar or identical rifle patterns that also follow these disassembly and reassembly directions. Covers the Argentine Mauser to Marlin Model 9 to Russian AK-47 to U.S. M-1 Garand to Winchester Model 1894.

Fireworks: A Gunsight Anthology, by Jeff Cooper, Paladin Press, Boulder, CO, 1998. 192 pp., illus. Paper cover. $27.00

A collection of wild, hilarious, shocking and always meaningful tales from the remarkable life of an American firearms legend.

From a Stranger's Doorstep to the Kremlin Gate, by Mikhail Kalashnikov, Ironside International Publishers, Inc., Alexandria, VA, 1999. 460 pp., illustrated. $34.95

A biography of the most influential rifle designer of the 20th century. His AK-47 assault rifle has become the most widely used (and copied) assault rifle of this century.

The Frontier Rifleman, by H.B. LaCrosse Jr., Pioneer Press, Union City, TN, 1989. 183 pp., illus. Soft covers. $17.50

The Frontier rifleman's clothing and equipment during the era of the American Revolution, 1760-1800.

The Gatling Gun: 19th Century Machine Gun to 21st Century Vulcan, by Joseph Berk, Paladin Press, Boulder, CO, 1991. 136 pp., illus. $34.95

Here is the fascinating on-going story of a truly timeless weapon, from its beginnings during the Civil War to its current role as a state-of-the-art modern combat system.

German Artillery of World War Two, by Ian V. Hogg, Stackpole Books, Mechanicsburg, PA, 1997. 304 pp., illus. $44.95

Complete details of German artillery use in WWII.

Gone Diggin: Memoirs Of A Civil War Relic Hunter, by Toby Law. Orange, VA: Publisher's Press, 2002. 1st edition signed. 151 pages, illustrated with b&w photos. $24.95

The true story of one relic hunter's life - The author kept exacting records of every relic hunt and every relic hunter he was with working with.

Grand Old Lady of No Man's Land: The Vickers Machine Gun, by Dolf L. Goldsmith, Collector Grade Publications, Cobourg, Canada, 1994. 600 pp., illus. $79.95.

Goldsmith brings his years of experience as a U.S. Army armourer, machine gun collector and shooter to bear on the Vickers, in a book sure to become a classic in its field.

Greenhill Military Manuals; Small Arms: Pistols and Rifles, by Ian Hogg; London: Greenhill Press, 2003. Revised. 160 pages, illustrated. Hardcover. $24.00

This handy reference guide, by the leading small arms author, provides descriptions, technical specifications and illustrations of 75 of the most important pistols and rifles, including the Heckler & Koch USP/SOCOM pistols, the FN Five-seveN 5.7mm pistol, the Heckler & Koch G36 rifle and much more.

Gun Digest 2004, 58th Edition, edited by Ken Ramage, DBI Books a division of Krause Publications, Iola, WI, 2002. 544 pp., illustrated. Paper covers. $27.95

This all new 58th edition continues the editorial excellence, quality, content and comprehensive cataloguing that firearms enthusiasts have come to know and expect. The most read gun book in the world for the last half century.

THE ARMS LIBRARY

Gun Engraving, by C. Austyn, Safari Press Publication, Huntington Beach, CA, 1998. 128 pp., plus 24 pages of color photos. $50.00

A well-illustrated book on fine English and European gun engravers. Includes a fantastic pictorial section that lists types of engravings and prices.

Gun Notes, Volume 1, by Elmer Keith, Safari Press, Huntington Beach, CA, 2002. 219 pp., illustrated Softcover. $24.95

A collection of Elmer Keith's most interesting columns and feature stories that appeared in "Guns & Ammo" magazine from 1961 to the late 1970's.

Gun Notes, Volume 2, by Elmer Keith, Safari Press, Huntington Beach, CA, 2002. 292 pp., illustrated. Softcover. $24.95

Covers articles from Keith's monthly column in "Guns & Ammo" magazine during the period from 1971 through Keith's passing in 1982.

Gun Talk, edited by Dave Moreton, Winchester Press, Piscataway, NJ, 1973. 256 pp., illus. $9.95

A treasury of original writing by the top gun writers and editors in America. Practical advice about every aspect of the shooting sports.

The Gun That Made the Twenties Roar, by Wm. J. Helmer, The Gun Room Press, Highland Park, NJ, 1977. Over 300 pp., illus. $24.95

Historical account of John T. Thompson and his invention, the infamous "Tommy Gun."

Gun Trader's Guide (2005 - 26th Edition), by Jarrett (ed.). Pocomoke, MD: Stoeger Publishing, 2004. 26th edition. Softcover. $21.99

The Gun Trader's Guide has been the standard reference for collectors, dealers, shooters and gun enthusiasts since 1953. This 592 page edition provides complete updated specifications, dates of manufacture and current market average values for over 6,000 handguns, rifles and shotguns, both foreign and domestic. A complete index is provided for easy reference to all guns plus handy thumb tabs help readers find, identify and price firearms with ease.

The Gunfighter, Man or Myth? by Joseph G. Rosa, Oklahoma Press, Norman, OK, 1969. 229 pp., illus. (including weapons). Paper covers. $14.95

A well-documented work on gunfights and gunfighters of the West and elsewhere. Great treat for all gunfighter buffs.

Guns Illustrated 2004, 24th Edition, edited by Ken Ramage, DBI Books a division of Krause Publications, Iola, WI, 2003. 388 pp., illustrated. Softcovers. $24.95

Highly informative, technical articles on a wide range of shooting topics by some of the top writers in the industry. A catalog section lists more than 3,000 firearms currently manufactured in or imported to the U.S.

Guns & Shooting: A Selected Bibliography, by Ray Riling, Ray Riling Arms Books Co., Phila., PA, 1982. 434 pp., illus. Limited, numbered edition. $75.00

A limited edition of this superb bibliographical work, the only modern listing of books devoted to guns and shooting.

Guns, Bullets, and Gunfighters, by Jim Cirillo, Paladin Press, Boulder, CO, 1996. 119 pp., illus. Paper covers. $16.00

Lessons and tales from a modern-day gunfighter.

The Guns of the Gunfighters: Lawmen, Outlaws & TV Cowboys, by Doc O'Meara. Iola, WI: Krause Publications, 2003. 1st edition. 16 page color section, 225 b&w photos. Hardcover. $34.95

Explores the romance of the Old West, focusing on the guns that the good guys & bad guys, real & fictional characters, carried with them. Profiles of more than 50 gunslingers, half from the Old West and half from Hollywood, include a brief biography of each gunfighter, along with the guns they carried. Fascinating stories about the TV and movie celebrities of the 1950s and 1960s detail their guns and the skill—or lack thereof—they displayed.

Gunstock Carving: A Step-by-Step Guide To Engraving Rifles and Shotguns, by Bill Janney. East Pertsburg, PA: Fox Chapel Publishing, October 2002.

Learn gunstock carving from an expert. Includes step-by-step projects and instructions, patterns, tips and techniques. 89 pages, illustrated in color. Softcover.$19.95

Hand-To-Hand Combat: United States Naval Institute, by U.S. Navy Boulder, CO: Paladin Press, 2003. 1st edition. 240 pages. Softcover. $25.00

Now you can own one of the classic publications in the history of U.S. military close-quarters combat training. The complete program shown in this book was designed to train sailors and naval aviators of World War II in the deadliest techniques of "commando tactics," jiu jitsu, boxing, wrestling and other fighting systems. Its goal was to teach "cold, efficient method[s] of overcoming your enemy in a manner most suitable to the performance of your mission or the saving of your life without any regard to the comfort or pleasure of the enemy." In 11 photo-heavy chapters, Hand-to-Hand Combat covers training tips; vulnerable targets; the brutal fundamentals of close-in fighting; frontal and rear attacks; prisoner search and control techniques; disarming pistols, rifles, clubs and knives; offensive means of "liquidating an enemy"; and much more. After reading this book (originally published by the United States Naval Institute in 1943), you will see why it has long been sought by collectors and historians of hand-to-hand combat.

Hidden in Plain Sight, "A Practical Guide to Concealed Handgun Carry" (Revised 2nd Edition), by Trey Bloodworth and Mike Raley, Paladin Press, Boulder, CO, 1997, softcover, photos, 176 pp. $20.00

Concerned with how to comfortably, discreetly and safely exercise the privileges granted by a CCW permit? This invaluable guide offers the latest advice on what to look for when choosing a CCW, how to dress for comfortable, effective concealed carry, traditional and more unconventional carry modes, accessory holsters, customized clothing and accessories, accessibility data based on draw-time comparisons and new holsters on the market. Includes 40 new manufacturer listings.

HK Assault Rifle Systems, by Duncan Long, Paladin Press, Boulder, CO, 1995. 110 pp., illus. Paper covers. $27.95

The little known history behind this fascinating family of weapons tracing its beginnings from the ashes of World War Two to the present time.

The Hunter's Guide to Accurate Shooting, by Wayne Van Zwoll, Guilford, CT: Lyons Press, 2002. 1st edition. 288 pp. Hardcover. $29.95

Firearms expert Van Zwoll explains exactly how to shoot the big-game rifle accurately. Taking into consideration every pertinent factor, he shows a step-by-step analysis of shooting and hunting with the big-game rifle.

The Hunting Time: Adventures In Pursuit Of North American Big Game: A Forty-Year Chronicle, by John E. Howard, Deforest, WI: Saint Huberts Press, 2002. 1st edition. 537 pages, illustrated with drawings. Hardcover. $29.95

From a novice's first hunt for whitetailed deer in his native Wisconsin, to a seasoned hunter's pursuit of a Boone and Crockett Club record book caribou in the northwest territories, the author carries the reader along on his forty year journey through the big game fields of North America.

I Remember Skeeter, compiled by Sally Jim Skelton, Wolfe Publishing Co., Prescott, AZ, 1998. 401 pp., illus. Paper covers. $19.95

A collection of some of the beloved storyteller's famous works interspersed with anecdotes and tales from the people who knew best.

Indian Tomahawks And Frontiersmen Belt Axes, by Daniel Hartzler & James Knowles. New Windsor, MD: Privately printed, 2002. 4th revised edition. 279 pages, illustrated with photos and drawings. Hardcover. $65.00

This fourth revised edition has over 160 new tomahawks and trade axes added since the first edition, also a list of 205 makers names. There are 15 chapters from the earliest known tomahawks to the present day. Some of the finest tomahawks in the country are shown in this book with 31 color plates. This comprehensive study is invaluable to any collector.

Jack O'Connor Catalogue of Letters, by Enzler-Herring, E. Cataloguer. Agoura CA: Trophy Room Books, 2002. 262 pages, 18 illustrations. Hardcover. $55.00

During a sixteen-year period beginning in 1960, O'Connor exchanged many letters with his pal, John Jobson. Material from nearly three hundred of these has been assembled and edited by Ellen Enzler Herring and published in chronological order. A number of the letters have been reproduced in full or part. They offer considerable insight into the beloved gun editor and "Dean of Outdoor Writers"over and beyond what we know about him from his books.

Jack O'Connor - The Legendary Life Of America's Greatest Gunwriter, by R. Anderson. Long Beach, CA: Safari Press, 2002. 1st edition. 240pp, profuse photos. Hardcover. $29.95

This is the book all hunters in North America have been waiting for--the long-awaited biography on Jack O'Connor! Jack O'Connor was the preeminent North American big-game hunter and gunwriter of the twentieth century, and Robert Anderson's masterfully written new work is a blockbuster filled with fascinating facts and stories about this controversial character. With the full cooperation of the O'Connor children, Anderson spent three years interviewing O'Connor's family and friends as well as delving into JOC's papers, photos, and letters, including the extensive correspondence between O'Connor and Bob Householder, and the O'Connor papers from Washington State University. O'Connor's lifelong friend Buck Buckner has contributed two chapters on his experiences with the master of North American hunting.

Joe Rychertinik Reflects on Guns, Hunting, and Days Gone by, by Joe Rychertinik, Precision Shooting, Inc., Manchester, CT, 1999. 281 pp., illustrated. Thirty articles by a master story-teller. Paper covers. $16.95.

Kill or Get Killed, by Col. Rex Applegate, Paladin Press, Boulder, CO, 1996. 400 pp., illus. $49.95

The best and longest-selling book on close combat in history.

Manual for H&R Reising Submachine Gun and Semi-Auto Rifle, edited by George P. Dillman, Desert Publications, El Dorado, AZ, 1994. 81 pp., illus. Paper covers. $14.95

A reprint of the Harrington & Richardson 1943 factory manual and the rare military manual on the H&R submachine gun and semi-auto rifle.

The Manufacture of Gunflints, by Sydney B.J. Skertchly, facsimile reprint with new introduction by Seymour de Lotbiniere, Museum Restoration Service, Ontario, Canada, 1984. 90 pp., illus. $24.50

Limited edition reprinting of the very scarce London edition of 1879.

Master Tips, by J. Winokur, Potshot Press, Pacific Palisades, CA, 1985. 96 pp., illus. Paper covers. $11.95

Basics of practical shooting.

The Military and Police Sniper, by Mike R. Lau, Precision Shooting, Inc., Manchester, CT, 1998. 352 pp., illustrated. Paper covers. $44.95

Advanced precision shooting for combat and law enforcement.

Military Rifle & Machine Gun Cartridges, by Jean Huon, Paladin Press, Boulder, CO, 1990. 392 pp., illus. $34.95

Describes the primary types of military cartridges and their principal loadings, as well as their characteristics, origin and use.

Military Small Arms of the 20th Century, 7th Edition, by Ian V. Hogg and John Weeks, DBI Books, a division of Krause Publications, Iola, WI, 2000. 416 pp., illustrated. Paper covers. Over 800 photographs and illustrations. $24.95

Cover small arms of 46 countries.

Modern Custom Guns, Walnut, Steel, and Uncommon Artistry, by Tom Turpin, Krause Publications, Iola, WI, 1997. 206 pp., illus. $49.95

From exquisite engraving to breathtaking exotic woods, the mystique of today's custom guns is expertly detailed in word and awe-inspiring color photos of rifles, shotguns and handguns.

Modern Gun Values: 12th Edition, edited by Ken Ramage, Krause Publications, Iola, WI 2003. 608 Pages, 3,000+ b&w photos. Softcover. $21.95

Back by popular demand, this all-new expanded edition helps collectors identify the firearm, evaluate condition and determine value. Detailed specifications—and current values from specialized experts—are provided for domestic and imported handguns, rifles, shotguns and commemorative firearms. Heavily illustrated. Over 7,500 arms described and valued, in three grades of condition, according to the NRA's Modern standards.

Modern Machine Guns, by John Walter, Stackpole Books, Inc. Mechanicsburg, PA, 2000. 144 pp., with 146 illustrations. $22.95

A compact and authoritative guide to post-war machine-guns. A gun-by-gun directory identifying individual variants and types including detailed evaluations and technical data.

Modern Sporting Guns, by Christopher Austyn, Safari Press, Huntington Beach, CA, 1994. 128 pp., illus. $40.00

A discussion of the "best" English guns; round action, over-and-under, boxlocks, hammer guns, bolt action and double rifles as well as accessories.

The More Complete Cannoneer, by M.C. Switlik, Museum & Collectors Specialties Co., Monroe, MI, 1990. 199 pp., illus. $19.95

Compiled agreeably to the regulations for the U.S. War Department, 1861, and containing current observations on the use of antique cannons.

The MP-40 Machine Gun, Desert Publications, El Dorado, AZ, 1995. 32 pp., illus. Paper covers. $11.95

A reprint of the hard-to-find operating and maintenance manual for one of the most famous machine guns of World War II.

Naval Percussion Locks and Primers, by Lt. J. A. Dahlgren, Museum Restoration Service, Bloomfield, Canada, 1996. 140 pp., illus. $35.00

First published as an Ordnance Memoranda in 1853, this is the finest existing study of percussion locks and primers origin and development.

THE ARMS LIBRARY

The Official Soviet AKM Manual, translated by Maj. James F. Gebhardt (Ret.), Paladin Press, Boulder, CO, 1999. 120 pp., illustrated. Paper covers. $18.00
This official military manual, available in English for the first time, was originally published by the Soviet Ministry of Defence. Covers the history, function, maintenance, assembly and disassembly, etc. of the 7.62mm AKM assault rifle.

The One-Round War: U.S.M.C. Scout-Snipers in Vietnam, by Peter Senich, Paladin Press, Boulder, CO, 1996. 384 pp., illus. Paper covers $59.95
Sniping in Vietnam focusing specifically on the Marine Corps program.

OSS Special Operations In China, by Col. F. Mills & John W. Brunner. Williamstown, NJ: Phillips Publications, 2003. 1st edition. 550 pages, illustrated with photos. Hardcover. $34.95

Parker Brothers: Knight Of The Trigger, by Ed Muderlak. A Fact-Based Historical Novel Describing The Life and Times of Captain Arthur William du Bray, 1848-1928. Davis, IL: Old Reliable Publishing, 2002. 223 pages. $25.00
Knight of the Trigger tells the story of the Old West when Parker's most famous gun saleman traveled the country by rail, competing in the pigeon ring, hunting with the rich and famous, and selling the "Old Reliable" Parker shotgun. The life and times of Captain Arthur William du Bray, Parker Brothers' on-the-road sales agent from 1884 to 1926, is described in a novelized version of his interesting life.

Powder Horns and their Architecture; And Decoration as Used by the Soldier, Indian, Sailor and Traders of the Era, by Madison Grant. York, PA: Privately Printed, 1987. 165 pages, profusely illustrated. Hardcover. $45.00
Covers homemade pieces from the late eighteenth and early nineteenth centuries.

Practically Speaking: An Illustrated Guide - The Game, Guns and Gear of the International Defensive Pistol Association, by Walt Rauch. Lafayette Hills, PA: Privately Printed, 2002. 1st edition. 79 pages, illustated with drawings and color photos. Softcover. $24.95
The game, guns and gear of the International Defensive Pistol Association with real-world applications.

Present Sabers: A Popular History of the U.S. Horse Cavalry, by Allan T. Heninger, Tucson, AZ: Excalibur Publications, 2002. 1st edition. 160 pages, with 148 photographs, 45 illustrations and 4 charts. Softcover. $24.95
An illustrated history of America's involvement with the horse cavalry, from it's earliest beginnings during the Revolutionary War through it's demise in World War 2. The book also contains several appendices, as well as depictions of the regular insignia of all the U.S. Cavalry units.

Principles of Personal Defense, by Jeff Cooper, Paladin Press, Boulder, CO, 1999. 56 pp., illustrated. Paper covers. $14.00
This revised edition of Jeff Cooper's classic on personal defense offers great new illustrations and a new preface while retaining the timeliness theory of individual defense behavior presented in the original book.

The Quotable Hunter, edited by Jay Cassell and Peter Fiduccia, The Lyons Press, N.Y., 1999. 224 pp., illustrated. $20.00
This collection of more than three hundred memorable quotes from hunters through the ages captures the essence of the sport, with all its joys idiosyncrasies, and challenges.

Renaissance Drill Book, by Jacob de Gheyn; edited by David J. Blackmore. Mechanicsburg, PA: Greenhill Books, 2003. 1st edition. 248 pages, 117 illustrations. Hardcover. $24.95
Jacob de Gheyn's Exercise of Armes was an immense success when first published in 1607. It is a fascinating 17th-century military manual, designed to instruct contemporary soldiers how to handle arms effectively, and correctly, and it makes for a unique glimpse into warfare as waged in the Thirty Years War and the English Civil War. manual uses illustrations to clearly demonstrate drill for soldiers employing calibers and muskets. It shows how to load and fire, or merely carry, a matchlock piece. In addition, detailed illustrations show the various movements and postures to be adopted during use of the pike.

A Rifleman Went to War, by H. W. McBride, Lancer Militaria, Mt. Ida, AR, 1987. 398 pp., illus. $29.95
The classic account of practical marksmanship on the battlefields of World War I.

Running Recon, by Frank Greco, Frank. A Photo Journey with SOG Special Ops Along the Ho Chi Minh Trail. Boulder, CO: Paladin Press, 2004. 1st edition. Hardcover. $79.95
Running Recon is a combination of military memoir and combat photography book. It reflects both the author's experience in Kontum, Vietnam, from April 1969 to April 1970 as part of the top-secret Studies and Observation Group (SOG) and the collective experience of SOG veterans in general. What sets it apart from other Vietnam books is its wealth of more than 700 photographs, many never before published, from the author's personal collection and those of his fellow SOG veterans.

Sharpshooting for Sport and War, by W.W. Greener, Wolfe Publishing Co., Prescott, AZ, 1995. 192 pp., illus. $30.00
This classic reprint explores the *first* expanding bullet; service rifles; shooting positions; trajectories; recoil; external ballistics; and other valuable information.

The Shooter's Bible 2004, No. 95, edited by William S. Jarrett, Stoeger Publishing Co., Wayne, NJ, 2003. 576 pp., illustrated. Paper covers. $23.95
Over 3,000 firearms currently offered by major American and foreign gunmakers. Represented are handguns, rifles, shotguns and black powder arms with complete specifications and retail prices.

The Shooter's Bible 2003, No. 94, edited by William S. Jarrett, Stoeger Publishing Co., Wayne, NJ, 2002. 576 pp., illustrated. Paper covers. $23.95
Over 3,000 firearms currently offered by major American and foreign gunmakers. Represented are handguns, rifles, shotguns and black powder arms with complete specifications and retail prices.

Shooting To Live, by Capt. W. E. Fairbairn & Capt. E. A. Sykes, Paladin Press, Boulder, CO, 1997, 4 1/2 x 7, soft cover, illus., 112 pp. $14.00
Shooting to Live is the product of Fairbairn's and Sykes' practical experience with the handgun. Hundreds of incidents provided the basis for the first true book on life-or-death shootouts with the pistol. Shooting to Live teaches all concepts, considerations and applications of combat pistol craft.

Shooting Buffalo Rifles Of The Old West, by Mike Venturino, MLV Enterprises, Livingston, MT, 2002. 278 pages, illustrated with b&w photos. Softcover. $30.00
This tome will take you through the history, the usage, the many models, and the actual shooting (and how to's) of the many guns that saw service on the Frontier and are lovingly called "Buffalo Rifles" today. If you love to shoot your Sharps, Ballards, Remingtons, or Springfield "Trapdoors" for hunting or competition, or simply love Old West history, your library WILL NOT be complete without this latest book from Mike Venturino!

Shooting Colt Single Actions, by Mike Venturino, MLV Enterprises, Livingston, MT 1997. 205 pp., illus. Softcover. $25.00
A complete examination of the Colt Single Action including styles, calibers and generations. Black & white photos throughout.

Shooting Lever Guns Of The Old West, by Mike Venturino, MLV Enterprises, Livingston, MT, 1999. 300 pp., illustrated. Softcover. $27.95
Shooting the lever action type repeating rifles of our American West.

Shooting Sixguns of the Old West, by Mike Venturino, MLV Enterprises, Livingston, MT, 1997. 221 pp., illus. Paper covers. $26.50.
A comprehensive look at the guns of the early West: Colts, Smith & Wesson and Remingtons, plus blackpowder and reloading specs.

Shooters Bible 2004 No. 95, by Jarrett (editor). The World's Standard Firearms Reference Book. Pocomoke, MD: Stoeger Publishing Company, 2003. 2004 edition. 576 pages. Pictorial softcover. $23.95
The new edition of the Shooter's Bible offers gun enthusi asts everything they need to know about some 3,000 firearms and related equipment produced by U.S. and foreign gunmakers. It includes complete specifications and updated retail prices for handguns, rifles, shotguns, black powder arms and scopes and sights, all heavily illustrated throughout. Comprehensive ballistics tables for all major rifle cartridges simplify the reader's search for the latest information in one 20-page section. In addition, the 2004 edition contains an array of original articles by noted outdoor writers. New for this edition is a special Web Directory designed to complement the regular Reference section, including the popular Gunfinder index.

Small Arms of World War II, by Chris Chant. St. Paul, MN: MBI Publishing Company, 2001. 1st edition. 96 pages, single page on each weapon with photograph, description, and a specifications table. Hardcover. New. $13.95
Detailing the design and development of each weapon, this book covers the most important infantry weapons used by both Allied and Axis soldiers between 1939 and 1945. These include both standard infantry bolt-action rifles, such as the German Kar 98 and the British Lee-Enfield, plus the automatic rifles that entered service toward the end of the war, such as the Stg 43. As well as rifles, this book also features submachine guns, machine guns and handguns and a specifications table for each weapon.

Sniper Training, FM 23-10, Reprint of the U.S. Army field manual of August, 1994, Paladin Press, Boulder, CO, 1995. 352pp., illus. Paper covers. $30.00
The most up-to-date U.S. military sniping information and doctrine.

Sniping in France, by Major H. Hesketh-Prichard, Lancer Militaria, Mt. Ida, AR, 1993. 224 pp., illus. $24.95
The author was a well-known British adventurer and big game hunter. He was called upon in the early days of "The Great War" to develop a program to offset an initial German advantage in sniping. How the British forces came to overcome this advantage.

Special Operations: Weapons and Tactics, by Timothy Mullin. London: Greenhill Press, 2003. 1st edition. 176 pages, with 189 illustrations. $39.95
The tactics and equipment of Special Forces explained in full, Contains 200 images of weaponry and training. This highly illustrated guide covers the full experience of special operations training from every possible angle. First-hand expert Mullin dissects the key components of special ops training and the variables that come into play when perfecting technique--from reducing ammo loading times to identifying weaknesses in an enemy's kit. His analysis, infused with personal anecdotes, takes in the full spectrum of military operations, including maritime missions, and the rural vs. urban battlefield. There is also considerable information on nonfirearm usage, such as specialized armor and ammunition.

The Sporting Craftsmen: A Complete Guide to Contemporary Makers of Custom-Built Sporting Equipment, by Art Carter, Countrysport Press, Traverse City, MI, 1994. 240 pp., illus. $35.00
Profiles leading makers of centerfire rifles; muzzleloading rifles; bamboo fly rods; fly reels; flies; waterfowl calls; decoys; handmade knives; and traditional longbows and recurves.

Standard Catalog of Military Firearms 2nd Edition: The Collector's Price & Reference Guide, by Ned Schwing. Iola, WI: Krause Publishing, 2003. 2nd edition. 448 pages. Softcover. $22.99
A companion volume to Standard Catalog of Firearms, this revised and expanded second edition comes complete with all the detailed information readers found useful and more. Listings beginning with the early cartridge models of the 1870s to the latest high-tech sniper rifles have been expanded to include more models, variations, historical information, and data, offering more detail for the military firearms collector, shooter, and history buff. Identification of specific firearms is easier with nearly 250 additional photographs. Plus, readers will enjoy "snap shots," small personal articles from experts relating real-life experiences with exclusive models. Revised to include every known military firearm available to the U.S. collector * More than 100 pages of expanded coverage * Special feature articles on focused aspects of collecting and shooting.

Stress Fire, Vol. 1: Stress Fighting for Police, by Massad Ayoob, Police Bookshelf, Concord, NH, 1984. 149 pp., illus. Paper covers. $11.95.
Gunfighting for police, advanced tactics and techniques.

Survival Guns, by Mel Tappan, Desert Publications, El Dorado, AZ, 1993. 456 pp., illus. Paper covers. $25.00
Discusses in a frank and forthright manner which handguns, rifles and shotguns to buy for personal defense and securing food, and the ones to avoid.

The Tactical Advantage, by Gabriel Suarez, Paladin Press, Boulder, CO, 1998. 216 pp., illustrated. Paper covers. $22.00
Learn combat tactics that have been tested in the world's toughest schools.

Tactical Marksman, by Dave M. Lauch, Paladin Press, Boulder, CO, 1996. 165 pp., illus. Paper covers. $35.00
A complete training manual for police and practical shooters.

Tim Murphy Rifleman Frontier Series Volume 3, by Roy Chandler. Jacksonville, NC: Iron Brigade Armory, 2003. 1st edition. 396 pages. Hardcover. $39.95
Tim Murphy may be our young nation's earliest recognized hero. Murphy was seized by Seneca Tribesmen during his infancy. Traded to the Huron, he was renamed and educated by Sir William Johnson, a British colonial officer Freed during the prisoner exchange of 1764, Murphy discovered his superior ability with a Pennsylvania longrifle. Still a youth he turned to frontier marksmanship competitions to provide a challenging if tenous livelihood. Murphy attained national prominence during our Revolutionary War while fighting in major battles, and by shooting a British General Officer during the Battle of Saratoga at a range so distant that the shot was believed by others to be impossible.An early volunteer in the Pennsylvania militia, Tim Murphy served valiantly in rifle companies including the justly famed Daniel Morgan's Riflemen. This is Murphy's story.

THE ARMS LIBRARY

To Ride, Shoot Straight, and Speak the Truth, by Jeff Cooper, Paladin Press, Boulder, CO, 1997, 5 1/2 x 8 1/2, soft-cover, illus., 384 pp. $32.00

Combat mind-set, proper sighting, tactical residential architecture, nuclear war - these are some of the many subjects explored by Jeff Cooper in this illustrated anthology. The author discusses various arms, fighting skills and the importance of knowing how to defend oneself, and one's honor, in our rapidly changing world.

Trailriders Guide to Cowboy Action Shooting, by James W. Barnard, Pioneer Press, Union City, TN, 1998. 134 pp., plus 91 photos, drawings and charts. Paper covers. $24.95

Covers the complete spectrum of this shooting discipline, from how to dress to authentic leather goods, which guns are legal, calibers, loads and ballistics.

The Ultimate Sniper, by Major John L. Plaster, Paladin Press, Boulder, CO, 1994. 464 pp., illus. Paper covers. $49.95

An advanced training manual for military and police snipers.

Uniforms And Equipment Of The Imperial Japanese Army In World War II, by Mike Hewitt. Atglen, PA: Schiffer Publications, 2002. 176 pages, with over 520 color and b&w photos. Hardcover. $59.95

Unrepentant Sinner, by Col. Charles Askins, Paladin Press, Boulder, CO, 2000. 322 pp., illustrated. $29.95

The autobiography of Colonel Charles Askins.

U.S. Marine Corp Rifle and Pistol Marksmanship, 1935, reprinting of a government publication, Lancer Militaria, Mt. Ida, AR, 1991. 99 pp., illus. Paper covers. $11.95

The old corps method of precision shooting.

U.S. Marine Corps Scout/Sniper Training Manual, Lancer Militaria, Mt. Ida, AR, 1989. Soft covers. $27.95

Reprint of the original sniper training manual used by the Marksmanship Training Unit of the Marine Corps Development and Education Command in Quantico, Virginia.

U.S. Marine Corps Scout-Sniper, World War II and Korea, by Peter R. Senich, Paladin Press, Boulder, CO, 1994. 236 pp., illus. $44.95

The most thorough and accurate account ever printed on the training, equipment and combat experiences of the U.S. Marine Corps Scout-Snipers.

U.S. Marine Corps Sniping, Lancer Militaria, Mt. Ida, AR, 1989. Irregular pagination. Soft covers. $18.95

A reprint of the official Marine Corps FMFM1-3B.

U.S. Marine Uniforms-1912-1940, by Jim Moran. Williamstown, NJ: Phillips Publications, 2001. 174 pages, illustrated with b&w photographs. Hardcover. $49.95

Weapons of Delta Force, by Fred Pushies. St. Paul, MN: MBI Publishing Company, 2002. 1st edition. 128 pgs., 100 b&w and 100 color illustrated. Hardcover. $24.95

America's elite counter-terrorist organization, Delta Force, is a handpicked group of the U.S. Army's finest soldiers. The group specializes in hostage rescues and other difficult procedures to protect the lives of Americans throughout the world. Delta uses some of the most sophisticated weapons in the field today, and all are detailed in this book. Pistols, sniper rifles, special mission aircraft, fast attack vehicles, SCUBA and paratrooper gear, and more are presented in this fully illustrated account of our country's heroes and their tools of the trade.

Weapons of the Waffen-SS, by Bruce Quarrie, Sterling Publishing Co., Inc., 1991. 168 pp., illus. $24.95

An in-depth look at the weapons that made Hitler's Waffen-SS the fearsome fighting machine it was.

Weatherby: The Man, The Gun, The Legend, by Grits and Tom Gresham, Cane River Publishing Co., Natchitoches, LA, 1992. 290 pp., illus. $24.95

A fascinating look at the life of the man who changed the course of firearms development in America.

The Winchester Era, by David Madis, Art & Reference House, Brownsville, TX, 1984. 100 pp., illus. $19.95

Story of the Winchester company, management, employees, etc.

With British Snipers to the Reich, by Capt. C. Shore, Lander Militaria, Mt. Ida, AR, 1988. 420 pp., illus. $29.95

One of the greatest books ever written on the art of combat sniping.

The World's Machine Pistols and Submachine Guns - Vol. 2a 1964 to 1980, by Nelson & Musgrave, Ironside International, Alexandria, VA, 2000. 673 pages. $59.95

Containing data, history and photographs of over 200 weapons. With a special section covering shoulder stocked automatic pistols, 100 additional photos.

The World's Sniping Rifles, by Ian V. Hogg, Stackpole Books, Mechanicsburg, 1998. 144 pp., illustrated. $24.00

A detailed manual with descriptions and illustrations of more than 50 high-precision rifles from 14 countries and a complete analysis of sights and systems.

Vietnam Order of Battle, by Shelby L. Stanton, William C. Westmoreland. Mechanicsburg, PA: Stackpole Books, 2003. 1st edition. 416 pages - 32 in full color, 101 pages halftones. Hardcover. $69.95

A monumental, encyclopedic work of immense detail concerning U.S. Army and allied forces that fought in the Vietnam War from 1962 through 1973. Extensive lists of units providing a record of every Army unit that served in Vietnam, down to and including separate companies, and also including U.S. Army aviation and riverine units. Shoulder patches and distinctive unit insignia of all divisions and battalions. Extensive maps portraying unit locations at each six-month interval. Photographs and descriptions of all major types of equipment employed in the conflict. Plus much more!

Wyatt Earp: A Biography of the Legend: Volume 1: The Cowtown Years, by Lee A. Silva. Santa Ana, CA: Privately printed, 2002. 1st edition signed. 995 pages, profusely illustrated, extensive biblio. and index, color jacket. Hardcover. $86.95

Fabulous new work on the Old West's most famous--or infamous--character. Lawman, gunman, gambler, mining speculator, the facts behind the real Wyatt Earp are told in this exhaustively researched, multi-volume work by award winning author and historian Lee A. Silva. The story of the Western cowtowns, their characters, and frontier guns is told, too, in chapters titled "The 'Buntline Special' Colt Controversy," "The Evolution of the Gunfighter," and much, much more! It's all in this thoroughly researched and detailed work. This is the first of a projected four volume set on Wyatt Earp. The first volume covers the years before the famous Tombstone years and Silva has done an incredible amount of research to show these early years.

GUNSMITHING

Accurizing the Factory Rifle, by M.L. McPhereson, Precision Shooting, Inc., Manchester, CT, 1999. 335 pp., illustrated. Paper covers. $44.95

A long-awaiting book, which bridges the gap between the rudimentary (mounting sling swivels, scope blocks and that general level of accomplishment) and the advanced (precision chambering, barrel fluting, and that general level of accomplishment) books that are currently available today.

The Art of Engraving, by James B. Meek, F. Brownell & Son, Montezuma, IA, 1973. 196 pp., illus. $42.95

A complete, authoritative, imaginative and detailed study in training for gun engraving. The first book of its kind—and a great one.

Checkering and Carving of Gun Stocks, by Monte Kennedy, Stackpole Books, Harrisburg, PA, 1962. 175 pp., illus. $39.95

Revised, enlarged cloth-bound edition of a much sought-after, dependable work.

Firearms Assembly/Disassembly, Part I: Automatic Pistols, 2nd Revised Edition, The Gun Digest Book of, by J.B. Wood, DBI Books, a division of Krause Publications, Iola, WI, 1999. 480 pp., illus. Paper covers. $24.95

Covers 58 popular autoloading pistols plus nearly 200 variants of those models integrated into the text and completely cross-referenced in the index.

Firearms Assembly/Disassembly Part II: Revolvers, Revised Edition, The Gun Digest Book of, by J.B. Wood, DBI Books, a division of Krause Publications, Iola, WI, 1997. 480 pp., illus. Paper covers. $27.95

Covers 49 popular revolvers plus 130 variants. The most comprehensive and professional presentation available to either hobbyist or gunsmith.

Firearms Assembly/Disassembly Part III: Rimfire Rifles, Revised Edition, The Gun Digest Book of, by J. B. Wood, DBI Books, a division of Krause Publications, Iola, WI., 1994. 480 pp., illus. Paper covers. $19.95

Greatly expanded edition covering 65 popular rimfire rifles plus over 100 variants all completely cross-referenced in the index.

Firearms Assembly/Disassembly Part IV: Centerfire Rifles, 3rd Revised Edition, The Gun Digest Book of, by J.B. Wood, Krause Publications, Iola, WI, 2004. 480 pp., illus. Paper covers. $24.95

Covers 54 popular centerfire rifles plus 300 variants. The most comprehensive and professional presentation available to either hobbyist or gunsmith.

Firearms Assembly/Disassembly, Part V: Shotguns, Revised Edition, The Gun Digest Book of, by J.B. Wood, Krause Publications, Iola, WI, 2002. 480 pp., illus. Paper covers. $24.95

Covers 46 popular shotguns plus over 250 variants with step-by-step instructions on how to dismantle and reassemble each. The most comprehensive and professional presentation available to either hobbyist or gunsmith.

Firearms Assembly 3: The NRA Guide to Rifle and Shotguns, NRA Books, Wash., DC, 1980. 264 pp., illus. Paper covers. $14.95

Text and illustrations explaining the takedown of 125 rifles and shotguns, domestic and foreign.

Firearms Assembly 4: The NRA Guide to Pistols and Revolvers, NRA Books, Wash., DC, 1980. 253 pp., illus. Paper covers. $13.95

Text and illustrations explaining the takedown of 124 pistol and revolver models, domestic and foreign.

Firearms Bluing and Browning, by R.H. Angier, Stackpole Books, Harrisburg, PA. 151 pp., illus. $19.95

A world master gunsmith reveals his secrets of building, repairing and renewing a gun, quite literally, lock, stock and barrel. A useful, concise text on chemical coloring methods for the gunsmith and mechanic.

Guns and Gunmaking Tools of Southern Appalachia, by John Rice Irwin, Schiffer Publishing Ltd., 1983. 118 pp., illus. Paper covers. $9.95

The story of the Kentucky rifle.

The Gunsmith Of Grenville County: Building The American Longrifle, by Peter Alexander, Texarkana, TX: Scurlock Publishing Co., 2002. 400 pages, with hundreds of illustrations, and six color photos of original rifles. Wire O Bind spine will lay flat on the workbench. Stiff paper covers. $45.00

The most extensive how to book on building longrifles ever published. Takes you through every step of building your own longrifle, from shop set up and tools to engraving, carving and finishing.

Gunsmithing: Pistols & Revolvers, by Patrick Sweeney, DBI Books, a division of Krause Publications, Iola, WI, 1998. 352 pp., illus. Paper covers. $24.95

Do-it-Yourself projects, diagnosis and repair for pistols and revolvers.

Gunsmithing: Rifles, by Patrick Sweeney, Krause Publications, Iola, WI, 1999. 352 pp., illustrated. Paper covers. $24.95

Tips for lever-action rifles. Building a custom Ruger 10/22. Building a better hunting rifle.

Gunsmithing Tips and Projects, a collection of the best articles from the *Handloader* and *Rifle* magazines, by various authors, Wolfe Publishing Co., Prescott, AZ, 1992. 443 pp., illus. Paper covers. $25.00

Includes such subjects as shop, stocks, actions, tuning, triggers, barrels, customizing, etc.

Gunsmith Kinks, by F.R. (Bob) Brownell, F. Brownell & Son, Montezuma, IA, 1st ed., 1969. 496 pp., well illus. $22.98

A widely useful accumulation of shop kinks, short cuts, techniques and pertinent comments by practicing gunsmiths from all over the world.

Gunsmith Kinks 2, by Bob Brownell, F. Brownell & Son, Publishers, Montezuma, IA, 1983. 496 pp., illus. $22.95

A collection of gunsmithing knowledge, shop kinks, new and old techniques, shortcuts and general know-how straight from those who do them best—the gunsmiths.

Gunsmith Kinks 3, edited by Frank Brownell, Brownells Inc., Montezuma, IA, 1993. 504 pp., illus. $24.95

Tricks, knacks and "kinks" by professional gunsmiths and gun tinkerers. Hundreds of valuable ideas are given in this volume.

Gunsmith Kinks 4, edited by Frank Brownell, Brownells Inc., Montezuma, IA, 2001. 564 pp., illus. $27.75

332 detailed illustrations. 560+ pages with 706 separate subject headings and over 5000 cross-indexed entries. An incredible gold mine of information.

Gunsmithing, by Roy F. Dunlap, Stackpole Books, Harrisburg, PA, 1990. 742 pp., illus. $34.95

A manual of firearm design, construction, alteration and remodeling. For amateur and professional gunsmiths and users of modern firearms.

Gunsmithing at Home: Lock, Stock and Barrel, by John Traister, Stoeger Publishing Co., Wayne, NJ, 1997. 320 pp., illus. Paper covers. $19.95

A complete step-by-step fully illustrated guide to the art of gunsmithing.

Home Gunsmithing the Colt Single Action Revolvers, by Loren W. Smith, Ray Riling Arms Books, Co., Phila., PA, 2001. 119 pp., illus. $29.95

Affords the Colt Single Action owner detailed, pertinent information on the operating and servicing of this famous and historic handgun.

How to Convert Military Rifles, Williams Gun Sight Co., Davision, MI, new and enlarged seventh edition, 1997. 76 pp., illus. Paper covers. $13.95

This latest edition updated the changes that have occured over the past thirty years. Tips, instructions and illustratons on how to convert popular military rifles as the Enfield, Mauser 96 nad SKS just to name a few are presented.

Mauser M98 & M96, by R.A. Walsh, Wolfe Publishing Co., Prescott, AR, 1998. 123 pp., illustrated. Paper covers. $32.50

How to build your own favorite custom Mauser rifle from two of the best bolt action rifle designs ever produced—the military Mauser Model 1898 and Model 1896 bolt rifles.

Mr. Single Shot's Gunsmithing-Idea-Book, by Frank de Haas, Mark de Haas, Orange City, IA, 1996. 168 pp., illus. Paper covers. $22.50

Offers easy to follow, step-by-step instructions for a wide variety of gunsmithing procedures all reinforced by plenty of photos.

Pistolsmithing, by George C. Nonte, Jr., Stackpole Books, Harrisburg, PA, 1974. 560 pp., illus. $34.95

A single source reference to handgun maintenance, repair, and modification at home, unequaled in value.

Professional Stockmaking, by D. Wesbrook, Wolfe Publishing Co., Prescott AZ, 1995. 308 pp., illus. $54.00

A step-by-step how-to with complete photographic support for every detail of the art of working wood into riflestocks.

Recreating the American Longrifle, by William Buchele, et al, George Shumway Publisher, York, Pa, 5th edition, 1999. 175 pp., illustrated. $40.00

Includes full size plans for building a Kentucky rifle.

The Story of Pope's Barrels, by Ray M. Smith, R&R Books, Livonia, NY, 1993. 203 pp., illus. $39.00

A reissue of a 1960 book whose author knew Pope personally. It will be of special interest to Schuetzen rifle fans, since Pope's greatest days were at the height of the Schuetzen-era before WWI.

Survival Gunsmithing, by J.B. Wood, Desert Publications, Cornville, AZ, 1986. 92 pp., illus. Paper covers. $11.95

A guide to repair and maintenance of the most popular rifles, shotguns and handguns.

The Tactical 1911, by Dave Lauck, Paladin Press, Boulder, CO, 1998. 137 pp., illus. Paper covers. $20.00

Here is the only book you will ever need to teach you how to select, modify, employ and maintain your Colt.

HANDGUNS

.22 Caliber Handguns; A Shooter's Guide. by Geiger, D. F Lincoln, RI: Andrew Mowbray, Inc., 2003. 1st edition.. Softcover. $21.95

Advanced Master Handgunning, by Charles Stephens, Paladin Press, Boulder, CO., 1994. 72 pp., illus. Paper covers. $14.00

Secrets and surefire techniques for winning handgun competitions.

Advanced Tactical Marksman More High Performance Techniques for Police, Military, and Practical Shooters, by Dave M. Lauck. Paladin Press, Boulder, CO 2002. 1st edition. 232 pages, photos, illus. Softcover $35.00

Lauck, one of the most respected names in high-performance shooting and gunsmithing, refines and updates his 1st book. Dispensing with overcomplicated mil-dot formulas and minute-of-angle calculations, Lauck shows you how to achieve superior accuracy and figure out angle shots, streamline the zero process, hit targets at 2,000 yards, deal with dawn and dusk shoots, train for real-world scenarios, choose optics and accessories and create a mobile shooting platform. He also demonstrates the advantages of his custom reticle design and describes important advancements in the MR-30PG shooting system.

American Beauty: The Prewar Colt National Match Government Model Pistol, by Timothy Mullin, Collector Grade Publications, Canada, 1999. 72 pp., 69 illus. $34.95

69 illustrations, 20 in full color photos of factory engraved guns and other authenticated upgrades, including rare 'double-carved' ivory grips.

The Ayoob Files: The Book, by Massad Ayoob, Police Bookshelf, Concord, NH, 1995. 223 pp., illus. Paper covers. $14.95

The best of Massad Ayoob's acclaimed series in American Handgunner magazine.

The Belgian Browning Pistols 1889-1949, by Anthony Vanderlinden. Wet Dog Publications, Geensboro, NC 2001. Limited edition of 2000 copies, signed by the author. 243 pages, plus index. Illustrated with b&w photos. Signed by the author. Hardcover. $65.00

Includes the 1899 compact, 1899 Large, 1900,01903, Grand Browning, 1910, 1922 Grand Rendement and high power pistols. Also includes a chapter on holsters.

Big Bore Handguns, by John Taffin, Krause Publishing, Iola, WI: 2002. 1st edition. 352 pages, 320 b&w photos with a 16-page color section. Hardcover. $39.95

Gives honest reviews and an inside look at shooting, hunting, and competing with the biggest handguns around. Covers handguns from major gunmakers, as well as handgun customizing, accessories, reloading, and cowboy activities. Significant coverage is also given to handgun customizing, accessories, reloading, and popular shooting hobbies including hunting and cowboy activities. Accessories consist of stocks, handgun holster rigs, and much more. Firearms include single-shot pistols, revolvers, and semi-automatics.

Big Bore Sixguns, by John Taffin, Krause Publications, Iola, WI, 1997. 336 pp., illus. $39.95

The author takes aim on the entire range of big bores from .357 Magnums to .500 Maximums, single actions and cap-and-ball sixguns to custom touches for big bores..

The Browning High Power Automatic Pistol (Expanded Edition), by Blake R. Stevens, Collector Grade Publications, Canada, 1996. 310 pages, with 313 illus. $49.95

An in-depth chronicle of seventy years of High Power history, from John M Browning's original 16-shot prototypes to the present. Profusely illustrated with rare original photos and drawings from the FN Archive to describe virtually every sporting and military version of the High Power. The numerous modifications made to the basic design over the years are, for the first time, accurately arranged in chronological order, thus permitting the dating of any High Power to within a few years of its production. Full details on the WWII Canadian-made Inglis Browning High Power pistol. The Expanded Edition contains 30 new pages on the interesting Argentine full-auto High Power, the latest FN 'MK3' and BDA9 pistols, plus FN's revolutionary P90 5.7x28mm Personal Defence Weapon, and more!

Browning Hi-Power Pistols, Desert Publications, Cornville, AZ, 1982. 20 pp., illus. Paper covers. $11.95

Covers all facets of the various military and civilian models of the Browning Hi-Power pistol.

Canadian Military Handguns 1855-1985, by Clive M. Law, Museum Restoration Service, Bloomfield, Ont. Canada, 1994. 130pp., illus. $40.00

A long-awaited and important history for arms historians and pistol collectors.

Collector's Guide To Colt .45 Service Pistols; Models of 1911 and 1911A1, by Charles W. Clawson. Fort Wayne, IN: Privately Printed, 2003. 3rd edition. 146 pages. Hardcover. $39.95

The 3rd edition has an addtional 16 pages of material. Complete Military Identification, Including all contractors.

Collecting U. S. Pistols & Revolvers, 1909-1945, by J. C. Harrison. The Arms Chest, Okla. City, OK. 1999. 2nd edition (revised). 185 pages, illus. Spiral bound. $35.00

Valuable and detailed reference book for the collector of U.S. Pistols & Revolvers. Identifies standard issue original military models of the M1911, M1911A1 and M1917Cal .45 Pistols and Revolvers as produced by all manufacturers from 1911 through 1945. Plus .22 ACE Models, National Match Models, and similar foreign military models produced by Colt or manufactured under Colt license. Plus Arsenal repair, refinish and Lend-Lease Models. 185 pages, illustratred with pictures and drawings.

The Colt .45 Auto Pistol, compiled from U.S. War Dept. Technical Manuals, and reprinted by Desert Publications, Cornville, AZ, 1978. 80 pp., illus. Paper covers. $12.95

Covers every facet of this famous pistol from mechanical training, manual of arms, disassembly, repair and replacement of parts.

Colt Automatic Pistols, by Donald B. Bady, Pioneer Press, Union City, TN, 1999. 368 pp., illustrated. Softcover. $19.95

A revised and enlarged edition of a key work on a fascinating subject. Complete information on every Colt automatic pistol.

The Combat Perspective; The Thinking Man's Guide to Self-Defense, by Gabriel Suarez. Boulder, CO Paladin Press, 2003. 1st edition. 112 pages. Softcover. $15.00

In The Combative Perspective, Suarez keys in on developing your knowledge about and properly organizing your mental attitude toward combat to improve your odds of winning – not just surviving – such a fight. The principles are as applicable to the bladesman as they are to the rifleman, to the unarmed fighter as they are to the sniper. Suarez' combative perspective has four basic components that he identifies as essential to winning any battle: desire for victory, elimination of uncertainty, development of situational awareness and willingness to act. In this book he examines each in a logical and scientific manner, demonstrating why, when it comes to defending your life, the mental edge is at least as critical to victory as the tactical advantage.

Combat Handgunnery, 5th Edition, by Chuck Taylor, Krause Publications, Iola, WI, 2002. 256 pp., illus. Paper covers. $21.95

This all-new edition looks at real world combat handgunnery from three different perspectives—military, police and civilian.

Complete Guide to Compact Handguns, by Gene Gangarosa, Jr., Stoeger Publishing Co., Wayne, NJ, 1997. 228 pp., illus. Paper covers. $22.95

Includes hundreds of compact firearms, along with text results conducted by the author.

Complete Guide to Service Handguns, by Gene Gangarosa, Jr., Stoeger Publishing Co., Wayne, NJ, 1998. 320 pp., illus. Paper covers. $22.95

The author explores the revolvers and pistols that are used around the globe by military, law enforcement and civilians.

Concealable Pocket Pistols: How to Choose and Use Small-Caliber Handguns, by Terence McLeod. Paladin Press, 2001. 1st edition. 80 pages. Softcover. $14.00

Small-caliber handguns are often maligned as too puny for serious self-defense, but millions of Americans own and carry these guns and have used them successfully to stop violent assaults. This is the first book ever devoted to eliminating the many misconceptions about the usefulness of these popular guns. "Pocket pistols" are small, easily concealed, inexpensive semiautomatic handguns in .22, .25, .32 and .380 calibers. Their small size and hammerless design enable them to be easily concealed and carried so they are immediately accessible in an emergency. Their purpose is not to knock an assailant off his feet with fire-breathing power (which no handgun is capable of doing) but simply to deter or stop his assault by putting firepower in your hands when you need it most. Concealable Pocket Pistols addresses every aspect of owning, carrying and shooting small-caliber handguns in a realistic manner. It cuts right to the chase and recommends a handful of the best pistols on the market today as well as the best ammunition for them. It then gets into the real-world issues of how to carry a concealed pocket pistol, how to shoot it under stress and how to deal with malfunctions quickly and efficiently. In an emergency, a small-caliber pistol in the pocket is better than the .357 Magnum left at home. Find out what millions of Americans already know about these practical self-defense tools.

The Custom Government Model Pistol, by Layne Simpson, Wolfe Publishing Co., Prescott, AZ, 1994. 639 pp., illus. Paper covers. $26.95

The book about one of the world's greatest firearms and the things pistolsmiths do to make it even greater.

The CZ-75 Family: The Ultimate Combat Handgun, by J.M. Ramos, Paladin Press, Boulder, CO, 1990. 100 pp., illus. Soft covers. $25.00

An in-depth discussion of the early-and-late model CZ-75s, as well as the many newest additions to the Czech pistol family.

Complete Encyclopedia of Pistols & Revolvers, by A.E. Hartnik, Knickerbocker Press, New York, NY, 2003. 272 pp., illus. $19.95

A comprehensive encyclopedia specially written for collectors and owners of pistols and revolvers.

Developmental Cartridge Handguns Of .22 Calibre, by John S. Laidacker, John S. As produced in the United States & abroad from 1855 to 1875. Atglen, PA: Schiffer

Publications, 2003. Reprint. 597 pages, with over 860 b&w photos, drawings, and charts. Hardcover. $100.00

This book is a reprint edition of the late John Laidacker's personal study of early .22 Cartridge Handguns from 1855-1875. Laidacker's primary aim was to offer a quick reference to the collector, and his commentary on the wide variety of types, variations and makers, as well as detailed photography, make this a superb addition to any firearm library.

Engraved Handguns Of .22 Calibre, by John S. Laidacker, Atglen, PA: Schiffer Publications, 2003. 1st edition. 192 pages, with over 400 color and b&w photos. $69.95

Experiments of a Handgunner, by Walter Roper, Wolfe Publishing Co., Prescott, AZ, 1989. 202 pp., illus. $37.00

A limited edition reprint. A listing of experiments with functioning parts of handguns, with targets, stocks, rests, handloading, etc.

The Farnam Method of Defensive Handgunning, by John S. Farnam, Police Bookshelf, 1999. 191 pp., illus. Paper covers. $24.00

A book intended to not only educate the new shooter, but also to serve as a guide and textbook for his and his instructor's training courses.

Fast and Fancy Revolver Shooting, by Ed. McGivern, Anniversary Edition, Winchester Press, Piscataway, NJ, 1984. 484 pp., illus. $19.95

A fascinating volume, packed with handgun lore and solid information by the acknowledged dean of revolver shooters.

German Handguns: The Complete Book of the Pistols and Revolvers of Germany, 1869 to the Present, by Ian Hogg. Greenhill Publishing, 2001. 320 pages, 270 illustrations. Hardcover. $49.95

Ian Hogg examines the full range of handguns produced in Germany from such classics as the Luger M1908, Mauser HsC and Walther PPK, to more unusual types such as the Reichsrevolver M1879 and the Dreyse 9mm. He presents the key data (length, weight, muzzle velocity, and range) for each weapon discussed and also gives its date of introduction and service record, evaluates and discusses peculiarities, and examines in detail particular strengths and weaknesses.

Glock: The New Wave in Combat Handguns, by Peter Alan Kasler, Paladin Press, Boulder, CO, 1993. 304 pp., illus. $27.00

Kasler debunks the myths that surround what is the most innovative handgun to be introduced in some time.

Glock's Handguns, by Duncan Long, Desert Publications, El Dorado, AR, 1996. 180 pp., illus. Paper covers. $19.95

An outstanding volume on one of the world's newest and most successful firearms of the century.

Greenhill Military Manual: Military Handguns of Two World Wars, by John Walter. London: Greenhill Publishing, 2003. 1st edition. 144 pages, illustrated. Hardcover. $24.00

A detailed description of each handgun and its key features is supported by technical data and specially selected illustrations. Details of relevant ammunition and accessories complete the work.

The Gun Digest Book of the 1911, by Patrick Sweeney. Krause Publications, Iola, WI, 2002. 336 pages, with 700 b&w photos. Softcover. $27.95

Compete guide of all models and variations of the Model 1911. The author also includes repair tips and information on buying a used 1911.

Gun Digest Book of Combat Handgunnery 5th Ed. by Massad Ayoob. Complete Guide To Combat Shooting. Iola, WI : Krause Publishing, 2002. 5th Edition. 256 pages, illustrated with 400 b&w photos. Originally published at $22.95 Softcover. $19.95

Tap into the knowledge of an international combat handgun expert for the latest in combat handgun designs, strengths and limitations; caliber, size, power and ability; training and technique; cover, concealment and hostage situations. Unparalleled!

The Gun Digest Book of the Glock; A Comprehensive Review, Design, History and Use. Iola, WI: Krause Publications, 2003. 1st edition. 303 pages, with 500 b&w photos. Softcover. 24.95

Examine the rich history and unique elements of the most important and influential firearms design of the past 50 years, the Glock autoloading pistol. This comprehensive review of the revolutionary pistol analyzes the performance of the various models and chamberings and features a complete guide to available accessories and little-known factory options. You'll see why it's the preferred pistol for law enforcement use and personal protection.

Hand Cannons: The World's Most Powerful Handguns, by Duncan Long, Paladin Press, Boulder, CO, 1995. 208 pp., illus. Paper covers. $22.00

Long describes and evaluates each powerful gun according to their features.

Handguns 2004: 16th Edition, by Dave Arnold. Iola, WI: Krause Publishing, 2003. 16th Edition. 320 pages, illustrated with 500 b&w photos. Softcover. $22.95

Target shooters, handgun hunters, collectors and those who rely upon handguns for self-defense will want to pack this value-loaded and entertaining volume in their home libraries. Shooters will find the latest pistol and revolver designs and accessories, plus test reports on several models. The handgun becomes an artist's canvas in a showcase of engraving talents. The catalog section – with comprehensive specs on every known handgun in production – includes a new display of semi-custom handguns, plus an expanded, illustrated section on the latest grips, sights, scopes and other aiming devices. Offer easy access to products, services and manufacturers.

Handguns of the Armed Organizations of the Soviet Occupation Zone and German Democratic Republic, by Dieter H. Marschall. Los Alamos, NM: Ucross Books, 2000. 128 pages, with 145 b&w illustrations, index. Softcover. 29.95

Translated from German this ground braking treatise covers the period from May 1945 through 1996. The organizations that used these pistols are described along with the guns and holsters. Included are the P08, P38, PP, PPK, P1001, PSM, Tokarev, Makarov, (including .22lr, cutaway, silenced, Suhl marked), Stechlin, plus Hungarian, Romanian and Czech pistols.

Handgun Stopping Power "The Definitive Study", by Evan P. Marshall & Edwin J. Sanow, Paladin Press, Boulder, CO, 1997, soft cover, photos, 240 pp. $45.00

Dramatic first-hand accounts of the results of handgun rounds fired into criminals by cops, storeowners, cabbies and others are the heart and soul of this long-awaited book. This is the definitive methodology for predicting the stopping power of handgun loads, the first to take into account what really happens when a bullet meets a man.

Heckler & Koch's Handguns, by Duncan Long, Desert Publications, El Dorado, AR, 1996. 142 pp., illus. Paper covers. $19.95

Traces the history and the evolution of H&K's pistols from the company's beginning at the end of WWII to the present.

Hidden in Plain Sight, by Trey Bloodworth & Mike Raley, Professional Press, Chapel Hill, NC, 1995. Paper covers. $19.95

A practical guide to concealed handgun carry.

High Standard: A Collectors Guide To The Hamden & Hartford Target Pistols, by Tom Dance. Andrew Mowbray, Inc., Lincoln, RI: 1999. 192 pp., Heavily illustrated with black & white photographs and technical drawings. $24.00

From Citation to Supermatic, all of the production models and specials made from 1951 to 1984 are covered according to model number or series, making it easy to understand the evolution to this favorite of shooters and collectors.

High Standard Automatic Pistols 1932-1950, by Charles E. Petty, The Gunroom Press, Highland Park, NJ, 1989. 124 pp., illus. $14.95

A definitive source of information for the collector of High Standard arms.

Hi-Standard Pistols and Revolvers, 1951-1984, by James Spacek, James Spacek, Chesire, CT, 1998. 128 pp., illustrated. Paper covers. $4.95

Technical details, marketing features and instruction/parts manual of every model High Standard pistol and revolver made between 1951 and 1984. Most accurate serial number information available.

History of Smith & Wesson Firearms, by Dean Boorman. New York: Lyons Press, 2002. 1st edition. 144 pages, illustrated in Full color. Hardcover. $29.95

The definitive guide to one of the world's best-known firearms makers. Takes the story through the years of the Military & Police .38 & of the Magnum cartridge, to today's wide range of products for law-enforcement customers.

How to Become a Master Handgunner: The Mechanics of X-Count Shooting, by Charles Stephens, Paladin Press, Boulder, CO, 1993. 64 pp., illus. Paper covers. $14.00

Offers a simple formula for success to the handgunner who strives to master the technique of shooting accurately.

Illustrated Encyclopedia of Handguns, by A.B. Zhuk, Stackpole Books, Mechanicsburg, PA, 2002. 256 pp., illus. Softcover, $24.95

Identifies more than 2,000 military and commercial pistols and revolvers with details of more than 100 popular handgun cartridges.

The Inglis Diamond: The Canadian High Power Pistol, by Clive M. Law, Collector Grade Publications, Canada, 2001. 312 pp., illustrated. $49.95

This definitive work on Canada's first and indeed only mass produced handgun, in production for a very brief span of time and consequently made in relatively few numbers, the venerable Inglis-made Browning High Power covers the pistol's initial history, the story of Chinese and British adoption, use post-war by Holland, Australia, Greece, Belgium, New Zealand, Peru, Brasil and other countries. All new information on the famous light-weights and the Inglis Diamond variations. Completely researched through official archives in a dozen countries. Many of the bewildering variety of markings have never been satisfactorily explained until now

Instinct Combat Shooting, by Chuck Klein, The Goose Creek, IN, 1989. 49 pp., illus. Paper covers. $12.00.

Defensive handgunning for police.

Japanese Military Cartridge Handguns 1893-1945, A Revised and Expanded Edition of Hand Cannons of Imperial Japan, by Harry L. Derby III & James D. Brown. Atglen, PA: Schiffer Publications, 2003. 1st edition. 350 pages, over 550 b&w and color photographs, drawings, and charts. Hardcover. $79.95

When originally published in 1981, The Hand Cannons of Imperial Japan was heralded as one of the most readable works on firearms ever produced. To arms collectors and scholars, it remains a prized source of information on Japanese handguns, their development, and their history. In this new Revised and Expanded edition, original author Harry Derby has teamed with Jim Brown to provide a thorough update reflecting twenty years of additional research. The authors have retained the format and much of the text of the original edition, focusing on military cartridge arms from the 1893-1945 period. Signal pistols, foreign-procured military handguns, ammunition, holsters, and accessories are also covered. Significant changes are included based on new findings, and a great deal of new information has been added, together with color illustrations of significant specimens. A number of newly discovered variants are identified and described, and expanded tables of reported serial numbers and production data are provided. Coverage and explanation of Japanese markings has been greatly enhanced, and a detailed study of inspection marks on the most widely known Types 14 and 94 is included. An appendix on valuation has also been added, using a relative scale that should remain relevant despite inflationary pressures. For the firearms collector, enthusiast, historian or dealer, this is the most complete and up-to-date work on Japanese military handguns ever written. Like its predecessor, it is certain to become a classic firearms reference and a benchmark for further research.

Know Your 45 Auto Pistols—Models 1911 & A1, by E.J. Hoffschmidt, Blacksmith Corp., Southport, CT, 1974. 58 pp., illus. Paper covers. $14.95

A concise history of the gun with a wide variety of types and copies.

Know Your Ruger Single Actions: The Second Decade 1963-1973, by John C. Dougan. Blacksmith Corp., North Hampton, OH, 1994. 143 pp., illus. Paper covers. $19.95

Know Your Ruger S/A Revolvers 1953-1963 (revised edition), by John C. Dougan. Blacksmith Corp., North Hampton, OH, 2002. 191 pp., illus. Paper covers. $19.95.

Know Your Walther P38 Pistols, by E.J. Hoffschmidt, Blacksmith Corp., Southport, CT, 1974. 77 pp., illus. Paper covers. $14.95

Covers the Walther models Armee, M.P., H.P., P.38—history and variations.

Know Your Walther PP & PPK Pistols, by E.J. Hoffschmidt, Blacksmith Corp., Southport, CT, 1975. 87 pp., illus. Paper covers. $14.95

A concise history of the guns with a guide to the variety and types.

La Connaissance du Luger, Tome 1, by Gerard Henrotin, H & L Publishing, Belguim, 1996. (The Knowledge of Luger, Volume 1, translated.) B&W and color photos. French text. 144 pages, illustrated. $45.00

Living With Glocks: The Complete Guide to the New Standard in Combat Handguns, by Robert H Boatman, Boulder, CO: Paladin Press, 2002. 1st edition. 184 pages, illustrated. Hardcover. $29.95

In this book he explains why in no uncertain terms. In addition to demystifying the enigmatic Glock trigger, Boatman describes and critiques each Glock model in production. Separate chapters on the G36, the enhanced G20 and the full-auto G18 emphasize the job-specific talents of these standout models for those seeking insight on which Glock pistol might best meet their needs. And for those interested in optimizing their Glock's capabilities, this book addresses all the peripherals – holsters, ammo, accessories, silencers, modifications and conversions, training programs and more. Whether your focus is on concealed carry, home protection, hunting, competition, training or law enforcement.

Luger Artiglieria: (The Luger Artillery: From the Prototypes Up to the Mauser Commemorative. The History and the Accessories.), by Mauro Baudino. Italy: Editoriale Olimpia, 2003. 1st edition. 112 pages, illustrated with color and black & white photos. ITALIAN TEXT with captions in English. Softcover. $31.95

In 1914, haunted by his dream of a "Greater Germany", the young Kaiser Wilhelm II launched his Armies confidently into war. In the years leading up to the conflict, German foreign policy had engineered a series of military and diplomatic provocations with the aim of redefining the European order. Germany's defence industry was growing at an alarming rate and during the war, this rapid growth would play a key role for the first time. In 1907, German Artillery planners asked for a semi-automatic pistol with a long barrel and a shoulder stock, which could be used like a carbine. In the same year, the "Prüfungskommission" held inconclusive trials using the Frommer, Borchardt and Mauser C.96 pistol. In February of the following year, the German Army formally accepted the semi-automatic Parabellum, which was named the P08 (Pistol Model 1908). Another three years were to pass, when in 1911, the "Kriegsministerium" decided it was time to consider supplying their Artillery men with a special weapon. Captain Adolf Fisher was ordered to study the feasibility of the project and, finally, on 3rd June, 1913, the LP08 (Lange Pistole 1908) was formally accepted, better known as - the Artillery Luger. The Baudino's book is the first one completely focused on the Artillery models. 112 pages, more than 200 colour and black & white pictures. Text written in Italian, all captions are translated into English summarizing the most important topics of each paragraph.

The Luger Handbook, by Aarron Davis, Krause Publications, Iola, WI, 1997. 112 pp., illus. Paper covers. $9.95.

Now you can identify any of the legendary Luger variations using a simple decision tree. Each model and variation includes pricing information, proof marks and detailed attributes in a handy, user-friendly format. Plus, it's fully indexed. Instantly identify that Luger!

Lugers at Random (Revised Format Edition), by Charles Kenyon, Jr., Handgun Press, Glenview, IL, 2000. 420 pp., illus. $59.95

A new printing of this classic, comprehensive reference for all Luger collectors.

The Luger Story, by John Walter, Stackpole Books, Mechanicsburg, PA, 2001. 256 pp., illus. Paper Covers. $19.95

The standard history of the world's most famous handgun.

The Mauser Self-Loading Pistol, by Belford & Dunlap, Borden Publ. Co., Alhambra, CA. Over 200 pp., 300 illus., large format. $29.95

The long-awaited book on the "Broom Handles," covering their inception in 1894 to the end of production. Complete and in detail: pocket pistols, Chinese and Spanish copies.

Mental Mechanics Of Shooting: How To Stay Calm at the Center, by Vishnu Karmakar and Thomas Whitney. Littleton, CO: Center Vision, Inc., 2001. 144 pages. Softcover. $19.95

Not only will this book help you stay free of trigger jerk, it will help you in all areas of your shooting.

9mm Parabellum; The History & Development of the World's 9mm Pistols & Ammunition, by Klaus-Peter Konig and Martin Hugo, Schiffer Publishing Ltd., Atglen, PA, 1993. 304 pp., illus. $39.95

Detailed history of 9mm weapons from Belguim, Italy, Germany, Israel, France, USA, Czechoslovakia, Hungary, Poland, Brazil, Finland and Spain.

The Official 9mm Markarov Pistol Manual, translated into English by Major James Gebhardt, U.S. Army (Ret.), Desert Publications, El Dorado, AR, 1996. 84 pp., illus. Paper covers. $14.95

The information found in this book will be of enormous benefit and interest to the owner or a prospective owner of one of these pistols.

The Official Soviet 7.62mm Handgun Manual, by Translation by Maj. James F. Gebhardt Ret.), Paladin Press, Boulder, CO, 1997, soft cover, illus., 104 pp. $20.00

This Soviet military manual, now available in English for the first time, covers instructions for use and maintenance of two side arms, the Nagant 7.62mm revolver, used by the Russian tsarist armed forces and later the Soviet armed forces, and the Tokarev 7.62mm semi-auto pistol, which replaced the Nagant.

The Operator's Tactical Pistol Shooting Manual; A Practical Guide to Combat Marksmanship, by Lawrence, Erik. Linesville, PA: Blackheart Publishing, 2003. 1st edition. 233 pages. Softcover. $24.50

This manual type book begins with the basic of safety with a pistol and progresses into advanced pistol handling. A self help guide for improving your capabilities with a pistol at your own pace. Over 200 pages and numerous descriptive photos. Subjects include: Combat Mindset, Pistol nomenclature and terms, Safety considerations, Shooting fundamentals, Shooting positions, Reloading techniques Malfunction drills, Combat marksmanship considerations, Training tips and drills, Shooting while wounded, Low light shooting, Left hand dominant shooter considerations, And appendixes that include various shooting standards, equipment supplies listing, progress worksheets, and emergency medical procedures for range injuries.

The P-08 Parabellum Luger Automatic Pistol, edited by J. David McFarland, Desert Publications, Cornville, AZ, 1982. 20 pp., illus. Paper covers. $14.95

Covers every facet of the Luger, plus a listing of all known Luger models.

The P08 Luger Pistol, by de Vries & Martens. Alexandria, VA: Ironside International, 2002. 152 pages, illustrated with 200 high quality b&w photos. Hardcover. $34.95

Covers all essential information on history and development, ammunition and accessories, codes and markings, and contains photos of nearly every model and accessory. Includes a unique selection of original German WWII propoganda photos, most never published before.

The P-38 Pistol: The Walther Pistols, 1930-1945. Volume 1. by Warren Buxton, Ucross Books, Los Alamos, MN 1999. $68.50

A limited run reprint of this scarce and sought-after work on the P-38 Pistol. 328 pp. with 160 illustrations.

The P-38 Pistol: The Contract Pistols, 1940-1945. Volume 2. by Warren Buxton, Ucross Books, Los Alamos, MN 1999. 256 pp. with 237 illustrations. $68.50

The P-38 Pistol: Postwar Distributions, 1945-1990. Volume 3. by Warren Buxton, Ucross Books, Los Alamos, MN 1999. Plus an addendum to Volumes 1 & 2. 272 pp. with 342 illustrations. $68.50

Pistols Of World War 1, by Adamek, Robert J. Pittsburgh: Pentagon Press, 2001. 1st edition signed and numbered. Over 90 pistols illustrated, technical data, designers, history, proof marks. 296 pages with illustations and photos. Softcover. $45.00

Over 25 pistol magazines illustrated with dimensions, serial number ranges. Over 35 cartridges illustrated with dimensions, manufactures, year of introduction. Weapons from 16 countries involved in WW1, statistics, quantities made, identification.

The Ruger "P" Family of Handguns, by Duncan Long, Desert Publications, El Dorado, AZ, 1993. 128 pp., illus. Paper covers. $14.95

A full-fledged documentary on a remarkable series of Sturm Ruger handguns.

The Ruger .22 Automatic Pistol, Standard/Mark I/Mark II Series, by Duncan Long, Paladin Press, Boulder, CO, 1989. 168 pp., illus. Paper covers. $16.00

The definitive book about the pistol that has served more than 1 million owners so well.

The Semiautomatic Pistols in Police Service and Self Defense, by Massad Ayoob, Police Bookshelf, Concord, NH, 1990. 25 pp., illus. Soft covers. $11.95

First quantitative, documented look at actual police experience with 9mm and 45 police service automatics.

Shooting Colt Single Actions, by Mike Venturino, Livingston, MT, 1997. 205 pp., illus. Paper covers. $25.00

A definitive work on the famous Colt SAA and the ammunition it shoots.

Sig Handguns, by Duncan Long, Desert Publications, El Dorado, AZ, 1995. 150 pp., illus. Paper covers. $19.95

The history of Sig/Sauer handguns, including Sig, Sig-Hammerli and Sig/Sauer variants.

Sixgun Cartridges and Loads, by Elmer Keith, reprint edition by The Gun Room Press, Highland Park, NJ, 1984. 151 pp., illus. $24.95

A manual covering the selection, use and loading of the most suitable and popular revolver cartridges.

Sixguns, by Elmer Keith, Wolfe Publishing Company, Prescott, AZ, 1992. 336 pp. Paper covers. $29.95. Hardcover $35.00

The history, selection, repair, care, loading, and use of this historic frontiersman's friend—the one-hand firearm.

Smith & Wesson's Automatics, by Larry Combs, Desert Publications, El Dorado, AZ, 1994. 143 pp., illus. Paper covers. $19.95

A must for every S&W auto owner or prospective owner.

Spanish Handguns: The History of Spanish Pistols and Revolvers, by Gene Gangarosa, Jr., Stoeger Publishing Co., Accokeek, MD, 2001. 320 pp., illustrated, b&w photos. Paper covers. $21.95

Standard Catalog Of Smith & Wesson; 2nd Edition, by Jim Supica and Richard Nahas. Krause Publications, Iola, WI: 2001. 2nd edition. 272 Pages, 350 b&w photos, with 16 page color section. Pictorial hardcover. $34.95

Clearly details 775 Smith & Wesson models, knives, holsters, ammunition and police items with complete pricing information, illustrated glossary and index.

Star Firearms, by Leonardo M. Antaris, Davenport, IA: Firac Publications Co., 2002. 640 pages, with over 1,100 b&w photos, 47 pages in full color. Hardcover. $119.95

The definitive work on Star's many models with a historical context, with a review of their mechanical features, & details their development throughout production plus tables of proof marks & codes, serial numbers, annual summaries, procurements by Spanish Guardia Civil & Spanish Police, exports to Bulgaria, Germany, & Switzerland during WW2; text also covers Star's .22 rifles & submachine guns & includes a comprehensive list of Spanish trade names matched to manufacturer for arms made prior to the Spanish Civil War (1936-1939).

Street Stoppers: The Latest Handgun Stopping Power Street Results, by Evan P. Marshall & Edwin J. Sandow, Paladin Press, Boulder, CO, 1997. 392 pp., illus. Paper covers. $42.95.

Compilation of the results of real-life shooting incidents involving every major handgun caliber.

The Tactical 1911, by Dave Lauck, Paladin Press, Boulder, CO, 1999. 152 pp., illustrated. Paper covers. $22.00

The cop's and SWAT operator's guide to employment and maintenance.

The Tactical Pistol, by Gabriel Suarez with a foreword by Jeff Cooper, Paladin Press, Boulder, CO, 1996. 216 pp., illus. Paper covers. $25.00

Advanced gunfighting concepts and techniques.

The Thompson/Center Contender Pistol, by Charles Tephens, Paladin Press, Boulder, CO, 1997. 58 pp., illus. Paper covers. $14.00

How to tune and time, load and shoot accurately with the Contender pistol.

The .380 Enfield No. 2 Revolver, by Mark Stamps and Ian Skennerton, I.D.S.A. Books, Piqua, OH, 1993. 124 pp., 80 illus. Paper covers. $19.95

The Truth About Handguns, by Duane Thomas, Paladin Press, Boulder, CO, 1997. 136 pp., illus. Paper covers. $18.00

Exploding the myths, hype, and misinformation about handguns.

Walther Pistols: Models 1 Through P99, Factory Variations and Copies, by Dieter H. Marschall, Ucross Books, Los Alamos, NM. 2000. 140 pages, with 140 b&w illustrations, index. Paper Covers. $19.95

This is the English translation, revised and updated, of the highly successful and widely acclaimed German language edition. This book provides the collector with a reference guide and overview of the entire line of the Walther military, police, and self-defense pistols from the very first to the very latest. Models 1-9, PP, PPK, MP, AP, HP, P.38, P1, P4, P38K, P5, P88, P99 and the Manurhin models. Variations, where issued, serial ranges, calibers, marks, proofs, logos, and design aspects in an astonishing quantity and variety are crammed into this very well researched and highly regarded work.

U.S. Handguns of World War 2, The Secondary Pistols and Revolvers, by Charles W. Pate, Mowbray Publishers, Lincoln, RI, 1997. 368 pp., illus. $39.00

This indispensable new book covers all of the American military handguns of W.W.2 except for the M1911A1.

HUNTING

NORTH AMERICA

Advanced Black Powder Hunting, by Toby Bridges, Stoeger Publishing Co., Wayne, NJ, 1998. 288 pp., illus. Paper covers. $21.95

The first modern day publication to be filled from cover to cover with guns, loads, projectiles, accessories and the techniques to get the most from today's front loading guns.

The Arms Library

Advanced Strategies for Trophy Whitetails, by David Morris, Safari Press, Inc., Huntington Beach, CA, 1999. 399 pp., illustrated. $29.95

This book is a must-have for any serious trophy hunter.

Adventures Of An Alaskan - You Can Do, by Dennis W. Confer. Foreword by Craig Boddington. Anchorage, AK : Wiley Ventures, 2003. 1st edition. 279 pages, illus. Softcover. $24.95

This book is about 45% fishing, 45% hunting, & 10% related adventures; travel, camping and boating. It is written to stimulate, encourage and motivate readers to make happy memories that they can do on an average income and to entertain, educate and inform readers of outdoor opportunities.

Aggressive Whitetail Hunting, by Greg Miller, Krause Publications, Iola, WI, 1995. 208 pp., illus. Paper covers. $14.95

Learn how to hunt trophy bucks in public forests, private farmlands and exclusive hunting grounds from one of America's foremost hunters.

Alaska Safari, by Harold Schetzle & Sam Fadala (designer). The most comprehensive guide to Alaska hunting. Anchorage, AK: Great Northwest Publishing, 2002. Revised 2nd edition. 366 pages, illus. with b&w photos. Softcover. $29.95

The author has brought a wealth of information to the hunter and anyone interested in Alaska. Harold Schetzle is a great guide and has also written another book called "Alaska Wilderness Hunter" which is a wonderful book of stories of Alaska hunting taken from many, many years of hunting and guiding.

Alaskan Yukon Trophies Won And Lost, by Young, G.O. Wolfe Publishing, Prescott, AZ. 2002. 273 pp. with b&w photographs and a five page epilogue by the publisher. Softcover. $35.00

A classic big game hunting tale.

American Duck Shooting, by George Bird Grinnell, Stackpole Books, Harrisburg, PA, 1991. 640 pp., illus. Paper covers. $19.95

First published in 1901 at the height of the author's career. Describes 50 species of waterfowl, and discusses hunting methods common at the turn of the century.

The American Wild Turkey, Hunting Tactics and Techniques, by John McDaniel, The Lyons Press, New York, NY, 2000. 240 pp., illustrated. $29.95

Loaded with turkey hunting anectdotes gleaned from a lifetime of experience.

Autumn Passages, Compiled by the editors of Ducks Unlimited Magazine, Willow Creek Press, Minocqua, WI, 1997. 320 pp. $27.50

An exceptional collection of duck hunting stories. Reminiscences of a hunter's life in rural America.

Bare November Days, by George Bird Evans et al, Down East Books, Camden, MA 2002. 136 pp., illus. $39.50

A new, original anthology, a tribute to ruffed grouse, king of upland birds.

Bear Attacks, by K. Etling, Safari Press, Long Beach, CA, 1998. 574 pp., illus. In 2 volumes. $75.00

Classic tales of dangerous North American bears.

The Best of Babcock, by Havilah Babcock, selected and with an introduction by Hugh Grey, The Gunnerman Press, Auburn Hills, MI, 1985. 262 pp., illus. $19.95.

A treasury of memorable pieces, 21 of which have never before appeared in book form.

Big Game Hunting, by Duncan Gilchrist, Outdoor Expeditions, books and videos, Corvallis, MT, 1999. 192 pp., illustrated. $14.95

Designed to be a warehouse of hunting information covering the major North American big game species.

Blacktail Trophy Tactics, by Boyd Iverson, Stoneydale Press, Stevensville, MI, 1992. 166 pp., illus. Paper covers. $14.95

A comprehensive analysis of blacktail deer habits, describing a deer's and man's use of scents, still hunting, tree techniques, etc.

Bowhunter's Handbook, Expert Strategies and Techniques, by M.R. James with Fred Asbell, Dave Holt, Dwight Schuh & Dave Samuel, DBI Books, a division of Krause Publications, Iola, WI, 1997. 256 pp., illus. Paper covers. $19.95

Tips from the top on taking your bowhunting skills to the next level.

The Buffalo Harvest, by Frank Mayer as told to Charles Roth, Pioneer Press, Union City, TN, 1995. 96 pp., illus. Paper covers. $12.50

The story of a hide hunter during his buffalo hunting days on the plains.

Call of the Quail: A Tribute to the Gentleman Game Bird, by Michael McIntosh, et al., Countrysport Press, Traverse City, MI, 1990. 175 pp., illus. $35.00

A new anthology on quail hunting.

Calling All Elk, by Jim Zumbo, Cody, WY, 1989. 169 pp., illus. Paper covers. $14.95

The only book on the subject of elk hunting that covers every aspect of elk vocalization.

The Complete Book of Grouse Hunting, by Frank Woolner, The Lyons Press, New York, NY, 2000. 192 pp., illustrated Paper covers. $24.95

The history, habits, and habitat of one of America's great game birds—and the methods used to hunt it.

The Complete Book of Mule Deer Hunting, by Walt Prothero, The Lyons Press, New York, NY, 2000. 192 pp., illustrated. Paper covers. $24.95

Field-tested practical advice on how to bag the trophy buck of a lifetime.

The Complete Book of Wild Turkey Hunting, by John Trout Jr., The Lyons Press, New York, NY, 2000. 192 pp., illustrated. Paper covers. $24.95

An illustrated guide to hunting for one of America's most popular game birds.

The Complete Book of Woodcock Hunting, by Frank Woolner, The Lyons Press, New York, NY, 2000. 192 pp., illustrated. Paper covers. $24.95

A thorough, practical guide to the American woodcock and to woodcock hunting.

The Complete Guide To Hunting Wild Boar in California, by Gary Kramer. Safari Press, 2002. 1st edition. Softcover. $15.95

Gary Kramer takes the hunter all over California, from north to south and east to west. He discusses natural history, calibers, bullets, rifles, pistols, shotguns, black powder, and bow and arrows. Other chapters discuss equipment, the six major systems of hunting hogs, the top hog-producing counties, and hunting areas--those with public access as well as private hog-hunting ranches and military bases that allow hunting. Suprisingly, there are quite a few areas in California that afford public access for hog hunters. The book is chock-a-block full with details, addresses, telephone numbers, Web sites, and relevant information that will help you bring the bacon home. Hints on photography, caring for the meat, as well as a good, thorough list of meat processors are also included to help with converting your hog into good memories and delightful dishes. And just when you thought Kramer would have nothing else to add, he divulges delicious recipes to appease your spouse and present her with a decent excuse as to why you went hunting! This is THE hogging best book on how to get your pig. 127pp, 37 photos.

The Complete Venison Cookbook from Field to Table, by Jim & Ann Casada, Krause Publications, Iola, WI, 1996. 208 pp., Comb-bound. $12.95

More than 200 kitchen tested recipes make this book the answer to a table full of hungry hunters or guests.

Coveys and Singles: The Handbook of Quail Hunting, by Robert Gooch, A.S. Barnes, San Diego, CA, 1981. 196 pp., illus. $11.95

The story of the quail in North America.

Coyote Hunting, by Phil Simonski, Stoneydale Press, Stevensville, MT, 1994. 126 pp., illus. Paper covers. $12.95

Probably the most thorough "How-to-do-it" book on coyote hunting ever written.

Dabblers & Divers: A Duck Hunter's Book, compiled by the editors of Ducks Unlimited Magazine, Willow Creek Press, Minocqua, WI, 1997. 160 pp., illus. $39.95

A word-and-photographic portrayal of waterfowl hunter's singular intimacy with, and passion for, watery haunts and wildfowl.

Dancers in the Sunset Sky, by Robert F. Jones, The Lyons Press, New York, NY, 1997. 192 pp., illus. $22.95

The musings of a bird hunter.

Deer & Deer Hunting, by Al Hofacker, Krause Publications, Iola, WI, 1993. 208 pp., illus. $34.95

Coffee-table volume packed full of how-to-information that will guide hunts for years to come.

Deer and Deer Hunting: The Serious Hunter's Guide, by Dr. Robert Wegner, Stackpole Books, Harrisburg, PA, 1984. 384 pp., illus. Paper covers. $18.95

In-depth information from the editor of "Deer & Deer Hunting" magazine. Major bibliography of English language books on deer and deer hunting from 1838-1984.

Deer and Deer Hunting Book 2, by Dr. Robert Wegner, Stackpole Books, Harrisburg, PA, 1987. 400 pp., illus. Paper covers. $18.95

Strategies and tactics for the advanced hunter.

Deer and Deer Hunting, Book 3, by Dr. Robert Wegner, Stackpole Books, Harrisburg, PA, 1990. 368 pp., illus. $18.95

This comprehensive volume covers natural history, deer hunting lore, profiles of deer hunters, and discussion of important issues facing deer hunters today.

The Deer Hunters: The Tactics, Lore, Legacy and Allure of American Deer Hunting, Edited by Patrick Durkin, Krause Publications, Iola, WI, 1997. 208 pp., illus. $29.95

More than twenty years of research from America's top whitetail hunters, researchers, and photographers have gone in to the making of this book.

Deer Hunting, by R. Smith, Stackpole Books, Harrisburg, PA, 1978. 224 pp., illus. Paper covers. $14.95

A professional guide leads the hunt for North America's most popular big game animal.

Dreaming the Lion, by Thomas McIntyre, Countrysport Press, Traverse City, MI, 1994. 309 pp., illus. $35.00

Reflections on hunting, fishing and a search for the wild. Twenty-three stories by *Sports Afield* editor, Tom McIntyre.

Elk and Elk Hunting, by Hart Wixom, Stackpole Books, Harrisburg, PA, 1986. 288 pp., illus. $34.95

Your practical guide to fundamentals and fine points of elk hunting.

Elk Hunting in the Northern Rockies, by Ed. Wolff, Stoneydale Press, Stevensville, MT, 1984. 162 pp., illus. $18.95

Helpful information about hunting the premier elk country of the northern Rocky Mountain states—Wyoming, Montana and Idaho.

Elk Hunting with the Experts, by Bob Robb, Stoneydale Press, Stevensville, MT, 1992. 176 pp., illus. Paper covers. $15.95

A complete guide to elk hunting in North America by America's top elk hunting expert.

Firelight, by Burton L. Spiller, Gunnerman Press, Auburn Hills, MI, 1990. 196 pp., illus. $19.95

Enjoyable tales of the outdoors and stalwart companions.

Getting a Stand, by Miles Gilbert, Pioneer Press, Union City, TN, 1993. 204 pp., illus. Paper covers. $13.95

An anthology of 18 short personal experiences by buffalo hunters of the late 1800s, specifically from 1870-1882.

Gordon MacQuarrie Trilogy: Stories of the Old Duck Hunters, by Gordon MacQuarrie, Willow Creek Press, Minocqua, WI, 1994. $49.00

A slip-cased three volume set of masterpieces by one of America's finest outdoor writers.

Greatest Elk; The Complete Historical and Illustrated Record of North America's Biggest Elk, by R. Selner, Safari Press, Huntington Beach, CA, 2000. 209 pages, profuse color illus. $39.95

Here is the book all elk hunters have been waiting for! This oversized book holds the stories and statistics of the biggest bulls ever killed in North America. Stunning, full-color photographs highlight over 40 world-class heads, including the old world records!

Grouse and Woodcock, A Gunner's Guide, by Don Johnson, Krause Publications, Iola, WI, 1995. 256 pp., illus. Paper covers. $14.95

Find out what you need in guns, ammo, equipment, dogs and terrain.

Gunning for Sea Ducks, by George Howard Gillelan, Tidewater Publishers, Centreville, MD, 1988. 144 pp., illus. $14.95

A book that introduces you to a practically untouched arena of waterfowling.

The Heck with Moose Hunting, by Jim Zumbo, Wapiti Valley Publishing Co., Cody, WY, 1996. 199 pp., illus. $17.95

Jim's hunts around the continent including encounters with moose, caribou, sheep, antelope and mountain goats.

High Pressure Elk Hunting, by Mike Lapinski, Stoneydale Press Publishing Co., Stevensville, MT, 1996. 192 pp., illus. $19.95

The secrets of hunting educated elk revealed.

Horns in the High Country, by Andy Russell, Alfred A. Knopf, NY, 1973. 259 pp., illus. Paper covers. $12.95

A many-sided view of wild sheep and their natural world.

How to Hunt, by Dave Bowring, Winchester Press, Piscataway, NJ, 1982. 208 pp., illus. Hardcover $15.00

A basic guide to hunting big game, small game, upland birds, and waterfowl.

Hunt High for Rocky Mountain Goats, Bighorn Sheep, Chamois & Tahr, by Duncan Gilchrist, Stoneydale Press, Stevensville, MT, 1992. 192 pp., illus. Paper covers. $19.95

The source book for hunting mountain goats.

THE ARMS LIBRARY

Hunting Adventure of Me and Joe, by Walt Prothero, Safari Press, Huntington Beach, CA, 1995. 220 pp., illus. $22.50
A collection of the author's best and favorite stories.

Hunting Mature Bucks, by Larry L. Weishuhn, Krause Publications, Iola, WI, 1995. 256 pp., illus. Paper covers. $14.95
One of North America's top white-tailed deer authorities shares his expertise on hunting those big, smart and elusive bucks.

Hunting Open-Country Mule Deer, by Dwight Schuh, Sage Press, Nampa, ID, 1989. 180 pp., illus. $18.95
A guide taking Western bucks with rifle and bow.

Hunting America's Wild Turkey, by Bridges, Toby, Stoeger Publishing Company, Pocomoke, MD, 2001. 256 pp., illus. $16.95
The techniques and tactics of hunting North America's largest, and most popular, woodland game bird.

Hunting the Rockies, Home of the Giants, by Kirk Darner, Marceline, MO, 1996. 291 pp., illus. $25.00
Understand how and where to hunt Western game in the Rockies.

Hunting Trips in North America, by F.C. Selous, Wolfe Publishing Co., Prescott, AZ, 1988. 395 pp., illus. $52.00
A limited edition reprint. Coverage of caribou, moose and other big game hunting in virgin wilds.

Hunting Trophy Deer, by John Wootters, The Lyons Press, New York, NY, 1997. 272 pp., illus. $24.95
A revised edition of the definitive manual for identifying, scouting, and successfully hunting a deer of a lifetime.

Hunting Trophy Whitetails, by David Morris, Stoneydale Press, Stevensville, MT, 1993. 483 pp., illus. $29.95
This is one of the best whitetail books published in the last two decades. The author is the former editor of *North American Whitetail* magazine.

Hunting Western Deer, by Jim and Wes Brown, Stoneydale Press, Stevensville, MT, 1994. 174 pp., illus. Paper covers. $14.95
A pair of expert Oregon hunters provide insight into hunting mule deer and blacktail deer in the western states.

Hunting Wild Turkeys in the West, by John Higley, Stoneydale Press, Stevensville, MT, 1992. 154 pp., illus. Paper covers. $12.95
Covers the basics of calling, locating and hunting turkeys in the western states.

Hunting with the Twenty-two, by Charles Singer Landis, R&R Books, Livonia, NY, 1994. 429 pp., illus. $35.00
A miscellany of articles touching on the hunting and shooting of small game.

I Don't Want to Shoot an Elephant, by Havilah Babcock, The Gunnerman Press, Auburn Hills, MI, 1985. 184 pp., illus. $19.95
Eighteen delightful stories that will enthrall the upland gunner for many pleasureable hours.

In Search of the Buffalo, by Charles G. Anderson, Pioneer Press, Union City, TN, 1996. 144 pp., illus. Paper covers. $13.95
The primary study of the life of J. Wright Mooar, one of the few hunters fortunate enough to kill a white buffalo.

In the Turkey Woods, by Jerome B. Robinson, The Lyons Press, N.Y., 1998. 207 pp., illustrated. $24.95
Practical expert advice on all aspects of turkey hunting—from calls to decoys to guns.

Jaybirds Go to Hell on Friday, by Havilah Babcock, The Gunnerman Press, Auburn Hills, MI, 1985. 149 pp., illus. $19.95
Sixteen jewels that reestablish the lost art of good old-fashioned yarn telling.

Measuring and Scoring North American Big Game Trophies, 2nd Edition, by Wm. H. Nesbitt and Philip L. Wright, The Boone & Crockett Club, Missoula, MT, 1999. 150 pp., illustrated. $34.95
The definitive manual for anyone wanting to learn the Club's world-famous big game measuring system.

Montana—Land of Giant Rams, Volume 2, by Duncan Gilchrist, Outdoor Expeditions and Books, Corvallis, MT, 1992. 208 pp., illus. $34.95
The reader will find stories of how many of the top-scoring trophies were taken.

Montana—Land of Giant Rams, Volume 3, by Duncan Gilchrist, Outdoor Expeditions, books and videos, Corvallis, MT, 1999. 224 pp., illus. Paper covers. $19.95
All new sheep information including over 70 photos. Learn about how Montana became the "Land of Giant Rams" and what the prospects of the future as we enter a new millenium.

More Tracks: 78 Years of Mountains, People & Happiness, by Howard Copenhaver, Stoneydale Press, Stevensville, MT, 1992. 150 pp., illus. $18.95
A collection of stories by one of the back country's best storytellers about the people who shared with Howard his great adventure in the high places and wild Montana country.

Mostly Huntin', by Bill Jordan, Everett Publishing Co., Bossier City, LA, 1987. 254 pp., illus. $21.95
Jordan's hunting adventures in North America, Africa, Australia, South America and Mexico.

Mule Deer: Hunting Today's Trophies, by Tom Carpenter and Jim Van Norman, Krause Publications, Iola, WI, 1998. 256 pp., illustrated. Paper covers. $19.95
A tribute to both the deer and the people who hunt them. Includes info on where to look for big deer, prime mule deer habitat and effective weapons for the hunt.

My Health is Better in November, by Havilah Babcock, University of S. Carolina Press, Columbia, SC, 1985. 284 pp., illus. $24.95
Adventures in the field set in the plantation country and backwater streams of SC.

The North American Waterfowler, by Paul S. Bernsen, Superior Publ. Co., Seattle, WA, 1972. 206 pp. Paper covers. $9.95
The complete inside and outside story of duck and goose shooting. Big and colorful, illustrations by Les Kouba.

The Old Man and the Boy, by Robert Ruark, Henry Holt & Co., New York, NY, 303 pp., illus. $24.95
A timeless classic, telling the story of a remarkable friendship between a young boy and his grandfather as they hunt and fish together.

The Old Man's Boy Grows Older, by Robert Ruark, Henry Holt & Co., Inc., New York, NY, 1993. 300 pp., illus. $24.95
The heartwarming sequel to the best-selling *The Old Man and the Boy.*

Old Wildfowling Tales, Volume 2, edited by Worth Mathewson, Sand Lake Press, Amity, OR, 1996. 240 pp. $21.95
A collection of duck and geese hunting stories based around accounts from the past.

One Man, One Rifle, One Land; Hunting all Species of Big Game in North America, by J.Y. Jones, Safari Press, Huntington Beach, CA, 2000. 400 pp., illustrated. $59.95
Journey with J.Y. Jones as he hunts each of the big-game animals of North America—from the polar bear of the high Artic to the jaguar of the low-lands of Mexico—with just one rifle.

161 Waterfowling Secrets, edited by Matt Young, Willow Creek Press, Minocqua, WI, 1997. 78 pp., Paper covers. $10.95
Time-honored, field-tested waterfowling tips and advice.

Outdoor Pastimes of an American Hunter, by Theodore Roosevelt, Stackpole Books, Mechanicsburg, PA, 1994. 480 pp., illus. Paper covers. $18.95
Stories of hunting big game in the West and notes about animals pursued and observed.

The Outlaw Gunner, by Harry M. Walsh, Tidewater Publishers, Cambridge, MD, 1973. 178 pp., illus. $22.95
A colorful story of market gunning in both its legal and illegal phases.

Pheasant Days, by Chris Dorsey, Voyageur Press, Stillwater, MN, 1992. 233 pp., illus. $24.95
The definitive resource on ringnecks. Includes everything from basic hunting techniques to the life cycle of the bird.

Pheasant Hunter's Harvest, by Steve Grooms, Lyons & Burford Publishers, New York, NY, 1990. 180 pp. $22.95
A celebration of pheasant, pheasant dogs and pheasant hunting. Practical advice from a passionate hunter.

A Pheasant Hunter's Notebook: Revised Second Edition, by Larry Brown. Camden, ME: Country Sport Press, 2003. 1st edition. 266 pages. Hardcover. $26.95
Larry Brown has spent a lifetime pursuing America's most colorful and raucous upland game bird, and the advice he presents here, based on written records of his hunts over the decades, is priceless. Though qualified to do so, the author doesn't lecture on his subject but shares his experiences as one hunter to another, coloring his information with interesting, informative, often amusing anecdotes. Particularly valuable are his strategies for hunting different kinds of cover in varying types of weather.

Pheasant Tales, by Gene Hill et al, Countrysport Press, Traverse City, MI, 1996. 202 pp., illus. $39.00
Charley Waterman, Michael McIntosh and Phil Bourjaily join the author to tell some of the stories that illustrate why the pheasant is America's favorite game bird.

Pheasants of the Mind, by Datus Proper, Wilderness Adventures Press, Bozeman, MT, 1994. 154 pp., illus. $25.00
No single title sums up the life of the solitary pheasant hunter like this masterful work.

Portraits of Elk Hunting, by Jim Zumbo, Safari Press, Huntington Beach, CA, 2001. 222 pp. illustrated. $39.95
Zumbo has captured in photos as well as in words the essence, charisma, and wonderful components of elk hunting: back-country wilderness camps, sweaty guides, happy hunters, favorite companions, elk woods, and, of course, the majestic elk. Join Zumbo in the uniqueness of the pursuit of the magnificent and noble elk.

Predator Calling with Gerry Blair, by Gerry Blair, Krause Publications, Iola, WI, 1996. 208 pp., illus. Paper covers. $14.95
Time-tested secrets lure predators closer to your camera or gun.

Proven Whitetail Tactics, by Greg Miller, Krause Publications, Iola, WI, 1997. 224 pp., illus. Paper covers. $19.95
Proven tactics for scouting, calling and still-hunting whitetail.

Quest for Dall Rams, by Duncan Gilchrist, Duncan Gilchrist Outdoor Expeditions and Books, Corvallis, MT, 1997. 224 pp., illus. Limited numbered edition. $34.95
The most complete book of Dall sheep ever written. Covers information on Alaska and provinces with Dall sheep and explains hunting techniques, equipment, etc.

Quest for Giant Bighorns, by Duncan Gilchrist, Outdoor Expeditions and Books, Corvallis, MT, 1994. 224 pp., illus. Paper covers. $19.95
How some of the most successful sheep hunters hunt and how some of the best bighorns were taken.

Radical Elk Hunting Strategies, by Mike Lapinski, Stoneydale Press Publishing Co., Stevensville, MT, 1988. 161 pp., illus. $18.95
Secrets of calling elk in close.

Rattling, Calling & Decoying Whitetails, by Gary Clancy, Edited by Patrick Durkin, Krause Publications, Iola, WI, 2000. 208 pp., illustrated. Paper covers. $19.95
How to consistently coax big bucks into range.

Records of North American Big Game 11th Edition, with hunting chapters by Craig Boddington, Tom McIntyre and Jim Zumbo, The Boone and Crockett Club, Missoula, MT, 1999. 700 pp., featuring a 32 page color section. $49.95
Listing over 17,150, of the top trophy big game animals ever recorded. Over 4,000 new listings are featured in this latest edition.

Records of North American Caribou and Moose, Craig Boddington et al, The Boone & Crockett Club, Missoula, MT, 1997. 250 pp., illus. $24.95
More than 1,800 caribou listings and more than 1,500 moose listings, organized by the state or Canadian province where they were taken.

Records of North American Elk and Mule Deer, 2nd Edition, edited by Jack and Susan Reneau, Boone & Crockett Club, Missoula, MT, 1996. 360 pp., illus. Paper cover, $18.95; hardcover, $24.95
Updated and expanded edition featuring more than 150 trophy, field and historical photos of the finest elk and mule deer trophies ever recorded.

Records of North American Sheep, Rocky Mountain Goats and Pronghorn edited by Jack and Susan Reneau, Boone & Crockett Club, Missoula, MT, 1996. 400 pp., illus. Paper cover, $18.95; hardcover, $24.95
The first B&C Club records book featuring all 3941 accepted wild sheep, Rocky Mountain goats and pronghorn trophies.

Reflections on Snipe, by Worth Mathewson. Camden, ME: Country Sport Press, 2003. Hardcover. $25.00
Reflections on Snipe is a delightful compendium of information on snipe behavior and habitats; gunning history; stories from the field; and the pleasures of hunting with good companions, whether human or canine. 144 pages, illustrated by Eldridge Hardie.

Return of Royalty; Wild Sheep of North America, by Dr. Dale E. Toweill and Dr. Valerius Geist, Boone and Crockett Club, Missoula, MT, 1999. 224 pp., illustrated. $59.95
A celebration of the return of the wild sheep to many of its historical ranges.

THE ARMS LIBRARY

Ringneck; A Tribute to Pheasants and Pheasant Hunting, by Steve Grooms, Russ Sewell and Dave Nomsen, The Lyons Press, New York, NY, 2000. 120 pp., illustrated. $40.00

A glorious full-color coffee-table tribute to the pheasant and those who hunt them.

Rooster! A Tribute to Pheasant Hunting, by Dale C. Spartas. Riverbend Publishing, 2003. 1st edition. 150+ glorious photos of pheasants, hunting dogs & hunting trips with family & friends. 128 pgs. Hardcover. $39.95

A very special, must-have book for the 2.3 million pheasant hunters across the country!

Rub-Line Secrets, by Greg Miller, edited by Patrick Durkin, Krause Publications, Iola, WI, 1999. 208 pp., illustrated. Paper covers. $19.95

Based on nearly 30 years experience. Proven tactics for finding, analyzing and hunting big bucks' rub-lines.

The Season, by Tom Kelly, Lyons & Burford, New York, NY, 1997. 160 pp., illus. $22.95

The delight and challenges of a turkey hunter's Spring season.

Secret Strategies from North America's Top Whitetail Hunters, compiled by Nick Sisley, Krause Publications, Iola, WI, 1995. 256 pp., illus. Paper covers. $14.95

Bow and gun hunters share their success stories.

Secrets of the Turkey Pros, by Glenn Sapir, North American Hunting Club, Minnetonka, MN, 1999. 176 pp., illustrated. $19.95

This work written by a seasoned turkey hunter draws on the collective knowledge and experience on some of the most renowned names in the world of wild turkey.

Sheep Hunting in Alaska—The Dall Sheep Hunter's Guide, by Tony Russ, Outdoor Expeditions and Books, Corvallis, MT, 1994. 160 pp., illus. Paper covers. $19.95

A how-to guide for the Dall sheep hunter.

Shots at Big Game, by Craig Boddington, Stackpole Books, Harrisburg, PA, 1989. 198 pp., illus. Softcover $15.95

How to shoot a rifle accurately under hunting conditions.

Southern Deer & Deer Hunting, by Larry Weishuhn and Bill Bynum, Krause Publications, Iola, WI, 1995. 256 pp., illus. Paper covers. $14.95

Mount a trophy southern whitetail on your wall with this firsthand account of stalking big bucks below the Mason-Dixon line.

Spring Gobbler Fever, by Michael Hanback, Krause Publications, Iola, WI, 1996. 256 pp., illus. Paper covers. $15.95

Your complete guide to spring turkey hunting.

Stand Hunting for Whitetails, by Richard P. Smith, Krause Publications, Iola, WI, 1996. 256 pp., illus. Paper covers. $14.95

The author explains the tricks and strategies for successful stand hunting.

The Sultan of Spring: A Hunter's Odyssey Through the World of the Wild Turkey, by Bob Saile, The Lyons Press, New York, NY, 1998. 176 pp., illus. $22.95

A literary salute to the magic and mysticism of spring turkey hunting.

Taking Big Bucks, by Ed Wolff, Stoneydale Press, Stevensville, MT, 1987. 169 pp., illus. $18.95

Solving the whitetail riddle.

Tales of Quails 'n Such, by Havilah Babcock, University of S. Carolina Press, Columbia, SC, 1985. 237 pp. $19.95

A group of hunting stories, told in informal style, on field experiences in the South in quest of small game.

They Left Their Tracks, by Howard Coperhaver, Stoneydale Press Publishing Co., Stevensville, MT, 1990. 190 pp., illus. $18.95

Recollections of 60 years as an outfitter in the Bob Marshall Wilderness.

Timberdoodle, by Frank Woolner, Nick Lyons Books, N. Y., NY, 1987. 168 pp., illus. $18.95

The classic guide to woodcock and woodcock hunting.

Timberdoodle Tales: Adventures of a Minnesota Woodcock Hunter, by T. Waters, Safari Press, Huntington Beach, CA, 1997. 220 pp., illus. $35.00

The life history and hunt of the American woodcock by the author. A fresh appreciation of this captivating bird and the ethics of its hunt.

To Heck with Moose Hunting, by Jim Zumbo, Wapiti Publishing Co., Cody, WY, 1996. 199 pp., illus. $17.95

Jim's hunts around the continent and even an African adventure.

Track Pack: Animal Tracks In Full Life Size, by Ed Gray. Mechanicsburg, PA: Stackpole Books, 2003. 1st edition. Spiral-bound: 34 pages. $7.95

An indispensable reference for hunters, trackers, and outdoor enthusiasts. This handy guide features the tracks of 38 common North American animals, from squirrels to grizzlies.

The Trickiest Thing in Feathers, by Corey Ford; compiled and edited by Laurie Morrow and illustrated by Christopher Smith, Wilderness Adventures, Gallatin Gateway, MT, 1998. 208 pp., illus. $29.95

Here is a collection of Corey Ford's best wing-shooting stories, many of them previously unpublished.

The Upland Equation: A Modern Bird-Hunter's Code, by Charles Fergus, Lyons & Burford Publishers, New York, NY, 1996. 86 pp. $18.00

A book that deserves space in every sportsman's library. Observations based on firsthand experience.

Upland Tales, by Worth Mathewson (Ed.), Sand Lake Press, Amity, OR, 1996. 271 pp., illus. $29.95

A collection of articles on grouse, snipe and quail.

A Varmint Hunter's Odyssey, by Steve Hanson with a guest chapter by Mike Johnson, Precision Shooting, Inc. Manchester, CT, 1999. 279 pp., illustrated. Paper covers. $39.95

A new classic by a writer who eats, drinks and sleeps varmint hunting and varmint rifles.

Waterfowler's World, by Bill Buckley, Ducks Unlimited, Inc., Memphis, TN, 1999. 192 pp., illustrated in color. $37.50

An unprecedented pictorial book on waterfowl and waterfowlers.

When the Duck Were Plenty, by Ed Muderlak, Safari Press, Inc., Huntington Beach, CA, 2000. 300 pp., illustrated.. $29.95

The golden age of waterfowling and duck hunting from 1840 till 1920. An anthology.

Whitetail: Behavior Through the Seasons, by Charles J. Alsheimer, Krause Publications, Iola, WI, 1996. 208 pp., illus. $34.95

In-depth coverage of whitetail behavior presented through striking portraits of the whitetail in every season.

Whitetail: The Ultimate Challenge, by Charles J. Alsheimer, Krause Publications, Iola, WI, 1995. 228 pp., illus. Paper covers. $14.95

Learn deer hunting's most intriguing secrets—fooling deer using decoys, scents and calls—from America's premier authority.

Whitetails by the Moon, by Charles J. Alsheimer, edited by Patrick Durkin, Krause Publications, Iola, WI, 1999. 208 pp., illustrated. Paper covers. $19.95

Predict peak times to hunt whitetails. Learn what triggers the rut.

Wildfowler's Season, by Chris Dorsey, Lyons & Burford Publishers, New York, NY, 1998. 224 pp., illus. $37.95

Modern methods for a classic sport.

Wildfowling Tales, by William C. Hazelton, Wilderness Adventures Press, Belgrade, MT, 1999. 117 pp., illustrated with etchings by Brett Smith. In a slipcase. $50.00

Tales from the great ducking resorts of the Continent.

Windward Crossings: A Treasury of Original Waterfowling Tales, by Chuck Petrie et al, Willow Creek Press, Minocqua, WI, 1999. 144 pp., 48 color art and etching reproductions. $35.00

An illustrated, modern anthology of previously unpublished waterfowl hunting (fiction and creative non fiction) stories by America's finest outdoor journalists.

Wings of Thunder: New Grouse Hunting Revisited, by Steven Mulak, Countrysport Books, Selma, AL, 1998. 168 pp. illustrated. $30.00

The author examines every aspect of New England grouse hunting as it is today - the bird and its habits, the hunter and his dog, guns and loads, shooting and hunting techniques, practice on clay targets, clothing and equipment.

Wisconsin Hunting, by Brian Lovett, Krause Publications, Iola, WI, 1997. 208 pp., illus. Paper covers. $16.95

A comprehensive guide to Wisconsin's public hunting lands.

The Woodchuck Hunter, by Paul C. Estey, R&R Books, Livonia, NY, 1994. 135 pp., illus. $25.00

This book contains information on woodchuck equipment, the rifle, telescopic sights and includes interesting stories.

The Working Retrievers, Tom Quinn, The Lyons Press, New York, NY, 1998. 257 pp., illus. $40.00

The author covers every aspect of the training of dogs for hunting and field trials - from the beginning to the most advanced levels - for Labradors, Chesapeakes, Goldens and others.

AFRICA/ASIA/ELSEWHERE

The Adventurous Life of a Vagabond Hunter, by Sten Cedergren, Safari Press, Inc., Huntington Beach, CA, 2000. 300 pp., illustrated. Limited edition, numbered, signed, and slipcased. $70.00

An unusual story in the safari business by a remarkable character.

African Adventures, by J.F. Burger, Safari Press, Huntington Beach, CA, 1993. 222 pp., illus. $35.00

The reader shares adventures on the trail of the lion, the elephant and buffalo.

African Adventures and Misadventures: Escapades in East Africa with Mau Mau and Giant Forest Hogs, by William York. Long Beach, CA: Safari Press, 2003. A limited edition of 1,000 copies. Signed and numbered. 250 pages, color and b&w photos. Hardcover in a Slipcase. $70.00

From his early days in Kenya when he and a companion trekked alone through the desert of the NFD and had to fend off marauding lions that ate his caravan ponies to encountering a Mau Mau terrorist who took potshots at his victims with a stolen elephant gun, the late Bill York gives an entertaining account of his life that will keep you turning the pages. York was there when the RAF bombed the rain forest to rid Kenya of the dreaded Mau Mau, and he gives an insider's view to the funny and outrageous behavior of some his famous acquaintances—Eric Rundgren, Ken Dawson, Frank Broadbent, and Iodine Ionides. There are stories about how York found a cache of rhino and elephant ivory that J. A. Hunter had stashed before his death, and how John Boyes managed to exasperate British authorities with his dastardly deeds! There is an entire chapter on hunting giant forest hogs, and there are encounters and adventures with crop-raiding elephant and ghost buffalo that could be seen but not killed. As with York's previous book, the pages are loaded with interesting anecdotes, fascinating tales, and well-written prose that give insight into East Africa and its more famous characters.

The African Adventures: A Return to the Silent Places, by Peter Hathaway Capstick, St. Martin's Press, New York, NY, 1992. 220 pp., illus. $22.95

This book brings to life four turn-of-the-century adventurers and the savage frontier they braved. Frederick Selous, Constatine "Iodine" Ionides, Johnny Boyes and Jim Sutherland.

African Camp-fire Nights, by J.E. Burger, Safari Press, Huntington Beach, CA, 1993. 192 pp., illus. $32.50

In this book the author writes of the men who made hunting their life's profession.

African Game Trails, by Theodore Roosevelt, Peter Capstick, Series Editor, St. Martin's Press, New York, NY 1988. 583 pp., illustrated. $24.95

The famed safari of the noted sportsman, conservationist, and President.

African Hunter, by James Mellon, Safari Press, Huntington Beach, CA, 1996. 522 pp., illus. Paper Covers, $75.00

Regarded as the most comprehensive title ever published on African hunting.

African Hunter II, by Boddington, Craig & Flack, Peter, editors Long Beach, CA: Safari Press, 2004. 1st edition. Foreword by Robin Hurt, introduction by James Mellon. 606pp, profuse color and b&w photos. Hardcover. $135.00

It is with considerable pride that after five years of work by the editors and publisher we are able to present the new African Hunter. Let us be the first to say that the original book can never be surpassed: James Mellon spent FIVE years hunting in every African country open to hunting during the late 1960s and early 1970s, making him uniquely qualified to write a book of such scope and breadth. He then spent several years producing his masterpiece. (His unlimited resources didn't hurt the project any, either.) Because so much has changed in today's Africa, however, it was necessary to update the original, and we feel proud to have equaled the standard set by the first book. To start, there is a total of twenty-five countries covered, with thorough in-depth overviews of their hunting areas, background information, and best times to hunt. Then we cover the game animals: It includes all the Big Five (lion, leopard, buffalo, rhino, and elephant); the nine spiral-horn antelope; game indigenous to only one region; game indigenous to most regions; the rarities; the plains game, and so on--all game animals throughout the entire African continent are given meticulous attention. There are hunting stories from each country that highlight hunting the game found in that particular area--these are thrilling stories written by people who have hunted and lived in the area for long periods of time. Moreover, you will read exiting stories of giant tuskers in Tanzania, huge leopards, obnoxious buffalo, a double on large maned lions, and a surprisingly nimble giant rhino. But the book goes beyond that with chapters on medical preparations, booking a safari, the rules, and the rifles for Africa; there is even a detailed checklist of game animals, country by country. You will also find detailed maps and numerous sidebars with immediate, at your fingertips information. In addition to the editors, a total of more than two-dozen contributors, too many to list all, endeavored to make this book the most complete it could be: The names include Gregor Woods, Tony Tomkinson, Joe Coogan, Rolf Rohwer, Piet Hougard, Volker Grellmann, Geoff Broom, Robin Hurt, Rudolf Sand, Tony Dyer, Franz Wegnert, Mike Murray, Tony Sanchez, Rudy Lubin, Angelo Dacey, Warren Parker, Reinald von Meurers, Beth Jones, and Steve Christenson. With over 500 full-color pages, hundreds of photographs, and updated tables on animals and where they are available, this is THE book to consult for the information on Africa today, and it is sure to become the industry "standard" for years to come.

African Jungle Memories, by J.F. Burger, Safari Press, Huntington Beach, CA, 1993. 192 pp., illus. $32.50.

A book of reminiscences in which the reader is taken on many exciting adventures on the trail of the buffalo, lion, elephant and leopard.

African Rifles & Cartridges, by John Taylor, The Gun Room Press, Highland Park, NJ, 1977. 431 pp., illus. $35.00.

Experiences and opinions of a professional ivory hunter in Africa describing his knowledge of numerous arms and cartridges for big game. A reprint.

African Safaris, by Major G.H. Anderson, Safari Press, Long Beach, CA, 1997. 173 pp., illus. $35.00.

A reprinting of one of the rarest books on African hunting, with a foreword by Tony Sanchez.

African Twilight, by Robert F. Jones, Wilderness Adventure Press, Bozeman, MT, 1994. 208 pp., illus. $36.00.

Details the hunt, danger and changing face of Africa over a span of three decades.

A Man Called Lion: The Life and Times of John Howard "Pondoro" Taylor, by P.H. Capstick, Safari Press, Huntington Beach, CA, 1994. 240 pp., illus. $27.95.

With the help of Brian Marsh, an old Taylor acquaintance, Peter Capstick has accumulated over ten years of research into the life of this mysterious man.

An Annotated Bibliography of African Big Game Hunting Books, 1785 to 1950, by Kenneth P. Czech, Land's Edge Press, St. Cloud, MN 2000. $50.00

This bibliography features over 600 big game hunting titles describing the regions the authors hunted, species of game bagged, and physical descriptions of the books (pages, maps, plates, bindings, etc.) It also features a suite of 16 colored plates depicting decorated bindings from some of the books. Limited to 700 numbered, signed copies.

Baron in Africa; The Remarkable Adventures of Werner von Alvensleben, by Brian Marsh, Safari Press, Huntington Beach, CA, 2001. Foreword by Ian Player. 288 pp., illus. $35.00

Follow his career as he hunts lion, goes after large kudu, kills a full-grown buffalo with a spear, and hunts for elephant and ivory in some of the densest brush in Africa. The adventure and the experience were what counted to this fascinating character, not the money or fame; indeed, in the end he left Mozambique with barely more than the clothes on his back. This is a must-read adventure story on one of the most interesting characters to have come out of Africa after World War II.

The Big Five; Hunting Adventures in Today's Africa, by Dr. S. Lloyd Newberry, Safari Press, Huntington Beach, CA, 2001. 214 pp., illus. Limited edition, numbered, signed and slipcased. $70.00.

Many books have been written about the old Africa and its fabled Big Five, but almost nothing exits in print that describes hunting the Big Five as its exists today.

Big Game and Big Game Rifles, by John "Pondoro" Taylor, Safari Press, Huntington Beach, CA, 1999. 215 pp., illus. $24.95.

Covers rifles and calibers for elephant, rhino, hippo, buffalo, and lion.

Campfire Lies of a Canadian Guide, by Fred Webb, Safari Press, Inc., Huntington Beach, CA, 2000. 250 pp., illustrated. Limited edition, numbered, signed and slipcased. $50.00.

Forty years in the life of a guide in the North Country.

Cottar: The Exception was the Rule, by Pat Cottar, Trophy Room Books, Agoura, CA, 1999. 350 pp., illustrated. Limited, numbered and signed edition. $135.00

The remarkable big game hunting stories of one of Kenya's most remarkable pioneers.

A Country Boy in Africa, by George Hoffman, Trophy Room Books, Agoura, CA, 1998. 267 pp., illustrated with over 100 photos. Limited, numbered edition signed by the author. $85.00

In addition to the author's long and successful hunting career, he is known for developing a most effective big game cartridge, the .416 Hoffman.

Death and Double Rifles, by Mark Sullivan, Nitro Express Safaris, Phoenix, AZ, 2000. 295 pages, illus. $85.00

Sullivan has captured every thrilling detail of hunting dangerous game in this lavishly illustrated book. Full of color pictures of African hunts & rifles.

Death in a Lonely Land, by Peter Capstick, St. Martin's Press, New York, NY, 1990. 284 pp., illus. $22.95

Twenty-three stories of hunting as only the master can tell them.

Death in the Dark Continent, by Peter Capstick, St. Martin's Press, New York, NY, 1983. 238 pp., illus. $22.95

A book that brings to life the suspense, fear and exhilaration of stalking ferocious killers under primitive, savage conditions, with the ever present threat of death.

Death in the Long Grass, by Peter Hathaway Capstick, St. Martin's Press, New York, NY, 1977. 297 pp., illus. $22.95

A big game hunter's adventures in the African bush.

Death in the Silent Places, by Peter Capstick, St. Martin's Press, New York, NY, 1981. 243 pp., illus. $23.95

The author recalls the extraordinary careers of legendary hunters such as Corbett, Karamojo Bell, Stigand and others.

Encounters with Lions, by Jan Hemsing, Trophy Room books, Agoura, CA, 1995. 302 pp., illus. $75.00

Some stories fierce, fatal, frightening and even humorous of when man and lion meet.

Fourteen Years in the African Bush, by A. Marsh, Safari Press Publication, Huntington Beach, CA, 1998. 312 pp., illus. Limited signed, numbered, slipcased. $70.00

An account of a Kenyan game warden. A graphic and well-written story.

From Sailor to Professional Hunter: The Autobiography of John Northcote, Trophy Room Books, Agoura, CA, 1997. 400 pp., illus. Limited edition, signed and numbered. $125.00

Only a handfull of men can boast of having a fifty-year professional hunting career throughout Africa as John Northcote has had.

Gone are the Days; Jungle Hunting for Tiger and other Game in India and Nepal 1953-1969, by Peter Byrne, Safari Press, Inc., Huntington Beach, CA, 2001. 225 pp., illus. Limited signed, numbered, slipcased. $70.00

Great Hunters: Their Trophy Rooms and Collections, Volume 1, compiled and published by Safari Press, Inc., Huntington Beach, CA, 1997. 172 pp., illustrated in color. $60.00

A rare glimpse into the trophy rooms of top international hunters. A few of these trophy rooms are museums.

Great Hunters: Their Trophy Rooms & Collections, Volume 2, compiled and published by Safari Press, Inc., Huntington Beach, CA, 1998. 224 pp., illustrated with 260 full-color photographs. $60.00

Volume two of the world's finest, best produced series of books on trophy rooms and game collections. 46 sportsmen sharing sights you'll never forget on this guided tour.

Great Hunters: Their Trophy Rooms & Collections, Volume 3, compiled and published by Safari Press, Inc., Huntington Beach, CA, 2000. 204 pp., illustrated with 260 full-color photographs. $60.00

At last, the long-awaited third volume in the best photographic series ever published of trophy room collections is finally available. Unbelievable as it may sound, this book tops all previous volumes. Besides some of the greatest North American trophy rooms ever seen, an extra effort was made to include European collections. Believe it or not, volume 3 includes the Sandringham Castle big-game collection, home of Queen Elizabeth II! Also included is the complete Don Cox African and Asian collection as displayed at his alma mater. This stupendous gallery contains the trophy collections of Prince D' Arenberg, Umberto D'Entreves, George and Edward Keller, Paul Roberts, Joe Bishop, and James Clark to name but a few. Whether it be castles, palaces, mansions, or museums, the finest of the finest in trophy room designs and collection unequaled anywhere will be found in this book. As before, each trophy room is accompanied by an informative text explaining the collection and giving you insights into the hunters who went to such great efforts to create their trophy rooms. All professionally photographed in the highest quality possible.

Horned Death, by John F. Burger, Safari Press, Huntington Beach, CA, 1992. 343 pp.illus. $35.00

The classic work on hunting the African buffalo.

Horn of the Hunter, by Robert Ruark, Safari Press, Long Beach, CA, 1987. 315 pp., illus. $35.00

Ruark's most sought-after title on African hunting, here in reprint.

Horned Giants, by Capt. John Brandt, Safari Press, Inc., Huntington Beach, CA, 1999. 288 pp., illustrated. Limited edition, numbered, signed and slipcased. $80.00

Hunting Eurasian wild cattle.

Hunter, by J.A. Hunter, Safari Press Publications, Huntington Beach, CA, 1999. 263 pp., illus. $24.95

Hunter's best known book on African big-game hunting. Internationally recognized as being one of the all-time African hunting classics.

A Hunter's Africa, by Gordon Cundill, Trophy Room Books, Agoura, CA, 1998. 298 pp., over 125 photographic illustrations. Limited numbered edition signed by the author. $125.00

A good look by the author at the African safari experience - elephant, lion, spiral-horned antelope, firearms, people and events, as well as the clients that make it worthwhile.

A Hunter's Wanderings in Africa, by Frederick Courteney Selous, Alexanders Books., Alexander, NC, 2003. 504 pp., illustrated. $28.50

A reprinting of the 1920 London edition. A narrative of nine years spent amongst the game of the far interior of South Africa.

Hunter's Tracks, by J.A. Hunter, Safari Press Publications, Huntington Beach, CA, 1999. 240 pp., illustrated. $24.95

This is the exciting story of John Hunter's efforts to capture the shady headman of a gang of ivory poachers and smugglers. The story is interwoven with the tale of one of East Africa's most grandiose safaris taken with an Indian maharaja.

Hunting Adventures Worldwide, by Jack Atcheson, Jack Atcheson & Sons, Butte, MT, 1995. 256 pp., illus. $29.95

The author chronicles the richest adventures of a lifetime spent in quest of big game across the world – including Africa, North America and Asia.

Hunting in Ethiopia, An Anthology, by Tony Sanchez-Arino, Safari Press, Huntington Beach, CA, 1996. 350 pp., illus. Limited, signed and numbered edition. $135.00

The finest selection of hunting stories ever compiled on hunting in this great game country.

The Hunting Instinct, by Phillip D. Rowter, Safari Press, Inc., Huntington Beach, CA, 1999. Limited edition signed and numbered and in a slipcase. $50.00

Safari chronicles from the Republic of South Africa and Namibia 1990-1998.

Hunting in Kenya, by Tony Sanchez-Arino, Safari Press, Inc., Huntington Beach, CA, 2000. 350 pp., illustrated. Limited, signed and numbered edition in a slipcase. $135.00

The finest selection of hunting stories ever compiled on hunting in this great game country make up this anthology.

Hunting in the Sudan, An Anthology, compiled by Tony Sanchez-Arino, Safari Press, Huntington Beach, CA, 1992. 350 pp., illus. Limited, signed and numbered edition in a slipcase. $125.00

The finest selection of hunting stories ever compiled on hunting in this great game country.

Hunting, Settling and Remembering, by Philip H. Percival, Trophy Room Books, Agoura, CA, 1997. 230 pp., illus. Limited, numbered and signed edition. $85.00

If Philip Percival is to come alive again, it will be through this, the first edition of his easy, intricate and magical book illustrated with some of the best historical big game hunting photos ever taken.

Hunting the Dangerous Game of Africa, by John Kingsley-Heath, Sycamore Island Books, Boulder, CO, 1998. 477 pp., illustrated. $95.00

Written by one of the most respected, successful, and ethical P.H.'s to trek the sunlit plains of Botswana, Kenya, Uganda, Tanganyika, Somaliland, Eritrea, Ethiopia, and Mozambique. Filled with some of the most gripping and terrifying tales ever to come out of Africa.

THE ARMS LIBRARY

In the Salt, by Lou Hallamore, Trophy Room Books, Agoura, CA, 1999. 227 pp., illustrated in black & white and full color. Limited, numbered and signed edition. $125.00

A book about people, animals and the big game hunt, about being outwitted and out maneuvered. It is about knowing that sooner or later your luck will change and your trophy will be "in the salt."

International Hunter 1945-1999, Hunting's Greatest Era, by Bert klineburger, Sportsmen on Film, Kerrville, TX, 1999. 400 pp., illustrated. A limited, numbered and signed edition. $125.00

The most important book of the greatest hunting era by the world's preeminent International hunter.

Jim Corbett, Master of the Jungle, by Tim Werling, Safari Press, Huntington Beach, CA, 1998. 215 pp., illus. $30.00

A biography of India's most famous hunter of man-eating tigers and leopards.

King of the Wa-Kikuyu, by John Boyes, St. Martin Press, New York, NY, 1993. 240 pp., illus. $19.95

In the 19th and 20th centuries, Africa drew to it a large number of great hunters, explorers, adventurers and rogues. Many have become legendary, but John Boyes (1874-1951) was the most legendary of them all.

Last Horizons: Hunting, Fishing and Shooting on Five Continents, by Peter Capstick, St. Martin's Press, New York, NY, 1989. 288 pp., illus. $19.95

The first in a two volume collection of hunting, fishing and shooting tales from the selected pages of The American Hunter, Guns & Ammo and Outdoor Life.

Last of the Ivory Hunters, by John Taylor, Safari Press, Long Beach, CA, 1990. 354 pp., illus. $29.95

Reprint of the classic book "Pondoro" by one of the most famous elephant hunters of all time.

Legends of the Field: More Early Hunters in Africa, by W.R. Foran, Trophy Room Press, Agoura, CA, 1997. 319 pp., illus. Limited edition. $100.00

This book contains the biographies of some very famous hunters: William Cotton Oswell, F.C. Selous, Sir Samuel Baker, Arthur Neumann, Jim Sutherland, W.D.M. Bell and others.

Lives Of A Professional Hunting Family, by Gerard Agoura Miller, AZ: Trophy Room Books, 2003. A limited edition of 1,000 copies. Signed and numbered. 303 pages, 230 black & white photogrphic illustrations. Hardcover. $135.00

Lives of a Professional Hunting Family encompasses nearly fifty years of professional hunting in East Africa. We expect this book to garner great demand and acclaim. There are more stories about hunting Africa's BIG FIVE than in most other books.

The Lost Classics, by Robert Ruark, Safari Press, Huntington Beach, CA, 1996. 260 pp., illus. $35.00

The magazine stories that Ruark wrote in the 1950s and 1960s finally in print in book form.

The Lost Wilderness; True Accounts of Hunters and Animals in East Africa, by Mohamed Ismail & Alice Pianfetti, Safari Press, Inc., Huntington Beach, CA, 2000. 216 pp, photos, illustrated. Limited edition signed and numbered and slipcased. $60.00

Mahonhboh, by Ron Thomson, Hartbeespoort, South Africa, 1997. 312 pp., illustrated. Limited signed and numbered edition. $50.00

Elephants and hunting in South Central Africa.

The Man-Eaters of Tsavo, by Lt. Colonel J.H. Patterson, Peter Capstick, series editor, St. Martin's Press, New York, NY, 1986, 5th printing. 346 pp., illus. $22.95

The classic man-eating story of the lions that halted construction of a railway line and reportedly killed one hundred people, told by the man who risked his life to successfully shoot them.

McElroy Hunts Asia, by C.J. McElroy, Safari Press, Inc., Huntington Beach, CA, 1989. 272 pp., illustrated. $50.00

From the founder of SCI comes a book on hunting the great continent of Asia for big game: tiger, bear, sheep and ibex. Includes the story of the all-time record Altai Argali as well as several markhor hunts in Pakistan.

Memoirs of an African Hunter, by Terry Irwin, Safari Press Publications, Huntington Beach, CA, 1998. 421 pp., illustrated. Limited numbered, signed and slipcased. $125.00

A narrative of a professional hunter's experiences in Africa.

Memoirs of a Sheep Hunter, by Rashid Jamsheed, Safari Press, Inc., Huntington Beach, CA, 1996. 330 pp., illustrated. $70.00

The author reveals his exciting accounts of obtaining world-record heads from his native Iran, and his eventual move to the U.S. where he procured a grand-slam of North American sheep.

Mundjamba: The Life Story of an African Hunter, by Hugo Seia, Trophy Room Books, Agoura, CA, 1996. 400 pp., illus. Limited, numbered and signed by the author. $125.00

An autobiography of one of the most respected and appreciated professional African hunters.

My Last Kambaku, by Leo Kroger, Safari Press, Huntington Beach, CA, 1997. 272 pp., illus. Limited edition signed and numbered and slipcased. $60.00

One of the most engaging hunting memoirs ever published.

The Nature of the Game, by Ben Hoskyns, Quiller Press, Ltd., London, England, 1994. 160 pp., illus. $37.50

The first complete guide to British, European and North American game.

On Target, by Christian Le Noel, Trophy Room Books, Agoura, CA, 1999. 275 pp., illustrated. Limited, numbered and signed edition. $85.00

History and hunting in Central Africa.

On Safari With Bwana Game, by Eric Balson. Long Beach, CA: Safari Press, 2003. Deluxe, 1st edn, ltd to 1000 signed copies. 210 pages, profusely illustrated. Hardcover in a Slipcase. $75.00

As a senior game warden, Eric Balson guided some of the most famous people on earth on their East African safaris--Prince Bernhard of the Netherlands, Marshall Tito of Yugoslavia, and famous wildlife artist Guy Coheleach--and their hunting adventures are all told in this book. On one safari, Balson and Prince Bernhard were charged five times in four days by a leopard, buffalo, crocodile, hippo, and the same croc again! In his youth, Balson had the extraordinary job of catching poisonous snakes for a living; as an adult he dispatched man-eating lions that were thought to be under a spell of witchcraft by the evil "lion-men of Singida." On other adventures he goes after hyena men and hunts with a Hanovarian hound named Artus. Balson devotes a special section of the book to the hundred-plus-pound elephants he hunted, some with success and others without, and he recounts the story of the biggest tusker he ever saw in the Rungwa Reserve--which his client refused to shoot! As a game warden, Balson was assigned to deal with problem animals and poachers alike and was at one time responsible for an area of 100,000 square miles. Then in the late 1990s, he was asked by the Mozambican government to establish a wildlife refuge there. After arriving, he was beseeched by some terrified natives to shoot a huge rogue tusker--an experience that ranked as the scariest episode in his long, full life as a hunter. When Balson decided to retire to Canada, he asked an artist to paint him a picture of elephants walking in front of Mt. Kilimanjaro, the scene he had kept so vividly in his mind from the time when he was a young boy in East Africa. A fascinating, exciting, colorful biography of a rewarding life full of amusing anecdotes and famous people.

One Long Safari, by Peter Hay, Trophy Room Books, Agoura, CA, 1998. 350 pp., with over 200 photographic illustrations and 7 maps. Limited numbered edition signed by the author. $100.00

Contains hunts for leopards, sitatunga, hippo, rhino, snakes and, of course, the general African big game bag.

Optics for the Hunter, by John Barsness, Safari Press, Inc., Huntington Beach, CA, 1999. 236 pp., illustrated. $24.95

An evaluation of binoculars, scopes, range finders, spotting scopes for use in the field.

Out in the Midday Shade, by William York, Safari Press, Inc., Huntington Beach, CA, 1999. Limited, signed and numbered edition in a slipcase. $70.00

Memoirs of an African Hunter 1949-1968.

The Path of a Hunter, by Gilles Tre-Hardy, Trophy Room Books, Agoura, CA, 1997. 318 pp., illus. Limited Edition, signed and numbered. $85.00

A most unusual hunting autobiography with much about elephant hunting in Africa.

The Perfect Shot; Shot Placement for African Big Game, by Kevin "Doctari" Robertson, Safari Press, Inc., Huntington Beach, CA, 1999. 230 pp., illustrated. $65.00

The most comprehensive work ever undertaken to show the anatomical features for all classes of African game. Includes caliber and bullet selection, rifle selection, trophy handling.

The Perfect Shot: Mini Edition For Africa, Long Beach, CA: Safari Press, 2002. A concise 126 page, pocket-size guide, which is a mini reference for making that "perfect shot." Softcover. $15.95

Here it finally is, the scaled-down version of Robertson's best-seller. As in the big book, the mini edition features animal tracks as well as ghost views of vital areas and point of aim for each animal. A brief essay on natural history, trophy assessment, and subspecies is included. In addition, the tables in the back list the minimum requirements for inclusion in the Rowland Ward and SCI record books. While nothing can replace the "big" book, this is a super handy item to throw in your backpack or place in your pocket for your next safari.

Peter Capstick's Africa: A Return to the Long Grass, by Peter Hathaway Capstick, St. Martin's Press, N. Y., NY, 1987. 213 pp., illus. $35.00

A first-person adventure in which the author returns to the long grass for his own dangerous and very personal excursion.

Pondoro, by John Taylor, Safari Press, Inc., Huntington Beach, CA, 1999. 354 pp., illustrated. $29.95

The author is considered one of the best storytellers in the hunting book world, and Pondoro is highly entertaining. A classic African big-game hunting title.

The Quotable Hunter, by Jay Cassell and Peter Fiduccia, The Lyons Press, N.Y., 1999. 288 pp., illustrated. $20.00

This collection of more than three hundred quotes from hunters through the ages captures the essence of the sport, with all its joys, idosyncrasies, and challenges.

The Recollections of an Elephant Hunter 1864-1875, by William Finaughty, Books of Zimbabwe, Bulawayo, Zimbabwe, 1980. 244 pp., illus. $45.00

Reprint of the scarce 1916 privately published edition. The early game hunting exploits of William Finaughty in Matabeleland and Nashonaland.

Return To Toonaklut - The Russell Annabel Story, by Jeff Davis. Long Beach, CA: Safari Press, 2002. 248pp, photos, illus. $34.95

Those of us who grew up after WW II cannot imagine the Alaskan frontier that Rusty Annabel walked into early in the twentieth century. The hardships, the resourcefulness, the natural beauty, not knowing what lay beyond the next horizon, all were a part of his existence. His extraordinary talent allows us even today to share in the excitement and experiences of Alaska in the first half of the twentieth century. This is the story of the man behind the legend, and it is as fascinating as any of the tales Rusty Annabel ever spun for the sporting magazines.

Rifles And Cartridges For Large Game - From Deer To Bear--Advice On The Choice Of A Rifle, by Layne Simpson. Long Beach, CA: Safari Press, 2002. Illustrated with 100 color photos, oversize book. 225pp, color illus. $39.95

Layne Simpson, who has been field editor for Shooting Times magazine for 20 years, draws from his hunting experiences on five continents to tell you what rifles, cartridges, bullets, loads, and scopes are best for various applications, and he explains why in plain English. Developer of the popular 7mm STW cartridge, Simpson has taken big game with rifle cartridges ranging in power from the .220 Swift to the .460 Weatherby Magnum, and he pulls no punches when describing their effectiveness in the field. A sample of the thirty chapters includes: "The Woods Rifle," "The Mountain Rifle," "Medicine For Dangerous Game," "The Custom Rifle," "The Beanfield Rifle," "The Saddle Rifle," "All About Rifle Barrels," "The Bolt-Action Rifle," "Hunting With Modern Single Shots," "The Lever-Action Rifle," "Pumps and Autoloaders," "Choosing An Optical Sight," "All About Scope Mounts," "The Trigger," "Notes On Open Sights," "The .22 Calibers On Deer," ".243 Through .458 Caliber Cartridges," "Wildcat Cartridges," "The Big-Game Bullet," "Handloading For Big Game," "Hunting With Factory Ammo," "Selecting The Big-Game Rifle Battery," and "When Old Rifles Go Afield." If you are interested in the equipment needed to successfully hunt white-tailed deer, pronghorn antelope, elk, mule deer, caribou, black bear, moose, Alaska brown bear, Cape buffalo, African lion, or any other big-game animal, this book is a must.

Rifles For Africa; Practical Advice On Rifles And Ammunition For An African Safari, by Gregor Woods. Long Beach, CA: Safari Press, 2002. 1st edition. 430 pages, illustrated. Photos. $39.95

Invaluable to the person who seeks advice and information on what rifles, calibers, and bullets work on African big game, be they the largest land mammals on earth or an antelope barely weighing in at 20 lbs.!

Robert Ruark's Africa, by Robert Ruark, edited by Michael McIntosh, Countrysport Press, Selma, AL, 1999. 256 pp illustrated with 19 original etchings by Bruce Langton. $32.00

These previously uncollected works of Robert Ruark make this a classic big-game hunting book.

Safari: A Dangerous Affair, by Walt Prothero, Safari Press, Huntington Beach, CA, 2000. 275 pp., illustrated. Limited edition, numbered, signed and slipcased. $60.00

True accounts of hunters and animals of Africa.

Safari Rifles: Double, Magazine Rifles and Cartridges for African Hunting, by Craig Boddington, Safari Press, Huntington Beach, CA, 1990. 416 pp., illus. $37.50

A wealth of knowledge on the safari rifle. Historical and present double-rifle makers, ballistics for the large bores, and much, much more.

THE ARMS LIBRARY

Safari: The Last Adventure, by Peter Capstick, St. Martin's Press, New York, NY, 1984. 291 pp., illus. $22.95

A modern comprehensive guide to the African Safari.

Sands of Silence, by Peter H. Capstick, Saint Martin's Press, New York, NY, 1991. 224 pp., illus. $35.00

Join the author on safari in Nambia for his latest big-game hunting adventures.

Solo Safari, by T. Cacek, Safari Press, Huntington Beach, CA, 1995. 270 pp., illus. $30.00

Here is the story of Terry Cacek who hunted elephant, buffalo, leopard and plains game in Zimbabwe and Botswana on his own.

Spiral-Horn Dreams, by Terry Wieland, Trophy Room Books, Agoura, CA, 1996. 362 pp., illus. Limited, numbered and signed by the author. $85.00

Everyone who goes to hunt in Africa is looking for something; this is for those who go to hunt the spiral-horned antelope—the bongo, myala, mountain nyala, greater and lesser kudu, etc.

Tales of the African Frontier, by J.A. Hunter, Safari Press Publications, Huntington Beach, CA, 1999. 308 pp., illus. $24.95

The early days of East Africa is the subject of this powerful John Hunter book.

To Heck With It - I'm Going Hunting - My First Eighteen Years as an International Big-Game, by Arnold Alward (with Bill Quimby) Long Beach, CA: Safari Press, 2003. Deluxe, 1st edn, ltd to 1000 signed copies. 308 pages, profusely illustrated. Hardcover in a slipcase. $80.00

During the course of his hunts, Arnold Alward, a Weatherby Award winner, shot a Grand Slam and a Super Slam of Sheep and the Big Five as well as all the spiral-horned antelope of Africa. His busiest year was 1988, when he made thirteen major hunts! One of his most grueling hunts was for a desert bighorn in Baja California, which completed his Grand Slam. When he went on safari to Ethiopia, he passed up a 75-pound elephant before taking a 110 x 115-pound tusker on the tenth day of the hunt; then he continued in that country to take a mountain nyala. After Ethiopia, he successfully hunted caribou in the Northwest Territories, the Yukon, and Quebec; a whitetail in Alberta; Columbia blacktails and brown bears on Alaska's Kodiak Island; and Coues deer in Mexico . . . all in the same year! During the rest of the eighteen years covered by this book, Alward hunted on six of the seven continents, and he visited the seventh continent, Antarctica. On his trip to Asia, he hunted most of the major sheep species that inhabit the High Altai, the Pamirs, and the Tibetan Plateau. During one of his trips to Mongolia, he slept in yurts, rode Mongol ponies, and took Altai and Gobi argali, Siberian roe deer, and maral stag.

Uganda Safaris, by Brian Herne, Winchester Press, Piscataway, NJ, 1979. 236 pp., illus. $24.95

The chronicle of a professional hunter's adventures in Africa.

Under the African Sun, by Dr. Frank Hibben, Safari Press, Inc., Huntington Beach, CA, 1999. Limited edition signed, numbered and in a slipcase. $85.00

Forty-eight years of hunting the African continent.

Under the Shadow of Man Eaters, by Jerry Jaleel, The Jim Corbett Foundation, Edmonton, Alberta, Canada, 1997. 152 pp., illus. A limited, numbered and signed edition. Paper covers. $35.00

The life and legend of Jim Corbett of Kumaon.

Use Enough Gun, by Robert Ruark, Safari Press, Huntington Beach, CA, 1997. 333 pp., illus. $35.00

Robert Ruark on big game hunting.

Warrior: The Legend of Col. Richard Meinertzhagen, by Peter H. Capstick, St. Martins Press, New York, NY, 1998. 320 pp., illus. $23.95

A stirring and vivid biography of the famous British colonial officer Richard Meinertzhagen, whose exploits earned him fame and notoriety as one of the most daring and ruthless men to serve during the glory days of the British Empire.

The Waterfowler's World, by Bill Buckley, Willow Creek Press, Minocqua, WI, 1999. 176 pp., 225 color photographs. $37.50

Waterfowl hunting from Canadian prairies, across the U.S. heartland, to the wilds of Mexico, from the Atlantic to the Pacific coasts and the Gulf of Mexico.

The Weatherby: Stories From the Premier Big-Game Hunters of the World, by Nancy Vokins (editor) 1956-2002. Long Beach, CA: Safari Press, 2004. Deluxe, Limited, Signed edition. 434pp, profuse color and b&w illus. Hardcover in a Slipcase. $200.00

For nearly fifty years, the Weatherby Award has been known as the Oscar of the hunting world in recognition of the achievements of the world's greatest hunters. From Herb Klein's first award in 1956 to Rex Baker's award in 2002, all the award winners to date have been included. The editor spent countless hours unearthing the best hunting stories from each of the Weatherby winners, so there are some hold-onto-the-edge-of-your-seat adventures described--tales of hunting on six continents for stunning trophies under the most difficult (and sometimes very amusing) conditions. The stories, many never before published, are by names you will recognize: Jack O'Connor (1957 recipient), Warren Page (1958), Prince Abdorreza of Iran (1962), Dr. Frank Hibben (1964), C. J. McElroy (1969), James Mellon (1972), Rudolf Sand (1976), Valentin de Madariaga (1977), Arthur Carlsberg (1978 posthumous recipient as he fell off a mountain while sheep hunting in Asia right before he was to receive his award), Watson Yoshimoto (1980), Jesus Yuren (1995), and all the other Weatherby winners. Here is your chance to read how Mellon pursued a giant markhor in Afghanistan with dogged determination; how Carlo Caldesi shot a gaur that gets singed in a brush fire; how Prince Abdorreza searched for a world-record Persian ibex; how Frank Hibben stalked an immense tiger, but ended up with the largest leopard ever taken in his time; how Thorton Snider (1985) found an elephant with monster tusks; how Rudolf Sand pursued an impossible-to-get mountain nyala; and what happened on C. J. McElroy's, founder of SCI, last safari in Africa. A grand total of 46 interesting stories and biographies, a historical introduction as to how the Weatherby originated, hundreds of fascinating photographs, and statistical information and background on the award are included. This limited edition has been signed by no less than sixteen living Weatherby winners, a unique feat in book publishing and sure to make this book a superb collector's item in years to come.

The Wheel of Life - Bunny Allen, A Life of Safaris and Sex, by Bunny Allen. Long Beach, CA: Safari Press, 2004. 1st edition. 300pp, illus, photos. Hardcover. $34.95

The Wheel of Life is his third complete book, and it contains some of Bunny's best stories never before published, as well as a highlights from the previous two books to set the stage for his later exploits. Bunny, together with his sons Anton and David, took out some of the most glamorous hunters ever to set foot in Africa, and The Wheel of Life tells it all. It can be safely argued that nowhere in Africa has there ever been a more interesting and colorful father-and-son team of PH hunters, and the pages of this book will sizzle under your fingertips. There are many sexually explicit stories in this latest volume, for Bunny was the ultimate ladies' man and known for his courtly manner and luck with women. Bunny is a wonderful raconteur, and his exciting tales of an adventurous life are sure to please.

Where Lions Roar: Ten More Years of African Hunting, by Craig Boddington, Safari Press, Huntington Beach, CA, 1997. 250 pp $35.00

The story of Boddington's hunts in the Dark Continent during the last ten years.

White Hunter, by J.A. Hunter, Safari Press Publications, Huntington Beach, CA, 1999. 282 pp., illustrated. $24.95

This book is a seldom-seen account of John Hunter's adventures in pre-WW2 Africa.

Wind, Dust and Snow, by Robert M. Anderson, Safari Press, Inc., Huntington Beach, CA, 1997. 240 pp., illustrated. $65.00

A complete chronology of modern exploratory and pioneering Asian sheep-hunting expeditions from 1960 until 1996, with wonderful background history and previously untold stories.

With a Gun in Good Country, by Ian Manning, Trophy Room Books, Agoura, CA, 1996. Limited, numbered and signed by the author. $85.00

A book written about that splendid period before the poaching onslaught which almost closed Zambia and continues to the granting of her independence. It then goes on to recount Manning's experiences in Botswana, Congo, and briefly in South Africa.

Yoshi - The Life and Travels of an International Trophy Hunter, by W. Yoshimoto (with Bill Quimby). Long Beach, CA: Safari Press, Inc., 2002. A limited edition of 1,000 copies, signed and numbered. 298pp, color and b&w photos. Hardcover in a Slipcase. $85.00

Watson T. Yoshimoto, a native Hawaiian, collected all sixteen major varieties of the world's wild sheep and most of the many types of goats, ibex, bears, antelopes, and antlered game of Asia, Europe, North America, South America, and the South Pacific . . . as well as the African Big Five. Follow Yoshi as he finds himself cut off from safety when the ice separates while he is hunting polar bears off the Russian coast. Experience his hunts for bharal at 18,000 feet in the Himalayas; tigers, gaurs, and wild Asian buffalo in India; an elephant with ivory weighing 127 and 123 pounds in Tanzania; and a near-world-record giant eland from the C.A.R. Yoshi visited many countries multiple times just because he liked the destinations or animals. He has collected all spiral-horned antelope, including many outstanding trophies of this tribe. His safari days go back to the 1950s when Yoshi had his rifles and supplies placed in huge wooden crates and shipped ahead via boat to East Africa, certainly a different era and time! All his life he shot with just two rifles: a .300 Weatherby and a .458 Winchester. When Yoshi ended a half century of hunting in 1995 at age 86, he had taken nearly 200 species of big game in forty-three countries on six continents. Along the way he earned the respect of his peers and was awarded hunting's highest achievement, the coveted Weatherby Award. His extensive big-game collection is now on display at the National Science Museum at Ueno Park in Tokyo. This is an interesting and highly readable book about the life of one of the best-known trophy hunters of the twentieth century.

RIFLES

The Accurate Rifle, by Warren Page, Claymore Publishing, Ohio, 1997. 254 pages, illustrated. Revised edition. Paper Covers. $17.95

Provides hunters & shooter alike with detailed practical information on the whole range of subjects affecting rifle accuracy, he explains techniques in ammo, sights & shooting methods. With a 1996 equipment update from Dave Brennan.

The Accurate Varmint Rifle, by Boyd Mace, Precision Shooting, Inc., Whitehall, NY, 1991. 184 pp., illus. $15.00

A long overdue and long needed work on what factors go into the selection of components for and the subsequent assembly of...the accurate varmint rifle.

The AK-47 Assault Rifle, Desert Publications, Cornville, AZ, 1981. 150 pp., illus. Paper covers. $15.95

Complete and practical technical information on the only weapon in history to be produced in an estimated 30,000,000 units.

American Hunting Rifles: Their Application in the Field for Practical Shooting, by Craig Boddington, Safari Press, Huntington Beach, CA, 1996. 446 pp., illus. Second printing trade edition. Softcover $24.95

Covers all the hunting rifles and calibers that are needed for North America's diverse game.

The American Krag Rifle and Carbine, by Joe Poyer. North Cape Publications, Tustin, CA: 2002. 1st edition. 317 pages, illustrated with hundreds of black & white drawings and photos. Softcover. $19.95

Provides the arms collector, historian and target shooter with a part by part analysis of what has been called the rifle with the smoothest bolt action ever designed. All changes to all parts are analyzed in detail and matched to serial number ranges. A monthly serial number chart by production year has been devised that will provide the collector with the year and month in which his gun was manufactured. A new and complete exploded view was produced for this book.

The AR-15 Complete Owner's Guide, Volume 1, 2nd Edition, by Walt Kuleck and Scott Duff. Export, PA: Scott A. Duff Publications, 2002. 224 pages, 164 photographs & line drawings. Softcover. $21.95

This book provides the prospective, new or experienced AR-15 owner with the in-depth knowledge he or she needs to select, configure, operate, maintain and troubleshoot his or her rifle. The Guide covers history, applications, details of components and subassemblies, operating, cleaning, maintenance, and future of perhaps the most versatile rifle system ever produced. A comprehensive Colt model number table and pre-/post-ban serial number information are included. This is the book I wish had existed prior to buying my first AR-15!

The AR-15 Complete Assembly Guide, Volume 2, by Walt Kuleck and Clint McKee. Export, PA: Scott A. Duff Publications, 2002. 1st edition. 155 pages, 164 photographs & line drawings. Softcover. $19.95

This book goes beyond the military manuals in depth and scope, using words and pictures to clearly guide the reader through every operation required to assemble their AR-15-type rifle. You'll learn the best and easiest ways to build your rifle. It won't make you an AR-15 armorer, but it will make you a more knowledgeable owner. You'll be able to do more with (and to) your rifle. You'll also be able to better judge the competence of those whom you choose to work on your rifle, and to discuss your needs more intelligently with them. In short, if you build it, you'll know how to repair it.

The AR-15/M16, A Practical Guide, by Duncan Long. Paladin Press, Boulder, CO, 1985. 168 pp., illus. Paper covers. $22.00

The definitive book on the rifle that has been the inspiration for so many modern assault rifles.

THE ARMS LIBRARY

Argentine Mauser Rifles 1871-1959, by Colin Atglen Webster, PA: Schiffer Publications, 2003. 1st edition. 304 pages, with over 400 b&w and color photographs, drawings, and charts. Hardcover. $79.95

This is the complete story of Argentina's contract Mauser rifles from the purchase of their first Model 1871s to the disposal of the last shipment of surplus rifles received in the United States in May 2002. Between 1891-1959 Argentina bought or manufactured nearly 500,000 Mauser rifles and carbines for itself as well as for its neighbors Peru, Bolivia, Uruguay and Paraguay. It also supplied Spain with rifles to help suppress the Melilla revolt in Morocco, which were eventually used against the United States during the Spanish American War of 1898. The Argentine Commission's relentless pursuit of tactical superiority resulted in a major contribution to the development of Mauser's now famous bolt-action system. The combined efforts of the Belgian, Turkish and Argentine arms commissions between 1889 and 1892 produced the origins of what became the Model 98 bolt-action system that is still in use today over 110 years later. Details include: thirty-seven identified variants; the history behind each purchase and the technical description of each variant; contract-by-contract, and in the case of the Model 1891, 1909 and 1947 weapons a month-by-month, detail of production and shipping data; over 400 pictures, illustrations, documents and blueprints; history and details of the manufacturing facilities in Europe and in Argentina as well as a description of the manufacturing process used by the "Matheu" (DGFM-FMAP) small arms factory in Argentina; interesting and colorful anecdotes about the people involved, including revelations about spying and secret alliances never before revealed.

The Art of Shooting with the Rifle, by Col. Sir H. St. John Halford, Excalibur Publications, Latham, NY, 1996. 96 pp., illus. Paper covers. $12.95

A facsimile edition of the 1888 book by a respected rifleman providing a wealth of detailed information.

The Art of the Rifle, by Jeff Cooper, Paladin Press, Boulder, CO, 1997. 104 pp., illus. $29.95

Everything you need to know about the rifle whether you use it for security, meat or target shooting.

Australian Military Rifles & Bayonets, 200 Years of, by Ian Skennerton, I.D.S.A. Books, Piqua, OH, 1988. 124 pp., 198 illus. Paper covers. $19.50

Australian Service Machine Guns, 100 Years of, by Ian Skennerton, I.D.S.A. Books, Piqua, OH, 1989. 122 pp., 150 illus. Paper covers. $19.50

Ballard: The Great American Single Shot Rifle, by Dutcher, John T., Denver, CO: Privately Printed, 2002. 1st edition. 380 pages, illustrated with black & white photos, with a 8 page color insert. Hardcover. $79.95

Benchrest Actions and Triggers, by Stuart Otteson. Rohnert Park, CA: Adams-Kane Press, July 2003. Limited edition. 64 pages. Softcover. $27.95

Stuart Otteson's Benchrest Actions and Triggers is truly a lost classic. Benchrest Actions and Triggers is a compilation of 17 articles Mr. Otteson wrote. The articles contained are of particular interest to the benchrest crowd. Reprinted by permission of Wolfe Publishing.

Black Magic: The Ultra Accurate AR-15, by John Feamster, Precision Shooting, Manchester, CT, 1998. 300 pp., illustrated. $29.95

The author has compiled his experiences pushing the accuracy envelope of the AR-15 to its maximum potential. A wealth of advice on AR-15 loads, modifications and accessories for everything from NRA Highpower and Service Rifle competitions to benchrest and varmint shooting.

The Black Rifle, M16 Retrospective, R. Blake Stevens and Edward C. Ezell, Collector Grade Publications, Toronto, Canada, 1987. 400 pp., illus. $59.95

The complete story of the M16 rifle and its development.

Blitzkrieg! - The MP40 Maschinenpistole of WWII, by Frank Iannamico. Harmony, ME: Moose Lake Publishing, 2003. 1st edition. Softcover. $29.95

It's back, now in a new larger 8x11 format with over 275 pages, 280 photos & documents. Lots of new info. and many unpublished photos. This book includes the history and development of the German machine pistol from the MP18,I to the MP40 to include; *The MP28.II the evolution begins *The Bergmann machine pistols *The Erma EMP *Steyr-Solothurn *The MP36 the missing link *The MP38 and MP40 *The Aberdeen Proving Ground trials *The German influences of U.S. weapon design *MP40 Production, contractors and subcontractors *Waffenamt-marks and proof marks and much more!

Bolt Action Rifles, Expanded 4th Edition, by Frank de Haas and Wayne van Zwoll, Krause Publications, Iola, WI 2003. 4th edition. 696 Pages, illustrated with 615 b&w photos. Softcover. $29.95

Work out all the details of every major design since the Mauser of 1871 with this essential volume. Author Frank de Haas analyzes 121 turnbolt actions -- how they function, takedown/assembly, strengths and weaknesses and dimensional specs.

The Book of the Garand, by Maj. Gen. J.S. Hatcher, The Gun Room Press, Highland Park, NJ, 1977. 292 pp., illus. $26.95

A new printing of the standard reference work on the U.S. Army M1 rifle.

Building Double Rifles on Shotgun Actions, by W. Ellis Brown. Ft. Collins, CO: Bunduki Publishing, 2001. 1st edition. 187 pages, including index and black & white photographs. Hardcover. $55.00

British .22RF Training Rifles, by Dennis Lewis and Robert Washburn, Excaliber Publications, Latham, NY, 1993. 64 pp., illus. Paper covers. $10.95

The story of Britain's training rifles from the early Aiming Tube models to the post-WWII trainers.

Classic Sporting Rifles, by Christopher Austyn, Safari Press, Huntington Beach, CA, 1997. 128 pp., illus. $50.00

As the head of the gun department at Christie's Auction House the author examines the "best" rifles built over the last 150 years.

The Collectable '03, by J. C. Harrison. The Arms Chest, Okla. City, OK. 1999. 2nd edition (revised). 234 pages, illus. Spiral bound. $35.00

Valuable and detailed reference book for the collector of the Model 1903 Springfield rifle. 234 pages, illustrated with drawings.

Collecting Classic Bolt Action Military Rifles, by Paul S. Scarlata. Andrew Mowbray, Inc. Lincoln, RI. 2001. 280 pages, illustrated. $39.95

Over 400 large photographs detail key features you will need to recognize in order to identify guns for your collection. Learn the original military configurations of these service rifles so that you can tell them apart from altered guns and bad restorations. The historical sections are particularly strong, giving readers a clear understanding of how and why these rifles were developed, and which troops used them. Advanced collectors will be fascinated by the countless historical photographs of these guns in the hands of troops.

Collecting the Garand, by J. C. Harrison. The Arms Chest, Okla. City, OK. 2001. 2nd edition (revised). 198 pages, illus. with pictures and drawings. Spiral bound. $35.00

Valuable and detailed reference book for the collector of the Garand.

Collecting the M1 Carbine, by J. C. Harrison. The Arms Chest, Okla. City, OK. 2000. 2nd edition (revised). 247 pages, illus. Spiral bound. $35.00

Valuable and detailed reference book for the collector of the M1 Carbine. Identifies standard issue original military models of M1 and M1A1 Models of 1942, '43, '44, and '45 Carbines as produced by each manufacturer. Plus Arsenal repair, refinish and Lend-Lease. 247 pages, illustratred with pictures and drawings.

The Complete AR15/M16 Sourcebook, Revised And Updated Edition. by Duncan Long, Paladin Press, Boulder, CO, 2002. 336 pp., illus. Paper covers. $39.95

The latest development of the AR15/M16 and the many spin-offs now available, selective-fire conversion systems for the 1990s, the vast selection of new accessories.

The Competitive AR15: The Mouse That Roared, by Glenn Zediker, Zediker Publishing, Oxford, MS, 1999. 286 pp., illustrated. Paper covers. $29.95

A thorough and detailed study of the newest precision rifle sensation.

Complete Guide To The M1 Garand and The M1 Carbine, by Bruce Canfield, Andrew Mowbray, Inc., Lincoln, RI, 1999. 296 pp., illustrated. $39.50

Covers all of the manufacturers of components, parts, variations and markings. Learn which parts are proper for which guns. The total story behind these guns, from their invention through WWII, Korea, Vietnam and beyond! 300+ photos show you features, markings, overall views and action shots. Thirty-three tables and charts give instant reference to serial numbers, markings, dates of issue and proper configurations. Special sections on Sniper guns, National Match Rifles, exotic variations, and more!

The Complete M1 Garand, by Jim Thompson, Paladin Press, Boulder, CO, 1998. 160 pp., illustrated. Paper cover. $24.00

A guide for the shooter and collector, heavily illustrated.

Crown Jewels: The Mauser In Sweden; A Century of Accuracy and Precision, by Dana Jones. Canada: Collector Grade Publications, 2003. 1st edition. 312 pages, 691 illustrations. Hardcover. $49.95

Here is the first in-depth study of all the Swedish Mausers - the 6.5mm m/94 carbines, m/96 long rifles, m/38 short rifles, Swedish K98Ks (called the m/39 in 7.92x57mm, then, after rechambering to fire the 8x63mm machinegun cartridge, the m/40); sniper rifles, and other military adaptations such as grenade launchers and artillery simulators. Then the focus shifts to the experimental prototypes and trial match rifles of the 1950s - some in .30-'06 - and finally to the precision competition rifles which became famous around the world. Also covers a wide variety of the micrometer-adjustment rear sight inserts and "diopter" receiver sights which were produced in order to allow shooters to take full advantage of the accuracy and precision of the Swedish Mauser. Full chapters on bayonets and the many accessories, both military and civilian.

The Emma Gees, by Capt. Herbert W McBride. Mt. Ida, AR: Lancer Publishing, 2003. Reprint. 224 pages, b&w photos. Softcover. $19.95

The Emma Gees is the rest of McBride's story. First published in 1918, this was McBride's first book about his service with the machine gun section in world war one. The Emma Gees was even rarer than A Rifleman went to War until this reprint that includes new biographical information from the National Archives of Canada. With chapters such as "A fine day for murder" and "Sniper Barn", this is an excellent companion to his other book.

The FAL Rifle, by R. Blake Stevens and Jean van Rutten, Collector Grade Publications, Cobourg, Canada, 1993. 848 pp., illus. $129.95

Originally published in three volumes, this classic edition covers North American, UK and Commonwealth and the metric FAL's.

The Fighting Rifle, by Chuck Taylor, Paladin Press, Boulder, CO, 1983. 184 pp., illus. Paper covers. $25.00

The difference between assault and battle rifles and auto and light machine guns.

Firearms Assembly/Disassembly Part III: Rimfire Rifles, Revised Edition, The Gun Digest Book of, by J. B. Wood, DBI Books, a division of Krause Publications, Iola, WI., 1994. 480 pp., illus. Paper covers. $19.95

Covers 65 popular rimfires plus over 100 variants, all cross-referenced in the index.

Firearms Assembly/Disassembly Part IV: Centerfire Rifles, 2nd Edition, The Gun Digest Book of, by J.B. Wood, Krause Publications, Iola, WI, 1991. 576 pages · 1,750 b&w photos.. Paper covers. $24.99

Covers 66 popular centerfire rifles plus 400 variants. The most comprehensive and professional presentation available to either hobbyist or gunsmith.

The FN-FAL Rifle, et al, by Duncan Long, Delta Press, El Dorado, AR, 1998. 148 pp., illustrated. Paper covers. $18.95

A comprehensive study of one of the classic assault weapons of all times. Detailed descriptions of the basic models plus the myriad of variants that evolved as a result of its universal acceptance.

Forty Years with the .45-70, second edition, revised and expanded, by Paul A. Matthews, Wolfe Publishing Co., Prescott, AZ, 1997. 184 pp., illus. Paper covers. $17.95

This book is pure gun lore-lore of the .45-70. It not only contains a history of the cartridge, but also years of the author's personal experiences.

F.N.-F.A.L. Auto Rifles, Desert Publications, Cornville, AZ, 1981. 130 pp., illus. Paper covers. $18.95

A definitive study of one of the free world's finest combat rifles.

German Sniper 1914-1945, by Peter R. Senich, Paladin Press, Boulder, CO, 1997 8 1/2 x 11, hardcover, photos, 468 pp. $69.95

The complete story of Germany's sniping arms development through both World Wars. Presents more than 600 photos of Mauser 98's, Selbstladegewehr 41s and 43s, optical sights by Goerz, Zeiss, etc., plus German snipers in action. An exceptional hardcover collector's edition for serious military historians everywhere.

The Great Remington 8 And Model 81 Autoloading Rifles, by John Henwood. Canada: Collector Grade Publications, 2003. 1st edition. 304 pages, 291 illustrations, 31 in color. Hardcover. $59.95

This first Collector Grade edition includes chapters on the genesis of the Remington Arms Company; Browning's five long recoil patents; the history of the Modèle 1900, the nearly identical clone produced by FN in Belgium, and the use of Browning, Remington and Winchester autoloading rifles by the French Air Service during World War I; the "cosmetic revamping" of the Model 8 which resulted in the Model 81; in-depth histories of production changes, markings, shipping dates, codes, and costs; deluxe-grade (engraved) and special models (factory experimentals, military, police and F.B.I. variants); contemporary autoloaders from around the world; notes on collecting the 8 and 81; how the long recoil autoloader works; disassembly, troubleshooting, and Model 8 and 81 component interchangeability; ammunition, ballistics, and reloading; factory options and aftermarket accessories (charger clips, magazine conversions, iron sights, scopes and mounts). The last chapter, titled "The Legend", is a fascinating study of Remington advertisements, posters and sporting art, which have become increasingly popular collectibles in recent times.

THE ARMS LIBRARY

Greenhill Military Manual: Military Rifles Of Two World Wars, by John Walter. London: Greenhill Publishing, 2003. 1st edition. 144 pages, illustrated. Hardcover. $24.00

Covers rifles from Britain, the USA, Germany, Russia, and elsewhere, Includes technical data and performance details. The twentieth century was a true testing ground for tactics, conducting warfare, and, inevitably, weaponry. The mainstay of all armies in the two great confrontations of that century was the military rifle. This informative book presents information on more than 60 weapons, including semiautomatics and auto-loaders, including the Mauser, Lee-Enfield, and Tokarev. A detailed description of each rifle and its key features is supported by technical data and specially selected illustrations. Details of relevant ammunition and accessories complete the work.

The Historic Henry Rifle: Oliver Winchester's Famous Civil War Repeater, by Wiley Sword. Andrew Mowbray, Inc., Lincoln, RI. 2002. Softcover. $29.95

It was perhaps the most important firearm of its era. Tested and proved in the fiery crucible of the Civil War, the Henry Rifle became the forerunner of the famous line of Winchester Repeating Rifles that "Won the West." Here is the fascinating story from the frustrations of early sales efforts aimed at the government to the inspired purchase of the Henry Rifle by veteran soldiers who wanted the best weapon.

Hitler's Garands: German Self-Loading Rifles Of World War II, by Darrin W. Weaver. Collector Grade Publications, Canada, 2001. 392 pages, 590 illustrations. $69.95

Hitler's Wehrmacht began World War II armed with the bolt action K98k, a rifle only cosmetically different from that with which Imperial Germany had fought the Great War a quarter-century earlier. Then in 1940, the Heereswaffenamt (HWaA, the Army Weapons Office) issued a requirement for a new self-loading rifle. The resulting Mauser G41(M) and flap-locked Walther G41(W) were both hampered by gas-takeoff at the muzzle, which resulted in arms which were overlong, clumsy, muzzle-heavy, unreliable, and consequently unpopular with the troops. Taking their lead from the Russians, Walther copied (and patented) the gas system of the Tokarev SVT self-loader, grafting it onto the flap-locked bolt of the G41 to create the G43, which was only produced during the last nineteen desperate months of World War II.

How-To's for the Black Powder Cartridge Rifle Shooter, by Paul A. Matthews, Wolfe Publishing Co., Prescott, AZ, 1996. 136 pp., illus. Paper covers. $22.50

Practices and procedures used in the reloading and shooting of blackpowder cartridges.

How to Convert Military Rifles, Davidson, MI: Williams Gun Sight Company, 1998. New revised enlarged Seventh Edition. 76 pages, illustrated. Softcover. $13.95

Explains the features that make certain models more desirable for conversion. Covers the steps to proper scope mounting, installing triggers and safeties; restocking and finishing. The exploded parts drawings are extremely useful and sight fitting charts can save hours of frustration. Revised and enlarged 7th edition presents information on 14 military and civilian rifles.

The Hunter's Guide to Accurate Shooting, by Wayne Van Zwoll. Guilford, CT: Lyons Press, 2002. 1st edition. 288 pp. Hardcover. $29.95

Firearms expert Van Zwoll explains exactly how to shoot the big-game rifle accurately. Taking into consideration every pertinent factor, he shows a step-by-step analysis of shooting and hunting with the big-game rifle.

Johnson Rifles and Machine Guns; The Story of Melvin Maynard Johnson, Jr. and his Guns, by Bruce N. Canfield, Lincoln, RI: Andrew Mowbray, Inc., 2002. 1st edition. 272 pages with over 285 photographs. Hardcover. $49.95

The M1941 Johnson Rifle is the hottest WW2 rifle on the collectors market today, and this new book covers them all! From invention and manufacture through issue to the troops.

Kalashnikov: The Arms and the Man, A Revised and Expanded Edition of the AK47 Story, by Edward C. Ezell. Canada: Collector Grade Publications, 2002. 312 pages, 356 illustrations. Hardcover. $59.95

The original edition of The AK47 Story was published in 1986, and the events of the intervening fifteen years have provided much fresh new material. Beginning with an introduction by Dr. Kalashnikov himself, we present a most comprehensive study of the "life and times" of the AK, starting with the early history of small arms manufacture in Czarist Russia and then the Soviet Union. We follow the development of the AK (originally designed in caliber 7.62x41mm) and all the offshoots and clones which make up the Kalashnikov "family" of small arms, including an important new summary of technical information on the numerous loadings of "intermediate" ammunition, right up to the "AK for the 21st Century" - the AK100 series, now being manufactured by the Joint Stock Company "Kalashnikov" in Izhevsk, Russia in three calibers: 7.62x39mm, 5.45x39mm, and 5.56x45mm NATO.

Know Your M1 Garand, by E. J. Hoffschmidt, Blacksmith Corp., Southport, CT, 1975, 84 pp., illus. Paper covers. $14.95

Facts about America's most famous infantry weapon. Covers test and experimental models, Japanese and Italian copies, National Match models.

Know Your Ruger 10/22 Carbine, by William E. Workman, Blacksmith Corp., Chino Valley, AZ, 1991. 96 pp., illus. Paper covers. $14.95

The story and facts about the most popular 22 autoloader ever made.

The Krag Rifle Story, by Frank Mallory with Ludwig Olson. Springfield Research Service, Silver Springs Md. 2001. $80.00

356 pages organized into 29 chapters dealing with each model and variation of Krag rifle and carbine, foreign as well as U.S., plus bayonets, accouterments, and ammunition. Twenty appendices provide data of interest to collectors on markings, finishes, production changes, serial numbers, etc. (Updated and expanded 2nd edition)

The Last Enfield: SA80 - The Reluctant Rifle, by Steve Raw, Collector Grade Publications, Canada 2003. 1st edition. 360 pages, with 382 illustrations. Hardcover. $49.95

In typical Collector Grade fashion, this book presents the entire, in-depth story of its subject firearm, in this case the controversial British SA80, right from the founding of what became the Royal Small Arms Factory (RSAF) Enfield in the early 1800s; briefly through two World Wars with Enfield at the forefront of small arms production for British forces; and covering the adoption of the 7.62mm NATO cartridge in 1954 and the L1A1 rifle in 1957. That's where this book begins to differ from the normal saga of a successful small arms development, for even though the SA80 has been the issue small arms system of the British Armed Forces for almost twenty years, the controversies surrounding it have never let up.

The Lee Enfield No. 1 Rifles, by Alan M. Petrillo, Excaliber Publications, Latham, NY, 1992. 64 pp., illus. Paper covers. $10.95

Highlights the SMLE rifles from the Mark 1-VI.

The Lee Enfield Number 4 Rifles, by Alan M. Petrillo, Excalibur Publications, Latham, NY, 1992. 64 pp., illus. Paper covers. $10.95

A pocket-sized, bare-bones reference devoted entirely to the .303 World War II and Korean War vintage service rifle.

Legendary Sporting Rifles, by Sam Fadala, Stoeger Publishing Co., So. Hackensack, NJ, 1992. 288 pp., illus. Paper covers. $16.95

Covers a vast span of time and technology beginning with the Kentucky Long-rifle.

The Li'l M1 .30 Cal. Carbine, by Duncan Long, Desert Publications, El Dorado, AZ, 1995. 203 pp., illus. Paper covers. $19.95

Traces the history of this little giant from its original creation.

A Master Gunmaker's Guide to Building Bolt-Action Rifles, by Bill Holmes. Boulder, CO: Paladin Press, 2003. Photos, illus., 152 pp. Softcover. $25.00

Many people today call themselves gunmakers, but very few have actually made a gun. Most buy parts wherever available and simply assemble them. During the past 50 years Bill Holmes has built from scratch countless rifles, shotguns and pistols of amazing artistry, ranging in caliber from .17 to .50. He has mastered the art of custom-making all the component parts himself and earned the right to call himself a gunmaker. In this book the esteemed gunmaker shows you step-by-step how to make (or modify) a custom bolt-action rifle in an inexpensive small shop. By following the simple instructions and mechanic's drawings, you will discover how to select the design, materials and tools; manufacture the bolt, trigger, safety and sights; fit, chamber, shape and finish the barrel; ensure that your heat-treating is done properly; design, checker and finish the stock; and everything else you need to know to be able to call yourself a gunmaker.

Mauser Smallbore Sporting, Target and Training Rifles, by Jon Speed, Collector Grade Publications, Inc., Cobourg, Ont., Canada, 1998. 372 pp., illustrated. $67.50

The history of all the smallbore sporting, target and training rifles produced by the legendary Mauser-Werke of Obendorf am Neckar.

Mauser: Original-Oberndorf Sporting Rifles, by Jon Speed, Collector Grade Publications, Inc., Cobourg, Ont., Canada, 1997. 508 pp., illustrated. $89.95

The most exhaustive study ever published of the design origins and manufacturing history of the original Oberndorf Mauser Sporter.

Mauser Military Rifles Of The World, 3rd Edition. by Robert Ball. Iola, WI: Krause Publications, 2003. 3rd edition. 304 pp., illus. With 1,000 b&w and 48-page color section. Hardcover. $39.95

This 3rd edition brings more than 200 new photos of these historical rifles and the wars in which they were carried. Mauser military rifles offer collectors almost unlimited variations, and author Bob Ball continues to find rare and interesting specimens. Every detail is presented, from the length and weight of the rifle to the manufacturer's markings. This book shows collectors precisely how to identify every model from 1871 to 1945 and provides production figures and the relative rarity of each model. Because Mauser rifles were produced under contract in so many different nations, the book is organized alphabetically by country and the year of production.

M14/M14A1 Rifles and Rifle Markmanship, Desert Publications, El Dorado, AZ, 1995. 236 pp., illus. Paper covers. $19.95

Contains a detailed description of the M14 and M14A1 rifles and their general characteristics, procedures for disassembly & assembly, operating and functioning of the rifles.

The M14 Owner's Guide and Match Conditioning Instructions, by Scott A. Duff and John M. Miller, Duff Publications, Export, PA, 1996. 180 pp., illus. Paper covers. $19.95

Traces the history and development from the T44 through the adoption and production of the M14 rifle.

The M-14 Rifle, facsimile reprint of FM 23-8, Desert Publications, Cornville, AZ, 50 pp., illus. Paper $11.95

Well illustrated and informative reprint covering the M-14 and M-14E2.

The M14-Type Rifle: A Shooter's and Collector's Guide, by Joe Poyer, North Cape Publications, Tustin, CA, 1997. 82 pp., illus. Paper covers. $14.95

Covers the history and development, commercial copies, cleaning and maintenance instructions, and targeting and shooting.

The M16/AR15 Rifle, by Joe Poyer, North Cape Publications, Tustin, CA, 1998. 150 pp., illustrated. Paper covers. $19.95

From its inception as the first American assault battle rifle to the firing lines of the National Matches, the M16/AR15 rifle in all its various models and guises has made a significant impact on the American rifleman.

Military Bolt Action Rifles, 1841-1918, by Donald B. Webster, Museum Restoration Service, Alexander Bay, NY, 1993. 150 pp., illus. $34.50

A photographic survey of the principal rifles and carbines of the European and Asiatic powers of the last half of the 19th century and the first years of the 20th century.

The Mini-14, by Duncan Long, Paladin Press, Boulder, CO, 1987. 120 pp., illus. Paper covers. $17.00

History of the Mini-14, the factory-produced models, specifications, accessories, suppliers, and much more.

Mr. Single Shot's Book of Rifle Plans, by Frank de Haas, Mark de Haas, Orange City, IA, 1996. 85 pp., illus. Paper covers. $22.50

Contains complete and detailed drawings, plans and instructions on how to build four different and unique breech-loading single shot rifles of the author's own proven design.

The MKB 42, MP43, MP44 and the Sturmgewehr 44, by de Vries & Martens. Alexandria, VA: Ironside International, 2003. 1st edition. 152 pages, illustrated with 200 high quality black & white photos. Hardcover. $39.95

Covers all essential information on history and development, ammunition and accessories, codes and markings, and contains photos of nearly every model and accessory. Includes a unique selection of original German WWII propoganda photos, most never published before.

M1 Carbine Owner's Manual, M1, M2 & M3 .30 Caliber Carbines, Firepower Publications, Cornville, AZ, 1984. 102 pp., illus. Paper covers. $9.95

The complete book for the owner of an M1 Carbine.

The M1 Garand Serial Numbers & Data Sheets, by Scott A. Duff, Scott A. Duff, Export, PA, 1995. 101 pp. Paper covers. $11.95

This pocket reference book includes serial number tables and data sheets on the Springfield Armory, Gas Trap Rifles, Gas Port Rifles, Winchester Repeating Arms, International Harvester and H&R Arms Co. and more.

The M1 Garand: Post World War, by Scott A. Duff, Scott A. Duff, Export, PA, 1990. 139 pp., illus. Soft covers. $21.95

A detailed account of the activities at Springfield Armory through this period. International Harvester, H&R, Korean War production and quantities delivered. Serial numbers.

THE ARMS LIBRARY

The M1 Garand: World War 2, by Scott A. Duff, Scott A. Duff, Export, PA, 1993. 210 pp., illus. Paper covers. $34.95

The most comprehensive study available to the collector and historian on the M1 Garand of World War II.

MG34-MG42 German Universal Machineguns, by Folke Myrvang. Collector Grade Publications, Canada. 2002. 496 pages, 646 illustrations. $79.95

This is the first-ever COMPETE study of the MG34 & MG42. Here the author presents in-depth coverage of the historical development, fielding, tactical use of and modifications made to these remarkable guns and their myriad accessories and ancillaries, plus authoritative tips on troubleshooting.

Modern Sniper Rifles, by Duncan Long, Paladin Press, Boulder, CO, 1997, 8 1/2 x 11, soft cover, photos, illus., 120 pp. $20.00

Noted weapons expert Duncan Long describes the .22 LR, single-shot, bolt-action, semiautomatic and large-caliber rifles that can be used for sniping purposes, including the U.S. M21, Ruger Mini-14, AUG and HK-94SG1. These and other models are evaluated on the basis of their features, accuracy, reliability and handiness in the field. The author also looks at the best scopes, ammunition and accessories.

More Single Shot Rifles and Actions, by Frank de Haas, Mark de Haas, Orange City, IA, 1996. 146 pp., illus. Paper covers. $22.50

Covers 45 different single shot rifles. Includes the history plus photos, drawings and personal comments.

The No. 4 (T) Sniper Rifle: An Armourer's Perspective, by Peter Laidler with Ian Skennerton, I.D.S.A. Books, Piqua, OH, 1993. 125 pp., 75 illus. Paper covers. $19.95

A reprint of the 1864 London edition. Captain Heaton was one of the great rifle shots from the earliest days of the Volunteer Movement.

The Official SKS Manual, Translation by Major James F. Gebhardt (Ret.), Paladin Press, Boulder, CO, 1997. 96 pp., illus. Paper covers. $16.00

This Soviet military manual covering the widely distributed SKS is now available in English.

Ordnance Tools, Accessories & Appendages of the M1 Rifle, by Pyle, Billy. Houston, TX: Privately printed, 2002. 2nd edition. 206 pages, illustrated with b&w photos. Softcover. $40.00

This is the new updated second edition with over 350 pictures and drawings - 30 of which are new. Part I contains accessories, appendages, and equipment including such items as bayonets, blank firing attachments, cheek pads, cleaning equipment, clips, flash hiders, grenade launchers, scabbards, slings, telescopes and mounts, winter triggers, and much more. Part II covers ammunition, grenades, and pyrotechnics. Part III shows the inspection gages. Part IV presents the ordnance tools, fixtures, and assemblies. Part V contains miscellaneous items related to the M1 Rifle such as arms racks, rifle racks, clip loading machine, and other devices.

Old German Target Arms: Alte Schiebenwaffen, by Jesse Thompson; C. Ron Dillon; Allen Hallock; Bill Loos. Rocester, NY: Tom Rowe Publications, 2003. 1st edition. 392 pages. Hardcover. $98.00

History of Schueten shooting from the middle ages through WWII. Hundreds of illustrations, most in color. History & Memorabilia of the Bundesschiessen (State or National Shoots), Bird Target rifles, American shooters in Germany. Schutzen rifles such as matchlocks, wheellocks, flintlocks, percussion, bader, bornmuller, rifles by Buchel and more.

Police Rifles, by Richard Fairburn, Paladin Press, Boulder, CO, 1994. 248 pp., illus. Paper covers. $35.00

Selecting the right rifle for street patrol and special tactical situations.

The Poor Man's Sniper Rifle, by D. Boone, Paladin Press, Boulder, CO, 1995. 152 pp., illus. Paper covers. $18.95

Here is a complete plan for converting readily available surplus military rifles to high-performance sniper weapons.

A Potpourri of Single Shot Rifles and Actions, by Frank de Haas, Mark de Haas, Ridgeway, MO, 1993. 153 pp., illus. Paper covers. $22.50

The author's 6th book on non-bolt-action single shots. Covers more than 40 single-shot rifles in historical and technical detail.

Precision Shooting with the M1 Garand, by Roy Baumgardner, Precision Shooting, Inc., Manchester, CT, 1999. 142 pp., illustrated. Paper covers. $12.95

Starts off with the ever popular ten-article series on accurinzing the M1 that originally appeared in Precision Shooting in the 1993-95 era. There follows nine more Baumgardner authored articles on the M1 Garand and finally a 1999 updating chapter.

Remington Autoloading And Pump Action Rifles, by Eugene Myszkowski, Tucson, AZ: Excalibur Publications, 2002. 132 pages, with 162 photographs, 6 illustrations and 18 charts. Softcover. $20.95

An illustrated history of Remington's centerfire Models 760, 740, 742, 7400 and 7600. The book is thoroughly researed and features many previously unpublished photos of the rifles, their accessories and accoutrements. Also covers high grade, unusual and experimental rifles. Contains information on collecting, serial numbers and barrel codes.

The Remington 700, by John F. Lacy, Taylor Publishing Co., Dallas, TX, 2002. 208 pp., illus. $49.95

Covers the different models, limited editions, chamberings, proofmarks, serial numbers, military models, and much more.

The Rifle Rules: Magic for the Ultimate Rifleman, by Don Paul. Kaua'i, HI: Pathfinder Publications, 2003. 1st edition. 116 pages, illus. Softcover. $14.95

A new method that shows you how to add hundreds of yards to your effective shooting ability. Ways for you to improve your rifle's accuracy which no factory can do. Lessons on what to do when being shot AT. A new system for determining the distance at which you never miss. A new cost-free way to practice. This book converts you and your rifle to a long distance influence, more accurate, and more powerful than any other. Not literary. Not complicated. Illustrations & photos added to make new concepts easy.

The Rifle Shooter, by G. David Tubb. Oxford Ms : Zediker Publishing, 2004. 1st edition. 416 pp softcover, 7x10 size, 400 photos and illustrations, very high quality printing. Softcover. $34.95

This is not just a revision of his landmark "Highpower Rifle" but an all-new, greatly expanded work that reveals David's thoughts and recommendations on all aspects of precision rifle shooting. Each shooting position and event is dissected and taken to extreme detail, as are the topics of ammunition, training, rifle design, event strategies, and wind shooting. Other segments in The Rifle Shooter include equipment selection and modifications, getting started in competitive shooting, ammunition loading and testing, shooting at Camp Perry, vision and the sighting system, and much, much more. You will learn the secrets of perhaps the greatest rifleman ever, and you'll learn how to put them to work for you!

Rifles of the World, 2nd Edition, by John Walter, DBI Books, a division of Krause Publications, Iola, WI, 1998. 384 pp., illus. $24.95

The definitive guide to the world's centerfire and rimfire rifles.

Ned H. Roberts and the Schuetzen Rifle, edited by Gerald O. Kelver, Brighton, CO, 1982. 99 pp., illus. $13.95

A compilation of the writings of Major Ned H. Roberts which appeared in various gun magazines.

Rock Island Rifle Model 1903, by C.S. Ferris. Export, PA: Scott A. Duff Publications, 2002. 177 pages, illustrated with b&w photographs. Foreword by Scott A. Duff. Softcover. $22.95

Schuetzen Rifles, History and Loading, by Gerald O. Kelver, Gerald O. Kelver, Publisher, Brighton, CO, 1972. Illus. $13.95

Reference work on these rifles, their bullets, loading, telescopic sights, accuracy, etc. A limited, numbered ed.

Shooting The .43 Spanish Rolling Block, by Croft Barker. Flatonia, TX: Cistern Publishing, 2003. 1st edition. 137 pages. Softcover. $25.50

The SOURCE for information on .43 caliber rolling blocks. Lots of photos and text covering Remington & Oveido actions, antique cartridges, etc. Features smokeless & black powder loads, rifle disassembly and maintenance, 11 mm bullets. Required reading for the rolling block owner.

Shooting the Blackpowder Cartridge Rifle, by Paul A. Matthews, Wolfe Publishing Co., Prescott, AZ, 1994. 129 pp., illus. Paper covers. $22.50

A general discourse on shooting the blackpowder cartridge rifle and the procedure required to make a particular rifle perform.

Shooting Lever Guns of the Old West, by Mike Venturino, MLV Enterprises, Livingston, MT, 1999. 300 pp., illustrated. Paper covers. $27.95

Shooting the lever action type repeating rifles of our American west.

Single Shot Rifles and Actions, by Frank de Haas, Orange City, IA, 1990. 352 pp., illus. Soft covers. $27.00

The definitive book on over 60 single shot rifles and actions.

S.L.R.—Australia's F.N. F.A.L. by Ian Skennerton and David Balmer, Arms & Militaria Press, 1989. 124 pp., 100 illus. Paper covers. $24.50

.577 Snider-Enfield Rifles & Carbines; British Service Longarms, by Ian Skennerton. 1866-C.1880. Australia: Arms & Militaria Press, 2003. 1st edition. 240 pp plus 8 colour plates, 100 illustrations. Marking Ribbon. Hardcover. $39.50

The definitive study of Britain's first breech-loading rifle, at first converted from Enfield muskets, then newly made with Mk III breech. The trials, development, rifle and carbine models are detailed; new information along with descriptions of the cartridges.

Small Arms Identification Series, No. 1—.303 Rifle, No. 1 S.M.L.E. Marks III and III*, by Ian Skennerton, I.D.S.A. Books, Piqua, OH, 1981. 48 pp. $10.50

Small Arms Identification Series, No. 2—.303 Rifle, No. 4 Marks I, & I*, Marks 1/2, 1/3 & 2, by Ian Skennerton, I.D.S.A. Books, Piqua, OH, 1994. 48 pp. $10.50

Small Arms Identification Series, No. 3—9mm Austen Mk I & 9mm Owen Mk I Sub-Machine Guns, by Ian Skennerton, I.D.S.A. Books, Piqua, OH, 1994. 48 pp. $10.50

Small Arms Identification Series, No. 4—.303 Rifle, No. 5 Mk I, by Ian Skennerton, I.D.S.A. Books, Piqua, OH, 1994. 48 pp. $10.50

Small Arms Identification Series, No. 5—.303-in. Bren Light Machine Gun, by Ian Skennerton, I.D.S.A. Books, Piqua, OH, 1994. 48 pp. $10.50

The '03 Springfield Rifles Era, by Campbell, Clark S.Richmond, VA: Privately Printed, 2003. 1st edition. 368 pages, 146 illustrations, drawn to scale by author. Hardcover. $58.00

A much-expanded version of this author's famous The '03 Springfield (1957) and The '03 Springfields (1971), representing forty years of research into all things 03. Part I is a complete and verifiably correct study of all standardized and special-purpose models of the U.S. M1903 Springfield rifle, in both .22 and .30 calibers, including those prototypes which led to standard models, and also all standardized .30 caliber cartridges, including National and International Match, and caliber .22. Part II is the result of the author's five years as a Research and Development Engineer with Remington Arms Co., and will be of inestimable value to anyone planning a custom sporter, whether or not based on the '03.

The Springfield Rifle M1903, M1903A1, M1903A3, M1903A4, Desert Publications, Cornville, AZ, 1982. 100 pp., illus. Paper covers. $14.95

Covers every aspect of disassembly and assembly, inspection, repair and maintenance.

Still More Single Shot Rifles, by James J. Grant, Pioneer Press, Union City, TN, 1995. 211 pp., illus. $29.95

This is Volume Four in a series of Single-Shot Rifles by America's foremost authority. It gives more in-depth information on those single-shot rifles which were presented in the first three books.

The Sturm, Ruger 10/22 Rifle and .44 Magnum Carbine, by Duncan Long, Paladin Press, Boulder, CO, 1988. 108 pp., illus. Paper covers. $15.00

An in-depth look at both weapons detailing the elegant simplicity of the Ruger design. Offers specifications, troubleshooting procedures and ammunition recommendations.

Swedish Mauser Rifles, by Kehaya, Steve and Joe Poyer. Tustin, CA: North Cape Publications, 2004. 2nd edition Revised. 267 pp., illustrated. Softcover. $19.95

Every known variation of the Swedish Mauser carbine and rifle is described including all match and target rifles and all sniper fersions. Includes serial number and production data.

Swiss Magazine Loading Rifles 1869 To 1958, by Poyer, Joe. Tustin, CA: North Cape Publications, 2003. 1st edition. 317 pages, illustrated with hundreds of black & white drawings and photos. Softcover. $19.95

It covers the K-31 on a part by part basis, as well as it's predecessor models of 1889 and 1911 and the first repeating magazine rifle ever adopted by a military, the Model 1869 Vetterli rifle and it's successor models. Also includes a history of the development and use of these fine rifles. Details regarding their ammunition, complete assembly/disassembly instructions as well as sections on cleaning, maintenance and trouble shooting.

The Tactical Rifle, by Gabriel Suarez, Paladin Press, Boulder, CO, 1999. 264 pp., illustrated. Paper covers. $25.00

The precision tool for urban police operations.

Target Rifle in Australia, by J.E. Corcoran, R&R, Livonia, NY, 1996. 160 pp., illus. $40.00

A most interesting study of the evolution of these rifles from 1860 - 1900. British rifles from the percussion period through the early smokeless era are discussed.

The Ultimate in Rifle Accuracy, by Glenn Newick, Stoeger Publishing Co., Wayne, N.J., 1999. 205 pp., illustrated. Paper covers. $11.95

This handbook contains the information you need to extract the best performance from your rifle.

THE ARMS LIBRARY

U.S. Marine Corps AR15/M16 A2 Manual, reprinted by Desert Publications, El Dorado, AZ, 1993. 262 pp., illus. Paper covers. $16.95

A reprint of TM05538C-23&P/2, August, 1987. The A-2 manual for the Colt AR15/M16.

U.S. Marine Corps Rifle Marksmanship, by U.S. Marine Corps. Boulder, CO: Paladin Press, 2002. Photos, illus., 120 pp. Softcover. $20.00

This manual is the very latest Marine doctrine on the art and science of shooting effectively in battle. Its 10 chapters teach the versatility, flexibility and skills needed to deal with a situation at any level of intensity across the entire range of military operations. Topics covered include the proper combat mind-set; cleaning your rifle under all weather conditions; rifle handling and marksmanship the Marine way; engaging targets from behind cover; obtaining a battlefield zero; engaging immediate threat, multiple and moving targets; shooting at night and at unknown distances; and much more.

U.S. Rifle M14—From John Garand to the M21, by R. Blake Stevens, Collector Grade Publications, Inc., Toronto, Canada, revised second edition, 1991. 350 pp., illus. $49.50

A classic, in-depth examination of the development, manufacture and fielding of the last wood-and-metal ("lock, stock, and barrel") battle rifle to be issued to U.S. troops.

War Baby!: The U.S. Caliber 30 Carbine, Volume I, by Larry Ruth, Collector Grade Publications, Toronto, Canada, 1992. 512 pp., illus. $69.95

Volume 1 of the in-depth story of the phenomenally popular U.S. caliber 30 carbine. Concentrates on design and production of the military 30 carbine during World War II.

War Baby Comes Home: The U.S. Caliber 30 Carbine, Volume 2, by Larry Ruth, Collector Grade Publications, Toronto, Canada, 1993. 386 pp., illus. $49.95

The triumphant competion of Larry Ruth's two-volume in-depth series on the most popular U.S. military small arm in history.

The Winchester Model 52, Perfection in Design, by Herbert G. Houze, Krause Publications, Iola, WI, 1997. 192 pp., illus. $34.95

This book covers the complete story of this technically superior gun.

SHOTGUNS

Advanced Combat Shotgun: Stress Fire 2, by Massad Ayoob, Police Bookshelf, Concord, NH, 1993. 197 pp., illus. Paper covers. $14.95

Advanced combat shotgun fighting for police.

The Best Of Holland & Holland, England's Premier Gunmaker, by Michael McIntosh & Jan G. Roosenburg. Long Beach, CA: Safari Press, Inc., 2002. 1st edition. 298 pages, profuse color illustrations. Hardcover. $69.95

Holland & Holland has had a long history of not only building London's "best" guns but also providing superior guns--the ultimate gun in finish, engraving, and embellishment. From the days of old in which a maharaja would order 100 fancifully engraved H&H shotguns for his guests to use at his duck shoot to the recent elaborately decorated sets depicting the Apollo 11 moon landing or the history of the British Empire, all of these guns represent the zenith in the art and craft of gunmaking and engraving. These and other H&H guns in the series named "Products of Excellence" are a cut above the ordinary H&H gun and hark back to a time when the British Empire ruled over one-third of the globe--a time when rulers, royalty, and the rich worldwide came to H&H for a gun that would elevate them above the crowd. In this book master gunwriter and acknowledged English gun expert Michael McIntosh and former H&H director Jan Roosenburg show us in words and pictures the finest products ever produced by H&H and, many would argue, by any gun company on earth. From a dainty and elegant .410 shotgun with gold relief engraving of scenes from Greek and Roman antiquity to the massive .700 Nitro Express double rifle, some of the most expensive and opulent guns ever produced on earth parade through these pages. An overview of the Products of Excellence series is given as well as a description and history of these special H&H guns. Never before have so many superlative guns from H&H--or any other maker for that manner--been displayed in one book. Many photos shown are firearms from private collections, which cannot be seen publicly anywhere except in this book. In addition, many interesting details and a general history of H&H are provided.

Best Guns, by Michael McIntosh, Countrysport Press, Selma, AL, 1999, revised edition. 418 pp. $45.00

Combines the best shotguns ever made in America with information on British and Continental makers.

The Better Shot, by Ken Davies, Quiller Press, London, England, 1992. 136 pp., illus. $39.95

Step-by-step shotgun technique with Holland and Holland.

Browning Auto-5 Shotguns: The Belgian FN Production, by H. M. Shirley Jr. and Anthony Vanderlinden. Geensboro, NC: Wet Dog Publications, 2003. Limited edition of 2000 copies, signed by the author. 233 pages, plus index. Over 400 quality b&w photographs and 24 color photographs. Signed by the author. Hardcover $59.95

This is the first book devoted to the history, model variations, accessories and production dates of this legendary gun. This publication is to date the only reference book on the Auto-5 (A-5) shotgun prepared entirely with the extensive cooperation and support of Browning, FN Herstal, the Browning Firearms Museum and the Liege Firearms Museum.

The Browning Superposed: John M. Browning's Last Legacy, by Ned Schwing, Krause Publications, Iola, WI, 1996. 496 pp., illus. $49.95

An exclusive story of the man, the company and the best-selling over-and-under shotgun in North America.

Cogswell & Harrison; Two Centuries of Gunmaking, by G. Cooley & J. Newton, Safari Press, Long Beach, CA, 2000. 128pp, 30 color photos, 100 b&w photos. $39.95

The authors have gathered a wealth of fascinating historical and technical material that will make the book indispensable, not only to many thousands of "Coggie" owners worldwide, but also to anyone interested in the general history of British gunmaking.

A Collector's Guide to United States Combat Shotguns, by Bruce N. Canfield, Andrew Mowbray Inc., Publishers, Lincoln, RI, 1993. 184 pp., illus. Paper covers. $24.00

Full coverage of the combat shotgun, from the earliest examples to the Gulf War and beyond.

Combat Shotgun and Submachine Gun, "A Special Weapons Analysis" by Chuck Taylor, Paladin Press, Boulder, CO, 1997, soft cover, photos, 176 pp. $25.00

From one of America's top shooting instructors comes an analysis of two controversial, misunderstood and misemployed small arms. Hundreds of photos detail field-testing of both, basic and advanced training drills, tactical rules, gun accessories and modifications. Loading procedures, carrying and fighting positions and malfunction clearance drills are included to promote weapon effectiveness.

The Defensive Shotgun, by Louis Awerbuck, S.W.A.T. Publications, Cornville, AZ, 1989. 77 pp., illus. Soft covers. $14.95

Cuts through the myths concerning the shotgun and its attendant ballistic effects.

The Ducks Unlimited Guide to Shotgunning, by Don Zutz, Willow Creek Press, Minocqua, WI, 2000. 166 pg. Illustrated. $24.50

This book covers everything from the grand old guns of yesterday to todays best shotguns and loads, from the basic shotgun fit and function to expert advice on ballistics, chocks, and shooting techniques.

Finding the Extra Target, by Coach John R. Linn & Stephen A. Blumenthal, Shotgun Sports, Inc., Auburn, CA, 1989. 126 pp., illus. Paper covers. $14.95

The ultimate training guide for all the clay target sports.

Fine European Gunmakers: Best Continental European Gunmakers & Engravers, by M. Nobili. Long Beach, CA: Safari Press, 2002. 250 pages, illustated in color. $69.95

Hundreds of books have been published about the British gun trade, but English speakers and publishers have largely ignored the European trade in fine guns until now! Many experts argue that Continental gunmakers produce guns equally as good or better than British makers. Marco Nobili's new work, Fine European Gunmakers, showcases the skills of the best craftsmen from continental Europe, and the author brings to life in words and pictures their finest sporting guns. The book covers the histories of the individual firms and looks at the guns they currently build, tracing the developments of their most influential models. Depicted with profuse color illustrations, it showcases the best guns ever made in Europe. All the greatest names are here, including Piotti, Beretta, Merkel, Kreighoff, Connecticut Shotgun, Perazzi, Hartmann & Weiss, Peter Hofer, Gamba, Fausti, Fanzoj, Lebeau & Courally, Fabbri and many others.

Fine Gunmaking: Double Shotguns, by Steven Dodd Hughes, Krause Publications Iola, WI, 1998. 167 pp., illustrated. $34.95

An in-depth look at the creation of fine shotguns.

Firearms Assembly/Disassembly, Part V: Shotguns, 2nd Edition, The Gun Digest Book of, by J.B. Wood, Krause Publications, Iola, WI, 2002. 560 pp., illus. $24.95 Covers 54 popular shotguns plus over 250 variants. The most comprehensive and professional presentation available to either hobbyist or gunsmith.

A.H. Fox "The Finest Gun in the World", revised and enlarged edition, by Michael McIntosh, Countrysport, Inc., New Albany, OH, 1995. 408 pp., illus. $49.00

The first detailed history of one of America's finest shotguns.

Game Shooting, by Robert Churchill, Countrysport Press, Selma, AL, 1998. 258 pp., illus. $30.00

The basis for every shotgun instructional technique devised and the foundation for all wingshooting and the game of sporting clays.

Greenhill Military Manual: Combat Shotguns, by Thompson, Leroy. London: Greenhill Publishing, 2002. 1st edition. 144 pages, illustrated. Hardcover. $24.00

The combat shotgun is one of the most devastating yet most misunderstood close-combat weapons. A great intimidator, the combat shotgun is widely used by military and police units for crowd control. This book traces the history of the combat shotgun, specialized tactics for its usage, the myriad ammunition choices, and the wealth of combat shotguns available to the military or police operator.

The Greener Story, by Graham Greener, Safari Press, Long Beach, CA, 2000. 231pp, color and b&w illustrations. $69.95

The history of the Greener Gunmakers and their guns.

Gun Digest Book of Sporting Clays, 2nd Edition, edited by Harold A. Murtz, Krause Publications, Iola, WI, 1999. 256 pp., illus. Paper covers. $21.95

A concise Gun Digest book that covers guns, ammo, chokes, targets and course layouts so you'll stay a step ahead.

The Gun Review Book, by Michael McIntosh, Countrysport Press, Selman, AL, 1999. Paper covers. $19.95

Compiled here for the first time are McIntosh's popular gun reviews from Shooting Sportsman; The Magazine of Wingshooting and Fine Shotguns. The author traces the history of gunmakes, then examines, analyzes, and critique the fine shotguns of England, Continental Europe and the United States.

The Heyday of the Shotgun, by David Baker, Safari Press, Inc., Huntington Beach, CA, 2000. 160 pp., illustrated. $39.95

The art of the gunmaker at the turn of the last century when British craftsmen brought forth the finest guns ever made.

Gunsmithing Shotguns: The Complete Guide To Care & Repair, by Henderson, David. New York: Globe Pequot, 2003. 1st edition. B&W photos & illus; 6x9 inches, 256 pages, illustrated. Hardcover. $24.95

An overview designed to provide insight, ideas, & techniques that will give the amateur gunsmith the confidence & skill to work on his own guns. General troubleshooting, common problems, stocks & woodworking, Soldering & brazing, barrel work, & more.

Holland & Holland: The "Royal" Gunmaker, by Dallas, Donald. London: Safari Press, 2004. 1st edition. 311 pages. Hardcover. $75.00

Donald Dallas tells the fascinating story of Holland & Holland from its very beginnings, and the history of the family is revealed for the first time. The terrific variety of the firm's guns and rifles is described in great detail and set within the historical context of their eras. From punt gun to boy's gun, from rook rifle to elephant gun, Holland & Holland supplied sporting firearms to every corner of the world. In May 1885, Holland & Holland advertised their new trademark as the "Royal," which the firm intended to apply to best guns and rifles only. Royal guns and rifles have been in production since that date, the choice of name symbolizing the excellence of the firm's output. And yet, gunmaking played no part in the early history of Holland & Holland. All fifty-one patents are described, the dating of Holland serial numbers is given from 1855 to the present day, all the trade labels are illustrated, and the rifle cartridges are examined in detail. The book is profusely illustrated with 112 color and 355 b&w photographs, mostly unpublished. In addition many rare guns and rifles are described and illustrated.

The House Of Churchill, by Don Masters. Safari Press, Long Beach, CA, 2002. 512 pages, profuse color and b&w illustrations. $79.95

This marvelous work on the house of Churchill contains serial numbers and dates of manufacture of its guns from 1891 forward, price lists from 1895 onward, a complete listing of all craftsmen employed at the company, as well as the prices realized at the famous Dallas auction where the "last" production guns were sold. The treatment of all aspects of this gunmaker is so thorough that it contains details that will defy even the greatest expert! This massive work is well illustrated with hundreds of color and b&w photos, period brochures, and gun labels, and it includes dozens of charts, tables, appendices, and a detailed index. It was written by Don Masters, a longtime Churchill employee, who is keeping the flame of Churchill alive.

THE ARMS LIBRARY

The Italian Gun, by Steve Smith & Laurie Morrow, wilderness Adventures, Gallatin Gateway, MT, 1997. 325 pp., illus. $49.95

The first book ever written entirely in English for American enthusiasts who own, aspire to own, or simply admire Italian guns.

The Ithaca Featherlight Repeater; the Best Gun Going, by Walter C. Snyder, Southern Pines, NC, 1998. 300 pp., illus. $89.95.

Describes the complete history of each model of the legendary Ithaca Model 37 and Model 87 Repeaters from their conception in 1930 throught 1997.

The Ithaca Gun Company from the Beginning, by Walter C. Snyder, Cook & Uline Publishing Co., Southern Pines, NC, 2nd Edition, 1999. 384 pp., illustrated in color and b&w. $90.00

The entire family of Ithaca Gun Company products is described along with new historical information and the serial number/date of manufacturing listing has been improved.

The Little Trapshooting Book, by Frank Little, Shotgun Sports Magazine, Auburn, CA, 1994. 168 pp., illus. Paper covers. $19.95

Packed with know-how from one of the greatest trapshooters of all time.

Lock, Stock, and Barrel, by C. Adams & R. Braden, Safari Press, Huntington Beach, CA, 1996. 254 pp., illus. $24.95

The process of making a best grade English gun from a lump of steel and a walnut tree trunk to the ultimate product plus practical advise on consistent field shooting with a double gun.

Mental Training for the Shotgun Sports, by Michael J. Keyes, Shotgun Sports, Auburn, CA, 1996. 160 pp., illus. Paper covers. $29.95

The most comprehensive book ever published on what it takes to shoot winning scores at trap, Skeet and Sporting Clays.

More Shotguns and Shooting, by Michael McIntosh, Countrysport Books, Selma, AL, 1998. 256 pp., illustrated. $30.00

From specifics of shotguns to shooting your way out of a slump, it's McIntosh at his best.

Mossberg Shotguns, by Duncan Long, Delta Press, El Dorado, AR, 2000. 120 pp., illustrated. $24.95

This book contains a brief history of the company and it's founder, full coverage of the pump and semiautomatic shotguns, rare products and a care and maintenance section.

The Mysteries of Shotgun Patterns, by George G. Oberfell and Charles E. Thompson, Oklahoma State University Press, Stillwater, OK, 1982. 164 pp., illus. Paper covers. $25.00

Shotgun ballistics for the hunter in non-technical language.

The Parker Gun, by Larry Baer, Gun Room Press, Highland Park, NJ, 1993. 195 pages, illustrated with b&w and Color photos. $35.00

Covers in detail, production of all models on this classic gun. Many fine specimens from great collections are illustrated.

Parker Gun Identification & Serialization, by S.P. Fjestad, Minneapolis, MN: Blue Book Publications, 2002. 1st edition. Softcover. $34.95

This new 608-page publication is the only book that provides an easy reference for Parker shotguns manufactured between 1866-1942. Included is a comprehensive 46-page section on Parker identification, with over 100 detailed images depicting serialization location and explanation, various Parker grades, extra features, stock configurations, action types, and barrel identification.

The Parker Story; Volumes 1 & 2, by Bill Mullins, "etal". The Double Gun Journal, East Jordan, MI, 2000. 1,025 pages of text and 1,500 color and monochrome illustrations. Hardbound in a gold-embossed cover. $295.00

The most complete and attractive "last word" on America's preeminent double gun maker. Includes tables showing the number of guns made by gauge, barrel length and special features for each grade.

Purdey Gun and Rifle Makers: The Definitive History, by Donald Dallas, Quiller Press, London 2000. 245 pages, illus. $100.00

245 colour plates, b&w photos, ills, bibliography. The definitive history. A limited edition of 3,000 copies. Signed and Numbered. With a PURDEY book plate.

Recreating The Double Barrel Muzzle Loading Shotgun, by William R. Brockway. York, PA: George Shumway, 2003. Revised 2nd edition. 175 pages, Illustrated. Includes full size drawings. Softcover. $40.00

This popular book, first published in 1985 and out of print for over a decade, has been updated by the author. This book treats the making of double guns of classic style, and is profusely illustrated, showing how to do it all. Many photos of old and contemporary shotguns.

Reloading for Shotgunners, 4th Edition, by Kurt D. Fackler and M.L. McPherson, DBI Books, a division of Krause Publications, Iola, WI, 1997. 320 pp., illus. Paper covers. $19.95

Expanded reloading tables with over 11,000 loads. Bushing charts for every major press and component maker. All new presentation on all aspects of shotshell reloading by two of the top experts in the field.

Remington Double Shotguns, by Charles G. Semer, Denver, CO, 1997. 617 pp., illus. $60.00

This book deals with the entire production and all grades of double shotguns made by Remington during the period of their production 1873-1910.

75 Years with the Shotgun, by C.T. (Buck) Buckman, Valley Publ., Fresno, CA, 1974. 141 pp., illus. $10.00

An expert hunter and trapshooter shares experiences of a lifetime.

The Shotgun Encyclopedia, by John Taylor, Safari Press, Inc., Huntington Beach, CA, 2000. 260 pp., illustrated. $34.95

A comprehensive reference work on all aspects of shotguns and shotgun shooting.

The Shotgun - A Shooting Instructor's Handbook, by Michael Yardley. Long Beach, CA: Safari Press, 2002. 272pp, b&w photos, line drawings. Hardcover. $29.95

This is one of the very few books intended to be read by shooting instructors and other advanced shots. In setting down a complete (but notably flexible) teaching system, Michael Yardley puts the greatest emphasis on safety, and he discusses the problems inherent in shooting because of individual fallibility. He sets out a "layer principal"--a series of checks and procedures to be used at all times--that provides a positive framework from which to build a solid, secure technique. After considering game- and clay-shooting safety comprehensively, he goes on to consider gun condition and proof (vital subjects for the instructor), and he explores shooting vision in unprecedented depth. In further chapters he analyzes the components and development of shooting technique by pointing out the styles of great instructors such as Percy Stanbury and Robert Churchill as well as the shooting techniques of some of the best-known modern competitors. There is practical advice on gunfit and on gun and cartridge selection.

The Shotgun: History and Development, by Geoffrey Boothroyd, Safari Press, Huntington Beach, CA, 1995. 240 pp., illus. $35.00

The first volume in a series that traces the development of the British shotgun from the 17th century onward.

The Shotgun Handbook, by Mike George, The Croswood Press, London, England, 1999. 128 pp., illus. $35.00

For all shotgun enthusiasts, this detailed guide ranges from design and selection of a gun to adjustment, cleaning, and maintenance.

Shotgun Stuff, by Don Zutz, Shotgun Sports, Inc., Auburn, CA, 1991. 172 pp., illus. Paper covers. $19.95

This book gives shotgunners all the "stuff" they need to achieve better performance and get more enjoyment from their favorite smoothbore.

Shotgun Technicana, by McIntosh, Michael and David Trevallion. Camden, ME: Down East Books, 2002. 272 pages, with 100 illustrations. Hardcover $28.00

Everything you wanted to know about fine double shotguns by the nations formost experts.

Shotguns & Shotgunning, by Simpson, Layne. Iola, WI: Krause Publications, 2003. 1st edition. High-quality color photography 224 pages, color illus. Hardcover. $36.95

This is the most comprehensive and valuable guide on the market devoted exclusively to shotguns. Part buyer's guide, part technical manual, and part loving tribute, shooters and hunters of all skill levels will enjoy this comprehensive reference tool. Excellent resource for shooters, gun hunters, and firearms collectors. Comprehensive guide covers the technical aspects of shotguns, hunting with shotguns, the evolution of shotguns, and popular shooting games.

Shotgunning: The Art and the Science, by Bob Brister, Winchester Press, Piscataway, NJ, 1976. 321 pp., illus. $18.95

Hundreds of specific tips and truly novel techniques to improve the field and target shooting of every shotgunner.

Shotguns and Shooting, by Michael McIntosh, Countrysport Press, New Albany, OH, 1995. 258 pp., illus. $30.00

The art of guns and gunmaking, this book is a celebration no lover of fine doubles should miss.

Spanish Best: The Fine Shotguns of Spain, 2nd Ed, by Terry Wieland, Down East Books, Traverse City, MI, 2001. 364 pp., illus. $60.00

A practical source of information for owners of Spanish shotguns and a guide for those considering buying a used shotgun.

Streetsweepers, "The Complete Book of Combat Shotguns", by Duncan Long, Paladin Press, Boulder, CO,1997, soft cover, 63 photos, illus., appendices, 160 pp. $24.95

Streetsweepers is the newest, most comprehensive book out on combat shotguns, covering single- and double-barreled, slide-action, semi-auto and rotary cylinder shotguns, plus a chapter on grenade launchers you can mount on your weapon and info about shotgun models not yet on the market. Noted gun writer Duncan Long also advises on which ammo to use, accessories and combat shotgun tactics.

Successful Shotgunning; How to Build Skill in the Field and Take More Birds in Competition, by Blakeley, Peter F. Mechanicsburg, PA: Stackpole Books, 2003. 1st edition. 305 pages, illustrated with 119 b&w photos & 4-page color section with 8 photos. Hardcover. $24.95

Successful Shotgunning focuses on wing-shooting and sporting clays techniques. Gain a better understanding of the shooting process as a whole as you sharpen your skills and become a better shot. How to evaluate moving targets in wing-shooting situations in the field, in a competitive environment, on a sporting clays course, or on a skeet field. Choose the correct gun and gun fit for you; learn to diagnose some common eye problems and correct your aim; tame recoil; and deal with the challenges of various sporting clays targets.

Suhler Luxusgewehre - Guns Deluxe 1973-2001, by Peter Arfmann. Suhl, Germany: Privately printed, 2001. 160 pages, illustrated with color photos. German and English Text. Hardcover. New. $100.00

The Tactical Shotgun, by Gabriel Suzrez, Paladin Press, Boulder, CO, 1996. 232 pp., illus. Paper covers. $25.00

The best techniques and tactics for employing the shotgun in personal combat.

Trap & Skeet Shooting, 4th Edition, by Chris Christian, DBI Books, a division of Krause Publications, Iola, WI, 1994. 288 pp., illus. Paper covers. $21.95

A detailed look at the contemporary world of Trap, Skeet and Sporting Clays.

Trapshooting is a Game of Opposites, by Dick Bennett, Shotgun Sports, Inc., Auburn, CA, 1996. 129 pp., illus. Paper covers. $19.95

Discover everything you need to know about shooting trap like the pros.

Uncle Dan Lefever, Master Gunmaker: Guns of Lasting Fame, by Robert W. Elliott. Privately Printed, 2002. Profusely illustrated with b&w photos, with a 45 page color section. 239 pages. Handsomely bound, with gilt titled spine and top cover. Hardcover. $60.00

U.S. Shotguns, All Types, reprint of TM9-285, Desert Publications, Cornville, AZ, 1987. 257 pp., illus. Paper covers. $16.95

Covers operation, assembly and disassembly of nine shotguns used by the U.S. armed forces.

U.S. Winchester Trench and Riot Guns and Other U.S. Military Combat Shotguns, by Joe Poyer, North Cape Publications, Tustin, CA, 1992. 124 pp., illus. Paper covers. $15.95

A detailed history of the use of military shotguns, and the acquisition procedures used by the U.S. Army's Ordnance Department in both World Wars.

The Winchester Model Twelve, by George Madis, David Madis, Dallas, TX, 1984. 176 pp., illus. $26.95

A definitive work on this famous American shotgun.

Winchester's Finest, the Model 21, by Ned Schwing, Krause Publications, Iola, WI, 1990. 360 pp., illus. $49.95

The classic beauty and the interesting history of the Model 21 Winchester shotgun.

The World's Fighting Shotguns, by Thomas F. Swearengen, T.B.N. Enterprises, Alexandria, VA, 1998. 500 pp., illus. $49.95

The complete military and police reference work from the shotgun's inception to date, with up-to-date developments.

ARMS ASSOCIATIONS

UNITED STATES

ALABAMA

Alabama Gun Collectors Assn.
Secretary, P.O. Box 70965, Tuscaloosa, AL 35407

ALASKA

Alaska Gun Collectors Assn., Inc.
C.W. Floyd, Pres., 5240 Little Tree, Anchorage, AK 99507

ARIZONA

Arizona Arms Assn.
Don DeBusk, President, 4837 Bryce Ave., Glendale, AZ 85301

CALIFORNIA

California Cartridge Collectors Assn.
Rick Montgomery, 1729 Christina, Stockton, CA 95204/209-463-7216 evs.
California Waterfowl Assn.
4630 Northgate Blvd., #150, Sacramento, CA 95834
Greater Calif. Arms & Collectors Assn.
Donald L. Bullock, 8291 Carburton St., Long Beach, CA 90808-3302
Los Angeles Gun Ctg. Collectors Assn.
F.H. Ruffra, 20810 Amie Ave., Apt. #9, Torrance, CA 90503
Stock Gun Players Assn.
6038 Appian Way, Long Beach, CA, 90803

COLORADO

Colorado Gun Collectors Assn.
L.E.(Bud) Greenwald, 2553 S. Quitman St., Denver, CO 80219/303-935-3850
Rocky Mountain Cartridge Collectors Assn.
John Roth, P.O. Box 757, Conifer, CO 80433

CONNECTICUT

Ye Connecticut Gun Guild, Inc.
Dick Fraser, P.O. Box 425, Windsor, CT 06095

FLORIDA

Unified Sportsmen of Florida
P.O. Box 6565, Tallahassee, FL 32314

GEORGIA

Georgia Arms Collectors Assn., Inc.
Michael Kindberg, President, P.O. Box 277, Alpharetta, GA 30239-0277

ILLINOIS

Illinois State Rifle Assn.
P.O. Box 637, Chatsworth, IL 60921
Mississippi Valley Gun & Cartridge Coll. Assn.
Bob Filbert, P.O. Box 61, Port Byron, IL 61275/309-523-2593
Sauk Trail Gun Collectors
Gordell M. Matson, P.O. Box 1113, Milan, IL 61264
Wabash Valley Gun Collectors Assn., Inc.
Roger L. Dorsett, 2601 Willow Rd., Urbana, IL 61801/217-384-7302

INDIANA

Indiana State Rifle & Pistol Assn.
Thos. Glancy, P.O. Box 552, Chesterton, IN 46304
Southern Indiana Gun Collectors Assn., Inc.
Sheila McClary, 309 W. Monroe St., Boonville, IN 47601/812-897-3742

IOWA

Beaver Creek Plainsmen Inc.
Steve Murphy, Secy., P.O. Box 298, Bondurant, IA 50035
Central States Gun Collectors Assn.
Dennis Greischar, Box 841, Mason City, IA 50402-0841

KANSAS

Kansas Cartridge Collectors Assn.
Bob Linder, Box 84, Plainville, KS 67663

KENTUCKY

Kentuckiana Arms Collectors Assn.
Charles Billips, President, Box 1776, Louisville, KY 40201
Kentucky Gun Collectors Assn., Inc.
Ruth Johnson, Box 64, Owensboro, KY 42302/502-729-4197

LOUISIANA

Washitaw River Renegades
Sandra Rushing, P.O. Box 256, Main St., Grayson, LA 71435

MARYLAND

Baltimore Antique Arms Assn.
Mr. Cillo, 1034 Main St., Darlington, MD 21304

MASSACHUSETTS

Bay Colony Weapons Collectors, Inc.
John Brandt, Box 111, Hingham, MA 02043
Massachusetts Arms Collectors
Bruce E. Skinner, P.O. Box 31, No. Carver, MA 02355/508-866-5259

MICHIGAN

Association for the Study and Research of .22 Caliber Rimfire Cartridges
George Kass, 4512 Nakoma Dr., Okemos, MI 48864

MINNESOTA

Sioux Empire Cartridge Collectors Assn.
Bob Cameron, 14597 Glendale Ave. SE, Prior Lake, MN 55372

MISSISSIPPI

Mississippi Gun Collectors Assn.
Jack E. Swinney, P.O. Box 16323, Hattiesburg, MS 39402

MISSOURI

Greater St. Louis Cartridge Collectors Assn.
Don MacChesney, 634 Scottsdale Rd., Kirkwood, MO 63122-1109
Mineral Belt Gun Collectors Assn.
D.F. Saunders, 1110 Cleveland Ave., Monett, MO 65708
Missouri Valley Arms Collectors Assn., Inc.
L.P Brammer II, Membership Secy., P.O. Box 33033, Kansas City, MO 64114

MONTANA

Montana Arms Collectors Assn.
Dean E. Yearout, Sr., Exec. Secy., 1516 21st Ave. S., Great Falls, MT 59405
Weapons Collectors Society of Montana
R.G. Schipf, Ex. Secy., 3100 Bancroft St., Missoula, MT 59801/406-728-2995

NEBRASKA

Nebraska Cartridge Collectors Club
Gary Muckel, P.O. Box 84442, Lincoln, NE 68501

NEW HAMPSHIRE

New Hampshire Arms Collectors, Inc.
James Stamatelos, Secy., P.O. Box 5, Cambridge, MA 02139

NEW JERSEY

Englishtown Benchrest Shooters Assn.
Michael Toth, 64 Cooke Ave., Carteret, NJ 07008
Jersey Shore Antique Arms Collectors
Joe Sisia, P.O. Box 100, Bayville, NJ 08721-0100
New Jersey Arms Collectors Club, Inc.
Angus Laidlaw, Vice President, 230 Valley Rd., Montclair, NJ 07042/201-746-0939; e-mail: acclaidlaw@juno.com

NEW YORK

Iroquois Arms Collectors Assn.
Bonnie Robinson, Show Secy., P.O. Box 142, Ransomville, NY 14131/716-791-4096
Mid-State Arms Coll. & Shooters Club
Jack Ackerman, 24 S. Mountain Terr., Binghamton, NY 13903

NORTH CAROLINA

North Carolina Gun Collectors Assn.
Jerry Ledford, 3231-7th St. Dr. NE, Hickory, NC 28601

OHIO

Ohio Gun Collectors Assn.
P.O. Box 9007, Maumee, OH 43537-9007/419-897-0861; Fax:419-897-0860
Shotshell Historical and Collectors Society
Madeline Bruemmer, 3886 Dawley Rd., Ravenna, OH 44266
The Stark Gun Collectors, Inc.
William I. Gann, 5666 Waynesburg Dr., Waynesburg, OH 44688

OREGON

Oregon Arms Collectors Assn., Inc.
Phil Bailey, P.O. Box 13000-A, Portland, OR 97213-0017/503-281-6864; off.:503-281-0918
Oregon Cartridge Collectors Assn.
Boyd Northrup, P.O. Box 285, Rhododendron, OR 97049

PENNSYLVANIA

Presque Isle Gun Collectors Assn.
James Welch, 156 E. 37 St., Erie, PA 16504

SOUTH CAROLINA

Belton Gun Club, Inc.
Attn. Secretary, P.O. Box 126, Belton, SC 29627/864-369-6767

Gun Owners of South Carolina
Membership Div.: William Strozier, Secretary, P.O. Box 70, Johns Island, SC 29457-0070/803-762-3240; Fax:803-795-0711; e-mail:76053.222@compuserve.com

SOUTH DAKOTA

Dakota Territory Gun Coll. Assn., Inc.
Curt Carter, Castlewood, SD 57223

TENNESSEE

Smoky Mountain Gun Coll. Assn., Inc.
Hugh W. Yabro, President, P.O. Box 23225, Knoxville, TN 37933
Tennessee Gun Collectors Assn., Inc.
M.H. Parks, 3556 Pleasant Valley Rd., Nashville, TN 37204-3419

TEXAS

Houston Gun Collectors Assn., Inc.
P.O. Box 741429, Houston, TX 77274-1429
Texas Gun Collectors Assn.
Bob Eder, Pres., P.O. Box 12067, El Paso, TX 79913/915-584-8183
Texas State Rifle Assn.
1131 Rockingham Dr., Suite 101, Richardson, TX 75080-4326

VIRGINIA

Virginia Gun Collectors Assn., Inc.
Addison Hurst, Secy., 38802 Charlestown Height, Waterford, VA 20197/540-882-3543

WASHINGTON

Association of Cartridge Collectors on the Pacific Northwest
Robert Jardin, 14214 Meadowlark Drive KPN, Gig Harbor, WA 98329
Washington Arms Collectors, Inc.
Joyce Boss, P.O. Box 389, Renton, WA, 98057-0389/206-255-8410

WISCONSIN

Great Lakes Arms Collectors Assn., Inc.
Edward C. Warnke, 2913 Woodridge Lane, Waukesha, WI 53188
Wisconsin Gun Collectors Assn., Inc.
Lulita Zellmer, P.O. Box 181, Sussex, WI 53089

WYOMING

Wyoming Weapons Collectors
P.O. Box 284, Laramie, WY 82073/307-745-4652 or 745-9530

NATIONAL ORGANIZATIONS

Amateur Trapshooting Assn.
David D. Bopp, Exec. Director, 601 W. National Rd., Vandalia, OH 45377/937-898-4638; Fax:937-898-5472
American Airgun Field Target Assn.
5911 Cherokee Ave., Tampa, FL 33604
American Coon Hunters Assn.
Opal Johnston, P.O. Cadet, Route 1, Box 492, Old Mines, MO 63630
American Custom Gunmakers Guild
Jan Billeb, Exec. Director, 22 Vista View Drive, Cody, WY 82414-9606 (307) 587-4297 (phone/fax). Email: acgg@acgg.org Website: www.acgg.org
American Defense Preparedness Assn.
Two Colonial Place, 2101 Wilson Blvd., Suite 400, Arlington, VA 22201-3061
American Paintball League
P.O. Box 3561, Johnson City, TN 37602/800-541-9169
American Pistolsmiths Guild
Alex B. Hamilton, Pres., 1449 Blue Crest Lane, San Antonio, TX 78232/210-494-3063
American Police Pistol & Rifle Assn.
3801 Biscayne Blvd., Miami, FL 33137
American Single Shot Rifle Assn.
Gary Staup, Secy., 709 Carolyn Dr., Delphos, OH 45833/419-692-3866. Website: www.assra.com
American Society of Arms Collectors
George E. Weatherly, P.O. Box 2567, Waxahachie, TX 75165
American Tactical Shooting Assn.(A.T.S.A.)
c/o Skip Gochenour, 2600 N. Third St., Harrisburg, PA 17110/717-233-0402; Fax:717-233-5340
Association of Firearm and Tool Mark Examiners
Lannie G. Emanuel, Secy., Southwest Institute of Forensic Sciences, P.O. Box 35728, Dallas, TX 75235/214-920-5979; Fax:214-920-5928; Membership Secy., Ann D. Jones, VA Div. of Forensic Science, P.O. Box 999, Richmond, VA 23208/804-786-4706; Fax:804-371-8328
Boone & Crockett Club
250 Station Dr., Missoula, MT 59801-2753
Browning Collectors Assn.
Secretary:Scherrie L. Brennac, 2749 Keith Dr., Villa Ridge, MO 63089/314-742-0571
The Cast Bullet Assn., Inc.
Ralland J. Fortier, Editor, 4103 Foxcraft Dr., Traverse City, MI 49684
Citizens Committee for the Right to Keep and Bear Arms
Natl. Hq., Liberty Park, 12500 NE Tenth Pl., Bellevue, WA 98005
Colt Collectors Assn.
25000 Highland Way, Los Gatos, CA 95030/408-353-2658.
Contemporary Longrifle Association
P.O. Box 2097, Staunton, VA 24402/540-886-6189. Website: www.CLA@longrifle.ws
Ducks Unlimited, Inc.
Natl. Headquarters, One Waterfowl Way, Memphis, TN 38120/901-758-3937
Fifty Caliber Shooters Assn.
PO Box 111, Monroe UT 84754-0111
Firearms Coalition/Neal Knox Associates
Box 6537, Silver Spring, MD 20906/301-871-3006
Firearms Engravers Guild of America
Rex C. Pedersen, Secy., 511 N. Rath Ave., Lundington, MI 49431/616-845-7695(Phone and Fax)
Foundation for North American Wild Sheep
720 Allen Ave., Cody, WY 82414-3402/web site: http://iigi.com/os/non/fnaws/fnaws.htm; e-mail: fnaws@wyoming.com
Freedom Arms Collectors Assn.
P.O. Box 160302, Miami, FL 33116-0302
Garand Collectors Assn.
P.O. Box 181, Richmond, KY 40475
Glock Collectors Association
P.O. Box 1063, Maryland Heights, MO 63043/314-878-2061 phone/FAX.
Glock Shooting Sports Foundation
BO Box 309, Smyrna GA 30081 770-432-1202 Website: www.gssfonline.com
Golden Eagle Collectors Assn. (G.E.C.A.)
Chris Showler, 11144 Slate Creek Rd., Grass Valley, CA 95945
Gun Owners of America
8001 Forbes Place, Suite 102, Springfield, VA 22151/703-321-8585
Handgun Hunters International
J.D. Jones, Director, P.O. Box 357

Arms Associations

MAG, Bloomingdale, OH 43910
Harrington & Richardson Gun Coll. Assn.
George L. Cardet, 330 S.W. 27th Ave., Suite 603, Miami, FL 33135
High Standard Collectors' Assn.
John J. Stimson, Jr., Pres., 540 W. 92nd St., Indianapolis, IN 46260 Website: www.highstandard.org
Hopkins & Allen Arms & Memorabilia Society (HAAMS)
P.O. Box 187, 1309 Pamela Circle, Delphos, OH 45833
International Ammunition Association, Inc.
C.R. Punnett, Secy., 8 Hillock Lane, Chadds Ford, PA 19317/610-358-1285;Fax:610-358-1560
International Benchrest Shooters
Joan Borden, RR1, Box 250BB, Springville, PA 18844/717-965-2366
International Blackpowder Hunting Assn.
P.O. Box 1180, Glenrock, WY 82637/307-436-9817
IHMSA (Intl. Handgun Metallic Silhouette Assn.)
PO Box 368, Burlington, IA 52601 Website: www.ihmsa.org
International Society of Mauser Arms Collectors
Michael Kindberg, Pres., P.O. Box 277, Alpharetta, GA 30239-0277
Jews for the Preservation of Firearms Ownership (JPFO) 501(c)(3)
2872 S. Wentworth Ave., Milwaukee, WI 53207/414-769-0760; Fax:414-483-8435
The Mannlicher Collectors Assn.
Membership Office: P.O. Box1249, The Dalles, Oregon 97058
Marlin Firearms Collectors Assn., Ltd.
Dick Paterson, Secy., 407 Lincoln Bldg., 44 Main St., Champaign, IL 61820
Merwin Hulbert Association,
2503 Kentwood Ct., High Point, NC 27265
Miniature Arms Collectors/Makers Society, Ltd.
Ralph Koebbeman, Pres., 4910 Kilburn Ave., Rockford, IL 61101/815-964-2569
M1 Carbine Collectors Assn. (M1-CCA)
623 Apaloosa Ln., Gardnerville, NV 89410-7840
National Association of Buckskinners (NAB)
Territorial Dispatch—1800s Historical Publication, 4701 Marion St., Suite 324, Livestock Exchange Bldg., Denver, CO 80216/303-297-9671
The National Association of Derringer Collectors
P.O. Box 20572, San Jose, CA 95160
National Assn. of Federally Licensed Firearms Dealers
Andrew Molchan, 2455 E. Sunrise, Ft. Lauderdale, FL 33304
National Association to Keep and Bear Arms
P.O. Box 78336, Seattle, WA 98178
National Automatic Pistol Collectors Assn.
Tom Knox, P.O. Box 15738, Tower Grove Station, St. Louis, MO 63163
National Bench Rest Shooters Assn., Inc.
Pat Ferrell, 2835 Guilford Lane, Oklahoma City, OK 73120-4404/405-842-9585; Fax: 405-842-9575
National Muzzle Loading Rifle Assn.
Box 67, Friendship, IN 47021 / 812-667-5131. Website: www.nmlra@nmlra.org
National Professional Paintball League (NPPL)
540 Main St., Mount Kisco, NY 10549/914-241-7400
National Reloading Manufacturers Assn.
One Centerpointe Dr., Suite 300, Lake Oswego, OR 97035
National Rifle Assn. of America
11250 Waples Mill Rd., Fairfax, VA 22030 / 703-267-1000. Website: www.nra.org
National Shooting Sports Foundation, Inc.
Doug Painter, President, Flintlock Ridge Office Center, 11 Mile Hill Rd., Newtown, CT 06470-2359/203-426-1320; FAX: 203-426-1087
National Skeet Shooting Assn.
Dan Snyuder, Director, 5931 Roft Road, San Antonio, TX 78253-9261/800-877-5338. Website: nssa-nsca.com
National Sporting Clays Association
Ann Myers, Director, 5931 Roft Road, San Antonio, TX 78253-9261/800-877-5338. Website: nssa-nsca.com
National Wild Turkey Federation, Inc.
P.O. Box 530, 770 Augusta Rd., Edgefield, SC 29824
North American Hunting Club
P.O. Box 3401, Minnetonka, MN 55343/612-936-9333; Fax: 612-936-9755
North American Paintball Referees Association (NAPRA)
584 Cestaric Dr., Milpitas, CA 95035
North-South Skirmish Assn., Inc.
Stevan F. Meserve, Exec. Secretary, 507 N. Brighton Court, Sterling, VA 20164-3919
Old West Shooter's Association
712 James Street, Hazel TX 76020 817-444-2049
Remington Society of America
Gordon Fosburg, Secretary, 11900 North Brinton Road, Lake, MI 48623
Rocky Mountain Elk Foundation
P.O. Box 8249, Missoula, MT 59807-8249/406-523-4500;Fax: 406-523-4581 Website: www.rmef.org
Ruger Collector's Assn., Inc.
P.O. Box 240, Greens Farms, CT 06436
Safari Club International
4800 W. Gates Pass Rd., Tucson, AZ 85745/520-620-1220
Sako Collectors Assn., Inc.
Jim Lutes, 202 N. Locust, Whitewater, KS 67154
Second Amendment Foundation
James Madison Building, 12500 NE 10th Pl., Bellevue, WA 98005
Single Action Shooting Society (SASS)
23255-A La Palma Avenue, Yorba Linda, CA 92887/714-694-1800; FAX: 714-694-1815/email: sasseot@aol.com Website: www.sassnet.com
Smith & Wesson Collectors Assn.
Cally Pletl, Admin. Asst.,PO Box 444, Afton, NY 13730
The Society of American Bayonet Collectors
P.O. Box 234, East Islip, NY 11730-0234
Southern California Schuetzen Society
Dean Lillard, 34657 Ave. E., Yucaipa, CA 92399
Sporting Arms and Ammunition Manufacturers' Institute (SAAMI)
Flintlock Ridge Office Center, 11 Mile Hill Rd., Newtown, CT 06470-2359/203-426-4358; FAX: 203-426-1087
Sporting Clays of America (SCA)
Ron L. Blosser, Pres., 9257 Buckeye Rd., Sugar Grove, OH 43155-9632/614-746-8334; Fax: 614-746-8605
Steel Challenge
23234 Via Barra, Valencia CA 91355 Website: www.steelchallenge.com
The Thompson/Center Assn.
Joe Wright, President, Box 792, Northboro, MA 01532/508-845-6960
U.S. Practical Shooting Assn./IPSC
Dave Thomas, P.O. Box 811, Sedro Woolley, WA 98284/360-855-2245 Website: www.uspsa.org
U.S. Revolver Assn.
Brian J. Barer, 40 Larchmont Ave., Taunton, MA 02780/508-824-4836
U.S.A. Shooting
U.S. Olympic Shooting Center, One Olympic Plaza, Colorado Springs, CO 80909/719-578-4670. Website: wwwusashooting.org
The Varmint Hunters Assn., Inc.
Box 759, Pierre, SD 57501/Member Services 800-528-4868
Weatherby Collectors Assn., Inc.
P.O. Box 478, Pacific, MO 63069 Website: www.weatherbycollectors.com Email: WCAsecretary@aol.com
The Wildcatters
P.O. Box 170, Greenville, WI 54942
Winchester Arms Collectors Assn.
P.O. Box 230, Brownsboro, TX 75756/903-852-4027
The Women's Shooting Sports Foundation (WSSF)
4620 Edison Avenue, Ste. C, Colorado Springs, CO 80915/719-638-1299; FAX: 719-638-1271/email: wssf@worldnet.att.net

ARGENTINA

Asociacion Argentina de Coleccionistas de Armes y Municiones
Castilla de Correos No. 28, Succursal I B, 1401 Buenos Aires, Republica Argentina

AUSTRALIA

Antique & Historical Arms Collectors of Australia
P.O. Box 5654, GCMC Queensland 9726, Australia
The Arms Collector's Guild of Queensland, Inc.
Ian Skennerton, P.O. Box 433, Ashmore City 4214, Queensland, Australia
Australian Cartridge Collectors Assn., Inc.
Bob Bennett, 126 Landscape Dr., E. Doncaster 3109, Victoria, Australia
Sporting Shooters Assn. of Australia, Inc.
P.O. Box 2066, Kent Town, SA 5071, Australia

BRAZIL

Associaçao de Armaria Coleçao e Tiro (ACOLTI)
Rua do Senado, 258 - 2 andar, Centro, Rio de Janeiro - RJ - 20231-002 Brazil / tel: 0055-21-31817989

CANADA

ALBERTA

Canadian Historical Arms Society
P.O. Box 901, Edmonton, Alb., Canada T5J 2L8
National Firearms Assn.
Natl. Hq: P.O. Box 1779, Edmonton, Alb., Canada T5J 2P1

BRITISH COLUMBIA

The Historical Arms Collectors of B.C. (Canada)
Harry Moon, Pres., P.O. Box 50117, South Slope RPO, Burnaby, BC V5J 5G3, Canada/604-438-0950; Fax:604-277-3646

ONTARIO

Association of Canadian Cartridge Collectors
Monica Wright, RR 1, Millgrove, ON, LOR IVO, Canada
Tri-County Antique Arms Fair
P.O. Box 122, RR #1, North Lancaster, Ont., Canada K0C 1Z0

EUROPE

BELGIUM

European Cartridge Research Assn.
Graham Irving, 21 Rue Schaltin, 4900 Spa, Belgium/32.87.77.43.40; Fax:32.87.77.27.51

CZECHOSLOVAKIA

Spolecnost Pro Studium Naboju (Czech Cartridge Research Assn.)
JUDr. Jaroslav Bubak, Pod Homolko 1439, 26601 Beroun 2, Czech Republic

DENMARK

Aquila Dansk Jagtpatron Historic Forening (Danish Historical Cartridge Collectors Club)
Steen Elgaard Møller, Ulriksdalsvej 7, 4840 Nr. Alslev, Denmark 10045-53846218;Fax:00455384 6209

ENGLAND

Arms and Armour Society
Hon. Secretary A. Dove, P.O. Box 10232, London, 5W19 2ZD, England
Dutch Paintball Federation
Aceville Publ., Castle House 97 High Street, Colchester, Essex C01 1TH, England/011-44-206-564840
European Paintball Sports Foundation
c/o Aceville Publ., Castle House 97 High St., Colchester, Essex, C01 1TH, England
Historical Breechloading Smallarms Assn.
D.J. Penn M.A., Secy., P.O. Box 12778, London SE1 6BX, England. Journal and newsletter are $23 a yr., including airmail.
National Rifle Assn.
(Great Britain) Bisley Camp, Brookwood, Woking Surrey GU24 OPB, England/01483.797777; Fax: 014730686275
United Kingdom Cartridge Club
Ian Southgate, 20 Millfield, Elmley Castle, Nr. Pershore, Worcestershire, WR10 3HR, England

FRANCE

STAC-Western Co.
3 Ave. Paul Doumer (N.311); 78360 Montesson, France/01.30.53-43-65; Fax: 01.30.53.19.10

GERMANY

Bund Deutscher Sportschützen e.v. (BDS)
Borsigallee 10, 53125 Bonn 1, Germany
Deutscher Schützenbund
Lahnstrasse 120, 65195 Wiesbaden, Germany

NORWAY

Scandinavian Ammunition Research Assn.
c/o Morten Stoen, Annerudstubben 3, N-1383 Asker, Norway

NEW ZEALAND

New Zealand Cartridge Collectors Club
Terry Castle, 70 Tiraumea Dr., Pakuranga, Auckland, New Zealand
New Zealand Deerstalkers Assn.
P.O. Box 6514 TE ARO, Wellington, New Zealand

SOUTH AFRICA

Historical Firearms Soc. of South Africa
P.O. Box 145, 7725 Newlands, Republic of South Africa
Republic of South Africa Cartridge Collectors Assn.
Arno Klee, 20 Eugene St., Malanshof Randburg, Gauteng 2194, Republic of South Africa
S.A.A.C.A. (Southern Africa Arms and Ammunition Assn.)
Gauteng office: P.O. Box 7597, Weltevreden Park, 1715, Republic of South Africa/011-679-1151; Fax: 011-679-1131; e-mail: saaaca@iafrica.com.
Kwa-Zulu Natal office: P.O. Box 4065, Northway, Kwazulu-Natal 4065, Republic of South Africa
SAGA (S.A. Gunowners' Assn.)
P.O. Box 35203, Northway, Kwazulu-Natal 4065, Republic of South Africa

SPAIN

Asociacion Espanola de Colleccionistas de Cartuchos (A.E.C.C.)
Secretary: Apdo. Correos No. 1086, 2880-Alcala de Henares (Madrid), Spain. President: Apdo. Correos No. 682, 50080 Zaragoza, Spain

2005 GUN DIGEST DIRECTORY OF THE ARMS TRADE

The **Product Directory** contains 84 product categories. The **Manufacturer's Directory** alphabetically lists the manufacturers with their addresses, phone numbers, FAX numbers and Internet addresses, if available.

DIRECTORY OF THE ARMS TRADE INDEX

PRODUCT & SERVICE DIRECTORY

AMMUNITION COMPONENTS, SHOTSHELL

A.W. Peterson Gun Shop, Inc.
Ballistic Products, Inc.
Blount, Inc., Sporting Equipment Div.
CCI/Speer Div of ATK
Cheddite, France S.A.
Claybuster Wads & Harvester Bullets
Garcia National Gun Traders, Inc.
Guncrafter Industries
Peterson Gun Shop, Inc., A.W.
Precision Reloading, Inc.
Ravell Ltd.
Tar-Hunt Custom Rifles, Inc.
The A.W. Peterson Gun Shop, Inc.
Vitt/Boos

AMMUNITION COMPONENTS--BULLETS, POWDER, PRIMERS, CASES

A.W. Peterson Gun Shop, Inc.
Acadian Ballistic Specialties
Accuracy Unlimited
Accurate Arms Co., Inc.
Action Bullets & Alloy Inc.
ADCO Sales, Inc.
Alaska Bullet Works, Inc.
Alex, Inc.
Alliant Techsystems Smokeless Powder Group
Allred Bullet Co.
Alpha LaFranck Enterprises
American Products, Inc.
Arizona Ammunition, Inc.
Armfield Custom Bullets
A-Square Co.
Atlantic Rose, Inc.
Baer's Hollows
Ballard Rifle & Cartridge Co., LLC
Barnes
Barnes Bullets, Inc.
Beartooth Bullets
Bell Reloading, Inc.
Berger Bullets Ltd.
Berry's Mfg., Inc.
Big Bore Bullets of Alaska
Big Bore Express
Bitterroot Bullet Co.
Black Belt Bullets
(See Big Bore Express)
Black Hills Shooters Supply
Black Powder Products
Blount, Inc., Sporting Equipment Div.
Blue Mountain Bullets
Brenneke GmbH
Briese Bullet Co., Inc.
Brown Co., E. Arthur
Brown Dog Ent.
BRP, Inc. High Performance Cast Bullets
Buck Stix-SOS Products Co.
Buckeye Custom Bullets
Buckskin Bullet Co.
Buffalo Arms Co.
Buffalo Bullet Co., Inc.
Buffalo Rock Shooters Supply
Bull-X, Inc.
Butler Enterprises
Calhoon Mfg.
Cambos Outdoorsman
Canyon Cartridge Corp.
Cascade Bullet Co., Inc.
Cast Performance Bullet Company
Casull Arms Corp.
CCI/Speer Div of ATK
Champion's Choice, Inc.
Cheddite, France S.A.
CheVron Bullets
Chuck's Gun Shop
Clean Shot Technologies
Competitor Corp., Inc.
Cook Engineering Service
Corbin Mfg. & Supply, Inc.
Cummings Bullets
Curtis Cast Bullets
Curtis Gun Shop
(See Curtis Cast Bullets)
Custom Bullets by Hoffman
D.L. Unmussig Bullets
Dakota Arms, Inc.
Davide Pedersoli and Co.
DKT, Inc.
Dohring Bullets
Dutchman's Firearms, Inc.
Eichelberger Bullets, Wm.
Federal Cartridge Co.
Fiocchi of America, Inc.
Forkin Custom Classics
Fowler Bullets
Fowler, Bob
(See Black Powder Products)
Freedom Arms, Inc.
Garcia National Gun Traders, Inc.
Gehmann, Walter
(See Huntington Die Specialties)
GOEX, Inc.
Golden Bear Bullets
Gotz Bullets
Grayback Wildcats
Green Mountain Rifle Barrel Co., Inc.
Grier's Hard Cast Bullets
GTB-Custom Bullets
Gun City
Harris Enterprises
Harrison Bullets
Hart & Son, Inc.
Hawk Laboratories, Inc.
(See Hawk, Inc.)
Hawk, Inc.
Heidenstrom Bullets
Hercules, Inc. (See Alliant Techsystems, Smokeless)
Hi-Performance Ammunition Company
Hirtenberger AG
Hobson Precision Mfg. Co.
Hodgdon Powder Co.
Hornady Mfg. Co.
HT Bullets
Hunters Supply, Inc.
Huntington Die Specialties
Impact Case & Container, Inc.
Imperial Magnum Corp.
IMR Powder Co.
Intercontinental Distributors, Ltd.
J&D Components
J&L Superior Bullets
(See Huntington Die Special)
J.R. Williams Bullet Co.
Jamison International
Jensen Bullets
Jensen's Firearms Academy
Jericho Tool & Die Co., Inc.
Jester Bullets
JLK Bullets
JRP Custom Bullets
Ka Pu Kapili
Kaswer Custom, Inc.
Keith's Bullets
Keng's Firearms Specialty, Inc./US Tactical Systems
Ken's Kustom Kartridges
Knight Rifles
Knight Rifles
(See Modern Muzzle Loading, Inc.)
Lapua Ltd.
Lawrence Brand Shot
(See Precision Reloading)
Liberty Shooting Supplies
Lightning Performance Innovations, Inc.
Lindsley Arms Cartridge Co.
Littleton, J. F.
Lomont Precision Bullets
Lyman Products Corp.
Magnus Bullets
Maine Custom Bullets
Marchmon Bullets
Markesbery Muzzle Loaders, Inc.
MarMik, Inc.
Marshall Fish Mfg. Gunsmith Sptg. Co.
MAST Technology, Inc.
McMurdo, Lynn
(See Specialty Gunsmithing)
Meister Bullets (See Gander Mountain)
Men-Metallwerk Elisenhuette GmbH
Merkuria Ltd.
Midway Arms, Inc.
Mitchell Bullets, R.F.
MI-TE Bullets
Montana Precision Swaging
Mountain State Muzzleloading Supplies, Inc.
Mulhern, Rick
Murmur Corp.
Nagel's Custom Bullets
National Bullet Co.
Naval Ordnance Works
North American Shooting Systems
North Devon Firearms Services
Northern Precision
Nosler, Inc.
OK Weber, Inc.
Oklahoma Ammunition Co.
Old Wagon Bullets
Old Western Scrounger Ammunition Inc.
Oregon Trail Bullet Company
Pacific Rifle Co.
Page Custom Bullets
Pease Accuracy
Penn Bullets
Peterson Gun Shop, Inc., A.W.
Petro-Explo Inc.
Phillippi Custom Bullets, Justin
Pinetree Bullets
PMC/Eldorado Cartridge Corp.
Polywad, Inc.
Pony Express Reloaders
Power Plus Enterprises, Inc.
Precision Delta Corp.
Prescott Projectile Co.
Price Bullets, Patrick W.
PRL Bullets, c/o Blackburn Enterprises
Professional Hunter Supplies
(See Star Custom Bullets)
Proofmark Corp.
PWM Sales Ltd.
Quality Cartridge
Quarton Beamshot
R.I.S. Co., Inc.
Rainier Bmiscallistics
Ramon B. Gonzalez Guns
Ravell Ltd.
Redwood Bullet Works
Reloading Specialties, Inc.
Remington Arms Co., Inc.
Rhino
Robinson H.V. Bullets
Rubright Bullets
Russ Haydon's Shooters' Supply
SAECO (See Redding Reloading Equipment)
Scharch Mfg., Inc.-Top Brass
Schneider Bullets
Schroeder Bullets
Schumakers Gun Shop
Scot Powder
Seebeck Assoc., R.E.
Shappy Bullets
Sharps Arms Co., Inc., C.
Shilen, Inc.
Sierra Bullets
SOS Products Co.
(See Buck Stix-SOS Products Co.)
Southern Ammunition Co., Inc.
Specialty Gunsmithing
Speer Bullets
Spencer's Rifle Barrels, Inc.
SSK Industries
Stanley Bullets
Star Ammunition, Inc.
Star Custom Bullets
Starke Bullet Company
Starline, Inc.
Stewart's Gunsmithing
Swift Bullet Co.
T.F.C. S.p.A.
Taracorp Industries, Inc.
Tar-Hunt Custom Rifles, Inc.
TCCI
TCSR
The A.W. Peterson Gun Shop, Inc.
The Gun Works
The Ordnance Works
Thompson Bullet Lube Co.
Thompson Precision
TMI Products
(See Haselbauer Products, Jerry)
Traditions Performance Firearms
Trico Plastics
True Flight Bullet Co.
Tucson Mold, Inc.
USAC
Vann Custom Bullets
Vihtavuori Oy/Kaltron-Pettibone
Vincent's Shop
Viper Bullet and Brass Works
Walters Wads
Warren Muzzleloading Co., Inc.
Watson Bullets
Western Nevada West Coast Bullets
Widener's Reloading & Shooting Supply, Inc.
Winchester Div. Olin Corp.
Winkle Bullets
Woodleigh
(See Huntington Die Specialties)
Worthy Products, Inc.
Wyant Bullets
Wyoming Custom Bullets
Zero Ammunition Co., Inc.

AMMUNITION, COMMERCIAL

3-Ten Corp.
A.W. Peterson Gun Shop, Inc.
Ace Custom 45's, Inc.
Ad Hominem
Air Arms
American Ammunition
Arizona Ammunition, Inc.
Arms Corporation of the Philippines
Arundel Arms & Ammunition, Inc., A.
A-Square Co.
Atlantic Rose, Inc.
Badger Shooters Supply, Inc.
Ballistic Products, Inc.
Benjamin/Sheridan Co., Crosman
Big Bear Arms & Sporting Goods, Inc.
Black Hills Ammunition, Inc.
Blammo Ammo
Blount, Inc., Sporting Equipment Div.
Brenneke GmbH
Buffalo Arms Co.
Buffalo Bullet Co., Inc.
Bull-X, Inc.
Cabela's
Cambos Outdoorsman
Casull Arms Corp.
CBC
CCI/Speer Div of ATK
Champion's Choice, Inc.
Cor-Bon Inc./Glaser LLC
Crosman Airguns
Cubic Shot Shell Co., Inc.
Daisy Outdoor Products
Dead Eye's Sport Center
Delta Arms Ltd.
Delta Frangible Ammunition LLC
Dutchman's Firearms, Inc.
Dynamit Nobel-RWS, Inc.
Effebi SNC-Dr. Franco Beretta
Eley Ltd.
Elite Ammunition
Estate Cartridge, Inc.
Federal Cartridge Co.
Fiocchi of America, Inc.
Garcia National Gun Traders, Inc.
Garrett Cartridges, Inc.
Garthwaite Pistolsmith, Inc., Jim
Gibbs Rifle Co., Inc.
Gil Hebard Guns, Inc.
Glaser LLC
Glaser Safety Slug, Inc.
GOEX, Inc.
Goodwin's Pawn Shop
Gun City
Guncrafter Industries
Hansen & Co.
Hart & Son, Inc.
Hi-Performance Ammunition Company
Hirtenberger AG
Hornady Mfg. Co.
Hunters Supply, Inc.
Intercontinental Distributors, Ltd.
Ion Industries, Inc.
Keng's Firearms Specialty, Inc./US Tactical Systems
Kent Cartridge America, Inc.
Knight Rifles
Lapua Ltd.
Lethal Force Institute
(See Police Bookshelf)
Lock's Philadelphia Gun Exchange
Lomont Precision Bullets
Magnum Research, Inc.
MagSafe Ammo Co.
Mandall Shooting Supplies Inc.
Markell, Inc.
Marshall Fish Mfg. Gunsmith Sptg. Co.
McBros Rifle Co.
Men-Metallwerk Elisenhuette GmbH
Mullins Ammunition
New England Ammunition Co.
Oklahoma Ammunition Co.
Old Western Scrounger Ammunition Inc.
Outdoor Sports Headquarters, Inc.
P.S.M.G. Gun Co.
Paragon Sales & Services, Inc.
Parker & Sons Shooting Supply
Peterson Gun Shop, Inc., A.W.
PMC/Eldorado Cartridge Corp.
Police Bookshelf
Polywad, Inc.
Pony Express Reloaders
Precision Delta Corp.
Pro Load Ammunition, Inc.
Quality Cartridge
R.E.I.
Ravell Ltd.
Remington Arms Co., Inc.
Rucker Dist. Inc.
RWS (See U.S. Importer-Dynamit Nobel-RWS, Inc.)
Sellier & Bellot, USA, Inc.
Southern Ammunition Co., Inc.
Speer Bullets
TCCI
The A.W. Peterson Gun Shop, Inc.
The BulletMakers Workshop
The Gun Room Press
The Gun Works
Thompson Bullet Lube Co.
USAC
VAM Distribution Co. LLC

PRODUCT & SERVICE DIRECTORY

Victory USA
Vihtavuori Oy/Kaltron-Pettibone
Visible Impact Targets
Voere-KGH GmbH
Weatherby, Inc.
Westley Richards & Co. Ltd.
Whitestone Lumber Corp.
Widener's Reloading & Shooting Supply, Inc.
William E. Phillips Firearms
Winchester Div. Olin Corp.
Zero Ammunition Co., Inc.

AMMUNITION, CUSTOM

3-Ten Corp.
A.W. Peterson Gun Shop, Inc.
Accuracy Unlimited
AFSCO Ammunition
Allred Bullet Co.
American Derringer Corp.
American Products, Inc.
Arizona Ammunition, Inc.
Arms Corporation of the Philippines
Atlantic Rose, Inc.
Ballard Rifle & Cartridge Co., LLC
Bear Arms
Belding's Custom Gun Shop
Berger Bullets Ltd.
Big Bore Bullets of Alaska
Black Hills Ammunition, Inc.
Blue Mountain Bullets
Brynin, Milton
Buckskin Bullet Co.
Buffalo Arms Co.
CBC
CFVentures
Champlin Firearms, Inc.
Cubic Shot Shell Co., Inc.
Custom Tackle and Ammo
D.L. Unmussig Bullets
Dakota Arms, Inc.
Dead Eye's Sport Center
Delta Frangible Ammunition LLC
DKT, Inc.
Dutchman's Firearms, Inc.
Elite Ammunition
Estate Cartridge, Inc.
GDL Enterprises
GOEX, Inc.
Grayback Wildcats
Hawk, Inc.
Hirtenberger AG
Hobson Precision Mfg. Co.
Horizons Unlimited
Hornady Mfg. Co.
Hunters Supply, Inc.
Jensen Bullets
Jensen's Custom Ammunition
Jensen's Firearms Academy
Kaswer Custom, Inc.
L. E. Jurras & Assoc.
L.A.R. Mfg., Inc.
Lethal Force Institute (See Police Bookshelf)
Lindsley Arms Cartridge Co.
Linebaugh Custom Sixguns
Loch Leven Industries/Convert-A-Pell
MagSafe Ammo Co.
MAST Technology, Inc.
McBros Rifle Co.
McMurdo, Lynn (See Specialty Gunsmithing)
Men-Metallwerk Elisenhuette GmbH
Milstor Corp.
Mullins Ammunition
Oklahoma Ammunition Co.
P.S.M.G. Gun Co.
Peterson Gun Shop, Inc., A.W.
Phillippi Custom Bullets, Justin
Police Bookshelf
Power Plus Enterprises, Inc.
Precision Delta Corp.
Professional Hunter Supplies (See Star Custom Bullets)
Quality Cartridge
R.E.I.
Ramon B. Gonzalez Guns
Sandia Die & Cartridge Co.
SOS Products Co. (See Buck Stix-SOS Products Co.)
Specialty Gunsmithing
Spencer's Rifle Barrels, Inc.
SSK Industries
Star Custom Bullets
Stewart's Gunsmithing
TCCI
The A.W. Peterson Gun Shop, Inc.
The BulletMakers Workshop
The Country Armourer
Vitt/Boos
Vulpes Ventures, Inc., Fox Cartridge Division
Warren Muzzleloading Co., Inc.
Watson Bullets
Worthy Products, Inc.
Zero Ammunition Co., Inc.

AMMUNITION, FOREIGN

A.W. Peterson Gun Shop, Inc.
Ad Hominem
AFSCO Ammunition
Armscorp USA, Inc.
Atlantic Rose, Inc.
B&P America
Cape Outfitters
CBC
Cheddite, France S.A.
Cubic Shot Shell Co., Inc.
Dead Eye's Sport Center
DKT, Inc.
Dynamit Nobel-RWS, Inc.
E. Arthur Brown Co.
Fiocchi of America, Inc.
Gamebore Division, Polywad, Inc.
Gibbs Rifle Co., Inc.
GOEX, Inc.
Goodwin's Pawn Shop
Gunsmithing, Inc.
Hansen & Co.
Heidenstrom Bullets
Hirtenberger AG
Hornady Mfg. Co.
I.S.S.
Intrac Arms International
Jack First, Inc.
K.B.I. Inc.
MagSafe Ammo Co.
Mandall Shooting Supplies Inc.
Marksman Products
MAST Technology, Inc.
Merkuria Ltd.
Mullins Ammunition
Navy Arms Company
Oklahoma Ammunition Co.
P.S.M.G. Gun Co.
Paragon Sales & Services, Inc.
Peterson Gun Shop, Inc., A.W.
Petro-Explo Inc.
Precision Delta Corp.
R.E.T. Enterprises
Ramon B. Gonzalez Guns
RWS (See U.S. Importer-Dynamit Nobel-RWS, Inc.)
Samco Global Arms, Inc.
Sentinel Arms
Southern Ammunition Co., Inc.
Speer Bullets
Stratco, Inc.
T.F.C. S.p.A.
The A.W. Peterson Gun Shop, Inc.
The BulletMakers Workshop
The Paul Co.
Victory Ammunition
Vihtavuori Oy/Kaltron-Pettibone
Wolf Performance Ammunition

ANTIQUE ARMS DEALER

Ackerman & Co.
Ad Hominem
Antique American Firearms
Antique Arms Co.
Aplan Antiques & Art, James O.
Armoury, Inc., The
Arundel Arms & Ammunition, Inc., A.
Ballard Rifle & Cartridge Co., LLC
Bear Mountain Gun & Tool
Bob's Tactical Indoor Shooting Range & Gun Shop
Buffalo Arms Co.
Cape Outfitters
Carlson, Douglas R, Antique American Firearms
CBC-BRAZIL
Chadick's Ltd.
Chambers Flintlocks Ltd., Jim
Champlin Firearms, Inc.
Chuck's Gun Shop
Clements' Custom Leathercraft, Chas
Cole's Gun Works
D&D Gunsmiths, Ltd.
David R. Chicoine
Dixie Gun Works
Dixon Muzzleloading Shop, Inc.
Duffy, Charles E. (See Guns Antique & Modern DBA)
Ed's Gun House
Enguix Import-Export
Fagan Arms
Flayderman & Co., Inc.
George Madis Winchester Consultants
Getz Barrel Company
Glass, Herb
Goergen's Gun Shop, Inc.
Golden Age Arms Co.
Goodwin's Pawn Shop
Gun Hunter Books (See Gun Hunter Trading Co.)
Gun Hunter Trading Co.
Guns Antique & Modern DBA / Charles E. Duffy
Hallowell & Co.
Hammans, Charles E.
HandCrafts Unltd. (See Clements' Custom Leather)
Handgun Press
Hansen & Co.
Hunkeler, A. (See Buckskin Machine Works)
Imperial Miniature Armory
James Wayne Firearms for Collectors and Investors
Kelley's
Knight's Mfg. Co.
Ledbetter Airguns, Riley
LeFever Arms Co., Inc.
Lever Arms Service Ltd.
Lock's Philadelphia Gun Exchange
Log Cabin Sport Shop
Logdewood Mfg.
Mandall Shooting Supplies Inc.
Marshall Fish Mfg. Gunsmith Sptg. Co.
Martin's Gun Shop
Michael's Antiques
Mid-America Recreation, Inc.
Montana Outfitters, Lewis E. Yearout
Muzzleloaders Etcetera, Inc.
Navy Arms Company
New England Arms Co.
Olathe Gun Shop
P.S.M.G. Gun Co.
Peter Dyson & Son Ltd.
Pony Express Sport Shop
Powder Horn Ltd.
Ravell Ltd.
Reno, Wayne
Retting, Inc., Martin B.
Robert Valade Engraving
Rutgers Book Center
Samco Global Arms, Inc.
Sarco, Inc.
Scott Fine Guns Inc., Thad
Shootin' Shack
Sportsmen's Exchange & Western Gun Traders, Inc.
Steves House of Guns
Stott's Creek Armory, Inc.
The Gun Room
The Gun Room Press
The Gun Works
Turnbull Restoration, Doug
Vic's Gun Refinishing
Wallace, Terry
Westley Richards & Co. Ltd.
Wild West Guns
Winchester Sutler, Inc., The
Wood, Frank (See Classic Guns, Inc.)
Yearout, Lewis E. (See Montana Outfitters)

APPRAISER - GUNS, ETC.

A.W. Peterson Gun Shop, Inc.
Ackerman & Co.
Antique Arms Co.
Armoury, Inc., The
Arundel Arms & Ammunition, Inc., A.
Barta's Gunsmithing
Beitzinger, George
Blue Book Publications, Inc.
Bob's Tactical Indoor Shooting Range & Gun Shop
Bonham's & Butterfields
Bullet N Press
Cape Outfitters
Chadick's Ltd.
Champlin Firearms, Inc.
Christie's East
Chuilli, Stephen
Clark Firearms Engraving
Clements' Custom Leathercraft, Chas
Cole's Gun Works
Colonial Arms, Inc.
Colonial Repair
Corry, John
Custom Tackle and Ammo
D&D Gunsmiths, Ltd.
David R. Chicoine
DGR Custom Rifles
Dietz Gun Shop & Range, Inc.
Dixie Gun Works
Dixon Muzzleloading Shop, Inc.
Duane's Gun Repair (See DGR Custom Rifles)
Ed's Gun House
Eversull Co., Inc.
Fagan Arms
Ferris Firearms
Flayderman & Co., Inc.
Forty-Five Ranch Enterprises
Francotte & Cie S.A. Auguste
Frontier Arms Co., Inc.
Gene's Custom Guns
George Madis Winchester Consultants
Getz Barrel Company
Gillmann, Edwin
Goergen's Gun Shop, Inc.
Golden Age Arms Co.
Goodwin's Pawn Shop
Griffin & Howe, Inc.
Griffin & Howe, Inc.
Griffin & Howe, Inc.
Groenewold, John
Gun City
Gun Hunter Books (See Gun Hunter Trading Co.)
Gun Hunter Trading Co.
Guncraft Books (See Guncraft Sports, Inc.)
Guncraft Sports, Inc.
Guncraft Sports, Inc.
Gunsmithing, Inc.
Hallowell & Co.
Hammans, Charles E.
HandCrafts Unltd. (See Clements' Custom Leather)
Handgun Press
Hank's Gun Shop
Hansen & Co.
Irwin, Campbell H.
Island Pond Gun Shop
Ithaca Classic Doubles
Jackalope Gun Shop
James Wayne Firearms for Collectors and Investors
Jensen's Custom Ammunition
Kelley's
L.L. Bean, Inc.
Lampert, Ron
LaRocca Gun Works
Ledbetter Airguns, Riley
LeFever Arms Co., Inc.
Lock's Philadelphia Gun Exchange
Log Cabin Sport Shop
Logdewood Mfg.
Long, George F.
Mahony, Philip Bruce
Mandall Shooting Supplies Inc.
Marshall Fish Mfg. Gunsmith Sptg. Co.
Martin's Gun Shop
Mathews Gun Shop & Gunsmithing, Inc.
McCann Industries
Mercer Custom Guns
Montana Outfitters, Lewis E. Yearout
Muzzleloaders Etcetera, Inc.
Navy Arms Company
New England Arms Co.
Nitex Gun Shop
Olathe Gun Shop
P&M Sales & Services, LLC
P.S.M.G. Gun Co.
Pasadena Gun Center
Pentheny de Pentheny
Perazone-Gunsmith, Brian
Peterson Gun Shop, Inc., A.W.
Pettinger Books, Gerald
Pony Express Sport Shop
Powder Horn Ltd.
R.A. Wells Custom Gunsmith
R.E.T. Enterprises
Ramon B. Gonzalez Guns
Retting, Inc., Martin B.
Robert Valade Engraving
Rutgers Book Center
Scott Fine Guns Inc., Thad
Shootin' Shack
Spencer Reblue Service
Sportsmen's Exchange & Western Gun Traders, Inc.
Steven Dodd Hughes
Stott's Creek Armory, Inc.
Stratco, Inc.
Ten-Ring Precision, Inc.
The A.W. Peterson Gun Shop, Inc.
The Gun Room Press
The Gun Shop
The Gun Works
The Orvis Co.
The Swampfire Shop (See Peterson Gun Shop, Inc.)
Thurston Sports, Inc.
Vic's Gun Refinishing
Walker Arms Co., Inc.
Wallace, Terry
Wasmundt, Jim
Weber & Markin Custom Gunsmiths
Werth, T. W.
Whildin & Sons Ltd, E.H.
Whitestone Lumber Corp.
Wild West Guns
Williams Shootin' Iron Service, The Lynx-Line
Winchester Sutler, Inc., The

PRODUCT & SERVICE DIRECTORY

Wood, Frank (See Classic Guns, Inc.)
Yearout, Lewis E.
(See Montana Outfitters)

AUCTIONEER - GUNS, ETC.

"Little John's" Antique Arms
Bonham's & Butterfields
Buck Stix-SOS Products Co.
Christie's East
Fagan Arms
Pete de Coux Auction House
Sotheby's

BOOKS & MANUALS (PUBLISHERS & DEALERS)

"Su-Press-On", Inc.
Alpha 1 Drop Zone
American Handgunner Magazine
Armory Publications
Arms & Armour Press
Ballistic Products, Inc.
Ballistic Products, Inc.
Barnes Bullets, Inc.
Bauska Barrels
Beartooth Bullets
Beeman Precision Airguns
Blacksmith Corp.
Blacktail Mountain Books
Blue Book Publications, Inc.
Blue Ridge Machinery & Tools, Inc.
Boone's Custom Ivory Grips, Inc.
Brown Co., E. Arthur
Brownells, Inc.
Bullet N Press
C. Sharps Arms Co. Inc./Montana Armory
Cape Outfitters
Cheyenne Pioneer Products
Collector's Armoury, Ltd.
Colonial Repair
Corbin Mfg. & Supply, Inc.
DBI Books Division of Krause Publications
deHaas Barrels
Dixon Muzzleloading Shop, Inc.
Excalibur Publications
Executive Protection Institute
Fulton Armory
Galati International
GAR
Golden Age Arms Co.
Gun City
Gun Hunter Books
(See Gun Hunter Trading Co.)
Gun Hunter Trading Co.
Gun List (See Krause Publications)
Guncraft Books
(See Guncraft Sports, Inc.)
Guncraft Sports, Inc.
Gunnerman Books
GUNS Magazine
Gunsmithing, Inc.
H&P Publishing
Handgun Press
Harris Publications
Hawk Laboratories, Inc.
(See Hawk, Inc.)
Hawk, Inc.
Heritage/VSP Gun Books
Hodgdon Powder Co.
Home Shop Machinist, The Village Press Publications
Hornady Mfg. Co.
Huntington Die Specialties
I.D.S.A. Books
Info-Arm
Ironside International Publishers, Inc.
Jantz Supply
Kelley's
King & Co.
Koval Knives
Krause Publications, Inc.
L.B.T.
Lapua Ltd.
Lebeau-Courally
Lethal Force Institute
(See Police Bookshelf)
Lyman Products Corp.
Madis Books
Magma Engineering Co.
Mandall Shooting Supplies Inc.
MarMik, Inc.
Marshall Fish Mfg. Gunsmith Sptg. Co.
Montana Armory, Inc.
(See C. Sharps Arms Co. Inc.)
Montana Precision Swaging
Mountain State Muzzleloading Supplies, Inc.
Mulberry House Publishing
Navy Arms Company
Numrich Gun Parts Corporation
OK Weber, Inc.
Outdoor Sports Headquarters, Inc.
Paintball Games International Magazine Aceville
Pansch, Robert F
Pejsa Ballistics
Pettinger Books, Gerald
PFRB Co.
Police Bookshelf
Precision Reloading, Inc.
Precision Shooting, Inc.
Primedia Publishing Co.
Professional Hunter Supplies
(See Star Custom Bullets)
Ravell Ltd.
Ray Riling Arms Books Co.
Remington Double Shotguns
Russ Haydon's Shooters' Supply
Rutgers Book Center
S&S Firearms
Safari Press, Inc.
Saunders Gun & Machine Shop
Scharch Mfg., Inc.-Top Brass
Scharch Mfg., Inc.-Top Brass
Semmer, Charles
(See Remington Double Shotguns)
Sharps Arms Co., Inc., C.
Shotgun Sports Magazine, dba Shootin' Accessories Ltd.
Sierra Bullets
Speer Bullets
SPG LLC
Stackpole Books
Star Custom Bullets
Stewart Game Calls, Inc., Johnny
Stoeger Industries
Stoeger Publishing Co.
(See Stoeger Industries)
Swift Bullet Co.
The A.W. Peterson Gun Shop, Inc.
The Gun Room Press
The Gun Works
The NgraveR Co.
Thomas, Charles C.
Track of the Wolf, Inc.
Trafalgar Square
Trotman, Ken
Tru-Balance Knife Co.
Vega Tool Co.
Vintage Industries, Inc.
VSP Publishers
(See Heritage/VSP Gun Books)
W.E. Brownell Checkering Tools
WAMCO-New Mexico
Wells Creek Knife & Gun Works
Wilderness Sound Products Ltd.
Williams Gun Sight Co.
Wolfe Publishing Co.
Wolf's Western Traders

BULLET CASTING, ACCESSORIES

Ballisti-Cast, Inc.
Buffalo Arms Co.
Bullet Metals
Cast Performance Bullet Company
CFVentures
Cooper-Woodward Perfect Lube
Davide Pedersoli and Co.
Ferguson, Bill
Huntington Die Specialties
Lee Precision, Inc.
Lithi Bee Bullet Lube
Lyman Products Corp.
MA Systems, Inc.
Magma Engineering Co.
Ox-Yoke Originals, Inc.
Rapine Bullet Mould Mfg. Co.
SPG LLC
The A.W. Peterson Gun Shop, Inc.
The Hanned Line
United States Products Co.

BULLET CASTING, FURNACES & POTS

Ballisti-Cast, Inc.
Buffalo Arms Co.
Bullet Metals
Ferguson, Bill
GAR
Lee Precision, Inc.
Lyman Products Corp.
Magma Engineering Co.
Rapine Bullet Mould Mfg. Co.
RCBS/ATK
The A.W. Peterson Gun Shop, Inc.
The Gun Works
Thompson Bullet Lube Co.

BULLET CASTING, LEAD

Action Bullets & Alloy Inc.
Ames Metal Products
Buckskin Bullet Co.
Buffalo Arms Co.
Bullet Metals
Hunters Supply, Inc.
Jericho Tool & Die Co., Inc.
Lee Precision, Inc.
Lithi Bee Bullet Lube
Magma Engineering Co.
Montana Precision Swaging
Ox-Yoke Originals, Inc.
Penn Bullets
Proofmark Corp.
SPG LLC
Splitfire Sporting Goods, L.L.C.
The A.W. Peterson Gun Shop, Inc.
The Gun Works
Walters Wads

BULLET PULLERS

Battenfeld Technologies Inc.
Davide Pedersoli and Co.
Hollywood Engineering
Huntington Die Specialties
Royal Arms Gunstocks
The A.W. Peterson Gun Shop, Inc.
The Gun Works

BULLET TOOLS

Brynin, Milton
Camdex, Inc.
Corbin Mfg. & Supply, Inc.
Cumberland Arms
Eagan, Donald V.
Holland's Gunsmithing
Hollywood Engineering
Lee Precision, Inc.
Niemi Engineering, W. B.
North Devon Firearms Services
Rorschach Precision Products
Sport Flite Manufacturing Co.
The A.W. Peterson Gun Shop, Inc.
The Hanned Line
WTA Manufacturing

BULLET, CASE & DIE LUBRICANTS

Beartooth Bullets
Bonanza (See Forster Products)
Brown Co., E. Arthur
Buckskin Bullet Co.
Buffalo Arms Co.
Camp-Cap Products
CFVentures
Cooper-Woodward Perfect Lube
CVA
E-Z-Way Systems
Ferguson, Bill
Forster Products
GAR
Guardsman Products
Heidenstrom Bullets
Hollywood Engineering
Hornady Mfg. Co.
Imperial (See E-Z-Way Systems)
Knoell, Doug
L.B.T.
Le Clear Industries
(See E-Z-Way Systems)
Lee Precision, Inc.
Lithi Bee Bullet Lube
MI-TE Bullets
Paco's (See Small Custom Mould & Bullet Co.)
RCBS Operations/ATK
Reardon Products
Rooster Laboratories
Shay's Gunsmithing
Small Custom Mould & Bullet Co.
Tamarack Products, Inc.
The Hanned Line
Uncle Mike's
(See Michaels of Oregon Co.)
Warren Muzzleloading Co., Inc.
Widener's Reloading & Shooting Supply, Inc.
Young Country Arms

CARTRIDGES FOR COLLECTORS

Ackerman & Co.
Ad Hominem
Armory Publications
Cameron's
Campbell, Dick
Cherry Creek State Park Shooting Center
Cole's Gun Works
Colonial Repair
Cubic Shot Shell Co., Inc.
Duane's Gun Repair
(See DGR Custom Rifles)
Ed's Gun House
Ed's Gun House
Enguix Import-Export
Forty-Five Ranch Enterprises
George Madis Winchester Consultants
Goergen's Gun Shop, Inc.
Goodwin's Pawn Shop
Grayback Wildcats
Gun City
Gun Hunter Books
(See Gun Hunter Trading Co.)
Gun Hunter Trading Co.
Jack First, Inc.
Kelley's
Liberty Shooting Supplies
Mandall Shooting Supplies Inc.
MAST Technology, Inc.
Michael's Antiques
Montana Outfitters, Lewis E. Yearout
Numrich Gun Parts Corporation
Pasadena Gun Center
Pete de Coux Auction House
Samco Global Arms, Inc.
SOS Products Co.
(See Buck Stix-SOS Products Co.)
Stone Enterprises Ltd.
The Country Armourer
The Gun Room Press
Ward & Van Valkenburg
Yearout, Lewis E.
(See Montana Outfitters)

CASE & AMMUNITION PROCESSORS, INSPECTORS, BOXERS

Ammo Load, Inc.
Hafner World Wide, Inc.
Scharch Mfg., Inc.-Top Brass
The A.W. Peterson Gun Shop, Inc.

CASE CLEANERS & POLISHING MEDIA

Battenfeld Technologies Inc.
Buffalo Arms Co.
G96 Products Co., Inc.
Huntington Die Specialties
Lee Precision, Inc.
Penn Bullets
The A.W. Peterson Gun Shop, Inc.
The Gun Works
Tru-Square Metal Products, Inc.
VibraShine, Inc.

CASE PREPARATION TOOLS

Battenfeld Technologies Inc.
High Precision
Hoehn Sales, Inc.
Huntington Die Specialties
J. Dewey Mfg. Co., Inc.
K&M Services
Lee Precision, Inc.
Match Prep-Doyle Gracey
Plum City Ballistic Range
PWM Sales Ltd.
RCBS Operations/ATK
Russ Haydon's Shooters' Supply
Sinclair International, Inc.
Stoney Point Products, Inc.
The A.W. Peterson Gun Shop, Inc.

CASE TRIMMERS, TRIM DIES & ACCESSORIES

Buffalo Arms Co.
Creedmoor Sports, Inc.
Fremont Tool Works
Goodwin's Pawn Shop
Hollywood Engineering
K&M Services
Lyman Products Corp.
Match Prep-Doyle Gracey
OK Weber, Inc.
Ozark Gun Works
PWM Sales Ltd.
RCBS/ATK
Redding Reloading Equipment
The A.W. Peterson Gun Shop, Inc.

PRODUCT & SERVICE DIRECTORY

CASE TUMBLERS, VIBRATORS, MEDIA & ACCESSORIES

4-D Custom Die Co.
Battenfeld Technologies Inc.
Berry's Mfg., Inc.
Dillon Precision Products, Inc.
Goodwin's Pawn Shop
Penn Bullets
Raytech Div. of Lyman Products Corp.
The A.W. Peterson Gun Shop, Inc.
Tru-Square Metal Products, Inc.
VibraShine, Inc.

CASES, CABINETS, RACKS & SAFES - GUN

All Rite Products, Inc.
Allen Co., Inc.
Alumna Sport by Dee Zee
American Display Co.
American Security Products Co.
Americase
Art Jewel Enterprises Ltd.
Bagmaster Mfg., Inc.
Barramundi Corp.
Berry's Mfg., Inc.
Big Spring Enterprises "Bore Stores"
Bison Studios
Black Sheep Brand
Brauer Bros.
Browning Arms Co.
Bushmaster Hunting & Fishing
Cannon Safe, Inc.
Chipmunk (See Oregon Arms, Inc.)
Connecticut Shotgun Mfg. Co.
D&L Industries (See D.J. Marketing)
D.J. Marketing
Dara-Nes, Inc.
(See Nesci Enterprises, Inc.)
Deepeeka Exports Pvt. Ltd.
Doskocil Mfg. Co., Inc.
DTM International, Inc.
EMF Co., Inc.
English, Inc., A.G.
Enhanced Presentations, Inc.
Eversull Co., Inc.
Flambeau, Inc.
Fort Knox Security Products
Freedom Arms, Inc.
Frontier Safe Co.
Galati International
GALCO International Ltd.
Gun-Ho Sports Cases
Hall Plastics, Inc., John
Hastings
Homak
Hoppe's Div. Penguin Industries, Inc.
Hunter Co., Inc.
Hydrosorbent Products
Impact Case & Container, Inc.
Johanssons Vapentillbehor, Bert
Johnston Bros. (See C&T Corp. TA Johnson Brothers)
Kalispel Case Line
KK Air International
(See Impact Case & Container Co.)
Knock on Wood Antiques
Kolpin Outdoors, Inc.
Lakewood Products LLC
Liberty Safe
Mandall Shooting Supplies Inc.
Marsh, Mike
McWelco Products
Morton Booth Co.
MPC
MTM Molded Products Co., Inc.
Nalpak
Necessary Concepts, Inc.
Nesci Enterprises Inc.
Oregon Arms, Inc.
(See Rogue Rifle Co., Inc.)
Outa-Site Gun Carriers
Pflumm Mfg. Co.
Poburka, Philip (See Bison Studios)
Powell & Son (Gunmakers) Ltd., William
Prototech Industries, Inc.
Rogue Rifle Co., Inc.
Schulz Industries
Silhouette Leathers
Southern Security
Sportsman's Communicators
Sun Welding Safe Co.
Sweet Home, Inc.
The Outdoor Connection, Inc.
The Surecase Co.
Tinks & Ben Lee Hunting Products
(See Wellington)
Trulock Tool
Universal Sports
W. Waller & Son, Inc.
Whitestone Lumber Corp.
Wilson Case, Inc.
Woodstream
Zanotti Armor, Inc.
Ziegel Engineering

CHOKE DEVICES, RECOIL ABSORBERS & RECOIL PADS

3-Ten Corp.
Action Products, Inc.
Answer Products Co.
Arundel Arms & Ammunition, Inc., A.
Bansner's Ultimate Rifles, LLC
Bartlett Engineering
Battenfeld Technologies Inc.
Bob Allen Sportswear
Briley Mfg. Inc.
Brooks Tactical Systems-Agrip
Brownells, Inc.
B-Square Company, Inc.
Buffer Technologies
Bull Mountain Rifle Co.
C&H Research
Cation
Chicasaw Gun Works
Clearview Products
Colonial Arms, Inc.
Connecticut Shotgun Mfg. Co.
CRR, Inc./Marble's Inc.
Danuser Machine Co.
Dina Arms Corporation
Gentry Custom LLC
Goodwin's Pawn Shop
Graybill's Gun Shop
Gruning Precision, Inc.
Harry Lawson Co.
Hastings
Haydel's Game Calls, Inc.
Hogue Grips
Holland's Gunsmithing
I.N.C. Inc. (See Kickeez I.N.C., Inc.)
J.P. Enterprises Inc.
Jackalope Gun Shop
Jenkins Recoil Pads
KDF, Inc.
Kickeez I.N.C., Inc.
Lawson Co., Harry
London Guns Ltd.
Lyman Products Corp.
Mag-Na-Port International, Inc.
Mandall Shooting Supplies Inc.
Marble Arms
(See CRR, Inc./Marble's Inc.)
Menck, Gunsmith Inc., T.W.
Middlebrooks Custom Shop
Morrow, Bud
Nu-Line Guns,Inc.
One Of A Kind
Original Box, Inc.
P.S.M.G. Gun Co.
Palsa Outdoor Products
Parker & Sons Shooting Supply
Pro-Port Ltd.
Que Industries, Inc.
Shotguns Unlimited
Simmons Gun Repair, Inc.
Stan Baker Sports
Stone Enterprises Ltd.
The A.W. Peterson Gun Shop, Inc.
Time Precision
Truglo, Inc.
Trulock Tool
Uncle Mike's
(See Michaels of Oregon Co.)
Universal Sports
Virgin Valley Custom Guns
Williams Gun Sight Co.
Wilson Combat
Wise Guns, Dale

CHRONOGRAPHS & PRESSURE TOOLS

Air Rifle Specialists
Brown Co., E. Arthur
C.W. Erickson's L.L.C.
Canons Delcour
Clearview Products
Competition Electronics, Inc.
Custom Chronograph, Inc.
D&H Precision Tooling
Hege Jagd-u. Sporthandels GmbH
Hutton Rifle Ranch
Mac-1 Airgun Distributors
Oehler Research, Inc.
P.A.C.T., Inc.
Romain's Custom Guns, Inc.
Savage Arms, Inc.
Stratco, Inc.
Tepeco

CLEANERS & DEGREASERS

Barnes Bullets, Inc.
Camp-Cap Products
Cubic Shot Shell Co., Inc.
G96 Products Co., Inc.
Goodwin's Pawn Shop
Hafner World Wide, Inc.
Half Moon Rifle Shop
Kleen-Bore, Inc.
LEM Gun Specialties, Inc. The Lewis Lead Remover
Modern Muzzleloading, Inc.
Northern Precision
Parker & Sons Shooting Supply
Parker Gun Finishes
PrOlixr Lubricants
R&S Industries Corp.
Ramon B. Gonzalez Guns
Rusteprufe Laboratories
Sheffield Knifemakers Supply, Inc.
Shooter's Choice Gun Care
Sierra Specialty Prod. Co.
Spencer's Rifle Barrels, Inc.
The A.W. Peterson Gun Shop, Inc.
The Gun Works
United States Products Co.

CLEANING & REFINISHING SUPPLIES

AC Dyna-tite Corp.
Alpha 1 Drop Zone
American Gas & Chemical Co., Ltd
Answer Products Co.
Armite Laboratories
Atlantic Mills, Inc.
Atsko/Sno-Seal, Inc.
Barnes Bullets, Inc.
Battenfeld Technologies Inc.
Beeman Precision Airguns
Bill's Gun Repair
Birchwood Casey
Blount, Inc., Sporting Equipment Div.
Blount/Outers ATK
Blue and Gray Products Inc.
(See Ox-Yoke Originals)
Break-Free, Inc.
Bridgers Best
Brown Co., E. Arthur
Brownells, Inc.
C.S. Van Gorden & Son, Inc.
Cambos Outdoorsman
Cambos Outdoorsman
Camp-Cap Products
CCI/Speer Div of ATK
Connecticut Shotgun Mfg. Co.
Creedmoor Sports, Inc.
CRR, Inc./Marble's Inc.
Custom Products
(See Jones Custom Products)
Cylinder & Slide, Inc., William R. Laughridge
Dara-Nes, Inc.
(See Nesci Enterprises, Inc.)
Deepeeka Exports Pvt. Ltd.
Desert Mountain Mfg.
Du-Lite Corp.
Dykstra, Doug
E&L Mfg., Inc.
Effebi SNC-Dr. Franco Beretta
Ekol Leather Care
Faith Associates
Flitz International Ltd.
Fluoramics, Inc.
Frontier Products Co.
G96 Products Co., Inc.
Golden Age Arms Co.
Guardsman Products
Gunsmithing, Inc.
Hafner World Wide, Inc.
Half Moon Rifle Shop
Hammans, Charles E.
Heatbath Corp.
Hoppe's Div. Penguin Industries, Inc.
Hornady Mfg. Co.
Hydrosorbent Products
Iosso Products
J. Dewey Mfg. Co., Inc.
Jantz Supply
Jantz Supply
Johnston Bros. (See C&T Corp. TA Johnson Brothers)
Jonad Corp.
K&M Industries, Inc.
Kellogg's Professional Products
Kesselring Gun Shop
Kleen-Bore, Inc.
Knight Rifles
Laurel Mountain Forge
Lee Supplies, Mark
LEM Gun Specialties, Inc. The Lewis Lead Remover
List Precision Engineering
LPS Laboratories, Inc.
Lyman Products Corp.
Mac-1 Airgun Distributors
Mandall Shooting Supplies Inc.
Marble Arms
(See CRR, Inc./Marble's Inc.)
Mark Lee Supplies
Micro Sight Co.
Minute Man High Tech Industries
Mountain State Muzzleloading Supplies, Inc.
MTM Molded Products Co., Inc.
Muscle Products Corp.
Nesci Enterprises Inc.
Northern Precision
October Country Muzzleloading
Old World Oil Products
Otis Technology, Inc.
Outers Laboratories Div. of ATK
Ox-Yoke Originals, Inc.
Parker & Sons Shooting Supply
Parker Gun Finishes
Pendleton Royal, c/o Swingler Buckland Ltd.
Pete Rickard, Inc.
Peter Dyson & Son Ltd.
Precision Airgun Sales, Inc.
Precision Reloading, Inc.
PrOlixr Lubricants
Pro-Shot Products, Inc.
R&S Industries Corp.
Radiator Specialty Co.
Rooster Laboratories
Russ Haydon's Shooters' Supply
Rusteprufe Laboratories
Rusty Duck Premium Gun Care Products
Saunders Gun & Machine Shop
Schumakers Gun Shop
Sheffield Knifemakers Supply, Inc.
Shooter's Choice Gun Care
Shotgun Sports Magazine, dba Shootin' Accessories Ltd.
Silencio/Safety Direct
Sinclair International, Inc.
Sno-Seal, Inc.
(See Atsko/Sno-Seal, Inc.)
Southern Bloomer Mfg. Co.
Splitfire Sporting Goods, L.L.C.
Starr Trading Co., Jedediah
Stoney Point Products, Inc.
Svon Corp.
T.F.C. S.p.A.
TDP Industries, Inc.
Tennessee Valley Mfg.
Tetra Gun Care
Texas Platers Supply Co.
The A.W. Peterson Gun Shop, Inc.
The Lewis Lead Remover
(See LEM Gun Specialties)
The Paul Co.
Track of the Wolf, Inc.
United States Products Co.
Van Gorden & Son Inc., C. S.
Venco Industries, Inc.
(See Shooter's Choice Gun Care)
VibraShine, Inc.
Volquartsen Custom Ltd.
Warren Muzzleloading Co., Inc.
Watson Bullets
WD-40 Co.
Wick, David E.
Willow Bend
Wolf's Western Traders
Young Country Arms

COMPUTER SOFTWARE - BALLISTICS

Action Target, Inc.
AmBr Software Group Ltd.
Arms Software
Arms, Programming Solutions
(See Arms Software)
Barnes Bullets, Inc.
Canons Delcour
Corbin Mfg. & Supply, Inc.
Data Tech Software Systems
Hodgdon Powder Co.
J.I.T. Ltd.
Jensen Bullets
Oehler Research, Inc.
Outdoor Sports Headquarters, Inc.
P.A.C.T., Inc.
Pejsa Ballistics
Powley Computer
(See Hutton Rifle Ranch)
RCBS Operations/ATK
Sierra Bullets
The Ballistic Program Co., Inc.
The Country Armourer
The Gun Works
Tioga Engineering Co., Inc.
W. Square Enterprises

PRODUCT & SERVICE DIRECTORY

CUSTOM GUNSMITH

A&W Repair
A.A. Arms, Inc.
Acadian Ballistic Specialties
Accuracy Unlimited
Ace Custom 45's, Inc.
Acra-Bond Laminates
Adair Custom Shop, Bill
Ahlman Guns
Aldis Gunsmithing & Shooting Supply
Alpha Precision, Inc.
Alpine Indoor Shooting Range
Amrine's Gun Shop
Answer Products Co.
Antique Arms Co.
Armament Gunsmithing Co., Inc.
Arms Craft Gunsmithing
Armscorp USA, Inc.
Artistry in Wood
Art's Gun & Sport Shop, Inc.
Arundel Arms & Ammunition, Inc., A.
Autauga Arms, Inc.
Badger Creek Studio
Baelder, Harry
Bain & Davis, Inc.
Bansner's Ultimate Rifles, LLC
Barnes Bullets, Inc.
Baron Technology
Barrel & Gunworks
Barta's Gunsmithing
Bear Arms
Bear Mountain Gun & Tool
Behlert Precision, Inc.
Beitzinger, George
Belding's Custom Gun Shop
Bengtson Arms Co., L.
Bill Adair Custom Shop
Billings Gunsmiths
BlackStar AccuMax Barrels
BlackStar Barrel Accurizing
(See BlackStar AccuMax)
Bob Rogers Gunsmithing
Bond Custom Firearms
Borden Ridges Rimrock Stocks
Borovnik KG, Ludwig
Bowen Classic Arms Corp.
Brace, Larry D.
Briese Bullet Co., Inc.
Briganti, A.J.
Briley Mfg. Inc.
Broad Creek Rifle Works, Ltd.
Brockman's Custom Gunsmithing
Broken Gun Ranch
Brown Precision, Inc.
Brown Products, Inc., Ed
Buchsenmachermeister
Buckhorn Gun Works
Budin, Dave
Bull Mountain Rifle Co.
Bullberry Barrel Works, Ltd.
Burkhart Gunsmithing, Don
Cache La Poudre Rifleworks
Calhoon Mfg.
Cambos Outdoorsman
Cambos Outdoorsman
Campbell, Dick
Carolina Precision Rifles
Carter's Gun Shop
Caywood, Shane J.
CBC-BRAZIL
Chambers Flintlocks Ltd., Jim
Champlin Firearms, Inc.
Chicasaw Gun Works
Chuck's Gun Shop
Chuilli, Stephen
Clark Custom Guns, Inc.
Clark Firearms Engraving
Classic Arms Company
Classic Arms Corp.
Clearview Products
Cleland's Outdoor World, Inc
Coffin, Charles H.
Cogar's Gunsmithing
Cole's Gun Works
Colonial Arms, Inc.
Colonial Repair
Colorado Gunsmithing Academy
Colorado School of Trades
Colt's Mfg. Co., Inc.
Conrad, C. A.
Corkys Gun Clinic
Cullity Restoration
Custom Single Shot Rifles
D&D Gunsmiths, Ltd.
D.L. Unmussig Bullets
Dangler, Homer L.
D'Arcy Echols & Co.
Darlington Gun Works, Inc.
Dave's Gun Shop
David Miller Co.
David R. Chicoine
David W. Schwartz Custom Guns
Davis, Don
Delorge, Ed
Del-Sports, Inc.
DGR Custom Rifles
DGS, Inc., Dale A. Storey
Dietz Gun Shop & Range, Inc.
Dilliott Gunsmithing, Inc.
Don Klein Custom Guns
Donnelly, C. P.
Duane A. Hobbie Gunsmithing
Duane's Gun Repair
(See DGR Custom Rifles)
Duffy, Charles E.
(See Guns Antique & Modern DBA)
Duncan's Gun Works, Inc.
E. Arthur Brown Co.
Eckelman Gunsmithing
Ed Brown Products, Inc.
Eggleston, Jere D.
Entre`prise Arms, Inc.
Erhardt, Dennis
Eversull Co., Inc.
Evolution Gun Works, Inc.
FERLIB
Ferris Firearms
Fisher, Jerry A.
Fisher Custom Firearms
Fleming Firearms
Flynn's Custom Guns
Forkin Custom Classics
Forster, Kathy
(See Custom Checkering)
Forster, Larry L.
Forthofer's Gunsmithing & Knifemaking
Francotte & Cie S.A. Auguste
Fred F. Wells/Wells Sport Store
Frontier Arms Co., Inc.
Fullmer, Geo. M.
Fulton Armory
G.G. & G.
Galaxy Imports Ltd., Inc.
Garthwaite Pistolsmith, Inc., Jim
Gary Reeder Custom Guns
Gator Guns & Repair
Genecco Gun Works
Gene's Custom Guns
Gentry Custom LLC
George Hoenig, Inc.
Gillmann, Edwin
Gilmore Sports Concepts, Inc.
Giron, Robert E.
Goens, Dale W.
Gonic Arms/North American Arms, Inc.
Goodling's Gunsmithing
Goodwin's Pawn Shop
Grace, Charles E.
Grayback Wildcats
Graybill's Gun Shop
Green, Roger M.
Greg Gunsmithing Repair
Gre-Tan Rifles
Griffin & Howe, Inc.
Griffin & Howe, Inc.
Griffin & Howe, Inc.
Gruning Precision, Inc.
Guncraft Books
(See Guncraft Sports, Inc.)
Guncraft Sports, Inc.
Guncraft Sports, Inc.
Guns Antique & Modern DBA / Charles E. Duffy
Gunsite Training Center
Gunsmithing Ltd.
Hamilton, Alex B.
(See Ten-Ring Precision, Inc.)
Hammans, Charles E.
Hammerli Service-Precision Mac
Hammond Custom Guns Ltd.
Hank's Gun Shop
Hanson's Gun Center, Dick
Harry Lawson Co.
Hart & Son, Inc.
Hart Rifle Barrels, Inc.
Hartmann & Weiss GmbH
Harwood, Jack O.
Hawken Shop, The
(See Dayton Traister)
Hecht, Hubert J., Waffen-Hecht
Heilmann, Stephen
Heinie Specialty Products
Hensley, Gunmaker, Darwin
High Bridge Arms, Inc.
High Performance International
High Precision
High Standard Mfg. Co./F.I., Inc.
Highline Machine Co.
Hill, Loring F.
Hiptmayer, Armurier
Hiptmayer, Klaus
Hoag, James W.
Hodgson, Richard
Hoehn Sales, Inc.
Hofer Jagdwaffen, P.
Holland's Gunsmithing
Huebner, Corey O.
Hunkeler, A.
(See Buckskin Machine Works)
Imperial Magnum Corp.
Irwin, Campbell H.
Island Pond Gun Shop
Israel Arms Inc.
Ivanoff, Thomas G.
(See Tom's Gun Repair)
J&S Heat Treat
J.J. Roberts / Engraver
Jack Dever Co.
Jackalope Gun Shop
Jamison's Forge Works
Jarrett Rifles, Inc.
Jarvis, Inc.
Jay McCament Custom Gunmaker
Jeffredo Gunsight
Jensen's Custom Ammunition
Jim Norman Custom Gunstocks
Jim's Precision, Jim Ketchum
John Rigby & Co.
Jones Custom Products, Neil A.
Juenke, Vern
K. Eversull Co., Inc.
KDF, Inc.
Keith's Custom Gunstocks
Ken Eyster Heritage Gunsmiths, Inc.
Ken Starnes Gunmaker
Ketchum, Jim (See Jim's Precision)
Kilham & Co.
King's Gun Works
Kleinendorst, K. W.
KOGOT
Korzinek Riflesmith, J.
L. E. Jurras & Assoc.
LaFrance Specialties
Lampert, Ron
LaRocca Gun Works
Larry Lyons Gunworks
Lathrop's, Inc.
Laughridge, William R.
(See Cylinder & Slide Inc.)
Lawson Co., Harry
Lazzeroni Arms Co.
LeFever Arms Co., Inc.
Les Baer Custom, Inc.
Linebaugh Custom Sixguns
List Precision Engineering
Lock's Philadelphia Gun Exchange
Lone Star Rifle Company
Long, George F.
Mag-Na-Port International, Inc.
Mahony, Philip Bruce
Mahony, Philip Bruce
Mahovsky's Metalife
Makinson, Nicholas
Mandall Shooting Supplies Inc.
Marshall Fish Mfg. Gunsmith Sptg. Co.
Martin's Gun Shop
Martz, John V.
Mathews Gun Shop & Gunsmithing, Inc.
Mazur Restoration, Pete
McCann, Tom
McCluskey Precision Rifles
McGowen Rifle Barrels
McMillan Rifle Barrels
MCS, Inc.
Mercer Custom Guns
Michael's Antiques
Mid-America Recreation, Inc.
Middlebrooks Custom Shop
Miller Arms, Inc.
Miller Custom
Mills Jr., Hugh B.
Moeller, Steve
Monell Custom Guns
Morrison Custom Rifles, J. W.
Morrow, Bud
Mo's Competitor Supplies
(See MCS, Inc.)
Mowrey's Guns & Gunsmithing
Mullis Guncraft
Muzzleloaders Etcetera, Inc.
NCP Products, Inc.
Neil A. Jones Custom Products
Nelson's Custom Guns, Inc.
Nettestad Gun Works
New England Arms Co.
New England Custom Gun Service
Newman Gunshop
Nicholson Custom
Nickels, Paul R.
Nicklas, Ted
Nitex Gun Shop
North American Shooting Systems
Nu-Line Guns,Inc.
Old World Gunsmithing
Olson, Vic
Ottmar, Maurice
Ox-Yoke Originals, Inc.
Ozark Gun Works
P&M Sales & Services, LLC
P.S.M.G. Gun Co.
PAC-NOR Barreling
Pagel Gun Works, Inc.
Parker & Sons Shooting Supply
Parker Gun Finishes
Pasadena Gun Center
Paterson Gunsmithing
Paulsen Gunstocks
Peacemaker Specialists
PEM's Mfg. Co.
Pence Precision Barrels
Pennsylvania Gunsmith School
Penrod Precision
Pentheny de Pentheny
Perazone-Gunsmith, Brian
Performance Specialists
Pete Mazur Restoration
Peter Dyson & Son Ltd.
Peterson Gun Shop, Inc., A.W.
Piquette's Custom Engraving
Plum City Ballistic Range
Powell & Son (Gunmakers) Ltd., William
Power Custom, Inc.
Professional Hunter Supplies
(See Star Custom Bullets)
Quality Custom Firearms
R&J Gun Shop
R.A. Wells Custom Gunsmith
Ramon B. Gonzalez Guns
Ray's Gunsmith Shop
Renfrew Guns & Supplies
Ridgetop Sporting Goods
Ries, Chuck
RMS Custom Gunsmithing
Robert Valade Engraving
Robinson, Don
Rocky Mountain Arms, Inc.
Romain's Custom Guns, Inc.
Ron Frank Custom Classic Arms
Ruger's Custom Guns
Rupert's Gun Shop
Savage Arms, Inc.
Schiffman, Mike
Schumakers Gun Shop
Score High Gunsmithing
Sharp Shooter Supply
Shaw, Inc., E. R.
(See Small Arms Mfg. Co.)
Shay's Gunsmithing
Shockley, Harold H.
Shooters Supply
Shootin' Shack
Shooting Specialties
(See Titus, Daniel)
Shotguns Unlimited
Silver Ridge Gun Shop
(See Goodwin, Fred)
Simmons Gun Repair, Inc.
Singletary, Kent
Siskiyou Gun Works
(See Donnelly, C. P.)
Skeoch, Brian R.
Sklany's Machine Shop
Slezak, Jerome F.
Small Arms Mfg. Co.
Small Arms Specialists
Smith, Art
Snapp's Gunshop
Speiser, Fred D.
Spencer Reblue Service
Spencer's Rifle Barrels, Inc.
Splitfire Sporting Goods, L.L.C.
Sportsmen's Exchange & Western Gun Traders, Inc.
Springfield Armory
Springfield, Inc.
SSK Industries
Star Custom Bullets
Steelman's Gun Shop
Steffens, Ron
Steven Dodd Hughes
Stiles Custom Guns
Stott's Creek Armory, Inc.
Sturgeon Valley Sporters
Sullivan, David S.
(See Westwind Rifles, Inc.)
Swann, D. J.
Swenson's 45 Shop, A. D.
Swift River Gunworks
Szweda, Robert
(See RMS Custom Gunsmithing)
Taconic Firearms Ltd., Perry Lane
Tank's Rifle Shop
Tar-Hunt Custom Rifles, Inc.
Tarnhelm Supply Co., Inc.
Taylor & Robbins
Tennessee Valley Mfg.
Ten-Ring Precision, Inc.

PRODUCT & SERVICE DIRECTORY

Terry K. Kopp Professional
Gunsmithing
The A.W. Peterson Gun Shop, Inc.
The Competitive Pistol Shop
The Custom Shop
The Gun Shop
The Gun Works
The Orvis Co.
The Robar Co., Inc.
The Swampfire Shop
(See Peterson Gun Shop, Inc.)
Theis, Terry
Thurston Sports, Inc.
Time Precision
Tom's Gun Repair, Thomas G. Ivanoff
Tom's Gunshop
Trevallion Gunstocks
Trulock Tool
Tucker, James C.
Turnbull Restoration, Doug
Upper Missouri Trading Co.
Van Horn, Gil
Van Patten, J. W.
Van's Gunsmith Service
Vest, John
Vic's Gun Refinishing
Virgin Valley Custom Guns
Volquartsen Custom Ltd.
Walker Arms Co., Inc.
Wallace, Terry
Wasmundt, Jim
Wayne E. Schwartz Custom Guns
Weatherby, Inc.
Weber & Markin Custom Gunsmiths
Weems, Cecil
Werth, T. W.
Wessinger Custom Guns & Engraving
Western Design
(See Alpha Gunsmith Division)
Westley Richards & Co. Ltd.
Westwind Rifles, Inc., David S.
Sullivan
White Barn Wor
White Rifles, Inc.
Wichita Arms, Inc.
Wiebe, Duane
Wild West Guns
William E. Phillips Firearms
Williams Gun Sight Co.
Williams Shootin' Iron Service, The
Lynx-Line
Williamson Precision Gunsmithing
Wilson Combat
Winter, Robert M.
Wise Guns, Dale
Wiseman and Co., Bill
Wood, Frank (See Classic Guns, Inc.)
Working Guns
Wright's Gunstock Blanks
Yankee Gunsmith "Just Glocks"
Zeeryp, Russ

CUSTOM METALSMITH

A&W Repair
Ackerman & Co.
Ahlman Guns
Alaskan Silversmith, The
Aldis Gunsmithing & Shooting Supply
Alpha Precision, Inc.
Amrine's Gun Shop
Answer Products Co.
Antique Arms Co.
Artistry in Wood
Baron Technology
Barrel & Gunworks
Bear Mountain Gun & Tool
Behlert Precision, Inc.
Beitzinger, George
Bengtson Arms Co., L.
Bill Adair Custom Shop
Billings Gunsmiths
Billingsley & Brownell
Bob Rogers Gunsmithing
Bowen Classic Arms Corp.
Brace, Larry D.
Briganti, A.J.
Broad Creek Rifle Works, Ltd.
Brown Precision, Inc.
Buckhorn Gun Works
Bull Mountain Rifle Co.
Bullberry Barrel Works, Ltd.
Carter's Gun Shop
Caywood, Shane J.
Checkmate Refinishing
Cleland's Outdoor World, Inc
Colonial Repair
Colorado Gunsmithing Academy
Craftguard
Crandall Tool & Machine Co.
Cullity Restoration
Custom Single Shot Rifles
D&D Gunsmiths, Ltd.
D&H Precision Tooling
D'Arcy Echols & Co.
Dave's Gun Shop
Delorge, Ed
DGS, Inc., Dale A. Storey
Dietz Gun Shop & Range, Inc.
Dilliott Gunsmithing, Inc.
Don Klein Custom Guns
Duane's Gun Repair
(See DGR Custom Rifles)
Duncan's Gun Works, Inc.
Erhardt, Dennis
Eversull Co., Inc.
Ferris Firearms
Fisher, Jerry A.
Forster, Larry L.
Forthofer's Gunsmithing &
Knifemaking
Fred F. Wells/Wells Sport Store
Fullmer, Geo. M.
Genecco Gun Works
Gentry Custom LLC
Grace, Charles E.
Grayback Wildcats
Graybill's Gun Shop
Green, Roger M.
Gunsmithing Ltd.
Hamilton, Alex B.
(See Ten-Ring Precision, Inc.)
Harry Lawson Co.
Hartmann & Weiss GmbH
Harwood, Jack O.
Hecht, Hubert J., Waffen-Hecht
Heilmann, Stephen
High Precision
Highline Machine Co.
Hiptmayer, Armurier
Hiptmayer, Klaus
Hoag, James W.
Holland's Gunsmithing
Island Pond Gun Shop
Ivanoff, Thomas G.
(See Tom's Gun Repair)
J J Roberts Firearm Engraver
J&S Heat Treat
J.J. Roberts / Engraver
Jamison's Forge Works
Jay McCament Custom Gunmaker
Jeffredo Gunsight
KDF, Inc.
Ken Eyster Heritage Gunsmiths, Inc.
Ken Starnes Gunmaker
Kilham & Co.
Kleinendorst, K. W.
Lampert, Ron
LaRocca Gun Works
Larry Lyons Gunworks
Lawson Co., Harry
Les Baer Custom, Inc.
List Precision Engineering
Lock's Philadelphia Gun Exchange
Mahovsky's Metalife
Makinson, Nicholas
Mandall Shooting Supplies Inc.
Mazur Restoration, Pete
McCann Industries
Mid-America Recreation, Inc.
Miller Arms, Inc.
Morrison Custom Rifles, J. W.
Morrow, Bud
Mullis Guncraft
Nelson's Custom Guns, Inc.
Nettestad Gun Works
New England Custom Gun Service
Nicholson Custom
Nitex Gun Shop
Noreen, Peter H.
Nu-Line Guns,Inc.
Olson, Vic
Ozark Gun Works
P.S.M.G. Gun Co.
Pagel Gun Works, Inc.
Parker & Sons Shooting Supply
Parker Gun Finishes
Pasadena Gun Center
Penrod Precision
Pete Mazur Restoration
Precision Specialties
Quality Custom Firearms
R.A. Wells Custom Gunsmith
Rice, Keith
(See White Rock Tool & Die)
Robert Valade Engraving
Robinson, Don
Rocky Mountain Arms, Inc.
Romain's Custom Guns, Inc.
Ron Frank Custom Classic Arms
Score High Gunsmithing
Simmons Gun Repair, Inc.
Singletary, Kent
Skeoch, Brian R.
Sklany's Machine Shop
Small Arms Specialists
Smith, Art
Smith, Sharmon
Snapp's Gunshop
Spencer Reblue Service
Spencer's Rifle Barrels, Inc.
Sportsmen's Exchange & Western
Gun Traders, Inc.
SSK Industries
Steffens, Ron
Stiles Custom Guns
Taylor & Robbins
Ten-Ring Precision, Inc.
The A.W. Peterson Gun Shop, Inc.
The Custom Shop
The Gun Shop
The Robar Co., Inc.
Tom's Gun Repair, Thomas G. Ivanoff
Turnbull Restoration, Doug
Van Horn, Gil
Van Patten, J. W.
Vic's Gun Refinishing
Waldron, Herman
Wallace, Terry
Weber & Markin Custom Gunsmiths
Werth, T. W.
Wessinger Custom Guns & Engraving
White Rock Tool & Die
Wiebe, Duane
Wild West Guns
Williams Shootin' Iron Service, The
Lynx-Line
Williamson Precision Gunsmithing
Winter, Robert M.
Wise Guns, Dale
Wood, Frank (See Classic Guns, Inc.)
Wright's Gunstock Blanks
Zufall, Joseph F.

DECOYS

Ad Hominem
Baekgaard Ltd.
Belding's Custom Gun Shop
Bill Russ Trading Post
Boyds' Gunstock Industries, Inc.
Carry-Lite, Inc.
Farm Form Decoys, Inc.
Feather, Flex Decoys
Flambeau, Inc.
G&H Decoys, Inc.
Grand Slam Hunting Products
Herter's Manufacturing Inc.
Klingler Woodcarving
Kolpin Outdoors, Inc.
L.L. Bean, Inc.
Molin Industries, Tru-Nord Division
Murphy, R.R. Co., Inc.
Original Deer Formula Co., The
Quack Decoy & Sporting Clays
Sports Innovations, Inc.
Tanglefree Industries
The A.W. Peterson Gun Shop, Inc.
Woods Wise Products

DIE ACCESSORIES, METALLIC

High Precision
King & Co.
MarMik, Inc.
Rapine Bullet Mould Mfg. Co.
Redding Reloading Equipment
Royal Arms Gunstocks
Sport Flite Manufacturing Co.
The A.W. Peterson Gun Shop, Inc.
Wolf's Western Traders

DIES, METALLIC

4-D Custom Die Co.
Badger Creek Studio
Buffalo Arms Co.
Competitor Corp., Inc.
Dakota Arms, Inc.
Dillon Precision Products, Inc.
Dixie Gun Works
Fremont Tool Works
Goodwin's Pawn Shop
Gruning Precision, Inc.
Jones Custom Products, Neil A.
King & Co.
Lee Precision, Inc.
Montana Precision Swaging
Neil A. Jones Custom Products
Ozark Gun Works
PWM Sales Ltd.
Rapine Bullet Mould Mfg. Co.
RCBS Operations/ATK
RCBS/ATK
Redding Reloading Equipment
Romain's Custom Guns, Inc.
Spencer's Rifle Barrels, Inc.
Sport Flite Manufacturing Co.
SSK Industries
The A.W. Peterson Gun Shop, Inc.
Vega Tool Co.
Wolf's Western Traders

DIES, SHOTSHELL

Goodwin's Pawn Shop
Hollywood Engineering
Lee Precision, Inc.
MEC, Inc.
The A.W. Peterson Gun Shop, Inc.

DIES, SWAGE

4-D Custom Die Co.
Bullet Swaging Supply, Inc.
Competitor Corp., Inc.
Corbin Mfg. & Supply, Inc.
D.L. Unmussig Bullets
Goodwin's Pawn Shop
Montana Precision Swaging
Sport Flite Manufacturing Co.
The A.W. Peterson Gun Shop, Inc.

ENGRAVER, ENGRAVING TOOLS

Ackerman & Co.
Adair Custom Shop, Bill
Ahlman Guns
Alaskan Silversmith, The
Alfano, Sam
Allard, Gary/Creek Side Metal &
Woodcrafters
Allen Firearm Engraving
Altamont Co.
American Pioneer Video
Baron Technology
Barraclough, John K.
Bates Engraving, Billy
Bill Adair Custom Shop
Billy Bates Engraving
Boessler, Erich
Brooker, Dennis
Buchsenmachermeister
Churchill, Winston G.
Clark Firearms Engraving
Collings, Ronald
Creek Side Metal & Woodcrafters
Cullity Restoration
Cupp, Alana, Custom Engraver
Dayton Traister
Delorge, Ed
Dolbare, Elizabeth
Drain, Mark
Dremel Mfg. Co.
Dubber, Michael W.
Engraving Artistry
Engraving Only
Eversull Co., Inc.
Firearms Engraver's Guild of America
Forty-Five Ranch Enterprises
Fountain Products
Francotte & Cie S.A. Auguste
Frank Knives
Fred F. Wells/Wells Sport Store
Gary Reeder Custom Guns
Gene's Custom Guns
George Madis Winchester Consultants
Glimm's Custom Gun Engraving
Golden Age Arms Co.
Gournet Artistic Engraving
Grant, Howard V.
GRS / Glendo Corp.
Gurney, F. R.
Half Moon Rifle Shop
Harris Hand Engraving, Paul A.
Harwood, Jack O.
Hawken Shop, The
(See Dayton Traister)
Hiptmayer, Armurier
Hiptmayer, Heidemarie
Hofer Jagdwaffen, P.
Ingle, Ralph W.
J J Roberts Firearm Engraver
J.J. Roberts / Engraver
Jantz Supply
Jeff Flannery Engraving
Jim Blair Engraving
John J. Adams & Son Engravers
Kane, Edward
Kehr, Roger
Kelly, Lance
Ken Eyster Heritage Gunsmiths, Inc.
Kenneth W. Warren Engraver
Klingler Woodcarving
Larry Lyons Gunworks
LeFever Arms Co., Inc.
Leibowitz, Leonard
Lindsay Engraving & Tools
Little Trees Ramble
(See Scott Pilkington)
McCombs, Leo

PRODUCT & SERVICE DIRECTORY

McDonald, Dennis
McKenzie, Lynton
Mele, Frank
Mid-America Recreation, Inc.
Nelson, Gary K.
New Orleans Jewelers Supply Co.
Pedersen, C. R.
Pedersen, Rex C.
Peter Hale/Engraver
Pilgrim Pewter, Inc.
(See Bell Originals Inc. Sid)
Pilkington, Scott
(See Little Trees Ramble)
Piquette's Custom Engraving
Potts, Wayne E.
Quality Custom Firearms
Rabeno, Martin
Ralph Bone Engraving
Reed, Dave
Reno, Wayne
Riggs, Jim
Robert Evans Engraving
Robert Valade Engraving
Robinson, Don
Rohner, Hans
Rohner, John
Rosser, Bob
Rundell's Gun Shop
Sam Welch Gun Engraving
Sampson, Roger
Schiffman, Mike
Sheffield Knifemakers Supply, Inc.
Sherwood, George
Singletary, Kent
Smith, Mark A.
Smith, Ron
Smokey Valley Rifles
SSK Industries
Steve Kamyk Engraver
Swanson, Mark
The Gun Room
The NgraveR Co.
Theis, Terry
Thiewes, George W.
Thirion Gun Engraving, Denise
Viramontez Engraving
Vorhes, David
W.E. Brownell Checkering Tools
Wagoner, Vernon G.
Wallace, Terry
Warenski Engraving
Weber & Markin Custom Gunsmiths
Wells, Rachel
Wessinger Custom Guns & Engraving
Ziegel Engineering

GAME CALLS

African Import Co.
Bill Russ Trading Post
Bostick Wildlife Calls, Inc.
Cedar Hill Game Calls, Inc.
Crit'R Call (See Rocky Mountain Wildlife Products)
Custom Calls
D-Boone Ent., Inc.
Deepeeka Exports Pvt. Ltd.
Dr. O's Products Ltd.
Duck Call Specialists
Faulhaber Wildlocker
Faulk's Game Call Co., Inc.
Fibron Products, Inc.
Flambeau, Inc.
Glynn Scobey Duck & Goose Calls
Goodwin's Pawn Shop
Grand Slam Hunting Products
Green Head Game Call Co.
Hally Caller
Haydel's Game Calls, Inc.
Herter's Manufacturing Inc.
Hunter's Specialties Inc.
Keowee Game Calls
Kolpin Outdoors, Inc.
Lohman Mfg. Co., Inc.
Mallardtone Game Calls
Moss Double Tone, Inc.
Oakman Turkey Calls
Original Deer Formula Co., The
Outdoor Sports Headquarters, Inc.
Pete Rickard, Inc.
Philip S. Olt Co.
Primos Hunting Calls
Protektor Model
Quaker Boy, Inc.
Rocky Mountain Wildlife Products
Sceery Game Calls
Sports Innovations, Inc.
Stewart Game Calls, Inc., Johnny
Sure-Shot Game Calls, Inc.
Tanglefree Industries
The A.W. Peterson Gun Shop, Inc.
Tinks & Ben Lee Hunting Products
(See Wellington)
Tink's Safariland Hunting Corp.
Wellington Outdoors
Wilderness Sound Products Ltd.
Woods Wise Products
Wyant's Outdoor Products, Inc.

GAUGES, CALIPERS & MICROMETERS

Blue Ridge Machinery & Tools, Inc.
Goodwin's Pawn Shop
Gruning Precision, Inc.
Huntington Die Specialties
K&M Services
King & Co.
Peter Dyson & Son Ltd.
Spencer's Rifle Barrels, Inc.
Starrett Co., L. S.
Stoney Point Products, Inc.

GUN PARTS, U.S. & FOREIGN

"Su-Press-On", Inc.
A.A. Arms, Inc.
Ahlman Guns
Amherst Arms
Antique Arms Co.
Armscorp USA, Inc.
Auto-Ordnance Corp.
B.A.C.
Badger Shooters Supply, Inc.
Ballard Rifle & Cartridge Co., LLC
Bar-Sto Precision Machine
Bear Mountain Gun & Tool
Billings Gunsmiths
Bill's Gun Repair
Bob's Gun Shop
Briese Bullet Co., Inc.
Brown Products, Inc., Ed
Brownells, Inc.
Bryan & Assoc.
Buffer Technologies
Cambos Outdoorsman
Cambos Outdoorsman
Cape Outfitters
Caspian Arms, Ltd.
CBC-BRAZIL
Century International Arms, Inc.
Chicasaw Gun Works
Chip McCormick Corp.
Cole's Gun Works
Colonial Arms, Inc.
Colonial Repair
Colt's Mfg. Co., Inc.
Custom Riflestocks, Inc., Michael M. Kokolus
Cylinder & Slide, Inc., William R. Laughridge
Dan Wesson Firearms
David R. Chicoine
Delta Arms Ltd.
DGR Custom Rifles
Dibble, Derek A.
Dixie Gun Works
Duane's Gun Repair
(See DGR Custom Rifles)
Duffy, Charles E.
(See Guns Antique & Modern DBA)
E.A.A. Corp.
Elliott, Inc., G. W.
EMF Co., Inc.
Enguix Import-Export
Entre`prise Arms, Inc.
European American Armory Corp.
(See E.A.A. Corp.)
Evolution Gun Works, Inc.
Falcon Industries, Inc.
Federal Arms Corp. of America
Felk Pistols, Inc.
Fleming Firearms
Fulton Armory
Gentry Custom LLC
Glimm's Custom Gun Engraving
Goodwin's Pawn Shop
Granite Mountain Arms, Inc.
Greider Precision
Gre-Tan Rifles
Groenewold, John
Gun Hunter Books
(See Gun Hunter Trading Co.)
Gun Hunter Trading Co.
Guns Antique & Modern DBA / Charles E. Duffy
Gunsmithing, Inc.
Hastings
Hawken Shop, The
(See Dayton Traister)
High Performance International
High Standard Mfg. Co./F.I., Inc.
I.S.S.
Irwin, Campbell H.
Jack First, Inc.
Jamison's Forge Works
Jonathan Arthur Ciener, Inc.
Kimber of America, Inc.
Knight's Mfg. Co.
Krico Deutschland GmbH
LaFrance Specialties
Lampert, Ron
LaPrade
Laughridge, William R.
(See Cylinder & Slide Inc.)
Leapers, Inc.
List Precision Engineering
Lodewick, Walter H.
Logdewood Mfg.
Lomont Precision Bullets
Long, George F.
Mandall Shooting Supplies Inc.
Markell, Inc.
Martin's Gun Shop
MCS, Inc.
Merkuria Ltd.
Mid-America Recreation, Inc.
Morrow, Bud
Mo's Competitor Supplies
(See MCS, Inc.)
North Star West
Northwest Arms
Nu-Line Guns,Inc.
Numrich Gun Parts Corporation
Nygord Precision Products, Inc.
Olathe Gun Shop
Olympic Arms Inc.
P.S.M.G. Gun Co.
Pacific Armament Corp
Perazone-Gunsmith, Brian
Performance Specialists
Peter Dyson & Son Ltd.
Peterson Gun Shop, Inc., A.W.
Ranch Products
Randco UK
Ravell Ltd.
Retting, Inc., Martin B.
Romain's Custom Guns, Inc.
Ruger (See Sturm, Ruger & Co., Inc.)
Rutgers Book Center
S&S Firearms
Sabatti SPA
Samco Global Arms, Inc.
Sarco, Inc.
Scherer Supplies
Shockley, Harold H.
Shootin' Shack
Silver Ridge Gun Shop
(See Goodwin, Fred)
Simmons Gun Repair, Inc.
Smires, C. L.
Smith & Wesson
Southern Ammunition Co., Inc.
Sportsmen's Exchange & Western Gun Traders, Inc.
Springfield Sporters, Inc.
Springfield, Inc.
Steyr Mannlicher GmbH & Co KG
STI International
Strayer-Voigt, Inc.
Sturm Ruger & Co. Inc.
Sunny Hill Enterprises, Inc.
T&S Industries, Inc.
Tank's Rifle Shop
Tarnhelm Supply Co., Inc.
Terry K. Kopp Professional Gunsmithing
The A.W. Peterson Gun Shop, Inc.
The Gun Room Press
The Gun Shop
The Gun Works
The Southern Armory
The Swampfire Shop
(See Peterson Gun Shop, Inc.)
Tom Forrest, Inc.
VAM Distribution Co. LLC
Vektor USA
W. Waller & Son, Inc.
W.C. Wolff Co.
Walker Arms Co., Inc.
Wescombe, Bill (See North Star West)
Wild West Guns
Williams Mfg. of Oregon
Winchester Sutler, Inc., The
Wise Guns, Dale
Wisners, Inc.

GUNS & GUN PARTS, REPLICA & ANTIQUE

Ackerman & Co.
Ahlman Guns
Armi San Paolo
Auto-Ordnance Corp.
Ballard Rifle & Cartridge Co., LLC
Bear Mountain Gun & Tool
Billings Gunsmiths
Bob's Gun Shop
Buffalo Arms Co.
Cache La Poudre Rifleworks
Campbell, Dick
Cash Mfg. Co., Inc.
CBC-BRAZIL
CCL Security Products
Chambers Flintlocks Ltd., Jim
Chicasaw Gun Works
Cimarron F.A. Co.
Cogar's Gunsmithing
Cole's Gun Works
Colonial Repair
Colt Blackpowder Arms Co.
Colt's Mfg. Co., Inc.
Custom Riflestocks, Inc., Michael M. Kokolus
Custom Single Shot Rifles
David R. Chicoine
Delhi Gun House
Delta Arms Ltd.
Dilliott Gunsmithing, Inc.
Dixie Gun Works
Dixon Muzzleloading Shop, Inc.
Ed's Gun House
Euroarms of America, Inc.
Flintlocks, Etc.
Getz Barrel Company
Golden Age Arms Co.
Goodwin's Pawn Shop
Groenewold, John
Gun Hunter Books
(See Gun Hunter Trading Co.)
Gun Hunter Trading Co.
Hastings
Heidenstrom Bullets
Hunkeler, A.
(See Buckskin Machine Works)
IAR Inc.
Imperial Miniature Armory
Ithaca Classic Doubles
Jack First, Inc.
Ken Starnes Gunmaker
L&R Lock Co.
Leonard Day
List Precision Engineering
Lock's Philadelphia Gun Exchange
Logdewood Mfg.
Lone Star Rifle Company
Lucas, Edward E
Mandall Shooting Supplies Inc.
Martin's Gun Shop
Mathews Gun Shop & Gunsmithing, Inc.
Mid-America Recreation, Inc.
Mountain State Muzzleloading Supplies, Inc.
Mowrey Gun Works
Navy Arms Company
Neumann GmbH
North Star West
Nu-Line Guns,Inc.
Numrich Gun Parts Corporation
Olathe Gun Shop
Parker & Sons Shooting Supply
Pasadena Gun Center
Pecatonica River Longrifle
PEM's Mfg. Co.
Peter Dyson & Son Ltd.
Pony Express Sport Shop
R.A. Wells Custom Gunsmith
Randco UK
Ravell Ltd.
Retting, Inc., Martin B.
Rutgers Book Center
S&S Firearms
Samco Global Arms, Inc.
Sarco, Inc.
Shootin' Shack
Silver Ridge Gun Shop
(See Goodwin, Fred)
Simmons Gun Repair, Inc.
Sklany's Machine Shop
Southern Ammunition Co., Inc.
Starr Trading Co., Jedediah
Stott's Creek Armory, Inc.
Taylor's & Co., Inc.
Tennessee Valley Mfg.
The A.W. Peterson Gun Shop, Inc.
The Gun Room Press
The Gun Works
Tiger-Hunt Gunstocks
Turnbull Restoration, Doug
Upper Missouri Trading Co.
Vintage Industries, Inc.
VTI Gun Parts
Weber & Markin Custom Gunsmiths
Wescombe, Bill (See North Star West)
Whitestone Lumber Corp.
Winchester Sutler, Inc., The

GUNS, AIR

Air Arms
Air Rifle Specialists
Air Venture Airguns

PRODUCT & SERVICE DIRECTORY

AirForce Airguns
Airrow
Allred Bullet Co.
Arms Corporation of the Philippines
BEC, Inc.
Beeman Precision Airguns
Benjamin/Sheridan Co., Crosman
Brass Eagle, Inc.
Brocock Ltd.
Bryan & Assoc.
BSA Guns Ltd.
Compasseco, Ltd.
Component Concepts, Inc.
Conetrol Scope Mounts
Crosman Airguns
Daisy Outdoor Products
Daystate Ltd.
Domino
Dynamit Nobel-RWS, Inc.
Effebi SNC-Dr. Franco Beretta
European American Armory Corp. (See E.A.A. Corp.)
Feinwerkbau Westinger & Altenburger
Gamo USA, Inc.
Gaucher Armes, S.A.
Great Lakes Airguns
Groenewold, John
Hammerli Service-Precision Mac
I.S.S.
IAR Inc.
J.G. Anschutz GmbH & Co. KG
Labanu, Inc.
Leapers, Inc.
List Precision Engineering
Mac-1 Airgun Distributors
Marksman Products
Maryland Paintball Supply
Merkuria Ltd.
Nationwide Airgun Repair
Nygord Precision Products, Inc.
Olympic Arms Inc.
Pardini Armi Srl
Precision Airgun Sales, Inc.
Precision Sales International, Inc.
Ripley Rifles
Robinson, Don
RWS (See U.S. Importer-Dynamit Nobel-RWS, Inc.)
Safari Arms/Schuetzen Pistol Works
Savage Arms, Inc.
Smart Parts
Smith & Wesson
Steyr Mannlicher GmbH & Co KG
Stone Enterprises Ltd.
The A.W. Peterson Gun Shop, Inc.
The Gun Room Press
The Park Rifle Co., Ltd.
Tippman Pneumatics, Inc.
Tristar Sporting Arms, Ltd.
Trooper Walsh
UltraSport Arms, Inc.
Visible Impact Targets
Walther GmbH, Carl
Webley and Scott Ltd.
Weihrauch KG, Hermann
Whiscombe (See U.S. Importer-Pelaire Products)

GUNS, FOREIGN MANUFACTURER U.S. IMPORTER

Accuracy Internationl Precision Rifles (See U.S.)
Accuracy Int'l. North America, Inc.
Ad Hominem
Air Arms
Armas Garbi, S.A.
Armas Kemen S. A. (See U.S. Importers)
Armi Perazzi S.P.A.
Armi San Marco (See U.S. Importers-Taylor's & Co.)
Armi Sport (See U.S. Importers-Cape Outfitters)
Arms Corporation of the Philippines
Armscorp USA, Inc.
Arrieta S.L.
Astra Sport, S.A.
Atamec-Bretton
AYA (See U.S. Importer-New England Custom Gun Serv)
B.A.C.
B.C. Outdoors
BEC, Inc.
Benelli Armi S.P.A.
Benelli USA Corp
Beretta S.P.A., Pietro
Beretta U.S.A. Corp.
Bernardelli, Vincenzo
Bersa S.A.
Bertuzzi (See U.S. Importer-New England Arms Co)
Bill Hanus Birdguns
Blaser Jagdwaffen GmbH
Borovnik KG, Ludwig
Bosis (See U.S. Importer-New England Arms Co.)
Brenneke GmbH
Browning Arms Co.
Bryan & Assoc.
BSA Guns Ltd.
Cabanas (See U.S. Importer-Mandall Shooting Supply)
Cabela's
Cape Outfitters
CBC
Champlin Firearms, Inc.
Chapuis Armes
Churchill (See U.S. Importer-Ellett Bros.)
Collector's Armoury, Ltd.
Conetrol Scope Mounts
Cosmi Americo & Figlio S.N.C.
Crucelegui, Hermanos (See U.S. Importer-Mandall)
Cubic Shot Shell Co., Inc.
Dakota (See U.S. Importer-EMF Co., Inc.)
Dakota Arms, Inc.
Daly, Charles/KBI
Davide Pedersoli and Co.
Domino
Dumoulin, Ernest
Eagle Imports, Inc.
EAW (See U.S. Importer-New England Custom Gun Serv)
Ed's Gun House
Effebi SNC-Dr. Franco Beretta
EMF Co., Inc.
Eversull Co., Inc.
F.A.I.R.
Fabarm S.p.A.
FEG
Feinwerkbau Westinger & Altenburger
Felk Pistols, Inc.
FERLIB
Fiocchi Munizioni S.P.A. (See U.S. Importer-Fiocch)
Firearms Co. Ltd. / Alpine (See U.S. Importer-Mandall
Firearms International
Flintlocks, Etc.
Galaxy Imports Ltd., Inc.
Gamba S.p.A. Societa Armi Bresciane Srl
Gamo (See U.S. Importers-Arms United Corp, Daisy M)
Gaucher Armes, S.A.
Gibbs Rifle Co., Inc.
Glock GmbH
Goergen's Gun Shop, Inc.
Griffin & Howe, Inc.
Griffin & Howe, Inc.
Griffin & Howe, Inc.
Grulla Armes
Hammerli Ltd.
Hammerli USA
Hartford (See U.S. Importer-EMF Co. Inc.)
Hartmann & Weiss GmbH
Heckler & Koch, Inc.
Hege Jagd-u. Sporthandels GmbH
Helwan (See U.S. Importer-Interarms)
Holland & Holland Ltd.
Howa Machinery, Ltd.
I.A.B. (See U.S. Importer-Taylor's & Co. Inc.)
IAR Inc.
IGA (See U.S. Importer-Stoeger Industries)
Imperial Magnum Corp.
Imperial Miniature Armory
Import Sports Inc.
Inter Ordnance of America LP
Intrac Arms International
J.G. Anschutz GmbH & Co. KG
JSL Ltd. (See U.S. Importer-Specialty Shooters)
K. Eversull Co., Inc.
Kimar (See U.S. Importer-IAR,Inc)
Korth Germany GmbH
Krico Deutschland GmbH
Krieghoff Gun Co., H.
Lakefield Arms Ltd. (See Savage Arms, Inc.)
Lapua Ltd.
Laurona Armas Eibar, S.A.L.
Lebeau-Courally
Lever Arms Service Ltd.
Llama Gabilondo Y Cia
Lomont Precision Bullets
London Guns Ltd.
Mandall Shooting Supplies Inc.
Marocchi F.lli S.p.A
Mauser Werke Oberndorf Waffensysteme GmbH
McCann Industries
MEC-Gar S.R.L.
Merkel
Mitchell's Mauser
Morini (See U.S. Importers-Mandall Shooting Supply)
New England Custom Gun Service
New SKB Arms Co.
Norica, Avnda Otaola
Norinco
Norma Precision AB (See U.S. Importers-Dynamit)
Northwest Arms
Nygord Precision Products, Inc.
OK Weber, Inc.
Para-Ordnance Mfg., Inc.
Pardini Armi Srl
Perugini Visini & Co. S.r.l.
Peters Stahl GmbH
Pietta (See U.S. Importers-Navy Arms Co, Taylor's)
Piotti (See U.S. Importer-Moore & Co., Wm. Larkin)
PMC/Eldorado Cartridge Corp.
Powell & Son (Gunmakers) Ltd., William
Prairie Gun Works
Ramon B. Gonzalez Guns
Rizzini F.lli (See U.S. Importers-Moore & C England)
Rizzini SNC
Robinson Armament Co.
Rossi Firearms
Rottweil Compe
Rutten (See U.S. Importer-Labanu Inc)
RWS (See U.S. Importer-Dynamit Nobel-RWS, Inc.)
S.A.R.L. G. Granger
S.I.A.C.E. (See U.S. Importer-IAR Inc)
Sabatti SPA
Sako Ltd (See U.S. Importer-Stoeger Industries)
San Marco (See U.S. Importers-Cape Outfitters-EMF)
Sarsilmaz Shotguns - Turkey (See B.C. Outdoors)
Sauer (See U.S. Importers-Paul Co., The, Sigarms I)
Savage Arms (Canada), Inc.
SIG
Sigarms, Inc.
SIG-Sauer (See U.S. Importer-Sigarms Inc.)
SKB Shotguns
Small Arms Specialists
Societa Armi Bresciane Srl (See U.S. Importer-Cape)
Sphinx Systems Ltd.
Springfield Armory
Springfield, Inc.
Starr Trading Co., Jedediah
Steyr Mannlicher GmbH & Co KG
T.F.C. S.p.A.
Tanfoglio Fratelli S.r.l.
Tanner (See U.S. Importer-Mandall Shooting Supply)
Taurus International Firearms (See U.S. Importer)
Taurus S.A. Forjas
Taylor's & Co., Inc.
Techno Arms (See U.S. Importer-Auto-Ordnance Corp
The A.W. Peterson Gun Shop, Inc.
Tikka (See U.S. Importer-Stoeger Industries)
TOZ (See U.S. Importer-Nygord Precision Products)
Ugartechea S. A., Ignacio
Ultralux (See U.S. Importer-Keng's Firearms)
Unique/M.A.P.F.
Valtro USA, Inc.
Verney-Carron
Voere-KGH GmbH
Walther GmbH, Carl
Webley and Scott Ltd.
Weihrauch KG, Hermann
Westley Richards & Co. Ltd.
Whiscombe (See U.S. Importer-Pelaire Products)
Wolf (See J.R. Distributing)
Yankee Gunsmith "Just Glocks"
Zabala Hermanos S.A.

GUNS, FOREIGN-IMPORTER

Accuracy International
AcuSport Corporation
Air Rifle Specialists
Auto-Ordnance Corp.
B.A.C.
B.C. Outdoors
Bell's Legendary Country Wear
Benelli USA Corp
Big Bear Arms & Sporting Goods, Inc.
Bill Hanus Birdguns
Bridgeman Products
British Sporting Arms
Browning Arms Co.
Cape Outfitters
Century International Arms, Inc.
Champion Shooters' Supply
Champion's Choice, Inc.
Chapuis USA
Cimarron F.A. Co.
CVA
CZ USA
Dixie Gun Works
Dynamit Nobel-RWS, Inc.
E&L Mfg., Inc.
E.A.A. Corp.
Eagle Imports, Inc.
Ellett Bros.
EMF Co., Inc.
Euroarms of America, Inc.
Eversull Co., Inc.
Fiocchi of America, Inc.
Flintlocks, Etc.
Franzen International, Inc. (See U.S. Importer)
G.U., Inc. (See U.S. Importer for New SKB Arms Co.)
Galaxy Imports Ltd., Inc.
Gamba, USA
Gamo USA, Inc.
Giacomo Sporting USA
Glock, Inc.
GSI, Inc.
Guncraft Books (See Guncraft Sports, Inc.)
Guncraft Sports, Inc.
Gunsite Training Center
Hammerli USA
I.S.S.
IAR Inc.
Imperial Magnum Corp.
Imperial Miniature Armory
Import Sports Inc.
Intrac Arms International
K. Eversull Co., Inc.
K.B.I. Inc.
Kemen America
Keng's Firearms Specialty, Inc./US Tactical Systems
Krieghoff International,Inc.
Labanu, Inc.
Legacy Sports International
Lion Country Supply
London Guns Ltd.
Magnum Research, Inc.
Marx, Harry (See U.S. Importer for FERLIB)
MCS, Inc.
MEC-Gar U.S.A., Inc.
Mitchell Mfg. Corp.
Navy Arms Company
New England Arms Co.
Nu-Line Guns,Inc.
Nygord Precision Products, Inc.
OK Weber, Inc.
P.S.M.G. Gun Co.
Para-Ordnance, Inc.
Pelaire Products
Perazone-Gunsmith, Brian
Perazzi U.S.A. Inc.
Powell Agency, William
Precision Sales International, Inc.
Rocky Mountain Armoury
S.D. Meacham
Safari Arms/Schuetzen Pistol Works
Samco Global Arms, Inc.
Savage Arms, Inc.
Scott Fine Guns Inc., Thad
Sigarms, Inc.
SKB Shotguns
Small Arms Specialists
Southern Ammunition Co., Inc.
Specialty Shooters Supply, Inc.
Springfield, Inc.
Stoeger Industries
Stone Enterprises Ltd.
Swarovski Optik North America Ltd.
Taurus Firearms, Inc.
Taylor's & Co., Inc.
The A.W. Peterson Gun Shop, Inc.
The Gun Shop
The Orvis Co.
The Paul Co.
Track of the Wolf, Inc.
Traditions Performance Firearms
Tristar Sporting Arms, Ltd.
Trooper Walsh
U.S. Importer-Wm. Larkin Moore
VAM Distribution Co. LLC
Vektor USA
VTI Gun Parts

PRODUCT & SERVICE DIRECTORY

Westley Richards Agency USA
(See U.S. Importer)
Wingshooting Adventures

GUNS, SURPLUS, PARTS & AMMUNITION

Ahlman Guns
Alpha 1 Drop Zone
Armscorp USA, Inc.
Arundel Arms & Ammunition, Inc., A.
B.A.C.
Bob's Gun Shop
Cambos Outdoorsman
Century International Arms, Inc.
Cole's Gun Works
Conetrol Scope Mounts
Delta Arms Ltd.
Ed's Gun House
Fleming Firearms
Fulton Armory
Garcia National Gun Traders, Inc.
Goodwin's Pawn Shop
Gun City
Gun Hunter Books
(See Gun Hunter Trading Co.)
Gun Hunter Trading Co.
Hank's Gun Shop
Hege Jagd-u. Sporthandels GmbH
Jackalope Gun Shop
Ken Starnes Gunmaker
LaRocca Gun Works
Lever Arms Service Ltd.
Log Cabin Sport Shop
Martin's Gun Shop
Navy Arms Company
Nevada Pistol Academy, Inc.
Northwest Arms
Numrich Gun Parts Corporation
Oil Rod and Gun Shop
Olathe Gun Shop
Paragon Sales & Services, Inc.
Pasadena Gun Center
Power Plus Enterprises, Inc.
Ravell Ltd.
Retting, Inc., Martin B.
Rutgers Book Center
Samco Global Arms, Inc.
Sarco, Inc.
Shootin' Shack
Silver Ridge Gun Shop
(See Goodwin, Fred)
Simmons Gun Repair, Inc.
Sportsmen's Exchange & Western
Gun Traders, Inc.
Springfield Sporters, Inc.
T.F.C. S.p.A.
Tarnhelm Supply Co., Inc.
The A.W. Peterson Gun Shop, Inc.
The Gun Room Press
Thurston Sports, Inc.
Whitestone Lumber Corp.
Williams Shootin' Iron Service, The
Lynx-Line

GUNS, U.S. MADE

3-Ten Corp.
A.A. Arms, Inc.
Accu-Tek
Ace Custom 45's, Inc.
Acra-Bond Laminates
Ad Hominem
Airrow
Allred Bullet Co.
American Derringer Corp.
AR-7 Industries, LLC
ArmaLite, Inc.
Armscorp USA, Inc.
Arundel Arms & Ammunition, Inc., A.
A-Square Co.
Austin & Halleck, Inc.
Autauga Arms, Inc.
Auto-Ordnance Corp.
Ballard Rifle & Cartridge Co., LLC
Barrett Firearms Manufacturer, Inc.
Bar-Sto Precision Machine
Benjamin/Sheridan Co., Crosman
Beretta S.P.A., Pietro
Beretta U.S.A. Corp.
Big Bear Arms & Sporting Goods, Inc.
Bill Russ Trading Post
Bond Arms, Inc.
Borden Ridges Rimrock Stocks
Borden Rifles Inc.
Brockman's Custom Gunsmithing
Brown Co., E. Arthur
Brown Products, Inc., Ed
Browning Arms Co.
Bryan & Assoc.
Bushmaster Firearms, Inc.
C. Sharps Arms Co. Inc./Montana
Armory
Cabela's
Calico Light Weapon Systems
Cambos Outdoorsman
Cape Outfitters
Casull Arms Corp.
CCL Security Products
Century Gun Dist. Inc.
Champlin Firearms, Inc.
Charter 2000
Cobra Enterprises, Inc.
Colt's Mfg. Co., Inc.
Competitor Corp., Inc.
Competitor Corp., Inc.
Conetrol Scope Mounts
Connecticut Shotgun Mfg. Co.
Connecticut Valley Classics
(See CVC, BPI)
Cooper Arms
Crosman Airguns
Cumberland Arms
Cumberland Mountain Arms
CVA
Daisy Outdoor Products
Dakota Arms, Inc.
Dan Wesson Firearms
Dayton Traister
Detonics USA
Dixie Gun Works
Downsizer Corp.
DS Arms, Inc.
DunLyon R&D, Inc.
Dutchman's Firearms, Inc.
E&L Mfg., Inc.
E. Arthur Brown Co.
Eagle Arms, Inc. (See ArmaLite, Inc.)
Ed Brown Products, Inc.
Emerging Technologies, Inc.
(See Laseraim Technologies, Inc.)
Entre`prise Arms, Inc.
Essex Arms
Excel Industries, Inc.
Fletcher-Bidwell, LLC.
FN Manufacturing
Freedom Arms, Inc.
Fulton Armory
Galena Industries AMT
Garcia National Gun Traders, Inc.
Gary Reeder Custom Guns
Genecco Gun Works
Gentry Custom LLC
George Hoenig, Inc.
George Madis Winchester Consultants
Gibbs Rifle Co., Inc.
Gil Hebard Guns, Inc.
Gilbert Equipment Co., Inc.
Goergen's Gun Shop, Inc.
Goodwin's Pawn Shop
Granite Mountain Arms, Inc.
Grayback Wildcats
Guncrafter Industries
H&R 1871.LLC
Hammans, Charles E.
Hammerli USA
Harrington & Richardson
(See H&R 1871, Inc.)
Hart & Son, Inc.
Hatfield Gun
Hawken Shop, The
(See Dayton Traister)
Heritage Firearms
(See Heritage Mfg., Inc.)
Heritage Manufacturing, Inc.
Hesco-Meprolight
High Precision
High Standard Mfg. Co./F.I., Inc.
Hi-Point Firearms/MKS Supply
HJS Arms, Inc.
H-S Precision, Inc.
Hutton Rifle Ranch
IAR Inc.
Imperial Miniature Armory
Israel Arms Inc.
Ithaca Classic Doubles
Ithaca Gun Company LLC
J.P. Enterprises Inc.
Jim Norman Custom Gunstocks
John Rigby & Co.
John's Custom Leather
K.B.I. Inc.
Kahr Arms
Kehr, Roger
Kelbly, Inc.
Kel-Tec CNC Industries, Inc.
Keystone Sporting Arms, Inc.
(Crickett Rifles)
Kimber of America, Inc.
Knight Rifles
Knight's Mfg. Co.
Kolar
L.A.R. Mfg., Inc.
L.W. Seecamp Co., Inc.
LaFrance Specialties
Lakefield Arms Ltd.
(See Savage Arms, Inc.)
Laseraim Technologies, Inc.
Les Baer Custom, Inc.
Lever Arms Service Ltd.
Ljutic Industries, Inc.
Lock's Philadelphia Gun Exchange
Lomont Precision Bullets
Lone Star Rifle Company
Mag-Na-Port International, Inc.
Magnum Research, Inc.
Mandall Shooting Supplies Inc.
Marlin Firearms Co.
Marshall Fish Mfg. Gunsmith Sptg. Co.
Mathews Gun Shop & Gunsmithing,
Inc.
Maverick Arms, Inc.
McBros Rifle Co.
McCann Industries
Mid-America Recreation, Inc.
Miller Arms, Inc.
MKS Supply, Inc.
(See Hi-Point Firearms)
MOA Corporation
Montana Armory, Inc.
(See C. Sharps Arms Co. Inc.)
MPI Stocks
Navy Arms Company
NCP Products, Inc.
New Ultra Light Arms, LLC
Noreen, Peter H.
North American Arms, Inc.
North Star West
Northwest Arms
Nowlin Mfg. Co.
Olympic Arms Inc.
Oregon Arms, Inc.
(See Rogue Rifle Co., Inc.)
P&M Sales & Services, LLC
Parker & Sons Shooting Supply
Parker Gun Finishes
Phillips & Rogers, Inc.
Phoenix Arms
Precision Small Arms Inc.
ProWare, Inc.
Ramon B. Gonzalez Guns
Rapine Bullet Mould Mfg. Co.
Remington Arms Co., Inc.
Rifles, Inc.
Robinson Armament Co.
Rock River Arms
Rocky Mountain Arms, Inc.
Rogue Rifle Co., Inc.
Rogue River Rifleworks
Rohrbaugh
Romain's Custom Guns, Inc.
RPM
Ruger (See Sturm, Ruger & Co., Inc.)
Safari Arms/Schuetzen Pistol Works
Savage Arms (Canada), Inc.
Schumakers Gun Shop
Searcy Enterprises
Sharps Arms Co., Inc., C.
Sigarms, Inc.
Sklany's Machine Shop
Small Arms Specialists
Smith & Wesson
Sound Tech Silencers
Spencer's Rifle Barrels, Inc.
Springfield Armory
Springfield, Inc.
SSK Industries
STI International
Stoeger Industries
Strayer-Voigt, Inc.
Sturm Ruger & Co. Inc.
Sunny Hill Enterprises, Inc.
T&S Industries, Inc.
Taconic Firearms Ltd., Perry Lane
Tank's Rifle Shop
Tar-Hunt Custom Rifles, Inc.
Taurus Firearms, Inc.
Texas Armory (See Bond Arms, Inc.)
The A.W. Peterson Gun Shop, Inc.
The Gun Room Press
The Gun Works
Thompson/Center Arms
Time Precision
Tristar Sporting Arms, Ltd.
U.S. Fire Arms Mfg. Co., Inc.
U.S. Repeating Arms Co., Inc.
Uselton/Arms, Inc.
Visible Impact Targets
Volquartsen Custom Ltd.
Wallace, Terry
Weatherby, Inc.
Wescombe, Bill (See North Star West)
Wessinger Custom Guns & Engraving
Whildin & Sons Ltd, E.H.
Whitestone Lumber Corp.
Wichita Arms, Inc.
Wildey, Inc.
Wilsom Combat
Z-M Weapons

GUNSMITH SCHOOL

American Gunsmithing Institute
Bull Mountain Rifle Co.
Colorado Gunsmithing Academy
Colorado School of Trades
Cylinder & Slide, Inc., William R.
Laughridge
Lassen Community College,
Gunsmithing Dept.
Laughridge, William R.
(See Cylinder & Slide Inc.)
Log Cabin Sport Shop
Modern Gun Repair School
Murray State College
North American Correspondence
Schools The Gun Pro
Nowlin Mfg. Co.
NRI Gunsmith School
Pennsylvania Gunsmith School
Piedmont Community College
Pine Technical College
Professional Gunsmiths of America
Smith & Wesson
Southeastern Community College
Spencer's Rifle Barrels, Inc.
Trinidad St. Jr. Col. Gunsmith Dept.
Wright's Gunstock Blanks
Yavapai College

GUNSMITH SUPPLIES, TOOLS & SERVICES

Ace Custom 45's, Inc.
Actions by "T" Teddy Jacobson
Alaskan Silversmith, The
Aldis Gunsmithing & Shooting Supply
Alley Supply Co.
Allred Bullet Co.
Alpec Team, Inc.
American Gunsmithing Institute
Ballard Rifle & Cartridge Co., LLC
Bar-Sto Precision Machine
Battenfeld Technologies Inc.
Bauska Barrels
Bear Mountain Gun & Tool
Bengtson Arms Co., L.
Bill's Gun Repair
Blue Ridge Machinery & Tools, Inc.
Boyds' Gunstock Industries, Inc.
Briley Mfg. Inc.
Brockman's Custom Gunsmithing
Brown Products, Inc., Ed
Brownells, Inc.
Bryan & Assoc.
B-Square Company, Inc.
Buffer Technologies
Bull Mountain Rifle Co.
Bushmaster Firearms, Inc.
C.S. Van Gorden & Son, Inc.
Carbide Checkering Tools
(See J&R Engineering)
Caywood, Shane J.
CBC-BRAZIL
Chapman Manufacturing Co.
Chicasaw Gun Works
Chip McCormick Corp.
Choate Machine & Tool Co., Inc.
Colonial Arms, Inc.
Colorado School of Trades
Colt's Mfg. Co., Inc.
Conetrol Scope Mounts
Corbin Mfg. & Supply, Inc.
CRR, Inc./Marble's Inc.
Cumberland Arms
Cumberland Mountain Arms
Custom Checkering Service, Kathy
Forster
Dan's Whetstone Co., Inc.
D'Arcy Echols & Co.
Dem-Bart Checkering Tools, Inc.
Dixie Gun Works
Dixie Gun Works
Dremel Mfg. Co.
Du-Lite Corp.
Entre`prise Arms, Inc.
Erhardt, Dennis
Evolution Gun Works, Inc.
Faith Associates
Falcon Industries, Inc.
FERLIB
Fisher, Jerry A.
Forgreens Tool & Mfg., Inc.
Forster, Kathy
(See Custom Checkering)
Gentry Custom LLC
Gilmore Sports Concepts, Inc.
Goodwin's Pawn Shop
Grace Metal Products
Gre-Tan Rifles
Gruning Precision, Inc.
Gunline Tools
Half Moon Rifle Shop
Hammond Custom Guns Ltd.

PRODUCT & SERVICE DIRECTORY

Hastings
Henriksen Tool Co., Inc.
High Performance International
High Precision
Holland's Gunsmithing
Import Sports Inc.
Ironsighter Co.
Israel Arms Inc.
Ivanoff, Thomas G.
(See Tom's Gun Repair)
J&R Engineering
J&S Heat Treat
J. Dewey Mfg. Co., Inc.
Jantz Supply
Jenkins Recoil Pads
JGS Precision Tool Mfg., LLC
Jonathan Arthur Ciener, Inc.
Jones Custom Products, Neil A.
Kailua Custom Guns Inc.
Kasenit Co., Inc.
Kleinendorst, K. W.
Korzinek Riflesmith, J.
LaBounty Precision Reboring, Inc
LaFrance Specialties
Laurel Mountain Forge
Lee Supplies, Mark
List Precision Engineering
Lock's Philadelphia Gun Exchange
London Guns Ltd.
Mahovsky's Metalife
Marble Arms
(See CRR, Inc./Marble's Inc.)
Mark Lee Supplies
Marsh, Mike
Martin's Gun Shop
McFarland, Stan
Menck, Gunsmith Inc., T.W.
Metalife Industries
(See Mahovsky's Metalife)
Michael's Antiques
Micro Sight Co.
Midway Arms, Inc.
MMC
Mo's Competitor Supplies
(See MCS, Inc.)
Mowrey's Guns & Gunsmithing
Neil A. Jones Custom Products
New England Custom Gun Service
Ole Frontier Gunsmith Shop
Olympic Arms Inc.
Parker & Sons Shooting Supply
Parker Gun Finishes
Parker Gun Finishes
Paulsen Gunstocks
PEM's Mfg. Co.
Perazone-Gunsmith, Brian
Peter Dyson & Son Ltd.
Power Custom, Inc.
Practical Tools, Inc.
Precision Specialties
R.A. Wells Custom Gunsmith
Ranch Products
Ransom International Corp.
Reardon Products
Rice, Keith
(See White Rock Tool & Die)
Robert Valade Engraving
Rocky Mountain Arms, Inc.
Romain's Custom Guns, Inc.
Royal Arms Gunstocks
Rusteprufe Laboratories
Sharp Shooter Supply
Shooter's Choice Gun Care
Simmons Gun Repair, Inc.
Smith Abrasives, Inc.
Southern Bloomer Mfg. Co.
Spencer Reblue Service
Spencer's Rifle Barrels, Inc.
Spradlin's
Starr Trading Co., Jedediah
Starrett Co., L. S.
Stiles Custom Guns
Stoney Point Products, Inc.
Sullivan, David S.
(See Westwind Rifles, Inc.)
Sunny Hill Enterprises, Inc.
T&S Industries, Inc.
T.W. Menck Gunsmith, Inc.
Tank's Rifle Shop
Tar-Hunt Custom Rifles, Inc.
Texas Platers Supply Co.
The A.W. Peterson Gun Shop, Inc.
The Gun Works
The NgraveR Co.
The Robar Co., Inc.
Theis, Terry
Tom's Gun Repair, Thomas G. Ivanoff
Track of the Wolf, Inc.
Trinidad St. Jr. Col. Gunsmith Dept.
Trulock Tool
Turnbull Restoration, Doug
United States Products Co.
Van Gorden & Son Inc., C. S.
Venco Industries, Inc.
(See Shooter's Choice Gun Care)
W.C. Wolff Co.
Warne Manufacturing Co.
Washita Mountain Whetstone Co.
Weigand Combat Handguns, Inc.
Wessinger Custom Guns & Engraving
White Rock Tool & Die
Wilcox All-Pro Tools & Supply
Wild West Guns
Will-Burt Co.
Williams Gun Sight Co.
Williams Shootin' Iron Service, The
Lynx-Line
Willow Bend
Windish, Jim
Wise Guns, Dale
Wright's Gunstock Blanks
Yavapai College
Ziegel Engineering

HANDGUN ACCESSORIES

"Su-Press-On", Inc.
A.A. Arms, Inc.
Ace Custom 45's, Inc.
Action Direct, Inc.
ADCO Sales, Inc.
Advantage Arms, Inc.
Aimtech Mount Systems
Ajax Custom Grips, Inc.
Alpha 1 Drop Zone
American Derringer Corp.
Arms Corporation of the Philippines
Astra Sport, S.A.
Autauga Arms, Inc.
Badger Creek Studio
Bagmaster Mfg., Inc.
Bar-Sto Precision Machine
Behlert Precision, Inc.
Berry's Mfg., Inc.
Blue and Gray Products Inc.
(See Ox-Yoke Originals)
Bond Custom Firearms
Bowen Classic Arms Corp.
Bridgeman Products
Broken Gun Ranch
Brooks Tactical Systems-Agrip
Brown Products, Inc., Ed
Bushmaster Hunting & Fishing
Butler Creek Corp.
Cannon Safe, Inc.
Centaur Systems, Inc.
Central Specialties Ltd
(See Trigger Lock Division
Charter 2000
Cheyenne Pioneer Products
Chicasaw Gun Works
Clark Custom Guns, Inc.
Classic Arms Company
Conetrol Scope Mounts
Crimson Trace Lasers
CRR, Inc./Marble's Inc.
Cylinder & Slide, Inc., William R.
Laughridge
D&L Industries (See D.J. Marketing)
D.J. Marketing
Dade Screw Machine Products
Dan Wesson Firearms
Delhi Gun House
DeSantis Holster & Leather Goods,
Inc.
Dixie Gun Works
Doskocil Mfg. Co., Inc.
E&L Mfg., Inc.
E. Arthur Brown Co.
E.A.A. Corp.
Eagle Imports, Inc.
Ed Brown Products, Inc.
Essex Arms
European American Armory Corp.
(See E.A.A. Corp.)
Evolution Gun Works, Inc.
Falcon Industries, Inc.
Federal Arms Corp. of America
Feinwerkbau Westinger & Altenburger
Fisher Custom Firearms
Fleming Firearms
Freedom Arms, Inc.
G.G. & G.
Galati International
GALCO International Ltd.
Garcia National Gun Traders, Inc.
Garthwaite Pistolsmith, Inc., Jim
Gil Hebard Guns, Inc.
Gilmore Sports Concepts, Inc.
Glock, Inc.
Goodwin's Pawn Shop
Gould & Goodrich
Gun-Alert
Gun-Ho Sports Cases
H.K.S. Products
Hafner World Wide, Inc.
Hammerli USA
Heinie Specialty Products
Henigson & Associates, Steve
High Standard Mfg. Co./F.I., Inc.
Hill Speed Leather, Ernie
HIP-GRIP Barami Corp.
Hi-Point Firearms/MKS Supply
Hobson Precision Mfg. Co.
Hoppe's Div. Penguin Industries, Inc.
H-S Precision, Inc.
Hume, Don
Hunter Co., Inc.
Impact Case & Container, Inc.
Import Sports Inc.
J.P. Enterprises Inc.
Jarvis, Inc.
JB Custom
Jeffredo Gunsight
Jim Noble Co.
John's Custom Leather
Jonathan Arthur Ciener, Inc.
Kalispel Case Line
KeeCo Impressions, Inc.
King's Gun Works
KK Air International
(See Impact Case & Container Co.)
Kolpin Outdoors, Inc.
L&S Technologies Inc.
(See Aimtech Mount Systems)
Lakewood Products LLC
LaserMax, Inc.
Les Baer Custom, Inc.
Loch Leven Industries/Convert-A-Pell
Lock's Philadelphia Gun Exchange
Lohman Mfg. Co., Inc.
Mag-Na-Port International, Inc.
Magnolia Sports, Inc.
Mag-Pack Corp.
Mahony, Philip Bruce
Mandall Shooting Supplies Inc.
Marble Arms
(See CRR, Inc./Marble's Inc.)
Markell, Inc.
MEC-Gar S.R.L.
Menck, Gunsmith Inc., T.W.
Merkuria Ltd.
Middlebrooks Custom Shop
Millett Sights
Mogul Co./Life Jacket
MTM Molded Products Co., Inc.
No-Sho Mfg. Co.
Numrich Gun Parts Corporation
Omega Sales
Outdoor Sports Headquarters, Inc.
Ox-Yoke Originals, Inc.
Pachmayr Div. Lyman Products
Pager Pal
Parker & Sons Shooting Supply
Pearce Grip, Inc.
Phoenix Arms
Practical Tools, Inc.
Precision Small Arms Inc.
Ram-Line ATK
Ranch Products
Ransom International Corp.
Ringler Custom Leather Co.
RPM
Seecamp Co. Inc., L. W.
Simmons Gun Repair, Inc.
Southern Bloomer Mfg. Co.
Springfield Armory
Springfield, Inc.
SSK Industries
Sturm Ruger & Co. Inc.
T.F.C. S.p.A.
Tactical Defense Institute
Tanfoglio Fratelli S.r.l.
The A.W. Peterson Gun Shop, Inc.
The Concealment Shop, Inc.
The Gun Works
The Keller Co.
The Protector Mfg. Co., Inc.
Thompson/Center Arms
Trigger Lock Division / Central
Specialties Ltd.
Trijicon, Inc.
Triple-K Mfg. Co., Inc.
Truglo, Inc.
Tyler Manufacturing & Distributing
United States Products Co.
Universal Sports
Volquartsen Custom Ltd.
W. Waller & Son, Inc.
W.C. Wolff Co.
Warne Manufacturing Co.
Weigand Combat Handguns, Inc.
Wessinger Custom Guns & Engraving
Western Design
(See Alpha Gunsmith Division)
Whitestone Lumber Corp.
Wichita Arms, Inc.
Wild West Guns
Williams Gun Sight Co.
Wilsom Combat
Yankee Gunsmith "Just Glocks"
Ziegel Engineering

HANDGUN GRIPS

A.A. Arms, Inc.
African Import Co.
Ahrends, Kim
(See Custom Firearms, Inc)
Ajax Custom Grips, Inc.
Altamont Co.
American Derringer Corp.
American Gripcraft
Arms Corporation of the Philippines
Art Jewel Enterprises Ltd.
Baelder, Harry
Big Bear Arms & Sporting Goods, Inc.
Bob's Gun Shop
Boone Trading Co., Inc.
Boone's Custom Ivory Grips, Inc.
Boyds' Gunstock Industries, Inc.
Brooks Tactical Systems-Agrip
Brown Products, Inc., Ed
Clark Custom Guns, Inc.
Claro Walnut Gunstock Co.
Cole-Grip
Colonial Repair
Crimson Trace Lasers
Custom Firearms (See Ahrends, Kim)
Cylinder & Slide, Inc., William R.
Laughridge
Dixie Gun Works
Dolbare, Elizabeth
E.A.A. Corp.
Eagle Imports, Inc.
EMF Co., Inc.
Essex Arms
European American Armory Corp.
(See E.A.A. Corp.)
Falcon Industries, Inc.
Feinwerkbau Westinger & Altenburger
Fibron Products, Inc.
Fisher Custom Firearms
Garthwaite Pistolsmith, Inc., Jim
Goodwin's Pawn Shop
Herrett's Stocks, Inc.
High Standard Mfg. Co./F.I., Inc.
HIP-GRIP Barami Corp.
Hogue Grips
H-S Precision, Inc.
Huebner, Corey O.
I.S.S.
Israel Arms Inc.
John Masen Co. Inc.
KeeCo Impressions, Inc.
Kim Ahrends Custom Firearms, Inc.
Korth Germany GmbH
Les Baer Custom, Inc.
Lett Custom Grips
Linebaugh Custom Sixguns
Lyman Products Corp.
Mandall Shooting Supplies Inc.
Michaels Of Oregon, Co.
Millett Sights
N.C. Ordnance Co.
Newell, Robert H.
Northern Precision
Pachmayr Div. Lyman Products
Pardini Armi Srl
Parker & Sons Shooting Supply
Pearce Grip, Inc.
Pilgrim Pewter, Inc.
(See Bell Originals Inc. Sid)
Precision Small Arms Inc.
Radical Concepts
Robinson, Don
Rosenberg & Son, Jack A.
Roy's Custom Grips
Spegel, Craig
Stoeger Industries
Sturm Ruger & Co. Inc.
Sunny Hill Enterprises, Inc.
Tactical Defense Institute
Taurus Firearms, Inc.
The A.W. Peterson Gun Shop, Inc.
Tirelli
Tom Forrest, Inc.
Triple-K Mfg. Co., Inc.
Tyler Manufacturing & Distributing
U.S. Fire Arms Mfg. Co., Inc.
Uncle Mike's
(See Michaels of Oregon Co.)
Vintage Industries, Inc.
Volquartsen Custom Ltd.
Western Mfg. Co.
Whitestone Lumber Corp.
Wright's Gunstock Blanks

HEARING PROTECTORS

Aero Peltor
Ajax Custom Grips, Inc.
Brown Co., E. Arthur
Browning Arms Co.

Creedmoor Sports, Inc.
David Clark Co., Inc.
Dillon Precision Products, Inc.
Dixie Gun Works
E-A-R, Inc.
Electronic Shooters Protection, Inc.
Gentex Corp.
Goodwin's Pawn Shop
Gunsmithing, Inc.
Hoppe's Div. Penguin Industries, Inc.
Kesselring Gun Shop
Mandall Shooting Supplies Inc.
Parker & Sons Shooting Supply
Paterson Gunsmithing
Peltor, Inc. (See Aero Peltor)
R.E.T. Enterprises
Ridgeline, Inc.
Rucker Dist. Inc.
Silencio/Safety Direct
Tactical Defense Institute
The A.W. Peterson Gun Shop, Inc.
The Gun Room Press
Triple-K Mfg. Co., Inc.
Watson Bullets
Whitestone Lumber Corp.

HOLSTERS & LEATHER GOODS

A&B Industries, Inc
(See Top-Line USA Inc.)
A.A. Arms, Inc.
Action Direct, Inc.
Action Products, Inc.
Aker International, Inc.
AKJ Concealco
Alessi Holsters, Inc.
Arratoonian, Andy
(See Horseshoe Leather Products)
Autauga Arms, Inc.
Bagmaster Mfg., Inc.
Baker's Leather Goods, Roy
Bandcor Industries, Div. of Man-Sew Corp.
Bang-Bang Boutique
(See Holster Shop, The)
Beretta S.P.A., Pietro
Bianchi International, Inc.
Bond Arms, Inc.
Brocock Ltd.
Brooks Tactical Systems-Agrip
Browning Arms Co.
Bull-X, Inc.
Cape Outfitters
Cathey Enterprises, Inc.
Chace Leather Products
Churchill Glove Co., James
Cimarron F.A. Co.
Classic Old West Styles
Clements' Custom Leathercraft, Chas
Cobra Sport S.R.I.
Collector's Armoury, Ltd.
Colonial Repair
Counter Assault
Delhi Gun House
DeSantis Holster & Leather Goods, Inc.
Dillon Precision Products, Inc.
Dixie Gun Works
Eagle Imports, Inc.
Ekol Leather Care
El Paso Saddlery Co.
EMF Co., Inc.
Faust Inc., T. G.
Freedom Arms, Inc.
Gage Manufacturing
GALCO International Ltd.
Garcia National Gun Traders, Inc.
Gil Hebard Guns, Inc.
Gilmore Sports Concepts, Inc.
GML Products, Inc.
Goodwin's Pawn Shop
Gould & Goodrich
Gun Leather Limited
Hafner World Wide, Inc.
HandCrafts Unltd.
(See Clements' Custom Leather)
Hank's Gun Shop
Heinie Specialty Products
Henigson & Associates, Steve
Hill Speed Leather, Ernie
HIP-GRIP Barami Corp.
Hobson Precision Mfg. Co.
Hogue Grips
Horseshoe Leather Products
Hume, Don
Hunter Co., Inc.
Import Sports Inc.
Jim Noble Co.
John's Custom Leather
K.L. Null Holsters Ltd.
Kirkpatrick Leather Co.
Kolpin Outdoors, Inc.
Korth Germany GmbH
Kramer Handgun Leather
L.A.R. Mfg., Inc.
Lawrence Leather Co.
Lock's Philadelphia Gun Exchange
Lone Star Gunleather
Magnolia Sports, Inc.
Mandall Shooting Supplies Inc.
Markell, Inc.
Marksman Products
Michaels Of Oregon, Co.
Minute Man High Tech Industries
Navy Arms Company
No-Sho Mfg. Co.
Null Holsters Ltd. K.L.
October Country Muzzleloading
Oklahoma Leather Products, Inc.
Old West Reproductions, Inc. R.M. Bachman
Pager Pal
Parker & Sons Shooting Supply
Pathfinder Sports Leather
Protektor Model
PWL Gunleather
Ramon B. Gonzalez Guns
Renegade
Ringler Custom Leather Co.
Rogue Rifle Co., Inc.
S&S Firearms
Safariland Ltd., Inc.
Safety Speed Holster, Inc.
Scharch Mfg., Inc.-Top Brass
Schulz Industries
Second Chance Body Armor
Silhouette Leathers
Smith Saddlery, Jesse W.
Sparks, Milt
Stalker, Inc.
Starr Trading Co., Jedediah
Strong Holster Co.
Stuart, V. Pat
Tabler Marketing
Tactical Defense Institute
Ted Blocker Holsters, Inc.
Tex Shoemaker & Sons, Inc.
Thad Rybka Custom Leather Equipment
The A.W. Peterson Gun Shop, Inc.
The Concealment Shop, Inc.
The Gun Works
The Keller Co.
The Outdoor Connection, Inc.
Torel, Inc.
Triple-K Mfg. Co., Inc.
Tristar Sporting Arms, Ltd.
Tyler Manufacturing & Distributing
Uncle Mike's
(See Michaels of Oregon Co.)
Venus Industries
W. Waller & Son, Inc.
Walt's Custom Leather, Walt Whinnery
Watson Bullets
Westley Richards & Co. Ltd.
Whinnery, Walt
(See Walt's Custom Leather)
Wild Bill's Originals
Wilsom Combat

HUNTING & CAMP GEAR, CLOTHING, ETC.

Action Direct, Inc.
Action Products, Inc.
Adventure 16, Inc.
All Rite Products, Inc.
Alpha 1 Drop Zone
Armor (See Buck Stop Lure Co., Inc.)
Atlanta Cutlery Corp.
Atsko/Sno-Seal, Inc.
B.B. Walker Co.
Baekgaard Ltd.
Bagmaster Mfg., Inc.
Barbour, Inc.
Bauer, Eddie
Bear Archery
Beaver Park Product, Inc.
Beretta S.P.A., Pietro
Better Concepts Co.
Bill Russ Trading Post
Bob Allen Sportswear
Boonie Packer Products
Boss Manufacturing Co.
Browning Arms Co.
Buck Stop Lure Co., Inc.
Bushmaster Hunting & Fishing
Cambos Outdoorsman
Cambos Outdoorsman
Camp-Cap Products
Carhartt, Inc.
Churchill Glove Co., James
Clarkfield Enterprises, Inc.
Classic Old West Styles
Clements' Custom Leathercraft, Chas
Coghlan's Ltd.
Cold Steel Inc.
Coleman Co., Inc.
Coulston Products, Inc.
Counter Assault
Dakota Corp.
Danner Shoe Mfg. Co.
Deepeeka Exports Pvt. Ltd.
Dr. O's Products Ltd.
Duofold, Inc.
Dynalite Products, Inc.
E-A-R, Inc.
Ekol Leather Care
Flambeau, Inc.
Forrest Tool Co.
Fox River Mills, Inc.
Frontier
G&H Decoys, Inc.
Gerber Legendary Blades
Glacier Glove
Grand Slam Hunting Products
HandCrafts Unltd.
(See Clements' Custom Leather)
High North Products, Inc.
Hinman Outfitters, Bob
Hodgman, Inc.
Houtz & Barwick
Hunter's Specialties Inc.
James Churchill Glove Co.
John's Custom Leather
K&M Industries, Inc.
Kamik Outdoor Footwear
Kolpin Outdoors, Inc.
L.L. Bean, Inc.
LaCrosse Footwear, Inc.
Leapers, Inc.
MAG Instrument, Inc.
Mag-Na-Port International, Inc.
McCann Industries
Molin Industries, Tru-Nord Division
Murphy, R.R. Co., Inc.
Northlake Outdoor Footwear
Original Deer Formula Co., The
Palsa Outdoor Products
Partridge Sales Ltd., John
Pointing Dog Journal, Village Press Publications
Powell & Son (Gunmakers) Ltd., William
Pro-Mark Div. of Wells Lamont
Ringler Custom Leather Co.
Robert Valade Engraving
Rocky Shoes & Boots
Scansport, Inc.
Sceery Game Calls
Schaefer Shooting Sports
Servus Footwear Co.
Simmons Outdoor Corp.
Sno-Seal, Inc.
(See Atsko/Sno-Seal, Inc.)
Swanndri New Zealand
TEN-X Products Group
The A.W. Peterson Gun Shop, Inc.
The Orvis Co.
The Outdoor Connection, Inc.
Tink's Safariland Hunting Corp.
Torel, Inc.
Triple-K Mfg. Co., Inc.
United Cutlery Corp.
Venus Industries
Wakina by Pic
Walls Industries, Inc.
Wideview Scope Mount Corp.
Wilderness Sound Products Ltd.
Winchester Sutler, Inc., The
Wolverine Footwear Group
Woolrich, Inc.
Wyoming Knife Corp.
Yellowstone Wilderness Supply

KNIVES & KNIFEMAKER'S SUPPLIES

A.G. Russell Knives, Inc.
Action Direct, Inc.
Adventure 16, Inc.
African Import Co.
Aitor-Cuchilleria Del Norte S.A.
American Target Knives
Art Jewel Enterprises Ltd.
Atlanta Cutlery Corp.
B&D Trading Co., Inc.
Barteaux Machete
Benchmark Knives
(See Gerber Legendary Blades)
Beretta S.P.A., Pietro
Beretta U.S.A. Corp.
Big Bear Arms & Sporting Goods, Inc.
Bill Russ Trading Post
Boker USA, Inc.
Boone Trading Co., Inc.
Boone's Custom Ivory Grips, Inc.
Bowen Knife Co., Inc.
Brooks Tactical Systems-Agrip
Browning Arms Co.
Buck Knives, Inc.
Buster's Custom Knives
Camillus Cutlery Co.
Campbell, Dick
Case & Sons Cutlery Co., W R
Chicago Cutlery Co.
Claro Walnut Gunstock Co.
Clements' Custom Leathercraft, Chas
Cold Steel Inc.
Coleman Co., Inc.
Collector's Armoury, Ltd.
Compass Industries, Inc.
Crosman Blades
(See Coleman Co., Inc.)
CRR, Inc./Marble's Inc.
Cutco Cutlery
damascususa@inteliport.com
Dan's Whetstone Co., Inc.
Deepeeka Exports Pvt. Ltd.
Degen Inc. (See Aristocrat Knives)
Delhi Gun House
DeSantis Holster & Leather Goods, Inc.
Diamond Machining Technology, Inc. (See DMT)
Dixie Gun Works
Dolbare, Elizabeth
EdgeCraft Corp., S. Weiner
Empire Cutlery Corp.
Eze-Lap Diamond Prods.
Flitz International Ltd.
Forrest Tool Co.
Forthofer's Gunsmithing & Knifemaking
Fortune Products, Inc.
Frank Knives
Frost Cutlery Co.
Galati International
George Ibberson (Sheffield) Ltd.
Gerber Legendary Blades
Glock, Inc.
Golden Age Arms Co.
H&B Forge Co.
Hafner World Wide, Inc.
Hammans, Charles E.
HandCrafts Unltd.
(See Clements' Custom Leather)
Harris Publications
High North Products, Inc.
Hoppe's Div. Penguin Industries, Inc.
Hunter Co., Inc.
Imperial Schrade Corp.
J.A. Blades, Inc.
(See Christopher Firearms Co.)
J.A. Henckels Zwillingswerk Inc.
Jackalope Gun Shop
Jantz Supply
Jenco Sales, Inc.
Jim Blair Engraving
Johnson Wood Products
KA-BAR Knives
Kasenit Co., Inc.
Kershaw Knives
Knifeware, Inc.
Koval Knives
Lamson & Goodnow Mfg. Co.
Lansky Sharpeners
Leapers, Inc.
Leatherman Tool Group, Inc.
Lethal Force Institute
(See Police Bookshelf)
Linder Solingen Knives
Mandall Shooting Supplies Inc.
Marble Arms
(See CRR, Inc./Marble's Inc.)
Marshall Fish Mfg. Gunsmith Sptg. Co.
Matthews Cutlery
McCann Industries
Molin Industries, Tru-Nord Division
Mountain State Muzzleloading Supplies, Inc.
Normark Corp.
October Country Muzzleloading
Outdoor Edge Cutlery Corp.
Pilgrim Pewter, Inc.
(See Bell Originals Inc. Sid)
Plaza Cutlery, Inc.
Police Bookshelf
Queen Cutlery Co.
R&C Knives & Such
R. Murphy Co., Inc.
Randall-Made Knives
Ringler Custom Leather Co.
Robert Valade Engraving
Scansport, Inc.
Schiffman, Mike
Sheffield Knifemakers Supply, Inc.
Smith Saddlery, Jesse W.
Springfield Armory
Spyderco, Inc.
T.F.C. S.p.A.
The A.W. Peterson Gun Shop, Inc.
The Creative Craftsman, Inc.

PRODUCT & SERVICE DIRECTORY

The Gun Room
The Gun Works
Theis, Terry
Traditions Performance Firearms
Traditions Performance Firearms
Tru-Balance Knife Co.
United Cutlery Corp.
Utica Cutlery Co.
Venus Industries
W.R. Case & Sons Cutlery Co.
Washita Mountain Whetstone Co.
Wells Creek Knife & Gun Works
Wenger North America/Precise Int'l.
Western Cutlery
(See Camillus Cutlery Co.)
Whinnery, Walt
(See Walt's Custom Leather)
Wideview Scope Mount Corp.
Wostenholm (See Ibberson [Sheffield] Ltd., George)
Wyoming Knife Corp.

LABELS, BOXES & CARTRIDGE HOLDERS

Ballistic Products, Inc.
Berry's Mfg., Inc.
Brocock Ltd.
Brown Co., E. Arthur
Cabinet Mtn. Outfitters Scents & Lures
Cheyenne Pioneer Products
Del Rey Products
DeSantis Holster & Leather Goods, Inc.
Flambeau, Inc.
Goodwin's Pawn Shop
Hafner World Wide, Inc.
J&J Products, Inc.
Kolpin Outdoors, Inc.
Liberty Shooting Supplies
Midway Arms, Inc.
MTM Molded Products Co., Inc.
Pendleton Royal, c/o Swingler Buckland Ltd.
Walt's Custom Leather, Walt Whinnery
Ziegel Engineering

LEAD WIRES & WIRE CUTTERS

Ames Metal Products
Big Bore Express
Bullet Swaging Supply, Inc.
D.L. Unmussig Bullets
Goodwin's Pawn Shop
Liberty Metals
Lightning Performance Innovations, Inc.
Montana Precision Swaging
Northern Precision
Sport Flite Manufacturing Co.
Star Ammunition, Inc.

LOAD TESTING & PRODUCT TESTING

Ballistic Research
Bridgeman Products
Briese Bullet Co., Inc.
Buckskin Bullet Co.
Bull Mountain Rifle Co.
CFVentures
Claybuster Wads & Harvester Bullets
Clearview Products
D&H Precision Tooling
Dead Eye's Sport Center
Defense Training International, Inc.
Duane's Gun Repair
(See DGR Custom Rifles)
Gruning Precision, Inc.
H.P. White Laboratory, Inc.
Hank's Gun Shop
Henigson & Associates, Steve
Hutton Rifle Ranch
J&J Sales
Jackalope Gun Shop
Jensen Bullets
Jonathan Arthur Ciener, Inc.
L. E. Jurras & Assoc.
Liberty Shooting Supplies
Linebaugh Custom Sixguns
Lomont Precision Bullets
MAST Technology, Inc.
McMurdo, Lynn
(See Specialty Gunsmithing)
Middlebrooks Custom Shop
Modern Gun Repair School
Multiplex International
Northwest Arms
Oil Rod and Gun Shop
Plum City Ballistic Range
R.A. Wells Custom Gunsmith
Ramon B. Gonzalez Guns
Rupert's Gun Shop
Small Custom Mould & Bullet Co.
SOS Products Co.
(See Buck Stix-SOS Products Co.)
Spencer's Rifle Barrels, Inc.
Tar-Hunt Custom Rifles, Inc.
Trinidad St. Jr. Col. Gunsmith Dept.
Vulpes Ventures, Inc., Fox Cartridge Division
W. Square Enterprises
X-Spand Target Systems

LOADING BLOCKS, METALLIC & SHOTSHELL

Battenfeld Technologies Inc.
Buffalo Arms Co.
Huntington Die Specialties
Jericho Tool & Die Co., Inc.
Sinclair International, Inc.
The A.W. Peterson Gun Shop, Inc.

LUBRISIZERS, DIES & ACCESSORIES

Ballisti-Cast, Inc.
Buffalo Arms Co.
Cast Performance Bullet Company
Cooper-Woodward Perfect Lube
Corbin Mfg. & Supply, Inc.
GAR
Hart & Son, Inc.
Javelina Lube Products
Lee Precision, Inc.
Lithi Bee Bullet Lube
Lyman Products Corp.
Magma Engineering Co.
PWM Sales Ltd.
RCBS Operations/ATK
Redding Reloading Equipment
S&S Firearms
SPG LLC
The A.W. Peterson Gun Shop, Inc.
Thompson Bullet Lube Co.
United States Products Co.
WTA Manufacturing

MOULDS & MOULD ACCESSORIES

Ad Hominem
American Products, Inc.
Ballisti-Cast, Inc.
Buffalo Arms Co.
Bullet Swaging Supply, Inc.
Cast Performance Bullet Company
Corbin Mfg. & Supply, Inc.
Davide Pedersoli and Co.
GAR
Huntington Die Specialties
Lee Precision, Inc.
Lyman Products Corp.
Magma Engineering Co.
Old West Bullet Moulds
Pacific Rifle Co.
Penn Bullets
Rapine Bullet Mould Mfg. Co.
RCBS Operations/ATK
Redding Reloading Equipment
S&S Firearms
Small Custom Mould & Bullet Co.
The A.W. Peterson Gun Shop, Inc.
The Gun Works
Wolf's Western Traders

MUZZLE-LOADING GUNS, BARRELS & EQUIPMENT

Accuracy Unlimited
Ackerman & Co.
Adkins, Luther
Allen Mfg.
Armi San Paolo
Armoury, Inc., The
Austin & Halleck, Inc.
Bauska Barrels
Bentley, John
Big Bore Express
Birdsong & Assoc., W. E.
Black Powder Products
Blount/Outers ATK
Blue and Gray Products Inc.
(See Ox-Yoke Originals)
Bridgers Best
Buckskin Bullet Co.
Bullberry Barrel Works, Ltd.
Butler Creek Corp.
Cabela's
Cache La Poudre Rifleworks
California Sights
(See Fautheree, Andy)
Cash Mfg. Co., Inc.
Caywood Gunmakers
CBC-BRAZIL
Chambers Flintlocks Ltd., Jim
Chicasaw Gun Works
Cimarron F.A. Co.
Claybuster Wads & Harvester Bullets
Cogar's Gunsmithing
Colonial Repair
Colt Blackpowder Arms Co.
Conetrol Scope Mounts
Cousin Bob's Mountain Products
Cumberland Arms
Cumberland Mountain Arms
Curly Maple Stock Blanks
(See Tiger-Hunt)
CVA
Dangler, Homer L.
Davide Pedersoli and Co.
Dayton Traister
deHaas Barrels
Delhi Gun House
Dixie Gun Works
Dixie Gun Works
Dixon Muzzleloading Shop, Inc.
Dolbare, Elizabeth
EMF Co., Inc.
Euroarms of America, Inc.
Feken, Dennis
Flintlocks, Etc.
Fort Hill Gunstocks
Fowler, Bob
(See Black Powder Products)
Frontier
Getz Barrel Company
Goergen's Gun Shop, Inc.
Golden Age Arms Co.
Gonic Arms/North American Arms, Inc.
Goodwin's Pawn Shop
Green Mountain Rifle Barrel Co., Inc.
H&R 1871.LLC
Hastings
Hawken Shop, The
(See Dayton Traister)
Hege Jagd-u. Sporthandels GmbH
Hodgdon Powder Co.
Hoppe's Div. Penguin Industries, Inc.
Hornady Mfg. Co.
House of Muskets, Inc., The
Hunkeler, A.
(See Buckskin Machine Works)
IAR Inc.
Impact Case & Container, Inc.
Ironsighter Co.
J. Dewey Mfg. Co., Inc.
Jamison's Forge Works
Jones Co., Dale
K&M Industries, Inc.
Kalispel Case Line
Kennedy Firearms
Knight Rifles
Knight Rifles
(See Modern Muzzle Loading, Inc.)
Kolar
L&R Lock Co.
L&S Technologies Inc.
(See Aimtech Mount Systems)
Lakewood Products LLC
Lodgewood Mfg.
Log Cabin Sport Shop
Lothar Walther Precision Tool Inc.
Lyman Products Corp.
Markesbery Muzzle Loaders, Inc.
Mathews Gun Shop & Gunsmithing, Inc.
McCann, Tom
Michaels Of Oregon, Co.
Millennium Designed Muzzleloaders
Modern Muzzleloading, Inc.
Mountain State Muzzleloading Supplies, Inc.
Mowrey Gun Works
Navy Arms Company
Newman Gunshop
North Star West
October Country Muzzleloading
Oklahoma Leather Products, Inc.
Olson, Myron
Orion Rifle Barrel Co.
Ox-Yoke Originals, Inc.
Pacific Rifle Co.
Parker & Sons Shooting Supply
Parker Gun Finishes
Pecatonica River Longrifle
Peter Dyson & Son Ltd.
Pioneer Arms Co.
Prairie River Arms
Rossi Firearms
Rusty Duck Premium Gun Care Products
S&S Firearms
Selsi Co., Inc.
Simmons Gun Repair, Inc.
Sklany's Machine Shop
Smokey Valley Rifles
South Bend Replicas, Inc.
Southern Bloomer Mfg. Co.
Splitfire Sporting Goods, L.L.C.
Starr Trading Co., Jedediah
Stone Mountain Arms
Sturm Ruger & Co. Inc.
Taylor's & Co., Inc.
Tennessee Valley Mfg.
The A.W. Peterson Gun Shop, Inc.
The Gun Works
The Hawken Shop
Thompson Bullet Lube Co.
Thompson/Center Arms
Tiger-Hunt Gunstocks
Track of the Wolf, Inc.
Traditions Performance Firearms
Truglo, Inc.
Uncle Mike's
(See Michaels of Oregon Co.)
Universal Sports
Upper Missouri Trading Co.
Venco Industries, Inc.
(See Shooter's Choice Gun Care)
Village Restorations & Consulting, Inc.
Virgin Valley Custom Guns
Voere-KGH GmbH
W.E. Birdsong & Assoc.
Warne Manufacturing Co.
Warren Muzzleloading Co., Inc.
Wescombe, Bill (See North Star West)
White Rifles, Inc.
William E. Phillips Firearms
Woodworker's Supply
Wright's Gunstock Blanks
Young Country Arms
Ziegel Engineering

PISTOLSMITH

A.W. Peterson Gun Shop, Inc.
Acadian Ballistic Specialties
Accuracy Unlimited
Ace Custom 45's, Inc.
Actions by "T" Teddy Jacobson
Adair Custom Shop, Bill
Ahlman Guns
Ahrends, Kim
(See Custom Firearms, Inc)
Aldis Gunsmithing & Shooting Supply
Alpha Precision, Inc.
Alpine Indoor Shooting Range
Armament Gunsmithing Co., Inc.
Arundel Arms & Ammunition, Inc., A.
Badger Creek Studio
Bain & Davis, Inc.
Bar-Sto Precision Machine
Behlert Precision, Inc.
Bengtson Arms Co., L.
Bill Adair Custom Shop
Billings Gunsmiths
Bob Rogers Gunsmithing
Bowen Classic Arms Corp.
Broken Gun Ranch
Caraville Manufacturing
Chicasaw Gun Works
Chip McCormick Corp.
Clark Custom Guns, Inc.
Cleland's Outdoor World, Inc
Colonial Repair
Colorado School of Trades
Colt's Mfg. Co., Inc.
Corkys Gun Clinic
Custom Firearms (See Ahrends, Kim)
Cylinder & Slide, Inc., William R. Laughridge
D&D Gunsmiths, Ltd.
D&L Sports
David R. Chicoine
Dayton Traister
Dilliott Gunsmithing, Inc.
Ellicott Arms, Inc. / Woods Pistolsmithing
Evolution Gun Works, Inc.
Ferris Firearms
Fisher Custom Firearms
Forkin Custom Classics
G.G. & G.
Garthwaite Pistolsmith, Inc., Jim
Gary Reeder Custom Guns
Genecco Gun Works
Gentry Custom LLC
Greider Precision
Guncraft Sports, Inc.
Guncraft Sports, Inc.
Gunsite Training Center
Hamilton, Alex B.
(See Ten-Ring Precision, Inc.)
Hammerli Service-Precision Mac
Hammond Custom Guns Ltd.
Hank's Gun Shop

Hanson's Gun Center, Dick
Harwood, Jack O.
Hawken Shop, The
  (See Dayton Traister)
Heinie Specialty Products
High Bridge Arms, Inc.
High Standard Mfg. Co./F.I., Inc.
Highline Machine Co.
Hoag, James W.
Irwin, Campbell H.
Island Pond Gun Shop
Ivanoff, Thomas G.
  (See Tom's Gun Repair)
J&S Heat Treat
Jarvis, Inc.
Jeffredo Gunsight
Jensen's Custom Ammunition
Jungkind, Reeves C.
Kaswer Custom, Inc.
Ken Starnes Gunmaker
Kilham & Co.
Kim Ahrends Custom Firearms, Inc.
King's Gun Works
La Clinique du .45
LaFrance Specialties
LaRocca Gun Works
Lathrop's, Inc.
Lawson, John G.
  (See Sight Shop, The)
Leckie Professional Gunsmithing
Les Baer Custom, Inc.
Linebaugh Custom Sixguns
List Precision Engineering
Long, George F.
Mag-Na-Port International, Inc.
Mahony, Philip Bruce
Mahovsky's Metalife
Mandall Shooting Supplies Inc.
Marvel, Alan
Mathews Gun Shop & Gunsmithing, Inc.
MCS, Inc.
Middlebrooks Custom Shop
Miller Custom
Mitchell's Accuracy Shop
MJK Gunsmithing, Inc.
Modern Gun Repair School
Mo's Competitor Supplies
  (See MCS, Inc.)
Mowrey's Guns & Gunsmithing
Mullis Guncraft
NCP Products, Inc.
Novak's, Inc.
Nowlin Mfg. Co.
Olathe Gun Shop
Paris, Frank J.
Pasadena Gun Center
Peacemaker Specialists
PEM's Mfg. Co.
Performance Specialists
Peterson Gun Shop, Inc., A.W.
Pierce Pistols
Piquette's Custom Engraving
Power Custom, Inc.
Precision Specialties
Ramon B. Gonzalez Guns
Randco UK
Ries, Chuck
Rim Pac Sports, Inc.
Rocky Mountain Arms, Inc.
RPM
Ruger's Custom Guns
Score High Gunsmithing
Shooters Supply
Shootin' Shack
Singletary, Kent
Springfield, Inc.
SSK Industries
Swenson's 45 Shop, A. D.
Swift River Gunworks
Ten-Ring Precision, Inc.
Terry K. Kopp Professional Gunsmithing
The A.W. Peterson Gun Shop, Inc.
The Gun Works
The Robar Co., Inc.
The Sight Shop
Thurston Sports, Inc.
Time Precision
Tom's Gun Repair, Thomas G. Ivanoff
Turnbull Restoration, Doug
Vic's Gun Refinishing
Volquartsen Custom Ltd.
Walker Arms Co., Inc.
Walters Industries
Wardell Precision Handguns Ltd.
Wessinger Custom Guns & Engraving
White Barn Wor
Wichita Arms, Inc.
Wild West Guns
Williams Gun Sight Co.
Williamson Precision Gunsmithing
Wilsom Combat
Wright's Gunstock Blanks

POWDER MEASURES, SCALES, FUNNELS & ACCESSORIES

4-D Custom Die Co.
Battenfeld Technologies Inc.
Buffalo Arms Co.
Davide Pedersoli and Co.
Dillon Precision Products, Inc.
Fremont Tool Works
Frontier
GAR
High Precision
Hoehn Sales, Inc.
Jones Custom Products, Neil A.
Modern Muzzleloading, Inc.
Neil A. Jones Custom Products
Pacific Rifle Co.
Peter Dyson & Son Ltd.
Precision Reloading, Inc.
Ramon B. Gonzalez Guns
RCBS Operations/ATK
RCBS/ATK
Redding Reloading Equipment
Saunders Gun & Machine Shop
Schumakers Gun Shop
Spencer's Rifle Barrels, Inc.
The A.W. Peterson Gun Shop, Inc.
Vega Tool Co.
VibraShine, Inc.
VTI Gun Parts

PRESS ACCESSORIES, METALLIC

Buffalo Arms Co.
Corbin Mfg. & Supply, Inc.
Hollywood Engineering
Huntington Die Specialties
MA Systems, Inc.
R.E.I.
Redding Reloading Equipment
Royal Arms Gunstocks
The A.W. Peterson Gun Shop, Inc.
Thompson Tool Mount
Vega Tool Co.

PRESS ACCESSORIES, SHOTSHELL

Hollywood Engineering
Lee Precision, Inc.
MEC, Inc.
Precision Reloading, Inc.
R.E.I.
The A.W. Peterson Gun Shop, Inc.

PRESSES, ARBOR

Blue Ridge Machinery & Tools, Inc.
Goodwin's Pawn Shop
Hoehn Sales, Inc.
K&M Services
RCBS Operations/ATK
Spencer's Rifle Barrels, Inc.
The A.W. Peterson Gun Shop, Inc.

PRESSES, METALLIC

4-D Custom Die Co.
Battenfeld Technologies Inc.
Dillon Precision Products, Inc.
Fremont Tool Works
Goodwin's Pawn Shop
Hornady Mfg. Co.
Huntington Die Specialties
Lee Precision, Inc.
Midway Arms, Inc.
R.E.I.
Ramon B. Gonzalez Guns
RCBS Operations/ATK
RCBS/ATK
Redding Reloading Equipment
Spencer's Rifle Barrels, Inc.
The A.W. Peterson Gun Shop, Inc.

PRESSES, SHOTSHELL

Ballistic Products, Inc.
Dillon Precision Products, Inc.
Goodwin's Pawn Shop
Hornady Mfg. Co.
MEC, Inc.
Precision Reloading, Inc.
Spolar Power Load, Inc.
The A.W. Peterson Gun Shop, Inc.

PRESSES, SWAGE

Bullet Swaging Supply, Inc.
The A.W. Peterson Gun Shop, Inc.

PRIMING TOOLS & ACCESSORIES

GAR
Goodwin's Pawn Shop
Hart & Son, Inc.
Huntington Die Specialties
K&M Services
RCBS Operations/ATK
Simmons, Jerry
Sinclair International, Inc.
The A.W. Peterson Gun Shop, Inc.

REBORING & RERIFLING

Ahlman Guns
Barrel & Gunworks
Bauska Barrels
BlackStar AccuMax Barrels
BlackStar Barrel Accurizing
  (See BlackStar AccuMax)
Buffalo Arms Co.
Champlin Firearms, Inc.
Ed's Gun House
Fred F. Wells/Wells Sport Store
Ivanoff, Thomas G.
  (See Tom's Gun Repair)
Jackalope Gun Shop
Jonathan Arthur Ciener, Inc.
LaBounty Precision Reboring, Inc
NCP Products, Inc.
Pence Precision Barrels
Redman's Rifling & Reboring
Rice, Keith
  (See White Rock Tool & Die)
Ridgetop Sporting Goods
Savage Arms, Inc.
Shaw, Inc., E. R.
  (See Small Arms Mfg. Co.)
Siegrist Gun Shop
Simmons Gun Repair, Inc.
Stratco, Inc.
Terry K. Kopp Professional Gunsmithing
The Gun Works
Time Precision
Tom's Gun Repair, Thomas G. Ivanoff
Turnbull Restoration, Doug
Van Patten, J. W.
White Rock Tool & Die
Zufall, Joseph F.

RELOADING TOOLS AND ACCESSORIES

4-D Custom Die Co.
Advance Car Mover Co., Rowell Div.
American Products, Inc.
Ammo Load, Inc.
Armfield Custom Bullets
Armite Laboratories
Arms Corporation of the Philippines
Atlantic Rose, Inc.
Atsko/Sno-Seal, Inc.
Bald Eagle Precision Machine Co.
Ballistic Products, Inc.
Berger Bullets Ltd.
Berry's Mfg., Inc.
Blount, Inc., Sporting Equipment Div.
Blue Mountain Bullets
Blue Ridge Machinery & Tools, Inc.
Bonanza (See Forster Products)
Brown Co., E. Arthur
BRP, Inc. High Performance Cast Bullets
Brynin, Milton
B-Square Company, Inc.
Buck Stix-SOS Products Co.
Buffalo Arms Co.
Bull Mountain Rifle Co.
C&D Special Products (See Claybuster Wads & Harvester Bullets)
Camdex, Inc.
Camp-Cap Products
Canyon Cartridge Corp.
Case Sorting System
CCI/Speer Div of ATK
CH Tool & Die Co.
  (See 4-D Custom Die Co.)
CheVron Bullets
Claybuster Wads & Harvester Bullets
Cook Engineering Service
Crouse's Country Cover
Cumberland Arms
Curtis Cast Bullets
Custom Products
  (See Jones Custom Products)
CVA
D.C.C. Enterprises
Davide Pedersoli and Co.
Davis, Don
Davis Products, Mike
Denver Instrument Co.
Dillon Precision Products, Inc.
Dropkick
E&L Mfg., Inc.
Eagan, Donald V.
Eichelberger Bullets, Wm.
Enguix Import-Export
Euroarms of America, Inc.
E-Z-Way Systems
Federated-Fry (See Fry Metals)
Feken, Dennis
Ferguson, Bill
Fisher Custom Firearms
Flambeau, Inc.
Flitz International Ltd.
Forster Products
Fremont Tool Works
Fry Metals
Gehmann, Walter
  (See Huntington Die Specialties)
Graf & Sons
Graphics Direct
Graves Co.
Green, Arthur S.
Greenwood Precision
GTB-Custom Bullets
Gun City
Hanned Precision
  (See The Hanned Line)
Harrell's Precision
Harris Enterprises
Harrison Bullets
Heidenstrom Bullets
High Precision
Hirtenberger AG
Hodgdon Powder Co.
Hoehn Sales, Inc.
Holland's Gunsmithing
Hondo Ind.
Hornady Mfg. Co.
Howell Machine
Hunters Supply, Inc.
Hutton Rifle Ranch
Image Ind. Inc.
Imperial Magnum Corp.
INTEC International, Inc.
Iosso Products
J&L Superior Bullets
  (See Huntington Die Special)
Jack First, Inc.
Javelina Lube Products
JGS Precision Tool Mfg., LLC
JLK Bullets
Jonad Corp.
Jones Custom Products, Neil A.
Jones Moulds, Paul
K&M Services
Kapro Mfg. Co. Inc. (See R.E.I.)
Knoell, Doug
Korzinek Riflesmith, J.
L.A.R. Mfg., Inc.
L.E. Wilson, Inc.
Lapua Ltd.
Le Clear Industries
  (See E-Z-Way Systems)
Lee Precision, Inc.
Liberty Metals
Liberty Shooting Supplies
Lightning Performance Innovations, Inc.
Lithi Bee Bullet Lube
Littleton, J. F.
Lock's Philadelphia Gun Exchange
Lortone Inc.
Lyman Instant Targets, Inc.
  (See Lyman Products)
Lyman Products Corp.
MA Systems, Inc.
Magma Engineering Co.
MarMik, Inc.
Marquart Precision Co.
Match Prep-Doyle Gracey
Mayville Engineering Co.
  (See MEC, Inc.)
MCS, Inc.
MEC, Inc.
Midway Arms, Inc.
MI-TE Bullets
Montana Armory, Inc.
  (See C. Sharps Arms Co. Inc.)
Mo's Competitor Supplies
  (See MCS, Inc.)
Mountain State Muzzleloading Supplies, Inc.
MTM Molded Products Co., Inc.
MWG Co.
Navy Arms Company
Newman Gunshop
North Devon Firearms Services
Old West Bullet Moulds

Original Box, Inc.
Outdoor Sports Headquarters, Inc.
Paco's (See Small Custom Mould & Bullet Co.)
Paragon Sales & Services, Inc.
Pease Accuracy
Pinetree Bullets
Ponsness/Warren
Prairie River Arms
Prime Reloading
Professional Hunter Supplies (See Star Custom Bullets)
Pro-Shot Products, Inc.
R.A. Wells Custom Gunsmith
R.E.I.
R.I.S. Co., Inc.
Rapine Bullet Mould Mfg. Co.
Reloading Specialties, Inc.
Rice, Keith (See White Rock Tool & Die)
Rochester Lead Works
Rooster Laboratories
Rorschach Precision Products
SAECO (See Redding Reloading Equipment)
Sandia Die & Cartridge Co.
Saunders Gun & Machine Shop
Saville Iron Co. (See Greenwood Precision)
Seebeck Assoc., R.E.
Sharp Shooter Supply
Sharps Arms Co., Inc., C.
Sierra Specialty Prod. Co.
Silver Eagle Machining
Skip's Machine
Small Custom Mould & Bullet Co.
Sno-Seal, Inc. (See Atsko/Sno-Seal, Inc.)
SOS Products Co. (See Buck Stix-SOS Products Co.)
Spencer's Rifle Barrels, Inc.
SPG LLC
SSK Industries
Stalwart Corporation
Star Custom Bullets
Starr Trading Co., Jedediah
Stillwell, Robert
Stoney Point Products, Inc.
Stratco, Inc.
Tamarack Products, Inc.
Taracorp Industries, Inc.
TCCI
TCSR
TDP Industries, Inc.
Tetra Gun Care
The Hanned Line
The Protector Mfg. Co., Inc.
Thompson/Center Arms
TMI Products (See Haselbauer Products, Jerry)
Vega Tool Co.
Venco Industries, Inc. (See Shooter's Choice Gun Care)
VibraShine, Inc.
Vibra-Tek Co.
Vihtavuori Oy/Kaltron-Pettibone
Vitt/Boos
W.B. Niemi Engineering
W.J. Riebe Co.
WD-40 Co.
Webster Scale Mfg. Co.
White Rock Tool & Die
Widener's Reloading & Shooting Supply, Inc.
Wise Custom Guns
Woodleigh (See Huntington Die Specialties)
Yesteryear Armory & Supply
Young Country Arms

RESTS BENCH, PORTABLE AND ACCESSORIES

Adventure 16, Inc.
Armor Metal Products
Bald Eagle Precision Machine Co.
Bartlett Engineering
Battenfeld Technologies Inc.
Blount/Outers ATK
Browning Arms Co.
B-Square Company, Inc.
Bull Mountain Rifle Co.
Canons Delcour
Clift Mfg., L. R.
Desert Mountain Mfg.
Greenwood Precision
Harris Engineering Inc.
Hart & Son, Inc.
Hidalgo, Tony
Hoehn Sales, Inc.
Hoppe's Div. Penguin Industries, Inc.
J&J Sales
Keng's Firearms Specialty, Inc./US Tactical Systems
Kolpin Outdoors, Inc.
Kramer Designs
Midway Arms, Inc.
Millett Sights
Protektor Model
Ransom International Corp.
Russ Haydon's Shooters' Supply
Saville Iron Co. (See Greenwood Precision)
Sinclair International, Inc.
Stoney Point Products, Inc.
The A.W. Peterson Gun Shop, Inc.
The Outdoor Connection, Inc.
Thompson Target Technology
Tonoloway Tack Drives
Varmint Masters, LLC
Wichita Arms, Inc.
Zanotti Armor, Inc.
Ziegel Engineering

RIFLE BARREL MAKER

Airrow
American Safe Arms, Inc.
Barrel & Gunworks
Bauska Barrels
BlackStar AccuMax Barrels
BlackStar Barrel Accurizing (See BlackStar AccuMax)
Border Barrels Ltd.
Brown Co., E. Arthur
Buchsenmachermeister
Bullberry Barrel Works, Ltd.
Bushmaster Firearms, Inc.
Canons Delcour
Carter's Gun Shop
Christensen Arms
Cincinnati Swaging
D.L. Unmussig Bullets
deHaas Barrels
Dilliott Gunsmithing, Inc.
DKT, Inc.
Donnelly, C. P.
Douglas Barrels, Inc.
Fred F. Wells/Wells Sport Store
Gaillard Barrels
Getz Barrel Company
Getz Barrel Company
Granite Mountain Arms, Inc.
Green Mountain Rifle Barrel Co., Inc.
Gruning Precision, Inc.
Half Moon Rifle Shop
Hart Rifle Barrels, Inc.
Hastings
Hofer Jagdwaffen, P.
H-S Precision, Inc.
Jackalope Gun Shop
Krieger Barrels, Inc.
Les Baer Custom, Inc.
Lilja Precision Rifle Barrels
Lothar Walther Precision Tool Inc.
McGowen Rifle Barrels
McMillan Rifle Barrels
Mid-America Recreation, Inc.
Modern Gun Repair School
Morrison Precision
N.C. Ordnance Co.
Obermeyer Rifled Barrels
Olympic Arms Inc.
Orion Rifle Barrel Co.
PAC-NOR Barreling
Pence Precision Barrels
Perazone-Gunsmith, Brian
Rogue Rifle Co., Inc.
Sabatti SPA
Savage Arms, Inc.
Schneider Rifle Barrels, Inc.
Shaw, Inc., E. R. (See Small Arms Mfg. Co.)
Shilen, Inc.
Siskiyou Gun Works (See Donnelly, C. P.)
Small Arms Mfg. Co.
Specialty Shooters Supply, Inc.
Spencer's Rifle Barrels, Inc.
Steyr Mannlicher GmbH & Co KG
Strutz Rifle Barrels, Inc., W. C.
Swift River Gunworks
Terry K. Kopp Professional Gunsmithing
The Gun Works
The Wilson Arms Co.
Turnbull Restoration, Doug
Verney-Carron
Virgin Valley Custom Guns
William E. Phillips Firearms
Wiseman and Co., Bill

SCOPES, MOUNTS, ACCESSORIES, OPTICAL EQUIPMENT

A.R.M.S., Inc.
Accu-Tek
Ackerman, Bill (See Optical Services Co.)
Action Direct, Inc.
ADCO Sales, Inc.
Aimtech Mount Systems
Air Rifle Specialists
Air Venture Airguns
All Rite Products, Inc.
Alley Supply Co.
Alpec Team, Inc.
Apel GmbH, Ernst
ArmaLite, Inc.
Arundel Arms & Ammunition, Inc., A.
B.A.C.
Badger Creek Studio
Bansner's Ultimate Rifles, LLC
Barrett Firearms Manufacturer, Inc.
Beaver Park Product, Inc.
BEC, Inc.
Beeman Precision Airguns
Benjamin/Sheridan Co., Crosman
Bill Russ Trading Post
BKL Technologies
Blount, Inc., Sporting Equipment Div.
Blount/Outers ATK
Borden Rifles Inc.
Broad Creek Rifle Works, Ltd.
Brockman's Custom Gunsmithing
Brocock Ltd.
Brown Co., E. Arthur
Brownells, Inc.
Brunton U.S.A.
BSA Optics
B-Square Company, Inc.
Bull Mountain Rifle Co.
Burris Co., Inc.
Bushmaster Firearms, Inc.
Bushnell Sports Optics Worldwide
Butler Creek Corp.
Cabela's
Carl Zeiss Inc.
Center Lock Scope Rings
Chuck's Gun Shop
Clark Custom Guns, Inc.
Clearview Mfg. Co., Inc.
Compass Industries, Inc.
Compasseco, Ltd.
Concept Development Corp.
Conetrol Scope Mounts
Creedmoor Sports, Inc.
Crimson Trace Lasers
Crosman Airguns
Custom Quality Products, Inc.
D.C.C. Enterprises
D.L. Unmussig Bullets
Daisy Outdoor Products
Del-Sports, Inc.
DHB Products
Dolbare, Elizabeth
E. Arthur Brown Co.
Eagle Imports, Inc.
Eclectic Technologies, Inc.
Edmund Scientific Co.
Ednar, Inc.
Eggleston, Jere D.
Emerging Technologies, Inc. (See Laseraim Technologies, Inc.)
Entre`prise Arms, Inc.
Euro-Imports
Evolution Gun Works, Inc.
Excalibur Electro Optics, Inc.
Excel Industries, Inc.
Falcon Industries, Inc.
Farr Studio, Inc.
Federal Arms Corp. of America
Freedom Arms, Inc.
Fujinon, Inc.
G.G. & G.
Galati International
Gentry Custom LLC
Gil Hebard Guns, Inc.
Gilmore Sports Concepts, Inc.
Goodwin's Pawn Shop
GSI, Inc.
Gun South, Inc. (See GSI, Inc.)
Guns Div. of D.C. Engineering, Inc.
Gunsmithing, Inc.
Hakko Co. Ltd.
Hammerli USA
Hart & Son, Inc.
Harvey, Frank
Highwood Special Products
Hiptmayer, Armurier
Hiptmayer, Klaus
Holland's Gunsmithing
Hunter Co., Inc.
Impact Case & Container, Inc.
Ironsighter Co.
Jeffredo Gunsight
Jena Eur
Jerry Phillips Optics
Jewell Triggers, Inc.
John Masen Co. Inc.
John's Custom Leather
Kahles A. Swarovski Company
Kalispel Case Line
KDF, Inc.
Keng's Firearms Specialty, Inc./US Tactical Systems
Kesselring Gun Shop
Kimber of America, Inc.
Knight's Mfg. Co.
Kowa Optimed, Inc.
KVH Industries, Inc.
Kwik-Site Co.
L&S Technologies Inc. (See Aimtech Mount Systems)
L.A.R. Mfg., Inc.
Laser Devices, Inc.
Laseraim Technologies, Inc.
LaserMax, Inc.
Leapers, Inc.
Leica USA, Inc.
Les Baer Custom, Inc.
Leupold & Stevens, Inc.
List Precision Engineering
Lohman Mfg. Co., Inc.
Lomont Precision Bullets
London Guns Ltd.
Mac-1 Airgun Distributors
Mag-Na-Port International, Inc.
Mandall Shooting Supplies Inc.
Marksman Products
Maxi-Mount Inc.
McBros Rifle Co.
McMillan Optical Gunsight Co.
MCS, Inc.
MDS
Merit Corp.
Military Armament Corp.
Millett Sights
Mirador Optical Corp.
Mitchell Optics, Inc.
MMC
Mo's Competitor Supplies (See MCS, Inc.)
MWG Co.
Navy Arms Company
New England Custom Gun Service
Nikon, Inc.
Norincoptics (See BEC, Inc.)
Olympic Optical Co.
Op-Tec
Optical Services Co.
Orchard Park Enterprise
Oregon Arms, Inc. (See Rogue Rifle Co., Inc.)
Ozark Gun Works
Parker & Sons Shooting Supply
Parsons Optical Mfg. Co.
PECAR Herbert Schwarz GmbH
PEM's Mfg. Co.
Pentax Corp.
PMC/Eldorado Cartridge Corp.
Precision Sport Optics
Premier Reticles
Quarton Beamshot
R.A. Wells Custom Gunsmith
Ram-Line ATK
Ramon B. Gonzalez Guns
Ranch Products
Randolph Engineering, Inc.
Rice, Keith (See White Rock Tool & Die)
Robinson Armament Co.
Rogue Rifle Co., Inc.
Romain's Custom Guns, Inc.
S&K Scope Mounts
Saunders Gun & Machine Shop
Schmidt & Bender, Inc.
Schumakers Gun Shop
Scope Control, Inc.
Score High Gunsmithing
Seecamp Co. Inc., L. W.
Segway Industries
Selsi Co., Inc.
Sharp Shooter Supply
Shepherd Enterprises, Inc.
Sightron, Inc.
Simmons Outdoor Corp.
Six Enterprises
Southern Bloomer Mfg. Co.
Spencer's Rifle Barrels, Inc.
Splitfire Sporting Goods, L.L.C.
Sportsmatch U.K. Ltd.
Springfield Armory
Springfield, Inc.
SSK Industries
Stiles Custom Guns
Stoeger Industries
Stoney Point Products, Inc.
Sturm Ruger & Co. Inc.
Sunny Hill Enterprises, Inc.

Swarovski Optik North America Ltd.
Swift Instruments, Inc.
T.K. Lee Co.
Talley, Dave
Tasco Sales, Inc.
Tele-Optics
The A.W. Peterson Gun Shop, Inc.
The Outdoor Connection, Inc.
Thompson/Center Arms
Traditions Performance Firearms
Trijicon, Inc.
Truglo, Inc.
U.S. Optics, A Division of Zeitz Optics U.S.A.
Ultra Dot Distribution
Uncle Mike's
(See Michaels of Oregon Co.)
Unertl Optical Co., Inc.
United Binocular Co.
Virgin Valley Custom Guns
Visible Impact Targets
Voere-KGH GmbH
Warne Manufacturing Co.
Warren Muzzleloading Co., Inc.
Watson Bullets
Weaver Products ATK
Weaver Scope Repair Service
Webley and Scott Ltd.
Weigand Combat Handguns, Inc.
Wessinger Custom Guns & Engraving
Westley Richards & Co. Ltd.
White Rifles, Inc.
White Rock Tool & Die
Whitestone Lumber Corp.
Wideview Scope Mount Corp.
Wilcox Industries Corp.
Wild West Guns
Williams Gun Sight Co.
York M-1 Conversion
Zanotti Armor, Inc.

SHELLHOLDERS

Corbin Mfg. & Supply, Inc.
Fremont Tool Works
GAR
Goodwin's Pawn Shop
Hart & Son, Inc.
Hollywood Engineering
Huntington Die Specialties
K&M Services
King & Co.
Protektor Model
PWM Sales Ltd.
RCBS Operations/ATK
Redding Reloading Equipment
The A.W. Peterson Gun Shop, Inc.
Vega Tool Co.

SHOOTING/TRAINING SCHOOL

Alpine Indoor Shooting Range
American Gunsmithing Institute
American Small Arms Academy
Auto Arms
Beretta U.S.A. Corp.
Bob's Tactical Indoor Shooting Range & Gun Shop
Bridgeman Products
Chapman Academy of Practical Shooting
Chelsea Gun Club of New York City Inc.
Cherry Creek State Park Shooting Center
Cleland's Outdoor World, Inc
CQB Training
Defense Training International, Inc.
Executive Protection Institute
Ferris Firearms
Front Sight Firearms Training Institute
G.H. Enterprises Ltd.
Gene's Custom Guns
Gilmore Sports Concepts, Inc.
Griffin & Howe, Inc.
Griffin & Howe, Inc.
Griffin & Howe, Inc.
Guncraft Books
(See Guncraft Sports, Inc.)
Guncraft Sports, Inc.
Guncraft Sports, Inc.
Gunsite Training Center
Henigson & Associates, Steve
Jensen's Custom Ammunition
Jensen's Firearms Academy
Kemen America
L.L. Bean, Inc.
Lethal Force Institute
(See Police Bookshelf)
Loch Leven Industries/Convert-A-Pell
Long, George F.
McMurdo, Lynn
(See Specialty Gunsmithing)
Mendez, John A.
NCP Products, Inc.
Nevada Pistol Academy, Inc.
North American Shooting Systems
North Mountain Pine Training Center
Nowlin Mfg. Co.
Paxton Quigley's Personal Protection Strategies
Pentheny de Pentheny
Performance Specialists
Police Bookshelf
Protektor Model
SAFE
Shoot Where You Look
Shooter's World
Shooters, Inc.
Sigarms, Inc.
Smith & Wesson
Specialty Gunsmithing
Starlight Training Center, Inc.
Tactical Defense Institute
The Firearm Training Center
The Midwest Shooting School
The Shooting Gallery
Thunden Ranch
Western Missouri Shooters Alliance
Yankee Gunsmith "Just Glocks"
Yavapai Firearms Academy Ltd.

SHOTSHELL MISCELLANY

American Products, Inc.
Ballistic Products, Inc.
Bridgeman Products
Goodwin's Pawn Shop
Lee Precision, Inc.
MEC, Inc.
Precision Reloading, Inc.
R.E.I.
RCBS Operations/ATK
T&S Industries, Inc.
The A.W. Peterson Gun Shop, Inc.
The Gun Works
Vitt/Boos
Ziegel Engineering

SIGHTS, METALLIC

100 Straight Products, Inc.
Accura-Site (See All's, The Jim Tembelis Co., Inc.)
Ad Hominem
Alley Supply Co.
All's, The Jim J. Tembelis Co., Inc.
Alpec Team, Inc.
Andela Tool & Machine, Inc.
AO Sight Systems
ArmaLite, Inc.
Ashley Outdoors, Inc.
Aspen Outfitting Co.
Axtell Rifle Co.
B.A.C.
Ballard Rifle & Cartridge Co., LLC
BEC, Inc.
Bob's Gun Shop
Bo-Mar Tool & Mfg. Co.
Bond Custom Firearms
Bowen Classic Arms Corp.
Brockman's Custom Gunsmithing
Brooks Tactical Systems-Agrip
Brown Co., E. Arthur
Brown Dog Ent.
Brownells, Inc.
Buffalo Arms Co.
Bushmaster Firearms, Inc.
C. Sharps Arms Co. Inc./Montana Armory
California Sights
(See Fautheree, Andy)
Campbell, Dick
Cape Outfitters
Cape Outfitters
Cash Mfg. Co., Inc.
Center Lock Scope Rings
Champion's Choice, Inc.
Chip McCormick Corp.
C-More Systems
Colonial Repair
CRR, Inc./Marble's Inc.
Davide Pedersoli and Co.
DHB Products
Dixie Gun Works
DPMS (Defense Procurement Manufacturing Services, Inc.)
E. Arthur Brown Co.
Effebi SNC-Dr. Franco Beretta
Evolution Gun Works, Inc.
Falcon Industries, Inc.
Farr Studio, Inc.
G.G. & G.
Garthwaite Pistolsmith, Inc., Jim
Goergen's Gun Shop, Inc.
Goodwin's Pawn Shop
Guns Div. of D.C. Engineering, Inc.
Gunsmithing, Inc.
Hank's Gun Shop
Heidenstrom Bullets
Heinie Specialty Products
Hesco-Meprolight
Hiptmayer, Armurier
Hiptmayer, Klaus
I.S.S.
Innovative Weaponry Inc.
J.G. Anschutz GmbH & Co. KG
J.P. Enterprises Inc.
Keng's Firearms Specialty, Inc./US Tactical Systems
Knight Rifles
Knight's Mfg. Co.
L.P.A. Inc.
Leapers, Inc.
Les Baer Custom, Inc.
List Precision Engineering
London Guns Ltd.
Lyman Instant Targets, Inc.
(See Lyman Products)
Mandall Shooting Supplies Inc.
Marble Arms
(See CRR, Inc./Marble's Inc.)
MCS, Inc.
MEC-Gar S.R.L.
Meprolight (See Hesco-Meprolight)
Merit Corp.
Mid-America Recreation, Inc.
Middlebrooks Custom Shop
Millett Sights
MMC
Modern Muzzleloading, Inc.
Montana Armory, Inc.
(See C. Sharps Arms Co. Inc.)
Montana Vintage Arms
Mo's Competitor Supplies
(See MCS, Inc.)
Navy Arms Company
New England Custom Gun Service
Newman Gunshop
Novak's, Inc.
OK Weber, Inc.
One Ragged Hole
Parker & Sons Shooting Supply
PEM's Mfg. Co.
Perazone-Gunsmith, Brian
RPM
Sharps Arms Co., Inc., C.
Slug Site
STI International
T.F.C. S.p.A.
Talley, Dave
Tank's Rifle Shop
The A.W. Peterson Gun Shop, Inc.
The Gun Doctor
Trijicon, Inc.
Truglo, Inc.
U.S. Optics, A Division of Zeitz Optics U.S.A.
Warne Manufacturing Co.
Weigand Combat Handguns, Inc.
Wichita Arms, Inc.
Wild West Guns
Williams Gun Sight Co.
Wilsom Combat
Wilsom Combat

STOCK MAKER

Acra-Bond Laminates
Amrine's Gun Shop
Antique Arms Co.
Artistry in Wood
Aspen Outfitting Co.
Bain & Davis, Inc.
Bansner's Ultimate Rifles, LLC
Baron Technology
Belding's Custom Gun Shop
Billings Gunsmiths
Bob Rogers Gunsmithing
Boltin, John M.
Borden Ridges Rimrock Stocks
Bowerly, Kent
Boyds' Gunstock Industries, Inc.
Brace, Larry D.
Briganti, A.J.
Broad Creek Rifle Works, Ltd.
Brown Precision, Inc.
Buchsenmachermeister
Bull Mountain Rifle Co.
Bullberry Barrel Works, Ltd.
Burkhart Gunsmithing, Don
Cambos Outdoorsman
Cambos Outdoorsman
Caywood, Shane J.
Chicasaw Gun Works
Chuck's Gun Shop
Claro Walnut Gunstock Co.
Coffin, Charles H.
Colorado Gunsmithing Academy
Custom Riflestocks, Inc., Michael M. Kokolus
Custom Single Shot Rifles
D&D Gunsmiths, Ltd.
Dangler, Homer L.
D'Arcy Echols & Co.
DGR Custom Rifles
DGR Custom Rifles
DGS, Inc., Dale A. Storey
Don Klein Custom Guns
Erhardt, Dennis
Eversull Co., Inc.
Fieldsport Ltd.
Fisher, Jerry A.
Forster, Larry L.
Fred F. Wells/Wells Sport Store
Gary Goudy Classic Stocks
Genecco Gun Works
Gene's Custom Guns
Gillmann, Edwin
Grace, Charles E.
Great American Gunstock Co.
Gruning Precision, Inc.
Gunsmithing Ltd.
Hank's Gun Shop
Harper's Custom Stocks
Harry Lawson Co.
Heilmann, Stephen
Hensley, Gunmaker, Darwin
Heydenberk, Warren R.
High Tech Specialties, Inc.
Hofer Jagdwaffen, P.
Huebner, Corey O.
Island Pond Gun Shop
Jack Dever Co.
Jamison's Forge Works
Jay McCament Custom Gunmaker
Jim Norman Custom Gunstocks
John Rigby & Co.
K. Eversull Co., Inc.
Keith's Custom Gunstocks
Ken Eyster Heritage Gunsmiths, Inc.
Larry Lyons Gunworks
Marshall Fish Mfg. Gunsmith Sptg. Co.
Mathews Gun Shop & Gunsmithing, Inc.
McGowen Rifle Barrels
Mercer Custom Guns
Mid-America Recreation, Inc.
Mike Yee Custom Stocking
Mitchell, Jack
Modern Gun Repair School
Morrow, Bud
Nelson's Custom Guns, Inc.
Nettestad Gun Works
Nickels, Paul R.
Paul and Sharon Dressel
Paul D. Hillmer Custom Gunstocks
Paulsen Gunstocks
Pawling Mountain Club
Pecatonica River Longrifle
Pentheny de Pentheny
Quality Custom Firearms
R&J Gun Shop
R.A. Wells Custom Gunsmith
Ralph Bone Engraving
RMS Custom Gunsmithing
Robinson, Don
Ron Frank Custom Classic Arms
Royal Arms Gunstocks
Royal Arms Gunstocks
Ruger's Custom Guns
Six Enterprises
Skeoch, Brian R.
Smith, Art
Smith, Sharmon
Speiser, Fred D.
Steven Dodd Hughes
Stott's Creek Armory, Inc.
Sturgeon Valley Sporters
Taylor & Robbins
Tennessee Valley Mfg.
The Custom Shop
Tiger-Hunt Gunstocks
Trico Plastics
Tucker, James C.
Turnbull Restoration, Doug
Vest, John
Walker Arms Co., Inc.
Wayne E. Schwartz Custom Guns
Weber & Markin Custom Gunsmiths
Wenig Custom Gunstocks
Wiebe, Duane
Wild West Guns
Williamson Precision Gunsmithing
Winter, Robert M.
Working Guns

PRODUCT & SERVICE DIRECTORY

STOCKS (COMMERCIAL)

Accuracy Unlimited
Acra-Bond Laminates
African Import Co.
Ahlman Guns
Aspen Outfitting Co.
B.A.C.
Baelder, Harry
Balickie, Joe
Bansner's Ultimate Rifles, LLC
Barnes Bullets, Inc.
Battenfeld Technologies Inc.
Beitzinger, George
Belding's Custom Gun Shop
Bell & Carlson, Inc.
Blount, Inc., Sporting Equipment Div.
Blount/Outers ATK
Bob's Gun Shop
Borden Ridges Rimrock Stocks
Borden Rifles Inc.
Bowerly, Kent
Boyds' Gunstock Industries, Inc.
Brockman's Custom Gunsmithing
Brown Co., E. Arthur
Buckhorn Gun Works
Bull Mountain Rifle Co.
Butler Creek Corp.
Cali'co Hardwoods, Inc.
Cape Outfitters
Caywood, Shane J.
Chambers Flintlocks Ltd., Jim
Chicasaw Gun Works
Chuilli, Stephen
Claro Walnut Gunstock Co.
Coffin, Charles H.
Coffin, Jim (See Working Guns)
Colonial Repair
Colorado Gunsmithing Academy
Colorado School of Trades
Conrad, C. A.
Curly Maple Stock Blanks
 (See Tiger-Hunt)
Custom Checkering Service, Kathy Forster
Custom Riflestocks, Inc., Michael M. Kokolus
D&D Gunsmiths, Ltd.
D&G Precision Duplicators
 (See Greene Precision)
David W. Schwartz Custom Guns
Davide Pedersoli and Co.
DGR Custom Rifles
Duane's Gun Repair
 (See DGR Custom Rifles)
Duncan's Gun Works, Inc.
Effebi SNC-Dr. Franco Beretta
Eggleston, Jere D.
Erhardt, Dennis
Eversull Co., Inc.
Falcon Industries, Inc.
Falcon Industries, Inc.
Fibron Products, Inc.
Fieldsport Ltd.
Fisher, Jerry A.
Folks, Donald E.
Forster, Kathy
 (See Custom Checkering)
Forthofer's Gunsmithing & Knifemaking
Francotte & Cie S.A. Auguste
Game Haven Gunstocks
George Hoenig, Inc.
Gervais, Mike
Gillmann, Edwin
Giron, Robert E.
Goens, Dale W.
Golden Age Arms Co.
Goodwin's Pawn Shop
Great American Gunstock Co.
Green, Roger M.
Greenwood Precision
Guns Div. of D.C. Engineering, Inc.
Hammerli USA
Hanson's Gun Center, Dick
Harper's Custom Stocks
Harry Lawson Co.
Harwood, Jack O.
Hecht, Hubert J., Waffen-Hecht
Hensley, Gunmaker, Darwin
High Tech Specialties, Inc.
Hiptmayer, Armurier
Hiptmayer, Klaus
Hogue Grips
H-S Precision, Inc.
Huebner, Corey O.
Island Pond Gun Shop
Israel Arms Inc.
Ivanoff, Thomas G.
 (See Tom's Gun Repair)
Jackalope Gun Shop
Jarrett Rifles, Inc.
Jim Norman Custom Gunstocks
John Masen Co. Inc.
Johnson Wood Products
KDF, Inc.
Keith's Custom Gunstocks
Kelbly, Inc.
Kilham & Co.
Klingler Woodcarving
Lawson Co., Harry
Mandall Shooting Supplies Inc.
McBros Rifle Co.
McDonald, Dennis
McMillan Fiberglass Stocks, Inc.
Michaels Of Oregon, Co.
Mid-America Recreation, Inc.
Miller Arms, Inc.
Mitchell, Jack
Morrison Custom Rifles, J. W.
MPI Stocks
MWG Co.
NCP Products, Inc.
Nelson's Custom Guns, Inc.
New England Arms Co.
New England Custom Gun Service
Newman Gunshop
Nickels, Paul R.
Oil Rod and Gun Shop
Old World Gunsmithing
One Of A Kind
Ottmar, Maurice
Pagel Gun Works, Inc.
Paragon Sales & Services, Inc.
Parker & Sons Shooting Supply
Paul and Sharon Dressel
Paul D. Hillmer Custom Gunstocks
Paulsen Gunstocks
Pawling Mountain Club
Pecatonica River Longrifle
PEM's Mfg. Co.
Perazone-Gunsmith, Brian
Powell & Son (Gunmakers) Ltd., William
Precision Gun Works
R&J Gun Shop
R.A. Wells Custom Gunsmith
Ram-Line ATK
Ramon B. Gonzalez Guns
Rampart International
Richards Micro-Fit Stocks
RMS Custom Gunsmithing
Robinson, Don
Robinson Armament Co.
Robinson Firearms Mfg. Ltd.
Romain's Custom Guns, Inc.
Ron Frank Custom Classic Arms
Royal Arms Gunstocks
Saville Iron Co.
 (See Greenwood Precision)
Schiffman, Mike
Score High Gunsmithing
Simmons Gun Repair, Inc.
Six Enterprises
Speiser, Fred D.
Stan De Treville & Co.
Stiles Custom Guns
Swann, D. J.
Swift River Gunworks
Szweda, Robert
 (See RMS Custom Gunsmithing)
T.F.C. S.p.A.
Tecnolegno S.p.A.
The A.W. Peterson Gun Shop, Inc.
The Gun Shop
The Orvis Co.
Tiger-Hunt Gunstocks
Tirelli
Tom's Gun Repair, Thomas G. Ivanoff
Track of the Wolf, Inc.
Trevallion Gunstocks
Tuttle, Dale
Vic's Gun Refinishing
Vintage Industries, Inc.
Virgin Valley Custom Guns
Volquartsen Custom Ltd.
Walker Arms Co., Inc.
Weber & Markin Custom Gunsmiths
Weems, Cecil
Wenig Custom Gunstocks
Werth, T. W.
Western Mfg. Co.
Wild West Guns
Williams Gun Sight Co.
Windish, Jim
Working Guns
Wright's Gunstock Blanks
Zeeryp, Russ

STUCK CASE REMOVERS

GAR
Goodwin's Pawn Shop
Huntington Die Specialties
MarMik, Inc.
The A.W. Peterson Gun Shop, Inc.
Tom's Gun Repair, Thomas G. Ivanoff

TARGETS, BULLET & CLAYBIRD TRAPS

Action Target, Inc.
Air Arms
American Target
Autauga Arms, Inc.
Beeman Precision Airguns
Benjamin/Sheridan Co., Crosman
Birchwood Casey
Blount, Inc., Sporting Equipment Div.
Blount/Outers ATK
Blue and Gray Products Inc.
 (See Ox-Yoke Originals)
Brown Precision, Inc.
Bull-X, Inc.
Caswell International
Champion Target Co.
Creedmoor Sports, Inc.
Crosman Airguns
D.C.C. Enterprises
Daisy Outdoor Products
Diamond Mfg. Co.
Federal Champion Target Co.
G.H. Enterprises Ltd.
H-S Precision, Inc.
Hunterjohn
J.G. Dapkus Co., Inc.
Kennebec Journal
Kleen-Bore, Inc.
Lakefield Arms Ltd.
 (See Savage Arms, Inc.)
Leapers, Inc.
Littler Sales Co.
Lyman Instant Targets, Inc.
 (See Lyman Products)
Marksman Products
Mendez, John A.
Mountain Plains Industries
MSR Targets
N.B.B., Inc.
National Target Co.
North American Shooting Systems
Outers Laboratories Div. of ATK
Ox-Yoke Originals, Inc.
Palsa Outdoor Products
Passive Bullet Traps, Inc.
 (See Savage Range Systems, Inc.)
PlumFire Press, Inc.
Precision Airgun Sales, Inc.
Protektor Model
Quack Decoy & Sporting Clays
Remington Arms Co., Inc.
Rockwood Corp.
Rocky Mountain Target Co.
Savage Range Systems, Inc.
Schaefer Shooting Sports
Seligman Shooting Products
Shooters Supply
Shoot-N-C Targets
 (See Birchwood Casey)
Target Shooting, Inc.
The A.W. Peterson Gun Shop, Inc.
Thompson Target Technology
Trius Traps, Inc.
Universal Sports
Visible Impact Targets
Watson Bullets
Woods Wise Products
World of Targets
 (See Birchwood Casey)
X-Spand Target Systems

TAXIDERMY

African Import Co.
Bill Russ Trading Post
Kulis Freeze Dry Taxidermy
World Trek, Inc.

TRAP & SKEET SHOOTER'S EQUIPMENT

American Products, Inc.
Bagmaster Mfg., Inc.
Ballistic Products, Inc.
Beretta S.P.A., Pietro
Blount/Outers ATK
Bob Allen Sportswear
Bridgeman Products
C&H Research
Cape Outfitters
Claybuster Wads & Harvester Bullets
Fiocchi of America, Inc.
G.H. Enterprises Ltd.
Hoppe's Div. Penguin Industries, Inc.
Jamison's Forge Works
Jenkins Recoil Pads
Jim Noble Co.
Kalispel Case Line
Kolar
Lakewood Products LLC
Ljutic Industries, Inc.
Mag-Na-Port International, Inc.
MEC, Inc.
Moneymaker Guncraft Corp.
MTM Molded Products Co., Inc.
NCP Products, Inc.
Pachmayr Div. Lyman Products
Palsa Outdoor Products
Pro-Port Ltd.
Protektor Model
Quack Decoy & Sporting Clays
Remington Arms Co., Inc.
Rhodeside, Inc.
Shooting Specialties
 (See Titus, Daniel)
Shotgun Sports Magazine, dba Shootin' Accessories Ltd.
Stan Baker Sports
T&S Industries, Inc.
TEN-X Products Group
The Gun Works
Trius Traps, Inc.
Truglo, Inc.
Universal Sports
Warne Manufacturing Co.
Weber & Markin Custom Gunsmiths
X-Spand Target Systems
Ziegel Engineering

TRIGGERS, RELATED EQUIPMENT

Actions by "T" Teddy Jacobson
B&D Trading Co., Inc.
Behlert Precision, Inc.
Bond Custom Firearms
Boyds' Gunstock Industries, Inc.
Broad Creek Rifle Works, Ltd.
Bull Mountain Rifle Co.
Chicasaw Gun Works
Dayton Traister
Dolbare, Elizabeth
Electronic Trigger Systems, Inc.
Eversull Co., Inc.
Feinwerkbau Westinger & Altenburger
Gentry Custom LLC
Goodwin's Pawn Shop
Hart & Son, Inc.
Hawken Shop, The
 (See Dayton Traister)
Hoehn Sales, Inc.
Holland's Gunsmithing
Impact Case & Container, Inc.
J.P. Enterprises Inc.
Jewell Triggers, Inc.
John Masen Co. Inc.
Jones Custom Products, Neil A.
K. Eversull Co., Inc.
KK Air International
 (See Impact Case & Container Co.)
Knight's Mfg. Co.
L&R Lock Co.
Les Baer Custom, Inc.
List Precision Engineering
London Guns Ltd.
M.H. Canjar Co.
Mahony, Philip Bruce
Master Lock Co.
Miller Single Trigger Mfg. Co.
NCP Products, Inc.
Neil A. Jones Custom Products
Nowlin Mfg. Co.
PEM's Mfg. Co.
Penrod Precision
Perazone-Gunsmith, Brian
Ramon B. Gonzalez Guns
Robinson Armament Co.
Sharp Shooter Supply
Shilen, Inc.
Simmons Gun Repair, Inc.
Spencer's Rifle Barrels, Inc.
Tank's Rifle Shop
Target Shooting, Inc.
The A.W. Peterson Gun Shop, Inc.
The Gun Works
Watson Bullets

MANUFACTURER'S DIRECTORY

A

A Zone Bullets, 2039 Walter Rd., Billings, MT 59105 / 800-252-3111; FAX: 406-248-1961
A&B Industries, Inc (See Top-Line USA Inc.)
A&W Repair, 2930 Schneider Dr., Arnold, MO 63010 / 617-287-3725
A.A. Arms, Inc., 4811 Persimmont Ct., Monroe, NC 28110 / 704-289-5356; or 800-935-1119; FAX: 704-289-5859
A.B.S. III, 9238 St. Morritz Dr., Fern Creek, KY 40291
A.G. Russell Knives, Inc., 1920 North 26th Street, Springdale, AR 72764 / 479-751-7341; FAX: 479-751-4520 ag@agrussell.com agrussell.com
A.R.M.S., Inc., 230 W. Center St., West Bridgewater, MA 02379-1620 / 508-584-7816; FAX: 508-588-8045
A.W. Peterson Gun Shop, Inc., 4255 W. Old U.S. 441, Mt. Dora, FL 32757-3299 / 352-383-4258; FAX: 352-735-1001
AC Dyna-tite Corp., 155 Kelly St., P.O. Box 0984, Elk Grove Village, IL 60007 / 847-593-5566; FAX: 847-593-1304
Acadian Ballistic Specialties, P.O. Box 787, Folsom, LA 70437 / 504-796-0078 gunsmith@neasolft.com
Accuracy International, Foster, PO Box 111, Wilsall, MT 59086 / 406-587-7922; FAX: 406-585-9434
Accuracy Internationl Precision Rifles (See U.S.)
Accuracy Int'l. North America, Inc., PO Box 5267, Oak Ridge, TN 37831 / 423-482-0330; FAX: 423-482-0336
Accuracy Unlimited, 16036 N. 49 Ave., Glendale, AZ 85306 / 602-978-9089; FAX: 602-978-9089 fglenn@cox.net www.glenncustom.com
Accuracy Unlimited, 7479 S. DePew St., Littleton, CO 80123
Accura-Site (See All's, The Jim Tembelis Co., Inc.)
Accurate Arms Co., Inc., 5891 Hwy. 230 West, McEwen, TN 37101 / 931-729-4207; FAX: 931-729-4211 burrensburg@aac-ca.com www.accuratepowder.com
Accu-Tek, 4510 Carter Ct., Chino, CA 91710
Ace Custom 45's, Inc., 1880 1/2 Upper Turtle Creek Rd., Kerrville, TX 78028 / 830-257-4290; FAX: 830-257-5724 www.acecustom45.com
Ackerman & Co., Box 133 US Highway Rt. 7, Pownal, VT 05261 / 802-823-9874 muskets@togsther.net
Ackerman, Bill (See Optical Services Co.)
Acra-Bond Laminates, 134 Zimmerman Rd., Kalispell, MT 59901 / 406-257-9003; FAX: 406-257-9003 merlins@digisys.net www.acrabondlaminates.com
Action Bullets & Alloy Inc., RR 1, P.O. Box 189, Quinter, KS 67752 / 785-754-3609; FAX: 785-754-3629 bullets@ruraltel.net
Action Direct, Inc., P.O. Box 770400, Miami, FL 33177 / 305-969-0056; FAX: 305-256-3541 www.action-direct.com
Action Products, Inc., 22 N. Mulberry St., Hagerstown, MD 21740 / 301-797-1414; FAX: 301-733-2073
Action Target, Inc., PO Box 636, Provo, UT 84603 / 801-377-8033; FAX: 801-377-8096
Actions by "T" Teddy Jacobson, 16315 Redwood Forest Ct., Sugar Land, TX 77478 / 281-277-4008; FAX: 281-277-9112 tjacobson@houston.rr.com www.actionsbyt.us
AcuSport Corporation, 1 Hunter Place, Bellefontaine, OH 43311-3001 / 513-593-7010; FAX: 513-592-5625
Ad Hominem, 3130 Gun Club Lane, RR #3, Orillia, ON L3V 6H3 CANADA / 705-689-5303; FAX: 705-689-5303
Adair Custom Shop, Bill, 2886 Westridge, Carrollton, TX 75006
ADCO Sales, Inc., 4 Draper St. #A, Woburn, MA 01801 / 781-935-1799; FAX: 781-935-1011
Adkins, Luther, 1292 E. McKay Rd., Shelbyville, IN 46176-8706 / 317-392-3795
Advance Car Mover Co., Rowell Div., P.O. Box 1, 240 N. Depot St., Juneau, WI 53039 / 414-386-4464; FAX: 414-386-4416
Advantage Arms, Inc., 25163 W. Ave. Stanford, Valencia, CA 91355 / 661-257-2290
Adventure 16, Inc., 4620 Alvarado Canyon Rd., San Diego, CA 92120 / 619-283-6314
Aero Peltor, 90 Mechanic St., Southbridge, MA 01550 / 508-764-5500; FAX: 508-764-0188
African Import Co., 22 Goodwin Rd, Plymouth, MA 02360 / 508-746-8552; FAX: 508-746-0404 africanimport@aol.com
AFSCO Ammunition, 731 W. Third St., P.O. Box L, Owen, WI 54460 / 715-229-2516 sailers@webtv.net
Ahlman Guns, 9525 W. 230th St., Morristown, MN 55052 / 507-685-4243; FAX: 507-685-4280 www.ahlmans.com
Ahrends, Kim (See Custom Firearms, Inc), Box 203, Clarion, IA 50525 / 515-532-3449; FAX: 515-532-3926
Aimtech Mount Systems, P.O. Box 223, Thomasville, GA 31799 / 229-226-4313; FAX: 229-227-0222 mail@aimtech-mounts.com www.aimtech-mounts.com
Air Arms, Hailsham Industrial Park, Diplocks Way, Hailsham, E. Sussex, BN27 3JF ENGLAND / 011-0323-845853
Air Rifle Specialists, P.O. Box 138, 130 Holden Rd., Pine City, NY 14871-0138 / 607-734-7340; FAX: 607-733-3261 ars@stny.rr.com www.air-rifles.com
Air Venture Airguns, 9752 E. Flower St., Bellflower, CA 90706 / 562-867-6355
AirForce Airguns, P.O. Box 2478, Fort Worth, TX 76113 / 817-451-8966; FAX: 817-451-1613 www.airforceairguns.com
Airrow, 11 Monitor Hill Rd., Newtown, CT 06470 / 203-270-6343
Aitor-Cuchilleria Del Norte S.A., Izelaieta, 17, 48260, Ermua, S SPAIN / 43-17-08-50 info@aitor.com www.ailor.com
Ajax Custom Grips, Inc., 9130 Viscount Row, Dallas, TX 75247 / 214-630-8893; FAX: 214-630-4942
Aker International, Inc., 2248 Main St., Suite 6, Chula Vista, CA 91911 / 619-423-5182; FAX: 619-423-1363 aker@akerleather.com www.akerleather.com
AKJ Concealco, P.O. Box 871596, Vancouver, WA 98687-1596 / 360-891-8222; FAX: 360-891-8221 Concealco@aol.com www.greatholsters.com
Alana Cupp Custom Engraver, P.O. Box 207, Annabella, UT 84711 / 801-896-4834
Alaska Bullet Works, Inc., 9978 Crazy Horse Drive, Juneau, AK 99801 / 907-789-3834; FAX: 907-789-3433
Alaskan Silversmith, The, 2145 Wagner Hollow Rd., Fort Plain, NY 13339 / 518-993-3983 sidbell@capital.net www.sidbell.cizland.com
Aldis Gunsmithing & Shooting Supply, 502 S. Montezuma St., Prescott, AZ 86303 / 602-445-6723; FAX: 602-445-6763
Alessi Holsters, Inc., 2465 Niagara Falls Blvd., Amherst, NY 14228-3527 / 716-691-5615
Alex, Inc., 3420 Cameron Bridge Rd., Manhattan, MT 59741-8523 / 406-282-7396; FAX: 406-282-7396
Alfano, Sam, 36180 Henry Gaines Rd., Pearl River, LA 70452 / 504-863-3364; FAX: 504-863-7715
All American Lead Shot Corp., P.O. Box 224566, Dallas, TX 75062
All Rite Products, Inc., 9554 Wells Circle, Suite D, West Jordan, UT 84088-6226 / 800-771-8471; FAX: 801-280-8302 info@allriteproducts.com www.allriteproducts.com
Allard, Gary/Creek Side Metal & Woodcrafters, Fishers Hill, VA 22626 / 703-465-3903
Allen Co., Inc., 525 Burbank St., Broomfield, CO 80020 / 303-469-1857; or 800-876-8600; FAX: 303-466-7437
Allen Firearm Engraving, P.O. Box 155, Camp Verde, AZ 86322 / 928-567-6711 rosebudmukco@netzero.com
Allen Mfg., 6449 Hodgson Rd., Circle Pines, MN 55014 / 612-429-8231
Alley Supply Co., PO Box 848, Gardnerville, NV 89410 / 775-782-3800; FAX: 775-782-3827 jetalley@aol.com www.alleysupplyco.com
Alliant Techsystems Smokeless Powder Group, P.O. Box 6, Rt. 114, Bldg. 229, Radford, VA 24141-0096 www.alliantpowder.com
Allred Bullet Co., 932 Evergreen Drive, Logan, UT 84321 / 435-752-6983; FAX: 435-752-6983
All's, The Jim J. Tembelis Co., Inc., 216 Loper Ct., Neenah, WI 54956 / 920-725-5251; FAX: 920-725-5251
Alpec Team, Inc., 201 Ricken Backer Cir., Livermore, CA 94550 / 510-606-8245; FAX: 510-606-4279
Alpha 1 Drop Zone, 2121 N. Tyler, Wichita, KS 67212 / 316-729-0800; FAX: 316-729-4262 www.alpha1dropzone.com
Alpha LaFranck Enterprises, P.O. Box 81072, Lincoln, NE 68501 / 402-466-3193
Alpha Precision, Inc., 3238 Della Slaton Rd., Comer, GA 30629-2212 / 706-783-2131 jim@alphaprecisioninc.com www.alphaprecisioninc.com
Alpine Indoor Shooting Range, 2401 Government Way, Coeur d'Alene, ID 83814 / 208-676-8824; FAX: 208-676-8824
Altamont Co., 901 N. Church St., P.O. Box 309, Thomasboro, IL 61878 / 217-643-3125; or 800-626-5774; FAX: 217-643-7973
Alumna Sport by Dee Zee, 1572 NE 58th Ave., P.O. Box 3090, Des Moines, IA 50316 / 800-798-9899
Amadeo Rossi S.A., Rua: Amadeo Rossi, 143, Sao Leopoldo, RS 93030-220 BRAZIL / 051-592-5566
AmBr Software Group Ltd., P.O. Box 301, Reistertown, MD 21136-0301 / 800-888-1917; FAX: 410-526-7212
American Ammunition, 3545 NW 71st St., Miami, FL 33147 / 305-835-7400; FAX: 305-694-0037
American Derringer Corp., 127 N. Lacy Dr., Waco, TX 76705 / 800-642-7817; or 254-799-9111; FAX: 254-799-7935
American Display Co., 55 Cromwell St., Providence, RI 02907 / 401-331-2464; FAX: 401-421-1264
American Gas & Chemical Co., Ltd, 220 Pegasus Ave, Northvale, NJ 07647 / 201-767-7300
American Gripcraft, 3230 S Dodge 2, Tucson, AZ 85713 / 602-790-1222
American Gunsmithing Institute, 1325 Imola Ave #504, Napa, CA 94559 / 707-253-0462; FAX: 707-253-7149
American Handgunner Magazine, 591 Camino de la Reina, Ste. 200, San Diego, CA 92108 / 619-297-5350; FAX: 619-297-5353
American Pioneer Video, PO Box 50049, Bowling Green, KY 42102-2649 / 800-743-4675
American Products, Inc., 14729 Spring Valley Road, Morrison, IL 61270 / 815-772-3336; FAX: 815-772-8046
American Safe Arms, Inc., 1240 Riverview Dr., Garland, UT 84312 / 801-257-7472; FAX: 801-785-8156
American Security Products Co., 11925 Pacific Ave., Fontana, CA 92337 / 909-685-9680; or 800-421-6142; FAX: 909-685-9685
American Small Arms Academy, P.O. Box 12111, Prescott, AZ 86304 / 602-778-5623
American Target, 1328 S. Jason St., Denver, CO 80223 / 303-733-0433; FAX: 303-777-0311
American Target Knives, 1030 Brownwood NW, Grand Rapids, MI 49504 / 616-453-1998
Americase, P.O. Box 271, 1610 E. Main, Waxahachie, TX 75165 / 800-880-3629; FAX: 214-937-8373
Ames Metal Products, 4323 S. Western Blvd., Chicago, IL 60609 / 773-523-3230; or 800-255-6937; FAX: 773-523-3854
Amherst Arms, P.O. Box 1457, Englewood, FL 34295 / 941-475-2020; FAX: 941-473-1212
Ammo Load, Inc., 1560 E. Edinger, Suite G, Santa Ana, CA 92705 / 714-558-8858; FAX: 714-569-0319
Amrine's Gun Shop, 937 La Luna, Ojai, CA 93023 / 805-646-2376
Amsec, 11925 Pacific Ave., Fontana, CA 92337
Analog Devices, Box 9106, Norwood, MA 02062
Andela Tool & Machine, Inc., RD3, Box 246, Richfield Springs, NY 13439
Anderson Manufacturing Co., Inc., 22602 53rd Ave. SE, Bothell, WA 98021 / 206-481-1858; FAX: 206-481-7839
Andres & Dworsky KG, Bergstrasse 18, A-3822 Karlstein, Thaya, AUSTRIA / 0 28 44-285; FAX: 02844 28619 andres.dnorsky@wvnet.as
Angelo & Little Custom Gun Stock Blanks, P.O. Box 240046, Dell, MT 59724-0046
Answer Products Co., 1519 Westbury Drive, Davison, MI 48423 / 810-653-2911
Antique American Firearms, P.O. Box 71035, Dept. GD, Des Moines, IA 50325 / 515-224-6552
Antique Arms Co., 1110 Cleveland Ave., Monett, MO 65708 / 417-235-6501
AO Sight Systems, 2401 Ludelle St., Fort Worth, TX 76105 / 888-744-4880; or 817-536-0136; FAX: 817-536-3517
Apel GmbH, Ernst, Am Kirschberg 3, D-97218, Gerbrunn, GERMANY / 0 (931) 707192 info@eaw.de www.eaw.de
Aplan Antiques & Art, James O., James O., HC 80, Box 793-25, Piedmont, SD 57769 / 605-347-5016
AR-7 Industries, LLC, 998 N. Colony Rd., Meriden, CT 06450 / 203-630-3536; FAX: 203-630-3637
Arizona Ammunition, Inc., 21421 No. 14th Ave., Suite E, Phoenix, AZ 85027 / 623-516-9004; FAX: 623-516-9012 www.azammo.com
ArmaLite, Inc., P.O. Box 299, Geneseo, IL 61254 / 800-336-0184; or 309-944-6939; FAX: 309-944-6949
Armament Gunsmithing Co., Inc., 525 Rt. 22, Hillside, NJ 07205 / 908-686-0960; FAX: 718-738-5019 armamentgunsmithing@worldnet.att.net
Armas Garbi, S.A., 12-14 20.600 Urki, 12, Eibar (Guipuzcoa), SPAIN / 943203873; FAX: 943203873 armosgarbi@euskalnet.n
Armas Kemen S. A. (See U.S. Importers)
Armfield Custom Bullets, 10584 County Road 100, Carthage, MO 64836 / 417-359-8480; FAX: 417-359-8497
Armi Perazzi S.P.A., Via Fontanelle 1/3, 1-25080, Botticino Mattina, ITALY / 030-2692591; FAX: 030 2692594
Armi San Marco (See U.S. Importers-Taylor's & Co.)
Armi San Paolo, 172-A, I-25062, via Europa, ITALY / 030-2751725
Armi Sport (See U.S. Importers-Cape Outfitters)
Armite Laboratories, 1560 Superior Ave., Costa Mesa, CA 92627 / 213-587-7768; FAX: 213-587-5075
Armoloy Co. of Ft. Worth, 204 E. Daggett St., Fort Worth, TX 76104 / 817-332-5604; FAX: 817-335-6517
Armor (See Buck Stop Lure Co., Inc.)

MANUFACTURER'S DIRECTORY

Armor Metal Products, P.O. Box 4609, Helena, MT 59604 / 406-442-5560; FAX: 406-442-5650
Armory Publications, 2120 S. Reserve St., PMB 253, Missoula, MT 59801 / 406-549-7670; FAX: 406-728-0597 armorypub@aol.com www.armorypub.com
Armoury, Inc., The, Rt. 202, Box 2340, New Preston, CT 06777 / 860-868-0001; FAX: 860-868-2919
Arms & Armour Press, Wellington House, 125 Strand, London, WC2R 0BB ENGLAND / 0171-420-5555; FAX: 0171-240-7265
Arms Corporation of the Philippines, Bo. Parang Marikina, Metro Manila, PHILIPPINES / 632-941-6243; or 632-941-6244; FAX: 632-942-0682
Arms Craft Gunsmithing, 1106 Linda Dr., Arroyo Grande, CA 93420 / 805-481-2830
Arms Software, 4851 SW Madrona St., Lake Oswego, OR 97035 / 800-366-5559; or 503-697-0533; FAX: 503-697-3337
Arms, Programming Solutions (See Arms Software)
Armscor Precision, 5740 S. Arville St. #219, Las Vegas, NV 89118 / 702-362-7750
Armscorp USA, Inc., 4424 John Ave., Baltimore, MD 21227 / 410-247-6200; FAX: 410-247-6205 info@armscorpusa.com www.armscorpusa.com
Arratoonian, Andy (See Horseshoe Leather Products)
Arrieta S.L., Morkaiko 5, 20870, Elgoibar, SPAIN / 34-43-743150; FAX: 34-43-743154
Art Jewel Enterprises Ltd., Eagle Business Ctr., 460 Randy Rd., Carol Stream, IL 60188 / 708-260-0400
Artistry in Wood, 134 Zimmerman Rd., Kalispell, MT 59901 / 406-257-9003; FAX: 406-257-9167 merlins@digisys.net www.acrabondlaminates.com
Art's Gun & Sport Shop, Inc., 6008 Hwy. Y, Hillsboro, MO 63050
Arundel Arms & Ammunition, Inc., A., 24A Defense St., Annapolis, MD 21401 / 410-224-8683
Ashley Outdoors, Inc., 2401 Ludelle St., Fort Worth, TX 76105 / 888-744-4880; FAX: 800-734-7939
Aspen Outfitting Co., Jon Hollinger, 9 Dean St., Aspen, CO 81611 / 970-925-3406
A-Square Co., 205 Fairfield Ave., Jeffersonville, IN 47130 / 812-283-0577; FAX: 812-283-0375
Astra Sport, S.A., Apartado 3, 48300 Guernica, Espagne, SPAIN / 34-4-6250100; FAX: 34-4-6255186
Atamec-Bretton, 19 rue Victor Grignard, F-42026, St.-Etienne (Cedex 1, FRANCE / 77-93-54-69; FAX: 33-77-93-57-98
Atlanta Cutlery Corp., 2143 Gees Mill Rd., Box 839 CIS, Conyers, GA 30207 / 800-883-0300; FAX: 404-388-0246
Atlantic Mills, Inc., 1295 Towbin Ave., Lakewood, NJ 08701-5934 / 800-242-7374
Atlantic Rose, Inc., P.O. Box 10717, Bradenton, FL 34282-0717
Atsko/Sno-Seal, Inc., 2664 Russell St., Orangeburg, SC 29115 / 803-531-1820; FAX: 803-531-2139 info@atsko.com www.atsko.com
Auguste Francotte & Cie S.A., rue du Trois Juin 109, 4400 Herstal-Liege, BELGIUM / 32-4-248-13-18; FAX: 32-4-948-11-79
Austin & Halleck, Inc., 2150 South 950 East, Provo, UT 84606-6285 / 877-543-3256; or 801-374-9990; FAX: 801-374-9998 www.austinhallek.com
Austin Sheridan USA, Inc., P.O. Box 577, 36 Haddam Quarter Rd., Durham, CT 06422 / 860-349-1772; FAX: 860-349-1771 swalzer@palm.net
Autauga Arms, Inc., Pratt Plaza Mall No. 13, Prattville, AL 36067 / 800-262-9563; FAX: 334-361-2961
Auto Arms, 738 Clearview, San Antonio, TX 78228 / 512-434-5450
Auto-Ordnance Corp., PO Box 220, Blauvelt, NY 10913 / 914-353-7770
Autumn Sales, Inc. (Blaser), 1320 Lake St., Fort Worth, TX 76102 / 817-335-1634; FAX: 817-338-0119
Avnda Otaola Norica, 16 Apartado 68, 20600, Eibar, SPAIN
AWC Systems Technology, P.O. Box 41938, Phoenix, AZ 85080-1938 / 623-780-1050; FAX: 623-780-2967 awc@awcsystech.com www.awcsystech.com
Axtell Rifle Co., 353 Mill Creek Road, Sheridan, MT 59749 / 406-842-5814
AYA (See U.S. Importer-New England Custom Gun Serv

B

B&D Trading Co., Inc., 3935 Fair Hill Rd., Fair Oaks, CA 95628 / 800-334-3790; or 916-967-9366; FAX: 916-967-4873
B&P America, 12321 Brittany Cir., Dallas, TX 75230 / 972-726-9069
B.A.C., 17101 Los Modelos St., Fountain Valley, CA 92708 / 435-586-3286
B.B. Walker Co., PO Box 1167, 414 E Dixie Dr, Asheboro, NC 27204 / 910-625-1380; FAX: 910-625-8125
B.C. Outdoors, Larry McGhee, PO Box 61497, Boulder City, NV 89006 / 702-294-3056; FAX: 702-294-0413 jdalton@pmcammo.com www.pmcammo.com
B.M.F. Activator, Inc., 12145 Mill Creek Run, Plantersville, TX 77363 / 936-894-2397; FAX: 936-894-2397 bmf25years@aol.com
Badger Creek Studio, 1629 Via Monserate, Fallbrook, CA 92028 / 760-723-9279; or 619-728-2663
Badger Shooters Supply, Inc., P.O. Box 397, Owen, WI 54460 / 800-424-9069; FAX: 715-229-2332
Baekgaard Ltd., 1855 Janke Dr., Northbrook, IL 60062 / 708-498-3040; FAX: 708-493-3106
Baelder, Harry, Alte Goennebeker Strasse 5, 24635, Rickling, GERMANY / 04328-722732; FAX: 04328-722733
Baer's Hollows, P.O. Box 284, Eads, CO 81036 / 719-438-5718
Bagmaster Mfg., Inc., 2731 Sutton Ave., St. Louis, MO 63143 / 314-781-8002; FAX: 314-781-3363 sales@bagmaster.com www.bagmaster.com
Bain & Davis, Inc., 307 E. Valley Blvd., San Gabriel, CA 91776-3522 / 626-573-4241 baindavis@aol.com
Baker, Stan. See: STAN BAKER SPORTS
Baker's Leather Goods, Roy, PO Box 893, Magnolia, AR 71754 / 870-234-0344 pholsters@ipa.net
Bald Eagle Precision Machine Co., 101-A Allison St., Lock Haven, PA 17745 / 570-748-6772; FAX: 570-748-4443
Balickie, Joe, 408 Trelawney Lane, Apex, NC 27502 / 919-362-5185
Ballard, Donald. See: BALLARD INDUSTRIES
Ballard Industries, Donald Ballard Sr., PO Box 2035, Arnold, CA 95223 / 408-996-0957; FAX: 408-257-6828
Ballard Rifle & Cartridge Co., LLC, 113 W. Yellowstone Ave., Cody, WY 82414 / 307-587-4914; FAX: 307-527-6097 ballard@wyoming.com www.ballardrifles.com
Ballistic Products, Inc., 20015 75th Ave. North, Corcoran, MN 55340-9456 / 763-494-9237; FAX: 763-494-9236 info@ballisticproducts.com www.ballisticproducts.com
Ballistic Research, 1108 W. May Ave., McHenry, IL 60050 / 815-385-0037
Ballisti-Cast, Inc., P.O. Box 1057, Minot, ND 58702-1057 / 701-497-3333; FAX: 701-497-3335
Bandcor Industries, Div. of Man-Sew Corp., 6108 Sherwin Dr., Port Richey, FL 34668 / 813-848-0432
Bang-Bang Boutique (See Holster Shop, The)
Bansner's Ultimate Rifles, LLC, P.O. Box 839, 261 E. Main St., Adamstown, PA 19501 / 717-484-2370; FAX: 717-484-0523 bansner@aol.com www.bansnersrifle.com
Barbour, Inc., 55 Meadowbrook Dr., Milford, NH 03055 / 603-673-1313; FAX: 603-673-6510
Barnes, 4347 Tweed Dr., Eau Claire, WI 54703-6302
Barnes Bullets, Inc., P.O. Box 215, American Fork, UT 84003 / 801-756-4222; or 800-574-9200; FAX: 801-756-2465 email@barnesbullets.com www.barnesbullets.com
Baron Technology, 62 Spring Hill Rd., Trumbull, CT 06611 / 203-452-0515; FAX: 203-452-0663 dbaron@baronengraving.com www.baronengraving.com
Barraclough, John K., 55 Merit Park Dr., Gardena, CA 90247 / 310-324-2574 johnbar120@aol.com
Barramundi Corp., P.O. Drawer 4259, Homosassa Springs, FL 32687 / 904-628-0200
Barrel & Gunworks, 2601 Lake Valley Rd., Prescott Valley, AZ 86314 / 928-772-4060 www.cutrifle.com
Barrett Firearms Manufacturer, Inc., P.O. Box 1077, Murfreesboro, TN 37133 / 615-896-2938; FAX: 615-896-7313
Bar-Sto Precision Machine, 73377 Sullivan Rd., PO Box 1838, Twentynine Palms, CA 92277 / 760-367-2747; FAX: 760-367-2407 barsto@eee.org www.barsto.com
Barta's Gunsmithing, 10231 US Hwy. 10, Cato, WI 54230 / 920-732-4472
Barteaux Machete, 1916 SE 50th Ave., Portland, OR 97215-3238 / 503-233-5880
Bartlett Engineering, 40 South 200 East, Smithfield, UT 84335-1645 / 801-563-5910
Bates Engraving, Billy, 2302 Winthrop Dr. SW, Decatur, AL 35603 / 256-355-3690 bbrn@aol.com
Battenfeld Technologies Inc., 5885 W. Van Horn Tavern Rd., Columbia, MO 65203 / 573-445-9200; FAX: 573-447-4158 battenfeldtechnologies.com
Bauer, Eddie, 15010 NE 36th St., Redmond, WA 98052
Baumgartner Bullets, 3011 S. Alane St., W. Valley City, UT 84120
Bauska Barrels, 105 9th Ave. W., Kalispell, MT 59901 / 406-752-7706
Bear Archery, RR 4, 4600 Southwest 41st Blvd., Gainesville, FL 32601 / 904-376-2327
Bear Arms, 374-A Carson Road, St. Mathews, SC 29135
Bear Mountain Gun & Tool, 120 N. Plymouth, New Plymouth, ID 83655 / 208-278-5221; FAX: 208-278-5221
Beartooth Bullets, PO Box 491, Dept. HLD, Dover, ID 83825-0491 / 208-448-1865 bullets@beartoothbullets.com beartoothbullets.com
Beaver Park Product, Inc., 840 J St., Penrose, CO 81240 / 719-372-6744
BEC, Inc., 1227 W. Valley Blvd., Suite 204, Alhambra, CA 91803 / 626-281-5751; FAX: 626-293-7073
Beeks, Mike. See: GRAYBACK WILDCATS
Beeman Precision Airguns, 5454 Argosy Dr., Huntington Beach, CA 92649 / 714-890-4808; FAX: 714-890-4808
Behlert Precision, Inc., P.O. Box 288, 7067 Easton Rd., Pipersville, PA 18947 / 215-766-8681; or 215-766-7301; FAX: 215-766-8681
Beitzinger, George, 116-20 Atlantic Ave., Richmond Hill, NY 11419 / 718-847-7661
Belding's Custom Gun Shop, 10691 Sayers Rd., Munith, MI 49259 / 517-596-2388
Bell & Carlson, Inc., Dodge City Industrial Park, 101 Allen Rd., Dodge City, KS 67801 / 800-634-8586; or 620-225-6688; FAX: 620-225-6688 email@bellandcarlson.com www.bellandcarlson.com
Bell Reloading, Inc., 1725 Harlin Lane Rd., Villa Rica, GA 30180
Bell's Gun & Sport Shop, 3309-19 Mannheim Rd, Franklin Park, IL 60131
Bell's Legendary Country Wear, 22 Circle Dr., Bellmore, NY 11710 / 516-679-1158
Benchmark Knives (See Gerber Legendary Blades)
Benelli Armi S.P.A., Via della Stazione, 61029, Urbino, ITALY / 39-722-307-1; FAX: 39-722-327427
Benelli USA Corp, 17603 Indian Head Hwy, Accokeek, MD 20607 / 301-283-6981; FAX: 301-283-6988 benelliusa.com
Bengtson Arms Co., L., 6345-B E. Akron St., Mesa, AZ 85205 / 602-981-6375
Benjamin/Sheridan Co., Crosman, Rts. 5 and 20, E. Bloomfield, NY 14443 / 716-657-6161; FAX: 716-657-5405 www.crosman.com
Bentley, John, 128-D Watson Dr., Turtle Creek, PA 15145
Beretta S.P.A., Pietro, Via Beretta, 18, 25063, Gardone Vae Trompia, ITALY / 39-30-8341-1 info@benetta.com www.benetta.com
Beretta U.S.A. Corp., 17601 Beretta Drive, Accokeek, MD 20607 / 301-283-2191; FAX: 301-283-0435
Berger Bullets Ltd., 5443 W. Westwind Dr., Glendale, AZ 85310 / 602-842-4001; FAX: 602-934-9083
Bernardelli, Vincenzo, P.O. Box 460243, Houston, TX 77056-8243 www.bernardelli.com
Bernardelli, Vincenzo, Via Grande, 10, Sede Legale Torbole Casaglia, Brescia, ITALY / 39-30-8912851-2-3; FAX: 39-030-2150963 bernardelli@bernardelli.com www.bernardelli.com
Berry's Mfg., Inc., 401 North 3050 East St., St. George, UT 84770 / 435-634-1682; FAX: 435-634-1683 sales@berrysmfg.com www.berrysmfg.com
Bersa S.A., Benso Bonadimani, Magallanes 775 B1704 FLC, Ramos Mejia, ARGENTINA / 011-4656-2377; FAX: 011-4656-2093+ info@bersa-sa.com.dr www.bersa-sa.com.ar
Bert Johanssons Vapentillbehor, S-430 20 Veddige, SWEDEN,
Bertuzzi (See U.S. Importer-New England Arms Co)
Better Concepts Co., 663 New Castle Rd., Butler, PA 16001 / 412-285-9000
Beverly, Mary, 3201 Horseshoe Trail, Tallahassee, FL 32312
Bianchi International, Inc., 100 Calle Cortez, Temecula, CA 92590 / 909-676-5621; FAX: 909-676-6777
Big Bear Arms & Sporting Goods, Inc., 1112 Milam Way, Carrollton, TX 75006 / 972-416-8051; or 800-400-BEAR; FAX: 972-416-0771
Big Bore Bullets of Alaska, PO Box 521455, Big Lake, AK 99652 / 907-373-2673; FAX: 907-373-2673 doug@mtaonline.net www.awloo.com/bbb/index.
Big Bore Express, 16345 Midway Rd., Nampa, ID 83651 / 208-466-9975; FAX: 208-466-6927 bigbore.com
Big Spring Enterprises "Bore Stores", P.O. Box 1115, Big Spring Rd., Yellville, AR 72687 / 870-449-5297; FAX: 870-449-4446
Bilal, Mustafa. See: TURK'S HEAD PRODUCTIONS
Bilinski, Bryan. See: FIELDSPORT LTD.
Bill Adair Custom Shop, 2886 Westridge, Carrollton, TX 75006 / 972-418-0950

MANUFACTURER'S DIRECTORY

Bill Austin's Calls, Box 284, Kaycee, WY 82639 / 307-738-2552
Bill Hanus Birdguns, P.O. Box 533, Newport, OR 97365 / 541-265-7433; FAX: 541-265-7400 www.billhanusbirdguns.com
Bill Russ Trading Post, William A. Russ, 25 William St., Addison, NY 14801-1326 / 607-359-3896
Bill Wiseman and Co., P.O. Box 3427, Bryan, TX 77805 / 409-690-3456; FAX: 409-690-0156
Billeb, Stepehn. See: QUALITY CUSTOM FIREARMS
Billings Gunsmiths, 1841 Grand Ave., Billings, MT 59102 / 406-256-8390; FAX: 406-256-6530 blgsgunsmiths@msn.com www.billingsgunsmiths.net
Billingsley & Brownell, P.O. Box 25, Dayton, WY 82836 / 307-655-9344
Bill's Gun Repair, 1007 Burlington St., Mendota, IL 61342 / 815-539-5786
Billy Bates Engraving, 2302 Winthrop Dr. SW, Decatur, AL 35603 / 256-355-3690 bbrn@aol.com
Birchwood Casey, 7900 Fuller Rd., Eden Prairie, MN 55344 / 800-328-6156; or 612-937-7933; FAX: 612-937-7979
Birdsong & Assoc., W. E., 1435 Monterey Rd, Florence, MS 39073-9748 / 601-366-8270
Bismuth Cartridge Co., 3500 Maple Ave., Suite 1650, Dallas, TX 75219 / 214-521-5880; FAX: 214-521-9035
Bison Studios, 1409 South Commerce St., Las Vegas, NV 89102 / 702-388-2891; FAX: 702-383-9967
Bitterroot Bullet Co., 2001 Cedar Ave., Lewiston, ID 83501-0412 / 208-743-5635 brootbil@lewiston.com
BKL Technologies, PO Box 5237, Brownsville, TX 78523
Black Belt Bullets (See Big Bore Express)
Black Hills Ammunition, Inc., P.O. Box 3090, Rapid City, SD 57709-3090 / 605-348-5150; FAX: 605-348-9827
Black Hills Shooters Supply, P.O. Box 4220, Rapid City, SD 57709 / 800-289-2506
Black Powder Products, 67 Township Rd. 1411, Chesapeake, OH 45619 / 614-867-8047
Black Sheep Brand, 3220 W. Gentry Parkway, Tyler, TX 75702 / 903-592-3853; FAX: 903-592-0527
Blacksmith Corp., P.O. Box 280, North Hampton, OH 45349 / 937-969-8389; FAX: 937-969-8399 sales@blacksmithcorp.com www.blacksmithcorp.com
BlackStar AccuMax Barrels, 11501 Brittmoore Park Drive, Houston, TX 77041 / 281-721-6040; FAX: 281-721-6041
BlackStar Barrel Accurizing (See BlackStar AccuMax)
Blacktail Mountain Books, 42 First Ave. W., Kalispell, MT 59901 / 406-257-5573
Blammo Ammo, P.O. Box 1677, Seneca, SC 29679 / 803-882-1768
Blaser Jagdwaffen GmbH, D-88316, Isny Im Allgau, GERMANY
Blount, Inc., Sporting Equipment Div., 2299 Snake River Ave., P.O. Box 856, Lewiston, ID 83501 / 800-627-3640; or 208-746-2351; FAX: 208-799-3904
Blount/Outers ATK, P.O. Box 39, Onalaska, WI 54650 / 608-781-5800; FAX: 608-781-0368
Blue and Gray Products Inc. (See Ox-Yoke Originals)
Blue Book Publications, Inc., 8009 34th Ave. S., Ste. 175, Minneapolis, MN 55425 / 952-854-5229; FAX: 952-853-1486 bluebook@bluebookinc.com www.bluebookinc.com
Blue Mountain Bullets, 64146 Quail Ln., Box 231, John Day, OR 97845 / 541-820-4594; FAX: 541-820-4594
Blue Ridge Machinery & Tools, Inc., P.O. Box 536-GD, Hurricane, WV 25526 / 800-872-6500; FAX: 304-562-5311 blueridgemachine@worldnet.att.net www.blueridgemachinery.com
BMC Supply, Inc., 26051 - 179th Ave. S.E., Kent, WA 98042
Bob Allen Co., P.O. Box 477, 214 SW Jackson, Des Moines, IA 50315 / 800-685-7020; FAX: 515-283-0779
Bob Allen Sportswear, 220 S. Main St., Osceola, IA 50213 / 210-344-8531; FAX: 210-342-2703 sales@bob-allen.com www.bob-allen.com
Bob Rogers Gunsmithing, P.O. Box 305, 344 S. Walnut St., Franklin Grove, IL 61031 / 815-456-2685; FAX: 815-456-2685
Bob's Gun Shop, P.O. Box 200, Royal, AR 71968 / 501-767-1970; FAX: 501-767-1970 gunparts@hsnp.com www.gun-parts.com
Bob's Tactical Indoor Shooting Range & Gun Shop, 90 Lafayette Rd., Salisbury, MA 01952 / 508-465-5561
Boessler, Erich, Am Vogeltal 3, 97702, Munnerstadt, GERMANY
Boker USA, Inc., 1550 Balsam Street, Lakewood, CO 80214 / 303-462-0662; FAX: 303-462-0668 sales@bokerusa.com bokerusa.com
Boltin, John M., P.O. Box 644, Estill, SC 29918 / 803-625-2185
Bo-Mar Tool & Mfg. Co., 6136 State Hwy. 300, Longview, TX 75604 / 903-759-4784; FAX: 903-759-9141 marykor@earthlink.net bo-mar.com
Bonadimani, Benso. See: BERSA S.A.
Bonanza (See Forster Products), 310 E. Lanark Ave., Lanark, IL 61046 / 815-493-6360; FAX: 815-493-2371
Bond Arms, Inc., P.O. Box 1296, Granbury, TX 76048 / 817-573-4445; FAX: 817-573-5636
Bond Custom Firearms, 8954 N. Lewis Ln., Bloomington, IN 47408 / 812-332-4519
Bonham's & Butterfields, 220 San Bruno Ave., San Francisco, CA 94103 / 415-861-7500; FAX: 415-861-0183 arms@butterfields.com www.butterfields.com
Boone Trading Co., Inc., PO Box 669, Brinnon, WA 98320 / 800-423-1945; or 360-796-4330; FAX: 360-796-4511 sales@boonetrading.com boonetrading.com
Boone's Custom Ivory Grips, Inc., 562 Coyote Rd., Brinnon, WA 98320 / 206-796-4330
Boonie Packer Products, P.O. Box 12517, Salem, OR 97309-0517 / 800-477-3244; or 503-581-3244; FAX: 503-581-3191 booniepacker@aol.com www.booniepacker.com
Borden Ridges Rimrock Stocks, RR 1 Box 250 BC, Springville, PA 18844 / 570-965-2505; FAX: 570-965-2328
Borden Rifles Inc., RD 1, Box 250BC, Springville, PA 18844 / 717-965-2505; FAX: 717-965-2328
Border Barrels Ltd., Riccarton Farm, Newcastleton, SCOTLAND UK
Borovnik KG, Ludwig, 9170 Ferlach, Bahnhofstrasse 7, AUSTRIA / 042 27 24 42; FAX: 042 26 43 49
Bosis (See U.S. Importer-New England Arms Co.)
Boss Manufacturing Co., 221 W. First St., Kewanee, IL 61443 / 309-852-2131; or 800-447-4581; FAX: 309-852-0848
Bostick Wildlife Calls, Inc., P.O. Box 728, Estill, SC 29918 / 803-625-2210; or 803-625-4512
Bowen Classic Arms Corp., P.O. Box 67, Louisville, TN 37777 / 865-984-3583 www.bowenclassicarms.com
Bowen Knife Co., Inc., P.O. Box 590, Blackshear, GA 31516 / 912-449-4794
Bowerly, Kent, 710 Golden Pheasant Dr., Redmond, OR 97756 / 541-923-3501 jkbowerly@aol.com
Boyds' Gunstock Industries, Inc., 25376 403 Rd. Ave., Mitchell, SD 57301 / 605-996-5011; FAX: 605-996-9878
Brace, Larry D., 771 Blackfoot Ave., Eugene, OR 97404 / 541-688-1278; FAX: 541-607-5833
Brass Eagle, Inc., 7050A Bramalea Rd., Unit 19, Mississauga,, ON L4Z 1C7 CANADA / 416-848-4844
Brauer Bros., 1520 Washington Avenue., St. Louis, MO 63103 / 314-231-2864; FAX: 314-249-4952 www.brauerbros.com
Break-Free, Inc., 13386 International Parkway, Jacksonville, FL 32218 / 800-428-0588; FAX: 904-741-5407 contactus@armorholdings.com www.break-free.com
Brenneke GmbH, P.O. Box 1646, 30837 Langenhagen, Langenhagen, GERMANY / +49-511-97262-0; FAX: +49-511-97262-62 info@brenneke.de brenneke.com
Bridgeman Products, Harry Jaffin, 153 B Cross Slope Court, Englishtown, NJ 07726 / 732-536-3604; FAX: 732-972-1004
Bridgers Best, P.O. Box 1410, Berthoud, CO 80513
Briese Bullet Co., Inc., 3442 42nd Ave. SE, Tappen, ND 58487 / 701-327-4578; FAX: 701-327-4579
Brigade Quartermasters, 1025 Cobb International Blvd., Dept. VH, Kennesaw, GA 30144-4300 / 404-428-1248; or 800-241-3125; FAX: 404-426-7726
Briganti, A.J., 512 Rt. 32, Highland Mills, NY 10930 / 914-928-9573
Briley Mfg. Inc., 1230 Lumpkin, Houston, TX 77043 / 800-331-5718; or 713-932-6995; FAX: 713-932-1043
Brill, R. See: ROYAL ARMS INTERNATIONAL
British Sporting Arms, RR1, Box 130, Millbrook, NY 12545 / 914-677-8303
Broad Creek Rifle Works, Ltd., 120 Horsey Ave., Laurel, DE 19956 / 302-875-5446; FAX: 302-875-1448 bcrw4guns@aol.com
Brockman's Custom Gunsmithing, P.O. Box 357, Gooding, ID 83330 / 208-934-5050
Brocock Ltd., 43 River Street, Digbeth, Birmingham, B5 5SA ENGLAND / 011-021-773-1200; FAX: 011-021-773-1211 sales@brocock.co.un www.brocock.co.uk
Broken Gun Ranch, 10739 126 Rd., Spearville, KS 67876 / 316-385-2587; FAX: 316-385-2597 nbowlin@ucom.net www.brokengunranch
Brooker, Dennis, Rt. 1, Box 12A, Derby, IA 50068 / 515-533-2103
Brooks Tactical Systems-Agrip, 279-C Shorewood Ct., Fox Island, WA 98333 / 253-549-2866 FAX: 253-549-2703 brooks@brookstactical.com www.brookstactical.com
Brown Co., E. Arthur, 3404 Pawnee Dr., Alexandria, MN 56308 / 320-762-8847
Brown Dog Ent., 2200 Calle Camelia, 1000 Oaks, CA 91360 / 805-497-2318; FAX: 805-497-1618
Brown Precision, Inc., 7786 Molinos Ave., Los Molinos, CA 96055 / 530-384-2506; FAX: 916-384-1638 www.brownprecision.com
Brown Products, Inc., Ed, 43825 Muldrow Trail, Perry, MO 63462 / 573-565-3261; FAX: 573-565-2791 edbrown@edbrown.com www.edbrown.com
Brownells, Inc., 200 S. Front St., Montezuma, IA 50171 / 800-741-0015; FAX: 800-264-3068 orderdesk@brownells.com www.brownells.com
Browning Arms Co., One Browning Place, Morgan, UT 84050 / 801-876-2711; FAX: 801-876-3331 www.browning.com
Browning Arms Co. (Parts & Service), 3005 Arnold Tenbrook Rd., Arnold, MO 63010 / 617-287-6800; FAX: 617-287-9751
BRP, Inc. High Performance Cast Bullets, 1210 Alexander Rd., Colorado Springs, CO 80909 / 719-633-0658
Brunton U.S.A., 620 E. Monroe Ave., Riverton, WY 82501 / 307-856-6559; FAX: 307-857-4702 info@brunton.com www.brunton.com
Bryan & Assoc., R D Sauls, PO Box 5772, Anderson, SC 29623-5772 / 864-261-6810 bryanandac@aol.com www.huntersweb.com/bryanandac
Brynin, Milton, P.O. Box 383, Yonkers, NY 10710 / 914-779-4333
BSA Guns Ltd., Armoury Rd. Small Heath, Birmingham B11 2PP, ENGLAND / 011-021-772-8543; FAX: 011-021-773-0845 sales@bsagun.com www.bsagun.com
BSA Optics, 3911 SW 47th Ave., Ste. 914, Ft. Lauderdale, FL 33314 / 954-581-2144; FAX: 954-581-3165 4info@basaoptics.com www.bsaoptics.com
B-Square Company, Inc., P.O. Box 11281, 2708 St. Louis Ave., Ft. Worth, TX 76110 / 817-923-0964 or 800-433-2909; FAX: 817-926-7012
Buchsenmachermeister, Peter Hofer Jagdwaffen, Buchsenmachermeister, Kirchgasse 24 A-9170, Ferlach, AUSTRIA / 43 4227 3683; FAX: 43 4227 368330 peterhofer@hoferwaffen.com www.hoferwaffen.com
Buck Knives, Inc., 1900 Weld Blvd., P.O. Box 1267, El Cajon, CA 92020 / 619-449-1100; or 800-326-2825; FAX: 619-562-5774
Buck Stix-SOS Products Co., Box 3, Neenah, WI 54956
Buck Stop Lure Co., Inc., 3600 Grow Rd. NW, P.O. Box 636, Stanton, MI 48888 / 989-762-5091; FAX: 989-762-5124 buckstop@nethawk.com www.buckstopscents.com
Buckeye Custom Bullets, 6490 Stewart Rd., Elida, OH 45807 / 419-641-4463
Buckhorn Gun Works, 8109 Woodland Dr., Black Hawk, SD 57718 / 605-787-6472
Buckskin Bullet Co., P.O. Box 1893, Cedar City, UT 84721 / 435-586-3286
Budin, Dave, 817 Main St., P.O. Box 685, Margaretville, NY 12455 / 914-568-4103; FAX: 914-586-4105
Budin, Dave. See: DEL-SPORTS, INC.
Buenger Enterprises/Goldenrod Dehumidifier, 3600 S. Harbor Blvd., Oxnard, CA 93035 / 800-451-6797; or 805-985-5828; FAX: 805-985-1534
Buffalo Arms Co., 660 Vermeer Ct., Ponderay, ID 83852 / 208-263-6953; FAX: 208-265-2096 www.buffaloarms.com
Buffalo Bullet Co., Inc., 12637 Los Nietos Rd., Unit A, Santa Fe Springs, CA 90670 / 800-423-8069; FAX: 562-944-5054
Buffalo Gun Center, 3385 Harlem Rd., Buffalo, NY 14225 / 716-833-2581; FAX: 716-833-2265 www.buffaloguncenter.com
Buffalo Rock Shooters Supply, R.R. 1, Ottawa, IL 61350 / 815-433-2471
Buffer Technologies, P.O. Box 104930, Jefferson City, MO 65110 / 573-634-8529; FAX: 573-634-8522
Bull Mountain Rifle Co., 6327 Golden West Terrace, Billings, MT 59106 / 406-656-0778
Bullberry Barrel Works, Ltd., 2430 W. Bullberry Ln., Hurricane, UT 84737 / 435-635-9866; FAX: 435-635-0348 fred@bullberry.com www.bullberry.com
Bullet Metals, Bill Ferguson, P.O. Box 1238, Sierra Vista, AZ 85636 / 520-458-5321; FAX: 520-458-1421 info@theantimonyman.com www.bullet-metals.com
Bullet N Press, 1210 Jones St., Gastonia, NC 28052 / 704-853-0265 bnpress@quik.com www.clt.quik.com/bnpress

MANUFACTURER'S DIRECTORY

Bullet Swaging Supply, Inc., P.O. Box 1056, 303 McMillan Rd., West Monroe, LA 71291 / 318-387-3266; FAX: 318-387-7779 leblackmon@colla.com
Bull-X, Inc., 411 E. Water St., Farmer City, IL 61842-1556 / 309-928-2574 or 800-248-3845; FAX: 309-928-2130
Burkhart Gunsmithing, Don, P.O. Box 852, Rawlins, WY 82301 / 307-324-6007
Burnham Bros., P.O. Box 1148, Menard, TX 78659 / 915-396-4572; FAX: 915-396-4574
Burris Co., Inc., PO Box 1747, 331 E. 8th St., Greeley, CO 80631 / 970-356-1670; FAX: 970-356-8702
Bushmaster Firearms, Inc., 999 Roosevelt Trail, Windham, ME 04062 / 800-998-7928; FAX: 207-892-8068 info@bushmaster.com www.bushmaster.com
Bushmaster Hunting & Fishing, 451 Alliance Ave., Toronto, ON M6N 2J1 CANADA / 416-763-4040; FAX: 416-763-0623
Bushnell Sports Optics Worldwide, 9200 Cody, Overland Park, KS 66214 / 913-752-3400 or 800-423-3537; FAX: 913-752-3550
Buster's Custom Knives, P.O. Box 214, Richfield, UT 84701 / 435-896-5319; FAX: 435-896-8333 www.warenskiknives.com
Butler Creek Corp., 2100 S. Silverstone Way, Meridian, ID 83642-8151 / 800-423-8327 or 406-388-1356; FAX: 406-388-7204
Butler Enterprises, 834 Oberting Rd., Lawrenceburg, IN 47025 / 812-537-3584
Buzz Fletcher Custom Stockmaker, 117 Silver Road, P.O. Box 189, Taos, NM 87571 / 505-758-3486

C

C&D Special Products (See Claybuster Wads & Harvester Bullets)
C&H Research, 115 Sunnyside Dr., Box 351, Lewis, KS 67552 / 316-324-5445; or 888-324-5445; FAX: 620-324-5984 info@mercuryrecoil.com www.mercuryrecoil.com
C. Palmer Manufacturing Co., Inc., P.O. Box 220, West Newton, PA 15089 / 412-872-8200; FAX: 412-872-8302
C. Sharps Arms Co. Inc./Montana Armory, 100 Centennial Dr., PO Box 885, Big Timber, MT 59011 / 406-932-4353; FAX: 406-932-4443
C.S. Van Gorden & Son, Inc., 1815 Main St., Bloomer, WI 54724 / 715-568-2612 vangorden@bloomer.net
C.W. Erickson's L.L.C., 530 Garrison Ave. NE, PO Box 522, Buffalo, MN 55313 / 763-682-3665; FAX: 763-682-4328 www.archerhunter.com
Cabanas (See U.S. Importer-Mandall Shooting Supply
Cabela's, One Cabela Drive, Sidney, NE 69160 / 308-254-5505; FAX: 308-254-8420
Cabinet Mtn. Outfitters Scents & Lures, P.O. Box 766, Plains, MT 59859 / 406-826-3970
Cache La Poudre Rifleworks, 140 N. College, Ft. Collins, CO 80524 / 920-482-6913
Calhoon Mfg., 4343 U.S. Highway 87, Havre, MT 59501 / 406-395-4079 www.jamescalhoon.com
Cali'co Hardwoods, Inc., 3580 Westwind Blvd., Santa Rosa, CA 95403 / 707-546-4045; FAX: 707-546-4027 calicohardwoods@msn.com
Calico Light Weapon Systems, 1489 Greg St., Sparks, NV 89431
California Sights (See Fautheree, Andy)
Cambos Outdoorsman, 532 E. Idaho Ave., Ontario, OR 97914 / 541-889-3135; FAX: 541-889-2633
Cambos Outdoorsman, Fritz Hallberg, 532 E. Idaho Ave, Ontario, OR 97914 / 541-889-3135; FAX: 541-889-2633
Camdex, Inc., 2330 Alger, Troy, MI 48083 / 810-528-2300; FAX: 810-528-0989
Cameron's, 16690 W. 11th Ave., Golden, CO 80401 / 303-279-7365; FAX: 303-628-5413 ncnoremac@aol.com
Camillus Cutlery Co., 54 Main St., Camillus, NY 13031 / 315-672-8111; FAX: 315-672-8832
Campbell, Dick, 20000 Silver Ranch Rd., Conifer, CO 80433 / 303-697-0150; FAX: 303-697-0150 dicksknives@aol.com
Camp-Cap Products, P.O. Box 3805, Chesterfield, MO 63006 / 314-532-4340; FAX: 314-532-4340
Cannon Safe, Inc., 216 S. 2nd Ave. #BLD-932, San Bernardino, CA 92400 / 310-692-0636; or 800-242-1055; FAX: 310-692-7252
Canons Delcour, Rue J.B. Cools, B-4040, Herstal, BELGIUM / 32.(0)42.40.61.40; FAX: 32(0)42.40.22.88
Canyon Cartridge Corp., P.O. Box 152, Albertson, NY 11507 FAX: 516-294-8946
Cape Outfitters, 599 County Rd. 206, Cape Girardeau, MO 63701 / 573-335-4103; FAX: 573-335-1555
Caraville Manufacturing, P.O. Box 4545, Thousand Oaks, CA 91359 / 805-499-1234
Carbide Checkering Tools (See J&R Engineering)
Carhartt, Inc., P.O. Box 600, 3 Parklane Blvd., Dearborn, MI 48121 / 800-358-3825; or 313-271-8460; FAX: 313-271-3455
Carl Walther GmbH, B.P. 4325, D-89033, Ulm, GERMANY
Carl Zeiss Inc., 13005 N. Kingston Ave., Chester, VA 23836 / 800-441-3005; FAX: 804-530-8481
Carlson, Douglas R, Antique American Firearms, P.O. Box 71035, Dept GD, Des Moines, IA 50325 / 515-224-6552
Carolina Precision Rifles, 1200 Old Jackson Hwy., Jackson, SC 29831 / 803-827-2069
Carrell, William. See: CARRELL'S PRECISION FIREARMS
Carrell's Precision Firearms, William Carrell, 1952 W.Silver Falls Ct., Meridian, ID 83642-3837
Carry-Lite, Inc., P.O. Box 1587, Fort Smith, AR 72902 / 479-782-8971; FAX: 479-783-0234
Carter's Gun Shop, 225 G St., Penrose, CO 81240 / 719-372-6240
Cascade Bullet Co., Inc., 2355 South 6th St., Klamath Falls, OR 97601 / 503-884-9316
Cascade Shooters, 2155 N.W. 12th St., Redwood, OR 97756
Case & Sons Cutlery Co., W R, Owens Way, Bradford, PA 16701 / 814-368-4123; or 800-523-6350; FAX: 814-768-5369
Case Sorting System, 12695 Cobblestone Creek Rd., Poway, CA 92064 / 619-486-9340
Cash Mfg. Co., Inc., P.O. Box 130, 201 S. Klein Dr., Waunakee, WI 53597-0130 / 608-849-5664; FAX: 608-849-5664
Caspian Arms, Ltd., 14 North Main St., Hardwick, VT 05843 / 802-472-6454; FAX: 802-472-6709
Cast Performance Bullet Company, P.O. Box 153, Riverton, WY 82501 / 307-857-2940; FAX: 307-857-3132 castperform@wyoming.com castperformance.com
Casull Arms Corp., P.O. Box 1629, Afton, WY 83110 / 307-886-0200
Caswell International, 720 Industrial Dr. No. 112, Cary, IL 60013 / 847-639-7666; FAX: 847-639-7694 www.caswellintl.com
Cathey Enterprises, Inc., P.O. Box 2202, Brownwood, TX 76804 / 915-643-2553; FAX: 915-643-3653
Cation, 2341 Alger St., Troy, MI 48083 / 810-689-0658; FAX: 810-689-7558
Caywood, Shane J., P.O. Box 321, Minocqua, WI 54548 / 715-277-3866
Caywood Gunmakers, 18 Kings Hill Estates, Berryville, AR 72616 / 870-423-4741 www.caywoodguns.com
CBC, Avenida Humberto de Campos 3220, 09400-000, Ribeirao Pires, SP, BRAZIL / 55 11 4822 8378; FAX: 55 11 4822 8323 export@cbc.com.bc www.cbc.com.bc
CBC-BRAZIL, 3 Cuckoo Lane, Honley, Yorkshire HD7 2BR, ENGLAND / 44-1484-661062; FAX: 44-1484-663709
CCG Enterprises, 5217 E. Belknap St., Halton City, TX 76117 / 800-819-7464
CCI/Speer Div of ATK, P.O. Box 856, 2299 Snake River Ave., Lewiston, ID 83501 / 800-627-3640 or 208-746-2351
CCL Security Products, 199 Whiting St, New Britain, CT 06051 / 800-733-8588
Cedar Hill Game Calls, Inc., 238 Vic Allen Rd, Downsville, LA 71234 / 318-982-5632; FAX: 318-368-2245
Centaur Systems, Inc., 1602 Foothill Rd., Kalispell, MT 59901 / 406-755-8609; FAX: 406-755-8609
Center Lock Scope Rings, 9901 France Ct., Lakeville, MN 55044 / 952-461-2114; FAX: 952-461-2194 marklee55044@usfamily.net
Central Specialties Ltd (See Trigger Lock Division
Century Gun Dist. Inc., 1467 Jason Rd., Greenfield, IN 46140 / 317-462-4524
Century International Arms, Inc., 1161 Holland Dr, Boca Raton, FL 33487 / 800-527-1252; FAX: 561-998-1993 support@centuryarms.com www.centuryarms.com
CFVentures, 509 Harvey Dr., Bloomington, IN 47403-1715 paladinwilltravel@yahoo.com www.caversam16.freeserve.co.uk
CH Tool & Die Co. (See 4-D Custom Die Co.), 711 N Sandusky St., P.O. Box 889, Mt. Vernon, OH 43050-0889 / 740-397-7214; FAX: 740-397-6600
Chace Leather Products, 507 Alden St., Fall River, MA 02722 / 508-678-7556; FAX: 508-675-9666 chacelea@aol.com www.chaceleather.com
Chadick's Ltd., P.O. Box 100, Terrell, TX 75160 / 214-563-7577
Chambers Flintlocks Ltd., Jim, 116 Sams Branch Rd., Candler, NC 28715 / 828-667-8361; FAX: 828-665-0852 www.flintlocks.com
Champion Shooters' Supply, P.O. Box 303, New Albany, OH 43054 / 614-855-1603; FAX: 614-855-1209
Champion Target Co., 232 Industrial Parkway, Richmond, IN 47374 / 800-441-4971
Champion's Choice, Inc., 201 International Blvd., LaVergne, TN 37086 / 615-793-4066; FAX: 615-793-4070 champ.choice@earthlink.net www.champchoice.com
Champlin Firearms, Inc., P.O. Box 3191, Woodring Airport, Enid, OK 73701 / 580-237-7388; FAX: 580-242-6922 info@champlinarms.com www.champlinarms.com
Chapman Academy of Practical Shooting, 4350 Academy Rd., Hallsville, MO 65255 / 573-696-5544; FAX: 573-696-2266 ha@chapmanacademy.com
Chapman, J Ken. See: OLD WEST BULLET MOULDS
Chapman Manufacturing Co., 471 New Haven Rd., P.O. Box 250, Durham, CT 06422 / 860-349-9228; FAX: 860-349-0084 sales@chapmanmfg.com www.chapmanmfg.com
Chapuis Armes, 21 La Gravoux, BP15, 42380, St. Bonnet-le-Chatea, FRANCE / (33)77.50.06.96
Chapuis USA, 416 Business Park, Bedford, KY 40006
Charter 2000, 273 Canal St, Shelton, CT 06484 / 203-922-1652
Checkmate Refinishing, 370 Champion Dr., Brooksville, FL 34601 / 352-799-5774; FAX: 352-799-2986 checkmatecustom.com
Cheddite, France S.A., 99 Route de Lyon, F-26501, Bourg-les-Valence, FRANCE / 33-75-56-4545; FAX: 33-75-56-3587 export@cheddite.com
Chelsea Gun Club of New York City Inc., 237 Ovington Ave., Apt. D53, Brooklyn, NY 11209 / 718-836-9422; or 718-833-2704
Cherry Creek State Park Shooting Center, 12500 E. Belleview Ave., Englewood, CO 80111 / 303-693-1765
CheVron Bullets, RR1, Ottawa, IL 61350 / 815-433-2471
Cheyenne Pioneer Products, PO Box 28425, Kansas City, MO 64188 / 816-413-9196; FAX: 816-455-2859 cheyennepp@aol.com www.cartridgeboxes.com
Chicago Cutlery Co., 1536 Beech St., Terre Haute, IN 47804 / 800-457-2665
Chicasaw Gun Works, 4 Mi. Mkr., Pluto Rd., Box 868, Shady Spring, WV 25918-0868 / 304-763-2848; FAX: 304-763-3725
Chip McCormick Corp., P.O. Box 1560, Manchaca, TX 78652 / 800-328-2447; FAX: 512-280-4282 www.chipmccormick.com
Chipmunk (See Oregon Arms, Inc.)
Choate Machine & Tool Co., Inc., P.O. Box 218, 116 Lovers Ln., Bald Knob, AR 72010 / 501-724-6193; or 800-972-6390; FAX: 501-724-5873
Christensen Arms, 192 East 100 North, Fayette, UT 84630 / 435-528-7999; FAX: 435-528-7494 www.christensenarms.com
Christie's East, 20 Rockefeller Plz., New York, NY 10020-1902 / 212-606-0406 christics.com
Chu Tani Ind., Inc., P.O. Box 2064, Cody, WY 82414-2064
Chuck's Gun Shop, P.O. Box 597, Waldo, FL 32694 / 904-468-2264
Chuilli, Stephen, 8895 N. Military Trl. Ste., Ste. 201E, Palm Beach Gardens, FL 33410
Churchill (See U.S. Importer-Ellett Bros.)
Churchill, Winston G., 2838 20 Mile Stream Rd., Proctorville, VT 05153 / 802-226-7772
Churchill Glove Co., James, PO Box 298, Centralia, WA 98531 / 360-736-2816; FAX: 360-330-0151
CIDCO, 21480 Pacific Blvd., Sterling, VA 22170 / 703-444-5353
Cimarron F.A. Co., P.O. Box 906, Fredericksburg, TX 78624-0906 / 830-997-9090; FAX: 830-997-0802 cimgraph@koc.com www.cimarron-firearms.com
Cincinnati Swaging, 2605 Marlington Ave., Cincinnati, OH 45208
Clark Custom Guns, Inc., 336 Shootout Lane, Princeton, LA 71067 / 318-949-9884; FAX: 318-949-9829
Clark Firearms Engraving, P.O. Box 80746, San Marino, CA 91118 / 818-287-1652
Clarkfield Enterprises, Inc., 1032 10th Ave., Clarkfield, MN 56223 / 612-669-7140
Claro Walnut Gunstock Co., 1235 Stanley Ave., Chico, CA 95928 / 530-342-5188; FAX: 530-342-5199 wally@clarowalnutgunstocks.com www.clarowalnutgunstocks.com
Classic Arms Company, Rt 1 Box 120F, Burnet, TX 78611 / 512-756-4001
Classic Arms Corp., P.O. Box 106, Dunsmuir, CA 96025-0106 / 530-235-2000
Classic Old West Styles, 1060 Doniphan Park Circle C, El Paso, TX 79936 / 915-587-0684

MANUFACTURER'S DIRECTORY

Claybuster Wads & Harvester Bullets, 309 Sequoya Dr., Hopkinsville, KY 42240 / 800-922-6287; or 800-284-1746; FAX: 502-885-8088
Clean Shot Technologies, 21218 St. Andrews Blvd. Ste 504, Boca Raton, FL 33433 / 888-866-2532
Clearview Mfg. Co., Inc., 413 S. Oakley St., Fordyce, AR 71742 / 501-352-8557; FAX: 501-352-7120
Clearview Products, 3021 N. Portland, Oklahoma City, OK 73107
Cleland's Outdoor World, Inc, 10306 Airport Hwy., Swanton, OH 43558 / 419-865-4713; FAX: 419-865-5865
Clements' Custom Leathercraft, Chas, 1741 Dallas St., Aurora, CO 80010-2018 / 303-364-0403; FAX: 303-739-9824 gryphons@home.com kuntaoslcat.com
Clenzoil Worldwide Corp, Jack Fitzgerald, 25670 1st St., Westlake, OH 44145-1430 / 440-899-0482; FAX: 440-899-0483
Clift Mfg., L. R., 3821 Hammonton Rd., Marysville, CA 95901 / 916-755-3390; FAX: 916-755-3393
Clymer Mfg. Co., 1645 W. Hamlin Rd., Rochester Hills, MI 48309-3312 / 248-853-5555; FAX: 248-853-1530
C-More Systems, P.O. Box 1750, 7553 Gary Rd., Manassas, VA 20108 / 703-361-2663; FAX: 703-361-5881
Cobra Enterprises, Inc., 1960 S. Milestone Drive, Suite F, Salt Lake City, UT 84104 FAX: 801-908-8301 www.cobrapistols@networld.com
Cobra Sport S.R.I., Via Caduti Nei Lager No. 1, 56020 San Romano, Montopoli v/Arno (Pi, ITALY / 0039-571-450490; FAX: 0039-571-450492
Coffin, Charles H., 3719 Scarlet Ave., Odessa, TX 79762 / 915-366-4729; FAX: 915-366-4729
Coffin, Jim (See Working Guns)
Coffin, Jim. See: WORKING GUNS
Cogar's Gunsmithing, 206 Redwine Dr., Houghton Lake, MI 48629 / 517-422-4591
Coghlan's Ltd., 121 Irene St., Winnipeg, MB R3T 4C7 CANADA / 204-284-9550; FAX: 204-475-4127
Cold Steel Inc., 3036 Seaborg Ave. Ste. A, Ventura, CA 93003 / 800-255-4716; or 800-624-2363; FAX: 805-642-9727
Cole-Grip, 16135 Cohasset St., Van Nuys, CA 91406 / 818-782-4424
Coleman Co., Inc., 3600 N. Hydraulic, Wichita, KS 67219 / 1-800-835-3278; www.coleman.com
Cole's Gun Works, Old Bank Building, Rt. 4 Box 250, Moyock, NC 27958 / 919-435-2345
Collector's Armoury, Ltd., Tom Nelson, 9404 Gunston Cove Rd., Lorton, VA 22079 / 703-493-9120; FAX: 703-493-9424 www.collectorsarmoury.com
Collings, Ronald, 1006 Cielta Linda, Vista, CA 92083
Colonial Arms, Inc., P.O. Box 636, Selma, AL 36702-0636 / 334-872-9455; FAX: 334-872-9540 colonialarms@mindspring.com www.colonialarms.com
Colonial Repair, 47 Navarre St., Roslindale, MA 02131-4725 / 617-469-4951
Colorado Gunsmithing Academy, RR 3 Box 79B, El Campo, TX 77437 / 719-336-4099; or 800-754-2046; FAX: 719-336-9642
Colorado School of Trades, 1575 Hoyt St., Lakewood, CO 80215 / 800-234-4594; FAX: 303-233-4723
Colt Blackpowder Arms Co., 110 8th Street, Brooklyn, NY 11215 / 718-499-4678; FAX: 718-768-8056
Colt's Mfg. Co., Inc., PO Box 1868, Hartford, CT 06144-1868 / 800-962-COLT; or 860-236-6311; FAX: 860-244-1449
Compass Industries, Inc., 104 East 25th St., New York, NY 10010 / 212-473-2614 or 800-221-9904; FAX: 212-353-0826
Compasseco, Ltd., 151 Atkinson Hill Ave., Bardtown, KY 40004 / 502-349-0910
Competition Electronics, Inc., 3469 Precision Dr., Rockford, IL 61109 / 815-874-8001; FAX: 815-874-8181
Competitor Corp., Inc., 26 Knight St. Unit 3, Jaffrey, NH 03452 / 603-532-9483; FAX: 603-532-8209 competitorcorp@aol.com competitor-pistol.com
Component Concepts, Inc., 530 S. Springbrook Road, Newberg, OR 97132 / 503-554-8095; FAX: 503-554-9370 cci@cybcon.com www.phantomonline.com
Concept Development Corp., 16610 E. Laser Drive, Suite 5, Fountain Hills, AZ 85268-6644
Conetrol Scope Mounts, 10225 Hwy. 123 S., Seguin, TX 78155 / 830-379-3030; or 800-CONETROL; FAX: 830-379-3030 email@conetrol.com www.conetrol.com
Connecticut Shotgun Mfg. Co., P.O. Box 1692, 35 Woodland St., New Britain, CT 06051 / 860-225-6581; FAX: 860-832-8707
Connecticut Valley Classics (See CVC, BPI)
Conrad, C. A., 3964 Ebert St., Winston-Salem, NC 27127 / 919-788-5469
Cook Engineering Service, 891 Highbury Rd., Vict, 3133 AUSTRALIA
Cooper Arms, P.O. Box 114, Stevensville, MT 59870 / 406-777-0373; FAX: 406-777-5228
Cooper-Woodward Perfect Lube, 4120 Oesterle Rd., Helena, MT 59602 / 406-459-2287 cwperfectlube@mt.net cwperfectlube.com
Corbin Mfg. & Supply, Inc., 600 Industrial Circle, P.O. Box 2659, White City, OR 97503 / 541-826-5211; FAX: 541-826-8669 sales@corbins.com www.corbins.com
Cor-Bon Inc./Glaser LLC, P.O. Box 173, 1311 Industry Rd., Sturgis, SD 57785 / 605-347-4544; or 800-221-3489; FAX: 605-347-5055 email@corbon.com www.corbon.com
Corkys Gun Clinic, 4401 Hot Springs Dr., Greeley, CO 80634-9226 / 970-330-0516
Corry, John, 861 Princeton Ct., Neshanic Station, NJ 08853 / 908-369-8019
Cosmi Americo & Figlio S.N.C., Via Flaminia 307, Ancona, ITALY / 071-888208; FAX: 39-071-887008
Coulston Products, Inc., P.O. Box 30, 201 Ferry St. Suite 212, Easton, PA 18044-0030 / 215-253-0167; or 800-445-9927; FAX: 215-252-1511
Counter Assault, 120 Industrial Court, Kalispell, MT 59901 / 406-257-4740; FAX: 406-257-6674
Cousin Bob's Mountain Products, 7119 Ohio River Blvd., Ben Avon, PA 15202 / 412-766-5114; FAX: 412-766-5114
CP Bullets, 1310 Industrial Hwy #5-6, South Hampton, PA 18966 / 215-953-7264; FAX: 215-953-7275
CQB Training, P.O. Box 1739, Manchester, MO 63011
Craftguard, 3624 Logan Ave., Waterloo, IA 50703 / 319-232-2959; FAX: 319-234-0804
Crandall Tool & Machine Co., 19163 21 Mile Rd., Tustin, MI 49688 / 616-829-4430
Creedmoor Sports, Inc., P.O. Box 1040, Oceanside, CA 92051 / 767-757-5529; FAX: 760-757-5558 shoot@creedmoorsports.com www.creedmoorsports.com
Creek Side Metal & Woodcrafters, Fishers Hill, VA 22626 / 703-465-3903
Creighton Audette, 19 Highland Circle, Springfield, VT 05156 / 802-885-2331
Crimson Trace Lasers, 8090 SW Cirrus Dr., Beverton, OR 97008 / 800-442-2406; FAX: 503-627-0166 www.crimsontrace.com
Crit'R Call (See Rocky Mountain Wildlife Products)
Crosman Airguns, Rts. 5 and 20, E. Bloomfield, NY 14443 / 716-657-6161; FAX: 716-657-5405
Crosman Blades (See Coleman Co., Inc.)
Crouse's Country Cover, P.O. Box 160, Storrs, CT 06268 / 860-423-8736
CRR, Inc./Marble's Inc., 420 Industrial Park, P.O. Box 111, Gladstone, MI 49837 / 906-428-3710; FAX: 906-428-3711
Crucelegui, Hermanos (See U.S. Importer-Mandall)
Cubic Shot Shell Co., Inc., 98 Fatima Dr., Campbell, OH 44405 / 330-755-0349
Cullity Restoration, 209 Old Country Rd., East Sandwich, MA 02537 / 508-888-1147
Cumberland Arms, 514 Shafer Road, Manchester, TN 37355 / 800-797-8414
Cumberland Mountain Arms, P.O. Box 710, Winchester, TN 37398 / 615-967-8414; FAX: 615-967-9199
Cummings Bullets, 1417 Esperanza Way, Escondido, CA 92027
Cupp, Alana, Custom Engraver, P.O. Box 207, Annabella, UT 84711 / 801-896-4834
Curly Maple Stock Blanks (See Tiger-Hunt)
Curtis Cast Bullets, 527 W. Babcock St., Bozeman, MT 59715 / 406-587-8117; FAX: 406-587-8117
Curtis Gun Shop (See Curtis Cast Bullets)
Custom Bullets by Hoffman, 2604 Peconic Ave., Seaford, NY 11783
Custom Calls, 607 N. 5th St., Burlington, IA 52601 / 319-752-4465
Custom Checkering Service, Kathy Forster, 2124 S.E. Yamhill St., Portland, OR 97214 / 503-236-5874
Custom Chronograph, Inc., 5305 Reese Hill Rd., Sumas, WA 98295 / 360-988-7801
Custom Firearms (See Ahrends, Kim)
Custom Products (See Jones Custom Products)
Custom Quality Products, Inc., 345 W. Girard Ave., P.O. Box 71129, Madison Heights, MI 48071 / 810-585-1616; FAX: 810-585-0644
Custom Riflestocks, Inc., Michael M. Kokolus, 7005 Herber Rd., New Tripoli, PA 18066 / 610-298-3013; FAX: 610-298-2431 mkokolus@prodigy.net
Custom Single Shot Rifles, 9651 Meadows Lane, Guthrie, OK 73044 / 405-282-3634
Custom Tackle and Ammo, P.O. Box 1886, Farmington, NM 87499 / 505-632-3539
Cutco Cutlery, P.O. Box 810, Olean, NY 14760 / 716-372-3111
CVA, 5988 Peachtree Corners East, Norcross, GA 30071 / 770-449-4687; FAX: 770-242-8546 info@cva.com www.cva.com
Cylinder & Slide, Inc., William R. Laughridge, 245 E. 4th St., Fremont, NE 68025 / 402-721-4277; FAX: 402-721-0263 bill@cylinder-slide.com www.clinder-slide.com
CZ USA, PO Box 171073, Kansas City, KS 66117 / 913-321-1811; FAX: 913-321-4901

D

D&D Gunsmiths, Ltd., 363 E. Elmwood, Troy, MI 48083 / 810-583-1512; FAX: 810-583-1524
D&G Precision Duplicators (See Greene Precision)
D&H Precision Tooling, 7522 Barnard Mill Rd., Ringwood, IL 60072 / 815-653-4011
D&L Industries (See D.J. Marketing)
D&L Sports, P.O. Box 651, Gillette, WY 82717 / 307-686-4008
D.C.C. Enterprises, 259 Wynburn Ave., Athens, GA 30601
D.J. Marketing, 10602 Horton Ave., Downey, CA 90241 / 310-806-0891; FAX: 310-806-6231
D.L. Unmussig Bullets, 7862 Brentford Dr., Richmond, VA 23225 / 804-320-1165; FAX: 804-320-4587
Dade Screw Machine Products, 2319 NW 7th Ave., Miami, FL 33127 / 305-573-5050
Daisy Outdoor Products, P.O. Box 220, Rogers, AR 72757 / 479-636-1200; FAX: 479-636-0573 www.daisy.com
Dakota (See U.S. Importer-EMF Co., Inc.)
Dakota Arms, Inc., 130 Industry Road, Sturgis, SD 57785 / 605-347-4686; FAX: 605-347-4459 info@dakotaarms.com www.dakotaarms.com
Dakota Corp., 77 Wales St., P.O. Box 543, Rutland, VT 05701 / 802-775-6062; or 800-451-4167; FAX: 802-773-3919
Daly, Charles/KBI, P.O. Box 6625, Harrisburg, PA 17112 / 866-DALY GUN
Da-Mar Gunsmith's, Inc., 102 1st St., Solvay, NY 13209
damascususa@inteliport.com, 149 Deans Farm Rd., Tyner, NC 27980 / 252-221-2010; FAX: 252-221-2010 damascususa@inteliport.com
Dan Wesson Firearms, 5169 Rt. 12 South, Norwich, NY 13815 / 607-336-1174; FAX: 607-336-2730 danwessonfirearms@citlink.net danwessonfirearms.com
Danforth, Mikael. See: VEKTOR USA
Dangler, Homer L., 2870 Lee Marie Dr., Adrian, MI 49221 / 517-266-1997
Danner Shoe Mfg. Co., 12722 NE Airport Way, Portland, OR 97230 / 503-251-1100; or 800-345-0430; FAX: 503-251-1119
Dan's Whetstone Co., Inc., 130 Timbs Place, Hot Springs, AR 71913 / 501-767-1616; FAX: 501-767-9598 questions@danswhetstone.com www.danswhetstone.com
Danuser Machine Co., 550 E. Third St., P.O. Box 368, Fulton, MO 65251 / 573-642-2246; FAX: 573-642-2240 sales@danuser.com www.danuser.com
Dara-Nes, Inc. (See Nesci Enterprises, Inc.)
D'Arcy Echols & Co., P.O. Box 421, Millville, UT 84326 / 435-755-6842
Darlington Gun Works, Inc., P.O. Box 698, 516 S. 52 Bypass, Darlington, SC 29532 / 803-393-3931
Dart Bell/Brass (See MAST Technology)
Darwin Hensley Gunmaker, P.O. Box 329, Brightwood, OR 97011 / 503-622-5411
Data Tech Software Systems, 19312 East Eldorado Drive, Aurora, CO 80013
Dave Norin Schrank's Smoke & Gun, 2010 Washington St., Waukegan, IL 60085 / 708-662-4034
Dave's Gun Shop, P.O. Box 2824, Casper, WY 82602-2824 / 307-754-9724
David Clark Co., Inc., P.O. Box 15054, Worcester, MA 01615 / 508-756-6216; FAX: 508-753-5827 sales@davidclark.com www.davidclark.com
David Condon, Inc., 109 E. Washington St., Middleburg, VA 22117 / 703-687-5642
David Miller Co., 3131 E. Greenlee Rd., Tucson, AZ 85716 / 520-326-3117
David R. Chicoine, 1210 Jones Street, Gastonia, NC 28052 / 704-853-0265 bnpress@quik.com www.icxquik.com/bnpress
David W. Schwartz Custom Guns, 2505 Waller St., Eau Claire, WI 54703 / 715-832-1735
Davide Pedersoli and Co., Via Artigiani 57, Gardone VT, Brescia 25063, ITALY / 030-8915000; FAX:

030-8911019 info@davidepedersoli.com www.davide_pedersoli.com
Davis, Don, 1619 Heights, Katy, TX 77493 / 713-391-3090
Davis Industries (See Cobra Enterprises, Inc.)
Davis Products, Mike, 643 Loop Dr., Moses Lake, WA 98837 / 509-765-6178; or 509-766-7281
Daystate Ltd., Birch House Lanee, Cotes Heath Staffs, ST15.022, ENGLAND / 01782-791755; FAX: 01782-791617
Dayton Traister, 4778 N. Monkey Hill Rd., P.O. Box 593, Oak Harbor, WA 98277 / 360-679-4657; FAX: 360-675-1114
DBI Books Division of Krause Publications, 700 E. State St., Iola, WI 54990-0001 / 715-445-2214
D-Boone Ent., Inc., 5900 Colwyn Dr., Harrisburg, PA 17109
Dead Eye's Sport Center, 76 Baer Rd., Shickshinny, PA 18655 / 570-256-7432 deadeyeprizz@aol.com
Deepeeka Exports Pvt. Ltd., D-78, Saket, Meerut-250-006, INDIA / 011-91-121-640363 or ; FAX: 011-91-121-640988 deepeeka@poboxes.com www.deepeeka.com
Defense Training International, Inc., 749 S. Lemay, Ste. A3-337, Ft. Collins, CO 80524 / 303-482-2520; FAX: 303-482-0548
Degen Inc. (See Aristocrat Knives)
deHaas Barrels, 20049 W. State Hwy. Z, Ridgeway, MO 64481 / 660-872-6308
Del Rey Products, P.O. Box 5134, Playa Del Rey, CA 90296-5134 / 213-823-0494
Delhi Gun House, 1374 Kashmere Gate, New Delhi 110 006, INDIA / 2940974; or 394-0974; FAX: 2917344 dgh@vsnl.com
Delorge, Ed, 6734 W. Main, Houma, LA 70360 / 985-223-0206 delorge@triparish.net www.eddelorge.com
Del-Sports, Inc., Dave Budin, Box 685, 817 Main St., Margaretville, NY 12455 / 845-586-4103; FAX: 845-586-4105
Delta Arms Ltd., P.O. Box 1000, Delta, VT 84624-1000
Delta Enterprises, 284 Hagemann Drive, Livermore, CA 94550
Delta Frangible Ammunition LLC, P.O. Box 2350, Stafford, VA 22555-2350 / 540-720-5778; or 800-339-1933; FAX: 540-720-5667 dfa@dfanet.com www.dfanet.com
Dem-Bart Checkering Tools, Inc., 1825 Bickford Ave., Snohomish, WA 98290 / 360-568-7356 walt@dembartco.com www.dembartco.com
Denver Instrument Co., 6542 Fig St., Arvada, CO 80004 / 800-321-1135; or 303-431-7255; FAX: 303-423-4831
DeSantis Holster & Leather Goods, Inc., P.O. Box 2039, 149 Denton Ave., New Hyde Park, NY 11040-0701 / 516-354-8000; FAX: 516-354-7501
Desert Mountain Mfg., P.O. Box 130184, Coram, MT 59913 / 800-477-0762; or 406-387-5361; FAX: 406-387-5361
Detonics USA, 53 Perimeter Center East #200, Atlanta, GA 30346 / 866-759-1169
DGR Custom Rifles, 4191 37th Ave. SE, Tappen, ND 58487 / 701-327-8135
DGS, Inc., Dale A. Storey, 1117 E. 12th, Casper, WY 82601 / 307-237-2414; FAX: 307-237-2414 dalest@trib.com www.dgsrifle.com
DHB Products, 336 River View Dr., Verona, VA 24482-2547 / 703-836-2648
Diamond Machining Technology, Inc. (See DMT)
Diamond Mfg. Co., P.O. Box 174, Wyoming, PA 18644 / 800-233-9601
Dibble, Derek A., 555 John Downey Dr., New Britain, CT 06051 / 203-224-2630
Dietz Gun Shop & Range, Inc., 421 Range Rd., New Braunfels, TX 78132 / 210-885-4662
Dilliott Gunsmithing, Inc., 657 Scarlett Rd., Dandridge, TN 37725 / 865-397-9204 gunsmithd@aol.com dilliottgunsmithing.com
Dillon Precision Products, Inc., 8009 East Dillon's Way, Scottsdale, AZ 85260 / 480-948-8009; or 800-762-3845; FAX: 480-998-2786 sales@dillonprecision.com www.dillonprecision.com
Dina Arms Corporation, P.O. Box 46, Royersford, PA 19468 / 610-287-0266; FAX: 610-287-0266
Dixie Gun Works, P.O. Box 130, Union City, TN 38281 / 731-885-0700; FAX: 731-885-0440 info@dixiegunworks.com www.dixiegunworks.com
Dixon Muzzleloading Shop, Inc., 9952 Kunkels Mill Rd., Kempton, PA 19529 / 610-756-6271 dixonmuzzleloading.com
DKT, Inc., 14623 Vera Drive, Union, MI 49130-9744 / 800-741-7083 orders; FAX: 616-641-2015
DLO Mfg., 10807 SE Foster Ave., Arcadia, FL 33821-7304
DMT--Diamond Machining Technology Inc., 85 Hayes Memorial Dr., Marlborough, MA 01752 FAX: 508-485-3924
Dohring Bullets, 100 W. 8 Mile Rd., Ferndale, MI 48220
Dolbare, Elizabeth, P.O. Box 502, Dubois, WY 82513-0502 / 307-450-7500 edolbare@hotmail.com www.scrimshaw-engraving.com
Domino, P.O. Box 108, 20019 Settimo Milanese, Milano, ITALY / 1-39-2-33512040; FAX: 1-39-2-33511587
Don Klein Custom Guns, 433 Murray Park Dr., Ripon, WI 54971 / 920-748-2931 daklein@charter.net www.donkleincustomguns.com
Donnelly, C. P., 405 Kubli Rd., Grants Pass, OR 97527 / 541-846-6604
Doskocil Mfg. Co., Inc., P.O. Box 1246, 4209 Barnett, Arlington, TX 76017 / 817-467-5116; FAX: 817-472-9810
Douglas Barrels, Inc., 5504 Big Tyler Rd., Charleston, WV 25313-1398 / 304-776-1341; FAX: 304-776-8560 www.benchrest.com/douglas
Downsizer Corp., P.O. Box 710316, Santee, CA 92072-0316 / 619-448-5510 www.downsizer.com
DPMS (Defense Procurement Manufacturing Services, Inc.), 13983 Industry Avenue, Becker, MN 55308 / 800-578-DPMS; or 763-261-5600; FAX: 763-261-5599
Dr. O's Products Ltd., P.O. Box 111, Niverville, NY 12130 / 518-784-3333; FAX: 518-784-2800
Drain, Mark, SE 3211 Kamilche Point Rd., Shelton, WA 98584 / 206-426-5452
Dremel Mfg. Co., 4915-21st St., Racine, WI 53406
Dri-Slide, Inc., 411 N. Darling, Fremont, MI 49412 / 616-924-3950
Dropkick, 1460 Washington Blvd., Williamsport, PA 17701 / 717-326-6561; FAX: 717-326-4950
DS Arms, Inc., P.O. Box 370, 27 West 990 Industrial Ave., Barrington, IL 60010 / 847-277-7258; FAX: 847-277-7259 www.dsarms.com
DTM International, Inc., 40 Joslyn Rd., P.O. Box 5, Lake Orion, MI 48362 / 313-693-6670
Duane A. Hobbie Gunsmithing, 2412 Pattie Ave., Wichita, KS 67216 / 316-264-8266
Duane's Gun Repair (See DGR Custom Rifles)
Dubber, Michael W., P.O. Box 312, Evansville, IN 47702 / 812-424-9000; FAX: 812-424-6551
Duck Call Specialists, P.O. Box 124, Jerseyville, IL 62052 / 618-498-9855
Duffy, Charles E. (See Guns Antique & Modern DBA), Williams Lane, P.O. Box 2, West Hurley, NY 12491 / 914-679-2997
Du-Lite Corp., 171 River Rd., Middletown, CT 06457 / 203-347-2505; FAX: 203-347-9404
Dumoulin, Ernest, Rue Florent Boclinville 8-10, 13-4041, Votten, BELGIUM / 41 27 78 92
Duncan's Gun Works, Inc., 1619 Grand Ave., San Marcos, CA 92069 / 760-727-0515
DunLyon R&D, Inc., 52151 E. US Hwy. 60, Miami, AZ 85539 / 928-473-9027
Duofold, Inc., RD 3 Rt. 309, Valley Square Mall, Tamaqua, PA 18252 / 717-386-2666; FAX: 717-386-3652
Dutchman's Firearms, Inc., 4143 Taylor Blvd., Louisville, KY 40215 / 502-366-0555
Dybala Gun Shop, P.O. Box 1024, FM 3156, Bay City, TX 77414 / 409-245-0866
Dykstra, Doug, 411 N. Darling, Fremont, MI 49412 / 616-924-3950
Dynalite Products, Inc., 215 S. Washington St., Greenfield, OH 45123 / 513-981-2124
Dynamit Nobel-RWS, Inc., 81 Ruckman Rd., Closter, NJ 07624 / 201-767-7971; FAX: 201-767-1589

E

E&L Mfg., Inc., 4177 Riddle Bypass Rd., Riddle, OR 97469 / 541-874-2137; FAX: 541-874-3107
E. Arthur Brown Co., 3404 Pawnee Dr., Alexandria, MN 56308 / 320-762-8847
E.A.A. Corp., P.O. Box 1299, Sharpes, FL 32959 / 407-639-4842; or 800-536-4442; FAX: 407-639-7006
Eagan, Donald V., P.O. Box 196, Benton, PA 17814 / 717-925-6134
Eagle Arms, Inc. (See ArmaLite, Inc.)
Eagle Grips, Eagle Business Center, 460 Randy Rd., Carol Stream, IL 60188 / 800-323-6144; or 708-260-0400; FAX: 708-260-0486
Eagle Imports, Inc., 1750 Brielle Ave., Unit B1, Wanamassa, NJ 07712 / 732-493-0333; FAX: 732-493-0301 gsodini@aol.com www.bersa-11ama.com
E-A-R, Inc., Div. of Cabot Safety Corp., 5457 W. 79th St., Indianapolis, IN 46268 / 800-327-3431; FAX: 800-488-8007
EAW (See U.S. Importer-New England Custom Gun Serv
Eckelman Gunsmithing, 3125 133rd St. SW, Fort Ripley, MN 56449 / 218-829-3176
Eclectic Technologies, Inc., 45 Grandview Dr., Suite A, Farmington, CT 06034
Ed Brown Products, Inc., P.O. Box 492, Perry, MO 63462 / 573-565-3261; FAX: 573-565-2791 edbrown@edbrown.com www.edbrown.com
Edenpine, Inc. c/o Six Enterprises, Inc., 320 D Turtle Creek Ct., San Jose, CA 95125 / 408-999-0201; FAX: 408-999-0216
EdgeCraft Corp., S. Weiner, 825 Southwood Road, Avondale, PA 19311 / 610-268-0500; or 800-342-3255; FAX: 610-268-3545 www.edgecraft.com
Edmisten Co., P.O. Box 1293, Boone, NC 28607
Edmund Scientific Co., 101 E. Gloucester Pike, Barrington, NJ 08033 / 609-543-6250
Ednar, Inc., 2-4-8 Kayabacho, Nihonbashi Chuo-ku, Tokyo, JAPAN / 81-3-3667-1651; FAX: 81-3-3661-8113
Ed's Gun House, Ed Kukowski, P.O. Box 62, Minnesota City, MN 55959 / 507-689-2925
Effebi SNC-Dr. Franco Beretta, via Rossa, 4, 25062, ITALY / 030-2751955; FAX: 030-2180414
Eggleston, Jere D., 400 Saluda Ave., Columbia, SC 29205 / 803-799-3402
Eichelberger Bullets, Wm., 158 Crossfield Rd., King Of Prussia, PA 19406
Ekol Leather Care, P.O. Box 2652, West Lafayette, IN 47906 / 317-463-2250; FAX: 317-463-7004
El Paso Saddlery Co., P.O. Box 27194, El Paso, TX 79926 / 915-544-2233; FAX: 915-544-2535 epsaddlery.com www.epsaddlery.com
Electro Prismatic Collimators, Inc., 1441 Manatt St., Lincoln, NE 68521
Electronic Shooters Protection, Inc., 15290 Gadsden Ct., Brighton, CO 80603 / 800-797-7791; FAX: 303-659-8668 esp@usa.net espamerican.com
Electronic Trigger Systems, Inc., P.O. Box 645, Park Rapids, MN 56470 / 218-732-5333
Eley Ltd., P.O. Box 705, Witton, Birmingham, B6 7UT ENGLAND / 021-356-8899; FAX: 021-331-4173
Elite Ammunition, P.O. Box 3251, Oakbrook, IL 60522 / 708-366-9006
Ellett Bros., 267 Columbia Ave., P.O. Box 128, Chapin, SC 29036 / 803-345-3751; or 800-845-3711; FAX: 803-345-1820
Ellicott Arms, Inc. / Woods Pistolsmithing, 8390 Sunset Dr., Ellicott City, MD 21043 / 410-465-7979
Elliott, Inc., G. W., 514 Burnside Ave, East Hartford, CT 06108 / 203-289-5741; FAX: 203-289-3137
EMAP USA, 6420 Wilshire Blvd., Los Angeles, CA 90048 / 213-782-2000; FAX: 213-782-2867
Emerging Technologies, Inc. (See Laseraim Technologies, Inc.)
EMF Co., Inc., 1900 E. Warner Ave., Suite 1-D, Santa Ana, CA 92705 / 949-261-6611; FAX: 949-756-0133
Empire Cutlery Corp., 12 Kruger Ct., Clifton, NJ 07013 / 201-472-5155; FAX: 201-779-0759
English, Inc., A.G., 708 S. 12th St., Broken Arrow, OK 74012 / 918-251-3399 agenglish@wedzone.net www.agenglish.com
Engraving Artistry, 36 Alto Rd., Burlington, CT 06013 / 860-673-6837 bobburt44@hotmail.com
Engraving Only, Box 55 Rabbit Gulch, Hill City, SD 57745 / 605-574-2239
Enguix Import-Export, Alpujarras 58, Alzira, Valencia, SPAIN / (96) 241 43 95; FAX: (96) 241 43 95
Enhanced Presentations, Inc., 5929 Market St., Wilmington, NC 28405 / 910-799-1622; FAX: 910-799-5004
Enlow, Charles, 895 Box, Beaver, OK 73932 / 405-625-4487
Entre`prise Arms, Inc., 15861 Business Center Dr., Irwindale, CA 91706
EPC, 1441 Manatt St., Lincoln, NE 68521 / 402-476-3946
Erhardt, Dennis, 4508 N. Montana Ave., Helena, MT 59602 / 406-442-4533
Essex Arms, P.O. Box 363, Island Pond, VT 05846 / 802-723-6203; FAX: 802-723-6203
Estate Cartridge, Inc., 900 Bob Ehlen Dr., Anoka, MN 55303-7502 / 409-856-7277; FAX: 409-856-5486
Euber Bullets, No. Orwell Rd., Orwell, VT 05760 / 802-948-2621
Euroarms of America, Inc., P.O. Box 3277, Winchester, VA 22604 / 540-662-1863; FAX: 540-662-4464 www.euroarms.net
Euro-Imports, 2221 Upland Ave. S., Pahrump, NV 89048 / 775-751-6671; FAX: 775-751-6671

MANUFACTURER'S DIRECTORY

European American Armory Corp. (See E.A.A. Corp.)
Eversull Co., Inc., 1 Tracemont, Boyce, LA 71409 / 318-793-8728; FAX: 318-793-5483 bestguns@aol.com
Evolution Gun Works, Inc., 4050 B-8 Skyron Dr., Doylestown, PA 18901 / 215-348-9892; FAX: 215-348-1056 egw@pil.net www.egw-guns.com
Excalibur Electro Optics, Inc., P.O. Box 400, Fogelsville, PA 18051-0400 / 610-391-9105; FAX: 610-391-9220
Excalibur Publications, P.O. Box 89667, Tucson, AZ 85752 / 520-575-9057 excalibureditor@earthlink.net
Excel Industries, Inc., 4510 Carter Ct., Chino, CA 91710 / 909-627-2404; FAX: 909-627-7817
Executive Protection Institute, P.O. Box 802, Berryville, VA 22611 / 540-554-2540; FAX: 540-554-2558 ruk@crosslink.net www.personalprotecion.com
Eze-Lap Diamond Prods., P.O. Box 2229, 15164 West State St., Westminster, CA 92683 / 714-847-1555; FAX: 714-897-0280
E-Z-Way Systems, P.O. Box 4310, Newark, OH 43058-4310 / 614-345-6645; or 800-848-2072; FAX: 614-345-6600

F

F.A.I.R., Via Gitti, 41, 25060 Marcheno Bresc, ITALY / 030/861162-8610344; FAX: 030/8610179 info@fair.it www.fair.it
Fabarm S.p.A., Via Averolda 31, 25039 Travagliato, Brescia, ITALY / 030-6863629; FAX: 030-6863684 info@fabarm.com www.fabarm.com
Fagan Arms, 22952 15 Mile Rd, Clinton Township, MI 48035 / 810-465-4637; FAX: 810-792-6996
Faith Associates, P.O. Box 549, Flat Rock, NC 28731-0549 FAX: 828-697-6827
Falcon Industries, Inc., P.O. Box 1060, Tijeras, NM 87059 / 505-281-3783; FAX: 505-281-3991 shines@ergogrips.net www.ergogrips.net
Far North Outfitters, Box 1252, Bethel, AK 99559
Farm Form Decoys, Inc., 1602 Biovu, P.O. Box 748, Galveston, TX 77553 / 409-744-0762; or 409-765-6361; FAX: 409-765-8513
Farr Studio, Inc., 183 Hunters Rd., Washington, VA 22747-2001 / 615-638-8825
Farrar Tool Co., Inc., 11855 Cog Hill Dr., Whittier, CA 90601-1902 / 310-863-4367; FAX: 310-863-5123
Faulhaber Wildlocker, Dipl.-Ing. Norbert Wittasek, Seilergasse 2, A-1010 Wien, AUSTRIA / 43-1-5137001; FAX: 43-1-5137001 faulhaber1@utanet.at
Faulk's Game Call Co., Inc., 616 18th St., Lake Charles, LA 70601 / 337-436-9726; FAX: 337-494-7205
Faust Inc., T. G., 544 Minor St, Reading, PA 19602 / 610-375-8549; FAX: 610-375-4488
Fautheree, Andy, P.O. Box 4607, Pagosa Springs, CO 81157 / 970-731-5003; FAX: 970-731-5009
Feather, Flex Decoys, 4500 Doniphan Dr., Neosho, MO 64850 / 318-746-8596; FAX: 318-742-4815
Federal Arms Corp. of America, 7928 University Ave., Fridley, MN 55432 / 612-780-8780; FAX: 612-780-8780
Federal Cartridge Co., 900 Ehlen Dr., Anoka, MN 55303 / 612-323-2300; FAX: 612-323-2506
Federal Champion Target Co., 232 Industrial Parkway, Richmond, IN 47374 / 800-441-4971; FAX: 317-966-7747
Federated-Fry (See Fry Metals)
FEG, Budapest, Soroksariut 158, H-1095, HUNGARY
Feinwerkbau Westinger & Altenburger, Neckarstrasse 43, 78727, Oberndorf a. N., GERMANY / 07423-814-00; FAX: 07423-814-200 info@feinwerkbau.de www.feinwerkbau.de
Feken, Dennis, Rt. 2, Box 124, Perry, OK 73077 / 405-336-5611
Felk Pistols, Inc., 2121 Castlebridge Rd., Midlothian, VA 23113 / 804-794-3744; FAX: 208-988-4834
Ferguson, Bill, P.O. Box 1238, Sierra Vista, AZ 85636 / 520-458-5321; FAX: 520-458-9125
Ferguson, Bill. See: BULLET METALS
FERLIB, Via Parte 33 Marcheno/BS, Marcheno/BS, ITALY / 00390308610191; FAX: 00390308966882 info@ferlib.com www.ferlib.com
Ferris Firearms, 7110 F.M. 1863, Bulverde, TX 78163 / 210-980-4424
Fibron Products, Inc., P.O. Box 430, Buffalo, NY 14209-0430 / 716-886-2378; FAX: 716-886-2394
Fieldsport Ltd., Bryan Bilinski, 3313 W. South Airport Rd., Traverse City, MI 49684 / 616-933-0767
Fiocchi Munizioni S.P.A. (See U.S. Importer-Fiocch
Fiocchi of America, Inc., 5030 Fremont Rd., Ozark, MO 65721 / 417-725-4118; or 800-721-2666; FAX: 417-725-1039
Firearms Co. Ltd. / Alpine (See U.S. Importer-Mandall
Firearms Engraver's Guild of America, 332 Vine St., Oregon City, OR 97045 / 503-656-5693
Firearms International, 5709 Hartsdale, Houston, TX 77036 / 713-460-2447
Fisher, Jerry A., 631 Crane Mt. Rd., Big Fork, MT 59911 / 406-837-2722
Fisher Custom Firearms, 2199 S. Kittredge Way, Aurora, CO 80013 / 303-755-3710
Fitzgerald, Jack. See: CLENZOIL WORLDWIDE CORP
Flambeau, Inc., 15981 Valplast Rd., Middlefield, OH 44062 / 216-632-1631; FAX: 216-632-1581 www.flambeau.com
Flayderman & Co., Inc., P.O. Box 2446, Ft. Lauderdale, FL 33303 / 954-761-8855
Fleming Firearms, 7720 E. 126th St. N., Collinsville, OK 74021-7016 / 918-665-3624
Fletcher-Bidwell, LLC., 305 E. Terhune St., Viroqua, WI 54665-1631 / 866-637-1860 fbguns@netscape.net
Flintlocks, Etc., 160 Rossiter Rd., P.O. Box 181, Richmond, MA 01254 / 413-698-3822; FAX: 413-698-3866 flintetc@berkshire.rr.com
Flitz International Ltd., 821 Mohr Ave., Waterford, WI 53185 / 414-534-5898; FAX: 414-534-2991
Fluoramics, Inc., 18 Industrial Ave., Mahwah, NJ 07430 / 800-922-0075; FAX: 201-825-7035
Flynn's Custom Guns, P.O. Box 7461, Alexandria, LA 71306 / 318-455-7130
FN Manufacturing, P.O. Box 24257, Columbia, SC 29224 / 803-736-0522
Folks, Donald E., 205 W. Lincoln St., Pontiac, IL 61764 / 815-844-7901
Foothills Video Productions, Inc., P.O. Box 651, Spartanburg, SC 29304 / 803-573-7023; or 800-782-5358
Foredom Electric Co., Rt. 6, 16 Stony Hill Rd., Bethel, CT 06801 / 203-792-8622
Forgett, Valmore. See: NAVY ARMS COMPANY
Forgreens Tool & Mfg., Inc., P.O. Box 955, Robert Lee, TX 76945 / 915-453-2800; FAX: 915-453-2460
Forkin Custom Classics, 205 10th Avenue S.W., White Sulphur Spring, MT 59645 / 406-547-2344
Forrest Tool Co., P.O. Box 768, 44380 Gordon Lane, Mendocino, CA 95460 / 707-937-2141; FAX: 717-937-1817
Forster, Kathy (See Custom Checkering)
Forster, Larry L., Box 212, 216 Highway 13 E., Gwinner, ND 58040-0212 / 701-678-2475
Forster Products, 310 E. Lanark Ave., Lanark, IL 61046 / 815-493-6360; FAX: 815-493-2371
Fort Hill Gunstocks, 12807 Fort Hill Rd., Hillsboro, OH 45133 / 513-466-2763
Fort Knox Security Products, 1051 N. Industrial Park Rd., Orem, UT 84057 / 801-224-7233; or 800-821-5216; FAX: 801-226-5493
Forthofer's Gunsmithing & Knifemaking, 5535 U.S. Hwy. 93S, Whitefish, MT 59937-8411 / 406-862-2674
Fortune Products, Inc., 205 Hickory Creek Rd., Marble Falls, TX 78654 / 210-693-6111; FAX: 210-693-6394 randy@accusharp.com
Forty-Five Ranch Enterprises, Box 1080, Miami, OK 74355-1080 / 918-542-5875
Foster, See: ACCURACY INTERNATIONAL
Fountain Products, 492 Prospect Ave., West Springfield, MA 01089 / 413-781-4651; FAX: 413-733-8217
4-D Custom Die Co., 711 N. Sandusky St., PO Box 889, Mt. Vernon, OH 43050-0889 / 740-397-7214; FAX: 740-397-6600 info@ch4d.com ch4d.com
Fowler Bullets, 806 Dogwood Dr., Gastonia, NC 28054 / 704-867-3259
Fowler, Bob (See Black Powder Products)
Fox River Mills, Inc., P.O. Box 298, 227 Poplar St., Osage, IA 50461 / 515-732-3798; FAX: 515-732-5128
Francotte & Cie S.A. Auguste, rue de Trois Juin 109, 4400 Herstal-Liege, BELGIUM / 32-4-248-13-18; FAX: 32-4-248-11-79
Frank Knives, 13868 NW Keleka Pl., Seal Rock, OR 97376 / 541-563-3041; FAX: 541-563-3041
Frank Mittermeier, Inc., P.O. Box 1, Bronx, NY 10465
Franzen International, Inc. (See U.S. Importer for)
Fred F. Wells/Wells Sport Store, 110 N Summit St., Prescott, AZ 86301 / 928-445-3655 www.wellssportstore@cableone-net
Freedom Arms, Inc., P.O. Box 150, Freedom, WY 83120 / 307-883-2468; FAX: 307-883-2005
Fremont Tool Works, 1214 Prairie, Ford, KS 67842 / 316-369-2327
Front Sight Firearms Training Institute, P.O. Box 2619, Aptos, CA 95001 / 800-987-7719; FAX: 408-684-2137
Frontier, 2910 San Bernardo, Laredo, TX 78040 / 956-723-5409; FAX: 956-723-1774
Frontier Arms Co., Inc., 401 W. Rio Santa Cruz, Green Valley, AZ 85614-3932
Frontier Products Co., 2401 Walker Rd., Roswell, NM 88201-8950 / 614-262-9357
Frontier Safe Co., 3201 S. Clinton St., Fort Wayne, IN 46806 / 219-744-7233; FAX: 219-744-6678
Frost Cutlery Co., P.O. Box 22636, Chattanooga, TN 37422 / 615-894-6079; FAX: 615-894-9576
Fry Metals, 4100 6th Ave., Altoona, PA 16602 / 814-946-1611
Fujinon, Inc., 10 High Point Dr., Wayne, NJ 07470 / 201-633-5600; FAX: 201-633-5216
Fullmer, Geo. M., 2499 Mavis St., Oakland, CA 94601 / 510-533-4193
Fulton Armory, 8725 Bollman Place No. 1, Savage, MD 20763 / 301-490-9485; FAX: 301-490-9547 www.fulton.armory.com
Furr Arms, 91 N. 970 W., Orem, UT 84057 / 801-226-3877; FAX: 801-226-3877

G

G&H Decoys, Inc., P.O. Box 1208, Hwy. 75 North, Henryetta, OK 74437 / 918-652-3314; FAX: 918-652-3400
G.C. Bullet Co., Inc., 40 Mokelumne River Dr., Lodi, CA 95240
G.G. & G., 3602 E. 42nd Stravenue, Tucson, AZ 85713 / 520-748-7167; FAX: 520-748-7583 ggg&3@aol.com www.ggg&3.com
G.H. Enterprises Ltd., Bag 10, Okotoks, AB T0L 1T0 CANADA / 403-938-6070
G.U., Inc. (See U.S. Importer for New SKB Arms Co.)
G.W. Elliott, Inc., 514 Burnside Ave., East Hartford, CT 06108 / 203-289-5741; FAX: 203-289-3137
G96 Products Co., Inc., 85 5th Ave., Bldg. #6, Paterson, NJ 07544 / 973-684-4050; FAX: 973-684-3848 g96prod@aol
Gage Manufacturing, 663 W. 7th St., A, San Pedro, CA 90731 / 310-832-3546
Gaillard Barrels, P.O. Box 21, Pathlow, SK S0K 3B0 CANADA / 306-752-3769; FAX: 306-752-5969
Gain Twist Barrel Co., Rifle Works and Armory, 707 12th St., Cody, WY 82414 / 307-587-4919; FAX: 307-527-6097
Galati International, P.O. Box 10, 616 Burley Ridge Rd., Wesco, MO 65586 / 636-584-0785; FAX: 573-775-4308 support@galatiinternational.com www.galatiinternational.com
Galaxy Imports Ltd., Inc., P.O. Box 3361, Victoria, TX 77903 / 361-573-4867; FAX: 361-576-9622 galaxy@cox-internet.com
GALCO International Ltd., 2019 W. Quail Ave., Phoenix, AZ 85027 / 623-474-7070; FAX: 623-582-6854 customerservice@usgalco.com www.usgalco.com
Galena Industries AMT, 5463 Diaz St., Irwindale, CA 91706 / 626-856-8883; FAX: 626-856-8878
Gamba S.p.A. Societa Armi Bresciane Srl, Renato, Via Artigiani 93, ITALY / 30-8911640; FAX: 30-8911648
Gamba, USA, P.O. Box 60452, Colorado Springs, CO 80960 / 719-578-1145; FAX: 719-444-0731
Game Haven Gunstocks, 13750 Shire Rd., Wolverine, MI 49799 / 616-525-8257
Gamebore Division, Polywad, Inc., P.O. Box 7916, Macon, GA 31209 / 478-477-0669; or 800-998-0669
Gamo (See U.S. Importers-Arms United Corp, Daisy M
Gamo USA, Inc., 3911 SW 47th Ave., Suite 914, Ft. Lauderdale, FL 33314 / 954-581-5822; FAX: 954-581-3165 gamousa@gate.net www.gamo.com
Gander Mountain, Inc., 12400 Fox River Rd., Wilmont, WI 53192 / 414-862-6848
GAR, 590 McBride Ave., West Paterson, NJ 07424 / 973-754-1114; FAX: 973-754-1114 garreloading@aol.com www.garreloading.com
Garcia National Gun Traders, Inc., 225 SW 22nd Ave., Miami, FL 33135 / 305-642-2355
Garrett Cartridges, Inc., P.O. Box 178, Chehalis, WA 98532 / 360-736-0702 www.garrettcartridges.com
Garthwaite Pistolsmith, Inc., Jim, 12130 State Route 405, Watsontown, PA 17777 / 570-538-1566; FAX: 570-538-2965 www.garthwaite.com
Gary Goudy Classic Stocks, 1512 S. 5th St., Dayton, WA 99328 / 509-382-2726 goudy@innw.net
Gary Reeder Custom Guns, 2601 7th Avenue East, Flagstaff, AZ 86004 / 928-526-3313; FAX: 928-527-0840 gary@reedercustomguns.com www.reedercustomguns.com
Gator Guns & Repair, 7952 Kenai Spur Hwy., Kenai, AK 99611-8311

MANUFACTURER'S DIRECTORY

Gaucher Armes, S.A., 46 rue Desjoyaux, 42000, Saint-Etienne, FRANCE / 04-77-33-38-92; FAX: 04-77-61-95-72
GDL Enterprises, 409 Le Gardeur, Slidell, LA 70460 / 504-649-0693
Gehmann, Walter (See Huntington Die Specialties)
Genco, P.O. Box 5704, Asheville, NC 28803
Genecco Gun Works, 10512 Lower Sacramento Rd., Stockton, CA 95210 / 209-951-0706; FAX: 209-931-3872
Gene's Custom Guns, P.O. Box 10534, White Bear Lake, MN 55110 / 651-429-5105; FAX: 651-429-7365
Gentex Corp., 5 Tinkham Ave., Derry, NH 03038 / 603-434-0311; FAX: 603-434-3002 sales@derry.gentexcorp.com www.derry.gentexcorp.com
Gentner Bullets, 109 Woodlawn Ave., Upper Darby, PA 19082 / 610-352-9396
Gentry Custom LLC, 314 N. Hoffman, Belgrade, MT 59714 / 406-388-GUNS davidgent@mcn.net www.gentrycustom.com
George & Roy's, P.O. Box 2125, Sisters, OR 97759-2125 / 503-228-5424; or 800-553-3022; FAX: 503-225-9409
George Hoenig, Inc., 6521 Morton Dr., Boise, ID 83704 / 208-375-1116; FAX: 208-375-1116
George Ibberson (Sheffield) Ltd., 25-31 Allen St., Sheffield, S3 7AW ENGLAND / 0114-2766123; FAX: 0114-2738465 sales@egging tongroupco.uk www.eggintongroup.co.uk
George Madis Winchester Consultants, George Madis, P.O. Box 545, Brownsboro, TX 75756 / 903-852-6480; FAX: 903-852-3045 gmadis@earthlink.com www.georgemadis.com
Gerber Legendary Blades, 14200 SW 72nd Ave., Portland, OR 97223 / 503-639-6161; or 800-950-6161; FAX: 503-684-7008
Gervais, Mike, 3804 S. Cruise Dr., Salt Lake City, UT 84109 / 801-277-7729
Getz Barrel Company, P.O. Box 88, 426 E. Market St., Beavertown, PA 17813 / 570-658-7263; FAX: 570-658-4110 www.getzbrl.com
Giacomo Sporting USA, 6234 Stokes Lee Center Rd., Lee Center, NY 13363
Gibbs Rifle Co., Inc., 219 Lawn St., Martinsburg, WV 25401 / 304-262-1651; FAX: 304-262-1658 support@gibbsrifle.com www.gibbsrifle.com
Gil Hebard Guns, Inc., 125 Public Square, Knoxville, IL 61448 / 309-289-2700; FAX: 309-289-2233
Gilbert Equipment Co., Inc., 960 Downtowner Rd., Mobile, AL 36609 / 205-344-3322
Gillmann, Edwin, 33 Valley View Dr., Hanover, PA 17331 / 717-632-1662 gillmaned@super-pa.net
Gilmore Sports Concepts, Inc., 5949 S. Garnett Rd., Tulsa, OK 74146 / 918-250-3810; FAX: 918-250-3845 info@gilmoresports.com www.gilmoresports.com
Giron, Robert E., 12671 Cousins Rd.., Peosta, IA 52068 / 412-731-6041
Glacier Glove, 4890 Aircenter Circle, Suite 210, Reno, NV 89502 / 702-825-8225; FAX: 702-825-6544
Glaser LLC, P.O. Box 173, Sturgis, SD 57785 / 605-347-4544; or 800-221-3489; FAX: 605-347-5055 email@corbon.com www.safetyslug.com
Glaser Safety Slug, Inc., P.O. Box 8223, Foster City, CA 94404 / 800-221-3489; FAX: 510-785-6685 safetyslug.com
Glass, Herb, P.O. Box 25, Bullville, NY 10915 / 914-361-3021
Glimm, Jerome. See: GLIMM'S CUSTOM GUN ENGRAVING
Glimm's Custom Gun Engraving, Jerome C. Glimm, 19 S. Maryland, Conrad, MT 59425 / 406-278-3574 jandlglimm@mcn.net
Glock GmbH, P.O. Box 50, A-2232, Deutsch Wagram, AUSTRIA
Glock, Inc., P.O. Box 369, Smyrna, GA 30081 / 770-432-1202; FAX: 770-433-8719
Glynn Scobey Duck & Goose Calls, Rt. 3, Box 37, Newbern, TN 38059 / 731-643-6128
GML Products, Inc., 394 Laredo Dr., Birmingham, AL 35226 / 205-979-4867
Gner's Hard Cast Bullets, 1107 11th St., LaGrande, OR 97850 / 503-963-8796
Goens, Dale W., P.O. Box 224, Cedar Crest, NM 87008 / 505-281-5419
Goergen's Gun Shop, Inc., 17985 538th Ave., Austin, MN 55912 / 507-433-9280
GOEX, Inc., P.O. Box 659, Doyline, LA 71023-0659 / 318-382-9300; FAX: 318-382-9303 mfahringer@goexpowder.com www.goexpowder.com
Golden Age Arms Co., 115 E. High St., Ashley, OH 43003 / 614-747-2488
Golden Bear Bullets, 3065 Fairfax Ave., San Jose, CA 95148 / 408-238-9515
Gonic Arms/North American Arms, Inc., 134 Flagg Rd., Gonic, NH 03839 / 603-332-8456; or 603-332-8457
Goodling's Gunsmithing, 1950 Stoverstown Rd., Spring Grove, PA 17362 / 717-225-3350
Goodwin, Fred. See: GOODWIN'S PAWN SHOP
Goodwin's Pawn Shop, Fred Goodwin, Silver Ridge, ME 04776 / 207-365-4451
Gotz Bullets, 11426 Edgemere Ter., Roscoe, IL 61073-8232
Gould & Goodrich, 709 E. McNeil, Lillington, NC 27546 / 910-893-2071; FAX: 910-893-4742
Gournet Artistic Engraving, Geoffroy Gournet, 820 Paxinosa Ave., Easton, PA 18042 / 610-559-0710 www.geoffroygournet.com
Gournet, Geoffroy. See: GOURNET ARTISTIC ENGRAVING
Grace, Charles E., 718 E. 2nd, Trinidad, CO 81082 / 719-846-9435 chuckgrace@sensonics.org
Grace Metal Products, P.O. Box 67, Elk Rapids, MI 49629 / 616-264-8133
Graf & Sons, 4050 S. Clark St., Mexico, MO 65265 / 573-581-2266; FAX: 573-581-2875 customerservice@grafs.com www.grafs.com
Grand Slam Hunting Products, Box 121, 25454 Military Rd., Cascade, MD 21719 / 301-241-4900; FAX: 301-241-4900 rlj6call@aol.com
Granite Mountain Arms, Inc., 3145 W. Hidden Acres Trail, Prescott, AZ 86305 / 520-541-9758; FAX: 520-445-6826
Grant, Howard V., Hiawatha 15, Woodruff, WI 54568 / 715-356-7146
Graphics Direct, P.O. Box 372421, Reseda, CA 91337-2421 / 818-344-9002
Graves Co., 1800 Andrews Ave., Pompano Beach, FL 33069 / 800-327-9103; FAX: 305-960-0301
Grayback Wildcats, Mike Beeks, 5306 Bryant Ave., Klamath Falls, OR 97603 / 541-884-1072; FAX: 541-884-1072 graybackwildcats@aol.com
Graybill's Gun Shop, 1035 Ironville Pike, Columbia, PA 17512 / 717-684-2739
Great American Gunstock Co., 3420 Industrial Drive, Yuba City, CA 95993 / 800-784-4867; FAX: 530-671-3906 gunstox@hotmail.com www.gunstocks.com
Great Lakes Airguns, 6175 S. Park Ave., Hamburg, NY 14075 / 716-648-6666; FAX: 716-648-6666 www.greatlakesairguns.com
Green, Arthur S., 485 S. Robertson Blvd., Beverly Hills, CA 90211 / 310-274-1283
Green, Roger M., P.O. Box 984, 435 E. Birch, Glenrock, WY 82637 / 307-436-9804
Green Head Game Call Co., RR 1, Box 33, Lacon, IL 61540 / 309-246-2155
Green Mountain Rifle Barrel Co., Inc., P.O. Box 2670, 153 West Main St., Conway, NH 03818 / 603-447-1095; FAX: 603-447-1099 www.gmriflebarrel.com
Greenwood Precision, P.O. Box 407, Rogersville, MO 65742 / 417-725-2330
Greg Gunsmithing Repair, 3732 26th Ave. North, Robbinsdale, MN 55422 / 612-529-8103
Greg's Superior Products, P.O. Box 46219, Seattle, WA 98146
Greider Precision, 431 Santa Marina Ct., Escondido, CA 92029 / 760-480-8892; FAX: 760-480-9800 greider@msn.com
Gre-Tan Rifles, 29742 W.C.R. 50, Kersey, CO 80644 / 970-353-6176; FAX: 970-356-5940 www.gtrtooling.com
Grier's Hard Cast Bullets, 1107 11th St., LaGrande, OR 97850 / 503-963-8796
Griffin & Howe, Inc., 36 W. 44th St., Suite 1011, New York, NY 10036 / 212-921-0980 info@griffinhowe.com www.griffinhowe.com
Griffin & Howe, Inc., 340 W. Putnam Ave., Greenwich, CT 06830 / 203-618-0270 info@griffinhowe.com www.griffinhowe.com
Griffin & Howe, Inc., 33 Claremont Rd., Bernardsville, NJ 07924 / 908-766-2287; FAX: 908-766-1068 info@griffinhowe.com www.griffinhowe.com
Grifon, Inc., 58 Guinam St., Waltham, MS 02154
Groenewold, John, P.O. Box 830, Mundelein, IL 60060 / 847-566-2365; FAX: 847-566-4065 jgairguns@direcway.com http://jgairguns.tripod.com/airgun
GRS / Glendo Corp., P.O. Box 1153, 900 Overlander St., Emporia, KS 66801 / 620-343-1084; or 800-836-3519; FAX: 620-343-9640 glendo@glendo.com www.glendo.com
Grulla Armes, Apartado 453, Avda Otaloa 12, Eiber, SPAIN
Gruning Precision, Inc., 7101 Jurupa Ave., No. 12, Riverside, CA 92504 / 909-289-4371; FAX: 909-689-7791 gruningprecision@earthlink.net www.gruningprecision.com
GSI, Inc., 7661 Commerce Ln., Trussville, AL 35173 / 205-655-8299
GTB-Custom Bullets, 482 Comerwood Court, S. San Francisco, CA 94080 / 650-583-1550
Guarasi, Robert. See: WILCOX INDUSTRIES CORP.
Guardsman Products, 411 N. Darling, Fremont, MI 49412 / 616-924-3950
Gun City, 212 W. Main Ave., Bismarck, ND 58501 / 701-223-2304
Gun Hunter Books (See Gun Hunter Trading Co.), 5075 Heisig St., Beaumont, TX 77705 / 409-835-3006; FAX: 409-838-2266 gunhuntertrading@hotmail.com
Gun Hunter Trading Co., 5075 Heisig St., Beaumont, TX 77705 / 409-835-3006; FAX: 409-838-2266 gunhuntertrading@hotmail.com
Gun Leather Limited, 116 Lipscomb, Ft. Worth, TX 76104 / 817-334-0225; FAX: 800-247-0609
Gun List (See Krause Publications), 700 E State St., Iola, WI 54990 / 715-445-2214; FAX: 715-445-4087
Gun South, Inc. (See GSI, Inc.)
Gun Vault, 7339 E. Acoma Dr., Ste. 7, Scottsdale, AZ 85260 / 602-951-6855
Gun-Alert, 1010 N. Maclay Ave., San Fernando, CA 91340 / 818-365-0864; FAX: 818-365-1308
Guncraft Books (See Guncraft Sports, Inc.), 10737 Dutchtown Rd., Knoxville, TN 37932 / 865-966-4545; FAX: 865-966-4500 findit@guncraft.com www.guncraft.com
Guncraft Sports, Inc., 10737 Dutchtown Rd., Knoxville, TN 37932 / 865-966-4545; FAX: 865-966-4500 findit@guncraft.com www.usit.net/guncraft
Guncraft Sports, Inc., Marie C. Wiest, 10737 Dutchtown Rd., Knoxville, TN 37932 / 865-966-4545; FAX: 865-966-4500 findit@guncraft.com www.guncraft.com
Guncrafter Industries, 171 Madison 1510, Huntsville, AR 72740 / 479-665-2466 www.guncrafterindustries.com
Gun-Ho Sports Cases, 110 E. 10th St., St. Paul, MN 55101 / 612-224-9491
Gunline Tools, 2950 Saturn St., "O", Brea, CA 92821 / 714-993-5100; FAX: 714-572-4128
Gunnerman Books, P.O. Box 81697, Rochester Hills, MI 48308 / 248-608-2856
Guns Antique & Modern DBA / Charles E. Duffy, Williams Lane, West Hurley, NY 12491 / 914-679-2997
Guns Div. of D.C. Engineering, Inc., 8633 Southfield Fwy., Detroit, MI 48228 / 313-271-7111; or 800-886-7623; FAX: 313-271-7112 guns@rifletech.com www.rifletech.com
GUNS Magazine, 591 Camino de la Reina, Suite 200, San Diego, CA 92108 / 619-297-5350; FAX: 619-297-5353
Gunsite Training Center, P.O. Box 700, Paulden, AZ 86334 / 520-636-4565; FAX: 520-636-1236
Gunsmithing Ltd., 57 Unquowa Rd., Fairfield, CT 06824 / 203-254-0436; FAX: 203-254-1535
Gunsmithing, Inc., 30 West Buchanan St., Colorado Springs, CO 80907 / 719-632-3795; FAX: 719-632-3493
Gurney, F. R., Box 13, Sooke, BC V0S 1N0 CANADA / 604-642-5282; FAX: 604-642-7859

H

H&B Forge Co., Rt. 2, Geisinger Rd., Shiloh, OH 44878 / 419-895-1856
H&P Publishing, 7174 Hoffman Rd., San Angelo, TX 76905 / 915-655-5953
H&R 1871.LLC, 60 Industrial Rowe, Gardner, MA 01440 / 508-632-9393; FAX: 508-632-2300 hr1871@hr1871.com www.hr1871.com
H. Krieghoff Gun Co., Boschstrasse 22, D-89079, Ulm, GERMANY / 731-401820; FAX: 731-4018270
H.K.S. Products, 7841 Founion Dr., Florence, KY 41042 / 606-342-7841; or 800-354-9814; FAX: 606-342-5865
H.P. White Laboratory, Inc., 3114 Scarboro Rd., Street, MD 21154 / 410-838-6550; FAX: 410-838-2802
Hafner World Wide, Inc., P.O. Box 1987, Lake City, FL 32055 / 904-755-6481; FAX: 904-755-6595 hafner@isgroupe.net
Hakko Co. Ltd., 1-13-12, Narimasu, Itabashiku Tokyo, JAPAN / 03-5997-7870/2; FAX: 81-3-5997-7840
Half Moon Rifle Shop, 490 Halfmoon Rd., Columbia Falls, MT 59912 / 406-892-4409 halfmoonrs@centurytel.net
Hall Manufacturing, 142 CR 406, Clanton, AL 35045 / 205-755-4094
Hall Plastics, Inc., John, P.O. Box 1526, Alvin, TX 77512 / 713-489-8709
Hallberg, Fritz. See: CAMBOS OUTDOORSMAN

MANUFACTURER'S DIRECTORY

Hallowell & Co., P.O. Box 1445, Livingston, MT 59047 / 406-222-4770; FAX: 406-222-4792 morris@hallowellco.com www.hallowellco.com
Hally Caller, 443 Wells Rd., Doylestown, PA 18901 / 215-345-6354; FAX: 215-345-8892 info@hallycaller.com www.hallycaller.com
Hamilton, Alex B. (See Ten-Ring Precision, Inc.)
Hammans, Charles E., P.O. Box 788, 2022 McCracken, Stuttgart, AR 72160-0788 / 870-673-1388
Hammerli Ltd., Seonerstrasse 37, CH-5600, SWITZERLAND / 064-50 11 44; FAX: 064-51 38 27
Hammerli Service-Precision Mac, Rudolf Marent, 9711 Tiltree St., Houston, TX 77075 / 713-946-7028 rmarent@webtv.net
Hammerli USA, 19296 Oak Grove Circle, Groveland, CA 95321 FAX: 209-962-5311
Hammond Custom Guns Ltd., 619 S. Pandora, Gilbert, AZ 85234 / 602-892-3437
HandCrafts Unltd. (See Clements' Custom Leather), 1741 Dallas St., Aurora, CO 80010-2018 / 303-364-0403; FAX: 303-739-9824 gryphons@home.com kuntaoslcat.com
Handgun Press, P.O. Box 406, Glenview, IL 60025 / 847-657-6500; FAX: 847-724-8831 handgunpress@earthlink.net
Hank's Gun Shop, Box 370, 50 West 100 South, Monroe, UT 84754 / 801-527-4456
Hanned Precision (See The Hanned Line)
Hansen & Co., 244-246 Old Post Rd., Southport, CT 06490 / 203-259-6222; FAX: 203-254-3832
Hanson's Gun Center, Dick, 233 Everett Dr., Colorado Springs, CO 80911
Harford (See U.S. Importer-EMF Co. Inc.)
Harper's Custom Stocks, 928 Lombrano St., San Antonio, TX 78207 / 210-732-7174
Harrell's Precision, 5756 Hickory Dr., Salem, VA 24153 / 540-380-2683
Harrington & Richardson (See H&R 1871, Inc.)
Harris Engineering Inc., Dept GD54, Barlow, KY 42024 / 502-334-3633; FAX: 502-334-3000
Harris Enterprises, P.O. Box 105, Bly, OR 97622 / 503-353-2625
Harris Hand Engraving, Paul A., 113 Rusty Ln., Boerne, TX 78006-5746 / 512-391-5121
Harris Publications, 1115 Broadway, New York, NY 10010 / 212-807-7100; FAX: 212-627-4678
Harrison Bullets, 6437 E. Hobart St., Mesa, AZ 85205
Harry Lawson Co., 3328 N. Richey Blvd., Tucson, AZ 85716 / 520-326-1117; FAX: 520-326-1117
Hart & Son, Inc., Robert W., 401 Montgomery St., Nescopeck, PA 18635 / 717-752-3655; FAX: 717-752-1088
Hart Rifle Barrels, Inc., P.O. Box 182, 1690 Apulia Rd., Lafayette, NY 13084 / 315-677-9841; FAX: 315-677-9610 hartrb@aol.com hartbarrels.com
Hartford (See U.S. Importer-EMF Co. Inc.)
Hartmann & Weiss GmbH, Rahlstedter Bahnhofstr. 47, 22143, Hamburg, GERMANY / (40) 677 55 85; FAX: (40) 677 55 92 hartmannundweisst-online.de
Harvey, Frank, 218 Nightfall, Terrace, NV 89015 / 702-558-6998
Harwood, Jack O., 1191 S. Pendlebury Lane, Blackfoot, ID 83221 / 208-785-5368
Hastings, P.O. Box 224, Clay Center, KS 67432 / 785-632-3169; FAX: 785-632-6554
Hatfield Gun, 224 N. 4th St., St. Joseph, MO 64501
Hawk Laboratories, Inc. (See Hawk, Inc.), 849 Hawks Bridge Rd., Salem, NJ 08079 / 609-299-2700; FAX: 609-299-2800
Hawk, Inc., 849 Hawks Bridge Rd., Salem, NJ 08079 / 609-299-2700; FAX: 609-299-2800 info@hawkbullets.com www.hawkbullets.com
Hawken Shop, The (See Dayton Traister)
Haydel's Game Calls, Inc., 5018 Hazel Jones Rd., Bossier City, LA 71111 / 318-746-3586; FAX: 318-746-3711
Heatbath Corp., P.O. Box 2978, Springfield, MA 01101 / 413-543-3381
Hecht, Hubert J., Waffen-Hecht, P.O. Box 2635, Fair Oaks, CA 95628 / 916-966-1020
Heckler & Koch GmbH, PO Box 1329, 78722 Oberndorf, Neckar, GERMANY / 49-7423179-0; FAX: 49-7423179-2406
Heckler & Koch, Inc., 21480 Pacific Blvd., Sterling, VA 20166-8900 / 703-450-1900; FAX: 703-450-8160 www.hecklerkoch-usa.com
Hege Jagd-u. Sporthandels GmbH, P.O. Box 101461, W-7770, Ueberlingen a. Boden, GERMANY
Heidenstrom Bullets, Dalghte 86-3660 Rjukan, 35091818, NORWAY, olau.joh@online.tuo
Heilmann, Stephen, P.O. Box 657, Grass Valley, CA 95945 / 530-272-8758; FAX: 530-274-0285 sheilmann@jps.net www.metalwood.com
Heinie Specialty Products, 301 Oak St., Quincy, IL 62301-2500 / 217-228-9500; FAX: 217-228-9502 rheinie@heinie.com www.heinie.com
Helwan (See U.S. Importer-Interarms)
Henigson & Associates, Steve, PO Box 2726, Culver City, CA 90231 / 310-305-8288; FAX: 310-305-1905
Henriksen Tool Co., Inc., 8515 Wagner Creek Rd., Talent, OR 97540 / 541-535-2309; FAX: 541-535-2309
Henry Repeating Arms Co., 110 8th St., Brooklyn, NY 11215 / 718-499-5600; FAX: 718-768-8056 info@henryrepeating.com www.henryrepeating.com
Hensley, Gunmaker, Darwin, PO Box 329, Brightwood, OR 97011 / 503-622-5411
Heppler, Keith. See: KEITH'S CUSTOM GUNSTOCKS
Hercules, Inc. (See Alliant Techsystems, Smokeless)
Heritage Firearms (See Heritage Mfg., Inc.)
Heritage Manufacturing, Inc., 4600 NW 135th St., Opa Locka, FL 33054 / 305-685-5966; FAX: 305-687-6721 infohmi@heritagemfg.com www.heritagemfg.com
Heritage/VSP Gun Books, P.O. Box 887, McCall, ID 83638 / 208-634-4104; FAX: 208-634-3101 heritage@gunbooks.com www.gunbooks.com
Herrett's Stocks, Inc., P.O. Box 741, Twin Falls, ID 83303 / 208-733-1498
Herter's Manufacturing Inc., 111 E. Burnett St., P.O. Box 518, Beaver Dam, WI 53916-1811 / 414-887-1765; FAX: 414-887-8444
Hesco-Meprolight, 2139 Greenville Rd., LaGrange, GA 30241 / 706-884-7967; FAX: 706-882-4683
Hesse Arms, Robert Hesse, 1126 70th Street E., Inver Grove Heights, MN 55077-2416 / 651-455-5760; FAX: 612-455-5760
Hesse, Robert. See: HESSE ARMS
Heydenberk, Warren R., 1059 W. Sawmill Rd., Quakertown, PA 18951 / 215-538-2682
Hickman, Jaclyn, Box 1900, Glenrock, WY 82637
Hidalgo, Tony, 12701 SW 9th Pl., Davie, FL 33325 / 954-476-7645
High Bridge Arms, Inc., 3185 Mission St., San Francisco, CA 94110 / 415-282-8358
High North Products, Inc., P.O. Box 2, Antigo, WI 54409 / 715-627-2331; FAX: 715-623-5451
High Performance International, 5734 W. Florist Ave., Milwaukee, WI 53218 / 414-466-9040
High Precision, Bud Welsh, 80 New Road, E. Amherst, NY 14051 / 716-688-6344; FAX: 716-688-0425 welsh5168@aol.com www.high-precision.com
High Standard Mfg. Co./F.I., Inc., 5200 Mitchelldale St., Ste. E17, Houston, TX 77092-7222 / 713-462-4200; or 800-272-7816; FAX: 713-681-5665 info@highstandard.com www.highstandard.com
High Tech Specialties, Inc., P.O. Box 839, 293 E Main St., Rear, Adamstown, PA 19501 / 717-484-0405; FAX: 717-484-0523 bansner@aol.com www.bansmersrifle.com/hightech
Highline Machine Co., Randall Thompson, Randall Thompson, 654 Lela Place, Grand Junction, CO 81504 / 970-434-4971
Highwood Special Products, 1531 E. Highwood, Pontiac, MI 48340
Hi-Grade Imports, 8655 Monterey Rd., Gilroy, CA 95021 / 408-842-9301; FAX: 408-842-2374
Hill, Loring F., 304 Cedar Rd., Elkins Park, PA 19027
Hill Speed Leather, Ernie, 4507 N 195th Ave., Litchfield Park, AZ 85340 / 602-853-9222; FAX: 602-853-9235
Hinman Outfitters, Bob, 107 N Sanderson Ave., Bartonville, IL 61607-1839 / 309-691-8132
Hi-Performance Ammunition Company, 484 State Route 366, Apollo, PA 15613 / 412-327-8100
HIP-GRIP Barami Corp., P.O. Box 252224, West Bloomfield, MI 48325-2224 / 248-738-0462; FAX: 248-738-2542 hipgripja@aol.com www.hipgrip.com
Hi-Point Firearms/MKS Supply, 8611-A North Dixie Dr., Dayton, OH 45414 / 877-425-4867; FAX: 937-454-0503 www.hi-pointfirearms.com
Hiptmayer, Armurier, RR 112 750, P.O. Box 136, Eastman, PQ J0E 1P0 CANADA / 514-297-2492
Hiptmayer, Heidemarie, RR 112 750, P.O. Box 136, Eastman, PQ J0E 1P0 CANADA / 514-297-2492
Hiptmayer, Klaus, RR 112 750, P.O. Box 136, Eastman, PQ J0E 1P0 CANADA / 514-297-2492
Hirtenberger AG, Leobersdorferstrasse 31, A-2552, Hirtenberg, AUSTRIA / 43(0)2256 81184; FAX: 43(0)2256 81808 www.hirtenberger.ot
HJS Arms, Inc., P.O. Box 3711, Brownsville, TX 78523-3711 / 956-542-2767; FAX: 956-542-2767
Hoag, James W., 8523 Canoga Ave., Suite C, Canoga Park, CA 91304 / 818-998-1510
Hobson Precision Mfg. Co., 210 Big Oak Ln., Brent, AL 35034 / 205-926-4662; FAX: 205-926-3193 cahobbob@dbtech.net
Hodgdon Powder Co., 6231 Robinson, Shawnee Mission, KS 66202 / 913-362-9455; FAX: 913-362-1307
Hodgman, Inc., 1750 Orchard Rd., Montgomery, IL 60538 / 708-897-7555; FAX: 708-897-7558
Hodgson, Richard, 9081 Tahoe Lane, Boulder, CO 80301
Hoehn Sales, Inc., 2045 Kohn Road, Wright City, MO 63390 / 636-745-8144; FAX: 636-745-7868 hoehnsal@usmo.com
Hofer Jagdwaffen, P., Buchsenmachermeister, Kirchgasse 24, A-9170 Ferlach, AUSTRIA / 43 4227 3683; FAX: 43 4227 368330 peterhofer@hoferwaffen.com www.hoferwaffen.com
Hoffman New Ideas, 821 Northmoor Rd., Lake Forest, IL 60045 / 312-234-4075
Hogue Grips, P.O. Box 1138, Paso Robles, CA 93447 / 800-438-4747 or 805-239-1440; FAX: 805-239-2553
Holland & Holland Ltd., 33 Bruton St., London, ENGLAND / 44-171-499-4411; FAX: 44-171-408-7962
Holland's Gunsmithing, P.O. Box 69, Powers, OR 97466 / 541-439-5155; FAX: 541-439-5155
Hollinger, Jon. See: ASPEN OUTFITTING CO.
Hollywood Engineering, 10642 Arminta St., Sun Valley, CA 91352 / 818-842-8376; FAX: 818-504-4168 cadqueenel1@aol.com
Homak, 5151 W. 73rd St., Chicago, IL 60638-6613 / 312-523-3100; FAX: 312-523-9455
Home Shop Machinist, The Village Press Publications, P.O. Box 1810, Traverse City, MI 49685 / 800-447-7367; FAX: 616-946-3289
Hondo Ind., 510 S. 52nd St., I04, Tempe, AZ 85281
Hoppe's Div. Penguin Industries, Inc., P.O. Box 1690, Oregon City, OR 97045-0690 / 610-384-6000
Horizons Unlimited, P.O. Box 426, Warm Springs, GA 31830 / 706-655-3603; FAX: 706-655-3603
Hornady Mfg. Co., P.O. Box 1848, Grand Island, NE 68802 / 800-338-3220 or 308-382-1390; FAX: 308-382-5761
Horseshoe Leather Products, Andy Arratoonian, The Cottage Sharow, Ripon U.K., ENGLAND U.K. / 44-1765-605858 andy@horseshoe.co.uk www.holsters.org
House of Muskets, Inc., The, PO Box 4640, Pagosa Springs, CO 81157 / 970-731-2295
Houtz & Barwick, P.O. Box 435, W. Church St., Elizabeth City, NC 27909 / 800-775-0337; or 919-335-4191; FAX: 919-335-1152
Howa Machinery, Ltd., Sukaguchi, Shinkawa-cho Nishikasugai-gun, Aichi 452-8601, JAPAN / 81-52-408-1231; FAX: 81-52-401-4999 howa@howa.co.jp http://www.howa.cojpl
Howell Machine, 815 1/2 D St., Lewiston, ID 83501 / 208-743-7418
H-S Precision, Inc., 1301 Turbine Dr., Rapid City, SD 57701 / 605-341-3006; FAX: 605-342-8964
HT Bullets, 244 Belleville Rd., New Bedford, MA 02745 / 508-999-3338
Hubert J. Hecht Waffen-Hecht, P.O. Box 2635, Fair Oaks, CA 95628 / 916-966-1020
Huebner, Corey O., P.O. Box 564, Frenchtown, MT 59834 / 406-721-7168 bugsboys@hotmail.com
Huey Gun Cases, 820 Indiana St., Lawrence, KS 66044-2645 / 816-444-1637; FAX: 816-444-1637 hueycases@aol.com www.hueycases.com
Hume, Don, P.O. Box 351, Miami, OK 74355 / 800-331-2686; FAX: 918-542-4340 info@donhume.com www.donhume.com
Hunkeler, A. (See Buckskin Machine Works), 3235 S 358th St., Auburn, WA 98001 / 206-927-5412
Hunter Co., Inc., 3300 W. 71st Ave., Westminster, CO 80030 / 303-427-4626; FAX: 303-428-3980 debbiet@huntercompany.com www.huntercompany.com
Hunterjohn, PO Box 771457, St. Louis, MO 63177 / 314-531-7250 www.hunterjohn.com
Hunter's Specialties Inc., 6000 Huntington Ct. NE, Cedar Rapids, IA 52402-1268 / 319-395-0321; FAX: 319-395-0326
Hunters Supply, Inc., P.O. Box 313, Tioga, TX 76271 / 940-437-2458; FAX: 940-437-2228 hunterssupply@hotmail.com www.hunterssupply.net
Huntington Die Specialties, 601 Oro Dam Blvd., Oroville, CA 95965 / 530-534-1210; FAX: 530-534-1212 buy@huntingtons.com www.huntingtons.com
Hutton Rifle Ranch, P.O. Box 170317, Boise, ID 83717 / 208-345-8781 www.martinbrevik@aol.com

MANUFACTURER'S DIRECTORY

Hydrosorbent Products, PO Box 437, Ashley Falls, MA 01222 / 800-448-7903; FAX: 413-229-8743 orders@dehumidify.com www.dehumidify.com

I

I.A.B. (See U.S. Importer-Taylor's & Co. Inc.)
I.D.S.A. Books, 1324 Stratford Drive, Piqua, OH 45356 / 937-773-4203; FAX: 937-778-1922
I.N.C. Inc. (See Kickeez I.N.C., Inc.)
I.S.S., P.O. Box 185234, Ft. Worth, TX 76181 / 817-595-2090; FAX: 817-595-2090 iss@concentric.net
I.S.W., 106 E. Cairo Dr., Tempe, AZ 85282
IAR Inc., 33171 Camino Capistrano, San Juan Capistrano, CA 92675 / 949-443-3642; FAX: 949-443-3647 sales@iar-arms.com iar-arms.com
Ide, Ken. See: STURGEON VALLEY SPORTERS
IGA (See U.S. Importer-Stoeger Industries)
Image Ind. Inc., 382 Balm Court, Wood Dale, IL 60191 / 630-766-2402; FAX: 630-766-7373
Impact Case & Container, Inc., P.O. Box 1129, Rathdrum, ID 83858 / 877-687-2452; FAX: 208-687-0632 bradk@icc-case.com www.icc-case.com
Imperial (See E-Z-Way Systems), P.O. Box 4310, Newark, OH 43058-4310 / 614-345-6645; FAX: 614-345-6600 ezway@infinet.com www.jcunald.com
Imperial Magnum Corp., P.O. Box 249, Oroville, WA 98844 / 604-495-3131; FAX: 604-495-2816
Imperial Miniature Armory, 10547 S. Post Oak Road, Houston, TX 77035-3305 / 713-729-8428; FAX: 713-729-2274 miniguns@aol.com www.1800miniature.com
Imperial Schrade Corp., 7 Schrade Ct., Box 7000, Ellenville, NY 12428 / 914-647-7601; FAX: 914-647-8701 csc@schradeknives.com www.schradeknives.com
Import Sports Inc., 1750 Brielle Ave., Unit B1, Wanamassa, NJ 07712 / 732-493-0302; FAX: 732-493-0301 gsodini@aol.com www.bersa-11ama.com
IMR Powder Co., 1080 Military Turnpike, Suite 2, Plattsburgh, NY 12901 / 518-563-2253; FAX: 518-563-6916
Info-Arm, P.O. Box 1262, Champlain, NY 12919 / 514-955-0355; FAX: 514-955-0357 infoarm@qc.aira.com
Ingle, Ralph W., Engraver, 112 Manchester Ct., Centerville, GA 31028 / 478-953-5824 riengraver@aol.com www.fega.com
Innovative Weaponry Inc., 2513 E. Loop 820 N., Fort Worth, TX 76118 / 817-284-0099 or 800-334-3573
INTEC International, Inc., P.O. Box 5708, Scottsdale, AZ 85261 / 602-483-1708
Inter Ordnance of America LP, 3305 Westwood Industrial Dr., Monroe, NC 28110-5204 / 704-821-8337; FAX: 704-821-8523
Intercontinental Distributors, Ltd., PO Box 815, Beulah, ND 58523
Intrac Arms International, 5005 Chapman Hwy., Knoxville, TN 37920
Ion Industries, Inc., 3508 E Allerton Ave., Cudahy, WI 53110 / 414-486-2007; FAX: 414-486-2017
Iosso Products, 1485 Lively Blvd., Elk Grove Village, IL 60007 / 847-437-8400; FAX: 847-437-8478
Iron Bench, 12619 Bailey Rd., Redding, CA 96003 / 916-241-4623
Ironside International Publishers, Inc., P.O. Box 1050, Lorton, VA 22199
Ironsighter Co., P.O. Box 85070, Westland, MI 48185 / 734-326-8731; FAX: 734-326-3378 www.ironsighter.com
Irwin, Campbell H., 140 Hartland Blvd., East Hartland, CT 06027 / 203-653-3901
Island Pond Gun Shop, Cross St., Island Pond, VT 05846 / 802-723-4546
Israel Arms Inc., 5625 Star Ln. #B, Houston, TX 77057 / 713-789-0745; FAX: 713-914-9515 www.israelarms.com
Ithaca Classic Doubles, Stephen Lamboy, No. 5 Railroad St., Victor, NY 14564 / 716-924-2710; FAX: 716-924-2737 ithacadoubles.com
Ithaca Gun Company LLC, 901 Rt. 34 B, King Ferry, NY 13081 / 315-364-7171; FAX: 315-364-5134 info@ithacagun.com
Ivanoff, Thomas G. (See Tom's Gun Repair)

J

J J Roberts Firearm Engraver, 7808 Lake Dr, Manassas, VA 20111 / 703-330-0448; FAX: 703-264-8600 james..roberts@angelfire.com www.angelfire.com/va2/engraver
J&D Components, 75 East 350 North, Orem, UT 84057-4719 / 801-225-7007 www.jdcomponents.com
J&J Products, Inc., 9240 Whitmore, El Monte, CA 91731 / 818-571-5228; FAX: 800-927-8361
J&J Sales, 1501 21st Ave. S., Great Falls, MT 59405 / 406-727-9789 mtshootingbench@yahoo.com www.j&jsales.us
J&L Superior Bullets (See Huntington Die Special)
J&R Engineering, P.O. Box 77, 200 Lyons Hill Rd., Athol, MA 01331 / 508-249-9241
J&R Enterprises, 4550 Scotts Valley Rd., Lakeport, CA 95453
J&S Heat Treat, 803 S. 16th St., Blue Springs, MO 64015 / 816-229-2149; FAX: 816-228-1135
J. Dewey Mfg. Co., Inc., P.O. Box 2014, Southbury, CT 06488 / 203-264-3064; FAX: 203-262-6907 deweyrods@worldnet.att.net www.deweyrods.com
J. Korzinek Riflesmith, RD 2, Box 73D, Canton, PA 17724 / 717-673-8512
J.A. Blades, Inc. (See Christopher Firearms Co.)
J.A. Henckels Zwillingswerk Inc., 9 Skyline Dr., Hawthorne, NY 10532 / 914-592-7370
J.G. Anschutz GmbH & Co. KG, Daimlerstr. 12, D-89079 Ulm, Ulm, GERMANY / 49 731 40120; FAX: 49 731 4012700 JGA-info@anschuetz-sport.com www.anschuetz-sport.com
J.G. Dapkus Co., Inc., Commerce Circle, P.O. Box 293, Durham, CT 06422 www.explodingtargets.com
J.I.T. Ltd., P.O. Box 230, Freedom, WY 83120 / 708-494-0937
J.J. Roberts / Engraver, 7808 Lake Dr., Manassas, VA 20111 / 703-330-0448 jjrengraver@aol.com www.angelfire.com/va2/engraver
J.P. Enterprises Inc., P.O. Box 378, Hugo, MN 55110 / 612-486-9064; FAX: 612-482-0970
J.R. Williams Bullet Co., 2008 Tucker Rd., Perry, GA 31069 / 912-987-0274
J.W. Morrison Custom Rifles, 4015 W. Sharon, Phoenix, AZ 85029 / 602-978-3754
J/B Adventures & Safaris Inc., 2275 E. Arapahoe Rd., Ste. 109, Littleton, CO 80122-1521 / 303-771-0977
Jack A. Rosenberg & Sons, 12229 Cox Ln., Dallas, TX 75234 / 214-241-6302
Jack Dever Co., 8520 NW 90th St., Oklahoma City, OK 73132 / 405-721-6393 jbdever1@home.com
Jack First, Inc., 1201 Turbine Dr., Rapid City, SD 57703 / 605-343-8481; FAX: 605-343-9420
Jack Jonas Appraisals & Taki, 13952 E. Marina Dr., #604, Aurora, CO 80014
Jackalope Gun Shop, 1048 S. 5th St., Douglas, WY 82633 / 307-358-3441
Jaffin, Harry. See: BRIDGEMAN PRODUCTS
Jagdwaffen, Peter. See: BUCHSENMACHERMEISTER
James Churchill Glove Co., PO Box 298, Centralia, WA 98531 / 360-736-2816; FAX: 360-330-0151 churchillglove@localaccess.com
James Wayne Firearms for Collectors and Investors, 2608 N. Laurent, Victoria, TX 77901 / 361-578-1258; FAX: 361-578-3559
Jamison International, Marc Jamison, 3551 Mayer Ave., Sturgis, SD 57785 / 605-347-5090; FAX: 605-347-4704 jbell2@masttechnology.com
Jamison, Marc. See: JAMISON INTERNATIONAL
Jamison's Forge Works, 4527 Rd. 6.5 NE, Moses Lake, WA 98837 / 509-762-2659
Jantz Supply, 309 West Main Dept HD, Davis, OK 73030-0584 / 580-369-2316; FAX: 580-369-3082 jantz@brightok.net www.knifemaking.com
Jarrett Rifles, Inc., 383 Brown Rd., Jackson, SC 29831 / 803-471-3616 www.jarrettrifles.com
Jarvis, Inc., 1123 Cherry Orchard Lane, Hamilton, MT 59840 / 406-961-4392
Javelina Lube Products, P.O. Box 337, San Bernardino, CA 92402 / 909-350-9556; FAX: 909-429-1211
Jay McCament Custom Gunmaker, Jay McCament, 1730-134th St. Ct. S., Tacoma, WA 98444 / 253-531-8832
JB Custom, P.O. Box 6912, Leawood, KS 66206 / 913-381-2329
Jeff Flannery Engraving, 11034 Riddles Run Rd., Union, KY 41091 / 859-384-3127; FAX: 859-384-2222 engraving@fuse.net http://home.fuse.net/engraving/
Jeffredo Gunsight, P.O. Box 669, San Marcos, CA 92079 / 760-728-2695
Jena Eur, PO Box 319, Dunmore, PA 18512
Jenco Sales, Inc., P.O. Box 1000, Manchaca, TX 78652 / 800-531-5301; FAX: 800-266-2373 jencosales@sbcglobal.net
Jenkins Recoil Pads, 5438 E. Frontage Ln., Olney, IL 62450 / 618-395-3416
Jensen Bullets, RR 1 Box 187, Arco, ID 83213 / 208-785-5590
Jensen's Custom Ammunition, 5146 E. Pima, Tucson, AZ 85712 / 602-325-3346; FAX: 602-322-5704
Jensen's Firearms Academy, 1280 W. Prince, Tucson, AZ 85705 / 602-293-8516
Jericho Tool & Die Co., Inc., 2917 St. Hwy. 7, Bainbridge, NY 13733 / 607-563-8222; FAX: 607-563-8560 jerichotool.com www.jerichotool.com
Jerry Phillips Optics, P.O. Box L632, Langhorne, PA 19047 / 215-757-5037; FAX: 215-757-7097
Jesse W. Smith Saddlery, 0499 County Road J, Pritchett, CO 81064 / 509-325-0622
Jester Bullets, Rt. 1 Box 27, Orienta, OK 73737
Jewell Triggers, Inc., 3620 Hwy. 123, San Marcos, TX 78666 / 512-353-2999; FAX: 512-392-0543
JGS Precision Tool Mfg., LLC, 60819 Selander Rd., Coos Bay, OR 97420 / 541-267-4331; FAX: 541-267-5996 jgstools@harborside.com www.jgstools.com
Jim Blair Engraving, P.O. Box 64, Glenrock, WY 82637 / 307-436-8115 jblairengrav@msn.com
Jim Noble Co., 1305 Columbia St., Vancouver, WA 98660 / 360-695-1309; FAX: 360-695-6835 jnobleco@aol.com
Jim Norman Custom Gunstocks, 14281 Cane Rd., Valley Center, CA 92082 / 619-749-6252
Jim's Precision, Jim Ketchum, 1725 Moclips Dr., Petaluma, CA 94952 / 707-762-3014
JLK Bullets, 414 Turner Rd., Dover, AR 72837 / 501-331-4194
Johanssons Vapentillbehor, Bert, S-430 20, Veddige, SWEDEN
John Hall Plastics, Inc., P.O. Box 1526, Alvin, TX 77512 / 713-489-8709
John J. Adams & Son Engravers, 7040 VT Rt 113, Vershire, VT 05079 / 802-685-0019
John Masen Co. Inc., 1305 Jelmak, Grand Prairie, TX 75050 / 817-430-8732; FAX: 817-430-1715
John Partridge Sales Ltd., Trent Meadows Rugeley, Staffordshire, WS15 2HS ENGLAND
John Rigby & Co., 500 Linne Rd. Ste. D, Paso Robles, CA 93446 / 805-227-4236; FAX: 805-227-4723 jribgy@calinet www.johnrigbyandco.com
John's Custom Leather, 523 S. Liberty St., Blairsville, PA 15717 / 724-459-6802; FAX: 724-459-5996
Johnson Wood Products, 34897 Crystal Road, Strawberry Point, IA 52076 / 563-933-6504 johnsonwoodproducts@yahoo.com
Johnston Bros. (See C&T Corp. TA Johnson Brothers)
Jonad Corp., 2091 Lakeland Ave., Lakewood, OH 44107 / 216-226-3161
Jonathan Arthur Ciener, Inc., 8700 Commerce St., Cape Canaveral, FL 32920 / 321-868-2200; FAX: 321-868-2201 www.22lrconversions.com
Jones Co., Dale, 680 Hoffman Draw, Kila, MT 59920 / 406-755-4684
Jones Custom Products, Neil A., 17217 Brookhouser Rd., Saegertown, PA 16433 / 814-763-2769; FAX: 814-763-4228
Jones, J. See: SSK INDUSTRIES
Jones Moulds, Paul, 4901 Telegraph Rd., Los Angeles, CA 90022 / 213-262-1510
JP Sales, Box 307, Anderson, TX 77830
JRP Custom Bullets, RR2 2233 Carlton Rd., Whitehall, NY 12887 / 518-282-0084 or 802-438-5548
JSL Ltd. (See U.S. Importer-Specialty Shooters)
Juenke, Vern, 25 Bitterbush Rd., Reno, NV 89523 / 702-345-0225
Jungkind, Reeves C., 509 E. Granite St., Llano, TX 78643-3055 / 325-247-1151
Jurras, L. See: L. E. JURRAS & ASSOC.
Justin Phillippi Custom Bullets, P.O. Box 773, Ligonier, PA 15658 / 412-238-9671

K

K&M Industries, Inc., Box 66, 510 S. Main, Troy, ID 83871 / 208-835-2281; FAX: 208-835-5211
K&M Services, 5430 Salmon Run Rd., Dover, PA 17315 / 717-292-3175; FAX: 717-292-3175
K. Eversull Co., Inc., 1 Tracemont, Boyce, LA 71409 / 318-793-8728; FAX: 318-793-5483 bestguns@aol.com

MANUFACTURER'S DIRECTORY

K.B.I. Inc., P.O. Box 6625, Harrisburg, PA 17112 / 717-540-8518; FAX: 717-540-8567
K.L. Null Holsters Ltd., 161 School St. NW, Hill City Station, Resaca, GA 30735 / 706-625-5643; FAX: 706-625-9392 ken@klnullholsters.com www.klnullholsters.com
Ka Pu Kapili, P.O. Box 745, Honokaa, HI 96727 / 808-776-1644; FAX: 808-776-1731
KA-BAR Knives, 200 Homer St., Olean, NY 14760 / 800-282-0130; FAX: 716-790-7188 info@ka-bar.com www.ka-bar.com
Kahles A. Swarovski Company, 2 Slater Rd., Cranston, RI 02920 / 401-946-2220; FAX: 401-946-2587
Kahr Arms, PO Box 220, 630 Route 303, Blauvelt, NY 10913 / 845-353-7770; FAX: 845-353-7833 www.kahr.com
Kailua Custom Guns Inc., 51 N. Dean Street, Coquille, OR 97423 / 541-396-5413 kailuacustom@aol.com www.kailuacustom.com
Kalispel Case Line, P.O. Box 267, Cusick, WA 99119 / 509-445-1121
Kamik Outdoor Footwear, 554 Montee de Liesse, Montreal, PQ H4T 1P1 CANADA / 514-341-3950; FAX: 514-341-1861
Kane, Edward, P.O. Box 385, Ukiah, CA 95482 / 707-462-2937
Kapro Mfg. Co. Inc. (See R.E.I.)
Kasenit Co., Inc., 39 Park Ave., Highland Mills, NY 10930 / 845-928-9595; FAX: 845-986-8038
Kaswer Custom, Inc., 13 Surrey Drive, Brookfield, CT 06804 / 203-775-0564; FAX: 203-775-6872
KDF, Inc., 2485 Hwy. 46 N., Seguin, TX 78155 / 830-379-8141; FAX: 830-379-5420
KeeCo Impressions, Inc., 346 Wood Ave., North Brunswick, NJ 08902 / 800-468-0546
Kehr, Roger, 2131 Agate Ct. SE, Lacy, WA 98503 / 360-491-0691
Keith's Bullets, 942 Twisted Oak, Algonquin, IL 60102 / 708-658-3520
Keith's Custom Gunstocks, Keith M. Heppler, 540 Banyan Circle, Walnut Creek, CA 94598 / 925-934-3509; FAX: 925-934-3143 kmheppler@hotmail.com
Kelbly, Inc., 7222 Dalton Fox Lake Rd., North Lawrence, OH 44666 / 216-683-4674; FAX: 216-683-7349
Kelley's, P.O. Box 125, Woburn, MA 01801-0125 / 800-879-7273; FAX: 781-272-7077 kels@star.net www.kelsmilitary.com
Kellogg's Professional Products, 325 Pearl St., Sandusky, OH 44870 / 419-625-6551; FAX: 419-625-6167 skwigton@aol.com
Kelly, Lance, 1723 Willow Oak Dr., Edgewater, FL 32132 / 904-423-4933
Kel-Tec CNC Industries, Inc., PO Box 236009, Cocoa, FL 32923 / 407-631-0068; FAX: 407-631-1169
Kemen America, 2550 Hwy. 23, Wrenshall, MN 55797 / 218-384-3670 patrickl@midwestshootingschool.com midwestshootingschool.com
Ken Eyster Heritage Gunsmiths, Inc., 6441 Bisop Rd., Centerburg, OH 43011 / 740-625-6131; FAX: 740-625-7811
Ken Starnes Gunmaker, 15940 SW Holly Hill Rd., Hillsboro, OR 97123-9033 / 503-628-0705; FAX: 503-443-2096 kstarnes@kdsa.com
Keng's Firearms Specialty, Inc./US Tactical Systems, 875 Wharton Dr., P.O. Box 44405, Atlanta, GA 30336-1405 / 404-691-7611; FAX: 404-505-8445
Kennebec Journal, 274 Western Ave., Augusta, ME 04330 / 207-622-6288
Kennedy Firearms, 10 N. Market St., Muncy, PA 17756 / 717-546-6695
Kenneth W. Warren Engraver, P.O. Box 2842, Wenatchee, WA 98807 / 509-663-6123; FAX: 509-665-6123
Ken's Kustom Kartridges, 331 Jacobs Rd., Hubbard, OH 44425 / 216-534-4595
Kent Cartridge America, Inc., PO Box 849, 1000 Zigor Rd., Kearneysville, WV 25430
Keowee Game Calls, 608 Hwy. 25 North, Travelers Rest, SC 29690 / 864-834-7204; FAX: 864-834-7831
Kershaw Knives, 25300 SW Parkway Ave., Wilsonville, OR 97070 / 503-682-1966; or 800-325-2891; FAX: 503-682-7168
Kesselring Gun Shop, 4024 Old Hwy. 99N, Burlington, WA 98233 / 360-724-3113; FAX: 360-724-7003 info@kesselrings.com www.kesselrings.com
Ketchum, Jim (See Jim's Precision)
Keystone Sporting Arms, Inc. (Crickett Rifles), 8920 State Route 405, Milton, PA 17847 / 800-742-2777; FAX: 570-742-1455
Kickeez I.N.C., Inc., 301 Industrial Dr., Carl Junction, MO 64834-8806 / 419-649-2100; FAX: 417-649-2200 kickey@ipa.net
Kilham & Co., Main St., P.O. Box 37, Lyme, NH 03768 / 603-795-4112
Kim Ahrends Custom Firearms, Inc., Box 203, Clarion, IA 50525 / 515-532-3449; FAX: 515-532-3926
Kimar (See U.S. Importer-IAR,Inc)
Kimber of America, Inc., 1 Lawton St., Yonkers, NY 10705 / 800-880-2418; FAX: 914-964-9340
King & Co., P.O. Box 1242, Bloomington, IL 61702 / 309-473-3964; FAX: 309-473-2161
King's Gun Works, 1837 W. Glenoaks Blvd., Glendale, CA 91201 / 818-956-6010; FAX: 818-548-8606
Kirkpatrick Leather Co., PO Box 677, Laredo, TX 78040 / 956-723-6631; FAX: 956-725-0672 mike@kirkpatrickleather.com www.kirkpatrickleather.com
KK Air International (See Impact Case & Container Co.)
Kleen-Bore, Inc., 16 Industrial Pkwy., Easthampton, MA 01027 / 413-527-0300; FAX: 413-527-2522 info@kleen-bore.com www.kleen-bore.com
Kleinendorst, K. W., RR 1, Box 1500, Hop Bottom, PA 18824 / 717-289-4687
Klingler Woodcarving, P.O. Box 141, Thistle Hill, Cabot, VT 05647 / 802-426-3811
Knifeware, Inc., P.O. Box 3, Greenville, WV 24945 / 304-832-6878
Knight Rifles, 21852 Hwy. J46, P.O. Box 130, Centerville, IA 52544 / 515-856-2626; FAX: 515-856-2628 www.knightrifles.com
Knight Rifles (See Modern Muzzle Loading, Inc.)
Knight's Mfg. Co., 7750 Ninth St. SW, Vero Beach, FL 32968 / 561-562-5697; FAX: 561-569-2955 civiliansales@knightarmco.com
Knock on Wood Antiques, 355 Post Rd., Darien, CT 06820 / 203-655-9031
Knoell, Doug, 9737 McCardle Way, Santee, CA 92071 / 619-449-5189
Knopp, Gary. See: SUPER 6 LLC
KOGOT, 410 College, Trinidad, CO 81082 / 719-846-9406; FAX: 719-846-9406
Kolar, 1925 Roosevelt Ave., Racine, WI 53406 / 414-554-0800; FAX: 414-554-9093
Kolpin Outdoors, Inc., P.O. Box 107, 205 Depot St., Fox Lake, WI 53933 / 414-928-3118; FAX: 414-928-3687 cdutton@kolpin.com www.kolpin.com
Korth Germany GmbH, Robert Bosch Strasse, 11, D-23909, 23909 Ratzeburg, GERMANY / 4541-840363; FAX: 4541-84 05 35 info@korthwaffen.de www.korthwaffen.com
Korth USA, 437R Chandler St., Tewksbury, MA 01876 / 978-851-8656; FAX: 978-851-9462 info@kortusa.com www.korthusa.com
Korzinek Riflesmith, J., RD 2 Box 73D, Canton, PA 17724 / 717-673-8512
Koval Knives, 5819 Zarley St., Suite A, New Albany, OH 43054 / 614-855-0777; FAX: 614-855-0945 koval@kovalknives.com www.kovalknives.com
Kowa Optimed, Inc., 20001 S. Vermont Ave., Torrance, CA 90502 / 310-327-1913; FAX: 310-327-4177 scopekowa@kowa.com www.kowascope.com
Kramer Designs, P.O. Box 129, Clancy, MT 59634 / 406-933-8658; FAX: 406-933-8658
Kramer Handgun Leather, P.O. Box 112154, Tacoma, WA 98411 / 800-510-2666; FAX: 253-564-1214 www.kramerleather.com
Krause Publications, Inc., 700 E. State St., Iola, WI 54990 / 715-445-2214; FAX: 715-445-4087
Krico Deutschland GmbH, Nurnbergerstrasse 6, D-90602, Pyrbaum, GERMANY / 09180-2780; FAX: 09180-2661
Krieger Barrels, Inc., 2024 Mayfield Rd, Richfield, WI 53076 / 262-628-8558; FAX: 262-628-8748
Krieghoff Gun Co., H., Boschstrasse 22, D-89079 Elm, GERMANY / 731-4018270
Krieghoff International,Inc., 7528 Easton Rd., Ottsville, PA 18942 / 610-847-5173; FAX: 610-847-8691
Kukowski, Ed. See: ED'S GUN HOUSE
Kulis Freeze Dry Taxidermy, 725 Broadway Ave., Bedford, OH 44146 / 216-232-8352; FAX: 216-232-7305 jkulis@kastaway.com kastaway.com
KVH Industries, Inc., 110 Enterprise Center, Middletown, RI 02842 / 401-847-3327; FAX: 401-849-0045
Kwik-Site Co., 5555 Treadwell St., Wayne, MI 48184 / 734-326-1500; FAX: 734-326-4120 kwiksiteco@aol.com

L

L&R Lock Co., 1137 Pocalla Rd., Sumter, SC 29150 / 803-775-6127; FAX: 803-775-5171
L&S Technologies Inc. (See Aimtech Mount Systems)
L. Bengtson Arms Co., 6345-B E. Akron St., Mesa, AZ 85205 / 602-981-6375
L. E. Jurras & Assoc., L. E. Jurras, P.O. Box 680, Washington, IN 47501 / 812-254-6170; FAX: 812-254-6170 jurasgun@rtcc.net
L.A.R. Mfg., Inc., 4133 W. Farm Rd., West Jordan, UT 84088 / 801-280-3505; FAX: 801-280-1972
L.B.T., Judy Smith, HCR 62, Box 145, Moyie Springs, ID 83845 / 208-267-3588
L.E. Wilson, Inc., Box 324, 404 Pioneer Ave., Cashmere, WA 98815 / 509-782-1328; FAX: 509-782-7200
L.L. Bean, Inc., Freeport, ME 04032 / 207-865-4761; FAX: 207-552-2802
L.P.A. Inc., Via Alfieri 26, Gardone V.T., Brescia, ITALY / 30-891-14-81; FAX: 30-891-09-51
L.R. Clift Mfg., 3821 Hammonton Rd., Marysville, CA 95901 / 916-755-3390; FAX: 916-755-3393
L.W. Seecamp Co., Inc., PO Box 255, New Haven, CT 06502 / 203-877-3429; FAX: 203-877-3429 seecamp@optonline.net
La Clinique du .45, 1432 Rougemont, Chambly, PQ J3L 2L8 CANADA / 514-658-1144
Labanu, Inc., 2201-F Fifth Ave., Ronkonkoma, NY 11779 / 516-467-6197; FAX: 516-981-4112
LaBoone, Pat. See: THE MIDWEST SHOOTING SCHOOL
LaBounty Precision Reboring, Inc, 7968 Silver Lake Rd., PO Box 186, Maple Falls, WA 98266 / 360-599-2047; FAX: 360-599-3018
LaCrosse Footwear, Inc., 18550 NE Riverside Parkway, Portland, OR 97230 / 503-766-1010; or 800-323-2668; FAX: 503-766-1015
LaFrance Specialties, P.O. Box 87933, San Diego, CA 92138 / 619-293-3373; FAX: 619-293-0819 timlafrance@att.net lafrancespecialties.com
Lake Center Marina, PO Box 670, St. Charles, MO 63302 / 314-946-7500
Lakefield Arms Ltd. (See Savage Arms, Inc.)
Lakewood Products LLC, 275 June St., Berlin, WI 54923 / 800-872-8458; FAX: 920-361-7719 lakewood@centurytel.net www.lakewoodproducts.com
Lamboy, Stephen. See: ITHACA CLASSIC DOUBLES
Lampert, Ron, Rt. 1, 44857 Schoolcraft Trl., Guthrie, MN 56461 / 218-854-7345
Lamson & Goodnow Mfg. Co., 45 Conway St., Shelburne Falls, MA 03170 / 413-625-6564; or 800-872-6564; FAX: 413-625-9816 www.lamsonsharp.com
Lansky Levine, Arthur. See: LANSKY SHARPENERS
Lansky Sharpeners, Arthur Lansky Levine, PO Box 50830, Las Vegas, NV 89016 / 702-361-7511; FAX: 702-896-9511
LaPrade, PO Box 250, Ewing, VA 24248 / 423-733-2615
Lapua Ltd., P.O. Box 5, Lapua, FINLAND / 6-310111; FAX: 6-4388991
LaRocca Gun Works, 51 Union Place, Worcester, MA 01608 / 508-754-2887; FAX: 508-754-2887 www.laroccagunworks.com
Larry Lyons Gunworks, 110 Hamilton St., Dowagiac, MI 49047 / 616-782-9478
Laser Devices, Inc., 2 Harris Ct. A-4, Monterey, CA 93940 / 831-373-0701; FAX: 831-373-0903 sales@laserdevices.com www.laserdevices.com
Laseraim Technologies, Inc., P.O. Box 3548, Little Rock, AR 72203 / 501-375-2227
Laserlyte, 2201 Amapola Ct., Torrance, CA 90501
LaserMax, Inc., 3495 Winton Place, Bldg. B, Rochester, NY 14623-2807 / 800-527-3703; FAX: 716-272-5427 customerservice@lasermax-inc.com www.lasermax-inc.com
Lassen Community College, Gunsmithing Dept., P.O. Box 3000, Hwy. 139, Susanville, CA 96130 / 916-251-8800; FAX: 916-251-8838
Lathrop's, Inc., 5146 E. Pima, Tucson, AZ 85712 / 520-881-0266; or 800-875-4867; FAX: 520-322-5704
Laughridge, William R. (See Cylinder & Slide Inc.)
Laurel Mountain Forge, P.O. Box 52, Crown Point, IN 46308 / 219-548-2950; FAX: 219-548-2950
Laurona Armas Eibar, S.A.L., Avenida de Otaola 25, P.O. Box 260, Eibar 20600, SPAIN / 34-43-700600; FAX: 34-43-700616
Lawrence Brand Shot (See Precision Reloading)
Lawrence Leather Co., P.O. Box 1479, Lillington, NC 27546 / 910-893-2071; FAX: 910-893-4742
Lawson Co., Harry, 3328 N Richey Blvd., Tucson, AZ 85716 / 520-326-1117; FAX: 520-326-1117
Lawson, John. See: THE SIGHT SHOP
Lawson, John G. (See Sight Shop, The)
Lazzeroni Arms Co., PO Box 26696, Tucson, AZ 85726 / 888-492-7247; FAX: 520-624-4250

Manufacturer's Directory

Le Clear Industries (See E-Z-Way Systems), P.O. Box 4310, Newark, OH 43058-4310 / 614-345-6645; FAX: 614-345-6600
Leapers, Inc., 7675 Five Mile Rd., Northville, MI 48167 / 248-486-1231; FAX: 248-486-1430
Leatherman Tool Group, Inc., 12106 NE Ainsworth Cir., P.O. Box 20595, Portland, OR 97294 / 503-253-7826; FAX: 503-253-7830
Lebeau-Courally, Rue St. Gilles, 386 4000, Liege, BELGIUM / 042-52-48-43; FAX: 32-4-252-2008 info@lebeau-courally.com www.lebeau-courally.com
Leckie Professional Gunsmithing, 546 Quarry Rd., Ottsville, PA 18942 / 215-847-8594
Ledbetter Airguns, Riley, 1804 E Sprague St, Winston Salem, NC 27107-3521 / 919-784-0676
Lee Precision, Inc., 4275 Hwy. U, Hartford, WI 53027 / 262-673-3075; FAX: 262-673-9273 info@leeprecision.com www.leeprecision.com
Lee Supplies, Mark, 9901 France Ct., Lakeville, MN 55044 / 612-461-2114
LeFever Arms Co., Inc., 6234 Stokes, Lee Center Rd., Lee Center, NY 13363 / 315-337-6722; FAX: 315-337-1543
Legacy Sports International, 206 S. Union St., Alexandria, VA 22314 / 703-548-4837 www.legacysports.com
Leibowitz, Leonard, 1205 Murrayhill Ave., Pittsburgh, PA 15217 / 412-361-5455
Leica USA, Inc., 156 Ludlow Ave., Northvale, NJ 07647 / 201-767-7500; FAX: 201-767-8666
LEM Gun Specialties, Inc. The Lewis Lead Remover, P.O. Box 2855, Peachtree City, GA 30269-2024 / 770-487-0556
Leonard Day, 6 Linseed Rd Box 1, West Hatfield, MA 01088-7505 / 413-337-8369
Les Baer Custom, Inc., 29601 34th Ave., Hillsdale, IL 61257 / 309-658-2716; FAX: 309-658-2610 www.lesbaer.com
LesMerises, Felix. See: ROCKY MOUNTAIN ARMOURY
Lethal Force Institute (See Police Bookshelf), PO Box 122, Concord, NH 03301 / 603-224-6814; FAX: 603-226-3554
Lett Custom Grips, 672 Currier Rd., Hopkinton, NH 03229-2652 / 800-421-5388; FAX: 603-226-4580 info@lettgrips.com www.lettgrips.com
Leupold & Stevens, Inc., 14400 NW Greenbrier Pky., Beaverton, OR 97006 / 503-646-9171; FAX: 503-526-1455
Lever Arms Service Ltd., 2131 Burrard St., Vancouver, BC V6J 3H7 CANADA / 604-736-2711; FAX: 604-738-3503 leverarms@leverarms.com www.leverarms.com
Lew Horton Dist. Co., Inc., 15 Walkup Dr., Westboro, MA 01581 / 508-366-7400; FAX: 508-366-5332
Liberty Metals, 2233 East 16th St., Los Angeles, CA 90021 / 213-581-9171; FAX: 213-581-9351 libertymfgsolder@hotmail.com
Liberty Safe, 999 W. Utah Ave., Payson, UT 84651-1744 / 800-247-5625; FAX: 801-489-6409
Liberty Shooting Supplies, P.O. Box 357, Hillsboro, OR 97123 / 503-640-5518; FAX: 503-640-5518 info@libertyshootingsupplies.com www.libertyshootingsupplies.com
Lightning Performance Innovations, Inc., RD1 Box 555, Mohawk, NY 13407 / 315-866-8819; FAX: 315-867-5701
Lilja Precision Rifle Barrels, P.O. Box 372, Plains, MT 59859 / 406-826-3084; FAX: 406-826-3083 lilja@riflebarrels.com www.riflebarrels.com
Lincoln, Dean, Box 1886, Farmington, NM 87401
Linder Solingen Knives, 4401 Sentry Dr. #B, Tucker, GA 30084 / 770-939-6915; FAX: 770-939-6738
Lindsay Engraving & Tools, Steve Lindsay, 3714 W. Cedar Hills, Kearney, NE 68845 / 308-236-7885 steve@lindsayengraving.com www.handgravers.com
Lindsay, Steve. See: LINDSAY ENGRAVING & TOOLS
Lindsley Arms Cartridge Co., P.O. Box 757, 20 College Hill Rd., Henniker, NH 03242 / 603-428-3127
Linebaugh Custom Sixguns, P.O. Box 455, Cody, WY 82414 / 307-645-3332 www.sixgunner.com
Lion Country Supply, P.O. Box 480, Port Matilda, PA 16870
List Precision Engineering, Unit 1 Ingley Works, 13 River Road, Barking, ENGLAND / 011-081-594-1686
Lithi Bee Bullet Lube, 1728 Carr Rd., Muskegon, MI 49442 / 616-788-4479 lithibee@att.net
"Little John's" Antique Arms, 1740 W. Laveta, Orange, CA 92668
Little Trees Ramble (See Scott Pilkington)
Littler Sales Co., 20815 W. Chicago, Detroit, MI 48228 / 313-273-6888; FAX: 313-273-1099 littlerptg@aol.com
Littleton, J. F., 275 Pinedale Ave., Oroville, CA 95966 / 916-533-6084
Ljutic Industries, Inc., 732 N. 16th Ave., Suite 22, Yakima, WA 98902 / 509-248-0476; FAX: 509-576-8233 ljuticgun@earthlink.net www.ljuticgun.com
Llama Gabilondo Y Cia, Apartado 290, E-01080, Victoria, SPAIN
Loch Leven Industries/Convert-A-Pell, P.O. Box 2751, Santa Rosa, CA 95405 / 707-573-8735; FAX: 707-573-0369
Lock's Philadelphia Gun Exchange, 6700 Rowland Ave., Philadelphia, PA 19149 / 215-332-6225; FAX: 215-332-4800 locks.gunshop@verizon.net
Lodewick, Walter H., 2816 NE Halsey St., Portland, OR 97232 / 503-284-2554 wlodewick@aol.com
Lodgewood Mfg., P.O. Box 611, Whitewater, WI 53190 / 262-473-5444; FAX: 262-473-6448 lodgewd@idcnet.com lodgewood.com
Log Cabin Sport Shop, 8010 Lafayette Rd., Lodi, OH 44254 / 330-948-1082; FAX: 330-948-4307 logcabin@logcabinshop.com www.logcabinshop.com
Logan, Harry M., Box 745, Honokaa, HI 96727 / 808-776-1644
Logdewood Mfg., P.O. Box 611, Whitewater, WI 53190 / 262-473-5444; FAX: 262-473-6448 lodgewd@idcnet.com www.lodgewood.com
Lohman Mfg. Co., Inc., 4500 Doniphan Dr., P.O. Box 220, Neosho, MO 64850 / 417-451-4438; FAX: 417-451-2576
Lomont Precision Bullets, 278 Sandy Creek Rd., Salmon, ID 83467 / 208-756-6819; FAX: 208-756-6824 www.klomont.com
London Guns Ltd., Box 3750, Santa Barbara, CA 93130 / 805-683-4141; FAX: 805-683-1712
Lone Star Gunleather, 1301 Brushy Bend Dr., Round Rock, TX 78681 / 512-255-1805
Lone Star Rifle Company, 11231 Rose Road, Conroe, TX 77303 / 936-856-3363; FAX: 936-856-3363 dave@lonestar.com
Long, George F., 1500 Rogue River Hwy., Ste. F, Grants Pass, OR 97527 / 541-476-7552
Lortone Inc., 2856 NW Market St., Seattle, WA 98107
Lothar Walther Precision Tool Inc., 3425 Hutchinson Rd., Cumming, GA 30040 / 770-889-9998; FAX: 770-889-4919 lotharwalther@mindspring.com www.lothar-walther.com
LPS Laboratories, Inc., 4647 Hugh Howell Rd., P.O. Box 3050, Tucker, GA 30084 / 404-934-7800
Lucas, Edward E, 32 Garfield Ave., East Brunswick, NJ 08816 / 201-251-5526
Lupton, Keith. See: PAWLING MOUNTAIN CLUB
Lyman Instant Targets, Inc. (See Lyman Products)
Lyman Products Corp., 475 Smith Street, Middletown, CT 06457-1541 / 800-423-9704; FAX: 860-632-1699 lymansales@cshore.com www.lymanproducts.com

M

M.H. Canjar Co., 6510 Raleigh St., Arvada, CO 80003 / 303-295-2638; FAX: 303-295-2638
MA Systems, Inc., P.O. Box 894, Pryor, OK 74362-0894 / 918-824-3705; FAX: 918-824-3710
Mac-1 Airgun Distributors, 13974 Van Ness Ave., Gardena, CA 90249-2900 / 310-327-3581; FAX: 310-327-0238 mac1@maclairgun.com www.mac1airgun.com
Madis Books, 2453 West Five Mile Pkwy., Dallas, TX 75233 / 214-330-7168
Madis, George. See: GEORGE MADIS WINCHESTER CONSULTANTS
MAG Instrument, Inc., 1635 S. Sacramento Ave., Ontario, CA 91761 / 909-947-1006; FAX: 909-947-3116
Magma Engineering Co., P.O. Box 161, 20955 E. Ocotillo Rd., Queen Creek, AZ 85242 / 602-987-9008; FAX: 602-987-0148
Mag-Na-Port International, Inc., 41302 Executive Dr., Harrison Twp., MI 48045-1306 / 586-469-6727; FAX: 586-469-0425 email@magnaport.com www.magnaport.com
Magnolia Sports, Inc., 211 W. Main, Magnolia, AR 71753 / 501-234-8410; or 800-530-7816; FAX: 501-234-8117
Magnum Power Products, Inc., P.O. Box 17768, Fountain Hills, AZ 85268
Magnum Research, Inc., 7110 University Ave. NE, Minneapolis, MN 55432 / 800-772-6168 or 763-574-1868; FAX: 763-574-0109 info@magnumresearch.com
Magnus Bullets, P.O. Box 239, Toney, AL 35773 / 256-420-8359; FAX: 256-420-8360
Mag-Pack Corp., P.O. Box 846, Chesterland, OH 44026 / 440-285-9480 magpack@hotmail.com
MagSafe Ammo Co., 4700 S US Highway 17/92, Casselberry, FL 32707-3814 / 407-834-9966; FAX: 407-834-8185 www.magsafeonline.com
Magtech Ammunition Co. Inc., 6845 20th Ave. S., Ste. 120, Centerville, MN 55038
Mahony, Philip Bruce, 67 White Hollow Rd., Lime Rock, CT 06039-2418 / 203-435-9341 filbalony-redbeard@snet.net
Mahovsky's Metalife, R.D. 1, Box 149a Eureka Road, Grand Valley, PA 16420 / 814-436-7747
Maine Custom Bullets, RFD 1, Box 1755, Brooks, ME 04921
Makinson, Nicholas, RR 3, Komoka, ON N0L 1R0 CANADA / 519-471-5462
Mallardtone Game Calls, 10406 96th St., Court West, Taylor Ridge, IL 61284 / 309-798-2481; FAX: 309-798-2501
Mandall Shooting Supplies Inc., 3616 N. Scottsdale Rd., Scottsdale, AZ 85251 / 480-945-2553; FAX: 480-949-0734
Marble Arms (See CRR, Inc./Marble's Inc.)
Marchmon Bullets, 6502 Riverdale Rd., Whitmore Lake, MI 48189
Marent, Rudolf. See: HAMMERLI SERVICE-PRECISION MAC
Mark Lee Supplies, 9901 France Ct., Lakeville, MN 55044 / 952-461-2114; FAX: 952-461-2194 marklee55044@usfamily.net
Markell, Inc., 422 Larkfield Center 235, Santa Rosa, CA 95403 / 707-573-0792; FAX: 707-573-9867
Markesbery Muzzle Loaders, Inc., 7785 Foundation Dr., Ste. 6, Florence, KY 41042 / 606-342-5553 or 606-342-2380
Marksman Products, 5482 Argosy Dr., Huntington Beach, CA 92649 / 714-898-7535; or 800-822-8005; FAX: 714-891-0782
Marlin Firearms Co., 100 Kenna Dr., North Haven, CT 06473 / 203-239-5621; FAX: 203-234-7991 www.marlinfirearms.com
MarMik, Inc., 2116 S. Woodland Ave., Michigan City, IN 46360 / 219-872-7231; FAX: 219-872-7231
Marocchi F.lli S.p.A, Via Galileo Galilei 8, I-25068 Zanano, ITALY
Marquart Precision Co., P.O. Box 1740, Prescott, AZ 86302 / 520-445-5646
Marsh, Mike, Croft Cottage, Main St., Derbyshire, DE4 2BY ENGLAND / 01629 650 669
Marshall Enterprises, 792 Canyon Rd., Redwood City, CA 94062
Marshall Fish Mfg. Gunsmith Sptg. Co., Rd. Box 2439, Westport, NY 12993 / 518-962-4897; FAX: 518-962-4897
Martin B. Retting Inc., 11029 Washington, Culver City, CA 90232 / 213-837-2412
Martini & Hagn, 1264 Jimsmith Lake Rd, Cranbrook, BC V1C 6V6 CANADA / 250-417-2926; FAX: 250-417-2928
Martin's Gun Shop, 937 S. Sheridan Blvd., Lakewood, CO 80226 / 303-922-2184
Martz, John V., 8060 Lakeview Lane, Lincoln, CA 95648 FAX: 916-645-3815
Marvel, Alan, 3922 Madonna Rd., Jarretsville, MD 21084 / 301-557-6545
Marx, Harry (See U.S. Importer for FERLIB)
Maryland Paintball Supply, 8507 Harford Rd., Parkville, MD 21234 / 410-882-5607
MAST Technology, Inc., 14555 US Hwy. 95 S., P.O. Box 60969, Boulder City, NV 89006 / 702-293-6969; FAX: 702-293-7255 info@masttechnology.com www.bellammo.com
Master Lock Co., 2600 N. 32nd St., Milwaukee, WI 53245 / 414-444-2800
Match Prep-Doyle Gracey, P.O. Box 155, Tehachapi, CA 93581 / 661-822-5383; FAX: 661-823-8680
Mathews Gun Shop & Gunsmithing, Inc., 10224 S. Paramount Blvd., Downey, CA 90241 / 562-928-2129; FAX: 562-928-8629
Matthews Cutlery, 4401 Sentry Dr. #B, Tucker, GA 30084 / 770-939-6915
Mauser Werke Oberndorf Waffensysteme GmbH, Postfach 1349, 78722, Oberndorf/N., GERMANY
Maverick Arms, Inc., 7 Grasso Ave., P.O. Box 497, North Haven, CT 06473 / 203-230-5300; FAX: 203-230-5420
Maxi-Mount Inc., P.O. Box 291, Willoughby Hills, OH 44096-0291 / 440-944-9456; FAX: 440-944-9456 maximount454@yahoo.com
Mayville Engineering Co. (See MEC, Inc.)
Mazur Restoration, Pete, 13083 Drummer Way, Grass Valley, CA 95949 / 530-268-2412
McBros Rifle Co., P.O. Box 86549, Phoenix, AZ 85080 / 602-582-3713; FAX: 602-581-3825
McCament, Jay. See: JAY MCCAMENT CUSTOM GUNMAKER
McCann, Tom, 14 Walton Dr., New Hope, PA 18938 / 215-862-2728

MANUFACTURER'S DIRECTORY

McCann Industries, P.O. Box 641, Spanaway, WA 98387 / 253-537-6919; FAX: 253-537-6919 mccann.machine@worldnet.att.net www.mccannindustries.com
McCluskey Precision Rifles, 10502 14th Ave. NW, Seattle, WA 98177 / 206-781-2776
McCombs, Leo, 1862 White Cemetery Rd., Patriot, OH 45658 / 740-256-1714
McDonald, Dennis, 8359 Brady St., Peosta, IA 52068 / 319-556-7940
McFarland, Stan, 2221 Idella Ct., Grand Junction, CO 81505 / 970-243-4704
McGhee, Larry. See: B.C. OUTDOORS
McGowen Rifle Barrels, 5961 Spruce Lane, St. Anne, IL 60964 / 815-937-9816; FAX: 815-937-4024
Mchalik, Gary. See: ROSSI FIREARMS
McKenzie, Lynton, 6940 N. Alvernon Way, Tucson, AZ 85718 / 520-299-5090
McMillan Fiberglass Stocks, Inc., 1638 W. Knudsen Dr. #102, Phoenix, AZ 85027 / 623-582-9635; FAX: 623-581-3825 mfsinc@mcmfamily.com www.mcmfamily.com
McMillan Optical Gunsight Co., 28638 N. 42nd St., Cave Creek, AZ 85331 / 602-585-7868; FAX: 602-585-7872
McMillan Rifle Barrels, P.O. Box 3427, Bryan, TX 77805 / 409-690-3456; FAX: 409-690-0156
McMurdo, Lynn (See Specialty Gunsmithing), PO Box 404, Afton, WY 83110 / 307-886-5535
MCS, Inc., 166 Pocono Rd., Brookfield, CT 06804-2023 / 203-775-1013; FAX: 203-775-9462
McWelco Products, 6730 Santa Fe Ave., Hesperia, CA 92345 / 619-244-8876; FAX: 619-244-9398 products@mcwelco.com www.mawelco.com
MDS, P.O. Box 1441, Brandon, FL 33509-1441 / 813-653-1180; FAX: 813-684-5953
Measurement Group Inc., Box 27777, Raleigh, NC 27611
Measures, Leon. See: SHOOT WHERE YOU LOOK
MEC, Inc., 715 South St., Mayville, WI 53050 / 414-387-4500; FAX: 414-387-5802 reloaders@mayul.com www.mayvl.com
MEC-Gar S.R.L., Via Madonnina 64, Gardone V.T. Brescia, ITALY / 39-30-8912687; FAX: 39-30-8910065
MEC-Gar U.S.A., Inc., Hurley Farms Industr. Park, 115, Hurley Road 6G, Oxford, CT 06478 / 203-262-1525; FAX: 203-262-1719 mecgar@aol.com www.mec-gar.com
Mech-Tech Systems, Inc., 1602 Foothill Rd., Kalispell, MT 59901 / 406-755-8055
Meister Bullets (See Gander Mountain)
Mele, Frank, 201 S. Wellow Ave., Cookeville, TN 38501 / 615-526-4860
Menck, Gunsmith Inc., T.W., 5703 S 77th St., Ralston, NE 68127
Mendez, John A., P.O. Box 620984, Orlando, FL 32862 / 407-344-2791
Men-Metallwerk Elisenhuette GmbH, P.O. Box 1263, Nassau/Lahn, D-56372 GERMANY / 2604-7819
Meprolight (See Hesco-Meprolight)
Mercer Custom Guns, 216 S. Whitewater Ave., Jefferson, WI 53549 / 920-674-3839
Merit Corp., PO Box 9044, Schenectady, NY 12309 / 518-346-1420 sales@meritcorporation.com www.meritcorporation.com
Merkel, Schutzenstrasse 26, D-98527 Suhl, Suhl, GERMANY FAX: 011-49-3681-854-203 www.merkel-waffen.de
Merkuria Ltd., Argentinska 38, 17005, Praha 7, CZECH REPUBLIC / 422-875117; FAX: 422-809152
Metal Merchants, PO Box 186, Walled Lake, MI 48390-0186
Metalife Industries (See Mahovsky's Metalife)
Michael's Antiques, Box 591, Waldoboro, ME 04572
Michaels Of Oregon, Co., P.O. Box 1690, Oregon City, OR 97045 www.michaels-oregon.com
Micro Sight Co., 242 Harbor Blvd., Belmont, CA 94002 / 415-591-0769; FAX: 415-591-7531
Microfusion Alfa S.A., Paseo San Andres N8, P.O. Box 271, Eibar, 20600 SPAIN / 34-43-11-89-16; FAX: 34-43-11-40-38
Mid-America Recreation, Inc., 1328 5th Ave., Moline, IL 61265 / 309-764-5089; FAX: 309-764-5089 fmilcusguns@aol.com www.midamericarecreation.com
Middlebrooks Custom Shop, 7366 Colonial Trail East, Surry, VA 23883 / 757-357-0881; FAX: 757-365-0442
Midway Arms, Inc., 5875 W. Van Horn Tavern Rd., Columbia, MO 65203 / 800-243-3220; or 573-445-6363; FAX: 573-446-1018
Midwest Gun Sport, 1108 Herbert Dr., Zebulon, NC 27597 / 919-269-5570
Midwest Sport Distributors, Box 129, Fayette, MO 65248
Mike Davis Products, 643 Loop Dr., Moses Lake, WA 98837 / 509-765-6178; or 509-766-7281
Mike Yee Custom Stocking, 29927 56 Pl. S., Auburn, WA 98001 / 253-839-3991
Military Armament Corp., P.O. Box 120, Mt. Zion Rd., Lingleville, TX 76461 / 817-965-3253
Millennium Designed Muzzleloaders, PO Box 536, Routes 11 & 25, Limington, ME 04049 / 207-637-2316
Miller Arms, Inc., P.O. Box 260 Purl St., St. Onge, SD 57779 / 605-642-5160; FAX: 605-642-5160
Miller Custom, 210 E. Julia, Clinton, IL 61727 / 217-935-9362
Miller Single Trigger Mfg. Co., 6680 Rt. 5-20, P.O. Box 471, Bloomfield, NY 14469 / 585-657-6338
Millett Sights, 7275 Murdy Circle, Adm. Office, Huntington Beach, CA 92647 / 714-842-5575 or 800-645-5388; FAX: 714-843-5707
Mills Jr., Hugh B., 3615 Canterbury Rd., New Bern, NC 28560 / 919-637-4631
Milstor Corp., 80-975 Indio Blvd. C-7, Indio, CA 92201 / 760-775-9998; FAX: 760-775-5229 milstor@webtv.net
Minute Man High Tech Industries, 10611 Canyon Rd. E., Suite 151, Puyallup, WA 98373 / 800-233-2734
Mirador Optical Corp., P.O. Box 11614, Marina Del Rey, CA 90295-7614 / 310-821-5587; FAX: 310-305-0386
Mitchell, Jack, c/o Geoff Gaebe, Addieville East Farm, 200 Pheasant Dr., Mapleville, RI 02839 / 401-568-3185
Mitchell Bullets, R.F., 430 Walnut St., Westernport, MD 21562
Mitchell Mfg. Corp., P.O. Box 9295, Fountain Valley, CA 92728 / 714-444-2220
Mitchell Optics, Inc., 2072 CR 1100 N, Sidney, IL 61877 / 217-688-2219; or 217-621-3018; FAX: 217-688-2505 mitche1@attglobal.net
Mitchell's Accuracy Shop, 68 Greenridge Dr., Stafford, VA 22554 / 703-659-0165
Mitchell's Mauser, P.O. Box 9295, Fountain Valley, CA 92728 / 714-979-7663; FAX: 714-899-3660
MI-TE Bullets, 1396 Ave. K, Ellsworth, KS 67439 / 785-472-4575; FAX: 785-472-5579
Mittleman, William, P.O. Box 65, Etna, CA 96027
Mixson Corp., 7635 W. 28th Ave., Hialeah, FL 33016 / 305-821-5190; or 800-327-0078; FAX: 305-558-9318
MJK Gunsmithing, Inc., 417 N. Huber Ct., E. Wenatchee, WA 98802 / 509-884-7683
MKS Supply, Inc. (See Hi-Point Firearms)
MMC, 5050 E. Belknap St., Haltom City, TX 76117 / 817-831-9557; FAX: 817-834-5508
MOA Corporation, 2451 Old Camden Pike, Eaton, OH 45320 / 937-456-3669 www.moaguns
Modern Gun Repair School, PO Box 846, Saint Albans, VT 05478 / 802-524-2223; FAX: 802-524-2053 jfwp@dlilearn.com www.mgsinfoadlifearn.com
Modern Muzzleloading, Inc., P.O. Box 130, Centerville, IA 52544 / 515-856-2626
Moeller, Steve, 1213 4th St., Fulton, IL 61252 / 815-589-2300
Mogul Co./Life Jacket, 500 N. Kimball Rd., Ste. 109, South Lake, TX 76092
Molin Industries, Tru-Nord Division, P.O. Box 365, 204 North 9th St., Brainerd, MN 56401 / 218-829-2870
Monell Custom Guns, 228 Red Mills Rd., Pine Bush, NY 12566 / 914-744-3021
Moneymaker Guncraft Corp., 1420 Military Ave., Omaha, NE 68131 / 402-556-0226
Montana Armory, Inc. (See C. Sharps Arms Co. Inc.), 100 Centennial Dr., P.O. Box 885, Big Timber, MT 59011 / 406-932-4353; FAX: 406-932-4443
Montana Outfitters, Lewis E. Yearout, 308 Riverview Dr. E., Great Falls, MT 59404 / 406-761-0859; or 406-727-4560
Montana Precision Swaging, P.O. Box 4746, Butte, MT 59702 / 406-494-0600; FAX: 406-494-0600
Montana Rifleman, Inc., 2593A Hwy. 2 East, Kalispell, MT 59901 / 406-755-4867
Montana Vintage Arms, 2354 Bear Canyon Rd., Bozeman, MT 59715
Morini (See U.S. Importers-Mandall Shooting Supply)
Morrison Custom Rifles, J. W., 4015 W Sharon, Phoenix, AZ 85029 / 602-978-3754
Morrison Precision, 6719 Calle Mango, Hereford, AZ 85615 / 520-378-6207 morprec@c2i2.com
Morrow, Bud, 11 Hillside Lane, Sheridan, WY 82801-9729 / 307-674-8360
Morton Booth Co., P.O. Box 123, Joplin, MO 64802 / 417-673-1962; FAX: 417-673-3642
Mo's Competitor Supplies (See MCS, Inc.)
Moss Double Tone, Inc., P.O. Box 1112, 2101 S. Kentucky, Sedalia, MO 65301 / 816-827-0827
Mountain Plains Industries, 3720 Otter Place, Lynchburg, VA 24503 / 800-687-3000; FAX: 434-845-6594 mpitargets@cstone.net
Mountain State Muzzleloading Supplies, Inc., Box 154-1, Rt. 2, Williamstown, WV 26187 / 304-375-7842; FAX: 304-375-3737
Mowrey Gun Works, P.O. Box 246, Waldron, IN 46182 / 317-525-6181; FAX: 317-525-9595
Mowrey's Guns & Gunsmithing, 119 Fredericks St., Canajoharie, NY 13317 / 518-673-3483
MPC, P.O. Box 450, McMinnville, TN 37110-0450 / 615-473-5513; FAX: 615-473-5516 thebox@blomand.net www.mpc-thebox.com
MPI Stocks, PO Box 83266, Portland, OR 97283 / 503-226-1215; FAX: 503-226-2661
MSR Targets, P.O. Box 1042, West Covina, CA 91793 / 818-331-7840
MTM Molded Products Co., Inc., 3370 Obco Ct., Dayton, OH 45414 / 937-890-7461; FAX: 937-890-1747
Mulberry House Publishing, P.O. Box 2180, Apache Junction, AZ 85217 / 888-738-1567; FAX: 480-671-1015
Mulhern, Rick, Rt. 5, Box 152, Rayville, LA 71269 / 318-728-2688
Mullins Ammunition, Rt. 2 Box 304N, Clintwood, VA 24228 / 276-926-6772; FAX: 276-926-6092 mammo@extremeshockusa.com www.extremeshockusa
Mullis Guncraft, 3523 Lawyers Road E., Monroe, NC 28110 / 704-283-6683
Multiplex International, 26 S. Main St., Concord, NH 03301 FAX: 603-796-2223
Multipropulseurs, La Bertrandiere, 42580, FRANCE / 77 74 01 30; FAX: 77 93 19 34
Mundy, Thomas A., 69 Robbins Road, Somerville, NJ 08876 / 201-722-2199
Murmur Corp., 2823 N. Westmoreland Ave., Dallas, TX 75222 / 214-630-5400
Murphy, R.R. Murphy Co., Inc. See: MURPHY, R.R. CO., INC.
Murphy, R.R. Co., Inc., R.R. Murphy Co., Inc. Murphy, P.O. Box 102, Ripley, TN 38063 / 901-635-4003; FAX: 901-635-2320
Murray State College, 1 Murray Campus St., Tishomingo, OK 73460 / 508-371-2371 darnold@mscok.edu
Muscle Products Corp., 112 Fennell Dr., Butler, PA 16002 / 800-227-7049; or 724-283-0567; FAX: 724-283-8310 mpc@mpc_home.com www.mpc_home.com
Muzzleloaders Etcetera, Inc., 9901 Lyndale Ave. S., Bloomington, MN 55420 / 952-884-1161 www.muzzleloaders-etcetera.com
MWG Co., P.O. Box 971202, Miami, FL 33197 / 800-428-9394; or 305-253-8393; FAX: 305-232-1247

N

N.B.B., Inc., 24 Elliot Rd., Sterling, MA 01564 / 508-422-7538; or 800-942-9444
N.C. Ordnance Co., P.O. Box 3254, Wilson, NC 27895 / 919-237-2440; FAX: 919-243-9845
Nagel's Custom Bullets, 100 Scott St., Baytown, TX 77520-2849
Nalpak, 1937-C Friendship Drive, El Cajon, CA 92020 / 619-258-1200
Nastoff, Steve. See: NASTOFFS 45 SHOP, INC.
Nastoffs 45 Shop, Inc., Steve Nastoff, 1057 Laverne Dr., Youngstown, OH 44511
National Bullet Co., 1585 E. 361 St., Eastlake, OH 44095 / 216-951-1854; FAX: 216-951-7761
National Target Co., 4690 Wyaconda Rd., Rockville, MD 20852 / 800-827-7060 or 301-770-7060; FAX: 301-770-7892
Nationwide Airgun Repair, 2310 Windsor Forest Dr., Louisville, KY 40272 / 502-937-2614; FAX: 812-637-1463 shortshoestring@insightbb.com
Naval Ordnance Works, Rt. 2, Box 919, Sheperdstown, WV 25443 / 304-876-0998
Navy Arms Co., 219 Lawn St., Martinsburg, WV 25401 / 304-262-9870; FAX: 304-262-1658
Navy Arms Company, Valmore J. Forgett Jr., 815 22nd Street, Union City, NJ 07087 / 201-863-7100; FAX: 201-863-8770 info@navyarms.com www.navyarms.com
NCP Products, Inc., 3500 12th St. N.W., Canton, OH 44708 / 330-456-5130; FAX: 330-456-5234
Necessary Concepts, Inc., P.O. Box 571, Deer Park, NY 11729 / 516-667-8509; FAX: 516-667-8588
NEI Handtools, Inc., 10960 Gary Player Dr., El Paso, TX 79935
Neil A. Jones Custom Products, 17217 Brookhouser Road, Saegertown, PA 16433 / 814-763-2769; FAX: 814-763-4228
Nelson, Gary K., 975 Terrace Dr., Oakdale, CA 95361 / 209-847-4590

MANUFACTURER'S DIRECTORY

Nelson, Stephen. See: NELSON'S CUSTOM GUNS, INC.
Nelson's Custom Guns, Inc., Stephen Nelson, 7430 Valley View Dr. N.W., Corvallis, OR 97330 / 541-745-5232 nelsons-custom@attbi.com
Nesci Enterprises Inc., P.O. Box 119, Summit St., East Hampton, CT 06424 / 203-267-2588
Nesika Bay Precision, 22239 Big Valley Rd., Poulsbo, WA 98370 / 206-697-3830
Nettestad Gun Works, 38962 160th Avenue, Pelican Rapids, MN 56572 / 218-863-4301
Neumann GmbH, Am Galgenberg 6, 90575, GERMANY / 09101/8258; FAX: 09101/6356
Nevada Pistol Academy, Inc., 4610 Blue Diamond Rd., Las Vegas, NV 89139 / 702-897-1100
New England Ammunition Co., 1771 Post Rd. East, Suite 223, Westport, CT 06880 / 203-254-8048
New England Arms Co., Box 278, Lawrence Lane, Kittery Point, ME 03905 / 207-439-0593; FAX: 207-439-0525 info@newenglandarms.com www.newenglandarms.com
New England Custom Gun Service, 438 Willow Brook Rd., Plainfield, NH 03781 / 603-469-3450; FAX: 603-469-3471 bestguns@cyborportal.net www.newenglandcustom.com
New Orleans Jewelers Supply Co., 206 Charters St., New Orleans, LA 70130 / 504-523-3839; FAX: 504-523-3836
New SKB Arms Co., C.P.O. Box 1401, Tokyo, JAPAN / 81-3-3943-9550; FAX: 81-3-3943-0695
New Ultra Light Arms, LLC, P.O. Box 340, Granville, WV 26534
Newark Electronics, 4801 N. Ravenswood Ave., Chicago, IL 60640
Newell, Robert H., 55 Coyote, Los Alamos, NM 87544 / 505-662-7135
Newman Gunshop, 2035 Chester Ave. #411, Ottumwa, IA 52501-3715 / 515-937-5775
Nicholson Custom, 17285 Thornlay Road, Hughesville, MO 65334 / 816-826-8746
Nickels, Paul R., 4328 Seville St., Las Vegas, NV 89121 / 702-435-5318
Nicklas, Ted, 5504 Hegel Rd., Goodrich, MI 48438 / 810-797-4493
Niemi Engineering, W. B., Box 126 Center Rd., Greensboro, VT 05841 / 802-533-7180; FAX: 802-533-7141
Nikon, Inc., 1300 Walt Whitman Rd., Melville, NY 11747 / 516-547-8623; FAX: 516-547-0309
Nitex Gun Shop, P.O. Box 1706, Uvalde, TX 78801 / 830-278-8843
Noreen, Peter H., 5075 Buena Vista Dr., Belgrade, MT 59714 / 406-586-7383
Norica, Avnda Otaola, 16 Apartado 68, Eibar, SPAIN
Norinco, 7A Yun Tan N, Beijing, CHINA
Norincoptics (See BEC, Inc.)
Norma Precision AB (See U.S. Importers-Dynamit)
Normark Corp., 10395 Yellow Circle Dr., Minnetonka, MN 55343-9101 / 612-933-7060; FAX: 612-933-0046
North American Arms, Inc., 2150 South 950 East, Provo, UT 84606-6285 / 800-821-5783; or 801-374-9990; FAX: 801-374-9998
North American Correspondence Schools The Gun Pro, Oak & Pawney St., Scranton, PA 18515 / 717-342-7701
North American Shooting Systems, P.O. Box 306, Osoyoos, BC V0H 1V0 CANADA / 250-495-3131; FAX: 250-495-3131 rifle@cablerocket.com
North Devon Firearms Services, 3 North St., Braunton, EX33 1AJ ENGLAND / 01271 813624; FAX: 01271 813624
North Mountain Pine Training Center (See Executive
North Star West, P.O. Box 488, Glencoe, CA 95232 / 209-293-7010 northstarwest.com
Northern Precision, 329 S. James St., Carthage, NY 13619 / 315-493-1711
Northlake Outdoor Footwear, P.O. Box 10, Franklin, TN 37065-0010 / 615-794-1556; FAX: 615-790-8005
Northside Gun Shop, 2725 NW 109th, Oklahoma City, OK 73120 / 405-840-2353
Northwest Arms, 26884 Pearl Rd., Parma, ID 83660 / 208-722-6771; FAX: 208-722-1062
No-Sho Mfg. Co., 10727 Glenfield Ct., Houston, TX 77096 / 713-723-5332
Nosler, Inc., P.O. Box 671, Bend, OR 97709 / 800-285-3701; or 541-382-3921; FAX: 541-388-4667 www.nosler.com
Novak's, Inc., 1206 1/2 30th St., P.O. Box 4045, Parkersburg, WV 26101 / 304-485-9295; FAX: 304-428-6722
Nowlin Mfg. Co., 20622 S 4092 Rd., Claremore, OK 74017 / 918-342-0689; FAX: 918-342-0624 nowlinguns@msn.com nowlinguns.com
NRI Gunsmith School, P.O. Box 182968, Columbus, OH 43218-2968
Nu-Line Guns,Inc., 1053 Caulks Hill Rd., Harvester, MO 63304 / 314-441-4500; or 314-447-4501; FAX: 314-447-5018
Null Holsters Ltd. K.L., 161 School St NW, Resaca, GA 30735 / 706-625-5643; FAX: 706-625-9392
Numrich Gun Parts Corporation, 226 Williams Lane, P.O. Box 299, West Hurley, NY 12491 / 866-686-7424; FAX: 877-GUNPART info@gunpartscorp.com www.@-gunparts.com
Nygord Precision Products, Inc., P.O. Box 12578, Prescott, AZ 86304 / 928-717-2315; FAX: 928-717-2198 nygords@northlink.com www.nygordprecision.com

O

O.F. Mossberg & Sons, Inc., 7 Grasso Ave., North Haven, CT 06473 / 203-230-5300; FAX: 203-230-5420
Oakman Turkey Calls, RD 1, Box 825, Harrisonville, PA 17228 / 717-485-4620
Obermeyer Rifled Barrels, 23122 60th St., Bristol, WI 53104 / 262-843-3537; FAX: 262-843-2129
October Country Muzzleloading, P.O. Box 969, Dept. GD, Hayden, ID 83835 / 208-772-2068; FAX: 208-772-9230 ocinfo@octobercountry.com www.octobercountry.com
Oehler Research, Inc., P.O. Box 9135, Austin, TX 78766 / 512-327-6900; or 800-531-5125; FAX: 512-327-6903 www.oehler-research.com
Oil Rod and Gun Shop, 69 Oak St., East Douglas, MA 01516 / 508-476-3687
OK Weber, Inc., P.O. Box 7485, Eugene, OR 97401 / 541-747-0458; FAX: 541-747-5927 okweber@pacinfo www.okweber.com
Oker's Engraving, P.O. Box 126, Shawnee, CO 80475 / 303-838-6042
Oklahoma Ammunition Co., 3701A S. Harvard Ave., No. 367, Tulsa, OK 74135-2265 / 918-396-3187; FAX: 918-396-4270
Oklahoma Leather Products, Inc., 500 26th NW, Miami, OK 74354 / 918-542-6651; FAX: 918-542-6653
Olathe Gun Shop, 716-A South Rogers Road, Olathe, KS 66062 / 913-782-6900; FAX: 913-782-6902 info@olathegunshop.com www.olathegunshop.com
Old Wagon Bullets, 32 Old Wagon Rd., Wilton, CT 06897
Old West Bullet Moulds, J Ken Chapman, P.O. Box 519, Flora Vista, NM 87415 / 505-334-6970
Old West Reproductions, Inc. R.M. Bachman, 446 Florence S. Loop, Florence, MT 59833 / 406-273-2615; FAX: 406-273-2615 rick@oldwestreproductions.com www.oldwestreproductions.com
Old Western Scrounger Ammunition Inc., 50 Industrial Parkway, Carson City, NV 89706 / 775-246-2091; FAX: 775-246-2095 www.ows-ammunition.com
Old World Gunsmithing, 2901 SE 122nd St., Portland, OR 97236 / 503-760-7681
Old World Oil Products, 3827 Queen Ave. N., Minneapolis, MN 55412 / 612-522-5037
Ole Frontier Gunsmith Shop, 2617 Hwy. 29 S., Cantonment, FL 32533 / 904-477-8074
Olson, Myron, 989 W. Kemp, Watertown, SD 57201 / 605-886-9787
Olson, Vic, 5002 Countryside Dr., Imperial, MO 63052 / 314-296-8086
Olympic Arms Inc., 620-626 Old Pacific Hwy. SE, Olympia, WA 98513 / 360-456-3471; FAX: 360-491-3447 info@olyarms.com www.olyarms.com
Olympic Optical Co., P.O. Box 752377, Memphis, TN 38175-2377 / 901-794-3890; or 800-238-7120; FAX: 901-794-0676 80
Omega Sales, P.O. Box 1066, Mt. Clemens, MI 48043 / 810-469-7323; FAX: 810-469-0425
100 Straight Products, Inc., P.O. Box 6148, Omaha, NE 68106 / 402-556-1055; FAX: 402-556-1055
One Of A Kind, 15610 Purple Sage, San Antonio, TX 78255 / 512-695-3364
One Ragged Hole, P.O. Box 13624, Tallahassee, FL 32317-3624
Op-Tec, P.O. Box L632, Langhorn, PA 19047 / 215-757-5037; FAX: 215-757-7097
Optical Services Co., P.O. Box 1174, Santa Teresa, NM 88008-1174 / 505-589-3833
Orchard Park Enterprise, P.O. Box 563, Orchard Park, NY 14127 / 616-656-0356
Oregon Arms, Inc. (See Rogue Rifle Co., Inc.)
Oregon Trail Bullet Company, PO Box 529, Dept. P, Baker City, OR 97814 / 800-811-0548; FAX: 514-523-1803
Original Box, Inc., 700 Linden Ave., York, PA 17404 / 717-854-2897; FAX: 717-845-4276
Original Deer Formula Co., The, P.O. Box 1705, Dickson, TN 37056 / 800-874-6965; FAX: 615-446-0646 deerformula1@aol.com www.deerformula
Orion Rifle Barrel Co., RR2, 137 Cobler Village, Kalispell, MT 59901 / 406-257-5649
Otis Technology, Inc., RR 1 Box 84, Boonville, NY 13309 / 315-942-3320
Ottmar, Maurice, Box 657, 113 E. Fir, Coulee City, WA 99115 / 509-632-5717
Outa-Site Gun Carriers, 219 Market St., Laredo, TX 78040 / 210-722-4678; or 800-880-9715; FAX: 210-726-4858
Outdoor Edge Cutlery Corp., 4699 Nautilus Ct. S. Ste. 503, Boulder, CO 80301-5310 / 303-652-8212; FAX: 303-652-8238
Outdoor Enthusiast, 3784 W. Woodland, Springfield, MO 65807 / 417-883-9841
Outdoor Sports Headquarters, Inc., 967 Watertower Ln., West Carrollton, OH 45449 / 513-865-5855; FAX: 513-865-5962
Outers Laboratories Div. of ATK, Route 2, P.O. Box 39, Onalaska, WI 54650 / 608-781-5800; FAX: 608-781-0368
Ox-Yoke Originals, Inc., 34 Main St., Milo, ME 04463 / 800-231-8313; or 207-943-7351; FAX: 207-943-2416
Ozark Gun Works, 11830 Cemetery Rd., Rogers, AR 72756 / 479-631-1024; FAX: 479-631-1024 ogw@hotmail.com www.eocities.com/ocarkgunworks

P

P&M Sales & Services, LLC, 4697 Tote Rd. Bldg. H-B, Comins, MI 48619 / 989-848-8364; FAX: 989-848-8364 info@pmsales-online.com
P.A.C.T., Inc., P.O. Box 531525, Grand Prairie, TX 75053 / 214-641-0049
P.S.M.G. Gun Co., 10 Park Ave., Arlington, MA 02174 / 781-646-1699; FAX: 781-643-7212 psmg2@aol.com
Pachmayr Div. Lyman Products, 475 Smith St., Middletown, CT 06457 / 860-632-2020; or 800-225-9626; FAX: 860-632-1699 lymansales@cshore.com www.pachmayr.com
Pacific Armament Corp, 4813 Enterprise Way, Unit K, Modesto, CA 95356 / 209-545-2800 gunsparts@att.net
Pacific Rifle Co., P.O. Box 841, Carlton, OR 97111 / 503-852-6276 pacificrifle@aol.com
PAC-NOR Barreling, 99299 Overlook Rd., P.O. Box 6188, Brookings, OR 97415 / 503-469-7330; FAX: 503-469-7331 info@pac-nor.com www.pac-nor.com
Paco's (See Small Custom Mould & Bullet Co.)
Page Custom Bullets, P.O. Box 25, Port Moresby, NEW GUINEA
Pagel Gun Works, Inc., 2 SE 1st St., Grand Rapids, MN 55744
Pager Pal, 200 W Pleasantview, Hurst, TX 76054 / 800-561-1603; FAX: 817-285-8769 www.pagerpal.com
Paintball Games International Magazine Aceville, Castle House 97 High St., Essex, ENGLAND / 011-44-206-564840
Palsa Outdoor Products, P.O. Box 81336, Lincoln, NE 68501 / 402-488-5288; FAX: 402-488-2321
Pansch, Robert F, 1004 Main St. #10, Neenah, WI 54956 / 920-725-8175
Paragon Sales & Services, Inc., 2501 Theodore St., Crest Hill, IL 60435-1613 / 815-725-9212; FAX: 815-725-8974
Para-Ordnance Mfg., Inc., 980 Tapscott Rd., Scarborough, ON M1X 1E7 CANADA / 416-297-7855; FAX: 416-297-1289
Para-Ordnance, Inc., 1919 NE 45th St., Ste 215, Ft. Lauderdale, FL 33308 info@paraord.com www.paraord.com
Pardini Armi Srl, Via Italica 154, 55043, Lido Di Camaiore Lu, ITALY / 584-90121; FAX: 584-90122
Paris, Frank J., 17417 Pershing St., Livonia, MI 48152-3822
Parker & Sons Shooting Supply, 9337 Smoky Row Road, Strawberry Plains, TN 37871 / 865-933-3286; FAX: 865-932-8586
Parker Gun Finishes, 9337 Smokey Row Rd., Strawberry Plains, TN 37871 / 865-933-3286; FAX: 865-932-8586
Parsons Optical Mfg. Co., PO Box 192, Ross, OH 45061 / 513-867-0820; FAX: 513-867-8380 psscopes@concentric.net
Partridge Sales Ltd., John, Trent Meadows, Rugeley, ENGLAND
Pasadena Gun Center, 206 E. Shaw, Pasadena, TX 77506 / 713-472-0417; FAX: 713-472-1322
Passive Bullet Traps, Inc. (See Savage Range Systems, Inc.)
Paterson Gunsmithing, 438 Main St., Paterson, NJ 07502 / 201-345-4100

MANUFACTURER'S DIRECTORY

Pathfinder Sports Leather, 2920 E. Chambers St., Phoenix, AZ 85040 / 602-276-0016
Patrick W. Price Bullets, 16520 Worthley Drive, San Lorenzo, CA 94580 / 510-278-1547
Pattern Control, 114 N. Third St., P.O. Box 462105, Garland, TX 75046 / 214-494-3551; FAX: 214-272-8447
Paul A. Harris Hand Engraving, 113 Rusty Lane, Boerne, TX 78006-5746 / 512-391-5121
Paul and Sharon Dressel, 209 N. 92nd Ave., Yakima, WA 98908 / 509-966-9233; FAX: 509-966-3365 dressels@nwinfo.net www.dressels.com
Paul D. Hillmer Custom Gunstocks, 7251 Hudson Heights, Hudson, IA 50643 / 319-988-3941
Paul Jones Moulds, 4901 Telegraph Rd., Los Angeles, CA 90022 / 213-262-1510
Paulsen Gunstocks, Rt. 71, Box 11, Chinook, MT 59523 / 406-357-3403
Pawling Mountain Club, Keith Lupton, PO Box 573, Pawling, NY 12564 / 914-855-3825
Paxton Quigley's Personal Protection Strategies, 9903 Santa Monica Blvd., 300, Beverly Hills, CA 90212 / 310-281-1762 www.defend-net.com/paxton
Payne Photography, Robert, Robert, P.O. Box 141471, Austin, TX 78714 / 512-272-4554
Peacemaker Specialists, P.O. Box 157, Whitmore, CA 96096 / 530-472-3438 www.peacemakerspecialists.com
Pearce Grip, Inc., P.O. Box 40367, Fort Worth, TX 76140 / 817-568-9704; FAX: 817-568-9707 info@pearcegrip.com www.pearcegrip.com
Pease Accuracy, Bob, P.O. Box 310787, New Braunfels, TX 78131 / 210-625-1342
PECAR Herbert Schwarz GmbH, Kreuzbergstrasse 6, 10965, Berlin, GERMANY / 004930-785-7383; FAX: 004930-785-1934 michael.schwart@pecar-berlin.de www.pecar-berlin.de
Pecatonica River Longrifle, 5205 Nottingham Dr., Rockford, IL 61111 / 815-968-1995; FAX: 815-968-1996
Pedersen, C. R., 2717 S. Pere Marquette Hwy., Ludington, MI 49431 / 231-843-2061; FAX: 231-845-7695 fega@fega.com
Pedersen, Rex C., 2717 S. Pere Marquette Hwy., Ludington, MI 49431 / 231-843-2061; FAX: 231-845-7695 fega@fega.com
Peifer Rifle Co., P.O. Box 220, Nokomis, IL 62075
Pejsa Ballistics, 1314 Marquette Ave., Apt 906, Minneapolis, MN 55403 / 612-332-5073; FAX: 612-332-5204 pejsa@sprintmail.com pejsa.com
Pelaire Products, 5346 Bonky Ct., W. Palm Beach, FL 33415 / 561-439-0691; FAX: 561-967-0052
Peltor, Inc. (See Aero Peltor)
PEM's Mfg. Co., 5063 Waterloo Rd., Atwater, OH 44201 / 216-947-3721
Pence Precision Barrels, 7567 E. 900 S., S. Whitley, IN 46787 / 219-839-4745
Pendleton Royal, c/o Swingler Buckland Ltd., 4/7 Highgate St., Birmingham, ENGLAND / 44 121 440 3060; or 44 121 446 5898; FAX: 44 121 446 4165
Pendleton Woolen Mills, P.O. Box 3030, 220 N.W. Broadway, Portland, OR 97208 / 503-226-4801
Penn Bullets, P.O. Box 756, Indianola, PA 15051
Pennsylvania Gun Parts Inc., RR 7 Box 150, Mount Pleasant, PA 15666
Pennsylvania Gunsmith School, 812 Ohio River Blvd., Avalon, Pittsburgh, PA 15202 / 412-766-1812; FAX: 412-766-0855 pgs@pagunsmith.com www.pagunsmith.com
Penrod Precision, 312 College Ave., P.O. Box 307, N. Manchester, IN 46962 / 260-982-8385; FAX: 260-982-1819
Pentax Corp., 35 Inverness Dr. E., Englewood, CO 80112 / 303-799-8000; FAX: 303-790-1131
Pentheny de Pentheny, c/o H.P. Okelly, 321 S. Main St., Sebastopol, CA 95472 / 707-824-1637; FAX: 707-824-1637
Perazone-Gunsmith, Brian, Cold Spring Rd., Roxbury, NY 12474 / 607-326-4088; FAX: 607-326-3140 bpgunsmith@catskill.net www.bpgunsmith@catskill.net
Perazzi U.S.A. Inc., 1010 West Tenth, Azusa, CA 91702 / 626-334-1234; FAX: 626-334-0344 perazziusa@aol.com
Performance Specialists, 308 Eanes School Rd., Austin, TX 78746 / 512-327-0119
Perugini Visini & Co. S.r.l., Via Camprelle, 126, 25080 Nuvolera, ITALY / 30-6897535; FAX: 30-6897821 peruvisi@virgilia.it
Pete de Coux Auction House, HC 30 Box 932 G, Prescott, AZ 86305-7447 / 928-776-8285; FAX: 928-776-8276 pdbullets@commspeed.net
Pete Mazur Restoration, 13083 Drummer Way, Grass Valley, CA 95949 / 530-268-2412; FAX: 530-268-2412
Pete Rickard, Inc., 115 Roy Walsh Rd, Cobleskill, NY 12043 / 518-234-2731: FAX: 518-234-2454 rickard@telenet.net www.peterickard.com
Peter Dyson & Son Ltd., 3 Cuckoo Lane, Honley, Holmfirth, Yorkshire, HD9 6AS ENGLAND / 44-1484-661062; FAX: 44-1484-663709 peter@peterdyson.co.uk www.peterdyson.co.uk
Peter Hale/Engraver, 800 E. Canyon Rd., Spanish Fork, UT 84660 / 801-798-8215
Peters Stahl GmbH, Stettiner Strasse 42, D-33106, Paderborn, GERMANY / 05251-750025; FAX: 05251-75611
Peterson Gun Shop, Inc., A.W., 4255 W. Old U.S. 441, Mt. Dora, FL 32757-3299 / 352-383-4258; FAX: 352-735-1001
Petro-Explo Inc., 7650 U.S. Hwy. 287, Suite 100, Arlington, TX 76017 / 817-478-8888
Pettinger Books, Gerald, 47827 300th Ave., Russell, IA 50238 / 641-535-2239 gpettinger@lisco.com
Pflumm Mfg. Co., 10662 Widmer Rd., Lenexa, KS 66215 / 800-888-4867; FAX: 913-451-7857
PFRB Co., P.O. Box 1242, Bloomington, IL 61702 / 309-473-3964; or 800-914-5464; FAX: 309-473-2161
Philip S. Olt Co., P.O. Box 550, 12662 Fifth St., Pekin, IL 61554 / 309-348-3633; FAX: 309-348-3300
Phillippi Custom Bullets, Justin, P.O. Box 773, Ligonier, PA 15658 / 724-238-2962; FAX: 724-238-9671 jrp@wpa.net http://www.wpa.net~jrphil
Phillips & Rogers, Inc., 100 Hilbig #C, Conroe, TX 77301 / 409-435-0011
Phoenix Arms, 4231 Brickell St., Ontario, CA 91761 / 909-937-6900; FAX: 909-937-0060
Photronic Systems Engineering Company, 6731 Via De La Reina, Bonsall, CA 92003 / 619-758-8000
Piedmont Community College, P.O. Box 1197, Roxboro, NC 27573 / 336-599-1181; FAX: 336-597-3817 www.piedmont.cc.nc.us
Pierce Pistols, 55 Sorrellwood Lane, Sharpsburg, GA 30277-9523 / 404-253-8192
Pietta (See U.S. Importers-Navy Arms Co, Taylor's
Pilgrim Pewter, Inc. (See Bell Originals Inc. Sid)
Pilkington, Scott (See Little Trees Ramble)
Pine Technical College, 1100 4th St., Pine City, MN 55063 / 800-521-7463; FAX: 612-629-6766
Pinetree Bullets, 133 Skeena St., Kitimat, BC V8C 1Z1 CANADA / 604-632-3768; FAX: 604-632-3768
Pioneer Arms Co., 355 Lawrence Rd., Broomall, PA 19008 / 215-356-5203
Piotti (See U.S. Importer-Moore & Co., Wm. Larkin)
Piquette, Paul. See: PIQUETTE'S CUSTOM ENGRAVING
Piquette's Custom Engraving, Paul R. Piquette, 80 Bradford Dr., Feeding Hills, MA 01030 / 413-789-4582; FAX: 413-786-8118 ppiquette@aol.com www.pistoldynamics.com
Plaza Cutlery, Inc., 3333 Bristol, 161 South Coast Plaza, Costa Mesa, CA 92626 / 714-549-3932
Plum City Ballistic Range, N2162 80th St., Plum City, WI 54761 / 715-647-2539
PlumFire Press, Inc., 30-A Grove Ave., Patchogue, NY 11772-4112 / 800-695-7246; FAX: 516-758-4071
PMC/Eldorado Cartridge Corp., P.O. Box 62508, 12801 U.S. Hwy. 95 S., Boulder City, NV 89005 / 702-294-0025; FAX: 702-294-0121 kbauer@pmcammo.com www.pmcammo.com
Poburka, Philip (See Bison Studios)
Pointing Dog Journal, Village Press Publications, P.O. Box 968, Dept. PGD, Traverse City, MI 49685 / 800-272-3246; FAX: 616-946-3289
Police Bookshelf, PO Box 122, Concord, NH 03301 / 603-224-6814; FAX: 603-226-3554
Polywad, Inc., P.O. Box 7916, Macon, GA 31209 / 478-477-0669; or 800-998-0669 FAX: 478-477-0666 polywadmpb@aol.com www.polywad.com
Ponsness/Warren, 768 Ohio St., Rathdrum, ID 83858 / 800-732-0706; FAX: 208-687-2233
Pony Express Reloaders, 608 E. Co. Rd. D, Suite 3, St. Paul, MN 55117 / 612-483-9406; FAX: 612-483-9884
Pony Express Sport Shop, 23404 Lyons Ave., PMB 448, Newhall, CA 91321-2511 / 818-895-1231
Potts, Wayne E., 912 Poplar St., Denver, CO 80220 / 303-355-5462
Powder Horn Ltd., PO Box 565, Glenview, IL 60025 / 305-565-6060
Powell & Son (Gunmakers) Ltd., William, 35-37 Carrs Lane, Birmingham, B4 7SX ENGLAND / 121-643-0689; FAX: 121-631-3504 sales@william-powell.co.uk www.william-powell.co.uk
Powell Agency, William, 22 Circle Dr., Bellmore, NY 11710 / 516-679-1158
Power Custom, Inc., 29739 Hwy. J, Gravois Mills, MO 65037 / 573-372-5684; FAX: 573-372-5799 rwpowers@laurie.net www.powercustom.com
Power Plus Enterprises, Inc., PO Box 38, Warm Springs, GA 31830 / 706-655-2132
Powley Computer (See Hutton Rifle Ranch)
Practical Tools, Inc., 7067 Easton Rd., P.O. Box 133, Pipersville, PA 18947 / 215-766-7301; FAX: 215-766-8681
Prairie Gun Works, 1-761 Marion St., Winnipeg, MB R2J 0K6 CANADA / 204-231-2976; FAX: 204-231-8566
Prairie River Arms, 1220 N. Sixth St., Princeton, IL 61356 / 815-875-1616; or 800-445-1541; FAX: 815-875-1402
Pranger, Ed G., 1414 7th St., Anacortes, WA 98221 / 206-293-3488
Precision Airgun Sales, Inc., 5247 Warrensville Ctr Rd., Maple Hts., OH 44137 / 216-587-5005; FAX: 216-587-5005
Precision Cast Bullets, 101 Mud Creek Lane, Ronan, MT 59864 / 406-676-5135
Precision Delta Corp., PO Box 128, Ruleville, MS 38771 / 662-756-2810; FAX: 662-756-2590
Precision Firearm Finishing, 25 N.W. 44th Avenue, Des Moines, IA 50313 / 515-288-8680; FAX: 515-244-3925
Precision Gun Works, 104 Sierra Rd., Dept. GD, Kerrville, TX 78028 / 830-367-4587
Precision Reloading, Inc., P.O. Box 122, Stafford Springs, CT 06076 / 860-684-7979; FAX: 860-684-6788 info@precisionreloading.com www.precisionreloading.com
Precision Sales International, Inc., PO Box 1776, Westfield, MA 01086 / 413-562-5055; FAX: 413-562-5056 precision-sales.com
Precision Shooting, Inc., 222 McKee St., Manchester, CT 06040 / 860-645-8776; FAX: 860-643-8215 www.theaccuraterifle.com
Precision Small Arms Inc., 9272 Jeronimo Rd, Ste 121, Irvine, CA 92618 / 800-554-5515; or 949-768-3530; FAX: 949-768-4808 www.tcbebe.com
Precision Specialties, 131 Hendom Dr., Feeding Hills, MA 01030 / 413-786-3365; FAX: 413-786-3365
Precision Sport Optics, 15571 Producer Lane, Unit G, Huntington Beach, CA 92649 / 714-891-1309; FAX: 714-892-6920
Premier Reticles, 920 Breckinridge Lane, Winchester, VA 22601-6707 / 540-722-0601; FAX: 540-722-3522
Prescott Projectile Co., 1808 Meadowbrook Road, Prescott, AZ 86303
Preslik's Gunstocks, 4245 Keith Ln., Chico, CA 95926 / 916-891-8236
Price Bullets, Patrick W., 16520 Worthley Dr., San Lorenzo, CA 94580 / 510-278-1547
Prime Reloading, 30 Chiswick End, Meldreth, ROYSTON UK / 0763-260636
Primedia Publishing Co., 6420 Wilshire Blvd., Los Angeles, CA 90048 / 213-782-2000; FAX: 213-782-2867
Primos Hunting Calls, 4436 North State St., Ste. A-7, Jackson, MS 39206 / 601-366-1288; FAX: 601-362-3274 www.primos.com
PRL Bullets, c/o Blackburn Enterprises, 114 Stuart Rd., Ste. 110, Cleveland, TN 37312 / 423-559-0340
Pro Load Ammunition, Inc., 5180 E. Seltice Way, Post Falls, ID 83854 / 208-773-9444; FAX: 208-773-9441
Professional Gunsmiths of America, Rt 1 Box 224, Lexington, MO 64067 / 660-259-2636
Professional Hunter Supplies (See Star Custom Bullets), P.O. Box 608, 468 Main St., Ferndale, CA 95536 / 707-786-9140; FAX: 707-786-9117 wmebride@humboldt.com
PrOlixr Lubricants, P.O. Box 1348, Victorville, CA 92393 / 760-243-3129; FAX: 760-241-0148 prolix@accex.net www.prolixlubricant.com
Pro-Mark Div. of Wells Lamont, 6640 W. Touhy, Chicago, IL 60648 / 312-647-8200
Proofmark Corp., P.O. Box 357, Burgess, VA 22432 / 804-453-4337; FAX: 804-453-4337 proofmark@rivnet.net www.proofmarkbullets.com
Pro-Port Ltd., 41302 Executive Dr., Harrison Twp., MI 48045-1306 / 586-469-6727; FAX: 586-469-0425 e-mail@magnaport.com www.magnaport.com
Pro-Shot Products, Inc., P.O. Box 763, Taylorville, IL 62568 / 217-824-9133; FAX: 217-824-8861 www.proshotproducts.com
Protektor Model, 1-11 Bridge St., Galeton, PA 16922 / 814-435-2442 mail@protektormodel.com www.protektormodel.com
Prototech Industries, Inc., 10532 E Road, Delia, KS 66418 / 785-771-3571 prototec@grapevine.net

Manufacturer's Directory

ProWare, Inc., 15847 NE Hancock St., Portland, OR 97230 / 503-239-0159
PWL Gunleather, P.O. Box 450432, Atlanta, GA 31145 / 800-960-4072; FAX: 770-822-1704 covert@pwlusa.com www.pwlusa.com
PWM Sales Ltd., N.D.F.S., Gowdall Lane, Pollington DN14 0AU, ENGLAND / 01405862688; FAX: 01405862622 Paulwelburn9@aol.com
Pyramyd Stone Inter. Corp., 2447 Suffolk Lane, Pepper Pike, OH 44124-4540

Q

Quack Decoy & Sporting Clays, 4 Ann & Hope Way, P.O. Box 98, Cumberland, RI 02864 / 401-723-8202; FAX: 401-722-5910
Quaker Boy, Inc., 5455 Webster Rd., Orchard Parks, NY 14127 / 716-662-3979; FAX: 716-662-9426
Quality Arms, Inc., Box 19477, Dept. GD, Houston, TX 77224 / 281-870-8377 arrieta2@excite.com www.gunshop.com
Quality Cartridge, P.O. Box 445, Hollywood, MD 20636 / 301-373-3719 www.qual-cart.com
Quality Custom Firearms, Stepehn Billeb, 22 Vista View Drive, Cody, WY 82414 / 307-587-4278; FAX: 307-587-4297 stevebilleb@wyoming.com
Quarton Beamshot, 4538 Centerview Dr., Ste. 149, San Antonio, TX 78228 / 800-520-8435; FAX: 210-735-1326 www.beamshot.com
Que Industries, Inc., PO Box 2471, Everett, WA 98203 / 425-303-9088; FAX: 206-514-3266 queinfo@queindustries.com
Queen Cutlery Co., PO Box 500, Franklinville, NY 14737 / 800-222-5233; FAX: 800-299-2618

R

R&C Knives & Such, 2136 CANDY CANE WALK, Manteca, CA 95336-9501 / 209-239-3722; FAX: 209-825-6947
R&D Gun Repair, Kenny Howell, RR1 Box 283, Beloit, WI 53511
R&J Gun Shop, 337 S. Humbolt St., Canyon City, OR 97820 / 541-575-2130 rjgunshop@highdestertnet.com
R&S Industries Corp., 8255 Brentwood Industrial Dr., St. Louis, MO 63144 / 314-781-5169 ron@miraclepolishingcloth.com www.miraclepolishingcloth.com
R. Murphy Co., Inc., 13 Groton-Harvard Rd., P.O. Box 376, Ayer, MA 01432 / 617-772-3481 www.r.murphyknives.com
R.A. Wells Custom Gunsmith, 3452 1st Ave., Racine, WI 53402 / 414-639-5223
R.E. Seebeck Assoc., P.O. Box 59752, Dallas, TX 75229
R.E.I., P.O. Box 88, Tallevast, FL 34270 / 813-755-0085
R.E.T. Enterprises, 2608 S. Chestnut, Broken Arrow, OK 74012 / 918-251-GUNS; FAX: 918-251-0587
R.F. Mitchell Bullets, 430 Walnut St., Westernport, MD 21562
R.I.S. Co., Inc., 718 Timberlake Circle, Richardson, TX 75080 / 214-235-0933
R.T. Eastman Products, P.O. Box 1531, Jackson, WY 83001 / 307-733-3217; or 800-624-4311
Rabeno, Martin, 530 The Eagle Pass, Durango, CO 81301 / 970-382-0353 fancygun@aol.com
Radack Photography, Lauren, 21140 Jib Court L-12, Aventura, FL 33180 / 305-931-3110
Radiator Specialty Co., 1900 Wilkinson Blvd., P.O. Box 34689, Charlotte, NC 28234 / 800-438-6947; FAX: 800-421-9525
Radical Concepts, P.O. Box 1473, Lake Grove, OR 97035 / 503-538-7437
Rainier Ballistics, 4500 15th St. East, Tacoma, WA 98424 / 800-638-8722; FAX: 253-922-7854 sales@rainierballistics.com www.rainierballistics.com
Ralph Bone Engraving, 718 N. Atlanta St., Owasso, OK 74055 / 918-272-9745
Ram-Line ATK, P.O. Box 39, Onalaska, WI 54650
Ramon B. Gonzalez Guns, P.O. Box 370, Monticello, NY 12701 / 914-794-4515; FAX: 914-794-4515
Rampart International, 2781 W. MacArthur Blvd., B-283, Santa Ana, CA 92704 / 800-976-7240 or 714-557-6405
Ranch Products, P.O. Box 145, Malinta, OH 43535 / 313-277-3118; FAX: 313-565-8536
Randall-Made Knives, P.O. Box 1988, Orlando, FL 32802 / 407-855-8075
Randco UK, 286 Gipsy Rd., Welling, DA16 1JJ ENGLAND / 44 81 303 4118
Randolph Engineering, Inc., Ranger Shooting Glasses, 26 Thomas Patten Dr., Randolph, MA 02368 / 800-541-1405; FAX: 781-986-0337 sales@randolphusa.com www.randolphusa.com
Randy Duane Custom Stocks, 7822 Church St., Middletown, VA 22645-9521
Range Brass Products Company, P.O. Box 218, Rockport, TX 78381
Ransom International Corp., 1027 Spire Dr, Prescott, AZ 86302 / 520-778-7899; FAX: 520-778-7993 ransom@primenet.com www.ransom-intl.com
Rapine Bullet Mould Mfg. Co., 9503 Landis Lane, East Greenville, PA 18041 / 215-679-5413; FAX: 215-679-9795
Ravell Ltd., 289 Diputacion St., 08009, Barcelona, SPAIN / 34(3) 4874486; FAX: 34(3) 4881394
Ray Riling Arms Books Co., 6844 Gorsten St., Philadelphia, PA 19119 / 215-438-2456; FAX: 215-438-5395 sales@rayrilingarmsbooks.com www.rayrilingarmsbooks.com
Ray's Gunsmith Shop, 3199 Elm Ave., Grand Junction, CO 81504 / 970-434-6162; FAX: 970-434-6162
Raytech Div. of Lyman Products Corp., 475 Smith Street, Middletown, CT 06457-1541 / 860-632-2020 or 800-225-9626; FAX: 860-632-1699 raysales@cshore.com www.raytech-ind.com
RCBS Operations/ATK, 605 Oro Dam Blvd., Oroville, CA 95965 / 530-533-5191 or 800-533-5000; FAX: 530-533-1647 www.rcbs.com
Reardon Products, P.O. Box 126, Morrison, IL 61270 / 815-772-3155
Red Diamond Dist. Co., 1304 Snowdon Dr., Knoxville, TN 37912
Redding Reloading Equipment, 1089 Starr Rd., Cortland, NY 13045 / 607-753-3331; FAX: 607-756-8445 techline@redding-reloading.com www.redding-reloading.com
Redfield Media Resource Center, 4607 N.E. Cedar Creek Rd., Woodland, WA 98674 / 360-225-5000; FAX: 360-225-7616
Redman's Rifling & Reboring, 189 Nichols Rd., Omak, WA 98841 / 509-826-5512
Redwood Bullet Works, 3559 Bay Rd., Redwood City, CA 94063 / 415-367-6741
Reed, Dave, Rt. 1, Box 374, Minnesota City, MN 55959 / 507-689-2944
Reimer Johannsen, Inc., 438 Willow Brook Rd., Plainfield, NH 03781 / 603-469-3450; FAX: 603-469-3471
Reloaders Equipment Co., 4680 High St., Ecorse, MI 48229
Reloading Specialties, Inc., Box 1130, Pine Island, MN 55463 / 507-356-8500; FAX: 507-356-8800
Remington Arms Co., Inc., 870 Remington Drive, P.O. Box 700, Madison, NC 27025-0700 / 800-243-9700; FAX: 910-548-8700
Remington Double Shotguns, 7885 Cyd Dr., Denver, CO 80221 / 303-429-6947
Renato Gamba S.p.A.-Societa Armi Bresciane Srl., Via Artigiani 93, 25063 Gardone, Val Trompia (BS), ITALY / 30-8911640; FAX: 30-8911648
Renegade, P.O. Box 31546, Phoenix, AZ 85046 / 602-482-6777; FAX: 602-482-1952
Renfrew Guns & Supplies, R.R. 4, Renfrew, ON K7V 3Z7 CANADA / 613-432-7080
Reno, Wayne, 2808 Stagestop Road, Jefferson, CO 80456
Republic Arms, Inc. (See Cobra Enterprises, Inc.)
Retting, Inc., Martin B., 11029 Washington, Culver City, CA 90232 / 213-837-2412
RG-G, Inc., P.O. Box 935, Trinidad, CO 81082 / 719-845-1436
RH Machine & Consulting Inc., P.O. Box 394, Pacific, MO 63069 / 314-271-8465
Rhino, P.O. Box 787, Locust, NC 28097 / 704-753-2198
Rhodeside, Inc., 1704 Commerce Dr., Piqua, OH 45356 / 513-773-5781
Rice, Keith (See White Rock Tool & Die)
Richards Micro-Fit Stocks, 8331 N. San Fernando Ave., Sun Valley, CA 91352 / 818-767-6097; FAX: 818-767-7121
Ridgeline, Inc., Bruce Sheldon, P.O. Box 930, Dewey, AZ 86327-0930 / 800-632-5900; FAX: 520-632-5900
Ridgetop Sporting Goods, P.O. Box 306, 42907 Hilligoss Ln. East, Eatonville, WA 98328 / 360-832-6422; FAX: 360-832-6422
Ries, Chuck, 415 Ridgecrest Dr., Grants Pass, OR 97527 / 503-476-5623
Rifles, Inc., 3580 Leal Rd., Pleasanton, TX 78064 / 830-569-2055; FAX: 830-569-2297
Riggs, Jim, 206 Azalea, Boerne, TX 78006 / 210-249-8567
Riley Ledbetter Airguns, 1804 E. Sprague St., Winston Salem, NC 27107-3521 / 919-784-0676
Rim Pac Sports, Inc., 1034 N. Soldano Ave., Azusa, CA 91702-2135
Ringler Custom Leather Co., 31 Shining Mtn. Rd., Powell, WY 82435 / 307-645-3255
Ripley Rifles, 42 Fletcher Street, Ripley, Derbyshire, DE5 3LP ENGLAND / 011-0773-748353
Rizzini F.lli (See U.S. Importers-Moore & C England)
Rizzini SNC, Via 2 Giugno, 7/7Bis-25060, Marcheno (Brescia), ITALY
RLCM Enterprises, 110 Hill Crest Drive, Burleson, TX 76028
RMS Custom Gunsmithing, 4120 N. Bitterwell, Prescott Valley, AZ 86314 / 520-772-7626
Robert Evans Engraving, 332 Vine St., Oregon City, OR 97045 / 503-656-5693
Robert Valade Engraving, 931 3rd Ave., Seaside, OR 97138 / 503-738-7672
Robinett, R. G., P.O. Box 72, Madrid, IA 50156 / 515-795-2906
Robinson, Don, Pennsylvania Hse, 36 Fairfax Crescent, W Yorkshire, ENGLAND / 0422-364458 donrobinsonuk@yahoo.co.uk www.guns4u2.co.uk
Robinson Armament Co., PO Box 16776, Salt Lake City, UT 84116 / 801-355-0401; FAX: 801-355-0402 zdf@robarm.com www.robarm.com
Robinson Firearms Mfg. Ltd., 1699 Blondeaux Crescent, Kelowna, BC V1Y 4J8 CANADA / 604-868-9596
Robinson H.V. Bullets, 3145 Church St., Zachary, LA 70791 / 504-654-4029
Rochester Lead Works, 76 Anderson Ave., Rochester, NY 14607 / 716-442-8500; FAX: 716-442-4712
Rock River Arms, 101 Noble St., Cleveland, IL 61241
Rockwood Corp., Speedwell Division, 136 Lincoln Blvd., Middlesex, NJ 08846 / 800-243-8274; FAX: 980-560-7475
Rocky Mountain Armoury, Mr. Felix LesMerises, 610 Main Street, P.O. Box 691, Frisco, CO 80443-0691 / 970-668-0136; FAX: 970-668-4484 felix@rockymountainarmoury.com
Rocky Mountain Arms, Inc., 1813 Sunset Pl, Unit D, Longmont, CO 80501 / 800-375-0846; FAX: 303-678-8766
Rocky Mountain Target Co., 3 Aloe Way, Leesburg, FL 34788 / 352-365-9598
Rocky Mountain Wildlife Products, P.O. Box 999, La Porte, CO 80535 / 970-484-2768; FAX: 970-484-0807 critrcall@earthlink.net www.critrcall.com
Rocky Shoes & Boots, 294 Harper St., Nelsonville, OH 45764 / 800-848-9452; or 614-753-1951; FAX: 614-753-4024
Rogue Rifle Co., Inc., 1140 36th St. N., Ste. B, Lewiston, ID 83501 / 208-743-4355; FAX: 208-743-4163
Rogue River Rifleworks, 500 Linne Road #D, Paso Robles, CA 93446 / 805-227-4706; FAX: 805-227-4723 rrrifles@calinet.com
Rohner, Hans, 1148 Twin Sisters Ranch Rd., Nederland, CO 80466-9600
Rohner, John, 186 Virginia Ave, Asheville, NC 28806 / 303-444-3841
Rohrbaugh, P.O. Box 785, Bayport, NY 11705 / 631-363-2843; FAX: 631-363-2681 API380@aol.com
Romain's Custom Guns, Inc., RD 1, Whetstone Rd., Brockport, PA 15823 / 814-265-1948 romwhetstone@penn.com
Ron Frank Custom Classic Arms, 7131 Richland Rd., Ft. Worth, TX 76118 / 817-284-9300; FAX: 817-284-9300 rfrank3974@aol.com
Rooster Laboratories, P.O. Box 414605, Kansas City, MO 64141 / 816-474-1622; FAX: 816-474-7622
Rorschach Precision Products, 417 Keats Cir., Irving, TX 75061 / 214-790-3487
Rosenberg & Son, Jack A., 12229 Cox Ln., Dallas, TX 75234 / 214-241-6302
Ross, Don, 12813 West 83 Terrace, Lenexa, KS 66215 / 913-492-6982
Rosser, Bob, 2809 Crescent Ave., Suite 20, Homewood, AL 35209 / 205-870-4422; FAX: 205-870-4421 www.hand-engravers.com
Rossi Firearms, Gary Mchalik, 16175 NW 49th Ave., Miami, FL 33014-6314 / 305-474-0401; FAX: 305-623-7506
Rottweil Compe, 1330 Glassell, Orange, CA 92667
Roy Baker's Leather Goods, PO Box 893, Magnolia, AR 71754 / 870-234-0344
Royal Arms Gunstocks, 919 8th Ave. NW, Great Falls, MT 59404 / 406-453-1149 royalarms@lmt.net www.lmt.net/~royalarms
Royal Arms International, R J Brill, P.O. Box 6083, Woodland Hills, CA 91365 / 818-704-5110; FAX: 818-887-2059 royalarms.com

MANUFACTURER'S DIRECTORY

Roy's Custom Grips, 793 Mt. Olivet Church Rd., Lynchburg, VA 24504 / 434-993-3470
RPM, 15481 N. Twin Lakes Dr., Tucson, AZ 85739 / 520-825-1233; FAX: 520-825-3333
Rubright Bullets, 1008 S. Quince Rd., Walnutport, PA 18088 / 215-767-1339
Rucker Dist. Inc., P.O. Box 479, Terrell, TX 75160 / 214-563-2094
Ruger (See Sturm, Ruger & Co., Inc.)
Ruger, Chris. See: RUGER'S CUSTOM GUNS
Ruger's Custom Guns, Chris Ruger, 1050 Morton Blvd., Kingston, NY 12401 / 845-336-7106; FAX: 845-336-7106 rugerscustom@outdrs.net rugergunsmith.com
Rundell's Gun Shop, 6198 Frances Rd., Clio, MI 48420 / 313-687-0559
Rupert's Gun Shop, 2202 Dick Rd., Suite B, Fenwick, MI 48834 / 517-248-3252 17rupert@pathwaynet.com
Russ Haydon's Shooters' Supply, 15018 Goodrich Dr. NW, Gig Harbor, WA 98329 / 877-663-6249; FAX: 253-857-7884 www.shooters-supply.com
Russ, William. See: BILL RUSS TRADING POST
Rusteprufe Laboratories, 1319 Jefferson Ave., Sparta, WI 54656 / 608-269-4144; FAX: 608-366-1972 rusteprufe@centurytel.net www.rusteprufe.com
Rusty Duck Premium Gun Care Products, 7785 Foundation Dr., Suite 6, Florence, KY 41042 / 606-342-5553; FAX: 606-342-5556
Rutgers Book Center, 127 Raritan Ave., Highland Park, NJ 08904 / 732-545-4344; FAX: 732-545-6686 gunbooks@rutgersgunbooks.com www.rutgersgunbooks.com
Rutten (See U.S. Importer-Labanu Inc)
RWS (See U.S. Importer-Dynamit Nobel-RWS, Inc.), 81 Ruckman Rd., Closter, NJ 07624 / 201-767-7971; FAX: 201-767-1589

S

S&K Scope Mounts, RD 2 Box 72E, Sugar Grove, PA 16350 / 814-489-3091; or 800-578-9862; FAX: 814-489-5466 comments@scopemounts.com www.scopemounts.com
S&S Firearms, 74-11 Myrtle Ave., Glendale, NY 11385 / 718-497-1100; FAX: 718-497-1105 info@ssfirearms.com ssfirearms.com
S.A.R.L. G. Granger, 66 cours Fauriel, 42100, Saint Etienne, FRANCE / 04 77 25 14 73; FAX: 04 77 38 66 99
S.C.R.C., P.O. Box 660, Katy, TX 77492-0660 FAX: 281-492-6332
S.D. Meacham, 1070 Angel Ridge, Peck, ID 83545
S.I.A.C.E. (See U.S. Importer-IAR Inc)
Sabatti SPA, Via A Volta 90, 25063 Gandome V.T.(BS), Brescia, ITALY / 030-8912207-831312; FAX: 030-8912059 info@sabatti.it www.sabatti.com
SAECO (See Redding Reloading Equipment)
Safari Arms/Schuetzen Pistol Works, 620-626 Old Pacific Hwy. SE, Olympia, WA 98513 / 360-459-3471; FAX: 360-491-3447 info@yarms.com www.olyarms.com
Safari Press, Inc., 15621 Chemical Lane B, Huntington Beach, CA 92649 / 714-894-9080; FAX: 714-894-4949 info@safaripress.com www.safaripress.com
Safariland Ltd., Inc., 3120 E. Mission Blvd., P.O. Box 51478, Ontario, CA 91761 / 909-923-7300; FAX: 909-923-7400
SAFE, PO Box 864, Post Falls, ID 83877 / 208-773-3624; FAX: 208-773-6819 staysafe@safe-llc.com www.safe-llc.com
Safety Speed Holster, Inc., 910 S. Vail Ave., Montebello, CA 90640 / 323-723-4140; FAX: 323-726-6973 e-mail@safetyspeedholster.com www.safetyspeedholster.com
Sako Ltd (See U.S. Importer-Stoeger Industries)
Sam Welch Gun Engraving, Sam Welch, HC 64 Box 2110, Moab, UT 84532 / 435-259-8131
Samco Global Arms, Inc., 6995 NW 43rd St., Miami, FL 33166 / 305-593-9782; FAX: 305-593-1014 samco@samcoglobal.com www.samcoglobal.com
Sampson, Roger, 2316 Mahogany St., Mora, MN 55051 / 612-679-4868
San Marco (See U.S. Importers-Cape Outfitters-EMF
Sandia Die & Cartridge Co., 37 Atancacio Rd. NE, Albuquerque, NM 87123 / 505-298-5729
Sarco, Inc., 323 Union St., Stirling, NJ 07980 / 908-647-3800; FAX: 908-647-9413
Sarsilmaz Shotguns - Turkey (see B.C. Outdoors)
Sauer (See U.S. Importers-Paul Co., The, Sigarms I
Sauls, R. See: BRYAN & ASSOC.
Saunders Gun & Machine Shop, 145 Delhi Rd, Manchester, IA 52057 / 563-927-4026
Savage Arms (Canada), Inc., 248 Water St., P.O. Box 1240, Lakefield, ON K0L 2H0 CANADA / 705-652-8000; FAX: 705-652-8431 www.savagearms.com
Savage Arms, Inc., 100 Springdale Rd., Westfield, MA 01085 / 413-568-7001; FAX: 413-562-7764
Savage Range Systems, Inc., 100 Springdale Rd., Westfield, MA 01085 / 413-568-7001; FAX: 413-562-1152 snailtraps@savagearms.com www.snailtraps.com
Saville Iron Co. (See Greenwood Precision)
Savino, Barbara J., P.O. Box 51, West Burke, VT 05871-0051
Scansport, Inc., P.O. Box 700, Enfield, NH 03748 / 603-632-7654
Sceery Game Calls, P.O. Box 6520, Sante Fe, NM 87502 / 505-471-9110; FAX: 505-471-3476
Schaefer Shooting Sports, P.O. Box 1515, Melville, NY 11747-0515 / 516-643-5466; FAX: 516-643-2426 robert@robertschaefer.com www.schaefershooting.com
Scharch Mfg., Inc.-Top Brass, 10325 Co. Rd. 120, Salida, CO 81201 / 719-539-7242; or 800-836-4683; FAX: 719-539-3021 scharch@chaffee.net www.topbraass.tv
Scherer, Liz. See: SCHERER SUPPLIES
Scherer Supplies, Liz Scherer, Box 250, Ewing, VA 24248 FAX: 423-733-2073
Schiffman, Curt, 2938 S. Greenwood, Mesa, AZ 85212
Schiffman, Mike, 8233 S. Crystal Springs, McCammon, ID 83250 / 208-254-9114
Schmidt & Bender, Inc., P.O. Box 134, Meriden, NH 03770 / 603-469-3565; FAX: 603-469-3471 scopes@cyberportal.net www.schmidtbender.com
Schmidtke Group, 17050 W. Salentine Dr., New Berlin, WI 53151-7349
Schneider Bullets, 3655 West 214th St., Fairview Park, OH 44126
Schneider Rifle Barrels, Inc., 1403 W Red Baron Rd., Payson, AZ 85541 / 602-948-2525
Schroeder Bullets, 1421 Thermal Ave., San Diego, CA 92154 / 619-423-3523; FAX: 619-423-8124
Schulz Industries, 16247 Minnesota Ave., Paramount, CA 90723 / 213-439-5903
Schumakers Gun Shop, 512 Prouty Corner Lp. A, Colville, WA 99114 / 509-684-4848
Scope Control, Inc., 5775 Co. Rd. 23 SE, Alexandria, MN 56308 / 612-762-7295
Score High Gunsmithing, 9812-A, Cochiti SE, Albuquerque, NM 087123 / 800-326-5632 or 505-292-5532; FAX: 505-292-2592
Scot Powder, Rt.1 Box 167, McEwen, TN 37101 / 800-416-3006; FAX: 615-729-4211
Scott Fine Guns Inc., Thad, P.O. Box 412, Indianola, MS 38751 / 601-887-5929
Searcy Enterprises, P.O. Box 584, Boron, CA 93596 / 760-762-6771; FAX: 760-762-0191
Second Chance Body Armor, P.O. Box 578, Central Lake, MI 49622 / 616-544-5721; FAX: 616-544-9824
Seebeck Assoc., R.E., P. O. Box 59752, Dallas, TX 75229
Seecamp Co. Inc., L. W., PO Box 255, New Haven, CT 06502 / 203-877-3429; FAX: 203-877-3429
Segway Industries, P.O. Box 783, Suffern, NY 10901-0783 / 914-357-5510
Seligman Shooting Products, Box 133, Seligman, AZ 86337 / 602-422-3607 shootssp@yahoo.com
Sellier & Bellot, USA, Inc., P.O. Box 27006, Shawnee Mission, KS 66225 / 913-685-0916; FAX: 913-685-0917
Selsi Co., Inc., P.O. Box 10, Midland Park, NJ 07432-0010 / 201-935-0388; FAX: 201-935-5851
Semmer, Charles (See Remington Double Shotguns), 7885 Cyd Dr, Denver, CO 80221 / 303-429-6947
Sentinel Arms, P.O. Box 57, Detroit, MI 48231 / 313-331-1951; FAX: 313-331-1456
Servus Footwear Co., 1136 2nd St., Rock Island, IL 61204 / 309-786-7741; FAX: 309-786-9808
Shappy Bullets, 76 Milldale Ave., Plantsville, CT 06479 / 203-621-3704
Sharp Shooter Supply, 4970 Lehman Road, Delphos, OH 45833 / 419-695-3179
Sharps Arms Co., Inc., C., 100 Centennial, Box 885, Big Timber, MT 59011 / 406-932-4353
Shaw, Inc., E. R. (See Small Arms Mfg. Co.)
Shay's Gunsmithing, 931 Marvin Ave., Lebanon, PA 17042
Sheffield Knifemakers Supply, Inc., P.O. Box 741107, Orange City, FL 32774-1107 / 386-775-6453; FAX: 386-774-5754
Sheldon, Bruce. See: RIDGELINE, INC.
Shepherd Enterprises, Inc., Box 189, Waterloo, NE 68069 / 402-779-2424; FAX: 402-779-4010 sshepherd@shepherdscopes.com www.shepherdscopes.com
Sherwood, George, 46 N. River Dr., Roseburg, OR 97470 / 541-672-3159
Shilen, Inc., 205 Metro Park Blvd., Ennis, TX 75119 / 972-875-5318; FAX: 972-875-5402
Shiloh Rifle Mfg., P.O. Box 279, Big Timber, MT 59011
Shockley, Harold H., 204 E. Farmington Rd., Hanna City, IL 61536 / 309-565-4524
Shoot Where You Look, Leon Measures, Dept GD, 408 Fair, Livingston, TX 77351
Shooters Arms Manufacturing, Inc., Rivergate Mall, Gen. Maxilom Ave., Cebu City 6000, PHILIPPINES / 6332-254-8478 www.shootersarms.com.ph
Shooter's Choice Gun Care, 15050 Berkshire Ind. Pky., Middlefield, OH 44062 / 440-834-8888; FAX: 440-834-3388 www.shooterschoice.com
Shooter's Edge Inc., 3313 Creekstone Dr., Fort Collins, CO 80525
Shooters Supply, 1120 Tieton Dr., Yakima, WA 98902 / 509-452-1181
Shooter's World, 3828 N. 28th Ave., Phoenix, AZ 85017 / 602-266-0170
Shooters, Inc., 5139 Stanart St., Norfolk, VA 23502 / 757-461-9152; FAX: 757-461-9155 gflocker@aol.com
Shootin' Shack, 357 Cypress Drive, No. 10, Tequesta, FL 33469 / 561-842-0990; FAX: 561-545-4861
Shooting Specialties (See Titus, Daniel)
Shooting Star, 1715 FM 1626 Ste 105, Manchaca, TX 78652 / 512-462-0009
Shoot-N-C Targets (See Birchwood Casey)
Shotgun Sports, P.O. Box 6810, Auburn, CA 95604 / 530-889-2220; FAX: 530-889-9106 custsrv@shotgunsportsmagazine.com shotgunsportsmagazine.com
Shotgun Sports Magazine, dba Shootin' Accessories Ltd., P.O. Box 6810, Auburn, CA 95604 / 916-889-2220 custsrv@shotgunsportsmagazine.com shotgunspotsmagazine.com
Shotguns Unlimited, 2307 Fon Du Lac Rd., Richmond, VA 23229 / 804-752-7115
Siegrist Gun Shop, 8752 Turtle Road, Whittemore, MI 48770 / 989-873-3929
Sierra Bullets, 1400 W. Henry St., Sedalia, MO 65301 / 816-827-6300; FAX: 816-827-6300
Sierra Specialty Prod. Co., 1344 Oakhurst Ave., Los Altos, CA 94024 FAX: 415-965-1536
SIG, CH-8212 Neuhausen, SWITZERLAND
Sigarms, Inc., 18 Industrial Dr., Exeter, NH 03833 / 603-772-2302; FAX: 603-772-9082 www.sigarms.com
Sightron, Inc., 1672B Hwy. 96, Franklinton, NC 27525 / 919-528-8783; FAX: 919-528-0995 info@sightron.com www.sightron.com
SIG-Sauer (See U.S. Importer-Sigarms Inc.)
Silencio/Safety Direct, 56 Coney Island Dr., Sparks, NV 89431 / 800-648-1812 or 702-354-4451; FAX: 702-359-1074
Silent Hunter, 1100 Newton Ave., W. Collingswood, NJ 08107 / 609-854-3276
Silhouette Leathers, P.O. Box 1161, Gunnison, CO 81230 / 970-641-6630 oldshooter@yahoo.com
Silver Eagle Machining, 18007 N. 69th Ave., Glendale, AZ 85308
Silver Ridge Gun Shop (See Goodwin, Fred)
Simmons, Jerry, 715 Middlebury St., Goshen, IN 46528-2717 / 574-533-8546
Simmons Gun Repair, Inc., 700 S. Rogers Rd., Olathe, KS 66062 / 913-782-3131; FAX: 913-782-4189
Simmons Outdoor Corp., 6001 Oak Canyon, Irvine, CA 92618 / 949-451-1450; FAX: 949-451-1460 www.meade.com
Sinclair International, Inc., 2330 Wayne Haven St., Fort Wayne, IN 46803 / 260-493-1858; FAX: 260-493-2530 sales@sinclairintl.com www.sinclairintl.com
Singletary, Kent, 4538 W Carol Ave., Glendale, AZ 85302 / 602-526-6836 kent@kscustom www.kscustom.com
Siskiyou Gun Works (See Donnelly, C. P.)
Six Enterprises, 320-D Turtle Creek Ct., San Jose, CA 95125 / 408-999-0201; FAX: 408-999-0216
SKB Shotguns, 4325 S. 120th St., Omaha, NE 68137 / 800-752-2767; FAX: 402-330-8040 skb@skbshotguns.com www.skbshotguns.com
Skeoch, Brian R., P.O. Box 279, Glenrock, WY 82637 / 307-436-9655 brianskeoch@aol.com
Skip's Machine, 364 29 Road, Grand Junction, CO 81501 / 303-245-5417
Sklany's Machine Shop, 566 Birch Grove Dr., Kalispell, MT 59901 / 406-755-4257
Slezak, Jerome F., 1290 Marlowe, Lakewood (Cleveland), OH 44107 / 216-221-1668
Slug Site, Ozark Wilds, 21300 Hwy. 5, Versailles, MO 65084 / 573-378-6430 john@ebeling.com john.ebeling.com
Small Arms Mfg. Co., 5312 Thoms Run Rd., Bridgeville, PA 15017 / 412-221-4343; FAX: 412-221-4303

MANUFACTURER'S DIRECTORY

Small Arms Specialists, 443 Firchburg Rd., Mason, NH 03048 / 603-878-0427; FAX: 603-878-3905 miniguns@empire.net miniguns.com
Small Custom Mould & Bullet Co., Box 17211, Tucson, AZ 85731
Smart Parts, 1203 Spring St., Latrobe, PA 15650 / 412-539-2660; FAX: 412-539-2298
Smires, C. L., 5222 Windmill Lane, Columbia, MD 21044-1328
Smith & Wesson, 2100 Roosevelt Ave., Springfield, MA 01104 / 413-781-8300; FAX: 413-731-8980
Smith, Art, P.O. Box 645, Park Rapids, MN 56470 / 218-732-5333;
Smith, Mark A., P.O. Box 182, Sinclair, WY 82334 / 307-324-7929
Smith, Michael, 2612 Ashmore Ave., Red Bank, TN 37415 / 615-267-8341
Smith, Ron, 5869 Straley, Ft. Worth, TX 76114 / 817-732-6768
Smith, Sharmon, 4545 Speas Rd., Fruitland, ID 83619 / 208-452-6329 sharmon@fmtc.com
Smith Abrasives, Inc., 1700 Sleepy Valley Rd., P.O. Box 5095, Hot Springs, AR 71902-5095 / 501-321-2244; FAX: 501-321-9232
Smith, Judy. See: L.B.T.
Smith Saddlery, Jesse W., 0499 County Road J, Pritchett, CO 81064 / 509-325-0622
Smokey Valley Rifles, E1976 Smokey Valley Rd., Scandinavia, WI 54977 / 715-467-2674
Snapp's Gunshop, 6911 E. Washington Rd., Clare, MI 48617 / 989-386-9226 snapp@glccomputers.com
Sno-Seal, Inc. (See Atsko/Sno-Seal, Inc.)
Societa Armi Bresciane Srl (See U.S. Importer-Cape
SOS Products Co. (See Buck Stix-SOS Products Co.), Box 3, Neenah, WI 54956
Sotheby's, 1334 York Ave. at 72nd St., New York, NY 10021 / 212-606-7260
Sound Tech Silencers, Box 391, Pelham, AL 35124 / 205-664-5860 silenceio@wmconnect.com www.soundtechsilencers.com
South Bend Replicas, Inc., 61650 Oak Rd.., South Bend, IN 46614 / 219-289-4500
Southeastern Community College, 1015 S. Gear Ave., West Burlington, IA 52655 / 319-752-2731
Southern Ammunition Co., Inc., 4232 Meadow St., Loris, SC 29569-3124 / 803-756-3262; FAX: 803-756-3583
Southern Bloomer Mfg. Co., P.O. Box 1621, Bristol, TN 37620 / 615-878-6660; FAX: 615-878-8761
Southern Security, 1700 Oak Hills Dr., Kingston, TN 37763 / 423-376-6297; FAX: 800-251-9992
Sparks, Milt, 605 E. 44th St. No. 2, Boise, ID 83714-4800
Spartan-Realtree Products, Inc., 1390 Box Circle, Columbus, GA 31907 / 706-569-9101; FAX: 706-569-0042
Specialty Gunsmithing, Lynn McMurdo, P.O. Box 404, Afton, WY 83110 / 307-886-5535
Specialty Shooters Supply, Inc., 3325 Griffin Rd., Suite 9mm, Fort Lauderdale, FL 33317
Speer Bullets, P.O. Box 856, Lewiston, ID 83501 / 208-746-2351; www.speer-bullets.com
Spegel, Craig, P.O. Box 387, Nehalem, OR 97131 / 503-368-5653
Speiser, Fred D., 2229 Dearborn, Missoula, MT 59801 / 406-549-8133
Spencer Reblue Service, 1820 Tupelo Trail, Holt, MI 48842 / 517-694-7474
Spencer's Rifle Barrels, Inc., 4107 Jacobs Creek Dr., Scottsville, VA 24590 / 804-293-6836; FAX: 804-293-6836 www.spencerriflebarrels.com
SPG LLC, P.O. Box 1625, Cody, WY 82414 / 307-587-7621; FAX: 307-587-7695 spg@cody.wtp.net www.blackpowderspg.com
Sphinx Systems Ltd., Gesteigtstrasse 12, CH-3800, Matten, BRNE, SWITZERLAND
Splitfire Sporting Goods, L.L.C., P.O. Box 1044, Orem, UT 84059-1044 / 801-932-7950; FAX: 801-932-7959 www.splitfireguns.com
Spolar Power Load, Inc., 17376 Filbert, Fontana, CA 92335 / 800-227-9667
Sport Flite Manufacturing Co., P.O. Box 1082, Bloomfield Hills, MI 48303 / 248-647-3747
Sporting Clays Of America, 9257 Bluckeye Rd, Sugar Grove, OH 43155-9632 / 740-746-8334; FAX: 740-746-8605
Sports Afield Magazine, 15621 Chemical Lane B, Huntington Beach, CA 92649 / 714-894-9080; FAX: 714-894-4949 info@sportsafield.com www.sportsafield.com
Sports Innovations, Inc., P.O. Box 5181, 8505 Jacksboro Hwy., Wichita Falls, TX 76307 / 817-723-6015
Sportsman Safe Mfg. Co., 6309-6311 Paramount Blvd., Long Beach, CA 90805 / 800-266-7150; or 310-984-5445
Sportsman's Communicators, 588 Radcliffe Ave., Pacific Palisades, CA 90272 / 800-538-3752
Sportsmatch U.K. Ltd., 16 Summer St. Leighton,, Buzzard Beds, Bedfordshire, LU7 8HT ENGLAND / 4401525-381638; FAX: 4401525-851236 info@sportsmatch-uk.com www.sportsmatch-uk.com
Sportsmen's Exchange & Western Gun Traders, Inc., 560 S. C St., Oxnard, CA 93030 / 805-483-1917
Spradlin's, 457 Shannon Rd., Texas CreekCotopaxi, CO 81223 / 719-275-7105; FAX: 719-275-3852 spradlins@prodigy.net www.spradlins.net
Springfield Armory, 420 W. Main St, Geneseo, IL 61254 / 309-944-5631; FAX: 309-944-3676 sales@springfield-armory.com www.springfieldarmory.com
Springfield Sporters, Inc., RD 1, Penn Run, PA 15765 / 412-254-2626; FAX: 412-254-9173
Springfield, Inc., 420 W. Main St., Geneseo, IL 61254 / 309-944-5631; FAX: 309-944-3676
Spyderco, Inc., 820 Spyderco Way, Golden, CO 80403 / 800-525-7770; or 800-525-7770; FAX: 303-278-2229 sales@spyderco.com www.spyderco.com
SSK Industries, J. D. Jones, 590 Woodvue Lane, Wintersville, OH 43953 / 740-264-0176; FAX: 740-264-2257 www.sskindustries.com
Stackpole Books, 5067 Ritter Rd., Mechanicsburg, PA 17055-6921 / 717-796-0411; or 800-732-3669; FAX: 717-796-0412 tmanney@stackpolebooks.com www.stackpolebooks.com
Stalker, Inc., P.O. Box 21, Fishermans Wharf Rd., Malakoff, TX 75148 / 903-489-1010
Stalwart Corporation, P.O. Box 46, Evanston, WY 82931 / 307-789-7687; FAX: 307-789-7688
Stan Baker Sports, Stan Baker, 10000 Lake City Way, Seattle, WA 98125 / 206-522-4575
Stan De Treville & Co., 4129 Normal St., San Diego, CA 92103 / 619-298-3393
Stanley Bullets, 2085 Heatheridge Ln., Reno, NV 89509
Star Ammunition, Inc., 5520 Rock Hampton Ct., Indianapolis, IN 46268 / 800-221-5927; FAX: 317-872-5847
Star Custom Bullets, P.O. Box 608, 468 Main St., Ferndale, CA 95536 / 707-786-9140; FAX: 707-786-9117 wmebridge@humboldt.com
Star Machine Works, P.O. Box 1872, Pioneer, CA 95666 / 209-295-5000
Starke Bullet Company, P.O. Box 400, 605 6th St. NW, Cooperstown, ND 58425 / 888-797-3431
Starkey Labs, 6700 Washington Ave. S., Eden Prairie, MN 55344
Starkey's Gun Shop, 9430 McCombs, El Paso, TX 79924 / 915-751-3030
Starlight Training Center, Inc., Rt. 1, P.O. Box 88, Bronaugh, MO 64728 / 417-843-3555
Starline, Inc., 1300 W. Henry St., Sedalia, MO 65301 / 660-827-6640; FAX: 660-827-6650 info@starlinebrass.com http://www.starlinebrass.com
Starr Trading Co., Jedediah, P.O. Box 2007, Farmington Hills, MI 48333 / 810-683-4343; FAX: 810-683-3282
Starrett Co., L. S., 121 Crescent St., Athol, MA 01331 / 978-249-3551; FAX: 978-249-8495
Steelman's Gun Shop, 10465 Beers Rd., Swartz Creek, MI 48473 / 810-735-4884
Steffens, Ron, 18396 Mariposa Creek Rd., Willits, CA 95490 / 707-485-0873
Stegall, James B., 26 Forest Rd., Wallkill, NY 12589
Steve Henigson & Associates, P.O. Box 2726, Culver City, CA 90231 / 310-305-8288; FAX: 310-305-1905
Steve Kamyk Engraver, 9 Grandview Dr., Westfield, MA 01085-1810 / 413-568-0457 stevek201@attbi
Steven Dodd Hughes, P.O. Box 545, Livingston, MT 59047 / 406-222-9377; FAX: 406-222-9377
Steves House of Guns, Rt. 1, Minnesota City, MN 55959 / 507-689-2573
Stewart Game Calls, Inc., Johnny, P.O. Box 7954, 5100 Fort Ave., Waco, TX 76714 / 817-772-3261; FAX: 817-772-3670
Stewart's Gunsmithing, P.O. Box 5854, Pietersburg North 0750, Transvaal, SOUTH AFRICA / 01521-89401
Steyr Mannlicher GmbH & Co KG, Mannlicherstrasse 1, 4400 Steyr, Steyr, AUSTRIA / 0043-7252-896-0; FAX: 0043-7252-78620 office@steyr-mannlicher.com www.steyr-mannlicher.com
STI International, 114 Halmar Cove, Georgetown, TX 78628 / 800-959-8201; FAX: 512-819-0465 www.stiguns.com
Stiles Custom Guns, 76 Cherry Run Rd., Box 1605, Homer City, PA 15748 / 712-479-9945
Stillwell, Robert, 421 Judith Ann Dr., Schertz, TX 78154
Stoeger Industries, 17603 Indian Head Hwy., Suite 200, Accokeek, MD 20607-2501 / 301-283-6300; FAX: 301-283-6986 www.stoegerindustries.com
Stoeger Publishing Co. (See Stoeger Industries)
Stone Enterprises Ltd., 426 Harveys Neck Rd., P.O. Box 335, Wicomico Church, VA 22579 / 804-580-5114; FAX: 804-580-8421
Stone Mountain Arms, 5988 Peachtree Corners E., Norcross, GA 30071 / 800-251-9412
Stoney Point Products, Inc., P.O. Box 234, 1822 N Minnesota St., New Ulm, MN 56073-0234 / 507-354-3360; FAX: 507-354-7236 stoney@newulmtel.net www.stoneypoint.com
Storm, Gary, P.O. Box 5211, Richardson, TX 75083 / 214-385-0862
Stott's Creek Armory, Inc., 2526 S. 475W, Morgantown, IN 46160 / 317-878-5489; FAX: 317-878-9489 sccalendar@aol.com www.Sccalendar.aol.com
Stratco, Inc., P.O. Box 2270, Kalispell, MT 59901 / 406-755-1221; FAX: 406-755-1226
Strayer, Sandy. See: STRAYER-VOIGT, INC.
Strayer-Voigt, Inc., Sandy Strayer, 3435 Ray Orr Blvd, Grand Prairie, TX 75050 / 972-513-0575
Strong Holster Co., 39 Grove St., Gloucester, MA 01930 / 508-281-3300; FAX: 508-281-6321
Strutz Rifle Barrels, Inc., W. C., P.O. Box 611, Eagle River, WI 54521 / 715-479-4766
Stuart, V. Pat, Rt.1, Box 447-S, Greenville, VA 24440 / 804-556-3845
Sturgeon Valley Sporters, Ken Ide, P.O. Box 283, Vanderbilt, MI 49795 / 517-983-4338 k.ide@mail.com
Sturm Ruger & Co. Inc., 200 Ruger Rd., Prescott, AZ 86301 / 928-541-8820; FAX: 520-541-8850 www.ruger.com
"Su-Press-On", Inc., P.O. Box 09161, Detroit, MI 48209 / 313-842-4222
Sullivan, David S. (See Westwind Rifles, Inc.)
Sun Welding Safe Co., 290 Easy St. No.3, Simi Valley, CA 93065 / 805-584-6678; or 800-729-SAFE; FAX: 805-584-6169 sunwelding.com
Sunny Hill Enterprises, Inc., W1790 Cty. HHH, Malone, WI 53049 / 920-795-4722; FAX: 920-795-4822
Super 6 LLC, Gary Knopp, 3806 W. Lisbon Ave., Milwaukee, WI 53208 / 414-344-3343; FAX: 414-344-0304
Sure-Shot Game Calls, Inc., P.O. Box 816, 6835 Capitol, Groves, TX 77619 / 409-962-1636; FAX: 409-962-5465
Svon Corp., 2107 W. Blue Heron Blvd., Riviera Beach, FL 33404 / 508-881-8852
Swann, D. J., 5 Orsova Close, Eltham North Vic., 3095 AUSTRALIA / 03-431-0323
Swanndri New Zealand, 152 Elm Ave., Burlingame, CA 94010 / 415-347-6158
Swanson, Mark, 975 Heap Avenue, Prescott, AZ 86301 / 928-778-4423
Swarovski Optik North America Ltd., 2 Slater Rd., Cranston, RI 02920 / 401-946-2220; or 800-426-3089; FAX: 401-946-2587
Sweet Home, Inc., P.O. Box 900, Orrville, OH 44667-0900
Swenson's 45 Shop, A. D., 3839 Ladera Vista Rd, Fallbrook, CA 92028-9431
Swift Bullet Co., P.O. Box 27, 201 Main St., Quinter, KS 67752 / 913-754-3959; FAX: 913-754-2359
Swift Instruments, Inc., 952 Dorchester Ave., Boston, MA 02125 / 617-436-2960; FAX: 617-436-3232
Swift River Gunworks, 450 State St., Belchertown, MA 01007 / 413-323-4052
Szweda, Robert (See RMS Custom Gunsmithing)

T

T&S Industries, Inc., 1027 Skyview Dr., W. Carrollton, OH 45449 / 513-859-8414
T.F.C. S.p.A., Via G. Marconi 118, B, Villa Carcina 25069, ITALY / 030-881271; FAX: 030-881826
T.G. Faust, Inc., 544 Minor St., Reading, PA 19602 / 610-375-8549; FAX: 610-375-4488
T.K. Lee Co., 1282 Branchwater Ln., Birmingham, AL 35216 / 205-913-5222 odonmich@aol.com www.scopedot.com
T.W. Menck Gunsmith, Inc., 5703 S. 77th St., Ralston, NE 68127 guntools@cox.net http://llwww.members.cox.net/guntools
Tabler Marketing, 2554 Lincoln Blvd., Suite 555, Marina Del Rey, CA 90291 / 818-755-4565; FAX: 818-755-0972
Taconic Firearms Ltd., Perry Lane, P.O. Box 553, Cambridge, NY 12816 / 518-677-2704; FAX: 518-677-5974
Tactical Defense Institute, 2174 Bethany Ridges, West Union, OH 45693 / 937-544-7228; FAX: 937-544-2887 tdiohio@dragonbbs.com www.tdiohio.com

MANUFACTURER'S DIRECTORY

Talley, Dave, P.O. Box 821, Glenrock, WY 82637 / 307-436-8724; or 307-436-9315
Talon Industries Inc. (See Cobra Enterprises, Inc.)
Tamarack Products, Inc., P.O. Box 625, Wauconda, IL 60084 / 708-526-9333; FAX: 708-526-9353
Tanfoglio Fratelli S.r.l., via Valtrompia 39, 41, Brescia, ITALY / 30-8910361; FAX: 30-8910183
Tanglefree Industries, 1261 Heavenly Dr., Martinez, CA 94553 / 800-982-4868; FAX: 510-825-3874
Tank's Rifle Shop, P.O. Box 474, Fremont, NE 68026-0474 / 402-727-1317 jtank@tanksrifleshop.com www.tanksrifleshop.com
Tanner (See U.S. Importer-Mandall Shooting Supply)
Taracorp Industries, Inc., 1200 Sixteenth St., Granite City, IL 62040 / 618-451-4400
Target Shooting, Inc., P.O. Box 773, Watertown, SD 57201 / 605-882-6955; FAX: 605-882-8840
Tar-Hunt Custom Rifles, Inc., 101 Dogtown Rd., Bloomsburg, PA 17815 / 570-784-6368; FAX: 570-389-9150 www.tar-hunt.com
Tarnhelm Supply Co., Inc., 431 High St., Boscawen, NH 03303 / 603-796-2551; FAX: 603-796-2918 info@tarnhelm.com www.tarnhelm.com
Tasco Sales, Inc., 2889 Commerce Pky., Miramar, FL 33025
Taurus Firearms, Inc., 16175 NW 49th Ave., Miami, FL 33014 / 305-624-1115; FAX: 305-623-7506
Taurus International Firearms (See U.S. Importer)
Taurus S.A. Forjas, Avenida Do Forte 511, Porto Alegre, RS BRAZIL 91360 / 55-51-347-4050; FAX: 55-51-347-3065
Taylor & Robbins, P.O. Box 164, Rixford, PA 16745 / 814-966-3233
Taylor's & Co., Inc., 304 Lenoir Dr., Winchester, VA 22603 / 540-722-2017; FAX: 540-722-2018
TCCI, P.O. Box 302, Phoenix, AZ 85001 / 602-237-3823; FAX: 602-237-3858
TCSR, 3998 Hoffman Rd., White Bear Lake, MN 55110-4626 / 800-328-5323; FAX: 612-429-0526
TDP Industries, Inc., P.O. Box 249, Ottsville, PA 18942-0249 / 215-345-8687; FAX: 215-345-6057
Techno Arms (See U.S. Importer- Auto-Ordnance Corp
Tecnolegno S.p.A., Via A. Locatelli, 6 10, 24019 Zogno, I ITALY / 0345-55111; FAX: 0345-55155
Ted Blocker Holsters, Inc., 9396 S.W. Tigard St., Tigard, OR 97223 / 800-650-9742; FAX: 503-670-9692 www.tedblocker.com
Tele-Optics, 630 E. Rockland Rd., P.O. Box 6313, Libertyville, IL 60048 / 847-362-7757; FAX: 847-362-7757
Tennessee Valley Mfg., 14 County Road 521, Corinth, MS 38834 / 601-286-5014 tvm@avsia.com www.avsia.com/tvm
Ten-Ring Precision, Inc., Alex B. Hamilton, 1449 Blue Crest Lane, San Antonio, TX 78232 / 210-494-3063; FAX: 210-494-3066
TEN-X Products Group, 1905 N Main St, Suite 133, Cleburne, TX 76031-1305 / 972-243-4016; or 800-433-2225; FAX: 972-243-4112
Tepeco, P.O. Box 342, Friendswood, TX 77546 / 713-482-2702
Terry K. Kopp Professional Gunsmithing, Rt 1 Box 224, Lexington, MO 64067 / 816-259-2636
Testing Systems, Inc., 220 Pegasus Ave., Northvale, NJ 07647
Tetra Gun Care, 8 Vreeland Rd., Florham Park, NJ 07932 / 973-443-0004; FAX: 973-443-0263
Tex Shoemaker & Sons, Inc., 714 W. Cienega Ave., San Dimas, CA 91773 / 909-592-2071; FAX: 909-592-2378 texshoemaker@texshoemaker.com www.texshoemaker.com
Texas Armory (See Bond Arms, Inc.)
Texas Platers Supply Co., 2453 W. Five Mile Parkway, Dallas, TX 75233 / 214-330-7168
Thad Rybka Custom Leather Equipment, 2050 Canoe Creek Rd., Springvale, AL 35146-6709
Thad Scott Fine Guns, Inc., P.O. Box 412, Indianola, MS 38751 / 601-887-5929
The A.W. Peterson Gun Shop, Inc., 4255 West Old U.S. 441, Mount Dora, FL 32757-3299 / 352-383-4258
The Accuracy Den, 25 Bitterbrush Rd., Reno, NV 89523 / 702-345-0225
The Ballistic Program Co., Inc., 2417 N. Patterson St., Thomasville, GA 31792 / 912-228-5739 or 800-368-0835
The BulletMakers Workshop, RFD 1 Box 1755, Brooks, ME 04921
The Competitive Pistol Shop, 5233 Palmer Dr., Ft. Worth, TX 76117-2433 / 817-834-8479
The Concealment Shop, Inc., 3550 E. Hwy. 80, Mesquite, TX 75149 / 972-289-8997; or 800-444-7090; FAX: 972-289-4410 info@theconcealmentshop.com www.theconcealmentshop.com
The Country Armourer, P.O. Box 308, Ashby, MA 01431-0308 / 508-827-6797; FAX: 508-827-4845
The Creative Craftsman, Inc., 95 Highway 29 North, P.O. Box 331, Lawrenceville, GA 30246 / 404-963-2112; FAX: 404-513-9488
The Custom Shop, 890 Cochrane Crescent, Peterborough, ON K9H 5N3 CANADA / 705-742-6693
The Ensign-Bickford Co., 660 Hopmeadow St., Simsbury, CT 06070
The Firearm Training Center, 9555 Blandville Rd., West Paducah, KY 42086 / 502-554-5886
The Fouling Shot, 6465 Parfet St., Arvada, CO 80004
The Gun Doctor, 435 East Maple, Roselle, IL 60172 / 708-894-0668
The Gun Room, 1121 Burlington, Muncie, IN 47302 / 765-282-9073; FAX: 765-282-5270 bshstleguns@aol.com
The Gun Room Press, 127 Raritan Ave., Highland Park, NJ 08904 / 732-545-4344; FAX: 732-545-6686 gunbooks@rutgersgunbooks.com www.rutgersgunbooks.com
The Gun Shop, 62778 Spring Creek Rd., Montrose, CO 81401
The Gun Shop, 5550 S. 900 East, Salt Lake City, UT 84117 / 801-263-3633
The Gun Works, 247 S. 2nd St., Springfield, OR 97477 / 541-741-4118; FAX: 541-988-1097 gunworks@worldnet.att.net www.thegunworks.com
The Gunsight, 1712 North Placentia Ave., Fullerton, CA 92631
The Hanned Line, 4463 Madoc Way, San Jose, CA 95130 smith@hanned.com www.hanned.com
The Hawken Shop, P.O. Box 593, Oak Harbor, WA 98277 / 206-679-4657; FAX: 206-675-1114
The Keller Co., P.O. Box 4057, Port Angeles, WA 98363-0997 / 214-770-8585
The Lewis Lead Remover (See LEM Gun Specialties)
The Midwest Shooting School, Pat LaBoone, 2550 Hwy. 23, Wrenshall, MN 55797 / 218-384-3670 shootingschool@starband.net
The NgraveR Co., 67 Wawecus Hill Rd., Bozrah, CT 06334 / 860-823-1533; FAX: 860-887-6252 ngraver98@aol.com www.ngraver.com
The Ordnance Works, 2969 Pidgeon Point Road, Eureka, CA 95501 / 707-443-3252
The Orvis Co., Rt. 7, Manchester, VT 05254 / 802-362-3622; FAX: 802-362-3525
The Outdoor Connection, Inc., 7901 Panther Way, Waco, TX 76712-6556 / 800-533-6076 or 254-772-5575; FAX: 254-776-3553 floyd@outdoorconnection.com www.outdoorconnection.com
The Park Rifle Co., Ltd., Unit 6a Dartford Trade Park, Power Mill Lane, Dartford DA7 7NX, ENGLAND / 011-0322-222512
The Paul Co., 27385 Pressonville Rd., Wellsville, KS 66092 / 785-883-4444; FAX: 785-883-2525
The Protector Mfg. Co., Inc., 443 Ashwood Place, Boca Raton, FL 33431 / 407-394-6011
The Robar Co., Inc., 21438 N. 7th Ave., Suite B, Phoenix, AZ 85027 / 623-581-2648; FAX: 623-582-0059 info@robarguns.com www.robarguns.com
The School of Gunsmithing, 6065 Roswell Rd., Atlanta, GA 30328 / 800-223-4542
The Shooting Gallery, 8070 Southern Blvd., Boardman, OH 44512 / 216-726-7788
The Sight Shop, John G. Lawson, 1802 E. Columbia Ave., Tacoma, WA 98404 / 253-474-5465 parahellum9@aol.com www.thesightshop.org
The Southern Armory, 25 Millstone Road, Woodlawn, VA 24381 / 703-238-1343; FAX: 703-238-1453
The Surecase Co., 233 Wilshire Blvd., Ste. 900, Santa Monica, CA 90401 / 800-92ARMLOC
The Swampfire Shop (See Peterson Gun Shop, Inc.)
The Wilson Arms Co., 63 Leetes Island Rd., Branford, CT 06405 / 203-488-7297; FAX: 203-488-0135
Theis, Terry, 21452 FM 2093, Harper, TX 78631 / 830-864-4438
Thiewes, George W., 14329 W. Parada Dr., Sun City West, AZ 85375
Things Unlimited, 235 N. Kimbau, Casper, WY 82601 / 307-234-5277
Thirion Gun Engraving, Denise, PO Box 408, Graton, CA 95444 / 707-829-1876
Thomas, Charles C., 2600 S. First St., Springfield, IL 62704 / 217-789-8980; FAX: 217-789-9130 books@ccthomas.com ccthomas.com
Thompson Bullet Lube Co., P.O. Box 409, Wills Point, TX 75169 / 866-476-1500; FAX: 866-476-1500 thompsonbulletlube.com www.thompsonbulletlube.com
Thompson Precision, 110 Mary St., P.O. Box 251, Warren, IL 61087 / 815-745-3625
Thompson, Randall. See: HIGHLINE MACHINE CO.
Thompson Target Technology, 4804 Sherman Church Ave. S.W., Canton, OH 44710 / 330-484-6480; FAX: 330-491-1087 www.thompsontarget.com
Thompson Tool Mount, 1550 Solomon Rd., Santa Maria, CA 93455 / 805-934-1281 ttm@pronet.net www.thompsontoolmount.com
Thompson/Center Arms, P.O. Box 5002, Rochester, NH 03866 / 603-332-2394; FAX: 603-332-5133 tech@tcarms.com www.tcarms.com
3-Ten Corp., P.O. Box 269, Feeding Hills, MA 01030 / 413-789-2086; FAX: 413-789-1549
Thunden Ranch, HCR 1, Box 53, Mt. Home, TX 78058 / 830-640-3138
Thurston Sports, Inc., RD 3 Donovan Rd., Auburn, NY 13021 / 315-253-0966
Tiger-Hunt Gunstocks, Box 379, Beaverdale, PA 15921 / 814-472-5161 tigerhunt4@aol.com www.gunstockwood.com
Tikka (See U.S. Importer-Stoeger Industries)
Time Precision, 4 Nicholas Sq., New Milford, CT 06776-3506 / 203-775-8343
Tinks & Ben Lee Hunting Products (See Wellington)
Tink's Safariland Hunting Corp., P.O. Box 244, 1140 Monticello Rd., Madison, GA 30650 / 706-342-4915; FAX: 706-342-7568
Tioga Engineering Co., Inc., P.O. Box 913, 13 Cone St., Wellsboro, PA 16901 / 570-724-3533; FAX: 570-724-3895 tiogaeng@epix.net
Tippman Pneumatics, Inc., 2955 Adams Center Rd., Fort Wayne, IN 46803
Tirelli, Snc Di Tirelli Primo E.C., Via Matteotti No. 359, Gardone V.T. Brescia, I ITALY / 030-8912819; FAX: 030-832240
TM Stockworks, 6355 Maplecrest Rd., Fort Wayne, IN 46835 / 219-485-5389
TMI Products (See Haselbauer Products, Jerry)
Tom Forrest, Inc., P.O. Box 326, Lakeside, CA 92040 / 619-561-5800; FAX: 888-GUN-CLIP info@gunmag.com www.gunmags.com
Tombstone Smoke`n' Deals, PO Box 31298, Phoenix, AZ 85046 / 602-905-7013; FAX: 602-443-1998
Tom's Gun Repair, Thomas G. Ivanoff, 76-6 Rt. Southfork Rd., Cody, WY 82414 / 307-587-6949
Tom's Gunshop, 3601 Central Ave., Hot Springs, AR 71913 / 501-624-3856
Tonoloway Tack Drives, HCR 81, Box 100, Needmore, PA 17238
Torel, Inc., 1708 N. South St., P.O. Box 592, Yoakum, TX 77995 / 512-293-2341; FAX: 512-293-3413
TOZ (See U.S. Importer-Nygord Precision Products)
Track of the Wolf, Inc., 18308 Joplin St. NW, Elk River, MN 55330-1773 / 763-633-2500; FAX: 763-633-2550
Traditions Performance Firearms, P.O. Box 776, 1375 Boston Post Rd., Old Saybrook, CT 06475 / 860-388-4656; FAX: 860-388-4657 info@traditionsfirearms.com www.traditionsfirearms.com
Trafalgar Square, P.O. Box 257, N. Pomfret, VT 05053 / 802-457-1911
Trail Visions, 5800 N. Ames Terrace, Glendale, WI 53209 / 414-228-1328
Trax America, Inc., PO Box 898, 1150 Eldridge, Forrest City, AR 72335 / 870-633-0410; or 800-232-2327; FAX: 870-633-4788 trax@ipa.net www.traxamerica.com
Treadlok Gun Safe, Inc., 1764 Granby St. NE, Roanoke, VA 24012 / 800-729-8732; or 703-982-6881; FAX: 703-982-1059
Treemaster, P.O. Box 247, Guntersville, AL 35976 / 205-878-3597
Trevallion Gunstocks, 9 Old Mountain Rd., Cape Neddick, ME 03902 / 207-361-1130
Trico Plastics, 28061 Diaz Rd., Temecula, CA 92590 / 909-676-7714; FAX: 909-676-0267 ustinfo@ustplastics.com www.tricoplastics.com
Trigger Lock Division / Central Specialties Ltd., 220-D Exchange Dr., Crystal Lake, IL 60014 / 847-639-3900; FAX: 847-639-3972
Trijicon, Inc., 49385 Shafer Ave., P.O. Box 930059, Wixom, MI 48393-0059 / 248-960-7700 or 800-338-0563
Trilby Sport Shop, 1623 Hagley Rd., Toledo, OH 43612-2024 / 419-472-6222
Trilux, Inc., P.O. Box 24608, Winston-Salem, NC 27114 / 910-659-9438; FAX: 910-768-7720

MANUFACTURER'S DIRECTORY

Trinidad St. Jr. Col. Gunsmith Dept., 600 Prospect St., Trinidad, CO 81082 / 719-846-5631; FAX: 719-846-5667
Triple-K Mfg. Co., Inc., 2222 Commercial St., San Diego, CA 92113 / 619-232-2066; FAX: 619-232-7675 sales@triplek.com www.triplek.com
Tristar Sporting Arms, Ltd., 1814 Linn St. #16, N. Kansas City, MO 64116-3627 / 816-421-1400; FAX: 816-421-4182 tristar@blitz-it.net www.tristarsportingarms
Trius Traps, Inc., P.O. Box 25, 221 S. Miami Ave., Cleves, OH 45002 / 513-941-5682; FAX: 513-941-7970 triustraps@fuse.net www.triustraps.com
Trooper Walsh, 2393 N. Edgewood St., Arlington, VA 22207
Trotman, Ken, 135 Ditton Walk, Unit 11, Cambridge, CB5 8PY ENGLAND / 01223-211030; FAX: 01223-212317 www.kentrolman.com
Tru-Balance Knife Co., P.O. Box 140555, Grand Rapids, MI 49514 / 616-647-1215
True Flight Bullet Co., 5581 Roosevelt St., Whitehall, PA 18052 / 610-262-7630; FAX: 610-262-7806
Truglo, Inc., P.O. Box 1612, McKinna, TX 75070 / 972-774-0300; FAX: 972-774-0323 www.truglosights.com
Trulock Tool, P.O. Box 530, Whigham, GA 31797 / 229-762-4678; FAX: 229-762-4050 trulockchokes@hotmail.com trulockchokes.com
Tru-Square Metal Products, Inc., 640 First St. SW, P.O. Box 585, Auburn, WA 98071 / 253-833-2310; or 800-225-1017; FAX: 253-833-2349 t-tumbler@qwest.net
Tucker, James C., P.O. Box 366, Medford, OR 97501 / 541-245-3887 jctstocker@yahoo.com
Tucson Mold, Inc., 930 S. Plumer Ave., Tucson, AZ 85719 / 520-792-1075; FAX: 520-792-1075
Turk's Head Productions, Mustafa Bilal, 908 NW 50th St., Seattle, WA 98107-3634 / 206-782-4164; FAX: 206-783-5677 info@turkshead.com www.turkshead.com
Turnbull Restoration, Doug, 6680 Rt. 5 & 20, P.O. Box 471, Bloomfield, NY 14469 / 585-657-6338; FAX: 585-657-6338 turnbullrest@mindspring.com www.turnbullrestoration.com
Tuttle, Dale, 4046 Russell Rd., Muskegon, MI 49445 / 616-766-2250
Tyler Manufacturing & Distributing, 3804 S. Eastern, Oklahoma City, OK 73129 / 405-677-1487; or 800-654-8415

U

U.S. Fire Arms Mfg. Co., Inc., 55 Van Dyke Ave., Hartford, CT 06106 / 877-227-6901; FAX: 800-644-7265 usfirearms.com
U.S. Importer-Wm. Larkin Moore, 8430 E. Raintree Ste. B-7, Scottsdale, AZ 85260
U.S. Optics, A Division of Zeitz Optics U.S.A., 5900 Dale St., Buena Park, CA 90621 / 714-994-4901; FAX: 714-994-4904 www.usoptics.com
U.S. Repeating Arms Co., Inc., 275 Winchester Ave., Morgan, UT 84050-9333 / 801-876-3440; FAX: 801-876-3737 www.winchester-guns.com
U.S. Tactical Systems (See Keng's Firearms Specialty)
Ugartechea S. A., Ignacio, Chonta 26, Eibar, SPAIN / 43-121257; FAX: 43-121669
Ultra Dot Distribution, P.O. Box 362, 6304 Riverside Dr., Yankeetown, FL 34498 / 352-447-2255; FAX: 352-447-2266
Ultralux (See U.S. Importer-Keng's Firearms)
UltraSport Arms, Inc., 1955 Norwood Ct., Racine, WI 53403 / 414-554-3237; FAX: 414-554-9731
Uncle Bud's, HCR 81, Box 100, Needmore, PA 17238 / 717-294-6000; FAX: 717-294-6005
Uncle Mike's (See Michaels of Oregon Co.)
Unertl Optical Co., Inc., 103 Grand Avenue, P.O. Box 895, Mars, PA 16046-0895 / 724-625-3810; FAX: 724-625-3819 unertl@nauticom.net www.unertloptics.net
Unique/M.A.P.F., 10 Les Allees, 64700, Hendaye, FRANCE / 33-59 20 71 93
UniTec, 1250 Bedford SW, Canton, OH 44710 / 216-452-4017
United Binocular Co., 9043 S. Western Ave., Chicago, IL 60620
United Cutlery Corp., 1425 United Blvd., Sevierville, TN 37876 / 865-428-2532; or 800-548-0835; FAX: 865-428-2267
United States Products Co., 518 Melwood Ave., Pittsburgh, PA 15213-1136 / 412-621-2130; FAX: 412-621-8740 sales@us-products.com www.us-products.com
Universal Sports, P.O. Box 532, Vincennes, IN 47591 / 812-882-8680; FAX: 812-882-8680
Upper Missouri Trading Co., P.O. Box 100, 304 Harold St., Crofton, NE 68730-0100 / 402-388-4844
USAC, 4500-15th St. East, Tacoma, WA 98424 / 206-922-7589
Uselton/Arms, Inc., 842 Conference Dr., Goodlettsville, TN 37072 / 615-851-4919
Utica Cutlery Co., 820 Noyes St., Utica, NY 13503 / 315-733-4663; FAX: 315-733-6602

V

V.H. Blackinton & Co., Inc., 221 John L. Dietsch, Attleboro Falls, MA 02763-0300 / 508-699-4436; FAX: 508-695-5349
Valdada Enterprises, P.O. Box 773122, 31733 County Road 35, Steamboat Springs, CO 80477 / 970-879-2983; FAX: 970-879-0851 www.valdada.com
Valtro USA, Inc., 1281 Andersen Dr., San Rafael, CA 94901 / 415-256-2575; FAX: 415-256-2576
VAM Distribution Co. LLC, 1141-B Mechanicsburg Rd., Wooster, OH 44691 www.rex10.com
Van Gorden & Son Inc., C. S., 1815 Main St., Bloomer, WI 54724 / 715-568-2612
Van Horn, Gil, P.O. Box 207, Llano, CA 93544
Van Patten, J. W., P.O. Box 145, Foster Hill, Milford, PA 18337 / 717-296-7069
Vann Custom Bullets, 2766 N. Willowside Way, Meridian, ID 83642
Van's Gunsmith Service, 224 Route 69-A, Parish, NY 13131 / 315-625-7251
Varmint Masters, LLC, Rick Vecqueray, P.O. Box 6724, Bend, OR 97708 / 541-318-7306; FAX: 541-318-7306 varmintmasters@bendcable.com www.varmintmasters.net
Vecqueray, Rick. See: VARMINT MASTERS, LLC
Vega Tool Co., c/o T.R. Ross, 4865 Tanglewood Ct., Boulder, CO 80301 / 303-530-0174 clanlaird@aol.com www.vegatool.com
Vektor USA, Mikael Danforth, 5139 Stanart St, Norfolk, VA 23502 / 888-740-0837; or 757-455-8895; FAX: 757-461-9155
Venco Industries, Inc. (See Shooter's Choice Gun Care)
Venus Industries, P.O. Box 246, Sialkot-1, PAKISTAN FAX: 92 432 85579
Verney-Carron, BP 72-54 Boulevard Thiers, 42002 St Etienne Cedex 1, St Etienne Cedex 1, FRANCE / 33-477791500; FAX: 33-477790702 email@verney-carron.com www.verney-carron.com
Vest, John, 1923 NE 7th St., Redmond, OR 97756 / 541-923-8898
VibraShine, Inc., P.O. Box 577, Taylorsville, MS 39168 / 601-785-9854; FAX: 601-785-9874 rdbekevibrashine.com www.vibrashine.com
Vibra-Tek Co., 1844 Arroya Rd., Colorado Springs, CO 80906 / 719-634-8611; FAX: 719-634-6886
Vic's Gun Refinishing, 6 Pineview Dr., Dover, NH 03820-6422 / 603-742-0013
Victory Ammunition, P.O. Box 1022, Milford, PA 18337 / 717-296-5768; FAX: 717-296-9298
Victory USA, P.O. Box 1021, Pine Bush, NY 12566 / 914-744-2060; FAX: 914-744-5181
Vihtavuori Oy, FIN-41330 Vihtavuori, FINLAND, / 358-41-3779211; FAX: 358-41-3771643
Vihtavuori Oy/Kaltron-Pettibone, 1241 Ellis St., Bensenville, IL 60106 / 708-350-1116; FAX: 708-350-1606
Viking Video Productions, P.O. Box 251, Roseburg, OR 97470
Village Restorations & Consulting, Inc., P.O. Box 569, Claysburg, PA 16625 / 814-239-8200; FAX: 814-239-2165 www.villagerestoration@yahoo.com
Vincent's Shop, 210 Antoinette, Fairbanks, AK 99701
Vintage Industries, Inc., 2772 Depot St., Sanford, FL 32773
Viper Bullet and Brass Works, 11 Brock St., Box 582, Norwich, ON N0J 1P0 CANADA
Viramontez Engraving, Ray Viramontez, 601 Springfield Dr., Albany, GA 31721 / 229-432-9683 sgtvira@aol.com
Viramontez, Ray. See: VIRAMONTEZ ENGRAVING
Virgin Valley Custom Guns, 450 E 800 N #20, Hurricane, UT 84737 / 435-635-8941; FAX: 435-635-8943 vvcguns@infowest.com www.virginvalleyguns.com
Visible Impact Targets, Rts. 5 & 20, E. Bloomfield, NY 14443 / 716-657-6161; FAX: 716-657-5405
Vitt/Boos, 1195 Buck Hill Rd., Townshend, VT 05353 / 802-365-9232
Voere-KGH GmbH, Untere Sparchen 56, A-6330 Kufstein, Tirol, AUSTRIA / 0043-5372-62547; FAX: 0043-5372-65752 voere@aon.com www.voere.com
Volquartsen Custom Ltd., 24276 240th Street, PO Box 397, Carroll, IA 51401 / 712-792-4238; FAX: 712-792-2542 vcl@netins.net www.volquartsen.com
Vorhes, David, 3042 Beecham St., Napa, CA 94558 / 707-226-9116; FAX: 707-253-7334
VSP Publishers (See Heritage/VSP Gun Books), P.O. Box 887, McCall, ID 83638 / 208-634-4104; FAX: 208-634-3101 heritage@gunbooks.com www.gunbooks.com
VTI Gun Parts, P.O. Box 509, Lakeville, CT 06039 / 860-435-8068; FAX: 860-435-8146 mail@vtigunparts.com www.vtigunparts.com
Vulpes Ventures, Inc., Fox Cartridge Division, P.O. Box 1363, Bolingbrook, IL 60440-7363 / 630-759-1229

W

W. Square Enterprises, 9826 Sagedale Dr., Houston, TX 77089 / 281-484-0935; FAX: 281-464-9940 lfdw@pdq.net www.loadammo.com
W. Waller & Son, Inc., 2221 Stoney Brook Rd., Grantham, NH 03753-7706 / 603-863-4177 www.wallerandson.com
W.B. Niemi Engineering, Box 126 Center Road, Greensboro, VT 05841 / 802-533-7180 or 802-533-7141
W.C. Wolff Co., P.O. Box 458, Newtown Square, PA 19073 / 610-359-9600; or 800-545-0077; mail@gunsprings.com www.gunsprings.com
W.E. Birdsong & Assoc., 1435 Monterey Rd., Florence, MS 39073-9748 / 601-366-8270
W.E. Brownell Checkering Tools, 9390 Twin Mountain Cir., San Diego, CA 92126 / 858-695-2479; FAX: 858-695-2479
W.J. Riebe Co., 3434 Tucker Rd., Boise, ID 83703
W.R. Case & Sons Cutlery Co., Owens Way, Bradford, PA 16701 / 814-368-4123; or 800-523-6350; FAX: 814-368-1736 jsullivan@wrcase.com www.wrcase.com
Wagoner, Vernon G., 2325 E. Encanto St., Mesa, AZ 85213-5917 / 480-835-1307
Wakina by Pic, 24813 Alderbrook Dr., Santa Clarita, CA 91321 / 800-295-8194
Waldron, Herman, Box 475, 80 N. 17th St., Pomeroy, WA 99347 / 509-843-1404
Walker Arms Co., Inc., 499 County Rd. 820, Selma, AL 36701 / 334-872-6231; FAX: 334-872-6262
Wallace, Terry, 385 San Marino, Vallejo, CA 94589 / 707-642-7041
Walls Industries, Inc., P.O. Box 98, 1905 N. Main, Cleburne, TX 76033 / 817-645-4366; FAX: 817-645-7946 www.wallsoutdoors.com
Walters Industries, 6226 Park Lane, Dallas, TX 75225 / 214-691-6973
Walters, John. See: WALTERS WADS
Walters Wads, John Walters, 500 N. Avery Dr., Moore, OK 73160 / 405-799-0376; FAX: 405-799-7727 www.tinwadman@cs.com
Walther America, P.O. Box 22, Springfield, MA 01102 / 413-747-3443 www.walther-usa.com
Walther GmbH, Carl, B.P. 4325, D-89033 Ulm, GERMANY
Walt's Custom Leather, Walt Whinnery, 1947 Meadow Creek Dr., Louisville, KY 40218 / 502-458-4361
WAMCO-New Mexico, P.O. Box 205, Peralta, NM 87042-0205 / 505-869-0826
Ward & Van Valkenburg, 114 32nd Ave. N., Fargo, ND 58102 / 701-232-2351
Ward Machine, 5620 Lexington Rd., Corpus Christi, TX 78412 / 512-992-1221
Wardell Precision Handguns Ltd., 48851 N. Fig Springs Rd., New River, AZ 85027-8513 / 602-465-7995
Warenski Engraving, Julie Warenski, 590 E. 500 N., Richfield, UT 84701 / 435-896-5319; FAX: 435-896-8333 julie@warenskiknives.com
Warenski, Julie. See: WARENSKI ENGRAVING
Warne Manufacturing Co., 9057 SE Jannsen Rd., Clackamas, OR 97015 / 503-657-5590 or 800-683-5590; FAX: 503-657-5695 info@warnescopemounts.com www.warnescopemounts.com
Warren Muzzleloading Co., Inc., Hwy. 21 North, P.O. Box 100, Ozone, AR 72854 / 501-292-3268
Washita Mountain Whetstone Co., P.O. Box 378, Lake Hamilton, AR 71951 / 501-525-3914
Wasmundt, Jim, P.O. Box 511, Fossil, OR 97830
Watson Bros., 39 Redcross Way, SE1 1H6, London, ENGLAND FAX: 44-171-403-336

MANUFACTURER'S DIRECTORY

Watson Bullets, 231 Allies Pass, Frostproof, FL 33843 / 863-635-7948 cbestbullet@aol.com
Wayne E. Schwartz Custom Guns, 970 E. Britton Rd., Morrice, MI 48857 / 517-625-4079
Wayne Firearms For Collectors & Investors
Wayne Specialty Services, 260 Waterford Drive, Florissant, MO 63033 / 413-831-7083
WD-40 Co., 1061 Cudahy Pl., San Diego, CA 92110 / 619-275-1400; FAX: 619-275-5823
Weatherby, Inc., 3100 El Camino Real, Atascadero, CA 93422 / 805-466-1767; FAX: 805-466-2527 www.weatherby.com
Weaver Products ATK, P.O. Box 39, Onalaska, WI 54650 / 800-648-9624 or 608-781-5800; FAX: 608-781-0368
Weaver Scope Repair Service, 1121 Larry Mahan Dr., Suite B, El Paso, TX 79925 / 915-593-1005
Webb, Bill, 6504 North Bellefontaine, Kansas City, MO 64119 / 816-453-7431
Weber & Markin Custom Gunsmiths, 4-1691 Powick Rd., Kelowna, BC V1X 4L1 CANADA / 250-762-7575; FAX: 250-861-3655 www.weberandmarkinguns.com
Webley and Scott Ltd., Frankley Industrial Park, Tay Rd., Birmingham, B45 0PA ENGLAND / 011-021-453-1864; FAX: 0121-457-7846 guns@webley.co.uk www.webley.co.uk
Webster Scale Mfg. Co., P.O. Box 188, Sebring, FL 33870 / 813-385-6362
Weems, Cecil, 510 W Hubbard St., Mineral Wells, TX 76067-4847 / 817-325-1462
Weigand Combat Handguns, Inc., 1057 South Main Rd., Mountain Top, PA 18707 / 570-868-8358; FAX: 570-868-5218 sales@jackweigand.com www.jackweigand.com
Weihrauch KG, Hermann, Industriestrasse 11, 8744 Mellrichstadt, Mellrichstadt, GERMANY
Welch, Sam. See: SAM WELCH GUN ENGRAVING
Wellington Outdoors, P.O. Box 244, 1140 Monticello Rd., Madison, GA 30650 / 706-342-4915; FAX: 706-342-7568
Wells, Rachel, 110 N. Summit St., Prescott, AZ 86301 / 928-445-3655 wellssportstore@cableone.net wellssportstore@cableone-net
Wells Creek Knife & Gun Works, 32956 State Hwy. 38, Scottsburg, OR 97473 / 541-587-4202; FAX: 541-587-4223
Welsh, Bud. See: HIGH PRECISION
Wenger North America/Precise Int'l., 15 Corporate Dr., Orangeburg, NY 10962 / 800-431-2996; FAX: 914-425-4700
Wenig Custom Gunstocks, 103 N. Market St., P.O. Box 249, Lincoln, MO 65338 / 660-547-3334; FAX: 660-547-2881 gustock@wenig.com www.wenig.com
Werth, T. W., 1203 Woodlawn Rd., Lincoln, IL 62656 / 217-732-1300
Wescombe, Bill (See North Star West)
Wessinger Custom Guns & Engraving, 268 Limestone Rd., Chapin, SC 29036 / 803-345-5677
West, Jack L., 1220 W. Fifth, P.O. Box 427, Arlington, OR 97812
Western Cutlery (See Camillus Cutlery Co.)
Western Design (See Alpha Gunsmith Division)
Western Mfg. Co., 550 Valencia School Rd., Aptos, CA 95003 / 831-688-5884 lotsabears@eathlink.net
Western Missouri Shooters Alliance, P.O. Box 11144, Kansas City, MO 64119 / 816-597-3950; FAX: 816-229-7350
Western Nevada West Coast Bullets, P.O. BOX 2270, DAYTON, NV 89403-2270 / 702-246-3941; FAX: 702-246-0836
Westley Richards & Co. Ltd., 40 Grange Rd., Birmingham, ENGLAND / 010-214722953; FAX: 010-214141138 sales@westleyrichards.com www.westleyrichards.com
Westley Richards Agency USA (See U.S. Importer for
Westwind Rifles, Inc., David S. Sullivan, P.O. Box 261, 640 Briggs St., Erie, CO 80516 / 303-828-3823
Weyer International, 2740 Nebraska Ave., Toledo, OH 43607 / 419-534-2020; FAX: 419-534-2697
Whildin & Sons Ltd, E.H., RR 2 Box 119, Tamaqua, PA 18252 / 717-668-6743; FAX: 717-668-6745
Whinnery, Walt (See Walt's Custom Leather)
Whiscombe (See U.S. Importer-Pelaire Products)
White Barn Wor, 431 County Road, Broadlands, IL 61816
White Pine Photographic Services, Hwy. 60, General Delivery, Wilno, ON K0J 2N0 CANADA / 613-756-3452
White Rifles, Inc., 234 S.1250 W., Linden, UT 84042 / 801-932-7950 www.whiterifles.com
White Rock Tool & Die, 6400 N. Brighton Ave., Kansas City, MO 64119 / 816-454-0478
Whitestone Lumber Corp., 148-02 14th Ave., Whitestone, NY 11357 / 718-746-4400; FAX: 718-767-1748 whstco@aol.com
Wichita Arms, Inc., 923 E. Gilbert, P.O. Box 11371, Wichita, KS 67211 / 316-265-0661; FAX: 316-265-0760 sales@wichitaarms.com www.wichitaarms.com
Wick, David E., 1504 Michigan Ave., Columbus, IN 47201 / 812-376-6960
Widener's Reloading & Shooting Supply, Inc., P.O. Box 3009 CRS, Johnson City, TN 37602 / 615-282-6786; FAX: 615-282-6651
Wideview Scope Mount Corp., 13535 S. Hwy. 16, Rapid City, SD 57702 / 605-341-3220; FAX: 605-341-9142 wvdon@rapidnet.com www.jii.to
Wiebe, Duane, 5300 Merchant Cir. #2, Placerville, CA 95667 / 530-344-1357; FAX: 530-344-1357 wiebe@d-wdb.com
Wiest, Marie. See: GUNCRAFT SPORTS, INC.
Wilcox All-Pro Tools & Supply, 4880 147th St., Montezuma, IA 50171 / 515-623-3138; FAX: 515-623-3104
Wilcox Industries Corp., Robert F Guarasi, 53 Durham St., Portsmouth, NH 03801 / 603-431-1331; FAX: 603-431-1221
Wild Bill's Originals, P.O. Box 13037, Burton, WA 98013 / 206-463-5738; FAX: 206-465-5925 wildbill@halcyon.com
Wild West Guns, 7521 Old Seward Hwy., Unit A, Anchorage, AK 99518 / 800-992-4570 or 907-344-4500; FAX: 907-344-4005 wwguns@ak.net www.wildwestguns.com
Wilderness Sound Products Ltd., 4015 Main St. A, Springfield, OR 97478 / 800-47-0006; FAX: 541-741-0263
Wildey, Inc., 45 Angevine Rd, Warren, CT 06754-1818 / 203-355-9000; FAX: 203-354-7759
Wildlife Research Center, Inc., 1050 McKinley St., Anoka, MN 55303 / 763-427-3350; or 800-USE-LURE; FAX: 763-427-8354
Will-Burt Co., 169 S. Main, Orrville, OH 44667
William E. Phillips Firearms, 38 Avondale Rd., Wigston, Leicester, ENGLAND / 0116 2886334; FAX: 0116 2810644 wephillips@aol.com
William Powell Agency, 22 Circle Dr., Bellmore, NY 11710 / 516-679-1158
Williams Gun Sight Co., 7389 Lapeer Rd., Box 329, Davison, MI 48423 / 810-653-2131 or 800-530-9028; FAX: 810-658-2140 williamsgunsight.com
Williams Mfg. of Oregon, 110 East B St., Drain, OR 97435 / 503-836-7461; FAX: 503-836-7245
Williams Shootin' Iron Service, The Lynx-Line, Rt. 2 Box 223A, Mountain Grove, MO 65711 / 417-948-0902; FAX: 417-948-0902
Williamson Precision Gunsmithing, 117 W. Pipeline, Hurst, TX 76053 / 817-285-0064; FAX: 817-280-0044
Willow Bend, P.O. Box 203, Chelmsford, MA 01824 / 978-256-8508; FAX: 978-256-8508
Wilsom Combat, 2234 CR 719, Berryville, AR 72616-4573 / 800-955-4856; FAX: 870-545-3310
Wilson Case, Inc., P.O. Box 1106, Hastings, NE 68902-1106 / 800-322-5493; FAX: 402-463-5276 sales@wilsoncase.com www.wilsoncase.com
Wilson Combat, 2234 CR 719, Berryville, AR 72616-4573 / 800-955-4856
Winchester Div. Olin Corp., 427 N. Shamrock, E. Alton, IL 62024 / 618-258-3566; FAX: 618-258-3599
Winchester Sutler, Inc., The, 270 Shadow Brook Lane, Winchester, VA 22603 / 540-888-3595; FAX: 540-888-4632
Windish, Jim, 2510 Dawn Dr., Alexandria, VA 22306 / 703-765-1994
Wingshooting Adventures, 0-1845 W. Leonard, Grand Rapids, MI 49544 / 616-677-1980; FAX: 616-677-1986
Winkle Bullets, R.R. 1, Box 316, Heyworth, IL 61745
Winter, Robert M., P.O. Box 484, 42975-287th St., Menno, SD 57045 / 605-387-5322
Wise Custom Guns, 1402 Blanco Rd., San Antonio, TX 78212-2716 / 210-828-3388
Wise Guns, Dale, 1402 Blanco Rd., San Antonio, TX 78212 / 210-734-9999
Wiseman and Co., Bill, P.O. Box 3427, Bryan, TX 77805 / 409-690-3456; FAX: 409-690-0156
Wisners, Inc., P.O. Box 58, Adna, WA 98522 / 360-748-4590; FAX: 360-748-6028 parts@gunpartsspecialist.com www.wisnersinc.com
Wolf (See J.R. Distributing)
Wolf Performance Ammunition, 2201 E. Winston Rd., Ste. K, Anaheim, CA 92806-5537 / 702-837-8506; FAX: 702-837-9250
Wolfe Publishing Co., 2625 Stearman Rd., Ste. A, Prescott, AZ 86301 / 928-445-7810; or 800-899-7810; FAX: 928-778-5124
Wolf's Western Traders, 1250 Santa Cora Ave. #613, Chula Vista, CA 91913 / 619-482-1701 patwolf4570book@aol.com
Wolverine Footwear Group, 9341 Courtland Dr. NE, Rockford, MI 49351 / 616-866-5500; FAX: 616-866-5658
Wood, Frank (See Classic Guns, Inc.), 5305 Peachtree Ind. Blvd., Norcross, GA 30092 / 404-242-7944
Woodleigh (See Huntington Die Specialties)
Woods Wise Products, P.O. Box 681552, Franklin, TN 37068 / 800-735-8182; FAX: 615-726-2637
Woodstream, P.O. Box 327, Lititz, PA 17543 / 717-626-2125; FAX: 717-626-1912
Woodworker's Supply, 1108 North Glenn Rd., Casper, WY 82601 / 307-237-5354
Woolrich, Inc., Mill St., Woolrich, PA 17701 / 800-995-1299; FAX: 717-769-6234/6259
Working Guns, Jim Coffin, 1224 NW Fernwood Cir., Corvallis, OR 97330-2909 / 541-928-4391
World of Targets (See Birchwood Casey)
World Trek, Inc., 7170 Turkey Creek Rd., Pueblo, CO 81007-1046 / 719-546-2121; FAX: 719-543-6886
Worthy Products, Inc., RR 1, P.O. Box 213, Martville, NY 13111 / 315-324-5298
Wostenholm (See Ibberson [Sheffield] Ltd., George)
Wright's Gunstock Blanks, 8540 SE Kane Rd., Gresham, OR 97080 / 503-666-1705 doyal@wrightsguns.com www.wrightsguns.com
WTA Manufacturing, P.O. Box 164, Kit Carson, CO 80825 / 800-700-3054; FAX: 719-962-3570 wta@rebeltec.net http://www.members.aol.com/ductman249/wta.html
Wyant Bullets, Gen. Del., Swan Lake, MT 59911
Wyant's Outdoor Products, Inc., P.O. Box 9, Broadway, VA 22815
Wyoming Custom Bullets, 1626 21st St., Cody, WY 82414
Wyoming Knife Corp., 101 Commerce Dr., Ft. Collins, CO 80524 / 303-224-3454

X

X-Spand Target Systems, 26-10th St. SE, Medicine Hat, AB T1A 1P7 CANADA / 403-526-7997; FAX: 403-528-2362

Y

Yankee Gunsmith "Just Glocks", 2901 Deer Flat Dr., Copperas Cove, TX 76522 / 817-547-8433; FAX: 254-547-8887 ed@justglocks.com www.justglocks.com
Yavapai College, 1100 E. Sheldon St., Prescott, AZ 86301 / 520-776-2353; FAX: 520-776-2355
Yavapai Firearms Academy Ltd., P.O. Box 27290, Prescott Valley, AZ 86312 / 928-772-8262; FAX: 928-772-0062 info@yfainc.corn www.yfainc.com
Yearout, Lewis E. (See Montana Outfitters), 308 Riverview Dr. E., Great Falls, MT 59404 / 406-761-0859; or 406-727-4569
Yellowstone Wilderness Supply, P.O. Box 129, W. Yellowstone, MT 59758 / 406-646-7613
Yesteryear Armory & Supply, P.O. Box 408, Carthage, TN 37030
York M-1 Conversion, 12145 Mill Creek Run, Plantersville, TX 77363 / 936-894-2397; FAX: 936-894-2397 bmf25years@aol.com
Young Country Arms, William, 1409 Kuehner Dr. #13, Simi Valley, CA 93063-4478

Z

Zabala Hermanos S.A., P.O. Box 97, 20600 Elbar, Elgueta, Guipuzcoa, 20600 SPAIN / 943-768076; FAX: 943-768201 imanol@zabalahermanos.com www.zabalabermanos.com
Zander's Sporting Goods, 7525 Hwy 154 West, Baldwin, IL 62217-9706 / 800-851-4373; FAX: 618-785-2320
Zanotti Armor, Inc., 123 W. Lone Tree Rd., Cedar Falls, IA 50613 / 319-232-9650 www.zanottiarmor.com
Zeeryp, Russ, 1601 Foard Dr., Lynn Ross Manor, Morristown, TN 37814 / 615-586-2357
Zero Ammunition Co., Inc., 1601 22nd St. SE, P.O. Box 1188, Cullman, AL 35056-1188 / 800-545-9376; FAX: 205-739-4683
Ziegel Engineering, 1390 E. Bunnett St. "F", Signal Hill, CA 90755 / 562-596-9481; FAX: 562-598-4734 ziegel@aol.com www.ziegeleng.com
Zim's, Inc., 4370 S. 3rd West, Salt Lake City, UT 84107 / 801-268-2505
Z-M Weapons, 203 South St., Bernardston, MA 01337 / 413-648-9501; FAX: 413-648-0219
Zufall, Joseph F., P.O. Box 304, Golden, CO 80402-0304